ALGEBRA

Teacher's Edition

HOUGHTON MIFFLIN HARCOURT
Supplemental Publishers

www.SaxonPublishers.com
800-531-5015

ISBN 13: 978-1-6027-7302-8
ISBN 10: 1-6027-7302-5

© 2009 Saxon®, an imprint of HMH Supplemental Publishers Inc.

All rights reserved. No part of this material protected by this copyright may be reproduced or utilized in any form or by any means, in whole or in part, without permission in writing from the copyright owner. Requests for permission should be mailed to: Paralegal Department, 6277 Sea Harbor Drive, Orlando, FL 32887.

Saxon® is a registered trademark of HMH Supplemental Publishers Inc.

Printed in the United States of America

If you have received these materials as examination copies free of charge, HMH Supplemental Publishers Inc. retains title to the materials and they may not be resold. Resale of examination copies is strictly prohibited and is illegal.

Possession of this publication in print format does not entitle users to convert this publication, or any portion of it, into electronic format.

6 7 8 0868 15 14 13 12
4500373810

Algebra 1 Content Overview

Saxon Secondary Mathematics

Research and Proven Results... T4
Consistent Lesson Structure... T8
Differentiated Instruction... T10
Adaptations for Saxon Math... T12
Ongoing Assessment and Intervention... T14
Components... T15
Components, Technology... T16

Table of Contents ... T17
Content by Strand ... T30
Pacing Guide ... T34

Section 1: Lessons 1–10, Investigation 1 ... 2A
Section 2: Lessons 11–20, Investigation 2 ... 56A
Section 3: Lessons 21–30, Investigation 3 ... 120A
Section 4: Lessons 31–40, Investigation 4 ... 190A
Section 5: Lessons 41–50, Investigation 5 ... 256A
Section 6: Lessons 51–60, Investigation 6 ... 322A
Section 7: Lessons 61–70, Investigation 7 ... 398A
Section 8: Lessons 71–80, Investigation 8 ... 464A
Section 9: Lessons 81–90, Investigation 9 ... 532A
Section 10: Lessons 91–100, Investigation 10 ... 602A
Section 11: Lessons 101–110, Investigation 11 ... 678A
Section 12: Lessons 111–120, Investigation 12 ... 754A

Appendix Lessons ... 830
Skills Bank ... 846
Properties and Formulas ... 884
English/Spanish Glossary ... T889
Additional Answers ... T899
Index ... T913

Saxon Secondary Mathematics Provides the Time to Learn, Process, and Master

Saxon Math's approach of distributed instruction, practice, and assessment gets results for today's standards, where mastery learning is required of all students. This approach makes the difference in helping high school students master the standards—with an understanding that lasts a lifetime—and is supported by research studies on effective teaching strategies.

Distributed Units of Instruction

Mastery of standards happens at different rates for different students.

Saxon's distributed approach breaks apart traditional units and then distributes and integrates the concepts across the year. This creates a learning curve that provides the time most students need to master every part of every standard. With this structure, no skills or concepts get dropped and students retain what they have learned well beyond the test.

The instruction of related concepts in Saxon is carefully distributed throughout each course.

The traditional chapter approach allows only a few weeks for student mastery of concepts

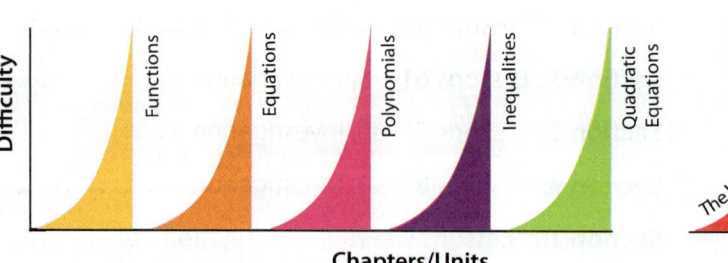

Research shows that there is value in a teaching method that uses small, easily digestible chunks of information within its lessons (Ausubel, 1969; Brophy & Everston, 1976). Studies by Rosenshine and Stevens (1986) and Brophy and Everston (1976) demonstrated the importance of using incremental steps when teaching new information.

Saxon's instructional approach to teaching mathematics is supported by Gagne's (1962, 1965) cumulative-learning theory and Anderson's (1983) ACT theory. Foundational research has also shown that distributed instruction results in greater student achievement (English, Wellburn, & Killian, 1934) and leads to a higher level of recall (Glenberg, 1979; Hintzman, 1974) than does massed instruction.

ALGEBRA 1 ■ GEOMETRY ■ ALGEBRA 2

Continual Practice

Review over time promotes long-term retention.

Students attain a depth of understanding on a particular concept by practicing it over time and in a variety of ways. Saxon Math provides that depth with its continual practice. Every day Saxon students practice not only the day's concept but also concepts and skills from previous lessons.

Saxon's continual practice provides cumulative review throughout the year.

- Skills and concepts are kept alive and reinforced through daily practice.
- Math connections are strengthened and made meaningful.
- Practice sets are rich and varied—just like state assessments and in real life.

The Saxon pedagogy of continual, distributed practice ensures that concepts are committed to students' long-term memory.

Research studies have shown that students, who are taught with a mathematics curriculum using continual practice and review, demonstrate greater math achievement and skill acquisition than do students who are taught with a massed approach (Good & Grouws, 1979; Hardesty, 1986; MacDonald, 1984; Mayfield & Chase, 2002; Ornstein, 1990; Usnick, 1991).

Long-term retention is best served if assignments about a particular skill are spread out in time, rather than concentrated within a short interval (Suydam, 1984). Additional studies have concluded that spaced (distributed) practice results in higher performance than massed practice (Dhaliwal, 1987).

Frequent, Cumulative Assessment

Progress is evaluated throughout the year.

Frequent, cumulative assessments are an integral part of Saxon Math, giving students the opportunity to demonstrate and communicate what they know and can do. Regular evaluation of skills helps teachers pinpoint areas where students may need further practice or reteaching before moving on to new concepts.

The consistently-placed assessments in Saxon Math are cumulative. This approach leads to greater understanding because students reflect on past concepts and make connections across all math strands. With a regular, cumulative method for testing and tracking student mastery, Saxon helps all students achieve the goal of long-term retention.

Research has indicated that well-designed classroom testing programs that are routine rather than an interruption (National Council of Teachers of Mathematics [NCTM], 2000) have a positive impact on later student achievement (Dempster, 1991). Dempster found that higher levels of achievement occur when testing is frequent and cumulative rather than infrequent or related only to content covered since the last test.

According to Fuchs (1995), cumulative assessment that is frequent and distributed has been found to be effective by a number of studies which show that students who are assessed frequently have higher test scores than do students who are assessed infrequently (Blair, 2000; Peckham & Roe, 1977; Rohm, Sparzo, & Bennett, 1986).

A History of Measurable Results

For more than 25 years, both classroom results and scientific research has shown *Saxon Math* to be effective. Saxon's approach to teaching mathematics has been found to be consistently successful for students of varying ability levels and socioeconomic backgrounds.

In addition, *Saxon Math* has been extensively field-tested to guarantee its grade-level appropriateness and effectiveness of explicit instruction.

> *Clopton, McKeown, McKeown, and Clopton (1999) concluded that*
>
> " the Saxon program has many high-quality features of presentation including clear statements of the lesson objectives, daily structure, [and] clear and explicit instructional materials."

Statistical analysis revealed that the average gain over the year was significantly higher for the Saxon group than the group using the traditional approach, despite the fact that the Saxon group began the year at a disadvantage.

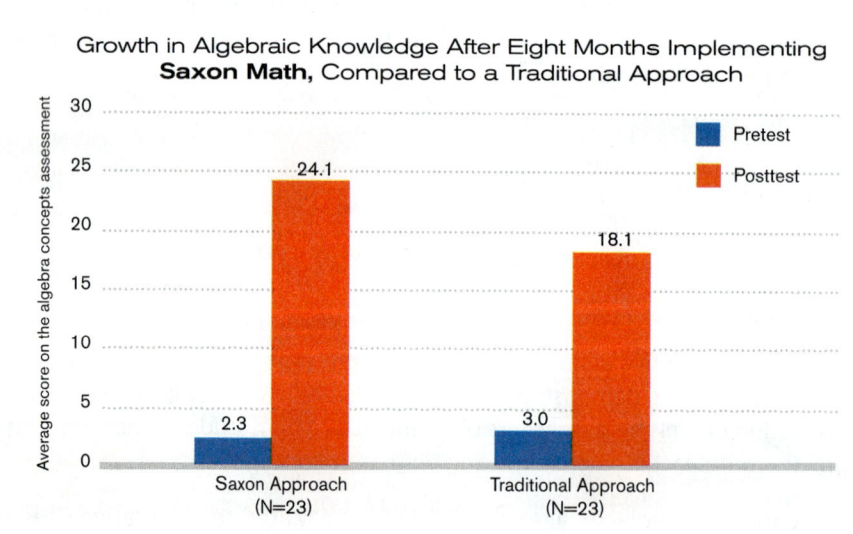

Gain from pretest to posttest was significantly higher for the Saxon approach at the 95% confidence interval. A post-hoc effect size was calculated from the existing data to be d=0.82.

ALGEBRA 1 ■ GEOMETRY ■ ALGEBRA 2

Program Efficacy Studies

Effectiveness of *Saxon Math* on the Achievement of High School Students' Math Performance

A quasi-experimental study by McBee (1982) also demonstrated the effects of the *Saxon Algebra 1* textbook in Oklahoma City Public Schools during one school year.

Data analysis showed that the Saxon group significantly outperformed the group using a traditional chapter text on 11 of the 21 subsections. A deeper analysis of the test scores showed that the Saxon students scored significantly higher than the other students at all ability levels (low, medium, and high).

Impact of *Saxon Math* on College Preparation

In a comparison-group study, Sanders (1997) investigated the differences in the math achievement of students preparing for college using *Saxon Math* and the math achievement of those using textbooks with more traditional methods of math instruction. In Georgia, 120 high school juniors from two schools participated in this comparison study. There were 81 students who used various textbooks and 39 students who used a Saxon textbook. At the end of the school year, these students were given the Georgia High School Graduation Tests which contained four math subsections.

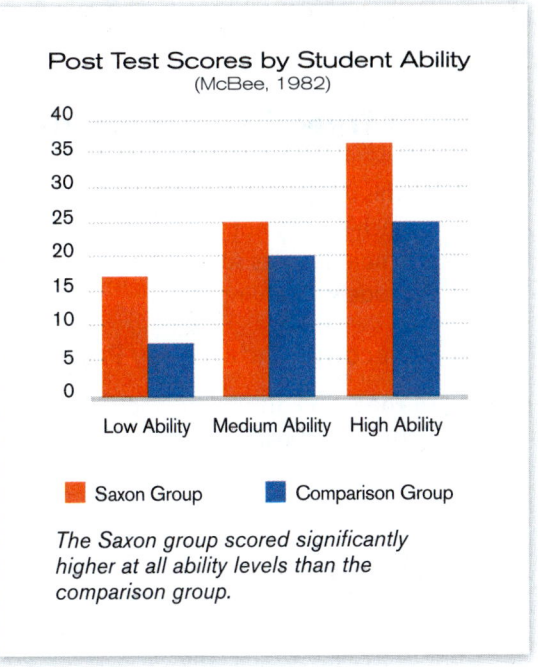

The Saxon group scored significantly higher at all ability levels than the comparison group.

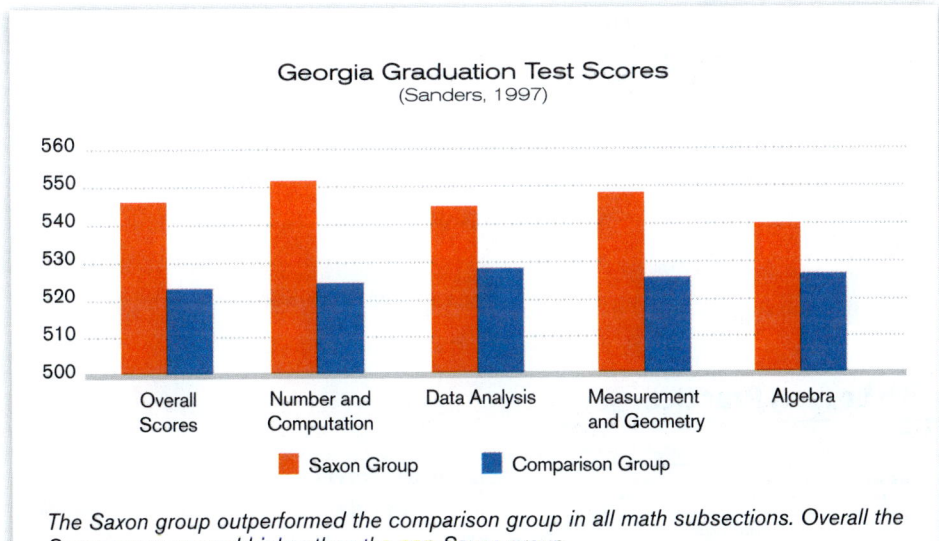

The Saxon group outperformed the comparison group in all math subsections. Overall the Saxon group scored higher than the non-Saxon group.

A comparison of the mean scores of both groups showed that the **Saxon group scored significantly higher** in all four math subsections of the graduation tests.

It is important to note that these research designs are among the most appropriate methods used to measure the effects of a curriculum on educational outcomes such as student performance (*What Works Clearinghouse*, 2003).

Consistent Lesson Structure That Enhances Mastery

A Three-Part Lesson Plan

This regular format allows students to become comfortable with the lessons and to know what to expect each day. By not including colorful distracting photographs, *Saxon Math* with its predictable format lets students focus solely on the mathematics. The color and vibrancy of mathematics comes from the students' learning.

Recommended Daily Pacing

The Saxon distributed approach is unique in that the focus of the day is mainly on the rich depth of content in the distributed Practice problems.

In a typical 60-min class period, it is suggested that you spend about half of the class period having the students complete the Practice problems. This allows you to have meaningful math conversations with students as they work out the problems.

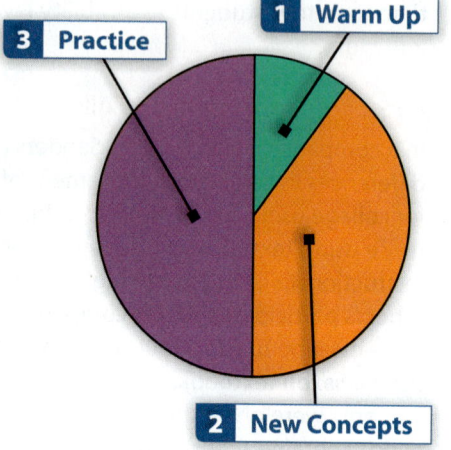

1 Warm Up — Prevention through Built-In Intervention

The **Warm Up** at the beginning of every lesson provides practice of those prerequisite skills, concepts, and vocabulary needed to be successful in that day's lesson.

> Lesson reference numbers with each problem show where students can go back to get additional help.

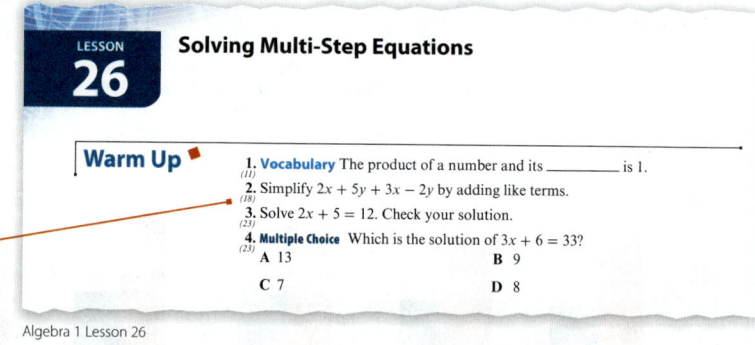

2 New Concepts with Lesson Practice — Increase Student Knowledge

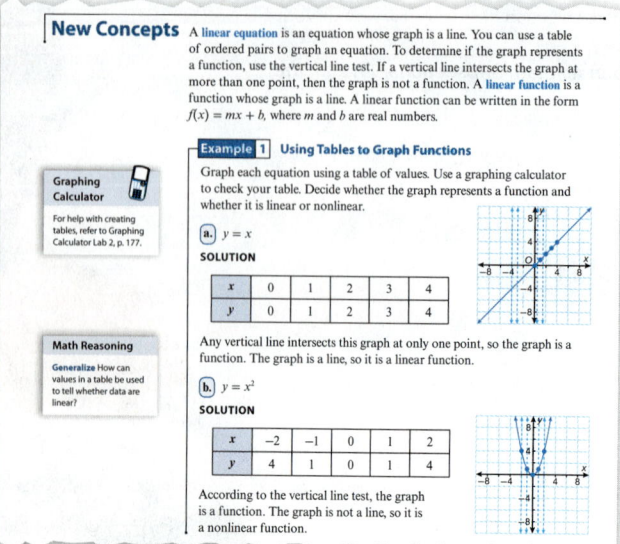

Each day the **New Concepts** introduces a new topic through clear explanations and Examples that build in-depth understanding and use a variety of methods and real-world applications.

Thinking and reasoning questions, reading math tips, math language notes, cautions, hints, graphing calculator tips—all help students understand how and why the math works.

ALGEBRA 1 ■ GEOMETRY ■ ALGEBRA 2

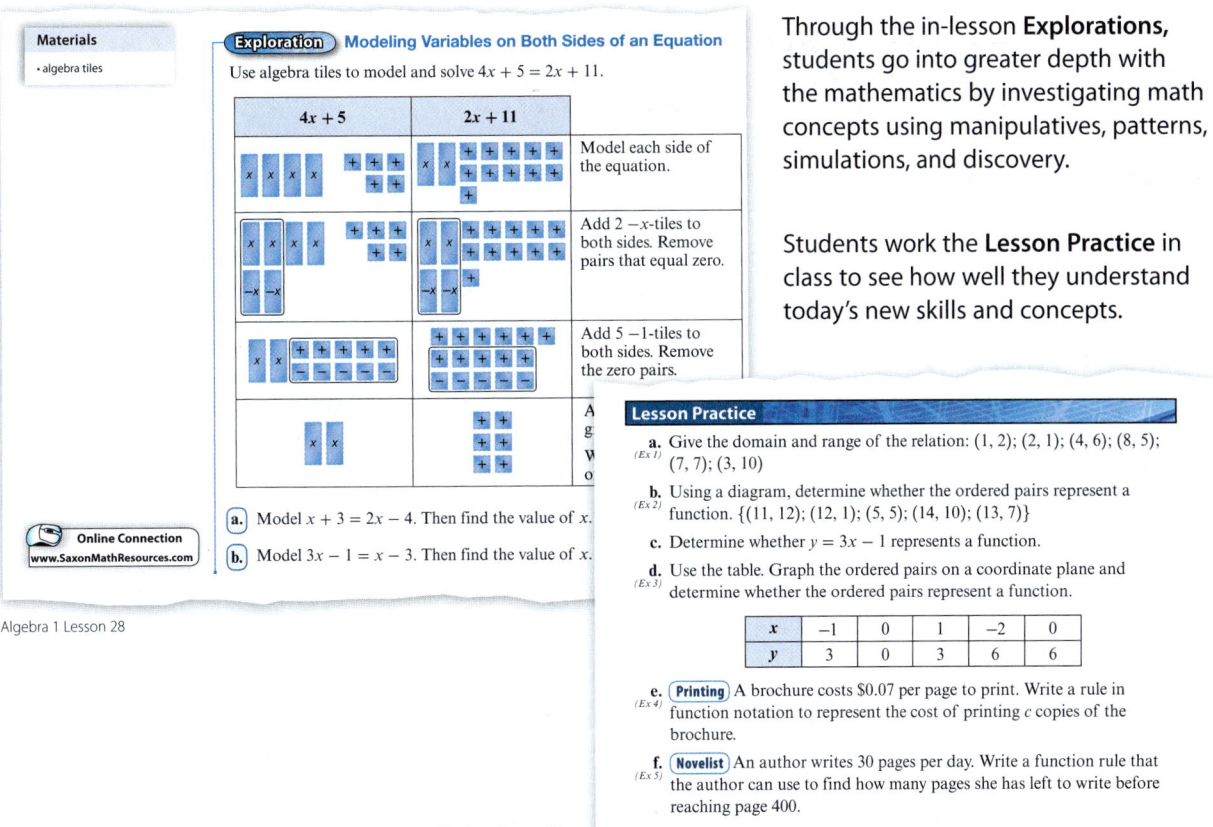

Through the in-lesson Explorations, students go into greater depth with the mathematics by investigating math concepts using manipulatives, patterns, simulations, and discovery.

Students work the **Lesson Practice** in class to see how well they understand today's new skills and concepts.

Lesson Practice

a. *(Ex 1)* Give the domain and range of the relation: (1, 2); (2, 1); (4, 6); (8, 5); (7, 7); (3, 10)

b. *(Ex 2)* Using a diagram, determine whether the ordered pairs represent a function. {(11, 12); (12, 1); (5, 5); (14, 10); (13, 7)}

c. Determine whether $y = 3x - 1$ represents a function.

d. *(Ex 3)* Use the table. Graph the ordered pairs on a coordinate plane and determine whether the ordered pairs represent a function.

x	−1	0	1	−2	0
y	3	0	3	6	6

e. *(Ex 4)* **Printing** A brochure costs $0.07 per page to print. Write a rule in function notation to represent the cost of printing c copies of the brochure.

f. *(Ex 5)* **Novelist** An author writes 30 pages per day. Write a function rule that the author can use to find how many pages she has left to write before reaching page 400.

Algebra 1 Lesson 25

3 Practice — Distributed and Integrated

The distributed **Practice** provides students with a depth of understanding. Because students practice the same topic over several lessons, they have "time to learn" the concept and have multiple opportunities to show that they understand.

The integrated nature of the **Practice** allows students to maintain and build on concepts and skills previously taught. By practicing problems from many lessons every day, students see how math concepts connect to each other and to the real world.

To help students build their mathematical language, *Saxon Math* provides continual exposure to and review of math vocabulary.

The distributed and mixed practice is unpredictable and therefore challenging. It mirrors the format of state tests.

*8. **Multi-Step** Three hundred people were surveyed as they left a movie theater.
(22) They were asked which type of movie they like best. The circle graph shows the survey results.
  a. Which type of movie was most popular?
  b. How many people liked horror movies the best?
  c. How many more people liked action movies than dramas?

*9. *(22)* Choose an appropriate graph to display the number of different types of DVDs sold at two video stores. Explain your answer.

*10. *(22)* A class of 20 students answered a survey about their favorite places to go on vacation. Use the data in the table to make a bar graph.

Beach	Amusement Park	Mountains	Museums
5	8	3	4

*11. **Geometry** A circle has a circumference of $\frac{8}{9}\pi$ meters. What is the radius of
(21) the circle?

12. **Multiple Choice** Which equation has solutions that are represented by the
(21) graphed points?
  A $y = 2x + 1$
  B $y = 2x + 3$
  C $y = -2x$
  D $y = -2x - 1$

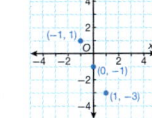

13. *(7)* **Coins** Jenny and Sam took the coins out of their pockets. Jenny has x quarters and y dimes. Sam has h half dollars and z nickels.
  a. Write expressions representing the value of the coins, in cents, in each person's pocket.
  b. Write an expression for the total number of cents they have.

14. *(17)* **Verify** "12 more than the product of x and 3" can be written as $3x + 12$ or $12 + 3x$. Substitute 2 for x and show that the expressions are equivalent.

15. *(7)* Use >, <, or = to compare the expressions.
$$24 + \frac{16}{4} - (4 + 3^2) \cdot 2 \; \bigcirc \; 24 + \left(\frac{16}{4} - 4\right) + 3^2 \cdot 2$$

Solve.

16. *(19)* $y - \frac{1}{2} = -2\frac{1}{2}$

*17. *(23)* $2x + 3 = 11$

*18. *(23)* $3x - 4 = 10$

*19. *(23)* Solve $2.2x + 2 = 8.6$

*20. *(Inv 1)* **Statistics** A basketball player attempted 1789 free throws. He made 801 of them. What is the probability that the player will make the next shot he attempts? Write the probability as a decimal rounded to the nearest hundredth.

Students get a **test prep** experience every day!

Algebra 1 Lesson 23

Differentiated Instruction:
Built-in support for all students

Lesson Structure *Saxon Math* provides a predictable routine that enables all learners to be successful. By focusing on the mathematics and not the "fluff" seen in other math texts, *Saxon Math* makes higher-level mathematical thinking accessible for every student.

For All Learners

Saxon Math provides additional support that can be valuable to all types of learners.

In the student text, there are **Hints** for extra help and **Cautions** to prevent common errors.

Explorations and **Labs** in the student edition allow students to investigate mathematics in more depth through manipulatives, technology, patterning, and other methods.

Alternate Method and **Manipulative Use** show different ways to solve the same problem.

Error Alerts in the teacher's edition offer additional ways that teachers can help students avoid common misunderstandings.

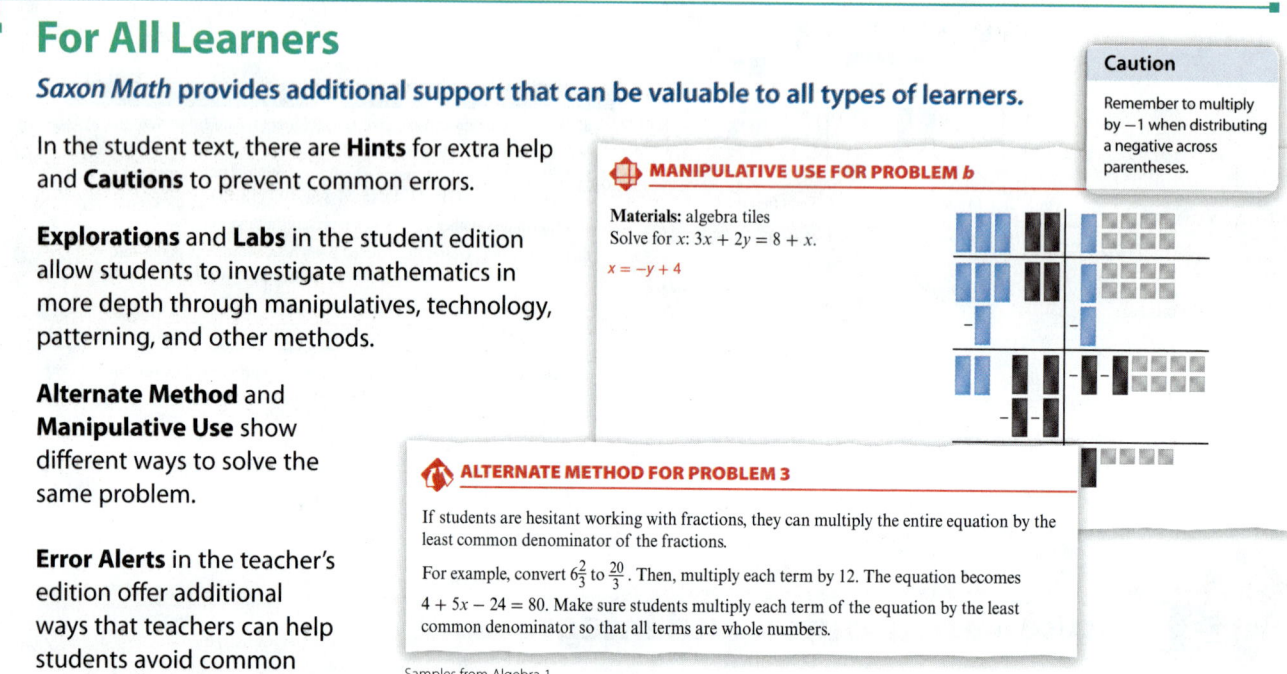

Samples from Algebra 1

English Learners

English learners will find structures in *Saxon Math* to help them acquire mathematical understanding and language. Visual models, activities and labs, math conversations, and language prompts all help students in their daily learning.

The **English Learners tips** focus on language acquisition, not on reteaching or simplifying the math. These tips are based on a proven approach with these steps:

- Define and Hear
- Model and Connect
- Discuss and Explain
- Apply and Use

The **Multilingual Glossary** provides math vocabulary and definitions in 13 languages: Armenian, Arabic, Cantonese, English, Hmong, Khmer, Korean, Punjabi, Russian, Spanish, Tagalog, Urdu, and Vietnamese.

The **English Learners Handbook** offers professional development and practical classroom tips on teaching mathematics to English learners.

The **Glossary** in the student textbook provides a Spanish translation of each math term and definition.

ENGLISH LEARNERS

Explain that a prefix is a word part that is added to the beginning of a word. Point out the word *misleading* in the title of the lesson. Tell students that the prefix *mis-* means "wrong." Say:

"The word *mislead* means to lead in the wrong direction."

Connect the definition of the word to the lesson by pointing out how the design of the graphs can lead someone to the wrong conclusions.

Have students brainstorm other words that begin with the prefix *mis-*, such as mistake, misunderstand, misfortune, and misbehave. Ask students to use the prefix to give each word's meaning.

Have students pick a graph in this lesson and explain why it is misleading.

Samples from Algebra 1

ALGEBRA 1 ■ GEOMETRY ■ ALGEBRA 2

Struggling Learners

Saxon Math includes a number of support features to help various categories of struggling learners.

The daily **Warm Up** exercises help students with prerequisite skills needed in order to be successful.

The **Skills Bank** in the student textbook offers instruction and practice on prerequisite skills.

Prerequisite Skills Intervention gives students more instruction and practice on prerequisite skills.

The **Reteaching Masters** provide intervention pages of instruction and stepped-out practice for the new concepts in every lesson.

Inclusion tips help teachers to accommodate special needs in the classroom.

Adaptations for Saxon Math provides complete and parallel support for special needs students.
See pp. T12–T13 for details.

INCLUSION

Some students have difficulty following multiple steps. Help these students by teaching them to focus on the first step. Point out that many problems can have several correct first steps, so they do not

Have them only describe what their first step would be, and why.

$3(x - 7) = 12$ Distributive Property, to clear parentheses

 $= -10$ Commutative
, so you can combine like

Combine like terms,
ging is necessary

INCLUSION

Some students will have trouble with logical reasoning when they try to identify the dependent and independent variables. Reinforce the difference by having students fill in the blanks in these sentences. Note that the order of the answers is intentionally reversed to assess student understanding.

I must know the _____ to find the _____. independent variable; dependent variable

The _____ depends on the _____.
dependent variable; independent variable

Samples from Algebra 1

Advanced Learners

Saxon Math provides advanced learners with many opportunities for expanding their concept development.

A **Challenge** problem is provided for every lesson.

Challenge and Enrichment Masters offer more in-depth extensions of the content.

The **Extend the Example, Extend the Problem,** and **Extend the Exploration** suggestions in the teacher's edition provide even more ways to engage the advanced learner.

CHALLENGE

Solve the equation by first multiplying by a reciprocal. Show each step.

$8(2x - 1) + 15 + 7x = 4(3x + 5) + 5x - 1$

Problem 20
Extend the Problem
Is the expression $|x - 3|$ equivalent to $|3 - x|$? Explain.

Samples from Algebra 1

CHALLENGE

Challenge students to make a table of values and graph of the equation $y = x^2 - 2x$. Is the graph a function? Is it linear?

Saxon

Adaptations for *Saxon Math*: Complete and Parallel Support for Special Populations

The flexible curriculum design of Adaptations for *Saxon Math* can be integrated into inclusion classrooms, pullout programs, or self-contained resource classrooms, ensuring that special needs students keep pace with the core curriculum.

Saxon Math Core Program

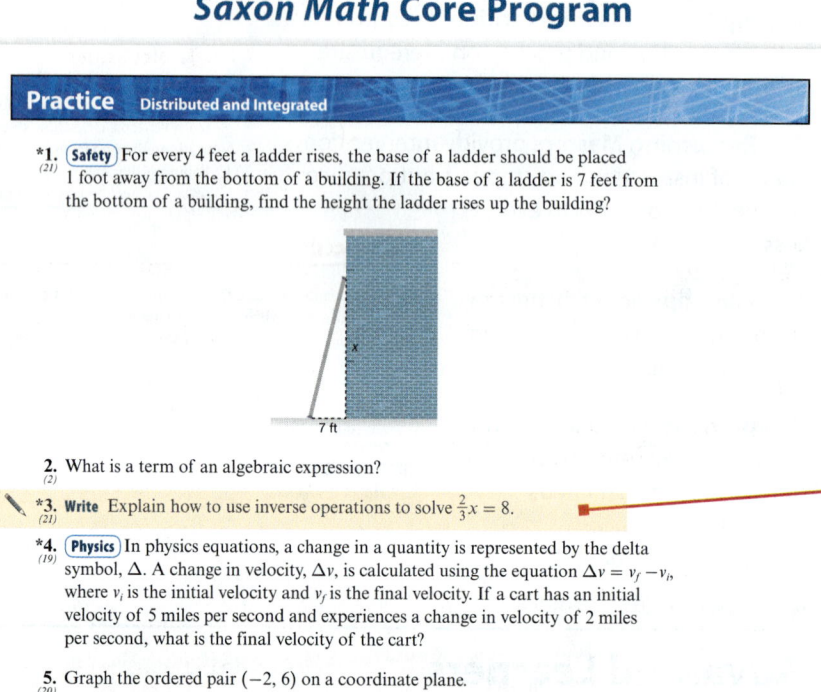

Practice Distributed and Integrated

*1. **(Safety)** For every 4 feet a ladder rises, the base of a ladder should be placed 1 foot away from the bottom of a building. If the base of a ladder is 7 feet from the bottom of a building, find the height the ladder rises up the building?

2. What is a term of an algebraic expression?

*3. **Write** Explain how to use inverse operations to solve $\frac{2}{3}x = 8$.

*4. **(Physics)** In physics equations, a change in a quantity is represented by the delta symbol, Δ. A change in velocity, Δv, is calculated using the equation $\Delta v = v_f - v_i$, where v_i is the initial velocity and v_f is the final velocity. If a cart has an initial velocity of 5 miles per second and experiences a change in velocity of 2 miles per second, what is the final velocity of the cart?

5. Graph the ordered pair $(-2, 6)$ on a coordinate plane.

6. **Geometry** The length of a rectangular picture frame is 3 times the width.
   a. Draw a picture of the picture frame and label the dimensions.
   b. Write an expression for the area of the frame.

7. Complete the table for $y = 2x + 7$.

x	−5	1	4
y			

*8. Solve $\frac{x}{3} = 5$.

*9. **Multiple-Choice** Which step can you use first to solve $-\frac{x}{9} = -52$?
   A Multiply both sides by 9.
   B Multiply both sides by −9.
   C Divide both sides by −52.
   D Divide both sides by 52.

*10. **Estimate** Alan makes $1 for each snow cone he sells. Alan calculates his profit by subtracting the daily cost of $195 to run the stand from the total number of snow cones he sells each day. How many snow cones does Alan need to sell to make a profit of $200 a day?

124 Saxon Algebra 1

Support for Learning Disabilities

The unique design organizes exercises in ways that allow success for students with learning disabilities, such as:

- Visual-motor integration
- Number reversal in reading
- Distractibility or lack of focus
- Verbal explanation
- Math anxiety
- Receptive language
- Spatial organization
- Number reversal in reading and copy work

ALGEBRA 1 ■ GEOMETRY ■ ALGEBRA 2

Adapted Practice Problems and Assessments

The carefully structured layout of the Practice pages helps special needs students focus on mastering the concept, rather than figuring out the directions.

Saxon Math Adapted Pages

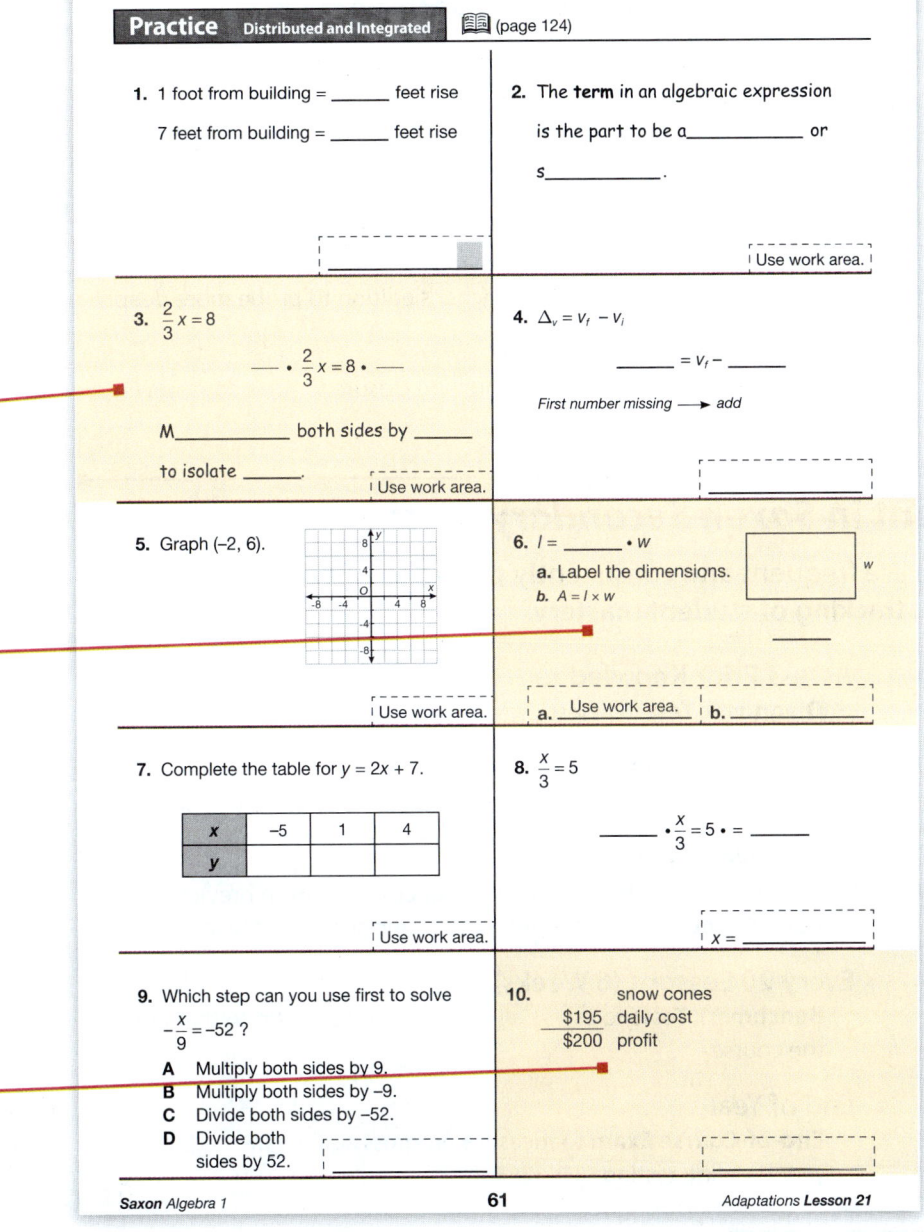

Adaptations for *Saxon Algebra 1, Geometry,* and *Algebra 2*

This unique program is available in these easy-to-use components:

- **Classroom Package**
  Teaching Guide, Student Reference Guide, CD of all adapted pages

- **Student Workbook**
  consumable workbook of all adapted practice pages

- **Assessment Masters**
  blackline masters of all adapted tests

- **Student Reference Guide**
  for each individual student

T13

Ongoing Assessment and Intervention

Assessments can be categorized in two ways, both of which are valuable and necessary in helping students succeed in mathematics.

Formative Assessment in *Saxon Secondary Math*

The instructional design of *Saxon Math* effectively helps you to identify immediately any learning gaps and to provide successful intervention to keep students on track.

Formative Assessment
• *Purpose:* Improvement
• Assess continuously **during** teaching to influence learning.
• Use for **immediate feedback** to intervene, if necessary, on a particular concept.

Before the Lesson
  Warm Up to check prerequisite skills and vocabulary

During the Lesson
  Reasoning questions to clarify students' thinking
  Lesson Practice to assess today's New Concepts
  Practice problems to check previously-taught content
  Math Conversations in the teacher's edition to probe more deeply

After the Lesson
  Check for understanding to provide closure for that day's new concept

Summative Assessment in *Saxon Secondary Math*

The assessments in *Saxon Math* are frequent and consistently placed to offer a regular method of ongoing testing and tracking of student mastery.

Summative Assessment
• *Purpose:* Accountability
• Assess periodically **after** teaching to gather evidence of learning.
• Use to **judge** learning, usually in the form of a grade or score.

Assess Prior Knowledge
  Diagnostic Test to assess previous year's content

Beginning of Year
  Baseline Test to benchmark knowledge of this year's course material

Every Five Lessons
  Cumulative Test to check mastery of concepts from previous lessons
  Performance Task a theme-based, rubric-scored assessment

Every 20 Lessons (6 Weeks)
  Benchmark Tests to assess all concepts and skills up to that point in the course

End of Year
  End-of-Course Exam to measure progress against the beginning-of-year baseline testing

Intervention Support

Use these resources to intervene when students are not showing progress on formative assessments or are scoring below 80% on summative assessments.

- Prerequisite Skills Intervention
- Skills Bank
- Reteaching Masters
- Scaffolding questions in teacher's edition
- Worked-out Examples in student text
- Additional Examples in teacher's edition
- Test and Practice Generator

ALGEBRA 1 ■ GEOMETRY ■ ALGEBRA 2

Components

Resources for Teaching

Student Edition

Teacher's Edition

turn page

Technology
— Student Edition eBook
— Teacher's Edition eBook
— Resources and Planner CD
— Instructional Presentations CD
— Online support

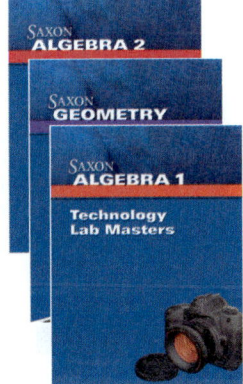

Instructional Masters
teaching tools and recording forms

Technology Lab Masters
activities for graphing calculator and geometry software

Warm Up and Teaching Transparencies
teaching tools and student edition Warm Up

Solutions Manual
full solutions to all problems in student text

Resources for Practice and Assessment

turn page

Technology
— Examview™ Test and Practice Generator
— Online support

Student Edition Practice Workbook
all Practice problems; no need to carry the textbook home

Course Assessments
diagnostic, baseline, cumulative, benchmark tests, and performance tasks

Standardized Test Practice
diagnostic test, standards practice, sample tests

College Entrance Exam Practice
practice tests for PSAT, SAT, ACT

Components   **T15**

ALGEBRA 1 ■ GEOMETRY ■ ALGEBRA 2

Components

For description of additional print components, turn back one page.

Resources for Differentiated Instruction

Reteaching Masters
one for every lesson and investigation

Challenge and Enrichment Masters
every challenge problem from TE plus additional enrichment sheets

Prerequisite Skills Intervention
pre-course skills and remediation

Adaptations for Saxon Math
A parallel program for special populations
(See pages T12–T13.)

Multilingual Glossary
terms and definitions in 13 languages

English Learners Handbook
guidance for modifying instruction for English learners; background on specific language issues

Technology

Student Edition eBook
complete student text on CD

Teacher's Edition eBook
complete teacher's edition on CD

Resources and Planner CD
electronic pacing calendar with standards, plus PDF resources

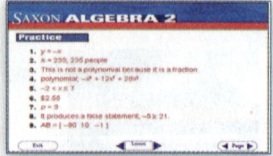

Instructional Presentations CD
Interactivities that model and demonstrate key concepts to engage students and enhance learning. These are correlated to program lessons.

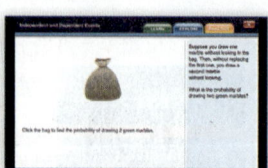

Online Support
Interactivities, graphing calculator tutorials and labs, multilingual glossary, math tools, homework help
www.SaxonMathResources.com

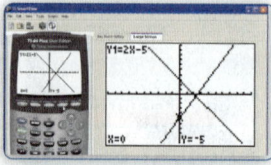

Texas Instruments (TI) Resources CD
keystroke tutorials, TI graphing calculator activities, TI application guides

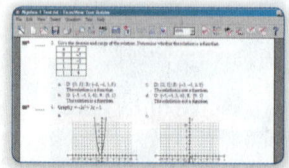

Test and Practice Generator—Examview™
LAN, web, or print based customizable testing with dynamic items; track student progress with reports

Components, Technology

Table of Contents

Section 1: Lessons 1-10, Investigation 1

			PAGE
	Section 1 Overview		2A
▫	1	Classifying Real Numbers	2
▫	2	Understanding Variables and Expressions	7
▫	3	Simplifying Expressions Using the Product Property of Exponents	12
▫	4	Using Order of Operations	17
▫	5	Finding Absolute Value and Adding Real Numbers **Exploration:** Modeling Real Number Addition	22
▫	6	Subtracting Real Numbers	27
▫	7	Simplifying and Comparing Expressions with Symbols of Inclusion	31
▫	8	Using Unit Analysis to Convert Measures **Exploration:** Using Unit Analysis	36
▫	9	Evaluating and Comparing Algebraic Expressions	43
▫	10	Adding and Subtracting Real Numbers	47
	Cumulative Assessment Cumulative Test 1, Performance Task 1		
▫	LAB 1	**Graphing Calculator:** Generating Random Numbers	52
▫	INV 1	**Investigation:** Determining the Probability of an Event **Exploration:** Conducting Experiments to Find Probabilities	53

DISTRIBUTED STRANDS

- Algebra Foundations
- Functions and Relations
- Equations
- Linear Equations and Functions
- Polynomials
- Rational Expressions and Functions
- Inequalities
- Systems of Equations and Inequalities
- Radical Expressions and Functions
- Quadratic Equations and Functions
- Absolute-Value Equations and Inequalities
- Probability and Data Analysis

Section 2: Lessons 11-20, Investigation 2

			PAGE
Section 2 Overview			56A
	11	Multiplying and Dividing Real Numbers	56
	12	Using the Properties of Real Numbers to Simplify Expressions	63
	13	Calculating and Comparing Square Roots	69
	14	Determining the Theoretical Probability of an Event **Exploration:** Finding Theoretical Probability	74
	15	Using the Distributive Property to Simplify Expressions	80
Cumulative Assessment		Cumulative Test 2, Performance Task 2	
	16	Simplifying and Evaluating Variable Expressions	86
	17	Translating Between Words and Algebraic Expressions	93
	18	Combining Like Terms	98
	19	Solving One-Step Equations by Adding or Subtracting **Exploration:** Using Algebra Tiles to Model One-Step Equations	103
	20	Graphing on a Coordinate Plane	110
Cumulative Assessment		Cumulative Test 3, Performance Task 3, Benchmark Test 1	
	INV 2	**Investigation:** Graphing a Relationship	117

Section 3: Lessons 21-30, Investigation 3

			PAGE
Section 3 Overview			120A
🟧	21	Solving One-Step Equations by Multiplying or Dividing **Exploration:** Using Inverse Operations	120
⬜	22	Analyzing and Comparing Statistical Graphs **Exploration:** Analyzing Bar Graphs	127
🟧	23	Solving Two-Step Equations	134
🟧	24	Solving Decimal Equations	140
🟨	25	Differentiating Between Relations and Functions	146
Cumulative Assessment		Cumulative Test 4, Performance Task 4	
🟧	26	Solving Multi-Step Equations	153
⬜	27	Identifying Misleading Representations of Data	159
🟧	28	Solving Equations with Variables on Both Sides **Exploration:** Modeling Variables on Both Sides of an Equation	164
🟧	29	Solving Literal Equations	171
🟨	LAB 2	**Graphing Calculator:** Creating a Table	177
🟨	30	Graphing Functions	179
Cumulative Assessment		Cumulative Test 5, Performance Task 5	
⬜	INV 3	**Investigation:** Analyzing the Effects of Bias in Sampling, Surveys, and Bar Graphs **Exploration:** Making and Analyzing Biased Graphs	187

DISTRIBUTED STRANDS

Section 4: Lessons 31-40, Investigation 4

			PAGE
Section 4 Overview			190A
	31	Using Rates, Ratios, and Proportions	190
	32	Simplifying and Evaluating Expressions with Integer and Zero Exponents	197
	33	Finding the Probability of Independent and Dependent Events	204
	34	Recognizing and Extending Arithmetic Sequences	211
	35	Locating and Using Intercepts	217
Cumulative Assessment		Cumulative Test 6, Performance Task 6	
	36	Writing and Solving Proportions **Exploration:** Changing Dimensions	223
	37	Using Scientific Notation **Exploration:** Applying Scientific Notation	230
	38	Simplifying Expressions Using the GCF	236
	39	Using the Distributive Property to Simplify Rational Expressions	243
	40	Simplifying and Evaluating Expressions Using the Power Property for Exponents **Exploration:** Raising a Power to a Power	249
Cumulative Assessment		Cumulative Test 7, Performance Task 7, Benchmark Test 2	
	INV 4	**Investigation:** Using Deductive and Inductive Reasoning	254

Section 5: Lessons 41-50, Investigation 5

			PAGE
Section 5 Overview			256A
🟥	41	Finding Rates of Change and Slope **Exploration:** Analyzing a Graph	256
🟧	42	Solving Percent Problems	263
🟪	43	Simplifying Rational Expressions	270
🟥	44	Finding Slope Using the Slope Formula	275
🟪	45	Translating Between Words and Inequalities	282
Cumulative Assessment		Cumulative Test 8, Performance Task 8	
🟨	46	Simplifying Expressions with Square Roots and Higher-Order Roots	288
🟧	47	Solving Problems Involving the Percent of Change	294
⬜	48	Analyzing Measures of Central Tendency	299
🟥	LAB 3	**Graphing Calculator:** Graphing Linear Functions	305
🟥	49	Writing Equations in Slope-Intercept Form	307
🟪	50	Graphing Inequalities	314
Cumulative Assessment		Cumulative Test 9, Performance Task 9	
🟨	INV 5	**Investigation:** Using Logical Reasoning	320

DISTRIBUTED STRANDS

- Algebra Foundations
- Functions and Relations
- Equations
- Linear Equations and Functions
- Polynomials
- Rational Expressions and Functions
- Inequalities
- Systems of Equations and Inequalities
- Radical Expressions and Functions
- Quadratic Equations and Functions
- Absolute-Value Equations and Inequalities
- Probability and Data Analysis

Section 6: Lessons 51-60, Investigation 6

			PAGE
Section 6 Overview			322A
	51	Simplifying Rational Expressions with Like Denominators	322
	52	Determining the Equation of a Line Given Two Points	329
	53	Adding and Subtracting Polynomials **Exploration:** Using Algebra Tiles to Add or Subtract Polynomials	335
	LAB 4	**Graphing Calculator:** Drawing Box-and-Whisker Plots	343
	54	Displaying Data in a Box-and-Whisker Plot	345
	LAB 5	**Graphing Calculator:** Calculating the Intersection of Two Lines	352
	55	Solving Systems of Linear Equations by Graphing	354
Cumulative Assessment		Cumulative Test 10, Performance Task 10	
	56	Identifying, Writing, and Graphing Direct Variation **Exploration:** Using Direct Variation	361
	57	Finding the Least Common Multiple	368
	58	Multiplying Polynomials **Exploration:** Modeling Products of Binomials	375
	59	Solving Systems of Linear Equations by Substitution	382
	60	Finding Special Products of Binomials **Exploration:** Multiplying Binomials	390
Cumulative Assessment		Cumulative Test 11, Performance Task 11, Benchmark Test 3	
	INV 6	**Investigation:** Transforming Linear Functions	396

Saxon Algebra 1

Section 7: Lessons 61-70, Investigation 7

			PAGE
Section 7 Overview			398A
	61	Simplifying Radical Expressions **Exploration:** Finding Products of Square Roots	398
	LAB 6	**Graphing Calculator:** Drawing Histograms	404
	62	Displaying Data in Stem-and-Leaf Plots and Histograms	406
	63	Solving Systems of Linear Equations by Elimination	412
	64	Identifying, Writing, and Graphing Inverse Variation **Exploration:** Modeling Inverse Variation	418
	65	Writing Equations of Parallel and Perpendicular Lines	424
Cumulative Assessment		Cumulative Test 12, Performance Task 12	
	66	Solving Inequalities by Adding or Subtracting	430
	67	Solving and Classifying Special Systems of Linear Equations	436
	68	Mutually Exclusive and Inclusive Events	443
	69	Adding and Subtracting Radical Expressions	449
	70	Solving Inequalities by Multiplying or Dividing	455
Cumulative Assessment		Cumulative Test 13, Performance Task 13	
	INV 7	**Investigation:** Comparing Direct and Inverse Variation **Exploration:** Determining Characteristics of Variation Graphs	462

DISTRIBUTED STRANDS

- Algebra Foundations
- Functions and Relations
- Equations
- Linear Equations and Functions
- Polynomials
- Rational Expressions and Functions
- Inequalities
- Systems of Equations and Inequalities
- Radical Expressions and Functions
- Quadratic Equations and Functions
- Absolute-Value Equations and Inequalities
- Probability and Data Analysis

Section 8: Lessons 71-80, Investigation 8

			PAGE
Section 8 Overview			464A
	LAB 7	**Graphing Calculator:** Finding the Line of Best Fit	464
	71	Making and Analyzing Scatter Plots	466
	72	Factoring Trinomials: $x^2 + bx + c$ **Exploration:** Representing Trinomials with Algebra Tiles	474
	73	Solving Compound Inequalities	481
	74	Solving Absolute-Value Equations	487
	75	Factoring Trinomials: $ax^2 + bx + c$	493
Cumulative Assessment		Cumulative Test 14, Performance Task 14	
	76	Multiplying Radical Expressions	500
	77	Solving Two-Step and Multi-Step Inequalities	505
	78	Graphing Rational Functions	510
	79	Factoring Trinomials by Using the GCF	517
	80	Calculating Frequency Distributions **Exploration:** Displaying Frequency Distributions	523
Cumulative Assessment		Cumulative Test 15, Performance Task 15, Benchmark Test 4	
	INV 8	**Investigation:** Identifying and Writing Joint Variation	529

Section 9: Lessons 81-90, Investigation 9

			PAGE
Section 9 Overview			532A
	81	Solving Inequalities with Variables on Both Sides	532
	82	Solving Multi-Step Compound Inequalities	538
	83	Factoring Special Products	543
	84	Identifying Quadratic Functions	550
	85	Solving Problems Using the Pythagorean Theorem **Exploration:** Justifying the Pythagorean Theorem	556
Cumulative Assessment		Cumulative Test 16, Performance Task 16	
	86	Calculating the Midpoint and Length of a Segment	563
	87	Factoring Polynomials by Grouping	570
	88	Multiplying and Dividing Rational Expressions	576
	LAB 8	**Graphing Calculator:** Characteristics of Parabolas	583
	89	Identifying Characteristics of Quadratic Functions	585
	90	Adding and Subtracting Rational Expressions	592
Cumulative Assessment		Cumulative Test 17, Performance Task 17	
	INV 9	**Investigation:** Choosing a Factoring Method **Exploration:** Factoring Trinomials of the Form $ax^2 + bx + c$ Using Algebra Tiles	598

DISTRIBUTED STRANDS

- Algebra Foundations
- Functions and Relations
- Equations
- Linear Equations and Functions
- Polynomials
- Rational Expressions and Functions

- Inequalities
- Systems of Equations and Inequalities
- Radical Expressions and Functions
- Quadratic Equations and Functions
- Absolute-Value Equations and Inequalities
- Probability and Data Analysis

Section 10: Lessons 91-100, Investigation 10

			PAGE
Section 10 Overview			602A
	91	Solving Absolute-Value Inequalities	602
	92	Simplifying Complex Fractions	609
	93	Dividing Polynomials	616
	94	Solving Multi-Step Absolute-Value Equations	624
	95	Combining Rational Expressions with Unlike Denominators	631
Cumulative Assessment		Cumulative Test 18, Performance Task 18	
	96	Graphing Quadratic Functions	638
	LAB 9	**Graphing Calculator:** Graphing Linear Inequalities	645
	97	Graphing Linear Inequalities **Exploration:** Graphing Inequalities	647
	98	Solving Quadratic Equations by Factoring	655
	99	Solving Rational Equations	662
	100	Solving Quadratic Equations by Graphing	669
Cumulative Assessment		Cumulative Test 19, Performance Task 19, Benchmark Test 5	
	INV 10	**Investigation:** Transforming Quadratic Functions	676

Section 11: Lessons 101-110, Investigation 11

		PAGE
Section 11 Overview		678A
101	Solving Multi-Step Absolute-Value Inequalities	678
102	Solving Quadratic Equations Using Square Roots	684
103	Dividing Radical Expressions	691
104	Solving Quadratic Equations by Completing the Square **Exploration:** Modeling Completing the Square	697
105	Recognizing and Extending Geometric Sequences	705
Cumulative Assessment	Cumulative Test 20, Performance Task 20	
106	Solving Radical Equations	712
107	Graphing Absolute-Value Functions	720
108	Identifying and Graphing Exponential Functions	727
109	Graphing Systems of Linear Inequalities	735
110	Using the Quadratic Formula	742
Cumulative Assessment	Cumulative Test 21, Performance Task 21	
INV 11	**Investigation:** Investigating Exponential Growth and Decay **Exploration:** Analyzing Different Values of k in the Exponential Growth Function	749

DISTRIBUTED STRANDS

- Algebra Foundations
- Functions and Relations
- Equations
- Linear Equations and Functions
- Polynomials
- Rational Expressions and Functions
- Inequalities
- Systems of Equations and Inequalities
- Radical Expressions and Functions
- Quadratic Equations and Functions
- Absolute-Value Equations and Inequalities
- Probability and Data Analysis

Section 12: Lessons 111-120, Investigation 12

		PAGE
Section 12 Overview		754A
111	Solving Problems Involving Permutations **Exploration:** Finding Possibilities When Order is Important	754
112	Graphing and Solving Systems of Linear and Quadratic Equations	761
113	Interpreting the Discriminant	769
LAB 10	**Graphing Calculator:** Graphing Radical Functions	775
114	Graphing Square-Root Functions	776
115	Graphing Cubic Functions	782
Cumulative Assessment Cumulative Test 22, Performance Task 22		
116	Solving Simple and Compound Interest Problems	788
117	Using Trigonometric Ratios	796
118	Solving Problems Involving Combinations	804
119	Graphing and Comparing Linear, Quadratic, and Exponential Functions	809
120	Using Geometric Formulas to Find the Probability of an Event	817
LAB 11	**Graphing Calculator:** Matrix Operations	824
Cumulative Assessment Cumulative Test 23, Performance Task 23, End-of-Course Exam		
INV 12	**Investigation:** Investigating Matrices **Exploration:** Using Matrix Addition to Transform Geometric Figures **Exploration:** Using Scalar Multiplication to Transform Geometric Figures	826

Saxon Algebra 1

Appendix — 830

LESSON		PAGE
1	Graphing and Solving Nonlinear Inequalities	830
2	Graphing Piecewise and Step Functions	833
3	Understanding Vectors	837
4	Using Variance and Standard Deviation to Analyze Data	840
5	Evaluating Expressions with Technology	843

Skills Bank — 846

LESSON		PAGE
1	Compare and Order Rational Numbers	846
2	Decimal Operations	847
3	Fraction Operations	848
4	Divisibility	849
5	Equivalent Decimals, Fractions, and Percents	850
6	Repeating Decimals and Equivalent Fractions	851
7	Equivalent Fractions	852
8	Estimation Strategies	853
9	Greatest Common Factor (GCF)	854
10	Least Common Multiple (LCM) and Least Common Denominator (LCD)	855
11	Mental Math	856
12	Prime and Composite Numbers and Prime Factorization	857
13	Classify Angles and Triangles	858
14	Classify Quadrilaterals	860
15	Complementary and Supplementary Angles	861
16	Congruence	862
17	Estimate the Perimeter and Area of Figures	863
18	Nets	864
19	Parts of a Circle	865
20	Perspective Drawing	866
21	Surface Area of Prisms and Pyramids	867
22	Tessellations	868
23	Three-Dimensional Figures	869
24	Transformations in the Coordinate Plane	870
25	Vertical Angles	871
26	Volume of Prisms and Cylinders	872
27	Making Bar and Line Graphs	873
28	Making Circle Graphs	874
29	Making Line Plots	875
30	Venn Diagrams	876
31	Problem-Solving Strategies	877

Properties and Formulas — 884

	PAGE
Properties	884
Formulas	886
Symbols	887
Metric Measures	888
Customary Measures	888

Glossary — T889

Additional Answers — T899

Index — T913

Content By Strand

LESSON

ALGEBRA FOUNDATIONS

Lesson	Title
1	Classifying Real Numbers
2	Understanding Variables and Expressions
3	Simplifying Expressions Using the Product Property of Exponents
4	Using Order of Operations
5	Finding Absolute Value and Adding Real Numbers
6	Subtracting Real Numbers
7	Simplifying and Comparing Expressions with Symbols of Inclusion
8	Using Unit Analysis to Convert Measures
9	Evaluating and Comparing Algebraic Expressions
10	Adding and Subtracting Real Numbers
11	Multiplying and Dividing Real Numbers
12	Using the Properties of Real Numbers to Simplify Expressions
13	Calculating and Comparing Square Roots
15	Using the Distributive Property to Simplify Expressions
16	Simplifying and Evaluating Variable Expressions
17	Translating Between Words and Algebraic Expressions
32	Simplifying and Evaluating Expressions with Integer and Zero Exponents
37	Using Scientific Notation
40	Simplifying and Evaluating Expressions Using the Power Property for Exponents
INV 4	Investigation: Using Deductive and Inductive Reasoning
46	Simplifying Expressions with Square Roots and Higher-Order Roots
INV 5	Investigation: Using Logical Reasoning

FUNCTIONS AND RELATIONS

Lesson	Title
20	Graphing on a Coordinate Plane
INV 2	Investigation: Graphing a Relationship
25	Differentiating Between Relationships and Functions
LAB 2	Graphing Calculator: Creating a Table
30	Graphing Functions
34	Recognizing and Extending Arithmetic Sequences
105	Recognizing and Extending Geometric Sequences
108	Identifying and Graphing Exponential Functions
INV 11	Investigation: Investigating Exponential Growth and Decay
115	Graphing Cubic Functions
116	Solving Simple and Compound Interest Problems
119	Graphing and Comparing Linear, Quadratic, and Exponential Functions

Saxon Algebra 1

LESSON	
EQUATIONS	
18	Combining Like Terms
19	Solving One-Step Equations by Adding or Subtracting
21	Solving One-Step Equations by Multiplying or Dividing
23	Solving Two-Step Equations
24	Solving Decimal Equations
26	Solving Multi-Step Equations
28	Solving Equations with Variables on Both Sides
29	Solving Literal Equations
31	Using Rates, Ratios, and Proportions
36	Writing and Solving Proportions
42	Solving Percent Problems
47	Solving Problems Involving the Percent of Change
117	Using Trigonometric Ratios
LINEAR EQUATIONS AND FUNCTIONS	
35	Locating and Using Intercepts
41	Finding Rates of Change and Slope
44	Finding Slope Using the Slope Formula
LAB 3	Graphing Calculator: Graphing Linear Functions
49	Writing Equations in Slope-Intercept Form
52	Determining the Equation of a Line Given Two Points
56	Identifying, Writing, and Graphing Direct Variation
INV 6	Investigation: Transforming Linear Functions
64	Identifying, Writing, and Graphing Inverse Variation
65	Writing Equations of Parallel and Perpendicular Lines
INV 7	Investigation: Comparing Direct and Inverse Variation
INV 8	Investigation: Identifying and Writing Joint Variation
POLYNOMIALS	
38	Simplifying Expressions Using the GCF
53	Adding and Subtracting Polynomials
58	Multiplying Polynomials
60	Finding Special Products of Binomials
72	Factoring Trinomials: $x^2 + bx + c$
75	Factoring Trinomials: $ax^2 + bx + c$
79	Factoring Trinomials by Using the GCF
83	Factoring Special Products
87	Factoring Polynomials by Grouping
INV 9	Investigation: Choosing a Factoring Method
93	Dividing Polynomials

LESSON	
RATIONAL EXPRESSIONS AND FUNCTIONS	
39	Using the Distributive Property to Simplify Rational Expressions
43	Simplifying Rational Expressions
51	Simplifying Rational Expressions with Like Denominators
57	Finding the Least Common Multiple
78	Graphing Rational Functions
88	Multiplying and Dividing Rational Expressions
90	Adding and Subtracting Rational Expressions
92	Simplifying Complex Fractions
95	Combining Rational Expressions with Unlike Denominators
99	Solving Rational Equations
INEQUALITIES	
45	Translating Between Words and Inequalities
50	Graphing Inequalities
66	Solving Inequalities by Adding or Subtracting
70	Solving Inequalities by Multiplying or Dividing
73	Solving Compound Inequalities
77	Solving Two-Step and Multi-Step Inequalities
81	Solving Inequalities with Variables on Both Sides
82	Solving Multi-Step Compound Inequalities
SYSTEMS OF EQUATIONS AND INEQUALITIES	
LAB 5	Graphing Calculator: Calculating the Intersection of Two Lines
55	Solving Systems of Linear Equations by Graphing
59	Solving Systems of Linear Equations by Substitution
63	Solving Systems of Linear Equations by Elimination
67	Solving and Classifying Special Systems of Linear Equations
LAB 9	Graphing Calculator: Graphing Linear Inequalities
97	Graphing Linear Inequalities
109	Graphing Systems of Linear Inequalities
112	Graphing and Solving Systems of Linear and Quadratic Equations
LAB 11	Graphing Calculator: Matrix Operations
INV 12	Investigation: Investigating Matrices
RADICAL EXPRESSIONS AND FUNCTIONS	
61	Simplifying Radical Expressions
69	Adding and Subtracting Radical Expressions
76	Multiplying Radical Expressions
103	Dividing Radical Expressions
106	Solving Radical Equations
LAB 10	Graphing Calculator: Graphing Radical Functions
114	Graphing Square-Root Functions

Saxon Algebra 1

LESSON	
QUADRATIC EQUATIONS AND FUNCTIONS	
84	Identifying Quadratic Functions
85	Solving Problems Using the Pythagorean Theorem
86	Calculating the Midpoint and Length of a Segment
LAB 8	Graphing Calculator: Characteristics of Parabolas
89	Identifying Characteristics of Quadratic Functions
96	Graphing Quadratic Functions
98	Solving Quadratic Equations by Factoring
100	Solving Quadratic Equations by Graphing
INV 10	Investigation: Transforming Quadratic Functions
102	Solving Quadratic Equations Using Square Roots
104	Solving Quadratic Equations by Completing the Square
110	Using the Quadratic Formula
113	Interpreting the Discriminant
ABSOLUTE-VALUE EQUATIONS AND INEQUALITIES	
74	Solving Absolute-Value Equations
91	Solving Absolute-Value Inequalities
94	Solving Multi-Step Absolute-Value Equations
101	Solving Multi-Step Absolute-Value Inequalities
107	Graphing Absolute-Value Functions
PROBABILITY AND DATA ANALYSIS	
LAB 1	Graphing Calculator: Generating Random Numbers
INV 1	Investigation: Determining the Probability of an Event
14	Determining the Theoretical Probability of an Event
22	Analyzing and Comparing Statistical Graphs
27	Identifying Misleading Representations of Data
INV 3	Investigation: Analyzing the Effects of Bias in Sampling, Surveys and Bar Graphs
33	Finding the Probability of Independent and Dependent Events
48	Analyzing Measures of Central Tendency
LAB 4	Graphing Calculator: Drawing Box-and-Whisker Plots
54	Displaying Data in a Box-and-Whisker Plot
LAB 6	Graphing Calculator: Drawing Histograms
62	Displaying Data in Stem-and-Leaf Plots and Histograms
68	Mutually Exclusive and Inclusive Events
LAB 7	Graphing Calculator: Finding the Line of Best Fit
71	Making and Analyzing Scatter Plots
80	Calculating Frequency Distributions
111	Solving Problems Involving Permutations
118	Solving Problems Involving Combinations
120	Using Geometric Formulas to Find the Probability of an Event

Pacing Guide

Pacing for the Year

The guide below will help you decide how to pace your instruction across the school year and how much time you have left in your schedule for other instructional or assessment options. For example, Benchmark Tests can be administered after every 20 lessons in order to check student progress. You can also assign Reteaching Masters or Challenge and Enrichment Masters to help struggling or advanced students.

Pacing Suggestions

The suggestions below for pacing each Section in a 45-minute class include one Lesson per day, one Investigation per day, and cumulative testing on two days. *See pages T8–T9 for more about the daily lesson structure.*

The suggestions on the next page will help you to sequence the instruction, practice, and assessment within a 90-minute block schedule.

Page A in each Section Overview gives day-by-day pacing for the lessons within that Section.

Section	Core Material to Cover	45-Minute Class	90-Minute Block *
1	Lessons 1–10; Investigation 1; Cumulative Test 1	12 days	6 days
2	Lessons 11–20; Investigation 2; Cumulative Tests 2, 3	13 days	7 days
3	Lessons 21–30; Investigation 3; Cumulative Tests 4, 5	13 days	6 days
4	Lessons 31–40; Investigation 4; Cumulative Tests 6, 7	13 days	7 days
5	Lessons 41–50; Investigation 5; Cumulative Tests 8, 9	13 days	6 days
6	Lessons 51–60; Investigation 6; Cumulative Tests 10, 11	13 days	7 days
7	Lessons 61–70; Investigation 7; Cumulative Tests 12, 13	13 days	6 days
8	Lessons 71–80; Investigation 8; Cumulative Tests 14, 15	13 days	7 days
9	Lessons 81–90; Investigation 9; Cumulative Tests 16, 17	13 days	6 days
10	Lessons 91–100; Investigation 10; Cumulative Tests 18, 19	13 days	7 days
11	Lessons 101–110; Investigation 11; Cumulative Tests 20, 21	13 days	6 days
12	Lessons 111–120; Investigation 12; Cumulative Tests 22, 23	13 days	7 days
	TOTAL	**155 days**	**78 days**

* For block scheduling, the pace is consistent. However, on some days, the suggested pacing calls for teaching an Investigation and the following lesson, which is in the next section.

You can use the Resources and Planner CD to map out your yearly schedule. The software can create a personalized schedule based on your school's calendar. If unexpected school cancellations or other events occur, you can easily use the pacing calendar in the software to produce a revised schedule.

Daily Pacing for Block Scheduling

For block class periods of 90 minutes, you should expect to (1) teach two lessons per class or (2) teach one lesson and give a Cumulative Test. Sometimes the lesson might be an Investigation so you may need to adjust your pacing accordingly. The charts below give just one suggestion on how to sequence your class instruction for each part of the class period.

Suggested Class Sequence for Non-Test Days

Two Lessons
Project the Warm Up from the first lesson. Have students work the problems as they enter the classroom.
Go over homework from the day before.
Instruct the New Concept from the first lesson.
Have students work the Lesson Practice from the first lesson.
Also have students work the problems for the first lesson that are in the Practice. These problems are indicated by the lesson's number in the student text.
If students have trouble sitting for the entire 90 minutes, you may want to have them work in groups or at the board.
Project the Warm Up from the second lesson.
Instruct the New Concept from the second lesson.
Have students work the Lesson Practice from the second lesson. Check their work while they are completing the problems.
Assign the remaining Practice problems from the first lesson and the Practice problems from the second lesson. Have students work some problems in class and complete the rest for homework.

One Lesson, One Investigation
Project the Warm Up from the lesson. Have students work the problems as they enter the classroom.
Go over homework from the day before.
Engage the students by working the Investigation in small groups or as a whole-class discussion activity.
Instruct the New Concept from the lesson.
Have students work the Lesson Practice from the lesson. Check their work while they are completing the problems.
Assign the Investigation Practice problems and the Practice problems from the lesson.
With the remaining time, have students begin work on the problems in class. Assign the rest as homework.

Suggested Class Sequence for Test Days

Cumulative Test, One Lesson
Have students take the Cumulative Test.
Project the Warm Up from the new lesson. Have students work the problems.
Go over homework from the day before.
Instruct the New Concept from the new lesson.
Have students work the Lesson Practice from the new lesson. Check their work while they are completing the problems.
Assign the Practice problems from the new lesson. Have students work some problems in class and complete the rest for homework. You can also assign the Performance Task, either as class work or homework.

Cumulative Test, One Investigation
Have students take the Cumulative Test.
Go over homework from the day before.
Engage the students by working the Investigation in small groups or as a whole-class discussion activity.
Assign the Investigation Practice problems. Have students begin work in class and complete the rest for homework. You can also assign the Performance Task, either as class work or homework.

Teaching Over Two Years

Sometimes Algebra 1 and Geometry are taught over two years. The pace is much slower and more time can be spent to explain concepts and to check thoroughly each homework Practice set. You can use additional program resources to adjust the pacing or to cover particular topics in more depth. Here is one suggested plan for each of the two years.

Year 1
Lessons 1–60
Investigations 1–6
Use Benchmark Test 3 after lesson 60 as the end-of-course exam for the first half of the book.

Year 2
Lessons 61–120
Investigations 7–12
Use the End-of-Course Exam to assess student progress on the entire course.

SECTION OVERVIEW
1

Lesson Planner

Lesson	New Concepts
1	Classifying Real Numbers
2	Understanding Variables and Expressions
3	Simplifying Expressions Using the Product Property of Exponents
4	Using Order of Operations
5	Finding Absolute Value and Adding Real Numbers
6	Subtracting Real Numbers
7	Simplifying and Comparing Expressions with Symbols of Inclusion
8	Using Unit Analysis to Convert Measures
9	Evaluating and Comparing Algebraic Expressions
10	Adding and Subtracting Real Numbers
LAB 1	Graphing Calculator: Generating Random Numbers
	Cumulative Test 1, Performance Task 1
INV 1	Investigation: Determining the Probability of an Event

Resources for Teaching
- Student Edition
- Teacher's Edition
- Student Edition eBook
- Teacher's Edition eBook
- Resources and Planner CD
- Solutions Manual
- Instructional Masters
- Technology Lab Masters
- Warm Up and Teaching Transparencies
- Instructional Presentations CD
- Online activities, tools, and homework help
  www.SaxonMathResources.com

Resources for Practice and Assessment
- Student Edition Practice Workbook
- Course Assessments
- Standardized Test Practice
- College Entrance Exam Practice
- Test and Practice Generator CD using ExamView™

Resources for Differentiated Instruction
- Reteaching Masters
- Challenge and Enrichment Masters
- Prerequisite Skills Intervention
- Adaptations for Saxon Algebra 1
- Multilingual Glossary
- English Learners Handbook
- TI Resources

Pacing Guide

 Resources and Planner CD for lesson planning support

45-Minute Class

Day 1	Day 2	Day 3	Day 4	Day 5	Day 6
Lesson 1	Lesson 2	Lesson 3	Lesson 4	Lesson 5	Lesson 6

Day 7	Day 8	Day 9	Day 10	Day 11	Day 12
Lesson 7	Lesson 8	Lesson 9	Lesson 10	Cumulative Test 1	Lab 1 Investigation 1

Block: 90-Minute Class

Day 1	Day 2	Day 3	Day 4	Day 5	Day 6
Lesson 1 Lesson 2	Lesson 3 Lesson 4	Lesson 5 Lesson 6	Lesson 7 Lesson 8	Lesson 9 Lesson 10	Cumulative Test 1 Lab 1 Investigation 1

* For suggestions on how to implement Saxon Math in a block schedule, see the Pacing section at the beginning of the Teacher's Edition.

Lessons 1–10, Investigation 1

Differentiated Instruction

Below Level

Warm Up	SE pp. 2, 7, 12, 17, 22, 27, 31, 36, 43, 47
Skills Bank	SE pp. 846–883
Reteaching Masters	Lessons 1–10, Investigation 1
Warm Up Transparencies	Lessons 1–10
Prerequisite Skills Intervention	Skills 7, 8, 11, 14, 16, 17, 18, 19, 20, 21, 43, 44, 51, 52, 54, 55, 59, 60, 89

Advanced Learners

Challenge	TE pp. 6, 10, 16, 21, 26, 30, 35, 41, 46, 51
Extend the Example	TE pp. 3, 8, 14, 19, 24, 28, 33, 39, 44, 48
Extend the Exploration	TE pp. 23, 37, 53
Extend the Problem	TE pp. 6, 10, 16, 21, 26, 29, 35, 41, 46, 50, 51, 54
Challenge and Enrichment Masters	Challenge 1–10; Enrichment 3, 4

English Learners

EL Tips	TE pp. 3, 8, 14, 18, 24, 28, 34, 37, 45, 48, 54
Multilingual Glossary	Booklet and Online
English Learners Handbook	

Special Needs

Inclusion Tips	TE pp. 3, 9, 15, 20, 25, 29, 33, 40, 45, 50
Adaptations for Saxon Algebra 1	Lessons 1–10; Cumulative Test 1

For All Learners

Exploration	SE pp. 23, 37, 53
Caution	SE pp. 12, 19
Hints	SE pp. 8, 18, 19, 23, 32, 36, 39, 47, 48, 54
Error Alert	TE pp. 3, 5, 6, 8, 9, 10, 11, 12, 14, 18, 19, 21, 24, 25, 26, 28, 29, 30, 33, 35, 39, 41, 43, 44, 45, 47, 49, 50, 54, 55
Alternate Method	TE pp. 4, 9, 13, 19, 24, 28, 32, 38, 44
Manipulative Use	TE pp. 5
Online Tools	

SE = Student Edition; TE = Teacher's Edition

Math Vocabulary

Lesson	New Vocabulary		Maintained	EL Tip in TE
1	closure counterexample empty set finite set infinite set integers intersection of sets	irrational numbers natural numbers rational numbers real numbers set union whole numbers	decimal difference digit fraction opposites simplest form sum Venn diagram	balance
2	coefficient constant factor	terms of an expression variable	expression product quotient	term
3	base of a power exponent	order of magnitude	factor repeated multiplication	base
4	order of operations simplify		exponent	operation
5	absolute value		counterexample integers real numbers	down
6	additive inverse opposites		absolute value	inverse
7			order of operations variable	innermost
8			area perimeter volume	unit
9	algebraic expression numeric expression		evaluate exponent	expression
10			rational	quarter
INV 1	event experimental probability outcome	probability random event simulation	as likely as not certain impossible likely unlikely	simulation

Section Overview 1   **2B**

SECTION OVERVIEW 1

Math Highlights

Enduring Understandings – The "Big Picture"
After completing Section 1, students will understand:
- How to classify real numbers and identify counterexamples.
- How to identify variables and constants in algebraic expressions.
- How to evaluate and simplify expressions using the order of operations and exponent rules.
- How to find the absolute value and add and subtract integers.
- How to convert units of measure.
- How to find probability by using experiments and simulations.

Essential Questions
- What is the difference between evaluating and simplifying algebraic expressions?
- What are real numbers and how do you perform operations with real numbers?
- When are exponent rules and the order of operations applied?
- What is the purpose of finding experimental probability?

Math Content Strands	Math Processes
Algebra Foundations	**Reasoning and Communication**
• Lesson 1 Classifying Real Numbers	*Lessons*
• Lesson 2 Understanding Variables and Expressions	• Analyze 6, 8, 9
• Lesson 3 Simplifying Expressions Using the Product Property of Exponents	• Error analysis 1, 2, 3, 4, 5, 6, 7, 8, 9, 10
	• Estimate 3, 5
• Lesson 4 Using Order of Operations	• Formulate 5
• Lesson 5 Finding Absolute Value and Adding Real Numbers	• Generalize 3
	• Justify 7, 8
• Lesson 6 Subtracting Real Numbers	• Math Reasoning 2, 3, 6, 8, 9
• Lesson 7 Simplifying and Comparing Expressions with Symbols of Inclusion	• Model 5, 6, 10
	• Multiple choice 1, 2, 3, 4, 5, 6, 7, 8, 9, 10
• Lesson 8 Using Unit Analysis to Convert Measures	• Multi–step 1, 2, 3, 4, 5, 6, 7, 8, 9, 10
• Lesson 9 Evaluating and Comparing Algebraic Expressions	• Predict Inv. 1
	• True or False 1, 3, 4, 5, 7, 8, 9, 10
• Lesson 10 Adding and Subtracting Real Numbers	• Verify 1, 2, 3, 4, 5, 7, 9, Inv. 1
	• Write 1, 2, 3, 4, 5, 6, 7, 8, 9, 10
Probability and Data Analysis	
• Lab 1 Graphing Calculator: Generating Random Numbers	• Graphing Calculator 7, Lab 1, Inv. 1
• Investigation 1 Determining the Probability of an Event	**Connections**
Connections in Practice Problems	**In Examples:** Comparing a crop circle to a soccer field, Converting units of currency, Dive depth, Football, Foreign travel, Half price sale, Investing, Phone charges, Speed of a supercomputer, Telecommunications
Lessons	
Data Analysis 9	
Geometry 1, 2, 3, 4, 5, 6, 7, 8, 9, 10	
Measurement 1, 2, 3, 4, 5, 6, 7, 10	**In Practice problems:** Anatomy, Aquarium, Astronomy, Attendance, Bacteria, Banking, Billing, Biology, Boating, Camping, Canoeing, Chemistry, Climate, Consumer Math, Cooking, Cost Analysis, Cycling, Economics, Entertainment, Fencing, Flight, Football, Golf, Health, Loans, Lunar rover, Manufacturing, Meteorology, Oceanography, Population, Quality Assurance, Remodeling, School supplies, Speed, Sports, Stocks, Swimming, Temperature, Time, Track practice, Transportation, Typing, Weather, Weather forecasting

Content Trace

Lessons 1–10, Investigation 1

Lesson	Warm Up: Prerequisite Skills	New Concepts	Where Practiced	Where Assessed	Looking Forward
1	Skills Bank 5, 30	Classifying Real Numbers	Lessons 2, 3, 4, 5, 6, 7, 8, 10, 11, 13, 14, 16, 17, 21, 22, 23, 24, 27, 28, 33, 34, 35, 39, 40, 50	Cumulative Tests 1, 2, 3, 6	Lessons 5, 6, 10, 11, 12
2	Skills Bank 2, 3	Understanding Variables and Expressions	Lessons 3, 4, 5, 6, 12, 14, 17, 20, 21, 24, 26, 29	Cumulative Tests 1, 2, 5, 10	Lessons 3, 4, 5, 23, 29
3	Lesson 2, Skills Bank 2, 3	Simplifying Expressions Using the Product Property of Exponents	Lessons 4, 5, 6, 8, 12, 15, 19, 21, 22, 23, 24, 25, 26, 29, 30, 37	Cumulative Tests 1, 2, 3, 5, 6	Lessons 4, 7, 9, 16
4	Lesson 3, Skills Bank 2, 3	Using Order of Operations	Lessons 5, 6, 7, 8, 9, 10, 11, 12, 13, 14, 16, 17, 18, 19, 20, 22, 23, 24, 26, 27, 30, 31, 36, 37, 45, 53	Cumulative Tests 1, 2, 3, 5, 6	Lessons 7, 9, 12, 16
5	Lesson 1, Skills Bank 2, 3	Finding Absolute Value and Adding Real Numbers	Lessons 6, 7, 8, 10, 11, 12, 13, 14, 15, 17, 18, 19, 20, 21, 23, 24, 27	Cumulative Tests 1, 2, 3, 4, 5, 6	Lessons 6, 7, 10, 11, 12
6	Lesson 1, Skills Bank 2, 3	Subtracting Real Numbers	Lessons 7, 8, 9, 11, 12, 13, 14, 15, 16, 18, 19, 21, 22, 25, 26, 27, 28, 29	Cumulative Tests 2, 3, 4, 8	Lessons 7, 16, 18, 19
7	Lessons 2, 4	Simplifying and Comparing Algebraic Expressions	Lessons 8, 9, 10, 11, 12, 13, 14, 15, 16, 20, 23, 26, 27, 29, 30, 68	Cumulative Tests 2, 4, 5, 14	Lessons 9, 12, 15, 16
8	Skills Bank 3, 26	Using Unit Analysis to Convert Measures	Lessons 9, 10, 11, 12, 13, 14, 15, 16, 17, 18, 20, 21, 23, 24, 26, 27, 28, 30, 45	Cumulative Tests 2, 3, 4, 5, 6, 7, 8	Lessons 11, 12, 16
9	Lessons 2, 3, 4, 7	Evaluating and Comparing Algebraic Expressions	Lessons 10, 11, 12, 13, 14, 15, 16, 17, 19, 21, 22, 23, 24, 25, 27, 28, 29, 35, 46, 47, 55	Cumulative Tests 2, 3, 5, 8	Lessons 12, 13, 15, 32
10	Lessons 1, 3, 4, 5	Adding and Subtracting Real Numbers	Lessons 11, 12, 13, 14, 15, 16, 17, 18, 19, 20, 22, 23, 24, 25, 26, 29, 30, 31	Cumulative Tests 2, 3, 4, 6, 7, 8	Lessons 13, 17, 32, 40
INV 1	N/A	Investigation: Determining the Experimental Probability of an Event	Lessons 11, 13, 15, 16, 22, 23, 24, 26, 29	Cumulative Tests 3, 4	Lessons 14, 33, 68, 80

SECTION OVERVIEW 1

Ongoing Assessment

	Type	Feature	Intervention *
BEFORE instruction	Assess Prior Knowledge	• Diagnostic Test	• Prerequisite Skills Intervention
BEFORE the lesson	Formative	• Warm Up	• Skills Bank • Reteaching Masters
DURING the lesson	Formative	• Lesson Practice • Math Conversations with the Practice problems	• Additional Examples in TE • Test and Practice Generator (for additional practice sheets)
AFTER the lesson	Formative	• Check for Understanding (closure)	• Scaffolding Questions in TE
AFTER 5 lessons	Summative	After Lesson 10 • Cumulative Test 1 • Performance Task 1	• Reteaching Masters • Test and Practice Generator (for additional tests and practice)
AFTER 20 lessons	Summative	• Benchmark Tests	• Reteaching Masters • Test and Practice Generator (for additional tests and practice)

* for students not showing progress during the formative stages or scoring below 80% on the summative assessments

Evidence of Learning – What Students Should Know

Because the Saxon philosophy is to provide students with sufficient time to learn and practice each concept, a lesson's topic will not be tested until at least five lessons after the topic is introduced.

On the Cumulative Test that is given during this section of ten lessons, students should be able to demonstrate the following competencies:
- Simplify and compare expressions using order of operations and exponent rules.
- Add real numbers.
- Find the absolute value.
- Identify variables, constants, and terms.
- Identify subsets of real numbers and a closed set under a given operation.

Test and Practice Generator CD using ExamView™

The Test and Practice Generator is an easy-to-use benchmark and assessment tool that creates unlimited practice and tests in multiple formats and allows you to customize questions or create new ones. A variety of reports are available to track student progress toward mastery of the standards throughout the year.

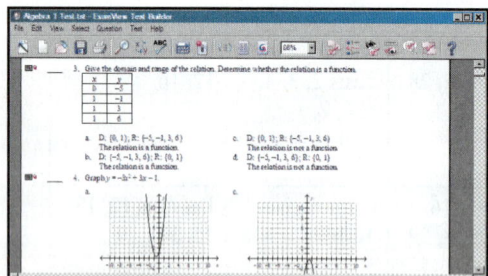 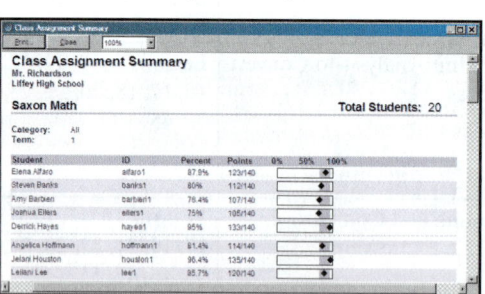

Saxon Algebra 1

Lessons 1–10, Investigation 1

Assessment Resources

Resources for Diagnosing and Assessing

- **Student Edition**
  - Warm Up
  - Lesson Practice

- **Teacher's Edition**
  - Math Conversations with the Practice problems
  - Check for Understanding (closure)

- **Course Assessments**
  - Diagnostic Test
  - Cumulative Tests
  - Performance Tasks
  - Benchmark Tests

Resources for Test Prep

- **Student Edition Practice**
  - Multiple-choice problems
  - Multiple-step and writing problems
  - Daily cumulative practice

- **Standardized Test Practice**

- **College Entrance Exam Practice**

- **Test and Practice Generator CD using ExamView™**

Resources for Intervention

- **Student Edition**
  - Skills Bank

- **Teacher's Edition**
  - Additional Examples
  - Scaffolding questions

- **Prerequisite Skills Intervention**
  - Worksheets

- **Reteaching Masters**
  - Lesson instruction and practice sheets

- **Test and Practice Generator CD using ExamView™**
  - Lesson practice problems
  - Additional tests

Cumulative Tests

The assessments in Saxon Math are frequent and consistently placed after every five lessons beginning with Cumulative Test 1 at the end of Section 1. These cumulative assessments offer a regular method of ongoing testing and check mastery of concepts from previous lessons.

Performance Tasks

The Performance Tasks can be used in conjunction with the Cumulative Tests and are scored using a rubric.

After Lesson 10   **For use with Performance Tasks**

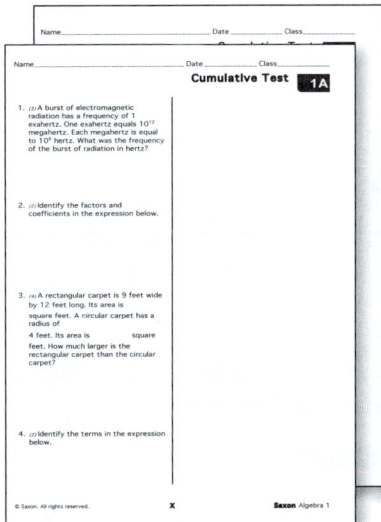

Section Overview 1   2F

LESSON 1

Warm Up

Problem 5
Write the digits to the right of the decimal point as a fraction over 100. Encourage students to use mental math to simplify the fraction. Think quarters.

$$\frac{75}{100} = \frac{25 \cdot 3}{25 \cdot 4} = \frac{3}{4}$$

2 New Concepts

In this lesson, students learn to classify real numbers.

Discuss the subsets of real numbers. Be sure to point out the relationships between the subsets. For example, every whole number is also an integer, but every integer is not a whole number.

TEACHER TIP
Use the Venn diagram to discuss how sets of numbers are related. Encourage students to copy the Venn diagram and to add common examples of each type of number.

LESSON RESOURCES

Student Edition Practice Workbook 1
Reteaching Master 1
Adaptations Master 1
Challenge and Enrichment Master C1

LESSON 1

Classifying Real Numbers

Warm Up

1. Vocabulary A _____ (Venn diagram, line plot) shows the relationship between sets.   **Venn diagram**

Write each fraction as a decimal.

2. $\frac{2}{9}$ $0.\overline{2}$

3. $4\frac{3}{8}$ 4.375

Write each decimal as a fraction in simplest form.

4. 0.6 $\frac{3}{5}$

5. 5.75 $5\frac{3}{4}$

New Concepts

A **set** is a collection of objects. Each object in the set is called an element. A set is written by enclosing the elements within braces. There are three types of sets. A set with no elements is called the null or **empty set**. A set with a finite number of elements is a **finite set**. An **infinite set** has an infinite number of elements.

{12, 24, 36}   {1, 3, 5,...}   { } or ∅
finite set   infinite set   null or empty set

The subsets of real numbers are infinite sets.

Subsets of Real Numbers	
Natural Numbers	The numbers used to count objects or things. {1, 2, 3, 4,...}
Whole Numbers	The set of natural numbers and zero. {0, 1, 2, 3, 4,...}
Integers	The set of whole numbers and the opposites of the natural numbers. {..., −4, −3, −2, −1, 0, 1, 2, 3, 4,...}
Rational Numbers	Numbers that can be written in the form $\frac{a}{b}$, where a and b are integers and $b \neq 0$. In decimal form, rational numbers either terminate or repeat. Examples: $\frac{1}{2}, 0.\overline{3}, -\frac{2}{3}, 0.125$
Irrational Numbers	Numbers that cannot be written as the quotient of two integers. In decimal form, irrational numbers neither terminate nor repeat. Examples: $\sqrt[3]{5}, \sqrt{2}, -\sqrt{2}, 3\sqrt{3}, \pi, 3\pi$
Real Numbers	The set including all rational and irrational numbers.

Reading Math
The three dots inside the braces are called an ellipsis. An ellipsis shows that the numbers in the set continue on without end.

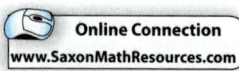
Online Connection
www.SaxonMathResources.com

MATH BACKGROUND

Using the Venn diagram, students can make logic proofs about set members. Students can use logic even if they do not know how to do formal proofs. Here is a formal proof that 3 is a real number:

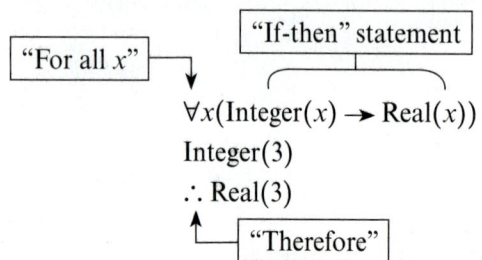

A common logical error is called affirming the consequent. For example:

$\forall x(\text{Integer}(x) \rightarrow \text{Real}(x))$

Real(3)

∴ Integer(3)

Although the conclusion is true, the argument is not valid. You can show this by applying the same proof for a counterexample such as $x = 3.25$.

2   *Saxon* Algebra 1

The Venn diagram below shows how the sets of numbers are related.

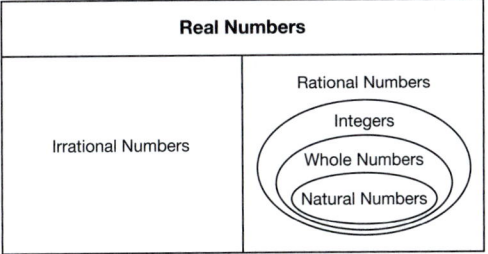

Example 1 Identifying Sets

For each number, identify the subsets of real numbers to which it belongs.

a. $\frac{1}{2}$

SOLUTION

{rational numbers, real numbers}

b. 5

SOLUTION

{natural numbers, whole numbers, integers, rational numbers, real numbers}

c. $3\sqrt{2}$

SOLUTION

{irrational numbers, real numbers}

Example 2 Identifying Sets for Real-World Situations

Identify the set of numbers that best describes each situation. Explain your choice.

a. the value of the bills in a person's wallet

SOLUTION The set of whole numbers best describes the situation. The wallet may contain no bills or any number of bills.

b. the balance of a checking account

SOLUTION The set of rational numbers best describes the situation. The balance could be positive or negative and may contain decimal amounts.

c. the circumference of a circular table when the diameter is a rational number

SOLUTION The set of irrational numbers describes the situation. Since circumference is equal to the diameter multiplied by pi, it will be an irrational number.

Math Language

The set of natural numbers is a **subset** of the set of real numbers because every natural number is a real number.

Each day brings you a **New Concept** where a new topic is introduced and explained through thorough **Examples** — using a variety of methods and real-world applications.

You will be reviewing and building on this concept throughout the year to gain a solid understanding and ensure mastery on the test.

Lesson 1   3

Example 1

Error Alert Students may only list some of the sets of which a number is a member. Encourage students to adopt a systematic approach. Suggest that they start working from the most specific set and that they work toward the most general set. Remind the students that a set is a subset of itself. Real numbers are therefore included in the solution.

Extend the Example

Identify the subsets of real numbers to which 2.3 and $2.\overline{3}$ belong. {rational numbers, real numbers}

Additional Example 1

For each number, identify the subsets of real numbers to which each number belongs.

a. 9 {natural numbers, whole numbers, integers, rational numbers, real numbers}

b. $5\sqrt{3}$ {irrational numbers, real numbers}

c. $\frac{1}{4}$ {rational numbers, real numbers}

Example 2

It may help students to think of specific numbers for each situation to make the connection with the appropriate set of numbers.

Additional Example 2

Identify the set of numbers that best describes each situation.

a. the cost of an item at a store rational numbers

b. the number of points a team scores in a football game whole numbers

c. the surface area of a sphere where the radius is a rational number irrational numbers

Lesson 1   3

INCLUSION

Students may benefit from creating tables to show set relationships. Read across the row to fill in the table. Make a column for each subset of real numbers.

Set	Natural	Whole
all natural numbers are	true	true
all whole numbers are	false	true
all integers are	false	false

ENGLISH LEARNERS

In Example 2, explain the meaning of the word **balance.** Say:

"The balance of a checking account is the amount of money in the account."

Ask students to give examples of actions that would change the balance of a checking account. Sample: writing a check, making a deposit

Ask:

"Anna has $223.15 in her checking account. If she writes a check for $37.50, what is the balance in her account?" $185.65

Example 3

Suggest that students circle the numbers that are in both sets. The circled numbers represent the intersection of the two sets. When writing the union of the two sets, the circled numbers should only be listed once.

Additional Example 3

Find $A \cap B$ and $A \cup B$.

a. $A = \{4, 8, 12, 16\}$;
   $B = \{5, 8, 11, 14, 17\}$
   $A \cap B = \{8\}; A \cup B =$
   $\{4, 5, 8, 11, 12, 14, 16, 17\}$

b. $A = \{1, 3, 5, 7, 9\}$;
   $B = \{2, 4, 6, 8\}$
   $A \cap B = \{\}$ or $\emptyset$; $A \cup B =$
   $\{1, 2, 3, 4, 5, 6, 7, 8, 9\}$

Example 4

Explain how a counterexample proves an assertion wrong.

"Suppose I claimed that all lobsters are red. What could you do to prove I was wrong?" Sample: show a green lobster

"What does a green lobster show?" Sample: There exists a lobster that is not red, so not all lobsters are red.

Additional Example 4

Determine whether each statement is true or false. Give a counterexample if false.

a. The set of integers is closed under addition. true

b. The set of natural numbers is closed under subtraction. Sample: $2 - 4 = -2$ is a counterexample. The difference is not a natural number. The statement is false.

The **intersection of sets** A and B, $A \cap B$, is the set of elements that are in A and B. The **union** of A and B, $A \cup B$, is the set of all elements that are in A or B.

Example 3 — Finding Intersections and Unions of Sets

Find $A \cap B$ and $A \cup B$.

a. $A = \{2, 4, 6, 8, 10, 12\}; B = \{3, 6, 9, 12\}$

SOLUTION

$A \cap B = \{6, 12\}; A \cup B = \{2, 3, 4, 6, 8, 9, 10, 12\}$

b. $A = \{11, 13, 15, 17\}; B = \{12, 14, 16, 18\}$

SOLUTION

$A \cap B = \{\ \}$ or $\emptyset$; $A \cup B = \{11, 12, 13, 14, 15, 16, 17, 18\}$

A set of numbers has **closure,** or is closed, under a given operation if the outcome of the operation on any two members of the set is also a member of the set. For example, the sum of any two natural numbers is also a natural number. Therefore, the set of natural numbers is closed under addition.

One example is all that is needed to prove that a statement is false. An example that proves a statement false is called a **counterexample**.

Example 4 — Identifying a Closed Set Under a Given Operation

Determine whether each statement is true or false. Give a counterexample for false statements.

a. The set of whole numbers is closed under addition.

SOLUTION

Verify the statement by adding two whole numbers.

$2 + 3 = 5$

$9 + 11 = 20$

$100 + 1000 = 1100$

The sum is always a whole number.

The statement is true.

b. The set of whole number is closed under subtraction.

SOLUTION

Verify the statement by subtracting two whole numbers.

$6 - 4 = 2$

$100 - 90 = 10$

$4 - 6 = -2$

$4 - 6$ is a counterexample. The difference is not a whole number.

The statement is false.

ALTERNATE METHOD FOR EXAMPLE 3

Make a Venn diagram to show the relationship between sets A and B. The numbers in the overlap of the two circles represent the intersection of the two sets. All the numbers included in either circle represent the union of the two sets.

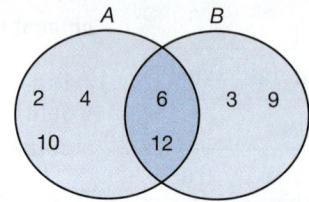

Lesson Practice

For each number, identify the subsets of real numbers to which it belongs.
(Ex 1)
a. -73
b. $\frac{5}{9}$
c. 18π

a. integers, rational numbers, real numbers
b. rational numbers, real numbers
c. irrational numbers, real numbers

Identify the set of numbers that best describes each situation. Explain your choice.
(Ex 2)
d. the number of people on a bus   whole numbers; Sample: There can be no people or any number of people.
e. the area of a circular platform   irrational numbers; Sample: Area is equal to pi times the radius squared, so the answer will be irrational.
f. the value of coins in a purse   rational numbers; Sample: The value of the coins will have tenths and hundredths places.

Find $C \cap D$ and $C \cup D$.
(Ex 3)
g. $C = \{4, 8, 12, 16, 20\}; D = \{5, 10, 15, 20\}$ g. $C \cap D = \{20\}; C \cup D = \{4, 5, 8, 10, 12, 15, 16, 20\}$
h. $C = \{6, 12, 18, 24\}; D = \{7, 14, 21, 28\}$
$C \cap D = \{\ \}$ or $\varnothing$; $C \cup D = \{6, 7, 12, 14, 18, 21, 24, 28\}$

Verify Determine whether each statement is true or false. Provide a counterexample for false statements.
(Ex 4)
i. The set of whole numbers is closed under multiplication.   true
j. The set of natural numbers is closed under division.
false; counterexample: $1 \div 2 = 0.5$

Practice   Distributed and Integrated

1. Multiply 26.1×6.15.   160.515
(SB 2)

2. Add $\frac{4}{7} + \frac{1}{8} + \frac{1}{2}$. $\frac{67}{56}$ or $1\frac{11}{56}$
(SB 3)

3. Divide $954 \div 0.9$.   1060
(SB 2)

4. Add $\frac{3}{5} + \frac{1}{8} + \frac{1}{8}$. $\frac{17}{20}$
(SB 3)

5. Write $\frac{3}{8}$ as a decimal.   0.375
(SB 5)

6. Write $0.66\overline{6}$ as a fraction. $\frac{2}{3}$
(SB 6)

7. Add $2\frac{1}{2} + 3\frac{1}{5}$. $5\frac{7}{10}$
(SB 3)

8. Name a fraction equivalent to $\frac{2}{5}$.
(SB 7) Sample: $\frac{4}{10}$

9. **Error Analysis** Two students determine the prime factorization of 72. Which student is correct? Explain the error.   Student B; Sample: Student A did not factor the 9 completely.
(SB 12)

Student A	Student B
72	72
$= 9 \cdot 8$	$= 9 \cdot 8$
$= 9 \cdot 4 \cdot 2$	$= 9 \cdot 4 \cdot 2$
$= 9 \cdot 2 \cdot 2 \cdot 2$	$= 3 \cdot 3 \cdot 2 \cdot 2 \cdot 2$

10. Find the prime factorization of 144. $2 \cdot 2 \cdot 2 \cdot 2 \cdot 3 \cdot 3$
(SB 12)

11. Write 0.15 as a percent. If necessary, round to the nearest tenth.   15%
(SB 5)

12. Write 7.2 as a percent. If necessary, round to the nearest tenth.   720%
(SB 5)

Lesson 1   5

MANIPULATIVE USE

Have students use index cards labeled with the subsets of real numbers. Write several numbers on the board. Then have students place the index cards underneath the numbers to show the sets to which each number belongs.

Lesson Practice

Problem a
Error Alert Students may have difficulty recognizing that an integer is also a rational number. Remind students that $x = \frac{x}{1}$.

Problem e
Scaffolding Encourage students to think about whether the units used in the example are discrete or continuous.

✓ Check for Understanding

The questions below help assess the concepts taught in this lesson.

"Is -36 a rational number? Explain why or why not." Sample: Yes, -36 is a rational number because it can be written as $\frac{-36}{1}$.

"Explain the differences between rational and irrational numbers." Sample: Rational numbers can be expressed as the quotient of two integers and irrational numbers cannot.

3 Practice

Math Conversations
Discussion to strengthen understanding

Problem 10
Point out that there is more than one way to find the prime factorization of a number.

"What methods can be used to find the prime factorization of a number?" Sample: using a factor tree or division by primes

"When making a factor tree, does it matter which pair of factors you choose first?" no

Lesson 1   5

Problem 19
Extend the Problem
"Suppose a second baby's head measures $5\frac{2}{8}$ inches long. How much longer is the second baby than the first?" The second baby is 2 inches longer than the first.

Problem 27
Error Alert
A common error students make is trying to line up decimal points when multiplying decimals. This usually results in the incorrect placement of the decimal point in the solution. Remind students to count the total number of decimal places in both factors; that will be the number of digits to the right of the decimal in the product.

---

*13. Use braces and digits to designate the set of natural numbers. {1, 2, 3,...}
(1)

*14. The set {0, 1, 2, 3,...} represents what set of numbers? whole numbers
(1)

*15. Represent the following numbers as being members of set K: 2, 4, 2, 0, 6, 0, 10, 8.
(1) K = {0, 2, 4, 6, 8, 10}

*16. **Multiple Choice** Which of the following numbers is an irrational number? B
(1)
  A 15   **B** $\sqrt{15}$ **C** 15.15151515...   **D** $-\frac{15}{3}$

*17. **Measurement** The surface area of a cube is defined as $6s^2$, where s is the length of
(1) the side of the cube. If s is an integer, then would the surface area of a cube be a rational or irrational number? rational number

18. **Verify** True or False: A right triangle can have an obtuse angle. Explain your
(SB 1) answer. false; Sample: A right angle and an obtuse angle have a sum of more than 180°.

19. **Anatomy** A baby's head is approximately one fourth of its total body length. If the
(SB 3) baby's body measures 19 inches, what does the baby's head measure? $4\frac{3}{4}$ inches

20. True or False: An acute triangle has 3 acute angles. Explain your answer. true;
(SB 13) Sample: By definition, an acute triangle has only acute angles.

21. True or False: A trapezoid has two pairs of parallel sides. Explain your answer.
(SB 14) false; A trapezoid has only one pair of parallel sides.

*22. **Track Practice** Tyrone ran 7 laps on the quarter-mile track during practice. Which
(1) subset of real numbers would include the distance Tyrone ran at practice?
  rational numbers

23. True or False: A parallelogram has two pairs of parallel sides. Explain your
(SB 14) answer. true; Sample: By definition, a parallelogram has two pairs of parallel sides.

24. **Write** Use the divisibility test to determine if 1248 is divisible by 2. Explain
(SB 4) your answer. yes; The ones digit is even.

*25. **Geometry** The diagram shows a right triangle. The length of the hypotenuse is
(1) a member of which subset(s) of real numbers? irrational numbers

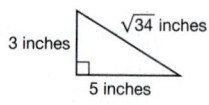

*26. **Multi-Step** The diagram shows a rectangle.
(1)
  a. Find the area of the rectangle. 18 square feet
  b. The number of square feet is a member of which subset(s) of real numbers? rational numbers, integers, whole numbers, and natural numbers

27. **Lunar Rover** The surface-speed record set by the lunar rover on the moon is
(SB 2) 10.56 miles per hour. At that speed, how far would the rover travel in 3.5 hours?
  36.96 miles

28. **Write** Use the divisibility test to determine if 207 is divisible by 3. Explain
(SB 4) your answer. yes; The sum of digits is 2 + 0 + 7 = 9, which is divisible by 3.

29. **Swimming** Vidiana and Jaime went swimming before school. Vidiana swam $\frac{3}{5}$ mile
(SB 1) and Jaime swam $\frac{4}{7}$ mile. Write a comparison to show who swam farther. Use <, >,
  or =. $\frac{3}{5} > \frac{4}{7}$

*30. **Banking** Shayla is balancing her checkbook. Which subset of real numbers best
(1) describes her balance? rational numbers

CHALLENGE

In problem 22, Tyrone runs 7 laps on a quarter-mile track. Determine whether or not the distance Tyrone runs during practice would remain in the same subset of real numbers if he runs 8, 9, or 10 laps. If not, identify any additional subsets. The distance Tyrone runs will also include natural numbers, whole numbers, and integers if he runs 8 laps.

LOOKING FORWARD

Classifying real numbers prepares students for

- **Lesson 5** Finding Absolute Value and Adding Real Numbers
- **Lesson 6** Subtracting Real Numbers
- **Lesson 10** Adding and Subtracting Real Numbers
- **Lesson 11** Multiplying and Dividing Real Numbers
- **Lesson 12** Using the Properties of Real Numbers to Simplify Expressions

LESSON 2

Understanding Variables and Expressions

Warm Up

1. **Vocabulary** When two numbers are multiplied, the result is called the _____. (*quotient, product*)   product

Add.

2. $\frac{2}{5} + \frac{1}{3}$ $\frac{11}{15}$

3. $654.1 + 78.39$ 732.49

Multiply.

4. $4.5(0.23)$ 1.035

5. $\frac{3}{8}\left(\frac{2}{9}\right)$ $\frac{1}{12}$

New Concepts

A symbol, usually a letter, used to represent an unknown number is called a **variable**. In the algebraic expression $4 + x$, x is a variable. The number 4 in this expression does not change value. A quantity whose value does not change is called a **constant**.

Example 1 Identifying Variables and Constants

Identify the constants and the variables in each expression.

a. $6 - 3x$

SOLUTION

The numbers 6 and 3 are constants because they never change. The letter x is a variable because it represents an unknown number.

b. $71wz + 28y$

SOLUTION

The numbers 71 and 28 are constants because they never change. The letters w, y, and z are variables because they represent unknown numbers.

The expression $4xy$ can also be written as $4 \cdot x \cdot y$. When two or more quantities are multiplied, each is a **factor** of the product. The numeric factor of a product including a variable is called the numeric coefficient, or simply the **coefficient**.

Math Reasoning

Connect What other term can be used to describe the coefficient in the expression $5mn$?

constant

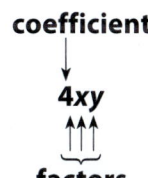

coefficient ↓ $4xy$ ↑↑↑ *factors*

Online Connection
www.SaxonMathResources.com

MATH BACKGROUND

There is overlap among the terms *variable, constant, factor, numeric coefficient,* and *term.* A Venn diagram helps to show this.

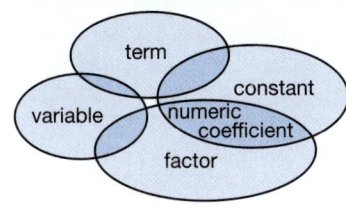

- A factor can be a variable, a constant, or a coefficient, but is never a term.

- A numeric coefficient is always a constant and a factor, but is never a variable or a term.

- A variable can be a term or a factor, but not a constant or a numeric coefficient.

- A constant can be a factor, a term, or a numeric coefficient, but not a variable.

- A term can be a variable or a constant, a combination of the two, but not a factor or a coefficient.

LESSON 2

1 Warm Up

Problem 2
Remind students to find a common denominator when adding fractions.

2 New Concepts

In this lesson, students learn different parts of an expression. Point out that variables can take on many different values, while a constant has a single value.

Example 1

Mention to students that any letter or symbol (other than an Arabic numeral), not just x, can represent a variable.

Additional Example 1

Identify the constants and variables in each expression.

a. $4 + 7x$ 4 and 7 are constants; x is a variable.

b. $24wz + 12y$ 24 and 12 are constants; w, z, and y are variables.

c. $4x + 7y = 36$ 4, 7, and 36 are constants; x and y are variables.

LESSON RESOURCES

Student Edition Practice Workbook 2
Reteaching Master 2
Adaptations Master 2
Challenge and Enrichment Master C2

Example 2

Error Alert Students often have difficulty recognizing an implied coefficient of 1. While identifying factors and coefficients, show that $ab = 1 \cdot a \cdot b$.

Extend the Example

Ask students to identify the constants and variables of each expression.

a. constant: 7, variables: v, w

b. constant: −5, variables: r, s, t

c. constant: $\frac{1}{3}$, variable: y

d. constant: 1, variables: c, d

Additional Example 2

Identify the factors and coefficients in each expression.

a. 6de The factors are 6, d, and e. The coefficient is 6.

b. −2qrs The factors are −2, q, r, and s. The coefficient is −2.

c. $\frac{y}{4}$ The factors are $\frac{1}{4}$ and y. The coefficient is $\frac{1}{4}$.

d. bc The factors are b and c. The expression bc has an implied coefficient of 1.

Example 2 Identifying Factors and Coefficients in Expressions

Identify the factors and coefficients in each expression.

a. 7vw

SOLUTION

The factors are 7, v, and w. The coefficient is 7.

b. −5rst

SOLUTION

The factors are −5, r, s, and t. The coefficient is −5.

c. $\frac{y}{3}$

SOLUTION

The factors are $\frac{1}{3}$ and y. The coefficient is $\frac{1}{3}$.

Hint
$\frac{y}{3} = \frac{1}{3}y$
$cd = 1cd$

d. cd

SOLUTION

The factors are c and d. The expression cd has an implied coefficient of 1.

Parts of an expression separated by + or − signs are called **terms of an expression**. A term that is in parentheses such as $(y + 2)$ can include a plus or minus sign.

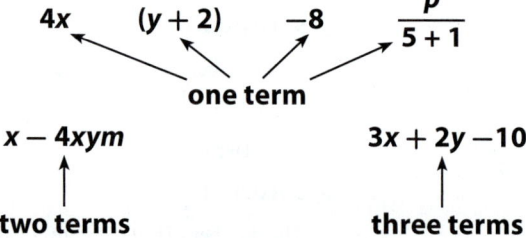

one term

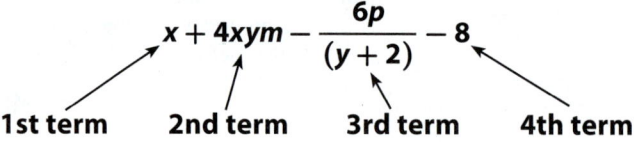

You can refer to a particular term of an expression by its placement within the expression. The terms of an expression are numbered from left to right, beginning with the first term.

$$x + 4xym - \frac{6p}{(y+2)} - 8$$

1st term   2nd term   3rd term   4th term

ENGLISH LEARNERS

In this lesson, explain the multiple meanings of **term**. Say:

"Term is a word that has many different meanings depending on the context. A term can refer to a period of time. For example, the president is elected for a term of four years. In school, a term can mean quarter or semester."

"Another meaning of term is to define the conditions, or terms, of an agreement. In this lesson, terms are different parts of an expression separated by + and − signs."

Example 3 Identifying Terms

Identify the terms in each expression.

a. $6xy + 57w - \dfrac{24x}{5y}$

SOLUTION

The first term is $6xy$.

The second term is $57w$.

The third term is $\dfrac{24x}{5y}$.

b. $m + 3mn - \dfrac{5t}{(d+8)} - 9$

SOLUTION

The first term is m.

The second term is $3mn$.

The third term is $\dfrac{5t}{(d+8)}$.

The fourth term is 9.

Example 4 Application: Telecommunications

The local telephone company uses the expression below to determine the monthly charges for individual customers.

$$0.1m + 4.95$$

a. How many terms are in the expression?

SOLUTION There are two terms.

b. Identify the constant(s).

SOLUTION The constants are 0.1 and 4.95.

c. Identify the variable(s).

SOLUTION The variable is m.

Lesson Practice

Identify the constants and variables in each expression.
(Ex 1)

a. $65qrs + 12x$ 65, 12; q, r, s, x   **b.** $4gh - 71yz$ 4, 71; g, h, y, z

Identify the factors and coefficients in each expression.
(Ex 2)

c. $17def$ 17, d, e, f; 17   **d.** $\dfrac{uv}{4}$ $\tfrac{1}{4}$, u, v; $\tfrac{1}{4}$

e. $-3st$ -3, s, t; -3 **f.** abc a, b, c; 1

Identify the terms in each expression.
(Ex 3)

g. $8v - 17yz + \dfrac{63b}{4gh}$ $8v, 17yz, \dfrac{63b}{4gh}$

h. $\dfrac{(4+2x)}{38q} + 18s - 47jkl$ $\dfrac{(4+2x)}{38q}, 18s, 47jkl$

Bill's Bikes uses the expression below to calculate rental fees.
(Ex 4)

$$6.50 + 3.25h - 0.75b$$

i. How many terms are in the expression?   3

j. Identify the constants.   6.50, 3.25, 0.75

k. Identify the variables.   h, b

Lesson 2   9

ALTERNATE METHOD FOR EXAMPLE 3

Have students identify the terms of each expression by drawing arrows to indicate which parts of the expression are the first, second, and third terms.

$6xy + 57w - \dfrac{24x}{5y}$

1st term   2nd term   3rd term

INCLUSION

Suggest that students use a graphic organizer like the grid below to organize the information in Example 4.

	Term	Constant	Variable
	$0.1m$	0.1	m
	4.95	4.95	
Number of Each	2 terms	2 constants	1 variable

Example 3
Additional Example 3

Identify the terms in each expression.

a. $5ax + 42v - \dfrac{10a}{3x}$ first term: 5ax; second term: 42v; third term: $\dfrac{10a}{3x}$

b. $x + 3xy - \dfrac{8d}{(j+4)} - 9$ first term: x; second term: 3xy; third term: $\dfrac{8d}{(j+4)}$; fourth term: 9

Example 4
Additional Example 4

A car rental company uses the formula below to determine the charge to rent a car.

$$29.95 + 19.95d$$

a. How many terms are in the expression? 2

b. Identify the constant(s). 19.95 and 29.95

c. Identify the variable(s). d

Lesson Practice

Problem c

Scaffolding Have students circle the factors and underline the coefficients; then have them make a list of the factors and the coefficients.

Problem d

Error Alert Students may write 4 as a factor instead of $\tfrac{1}{4}$. Remind them that $\dfrac{uv}{4}$ is the same as $\tfrac{1}{4}uv$.

Check for Understanding

The questions below help assess the concepts taught in this lesson.

"Is -36 a coefficient in the expression $-36 + 12y$?" No: It is a constant.

"How do you find the number of terms in an expression?" Sample: Count the number of parts separated by + and − signs.

Lesson 2   9

3 Practice

Math Conversations

Discussion to strengthen understanding

Problem 1

Guide students by asking them the following questions:

"What does GCF stand for?" greatest common factor

"How do you find the greatest common factor? Sample: List the factors for each number and find the greatest number that is in both lists.

Problem 6

Error Alert

Students may forget to change the divisor to its reciprocal when they change the division to multiplication. Suggest that students circle the division sign and then circle the multiplication sign when they rewrite the expression.

Problem 16

Extend the Problem

"$2 \cdot 2 \cdot 3 \cdot 3 \cdot 5$ is the prime factorization of which number?" 180

"What is the prime factorization of 36?" $2 \cdot 2 \cdot 3 \cdot 3$

Practice Distributed and Integrated

Find the GCF of each pair of numbers.

1. (SB 9) 24, 32 8
2. (SB 9) 28, 42 14

Find the LCM of each group of numbers.

3. (SB 10) 9, 12 36
4. (SB 10) 3, 5, 6 30

Multiply or divide.

5. (SB 3) $\frac{3}{4} \cdot \frac{8}{15}$ $\frac{2}{5}$
6. (SB 3) $\frac{7}{15} \div \frac{21}{25}$ $\frac{5}{9}$

Identify the coefficients and variables in each expression.

*7. (2) $rst - 12v$ coefficients: 1, 12; variables: r, s, t, v

*8. (2) $2xy + 7w - 8$ coefficients: 2, 7; variables: x, y, w

*9. (2) $47s + \frac{2}{5}t$ coefficients: 47, $\frac{2}{5}$; variables: s, t

Identify the following statements as true or false. Explain your choice.

*10. (1) **Verify** All whole numbers are natural numbers. false; Sample: Zero is a whole number, but it is not a natural number.

11. (1) **Verify** All integers are real numbers. true; Sample: The set of integers is a subset of real numbers.

12. (1) **Verify** A number can be a member of the set of rational numbers and the set of irrational numbers. false; Sample: By definition, the sets of rational and irrational numbers do not have any members in common.

13. (SB 29) **Multi-Step** Use the following set of data.

    3, 6, 4, 3, 6, 5, 6, 7, 4, 3, 2, 4, 6

    a. What is the frequency of each number? 1 two; 3 threes; 3 fours; 1 five; 4 sixes; 1 seven
    b. Display the set of data in a line plot. 13b.

14. (1) All natural numbers are members of which other subsets of real numbers? whole numbers, integers, and rational numbers

15. (1, SB 3) **Measurement** Add $7\frac{3}{8}$ meters + $6\frac{1}{3}$ meters. Does the sum belong to the set of rational numbers, integers, or whole numbers? $13\frac{17}{24}$ meters; rational numbers

16. (SB 12) Find the prime factorization of 153. $3 \cdot 3 \cdot 17$

17. (SB 13) **Verify** True or False: An obtuse triangle can have more than one obtuse angle. Explain your choice. false; Sample: The sum of two obtuse angles is greater than 180°.

18. (SB 13) **Geometry** A line can be classified as a _____ angle. straight

19. (SB 4) **Write** Use the divisibility test to determine if 2345 is divisible by 4. Explain your answer. no; The number formed by the last two digits is not divisible by 4.

20. (SB 5) Write 0.003 as a percent. If necessary, round to the nearest tenth. 0.3%

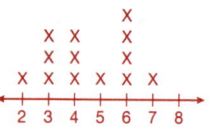

Frequency of Numbers

Numbers

🟥 CHALLENGE

"The variable h represents the number of hours in problem 29. To find the charges for a bike rental for 3 hours, let $h = 3$. In other words, the charge for 3 hours is $\$5 + \$2.25 \cdot 3$. Identify the variables and constants in this expression." The constants are 5, 2.25, and 3. There are no variables.

"What will the bicycle store charge for 3 hours?" $\$5 + \$2.25 \cdot 3 = \$5 + \$6.75 = \$11.75$

21. Use braces and digits to designate the set of whole numbers. {0, 1, 2, 3,...}

22. The set {1, 2, 3,...} represents what set of numbers? natural numbers

*23. Multiple Choice What is the second term in the expression
$\sqrt{8} + \frac{gh}{5} + (3x + y) + 15gh$? **D**

A $(3x + y)$ **B** $15gh$ **C** $\sqrt{8}$ **D** $\frac{gh}{5}$

*24. Astronomy To calculate the amount of time it takes for a planet to travel around the sun, you use the following expression: $\frac{2\pi r}{v}$. Which values are constants, which are variables, and which are coefficients? constants: 2 and π; variables r and v; coefficient: 2π

*25. Entertainment Admission price for a matinee movie is $5.75 for children and $6.25 for adults. Brad uses the expression $5.75c + $6.25a to calculate the cost for his family. What are the variables in the expression? c and a

*26. Error Analysis The surface area of a rectangular prism is $2lw + 2lh + 2wh$. Two students determined the variables in the formula. Which student is correct? What was the error of the other student? Student B; Student A listed two terms.

Student A	Student B
variables: $2lw$, $2lh$	variables: l, w, h

*27. Cost Analysis A large medical organization wants to put two cylindrical aquariums in the pharmacy area. It will cost the pharmacy 53 cents per cubic inch of aquarium. This is the formula for figuring out the cost: $P = (\pi r^2 h)(\$0.53)$.
  a. Find the coefficients of the expression. $0.53, \pi$
  b. Find the variables of the expression. r, h

28. Multiple Choice Which shape is not a parallelogram? **C**

A square   **B** rectangle   **C** trapezoid   **D** rhombus

*29. Cycling A bicycle shop uses the expression $5 + $2.25h to determine the charges for bike rentals. How many terms are in the expression? 2 terms

30. Attendance The attendance clerk keeps records of students' attendance. Which subset of real numbers would include the number of students in attendance each school day? whole numbers

Lesson 2   11

LOOKING FORWARD

Understanding variables and expressions prepares students for

• **Lesson 3** Simplifying Expressions Using the Product Property of Exponents

• **Lesson 4** Using Order of Operations

• **Lesson 5** Finding Absolute Value and Adding Real Numbers

• **Lesson 23** Solving Two-Step Equations

• **Lesson 29** Solving Literal Equations

LESSON
3

1 Warm Up

Problem 4
Students can write using prime factorization, or they can multiply and then simplify.

2 New Concepts

In this lesson, students simplify exponential expressions.

Discuss the definitions of base, power, and exponent. A power is the entire expression. For example, 10^2 is a power of 10.

Example 1

Error Alert Students may only multiply the numerator when a fraction is raised to a power. Remind them to multiply both the numerator and the denominator to find a power of a fraction.

Additional Example 1
Simplify each expression.

a. 6^4 1296
b. $(0.8)^3$ 0.512
c. $\left(\frac{1}{3}\right)^6$ $\frac{1}{729}$
d. 10^5 100,000

LESSON RESOURCES

Student Edition Practice Workbook 3
Reteaching Master 3
Adaptations Master 3
Challenge and Enrichment Master C3, E3

LESSON
3

Simplifying Expressions Using the Product Property of Exponents

Warm Up

1. **Vocabulary** In the term $4x$, x is the _____. (*variable*, *coefficient*)
   (2) variable

   Simplify.

2. $(1.2)(0.7)$ 0.84
   (SB 2)

3. $(0.5)(11)(0.9)$ 4.95
   (SB 2)

4. $\left(\frac{2}{3}\right)\left(\frac{6}{7}\right)$ $\left(\frac{4}{7}\right)$
   (SB 3)

5. $\left(\frac{1}{2}\right)\left(\frac{4}{5}\right)\left(\frac{15}{16}\right)$ $\left(\frac{3}{8}\right)$
   (SB 3)

New Concepts

An exponent can be used to show repeated multiplication.

base → 5^3 ← exponent

The **base of a power** is the number used as a factor. If the **exponent** is a natural number, it indicates how many times the base is used as a factor.

Words	Power	Multiplication	Value
five to the first power	5^1	5	5
five to the second power or five squared	5^2	$5 \cdot 5$	25
five to the third power or five cubed	5^3	$5 \cdot 5 \cdot 5$	125
five to the fourth power	5^4	$5 \cdot 5 \cdot 5 \cdot 5$	625

Caution
Be careful not to multiply the base and the exponent when simplifying powers.

Online Connection
www.SaxonMathResources.com

Example 1 Simplifying Expressions with Exponents

Simplify each expression.

a. 7^3

SOLUTION

The exponent 3 indicates that the base is a factor three times.

7^3
$= 7 \cdot 7 \cdot 7$
$= 343$

b. $(0.3)^4$

SOLUTION

The exponent 4 indicates that the base is a factor four times.

$(0.3)^4$
$= (0.3)(0.3)(0.3)(0.3)$
$= 0.0081$

MATH BACKGROUND

Two special cases for exponents are related to the Product Property of Exponents.

- Any number raised to the power of 1 equals itself: $a^1 = a$. This can be shown as follows:

  $a^2 = a \cdot a$ and $a^2 = a^{1+1} = a^1 \cdot a^1$

  so $a \cdot a = a^1 \cdot a^1$

  therefore $a = a^1$

- 1 raised to any power is 1: $1^b = 1$. You can show this with a pattern:

  $1^2 = 1 \cdot 1 = 1$

  $1^3 = 1 \cdot 1 \cdot 1 = 1$

  $1^b = \underbrace{1 \cdot 1 \cdot \ldots \cdot 1 \cdot 1}_{b \text{ times}} = 1$

Math Reasoning

Generalize Examine the powers of 10. What pattern do you see?

The exponent matches the number of zeros when the expression is simplified.

 c. $\left(\frac{1}{2}\right)^5$

SOLUTION

The exponent 5 indicates that the base is a factor five times.

$\left(\frac{1}{2}\right)^5$
$= \frac{1}{2} \cdot \frac{1}{2} \cdot \frac{1}{2} \cdot \frac{1}{2} \cdot \frac{1}{2}$
$= \frac{1}{32}$

 d. 10^3

SOLUTION

The exponent 3 indicates that the base is a factor three times.

10^3
$= 10 \cdot 10 \cdot 10$
$= 1000$

The product of powers whose bases are the same can be found by writing each power as repeated multiplication.

$$5^4 \cdot 5^5 = (5 \cdot 5 \cdot 5 \cdot 5) \cdot (5 \cdot 5 \cdot 5 \cdot 5 \cdot 5) = 5^9$$

The sum of the exponents in the factors is equal to the exponent in the product.

Product Property of Exponents
If m and n are real numbers and $x \neq 0$, then $x^m \cdot x^n = x^{m+n}$.

Example 2 Applying the Product Property of Exponents

Simplify each expression.

 a. $x^5 \cdot x^7 \cdot x^2$

SOLUTION

Since each of the factors has the same base, the exponents can be added to find the power of the product.

$x^{5+7+2} = x^{14}$

b. $m^3 \cdot m^2 \cdot m^4 \cdot n^6 \cdot n^7$

SOLUTION

The first three factors have m as the base. The exponents can be added to find the product of those three factors. The last two factors have n as the base. The exponents can be added to find the product of the last two factors.

$m^{3+2+4} \cdot n^{6+7} = m^9 n^{13}$

The **order of magnitude** is defined as the nearest power of ten to a given quantity. The order of magnitude can be used to estimate when performing calculations mentally.

Math Reasoning

Estimate Use the order of magnitude to estimate 1,127,000 times 108.

Sample:
$10^6 \cdot 10^2 = 10^8$

Example 2

Remind students that the base of each factor must be the same to add exponents.

"How do you know if an expression containing exponents is simplified completely?" Sample: The expression is simplified completely if it no longer contains exponents or if there are no factors with the same base.

"How do you know which factors to group together?" Sample: Group powers with the same base because their exponents can be combined.

Additional Example 2

Simplify each expression.

a. $b^5 \cdot b^4 \cdot b^2$ b^{11}

b. $v^3 \cdot v^5 \cdot v^7 \cdot w^2 \cdot w^4$ $v^{15} w^6$

Lesson 3   13

ALTERNATE METHOD FOR EXAMPLE 2

a. Ask students to write $x^5 \cdot x^7 \cdot x^2$ using only multiplication.
$(x \cdot x \cdot x \cdot x \cdot x)(x \cdot x \cdot x \cdot x \cdot x \cdot x \cdot x)(x \cdot x)$

Then have students count the x's to find the exponent for the product. Sample: There are 14 x's, so the answer is x^{14}.

b. Ask students to write $m^3 \cdot m^5 \cdot m^7 \cdot n^2 \cdot n^4$ using only multiplication.
$(m \cdot m \cdot m)(m \cdot m \cdot m \cdot m \cdot m)(m \cdot m \cdot m \cdot m \cdot m \cdot m \cdot m)(n \cdot n)(n \cdot n \cdot n \cdot n)$

Then have students count the m's and n's to find the product. Sample: There are 15 m's and 6 n's, so the answer is $m^{15} n^6$.

Lesson 3   13

Example 3
Extend the Example
"1 TFLOP is 10^6 MFLOPS. How many MFLOPS are in 1 PFLOP?" 10^9 MFLOPS

Additional Example 3
There are 10^6 exabytes in a yottabyte. There are 10^9 gigabytes in an exabyte. How many gigabytes are in a yottabyte? 10^{15}

Lesson Practice
Problem c
Error Alert Students may not multiply the whole fraction by itself. Encourage students to write out .

Problem f
Scaffolding Suggest that students circle the y's and z's before adding the exponents.

Check for Understanding
The questions below help assess the concepts taught in this lesson.

"How do you simplify a power?"
Write the power as multiplication of the base times itself and then simplify.

"Explain why you add exponents only if the bases are the same."
Sample: The exponents show how many times a single number, the base, is used as a factor.

Example 3 Application: Speed of a Supercomputer

In 2006, the fastest supercomputer's performance topped out at about one PFLOPS. One PFLOPS is equal to 10^3 TFLOPS. Each TFLOPS is equal to 10^{12} FLOPS. What was the computer's speed in FLOPS?

SOLUTION

Understand

1 PFLOPS = 10^3 TFLOPS

1 TFLOPS = 10^{12} FLOPS

Find the number of FLOPS in one PFLOPS.

Plan

Write an expression to find the number of FLOPS in one PFLOPS.

Solve

To find the speed in FLOPS, find the product of the number of TFLOPS, 10^3, and the number of FLOPS in a TFLOPS, 10^{12}.

$10^3 \cdot 10^{12}$

$= 10^{3+12}$

$= 10^{15}$

The computer performed at a speed of 10^{15} FLOPS.

Check

$$10^3 \cdot 10^{12} \stackrel{?}{=} 10^{15}$$

$$(10 \cdot 10 \cdot 10)(10 \cdot 10 \cdot 10 \cdot 10 \cdot 10 \cdot 10 \cdot 10 \cdot 10 \cdot 10 \cdot 10 \cdot 10 \cdot 10) \stackrel{?}{=} 10^{15}$$

$$10^{15} = 10^{15} \checkmark$$

Lesson Practice
Simplify each expression.

a. 6^4 1296   (Ex 1)

b. $(1.4)^2$ 1.96   (Ex 1)

c. $\left(\frac{2}{5}\right)^3$ $\frac{8}{125}$ (Ex 1)

d. 10^6 1,000,000   (Ex 1)

e. $w^3 \cdot w^5 \cdot w^4$ w^{12} (Ex 2)

f. $y^6 \cdot y^5 \cdot z^3 \cdot z^{11} \cdot z^2$ $y^{11}z^{16}$ (Ex 2)

g. If a supercomputer has a top speed of one EFLOPS which is equal to 10^9 GFLOPS, and if one GFLOPS is 10^9 FLOPS, what is the computer's speed in FLOPS? 10^{18} (Ex 3)

Practice   Distributed and Integrated

Find the GCF for each pair of numbers.

1. 15, 35   5   (SB 9)

2. 32, 48   16   (SB 9)

ENGLISH LEARNERS

For this lesson, explain the meaning of the word **base**. Students may be more familiar with the word in terms of baseball bases, military bases, or as the bottom support of a bridge. Write 5^3 on the chalkboard. Say:

"The word base has many different meanings. In mathematics, the base of a power is the number used as a factor. It tells you what you are going to multiply."

Write $5 \cdot 5 \cdot 5$ on the chalkboard under 5^3. Ask:

"What is the base?"   5

Have a volunteer write an expression with a base and a power on the chalkboard. Then have other volunteers identify the base.

Find the LCM for each group of numbers.

3. 8, 12   24 (SB 10)

4. 2, 4, 7   28 (SB 10)

Multiply or divide.

5. $\frac{9}{16} \cdot \frac{12}{15}$ $\frac{9}{20}$ (SB 3)

6. $\frac{6}{15} \div \frac{24}{30}$ $\frac{1}{2}$ (SB 3)

Identify the coefficients and variables in each expression.

7. $6mn + 4b$ coefficients: 6, 4; variables: m, n, b (2)

8. $5j - 9cd + 2$ coefficients: 5, 9; variables: j, c, d (2)

9. $23t + \frac{4}{7}w$ coefficients: 23, $\frac{4}{7}$; variables: t, w (2)

Identify the following statements as true or false. Explain your choice.

*10. Verify All real numbers are integers.   false; Sample: Fractions are real numbers, but they are not integers. (1)

11. Verify All natural numbers are whole numbers.   true; Sample: The set of whole numbers contains all the natural numbers and zero. (2)

12. Verify All irrational numbers are real numbers.   true; Sample: By definition, the set of irrational numbers is a subset of the set of real numbers. (2)

Complete the comparisons. Use <, >, or =.

13. 42.53 42.35 (SB 1)

14. $\frac{5}{9}$ $\frac{7}{12}$ (SB 1)

15. Add $1\frac{1}{8} + 7\frac{2}{5}$. $8\frac{21}{40}$ (SB 3)

16. Measurement Use braces and digits to designate the set of integers. Which measurement can be described by the set of integers: temperature or volume? {..., −3, −2, −1, 0, 1, 2, 3,...}; temperature (1)

17. Find the prime factorization of 98. $2 \cdot 7 \cdot 7$ (SB 12)

*18. Error Analysis Two students are trying to simplify the expression $x^2 \cdot x^5$. Which student is correct? Explain the error. (3)

Student A	Student B
$x^2 \cdot x^5$	$x^2 \cdot x^5$
$x^{2 \cdot 5} = x^{10}$	$x^{2+5} = x^7$

18. Student B; Sample: Student A multiplied the exponents instead of adding them.

19. Verify True or False: A rhombus is always a square. Explain your choice. (SB 14)

20. Write Use the divisibility test to determine if 306 is divisible by 6. Explain your answer.   yes; The number is divisible by 2 and by 3. (SB 4)

19. false; Sample: A rhombus does not always have 4 right angles to make it a square.

*21. The expression 3^6 indicates the number of times 3 is used as a factor. (3)

  a. Which number in the expression is the base?   3

  b. Which number is the exponent?   6

  c. What is the simplified value of this expression?   729

Lesson 3   15

Problem 25

Guide students by asking them the following questions:

"How many decades are there between 2000 and 2030?"
3 decades

"How do you find the population after 1 decade?" Multiply the original population by 3.

"How do you find the population after 3 decades?" Multiply the original population by 3 three times.

"What is another way to say multiply by 3 three times?"
Multiply the original population by 3^3.

Problem 27
Extend the Problem

"How many bacteria will there be after 15 hours?" 32

"How many bacteria will there be after 1 day 21 hours?" 32,768

---

*22. **Multiple Choice** MFLOPS, TFLOPS, and PFLOPS are used to measure the speed of a computer. One PFLOP is equal to 10^3 TFLOPS. Each TFLOP is equal to 10^6 MFLOPS. How many MFLOPS are in a PFLOP? **B**
(3)
  A 10^{18} **B** 10^9 **C** 10^6 **D** 10^3

*23. (Cooking) A cooking magazine advertises 4^4 recipes in every issue. How many recipes are in 4^2 issues?   4096 recipes
(3)

*24. **Multi-Step** A business is worth 10^6 dollars this year. The business expects to be 10^3 more valuable in five years.
(3)
  a. Simplify 10^3 to determine how many times more valuable the business will be.   1000
  b. What will the business be worth in five years? Express your answer in exponential form, then simplify your answer. 10^9 dollars; $1,000,000,000

*25. (Population) The population of Bridgetown triples every decade. If the population in the year 2000 was 25,000, how many people will be living in Bridgetown in 2030?   675,000 people
(3)

26. **Multiple Choice** Which triangle is a right triangle?   **A**
(SB 13)
  A a triangle with angle measures of 45°, 45°, and 90°
  B a triangle with angle measures of 40°, 110°, and 30°
  C a triangle with angle measures of 55°, 45°, and 80°
  D a triangle with angle measures of 60°, 60°, and 60°

*27. (Bacteria) The population of a certain bacteria doubles in size every 3 hours. If a population begins with one bacterium, how many will there be after one day? Simplify the expression $1 \cdot (2)^8$ to determine the population after one day.
(3)
  256 bacteria

 28. **Geometry** You can calculate the area of a trapezoid using the following equation:
(2)
$A = h \times \frac{b_1 + b_2}{2}$. Identify the constant(s) in the equation. $\frac{1}{2}$

*29. (Aquarium) A fish tank is in the shape of a cube. Each side measures 3 feet. What is the volume of the fish tank?   27 ft³
(SB 26)

*30. (Remodeling) Vanessa is remodeling her bathroom. She uses the expression $2l + 2w$ to determine the amount of wallpaper border she needs.
(2)
  a. How many terms are in the expression?   2 terms
  b. What are the variables? l and w

16   Saxon Algebra 1

⭐ CHALLENGE

Have students simplify
$\left(\frac{2}{3}\right)^2 \left(\frac{2}{3}\right)^2 \left(\frac{9}{4}\right)\left(\frac{9}{4}\right)$ using the Product Property of Exponents and then check using the order of operations. Have them show their work.

Sample: $\left(\frac{2}{3}\right)^2\left(\frac{2}{3}\right)^2\left(\frac{9}{4}\right)\left(\frac{9}{4}\right) = \left(\frac{2}{3}\right)^{2+2}\left(\frac{9}{4}\right)^{1+1} =$
$\left(\frac{2}{3}\right)^4\left(\frac{9}{4}\right)^2 = \left(\frac{16}{81}\right)\left(\frac{81}{16}\right) = 1$;
$\left(\frac{2}{3}\right)^2\left(\frac{2}{3}\right)^2\left(\frac{9}{4}\right)\left(\frac{9}{4}\right) = \left(\frac{4}{9}\right)\left(\frac{4}{9}\right)\left(\frac{9}{4}\right)\left(\frac{9}{4}\right) =$
$\left(\frac{16}{81}\right)\left(\frac{9}{4}\right)\left(\frac{9}{4}\right) = \left(\frac{144}{324}\right)\left(\frac{9}{4}\right) = \left(\frac{1296}{1296}\right) = 1$

LOOKING FORWARD

Simplifying expressions with exponents prepares students for

- **Lesson 4** Using Order of Operations
- **Lesson 7** Simplifying and Comparing Expressions with Symbols of Inclusion
- **Lesson 9** Evaluating and Comparing Algebraic Expressions
- **Lesson 16** Simplifying and Evaluating Variable Expressions

LESSON 4

Using Order of Operations

Warm Up

1. **Vocabulary** A(n) _____ can be used to show repeated multiplication.
   (3) **exponent**

Simplify.

2. $28.75 + 13.5$ **42.25**
   (SB 2)

3. $89.6 - 7.4$ **82.2**
   (SB 2)

4. $\dfrac{2}{3} \cdot \dfrac{9}{16}$ $\dfrac{3}{8}$
   (SB 3)

5. $4\dfrac{1}{5} \div 3\dfrac{1}{2}$ $1\dfrac{1}{5}$
   (SB 3)

New Concepts

To **simplify** an expression means to perform all indicated operations. Simplifying an expression could produce multiple answers without rules concerning the order in which operations are performed. Consider the example below.

Method 1: $\dfrac{2 \cdot (3)^2}{6} = \dfrac{2 \cdot 9}{6} = \dfrac{18}{6} = 3$

Method 2: $\dfrac{2 \cdot (3)^2}{6} = \dfrac{(2 \cdot 3)^2}{6} = \dfrac{6^2}{6} = \dfrac{36}{6} = 6$

To avoid confusion, mathematicians have agreed to use the order of operations. The **order of operations** is a set of rules for simplifying expressions. Method 1 followed the order of operations.

Order of Operations
1. Work inside grouping symbols.
2. Simplify powers and roots.
3. Multiply and divide from left to right.
4. Add and subtract from left to right.

Example 1   **Simplifying Expressions with Parentheses**

Simplify. Justify each step.

$(10 \cdot 3) + 7 \cdot (5 + 4)$

SOLUTION

Write the expression. Then use the order of operations to simplify.

$(10 \cdot 3) + 7 \cdot (5 + 4)$

$= 30 + 7 \cdot 9$ Simplify inside the parentheses.

$= 30 + 63$ Multiply.

$= 93$ Add.

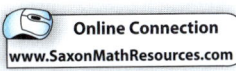
Online Connection
www.SaxonMathResources.com

Lesson 4   17

---

1 Warm Up

Problem 5

Remind students to write the mixed numbers as improper fractions before multiplying by the reciprocal.

2 New Concepts

In this lesson, students learn to simplify expressions using the order of operations.

Example 1

Have students refer to the Order of Operations chart.

Additional Example 1

Simplify. Justify each step.
$(4 \cdot 5) + 3 \cdot (6 + 2)$
$= 20 + 3 \cdot 8$
Simplify inside the parentheses.
$= 20 + 24$ Multiply.
$= 44$ Add.

TEACHER TIP

To help students remember the order of operations, introduce the mnemonic PEMDAS: "**P**lease **E**xcuse **M**y **D**ear **A**unt **S**ally." (Parentheses, Exponents, Multiplication/Division, Addition/Subtraction)

LESSON RESOURCES

Student Edition Practice Workbook 4
Reteaching Master 4
Adaptations Master 4
Challenge and Enrichment Master C4, E4
Technology Lab Master 4

MATH BACKGROUND

Computer programming is one area in which people use the order of operations. If a formula is not entered correctly in a spreadsheet, then the result is different from what was expected.

A graphing calculator is another good way to show the effect of order of operations. After showing one graph, add parentheses to see how they change the graph.

Lesson 4   17

Example 2

Error Alert

Students may be tempted to simplify from left to right. Remind students that they must follow the order of operations.

Additional Example 2

Simplify each expression. Justify each step.

a. $5^2 + 8 \div 2 - 3 \cdot (2)^3$
$= 25 + 8 \div 2 - 3 \cdot 8$
Simplify the exponents.
$= 25 + 4 - 24$
Multiply and divide.
$= 5$
Add and subtract.

b. $\dfrac{(3 \cdot 4 - 3)^2}{3}$

$= \dfrac{(12 - 3)^2}{3}$
Multiply inside the parentheses.

$= \dfrac{(9)^2}{3}$
Subtract inside the parentheses.

$= \dfrac{81}{3}$
Simplify the exponent.

$= 27$
Divide.

Example 3

Remind students to simplify each expression before they compare.

Additional Example 3

Compare the expressions. Use $<, >,$ or $=$.

$(2.5 + 5) \div 3 + 4^2 \; \boxed{>} \; \dfrac{(22 + 5)}{3} - 9 \quad 18.5 > 0$

Example 2 Simplifying Expressions with Exponents

Simplify each expression. Justify each step.

a. $4^3 + 9 \div 3 - 2 \cdot (3)^2$

SOLUTION Write the expression. Then use the order of operations to simplify.

$4^3 + 9 \div 3 - 2 \cdot (3)^2$
$= 64 + 9 \div 3 - 2 \cdot 9$ Simplify exponents.
$= 64 + 3 - 18$ Multiply and divide from left to right.
$= 49$ Add and subtract from left to right.

b. $\dfrac{(2 \cdot 3 - 2)^2}{2}$

Hint
Remember to use the order of operations inside parentheses as well.

SOLUTION Write the expression. Then use the order of operations to simplify.

$\dfrac{(2 \cdot 3 - 2)^2}{2}$

$= \dfrac{(6 - 2)^2}{2}$ Multiply inside the parentheses.

$= \dfrac{(4)^2}{2}$ Subtract inside the parentheses.

$= \dfrac{16}{2}$ Simplify the exponent.

$= 8$ Divide.

Example 3 Comparing Expressions

Compare the expressions. Use $<, >,$ or $=$.

$(1.5 + 3) \div 9 + 3^3 \; \bigcirc \; \dfrac{(18 + 8)}{2} - 8 \div 4$

SOLUTION

Use the order of operations to simplify the two expressions.

$(1.5 + 3) \div 9 + 3^3$ $\dfrac{(18 + 8)}{2} - 8 \div 4$

$= (4.5) \div 9 + 3^3$ $= \dfrac{26}{2} - 8 \div 4$

$= 4.5 \div 9 + 27$ $= 13 - 8 \div 4$

$= 0.5 + 27$ $= 13 - 2$

$= 27.5$ $= 11$

Hint
Remember to compare the original expressions in the inequality.

Since $27.5 > 11$, $(1.5 + 3) \div 9 + 3^3 \; \boxed{>} \; \dfrac{(18 + 8)}{2} - 8 \div 4$.

ENGLISH LEARNERS

Ask students for meanings of the word **operation.** Sample: "surgery," "a military campaign or mission," or "procedures for making a machine work"

Explain by saying:

"The word operation has many meanings. In mathematics, an operation is a mathematical process, such as addition or multiplication. The order of operations is the set of rules for the order in which the processes should be completed."

Ask students to make an order of operations for washing a car. Sample:
1. Get the car wet.
2. Scrub the car with soap.
3. Rinse the car with water.
4. Dry off the car.

Say:

"If you did not follow these rules in the correct order, you might not get the desired result—a clean car."

Example 4 Application: Comparing a Crop Circle to a Soccer Field

A crop circle in a wheat field has a diameter of 100 yards. Its area is $3.14 \cdot \left(\frac{100}{2}\right)^2$ square yards. A World Cup soccer field is 70 yards by 110 yards. Its area is $(70 \cdot 110)$ square yards. How much larger is the crop circle than the soccer field?

Hint
Remember that the formula for the area of a circle is πr^2.

SOLUTION

Find each area and subtract to find the difference.

Area of crop circle: $3.14 \cdot \left(\frac{100}{2}\right)^2$

Area of soccer field: $(70 \cdot 110)$

Difference in area: $3.14 \cdot \left(\frac{100}{2}\right)^2 - (70 \cdot 110)$

Simplify the expression.

$3.14 \cdot \left(\frac{100}{2}\right)^2 - (70 \cdot 110)$

$= 3.14 \cdot (50)^2 - (7700)$ Evaluate inside the parentheses.

$= 3.14 \cdot 2500 - 7700$ Simplify the exponent.

$= 7850 - 7700$ Multiply.

$= 150$ Subtract.

The crop circle is 150 yd² larger than the soccer field.

Lesson Practice

a. Simplify $45 - (2 + 4) \cdot 5 - 3$. Justify each step.   See Additional Answers.
(Ex 1)

Simplify each expression. Justify each step.
(Ex 2)

b. $9 \cdot 2^3 - 9 \div 3$ See Additional Answers.

c. $\frac{15 - 3^2 + 4 \cdot 2}{7}$ See Additional Answers.

d. Compare the expressions. Use <, >, or =.
(Ex 3)

$\frac{1}{4} + 3^2 + 6$ $5 - 2 + 2 \cdot 4 + 3 \div 9$

Caution
Do not forget to cube $\frac{3}{2}$ in the expression for the model moon's volume.

e. Jonah is making a model of the moon using plastic foam. He uses
(Ex 4) the formula $\frac{4}{3}\pi r^3$ to find the volume. The model moon's radius is $\frac{3}{2}$ inches. What is the volume of the model moon? Give the answer in terms of π. $\frac{9}{2}\pi$ in³

Lesson 4   19

Example 4

Make sure students find the area first and then subtract to find the answer.

Extend the Example
"If the crop circle's diameter was increased by 20 yards, how much larger would the crop circle be than the soccer field?" 3604 yd²

Additional Example 4
Use the drawing to write an expression and to find the area of the shaded region. $10^2 - \pi 5^2 = 21.5$ in²

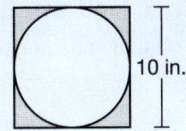

Lesson Practice

Problem d
Scaffolding Direct students to first simplify each expression before comparing.

Problem e
Error Alert Students may not cube the fraction properly. Remind them to cube both the numerator and denominator.

Check for Understanding

The questions below help assess the concepts taught in this lesson.

"What is the first step in simplifying the expression $8 \cdot 7 + 2 \cdot 2$? Explain." Sample: Multiply $8 \cdot 7$ first because you multiply from left to right before adding.

"What is the first step in simplifying $8 \cdot (7 + 2) \cdot 2$? Explain." Add $7 + 2$ because numbers in grouping symbols are simplified first.

⚠ ALTERNATE METHOD FOR EXAMPLE 4

Have students find the area of the crop circle and the area of the soccer field. After they find each area, they can subtract to find the difference.

Lesson 4   19

Practice Distributed and Integrated

Add, subtract, multiply, or divide.

1. (SB 3) $2\frac{1}{4} + 4\frac{1}{2}$ $6\frac{3}{4}$
2. (SB 3) $5\frac{2}{5} - 3\frac{1}{4}$ $2\frac{3}{20}$
3. (SB 3) $1\frac{3}{4} + 4\frac{1}{8} - 2\frac{1}{2}$ $3\frac{3}{8}$
4. (SB 3) $4\frac{1}{3} \div 2\frac{1}{6}$ 2
5. (SB 2) $3.519 \div 0.3$ 11.73
6. (SB 2) $4.16 \cdot 2.3$ 9.568

7. (2) How many terms are in the algebraic expression $14x^2 + 7x + \frac{x}{4}$?   3

8. (SB 12) Find the prime factorization of 225. $3 \cdot 3 \cdot 5 \cdot 5$

9. (SB 4) **Write** Use the divisibility test to determine if 124,302 is divisible by 3. Explain your answer.   124,302 is divisible by 3; Sample: The sum of the digits is 12, which is divisible by 3.

10. (1) Represent the following numbers as being members of set L: $-15, 1, 7, 3, -8, 7, 0, 12, 6, 12$ $L = \{-15, -8, 0, 1, 3, 6, 7, 12\}$

*11. (1) **Verify** True or False: All whole numbers are integers. Explain your answer.   true; Sample: The set of whole numbers is a subset of the set of integers.

*12. (1) To which set(s) of numbers does $\sqrt{5}$ belong?   irrationals and reals

13. (SB 5) Write $\frac{1}{6}$ as a percent. If necessary, round to the nearest tenth.   16.7%

14. (SB 5) Write $\frac{5}{9}$ as a percent. If necessary, round to the nearest tenth.   55.6%

*15. (4) Compare $3 \cdot 4^2 + 4^2 \bigcirc 3 \cdot (16 + 16)$ using $<$, $>$, or $=$. Explain.   Sample: The value of the first expression is 64, and the value of the second expression is 96.

16. (SB 13) **Multiple Choice** Which triangle is an obtuse triangle?   B
   A a triangle with angle measures of 45°, 45°, and 90°
   B a triangle with angle measures of 40°, 120°, and 20°
   C a triangle with angle measures of 55°, 45°, and 80°
   D a triangle with angle measures of 60°, 60°, and 60°

17. (SB 29) Display the following set of data in a line plot:
   6, 7, 8, 4, 5, 4, 3, 4, 5, 3, 2, 6, 2, 7

17. Frequency of Numbers
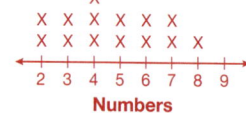

18. (SB 14) **Verify** True or False: A square is a rectangle. Explain your choice.   true; A square has 4 right angles and its opposite sides are parallel and congruent.

19. (SB 3) **Measurement** Subtract $15\frac{1}{3}$ yards $- 7\frac{4}{5}$ yards. $7\frac{8}{15}$ yards

20. (SB 12) **Error Analysis** Two students determine the prime factorization of 108. Which student is correct? Explain the error.   Student B; Sample: Student A has an extra factor of 3, which results in a product of 324.

Student A	Student B
$108 = 2 \cdot 2 \cdot 3 \cdot 3 \cdot 3 \cdot 3$	$108 = 2^2 \cdot 3^3$

21. (SB 4) **Write** Use the divisibility test to determine if 1116 is divisible by 9. Explain your answer.   yes; The sum of the digits $1 + 1 + 1 + 6 = 9$, which is divisible by 9.

20   Saxon Algebra 1

22. $\frac{n}{6} + 3xy - 19$
  a. Find the variables of the expression. *n, x, y*
  b. Find the terms of the expression. $\frac{n}{6}$, *3xy*, *19*

*23. **Biology** A survey found that there were 1100 gray wolves in Minnesota in 1976. By 2003, the number of gray wolves had increased to 2300. What was the average growth of the wolf population in one year? (Round to the nearest whole number.)
$(2300 - 1100) \div (2003 - 1976) = 1200 \div 27 \approx 44$ wolves

*24. **Multiple Choice** A bouquet is made from nine red roses that cost $1.75 each and five white roses that cost $1.50 each. Use the expression $9 \cdot (\$1.75) + 5 \cdot (\$1.50)$ to find the cost of the bouquet. **B**
  A $31.00   **B** $23.25
  C $25.25   **D** $21.75

*25. A can of soup in the shape of a cylinder has a radius of 3.8 cm and a height of 11 cm. What is the surface area of the can to the nearest tenth? Use 3.14 for π.   353.2 cm²

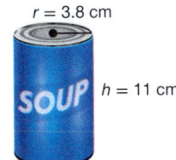

r = 3.8 cm
h = 11 cm

*26. **Multi-Step** Two friends compare the amount of change they have in their pockets. Ashley has 12 nickels, 2 dimes, and 4 quarters. Beto has 10 nickels, 4 dimes, and 3 quarters. Who has more money?
  a. Write an expression to represent the value of Ashley's money. (Hint: Use 10¢ to represent the value of each dime, 5¢ for each nickel, and so on). Simplify the expression. $12 \cdot 5¢ + 2 \cdot 10¢ + 4 \cdot 25¢ = 60¢ + 20¢ + 100¢ = 180¢$
  b. Write an expression to represent the value of Beto's money. Simplify the expression. $10 \cdot 5¢ + 4 \cdot 10¢ + 3 \cdot 25¢ = 50¢ + 40¢ + 75¢ = 165¢$
  c. Compare the value of money that each friend has. Who has more?   Ashley

*27. **School Supplies** Anthony had 10 packages of markers. Each package contained 8 markers. He gave 2 packages to each of the other 3 people in his group. Use the expression $8(10 - 3 \cdot 2)$ to determine how many markers Anthony kept for himself.   32 markers

28. **Geometry** Use the cube shown to write a formula for the volume of any cube.   Volume of cube = s^3

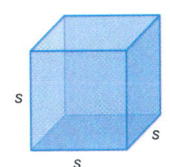

*29. **Temperature** The hottest day in Florida's history was 109°F, which occurred on June 29, 1931 in Monticello. Use the expression $\frac{5}{9}(F - 32)$ to convert this temperature to degrees Celsius. Round your answer to the nearest tenth of a degree.   42.8°C

*30. **Billing** Each month Mrs. Li pays her phone company $28 for phone service and $0.07 per minute for long-distance calls. Use the expression $28 + 0.07m$ to find the amount she was billed if her long-distance calls totaled 223 minutes. $43.61

CHALLENGE

Give students an expression that uses the order of operations without the grouping symbols. Ask them to insert grouping symbols to make the equations true.

For example, add parentheses in the equations below to make the number sentences true.

a. $9 + 12 \div 3 - 1 = 15$ $9 + 12 \div (3 - 1) = 15$

b. $3 \cdot 4^2 - 2^3 + 3^2 = 23$ $(3 \cdot 4)^2 - (2^3 + 3)^2 = 23$

LOOKING FORWARD

Simplifying expressions using the order of operations prepares students for

- **Lesson 7** Simplifying and Comparing Expressions with Symbols of Inclusion
- **Lesson 9** Evaluating and Comparing Algebraic Expressions
- **Lesson 12** Using the Properties of Real Numbers to Simplify Expressions
- **Lesson 16** Simplifying and Evaluating Variable Expressions

---

Problem 23
Error Alert
A common error in multi-step problems is forgetting to do the last step. Remind students that after they find the difference in population, they still need to divide by the number of years and round to the nearest whole number.

Guide the students by asking them the following questions:

"How many years are between 1976 and 2003?" 27

"How do you find how much the population has grown?" Subtract the population in 1976 from the population in 2003.

"What is the next step?" Divide the change in population by the number of years.

Problem 23
Extend the Problem
"If the growth rate stays the same, how many gray wolves will be in Minnesota in 2010?" 2608 wolves

Problem 28
Ask, "How do you find volume?" Multiply $\ell \cdot w \cdot h$, or in this example, $s \cdot s \cdot s$.

"What is another way to write $s \cdot s \cdot s$?" s^3

Problem 30
Remind students to put the decimal point in the correct place after multiplying the long-distance phone rate by the number of minutes.

LESSON 5

1 Warm Up

Problem 2
Remind students to line up the decimals before subtracting.

2 New Concepts

In this lesson, students learn how to find absolute value and how to add signed numbers.

Emphasize that absolute value is a measure of distance. Specifically, it is the distance from zero to another number on the number line. The absolute value of a number must therefore always be positive.

Example 1

Explain that a number line shows the location of numbers as the distance and direction from 0.

Additional Example 1
Simplify.

a. $|-5|$ 5

b. $|3.9|$ 3.9

c. $\left|2 - \frac{1}{3}\right|$ $\frac{5}{3}$ or $1\frac{2}{3}$

d. $-|17 + 24|$ -41

LESSON RESOURCES

Student Edition Practice Workbook 5
Reteaching Master 5
Adaptations Master 5
Challenge and Enrichment Master C5

LESSON 5

Finding Absolute Value and Adding Real Numbers

Warm Up

1. **Vocabulary** The set of _____ (integers, real numbers) includes all rational or irrational numbers. **real numbers**

Simplify.

2. $54.2 - 27.38$ **26.82**

3. $\frac{1}{2} + \frac{3}{8}$ **$\frac{7}{8}$**

4. $1.09 + 76.9$ **77.99**

5. $\frac{3}{4} - \frac{3}{8}$ **$\frac{3}{8}$**

New Concepts

The **absolute value** of a number is the distance from the number to zero on a number line. The absolute value of 4 is written $|4|$.

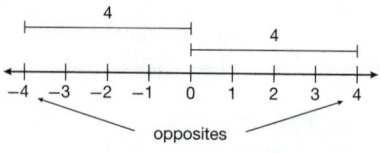

$|-4| = 4$ $|4| = 4$

> **Absolute Value**
> The absolute value of a number n is the distance from n to 0 on a number line.

Example 1 Finding the Absolute Value

Simplify.

a. $|0|$

SOLUTION
The absolute value of 0 is 0.

b. $|7.12|$

SOLUTION
The distance from 7.12 to 0 is 7.12. So the absolute value is 7.12.

c. $\left|1 - \frac{3}{4}\right|$

SOLUTION
First simplify within the absolute-value bars. Then find the absolute value.

$\left|1 - \frac{3}{4}\right| = \left|\frac{1}{4}\right| = \frac{1}{4}$

d. $-|11 - 2|$

SOLUTION
First simplify within the absolute-value bars. Then find the absolute value.

$-|11 - 2| = -|9| = -9$

Reading Math
Read $-|9|$ as the opposite of the absolute value of 9.

22   *Saxon Algebra 1*

MATH BACKGROUND

Scalars and vectors are useful for understanding absolute value. Scalars are quantities which are described by a magnitude (or positive numeric value). Vectors are quantities which are described by both magnitude and direction. Distance is a scalar; it is always positive. Displacement is a vector. It shows the distance and direction to an object from a reference point. It can be positive or negative. Distance equals the magnitude of the displacement.

Addition of real numbers can be shown with vectors. Place the two vectors, head to tail as shown here in blue. Then draw a resultant vector from the tail of the first vector to the head of the second vector.

$6 + (-11) = -5$

Hint

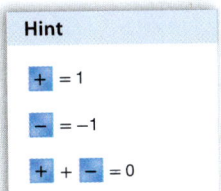

Exploration Modeling Real Number Addition

Find the sum $-5 + 3$.

Model -5 and 3 using algebra tiles.

Group positive and negative tiles to make zero pairs.

Count the remaining tiles.

$$-5 + 3 = -2$$

Model $-5 + 3$ on a number line.

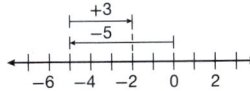

Use algebra tiles to find the sum. Then model each problem on a number line.

a. $4 + (-3)$ 1 **b.** $-2 + -6$ -8 **c.** $(-7) + 7$ 0

Generalize Determine whether each statement is true or false. Provide a counterexample for false statements.

d. The sum of two positive numbers is always positive. true

e. The sum of two negative numbers is always negative. true

f. The sum of a positive and a negative number is always negative. false; counterexample: $6 + (-4) = 2$

The sum of two numbers can also be found using the rules for adding real numbers. These rules apply to all real-number addends.

Rules for Adding Real Numbers
Adding Numbers With the Same Sign
To add numbers with the same sign, add their absolute values. The sum will have the same sign as the addends.
Examples $3 + 2 = 5$ $-3 + (-2) = -5$
Adding Numbers With Different Signs
To add numbers with different signs, find the difference of their absolute values. The sum will have the sign of the addend with the greater absolute value.
Examples $3 + (-2) = 1$ $(-3) + 2 = -1$

a.
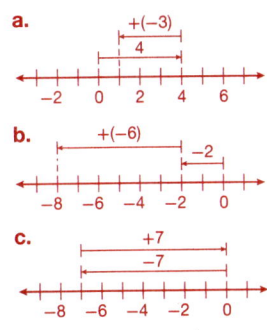

Online Connection
www.SaxonMathResources.com

Exploration

In the Exploration, students use algebra tiles to model addition and subtraction with integers. Students may gain insight by working with multiple representations of the same problem. For example, they can use algebra tiles, a number line, and an algorithm. Using manipulatives can help reinforce why an algorithm works.

Extend the Exploration

Use algebra tiles to find the sum.

a. $3 + (-3)$ 0

b. $-2 + 7$ 5

c. $9 + (-1)$ 8

Lesson 5   23

Example 2

Restate the rules for adding real numbers with the same sign and with different signs.

Additional Example 2

Find each sum.

a. $17 + (-52)$ -35

b. $(-4) + (-31)$ -35

c. $(-2.7) + 3.1$ 0.4

d. $-\left(\frac{1}{2}\right) + \left(\frac{2}{3}\right)$ $\frac{1}{6}$

Example 3

Error Alert

Students may not know where to begin. Remind them that if a set is closed under addition, the sum will be contained in the same set as the addends. It may be helpful to try to think of counterexamples.

Extend the Example

"If an integer x is added to itself x times, is the sum a member of the set of all real numbers?" yes

Additional Example 3

Determine whether each statement is true or false. Give a counterexample for false statements.

a. The set of whole numbers is closed under addition. true

b. The set of natural numbers is closed under addition. true

Example 4

Remind students that words such as gain or loss indicate positive and negative values.

Additional Example 4

Daryl walks 10 yards from his house to the bus stop. Realizing he dropped his keys, he walks back 4 yards. How far from his house is he? Use addition to find how far Daryl is from his house. 6 yards

---

Example 2 Adding Real Numbers

Find the sum.

a. $(-12) + 21$

SOLUTION Since the numbers have different signs, find the difference of their absolute values. The sum is positive because $|-12| < |21|$.

$(-12) + 21 = 9$

b. $(-19) + (-8)$

SOLUTION Since the numbers have the same sign, find the sum of their absolute values. The sum is negative because both addends are negative.

$(-19) + (-8) = -27$

c. $(3.2) + (-5.1)$

SOLUTION Since the numbers have different signs, find the difference of their absolute values. The sum is negative because $|3.2| < |-5.1|$.

$(3.2) + (-5.1) = -1.9$

d. $\left(-\frac{3}{5}\right) + \left(-\frac{1}{5}\right)$

SOLUTION Since the numbers have the same sign, find the sum of their absolute values. The sum is negative because both addends are negative.

$\left(-\frac{3}{5}\right) + \left(-\frac{1}{5}\right) = \left(-\frac{4}{5}\right)$

Math Language

A set of numbers is **closed** under a given operation if the outcome of the operation on any two members of the set is also a member of the set.

Example 3 Identifying Sets of Real Numbers Closed Under Addition

Determine whether each statement is true or false. Give a counterexample for false statements.

a. The set of integers is closed under addition.

SOLUTION The statement is true because the sum of any two integers will be an integer.

b. The set of real numbers is closed under addition.

SOLUTION The statement is true because the sum of any two real numbers will be a real number.

Example 4 Application: Football

On the first down, the Cougars lost 4 yards. They gained 7 yards on the second down. Use addition to find the total number of yards lost or gained on the first two downs.

SOLUTION A loss of 4 yards can be expressed as -4.

$(-4) + 7 = 3$

The Cougars gained a total of 3 yards on the first two downs.

ALTERNATE METHOD FOR EXAMPLE 2

Use a number line to show each expression. For example, $(-12) + 21$ is shown on the number line below.

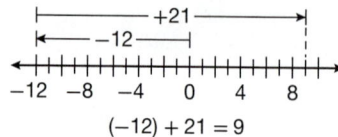

$(-12) + 21 = 9$

ENGLISH LEARNERS

Explain the meaning of the word **down**. Say:

"A down is an attempt, or try, to get the football past a certain point on the field."

Ask a volunteer to tell about a play they know of or exprerienced using the word down. Sample: I made a touchdown on the second down of a game.

Lesson Practice

Simplify.
(Ex 1)
a. $|-3.4|$ 3.4
b. $\left|\frac{6}{7}\right|$ $\frac{6}{7}$
c. $|14 + (-22)|$ 8
d. $-|7 + 16|$ -23

Find the sum.
(Ex 2)
e. $(-23.4) + 18.72$ -4.68
f. $\left(-\frac{2}{3}\right) + \left(-\frac{1}{6}\right)$ $-\frac{5}{6}$

Determine whether each statement is true or false. Give a counterexample for false statements.
(Ex 3)
g. The set of rational numbers is closed under addition. true
h. The set of positive integers is closed under addition. true

i. The temperature at 7:00 p.m. was 34°F. The temperature fell 12°F by
(Ex 4) midnight. Use addition to find the temperature at midnight. 22°F

Practice Distributed and Integrated

Add, subtract, multiply, or divide.

1. $1\frac{1}{6} + 3\frac{1}{3}$ $4\frac{1}{2}$
(SB 3)
2. $2\frac{3}{8} - 1\frac{1}{4}$ $1\frac{1}{8}$
(SB 3)
3. $3\frac{2}{3} + 1\frac{5}{8} - 1\frac{3}{4}$ $3\frac{13}{24}$
(SB 3)
4. $3\frac{1}{3} \div 1\frac{3}{5}$ $2\frac{1}{12}$
(SB 3)
5. $1.506 \div 0.2$ 7.53
(SB 2)
6. $2.89 \cdot 1.2$ 3.468
(SB 2)

7. How many terms are in the algebraic expression $2x^2 + 3x + 7$? 3
(2)

8. Find the prime factorization of 150. $2 \cdot 3 \cdot 5 \cdot 5$
(SB 12)

9. **Write** Use the divisibility test to determine if 125,000 is divisible by 10.
(SB 4) Explain your answer. yes; The ones digit is 0.

10. **Model** Represent the following numbers as being members of set L: $-12, 0, -8, 4,$
(1) $-4, 4, 0, 8, 8, 12$. $L = \{-12, -8, -4, 0, 4, 8, 12\}$

11. **Verify** True or False: All integers are rational numbers. Explain your answer.
(1) true; All integers can be expressed as fractions.

12. **Error Analysis** Student A said that $\frac{\sqrt{2}}{1}$ is a rational number. Student B said that it is
(1) an irrational number. Which student is correct? Explain your answer. Student B; Sample: The $\sqrt{2}$ is irrational.

13. Write $\frac{5}{8}$ as a decimal and a percent. 0.625; 62.5%
(SB 5)

14. **Measurement** Order the lengths 1.25 yards, 3 feet, $1\frac{1}{3}$ yards from least to greatest.
(SB 1) 3 feet, 1.25 yards, $1\frac{1}{3}$ yards

15. Write 7% as a fraction in simplest form and as a decimal. $\frac{7}{100}$; 0.07
(SB 5)

16. **Formulate** Write an equation using absolute values to represent the sentence.
(5) "The distance from -11 to 0 is 11." $|-11| = 11$

Lesson 5   25

INCLUSION

Students may struggle with word problems. They may benefit from using a table when adding real numbers. Encourage students to identify keywords that, in the context of a problem like problem **i**, show whether a number is positive or negative.

Keywords	temperature **was** 34°F	temperature **fell** 12°F
Positive	+34	
Negative		−12

Problem 22
Ask, "How is a thermometer similar to a number line?"
Sample: Both have sections on either side of zero.

Problem 24
Ask students to explain the meaning of the phrase "closed under addition." Sample: A set of numbers is closed under addition if the sum of any two numbers in the set is also one of the numbers in the set.

Problem 26
Extend the Problem
"Suppose Martha needs to pay $550 for rent. How much money does she have to deposit so that she can write a check for $550? Write an addition sentence and use absolute value to find the answer."
Sample: $500 + (-34.65) + (-550) = -84.65$; $|-84.65| = 84.65$; $84.65

Problem 29
Error Alert
Students may confuse exponents with repeated addition. An analogy may help them remember the difference:

"Multiplication is to repeated addition as exponents are to repeated multiplication."

---

17. Multiple Choice Which angle measures form an acute triangle? **C**
(SB 13)
A 45°, 45°, and 90°   B 40°, 110°, and 20°
C 55°, 45°, and 80°   D 30°, 30°, and 120°

18. Estimate: $1.48 + $0.12 − $0.27. **$1.30**
(SB 8)

19. Write Use the definition of absolute value to write $|-5| = 5$ in words.
(5) The distance from −5 to 0 is 5.

20. Verify True or False: A rectangle is a parallelogram. Explain your choice **true;**
(SB 14) The opposite sides of rectangles are congruent and parallel.

*__**21. Geometry**__ The hypotenuse squared (c^2) can be determined by solving for $a^2 + b^2$ in
(4) the Pythagorean Theorem. Using the order of operations, decide if the expression
$(a + b)$ should be determined before a^2? **No, a^2 should be determined first.**

*__**22.**__ (Weather) One winter day the temperature rose 29°F from a low of −3°F in the
(5) morning. What was the day's high temperature? **26°F.**

*__**23.**__ (Football) On the first down, the Tigers gained 8 yards. Then they were pushed back
(5) for a loss of $13\frac{1}{2}$ yards on the second down. Write and solve an addition problem
to find the total number of yards lost or gained on the first two downs.
$8 + (-13\frac{1}{2}) = -5\frac{1}{2}$ yards

*__**24. Multiple Choice**__ Which of these sets of numbers is closed under addition? **D**
(5)
A integers   B rational numbers
C real numbers   D all of these

*__**25. Multi-Step**__ Airplane A took off from an airport that is 43 feet below sea level, and
(5) then climbed 20,512 feet to its cruising altitude. Airplane B took off at the same time
from an airport that was 1924 feet above sea level, and then climbed 18,527 feet to its
cruising altitude. Which airplane is currently cruising at a higher altitude? **Airplane A**

*__**26.**__ (Banking) Martha had $500 in her checking account. She made a withdrawal of $34.65.
(5) Write and solve an addition problem to find Martha's balance after the withdrawal.
$500 + (-$34.65) = $465.35

*__**27. Multi-Step**__ A china cup-and-saucer set sells for $15.25 and a plate sells for $25.
(4) A woman buys 3 cup-and-saucer sets and 4 plates. If she pays a 5% sales tax, how
much does she pay for her purchase?
a. Determine how much the woman spends before sales tax. Use the expression
$3 \cdot (\$15.25) + 4 \cdot (\$25)$ to solve. **$145.75**
b. How much does she pay with sales tax included? Round your answer to the nearest
hundredth. Use the expression $\$145.75 + (0.05) \cdot (\$145.75)$ to solve. **$153.04**

*__**28.**__ (Stocks) Stock in the ABC Company fell 12.67 points on Monday and 31.51 points
(5) on Tuesday. Determine the total change in the stock for the two days.
−44.18 points

*__**29. Multiple Choice**__ Which expression correctly represents 1.6^5? **A**
(3)
A $1.6 \times 1.6 \times 1.6 \times 1.6 \times 1.6$ B $1.6 + 1.6 + 1.6 + 1.6 + 1.6$
C $0.6 \times 0.6 \times 0.6 \times 0.6 \times 0.6 + 1$ D $1 \times 1 \times 1 \times 1 \times 1 + 0.6$

*__**30.**__ (Temperature) At midnight the temperature was −7°F. By noon the temperature had
(5) risen 23°F. What was the temperature at noon? **16°F**

26 Saxon Algebra 1

CHALLENGE

Absolute-value expressions can be nested. Have students solve the following nested absolute-value expression.

$-3 + |-5|-7-4-|(-2) + |1 + (-3)||$
−9

LOOKING FORWARD

Finding absolute value and adding real numbers prepares students for

- **Lesson 6** Subtracting Real Numbers
- **Lesson 7** Simplifying and Comparing Expressions with Symbols of Inclusion
- **Lesson 10** Adding and Subtracting Real Numbers
- **Lesson 11** Multiplying and Dividing Real Numbers
- **Lesson 12** Using the Properties of Real Numbers to Simplify Expressions

LESSON 6

Subtracting Real Numbers

Warm Up

1. **Vocabulary** The _____ of a number is the distance from the
   (1) number to 0 on a number line. **absolute value**

   Simplify.

   2. $86.9 - 18.94$ **67.96**
      (SB2)

   3. $\frac{1}{3} + \frac{4}{9}$ $\frac{7}{9}$
      (SB3)

   4. $41.06 + 83.7$ **124.76**
      (SB2)

   5. $\frac{5}{6} - \frac{5}{12}$ $\frac{5}{12}$
      (SB3)

New Concepts

Two numbers with the same absolute value but different signs are called **opposites**. Another name for the opposite of a number is **additive inverse**. The sum of a number and its opposite is 0.

Inverse Property of Addition
For every real number a, $a + (-a) = (-a) + a = 0$.
Example $5 + (-5) = 0$

Addition and subtraction are inverse operations. Subtracting a number is the same as adding the inverse of the number.

Rules for Subtracting Real Numbers
To subtract a number, add its inverse. Then follow the rules for adding real numbers.
Example $3 - 5 = 3 + (-5) = -2$

Example 1 Subtracting Real Numbers

Find each difference.

Math Reasoning

Analyze What is the meaning of $-(-8)$?

Sample: It means the opposite of negative 8 which is 8.

a. $(-12) - 21$

SOLUTION

$(-12) - 21$
$(-12) + (-21) = -33$

b. $(-19) - (-8)$

SOLUTION

$(-19) - (-8)$
$(-19) + (+8) = -11$

c. $3.2 - (-5.1)$

SOLUTION

$3.2 - (-5.1)$
$3.2 + (+5.1) = 8.3$

d. $\left(-\frac{3}{5}\right) - \left(-\frac{1}{5}\right)$

SOLUTION

$\left(-\frac{3}{5}\right) - \left(-\frac{1}{5}\right)$
$\left(-\frac{3}{5}\right) + \left(+\frac{1}{5}\right) = -\frac{2}{5}$

Online Connection
www.SaxonMathResources.com

Lesson 6   27

LESSON 6

1 Warm Up

Problem 5
Remind students to find a common denominator before subtracting.

2 New Concepts

In this lesson, students learn to subtract real numbers. Discuss the definition of additive inverse. Explain that subtracting real numbers means writing an equivalent addition statement.

Example 1

Remind students that any subtraction problem can be turned into an addition problem by adding the opposite.

Additional Example 1

Find each difference.

a. $(-13) - 8$ **–21**

b. $(-32) - (-22)$ **–10**

c. $4.5 - (-8.2)$ **12.7**

d. $\left(-\frac{6}{7}\right) - \left(-\frac{1}{7}\right)$ $-\frac{5}{7}$

TEACHER TIP

Students may benefit from modeling the subtraction on a number line.

LESSON RESOURCES

Student Edition Practice
   Workbook 6
Reteaching Master 6
Adaptations Master 6
Challenge and Enrichment
   Master C6
Technology Lab Master 6

MATH BACKGROUND

Extending patterns with subtraction problems can clarify what it means to subtract a negative number. In the patterns below, each time the subtrahend decreases by 1, the difference increases by 1.

$3 - 3 = 0$ $-1 - 3 = -4$

$3 - 2 = 1$ $-1 - 2 = -3$

$3 - 1 = 2$ $-1 - 1 = -2$

$3 - 0 = 3$ $-1 - 0 = -1$

These patterns can be extended to differences with negative subtrahends.

$3 - (-1) = 4$ $-1 - (-1) = 0$

$3 - (-2) = 5$ $-1 - (-2) = 1$

Lesson 6   27

Example 2
Have students theorize and test each statement.

Additional Example 2
Determine whether each statement is true or false. Give a counterexample for false statements.

a. The set of negative integers is closed under subtraction.
false; Sample: $(-1) - (-2) = 1$

b. The set of rational numbers is closed under subtraction. true

Example 3
Error Alert
Students may write the opposite of the number being subtracted, but might forget to change the problem to addition. Remind students to add the opposite.

Additional Example 3
Death Valley is 282 feet below sea level. If Nayip is standing in Death Valley and is 6 feet tall, what is the altitude at the top of Nayip's head? 276 ft below sea level

Extend the Example
Nayip descends 15 more meters to collect an additional sample, and then rises 6 meters. Where is Nayip in relation to the surface?
44 m below the surface

Lesson Practice
Problem a
Scaffolding Write the problem as an addition problem. Then solve.

Problem d
Error Alert When subtracting fractions, remember to find a common denominator.

Math Language
A set of numbers is **closed** under a given operation if the outcome of the operation on any two members of the set is also a member of the set.

Example 2 Determining Closure Over Subtraction
Determine whether each statement is true or false. Give a counterexample for false statements.

a. The set of integers is closed under subtraction.
SOLUTION
The statement is true because the difference of any two integers will be an integer.

b. The set of real numbers is closed under subtraction.
SOLUTION
The statement is true because the difference of any two real numbers will be a real number.

Example 3 Application: Dive Depth
Nayip collected a water sample at a depth of 23 meters from the surface. He descended another 12 meters to collect a plant sample. Where was Nayip in relation to the surface when he retrieved the plant sample?

SOLUTION
A depth of 23 meters can be written as (-23).
$(-23) - 12$
$= (-23) + (-12)$
$= -35$

Nayip was at 35 meters below the surface when he collected the plant sample.

Lesson Practice
Find each difference.
(Ex 1)
a. $14 - (-22)$ 36
b. $(-7) - 16$ -23
c. $(-23.4) - 18.72$ -42.12
d. $\left(-\frac{2}{3}\right) - \left(-\frac{1}{6}\right)$ $-\frac{1}{2}$

Determine whether each statement is true or false. Give a counterexample for false statements.
(Ex 2)
e. The set of whole numbers is closed under subtraction. false; Sample: counterexample: $5 - 12 = -7$
f. The set of rational numbers is closed under subtraction. true

g. On January 23, 1960, the Trieste dove to a record depth of 37,800 feet below sea level. The record set previously, on January 7th of the same year, was 13,800 feet less than the dive on January 23rd. What was the record set on January 7th in relation to sea level? $-24,000$ feet
(Ex 3)

28 Saxon Algebra 1

ALTERNATE METHOD FOR EXAMPLE 3
Have students draw a vertical number line to model Nayip's location.

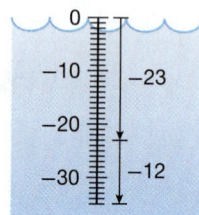

ENGLISH LEARNERS
Explain that **inverse** means opposite, almost like a mirror image. Ask students to come up with concrete examples of inverse, such as right hand and left hand, attic and basement, or even yesterday and tomorrow. Then draw a number line on the board, and point out that the positive side is the inverse of the negative, and that the negative side is the inverse of the positive.

Practice Distributed and Integrated

Add, subtract, multiply, or divide.

1. (SB 3) $5\frac{1}{3} \div 2\frac{1}{3}$ $2\frac{2}{7}$
2. (SB 3) $40\frac{1}{8} - 21\frac{1}{4}$ $18\frac{7}{8}$
3. (5) $5\frac{2}{3} + 2\frac{5}{6} + (-2\frac{1}{6})$ $6\frac{1}{3}$
4. (SB 3) $1\frac{2}{3} \div 1\frac{1}{4} \cdot 1\frac{1}{2}$ 2
5. (SB 2) $0.74 \div 0.2 \cdot 0.3$ 1.11
6. (SB 2) $5.4 \cdot 0.3 \div 0.4$ 4.05
7. (SB 2) $1.24 \cdot 0.2 \div 0.1$ 2.48
8. (SB 2) $112.4 \div 3.2$ 35.125

9. (SB 12) Find the prime factorization of 592. $2 \cdot 2 \cdot 2 \cdot 2 \cdot 37$
10. (SB 12) Find the prime factorization of 168. $2 \cdot 2 \cdot 2 \cdot 3 \cdot 7$

11. **Model** Display the following set of data in a line plot.
(SB 29)
8, 6, 9, 7, 5, 4, 6, 7, 9, 8, 5, 6, 6, 8

11. Frequency of Numbers

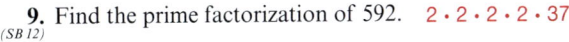

12. **Write** Use the divisibility test to determine if 2326 is divisible by 3. Explain your
(SB 4) answer.   no; The sum of the digits is 2 + 3 + 2 + 6 = 13, which is not divisible by 3.

13. (SB 5) Write 6% as a fraction in simplest form and as a decimal. $\frac{3}{50}$; 0.06

14. **Measurement** Write 1.25 feet as a fraction in simplest form and compare it to $\frac{5}{3}$ feet.
(SB 5) Which is greater? $1\frac{1}{4}$; $\frac{5}{3}$ feet

15. (SB 5) Write $\frac{3}{5}$ as a decimal and as a percent.   0.6; 60%

16. **Multiple Choice** What is the value of the expression below?   **D**
(4)
$$\frac{(3 \cdot 20 + 2 \cdot 20) \cdot 6 - 20}{10^2}$$

  A 2.8   **B** 58   **C** −14   **D** 5.8

17. Simplify $\frac{(45 + 39 + 47 + 40 + 33 + 39 + 41)}{(2 \cdot 2)^2 - 12}$.   71
(4)

*18. **Multiple Choice** Which of these differences will be negative?   **B**
(6)
  A −4.8 − (−5.2)   **B** 4.8 − 5.2
  C 4.8 − 3.2   **D** 6.7 − (−7.8)

*19. **Football** Ryan's varsity football team is on its own 25-yard line. The quarterback
(6) stumbles for a loss of 15 yards. What line is Ryan's varsity football team on now?
10-yard line

*20. **Geometry** If one angle in a triangle measures 105.5° and another measures 38.2°,
(6) what is the measurement of the third angle? Use the expression 180 − 105.5 − 38.2
to solve.   36.3°

*21. **Temperature** On a winter day, a wind gust makes the temperature in Antarctica
(6) feel sixteen degrees colder than the actual temperature. If the temperature is −5°C,
how cold did it feel?   −21°C

Lesson 6   29

INCLUSION

Students may benefit from a concrete example of subtracting integers. Use two-color counters to model the following problem:

$$-7 - 14.$$

Lay out 7 negatives (red side up) and 14 positives (yellow side up). To subtract, flip the 14 positives over and add.

Repeat this activity with different numbers.

Check for Understanding

The questions below help assess the concepts taught in the lesson.

"How do you find the opposite of a real number?"
Sample: Change the sign.

"Explain how to solve (−9) − 15." Sample: Change the subtraction to addition using the additive inverse of 15.

3 Practice

Math Conversations
Discussion to strengthen understanding

Problem 2
"What is the additive inverse of $21\frac{1}{4}$?" $-21\frac{1}{4}$

"How can you rewrite the subtraction problem $40\frac{1}{8} - 21\frac{1}{4}$?"
$40\frac{1}{8} + (-21\frac{1}{4}) = 18\frac{7}{8}$

Problem 3
Suggest that it might be easier to first add the addends with common denominators.

$2\frac{5}{6} + (-2\frac{1}{6}) = \frac{2}{3}$

$\frac{2}{3} + 5\frac{2}{3} = 6\frac{1}{3}$

Problem 12
Error Alert
A common error in using the divisibility test is that students just look at the last digit instead of adding all of the digits. Remind students to add all the digits: 2 + 3 + 2 + 6 = 13.

If the sum is not divisible by 3, then 2326 is not divisible by 3.

Problem 19
Extend the Problem
"If Ryan's football team gains 5 yards instead of losing 15, what line will the team be on?"
30-yard line

Lesson 6   29

Problem 23

Discuss the meaning of equiangular. Point out that the first part of the word sounds like equal and the last part sounds like angle. The word means equal angles.

Problem 29

Error Alert

Students may think that $-9.09090\overline{909}$ is an irrational number because it is a repeating decimal. Explain that this number can be written as a fraction, $-9\frac{1}{11}$, and therefore is rational.

*22. (Consumer Math) Leila issued a check for $149.99 and deposited $84.50 in her
 (6) account. What is the net change in her account? −$65.49

23. **Multiple Choice** Which triangle is an equiangular triangle? **B**
(SB 13)
 A a triangle with angle measures of 45°, 45°, and 90°
 B a triangle with angle measures of 60°, 60°, and 60°
 C a triangle with angle measures of 55°, 35°, and 90°
 D a triangle with angle measures of 30°, 30°, and 120°

24. (Boating) The tour boat can leave the dock only if the level of the lake is no more
 (5) than 2 feet below normal. Before the recent rainfall, the level of the lake was
 $5\frac{1}{3}$ feet below normal. After the recent rainfall, the level of the lake rose $3\frac{1}{4}$ feet.
 Can the tour boat leave the dock? Explain. no; Sample: After the rainfall, the lake
 level is at $-2\frac{1}{12}$ feet, which is more than 2 feet below normal.

*25. **Geometry** The triangle inequality is a theorem from geometry stating that for any
 (5) two real numbers a and b, $|a + b| \leq |a| + |b|$. Verify the triangle inequality by
 simplifying $|-18.5 + 4.75| \leq |-18.5| + |4.75|$. $13.75 \leq 23.25$

*26. **Error Analysis** Two students solved this problem. Which student is correct? Explain
 (5) the error. Student A; Sample: Student B added 11 floors instead of subtracting.

The elevator started on the second floor and went up 8 floors, then down 11 floors to the garage level, and then up 6 floors. Which floor is the elevator on now?

Student A	Student B
$2 + 8 + (-11) + 6 = 5$	$2 + 8 - (-11) + 6 = 27$
The 5th floor	The 27th floor

27. **Multi-Step** A bit is a binary digit and can have a value of either 0 or 1. A byte is a
 (3) string of 8 bits.
 a. Write the number of bits in one byte as a power of 2. 2^3
 b. Write 32 as a power of 2. 2^5
 c. Write the number of bits in 32 bytes as a power of 2. 2^8

*28. $16c + (-4d) + \frac{8\pi}{15} + 21efg$
 (2)
 a. Find the coefficients of the expression. 16, −4, 21
 b. Find the number of terms in the expression. 4
 c. **Justify** Rewrite the expression so that there are no parentheses. Justify your change.
 $16c - 4d + \frac{8\pi}{15} + 21efg$; Subtracting a number is the same as adding its inverse.

*29. **Multiple Choice** What subset of numbers does the number $-9.0909090\overline{909}$ belong to? **D**
 (1)
 A integers   **B** irrational numbers
 C natural numbers   **D** rational numbers

*30. (Oceanography) The Pacific Ocean has an average depth of 12,925 feet, while the
 (6) Atlantic Ocean has as average depth of 11,730 feet. Find the difference in average
 depths. 1195 ft

30 *Saxon Algebra 1*

⭐ **CHALLENGE**

Challenge students to simplify the expression.

$25 - (-28) - [57 - (-86 - 19)]$ −109

LOOKING FORWARD

Subtracting real numbers prepares students for

• **Lesson 7** Simplifying and Comparing Expressions with Symbols of Inclusion

• **Lesson 16** Simplifying and Evaluating Variable Expressions

• **Lesson 18** Combining Like Terms

• **Lesson 19** Solving One-Step Equations by Adding or Subtracting

LESSON 7

Simplifying and Comparing Expressions with Symbols of Inclusion

Warm Up

1. **Vocabulary** A _____ is used to represent an unknown number.
   (2) variable

   Simplify.

   2. $-1.5 + 3^2 - (3 - 5)$ 9.5
      (4)
   3. $12 - 4 \cdot 0.5 + (3.4 - 1.7)$ 11.7
      (4)
   4. $\left(\frac{2}{3}\right)^2 - \left(\frac{1}{3}\right)^2 + \frac{5}{6}$ $\frac{7}{6}$ or $1\frac{1}{6}$
      (4)

New Concepts

A mathematical expression can include numbers, variables, operations, and symbols of inclusion. Symbols of inclusion, such as fraction bars, absolute-value symbols, parentheses, braces, and brackets indicate which numbers, variables, and operations are parts of the same term. An example is shown below.

$$\left(\frac{2x}{3} + 3\frac{1}{5}\right) - 2y$$

The expression inside the parentheses is considered a single term. To simplify an expression with multiple symbols of inclusion, begin inside the innermost symbol of inclusion and work outward.

Example 1 Expressions with Absolute-Value Symbols and Parentheses

Simplify each expression.

a. $9 - |4 - 6|$

SOLUTION

$9 - |4 - 6|$
$= 9 - |-2|$ Subtract inside absolute-value symbols.
$= 9 - 2$ Simplify the absolute value.
$= 7$ Subtract.

b. $5 \cdot 2 + [3 + (6 - 8)]$

SOLUTION Begin simplifying inside the innermost symbol of inclusion.

$5 \cdot 2 + [3 + (6 - 8)]$
$= 5 \cdot 2 + [3 + (-2)]$ Subtract inside parentheses.
$= 5 \cdot 2 + 1$ Add inside brackets.
$= 10 + 1$ Multiply.
$= 11$ Add.

Math Language

( )	parentheses
[ ]	brackets
{ }	braces
$\frac{a}{b}$	fraction bar
$|x|$	absolute-value symbols

Online Connection
www.SaxonMathResources.com

Lesson 7   31

LESSON 7

1 Warm Up

Problem 2
Remind students to simplify the exponent before adding or subtracting.

2 New Concepts

In this lesson, students will apply the order of operations to numeric and algebraic expressions with symbols of inclusion. Note the symbols of inclusion in the Math Language box.

Example 1

Explain to students that they can think of symbols of inclusion as layers of a problem, and that to solve the problem correctly, they must start with the innermost layer, or symbol of inclusion.

Additional Example 1
Simplify.

a. $|3 - 9| - |5 - 2|$ 3
b. $4 \cdot 3 - [6 - (5 + 9)]$ 20

LESSON RESOURCES

Student Edition Practice Workbook 7
Reteaching Master 7
Adaptations Master 7
Challenge and Enrichment Master C7

Lesson 7   31

MATH BACKGROUND

One of the roles of mathematics is to be a form of communication. As with any language, math has its own set of rules. A zero following a 1 means something altogether different from a zero placed before it, just as the placement of words in a sentence can change its meaning. Without rules, both English and mathematics would be a chaotic, uncommunicative jumble.

The order of operations is a form of mathematical "grammar," with symbols of inclusion helping to form more complex "sentences." Understanding the grammar of mathematics enables students to communicate mathematically.

It is important to follow the order of operations at all times, even when working inside symbols of inclusion.

Example 2 Simplifying Expressions with Brackets

Simplify.

$3 + 5 \cdot [(9 - 3)^2 - 6]$

SOLUTION

Begin inside the innermost symbol of inclusion and work outward.

$3 + 5 \cdot [(9 - 3)^2 - 6]$

$= 3 + 5 \cdot [6^2 - 6]$	Simplify inside the parentheses.
$= 3 + 5 \cdot [36 - 6]$	Evaluate the exponent.
$= 3 + 5 \cdot 30$	Subtract inside the brackets.
$= 3 + 150$	Multiply.
$= 153$	Add.

Hint

Use the order of operations:
1. symbols of inclusion;
2. powers and roots;
3. multiply or divide;
4. add or subtract.

To simplify a rational expression such as $\frac{6 \cdot 3}{4 - 2}$, the numerator and denominator must be simplified first.

Example 3 Simplifying Expressions with Rational Numbers

Simplify. Justify each step.

$[5 \cdot (4 + 2)^2] + \frac{4 \cdot 5}{2}$

SOLUTION

Justify each step using the order of operations or mathematical properties.

$[5 \cdot (4 + 2)^2] + \frac{4 \cdot 5}{2}$

$= [5 \cdot (6)^2] + \frac{4 \cdot 5}{2}$	Add inside the parentheses.
$= [5 \cdot 36] + \frac{4 \cdot 5}{2}$	Simplify the exponent.
$= 180 + \frac{4 \cdot 5}{2}$	Multiply inside the brackets.
$= 180 + \frac{20}{2}$	Simplify the numerator.
$= 180 + 10$	Simplify the fraction.
$= 190$	Add.

Example 4 Compare Expressions with Symbols of Inclusion

Compare the expressions. Use <, >, or =.

$12 + [5(7 - 5)^3 - 14] \; \bigcirc \; [(9 - 5)^2 + 7] - 3^3$

Example 2

Point out that operations within grouping symbols (parentheses, brackets, and braces) can be the base of an exponent. Students must simplify the expression within the grouping symbol first before finding the power.

Additional Example 2

Simplify.

$-4 + [6 - (-2 + 4)^2]$ -2

Example 3

Mathematical concepts such as fractions, absolute value, and radicals also create groupings of expressions that students need to simplify before completing other operations.

Additional Example 3

Simplify.

$\frac{4 + 5}{3} - (2 \cdot 3^2 - 4)$ -11

Example 4

When students compare two numeric expressions, remind them to simplify each side separately using the order of operations. Then have them compare the values.

Additional Example 4

Compare the expressions. Use <, >, or =.

$14 + [(3 - 5)^3 + 7] \; \bigcirc \; 4^2 - [20 - (5)^2]$ $13 < 21$

ALTERNATE METHOD FOR EXAMPLE 3

Have students rewrite the fraction as division with grouping symbols for the numerator.

$[5 \cdot (4 + 2)^2] + \frac{4 \cdot 5}{2}$

$= [5 \cdot (4 + 2)^2] + (4 \cdot 5) \div 2$

$= (5 \cdot 6^2) + (4 \cdot 5) \div 2$

$= (5 \cdot 36) + (4 \cdot 5) \div 2$

$= 180 + 20 \div 2$

$= 180 + 10$

$= 190$

SOLUTION Simplify each expression. Then compare.

$12 + [5(7-5)^3 - 14]$ $[(9-5)^2 + 7] - 3^3$
$= 12 + [5(2)^3 - 14]$ $= [(4)^2 + 7] - 3^3$
$= 12 + [5 \cdot 8 - 14]$ $= [16 + 7] - 3^3$
$= 12 + [40 - 14]$ $= 23 - 3^3$
$= 12 + 26$ $= 23 - 27$
$= 38$ $= -4$

Since $38 > -4$, $12 + [5(7-5)^3 - 14]$ $[(9-5)^2 + 7] - 3^3$.

Example 5 Application: Half Price Sale

Beatrice wants to buy 3 DVDs marked $7 each and 4 CDs marked $12 each. Everything in the store is on sale for half off the marked price. Beatrice has $31.50 to spend and a coupon good for $1 off each CD. Use the expression below to determine if Beatrice has enough money to buy all the items she wants.

$$\$31.50 - \left[\frac{3 \cdot \$7}{2} + \frac{4 \cdot \$12}{2} - (4 \cdot \$1)\right]$$

SOLUTION Begin inside the innermost symbols of inclusion to simplify the expression.

$\$31.50 - \left[\frac{3 \cdot \$7}{2} + \frac{4 \cdot \$12}{2} - (4 \cdot \$1)\right]$

$= \$31.50 - \left[\frac{3 \cdot \$7}{2} + \frac{4 \cdot \$12}{2} - \$4\right]$ Multiply inside the parentheses.

$= \$31.50 - \left[\frac{\$21}{2} + \frac{\$48}{2} - \$4\right]$ Simplify the numerators.

$= \$31.50 - [\$10.50 + \$24 - \$4]$ Simplify the fractions.

$= \$31.50 - \$30.50$ Simplify inside the brackets.

$= \$1.00$ Subtract.

Beatrice has enough money.

Graphing Calculator

Enter the expression $10 + 8 \div 2^2$ into your calculator. If the calculator follows the order of operations, the answer will be 12.

Lesson Practice

Simplify each expression.
(Ex 1)
a. $12 + |5 - 11|$ 18
b. $5(8 + 4) \div (15 - 5 - 4)$ 10
c. $5 + [6 \cdot (2^3 + 4)]$ 77
d. **Justify** Simplify the expression. Justify each step.   See Additional Answers.
(Ex 3)
$$4(1 + 2)^2 \div 6 + \frac{8 \cdot 3}{2}$$

Lesson 7   33

Check for Understanding

The questions below help assess the concepts taught in this lesson.

"What is the order of operations?"
symbols of inclusion, powers and roots, multiplication or division, addition or subtraction

"Explain how to rewrite $4 + 3^3$ so that the addition is completed before the power."
Place parentheses around the expression $4 + 3$.

3 Practice

Math Conversations
Discussion to strengthen understanding

Problem 3
Remind students to write equivalent fractions using the least common denominator before adding or subtracting. Ask, "What is the least common denominator?" 12

Problem 20
Guide students by asking, "What is the formula for finding circumference?" $C = 2\pi r$

"Which property of multiplication is useful in this situation?"
commutative

---

f. Sample: Begin inside the parentheses. Square the height. Next, divide the weight by the new denominator. Then multiply the quotient by 703.

e. Compare the expressions. Use $<$, $>$, or $=$.
(Ex 4)
$(13 + 5) - [5 \cdot 2^2]$ ⊘ $[(7 + 11) - 5] - 2^3$.

f. (Health) Body Mass Index (BMI) is the relation of weight to height. The
(Ex. 5) expression $\left(\dfrac{W}{H^2}\right) \cdot 703$, where W is weight in pounds and H is height in inches, is used to calculate BMI. Explain the steps that are necessary to simplify this expression.

Practice   Distributed and Integrated

Add, subtract, multiply, or divide.

1. $(5 + 2)^2 - 50$ -1
(4)

2. $(3 - 5) + 7^2$ 47
(4)

3. $3\dfrac{1}{3} - 1\dfrac{1}{6} - 5\dfrac{1}{4}$ $-3\dfrac{1}{12}$
(6)

4. $2\dfrac{1}{3} \cdot 3\dfrac{1}{4} \cdot 1\dfrac{1}{2}$ $11\dfrac{3}{8}$
(SB 3)

5. $(0.56 + 0.3) \cdot 0.2$ 0.172
(4)

6. $3.25 \cdot 0.4 + 0.1$ 1.4
(4)

7. $1.2 \div 0.1 \div 0.1$ 120
(SB 2)

8. $20.2 \cdot 0.1 \cdot 0.1$ 0.202
(SB 2)

9. **Verify** True or False: All whole numbers are counting numbers. If true, explain
(1) your answer. If false, give a counterexample.   false; 0 is a whole number but not a counting number.

10. The set $\{\ldots, -3, -2, -1, 0, 1, 2, 3, \ldots\}$ represents which set of numbers?   integers
(1)

11. **Justify** True or False: An obtuse triangle has two obtuse angles. Explain your choice.
(SB 13) false; A triangle can only have one obtuse angle.

12. Find the prime factorization of 207. $3 \cdot 3 \cdot 23$
(SB 12)

13. Find the prime factorization of 37. $1 \cdot 37$
(SB 12)

14. **Write** Use the divisibility test to determine if 10,048 is divisible by 8. Explain.
(SB 4) yes; The number formed by the last three digits is divisible by 8.

15. Write 0.345 as a fraction in simplest form and as a percent. $\dfrac{69}{200}$; 34.5%
(SB 5)

16. Write 0.07% as a fraction in simplest form and as a decimal. $\dfrac{7}{10,000}$; 0.0007
(SB 5)

*17. Evaluate $(|-3| \cdot 4) + \left[\left(\dfrac{1}{2} + \dfrac{1}{4}\right) \div \dfrac{1}{3}\right]$. $14\dfrac{1}{4}$
(7)

*18. Compare: $\dfrac{1}{3} + \dfrac{1}{5} \cdot \dfrac{2}{15}$ ⊘ $\left(\dfrac{1}{3} + \dfrac{1}{5}\right) \cdot \dfrac{2}{15}$.
(7)

*19. (Temperature) The following two formulas are used to convert degrees Celsius (°C) to
(7) degrees Fahrenheit (°F) and vise versa: $C = \dfrac{5}{9}(F - 32)$ and $F = \dfrac{9}{5}C + 32$. Explain how the equations are different.   Sample: The two formulas contain opposite operations.

*20. (Fencing) The diagram represents the fencing around a backyard. The fence
(7) is formed with parallel lines and a half-circle. Write and solve an equation to determine how many feet of fencing are needed. Round the answer to the nearest tenth.   Sample: Perimeter $= (2 \cdot 40) + \dfrac{1}{2}(2\pi \cdot 15) = 80 + 47.1 = 127.1$ ft

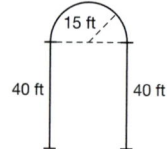

ENGLISH LEARNERS

For this lesson, discuss the meaning of the word *innermost* with students.

"Innermost means the inner group of symbols."

Have students identify the innermost group in each example.

*21. **Multiple Choice** Simplify $[(10-8)^2 - (-1)] + (5-3)$. **B**
(7)
   A -38 B 7   C -80 D 37

*22. (Manufacturing) A company produces two different types of 6-sided boxes. Box A is
(7) 12 inches long, 12 inches wide, and 12 inches tall. Box B is 16 inches long,
16 inches wide, and 6.75 inches tall. Both boxes have the same volume, but the
company wants to know which box uses less material to produce.
   a. Write and solve an expression to find the surface area of Box A. $6 \cdot 12^2 = 864$ in²
   b. Write and solve an expression to find the surface area of Box B. $(2 \cdot 16^2) + 4(16 \cdot 6.75) = 944$ in²
   c. Compare the box sizes. Which box uses less material?   864 < 944; Box A

*23. **Multi-Step** A ball is dropped from a height of 25.6 feet. After it hits the ground, it
(6) bounces to 12.8 feet and falls back to the ground. Next it bounces to 6.4 feet and
falls back to the ground. Then it bounces to 3.2 feet and falls back to the ground.
   a. Find the difference in heights between each consecutive bounce.   12.8 feet, 6.4 feet, 3.2 feet
   b. If the pattern continues, will the ball ever stop bouncing? Explain.
      no; Sample: The ball is bouncing back up halfway each time.

24. **Geometry** What is the perimeter of the rectangle?   61.464 units
(6)

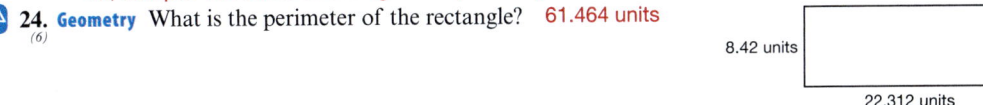

25. **Measurement** A valley is 250 below sea level and a small hill is 78 feet above sea
(5) level. Solve $|-250| + 78$ to determine the distance from the bottom of the valley
to the top of the hill.   328 ft

*26. (Transportation) In the last hour, 7 planes have landed at the airport and 11 planes
(5) have taken off. Use addition to find the change in the total number of planes at
the airport in the last hour. -4 planes

27. **Error Analysis** The temperature in the morning was $-18°$F. It increased by 5° by noon
(4) and dropped 10° in the evening. Two students determined the temperature in the
evening. Which student is correct? Explain the error.   Student B; Student A should
have subtracted 10.

Student A	Student B
$-18 + 5 + 10 = -3$	$-18 + 5 + (-10) = -23$

*28. (Meteorology) The water level of the reservoir in Purcellville, Virginia was 2 feet
(6) below normal. After a heavy rainstorm, the water level increased to 5 feet above
normal. Write and solve a subtraction problem to find the change in the water
level caused by the rainstorm. $5 - (-2) = 7$ feet

29. **Multiple Choice** Which term in the expression $\frac{\sqrt{9}ny}{nx} + a^2 - \frac{n}{4} + \frac{3\pi}{8}$ contains an
(1) irrational constant? **B**
   A $\frac{\sqrt{9}ny}{nx}$ B $\frac{3\pi}{8}$ C $\frac{n}{4}$ D a^2

*30. **Geometry** The measure of each interior angle of a hexagon is given by the
(7) expression $\frac{180(6-2)°}{6}$. What is the measure of an interior angle of a
hexagon?   120°

Problem 22
Extend the Problem
Have students experiment to find some other possible dimensions, and the associated surface areas, of boxes with the same volume.

"Can you draw a conclusion about which shape of box would have the least surface area for a given volume?" A cube has the least surface area.

Problem 25
Error Alert
Remind students that the absolute value is the distance from zero to a number on a number line and therefore is always positive.

Lesson 7

CHALLENGE

Grouping symbols can be added in a variety of places to change the value of a numeric expression. Have students insert grouping symbols into the following expression to create several different values. Students can work in pairs and challenge each other to find their grouping-symbol arrangement for a given value.

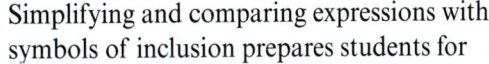

Sample: $(3 + 4 \cdot 6^2) - (5 \cdot 7 + 11) = 101$
$3 + (4 \cdot 6^2 - 5 \cdot 7) + 11 = 123$

LOOKING FORWARD

Simplifying and comparing expressions with symbols of inclusion prepares students for

- **Lesson 9** Evaluating and Comparing Algebraic Expressions
- **Lesson 12** Using Properties of Real Numbers to Simplify Expressions
- **Lesson 15** Using the Distributive Property to Simplify Expressions
- **Lesson 16** Simplifying and Evaluating Variable Expressions

LESSON 8

1 Warm Up

Problems 2–5
Remind students that they can use prime factorization to identify common factors. If students cancel all common factors before multiplying, their product will be in simplest form.

2 New Concepts

In this lesson, students learn to convert a variety of units. Familiarity with common unit equivalents, especially for length, will be helpful.

Example 1

Point out to students that when they find the unit equivalency, they should write it as a fraction with the current unit of measure (yards) in the denominator; this is so the unit of yards will cancel and leave the desired unit of measure (miles) in the numerator.

Additional Example 1
An elephant can charge at speeds of about 25 miles per hour. How fast can an elephant charge in feet per hour? **132,000 ft/hr**

LESSON RESOURCES

Student Edition Practice Workbook 8
Reteaching Master 8
Adaptations Master 8
Challenge and Enrichment Master C8

LESSON 8 — Using Unit Analysis to Convert Measures

Warm Up

1. **Vocabulary** The amount of space a solid figure occupies is called the _____ (area, volume). **volume**

Simplify.

2. $\dfrac{7}{12} \cdot \dfrac{36}{49}$ $\dfrac{3}{7}$

3. $\dfrac{8}{9} \cdot \dfrac{15}{36}$ $\dfrac{10}{27}$

4. $\dfrac{2}{5} \cdot \dfrac{15}{16} \cdot \dfrac{6}{7}$ $\dfrac{9}{28}$

5. $\dfrac{12}{13} \cdot \dfrac{1}{4} \cdot \dfrac{39}{48}$ $\dfrac{3}{16}$

New Concepts

Unit analysis is a process for converting measures into different units. A unit ratio, or conversion factor, compares 2 measures that name the same amount.

$$\dfrac{12 \text{ in.}}{1 \text{ ft}} \qquad \dfrac{1 \text{ m}}{100 \text{ cm}} \qquad \dfrac{3 \text{ ft}}{1 \text{ yd}}$$

Since the amounts used in a unit ratio are equal to each other, a unit ratio is always equal to 1. Since the product of 1 and a number is that number, a unit ratio multiplied by a measure will always name the same amount.

Example 1 Converting Units of Length

A cheetah ran at a rate of 105,600 yards per hour. How fast did the cheetah run in miles per hour?

Hint
A mile is equal to 1760 yards.

SOLUTION Find a unit ratio and multiply.

$\dfrac{105{,}600 \text{ yd}}{1 \text{ hour}} = \dfrac{? \text{ mi}}{1 \text{ hour}}$ Identify known and missing information.

$105{,}600 \text{ yd} \rightarrow ? \text{ mi}$ Write the conversion.

$1 \text{ mi} = 1{,}760 \text{ yd}$ Equate units.

$\dfrac{1 \text{ mi}}{1760 \text{ yd}}$ Write a unit ratio.

$\dfrac{105{,}600 \text{ yd}}{1 \text{ hr}} \cdot \dfrac{1 \text{ mi}}{1760 \text{ yd}}$ Write the multiplication sentence.

$= \dfrac{\cancel{105{,}600}^{60} \text{ yd}}{1 \text{ hr}} \cdot \dfrac{1 \text{ mi}}{\cancel{1760}_{1} \text{ yd}}$ Cancel out common factors.

$= \dfrac{60 \text{ mi}}{1 \text{ hr}}$ Multiply.

$\dfrac{105{,}600 \text{ yd}}{1 \text{ hr}} = \dfrac{60 \text{ mi}}{1 \text{ hr}}$ Write the ratio of miles per hour.

The cheetah ran at a rate of 60 miles per hour.

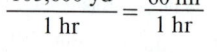
Online Connection
www.SaxonMathResources.com

36 Saxon Algebra 1

MATH BACKGROUND

Many real-world applications require the conversion of measurements between different units in order to solve the problem. Unit analysis is often called dimensional analysis. Conversions can be made within unit systems (customary and metric) and between the systems.

It is important to write the components of derived units like speed and density carefully as fractions and to place the correct units in the numerator and denominator. For example, a speed in miles per hour should be written as $\dfrac{\text{mi}}{\text{hr}}$, and density in kilograms per liter should be written as $\dfrac{\text{kg}}{l}$.

Exploration: Using Unit Analysis

If a measure of length changes, then the unit analysis occurs in one dimension. If a measure of area changes, the units for the dimensions of both length and width must change.

Draw two congruent squares with side lengths of 3 inches on a sheet of paper. Label the sides of the first square 1 yard. Divide both the length and width of the second square into 3 equal sections. This will divide the square into 9 congruent smaller squares. Label the sides of the second square 3 feet.

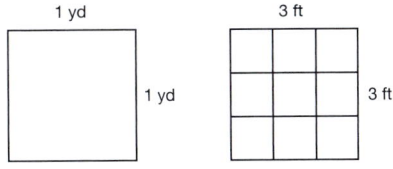

a. What is the area of the first square? Show your calculation.
1 yd × 1 yd = 1 yd²

b. What is the area of the second square? Show your calculation.
3 ft × 3 ft = 9 ft²

c. Write two unit ratios for converting between feet and yards. $\frac{1\text{ yd}}{3\text{ ft}}, \frac{3\text{ ft}}{1\text{ yd}}$

d. Which unit ratio should be used for converting yards to feet? Explain your choice. Sample: The unit ratio, $\frac{3\text{ ft}}{1\text{ yd}}$, should be used so that yards will cancel and the answer will be in feet.

e. Justify Use a unit ratio to convert the area of the first square into square feet. Show your calculation. $1\text{ yd}^2 \cdot \frac{3\text{ ft}}{1\text{ yd}} \cdot \frac{3\text{ ft}}{1\text{ yd}} = 9\text{ ft}^2$

f. Write Why is it necessary to multiply by the unit ratio twice to convert square yards to square feet? Sample: Both the length and width must be converted from yards to feet.

Extend the example of the area of squares to the volume of cubes. Draw two cubes, one with dimensions of 1 yard and one with dimensions of 3 feet.

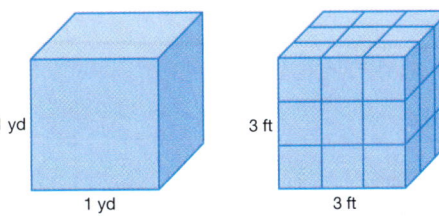

g. What is the volume of the first cube? Show your calculation.
1 yd × 1 yd × 1 yd = 1 yd³

h. What is the volume of the second cube? Show your calculation.
3 ft × 3 ft × 3 ft = 27 ft³

i. Justify Use a unit ratio to convert the volume of the first cube into cubic feet. Show your calculation. $1\text{ yd}^3 \cdot \frac{3\text{ ft}}{1\text{ yd}} \cdot \frac{3\text{ ft}}{1\text{ yd}} \cdot \frac{3\text{ ft}}{1\text{ yd}} = 27\text{ ft}^3$

j. Write Why is it necessary to multiply by the unit ratio three times to convert cubic yards to cubic feet? Sample: The length, width, and height must all be converted from yards to feet.

Math Reasoning

Write How could a single unit ratio be used to perform the area conversion?

Multiply the unit ratios for each dimension together to get a unit ratio.

Exploration

Note that the lengths of the sides and the areas of the congruent squares are equivalent measures, but that the change in units causes a change in the numeric values.

Have students write unit equivalencies for square yards and square feet and for cubic yards and cubic feet. Explore the pattern in the exponent of the unit and in the numeric equivalency of the units expressed in feet.

Extend the Exploration

"Write area and volume with equivalent measures of meters and centimeters and equivalent measures of inches and feet."
1 m² = 10,000 cm²
1 m³ = 1,000,000 cm³
1 ft² = 144 in²
1 ft³ = 1728 in³

ENGLISH LEARNERS

Discuss with students the meaning of the word **unit.** Say:

"A unit is an exact amount of a particular type of measurement. There are many types of units of measure. For example, distance can be measured in the unit "miles" or the unit "kilometers."

Have a volunteer give an example of other types of units of measure and how they are used. Sample: A bucket of water can be measured in the unit "cups" or "liters".

Provide students with some unit equivalency statements and if possible, show them a device used to measure some of the units, such as a ruler, meter or yard stick, or measuring cup.

Example 2

Tell students that they can also express the area of the room as square meters (m²). This means they would have to use the conversion factor $1\text{ m}^2 = 10{,}000\text{ cm}^2$.

Additional Example 2

Suppose that a gallon of paint will cover 57,600 in². Mary Alice wants to paint the solid wall of her hallway with two coats. The wall is 36 ft long and $10\frac{1}{2}$ ft tall. Will 2 gal of the paint be enough to cover the wall? Explain. yes; Sample: The hallway requires 756 ft² of paint for two coats. Two gallons of paint will cover 800 ft².

Example 3

Explain that rates such as speed, density, and pressure are called *derived units*. Derived units usually combine units that measure different dimensions; for example, speed gives information about distance or length over time.

Additional Example 3

A spray-painting apparatus is designed to spray 1000 cubic centimeters of paint per minute. How long would it take to empty a container that is 0.2 m³? 200 min

TEACHER TIP

In Example 2, there is more than one way to make the conversion. In Example 2, students can express the length in meters and area in square meters; this will allow them to work with decimals. Have students discuss whether they feel more comfortable working with large numbers or decimal numbers.

Math Reasoning

Each mat is 110 **centimeters square.** This means that the length and width are 110 centimeters each.

Math Reasoning

Analyze Compare the process of converting feet to inches with the process of converting feet per minute to inches per minute.

former uses one conversion factor, latter uses two conversion factors

---

Example 2   **Converting Units of Area**

A gym measures 8.5 meters by 14 meters. The owner bought mats to cover the floor. Each mat is 110 centimeters square. If 95 mats were purchased, are there enough mats to cover the floor?

SOLUTION Find the area and convert the unit of measure.

$8.5 \text{ m} \cdot 14 \text{ m} = 119 \text{ m}^2$ Find the area of the room.

$119 \text{ m}^2 \rightarrow ?\text{ cm}^2$ Write the conversion.

$1 \text{ m} = 100 \text{ cm}$ Equate units.

$\dfrac{100 \text{ cm}}{1 \text{ m}}$ Write a unit ratio.

$119 \text{ m} \cdot \text{m} \cdot \dfrac{100 \text{ cm}}{1 \text{ m}} \cdot \dfrac{100 \text{ cm}}{1 \text{ m}}$ Write the multiplication sentence.

$= 119\, \cancel{\text{m}} \cdot \cancel{\text{m}} \cdot \dfrac{100 \text{ cm}}{1\, \cancel{\text{m}}} \cdot \dfrac{100 \text{ cm}}{1\, \cancel{\text{m}}}$ Cancel out common factors.

$= \dfrac{119 \cdot 100 \text{ cm} \cdot 100 \text{ cm}}{1} = 1{,}190{,}000 \text{ cm}^2$ Multiply.

$95(110 \text{ cm} \cdot 110 \text{ cm}) = 1{,}149{,}500 \text{ cm}^2$ Find the area of 95 mats.

$1{,}149{,}500 \text{ cm}^2 < 1{,}190{,}000 \text{ cm}^2$ Compare the areas.

The area covered by 95 mats is less than the area of the floor, so there are not enough mats to cover the floor.

Example 3   **Application: Converting Units of Volume**

A hose with a flow rate of 41,472 cubic inches per hour is filling up a pool. The volume of the pool is 1,104 cubic feet. How many hours will it take to fill the pool?

SOLUTION Find the volume and convert the unit of measure.

$\dfrac{41{,}472 \text{ in}^3}{1 \text{ hour}} \rightarrow \dfrac{?\text{ ft}^3}{1 \text{ hour}}$ Identify known and missing information.

$1 \text{ ft} = 12 \text{ in.}$ Equate units.

$\dfrac{1 \text{ ft}}{12 \text{ in.}}$ Write a unit ratio.

$\dfrac{41{,}472 \text{ in.} \cdot \text{in.} \cdot \text{in.}}{1 \text{ hr}} \cdot \dfrac{1 \text{ ft}}{12 \text{ in.}} \cdot \dfrac{1 \text{ ft}}{12 \text{ in.}} \cdot \dfrac{1 \text{ ft}}{12 \text{ in.}}$ Write the multiplication sentence.

$= \dfrac{\overset{24}{\cancel{41{,}472}}\, \cancel{\text{in.}} \cdot \cancel{\text{in.}} \cdot \cancel{\text{in.}}}{1 \text{ hr}} \cdot \dfrac{1 \text{ ft}}{\underset{1}{\cancel{12 \text{ in.}}}} \cdot \dfrac{1 \text{ ft}}{\underset{1}{\cancel{12 \text{ in.}}}} \cdot \dfrac{1 \text{ ft}}{\underset{1}{\cancel{12 \text{ in.}}}}$ Cancel out common factors.

$= \dfrac{24 \text{ ft} \cdot \text{ft} \cdot \text{ft}}{1 \text{ hr}} = \dfrac{24 \text{ ft}^3}{1 \text{ hr}}$ Multiply.

$1{,}104 \div 24 = 46 \text{ hours}$

It will take 46 hours to fill the pool.

 ALTERNATE METHOD FOR EXAMPLE 2

Use the conversion factor $1 \text{ m}^2 = 10{,}000 \text{ cm}^2$ to convert the area of the gym floor.

$119 \text{ m}^2 \cdot \dfrac{10{,}000 \text{ cm}^2}{1 \text{ m}^2} = 1{,}190{,}000 \text{ cm}^2$

OR: Use meters for all measurements.

Area of gym floor: 119 m^2

Area of one mat: $1.1 \text{ m} \cdot 1.1 \text{ m} = 1.21 \text{ m}^2$

Total area of mats: $95 \cdot 1.21 \text{ m}^2 = 114.95 \text{ m}^2$

$114.95 < 119$

Unit analysis can be used for more than just converting units of length. It can also be used to convert units of mass, density, temperature, capacity, or even money. In economics, the value of money is defined by what people are willing to exchange for it. This means that the value of a currency can change relative to the value of other currencies. An exchange-rate listing shows what a currency is worth compared to other currencies at that moment.

Example 4 Foreign Travel: Converting Units of Currency

Jared and his family are going on a vacation to Europe. He takes $225 with him. He needs to exchange this amount for its equivalent value in euros. If the current exchange rate is 1 euro = $1.36, what is the value of Jared's $225 in euros?

SOLUTION

Convert the unit of measure.

225 dollars → ? euros	Write the conversion.
1 euro = 1.36 dollars	Equate units.
$\dfrac{1 \text{ euro}}{1.36 \text{ dollars}}$	Write a unit ratio.
225 dollars · $\dfrac{1 \text{ euro}}{1.36 \text{ dollars}}$	Write the multiplication sentence.
= 165.44 euros	Multiply and cancel.

Check Since a euro is worth more than a dollar, Jared should have fewer euros than dollars after the exchange.

225 > 165.44   The answer is reasonable.

Hint
Choose a unit conversion factor that cancels the units you want to change and replaces them with the units you want.

Lesson Practice

a. A Mourning Dove can reach speeds up to 35 miles per hour. How fast is this in feet per hour?   **184,800 feet per hour**
(Ex 1)

b. An interior wall measures 4.5 yards by 3.25 yards. What is the size of the wall in square feet?   **131.625 ft²**
(Ex 2)

c. Della has a small bag containing 50 cubic centimeters of potting soil. Her planter has a volume of 46,300 cubic millimeters. Does Della have enough soil to fill the planter? Explain.
(Ex 3)

c. yes; Sample: 46,300 mm³ = 46.3 cm³

d. Arthur just returned from London. He has 16 British pounds to convert to American dollars. If the exchange rate is 1 pound = $2.016, what is the value of Arthur's 16 pounds in dollars?   **$32.26**
(Ex 4)

Lesson 8   39

3 Practice

Math Conversations

Discussion to strengthen understanding

Problem 1

Guide students by asking, "How do you write the mixed numbers as improper fractions?" $\frac{13}{3}, \frac{4}{3}, \frac{10}{3}$

Problem 17

Have students use elimination to arrive at the correct answer. Remind students that any time the subtrahend is greater than the minuend, the difference will be negative. Use simpler numbers to reinforce this. Sample: $7 - 10$ and $-2 - 6$

Practice Distributed and Integrated

Add, subtract, multiply, or divide.

1. (4) $4\frac{1}{3} \div 1\frac{1}{3} + 3\frac{1}{3}$ $6\frac{7}{12}$

2. (4) $2\frac{3}{8} - 1\frac{3}{4} \div 1\frac{1}{2}$ $1\frac{5}{24}$

3. (6) $2\frac{2}{3} + 1\frac{5}{6} - 6\frac{3}{4}$ $-2\frac{1}{4}$

4. (4) $3\frac{1}{3} \div 1\frac{1}{4} \cdot \frac{1}{2}$ $1\frac{1}{3}$

5. (6) $0.37 \div 0.2 \cdot 0.1$ 0.185

6. (SB 2) $1.74 \cdot 0.3 \div 0.2$ 2.61

7. (1) Given the sets $A = \{1, 3, 5\}$, $B = \{0, 2, 4, 6\}$, and $C = \{1, 2, 3, 4\}$, are the following statements true or false?
   a. $A \cup B = \{0, 1, 2, 3, 4, 5, 6\}$ true
   b. $A \cap B = \{0, 1, 2, 3, 4, 5, 6\}$ false
   c. $B \cup C = \{2, 4\}$ false
   d. $A \cap C = \{1, 3\}$ true

8. (4) Compare the expressions using $<$, $>$, or $=$. Explain.
   $8^2 \div 4 - 6^2$ $<$ $(6 \cdot 7 \cdot 5) \div 6 - 15$ $-20 < 20$

9. (SB 29) Draw a line plot for the frequency table.

Number	2	3	4	5	6	7
Frequency	4	3	2	1	4	3

9. Frequency of Numbers

10. (SB 2) Subtract $78\frac{2}{5} - 14\frac{7}{10}$. $63\frac{7}{10}$

11. (SB 12) Find the prime factorization of 484. $2 \cdot 2 \cdot 11 \cdot 11$

12. (SB 4) **Write** Use the divisibility test to determine if 22,993 is divisible by 5. Explain your answer.   no; The ones digit is not a 0 or a 5.

13. (SB 5) Write 125% as a fraction in simplest form and as a decimal. $1\frac{1}{4}$; 1.25

14. (8) Convert 105 kilometers per hour to kilometers per minute.   1.75 km per minute

*15. (8) Convert 74 square meters to square centimeters.   740,000 cm²

*16. (8) (Camping) Norman's camping tent has a volume of 72,576 cubic inches. What is the volume of the tent in cubic feet?   42 ft³

17. (6) **Multiple Choice** Which of these differences will be positive?   C

   A $-\frac{1}{2} - \frac{1}{8}$

   B $\frac{9}{12} - 1$

   C $\frac{5}{7} - \frac{3}{10}$

   D $-\frac{14}{15} - \left(\frac{4}{15}\right)$

INCLUSION

Problems requiring two conversions, such as rate, may be more difficult for students. Help them first set up the ratios using words only. Write the given ratio and the required ratio, with a few empty ratio boxes between to fill in the necessary unit rates. For example, convert yards per minute to feet per second.

$$\frac{yd}{min} = \frac{\square}{\square} = \frac{\square}{\square} = \frac{ft}{sec}$$

Have the students fill in the ratio boxes to make the necessary conversions. Tell them to cancel the matching factors in the numerator and denominator as they work through the problem.

$$\frac{\cancel{yd}}{\cancel{min}} = \frac{\boxed{min}}{\boxed{sec}} = \frac{\boxed{ft}}{\boxed{yd}} = \frac{ft}{sec}.$$

Once students have worked through a few conversions in words only, give them problems that require specific conversions.

18. Error Analysis Two students used unit analysis to convert a measurement of length. Which student is correct? Explain the error.

Student A	Student B
1 cm = 10 mm	1 cm = 10 mm
5540 mm = 5540 mm × $\frac{1 \text{ cm}}{10 \text{ mm}}$	5540 mm = 5540 mm × $\frac{10 \text{ mm}}{1 \text{ cm}}$
5540 mm = 554 cm	5540 mm = 55400 cm

18. Student A; Sample: Student B incorrectly wrote the unit ratio, multiplying by 10 to cancel the units instead of dividing by 10.

*19. **Multiple Choice** Which one of the following ratios can be used to convert 120 cm into an equivalent measure in inches? (Hint: There are 2.54 cm in one inch.) **B**

A $\frac{2.54 \text{ cm}}{1 \text{ in.}}$

B $\frac{1 \text{ in.}}{2.54 \text{ cm}}$

C $\frac{2.54 \text{ cm}}{1 \text{ in.}} \cdot \frac{2.54 \text{ cm}}{1 \text{ in.}}$

D $\frac{1 \text{ in.}}{2.54 \text{ cm}} \cdot \frac{1 \text{ in.}}{2.54 \text{ in.}}$

*20. **Weather Forecasting** One knot is exactly 1.852 kilometers per hour. The highest wind gust for the day was measured at 38 knots.
  a. How many km/hr was the recorded wind gust? (Hint: 1 knot = 1.852 km/hr)
  70.376 km/hr
  b. How many mph was the recorded wind gust? (Hint: 1 mi = 1.609 km)
  43.74 mph

*21. **Multi-Step** How can you find the area of the triangle in square inches?

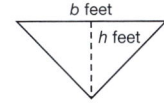
b feet
h feet

  a. Write a formula for computing the area of the triangle in units of square feet. $A = \frac{1}{2}b \cdot h$ ft²
  b. Write a new formula that computes the area of the triangle in units of square inches.   Sample: $A = \frac{1}{2}b \cdot h \cdot \frac{12}{1} \cdot \frac{12}{1}$ in²
  c. What is the area of the triangle in square inches if $b = 3$ ft and $h = 2.2$ ft?
  475.2 in²

*22. **Chemistry** Water has a density of 1 gram per cubic centimeter. What is the density of water in grams per cubic inch?   16.39 grams per cubic inch

*23. **Justify** True or False: A right triangle has one right angle, one obtuse angle, and one acute angle. If false, explain why.   false; A right triangle contains one right angle and two acute angles.

Problem 20
Guide students by asking the following questions:

"How would you write the conversion factor with knots in the denominator?" $\frac{1.852 \text{ km/hr}}{1 \text{ knot}}$

"What is the correct way to write km/hr in fraction form?" $\frac{1.852 \text{ km}}{1 \text{ hr}}$

Problem 21
Error Alert
Check that students are correctly recalling and applying the formula for the area of a triangle.

Problem 21
Extend the Problem
"What is the area of the triangle in square yards? Round the answer to the nearest tenth." 0.4 yd²

Lesson 8   41

CHALLENGE

Many unit analysis problems include the conversion of more than one unit. For example, a unit of speed may be converted from miles per hour to feet per second. Challenge students to convert 44 miles per hour to feet per second. about 65 ft/sec

Lesson 8   41

Problem 24
Remind students that $(2+4)^2$ and $2^2 + 4^2$ are not equivalent. Show them using the order of operations that $(2+4)^2 = 6^2 = 36$ and that $2^2 + 4^2 = 4 + 16 = 20$.

Problem 26
Tell students that it is common accounting practice to place a loss in parentheses.

Problem 28
Remind students that if any number or variable does not have an exponent, then it is understood that the exponent is 1.

Problem 30
Encourage students to make a drawing of the photograph with the 2-inch-wide frame.

---

24. Error Analysis Student A and Student B simplified the expression $\frac{24}{8} + (2+4)^2$. Which student is correct? Explain the error.   Student A; Sample: Student B needed to simplify inside the parentheses first.

Student A	Student B
$\frac{24}{8} + (2+4)^2$	$\frac{24}{8} + (2+4)^2$
$3 + 6^2$	$3 + (2+16)$
$3 + 36 = 39$	$3 + 18 = 21$

25. Geometry A square pyramid has a base with edges of 8 inches and a height of 12 inches.

25b. Sample: I simplified the s^2 first, because the order of operations tells us to simplify exponents before multiplying or adding.

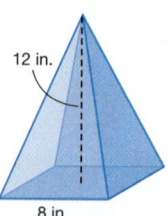

a. Use the following formula to find the volume: $V = \frac{1}{3}s^2h$.   256 in³

b. **Analyze** Which term did you simplify first? Why?

*26. Economics Use the table of the Profit and Loss Report of ABC Company. What was the total profit or loss for the year? [( ) indicates a loss.]

	1st Quarter	2nd Quarter	3rd Quarter	4th Quarter
Profit or Loss	$6 million	($3.5 million)	($2 million)	$5 million

profit of 5.5 million

*27. Multi-Step Two groups of students measured the length of a tabletop. Group A's measurement was $56\frac{3}{4}$ inches. Group B's measurement was $57\frac{3}{4}$ inches. If the actual length of the tabletop was $57\frac{1}{2}$ inches, which group's measurement had the smaller error?   Group B

28. Error Analysis Two students simplified an expression containing an exponent. Which student is correct? Explain the error.

28. Student A; Sample: Student B incorrectly used b as b^0 and c as c^0.

Student A	Student B
$b^2 \cdot c^2 \cdot c \cdot b^2 \cdot b =$	$b^2 \cdot c^2 \cdot c \cdot b^2 \cdot b =$
$b^2 \cdot b^2 \cdot b \cdot c^2 \cdot c = b^5 c^3$	$b^2 \cdot b^2 \cdot b \cdot c^2 \cdot c = b^4 c^2$

29. Speed A giraffe can run 32 miles per hour. What is the speed in feet per hour?   168,960 feet per hour

30. Geometry A square photograph measuring 8 inches by 8 inches is positioned within a 1-inch-wide picture frame as shown.

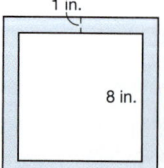

a. What is the area of the photograph?   64 sq. in.

b. What is the combined area of the photograph and frame?   100 sq. in.

c. What is the area of the frame alone?   36 sq. in.

d. If the 1-inch-wide frame is replaced with a 2-inch-wide frame, how much more wall space will be needed to hang the framed photograph?   44 sq. in.

42   Saxon Algebra 1

LOOKING FORWARD

Using unit analysis to convert measures prepares students for

- **Lesson 11** Multiplying and Dividing Rational Numbers

- **Lesson 12** Using the Properties of Real Numbers to Simplify Expressions

- **Lesson 16** Simplifying and Evaluating Variable Expressions

LESSON 9

Evaluating and Comparing Algebraic Expressions

Warm Up

1. **Vocabulary** When two numbers are divided, the result is called the _____. (quotient, product). **quotient**

Simplify.

2. $x^5 b^2 \cdot 3b^3 x$ $3x^6 b^5$

3. $\dfrac{4^3}{2^3} + 7^2$ 57

4. $\dfrac{5^3}{3^2 + 4^2}$ 5

5. $32 \div [2 \cdot (8 - 7)]$ 16

New Concepts

Any expression containing only numbers and operations is a **numeric expression**. An **algebraic expression** is an expression with variables and/or numbers that uses operations (e.g., $+$, $-$, $\times$, or $\div$). An algebraic expression is also called a variable expression.

Math Language

Evaluate means to substitute values for the variables and to simplify using the order of operations.

Example 1 Evaluating Algebraic Expressions

Evaluate the expression when $x = 3$ and $a = 1$.

$$3x - 4x + ax$$

SOLUTION Substitute 3 for x and 1 for a in the expression. Then simplify.

$3x - 4x + ax$
$= 3 \cdot 3 - 4 \cdot 3 + 1 \cdot 3$
$= 9 - 12 + 3$
$= 0$

When the variables in algebraic expressions have exponents, it is helpful to write the value in parentheses.

Example 2 Evaluating Algebraic Expressions with Exponents

Evaluate the expression for $y = 2$ and $z = 4$.

$$3(z - y)^2 - 4y^3$$

SOLUTION Substitute 2 for y and 4 for z in the expression. Then simplify.

$3(z - y)^2 + 4y^3$
$= 3(4 - 2)^2 - 4(2)^3$
$= 3(2)^2 - 4(2)^3$
$= 3 \cdot 4 - 4(8)$
$= 12 - (32)$
$= -20$

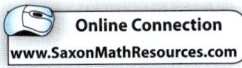
Online Connection
www.SaxonMathResources.com

Lesson 9   43

LESSON 9

1 Warm Up

Problem 4
Remind students that the fraction bar is a grouping symbol. In this problem, students need to add $3^3 + 4^2$ before dividing.

2 New Concepts

In this lesson, students learn to evaluate algebraic expressions and compare them.

Example 1

Remind students to be sure they substituted the correct value for x and the correct value for a.

Additional Example 1

Evaluate the expression $2x + 3y - xy$ for $x = 2$ and $y = 5$. **9**

Example 2

Error Alert Make sure students follow the order of operations when simplifying the expression.

Additional Example 2

Evaluate the expression $2(a + z)^3 - z^2$ for $a = 3$ and $z = 2$. **246**

LESSON RESOURCES

Student Edition Practice Workbook 9
Reteaching Master 9
Adaptations Master 9
Challenge and Enrichment Master C9

MATH BACKGROUND

Careful use of terminology is important in this lesson. Emphasize that you simplify a numeric expression and evaluate an algebraic expression.

To simplify a numeric expression means to carry out the operations to produce a simpler, but equivalent, expression. To evaluate an algebraic expression means to find its value when given the values of the variables in the expression. When you teach students to evaluate, make it clear that you also want them to simplify the resulting numeric expression.

Note that you do not solve a numeric expression or algebraic expression. To find a solution, there must be an equation or an inequality. In this lesson, students will see an equation or inequality when they compare two expressions, but they do not solve equations until Lesson 19.

Lesson 9   43

Example 3

Point out that the open end of the inequality sign faces the expression with a greater value.

Additional Example 3

Compare the expressions when $b = 5$ and $c = 2$.

$4b^3 - 3c + 2b^2 \; \boxed{<} \; 3b^2c^3$

$544 < 600$

Example 4

Error Alert Students may think the m in $0.45m$ is a digit in the thousandths place. Emphasize that $0.45m$ is 0.45 times m.

Extend the Example

Have students evaluate how much the company charges for using 175 minutes. $98.75

Additional Example 4

A company charges $60 per month and $4 per movie rented. How much will it cost if 7 movies are rented in a month? $88

Lesson Practice

Problem a

Scaffolding Before evaluating, have students write the expression with the correct values substituted.

Problem c

Error Alert Remind students to square the value of x before multiplying by 6.

Check for Understanding

The following questions help assess the concepts taught in this lesson:

"Explain how to evaluate an expression." Sample: Substitute the values and simplify.

"Explain how to compare algebraic expressions." Sample: Evaluate and then compare using the symbols <, >, or =.

44 Saxon Algebra 1

Two algebraic expressions are equivalent if they can be simplified to the same value. For example, $2 \cdot 2 - 1$ is equivalent to $15 \div 5$. Both expressions have a simplified value of 3.

Example 3 Comparing Algebraic Expressions

Compare the expressions when $a = 4$ and $b = 3$. Use <, >, or =.

$3a^2 + 2b - 4b^3 \bigcirc 2a^2b^2$

SOLUTION Simplify the expression on the left and then compare.

$3a^2 + 2b - 4b^3$ $2a^2b^2$
$3(4)^2 + 2(3) - 4(3)^3$ $2(4)^2(3)^2$
$= 3(16) + 2(3) - 4(27)$ $= 2(16)(9)$
$= 48 + 6 - 108$ $= 288$
$= 54 - 108$
$= -54$

Since $-54 < 288$, $3a^2 + 2b - 4b^3 < 2a^2b^2$ when $a = 4$ and $b = 3$.

Many real-world situations can be described using math. Algebraic expressions can be used to represent relationships between quantities.

Example 4 Application: Phone Charges

Math Reasoning

Analyze In the expression $20 + 0.45m$, what does the variable m represent?

the number of minutes used in one month

A cell phone company charges a $20 monthly fee and then 45 cents per minute. The company uses the expression $20 + 0.45m$ to find the total amount to charge for each month. How much would the company charge for 200 minutes?

SOLUTION Substitute 200 for m in the expression and simplify.

$20 + 0.45m$
$= 20 + 0.45(200)$
$= 20 + 90$
$= 110$

The cell phone company would charge $110.

Lesson Practice

Evaluate each expression for the given values.

a. $3x - 4b + 2bx$; $x = 10, b = 2$ 62
(Ex 1)

b. $2ab - 4a^2 + 10$; $a = -1, b = 8$ -10
(Ex 2)

c. Compare the expressions when $x = 2$ and $y = 5$. Use <, >, or =.
(Ex 3)
$(6x^2 + y^3) - 3x^6 \; \boxed{<} \; 8x^4 - y^3$

d. **Climate** The lowest recorded temperature is $-89.4°C$ in Antarctica.
(Ex 4) The expression $\frac{9}{5}C + 32$ can be used to convert Celsius measurements to Fahrenheit. What is the lowest recorded temperature in degrees Fahrenheit? $-128.92°F$

44 Saxon Algebra 1

 **ALTERNATE METHOD FOR EXAMPLE 4**

Have students think about the problem as a two-step process. Determine the cost for using 200 minutes. Add on $20 to the cost of the minutes.

$(200)(0.45) = 90$
$90 + 20 = 110$

Practice Distributed and Integrated

Add, subtract, multiply, or divide.

1. (SB 3) $4\frac{1}{3} \div 2\frac{1}{3}$ $1\frac{6}{7}$
2. (SB 3) $42\frac{3}{8} - 21\frac{3}{4}$ $20\frac{5}{8}$
3. (SB 3) $1\frac{2}{3} + 2\frac{5}{6}$ $4\frac{1}{2}$
4. (SB 3) $2\frac{2}{3} \div 1\frac{3}{4}$ $1\frac{11}{21}$
5. (SB 2) $0.75 \div 0.2$ 3.75
6. (SB 2) $1.74 \div 0.3$ 5.8
7. (SB 2) $1.25 \cdot 0.2$ 0.25
8. (SB 2) 12.2×3.2 39.04

9. (SB 14) **Verify** True or False: A square is a rhombus. Explain your choice.   true; A square has 2 pairs of parallel sides and its sides are congruent.

10. (7) Simplify $4[(6-4)^3 - 5]$. 12

11. (8) Convert 1.86 km^2 to m^2. $1,860,000$ m^2

*12. (9) Evaluate the expression $14c + 28 - 12cd$ for the given values $c = 4$ and $d = 5$. -156

13. (SB 13) A straight angle measures _____. $180°$

14. (SB 12) Find the prime factorization of 125. $5 \cdot 5 \cdot 5$

*15. (9) Find the value of the expression $\frac{t-36}{36} + l$ if $t = 72$ and $l = 1$. 2

16. (7) **Multiple Choice** Evaluate the expression $14 + \frac{36}{9} \cdot (2 + 5)$.   **C**
  A 126   **B** 21   **C** 42   **D** 140

17. (7) Simplify $(3 + 12) + (|-4| - 2)^3 + 1$. 24

*18. (9) **Flight** A rocket is fired upward at an initial speed of 112 feet per second (ft/sec). It travels at a speed of $112 - 32t$ ft/sec, where t is the flight time in seconds.
  a. What is the rocket's speed after 1 second?   80 ft/sec
  b. What is the rocket's speed after 2 seconds?   48 ft/sec

*19. (9) **Canoeing** Rachel wants to rent a canoe for 3 hours. Use the expression $\$6.50 + \$1.75h$, where h represents the number of hours, to calculate the cost of renting the canoe. $\$11.75$

*20. (9) **Error Analysis** Two students were asked to evaluate when x is 5 and y is -5. Which student is correct? Explain the error.   Student B; Sample: Student A made an error in evaluating the negative number raised to a power.

Student A	Student B
$\frac{y^2}{-x} = \frac{-5^2}{-(5)} = \frac{-25}{-5} = 5$	$\frac{y^2}{-x} = \frac{(-5)^2}{-(5)} = \frac{25}{-5} = -5$

*21. (9) **Data Analysis** The variance of a set of data can be found with the expression $\frac{s}{n}$, where s is the sum of the squared deviation and n is the total number of data items in the set. What is the variance for a set of data with 12 items and a sum of the squared deviations equal to 30? 2.5

Lesson 9   45

Problem 25

Discuss with students how the ratio they found in part **c** relates to the unit conversion factor from millimeters to centimeters.
Sample: The ratio is the square of the conversion factor.

Problem 26

Before students calculate the volume, ask:

"What information do you need to find the volume?" area of the base and height of the cylinder

Problem 30

Extend the Problem

"Suppose Jared starts with 450 words and then types for 20 minutes at 35 words per minute. What is the total number of words that he will have typed?"
1150 words

---

*22. (**Sports**) In volleyball, the statistic for total blocks at the net is calculated with the expression $s + 0.5a$, where s is the number of solo blocks and a is the number of assisted blocks. What is the total-blocks statistic for a player who has 80 solo blocks and 53 assisted blocks?   106.5 total blocks

23. **Write** Use the divisibility test to determine if 224 is divisible by 6. Explain your answer.   no; The number is divisible by 2, but not divisible by 3.

24. Write 35.2% as a fraction in simplest form and as a decimal. $\frac{44}{125}$; 0.352

*25. **Multi-Step** The rectangle has dimensions measured in centimeters. What is the ratio of the area of the rectangle in centimeters to the area of the rectangle in millimeters?

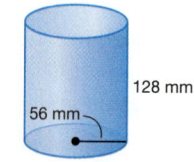

a. Calculate the area of the rectangle.   2112 cm²

b. Find the area of the rectangle in square millimeters.   211,200 mm²

c. Find the ratio of square centimeters to square millimeters for the rectangle.   1:100

*26. **Geometry** A right circular cylinder has a base radius of 56 mm and a height of 128 mm. What is its volume in cubic centimeters? Round the answer to the nearest hundredth. Use 3.14 for π.   1260.42 cm³

27. (**Loans**) The formula for long-term loans is $F = P(1 + i)^{n \div 12}$, where F is the future value of money, P is the present value, i is the interest rate, and n is the length of time the money is borrowed in months. When solving this equation for F, what step would you perform after adding 1 and i?   Divide n by 12.

28. (**Golf**) Below is Rickie's golf score for two golf tournaments. What is the difference in his final score for the 1st and 2nd tournament?   1

1st Tournament	1	−2	−3	2
2nd Tournament	−2	−1	1	−1

29. **Error Analysis** Two students were asked to evaluate $(30 − 10)^2$. Student A answered 400, and Student B answered −70. Which student is correct? Explain the error.

Student A	Student B
$(30 − 10)^2$	$(30 − 10)^2$
$= 20^2$	$= (30 − 10 \cdot 10)$
$= 400$	$= (30 − 100)$
	$= −70$

Student A; Sample: Student B did not follow the order of operations and did not work inside the parentheses first.

*30. (**Typing**) Jared can type 35 words per minute. Use the expression $35m$ to find the number of words he can type in 15 minutes.   525 words

46   Saxon Algebra 1

 CHALLENGE

Sometimes an expression will include more than two variables. Evaluate the expression $2(z − x)^2 + 2v^2 − 2wy$ for $v = 4$, $w = 9$, $x = 13$, $y = 3$, and $z = 20$.   76

 LOOKING FORWARD

Evaluating and comparing algebraic expressions prepares students for

• **Lesson 12** Using the Properties of Real Numbers to Simplify Expressions

• **Lesson 13** Calculating and Comparing Square Roots

• **Lesson 15** Using the Distributive Property to Simplify Expressions

• **Lesson 32** Simplifying and Evaluating Expressions with Integer and Zero Exponents

LESSON 10

Adding and Subtracting Real Numbers

Warm Up

1. **Vocabulary** Any real number that cannot be written as a quotient of integers is called a(n) _____ number. **irrational**

Simplify.

2. $(25 \div 5) - (30 \div 10)$ **2**
3. $-4 + (-9) + (-6)$ **−19**
4. $(2.45 + 5.75) - (4.85 - 3.75)$ **7.1**
5. $(j^4k^5)(4kj^2)(3k^3)$ **$12j^6k^9$**

New Concepts

When solving a problem containing addition and subtraction of signed numbers, begin by writing the problem as addition only. Next, group and add the terms with like signs. Then add the terms with unlike signs.

Example 1 Adding and Subtracting Fractions and Decimals

Simplify.

a. $-\dfrac{1}{5} + \dfrac{3}{5} - \dfrac{2}{5} - \left(-\dfrac{4}{5}\right)$

Hint
Use the rules below for adding integers.
1. Like signs: Add and keep the sign.
2. Unlike signs: Subtract and keep the sign of the greater absolute value.

SOLUTION

$-\dfrac{1}{5} + \dfrac{3}{5} - \dfrac{2}{5} - \left(-\dfrac{4}{5}\right)$

$= -\dfrac{1}{5} + \dfrac{3}{5} + \left(-\dfrac{2}{5}\right) + \dfrac{4}{5}$ Write the problem as addition.

$= -\dfrac{1}{5} + \left(-\dfrac{2}{5}\right) + \dfrac{3}{5} + \dfrac{4}{5}$ Group the terms with like signs.

$= -\dfrac{3}{5} + \dfrac{7}{5}$ Add numbers with like signs.

$= \dfrac{4}{5}$ Add.

b. $3.16 + (-1.22) - 4.73 + 5.6$

SOLUTION

$3.16 + (-1.22) - 4.73 + 5.6$

$= 3.16 + (-1.22) + (-4.73) + 5.6$ Write the problem as addition.
$= 3.16 + 5.6 + (-1.22) + (-4.73)$ Group the terms with the same signs.
$= 8.76 + (-5.95)$ Add numbers with like signs.
$= 2.81$ Add.

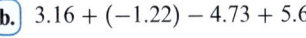
Online Connection
www.SaxonMathResources.com

Lesson 10   47

MATH BACKGROUND

A number line represents real numbers, which consist of all the rational numbers and irrational numbers. Between any two consecutive integers on a number line, there are infinitely many rational numbers and infinitely many irrational numbers.

As students compare and order fraction and decimal values, have them subdivide number lines into appropriate units to model the problems. It may be necessary to find common denominators before subdividing the number lines. In this way, students may begin to understand the concept of infinitely many numbers between any two integers on the number line.

---

1 Warm Up

Problem 4
Remind students to follow the order of operations and to work inside the parentheses first.

2 New Concepts

In this lesson, students learn to add and subtract real numbers.

Example 1
Remind students to group terms with like signs; this will make it easier to solve the problem.

Error Alert Students may have difficulty perceiving the subtraction of a negative number as addition, a "double negative." Ask students when they have heard the phrase "double negative" and how it would relate to subtracting a negative number.

Additional Example 1
Simplify.

a. $\dfrac{3}{7} + \dfrac{1}{7} - \dfrac{2}{7} - \left(-\dfrac{4}{7}\right)$ $\dfrac{6}{7}$

b. $79.5 + (-3.12) + 7.34 - 6.18$
77.54

LESSON RESOURCES

Student Edition Practice Workbook 10
Reteaching Master 10
Adaptations Master 10
Challenge and Enrichment Master C10

Example 2

Explain that it will be easier to order numbers if students write the fractions as decimals or the decimals as fractions.

Additional Example 2

Order the numbers from least to greatest.

$\frac{3}{5}, -\frac{1}{4}, -0.75, 0$

$-0.75, -\frac{1}{4}, 0, \frac{3}{5}$

Example 3

Remind students that they can write a fraction as a decimal by dividing the numerator by the denominator.

Additional Example 3

Complete the comparison. Use $<$, $>$, or $=$.

$\frac{7}{9} - \frac{1}{9} + \left(-\frac{2}{9}\right) \bigcirc$
$2.15 - 4.27 + 2.56$ $0.\overline{4} > 0.44$

Example 4

Suggest to students that they set up each problem vertically.

Extend the Example

In which quarter did Investment A grow the most?
the first quarter, $255.75 − $250 = $5.75

Additional Example 4

In January Rich invested $475 in two accounts. The table below shows the growth of each account.

Invest.	June	December
A	$495.78	$521.36
B	$482.17	$515.98

a. Which investment grew more?
   Investment A

b. During which span of time did Investment B grow more?
   June to December

Example 2 Ordering Rational Numbers

Order the numbers from least to greatest.

$\frac{7}{8}, -2, 0.125, \frac{1}{2}$

SOLUTION

Use a number line to order the numbers. Place each number on the number line.

To order these numbers from least to greatest, read the numbers on the number line from left to right.

$-2, 0.125, \frac{1}{2}, \frac{7}{8}$

Example 3 Comparing Rational Expressions

Complete the comparison. Use $<$, $>$, or $=$.

$\frac{3}{8} + \left(-\frac{5}{8}\right) - \frac{1}{8} \bigcirc -2.75 + 6.25 - 3.75$

SOLUTION

Simplify each expression. Then compare.

$\frac{3}{8} + \left(-\frac{5}{8}\right) - \frac{1}{8}$ $-2.75 + 6.25 - 3.75$

$= \frac{3}{8} + \left(-\frac{5}{8}\right) + \left(-\frac{1}{8}\right)$ $= -2.75 + 6.25 + (-3.75)$

$= \frac{3}{8} + \left(-\frac{6}{8}\right)$ $= -2.75 + (-3.75) + 6.25$

$= -\frac{3}{8}$ $= -6.50 + 6.25$

$= -0.25$

Hint
Convert $-\frac{3}{8}$ to a decimal or -0.25 to a fraction to make comparing the values easier.

Since $-\frac{3}{8} < -0.25$, $\frac{3}{8} + \left(-\frac{5}{8}\right) - \frac{1}{8} < -2.75 + 6.25 - 3.75$.

Example 4 Application: Investing

Carly invested $250 in two accounts. The table below shows the ending balance per quarter.

	1st Quarter	2nd Quarter	3rd Quarter	4th Quarter
Investment A	$255.75	$258.81	$260.25	$262.99
Investment B	$260.66	$274.22	$268.92	$290.07

ENGLISH LEARNERS

For Example 4, explain the meaning of the word **quarter**.

Say, "A quarter is a coin worth $\frac{1}{4}$ of a dollar. It is also a term used in business that means 3 months, or $\frac{1}{4}$ of a year."

Have students find other examples of things that are divided into quarters, such as a quarter of an hour, or a quarter in American football. Explain that all of these examples represent something that is $\frac{1}{4}$ of a whole.

a. Which investment grew more?

SOLUTION

Find the differences and compare.

Investment A	Investment B
$262.99 − $250 = $12.99	$290.07 − $250 = $40.07

Investment B grew more.

b. In which quarter did Investment B grow the most?

SOLUTION

$260.66 − $250.00 = $10.66
$274.22 − $260.66 = $13.56
$268.92 − $274.22 = −$5.30
$290.07 − $268.92 = $21.15

The greatest difference is $21.15, which occurred in the 4th quarter.

Lesson Practice

Simplify.

a. (Ex 1) $\frac{4}{9} + \frac{2}{9} - \frac{5}{9}$ $\frac{1}{9}$

b. $16.21 - 21.54 + 12.72$ 7.39

c. (Ex 2) Order the numbers from least to greatest.

$\frac{3}{4}, -1, 0.85, \frac{5}{8}$ $-1, \frac{5}{8}, \frac{6}{8}, 0.85$

d. (Ex 3) Complete the comparison. Use <, >, or =.

$3.2 + (-2.8) - 5.2$ $<$ $\frac{7}{12} - \frac{5}{12} + \left(-\frac{11}{12}\right)$

e. (Ex 4) Jonah ran a race in 32.68 seconds. Jarrod finished 1.92 seconds before Jonah. Gayle finished 3.01 seconds after Jonah. How many seconds did it take Gayle to run the race?   35.69 seconds

Practice Distributed and Integrated

Add, subtract, multiply, or divide.

1. (SB 3) $\frac{1}{2} + \frac{3}{5}$ $\frac{11}{10}$ or $1\frac{1}{10}$

2. (SB 3) $15\frac{1}{3} - 7\frac{4}{5}$ $7\frac{8}{15}$

3. (SB 3) $3\frac{2}{3} \cdot 2\frac{1}{4}$ $8\frac{1}{4}$

4. (SB 3) $3\frac{2}{5} \div 1\frac{2}{3}$ $2\frac{1}{25}$

5. (SB 3) $78\frac{2}{5} - 14\frac{7}{10}$ $63\frac{7}{10}$

6. (SB 3) $2\frac{1}{3} \cdot 1\frac{1}{4}$ $2\frac{11}{12}$

7. (SB 2) $10.2 \cdot 3.15$ 32.13

8. (SB 2) $20.46 \div 2.2$ 9.3

Lesson 10   49

9. $12.3 \cdot 2.02$ 24.846
(SB 2)

10. $0.8 \div 0.25$ 3.2
(SB 2)

*11. Order from greatest to least: $\frac{6}{7}, \frac{3}{5}, \frac{1}{7}, -\frac{4}{3}$. $\frac{6}{7}, \frac{3}{5}, \frac{1}{7}, -\frac{4}{3}$
(10)

12. A(n) _____ angle measures less than 90°.   acute
(SB 1)

13. Convert 8673 g to kg.   8.673 kg
(8)

14. Convert 26 mi to km. Round your answer to the nearest tenth.   41.8 km
(8)

15. True or False: $(2 + 5) - (3 \cdot 4) = 2 + 5 - 3 \cdot 4$. Explain.   true; Sample: The value of each expression is -5.
(4)

*16. **Multiple Choice** Simplify $1.29 + 3.9 - 4.2 - 9.99 + 6.1$.   A
(10)
  A -2.9 B -1 C 1 D 2.9

*17. **Error Analysis** Which student is correct? Explain the error.   Student A; Sample: Student B did not complete the operations in parentheses first.
(10)

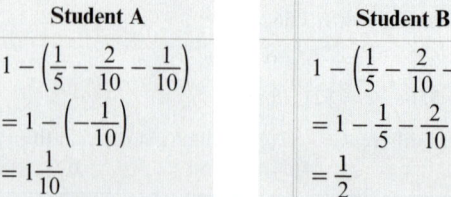

*18. (Time) A ship sailed northeast for $2\frac{1}{4}$ hours. It then sailed east for $1\frac{1}{3}$ hours. How much longer did it sail northeast than east? $\frac{11}{12}$ hour or 55 minutes
(10)

19. **Model** Draw a line plot for the frequency table.
(SB 29)

Number	9	10	11	12	13	14
Frequency	4	3	2	1	0	4

Frequency of Numbers

*20. **Multi-Step** A map shows streets $\frac{1}{1000}$ of their size.
(9)
  a. Write an expression that represents the real length of a block if the length of the block on the map is b.   Sample: $1000b$
  b. Find the actual length of a block that is 0.4 feet on the map.   400 feet

*21. **Geometry** A parallelogram has a base of z and a height of $2z$. Write an expression to find the area of the parallelogram. If z is equal to 12 cm, what is the area of the parallelogram? $A = 2z^2$; 288 cm²
(9)

22. **Error Analysis** Two students used unit analysis to convert a measurement of area to a different unit. Which student is correct? Explain the error.
(8)

22. Student B; Sample: Student A only multiplied by the unit ratio once instead of twice.

Student A	Student B
1 ft = 12 in.	1 ft = 12 in.
$9 \text{ ft}^2 = 9 \text{ ft}^2 \times \frac{12 \text{ in.}}{1 \text{ ft}}$	$9 \text{ ft}^2 = 9 \text{ ft}^2 \times \frac{12 \text{ in.}}{1 \text{ ft}} \times \frac{12 \text{ in.}}{1 \text{ ft}}$
$9 \text{ ft}^2 = 108 \text{ in}^2$	$9 \text{ ft}^2 = 1{,}296 \text{ in}^2$

---

3 Practice

Math Conversations
Discussions to strengthen understanding

Problem 11
Guide students through the problem by asking the following questions:

"How can you compare the fractions, without finding common denominators?" You can write the fractions as decimals.

"How do you write fractions as decimals?" You divide the numerator by the denominator.

"Write the fractions as decimals. Round to the nearest hundredth."
0.86, 0.6, 0.14, −1.33

Problem 15
Error Alert Some students may forget to use the order of operations for this problem. Remind students that they should start by working inside the parentheses, and then multiply before adding and subtracting.

Problem 20
Extend the Problem
"Suppose you are going to walk to a grocery store that is 12 blocks away. If each block length is 0.4 feet on the map, how many feet will you walk to get to the grocery store and back?" 9600 ft

"How far is this in miles? (Round to the nearest tenth.)" 1.8 mi

---

INCLUSION

Students may benefit from visualizing the addition and subtraction of fractions. Have them use fraction strips to find the answer to $\frac{1}{6} + \frac{4}{6} - \frac{3}{6} + \frac{2}{6}$.

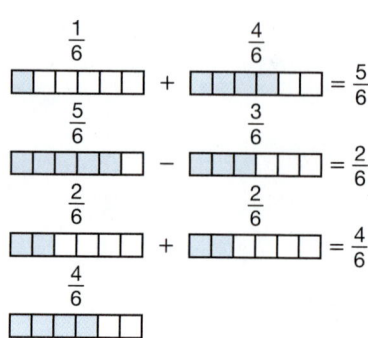

23. **Meteorology** When a weather system passes through, a barometer can be used to measure the change in atmospheric pressure in millimeters of mercury. What is the pressure difference in inches of mercury for a measured change of +4.5 mm of mercury? Round the answer to the nearest thousandth. +0.177 in. of mercury

*24. **Multi-Step** A plot of land contains a rectangular building that is 9 yards long and 6 yards wide and a circular building with a diameter of 4 yards.

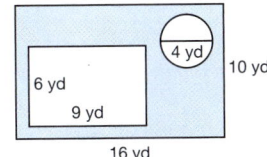

a. Write an expression for the area of the two buildings.

b. Write an expression and solve for how much area on the plot of land is not being taken up by the buildings. Round the answer to the nearest hundredth yard. $16 \cdot 10 - \left[9 \cdot 6 + \pi\left(\frac{4}{2}\right)^2\right] \approx 93.44$ yd²

24a. $9 \cdot 6 + \pi\left(\frac{4}{2}\right)^2$

*25. **Error Analysis** Student A and Student B each added the numbers −4.8 and 3.6 as shown below. Which student is correct? Explain the error.

Student A	Student B
−4.8 + 3.6	−4.8 + 3.6
|−4.8| = 4.8	|−4.8| = 4.8
|+3.6| = 3.6	|+3.6| = 3.6
4.8	4.8
+3.6	−3.6
8.4	1.2
8.4	−1.2

25. Student B; Sample: Student A added the absolute values of the numbers rather than subtracting them.

26. **Banking** Raul had $500 in his checking account. He wrote checks for $157.62 and $43.96. Then he deposited $225. Find Raul's balance after these three transactions. $523.42

27. **Write** Mutually exclusive means that two sets of numbers have no numbers in common. Name two subsets of real numbers that are mutually exclusive. Explain.

27. Rational and irrational numbers; Sample: By definition, the sets of rational and irrational numbers do not contain the same numbers.

*28. **Stocks** Stock in the 123 Company fell 8.2 points on Monday and 5.3 points on Tuesday. On Wednesday the stock rose 9.1 points. Determine the total change in the stock for the three days.   −4.4 points

*29. **Football** The Rams gained 4 yards on the first down, lost 6 yards on the second down, and gained 14 yards on the third down. How many total yards did the Rams gain on the three downs?   12 yards

30. **Measurement** A kite flies 74 feet above the ground. The person flying the kite is 5 feet 6 inches tall. How far above the person is the kite?   68 feet 6 inches

Lesson 10   51

Problem 24a
Guide students by asking the following questions.

"What is an expression for the area of the rectangular building?"
$6 \cdot 9$

"What is an expression for the area of the circular building?"
$\pi\left(\frac{4}{2}\right)^2$

"What is an expression for the total area of both building?"
$6 \cdot 9 + \pi\left(\frac{4}{2}\right)^2$

Problem 24b
Guide students by asking the following questions.

"What is an expression for the area of the plot of land?" $16 \cdot 10$

"What is an expression for the area of the plot of land without the buildings?"
$16 \cdot 10 - \left[6 \cdot 9 + \pi\left(\frac{4}{2}\right)^2\right]$

Problem 29
Extend the Problem
If the Rams started on their own 10-yard line, what yard line were they on after the third down?
their own 22-yard line

CHALLENGE

Challenge students to order the list of numbers and expressions from the greatest to the least.

$(-0.30 - 0.02),\ 0.34,\ \frac{1}{3},\ \left(-\frac{1}{6} - \frac{1}{6}\right)$

$0.34,\ \frac{1}{3},\ (-0.30 - 0.02),\ \left(-\frac{1}{6} - \frac{1}{6}\right)$

LOOKING FORWARD

Adding and subtracting real numbers prepares students for

- **Lesson 13** Calculating and Comparing Square Roots
- **Lesson 17** Translating Between Words and Algebraic Expression
- **Lesson 32** Simplifying and Evaluating Expressions with Integer and Zero Exponents
- **Lesson 40** Simplifying and Evaluating Expressions Using the Power Property for Exponents

Lesson 10   51

LAB 1

Materials
- graphing calculator

Discuss

Many real-world events can have random outcomes. For instance, tossing a coin has a random outcome. In this lab, students will use a graphing calculator to simulate a random outcome without physically performing the event itself.

LAB 1

Generating Random Numbers

Graphing Calculator Lab (*Use with Investigation 1*)

A set of random integers has no pattern. Some common methods for generating random integers include rolling a number cube or drawing numbers out of a hat. A graphing calculator can also be used to generate random integers.

Generate three random integers between 1 and 12.

1. Press **MATH** and then press the ▶ key three times to highlight **PRB**.

   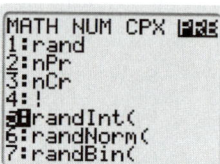

2. Select **5:randInt(** by pressing **5**.

3. Identify the range of values. The lowest possible value is 1 and the highest is 12. So, press **1** [**,**] **12** [**)**].

   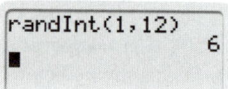

4. Press **ENTER** to generate one integer between 1 and 12. An integer between 1 and 12 is 6.

5. Press **ENTER** two more times to generate two more integers between 1 and 12. Three integers between 1 and 12 are 6, 12, and 9.

   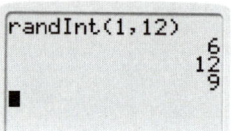

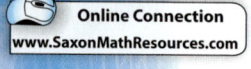

Lab Practice

Jared lost the number cubes to his favorite board game, but he does have his graphing calculator. According to the rules, the player should throw two number cubes and move the total number of spaces shown on the top faces of the cubes.

a. What range of numbers does a single number cube generate? What would Jared enter into the calculator to simulate a number cube?
   1–6; randInt (1, 6)

b. How would Jared simulate rolling two number cubes? How would Jared know how many spaces to move? Enter randInt (1, 6) and press **ENTER** twice; Add the two random numbers that were generated.

c. Simulate Jared taking three turns. What number of spaces will he move in each turn? What is the total number of spaces moved?
   Answers will vary, but there should be three answers between 2 and 12. Sample: 8, 4, 8; 20 spaces

INVESTIGATION 1

Determining the Probability of an Event

Probability is the measure of how likely a given event, or outcome, will occur. The probability of an event can be written as a fraction or decimal ranging from 0 to 1, or as a percent from 0% to 100%.

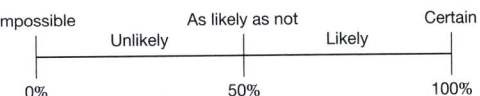

Range of Probability

Impossible — Unlikely — As likely as not — Likely — Certain
0% — 50% — 100%

Math Language
An **outcome** is a possible result of a probability experiment.
An **event** is an outcome or set of outcomes in a probability experiment.

Describe each of the events below as impossible, unlikely, as likely as not, likely, or certain.

1. Jake rolls a number less than 7 on a number cube.   **certain**
2. February will have 30 days.   **impossible**
3. A tossed coin will land on tails.   **as likely as not**
4. Shayla correctly guesses a number between 1 and 100.   **unlikely**

Experimental probability is the measure of how likely a given event will occur based on repeated trials.

$$\text{experimental probability} = \frac{\text{number of times an event occurs}}{\text{number of trials}}$$

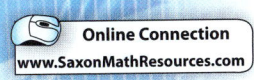

Online Connection
www.SaxonMathResources.com

Materials
- small paper sacks
- small red, blue, green, and yellow paper squares

Exploration: Conducting Experiments to Find Probabilities

Place a small handful of colored squares into a paper sack. Draw out a square of paper without looking. Record the color in a frequency table like the one below.

Color	Tally	Frequency
Red		
Blue		
Green		
Yellow		

Repeat the experiment 50 times, replacing the square after each draw.

5. What is the experimental probability of drawing a red square? a blue square? a green square? a yellow square? Express each probability as a fraction and as a percent.   **See student work.**

6. **Predict** Which color are you most likely to draw? Explain your reasoning.   **See student work.**

Investigation 1   53

INVESTIGATION 1

Materials
- small paper sacks
- small red, blue, green, and yellow paper squares
- graphing calculator
- **Alternate Materials** A spinner with four equal sectors can be used instead of squares of colored paper.

Discuss
In this investigation, students learn how to determine the experimental probability of an event by performing an experiment and by using a graphing calculator to simulate an event.

Extend the Exploration
After students answer problem **6**, have them add some purple squares to the sack and perform the experiment again reanswering problems **5** and **6**.

INVESTIGATION RESOURCES

Reteaching Master
Investigation 1

MATH BACKGROUND

Experimental probability should be distinguished from theoretical probability. Theoretical probability is the fraction of times an event is expected to occur. For example, you may roll a number cube, labeled 1–6, 10 times and roll a four 3 times. Your experimental probability of rolling a four would be $\frac{3}{10}$. Your theoretical probability of rolling a four is $\frac{1}{6}$ since there is only 1 four on a number cube out of the 6 numbers on the cube altogether.

When you are calculating experimental probability, it is essential that the experiment is repeated many times under unchanged conditions. The experimental probability of an event approaches the theoretical probability of an event as the number of trials in the experiment increases.

Investigation 1   53

Problem 8b
Error Alert

Students may try to multiply 3.2 by 3000 to get their answer. Remind them that they must change 3.2% to the decimal 0.032 when multiplying by 3000 to get the correct answer.

Problem 8c

Guide students by asking the following questions.

"How much would is cost to make all of the pistons?" $75,000

"How many pistons are defective?" 96

"How many pistons are not defective?" 2904

"How much revenue can be made if all of the good piston were sold?" $101,640

"How much profit can be made from making 3000 pistons?" $26,640

Problems 9–10
Extend the Problem

Have students simulate the problem if 1 in 5 prize pieces is a winner.

Experimental probability is widely used in sports. In baseball, a player's batting average is the probability of a player getting a hit based on his previous at bats. It is typically expressed as a decimal to the thousandths place. For instance, if a player has made 3 hits after coming to bat 10 times, his batting average is .300.

7. (**Sports**) If a player gets 8 hits in 25 at bats, what is the probability that he will get a hit on his next at bat? Express the answer as a decimal number to the thousandths place.   .320

In addition to sports, experimental probability is often used in banking, insurance, weather forecasting, and business.

8. (**Quality Assurance**) A piston manufacturer is concerned with the likelihood of defects, as this affects costs and profits. The manufacturer inspects 250 pistons and finds that 8 have defects.

   a. What is the probability a piston will have a defect? Express the probability as a percent.   3.2%

   b. If the same manufacturer produces 3000 pistons, about how many will likely have defects?   96 pistons

   c. **Evaluate** Pistons sell for $35 and it costs $25 in materials to make each piston. How much profit would the manufacturer likely make on 3000 pistons if defective ones cannot be sold? $26,640

Hint
Manufacturing costs must be paid for all pistons made, but only the ones that pass inspection can be sold.

A *random event* is an event whose outcome cannot be predicted. For example, drawing a card labeled 8 from a bin of cards, each labeled with a number from 1 to 100, represents a random event. An experiment could be conducted to determine the experimental probability of drawing a card labeled 8, however, it is not always practical to conduct an experiment to determine an experimental probability. In some instances it makes sense to perform a *simulation* of a random event using models such as number cubes, spinners, coins, or random number generators.

Graphing Calculator
For help with generating random numbers, see Graphing Calculator Lab 1 on page 52.

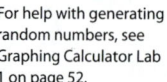 **Exploration** Using a Simulation to Find Probabilities

Saxon O's cereal is having a contest. Each box of cereal contains a prize piece and claims that 1 in 8 pieces is a winner. Conduct a simulation to determine the experimental probability of winning a prize piece within 50 boxes of cereal.

To simulate this problem, use the digits 1 through 8, with 1 representing a winning prize piece. Use your calculator to generate 50 random numbers.

9. According to your simulation, what is the probability of winning a prize in the Saxon O's contest? Express your answer as a fraction and as a percent.   See student work.

10. **Verify** How does your answer in problem 9 compare to the likelihood stated on the cereal box?   See student work.

54   *Saxon* Algebra 1

 ENGLISH LEARNERS

Students may be unfamiliar with the term **simulation.** Say:

"A simulation imitates an experiment. Simulations are used when it is difficult to do the real experiment."

Discuss how simulations are used to train people how to work something or to understand how something functions. For example, pilots are taught to fly planes using software that simulates flying a plane.

Dummies or models are used to simulate car accidents and to help make cars safer to drive.

Be sure students understand how a simulation using random numbers can be used to determine the experimental probability of winning a prize piece within any given number of boxes of cereal.

Have students explain how to model a simulation for problems **9** and **10** using a spinner instead of a graphing calculator.

Investigation Practice

Describe each of the following events as impossible, unlikely, as likely as not, likely, or certain.

a. Gavin rolls an even number on a number cube.   **as likely as not**

b. In the northern hemisphere, the temperature will get above 90°F in the month of July.   **likely**

c. The first person that Sonya meets is a left-handed person.   **unlikely**

d. A player with a batting average of .875 gets a hit on his next at bat.   **likely**

Jamie spun a game spinner and recorded the results in the table.

Outcome	Frequency
A	9
B	6
C	10

e. What is the probability of landing on A? on B? on C? Express each probability as a fraction and as a percent. $\frac{9}{25}$, 36%; $\frac{6}{25}$, 24%; $\frac{2}{5}$, 40%

f. **Predict** Which letter will Jamie most likely spin? Explain your reasoning.
C; Sample: The letter C has the greatest probability of occurring.

g. **(Sports)** If a baseball player has 18 hits in 50 at bats, what is the probability that he will get a hit in his next at bat? Express your answer as a decimal number in the thousandths place.   .360

h. According to a survey at Johnson High School, 1 in 4 students has a part-time job. Conduct a simulation to determine the experimental probability of a student having a part-time job in a random group of 25 students.
See student work.

Investigation 1   55

Investigation Practice

Math Conversations
Discussion to strengthen understanding

Problem b

Error Alert
Some students may assume that the temperature always gets above 90°F in July and think that the answer is certain. Remind students that although it is likely for July to be hot in the northern hemisphere, it is not certain that temperatures will be above 90°F.

Problem g

Scaffolding Guide students by asking the following questions.

"What is the formula for finding experimental probability?"
experimental probability = $\frac{\text{number of times an event occurs}}{\text{number of trials}}$

"What number represents the number of times the event occurs?" 18 hits

"What number represents the number of trials?" 50 at bats

"How would you find the probability in decimal form?"
Divide the number of hits by the number of at bats.

LOOKING FORWARD

Determining the experimental probability of an event prepares students for

- **Lesson 14** Determining the Theoretical Probability of an Event

- **Lesson 33** Finding the Probability of Independent and Dependent Events

- **Lesson 68** Mutually Exclusive and Inclusive Events

- **Lesson 80** Calculating Probability Distributions

Investigation 1   55

SECTION OVERVIEW 2

Lesson Planner

Lesson	New Concepts
11	Multiplying and Dividing Real Numbers
12	Using the Properties of Real Numbers to Simplify Expressions
13	Calculating and Comparing Square Roots
14	Determining the Theoretical Probability of an Event
15	Using the Distributive Property to Simplify Expressions
	Cumulative Test 2, Performance Task 2
16	Simplifying and Evaluating Variable Expressions
17	Translating Between Words and Algebraic Expressions
18	Combining Like Terms
19	Solving One-Step Equations by Adding or Subtracting
20	Graphing on a Coordinate Plane
	Cumulative Test 3, Performance Task 3
INV 2	Investigation: Graphing a Relationship

Resources for Teaching
- Student Edition
- Teacher's Edition
- Student Edition eBook
- Teacher's Edition eBook
- Resources and Planner CD
- Solutions Manual
- Instructional Masters
- Technology Lab Masters
- Warm Up and Teaching Transparencies
- Instructional Presentations CD
- Online activities, tools, and homework help
  www.SaxonMathResources.com

Resources for Practice and Assessment
- Student Edition Practice Workbook
- Course Assessments
- Standardized Test Practice
- College Entrance Exam Practice
- Test and Practice Generator CD using ExamView™

Resources for Differentiated Instruction
- Reteaching Masters
- Challenge and Enrichment Masters
- Prerequisite Skills Intervention
- Adaptations for Saxon Algebra 1
- Multilingual Glossary
- English Learners Handbook
- TI Resources

Pacing Guide

 Resources and Planner CD for lesson planning support

45-Minute Class

Day 1	Day 2	Day 3	Day 4	Day 5	Day 6
Lesson 11	Lesson 12	Lesson 13	Lesson 14	Lesson 15	Cumulative Test 2
Day 7	**Day 8**	**Day 9**	**Day 10**	**Day 11**	**Day 12**
Lesson 16	Lesson 17	Lesson 18	Lesson 19	Lesson 20	Cumulative Test 3
Day 13					
Investigation 2					

Block: 90-Minute Class

Day 1	Day 2	Day 3	Day 4	Day 5	Day 6
Lesson 11 Lesson 12	Lesson 13 Lesson 14	Lesson 15 Cumulative Test 2	Lesson 16 Lesson 17	Lesson 18 Lesson 19	Lesson 20 Cumulative Test 3
Day 7					
Investigation 2 Lesson 21					

* For suggestions on how to implement Saxon Math in a block schedule, see the Pacing section at the beginning of the Teacher's Edition.

56A   Saxon Algebra 1

Lessons 11–20, Investigation 2

Differentiated Instruction

Below Level		Advanced Learners	
Warm Up	SE pp. 56, 63, 69, 74, 80, 86, 93, 98, 103, 110	Challenge	TE pp. 61, 68, 72, 79, 85, 91, 96, 101, 108, 116
Skills Bank	SE pp. 846–883	Extend the Example	TE pp. 59, 65, 69, 75, 82, 88, 93, 99, 106, 111, 112
Reteaching Masters	Lessons 11–20, Investigation 2	Extend the Problem	TE pp. 60, 68, 73, 78, 85, 91, 95, 97, 101, 102, 108, 109, 116, 118
Warm Up Transparencies	Lessons 11–20		
Prerequisite Skills Intervention	Skills 6, 11, 14, 16, 18, 43, 44, 45, 46, 47, 48, 52, 56, 57, 58, 68, 71, 79, 90	Challenge and Enrichment Masters	Challenge: 11–20, Enrichment: 11, 13, 17, 20

English Learners		Special Needs	
EL Tips	TE pp. 56, 64, 69, 75, 81, 88, 94, 98, 104, 113, 118	Inclusion Tips	TE pp. 59, 66, 71, 78, 82, 89, 95, 100, 106, 111
Multilingual Glossary	Booklet and Online	Adaptations for Saxon Algebra 1	Lessons 11–20, Cumulative Tests 2, 3
English Learners Handbook			

For All Learners			
Exploration	SE pp. 74, 104	Alternate Method	TE pp. 57, 70, 76, 99
Caution	SE pp. 65, 70, 88, 89, 94, 105, 112, 118	Manipulative Use	TE pp. 60, 77, 105
Hints	SE pp. 58, 64, 75, 81, 82, 86, 93, 98, 99, 104, 106, 111	Online Tools	
Error Alert	TE pp. 57, 59, 60, 64, 66, 70, 71, 73, 76, 77, 79, 80, 81, 82, 85, 88, 89, 90, 92, 94, 95, 97, 99, 100, 102, 105, 106, 107, 109, 110, 113, 114, 115, 118, 119		

SE = Student Edition; TE = Teacher's Edition

Math Vocabulary

Lesson	New Vocabulary		Maintained	EL Tip in TE
11	multiplicative inverse	reciprocal	repeated addition	property
12			factor term	identity
13	perfect square radicand	square root	exponent estimate	radical
14	complement of an event sample space	simple event theoretical probability	outcome event	favorable
15			algebraic expression integer numeric expression	distribute
16			evaluate substitute	principal
17			difference product quotient sum	reverse
18	like terms unlike terms		coefficient Distributive Property variable	combine
19	equation equivalent equations inverse operations solution of an equation in one variable		equivalent variable	isolate
20	coordinate coordinate plane dependent variable independent variable ordered pair origin	quadrants x-axis x-coordinate y-axis y-coordinate	intersection perpendicular horizontal axis vertical axis	substitute
INV 2	continuous graph discrete data discrete graph		scale intervals increase decrease	discrete

SECTION OVERVIEW 2

Math Highlights

Enduring Understandings – The "Big Picture"

After completing Section 2, students will understand:

- How to perform operations with real numbers and find the square root of a number.
- How to translate words into algebraic expressions.
- How to solve equations and graph ordered pairs on a coordinate plane.
- How to determine the independent and dependent variable in a relationship.
- How to simplify, evaluate, and compare algebraic expressions using properties.
- How to find the theoretical probability of a simple event and the complement of an event.

Essential Questions

- How can the properties of real numbers be used to justify the simplification of algebraic expressions and solutions of equations?
- What is the relationship between the ordered pairs on a graph and the solutions of an equation?
- When a relationship has two variable quantities, which variable is dependent and which is independent?
- Why do the possible values of the theoretical probability of an event range from 0 to 1, and how does this help to find the complement of an event?

Math Content Strands

Algebra Foundations
- Lesson 11 — Multiplying and Dividing Real Numbers
- Lesson 12 — Using the Properties of Real Numbers to Simplify Expressions
- Lesson 13 — Calculating and Comparing Square Roots
- Lesson 15 — Using the Distributive Property to Simplify Expressions
- Lesson 16 — Simplifying and Evaluating Variable Expressions
- Lesson 17 — Translating Between Words and Algebraic Expressions

Equations
- Lesson 18 — Combining Like Terms
- Lesson 19 — Solving One-Step Equations by Adding or Subtracting
- Investigation 2 — Graphing a Relationship

Functions and Relations
- Lesson 20 — Graphing on a Coordinate Plane

Probability and Data Analysis
- Lesson 14 — Determining the Theoretical Probability of an Event

Connections in Practice Problems

	Lessons
Geometry	11, 12, 14, 15, 16, 17, 18, 19, 20
Measurement	16, 17, 18
Probability	11, 13, 15, 17, 18, 19
Statistics	20

Math Processes

Reasoning and Communication

	Lessons
Analyze	11, 12, 13, 14, 16, 20, Inv. 2
Error analysis	11, 12, 13, 14, 15, 16, 17, 18, 19, 20
Estimate	16, Inv. 2
Formulate	13
Generalize	11, 14, 17, 20
Justify	11, 12, 13, 14, 15, 16, 17, 18, 19, Inv. 2
Math Reasoning	11, 12, 13, 14, 15, 16, 17, 18, 19, 20, Inv. 2
Model	11, 13, 14, 15, 20
Multiple choice	11, 12, 13, 14, 15, 16, 17, 18, 19, 20, Inv. 2
Multi-step	11, 12, 13, 15, 16, 17, 18, 19, 20
Predict	18, 20, Inv. 2
True or False	11, 12, 13, 15, 16, 17, 18, 19
Verify	11, 12, 13, 14, 15, 16, 18, 19, 20
Write	12, 14, 15, 16, 17, 19, 20, Inv. 2
Graphing Calculator	13, 16

Connections

In Examples: Ballroom dancing, Cave exploration, Consumer math, Investments, Landscaping, Measurement, Savings, State fair, Wages, Weather

In Practice problems: Air travel, Age, Astronomy, Babysitting, Banking, Bowling, Braking distance, Budgeting, Business, Carpentry, Chemistry, Construction, Cost of pecans, Energy conservation, Finance, Fundraising, Geography, Horse's speed, Interior decorating, International banking, Investing, Investments, Landscaping, Manufacturing, Meteorology, Nutrition, Ocean travel, Oceanography, Payroll accountancy, Personal finance, Phone charges, Photography, Physics, Racing, Reading, Retailing, Savings, Savings accounts, Science, Sewing, Sites, Stocks, Surveying, Travel, Temperature, Tiling, Tug of war, World records

Content Trace

Lesson	Warm Up: Prerequisite Skills	New Concepts	Where Practiced	Where Assessed	Looking Forward
11	Lessons 3, 5, 6	Multiplying and Dividing Real Numbers	Lessons 12, 13, 14, 16, 17, 19, 20, 23, 24, 27, 30, 31, 33	Cumulative Tests 3, 4, 5, 8	Lessons 12, 15, 16, 37
12	Lessons 5, 9, 11	Using the Properties of Real Numbers to Simplify Expressions	Lessons 13, 14, 15, 16, 17, 18, 19, 20, 21, 22, 24, 25, 26, 27, 28, 30	Cumulative Tests 3, 7, 9	Lessons 15, 16, 17, 18
13	Lessons 3, 10, 11	Calculating and Comparing Square Roots	Lessons 14, 15, 16, 17, 18, 19, 20, 21, 23, 24, 25, 26, 28, 29, 31, 33, 42, 59	Cumulative Tests 3, 4, 5, 7	Lessons 16, 17, 46
14	Lessons 4, 5, 6, 10, Inv. 1	Determining the Theoretical Probability of an Event	Lessons 15, 16, 17, 18, 19, 20, 21, 22, 23, 24, 26, 27, 30	Cumulative Tests 3, 4, 5, 6	Lessons 33, 68, 80
15	Lessons 2, 4, 9, 11	Using the Distributive Property to Simplify Expressions	Lessons 16, 17, 18, 19, 21, 22, 24, 25, 27, 28, 31, 32, 48, 49	Cumulative Tests 3, 4, 5	Lessons 16, 26, 29, 32
16	Lessons 6, 7, 11, 13, 15	Simplifying and Evaluating Variable Expressions	Lessons 17, 18, 19, 20, 22, 24, 25, 26, 29, 31, 41, 49	Cumulative Tests 4, 5, 6, 7	Lessons 17, 37, 40, 46
17	Lessons 6, 9, 11, 15	Translating Between Words and Algebraic Expressions	Lessons 18, 19, 20, 21, 22, 23, 25, 26, 28, 29, 31, 32, 39	Cumulative Tests 4, 6, 7, 8	Lessons 26, 42, 45, 56
18	Lessons 2, 3, 17	Combining Like Terms	Lessons 19, 20, 21, 22, 24, 26, 28, 29, 31, 35, 36, 37, 46	Cumulative Tests 4, 5, 6, 8, 9, 11, 13	Lessons 19, 23, 26, 28, 29, 117
19	Lessons 5, 6, 9, 16	Solving One-Step Equations by Adding or Subtracting	Lessons 20, 21, 22, 23, 25, 27, 28, 30, 32	Cumulative Tests 4, 5, 9	Lessons 21, 23, 24, 26, 28
20	Lessons 5, 7, 15, 18	Graphing on a Coordinate Plane	Lessons 21, 22, 23, 24, 25, 27, 28, 29, 32, 33, 35, 36, 46	Cumulative Tests 4, 5, 7	Lessons 25, 30, 34, 71, Inv. 2
INV 2	N/A	Investigation: Graphing a Relationship	Lessons 21, 25, 28, 30, 38	Cumulative Test 7	Lessons 25, 30, 41, 71

SECTION OVERVIEW 2

Ongoing Assessment

	Type	Feature	Intervention *
BEFORE instruction	Assess Prior Knowledge	• Diagnostic Test	• Prerequisite Skills Intervention
BEFORE the lesson	Formative	• Warm Up	• Skills Bank • Reteaching Masters
DURING the lesson	Formative	• Lesson Practice • Math Conversations with the Practice problems	• Additional Examples in TE • Test and Practice Generator (for additional practice sheets)
AFTER the lesson	Formative	• Check for Understanding (closure)	• Scaffolding Questions in TE
AFTER 5 lessons	Summative	After Lesson 15 • Cumulative Test 2 • Performance Task 2 After Lesson 20 • Cumulative Test 3 • Performance Task 3	• Reteaching Masters • Test and Practice Generator (for additional tests and practice)
AFTER 20 lessons	Summative	• Benchmark Tests	• Reteaching Masters • Test and Practice Generator (for additional tests and practice)

* for students not showing progress during the formative stages or scoring below 80% on the summative assessments

Evidence of Learning – What Students Should Know

Because the Saxon philosophy is to provide students with sufficient time to learn and practice each concept, a lesson's topic will not be tested until at least five lessons after the topic is introduced.

On the Cumulative Tests that are given during this section of ten lessons, students should be able to demonstrate the following competencies:
- Identify variables and constants.
- Identify subsets of real numbers.
- Find the absolute value, and add and subtract real numbers.
- Order and multiply rational numbers.
- Identify properties, and use properties to simplify algebraic expressions with and without exponents.
- Estimate square roots, find the square roots of perfect squares, and compare square roots.
- Convert units of measure.
- Find the probability of an event.

Test and Practice Generator CD using ExamView™

The Test and Practice Generator is an easy-to-use benchmark and assessment tool that creates unlimited practice and tests in multiple formats and allows you to customize questions or create new ones. A variety of reports are available to track student progress toward mastery of the standards throughout the year.

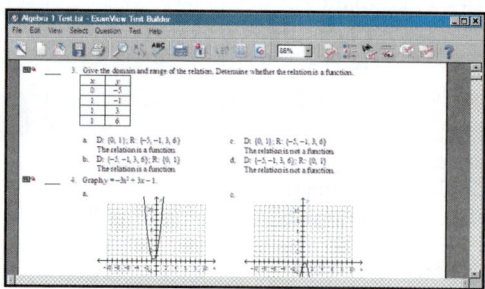
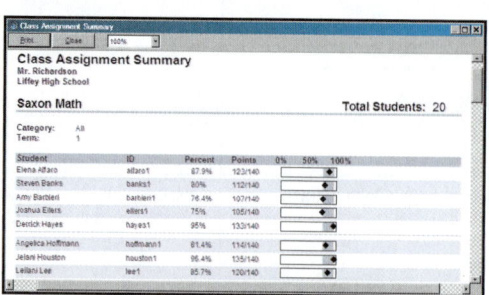

Saxon Algebra 1

Assessment Resources

Resources for Diagnosing and Assessing

- **Student Edition**
  - Warm Up
  - Lesson Practice

- **Teacher's Edition**
  - Math Conversations with the Practice problems
  - Check for Understanding (closure)

- **Course Assessments**
  - Diagnostic Test
  - Cumulative Tests
  - Performance Tasks
  - Benchmark Tests

Resources for Test Prep

- **Student Edition Practice**
  - Multiple-choice problems
  - Multiple-step and writing problems
  - Daily cumulative practice

- **Standardized Test Practice**

- **College Entrance Exam Practice**

- **Test and Practice Generator CD using ExamView™**

Resources for Intervention

- **Student Edition**
  - Skills Bank

- **Teacher's Edition**
  - Additional Examples
  - Scaffolding questions

- **Prerequisite Skills Intervention**
  - Worksheets

- **Reteaching Masters**
  - Lesson instruction and practice sheets

- **Test and Practice Generator CD using ExamView™**
  - Lesson practice problems
  - Additional tests

Cumulative Tests

The assessments in Saxon Math are frequent and consistently placed after every five lessons to offer a regular method of ongoing testing. These cumulative assessments check mastery of concepts from previous lessons.

Performance Tasks

The Performance Tasks can be used in conjunction with the Cumulative Tests and are scored using a rubric.

After Lesson 15

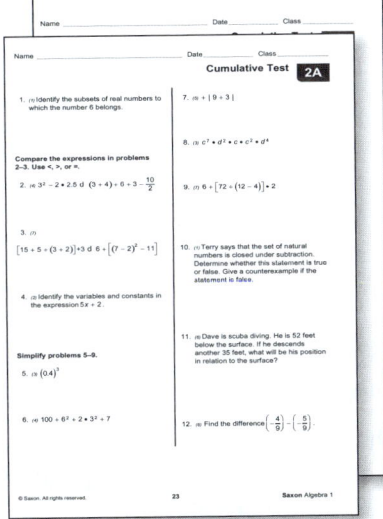

After Lesson 20

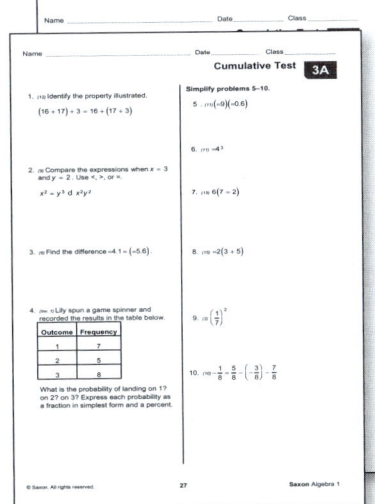

For use with Performance Tasks

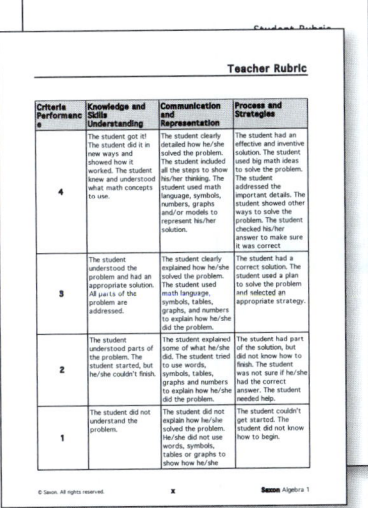

Section Overview 2   56F

LESSON 11

1 Warm Up

Problem 3
Remind students that in algebra, the subtraction sign means "to add the opposite."

2 New Concepts

In this lesson, students learn to multiply and divide signed numbers.

Discuss the properties of real numbers that apply specifically to multiplication. Explain the rules for multiplying and dividing real numbers.

LESSON RESOURCES

Student Edition Practice Workbook 11
Reteaching Master 11
Adaptations Master 11
Challenge and Enrichment Master C11, E11

LESSON 11 — Multiplying and Dividing Real Numbers

Warm Up

1. **Vocabulary** Two numbers with the same absolute value but different signs are called _____ (integers, opposites).   **opposites**

Simplify each expression.

2. $(-4) + (-4) + (-4)$ **−12**
3. $-8 - 8 - 8 - 8 - 8 - 8$ **−48**
4. 5^4 **625**
5. 2^5 **32**

New Concepts

The sum of three 2's is 6 and the sum of two 3's is 6.

$$2 + 2 + 2 = 6 \qquad 3 + 3 = 6$$

Multiplication is a way to show repeated addition of the same number. The repeated addition above can be shown as multiplication of the same number.

$$3 \cdot 2 = 6 \quad \text{or} \quad 2 \cdot 3 = 6$$

The properties of real numbers apply to all real numbers, rational and irrational. Use these properties when evaluating and simplifying numeric and algebraic expressions.

The table shows some properties of multiplication when a and b are real numbers.

Math Reasoning

Analyze How are the Identity Property of Multiplication and the Identity Property of Addition alike?

Sample: When either property is applied, the number retains its identity. The value of the number does not change.

Online Connection
www.SaxonMathResources.com

Properties of Real Numbers
Multiplication Property of −1
For every real number a, $$a \cdot -1 = -1 \cdot a = -a$$
Example $9 \cdot -1 = -1 \cdot 9 = -9$
Multiplication Property of Zero
For every real number a, $$a \cdot 0 = 0$$
Example $9 \cdot 0 = 0$
Inverse Property of Multiplication
For every real number a, where $a \neq 0$, $$a \cdot \frac{1}{a} = \frac{1}{a} \cdot a = 1$$
Example $3 \cdot \frac{1}{3} = \frac{1}{3} \cdot 3 = 1$

MATH BACKGROUND

Connect the rules for multiplying and dividing integers to the following three points.

- Multiplication can be thought of as repeated addition. For example, 3×4 means $4 + 4 + 4$.
- The Commutative Property holds for the multiplication operation. For example, $12 \times 4 = 4 \times 12$.
- Division and multiplication are inverse operations. For example, $4 \times 7 = 28$ and $28 \div 7 = 4$.

ENGLISH LEARNERS

Discuss with students the meaning of the word **property**. Say:

"The things that belong to people are referred to as their property. For example, people may own their own car or clothing."

Have volunteers give other examples of property. Sample: bicycle, pet, school supplies, games, etc.

To multiply signed numbers, use the rules in the table below.

Multiplying Signed Numbers	
The product of two numbers with the same sign is a positive number.	
Examples	$(3)(4) = 12 \quad (-5)(-3) = 15$
The product of two numbers with opposite signs is a negative number.	
Examples	$(-2)(4) = -8 \quad 6(-2) = -12$

Example 1 Multiplying Rational Numbers

Simplify each expression. Justify your answer.

a. $4(-8)$

SOLUTION

$4(-8) = -32$ The product of two numbers with opposite signs is negative.

b. $(-6)(-0.7)$

SOLUTION

$(-6)(-0.7) = 4.2$ The product of two numbers with the same sign is positive.

To raise a number to a power, use repeated multiplication to simplify.

Example 2 Raising a Number to a Power

Simplify each expression.

a. $(-3)^4$

SOLUTION

$(-3)^4$
$= (-3)(-3)(-3)(-3)$ Use repeated multiplication.
$= 81$

b. $(-3)^3$

SOLUTION

$(-3)^3$
$= (-3)(-3)(-3)$ Use repeated multiplication.
$= -27$

c. -3^4

SOLUTION

-3^4
$= -1 \cdot 3^4$
$= -1[(3)(3)(3)(3)]$ Use repeated multiplication.
$= -1(81)$ Find the product inside the brackets.
$= -81$ Multiplication Property of -1

Math Reasoning

Generalize How does an even or odd exponent affect the product of the power of a negative number?

Sample: When you simplify a power of a negative number with an even exponent, the product is always positive. When you simplify a power of a negative number with an odd exponent, the product is always negative.

Example 1

Students apply the rules for multiplying signed numbers.

Additional Example 1

Students should see that the sign of the product is determined by the sign of the factors.

Simplify each expression. Justify your answer.

a. $12(-8)$ -96; Sample: The product of two numbers with opposite signs is negative.

b. $(-5.2)(-3)$ 15.6; Sample: The product of two numbers with the same signs is positive.

TEACHER TIP

The product of any pair of negative numbers is positive. An even number of negative factors can be paired to produce a positive result. An odd number of negative factors cannot be paired, so a negative result is produced.

Example 2

Students should see raising a power as repeated multiplication. So, the rules for multiplying signed numbers apply to powers, also.

Additional Example 2

Simplify each expression.

a. $(-2)^3$ -8

b. $(-4)^4$ 256

c. -5^3 -125

Error Alert Students may have difficulty understanding the difference between -2^5 and $(-2)^5$. Have students rewrite -2^5 as $-1 \cdot 2^5$. Then remind them to use the order of operations, simplifying the exponent before multiplication.

ALTERNATE METHOD FOR EXAMPLE 2

Explain to students that another meaning of a negative sign is "the opposite of."

When students simplify the expression $(-3)^4$, they can multiply $(3)(3)(3)(3) = 81$. The answer is temporarily positive. Then students can count the number of negative signs in the factors. Because there are four negative signs in the problem, the final answer is positive.

When simplifying the expression $(-3)^3$, they can multiply $(3)(3)(3) = 27$. The answer is temporarily positive. Then, because there are three negative sign in the problem, the final answer is negative.

Lesson 11   57

Example 3

Students use the rules for dividing signed numbers.

Additional Example 3

Simplify each expression. Justify your answer.

a. $-72 \div (-24)$ **3; Sample: The quotient of two numbers with the same sign is positive**

b. $12.1 \div (-11)$ **−1.1; Sample: The quotient of two numbers with opposite signs is negative.**

Example 4

Students apply the rules for dividing signed numbers to fractions.

Additional Example 4

Evaluate each expression.

a. $-\dfrac{5}{6} \div \left(-\dfrac{2}{9}\right)$ $\dfrac{15}{4}$

b. $-\dfrac{12}{5} \div \left(\dfrac{18}{25}\right)$ $-\dfrac{10}{3}$

To divide signed numbers, use the rules in the table below.

Dividing Signed Numbers
The quotient of two numbers with the same sign is a positive number.
Examples $6 \div 3 = 2$ $-8 \div (-2) = 4$ $\dfrac{6}{3} = 2$ $\dfrac{-8}{-2} = 4$
The quotient of two numbers with opposite signs is a negative number.
Examples $10 \div (-5) = -2$ $-12 \div 3 = -4$ $\dfrac{10}{-5} = -2$ $\dfrac{-12}{3} = -4$

Example 3 Dividing Real Numbers

Simplify each expression. Justify your answer.

a. $-16 \div (-2)$

SOLUTION

$-16 \div (-2) = 8$ The quotient of two numbers with the same sign is positive.

b. $2.8 \div (-7)$

SOLUTION

$2.8 \div (-7) = -0.4$ The quotient of two numbers with opposite signs is negative.

Dividing by a number a is the same as multiplying by the **reciprocal** $\dfrac{1}{a}$, or **multiplicative inverse,** of the divisor.

$$12 \div 2 = 12 \cdot \dfrac{1}{2} = 6$$

The reciprocal of 2 is $\dfrac{1}{2}$. Multiplying 12 by $\dfrac{1}{2}$ is the same as dividing 12 by 2.

Hint

The product of a number and its reciprocal is always 1. So, both the number and its reciprocal have the same sign.

$2 \cdot \dfrac{1}{2} = 1$ and $-2 \cdot \left(-\dfrac{1}{2}\right) = 1$

Example 4 Dividing Positive and Negative Fractions

Evaluate each expression.

a. $-\dfrac{2}{3} \div \left(-\dfrac{3}{4}\right)$

SOLUTION

$-\dfrac{2}{3} \div \left(-\dfrac{3}{4}\right)$

$-\dfrac{2}{3} \cdot \left(-\dfrac{4}{3}\right)$ Multiply by the reciprocal of $-\dfrac{3}{4}$.

$-\dfrac{2}{3} \cdot \left(-\dfrac{4}{3}\right) = \dfrac{8}{9}$ The product of two fractions with the same sign is positive.

Reading Math

You can write $-\frac{3}{5}$ as $\frac{-3}{5}$ or $\frac{3}{-5}$.

b. $\frac{2}{9} \div \left(-\frac{3}{5}\right)$

SOLUTION

$\frac{2}{9} \div \left(-\frac{3}{5}\right)$

$\frac{2}{9} \cdot \left(-\frac{5}{3}\right)$ Multiply by the reciprocal of $-\frac{3}{5}$.

$\frac{2}{9} \cdot \left(-\frac{5}{3}\right) = -\frac{10}{27}$ The product of two fractions with different signs is negative.

Example 5   **Application: Cave Exploration**

The Voronya Cave in Abkhazia, Georgia is the deepest known cave in the world. At an elevation of -2140 meters, Voronya is a challenge for experienced cavers. If it takes 8 days to travel to the bottom of the cave, what is the average number of meters the cavers would travel each day?

SOLUTION

Write an expression.

elevation of cave		number of days to travel
-2140 m	$\div$	8 days

$-2140 \div 8 = -267.5$

The cavers would travel an average of -267.5 meters per day.

Lesson Practice

Simplify each expression. Justify your answer.
(Ex 1)
a. $9(-0.8)$

b. $-12(-2.5)$ 30; Sample: Multiplying two numbers with like signs results in a positive product.

Simplify each expression.
(Ex 2)
c. $(-4)^3$ -64

d. $(-8)^4$ 4096

e. -5^4 -625

Simplify each expression. Justify your answer.
(Ex 3)
f. $-105 \div (-7)$ 15; Sample: Dividing two numbers with like signs results in a positive quotient.

g. $63.9 \div (-3)$ -21.3; Sample: Dividing two numbers with different signs results in a negative quotient.

Evaluate each expression.
(Ex 4)
h. $-\frac{4}{5} \div \left(-\frac{9}{10}\right)$ $\frac{8}{9}$

i. $\frac{3}{8} \div \left(-\frac{3}{4}\right)$ $-\frac{1}{2}$

j. (Science) During a cold spell in January 1989, Homer, Alaska, recorded
(Ex 5) a low temperature of $-24°F$. The city of Bethel, Alaska, recorded a low temperature twice as cold as the low in Homer. What was the temperature in Bethel, Alaska? $-48°F$

a. -7.2; Sample: Multiplying two numbers with different signs results in a negative product.

Lesson 11   59

Example 5

Students use division of signed numbers to solve a real-world problem.

Extend the Example

"If another team of cavers travels an average of -194.5 feet per day, about how many days will it take them to reach the bottom of the cave?" It would take about 11 days to reach the bottom at an average rate of -194.5 feet per day.

Additional Example 5

After an event, 5 students will equally share the profits or debt. The event ended with a debt, represented by $-\$100$. What value represents each student's share? $-\$20$

Lesson Practice

Problem a

Scaffolding After simplifying the expression, be sure students state the applicable rule for multiplying signed numbers.

Problem h

Error Alert Some students may try to divide fractions by dividing the numerators and dividing the denominators. Remind them to multiply by the reciprocal.

Check for Understanding

The questions below help assess the concepts taught in this lesson.

"Explain how to determine the sign of the product or quotient of two numbers." Sample: If the two numbers have like signs, the answer is positive. If the two numbers have different signs, the answer is negative.

"Explain the difference in finding the solution to $(-2)^2$ and -2^2."
Sample: In $(-2)^2$, negative two is raised to the 2nd power. In -2^2, only the 2 is raised to the 2nd power.

INCLUSION

Students may need help remembering products of common powers. Have students use index cards to create flash cards of common powers. ($2^2, 2^3, 2^4, 2^5, 3^2, 3^3$, etc.) The flash cards should include the value of each power on the back of the card. Have students practice recalling each value from memory.

Lesson 11   59

3 Practice

Math Conversations

Discussion to strengthen understanding

Problem 2
Error Alert
Some students may take the opposite of −4 before squaring which will result in a sign error. Remind them to follow the order of operations.

Problem 3
Encourage students to use estimation to see which answer is more reasonable. Student B subtracts $\frac{2}{4}$ or half from $\frac{11}{12}$. Yet when the computation inside the parentheses is finished, the answer is not significantly lower than $\frac{11}{12}$.

Problem 8
Extend the Problem
Evaluate the expression if $x = -2$. −42

Problem 11
Guide the students by asking them the following questions.

"What time is noon?" 12:00 p.m.

"What extra information is provided?" 3:00 a.m.

"How many hours did the temperature fall until 11 p.m.?" 11 hours

"How many degrees did the temperature fall?" −22°C

Practice Distributed and Integrated

*1. **Verify** True or False: The product of a number and its reciprocal is equal to one.
(11) Verify your answer.   true; Sample: $7 \times \frac{1}{7} = \frac{7}{1} \times \frac{1}{7} = \frac{7}{7} = 1$

*2. Simplify $-(-4)^2$.   −16
(11)

3. **Error Analysis** Which student is correct? Explain the error.   Student A;
(10) Sample: Student B did not find a common denominator.

Student A	Student B
$\left(\frac{11}{12} - \frac{2}{4} - \frac{1}{3}\right) + \frac{11}{12}$	$\left(\frac{11}{12} - \frac{2}{4} - \frac{1}{3}\right) + \frac{11}{12}$
$= \frac{1}{12} + \frac{11}{12}$	$= \frac{8}{12} + \frac{11}{12}$
$= 1$	$= \frac{19}{12}$

4. Simplify $\frac{2 \cdot 14 + 3 \cdot 7}{71 - 15}$. $\frac{7}{8}$
(4)

5. Draw a line plot for the frequency table.
(SB 29)

Number	5	6	7	8	9	10
Frequency	4	2	0	1	0	3

5.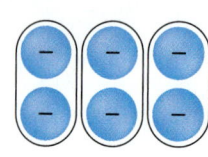

6. A(n) _____ angle measures more than 90° and less than 180°.   obtuse
(SB 13)

7. Evaluate $3(x + 4) + y$ when $x = 8$ and $y = 7$.   43
(9)

8. Evaluate the expression $3x^2 + 2(x - 1)^3$ for the given value $x = 6$.   358
(9)

9. **Multiple Choice** Which rate is the fastest?   B
(8)
A 660 ft/15 s
B 645 ft/11 s
C 616 ft/12 s
D 1100 ft/30 s

10. $5 + \frac{9}{3}\left[4\left(\frac{1}{2} + 4\right)\right]$

$5 + \frac{9}{3}\left[4\left(\frac{9}{2}\right)\right]$ symbols of Inclusion
$5 + \frac{9}{3}[18]$ symbols of Inclusion
$5 + 54$ Multiply.
59 Add.

10. **Justify** Simplify $5 + \frac{9}{3}[4(\frac{1}{2} + 4)]$. Justify each step.
(7)

*11. **Multiple Choice** The temperature at noon was 20°C. The temperature fell 2 degrees
(11) every hour until 3 a.m. the next day. What was the temperature at 11 p.m. that evening?   B
A 22°C
B −2°C
C −30°C
D −22°C

60   *Saxon* Algebra 1

🔶 MANIPULATIVE USE

Materials: two-color counters

Model the expression. $-6 \div 3 = -2$.

Divide the six negative counters into 3 groups. In each group there are two negative counters.

Now model $-6 \div (-3) = 2$.

Divide the six negative counters into 3 groups. Then, because the divisor is −3, the opposite of 3, take the opposite by flipping the counters to be positive.

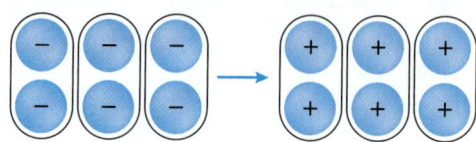

*12. (Physics) The magnitude of the instant acceleration of an object in uniform circular motion is found using the formula $a = \frac{v^2}{r}$, where r is the radius of the circle and v is the constant speed. Evaluate $a = \frac{v^2}{r}$ if $v = 35$ cm/s and $r = 200$ cm. $a = 6.125$ cm/s^2

*13. (Retailing) A grocery store is having a sale on strawberries. Suppose 560 pints of strawberries are sold at a loss of $0.16 for each pint. How much money does the store lose on the sale of the strawberries? $89.60

*14. (Ocean Travel) The deepest point of the Kermandec trench in the Pacific Ocean is 10,047 meters below sea level. A submarine made two dives from above the deepest point of the trench at a rate of 400 meters per minute. The first of the two dives was 10 minutes long and the second was 4 minutes. How far did the submarine travel in each dive? -4000 m, -1600 m

15. Add $-1.06 + 2.01 + 4.13$.   5.08

16. **Multi-Step** A purple string is 0.99 m long. A green string is 0.23 m long. What is the difference in length of the two pieces?
   a. **Estimate** Estimate the difference using fractions.   Sample: $1 - \frac{1}{4} = \frac{3}{4}$, about $\frac{3}{4}$ m
   b. Find the exact value of the difference using fractions. $\frac{99}{100} - \frac{23}{100} = \frac{76}{100} = \frac{19}{25}$

17. **Error Analysis** Two students solved a homework problem as shown below. Which student is correct? Explain the error.   Student B; Sample: Student A should have multiplied 4 and 17 together first.

Student A	Student B
Evaluate $3g - 4(g + 2b)$; $g = 9$ and $b = 4$.	Evaluate $3g - 4(g + 2b)$; $g = 9$ and $b = 4$.
$3(9) - 4(9 + 2(4))$	$3(9) - 4(9 + 2(4))$
$27 - 4(17)$	$27 - 4(17)$
$23(17)$	$27 - 68$
391	-41

18. (Science) Scientists can use the expression $2.6f + 65$ to estimate the height of a person if they know the length of the femur bone, f. What is the approximate height of a person if the femur bone is 40 centimeters long?   169 cm

19. **Error Analysis** The highest point in North America, Mount McKinley, in the Alaska Range, is 20,320 feet above sea level. The lowest point in North America is 282 feet below sea level and is in Death Valley in California. Which student correctly calculated the difference in elevations? Explain the error.   Student B; Sample: Student A subtracted 282 instead of -282.

Student A	Student B
$20{,}320 - 282$	$20{,}320 - (-282)$
$20{,}320 + (-282)$	$20{,}320 + (+282)$
$20{,}038$ feet	$20{,}602$ feet

Lesson 11   61

Problem 12
Encourage students to use unit analysis as they evaluate this expression. It may be helpful to work through the problem as a class showing the following steps:

$$\frac{\left(\frac{cm}{s}\right)^2}{cm} = \frac{\left(\frac{cm^2}{s^2}\right)}{cm}$$
$$= \frac{cm^2}{s^2} \div cm = \frac{cm^2}{s^2} \cdot \frac{1}{cm}$$
$$= \frac{cm^2}{s^2} \cdot \frac{1}{cm} = \frac{cm}{s^2}.$$

Problem 15
Have students rewrite the problem vertically, lining up the decimal points before adding.

Problem 19
Point out that "below sea level" is represented by a negative number.

CHALLENGE

Have students explain how to simplify the expression $-4(-2)^3$. Sample: Simplify the power $(-2)^3 = -8$, and then multiply $-4 \cdot -8 = 32$.

Lesson 11   61

Problem 26
Discuss that perimeter is the distance around something. Ask, **"Why can't a distance ever be negative?"** Sample: If there is something to measure, it exists and is therefore positive. Negative distance is impossible.

 20. Probability Describe each of the events below as impossible, unlikely, as likely as
(Inv.1) not, likely, or certain.
   a. Joshua rolls an odd number on a standard number cube.   as likely as not
   b. Maria's birthday is September 31st.   impossible
   c. The basketball team has won 11 of their last 12 games. The team will win the next game.   likely

Simplify each expression.

*21. $5(-2)$ -10
(11)

*22. $(-3)(-5)$ 15
(11)

23. $-|-15 + 5|$ -10
(5)

*24. $(-3)(-6)(-2)(5)$ -180
(11)

*25. $(3)(5)$ 15
(11)

27a.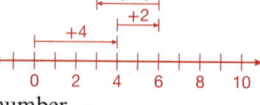

26. Geometry Can the perimeter of a rectangle be any integer value?
(1) No, the perimeter of a rectangle cannot be a negative integer.

27. Model Mary is playing a board game using a number cube to decide the number
(10) of spaces she moves. She moves forward on an even number and backward on an odd number. Her first 5 rolls were 4, 2, 3, 6, 1.
   a. Model her moves on a number line with zero being the starting point.
   b. Using addition and subtraction, write an expression showing her moves.
      $4 + 2 - 3 + 6 - 1$
   c. At a the end of 5 rolls, how many spaces is she away from the starting point?
      8 spaces

*28. **Analyze** Jan bought 2 yards of ribbon. She needs 64 inches of ribbon to make a bow.
(8) Does she have enough ribbon? Explain your answer.   yes; 2 yards is 72 inches.

29. **Meteorology** A meteorologist reported the day's low temperature of $-5°F$ at 7 a.m.
(6) and the day's high temperature of $20°F$ at 5 p.m. How much did the temperature rise from 7 a.m. to 5 p.m.? $25°F$

30. **Phone Charges** Fast Talk Phone Company charges an initial fee of $20 plus
(9) 10¢ per minute used. The total bill is expressed as $20 + 0.10m$, where m is the minutes used. If 200 minutes are used, what is the amount of the bill? $40

LOOKING FORWARD

Multiplying and dividing real numbers prepares students for

- **Lesson 12** Using the Properties of Real Numbers to Simplify Expressions

- **Lesson 15** Using the Distributive Property to Simplify Expressions

- **Lesson 16** Simplifying and Evaluating Variable Expressions

- **Lesson 37** Using Scientific Notation

LESSON 12

Using the Properties of Real Numbers to Simplify Expressions

Warm Up

1. **Vocabulary** A(n) _____ expression is an expression with constants and/or variables that uses the operations +, −, ×, or ÷.   **algebraic**
2. Simplify $6 - |-6| + (-4)$.   **−4**
3. Divide $-\frac{4}{5} \div \left(-\frac{8}{9}\right)$. $\frac{9}{10}$
4. Evaluate $2|y| - 2|x| + m$ for $x = -1.5$, $y = -3$, and $m = -1.3$.   **1.7**

New Concepts

The properties of real numbers are used to simplify expressions and write equivalent expressions. The table shows properties of addition and multiplication when a, b, and c are real numbers.

Math Language

0 is the **additive identity**.

1 is the **multiplicative identity**.

Properties of Addition and Multiplication	
Identity Property of Addition	
For every real number a, $a + 0 = a$	Example: $5 + 0 = 5$
Identity Property of Multiplication	
For every real number a, $a \cdot 1 = a$	Example: $5 \cdot 1 = 5$
Commutative Property of Addition	
For every real number a and b, $a + b = b + a$	Example: $5 + 2 = 2 + 5$ $7 = 7$
Commutative Property of Multiplication	
For every real number a and b, $a \cdot b = b \cdot a$ $ab = ba$	Example: $5 \cdot 2 = 2 \cdot 5$ $10 = 10$
Associative Property of Addition	
For every real number a, b, and c, $(a + b) + c = a + (b + c)$ $a + b + c = a + b + c$	Example: $(1 + 2) + 3 = 1 + (2 + 3)$ $3 + 3 = 1 + 5$ $6 = 6$
Associative Property of Multiplication	
For every real number a, b, and c, $(a \cdot b) \cdot c = a \cdot (b \cdot c)$ $abc = abc$	Example: $(1 \cdot 2) \cdot 3 = 1 \cdot (2 \cdot 3)$ $2 \cdot 3 = 1 \cdot 6$ $6 = 6$

Online Connection
www.SaxonMathResources.com

LESSON 12

1 Warm Up

Problem 3
Check that students remember how to divide negative numbers.

2 New Concepts

In this lesson, students learn to simplify expressions using the properties of real numbers.

Discuss the numeric example for each property and relate it to the general statement.

Point out that the Associative Property does not change the order of the numbers, but the Commutative Property does.

TEACHER TIP

Help students remember the Associative and Commutative Properties by defining related words. The word associate means group and the Associative Property regroups numbers. The word commute means move and the Commutative Property moves the position of the numbers.

MATH BACKGROUND

Students intuitively know many of the properties or they may know them through experiments. They know that $2 \cdot 3 = 3 \cdot 2$ and that the order in which you multiply two numbers does not change the product. After this connection is made, the next step is to use the properties.

Students are learning to explain their reasoning and to show why their work is correct. Identifying properties as they are used in problems gives them the opportunity to justify their work mathematically.

The properties allow students to simplify numeric and algebraic expressions. The properties help students break a problem into smaller steps. Students learn to look at every detail in a problem while putting several steps together to reach a desired result.

LESSON RESOURCES

Student Edition Practice Workbook 12
Reteaching Master 12
Adaptations Master 12
Challenge and Enrichment Master C12

Example 1

Error Alert Recognizing the properties is the first step for students to be able to utilize them to justify their work. In **d**, some students may use the Associative Property because there are parentheses. Have students check for the Commutative Property, first.

Additional Example 1

Identify each property illustrated.

a. $1 \cdot 4 = 4$ Identity Property of Multiplication

b. $6 + 9 = 9 + 6$ Commutative Property of Addition

c. $(2 \cdot 5) \cdot 4 = 2 \cdot (5 \cdot 4)$ Associative Property of Multiplication

d. $(7 + 1) + 3 = (1 + 7) + 3$ Commutative Property of Addition

Example 2

Determining the validity of statements through evaluation helps students recognize and apply the properties.

Additional Example 2

Tell whether each statement is true or false. Justify your answer using the properties. Assume all variables represent real numbers.

a. $d \cdot 0 = d$ false; Identity Property of Multiplication states that $d \cdot 1 = d$

b. $(er)b = (re)b$ true; Commutative Property of Multiplication

c. $x(y + z) = (x + y)z$ false; The Associative Property of Multiplication states that $x(yz) = (xy)z$. The Associative Property of Addition states that $x + (y + z) = (x + y) + z$. Neither applies to more than one operation at a time.

Hint

Compare the left side of the equation to the right side. Determine what changes have been made.

Math Reasoning

Analyze Why does the Commutative Property not apply to subtraction?

Sample: Reversing the terms in a subtraction problem changes the sign of each number; $3 - 5 \neq 5 - 3$

Write

Explain why it is necessary to substitute only one value for the variable to show that the statement is false.

Sample: Since the statement must be true for all values substituted for the variable, it takes only one counterexample to make the statement false.

Example 1   Identifying Properties

Identify the property illustrated in each equation.

a. $1 \cdot 8 = 8$

SOLUTION Since 8 is multiplied by 1, its value does not change. This is the Identity Property of Multiplication.

b. $13 + 5 = 5 + 13$

SOLUTION The order of the terms is changed. This is the Commutative Property of Addition.

c. $(3 \cdot 4) \cdot 7 = 3 \cdot (4 \cdot 7)$

SOLUTION The terms and the order are not changed; only the grouping of the factors is changed. This is the Associative Property of Multiplication.

d. $(12 + 9) + 5 = (9 + 12) + 5$

SOLUTION The terms are the same and the same two terms are grouped. However, the order of the grouped terms has changed. This is the Commutative Property of Addition.

Example 2   Using Properties to Justify Statements

Tell whether each statement is true or false. Justify your answer using the properties. Assume all variables represent real numbers.

a. $gh = hg$

SOLUTION The statement is true. It illustrates the Commutative Property of Multiplication.

Check Substitute a value for each variable to determine whether the statement is true.

Let $g = 6$ and $h = 7$.

$6 \cdot 7 \stackrel{?}{=} 7 \cdot 6$

$42 = 42$ ✓

b. $b + 1 = b$

SOLUTION The statement is false. To illustrate the Identity Property of Addition, the equation should be $b + 0 = b$.

Check Substitute a value for the variable to determine whether the statement is true.

Let $b = 13$.

$13 + 1 \neq 13$ ✗

ENGLISH LEARNERS

For this lesson, discuss what **identity** means. Your identity does not change. The Identity Properties show operations that do not change the identity of the original number.

Adding 0 to any number does not change its identity.

For example, $6 + 0 = 6$.

Multiplying any number by 1 does not change its identity.

For example, $4 \cdot 1 = 4$.

c. $d + (e + f) = (d + e) + f$

SOLUTION Substitute a value for the variables to determine whether the statement is true.

Let $d = 5$, $e = 7$, and $f = 9$.

$5 + (7 + 9) \stackrel{?}{=} (5 + 7) + 9$
$5 + 16 \stackrel{?}{=} 12 + 9$
$21 = 21$ ✓

The statement is true by the Associative Property of Addition.

Example 3 Justifying Steps to Simplify an Expression

Simplify each expression. Justify each step.

a. $16 + 3x + 4$

SOLUTION

$16 + 3x + 4$
$= 3x + 16 + 4$ Commutative Property of Addition
$= 3x + (16 + 4)$ Associative Property of Addition
$= 3x + 20$ Add.

b. $(25) \cdot y \cdot \left(\dfrac{1}{25}\right)$

SOLUTION

$(25) \cdot y \cdot \left(\dfrac{1}{25}\right)$
$= (25) \cdot \left(\dfrac{1}{25}\right) \cdot y$ Commutative Property of Multiplication
$= 1 \cdot y$ Multiply
$= y$ Identity Property of Multiplication

> **Caution**
> Don't skip or combine steps. For each property necessary to simplify the expression, a step must be shown.

Example 4 Application: Consumer Math

Envelopes, pens, and correction tape can be purchased at an office supply store for the following prices respectively: $2.85, $5.35, and $2.15. Find the total cost of the supplies. Justify each step.

SOLUTION

$\$2.85 + \$5.35 + \$2.15$
$= \$2.85 + \$2.15 + \$5.35$ Commutative Property of Addition
$= (\$2.85 + \$2.15) + \$5.35$ Associative Property of Addition
$= \$5.00 + \$5.35$ Add within the parentheses.
$= \$10.35$ Add.

The supplies will cost $10.35.

Lesson Practice

Problem a

Scaffolding State the difference between the left and right side of the equation; for example, "The parentheses moved to group different numbers."

Problem f

Error Alert Some students may apply the properties to all operations. To see that the Commutative Property does not apply to subtraction, have students evaluate the equation with whole numbers.

Check for Understanding

The questions below help assess the concepts taught in this lesson.

"Why should you know the names of the properties?" Sample: They allow you to justify your work.

"How do properties help you simplify expressions?" Sample: They are like rules to follow so that you do not change the problem in a way that is not mathematically correct.

3 Practice

Math Conversations

Discussions to strengthen understanding

Problem 4

Error Alert

A common error is for students to assume that the answer will be negative because all of the factors are negative. Have students simplify the expression, two numbers at a time, using the rules for multiplying real numbers to justify the sign on their answer.

66   Saxon Algebra 1

---

h.
$18 + 7x + 4$
$= 7x + 18 + 4$ Commutative Property of Addition
$= 7x + (18 + 4)$ Associative Property of Addition
$= 7x + 22$ Add.

i.
$\frac{1}{3} d \cdot 3$
$= \frac{1}{3} \cdot 3 \cdot d$ Commutative Property of Multiplication
$= \left(\frac{1}{3} \cdot 3\right) \cdot d$ Associative Property of Multiplication
$= 1 \cdot d$ Multiply.
$= d$ Identity Property of Multiplication

Lesson Practice

Identify each property illustrated. (Ex 1)

a. $5 + (9 + 8) = (5 + 9) + 8$ Associative Property of Addition

b. $0 + 10 = 10$ Identity Property of Addition

c. $15 \cdot 3 = 3 \cdot 15$ Commutative Property of Multiplication

d. $17 \cdot 1 = 17$ Identity Property of Multiplication

Tell whether each statement is true or false. Justify your answer using the properties. Assume all variables represent real numbers. (Ex 2)

e. $(ab)c = a(bc)$ true; Associative Property of Multiplication

f. $m - z = z - m$ false; Commutative Property does not work for subtraction

g. $w + 0 = w$ true; Identity Property of Addition

Simplify each expression. Justify each step. (Ex 3)

h. $18 + 7x + 4$

i. $\frac{1}{3} d \cdot 3$

j. Erasers, markers, and paper can be purchased at the school store for (Ex 4) the following prices, respectively: $1.45, $3.35, and $2.65. Find the total cost of the supplies. Justify each step.

j. $1.45 + $3.35 + $2.65
= $1.45 + ($3.35 + $2.65) Associative Property of Addition
= $1.45 + $6.00   Add within the parentheses.
= $7.45   Add.

Practice   Distributed and Integrated

*1. Identify the property illustrated in the equation $100 \cdot 1 = 100$.   Identity Property of Multiplication
(12)

Simplify each expression.

2. $-18 \div 3$ -6
(11)

3. $|12 - 30|$ 18
(5)

4. $(-3)(-2)(-1)(-8)$ 48
(11)

*5. True or False: $p(q + r) = (p + q)r$. Justify your answer using the properties.
(12)

5. false; The Associative Property only applies when the operations are all addition or all multiplication.

6. Write a fraction equivalent to $\frac{2}{3}$.   Sample: $\frac{4}{6}$
(SB 7)

7. True or False: The sum of the measures of complementary angles is 90°.   true
(SB 15)

*8. **Multiple Choice** Which equation demonstrates the Identity Property of Addition?   B
(12)

A $a \cdot 0 = 0$

B $a + 0 = a$

C $a \cdot \frac{1}{a} = 1$

D $a + 1 = 1 + a$

9. Add $\frac{11}{15} + \frac{1}{30} + \frac{3}{60}$. $\frac{49}{60}$
(10)

66   Saxon Algebra 1

 INCLUSION

Materials: counters

Model the expression $3 \cdot 4$ by making 3 groups of 4 counters.

Have the students count the counters.

Then model $4 \cdot 3$ by making 4 groups of 3 counters.

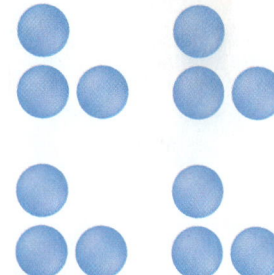

Have the students count the counters. Ask, "Does it matter the order in multiplying two numbers?" no

10. **Error Analysis** Students were asked to simplify $\frac{5}{6} \div \left(-\frac{3}{2}\right)$. Which student is correct?
    (11) Explain the error.   Student A; Sample: The quotient of a positive and a negative number is negative.

Student A	Student B
$\frac{5}{6} \div \left(-\frac{3}{2}\right)$	$\frac{5}{6} \div \left(-\frac{3}{2}\right)$
$= \frac{5}{6} \cdot \left(-\frac{2}{3}\right)$	$= \frac{5}{6} \cdot \left(-\frac{2}{3}\right)$
$= -\frac{5}{9}$	$= \frac{5}{9}$

*11. Jon has 5 marbles. His best friend gives him some more. Then he buys 15 more
(12) marbles. The expression $5 + x + 15$ shows the total number of marbles Jon now has. Show two ways to simplify this expression and justify each step.
See Additional Answers.

12. **Multiple Choice** What is the value of $\frac{(5x + x)^2(6 - x)}{x}$ when $x = 2$?   A
(9)
    A 288   B 200   C 400   D 28

*13. Find the value of $(4x^3y^2)^2$ when $x = 2$ and $y = 1$.   1024
(9)

14. Convert 588 ounces to pounds. (Hint: 1 lb = 16 oz)   36.75 lb
(8)

*15. **Geometry** A wall in a rectangular room is 12 feet by 8 feet. Jose calculated the area
(12) using the equations $A = 12 \cdot 8$ and $A = 8 \cdot 12$. Explain why each expression will give him the same answer.   Sample: The Commutative Property of Multiplication says that the order of the factors does not change the product.

*16. (**Interior Decorating**) Tim is building a picture frame that is 10 inches long and
(12) 6 inches wide. He calculated the perimeter using $P = 2(10 + 6)$. His brother calculated the perimeter for the same frame using $P = 2(6 + 10)$. Will the measurements be the same? Explain.   yes; Sample: The Commutative Property of Addition states that the order of the terms does not affect the sum.

*17. (**Temperature**) To convert a temperature from Celsius to Fahrenheit, Marc uses the
(12) formula $F = \frac{9}{5}C + 32$. He also uses the formula $F = 32 + \frac{9}{5}C$. Which calculation is correct? Explain.   Both are correct; Sample: The Commutative Property of Addition states that the order of the terms can be changed without changing the sum.

18. **Geometry** A rectangle is twice as long as it is wide. If the width of the
(11) rectangle measures 2.3 inches, what is the area of the rectangle?
10.58 sq. in.

19. **Multi-Step** In each of the first five rounds of a game, Tyra scored 28 points. In
(11) each of the next three rounds, she scored −41 points. Then she scored two rounds of −16 points. What is the total number of points that Tyra scored? Explain.
−15; Sample: $5(28) + 3(-41) + 2(-16) = 140 - 123 - 32 = -15$

*20. **Multiple Choice** Order from greatest to least: $\frac{1}{4}, 0.23, -0.24, \frac{1}{3}$.   D
(10)
    A $-0.24, 0.23, \frac{1}{4}, \frac{1}{3}$ B $\frac{1}{4}, \frac{1}{3}, 0.23, -0.24$
    C $-0.24, 0.23, \frac{1}{3}, \frac{1}{4}$ D $\frac{1}{3}, \frac{1}{4}, 0.23, -0.24$

21. (**Sewing**) Maria is sewing curtains that require 124 inches of ribbon trim. She can
(8) only buy the ribbon in whole yard lengths. How many yards does she need to buy?
4 yards

Lesson 12   67

Problem 10
Before simplifying the expression, ask, "When two real numbers have opposite signs, what is the sign of their quotient?" negative

Problem 17
Explain that the Commutative Property applies to terms that are added. The expressions are the same due to the order of operations.

Problem 19
Guide the students by asking them the following questions.

"How many points are scored in the first five rounds?" 140

"How many points are scored in the next three rounds?" −123

"How many points are scored in the last two rounds?" −32

"How is the total score determined?" Add all of the points together.

Problem 21
Remind students that there are 36 inches in a yard.

Problem 26

Guide the students by asking them the following questions.

"What is a balance?" Sample: how much money is in an account

"What does it mean to make a withdrawal?" Sample: take money out of an account

"What does it mean to make a deposit?" Sample: put money into an account

"Explain interest and how it affects an account." Sample: Interest is money that the bank pays you to keep your money in that particular bank. Interest is a deposit into the account that increases the balance in the account

Problem 28
Extend the Problem

"Bill rides a bus for 3.25 hours to visit a friend who lives 180.7 miles away. How fast was the bus traveling?" 55.6 miles per hour

"Bill travels on a bus to see his friend who lives 233.6 miles away. The bus travels at 58.4 miles per hour. How many hours will he be on the bus?" 4 hours

---

22. Error Analysis Student A and Student B simplified the expression $9 - 4 \cdot 2$. Which student is correct? Explain the error. Student B; Sample: Student A did not follow the order of operations.

Student A	Student B
$9 - 4 \cdot 2$	$9 - 4 \cdot 2$
$= 5 \cdot 2$	$= 9 - 8$
$= 10$	$= 1$

23. Write Explain how to use the order of operations to simplify $4(8 - 9 \div 3)^2$.

23. Sample: First you have to work inside the parentheses and divide 9 by 3 to get 3. Next, take that 3 away from 8 to get 5. Then square 5 to get 25 and multiply by 4 to get 100.

24. Simplify $x^2 k x k^2 x^2 y k x^2$. $k^4 x^7 y$

25. Error Analysis Two students evaluate the expression $4t + 5x - \frac{1}{x}$ when $x = 3$. Which student is correct? Explain the error.

Student A	Student B
$4t + 5x - \frac{1}{x}; x = 3$	$4t + 5x - \frac{1}{x}; x = 3$
$= 4t + 5(3) - \frac{1}{3}$	$= 4t + 53 - \frac{1}{3}$
$= 4t + 15 - \frac{1}{3}$	$= 4t + 52\frac{2}{3}$
$= 4t + 14\frac{2}{3}$	

25. Sample: Student A; Student B did not treat the constant and variable in the second term as factors. Instead of multiplying, Student B treated x as a digit in the ones place.

26. Savings Accounts The table below shows the transactions Jennifer made to her savings account during one month. Find the balance of her account. $473.75

Jennifer's Bank Account	
Beginning Balance	$396.25
Withdrawal	$150.50
Deposit	$220.00
Interest (deposit)	$8.00

***27. Tug of War** In a game of Tug of War, Team A pulls the center of the rope three and a half feet in their direction. Then Team B pulls back five feet before Team A pulls for another eight feet. How far from the starting point is the center of the rope? 6.5 feet

28. Travel Bill rides a bus for 2.5 hours to visit a friend. If the bus travels at about 60 to 63 miles per hour, how far away does Bill's friend live? (Hint: To find distance, multiply rate by time.) between 150 and 157.5 miles

29. Justify Simplify $2^2 + 24 - (3 - 12)$. Explain your steps.

30. Verify Give an example that illustrates that the sum of a number and its opposite is zero. Sample: $7 + (-7) = 0$

29.
$2^2 + 24 - (3 - 12)$
$= 2^2 + 24 - (-9)$ symbols of inclusion
$= 4 + 24 - (-9)$ powers
$= 37$ algebraic addition

68   Saxon Algebra 1

CHALLENGE

Have students explain why the Identity Property applies to subtraction but the Commutative Property does not. Sample: Subtraction is the same as adding the opposite. Zero is its own opposite; therefore, it has the same identity as addition.

$$5 - 0 = 5$$

The Commutative Property does not apply to subtraction because the sign of the minuend and subtrahend change.

LOOKING FORWARD

Using properties to simplify expressions prepares students for

• **Lesson 15** Using the Distributive Property to Simplify Expressions

• **Lesson 16** Simplifying and Evaluating Variable Expressions

• **Lesson 17** Translating Between Words and Algebraic Expressions

• **Lesson 18** Combining Like Terms

LESSON 13

Calculating and Comparing Square Roots

Warm Up

1. **Vocabulary** The number that tells how many times the base of a power is used as a factor is called the _____ (*variable*, *exponent*). **exponent**

Simplify each expression.

2. $-3 + (-4) - (-8)$ **1**

3. $[-(-4)^3]$ **64**

4. $a^3 \cdot x^4 \cdot x^8 \cdot a^4 \cdot z^4$ $a^7x^{12}z^4$

5. $\left(-\dfrac{2}{6}\right) \div \left(-\dfrac{3}{8}\right)$ $\dfrac{8}{9}$

New Concepts

A **perfect square** is a number that is the square of an integer. The product of an integer and itself is a perfect square.

$2^2 =$ ▢ $3^2 =$ ▢

A square root is indicated by a radical symbol $\sqrt{}$. A **radicand** is the number or expression under a radical symbol.

$$\sqrt{50} \qquad\qquad 2\sqrt{7}$$

50 is the radicand.   7 is the radicand.

The **square root** of x, written $\sqrt{x}$, is the number whose square is x.

$$4^2 = 16$$
$$\sqrt{16} = 4$$

A square number can only end with the digits: zero, one, four, five, six, and nine. However, not all numbers ending in these digits will be perfect squares.

Math Reasoning

Formulate What is the inverse of x^2?

The inverse of x^2 is $\pm\sqrt{x}$.

Example 1   Finding Square Roots of Perfect Squares

a. Is the radicand in $\sqrt{50}$ a perfect square? Explain.

SOLUTION

50 is not a perfect square. There is no integer multiplied by itself that equals 50.

b. Is the radicand in $\sqrt{64}$ a perfect square? Explain.

SOLUTION

64 is a perfect square; $8 \cdot 8 = 8^2 = 64$. The product of an integer and itself is a perfect square.

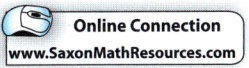
Online Connection
www.SaxonMathResources.com

Lesson 13   69

MATH BACKGROUND

The inverse process of squaring a number is finding a square root; for example, $12^2 = 144$ and $\sqrt{144} = 12$. Since $(-12)^2 = 144$, then -12 is also a square root of 144, Thus, every positive real number has two square roots, one positive and one negative. The positive square root is called the principal square root and is shown by the radical expression $\sqrt{n}$. The negative square root is written $-\sqrt{n}$.

ENGLISH LEARNERS

The word **radical** is a multiple-meaning word. In math, a radical is a symbol used to show a square root.

Have students complete these sentences to contrast different meanings of radical.

"Use a radical symbol over the number _____ to show the square root of nine." **nine**

"Her radical _____ for reorganizing the chess club upset many members." **ideas**

---

1   Warm Up

Problem 4
Remind students that only the bases that are the same can be multiplied.

2   New Concepts

In this lesson, students learn to calculate square roots of perfect squares and to approximate square roots of non-perfect squares.

Example 1

Have students make a list of the square numbers from 1^2 to 20^2.

Extend the Example
Ask students to explain why the radicand in $\sqrt{-16}$ is not a perfect square. Sample: There is no integer that when multiplied by itself gives a product of -16.

Additional Example 1

a. Is the radicand in $\sqrt{200}$ a perfect square? Explain. no; No integer multiplied by itself equals 200.

b. Is the radicand in $\sqrt{225}$ a perfect square? Explain. Yes, $\sqrt{225}$ is a perfect square because $15^2 = 225$.

LESSON RESOURCES

Student Edition Practice Workbook 13
Reteaching Master 13
Adaptations Master 13
Challenge and Enrichment Master C13, E13
Technology Lab Master 13

Example 2

If a number is not a perfect square, the square root will be irrational and can only be approximated.

Additional Example 2
Estimate the value of $\sqrt{75}$ to the nearest integer. Explain your reasoning. $\sqrt{75} \approx 9$; Since 75 is closer to 81 than to 64, $\sqrt{75}$ is closer to 9 than to 8.

TEACHER TIP
A list of the first twenty perfect squares will help students estimate square roots.

Example 3

Error Alert Emphasize that students take the square roots before adding. Show them that $\sqrt{4} + \sqrt{36} \neq \sqrt{40}$, $\sqrt{4} + \sqrt{36} = 2 + 6 = 8$, and $8 = \sqrt{64}$, not $\sqrt{40}$.

Additional Example 3
Compare the expressions. Use <, >, or =.
$\sqrt{81} - \sqrt{16}$ ⊗ $\sqrt{25} + \sqrt{4}$

Example 4

To help students visualize the problem, sketch two squares, one 10 feet on each side and one 20 feet on each side. Have a volunteer explain why the dance floor area must be between the areas of the two squares. The squares in the sketches have areas of 100 ft² and 400 ft², and 289 is between 100 and 400.

Additional Example 4
A shopper got a bargain on 361 brick patio tiles, each 1-foot square. What is the side length of a square patio made with the tiles? Explain. Sample: 19 ft; The square of 19 is 361.

Math Reasoning

Analyze Is 1.44 a perfect square?

no; Sample: A perfect square must be the square of a integer. 1.44 is the square of 1.2 which is not an integer.

Caution

Square roots must be simplified before performing any other operations. For example, $\sqrt{4} + \sqrt{36} \neq \sqrt{40}$.

Not all numbers are perfect squares, but their square roots can be estimated.

Example 2 Estimating Square Roots

Estimate the value $\sqrt{50}$ to the nearest integer. Explain your reasoning.

SOLUTION

$\sqrt{50}$ is not a perfect square.

Determine which two perfect squares 50 falls between on the number line.

50 is between the perfect squares 49 and 64.

Then determine which perfect square $\sqrt{50}$ is closest to.

$\sqrt{50}$ is between the numbers 7 and 8 because $\sqrt{49} = 7$ and $\sqrt{64} = 8$.

$\sqrt{50}$ is closer to the number 7 because 50 is closer to 49 than 64.

$\sqrt{50} \approx 7$

When comparing expressions that contain radicals, simplify the expressions with radicals first. Next, perform any operations necessary. Then compare the expressions.

Example 3 Comparing Expressions Involving Square Roots

Compare the expressions. Use <, >, or =.

$$\sqrt{4} + \sqrt{36} \bigcirc \sqrt{9} + \sqrt{25}$$

SOLUTION

$\sqrt{4} + \sqrt{36} \bigcirc \sqrt{9} + \sqrt{25}$

$2 + 6 \bigcirc 3 + 5$ Simplify the expressions.

$8 = 8$ Add.

Example 4 Application: Ballroom Dancing

The area of a dance floor that is in the shape of a square is 289 square feet. What is the side length of the dance floor? Explain.

SOLUTION

The side length can be found by finding the square root of the area.

Area of a square = side length × side length

$A = s^2$ Write the formula.

$289 = s^2$ Substitute 289 for A.

$\sqrt{289} = s$ Find the square root of 289.

$17 = s$

Each side length of the dance floor is 17 feet.

ALTERNATE METHOD FOR EXAMPLE 2

A divide-and-average strategy can be used to estimate square roots.

Step 1: Try any reasonable guess for the square root; for example, guess 6 for $\sqrt{50}$.

Step 2: Divide the radicand by the guess.

$$50 \div 6 \approx 8$$

Step 3: Average the guess and the quotient.

$$(6 + 8) \div 2 \approx 7$$

Have students try the divide-and-average method for $\sqrt{300}$. Sample: Guess 20. $300 \div 20 = 15$. $(20 + 15) \div 2 = 17.5$.

a. yes; Sample: $15^2 = 225$; The product of an integer and itself is a perfect square.

b. no; Sample: There is no integer multiplied by itself that equals 350.

c. Sample: $\sqrt{37} \approx 6$; 37 is between the perfect squares 36 and 49. $\sqrt{36} = 6$ and $\sqrt{49} = 7$, so $\sqrt{37}$ is between 6 and 7, but closer to 6.

Lesson Practice

a. Is the radicand in $\sqrt{225}$ a perfect square? Explain.
(Ex 1)

b. Is the radicand in $\sqrt{350}$ a perfect square? Explain.
(Ex 1)

c. Estimate the value of $\sqrt{37}$ to the nearest integer. Explain your reasoning.
(Ex 2)

d. Compare the expressions. Use <, >, or =.
(Ex 3)

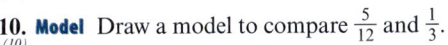
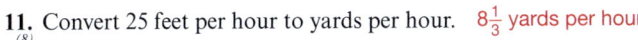
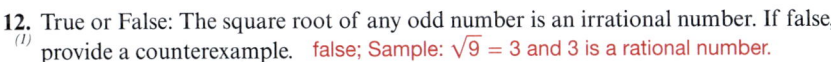

e. The city park has a new sandbox in the shape of a square. The area of the sandbox is 169 square feet. What is the side length of the sandbox? Explain. 13 feet; To find the side length, find the square root of the area: $\sqrt{169} = 13$.
(Ex 4)

Practice   Distributed and Integrated

Simplify each expression.

1. $-16 \div -2$ 8
(11)

2. $\dfrac{4 + 7 - 6}{2 + 7 - 3}$ $\dfrac{5}{6}$
(11)

3. $-2 + 11 - 4 + 3 - 8$ 0
(6)

4. $(-2)(-3) + 11(2) - 3 - 6$ 19
(6)

Evaluate each expression for the given values.

*5. $3p - 4g - 2x$ for $p = 2$, $g = -3$, and $x = 4$ 10
(9)

6. $3xy - 2yz$ for $x = 3$, $y = 4$, and $z = 3$ 12
(9)

*7. $\sqrt{40}$ is between which two whole numbers?   6 and 7
(13)

*8. **Multiple Choice** Which of the following numbers is a perfect square?   B
(13)
A 200   B 289
C 410   D 150

*9. Solve $b = \sqrt{4}$. $b = 2$
(13)

10. **Model** Draw a model to compare $\dfrac{5}{12}$ and $\dfrac{1}{3}$.
(10)

11. Convert 25 feet per hour to yards per hour. $8\dfrac{1}{3}$ yards per hour
(8)

12. True or False: The square root of any odd number is an irrational number. If false, provide a counterexample.   false; Sample: $\sqrt{9} = 3$ and 3 is a rational number.
(1)

Lesson 13   71

INCLUSION

When finding square roots, some students may simply rewrite the perfect square without the radical symbol. It may be helpful to show them $\sqrt[2]{}$ that $\sqrt{}$ have the same meaning. Have them write the index number 2 as a reminder that they are looking for a number that when multiplied by itself, or when raised to the second power, will equal the radicand.

Write on the chalkboard:

$8^2 = 8 \cdot 8 = 64$, so

$\sqrt[2]{64} = \sqrt[2]{8^2} = \sqrt[2]{8 \cdot 8} = 8$

Emphasize that the square root symbol "undoes" the squaring. Give students a few perfect squares to write as 64 was written.

Lesson Practice

Problem d

Error Alert Remind students that they cannot add before taking the square roots. The square roots must be taken first.

Problem e

Scaffolding Help students use successive approximation to find $\sqrt{169}$. Ask:

"Is the side length greater than 10 feet?" Explain. Yes, $169 > 100$.

"Is it greater than 12 feet?" Explain. Yes, $169 > 144$.

"Is it less than 20 feet?" Explain. Yes, $169 < 400$.

✓ Check for Understanding

The questions below help assess the concepts taught in this lesson.

"Explain how to prove that a number n is a perfect square."
Sample: Find some number that, when squared, is equal to n.

"If you are given the area of a square, how can you find the length of one side? Explain."
Sample: Take the square root of the area. The square of the side length equals the area, so the square root of the area equals the side length.

3 Practice

Math Conversations
Discussion to strengthen understanding

Problem 12
Remind students that to prove the statement false, they must find at least one odd number that is a perfect square. Listing the odd numbers up to 30 will result in the perfect squares 9 and 25.

Lesson 13   71

*13. **Multiple Choice** The area of a square is 392 square meters. The area of a second square is half the area of the first square. What is the side length of the second square? A
    A 14 meters
    B ≈ 20 meters
    C 196 meters
    D 96 meters

*14. True or False: $xyz = yxz$. Justify your answer using the properties. true; Commutative Property of Multiplication

15. **Verify** Determine whether each statement below is true or false. If false, explain why.
    a. $4^2 + 15 \cdot 20$ is equal to 316. true
    b. $(4 + 5)^2$ is the same as $4 + 5^2$. false; $(4 + 5)^2$ is equal to 9^2, or 81, whereas $4 + 5^2$ is equal to $4 + 25$, or 29.

16. **Multi-Step** Kristin has several ropes measuring $8\frac{1}{4}$ in., $8\frac{3}{16}$ in., $8\frac{5}{8}$ in., and $8\frac{1}{16}$ in. How should she order them from least to greatest?
    a. Find a common denominator for each measure. $8\frac{4}{16}$ in., $8\frac{3}{16}$ in., $8\frac{10}{16}$ in., and $8\frac{1}{16}$ in.
    b. Order the measures from least to greatest. $8\frac{1}{16}$ in., $8\frac{3}{16}$ in., $8\frac{4}{16}$ in., and $8\frac{10}{16}$ in.

17. Arrange in order from least to greatest:
    1.11, 1.5, 1.09, 1.05   1.05, 1.09, 1.11, 1.5

*18. Are the expressions $(20k^3 \cdot 5v^5)9k^2$ and $900k^3v^5$ equivalent? Explain. no; Sample: The first expression simplified is $900k^5v^5$.

*19. **Science** The Barringer Meteor Crater in Winslow, Arizona, is very close to a square in shape. The crater covers an area of about 1,690,000 square meters. What is the approximate side length of the crater? about 1300 meters

20. **Science** The time, t, in seconds it takes for an object dropped to travel a distance, d, in feet can be found using the formula $t = \frac{\sqrt{d}}{4}$. Determine the time it takes for an object to drop 169 feet. 3.25 seconds

*21. **Multi-Step** The flow rate for a particular fire hose can be found using $f = 120\sqrt{p}$, where f is the flow rate in gallons per minute and p is the nozzle pressure in pounds per square inch. When the nozzle pressure is 169 pounds per square inch, what is the flow rate? 1560 gal/min

22. **World Records** The world's largest cherry pie was baked in Michigan. It had a diameter of 210 inches. If the diameter was converted to feet, would it be a rational number? Explain. yes; Sample: Divide 210 by 12 to convert it into feet. It is 17.5 feet in diameter.

 23. Find the area of the shaded portion of the circle. The radius of the circle is 4 inches. (Use 3.14 for π.) 32.1775 in²

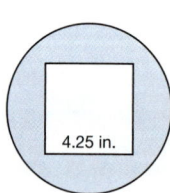

4.25 in.

CHALLENGE

Compare the expressions using estimation.

$\sqrt{800}$ ○ $\sqrt{170} + \sqrt{330}$ 28 ⊘ 13 + 18

24. Banking Frank deposited $104.67 into his bank account. Later that day, he spent $113.82 from the same account. Estimate the change in Frank's account balance for that day.   Sample: +$105 + (−$114) = −$9

25. Justify Simplify $52 + (1+3)^2 \cdot (16-14)^3 - 20$. Justify each step.

26. Error Analysis Two students simplify the expression $2 + 3x + 1$. Which student is correct? Explain the error.   Student A; Sample: Student B incorrectly used the Associative Property when adding 2 + 3x.

Student A	Student B
$2 + 3x + 1$	$2 + 3x + 1$
$= 2 + 1 + 3x$	$= (2 + 3)x + 1$
$= (2 + 1) + 3x$	$= 5x + 1$
$= 3 + 3x$	

*27. Justify Arlene has 30 buttons and buys x packages of buttons. There are 7 buttons in each package. She uses 12 buttons. The number of buttons she now has is represented by the expression $30 + 7x - 12$. Simplify the expression and justify each step using the properties.

28. Multiple Choice Which of the following expressions will result in a negative number?   **D**

A $(-6)^2$

B $(-6) \div (-6)$

C $-\dfrac{3}{4}(6) \div (-4)$

D $-1 \cdot (-6)^2$

29. International Banking A Greek company needs to purchase some products from a U.S. corporation. First, the company must open an account in U.S. dollars. If the account is to hold $1,295,800, how many drachma, the Greek currency, should the company deposit? Use the exchange rate of one Greek drachma for every $0.004 in U.S. currency.   323,950,000 drachmae

30. Probability Describe each of the following events as impossible, unlikely, as likely as not, likely, or certain.

a. Jim rolls a 10 on a standard number cube.   impossible

b. Sarah guesses a number correctly between 1 and 900.   unlikely

c. Mayra dropped a coin and it landed heads up.   as likely as not

25. $52 + (1+3)^2 \cdot (16-14)^3 - 20$
$= 52 + 4^2 \cdot 2^3 - 20$ symbols of inclusion
$= 52 + 16 \cdot 8 - 20$ powers
$= 52 + 128 - 20$ multiplication
$= 160$ addition and subtraction

27. $30 + 7x + (-12)$
$= 30 + (-12) + 7x$ Commutative Property of Addition
$= [30 + (-12)] + 7x$ Associative Property of Addition
$= 18 + 7x$ Add.

Lesson 13   73

Problem 25
Error Alert
If students do not simplify $52 + (1+3)^2 \cdot (16-14)^3 - 20$ correctly, review the order of operations using the mnemonic PEMDAS: Please Excuse My Dear Aunt Sally. The operation in parentheses (the P in Please) comes before exponents (the E in Excuse).

Problem 28
Error Alert
Emphasize the difference between $(-6)^2$ and -6^2. The first expression equals $(-6) \times (-6)$. The second equals $-1(6)^2$ or $-(6 \times 6)$ or $-1 \times 6 \times 6$.

Problem 30
For students who have difficulty with the vagueness of the terms likely and unlikely, suggest that they label an event unlikely if it has a probability less than $\frac{1}{4}$, and likely if the probability is greater than $\frac{3}{4}$.

Extend the Problem
Describe each event as impossible, unlikely, as likely as not, likely, or certain.

rolling a number divisible by 5 on a number cube unlikely

pulling a red marble from a bag of 4 red marbles and 1 green marble likely

---

LOOKING FORWARD

Calculating and comparing square roots prepares students for

- **Lesson 16** Simplifying and Evaluating Variable Expressions

- **Lesson 17** Translating Between Words and Algebraic Expressions

- **Lesson 46** Simplifying Expressions with Square Roots and Higher Order Roots

LESSON 14

1. Warm Up

Problem 4
Remind students that since the absolute value of a number is its distance from zero, it is always positive.

2. New Concepts

In this lesson, students learn to calculate probabilities of simple events, expressing the results as fractions, decimals, or percents. They also learn that two complementary events have probabilities with a sum of 1.

The Exploration may be done before discussing the vocabulary presented in the lesson.

Exploration

Have students work in pairs or small groups. If time is limited, have each group do the experiment 20 times, and then have them compile all the results. Students will find that the experimental probabilities for the entire class are closer to $\frac{1}{4}$ for each color than the results for any individual group or pair.

LESSON RESOURCES

Student Edition Practice
   Workbook 14
Reteaching Master 14
Adaptations Master 14
Challenge and Enrichment
   Master C14

LESSON 14 — Determining the Theoretical Probability of an Event

Warm Up

1. **Vocabulary** _____ (Closure, Probability) is the measure of how likely it is that an event will occur. **Probability**

Simplify each expression.

2. $5 \times 7 - 27 \div 9 + 6$ **38**
3. $6.3 + (-2.4) + (-8.9)$ **−5**
4. $6 + |-72| + |-5|$ **83**
5. Write a number to represent the opposite of "twelve floors up." **−12**

New Concepts

Math Language
A fair coin has an equally likely chance of landing on heads or tails. The coin is not weighted so that one outcome is more likely than another.

A **sample space** is the set of all possible outcomes of an event. For example, a toss of a fair coin has two equally likely outcomes. The two possible outcomes, heads and tails, is the sample space.

A **simple event** is an event having only one outcome. For example, rolling a 5 on a number cube is a simple event.

The **theoretical probability** of an outcome is found by analyzing a situation in which all outcomes are equally likely, and then finding the ratio of favorable outcomes to all possible outcomes. For example, the probability of tossing a coin and it landing on heads is $\frac{1}{2}$ or 0.5 or 50%.

Exploration — Finding Theoretical Probability

Materials
- small paper sacks
- colored marbles

Place 4 different-colored marbles in a sack. Without looking, draw one marble out of the sack. Record the color in a frequency table.

Color	Tally	Frequency
Red		
Green		
Yellow		
Blue		

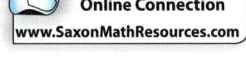
Online Connection
www.SaxonMathResources.com

a. Repeat the experiment 10 times, 20 times, 50 times and 100 times, replacing the marble after each draw. **See student work.**

b. Divide the number of times a red marble is picked by the total number of times you pick a marble. Write this as a probability. **See student work.**

c. **Generalize** What do you notice about the probabilities as the number of times you pick a marble is increased? **Sample: As the number of trials increase, the probability that red is chosen gets closer to $\frac{1}{4}$ or 25%.**

MATH BACKGROUND

The type of probability that students will study deals principally with well-defined random physical experiments. Exactly one outcome from a set of n equally likely outcomes will occur. The set of all outcomes is the sample space; any subset of the sample space is an event. Thus, a spinner with four equal parts—2 red, 1 blue, 1 yellow—can be used for a probability experiment with 4 outcomes, but only 3 simple events.

Probability is a measure of the likelihood of an event. A number from 0 to 1 is assigned to each event to describe its likelihood. Probability does not tell anything about what will actually happen. If there is a $\frac{1}{4}$ chance of spinning the color blue, this does not mean that you will get blue exactly 1 time out of every 4 spins. However, if the experiment is repeated a great number of times, it is reasonable to expect that the fraction of blue results will probably come close to $\frac{1}{4}$.

Example 1 Identifying Sample Spaces

A number cube labeled 1–6 is rolled. List the outcomes for each event.

a. a number less than or equal to 3

SOLUTION

{3, 2, 1}

b. an odd number

SOLUTION

{1, 3, 5}

c. a number greater than 4

SOLUTION

{5, 6}

Theoretical probability can be determined using the following formula:

$$P(\text{event}) = \frac{\text{number of favorable outcomes}}{\text{total number of outcomes}}$$

A **complement of an event** is a set of all outcomes of an experiment that are not in a given event. For example, if heads is the desired event when tossing a coin, tails is the complement of the event. The sum of an event and its complement equals 1.

$$P(\text{event}) + P(\text{not event}) = 1$$
$$P(\text{not event}) = 1 - P(\text{event})$$

Example 2 Calculating Theoretical Probability

There are 4 green, 3 blue, and 3 red marbles in a bag.

Give each answer as a decimal and as a percent.

a. What is the probability of randomly choosing a red marble?

SOLUTION

$$P(\text{red}) = \frac{3 \text{ red marbles}}{10 \text{ marbles in all}}$$

$$P(\text{red}) = \frac{3}{10}$$

The probability of choosing a red marble is 0.3 or 30%.

b. What is the probability of randomly choosing a marble that is not green?

SOLUTION

$$P(\text{green marble}) + P(\text{not green marble}) = 1$$
$$P(\text{not green marble}) = 1 - P(\text{green marble})$$
$$P(\text{not green marble}) = 1 - \frac{4}{10}$$
$$P(\text{not green marble}) = \frac{6}{10} = \frac{3}{5}$$

The probability of not choosing a green marble is 0.6 or 60%.

Math Language

A spinner is divided into four equal parts: blue, yellow, green, and red. If the spinner lands on yellow, then the **outcome** is yellow.

Reading Math

The probability of an event can be written $P(\text{event})$. The probability of picking a red marble can be written $P(\text{red})$.

Hint

Probability can be expressed as a fraction, decimal, or percent.

Example 1

Use the example to contrast the use of the terms outcome and event. There are 6 different outcomes for rolling the cube. The event of getting a number less than or equal to 3 includes 3 out of the 6 outcomes.

Additional Example 1

A number cube labeled 1–6 is rolled. List the outcomes for each event.

a. rolling an even number {2, 4, 6}

b. rolling a multiple of 3 {3, 6}

c. rolling a prime number {2, 3, 5}

Extend the Example

Have students list the outcomes for a 6-part spinner with 3 parts red, 2 blue, and 1 white. {red, red, red, blue, blue, white}

Emphasize that it is important to show all 6 outcomes even though some of them are the same. All of the outcomes are needed so that the denominators of the probability fractions will be correct.

Example 2

To make a model for the example, draw 10 circles on the board and label them with their color names.

Additional Example 2

There are 4 green marbles, 3 blue marbles, and 3 red marbles in a bag. Give each answer as a decimal and as a percent.

a. What is the probability of randomly choosing a green or red marble? $\frac{7}{10}$, 0.7, or 70%

b. What is the probability of randomly choosing a marble that is not blue? $\frac{7}{10}$, 0.7, or 70%

ENGLISH LEARNERS

Explain the meaning of the word **favorable**. Say:

"The word favorable means pleasing or wanted. For example, the plane flew faster because the winds were favorable."

Ask a volunteer to define the word favorable in their own words. Sample: It is something I would like to happen.

Have students use the word favorable in a sentence. Sample: The weather report is favorable for a picnic tomorrow.

Chance, like probability, is the likelihood of an event occurring.

Example 3 Calculating Chance

In a bucket there are 10 balls numbered as follows: 1, 1, 2, 3, 4, 4, 4, 5, 6, and 6. A single ball is randomly chosen from the bucket. What is the probability of drawing a ball with a number greater than 4? Is there a greater chance of drawing a number greater than 4 or a 1?

SOLUTION

$P(\text{greater than } 4) = \frac{3}{10}$ 3 out of the 10 balls have a number greater than 4.

The probability of drawing a ball with a number greater than 4 is 0.3, or 30%.

$P(1) = \frac{2}{10} = \frac{1}{5}$ 2 out of the 10 balls are numbered 1.

$\frac{3}{10} > \frac{1}{5}$ Compare $\frac{3}{10}$ and $\frac{1}{5}$.

There is a greater chance of drawing a number greater than 4 than drawing a 1.

Example 4 Application: State Fair

At a carnival game, you drop a ball into the top of the device shown below. As the ball falls, it goes either left or right as it hits each peg. In total, the ball can follow 16 different paths. The ball eventually lands in one of the bins at the bottom and you win that amount of money. (One path to $0 is shown.) What is the probability of winning $2?

Math Reasoning

Analyze If you drop the ball once, is there less than or greater than a 20% probability of not winning $2?

greater than 20%;
$P(\text{not } \$2) = 1 - \frac{1}{8} = \frac{7}{8} = 0.875$ or 87.5%

SOLUTION

total number of paths = 16

number of paths to $2 bins = 2

$P(\$2) = \dfrac{\text{number of paths to \$2 bins}}{\text{total number of paths to win}} = \dfrac{2}{16}$

$P(\$2) = \dfrac{1}{8}$

The probability of winning $2 is $\frac{1}{8}$.

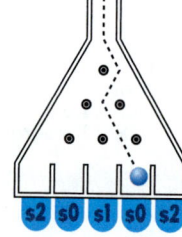

Lesson Practice

A number cube labeled 1–6 is rolled. List the outcome for each event.
(Ex 1)

a. a number less than or equal to 4   {1, 2, 3, 4}

b. an even number   {2, 4, 6}

c. a number greater than 2   {3, 4, 5, 6}

There are 4 green, 3 blue, and 3 red marbles in a bag.
(Ex 2)

d. $\frac{3}{10}$ or 0.3 or 30%

d. What is the probability of randomly choosing a blue marble?

e. What is the probability of randomly not choosing a red marble? $\frac{7}{10}$ or 0.7 or 70%

76   Saxon Algebra 1

Example 3

Point out that it may be easier to use decimals rather than fractions when comparisons are needed.

Additional Example 3

A bucket has 10 balls numbered 1, 1, 2, 3, 4, 4, 4, 5, 6, and 6. If one ball is drawn at random, is there a greater chance of getting an even number or a multiple of 5? Explain. an even number; The probability of drawing a multiple of 5 is $\frac{1}{10}$. The probability of drawing an even number is $\frac{3}{5}$; $\frac{3}{5} > \frac{1}{10}$.

Error Alert Some students may use 2 as the numerator of the probability fraction because there are only two numbers greater than 4. Emphasize that the number of outcomes is the total number of balls, not the number of different numbers.

Example 4

TEACHER TIP

Explain to students that the results of previous plays do not affect the current outcome. If a person plays the game 100 times and gets no money, the chances of winning $2 on the next play are still $\frac{1}{8}$.

Additional Example 4

What is the probability of winning $1? $\frac{3}{8}$

Lesson Practice

Problem c

Error Alert Make sure students understand that a number greater than 2 does not include 2.

76   Saxon Algebra 1

ALTERNATE METHOD FOR EXAMPLE 3

Sketch two circles each evenly divided into 10 sections. Label the sections of each circle 1, 1, 2, 3, 4, 4, 4, 5, 6, 6. Have two volunteers shade one circle to show the sections with numbers greater than 4, and the other circle to show sections with the number 1.

Ask:

"Which circle has a greater part shaded?"
the one showing numbers greater than 4

"Which event has the greater chance of happening?" landing on a number greater than 4

Point out that the shaded circles are a visual representation of the two probabilities described in Example 3.

f. $\frac{5}{8}$ or 0.625 or 62.5%; The chance of drawing a 6 is $\frac{1}{8}$, which is less than the chance of drawing a 7, which is $\frac{1}{4}$.

f. (Ex 3) Suppose there are 8 balls in a bucket numbered as follows; 1, 2, 3, 5, 5, 6, 7, and 7. A single ball is randomly chosen from the bucket. What is the probability of drawing a ball with a number less than 6? Do you have a greater chance of drawing a 7 or a 6?

g. (Ex 4) A 52-card deck has 4 kings in the deck. What is the probability of randomly drawing a king out of the deck? $\frac{1}{13}$

Practice   Distributed and Integrated

*1. (14) A number cube labeled 1–6 is rolled three times. What is the probability that the next roll will produce a number greater than 4? $\frac{1}{3}$

*2. (14) An jar contains 5 green marbles and 9 purple marbles. A marble is drawn and dropped back into the jar. Then a second marble is drawn and dropped back into the jar. Both marbles are green. If another marble is drawn, what is the probability that it will be green? $\frac{5}{14}$

3. (8) Convert 20 inches to centimeters (2.54 cm = 1 in.).   50.8 cm

4. (8) Convert 25 feet to centimeters. (Hint: Convert from feet to inches to centimeters.) 762 cm

Simplify.

5. (4) $3 - 2 \cdot 4 + 3 \cdot 2$ 1

6. (11) $-3(-2)(-3) - 2$ -20

7. (4) $5(9 + 2) - 4(5 + 1)$ 31

8. (4) $3(6 + 2) + 3(5 - 2)$ 33

9. (13) Evaluate $\sqrt{31 + z}$ when $z = 5$.   6

10. (10) Use <, > or = to compare $\frac{4}{5}$ and $\frac{5}{6}$. $\frac{4}{5} < \frac{5}{6}$

*11. (13) **Geometry** What is the length of the side of a square that has an area of 49 square centimeters?   7 centimeters

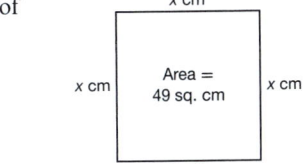

12. (12) **Multiple Choice** Which equation demonstrates the Associative Property of Addition?   **A**

A $(a + b) + c = a + (b + c)$

B $ab + c = ba + c$

C $a(b + c) = ab + ac$

D $a + (b + c) = a + (c + b)$

Lesson 14   77

MANIPULATIVE USE FOR Lesson Practice a–c

Materials: 6-part spinner about 3 in. in diameter and a paper clip for each pair of students

Have students work in pairs. Each pair needs a paper clip and one 6-part spinner about 3 in. in diameter. Have students write the numbers 1–6 in the sectors. Explain that they are going to simulate rolling a 1–6 number cube by spinning the paper clip around the point of a pencil. One partner spins; the other records results.

Have student pairs spin and record for 15 minutes, and compile all results in a class chart. Then have students find the fractional part of the total number of spins for each number and convert their fractions to decimals. The theoretical probability of spinning each number is $\frac{1}{6}$ or $0.1\overline{66}$. By using such a large number of spins, the experimental results should come close to the theoretical results.

Problem 13

Extend the Problem

"If each of the two variables can be positive, zero, or negative, how many possibilities are there? Give an example of each and organize the results in the three categories positive, zero, and negative." 9; Sample: positive: $-(2)(-3)$, $-(-2)(3)$; zero: $-(2)(0)$, $-(0)(3)$, $-(0)(0)$, $-(0)(-3)$, $-(-2)(0)$; negative: $-(2)(3)$, $-(-2)(-3)$

Problem 16

Guide students by asking them the following questions.

"How many outcomes are there?" 11, one for each letter in the word probability

"How many favorable outcomes are there?" 2

Problem 17

Extend the Problem

Ask students to explain why answer choice B is impossible. Sample: There are 16 marbles, so the denominator must be a factor.

*13. (11) **Justify** What must be true of each of the values of x and y if $-xy$ is positive? zero? negative? Either x or y is positive and the other is negative; Either x or y is zero; Both x and y are positive or both x and y are negative.

14. (12) Identify the property illustrated in the expression $5 \cdot 6 = 6 \cdot 5$. Commutative Property of Multiplication

*15. (14) **Multiple Choice** A number cube labeled 1–6 is tossed. What is the theoretical probability of rolling an odd number? A

A $\frac{1}{2}$

B $\frac{1}{3}$

C $\frac{1}{4}$

D $\frac{2}{3}$

*16. (14) A letter is chosen at random from the word probability. What is the probability of randomly choosing the letter b? $\frac{2}{11}$

*17. (14) **Multiple Choice** A bag contains 4 blue, 6 red, 5 yellow, and 1 orange marble. What is the probability of randomly choosing a blue marble? C

A $\frac{1}{16}$

B $\frac{4}{15}$

C $\frac{1}{4}$

D $\frac{4}{32}$

18. (13) **Error Analysis** Students were asked to find the square root of 16. Which student is correct? Explain the error.

Student A	Student B
$\sqrt{16} = 4$	$\sqrt{16} = 8$
$4 \times 4 = 16$	$8 \times 2 = 16$

18. Student A; Sample: Student B found two different numbers that have a product of 16 instead of one number that, when multiplied by itself, equals 16.

*19. (13) **Braking Distance** The speed a vehicle was traveling when the brakes were first applied can be estimated using the formula $s = \sqrt{\frac{d}{0.04}}$, where d is the length of the vehicle's skid marks in feet and s is the speed of the vehicle in miles per hour. Determine the speed of a car whose skid marks were 4^2 feet long. about 20 miles per hour

*20. (9) **Physics** The centripetal force of an object in circular motion can be expressed as $\frac{mv^2}{r}$, where m is mass, v is tangential velocity, and r is the radius of the circular path. What is the centripetal force of a 2-kg object traveling at 50 cm/s in a circular path with a radius of 25 centimeters? 200 kg • cm/s^2

78 **Saxon** *Algebra 1*

INCLUSION

Some students may need a review of converting fractions to equivalent decimals and percents. Use a 10 × 10 grid as a visual model. Point out that each small square is $\frac{1}{100}$ or 0.01 of the total square. Since a percent is a ratio to one hundred, each small square is also 1% of the total.

Have students use the 10 × 10 grid model to convert the fractions $\frac{1}{2}$, $\frac{3}{4}$, $\frac{2}{5}$, $\frac{7}{10}$, $\frac{3}{100}$, and $\frac{33}{100}$ to decimals and percents. 0.5, 50%; 0.75, 75%; 0.4, 40%; 0.7, 70%; 0.03, 3%; 0.33, 33% Then use the same fractions to review the general method of converting a fraction to a decimal: divide the numerator by the denominator. To convert these decimals to percents, students move the decimal point two places to the right and add the percent symbol.

21. Verify Convert 2.35 pounds to ounces (1 lb = 16 oz). Check to see if your answer
(8)   is reasonable. **37.6 oz; Sample: 2.35 rounds down to 2 and 2 · 16 = 32. The answer 37.6 oz is reasonable, as it is close to the estimate of 32 oz.**

22. Write If a computer program is designed to run until it reaches the end of the
(1)   number pi (π), will the program ever end? Explain. **no; Sample: Since π is an irrational number and will never end, the program will never end.**

23. Geography The lowest point in elevation in the United States is Death Valley,
(1)   California. Death Valley is 86 meters below sea level. Which set of numbers best describes elevations in Death Valley? **real numbers**

24. Temperature To convert degrees Celsius to degrees Fahrenheit, use the
(2)   equation $C = \frac{5}{9}(F - 32)$.
  a. How many terms are in the expression $\frac{5}{9}(F - 32)$? **1**
  b. Identify the constants in the expression. **$\frac{5}{9}$, 32**

25. Simplify $-7 + 3 - 2 - 5 + (-6)$. **−17**
(6)

26. Error Analysis Ms. Mahoney, the algebra teacher, has two cakes that weigh 3 pounds
(4)   and 5 pounds. She cuts the cakes into 16 equal pieces. She asks the students to write an expression that represents the weight of each piece. Which student is correct? Explain the error.

26. Student B; Sample: The weight of each piece is the weight of the cakes divided by 16. The weight of the cakes is 3 + 5. Student B put parentheses around 3 + 5, grouping 3 and 5. Student A did not put parentheses around 3 + 5, and without these grouping symbols, 5 ÷ 16 is the operation performed first.

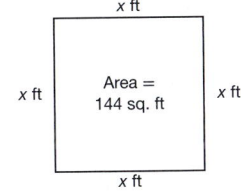

Student A	Student B
uses the expression $3 + 5 \div 16$	uses the expression $(3 + 5) \div 16$

27. Model While the Petersen family was waiting for their table, 9 people left the
(5)   restaurant and 15 people entered. Find the sum of −9 and 15 to determine the change in the number of people in the restaurant. Use algebra tiles to model the situation. **+6 people**

28. Justify Simplify $22 - (-11) - 11 - (-22)$. Justify your answer. **44; Sample: This is the same as $22 + 11 - 11 + 22$.**
(6)

29. Write Why is the order of operations important when simplifying an expression
(7)   like $(5 + 7)^2 \div (14 - 2)$? **Sample: If you don't complete the problem in the correct order, you get the wrong answer.**

*30. Landscaping Tanisha is building a fence around a square flower bed that has an
(13) area of 144 square feet. How many feet of fencing does she need? **48 feet**

Problem 27
Error Alert Stress that the problem asks for the change in the number of people and not the actual number. So, it makes no difference how many people are in the Petersen family or in the rest of the restaurant.

Problem 30
Ask students, "What information is needed to solve the problem?" Sample: the side length of the square

"Why is the side length needed?" Sample: The sum of the side lengths will equal the perimeter. The perimeter equals the number of feet of fencing needed.

Lesson 14   79

◆ CHALLENGE

Explain that the odds in favor of an event is the ratio of the probability of the event to the probability of its complement. If the event is A, and its complement is $\overline{A}$, then the odds for A are $P(A) : P(\overline{A})$ or $\frac{P(A)}{P(\overline{A})}$.
Challenge students to find the odds of an event with 2 equally likely outcomes.
Sample: 1 to 1; $P(A) = 50\%$, $P(\overline{A}) = 50\%$, and $\frac{P(A)}{P(\overline{A})} = \frac{0.5}{0.5}$, or 1 to 1.

LOOKING FORWARD

Determining the theoretical probability of an event prepares students for

- **Lesson 33** Finding the Probability of Independent and Dependent Events
- **Lesson 68** Mutually Exclusive and Inclusive Events
- **Lesson 80** Calculating Frequency Distributions

Lesson 14   79

LESSON 15

1 Warm Up

Problem 3
Remind students that following the order of operations requires that the expression in the absolute-value symbols be simplified before taking the absolute value of the expression.

2 New Concepts

In this lesson, students learn to use the Distributive Property to simplify expressions.

Example 1

Students should use the Distributive Property rather than the order of operations to simplify the expressions in this lesson.

Error Alert Students may forget to distribute the factor outside the parentheses to all the terms in the parentheses. Remind them to multiply each term in the parentheses by the factor outside the parentheses.

Additional Example 1
Simplify each expression.

a. $5(3 + 9)$ 60

b. $6(2 - 7)$ −30

LESSON RESOURCES

Student Edition Practice Workbook 15
Reteaching Master 15
Adaptations Master 15
Challenge and Enrichment Master C15

LESSON 15 — Using the Distributive Property to Simplify Expressions

Warm Up

1. **Vocabulary** In the expression $3x + 5$, $3x$ is a _____ (variable, term) of the expression.   term

Simplify each expression.

2. $5 - 7 + 5(3)$ 13

3. $(-5) + (-2) + |(-5) + (-2)|$ 0

4. Evaluate $7x + 4y$ for $x = 2.1$ and $y = -0.7$.   11.9

5. Find the product of $\frac{3}{8}$, $\frac{4}{5}$, and $\frac{2}{3}$. $\frac{1}{5}$

New Concepts

The Distributive Property can be used to simplify expressions. Since subtraction is the same as adding the opposite, the Distributive Property will also work with subtraction.

The Distributive Property
For all real numbers a, b, c,
$a(b + c) = ab + ac$ and $a(b - c) = ab - ac$
Examples
$5(2 + 1) = 5 \cdot 2 + 5 \cdot 1 = 15 \qquad 5(2 - 1) = 5 \cdot 2 - 5 \cdot 1 = 5$

Example 1 Distributing a Positive Integer

Simplify each expression.

Math Reasoning

Verify Use the order of operations to show that $4(5 - 3) = 8$.

Subtract 3 from 5, and then multiply by 4; $(4)(2) = 8$

a. $6(4 + 8)$

SOLUTION

$6(4 + 8)$
$= 6(4) + 6(8)$ Distribute the 6.
$= 24 + 48$ Multiply.
$= 72$ Add.

b. $4(5 - 3)$

SOLUTION

$4(5 - 3)$
$= 4(5) + 4(-3)$ Distribute the 4.
$= 20 - 12$ Multiply.
$= 8$ Subtract.

Online Connection
www.SaxonMathResources.com

80   Saxon Algebra 1

MATH BACKGROUND

Students have learned to simplify expressions by distributing factors with only one term. To extend this method, distribute a factor with two terms over the set of numbers in parentheses. For example, the expression $(3 + 4)(5 + 2)$ can be simplified using distribution.

Distribute each term in the first parentheses over the second parentheses. The result is the expanded form $3(5 + 2) + 4(5 + 2)$. Apply the basic rules for distribution to each term in the expanded expression, and then simplify $(3 \cdot 5) + (3 \cdot 2) + (4 \cdot 5) + (4 \cdot 2)$.

Use the Multiplication Property of −1 to simplify an expression like −(5 + 2). Rewrite the expression as −1(5 + 2) and then distribute.

Example 2 Distributing a Negative Integer

Simplify each expression.

a. −(9 + 4)

SOLUTION

−(9 + 4)
= (−1)(9) + (−1)(4)   Distribute.
= −9 − 4   Multiply.
= −13   Simplify.

b. −9(−6 − 3)

SOLUTION

−9(−6 − 3)
= (−9)(−6) + (−9)(−3)
= 54 + 27
= 81

Hint
The product of a real number and 1 is the real number.

The Distributive Property applies not only to numeric expressions but also to algebraic expressions.

Example 3 Simplifying Algebraic Expressions

Simplify each expression.

a. −4(x + 7)

SOLUTION

−4(x + 7)
= (−4)(x) + (−4)(7)   Distribute.
= −4x − 28   Multiply.

b. (5 − x)6

SOLUTION

(5 − x)6
= 6(5) + 6(−x)
= 30 − 6x

Reading Math
There are different ways to write the same expression:
6 · (5 − x)
(5 − x) · 6
6(5 − x)
(5 − x)6

Example 4 Simplifying Algebraic Expressions with Exponents

Simplify each expression.

a. $mn(mx + ny + 2p)$

SOLUTION

$mn(mx + ny + 2p)$
$= m^2nx + mn^2y + 2mnp$ Multiply.

b. $-xy(y^2 - x^2z)$

SOLUTION

$-xy(y^2 - x^2z)$
$= (-xy)(y^2) + (-xy)(-x^2z)$ Distribute. Combine like terms.
$= -xy^3 + x^3yz$

Hint
When multiplying, add the exponents of powers with the same base.
$y(y^2) = y^{1+2} = y^3$

Lesson 15 81

ENGLISH LEARNERS

Explain the meaning of the word **distribute**. Say:

"To distribute something is to share it with others. The number or variable that is distributed is shared among the terms in the parentheses."

Discuss the idea of distributing papers to the whole class. A piece of paper is given to each person in class.

Example 5

Multiplication involving a factor with more than one term can be determined using the Distributive Property.

Extend the Example
Challenge students to find the area of one end zone and then both end zones combined.
4800, 9600

Additional Example 5
A standard tennis court is 78 feet long and 27 feet wide for singles matches. For doubles matches, each of two alleys add $4\frac{1}{2}$ feet to the width. What is the area of a tennis court for doubles?
2808 ft²

Lesson Practice

Problem g
Error Alert Students may not consider the variables without exponents. Remind them that the exponent is understood to be one.

Problem h
Scaffolding Suggest that students determine how many different variables are in the expression before simplifying.

Check for Understanding

The questions below help assess the concepts taught in this lesson.

"Give an example of an expression that can be simplified using the Distributive Property."
Sample: 3(x+2)

"Explain how to use the Distributive Property to simplify expressions." Each individual term in the parentheses is multiplied by the factor(s) outside of the parentheses.

Hint
To find the area of a rectangle, multiply length times width.

Example 5 Application: Landscaping

The turf on a football field is being replaced. The field is 300 feet long and 160 feet wide, not including the two end zones. Each end zone adds an additional 30 feet to the field's length. Write an expression using the Distributive Property to show the entire area of the field. Simplify the expression.

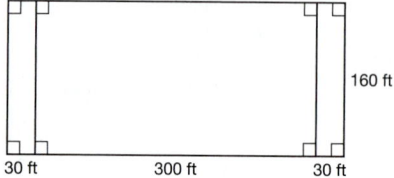

SOLUTION

width	×	length
= 160	×	(30 + 300 + 30)

$= 160(30 + 300 + 30)$
$= 160(30) + 160(300) + 160(30)$ Use the Distributive Property.
$= 4800 + 48{,}000 + 4800$ Multiply.
$= 57{,}600$ Add.

Check Use the order of operations.
$160(30 + 300 + 30)$ Perform the operation inside the parentheses.
$= 160(360)$ Multiply.
$= 57{,}600$ ✓

The area of the football field is 57,600 ft².

Lesson Practice

Simplify each expression.

a. $8(2 + 7)$ 72 (Ex 1)
b. $4(6 - 2)$ 16 (Ex 1)
c. $-(9 + 3)$ −12 (Ex 2)
d. $-14(4 - 2)$ −28 (Ex 2)
e. $-10(m + 4)$ −10m − 40 (Ex 3)
f. $(7 - y)8$ 56 − 8y (Ex 3)
g. $4xy^3(x^4y - 5x)$ $4x^5y^4 - 20x^2y^3$ (Ex 4)
h. $-2x^2m^2(m^2 - 4m)$ $-2x^2m^4 + 8x^2m^3$ (Ex 4)
i. A group of 4 adults and 8 children are buying tickets to an amusement park. Tickets are $15 each. Write an expression using the Distributive Property to show the total cost of the tickets. Simplify the expression. (Ex 5)
15(4 + 8); $180

INCLUSION

For students who forget to multiply all terms in the parentheses by the factor outside the parentheses, have them try multiplying the factors vertically. Simplify. $xy(4x - 3y^2)$.

Write the problem vertically.
$4x - 3y^2$
$\times \quad xy$

Multiply each term by xy, crossing off each term as it is multiplied.

$$\begin{array}{r} 4x - 3y^2 \\ \times \quad xy \\ \hline -3xy^3 \end{array} \Rightarrow \begin{array}{r} \cancel{4x} - \cancel{3y^2} \\ \times \quad xy \\ \hline 4x^2y - 3xy^3 \end{array}$$

Tell students that the final answer will have the same number of terms as the original expression in parentheses.

Practice Distributed and Integrated

Evaluate.

1. $-7(-8 + 3)$ 35
2. $5(-3 - 6)$ -45
3. Evaluate $\sqrt{10{,}000}$. 100
4. Solve $c = \sqrt{25}$. $c = 5$

*5. **Multi-Step** In a shipment of 800 eggs, the probability of an egg breaking is $\frac{2}{25}$. How many are likely to be broken in the shipment? Justify the answer. 64 eggs; Sample: $\frac{2}{25} = \frac{b}{800}$; $25b = 1600$; $b = 64$

6. The digits 0, 1, 2, 3, 4, 5, 6, 7, 8 and 9 are written on cards that are shuffled and placed face down in a stack. One card is selected at random. What is the probability that the digit is odd and greater than 5? $\frac{2}{10} = \frac{1}{5}$

*7. In a bucket there are 10 balls in a bucket numbered 1, 1, 2, 3, 4, 4, 4, 5, 6, and 6. A single ball is randomly chosen from the bucket. What is the probability of drawing a ball with a number less than 7? Explain.   7. 1; Sample: An event that is certain to happen has a probability of 1. All 10 of the balls have a number label less than 7, so the event is certain.

*8. **Multiple Choice** Simplify the expression $-5(x + 6)$. Which is the correct simplification? D
   A $-5 + x - 11$ B $-5x + 1$ C $-5x + 30$ D $-5x - 30$

*9. Find the value of y in the equation $18 - x = y$ if $x = -4$. $y = 22$

10. The water level of the reservoir in Austin, Texas, was 3 feet below normal. After a heavy rain storm, the water level increased to 5 feet above normal. How much did the rain storm change the water level? 8 ft

11. **Error Analysis** Two students evaluated a numeric expression. Which student is correct? Explain the error.

Student A	Student B
$-8(-5 + 14)$	$-8(-5 + 14)$
$= 40 - 112$	$= -13 + 6$
$= -72$	$= -7$

Student A; Sample: Student B added the numbers instead of multiplying when using the Distributive Property.

12. **Write** Evaluate the expression $-8(9 - 15)$ using the Distributive Property. Explain.   48; Sample: I multiplied -8 by each number in parentheses and added the products.

*13. (**Surveying**) The county surveyed a piece of property and divided it into equal-sized lots. Use the diagram to write an expression that requires the Distributive Property to evaluate it. Evaluate the expression to find the total number of lots on the property. $6(4 + 7)$; $6(4 + 7) = 6(4) + 6(7) = 24 + 42 = 66$ lots

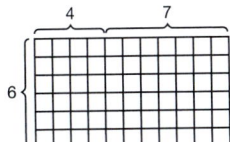

*14. True or False: $m + 0 = m$. Justify your answer using the properties. true; Identity Property of Addition

Lesson 15 83

Problem 19

Remind students to treat the radicand as an expression within parentheses and the square root as a exponent. That is, substitute 13 for z, add 36 and 13, then take the square root of 49.

Problem 21

Guide the students by asking them the following questions.

"What operation is used to form the expression?" multiplication

"Which property involves multiplication and changes the order of a factor?" Commutative Property of Multiplication

"Which property involves multiplication and grouping?" Associative Property of Multiplication

---

15. Convert 3.4 yd³ to ft³. 91.8 ft³
(8)

16. **Multi-Step** Travis plans to divide his collection of baseball cards among
(15) 8 grandchildren. He will give each child the same number of cards. Each card is worth $14. Write an expression to represent the value of each child's cards. Let c equal the total number of cards in Travis's collection. $14\left(\frac{c}{8}\right)$

17. (**Budgeting**) Kennedy's teacher asked her to plan the budget for the class party.
(15) Kennedy began by writing the expression $g = b + 7$ to represent that the number of girls equals the number of boys plus seven. Each girl will need $6. Write and simplify an algebraic expression that uses the Distributive Property to show the total cost for girls at the class party. $6(b + 7) = 6b + 42$

*18. If a number cube is rolled, what is the probability of it landing on the number
(14) 5 or 6? $\frac{2}{6}$ or $\frac{1}{3}$

*19. **Error Analysis** Two students are evaluating the expression $\sqrt{36 + z}$ for $z = 13$.
(13) Which student is correct? Explain the error. Student A; Sample: Student B incorrectly applied the square root.

Student A	Student B
$\sqrt{36 + z}$	$\sqrt{36 + z}$
$= \sqrt{36 + 13}$	$= \sqrt{36} + z$
$= \sqrt{49}$	$= 6 + 13$
$= 7$	$= 19$

20. **Justify** The expression 6 • 2 • 4 would be simplified from left to right using the order
(12) of operations. What property would allow this expression to be simplified from right to left? Commutative Property of Multiplication

*21. (**Investments**) Susan invests the same amount of money in each of 7 stocks. In one
(12) year, her money increased 8 times. The value of her investment is represented by the expression $7x • 8$. Show two methods to simplify the expression and justify each step using the properties. See Additional Answers.

22. (**Age**) Rickie is $3\frac{3}{4}$ years older than Raymond. Raymond is $2\frac{1}{2}$ years younger
(10) than Ryan. If Ryan is $14\frac{1}{4}$ years old, how old is Rickie? $15\frac{1}{2}$ years

23. **Write** Write the procedure for evaluating the expression $16f^2 g^3 - 4f^8 + 12$ for
(9) $f = 3$ and $g = 5$. Sample: Substitute the value 3 for f and the value 5 for g. Evaluate exponents from left to right. Multiply from left to right. Subtract and add from left to right.

24. **Model** Use the number line to model $x - 8$ when $x = -6$. See Additional Answers.
(6)

25. (**Astronomy**) In astronomy, brightness is given in a value called magnitude. A
(3) -2-magnitude star is 2.512 times brighter than a -1-magnitude star, a -3-magnitude star is 2.512 times brighter than a -2-magnitude star, and so on. If Sirius is magnitude -1.5 and the full moon is magnitude -12.5, how much brighter is the full moon? 2.512^{11} or about 25,131 times brighter

84 Saxon Algebra 1

26. **Error Analysis** Student A and Student B each solved the absolute-value problem as shown below. Which student is correct? Explain the error.

Student A	Student B
$-\|12 - 15\|$	$-\|12 - 15\|$
$= -\|-3\|$	$= -\|-3\|$
$= -(3)$	$= \|+3\|$
$= -3$	$= 3$

Student A; Sample: Student B combined the two negative signs before taking the absolute value, but should have taken the absolute value first.

*27. Find the value of y in the equation $x - |x - 2| = y$ if $x = -3$. $y = -8$

28. **Verify** When simplified, will the expression $3 + \frac{2}{3} + |-5|$ be positive or negative? Explain.   Sample: It will be positive because every part is positive; the negative value in the absolute value symbols will become positive.

29. **Probability** Thomas spun a game spinner and recorded the results in the table below.

Outcome	Frequency
Red	3
Blue	5
Yellow	9
Green	8

Use the table to find the experimental probability of each event. Express each probability as a fraction and as a percent.

a. landing on red $\frac{3}{25}$, 12%

b. landing on green $\frac{8}{25}$, 32%

c. not landing on green $\frac{17}{25}$, 68%

30. **Geometry** What is the perimeter of a square with an area of 121 sq. in.?   44 in.

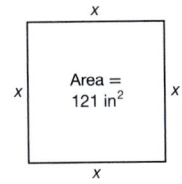

Problem 26
Error Alert
A common error when simplifying expressions with absolute values is to treat the absolute-value bars like parentheses. Remind students to first simplify the expression inside the absolute-value bars, take the absolute value, and then determine whether the answer should be positive or negative depending on the sign in front of the absolute-value bars.

Problem 29
Extend the Problem
"Suppose Thomas spun the game spinner 50 more times. How many more times is he likely to land on red?"   6

Lesson 15   85

CHALLENGE

Sometimes factors will involve multiple terms in separate parentheses. The method to simplify the expression using the Distributive Property is still the same. Simplify the expression:

$(x - 2y)(m + y)$ $mx + xy - 2my - 2y^2$

LOOKING FORWARD

Understanding the Distributive Property prepares students for

- **Lesson 16** Simplifying and Evaluating expressions with Positive Exponents
- **Lesson 26** Solving Multi-Step Equations
- **Lesson 29** Solving Literal Equations
- **Lesson 32** Simplifying and Evaluating Expressions with Integer and Zero Exponents

LESSON 16

1 Warm Up

Problem 4
Remind students to simplify the absolute-value expression before subtracting.

2 New Concepts

In this lesson, students learn to simplify and evaluate expressions containing variables.

Review the meanings of the words variable and exponent. Explain that variables can be substituted with numbers.

Example 1

Remind students that the order of operations requires subtraction inside the parentheses first, then multiplication inside the brackets, and finally multiplication outside of the brackets.

Additional Example 1
Evaluate each expression for the given values of the variables.

a. $-a[-a(p - a)]$ for $a = 5$ and $p = 7$ **50**

b. $(-x + a) - (x - a)$ for $a = -8$ and $x = 14$ **−44**

LESSON RESOURCES

Student Edition Practice
 Workbook 16
Reteaching Master 16
Adaptations Master 16
Challenge and Enrichment
 Master C16

LESSON 16 — Simplifying and Evaluating Variable Expressions

Warm Up

1. **Vocabulary** The set of whole numbers and their opposites {..., −4, −3, −2, −1, 0, 1, 2, 3, 4,...} is the set of _____. **integers**
   (6)

Simplify.

2. $-ax^2(dx^3 - a^5x)$ **$-adx^5 + a^6x^3$**
   (15)

3. $\sqrt{36} + \sqrt{81} - 4^2$ **−1**
   (13)

4. $[-(-5)] - |-7|$ **−2**
   (7)

5. Which value is equivalent to $\frac{9}{10}\left(-\frac{1}{12}\right)$? **B**
   (11)

   A $-\frac{49}{60}$ B $-\frac{3}{40}$ C $\frac{3}{60}$ D $\frac{3}{40}$

New Concepts

To evaluate an expression that contains variables, substitute each variable in the expression with a given numeric value, and then find the value of the expression.

Example 1 Evaluating Expressions with Two Variables

Evaluate each expression for the given values of the variables.

a. $-a[-a(p - a)]$ for $a = 3$ and $p = 4$

SOLUTION

$-a[-a(p - a)]$
$= -3[-3(4 - 3)]$ Substitute each variable with the given value.
$= -3[-3(1)]$ Subtract.
$= -3[-3]$ Multiply inside the brackets.
$= 9$ Multiply.

b. $(-x + a) - (x - a)$ for $a = -2$ and $x = 7$

SOLUTION

$(-x + a) - (x - a)$
$= [-7 + (-2)] - [7 - (-2)]$ Substitute each variable with the given value.
$= [-7 + (-2)] - [7 + 2]$ Take the opposite of −2.
$= (-9) - (9)$ Evaluate inside the brackets.
$= -18$ Subtract.

Hint
Use parentheses when substituting a number for a variable, so that the negative signs and the subtraction signs are not confused.

MATH BACKGROUND

Simplifying and evaluating expressions with multiple variables and exponents are important skills to have in solving problems in everyday life. Since students have already learned how to set up linear expressions from word problems, they can now be introduced to nonlinear ones involving multiple variables.

For example, the amount of interest earned on a $1000 deposit after 5 years at a rate of 5% per year can be expressed by:

$$I = [x(1.00 + y)^z - x]$$

where I is the amount of interest earned, x is the initial deposit, y is the annual interest rate, and z is the time in years. Students can apply this expression to other similar problems.

Example 2 Evaluating Expressions with Three Variables

Evaluate each expression for the given values of the variables.

a. $(yx)(zyx)$ for $x = 2$, $y = -1$, and $z = 4$

SOLUTION

$(yx)(zyx)$
$= [(-1)(2)][(4)(-1)(2)]$ Substitute each variable with the given value.
$= (-2)(-8)$ Multiply inside the brackets.
$= 16$ Multiply.

b. $\dfrac{x(4ap)}{xp}$ for $a = 1$, $p = 5$, and $x = -3$

SOLUTION

$\dfrac{x(4ap)}{xp}$

$= \dfrac{(-3)(4)(1)(5)}{(-3)(5)}$ Substitute each variable with the given value.

$= \dfrac{-60}{-15} = 4$ Multiply and simplify.

An expression can be simplified before it is evaluated.

Example 3 Simplifying Before Evaluating Expressions

Simplify each expression. Then evaluate it. Justify each step.

a. $-x(y - 3) + y$ for $x = 0.5$ and $y = -1.75$

SOLUTION

$-x(y - 3) + y$
$= -xy + 3x + y$ Distributive Property
$= -(0.5)(-1.75) + 3(0.5) + (-1.75)$ Substitute.
$= 0.875 + 1.5 - 1.75$ Multiply and add.
$= 0.625$

b. $x(x + 2y) - x$ for $x = \dfrac{1}{2}$ and $y = \dfrac{1}{4}$

SOLUTION

$x(x + 2y) - x$
$= x^2 + 2xy - x$ Distributive Property
$= \left(\dfrac{1}{2}\right)^2 + 2\left(\dfrac{1}{2}\right)\left(\dfrac{1}{4}\right) - \left(\dfrac{1}{2}\right)$ Substitute.
$= \dfrac{1}{4} + \dfrac{1}{4} - \dfrac{1}{2} = 0$ Use order of operations to simplify.

Math Reasoning

Verify Evaluate Example 3a without simplifying first to show that the answer is the same.

Sample: $-x(y - 3) + y$
$= -0.5(-1.75 - 3) + (-1.75)$
$= -0.5(-4.75) + (-1.75)$
$= 2.375 + (-1.75)$
$= 0.625$

Online Connection
www.SaxonMathResources.com

Example 2

Generally, parentheses are changed to brackets when numbers are substituted for variables. Since only multiplication is involved in this example, the brackets can be dropped.

Additional Example 2

Evaluate each expression for the given values of the variables.

a. $cb(abc^2)$ for $a = 2$, $b = -1$, $c = 3$ 54

b. $\dfrac{xy(7z)}{x^2y}$ for $x = -1$, $y = 3$, $z = 2$ -14

Example 3

When fractions and decimals are involved, it is sometimes easier to simplify an expression before evaluating it.

Additional Example 3

Simplify each expression. Then evaluate. Justify each step.

a. $-x(y - 3) + y$ for $x = 0.75$ and $y = -2.5$
$-x(y - 3) + y$
$= -xy + 3x + y$ Distribute.
$= -0.75(-2.5)$
  $+ 3(0.75) + (-2.5)$ Substitute.
$= 1.875 + 2.25$
  $+ (-2.5)$ Multiply.
$= 1.625$ Simplify.

b. $x(x + 2y) - x$ for $x = \dfrac{1}{3}$ and $y = \dfrac{1}{2}$

$x(x + 2y) - x$
$= x^2 + 2xy - x$ Distribute
$= \left(\dfrac{1}{3}\right)^2 + 2\left(\dfrac{1}{3}\right)\left(\dfrac{1}{2}\right) - \left(\dfrac{1}{3}\right)$ Substitute
$= \left(\dfrac{1}{9}\right) + \left(\dfrac{1}{3}\right) - \left(\dfrac{1}{3}\right)$ Simplify.
$= \dfrac{1}{9}$ Simplify.

Example 4

Error Alert A common error when applying the laws of exponents is applying the exponent to all variables in an expression such as ym^3. Point out to students that in ym^3, only m is raised to the power. In $(ym)^3$, both variables are raised to the power.

Additional Example 4

Evaluate each expression for the given values of the variables.

a. If $b = -3$ and $z = 6$, what is the value of zb^3? -162

b. If $x = 2$ and $y = -2$, what is the value of $3\left(\frac{x}{3-y}\right)^2$? $\frac{12}{25}$

c. If $m = 5$, what is the value of $|(-m)^3|$? 125

Example 5

In this example, the current-year principal is found by multiplying 1.04, the interest rate plus 1, times the principal accumulated in the previous year. By multiplying by 1.04, the total principal, rather than just the interest, is calculated for the current year.

Extend the Example

Determine the value of a 3-year-old car to the nearest dollar if the original price was $20,000. The current-year value is 85% of the previous-year value. $12,283.

Additional Example 5

If the principal balance after 4 years is $1675, how much is the principal balance after 6 years? $1811.68

Example 4 Evaluating Expressions with Exponents

Evaluate each expression for the given values of the variables.

a. If $m = -2$ and $y = 2.5$, what is the value of ym^3?

SOLUTION

ym^3

$= (2.5)(-2)^3$ Substitute each variable with the given value.

$= (2.5)(-8)$ Evaluate the exponent.

$= -20$ Multiply.

Caution Since there are no parentheses around ym in the expression ym^3, only m is raised to the third power.

b. If $a = 3$ and $b = -1$, what is the value of $2\left(\frac{a}{5-b}\right)^2$?

SOLUTION

$2\left(\frac{a}{5-b}\right)^2$

$= 2\left(\frac{3}{5-(-1)}\right)^2$ Substitute each variable with the given value.

$= 2\left(\frac{3}{5+1}\right)^2$ Take the opposite of -1.

$= 2\left(\frac{3}{6}\right)^2$ Perform operations inside the parentheses.

$= 2\left(\frac{1}{2}\right)^2$ Write the fraction in simplest form.

$= 2\left(\frac{1}{4}\right)$ Evaluate the exponent.

$= \frac{1}{2}$ Multiply.

c. If $a = 3$, what is the value of $|(-a)^3|$?

SOLUTION

$|(-a)^3|$

$= |(-3)^3|$ Substitute the variable with the given value.

$= |(-3)(-3)(-3)|$ Evaluate the exponent.

$= |-27|$ Multiply.

$= 27$ Take the absolute value.

Example 5 Application: Investments

A savings account increases as interest accumulates according to the formula $P_y = 1.04(P_{y-1})$, where P_y is the principal balance at the end of y years and P_{y-1} is the principal balance after $y-1$ years. After 6 years, there is a principal balance of $1450.00. How much is the principal balance after 8 years?

ENGLISH LEARNERS

Explain the meaning of the word **principal**. Say:

"Principal is an amount of money invested or borrowed. For example, the amount of money put into a savings account is the principal."

Have a volunteer use the word principal in a sentence. Sample: The principal in my savings account was $250.

Ask students to share other experiences that they have had involving principal.

Caution

In the equation $P_y = 1.04(P_{y-1})$, the subscript y refers to a particular number of years. So, $y - 1$ refers to 1 year less than y.

SOLUTION

P_{7-1} or P_6	represents the principal balance after 6 years
P_{7-1} or $P_6 = \$1450$	
$P_7 = 1.04(P_{7-1})$	Write the formula for the principal balance after 7 years.
$P_7 = 1.04(1450)$	Substitute 1450 for P_{7-1}.
$P_7 = \$1508$	
$P_8 = 1.04(P_{8-1})$	Write the formula for the principal balance after 8 years.
P_{8-1} or P_7	represents the principal balance after 7 years
$P_8 = 1.04(1508)$	Substitute 1508 for P_{8-1}.
$P_8 = \$1568.32$	

Her principal balance is $1568.32 after 8 years.

Lesson Practice

Evaluate each expression for the given values of the variables.

a. (Ex 1) $ax[-a(a - x)]$ for $a = 2$ and $x = -1$ 12

b. (Ex 1) $-b[-b(b - c) - (c - b)]$ for $b = -2$ and $c = 0$ -12

c. (Ex 2) $(5y)(2z)4xy$ for $x = 3$, $y = -1$, and $z = \frac{1}{2}$ 60

d. (Ex 2) $\frac{4rs}{6st}$ for $r = -1$, $s = -3$, and $t = -2$ $\frac{1}{3}$

Simplify each expression. Then evaluate for $a = 2$ and $b = -1$. Justify each step.

e. (Ex 3) $-b(a - 3) + a$

f. $-a(-b - a) - b$

Evaluate each expression for the given values of the variable.

g. (Ex 4) If $a = -2$ and $b = 25$, what is the value of $\frac{-b(a - 4) + b}{b}$?   7

h. If $x = -4$ and $y = -2$, what is the value of $\frac{x^2 - x|y|}{x^3}$? $-\frac{3}{8}$

i. (Ex 5) A savings account grows according to the formula $P_y = 1.04(P_{y-1})$, where P_y is the principal balance at the end of y years and P_{y-1} is the principal balance after $y - 1$ years. After 6 years, there is a principal balance of $1600.00. How much is the principal balance after 8 years? $1730.56

e. Sample:
$-b(a - 3) + a$,
$-ba + 3b + a$, Distribute;
$-(-1)(2) + 3(-1) + 2$, Substitute; $2 - 3 + 2 = 1$, Simplify.

f. Sample:
$-a(-b - a) - b$,
$ab + a^2 - b$, Distribute;
$2(-1) + (2)^2 - (-1)$, Substitute; $-2 + 4 + 1 = 3$, Simplify.

Lesson Practice

Problem f

Error Alert Students must distribute twice in this problem. Remind them to distribute over both terms in the expressions, not just the first terms.

Problem g

Scaffolding Students should distribute b, add like terms to simplify the expression, and substitute the given values to find the answer. Suggest checking the answer by substituting before simplifying. The result should be the same.

Check for Understanding

The questions below help assess the concepts taught in this lesson.

"Name two methods for evaluating an expression with variables." Sample: You can simplify first and then substitute the numbers, or substitute first and then simplify. The order depends on the expression and the values substituted for the variables.

"Whether simplifying first or evaluating first, what mathematical process is required to solve the problem correctly?" Sample: following the order of operations

Lesson 16   89

INCLUSION

Using grid paper may help students organize their work. Accuracy may also improve by clearly showing each step. Have students write the original problem and place each variable or number in its own cell. Just below the original problem, have them make the needed substitutions, keeping the values aligned with the variables in the respective unit square above them.

Students should then simplify the problem keeping the work aligned vertically. For example evaluate $-x(y + x)$ for $x = -2$ and $y = 3$.

$-x$	$(y$	$+$	$x)$
$-(-2)$	$(3$	$+$	$(-2))$
2		(1)	
	2		

The answer is 2.

Lesson 16   89

Practice Distributed and Integrated

Simplify.

1. $2 + 5 - 3 + 7 - (-3) + 5$ 19
(10)

2. $3(7) + 5 - 3 + 7 - 9 \div 2$ 25.5
(4)

3. Represent the following numbers as being members of set K: $-2, -1, -4, -1, -3,$
(1) $-1, -5, -3$. $K = \{-5, -4, -3, -2, -1\}$

Determine if each statement is true or false. If true, explain why. If false, give a counterexample.

4. The set of whole numbers is closed under multiplication.   true; The product of any
(1) two whole numbers is contained within the set of whole numbers.

5. All integers are whole numbers.   false; Sample: -7 is an integer, but it is not a
(1) whole number.

Simplify by using the Distributive Property.

6. $-4y(d + cx)$ $-4yd - 4ycx$
(15)

7. $(a + bc)2x$ $2xa + 2xbc$
(15)

Evaluate the expression for the given values.

*8. $pa[-a(-a)]$ when $p = 2$ and $a = -1$ -2
(16)

*9. $x(x - y)$ when $x = \frac{1}{5}$ and $y = \frac{6}{5}$ $-\frac{1}{5}$
(16)

*10. $\left(\frac{x-3}{y}\right)^2$ when $x = -5$ and $y = 2$ 16
(16)

11. $4(b + 1)^2 - 6(c - b)^4$ when $b = 2$ and $c = 7$ -3714
(9)

12. $20x + 4$; Sample: Since a square has four equal sides, $4(5x + 1) = 4(5x) + 4(1) = 20x + 4$ would be used to find the perimeter.

12. **Geometry** The measure of one side of a square is $5x + 1$ meters. What expression
(15) would be used for the perimeter of the square? Explain.

13. Identify the property illustrated in the equation $2 + (1 + 7) = (2 + 1) + 7$.
(12) Associative Property of Addition

*14. **Multiple Choice** A fish tank empties at a rate of $v = 195 - 0.5t$, where v is the
(16) number of liters remaining after t seconds have passed. If the fish tank empties for 20 seconds, how many liters remain?   **B**

A 205 **B** 185

C 175 **D** 174.5

*15. **Multi-Step** A solid, plastic machine part is shaped like a cone that is 8 centimeters
(16) high and has a radius of 2 centimeters. A machinist has removed some of the plastic by drilling a cylindrical hole into the part's base. The hole is 4 centimeters deep and has a diameter of 1 centimeter.

a. Determine the volume of the cone. Use the formula $V = \frac{1}{3}\pi r^2 h$.   33.49 cm³

b. Determine the volume of the cylindrical hole. Use the formula $V = \pi r^2 h$.   3.14 cm³

c. Determine the volume of the plastic machine part by subtracting the volume of the cylindrical hole from the volume of the cone.   30.35 cm³

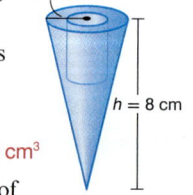

90   *Saxon Algebra 1*

*16. (Chemistry) Boyle's law relates the pressure and volume of a gas held at a constant
(16) temperature. This relationship is represented by the equation $P_f = \frac{P_i V_i}{V_f}$. In this
equation, P_i and V_i represent the gas's initial pressure and volume. P_f and V_f
represent the gas's final pressure and volume. What is the final pressure of the
gas if a 3-liter volume of gas at a pressure of 1 atmosphere is expanded to a final
volume of 6 liters?   0.5 atmosphere

*17. (Investing) Jamie wants to determine how much she should invest in a stock. She uses
(16) the equation for present value, $V_p = \frac{V_f}{(1+i)^t}$, in which V_f is the future value, i is the
interest rate, and t is the number of years. How much should her present value be
if she wants the future value of the stock to be $2000 in 10 years at an interest rate
of 0.02? Round the answer to the nearest dollar. $1641

*18. **Multiple Choice** Given the information in the table, which
(16) equation best relates x and y?   **C**

A $y = x^3 + 5$

B $y = \frac{x^2 + 5}{x}$

C $y = |x^3 + 5|$

D $y = \frac{x^3 + 5}{x}$

x	y
2	13
1	6
−1	4
−2	3

*19. **Measurement** A party planner use the equation $A = Nx^2$ to estimate how much cake
(16) is needed for a party with N guests, where x is the width of a square piece of cake.
If each piece of cake will be about 3 inches wide, approximate the area of the base
of a cake pan for the given number of guests.
a. 50 guests   450 in²
b. 150 guests   1350 in²
c. 350 guests   3150 in²

*20. **Multi-Step** Two teams of students were riding bikes for charity. There were a total
(15) of b students on the blue team and they each rode 15 miles. There were a total of
r students on the red team and they each rode 3 miles. The students collected $2
for each mile.
a. Write an expression for the total number of miles ridden by both teams. $15b + 3r$
b. Write and simplify an expression that uses the Distributive Property to show the
total amount of money collected. $2(15b + 3r) = 30b + 6r$

21. **Error Analysis** A bucket contains 10 balls numbered 1, 1, 2, 3, 4, 4, 5, 6, and 6. A
(14) single ball is randomly chosen from the bucket. What is the probability of drawing
a ball with a number greater than or equal to 5? Which student is correct? Explain
the error.   Student A; Sample: Student B only considered numbers greater than 5.

Student A

$P(5 \text{ or } 6) = \frac{3}{10}$

Student B

$P(5 \text{ or } 6) = \frac{2}{10}$ or $\frac{1}{5}$

22. **Estimate** $\sqrt{36} + \sqrt{40}$ ◯ $\sqrt{25} + \sqrt{80}$. Verify the answer.
(13)

22. <; Sample:
$\sqrt{36} + \sqrt{40}$ ◯ $\sqrt{25} + \sqrt{80}$
$6 + 6$ ◯ $5 + 9$
12 ◯ 14
$12 < 14$

Problem 16
Guide students by asking the following questions.

"What is the value of P_i?"
1 atmosphere

"What is the value of V_i?" 3 liters

"What is the value of V_f?" 6 liters

Problem 17
Extend the Problem
Suppose Jamie wants the future value of the stock to be $2000 in 5 fewer years, how much should the present value be? $1811.46

Problem 18
A strategy for solving this problem would be to choose one pair of x- and y-values. Find the choice that the pair satisfies. Then check all other pairs in that choice.

Problem 22
Guide the students by asking them the following questions.

"What is the square root of 36?" 6

"The square root of 40 is close to the square root of what number?" 36

"What is the square root of 25?" 5

"The square root of 80 is very close to the square root of what number?" 81

Lesson 16   91

CHALLENGE

Square roots and cubic roots can also be expressed as fractional exponents. For example,

$\sqrt{x} = x^{\frac{1}{2}}$ and $\sqrt[3]{x} = x^{\frac{1}{3}}$

Evaluate the following expression for the given values of the variables:

$[(x^{\frac{1}{2}} + y)z]^{\frac{1}{3}}$ for $x = 9, y = 2, z = 25$ 5

Problem 23
Error Alert
In problems that use different units, remind students to make sure that the appropriate conversions are used to solve the problem.

Problem 30
Error Alert
Students may use the total number of outcomes as only those sent to Zippy Lanes. Point out that a total of 500 balls were manufactured in one day.

23. **Multi-Step** John is using square ceramic floor tiles that are each 18 inches long. How many of these tiles will John need to cover a floor with an area of 81 square feet?   36 tiles

24. **Oceanography** *Alvin* (DSV-2), a 16-ton manned research submersible, is used to observe life forms at depths of up to 8000 feet below sea level. After the hull was replaced, *Alvin* was able to dive about 2.6 times the distance as before the hull replacement. About how far was it able to travel after the hull was replaced?   ≈ −20,800 feet

25. **Analyze** What is the sign of the sum of −8 + 7? Explain how the sign is determined.   Sample: The sign of the sum is negative because the number with the greater absolute value is negative.

26. **Write** Why would you want to convert measures from one unit to another when working with a recipe found in a French cookbook?   Sample: France uses metric measures in their recipes, but the United States uses customary measures.

27. **Justify** Evaluate $10(8-6)^3 + 4(|-5 + (-2)| + 2)$. Justify each step.

28. **Error Analysis** Two students wanted to find out the change in temperature in Calgary, Canada. It was −1°C in the morning and was −20°C by nighttime. Which student is correct? Explain the error.

Student A	Student B
−20 − 1	−20 − (−1)
−20 + (−1)	−20 + 1
−21	−19

29. **Construction** A father builds a playhouse in the shape of a rectangular prism with a triangular prism on top, as shown in the figure. The volume of the rectangular prism is $(10 \cdot 5.8 \cdot 8)$ ft³, and the volume of the triangular prism is $[\frac{1}{2} \cdot (10 \cdot 5.8)] \cdot 4$ ft³. What is the volume of the whole structure?   580 ft³

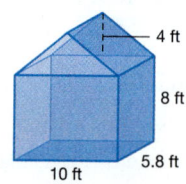

30. **Manufacturing** A manufacturing company produced 500 bowling balls in one day. Of those, 10 were found to be defective. The manufacturer sent a shipment of 250 balls to Zippy Lanes.
    a. What is the experimental probability that a bowling ball with have a defect?
    b. Predict the number of balls in the shipment to Zippy Lanes that will have a defect.   5 balls

27. $10 \cdot 2^3 + 4(7 + 2)$ Simplify grouping symbols.
    $= 10 \cdot 2^3 + 4 \cdot 9$ Simplify inside parentheses.
    $= 10 \cdot 8 + 4 \cdot 9$ Simplify exponents.
    $= 80 + 36$ Multiply.
    $= 116$ Add.

28. Student B; Sample: Student A added the two temperatures instead of subtracting to find the change.

92   *Saxon Algebra 1*

LOOKING FORWARD

Simplifying and evaluating variable expressions prepares students for

- **Lesson 17** Translating Between Words and Algebraic Expressions
- **Lesson 37** Using Scientific Notation
- **Lesson 40** Simplifying and Evaluating Expressions Using the Power Property for Exponents
- **Lesson 46** Simplifying Expressions with Square Roots and Higher Order Roots

LESSON 17

Translating Between Words and Algebraic Expressions

Warm Up

1. **Vocabulary** An expression that has only numbers and operations is a _____ (*numeric, variable*) expression.   numeric

Simplify each expression.

2. $5 - 7 + 5 - (-3)$ 6
3. $(5 + 7)4 + 7(5 - 3)$ 62
4. $(x^3 + m^5)x^2m^2$ $x^5m^2 + x^2m^7$
5. Which value is equivalent to $-(-6)^3$?   B
   A -216 B 216 C 18 D -18

New Concepts

Algebraic expressions, or variable expressions, are expressions that contain at least one variable. A numeric expression contains only numbers and operations.

Translating Word and Phrases into Algebraic Expressions

Words	Phrases	Expressions
Addition sum, total, more than, added, increased, plus	4 added to a number 7 increased by a number	$x + 4$ $7 + x$
Subtraction less, minus, decreased by, difference, less than	the difference of 5 and a number 8 less than a number	$5 - x$ $x - 8$
Multiplication product, times, multiplied	the product of a number and 12 a number times 3	$12(x)$ $3x$
Division quotient, divided by, divided into	the quotient of a number and 6 10 divided by a number	$x \div 6$ $\frac{10}{x}$

Hint

Remember that in multiplication, the coefficient is usually written before the variable.

Hint

"Years younger than" means less than.

Online Connection
www.SaxonMathResources.com

Example 1   Translating Words into Algebraic Expressions

Write an algebraic expression for each phrase.

a. y increased by 12

SOLUTION $y + 12$

b. the product of x and 4

SOLUTION $4x$

c. 8 less than the quotient of m and 15

SOLUTION $\frac{m}{15} - 8$

d. James is 6 years younger than Lydia, who is x years old. Write the expression that shows James's age.

SOLUTION If x represents Lydia's age, then $x - 6$ represents James's age.

Lesson 17   93

MATH BACKGROUND

Being able to translate between words, phrases, and algebraic expressions is the cornerstone of applying formulas and solving word problems. Students will be required to recognize several standard phrases (added to, minus) as well as some uncommon phrases (quadrupled, decreased by) and to understand their implications. The real challenge is in understanding the nuances of the English language. Care must be taken when writing expressions to be translated by students. Some phrases, such as 3 times a number subtracted from 8, can be confusing. Two interpretations are possible. In one case, subtraction is the second operation mentioned but the first to be written in the corresponding expression $8 - 3x$. In the other case, the same holds true; however, the product can be interpreted as $3(8 - x)$.

---

1   Warm Up

Problem 5

Remind students to follow the order of operations.

2   New Concepts

In this lesson, students will learn to equate words and phrases with operations.

Example 1

Determine how the variables and numbers are affected by operations.

Additional Example 1

Write each phrase as an algebraic expression.

a. x decreased by 7 $x - 7$

b. the product of 12 and n $12n$

c. 3 less than the quotient of z and 24 $\frac{z}{24} - 3$

d. Sylvia is 4 years younger than Omar, who is y years old. Write the expression that will show Sylvia's age. $y - 4$

Extend the Example

In part d, Maria is twice James' age. Write an expression to show Maria's age. $2(x - 6)$

LESSON RESOURCES

Student Edition Practice Workbook 17
Reteaching Master 17
Adaptations Master 17
Challenge and Enrichment Master C17, E17

Example 2
Error Alert When translating algebraic expressions, students may forget that subtraction is not commutative. For problems involving subtraction, have students determine which number is the minuend.

Additional Example 2
Use words to write each algebraic expression in two different ways.

a. $b + 12$ 12 more than b; the sum of 12 and b

b. $p - 7$ 7 less than p; the difference of p and 7

c. $21 \cdot x$ the product of 21 and x; 21 times x

d. $y \div 8$ y divided by 8; the quotient of y and 8

e. $10 - \frac{1}{2}(14)$ the difference of 10 and one-half of 14; 10 minus 14 divided by 2

Example 3
Additional Example 3
Jayne has saved x dollars. Write an algebraic expression to represent the total amount of money she will have saved if she saves $75 per week for y number of weeks. $x + 75y$

Lesson Practice
Problem a
Scaffolding Before writing the expression, have students identify the operation to be used.

Problem c
Error Alert Some students may identify only one operation for the expression. Remind them that more than describes addition and times describes multiplication.

Caution
"Less than" phrases are written in the reverse order of the given form.
two less than x: $x - 2$

Math Reasoning
Generalize Using the operations multiplication and division, explain the relationship between a number and its reciprocal.
Sample: Multiplying by a number is the same as dividing by its reciprocal, and vice versa.

Example 2 Translating Algebraic Expressions into Words
Use words to write each algebraic expression in two different ways.

a. $m + 7$
SOLUTION
7 more than m;
the sum of 7 and m

b. $y - 9$
SOLUTION
9 less than y;
the difference of y and 9

c. $5 \cdot n$
SOLUTION
the product of 5 and n;
5 times n

d. $x \div 3$
SOLUTION
x divided by 3;
the quotient of x and 3

e. $27 - \frac{1}{2}(18)$
SOLUTION
the difference of 27 and one-half of 18;
27 minus 18 divided by 2

Example 3 Application: Savings
Jayne is saving money to buy a car. She has x dollars saved and is saving y dollars per week. Write an algebraic expression to represent the total amount of money she will have saved after 52 weeks.

SOLUTION

dollars saved	dollars saved each week	amount saved after 52 weeks
x	y	$x + 52y$

Jayne will have $x + 52y$ dollars saved after 52 weeks.

Lesson Practice
Write each phrase as an algebraic expression.
(Ex 1)
a. the product of x and 8 $8x$
b. 18 minus y $18 - y$
c. 7 more than 5 times x $5x + 7$
d. Raquel is 2 years older than Monica, who is x years old. Write the expression that shows Raquel's age. $x + 2$

Use words to write each algebraic expression in two different ways.
(Ex 2)
e.   Sample: 10 divided by s; the quotient of 10 and s
f. $5 - r$ Sample: r less than 5; the difference of 5 and r
g. $3m + 7$ Sample: 7 more than 3 times m; the sum of 3 times m and 7

ENGLISH LEARNERS

The word **reverse** means opposite.

Say:
"The car was going forward, but now the car is going in the reverse direction."

Ask:
"What direction is the car going?" backward

Ask:
"What is the reverse order of the set of letters A, B, C, and D?" D, C, B, and A

Say:
"Some objects cannot be reversed, like right and left shoes. Name something that is not reversible." Sample: gloves

h. $\frac{3}{4}x + 9$ Sample: three-fourths x plus 9; the sum of three-fourths of x and 9

i. $\frac{x-3}{2}$ Sample: the quotient of three less than x and 2; the difference of x and 3 divided by 2

j. **(Savings)** Jon has d dollars in a savings account. He withdraws x dollars each week for 15 weeks. Write an algebraic expression to represent the amount of money that will be left in the savings account at the end of the 15 weeks. $d - 15x$

Practice   Distributed and Integrated

Expand each algebraic expression by using the Distributive Property.

1. $(4 + 2y)x$ $4x + 2xy$
(15)

2. $-2(x - 4y)$ $-2x + 8y$
(15)

3. **Write** What is a term of an algebraic expression?   Sample: a part of an expression that is added to or subtracted from the other parts
(2)

4. Given the sets $A = \{-3, -2, -1\}$, $B = \{1, 2, 3\}$, and $C = \{-1, 1, -2, 2, -3, 3\}$,
(1) are the following statements true or false?
   a. $A \cap C = \{-3, -2, -1\}$ true
   b. $A \cap B = \{-3, -2, -1, 1, 2, 3\}$ false
   c. $B \cup C = \{-3, -2, -1, 1, 2, 3\}$ true
   d. $A \cup B = \{-3, -2, -1\}$ false

Write the algebraic expressions for each statement.

*5. three times the sum of the opposite of a number and -7 $3(-x + (-7))$
(17)

*6. 0.18 of what number is 4.68? $0.18x = 4.68$
(17)

7. Add $4.7 + (-9.2) - 1.9$. -6.4
(10)

8. Compare $\sqrt{36} + \sqrt{121}$ ⊖ $\sqrt{100} + \sqrt{49}$ using <, >, or =.
(13)

9. Between which two whole numbers is $\sqrt{15}$?   3 and 4
(13)

10. **Justify** True or False: $k = 0 \cdot k$, where k is any real number except for zero. Justify your
(12) answer using the properties.   false; Identity Property of Multiplication states that $k \cdot 1 = k$.

11. Evaluate $(a + 4)^3 + 5x^2$ when $a = -3$ and $x = -1$.   6
(16)

*12. **Justify** True or False: $yx^2m^3 = -4$ when $x = -1$, $y = 2$, and $m = -2$. Justify your
(16) answer.   false; $yx^2m^3 = (2)(-1)^2(-2)^3 = (2)(1)(-8) = -16$

*13. Translate $3(x + 6)$ into word form.   Sample: three times the sum of a number and 6
(17)

*14. **Multiple Choice** Which expression is the algebraic translation of "4 times the sum of
(17) 9 and g"?   **B**
   A $4 + 9g$ **B** $4(9 + g)$ **C** $4 \cdot 9g$ **D** $(4 + 9)g$

Lesson 17   95

 **INCLUSION**

Materials: 3 × 5 note cards; paper

When translating word phrases to algebraic expressions, students might benefit from writing each important word on a note card. Ask them to arrange the words on the note cards in the same order as the original phrase.

Example: $\boxed{-3}$ $\boxed{\text{less}}$ $\boxed{\text{than}}$ $\boxed{5}$ $\boxed{\text{times}}$ $\boxed{\text{a number}}$

Ask students to group the cards that show "5 times a number." Ask, **"What operation is shown by the word *times*?"** Sample: multiplication

Have students write that as the term, $5x$. Now have students examine the phrase "-3 less than." Ask, **"Is $5x$ being subtracted from -3, or is -3 being subtracted from $5x$?"** Guide students to understand that -3 less than shows that -3 is being subtracted from $5x$. Students should complete the expression as $5x - (-3)$, or $5x + 3$.

Lesson 17   95

Problem 16

Encourage students to first find the amount of money that Miles had left after spending $7. $m - 7$ Then double that amount.

Problem 18

Guide the students by asking the following questions.

"Which step did Student A and Student B perform first?" Each substituted the given values into the expression.

"Which student made an error in the second step?" Student B

"What error was made?" Sample: The student raised -2 to an even power and the result was a negative number, -4. It should have been positive 4.

---

*15. (Age) Mary is one year younger than twice Paul's age. Write an expression for Mary's age. $2p - 1$

*16. (Finance) Miles spent $7 and then received a paycheck that doubled the money he had left. Write an expression to represent how much money he has now. $2(m-7)$

*17. **Multi-Step** A produce stand sells apples and bananas. Apples cost $0.20 each and bananas cost $0.10 each.
   a. Choose variables to represent apples and bananas.
   b. Write an expression to represent the total pieces of fruit. $a + b$
   c. Write an expression to represent how much the fruit costs in dollars. $0.2a + 0.1b$

17a. Sample: a is the number of apples and b is the number of bananas.

18. **Error Analysis** Students are asked to evaluate $\frac{x^2 - 4x}{xy}$ when $x = -2$ and $y = 3$. Which student is correct? Explain the error. Student A; Student B should have found that $(-2)^2 = 4$.

Student A	Student B
$\frac{x^2 - 4x}{xy}$	$\frac{x^2 - 4x}{xy}$
$\frac{(-2)^2 - 4(-2)}{(-2)(3)}$	$\frac{(-2)^2 - 4(-2)}{(-2)(3)}$
$= \frac{4 + 8}{-6}$	$= \frac{-4 - (-8)}{-6}$
$= \frac{12}{-6} = -2$	$= \frac{4}{-6}$
	$= \frac{-2}{3}$

*19. **Geometry** The figure below has corners that are square and a curved section that is a half circle. The dimensions given are in meters. What is the area of the figure? Use 3.14 for π. 297 m²

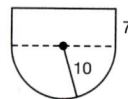

*20. **Multi-Step** A painter estimates that one gallon of a certain kind of paint will cover 305 square feet of wall. How many gallons of the paint will cover the wall described by the diagram below? (Dimensions given are in feet.) 2 gallons

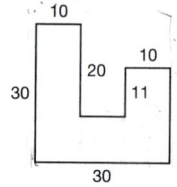

CHALLENGE

Demonstrate how to use the phrase "the quantity. ..." to translate an expression in parentheses. For example, $18 - (4 + x)$ translates "eighteen minus the quantity four plus x."

Challenge students to translate the following phrases:

"the product of five and the quantity two less than a number" $5(n - 2)$

"the difference of seven and the quantity three times a number plus two" $7 - (3x + 2)$

*21. **Error Analysis** Two students simplified an algebraic expression. Which student is correct? Explain the error.   Student B; Student A multiplied the exponents of the like variables instead of adding.

Student A	Student B
$2r^3t(r^5t^2 + 4r^3t^3)$ $= 2r^{15}t^2 + 8r^9t^3$	$2r^3t(r^5t^2 + 4r^3t^3)$ $= 2r^8t^3 + 8r^6t^4$

22. **Probability** There are 400 students in the cafeteria. Of these students, 120 are tenth-graders. What is the probability of randomly selecting a tenth-grader? Express the answer as a percent.   30%

23. **Error Analysis** Two students simplify the expression $-7 - x + 7$. Which student is correct? Explain the error.

Student A	Student B
$-7 - x + 7$ $= x + (-7) + 7$ $= x + (-7 + 7)$ $= x + 0$ $= x$	$-7 - x + 7$ $= -7 + 7 - x$ $= (-7 + 7) - x$ $= 0 - x$ $= -x$

23. Student B; Sample: Student A did not move the negative sign with the variable when the Commutative Property was used.

24. **Justify** Simplify $-\frac{2}{3} \div \left(-\frac{8}{9}\right)$. Show your steps.

25. **Write** Must the algebraic expression $x + 7y$ have only one value? Explain.

26. **Measurement** Madison used a scale and measured her weight at 85 pounds. How many kilograms does Madison weigh? (Hint: 1 kilogram = 2.2 pounds.)   38.64 kg

27. **Energy Conservation** Wind turbines take the energy from the wind and convert it to electrical energy. Use the formula $P = ad^2v^3 \frac{\pi}{4} e$ to find the amount of available energy in the air. Describe the steps you would take to simplify the formula.

28. **Finance** Tonia deposited a total of $174.52 into her checking account. She also withdrew a total of $186.15. Use addition to find the net change in Tonia's checking account.   −$11.63

29. **Justify** What is the first step in simplifying the expression $2 \cdot 4 + 5^2 + (23 - 2)^2$?   Subtract 2 from 23.

30. **Payroll Accounting** Employees at Wilkinson Glass Company earn x number of dollars per hour. Executives make y number of dollars per hour. Each employee and executive works 40 hours per week. Write and simplify an algebraic expression that uses the Distributive Property to show a weekly payroll for one employee and one executive. $40(x + y) = 40x + 40y$

25. no; Sample: The variables x and y can have many different values, so the expression does not have to represent just one value.

27. Sample: Simplify the fraction, raise base numbers to their exponents, and multiply.

24. $\left(\frac{3}{4}\right)$; Sample: $-\frac{2}{3} \div \left(-\frac{8}{9}\right) = -\frac{2}{3} \cdot \left(-\frac{9}{8}\right) = \frac{18}{24} = \frac{3}{4}$

Lesson 17   97

Problem 22
Extend the Problem
"Suppose there were 95 ninth-graders in the cafeteria. What is the probability of randomly selecting a ninth-grader? Express your answer as a percent."   23.75%

Problem 25
Error Alert
Watch for students who assume there is one value for x and one value for y. Point out that since values are not given in this problem, either variable could be any number. Demonstrate that the expression can have more than one value. For example, evaluate the expression for $x = 2$ and $y = -3$, and then for $x = -5$ and $y = 4$. Use different combinations of the values as well.

Problem 28
"How can you tell whether the net change in Tonia's account will be positive or negative before you begin to solve the problem?" The absolute value of the withdrawal is greater than the absolute value of the deposit, so the net change will be negative.

LOOKING FORWARD

Translating between words and algebraic expressions prepares students for

- **Lesson 26** Solving Multi-Step Equations
- **Lesson 42** Solving Percent Problems
- **Lesson 45** Translating Between Words and Inequalities
- **Lesson 56** Identifying, Writing, and Graphing Direct Variation

LESSON 18

1 Warm Up

Problem 3
Briefly review the product rule of exponents.

2 New Concepts

In this lesson, students will learn to identify and combine like terms within a variable expression.

Throughout the lesson, use the terms algebraic expression and variable expression to describe an expression with at least one variable.

Example 1

Review the Distributive Property and the Associative Property of Addition to prepare students to follow the examples. You may ask students to underline like terms before simplifying.

Additional Example 1
Simplify each expression.

a. $4y + 9y$ $13y$

b. $-3n - (-10n) + 8n$ $15n$

c. $12xy - 4a + 2yx$ $14xy - 4a$

LESSON RESOURCES

Student Edition Practice Workbook 18
Reteaching Master 18
Adaptations Master 18
Challenge and Enrichment Master C18

LESSON 18 Combining Like Terms

Warm Up

1. **Vocabulary** A _____ (constant, variable) is a symbol, usually a letter used to represent an unknown number. **variable**

Simplify each expression.

2. $(0.2)^5$ **0.00032**

3. $y^3 \cdot x^4 \cdot y^2 \cdot x^5 \cdot y$ **$x^9 y^6$**

4. Write the phrase "six more than twice a number" as an algebraic expression. **$2x + 6$**

New Concepts

Two or more terms that have the same variable or variables raised to the same power are **like terms.** Terms with different variables or terms with the same variable or variables raised to a different power are **unlike terms.**

$$\boxed{3x^4} + 5y^4 + \boxed{5x^4}$$

Because the variable x has the same power, $3x^4$ and $5x^4$ are like terms. Because the variables are not the same, $5y^4$ and $5x^4$ are unlike terms. The coefficient is not used to establish whether the terms are like or unlike.

Hint
It may be helpful to circle, box, or underline the terms that are alike before combining like terms.

Example 1 Combining Like Terms Without Exponents

Simplify each expression.

a. $5x + 7x$

SOLUTION

$5x + 7x$
$= (5 + 7)x$ Use the Distributive Property.
$= 12x$ Simplify.

b. $-4y - (-3y) + 5y$

SOLUTION

$-4y - (-3y) + 5y$
$= (-4 + 3 + 5)y$ Take the opposite of -3, and then use the Distributive Property.
$= 4y$ Simplify.

c. $6xy - 3a + 4yx$

SOLUTION

$6xy - 3a + 4yx$
$= 6xy + 4yx - 3a$ Rearrange the terms.
$= 6xy + 4xy - 3a$ Rearrange the factors.
$= 10xy - 3a$ Add the like terms.

Math Reasoning

Justify Why can the order of the factors in a term be rearranged?

Commutative Property of Multiplication; $4 \cdot x \cdot y = 4 \cdot y \cdot x$

MATH BACKGROUND

Expressions can be grouped into like terms by using the Associative and Commutative Properties of Addition. Once like terms have been grouped, then the reverse of the Distributive property can be applied to the group. Since like terms are being multiplied by a common factor, the factor can be divided out or "undistributed." Essentially, the distribution of a factor can be "undone" by dividing out a common factor.

ENGLISH LEARNERS

Combine means to join or bring together in unity. Say,

"We can combine the color blue and the color yellow to form the color green."

Combining objects can be similar to combining like terms. Say,

"Craig has 5 pens, 3 books, and 2 markers. Liza has 4 books and 1 marker. If the supplies are combined, how many of each type of supply do they have altogether?" 5 pens, 7 books, and 3 markers

Example 2 Combining Like Terms With Exponents

Simplify each expression.

a. $x^5 + y^3 + x^5 + y^3$

SOLUTION

$x^5 + y^3 + x^5 + y^3$
$= x^5 + x^5 + y^3 + y^3$ Rearrange the terms.
$= (1 + 1)x^5 + (1 + 1)y^3$ Use the Distributive Property.
$= 2x^5 + 2y^3$ Simplify.

b. $3k^2 - 2k^2 + 4k^2 + 2kx^4 + kx^4$

SOLUTION

$3k^2 - 2k^2 + 4k^2 + 2kx^4 + kx^4$
$= (3 - 2 + 4)k^2 + (2 + 1)kx^4$ Use the Distributive Property.
$= 5k^2 + 3kx^4$ Simplify.

c. $2x^2y^3 + xy - 8y^3x^2 - 5yx$

SOLUTION

$2x^2y^3 + xy - 8y^3x^2 - 5yx$
$= 2x^2y^3 - 8y^3x^2 + xy - 5xy$ Rearrange the terms.
$= 2x^2y^3 - 8x^2y^3 + xy - 5xy$ Rearrange the factors.
$= (2 - 8)x^2y^3 + (1 - 5)xy$ Use the Distributive Property.
$= -6x^2y^3 - 4xy$ Simplify.

Hint
The coefficient of x is 1.
The coefficient of $-x$ is -1.

Reading Math
It is customary to write the factors of a term in alphabetical order. So, x^2zy^3 is written x^2y^3z.

Example 3 Application: Measurement

Olympic competition offers three equestrian disciplines: dressage, show jumping, and endurance. The diagram represents the measurements for a regulation dressage arena.

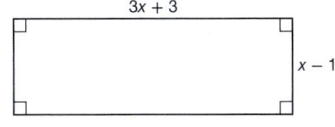

Find the perimeter of the arena as a simplified variable expression. Then evaluate the expression for $x = 19.5$ meters.

SOLUTION

$P = 2l + 2w$ Write the formula for the perimeter of a rectangle.
$P = 2(3x + 3) + 2(x - 1)$ Substitute for l and w.
$P = 6x + 6 + 2x - 2$ Use the Distributive Property.
$P = 8x + 4$ Combine like terms.
$P = 8(19.5) + 4$ Substitute 19.5 for x.
$P = 156 + 4 = 160$ Multiply. Then add.

The perimeter of the dressage arena is $8x + 4$ or 160 meters.

Online Connection
www.SaxonMathResources.com

Lesson 18   99

ALTERNATE METHOD FOR EXAMPLE 2

Have students write the like terms vertically. Visually, the like terms may stand out more clearly. For example, simplify $xy + 4x^2y - 3xy - 7x^2y$.

Write the like terms vertically.

$\begin{array}{r}xy\\-3xy\\\hline\end{array}$ and $\begin{array}{r}4x^2y\\-7x^2y\\\hline\end{array}$

Students can then add the like terms and combine them into one expression.

$\begin{array}{r}xy\\-3xy\\\hline -2xy\end{array}$ and $\begin{array}{r}4x^2y\\-7x^2y\\\hline (-3x^2y)\end{array}$ $-2xy - 3x^2y$

Example 2
Point out to students that since this example does not use multiplication, they should not add exponents.

Additional Example 2
Simplify each expression.

a. $x^3 + z^2 + x^3 + z^2$ $2x^3 + 2z^2$

b. $5n^3 + 2n^3 + 4nx^2 + nx^2$
$7n^3 + 5nx^2$

c. $2xy + 4x^2z + 3xy - 5x^2z$
$5xy - x^2z$

Error Alert Students may not consider terms that have implied coefficients. Suggest that students write the number one on these terms before simplifying.

Example 3
Throughout the study of Algebra, students will often apply geometric formulas to solve problems and in doing so will combine like terms.

Extend the Example
Have students find the length and width of the arena.
$l = 61.5$, $w = 18.5$

Additional Example 3
The Olympics uses a standard size pool for swimming competitions. Find the perimeter of an Olympic-size swimming pool if $l = 10x$, $w = 5x$, and $x = 5$ meters. 150 meters

TEACHER TIP
Have students who have difficulty identifying like terms underline terms with variables that are alike. They can circle or box other like terms and then simplify the expression.

Lesson 18   99

Lesson Practice

Problem c

Scaffolding Before students simplify this expression, have them identify the like terms within the expression.

Problem e

Error Alert Some students may not identify x^2y and yx^2 as like terms. Review the Commutative Property of Multiplication with these students.

Check for Understanding

The questions below help assess the concepts taught in this lesson.

"**How can you identify like terms?**" The variables should be the same or the variable(s) should form the same product

"**How are coefficients included in the process of collecting like terms?**" Sample: Coefficients are not used to identify like terms, but are added or subtracted when like terms are combined.

3 Practice

Math Conversations

Discussion to strengthen understanding

Problem 1

Guide the students by asking them the following questions.

"**What is '5 times a number' translated into an algebraic expression?**" $5x$

"**Which two terms are being added?**" $5x$ and -8

Lesson Practice

Simplify each expression.

a. (Ex 1) $-2xy - 3x + 4 - 4xy - 2x$ $-6xy - 5x + 4$
b. (Ex 1) $7m - (-8m) + 9m$ $24m$
c. (Ex 1) $3yac - 2ac + 6acy$ $9acy - 2ac$
d. (Ex 2) $x^4y + 3x^4y + 2x^4y$ $6x^4y$
e. (Ex 2) $x^2y - 3yx + 2yx^2 - 2xy + yx$ $3x^2y - 4xy$
f. (Ex 2) $m^3n + m^3n - x^2y^7 + x^2y^7$ $2m^3n$
g. (Ex 3) A triangular-shaped display case has the dimensions shown on the diagram. Find the perimeter of the display case as a simplified variable expression. Then evaluate the expression for $x = 2$ feet. $2x^2 + x + 2$ feet; 12 feet

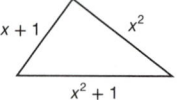

Practice   Distributed and Integrated

1. (17) Write an algebraic expression for this statement: The sum of 5 times a number and -8. $5x + (-8)$

Simplify each expression by adding like terms.

*2. (18) $m + 4 + 3m - 6 - 2m + mc - 4mc$ $2m - 2 - 3cm$

*3. (18) $xy - 3xy^2 + 5y^2x - 4xy$ $-3xy + 2xy^2$

*4. (18) **Multiple Choice** Simplify $2x^2 + 3x$.   **D**
   A $5x^2$
   B $5x^3$
   C $6x^3$
   D cannot be simplified

*5. (18) (**Reading**) Two classes are keeping track of how many pages they can read. In one class, the boys read 15 pages per night and the girls read 12 pages per night. In another class, the boys read 7 pages per night and the girls read 9 pages per night. Each class has x girls and y boys.
   a. Write expressions representing the number of pages each class read per night. $12x + 15y$ and $9x + 7y$
   b. Write an expression for the number they read altogether. $21x + 22y$

6. (5) **Justify** After doing three addition problems that included negative numbers, John found that all three answers were negative. John concluded that any addition problem involving a negative number must have a negative answer. Is John correct? Explain. Give a counterexample if necessary.

6. no; Sample: Many addition problems with negative numbers have positive answers. For example, $-2 + 3 = 1$ or $6 + (-2) = 4$.

7. (6) (**Geography**) The retention pond at Martha's summer home in Florida changed -3 inches every day for 5 days. After 5 days, the water level was -40 inches. What was the original water level 5 days ago? -25 inches

---

 INCLUSION

Have students who struggle combining like terms, write the factors of each term in alphabetical order.

Be sure students understand that the Commutative Property of Multiplication allows you to rearrange to order of the factors of a term without changing the value of the term: $4ab = 4ba$.

See problem c in the Lesson Practice: $3yac - 2ac + 6acy$. Students can write the first term as $3acy$. This should help them identify like terms without difficulty.

Have students rewrite the factors in Lesson Practice e. Encourage them to use this method if they have any doubt about like terms.

8. **Bowling** A ten-pin bowling ball has a volume of about 5274 cm³. A candlepin bowling ball has a volume of about 48 in³. About how much greater is the volume of a ten-pin bowling ball than the volume of a candlepin bowling ball? **about 274 in³ or 4487 cm³ greater**

Simplify.

9. $\dfrac{-16 + 4}{2(\sqrt{13 - 4})}$ **−2**

10. $-7 - (2^4 \div 8)$ **−9**

*11. $6bac - 7ac + 8acb$ **$14abc - 7ac$**

*12. $2x^3y + 4x^3y + 9x^3y$ **$15x^3y$**

13. $|-15 + \sqrt{81}|^2$ **36**

14. $\dfrac{\sqrt{6-2}}{2 \cdot |-7+3|}$ **$\dfrac{1}{4}$**

*15. **Sewing** Susan started with 11 bows. She can tie 4 bows per minute. Analise ties twice as many per minute.
   a. Write expressions representing the number of bows each girl will have after x minutes. **$11 + 4x$; $8x$**
   b. Write an expression for the number they will have altogether after x minutes. **$12x + 11$**

16. **Multi-Step** Marshall, Hank, and Jean are all cousins. Marshall is 3 years older than Hank. Hank is twice the age of Jean.
   a. Write expressions to represent the ages of the cousins. Assign the variable j to represent Jean. **Sample: Marshall = $2j + 3$; Hank = $2j$; Jean = j**
   b. If Jean is 12 years old, how old are the other cousins? **Hank is 24; Marshall is 27.**
   c. If Hank was 14, how old would Jean be? **7**

*17. **Justify** Simplify $8x + x(2x + 5)$ and explain each step.

18. Evaluate $\dfrac{8ak}{4k(2a - 2c + 8)}$ when $a = \dfrac{1}{2}$, $c = 3$, and $k = -2$. **$\dfrac{1}{3}$**

17. $8x + 2x^2 + 5x$, Distributive Property; $2x^2 + 8x + 5x$, Commutative Property of Addition; $2x^2 + 13x$, Add.

*19. True or False: $pm^2 - z^3 = 27$ when $p = -5$, $m = 0$, and $z = -3$. Justify your answer. **true; $pm^2 - z^3 = (-5)0^2 - (-3)^3 = 0 - (-27) = 27$**

20. **Error Analysis** Two students are asked to evaluate $x^2y - |4x|^2z$ when $x = -2$, $y = \dfrac{1}{2}$, and $z = -1$. Which student is correct? Explain the error.

20. Student A; Sample: Student B substituted the wrong values for y and z.

Student A	Student B
$x^2y - |4x|^2 z$	$x^2y - |4x|^2 z$
$(-2)^2\left(\dfrac{1}{2}\right) - |4(-2)|^2(-1)$	$(-2)^2(-1) - |4(-2)|^2\left(\dfrac{1}{2}\right)$
$= 4\left(\dfrac{1}{2}\right) - |-8|^2(-1)$	$= 4(-1) - |-8|^2\left(\dfrac{1}{2}\right)$
$= 2 - (8)^2(-1) = 66$	$= -4 - (8)^2\left(\dfrac{1}{2}\right) = -36$

21. **Predict** How can finding a common denominator tell you that $\dfrac{1}{9} - \dfrac{2}{20}$ will result in a positive number?

21. Finding a common denominator shows you that the first fraction is greater than the second fraction, and that a greater positive number minus a lesser positive number results in a positive number.

Lesson 18   101

Problem 15
Extend the Problem
How many bows would both girls have tied altogether after 6 minutes? 15 minutes? **83 bows; 191 bows**

Problem 16
Students may not know how to begin the problem. Use the following question to help guide them.

"If j represents the age of Jean, what is the age of Hank?" **$2j$**

"What is the age of Marshall?"
$h + 3 = 2j + 3$

Extend the Problem
Melissa, another cousin is 8 years younger than Hank. How old is Melissa if Jean is 9 years old? **10 years old**

CHALLENGE

Challenge students to use the reverse of the Distributive Property to divide out constants and variables from $3x^2y - 4xy$. Then have students distribute the factor to check their work. **$xy(3x - 4)$**

Lesson 18   101

Problem 24
Extend the Problem

If two openings, each *y* feet wide, are left for steps in the original railing, what is the length of railing needed? $(2w + 2l) - 2y$

Problem 28

Guide the students by asking them the following questions.

"What is the total area of the office?" $140 + 4 = 144$ ft^2

"What is the formula for area of a square?" $A = s^2$

"How can you find the length of one side if you know the area of a square?" Find the square root of the area.

Problem 29
Error Alert

For students who have difficulty with translating the phrase "the sum of the squares of 8 and *p*," contrast it with the phrase "the square of the sum of 8 and *p*."

---

*22. **Multi-Step** Tamatha picks 10 peaches a minute for *x* minutes. Her grandmother picks 12 peaches a minute for 3 fewer minutes.
(18)
    a. Write an expression to represent the number of minutes the grandmother picks peaches. $x - 3$
    b. Write an expression for the number of peaches they pick together and then simplify. $10x + 12(x - 3); 22x - 36$

23. **Geometry** Translate the Pythagorean Theorem into symbols. In a right triangle, the sum of the squares of the legs of the triangle is equal to the square of the hypotenuse. Let *a* and *b* be the legs of the triangle and *c* be the hypotenuse.
(17)
$a^2 + b^2 = c^2$

24. **Measurement** A railing is being built around a rectangular deck.
(17)

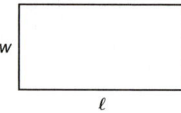

    a. Write an expression to represent the number of feet of railing needed. $2w + 2l$
    b. The width is doubled. The length is tripled. Write an expression to represent the number of feet of railing needed. $4w + 6l$

25. **Multiple Choice** Simplify the expression $7(10 - y)$. Which expression is correct? **B**
(15)
    A $70 - y$ **B** $70 - 7y$
    C $70 - 7 + y$ **D** $70y - 7y$

26. **Justify** Simplify the expression $-m(mn^2 - m^2n)$ and explain your method for simplifying. $-m^2n^2 + m^3n$; Sample: Using the Distributive Property, each term is multiplied by $-m$: $-m(mn^2) -m(-m^2n)$.
(15)

27. **Probability** A number is chosen at random from the numbers 1 through 5. What is the probability that an odd number will be chosen? $\frac{3}{5}$
(14)

28. **Carpentry** A new company buys 140 square feet of carpet to cover the floor in one of its square offices. The carpet is 4 square feet too small. What is the length of the office floor? 12 feet
(13)

29. **Verify** The Commutative Property states that $6 \cdot 4 = 4 \cdot 6$. Show that the Commutative Property does not apply to division. Sample: $24 \div 4 = 6$, $4 \div 24 = \frac{1}{6}$, and $6 \neq \frac{1}{6}$.
(12)

30. **Error Analysis** Two students translate the phrase "the sum of the squares of 8 and *p*" into an algebraic expression. Which student is correct? Explain the error. Student B; Sample: Student A squared the sum instead of finding the sum of the squares.
(17)

Student A	Student B
$(p + 8)^2$	$p^2 + 8^2$

102   *Saxon* Algebra 1

LOOKING FORWARD

Combining like terms prepares students for

- **Lesson 19** Solving One-Step Equations by Adding or Subtracting
- **Lesson 23** Solving Two-Step Equations
- **Lesson 26** Solving Multi-Step Equations
- **Lesson 28** Solving Equations with Variables on Both Sides
- **Lesson 29** Solving Literal Equations
- **Lesson 117** Using Trigonometric Ratios

LESSON 19

Solving One-Step Equations by Adding or Subtracting

Warm Up

1. **Vocabulary** −4 and 4 are _____ because they have the same absolute value but different signs. **opposites**

2. Add $7.5 + (-1.25)$. **6.25**

3. Subtract $12.75 − (−1.05)$. **13.8**

4. Use $<$, $>$, or $=$ to compare $6x + 3$ and $-2x + 4$ when $x = -3$.

4. $6(-3) + 3 = -15$ and $-2(-3) + 4 = 10$, so $6x + 3 < -2x + 4$ when $x = -3$

5. Evaluate $w - (wy - y)$ for $w = -4$ and $y = -1$. **C**
   A 1   B −1   C −9   D 9

New Concepts

An **equation** is a statement that uses an equal sign to show that two quantities are equal. A **solution of an equation in one variable** is a value of the variable that makes the equation true.

Example 1 Identifying Solutions

State whether the value of the variable is a solution of the equation.

a. $x + 6 = 9$ for $x = 3$

SOLUTION

$x + 6 = 9$

$(3) + 6 \stackrel{?}{=} 9$ Substitute 3 for x.

$9 = 9$ ✓

Solution, $3 + 6 = 9$

b. $x − 6 = 9$ for $x = 3$

SOLUTION

$x − 6 = 9$

$(3) − 6 \stackrel{?}{=} 9$ Substitute 3 for x.

$-3 \neq 9$ ✗

Not a solution, $3 − 6 \neq 9$

Math Reasoning

Verify If the same quantity is added to both sides of $x − 7 = 15$, show that the resulting equation is equivalent to $x − 7 = 15$.

Sample: $x − 7 = 15$ is equivalent to $x − 7 + 7 = 15 + 7$ because 22 is the solution to both equations.

An equation is like a balance scale.

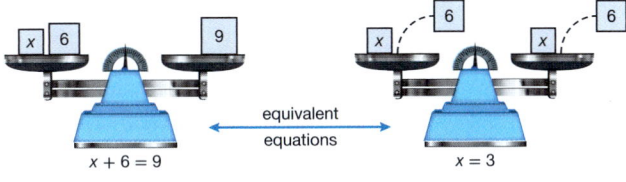

equivalent equations

$x + 6 = 9$ $x = 3$

The scale remains balanced when the same quantity is added to both sides, or when the same quantity is subtracted from both sides.

Equivalent equations have the same solution set. By adding or subtracting the same quantity from both sides of an equation, each equation remains equivalent to the original equation. Furthermore, each side of the equation remains balanced as the equation is solved.

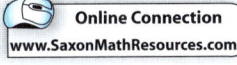
Online Connection
www.SaxonMathResources.com

Lesson 19   103

MATH BACKGROUND

As students begin solving equations, the skill-building aspects of the study of algebra become more apparent. Many skills and concepts that students have previously studied will be applied to finding the solutions of equations. Students who are familiar with these rules and concepts may find solving equations less frustrating than those who are not proficient in these crucial skills.

The rules regarding signed numbers, the properties of equality, and the inverse operations will all be necessary to solve equations with accuracy. Continue to remind students of the skills and concepts that they have already learned.

TEACHER TIP

In part **d** of the Exploration, students will need to remove zero pairs of tiles to solve the equation. Review how making pairs of +1 and −1 tiles form a zero pair that can be removed from one side or both sides without consequence. Students may also think that removing zero pairs from one side of the equation means that they should remove tiles from the other side of the equation. Have them write the value of each pair they remove and instruct them to remove tiles that are equal in value. Students should see that removing zero pairs requires no movement on the other side of the equation.

a.
b.
c.
d.

The Addition and Subtraction Properties of Equality hold for every real number a, b, and c.

Addition and Subtraction Properties of Equality
Addition Property of Equality
You can add the same number to both sides of an equation and the statement will still be true.

Examples $2 = 2$ $a = b$
                $3 + 2 = 2 + 3$ $a + c = b + c$
                $5 = 5$

Subtraction Property of Equality
You can subtract the same number from both sides of an equation and the statement will still be true.

Examples $10 = 10$ $a = b$
                $10 - 4 = 10 - 4$ $a - c = b - c$
                $6 = 6$

On the first page of the lesson the Subtraction Property of Equality is illustrated with balance scales. Below, the Addition Property of Equality is illustrated.

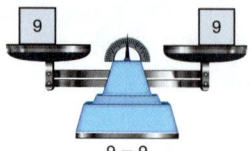
$9 = 9$

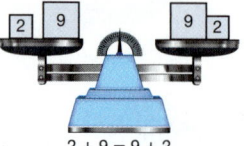
$2 + 9 = 9 + 2$

Inverse operations are operations that undo each other. To solve an equation, isolate the variable on one side of the equal sign by using inverse operations. Use the same inverse operation on each side of the equation.

Inverse Operations

Addition ⟷ Subtraction

Multiplication ⟷ Division

Materials

algebra tiles

Hint

The + and − algebra tiles that are the same shape are opposites and undo each other.

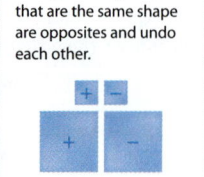

Exploration   Using Algebra Tiles to Model One-Step Equations

Use algebra tiles to model $x + 6 = 9$.

a. Model each side of the equation.

b. Isolate the x-tile. Add six negative 1-tiles to both sides. Remove pairs that equal zero.

c. What is the solution? $x = 3$

d. Use algebra tiles to model $x - 2 = 4$. What is the solution? $x = 6$

104   **Saxon** Algebra 1

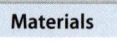 ENGLISH LEARNERS

Explain the meaning of the word **isolate**. Place a stack of books on a table. Lift one book off of the stack and set it to the side of the other books. Say:

"**Isolate means to set apart or cut off from others. By isolating this book from the stack, it has been set to the side of the stack.**"

Use other objects to show the meaning of the word. Have volunteers describe the action using the word isolate.

Example 2 Solving Equations by Adding

Solve. Then check the solution.

a. $x - 3 = 12$

SOLUTION

$x - 3 = 12$
$\underline{+3 = +3}$ Add 3 to both sides to undo the subtraction.
$x = 15$

Check Substitute 15 for x.

$x - 3 \stackrel{?}{=} 12$
$(15) - 3 \stackrel{?}{=} 12$
$12 = 12$ ✓

b. $-15 = n - 8$

SOLUTION

$-15 = n - 8$
$\underline{+8 = +8}$ Add 8 to both sides.
$-7 = n$

Check Substitute -7 for n.

$-15 \stackrel{?}{=} (-7) - 8$
$-15 = -15$ ✓

Example 3 Solve Equations by Subtracting

Solve.

a. $k + 7 = 13$

SOLUTION

$k + 7 = 13$
$\underline{-7 = -7}$ Subtract 7 from both sides.
$k = 6$

b. $-21 = p + 9$

SOLUTION

$-21 = p + 9$
$\underline{-9 = -9}$ Subtract 9 from both sides.
$-30 = p$

Caution

Sometimes the variable is on the right side of the equal sign. Use inverse operations to isolate the variable.

Math Reasoning

Justify Does it matter if you add (−7) to each side or subtract 7 from each side? Explain.

no; Sample: Adding negative seven is the same as subtracting positive seven.

Example 2

Error Alert When the variable is on the right side of the equation as in Example 2b, some students may continue to apply the inverse operation on the left side of the equation. Remind them that it is the variable that must be isolated. Tell students to begin solving on the side of the equation where the variable is located. Otherwise, a sign error will most likely result due to students dropping the transformation that isolates the variable.

Additional Example 2

Solve each equation. Then check the solution.

a. $n + 17 = 20$ $n = 3, 3 + 17 = 20$

b. $10 = y - 3$ $y = 13, 10 = 13 - 3$

Example 3

Have students identify the operation they will use to solve each equation before they begin.

Additional Example 3

Solve.

a. $-5 = x - 7$
$-5 + 7 = x - 7 + 7$
$2 = x$

b. $6 + x = -1$
$6 - 6 + x = -1 - 6$
$x = -7$

MANIPULATIVE USE

Materials: algebra tiles

For Example 2a, have students use algebra tiles to model the equation $x - 3 = 12$. Have them write an equal sign in the middle of a piece of paper. The left side of the paper represents the left side of the equation, and the right side represents the right side of the equation.

Model the left side of the equation with one x-tile and three -1-tiles and the right side with twelve $+1$-tiles. For the inverse operation, place three $+1$-tiles on each side of the equation.

Students can remove the zero pairs on the left side of the equation, then read the solution: $x = 15$.

Have students continue to model Example 2b and 2c. This activity can be carried over to solving equations by subtracting in Example 3 as well.

Example 4
Students will have to rewrite the fractions with a common denominator. Encourage them to do this before subtracting to solve the equation.

Additional Example 4
Solve.

a. $x + \frac{1}{2} = \frac{3}{4}$ $x = \frac{1}{4}$

Example 5
Draw students' attention to the table that accompanies the problem. They will need to get some information from this table to be able to solve the problem.

Extend the Example
Have students find how many degrees the temperature rose if it was 32°F by 8:00 a.m.
24°F; $8 + x = 32$; $x = 24$

Additional Example 5
The temperature in Lubbock, Texas, rose 16°F in one week to 97°F. At what temperature did the week begin? 81°F; $x + 16 = 97$; $x = 81$

Lesson Practice

Problem f
Error Alert Because both a negative sign and a positive sign are involved, some students may get confused as to which operation to use. Help them understand that the goal is to isolate the variable, so they should use the operation that is the inverse of the operation on the same side as the variable.

Problem g
Scaffolding Before subtracting to solve the equation, suggest that students find a common denominator for the fractions and write the problem using the LCD.

Reading Math
Here is another way to show steps leading to the solution:
$$x + \frac{1}{4} - \frac{1}{4} = -\frac{3}{8} - \frac{1}{4}$$
$$x = -\frac{5}{8}$$

Example 4 Solve Fraction Equations by Adding or Subtracting

Solve.
$$x + \frac{1}{4} = -\frac{3}{8}$$

SOLUTION

$$x + \frac{1}{4} = -\frac{3}{8}$$
$$-\frac{1}{4} = -\frac{1}{4}$$ Subtract $\frac{1}{4}$ from both sides.
$$x = -\frac{5}{8}$$

Example 5 Application: Weather

On January 10, 1911, the temperature in Rapid City, South Dakota, fell 47°F in 15 minutes. What was the temperature at 7:00 a.m.?

Temperature in Rapid City, SD	
7:00 a.m.	
7:15 a.m.	8°F

SOLUTION

Let x = the temperature at 7:00 a.m.

Write an equation.

$$x - 47 = 8$$
$$+47 = +47$$ To isolate the variable, add 47 to each side.
$$x = 55$$

At 7:00 a.m. the temperature was 55°F.

Lesson Practice

State whether the value of each variable is a solution of the equation. (Ex 1)

a. $h - 14 = 2$ for $h = 12$ not a solution, $12 - 14 = -2$

b. $-11 = j - 4$ for $j = -7$ solution, $-11 = -7 - 4$

Solve. Then check the solution. (Ex 2)

c. $x - 5 = 17$ $x = 22$, $22 - 5 = 17$; $17 = 17$

d. $-30 = m - 12$ $m = -18$; $-30 = -18 - 12$; $-30 = -30$

Solve.

e. $p + 3 = 37$ $p = 34$ (Ex 3)

f. $-14 = y + 8$ $y = -22$ (Ex 3)

g. $d + 4\frac{1}{2} = 3\frac{1}{6}$. $d = -1\frac{1}{3}$ (Ex 4)

h. Jagdeesh took the same test twice. On the second test he scored 87, which was 13 points higher than on the first test. What was his first test score?   74 (Ex 5)

Hint
Always give fractions in simplest form unless instructed otherwise.

106   Saxon Algebra 1

INCLUSION

Help students see how to sort the information in word problems by asking these questions about Example 5:

"How many degrees did the temperature fall?" 47°F

"How can the change be represented in an algebraic expression?" −47°F

"What was the temperature at 7:15 a.m.?" 8°F

"What variable is used to represent the unknown temperature?" x

"What expression represents the fall in temperature?" $x - 47$

"What temperature is equal to $x - 47$?" 8°F

"What equation is used to solve the problem?" $x - 47 = 8$

"What inverse operation is used to isolate x?" addition

"What number is added to each side of the equation?" 47

"What is the solution?" 55°F

Practice   Distributed and Integrated

1. Simplify $-3x^2ym + 7x - 5ymx^2 + 16x$. $-8mx^2y + 23x$
   (18)

Solve each equation.

*2. $x + 5 = 7$ $x = 2$
(19)

*3. $x + 5 = -8$ $x = -13$
(19)

*4. $x - 6 = 4$ $x = 10$
(19)

5. Write the algebraic expression for the phrase "seven times the sum of a number and -5." $7(x + (-5))$
(17)

6. Expand the expression $-3(-x - 4)$ by using the Distributive Property. $3x + 12$
(15)

7. Simplify $xm^2xm^3x^3m$. m^6x^5
(3)

8. Identify the property illustrated by $3 + 8 = 8 + 3$.   Commutative Property of Addition
(12)

9. **Write** True or False: $-5^4 = (-5)^4$. Explain.   false; Sample: The answers are opposites; $-5^4 = -1 \times 5^4 = -1 \times 625 = -625$; $(-5)^4 = (-5)(-5)(-5)(-5) = 625$
(11)

10. Sandra lost 8 points for incorrect answers on her quiz, but gained 5 points for a bonus question. What is the sum of points Sandra lost and gained? -3
(10)

*11. **Error Analysis** A teacher asked two students to solve the following equation for x: $x + \frac{1}{3} = \frac{4}{9}$. Which student is correct? Explain the error.
(19)

11. Student B; Student A should have subtracted $\frac{1}{3}$ from both sides of the equation to isolate x.

Student A	Student B
$x + \frac{1}{3} + \frac{1}{3} = \frac{4}{9} + \frac{1}{3}$	$x + \frac{1}{3} - \frac{1}{3} = \frac{4}{9} - \frac{1}{3}$
$x = \frac{4}{9} + \frac{3}{9}$	$x = \frac{4}{9} - \frac{3}{9}$
$x = \frac{7}{9}$	$x = \frac{1}{9}$

*12. **Multiple Choice** A swimming pool is $\frac{4}{5}$ full. A maintenance man removes some of the water so that the pool is $\frac{1}{3}$ full. As a fraction of the pool's total capacity, how much water did the maintenance man remove?   **C**
(19)

   A $\frac{1}{5}$ **B** $\frac{3}{2}$ **C** $\frac{7}{15}$ **D** $\frac{17}{15}$

*13. (**Chemistry**) Many chemists use kelvins to describe temperatures. To convert from a temperature in degrees Celsius to kelvins, a chemist will use the equation $T_{\text{Celsius}} + 273.15 = T_{\text{kelvin}}$. If a gas cools to a temperature of 325.20K, what is its temperature in degrees Celsius? $52.05°C$
(19)

*14. (**Business**) A movie theater needs to sell 3500 tickets over a single weekend to cover its operating expenses before it starts making a profit. If it sells 1278 tickets on Friday, what is the minimum number of tickets it needs to sell over the rest of the weekend in order to make a profit? Write an equation and then solve it.
(19)
   $3500 - x = 1278$; 2222 tickets

Lesson 19   107

Check for Understanding

The questions below help assess the concepts taught in this lesson.

"Why is the inverse operation used to solve an equation?" Sample: It is used to isolate the variable on one side of the equal sign.

"How can you check if your solution is correct?" Sample: Substitute the solution into the original equation and simplify.

3 Practice

Math Conversations

Discussion to strengthen understanding

Problem 1

Error Alert
Some students may not recognize that x^2ym is the same term as ymx^2. Remind them of the Commutative Property of Multiplication, which states that factors may be multiplied in any order. Thus, $x^2ym = ymx^2$ and the terms can be combined.

Problem 7

Guide the students by asking them the following questions.

"How can you combine the terms of this expression?" Add the exponents for each variable, then write each variable with the total of the exponents for that variable.

"Why can the exponents of like bases be added?" Exponents represent multiplication of the same value.

"What is the exponent of the last variable in the expression?" There is no exponent, so it is considered to be 1.

Lesson 19   107

*15. **Write** Jeremy is solving the equation $x - 2.5 = 7.0$. What must he do to both sides of the equation in order to isolate x?

15. Add 2.5 to both sides of the equal sign.

*16. **Multiple Choice** Given the information in the table, which equation best relates a and b?

a	b
−5	0
0	−5
5	−10
−10	5

A $a - b = 5$ **B** $a - b = -5$ **C** $-5 - b = a$ **D** $a - 5 = b$ **C**

17. **Error Analysis** Two students simplify the expression $6x + 8 - 4x - 2$. Which student is correct? Explain the error.   Student B; Sample: Student A added unlike terms.

Student A	Student B
$2x + 6$ $= 8x$	$2x + 6$

18. **Geometry** Write an expression to represent the sum of the degrees in the triangle. $2x - 5$

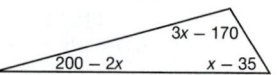

19. **Multi-Step** At a family camp, the big race is on the final day. Each family member runs for t hours and the family that runs the farthest wins. The rate each person ran is shown in the chart. To find how far they ran, multiply their rate by the amount of time they ran.
a. Write an expression to represent how far each person ran.
b. Write an expression to represent how far the family ran.
c. How far did they run if each person ran hour?

Family Member	Rate (mph)
Julio	4
Jorge	5
Sam	3

20. **Error Analysis** Two students translate the phrase "five more than the product of a number and three" into an algebraic expression. Which student is correct? Explain the error.

Student A	Student B
$\frac{x}{3} + 5$	$3x + 5$

*21. When $x = 1.5$ and $y = -2$, what is the value of $|x^2 + y^3|$?   5.75

19a. $4t$; $5t$; $3t$

19b. $12t$

19c. 2 miles

20. Student B; Sample: Student A translated it into an expression using a quotient rather than the product.

22. **Multiple Choice** A store owner makes a pyramid-shaped display using a stack of soup cans. She arranges the cans so that the highest level of the stack has one can. The second-highest level has four cans arranged in a square supporting the top can. The third-highest level has nine cans arranged in a square that supports the second-highest level. Which of the following expressions best represents the number of cans in the lowest level of a display that is l levels high? **C**
    A $3l$ B $4l$ C l^2 D l^3

23. **Write** a. What is the sign of the result when a negative value is cubed? The resulting value is negative.
    b. What is the sign of the result when the absolute value of an expression is taken? The resulting value is positive.

24. **Sites** Use the table to answer the questions.
    a. If a building is randomly chosen, what is the probability that it is exactly 1250 feet tall? $\frac{1}{7}$
    b. What is the probability that a building exactly 1046 feet tall is chosen? $\frac{2}{7}$
    c. What is the probability that a building that was built between 1960 and 1980 is chosen? $\frac{3}{7}$

Building	Height (ft)	Year Built
Sears Tower	1451	1974
Empire State Building	1250	1931
Aon Center	1136	1973
John Hancock Center	1127	1969
Chrysler Building	1046	1930
New York Times Building	1046	2007
Bank of America Plaza	1023	1992

25. **Write** What is a perfect square? Sample: a number that is the square of an integer

26. **Personal Finance** The expression $P(1 + i)^2$ can be used to find the value of an investment P after 2 years at an interest rate of i. What is the value of an investment of $500 deposited in an account with a 3% interest rate after 2 years? (Hint: Remember to convert the percent to a decimal before calculating.) $530.45

27. **Racing** The formula for the cylindrical volume of an engine on a dragster is $\left(\frac{\pi}{4}\right)b^2 s$, where b is the inside diameter (the bore) and s is the distance that the piston moves from its highest position to its lowest position (the stroke). Following the order of operations, describe the steps you would take to simplify the formula. Sample: First I would divide π by 4. Then I would find b^2. Finally, I would multiply to find the solution.

28. **Justify** What is the additive inverse of 12? Justify your answer. −12; Sample: When a number is added with its additive inverse, the sum is 0; $12 + (-12) = 0$

29. **Multi-Step** Theater tickets cost $14 dollars for adults, a, and $8 for children, c. Additionally, each person who went to the theater on Thursday made a $5 contribution to charity. Write an expression using the Distributive Property to show the amount of money that the theater received on Thursday. Simplify the expression. $5(a + c) + (14a + 8c)$; $19a + 13c$

30. **Probability** What is the probability that an ace will be chosen from a full deck of 52 playing cards? What is the probability of another ace being drawn if the first ace drawn is not returned to the deck? $\frac{4}{52} = \frac{1}{13}$; $\frac{3}{51} = \frac{1}{17}$

Lesson 19   109

LOOKING FORWARD

Solving one-step equations by adding or subtracting prepares students for

- **Lesson 21** Solving One-Step Equations by Multiplying or Dividing
- **Lesson 23** Solving Two-Step Equations
- **Lesson 24** Solving Decimal Equations
- **Lesson 26** Solving Multi-Step Equations
- **Lesson 28** Solving Equations with Variables on Both Sides

LESSON 20

1 Warm Up

Problem 4

Make sure that students remember to distribute the 4 over both terms.

2 New Concepts

In this lesson, students learn to graph on a coordinate plane.

Discuss the definition of a **coordinate plane.** Explain that a coordinate plane needs both an x-axis and a y-axis.

Remind students that a coordinate plane consists of coordinates. Coordinates, also known as ordered pairs, must have both an x- and y-value.

Coordinates or ordered pairs need to be in parentheses: (3, 2). If they are not in parentheses, they are a list or sequence of numbers: 3, 5.

Error Alert Tell students to use Roman numerals (I, II, III, IV) when identifying quadrants rather than numbers (1, 2, 3, 4).

TEACHER TIP

Tell the students that x comes before y in the alphabet to help them remember that it is the same for ordered pairs: (x, y).

LESSON RESOURCES

Student Edition Practice Workbook 20
Reteaching Master 20
Adaptations Master 20
Challenge and Enrichment Master C20, E20

LESSON 20 Graphing on a Coordinate Plane

Warm Up

1. **Vocabulary** The distance from a number to 0 on the number line is the _____. **absolute value**
   (5)

Simplify.

2. $|3 + (-5) - (-7)|$ **5**
   (7)

3. $|3 + (-5) + (-7)|$ **9**
   (7)

4. $4(8 + c) + 5$ **37 + 4c**
   (15)

5. $5y^2 + 3x^4 - 5y^2 - 5x^4$ **$-2x^4$**
   (18)

New Concepts

Math Language

Perpendicular lines intersect at right angles. The sides of a book are perpendicular. They intersect and form a right angle at the corner of the book.

A **coordinate plane** is made of two perpendicular number lines, one horizontal and one vertical. The horizontal line is called the **x-axis,** and the vertical line is called the **y-axis.** The number lines divide the plane into four **quadrants,** numbered and named as shown. The intersection of the x- and y-axis is called the **origin**.

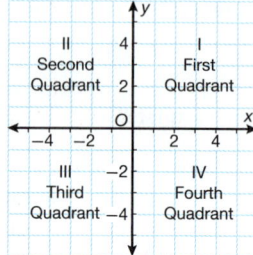

Each point on the coordinate plane is identified by an **ordered pair,** or two numbers in parentheses, separated by a comma. An ordered pair is written as follows: (x, y). The ordered pair that represents the origin is (0, 0).

The first number in an ordered pair is called the **x-coordinate** and indicates the distance to the right or left of the origin. The second number, the **y-coordinate,** is the distance above or below the horizontal axis. A **coordinate** is a number that helps locate a point on a graph.

To find or graph a point, always start at the origin. Then use the sign of the coordinate to determine the location of the point.

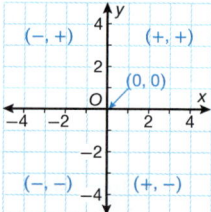

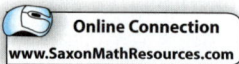
Online Connection
www.SaxonMathResources.com

110 Saxon Algebra 1

MATH BACKGROUND

A plane is a two-dimensional surface that is flat. A coordinate plane is a plane that has been labeled by lines. Coordinate planes are often used for mapping. A polar coordinate system is another two-dimensional coordinate system. A point on a polar coordinate system is determined by a given angle and distance.

The coordinate systems in this lesson are called Cartesian coordinate systems. The four quadrants are formed by the x-axis and the y-axis. On the coordinate plane there are points in the form (x, y) where the x-coordinate is the abscissa and the y-coordinate is the ordinate.

Hint

When graphing a point, always move left or right first.

Example 1 — Graphing Ordered Pairs on a Coordinate Plane

Graph each ordered pair on a coordinate plane. Label each point.

a. (4, 2)

SOLUTION

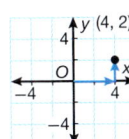

Point (4, 2) is located in the first quadrant, 4 units to the right of the origin and 2 units above the horizontal axis.

b. (−3, 0)

SOLUTION

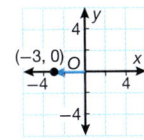

Point (−3, 0) is on the *x*-axis. It is located 3 units to the left of the origin.

Reading Math

In an ordered pair (*x*, *y*), *x* is the independent variable and *y* is the dependent variable.

When there is a relationship between two variable quantities, one variable is the independent variable and the other is the dependent variable.

Variables
Independent variable: The variable whose value can be chosen. Also called the input variable.
Dependent variable: The variable whose value is determined by the input value of another variable. Also called the output value.

The dependent variable always depends on what value is chosen for the independent variable.

Math Reasoning

Analyze The total charge on a bill is usually a dependent variable. Explain.

Sample: The total charge is dependent on the number of items purchased.

Example 2 — Identifying Independent and Dependent Variables

For each pair of variables, identify the independent variable and the dependent variables.

a. number of traffic violations, cost of auto insurance

SOLUTION

independent variable: number of traffic violations; dependent variable: cost of auto insurance

The cost of auto insurance depends upon the number of traffic violations.

b. electric bill total, kilowatts of electricity used

SOLUTION

independent variable: kilowatts of electricity used; dependent variable: electric bill total

Electric bills are based, or dependent, on the electricity usage. The kilowatts of electricity determine the electric bill total.

Lesson 20   111

Example 1

Students graph ordered pairs on a coordinate plane.

Additional Example 1

Graph each ordered pair on a coordinate plane. Label each point.

a. (2, 3)

b. (0, −5)

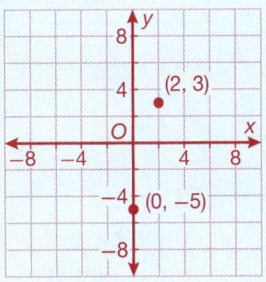

Extend the Example

Have students identify what quadrants the coordinates (3, 6), (−6, 0), and (2, −4) are in. I, *x*-axis, IV

Example 2

The word dependent means to rely on something for support. The word independent means to not rely or be influenced by something.

Additional Example 2

For each pair of variables, identify the independent variable and the dependent variables.

a. the distance traveled, the amount of gas used
independent variable; the distance traveled; dependent variable: amount of gas used

b. the water bill, gallons of water used independent variable: gallons of water used; dependent variable: the water bill

---

INCLUSION

For students having problems plotting points on the coordinate grid, have them draw a vertical line through the *x*-value of the point and a horizontal line through the *y*-value of the point to locate the point.

Graph the ordered pair (−3, −5).

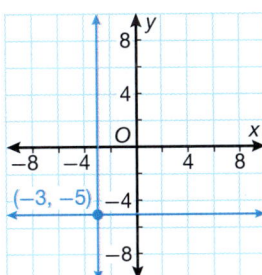

Lesson 20   111

Example 3

Students will substitute given independent values to determine dependent values.

Additional Example 3

Complete the table for the equation $y = 3x - 4$.

x	y
-1	-7
0	-4
2	2
$\frac{1}{3}$	-3

Extend the Example

Have students graph the points from the table and draw a line through them. Ask them to verify that another point on the line could be included in the table. Sample: $(-3, -10)$

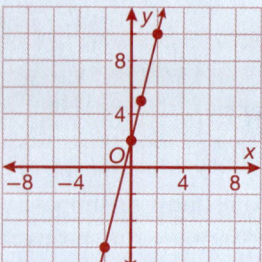

A solution to an equation with two variables is an ordered pair that makes the equation true. There are infinite solutions to the equation $y = 4x + 2$. Solutions can be found by substituting values for the independent variable, x, to find the corresponding value of the dependent variable, y.

Example 3 Determining the Dependent Variable

Complete the table for the equation $y = 4x + 2$.

x	y
-2	
0	
2	
$\frac{3}{4}$	

Caution

Be sure to use the order of operations when simplifying either side of an equation.

SOLUTION

Substitute the x-values into the equation to determine the y-values.

First substitute -2 for x in the equation.

$y = 4x + 2$ Write the equation.
$y = 4(-2) + 2$ Substitute -2 for x.
$y = -8 + 2$ Evaluate.
$y = -6$

One solution to the equation is the ordered pair $(-2, -6)$.

Then substitute the other values to complete the table.

Math Reasoning

Generalize How are the independent and dependent variables graphed on the coordinate plane?

Sample: The independent variable is graphed as the x-coordinate. The dependent variable is graphed as the y-coordinate.

$x = 0$
$y = 4x + 2$
$y = 4(0) + 2$
$y = 0 + 2$
$y = 2$

$x = 2$
$y = 4x + 2$
$y = 4(2) + 2$
$y = 8 + 2$
$y = 10$

$x = \frac{3}{4}$
$y = 4x + 2$
$y = 4\left(\frac{3}{4}\right) + 2$
$y = 5$

The completed table shows the ordered pairs for the given values of x.

x	y
-2	-6
0	2
2	10
$\frac{3}{4}$	5

Values are assigned to the variable x. The value of the variable y is dependent on the value chosen for the variable x.

Example 4 Application: Wages

The federal minimum wage is about $5 per hour. The total on a minimum-wage worker's paycheck is dependent on the number of hours worked. The paycheck total can be calculated using the equation $y = 5x$.

Find the pay for 1, 3, 5, and 8 hours of. Make a graph to represent the equation $y = 5x$.

SOLUTION

Understand Since a worker makes $5 per hour, a worker's pay is calculated by multiplying the number of hours worked by 5.

Plan Find the amount of pay, y, when x is equal to 1, 3, 5, and 8 hours. Then graph the ordered pairs.

Solve Substitute 1, 3, 5, and 8 for x.

$y = 5x$	$y = 5x$	$y = 5x$	$y = 5x$
$y = 5(1)$	$y = 5(3)$	$y = 5(5)$	$y = 5(8)$
$y = 5$	$y = 15$	$y = 25$	$y = 40$

The pay for 1, 3, 5, and 8 hours is $5, $15, $25, and $40 respectively.

The ordered pairs are (1, 5), (3, 15), (5, 25), and (8, 40).

Graph the ordered pairs. Connect the points with a smooth line.

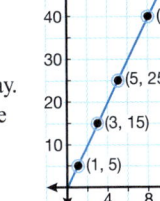

Check As the number of hours increases; so does the pay. The pay should increase steadily, which is shown by the straight line on the graph.

Math Reasoning

Predict How many hours would someone have worked if they are paid $122.50?

24.5 hours

Lesson Practice

a.–f. See Additional Answers.

Graph each ordered pair on a coordinate plane. Label each point.
(Ex 1)
a. (0, 5)
b. (−1, −6)
c. (−2, 0)
d. (−3, 4)
e. (5, −1)
f. (2, −4)

For each pair of variables, identify the independent variable and the dependent variable.
(Ex 2)
g. the amount paid, the number of toys purchased   The amount paid is dependent, and the number of toys purchased is independent.
h. the number of hours worked, the number of yards mowed   The number of hours worked is dependent, and the number of yards mowed is independent.
i. Complete the table for the equation $y = 2x - 1$.
(Ex 3)

x	−3	−2	−1
y	−7	−5	−3

Lesson 20   113

Example 4
Students calculate the amount of a paycheck that depends on the hours worked for minimum wage.

Additional Example 4
A friend's allowance wages are about $15 per day. His allowance payment from his parents is dependent on him completing all of his given chores for the day. The total allowance can be calculated using the equation $y = 15x$. Find the pay when he works 5, 7, 10, and 12 days. $75, $105, $150, $180

Lesson Practice

Problem b

Error Alert Students might start on the y-axis for the abscissa instead of the x-axis. Remind students to draw arrows above the coordinates to help them.

Problem g

Scaffolding Ask the following questions:

"When purchasing items is the amount paid determined before or after you pick out the items? after, so amount paid depends on items purchased

Check for Understanding

The questions below help assess the concepts taught in this lesson.

"The points (−2, −7) and (−500, 3) are found in which quadrants?" (−2, −7) is in Quadrant III; (−500, 3) is in Quadrant II.

"Which direction is described by the independent variable for an ordered pair?" left or right

"How is a ordered pair determined for a given equation?" A independent value is chosen and evaluated in the given equation. The input and output values form an ordered pair.

 ENGLISH LEARNERS

For this lesson, explain the meaning of the word **substitute**. Say:

"The word substitute means to take the place of another."

Connect the meaning of substitute with the mathematical meaning of being replaced or plugged into when simplifying.

Discuss examples of substitutes that exist, like substitute teachers, food substitutes, and sugar substitutes.

Have students identify what the substitutes are in the table in Example 3 and explain how the substitutes change an equation by comparing the y-values in the table.

Lesson 20   113

j.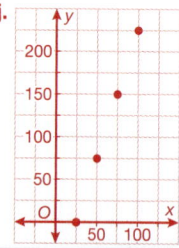

j. **Fundraising** The prom committee raises money for the prom by selling
(Ex 4) flowers. The money earned for the prom is dependent on the number of
flowers sold. Money earned is represented by the equation $y = 3x - 75$.

Find the amount of money raised when 25, 50, 75, and 100 flowers
are sold. Make a graph to represent the equation $y = 3x - 75$.
$0, $75, $150, $225

Practice   Distributed and Integrated

Simplify.

1. (+3) + (−14)   −11
(5)

2. $4xyz - 3yz + zxy$ $5xyz - 3yz$
(18)

3. $3xyz - 3xyz + zxy$ xyz
(18)

Solve.

4. $x - 4 = 10$ $x = 14$
(19)

5. $x + \frac{1}{5} = -\frac{1}{10}$ $x = -\frac{3}{10}$
(19)

*6. Graph the ordered pair (3, −4) on a coordinate plane.
(20)

*7. Graph the ordered pair (0, 5) on a coordinate plane.
(20)

*8. **Multiple Choice** Which ordered pair is associated
(20) with point Z? **C**

   A (3, 0)   **B** (0, 3)

   C (−3, 0)   **D** (0, −3)

6.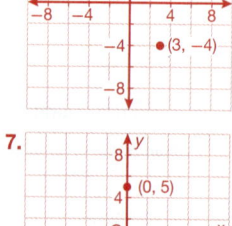

7.

*9. **Babysitting** Ellen charges $3 plus $1 per child for an hour of
(20) babysitting. To determine her hourly rate, she uses the formula
$r = 3 + c$, where r is the rate and c is the number of children
Complete the table and graph the solutions.

c	r
1	4
2	5
3	6
4	7

9.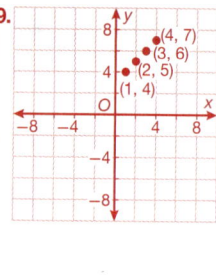

*10. **Reading** Thomas read 10 pages in a book before starting his
(20) speed-reading lessons. After his lessons, he could read 3 pages
per minute. The equation $y = 3x + 10$ calculates the total
number of pages read after x minutes. Complete the table.

x	y
15	55
20	70
30	100
50	160

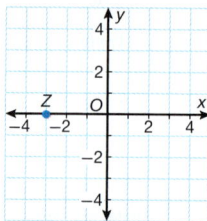

114   Saxon Algebra 1

*11. Error Analysis Two students completed an *x/y* chart for the equation $y = 3 + 2x$ to find a solution to the equation. Which student is correct? Explain the error.
(20)

11. Student B; Sample: Student A should have determined the product of 2 and 2 first.

Student A

x	y
2	10

$y = 3 + 2(2)$
$y = 5(2)$
$y = 10$
(2, 10) is a solution.

Student B

x	y
2	7

$y = 3 + 2(2)$
$y = 3 + 4$
$y = 7$
(2, 7) is a solution.

*12. Multi-Step For a lemonade stand, profit depends on the number of cups sold. Profit is represented by the equation $y = x - 5$, where x is the number of cups sold and y is the profit in dollars.
(20)

x	5	10	20	50
y	0	5	15	45

a. Complete the table and graph the solutions.   See Additional Answers.

b. How would you find the profit if 30 cups were sold?   Sample: Substitute $x = 30$ into the equation

13. Geometry The triangle has a perimeter of 24 centimeters. Find the value for x.
(19) $x = 6$ cm

*14. Multi-Step To climb to the highest observation deck in the Empire State Building, you have to walk up 1860 steps. Starting at the lowest step, a security guard walks up $\frac{1}{4}$ the total number of steps during his morning rounds. At the end of his afternoon rounds, he stands on the 310th step. How many steps did he walk down during the afternoon rounds?   155 steps
(19)

*15. Error Analysis Two students simplify the expression $5x^2 + 7x^2$. Which student is correct? Explain the error.   Student A; Sample: Student B added the exponents of x.
(18)

Student A	Student B
$12x^2$	$12x^4$

16. Write Why do mathematicians use symbols rather than words?
(17)

16. Sample: Mathematicians use symbols to express briefly and accurately what might take longer to express in words.

17. Multiple Choice Which equation demonstrates the Associative Property of Addition?   **D**
(12)

A $6 - 3c = 3c - 6$
B $c^3 - 6 = c^3 + 6$
C $(6 - c)^3 = (c - 6)^3$
D $(6 + c^3) - 4 = 6 + (c^3 - 4)$

18. Evaluate each of the following expressions when $a = 2$.
(16)
a. a^2 **b.** $-a^2$ **c.** $-a^3$ **d.** $(-a)^3$ **e.** $|(-a)^2|$
a. 4, **b.** −4, **c.** −8, **d.** −8, and **e.** 4

19. Analyze A school is holding a blood drive. If 3 students out of the 50 who give blood are Type A, what is the probability that a randomly selected student is Type A? Write the probability as a decimal.   0.06
(14)

20. Evaluate $\sqrt{441} + \sqrt{1089}$.   54
(13)

Lesson 20   115

Problem 12
Students may assume that there is a pattern for the *x*-values. This assumption will affect the *y*-values.

Point out to students to pay attention to the *x* values before computing the *y* values to help avoid an error.

Problem 15
Error Alert
A common error when combining like terms is to add the exponents instead or in addition to the coefficients of the variables.

Remind students to leave the exponents unchanged when they are adding like terms.

$5x^2 + 7x^2 = (5 + 7)x^2 = 12x^2$.

Problem 18
Error Alert
Remind the students of the following statements when multiplying:

negative × negative = positive

negative × positive = negative

Problem 21
Extend the Problem
Have the students change their multiplication problem to division and decide if the Associative Property holds for division.

Problem 30
Extend the Problem
Have students use their graphs to predict the distance the person ran in 3 hours. **15 mi**

Ask students which quadrants the points would be plotted in to represent this situation. Sample: Quadrant 1; only because time and distance are both positive

---

21. Analyze Use an example to show that the Associative Property holds true for multiplication.
(12)

21. Sample:
$(3 \cdot 2) \cdot 4 = 3 \cdot (2 \cdot 4)$
$6 \cdot 4 = 3 \cdot 8$
$24 = 24$

22. Statistics Use the data in the table to find the average yearly change in the deer population during a five-year period. **−9.6 deer**
(11)

Deer Population

Year	Decrease in Number of Deer
2000	10
2001	7
2002	9
2003	10
2004	12

23. Stocks A Stock Market Report shows the value of stocks in points. The value of the stock is determined by the number of points. If a stock is at $79\frac{5}{7}$ points and it drops 3 points, what is the value of stock? $76\frac{5}{7}$ **points**
(10)

24. Nutrition One hundred grams of honey contains about 0.3 grams of protein. How many milligrams is 0.3 grams of protein? **300 mg**
(8)

25. Tiling A contractor lays patterned tile floors. He often begins with a polygon and makes diagonal lines that pass from corner to corner of the polygon. He uses the following expression $\frac{n^2 - 3n}{2}$, where n equals the number of sides of the polygon to find the number of diagonal lines for any given polygon.
(7)
a. Find the number of diagonals for a hexagon. **9**
b. **Model** Check your work by drawing the diagonals in a hexagon.

25b.

26. Write and simplify a mathematical expression that shows "fourteen minus the quotient of three squared and the sum of three plus six." $14 - \frac{(3)^2}{3+6}$; **13**
(4)

27. Verify Indicate whether each statement is true or false. If the statement is false, explain why.
(2)
a. The coefficient of x in the expression $x + 3$ is 3. **false; Sample: The coefficient of x is 1.**
b. The factors of the expression $\frac{2mn}{5}$ are $\frac{2}{5}$, m, and n. **true**

28. Name the coefficient(s), variables, and number of terms in the expression $b^2 - 4ac$. **coefficients 1 and −4; variables b, a, and c; There are 2 terms.**
(2)

29. Multi-Step Pencils cost ten cents and erasers cost five cents.
(17)
a. Write an expression to represent the total number of school supplies purchased. $p + e$
b. Write an expression to represent how much the supplies cost in cents. $10p + 5e$

***30. Analyze** A person runs 5 miles per hour. The equation $d = 5t$ tells how far the person has run in t hours. Make a table when $t = 0, 1, 2,$ and 4 hours. Graph the ordered pairs in a graph and connect all the points. What do you notice? **The graph is linear.**
(20)

x	0	1	2	4
y	0	5	10	20

116 Saxon Algebra 1

CHALLENGE

Create a square on a coordinate plane by having all of the coordinates be in a different quadrant. Name each coordinate.
Sample: (3, 3) in quadrant I, (−1, 3) in quadrant II, (−1, −1) in quadrant III, and (3, −1) in quadrant IV

Other geometric figures can be created.

LOOKING FORWARD

Graphing on a coordinate plane prepares students for

- **Investigation 2** Graphing a Relationship
- **Lesson 25** Differentiating Between Relations and Functions
- **Lesson 30** Graphing Functions
- **Lesson 34** Recognizing and Extending Arithmetic Sequences
- **Lesson 71** Making and Analyzing Scatter Plots

INVESTIGATION 2

Graphing a Relationship

A graph is a visual representation of how data change and relate to each other. A graph can convey the numeric relationship between data like time and distance.

Beach Trip Maria takes a trip to the beach. She stays at the beach all day before driving back home. As Maria drives to the beach, her distance from home increases. While she is at the beach, there is no change in her distance from home. As she returns home, her distance from home decreases.

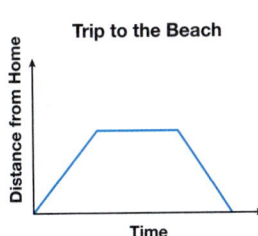

Horse's Speed The graph shows the various speeds at which a horse travels.

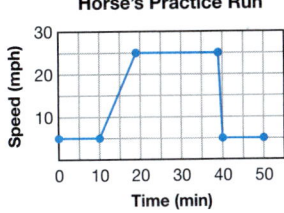

1. **Analyze** Use the graph to complete the table. Describe the horse's speed in each of the time intervals as increasing, no change, or decreasing.

Interval	Description
0 to 10 minutes	no change
10 to 18 minutes	increasing
18 to 38 minutes	no change
38 to 40 minutes	decreasing
40 to 50 minutes	no change

Math Reasoning

Analyze How does the increase in the horse's speed compare to the decrease in its speed? Explain. **See below.**

You can use a graph to show how data change. When drawing a graph to represent a real-world situation,

- choose appropriate intervals for the units on the axes;
- be sure to space the intervals equally;
- only use values that make sense, such as positive numbers of books or whole numbers of people.

Sample: The speed of the horse increases more slowly than it decreases. The line showing the increase in speed is not as steep as the line showing the decrease in speed.

Investigation 2   117

INVESTIGATION 2

Discuss

In this investigation, students read and draw graphs to represent data change.

Define **discrete graph** and **continuous graph.** Discrete graphs will be applied further when students study trend lines and scatter plots.

Problem 1

In class discussion about the horse's speed, help students to understand that the steepness of the graph gives information about how quickly the horse speeds up and slows down. Begin the discussion by calling the students' attention to the Math Reasoning on the first page of the lesson.

INVESTIGATION RESOURCES

Reteaching Master
   Investigation 2
Technology Lab Master
   Investigation 2

MATH BACKGROUND

Graphs are used to represent and compare two quantities. Continuous graphs are associated with quantities such as time, which can take on fractional values. Discrete graphs are usually associated with whole numbers and do not take on fractional values. For example, pencils can only be purchased in whole-number quantities. Also remember that in graphs, the dependent variable is represented on the vertical axis and the independent variable is represented on the horizontal axis.

Investigation 2   117

Problem 2
Error Alert
Some students may use the cost of pecans as the independent variable. Remind students that the cost depends on the number of pounds purchased. Therefore, the vertical axis should represent the cost.

Problem 8
Extend the Problem
Have students draw a graph to represent an increase in price to $8 per sheet.

Problem 9
Show students that when reading a graph from left to right, increasing corresponds to sections of the graph that slant up to the right or go uphill and decreasing corresponds to sections of the graph that slant down to the right or go downhill.

Problem 11
Draw students' attention to the difference in the graph of the plane's altitude and the other graphs in this lesson. Explain that the plane's altitude is shown with a smooth curve rather than with sharp corners because the plane's altitude changes gradually over time.

---

3. Accept reasonable answers.
4. $3.00; $13.50
5.

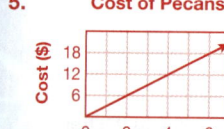
Cost of Pecans

6. Sample: Disconnected points that lie along a line.

Math Reasoning
Analyze Identify the dependent and independent variables. Explain

Sample: The cost depends on the number of sheets purchased. The independent variable is the number of sheets. The dependent variable is the cost.

Caution
The phrases increasing, no change, and decreasing describe the elevation of the hiker, not the speed.

8.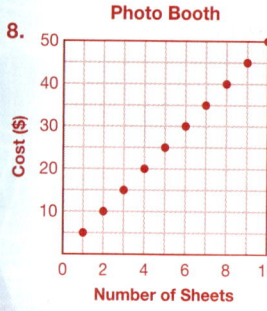
Photo Booth

11. Sample: Since the plane begins and ends it journey at ground level, its altitude will be 0 miles at the beginning and end of the flight.

Cost of Pecans Customers at a local grocery store pay $3.00 per pound for pecans. They can purchase the pecans in fractions of a pound.

2. **Justify** Should the graph representing this situation display negative values for pounds of pecans? Explain.   no; Sample: A negative number of pounds does not make sense.
3. **Estimate** What is a reasonable maximum number of pounds to graph?
4. What is the cost of purchasing 1 pound of pecans? 4.5 pounds?
5. Draw a graph to represent the situation.

The cost-per-pound data modeled in the graph are continuous. Continuous data are data where numbers between any two data values have meaning. A graph of this data is drawn with a solid line. A **continuous graph** is a graph that has no gaps, jumps, or asymptotes.

Data that involve a count of items, such as a number of people, are called **discrete data**. A **discrete graph** is made up of separate, disconnected points determined by a set of discrete data.

Photography A sheet of photos at an automatic photo booth costs $5. Patrons may purchase only full sheets of photos. The photo booth can print up to 10 sheets per patron.

6. **Predict** What will the graph look like?
7. What is the least number of photo sheets for purchase? The greatest number of sheets?   1 sheet; 10 sheets
8. Draw a graph that represents the situation.
9. **Write** Use the graph to describe Maura's hike on Windy Hill. In the description, use the phrases increasing, no change, and decreasing.

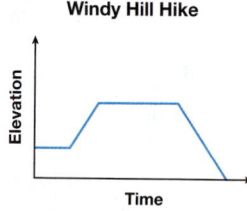
Windy Hill Hike

Sample: Maura walks along a flat trail for some time with no change in her elevation. Then her elevation increases as she walks up a hill. There is no change in her elevation as she walks along the top of the hill. Her elevation decreases when she walks down the hill to the base of the hill.

A graph represents the relationship between two quantities. The "Windy Hill Hike" graph shows the relationship between a hiker's time and altitude.

10. **Analyze** Describe another set of data that could be related to the hiker's time.   Sample: the hiker's distance from the starting point

Many quantities can be measured and compared, such as a plane's traveling speed and its altitude.

Air Travel A commercial airplane travels at 600 miles per hour and typically flies at a height of about 6 miles. The graph shows the flight time and the altitude of an airplane.

11. What is the plane's altitude at the beginning and end of its 6-hour trip? Explain.

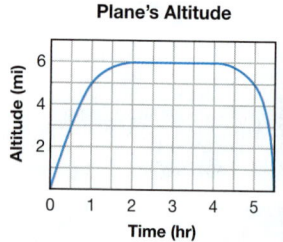
Plane's Altitude

118   Saxon Algebra 1

🌐 ENGLISH LEARNERS

For this lesson, explain the meaning of the word **discrete**. Say:

"**Discrete means a countable set of values that represent a whole. In many situations, a fractional part of something doesn't make sense.**"

Discuss how purchasing a box of cereal or canned goods is different than buying an item by the pound. Because boxes or cans can only be purchased in whole-number quantities, the number of items is discrete.

The number of pounds does not have to be a whole number. When purchasing by the pound, the number of pounds is continuous. Say,

"**Is the number of pencils in a pencil holder discrete or continuous?**" discrete

"**Is the number of ounces of flour scooped from a canister discrete or continuous?**"
continuous

12. **Write** Describe the plane's flight in the first and last hour of the trip.

13. **Write** Explain why the graph of the plane's flight is relatively flat between 2 and 4 hours of the flight.   Sample: For the middle part of the trip, there is no change in altitude.

12. Sample: Within the first and last hour of the trip, the altitude of the plane quickly increases and decreases, respectively.

Investigation Practice

Graph each situation. Indicate whether the graph is continuous or discrete. Then describe the graph as increasing, no change, and/or decreasing.

a. Boxes of greeting cards sell for $5 a box. Income is calculated based on the number of boxes sold.   discrete, increasing

b. A scuba diver dives to a depth of 100 feet below sea level, then spends some time exploring the aquatic life at that level. The diver then descends to 250 feet below sea level for the remainder of the dive. (Hint: Assume the diver descends about 100 ft per 5 minutes.)

c. A driver brakes as she approaches an intersection. She stops to watch for traffic and pedestrians. The driver continues when the way is clear.   continuous, decreasing, no change, increasing

d. **Multiple Choice** The temperature of an ice cube increases until it starts to melt. While it melts, its temperature stays constant. Which graph best represents the situation?   A

a. *(Greeting Card Sales graph)*

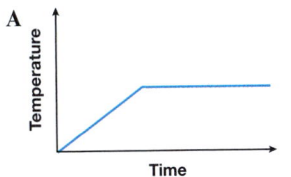
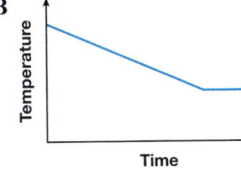
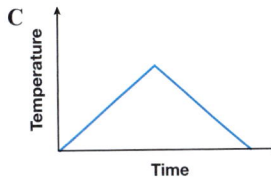

Describe the shape of the graph representing each situation.

e. **Write** A rocket is launched into orbit and, in time, returns to Earth. The graph relates time to the rocket's distance from Earth.

f. **Write** The ink in a printer is used until the ink cartridge is empty. The graph relates time used to the amount of ink in the cartridge.

g. **Write** An employee of a delivery service earns $3 for every package she delivers. The graph shows the employee's total earnings based on the number of packages delivered.   Sample: The graph is a series of points that fall in a line that increases from left to right.

e. Sample: The graph is an upside-down U.

f. Sample: The graph is a line that decreases from left to right.

b. continuous, increasing, no change, increasing, no change

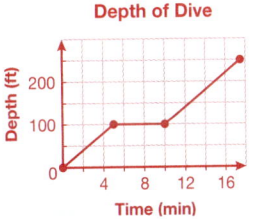

c. *(Driving Speed graph)*

Investigation 2   119

LOOKING FORWARD

Graphing relationships prepares students for

- **Lesson 25** Differentiating Between Relations and Functions
- **Lesson 30** Graphing Functions
- **Lesson 41** Finding Rates of Change and Slope
- **Lesson 71** Making and Analyzing Scatter Plots

Investigation Practice

Math Conversations
Discussion to strengthen understanding

Problem d
Error Alert
Some students may visualize the size of the ice cube rather than the temperature. Encourage students to read the axes to avoid confusion. It may be helpful for students to sketch the graph before looking at the possible answers.

Problem e
Scaffolding Ask students the following questions to guide them to their answers.

"Before the rocket is launched, what is its distance from Earth?" Because it is still on the ground, the distance is zero.

"As the rocket is launched, what happens to the distances from Earth?" The distances increase.

"As the rocket begins to return to Earth, what happens to the distances from Earth?" The distances decrease.

"What is the distance from Earth when the rocket lands?" The distance is zero.

"Draw a graph that starts at zero, increases, and then decreases back to zero." See student work.

Investigation 2   119

SECTION OVERVIEW

3

Lesson Planner

Lesson	New Concepts
21	Solving One-Step Equations by Multiplying or Dividing
22	Analyzing and Comparing Statistical Graphs
23	Solving Two-Step Equations
24	Solving Decimal Equations
25	Differentiating Between Relations and Functions
	Cumulative Test 4, Performance Task 4
26	Solving Multi-Step Equations
27	Identifying Misleading Representations of Data
28	Solving Equations with Variables on Both Sides
29	Solving Literal Equations
LAB 2	Graphing Calculator Lab: Creating a Table
30	Graphing Functions
	Cumulative Test 5, Performance Task 5
INV 3	Investigation: Analyzing the Effects of Bias in Sampling, Surveys, and Bar Graphs

Resources for Teaching

- Student Edition
- Teacher's Edition
- Student Edition eBook
- Teacher's Edition eBook
- Resources and Planner CD
- Solutions Manual
- Instructional Masters
- Technology Lab Masters
- Warm Up and Teaching Transparencies
- Instructional Presentations CD
- Online activities, tools, and homework help
  www.SaxonMathResources.com

Resources for Practice and Assessment

- Student Edition Practice Workbook
- Course Assessments
- Standardized Test Practice
- College Entrance Exam Practice
- Test and Practice Generator CD using ExamView™

Resources for Differentiated Instruction

- Reteaching Masters
- Challenge and Enrichment Masters
- Prerequisite Skills Intervention
- Adaptations for Saxon Algebra 1
- Multilingual Glossary
- English Learners Handbook
- TI Resources

Pacing Guide

 Resources and Planner CD for lesson planning support

45-Minute Class

Day 1	Day 2	Day 3	Day 4	Day 5	Day 6
Lesson 21	Lesson 22	Lesson 23	Lesson 24	Lesson 25	Cumulative Test 4
Day 7	**Day 8**	**Day 9**	**Day 10**	**Day 11**	**Day 12**
Lesson 26	Lesson 27	Lesson 28	Lesson 29	Lab 2 Lesson 30	Cumulative Test 5
Day 13					
Investigation 3					

Block: 90-Minute Class

Day 1	Day 2	Day 3	Day 4	Day 5	Day 6
Investigation 2 Lesson 21	Lesson 22 Lesson 23	Lesson 24 Lesson 25	Cumulative Test 4 Lesson 26	Lesson 27 Lesson 28	Lesson 29 Lab 2 Lesson 30
Day 7					
Cumulative Test 5 Investigation 3					

* For suggestions on how to implement Saxon Math in a block schedule, see the Pacing section at the beginning of the Teacher's Edition.

120A   Saxon Algebra 1

Lessons 21–30, Investigation 3

Differentiated Instruction

Below Level		Advanced Learners	
Warm Up	SE pp. 120, 127, 134, 140, 146, 153, 159, 164, 171, 179	Challenge	TE pp. 126, 131, 139, 144, 152, 158, 162, 169, 176, 186, 189
Skills Bank	SE pp. 846–883	Extend the Example	TE pp. 123, 129, 136, 142, 148, 155, 160, 166, 172, 182
Reteaching Masters	Lessons 21–30, Investigation 3	Extend the Exploration	TE pp. 121, 127
Warm Up Transparencies	Lessons 21–30	Extend the Problem	TE pp. 124, 131, 133, 138, 144, 150, 151, 157, 158, 162, 163, 174, 176, 184, 186, 187
Prerequisite Skills Intervention	Skills 11, 14, 22, 68, 69, 70, 71, 72, 78, 80, 83, 85, 86	Challenge and Enrichment Masters	Challenge: 21–30; Enrichment: 23, 25, 26, 28, 30

English Learners		Special Needs	
EL Tips	TE pp. 124, 130, 138, 143, 148, 155, 161, 168, 172, 181, 188	Inclusion Tips	TE pp. 121, 123, 128, 137, 142, 147, 151, 156, 160, 165, 173, 182
Multilingual Glossary	Booklet and Online English Learners Handbook	Adaptations for Saxon Algebra 1	Lessons 21–30, Cumulative Tests 4, 5

For All Learners			
Exploration	SE pp. 121, 127, 164, 189	Alternate Method	TE pp. 122, 129, 149, 154, 166, 167, 180, 183, 184,
Caution	SE pp. 130, 136, 154	Manipulative Use	TE pp. 135, 136, 141, 150, 174
Hints	SE pp. 121, 140, 142, 147, 148, 155, 159, 172, 173, 174, 188	Online Tools	
Error Alert	TE pp. 122, 123, 124, 128, 130, 133, 136, 137, 139, 141, 142, 143, 145, 147, 149, 151, 155, 157, 158, 161, 163, 165, 167, 169, 172, 174, 175, 182, 183, 184, 188		

SE = Student Edition; TE = Teacher's Edition

Math Vocabulary

Lesson	New Vocabulary		Maintained	EL Tip in TE
21			inverse operations variable	initial velocity final velocity
22	bar graph circle graph double-bar graph	double-line graph line graph stem-and-leaf plot	horizontal axis vertical axis	circle graphs pie graphs
23			coefficient order of operations reciprocal	substitute
24			power	like
25	domain function range	relation vertical-line test	dependent variable independent variable ordered pair x-value y-value	dependent independent
26			like terms	acute right
27			vertical scale	misleading
28	identity		like terms inverse operations	isolate
29	literal equation		variable	solve
30	linear equation linear function		relation vertical-line test	function
INV 3	convenience sampling method simple random sampling method stratified random sampling method systematic random sampling method voluntary sampling method		population sample random	bias

Section Overview 3

SECTION OVERVIEW 3

Math Highlights

Enduring Understandings – The "Big Picture"

After completing Section 3, students will understand:

- How to solve multi-step equations and literal equations.
- How to identify functions, independent and dependent variables, and the domain and range.
- How to write functions.
- How to choose appropriate graphs to display data and identify misleading graphs.

Essential Questions

- How do functions and equations relate to each other?
- What is the nature of equality and how is it represented through mathematical symbols?
- What is the purpose of displaying data?

Math Content Strands	Math Processes

Math Content Strands

Equations
- Lesson 21 — Solving One-Step Equations by Multiplying or Dividing
- Lesson 23 — Solving Two-Step Equations
- Lesson 24 — Solving Decimal Equations
- Lesson 26 — Solving Multi-Step Equations
- Lesson 28 — Solving Equations with Variables on Both Sides
- Lesson 29 — Solving Literal Equations

Functions and Relations
- Lesson 25 — Differentiating Between Relations and Functions
- Lesson 30 — Graphing Functions
- Lab 2 — Graphing Calculator: Creating a Table

Probability and Data Analysis
- Lesson 22 — Analyzing and Comparing Statistical Graphs
- Lesson 27 — Identifying Misleading Representations of Data
- Investigation 3 — Analyzing the Effects of Bias in Sampling, Surveys, and Bar Graphs

Connections in Practice Problems

	Lessons
Geometry	21, 22, 23, 24, 25, 26, 27, 28, 29, 30
Measurement	21, 24, 25, 27, 28, 29, 30
Probability	21, 22, 23, 24, 26, 28, 29
Statistics	23, 27

Math Processes

Reasoning and Communication

	Lessons
Analyze	21, 22, 25, 26, 27, 29, 30, Inv 3
Connect	29
Error analysis	21, 22, 23, 24, 25, 26, 28, 29, 30
Estimate	21, 28
Formulate	28
Generalize	22, 24, 25, 28, 29, 30
Justify	21, 23, 24, 26, 27, 29, 30, Inv 3
Math Reasoning	21, 22, 23, 24, 25, 26, 28, 29, 30
Model	23, 26, 30
Multiple choice	21, 22, 23, 24, 25, 26, 27, 28, 29, 30
Multi-step	21, 22, 23, 24, 25, 26, 27, 28, 29, 30
Predict	22, 30
True or False	22, 27, 28
Verify	21, 22, 23, 24, 25, 26, 27, 28, 29, 30
Write	21, 22, 23, 24, 25, 26, 27, 28, 29, 30, Inv. 3
Graphing Calculator	22, 24, 26, 29, 30, Lab 2

Connections

In Examples: Architecture, Car wash fundraiser, Fitness, Geometry Landscaping, Reading, Telephone rates, Television prices, Travel plans, Yearly sales, Zoology

In Practice problems: Accounting, Altitude, Architecture, Astronomical unit, Astronomy, Automotive safety, Average cost, Basketball, Biased questions, Biology, Carpentry, Coins, Computer engineering, Construction, Consumer economics, Consumer math, Contests, Cooking, Digital technology, Emails to Congress, Employment, Endangered animals, Energy conservation, Fundraising, Golf, Grades, Hair growth, Highway mileage, Hiking, Internet access, Internet usage, Investing, Kangaroos, Landscape design, Luggage survey, Marketing, Membership rates, Meteorology, Movie club, Novelist, Phone charges, Photography, Physics, Population growth, Presidential facts, Pricing, Printing, Production, Quality control, Racing, Retailing, Safety, Sales, Savings, Stock market, Temperature, Travel, Traveling costs, Wages, Zoo survey

Content Trace

Lesson	Warm Up: Prerequisite Skills	New Concepts	Where Practiced	Where Assessed	Looking Forward
21	Lessons 2, 9, 11, 19	Solving One-Step Equations by Multiplying or Dividing	Lessons 22, 23, 24, 25, 26, 27, 28, 30, 31, 33	Cumulative Tests 5, 6, 7	Lessons 23, 24, 26, 28, 29, 31
22	Lessons 1, 7, Skills Bank 1	Analyzing and Comparing Statistical Graphs	Lessons 23, 24, 25, 26, 27, 28, 29, 30, 31, 32, 37, 38, 40, 42	Cumulative Tests 5, 6	Lessons 27, 48, 54, 62, Investigation 3
23	Lessons 2, 9, 15, 18, 19	Solving Two-Step Equations	Lessons 25, 26, 27, 28, 29, 30, 31, 32, 34, 35, 36, 41, 43	Cumulative Tests 5, 6, 7, 9, 11	Lessons 24, 26, 28, 29
24	Lessons 3, 16, Skills Bank 1	Solving Decimal Equations	Lessons 25, 26, 27, 28, 29, 31, 32, 33, 34, 40, 42, 43, 44, 54, 55, 85	Cumulative Tests 5, 6, 7, 8	Lessons 26, 28, 29, 36, 42
25	Lessons 3, 17, 20, 24	Differentiating Between Relations and Functions	Lessons 26, 27, 28, 29, 30, 31, 32, 33, 34, 35, 36, 37, 39, 40, 41, 43, 44, 52	Cumulative Tests 5, 6	Lessons 30, 34, 71
26	Lessons 11, 18, 23	Solving Multi-Step Equations	Lessons 27, 28, 29, 30, 31, 32, 33, 34, 36, 37, 38, 39, 41, 47, 48, 54, 56, 59	Cumulative Tests 6, 7, 8, 9	Lessons 28, 29, 31, 36, 42, 47
27	Lessons 22, 26, Inv. 2	Identifying Misleading Representations of Data	Lessons 28, 29, 30, 32, 33, 34, 36, 37, 39, 40, 42	Cumulative Tests 6, 8, 9	Lessons 48, 54, 62
28	Lessons 2, 7, 26	Solving Equations with Variables on Both Sides	Lessons 29, 30, 31, 32, 33, 34, 35, 36, 37, 38, 41, 44, 47, 49, 52, 54, 55, 58, 59, 85	Cumulative Tests 6, 7, 8, 9, 10, 11	Lessons 29, 31, 36, 42, 47, 117
29	Lessons 2, 9, 26, 28	Solving Literal Equations	Lessons 30, 31, 32, 34, 37, 38, 42, 57	Cumulative Tests 6, 7, 8	Lessons 31, 36, 42, 47, 55
30	Lessons 9, 20, 25	Graphing Functions	Lessons 31, 32, 34, 37, 38, 39, 42, 43, 45, 46	Cumulative Tests 6, 7	Lessons 34, 50, 55, 71, 78, 96
INV 3	N/A	Investigation: Analyzing the Effects of Bias in Sampling, Surveys, and Bar Graphs	Lessons 35, 38	Cumulative Tests 8, 10	Lessons 48, 54, 62

SECTION OVERVIEW 3

Ongoing Assessment

	Type	Feature	Intervention *
BEFORE instruction	Assess Prior Knowledge	• Diagnostic Test	• Prerequisite Skills Intervention
BEFORE the lesson	Formative	• Warm Up	• Skills Bank • Reteaching Masters
DURING the lesson	Formative	• Lesson Practice • Math Conversations with the Practice problems	• Additional Examples in TE • Test and Practice Generator (for additional practice sheets)
AFTER the lesson	Formative	• Check for Understanding (closure)	• Scaffolding Questions in TE
AFTER 5 lessons	Summative	After Lesson 25 • Cumulative Test 4 • Performance Task 4 After Lesson 30 • Cumulative Test 5 • Performance Task 5	• Reteaching Masters • Test and Practice Generator (for additional tests and practice)
AFTER 20 lessons	Summative	• Benchmark Tests	• Reteaching Masters • Test and Practice Generator (for additional tests and practice)

* for students not showing progress during the formative stages or scoring below 80% on the summative assessments

Evidence of Learning – What Students Should Know

Because the Saxon philosophy is to provide students with sufficient time to learn and practice each concept, a lesson's topic will not be tested until at least five lessons after the topic is introduced.

On the Cumulative Tests that are given during this section of ten lessons, students should be able to demonstrate the following competencies:
- Simplify and evaluate algebraic expressions with two or three variables.
- Combine like terms in algebraic expressions with and without exponents. Add real numbers.
- Translate words into algebraic expressions.
- Solve two-step equations with fractions and decimals.
- Identify the dependent variable and graph ordered pairs on a coordinate plane.
- Calculate theoretical probability of an event.
- Compare expressions involving square roots.
- Analyze stem-and-leaf plots.
- Convert units of measure.

Test and Practice Generator CD using ExamView™

The Test and Practice Generator is an easy-to-use benchmark and assessment tool that creates unlimited practice and tests in multiple formats and allows you to customize questions or create new ones. A variety of reports are available to track student progress toward mastery of the standards throughout the year.

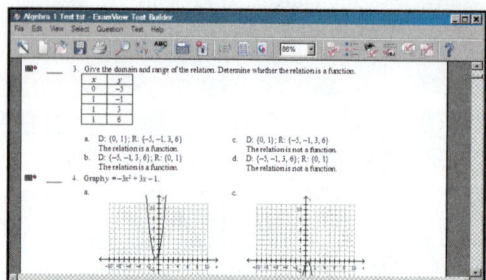
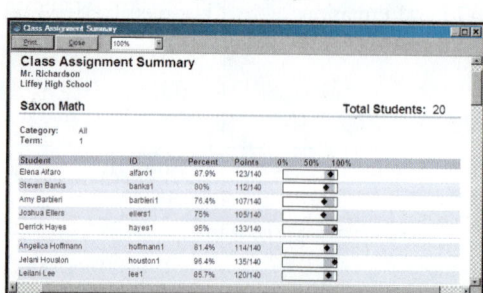

Saxon *Algebra 1*

Assessment Resources

Resources for Diagnosing and Assessing

- **Student Edition**
  - Warm Up
  - Lesson Practice

- **Teacher's Edition**
  - Math Conversations with the Practice problems
  - Check for Understanding (closure)

- **Course Assessments**
  - Diagnostic Test
  - Cumulative Tests
  - Performance Tasks
  - Benchmark Tests

Resources for Test Prep

- **Student Edition Practice**
  - Multiple-choice problems
  - Multiple-step and writing problems
  - Daily cumulative practice

- **Standardized Test Practice**

- **College Entrance Exam Practice**

- **Test and Practice Generator CD using ExamView™**

Resources for Intervention

- **Student Edition**
  - Skills Bank

- **Teacher's Edition**
  - Additional Examples
  - Scaffolding questions

- **Prerequisite Skills Intervention**
  - Worksheets

- **Reteaching Masters**
  - Lesson instruction and practice sheets

- **Test and Practice Generator CD using ExamView™**
  - Lesson practice problems
  - Additional tests

Cumulative Tests

The assessments in Saxon Math are frequent and consistently placed after every five lessons to offer a regular method of ongoing testing. These cumulative assessments check mastery of concepts from previous lessons.

Performance Tasks

The Performance Tasks can be used in conjunction with the Cumulative Tests and are scored using a rubric.

After Lesson 25
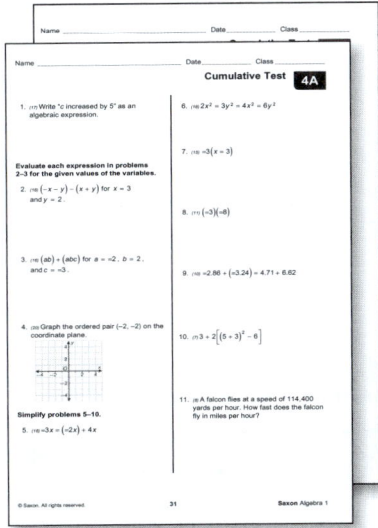

After Lesson 30
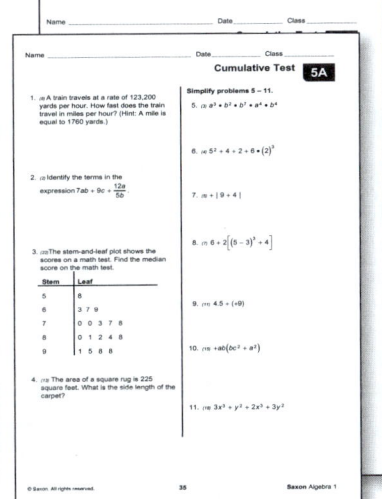

For use with Performance Tasks
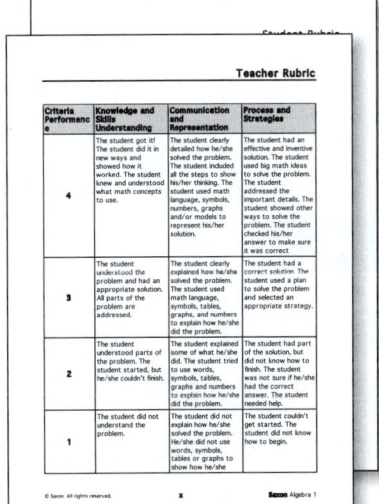

LESSON 21

1 Warm Up

Problem 5

In order for the equation to remain true, an operation applied to the left side of the equation must also be applied to the right side of the equation. Remind students that addition and subtraction are inverse operations. In this problem, they must subtract 5 to "undo" adding 5.

2 New Concepts

In this lesson, students learn how to solve one-step equations by multiplying or dividing.

Discuss with students how they have solved one-step equations before with addition and subtraction. Remind them that they used inverse operations to isolate variables.

Have students make connections between the Addition and Subtraction Properties of Equality and the Multiplication and Division Properties of Equality.

LESSON RESOURCES

Student Edition Practice
  Workbook 21
Reteaching Master 21
Adaptations Master 21
Challenge and Enrichment
  Master C21

120 *Saxon* Algebra 1

LESSON 21

Solving One-Step Equations by Multiplying or Dividing

Warm Up

1. **Vocabulary** In the equation $5x = 10$, x is the _____. (*variable, coefficient*) **variable**
(2)
2. Multiply $\frac{4}{5}$ and $\frac{1}{2}$. Give the answer in simplest form. $\frac{2}{5}$
(11)
3. Divide $\frac{3}{4}$ by $\frac{1}{2}$. Give the answer in simplest form. $\frac{3}{2}$ or $1\frac{1}{2}$
(11)
4. Evaluate $8n + 2$ for $n = 0.5$. **6**
(9)
5. **Multiple Choice** Which is the solution? **D**
(19)
   $5 + x = 7$
   A 12   **B** 7
   C 5   **D** 2

New Concepts

To find the solution of an equation, isolate the variable by using inverse operations. You must use the same inverse operation on each side of the equation.

Math Language

An **inverse operation** undoes another operation.

Inverse Operations

Add ⟷ Subtract
Multiply ⟷ Divide

Multiplication and Division Properties of Equality
Multiplication Property of Equality
Both sides of an equation can be multiplied by the same number, and the statement will still be true.
Examples $2 = 2$ $a = b$
$3 \cdot 2 = 3 \cdot 2$ $a \cdot c = b \cdot c$
$6 = 6$ $ac = bc$
Division Property of Equality
Both sides of an equation can be divided by the same number, and the statement will still be true.
Examples $10 = 10$ $a = b$
$\frac{10}{2} = \frac{10}{2}$ $\frac{a}{c} = \frac{b}{c} (c \neq 0)$
$5 = 5$

Online Connection
www.SaxonMathResources.com

120 *Saxon* Algebra 1

MATH BACKGROUND

For an equation of the form $ax = b$, the solution is:

$$ax = b$$
$$ax \cdot \frac{1}{a} = b \cdot \frac{1}{a}$$
$$x = \frac{b}{a}$$

Substitute $\frac{b}{a}$ into the original equation to verify that it is the correct solution.

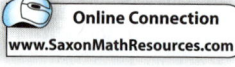 The statement is true.

Equations can have many equivalent forms. Here are a few examples.

Equation		Equivalent form
$a = bx$	Divide both sides by b.	$\frac{a}{b} = x$
$bx = a$	Swap left and right sides.	$a = bx$
$-a = bx$	Multiply both sides by -1.	$a = -bx$

Exploration: Using Inverse Operations

Copy and complete each table. Find the value of x by using the given values for the expression. Then explain how you found the values in the first column.

a.

x	$\frac{60}{x}$
60	1
30	2
20	3
15	4
12	5
10	6

Sample: Divide 60 by the given value.

b.

x	$4x$
2	8
5	20
8	32
9	36
12	48
15	60

Sample: Divide the given value by 4.

c. Justify Is 20 a solution of the equation $\frac{60}{x} = 3$? Explain.   Sample: Yes, 60 divided by 20 is equal to 3.

d. Justify Is 7 a solution of the equation $4x = 54$? Explain.   Sample: No, $4(7) = 28$

Example 1 Solving Equations by Multiplying

Solve each equation. Then check the solution.

a. $\frac{x}{6} = 8$

SOLUTION

$$\frac{x}{6} = 8$$

$$6 \cdot \frac{x}{6} = 8 \cdot 6 \quad \text{Multiplication Property of Equality}$$

$$x = 48$$

Check Substitute 6 for x.

$$\frac{48}{6} \stackrel{?}{=} 8$$

$$8 = 8 \checkmark$$

b. $-11 = \frac{1}{4}w$

SOLUTION

$$\frac{4}{1} \cdot -11 = \frac{4}{1} \cdot \frac{1}{4}w \quad \text{Multiplication Property of Equality}$$

$$-44 = w \quad \text{Simplify.}$$

Check Substitute -44 for w.

$$-11 = \frac{1}{4}w$$

$$-11 \stackrel{?}{=} \frac{1}{4}(-44)$$

$$-11 = -11 \checkmark$$

Hint
Inverse operations "undo" each other. Multiplying by 6 "undoes" dividing by 6.

Math Reasoning

Verify Show that dividing both sides of the equation by 5 or multiplying both sides of the equation by $\frac{1}{5}$, will result in the same solution.

$\frac{1}{5} \cdot 5x = 20 \cdot \frac{1}{5}$, $x = 4$

Lesson 21   121

Exploration

Students evaluate an expression using multiplication and division to generate a table of values. This teaches students to reason about solutions without using an algorithm. For example, in Problem d they are asked if 7 is a solution of $4x = 54$. Although students did not evaluate the expression for $x = 7$, they can estimate that the solution must be between 12 and 15 ($4 \cdot 12 = 48$ and $4 \cdot 15 = 60$), so $x = 7$ cannot be a solution.

Extend the Exploration

Is 17 a solution of the equation $4x = 65$? Explain.
Sample: no, $4 \cdot 17 = 68$.

Example 1

In Lesson 19, students used inverse operations to solve addition and subtraction equations. Now they solve multiplication and division equations.

TEACHER TIP

In Example 1a students who have difficulty with fractions in equations may benefit from rewriting $\frac{x}{6}$ as $\frac{1}{6}x$. This will help students see that multiplying both sides by 6 will isolate x.

Additional Example 1

Solve. Check the solution.

a. $\frac{x}{7} = 8$ $x = 56$; $\frac{56}{7} = 8$

b. $-3 = \frac{3}{2}x$ $x = -2$; $\frac{3}{2} \cdot -2 = \frac{-6}{2} = -3$

INCLUSION

In the Exploration, students may have difficulty with directionality (working from right to left). Point out that the two tables are similar. In the first table, you divide to find the answer. In the second table, it looks like you should multiply, but because you are working from right to left, you divide to find the missing values.

In each table, guide students by asking for the first two values.

"60 divided by 1 equals what number?" 60

"60 divided by 2 equals what number?" 30

"What number times 4 equals 8?" 2

"What number times 4 equals 20?" 5

Lesson 21   121

Example 2

Point out that division is the same as multiplying by a reciprocal.

Error Alert When the coefficient of the variable is a fraction, such as in Example 2c, students may multiply the other side by that fraction instead of by the reciprocal. Remind students to be sure to multiply or divide both sides by the same number.

Additional Example 2

Solve each equation. Then check the solution.

a. $12x = 132$ $x = 11$

b. $-8x = 60$
$x = -\frac{15}{2}$ or $x = -7\frac{1}{2}$

c. $\frac{4}{7}x = \frac{9}{14}$
$x = \frac{9}{8}$ or $x = 1\frac{1}{8}$

Example 2 Solving Equations by Dividing

Solve each equation. Then check the solution.

a. $5x = 20$

SOLUTION

$5x = 20$

$\frac{5x}{5} = \frac{20}{5}$ Division Property of Equality

$x = 4$ Simplify.

Check Substitute 4 for x.

$5x = 20$
$5(4) \stackrel{?}{=} 20$
$20 = 20$ ✓

b. $-12 = 3n$

SOLUTION

$-12 = 3n$

$-\frac{12}{3} = \frac{3n}{3}$ Division Property of Equality

$-4 = n$ Simplify.

Check Substitute -4 for n.

$-12 = 3n$
$-12 \stackrel{?}{=} 3(-4)$
$-12 = -12$ ✓

Reading Math

$\frac{2}{5}p$ can be written as $\frac{2p}{5}$, $\left(\frac{2}{5}\right)p$, $\frac{2}{5} \cdot p$, or $\frac{2}{5} \times p$.

c. $\frac{2}{5}p = 7$

SOLUTION

$\frac{2}{5}p = 7$

$\left(\frac{2}{5} \div \frac{2}{5}\right)p = \left(7 \div \frac{2}{5}\right)$ Divide both sides by $\frac{2}{5}$.

$\left(\frac{\overset{1}{\cancel{2}}}{\underset{1}{\cancel{5}}} \cdot \frac{\overset{1}{\cancel{5}}}{\underset{1}{\cancel{2}}}\right)p = \left(7 \cdot \frac{5}{2}\right)$ Divide by multiplying by the reciprocal of $\frac{2}{5}$, which is $\frac{5}{2}$.

$p = \frac{35}{2}$

Check Substitute $\frac{35}{2}$ for p.

$\left(\frac{\overset{1}{\cancel{2}}}{\underset{1}{\cancel{5}}}\right)\left(\frac{\overset{7}{\cancel{35}}}{\underset{1}{\cancel{2}}}\right) \stackrel{?}{=} 7$

$7 = 7$ ✓

ALTERNATE METHOD FOR EXAMPLE 2b

Have students solve the equation by multiplying both sides by $\frac{1}{3}$.

$-12 = 3n$

$-12 \cdot \frac{1}{3} = 3n \cdot \frac{1}{3}$

$-4 = n$

Write equations to solve real-world problems.

Example 3 — Application: Architecture

Anita is an architect. She is designing a rectangular room that has an area of 126 square feet. If the length of the room is 12 feet, what is its width?

Understand

The answer will be the width of the room in feet.

List the important information:
- The room is a rectangle.
- The area is 126 square feet.
- The length is 12 feet.

Plan

To find the area of a rectangle, multiply the length by the width.

Solve

$A = lw$ Write the formula.

$126 = 12w$ Substitute 126 for A and 12 for l.

$\dfrac{126}{12} = \dfrac{12w}{12}$ Division Property of Equality

$10\dfrac{6}{12} = w$ Simplify.

The width will be $10\dfrac{1}{2}$ feet.

Check

Area of a rectangle = length × width

$126 \stackrel{?}{=} 12 \times 10\dfrac{1}{2}$

$126 = 126$ ✓

Lesson Practice

Solve each equation. Then check the solution.

a. (Ex 1) $\dfrac{k}{9} = 3$ $k = 27$

b. (Ex 1) $-20 = \dfrac{1}{5}m$ $m = -100$

c. (Ex 2) $8y = 24$ $y = 3$

d. (Ex 2) $-15 = 3x$ $x = -5$

e. (Ex 2) $\dfrac{3}{4}y = 11$ $y = \dfrac{44}{3}$

f. (Ex 2) $8 = -\dfrac{5}{12}n$ $n = -\dfrac{96}{5}$

g. (Ex 3) A rectangular pool has an area of 140 square feet. If the length of the pool is 16 feet, what is its width? $8\dfrac{3}{4}$ ft

Lesson 21

Example 3

Extend the Example

"Anita is designing a square storage room. The perimeter is 40 feet. Write and solve an equation to find the dimensions of the storage room floor."
$40 = 4s$; 10 feet by 10 feet

Additional Example 3

Find the width of a rectangular rug, if the area is 44 square inches and the length is 8 inches. $5\dfrac{1}{2}$ in.

Lesson Practice

Problem e

Scaffolding First ask students to identify the reciprocal of $\dfrac{3}{4}$.

Problem f

Error Alert Students may forget that when the coefficient is negative, the reciprocal is also negative. Encourage students to check their solutions.

Check for Understanding

The following questions help assess the concepts taught in this lesson.

"If the product of two factors equals 1, what do you know about the factors?" Sample: The factors are reciprocals of each other.

"How can the Multiplication Property of Equality be used to solve $\dfrac{1}{2}y = 2$?"

Sample: Multiplying each side of the equation by the reciprocal of the fraction keeps the equation true and isolates the variable.

 INCLUSION

Materials: grid paper

For Example 3, guide students to model the problem by drawing a rectangle and using a guess-and-check strategy.

"If each row is 12 ft long, how many 1-inch squares would be in each row?" 12

"Suppose you guess that there are 10 rows. What will the area be? 120 ft²

"How can you revise your guess to increase the area by 6 ft²?" Add another half row: $10\dfrac{1}{2}$ ft · 12 ft = 126 ft²

"How do you find the area of a rectangle?" Multiply the length by the width.

"How can you use the area of the rectangle and the length to find the width?" Divide the area by the length.

3 Practice

Math Conversations
Discussion to strengthen understanding

Problem 6
Extend the Problem
"The picture frame has a perimeter of 28 inches. Write and solve an equation to find the width of the picture frame." $2(3w + w) = 28$; $w = 3\frac{1}{2}$ in.

Problem 9
Error Alert
Some students may not notice the negative signs and may multiply by 9 instead of multiplying by -9.

Practice Distributed and Integrated

*1. (Safety) For every 4 feet a ladder rises, the base of the ladder should be placed 1 foot away from the bottom of a building. If the base of the ladder is 7 feet from the bottom of a building, find the height the ladder rises up the building? $\frac{x}{4} = 7$; The ladder rises 28 feet.
(21)

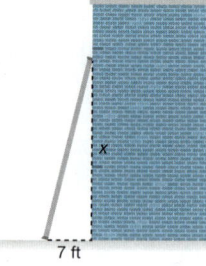

2. What is a term of an algebraic expression? Sample: The term in an algebraic expression is the part to be added or subtracted.
(2)

*3. **Write** Explain how to use inverse operations to solve $\frac{2}{3}x = 8$.
(21)

3. Sample: Multiply both sides by the multiplicative inverse of $\frac{2}{3}$, which is $\frac{3}{2}$, in order to isolate x. $\frac{3}{2} \cdot \frac{2}{3}x = 8 \cdot \frac{3}{2}$, $x = 12$.

*4. (Physics) In physics equations, a change in a quantity is represented by the delta symbol, Δ. A change in velocity, Δv, is calculated using the equation $\Delta v = v_f - v_i$, where v_i is the initial velocity and v_f is the final velocity. If a cart has an initial velocity of 5 miles per second and experiences a change in velocity of 2 miles per second, what is the final velocity of the cart? 7 miles per second
(19)

5. Graph the ordered pair $(-2, 6)$ on a coordinate plane.
(20)

6. **Geometry** The length of a rectangular picture frame is 3 times the width.
(3)
   a. Draw a picture of the picture frame and label the dimensions.
   b. Write an expression for the area of the frame. $3w^2$

7. Complete the table for $y = 2x + 7$.
(20)

x	−5	1	4
y	−3	9	15

5.

6a.

*8. Solve $\frac{x}{3} = 5$. $x = 15$
(21)

*9. **Multiple-Choice** Which step can you use first to solve $-\frac{x}{9} = -52$? B
(21)
  A Multiply both sides by $\frac{1}{9}$.
  B Multiply both sides by -9.
  C Divide both sides by -52.
  D Divide both sides by 52.

*10. **Estimate** Alan makes $1 for each snow cone he sells. Alan calculates his profit by subtracting the daily cost of $195 to run the stand from the amount he makes on the snow cones that he sells each day. How many snow cones does Alan need to sell to make a profit of $200 a day? 395 snow cones
(19)

124 Saxon Algebra 1

ENGLISH LEARNERS

For Problem 4, explain the meaning of **initial velocity** and **final velocity**. Say: "Initial velocity means the starting speed. Final velocity means the ending speed."

Have students identify the initial and final velocity in the exercise. Say:

"In physics, velocity is speed in a given direction. Change in velocity usually means speeding up or slowing down."

Have students suggest situations that could represent a change in velocity. Sample: a car driving on the freeway then slowing down on the off ramp, a bus stopping and then going back into the traffic.

11. **Write** Explain which terms in $3z^2y + 2yz - 4y^2z - z^2y + 8yz$ can be combined.

12. **Astronomy** The relative weight of an object on the surface of Jupiter can be found using $2.364w$, where w is the weight of the object on Earth. The space shuttle weighs about 4,500,000 pounds on earth. What would be the weight of the space shuttle on Jupiter? 10,638,000 lb

13. **Geometry** The length of a frame is 8 inches. Let w be the width of the frame. The formula $A = 8w$ calculates the area of backing needed for a framed picture. Complete the table and graph the solutions.

w	A
2	16
4	32
6	48
8	64

13.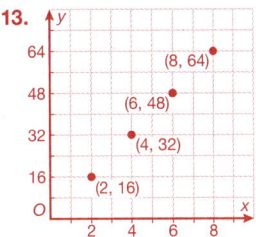

14. Simplify $-4 - 3 + 2 - 4 - 3 - 8$. -20

15. **Multiple Choice** Simplify $5p + 7 - 8p + 2$. **A**
   A $9 - 3p$ B $3p - 9$ C $13p + 5$ D $13p - 9$

16. **Verify** Evaluate $\frac{2}{3}(4 + \frac{3}{4})$ using two different methods. Verify the solution of each method.

17. **Probability** A letter of the alphabet is randomly chosen. What is the probability that the letter is a vowel? $\frac{5}{26}$

18. **Justify** The area of a square is 100 square feet, what is the length of each side? Explain. 10 feet; Sample: A square has equal sides and $A = s^2$, so the length of one side is $\sqrt{100} = 10$.

19. **Measurement** A picture framer calculates the amount of materials needed using $2l + 2w$. If the framer used $2w + 2l$, would the results be the same? Explain.

*20. **Multi-Step** Alda's school is 1200 yards from her house. She walks 150 yards per minute. The equation $y = 1200 - 150x$ represents how far she will be from the school after x minutes.
   a. Complete the table and graph the solutions. See Additional Answers.

x	y
1	1050
4	600
6	300
8	0

   b. What does it mean to say that after 8 minutes, she is 0 yards from the school? See Additional Answers.

*21. **Analyze** A student says that to solve $-\frac{3}{4}x = 12$ you should divide each side by $-\frac{3}{4}$. Another student says that to solve the equation you should multiply each side by $-\frac{4}{3}$. Will both methods result in the correct solution? Explain.

---

11. Sample: $3z^2y$ and $-z^2y$ can be combined. $2yz$ and $8yz$ can be combined. Each pair has the same variables and the same powers of variables. $-4y^2z$ cannot be combined with any other term because no other term has y^2z.

16. **Method 1**
$$\frac{2}{3}(4 + \frac{3}{4})$$
$$= \frac{2}{3}(4) + \frac{2}{3}(\frac{3}{4})$$
$$= \frac{8}{3} + \frac{1}{2}$$
$$= \frac{19}{6}$$

Method 2
$$\frac{2}{3}(4 + \frac{3}{4})$$
$$= \frac{2}{3}(\frac{19}{4})$$
$$= \frac{19}{6}$$

19. yes; Sample: The Commutative Property of Addition allows the order of the addends to be changed without affecting the result.

21. yes; Sample: Dividing by a number is the same as multiplying by its reciprocal. Dividing by $-\frac{3}{4}$ is the same as multiplying by $-\frac{4}{3}$.

Problem 16
Guide students by asking, "If you used the order of operations, what would you do first?" Add to simplify inside the parentheses.

"If you used the Distributive Property, what would you do first? Multiply. What would you do next?" Add.

Lesson 21   125

Problem 22
Guide the students by asking them the following questions.

"How can you use repeated multiplication to write 4^3?"
$4 \cdot 4 \cdot 4$

"How can you use repeated multiplication to write $\left(\frac{1}{4}\right)^3$?"
$\frac{1}{4} \cdot \frac{1}{4} \cdot \frac{1}{4}$

"If you know that $4 \cdot \frac{1}{4} = 1$, what does $4 \cdot 4 \cdot 4 \cdot \frac{1}{4} \cdot \frac{1}{4} \cdot \frac{1}{4}$ equal?" 1

Problem 30
If students are having trouble, ask, "What do you have to do to $x - 5$ to isolate the x?" Add 5.

---

22. Multi-Step Determine whether $4^3 \cdot \left(\frac{1}{4}\right)^3 = 1$.
(3)
  a. Simplify the expressions 4^3 and $\left(\frac{1}{4}\right)^3$. $64, \frac{1}{64}$
  b. Write an expression for the multiplication of 4^3 and $\left(\frac{1}{4}\right)^3$ without using exponents. Then check to see if the product of the expressions is 1.
  Sample: $4 \cdot 4 \cdot 4 \cdot \frac{1}{4} \cdot \frac{1}{4} \cdot \frac{1}{4} = 64 \cdot \frac{1}{64} = 1$

23. Write Will dividing two integers ever produce an irrational number? Explain.
(1) Sample: no; A rational number can be expressed as a ratio of two integers.

24. Analyze If a student is converting from 225 square units to 22,500 square units,
(8) what units of measure is he or she most likely converting?   Sample: metric units of measure, such as cm² to mm² or dm² to cm²

25. Golf A round of golf takes 4.5 hours and each hole takes 0.25 hours. In the
(20) equation $y = 4.5 - 0.25x$, x is the number of holes played and y is the remaining time to finish the round. Make a table for 4, 8, 12, and 16 holes and then graph the ordered pairs in your table.   See Additional Answers.

26. Simplify $-|15 - 5|$. -10
(5)

*27. Pricing One fruit stand has s strawberries and k kiwis to sell. Another stand has
(18) twice as many strawberries and four times as many kiwis to sell.
  a. Write expressions representing the number of strawberries and kiwis each stand has to sell. $s + k$ and $2s + 4k$
  b. Write an expression for the total number of pieces of fruit. $3s + 5k$

*28. Sketch a graph to represent the following situation: A tomato plant grows at a
(Inv 2) slow rate, and then grows rapidly with more sun and water.

29. Write an algebraic expression for "0.21 of what number is 7.98?" $0.21x = 7.98$
(17)

30. Error Analysis Two students solve $x - 5 = 11$. Which student is correct? Explain
(19) the error.   Student A; Sample: Student B should have added 5 to both sides of the equation to isolate x.

Student A	Student B
$x - 5 = 11$	$x - 5 = 11$
$+5 = +5$	$-5 = -5$
$x = 16$	$x = 6$

28. Tomato Plant Growth

---

126   Saxon Algebra 1

CHALLENGE

"Sometimes you have to use more than one equation to find the answer to a problem. The combined area of 4 equal-sized squares is 324 ft². What is the perimeter of each square? Write and solve equations to find the answer."

$4A = 324$ ft²
$A = 81$ ft²   Area of one square
$A = s^2 = 81$ ft²
$s = \sqrt{81\text{ ft}^2}$
$s = 9$ ft   Length of one side
$P = 4s$
$P = 4(9\text{ ft}) = 36$ ft

LOOKING FORWARD

Solving one-step multiplication and division equations prepares students for

- **Lesson 23** Solving Two-Step Equations
- **Lesson 24** Solving Decimal Equations
- **Lesson 26** Solving Multi-Step Equations
- **Lesson 28** Solving Equations with Variables on Both Sides
- **Lesson 29** Solving Literal Equations
- **Lesson 31** Using Rates, Ratios, and Proportions

LESSON 22

Analyzing and Comparing Statistical Graphs

Warm Up

1. **Vocabulary** The set of real numbers includes all _____ numbers and all _____ numbers. **rational, irrational**

Name the point on the number line that corresponds to each given value.

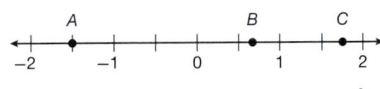

2. -1.5 **point A**
3. 1.75 **point C**
4. $\frac{2}{3}$ **point B**

5. Find the difference between 12.3 million and 20,000. **12,280,000**

New Concepts

Numerical data can be displayed in different ways. **Bar graphs** use vertical and horizontal bars to represent data.

Exploration Analyzing Bar Graphs

A sample survey asked students to name their favorite type of pet. The results are shown in the bar graph.

Math Reasoning

Predict If 1000 students are surveyed, how many are likely to pick dogs as their favorite pets?

320 students

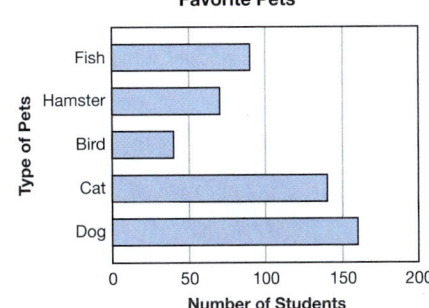

a. types of pets; number of students

a. What information is shown on the vertical axis? the horizontal axis?

b. Use the graph to complete the table.

Pet	Dog	Cat	Bird	Hamster	Fish
Number of Students	160	140	40	70	90

c. How many students were surveyed? $160 + 140 + 40 + 70 + 90 = 500$

d. **Analyze** Which pet did students choose twice as often as the hamster? Explain. cat; Sample: 70 students chose hamster and 140 chose cat. 140 is twice as many as 70.

Online Connection
www.SaxonMathResources.com

LESSON 22

1 Warm Up

Problem 2
Remind students that -1.5 can be written as a mixed number, $-1\frac{1}{2}$. On a number line, -1.5 is less than -1, so it will be to the left of -1.

2 New Concepts

In this lesson, students will interpret various data displays, including double-bar graphs, stem-and-leaf plots, double-line graphs, and circle graphs.

Exploration

Before moving to double-bar graphs, make sure students are proficient at reading bar graphs.

Extend the Exploration

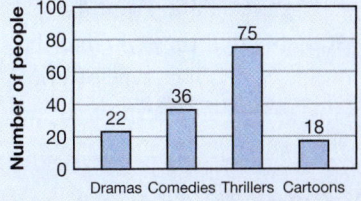

a. How many people were surveyed? **151 people**

b. Which kind of movie was most popular? **thrillers**

LESSON RESOURCES

Student Edition Practice Workbook 22
Reteaching Master 22
Adaptations Master 22
Challenge and Enrichment Master C22
Technology Lab Master 22

MATH BACKGROUND

An important skill for students to practice is choosing an appropriate data display. Double-bar graphs and double-line graphs are useful for comparing two sets of data. Stem-and-leaf plots are useful for visualizing measures of central tendency. Circle graphs are best for analyzing parts of a whole.

Each type of graph also has weaknesses. It often is difficult to read exact data from a bar graph or line graph. A circle graph can be misleading. A circle graph based on data from 30 people could look identical to a graph of data collected from 1500 people.

A **double-bar graph** shows groups of two bars side by side. This allows easier comparison of two related sets of data.

Example 1 Interpreting Double-Bar Graphs

Sal and Harry both own sandwich shops. The double-bar graph shows the number of shops they owned at the end of each year. What conclusions can be made from the graph?

SOLUTION

- Harry always had more shops open than Sal, except in 2004, when they both had the same number of shops open.
- The number of shops Harry owned increased from the years 2001 to 2006.
- The number of shops Sal owned increased from the years 2001 to 2004, but decreased from the years 2004 to 2006.

A **stem-and-leaf plot** is a data display that uses some digits as "stems" and others as "leaves." The "stems" have a greater place value than the "leaves." Stem-and-leaf plots are useful for organizing and ordering data.

Example 2 Interpreting Stem-and-Leaf Plots

The stem-and-leaf plot shows the ages of members of a hiking club.

Find the age of members at the hiking club that occurs most often.

SOLUTION Look at the key. The stems represent tens and the leaves represent ones. So 3|2 represents 3 tens 2 ones, which is 32.

The data set:

10, 10, 17, 24, 26, 32, 33, 34, 41, 41, 41, 43, 53, 56, 56, 59

41 is the data value that occurs most often.

The age that occurs most often is 41 years.

Age of Hiking Club Members

Stem	Leaf
1	0 0 7
2	4 6
3	2 3 4
4	1 1 1 3
5	3 6 6 9

Key: 1|0 means 10

In a **line graph,** a line is drawn through points on a grid to show trends and changes in data over time. As with bar graphs, two related data sets can be compared in a **double-line graph.**

Math Reasoning

Verify How many data values should be in your list?

Sample: There should be the same number of data values as there are leaves in the stem-and-leaf plot.

128 Saxon Algebra 1

 INCLUSION

In Example 1, students who have difficulty with mental processing may have trouble focusing on subsets of the data. Help these students by asking specific questions about subsets of the data.

"What can you conclude if you compare each light blue bar to the dark blue bar touching it?" Sample: The number of shops Harry owns is always greater than or equal to the number Sal owns.

"Look only at the dark blue bars. What trend do you see?" Sample: The number of shops Harry owns increases each year.

Example 3 Interpreting Line and Double-line Graphs

The double-line graph shows the same data as the double-bar graph in Example 1.

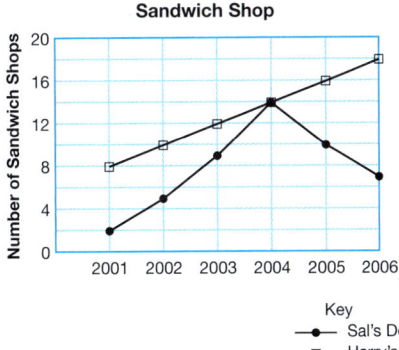

What conclusions can you make from each graph?

SOLUTION

- Sal had fewer sandwich shops than Harry in 2001, but in 2004 they both had the same number of sandwich shops.
- The graph of Harry's shops is a straight line that shows a steady increase in the number of shops each year.
- Harry had 6 more shops than Sal in 2001, they both had 14 shops in 2004, and Harry had 11 more shops than Sal in 2006.

Math Reasoning

Predict If the number of shops Harry owns increases at the same yearly rate, how many shops will he own in 2010?

26 shops

Example 4 Comparing Data using Double-Bar Graphs

The table shows Andre's bank account transactions.

Month	January	February	March	April	May	June
Deposits	$475	$200	$350	$425	$500	$150
Withdrawals	$100	$275	$350	$400	$200	$225

Make a graph to compare the deposits and withdrawals.

SOLUTION Use a double-bar graph to compare the deposits and withdrawals.

- The graph shows that the deposits were greater than the withdrawals in January, April, and May.
- The withdrawals were greater than the deposits in February and June.
- Andre deposited and withdrew the same amount of money in March.

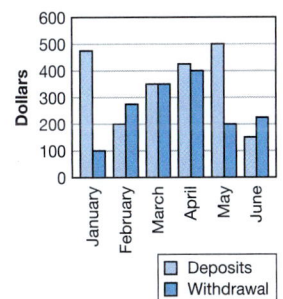

Lesson 22 **129**

Example 3

Students will see an alternative display of the data from the double-bar graph in Example 1. Point out to students that the double-line graph makes it easier to see different trends between the data sets.

Additional Example 3

How many more shops than Sal did Harry have in 2002? in 2005? 5; 6

Example 4

Students learn how to choose an appropriate graph to compare data.

Extend the Example

"Andre would like to make a graph to display his account balance at the end of each month. Which type of graph could he use?" line graph or bar graph

Additional Example 4

What was the next to the greatest difference between the deposits and withdrawals Andre made in a month? $300 in May

---

ALTERNATE METHOD FOR EXAMPLE 4

Have students make a double-line graph to compare the data. Then have students identify in which two months were the deposits and withdrawals almost the same amount. March and April

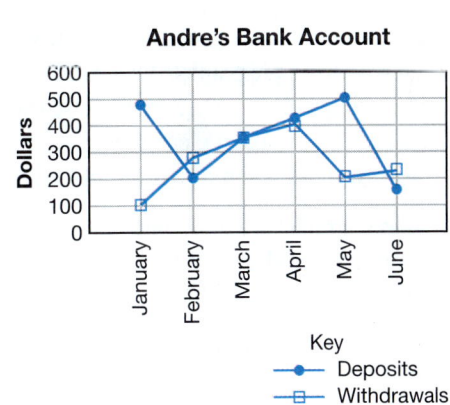

Lesson 22 **129**

Example 5

Students will use a circle graph showing percents of sales by quarter to find amounts of sales each quarter. Make sure that students understand that in real-world problems, the percents may total to 99% or 101% because of rounding errors. This will affect their results when they check their answers.

Additional Example 5

Suppose that next year Art Online has $32 million in sales. If the sales follow the same pattern as this year's sales, what will be the earnings in each quarter? **$3.84 million; $10.24 million; $4.16 million; $13.76 million**

Lesson Practice

Problem b

Error Alert Students may read the greatest value on the graph. Remind them to read the question carefully and to use the key.

Problem c

Scaffolding Have students list the data in order. Then ask what numbers they will use for the stems.

 Check for Understanding

The questions below help assess the concepts taught in this lesson.

"Which type of graph would best display the percents of votes won by each candidate in an election?" **circle graph**

"Which type of graph would best compare changes in two sets of data over time?" **double-line graph**

A **circle graph** uses sections of a circle to compare parts of the circle to the whole circle. The whole circle represents the entire set of data.

Example 5 **Application: Yearly Sales**

The circle graph shows Art Online's total yearly sales by quarter. The total amount of sales for the year was $20 million. Find the sales for each quarter.

Caution
Circle graphs are sometimes labeled with actual data values instead of percents. Always check the labels and keys of a graph.

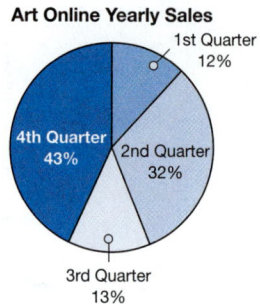

Art Online Yearly Sales
- 1st Quarter 12%
- 2nd Quarter 32%
- 3rd Quarter 13%
- 4th Quarter 43%

SOLUTION

Multiply the percent of sales for each quarter by the total amount for the year.

1st Quarter: $12\% \times 20$ million $= 0.12 \times 20$ million $= 2.4$ million
2nd Quarter: $32\% \times 20$ million $= 0.32 \times 20$ million $= 6.4$ million
3rd Quarter: $13\% \times 20$ million $= 0.13 \times 20$ million $= 2.6$ million
4th Quarter: $43\% \times 20$ million $= 0.43 \times 20$ million $= 8.6$ million

Check Find the sum of the amounts calculated for each quarter.

$2,400,000 + 6,400,000 + 2,600,000 + 8,600,000 = 20,000,000$

Lesson Practice

a. (Ex 1) Use the double-bar graph in Example 1. What year shows the greatest difference between the number of shops Sal and Harry owned? **2006**

b. (Ex 3) Use the double-line graph in Example 3. What was the greatest number of shops Sal opened in one year? **5**

c. (Ex 2) Make a stem-and-leaf plot of the data showing the height in inches of grandchildren in the Jackson family: 56, 52, 68, 49, 49, 40, 72, 71, 43, 54. What height occurs most often? **49 in.**

c. Height of Jackson Grandchildren (in inches)

Stem	Leaf
4	0 3 9 9
5	2 4 6
6	8
7	1 2

Key: 6|8 = 68

d. (Ex 4) Use the data in Example 4. Which month shows the greatest difference between deposits and withdrawals? **January**

e. Predict (Ex 5) Use the circle graph from Example 5. If first quarter sales the next year are $3,000,000, predict the total sales for the year. **$25,000,000**

130 Saxon Algebra 1

ENGLISH LEARNERS

Students may sometimes hear **circle graphs** referred to as **pie graphs.** This can be confusing to English Learners. Use these questions to make it clear how dividing a pie into slices is similar to a circle graph.

"Circle graphs are sometimes called pie graphs, or pie charts. What is the shape of a pie?" **a circle**

"Does a pie have to be cut into equal-sized slices?" **no**

"Suppose I cut a pie into four different-sized slices. I label each slice for a different person. How could I show this same information in a circle graph?" **Sample: Make a circle graph that looks like the pie. Label each slice with a name and a fraction or percent.**

Have students look at the circle graph in Example 5 and identify the segment that represents about one-third of the graph. **2nd Quarter Sales: 32%**

Practice   Distributed and Integrated

*1. True or False: A stem-and-leaf plot can help analyze change over time. If false,
(22) explain why.   False; stem-and-leaf plots help organize data.

2. Complete the table for $y = -3x - 9$.
(20)

x	−1	0	1
y	−6	−9	−12

3. Simplify $2p(xy - 3k)$. $2pxy - 6pk$
(15)

4. Solve $y - 3 = 2$. $y = 5$
(19)

*5. Solve $x - \frac{1}{4} = \frac{7}{8}$. $x = \frac{9}{8}$ or $1\frac{1}{8}$
(19)

6. Solve $4x = 2\frac{2}{3}$. $x = \frac{2}{3}$
(21)

7. Solve $7x = 49$. $x = 7$
(21)

*8. Choose an appropriate graph to display the change in profit of a company over
(22) several years. Explain your choice.   line graph; Sample: Line graphs show changes in data over time.

9. **Verify** Determine whether each statement below is true or false. If false, provide a
(1) counterexample.
   a. The set of integers is closed under division.   false; Sample: 3 ÷ 4 is not an integer.
   b. The set of irrational numbers is closed under division.   false; Sample: $\sqrt{3} \div \sqrt{3}$ is a whole number.
   c. The set of integers is closed under addition.   true

*10. (Racing) The table shows the Indianapolis 500 fastest lap times to the nearest
(22) second, every 5 years since 1960. Make an appropriate graph to display the
data. Then make a conclusion about the data.   See Additional Answers.

Fastest Lap Times in the Indianapolis 500

Year	1960	1965	1970	1975	1980	1985	1990	1995	2000	2005
Time (seconds)	62	57	54	48	47	44	40	40	41	39

11. Graph the ordered pair $(-4, -1)$ on a coordinate plane.
(20)

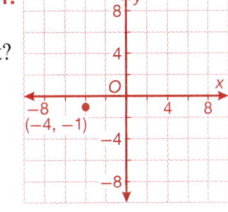

12. **Error Analysis** Two students plotted the point $(-4, 3)$. Which student is correct?
(20) Explain the error.

Student A
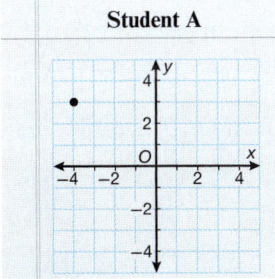

Student B
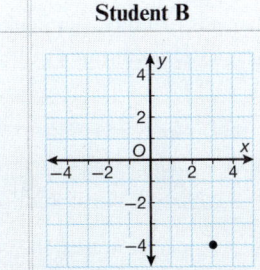

12. Student A; Sample: Student B graphed the point $(3, -4)$ by first moving vertically, then horizontally.

Lesson 22   131

3 Practice

Math Conversations
Discussion to strengthen understanding

Problem 9
Students may need to review closure properties. Remind them that they need only one counterexample, which is one example in which the result of the operation is not part of the set.

Problem 11
Extend the Problem
Have students plot the ordered pairs $(-2.5, 3)$ and $\left(1, -3\frac{1}{2}\right)$ on a coordinate plane.

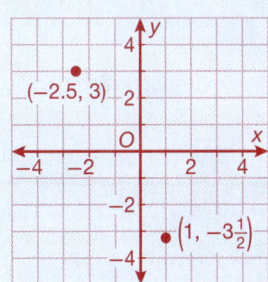

⭐ CHALLENGE

Example 4 discusses Andre's finances. Have students make a graph that displays his account balance at the end of each month.

(Assume there was no money in Andre's account before January.)

Andre's Bank Account

Lesson 22   131

Problem 14
Suggest that students try various numbers that satisfy each part of the question. Then look for a pattern or generalization about the set of answers they generate.

Problem 19
Guide the students by asking them the following questions.

"What would a graph of the data show?" Sample: It would compare the numbers of endangered animals by type for U.S. and other countries.

"What type of graph would display this data well?" double-bar graph

---

13. Multiple Choice A baker needs 25 eggs for all the cakes she plans to bake. She only has 12 eggs. If x is the number of eggs she will buy to complete her ingredients list, which of the following equations best represents how she can find x? **B**
(19)
A $12 - x = 25$ **B** $12 + x = 25$ **C** $25 + x = 12$ **D** $x - 12 = 25$

*14. **Analyze** For the equation $x = 14 - y$, what must be true of each value of x if y is
(19)
a. greater than 14? x must be negative.
b. equal to 14? x must be zero.
c. less than 14? x must be positive.

*15. **Multiple Choice** Which graph would best compare the ages of people living in
(22) two different cities? **D**
A circle graph   B stem-and-leaf plot
C double-line graph   D double-bar graph

16. **Travel** A man travels 25 miles to work. On his way home, he stops to fill up
(17) with gas after going d miles. Write an expression to represent his distance from home. $25 - d$

17. **Verify** Show that each equation is true for the given values of x and y.
(16)
a. $x\left(\dfrac{y}{y-x}\right)^2 = -\dfrac{4}{9}$; $x = -4$ and $y = 2$ b. $|(x-y)^3| = 27$; $x = -1$ and $y = 2$

17a. Sample: True;
$x\left(\dfrac{y}{y-x}\right)^2$
$= -4\left(\dfrac{2}{2-(-4)}\right)^2$
$= -4\left(\dfrac{2}{6}\right)^2$
$= -4\left(\dfrac{1}{3}\right)^2$
$= -4\left(\dfrac{1}{9}\right) = -\dfrac{4}{9}$

17.b. Sample: True;
$|(-1-2)^3| = |(-3)^3| = |-27| = 27$

18. **Write** What is a sample space? Sample: A sample space is the set of all possible outcomes.
(14)

*19. **Endangered Animals** The table shows the number of threatened or endangered
(22) animal species as of July 22, 2007. Make an appropriate graph to display the data. Then make a conclusion about the data. See Additional Answers.

Number of Threatened or Endangered Species in the U.S. and Foreign Countries

	Mammals	Birds	Reptiles	Amphibians	Fish	Clams	Snails	Insects	Arachnids	Crustaceans
U.S.	81	89	37	23	139	70	76	57	12	22
Foreign	276	182	81	9	12	2	1	4	0	0

20. **Generalize** Use the pairs of equations. What can be concluded about the Commutative
(12) Property? Sample: The Commutative Property does not apply to subtraction.

$9 - 5 = 4$ and $5 - 9 = -4$
$12 - 6 = 6$ and $6 - 12 = -6$
$7 - 3 = 4$ and $3 - 7 = -4$

21. **Landscape Design** Wanchen is planting a garden the shape of a trapezoid in
(4) her yard. Use the diagram to find the area of her garden. 26.35 ft²

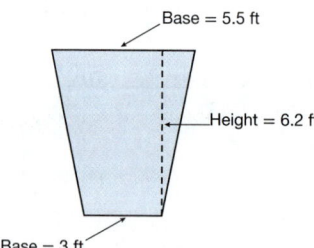

Base = 5.5 ft
Height = 6.2 ft
Base = 3 ft

132   Saxon Algebra 1

22. Simplify $-7 + (-3) + 4 - 3 + (-2)$. -11
(6)

*23. **Geometry** An arc of a circle is a segment of the circumference of a circle. If
(21) an arc measures 16 inches and is $\frac{4}{9}$ the circumference of a circle, what is the
circumference of the circle? $\frac{4}{9}c = 16$; $c = 36$ inches. The circumference is 36 inches.

24. **Multi-Step** A house has an area of 1200 square feet. The owners add on a new
(4) room that is 15 feet long and 20 feet wide. What is the area of the house now?
   a. Write an expression to represent the area of the new room. $15 \cdot 20$
   b. Write an expression to represent the total area of the house now. $1200 + (15 \cdot 20)$
   c. Find the area of the house now. 1500 ft^2

25. **Write** Describe a situation that could be represented by the expression $2d - w$.
(9) Sample: A man makes 2 bank deposits of d dollars and withdraws w dollars.

26. Simplify $3ab^2 - 2ab + 5b^2a - ba$. $8ab^2 - 3ab$
(18)

*27. The circle graph shows the result of a poll on the sleeping habits of children ages
(22) 9–12. What portion of the children said they slept the recommended $9\frac{1}{2}$ to $10\frac{1}{2}$
hours for their age group? Express the answer as a decimal rounded to the nearest
hundredth.   0.32

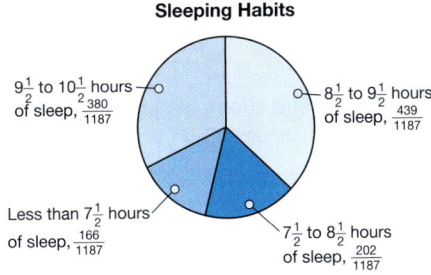

28. Simplify x^2yyyx^3yx. x^6y^4
(3)

*29. **Multi-Step** Enrique pays $31.92 (not including tax) for 6 books that are on sale. Each
(21) book costs the same amount. Enrique pays $\frac{4}{5}$ of the original cost of the books.
   a. What is the sale price of each book? $6x = \$31.92$; $x = \$5.32$
   b. What was the original cost of each book? $\frac{4}{5}x = \$5.32$; $x = \$6.65$

30. **Probability** In a standard deck of cards, there are 13 cards in each
(Inv 1) of four suits: hearts, diamonds, clubs, and spades. Jose randomly
draws a card from a deck and replaces it after each draw. His
results are recorded in the table. Find the experimental probability
of each event.
   a. drawing a heart $\frac{4}{13}$
   b. not drawing a club $\frac{10}{13}$

Outcome	Frequency
Hearts	8
Diamonds	8
Clubs	6
Spades	4

Problem 27
Extend the Problem
"Out of 2500 children aged 9 through 12, about how many would you expect do not get the recommended amount of sleep?"
about 1700 children

Problem 30
Error Alert
Students might use the numbers in "13 cards of 4 suits" instead of the numbers in the table. Remind students that

$P(\text{hearts}) = \frac{\text{number of hearts picked}}{\text{total number of cards picked}}$

not

$P(\text{hearts}) = \frac{\text{number of hearts in deck}}{\text{total number of cards in deck}}$.

Lesson 22   133

LOOKING FORWARD

Analyzing and comparing statistical graphs prepares students for

- **Lesson 27** Identifying Misleading Representations of Data
- **Investigation 3** Analyzing the Effects of Bias in Sampling, Surveys, and Bar Graphs
- **Lesson 48** Analyzing Measures of Central Tendency
- **Lesson 54** Displaying Data in Box-and-Whisker Plots
- **Lesson 62** Displaying Data in Stem-and-Leaf Plots and Histograms

LESSON 23

1 Warm Up

Use the Warm Up to review the prerequisite skills for this lesson such as simplifying expressions. In Problem 2 students use the Distributive Property to simplify.

2 New Concepts

In this lesson, students learn to solve two-step equations.

Discuss why it is necessary to use inverse operations when an equation has two operations, and explain the importance of reversing the order of operations.

Example 1

Remind students that in Lesson 9 they learned to evaluate expressions by substituting a given value in place of the variable and then using the order of operations. Explain that the order of operations must be reversed when solving equations.

Additional Example 1

a. Evaluate $5x + 4$ for $x = 2$. **14**

b. Solve $5x + 4 = 14$. **$x = 2$**

LESSON RESOURCES

Student Edition Practice Workbook 23
Reteaching Master 23
Adaptations Master 23
Challenge and Enrichment Master C23, E23

LESSON 23

Solving Two-Step Equations

Warm Up

1. **Vocabulary** In the equation $-5x = 20$, -5 is the _____ (*variable, coefficient*). **coefficient**

Simplify.

2. $3(x - 4)$ **$3x - 12$**

3. $-2(x - 3) + 4(x + 1)$ **$2x + 10$**

4. Evaluate $\frac{3}{4}n + \frac{5}{6}$ for $n = \frac{2}{9}$. **1**

5. **Multiple Choice** What is the solution of $-7 + x = 14$? **D**
   A -2
   B 2
   C 7
   D 21

New Concepts

If an equation has two operations, use inverse operations and work backward to undo each operation one at a time.

To reverse the order of operations:
- First add or subtract.
- Then multiply or divide.

Example 1 Evaluating Expressions and Solving Equations

a. Evaluate $3x - 2$ for $x = 4$.

SOLUTION Substitute 4 for x and use the order of operations.

$3(4) - 2$ Multiply first.
$12 - 2 = 10$ Then subtract.

b. Solve $3x - 2 = 10$.

SOLUTION Reverse the order of operations.

$$3x - 2 = 10$$
$$\underline{+2 = +2}$$ Undo the subtraction by adding.
$$3x = 12$$
$$\frac{3x}{3} = \frac{12}{3}$$ Undo the multiplication by dividing.
$$x = 4$$

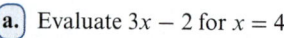
Online Connection
www.SaxonMathResources.com

134   Saxon Algebra 1

MATH BACKGROUND

Isolating a variable is an undoing process, handled by working backward. If students have difficulty understanding why they need to reverse the order of operations, use a story problem to explain. For example, a farmer has x chickens that each lay a dozen eggs. She sells 24 eggs. Now she has 36 eggs. How many chickens does the farmer have? You can write an equation, and underneath write the corresponding parts of the story:

$12x$	$-$	24	$=$	36
x chickens lay eggs		24 eggs sold		36 eggs remaining

First, you must undo the last thing that happened in the story, which is selling the 24 eggs. So, addition is the first step you use to solve this two-step equation.

Math Reasoning

Write Explain why the first step in checking the solution is to multiply by 4 and the last step in solving the equation is to divide by 4.

Sample: When you check the solution you use the order of operations, so you multiply first. When you solve the equation you use inverse operations and reverse the order of operations, so you divide last.

Example 2 Solving Two-Step Equations with Positive Coefficients

Solve the equation. Then check the solution.

$4x + 5 = 17$

SOLUTION To isolate x, first eliminate 5 and then eliminate the 4.

$$4x + 5 = 17$$
$$\underline{-5 = -5} \quad \text{Subtraction Property of Equality}$$
$$4x = 12 \quad \text{Simplify.}$$
$$\frac{4x}{4} = \frac{12}{4} \quad \text{Division Property of Equality}$$
$$x = 3$$

Check Substitute 3 for x in the original equation.

$$4(3) + 5 \stackrel{?}{=} 17$$
$$12 + 5 \stackrel{?}{=} 17$$
$$17 = 17 \checkmark$$

Example 3 Solving Two-Step Equations with Negative Coefficients

Solve the equation. Then check the solution.

$8 = -5m + 6$

SOLUTION To isolate m, first eliminate the 6 and then eliminate the -5.

$$8 = -5m + 6$$
$$\underline{-6 = -6} \quad \text{Subtraction Property of Equality}$$
$$2 = -5m \quad \text{Simplify.}$$
$$\frac{2}{-5} = \frac{-5}{-5}m \quad \text{Division Property of Equality}$$
$$-\frac{2}{5} = m \quad \text{Simplify.}$$

Check Substitute $-\frac{2}{5}$ for m.

$$8 \stackrel{?}{=} -5\left(-\frac{2}{5}\right) + 6$$
$$8 \stackrel{?}{=} 2 + 6$$
$$8 = 8 \checkmark$$

Lesson 23

Example 2
Discuss how the steps for solving and checking equations are related to the order of operations. Have students work in pairs. Each student solves the problem and then checks their partner's answer to see if it is a solution.

Additional Example 2
Solve $6r + 12 = 42$. Then check the solution. $r = 5$, Check:
$6(5) + 12 \stackrel{?}{=} 42$
$30 + 12 \stackrel{?}{=} 42$
$42 = 42$

TEACHER TIP
Point out that students must reverse the order of operations when solving equations, but must follow the order of operations when checking solutions, since this involves simplifying.

Example 3
Error Alert Students may get confused when they see the equation written as $8 = -5m + 6$. If they start by subtracting the 8, remind them to first get rid of the variable's "neighbor," in this case the 6, no matter which side of the equal sign it is on. Rewriting the equation as $-5m + 6 = 8$ can make it easier for students to solve.

Additional Example 3
Solve $32 = -4q + 8$. Then check the solution. $q = -6$, Check:
$32 \stackrel{?}{=} -4(-6) + 8$
$32 \stackrel{?}{=} 24 + 8$
$32 = 32$

Example 4
Ask for volunteers to explain how they used estimation to determine whether their solution was reasonable.

Additional Example 4
Solve the equation.
$\frac{2}{5}x - \frac{1}{4} = \frac{3}{10}$ $x = \frac{11}{8}$

Example 5
Error Alert Students often have difficulty with word problems, especially in a case like this where the cost is given per month, not per year. Help students to identify key words in the given information to make sure they answer the question.

Extend the Example
Ask students to write an equation if the cost were $47 per month instead of $30 per month. Then find the number of months it would take for the charges at the first gym to reach $1500.
$47x + 90 = 1500$, $x = 30$ months

Additional Example 5
Perfect Painters will charge $25 for paint and materials and $25 per hour to paint a room. Classic Painters will charge $250 to paint the same room. How many hours will it take for Perfect Painters charge to be the same as Classic Painters? 9 hours

---

Math Language
When you multiply a number by its **reciprocal**, the product is 1.
$\frac{2}{1} \cdot \frac{1}{2} = 1$

Caution
Read the problem carefully. The number of months is unknown, but the question asks for the number of years.

Example 4 Solving Two-Step Equations with Fractions
Solve the equation. Then check the solution to see if it is reasonable.
$$\frac{1}{2}n - \frac{1}{3} = \frac{3}{4}$$

SOLUTION

To isolate n, first eliminate the $\frac{1}{3}$ and then eliminate the $\frac{1}{2}$.

$$\frac{1}{2}n - \frac{1}{3} = \frac{3}{4}$$
$$+\frac{1}{3} = +\frac{1}{3} \quad \text{Addition Property of Equality}$$
$$\frac{1}{2}n = \frac{13}{12} \quad \text{Simplify.}$$
$$\frac{2}{1} \cdot \frac{1}{2}n = \frac{13}{12} \cdot \frac{2}{1} \quad \text{Multiplication Property of Equality}$$
$$n = \frac{13}{6} \quad \text{Simplify.}$$

Estimate to verify that the solution is reasonable.
$\frac{13}{6}$ is about 2. Substitute 2 for n. $\frac{1}{2}$ of 2 is 1.
$\frac{1}{3}$ subtracted from 1 is $\frac{2}{3}$, which is close to $\frac{3}{4}$.
So, the solution $\frac{13}{6}$ is reasonable.

Example 5 Application: Fitness
A gym charges a $90 fee plus $30 per month. Another gym charges a fee of $1500. How many years will it take for the charges at the first gym to reach $1500?

SOLUTION Write an expression to represent the total cost at the first gym.

monthly cost times the number of months plus the membership fee
30 · x + 90

Use the expression to write an equation equal to the total cost of $1500.

$30x + 90 = 1500$
$-90 = -90$ Subtraction Property of Equality
$30x = 1410$ Simplify.
$\frac{30}{30}x = \frac{1410}{30}$ Division Property of Equality
$x = 47$ Simplify.

47 months is about 4 years. It will take about 4 years for the total charges at the first gym to reach $1500.

136 *Saxon* Algebra 1

 MANIPULATIVE USE FOR EXAMPLE 4

Materials: fraction strips

Help students work with fraction strips to check if their solution is reasonable.

They can begin with 13 sixths and then see that half of 13 sixths is about 6 sixths, or 1. Then they can subtract $\frac{1}{3}$ from 1, which results in $\frac{2}{3}$.

Finally they can compare two $\frac{1}{3}$ strips with three $\frac{1}{4}$ strips to see that they are about equal, so the solution $\frac{13}{6}$ is reasonable.

136 *Saxon* Algebra 1

b. Sample: Use the order of operations in reverse, and subtract to undo the addition. First subtract 6.

c. $w = 4$; $8(4) - 4 = 32 - 4 = 28$

d. $x = 11$; $-2(11) + 12 = -22 + 12 = -10$

e. $m = -\frac{4}{3}$

Lesson Practice

a. Justify Which step would you use first to evaluate $9y + 6$ for $y = 2$? (Ex 1) Explain. Sample: Use the order of operations and first multiply 9 by 2.

b. Justify Which step would you use first to solve $9y + 6 = 24$? Explain. (Ex 1)

Solve each equation. Then check the solution.

c. $8w - 4 = 28$ (Ex 2)

d. $-10 = -2x + 12$ (Ex 3)

e. Solve $\frac{1}{8}m + \frac{3}{4} = \frac{7}{12}$. Then check the solution to see if it is reasonable. (Ex 4)

f. (Energy Conservation) The Green family conserves energy by using energy-efficient bulbs. They pay $125 for energy-efficient bulbs. If the family saves $7 per month on their electricity bill, and the power company gives them a rebate of $25, in about how many months will they have paid for the bulbs? about 14 months

Practice Distributed and Integrated

1. Evaluate $(x - y) - (x - y)$ for $x = 3.5$ and $y = 2.5$. 0
   (9)

2. **Write** Explain how to graph the point $(-2, 4)$. Sample: Start at the origin. Go
   (20) 2 units left and then 4 units up. Mark the point.

*3. **Multiple Choice** What is the value of x in the equation $3x + 5 = 32$? **B**
   (23)
   A 24   **B** 9   **C** 81   **D** $12\frac{1}{3}$

4. **Error Analysis** Two students solve $-12x = -72$. Which student is correct? Explain the error.
   (21)

Student A	Student B
$-12x = -72$	$-12x = -72$
$-\frac{12x}{12} = -\frac{72}{12}$	$\frac{-12x}{-12} = \frac{-72}{-12}$
$x = -6$	$x = 6$

4. Student B; Sample: Student A divided both sides of the equation by 12 instead of −12.

*5. **(Altitude)** A plane increases altitude by 350 meters every minute. If the plane
   (17) started at an altitude of 750 meters above sea level, what is the plane's altitude after 6 minutes? 2850 meters

6. **Verify** Is $x = 9$ the solution for $3x - 8 = 22$? Explain. If false, provide a correct
   (23) solution and check. false; $3(9) - 8 \neq 22$; $x = 10$; Check: $3(10) - 8 = 22$, $30 - 8 = 22$

7. **Justify** Find a counterexample to the following statement: A rational number
   (1) that is not an integer, such as $\frac{3}{5}$, multiplied by any integer will produce a rational number that is not an integer. Sample: $\frac{3}{5} \cdot 5 = 3$

Lesson 23   137

INCLUSION

In problem e, students who have difficulty with mental processing may be overwhelmed. Help students by breaking the problem into two parts. Clearly state the goal and each step and method.

Goal: Get the variable m by itself.

a. • Clear the denominators.
   • Multiply by a common denominator.
   $$24\left(\frac{1}{8}m + \frac{3}{4}\right) = 24\left(\frac{7}{12}\right)$$
   $$3m + 18 = 14$$

b. • Solve a two-step problem.
   • Use order of operations in reverse.
   • Subtract to undo +18.
   • Divide to undo $3 \times m$.
   $$3m + 18 = 14$$
   $$3m = -4$$
   $$m = -\frac{4}{3}$$

Lesson Practice

Problem d

Error Alert Some students may not notice the negative coefficient and divide by 2 instead of −2.

Problem d

Scaffolding Suggest that students swap the left and right sides of the equation if they are more comfortable with the variable on the left side: $-2x + 12 = -10$. Then solve.

✓ Check for Understanding

The questions below help assess the concepts taught in this lesson.

"Explain why you reverse the order of operations to solve $2x - 5 = 3$." Sample: Isolate the variable. First add 5 and then divide by 2. You could divide by 2 first and then add $\frac{5}{2}$ to $\frac{3}{2}$, and then simplify $\frac{8}{2}$. The second method is more complicated.

"Describe how you can check that $x = 4$ is the solution of $2x - 5 = 3$." Sample: Substitute 4 for x in the equation and see if the resulting equation is true.

3 Practice

Math Conversations

Discussion to strengthen understanding

Problem 4

Students may have trouble identifying which answer is incorrect because both approaches are so similar. Suggest that students compare each solution step to identify when the methods differ.

Lesson 23   137

Problem 11
Extend the Problem
"Find the area of the circle using the radius you found in Problem 11. Give the answer in terms of pi." $\frac{16}{81}\pi$ m²

Problem 16
"What would be the advantage of first multiplying both sides of the equation by 2?" This would remove the fractions.

"What would you do after multiplying by 2?" Add 1 to both sides of the equation.

"If you found a solution of $y = -4$ what did you forget to do?" Multiply the y by 2 to get $2y - 1 = -5$.

"What is the solution?" $y = -2$

"Is this a one-step or a two-step problem?" Sample: It is a one-step problem because the given equation has only one operation.

---

*8. **Multi-Step** Three hundred people were surveyed as they left a movie theater. They were asked which type of movie they like best. The circle graph shows the survey results.
  a. Which type of movie was most popular? comedy
  b. How many people liked horror movies the best? 45 people
  c. How many more people liked action movies than dramas? 30 people

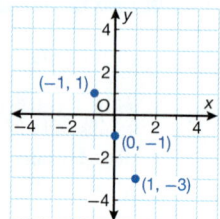

*9. Choose an appropriate graph to display the number of different types of DVDs sold at two video stores. Explain your answer. double-bar graph; Sample: Double-bar graphs can compare two different sets of data side by side.

*10. A class of 20 students answered a survey about their favorite places to go on vacation. Use the data in the table to make a bar graph. See Additional Answers.

Beach	Amusement Park	Mountains	Museums
5	8	3	4

*11. **Geometry** A circle has a circumference of $\frac{8}{9}\pi$ meters. What is the radius of the circle? $\frac{4}{9}$ meters

12. **Multiple Choice** Which equation has solutions that are represented by the graphed points? D
  A $y = 2x + 1$
  B $y = 2x + 3$
  C $y = -2x$
  D $y = -2x - 1$

  Points: $(-1, 1)$, $(0, -1)$, $(1, -3)$

13. **(Coins)** Jenny and Sam took the coins out of their pockets. Jenny has x quarters and y dimes. Sam has h half dollars and z nickels.
  a. Write expressions representing the value of the coins, in cents, in each person's pocket. $25x + 10y$; $50h + 5z$
  b. Write an expression for the total number of cents they have. $25x + 50h + 10y + 5z$

14. **Verify** "12 more than the product of x and 3" can be written as $3x + 12$ or $12 + 3x$. Substitute 2 for x and show that the expressions are equivalent. $3x + 12 = 3(2) + 12 = 6 + 12 = 18$; $12 + 3x = 12 + 3(2) = 12 + 6 = 18$

15. Use $>$, $<$, or $=$ to compare the expressions.
$$24 + \frac{16}{4} - (4 + 3^2) \cdot 2 \; < \; 24 + \left(\frac{16}{4} - 4\right) + 3^2 \cdot 2$$

Solve.

16. $y - \frac{1}{2} = -2\frac{1}{2}$ $y = -2$

*17. $2x + 3 = 11$ $x = 4$

*18. $3x - 4 = 10$ $x = 4\frac{2}{3}$

*19. Solve $2.2x + 2 = 8.6$ $x = 3$

*20. **Statistics** A basketball player attempted 1789 free throws. He made 801 of them. What is the probability that the player will make the next shot he attempts? Write the probability as a decimal rounded to the nearest hundredth. 0.45

138   Saxon Algebra 1

ENGLISH LEARNERS

In this lesson, explain the meaning of the word **substitute.** Say:

"To substitute is to put someone or something where someone else or something else would otherwise be."

For example, when a teacher is absent from school, another person substitutes for the teacher.

In this lesson, students substitute a number for a variable. This is one way to check that a solution is correct.

Write $2m + 4 = 10$ on the board. Point to m and say:

"To check if $m = 3$ is a solution of $2m + 4 = 10$, substitute 3 for m in the equation."

$$2m + 4 = 10$$
$$2(3) + 4 \stackrel{?}{=} 10$$
$$6 + 4 \stackrel{?}{=} 10$$
$$10 = 10$$

21. **Presidential Facts** Many of our first 43 U.S. Presidents had the same first name. Use the table.
    a. If a U.S President is chosen at random, what is the theoretical probability of choosing one whose name is George? $\frac{3}{43}$
    b. What is the probability of choosing one whose name is William or John? $\frac{8}{43}$
    c. What is the probability of choosing a president whose name is not shown in the table? $\frac{26}{43}$

Names	Number of Presidents
James	6
John	4
William	4
George	3

22. **Carpentry** Alice wants to add a square porch to the back of her house. The area of the porch is 361 square feet. What is the length of each side of the porch? 19 feet

23. **Meteorology** The highest temperature ever recorded at the South Pole is −13.6°C. The lowest temperature is about 6 times lower than the highest temperature recorded. Approximately what is the lowest temperature recorded? ≈ −81.6°C

24. **Model** On Monday the low temperature was −4°F. The temperature rose 21°F to the high temperature for that day. What was the high temperature on Monday? Use a number line or thermometer to model the addition. 17°F

25. **Multi-Step** Paula's bank statement showed the following transactions for last month. The beginning balance was $138.24. There was a withdrawal of $46.59, then a deposit of $29.83, plus $1.87 in interest added. What was the balance after these transactions? $123.35

26. Simplify $4 \div 2 + 6^2 - 22$. 16

27. **Write** Explain how to simplify $a^3b^2ac^5a^4b$. $a^8b^3c^5$; Sample: Use the Product Rule for Exponents by adding together the exponents of like bases.

28. Convert 332 meters per second to centimeters per second. 33,200 cm/sec

29. **Multiple Choice** In 2000, the U.S. economy gained $111,349 million from the sale of goods exported to Mexico. However, the U.S. economy lost $135,926 million from the sale of goods imported from Mexico. What was the U.S. balance of trade with Mexico in the year 2000? D
    A $247,275 million
    B $24,926 million
    C $1.2 million
    D −$24,577 million

30. **Probability** Describe each of the following events as impossible, unlikely, as likely as not, likely, or certain.
    a. Tanisha buys a new pair of shoes and the first shoe she pulls out of the box is for the left foot. as likely as not
    b. Ralph rolls a number less than 7 on a standard number cube. certain
    c. November will have 31 days. impossible

Problem 21
Error Alert
Remind students that they should use the facts in the problem and the table. The total number of Presidents is 43. If they only look at the table they will use 17 instead of 43.

Problem 22
Error Alert
Some students may think the length of a side is about 60 ft, because $6^2 = 36$. Point out that 60^2 is 3600, not 360.

Problem 27
Error Alert
Students may forget to add the exponent "1" when it is implied. Have students rewrite the expression as $a^3b^2a^1c^5a^4b^1$ and then simplify.

CHALLENGE

Some equations will require combining like terms before using the inverse operations of addition or subtraction. Solve the following equation by first combining like terms that are on the same side of the equal sign.

$$5x - 6 - 2x = 3$$

$3x - 6 = 9$
$3x = 15$
$x = 5$

LOOKING FORWARD

Solving two-step equations prepares students for

- **Lesson 24** Solving Decimal Equations
- **Lesson 26** Solving Multi-Step Equations
- **Lesson 28** Solving Equations with Variables on Both Sides
- **Lesson 29** Solving Literal Equations

LESSON 24

1 Warm Up

Problem 2
If students list 2.85 as the greatest number, ask them to identify a detail they missed (the negative sign in −2.85).

2 New Concepts

In this lesson, students learn to solve decimal equations.

All of the methods students used to solve equations in previous lessons will work with decimal equations.

Example 1
In Lesson 23 students learned to solve an equation with fractions by multiplying by the least common denominator. In this example students multiply by the power of 10 that will eliminate all of the decimals. To help them find the correct power of 10, guide students to find the decimal with the most digits to the right of the decimal point.

Additional Example 1
Solve each equation.

a. $4 + 0.2x = 8.6$ $x = 23$

b. $0.004m + 0.06 = 0.8$ $m = 185$

LESSON RESOURCES

Student Edition Practice Workbook 24
Reteaching Master 24
Adaptations Master 24
Challenge and Enrichment Master C24

LESSON 24 — Solving Decimal Equations

Warm Up

1. **Vocabulary** If $10^3 = 1{,}000$, then $1{,}000$ is the third _____ of 10. **C**
   A exponent   B base   C power   D factor

2. Write the numbers below in order from least to greatest.
   $-2.85, \frac{5}{8}, 0.58, -0.8$ $-2.85, -0.8, 0.58, \frac{5}{8}$

3. Simplify $4x - 3x^2 + 7x$. $-3x^2 + 11x$

New Concepts

To write decimals as integers, multiply by a power of 10.

Example 1 Solving by Multiplying by a Power of 10

Solve.

a. $8 + 0.5x = 10.5$

SOLUTION

$8 + 0.5x = 10.5$
$10(8) + 10(0.5)x = 10(10.5)$ Multiply each term by 10.
$80 + 5x = 105$ Multiply.
$\quad -80 \quad\quad -80$ Subtraction Property of Equality
$5x = 25$ Simplify.
$\frac{5x}{5} = \frac{25}{5}$ Division Property of Equality
$x = 5$ Simplify.

b. $0.006a + 0.02 = 0.2$

SOLUTION

$0.006a + 0.02 = 0.2$
$1000(0.006a) + 1000(0.02) = 1000(0.2)$ Multiply each term by 1,000.
$6a + 20 = 200$ Multiply.
$\quad -20 \quad -20$ Subtraction Property of Equality
$6a = 180$ Simplify.
$\frac{6a}{6} = \frac{180}{6}$ Division Property of Equality
$a = 30$ Simplify.

Hint
If the decimals are in the thousandths, hundredths, and tenths places, multiply by a power of 10 that will make the decimal with the least value an integer. $0.006 \times 1000 = 6$

MATH BACKGROUND

Using a technique learned in this lesson, you can use decimal equations to prove that a repeating decimal is rational. Start with a decimal equation:

$$x = 0.2\overline{626}$$

Multiply this equation by 100:

$$100x = 26.2\overline{626}$$

Subtract x from both sides:

$$100x - x = 26.2\overline{626} - x$$

On the right side only, substitute $x = 0.2\overline{626}$:

$$100x - x = 26.2\overline{626} - 0.2\overline{626}$$

Simplify both sides and solve for x:

$$99x = 26$$

$$x = \frac{26}{99}$$

You can apply this technique to any repeating decimal.

A decimal equation can also be solved by using inverse operations without multiplying by a power of 10 first.

Example 2 Solving Two-Step Decimal Equations

Solve.

a. $0.2m + 0.8 = 1.8$

SOLUTION

$$0.2m + 0.8 = 1.8$$
$$\underline{-0.8 \quad -0.8} \quad \text{Subtraction Property of Equality}$$
$$0.2m = 1 \quad \text{Simplify.}$$
$$\frac{0.2m}{0.2} = \frac{1}{0.2} \quad \text{Division Property of Equality}$$
$$m = 5 \quad \text{Simplify.}$$

b. $-0.03n - 1.2 = -1.44$

SOLUTION

$$-0.03n - 1.2 = -1.44$$
$$\underline{+1.2 \quad +1.2} \quad \text{Addition Property of Equality}$$
$$-0.03n = -0.24 \quad \text{Simplify.}$$
$$\frac{-0.03n}{-0.03} = \frac{-0.24}{-0.03} \quad \text{Division Property of Equality}$$
$$n = 8 \quad \text{Simplify.}$$

Finding a decimal part of a number is the same as finding a fraction or percent of a number.

Example 3 Finding Decimal Parts of Numbers

0.48 of 86 is what number?

SOLUTION

decimal number	of	given number	is	what number
0.48	·	86	=	n

$0.48 \cdot 86 = n$ Multiply.

$41.28 = n$

Estimate the answer to see if it is reasonable.

0.48 is less than 0.50 or $\frac{1}{2}$.

$\frac{1}{2}$ of 86 is 43.

41.28 is close to 43, so the answer is reasonable.

Math Reasoning

Verify Are $0.2m + 0.8 = 1.8$ and $2m + 8 = 18$ equivalent equations? Explain.

Sample: Yes, they are equivalent. Use the Multiplication Property of Equality and multiply each term in the equation by the same power of 10. $10(0.2) + 10(0.8) = 10(1.8)$

Math Language

$\frac{1}{2}$ **of** $100 = \frac{1}{2} \times 100 = 50$
0.5 **of** $100 = 0.5 \times 100 = 50$
50% **of** $100 = 0.5 \times 100 = 50$
"Of" means to multiply.

Lesson 24   141

MANIPULATIVE USE

Materials: coins or discs to represent coins

Use coins or discs to model the equation and check the answer in Example 2:

| m groups of 2 dimes | + | 8 dimes | = | 18 dimes |

"How many groups of 2 dimes will you have, if you remove 8 dimes from each side of the equation?" 5 groups of 2 dimes

Check $m = 5$ groups of 2 dimes.

| 10 dimes | + | 8 dimes | = | 18 dimes |

Lesson 24   141

Example 4

Error Alert Check students can visualize the problem. Have them draw a diagram and correctly label the height and length of the tail.

Extend the Example

"What is the length of a mandrill's tail if the mandrill is 70.1 cm long?" $t = 5.63$ cm

Additional Example 4

Find the distance from Town *A* to Town *B*, if the distance from Town *A* to Town *C* is 26.2 km, and the distance from Town *B* to Town *C* is 8.9 km. 17.3 km

Lesson Practice

Problem a

Scaffolding Suggest that students multiply each term by 100 to clear the decimals. Then solve.

Problem c

Error Alert Remind students that the coefficient of *n* is negative.

Check for Understanding

The questions below help assess the concepts taught in this lesson.

"Does multiplying by 100 always clear the decimals in a decimal equation? Explain." No; Sample: It will not clear decimals in the thousandths.

"In $0.035n = 28$, how can you check if the solution is reasonable?" Sample: Round 0.035 to 0.04. Divide 2800 by 4. The answer should be in the hundreds.

Example 4 Application: Zoology

The height of an average mandrill (a large species of baboon) is 2.54 cm more than 12 times the length of its tail. If the height of a mandrill is 78.74 centimeters, then what is the length of its tail?

Hint Draw a diagram to help visualize the problem.

SOLUTION

height of mandrill = (12 times the tail length) plus 2.54 cm

Write and solve an equation to find the length of the mandrill's tail.

$12t + 2.54 = 78.74$

$\underline{-2.54 = -2.54}$ Subtraction Property of Equality

$12t = 76.20$ Simplify.

$\dfrac{12t}{12} = \dfrac{76.20}{12}$ Division Property of Equality

$t = 6.35$ cm Simplify.

Check

$12t + 2.54 = 78.74$

$12(6.35) + 2.54 \stackrel{?}{=} 78.74$ Substitute 6.35 for *t*.

$76.20 + 2.54 \stackrel{?}{=} 78.74$ Multiply.

$78.74 = 78.74$ ✓ Add.

The mandrill's tail is 6.35 cm long.

Lesson Practice

Solve each equation.

a. $0.25 + 0.18y = 0.97$ $y = 4$ (Ex 1)

b. $0.05 = 0.5 - 0.15q$ $q = 3$ (Ex 1)

c. $-0.5n + 1.4 = 8.9$ $n = -15$ (Ex 2)

d. 0.6 of 24 is what number? 14.4 (Ex 3)

e. **Highway Mileages** Use the diagram. The distance from Town A to Town C is 52.8 kilometers. What is the distance from Town B to Town C? 35.2 km (Ex 4)

Practice Distributed and Integrated

1. **Multiple Choice** What is the solution of $\frac{4}{5}x = -24$ for *x*? A
   (21)

   A -30 B $-\dfrac{96}{5}$ C $\dfrac{96}{5}$ D 30

142 *Saxon* Algebra 1

INCLUSION

Encourage students with visual impairment to use a grid to help them line up decimals correctly and organize the information given in the problem. For example, they can solve Example 4 using the following grid.

12t	+	2	•	54	=		78	•	74
	−	2	•	54	=	−	2	•	54
12t					=		76	•	20

$12t = 76.20$

6.35
$12\overline{)76.20}$

2. Simplify $3(2x + 5x)$ using the two different methods shown below.
   (18)
   a. Combine like terms, and then multiply. $3(2x + 5x) = 3(7x) = 21x$
   b. Distribute, and then combine like terms. $3(2x + 5x) = 6x + 15x = 21x$

*3. Solve $0.45x - 0.002 = 8.098$. $x = 18$
(24)

*4. **Justify** If you multiply both sides of an equation by a constant c, what happens
(21) to the solution? Explain your answer.

4. The solution remains the same. Sample: The Multiplication Property of Equality states that you can multiply both sides of an equation by the same number and the statement will still be true.

*5. (**Stock Market**) An investor buys some stock at $6.57 a share. She spends $846.25
(24) which includes a transaction fee of $25. How many shares of stock did she buy?
125 shares of stock

*6. **Multiple Choice** 0.8 is 0.32 of what number? **A**
(24) **A** 2.5   **B** 0.25   **C** 0.4   **D** 4

*7. **Verify** Solve $0.45x + 0.9 = 1.008$. Will both methods shown below result in the
(24) same solution? Verify by using both methods to solve.

Method I: Multiply both sides of the equation by 1000 first.

Method II: Subtract 0.9 from both sides first.

7. Sample: Multiplying both sides by 1,000 and then subtracting 900 from both sides will result in $450x = 108$, $x = 0.24$; Subtracting 0.9 from both sides, will result in $0.45x = 0.108$, $x = 0.24$.

8. Identify the coefficient, the variable(s), and the number of terms in the
(2) expression $\frac{9}{5}C + 32$.   coefficient $\frac{9}{5}$, variable C, number of terms = 2

*9. **Verify** Solve $0.25x + \frac{1}{2} = 0.075$. Will both methods shown below result in the same
(24) solution? Explain. $x = -1.7$; Sample: $0.25x + 0.5 = 0.075$ is equivalent to $\frac{x}{4} + \frac{1}{2} = \frac{3}{40}$.

Method I: First write the fraction as a decimal.

Method II: First write the decimals as fractions.

*10. **Error Analysis** Two students use the circle graph to find the total percent
(22) of students who have fewer than two siblings. Which student is correct? Explain the error.

Student A	Student B
0 siblings or 1 sibling = 20 20% of the students	Total students: $8 + 12 + 6 + 4 = 30$ 0 siblings or 1 sibling = 20 $\frac{20}{30} \approx 67\%$ of the students

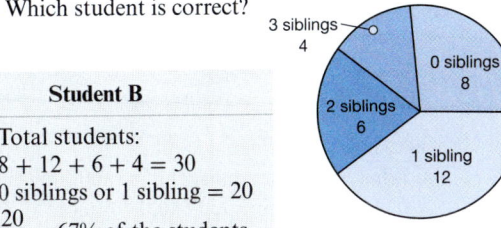

Students' Siblings

*11. **Measurement** The graph shows an estimation of the changes
(22) in the diameter of a tree, in inches, every 20 years. What
was the approximate circumference of the tree when the
tree was 100 years old? Use 3.14 for π. Round the answer
to the nearest tenth.   62.8 inches

Growth of Tree

10. Student B; Sample: The circle graph shows the number of students, not the percentages. Student A found the total number of students and wrote that number as a percent.

Lesson 24

---

3 Practice

Math Conversations
Discussion to strengthen understanding

Problem 2
Discuss the two different methods and ask students:

"Do you prefer one method more than the other? If so, explain."
Sample: I prefer the first method because I can mentally compute the answer.

"Can you use the first method to simplify $7(3n + 4)$? Explain." No; Sample: I cannot combine $3n$ and 4 because these are not like terms.

Problem 6
Error Alert
One typical error is that students just divide 0.32 by 0.8 or know that $8 \cdot 4 = 32$, so they choose either C or D. Answer choice B represents the common mistake of incorrect placement of the decimal point. Remind students to translate the words in the problem into math symbols in order to find the correct solution.

ENGLISH LEARNERS

The word **like** has two different meanings depending on the context in which it is used. In mathematics, when a problem such as Problem 2 says to combine like terms, it means to combine similar terms. Write $3(2x + 5x)$ on the board.

Say:

"Are $2x$ and $5x$ like terms?" yes

"Are 3 and $23x$ like terms?" no

People use this meaning when they say that one person is like another person. Point out that in this usage *like* is an adjective.

Like also is a verb that means to be fond of or to be attracted to. "Do you like sports?" "I like to eat ice cream." Ask students to brainstorm other examples of both meanings of the word *like*.

Problem 12

Extend the Problem

"If Will spent a total of $20, what did he spend on each item?"
apples: $2.00, peanut butter: $8.00; juice: $4.00; strawberries: $6.00

Problem 16

Guide students by asking the following questions.

"What should you do first to simplify the equation?" Sample: Rewrite the equation by grouping like terms together:
$(11 \cdot 3 \cdot 2)w^4w^7z^9z^2 \stackrel{?}{=} 66w^{11}z^{11}$

"What should you do next?" Sample: Simplify the like terms on the left side of the equation:
$66w^{11}z^{11} = 66w^{11}z^{11}$

Problem 19

Extend the Problem

"Write two more formulas you could use to find the perimeter."
Sample: $P = 2\ell + 2w$ and $P = 2w + 2\ell$

"Which property did you use to write these formulas?" Sample: Distributive Property

---

*12. The circle graph shows the amount of money Will spent on different snacks at a store. If Will spent $12, how much money did he spend on each item?

12. Will spent $1.20 on apples, $4.80 on peanut butter, $2.40 on juice, and $3.60 on strawberries.

Will's Spendings

13. Graph the ordered pair on a coordinate plane (2, 1). See Additional Answers.

14. **Probability** A spinner is divided in equal sections and labeled as shown in the diagram.
   a. If x is an even number, what is the probability the spinner will land on an even number? $\frac{5}{8}$
   b. If x is an odd number, what is the probability the spinner will land on an odd number? $\frac{1}{2}$
   c. If $x = 20$, what is the probability the spinner will land on a number less than 20? $\frac{1}{4}$

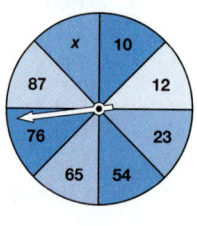

15. **Multi-Step** Each camp counselor at Camp Wallaby walked 6 miles for a health and fitness activity. Each camper walked 2 miles. The camp leader paid $0.50 into a Fun Day account for every mile walked. Write an expression to represent the total amount of money earned from walking by counselors and campers. $0.50(6c + 2d) = 3c + d$

16. **Verify** Are the expressions below equivalent? Explain.
$(11w^4 \cdot 3z^9)(2w^7z^2) \stackrel{?}{=} 66w^{11}z^{11}$

16. Sample: Yes; Using the Product Rule of Exponents the left side simplified is the same as the right.

17. **Contests** Miguel entered a contest offering prizes to the top 3 finishers. The probability of winning 1st is 12%, the probability of winning 2nd is 18%, and the probability of winning 3rd is 20%. What is the probability that Miguel will not win any prize? 50%

18. **Retailing** Use the circle graph.
   a. What is the probability that a randomly chosen person who purchased a shirt paid $40.00 or more? $\frac{8}{100} = \frac{2}{25}$
   b. What is the probability that a randomly chosen person who purchased a shirt paid $30 or less? $\frac{17}{25}$

Shirt Sales

19. **Construction** To calculate the amount of fencing for a rectangular area, Kelvin uses the formula $P = 2(l + w)$. Bonnie uses the formula $P = 2(w + l)$. Will their calculations of the perimeter be the same? Explain.

19. Yes; Sample: The Commutative Property of Addition allows the order of the addends to be changed without affecting the sum.

20. **Write** Explain how to simplify $\frac{4}{7} \div \left[\left(-\frac{3}{8}\right) \cdot \left(-\frac{8}{3}\right)\right]$.

20. $\left(\frac{4}{7}\right)$; Sample explanation: A fraction multiplied by its reciprocal equals 1; $\frac{4}{7} \div 1 = \frac{4}{7}$

144 Saxon Algebra 1

⭐ CHALLENGE

In some problems, you need to find the decimal part of a decimal number. Solve and check that your answer is reasonable.

0.35 of 12.6 is what number?

4.41; 0.35 is a little more than $\frac{1}{3}$, and $\frac{1}{3} \cdot 12.6 = 4.2$. Since 4.41 is close to 4.2, the answer is reasonable.

21. Simplify $\frac{2}{5} \div \left(-\frac{7}{2}\right) \cdot \left(-\frac{5}{2}\right)$. $\frac{2}{7}$
(4)

22. **Write** Explain why $k^2 \cdot m \cdot b^4 \cdot c^3$ cannot be simplified using the Product Rule
(3) of Exponents.   Sample: To simplify the expression, some of the bases would need to be the same in order to add the exponents.

23. **Justify** Write the expression so there are no parentheses. Justify your change
(15) with a property. $6(ab + ef)$ $6ab + 6ef$; Distributive Property

24. **Generalize** Some real numbers can contain patterns within them, such as
(1) 21.12122122212222...
   a. Find a pattern in the number above. Is the pattern you found a repeating pattern?
   b. Is this number a rational number or an irrational number? Explain.

24a. Sample: After the decimal place a 1 is followed by an increasing number of 2s each separated by a 1.; no

24b. Sample: Irrational, no section of the decimal repeats nor does it terminate.

25. Convert 630 cubic centimeters to cubic inches. (Hint: 1 in. = 2.54 cm)   38.44 in³
(8)

26. **Multi-Step** The temperature at 6 a.m. was 30°C. If the temperature increases by
(10) 2 degrees every half hour, what will the temperature be by 9 a.m.? What time will it be when the temperature is 50°C?   42°C, 11 a.m.

27. Simplify $-|10 - 7|$. -3
(5)

*28. **Internet Usage** The circle graph shows
(22) approximate total Internet usage in the world.
   a. The estimated number of Internet users worldwide is 1,154,358,778. About how many people in North America use the Internet?   about 230,871,756 people
   b. About how many more people use the Internet in Asia than in North America?   about 173,153,816 more people

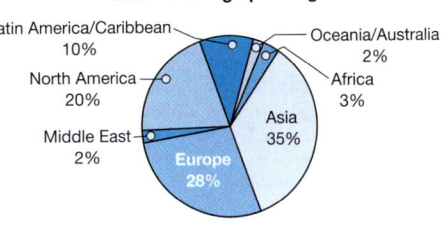

Internet Usage per Region
Latin America/Caribbean 10%
Oceania/Australia 2%
North America 20%
Africa 3%
Middle East 2%
Asia 35%
Europe 28%

29. **Geometry** A small square park is 784 square yards. A row of trees was planted
(13) on one side of the park. One tree was planted at each corner. Then one tree was planted every seven yards between the corner trees. How many trees were planted in the row?   5 trees

30. **Quality Control** Elite Style inspects 500 hair dryers manufactured and finds 495 to
(Inv 1) have no defects. There are 20,000 hair dryers in their warehouse.
   a. What is the experimental probability that a hair dryer will have no defects? $\frac{99}{100}$
   b. Predict the number of hair dryers that will have no defects in the warehouse.   19,800 hair dryers

Problem 21
Error Alert
If students give a negative answer, they did not correctly keep track of the negative signs. In the division step of solving this problem, students may forget the negative sign when they multiply by the reciprocal. Remind students that the reciprocal of $-\frac{7}{2}$ is $-\frac{2}{7}$.

Lesson 24   145

LOOKING FORWARD

Solving decimal equations prepares students for

- **Lesson 26** Solving Multi-Step Equations
- **Lesson 28** Solving Equations with Variables on Both Sides
- **Lesson 29** Solving Literal Equations
- **Lesson 36** Writing and Solving Proportions
- **Lesson 42** Solving Percent Problems

LESSON 25

1 Warm Up

Problem 4
In this problem, students will substitute -0.4 for y before solving for x.

2 New Concepts

In this lesson, students learn how to determine if a relation is a function. Stress that for a function no x-value is paired with more than one y-value.

Example 1

Mapping diagrams can be used to sort domain and range values. The domain and range can have a different number of elements because values may repeat.

Additional Example 1
Give the domain and range of the relation.
$\{(-2, 0), (-3, 0), (-1, 3), (0, 1)\}$
Domain: $\{-3, -2, -1, 0\}$
Range: $\{0, 1, 3\}$

TEACHER TIP

Point out that just as x comes before y in the alphabet, d comes before r, so the **d**omain is the set of x-values and the **r**ange is the set of y-values.

LESSON RESOURCES

Student Edition Practice Workbook 25
Reteaching Master 25
Adaptations Master 25
Challenge and Enrichment Master C25, E25

LESSON 25

Differentiating Between Relations and Functions

Warm Up

1. **Vocabulary** In the _____ $(-5, 2)$, -5 is the _____ and 2 is the _____. **ordered pair, x-value, y-value**

2. Simplify $(-4)^2 + 3^2 - 2^3$. **17**

3. Find the value of y when $x = 8$.
   $5y = -3x - 6$ **-6**

4. Find the value of x when $y = -0.4$.
   $x - 8y = 1.6$ **-1.6**

5. **Multiple Choice** Jenny has n dollars in her savings account. If she deposits d dollars in her savings account each week, which expression represents the amount she will have in her savings account at the end of a year? **A**
   A $n + 52d$ **B** $52d - n$ **C** $n + d$ **D** $52n + d$

New Concepts

The **domain** is the set of possible values for the independent variable (input values) of a set of ordered pairs.

The **range** is the set of values for the dependent variable (output values) of a set of ordered pairs.

Math Language
In an ordered pair (x, y), x is the **independent variable** and y is the **dependent variable**.

A **relation** is a set of ordered pairs where each number in the domain is matched to one or more numbers in the range. Relations can also be represented using set notation, tables, diagrams, or equations.

Example 1   Determining the Domain and Range of a Relation

Give the domain and range of the relation.
$\{(2, 6), (2, 10), (8, 6), (5, 1), (4, 6), (3, 9)\}$

SOLUTION

Use a mapping diagram. Place the x-values in the oval on the left, and the y-values in the oval on the right.

The domain is all the x-values.

The range is all the y-values.

Domain: $\{2, 3, 4, 5, 8\}$

Range: $\{1, 6, 9, 10\}$

Online Connection
www.SaxonMathResources.com

A **function** is a mathematical relationship pairing each value in the domain with exactly one value in the range.

146   *Saxon Algebra 1*

MATH BACKGROUND

A relation is a correspondence between two sets, the domain and range. Functions are a subset of relations, so while every function is a relation, not every relation is a function.

When a relation is a function, every domain value corresponds to only one range value. Conversely, when a relation is not a function, there will be one or more domain values that correspond to more than one range value.

There is a subset of functions in which every range value corresponds to only one domain value. Another way of stating that a function is one-to-one is to say that the following statement is always true:
if $f(a) = f(b)$, then $a = b$.

The function $y = f(x)$ is a function if it passes the *vertical line test*. It is a one-to-one function if it passes both the *vertical line test* and the *horizontal line test*.

Hint

When you write the domain and range, only write 10 and 3 once.

Domain: {0, 3, 4, 8, 10}

Range: {1, 2, 3, 4, 9}

Example 2 Identifying a Set of Ordered Pairs as a Function

a. Determine whether {(3, 3), (10, 1), (0, 3), (8, 9), (4, 4), (10, 2)} represents a function.

SOLUTION

Each domain value must map with exactly one range value.

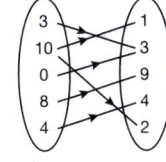

The diagram shows that the domain value of 10 maps to the range values 1 and 2.

The relation is not a function. Each domain value does not have exactly one range value.

b. Determine whether $y = \frac{1}{2}x - 1$ represents a function.

SOLUTION

No matter what value is substituted for the independent variable x, the equation outputs exactly one value for the dependent variable y.

Domain (x)	-6	0	2	5	7	10
Range (y)	-4	-1	0	$\frac{3}{2}$	$\frac{5}{2}$	4

The equation represents a function.

If a relation is graphed on a coordinate grid, the **vertical-line test** can be used to determine if the relation is a function.

Vertical-Line Test

A graph on the coordinate plane represents a function if any vertical line intersects the graph in exactly one point.

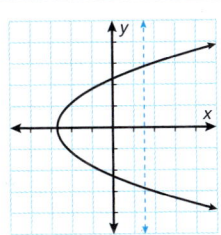
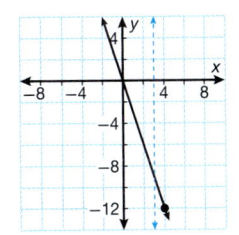

The relation is not a function. The vertical-line cuts the graph in more than one place.

The relation is a function. The vertical-line cuts the graph in exactly one place.

Lesson 25   147

Example 3

When the graph is a set of points, have students draw a vertical line at each point to see if it touches another point.

Extend the Example

Ask students to name an ordered pair they could add so that the set would still be a function. Then ask for an ordered pair they could add so it would no longer be a function. Sample: function (4, 0); not a function (2, 5)

Additional Example 3

"Graph the ordered pairs and use the vertical-line test to see if the set is a function." not a function

x	3	−2	4	1	−4	−2
y	−4	1	3	0	1.5	−3

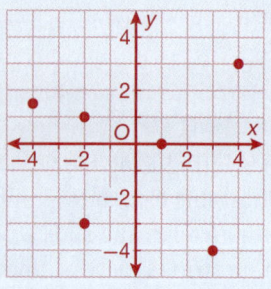

Example 4

Tell students the independent variable is what gets substituted into the function rule and the result is the dependent variable.

Additional Example 4

a. Write $x - 3y = 4$ in function form. $y = \frac{x}{3} - \frac{4}{3}$

b. Mass in kilograms is related to weight in pounds. There are about 2.2 lb per kg. Write a rule in function notation to represent the weight, in pounds, of a dog whose mass is x kilograms.
$f(x) = 2.2x$

Hint

More than one vertical line should be drawn along the x-axis to check using the vertical-line test.

Reading Math

$f(x)$ is read as "f of x."

Example 3 Identifying a Graph as a Function

Use the table. Graph the ordered pairs on a coordinate grid and determine whether the ordered pairs represent a function.

SOLUTION

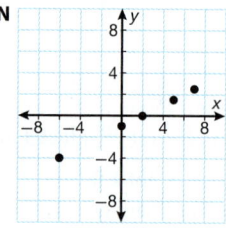

Domain (x)	Range (y)
−6	−4
0	−1
2	0
5	$\frac{3}{2}$
7	$\frac{5}{2}$

No matter what vertical line is drawn, the graph is intersected at only one point by each line. The ordered pairs represent a function.

In a function, the independent variable determines the value of the dependent variable. This means the dependent variable y is a function of the independent variable x. In terms of the variables, y is a function of x and can be written like the following example:

$$y = f(x)$$
$$y = 6x + 3$$
$$f(x) = 6x + 3$$

Example 4 Writing a Function

a. Write $x + 2y = 5$ in function form.

SOLUTION

$x + 2y = 5$

$y = -\frac{x}{2} + \frac{5}{2}$ Solve for y.

$f(x) = -\frac{x}{2} + \frac{5}{2}$

b. Food labels list the grams of fats, carbohydrates, and proteins in a single serving. Proteins convert to 4 calories per gram. Write a rule in function notation to represent the number of calories from protein.

SOLUTION

The number of calories depends on the number of grams of protein eaten.

dependent variable: number of calories

independent variable: number of grams of protein

Let p represent the number of grams of protein.

$y = 4p$

$f(p) = 4p$ Use function notation.

ENGLISH LEARNERS

For this lesson, explain how the words dependent and independent are related. Say:

"The word **dependent** means depends on, or relies on. The word **independent** means does not depend on because the prefix *in* means *not*."

Discuss common uses of these terms. For example, children are considered dependents until they become 18; then they gain their independence. Point out again that the prefix *in* means *not*.

Discuss how the range values depend on the domain values. For the function $f(x) = 2x$, there are choices in what to substitute for x; it relies on nothing. However, after you choose x, there is no choice for $f(x)$; it must be twice x. The value of $f(x)$ depends on the value of x, so $f(x)$ is the dependent variable.

Example 5 Application: Reading

A student reads an average of 25 pages per day while reading a 544-page novel. Write a rule in function notation to find the number of pages she has left to read at the end of any given day.

SOLUTION

Let d represent the days spent reading.

$25d$	number of pages read
$544 - 25d$	number of pages that have not been read

The number of pages left to read depends on the number of days the student has been reading.

$y = 544 - 25d$

$f(d) = 544 - 25d$ Use function notation.

Math Reasoning

Write Does it make sense for d to be greater than 21? Explain.

no, Sample: The values of d greater than 21 make $25d$ greater than 544.

Lesson Practice

a. Give the domain and range of the relation: (1, 2); (2, 1); (4, 6); (8, 5); (7, 7); (3, 10)   domain: {1, 2, 3, 4, 7, 8}; range: {1, 2, 5, 6, 7, 10}
(Ex 1)

b. Using a diagram, determine whether the ordered pairs represent a function. {(11, 12); (12, 1); (5, 5); (14, 10); (13, 7)}
(Ex 2)

c. Determine whether $y = 3x - 1$ represents a function.   Function

d. Use the table. Graph the ordered pairs on a coordinate plane and determine whether the ordered pairs represent a function.
(Ex 3)

x	-1	0	1	-2	0
y	3	0	3	6	6

e. (Printing) A brochure costs $0.07 per page to print. Write a rule in function notation to represent the cost of printing c copies of the brochure. $f(c) = \$0.07c$
(Ex 4)

f. (Novelist) An author writes 30 pages per day. Write a function rule that the author can use to find how many pages she has left to write before reaching page 400. $f(d) = 400 - 30d$
(Ex 5)

b.
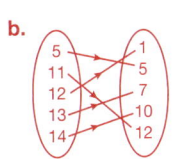
Function

d.
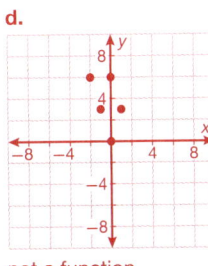
not a function

Practice   Distributed and Integrated

1. Solve $0.3 + 0.05y = 0.65$. $y = 7$
(24)

2. **Verify** Verify that the following solutions are correct for each equation given.   See Additional Answers.
(19)
   a. $103 + x = 99$ when $x = -4$
   b. $\frac{1}{2} - x = \frac{3}{4}$ when $x = -\frac{1}{4}$

*3. Make a table to determine whether $y = x + 2$ represents a function.
(25)   See Additional Answers.

ALTERNATIVE METHOD FOR EXAMPLE 5

Students may confuse the dependent and independent variables. To avoid this confusion, it may help to find the function rule step by step using a table.

d	1	2	3
$25d$	25	50	75
$f(d) = 544 - 25d$	519	494	469

Students can also use the table to check that this relation is a function.

3 Practice

Math Conversations

Discussion to strengthen understanding

Problem 6

Students can determine the answer just by looking at the *x*-values. If all the *x*-values are different, then the set must be a function.

Problem 7

Guide the students by asking them the following questions.

"How many sides does a square have?" 4

"What is true about the lengths of the sides?" They are all the same length.

"What is perimeter?" The distance around an object.

"Does perimeter depend on the side lengths or do the side lengths depend on the perimeter?" Perimeter depends on the side lengths.

Problem 13

Extend the Problem

Suppose that the annual fee increases to $44.90 for the next year. How many fewer movies would Stephen be able to rent for the same amount of money he spent the previous year?
5 fewer DVDs

---

*4. **Hiking** A hiker can average 15 minutes per mile. Write a rule in function notation to describe the time it takes the hiker to walk *m* miles. $f(m) = 15m$

5. Subtract $3.16 - 1.01 - 0.11$. 2.04

*6. **Multiple Choice** Which set of ordered pairs represents a function? A

   A $\{(1, 1); (2, 2); (3, 3); (4, 4)\}$

   B $\{(1, 0); (2, 1); (1, 3); (2, 4)\}$

   C $\{(1, 1); (1, 2); (1, 3); (1, 4)\}$

   D $\{(10, 1); (10, 2); (12, 3); (12, 4)\}$

*7. A square has a side length of *s*. Write a rule in function notation to represent the perimeter. $f(s) = 4s$

*8. **Generalize** If a set of ordered pairs is a function, are the ordered pairs also a relation? Explain. Sample: Yes, because all functions also meet the criteria for a relation.

*9. **Analyze** A student draws a circle on a coordinate plane. The center of the circle is at the origin. Is this circle a function or a relation? Explain.

9. Relation. Sample: If you draw a vertical line through the circle it will show that several domain values have more than one range value. So a graph of circle does not represent a function.

*10. **Photography** A student is making a pinhole camera. What is the circumference of the pinhole in the box? Use 3.14 for π and round to the nearest hundredth.

$C = \pi d$
$= 3.14(0.45)$
$= 1.413$
The circumference is 1.41 mm.

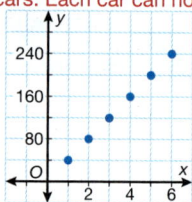

diameter = 0.45 mm

*11. **Astronomical Unit** An astronomical unit is the average distance from the Sun to the Earth. 1 AU (astronomical unit) is approximately equal to 93 million miles. If Jupiter is about 5.2 AU from the Sun, about how many miles is it from the Sun? about 483,600,000 miles

 12. **Write** Describe a possible situation for the discrete graph. Sample: A subway train can hold up to 6 cars. Each car can hold 40 passengers.

*13. **Movie Club** Stephen belongs to a movie club in which he pays an annual fee of $39.95 and then rents DVDs for $0.99 each. In one year, Stephen spent $55.79. Write and solve an equation to find how many DVDs he rented.
$39.95 + 0.99x = 55.79$; 16 DVDs.

150 *Saxon Algebra 1*

MANIPULATIVE USE

Materials: coordinate plane transparency, colored overhead markers, ruler

Demonstrate a vertical-line test by plotting the sets of ordered pairs in Problem 6 on a coordinate grid. Then use the ruler to represent the vertical-line test for each set of ordered pairs.

14. Error Analysis Two students solve $5a + 4 = 34$. Which student is correct? Explain the error.

Student A	Student B
$5a + 4 = 34$	$5a + 4 = 34$
$\dfrac{5a+4}{5} = \dfrac{34}{5}$	$+4 +4$
$a + \dfrac{4}{5} = \dfrac{34}{5}$	$5a = 38$
$a = \dfrac{34}{5} - \dfrac{4}{5}$	$a = \dfrac{38}{5}$
$a = \dfrac{30}{5}$	
$a = 6$	

14. Student A: Student B did not use inverse operations to "undo" +4. Student B should have subtracted 4 from both sides instead of adding 4 to both sides.

15. Multiple Choice The graph shows the points scored by Michaela and Jessie during the first five basketball games of the season. What conclusion can you make from the graph? **B**

A Michaela is the best player on the team.

B Michaela usually scores more points than Jessie.

C Neither player will score more than 18 points in the next game.

D Jessie does not play as much as Michaela.

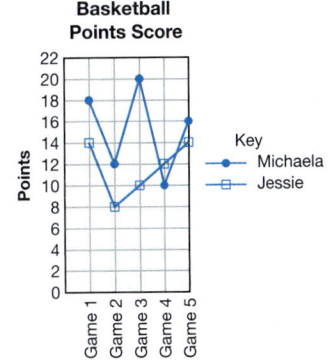

*16. Write Two sets of data represent the number of bottles of water and the number of bottles of juice a store sells each month. Give reasons why the following types of graphs would be appropriate to represent the data: a double-bar graph, a double-line graph, and two stem-and-leaf plots.

16. Sample: A double-bar graph would compare the amounts of each beverage sold each month. A double-line graph would show the changes in the amounts of each beverage sold. A stem-and-leaf plot can help to quickly organize the data and show the middle of the data.

17. Choose an appropriate graph to display the portion of students in a class who have birthdays in each month. Explain your choice.   circle graph; Sample: Circle graphs best compare parts to a whole.

18. Find the value of $3z - 2(z - 1)^2 + 2$ for $z = 4$. -4

19. Cooking A recipe calls for 2.5 cups of orange juice for a batch of fruit drink. In the equation, $y = 2.5x$, y represents the number of cups of orange juice and x represents number of batches of fruit drink. Make a table when $x = 1, 2, 3,$ and 4 batches of fruit drink. Then graph the ordered pairs in your table. See Additional Answers.

20. Analyze "Three more than x" can be written as $x + 3$ or $3 + x$. Can "three less than x" be written as $x - 3$ or $3 - x$? Explain.   no, Sample: Subtraction is not commutative. The correct expression is $x - 3$.

21. Multi-Step Population growth for a certain type of animal is determined by the formula $N_n = N_i 2^n$, where N_i is the initial population size and N_n is the population size after n generations. If the initial population is 45, what is the difference between the population size after the fourth generation and the population size after the sixth generation?   2160

Lesson 25   151

Problem 17
Error Alert
Students may answer line graph because the problem refers to "each month," and month is a measure of time. Stress that they should use a line graph to track changes of the same item(s) over time, not to compare different amounts.

Problem 20
Extend the Problem
Is the expression $|x - 3|$ equivalent to $|3 - x|$? Explain. Yes, they are equivalent. Sample: For every value of x substituted, the expressions inside the absolute value signs are opposites. The expressions are equivalent because the absolute values of opposites are equivalent.

INCLUSION

Some students will have trouble with logical reasoning when they try to identify the dependent and independent variables. Reinforce the difference by having students fill in the blanks in these sentences. Note that the order of the answers is intentionally reversed to assess student understanding.

I must know the _____ to find the _____.   independent variable; dependent variable

The _____ depends on the _____.   dependent variable; independent variable

Lesson 25   151

Problem 28

Guide the students by asking them the following questions.

"How do you write 64 in exponential form with a base of 2?" $(2^3)^2 = 2^6$

"How do you write 64 times 8 in exponential form with a base of 2?" 1 byte = 8 bits = 2^3 bits, 64 bytes = (64)(8) = $(2^3)^2(2^3)$ bits

"How do you multiply powers with like bases, such as $2^6 \cdot 2^3$?" Keep the base the same and add the exponents, 2^9.

---

22. (Architecture) An architect is designing a very large square mall. Estimate the total area of the mall, if each side length is approximately 4890 feet. 2.4 million ft²

23. Write True or False. The expression 12 − 8 − 2 could be simplified using the Associative Property. Explain. false; Sample: The Associative Property applies only to multiplication and addition.

24. Solve $1\frac{1}{2}y = 6\frac{3}{4}$. $y = 4\frac{1}{2}$

25. Solve $\frac{1}{8}m - \frac{1}{4} = \frac{3}{4}$. $m = 8$

26. Verify Determine if each statement below is true or false. If false, explain why.

a. $\dfrac{(5-x)^3 + 12}{(4x)} = \dfrac{41 - x}{x^3}$ for $x = 2$. true

b. $\dfrac{(5-x)^3 + 12}{(4x)} = \dfrac{41 - x}{x^3}$ for $x = 3$.

26b. false; Sample: The value of the first expression is $\frac{5}{3}$ and the value of the second expression is $\frac{38}{27}$.

27. Measurement The distance between City A and City C is 312.78 miles. City B lies on a point on a direct line between Cities A and C. If the distance between City C and City B is 191.9 miles, what is the distance between Cities A and B? 120.88 miles

28. (Computer Engineering) Eight bits, or 2^3 bits, equal one byte. How many bits are in 64, or 2^6, bytes? 2^9 or 512 bits

29. Geometry The measure of the length of a rectangle is $4x - y$ feet and the width is xy. What expression would show the area of the rectangle? Explain.

29. $4x^2y - xy^2$; Sample: The area of the rectangle would be found using $A = lw = xy(4x - y) = 4x^2y - xy^2$.

30. Simplify $|-2 - 3| - 4 + (-8)$. −7

CHALLENGE

Division by zero is undefined. Sometimes certain values cannot be used for the domain of a function because they will cause the expression to be undefined. Tell which values cannot be used for the domain of each function and why.

$f(x) = \dfrac{2}{x}, \; g(x) = \dfrac{x+1}{x-6}, \; h(x) = \dfrac{1}{(x+1)^2}$

0, 6, and −1; Sample: These values will make the respective denominators equal to 0, and division by 0 is undefined.

LOOKING FORWARD

Analyzing and comparing functions and relations prepares students for

- **Lesson 30** Graphing Functions
- **Lesson 34** Recognizing and Extending Arithmetic Sequences
- **Lesson 71** Making and Analyzing Scatter Plots

LESSON 26

Solving Multi-Step Equations

Warm Up

1. **Vocabulary** The product of a number and its _____ is 1.   **reciprocal**
   (11)
2. Simplify $2x + 5y + 3x - 2y$ by adding like terms.   **$5x + 3y$**
   (18)
3. Solve $2x + 5 = 12$. Check your solution.   **3.5**
   (23)
4. **Multiple Choice** Which is the solution of $3x + 6 = 33$?   **B**
   (23)
      A 13   B 9
      C 7   D 8

New Concepts

Equations that are more complex may have to be simplified before they can be solved. More than two steps may be required to solve them. If there are like terms on one side of an equation, combine them first. Then apply inverse operations and the properties of equality to continue solving the equation.

Example 1   Combining Like Terms

Solve $5x + 8 - 3x + 2 = 20$. Justify each step. Check the solution.

SOLUTION

$5x + 8 - 3x + 2 = 20$	
$5x - 3x + 8 + 2 = 20$	Commutative Property of Addition
$2x + 10 = 20$	Combine like terms.
$-10 = -10$	Subtraction Property of Equality
$2x = 10$	Simplify.
$\dfrac{2x}{2} = \dfrac{10}{2}$	Division Property of Equality
$x = 5$	Simplify.

Math Language

Like terms have the same variable(s) raised to the same power(s).

Check Substitute 5 for x.

$5x + 8 - 3x + 2 = 20$
$5(5) + 8 - 3(5) + 2 \stackrel{?}{=} 20$
$25 + 8 - 15 + 2 \stackrel{?}{=} 20$
$20 = 20$ ✓

Complex equations can contain symbols of inclusion such as parentheses and brackets. Eliminate the symbols of inclusion first. Use the Distributive Property if multiplication is indicated by the symbols of inclusion. Then combine like terms on each side of the equation. Continue to solve the equation by applying inverse operations and the properties of equality.

Online Connection
www.SaxonMathResources.com

Lesson 26   153

MATH BACKGROUND

Most equations in this lesson have two or three terms on one side of the equal sign and a single term on the other side. Note that during solving, the number of terms may increase, for example after using the Distributive Property. Students may find this confusing if they expect each step to produce a simpler, equivalent equation. An analogy with sacrificing a piece in chess may be helpful for explaining this. In chess, a short term goal is to win pieces, but sometimes you intentionally lose a piece because you can get it back (plus more) a few moves later. In the same way, a solution to an equation may have intermediate steps that produce a more complex equation. Although the ultimate goal is to isolate the variable, not every step has to produce a simpler equation.

LESSON 26

1 Warm Up

Problem 1

Discuss with students that multiplicative inverse is another name for reciprocal.

2 New Concepts

In this lesson, students continue to solve equations by using inverse operations and the Properties of Equality, but now they must first simplify one of the expressions using the Distributive Property and/or by combining like terms.

Example 1

Like terms will be combined before using inverse operations to solve the equation.

Additional Example 1

Solve $3 + x - 10 + 4x = 28$. Justify each step. Check the solution.

$3 - 10 + x + 4x = 28$ Commutative Property of Addition

$-7 + 5x = 28$ Combine like terms.

$5x = 35$ Add 7.

$x = 7$ Divide by 5.

Check: $3 + 7 - 10 + 4(7) \stackrel{?}{=} 28$

$28 = 28$

LESSON RESOURCES

Student Edition Practice Workbook 26
Reteaching Master 26
Adaptations Master 26
Challenge and Enrichment Master C26, E26

Lesson 26   153

Example 2

Just as in simplifying a numeric expression, the first step in simplifying an algebraic expression is to clear the grouping symbols.

Additional Example 2

Solve $-2(x - 2) + x = 16$. Justify each step. Check the solution.

$-2x + 4 + x = 16$	Distributive Property
$-2x + x + 4 = 16$	Commutative Property
$-x + 4 = 16$	Combine like terms.
$-x = 12$	Subtract 4.
$x = -12$	Divide by -1.

Check: $-2(-12 - 2) + (-12) \stackrel{?}{=} 16$
$16 = 16$

Example 3

In this example students use the Distributive Property and combine two sets of like terms before applying inverse operations.

Additional Example 3

Solve $6x + 2(7 - x) + 10 = 20$. Justify each step. Check the solution.

$6x + 14 - 2x + 10 = 20$	Distributive Property
$4x + 24 = 20$	Combine like terms.
$4x = -4$	Subtract 24.
$x = -1$	Divide by 4.

Check:
$6(-1) + 2[7 - (-1)] + 10 \stackrel{?}{=} 20$
$20 = 20$

TEACHER TIP

Tell students to align the equal signs when solving equations. This will help them avoid errors when applying inverse operations to both sides of the equation.

Math Reasoning

Write What is another way to eliminate the coefficient 7 from $7x$?

Multiply both sides by the reciprocal $\frac{1}{7}$.

Caution

Remember to multiply by -1 when distributing a negative across parentheses.

Example 2 Using Distributive Property

Solve $x + 3(2x + 4) = 47$. Justify each step. Check the solution.

SOLUTION

$x + 3(2x + 4) = 47$	
$x + 6x + 12 = 47$	Distributive Property
$7x + 12 = 47$	Combine like terms.
$-12 = -12$	Subtraction Property of Equality
$7x = 35$	Simplify.
$\frac{7x}{7} = \frac{35}{7}$	Division Property of Equality
$x = 5$	Simplify.

Check Substitute 5 for x.
$x + 3(2x + 4) = 47$
$5 + 3[2(5) + 4] \stackrel{?}{=} 47$
$5 + 3[10 + 4] \stackrel{?}{=} 47$
$5 + 3[14] \stackrel{?}{=} 47$
$47 = 47$ ✓

When equations contain symbols of inclusion and like terms, first apply the Distributive Property. Next, add like terms. Then apply inverse operations and the properties of equality to solve the equation.

Example 3 Simplifying before Solving

Solve $5x - (x - 3) - 1 = 18$. Justify each step. Check the solution.

SOLUTION

$5x - (x - 3) - 1 = 18$	
$5x - x + 3 - 1 = 18$	Distributive Property
$4x + 2 = 18$	Combine like terms.
$-2 = -2$	Subtraction Property of Equality
$4x = 16$	Simplify.
$\frac{1}{4} \cdot 4x = 16 \cdot \frac{1}{4}$	Multiplication Property of Equality
$x = 4$	Simplify.

Check Substitute 4 for x.
$5x - (x - 3) - 1 = 18$
$5(4) - (4 - 3) - 1 \stackrel{?}{=} 18$
$20 - 1 - 1 \stackrel{?}{=} 18$
$18 = 18$ ✓

ALTERNATE METHOD FOR EXAMPLE 2

Have students guess and check to find the value of x.

"First, set the value of x equal to zero."

$0 + 3(2 \cdot 0 + 4) \stackrel{?}{=} 47$
$3(0 + 4) \stackrel{?}{=} 47$
$12 \neq 47$

"You now know that $x > 0$. Now try substituting 10 for x."

$10 + 3(2 \cdot 10 + 4) \stackrel{?}{=} 47$
$10 + 3(20 + 4) \stackrel{?}{=} 47$
$10 + 72 \stackrel{?}{=} 47$
$82 \neq 47$

"You also know that $x < 10$. Try a value between 0 and 10."

Have students repeat the guess-and-check method until they find the answer of $x = 5$.

Example 4 Application: Landscaping

Jim is building a right triangular flower bed. One of the acute angles will measure twice the other acute angle. What are the measures of the two acute angles?

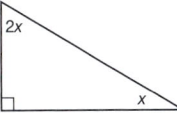

Hint
The sum of the measures of the angles of a triangle is 180°.

SOLUTION

$x + 2x + 90 = 180$	Sum of the angle measures
$3x + 90 = 180$	Combine like terms.
$-90 = -90$	Subtraction Property of Equality
$3x = 90$	Simplify.
$\dfrac{3x}{3} = \dfrac{90}{3}$	Division Property of Equality
$x = 30$	Simplify.

The measures of the angles are 30° and 60°.

Lesson Practice

Solve. Justify each step. Check the solution.

a. (Ex 1) $3x + 2 - x + 7 = 16$ 3.5; See Additional Answers.

b. (Ex 2) $6(x - 1) = 36$ 7; See Additional Answers.

c. (Ex 3) $5x - 3(x - 4) = 22$ 5; See Additional Answers.

 d. (Ex 4) **Geometry** Juan is building a triangular shelf. He wants one angle to be a right angle and the other two angles to have the same measure. What are the measures of the angles? 45°, 45°, 90°

Practice Distributed and Integrated

*1. (26) Solve for x in the equation $\dfrac{3}{4} + \dfrac{1}{2}x + 2 = 0$. $x = -5\dfrac{1}{2}$

*2. (25) **Multiple Choice** A vending machine will only accept quarters in change. What are the independent and dependent variables that describe the amount of money in change held by the vending machine? **D**

A Independent variable: value of 1 quarter; dependent variable: number of quarters

B Independent variable: value of 1 quarter; dependent variable: value of the quarters

C Independent variable: value of the quarters; dependent variable: number of quarters

D Independent variable: number of quarters; dependent variable: value of the quarters

Example 4

Remind students that in a triangle the sum of the measures of the angles is 180°.

Extend the Example
"A triangle cannot have two right angles. Why?" Two right angles sum to 180°, so the third angle would be 0°.

Additional Example 4
"Lara cuts a triangle with angles x, $5x$, and $x + 40$. What are the measures of the angles?" 20°, 100°, and 60°

Lesson Practice

Problem a
Error Alert Students might combine the x-terms to be $4x$. Help students catch the negative sign by having them circle each term with its sign.

Problem d
Scaffolding Guide students to first write an equation using x for each unknown angle.
$90 + x + x = 180$

Then combine like terms and solve.

###

The questions below help assess the concepts taught in this lesson.

"Why would you use the Distributive Property to solve $16x - 4(3x - 2) = 40$?" Sample: The Distributive Property makes it possible to combine like terms.

"How could you use the Commutative Property to solve $7x - 8 + 5x + 2 = 30$?" Sample: Move like terms next to each other and simplify.

ENGLISH LEARNERS

For Example 4, explain the meanings of **acute** and **right**. Say:

"Acute angles measure less than 90° and right angles measure 90° exactly."

Connect the meaning of acute and right by pointing to each angle in diagrams of the triangles.

Discuss other ways the word *acute* is used, such as experiencing acute pains. In this phrase, *acute* means sharp and intense. Compare this to an acute triangle, whose angles have a sharper point than right angles or obtuse angles.

Have students find other acute and right triangles in the classroom. Ask them if the top of a desk and its legs form a right or acute angle, or if the point of a pencil is acute. Sample answer: right angle; acute angle

3 Practice

Math Conversations
Discussion to strengthen understanding

Problem 8
Guide the students by asking them the following questions.

"Does it matter if your graph is a set of points or a continuous line or curve?" No.

"What do you have to make sure will happen?" Sample: No two x-values will be paired with the same y-value.

Problem 11
Guide the students by asking them the following questions.

"What rule is applied in the first step?" Multiplication Property of Equality

"Where do student A and Student B differ in this step?" Student A multiplied the first term by 10, while student B multiplied the first term by 100.

"Which student did not apply the rule correctly? Explain." Student A; All terms were not multiplied by the same number.

---

*3. **Multiple Choice** Which one of the expressions below can be simplified by combining like terms? B
(18)
  A $6(5x + 1)$ B $2x(3 + 8)$
  C $7x + 5$ D $9x - 6y + 4$

4. A table shows temperature changes over a period of a week.
(22)
  a. Why would a circle graph inaccurately display the data?
  b. Which type of graph would best display the data?

*5. **Digital Technology** The average size for the memory storage of an mp3 player is
(26) 2 gigabytes (GB). The average size of an mp3 song is 5.5 megabytes (MB). About how many songs can you store on a 2-gigabyte player if the player requires 16 megabytes for its own use? (Hint: 1gigabyte = 1024 megabytes) about 370 mp3 songs

*6. **Write** Describe two different methods for solving $12(x + 7) = 96$.
(26)

*7. **Justify** Solve $-5(3x - 7) + 11 = 1$. Justify each step with an operation or property.
(26) See Additional Answers.

*8. **Verify** Draw the graph of a function. Check to see if your graph is truly a function.
(25)

*9. Use the graph. Determine whether the relation is a function.   no
(25)

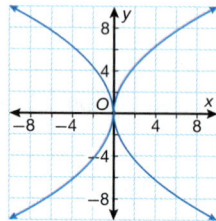

10. Solve $0.4m + 2.05 = 10.45$. $m = 21$
(24)

11. **Error Analysis** Two students solved $0.4x - 0.08 = 6.32$. Which student is correct?
(24) Explain the error.   Student B; Sample: Student A did not multiply each term by the correct power of ten, 100.

Student A	Student B
$0.4x - 0.08 = 6.32$	$0.4x - 0.08 = 6.32$
$10(0.4x) - 100(0.08) = 100(6.32)$	$100(0.4x) - 100(0.08) = 100(6.32)$
$4x - 8 = 632$	$40x - 8 = 632$
$+8 \quad +8$	$+8 \quad +8$
$4x = 640$	$40x = 640$
$\frac{4x}{4} = \frac{640}{4}$	$\frac{40x}{40} = \frac{640}{40}$
$x = 160$	$x = 16$

12. **Verify** Is $x = 8$ a solution for $7x - 12 = 44$? Explain. If false, provide a correct
(23) solution and check.   true; $7(8) - 12 = 44$; $56 - 12 = 44$

156   Saxon Algebra 1

4a. Sample: A circle graph is used to show percentages of a whole.

4b. Sample: A line graph would best represent the change in temperature over a period of time.

6. Sample: You can either divide both sides of the equation by 12 or use the Distributive Property and then solve.

8. See student work. Students should draw vertical lines across their graphs to check that the lines do not intersect the graph in more than one place.

INCLUSION

Some students have difficulty following multiple steps. Help these students by teaching them to focus on the first step. Point out that many problems can have several correct first steps, so they do not have to use the same first step on every problem. Once students realize this, they will be more confident, and they should be able to solve problems more quickly.

Give students practice identifying the first step with equations such as the following.

Have them only describe what their first step would be, and why.

$3(x - 7) = 12$ Distributive Property, to clear parentheses

$5x + 1 - 6x + 9 = -10$ Commutative Property of Addition, so you can combine like terms

$2x + x + 7x = 14$ Combine like terms, because no rearranging is necessary

156   Saxon Algebra 1

*13. **Multi-Step** Emil cooks 64 hot dogs. He uses 5 packages of hot dogs plus 4 hot dogs
(23) left over from a meal earlier in the week. How many hot dogs are in each package?
   a. Write an equation to find the number of hot dogs in a package. $5h + 4 = 64$
   b. Solve the equation, and then check the solution. $h = 12$; 12 hot dogs in
      each package.; $5(12) + 4 = 64$

*14. (Kangaroos) A large kangaroo can travel 15 feet in each hop. Write and solve an
(21) equation to find how many hops it takes for the kangaroo to travel one mile.
   (Hint: 5,280 feet = 1 mile) $15x = 5,280$; 352 hops

15. **Verify** Show that the graphed point is a solution to the equation $y = 2x + 9$.
(12)

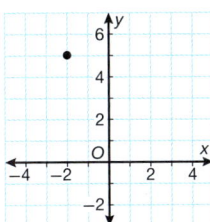

Sample: The point is $(-2, 5)$.
Substitute $x = -2$
into the equation, and the result should be 5;
$y = 2(-2) + 9 = -4 + 9 = 5$

16. **Analyze** Determine whether $3p^2qd^3$ and $(2qdp \cdot -5d^2p)$ are terms that can be
(18) combined. Explain your reasoning. Sample: Yes, they can be combined. When the
second one is simplified, they are like terms.

17. **Probability** The probability of rain on Monday is a. It is twice as likely to
(17) rain on Tuesday. Write an expression to represent the probability of rain on
Tuesday. P(rain on Tues.) = $2a$

18. (Biology) A biologist wants to calculate the volume of a spherical cell. She uses the
(16) equation for the volume of a sphere, which is $V = \frac{4}{3}\pi r^3$. If the cell has a radius of
2 micrometers, what is its volume? Use 3.14 for π and round to the nearest tenth.
about 33.5 micrometers^3

19. (Employment) Jim manages a restaurant that is currently hiring employees. On
(14) Tuesday, he interviewed 2 waiters, 2 line cooks, 3 dishwashers, and 1 chef. On
Thursday, he interviewed 2 waiters, 1 line cook, 2 dishwashers, and 3 chefs. What
is the probability that a randomly selected person interviewed applied to be a
waiter? $\frac{1}{4}$

20. **Verify** Compare the following expression using $<, >, =$. Verify your answer.
(13)
$\sqrt{324} - \sqrt{144}$ ⊙ $\sqrt{400} - \sqrt{289}$ Sample: $\sqrt{324} - \sqrt{144}$ ○ $\sqrt{400} - \sqrt{289}$
                                                        18 −   12   20 −   17
                                                              6 >   3

21. Evaluate.
(7)
$\frac{6}{2}[5(3 + 4)]$ 105

22. **Model** Use a number line to model $-8 - (-4) - (-6)$. Then simplify the
(6) expression. 2

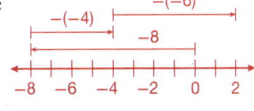

23. Simplify.
(4)
$2 \cdot (3 + 4)^2 + 15$ 113

Lesson 26   157

Problem 26
Error Alert
In part a, students might think that there are two terms because they see a plus sign. Point out that the sum is enclosed in grouping symbols, and further that it is raised to a power, so there is just one term in the expression on the right side of the equal sign.

Problem 29
Extend the Problem
"What does the *lw* in the volume formula represent?" area of the base

"What would be another form for the volume formula of a rectangular prism?" Sample: area of the base times the height

24. Subtract $\frac{1}{4} - \frac{1}{3}$. $-\frac{1}{12}$
(10)

25. **Probability** The probability of rolling a 4 on a six-sided number cube is $\frac{1}{6}$. To find
(3) the probability of rolling a 6-sided number cube and getting a 4 five times in a row, multiply the probability $\frac{1}{6}$ by itself five times. Write the answer using an exponent. $\left(\frac{1}{6}\right)^5$

26. **Investing** To find the amount of money earned on a bank deposit that earns
(2) quarterly compounded interest, the formula $A = P\left(1 + \frac{r}{4}\right)^{4t}$ is used.

   P = principal, (the amount originally deposited)

   r = the interest rate

   t = time in years.

   a. How many terms are in $P\left(1 + \frac{r}{4}\right)^{4t}$?   1

   b. How many variables are in $P\left(1 + \frac{r}{4}\right)^{4t}$?   3

   c. What is the coefficient of t?   4

27. Identify the coefficient, the variable(s), and the number of terms in $\frac{1}{3}Bh$.
(2) coefficient $\frac{1}{3}$, variables B and h, 1 term

28. **Multi-Step** The Noatak National Preserve in Alaska covers 6,574,481 acres. One
(8) acre is equal to 4840 square yards. What is the area of the preserve in square miles?

   a. Find the area of the preserve in square yards.   31,820,488,040 yd²

   b. Convert square yards to square miles. (Hint: 1 mile = 1760 yards)
   10,272.62656 mi²

29. **Geometry** To find the volume of a rectangular-prism shaped–
(12) sunscreen bottle, Jagdeesh uses the formula $V = lwh$. Betty uses the formula $V = wlh$. Will the volume of the bottle be the same? Explain.   yes; Sample: The Commutative Property of Multiplication allows the terms to be multiplied in a different order without changing the product.

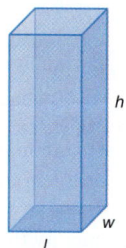

30. The spinner in a board game is divided into four equal sections colored blue, red,
(Inv 1) green, and yellow. Conduct a simulation using random numbers to determine the number of times the spinner lands on blue in 30 spins. Use the random number generator in a graphing calculator to simulate the spins.   See student work.

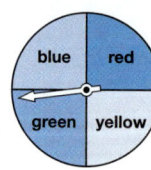

158   *Saxon Algebra 1*

CHALLENGE

An equation can have more than one set of grouping symbols. Start by using the Distributive Property on the innermost set of grouping symbols and work outward.

Solve: $3[x - (2x + 1)] + 4(x + 7) = -100$
$x = -125$

LOOKING FORWARD

Solving multi-step equations prepares students for

- **Lesson 28** Solving Equations with Variables on Both Sides
- **Lesson 29** Solving Literal Equations
- **Lesson 31** Using Rates, Ratios, And Proportions
- **Lesson 36** Writing and Solving Proportions
- **Lesson 42** Solving Percent Problems
- **Lesson 47** Solving Problems Involving the Percent of Change

LESSON 27

Identifying Misleading Representations of Data

Warm Up

3. Sample:

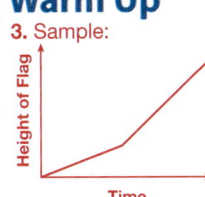

1. **Vocabulary** A bar graph uses _____ to represent data.
   (22) horizontal or vertical bars
2. True or False: A circle graph shows how data change.   False
   (22)
3. Draw a graph that represents a flag being raised up a flagpole slowly at the beginning and quickly at the end.
   (Inv 2)
4. Solve $2(2x + 3) = 24$.   4.5
   (26)

New Concepts

When displaying data, components such as the scale or labels can make a graph misleading.

Example 1 Identifying Misleading Line Graphs

The line graph shows the number of members of a health club each month since it opened. Explain why the graph may be misleading.

Hint
When there is a large gap between data values, a graph may use a broken axis. In the graph showing memberships, the vertical axis has a broken scale.

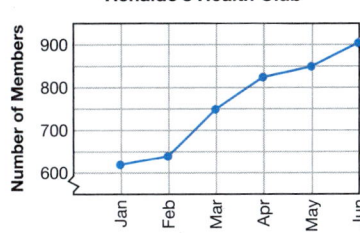

SOLUTION Because the scale does not start at zero, the membership appears to have increased much more than it actually did.

Another characteristic that may create a misleading graph is the size of the increments in the scale.

Example 2 Identifying Misleading Bar Graphs

A radio station conducted a survey of music preferences of listeners. The bar graph shows the results. Explain why the graph may be misleading.

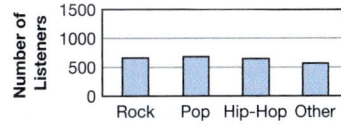

SOLUTION
The large increments of the scale make the data values appear to be closer than they actually are.

Lesson 27   **159**

MATH BACKGROUND

One good way to determine whether a bar graph is misleading is to look at the ratio of two data points. Suppose that a bar graph shows a cow weighing 2000 lb and an elephant weighing 4000 lb. The bar for the elephant should appear twice as high as the bar for the cow.

In a line graph, the slope of the graph indicates whether the changes in the *y*-values are significant. The units and intervals chosen for both scales affect the appearance of the slope.

Sometimes data are unintentionally represented in a misleading manner. If you make a graph with a software program, you might accidentally stretch the graph vertically or horizontally, which makes the graph misleading. For example, if you stretch a graph horizontally, the slope will appear to be less steep.

LESSON 27

1 Warm Up

Problem 3
Remind students that line graphs show change over time.

2 New Concepts

In this lesson, students analyze how graphs can be misleading.

Example 1
Changes in data may seem more significant depending on where the vertical scale starts.

Additional Example 1
"Explain why the graph may be misleading?" The scale does not start at zero.

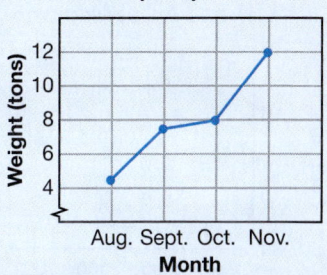

Example 2
The vertical scale can minimize differences in bar heights.

LESSON RESOURCES

Student Edition Practice
 Workbook 27
Reteaching Master 27
Adaptations Master 27
Challenge and Enrichment
 Master C27

Lesson 27   **159**

Example 3

Point out that a circle graph must show parts of a whole. If a category is missing, then the percentages are misleading.

Extend the Example

"Find the percentage for each category if the deli sold a total of 400 sandwiches (including 176 chicken salad). turkey: 13%; ham: 21%; roast beef: 10%; tuna: 12%; chicken salad: 44%

Example 4

A misleading graph can persuade people that significant changes are insignificant.

Additional Example 4

Ask students how this graph is misleading. Have them make a graph that is not misleading.
The scale makes the change in cost seem less.

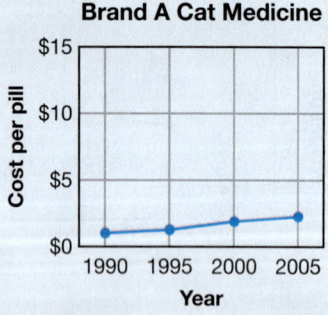

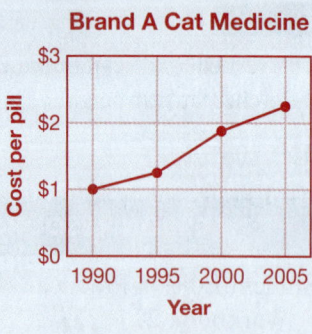

Example 3 **Identifying Misleading Circle Graphs**

The circle graph shows the number of some types of sandwiches a deli sells in one day. Explain why the graph may be misleading.

SOLUTION The title does not specify that these were the only sandwiches the deli sold, and it may not represent all categories. The deli may also have served a chicken salad or other type of sandwich, making the graph misleading.

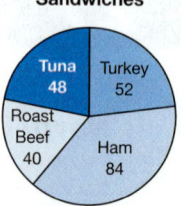

Example 4 **Application: Television Prices**

An electronics store created the graph to show the average selling price of a television each year.

a. Explain why the graph may be misleading.

SOLUTION The large increments make the data values appear to be closer than they actually are.

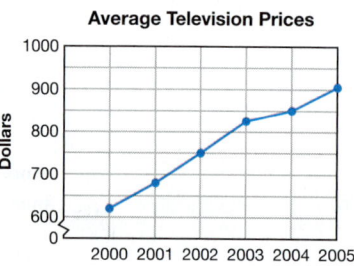

Math Reasoning

Analyze What increments could be used for the vertical axis of the graph in Example 4a so that the graph is not misleading?

increments of 50

b. What conclusion might be made from the graph? Why might the store have created this graph?

SOLUTION The graph seems to show that the prices have not increased much over the past five years. The store may want it to appear as though prices have not increased significantly; when in reality they have actually increased by almost 50 percent.

c. Make a graph of the sales data that is not misleading.

SOLUTION Use a broken axis and smaller increments.

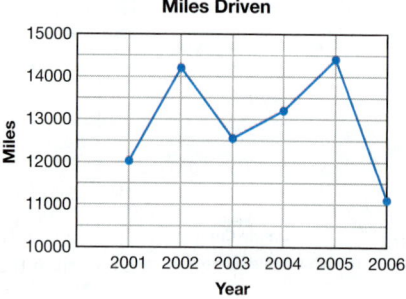

Lesson Practice

a. The graph at right shows the number of miles a car traveled each year. Explain why the graph may be misleading.
(Ex 1)
The vertical scale does not begin at 0. The title does not specify whether the car or the driver traveled all the miles.

INCLUSION

Materials: graph paper, colored markers

In Example 4c, students who have difficulty following multiple steps may need help making the graph. Students need to decide on the scale, but first they must find the least and greatest y-values, and before they can find these, they need to list all of the data points. Help students use these steps to make the graph:

1. List the data points for the existing graph. Use these values if students have trouble reading the graph: (2000, 620); (2001, 680); (2002, 750); (2003, 825); (2004, 850); and (2005, 905).

2. List the least and the greatest y-values.

3. Use the least and greatest y-values to decide on a scale. Label the scales.

4. Plot the data points on the grid.

5. Add all necessary labels and a title.

b. The graph below shows baking temperatures of various foods. Explain why the graph may be misleading.
(Ex 2)

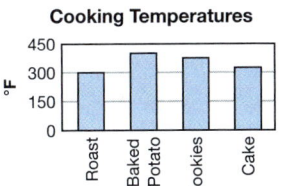

Sample: The large increments make the temperatures appear to be closer than they actually are.

c. The circle graph below shows the number of some kinds of dogs that were sold by the pet store. Explain why the graph may be misleading.
(Ex 3)

d. Sample: The vertical axis has a broken scale, so it appears that the number of products sold throughout the year changed more than it actually did.

e. Sample: The salesman may want it to appear that his sales increased a large amount from the beginning of the year to the end.

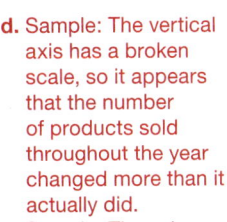

Sample: The title does not specify that these were the only dogs the pet shop sold and may not represent all breeds sold.

A salesperson created the graph at right to display the number of products he sold each month.
(Ex 4)

d. Explain why the graph may be misleading.

e. What conclusion might be made from the graph? Why might the salesman have created this graph?

f. Make a graph of the sales data that is not misleading.

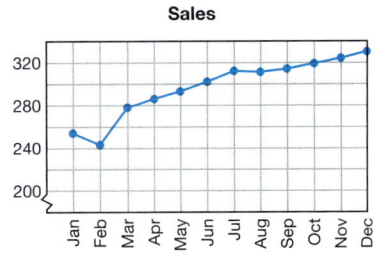

Practice   Distributed and Integrated

1. Simplify $(-2 + 3) \div (4 - 5 + 3)$. $\frac{1}{2}$
(11)

Solve.

2. $0.5x - 0.2 = 0.15$ $x = 0.7$
(23)

3. $\frac{1}{4} + \frac{2}{5}x + 1 = 2\frac{1}{4}$ $x = \frac{5}{2}$
(26)

4. **Multiple Choice** Which is the solution to the equation below?   **A**
(24)
$-0.4n + 0.305 = 0.295$

A 0.025   B −0.025   C 0.0004   D −0.7375

Lesson 27   161

Problem 11

Guide students by asking them the following questions.

"What do the data values have in common?" Sample: Each is a multiple of 1000.

"How would you label the vertical axis of the graph?" Sample: I would make the scale from 0 to 200 in intervals of 25.

"What would you need to include on the label of the vertical axis?" Sample: Whatever the unit is for the data values, I would need to add "(in thousands)" after it.

Problem 14
Extend the Problem

"Suppose 4 more friends arrive in a separate car to join the first 3. The total cost for both groups was $104. Write an equation to solve for the number of hours kayaked." $7(4x + 2) + 12 = 104$

"How many hours did they go kayaking?" 3 hours

"How much would it cost for the same group of 7 friends to kayak for 5 hours?" $160

Problem 15

Remind students that the variable h in the formula represents the slant height of the pyramid.

"What variable do you need to solve for?" h

"What values do you know that you can substitute into the formula?" $A = 150$ m²; $b = 5$ m

---

5. **Analyze** On a coordinate plane, a student draws a graph of two parallel lines perpendicular to the y-axis. Does the graph represent a function? **no**

6. Identify the property illustrated by $3 \cdot (9 \cdot 5) = (3 \cdot 9) \cdot 5$. **Associative Property of Multiplication**

*7. **Automotive Safety** The stopping distance d required by a moving vehicle is dependent on the square of its speed s. Write a rule in function notation to represent this information. **Sample: $d(s) = s^2$ or $f(s) = s^2$**

*8. A petting zoo contains 10 species of animals. The graph shows percentages of the 5 most numerous types of animals at the zoo. Give reasons why the circle graph may be misleading. **See Additional Answers.**

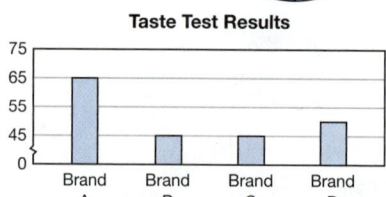

Petting Zoo

*9. **Justify** Is 4 a solution to the equation $5x + 8 - 3x + 4 = 20$? Justify your answer. **yes; $5(4) + 8 - 3(4) + 4 = 20$ is true**

*10. The bar graph shows results of a taste test of four different brands of yogurt. True or False. Twice as many people preferred Brand A over Brand D. **false**

Taste Test Results

*11. **Analyze** Using the set of data values 125,000, 105,000, 162,000, 112,000, and 148,000 without using a broken axis or very large intervals, how could a student make a reasonably sized graph of the data? **Sample: The student could use a scale of 0 to 200 and state that the data is in thousands.**

*12. **Production** A company has 6 machines to produce parts for its product. A manager uses the bar graph showing the number of parts produced by each machine each day. What incorrect conclusions might the manager make about the efficiency of the machines? **See Additional Answers.**

Machine Production

*13. True or False: Large intervals on a scale can make changes in data appear less than they actually are. If false, explain why. **true**

*14. **Multi-Step** Three friends rented a kayak. It cost $4 per hour per person to rent the kayak, plus $2 for each life jacket, and $3 to park the car. It cost $57 in all. How many hours did they spend kayaking? **4 hours**

*15. **Geometry** The formula for the surface area of a square pyramid is $S = \left(4 \cdot \frac{1}{2}bh\right) + b^2$. If the measure of b is 5 m, what is the largest slant height possible for the total surface area to be no more than 150 m²? **$h = 12.5$ m**

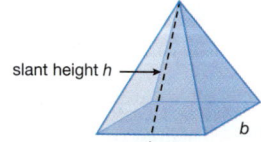

slant height h

162 Saxon Algebra 1

CHALLENGE

Give students the following data for the average gas price of regular gasoline per gallon over a time span of 7 years.

1999: $1.17; 2000: $1.51; 2001: $1.46; 2002: $1.36; 2003: $1.59; 2004: $1.88; 2005: $2.30

Have students create two different graphs of the data. One graph would imply that gasoline prices skyrocketed during the 7 years, and the other would make it seem that there was little change in gasoline prices over the same period. Then have students decide who might make each type of graph and why.

16. Justify What is the first step in solving $0.35 + 0.22x = 1.67$?
(24) Sample: Work in reverse order of operations, subtracting 0.35 from both sides of the equation.

*17. Phone Charges The length of the first ten calls Tyrese made one month were 13, 28,
(22) 6, 10, 13, 22, 31, 12, 2, and 9 minutes. In a stem-and-leaf plot of the data which digit would appear the most in the leaves column? 2

18. Verify Show that $-\frac{3}{4}x = 12$ and $\frac{5}{32}x = -2\frac{1}{2}$ have the same solution.
(21)

19. Graph the ordered pair $(-1, 0)$ on a coordinate plane.
(20)

19.

20. Measurement To measure the length of a steel rod, an engineer uses a reference
(19) point a few millimeters from the end of the ruler. She then subtracts this reference point from her final measurement of 325 mm. If the rod's length is 318 mm, what reference point did she use? 7 millimeters

21. Convert 37 American dollars to Indian rupees. (Hint: 1 rupee = $0.025)
(8) 1480 Indian rupees

22. Statistics Absolute deviation is the absolute value of the difference between a
(5) value in a data set and the mean of the data set. For the data set {8, 9, 11, 12, 15}, the mean is 11, so the absolute deviation for the value 15 is $|15-11| = |4| = 4$. What is the absolute deviation for each of the other numbers in the above data set?

22. For 8, the absolute deviation is 3. For 9, the absolute deviation is 2. For 11, the absolute deviation is 0. For 12, the absolute deviation is 1.

23. Fundraising The cheerleaders made $3 profit on each item sold in a fundraiser.
(15) They sold x calendars and y candles in total. Write and simplify an algebraic expression to find the total profit. Sample: $3(x+y) = 3x + 3y$

24. Write A coin is tossed 8 times. What is the probability that the next time the coin
(14) is tossed the result will be heads? Explain. $\frac{1}{2}$; Sample: The probability that the results will be heads will remain the same.

25. Simplify $11 \cdot 3 + 7$. 40
(4)

26. Multi-Step A vending machine has q quarters and d dimes.
(9)
  a. Write an expression with variables to represent the value of the money. Sample: $q \cdot \$0.25 + d \cdot \$0.10$
  b. Find the value of the change in the machine if there are 21 quarters and 13 dimes. $6.55

27. Use <, >, or = to compare the expressions. $\frac{1}{3} + \frac{1}{5} \cdot \frac{2}{15}$ ⊘ $(\frac{1}{3} + \frac{1}{5}) \cdot \frac{2}{15}$
(7)

28. Write A man runs up and down stairs. If the number of stairs he runs up plus the
(6) number of stairs he runs down is the total number of stairs, describe his position at the end of his run. Sample: The number of stairs he ran up minus the number of stairs he ran down describes his position at the end of his run.

29. Write Show the steps for simplifying $10 \cdot 4^2 + 72 \div 2^3$.
(4)

30. Accounting Accountants prepare financial reports for businesses. Identify the set
(1) of numbers that best describes the numbers in a financial report. Explain your choice. Sample: rational numbers, because irrational numbers cannot be shown as fractions or ratios.

18. Sample:

Solve Equation 1	Substitute
$-\frac{3}{4}x = 12$	$\frac{5}{32}(-16) = -2\frac{1}{2}$
$x = -16$	$-2\frac{1}{2} = -2\frac{1}{2}$

29.
$10 \cdot 4^2 + 72 \div 2^3$
$10 \cdot 16 + 72 \div 8$ Simplify the exponents.
$160 + 9$ Multiply and divide from left to right.
169 Add.

Lesson 27   163

Problem 21
Error Alert

A common error students may make is to multiply the American dollars by the amount each Indian rupee is worth, instead of dividing by that amount.

$\$37 \cdot \frac{\$0.025}{\text{rupee}} \neq 0.93$ rupees

$\$37 \div \frac{\$0.025}{\text{rupee}} = 1480$ rupees

Remind students to check their answers to make sure they make sense. If 1 Indian rupee is worth about 3 cents, could less than 1 rupee be worth $37? no

Problem 26
Extend the Problem

"A second vending machine has quarters (q), dimes (d), and nickels (n). Write an expression with variables to represent the value of the money." Sample: $0.25q + 0.10d + 0.05n$

"Find the number of nickels in the machine if there are 16 quarters and 50 dimes, and the total value of the money in the machine is $10.00." 20 nickels

Problem 29
Guide the students by reminding them of the order of operations.

"What step would you perform first when simplifying the expression? Evaluate the exponents.

"What two steps would you perform next?" Sample: I would multiply 10 and 16 and divide 72 by 8.

"What two addends would you be left with?" 160 and 9

LOOKING FORWARD

Identifying misleading representations of data prepares students for

- **Lesson 48** Analyzing Measures of Central Tendency
- **Lesson 54** Displaying Data in Box-and-Whisker Plots
- **Lesson 62** Displaying Data in Stem-and-Leaf Plots and Histograms

LESSON 28

Solving Equations with Variables on Both Sides

1 Warm Up

Problem 2
Remind students to use the order of operations to simplify the expression.

2 New Concepts

Discuss the definition of an identity equation. Explain that if the variables can be eliminated and the resulting equation is true, then there are infinitely many solutions because any value for the variable will make the equation true.

Exploration

Students gain insight by modeling different equations with algebra tiles. In each case, the goal is to isolate the variable.

Additional Exploration

"Describe how you would set up algebra tiles to solve $4x + 4 = 5x + 5$." Then solve. Sample: Put 4 x-tiles on the left side and 5 x-tiles on the right side. Put 4 1-tiles on the left and 5 1-tiles on the right. The solution is $x = -1$.

LESSON RESOURCES

Student Edition Practice Workbook 28
Reteaching Master 28
Adaptations Master 28
Challenge and Enrichment Master C28, E28
Technology Lab Master 28

Warm Up

1. **Vocabulary** In the expression $-5x + 2 + 3x$, $-5x$ and $3x$ are _____ terms. like

2. Simplify $10 - 4(5 + 3) + 2^3$. -14

Solve.

3. $2(3 - x) = 10$ -2

4. $-3(1 + 2x) + x = 32$ -7

5. **Multiple Choice** Which value is a solution to the equation $3(x - 4) - x = 30$? D
   A 14   B 9   C 6   D 21

New Concepts

To solve an equation with variables on both sides, use inverse operations to bring the variables together on one side of the equation.

Materials
- algebra tiles

Exploration Modeling Variables on Both Sides of an Equation

Use algebra tiles to model and solve $4x + 5 = 2x + 11$.

$4x + 5$	$2x + 11$	
(tiles)	(tiles)	Model each side of the equation.
(tiles with $-x$ $-x$)	(tiles with $-x$ $-x$)	Add 2 $-x$-tiles to both sides. Remove pairs that equal zero.
(tiles)	(tiles)	Add 5 -1-tiles to both sides. Remove the zero pairs.
x x	(6 tiles)	Arrange into 2 equal groups. What is the value of x? $x = 3$

a. Model $x + 3 = 2x - 4$. Then find the value of x. See student work. $x = 7$

b. Model $3x - 1 = x - 3$. Then find the value of x. See student work. $x = -1$

164 Saxon Algebra 1

MATH BACKGROUND

Students can use what they learned in previous lessons to solve equations that have the variable on both sides.

The simplest case of an identity equation is $x = x$. Other simple examples are:

$$x + 10 = x + 10$$
$$5x = 5x$$

Students can see these are identity equations by inspection.

It is less obvious that 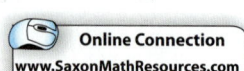 $4x + 8 = \frac{12(2 + x)}{3}$ is an identity because it takes several steps to change the right side to be the same expression as the left side.

A good exercise is to challenge students to make up their own identities by working backwards from a simple identity. You can also have students generate equations that have no solution by starting from an inequality such as $5 \neq 3$.

Math Language

Inverse operations undo each other. Addition and subtraction are inverse operations. Multiplication and division are inverse operations.

Example 1 Using Inverse Operations

Solve $6x = 4x - 10$. Justify each step. Check the solution.

SOLUTION

$$6x = 4x - 10$$
$$\underline{-4x = -4x} \qquad \text{Subtraction Property of Equality}$$
$$2x = -10 \qquad \text{Combine like terms.}$$
$$\frac{2x}{2} = \frac{-10}{2} \qquad \text{Division Property of Equality}$$
$$x = -5$$

Check Substitute -5 for x in the original equation.

$$6x = 4x - 10$$
$$6(-5) \stackrel{?}{=} 4(-5) - 10$$
$$-30 \stackrel{?}{=} -20 - 10$$
$$-30 = -30 \checkmark$$

Equations with variables on both sides might also contain symbols of inclusion and like terms. The first step is to apply the Distributive Property. The second step is to add like terms. Then apply inverse operations and the properties of equality to solve the equation.

Example 2 Simplifying Before Solving

Solve $5(2x + 4) - 2x = 6 + 2(3x + 12)$. Justify each step.

SOLUTION

$$5(2x + 4) - 2x = 6 + 2(3x + 12)$$
$$10x + 20 - 2x = 6 + 6x + 24 \qquad \text{Distributive Property}$$
$$10x - 2x + 20 = 6 + 6x + 24 \qquad \text{Commutative Property}$$
$$8x + 20 = 6x + 30 \qquad \text{Combine like terms.}$$
$$\underline{-6x \qquad\quad = -6x} \qquad \text{Subtraction Property of Equality}$$
$$2x + 20 = 30 \qquad \text{Simplify.}$$
$$\underline{-20 = -20} \qquad \text{Subtraction Property of Equality}$$
$$2x = 10 \qquad \text{Simplify.}$$
$$\frac{1}{2} \cdot 2x = 10 \cdot \frac{1}{2} \qquad \text{Multiplication Property of Equality}$$
$$x = 5 \qquad \text{Simplify.}$$

Math Reasoning

Write What is another way to eliminate the coefficient 2 from $2x$?

Divide both sides by 2.

An **identity** is an equation that is always true. It has infinitely many solutions. If no value of the variable makes an equation true, then the equation has no solution.

Example 1

Remind students they have already learned how to use inverse operations to isolate the variable in the equation.

Additional Example 1

Solve $8x = 3x + 20$. Justify each step. Check the solution.

$5x = 20$ Subtract $3x$.
$x = 4$ Divide by 4.
Check:
$8 \cdot 4 \stackrel{?}{=} 3 \cdot 4 + 20$
$32 = 32$

Example 2

Explain to students that they may need to simplify the expression on each side of the equal sign before solving.

Error Alert Students may find an incorrect solution because they try to solve the equation using mental math. Suggest that they write down the steps needed to solve the equation so they can go back and find an error if their solution does not check.

Additional Example 2

Solve.
$3x + 4(2 - 2x) = 3(5x + 1) - 15$. Justify each step. Check the solution.

$3x + 8 - 8x = 15x + 3 - 15$
            Distributive Property
$8 - 5x = 15x - 12$
            Combine like terms.
$8 = 20x - 12$ Add $5x$.
$20 = 20x$ Add 12.
$1 = x$ Divide by 20.

Lesson 28   165

🔶 INCLUSION

Materials: balance scales, color markers

Some students have trouble because they tend to transpose numbers and sequences. Help these students by modeling how to keep operations on the left and right sides separated as they solve Example 1.

Example 3

Point out to students that an equation may have infinitely many solutions or no solution.

Additional Example 3

Solve each equation. Justify each step.

a. $2x + 4(x + 3) = 2(3x + 6)$
The equation has infinite solutions because it is true for every value of x.

b. $9x - 5(2x + 1) = 2(3x - 6) - 7x$
The equation has no solutions.

TEACHER TIP

Emphasize the use of inverse operations in solving the equations. Students at this level should not try to solve by guessing and checking.

Example 4

This real-world example describes two expressions with the same variable equal to each other. There is one solution.

Extend the Example

"What does each company charge for 200 long-distance minutes?"
Company A: $26.95; Company B: $25.95

"If you use 200 long-distance minutes, how much do you save by using Company B?" $1.00

Additional Example 4

A clerk at one store is paid $400 per week plus $0.75 for every item she sells. At another store, a clerk is paid $500 per week plus $0.50 for every item she sells. For how many sold items are the clerks paid the same amount?
400 items

Math Reasoning

Analyze When the simplified equation is an identity, what values of the variable will satisfy the original equation?

all real numbers

Math Reasoning

Analyze When all variables are eliminated in an equation, resulting in a false statement, what values of the variable satisfy the original equation?

none

Example 3   **No Solutions or Infinitely Many Solutions**

Solve each equation. Justify each step.

a. $10 - 6x = -2(3x - 5)$

SOLUTION

$10 - 6x = -2(3x - 5)$
$10 - 6x = -6x + 10$ Distributive Property
$\underline{+6x = +6x}$ Addition Property of Equality
$10 = 10$ Simplify. Always true.

Since $10 = 10$ is always true, the equation is an identity.

b. $7x - 2 = 9x - 5 - 2x$

SOLUTION

$7x - 2 = 9x - 5 - 2x$
$7x - 2 = 7x - 5$ Combine like terms.
$\underline{-7x = -7x}$ Addition Property of Equality
$-2 = -5$ Simplify. Never true.

Since $-2 = -5$ is never true, the equation has no solutions.

Example 4   **Application: Telephone Rates**

Telephone Company A charges $18.95 per month for local calls and $0.04 per minute for long-distance calls. Telephone Company B charges $21.95 per month for local calls and $0.02 per minute for long-distance calls. For what number of minutes of long-distance calls per month is the cost of the plans the same?

SOLUTION

Let m = the number of minutes of long distance calls.

Company A's monthly charge = $18.95 + $0.04m

Company B's monthly charge = $21.95 + $0.02m

$18.95 + 0.04m = 21.95 + 0.02m$ Write an equation.
$\underline{-0.02m = -0.02m}$ Subtraction Property of Equality
$18.95 + 0.02m = 21.95$ Simplify.
$\underline{-18.95 = -18.95}$ Subtraction Property of Equality
$0.02m = 3.00$ Simplify.
$\dfrac{0.02m}{0.02m} = \dfrac{3.00}{0.02}$ Division Property of Equality
$m = 150$ Simplify.

The costs will be same for 150 minutes.

⚠️ ALTERNATE METHOD FOR EXAMPLE 3

In Part a, have students multiply both sides by the reciprocal of -2 instead of using the Distributive Property.

$$10 - 6x = -2(3x - 5)$$
$$-\tfrac{1}{2} \cdot 10 - \left(-\tfrac{1}{2}\right) \cdot 6x = -\tfrac{1}{2} \cdot -2(3x - 5)$$
$$-5 + 3x = 3x - 5$$
$$-5 = -5$$

The resulting equation is still always true, so this method confirms that the equation is an identity.

Lesson Practice

Solve each equation. Justify each step. Check the solution.

a. $6x = 3x + 27$ 9; See Additional Answers.
(Ex 1)

b. $2 + 3(3x - 6) = 5(x - 3) + 15$ 4; See Additional Answers.
(Ex 2)

Solve each equation. Justify each step. If the equation is an identity, write identity. If the equation has no solution, write no solution.
(Ex 3)

c. $2(x + 3) = 3(2x + 2) - 4x$ identity; See Additional Answers.

d. $3(x + 4) = 2(x + 5) + x$ no solution; See Additional Answers.

e. (Ex 4) **Membership Rates** A fitness center has a membership fee of $125. Members only pay $5 per day to work out at the center. A nonmember pays $10 per day to work out. After how many work-out days is the total cost for members, including the membership fee, the same as the total cost for nonmembers?   25 days

Practice   Distributed and Integrated

1. Solve for y: $\frac{3}{4}y = 4\frac{7}{8}$. $y = 6\frac{1}{2}$
(21)

*2. Solve for p: $3p - 4 - 6 = 2(p - 5)$. $p = 0$
(38)

*3. **Formulate** You have $3 in bills and a certain number of nickels in one pocket. In
(28) the other pocket you have $2 in bills and a certain number of dimes. You have the same number of dimes as nickels and the same amount of money in each pocket. Write an equation to find the number of dimes and nickels you have.
$3 + 0.05n = 2 + 0.10n$, $n = 20$; 20 dimes and 20 nickels

4. **Error Analysis** Two students used the Distributive Property to solve the same
(26) multi-step equation. Which student is correct? Explain the error.   Student B;
Sample: Student A incorrectly distributed in step 1.

Student A	Student B
$4x - 2(12 - x) = 18$	$4x - 2(12 - x) = 18$
$4x - 24 - x = 18$	$4x - 24 + 2x = 18$
$3x - 24 = 18$	$6x - 24 = 18$
$3x = 42$	$6x = 42$
$x = 14$	$x = 7$

*5. (**Wages**) A worker at one farm is paid $486 for the week, plus $0.03 for every pound
(28) of apples she picks. At another farm, a worker is paid $490 for the week, plus $0.02 for every pound of apples. For how many pounds of apples are the workers paid the same amount?   400 lb

*6. **Multiple Choice** What is the value of x when $(x + 15)\frac{1}{3} = 2x - 1$?   A
(28)

A $\frac{18}{5}$ B $\frac{5}{18}$ C $\frac{18}{7}$ D $\frac{7}{18}$

Lesson 28   167

Problem 7

Remind students that subtracting an expression that is inside parentheses is the same as multiplying the expression by −1. Encourage students to use the Distributive Property to avoid making errors with the negative signs.

Problem 12

After students find the domain and range of the relation in Part a, ask, "For every domain value of the function, is there exactly one range value?" yes

"How can you tell just by looking at the graph?" Sample: Use the vertical line test and see that any vertical line would only pass through one point of the function.

---

*7. **Error Analysis** Two students solved the same multi-step equation. Which student
(28) is correct? Explain the error.   Student B is correct. Sample: Student A didn't distribute properly.

Student A	Student B
$3x - 4 = 2x - (4 + x)$	$3x - 4 = 2x - (4 + x)$
$3x - 4 = 2x - 4 + x$	$3x - 4 = 2x - 4 - x$
$3x - 4 = 3x - 4$	$3x - 4 = x - 4$
$0 = 0$	$2x = 0$
All real numbers.	$x = 0$

*8. **Generalize** If the equation $yx = zx$ is true, when yx is positive, $x \neq 0$, and z is
(26) a negative integer. Will x be positive or negative? Sample: zx must be positive; therefore, x must be a negative number.

9. **Geometry** The graph shows areas of several square
(27) sheets of paper.

a. About how many times greater does the area of Sheet 4 appear to be than that of Sheet 3?   about 4

b. The squares have side lengths of 9, 10, 8, and 11 inches. About how many times greater is the area of Sheet 4 than the area of Sheet 3? about 2

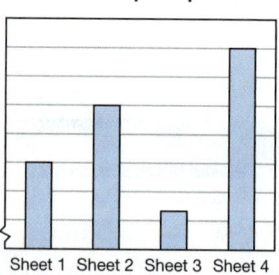
Area of Paper Squares

10. True or False: A broken scale can make changes in data appear less than they
(27) actually are. If false, explain why.   false; Sample: A broken scale makes data changes appear greater than they are.

11. **Multi-Step** Average home prices in several cities are shown in the table.
(27)

City	Woodside	Reefville	Boynton	Dunston	York
Average Home Price (in thousands)	$265	$210	$320	$375	$350

a. Make a bar graph with a scale from 200 to 400. Use intervals of 40.
See Additional Answers.
b. Without looking at the scale, what conclusions might the graph lead to?
c. Why might a real estate agent who sells houses only in Reefville want to show potential clients a graph like this?   Sample: The clients are likely to conclude that home prices in Reefville are much less than in the other cities.

*12. **Multi-Step** Use the graph.
(25)
a. Give the domain and range of the relation.
b. Determine whether the relation is a function. Explain.
The relation is a function. Sample: Each domain value is paired with exactly one range value.

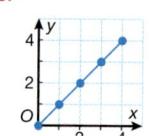

11b. Sample: The average home price in Dunston is much greater than most others. On average a house in Dunston would cost about 4 times more than one in Reefville.

12a. D: $\{0 \leq x \leq 4\}$; R: $\{0 \leq y \leq 4\}$

168   Saxon Algebra 1

---

eL ENGLISH LEARNERS

Explain the meaning of the word **isolate**. Say:

"**To isolate something means to set it apart from other things.**"

Explain that to isolate a variable is to set it apart from the other terms in the equation. Point out that in the equation $x = 5$, the variable is isolated, or set apart, from the constant by the equal sign. It is alone on one side of the equation.

Discuss other examples of isolation, like when an ill person is isolated to keep germs from spreading. Have students share a word from their culture that has a similar meaning to the word *isolate*.

*13. **Multiple Choice** Use the graph shown. A conservation group
(25) has been working to increase the population of a herd of
Asian elephants. The graph shows the results of their
efforts. Which relations represent the data in the graph? **B**

A {(1, 4.5), (2, 6), (3, 10), (4, 14.5)}

B {(1, 5), (2, 6), (3, 10), (4, 15)}

C {(4.5, 1), (6, 2), (10, 3), (14.5, 4)}

D {(5, 1), (6, 2), (10, 3), (15, 4)}

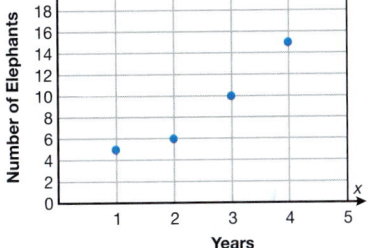

14. 0.28 of what number is 18.2?   65
(24)

15. **(Internet Access)** At a local diner, customers can enjoy wireless
(23) Internet access.

a. Write an equation that can be used to find the cost of being online
for m minutes.   Sample: $C = \$0.05m + \$3.95$

b. **Estimate** You know it will require $1\frac{1}{2}$ to 2 hours to get your research
done online. About how much will it cost to do your work
at the diner?   from $8.50 to $10.00

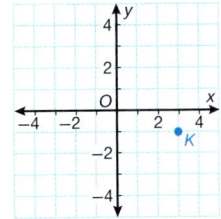

16. Determine whether the statement is true or false. If false, explain why.
(22) A line graph can help analyze change over time.   true

17. Use the coordinate grid.
(20) Find the coordinates of point K.   Sample: (3, −1)

*18. Silvia had $247 in her savings account. She made a deposit into her savings
(19) account. Now, her account has $472. Write an equation that shows the amount
of money that is currently in her account. Determine how much money was
deposited. $247 + x = \$472$; $225

19. **(Cooking)** George has already sliced 1 carrot and continues to slice 6 carrots per
(18) minute. Frank has already sliced 16 carrots and continues to slice 4 carrots
per minute.

a. Write expressions representing the number of carrots sliced by each person in
m minutes. $6m + 1$ and $4m + 16$

b. Write an expression for the total number of carrots sliced. $10m + 17$

20. **(Grades)** A student raised her grade by 13 points. Write an expression to represent
(17) her new grade. $g + 13$

Lesson 28   169

Problem 14

Error Alert
Students may not recognize this as a percent problem. Remind students that 0.28 is the same as 28% and suggest that they set up a proportion to solve.

$$\frac{\text{is}}{\text{of}} = \frac{\%}{100} \rightarrow \frac{18.2}{x} = \frac{28}{100}$$

Problem 15

Before students write the equation, ask, "What is the constant of the equation?" 3.95

"What will be the coefficient of the variable m?" 0.05

Before students estimate the cost, ask, "How many minutes are in $1\frac{1}{2}$ hours? In 2 hours?" 90 minutes; 120 minutes

---

CHALLENGE

Solve the equation by first multiplying by a reciprocal. Show each step.

$8(2x − 1) + 15 + 7x = 4(3x + 5) + 5x − 1$

$\quad 8(2x − 1) + 15 + 7x = 4(3x + 5) + 5x − 1$

$\quad \frac{1}{4} \cdot 8(2x − 1) + \frac{1}{4} \cdot 15 + \frac{1}{4} \cdot 7x$

$\quad = \frac{1}{4} \cdot 4(3x + 5) + \frac{1}{4} \cdot 5x − \frac{1}{4} \cdot 1$

$\quad 2(2x − 1) + \frac{15}{4} + \frac{7}{4}x = 3x + 5 + \frac{5}{4}x − \frac{1}{4}$

$\quad 4x − 2 + \frac{15}{4} + \frac{7}{4}x = 3x + 5 + \frac{5}{4}x − \frac{1}{4}$

$\quad \frac{23}{4}x + \frac{7}{4} = \frac{17}{4}x + \frac{19}{4}$

$\quad \frac{6}{4}x = \frac{12}{4}$

$\quad x = 2$

Lesson 28   169

Problem 27

Remind students how to find the perimeter of a polygon. When adding the lengths of the sides, have them combine like terms to simplify the answer.

Problem 29

Guide students by asking the following questions.

"How many feet are in 1 mile?" 5280 feet

"Are you converting from a larger unit of measurement to a smaller unit, or from a smaller unit to a larger unit?" from a larger unit to a smaller unit

"When changing to smaller units, will you need a greater number of them or a fewer number of them?" greater

"Should you multiply or divide?" multiply

---

*21. **Astronomy** The gravitational force between two objects can be approximated by using $F = \frac{m_1 m_2}{d^2}$, where F is the gravitational force in newtons, m_1 is the mass in kilograms of the first object, m_2 is the mass in kilograms of the second object, and d is the distance between them expressed in meters. If the mass of a satellite is 500 kilograms, the mass of a small asteroid is 1500 kilograms, and the distance between them is 1000 meters, what is the gravitational force between the satellite and the asteroid?   about 0.75 N

22. **Verify** Use two different methods to evaluate $8(10 - 4)$. Verify that each method gives the same result.   See Additional Answers.

23. Evaluate $\sqrt{49} + 4^2$.   23

24. True or False: $(b + c) + d = b + (c + d)$. Justify your answer.   true; Associative Property of Addition

25. Evaluate the expression $3n^2p^5 + 4(n - 8)^2$ for the given values $n = -3$ and $p = 1$.   511

26. **Write** Give a counterexample for the following statement: The set of irrational numbers is closed under subtraction.   Any irrational number subtracted from itself will equal 0, which is not an irrational number; Sample: $\sqrt{3} - \sqrt{3} = 0$

27. **Measurement** Find the perimeter of the polygon. $17x + 13$

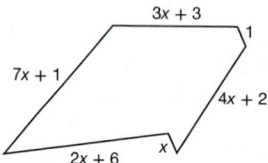

28. **Probability** A coin is tossed 3 times.
   a. What set of numbers could be used to express the different probabilities of how the coin is tossed?   rational numbers
   b. Could the probability ever be a whole number? Explain.   Sample: yes; 0 and 1 can be a probability.

29. **Write** When a student converts from miles to feet, will the student multiply or divide? Explain.   Sample: 1 mi = 5280 ft, so the student will multiply because the conversion is from a larger unit of measure to a smaller unit of measure.

*30. **Write** Describe a situation that could be represented by a continuous graph.   Sample: A graph that shows changes over time. For example: The salaries of women from 1990 to 2010.

LOOKING FORWARD

Solving equations with variables on both sides prepares students for

• **Lesson 29** Solving Literal Equations

• **Lesson 31** Using Rates, Ratios, and Proportions

• **Lesson 36** Writing and Solving Proportions

• **Lesson 42** Solving Percent Problems

• **Lesson 47** Solving Problems Involving the Percent of Change

• **Lesson 117** Using Trigonometric Ratios

LESSON 29

Solving Literal Equations

Warm Up

1. **Vocabulary** A _____ (constant, variable) is a letter used to represent an unknown.   **variable**
2. Evaluate the expression rt if $r = 4$ and $t = 7$.   **28**
3. Solve the equation $3x - 24 = 6$.   **10**
4. Solve the equation $4x + 14 = 2x + 20$.   **3**
5. Solve the equation $5x + 2 = 2x - 9$. $-\frac{11}{3}$

New Concepts

Recall when solving an equation with one variable, inverse operations are used to isolate the variable as shown below.

$2x - 6 = 14$

$\underline{+6 = +6}$ Add 6 to undo subtracting 6.

$2x = 20$ Simplify.

$\dfrac{2x}{2} = \dfrac{20}{2}$ Divide by 2 to undo multiplication.

$x = 10$ Simplify.

A **literal equation** is an equation with more than one variable. As in an equation with one variable, use inverse operations and properties of equalities to solve for a specific variable in a literal equation. The solution for the specific variable will be in the terms of the other variables and numbers.

Math Reasoning

Connect Give an example of an equation that would contain more than one variable.

formula for area of a rectangle

Example 1 Solving for a Variable

Solve for y: $2x + 3y = 10$. Justify each step.

SOLUTION

$2x + 3y = 10$ Find y in the equation.

$\underline{-2x = -2x}$ Subtract $2x$ to eliminate from the y side.

$3y = -2x + 10$ Simplify.

$\dfrac{3y}{3} = \dfrac{-2x}{3} + \dfrac{10}{3}$ Divide by 3 to eliminate the coefficient of y.

$y = \dfrac{-2x}{3} + \dfrac{10}{3}$ Simplify.

If the variable being solved for is on both sides of the equation, the first step is to eliminate the variable on one side or the other.

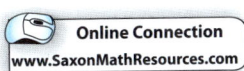
Online Connection
www.SaxonMathResources.com

Lesson 29   171

MATH BACKGROUND

Solving literal equations helps to show the relationship of the variables in the equation. For example, the formula for the area of a triangle is $A = \dfrac{bh}{2}$. To find the relationship of the base to the area of the triangle, solve the equation for b:

$b = \dfrac{2A}{h}$

So, the base of a triangle is twice the area divided by the height. This can be useful when finding an unknown measurement for a triangle if you are given the area.

LESSON 29

1 Warm Up

Problem 4
Solve the equation by isolating the variable on one side of the equal sign.

2 New Concepts

In this lesson, students solve for one variable in equations with multiple variables.

A **literal equation** is an equation with more than one variable. It can be solved for any of the variables. An equation in the form $y = mx + b$ is a solution for y of a literal equation. The solution for x is $x = \dfrac{y - b}{m}$.

Example 1

Remind students that to solve an equation for a given variable they must isolate that variable on one side of the equal sign.

Additional Example 1

Solve for x: $y = -3x - 5$.
Justify each step.

$y + 5 = -3x$ Add 5 to both sides.

$\dfrac{y + 5}{-3} = x$ Divide both sides by 3.

$-\dfrac{y + 5}{3} = x$ Move the negative sign.

LESSON RESOURCES

Student Edition Practice
  Workbook 29
Reteaching Master 29
Adaptations Master 29
Challenge and Enrichment
  Master C29

Lesson 29   171

Example 2

Error Alert Students might incorrectly combine unlike terms. Remind them that $3p + 2a$ are unlike terms and cannot be combined.

Additional Example 2
Solve for r and justify each step.
$3r + 2s - 7 = -4s + 4r - 8$.

$3r = -6s + 4r - 1$	Add $-2s + 7$.
$-r = -6s - 1$	Subtract $4r$.
$r = 6s + 1$	Divide by -1.

Example 3

Have a volunteer explain how solving the equation for F is a method for converting Celsius temperatures to Fahrenheit.

Extend the Example
Explain that the Celsius and Fahrenheit temperatures are equal at $-40°$.

"Verify that $-40°C = -40°F$ by substituting -40 into one of the formulas."

$F = \frac{9}{5}(-40) + 32$

$F = -72 + 32$

$F = -40$

Additional Example 3
Find the Fahrenheit temperature when the Celsius temperature is $25°$. **77°F**

Example 2 Solving for Variables on Both Sides

Solve for p: $4p + 2a - 5 = 6a + p$. Justify each step.

SOLUTION

$$4p + 2a - 5 = 6a + p$$

$\underline{-p \qquad\qquad\quad = \qquad -p}$	Eliminate the p on the right side.
$3p + 2a - 5 = 6a$	Combine like terms.
$\underline{\quad -2a + 5 = -2a + 5}$	Eliminate the $2a$ and -5 from the left side.
$3p = 4a + 5$	Combine like terms.
$\frac{3p}{3} = \frac{4a}{3} + \frac{5}{3}$	Divide both sides by 3.
$p = \frac{4a}{3} + \frac{5}{3}$	Simplify.

A formula is a type of literal equation. Use inverse operations to isolate any variable in the formula.

Example 3 Solving a Formula for a Variable

The formula $C = \frac{5}{9}(F - 32)$ expresses Celsius temperature in terms of Fahrenheit temperature. Find the Fahrenheit temperature when the Celsius temperature is 20°.

SOLUTION

Step 1: Solve for F. Justify each step.

$C = \frac{5}{9}(F - 32)$	
$\frac{9}{5} \cdot C = \frac{9}{5} \cdot \frac{5}{9}(F - 32)$	Multiplication Property of Equality
$\frac{9}{5}C = F - 32$	Simplify.
$\underline{\quad +32 = \quad +32}$	Addition Property of Equality
$\frac{9}{5}C + 32 = F$	Simplify.

Hint
Remember that dividing by a fraction is the same as multiplying by the reciprocal.

Step 2: Substitute 20 for C.

$\frac{9}{5}C + 32 = F$

$\frac{9}{5}(20) + 32 = F$

$36 + 32 = F$

$68 = F$

20°C is equivalent to 68°F.

ENGLISH LEARNERS

Explain the meaning of the word **solve.** The student has solved an equation for a variable when that variable is isolated by itself on one side of the equal sign.

Some students may think that $y = 4a + 5b$ is not a solution to an equation because there are still unknowns. Discuss with students that they have solved the equation for y because there are no more steps they can take to solve for the variable.

Ask students to come up with other examples of solving, such as word or number puzzles, riddles, problems, and situations in life. Ask,

"When is a riddle or puzzle solved?" Sample: When all of the blanks are filled in.

Example 4 Application: Geometry

The formula for the circumference of a circle is $C = 2\pi r$. If the circle's circumference is 24 inches, what is the radius? Leave the symbol π in the answer.

SOLUTION

Step 1: Since the question asked for the radius, the first step is to solve the formula for r.

$C = 2\pi r$

$\dfrac{C}{2\pi} = \dfrac{2\pi r}{2\pi}$ Isolate the variable r.

$\dfrac{C}{2\pi} = r$ Simplify.

Step 2: Substitute 24 for C.

$\dfrac{24}{2\pi} = r$

$\dfrac{12}{\pi} = r$ Simplify.

The radius of the circle is $\dfrac{12}{\pi}$ inches.

Example 5 Application: Travel Plans

The Ramirez family is taking a trip to the coast. They live 270 miles from the coast. They want to make the trip in $4\tfrac{1}{2}$ hours. Use the distance formula $d = rt$ to determine the average speed the family needs to drive.

SOLUTION

Step 1: The answer will be the speed they are driving, so solve the formula for r.

$d = rt$

$\dfrac{d}{t} = \dfrac{rt}{t}$ Divide both sides by t.

$\dfrac{d}{t} = r$ Simplify.

Step 2: Substitute 270 for d and 4.5 for t.

$\dfrac{d}{t} = r$

$\dfrac{270}{4.5} = r$

$60 = r$

The Ramirez family needs to average a speed of 60 mph to make the trip in $4\tfrac{1}{2}$ hours.

Hint

In the formula $d = rt$;

d is distance, r is rate or speed, and t is time.

Example 4

Remind students that π is a constant, not a variable, and that it is approximately 3.14.

Additional Example 4

The formula for the area of a rectangle is $A = \ell w$. If a rectangle's area measures 64 cm², and the width measures 16 cm, what is the measure of the length of the rectangle? $\ell = 4$ cm

Example 5

Make sure students understand that the distance is measured in miles and the time is measured in hours, so the rate will be measured in miles per hour, or mi/hr.

Additional Example 5

The Chu family is taking a camping trip. They live 176 miles from the campsite. If they travel 55 miles per hour, how long will it take them to reach the campsite? $t = \dfrac{d}{r}$; 3.2 hr

TEACHER TIP

Because students are solving for r, they may be tempted to divide both sides of the equation by r. Show students that although it is not wrong to divide both sides by r, they will be adding extra steps.

Lesson 29   173

INCLUSION FOR EXAMPLE 5

Help students who have difficulty with temporal concepts by working through a concrete example. Have students find the distance in miles between two cities. Explain that they are traveling from the first city to the second. Work problems with speeds that are an easy multiple of the distance.

For example, the distance between Middletown and Springdale is 150 miles.

Ask how long it will take to travel this far at a rate of 50 miles per hour. **3 hours**

Then, ask students to find the distance between two locations if they ride a bicycle at 18 mi/hr for 3 hours. **54 miles**
If students answer 6 miles, have them compare that to 18 mi/hr. Point out that it will take less than, not more than, 1 hr to travel 6 mi at this speed.

Lesson Practice

a. Solve for n: $3m + 2n = 8$. $n = -\frac{3}{2}m + 4$
(Ex 1)

b. Solve for x: $3x + 2y = 8 + x$. $x = -y + 4$
(Ex 2)

c. (Temperature) The formula $F = \frac{9}{5}C + 32$ expresses a Fahrenheit temperature in terms of Celsius temperature. Find the Celsius temperature when the Fahrenheit temperature is 86°. $C = \frac{5}{9}(F - 32)$, 30°C
(Ex 3)

d. $\frac{V}{lw} = h$, 36 in.

d. (Geometry) The formula for the volume of a rectangular prism with length l, width w, and height h, is $V = lwh$. Find the height in inches of a rectangular prism with volume 6 ft³, width 12 in., and length 24 in.
(Ex 4)

Hint
Since the question asks for gallons, the first step is to solve the formula for g.

e. (Traveling Costs) The fuel economy rating of a vehicle is determined by the formula $F = \frac{m}{g}$. In the formula, F is fuel economy, m is miles traveled, and g is gallons of fuel. Felicia's car has a fuel rating of 28 miles per gallon. Her trip is 350 miles. How many gallons of fuel does she need? $g = \frac{m}{F}$, 12.5 gallons
(Ex 5)

Practice   Distributed and Integrated

*1. Solve $3x + 2y = 5 - y$ for y.   ***2.** Solve $-2y + 6y - x - 4 = 0$ for y. $y = \frac{1}{4}x + 1$
(29) $y = -x + \frac{5}{3}$ (29)

3. (Average Cost) Boris uses a coupon for $35 off any framing order of $50 or more. He wants to frame 5 photographs. With the coupon it will cost $107.50 not including tax. What is the average cost to frame a photograph without the coupon? $28.50
(24)

*4. Multiple Choice The floor area of recreation center will be a rectangle with a length of 130 feet and a width of 110 feet. Which formula can be used to find the area of the recreation center? **C**
(29)

A $A = s^2$ **B** $A \cdot l = w$

C $A = lw$ **D** $A = \frac{1}{2}ab$

5. Give the domain and range of the relation.
(25)
$\{(9, 3); (8, 1); (8, 2); (8, 3); (7, 0); (7, 4); (6, 2)\}$ domain: {6, 7, 8, 9}; range: {0, 1, 2, 3, 4}

*6. Multiple Choice Which operation should be performed first when solving the multi-step equation $12x + 6(2x - 1) + 7 = 37$? **B**
(26)
A Divide both sides of the equation by 12.
B Multiply $(2x - 1)$ by 6.
C Add 1 to both sides of the equation.
D Subtract 37 from both sides of the equation.

7. Sample: Add or subtract terms so that the terms with an x-variable are isolated on one side of the equation. Simplify the equation by collecting like terms. Multiply or divide so that the x-variable has a coefficient of 1.

*7. Write Explain how to solve $5x + 4z = 10z - 2x$ for x.
(29)

*8. (Basketball) Lee's basketball team played 22 games this season. Lee scored an average of t three-pointers and s two-pointers per game during the season. Write an expression to show how many total points he scored during the season. $22(3t + 2s)$
(17)

174   Saxon Algebra 1

MANIPULATIVE USE FOR PROBLEM b

Materials: algebra tiles
Solve for x: $3x + 2y = 8 + x$.

$x = -y + 4$

9. **Analyze** The measures of the angles in the two triangles can be found
(26) using the equations $x + x + 90 = 180$ and $3y + y + 90 = 180$.
Which triangle will contain the smallest angle?   Triangle B

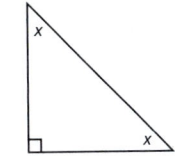
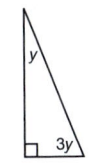

*10. **Error Analysis** Two students are making a bar graph of test scores ranging from
(27) 85 through 100. They want to emphasize the difference in the range of scores.
Which student is correct? Explain the error.   Student A: Sample: Student B in using larger increments does not emphasize the differences.

Student A	Student B
Use a vertical scale from 75 to 100 in increments of 5.	Use a vertical scale from 0 through 100 in increments of 10.

11. **Analyze** The expression xy^3 has a positive value. What must be true of the value
(16) of x if y is negative? x must be negative.

*12. What should you watch for when analyzing a circle graph?   Sample: All categories
(27) of the data set should be represented.

13. Round $\sqrt{26}$ to the nearest integer.   5
(13)

*14. **Geometry** A triangle and a rectangle have the same area. Use the diagrams to find
(28) the area.   Each has an area of 40 square units

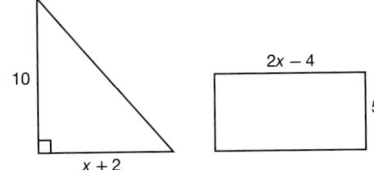

*15. **Multi-Step** A gym charges for attending exercise classes. Raquel pays $10 to attend
(28) each class because she is a non-member. Since Viola is a member, she pays $15 per month for a membership fee, but only $5 for each class.

  a. Write an expression to show how much it cost Raquel per month for c exercise classes. $10c$

  b. Write an expression to show how much it cost Viola per month for membership and c exercise classes. $5c + 15$

  c. Set the two expressions equal to each other. Solve this equation to determine how many classes they would each have to attend to have the same cost. $10c = 5c + 15$; $c = 3$

16. **Verify** Is $x = 11$ a solution for $6x + 8 = 74$? Explain. If false, provide a correct
(23) solution and check.

17. Choose an appropriate graph to display the grade received by each of the students
(22) on a science test. Explain your choice.   stem-and-leaf plot; Sample: Stem-and-leaf plots are best for ordering data.

16. true; Sample:
$6x + 8 = 74$
$6x = 66$
$x = 11$

Problem 11
Error Alert
When multiplying negative numbers, students sometimes perform the calculations in their heads, which can lead to errors in their math.

For xy^3, when y is a negative number, encourage students to choose a negative number and perform the calculation on paper or with a calculator.

If $y = -2$ then
$xy^3 = x \cdot (-2) \cdot (-2) \cdot (-2)$
$xy^3 = x \cdot (4) \cdot (-2)$
$xy^3 = x(-8)$

Problem 18

Guide students by asking them the following questions.

"What are the ordered pairs that you will plot?" (3, 36), (5, 60), (8, 96), (10, 120)

"What will the *x*-axis of your coordinate grid measure? What is the scale?" feet; by ones

"What will the *y*-axis of your coordinate grid measure? What is the scale?" inches; by 10s or 12s

Problem 21
Extend the Problem

"Suppose Jocelyn buys two containers of strawberries. The first container holds $2\frac{1}{2}$ pounds and the second container holds $5\frac{1}{4}$ pounds. How much will Jocelyn spend?" $17.50

"Suppose you buy grapes and strawberries. If grapes cost $3.50 per pound, write a new expression to represent the total cost for a container with *s* pounds of strawberries and *g* pounds of grapes." $1 + 2s + 3.5g$

---

  18. Measurement To convert between feet and inches, use the equation $i = 12f$ where i is the number of inches and f is the number of feet. Complete the table and graph the solutions.

f	i
3	36
5	60
8	96
10	120

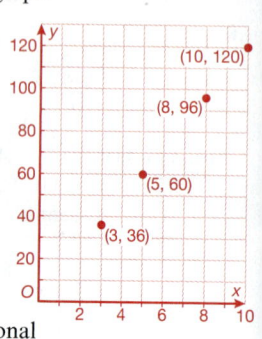

19. Verify True or False. A repeating decimal multiplied by a variable is an irrational number. If the statement is false, give a counterexample.

20. Astronomy The temperature on the surface of Mars varies by 148°F. The highest temperature is about 23°F. What is that lowest temperature on the surface of Mars? $-125°F$

21. Consumer Economics A strawberry container costs $1 and the strawberries cost $2 per pound. Write an expression to represent the total cost for a container with *s* pounds of strawberries. $1 + 2s$

22. Simplify $x^2 - 3yx + 2yx^2 - 2xy + yx$. $x^2 + 2x^2y - 4xy$

23. Solve $-3y + \frac{1}{2} = \frac{5}{7}$. $y = -\frac{1}{14}$

24. Solve $k + 4 - 5(k + 2) = 3k - 2$. $k = -\frac{4}{7}$

25. Generalize The value of $z + 2$ is an odd integer. What generalizations can be made about *z* using this information? Sample: The number represented by *z* is odd, and it is an integer.

26. Which expression is greater: $\frac{1}{3} - 1$ or $\frac{1}{2} - 1$. $\frac{1}{2} - 1$

27. Justify Simplify $(3 + 5) - 2^3$. Justify each step using the order of operations or mathematical properties.
$8 - 2^3$ Parenthesis first.
$8 - 8$ Simplify Exponents.
0 Subtract.

28. Analyze Find the value of *y* when $x = 2$.
$-x - (-2) = y$ $y = 0$

 29. Population Growth The expression $303{,}000{,}000 \times (1.015)^t$, where *t* stands for years, represents the population growth of the U.S.A. Based on this expression, about how many people will live in the U.S.A. eight years from now? about 341,327,254

30. Probability On the first street in Hidden Oaks subdivision, 5 out of 20 families own trucks.
  a. What is the probability that a randomly selected family in the subdivision owns a truck? $\frac{1}{4}$
  b. Predict the number of truck-owning families you can expect among the 140 families living in the subdivision. 35 families

19. false; Sample: Repeating decimals are rational numbers because they can be expressed as fractions. For example, $0.\overline{33}$ can be expressed as $\frac{1}{3}$. A repeating number multiplied by a variable could be a rational number.

176   Saxon Algebra 1

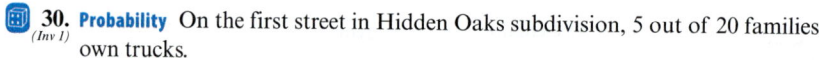

 CHALLENGE

The formula for the area of a circle is $A = \pi r^2$. If the circle's area measures 81 m^2, what is the radius? Leave the symbol π in the answer.

$A = \pi r^2$
$\frac{A}{\pi} = r^2$
$\sqrt{\frac{A}{\pi}} = \sqrt{r^2}$
$\frac{\sqrt{A}}{\sqrt{\pi}} = r$

$\frac{\sqrt{81}}{\sqrt{\pi}} = r$
$\frac{9}{\sqrt{\pi}} = r$

 LOOKING FORWARD

Solving literal equations prepares students for

Lesson 31 Using Rates, Ratios, and Proportions

Lesson 36 Writing and Solving Proportions

Lesson 42 Solving Percent Problems

Lesson 47 Solving Problems Involving the Percent of Change

Lesson 55 Solving Systems of Linear Equations by Graphing

LAB 2

Creating a Table

Graphing Calculator Lab *(Use with Lesson 30)*

An equation describes a relationship between two quantities. Sometimes it is inconvenient to calculate a large quantity of outputs by substituting given values into the equation. Instead, use your graphing calculator to quickly make a table of values.

Find the value of *y* for the equation $y = 3x + 5$ when $x = 15, 45, 75, 105,$ and 135.

1. To enter the equation into the Y = editor, press the [Y=] key. Then press **3** [X,T,θ,n] [+] **5**.

2. Open the Table Setup menu by pressing [2nd] [WINDOW] (TBLSET). TblStart is the value of *x* to start the table of values. ΔTbl is the increment by which *x*-values in the table should increase.

   Since the smallest value of *x* is 15, press **1 5** [ENTER]. Consecutive *x*-values increase by 30, so for ΔTbl, press **3 0** [ENTER].

   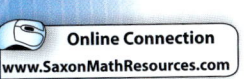

3. Press [2nd] [GRAPH] (TABLE) to view the table of values.

   From this screen's table of values, you can see that $y = 50$ when $x = 15$, $y = 140$ when $x = 45$, $y = 230$ when $x = 75$, $y = 320$ when $x = 105$, and $y = 410$ when $x = 135$.

4. Press the [▼] key repeatedly to see larger values of *x* and *y*.

   For $x = 405$, $y = 1220$.

   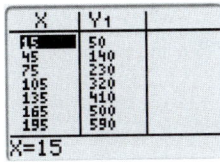

Materials
- graphing calculator

Discuss
The graphing calculator can quickly display a table of values for an equation. Students can use the table of values to solve an equation for any value, find coordinate pairs for the graph of the equation, or to simply check their answers. To calculate the table of values, equations must be in slope-intercept ($y = mx + b$) form. Instead of creating long lists of values, students can also input their own values for *x* and have the calculator compute the corresponding *y* values. In the [TBLSET] menu, students can highlight the "Ask" function for the "Indpnt" – or *x* – variable. They can then go to the [TABLE] function and input any value for *x* and press [ENTER]. The calculator will compute the *y* value.

Online Connection
www.SaxonMathResources.com

Lab 2   177

You can compare y-values for more than one equation for a given set of x-values. Enter equations into the [Y=] editor for Y_1, Y_2, and so on, for as many equations as you have. Then set TblStart and ΔTbl values in the Table Setup menu and press [2nd] [GRAPH] (TABLE) to view the table of values. Use the [◄] and [►] keys to navigate across the equations and the [▲] and [▼] keys to scroll through values of x in the table.

Lab Practice

Use a table to find y for the equation for the given values of x. Indicate the TblStart and ΔTbl values you use.

a. $y = 2x - 2$ for $x = 2, 5, 8,$ and 11

b. $y = 4x$ for $x = 1, 8, 15,$ and 22

Stephanie is growing two varieties of flowers for a show taking place in three months. The height y in inches of Flower A after x months can be modeled by the equation $y = 2x + 1$. Flower B grows according to the equation $y = 3x - 2$. Stephanie will plant the flowers at the same time and monitor their height at the end of each month. If Flower A and Flower B are the same height, she will use them to make an arrangement to present at the flower show.

c. How would Stephanie simulate the growth of each flower?

d. What would Stephanie enter into the calculator to simultaneously model the growth of Flower A and Flower B?

e. What TblStart value should Stephanie use?

f. What ΔTbl value should she use?

g. How tall are Flower A and Flower B at the end of each month?

h. Will Stephanie be able to create an arrangement of Flowers A and B for the flower show? Explain.

---

a. $y = 2, 8, 14$ and 20, respectively; TblStart $= 2$; ΔTbl $= 3$

b. $y = 4, 32, 60,$ and 88, respectively; TblStart $= 1$; ΔTbl $= 7$

c. Enter the equation that models the growth of the flower into the [Y=] editor.

d. Enter $y = 2x + 1$ for Y_1 and $y = 3x - 2$ for Y_2.

e. She should use TblStart=1, because she will grow the flowers for at least one month.

f. ΔTbl=1, because she will measure their height at the end of every month.

g. Flower A: 3 inches after 1 month, 5 inches tall after 2 months, 7 inches tall after 3 months; Flower B: 1 inch after 1 month, 4 inches after 2 months, 7 inches after 3 months

h. yes; They will both be 7 inches tall in 3 months.

LESSON 30

Graphing Functions

Warm Up

1. **Vocabulary** A ___relation___ (relation, function) is a set of ordered pairs where each number in the domain is matched to one or more numbers in the range.

Determine the coordinates of each point labeled on the coordinate grid.

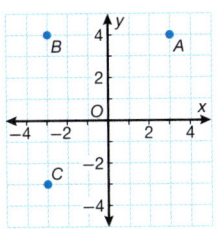

2. Point A (3, 4)
3. Point B (−3, 4)
4. Point C (−3, −3)
5. Evaluate $2x + 3$ for $x = 4$.   11

New Concepts

A **linear equation** is an equation whose graph is a line. You can use a table of ordered pairs to graph an equation. To determine if the graph represents a function, use the vertical line test. If a vertical line intersects the graph at more than one point, then the graph is not a function. A **linear function** is a function whose graph is a line. A linear function can be written in the form $f(x) = mx + b$, where m and b are real numbers.

Example 1 Using Tables to Graph Functions

Graph each equation using a table of values. Use a graphing calculator to check your table. Decide whether the graph represents a function and whether it is linear or nonlinear.

a. $y = x$

SOLUTION

x	0	1	2	3	4
y	0	1	2	3	4

Any vertical line intersects this graph at only one point, so the graph is a function. The graph is a line, so it is a linear function.

b. $y = x^2$

SOLUTION

x	−2	−1	0	1	2
y	4	1	0	1	4

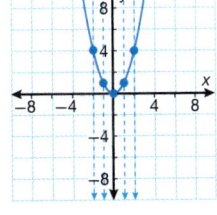

According to the vertical line test, the graph is a function. The graph is not a line, so it is a nonlinear function.

Graphing Calculator

For help with creating tables, refer to Graphing Calculator Lab 2, p. 177.

Math Reasoning

Generalize How can values in a table be used to tell whether data are linear?

If the change in y-values is always the same for a given change in x-values, then the data are linear.

LESSON 30

1 Warm Up

Problem 5

Evaluate for the given value and use the order of operations.

2 New Concepts

In this lesson, students make graphs and decide if they represent functions. A graph of a linear equation or linear function is a straight line.

Example 1

Remind students to choose x values and evaluate to find y.

Additional Example 1

Make a graph and decide if it is a function and if it is linear.

a. $y = 2x − 5$

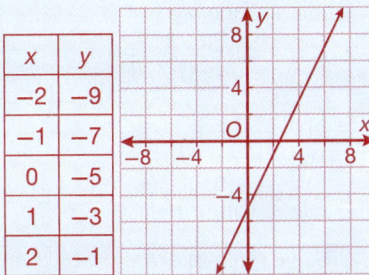

x	y
−2	−9
−1	−7
0	−5
1	−3
2	−1

linear function

b. $y = 3x^2$ nonlinear function; See Additional Answers.

Lesson 30   179

LESSON RESOURCES

Student Edition Practice
  Workbook 30
Reteaching Master 30
Adaptations Master 30
Challenge and Enrichment
  Master C30, E30
Technology Lab Master 30

MATH BACKGROUND

Functions can take different forms when graphed on a coordinate plane. A linear function, in the form $f(x) = mx + b$, is always a straight line with a constant slope. If the slope m is positive, the line rises upward to the right; if m is negative, the line falls downward to the right. Note that if the line is horizontal, the slope is 0, and it is a function. If the line is vertical, the slope is undefined, and it is not a function.

Nonlinear functions include quadratic functions, such as $f(x) = x^2 + 3$, and absolute-value functions, such as $f(x) = |x| + 1$. The graph of a quadratic function is a U-shaped parabola and the graph of an absolute-value function is V-shaped.

Lesson 30   179

Example 2
Additional Example 2

Use the coordinates in each table to match each graph with one of the tables.

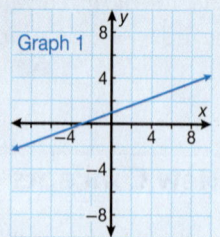
Graph 1

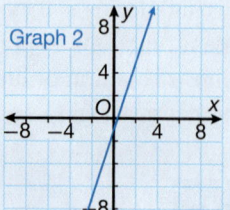
Graph 2

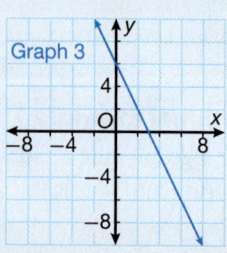
Graph 3

Table 1. Rule: $f(x) = 3x - 1$

x	−2	−1	0	1	2
f(x)	−7	−4	−1	2	5

Graph 2

Table 2. Rule: $f(x) = -2x + 6$

x	−1	1	2	5	7
f(x)	8	4	2	−4	−8

Graph 3

Table 3. Rule: $f(x) = \frac{1}{3}x + 1$

x	−6	−3	0	3	6
f(x)	−1	0	1	2	−6

Graph 1

TEACHER TIP

Encourage students who find it hard to translate from the table of values to a graph to first write the values as ordered pairs. In Example 2, have students write the values in Table 1 as (−3, 3), (0, 4), (3, 5), (6, 6), and (9, 7).

Example 2 — Matching a Graph to a Table

Use the coordinates in each table to match each graph with one of the tables.

Table 1 Rule: $f(x) = \frac{1}{3}x + 4$

x	−3	0	3	6	9
f(x)	3	4	5	6	7

Table 2 Rule: $f(x) = 5x - 1$

x	−2	−1	0	1	2
f(x)	−11	−6	−1	4	9

Table 3 Rule: $f(x) = -\frac{1}{2}x + 2$

x	−4	−2	0	2	4
f(x)	4	3	2	1	0

Graph 1

Graph 2

Graph 3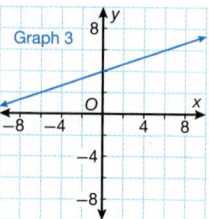

Math Reasoning

Analyze To match an equation to a graph, what characteristic(s) of the graph can often be most easily identified in the equation?

the y-intercept

SOLUTION

Table 1 has the ordered pair (0, 4). The graph in Graph 3 is the only graph that includes this point. The ordered pairs (3, 5) and (6, 6) also are on the graph. Graph 3 matches the values in Table 1.

For Table 2, look at the ordered pair (0, −1). This ordered pair only occurs in Graph 1. The ordered pairs (−1, −6) and (1, 4) also are on the graph. Graph 1 matches the values in Table 2.

Graph 2 matches Table 3. The ordered pairs (−4, 4), (0, 2), and (4, 0) are on Graph 2.

Example 3 — Matching an Equation to a Graph

Match the three equations below to the three graphs shown.

Equation A: $y = x + 3$

Equation B: $y = |x| + 3$

Equation C: $y = \sqrt{x} + 3$

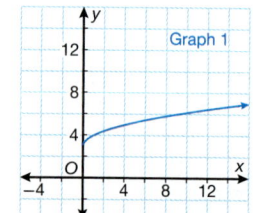
Graph 1

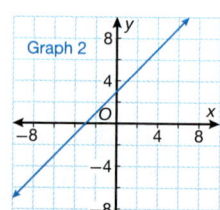
Graph 2

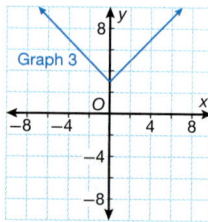
Graph 3

ALTERNATE METHOD FOR EXAMPLE 2

Introduce the y-intercept to students. For linear functions in the form $f(x) = mx + b$, b represents the y-intercept, or where the graph of the line intercepts the y-axis.

The first function in Example 2 has a y-intercept of 4. Graph 3 shows the only line that intersects the y-axis at (0, 4).

The second function has a y-intercept of −1. Graph 1 shows the only line that intersects the y-axis at (0, −1).

The third function has a y-intercept of 2. Graph 2 shows the only line that intersects the y-axis at (0, 2).

The y-intercept is also useful as a way for students to check their answers after they have matched the tables with the graphs.

SOLUTION

Find three ordered pairs for each equation. Check to see which graph includes the ordered pairs.

Equation A: Substituting different values of x into $y = x + 3$ results in the following ordered pairs: (0, 3), (1, 4) and (2, 5). Only Graph 2 includes these ordered pairs, so Equation A matches Graph 2.

Equation B: For $y = |x| + 3$, any value for x will have a positive y-value. Equation B matches Graph 3.

Equation C: For $y = \sqrt{x} + 3$, there cannot be x-values that are negative. Equation C matches Graph 1.

Example 4 Identifying the Domain and Range

Use the graphs to identify the domain and range of each function.

a.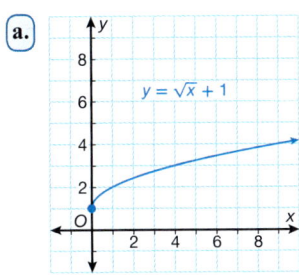

SOLUTION

The domain is $x \geq 0$ because you cannot take the square root of a negative number. By inspection of the graph, the range is $y \geq 1$.

b.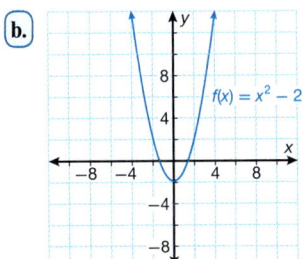

SOLUTION

By inspection of the graph, the domain is all real numbers and the range is $y \geq -2$.

Example 3

Have students use what they know about functions and equations to match the graphs with the equations.

Additional Example 3

Match the two equations below with the two graphs shown.

Equation A: $y = 5x - 4$

Equation B: $y = x^2 + 3$

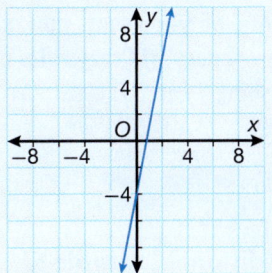

Equation A

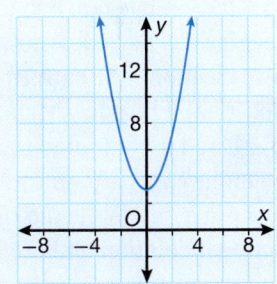

Equation B

Example 4

The x-values on a graph show the domain. The y-values on the graph show the range.

Additional Example 4

Use the graph to identify the domain and range of the function.

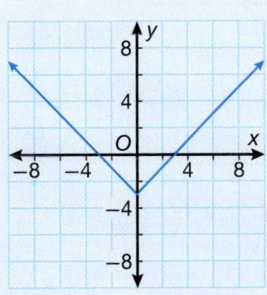

The domain is all real numbers. The range is $y \geq -3$.

Lesson 30   181

ENGLISH LEARNERS

Explain the meaning of the word **function**. The term has several meanings in the English language. In the mathematical context, a function is a relation of the dependent variable to the independent variable.

Discuss other meanings of the word *function*. Say that a function can also mean a job or duty. For example, the stomach's function is to digest food. A machine has a function, and this is the meaning closest to the mathematical meaning of a function rule.

To write the equation $y = 2x - 7$ as a function, replace y with $f(x)$. The equation becomes the function $f(x) = 2x - 7$.

Lesson 30   181

Example 5

Error Alert Some students may try to write an equation with only one operation. Remind students that the team needs to purchase soap (subtraction), and then they earn money washing the cars (multiplication).

Extend the Example

"If the soccer team decides to charge $7 per car and still spends a total of $4 on soap, how much more money will they raise by washing 7 cars? **They will earn $14 more. The function is:**
$f(x) = (7x - 4) - (5x - 4)$
$f(x) = 2x$

Additional Example 5

Carlos mows lawns. He spends $5 per day on bus fare and earns $6 per lawn. The table below shows the money he earns for lawns mowed in a day. Make a graph and use it to find the amount he earns after mowing 5 lawns in a day. Write the rule in functional notation and use it to check the answer.

Lawns mowed, x	0	1	2	3
Money earned, $f(x)$	−5	1	7	13

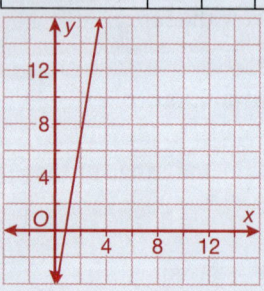

$f(x) = 6x - 5$; $25

Math Reasoning

Verify Why is the money raised for 0 cars −$4.00?

Sample: The soap was bought before any cars were washed.

a.

x	0	2	−2
y	5	9	1

The graph is a function and it is linear.

b.

x	0	−1	1
y	1	2	2

The graph is a function and it is not linear.

Example 5 Application: Car Wash Fundraiser

The soccer team raises money by washing cars. They charge $5 per car and spend a total of $4 on soap. The table shows the money they raise. Make a graph and use it to find the amount they raise by washing 7 cars. Write the rule in functional notation and use it to check the answer.

Number of Cars Washed, x	0	1	2	3	4	5
Money Raised, $f(x)$	−4	1	6	11	16	21

SOLUTION

Use the ordered pairs to make a graph. Extend the line beyond $x = 7$. The y-value on the line is 31 when $x = 7$, so the soccer team raises $31 by washing 7 cars.

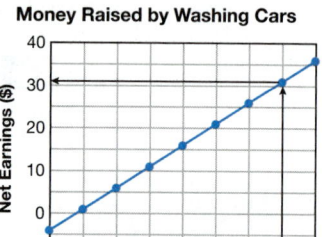

Check the answer by evaluating the function for $x = 7$. The rule is $5 times the number of cars x minus $4, or

$f(x) = 5x - 4$.

$f(x) = 5x - 4$
$f(7) = 5(7) - 4$
$= 35 - 4$
$= 31$

Lesson Practice

a. Graph $y = 2x + 5$ using a table of values. Use a graphing calculator to check your table. Decide whether the graph represents a function and whether it is linear or nonlinear. *(Ex 1)*

b. Graph $y = x^2 + 1$ using a table of values. Use a graphing calculator to check your table. Decide whether the graph represents a function and whether it is linear or nonlinear. *(Ex 1)*

c. Match the equation $y = -2x^2$ to the correct graph. **Graph 2** *(Ex 3)*

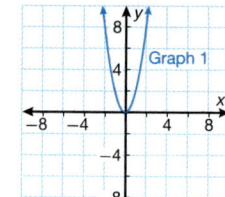
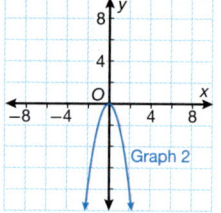

INCLUSION FOR EXAMPLE 5

Materials: play money, counters, paper clips

Try a group activity to help students who have difficulty with money concepts. Give each group 4 paper clips, 6 counters, and 25 play dollars. Have them mark 4 dollars as "negative dollars" with paper clips.

Have students draw a table and coordinate grid. Tell them to take 0 counters and the 4 negative dollars. This corresponds to the money spent for soap. They have washed no cars yet, so they just have −$4. Have them enter (0, −4), in their table and plot this point on the grid.

Have students add a counter and 5 play dollars. Have them enter this new entry (1, 1) and plot the point on the grid. Continue in this way to plot points for 2 cars, 3 cars, etc. Ask students to name the function they have graphed. $f(x) = 5x - 4$

Use the coordinates in the tables to match the graph with each table.
(Ex 2)

d. $y = \frac{1}{3}x + 1$ Graph 2

x	−6	−3	0	3	6
y	−1	0	1	2	3

e. $y = 3x + 1$ Graph 1

x	−3	−2	0	1	2
y	−8	−5	1	4	7

h.
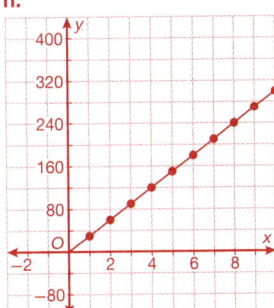

8 classes send 240 emails; $f(x) = 30x$; $240 = 30(8)$

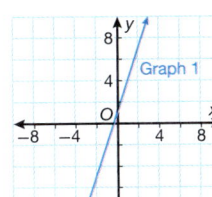 Graph 1

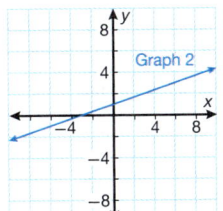 Graph 2

Identify the domain and range of the function shown in each graph.
(Ex 4)

f. 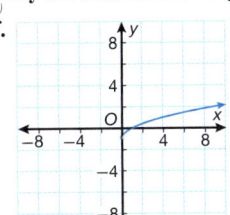   The domain is $x \geq 0$ and the range is $y \geq -1$.

g. 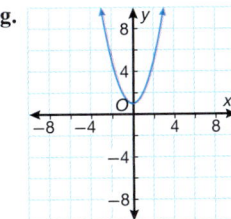   The domain is all real numbers and the range is $y \geq 1$.

h. **Emails to Congress** The table shows the number of emails history classes
(Ex 5) send to their senators. Make a graph and use it to find how many emails were sent from 8 classes. Write the rule in function notation and use it to check your answer. $f(x) = 30x$

Number of Classes, x	1	2	3	4
Emails Sent, $f(x)$	30	60	90	120

Practice   Distributed and Integrated

Solve.

1. $x + \frac{1}{2} = 2\frac{1}{5}$ $x = 1\frac{7}{10}$
(19)

2. $0.4x - 0.3 = -0.14$ $x = 0.4$
(23)

3. $\frac{1}{3} + \frac{5}{12}x - 2 = 6\frac{2}{3}$ $x = 20$
(26)

4. $\frac{2}{3} - \frac{4}{9}x + 1 = 2\frac{7}{9}$ $x = -\frac{5}{2}$
(26)

*5. Solve and check $x - 4(x - 3) + 7 = 6 - (x - 4)$. $x = \frac{9}{2}$; $\frac{9}{2} - 4(\frac{9}{2} - 3) + 7 \stackrel{?}{=} 6 - (\frac{9}{2} - 4)$
(28)
$\frac{9}{2} - 4(\frac{3}{2}) + 7 \stackrel{?}{=} 6 - (\frac{1}{2})$
$\frac{9}{2} - 6 + 7 \stackrel{?}{=} 6 - \frac{1}{2}$
$\frac{11}{2} = \frac{11}{2}$

Lesson 30   183

Lesson Practice

Problem d

Scaffolding Have students make a table of values for the equation. Make sure they use at least 5 values for *x* in their tables and that at least 2 of the values are negative and at least 2 are positive.

Problem h

Error Alert Make sure students check their answers by substituting the number of emails for 8 classes (240) into the function. If the values are not equal, then the function and the answer are incorrect.

Check for Understanding

The questions below help assess the concepts taught in this lesson.

"How can you tell that an equation is linear?" Sample: An equation is linear if it is in the format $y = mx + b$. Graphing the equation will also show if it is a straight line.

"How can you represent a function as a graph?" Sample: Make a table of values and evaluate values of *x* for $f(x)$. Then plot the values from the table as coordinate points on a grid.

ALTERNATE METHOD FOR PROBLEM 3

If students are hesitant working with fractions, they can multiply the entire equation by the least common denominator of the fractions.

For example, convert $6\frac{2}{3}$ to $\frac{20}{3}$. Then, multiply each term by 12. The equation becomes $4 + 5x - 24 = 80$. Make sure students multiply each term of the equation by the least common denominator so that all terms are whole numbers.

Lesson 30   183

3 Practice

Math Conversations

Discussion to strengthen understanding

Problem 8
Error Alert
A common error when matching equations with graphs is working with equations in different forms. Remind students to put all equations into the same form, isolating the *y* variable. Have them solve for *y*. For example, choice B becomes $y = x + 10$.

Problem 10
Extend the Problem
"What is a rule for the table?"
$y = 3x + 4$

"What is the value for *y* if $x = -1$? -5?" 1; -11

---

*6. Verify Is the statement below true or false? Explain.
(25)
The graph of a circle shows that the equation of the circle, $x^2 + y^2 = 1$, is a function.

false; A vertical line crosses the circle at two points so the equation is not a function.

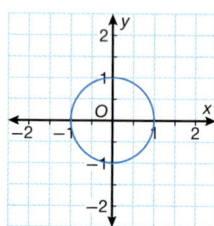

*7. (Savings) For every dollar Mirand deposits into her checking account, she deposits
(30) 1.5 times as much into her savings account, which started with $50. So, $s = 1.5c + 50$, where *s* is the amount in savings and *c* is the amount deposited in checking. Which graph represents this equation? Graph 1

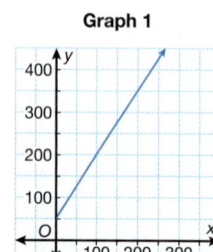 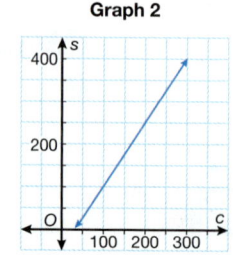 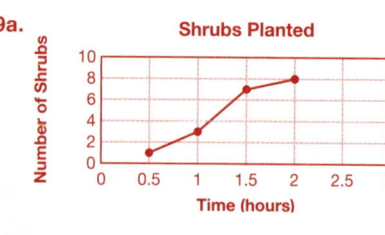

9a.

*8. Multiple Choice Which equation represents the line on the graph? D
(30)
A $y = x + 10$

B $y - x = 10$

C $-x = 10 + y$

D $y = -x + 10$

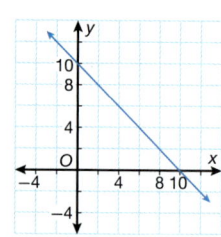

*9. Multi-Step The table shows the total number of shrubs a gardener plants after each
(30) half hour.

Time (hours)	0.5	1	1.5	2
Number of Shrubs	1	3	7	8

a. Plot these data on a coordinate grid.
b. Is the graph a function? Explain. yes; A vertical line will cross the graph at one point only.
c. **Predict** Can you predict the number of shrubs the gardener will plant in 3 hours? Why or why not? no; This is not a linear function.

*10. Use the table to make a graph. Is the graph linear? Explain.
(30)

x	0	1	2	3
y	4	7	10	13

10.

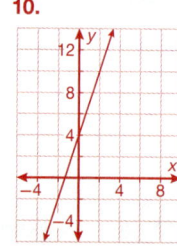

yes; It is linear because the graph is a line.

184 Saxon Algebra 1

ALTERNATE METHOD FOR PROBLEM 7

Have students find the *y*-intercept of the equation.

Solve for *s* if $c = 0$.

$s = 1.5(0) + 50$

$s = 50$

The *y*-intercept is (0, 50).

Find the graph that intersects the axes at the point you found. Graph 1

11. **Error Analysis** Two students solved $2x - y = 6$ for y. Which student is correct? Explain the error.

Student A	Student B
$2x - y = 6$	$2x - y = 6$
$2x = y + 6$	$2x = y + 6$
$2x - 6 = y$	$2x + 6 = y$

11. Student A Sample: Student B did not subtract 6 on both sides.

12. **Geometry** What is the area of the shaded part of the rectangle?   area of the shaded part: $14x - 24$

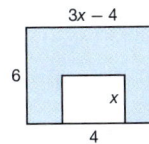

*13. **Multi-Step** Solve $\frac{x}{2} + \frac{y}{3} = 2$ for y. Find y when $x = 3$. $y = -\frac{3}{2}x + 6$; $y = 1\frac{1}{2}$

*14. **Consumer Math** Joel deposited money in an account that has a certain annual interest rate. Using the formula $i = prt$, or interest = principal · rate · time, how could he compute for the rate if the numeric values of the other items were given? $r = \frac{i}{pt}$

15. Simplify $\frac{3 + 7(-3)}{-7 - 2(-3)}$.   18

16. **Error Analysis** Two students solved the same multi-step equation. Which student is correct? Explain the error.   Student B is correct; Sample: Student A did not distribute the -4 and -6 over both terms.

Student A	Student B
$2x - 4(3x + 6) = -6(2x + 1) - 4$	$2x - 4(3x + 6) = -6(2x + 1) - 4$
$2x - 12x + 6 = -12x + 1 - 4$	$2x - 12x - 24 = -12x - 6 - 4$
$-10x + 6 = -12x - 3$	$-10x - 24 = -12x - 10$
$2x = -9$	$2x = 14$
$x = -4\frac{1}{2}$	$x = 7$

17. **Measurement** On a map, 1 centimeter represents 50 kilometers. The actual distance between two cities is 675 kilometers. Find the distance between the two cities on the map.   13.5 cm

*18. **Multiple Choice** What would make the graph of basketball scores less misleading?   D
 A Using a broken scale on the horizontal axis
 B Using a broken scale on the vertical axis
 C Using larger intervals
 D Using smaller intervals

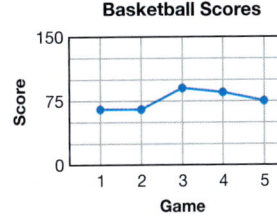

Lesson 30   185

Problem 13
Guide students by asking them the following questions.

"What is another way to write $\frac{y}{3}$?" $\frac{1}{3}y$

"What can you do to make the coefficient for y equal to 1?" Multiply $\frac{1}{3}$ by its reciprocal.

"Should you multiply the other terms in the equation by 3?"   yes

"What is the new equation?" $\frac{3}{2}x + y = 6$

"What is the next step needed to solve for y?"   Subtract $\frac{3}{2}x$ from both sides of the equal sign.

Lesson 30   185

Problem 22
Extend the Problem
"What would the length of John's hair be if he let it grow for three years?" $h = 20$ in.

"Joanne's hair is 3 inches long. It only grows 0.4 inches per month. After how many months would John and Joanne's hair be the same length?" after 10 months

Problem 23
Guide students by asking them the following questions.

"How many different possible outcomes, or keys, can be chosen? What are they?" 10; 0, 1, 2, 3, 4, 5, 6, 7, 8, 9

"How many keys show 5?" 1

"What is the probability of choosing channel 5 written as a fraction?" $\frac{1}{10}$

"What is the fraction written as a decimal and percent?" 0.1; 10%

Problem 25
Before adding and subtracting decimal numbers, ask students

"How do you line up the digits in the numbers?" Align the decimal points.

---

19. Generalize What effect do large intervals have on the appearance of a graph?
(27) Sample: Changes in data appear less than they actually are.

*20. Sales The circle graph shows the amounts of orange juice and fruit punch sold each month. Explain why this graph is misleading and determine what may be a more appropriate graph to compare the sales of the two beverages. Sample: The circle graph may make it appear that orange juice and fruit punch are the only drinks sold at the store and that fruit punch is the drink most sold by the store. A bar graph would be a more appropriate graph, as it does not represent parts of a whole.

Fruit Juice Sales
Orange Juice 42%
Fruit Punch 58%

21. Model Make a stem-and-leaf plot of the following temperatures in Woodmont:
(22) 72°F, 74°F, 63°F, 62°F, 63°F, 78°F, 65°F, 51°F, 53°F, 53°F, 61°F, 80°F.

22. Hair Growth Hair grows approximately half an inch each month.
(12) John's hair is 2 inches long. Let m be the number of months. The formula $h = 2 + 0.5m$ calculates the length John's hair will be in m months if he does not cut it. Complete the table and graph the solutions. See Additional Answers.

m	h
4	4
6	5
10	7
20	12

23. A television remote has a key for each of the channels 0 through 9. If one key is
(14) chosen at random, what is the chance that channel 5 is chosen? Write your answer as a percent. 10%

21. Woodmont Temperatures (°F)

Stem	Leaves
5	1, 3, 3
6	1, 2, 3, 3, 5
7	2, 4, 8
8	0

Key: 7|2 means 72

24. Multi-Step Todd has 18 boxes of cards with x cards in each box. He divides the cards
(12) equally with 5 friends. The expression $18x \div 6$ represents the number of cards each person has. Simplify the expression and justify each step. See Additional Answers.

25. Justify Evaluate $5.2 - 1.6 + 4.08 + 8$. Justify each step. See Additional Answers.
(10)

26. Generalize In unit analysis, you often need to apply unit ratios multiple times to
(8) convert to the desired units. For example, $4518 \text{ cm}^2 \cdot \frac{1 \text{ m}}{100 \text{ cm}} \cdot \frac{1 \text{ m}}{100 \text{ cm}} = 0.4518 \text{ m}^2$ converts from square centimeters to square meters. State a general rule for applying a unit ratio the correct number of times to perform a unit conversion.

26. Sample: When I use a unit as a factor n times, I need to apply a unit ratio for converting that unit n times.

27. Justify Evaluate $3 + \left(\frac{5-2}{4} + 2^2\right)$. Justify each step. See Additional Answers.
(7)

28. Consumer Economics A gym charges $2 a visit for the first 15 visits in a month.
(4) After that, the cost is reduced to $\frac{1}{4}$ of the price per visit. Use the expression $15 \cdot \$2 + (23 - 15) \cdot \frac{1}{4} \cdot \$2$ to show how much someone will pay if they go to this gym 23 times in a month. $34

29. Analyze Given the equations $a = (1.01)^x$ and $b = (0.99)^x$, which value, a or b,
(3) grows smaller as the exponent x grows larger? Sample: b, because any number less than one multiplied by itself will decrease

30. Write Write a possible situation that could be represented by the graph at the right.
(Inv 2) Samples: An airplane descends at a steady rate. An item loses value steadily over time.

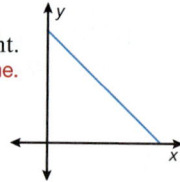

186 Saxon Algebra 1

CHALLENGE

Challenge students to make a table of values and graph of the equation $y = x^2 - 2x$. Is the graph a function? Is it linear?

x	−1	0	1	2	3
y	3	0	−1	0	3

See Additional Answers.

LOOKING FORWARD

Graphing functions prepares students for

• **Lesson 34** Locating and Using Intercepts

• **Lesson 50** Graphing Inequalities

• **Lesson 55** Solving Systems of Linear Equations by Graphing

• **Lesson 71** Making and Analyzing Scatter Plots

• **Lesson 78** Graphing Rational Functions

• **Lesson 96** Graphing Quadratic Functions

INVESTIGATION 3

Analyzing the Effects of Bias in Sampling, Surveys, and Bar Graphs

To gather complete and accurate information about a particular population, researchers need to collect data from all of the population's members.

Sampling It is not always practical to survey every individual in the population, so researchers use data from the sample to draw conclusions about the entire population. The table below identifies five sampling methods.

> **Math Language**
> A **population** is a group that someone is gathering information about.
> A **sample** is part of a population.
> A sample is **random** if every member of the population has an equal chance of being chosen.

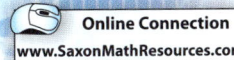
Online Connection
www.SaxonMathResources.com

	Sampling Method	Example
Simple Random	Select a group at random from the larger population.	Draw names of people to survey from a hat.
Stratified Random	Separate a population into smaller groups that have a certain characteristic. Then survey at random within each group.	Separate a herd of cows by breed; then survey a random sample from each breed.
Systematic Random	After calculating the required sample size, survey every nth member.	Choose the number 5 at random. Survey every 5th person.
Convenience	Select individuals from the population based on easy availability and/or accessibility.	Survey the first five people who arrive at a local mall.
Voluntary	Sample individuals who self-select into a survey by responding to a general appeal.	A news program asks viewers to participate in an online poll.

Luggage Survey A luggage company wants to know the most popular backpack color among high school students. Company representatives record the color of backpacks carried by boys in the cafeteria during lunch. Since the survey excludes high school girls, the sample is biased. It does not include some members of the population.

Analyze Give a reason why the sampling method may be biased.

1. A chef asks the first four customers who order the new cheese sauce if they like it.
2. At a convention of science teachers, attendees are asked to identify what their favorite subject was in high school.
3. A librarian sends questionnaires about library usage to families with children.   Sample: Families without children have no chance to respond.

1. Sample: Customers who ordered the cheese sauce probably like cheese.
2. Sample: Most science teachers' favorite subject is science.

Investigation 3   **187**

INVESTIGATION 3

Materials
- paper bag
- small squares of blue paper
- large squares of white paper
- graph paper

Discuss
In this investigation, students learn how surveys can be biased. They will determine what makes a survey question biased, write their own biased and unbiased questions, and be shown misleading graphs.

Problems 1–3
Extend the Problems
Have students suggest ways to fix the sampling method to eliminate bias.
1. Sample: Offer the cheese sauce to random customers and ask if they like it.
2. Sample: Survey people in a shopping mall.
3. Sample: Send questionnaires to people with and without children.

INVESTIGATION RESOURCES

Reteaching Master
   Investigation 3

MATH BACKGROUND

Surveys have many purposes. Companies survey consumers on the products they buy, politicians survey voters on the issues they support and the candidates they vote for, and media companies survey people on the television shows they watch and the radio stations they listen to.

A survey collects data from a population of people. A population is the entire set of persons, objects, or events that the surveyor intends to study.

If a population is too large, the surveyor may take a sample of the population to represent the entire group. The most practical way to take a representative sample is to take a random sample of a percentage of the population.

Investigation 3   **187**

Discuss

A person conducting a survey can introduce bias by asking questions that lead people to answer a certain way. A survey question should be neutral.

Error Alert

Students may ask survey questions that they may not realize are biased. Ask the students to list words or phrases that would appear in biased questions. For example, the use of negative contractions such as *aren't, didn't,* and *don't* can lead to biased questions. Adjectives such as *ugly, pretty, beautiful, bland,* and *delicious* can also influence questions.

---

4. Sample: Randomly survey visitors leaving the zoo.

5. Sample: Survey every fifth visitor leaving the zoo.

6. Sample: Yes; People visiting with children might only visit the zoo because they have children.

> **Hints**
> Biased sampling methods exclude certain members of the population.
>
> Biased questions exclude unsatisfactory responses.

7. Sample: Bias: Didn't you like the special tonight? Unbiased: How was the special?

8. Sample: Bias: Do you prefer listening to noisy, ear-splitting rock music or quiet, relaxing classical music? Unbiased: What type of music do you prefer to listen to?

(**Zoo Survey**) Researchers for an advertising campaign survey people to find out why they like to visit the zoo.

4. Give an example of an unbiased sample for this survey.

5. Describe a systematic sampling method.

6. **Justify** Would it be biased to only survey families with children? Explain.

(**Biased Questions**) Occasionally, researchers ask biased questions that force the person being questioned to respond with a particular answer. For instance, "Didn't you eat enough?" uses a negative question, which indicates that the person who is being questioned has eaten enough.

Write Create one biased and one non-biased question for each survey.

7. A restaurant owner polls ten patrons on whether they enjoyed the chef's special.

8. A music store questions five customers about their listening habits.

(**Marketing**) Advertisers may accidentally or intentionally present data in a misleading way. Consider these graphs of the data collected from a survey of pet owners.

Graph A: This could be misleading because of the break in the graph. It appears that the number of people who have dogs is much greater than those who have cats, birds, or fish.

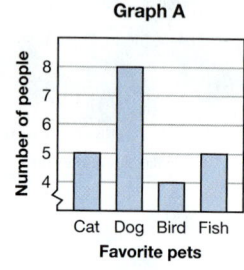

Graph B: This could be misleading because there are no labels on the vertical axis. It is not possible to determine whether each grid represents 1 person or 100 people.

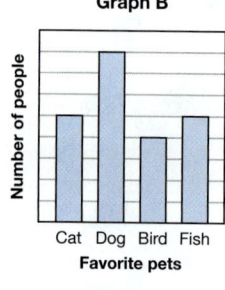

Graph C: This is not misleading. The vertical scale starts at 0 and the intervals are equal.

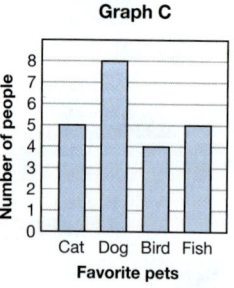

ENGLISH LEARNERS

Discuss the meaning of the word **bias.** Say, **"A person who has already formed an opinion, whether favorable or unfavorable, toward a person or thing, has a bias."**

People, groups, or companies can have a bias toward their views or products. When conducting a survey, they may try to lead a person's answer to a desirable response by asking a biased question.

Write the question, **"Do you like Brand X pizza?"** on the board. Below it, write, **"Doesn't Brand X pizza taste good?"** Ask students what they notice about the questions. Ask them if they are inclined to answer a certain way for the second question.

Ask students how they form leading questions in their language. Have them give examples in their language.

Exploration: Making and Analyzing Biased Graphs

Your school district is discussing the possibility of requiring students to wear school uniforms. Your class was chosen to select the colors for the uniforms. They will be either blue or white. Each student should indicate a color preference.

Materials
- paper bag
- small squares of blue paper
- large squares of white paper

9. Record the results in a table. *See student work.*
10. Make a bar graph of the data.
11. Draw a set of axes. Label the horizontal axis with the uniform colors. Label the vertical axis with the number of students. *See student work.*
12. Draw two bars, each with a height equal to the number of people who chose the color. *See student work.*

Create a biased bar graph of the data.

13. Draw a set of axes. Label the horizontal axis with the uniform colors. *See student work.*
14. Use the colored squares of paper to create a blue or white column. If 5 students chose blue, then build a bar with 5 blue squares. *See student work.*
15. **Analyze** What is the difference between the two graphs you created?

15. Sample: The units on the vertical axis are different. The different sizes of paper in the second graph distort the comparison between the numbers of students who voted for each color.

Investigation Practice

Managers of an apartment complex want to know what visitors to the complex think of the complex and the management office employees. They survey every fifth person who signs a lease.

a. What is the population? *People who visit the complex*
b. Identify the sample. *Every fifth person who signs a lease*
c. Which of the following is the sampling method used? **B**
   A random B systematic
   C stratified D voluntary
d. What is a possible bias for this survey?

d. Sample: People who visit the complex but do not sign a lease will not be included.

e. The approximate areas of four different oceans are listed below. Create a graph of the data that is misleading. Then redraw your graph so it is not misleading.
See student's work.

Ocean	Approximate area (million mi^2)
Arctic	5
Indian	27
Atlantic	30
Pacific	60

Discuss
The presentation of the results of a survey can also be biased. Discuss some ways that a person can manipulate a graph or table to skew the results of a survey. Examples include different scales for the x- and y-axes on a graph, starting one of the axes at some point other than zero, or inserting a break in the numbering of an axis.

Investigation Practice

Math Conversations
Discussion to strengthen understanding

Problem e
Scaffolding Ask students the following questions to guide them to their answers.

"What type of graph will you make?" Sample: bar graph

"What is the range of areas? What scale will you use for your misleading graph?" 55 million mi^2; Sample: 5 to 60 by fives

"What scale will you use for your appropriate graph?" Sample: 0 to 65 by fives

Investigation 3   189

CHALLENGE

Have students create their own short survey. First, have them create the survey with biased questions, and then have them write the same survey with unbiased questions. Have them explain what they did to change their survey from biased to unbiased.

Examples: Students could survey favorite types of sports. They could bias their survey by only asking students on the baseball team, or only asking boys. They could make the survey unbiased by asking a random sample of people, or ask both boys and girls.

LOOKING FORWARD

Analyzing the effects of bias in surveys and sampling prepares students for

Lesson 48 Analyzing Measures of Central Tendency

Lesson 54 Displaying Data in Box-and-Whisker Plots

Lesson 62 Displaying Data in Stem-and-leaf Plots and Histograms

SECTION OVERVIEW
4

Lesson Planner

Lesson	New Concepts
31	Using Rates, Ratios, and Proportions
32	Simplifying and Evaluating Expressions with Integer and Zero Exponents
33	Finding the Probability of Independent and Dependent Events
34	Recognizing and Extending Arithmetic Sequences
35	Locating and Using Intercepts
	Cumulative Test 6, Performance Task 6
36	Writing and Solving Proportions
37	Using Scientific Notation
38	Simplifying Expressions Using the GCF
39	Using the Distributive Property to Simplify Rational Expressions
40	Simplifying and Evaluating Expressions Using the Power Property of Exponents
	Cumulative Test 7, Performance Task 7
INV 4	Investigation: Using Deductive and Inductive Reasoning

Resources for Teaching
- Student Edition
- Teacher's Edition
- Student Edition eBook
- Teacher's Edition eBook
- Resources and Planner CD
- Solutions Manual
- Instructional Masters
- Technology Lab Masters
- Warm Up and Teaching Transparencies
- Instructional Presentations CD
- Online activities, tools, and homework help
  www.SaxonMathResources.com

Resources for Practice and Assessment
- Student Edition Practice Workbook
- Course Assessments
- Standardized Test Practice
- College Entrance Exam Practice
- Test and Practice Generator CD using ExamView™

Resources for Differentiated Instruction
- Reteaching Masters
- Challenge and Enrichment Masters
- Prerequisite Skills Intervention
- Adaptations for Saxon Algebra 1
- Multilingual Glossary
- English Learners Handbook
- TI Resources

Pacing Guide

 Resources and Planner CD for lesson planning support

45-Minute Class

Day 1	Day 2	Day 3	Day 4	Day 5	Day 6
Lesson 31	Lesson 32	Lesson 33	Lesson 34	Lesson 35	Cumulative Test 6
Day 7	**Day 8**	**Day 9**	**Day 10**	**Day 11**	**Day 12**
Lesson 36	Lesson 37	Lesson 38	Lesson 39	Lesson 40	Cumulative Test 7
Day 13					
Investigation 4					

Block: 90-Minute Class

Day 1	Day 2	Day 3	Day 4	Day 5	Day 6
Lesson 31 Lesson 32	Lesson 33 Lesson 34	Lesson 35 Cumulative Test 6	Lesson 36 Lesson 37	Lesson 38 Lesson 39	Lesson 40 Cumulative Test 7
Day 7					
Investigation 4 Lesson 41					

* For suggestions on how to implement Saxon Math in a block schedule, see the Pacing section at the beginning of the Teacher's Edition.

Lessons 31–40, Investigation 4

Differentiated Instruction

Below Level		Advanced Learners	
Warm Up	SE pp. 190, 197, 204, 211, 217, 223, 230, 236, 243, 249	Challenge	TE pp. 196, 203, 209, 216, 222, 228, 235, 242, 248, 253
Skills Bank	SE pp. 846–883	Extend the Example	TE pp. 193, 200, 206, 214, 220, 225, 226, 232, 240, 245, 251
Reteaching Masters	Lessons 31–40, Investigation 4		
Warm Up Transparencies	Lessons 31–40	Extend the Problem	TE pp. 195, 203, 210, 215, 222, 228, 233, 234, 235, 241, 248, 255
Prerequisite Skills Intervention	Skills 7, 8, 10, 12, 15, 35, 59, 77	Challenge and Enrichment Masters	Challenge: 31–40 Enrichment: 31

English Learners		Special Needs	
EL Tips	TE pp. 193, 200, 208, 212, 218, 224, 230, 237, 245, 251	Inclusion Tips	TE pp. 192, 199, 206, 213, 220, 225, 232, 240, 246, 252
Multilingual Glossary	Booklet and Online English Learners Handbook	Adaptations for Saxon Algebra 1	Lessons 31–40, Cumulative Tests 6, 7

For All Learners			
Exploration	SE pp. 225, 230, 249	Alternate Method	TE pp. 191, 205, 212, 214, 219, 233, 238, 239, 244, 250
Caution	SE pp. 191, 198, 208, 218, 231, 239	Manipulative Use	TE pp. 241
Hints	SE pp. 190, 205, 207, 219, 224, 231, 232, 237, 238, 243, 245, 249, 254	Online Tools	
Error Alert	TE pp. 191, 192, 193, 194, 195, 196, 198, 200, 202, 207, 208, 210, 213, 214, 215, 216, 218, 220, 222, 225, 227, 231, 233, 234, 235, 237, 240, 241, 243, 246, 250, 251, 252, 254, 255		

SE = Student Edition; TE = Teacher's Edition

Math Vocabulary

Lesson	New Vocabulary		Maintained	EL Tip in TE
31	cross products proportion rate	ratio unit rate	conversion factor	actual
32			exponential form standard form	intense
33	dependent events independent events	odds	event outcome	camper
34	arithmetic sequence common difference	sequence term of a sequence	order of operations substitute	recursive
35	solution of a linear equation in two variables standard form of a linear equation x-intercept y-intercept		linear equation ordered pair origin x-axis y-axis	intercept intersect
36	congruent scale scale drawing	scale factor similar	proportion ratio	cast
37	scientific notation		decimal exponent power of ten	pattern
38	greatest common factor (GCF) of monomials		composite number factor tree prime factorization prime number	prime
39	rational expression		exponent variable	implied
40			exponent	justify
INV 4	conclusion conditional statement deductive reasoning hypothesis inductive reasoning		counterexample premise	

SECTION OVERVIEW 4

Math Highlights

Enduring Understandings – The "Big Picture"

After completing Section 4, students will understand:

- How to solve problems using rates, ratios, and proportions.
- Recognize and extend arithmetic sequences.
- How to use the x- and y-intercepts to graph linear equations.
- How to simplify rational expressions by factoring and applying exponent rules.
- Identify independent and dependent events and find the probability.

Essential Questions

- How can exponent rules be used to simplify algebraic expressions?
- What are the intercepts of a linear equation?
- How does finding the probability of an independent event differ from the finding the probability of a dependent event?
- How do ratios and rates differ and how can proportions be used to solve problems?

Math Content Strands	Math Processes

Algebra Foundations
- Lesson 32 — Simplifying and Evaluating Expressions with Integer and Zero Exponents
- Lesson 37 — Using Scientific Notation
- Lesson 40 — Simplifying and Evaluating Expressions Using the Power Property of Exponents
- Investigation 4 — Using Deductive and Inductive Reasoning

Equations
- Lesson 31 — Using Rates, Ratios, and Proportions
- Lesson 36 — Writing and Solving Proportions

Functions and Relations
- Lesson 34 — Recognizing and Extending Arithmetic Sequences

Linear Equations and Functions
- Lesson 35 — Locating and Using Intercepts

Polynomials
- Lesson 38 — Simplifying Expressions Using the GCF

Probability and Data Analysis
- Lesson 33 — Finding the Probability of Independent and Dependent Events

Rational Expressions and Functions
- Lesson 39 — Using the Distributive Property to Simplify Rational Expressions

Connections in Practice Problems

	Lessons
Data Analysis	35
Geometry	31, 32, 33, 34, 35, 36, 37, 38, 39, 40
Measurement	36, 37, 38, 40
Probability	31, 35, 39
Statistics	34

Reasoning and Communication

	Lessons
Analyze	31, 32, 33, 37, 38, 39, 40
Error analysis	31, 32, 33, 34, 35, 36, 37, 39, 40
Estimate	31, 37
Formulate	37, 38, 39
Generalize	34, 36, 38, 39, 40
Justify	31, 33, 34, 36, 37, 38, 39, 40
Math Reasoning	31, 32, 33, 34, 35, 36, 37, 38, 39, 40
Model	33
Multiple choice	31, 32, 33, 34, 35, 36, 37, 38, 39, 40
Multi-step	31, 32, 33, 34, 35, 36, 37, 38, 39
Predict	31, 32, 33, 34, 37, 38
True or False	33, 36, 39, 40
Verify	31, 32, 34, 35, 36, 37, 38, 39, 40
Write	31, 32, 33, 34, 35, 37, 38, 39, 40, Inv. 4
Graphing Calculator	31, 33, 34

Connections

In Examples: Changing dimensions, Finding the height of an object, Furniture, Interior design, Play tickets, Seating for a reception, Speed of light, Sound intensity, Trucking

In Practice problems: Architecture, Astronomy, Athletics, Biology, Car rental, Carpentry, Chemistry, Construction, Cooking, Dog breeds, Drama, Economics, Entertainment, Entrepreneurship, Exercising, Finance, Fishery, Free fall, Fuel costs, Fundraising, Geography, Health, Homework, Keeping cool, Landscaping, Marathons, Meteorology, Mileage, Painting, Physical science, Physiology, Piano lessons, Pool charges, Roller coasters, Salaries, Savings, Shipping, Shopping, Soccer, Stamp collecting, Stock market, Temperature, The Great Pyramid, Time, Vehicle rental

Saxon Algebra 1

Lessons 31–40, Investigation 4

Content Trace

Lesson	Warm Up: Prerequisite Skills	New Concepts	Where Practiced	Where Assessed	Looking Forward
31	Lessons 4, 21	Using Rates, Ratios, and Proportions	Lessons 32, 33, 34, 35, 36, 37, 38, 39, 40, 41, 43, 44, 46, 47, 96	Cumulative Tests 7, 9, 10, 11, 14	Lessons 36, 42, 44, 99
32	Lessons 3, 5, 6	Simplifying and Evaluating Expressions with Integer and Zero Exponents	Lessons 33, 34, 35, 36, 37, 38, 39, 40, 42, 45, 47, 48, 55, 97	Cumulative Tests 7, 9, 11, 14	Lessons 37, 40, 46
33	Lessons 11, 14	Finding the Probability of Independent and Dependent Events	Lessons 34, 35, 36, 37, 38, 39, 40, 41, 42, 43, 45, 46, 48, 49, 50, 70, 104	Cumulative Tests 7, 8, 10	Lessons 68, 80, 111, 118
34	Lessons 2, 6, 11	Recognizing and Extending Arithmetic Sequences	Lessons 35, 36, 37, 38, 39, 40, 41, 42, 43, 44, 47, 49, 50, 51, 105	Cumulative Tests 7, 8, 10, 11, 15	Lesson 71
35	Lessons 16, 20, 23	Locating and Using Intercepts	Lessons 36, 37, 38, 39, 40, 41, 42, 43, 44, 45, 48, 49, 50, 51, 107	Cumulative Tests 7, 9	Lessons 41, 44, 49, 52
36	Lessons 23, 31	Writing and Solving Proportions	Lessons 37, 38, 39, 40, 41, 42, 43, 45, 46, 49, 51, 52, 57, 99, 108	Cumulative Tests 8, 9, 13, 14	Lessons 42, 47, 56, 117
37	Lessons 3, 11, 32	Using Scientific Notation	Lessons 38, 39, 40, 41, 42, 43, 44, 45, 46, 47, 50, 52, 53, 110	Cumulative Tests 8, 10	Lessons 40, 46
38	Lessons 2, 16, 32	Simplifying Expressions Using the GCF	Lessons 39, 40, 41, 42, 43, 44, 45, 46, 47, 48, 50, 51, 53, 54, 56, 57	Cumulative Tests 8, 9, 10, 13	Lessons 58, 60, 72, 75, 79
39	Lessons 1, 15, 38	Using the Distributive Property to Simplify Rational Expressions	Lessons 40, 41, 42, 43, 45, 46, 48, 52, 54, 55, 63, 85, 101	Cumulative Tests 8, 9, 10, 11, 12, 15	Lessons 43, 51, 57, 78, 88
40	Lessons 3, 11, 13, 32	Simplifying and Evaluating Expressions Using the Power Property of Exponents	Lessons 41, 42, 43, 44, 45, 46, 47, 48, 49, 50, 53, 54, 55, 56, 63, 98, 102	Cumulative Tests 8, 9, 10, 11, 14, 15	Lessons 46, 60, 88, 92
INV 4	N/A	Investigation: Using Deductive and Inductive Reasoning	Lessons 48, 49, 51, 54, 58, 59	Cumulative Test 9	Lesson 41 Investigations 5, 6, 7, 8, 9, 10, 11, 12

Section Overview 4   190D

SECTION OVERVIEW 4

Ongoing Assessment

	Type	Feature	Intervention *
BEFORE instruction	Assess Prior Knowledge	• Diagnostic Test	• Prerequisite Skills Intervention
BEFORE the lesson	Formative	• Warm Up	• Skills Bank • Reteaching Masters
DURING the lesson	Formative	• Lesson Practice • Math Conversations with the Practice problems	• Additional Examples in TE • Test and Practice Generator (for additional practice sheets)
AFTER the lesson	Formative	• Check for Understanding (closure)	• Scaffolding Questions in TE
AFTER 5 lessons	Summative	After Lesson 35 • Cumulative Test 6 • Performance Task 6 After Lesson 40 • Cumulative Test 7 • Performance Task 7	• Reteaching Masters • Test and Practice Generator (for additional tests and practice)
AFTER 20 lessons	Summative	• Benchmark Tests	• Reteaching Masters • Test and Practice Generator (for additional tests and practice)

* for students not showing progress during the formative stages or scoring below 80% on the summative assessments

Evidence of Learning – What Students Should Know

Because the Saxon philosophy is to provide students with sufficient time to learn and practice each concept, a lesson's topic will not be tested until at least five lessons after the topic is introduced.

On the Cumulative Tests that are given during this section of ten lessons, students should be able to demonstrate the following competencies:
- Use exponent rules to simplify algebraic expressions with integer exponents.
- Solve one- and two-step equations.
- Find unit rates.
- Determine the domain and range of a relation.
- Find x- and y-intercepts and use them to graph linear equations.
- Analyze circle graphs and interpret misleading graphs.
- Use a tree-diagram to find sample spaces.

Test and Practice Generator CD using ExamView™

The Test and Practice Generator is an easy-to-use benchmark and assessment tool that creates unlimited practice and tests in multiple formats and allows you to customize questions or create new ones. A variety of reports are available to track student progress toward mastery of the standards throughout the year.

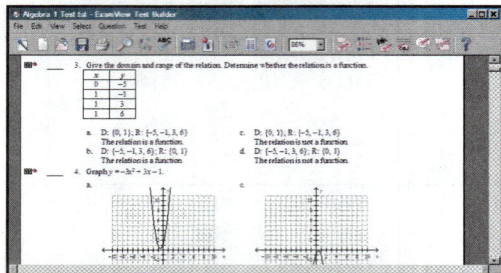
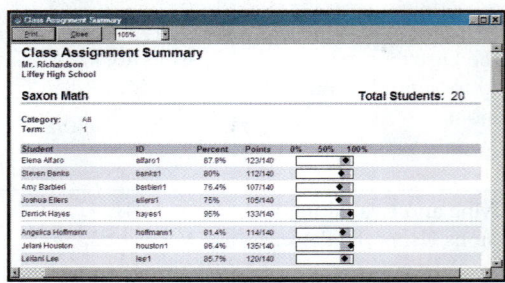

Saxon Algebra 1

Lessons 31–40, Investigation 4

Assessment Resources

Resources for Diagnosing and Assessing

- **Student Edition**
  - Warm Up
  - Lesson Practice

- **Teacher's Edition**
  - Math Conversations with the Practice problems
  - Check for Understanding (closure)

- **Course Assessments**
  - Diagnostic Test
  - Cumulative Tests
  - Performance Tasks
  - Benchmark Tests

Resources for Test Prep

- **Student Edition Practice**
  - Multiple-choice practice problems
  - Multiple-step and writing problems
  - Daily cumulative practice

- **Standardized Test Practice**

- **College Entrance Exam Practice**

- **Test and Practice Generator CD using ExamView™**

Resources for Intervention

- **Student Edition**
  - Skills Bank

- **Teacher's Edition**
  - Additional Examples
  - Scaffolding questions

- **Prerequisite Skills Intervention**
  - Worksheets

- **Reteaching Masters**
  - Lesson instruction and practice sheets

- **Test and Practice Generator CD using ExamView™**
  - Lesson practice problems
  - Additional tests

Cumulative Tests

The assessments in Saxon Math are frequent and consistently placed after every five lessons to offer a regular method of ongoing testing. These cumulative assessments check mastery of concepts from previous lessons.

Performance Tasks

The Performance Tasks can be used in conjunction with the Cumulative Tests and are scored using a rubric.

After Lesson 35

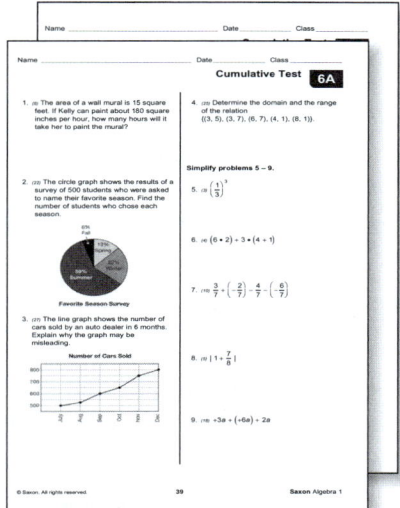

After Lesson 40

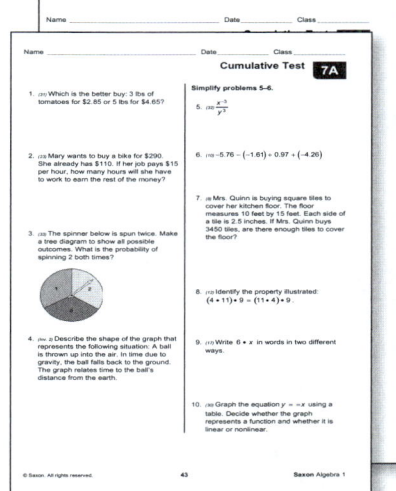

For use with Performance Tasks

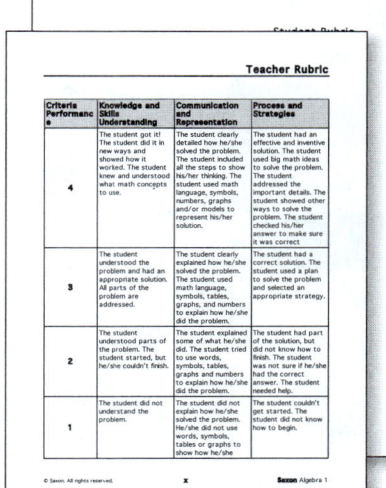

SECTION OVERVIEW 4

Section Overview 4   190F

LESSON 31

Using Rates, Ratios, and Proportions

Warm Up

1. **Vocabulary** The simplest form of $\frac{3}{6}$ is $\frac{1}{2}$. When you _____ a fraction, you are writing it in simplest form.   **simplify**

Simplify.

2. $2.3 - 3.6 \div 4 - 1.7$ -0.3

3. $\dfrac{-0.4 + 1.3 \cdot 4}{0.5 - 5.1 \div 3}$ -4

Solve.

4. $8x = 112$ 14

5. $2.5y = 62.5$ 25

New Concepts

A **ratio** is a comparison of two quantities using division.

Examples: 2 boys to 3 girls   2 to 3, 2:3, $\frac{2}{3}$

A **rate** is a ratio that compares quantities measured in different units.

Examples: 5 feet per 30 seconds   15 apples for $6.00   25,000 hits per month

A **unit rate** is a rate whose denominator is 1. A unit price is the cost per unit.

Examples: 55 miles per hour $2.50 per box

Example 1 Finding Unit Rates

Which is the better buy: 5 cans of tuna for $4.95 or 6 cans for $5.75?

SOLUTION

$\dfrac{\text{total cost}}{\text{number of cans}} = \dfrac{\$4.95}{5} = \$0.99$ per can   Find the unit price.

$\dfrac{\text{total cost}}{\text{number of cans}} = \dfrac{\$5.75}{6} = 0.96$ per can   Find the unit price.

$\$0.96 < \$0.99$ Compare the unit prices.

6 cans for $5.75 is the better buy.

Hint

When working with rates, usually you will see the words *per, for,* and *each* indicated by a forward slash (/).

1 mile per 2 minutes

1 mi/2 min

Example 2 Converting Rates

a. A bus driver drives at 30 miles per hour. What is the rate of the bus in miles per minute?

SOLUTION

$\dfrac{30 \text{ miles}}{1 \text{ hour}} \cdot \dfrac{1 \text{ hour}}{60 \text{ minutes}}$ Multiply by a conversion factor.

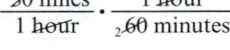

$\dfrac{{}^{1}\cancel{30} \text{ miles}}{1 \cancel{\text{hour}}} \cdot \dfrac{1 \cancel{\text{hour}}}{{}_{2}\cancel{60} \text{ minutes}}$ Cancel like units of measure.

If the driver drives 1 mi/2 min, then he drives $\frac{1}{2}$ mi/min.

MATH BACKGROUND

This method for converting rates is sometimes called unit analysis. In this method, the value of the rate does not change. Since the numerator and denominator of the conversion factor are equal, the rate multiplies by 1. The Identity Property for Multiplication states that multiplying by 1 does not change the value.

When multiplying fractions, units can be cancelled like common factors. To be sure the units will cancel, first set up the expression using only units.

Be sure the numerator of a conversion factor is the desired numerator, and the denominator of a conversion factor is the desired denominator.

After setting up the units of the conversion factor(s), fill in the numeric measurements. The numeric factors in the conversion expression may cancel. Simplifying the numbers helps eliminate computation errors.

b. An engineer opens a valve that drains 60 gallons of water per minute from a tank. How many quarts were drained per second?

SOLUTION

$$\frac{60 \text{ gallons}}{1 \text{ minute}} = \frac{? \text{ quarts}}{1 \text{ second}}$$

$$\frac{60 \text{ gallons}}{1 \text{ minute}} \cdot \frac{4 \text{ quarts}}{1 \text{ gallon}} = \frac{240 \text{ quarts}}{1 \text{ minute}}$$

Use a conversion factor to change gallons to quarts. Then simplify.

$$\frac{240 \text{ quarts}}{1 \text{ minute}} \cdot \frac{1 \text{ minute}}{60 \text{ seconds}} = \frac{240^{\,4} \text{ quarts}}{60^{\,1} \text{ seconds}}$$

Use a conversion factor to change minutes to seconds. Then simplify.

The tank drains at a rate of 4 quarts per second.

Caution

Set up the conversion factor so the units of measure cancel.

Use the factor $\frac{4 \text{ quarts}}{1 \text{ gallon}}$, not $\frac{1 \text{ gallon}}{4 \text{ quarts}}$.

A **proportion** is an equation that shows two ratios are equal. The equation $\frac{3}{5} = \frac{9}{15}$ is a proportion.

> **Cross Products Property**
>
> If $\frac{a}{b} = \frac{c}{d}$ and $b \neq 0$ and $d \neq 0$, then $ad = bc$.
>
> In $\frac{a}{b} \bowtie \frac{c}{d}$, ad and bc are the **cross products**.

Example 3 Solving Proportions Using Cross Products

Solve each proportion.

a. $\frac{x}{15} = \frac{2}{3}$

SOLUTION

$$\frac{x}{15} = \frac{2}{3}$$

$3 \cdot x = 15 \cdot 2$ Write the cross products.

$3x = 30$ Simplify.

$x = 10$ Solve.

b. $\frac{x-1}{12} = \frac{1}{6}$

SOLUTION

$$\frac{x-1}{12} = \frac{1}{6}$$

$6(x - 1) = 12(1)$ Write the cross products.

$6x - 6 = 12$ Distribute and multiply.

$6x = 18$ Simplify.

$x = 3$ Solve.

Lesson 31   191

ALTERNATE METHOD FOR EXAMPLE 3

Students can also use equivalent fractions to solve proportions. To solve $\frac{x}{15} = \frac{2}{3}$, look at the constants in the denominator.

Ask, "What factor will make a fraction equivalent to $\frac{2}{3}$ with a denominator of 15? **5** What is the product of $\frac{2}{3}$ and $\frac{5}{5}$? **$\frac{10}{15}$**"

Write $\frac{x}{15} = \frac{10}{15}$ on the chalkboard. Ask, "Since the denominators of both fractions are the same, what value must x equal?" **10**

Example 4

Students use the Cross Products Property to solve real-world problems using ratios.

Additional Example 4
a. The ratio of pencils to erasers is 1:2. There are 24 pencils and erasers in all. How many pencils and erasers are there?
8 pencils and 16 erasers

b. A scale on a map is equal to the ratio 1 cm:30 km. If a distance on the map is 4.5 cm, what is the actual distance?
135 km

Error Alert Students may form a proportion with incorrect ratios. Be sure that the ratios include the quantity of what is given and the quantity of what is being determined.

Proportions are used to represent many real-world situations that require finding a missing value. Using the cross products is an efficient method for solving the proportions.

Example 4 Solving Multi-Step Proportions

a. The ratio of boys to girls in a math class is 3:2. The class has 25 students in all. How many boys and how many girls are in the class?

SOLUTION

The ratio of boys to girls is 3 to 2. There are 3 boys in each group of 5 students.

$$\frac{\text{number of boys}}{\text{total in group}} = \frac{3}{5}$$ Write a ratio.

Write and solve a proportion. Let b represent the number of boys in the class.

$\frac{3}{5} = \frac{b}{25}$ There are b boys to 25 students.

$3 \cdot 25 = 5 \cdot b$ Write the cross products.

$5b = 75$ Simplify.

$b = 15$ Solve.

There are 15 boys in the class. So, there are $25 - 15$ or 10 girls in the class.

Math Reasoning

Analyze Would you get the same answer for Example 4a if your ratio compared girls to the total group? Explain.

yes; Sample: $\frac{2}{5} = \frac{g}{25}$, $50 = 5g$, $g = 10$

b. On the map, Albany to Jamestown measures 12.6 centimeters, Jamestown to Springfield measures 9 centimeters, and Springfield to Albany measures 4.75 centimeters. What is the actual distance from Albany to Jamestown to Springfield and back to Albany?

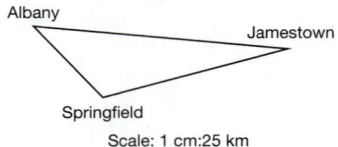

Scale: 1 cm:25 km

SOLUTION

$12.6 + 9 + 4.75 = 26.35$ cm   Find the total distance on the map.

$\frac{26.35 \text{ cm}}{x \text{ km}} = \frac{1 \text{ cm}}{25 \text{ km}}$ Set up a proportion using the map scale.

$26.35 \cdot 25 = 1 \cdot x$ Write the cross products.

$658.75 = x$ Solve.

The actual distance is 658.75 kilometers.

Proportions are frequently used to solve problems involving variations of the distance formula $d = rt$.

$$\text{rate} = \frac{\text{distance}}{\text{time}} \quad \text{or} \quad \text{time} = \frac{\text{distance}}{\text{rate}}$$

 INCLUSION

Use this strategy with students who have difficulty with logical reasoning. When setting up proportions, begin with word ratios. Have students identify the two units being compared. Then have them write the words in a proportion. For example,

$$\frac{\text{boys}}{\text{girls}} = \frac{\text{boys}}{\text{girls}} \quad \text{or} \quad \frac{\text{boys}}{\text{total}} = \frac{\text{boys}}{\text{total}}.$$

Then, numbers and the variable can be included in the proportion. To help students make sure they answer the question, have them keep the labels in the proportion. They can check to be sure the solution to the proportion satisfies the question.

Math Reasoning

Estimate It takes 5.75 hours to drive about 300 miles. How long will it take to drive about 580 miles at the same rate?

Sample: Round 5.75 to 6 hr and 580 mi to 600 mi. It will take almost twice as long to drive 580 mi as it will to drive 300 mi. It will take about 12 hr.

Example 5 Application: Trucking

Mr. Jackson drove a truck 300 miles in 6 hours. If he drives at a constant speed, how long will it take him to drive 450 miles?

SOLUTION

Let x represent the number of hours it will take to drive 450 miles.

$$\text{rate} = \frac{\text{distance}}{\text{time}}$$

$\dfrac{300 \text{ miles}}{6 \text{ hours}} = \dfrac{450 \text{ miles}}{x \text{ hours}}$ Set up a proportion.

$300 \cdot x = 450 \cdot 6$ Write cross products.

$300x = 2700$ Solve.

$x = 9$

Mr. Jackson will drive 450 miles in 9 hours.

Lesson Practice

a. 0.62 < 0.65; 8 boxes for $4.96 is the better buy.

a. Which is the better buy: 8 boxes for $4.96 or 5 boxes for $3.25? (Ex 1)

b. A chemist raised the temperature of a liquid 45°F in 1 minute. What is this amount in degrees Fahrenheit per second? $\frac{3}{4}$°F/s (Ex 2)

c. Jamie typed 20 pages of a document in 2 hours. How many pages did she type in 1 minute? $\frac{1}{6}$ of a page per min (Ex 2)

Solve each proportion. (Ex 3)

d. $\dfrac{c}{7} = \dfrac{3}{21}$ 1

e. $\dfrac{5}{n+2} = \dfrac{10}{16}$ 6

f. 25 blue chips and 35 red chips

f. The ratio of blue chips to red chips in a bag is 5:7. The bag has 60 chips in all. How many blue chips and how many red chips are in the bag? (Ex 4)

g. A map shows a 5.5-inch distance between Orange City and Newtown, and a 3.75-inch distance from Newtown to Westville. The scale on the map is 1 inch:100 miles. What is the actual distance, if you drive from Orange City via Newtown to Westville? 925 miles (Ex 4)

h. If Jeff walks 4 miles in 48 minutes, how far can he walk in 72 minutes? 6 miles (Ex 5)

Practice   Distributed and Integrated

Simplify.

1. $7 - 4 - 5 + 12 - 2 - |-2|$ 6
(10)

2. $-6 \cdot 3 + |-3(-4 + 2^3)|$ -6
(11)

Lesson 31   **193**

 ENGLISH LEARNERS

Discuss the word **actual**.

Say:

"Actual means real. For example, a fake diamond is not an actual diamond."

Say:

"A map does not represent the actual size because it would be too large to hold."

Ask:

"What are some situations that are not actual events?" plays, movies, fictional books

Ask:

"What are some other situations that are actual events?" reports in the newspaper, events in the almanac

---

Example 5

Students use the Cross Products Property to solve rate problems.

Extend the Example
Find the unit rate to determine the speed that Mr. Jackson was driving. 50 miles per hour

Additional Example 5
Susan ran 12 miles in 2 hours during her marathon training. If she runs at a constant speed, how long will it take her to complete a marathon that is 26.2 miles?
4 hours 22 minutes

Lesson Practice

Problem f
Error Alert Students may not add the two parts in the ratio to get a total to use in the proportion.

Problem g
Scaffolding Have students add the distances on the map. Then have them set up a proportion to find the actual number of miles traveled.

 **Check for Understanding**

The questions below help assess the concepts taught in this lesson.

"Why would you use a unit price?" Sample: A unit price can be used to determine the better buy.

"Explain how to convert a rate to different units." Sample: Multiply a rate by a conversion factor(s) that is set up so that units cancel.

"When would you use cross-multiplication?" Sample: To solve a proportion.

Lesson 31   **193**

3 Practice

Math Conversations
Discussion to strengthen understanding

Problem 12
Guide the students by asking them the following questions.

"What are you asked to find?"
the total number of foxes

"How many tagged foxes were recorded?" 21 tagged foxes

"What should the ratios in a proportion compare?" the number of tagged foxes to the total number of foxes

Error Alert
Students may add the number of tagged foxes with the total. Remind students that the total is given and that the next step is to set up the proportion.

Solve.

3. $-0.05n + 1.8 = 1.74$ $n = 1.2$
   (24)

4. $-y - 8 + 6y = -9 + 5y + 2$ no solution
   (28)

*5. **Multiple Choice** What is the value of x when $2x - 4.5 = \frac{1}{2}(x + 3)$?   D
   (28)
   A 9   B 2.4   C 2   D 4

6. Solve for y: $4 + 2x + 2y - 3 = 5$. $y = -x + 2$
   (29)

7. Simplify $4k(2c - a + 3m)$. $8ck - 4ak + 12km$
   (15)

Evaluate.

8. $3x^2 + 2y$ when $x = -2$ and $y = 5$ 22
   (16)

9. $2(a^2 - b)^2 + 3a^3b$ when $a = -3$ and $b = 2$ -64
   (16)

*10. If 10 boxes of cereal sell for $42.50, what is the unit price? $4.25 per box
   (31)

*11. **Geometry** In the diagram, $\triangle ABC$ and $\triangle XYZ$ are similar triangles. What is the
   (31) value of n?   6

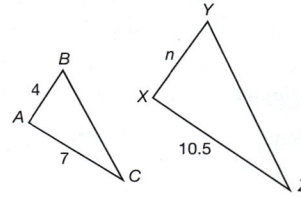

*12. **Predict** An estimate of the number of tagged foxes to the total number of foxes in
   (31) a forest is 3:13. A forest warden recorded 21 tagged foxes. About how many foxes are in the forest? $\frac{21}{x} = \frac{3}{13}$, 91 foxes

13. **Multi-Step** A skydiver falls at a rate given by $s = 1.05\sqrt{w}$, where s is the falling
   (13) speed in feet per second and w is the weight of the skydiver with gear in pounds. What is the approximate falling speed of a 170-pound man with 40 pounds of gear? (Round to the nearest whole number.) ≈ 15 ft/sec

14. Copy and complete the table for $y = x^2 + 2$. Then use the table to graph the
   (30) equation.

x	-3	-1	0	1	3
y	11	3	2	3	11

14.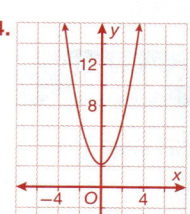

*15. **Shopping** Glenn buys 4 computers for $2800. How much will
   (31) 6 computers cost? $4200

194   Saxon Algebra 1

16. Probability A spinner is divided into 5 sections labeled *A* through *E*. The bar graph shows the results of 50 spins. What is the experimental probability that the next spin will land on *A* or *D*? 2 out of 5

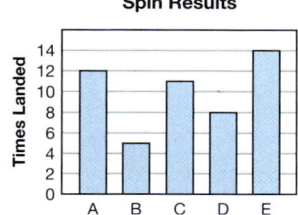

Spin Results

17. (Mileage) The table shows how far a car travels for each gallon of gasoline it uses.

Number of Gallons, x	1	2	3	4
Miles Traveled, f(x)	33	66	99	132

a. Use the table to make a graph.
b. Write a rule for the function. $f(x) = 33x$
c. How far will the car travel using 10 gallons of gasoline? 330 miles

17a.

18. Multi-Step Students are paid *d* dollars per hour for gardening and *g* dollars per hour for babysitting and housework. Sally babysat for 6 hours and mowed lawns for 3 hours. Her brother weeded gardens for 5 hours and mopped floors for 1 hour.
a. Write an expression to represent the amount each student earned. $3d + 6g, 5d + g$
b. Write expressions for the total amount they earned together. $8d + 7g$
c. If they are paid $5 an hour for gardening and $4 an hour for babysitting and housework, how much did they earn together? $68

*19. (Carpentry) A carpenter has propped a board up against a wall. The wall, board, and ground form a right triangle. What will be the measures of the three angles?
90°, 60°, 30°

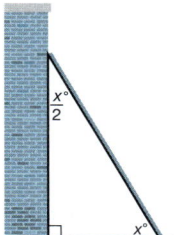

20. Give the domain and range of the relation.

$$\{(12, 2); (11, 10); (18, 0); (19, 1); (13, 4)\}$$

domain: {11, 12, 13, 18, 19}; range: {0, 1, 2, 4, 10}

*21. Use a graphing calculator to make a table of values for $f(x) = x^2 - 1$. Graph the function and determine the domain and range. See Additional Answers.

Lesson 31   195

Problem 16
Extend the Problem
If you spin the spinner 200 times, how many times would you expect it to land on *C* or *E*? 100 times

Problem 17
Guide the students by asking them the following questions.

"What type of function is this?" linear

"The function values are increasing. Which two operations are possible?" addition, multiplication

"How will you find the distance the car will travel using ten gallons?" Substitute $x = 10$ into $f(x) = 33x$, and simplify.

Problem 18b
Error Alert
Students may forget that there is a coefficient of 1 in front of *g*. If needed, have students write the coefficient before combining like terms.

Problem 20
To help associate domain and range with the appropriate *x*-values and *y*-values, alphabetize the terms. The domain refers to the *x*-values and each comes first alphabetically.

Lesson 31   195

Problem 26

Error Alert

Students may substitute 5.5 for r. Remind them to convert 5.5% to a decimal before substituting for r.

Problem 29

Use the order of operations. Multiplication always should be simplified before addition.

Problem 30

Guide the students by asking them the following questions.

"What are you asked to find?" the length of the side of the pyramid

"What has been given?" the perimeter of the pyramid

"What is the formula for the perimeter of a square?" $P = 4s$

"What is the equation for the perimeter of the pyramid's base?" $916 = 4s$

---

*22. **Write** Why is there no conclusive value for x in the equation
(28) $\frac{3}{2}x + 5 = 2x - \frac{1}{2}x + 5$? Explain.   In the equation $x = x$, x can have any value.

23. **Multi-Step** Amy works in a kitchen appliance store. She earns $65 daily and a
(17) commission worth $10 less than one-fifth of the value of each appliance she sells. Let m equal the value of an appliance.

a. Write an expression for Amy's daily salary if she sells one appliance every day.

b. Write an expression for Amy's daily salary if she sells n appliances every day.

c. If you know the value of m and n, which part of the expression would you solve first?   Divide m by 5.

23a. Sample: $65 + (\frac{m}{5} - 10)$

23b. Sample: $65 + n(\frac{m}{5} - 10)$

24. **Multiple-Choice** Which expression is equivalent to $4(x^2 - 4) + 3z^3(4z^7)$?   **B**
(15)
A $4x^2 - 16 + 3z^{10}$ B $4x^2 - 16 + 12z^{10}$

C $4x^2 - 16 + 12z^{21}$ D $4x - 16 + 12z^{10}$

*25. **Error Analysis** Two students solved $\frac{3z}{2} - \frac{4q}{3} = 6$ for z. Which student is correct?
(29) Explain the error.

Student A	Student B
$\frac{3z}{2} - \frac{4q}{3} = 6$	$\frac{3z}{2} - \frac{4q}{3} = 6$
$3(3z) - 2(4q) = 6$	$3(3z) - 2(4q) = 6(6)$
$9z - 8q = 6$	$9z - 8q = 36$
$9z = 6 + 8q$	$9z = 36 + 8q$
$z = \frac{6 + 8q}{9}$	$z = 4 + \frac{8}{9}q$

25. Student B; Sample: Student A did not multiply both sides by 6.

26. **Finance** Compound interest is calculated using the formula $A = P(1 + \frac{r}{1})^t$, where
(16) P = principal (amount originally deposited), r = the interest rate, and t = time in years. If $1500 is deposited into an account and compounded annually at 5.5%, how much money will be in the account after 10 years? $2562.22

*27. **Verify** Suppose that $\frac{3}{4} = \frac{x}{100}$. Show that x equals 75. $4x = 300$; Divide by 4 to get 75.
(31)

28. **Verify** Is $m = \frac{2}{3}$ a solution for $\frac{1}{3}m + \frac{5}{6} = \frac{11}{18}$? Explain. If false, provide a correct
(23) solution and check.   false, $\frac{1}{3}(\frac{2}{3}) + \frac{5}{6} = \frac{19}{18} \neq \frac{11}{18}$; $m = -\frac{2}{3}$; Check: $\frac{1}{3}(\frac{-2}{3}) + \frac{5}{6} = \frac{11}{18}$

29. **Justify** Simplify $20 \cdot \$9 + 10 \cdot \$13$. Justify each step.
(4)

30. **The Great Pyramid** The base of the great Pyramid of Giza is almost a perfect
(21) square. The perimeter of the base measures about 916 meters. What is the length of each side of the pyramid's base? $4s = 916$; $s = 229$ m

29. $20 \cdot \$9 + 10 \cdot \$13$
    $\$180 + \$130$ Multiply from left to right.
    $\$310$ Add.

196   Saxon Algebra 1

 CHALLENGE

The ratio of four times a number to the sum of the same number and three is 5:2. What is the number?   5

 LOOKING FORWARD

Using rates, ratios, and proportions prepares students for

• **Lesson 36** Writing and Solving Proportions

• **Lesson 42** Solving Percent Problems

• **Lesson 44** Finding Slope Using the Slope Formula

• **Lesson 99** Solving Rational Equations

LESSON 32

Simplifying and Evaluating Expressions with Integer and Zero Exponents

Warm Up

1. **Vocabulary** The _____ of a power is the number used as a factor.
   (3) **base**

   Simplify.

   2. 3^4 **81**
   (3)

   3. $x^5 \cdot x^6$ x^{11}
   (3)

   4. $26 + (-18)$ **8**
   (5)

   5. $-34 - 19$ **−53**
   (6)

New Concepts

Algebraic expressions may contain exponents that are positive, negative, or zero. The relationship between the different exponents can be understood by looking at successive powers of a positive integer greater than 1. Look at the powers of 2.

> **Math Reasoning**
> **Verify** Show why $2^4 = 16$.
>
> Sample: $2^4 =$
> $2 \cdot 2 \cdot 2 \cdot 2 = 16$

Power of 2		Value
2^4	=	16
2^3	=	8
2^2	=	4
2^1	=	2

In the left column, each entry is found by decreasing the exponent in the previous entry by one. In the right column, each entry is found by halving the previous entry, or by dividing it by 2. Use this pattern to find the next three powers.

Power of 2		Value
2^4	=	16
2^3	=	8
2^2	=	4
2^1	=	2
2^0	=	1
2^{-1}	=	$\frac{1}{2}$ or $\frac{1}{2^1}$
2^{-2}	=	$\frac{1}{4}$ or $\frac{1}{2^2}$

The pattern illustrates the properties for negative and zero exponents.

Negative and Zero Exponent Properties
Negative Exponent Property
For every nonzero number x, $x^{-n} = \frac{1}{x^n}$ and $x^n = \frac{1}{x^{-n}}$.
Zero Exponent Property
For every nonzero number x, $x^0 = 1$.

> **Math Language**
> **The Product Property of Exponents** states that the exponents of powers with the same base are added.
> $x^3 \cdot x^4 = x^{3+4} = x^7$

An algebraic expression is not considered simplified if it contains negative or zero exponents. The Product Property of Exponents applies to negative and zero exponents.

---

1 Warm Up

Problem 3
Remind students that to multiply powers with like bases, they need to add the exponents and keep the base.

2 New Concepts

In this lesson, students learn to simplify expressions containing integer and zero exponents. They also learn the Quotient Property of Exponents.

Discuss the properties for negative and zero exponents. Point out that x cannot equal zero.

TEACHER TIP

Complete the power pattern with bases other than 2. Include -2 in the other examples so that students can see the difference between a negative base and a negative exponent.

LESSON RESOURCES

Student Edition Practice Workbook 32
Reteaching Master 32
Adaptations Master 32
Challenge and Enrichment Master C32

MATH BACKGROUND

In addition to the patterns shown in the lesson, the definition of zero and negative exponents can be derived using the quotient property. The quotient property states that if m and n are real numbers and $x \neq 0$, then

$$\frac{x^m}{x^n} = x^{m-n}$$

If $m = n$, then $x^m = x^n$ and $\frac{x^m}{x^n} = 1$. Also, $m - n = 0$. So, $1 = x^0$.

Look at an example to better understand negative exponents.

Using the Quotient Property of Exponents, $\frac{x^5}{x^8} = x^{5-8} = x^{-3}$. Then write the powers using repeated multiplication and simplify.

$$\frac{x^5}{x^8} = \frac{x \cdot x \cdot x \cdot x \cdot x}{x \cdot x \cdot x \cdot x \cdot x \cdot x \cdot x \cdot x} = \frac{1}{x^3}$$

Combine these two facts and conclude that $x^{-3} = \frac{1}{x^3}$.

Example 1

Students use their understanding of negative exponents to simplify expressions.

Error Alert Students may write x^{-3} as $-x^3$. Emphasize the meaning of a negative exponent by having students write the Negative Exponent Property before they use it.

Additional Example 1

Simplify each expression. All variables represent nonzero real numbers.

a. x^{-9} $\frac{1}{x^9}$

b. $\frac{d^{-2}}{c^3}$ $\frac{1}{c^3 d^2}$

c. $\frac{1}{a^{-5}}$ a^5

Example 2

Students evaluate expressions with negative and zero exponents.

Additional Example 2

Evaluate each expression for $a = -7$ and $b = -4$.

a. $a^0 b^2$ 16

b. $8b^{-2} \cdot b^1$ -2

Example 1 Simplifying Expressions with Negative Exponents

Simplify each expression. All variables represent nonzero real numbers.

a. x^{-3}

SOLUTION

$x^{-3} = \frac{1}{x^3}$ Write with only positive exponents.

b. $\frac{y^{-4}}{x^2}$

SOLUTION

$\frac{y^{-4}}{x^2} = \frac{1}{x^2 \cdot y^4} = \frac{1}{x^2 y^4}$ Write with only positive exponents.

c. $\frac{1}{w^{-4}}$

SOLUTION

$\frac{1}{w^{-4}} = w^4$ Write with only positive exponents.

Example 2 Evaluating Expressions with Negative and Zero Exponents

Evaluate each expression for $a = -2$ and $b = -3$.

a. $a^2 b^0$

SOLUTION

$a^2 b^0$
$= a^2 \cdot 1$ Simplify using the Zero Exponent Property.
$= a^2$ Multiplicative Identity
$= (-2)^2$ Substitute -2 for a.
$= 4$ Simplify.

b. $3b^{-3} \cdot b$

SOLUTION

$3b^{-3} \cdot b$
$= 3b^{-2}$ Product Property of Exponents
$= \frac{3}{b^2}$ Simplify using the Negative Exponent Property.
$= \frac{3}{(-3)^2}$ Substitute -3 for b. Then simplify.
$= \frac{3}{9} = \frac{1}{3}$ Simplify.

Caution

When working through problems, you may incorrectly replace b^0 with 0 instead of 1.

Online Connection
www.SaxonMathResources.com

The Quotient Property of Exponents is used when dividing algebraic expressions. This property states that to divide two algebraic expressions with the same base, subtract their exponents.

Quotient Property of Exponents

If m and n are real numbers and $x \neq 0$, then

$$\frac{x^m}{x^n} = x^{m-n} = \frac{1}{x^{n-m}}$$

$$\frac{5^4}{5^2} = 5^{4-2} = 5^2 = 25 \qquad \frac{5^2}{5^4} = \frac{1}{5^{4-2}} = \frac{1}{5^2} = \frac{1}{25}$$

Example 3 Using the Quotient Property of Exponents

Simplify each expression. All variables represent nonzero real numbers.

a. $\dfrac{x^7}{x^3}$

SOLUTION

$\dfrac{x^7}{x^3}$

$= x^{7-3}$ Quotient Property of Exponents

$= x^4$ Simplify.

b. $\dfrac{x^3}{x^{-7}}$

SOLUTION

$\dfrac{x^3}{x^{-7}}$

$= x^{3-(-7)}$ Quotient Property of Exponents

$= x^{10}$ Simplify.

c. $\dfrac{x^{-5}y^6z}{z^{-3}y^2x}$

SOLUTION

$\dfrac{x^{-5}y^6z}{z^{-3}y^2x}$

$= x^{-5-1}y^{6-2}z^{1-(-3)}$ Quotient Property of Exponents

$= x^{-6}y^4z^4$ Simplify.

$= \dfrac{y^4z^4}{x^6}$ Write with only positive exponents.

Math Reasoning

Analyze Why is $\dfrac{x^5}{x} = x^4$?

Sample: $\dfrac{x^5}{x} = \dfrac{x \cdot x \cdot x \cdot x \cdot x}{x} = x^4$. Since $x = x^1$, you subtract $5 - 1 = 4$ to get x^4.

Math Reasoning

Analyze Use the Quotient Property of Exponents to show another method for simplifying $\dfrac{x^{-5}}{x}$.

$\dfrac{x^{-5}}{x} = \dfrac{1}{x^{1-(-5)}}$

$= \dfrac{1}{x^{1+5}}$

$= \dfrac{1}{x^6}$

Lesson 32   199

Example 4

Students apply the Quotient Property of Exponents to compare the intensity levels of sounds.

Extend the Example

Using the equation $\frac{x}{10^{-7}} = 10^2$, find the sound that is 10^2 times more intense than that of regular speech at 10^{-7} watts per square meter. **vacuum cleaner**

Additional Example 4

A kilometer is 10^3 meters. A millimeter is 10^{-3} meters. How many times larger is a kilometer than a millimeter? Express the answer in exponential and standard form. **10^6 or 1,000,000 times larger**

Lesson Practice

Problem d

Error Alert Students may think that the answer is 0. Remind them that any nonzero number to the zero power is 1.

Problem i

Scaffolding Have students use the quotient property to simplify the expression. Then have them write all powers with positive exponents.

Check for Understanding

The questions below help assess the concepts taught in this lesson.

"Explain how to simplify an expression that contains a negative exponent in the numerator." **Sample: If a variable in the numerator is raised to a negative exponent, move the variable to the denominator and change the sign of the exponent. Then simplify.**

"Explain how the Quotient Property of Exponents works." **Sample: Subtract the exponents and keep the base.**

Math Reasoning

Write Which value is greater, 10^{-2} or 10^1? Explain.

10^1; $10^1 = 10$ and $10^{-2} = \frac{1}{100}$; $\frac{1}{100} < 10$

Math Language

10^{10} is in **exponential form**. 10,000,000,000 is in **standard form**.

Example 4 Application: The Intensity of Sound

The intensity of sound can be measured in watts per square meter. The table below lists intensity levels for some common sounds.

Intensity of Sound

Watts/Square Meter	Common Sound
10^3 to 10^7	Rocket Liftoff
10^0 to 10^2	Jet Liftoff
10^{-2} to 10^0	Loud Music
10^{-6} to 10^{-4}	Vacuum Cleaner
10^{-9} to 10^{-6}	Regular Speech
10^{-10} to 10^{-9}	Soft Whisper

How many times more intense is the sound of a rocket liftoff at 10^3 watts per square meter than that of regular speech at 10^{-7} watts per square meter?

Express the answer in exponential and standard form.

SOLUTION

$\dfrac{10^3}{10^{-7}}$ Write a ratio to compare the sound intensities.

$= 10^{3-(-7)}$ Quotient Property of Exponents

$= 10^{10}$ Simplify the exponent.

$= 10,000,000,000$ Simplify.

The sound of a rocket liftoff is 10^{10} or 10,000,000,000 times more intense than that of regular speech.

Lesson Practice

Simplify each expression. All variables represent nonzero real numbers. *(Ex 1)*

a. x^{-5} $\;\frac{1}{x^5}$
b. $\dfrac{p^{-8}}{q^4}$ $\;\frac{1}{p^8 q^4}$
c. $\dfrac{1}{d^{-8}}$ $\;d^8$

Evaluate each expression for $a = 4$, $b = 6$, and $c = 3$. *(Ex 2)*

d. $a^0 b c^2$ **54**
e. $4a^{-2}$ $\;\frac{1}{4}$

Simplify each expression. All variables represent nonzero real numbers. *(Ex 3)*

f. $\dfrac{x^{10}}{x^4}$ $\;x^6$
g. $\dfrac{x^9}{x^{-2}}$ $\;x^{11}$
h. $\dfrac{xy^{-3}z^5}{y^2 x^2 z}$ $\;\frac{z^4}{xy^5}$

i. Refer to the table in Example 4. How many times more intense is the sound of a jet liftoff at 10^1 watts per square meter than that of a vacuum cleaner at 10^{-5} watts per square meter? Express the answer in exponential and standard form. **10^6 or 1,000,000 times more intense**
(Ex 4)

ENGLISH LEARNERS

In Example 4, explain the meaning of **intense**. Say:

"Intense means strong or powerful. If a sound is more intense, it is stronger, more powerful, or louder."

Discuss examples of things that could be described as intense, such as feelings, lights, and activities.

Ask students to describe each sound in Example 4 as more or less intense than the sound of a car horn.

Practice   Distributed and Integrated

Simplify.

*1. $y^0 \dfrac{y^6}{y^5}$ y
(32)

*2. $\dfrac{m^3 p^2 q^{10}}{m^{-2} p^4 q^{-6}}$ $\dfrac{m^5 q^{16}}{p^2}$
(32)

Solve.

3. $9x - 2 = 2x + 12$ $x = 2$
(28)

*4. $3y - y + 2y - 5 = 7 - 2y + 5$ $y = \dfrac{17}{6}$
(28)

5. $2y + 3 = 3(y + 7)$ $y = -18$
(28)

6. $5(r - 1) = 2(r - 4) - 6$ $r = -3$
(28)

 *7. **Geometry** Express the ratio of the area of the circle to the area of the square. $\dfrac{\pi}{4}$
(32)

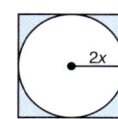

8. The sum of twice a number and 17 is 55. Find the number.   19
(17)

*9. **Error Analysis** Two students solved the proportion $\dfrac{3}{8} = \dfrac{x}{4}$. Which student is correct?
(31) Explain the error.

Student B; Sample: Student A did not find the cross products of the proportion.

Student A	Student B
$\dfrac{3}{8} = \dfrac{x}{4}$	$\dfrac{3}{8} = \dfrac{x}{4}$
$3 \cdot x = 8 \cdot 4$	$8 \cdot x = 3 \cdot 4$
$x = 10\dfrac{2}{3}$	$x = 1\dfrac{1}{2}$

*10. **Health** The circle graph shows the prevalence of all listed types of allergies among
(27) people who suffer from allergies. What about the graph may lead someone to an inaccurate conclusion?

Allergy Prevalence

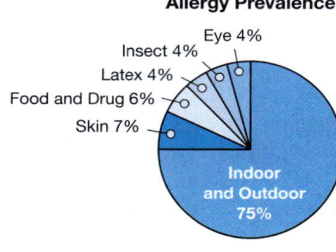

Eye 4%
Insect 4%
Latex 4%
Food and Drug 6%
Skin 7%
Indoor and Outdoor 75%

Sample: The title of the graph does not specify that the data only apply to those who suffer from allergies. Someone may conclude that 75% of people suffer from indoor and outdoor allergies.

 11. **Write** Why is it best to combine like terms in an equation, such as
(26) $3n + 9 - 2n = 6 - 2n + 12$, before attempting to isolate the variable?

11. Sample: By combining like terms, the equation becomes simpler and easier to deal with. Combining contributes to the process of isolating the variable.

12. **Verify** Is $n = 9$ a solution for $-28 = -4n + 8$? Explain. If false, provide a correct
(23) solution and check.   true, $-28 = -4(9) + 8$; $-28 = -36 + 8$; $-28 = -28$

Lesson 32   201

---

3 Practice

Math Conversations
Discussion to strengthen understanding

Problem 4
Remind students to begin by collecting like terms. Encourage them to isolate the variable on the side with the greater coefficient to avoid dealing with negative coefficients.

Problem 7
Review the formulas for finding the area of a circle and the area of a square. Encourage students to begin by writing the ratio $\dfrac{\pi r^2}{s^2}$ and then have them substitute the values for r and s.

Problem 8
Remind students that a sum is the answer to an addition problem.

Lesson 32   201

Problem 13
To be a function, there can only be one *y*-value associated with any *x*-value. Here there are two *y*-values associated with $x = 1$.

Problem 17
Guide the students by asking them the following questions.

"How would you determine the number of pencils in 10 cartons?"
Use a proportion.

"How many pencils are in 10 cartons?" 1200 pencils

"How many pencils are in a dozen?" 12 pencils

"How many dozen pencils are in 10 cartons?" 100 dozen pencils

Problem 18
Review with students that 1 meter is equal to 100 centimeters and that 1000 meters is equal to 1 kilometer.

Problem 20
Error Alert
Students may take the absolute value after adding 10. Remind them that absolute-value bars are grouping symbols, and that grouping symbols are the first step according to the order of operations.

---

13. The table lists the ordered pairs from a relation. Determine whether the relation represents a function. Explain why or why not

Domain (x)	Range (y)
1	5
0	6
2	4
1	8
3	3

no; Sample: For the input, 1, there are two outputs, 5 and 8. For the relation to be a function, each input would only have one output.

14. If there are 60 dozen pencils in 12 cartons, how many are in 1 carton? 5 dozen pencils

15. Multi-Step How many seconds are in 1 day? 86,400

16. Roller Coasters The table shows the number of roller coasters in several countries. Suppose one student displays the data in a bar graph, and another student makes a circle graph of the data. Compare the information that each type of display shows.

Roller Coasters Worldwide

Country	Japan	United Kingdom	Germany	France	China	South Korea	Canada	United States
Number	240	160	108	65	60	54	51	624

16. Sample: The bar graph will show the exact number of roller coasters in each country and will compare the number of roller coasters in each country. The circle graph will show the relative number of coasters in each country to the total number of coasters.

17. If there are 720 pencils in 6 cartons, how many dozen pencils are in 10 cartons? 100 dozen

18. Multi-Step How many centimeters are in 1 kilometer? 100,000 cm

*19. Geography On a map, Brownsville and Evanstown are 2.5 inches apart. The scale on the map is 1 inch:25 miles. How far apart are the two towns?
62.5 miles

20. Copy and complete the table for $y = |x| + 10$. Then use the table to graph the equation. Is the graph of the equation a function? yes

x	−3	−2	−1	0	1	2
y	13	12	11	10	11	12

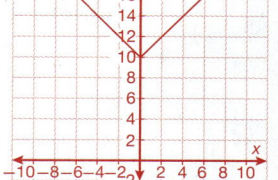

*21. Multiple Choice Which expression is simplified? **C**

A $\dfrac{6xy^2}{z^0}$ B $\dfrac{6x^3y^{-2}}{z}$ C $\dfrac{6x^3y^2}{z}$ D $\dfrac{6x^3y^2z}{z}$

*22. Chemistry An electron has a mass of 10^{-28} grams and a proton has a mass of 10^{-24} grams. How many times greater is the mass of a proton than the mass of an electron? $10^4 = 10,000$ times greater

202 *Saxon Algebra 1*

23. Multi-Step A border is being built along two sides of a triangular garden. The third side is next to the house.

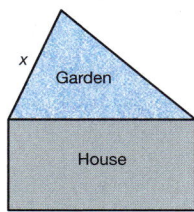

a. The second side of the garden is 4 feet longer than first side. Write an expression for the length of the second side. $x + 4$

b. If the total amount of border is 28 feet, how long are the sides of the garden that are not next to the house?   12 ft, 16 ft

24. Multi-Step The temperature of a liquid is 72°F. The first step of a set of instructions requires that a scientist cools the liquid by 15°F. The second step requires that she warms it until it reaches 85°F. By how many degrees will she warm the liquid in the second step?   28°F

25. Analyze Megan and Molly have an age gap of 6 years. Megan is older. If Molly is 8 years old, then how old is Megan?   14 years old

26. Fuel Costs It cost Rayna $73.25 to fill her truck with gas, not including tax. The gasoline tax is $0.32 per gallon. If the price for gasoline including tax is $3.25 per gallon, how many gallons of gas did she buy?

a. Write an equation to represent the problem.   Sample: $(\$3.25 − 0.32)x = 73.25$

b. How many gallons of gas did she buy?   25 gallons of gas

27. Expand the expression $(5p − 2c)4xy$ by using the Distributive Property.
$20pxy − 8cxy$

Solve each proportion.

28. $\dfrac{7}{x} = \dfrac{1}{0.5}$ $x = 3.5$

*29. $\dfrac{1}{x} = \dfrac{-3}{x + 2}$ $x = -0.5$

30. Multi-Step How far Sam bikes in two hours depends on the rate at which he rides. His distance is represented by the equation $y = 25x$, where x is the time in hours and y is the distance in miles.

a. Copy and complete the table and graph the solutions.

x	1	2	3	4	5
y	25	50	75	100	125

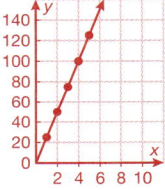

b. Connect the points. What do you notice?   They all lie on the same line.

c. **Predict** If Sam rides at the same rate, how long will it take him to ride 80 miles?
3.2 hr or 3 hr and 12 min

Problem 23
Extend the Problem
If the second side is 32 feet, how many total feet of border is needed?   60 feet

Problem 24
Guide the students by asking them the following questions.

"What will the temperature of the liquid be after the scientist cools it by 15°F?"   57°F

"What equation could you use to find the number of degrees the scientist should warm the liquid in the second step?"   Sample: $57 + x = 85$

Lesson 32   203

CHALLENGE

Simplify the expression.

$\dfrac{a^{-2}b^6c^{-3}}{\dfrac{a^4b^8c^{-5}}{b^{-5}}}$

$\dfrac{b^3c^2}{a^6}$

LOOKING FORWARD

Simplifying and evaluating expressions with integer and zero exponents prepares students for

Lesson 37 Using Scientific Notation

Lesson 40 Simplifying and Evaluating Expressions Using the Power Property of Exponents

Lesson 46 Simplifying Expressions with Square Roots and Higher Order Roots

LESSON 33

1 Warm Up

Problem 3
Remind students that the probability of an event is the number of favorable outcomes divided by the number of total possible outcomes.

2 New Concepts

In this lesson, students learn to identify whether events are independent or dependent. Students learn to apply the rules of probability to determine the probability of an event.

Discuss finding the probability of a single event, using a number from 0 to 1 to express the likelihood that an event will occur. Remind students how to determine the probability of an event.

Review that the notation $P(A)$ means the probability of event A. Then discuss the two cases for $P(A \text{ and } B)$—when events A and B are independent and when they are dependent.

Explain that the probability of two events occurring is equal to or less than the probability of either event occurring by itself.

LESSON RESOURCES

Student Edition Practice Workbook 33
Reteaching Master 33
Adaptations Master 33
Challenge and Enrichment Master C33

LESSON 33

Finding the Probability of Independent and Dependent Events

Warm Up

1. **Vocabulary** A _____ is the set of all possible outcomes of an event. **sample space**

A number cube is labeled 1–6. Suppose the number cube is rolled once.
2. List all the possible outcomes. **1, 2, 3, 4, 5, 6**
3. What is the probability of rolling a prime number? $\frac{3}{6}$ or $\frac{1}{2}$

Simplify.
4. $\frac{4}{5} \cdot \frac{15}{22}$ $\frac{6}{11}$
5. $\frac{18}{55}\left(-\frac{33}{54}\right)$ $-\frac{1}{5}$

New Concepts

Events where the outcome of one does not affect the probability of the other are called **independent events**. To find the probability of two independent events, multiply the probabilities of the two events.

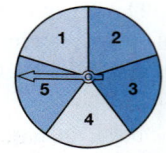 

Spinning a spinner and flipping a coin are independent events. The result of one does not affect the result of the other. What is the probability of spinning a 3 and landing on heads?

$$P(3 \text{ and heads}) = P(3) \cdot P(\text{heads})$$
$$= \frac{1}{5} \cdot \frac{1}{2}$$
$$= \frac{1}{10}$$

Math Reasoning

Write Explain why the first spin does not affect the second spin.

Sample: All of the same outcomes are still available for the second spin.

Spinning the spinner twice also creates two independent events. The first spin does not affect the second spin. What is the probability of spinning a 5 and then a 1?

$$P(5 \text{ and } 1) = P(5) \cdot P(1)$$
$$= \frac{1}{5} \cdot \frac{1}{5}$$
$$= \frac{1}{25}$$

Online Connection
www.SaxonMathResources.com

With **dependent events**, the outcome of one event does affect the probability of the other event. To find the probability of two dependent events, you multiply the probability of the first event by the probability of the second event, given the results of the first event.

204   Saxon Algebra 1

MATH BACKGROUND

Associate the word simultaneous with independent events. Associate the word rely with dependent events.

Consider the following events: a coin landing on heads and rolling a 3 on a number cube. Both events can occur simultaneously. Since each event can be performed independently, without the other event, these events are considered independent.

Consider the following events: choosing a card with a heart from a deck without replacing it and choosing a second card with a heart. The sample space for the probability of the second event is different than the first because the card was not replaced. Since the probability of the second event relies on the first event, the events are considered dependent.

Type of Events	Definition	Calculating the Probability
Independent Events	The outcome of the first event does not affect the second event.	$P(A \text{ and } B) = P(A) \cdot P(B)$
Dependent Events	The outcome of the first event does affect the second event.	$P(A \text{ and } B) = P(A) \cdot P(B)$, where $P(B)$ is calculated under the new conditions.

Example 1 Identifying Situations Involving Independent and Dependent Events

Identify each set of events as independent or dependent.

a. rolling a 6 on one number cube and a 4 on another number cube

SOLUTION These events are independent. Rolling one number cube does not affect the outcome of rolling the other number cube.

b. rolling a 6 on a number cube and then a 4 on the same number cube

SOLUTION These events are independent. Both rolls of this number cube have the same possible outcomes, and the result of the first roll does not affect the second roll.

c. drawing a red marble from a bag, keeping it out of the bag, and then drawing a blue marble

SOLUTION These events are dependent. By not replacing the first marble, the outcome of the second draw is affected. There are fewer marbles to choose from.

d. drawing a red marble from a bag, putting it back in the bag, and then drawing a blue marble

SOLUTION These events are independent. Because the first marble is replaced, the second draw is not affected. It has the same choices as the first.

Hint
Sometimes independent events are described as events with replacement. Dependent events are without replacement.

A tree diagram can help demonstrate the sample space for events.

Example 2 Using a Tree Diagram

A coin is flipped twice. Make a tree diagram showing all possible outcomes. What is the probability of the coin landing on heads both times?

SOLUTION

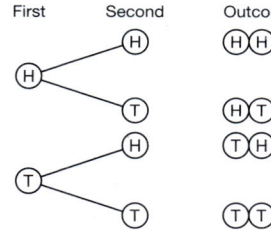

$P(H, H) = \frac{1}{4}$

Lesson 33   205

TEACHER TIP
A distinction can be made between the formulas for dependent and independent events by using the expression "B after A" in the second formula.

Independent Events
$P(A \text{ and } B) = P(A) \cdot P(B)$

Dependent Events
$P(A \text{ and } B) = P(A) \cdot P(B \text{ after } A)$

Example 1
Students identify independent and dependent events. Use Example 1c and 1d to emphasize the key idea of replacement.

Additional Example 1
Identify each set of events as independent or dependent.

a. tossing two coins, a dime and a quarter independent

b. tossing the same coin twice independent

c. putting 10 students' names in a bag and drawing two names without replacement dependent

d. putting 10 students' names in a bag and drawing one name per week to choose a room monitor. A student can be chosen more than once. independent

Example 2
Students use a tree diagram to illustrate all the outcomes in a sample and to find the probability of an event.

Additional Example 2
A coin is flipped twice. Make a tree diagram showing all possible outcomes. What is the probability of the coin landing on heads and then tails?
$P(H, T) = \frac{1}{4}$

ALTERNATE METHOD FOR EXAMPLE 2

For probability situations with two events, a table can be used instead of a tree diagram to show all the possible outcomes. Have students list the outcomes of the first event in the boxes on the left of the table and the outcomes of the second event in the boxes along the top. Then have them complete the table to find all possible outcomes for the two events.

	Heads	Tails
Heads	Heads, Heads	Heads, Tails
Tails	Tails, Heads	Tails, Tails

Example 3
Students calculate the probability of dependent events.

Additional Example 3

A bag has 5 ten-dollar bills and 15 one-dollar bills.

a. Find the probability of drawing a one-dollar bill, keeping it, and then drawing a ten-dollar bill.
$\frac{15}{20} \cdot \frac{5}{19} = \frac{15}{76}$

b. Find the probability of drawing a ten-dollar bill, keeping it, and then drawing another ten-dollar bill.
$\frac{5}{20} \cdot \frac{4}{19} = \frac{1}{19}$

Extend the Example

A bag of shapes has 3 circles and 2 squares. Find the probability of drawing a circle, keeping it, drawing another circle, keeping it, and then drawing a third circle. $\frac{3}{5} \cdot \frac{2}{4} \cdot \frac{1}{3} = \frac{1}{10}$

Example 3 Calculating the Probability of Dependent Events

Natalia has two squares and three circles in a bag.

a. Find the probability of drawing a circle, keeping it, and then drawing another circle without the use of a tree diagram.

SOLUTION

For the first draw, the bag has 5 shapes and 3 are circles.

$$P(\text{1st circle}) = \frac{3}{5}$$

For the second draw, a circle has been removed. There is one less circle and one less shape.

$$P(\text{2nd circle}) = \frac{2}{4}$$

To find the probability of these two events, multiply their probabilities.

$$P(\text{1st circle}) \cdot P(\text{2nd circle}) = \frac{3}{5} \cdot \frac{2}{4} = \frac{6}{20} = \frac{3}{10}$$

b. Find the probability of drawing a square, keeping it, and then drawing a circle.

SOLUTION

For the first draw, the bag has 5 shapes and 2 are squares.

$$P(\text{square}) = \frac{2}{5}$$

For the second draw, a square has been removed. There is one less shape, but the number of circles is the same.

$$P(\text{circle}) = \frac{3}{4}$$

To find the probability of these two events, multiply their probabilities.

$$P(\text{square}) \cdot P(\text{circle}) = \frac{2}{5} \cdot \frac{3}{4} = \frac{6}{20} = \frac{3}{10}$$

Math Reasoning

Justify Why do both the numerator and the denominator change for the second event?

There is one less shape and one less circle because a circle was removed.

Odds are another way of describing the likelihood of an event. Odds are expressed as a ratio, usually written with a colon. Odds can be calculated for something or against something happening.

Definition of Odds
Odds of an event: A ratio expressing the likelihood of an event.
Assume that all outcomes are equally likely, and that there are m favorable and n unfavorable outcomes.
The odds for the event are $m:n$.   The odds against the event are $n:m$.

INCLUSION

Students may have difficulty visualizing the outcomes in the sample spaces for these examples. Use spinners to make visual models. For instance, for the first problem in Example 3, draw two spinners to represent the first and second draws.

Have students spin a paper clip around the tip of a pencil centered on the spinner, to better understand the basic concepts underlying the example.

First Draw   **Second Draw**

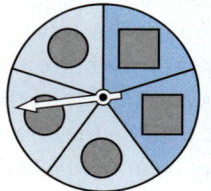 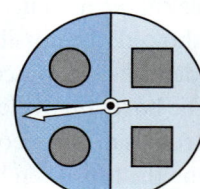

Example 4 Calculating Odds

A bag contains 6 red marbles, 2 yellow marbles, and 1 blue marble.

a. What are the odds of drawing a red marble?

SOLUTION

Look at the favorable outcomes and the unfavorable outcomes.

There are 6 red marbles (favorable outcomes).

There are 3 marbles that are not red (unfavorable outcomes).

The odds of drawing a red marble are 6:3 or 2:1.

b. What are the odds against drawing a blue marble?

SOLUTION

Look at the favorable and the unfavorable outcomes.

There are 8 marbles that are not blue (unfavorable outcome).

There is 1 blue marble (favorable outcome).

The odds against drawing a blue marble are 8:1.

Hint
The sum of the favorable and unfavorable outcomes should be the same as the total possible outcomes.

Example 5 Solving Multi-Step Problems Involving Probability

Isaac has 6 blue and 4 white shirts in his closet. There are also 2 pairs of navy pants and 3 pairs of khaki pants in his closet.

a. What is the probability Isaac will choose khaki pants and a white shirt from his closet?

SOLUTION

$P(\text{khaki pants}) = \frac{3}{5}$

$P(\text{white shirt}) = \frac{4}{10} = \frac{2}{5}$

$P(\text{khaki pants and white shirt}) = \frac{3}{5} \cdot \frac{2}{5} = \frac{6}{25}$

b. Assume that after the pants and shirt are worn, they are put in the laundry hamper. What is the probability that he will choose khaki pants and a white shirt from the closet to wear the next day?

SOLUTION

$P(\text{khaki pants}) = \frac{2}{4} = \frac{1}{2}$

$P(\text{white shirt}) = \frac{3}{9} = \frac{1}{3}$

$P(\text{khaki pants and white shirt}) = \frac{1}{2} \cdot \frac{1}{3} = \frac{1}{6}$

Example 4

Students calculate odds of an event happening. Point out that the odds for an event and the odds against an event are reciprocals of each other.

Error Alert If students have difficulty simplifying odds to lowest terms, remind them to divide both terms of the ratio by the greatest common factor.

Additional Example 4
A box contains 3 pink, 4 yellow, and 5 blue highlighters. One highlighter is chosen at random.

a. What are the odds of choosing a yellow highlighter? 4:8 or 1:2

b. What are the odds against choosing a blue highlighter? 7:5

Example 5

Students solve a two-step probability problem. Point out how the probability of choosing a white shirt changes from 4 out of 10 to 3 out of 9 after one shirt is put in the laundry. Ask students how the probability of choosing khaki pants changes. Sample: First it is 3 out of 5; then it is 2 out of 4.

Additional Example 5
The computer club has 10 boys and 12 girls. The chess club has 15 boys and 5 girls. Each club will chose a member at random to be club treasurer.

a. What is the probability that both treasurers will be girls? $\frac{3}{22}$

b. Both girls resign and a different pair of students is chosen. What is the probability that both treasurers will again be girls? $\frac{44}{399}$

Lesson Practice

Problem f
Scaffolding Review the steps in solving the problem: (1) Find the probability of drawing red on the first draw; (2) Find the probability of drawing red on the second draw; (3) Multiply the two fractions from the preceding steps.

Problem h
Error Alert Students may compute probability instead of odds. Contrast odds with probability. With odds, the sum of the numerator and denominator in the unreduced ratio will equal the total number of outcomes. With probability, the denominator will equal the total number of outcomes.

Problem j
Emphasize that the activities are chosen at random. If students have trouble understanding the conditions of the problem, have them create a tree diagram to model the situation.

Check for Understanding
The questions below help assess the concepts taught in this lesson.

"How are independent events different from dependent events?" Sample: In independent events, the results of the second event are not affected by what happens in the first event.

"What is the difference between finding a probability and finding odds?" Sample: Probability is the ratio of the number of outcomes in the event to the number of outcomes in the sample space. Odds for the event is the ratio of the number of favorable outcomes to the number of unfavorable outcomes.

Lesson Practice

Identify each set of events as independent or dependent.

a. (Ex 1) A card is chosen from a deck of cards, replaced, and then a second card is chosen.   **independent**

b. (Ex 1) A marble is drawn from a bag, kept, and then a second marble is drawn.   **dependent**

c. (Ex 1) A coin is flipped, and a number cube is rolled.   **independent**

d. (Ex 1) A spinner is spun and the result is recorded. Then the spinner is spun a second time.   **independent**

e. (Ex 2) A coin is flipped and a six-sided number cube is tossed. Make a tree diagram showing all possible outcomes. What is the probability of landing on tails and on an even number? $\frac{1}{4}$

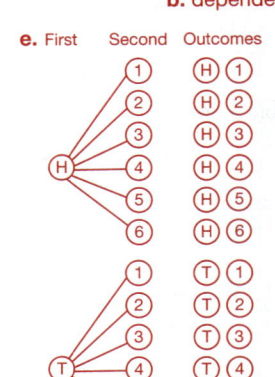

First   Second   Outcomes

A bag contains 4 red blocks and 3 blue blocks. (Ex 3)

f. Find the probability of drawing a red block, keeping it, and then drawing another red block. $\frac{2}{7}$

g. Find the probability of drawing a blue block, keeping it, and then drawing a red block. $\frac{2}{7}$

Use the spinner to answer the problems. (Ex 4)

h. What are the odds of spinning black?   2:6 or 1:3

i. What are the odds against spinning gray?   5:3

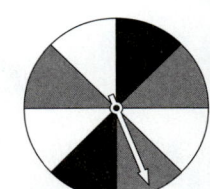

Campers select one inside activity and one outside activity daily. There are 5 inside activities and 8 outside activities. (Ex 5)

j. What is the probability of choosing pottery and horseback riding on the first day? $\frac{1}{40}$

k. Inside activities can be repeated, but outside activities cannot be repeated. What is the probability of choosing pottery and swimming the second day? $\frac{1}{35}$

Caution
The outside events are dependent, so the total number of outcomes changes.

Practice   Distributed and Integrated

Solve.

1. (28) $-5v = 6v + 5 - v$ $v = -\frac{1}{2}$

2. (26) $-3(b + 9) = -6$ $b = -7$

3. (26) $-22 = -p - 12$ $p = 10$

4. (26) $-\frac{2}{5} = -\frac{1}{3}m + \frac{3}{5}$ $m = 3$

5. (31) $\frac{2}{x} = \frac{30}{-6}$ $x = -0.4$

6. (31) $\frac{x-4}{6} = \frac{x+2}{12}$ $x = 10$

Simplify.

7. (32) $\frac{y^6 x^5}{y^5 x^7}$ $\frac{y}{x^2}$

*8. (32) $\frac{w^{-5} z^{-3}}{w^{-3} z^2}$ $\frac{1}{w^2 z^5}$

9. (32) $\frac{4x^2 z^0}{2x^3 z}$ $\frac{2}{xz}$

208   *Saxon Algebra 1*

ENGLISH LEARNERS

Explain what it means to be a **camper.**
Say:

"A camper is a person who spends time in the forest or mountains for enjoyment. Usually campers spend more than 1 day camping, so they sleep in tents." "Campers often go fishing." "What are some other camping activities?" Sample: hiking, cooking, swimming

*10. **Model** There are 10 little marbles and 4 big marbles in a bag. A big marble is drawn and not replaced. Draw a picture that represents how the contents of the bag change between the first draw and the second draw. 10. Sample:

Before draw / After draw

*11. **Write** Explain the difference between probability and odds.

11. Sample: Probability is the ratio of favorable outcomes to total outcomes (or sample space). Odds is the ratio of favorable to unfavorable outcomes.

*12. **True or False:** Two rolls of a number cube are independent events. true

*13. Is the set of whole numbers closed under subtraction? Explain. No, because $3 - 7 = -4$ and -4 is not a whole number.

*14. **Multiple Choice** A bag contains 3 blue stones, 5 red stones, and 2 white stones. What is the probability of picking a blue stone, keeping it, and then picking a white stone? **B**

   A $\frac{3}{50}$ **B** $\frac{1}{15}$ **C** $\frac{3}{28}$ **D** $\frac{1}{2}$

15. (**Stock Market**) The value of an investor's stock changed by $-1\frac{3}{4}$ points last week. This week the value changed by 3 times as much. How much did the value of the investor's stock change this week? $-5\frac{1}{4}$ points

*16. **Predict** What is the probability of rolling a 3 twice in a row on a six-sided number cube? $\frac{1}{36}$

17. **Write** Give an example of a situation in which someone may want to use large intervals on a graph to persuade people to come to a certain conclusion.

17. Sample: A student who wants to make it appear that test grades have not dropped dramatically could use large intervals on the graph to persuade people to make this conclusion.

*18. **Analyze** Simplify $x^3 \cdot x^{-3}$. What is the mathematical relationship between x^n and x^{-n}? 1; They are reciprocals.

19. (**Time**) A nanosecond is 10^{-9} times as fast as 1 second and a microsecond is 10^{-6} times as fast as 1 second. How much faster is the nanosecond than the microsecond? $10^3 = 1000$ times faster

20. Convert 30 quarts per mile to gallons per mile. 7.5 gal/mi

*21. **Error Analysis** Two students solved the proportion $\frac{5}{9} = \frac{c}{45}$. Which student is correct? Explain the error.

Student A	Student B
$\frac{5}{9} = \frac{c}{45}$	$\frac{5}{9} = \frac{c}{45}$
$9c = 225$	$9c = 225$
$c = 25$	$c = 2025$

Student A; Student B multiplied 9 by 225 instead of dividing 225 by 9.

*22. (**Vehicle Rental**) One moving company charges $19.85 plus $0.20 per mile to rent a van. The company also rents trucks for $24.95 plus $0.17 per mile. At how many miles is the price the same for renting the vehicles? 170 mi

23. If a set of ordered pairs is not a relation, can the set still be a function? Explain. Sample: No, the set cannot be a function because all functions are also relations.

Lesson 33   209

3 Practice

Math Conversations
Discussion to strengthen understanding

Problem 13
Guide the students by asking them the following questions.

"What happens when you subtract a greater number from a smaller one?" You get a negative number.

"Is a negative number a whole number?" no

Problem 17
If students need help getting started, remind them that using large intervals on the vertical axis of a graph will flatten out the graph. Smaller intervals on the vertical axis make the slope seem steeper than the same line graphed using larger intervals.

Problem 22
Guide the students by asking them the following questions.

"What equation shows the cost of renting the van?" $y = 0.2x + 19.85$

"What does x represent in this equation? number of miles driven

"What does y represent in this equation? total cost for renting the van

"What equation shows the cost of renting the truck?" $y = 0.17x + 24.95$

 CHALLENGE

A bag of shapes has 3 circles, 2 squares, and 4 triangles. Three shapes are drawn at random from the bag. The first shape is drawn and is not returned to the bag; the second shape is drawn and is returned to the bag. What is the probability of drawing the shapes in the following order: square, circle, triangle? Show your work. $\frac{2}{9} \cdot \frac{3}{8} \cdot \frac{4}{8} = \frac{1}{24}$

Lesson 33   209

Problem 27

Error Alert

Students may not know how to begin the problem. Point out that there are two ways to solve the problem: find the qualifying average speed r necessary to complete the Boston marathon in $3\frac{2}{3}$ hours, or find the time t it took Jill to finish her last marathon.

Extend the Problem

Greg hopes to finish his next marathon at an average pace of 8 miles per hour. How long, in hours and minutes, will it take him to finish? 3 hours, 16.5 minutes

Problem 29

Extend the Problem

How much fence should he buy if he plans to use the side of the garage for one side of the dog pen? 36 ft

---

24. **Write** Explain how to find the solution of $0.09n + 0.2 = 2.9$.

24. Sample: First multiply each term by 100. Then add –20 to both sides of the equation. Finally divide both sides by 9 to get the answer $n = 30$.

25. **Keeping Cool** The British thermal unit (BTU) is a unit of energy used globally in air conditioning industries. The number of BTUs needed to cool a room depends on the area of the room. To find the number of BTUs recommended for any size room, use the formula $B = 377lw$, where B is the number of BTUs, l is the length of the room, and w is the width of the room. The room you want to cool uses the recomended number of 12,252.5 BTUs and is 5 meters wide. Find the area of the room. 32.5 m²

26. **Multi-Step** A quarterback throws the ball approximately 30 times per game. He has already thrown the ball 125 times this season. The equation $y = 30x + 125$ predicts how many times he will have thrown the ball after x more games.

x	y
2	185
3	215
4	245
5	275

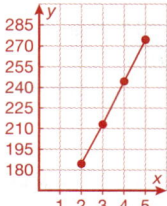

a. Copy and complete the table using a graphing calculator and then graph the solutions.

b. When will he have thrown the ball more than 300 times? after 6 more games

27. **Marathons** A marathon is 26.2 miles long. In order to qualify for the Boston Marathon, Jill must first complete a different marathon within $3\frac{2}{3}$ hours. Her average speed in the last marathon she completed was 7.8 miles per hour. Did she qualify for the Boston Marathon? Explain. yes; Sample: The qualifying average speed is about 7.15 miles per hour.

28. **Geometry** The rectangles shown are similar.

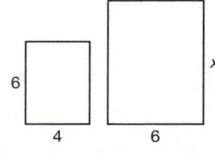

a. Find the ratio of the side lengths of the smaller rectangle to the larger rectangle. $\frac{2}{3}$

b. Find the longer side length of the larger rectangle using proportions. $x = 9$

29. Jack is building a square pen for his dog. If he wants the area of the pen to be 144 square feet, how long should he make each side of the pen? 12 ft

30. True or False: Whole numbers include negative numbers. false

210 Saxon Algebra 1

LOOKING FORWARD

Finding the probability of independent and dependent events prepares students for

- **Lesson 68** Mutually Exclusive and Inclusive Events
- **Lesson 80** Calculating Frequency Distributions
- **Lesson 111** Solving Problems Involving Permutations
- **Lesson 118** Solving Problems Involving Combinations

LESSON 34

Recognizing and Extending Arithmetic Sequences

Warm Up

1. **Vocabulary** Any quantity whose value does not change is called a _____. **constant**

Simplify.

2. $7.2 - 5.8 - (-15)$ **16.4**
3. $-0.12 - (-43.7) - 73.5$ **−29.92**
4. $6(-2.5)$ **−15**
5. $(-15)(-4.2)$ **63**

New Concepts

Sequences of numbers can be formed using a variety of patterns and operations. A **sequence** is a list of numbers that follow a rule, and each number in the sequence is called a **term of the sequence.** Here are a few examples of sequences:

1, 3, 5, 7, …

7, 4, 1, −2, …

2, 6, 18, 54, …

1, 4, 9, 16, …

Math Language

The symbol "..." is an **ellipsis** and is read "and so on." In mathematics, the symbol means the pattern continues without end.

In the above examples, the first two sequences are a special type of sequence called an arithmetic sequence. An **arithmetic sequence** is a sequence that has a constant difference between two consecutive terms called the **common difference.**

To find the common difference, choose any term and subtract the previous term. In the first sequence above, the common difference is 2, while in the second sequence, the common difference is −3.

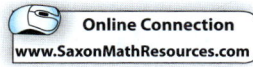  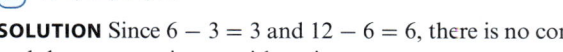

If the sequence does not have a common difference, then it is not arithmetic.

Example 1 Recognizing Arithmetic Sequences

Determine if each sequence is an arithmetic sequence. If yes, find the common difference and the next two terms.

a. 7, 12, 17, 22, …

SOLUTION Since $12 - 7 = 5$, $17 - 12 = 5$, and $22 - 17 = 5$, the sequence is arithmetic with a common difference of 5. The next two terms are $22 + 5 = 27$ and $27 + 5 = 32$.

b. 3, 6, 12, 24, …

SOLUTION Since $6 - 3 = 3$ and $12 - 6 = 6$, there is no common difference and the sequence is not arithmetic.

Lesson 34   211

MATH BACKGROUND

The general term a_n of a sequence can be specified by an explicit formula which gives a_n as a function of n, or by a recursive formula expressing a_n as a function of the preceding term a_{n-1}. Adjacent terms in an arithmetic sequence, also called an arithmetic progression, are related by a common difference. The terms between two given terms of an arithmetic sequence are called the arithmetic means between the given terms. A single arithmetic mean between two numbers is the average of those numbers.

In the sequence $4, 2, 1, \frac{1}{2}, \frac{1}{4}, \frac{1}{8}, \ldots$, each term is half of the previous term. The terms are getting closer and closer to 0, so we say the limit of the sequence is 0. An infinite sequence with a limit is said to converge or be convergent. An infinite sequence that does not have a limit is divergent.

TEACHER TIP

Students are shown the subscript notation a_n for indicating the nth term of a sequence. An alternative notation uses parentheses, with $a(1)$ representing the first term and $a(n)$ representing the nth term. Some students may find the parentheses easier to use than the subscripts.

Example 2

Students use the initial term and the common difference to write four terms of an arithmetic sequence. Emphasize that the common difference d can be any real number, positive or negative. The text presents the recursive formula $a_n = a_{n-1} + d$. The formula $a_{n+1} = a_n + d$ can also be used. If it is helpful to students, have them compare the two formulas.

Additional Example 2

Use a recursive formula to find the first four terms of an arithmetic sequence where $a_1 = 5$ and the common difference $d = -8$. **5, −3, −11, −19**

The first term of a sequence is denoted as a_1, the second term as a_2, the third term a_3, and so on. The nth term of an arithmetic sequence is denoted a_n. The term preceding a_n is denoted a_{n-1}. For example, if $n = 6$, then the term preceding a_6 is a_{6-1} or a_5.

Term Number (n)	Term	Sequence Pattern	Description
1	1st or a_1	7	a_1
2	2nd or a_2	$(7) + 4$	$a_1 + d$
3	3rd or a_3	$(7 + 4) + 4$	$a_2 + d$
4	4th or a_4	$(7 + 4 + 4) + 4$	$a_3 + d$
5	5th or a_5	$(7 + 4 + 4 + 4) + 4$	$a_4 + d$
n	n^{th} or a_n	$a_{n-1} + 4$	$a_{n-1} + d$

Math Reasoning

Generalize Give an example of an arithmetic sequence. State the first 4 terms and the common difference.

Sample: 6, 9, 12, 15, …; The common difference is 3.

Arithmetic sequences can be represented using a formula.

Arithmetic Sequence Formula

Use the formula below to find the next term in a sequence.

$$a_n = a_{n-1} + d$$

a_1 = first term
d = common difference
n = term number

In the arithmetic sequence 7, 11, 15, 19, …, $a_1 = 7$, $a_2 = 11$, $a_3 = 15$, and $a_4 = 19$. The common difference is 4.

Example 2 Using a Recursive Formula

Use a recursive formula to find the first four terms of an arithmetic sequence where $a_1 = -2$ and the common difference $d = 7$.

SOLUTION

$a_n = a_{n-1} + d$	Write the formula.
$a_n = a_{n-1} + 7$	Substitute 7 for d.
$a_1 = -2$	Write the first term.
$a_2 = -2 + 7 = 5$	Find the second term.
$a_3 = 5 + 7 = 12$	Find the third term.
$a_4 = 12 + 7 = 19$	Find the fourth term.

The first four terms of the sequence are −2, 5, 12, and 19.

A rule for finding any term in an arithmetic sequence can be developed by looking at a different pattern in the sequence 7, 11, 15, 19, ….

212 *Saxon* Algebra 1

⚠ ALTERNATE METHOD FOR EXAMPLE 2

Illustrate finding the terms of an arithmetic sequence using this diagram:

Have students copy the diagram and fill in the boxes. Make sure that students include the labels a_1, a_2, a_3, and a_4 to emphasize that $a_n = a_{n-1} + 7$.

eL ENGLISH LEARNERS

Discuss the meaning of the word **recursive**. Draw a pattern of a bouncing ball on the chalkboard. Say:

"If something is recursive, then it repeats itself. For example, the path of a bouncing ball makes a recursive pattern."

Ask students to give other examples using the word recursive. Sample: When a stone is thrown into water, the ripples make a recursive pattern.

Math Reasoning

Write Explain the difference between a^1 and a_1.

Sample: a^1 is read "a to the first power" and simplifies to a while a_1 is read "a sub one" and means the first term of an arithmetic sequence.

Term	Term Number (n)	Sequence Pattern	Description
1st or a_1	1	7	a_1
2nd or a_2	2	$7 + 4 = 7 + (1)4$	$a_1 + (1)d$
3rd or a_3	3	$7 + 4 + 4 = 7 + (2)4$	$a_1 + (2)d$
4th or a_4	4	$7 + 4 + 4 + 4 = 7 + (3)4$	$a_1 + (3)d$
5th or a_5	5	$7 + 4 + 4 + 4 + 4 = 7 + 4(4)$	$a_1 + (4)d$
nth or a_n	n	$7 + (n - 1)4$	$a_1 + (n - 1)d$

Finding the nth Term of an Arithmetic Sequence

$$a_n = a_1 + (n - 1)d$$

$a_1 =$ first term $\quad d =$ common difference

Example 3 Finding the nth Term in Arithmetic Sequences

a. Use the rule $a_n = 6 + (n - 1)2$ to find the 4th and 11th terms of the sequence.

SOLUTION

4th term:
$a_4 = 6 + (4 - 1)2$
$= 6 + (3)2$
$= 6 + 6$
$= 12$

11th term:
$a_{11} = 6 + (11 - 1)2$
$= 6 + (10)2$
$= 6 + 20$
$= 26$

b. Find the 10th term of the sequence 3, 11, 19, 27, ...

SOLUTION

$a_1 = 3$ and the common difference $d = 11 - 3 = 8$

$a_n = 3 + (n - 1)8 \quad$ Write the rule, substituting for a, and d.
$a_{10} = 3 + (10 - 1)8 \quad$ Substitute the value for n.
$a_{10} = 75 \quad$ Simplify using the order of operations.

c. Find the 10th term of the sequence $\frac{1}{4}, \frac{3}{4}, \frac{5}{4}, \frac{7}{4}, ...$

SOLUTION

$a_1 = \frac{1}{4}$ and $d = \frac{3}{4} - \frac{1}{4} = \frac{2}{4} = \frac{1}{2}$

$a_n = \frac{1}{4} + (n - 1)\frac{1}{2} \quad$ Write the rule, substituting for a, and d.
$a_{10} = \frac{1}{4} + (10 - 1)\frac{1}{2} \quad$ Substitute the value for n.
$a_{10} = \frac{19}{4} \quad$ Simplify using the order of operations.

Example 3

Students use the explicit formula $a_n = a_1 + (n - 1)d$ to find the nth term of an arithmetic sequence.

Error Alert When students are using the formula $a_n = a_1 + (n - 1)d$, emphasize that they follow the order of operations.

TEACHER TIP

Contrast the formulas $a_n = a_1 + (n - 1)d$ and $a_n = a_{n-1} + d$ with students. The latter is a rule showing how to use any term in the sequence to compute the next term provided that d is given. The former provides a way to compute any term given a_1, n, and d.

Additional Example 3

a. Use the rule $a_n = -5 + (n - 1)(-2)$ to find the 8th and 20th terms of the sequence. $-19, -43$

b. Find the 12th term of the sequence 3, 10, 17, ... 80

c. Find the 45th term of the sequence 3, $3\frac{1}{4}$, $3\frac{1}{2}$, $3\frac{3}{4}$, ... 14

Lesson 34   213

🛆 INCLUSION

Explain how the formulas $a_n = a_{n-1} + d$ and $a_n = a_1 + (n - 1)d$ work and what the variables mean using a familiar sequence such as the even numbers. Put this chart on the board.

Even Numbers

Term	2	4	6	8	10
Term Name	a_1	a_2	a_3	a_4	a_5
Place in Sequence	1st	2nd	3rd	4th	5th
Term Number	1	2	3	4	5

Help students read the subscripted variables $a_1, a_2, a_3,$ etc. Explain that a_1 is read "a-sub-one." Then add 5 blank columns to the right of the chart. Have students fill them in beginning with the 6th term. Introduce the idea of using nth to name any place in the sequence and a_n to name any term. Use the chart for additional practice on the notation and vocabulary. Ask questions such as, "What is a-sub-four?" and "What is the third term?"

Lesson 34   213

Example 4

Students use the *n*th term, or explicit, formula to solve a problem about an arithmetic sequence. Have students begin by identifying the initial term and the common difference. $a_1 = 9$, $d = 6$

Error Alert Students may find all the terms in the sequence to solve the problem rather than use the formula. Emphasize that finding the *n*th term for large values of *n* may be difficult if students do not learn to use the formula $a_n = a_1 + (n - 1)d$.

Extend the Example

If the first table seats 9 guests and each additional table seats 6 guests, how many tables do you need for 201 guests? (Hint: Use the formula $a_n = a_1 + (n - 1)d$ and solve for *n*.) 33 tables

Additional Example 4

The first table seats 10 guests and each additional table seats 8 guests.

a. Write a rule to model the situation. $a_n = 10 + (n - 1)8$

b. Use the rule to find how many guests can be seated with 15 tables. 122

Lesson Practice

Problem b

Error Alert Remind students that unless all of the differences between adjacent terms are the same, the sequence is not arithmetic. Have them find the differences until they find two that are not equal.

Problem g

Scaffolding Have students identify the first term 12 and the common difference 6. Then have them write the formula, substituting the values for a_1 and d. Last, solve for a_{15}.

214   Saxon Algebra 1

Math Reasoning

Verify Is the sequence $-1, -5, -9, -13, \ldots$ an arithmetic sequence?

Sample:
$-5 - (-1) = -4$,
$-9 - (-5) = -4$,
$-13 - (-9) = -4$;
The sequence is arithmetic. It has a common difference of -4.

a. yes; common difference $= -1$; 3, 2

Example 4 **Application: Seating for a Reception**

The first table at a reception will seat 9 guests while each additional table will seat 6 more guests.

a. Write a rule to model the situation.

SOLUTION $a_1 = 9$ and $d = 6$. The rule is $a_n = 9 + (n - 1)6$.

b. Use the rule to find how many guests can be seated with 10 tables.

SOLUTION

$a_n = 9 + (n - 1)6$

$a_{10} = 9 + (10 - 1)6$

$a_{10} = 63$

63 guests can be seated with 10 tables.

Lesson Practice

Determine if each sequence is an arithmetic sequence. If yes, find the common difference and the next two terms.

a. 7, 6, 5, 4, ... *(Ex 1)*   **b.** 10, 12, 15, 19, ...   no

c. Use a recursive formula to find the first four terms of an arithmetic *(Ex 2)* sequence where $a_1 = -3$ and the common difference $d = 4$. $-3, 1, 5, 9$

d. Use the rule $a_n = 14 + (n - 1)(-3)$ to find the 4th and 11th terms of an *(Ex 3)* arithmetic sequence.   4th term: 5; 11th term: -16

e. Find the 10th term of the sequence 1, 10, 19, 28, ... $a_{10} = 82$ *(Ex 3)*

f. Find the 11th term of the sequence $\frac{2}{3}, 1, 1\frac{1}{3}, 1\frac{2}{3}, \ldots$ $a_{11} = 4$ *(Ex 3)*

Flowers are purchased to put on tables at a reception. The head table needs to have 12 flowers and the other tables need to have 6 flowers each. *(Ex 4)*

g. Write a rule to model the situation. $a_n = 12 + (n - 1)6$

h. Use the rule to find the number of flowers needed for 15 tables.   96

Practice   Distributed and Integrated

Solve each proportion

1. $\frac{2}{10} = \frac{x}{-20}$ $x = -4$ *(31)*

2. $\frac{32}{4} = \frac{x + 4}{3}$ $x = 20$ *(31)*

*3. **(Construction)** An amphitheater with tiered rows is being constructed. The first row *(34)* will have 24 seats and each row after that will have an additional 2 seats. If there will be a total of 15 rows, how many seats will be in the last row?   52 seats

214   Saxon Algebra 1

ALTERNATE METHOD FOR EXAMPLE 4

Have students solve the problem using the recursive formula $a_n = a_{n-1} + d$.

$a_n = a_{n-1} + d$

$a_2 = 9 + 6 = 15$

$a_3 = 15 + 6 = 21$

$a_4 = 21 + 6 = 27$

$a_5 = 27 + 6 = 33$

$a_6 = 33 + 6 = 39$

$a_7 = 39 + 6 = 45$

$a_8 = 45 + 6 = 51$

$a_9 = 51 + 6 = 57$

$a_{10} = 57 + 6 = 63$

63 guests can be seated at 10 tables.

*4. Use a graphing calculator to complete the table of values for the function $f(x) = 2x^2 - 5$. Graph the function.
(30)

x	y
-2	3
-1	-3
0	-5
1	-3
2	3

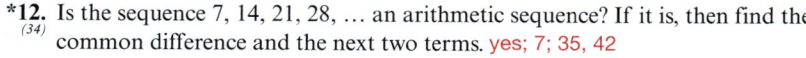

*5. Solve $y = x + \frac{z}{3}$ for z. $z = 3(y - x)$
(29)

Solve each equation. Check your answer.

6. $4x + 2 = 5(x + 10)$ $x = -48$
(28)

7. $2\left(n + \frac{1}{3}\right) = \frac{3}{2}n + 1 + \frac{1}{2}n - \frac{1}{3}$ all real numbers
(28)

8. A bead is drawn from a bag, kept, and then a second bead is drawn. Identify these events as independent or dependent.   dependent
(33)

*9. **Justify** Is the sequence 0.3, −0.5, −1.3, −2.1, … an arithmetic sequence? Justify your answer.   yes; The sequence has a common difference of −0.8.
(34)

*10. **Write** Explain why the sequence 2, 4, 8, 12, 16, … is not an arithmetic sequence.   10. Sample: The first two terms have a difference of 2 while all of the other terms have a difference of 4.
(34)

*11. **Multiple Choice** In the rule for the nth term of an arithmetic sequence $a_n = a_1 + (n - 1)d$, what does d represent?   **D**
(34)
A the number of terms   **B** the first term
C the nth term   **D** the common difference

*12. Is the sequence 7, 14, 21, 28, … an arithmetic sequence? If it is, then find the common difference and the next two terms.   yes; 7; 35, 42
(34)

13. **Statistics** A poll is taken and each person is asked two questions. The results are shown in the table. What is the probability that someone answered "yes" to both questions? $\frac{33}{200}$
(33)

	Question 1	Question 2
Yes	55	30
No	45	70

14. **Predict** A number cube labeled 1–6 is rolled two times. What is the probability of rolling a 2 and then a 3? $\frac{1}{36}$
(33)

*15. **Geometry** A rectangle with perimeter 10 units has a length of 3 units and a width of 2 units. Additional rectangles are added as shown below.
(34)

 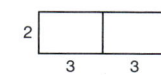 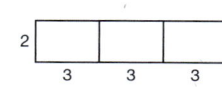 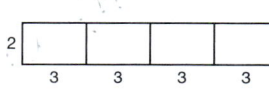

P = 10 units   P = 16 units   P = 22 units   P = 28 units

a. Write a rule for the perimeter of n rectangles. $a_n = 10 + (n - 1)6$
b. Use the rule to find the perimeter of 12 rectangles.   76

*16. Work uniforms include pants or a skirt, a shirt, and a tie or a vest. There are 3 pairs of pants, 5 skirts, 10 shirts, 2 ties, and 1 vest in a wardrobe.
(33)
a. What is the probability of choosing a pair of pants, a shirt, and a tie? $\frac{1}{4}$
b. The pants and shirt from the previous day must be washed, but the tie returns to the wardrobe. What is the probability of choosing pants, a shirt, and a tie the next day? $\frac{4}{21}$

Lesson 34   215

Problem 17
Error Alert
If students divide 6 by 4, they may need a review of the meaning of negative exponents. Remind them that the definition of c^{-2} is $\frac{1}{c^2}$. So, it is also true that $\frac{1}{c^{-2}} = c^2$.

Problem 23
Guide the students by asking them the following questions.

"Is the tuition increasing or decreasing?" increasing

"If you used 5000-dollar intervals on the vertical axis, what would happen to the graph?" It would appear that the tuition was increasing more quickly because the line on the graph would look steeper.

"Does changing the intervals on the vertical axis change the rate at which the tuition increases? Explain." No. It just changes the way the graph looks.

Problem 27
Suggest that students first write an equation for the situation using w for the number of weeks and s for the total savings.
$s = (612.50 - 250)w + 400$

Students can then substitute 5500 for s, solve for the number of weeks w, and convert weeks to months.

---

17. Evaluate the expression $d = 6 \cdot \frac{1}{c^{-2}}$ for $c = 2$.   24
(32)

18. (Physical Science) The wavelengths of microwaves can range from 10^{-3} m to 10^{-1} m.
(32) Express the range of wavelengths using positive exponents. $\frac{1}{10}$m to $\frac{1}{10^3}$m

20. yes; Sample: For every value of x, there is only one value of y. A vertical line drawn through the graph of the equation also strikes the graph only once.

19. **Multiple Choice** Ms. Markelsden baked 36 cookies in 45 minutes. How many cookies
(31) can she bake in 3 hours?   **D**

  A 45 cookies   **B** 81 cookies
  C 64 cookies   **D** 144 cookies

20. Does $y = x^2 + 2$ represent a function? Explain how you know.
(30)

21. (Architecture) A model of a building is 15 inches tall. In the scale drawing, 1 inch
(31) represents 20 feet. How tall is the building?   300 feet

*22. **Generalize** Given $\frac{2}{b} = \frac{1}{a}$, where a and b are positive numbers, write an equation
(31) that shows how to find a. $a = \frac{b}{2}$

23. The line graph at right shows the costs of tuition at a
(27) university over the past 5 years. How might this graph be misleading?   Sample: The increments are large, making the increase in tuition costs seem less than they actually are.

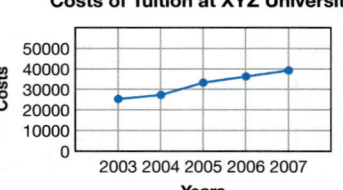

Costs of Tuition at XYZ University

24. **Write** The equation $x + 5 = x - 5$ has no solution. Explain
(28) why it has no solution.   Sample: The resulting equation $5 = -5$ is a false statement.

25. **Verify** Solve $16x + 4(2x - 6) = 60$ for x. Check your answer.
(26) $x = 3.5$; $16(3.5) + 4(2(3.5) - 6) = 56 + 4(7 - 6) = 56 + 4 = 60$

26. True or False: Any irrational number divided by an irrational number will be
(1) an irrational number. Explain your answer.   false; Sample: $\sqrt{5} \div \sqrt{5} = 1$; Any number divided by itself, even an irrational number, will equal 1.

27. (Savings) Hector has $400 in his savings account. Each week he deposits his $612.50
(23) paycheck and takes out $250 to live on for the week. If he wants to buy a car for $5500, about how many months will it take him to save up for the car?
$612.50x - 250x + 400 = 5500$; It will take about 4 months.

28. **Multi-Step** Jamal is riding his bike at a rate of about 8 miles per hour. How many
(31) hours will it take Jamal to ride 50 miles? $8t = 50$: It will take him about $6\frac{1}{4}$ hours.

29. (Car Rental) A family rented a car that cost $45 per day plus $0.23 per mile. If the
(24) family rented the car for 7 days and paid $395.50 altogether, how many miles did they drive?   350 miles

30. **Error Analysis** Two students determine whether the ordered pairs in the table
(25) represent a function. Which student is correct? Explain the error.

Student A	Student B
(7, 12) and (7, 10) The x-values are the same, so it is not a function.	All the y-values are different, so it is not a function.

x	y
7	10
−2	−3
7	12
5	4

Student A; Sample: Student B confused the dependent and independent variables.

216   *Saxon* Algebra 1

CHALLENGE

Present this formula for the sum of the first n terms of an arithmetic sequence with first term a_1 and nth term a_n:

$$S_n = \frac{n}{2}(a_1 + a_n)$$

"Find the sum of the positive integers less than 100 and divisible by 6. Explain your solution."   816; Sample: The sequence is 6, 12, 18, . . . , 96. Since $96 \div 6 = 16$, there are 16 terms in the sequence. Students should use the formula with $n = 16$, $a_1 = 6$, and $a_n = 96$.

LOOKING FORWARD

Recognizing and extending arithmetic sequences prepares students for

• **Investigation 4** Using Deductive and Inductive Reasoning

• **Lesson 41** Finding Rates of Change and Slope

• **Lesson 56** Identifying, Writing, and Graphing Direct Variation

• **Investigation 7** Comparing Direct and Inverse Variation

LESSON 35

Locating and Using Intercepts

Warm Up

1. **Vocabulary** A pair of numbers that can be used to locate a point on a coordinate plane is called a(n) _____.   ordered pair

Evaluate.

2. $3x + 14; x = -9$ -13

3. $7.5w - 84.3; w = 15$ 28.2

Solve.

4. $7x - 18 = -74$ -8

5. $57 + 19y = -76$ -7

New Concepts

Linear equations can be graphed by making a table of ordered pairs that satisfy the equation and then graphing the corresponding points (x, y). An ordered pair or set of ordered pairs that satisfy an equation is called the **solution of a linear equation in two variables.** When an equation is in standard form, the linear equation can be graphed another way.

Math Language

An **ordered pair** can be used to locate a point on a coordinate plane.

Standard Form of a Linear Equation
The **standard form of a linear equation** is $Ax + By = C$, where A, B, and C are real numbers and A and B are not both zero.

The x-coordinate of the point where the graph of an equation intersects the x-axis is called the **x-intercept**. The y-coordinate of the point where the graph of an equation intersects the y-axis is called the **y-intercept**. The coordinate pairs $(x, 0)$ and $(0, y)$ that satisfy a linear equation are two solutions of the linear equation in two variables.

Example 1   Finding x- and y-Intercepts

Find the x- and y-intercepts for $3x + 4y = 24$.

SOLUTION

To find the intercepts, make a table. Substitute 0 for y and solve for x. Substitute 0 for x and solve for y.

$3x + 4y = 24$ $3x + 4y = 24$
$3x + 4(0) = 24$ $3(0) + 4y = 24$
$3x = 24$ $4y = 24$
$\frac{3x}{3} = \frac{24}{3}$ $\frac{4y}{4} = \frac{24}{4}$
$x = 8$ $y = 6$

x	y
8	0
0	6

The x-intercept is 8. The y-intercept is 6.

---

1 Warm Up

Problems 4 and 5
Remind students to solve the equations using inverse operations.

2 New Concepts

In this lesson, students learn to find the x- and y-intercepts of a linear equation algebraically, to locate them on a graph, and to use them to graph a linear equation.

Example 1

The x-intercept is the x-coordinate of a point that lies on the x-axis. The y-intercept is the y-coordinate of a point that lies on the y-axis.

Additional Example 1
Find the x- and y-intercepts for $2x + 5y = 10$. The x-intercept is 5. The y-intercept is 2.

TEACHER TIP

To quickly find the y-intercept, cover the x-term with a pencil or finger so that only the y-term is visible. Solve for y. Then cover the y-term and solve for x to find the x-intercept.

Lesson 35   217

MATH BACKGROUND

Equations of the form

$$Ax + By = C$$
$$y = mx + b,$$

where A, B, C, m, and b are real numbers, are linear. The graphs of such equations with only two variables are always two-dimensional, and each dimension is represented by a variable.

When A or B is zero, the graph of such an equation still exists on the coordinate plane. The line is either horizontal (when the x-term is missing) or vertical (when the y-term is missing). After students become proficient with the 2-dimensional coordinate plane, they will be prepared to learn about adding a third variable to work in three dimensions.

LESSON RESOURCES

Student Edition Practice Workbook 35
Reteaching Master 35
Adaptations Master 35
Challenge and Enrichment Master C35

Example 2

Point out that any two points on the coordinate plane define a line. The x- and y-intercepts give two ordered pairs that are easy to find and graph.

Additional Example 2

Graph $3x - 7y = 21$ using the x- and y-intercepts.

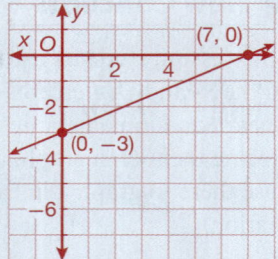

Error Alert When graphing a linear equation, remind students to draw arrowheads at both ends of the line since the line extends out to the entire coordinate plane.

Example 3

By convention, the horizontal axis is the x-axis and the vertical axis is the y-axis.

Additional Example 3

Find the x- and y-intercepts on the graph. The x-intercept is −2. The y-intercept is 9.

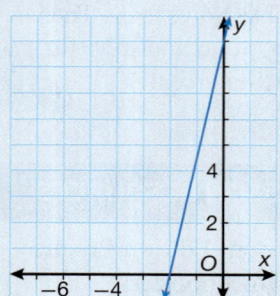

An efficient method for graphing a linear equation in two variables is to plot the x- and y-intercepts and then to draw a line through them.

Example 2 Graphing Using the x- and y-Intercepts

Graph $5x - 6y = 30$ using the x- and y-intercepts.

Math Reasoning

Write Explain why the y-value of the x-intercept is 0 and the x-value of the y-intercept is 0.

Sample: The x-intercept is on the x-axis. Every point on the x-axis has a y-value of 0. The y-intercept is on the y-axis. Every point on the y-axis has an x-value of 0.

SOLUTION

To find the intercepts, make a table. Substitute 0 for y and solve for x. Substitute 0 for x and solve for y.

$$5x - 6y = 30 \qquad\qquad 5x - 6y = 30$$
$$5x - 6(0) = 30 \qquad\quad 5(0) - 6y = 30$$
$$5x = 30 \qquad\qquad\qquad -6y = 30$$
$$\frac{5x}{5} = \frac{30}{5} \qquad\qquad\quad \frac{-6y}{-6} = \frac{30}{-6}$$
$$x = 6 \qquad\qquad\qquad\quad y = -5$$

x	y
6	0
0	−5

The x-intercept is 6. The y-intercept is −5.

To graph the equation, plot the points $(6, 0)$ and $(0, -5)$. Then draw a line through them.

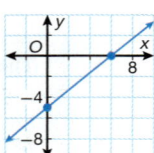

Example 3 Locating x- and y-Intercepts on a Graph

Caution

The interval used on the x- and y-axis varies. Check the labels before naming the coordinates of a point.

Find the x- and y-intercepts on the graph.

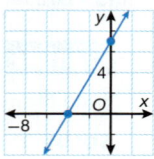

SOLUTION

The x-intercept is the x-coordinate of the point where the line crosses the x-axis. The point where the line crosses the x-axis is $(-4, 0)$. The x-intercept is −4.

The y-intercept is the y-coordinate of the point where the line crosses the y-axis. The point where the line crosses the y-axis is $(0, 7)$. The y-intercept is 7.

ENGLISH LEARNERS

Explain the meaning of the words **intercept** and **intersect.** If possible, show students a drawing or photograph of a soccer or football player intercepting a pass. Say:

"**Intercept means to mark or gain possession of. Intersect means to cross or to cut. If a ball intersects the path of a player, the ball may be intercepted.**"

Have volunteers use the words in sentences describing real-world situations. Sample: Two streets intersect. A football player intercepts a forward.

Any linear equation can be rearranged into standard form. Put both variables and their coefficients on one side of the equal sign and the constants on the other side.

Example 4 Using Standard Form to Graph

Write the equation $y = -\frac{2}{3}x + 5$ in standard form. Then graph the equation using the x- and y-intercepts.

SOLUTION

Write the equation in standard form.

$$y = -\frac{2}{3}x + 5$$

$$+\frac{2}{3}x = +\frac{2}{3}x$$

$$\frac{2}{3}x + y = 5$$

To find the x-intercept, substitute 0 for y and solve for x.

$$\frac{2}{3}x + y = 5$$

$$\frac{2}{3}x + 0 = 5$$

$$\frac{2}{3}x = 5$$

$$\left(\frac{3}{2}\right)\frac{2}{3}x = 5\left(\frac{3}{2}\right)$$

$$x = 7\frac{1}{2}$$

The x-intercept is $7\frac{1}{2}$.

To find the y-intercept, substitute 0 for x and solve for y.

$$\frac{2}{3}x + y = 5$$

$$\frac{2}{3}(0) + y = 5$$

$$y = 5$$

The y-intercept is 5.

Graph the x- and y-intercepts and draw a line through them.

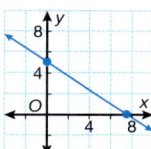

> **Hint**
> Use inverse operations to write the equation so that both variables are on the same side.

Example 4

Graphing lines using the x- and y-intercepts will prepare students for finding and using the slope of a line.

Additional Example 4

Write the equation $y = -\frac{1}{2}x + 4$ in standard form. Then graph the equation using the x- and y-intercepts. $x + 2y = 8$; The x-intercept is 8. The y-intercept is 4.

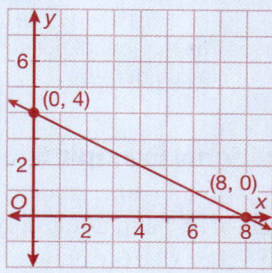

TEACHER TIP

Plot one point on a chalkboard or overhead grid and show students that many lines can be drawn through one point. Emphasize that any two points on the coordinate plane define a unique line. The x- and y-intercepts are two ordered pairs that are easy to find and graph.

Lesson 35 219

ALTERNATE METHOD FOR EXAMPLE 4

Have students graph the equation $y = -\frac{2}{3}x + 5$ using any two points other than the x- and y-intercepts. Encourage them to use negative and positive values of x.

Students can substitute any number for x and solve for y. However, since x is multiplied by $-\frac{2}{3}$, picking multiples of 3 can make evaluating y much easier.

Have students copy and complete the table.

x	y
-3	7
3	3
6	1

Have students locate the intercepts on the graph and confirm that they are the same as those that were found in the example.

Lesson 35 219

Example 5

Remind students that when solving word problems, it is necessary to think about whether negative and fractional numbers are reasonable solutions.

Extend the Example

"Could the drama club member have sold the same number of adult and student tickets? Explain." No. Substituting x for y and solving for x results in $x = \frac{400}{13}$, which is not a whole number. The number of tickets must be a whole number.

Additional Example 5

At a football game, student tickets are $3 and adult tickets are $5. Let x be the number of student tickets sold. Let y be the number of adult tickets sold. The equation $3x + 5y = 630$ shows that $630 was raised from ticket sales. Find the intercepts and explain what each means. $x = 210$, $y = 126$; If only students attended the game, 210 tickets were sold. If only adults attended the game, 126 tickets were sold.

Lesson Practice

Problem b

Scaffolding Suggest that students create a table with $x = 0$ and $y = 0$. Then have them plot the two points and draw a line through them.

Problem e

Error Alert Some students may switch the solutions for x and y. Encourage them to check their work by substituting the values into the equation.

220   *Saxon* Algebra 1

Example 5 Application: Play Tickets

At a school play, student tickets are $5 and adult tickets are $8. Let x be the number of student tickets sold. Let y be the number of adult tickets sold. The equation $5x + 8y = 400$ shows that one drama club member raised $400 from ticket sales. Find the intercepts and explain what each means.

SOLUTION

> **Math Reasoning**
>
> **Verify** Use the facts of the problem to show that the solution is correct.
>
> The members raised $400 in ticket sales. 80 student tickets at $5 each equals $400. 50 adult tickets at $8 each equals $400.

Substitute 0 for y and solve for x. Then substitute 0 for x and solve for y.

$$5x + 8y = 400 \qquad\qquad 5x + 8y = 400$$
$$5x + 8(0) = 400 \qquad\qquad 5(0) + 8y = 400$$
$$5x = 400 \qquad\qquad 8y = 400$$
$$\frac{5x}{5} = \frac{400}{5} \qquad\qquad \frac{8y}{8} = \frac{400}{8}$$
$$x = 80 \qquad\qquad y = 50$$

The x-intercept is 80. The y-intercept is 50.

The x-intercept shows that if the drama club member sold no adult tickets, 80 student tickets were sold. The y-intercept shows that if no student tickets were sold, 50 adult tickets were sold.

Lesson Practice

a. Find the x- and y-intercepts for $-6x + 9y = 36$.   The x-intercept is –6 and
   (Ex 1)   the y-intercept is 4.

b. Graph $4x + 7y = 28$ using the x- and
   (Ex 2) y-intercepts.

c. Find the x- and y-intercepts on the graph.   The x-intercept is –8 and
   (Ex 3)   the y-intercept is –9.

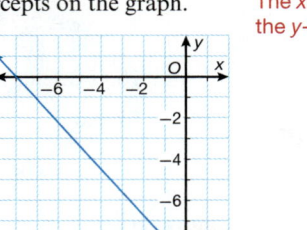

d. Write $4y = 12x - 12$ in standard form. Then graph the equation using
   (Ex 4) the x- and y-intercepts.

e. (**Athletics**) Hirva jogs 6 miles per hour and bikes 12 miles per hour. The
   (Ex 5) equation $6x + 12y = 24$ shows that she has gone a total of 24 miles.
   Find the intercepts and explain what each means.   The x-intercept is 4 and the y-intercept is 2. They mean that to go 24 miles by one mode, she could run for 4 hours or bike for 2 hours.

b.

d. $-12x + 4y = -12$

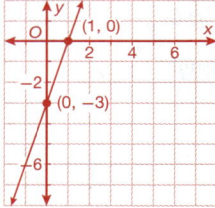

INCLUSION

Have students work in pairs. Using coordinate grids, have each student choose a point on the x-axis and a point on the y-axis and draw a line through the points. Then have them trade grids and identify the x- and y-intercepts on the lines drawn by their partner.

Practice Distributed and Integrated

Solve.

1. (31) $\dfrac{-2.25}{x} = \dfrac{9}{6}$ $x = -1.5$

*2. (31) $\dfrac{y+2}{y+7} = \dfrac{11}{31}$ $y = \dfrac{3}{4}$

3. (28) $2(f+3) + 4f = 6 + 6f$ all real numbers

4. (28) $3x + 7 - 2x = 4x + 10$ $x = -1$

Evaluate each expression for the given value of the variable.

5. (9) $(m + 6) \div (2 - 5)$ for $m = 9$ -5

6. (9) $-3(x + 12 \cdot 2)$ for $x = -8$ -48

Simplify by combining like terms.

7. (18) $10y^3 + 5y - 4y^3$ $6y^3 + 5y$

8. (18) $10xy^2 - 5x^2y + 3y^2x$ $13xy^2 - 5x^2y$

9. (1) Identify the subsets of real numbers to which the number $\sqrt{7}$ belongs.
real numbers, irrational numbers

*10. (35) Find the x- and y-intercepts for $5x + 10y = -20$.   The x-intercept is -4 and the y-intercept is -2.

*11. (35) Find the x- and y-intercepts for $-8x + 20y = 40$.   The x-intercept is -5 and the y-intercept is 2.

*12. (35) **Write** Explain how knowing the x- and y-intercepts is helpful in graphing a linear equation.   Sample: They give you 2 points that are easy to find and graph because they lie on the x- and y-axis.

*13. (35) **Multiple Choice** What is the x-intercept for the equation $15x + 9y = 45$?   **B**
 A $(0, 3)$ B $(3, 0)$ C $(5, 0)$ D $(0, 5)$

*14. (35) (**Fishery**) A Pacific salmon can swim at a maximum speed of 8 miles per hour. The function $y = 8x$ describes how many miles y the fish swims in x hours. Graph the function. Use the graph to estimate the number of miles the fish swims in 2.5 hours.
See Additional Answers; 20 miles

15. (34) Determine if the sequence 34, 29, 24, 19, ... is an arithmetic sequence or not. If yes, find the common difference and the next two terms. If no, find the next two terms.
yes; -5; 14, 9

16. (34) **Error Analysis** Two students are finding the common difference for the arithmetic sequence 18, 15, 12, 9, ... Which student is correct? Explain the error.   Student B; Student A subtracted the second term from the first term instead of the first term from the second term.

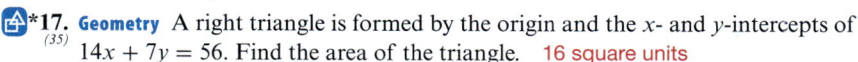

Student A	Student B
$18 - 15 = 3$	$15 - 18 = -3$
$15 - 12 = 3$	$12 - 15 = -3$
$12 - 9 = 3$	$9 - 12 = -3$

*17. (35) **Geometry** A right triangle is formed by the origin and the x- and y-intercepts of $14x + 7y = 56$. Find the area of the triangle.   16 square units

---

Check for Understanding

The questions below help assess the concepts taught in this lesson.

"Explain what the x- and y-intercepts are." Sample: The x-intercept is where the graph of a linear equation intersects the x-axis. The y-intercept is where the graph of a linear equation intersects the y-axis.

"What is the value of the x-coordinate in the ordered pair that represents the y-intercept?" Sample: The y-intercept always has the ordered pair $(0, y)$, so the x-coordinate is always 0.

3 Practice

Math Conversations
Discussion to strengthen understanding

Problem 8
Before combining like terms, ask, "What are like terms?" terms having the same variables with the same exponents

Lesson 35   221

Problem 18
Have students graph the ordered pairs given in the table so that they see the relationship between an arithmetic sequence and a linear equation. Then help them see that the common difference is the slope of the line.

Problem 19
Error Alert
Some students may think that the common difference is 7. Show them that since each number is to the left of the previous number, the common difference must be negative.

Problem 22
Guide the students by asking them the following questions.

"How many marbles are in the bag before any one is drawn?" 10

"After removing one white marble, what is the probability of drawing a white marble on the second draw?" $\frac{2}{9}$

"How is the probability of both events happening determined?"
Multiply their individual probabilities.

Problem 28
Extend the Problem
The Celsius-temperature scale was defined to have water freeze at 0°C and boil at 100°C at atmospheric pressure.

"What is the freezing and boiling points of water in Fahrenheit?"
The freezing point is 32°F. The boiling point is 212°F.

"Find the Celsius temperature when the Fahrenheit temperature is −40°." −40°C

---

18. **Data Analysis** The table shows the weights of a newborn baby who was 7.5 lb at birth.
    a. Write a recursive formula for the baby's weight gain. $a_1 = 9, a_n = a_{n-1} + 1.5$
    b. If the pattern continues, how much will the baby weigh after 7 weeks? 18 lb

Week Number	Weight (lb)
1	9
2	10.5
3	12
4	13.5

*19. **Multi-Step** Use the arithmetic sequence −65, −72, −79, −86, ...
   a. What is the value of a_1? −65
   b. What is the common difference d? −7
   c. Write a rule for the nth term of the sequence. $a_n = -65 + (n-1)(-7)$

20. **Write** A coin is flipped and lands on heads. It is flipped again and lands on tails. Identify these events as independent or dependent. independent

21. (**Economics**) You have agreed to a babysitting job that will last 14 days. On the first day, you earn $25, but on each day after that you will earn $15. How much will you earn if you babysit for 7 days? $115

22. **Probability** A bag holds 5 red marbles, 3 white marbles, and 2 green marbles. A marble is drawn, kept out, and then another marble is drawn. What is the probability of drawing two white marbles? $\frac{1}{15}$

*23. **Multiple Choice** Which of the following expressions is the simplified solution of $\frac{m^3 n^{-10} p^5}{mn^0 p^{-2}}$? D

   A $\frac{m^3 p^3}{n^{10}}$ B $\frac{m^3 p^7}{n^{10}}$ C $\frac{m^2 p^3}{n^9}$ D $\frac{m^2 p^7}{n^{10}}$

*24. **Verify** Is the statement $4^{-2} = -16$ correct? Explain your reasoning.

25. Convert 45 miles per hour to miles per minute. 0.75 mi/min

26. Rewrite the following question so it is not biased: Would you rather buy a brand new luxury SUV or a cheap used car? Sample: Do you prefer SUVs or passenger cars?

27. Identify the independent variable and the dependent variable: money earned, hours worked. The money earned is dependent, and the hours worked is independent.

28. (**Temperature**) Use the formula $F = \frac{9}{5}C + 32$ to find an equivalent Fahrenheit temperature when the temperature is −12°C. 10.4°F

29. (**Homework**) A student has to write a book report on a book that contains 1440 pages. Suppose she plans to read 32 pages per day. Using function notation, express how many pages remain after reading for d days. $f(d) = 1440 - 32d$

30. (**Soccer**) For every hour a player practices soccer, he must drink 8 fluid ounces of liquid to stay hydrated. Write an equation describing this relation and determine whether it is a function. Sample: $f = 8h$; The relation is a function.

24. no; The base of 4 was correctly raised to the second power, but the rule for negative exponents was not correctly followed. The correct solution is $4^{-2} = \frac{1}{16}$.

CHALLENGE

Describe the graph of a line drawn through the following points: (5, −2), (5, 3). Draw a line through the points and determine the x- and y-intercepts. Write an equation in standard form representing the graph of the line. The graph is a vertical line passing through each point. The x-intercept is 5. There is no y-intercept. The equation is $x + 0y = 5$.

LOOKING FORWARD

Locating and using intercepts prepares students for

- **Lesson 41** Finding Rates of Change and Slope
- **Lesson 44** Finding Slope Using the Slope Formula
- **Lesson 49** Writing Equations in Slope-Intercept Form
- **Lesson 52** Determining the Equation of a Line Given Two Points

LESSON 36

Writing and Solving Proportions

Warm Up

1. **Vocabulary** A _____ is a comparison of two quantities using division. **ratio**

Solve.

2. $\frac{13}{52} = \frac{x}{36}$ **9**

3. $\frac{42}{56} = \frac{63}{w}$ **84**

4. $15x - 37 = 143$ **12**

5. $78 + 22y = -230$ **−14**

New Concepts

Proportions are frequently used to solve problems in mathematics. Proportional reasoning can be applied in many situations, including reading and drawing maps, architecture, and construction. Solving problems in these situations requires knowledge of similar figures.

Reading Math

The ~ symbol indicates similar figures and reads "is similar to."
The ≅ symbol indicates congruent figures and reads "is congruent to."

If two geometric objects or figures are **similar**, they have the same shape but are not necessarily the same size. The triangles below are similar.

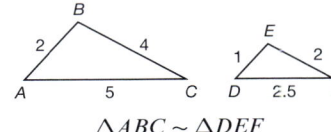

$\triangle ABC \sim \triangle DEF$

When two figures are similar, they have sides and angles that correspond. Corresponding sides and angles are found using the order of the letters in the similarity statement. In the triangles above, $\angle A$ and $\angle D$ correspond, $\angle B$ and $\angle E$ correspond, and $\angle C$ and $\angle F$ correspond. Corresponding angles of similar figures are **congruent**, or have the same measure.

$\angle A \cong \angle D \qquad \angle B \cong \angle E \qquad \angle C \cong \angle F$

Reading Math

$\overline{AB}$ is read "segment AB."

Sides of similar figures also correspond. In the example above, $\overline{AB}$ and $\overline{DE}$ correspond, $\overline{BC}$ and $\overline{EF}$ correspond, and $\overline{AC}$ and $\overline{DF}$ correspond. Corresponding sides of similar figures do not have to be congruent. However, they do have to be in proportion. The ratio of the all pairs of corresponding sides must be the same.

$$\frac{AB}{DE} = \frac{BC}{EF} = \frac{AC}{DF}$$

In the example above, the ratio of the sides of $\triangle ABC$ to $\triangle DEF$ is 2 to 1. This ratio, which can also be written as $\frac{2}{1}$ or 2:1, is called the scale factor of $\triangle ABC$ to $\triangle DEF$.

$$\frac{AB}{DE} = \frac{BC}{EF} = \frac{AC}{DF} = \frac{2}{1}$$

A **scale factor** is the ratio of a side length of a figure to the side length of a similiar figure. The scale factor of $\triangle DEF$ to $\triangle ABC$ is 1 to 2.

Online Connection
www.SaxonMathResources.com

MATH BACKGROUND

Although proportions can be solved using the LCD of the ratios in the proportion, it is customary to use the cross products instead. The cross product method is derived using the LCD.

$\frac{a}{b} = \frac{c}{d} \quad b \neq 0, d \neq 0$

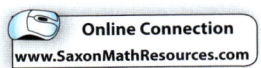

The least common denominator is bd. Multiply each ratio in the proportion by bd and then cancel the common factors.

$\frac{a}{b} = \frac{c}{d}$

$\frac{(\cancel{b}d)a}{\cancel{b}} = \frac{(b\cancel{d})c}{\cancel{d}}$ Multiply by the LCD.

$da = bc$ Simplify.

$ad = bc$ Commutative Property

So, the use of cross products to solve proportions is justified.

Example 1

Remind students that when they are given two similar figures, it is helpful to make sure that the orientations of the figures are the same before solving the problem.

Additional Example 1

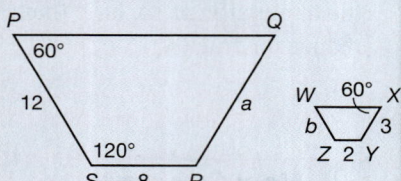

$PQRS \sim WXYZ$

a. Find m∠Q and m∠Z.
   m∠Q = 60°; m∠Z = 120°

b. Find the scale factor of $PQRS$ to $WXYZ$. $\frac{4}{1}$

c. Use the scale factor to find QR and WZ. $QR = 12$; $WZ = 3$

Example 2

Since the sun is so far away, every triangle formed by an object and its shadow is similar to other triangles created by objects and their shadows at the same time of day in the same vicinity.

Additional Example 2

Triangles drawn with the same 5.5-foot-tall woman and a basketball player with a 5-foot-long shadow are similar. How tall is the basketball player? He is 6.875 feet tall.

Reading Math

The notation m∠Q is read "the measure of angle Q."

Hint

To avoid confusion, write the ratios with all sides from one figure in the numerator and all corresponding sides from the other figure in the denominator.

Example 1 Finding Measures in Similar Figures

$PQRS \sim WXYZ$

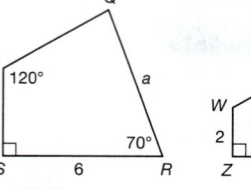
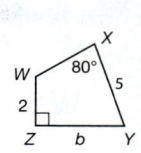

a. Find m∠Q and m∠W.

SOLUTION

∠Q and ∠X correspond, so they are equal, and m∠Q = 80°. ∠W and ∠P correspond, so they are equal and m∠W = 120°.

b. Find the scale factor of $PQRS$ to $WXYZ$.

SOLUTION

$\overline{PS}$ and $\overline{WZ}$ correspond, so the scale factor of $PQRS$ to $WXYZ$ is $\frac{PS}{WZ} = \frac{3}{2}$.

c. Use the scale factor to find QR and ZY.

SOLUTION

All corresponding side lengths must be in a ratio of 3 to 2. $\overline{QR}$ corresponds with $\overline{XY}$ and $\overline{ZY}$ corresponds with $\overline{SR}$.

$$\frac{PS}{WZ} = \frac{QR}{XY} \qquad \frac{PS}{WZ} = \frac{SR}{ZY}$$

$$\frac{3}{2} = \frac{a}{5} \qquad \frac{3}{2} = \frac{6}{b}$$

$$2a = 15 \qquad 3b = 12$$

$$a = 7.5 \qquad b = 4$$

So, $QR = 7.5$ and $ZY = 4$.

Another application of proportional reasoning is indirect measurement. Indirect measurement involves using similar figures to find unknown lengths.

Example 2 Using Indirect Measurement

A radio tower casts a shadow 10 feet long. A woman who is 5.5 feet tall casts a shadow 4 feet long. The triangle drawn with the tower and its shadow is similar to the triangle drawn with the woman and her shadow. How tall is the radio tower?

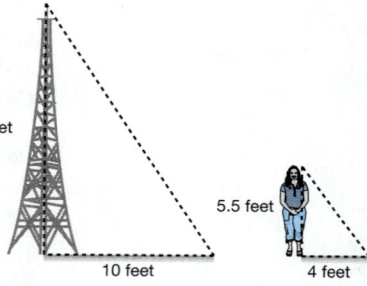

SOLUTION Set up a proportion to solve the problem.

$$\frac{10}{4} = \frac{x}{5.5}$$

$$10(5.5) = 4 \cdot x$$

$$55 = 4x$$

$$13.75 = x$$

The radio tower is 13.75 feet tall.

ENGLISH LEARNERS

Explain the meaning of the word **cast**.

Say:
"Shadows are cast, or caused by objects."

Say:
"A shadow is formed by an object that blocks a light source. The object casts, or causes a shadow to appear on a surface."

Ask:
"If a building casts a 10-foot shadow, what does the shadow resemble? Explain." Sample: The shadow resembles the building since the building caused the shadow on the surface.

Math Reasoning

Generalize Will the proportions $\frac{x}{4} = \frac{5}{6}$ and $\frac{4}{x} = \frac{6}{5}$ give the same values for x? Explain your reasoning.

yes; The first proportion simplifies to $6 \cdot x = 4 \cdot 5$, and the second proportion simplifies to $6 \cdot x = 4 \cdot 5$. The value of x in both proportions is $3\frac{1}{3}$.

A **scale drawing** is a drawing that reduces or enlarges the dimensions of an object by a constant factor. Maps and blueprints are examples of scale drawings. The **scale** is a ratio showing the relationship between a scale drawing or model and the actual object.

Example 3 Application: Scale Drawings

A desk is designed to have three drawers on the right side. In the scaled design drawing, the width of the drawers is 4 centimeters. If the scale of the drawing is 1 cm:7 cm, how wide will the actual desk drawers be?

SOLUTION Set up a proportion to solve the problem.

$$\frac{\text{drawing length}}{\text{actual length}} = \frac{1}{7} = \frac{4}{x}$$

$$1 \cdot x = 4 \cdot 7$$

$$x = 28$$

The width of the actual desk drawers will be 28 centimeters.

Scale factors of side lengths can also be used to determine the ratios of perimeters, areas, and volumes of figures and solids.

Exploration Changing Dimensions

Students may work in groups of two or three.

Materials
- 64 cubes per pair or group

Alternate Materials (blocks, cheese or sugar cubes are possible examples)

a. Begin with 1 cube and let the length of an edge equal 1 unit. Then the perimeter of the base of the cube is $4 \cdot 1 = 4$ units, the area of the base of the cube is $1 \cdot 1 = 1$ square unit, and the volume of the cube is $1 \cdot 1 \cdot 1 = 1$ cubic unit. Copy and complete the table below.

Length of Edge (units)	Perimeter of the Base (units)	Area of the Base (square units)	Volume of the Base (cubic units)
1	4	1	1
2	8	4	8
3	12	9	27

b. Use the cubes to build another cube with edge lengths of 2 units. Record your answers in the table.

c. Repeat for a cube with a side length of 3 units. Record your answers in the table.

Use the rows with edge lengths of 2 and 3 from the table.

d. What is the scale factor of the edge lengths? $\frac{2}{3}$

e. Find the ratio of the perimeters. How does this ratio compare to the scale factor? $\frac{8}{12} = \frac{2}{3}$; Sample: It is the same ratio.

f. Find the ratio of the areas. How does this ratio compare to the scale factor? $\frac{4}{9}$; Sample: It is the scale factor squared, or $\frac{2^2}{3^2} = \frac{4}{9}$.

Lesson 36 225

Example 3
Scale drawings are an integral part of designing.

Error Alert A common mistake in writing proportions is to invert one of the fractions. Encourage students to describe in words the values in the numerator and the denominator.

Extend the Example
The design is expanded to include the entire room. Using the same scale factor, what are the dimensions of the room in the design if its actual dimensions are 420 centimeters by 700 centimeters? 60 cm by 100 cm

Additional Example 3
In a scale drawing, a kite is designed so that the length of the tail is 9 centimeters. If the scale of the drawing is 1 cm:10 cm, what is the length of the actual kite tail? 90 cm

Exploration
Students compare the scale factor of two similar figures to the ratio of their perimeters, areas, and volumes. This will lead them to discover how scale factor is related to perimeter, area, and volume.

 INCLUSION

For scale-drawing problems, have students make a proportion table like the one shown below for Example 3.

	Scale Ratio	Equivalent Ratio
Drawing Length	1	4
Actual Length	7	x

Label the rows with a description for the numerator and the denominator. Label the columns with a description for each ratio. The table will ensure that the ratios are setup correctly. $\frac{1}{7} = \frac{4}{x}$

Lesson 36 225

Example 4

Remind students that the formula for the area of a circle with radius r is $A = \pi r^2$.

Additional Example 4

a. What is the ratio of the radius of the innermost circle to the radius of the outermost circle? $\frac{1}{5}$

b. What is the ratio of the area of the innermost circle to the area of the outermost circle? $\frac{1}{25}$

Extend the Example

"If you threw 100 darts randomly at the board and all of them hit the board, how many will hit the bulls eye?" By the ratio of the areas, 4 will be inside the smallest inner circle.

Lesson Practice

Problem b

Scaffolding Before writing the proportion using values from the triangles, suggest that students write the proportion in words first. Use words like height and base.

Math Language

Perimeter is the distance around a closed plane figure. **Circumference** is the distance around a circle.

Math Reasoning

Verify Use Example 3 to show that if similar figures have a scale factor of $\frac{a}{b}$, then the ratio of their areas is $\frac{a^2}{b^2}$.

---

g. Find the ratio of the volumes. How does this ratio compare to the scale factor? $\frac{8}{27}$; Sample: It is the scale factor cubed, or $\frac{2^3}{3^3} = \frac{8}{27}$.

Ratios of the Perimeter, Area, and Volume of Similar Figures

If two similar figures have a scale factor of $\frac{a}{b}$, then the ratio of their perimeters is $\frac{a}{b}$, the ratio of their areas is $\frac{a^2}{b^2}$, and the ratio of their volumes is $\frac{a^3}{b^3}$.

Example 4 Application: Changing Dimensions

A dartboard is composed of concentric circles. The radius of the smallest inner circle is 1 inch, and with each consecutive circle, the radius increases by 1 inch.

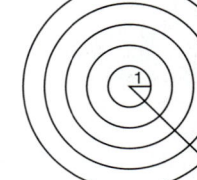

a. What is the ratio of the circumference of the two inner circles to the circumference of the outermost circle?

SOLUTION

$$\frac{\text{circumference of two inner circles}}{\text{circumference of outermost circle}} = \frac{2\pi(2)}{2\pi(5)} = \frac{2}{5}$$

b. What is the ratio of the area of the two inner circles to the area of the outermost circle?

SOLUTION

$$\frac{\text{area of two inner circles}}{\text{area of outermost circle}} = \frac{\pi(2)^2}{\pi(5)^2}$$
$$= \frac{4\pi}{25\pi}$$
$$= \frac{4}{25}$$

Lesson Practice

a. $\triangle ABC \sim \triangle LKM$. Find m$\angle K$ and m$\angle C$. 25°; 20°
(Ex 1)

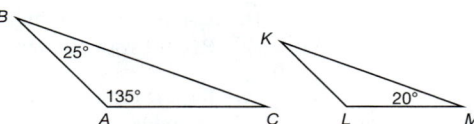

b. The figures are similar. Find the scale factor. Then use the scale factor
(Ex 1) to find x. $\frac{5}{3}$; $\frac{25}{3}$

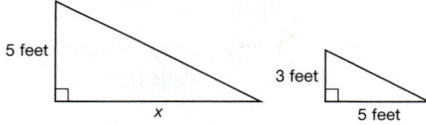

c. (Ex 2) The side of a building casts a shadow 21 meters long. A statue that is 5 meters tall casts a shadow 4 meters long. The triangles are similar. How tall is the building? 26.25 meters

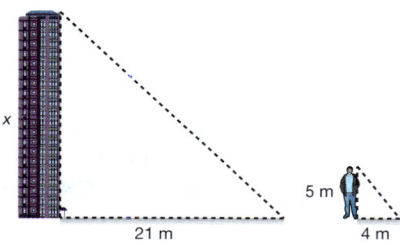

d. (Ex 3) The scale drawing of the kitchen tabletop has dimensions 5 inches by 2.5 inches. If the scale factor of the drawing to the actual table is 1 in.:18 in., what are the dimensions of the actual table?
90 in. by 45 in.

e. (Ex 4) Small toy cars are constructed using a scale factor of 1 in.:64 in. What is the ratio of the areas of the toy car and the actual car?
1 sq. in. :4096 sq. in.

Practice   Distributed and Integrated

Solve each proportion.

*1. (36) $\frac{3}{4} = \frac{x}{100}$ $x = 75$

*2. (36) $\frac{5.5}{x} = \frac{1.375}{11}$ $x = 44$

Simplify each expression.

3. (4) $2^2 + 6(8 - 5) \div 2$ 13

4. (4) $\frac{(3 + 2)(4 + 3) + 5^2}{6 - 2^2}$ 30

5. (4) $\frac{14 - 8}{-2^2 + 1}$ -2

6. (20) The point (3, 5) is graphed in which quadrant of a coordinate plane?   first

7. (25) True or False: The set of ordered pairs below defines a function.   true

$\{(1, 3), (2, 3), (3, 3), (4, 3)\}$

*8. (36) The triangles at right are similar. Find the missing length.   6.75

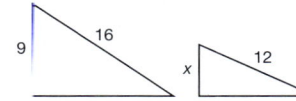

*9. (36) **Multiple Choice** One triangle has side lengths 3, 5, and 6. A similar triangle has side lengths 18, 15, and 9. Which of the following ratios is the scale factor of the triangles?   **B**

A $\frac{1}{6}$ B $\frac{1}{3}$ C $\frac{1}{5}$ D $\frac{2}{3}$

*10. (36) (Landscaping) A landscaping company needs to measure the height of a tree. The tree casts a shadow that is 6 feet long. A person who is 5 feet tall casts a shadow that is 2 feet long.
   a. Draw a picture to represent the problem.   See student work.
   b. Use your picture to find the height of the tree.   15 feet

Lesson 36   227

Problem 16
Guide the students by asking them the following questions.

"What is needed first to begin solving the problem?" Sample: the length of the base and the height of the triangle.

"How can the length of the base and the height of the triangle be found? Explain." Sample: Find the *x*- and *y*-intercepts. The distance from the origin to the *x*-intercept is the length of the base of the triangle. The distance from the origin to the *y*-intercept is the length of the height of the triangle.

Problem 21
Extend the Problem

"How many more pounds would the object weigh on Earth if its weight on the moon is $41\frac{2}{3}$ pounds?" 50 pounds more

The force of gravity on Mars is about 37% of that on Earth, 236% greater on Jupiter than on Earth, and 2700% greater on the surface of the sun than on Earth.

"What is the 200-pound object's weight on Mars, Jupiter, and the Sun?" about 74 lb on Mars, about 472 lb on Jupiter, about 5400 lb on the Sun

---

*11. A real estate company sells small models of houses. The scale factor of the models to the actual houses is 0.5 ft:10 ft. Find the ratio of the areas of the model to the actual house.   0.25 sq. ft:100 sq. ft

12. (Entrepreneurship) A small child decided to sell his artwork. He sold black-and-white drawings for $2 and colored drawings for $3. The equation $2x + 3y = 24$ shows that he earned $24. Find the *x*- and *y*-intercepts.   The *x*-intercept is 12 and the *y*-intercept is 8.

*13. **Verify** A tree casts a shadow 14 feet long. A flagpole that is 20 feet tall casts a shadow 8 feet long. The triangle formed by the tree and its shadow is similar to the triangle formed by the flagpole and its shadow. Verify that the tree is 35 feet tall. $\frac{20}{8} = \frac{x}{14}$, $8x = 280$, $x = 35$

14. Find the *x*-intercept for $11x - 33y = 99$.   9

15. Find the *y*-intercept for $-7x - 8y = 56$. -7

*16. **Geometry** A right triangle is formed by the origin and the *x*- and *y*-intercepts of the line $11x - 4y = 22$. Find the area of the triangle.   5.5 square units

17. **Multi-Step** A car wash is held as a school fundraiser to earn $280 for a field trip. The charge is $7 for a car and $10 for an SUV. Let *x* be the number of cars and *y* be the number of SUVs washed. The profits are calculated using the equation $7x = -10y + 280$.
   a. Rewrite the profit equation in standard form. $7x + 10y = 280$
   b. Calculate the *y*-intercept and explain its real-world meaning.   28; Sample: To earn $280 by only washing SUVs, 28 SUVs would have to be washed.
   c. Calculate the *x*-intercept and explain its real-world meaning.   40; To earn $280 by washing only cars, 40 cars would have to be washed.

18. Determine if the sequence 0.4, 0.1, -0.2, -0.5, ... is an arithmetic sequence or not. If yes, find the common difference and the next two terms. If no, find the next two terms.   yes; -0.3; -0.8, -1.1

*19. **Error Analysis** Two students are writing an example of an arithmetic sequence. Which student is correct? Explain the error.   Student A; Student B's sequence does not have a common difference.

Student A	Student B
5, 1, -3, -7, ...	1, 4, 16, 44, ...

*20. **Verify** At a raffle, 5 students' names are in a hat. There are 3 prizes in a bag: 2 books and a free lunch. Once the name and a prize are drawn, they are not replaced. After giving out a book in the first drawing, a remaining student quickly calculates her probability of winning a book in the second drawing as $\frac{1}{8}$. Show that she is correct.   Sample: There are 4 students left and 2 prizes, 1 of which is a book. P(student and book) = $\frac{1}{4} \cdot \frac{1}{2} = \frac{1}{8}$

21. (Astronomy) The force of gravity on the moon is about one-sixth of that on Earth. If an object on Earth weighs 200 pounds, about how much does it weigh on the moon?   about $33\frac{1}{3}$ pounds

228   Saxon Algebra 1

CHALLENGE

If a triangle has sides lengths *x*, *y*, and *z*, and a similar triangle has lengths $2.5x$, $2.5y$, $2.5z$, what is the ratio of the area of the triangle to the similar triangle?   1:6.25

22. **Multiple Choice** What are the odds against spinning a B on the spinner? **C**
    A 1:2 **B** 1:3 **C** 2:1 **D** 3:1

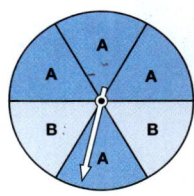

23. **Multi-Step** Steve has $300 in the bank. Each week he spends $10. Mario has $100 in the bank and deposits $5 each week.
    a. Write expressions to represent how many dollars each person has in the bank after w weeks. $300 - 10w$, $100 + 5w$
    b. Write an expression that represents how many dollars they have altogether. $400 - 5w$
    c. After 6 weeks, how much money do they have? $370

24. Identify the independent variable and the dependent variable in the following statement: The fire was very large, so many firefighters were there. The number of firefighters is dependent, and the size of the fire is independent.

25. **Multi-Step** The measure of angle B is three times the measure of angle A. The sum of the angle measures is 128°. Find the value of x.
    $3(x + 2) + (x + 2) = 128$, $x = 30$

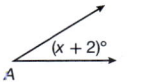

26. (**Piano Lessons**) A piano student has a $250 scholarship and an additional $422 saved for piano lessons. If each lesson costs $42, how many lessons will he have?
    16 lessons

27. Simplify $\frac{4x^2z^0}{2x^3z}$. $\frac{2}{xz}$

28. (**Meteorology**) Meteorologists sometimes use a measure known as virtual temperature (T_v) in kelvins (K) to compare dry and moist air. It can be calculated as $T_v = T(1 + 0.61r)$, where T is the temperature of the air and r is the mixing ratio of water vapor and dry air. For temperatures of $T = 282.5$ K and $T_v = 285$ K, find the mixing ratio to the nearest thousandth. $r = 0.015$

29. **Measurement** For a science project, Joe must measure out 5 samples of a liquid. The graph shows the size of his samples. Why might the data require smaller intervals on the graph? Sample: The samples are measured precisely. Smaller intervals would better show the differences.

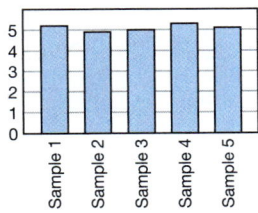

30. **Justify** Solve the equation $34 - 2(x + 17) = 23x - 15 - 3x$. Write out and justify each step. See Additional Answers.

Problem 23
Guide the students by asking them the following questions.

"When calculating the amount of money in the bank, what operation indicates a withdrawal?" Spending money lessens the amount in the acccunt, so the operation is subtraction.

"How is the expression written to represent the amount that Steve has in the bank after w weeks?" $300 - 10w$

"How about for Mario?" $100 + 5w$

LOOKING FORWARD

Writing and solving proportions prepares students for

- **Lesson 42** Solving Percent Problems
- **Lesson 47** Solving Problems Involving the Percent of Change
- **Lesson 56** Identifying, Writing, and Graphing Direct Variation
- **Lesson 117** Using Trigonometric Ratios

LESSON 37

1 Warm Up

Problem 5
Explain to students that the definition of negative exponents and either the Quotient Property or the Product Property of Exponents are used to solve this problem.

2 New Concepts

In this lesson, students review how to write large and small numbers in scientific notation. Students also multiply and divide numbers written in scientific notation by applying the rules of exponents.

Exploration

In this Exploration, students use patterns to generalize the movement of a decimal when a number is multiplied by a power of ten.

LESSON RESOURCES

Student Edition Practice Workbook 37
Reteaching Master 37
Adaptations Master 37
Challenge and Enrichment Master C37
Technology Lab Master 37

LESSON 37

Using Scientific Notation

Warm Up

1. **Vocabulary** The _____ tells how many times the base of a power is used as a factor. **exponent**

Simplify.

2. 7^4 **2401**

3. $(8.34)(-4)(100)$ **−3336**

4. 5^{-5} $\dfrac{1}{3125}$

5. $\dfrac{3x^{-3}}{5xy^{-5}}$ $\dfrac{3y^5}{5x^4}$

New Concepts

Very large or very small numbers are often written in **scientific notation**, a method of writing a number as the product of a number greater than or equal to 1 but less than 10 and a power of ten.

Exploration Applying Scientific Notation

a. Copy the table. Multiply to find each number in standard form.

Scientific Notation	Standard Form
1.08×10^2	108
1.08×10^3	1080
1.08×10^4	10,800
1.08×10^5	108,000

b. What pattern do you see in the table? Sample: The exponent and the number of places the decimal moved to the right are the same.

c. Copy the table. Multiply to find each number in standard form.

Scientific Notation	Standard Form
1.08×10^{-1}	0.108
1.08×10^{-2}	0.0108
1.08×10^{-3}	0.00108
1.08×10^{-4}	0.000108

d. What pattern do you see in the table? Sample: The absolute value of the exponent and the number of places the decimal moved to the left are the same.

e. Which direction does the decimal move when the exponent is positive? **right**

f. Which direction does the decimal move when the exponent is negative? **left**

Online Connection
www.SaxonMathResources.com

MATH BACKGROUND

Scientific notation is written as the product of a number greater than or equal to 1 and less than 10 times a power of 10. It enables mathematicians, scientists, and engineers to easily write and work with numbers that are either very large or very small. The name scientific notation is used because very large and very small numbers are used often in scientific work. Characteristics such as the distance of astronomical bodies from Earth or the size of atoms require very large or small numbers, respectively.

ENGLISH LEARNERS

Explain the meaning of the word **pattern**. Point out to students that the desks in the classroom make a pattern. Say:

"**A pattern is an arrangement of things that repeat in a certain way. Describe the pattern of desks in this classroom.**" Sample: The pattern is 4 vertical rows of 6 desks each.

Have students find and describe other patterns found in the classroom.

Scientific Notation

A number written as the product of two factors in the form $a \times 10^n$, where $1 \leq a < 10$ and n is an integer.

Example 1 Writing Numbers in Scientific Notation

Write each number in scientific notation.

a. 856,000

SOLUTION

Because this is a number greater than 1, the exponent will be positive.

The decimal point moves to be after the 8 so that there is one digit to the left of the decimal.

$$856{,}000.$$
$$5\,4\,3\,2\,1$$

Move the decimal five places, and write the number as 8.56000×10^5.

So, $856{,}000 = 8.56 \times 10^5$.

b. 0.0005

SOLUTION

Because this is a number between 0 and 1, the exponent will be negative.

The decimal point moves to be after the 5, so that there is one digit to its left.

$$0.0005.$$
$$1\,2\,3\,4$$

Move the decimal four places, and write the number as 5×10^{-4}.

To multiply numbers in scientific notation, multiply the coefficients and then multiply the powers. If the result is not in scientific notation, adjust it so that it is.

Example 2 Multiplying Numbers in Scientific Notation

Find the product. Write the answer in scientific notation.

$(5.7 \times 10^5)(1.8 \times 10^3)$

SOLUTION

$(5.7 \times 10^5)(1.8 \times 10^3)$

$= (5.7 \cdot 1.8)(10^5 \cdot 10^3)$ Use the Commutative and Associative Properties of Multiplication to group the numbers and the powers.

$= 10.26 \times 10^8$ Simplify.

Notice that the result is not in scientific notation. There is more than one digit before the decimal point. Move the decimal to the left one place and add one to the exponent.

$10.26 \times 10^8 = 1.026 \times 10^9$

Caution

8.56×10^5 is in scientific notation.
85.6×10^4 is not in scientific notation.

Math Reasoning

Analyze Why is there no decimal point in the answer?

Sample: A decimal point is at the end of a whole number, but does not need to be written.

Hint

When you multiply powers with like bases, keep the base the same and add the exponents.
$10^5 \cdot 10^3 = 10^{5+3}$

Example 1

In this example, students write large and small numbers in scientific notation using positive exponents.

Additional Example

Write each number in scientific notation.

a. 4,900,000 4.9×10^6

b. 0.00000093 9.3×10^{-7}

Example 2

In this example, students are introduced to multiplying numbers written in scientific notation.

Error Alert When alternating between writing numbers in standard form and scientific notation, students may confuse the direction that the decimal point moves and confuse the use of positive and negative exponents. Remind them that when given a number in scientific notation, a positive exponent indicates that the decimal point moves to the right in order to express the number in standard form. When the number in scientific notation has a negative exponent, the decimal point moves to the left in order to express the number in standard form.

Additional Example

Find the product of $(3.2 \times 10^7)(4.3 \times 10^2)$. Write the answer in scientific notation. 13.76×10^9, 1.376×10^{10}

Example 3

In this example, students are introduced to dividing numbers written in scientific notation.

Additional Example

Find the quotient. Write the answer in scientific notation.

$\dfrac{(6.8 \times 10^5)}{(2.5 \times 10^8)}$ 2.72×10^{-3}

Example 4

In this example, students evaluate two expressions written in scientific notation and compare the values.

Additional Example

Compare. Use $<$, $>$, or $=$.

$\dfrac{(8.3 \times 10^4)}{(5.7 \times 10^8)}$ $\dfrac{(7.2 \times 10^5)}{(4.4 \times 10^9)}$

$(1.46 \times 10^{-4}) < (1.64 \times 10^{-4})$

Example 5

In this example, students use scientific notation in a real-world application.

Extend the Example

The average distance from Earth to the Sun is about 150,000,000,000 astronomical units (about 92 million miles). Write the distance in scientific notation. 1.5×10^{11}

Additional Example 5

The speed of light is 3×10^8 meters per second. If Venus is 1.08×10^5 meters from the Sun, how many seconds does it take light to reach Venus from the Sun? Write the answer in scientific notation. 0.36×10^{-3}; 3.6×10^{-4} seconds

---

To divide numbers in scientific notation, divide the coefficients, and then divide the powers. If the result is not in scientific notation, adjust it so that it is.

Example 3 Dividing Numbers in Scientific Notation

Find the quotient. Write the answer in scientific notation.

$\dfrac{1.2 \times 10^3}{9.6 \times 10^6}$

SOLUTION

$\dfrac{1.2 \times 10^3}{9.6 \times 10^6}$

Hint
When you divide powers with like bases, keep the base the same and subtract the exponents.
$\dfrac{10^3}{10^6} = 10^{3-6}$

$= \dfrac{1.2}{9.6} \times \dfrac{10^3}{10^6}$ Divide the coefficients and divide the powers.

$= 0.125 \times 10^{-3}$ Simplify.

Notice that this number is not in scientific notation. There is not one nonzero digit before the decimal point. Move the decimal to the right one place and subtract one from the exponent.

$0.125 \times 10^{-3} = 1.25 \times 10^{-4}$

Example 4 Comparing Expressions with Scientific Notation

Compare. Use $<$, $>$, or $=$.

$\dfrac{7.2 \times 10^6}{3.6 \times 10^4}$ ◯ $\dfrac{1.05 \times 10^7}{3.5 \times 10^5}$

SOLUTION

$\dfrac{7.2 \times 10^6}{3.6 \times 10^4}$ $\dfrac{1.05 \times 10^7}{3.5 \times 10^5}$

$= \dfrac{7.2}{3.6} \times \dfrac{10^6}{10^4}$ $= \dfrac{1.05}{3.5} \times \dfrac{10^7}{10^5}$

$= 2 \times 10^2 = 200$ $= 0.3 \times 10^2 = 30$

Since $200 > 30$, then $\dfrac{7.2 \times 10^6}{3.6 \times 10^4} > \dfrac{1.05 \times 10^7}{3.5 \times 10^5}$.

Example 5 Application: Speed of Light

The speed of light is 3×10^8 meters per second. If Earth is 1.47×10^{11} meters from the sun, how many seconds does it take light to reach Earth from the sun? Write the answer in scientific notation.

SOLUTION Divide the earth's distance from the sun by the speed of light.

$\dfrac{1.47 \times 10^{11}}{3 \times 10^8} = 0.49 \times 10^3$

$= 4.9 \times 10^2$ Write the answer in scientific notation.

It takes light about 4.9×10^2 seconds to reach the earth from the sun.

INCLUSION

Allow students to write exponents using a red pencil throughout the lesson. This will remind them of the correct position of the exponent and alleviate any possible misreading of the number or term.

Lesson Practice

Write each number in scientific notation.

a. (Ex 1) 1,234,000. 1.234×10^6

b. 0.0306. 3.06×10^{-2}

c. (Ex 2) Find the product. Write the answer in scientific notation.
$(5.82 \times 10^3)(6.13 \times 10^{11})$ 35.6766×10^{14}; 3.56766×10^{15}

d. (Ex 3) Find the quotient. Write the answer in scientific notation.
$\dfrac{(7.29 \times 10^{-2})}{(8.1 \times 10^{-6})}$ 9×10^3

e. (Ex 4) Compare. Use $<$, $>$, or $=$.
$\dfrac{4.56 \times 10^9}{3 \times 10^5}$ $>$ $\dfrac{5.2 \times 10^8}{1.3 \times 10^5}$

f. (Ex 5) **Astronomy** The speed of light is 3×10^8 meters per second. If Mars is 2.25×10^{11} meters from the Sun, how many seconds does it take light to reach Mars from the Sun? Write the answer in scientific notation.
7.5×10^2 seconds

Practice   Distributed and Integrated

Simplify each expression.

1. (4) $18 \div 3^2 - 5 + 2$ -1

2. (4) $7^2 + 4^2 + 3$ 68

3. (4) $3[-2(8 - 13)]$ 30

Simplify each expression by combining like terms.

4. (18) $13b^2 + 5b - b^2$ $12b^2 + 5b$

5. (18) $-3(8x + 4) + \dfrac{1}{2}(6x - 24)$ $-21x - 24$

*6. (37) Write 7.4×10^{-9} in standard form. 0.0000000074

*7. (37) **Write** Explain how to recognize if a number is in scientific notation.   Sample: It has to be of the form $a \times 10^b$, and a has to be greater than or equal to 1 and less than 10.

*8. (37) **Write** Explain why anyone would want to use scientific notation.   Sample: It quickly shows how large or small a number is without having to count zeros.

*9. (37) **Multiple Choice** What is $(3.4 \times 10^{10})(4.8 \times 10^5)$ in scientific notation?   **B**
   A 1.632×10^{15} **B** 1.632×10^{16} **C** 16.32×10^{15} **D** 16.32×10^{16}

*10. (37) **Physiology** The diameter of a red blood cell is about 4×10^{-5} inches. Write this number in standard notation. 0.00004

11. (36) The triangles shown are similar. Find the missing length. $13\dfrac{1}{3}$

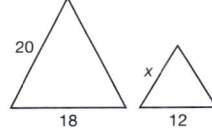

12. (26) A student's final grade is determined by adding four test grades and dividing by 4. The student's first three test grades are 79, 88, and 94. What must the student make on the last test to get a final grade of 90? $x = 99$

Lesson 37   233

ALTERNATE METHOD

To check their solutions, you may have students use scientific calculators. Students should be aware that they will need to enter parentheses and use the ^ button to enter exponents.

Some calculators will show answers in scientific notation; some will not. Check the settings of the calculator to see if this option is available. If not, students will have to write the results in scientific notation on their own to check.

$(2.6 \times 10^3) \times (4.1 \times 10^5)$

$1066000000 = 1.066 \times 10^9$

Problem 17

Guide the students by asking them the following questions.

"Is it necessary to find the area of each circle to find the ratio of the areas?" no

"How can you easily find the ratio of the areas with the given information of the two radii?" Sample: The formula for the area of a circle is $A = \pi r^2$. Since π can be cancelled out of the ratio, it doesn't need to be written it in the first place. Just square each radius and write a ratio.

Problem 20

Error Alert

Students may not notice that the problem does not ask for the number of untagged foxes, only for the proportion that would allow them to find the number of untagged foxes.

Problem 22

Extend the Problem

The wavelength of green visible light is 510 nanometers. A nanometer is one-billionth of a meter. Write this measure in scientific notation. 5.1×10^{-7}

234 *Saxon Algebra 1*

---

*13. Graph $50x - 100y = 300$ using the x- and y-intercepts. See Additional Answers.
(35)

14. **Geometry** A square has side lengths of 3 centimeters. Another square has side
(36) lengths of 6 centimeters.
   a. What is the scale factor of the sides of the smaller square to the larger square? 1 to 2
   b. What is the perimeter of each square? smaller: 12 cm; larger: 24 cm
   c. What is the ratio of the perimeter of the smaller square to the perimeter of the larger square? 1 to 2
   d. What is the area of each square? smaller: 9 sq. cm; larger: 36 sq. cm
   e. What is the ratio of the area of the smaller square to the area of the larger square? 1 to 4

*15. **Error Analysis** In the figures at right, $\angle A$ and $\angle F$ correspond. Two students
(36) are finding the measure of $\angle F$. Which student is correct? Explain the error.

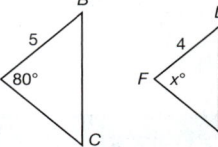

Student A	Student B
$\frac{5}{4} = \frac{80}{x}$	$m\angle A = m\angle F$
$5x = 320$	$80° = m\angle F$
$x = 64$	
$m\angle F = 64°$	

Student B; Sample: Corresponding angles of similar triangles are congruent. They are not in proportion.

16. **Architecture** A room is 10 feet by 12 feet. If the scale of the blueprints to the room
(36) is 1 inch to 2 feet, find the dimensions of the room on the blueprints. 5 inches by 6 inches

*17. **Measurement** What is the ratio of the area of the smaller circle to the area of the
(36) larger circle? $\frac{4}{9}$

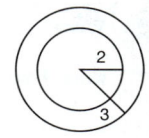

18. **Verify** Verify that the sequence 4, $2\frac{2}{3}$, $1\frac{1}{3}$, 0, … is an arithmetic sequence.
(34)

19. A piece of fruit is chosen from a box, eaten, and then a second piece of fruit is
(33) chosen. Identify these events as independent or dependent. dependent

20. **Predict** An estimate of the number of tagged foxes to the total number of foxes
(31) in a forest is 3 to 13. A forest warden noted 21 tagged foxes during a trip in the forest. Write a proportion to indicate the total number of foxes that might be in the forest. Sample: $\frac{21}{x} = \frac{3}{13}$

21. **Multiple Choice** In the rule for the nth term of arithmetic sequence
(34) $a_n = a_1 + (n - 1)d$, what does a_1 represent? **B**
   A the number of terms   **B** the first term
   C the nth term   **D** the common difference

*22. **Physical Science** The wavelengths of ultraviolet light can range from 10^{-9} meter to
(32) 10^{-7} meter. Express the range of wavelengths using positive exponents. $\frac{1}{10^9}$ m to $\frac{1}{10^7}$ m

18. $2\frac{2}{3} - 4 = -\frac{4}{3}$
$1\frac{1}{3} - 2\frac{2}{3} = -\frac{4}{3}$ and
$0 - 1\frac{1}{3} = -\frac{4}{3}$
The sequence is arithmetic with a common difference of $-\frac{4}{3}$.

234 *Saxon Algebra 1*

23. Estimate Between which two whole numbers is the solution to $\frac{13}{14} = \frac{x}{10}$? **9 and 10**

24. Dog Breeds The table shows the number of dogs of the top five breeds registered with the American Kennel Club in 2006. Describe how the data could be displayed in a potentially misleading way.

24. Sample: The data could be displayed in a circle graph even though the given breeds do not represent the entire data set, which could lead to incorrect conclusions.

Breed	Labrador Retriever	Yorkshire Terrier	German Shepherd	Golden Retriever	Beagle
Number	123,760	48,346	43,575	42,962	39,484

25. Choose an appropriate graph to display a survey showing what type of sport most people like. Explain your answer. **bar graph;** Sample: Bar graphs can clearly display information gathered in surveys to compare different categories of data.

26. Exercising A weightlifter averages 2 minutes on each exercise. Each workout includes a 20-minute swim. Write a rule in function notation to describe the time it takes to complete w exercises and the swim. $f(w) = 2w + 20$

27. Estimate Using the order of magnitude, estimate the value of 89,678 multiplied by 11,004,734. $(10^5) \times (10^7) = 10^{12}$

28. Justify Solve for x: $7x + 9 = 2(4x + 2)$. Justify each step.

*29. An oceanographer wants to convert measurements that are above and below sea level from yards to feet. He takes measurements of depths and heights in yards and feet.

yards	−679	−125	32	79
feet	−2037	−375	96	237

  a. Formulate Use the table to write a formula to convert from yards to feet. $f = 3y$
  b. Predict Use the formula to convert 27.5 yards to feet. **82.5 ft**
  c. Write a formula to convert yards to inches. $N = 36y$

30. Multi-Step A rectangle has a perimeter of $38 + x$ centimeters. The rectangle has a length of $3x - 2$ centimeters and a width of x centimeters. What is the length of the rectangle?
  a. Substitute the dimensions of the rectangle into the perimeter formula $P = 2w + 2l$. $2x + 2(3x - 2) = 38 + x$
  b. Solve for x. $x = 6$
  c. Find the length of the rectangle. length = $3(6) - 2 = 16$ cm

28.
$7x + 9 = 2(4x + 2)$
$7x + 9 = 8x + 4$ Distributive Property
$\underline{-7x \qquad -7x}$ Subtraction Property of Equality
$9 = x + 4$
$\underline{-4 \qquad -4}$ Subtraction Property of Equality
$5 = x$

Lesson 37   235

CHALLENGE

Have students write each number in scientific notation and then simplify the expression.

$$\dfrac{\dfrac{35,000,000}{20,000} \times \dfrac{81,000}{15,000}}{16,000,000 \times 74,000}$$

$$\dfrac{\dfrac{3.5 \times 10^7}{2 \times 10^4} \times \dfrac{8.1 \times 10^4}{1.5 \times 10^4}}{(1.6 \times 10^7) \times (7.4 \times 10^4)} = 7.981 \times 10^{-9}$$

LOOKING FORWARD

Using scientific notation prepares students for

- **Lesson 40** Simplifying and Evaluating Expressions Using the Power Property of Exponents
- **Lesson 46** Simplifying Expressions with Square Roots and Higher-Order Roots

---

Problem 28
Guide the students by asking them the following questions.
"What is the first step you should take to solve the equation?" Sample: Use the Distributive Property to multiply the expression in the parentheses by 2.
"What is the second step you should take to solve the equation?" Sample: Either move the numerical terms to one side of the equation or move the variable terms to one side of the equation.

Problem 29
Extend the Problem
Use the formula written in part c to convert −679 yards to inches. −24,444 in.

Problem 30
Error Alert
Students may not complete the problem, thinking that the value of x is the length of the rectangle. Encourage them to read the problem carefully to see what they are asked to find.

Lesson 37   235

LESSON 38

1 Warm Up

Problem 4
Students may simplify the term with the negative exponent first and then apply the Product Property of Exponents.

2 New Concepts

In this lesson, students learn to simplify expressions using the greatest common factor or GCF.

Discuss the idea that a quantity can be factored out of more than one term in an algebraic expression if every term in the expression has that quantity as a factor. In this lesson, students learn to identify those factors.

LESSON RESOURCES

Student Edition Practice
   Workbook 38
Reteaching Master 38
Adaptations Master 38
Challenge and Enrichment
   Master C38

LESSON 38 — Simplifying Expressions Using the GCF

Warm Up

1. **Vocabulary** When two or more quantities are multiplied, each is a _____ (*term, factor*) of the product. *factor*

Simplify.

2. $2x(3x - 5)$ $6x^2 - 10x$

3. $-3x^2y(4x^2 - 7xy)$ $-12x^4y + 21x^3y^2$

4. $\dfrac{x^5}{x^{-3}}$ x^8

5. $\dfrac{1}{-(-4)^3}$ $\dfrac{1}{64}$

New Concepts

Simplifying expressions that contain numbers often requires knowledge of prime numbers and factors. Recall that a prime number is a whole number that is only divisible by itself and 1.

$$2 = 1 \cdot 2 \quad 5 = 1 \cdot 5 \quad 13 = 1 \cdot 13 \quad 19 = 1 \cdot 19$$

All whole numbers other than 1 that are not prime are composite numbers. Composite numbers have whole-number factors other than 1 and the number itself. They can be written as a product of prime numbers, which is called the prime factorization of a number.

$$4 = 2 \cdot 2 \quad 6 = 2 \cdot 3 \quad 8 = 2 \cdot 2 \cdot 2$$

Math Reasoning

Formulate Find all of the prime numbers that are less than 100.

2, 3, 5, 7, 11, 13, 17, 19, 23, 29, 31, 37, 41, 43, 47, 53, 59, 61, 67, 71, 73, 79, 83, 89, 97

Several methods can be used to find the prime factorization of a number. The process requires breaking down the composite numbers until all the factors are prime numbers.

The prime factorization for the number 24 can be found in at least three ways.

$$24 = 2 \cdot 12$$
$$= 2 \cdot 2 \cdot 6$$
$$= 2 \cdot 2 \cdot 2 \cdot 3$$

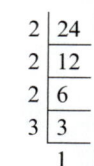

It does not matter which method is used to find a prime factorization. The final product, however, must consist of only prime numbers. The factors are usually written in ascending order.

MATH BACKGROUND

If the greatest common factor, or GCF, of two or more numbers is 1, the numbers are said to be relatively prime.

For example, 8 and 13 are relatively prime numbers. The factors of 8 are 1, 2, 4, and 8. The factors of 13 are 1 and 13. The only factor that is common to both numbers is 1.

The concept of relatively prime numbers is applied each time a fraction is reduced to lowest terms. The only common factor of the numerator and the denominator of a fraction in lowest terms is 1.

Example 1 **Finding the Prime Factorization of a Number**

Find the prime factorization of each number.

 120

SOLUTION

Method 1: List the factors and then the prime factors.

$$120 = 2 \cdot 60$$
$$= 2 \cdot 2 \cdot 30$$
$$= 2 \cdot 2 \cdot 2 \cdot 15$$
$$= 2 \cdot 2 \cdot 2 \cdot 3 \cdot 5$$

> **Hint**
> One method for finding the prime factorization of a number is to divide out all 2's first, then all 3's, then all 5's, and so on, if they are factors.

Method 2: Use a factor tree.

```
        120
       /   \
      10    12
     / \   / \
    2   5 3   4
             / \
            2   2
```

The prime factors are 2, 2, 2, 3, and 5.

Method 3: Use division by primes.

```
2 | 120
2 |  60
2 |  30
3 |  15
5 |   5
      1
```

The prime factors are 2, 2, 2, 3, and 5.

The prime factorization of $120 = 2 \cdot 2 \cdot 2 \cdot 3 \cdot 5$.

 924

SOLUTION

$$924 = 2 \cdot 462$$
$$= 2 \cdot 2 \cdot 231$$
$$= 2 \cdot 2 \cdot 3 \cdot 77$$
$$= 2 \cdot 2 \cdot 3 \cdot 7 \cdot 11$$

The prime factorization of $924 = 2 \cdot 2 \cdot 3 \cdot 7 \cdot 11$.

Prime factorization can be used when determining the **greatest common factor (GCF) of monomials,** which is the product of the greatest integer that divides without a remainder into the coefficients and the greatest power of each variable that divides without a remainder into each term.

Finding the GCF means finding the largest monomial that divides without a remainder into each term of a polynomial.

Example 1

This example shows how to find the prime factorization of a number by listing the factors, making a factor tree, or by making a table.

Error Alert Students may draw out only sections of the factor tree, and then overlook factors when writing the prime factorization of a number. Encourage them to complete the factor tree to avoid this type of error.

Additional Example 1

a. Find the prime factorization of 180. $180 = 2 \times 2 \times 3 \times 3 \times 5$

b. Find the prime factorization of 2730. $2730 = 2 \times 3 \times 5 \times 7 \times 13$

TEACHER TIP

Use the Sieve of Eratosthenes to find the prime numbers from 1 to 100. Write down the numbers from 1 to 100. Start with two, the first prime number. Eliminate all its multiples. Move to the next prime, eliminating all of its multiples. Repeat this process until only prime numbers remain.

 ENGLISH LEARNERS

Explain the meaning of the word **prime.** Say:

"The word prime means first. For example, it means first in time or it means the original version. Give other examples of being first."
Sample: first in importance or rank, first in quality, first in value

Ask volunteers to use the word prime in a sentence. Sample: The prime minister is the chief officer in a government.

Example 2

This example provides instruction in finding the GCF of algebraic terms in expressions.

Additional Example 2

a. Find the GCF of $9a^4b^7 + 12a^2b^5$. $3a^2b^5$

b. Find the GCF of $4m^3n^4p^6 - 6m^2n^6p^4$. $2m^2n^4p^4$

Example 3

This example demonstrates factoring a polynomial using the GCF of the terms and then checking the solution.

Additional Example 3

a. Factor $9x^4 - 3x^2 + x$ completely. $x(9x^3 - 3x + 1)$

Example 2 Determining the GCF of Algebraic Expressions

Find the GCF of each expression.

a. $6a^2b^3 + 8a^2b^2c$

SOLUTION

Write the prime factorization for both terms.

$6a^2b^3 = 2 \cdot 3 \cdot a \cdot a \cdot b \cdot b \cdot b$ $\qquad$ $8a^2b^2c = 2 \cdot 2 \cdot 2 \cdot a \cdot a \cdot b \cdot b \cdot c$

Find all factors that are common to both terms.

$6a^2b^3 = 2 \cdot 3 \cdot a \cdot a \cdot b \cdot b \cdot b$
$8a^2b^2c = 2 \cdot 2 \cdot 2 \cdot a \cdot a \cdot b \cdot b \cdot c$

Each term has one factor of 2, two factors of a and two factors of b, so the GCF of $6a^2b^3$ and $8a^2b^2c$ is $2 \cdot a \cdot a \cdot b \cdot b = 2a^2b^2$.

b. $8c^4d^2e - 12c^3d^4e^2$

SOLUTION

$8c^4d^2e = 2 \cdot 2 \cdot 2 \cdot c \cdot c \cdot c \cdot c \cdot d \cdot d \cdot e$
$12c^3d^4e^2 = 2 \cdot 2 \cdot 3 \cdot c \cdot c \cdot c \cdot d \cdot d \cdot d \cdot d \cdot e \cdot e$

The GCF is $4c^3d^2e$.

Finding the GCF of a polynomial allows you to factor it and to write the polynomial as a product of factors instead of the sum or difference of monomials.

Factoring a polynomial is the inverse of the Distributive Property. Using the Distributive Property will "undo" the factoring of the GCF.

Example 3 Factoring a Polynomial

Factor each polynomial completely.

a. $6x^3 + 8x^2 - 2x$

SOLUTION

Find the GCF of the terms. The GCF is $2x$.

Write each term of the polynomial with the GCF as a factor.

$6x^3 + 8x^2 - 2x = 2x \cdot 3x^2 + 2x \cdot 4x - 2x \cdot 1$
$2x(3x^2 + 4x - 1)$

Hint

You can also divide each term by the GCF.
$\frac{6x^3}{2x} = 3x^2$

Check

$2x(3x^2 + 4x - 1)$
$2x(3x^2) + 2x(4x) - 2x(1)$ $\qquad$ Use the Distributive Property.
$6x^3 + 8x^2 - 2x$ $\qquad$ Multiply each term by the GCF.

The factored polynomial is the same as the original polynomial.

238 Saxon Algebra 1

ALTERNATE METHOD FOR EXAMPLE 3

The method shown in Example 2 can be extended in Example 3 to help students factor a polynomial. Factor $4x^2y + 8x^3y^2 - 2x^2y^3$ completely.

Find the prime factorization of each term.

$4x^2y = 2 \times 2 \times x \times x \times y$

$8x^3y^2 = 2 \times 2 \times 2 \times x \times x \times x \times y \times y$

$2x^2y^3 = 2 \times x \times x \times y \times y \times y$

Circle the factors that are common to all the terms. By the method in Example 2, the GCF is $2x^2y$.

Now extend the example. Multiply the uncircled factors of the terms to find the reduced terms.

$2 = 2$
$2 \times 2 \times x \times y = 4xy$
$y \times y = y^2$

Rewrite the expression as the product of the GCF and the reduced terms.

$2x^2y(2 + 4xy - y^2)$

Caution

To completely factor a polynomial, you must factor out the greatest common factor, not just a common factor.

b. $9x^4y^2 - 9x^6y$

SOLUTION

The GCF of the polynomial is $9x^4y$.

$9x^4y^2 - 9x^6y = 9x^4y \cdot y - 9x^4y \cdot x^2$

The factored polynomial is $9x^4y(y - x^2)$.

Fractions can be simplified if the numerator and denominator contain common factors. This is because the operations of multiplication and division undo each other.

numeric fractions: $\frac{4}{10} = \frac{2}{5}$ and $\frac{8}{4} = \frac{2}{1}$ or 2

algebraic fractions: $\frac{4x}{10} = \frac{2x}{5}$ and $\frac{8x}{4} = 2x$

Notice that there is no addition or subtraction involved in the fractions above. Simplifying fractions with addition or subtraction in the numerator follows similar rules to adding or subtracting numeric fractions. A fraction can only be simplified if the numerator and the denominator have common factors.

Example 4 **Simplifying Algebraic Fractions**

Simplify each expression.

a. $\frac{3p + 3}{3}$

SOLUTION

$\frac{3p + 3}{3}$

$= \frac{3(p + 1)}{3}$ Factor out the GCF.

$= p + 1$ Simplify.

Math Reasoning

Write Explain why you cannot reduce the fraction $\frac{5x - 2}{5}$.

Sample: The numerator of the fraction cannot be factored, and therefore cannot be reduced, because division does not undo subtraction.

b. $\frac{5x - 25x^2}{5xy}$

SOLUTION

$\frac{5x - 25x^2}{5xy}$

$= \frac{5x(1 - 5x)}{5xy}$ Factor out the GCF.

$= \frac{1 - 5x}{y}$ Simplify.

Additional Example 3

b. Factor $8x^5y^3 - 6x^2y^8$ completely. $(2x^2y^3)(4x^3 - 3y^5)$

Example 4

This example provides instruction on using the GCF to simplify an algebraic expression.

Additional Example 4

Simplify each expression.

a. Simplify $\frac{4x + 8}{4}$. $x + 2$

b. Simplify $\frac{6a - 36a^2}{6ab}$. $\frac{1 - 6a}{b}$

Lesson 38   239

ALTERNATE METHOD FOR EXAMPLE 4

Rewrite the expression to be simplified as two or more separate fractions with a common denominator.

$\frac{3x + 1}{3} = \frac{3x}{3} + \frac{1}{3}$

Using the expression on the right side of the equal sign, it may be clearer that one part of the fraction can be simplified, but that the other cannot. The fraction is simplified $x + \frac{1}{3}$.

The method can also be used to identify numerators and denominators with common factors.

$\frac{3x + 6}{3} = \frac{3x}{3} + \frac{6}{3}$

$\frac{\cancel{3}x}{\cancel{3}} + \frac{\overset{2}{\cancel{6}}}{\cancel{3}} = \frac{x}{1} + \frac{2}{1} = x + 2$

Lesson 38   239

Example 5

This example demonstrates the use of factoring with the GCF.

Extend the Example

Suppose that the initial velocity is increased by 4 feet/second. Find the new formula. Then rewrite the formula by factoring the right side using the GCF and making the t^2-term positive.
$h = -16t^2 + 76t + 12;$
$h = -4(4t^2 - 19t - 3)$

Additional Example 5

The formula $h = -16t^2 + 76t + 16$ can be used to represent the height of an object that is launched into the air from 16 feet off the ground with an initial velocity of 76 ft/s. Rewrite the equation by factoring the right side using the GCF and making the t^2 term positive. $-4(4t^2 - 19t - 4)$

Lesson Practice

Problems a and b

Error Alert Some students may not completely factor the numbers using prime factors. Have students check their answers for numbers that have factors other than themselves and 1.

Problems c and d

Scaffolding Suggest that students write out the prime factorization of each term before finding the GCF.

Math Reasoning

Verify Show that the polynomial $-2x^3y - 6xy^3$ equivalent to $-2xy(x^2 + 3y^2)$?

Using the Distributive Property,
$-2xy(x^2 + 3y^2)$
$= -2xy \cdot x^2 + (-2xy)(3y^2)$
$= -2x^3y - 6xy^3$.

Example 5 Application: Finding the Height of an Object

The formula $h = -16t^2 + 72t + 12$ can be used to represent the height of an object that is launched into the air from 12 feet off the ground with an initial velocity of 72 feet/second. Rewrite the formula by factoring the right side using the GCF and making the t^2-term positive.

SOLUTION

The GCF of the monomials is 4. To keep the t^2-term positive, factor out -4. So $h = -4(4t^2 - 18t - 3)$.

Lesson Practice

Find the prime factorization of each number.
(Ex 1)
a. 100 $2 \cdot 2 \cdot 5 \cdot 5$ b. 51 $3 \cdot 17$

Find the GCF of each expression.
(Ex 2)
c. $24m^3n^4 + 32mn^5p$ $8mn^4$ d. $5p^2q^5r^2 - 10pq^2r^2$ $5pq^2r^2$

Factor each polynomial completely.
(Ex 3)
e. $8d^2e^3 + 12d^3e^2$ $4d^2e^2(2e + 3d)$ f. $12x^4y^2z - 42x^3y^3z^2$ $6x^3y^2z(2x - 7yz)$

Factor each expression completely.
(Ex 4)
g. $\dfrac{6x + 18}{6}$ $x + 3$ h. $\dfrac{18x + 45x^3}{9x}$ $2 + 5x^2$

i. The formula $h = -16t^2 + 60t + 4$ can be used to find the height of an
(Ex 5) object that is launched into the air from 4 feet off the ground with an initial velocity of 60 feet/second. Rewrite the formula by factoring the right side of the equation using the GCF and making the t^2-term positive. $h = -4(4t^2 - 15t - 1)$

Practice   Distributed and Integrated

Solve each equation for the variable indicated.

1. $6 = hj + k$ for j $j = \dfrac{6 - k}{h}$ 2. $\dfrac{a + 3}{b} = c$ for a $a = bc - 3$
(29)   (29)

Draw a graph that represents each situation.

3. A tomato plant grows taller at a steady pace.
(Inv 2)

4. A tomato plant grows at a slow pace, and then grows rapidly with more sun and
(Inv 2) water.   See Additional Answers.

5. A tomato plant grows slowly at first, remains a constant height during a dry spell,
(Inv 2) and then grows rapidly with more sun and water.   See Additional Answers.

Find each unit rate.

6. Thirty textbooks weigh 144 pounds.   7. Doug makes $43.45 in 5.5 hours. $7.90/hour
(31) 4.8 lb/book   (31)

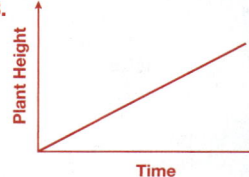
3.
Plant Height
Time

240   *Saxon Algebra 1*

INCLUSION

To help students with factoring algebraic expressions, have them use a grid to list the terms and the prime factorization of each variable in the terms m^3p^2s and mp^2s^4. Then have students circle each pair of like variables.

Students can now find the factors of the GCF, mp^2s. Remind them to multiply the circled variables to form one term. The variables that are not circled are terms in the factored form of the expression $m^3p^2s + mp^2s^4$, or $mp^2s(m^2 + s^3)$.

8. Write 2×10^6 in standard notation. **2,000,000**

9. Solve $\frac{p}{3} = \frac{18}{21}$. $\frac{18}{7}$ or ≈ 2.57

*10. Find the prime factorization of 140. $2 \cdot 2 \cdot 5 \cdot 7$

*11. Multiple Choice Which of the following expressions is the correct simplification of $\frac{10x + 5}{5}$? **B**
- **A** $2x + 5$
- **B** $2x + 1$
- **C** $10x + 1$
- **D** $5x$

*12. (Free Fall) The function $h = 40 - 16t^2$ can be used to find the height of an object as it falls to the ground after being dropped from 40 feet in the air. Rewrite the equation by factoring the right side. $h = 8(5 - 2t^2)$

*13. Write Explain how the Distributive Property and factoring a polynomial are related.

13. Sample: They use opposite operations. The Distributive Property uses multiplication to rewrite a product as a polynomial. Factoring divides out the GCF to write a polynomial as a product of its factors.

*14. Generalize Explain why the algebraic fraction $\frac{6(x-1)}{6}$ can be reduced, and why the fraction $\frac{6x-1}{6}$ cannot be reduced.

14. Sample: The fraction $\frac{6(x-1)}{6}$ can be reduced because the division of 6 undoes the multiplication of 6 in the numerator. The numerator of the fraction $\frac{6x-1}{6}$ cannot be factored and therefore cannot be reduced because division does not undo subtraction.

15. (Biology) The approximate diameter of a DNA helix is 0.000000002 meters. Write this number in scientific notation. 2×10^{-9}

16. Measurement A nanosecond is one-billionth of a second. Write this number in scientific notation. 1×10^{-9}

17. Write 78,000,000 in scientific notation. 7.8×10^7

*18. Geometry A square has side length 6.04×10^{-5} meters. What is its area? 3.64816×10^{-9} square meters

*19. The triangles are similar. Find the missing length. **16**

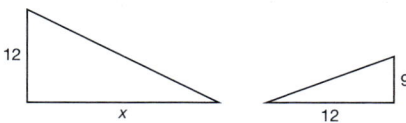

20. Multi-Step An adult brain weighs about 3 pounds.
a. There are about 100 billion brain cells in the brain. Write this number in scientific notation. 1×10^{11}
b. Divide the weight of an adult brain by the number of cells and find how many pounds one brain cell weighs. Write the answer in scientific notation. 3×10^{-11} lb

*21. Analyze Find the x- and y-intercepts for $y = 12x$ and explain how they relate to the graph of the equation.

21. Sample: When $y = 0$, $0 = 12x$, so $0 = x$. When $x = 0$, $y = 12(0)$, so $y = 0$. The x-intercept and the y-intercept are the same, the origin.

22. (Fundraising) The math club has a carwash to raise money. Out of the first 40 vehicles, 22 are SUVs and 18 are cars. What are the odds against the next one being a car? **11:9**

*23. Justify Explain why the statement $3^{-2} = -6$ is false. The base of 3 and the exponent of -2 were multiplied; the rule for negative exponents was not used. The correct solution is $3^{-2} = \frac{1}{9}$.

Lesson 38   241

Check for Understanding

The questions below help assess the concepts taught in this lesson.

"How can the GCF of the variable terms be found quickly in the terms of an algebraic expression?" The GCF for any variable in the terms will be the variable with the least power.

"Why is this factor of the expression called the greatest common factor, or GCF?" It is the largest factor of each of the terms of an expression.

3 Practice

Math Conversations

Discussion to strengthen understanding

Problems 6 and 7
Error Alert Students may write a ratio rather than the unit rate. Remind students that the unit rate compares one of something to another quantity.

Problem 13
Extend the Problem
"Show how factoring and the Distributive Property are related using the expression $4m^2n^8 - 6m^4n^3$." Sample: Distribute the GCF $2m^2n^3$ over $(2n^5 - 3m^2)$. The product is $4m^2n^8 - 6m^4n^3$.

Problem 20
Extend the Problem
"Write the weight of one brain cell in pounds in standard notation." 0.00000000003 lb

 MANIPULATIVE USE

Materials: algebra tiles

Have students model the algebraic terms using algebra tiles.

$4x^6y^3 + 6x^3y^2$

Students can physically stack the tiles by placing one of the same kind of tile on top of each other. Only the stacked tiles will be a factor used to calculate the GCF.

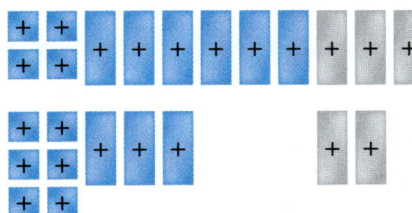

Lesson 38   241

Problem 28

Guide the students by asking them the following questions.

"What does the variable represent?" the number of visits per month

"What expression represents the cost of the visits to Barton Springs Pool without the membership fee?" 2x

"What expression represents the total monthly cost of the visits to Barton Springs Pool?" 2x + $20.90

---

24. Analysis A bookstore wants to show the number of different types of books that were sold on a given day. Why is this graph misleading? Sample: The break in the graph is distorting the number of books sold.

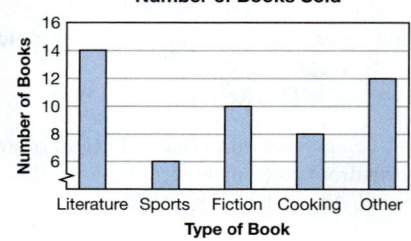

Number of Books Sold

*25. Determine if the sequence $\frac{5}{4}, 2, \frac{11}{4}, \frac{7}{2}, \ldots$ is an arithmetic sequence. If yes, find the common difference and the next two terms. yes; $\frac{3}{4}; \frac{17}{4}, 5$

26. Multiple Choice Which equation is in standard form? **D**
- **A** $y - 6 = 3(x + 4)$
- **B** $y = -6x + 13$
- **C** $10y = 12y + 25$
- **D** $9x + 11y = 65$

27. How is the value 30 represented in a stem-and-leaf plot? 3|0

28. (Pool Charges) Barton Springs Pool charges $2 a visit plus a membership fee of $20.90 a month. Blue Danube Pool charges $2.95 a visit, with no membership fee. At what number of visits per month will the total fees for each pool be the same? 22 visits

29. (Stock Market) On a day of heavy trading, one share of ABC Industries' stock originally decreased by $5 only to increase later in the day by twice the original value. The stock ended the day at $43 a share. What was the starting price of one share? $16

30. Multi-Step The table shows the total number of shrubs a gardener planted after each half hour.

Time (hr)	0.5	1	1.5	2
Number of Shrubs	1	3	7	8

a. Plot this data on a coordinate grid.

b. Determine if the graph is a function. Explain. yes; A vertical line will cross the graph at one point only.

c. **Predict** Can you predict the number of shrubs the gardener will plant in 3 hours? Why or why not? no; This is not a linear function.

30a.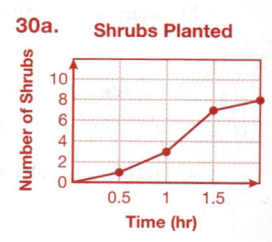

Shrubs Planted

242 *Saxon* Algebra 1

CHALLENGE

Challenge students to write a 4-term expression that can be factored using the GCF $6g^4h^7k^2$. Then have students factor the expression that they wrote.
Sample:
$12g^4h^8k^4 - 30g^5h^7k^3 + 18g^7h^9k^2 - 6g^4h^{10}k^6$;
$(6g^4h^7k^2)(2hk^2 - 5gk + 3g^3h^2 - h^3k^4)$

LOOKING FORWARD

Simplifying expressions using the GCF will prepare students for

- **Lesson 58** Multiplying Polynomials
- **Lesson 60** Finding Special Products of Binomials
- **Lesson 72** Factoring Trinomials: $x^2 + bx + c$
- **Lesson 75** Factoring Trinomials: $ax^2 + bx + c$
- **Lesson 79** Factoring Trinomials by Using the GCF

LESSON 39

Using the Distributive Property to Simplify Rational Expressions

Warm Up

1. **Vocabulary** The set of _____ numbers includes all rational and irrational numbers.   **real**

Simplify.

2. $-3x^2y(4x^2y^{-1} - xy)$ $-12x^4 + 3x^3y^2$

3. $mn(2x - 3my + 5ny)$ $2mnx - 3m^2ny + 5mn^2y$

4. $\dfrac{5x - 25x^2}{5x}$ $1 - 5x$

5. Factor. $3a^2b^3 - 6a^4b + 12ab$ $3ab(ab^2 - 2a^3 + 4)$

New Concepts

A **rational expression** is an expression with a variable in the denominator. Rational expressions can be treated just like fractions. As with fractions, the denominator cannot equal zero. Therefore, any value of the variable that makes the denominator equal to zero is not permitted.

Variables stand for unknown real numbers. So, all properties that apply to real numbers also apply to rational expressions. The Distributive Property can be used to simplify rational expressions.

Math Reasoning

Write Why isn't division by zero allowed?

Sample: The number 0 has no reciprocal because no number can be multiplied by 0 to give a product of 1. Therefore, division by zero is impossible.

Hint

When multiplying powers, add the exponents. When dividing powers, subtract the exponents.

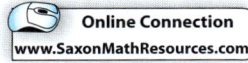

Example 1 Distributing Over Addition

Simplify $\dfrac{x^2}{y^2}\left(\dfrac{x^2}{y} + \dfrac{3y^3}{m}\right)$.

SOLUTION

$\dfrac{x^2}{y^2}\left(\dfrac{x^2}{y} + \dfrac{3y^3}{m}\right)$

$= \left(\dfrac{x^2}{y^2} \cdot \dfrac{x^2}{y}\right) + \left(\dfrac{x^2}{y^2} \cdot \dfrac{3y^3}{m}\right)$ Multiply $\dfrac{x^2}{y^2}$ by each term inside the parentheses.

$= \dfrac{x^4}{y^3} + \dfrac{3x^2y^3}{y^2m}$ Simplify.

$\dfrac{x^4}{y^3} + \dfrac{3x^2y}{m}; y \ne 0, m \ne 0$

Note that $y \ne 0$ and $m \ne 0$ because either value would make the denominator equal to zero.

---

1 Warm Up

Problem 4
Watch for students who cancel the term $5x$ in the numerator and denominator. Remind them that the common factor $5x$ must be factored out of the numerator and then canceled.

2 New Concepts

In this lesson, students learn to use the Distributive Property to simplify rational expressions.

Emphasize that, like a fraction, the denominator of a rational expression cannot equal zero.

Example 1

Error Alert When simplifying the expression, some students may cancel the y in the denominator of the first term inside the parentheses with the y^3 in the numerator of the second term inside of the parentheses. Remind them that only factors are canceled. Cancellation across addition or subtraction will result in errors.

Additional Example 1

Simplify $\dfrac{a}{b^3}\left(\dfrac{a^2}{b} + \dfrac{3b^2}{z}\right)$. $\dfrac{a^3}{b^4} + \dfrac{3a}{bz}$

LESSON RESOURCES

Student Edition Practice Workbook 39
Reteaching Master 39
Adaptations Master 39
Challenge & Enrichment Master C39

MATH BACKGROUND

The problems in this lesson require a clear understanding of the Distributive Property. A goal of simplification is to eliminate parentheses. By multiplying through, or over, parentheses, the Distributive Property accomplishes that goal.

The rules for exponents must also be followed. An expression is not considered simplified if any of the variables have a negative exponent, regardless of whether they appear in the numerator or the denominator.

Because rational expressions have a variable(s) in the denominator, it is important to remember that the value of the variables in the denominator cannot cause the denominator to equal zero. For those values of the variable, the fraction is undefined. (Note: A variable with a value of zero can appear in the denominator if the exponent is negative because when the expression is simplified, that variable will be in the numerator.)

Lesson 39   243

Example 2

Note that values of the variables that cause the denominator of the original problem, as well as the simplified expression, to equal zero are given with the solution. This is because the original fraction would be undefined if these values were allowed.

Additional Example 2

Simplify $\frac{x^2}{c^2}\left(\frac{dmy}{x^2a} - 2x^3y\right)$.

$\frac{dmy}{c^2a} - \frac{2x^5y}{c^2}, a \neq 0, c \neq 0, x \neq 0$

Example 3

These problems introduce negative exponents into the distributive and simplification processes.

TEACHER TIP

Tell students to show all the steps when solving. This will allow for errors to be recognized when multiplying or dividing powers.

Additional Example 3

Simplify each expression.

a. $\frac{x^2}{y^{-3}}\left(\frac{x^2}{y} - \frac{3z^{-2}y}{x}\right) x^4y^2 - \frac{3y^4x}{z^2}$,
$x \neq 0, y \neq 0, z \neq 0$

b. $\frac{a^{-1}}{b^2}\left(\frac{3bm}{da^{-2}c^{-4}} + a^{-3}c^{-4}\right)$
$\frac{3mc^4a}{db} + \frac{1}{b^2a^4c^4}, a \neq 0, b \neq 0,$
$c \neq 0, d \neq 0$

Math Reasoning

Justify Why can the final expression not be simplified further?

Sample: As with fractions, the terms cannot be added because they do not have like denominators.

Example 2 Distributing Over Subtraction

Simplify $\frac{m}{z}\left(\frac{axp}{mk} - 2m^4p^4\right)$.

SOLUTION

$\frac{m}{z}\left(\frac{apx}{mk} - 2m^4p^4\right)$

$= \frac{mapx}{zmk} - \frac{m \cdot 2m^4p^4}{z}$ Distribute $\frac{m}{z}$.

$= \frac{apx}{zk} - \frac{2m^5p^4}{z}; z \neq 0, k \neq 0, m \neq 0$ Simplify.

Note that $z \neq 0$, $k \neq 0$, and $m \neq 0$ because any of those values would make a denominator equal to zero. Although there is not an m in the denominator of the final expression, there is one in the denominator of the original expression; that is why $m \neq 0$.

When simplifying an expression with negative exponents, the final expression should not have negative exponents.

Example 3 Simplifying with Negative Exponents

Simplify each expression.

a. $\frac{b^3}{d^{-3}}\left(\frac{2b^2}{d} - \frac{f^{-3}d}{b}\right)$

SOLUTION

$\frac{b^3}{d^{-3}}\left(\frac{2b^2}{d} - \frac{f^{-3}d}{b}\right)$

$= \frac{b^3 \cdot 2b^2}{d^{-3} \cdot d} - \frac{b^3 \cdot f^{-3}d}{d^{-3}b}$ Distribute $\frac{b^3}{d^{-3}}$.

$= \frac{2b^5}{d^{-2}} - \frac{b^3f^{-3}d}{d^{-3}b}$ Product Property of Exponents

$= 2b^5d^2 - \frac{b^2d^4}{f^3}; d \neq 0, b \neq 0, f \neq 0$ Simplify.

b. $\frac{n^{-1}}{m}\left(\frac{mx}{cn^{-3}p^{-5}} + 5n^{-4}p^{-5}\right)$

SOLUTION

$\frac{n^{-1}}{m}\left(\frac{mx}{cn^{-3}p^{-5}} + 5n^{-4}p^{-5}\right)$

$= \frac{n^{-1}mx}{mcn^{-3}p^{-5}} + \frac{n^{-1} \cdot 5n^{-4}p^{-5}}{m}$ Distribute $\frac{n^{-1}}{m}$.

$= \frac{n^{-1}x}{cn^{-3}p^{-5}} + \frac{5n^{-5}p^{-5}}{m}$ Simplify.

$= \frac{n^2xp^5}{c} + \frac{5}{mn^5p^5}; c \neq 0, m \neq 0, n \neq 0, p \neq 0$ Simplify.

ALTERNATE METHOD FOR EXAMPLE 3b

Before students distribute, have them change any factors with negative exponents to factors with positive exponents. Then have them distribute and, if necessary, cancel.

$\frac{n^{-1}}{m}\left(\frac{mx}{cn^{-3}p^{-5}} + 5n^{-4}p^{-5}\right) = \frac{1}{nm}\left(\frac{mxn^3p^5}{c} + \frac{5}{n^4p^5}\right)$

$= \frac{mxn^3p^5}{nmc} + \frac{5}{nmn^4p^5}$

$= \frac{xn^2p^5}{c} + \frac{5}{mn^5p^5}; c \neq 0, m \neq 0, n \neq 0, p \neq 0$

Example 4 **Distributing Over Multiple Operations**

Simplify each expression.

a. $\dfrac{ab}{c^2}\left(\dfrac{axb}{c} + 2bx - \dfrac{4}{c^2}\right)$

SOLUTION

$\dfrac{ab}{c^2}\left(\dfrac{axb}{c} + 2bx - \dfrac{4}{c^2}\right)$

$= \dfrac{ab \cdot axb}{c^2 \cdot c} + \dfrac{ab \cdot 2bx}{c^2} - \dfrac{ab \cdot 4}{c^2 \cdot c^2}$ Distribute $\dfrac{ab}{c^2}$.

$= \dfrac{a^2b^2x}{c^3} + \dfrac{2ab^2x}{c^2} - \dfrac{4ab}{c^4}$; $c \neq 0$ Simplify.

b. $\dfrac{g^2h}{d^2}\left(\dfrac{g^{-2}xh}{d^{-1}} - 2h^4x^{-1} + \dfrac{9}{d^{-3}}\right)$

SOLUTION

$\dfrac{g^2h}{d^2}\left(\dfrac{g^{-2}xh}{d^{-1}} - 2h^4x^{-1} + \dfrac{9}{d^{-3}}\right)$

$= \dfrac{g^0xh^2}{d} - \dfrac{2h^5x^{-1}g^2}{d^2} + \dfrac{9g^2h}{d^{-1}}$ Distribute $\dfrac{g^2h}{d^2}$.

$= \dfrac{xh^2}{d} - \dfrac{2h^5g^2}{xd^2} + 9dg^2h$; $d \neq 0$ and $x \neq 0$ Simplify.

Hint

When a variable has no exponent, it is implied that the exponent is 1.

Any variable or number raised to the 0 power equals 1.

Example 5 **Application: Furniture**

A tabletop that is in the shape of a trapezoid has height $\dfrac{a^2c}{b}$, and bases $\dfrac{b^3}{c}$ and $\dfrac{da}{c^2}$. The area of the tabletop is represented by the expression $\dfrac{a^2c}{2b}\left(\dfrac{b^3}{c} + \dfrac{da}{c^2}\right)$. Simplify the expression.

SOLUTION

$\dfrac{a^2c}{2b}\left(\dfrac{b^3}{c} + \dfrac{da}{c^2}\right)$

$= \dfrac{a^2cb^3}{2bc} + \dfrac{a^2c \cdot da}{2bc^2}$ Distribute.

$= \dfrac{a^2b^3c}{2bc} + \dfrac{a^3cd}{2bc^2}$ Multiply.

$= \dfrac{a^2b^2}{2} + \dfrac{a^3d}{2bc}$ Simplify.

The area of the tabletop can be represented by the simplified expression $\dfrac{a^2b^2}{2} + \dfrac{a^3d}{2bc}$ where b and $c \neq 0$.

Hint

The formula for the area of a trapezoid is $A = \dfrac{1}{2}h(b_1 + b_2)$.

Lesson 39   245

Example 4

When distributing over several operations it may be helpful for students to show each term in parentheses multiplied by the factor outside of the parentheses.

Additional Example 4

a. $\dfrac{fg^2}{h}\left(\dfrac{fxg}{h} + \dfrac{4}{h^2} - 2gx\right)$

$\dfrac{f^2xg^3}{h^2} + \dfrac{4fg^2}{h^3} - \dfrac{2fg^3x}{h}$, $h \neq 0$

b. $\dfrac{mn^4}{p^{-2}}\left(\dfrac{m^{-2}rn}{p^3} - n^4r^2 + \dfrac{8m}{p}\right)$

$\dfrac{r}{mn^3p} - \dfrac{mp^2}{r^2} + \dfrac{8m^2p}{n^4}$, $m \neq 0$, $n \neq 0$, $p \neq 0$, $r \neq 0$

Example 5

This problem relates the use of the distributive property to geometric formulas.

Extend the Example

"If another table in the shape of a trapezoid with the same-size bases has a height $\dfrac{c^2a^{-1}}{b^2}$ what is the area of that table in simplest form?" $\dfrac{cb}{2a} + \dfrac{d}{2b^2}$

Additional Example 5

A triangular section of a building has an area represented by the expression $\dfrac{r^4f}{2}\left(\dfrac{qr^1}{f^2t} - \dfrac{6t^3q}{r^1f^6}\right)$. Simplify the expression."

$\dfrac{r^3qf^3}{2t} + \dfrac{3r^5qt^3}{f^5}$, $f \neq 0$, $r \neq 0$, $t \neq 0$

ENGLISH LEARNERS

Explain the meaning of the word **implied.** Discuss that implied refers to something that is suggested or understood. Say:

"Implied means that something is understood without being said. For example, happiness is implied with a smile."

Ask a volunteer to use the word in a sentence. Sample: Sadness can be implied with a tear.

Lesson 39   245

Lesson Practice

Problems c and f
Error Alert When there is no common variable in the numerator from which to subtract the exponent of the variable in the denominator, some students may leave the variable in the denominator even if it has a negative exponent. Remind them that the term is not simplified if it has a negative exponent in the denominator.

Problems b, d, e, and f
Scaffolding Before students distribute, suggest that they write the second term in the parentheses in fraction form.

 Check for Understanding
The questions below help assess the concepts taught in this lesson.

"Explain how to use the **Distributive Property to simplify a rational expression.**" The term outside the parentheses must be multiplied by each term inside the parentheses so that the parentheses can be removed.

"For which values is the denominator undefined in the expression $\frac{2x^2y}{xy}$?" $x = 0; y = 0$

3 Practice

Math Conversations
Discussion to strengthen understanding

Problem 6
Error Alert
Students will often write the algebraic expression in the order that it is read: $3 - x$. Remind students of the meaning of less than.

Lesson Practice

Simplify each expression.

a. (Ex 1) $\dfrac{r^2}{q}\left(\dfrac{r^2}{q^3} + \dfrac{7q^3}{w}\right)$ $\quad \dfrac{r^4}{q^4} + \dfrac{7q^2r^2}{w}, q \neq 0, w \neq 0$

b. (Ex 2) $\dfrac{t}{z}\left(\dfrac{uay}{tq} - 2t^3y^2\right)$ $\quad \dfrac{uay}{zq} - \dfrac{2t^4y^2}{z}, q \neq 0, t \neq 0, z \neq 0$

Math Reasoning
Generalize For problem f, which variable in the numerator cannot equal zero? Explain.

Sample: The variable d has a negative exponent, so $d \neq 0$ because $d^{-2} = \frac{1}{d^2}$. If $d = 0$, the expression will be undefined.

c. (Ex 3) $\dfrac{j^{-2}}{m}\left(\dfrac{j^{-3}}{m^{-2}} + \dfrac{9m^3}{k}\right)$ $\quad \dfrac{m}{j^5} + \dfrac{9m^2}{kj^2}, j \neq 0, k \neq 0, m \neq 0$

d. (Ex 3) $\dfrac{n^{-2}}{z}\left(\dfrac{v^{-2}cb}{nv^{-1}} - 4n^5b^{-3}\right)$ $\quad \dfrac{cb}{n^3zv} - \dfrac{4n^3}{zb^3}, b \neq 0, n \neq 0, v \neq 0, z \neq 0$

e. (Ex 4) $\dfrac{fs}{d^4}\left(\dfrac{fhs}{d} + 2sk - \dfrac{7}{d^6}\right)$ $\quad \dfrac{f^2hs^2}{d^5} + \dfrac{2fs^2k}{d^4} - \dfrac{7fs}{d^{10}}, d \neq 0$

f. (Ex 4) $\dfrac{zx}{w^{-2}}\left(\dfrac{zd^{-2}x}{w} + 5tz - \dfrac{2}{w^{-4}}\right)$ $\quad \dfrac{z^2x^2w}{d^2} + 5tz^2xw^2 - 2zxw^6, d \neq 0, w \neq 0$

g. (Ex 5) **(Painting)** A rectangular canvas is to be painted. The area of the canvas with length $\left(\dfrac{t^{-3}}{y^{-2}} + \dfrac{z^{-4}}{y^5t}\right)$ and width $\dfrac{t^2y}{z}$ is represented by the expression $\dfrac{t^2y}{z}\left(\dfrac{t^{-3}}{y^{-2}} + \dfrac{z^{-4}}{y^5t}\right)$ where t, y and $z \neq 0$. Simplify the expression. $\dfrac{y^3}{tz} + \dfrac{t}{y^4z^5}, t \neq 0, y$

Practice Distributed and Integrated

Solve each equation. Check your answer.

1. (26) $4\left(y + \dfrac{3}{2}\right) = -18$ $y = -6$

2. (26) $x - 4 + 2x = 14$ $x = 6$

3. (1) True or False: The set of integers is closed under division. If false, give a counterexample. false; Sample: $2 \div 3$ is not an integer.

Translate words into algebraic expressions.

4. (17) the sum of a and 3 $a + 3$

5. (17) 2.5 more than k $k + 2.5$

6. (17) 3 less than x $x - 3$

7. (17) 2 more than the product of 3 and y $3y + 2$

*8. (39) Simplify $\dfrac{d^2}{s^2}\left(\dfrac{d^2}{s} + \dfrac{9s^3}{h}\right)$. $\dfrac{d^4}{s^3} + \dfrac{9d^2s}{h}, h \neq 0, s \neq 0$

*9. (39) **Write** Why isn't division by zero allowed? Sample: Division by zero is undefined. A number cannot be divided into groups of zero and zero has no reciprocal.

*10. (39) **Justify** Simplify $\dfrac{x^{-2}}{n^{-1}}(2x^{-4} + n^{-3})$ and explain each step.

10. Sample:
$\dfrac{x^{-2}}{n^{-1}}(2x^{-4} + n^{-3})$
$= \dfrac{2x^{-4} \cdot x^{-2}}{n^{-1}} + \dfrac{x^{-2}n^{-3}}{n^{-1}}$ Distributive Property
$= \dfrac{2x^{-6}}{n^{-1}} + n^{-2}x^{-2}$ Rules of Exponents
$= \dfrac{2n}{x^6} + \dfrac{1}{n^2x^2}$ Rules of Exponents
$n \neq 0, x \neq 0$

*11. (39) **Multiple Choice** Simplify $\dfrac{g^{-2}s}{b^2}\left(\dfrac{g^{-3}s^{-1}}{b^{-1}} + \dfrac{4}{b^3}\right)$ where b, g and $s \neq 0$. **D**

A $\dfrac{4g^{-5}s^{-1}}{b^4}$

B $\dfrac{g^{-5}s^{-1}}{b} + \dfrac{4g^{-2}s}{b^5}$

C $\dfrac{g^{-5}}{b} + \dfrac{4g^{-2}s}{b^5}$

D $\dfrac{1}{bg^5} + \dfrac{4s}{b^5g^2}$

246 Saxon Algebra 1

INCLUSION

For students having difficulty keeping track of the factors when distributing, have them use a highlighter to color-code the factor that is being distributed over the addition (or subtraction). Then, they can confirm visually that the factor is being applied to each term in the parentheses.

Example 1:

$\dfrac{x^2}{y^2}\left(\dfrac{x^2}{y} + \dfrac{3y^3}{m}\right) = \left(\dfrac{x^2}{y^2} \cdot \dfrac{x^2}{y}\right) + \left(\dfrac{x^2}{y^2} \cdot \dfrac{3y^3}{m}\right)$

For students having difficulty keeping track of the factors when simplifying rational expressions, have them use a highlighter to color-code common factors.

Example 2: $\dfrac{mapx}{zmk} - \dfrac{m \cdot 2m^4p^4}{z}$

*12. Simplify the expression $\frac{w^2p}{t}\left(\frac{4}{w^4} - \frac{t^2}{p^5}\right)$. $\frac{4p}{tw^2} - \frac{w^2t}{p^4}, p \neq 0, t \neq 0, w \neq 0$
(39)

*13. Find the prime factorization of 918. $2 \cdot 3 \cdot 3 \cdot 3 \cdot 17$
(38)

*14. **Error Analysis** Two students factor the polynomial $16x^4y^2z + 28x^3y^4z^2 + 4x^3y^2z$ as shown below. Which student is correct? Explain the error.
(38)

Student A	Student B
$4x^3y^2z(4x + 7y^2z)$	$4x^3y^2z(4x + 7y^2z + 1)$

14. Student B; Sample: The third term of the polynomial is the same as the GCF, and factoring results in a monomial divided by itself, which is 1. Student A represented the third term with 0, not 1.

15. **Geometry** The area of a rectangle is represented by the polynomial $6a^2b + 15ab$. Find two factors that could be used to represent the length and width of the rectangle. $3ab(2a + 5)$; Sample: $3ab$ and $2a + 5$
(38)

16. **Multiple Choice** Complete the following statement: The side lengths of similar figures _____. **C**
(36)
  A must be congruent
  B cannot be congruent
  C are in proportion
  D must be whole numbers

17. **Multi-Step** Use the expression $24x^2y^3 + 18xy^2 + 6xy$.
(38)
  a. What is the GCF of the polynomial? $6xy$
  b. Use the GCF to factor the polynomial completely. $6xy(4xy^2 + 3y + 1)$

*18. **Probability** The probability that a point selected at random is in the shaded region of the figure is represented by the fraction $\frac{\text{area of shaded rectangle}}{\text{area of entire rectangle}}$. Find the probability. Write your answer in simplest form. $\frac{6(x+4)}{9 \cdot 15} = \frac{6(x+4)}{135} = \frac{2(x+4)}{45}$
(38)

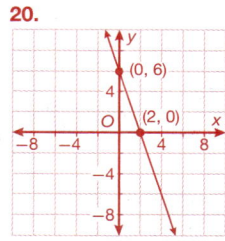

*19. **Analyze** In order to double the volume of water in a fish tank, is it necessary to double the length, width, and height of the tank? If yes, explain why. If no, explain how to double the volume of water. no; Sample: Double only one of the dimensions to double the volume.
(36)

*20. Graph $27x + 9y = 54$ using the x- and y-intercepts.
(35)

*21. **Fundraising** For a fundraiser, the science club sold posters for $5 and mugs for $8. The equation $5x + 8y = 480$ shows that they made $480. Find the x- and y-intercepts. The x-intercept is 96 and the y-intercept is 60.
(35)

20. (graph showing line through (0, 6) and (2, 0))

22. **Entertainment** A contestant is in the bonus round of a game show where she can win $1500 for answering the first question correctly and then an additional $500 for each correct response to each of the next five questions. If she answers all of the questions correctly, how much money will she receive when she answers the sixth question? $4000
(34)

Lesson 39 247

Problem 13
Point out to students that the factorization may begin with any two factors whose product is 918. Here, knowledge of the divisibility rules can be helpful. The prime factorization will be the same regardless of the beginning factors. Only the order of the factors in the prime factorization may vary.

Problem 14
Guide the students by asking them the following questions.

"What is the GCF of the terms in the polynomial?" $4x^3y^2z$

"What is the quotient of any number, except zero, and itself?" 1

Lesson 39 247

Problem 27

Guide the student by asking them the following questions.

"What does it mean in terms of outcomes that the odds of winning are 3 to 7?" The number of favorable outcomes is 3 and the number of unfavorable outcomes is 7.

"How would you find the total number of possible outcomes?" Add the number of favorable and unfavorable outcomes.

"How many total outcomes are there?" 10

"If the odds of winning a CD are 3:7, how many outcomes are there for not winning a CD?" 7

"Probability is the ratio of favorable outcomes to total outcomes. How many favorable outcomes are there for winning something other than a CD?" 7

Problem 30

Extend the Problem

Use the rule to find $f(18)$. 9.5

---

23. Write 0.00608 in scientific notation. 6.08×10^{-3}
(37)

24. **Error Analysis** Two students write 1.32×10^{-5} in standard form. Which student is correct? Explain the error.
(37)

Student A	Student B
0.00000132	0.0000132

24. Student B; Sample: Student A wrote 5 zeros and moved the decimal point 6 places instead of 5.

25. **Verify** Show that $4\frac{3}{4}$ is the solution to $\frac{1}{n-1} = \frac{4}{15}$.
(31)

25. $\frac{1}{4\frac{3}{4} - 1} \stackrel{?}{=} \frac{4}{15}$
$4\left(4\frac{3}{4} - 1\right) \stackrel{?}{=} 15(1)$
$19 - 4 \stackrel{?}{=} 15$
$15 = 15$

26. Evaluate the expression $\frac{x^2 y^{-2}}{z^2}$ if $x = 3$, $y = 4$, and $z = -2$. $\frac{9}{64}$
(32)

27. **Analyze** The odds of winning a CD in a raffle are 3:7. Explain how to find the probability of not winning a CD.
(33)

27. Sample: Odds are the ratio of favorable to unfavorable outcomes, so added together they equal the total number of outcomes ($3 + 7 = 10$). If the odds of winning a CD are 3:7, then there are 7 outcomes for not winning a CD. So the probability of not winning a CD is $\frac{7}{10}$.

28. **Stamp Collecting** The table shows some collectible stamps with their estimated values. Explain whether the ordered pairs, such as (2, $2) and (2, $3), will be a function. Sample: The ordered pairs will form a relation but not a function because a given stamp will have more than one possible value.
(25)

Number	Stamp	Value (low)	Value (high)
1	11¢ President Hayes (1931)	$2	$4
2	14¢ American Indian (1931)	$2	$3
3	4¢ President Taft (1930)	$1	$3
4	1¢ Benjamin Franklin (1911)	$5	$50

29. **Salaries** In an interview with a potential employee, an employer shows a line graph displaying the average salary of employees over several years. Explain why the graph is potentially misleading and why the employer might have shown this graph. Sample: The vertical axis has a broken scale, making the data appear to increase dramatically. The employer may want the candidate to feel the employer gives large raises.
(27)

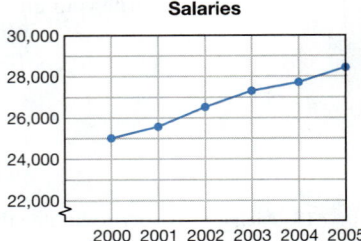
Salaries

30. **Formulate** Write a rule for the table in function notation.
(30) $f(g) = 0.5g + 0.5$

g	2	4	6	8	10
$f(g)$	1.5	2.5	3.5	4.5	5.5

248 *Saxon* Algebra 1

 CHALLENGE

Some problems require distributing more than one factor. Simplify the expression.

$\left(\dfrac{ab^{-2}}{c^2} + 4b^{-1}d^{-2}\right)\left(\dfrac{a^{-3}db^4}{c^{-7}} - \dfrac{5b^{-2}}{c^{-3}}\right)$

$\dfrac{b^2 c^5 d}{a^2} - \dfrac{5ac}{b^4} + \dfrac{4b^3 c^7}{a^3 d} - \dfrac{20c^3}{b^3 d^2}, a \neq 0, b \neq 0, c \neq 0,$
$d \neq 0$

 LOOKING FORWARD

Using the Distributive Property to simplify rational expressions prepares students for

• **Lesson 43** Simplifying Rational Expressions

• **Lesson 51** Simplifying Rational Expressions with Like Denominators.

• **Lesson 57** Finding the Least Common Multiple

• **Lesson 78** Graphing Rational Functions

• **Lesson 88** Multiplying and Dividing Rational Expressions

LESSON 40

Simplifying and Evaluating Expressions Using the Power Property of Exponents

Warm Up

1. **Vocabulary** The _____ is the number that tells how many times the base of a power is used as a factor.   **exponent**

Simplify.

2. $(4x^2y^3)(5x^4y^4)$ $20x^6y^7$

3. $\dfrac{24x^3y^6}{36x^5y^3}$ $\dfrac{2y^3}{3x^2}$

4. $(-3)^2 - 3^2$ 0

5. Compare: $4^2 + \sqrt{36}$ $>$ $-(-3)^2 + \sqrt{25}$. Use >, <, or =.

New Concepts

Previous lessons have explored expressions involving exponents. Several rules and definitions have been developed.

$$x^0 = 1 \qquad x^m \cdot x^n = x^{m+n}$$

$$x^1 = x \qquad x^{-n} = \dfrac{1}{x^n}$$

$$\dfrac{x^m}{x^n} = x^{m-n}$$

There is another property of exponents that involves raising a power to a power.

Exploration Raising a Power to a Power

This Exploration shows how to raise a power to a power.

The expression $(2^4)^3$ means to use 2^4 as a factor three times.

$$(2^4)^3 = 2^4 \cdot 2^4 \cdot 2^4 = 2^{12}$$

Hint
Write in a 1 if there is no exponent for variables or numbers. For example, $4 = 4^1$ and $x = x^1$.

Simplify.

a. $(3^2)^3$ $3^2 \cdot 3^2 \cdot 3^2 = 3^6$

b. $(4^5)^2$ $4^5 \cdot 4^5 = 4^{10}$

c. $(7^2)^4$ $7^2 \cdot 7^2 \cdot 7^2 \cdot 7^2 = 7^8$

d. Are there any patterns? What conclusions can you draw from the patterns?   Sample: $2 \cdot 3 = 6$, $5 \cdot 2 = 10$, $2 \cdot 4 = 8$; The two exponents are multiplied together.

The expression $(a^2)^3$ means to use a^2 as a factor three times.

$$(a^2)^3 = a^2 \cdot a^2 \cdot a^2 = a^6$$

Math Reasoning

Generalize Use the meaning of powers and exponents to explain why $(a^2)^3 = a^6$.

Sample: Raising to the third power means multiplying the base three times, so $(a^2)^3 = a^2 \cdot a^2 \cdot a^2$ or $a \cdot a \cdot a \cdot a \cdot a \cdot a = a^6$.

Simplify.

e. $(a^3)^5$ $a^3 \cdot a^3 \cdot a^3 \cdot a^3 \cdot a^3 = a^{15}$

f. $(b^6)^2$ $b^6 \cdot b^6 = b^{12}$

g. $(d^4)^4$ $d^4 \cdot d^4 \cdot d^4 \cdot d^4 = d^{16}$

h. Using the results from **a** through **g** above, write a rule for raising a power to a power.   Sample: When raising a power to a power, multiply the exponents.

Online Connection
www.SaxonMathResources.com

Lesson 40   **249**

LESSON 40

1 Warm Up

Problem 4
Ask students what number is being raised to the second power in each of the two terms.

2 New Concepts

In this lesson, students learn to simplify expressions by using three new properties for exponents: the Power of a Power Property, the Power of a Product Property, and the Power of a Quotient Property.

Review the rules of exponents. Remind students that the rule $x^m \cdot x^n = x^{m+n}$ is called the Product Property of Exponents.

Exploration

Students have learned how to multiply and divide powers, now they will discover how to raise a power to a power.

Additional Exploration
Simplify.

a. $(2^3)^4$ 2^{12}

b. $(10^2)^3$ 10^6

c. $(x^3)^2$ x^6

d. $(s^3)^2$ s^6

LESSON RESOURCES

Student Edition Practice Workbook 40
Reteaching Master 40
Adaptations Master 40
Challenge & Enrichment Master C40

MATH BACKGROUND

This lesson introduces three new properties for exponents. The Power of a Power Property is an extension of the basic definition of a power: the result of raising a base to an exponent. In the case of the Power of a Power Property, the base is itself a power.

The Power of a Product Property is a combination of the basic definition of a power and the Product Property for Exponents. In the case of the Power of a Product Property, the base is a product of factors, one or more of which may be in exponential form. The Power of a Quotient Property is an extension of the Power of a Product Property.

TEACHER TIP

Point out that $(3^2)^3 = (3^3)^2$. Have students verify this statement.

Example 1

Students should start to develop a facility for simplifying a power of a power using the rule rather than using multiple factors.

Additional Example 1

Simplify each expression.

a. $(3^4)^2$ 3^8

b. $(z^5)^3$ z^{15}

Example 2

In this example, students extend the Power of a Power Property to bases that are products. Point out that this rule applies only when the base is a product. The property would not apply to $(5 + x^2)^3$.

$(5 + x^2)^3 \neq 5^3 + x^6$

Error Alert Some students may raise 2 to the third power in Example 2b instead of raising -2 to the third power. Point out that -2 means negative two, not subtract two.

Additional Example 2

Simplify each expression.

a. $(3g^4)^3$ $27g^{12}$

b. $(-4m^2n^3)^2$ $16m^4n^6$

Example 3

Extend the Example

"If the length of one side of the room is $3ab^3c^2$ feet, what is the area of the room?" $9a^2b^6c^4$

Additional Example 3

Use the formula $A = \pi r^2$ to find the area of a circle with radius $2x^2y^3$. $4x^4y^6\pi$

250 Saxon Algebra 1

The pattern in the Exploration leads to the Power of a Power Property.

Power of a Power Property
If m and n are real numbers and $x \neq 0$, then $(x^m)^n = x^{mn}$.

Example 1 Simplifying a Power of a Power

Simplify each expression.

a. $(2^3)^2$

SOLUTION

$(2^3)^2$
$= 2^{3 \cdot 2}$
$= 2^6$

b. $(a^6)^3$

SOLUTION

$(a^6)^3$
$= a^{6 \cdot 3}$
$= a^{18}$

The Power of a Power Property and the Product Property of Exponents can be used together to formulate a rule for the power of a product. Look at the expression $(5x^2)^3$. The outer exponent of 3 means to use everything inside the parentheses as a factor three times, or to multiply $5x^2$ three times.

$(5x^2)^3 = 5x^2 \cdot 5x^2 \cdot 5x^2$
$= (5 \cdot 5 \cdot 5) \cdot (x^2 \cdot x^2 \cdot x^2) = 5^3 \cdot x^6 = 125x^6$

This pattern is summarized in the Power of a Product Property.

Power of a Product Property
If m is a real number with $x \neq 0$ and $y \neq 0$, then $(xy)^m = x^m y^m$.

Example 2 Simplifying a Power of a Product

Simplify each expression.

Math Reasoning

Write Explain the difference between the expression $x^m \cdot x^n$ and $(x^m)^n$.

Sample:
$x^m \cdot x^n = x^{m+n}$ is the product of powers and is simplified by adding exponents; $(x^m)^n = x^{mn}$ is the power of a power and is simplified by multiplying exponents.

a. $(7a^3b^5)^3$

SOLUTION

$(7a^3b^5)^3$
$= 7^3 \cdot a^{3 \cdot 3} \cdot b^{5 \cdot 3}$
$= 343a^9b^{15}$

b. $(-2y^4)^3$

SOLUTION

$(-2y^4)^3$
$= (-2)^3 \cdot y^{4 \cdot 3}$
$= -8y^{12}$

Example 3 Application: Interior Design

A square family room is being measured for carpeting. If the length of one side of the room is $2x$ feet, what is the area of the room?

SOLUTION

The area is $(2x)^2 = 4x^2$ square feet.

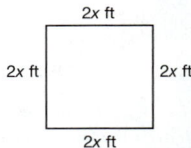

250 Saxon Algebra 1

🔺 **ALTERNATE METHOD FOR EXAMPLE 2**

Although the Power of a Product Property is a convenient shortcut, some students may benefit from writing the base as a factor multiple times. Example 2a becomes $(7a^3b^5)(7a^3b^5)(7a^3b^5) = 343a^9b^{15}$.

A few students may even need to use the Associative and Commutative Properties to reorganize the factors before applying the Product Property of Exponents.

$(7 \cdot 7 \cdot 7)(a^3 \cdot a^3 \cdot a^3)(b^5 \cdot b^5 \cdot b^5) = 343a^9b^{15}$

Power of a Quotient Property

If x and y are any nonzero real numbers and m is an integer, then
$$\left(\frac{x}{y}\right)^m = \frac{x^m}{y^m}.$$

Example 4 Simplifying a Power of a Quotient

Simplify each expression.

a. $\left(\dfrac{2x}{5}\right)^2$

SOLUTION

$\left(\dfrac{2x}{5}\right)^2$

$= \dfrac{2^2 x^2}{5^2}$

$= \dfrac{4x^2}{25}$

b. $\left(\dfrac{-x^2}{3y^3}\right)^4$

SOLUTION

$\left(\dfrac{-x^2}{3y^3}\right)^4$

$= \dfrac{(-1)^4 (x^2)^4}{(3)^4 (y^3)^4}$

$= \dfrac{x^8}{81 y^{12}}$

The rules for exponents apply to many expressions with powers. When simplifying expressions, be sure to follow the order of operations.

Example 5 Simplifying Expressions with Powers

Simplify each expression.

a. $(4xy^2)^2 (2x^3 y)^2$

SOLUTION

$(4xy^2)^2 (2x^3 y)^2$

$= (4^2 x^2 y^4)(2^2 x^6 y^2)$

$= (16 x^2 y^4)(4 x^6 y^2)$

$= 64 x^8 y^6$

b. $(-5x^{-2})^2 (3xy^2)^4$

SOLUTION

$(-5x^{-2})^2 (3xy^2)^4$

$= (-5^2 x^{-4})(3^4 x^4 y^8)$

$= (25 x^{-4})(81 x^4 y^8)$

$= 2025 x^0 y^8$

$= 2025 y^8$

Math Reasoning

Justify Is $5(x^2)^3$ equivalent to $(5x^2)^3$? Justify your answer.

no; The number 5 is only cubed when it is inside the parentheses. $5(x^2)^3 = 5x^6$ and $(5x^2)^3 = 125x^6$.

Lesson Practice

Simplify each expression.

a. (Ex 1) $(5^2)^2$ $\quad 5^4 = 625$

b. (Ex 1) $(b^4)^7$ $\quad b^{28}$

c. (Ex 2) $(-3n^4)^2$ $\quad 9n^8$

d. (Ex 5) $(9ab^{-2})^2 (2a^2 b^4)$ $\quad 162a^4$

e. (Ex 4) $\left(\dfrac{3y^4}{4}\right)^3$ $\quad \dfrac{27y^{12}}{64}$

f. (Ex 4) $\left(\dfrac{-x}{7y^5}\right)^2$ $\quad \dfrac{x^2}{49 y^{10}}$

g. (Ex 3) A shipping container is in the shape of a cube with a side length of $3x$ inches. What is the volume of the container? $27x^3$ cubic inches

Lesson 40 251

3 Practice

Math Conversations
Discussion to strengthen understanding

Problem 6
Guide the students by asking them the following questions.

"Which expressions result in a negative number?" **B, C,** and **D**

"Which of those three expressions result in x^4?" **B** and **C**

"Which of those two expressions result in a coefficient of -24?" **C**

Problems 11–13
Error Alert
Remind students that an expression in not simplified if it contains negative exponents.

Problem 11
Error Alert
A common error is to eliminate the fraction when it simplifies to a numerator of 1. Students may write the answer as $c^3 d^4$ instead of $\frac{1}{c^3 d^4}$. Remind them that the coefficient of the numerator is still 1.

Problem 12
Remind student that $a^0 = 1$

Practice Distributed and Integrated

Solve each proportion.

1. (31) $\frac{3}{12} = \frac{-24}{m}$ $m = -96$
2. (31) $\frac{-4}{0.8} = \frac{2}{x-1}$ $x = 0.6$
3. (31) $\frac{5}{12} = \frac{1.25}{k}$ $k = 3$

4. (1) True or False: All whole numbers are integers. If false, give a counterexample. **true**

*5. (40) Simplify $(4^4)^5$ using exponents. 4^{20}

*6. (40) **Multiple Choice** Which expression simplifies to $-24x^4 y^3$? **C**
   A $(-2x^2 y)^2 (6y)$
   B $-2(x^2 y)^2 (6y)$
   C $-(2x^2 y)^2 (6y)$
   D $(-2xy)^3 (3)$

7. (39) Simplify $\frac{e^3}{r^5}\left(\frac{e^2}{4r} + \frac{r^9}{k}\right)$. $\frac{e^5}{4r^6} + \frac{e^3 r^4}{k}, k \neq 0, r \neq 0$

*8. (40) **Cooking** Use the formula $A = \pi r^2$ for the area of a circle. A 6-inch pizza covers an area of $\pi(6)^2 = 36\pi$ square inches. What happens to the area of the pizza if you double the radius and make a 12-inch pizza? The area of the pizza will be quadrupled; $A = \pi(12)^2 = 144\pi$

*9. (40) **Verify** Is the statement $(a + b)^n = a^n + b^n$ true? Verify your answer with a numeric example. no; Sample: Let $a = 3$, $b = 4$, and $n = 2$. $(3 + 4)^2 = 7^2 = 49$, but $3^2 + 4^2 = 9 + 16 = 25$.

*10. (40) **Generalize** When do you know to add exponents and when to multiply exponents? **10.** Sample: You add exponents when you are multiplying two powers with the same base. You multiply exponents when you are raising a power to a power.

11. (39) **Painting** A rectangular top on a bench is to be painted. Its area is $\frac{wd^{-3}}{c}\left(\frac{d}{w^{-4}} + \frac{c^{-2}}{wd}\right)$. Simplify. $\frac{w^5}{d^2 c} + \frac{1}{c^3 d^4}$

12. (39) Simplify $\frac{a^2}{d^2}\left(\frac{a^{-2} x}{d^{-1}} - \frac{2x}{d^{-3}}\right)$ where d and $a \neq 0$. $\frac{x}{d} - 2a^2 dx, d \neq 0, a \neq 0$

*13. (39) **Geometry** The equation of an ellipse is $\frac{wx^2}{g^2} + \frac{gy^2}{w^2} = 1$. To enlarge the ellipse, the left side is multiplied by $\frac{g^5}{w^{-2}}$. This expression is $\frac{g^5}{w^{-2}}\left(\frac{wx^2}{g^2} + \frac{gy^2}{w^2}\right)$. Simplify. $g^3 w^3 x^2 + g^6 y^2$

14. (39) The trim around a window has a total length of $\frac{rt}{w^3}\left(\frac{rty}{w} + 2ty - \frac{8}{w^2}\right)$.
   a. Simplify the expression. $\frac{r^2 t^2 y}{w^4} + \frac{2rt^2 y}{w^3} - \frac{8rt}{w^5}$
   b. Identify the variables that cannot equal zero. $w \neq 0$

*15. (38) Find the GCF of $4xy^2 z^4 - 2x^2 y^3 z^2 + 6x^3 y^4 z$. $2xy^2 z$

16. (38) **Error Analysis** Two students are simplifying the fraction $\frac{3x-6}{9}$ as shown below. Which student is correct? Explain the error.

Student A	Student B
$\frac{3x-6}{9} = \frac{\cancel{3}(x-2)}{\cancel{9}_3} = \frac{x-2}{3}$	$\frac{\cancel{3}x-6}{\cancel{9}_3} = \frac{x-\cancel{6}^2}{\cancel{3}} = x-2$

16. Student A; Sample: Student B canceled without first writing the numerator as a product. The factor that is canceled in the denominator must be the same factor that is canceled in the numerator and, therefore, must be a common factor.

252 Saxon Algebra 1

INCLUSION

When students are simplifying expressions with bases that are products, help them organize their work by having them draw one box for each factor (or base). For example, since there are 3 bases in the expression $(7a^3 b^5)^3$, have students draw three boxes and write the bases 7, a^3, and b^5 in each box, respectively. Between the boxes, have students place a dot to indicate multiplication. On the outside of each box at the top right-hand corner, have students write the exponent.

Students can then work through the problem applying the Power of a Power Property.

This method will also help students understand the term *base*, as each base must have its own box. The number of boxes will equal the number of different bases in the problem.

*17. (**Shipping**) A shipping container is in the shape of a rectangular box that has a length of $10x + 15$ units, a width of $5x$ units, and a height of 2 units.
   a. Write an expression that can be used to find the volume of the box. $2 \cdot 5x(10x + 15)$
   b. Factor the expression completely. $50x(2x + 3)$

18. 0.78 of 250 is what number? 195

19. Give the domain and range of $\{(4, 9); (4, 7); (2, 4); (5, 12); (9, 4)\}$.
    domain: $\{2, 4, 5, 9\}$, range: $\{4, 7, 9, 12\}$

20. The heights of 8 trees were 250, 190, 225, 205, 180, 240, 210, and 220 feet. How could a misleading graph make you think the trees are all very similar in size?
    a. Make a bar graph of the data using a broken axis. See Additional Answers.
    b. Make a bar graph of the data using large increments. See Additional Answers.
    c. Compare the two graphs.

    20c. Sample: The heights appear to vary greatly in the graph with the broken scale. The heights appear very close to each other in the graph with large increments.

21. **Justify** Without changing the number to standard form, explain how you can tell that $-10 < 1 \times 10^{-4}$. Sample: 1×10^{-4} is a small number, but it is greater than 0, so it is greater than -10.

*22. **Multiple Choice** What is $\frac{1.6 \times 10^7}{6.4 \times 10^2}$ in scientific notation? **A**
    A 2.5×10^4 **B** 0.25×10^5 **C** 2.5×10^6 **D** 4×10^5

23. (**Astronomy**) The diameter of the moon is approximately 3,480,000 meters. Write this distance in scientific notation. 3.48×10^6

24. The rectangles below are similar. Find the missing length. 80

25.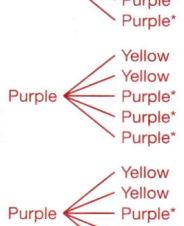

*25. (**Drama**) The equation $11x - 2y = 110$ represents the profit per ticket sold for the school play. Graph this equation using the intercepts.

26. **Justify** Is the sequence 0.2, 2, 20, 200, ... an arithmetic sequence? Justify your answer. no; The sequence does not have a common difference. $2 - 0.2 = 1.8$ but $20 - 2 = 18$.

27. There are 2 yellow stickers and 4 purple stickers. Make a tree diagram showing all possible outcomes of drawing two stickers. How many possible ways are there to draw a purple sticker, keep it, and then draw another purple sticker?

28. In a stem-and-leaf plot, which digit of the number 65 would be a leaf? 5

29. **Measurement** How many inches are there in 18 yards? 648 inches

30. **Analyze** The rule for negative exponents states that for every nonzero number x, $x^{-n} = \frac{1}{x^n}$. Explain why the base, x, cannot be zero. Sample: If x is zero, then the rule would be $0^{-n} = \frac{1}{0^n}$, but $0^n = 0$ since zero multiplied any number of times is zero. This would mean dividing by zero, which is undefined.

27.

12 ways

Problem 29
Guide the students by asking them the following questions.

"How many feet are in a yard?" 3

"How many inches are in a foot?" 12

"How would you find the number of inches in a yard?" Multiply 12 by 3.

"How many inches are in a yard?" 36

"How would you find the number of inches in 18 yards?" Multiply 36 by 18.

CHALLENGE

a. Fill in the boxes with values that will make the equation true.
$(x^9 y^6 z^3) = (x^\square y^\square z^\square)^{-3} (x^{-3} y^{-2} z^{-1})^{-3}$

b. Simplify $(x^{-4} y^2 z^6)^2 (x^2 y^{-1} z^{-3})^4$. 1

LOOKING FORWARD

Simplifying and evaluating expressions using the power rule for exponents prepares students for

- **Lesson 46** Simplifying Expressions with Square Roots and Higher-Order Roots
- **Lesson 60** Finding Special Products of Binomials
- **Lesson 88** Multiplying and Dividing Rational Expressions
- **Lesson 92** Simplifying Complex Fractions

INVESTIGATION 4

Discuss

In the activity on this page, students learn the difference between deductive and inductive reasoning. Be sure students are comfortable with the definitions of premise and conclusion.

Error Alert

Some students may assume that if a premise shows a valid pattern, a conclusion based on that pattern uses deductive reasoning. Point out that the difference between the two premises below is that in the first one, you assume the pattern will continue and that may not be the case; in the second, the rule guarantees the pattern will continue.
Premise 1: 2, 4, 6, 8,…
Premise 2: $y = x + 2$
Encourage students to ask themselves "Is the premise based on a few cases or is it based on a definition, fact or other rule?"

Problems 1–3
Extend the Problem

Identify the type of reasoning used. Explain your answer.
Premise: $y = 2x + 4$
Conclusion: If $x = 2$, then $y = 8$.
deductive reasoning; Sample: The conclusion is based on a rule.

INVESTIGATION RESOURCES

Reteaching Master
Investigation 4

INVESTIGATION 4

Using Deductive and Inductive Reasoning

Math Language
A **premise** is the foundation for an argument. It is used as evidence for the conclusion. A **conclusion** is an opinion or decision that logically follows the premise.

There are two basic kinds of reasoning: deductive and inductive. **Deductive reasoning** bases a conclusion on laws or rules. **Inductive reasoning** bases a conclusion on an observed pattern. Both types of reasoning can be used to support or justify conclusions.

All fruit have seeds. An apple is a fruit.

The two statements form an argument. The first statement is the premise, and the second statement is the conclusion. In deductive reasoning, if the argument is solid, the conclusion is guaranteed. In inductive reasoning, if the argument is solid, the conclusion is supported but not guaranteed. Consider the following examples:

Daryl	Aliya
According to Newton's First Law, every object will remain in uniform motion in a straight line unless compelled to change its state by the action of an external force. So, if I kick a ball, it will travel forward at a constant speed until it hits the wall.	In the past, I've noticed that every time I kick a soccer ball, it travels forward at a constant speed until it hits the wall. The next time I kick a ball, it will keep going until it hits the wall.

Daryl's reasoning is deductive because it is based on his knowledge of Newton's First Law of Motion. Aliya reasons inductively, basing her conclusions on her observations.

Identify the type of reasoning used. Explain your answer.

1. Premise: A student has earned a score of 100 on the last five math tests.
   Conclusion: The student will earn a score of 100 on the next math test.
   See Additional Answers.
2. Premise: The measures of three angles of a rectangle are all 90°.
   Conclusion: The measure of the fourth angle is 90°.
3. Premise: A number pattern begins with 3, 5, 7, 9, 11, ….
   Conclusion: The next number in the pattern will be 13.

Each premise and conclusion above can be written as one sentence. For instance, the second set could be restated as, "If the measures of three angles of a rectangle are all 90°, then the measure of the fourth angle is 90°." This is called a conditional statement. A **conditional statement** is a logical statement that can be written in "if-then" form.

Hint
If a conditional statement is true and you apply it to a situation in which the hypothesis is true, then you can state that the conclusion is true by deductive reasoning.

A conditional statement is made up of two parts: a hypothesis and a conclusion. The **hypothesis** is the condition. It follows the word "if." The **conclusion** is the judgment. It follows the word "then." A conditional statement can either be true or false.

2. deductive reasoning; Sample: Since the measures of a rectangle's angles are all the same, the fourth angle must also measure 90°.
3. inductive reasoning; Sample: The conclusion is based on the pattern established by the first five terms in the sequence.

Online Connection
www.SaxonMathResources.com

MATH BACKGROUND

Conclusions can be made using inductive or deductive reasoning. Inductive reasoning is used to form a general conclusion based on a limited number of observations. Deductive reasoning is used to form conclusions based on facts that are accepted to be true. Consequently, conclusions based on inductive reasoning are open to interpretation and may become inaccurate as additional information is gathered.

Conclusions based on deductive reasoning are a consequence of the accepted facts. Inductive reasoning addresses what may be true based on observation, while deductive reasoning addresses what must be true.

4. Sample: If you stay in the sun too long, then you will get a sunburn.

5. Sample: If a student has a temperature higher than 101 degrees, then the student should stay home from school.

✎ **Write** Use the given hypothesis to write a true or false conditional statement.

4. Write a true conditional statement: If you stay in the sun too long, ….

5. Write a true conditional statement: If a student has a temperature higher than 101 degrees, ….

6. Write a false conditional statement: If a number is divisible by 5, ….
Sample: If a number is divisible by 5, then it is prime.

The statement "If a figure has four sides, then it is a square" is false. It is not true because a rectangle has four sides, but a rectangle is not a square. An example that contradicts a statement is called a counterexample. One counterexample is sufficient to show that a statement is false.

Provide a counterexample for each statement.

7. The sum of a positive number and a negative number is negative.
Sample: The sum of 10 and −5 is 5.

8. If a student is a teenager, then she is 14 years old.   Sample: A 15-year-old is a teenager but is not 14 years old.

Investigation Practice

Identify the type of reasoning used. Explain your answer.

a. My friend has an allergic reaction when he eats peanuts.   inductive, based on an observed pattern

b. If a driver sees a red light, she should stop.   deductive, based on a rule

Use the given hypothesis to write a true or false conditional statement.

c. Write a true conditional statement: If it rains today, ….   Sample: If it rains today, then the game will be postponed.

d. Write a false conditional statement: If $x = 2$, ….   Sample: If $x = 2$, then x is negative.

Use the diagram to write a counterexample for each statement.

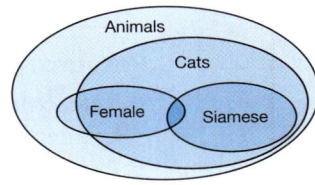

e. If an animal is a cat, then it is Siamese.   Sample: Cats are animals, but not all cats are Siamese.

f. All female cats are Siamese.   Sample: Some female cats are not Siamese.

Discuss
In the first activity on this page, students are introduced to conditional statements and the two parts to a conditional statement: hypothesis and conclusion. Point out that the conclusion depends on the hypothesis.

Discuss
In the second activity on this page, students learn that a single example that shows that the conclusion is not true is all that is needed to prove a conditional statement false.

Problem 7
Extend the Problem
Before going over problem 7, ask students to state it in conditional form using if and then. If a positive and negative number are added, then the sum is negative.

Error Alert
Some students may find an example that makes the conditional statement true. Remind them that it doesn't matter how many cases make the statement true, land that it takes only one counterexample to make the conditional statement false.

Investigation Practice

Math Conversations
Discussion to strengthen understanding

Problem e
TEACHER TIP
Remind students that an oval completely inside another oval in a Venn diagram indicates that all the elements of the inner oval are also elements of the outer oval, but not vice versa.

LOOKING FORWARD

Using inductive and deductive reasoning prepares students for

- **Lesson 41** Finding Rates of Change and Slope
- **Investigation 5** Using Logical Reasoning
- **Investigation 6** Transforming Linear Functions
- **Investigation 7** Comparing Direct and Inverse Variation
- **Investigation 8** Identifying and Writing Joint Variation
- **Investigation 9** Choosing a Factoring Model
- **Investigation 10** Transforming Quadratic Functions
- **Investigation 11** Investigating Exponential Growth and Decay
- **Investigation 12** Investigating Matrices

SECTION OVERVIEW 5

Lesson Planner

Lesson	New Concepts
41	Finding Rates of Change and Slope
42	Solving Percent Problems
43	Simplifying Rational Expressions
44	Finding Slope Using the Slope Formula
45	Translating Between Words and Inequalities
	Cumulative Test 8, Performance Task 8
46	Simplifying Expressions with Square Roots and Higher-Order Roots
47	Solving Problems Involving the Percent of Change
48	Analyzing Measures of Central Tendency
LAB 3	Graphing Calculator Lab: Graphing Linear Functions
49	Writing Equations in Slope-Intercept Form
50	Graphing Inequalities
	Cumulative Test 9, Performance Task 9
INV 5	Investigation: Using Logical Reasoning

Resources for Teaching
- Student Edition
- Teacher's Edition
- Student Edition eBook
- Teacher's Edition eBook
- Resources and Planner CD
- Solutions Manual
- Instructional Masters
- Technology Lab Masters
- Warm Up and Teaching Transparencies
- Instructional Presentations CD
- Online activities, tools, and homework help
  www.SaxonMathResources.com

Resources for Practice and Assessment
- Student Edition Practice Workbook
- Course Assessments
- Standardized Test Practice
- College Entrance Exam Practice
- Test and Practice Generator CD using ExamView™

Resources for Differentiated Instruction
- Reteaching Masters
- Challenge and Enrichment Masters
- Prerequisite Skills Intervention
- Adaptations for Saxon Algebra 1
- Multilingual Glossary
- English Learners Handbook
- TI Resources

Pacing Guide

 Resources and Planner CD for lesson planning support

45-Minute Class

Day 1	Day 2	Day 3	Day 4	Day 5	Day 6
Lesson 41	Lesson 42	Lesson 43	Lesson 44	Lesson 45	Cumulative Test 8
Day 7	**Day 8**	**Day 9**	**Day 10**	**Day 11**	**Day 12**
Lesson 46	Lesson 47	Lesson 48	Lab 3 Lesson 49	Lesson 50	Cumulative Test 9
Day 13					
Investigation 5					

Block: 90-Minute Class

Day 1	Day 2	Day 3	Day 4	Day 5	Day 6
Investigation 4 Lesson 41	Lesson 42 Lesson 43	Lesson 44 Lesson 45	Cumulative Test 8 Lesson 46	Lesson 47 Lesson 48	Lab 3 Lesson 49 Lesson 50
Day 7					
Cumulative Test 9 Investigation 5					

*For suggestions on how to implement Saxon Math in a block schedule, see the Pacing section at the beginning of the Teacher's Edition.

Lessons 41–50, Investigation 5

Differentiated Instruction

Below Level	
Warm Up	SE pp. 256, 263, 270, 275, 282, 288, 294, 299, 307, 314
Skills Bank	SE pp. 846–883
Reteaching Masters	Lessons 41–50, Investigation 5
Warm Up Transparencies	Lessons 41–50
Prerequisite Skills Intervention	Skills 6, 14, 49, 58, 74, 75, 84, 87, 88

Advanced Learners	
Challenge	TE pp. 262, 269, 273, 281, 287, 292, 298, 303, 312, 318
Extend the Example	TE pp. 257, 258, 264, 270, 278, 284, 290, 295, 301, 310, 316
Extend the Problem	TE pp. 261, 267, 268, 274, 279, 280, 286, 287, 292, 297, 303, 304, 312, 318, 320
Challenge and Enrichment Masters	Challenge: 41–50; Enrichment: 42, 44, 45

English Learners	
EL Tips	TE pp. 257, 265, 272, 280, 284, 290, 296, 301, 310, 315, 321
Multilingual Glossary	Booklet and Online
English Learners Handbook	

Special Needs	
Inclusion Tips	TE pp. 259, 267, 271, 276, 283, 291, 297, 302, 308, 316
Adaptations for Saxon Algebra 1	Lessons 41–50, Cumulative Tests 8, 9

For All Learners			
Exploration	SE pp. 256	Alternate Method	TE pp. 258, 264, 278, 289, 295, 300, 309
Caution	SE pp. 264, 270, 271, 310, 315	Online Tools	
Hints	SE pp. 256, 259, 265, 278, 282, 284, 288, 289, 294, 299, 308		
Error Alert	TE pp. 257, 259, 260, 264, 266, 268, 271, 272, 273, 274, 276, 278, 280, 281, 283, 284, 285, 287, 288, 289, 290, 293, 294, 296, 297, 301, 303, 308, 310, 311, 313, 314, 316, 317, 321		

SE = Student Edition; TE = Teacher's Edition

Math Vocabulary

Lesson	New Vocabulary	Maintained	EL Tip in TE
41	rate of change slope	linear equation	rise run
42	percent	proportion	economy
43		greatest common factor (GCF) rational expression	acceleration
44	rate of change slope	coordinate ordered pair	laps
45	inequality	algebraic expression	set-up fee
46	cube root principal square root	perfect square square root	root
47	percent of change	percent	medal
48	mean measure of central tendency median mode outlier range of a set of data	data value	average
49	slope-intercept form solution of an equation in two variables	coefficient variable y-intercept	flat fee
50	equivalent inequalities linear inequality in one variable solution of an inequality in one variable	endpoint inequality solution set	symbolic form
INV 5	converse contrapositive inverse	conclusion conditional statement counterexample hypothesis	original

Section Overview 5   256B

SECTION OVERVIEW 5

Math Highlights

Enduring Understandings – The "Big Picture"
After completing Section 5, students will understand:
- How to describe rates of change, find the slope of a line, and write equations in slope-intercept form.
- How to translate between words and inequalities and to graph inequalities.
- How to solve percent problems and find percent increase or decrease.
- How to analyze measures of central tendency and identify outliers.
- How to simplify rational expressions.

Essential Questions
- When is an expression undefined?
- What is the connection between rate of change and slope?
- Which measures of central tendency best describe a data set, and what is the meaning of an outlier?
- What is the connection between higher-order roots and exponents?

Math Content Strands

Algebra Foundations
- Lesson 46 — Simplifying Expressions with Square Roots and Higher-Order Roots
- Investigation 5 — Using Logical Reasoning

Equations
- Lesson 42 — Solving Percent Problems
- Lesson 47 — Solving Problems Involving the Percent of Change

Inequalities
- Lesson 45 — Translating Between Words and Inequalities
- Lesson 50 — Graphing Inequalities

Linear Equations and Functions
- Lesson 41 — Finding Rates of Change and Slope
- Lesson 44 — Finding Slope Using the Slope Formula
- Lesson 49 — Writing Equations in Slope-Intercept Form
- Lab 3 — Graphing Calculator Lab: Graphing Linear Functions

Rational Expressions and Functions
- Lesson 43 — Simplifying Rational Expressions

Probability and Data Analysis
- Lesson 48 — Analyzing Measures of Central Tendency

Connections in Practice Problems

	Lessons
Coordinate Geometry	47
Data Analysis	47, 48
Geometry	41, 42, 43, 44, 45, 46, 48, 49, 50
Measurement	41, 46
Probability	43, 44, 49, 50
Statistics	48

Math Processes

Reasoning and Communication

	Lessons
Analyze	41, 43, 44, 45, 46, 47, 48, 49, 50
Error analysis	41, 42, 43, 44, 45, 46, 47, 48, 49, 50
Estimate	46, 49
Formulate	43, 48, 50
Generalize	42, 44, 45, 48, 49, Inv. 5
Justify	46, 50
Math Reasoning	41, 42, 43, 44, 45, 46, 47, 48, 49, 50
Model	45
Multiple choice	41, 42, 43, 44, 45, 46, 47, 48, 49, 50
Multi-step	41, 42, 43, 44, 45, 46, 47, 48, 49, 50
Predict	41, 44, Inv. 5
True or False	50
Verify	41, 42, 43, 44
Write	41, 42, 43, 44, 45, 47, 48, 49, 50
Graphing Calculator	42, 45, 50

Connections

In Examples: Advertising, Calculating rental rates, Calculating wages, Cooking, Determining rates of change, Finances, Moving objects, Olympics, Practice times, Raising funds, Soccer team clothing, Volume

In Practice problems: Architecture, Astronomy, Atmospheric science, Basketball rules, Budgeting, Chemistry, Computers, Cooking, Digital signal processing, Earth science, Exercising, Farming, Fill rate, Finances, Fuel efficiency, Fuel prices, Fundraising, Gas prices, Geography, Hobbies, Hockey, Measurement conversion, Membership dues, Music, Names, Packaging, Packing, Painting, Personal finance, Pet care, Phone numbers, Physical science, Planting, Pricing, Recreation, Remote sensing, Restoration, Sale prices, Scale models, Scheduling, Sports, Taxi fares, Tourism, Transporting freight, Travel, Vacation, Wages, Woodworking, Zoology

Content Trace

Lesson	Warm Up: Prerequisite Skills	New Concepts	Where Practiced	Where Assessed	Looking Forward
41	Lessons 20, 25, 30	Finding Rates of Change and Slope	Lessons 42, 43, 44, 45, 46, 47, 49, 50, 51, 54, 55, 57	Cumulative Tests 9, 10, 11, 12, 14	Lessons 44, 49, 52, 56
42	Lessons 23, 31, 36	Solving Percent Problems	Lessons 43, 44, 45, 46, 48, 49, 50, 51, 52, 55, 56, 58, 103	Cumulative Tests 9, 12, 16	Lessons 47, 56, 117
43	Lessons 32, 38 Skills Bank 9	Simplifying Rational Expressions	Lessons 44, 45, 46, 47, 48, 49, 50, 51, 52, 53, 56, 58, 59, 104, 105	Cumulative Tests 9, 10, 12, 13, 15	Lessons 51, 57, 78, 88
44	Lessons 20, 41	Finding Slope Using the Slope Formula	Lessons 45, 46, 47, 48, 49, 50, 51, 52, 53, 54, 57, 59, 60	Cumulative Tests 9, 10, 11, 12, 14	Lessons 49, 52, 56
45	Lessons 9, 13, 32	Translating Between Words and Inequalities	Lessons 46, 47, 48, 49, 50, 52, 53, 55, 58, 60, 61, 106, 107	Cumulative Tests 9, 10, 11, 12, 13, 15	Lessons 50, 66, 70, 73, 77
46	Lessons 11, 13	Simplifying Expressions with Square Roots and Higher-Order Roots	Lessons 47, 48, 49, 50, 51, 52, 53, 54, 55, 56, 59, 61, 62, 108	Cumulative Tests 10, 11, 12, 13, 15	Lessons 61, 69, 76, 103, 105
47	Lesson 42 Skills Bank 5	Solving Problems Involving the Percent of Change	Lessons 48, 49, 50, 51, 53, 54, 55, 57, 60, 62, 63, 100, 109	Cumulative Tests 10, 11, 12, 13, 14, 15	Lesson 116
48	Lessons 4, 28, Inv. 1 Skills Bank 1	Analyzing Measures of Central Tendency	Lessons 49, 50, 51, 52, 53, 54, 55, 56, 57, 58, 61, 63, 64, 97, 110	Cumulative Tests 10, 11, 12, 13	Lessons 54, 62
49	Lessons 29, 30, 35	Writing Equations in Slope-Intercept Form	Lessons 50, 51, 52, 53, 54, 55, 56, 57, 58, 59, 62, 64, 65	Cumulative Tests 10, 11, 12, 13	Lessons 52, 56, 64, 65
50	Lessons 23, 45	Graphing Inequalities	Lessons 51, 52, 53, 54, 55, 56, 57, 58, 60, 65, 66	Cumulative Tests 10, 12	Lessons 66, 70, 73, 77
INV 5	N/A	Investigation: Using Logical Reasoning	Lessons 51, 52, 59, 64, 67	Cumulative Test 10	Investigations 10, 11, 12

SECTION OVERVIEW 5

Ongoing Assessment

	Type	Feature	Intervention *
BEFORE instruction	Assess Prior Knowledge	• Diagnostic Test	• Prerequisite Skills Intervention
BEFORE the lesson	Formative	• Warm Up	• Skills Bank • Reteaching Masters
DURING the lesson	Formative	• Lesson Practice • Math Conversations with the Practice problems	• Additional Examples in TE • Test and Practice Generator (for additional practice sheets)
AFTER the lesson	Formative	• Check for Understanding (closure)	• Scaffolding Questions in TE
AFTER 5 lessons	Summative	After Lesson 45 • Cumulative Test 8 • Performance Task 8 After Lesson 50 • Cumulative Test 9 • Performance Task 9	• Reteaching Masters • Test and Practice Generator (for additional tests and practice)
AFTER 20 lessons	Summative	• Benchmark Tests	• Reteaching Masters • Test and Practice Generator (for additional tests and practice)

* for students not showing progress during the formative stages or scoring below 80% on the summative assessments

Evidence of Learning – What Students Should Know

Because the Saxon philosophy is to provide students with sufficient time to learn and practice each concept, a lesson's topic will not be tested until at least five lessons after the topic is introduced.

On the Cumulative Tests that are given during this section of ten lessons, students should be able to demonstrate the following competencies:
- Find the prime factorization of a number.
- Use the power rule of exponents, and simplify expressions with negative exponents.
- Solve multi-step equations, and literal equations.
- Recognize and extend arithmetic sequences.
- Simplify rational expressions by using the GCF and the Distributive Property.
- Write and solve proportions, and use conversion factors to find rates.
- Determine slope from a graph.
- Calculate the probability of an event.
- Identify misleading graphs, and choose appropriate graphs to represent data.

Test and Practice Generator CD using ExamView™

The Test and Practice Generator is an easy-to-use benchmark and assessment tool that creates unlimited practice and tests in multiple formats and allows you to customize questions or create new ones. A variety of reports are available to track student progress toward mastery of the standards throughout the year.

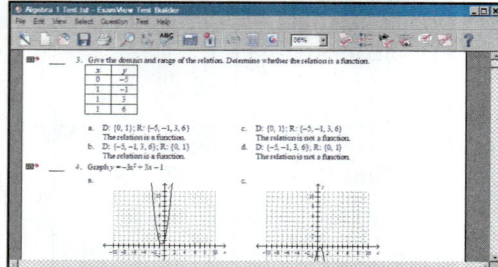
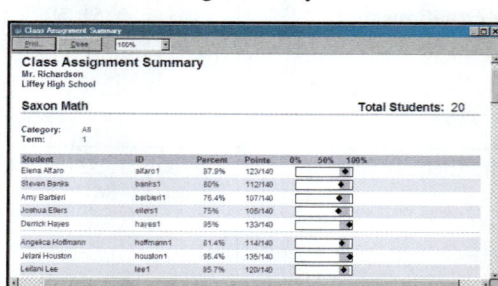

256E *Saxon Algebra 1*

Lessons 41–50, Investigation 5

Assessment Resources

Resources for Diagnosing and Assessing

- **Student Edition**
  - Warm Up
  - Lesson Practice

- **Teacher's Edition**
  - Math Conversations with the Practice problems
  - Check for Understanding (closure)

- **Course Assessments**
  - Diagnostic Test
  - Cumulative Tests
  - Performance Tasks
  - Benchmark Tests

Resources for Test Prep

- **Student Edition Practice**
  - Multiple-choice problems
  - Multiple-step and writing problems
  - Daily cumulative practice

- **Standardized Test Practice**

- **College Entrance Exam Practice**

- **Test and Practice Generator CD using ExamView™**

Resources for Intervention

- **Student Edition**
  - Skills Bank

- **Teacher's Edition**
  - Additional Examples
  - Scaffolding questions

- **Prerequisite Skills Intervention**
  - Worksheets

- **Reteaching Masters**
  - Lesson instruction and practice sheets

- **Test and Practice Generator CD using ExamView™**
  - Lesson practice problems
  - Additional tests

Cumulative Tests

The assessments in Saxon Math are frequent and consistently placed after every five lessons to offer a regular method of ongoing testing. These cumulative assessments check mastery of concepts from previous lessons.

Performance Tasks

The Performance Tasks can be used in conjunction with the Cumulative Tests and are scored using a rubric.

After Lesson 45

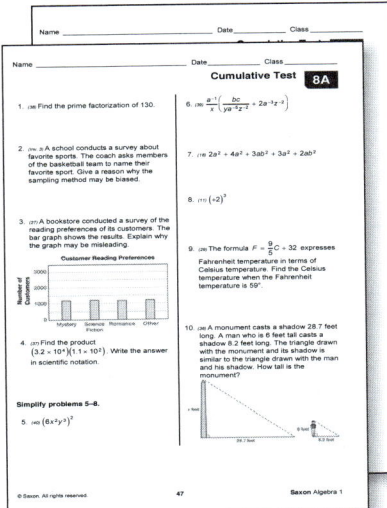

After Lesson 50

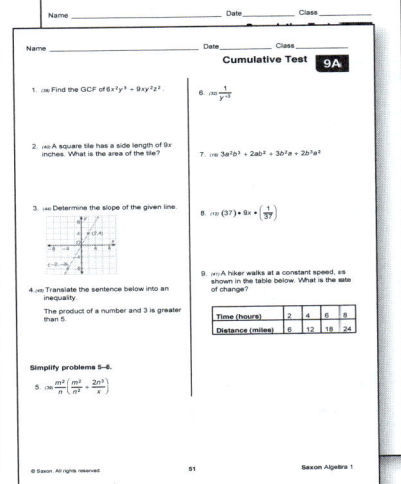

For use with Performance Tasks

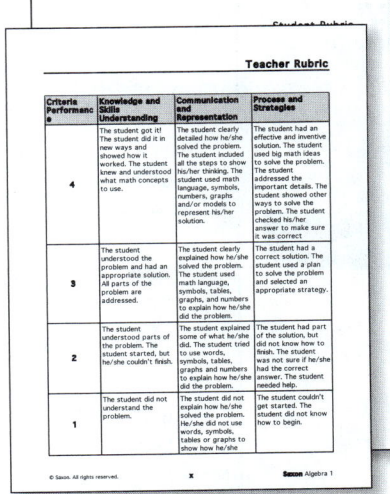

Section Overview 5 **256F**

LESSON 41

1 Warm Up

Problems 3–5
Remind students that the coordinate plane is divided into four quadrants. The quadrants are named counterclockwise, starting from I.

2 New Concepts

In this lesson, students will find the slope of a line and will interpret it as a rate of change.

Exploration

The Exploration prepares students to interpret slopes by looking at a graph. They will discover that a steeper line means a greater rate.

Example 1

Explain to students that they can use a graph to find a rate. Point out that the rate will be miles per hour, since they must find the ratio of distance to time.

Additional Example 1
Use the graph. Find the rate of change from the start time to 2 hours. (0, 0) to (2, 120), $\frac{120-0}{2-0} = 60$ mi/hr

LESSON RESOURCES

Student Edition Practice Workbook 41
Reteaching Master 41
Adaptations Master 41
Challenge and Enrichment Master C41

LESSON 41 — Finding Rates of Change and Slope

Warm Up

1. **Vocabulary** A _____ (*literal, linear*) equation is an equation whose graph is a straight line. **linear**

2. Find the range of the function $f(x) = 2x + 3$ for the domain {0, 1, 2}. **3, 5, 7**

Name the quadrant on the coordinate plane in which the following points are located:

3. (3, −5) **quadrant IV**   4. (−3, −5) **quadrant III**   5. (−5, 3) **quadrant II**

New Concepts

A **rate of change** is a ratio that compares the change in one quantity with the change in another. For example, the speed of a car is a rate of change that compares the distance and the time traveled.

Exploration — Analyzing a Graph

Arvand leaves his house and jogs to Cory's house. Later they walk to a local pizza shop. The graph shows the distance Arvand traveled between the time he left home and when he arrived at the pizza shop.

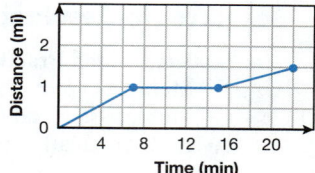

a. When was Arvand traveling the fastest? **during the first 7 minutes**

b. How long was Arvand at Cory's house? How can you tell? **8 minutes; Sample: The distance did not change between 7 and 15 minutes.**

c. Compare the graph during the times Arvand was jogging to Cory's and when they were walking to the pizza shop. **Sample: The graph is steeper during the time when Arvand was jogging than the time when they were both walking.**

Example 1 — Determining Rate of Change from a Graph

A car travels on a highway at a constant speed. The graph shows the relationship between the distance traveled and the time traveled. Find the rate of change.

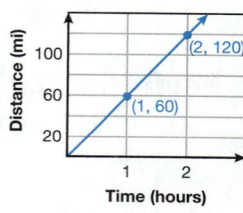

SOLUTION Choose two points on the graph and find the ratio of the change in distance to the change in time.

$$\frac{\text{change in distance}}{\text{change in time}} = \frac{120 - 60}{2 - 1}$$
$$= 60$$

The rate of change is 60 miles per hour.

Hint
You can use any two points on the line to determine the rate of change.

Online Connection
www.SaxonMathResources.com

MATH BACKGROUND

In Lesson 31, students learned to use rates, ratios, and proportions. In Lesson 35, they learned how to graph linear functions. This lesson extends these concepts. The functions in this lesson are all linear. Because of this, the ratio of the vertical change to the horizontal change will be constant for any two points chosen on a graph. It should be mentioned that this may not be true for other graphs.

In the Exploration, each line segment will have the same slope when the student chooses two points of the same segment.

Example 2 Determining Rate of Change from a Table

A shop charges a fee for renting kayaks. What is the rate of change for the rental fees?

Time (hours)	2	4	6	8
Cost	$32.50	$60.50	$88.50	$116.50

SOLUTION Notice that the costs increase the same amount every 2 hours. Choose two sets of values from the table to find the ratio of the change in cost to the change in time.

$$\frac{\text{change in cost}}{\text{change in time}} = \frac{60.5 - 32.5}{4 - 2} = \frac{28}{2}$$

The rate of change is $14 per hour.

Math Reasoning

Predict The rate of change is $14 per hour. How much would it cost to rent a kayak for 10 hours?

$144.50

Slope of a Line

The **slope** of a line is a rate of change. It is equal to the ratio of the vertical change (rise) to the horizontal change (run).

$$\text{slope} = \frac{\text{rise}}{\text{run}}$$

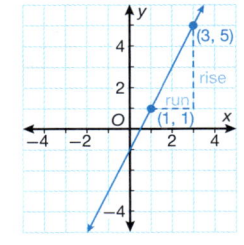

Example 3 Determining Slope from a Graph

Find the slope of each line.

a.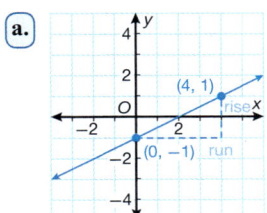

b.

SOLUTION Find the ratio of the rise to the run.

$$\text{slope} = \frac{\text{rise}}{\text{run}} = \frac{2}{4}$$
$$= \frac{1}{2}$$

SOLUTION Find the ratio of the rise to the run.

$$\text{slope} = \frac{\text{rise}}{\text{run}} = \frac{-9}{3}$$
$$= -3$$

Example 2

In this example, students will find a rate of change from a table. Point out that the rate will be cost per hour.

Extend the Example

"How many hours can you rent the kayak for $200.50?" 14 hours

Additional Example 2

The fees shown below are for canoe rentals. What is the rate of change for the rental fees?

Time (hr)	3	6	9
Cost	$22.15	$37.15	$52.15

$5 per hour

Example 3

In this example, students will find the slope of the graph of a linear equation.

Error Alert Students will sometimes find the ratio of the run to the rise. Remind students that because in a function the y-value is dependent on the x-value, they are comparing how much the y-value changes depending on the x-value.

Additional Example 3

Find the slope of the line.

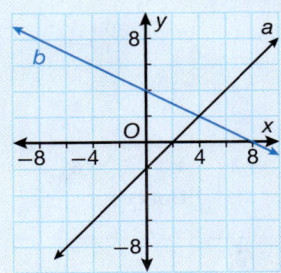

a. 1

b. $-\frac{1}{2}$

ENGLISH LEARNERS

Discuss the meaning of the words **rise** and **run**. Rise means to move from a lower to a higher position. Run means to move quickly. Say:

"For example, a person may rise from a chair. Run is a way to move across the ground quickly."

Have a volunteer explain the meaning of run and rise using the terms up, down, right, and left. Sample: Run means to move right or left. Rise means to move up or down.

Have students write and read a sentence using the words rise and run.

Example 4

This example explains to students why the slope of a horizontal line is 0 and the slope of a vertical line is undefined.

Additional Example 4

Determine whether each pair of points lies on a horizontal or vertical line. Then find the slope.

a. (5, 1) (8, 1) horizontal; 0

b. (3, 1) (3, 9) vertical, undefined

Example 5

Explain that students can find the rate of change using a table or a graph.

Extend the Example

"Use the rate of change to find the additional amount of beans you will need to make 24 servings if you have enough to make 18." 15 ounces

Additional Example 5

The graph shows the relationship between the distance a car drives and the time it takes to drive that distance. This data is shown in the table below.

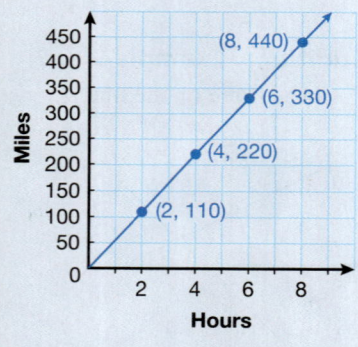

Hours	2	4	6	8
Miles	110	220	330	440

a. Use the table or graph to find the slope of the line. $\frac{55}{1}$

258   **Saxon** Algebra 1

A line with a positive slope rises from left to right. A line with a negative slope falls from left to right. There are two other cases to consider: horizontal and vertical lines.

Horizontal and Vertical Lines

The graph of the equation $y = c$, where c is a constant, is a horizontal line. The slope of a horizontal line is 0.

The graph of the equation $x = c$, where c is a constant, is a vertical line. The slope of a vertical line is undefined.

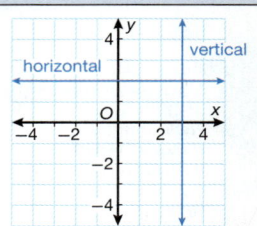

Example 4 Graphing Horizontal and Vertical Lines

a. Find the slope of the horizontal line.

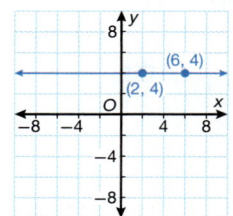

SOLUTION Find the ratio of the rise to the run.

$$\text{slope} = \frac{\text{rise}}{\text{run}} = \frac{4 - 4}{6 - 2}$$

$$= \frac{0}{4}$$

The slope is 0 because 0 divided by any nonzero number is 0.

b. Find the slope of the vertical line.

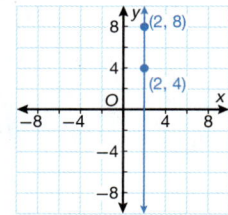

SOLUTION Find the ratio of the rise to the run.

$$\text{slope} = \frac{\text{rise}}{\text{run}} = \frac{8 - 4}{2 - 2}$$

$$= \frac{4}{0}$$

The slope is undefined because any number divided by 0 is undefined.

Example 5 Application: Cooking

The graph and table show the relationship between the number of servings a salsa recipe makes and the ounces of black beans used to make this recipe.

Servings	4	6	10	18
Black Beans (oz)	10	15	25	45

a. Use the table or graph to find the slope of the line.

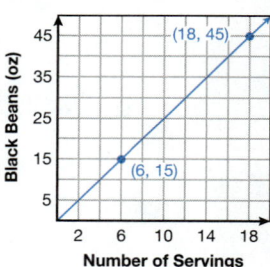

258   **Saxon** Algebra 1

ALTERNATE METHOD FOR EXAMPLE 5

Because this function is linear, $y = \frac{5}{2}x$, and $f(0) = 0$, students can find the unit rate of beans per serving using one set of values: $\frac{10}{4} = \frac{5}{2}$. If a graph of the data is given, students can quickly check to see if the graph passes through the origin to use this method.

Hint

Notice that the value of the rate of change is equal to the slope of the line.

SOLUTION Find the ratio of the change in amount of beans to the change in servings.

$$\frac{\text{change in amount of beans}}{\text{change in servings}} = \frac{15 - 10}{6 - 4} = \frac{5}{2}$$

The slope is $\frac{5}{2}$.

b. What does the rate of change mean in this example?

SOLUTION Explain how the variables are related in this ratio.

For every 5 ounces of black beans, 2 servings of salsa can be made.

Lesson Practice

a. Use the graph to find the rate of change.   4 kicks/measure
(Ex 1)

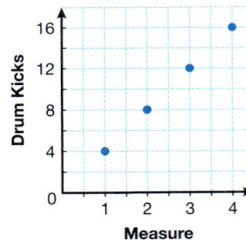

b. Use the table to find the rate of change.   5280 ft/mi
(Ex 2)

Miles	3	5	7	9
Feet	15,840	26,400	36,960	47,520

Find the slope of each line.

c. 3 **d.** $-\frac{2}{5}$
(Ex 3)   (Ex 3)

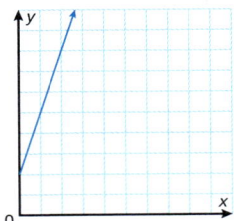 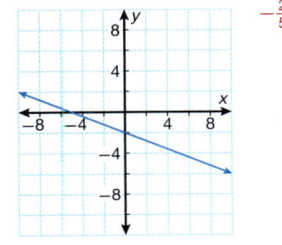

e. Find the slope of the horizontal line that passes through the points
(Ex 4) (5, 3) and (8, 3). $\frac{0}{3}$; 0

f. Find the slope of the vertical line that passes through the points (6, 5)
(Ex 4) and (6, 10). $\frac{5}{0}$; undefined

Lesson 41   259

b. What does the rate of change mean in this example? Sample: The car is going 55 miles per hour.

Lesson Practice

Problem b

Scaffolding Have students first identify what rate of change they are finding (ft/mi). Then have them choose two points and identify what units each coordinate represents.

Problem f

Error Alert Students will often say that the slope of a vertical line is 0. Encourage them to use two points to find the slope and see that they are dividing by 0.

Check for Understanding

The questions below help assess the concepts taught in this lesson.

"Explain how finding a rate of change from a graph is similar to finding a rate of change from a table." Sample: Both require finding two pairs of values and using them to find the ratio of the changes. Finding the rate of change from a graph requires finding two points that are on the line.

"Explain why the slope of a horizontal line is 0." Sample: The y-values on a horizontal line are the same for all x-values, so the rise is always equal to 0. Zero divided by any number, besides 0, is equal to 0.

"Explain why the slope of a vertical line is not 0." Sample: The x-values on a vertical line are the same for all y-values, so the run is always equal to 0. Any number divided by 0 is undefined.

INCLUSION

For some students, it may be easier to find slopes or rates of change by using a graph rather than by using a table. Encourage these students to plot points from the table on graph paper to help them visualize the vertical and horizontal changes. Help them to label the rise and run.

Lesson 41   259

3 Practice

Math Conversations
Discussion to strengthen understanding

Problem 5
Remind students that the graph of lines that have a negative slope will slant down to the right.

Problem 8
Error Alert
Students may move the decimal before the last two zeros. Remind them that scientific notation requires multiplying a number between 1 and 10 by a power of 10.

(Music) The table shows the number of times Iliana kicked her bass drum during each measure in a song.

Measure	1	2	3	4
Drum Kicks	4	8	12	16

g. (Ex 5) Use the table or graph to find the slope of the line.   4

h. (Ex 5) What does the rate of change mean in this problem?   During each measure, Iliana kicked the drum 4 times.

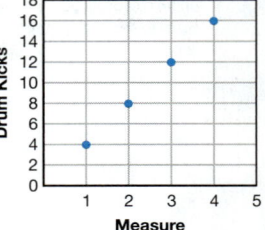

Practice   Distributed and Integrated

Solve each equation. Check your answer.

1. (26) $-2(b + 5) = -6$ $b = -2$
2. (26) $4(y + 1) = -8$ $y = -3$
3. (26) $\frac{5}{8} = 2m + \frac{3}{8}$ $m = \frac{1}{8}$

Find the slope of the line.

*4. (41) line a $1\frac{1}{4}$

*5. (41) line b $-\frac{1}{3}$

*6. (41) line c 0

*7. (41) line d undefined

8. (37) Write 110,400 in scientific notation. 1.104×10^5

*9. (38) **Multiple Choice** Which of the following expressions is the GCF of $45a^3b^4c^2 + 30a^2bc^3$?   **A**

A $15a^2bc^2$ **B** $5a^2bc^2$ **C** $3a^3b^4c^3$ **D** $15a^3b^4c^3$

10. (38) **Verify** Is $2x(5x^3 + 6x^2 - 3x)$ completely factored? Explain why or why not. If no, factor the polynomial completely.

10. no; The terms $5x^3$, $6x^2$, and $3x$ all have a common factor of x; $2x^2(5x^2 + 6x - 3)$

*11. (41) (Finances) The graph shows the amount of money Siobhan has in her bank account over time. What is the rate of change in her balance over time? $66.67 per year

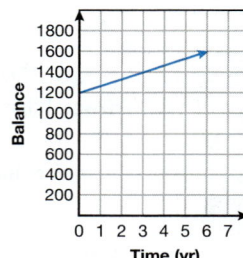

*12. (41) **Analyze** At some point on Mindy's mountain climbing trip, a graph relating her distance up the mountain over her climbing time shows a line with a negative slope. Why might this be?   Sample: Mindy is descending the mountain.

260   Saxon Algebra 1

13. Simplify $(b^3)^5$ using exponents. b^{15}
(40)

14. **Error Analysis** Two students simplify the expression $(-2x^7)^5$ as shown below. Which
(40) student is correct? Explain the error.   Student B; $(-2)^5 = -32$, not -10. Student A multiplied the coefficient by the exponent, which is incorrect.

Student A	Student B
$(-2x^7)^5 = -10x^{35}$	$(-2x^7)^5 = -32x^{35}$

*15. **Geometry** Use the formula $A = s^2$ to find the area of the square. $A = 16x^2y^2$
(40)

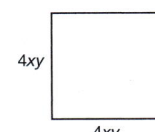

4xy

4xy

16. **Multi-Step** There are 10 millimeters in a centimeter. Therefore, there are 10^3 cubic
(40) millimeters in one cubic centimeter.
   a. There are 10^2 centimeters in a meter. How many cubic centimeters are in one cubic meter? 10^6
   b. How many cubic millimeters are in one cubic meter? 10^9

17. (**Packing**) The sides of a box in the shape of a cube are $5ab$ inches long. What is the
(40) volume of the box? $125a^3b^3$ cubic inches

Simplify

18. $\dfrac{fr}{d^3}\left(\dfrac{fsr}{d^2} + 3fs - \dfrac{8}{d}\right)$ $\dfrac{f^2sr^2}{d^5} + \dfrac{3f^2rs}{d^3} - \dfrac{8fr}{d^4}$ *19. $\dfrac{rt^{-2}}{g^{-3}h}\left(\dfrac{tg^4}{r^3h^{-2}} - \dfrac{r^3h}{g^{-2}r^{-2}}\right)$ $\dfrac{g^7h}{tr^2} - \dfrac{r^6g^5}{t^2}$
(39)   (39)

*20. (**Woodworking**) You are making furniture for a miniature dollhouse with a scale of
(36) 1 in.:12 in. If an actual chair measures 3 feet high, what will be the height of the chair in the dollhouse?   3 inches

21. Find the x- and y-intercepts on the graph.
(35) The x-intercept is 2. The y-intercept is 5.

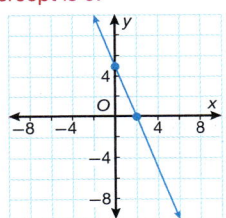

22. **Measurement** The formula $F = \dfrac{9}{5}C + 32$ calculates the number of degrees
(35) Fahrenheit from the degrees Celcius. Write this formula in standard form.
$5F - 9C = 160$ or $-9C + 5F = 160$

23. Write a recursive formula for the arithmetic sequence 8, 19, 30, 41,…. Then find
(34) the next two terms of the sequence. $a_1 = 8$, $a_n = a_{n-1} + 11$; 52, 63

24. **Write** Explain the difference between dependent and independent events.
(33)

24. Sample: When looking at two events, if they are dependent, the first will affect the probability of the second. If they are independent, the first does not affect the second.

Lesson 41   261

25. (**Cooking**) To make two batches of cookies, Ralph needs $\frac{3}{4}$ cup molasses. How many cups would he need to make 6 batches of cookies? $2\frac{1}{4}$ cups

26. (**Painting**) It will cost $2.50 per square foot to paint the walls of a storage shed. Write a rule in function notation to describe the cost of painting x square feet of outside wall space. $f(x) = \$2.50x$

27. The two parabolas have the same shape but different orientations. Determine whether each parabola is a function. Parabola A is a function; Parabola B is not a function.

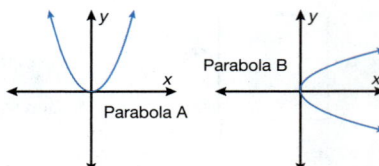

28. **Multi-Step** A physicist wants to find the kinetic energy of a ball that has a mass of 2.5 kg and travels a distance of 5.8 meters in 2.5 seconds. The formula for kinetic energy is $E_K = \frac{1}{2}mv^2$, where m is the mass of the object and v is the object's velocity. The formula for velocity is $v = \frac{d}{t}$, where d is distance traveled and t is the amount of time. What are the velocity and the kinetic energy of the ball? $v = 2.32$ m/s, $E_k = 6.728$ kg · m²/s²

29. **Multi-Step** Two cars travel the same distance. Car 1 travels at 50 mph and Car 2 at 65 mph. If it takes Car 1 one more hour to travel than Car 2, how far did the cars travel? Remember, $d = rt$.
    a. Write an expression to represent the distance Car 2 travels. $65x$
    b. Write an expression to represent the distance Car 1 travels. $50(x + 1)$
    c. Use these expressions to find the time Car 2 traveled. $65x = 50(x + 1); x = 3\frac{1}{3}$
    d. Use this information to determine the distance traveled. 216.7 miles

30. **Multi-Step** The length of a rectangle is 5 inches less than 3 times the width. The perimeter of the rectangle is 14 inches. Find the length and width of the rectangle. length = 4 in., width = 3 in.

CHALLENGE

Graph the line that passes through the point $(-2, 3)$ and has a slope of -3. (Hint: Write -3 as a fraction.)

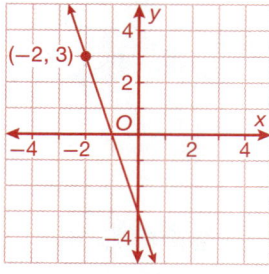

LOOKING FORWARD

Finding slopes and rates of change prepares students for

- **Lesson 44** Finding Slope Using the Slope Formula
- **Lesson 49** Writing Equations in Slope-Intercept Form
- **Lesson 52** Determining the Equation of a Line Given Two Points
- **Lesson 56** Identifying, Writing, and Graphing Direct Variation

LESSON 42

Solving Percent Problems

Warm Up

1. **Vocabulary** Two equivalent ratios form a _____.   proportion
   (31)

   Solve the equation.

2. $3x + 8 = 32$ 8
   (23)

3. $-6y - 7 = 29$ -6
   (23)

4. A team's ratio of wins to losses in football games is 5 to 4. If the team wins
   (36) 25 games, how many games did the team lose?   20 games

5. The ratio of white marbles to black marbles is 7 to 10. There are
   (36) 136 marbles in the bag. How many marbles are white?   56 white marbles

New Concepts

A **percent** is a ratio that compares a number to 100. For example, 50% is the ratio $\frac{50}{100}$. There are three components that form a percent statement: the whole is the total amount; the percent is a rate that quantifies an amount measured with respect to the whole; the percentage is a number that represents a percent of the whole.

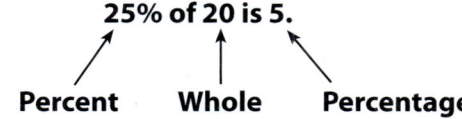

Percent   Whole   Percentage

If two of the components are known, then the third component can be determined.

Example 1 Using an Equation to Find a Percentage

a. What number is 25% of 50?

SOLUTION

$c = 0.25 \cdot 50$ Change the percent to its decimal form.

$ = 12.5$ Multiply the percent by the whole.

Check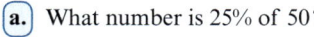

b. What number is 125% of 64?

SOLUTION

$n = 1.25 \cdot 64$ Change the percent to its decimal form.

$ = 80$ Multiply the percent by the whole.

Check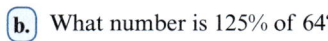

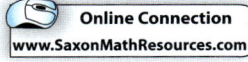

Lesson 42   **263**

MATH BACKGROUND

A percent is a special kind of ratio that compares a number to one hundred. This ratio uses a percent sign.

In order to solve problems with percents, students should be able to convert between percents, decimals, and fractions. For example, they should be able to understand that $\frac{1}{4}$, 0.25, and 25% all represent the same part of a whole.

There are two important skills needed to solve percent problems. Translating words into equations and converting numbers into different forms allow students to set up proportions to solve percent problems.

Example 2

Error Alert Students may have difficulty writing the proportion. Encourage them to label the part and the whole as they write proportions.

Additional Example 2

a. What number is 120% of 25?
   30

b. 12 is what percent of 72?
   $16\frac{2}{3}$ %

Example 3

A percent statement is used to determine net pay in a real-world situation.

Extend the Example

"Suppose Ana saves 20% of her net pay. How much will she save every two weeks? $165.99

Additional Example 3

Lee receives $1278.91 in gross wages every week. However, 33.85% of the gross earning is removed for taxes and other deductions. Using an equation, determine the net pay. $846.00

A percent statement can be set up as a proportion. One ratio compares the part of a quantity to the whole quantity. The other ratio is the percent rate written in the form of a ratio.

$$\frac{\text{part}}{\text{whole}} = \text{percent rate}$$

For example, 10% of 50 is 5 can be written as a proportion.

Whole → $\frac{5}{50} = \frac{10}{100}$ ← Percent (Part, Percent labeled)

Example 2 Using a Proportion

a. What number is 125% of 48?

SOLUTION

Set up a proportion to find the percentage.

$\frac{c}{48} = \frac{125}{100}$ Write a proportion.

$6000 = 100c$ Cross multiply.

$60 = c$ Solve for c.

60 is 125% of 48.

Check 125% is $\frac{5}{4}$. So, $\left(\frac{5}{4}\right)(48) = 60$.

Caution
When setting up a proportion, make sure you know which is the part and which is the whole.

b. 15 is what percent of 45?

SOLUTION

Set up a proportion to find the percent.

$\frac{15}{45} = \frac{x}{100}$ Write a proportion.

$45x = 1500$ Cross multiply.

$x = 33.\overline{3}$ Solve for x.

15 is $33\frac{1}{3}$% of 45.

Check $33\frac{1}{3}$% is $\frac{1}{3}$. So, $\left(\frac{1}{3}\right)(45) = 15$.

Example 3 Application: Calculating Wages

Ana receives $1153.84 in gross earnings every two weeks. However, 28.07% of the gross earnings is removed for taxes and other deductions. Using an equation, determine the net pay.

264   Saxon Algebra 1

 ALTERNATE METHOD FOR EXAMPLE 3

Instead of having students find the percentage that is deducted, have them find the percentage that is received. First, have the students find the percent that is received by subtracting the percent deducted from 100%.
$100\% - 28.07\% = 71.93\%$

Then, have students answer the question, "What is 71.93% of $1153.84?"
$n = (0.7193)(\$1153.84)$
$\approx \$829.96$

Hint

Gross earning is the amount of money earned by a worker before any deductions, like taxes, are taken out. Net pay is actual amount of money a worker receives after deductions.

SOLUTION First, find the total amount of money that will be deducted. Then subtract the deductions from the gross earnings to determine that net pay.

$28.07\% \cdot \$1153.84 = d$

$0.2807 \cdot \$1153.84 = d$

$\$323.88 \approx d$

Now $323.88 of deductions is subtracted from the gross earnings.

(gross earnings) − (deductions) = (net pay)

$\$1153.84 \quad - \quad \$323.88 \quad = \$829.96$

The amount that Ana receives in net pay is $829.96.

Check Use estimation. Since about 30% is deducted from about $1200, then she receives about 70% of $1200 in net pay. Use an equation to find 70% of $1200.

$(0.70)(\$1200) = \$840$

$829.96 is a reasonable answer because $829.96 is about $840.

Example 4 Application: Finances

Dominic earns $9.25 an hour working part-time. The circle graph shows how he divides his earnings. This month Dominic has worked a total of 54 hours.

Find the amount of Dominic's earnings that will be put into savings this month.

Division of Earnings
- 10% Charity
- Savings 40%
- 50% Personal Spending

SOLUTION Find the total amount that Dominic earned this month. Then find 40% of the total amount earned.

$(\$9.25)(54) = \$499.50$ — Multiply the rate by the hours.

Dominic earned $499.50 this month. Now find 40% of $499.50 to determine how much money will be put into savings. Set up a proportion to find the percentage.

$\dfrac{c}{\$499.50} = \dfrac{40}{100}$ — Write a proportion.

$40 \cdot \$499.50 = 100c$ — Cross multiply.

$\dfrac{\$19{,}980}{100} = \dfrac{100c}{100}$ — Divide both sides by 100.

$\$199.80 = c$ — Solve for c.

Dominic puts $199.80 into savings this month.

Math Reasoning

Why is it necessary to determine the total amount earned first?

It is necessary to have two out of the three components to solve a percent problem.

Example 4

A percent statement is used to solve a division-of-earnings problem.

Additional Example 4

Raul worked 45 hours at $7.50 per hour during this month. If he saves 30% of his monthly earnings, how much will save this month? $101.25

Lesson 42   265

 ENGLISH LEARNERS

Discuss the meaning of the *economy*. Say:

"Economy is the way that people use money, materials, or labor. If a household economy is good, then the money is being spent carefully."

Ask:

"Car A has excellent fuel economy and Car B has poor fuel economy. If the cars drive the same distance, which car would use less gas?" Car A

Have students compare the number of miles a small car can travel on a gallon to the number of miles a large truck can travel on a gallon. Have them determine which types of vehicles have better fuel economy.

Lesson Practice

a. What number is 35% of 70. 24.5
(Ex 1)

b. What number is 150% of 24? 36
(Ex 1)

c. Using a proportion, find 315% of 21. $\frac{315}{100} = \frac{x}{21}; x = 66.15$
(Ex 2)

d. 59.5 is what percent of 17? $\frac{59.5}{17} = \frac{p}{100}; 350\%$
(Ex 2)

e. **Fuel Economy** A driver who accelerates quickly and brakes heavily reduces his car's fuel economy by as much as 33%. The car is supposed to get 32 miles per gallon. Using an equation, find the actual fuel economy of the car.
(Ex 3)

e. (0.33)(32) = 10.56 miles per gallon;
32 − 10.56 = 21.44 miles per gallon

f. **Fund-Raising** A school raised $15,432 for a new computer lab. The money will be allotted as follows: 50% for construction costs, 45% for technology purchases, and 5% for incidental expenses. Using a proportion, find the amount that will be spent on technology purchases. $\frac{t}{15,432} = \frac{45}{100}; \$6944.40$
(Ex 4)

Practice   Distributed and Integrated

Solve each equation. Check your answer.

1. $5d - 8 = 3 + 7d$ $d = -\frac{11}{2}$
(28)

2. $9 + 2.7t = -4.8t - 6$ $t = -2$
(28)

Solve each equation for the indicated variable.

3. $V = \frac{1}{3}lwh$ for w $w = \frac{3V}{lh}$
(29)

4. $d = rt$ for t $t = \frac{d}{r}$
(29)

5. $\sqrt{42}$ is between which two integers? between 6 and 7
(13)

6. What is 18% of 340? 61.2
(42)

*7. What is 270% of 93? 251.1
(42)

8. Simplify $(6mn^3)^2$. $36m^2n^6$
(40)

*9. **Multiple Choice** What is 54% of 1200? C
(42)
A 64.8   B 600   C 648   D 1254

*10. **Gas Prices** Shoshannah researched gasoline prices and found that gas was 224% more expensive than it had been during the same week 5 years previously, when the average price of regular gasoline was $1.36 per gallon. What was the new price?
(42) $3.05 per gallon

*11. **Write** Explain how fractions, percentages, and decimals are all related. All of them are used to express a part of a whole.
(42)

266   Saxon Algebra 1

12. **Multi-Step** The graph shows the number of pitches thrown in each inning of a baseball game.

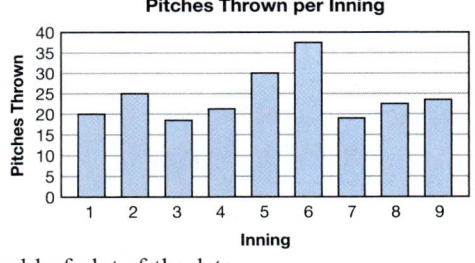

Pitches Thrown per Inning

12a. **Numbers of Pitches Thrown per Inning**

Stem	Leaves
1	9, 9
2	0, 1, 2, 3, 5
3	0, 8

Key: 1 | 9 means 19

a. Make a stem-and-leaf plot of the data.
b. Find the greatest and least number of pitches thrown during the game.
 greatest: 38; least: 19

13. (**Wages**) Maria earned $10.50 per hour working at an ice cream shop. She earned $147 each week before taxes. Find the number of hours she worked each week. 14 hours

14. (**Computers**) One megabyte holds 10^6 pieces of information and one terabyte holds 10^{12} pieces of information. A terabyte holds how many times more information than a megabyte? 10^6 = 1,000,000 times more information

15. **Verify** For $6x + \frac{1}{4}(y) = 44$, is $y = 88 - 24x$? If the solution for y is incorrect, give the correct solution for y. incorrect; $y = 176 - 24x$

16. (**Pricing**) A baker sells 2 pies for $5, 4 pies for $10, and 6 pies for $15. What is the price of 14 pies? $35
 a. Create a table comparing the number of pies sold to the total cost.
 b. Illustrate the data using a graph. Does the graph show a function?
 c. Determine a rule for the function. $y = 2.50x$
 d. Graph the function using a graphing calculator and determine the price of 14 pies. $35.00

16a.
x (Number of Pies)	2	4	6
y (Total Cost)	$5	$10	$15

17. How could a company use a line graph to make it appear as though they had a larger profit? Sample: They could draw the graph with a broken axis.

18. **Multi-Step** A family plans to take a road trip. They leave Town A, go to Town B, and then end at Town C. On the way back, they decide to travel different roads for a change of scenery.

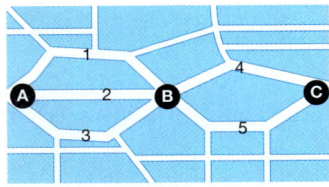

16b. (graph of Price ($) vs Number of Pies) yes

a. What is the probability they took Road 1 and Road 4 on the way to Town C? $\frac{1}{6}$
b. What is the probability they will take Road 2 and Road 5 on the way back? $\frac{1}{2}$

Lesson 42 267

INCLUSION

Students may have difficulty conceptualizing percents higher than 100%. Describe a class of 5 students growing by 400%. Then have students copy and complete the table.

Percent	Number of students
100%	5
200%	10
300%	15
400%	20

Explain to the students that multiplying by percents greater than 100% is the same as multiplying by a number greater than 1.

Write this sentence on the chalkboard: "The weight of an 8-pound baby increases by 20 times as it grows to adulthood."

Ask students to write the sentence replacing "20 times" with a percent. Sample: The weight of an 8-pound baby increases by 2000% as it grows to adulthood.

Problem 5
Guide students by asking them the following questions.

"The number 42 is between which perfect squares?" 36 and 49

"What is the square root of 36?" 6

"What is the square root of 49?" 7

Problem 13
Extend the Problem
"Suppose Maria earned the same hourly rate and worked the same weekly hours for a month (4 weeks). How much would she earn before taxes?" $588

"If Maria received a $1 more per hour raise, how much would she earn for the same weekly hours before taxes?" $161

Problem 17
Guide students by asking them the following questions.

"On which axis would you show profit on a line graph?" y-axis

"On which axis would you show time on a line graph?" x-axis

"How might you make the profit appear larger at first glance?" Sample: Use a break in the y-axis.

Problem 20
Error Alert
Students may not carefully read the intervals on the *x*- and *y*-axis. Direct them to notice that in this problem, each interval represents two units.

Problem 24
Guide the students by asking them the following questions.

"In which direction will the decimal point move?" to the right

"How many places will the decimal point move?" three

"What sign will the exponent in scientific notation have?" negative

Problem 25
Guide the students by asking them the following questions.

"Will a variable that causes a fraction to be undefined be in the numerator or denominator of the fraction?" the denominator

"Which variable has the potential to cause the fractions to be undefined?" s

Problem 27
Remind students that to raise a power to a power the exponents are multiplied.

---

19. Generalize During the past 4 years you have grown 3 inches per year.
(34)
  a. Write a recursive formula that describes the sequence. $a_n = a_{n-1} + 3$
  b. If you were 52 inches tall 4 years ago, how tall are you now? 64 in.
  c. Would you expect this pattern of growth to continue for a long time? Explain your reasoning. no; Sample: Humans eventually stop growing.

*20. Find the *x*- and *y*-intercepts on the graph. The *x*-intercept is −8 and the
(35) *y*-intercept is −7.

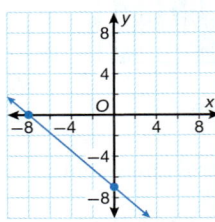

*21. **Generalize** A gerbil cage measures 24 inches by 10 inches by 18 inches. If you
(36) double the lengths of each side of the cage, how will this increase affect the volume of the cage? The volume will increase by 8 times.

*22. Find the GCF of $14p^5qr^2 - 28p^2q^2r^3$. $14p^2qr^2$
(38)

23. **Verify** Show that $\frac{r^{-2}}{s^{-3}}\left(\frac{rs^{-2}}{sr^{-1}} - \frac{s^{-3}r^{-1}}{r^{-3}}\right) = 0$. Sample: $\frac{r^{-2}}{s^{-3}}\left(\frac{rs^{-2}}{sr^{-1}} - \frac{s^{-3}r^{-1}}{r^{-3}}\right) = \left(\frac{r^{-1}s^{-2}}{s^{-2}r^{-1}} - \frac{s^{-3}r^{-3}}{s^{-3}r^{-3}}\right) = 1 - 1 = 0$
(39)

24. **Earth Science** A grain of sand is approximately 0.002 meters in diameter. Write this
(37) number in scientific notation. 2×10^{-3}

*25. **Multiple Choice** In the expression $\frac{pg^3}{s}\left(\frac{g^2p^3}{s^4} + \frac{9p}{s^2} - n\right)$, which variable cannot
(39) equal 0? C
  A p   **B** g   **C** s   **D** n

26. **Fuel Efficiency** The graph represents the amount of gasoline used and the number
(41) of miles driven. What is the rate of change? 25 miles per gallon

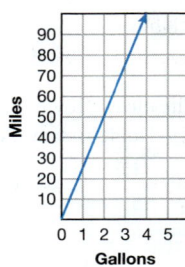

27. **Error Analysis** Two students simplify the expression $(3^4)^2$ as shown below. Which
(40) student is correct? Explain the error.

27. Student A; Sample: Student B raised the base to the second power.

Student A	Student B
$(3^4)^2 = 3^{4 \cdot 2} = 3^8$	$(3^4)^2 = 9^{4 \cdot 2} = 9^8$

268   Saxon Algebra 1

*28. Find the rate of change from the graph. $\frac{1}{4}$ mile/inch

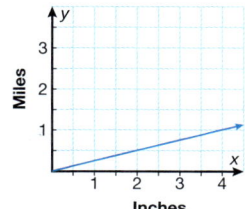

*29. **Multi-Step** A mountain resort charges a set fee for cabin rentals as well as for each day of snowboard rentals.

Days of Cabin and Snowboard Rentals	1	2	3	4
Cost	$405	$427	$449	$471

a. What is the rate of change in the rental costs? $22 per 1 day

b. What will the mountain resort charge for 7 days? $537

30. **Geometry** A right triangle has side lengths 6 cm, 8 cm, and 10 cm. Use the shorter leg as the base of the triangle and find the slope of the hypotenuse. Then use the longer leg as the base of the triangle and find the slope of the hypotenuse. Assume the slopes are positive. $\frac{4}{3}$; $\frac{3}{4}$

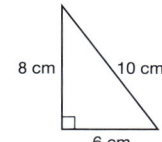

Problem 28
Extend the Problem
"Suppose the current rate of change is a ratio that describes a scale on a map. Find the number of miles that is represented by a foot on the map." 3 miles

Lesson 42   269

CHALLENGE

An after-school program received a grant for $21,327. Program administrators want to use $\frac{1}{4}$ of the funds to pay tutors, 0.5 of the funds for a new facility, 12% of the funds for a parent-student program, and 13% of the funds for materials. Estimate the amount of funds available for each category. Paying tutors: $5000; new facility: $10,000; parent-student program: $2400; materials: $2600

LOOKING FORWARD

Solving percent problems prepares students for

• **Lesson 47** Solving Problems Involving the Percent of Change

• **Lesson 56** Identifying, Writing, and Graphing Direct Variation

• **Lesson 117** Using Trigonometric Ratios

Lesson 42   269

LESSON 43

1 Warm Up

Problem 5
Remind students that they can use the Distributive Property to factor polynomials.

2 New Concepts

In this lesson, students learn how to simplify rational expressions and find undefined, or excluded, values for rational expressions.

Example 1

Remind students that division by zero is undefined.

Extend the Example

Ask students if changing the denominator in Example 1a to x^2 will affect the undefined values. Have them explain their answer.
no; Sample: The only number that equals zero when squared is zero, so the expression is only undefined at $x = 0$.

Additional Example 1

Determine the values for which each rational expression is undefined.

a. $\dfrac{2+x}{3x}$ $x = 0$ b. $\dfrac{7x+1}{x-7}$ $x = 7$

c. $\dfrac{(2x+1)(x-1)}{5x-15}$ $x = 3$

LESSON RESOURCES

Student Edition Practice
   Workbook 43
Reteaching Master 43
Adaptations Master 43
Challenge and Enrichment
   Master C43

LESSON 43

Simplifying Rational Expressions

Warm Up

1. **Vocabulary** The largest whole number that is a factor of two or more indicated numbers is the _____. **greatest common factor**

Simplify.

2. $\dfrac{36}{48}$ $\dfrac{3}{4}$ 3. $\dfrac{32x^5}{48x^7}$ $\dfrac{2}{3x^2}$ 4. $\dfrac{7x - 49x^2}{7x}$ $1 - 7x$

5. Factor $3x^2 + 6x^3$ completely. $3x^2(1 + 2x)$

New Concepts

Rational expressions are fractions with a variable in the denominator. Since division by 0 in mathematics is undefined, the denominator of a rational expression must not equal 0.

Example 1 Determining When an Expression is Undefined

Determine the values for which each rational expression is undefined.

a. $\dfrac{x+8}{4x}$

Caution
Some students may mistakenly think that if the numerator equals zero, the fraction is undefined. Remind them that dividing zero by a nonzero number always results in a quotient equal to zero.

SOLUTION

denominator $= 4x$ Start with the denominator.
$4x = 0$ when $x = 0$ The expression is undefined at $x = 0$.

b. $\dfrac{2x+1}{x-4}$

SOLUTION

denominator $= x - 4$ Start with the denominator.
$x - 4 = 0$ when $x = 4$ The expression is undefined at $x = 4$.

c. $\dfrac{(x+5)(x-3)}{3x+21}$

SOLUTION

denominator $= 3x + 21$ Start with the denominator.
$3x + 21 = 0$ Find its zero value.
$x + 7 = 0$ Divide by 3.
$x = -7$ The expression is undefined at $x = -7$.

Online Connection
www.SaxonMathResources.com

MATH BACKGROUND

Rational numbers are in the form $\dfrac{a}{b}$, where a and b are integers and $b \neq 0$. Likewise, rational expressions are in the form $\dfrac{a}{b}$, where a and b are polynomials and $b \neq 0$, and the degree of b is greater than or equal to 1. Factoring is important when finding values of the variable that cause the denominator to equal zero.

Factoring polynomials is also important for operations with rational expressions. First of all, factoring and dividing out like factors make it easier to identify common denominators; this is useful for adding and subtracting rational expressions. Secondly, factoring and dividing out like factors make it easier to simplify products and quotients of rational expressions.

Example 2 Simplifying Using a Common Factor

Simplify each rational expression. Determine undefined values.

a. $\dfrac{54x + 9}{4 + x}$

SOLUTION

$\dfrac{54x + 9}{4 + x}, x \neq -4$	Determine undefined values.
GCF = 9	Find the numerator's GCF.
GCF = none	Find the denominator's GCF.
$\dfrac{54x + 9}{4 + x} = \dfrac{9(6x + 1)}{4 + x}$	Factor.
$\dfrac{9(6x + 1)}{4 + x}, x \neq -4$	Include undefined values in the answer.

b. $\dfrac{2x^2 - 10x}{4x^2 + 6x}$

SOLUTION

GCF = 2x	Find the numerator's GCF.
GCF = 2x	Find the denominator's GCF.
$\dfrac{2x^2 - 10x}{4x^2 + 6x} = \dfrac{2x(x - 5)}{2x(2x + 3)}; x \neq -\dfrac{3}{2}; x \neq 0$	Factor. Determine undefined values.
$\dfrac{\overset{1}{\cancel{2x}}(x - 5)}{\underset{1}{\cancel{2x}}(2x + 3)} = \dfrac{x - 5}{2x + 3}$	Simplify by dividing out like monomials.
$\dfrac{x - 5}{2x + 3}, x \neq -\dfrac{3}{2}; x \neq 0$	Include undefined values in the answer.

c. $\dfrac{2x^2 - 14x}{4x - 28}$

SOLUTION

GCF = 2x	Find the numerator's GCF.
GCF = 4	Find the denominator's GCF.
$\dfrac{2x^2 - 14x}{4x - 28} = \dfrac{2x(x - 7)}{4(x - 7)}; x \neq 7$	Factor. Determine undefined values.
$\dfrac{2x\cancel{(x - 7)}}{4\cancel{(x - 7)}} = \dfrac{2x}{4}$	Simplify by dividing out like binomials.
$\dfrac{\overset{1}{\cancel{2x}}}{\underset{2}{\cancel{4}}} = \dfrac{x}{2}$	Simplify.
$\dfrac{x}{2}; x \neq 7$	Include undefined values in the answer.

Caution

Determine values that cause the denominator to equal zero before the fraction is simplified.

Example 2

Error Alert Students may simplify before finding the undefined values. Remind them to identify the undefined values before simplifying.

Additional Example 2

Simplify each rational expression. Determine undefined values.

a. $\dfrac{27x + 9}{x - 10} \quad \dfrac{9(3x + 1)}{x - 10}, x \neq 10$

b. $\dfrac{8x^2 - 4x}{12x^2 + 8x} \quad \dfrac{2x - 1}{3x + 2}, x \neq 0, x \neq -\dfrac{2}{3}$

c. $\dfrac{7x^2 + 21x}{5x + 15} \quad \dfrac{7x}{5}, x \neq -3$

TEACHER TIP

Students may simplify the rational expression first and then find undefined values of the variable. Emphasize that they use the original denominator when finding those values; this is because the original fraction is not defined for values that cause the denominator to equal zero.

Lesson 43

  INCLUSION

Have students simplify a rational expression using prime factorization. Tell them to copy and complete the table.

Term	Prime Factorization
$2x^2$	$2 \cdot x \cdot x$
$10x$	$2 \cdot 5 \cdot x$
$4x^2$	$2 \cdot 2 \cdot x \cdot x$
$6x$	$2 \cdot 3 \cdot x$

Copy the factors into the fraction.

$$\dfrac{2x^2 - 10x}{4x^2 + 6x} = \dfrac{2 \cdot x \cdot x - 2 \cdot 5 \cdot x}{2 \cdot 2 \cdot x \cdot x + 2 \cdot 3 \cdot x}$$

Group the common factors in the numerator and the denominator.

$$\dfrac{2x^2 - 10x}{4x^2 + 6x} = \dfrac{(2x) \cdot x - (2x) \cdot 5}{(2x) \cdot 2x + (2x) \cdot 3}$$

Then factor out the common factors and divide out like terms.

$$\dfrac{\cancel{2x}(x - 5)}{\cancel{2x}(2x + 3)} = \dfrac{x - 5}{2x + 3}$$

Lesson 43   271

Example 3

Students determine the simplest form of a rational expression in a real-world application.

Additional Example 3

The distance a car has traveled is equal to $8.1t + 0.9t^2$. It took $1.8t^2$ seconds to travel that far. What is the velocity of the car in simplest form? $\frac{9+t}{2t}, t \neq 0$

Lesson Practice

Problem c

Scaffolding Suggest that students use mental math to find the undefined values. Mentally determine that $42 - 42 = 0$, so $6x = 42$. Then $x = 7$.

Problem e

Error Alert Students may not find all values of x for which the expression is undefined. Remind students to factor the denominator first. Suggest that they try both substituting 0 for x and solving $ax + b = 0$.

✓ Check for Understanding

The questions below help assess the concepts taught in this lesson.

"**Explain how to determine when a rational expression is undefined.**" Sample: Find the values of the variable that cause the denominator to equal zero.

"**Explain how to simplify a rational expression.**" Sample: Find common factors in the denominator and numerator and divide out like terms.

Example 3 **Application: Moving Objects**

The expression $3.5t + 0.7t^2$ represents the distance a moving object travels through time t. The expression $1.4t^2$ represents the distance the same object moves from rest with twice the acceleration.

Simplify $\frac{3.5t + 0.7t^2}{1.4t^2}$.

Math Reasoning

Analyze Determine the undefined value for the rational expression $\frac{3.5t + 0.7t^2}{1.4t^2}$. What is its meaning in the context of the problem?

Sample: The undefined value is $t = 0$. At time $t = 0$ the objects are not moving.

SOLUTION

$1.4t^2$	Identify the denominator.
$t \neq 0$	Determine undefined values.
$\frac{3.5t + 0.7t^2}{1.4t^2} = \frac{0.7t(5 + t)}{1.4t^2}$	Factor the numerator.
$= \frac{0.7t(5 + t)}{0.7t(2t)}$	Factor the denominator.
$= \frac{5 + t}{2t}$	Simplify.

The simplified expression is $\frac{5+t}{2t}, t \neq 0$.

Lesson Practice

Determine the values for which each rational expression is undefined. (Ex 1)

a. $\frac{16x - 7}{5x}$ $x = 0$ b. $\frac{1 + 3x}{x + 8}$ $x = -8$ c. $\frac{11 - x}{6x - 42}$ $x = 7$

Simplify each rational expression. Determine undefined values. (Ex 2)

d. $\frac{7x - 27}{5x}$ e. $\frac{3x^2 - 3x}{9x^2 + 15x}$ f. $\frac{4x + 28}{3x^2 + 21x}$

d. $\frac{7x - 27}{5x}, x \neq 0$

e. $\frac{x - 1}{3x + 5}, x \neq -\frac{5}{3}; x \neq 0$

f. , $x \neq 0; x \neq -7$

A package is needed that uses the least amount of material to hold the greatest volume of product. A container in the shape of a right circular cylinder has a surface area of $S = 2\pi rh + 2\pi r^2$ and a volume of $V = \pi r^2 h$.

g. Simplify $\frac{2\pi rh + 2\pi r^2}{\pi r^2 h}$. $\frac{2(h+r)}{rh}; h \neq 0, r \neq 0$

Practice   Distributed and Integrated

Evaluate each function for the given input value.

1. $f(x) = -2x$ for $x = -5$ 10
(30)

2. $h(x) = 3x - 1$ for $x = 7$ 20
(30)

Find the indicated term of each arithmetic sequence.

3. $a_n = 16 + (n - 1)(-0.5)$, 15th term   9
(34)

4. $-8, -6, -4, -2, \ldots$, 100th term   190
(34)

272   *Saxon* Algebra 1

🇪🇱 ENGLISH LEARNERS

Explain the meaning of the word **acceleration**. Acceleration, or accelerate, means to speed up. Say:

"When the gas pedal of a car is pressed down, the car accelerates. What happens to the car's speed when the gas pedal is pressed down?"
Sample: The car speeds up.

Have students list objects that might accelerate. Sample: a rocket, a swimmer, a go-cart, a bicycle, a runner

Identify the values that make the rational expressions below undefined.

*5. $\dfrac{25}{x+10}$ $x = -10$
(43)

*6. $\dfrac{12+3x}{5-x}$ $x = 5$
(43)

7. What is 14% of 120?   16.8
(42)

8. What is 75% of 60?   45
(42)

9. A school needs to raise $2700. A nearby store promises to donate twice the amount the students raise. How much money do the students need to raise?
(23) $900; $x + 2x = \$2700$, $x = \$900$

10. Ann-Marie has $2.55 in nickels and dimes. She has $1.80 in dimes. How many nickels does Ann-Marie have?
(24)
   a. Write an equation to represent the situation. $1.8 + 0.05n = 2.55$
   b. How many nickels does she have?   15 nickels

11. **Error Analysis** Two students use the diagram to determine whether the relation is a function. Which student is correct? Explain the error.
(25)

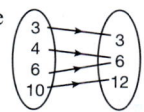

11. Student B; Sample: Student A confused the dependent and independent variables. If any of the x-values were the same, the relation would not be a function.

Student A	Student B
$\{(3, 3), (4, 6), (6, 6), (10, 12)\}$ The y-values are not all different; y equals 6 twice. So, it is not a function.	$\{(3, 3), (4, 6), (6, 6), (10, 12)\}$ All the x-values are different, so it is a function.

12. **Write** Explain how you can use a graph to tell whether a relation is a function.
(30)

13. **Geography** A map shows a 2.5-inch distance between Brownsville and Evanstown. The scale on the map is 1 inch:25 miles. How far apart are the two towns?
(31) 62.5 miles

12. Sample: Use a vertical line test. If a vertical line passes through more than one point on the graph, the relation is not a function.

*14. **Multiple Choice** Which of the following rational expressions is undefined at $x = -6$?   A
(43)

A $\dfrac{x-6}{12x+72}$ B $\dfrac{x}{2(x+12)}$

C $\dfrac{x+6}{72-12x}$ D $\dfrac{2x+12}{x}$

*15. **Digital Signal Processing** In digital signal processing, electronic signals are often represented as rational expressions. The rational expression $\dfrac{3z^2 + 2.7z}{(z+0.9)(z-0.9)}$ models a digital signal. What is the simplified form of this signal representation? $\dfrac{3z}{(z-0.9)}, z \neq 0.9, z \neq -0.9$
(43)

*16. **Analyze** Given the rational expression $\dfrac{8x}{2x+16}$, for what values of x would its reciprocal be undefined?   undefined at $x = 0$
(43)

17. **Phone Numbers** A student forgets the last two digits of her friend's phone number. She does remember that the digits are different. What is the probability of guessing the last two digits correctly on the first try? $\dfrac{1}{90}$
(33)

18. **Multi-Step** In an arithmetic sequence, $a_1 = 17$ and $d = 10$.
(34)
   a. Write a rule for the nth term of the sequence. $a_n = 17 + (n-1)10$
   b. Use the rule to find the fourth and eleventh terms of the sequence.   47; 117

Lesson 43   273

3 Practice

Math Conversations
Discussion to strengthen understanding

Problem 9
Show students a division diagram to help them write an equation.

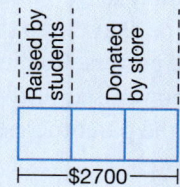

So, $3x = \$2700$.

Problem 10
Error Alert
Students may not correctly calculate decimal placement when solving an equation using dollar amounts. Converting dollar amounts to cents before solving the problem may help eliminate decimal placement errors.

Problem 14
Rather than students solving each denominator for the undefined value, suggest that they substitute the given value in each denominator to find the expression that is undefined at $x = -6$.

Problem 16
Students may take the opposite of 8 to determine the undefined value as -8. Some students may need to write the expression $8x = 0$ on paper to emphasize that the operation used to find the undefined value is division.

CHALLENGE

Have students use guess and check to find undefined values of the variables. Then have them simplify the rational expression.

$\dfrac{x^2 - 1}{2x^2 - 2}$ $\dfrac{1}{2}$; The expression is undefined when $x = 1$ or $x = -1$.

Lesson 43   273

Problem 22
Extend the Problem
"If the height of the box is $6x + 4$, write an expression to represent the volume of the box." $32x(3x + 2)^2$

Problem 23
Error Alert
Students may forget to raise the coefficients 10 and 3 to their respective powers. Remind them that the power is applied to each factor in the parentheses.

Problem 29
Guide the students by asking them the following questions.

"The lean was reduced by 10%. What percent of the original lean does the tower have now?" 90%

"How can 90% be used to find the number of feet past center that the tower now leans?" Sample: Multiply 14.5 by 0.90.

---

19. Verify Verify that $5x + 6y = -12$ is the standard form of the equation $y = -\frac{5}{6}x - 2$. Sample: Multiply both sides by 6 to get $6y = -5x - 12$ and then add $5x$ to both sides; $5x + 6y = -12$.

20. Name the corresponding sides and angles of the two similar triangles shown at right. $\overline{MN}$ and $\overline{KL}$; $\overline{MP}$ and $\overline{KJ}$; $\overline{NP}$ and $\overline{LJ}$; $\angle M$ and $\angle K$; $\angle N$ and $\angle L$; $\angle P$ and $\angle J$

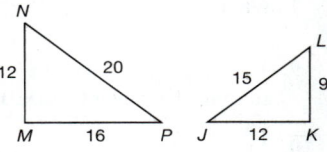

*21. Multiply $(1.6 \times 10^{-5})(2.2 \times 10^3)$ and write the answer in scientific notation. 3.52×10^{-2}

22. Packaging The bottom of a rectangular box has a length of $6x + 4$ inches and a width of $8x$ inches.
   a. Write an expression that can be used to find the area of the bottom of the box. $8x(6x + 4)$
   b. Factor the expression completely. $16x(3x + 2)$

*23. Multiple Choice Simplify $(10g^3h^{-4})^2 (3gh^6)^3$. **A**
   A $2700g^9h^{10}$ **B** $180g^9h^{10}$ **C** $180g^5h^7$ **D** $2700g^{18}h^{16}$

24. Formulate Multiply $(8x^3)(2x)^{-3}$. What is true about $(8x^3)$ and $(2x)^{-3}$? (Hint: Simplify the expression.) They are multiplicative inverses of each other.

25. Simplify $\frac{k}{g}\left(\frac{rtw}{nk} - 5k^2w^6\right)$. $\frac{rtw}{ng} - \frac{5k^3w^6}{g}$

*26. Probability $P(A) = \frac{r^2}{t}$, $P(B) = \frac{t}{s}$, and $P(C) = \frac{s^2}{rt}$. $P(A \text{ and } (B \text{ or } C))$ is represented by the expression $\frac{r^2}{t}\left(\frac{t}{s} + \frac{s^2}{rt}\right)$. Simplify. $\frac{r^2}{s} + \frac{rs^2}{t^2}$

27. Use the table to find the rate of change. 12 guests/table

Tables	3	5	7	9
Guests	36	60	84	108

*28. Multi-Step A plant in Selena's garden will eventually reach a height of 134.4 centimeters. Today the plant measures 42 centimeters in height. What percent of the present height of Selena's plant is the final height of the plant?
   a. Write a proportion to solve the problem. Sample: $\frac{x}{100} = \frac{134.4}{42}$
   b. Find the solution. 320%
   c. Choose a method with which to check your work and determine the reasonableness of your solution.

28c. Sample: $320\% = 3.2$ times a number; $42 \cdot 3.2 = 134.4$

29. Restoration At the beginning of 1999, the Leaning Tower of Pisa leaned 14.5 feet past center and was in danger of falling over. Engineers tried removing dirt from the side of the tower opposite from the direction in which it leans, and were able to reduce the lean by about 10%. About how far past center did the tower lean after the dirt was removed? about 13 ft

*30. Geometry Two similar triangles are shown at right. The sides on the larger triangle are 130% of those on the smaller triangle. What is the length of side x? 15.6

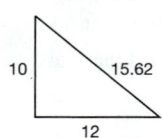 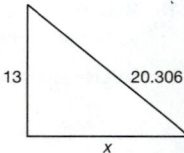

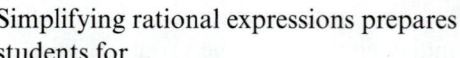

LESSON 44

Finding Slope Using the Slope Formula

Warm Up

1. **Vocabulary** The _____ of a line is the steepness of the line. **slope**
   (41)

Name the coordinates of each point.
   (20)
2. W $(-6, -4)$
3. X $(4, -5)$
4. Y $(5, 3)$

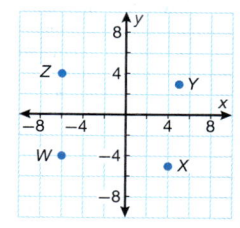

5. Use the table to find the rate of change. $\frac{4}{1}$
   (41)

Servings	2	4	8	12
Corn (oz)	8	16	32	48

New Concepts

Any two ordered pairs on a line can be used to determine the slope of the line. The **slope** is a measure of the steepness of a line. The slope m of a line containing points (x_1, y_1) and (x_2, y_2) is $m = \frac{y_2 - y_1}{x_2 - x_1}$.

Math Reasoning

Write Describe the formula for slope using only words.

Sample: The slope is equal to the ratio of the rise over the run.

Math Reasoning

Analyze When is the slope an improper fraction?

when the change in y-values is greater than the change in the x-values

Example 1 Determining Slope from Two Points

Determine the slope of the line that contains the given points.

a. $(2, 4)$ and $(6, 6)$

SOLUTION

$m = \frac{y_2 - y_1}{x_2 - x_1}$ slope formula

$= \frac{6 - 4}{6 - 2}$ Substitute x- and y-values.

$= \frac{1}{2}$ Simplify.

The slope of the line is $\frac{1}{2}$.

b. $(-4, 4)$ and $(4, -2)$

SOLUTION

$m = \frac{y_2 - y_1}{x_2 - x_1}$

$= \frac{(-2) - 4}{4 - (-4)}$

$= -\frac{3}{4}$

The slope of the line is $-\frac{3}{4}$.

c. $(0, -5)$ and $(5, 10)$

SOLUTION

$m = \frac{y_2 - y_1}{x_2 - x_1}$ slope formula

$= \frac{10 - (-5)}{5 - 0}$ Substitute x- and y-values.

$= 3$ Simplify.

The slope of the line is 3.

d. $(-6, 5)$ and $(3, -13)$

SOLUTION

$m = \frac{y_2 - y_1}{x_2 - x_1}$

$= \frac{(-13) - 5}{3 - (-6)}$

$= -2$

The slope of the line is -2.

Online Connection
www.SaxonMathResources.com

Lesson 44   275

MATH BACKGROUND

Another way to define the slope of a line is by the angle formed by the line and the horizon. A horizontal line and the horizon form a 0° angle, and the slope of the line is 0. A vertical line and the horizon form a 90° angle, and the slope of the line is undefined. All other lines have either a negative or positive slope.

A surface with a 0° incline is not steep and is represented by a horizontal line. A surface with a 90° incline could be represent by a cliff or a wall. The concepts of inclines and slopes are related and can be used to explain vertical and horizontal lines.

Example 2

In this example, students determine the slope of a line using points from a table and the slope formula.

Remind students that they can pick any two points on a line to find the slope.

Error Alert Students may reverse the x and y in the formula. Remind students to write the formula and then substitute.

Additional Example 2

Determine the slope of the line that contains the given points.

x	y
−2	3
1	−3
0	−1

The slope of the line is −2.

Example 3

In this example, students determine the slope of a line from the graph of the line and the slope formula.

Additional Example 3

Determine the slope of given line.

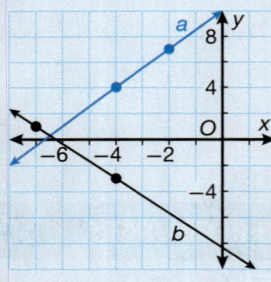

line a: $\frac{3}{2}$
line b: $-\frac{4}{3}$

Two points are not always given explicitly as coordinates to determine the slope. If given a table or graph then two points must be chosen in order to use the slope formula.

Example 2 Determining Slope From a Table

Determine the slope of the line that contains the given points shown in the table.

x	y
−5	6
10	0
40	−12

SOLUTION

$m = \dfrac{y_2 - y_1}{x_2 - x_1}$ slope formula

$= \dfrac{0 - 6}{10 - (-5)}$ Substitute coordinates of 2 ordered pairs.

$= \dfrac{-6}{15}$

$= -\dfrac{2}{5}$ Simplify.

The slope of the line is $-\dfrac{2}{5}$.

Math Reasoning

Verify Choose another set of points from the table to verify that the slope is $-\dfrac{2}{5}$.

Sample:
$\dfrac{-12 - 0}{40 - 10} =$
$-\dfrac{12}{30} = -\dfrac{2}{5}$

Example 3 Determining Slope from a Graph

Determine the slope of the given line.

a.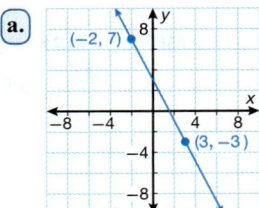

b.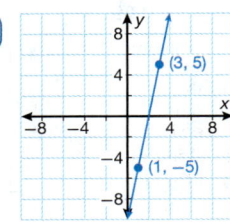

SOLUTION

$m = \dfrac{y_2 - y_1}{x_2 - x_1}$ slope formula

$= \dfrac{(-3) - 7}{3 - (-2)}$ Substitute in x- and y-values.

$= \dfrac{-10}{5}$

$= -2$ Simplify.

The slope of the line is −2.

SOLUTION

$m = \dfrac{y_2 - y_1}{x_2 - x_1}$

$= \dfrac{5 - (-5)}{3 - 1}$

$= \dfrac{10}{2}$

$= 5$

The slope of the line is 5.

🔷 INCLUSION

Students can use the Coordinate Grid transparency to graph the line in Example 2 using the values in the table. This shows that lines that fall from left to right have negative slopes.

Example 4 Determining Slopes of Horizontal and Vertical Lines

Determine the slope of the given line.

a.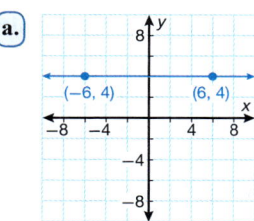

SOLUTION

$m = \dfrac{y_2 - y_1}{x_2 - x_1}$ slope formula

$= \dfrac{4 - 4}{6 - (-6)}$ Substitute the x- and y-values.

$= \dfrac{0}{12}$

$= 0$ Simplify.

The slope is 0, or no slope.

b.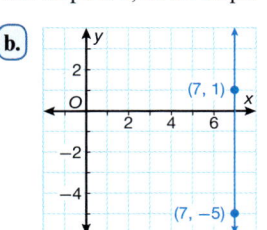

SOLUTION

$m = \dfrac{y_2 - y_1}{x_2 - x_1}$ slope formula

$= \dfrac{(-5) - 1}{7 - 7}$ Substitute the x- and y-values.

$= \dfrac{-6}{0}$ Simplify.

The slope is undefined.

The slope of a vertical line is undefined because it has a zero in the denominator. The slope of a horizontal line has a zero in the numerator, therefore its slope is zero.

Math Reasoning

Generalize What is true about the x-coordinates of any line with an undefined slope?

Sample: The x-coordinates are all the same because the line is a vertical line.

Example 4

Students learn to compute the slopes of horizontal lines and show that vertical lines have undefined slopes.

Additional Example 4

Determine the slope of the given line.

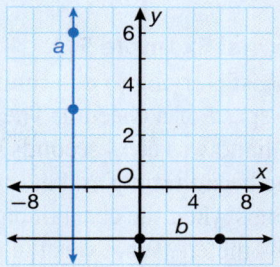

line a: $m =$ undefined slope
line b: 0

Lesson 44   277

Example 5

Students learn to find the speed of a moving object.

Extend the Example
If the train continues at the same speed, how many seconds would be on the clock after another $\frac{1}{8}$ mile? **51 seconds**

Additional Example 5
A biologist is trying to determine the top speed of a cheetah. The second hand was at 14 seconds when he began timing and at 51 seconds when the cheetah had run 1184 meters. What was the speed of the cheetah in meters per second? **32 m/s**

Lesson Practice

Problem a
Error Alert Students may subtract negative numbers incorrectly. Remind them to check their work by working backward.

Problem j
Scaffolding Suggest that students use unit analysis before working through the problem.

Check for Understanding

The questions below help assess the concepts taught in this lesson.

"What is the slope of a horizontal line?" A horizontal line has a slope of 0.

"Why does a vertical line have an undefined slope?" because on vertical lines, any two points have the same x coordinate, so $x_2 - x_1$ will always be 0 and division by 0 is undefined

"How can you tell if the slope of a line is positive or negative just by looking at a graph of the line?" If the line slopes up to the right, it has a positive slope; if it slopes down to the right, it has a negative slope.

278 **Saxon** Algebra 1

A **rate of change** is a ratio that compares the change in one quantity with the change in another. The slope of a line represents a rate of change.

Example 5   **Application: Determining Rates of Change**

Alyssa used the second hand of a clock to record the time it took a train to travel the distance from her house to a friend's house. The second hand of the clock was at 12 seconds when she began timing and at 38 seconds when the train had traveled the one-quarter-mile distance to her friend's house. What was the speed of the train in feet per second?

SOLUTION

Understand Alyssa is trying to calculate the speed of the train based on changes in both time and distance. The speed can be expressed as a ratio of the changes in each quantity.

$$\text{speed} = \frac{\text{change in distance}}{\text{change in time}}$$

Hint
Remind students that there are 5280 feet in 1 mile. So, a quarter mile is 1320 feet.

Plan Represent the original distance and time as one point on a line and the final time and distance as the second point. Then find the slope of the line connecting these two points.

Solve Use the slope formula to find the speed.

Label the points. $(x_1, y_1) \rightarrow (12, 0)$ and $(x_2, y_2) \rightarrow (38, 1320)$.

Apply the slope formula. $m = \dfrac{y_2 - y_1}{x_2 - x_1} = \dfrac{1320 - 0}{38 - 12}$

Simplify. $m = \dfrac{1320}{26} = 50.8 \text{ ft/s}$

Check

$$50.8 \frac{\text{ft}}{\text{s}} \cdot \frac{1 \text{ mile}}{5280 \text{ ft}} \cdot 3600 \frac{\text{s}}{\text{hour}} = 34.6 \text{ mph}$$

The speed of 34.6 mph is reasonable for a train.

Lesson Practice

Determine the slope of the line that contains the given points.
(Ex 1)

a. $(-3, -4)$ and $(3, 0)$ $\frac{2}{3}$

b. $(-5, 8)$ and $(5, 6)$ $-\frac{1}{5}$

c. $(0, 6)$ and $(1, 12)$ 6

d. $(-2, 7)$ and $(2, -9)$ -4

Math Reasoning
Generalize What pattern do you notice in lines that have a positive slope? a negative slope?

Sample: The lines slope up to the right; the lines slope down to the right.

Determine the slope of the line that contains the points shown in the table.

e. *(Ex 2)*   7

x	y
−4	−27
−2	−13
0	1

278 **Saxon** Algebra 1

ALTERNATE METHOD FOR EXAMPLE 5

Find the speed in miles per second and then convert it to feet per second.

38 seconds − 12 seconds = 26 seconds

$$\frac{0.25 \text{ mi}}{26 \text{ s}} = \frac{1 \text{ mi}}{104 \text{ s}}$$

$$\frac{1 \text{ mi}}{104 \text{ s}} = \frac{1 \text{ mi}}{104 \text{ s}} \cdot \frac{5280 \text{ ft}}{1 \text{ mi}} = \frac{5280 \text{ ft}}{104 \text{ s}}$$

$$\frac{5280 \text{ ft}}{104 \text{ s}} \approx 50.8 \text{ ft/s}$$

Determine the slope of the given line.

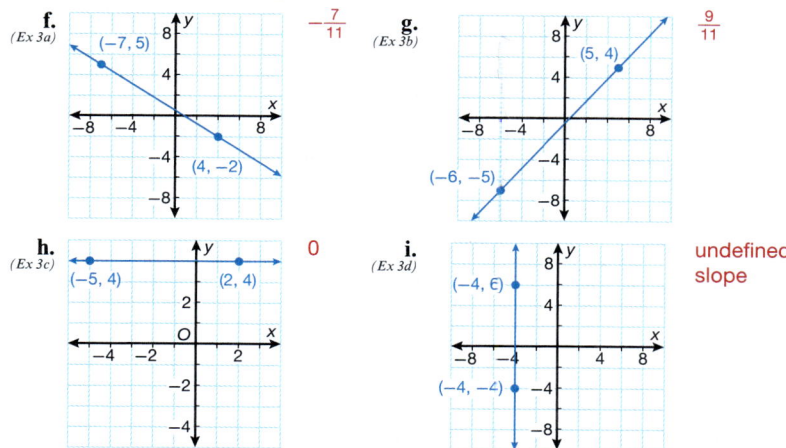

j. Michael timed a train using a clock. The train traveled a distance of one
(Ex 4) half mile from $t = 10$ seconds to $t = 55$ seconds. What was the speed of
the train in feet per second? (Round the answer to the nearest tenth.)
58.7 ft/s

Practice   Distributed and Integrated

Write each number in standard notation.

1. 8.2×10^{-9} 0.0000000082
(37)

2. 0.23×10^6 230,000
(37)

Write each number in scientific notation.

3. 112,500 1.125×10^5
(37)

4. 0.00058 5.8×10^{-4}
(37)

List the domain and range of the following relations.

5. (1, 2), (3, 4), (5, 6) (7, 8)   domain: {1, 3, 5, 7}; range: {2, 4, 6, 8}
(25)

6. (3, 4), (3, 5), (4, 4) (4, 5)   domain: {3, 4}; range: {4, 5}
(25)

7. **(Exercising)** A gymnast spends 20 minutes on each stretching exercise. She completes
(25) the workout with a 3-hour practice session. Write a function to describe the time it
takes to complete x exercises and the practice session. $f(x) = 20x + 180$

8. What percent of 520 is 26?   5%
(42)

9. Find 35% more than 90.   121.50
(42)

10. Find the value that makes the expression $\frac{22 + x}{16 + 8x}$ undefined. $x = -2$
(43)

Lesson 44   279

3 Practice

Math Conversations
Discussion to strengthen understanding

Problem 5
Extend the Problem
"Is this relation a function? Explain." yes; Sample: For every x-value, there is only one y-value.

Problem 6
Extend the Problem
"Is this relation a function? Explain." no; Sample: For every x-value, there is more than one y-value.

Problem 7
Extend the Problem
"If the gymnast completes 5 stretching exercises, how long will it take her to complete the workout?" 280 minutes

"If the gymnast completes her workout in 260 minutes, how many stretching exercises did she do? 4 exercises

Problem 10
Extend the Problem
"What value will make the expression equal zero? Explain."
−22; Sample: A fraction has a value of zero when only the numerator equals zero.

Problem 14
Guide students by asking them the following questions.

"What is (x_1, y_1)?" (2, 22)

"To what do you convert 1 year?" 12 months

"What is (x_2, y_2)?" (12, 42)

"What is the next step?" Use the slope formula, $m = \frac{y_2 - y_1}{x_2 - x_1}$.

Extend the Problem
"If the growth rate stays the same, what will the length of the red-tailed boa be at 2 years of age?" 66 inches

Problem 17
Error Alert
Students may multiply 12 · $13.80 to find the cost of hamburger. Remind students that since the price of hamburger is per 4 pounds, they need to figure out how many 4-pound batches of hamburger are needed.

Problem 22
Ask, "How can you check that the factors are correct?" Sample: Compare the product of the factors to the original polynomial.

Use the formula for slope to determine the slope of the line connecting the given points.

*11. (−5, 1) and (5, 7) $m = \frac{3}{5}$
(44)

*12. (−3, −4) and (3, −6) $m = -\frac{1}{3}$
(44)

*13. Find the slope of a line containing (3, −6) and (3, 4). undefined
(44)

*14. (Zoology) If a red-tailed boa, a western hemisphere constrictor snake, grows from 22 inches at 2 months of age to 42 inches at 1 year of age, what is its average growth rate? 2 inches per month
(44)

15. **Predict** The points in the table all lie on the same line. What is the missing y-value?
(44) −14

x	y
7	66
5	46
3	26
1	6
0	

16. (Planting) An orchard has enough space to plant 21 rows with y trees in each row, or 18 rows with $y + 7$ trees in each row. If each orchard plan contains the same number of trees, how many trees can each orchard contain? 882 trees
(28)

17. **Multi-Step** The price of 4 pounds of hamburger is $13.80. The price of a pound of potato salad is $3.75. How much would it cost to buy 12 pounds of hamburger and 3 pounds of potato salad? $52.65
(31)

18. (Architecture) Plans for the construction of an eight-floor hotel call for the first floor to be 16 feet high and each additional floor to be 10.5 feet high. What is the height of the building? 89.5 ft
(34)

19. **Multi-Step** Pencils and T-shirts were bought to sell at the school bookstore. The bookstore's profits are calculated using the equation $2y - 500 = -20x$, where y is the number of boxes of pencils sold and x is the number of T-shirts sold.
(35)
a. Rewrite the profit equation in standard form. $20x + 2y = 500$
b. Calculate the y-intercept and explain its real-world meaning.
c. Calculate the x-intercept and explain its real-world meaning. 25; Sample: To earn all profits with just T-shirt sales, 25 T-shirts would have to be sold.

19b. 250; Sample: To earn all profits with just pencil sales, 250 boxes of pencils would have to be sold.

20. **Multi-Step** A swimmer's average time per lap is $\frac{3}{4}$ minute. If he swims for $10\frac{1}{2}$ minutes, how many laps does he swim?
(24)
a. Write an equation to find the number of laps. Sample: $0.75x = 10.5$
b. **Write** Explain how to solve the problem in two different ways.

20b. Sample: To get rid of the decimal, multiply both sides by 100 and then solve $100 \cdot 0.75x = 10.5 \cdot 100$. Isolate the variable by dividing by 0.75, $x = 14$ laps

21. Multiply $(4.2 \times 10^{12})(3.14 \times 10^{-4})$ and write the answer in scientific notation.
(37) 1.3188×10^9

22. Factor the polynomial $3x^2y^2 + 3xy^3 - 6x^3y^6$ completely. $3xy^2(x + y - 2x^2y^4)$
(38)

23. Simplify $(-2^3)^3$ using exponents. -2^9
(40)

280 Saxon Algebra 1

ENGLISH LEARNERS

Students trying to solve Problem 20 might be unfamiliar with the term **laps.** Say:

"A lap is the distance a person swims when going from one end of a pool to the other end and back again."

Explain that the term is also used in running, meaning one circuit of a track.

*24. **Probability** A student takes a quiz that has 5 true/false questions and 5 multiple-choice questions with four choices for each question. This means there are 2^5 possible ways to answer the true/false questions and 2^{10} ways to answer the multiple-choice questions. The student guesses on every question.
   a. How many ways are there to answer all of the questions?   32,768 ways
   b. What is the probability that the student will get every question right? $\frac{1}{32,768}$

*25. **Multiple Choice** What is the slope of the line that passes through the points $(-5, 8)$ and $(5, 2)$?   **B**

   A $-1\frac{2}{3}$ **B** $-\frac{3}{5}$

   C $\frac{3}{5}$ **D** $1\frac{2}{3}$

26. **Generalize** Give an example of a real-world situation that could be represented by a graph with a negative slope.   Sample: number of ice cream cones sold from August to November

*27. (**Taxi Fares**) A taxi company charges \$0.75 per mile (\$0.75m) on the weekends. During the week, the company charges a base fee of \$2.50 plus \$0.50 a mile (\$2.50 + \$0.50m). Write a simplified rational expression for the ratio of the weekend charge to the weekday charge. $\frac{0.75m}{2.50 + 0.50m} = \frac{3m}{10 + 2m}$

*28. **Error Analysis** Two students found the value at which $\frac{x+5}{x+3}$ is undefined. Which student is correct? Explain the error.   Student A; Sample: Student B did not add the inverse of 3 when solving for the undefined value.

Student A	Student B
$\frac{x+5}{x+3}$	$\frac{x+5}{x+3}$
denominator $= x + 3$	denominator $= x + 3$
$x + 3 = 0$ when $x = -3$	$x + 3 = 0$ when $x = 3$
$\frac{x+5}{x+3}, x \neq -3$	$\frac{x+5}{x+3}, x \neq 3$

29. **Multi-Step** To make a rope that is x^2 units long requires that 4 strands be twisted together. Each strand must be $x^2 + 6x$ units in length.
   a. What is the total length of the 4 strands? $4x^2 + 24x$ units
   b. Write a rational expression for the length of the rope divided by the total length of the strands. $\frac{x^2}{4x^2 + 24x}$
   c. Simplify the rational expression. $\frac{x}{4(x+6)}$

30. **Geometry** The right circular cylinder shown has a height that is 2 units more than the radius of its bases.
   The ratio $\frac{2\pi r^2 + 4\pi r}{2\pi r^2}$ gives the surface area around the cylinder to the surface area of both bases. Simplify. $\frac{r+2}{r}$

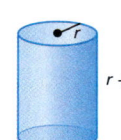

Problem 26
Ask, "What would the graph of a line with a negative slope look like?" Sample: It would go down from left to right.

Problem 30
Error Alert
Some students may try to substitute an approximation for π. Encourage them to leave π unconverted to avoid introducing inaccuracy and adding steps to the task of simplifying.

Lesson 44   281

CHALLENGE

Car A traveled a farther distance than Car B over the same amount of time. Which car traveled at a faster speed? Explain.   Car A traveled at a faster speed because it has the greater numerator in the formula for speed.

LOOKING FORWARD

Finding slope using the slope formula prepares students for

• **Lesson 49** Writing Equations in Slope-Intercept Form

• **Lesson 52** Determining the Equation of a Line Given Two Points

• **Lesson 56** Identifying, Writing, and Graphing Direct Variation

LESSON 45

1 Warm Up

Problem 4
Remind students that when they divide expressions with the same base, they should subtract the exponents.

2 New Concepts

Students will learn to translate between words and inequalities in preparation for solving word problems.

Example 1

Students have learned to translate words into algebraic expressions and equations. They will now translate words into algebraic expressions with inequality symbols.

Additional Example 1

Translate each sentence into an inequality.

a. The difference of 3 and a number is less than 0. $3 - n < 0$

b. The sum of a number and $\frac{1}{3}$ is at most $\frac{5}{6}$. $n + \frac{1}{3} \leq \frac{5}{6}$

c. The quotient of 1 and a number is at least 8. $\frac{1}{n} \geq 8$

d. The product of 3 and the sum of a number and 7 is at least 1. $3(n + 7) \geq 1$

LESSON RESOURCES

Student Edition Practice
　Workbook 45
Reteaching Master 45
Adaptations Master 45
Challenge and Enrichment
　Master C45, E45

LESSON 45

Translating Between Words and Inequalities

Warm Up

1. (9) A(n) _____ is an expression with constants and/or variables that uses the operations $+, -, \times$, or $\div$. **algebraic expression**

Simplify.

2. (13) $-1 + (-2)^2 - \sqrt{9}$　**0**

3. (13) $\sqrt{400} + \sqrt{225} - \sqrt{81} - \sqrt{100}$　**16**

4. (32) $\dfrac{x^3y^2}{xy^4}$　$\dfrac{x^2}{y^2}$

5. (32) $\dfrac{x^3y^{-3}z}{x^2yz^5}$　$\dfrac{x}{y^4z^4}$

New Concepts

An **inequality** is a mathematical statement comparing quantities that are not equal.

To translate between words and symbolic forms of inequalities, it helps to be familiar with the meaning of terms and symbols. Inequalities can have any number of operations and variables.

Reading Math

The inequality symbols and their meanings are shown below.
< less than
> greater than
≤ less than or equal to
≥ greater than or equal to
≠ does not equal

Hint

Remember that division can be shown using a fraction. The first term, n, in the statement "the quotient of a number and 2" is the numerator. The second term, 2, is the denominator.

Example 1 Translating Sentences into Inequalities

Translate each sentence into an inequality.

a. The quotient of a number and 2 is less than or equal to 6.
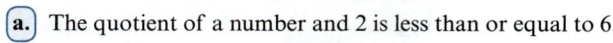
operation: division　inequality: ≤

SOLUTION

$\dfrac{n}{2} \leq 6$

b. $\frac{1}{2}$ is greater than the product of a number and $\frac{3}{4}$.
operation: multiplication　inequality: >

SOLUTION

$\dfrac{1}{2} > \dfrac{3}{4}y$

c. The difference of a number and 2.8 does not equal 8.2.
operation: subtraction　inequality: ≠

SOLUTION

$g - 2.8 \neq 8.2$

d. The sum of the product of 20 and a number and 75 is at least 195.
　addition　　　　　20x　　　　75　≥　195

SOLUTION

$20x + 75 \geq 195$

282　Saxon Algebra 1

MATH BACKGROUND

Given any two real numbers, there are three possibilities: the first number is less than the second number, the numbers are equal, or the first number is greater than the second number.

Strict inequalities use > and <, and never allow the expressions to be equal in value. $2 > 2$ is a false statement.

Nonstrict inequalities use ≤ or ≥. In addition to allowing one expression to be greater or less than the other, nonstrict inequalities allow the expressions to be equal in value. $2 \geq 2$ is a true statement.

The Symmetric Property does not hold for inequalities. If the two sides of the inequality are exchanged, the direction, or order, of the inequality symbol must be switched as well. $2 < 3$ becomes $3 > 2$.

Example 2 Translating Inequalities into Words

Write each inequality as a sentence.

a. $6 > x + 8$

Determine the words or phrases you want to use for each operation symbol and the inequality symbol.

The symbol "+" indicates addition which can be written as "the sum of."

The symbol ">" can be written as "greater than."

SOLUTION

6 is greater than the sum of a number and 8.

b. $2.5z < 15$

Determine the words or phrases you want to use.

There is no operation symbol between the number and the variable, so multiplication is understood. Multiplication can be written as "the product of."

The symbol "<" can be written as "less than."

SOLUTION

The product of a number and 2.5 is less than 15.

c. $-2x + 4 \geq -8$

Determine the words or phrases you want to use.

There is no operation symbol between the number and the variable, so multiplication is understood. Multiplication can be written as "the product of."

The symbol "+" indicates addition which can be written as "the sum of."

The symbol "$\geq$" can be written as "at least."

SOLUTION

The sum of the product of a number and -2 and 4 is at least -8.

d. $3x - 6 \leq -30$

Determine the words or phrases you want to use.

There is no operation symbol between the number and the variable, so multiplication is understood. Multiplication can be written as "times."

The symbol "$-$" indicates subtraction, which can be written as "the difference of."

The symbol "$\leq$" can be written as "less than or equal to."

SOLUTION

The difference of 3 times a number and 6 is less than or equal to -30.

Reading Math

Phrases like "at least" and "at most" are sometimes confusing. "At least" means that the value is the lowest possible, so the inequality to translate to is "greater than or equal to" ($\geq$).

Math Reasoning

Analyze Write $3x - 6 \leq -30$ as a sentence using "at most."

The difference between 3 times a number and 6 is at most -30.

Example 2

Different words and phrases can sometimes be used to represent inequality symbols. Encourage students to try different phrases, and let them share their sentences with the rest of the class.

Additional Example 2

Write each inequality as a sentence.

a. $\dfrac{n + 3}{-2} > -3$ Sample: The sum of a number and 3 divided by -2 is greater than -3.

b. $m - 5 < 8$ Sample: 5 less than a number is less than 8.

c. $\dfrac{a}{7.2} \geq 4.6$ Sample: The quotient of a number and 7.2 is at least 4.6.

d. $6(-5 - z) \leq 15$ Sample: The product of 6 and the difference of -5 and z is less than or equal to 15.

Error Alert Students often miss the subtle difference between "less than" and "is less than" and use the wrong symbol for each. Write the following examples on the board to show the difference.

3 less than 6: $6 - 3$

3 is less than 6: $3 < 6$

TEACHER TIP

To remind students that $\geq$ means greater than or equal to, write $>$ on one transparency and $=$ on another. Lay the second one over the first one to display $>\!\!=$, and then $\overset{>}{=}$. Slide the top transparency up until it looks closer to $\geq$.

INCLUSION

Completing these charts with *yes* and *no* will help students make a meaningful connection between the words and the symbols. The tables can be extended to include values greater than 3.

x is at most 2. Can x be …			Write the inequality.
1?	2?	3?	$x \leq 2$
yes	yes	no	

x is at least 2. Can x be …			Write the inequality.
1?	2?	3?	$x \geq 2$
no	yes	yes	

x is less than 2. Can x be …			Write the inequality.
1?	2?	3?	$x < 2$
yes	no	no	

x is more than 2. Can x be …			Write the inequality.
1?	2?	3?	$x > 2$
no	no	yes	

Example 3

Students use inequalities to solve real-world problems.

Extend the Example

"Substitute 50, 60, and 70 for c in the left side of the inequality to see if Jonas can afford suits costing $50, $60, and $70." He can afford $50 and $60 suits, but not $70 suits.

Additional Example 3

Carol buys a large bottle of juice for $4.50 and apples for 25¢ each. Write an inequality for how many apples she can buy if she can spend no more than $15. $0.25a + 4.50 \leq 15$

Lesson Practice

Problem c

Scaffolding Have students first write ___ + ___ to indicate a sum. Then have them write each addend. For "does not equal 15", ask if 15 is included. Since it is not, finish the statement with $\neq$ 15.

Problem i

Error Alert Students may use $<$ or $\leq$ because of the word lowest. Explain that if 140° is the lowest temperature, the other temperatures are higher.

Check for Understanding

The questions below help assess the concepts taught in this lesson.

"What is the difference between an equation and an inequality?" Sample: The expressions in an equation have the same value. The expressions in an inequality do not necessarily have the same value.

"Which represents "not more than", $<$ or $\leq$? Why?" $\leq$; Sample: A number not more than 20 is any number up to and including 20.

Inequalities are used to solve a variety of real-world problems. First determine the unknowns and the inequality symbol needed. Then translate the words into symbols and solve the inequality.

Example 3 Application: Soccer Team Clothing

Jonas is purchasing 15 screen-printed warm-up suits for his soccer team. He can spend $1000 at most. There is a set-up fee of $25 for the screen-printing. What can he spend at most on each suit including tax and printing costs?

15, $1000 at most, set-up fee of $25	Identify the needed information.
unknown: cost of one suit variable: c	Identify the unknown and assign a variable.
15 times the cost of a suit plus the $25 set up fee is at most $1000.	Organize the given information.
$15c + 25 \leq 1000$	Translate the sentence into an inequality.

Hint When assigning variables to represent an unknown, it is useful to select letters that relate to the unknown.

SOLUTION

$15c + 25 \leq 1000$, where c is the cost of one suit.

Lesson Practice

Translate each sentence into an inequality. (Ex 1)

a. The quotient of an unknown number and -2 is greater than the opposite of 9. $\frac{x}{-2} > -9$

b. 0 is less than or equal to the difference of twice a number and 8. $0 \leq 2n - 8$

c. The sum of half a number and 3 does not equal 15. $\frac{1}{2}n + 3 \neq 15$

d. The product of 11 and a number is less than 121. $11n < 121$

Write each inequality as a sentence. (Ex 2)

e. $12b \geq -8$ Sample: The product of 12 and an unknown is at least -8.

f. $1.5x + 2.5 < 11.5$ Sample: The sum of the product of 1.5 and a number and 2.5 is less than 11.5.

g. $9 > \frac{1}{3}x - 8$ 9 is greater than the difference of one-third of a number and 8.

h. $\frac{a}{7} \leq 8$ A number divided by 7 is at most 8.

i.  The lowest temperature at which a piece of beef can be cooked rare is 140°F. The formula used to convert degrees Celsius to degrees Fahrenheit is $\frac{9}{5}°C + 32 = °F$. Write an inequality for an equivalent reading in degrees Celsius for a piece of beef cooked rare. (Ex 3)
$\frac{9}{5}°C + 32 \geq 140$

ENGLISH LEARNERS

Discuss with students the meaning of the phrase **set-up fee.** Say:

"A set-up fee is a one-time charge for preparing the equipment."

Explain that the set-up fee is the same regardless of the number of items made.

Say:

"Jonas would pay a $25 set-up fee even if he wanted to have 50 warm-up suits made."

Have students describe any set-up fees with which they are familiar. Sample: The Chess Club was charged a set-up fee to print posters for a tournament.

Practice Distributed and Integrated

Use unit analysis to convert each measurement.

1. (8) 42 feet to centimeters   1280.16 cm
2. (8) 2 miles to inches   126,720 in.

5,280 × 2 × 12 =

Simplify.

3. (4) $-2(-3-3)(-2-4)-(-3-2)+3(4-2)$ -61

4. (4) $\dfrac{5(-5+3)+7(-5+9)+2}{(4-2)+3+5}$ 2

Translate each sentence into an inequality.

*5. (45) The product of 6 and an unknown number is less than or equal to 15. $6x \leq 15$

*6. (45) Josephine sleeps more than 7 hours each night. $x > 7$

Translate each inequality into a sentence.

*7. (45) $-4b \geq 7$ Sample: The product of -4 and b is at least 7.

*8. (45) $\dfrac{t}{7} - 4 < 8$ Sample: Four less than the quotient of t and 7 is less than 8.

9. (41) **Geometry** On a separate sheet of paper, plot the points $(1, 3)$, $(3, 2)$, $(5, -1)$, and $(2, 1)$. Connect the points, in order, to form a quadrilateral. Find the slope of each side. $-\tfrac{1}{2}, -\tfrac{3}{2}, -2, -\tfrac{2}{3}$

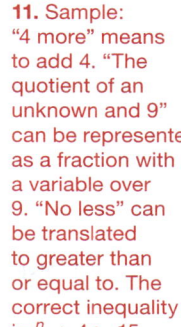

10. (42) **Multiple Choice** What percent of 160 is 24?   **B**
    A 6.67%   B 15%   C 136%   D 184%

*11. (45) **Write** Explain how to translate the phrase "4 more than the quotient of an unknown and 9 is no less than 15."

11. Sample: "4 more" means to add 4. "The quotient of an unknown and 9" can be represented as a fraction with a variable over 9. "No less" can be translated to greater than or equal to. The correct inequality is $\tfrac{n}{9} + 4 \geq 15$.

*12. (45) **Sports** Harriet's current score after two rounds in a freestyle skating contest is 45.7 points. She needs to have a score of 83.2 or better to win first place. Write an inequality that expresses the possible scores she can achieve to win first place. $s + 45.7 \geq 83.2$, where s is the score of the third round.

*13. (45) **Multiple Choice** Which of the following inequalities represents "Five less than an unknown is at most seven"?   **C**
    A $x + 5 \leq 7$ B $x + 5 > 7$ C $x - 5 \leq 7$ D $x - 5 > 7$

14. (44) Find the slope of a line containing the two points $(-5, -6)$ and $(8, 7)$. $m = 1$

Lesson 45   285

3 Practice

Math Conversations
Discussion to strengthen understanding

Problem 10
Because 24 is less than 160, answer choices **C** and **D** can be eliminated.

Problem 12
Guide the students by asking them the following questions

"How many points were made in Rounds 1 and 2?" 45.7

"What score is needed to win first place?" 83.2 or more

"What is the score in the third round?" s

"What inequality symbol represents 83.2 or better?" $\geq$

Problem 14
Error Alert
Students may answer $\tfrac{1}{3}$ by subtracting 6 from 7 in the numerator and 5 from 8 in the denominator. Remind them that they are subtracting negative numbers, which is the same as adding the opposite.

Lesson 45   285

Problem 17
Remind students that the hypotenuse is the side opposite the right angle.

Problem 18
Have students check the answer by using the Distributive Property. Discuss with students that the number of terms in the parentheses should be the same as the original number of terms.

Problem 20
Extend the Problem
Ask the students the meaning of the *y*-intercept.
The *y*-intercept is the monthly bill when no classes are taken.

Ask students to determine the domain for this situation.
The domain is $x \geq 0$ because you cannot enroll in a negative number of classes.

---

*15. **Multi-Step** Stock A and Stock B have both experienced rapid growth on the market
(44) over the past several days. The graph shows the growth of both stocks over 9 days.

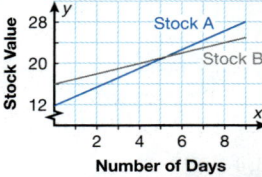

a. After 9 days, what was the average rate of increase for Stock A? $1.78 per day
b. What was the average rate of increase for Stock B? $1.00 per day
c. **Write** Explain which stock was the better buy based on the graphs shown.

15c. Sample: Stock A is the better buy. Its graph shows a larger rate of increase in value over the 9 days.

16. (**Atmospheric Science**) Scientists at Mauna Loa Observatory in Hawaii have measured
(44) the levels of carbon dioxide present in the atmosphere for many years. In 1962 the level was measured at 315 parts per million. It had increased to 320 parts per million by 1969. What was the average rate of increase for carbon dioxide between 1962 and 1969 to two decimal places? 0.71 parts per million per year

17. **Geometry** A student draws a right triangle on a coordinate plane. What is the slope
(44) of the triangle's hypotenuse? $m = \frac{6}{5}$

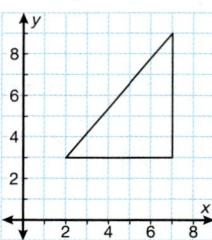

18. Factor the polynomial $5m^2n^4 + 10m^3n$ completely. $5m^2n(n^3 + 2m)$
(38)

19. Simplify $\frac{x^{-3}}{w^2}\left(\frac{4x^2}{w} - \frac{j^{-3}w}{x}\right)$. $\frac{4}{xw^3} - \frac{1}{j^3wx^4}$
(39)

20. (**Membership Dues**) A local gym charges a monthly fee of $12 plus $4 for each
(35) class attended. The equation $y = 4x + 12$ can be used to calculate the monthly bill. Find the intercepts. (0, 12), (−3, 0)

21. **Multi-Step** You and a friend are taking a trip. The scale on your map is
(36) 1 inch:16 miles.
  a. If the first leg of the trip measures 5 inches on the map, how many miles will you be driving? 80 miles
  b. If the second leg of the trip measures 17.5 inches on the map, how many miles will you be driving on this leg? 280 miles
  c. If you find a shorter route for the two legs that totals 20 inches on the map, how many miles shorter will the shorter route be? 40 miles
  d. Will the shorter route always be the faster route? Explain your reasoning. no; Sample: The shorter route may have more traffic or a slower speed limit for driving.

22. **(Astronomy)** The radius of the moon is about 1.75×10^3 kilometers. Use the formula $A = 4\pi r^2$ to find the surface area of the moon. Write your answer in terms of π. $1.225\pi \times 10^7$ square kilometers

23. Use the table to find the rate of change. $6.75/hour

Hours	2	4	6	8
Earnings	$13.50	$27	$40.50	$54

*24. **Model** A dog digs a conical hole that has a volume of 803 in³. The next day the dog increases the volume by another 25%. Write an equation or proportion to find the new volume and draw a model to represent the problem.
Sample: $V = 803 + (803 \cdot 25\%) = 1003.75$ in³; See student work.

25. Simplify $\frac{24 + 9x}{x}$. Identify any excluded values. $\frac{24 + 9x}{x}$; $x \neq 0$

*26. **Error Analysis** Two students simplified the following rational expression: $\frac{x^2 - 11x}{2x^2 - 6x}$. Which student is correct? Explain the error.

26. Student B; Sample: Student A did not factor the GCF from the numerator correctly.

Student A
$\frac{x^2 - 11x}{2x^2 - 6x}$
numerator GCF = x
denominator GCF = $2x$
$\frac{x^2 - 11x}{2x^2 - 6x} = \frac{2x(x-11)}{2x(x-3)} = \frac{x-11}{x-3}$
$\frac{x^2 - 11x}{2x^2 - 6x} = \frac{x-11}{x-3}, x \neq 3$

Student B
$\frac{x^2 - 11x}{2x^2 - 6x}$
numerator GCF = x
denominator GCF = $2x$
$\frac{x^2 - 11x}{2x^2 - 6x} = \frac{x(x-11)}{2x(x-3)} = \frac{x-11}{2(x-3)}$
$\frac{x^2 - 11x}{2x^2 - 6x} = \frac{x-11}{2(x-3)}, x \neq 3$

27. Use the information in the graph to complete the table below.

x	0	1	−1	2	4
y	1	0.5	1.5	0	−1

28. **Multi-step** A centimeter is 10^{-2} times the length of a meter and a kilometer is 10^3 times the length of a meter.
   a. Using the Quotient Property of Exponents, how many times longer is the length of a kilometer than the length of a centimeter? $10^5 = 100{,}000$ times longer
   b. First, using exponents, express how many times longer a meter is then a centimeter. Then use that answer to find how many times longer a kilometer is than a centimeter. Are the results the same as for part **a**? 10^2 times longer; $10^2 \cdot 10^3 = 10^5 = 100{,}000$ times longer; yes

29. **(Names)** A new baby girl arrives. The parents have 6 names they really like, including Maria and Gail. They are going to pick one of the 6 names for a first name and one for a middle name. What is the probability that the baby will be named Maria Gail? $\frac{1}{30}$

30. **Generalize** Is there a pattern in the number of zeros in standard notation and the exponent in scientific notation? Consider 0.0204, 8,000,000, and 6700.   For 8,000,000, the number of zeros equals the exponent, but that does not hold true for the other examples. The pattern only exists if there is one digit followed by zeros.

Lesson 45   287

CHALLENGE

Translate these sentences into algebraic inequalities:

The absolute value of the difference of twice a number and 5 is not less than the square of the sum of 7 and the number.
$|2x - 5| \geq (7 + x)^2$

Twice the square of the difference of the cube of a number and 1 is not more than the sum of half the number and 1.
$2(x^3 - 1)^2 \leq \frac{x}{2} + 1$

LOOKING FORWARD

Translating between words and inequalities prepares students for

- **Lesson 50** Graphing Inequalities
- **Lesson 66** Solving Inequalities by Adding or Subtracting
- **Lesson 70** Solving Inequalities by Multiplying or Dividing
- **Lesson 73** Solving Compound Inequalities
- **Lesson 77** Solving Two-Step and Multi-Step Inequalities

LESSON 46

1 Warm Up

Problem 5
Remind students that
$a^b = \underbrace{a \cdot a \cdot \ldots \cdot a \cdot a}_{b \text{ factors}}$, not $a \times b$.

2 New Concepts

In this lesson, students simplify expressions with square roots and higher order roots. All of the roots students find in this lesson will be integers.

Example 1

Students simplify basic square root expressions. Suggest that students rewrite an expression like $-\sqrt{9}$ as $-1 \cdot \sqrt{9}$.

Error Alert If students think the root is defined in problem **e**, stress that $\sqrt{-36} \neq -\sqrt{36}$.

Additional Example 1
Simplify each expression.

a. $\sqrt{81}$ 9

b. $-\sqrt{16}$ –4

c. $\sqrt{1}$ 1

d. $\sqrt{\frac{49}{64}}$ $\frac{7}{8}$

e. $\sqrt{-9}$ no real solution

LESSON RESOURCES

Student Edition Practice
   Workbook 46
Reteaching Master 46
Adaptations Master 46
Challenge and Enrichment
   Master C46

LESSON 46

Simplifying Expressions with Square Roots and Higher-Order Roots

Warm Up

1. **Vocabulary** A _____ is a number that is the square of an integer. *perfect square*

Tell whether each number represents a perfect square. Justify your answer.

2. 25   yes; $\sqrt{25} = 5$

3. 12   no; Sample: There is not a whole number squared that equals 12.

4. 49   yes: $\sqrt{49} = 7$

Simplify.

5. 5^3 125

6. $(-3)^4$ 81

New Concepts

A number has both a positive and a negative square root. The **principal square root** is the positive square root of a number. Typically, if no negative sign is present, the principal square root is calculated.

Hint
Any positive number x has both a positive and negative square root. These can be written as $\pm\sqrt{x}$.

Example 1 Simplifying Expressions Using the Positive and Negative Values of the Square Root

Simplify each expression.

a. $\sqrt{64}$

SOLUTION
$\sqrt{64} = \sqrt{8^2}$
$= \sqrt{8 \cdot 8}$
$= 8$

b. $-\sqrt{9}$

SOLUTION
$-\sqrt{9} = -\sqrt{3^2}$
$= -\sqrt{3 \cdot 3}$
$= -3$

c. $\sqrt{0}$

SOLUTION
$\sqrt{0} = 0$

d. $\sqrt{\frac{4}{25}}$

SOLUTION
$\sqrt{\frac{4}{25}} = \frac{\sqrt{4}}{\sqrt{25}}$
$= \frac{\sqrt{2^2}}{\sqrt{5^2}}$
$= \frac{2}{5}$

e. $\sqrt{-36}$

SOLUTION
$\sqrt{-36}$ has no real solution. There is no real number a such that $a^2 = -36$.

Online Connection
www.SaxonMathResources.com

288   *Saxon Algebra 1*

MATH BACKGROUND

The fourth root is the same as the "square root of the square root." Show this using the power rule of exponents.

$\sqrt[4]{x} = x^{\frac{1}{4}}$
$= x^{\left(\frac{1}{2} \cdot \frac{1}{2}\right)}$
$= \left(x^{\frac{1}{2}}\right)^{\frac{1}{2}}$
$= \left(\sqrt{x}\right)^{\frac{1}{2}}$
$= \sqrt{\sqrt{x}}$

Note that the expression $x^{\frac{1}{4}}$ is not the same as $\frac{1}{x^4}$. The expression $\frac{1}{x^4} = x^{-4}$ by the definition of negative exponents. Since $-4 \neq \frac{1}{4}$, $x^{\frac{1}{4}} \neq x^{-4}$.

Higher order roots can be calculated in a similiar way that square roots are calculated. The **cube root** is a number, written as $\sqrt[3]{x}$, whose cube is x. For example, the cube root of 8 is 2 because $2^3 = 8$. The cube root of 8 is written as $\sqrt[3]{8}$. In general, $\sqrt[n]{c^n} = c$.

Higher–Order Roots
If $a^n = b$, then the nth root of b is a, or $\sqrt[n]{b} = a$. The n to the left of the radical sign in the expression is the index of the radical. The index is an integer greater than or equal to 2.

In the case of square roots, the index is not written and is understood to be 2.

Example 2 Simplifying Roots

Simplify each expression.

a. $\sqrt[3]{64}$

SOLUTION

$\sqrt[3]{64} = \sqrt[3]{4^3}$
$= \sqrt[3]{4 \cdot 4 \cdot 4} = 4$

b. $\sqrt[3]{-8}$

SOLUTION

$\sqrt[3]{-8} = \sqrt[3]{(-2)^3}$
$= \sqrt[3]{(-2) \cdot (-2) \cdot (-2)} = -2$

c. $\sqrt[4]{81}$

SOLUTION

$\sqrt[4]{81} = \sqrt[4]{3^4}$
$= \sqrt[4]{3 \cdot 3 \cdot 3 \cdot 3} = 3$

d. $\sqrt[4]{-1}$

SOLUTION

$\sqrt[4]{-1}$ has no real solution.

Math Reasoning

Analyze Why does $\sqrt[4]{-1}$ have no real solution?

There is no real number that equals −1 when raised to the fourth power.

Roots can be written as fractional exponents. Consider the expression $\left(x^{\frac{1}{2}}\right)^2$. Using the Power of a Power Property, the expression simplifies to x. This is equivalent to the statement $(\sqrt{x})^2 = x$.

Fractional Exponents
$\sqrt[n]{b} = b^{\frac{1}{n}}$

Example 3 Simplifying Expressions with Fractional Exponents

Simplify each expression.

a. $(216)^{\frac{1}{3}}$

SOLUTION

$(216)^{\frac{1}{3}} = \sqrt[3]{216}$
$= \sqrt[3]{6^3}$
$= 6$

b. $(-27)^{\frac{1}{3}}$

SOLUTION

$(-27)^{\frac{1}{3}} = \sqrt[3]{-27}$
$= \sqrt[3]{(-3)^3}$
$= -3$

c. $(10,000)^{\frac{1}{4}}$

SOLUTION

$(10,000)^{\frac{1}{4}} = \sqrt[4]{10,000}$
$= \sqrt[4]{10^4} = 10$

d. $(-256)^{\frac{1}{4}}$

SOLUTION

$(-256)^{\frac{1}{4}} = \sqrt[4]{-256}$ has no real solution.

Hint

In part **c**, notice that $10,000 = 100^2$, which equals $(10^2)^2$ or 10^4. Sometimes it may be helpful to find the square root in order to find the nth root.

Example 2

Point out that the root of a negative number is undefined if the index is even, but that the root of a negative number is defined if the index is odd.

TEACHER TIP

To get started finding roots, suggest that students think of the rules of divisibility as they guess and check to find the higher order roots of numbers.

Additional Example 2

Simplify each expression.

a. $\sqrt[3]{125}$ 5

b. $\sqrt[3]{-1000}$ −10

c. $\sqrt[4]{16}$ 2

d. $\sqrt[4]{-81}$ no real solution

Example 3

It may help to show students fractional roots using the Product Property of Exponents:
$b^{\frac{1}{3}} \cdot b^{\frac{1}{3}} \cdot b^{\frac{1}{3}} = b^{\left(\frac{1}{3}+\frac{1}{3}+\frac{1}{3}\right)} = b^1$. Or,
$8^{\frac{1}{3}} \cdot 8^{\frac{1}{3}} \cdot 8^{\frac{1}{3}} = 8^{\left(\frac{1}{3}+\frac{1}{3}+\frac{1}{3}\right)}$
$2 \cdot 2 \cdot 2 = 8$

Error Alert Some students may think that $216^{\frac{1}{3}}$ means $\frac{1}{216^3}$. Remind them that 216^{-3} means $\frac{1}{216^3}$.

Additional Example 3

Simplify each expression.

a. $(343)^{\frac{1}{3}}$ 7

b. $(-8)^{\frac{1}{3}}$ −2

c. $(625)^{\frac{1}{4}}$ 5

d. $(-1296)^{\frac{1}{4}}$ no real solution

ALTERNATE METHOD FOR EXAMPLE 3

To find $\sqrt[3]{216}$, have students factor 216 into prime factors.

216

2×108

$2 \times 2 \times 54$

$2 \times 2 \times 2 \times 27$

$2 \times 2 \times 2 \times 3 \times 9$

$2 \times 2 \times 2 \times 3 \times 3 \times 3$

Write the prime factorization under the radical sign. Group every three factors that are the same using boxes or circles.

$\sqrt[3]{216} = \sqrt[3]{\boxed{2 \times 2 \times 2} \times \boxed{3 \times 3 \times 3}}$

The product of three identical factors equals a perfect cube. Simplify the root by replacing a triple-factor group under the radical with a single factor outside of the radical.

$\sqrt[3]{216} = 2\sqrt[3]{\boxed{3 \times 3 \times 3}} = 2 \times 3 = 6$

Example 4

Explain that since the sides of a cube are all the same length, the cube root of the volume is equal to the length of one side.

Extend the Example

A second gift box has a volume that is 631 cubic inches less than the volume of the first box. What is the side length of the second box? **14 in.**

Additional Example 4

A box has a volume of 6859 cubic inches. What is the length of the side of the box? **19 in.**

Lesson Practice

Problem g

Error Alert Students may think the root of a negative number never has a real solution. Explain that it has no real solution only if the index is even.

Problem m

Scaffolding Guide students to first find the index. Then have them identify the index as even or odd.

Check for Understanding

The questions below help assess the concepts taught in this lesson.

"What is a principal square root? Explain." Sample: It's the positive square root of a number. The square roots of 100 () are 10 and −10, but $\sqrt{100}$ means to find only the positive square root, 10.

"What is the difference between $-\sqrt{121}$ and $\sqrt{-121}$?" Sample: $-\sqrt{121}$ is the negative of a square root; $\sqrt{-121}$ is the square root of a negative number. It has no real solution.

Example 4 **Application: Volume**

A gift box in the shape of a cube has a volume of 3375 cubic inches. What is the side length of the box?

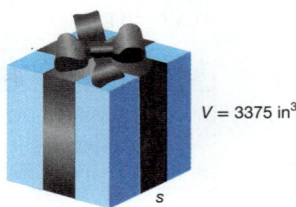

$V = 3375$ in³

SOLUTION

Use the formula for the volume of a cube.

$V = s^3 = 3375$

The side length of the box is equal to the cube root of the volume.

$s = \sqrt[3]{3375}$
$ = \sqrt[3]{15^3}$
$ = 15$

The side length of the box is 15 inches.

Check $V = 15^3 = 3375$

Lesson Practice

Simplify each expression.

a. $\sqrt{196}$ **14**   (Ex 1)
b. $-\sqrt{64}$ **−8**   (Ex 1)
c. $\sqrt{1}$ **1**   (Ex 1)
d. $\sqrt{-64}$ **no real solution**   (Ex 1)
e. $\sqrt{\dfrac{81}{144}}$ **$\dfrac{9}{12}$, or $\dfrac{3}{4}$**   (Ex 1)
f. $\sqrt[3]{1728}$ **12**   (Ex 2)
g. $\sqrt[3]{-343}$ **−7**   (Ex 2)
h. $\sqrt[4]{160{,}000}$ **20**   (Ex 2)
i. $\sqrt[4]{-16}$ **no real solution**   (Ex 2)
j. $(125)^{\frac{1}{3}}$ **5**   (Ex 3)
k. $(-8)^{\frac{1}{3}}$ **−2**   (Ex 3)
l. $(81)^{\frac{1}{4}}$ **3**   (Ex 3)
m. $(-625)^{\frac{1}{4}}$ **no real solution**   (Ex 3)

n. A sculpture in the shape of a cube has a volume of 1728 cubic feet. What is the side length of the block? **12 ft**   (Ex 4)

ENGLISH LEARNERS

Discuss with students the meaning of the word **root**. Say:

"Root means the beginning, origin, or source. For example, the roots of a plant are its source for getting water and nutrients."

Ask for volunteers to explain any similarities between the mathematical definition and the other definitions of this word. Sample: The root is a factor, or source, of the number under the radical.

Ask students if they can think of any other kinds of roots. Sample: cultural roots, roots of teeth and hair, roots of a problem

Practice Distributed and Integrated

Evaluate each expression for the indicated values.

1. $(p - x)(a - px)$ for $a = -3$, $p = 3$, and $x = -4$ 63
   (9)
2. $-a[-a(x - a)]$ for $a = -2$ and $x = 3$ 20
   (9)

Evaluate each expression.

*3. $\sqrt{-10{,}000}$ no real solution
   (46)

*4. $-\sqrt[4]{10{,}000}$ -10
   (46)

5. Simplify the following expression by adding like terms:
   (18) $xym^2 + 3xy^2m - 4m^2xy + 5mxy^2$. $-3m^2xy + 8mxy^2$

*6. **Multiple Choice** Evaluate $-\sqrt[3]{-\dfrac{27}{64}}$.   **C**
   (46)

   A $-\dfrac{3}{4}$ **B** $\dfrac{9}{16}$ **C** $\dfrac{3}{4}$ **D** no real solution

Translate each sentence into an inequality.

7. The opposite of 2 is less than or equal to the difference of a number and 7. $-2 \leq x - 7$
   (45)
8. A U.S. citizen must be at least 35 years old in order to run for President. $a \geq 35$
   (45)

*9. **Estimate** Find the two whole numbers that $\sqrt[3]{1500}$ is between.   11 and 12
   (46)

10. **Farming** For every 15 cows, a farmer puts out 1 mineral block for them to eat as a source of additional nutrients. What are the dependent and independent variables?
    (20)
    10. independent variable: number of cattle as a multiple of 15; dependent variable: number of mineral blocks

11. Use the table of ordered pairs below to make a graph.
    (30)

x	0	1	3	4	5
y	-1	2	8	11	14

12. Solve $\dfrac{5}{7} = \dfrac{h}{49}$.   35
    (31)

13. **Multi-Step** Work uniforms include pants or a skirt, a shirt, and a tie or a vest. There are 3 pairs of pants, 5 skirts, 10 shirts, 2 ties, and 1 vest in a wardrobe.
    (33)
    a. What is the probability of choosing a skirt, a shirt, and a vest? $\dfrac{5}{24}$
    b. The skirt and shirt from the previous day must be washed, but the vest returns to the wardrobe. What is the probability of choosing pants, a shirt, and a tie the next day? $\dfrac{2}{7}$

*14. **Multi-Step** A student earns $10 for every yard he mows in his neighborhood. He wants to buy a new MP3 player for $180 including tax. At least how many yards will he need to mow in order to earn the money for the MP3 player?
    (45)
    a. Write an inequality that could be used to solve the problem. $10y \geq 180$
    b. Solve the inequality. $y \geq 18$

Lesson 46   291

---

3 Practice

Math Conversations
Discussion to strengthen understanding

Problem 5
Remind students that the Commutative Property of Multiplication justifies that $xy^2m = mxy^2$.

Problem 9
Guide students by asking them the following questions.

"What cubed number is close to 1500?" Sample: $10^3 = 1000$

"Is $\sqrt[3]{1500}$ greater than or less than 10?" greater than

"What is the next number you will try?" Sample: 11

"Is $\sqrt[3]{1500}$ greater than or less than 11?" greater than

"Is $\sqrt[3]{1500}$ greater than or less than 12?" less than

---

INCLUSION

Students may find it helpful to make a table with perfect squares and perfect cubes. Have students refer to their tables when simplifying expressions.

Perfect Squares	Perfect Cubes
$1 = 1^2$	$1 = 1^3$
$4 = 2^2$	$8 = 2^3$
$9 = 3^2$	$27 = 3^3$
$16 = 4^2$	$64 = 4^3$
$25 = 5^2$	$125 = 5^3$
$36 = 6^2$	$216 = 6^3$
$49 = 7^2$	$343 = 7^3$
$64 = 8^2$	$512 = 8^3$
$81 = 9^2$	$729 = 9^3$
$100 = 10^2$	$1000 = 10^3$

Lesson 46   291

Problem 18
Extend the Problem
"Suppose the same model represents a different room, but that the scale factor is now 1 in.: 12 in."

"What are the dimensions of the second room?" The dimensions are 108 inches by 180 inches, or 9 feet by 15 feet.

Problem 19
Some students may find it helpful to write each number in standard form first and then write the numbers in scientific notation.

Problem 20
Point out to students that the GCF of bases that are the same will be the base with the smallest exponent.

Problem 25
Guide the students by asking them the following questions.

"What is the formula for finding the slope of a line?" Sample: The ratio of the difference in the y-coordinates over the difference in the x-coordinates.

"Name a pair of x- and y-coordinates to find the slope of the line in this problem." Sample: x-coordinates: 0 and 4; y-coordinates: −3 and −4

Simplify.

15. $\frac{gt}{d^2}\left(\frac{gth}{d} - 3th + \frac{t}{5}\right)$ $\frac{g^2t^2h}{d^3} - \frac{3gt^2h}{d^2} + \frac{gt^2}{5d^2}$

16. $\left(\frac{-8x^4}{3}\right)^2$ $\frac{64x^8}{9}$

*17. **Measurement** Write an inequality to represent the value of the diameter of a circle that has a circumference greater than 5 inches. $d > \frac{5}{\pi}$, where d is the diameter.

18. (**Scale Models**) A designer is making a model of a room. The model is 9 inches by 15 inches. If the scale factor is 1 in.:10 in., what are the dimensions of the room? 90 inches by 150 inches or 7.5 feet by 12.5 feet

19. **Multi-Step** At the end of 2006, the U.S. debt was $4.9 trillion. The population was approximately 300 million.
   a. Write these amounts in scientific notation. 4.9×10^{12}; 3×10^8
   b. Divide the debt by the population to find the approximate debt per person in the United States. about 1.63×10^4 per person

20. **Justify** Show that the GCF of the polynomial $27x^2y^3z + 12xy^2z$ is $3xy^2z$. Then factor the polynomial. See Additional Answers.

21. (**Fill Rate**) Ailani places a hose in a partially filled swimming pool to fill it. The table shows the number of gallons in the pool over time. Find the rate at which the hose adds water. 4.85 gallons per minute

Time (min)	10	15	30	60
Water (gal)	15,048.5	15,072.75	15,145.51	15,291

22. What is 120% of 250? 300

23. **Multiple Choice** Which one of the following rational expressions cannot be further simplified? B

   A $\frac{7x+1}{5x^2-x}$
   B $\frac{x^2}{15-x}$
   C $\frac{x^2+1}{x^2-3x}$
   D $\frac{8(2-x)}{6-3x}$

*24. **Justify** Simplify the rational expression $\frac{6-6x}{9-9x}$. Explain your reasoning. 24. $\frac{2}{3}$; Sample: I factored out a 6 in the numerator and a 9 in the denominator. Then I canceled the $1-x$ binomial and simplified the remaining fraction.

25. Find the slope of the line containing the points in the table. $m = -\frac{1}{4}$

x	y
−8	−1
−4	−2
0	−3
4	−4
8	−5

26. Find the slope of a line containing the points $(1, 7)$ and $(5, 8)$. $m = \frac{1}{4}$

292 Saxon Algebra 1

CHALLENGE

In Example 4, suppose a second gift box has a volume that is 8 times greater, so that $V = 8 \cdot 3375$ in³; the length of each side is $s = \sqrt[3]{8 \cdot 3375}$ inches. Without using a calculator, find the length of each side. 30 in.

If students have difficulty, guide them with the following instructions.

"Rewrite $\sqrt[3]{8 \cdot 3375}$ using fractional exponents."

$(8 \cdot 3375)^{\frac{1}{3}}$

"Use $\sqrt[3]{a \cdot b} = \sqrt[3]{a} \cdot \sqrt[3]{b}$ to rewrite the expression as the product of two factors."

$8^{\frac{1}{3}} \cdot 3375^{\frac{1}{3}}$

"Simplify to find the length of each side without using a calculator."

$8^{\frac{1}{3}} \cdot 3375^{\frac{1}{3}} = 2 \cdot 15 = 30$ in.

27. Error Analysis Two students translate the sentence "The product of 25 and an unknown number is at most 150." Which student is correct? Explain the error.

Student A	Student B
$25x \leq 150$	$25x \geq 150$

27. Student A; Sample: Student B incorrectly translated "at most" as greater than or equal to instead of less than or equal to.

*28. Geometry Gretchen wants to design a rectangular flower bed so that the length is twice the width. She has 45 feet of edging. Write an inequality that represents the greatest possible width of the flower bed. $6w \leq 45$

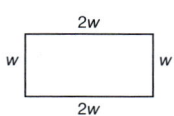

*29. Scheduling Marcy needs to read a 400-page book for her literature class. She has already read 255 pages. If she has 8 more days to read the book, about how many pages does she need to read each day to complete the reading assignment on or before time? about 18 pages

*30. Sports A can containing 3 tennis balls has a volume of $\frac{128}{9}\pi$ cubic inches. What is the diameter of each tennis ball? (Hint: The formula for the volume of a cylinder is $V = \pi r^2 h$.) $2\frac{2}{3}$ inches

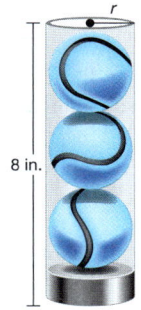

Problem 27
Error Alert
A common error students make is to confuse "at most" with "greater than." Point out that at most means not more than, which is the same as "less than or equal to."

Problem 30
Guide the students by asking them the following questions.

"What number equals r^2h?" $\frac{128}{9}$

"What is the height of the cylinder?" 8 inches

"What is r^2?" $\frac{16}{9}$

Lesson 46 293

LOOKING FORWARD

Simplifying expressions with square roots and higher order roots prepares students for

- **Lesson 61** Simplifying Radical Expressions
- **Lesson 69** Adding and Subtracting Radical Expressions
- **Lesson 76** Multiplying Radical Expressions
- **Lesson 103** Dividing Radical Expressions
- **Lesson 105** Recognizing and Extending Geometric Sequences

LESSON 47

1 Warm Up

Problems 2–5
Solve these problems using a proportion.

2 New Concepts

In this lesson, students learn how to find the percent of increase or decrease of a number.

Example 1

Error Alert Students may try to divide the new amount by the original amount to find the percent of change. Explain that the difference of the two amounts must be divided by the original amount.

Additional Example 1

Find the percent of change.

a. number of hats Juana's company sold in 1999: 14,260
number of hats Juana's company sold in 2007: 25,491
The percent of increase is 79%.

b. number of banks in the United States in 1990: 15,158
number of banks in the United States in 2004: 8975
The percent of decrease is 41%.

LESSON RESOURCES

Student Edition Practice Workbook 47
Reteaching Master 47
Adaptations Master 47
Challenge and Enrichment Master C47
Technology Lab Master 47

LESSON 47

Solving Problems Involving the Percent of Change

Warm Up

1. Vocabulary A number that is part of 100 is the _____ of the number.   **percent**

Solve.

2. 60 is what percent of 80?   **75%**
3. 20% of 40 is what number?   **8**
4. 7 is 5% of what number?   **140**
5. 25 is what percent of 80?   **31.25%**

New Concepts

The **percent of change** is the ratio of the amount of change in a quantity to the original amount, expressed as a percent. The percent of change can be a percent of increase or percent of decrease.

Example 1 Finding the Percent of Increase or Decrease

Find the percent of change.

Hint
Always subtract the original number from the new number to determine if the amount of change is an increase or decrease.

a. number of United States airports in 1985: 15,161
number of United States airports in 2005: 19,854

SOLUTION

$19{,}854 - 15{,}161 = 4693$ The difference is positive, so the percent of change is a percent of increase.

$$\frac{\text{amount of increase}}{\text{original amount}} = \frac{4693}{15{,}161}$$

≈ 0.31, or 31%

The percent of increase is 31%.

b. number of taxicabs in the United States in 2001: 31,800
number of taxicabs in the United States in 2002: 30,800

SOLUTION

$30{,}800 - 31{,}800 = -1000$ The difference is negative, so the percent of change is a percent of decrease.

$$\frac{\text{amount of decrease}}{\text{original amount}} = \frac{-1000}{31{,}800}$$

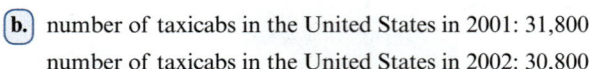

≈ -0.03, or -3%

Online Connection
www.SaxonMathResources.com

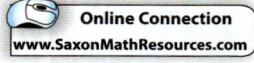

The percent of decrease is 3%.

294   *Saxon Algebra 1*

MATH BACKGROUND

The percent of change is used extensively in real-world applications, especially in the business world. Companies track their sales, customers, and profits, and then determine the percent of change to see the amount of increase or decrease.

The percent of change is used daily in stock market reports. To find the percent of change for a stock price, analysts subtract yesterday's price from today's price and then divide by yesterday's amount. If a company's shares sold at $10 apiece yesterday, and reached the value of $15 at the closing bell of the New York Stock Exchange today, then each share has increased in value by $5.

A markup results when a percent of increase is applied to a cost. A discount results when a percent of decrease is applied to a cost.

Example 2 Finding Markups and Discounts

a. A music store marks up the price of CDs they purchased at $9.00 each by 70%. What is the markup and new price of each CD?

SOLUTION

70% is a percent of increase in the $9.00 cost.

$n = 0.70 \cdot \$9$ Use an equation to find 70% of $9.

$n = \$6.30$

The markup is $6.30.

$\$9 + \$6.30 = \$15.30$ Add the markup to the original price.

The new price of each CD is $15.30.

b. A bookstore is having a sale of 40% off all items. What is the discount and new price of a book that originally cost $12?

SOLUTION

40% is a percent of decrease in the $12 cost.

What is 40% of $12?

$0.40 \cdot \$12 = n$ Use an equation to find 40% of $12.

$n = \$4.80$

The discount is $4.80.

$\$12 - \$4.80 = \$7.20$ Subtract the discount from the original price to find the new price, $7.20.

The new price of the book is $7.20.

Example 3 Application: Raising Funds

In 2006, the 100 Mile BEADS Walkathon for Education, Advancement, Development, and Success raised $36,000 for girls in Africa. The organizers hope to raise $100,000 in 2007. What will be the percent of increase in the amount raised?

SOLUTION

36,000   original amount

$100,000 - 36,000 = 64,000$ Find the amount of increase.

$\dfrac{64,000}{36,000} \approx 1.78$ $\dfrac{\text{amount of increase}}{\text{original amount}}$

$= 178\%$ Write the decimal as a percent.

The percent of increase is 178%.

Math Reasoning

Analyze Why does the pen-and-pencil set cost 60% of the original price if the discount is 40%?

Sample: because percent means per 100 and $40 + 60 = 100$

Lesson 47   295

ALTERNATE METHOD FOR EXAMPLE 2

When an amount increases by a percentage, the amount is 100% plus the percent increase.

For example, if the price of the CD increases by 70%, then the new price of the CD is 170% of $9.00. By multiplying 1.7 by 9, one step is removed when finding the new cost of the CD: $1.7 \cdot \$9 = \$15.30$.

When an amount decreases by a percentage, the new amount can be found by multiplying 100% minus the percent of decrease times the original amount.

For example, $100\% - 40\% = 60\%$. The original amount of $12 multiplied by 0.6 is $7.20. With this method, one step is removed when finding the new cost.

Example 4
Have students check their answers when finding percent of change.

Additional Example 4
In the 2000 Summer Olympics, U.S. athletes earned a total of 97 medals. In 2004, U.S. athletes earned a total of 102 medals. What is the percent of increase in the number of U.S. medals?
about 5%

Lesson Practice
Problems a and b
Scaffolding Have students determine if there is a percent of increase or decrease and have them identify the original amount. Then have them find the amount of change and write the ratio to find the percent of change.

Problem c
Error Alert After students find the markup, they may overlook finding the new price. Suggest that students begin by writing "1) Markup" and "2) New Price" on their paper to organize their work.

Check for Understanding
The questions below help assess the concepts taught in this lesson.

"How can an amount change after a percent of change is applied to it?" Sample: An amount either increases or decreases by a percentage. The greater the percent of change, the greater the increase or decrease.

"Is finding the percent of change like finding the percent of a number? Explain." Sample: Yes, finding the percent of change is finding what percent the amount of increase or decrease is of the original amount.

296 *Saxon* Algebra 1

Example 4 Olympics
In the 2002 Winter Olympics, U.S. athletes received a total of 34 medals. In the 2006 Winter Olympics, U.S. athletes received a total of 25 medals. What is the percent of decrease in the number of U.S. Winter Olympic medals?

SOLUTION

34	original amount
$34 - 25 = 9$	Find the amount of decrease.
$\frac{9}{34} \approx 0.26$	$\frac{\text{amount of decrease}}{\text{original amount}}$
$\approx 26\%$	Write the decimal as a percent.

The percent of decrease is about 26%.

Lesson Practice

Find the percent of change.
(Ex 1)
a. January 2006 salary: $600/week
   January 2007 salary: $630/week   % of increase: 5%
b. number of words in the first draft of an essay: 1032
   number of words in the final draft of an essay: 774   % of decrease: 25%

c. $19.80; $63.80
(Ex 2)
c. A shoe store marks up the price of a pair of boots that cost the store $44.00 by 45%. What is the markup and new price of the pair of boots?

d. $75,680; $268,320
(Ex 2)
d. A real estate agency is selling a house at 22% off the original cost of $344,000. What is the discount and new price of the house?

e. A weightlifter can lift 90 pounds. After six months he can lift
(Ex 3) 125 pounds. What is the percent of increase in the amount of weight he can lift?   39%

f. Binders that originally sold for $4.95 each are now selling for $3.87
(Ex 4) each. What is the percent of decrease in the price of the binders?   22%

Practice Distributed and Integrated

Solve the equations. Check your answers.
1. $-(x - 3) - 2(x - 4) = 7$ $x = \frac{4}{3}$
(26)
2. $3p - 4 - 6 = -2(p - 5)$ $p = 4$
(28)
3. $k + 4 - 5(k + 2) = 3k - 2$ $k = -\frac{4}{7}$
(28)
4. Write an inequality for the product of 3.6 and an unknown number that is greater
(45) than 18. $3.6x > 18$
5. Simplify $a^3x - |x^3|$ for $a = -3$ and $x = -2$.   46
(9)

296 *Saxon* Algebra 1

ENGLISH LEARNERS

Discuss the meaning of the word **medal.** Write "metal" and "medal" on the chalkboard. Emphasize their different spellings and meanings. Say:

"A medal is an award given to people for accomplishments or bravery. Metal is a material such as steel or gold."

Ask students to come up with other words that are pronounced the same, or similarly, but have different spellings and meanings. Give students examples such as sum and some.

6. If 15 boxes of cereal costs $67.50, what is the unit price? $4.50 per box
(31)

7. Evaluate $\sqrt[3]{-512}$. -8
(46)

*8. Find the percentage of increase or decrease from an original price of $35 to a new price of $49.   40% increase
(47)

*9. **Multiple Choice** 78 changes to 88. Find the percent of increase or decrease.   C
(47)
  A 10%   B 12%   C 13%   D 11%

*10. **Analyze** Is it possible to have a percent of increase of more than 100%? Is it possible to have a percent of decrease of more than 100%? Explain.
(47)

*11. The first 3 numbers in a sequence are 30,000, 12,000, and 4800. Use percent to describe the pattern of the sequence. List the next 2 terms.
(47)

12. **Multiple Choice** Which points are connected by a line with an undefined slope?   D
(44)
  A $(-16, 8)$ and $(-1, 10)$ B $(-5, -15)$ and $(18, 6)$
  C $(1, 1)$ and $(-1, -1)$ D $(-1, -4)$ and $(-1, 15)$

13. **Write** Based on the slope formula, why is the slope often described as rise over run $(m = \frac{rise}{run})$?
(44)

*14. (**Sale Prices**) A holiday weekend sale advertised a 25% discount on a TV that regularly sells for $500. After the holiday weekend, the sale price was increased by 25%. The management said this should put the new price back to its original price of $500. Is the management correct? If not, which price is higher? Explain.
(47)

15. **Error Analysis** Two students evaluate the expression $16^{\frac{1}{4}}$. Which student is correct? Explain the error.
(46)

Student A	Student B
$16^{\frac{1}{4}} = 2$	$16^{\frac{1}{4}} = \frac{1}{64}$

10. Sample: It is possible to have a percent of increase more than 100%; this could be when a price more than doubles. However, it is not possible to have a percent of decrease more than 100%.

11. Sample: There is a 60% decrease from one number to the next number. 1920, 768

13. Sample: Rise over run refers to a change in the vertical position of a line divided by the corresponding change in the horizontal position.

Student A; Sample: The expression is equal to the fourth root of 16, which is 2.

14. not correct Sample: discounted price: $500 - $125 = $375; new price: $375 + $93.75 = $468.75; The original price is higher.

*16. (**Basketball Rules**) In the NBA, the inner part of a basketball hoop has an area of 81π square inches. What is the circumference of the hoop? (Hint: The formula for the area of a circle is $A = \pi r^2$.) 18π inches
(46)

*17. **Data Analysis** The geometric mean is the nth root of the product of n numbers. For example, the geometric mean of 1, 2, and 4 is $\sqrt[3]{1 \cdot 2 \cdot 4} = 2$. Find the geometric mean of 2, 4, 25, and 50.   10
(46)

18. On average, the ratio of sparrows to doves who come to Jenn's birdbath is 7 to 8. On Tuesday 45 birds came to bathe. How many sparrows and how many doves came to bathe that day?   21 sparrows and 24 doves
(31)

19. Evaluate the expression $\frac{3n^0}{m^{-2}}$ if $m = -3$ and $n = 8$.   27
(32)

20. **Multi-Step** In an arithmetic sequence, $a_1 = 9$ and $d = 13$.
(34)
  a. Write a recursive formula for the sequence. $a_1 = 9, a_n = a_{n-1} + 13$
  b. Using that formula, find the first four terms of the sequence.   9, 22, 35, 48

Lesson 47   297

3 Practice

Math Conversations
Discussion to strengthen understanding

Problem 3
Guide students by asking them the following questions.

"What is the first step in solving the equation?" Use the Distributive Property to multiply $k + 2$ by -5.

"What is the next step?" Combine like terms.

"How can you check your answer?" Substitute the value for k into the original equation and evaluate.

Problem 8
Guide students by asking them the following questions.

"Is there a percent of increase or of decrease in the price?" increase

"What is the change in price?" $14

"Which amount will you divide into 14?" the original amount, $35

Problem 14
Error Alert
Students may think that the management is correct since the same percent is applied after the sale. Have students find the discounted price of the TV and the new price of the TV after the increase. Point out that the price after the sale is a percent of the sale price, not the original price, so it is less than the original price.

Problem 18
Extend the Problem
"The next day there were 5 more doves than sparrows at the birdbath. How many sparrows and how many doves came to bathe that day?" 35 sparrows and 40 doves

INCLUSION

Have each student copy and complete the first two columns of the table. Then have them describe any patterns that they notice. Sample: For each 10%, the amount increases by 6.

% of 60	Amount	Decrease	Increase
10% of 60	= 6	54	66
20% of 60	= 12	48	72
30% of 60	= 18	42	78
90% of 60	= 54	6	114
100% of 60	= 60	0	120

Have the students work in pairs to complete the table. One student in each pair will find the percent of increase of the number and the other will find the percent of decrease of the original number. Then have the students explain their results. Sample: A 100% increase doubles the original amount; a 100% decrease results in 0. Each amount of 10% increase or decrease is 6 more or less, respectively, than the previous amount.

Lesson 47   297

Problem 22
Guide students by asking them the following questions.

"What is the formula for the slope of a line?"
$m = \frac{y_2 - y_1}{x_2 - x_1}$

"What are the coordinates of the vertices of the figure?" (0, 6), (4, 0), (0, −5), (−4, 0)

"What are the slopes of all four sides?"
$m = \frac{3}{2}, m = -\frac{3}{2},$
$m = \frac{5}{4}, m = -\frac{5}{4}$

Problem 30
Guide students by asking them the following questions.

"What equation can be used to represent the amount of money that Shari deposited?"
$220.25 + $318.12 + 2x = $854.71

"What is the first step to solving the equation?" Add; $220.25 + $318.12 = $538.37

"What is the total amount of the two deposits?" $316.34

---

21. Error Analysis Two students translate the sentence "twice a number is less than or equal to 5" as shown below. Which student is correct? Explain the error.

Student A	Student B
$2 + x \leq 5$	$2x \leq 5$

Student B; Sample: Twice a number means 2 times a number; Student A added instead of multiplying

*22. Coordinate Geometry A diamond is centered on a coordinate axis. What are the slopes of its two steepest sides? $m = \pm\frac{3}{2}$

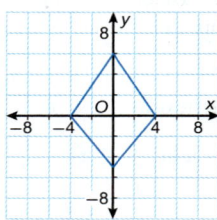

*23. Determine any values where the rational expression $\frac{x + 4x^2}{16}$ is undefined. The expression is defined for all values of x.

*24. Budgeting A family wants to write a budget where they put a total of 15% of their income each month into retirement savings. They are already putting 6% of their income into a retirement account. If the family's income each month is $3484.00, how much more do they need to put into retirement each month? $313.56

25. Use the graph to find the rate of change. −4 eggs/omelet

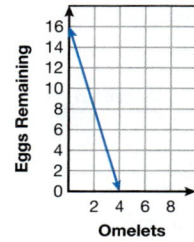

26. Simplify $(-4ab^2c^2)^3$. $-64a^3b^6c^6$

27. Analyze For the expression $\frac{3x^{-2}}{f}$, why can x not equal zero?

28. Chemistry The approximate radius of an electron is 2.817939×10^{-15} meter. Write this number in standard notation. 0.000000000000002817939

29. Multi-Step Use the expression $4a + 4ab + 4bc$.
  a. Is the expression $2(2a + 2ab + 2bc)$ a correct factorization of the polynomial? Explain.
  b. Does the expression $2(2a + 2ab + 2bc)$ factor the polynomial completely?

30. Finance Over the past six months, Shari made four deposits for a total of $854.71. She wrote down the first two deposits of $220.25 and $318.12 in her register. The final two deposits were of equal amounts that she forgot to write down. What amount should Shari write in her register for each of those deposits? $158.17

27. Sample: Because if $x = 0$, then $x^2 = 0$, and you can not have a zero denominator.

29a. yes; Sample: Using the Distributive Property, $2(2a + 2ab + 2bc) = 4a + 4ab + 4bc$, which is the original polynomial.

29b. no; Sample: The polynomial in parentheses, $2a + 2ab + 2bc$, still has a common factor of 2. The complete factorization would be $4(a + ab + bc)$.

 CHALLENGE

Maria received a gift of shares in a company stock with a total value of $65. Fifteen years later, the stock is worth $868.39. What is the percent of increase of the stock price?
about 1236%

Another stock that Maria owns fell in value from $74.08 to $73.63 in two years. What is the percent of decrease? about 0.6%

LOOKING FORWARD

Finding the percent of increase or decrease prepares students for

• **Lesson 116** Solving Simple and Compound Interest Problems

LESSON 48

Analyzing Measures of Central Tendency

Warm Up

1. **Vocabulary** A possible result in a probability experiment is called a(n) _____. **outcome**
   (Inv 1)

   Order the numbers from least to greatest.

2. $\frac{4}{9}, 1\frac{4}{5}, \frac{3}{8}, 1\frac{2}{3}, \frac{2}{5}$ $\frac{3}{8}, \frac{2}{5}, \frac{4}{9}, 1\frac{2}{3}, 1\frac{4}{5}$
   (SB 1)

3. 2.75, 2.59, 2.337, 2.5   **2.337, 2.5, 2.59, 2.75**
   (SB 1)

4. Simplify $\frac{6-3+5}{10-2}$.   **1**
   (4)

5. Solve $3x + 7 = 5x + 11$.   **−2**
   (28)

New Concepts

A **measure of central tendency** is a value that describes the center of a data set. Measures of central tendency include the mean, median, and mode.

The **mean** is the sum of values in a data set divided by the number of data values.

The **median** is the middle number in a set of numbers when they are arranged in order. If there is an even number of data values in the set, the median is the mean of the two middle numbers.

The **mode** is the value or values that occur most frequently in a data set. If all values occur the same number of times, the data set has no mode.

Example 1 Finding the Mean, Median, and Mode

Find the mean, median, and mode of the values in the data set, rounded to the nearest whole.

$$35, 36, 33, 38, 36, 34, 35, 35, 33$$

SOLUTION

mean: $\frac{35 + 36 + 33 + 38 + 36 + 34 + 35 + 35 + 33}{9}$

$= \frac{315}{9}$

$= 35$

The mean of the values is 35.

median: 33, 33, 34, 35, ㉟, 35, 36, 36, 38

The median is 35.

mode: The number 35 occurs more often than any other number.

The mode is 35.

Hint

Find the me**a**n of the values by finding the **a**verage. The me**di**an is the mi**d**dle number of the values, like the median is the middle stripe on a road. The m**o**de is the value that occurs m**o**st frequently.

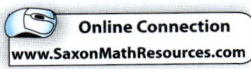
Online Connection
www.SaxonMathResources.com

Lesson 48   299

MATH BACKGROUND

Students have used graphs as a way to describe and analyze data visually. Now they will learn how to measure data using statistics. Statistics is a science that uses mathematical methods of collection, organization, and interpretation of data, and it has applications in many fields of study.

Common measures of data are the mean, median, mode, and range. People often refer to the mean as the average, although median and mode are also types of averages. Students will need to understand how to measure the mean of data when later computing other statistics, like standard deviation.

1 Warm Up

Problem 4
Remind students that they must subtract and add from left to right when simplifying the numerator.

2 New Concepts

In this lesson, students will learn that mean, median, mode, and range can be used to describe a larger set of data. They will also learn how an outlier can affect measures of central tendency.

Example 1

In this example, students will find the mean, median, and mode of a set of data.

Additional Example 1

The following data show the mean age (rounded to the nearest whole) of the populations of 11 northeastern states in the United States in 2000.

39, 37, 38, 37, 37, 37, 36, 38, 37, 36, 36

Find the mean, median, and mode of the values in the data set, and round them to the nearest whole. **mean: 37; median: 37; mode: 37**

LESSON RESOURCES

Student Edition Practice
   Workbook 48
Reteaching Master 48
Adaptations Master 48
Challenge and Enrichment
   Master C48
Technology Lab Master 48

Example 2

In this example, students compare sets of data using the range. Remind students that the larger the range is for a set group of numbers, the more spread out the data values are in the set.

Additional Example 2

The table lists the total points teams scored in the two divisions of the **All-Star** Football League for the 1981 regular season.

Total Points Scored in the 1981 Regular Season

North	357, 367, 368, 295, 315, 324, 347, 397, 315, 426, 325, 253, 303, 207
South	421, 345, 355, 478, 321, 311, 343, 356, 281, 273, 322, 276, 259, 322

Did the North or the South have a greater range of points over the 1981 regular season? **neither; Both had an equal range.**

Example 3

In this example, students analyze the effect of outliers on the measures of central tendency for a set of data. The effects of an outlier vary with the size of the data set and the amount of the difference between the outlier and the other data.

Additional Example 3

The following data show the high temperatures (in degrees Fahrenheit) for the first week of April 2007 in Austin, Texas.

84, 85, 84, 74, 73, 69, 50

Identify any outliers in the data set. Describe how any outliers affect the measures of central tendency. **50; Sample: Without the outlier, the mean is about 4 degrees higher and the median is 5 degrees higher.**

Another way to analyze a set of numbers is by looking at its range. The **range of a set of data** is the difference between the greatest and least values in the data set.

Example 2 Comparing Data

The table lists the total points teams scored in the two divisions of the All-Star Football League for the 2006 regular season.

Total Points Scored in the 2006 Regular Season

North	398, 425, 355, 307, 427, 301, 282, 305, 413, 270, 292, 211, 335, 367, 298, 314
South	385, 316, 300, 260, 353, 373, 353, 238, 427, 324, 371, 267, 492, 331, 319, 168

Does the North or the South have a greater range of points over the 2006 regular season?

SOLUTION

Find the range of values for each data set by determining the greatest and least values in each set and finding the difference between them.

North   greatest value: 427; least value: 211 $427 - 211 = 216$
South   greatest value: 492; least value: 168 $492 - 168 = 324$

Compare the ranges of the two data sets.

$$324 > 216$$

The data for the South has a greater range of values. Therefore, the values in this data set are more spread out than the values in the data set for the North.

Certain values in a data set can affect the measures of central tendency. An **outlier** is a data value that is much greater than or less than the other values in the data set.

Example 3 Analyzing the Effects of an Outlier

The following data show the high temperatures (in degrees Fahrenheit) for the first fifteen days in July 2007 for Seattle, Washington.

75, 79, 81, 81, 84, 81, 81, 78, 76, 78, 89, 98, 81, 78, 86

a. Identify any outliers in the data set.

SOLUTION

Write the data in numeric order and observe any patterns.

75, 76, 78, 78, 78, 79, 81, 81, 81, 81, 81, 84, 86, 89, 98

The outlier value of 98 is much greater than the other values in the data set.

ALTERNATE METHOD FOR EXAMPLE 2

Compare the greatest data values from each set and the least data values from each set individually.

greatest values

  North: 427   South: 492

$$427 < 492$$

least values

  North: 211   South: 168

$$211 > 168$$

Compare side by side.

  least values   greatest values

  $168 < 211$ $427 < 492$

The greatest value in the data set for the South is greater than the greatest value for the North, and the least value in the data set for the South is less than the least value for the North. Therefore, the South had a greater range of points for the 2006 season.

b. Describe how the outlier affects the measures of central tendency.

SOLUTION

Find the mean, median, and mode with and without the outlier and compare.

With the outlier:

mean: $\frac{1226}{15} \approx 82$ median: 81   mode: 81

Without the outlier:

mean: $\frac{1128}{14} \approx 81$ median: 81   mode: 81

The outlier value of 98 raised the mean temperature by 1 degree.

Example 4 Application: Advertising

Super-Grow Fertilizer placed this advertisement in the newspaper. Is the statement in the advertisement true? Does the statement accurately describe the data? Explain.

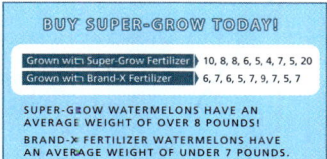

BUY SUPER-GROW TODAY!

Grown with Super-Grow Fertilizer) 10, 8, 8, 6, 5, 4, 7, 5, 20
Grown with Brand-X Fertilizer) 6, 7, 6, 5, 7, 9, 7, 5, 7

SUPER-GROW WATERMELONS HAVE AN AVERAGE WEIGHT OF OVER 8 POUNDS!
BRAND-X FERTILIZER WATERMELONS HAVE AN AVERAGE WEIGHT OF UNDER 7 POUNDS.

SOLUTION

Find the mean, median, and mode of the values for each data set.

Super-Grow: mean = $\frac{73}{9} \approx 8.1$; median = 7; mode = 5 and 8; outlier = 20

Brand-X: mean = $\frac{59}{9} \approx 6.6$; median = 7; mode = 7; no outliers

The statement is true since it lists the correct mean of each data set, but the outlier in the data for Super-Grow raises the mean for that data set. Without the outlier, the mean is 6.625.

Lesson Practice

a. Find the mean, median, and mode of the values in the data set.
(Ex 1)   mean: 29; median: 28; mode: 25
46, 33, 25, 21, 38, 25, 30, 15, 28

b. Do trucks or convertibles have a greater range of sales over the 8-week
(Ex 2)   period?   trucks

Weekly Car Sales at AutoMart (in thousands of dollars)

Trucks	350, 125, 415, 370, 560, 280, 265, 430
Convertibles	640, 720, 600, 640, 310, 755, 780, 660

The following data show the ages of 20 students graduating from college.
(Ex 3)
22, 22, 23, 22, 25, 26, 22, 21, 22, 26, 64, 22, 23, 24, 22, 25, 22, 22, 24, 59

c. Identify any outliers in the data set.   59 and 64

d. Describe how any outliers affect the measures of central tendency.

Lesson 48   301

Check for Understanding

The questions below help assess the concepts taught in this lesson.

"Explain how a data set could have no mode but still have repeated values in the set."
Sample: If every value in the data set is repeated equally, there will be no mode, because no number occurs more than another.

"Which measure of central tendency do you think best describes a data set? Explain."
Sample: The best measure of central tendency of a data set changes with each type of data set.

3 Practice

Math Conversations
Discussion to strengthen understanding

Problem 7
Guide the students by asking them the following questions.

"What is the formula for finding the mean of a set of data?"
mean = $\frac{\text{sum of data values}}{\text{number of data values}}$

"How can you represent the addition of four identical values to the data set?" $+4x$

"What equation can you write to find the new values?"
$19 = \frac{105 + 4x}{10}$

---

e. **Fuel Prices** The following data show the annual mean price of regular
(Ex 2) gasoline for 10 cities across the United States in 2005: $2.26, $2.32, $2.22, $2.24, $2.27, $2.49, $2.39, $2.30, $2.48, $2.36. What was the median price of a gallon of regular gasoline among these cities in 2005 in dollars? If budgeting money for gasoline, would you use this measure of central tendency? Explain. $2.31; Sample: no; If I lived in 1 of the 10 cities, I would use the mean, $2.33, since it might be better to use the higher price when budgeting.

Practice Distributed and Integrated

Find the greatest common factor.

1. $4ab^2c^4 - 2a^2b^3c^2 + 6a^3b^4c$ $2ab^2c$
(38)

2. $5m^2x^2y^5 - 10m^2xy^2 + 15m^2x^2y^4$ $5m^2xy^2$
(38)

Simplify.

3. $4x^2(ax - 2)$ $4ax^3 - 8x^2$
(15)

4. $\frac{6a^{-3}c^{-3}}{a^{-2}cd^0}$ $\frac{6}{ac^4}$
(32)

5. A deck of cards contains 6 green cards and 2 yellow cards. What is the probability
(33) of drawing a green card, keeping it, and then drawing another green card? $\frac{15}{28}$

*6. Find the mean, median, and mode of the following data set:
(48)
number of kittens in 11 litters: 3, 5, 4, 2, 6, 6, 2, 1, 4, 6, 5.   mean: 4; median: 4; mode: 6

 7. **Statistics** The numbers below have a mean of 17.5. What four identical values
(26) could be added to this set of numbers to increase the mean to 19?   21.25

$$\{19, 18, 17, 17, 19, 15\}$$

8. **Multi-Step** The area of a square game board is represented by the
(39) expression $\left(\frac{x}{y} - \frac{r}{x}\right)^2$.
   a. Write this expression as a product of two terms. $\left(\frac{x}{y} - \frac{r}{x}\right)\left(\frac{x}{y} - \frac{r}{x}\right)$
   b. Distribute both fractions in the first factor, $\frac{x}{y}$ and $-\frac{r}{x}$, one at a time, as if it were two separate problems: $\frac{x}{y}\left(\frac{x}{y} - \frac{r}{x}\right)$ and $-\frac{r}{x}\left(\frac{x}{y} - \frac{r}{x}\right)$. $\frac{x^2}{y^2} - \frac{r}{y} - \frac{r}{y} + \frac{r^2}{x^2}$ or $\frac{x^2}{y^2} - \frac{xr}{yx} - \frac{rx}{xy} + \frac{r^2}{x^2}$
   c. Simplify the result of part b. $\frac{x^2}{y^2} - \frac{2r}{y} + \frac{r^2}{x^2}$

9. **Write** When is the statement $(-2)^n = 2^n$ true for a positive integer n? When is it
(40) false? Explain.

9. true when n is even and false when n is odd; Sample: Multiplying a negative number an even number of times results in a positive number, while multiplying a negative number an odd number of times results in a negative number.

10. **Data Analysis** If $x + 12$ represents the number of data values in a set of data, the
(48) mean of this data is 9, and the sum of all the data values is 216, how many data values are in the set?
   a. Write an equation to find the value of x. Start with the formula for finding the mean. $9 = \frac{216}{x + 12}$, so $9(x + 12) = 216$.
   b. Solve for x. $x = 12$
   c. Find the number of data values in the set.   24

302 Saxon Algebra 1

INCLUSION

Materials: graph paper, or centimeter grid paper from Teacher Tools, scissors, tape

Help students find the mean of a data set by completing the activity. Use the following data set, or provide your own, as long as the mean works out to be a whole number.

9, 4, 11, 8, 7, 8, 12, 5

On graph or centimeter grid paper, have students shade in columns or bars the height or length of each data value using one square per unit.

Have students cut out each of the shaded bars and tape them together end to end. Guide the students to fold the long strip into as many equal sections as there are data values, allowing them to guess and check.

"What is the length of each section?" 8

"What does the number represent?"
the mean

*11. **Multiple Choice** The following data set shows the number of minutes 8 students spent studying last night: 30, 90, 60, 30, 90, 40, 90, 50. Which measure has a value of 55? **B**
A mean   B median   C mode   D range

*12. **Write** Can 7 be the mode of 1, 2, 3, 4, 7, 7 even though it fails to occur in the middle of the data set? Explain.   yes; Sample: It is possible for the mode to be the highest or lowest value in the data set.

*13. **Multi-Step** Matthew opened a checking account last year for $150. Since then, the balance has increased by 15%, decreased by 8%, and then increased again by 25%.
  a. What is the account balance now? $198.38
  b. Did the balance increase or decrease over the original amount? By what percent?   increase by 32%

*14. (**Travel**) A round-trip plane fare from Orlando, Florida, to Manila, Philippines, during autumn costs $1689. However, the same round-trip flight during winter costs $3474. Find the percent of change.   percent increase of 106%

*15. Provide a counterexample for this statement: The sum of an even number and an odd number is an even number.   Sample: The sum of 8 and 7 is 15, which is odd.

*16. **Analyze** Juan recorded the number of points he scored individually in the last 13 basketball games his team played: 33, 12, 18, 21, 10, 18, 14, 20, 11, 24, 0, 0, 0. Tell why the mode is not the best measure of central tendency to describe the data set.

16. Sample: The mode of the data set is 0, but this is not representative of Juan's average score. He may have missed the last three games, so the median or mean would better describe the set.

*17. (**Hockey**) In hockey, a goalie gets a shutout if he or she can prevent the opposing team from scoring for the entire game. Study the data in the table. Identify the outlier. What would this outlier represent in the data?   12; Sample: The outlier represents a goalie who performed very well for the season.

Shutouts for the 2006–2007 Regular Hockey Season
2 5 8 3 5 2 4 7 5 4 6 2 5 4 12
5 3 5 2 7 4 5 3 3 5 4 2 5 2 2

18. **Multi-Step** A cell phone bill can be calculated using the equation $10y = 3x + 360$, where x is the number of minutes used and y is the amount of the bill.
  a. Rewrite this equation in standard form. $-3x + 10y = 360$
  b. Calculate the y-intercept and explain its real-world meaning.
  c. Calculate the x-intercept and explain its real-world meaning.

18b. 36; Sample; If 0 minutes are used, the bill is $36. In other words, even if the phone has not been used, the person will still be charged $36.

18c. –120; Sample: In order to have a $0 bill, –120 minutes would have to be used. This is impossible.

19. (**Recreation**) The formula $h = -16t^2 + 12t + 2$ can be used to find the height of a ball that is kicked into the air from 2 feet off the ground with an initial velocity of 12 feet/second. Rewrite the formula by factoring the right side of the equation using the GCF and making the t^2-term positive. $h = -2(8t^2 - 6t - 1)$

20. Find 93% of 24 using a proportion.   22.32

21. (**Transporting Freight**) Ramps are often used to load freight on to trucks for transporting. The figure at right shows one possible structure of a ramp. The ratio comparing the area of the top of the ramp to the area of one of its sides is $\frac{x\ell}{0.5(x^2 + 4x)}$. Simplify this expression. $\frac{2\ell}{x+4}$

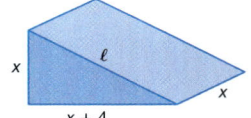

Lesson 48   303

CHALLENGE

Give students the following data for the mean price per pound of ten different fresh fruits and vegetables in 2005.

$0.97, $0.48, $0.89, $1.10, $2.76, $1.51, $0.99, $0.50, $0.85, $1.85

Have students estimate the mean of the data by simply looking at the values. $1.25

"How can you check your estimate with only addition and subtraction?" Sample: I can add up the values higher than my estimate, and subtract my estimate from them. Then I can add up the lower values, and subtract my estimate from them. The sum of the differences above and below my estimate should be equal.

Problem 14
Error Alert
A common error when solving percent of change problems is dividing the amount of change by the wrong value.

$3474 - 1689 = 1785$

$\frac{1785}{3474} = 0.51 = 51\%$

Remind students to divide by the original amount, and to check their answers to see if they make sense. If the price changed by about 50%, then

$1689 \cdot 0.5 = 844.50$

$1689 + 844.50 = 2533.50$

$2533.50 \neq 3474$

Problem 18
Extend the Problem
"Find the cost of the phone bill if the consumer uses 250 minutes." $111

"If the phone bill comes out to $72, how many minutes has the consumer used?" 120 minutes

Problem 21
Guide the students by reminding them how to factor out common terms.

"What common term can you factor out of the expression $x^2 + 4x$?" x

"Can you divide out any terms?" yes; the x in the numerator and denominator

"Can you leave 0.5 in the denominator?" no; Sample: 0.5 is the decimal representation of the fraction $\frac{1}{2}$, and you cannot leave a fraction in the denominator when simplifying.

Lesson 48   303

22. Determine the slope of the line containing the two points (2, −9) and (4, −25).
    $m = -8$

23. **Formulate** Translate "the sum of $\frac{1}{2}$ an unknown and the opposite of 4 is less than 6." $\frac{1}{2}x + (-4) < 6$

24. **Multiple Choice** Marshall deposits $45 into his savings account every month. His current balance is $215. After how many months will his balance exceed $500? Write an inequality to represent the situation. **A**

    A $45w + 215 > 500$ **B** $45w + 500 \leq 215$

    C $45w + 215 \leq 500$ **D** $45w + 500 > 215$

25. Write $\sqrt[6]{m}$ with a fractional exponent. $m^{\frac{1}{6}}$

*26. **Multiple Choice** Which expression is equal to $-15^{\frac{1}{4}}$? **B**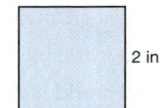

    A $\sqrt[4]{-15}$ **B** $-\sqrt[4]{15}$

    C $\dfrac{1}{\sqrt[4]{-15}}$ **D** $-\dfrac{1}{\sqrt[4]{15}}$

27. Find the percent of increase or decrease from an original price of $500 to a new price of $400. 20% decrease

*28. **Error Analysis** Student A and Student B computed the percent of increase of the price of gasoline in Idaho at $3.25 in June 2007, from the nationwide average of $3.07. Which student is correct? Explain the error. Student A; Sample: Student B calculated a percent decrease.

Student A	Student B
$\dfrac{\$3.25 - \$3.07}{\$3.07} = \dfrac{\$0.18}{\$3.07}$	$\dfrac{\$3.07 - \$3.25}{\$3.25} = -\dfrac{\$0.18}{\$3.25}$
≈ 0.06	≈ -0.06
$= 6\%$	$= -6\%$

*29. **Geometry** Draw a similar figure whose perimeter is 75% more than the perimeter of the square below. Square with side length 3.5 inches

2 in.

30. **Analyze** Determine if the premise and the conclusion use inductive or deductive reasoning. Explain your choice. inductive reasoning; The conclusion is based on an observed pattern.

    Premise: The light turned on the last 50 times the switch was flipped.

    Conclusion: The light will turn on the next time the switch is flipped.

LOOKING FORWARD

Analyzing measures of central tendency prepares students for

- **Lesson 54** Displaying Data in Box-and-Whisker Plots
- **Lesson 62** Displaying Data in Stem-and-Leaf Plots and Histograms

LAB 3

Graphing Linear Functions

Graphing Calculator Lab (*Use with Lesson 49*)

While the graph of an equation can be drawn by hand, this method may be time-consuming. Also, it can be difficult to read exact values on a hand-drawn graph. A graphing calculator quickly creates an accurate graph of an equation.

Graph the line $y = 2x + 7$.

1. Enter the equation into the Y= editor. Press the **Y=** key. Then press 2 **X,T,θ,n** **+** 7.

   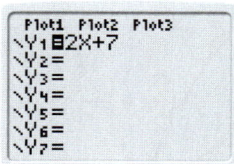

2. Press **ZOOM** and choose **6: ZStandard** to view the graph of the equation in the standard viewing window.

   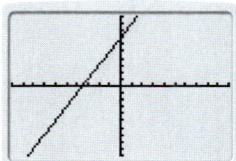

3. Place the cursor on the *y*-intercept by pressing **TRACE**. The cursor will automatically appear on the *y*-intercept the first time the function is traced. The coordinates of the cursor are located at the bottom of the screen. The *y*-intercept for the line $y = 2x + 7$ is (0, 7).

   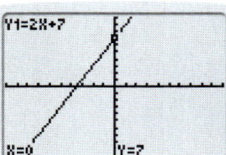

4. While the cursor is tracing the *y*-intercept, press **ENTER**. This will center the viewing window on the *y*-intercept.

   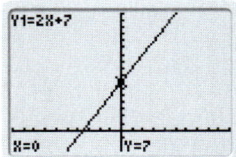

5. Press **ZOOM** and select **5: ZSquare**. The graph now appears to have a steeper incline. This is the most accurate picture of the graph of $y = 2x + 7$.

   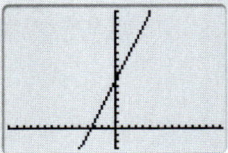

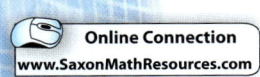
Online Connection
www.SaxonMathResources.com

Materials
- graphing calculator

Discuss
A graphing calculator is an effective tool that can be used to save time and check answers by graphing lines on the display screen. To graph a line, equations must be in slope-intercept ($y = mx + b$) form. Students can use the **TRACE** function to view ordered pairs anywhere on the line. If they prefer a numeric view of the ordered pairs, they can use the **2nd** **GRAPH** (TABLE) keys to display a table of ordered pairs.

Lab 3   305

6. Trace the line to locate other points on the graph by pressing TRACE. Use the ◄ and ► keys to move the cursor along the line. The coordinates of the cursor are displayed at the bottom of the screen.

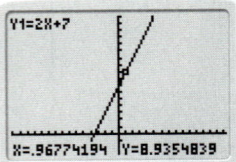

Lab Practice

Use the line $y = 3x + 6$ to complete the problems.

a. Graph the equation in the standard viewing window.
b. Find the y-intercept of the line.   (0, 6)
c. Use the trace feature to find the coordinates of 3 other points on the line. Round to the nearest hundredth.   Sample: $(-0.65, 4.05)$, $(1.29, 9.87)$, $(2.26, 12.78)$

a.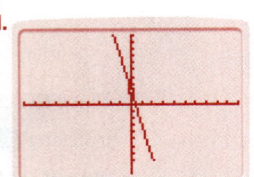

Use the line $y = -5x + 2$ to complete the problems.

d. Graph the equation in the standard viewing window.
e. Find the y-intercept of the line.   (0, 2)
f. Use the trace feature to find the coordinates of 3 other points on the line. Round to the nearest hundredth.   Sample: $(-1.61, 10.05)$, $(-0.65, 5.25)$, $(0.97, -2.85)$

LESSON 49

Writing Equations in Slope-Intercept Form

Warm Up

1. **Vocabulary** Which ordered pair could be the coordinates of the y-intercept of a graph? **B**
   A (3, 0)   B (0, 4)   C (1, 2)   D (−1, −6)

   Solve for y.

2. $x + 3y - 4 = 0$ $y = -\frac{1}{3}x + \frac{4}{3}$

3. $3x - 2y - 7 = 0$ $y = \frac{3}{2}x - \frac{7}{2}$

   Find the y-value given the x-value.

4. $y = 2x + 10;\ x = 4$ $y = 18$

5. $y = x^2;\ x = -9$ $y = 81$

New Concepts

The slope-intercept form of a linear equation can be used to graph lines quickly because it gives information about the characteristics of the graph of the equation.

Math Language

The *y-intercept* is the y-value where a graph intersects the y-axis, and is usually represented by the variable b. The coordinate is $(0, b)$.

Slope-Intercept Form of an Equation
The **slope-intercept form** is $y = mx + b$, where the value of m is the slope of the line and the value of b is the y-intercept.

Example 1 Determining the Slope and y-Intercept of a Line

Determine the slope and the y-intercept of each equation.

a. $y = 3x - 4$

SOLUTION The equation is already written in slope-intercept form. The slope (m) is the coefficient of x, and the y-intercept is the constant value in the equation. Write the equation so that the operation with the constant is addition.

$y = 3x + (-4)$

slope: 3 y-intercept: −4

b. $2x + 3y - 9 = 0$

SOLUTION Isolate the variable y to write the equation in slope-intercept form.

$2x + 3y - 9 = 0$

$\begin{array}{rr} -2x & -2x \end{array}$ Subtraction Property of Equality

$3y - 9 = -2x$

$\begin{array}{rr} +9 & +9 \end{array}$ Addition Property of Equality

$\dfrac{3y}{3} = \dfrac{-2x + 9}{3}$ Division Property of Equality

$y = -\dfrac{2}{3}x + 3$

slope: $-\dfrac{2}{3}$ y-intercept: 3

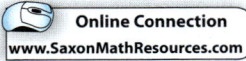
Online Connection
www.SaxonMathResources.com

Lesson 49   307

MATH BACKGROUND

For any linear equation expressed in slope-intercept form, the coefficient of x is equal to $\dfrac{\Delta y}{\Delta x}$. This ratio describes a rate of change.

For linear equations, the rate of change is constant. The study of nonconstant rates of change requires calculus. Each kind of rate of change has a different application.

For instance, velocity describes a constant rate of change and acceleration describes a nonconstant rate of change.

---

1 Warm Up

Problems 2 and 3

Remind students use inverse operations when isolating the y variable.

2 New Concepts

In this lesson, students learn to write equations in slope-intercept form.

Discuss with students the characteristics of a line. Explain how a steeper slope indicates a greater rate of change.

Example 1

Point out to students that writing an equation in slope-intercept form is the same as solving for y.

Additional Example 1

Determine the slope and the y-intercept of each equation.

a. $y = 5x + 7$ slope: 5; y-intercept: 7

b. $6x - 3y + 3 = 0$ slope: 2; y-intercept: 1

TEACHER TIP

Help students understand that $y = mx + b$ is the general form.

LESSON RESOURCES

Student Edition Practice Workbook 49
Reteaching Master 49
Adaptations Master 49
Challenge and Enrichment Master C49

Example 2

Error Alert Students may confuse rise and run when graphing equations. The mnemonic "rise up, run across" may help them remember that $\frac{\text{rise}}{\text{run}} = \frac{\Delta y}{\Delta x}$.

Additional Example 2

Graph each line using the equation that is in slope-intercept form.

a. $y = 6x$

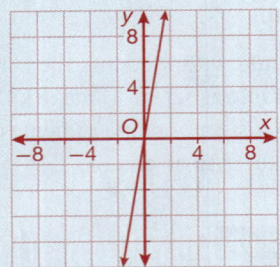

b. $3y + 5x + 9 = 0$

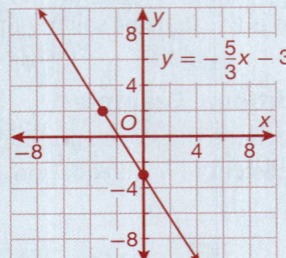

The **solution of an equation in two variables** is an ordered pair or set of ordered pairs that satisfies the equation. Solutions of equations in two variables can be represented in a table of values or as a graph on a coordinate plane.

Example 2 Graphing an Equation of a Line in Slope-Intercept Form

Graph each line using the equation that is in slope-intercept form.

a. $y = \frac{2}{3}x$

SOLUTION

Identify the slope and y-intercept from the equation. There is no constant, so the value of b is 0.

slope: $\frac{2}{3}$ y-intercept: 0

Graph the y-intercept on the coordinate plane at point $(0, 0)$.

Use the value of the slope to plot another point on the line. The slope is $\frac{2}{3}$, so this means a rise of 2 over a run of 3. Starting at the y-intercept, $(0, 0)$, move 2 units up and 3 units to the right. A second point on the line is $(3, 2)$.

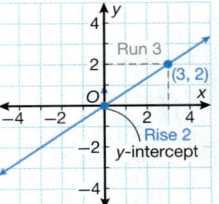

Draw a line through the two points.

b. $2x + y + 5 = 0$

SOLUTION

Write the equation in slope-intercept form.

$y = -2x - 5$

Identify the slope and y-intercept from the equation.

slope: -2 y-intercept: -5

Hint

Slope is often written as $\frac{\text{rise}}{\text{run}}$ or "rise over run." When the value of m is a whole number, think about it in rational form. For example, $6 = \frac{6}{1}$.

Graph the y-intercept on the coordinate plane at point $(0, -5)$.

Use the value of the slope to plot another point on the line. The slope is -2, or $-\frac{2}{1}$, so this means a negative rise of 2 over a run of 1. Starting at the y-intercept, $(0, -5)$, move 2 units down and 1 unit to the right. A second point on the line is $(1, -7)$.

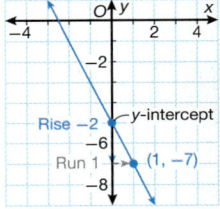

Draw a line through the two points.

INCLUSION

For Example 2, have students make a table of values.

x	y
0	0
3	2
6	4

Then have students plot the ordered pairs to make the graph.

You can use a graph to write an equation of the line in slope-intercept form.

Example 3 Writing the Equation of a Line from a Graph

a. Write the equation of the graphed line in slope-intercept form.

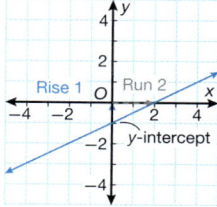

SOLUTION

Identify the y-intercept from the graph by identifying the y-value where the line crosses the y-axis.

y-intercept: -1

Identify the slope by determining how to move from one point to another.

rise = 1

run = 2

slope: $\frac{1}{2}$

Write the equation in slope-intercept form.

$y = \frac{1}{2}x - 1$

b. Write the equation of the graphed line in slope-intercept form.

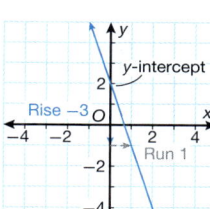

SOLUTION

Identify the y-intercept from the graph by identifying the y-value where the line crosses the y-axis.

y-intercept: 2

Identify the slope by determining how to move from one point to another.

rise = -3

run = 1

slope: -3

Write the equation in slope-intercept form.

$y = -3x + 2$

Check Verify the solution by graphing the equation on a graphing calculator and comparing it to the original graph.

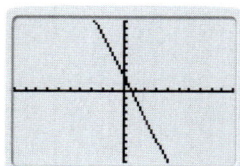

Math Reasoning

Generalize What is the slope of a horizontal line? What is the slope-intercept form of the equation of a horizontal line? $0; y = 0x + b$

Lesson 49   309

Example 3

Make sure students do not confuse the y-intercept with the x-intercept.

Additional Example 3

Write the equation of the graphed line in slope-intercept form.

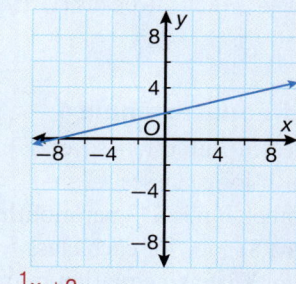

$y = \frac{1}{4}x + 2$

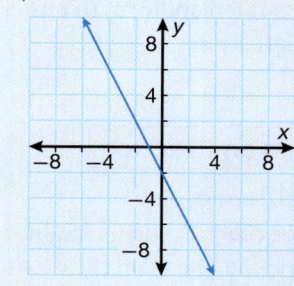

$y = -2x - 2$

ALTERNATE METHOD FOR EXAMPLE 3

After students identify the y-intercept, have them use the equation $\frac{y_2 - y_1}{x_2 - x_1}$ to find the slope.

Lesson 49   309

Example 4

Students translate a rate of change problem into an equation that is in slope-intercept form.

Extend the Example

Ask students, "Without finding the equation, how could you draw the graph of the situation?" Sample: Graph the points (1, 35) and (2, 45).

Additional Example 4

A health club offers several month-long classes. Club membership is $40 per month plus a $15 fee for each class taken. Write an equation in slope-intercept form to represent the situation.
$y = 15x + 40$

Lesson Practice

Problem d

Error Alert Students might graph the line from the origin instead of the y-intercept. Remind students to identify the correct starting point.

Problem e

Scaffolding Suggest that students identify the y-intercept before finding the slope.

Check for Understanding

The questions below help assess the concepts taught in this lesson.

"Explain how slope-intercept form describes the graph of an equation." Sample: The coefficient of the variable x represents the slope of the line and the constant represents the y-intercept.

"Explain how to find the slope of a line when given the graph." Sample: Find the ratio of units moving up or down to units moving across.

When working with a real-world application of linear equations, it is important to correctly identify all of the values. The y-intercept is often a starting value. The slope of a line is the rate of change, so the value that is the rate of change in the problem will be substituted for m.

Example 4 Calculating Rental Rates

Monica is helping prepare a budget for her family vacation. The family has decided to rent canoes for a day on the lake. The rental for a canoe is a $25 flat fee plus $10 per hour. Write an equation in slope-intercept form to represent this situation and then graph it.

SOLUTION

Define the variables.

Let y represent the total rental cost and x represent the number of hours of canoe rental.

Math Reasoning

Analyze Why is the graph of the line shown only in the first quadrant?

Sample: because canoes cannot be rented for negative hours or negative amounts of money

Caution

Even though a linear equation is often used to represent a real-world problem, pay attention to restrictions on the domain and range.

Identify the slope and y-intercept from the information in the problem.

The slope is 10 because it is the rate of change based on the number of hours the canoe is rented. The y-intercept is 25, the flat fee or cost, of renting the canoe for 0 hours.

Write the equation in slope-intercept form.

$$y = 10x + 25$$

Graph the equation of the line.

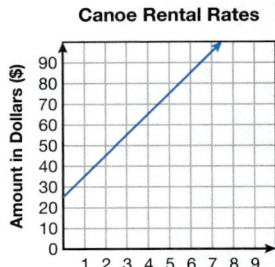
Canoe Rental Rates

Lesson Practice

Determine the slope and the y-intercept of the equation. (Ex 1)

a. $y = 0.7x - 4.9$
$m = 0.7; b = -4.9$

b. $-9x + 3y = 12$
$m = 3; b = 4$

Graph each line using the equation that is in slope-intercept form. (Ex 2)

c. $y = \dfrac{3}{5}x$

d. $x - 4y - 20 = 0$

Write the equation of the graphed line in slope-intercept form. (Ex 3)

e. Write the equation of the graphed line in slope-intercept form. $y = x + 4$

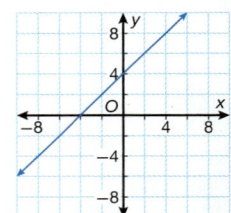

c.

d. (graph showing $y = \dfrac{1}{4}x - 5$)

310 Saxon Algebra 1

ENGLISH LEARNERS

English learners may not be familiar with the phrase **flat fee.** Say:

"A flat fee is a cost for a service that does not change with how much of the service is used."

Ask students to come up with examples of flat fees. Relate flat fees to constants and emphasize that they do not change.

f. Write the equation of the graphed line in slope-intercept form $y = -\frac{1}{3}x - 2$

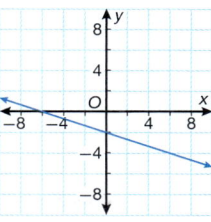

g. Monica's family will be renting a car on their vacation. The car rents for an initial fee of $50 plus $0.50 per mile. Write a linear equation in slope-intercept form to represent this situation and then graph it. $y = 0.5x + 50$; See Additional Answers.

Practice Distributed and Integrated

Expand each expression by using the Distributive Property.

1. $x^2y^3(3xy - 5y)$ $3x^3y^4 - 5x^2y^4$
2. $-2x^3y^3(4x^2y - 3xy)$ $-8x^5y^4 + 6x^4y^4$

Evaluate each expression for the given values.

3. x^2y^3z if $x = 3$, $y = -2$, and $z = 4$ -288
4. $-x^2 - y^3$ if $x = -3$ and $y = -2$ -1

5. Find the x-intercept of the line $3x + 2y - 10 = 0$. $\left(\frac{10}{3}, 0\right)$

*6. Identify the slope and y-intercept of the line $2x - 5y - 6 = 0$. $m = \frac{2}{5}$; $b = -\frac{6}{5}$

*7. **Multiple Choice** What is the equation of the graphed line? **B**

A $y = -\frac{1}{3}x + 3$
B $y = -\frac{1}{3}x - 3$
C $y = -3x + 3$
D $y = -3x - 3$

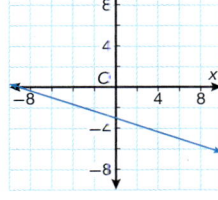

*8. **Multi-Step** The directions on a box of frozen biscuits state to cook one biscuit for 90 seconds on high and to add 15 seconds of cooking time for each additional biscuit.
a. Write a linear equation in slope-intercept form to represent the situation. Identify what the variables y and x represent.

8a. $y = 15x + 75$; y represents the total cooking time and x represents the number of biscuits.

b. **Analyze** What is the y-intercept of the graph? Does it have any meaning? Why or why not? 75; no; Sample: You would not cook 0 biscuits for 75 seconds

*9. (Measurement Conversion) The formula for converting from Celsius to Fahrenheit is $F = \frac{9}{5}C + 32$, where C is the temperature in degrees Celsius and F is the temperature in degrees Fahrenheit. Identify the slope and the y-intercept of the equation and then graph it. slope: $\frac{9}{5}$; y-intercept: 32

9.
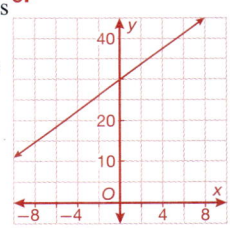

Lesson 49   311

Problem 13

Extend the Problem

"Suppose Hari surveys 20 more people and each new person surveyed has at least 4 pets. How would this affect how likely it is for the next person surveyed to have more than 4 pets?" Sample: It would increase the likelihood of the next person surveyed having more than 4 pets.

Problem 15

Have students check their answers by using another method. First have them convert the percent to a decimal. Then have them multiply the decimal by 80.

---

*10. **Pet Care** The table shows a feeding chart on the bag of a certain brand of cat food.
(49)

Maximum Weight of Cat	Amount of Food Per Day
6 lb	$\frac{3}{4}$ cup
9 lb	$1\frac{1}{4}$ cups
12 lb	$1\frac{3}{4}$ cups

a. Write an equation in slope-intercept form. $y = \frac{1}{6}x - \frac{1}{4}$

b. **Write** The three points in the table show that this is a linear equation. Do you think this relationship would be a linear equation? Explain.

10b. no; Sample: According to the x-intercept, a cat that weighs $1\frac{1}{2}$ lb should get zero cups of food a day.

11. Find the mean, median, and mode of the set of data below.
(48) number of pockets in 8 pairs of pants: 4, 2, 0, 4, 5, 4, 2, 3   mean: 3; median: 3.5; mode: 4

12. **Error Analysis** Two students studied the table of data.
(48) Student A says that the median lowest temperature per month for San Diego, California, is 38.5°F. Student B says that the median is 52.5°F. Which student is correct? Explain the error.   Student B; Sample: Student A failed to list the data in numeric order before finding the median.

Lowest Recorded Temperature in San Diego (in °F)			
July 2006	68	Jan 2007	35
Aug 2006	63	Feb 2007	45
Sep 2006	61	Mar 2007	45
Oct 2006	55	Apr 2007	50
Nov 2006	42	May 2007	55
Dec 2006	42	Jun 2007	58

*13. **Probability** Hari surveyed the first 15 students who came to
(48) class about the number of pets they owned. According to the data he collected, is the next person he surveys likely to have more than 4 pets? Explain.

2, 1, 3, 1, 1, 0, 2, 2, 3, 7, 0, 4, 2, 1, 1

14. Simplify $\frac{x^2 - 12x}{2x^2 - x} \cdot \frac{x - 12}{2x - 1}$
(43)

13. no; Sample: The data centers around the values 2 (mean and median) and 1 (mode). It is more likely that the next person surveyed will have 1 or 2 pets.

15. Find 22% of 80 using a proportion.   17.6
(42)

16. **Estimate** Approximate the slope of the line shown in the graph.   Sample: −6
(41)

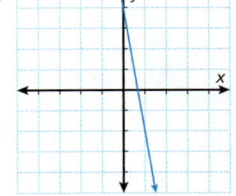

17. **Travel** Quick Cab charges a $5 fee for a ride, plus $0.15 for every block.
(28) Speedy Cab charges $7 for a ride, but only $0.05 every block. For what number of blocks is the cost of travel the same?   20 blocks

18. A deck of cards contains 15 cards, five of each number 1, 2, and 3. What
(33) are the odds of getting a 1? What are the odds against getting a 3?
5:10 or 1:2; 10:5 or 2:1

19. Write a recursive formula for the arithmetic sequence with $a_1 = -3$ and common
(34) difference $d = 9$. Then find the first four terms of the sequence.
$a_1 = -3, a_n = a_{n-1} + 9; -3, 6, 15, 24$

20. **Multi-Step** Use the similar triangles shown.
(36)
a. What angle corresponds with ∠M?   ∠Q
b. Find m∠Q.   110°
c. What is the scale factor of the triangles?   3:2 or 2:3
d. Use the scale factor to find the value of x. $\frac{20}{3}$

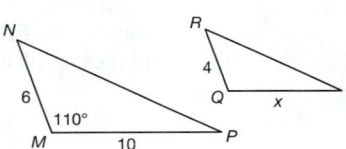

312   Saxon Algebra 1

🟥 CHALLENGE

The ordered pairs (0, 0) and (1, 4) fall on the graph of an equation. Determine the equation for the line and another point that lies on the line within quadrant III. $y = 4x$; Sample: (−3, −12)

21. (Tourism) The number of visitors to national parks in the United States each year for the years 1990 to 2005 (in millions) are as follows: 258.7, 267.8, 274.7, 273.1, 268.6, 269.6, 265.8, 275.3, 286.7, 287.1, 285.9, 279.9, 277.3, 266.1, 276.9, 273.5. Find the range of the data.   **28.4 million**

*22. Geometry Ferdinand found the areas of seven triangles. This was his data set: 7 cm², 8 cm², 12 cm², 6 cm², 7 cm², 10 cm², 6 cm². If the triangle at right has the same area as the mean value in the data set, what is the height (h) of the triangle?   **4 cm**

23. Error Analysis A box of chocolates sells for $12.50. The price of the chocolates decreased by 15% from last year. Student A and Student B tried to find the price from last year. Which student is correct? Explain the error.

23. Student B; Sample: Since the price decreased by 15%, 85% of the original price would be the current price.

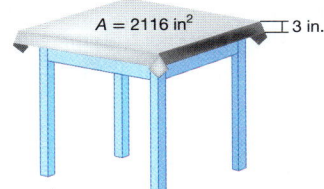

*24. Multi-Step A square table has an area of 2116 square inches. A tablecloth hangs 3 inches over each end of the table.
  a. What is the length of one side of the table?   **46 inches**
  b. What is the area of the tablecloth?   **2704 square inches**
  c. What is the area of the part of the tablecloth that hangs over the table?   **588 square inches**

*25. Analyze Copy and complete the statement with $\sqrt[4]{\sqrt{256}}$ __?__ $\sqrt{\sqrt[4]{256}}$ >, <, or =.   **=**

26. Find the percent of increase or decrease to the nearest percent from an original price of $20 to a new price of $23.   **15% increase**

27. Write an inequality for the following sentence: The sum of twice a number and $\frac{1}{3}$ is less than $1\frac{2}{3}$. $2x + \frac{1}{3} < 1\frac{2}{3}$

*28. (Remote Sensing) Satellites perform sophisticated data collection, but over time their orbits decay, affecting their measurements. In 1980 the NOAA-06 satellite was holding an orbit of 826 km. By 1996 the orbit had decayed to 804 km. What was the average rate of orbital decay for NOAA-06?   **−1.375 km/yr**

29. Analyze Determine if the following statement uses inductive or deductive reasoning. Explain your choice.   **inductive reasoning; The conclusion is based on an observed pattern.**

"If Sharon made at least one goal at each of her last soccer games, then she will make at least one goal at her next soccer game."

30. Multi-Step A leather footstool in the shape of a cube is being made for a living room. The length of one side of the footstool is $2x$ inches.
  a. What is the area of one side of the footstool? $(2x)^2$ **or** $4x^2$ **square inches**
  b. What is the surface area of leather needed to make the footstool? $5(4x^2)$ **or** $20x^2$ **square inches**

Lesson 49   313

Problem 23
Guide students by asking the following questions.

"What percent of last year's price is this year's price?" **85%**

"Is it reasonable for an amount that is 85% of an original amount to be about 10 times less the original amount?" No; Sample: If the new amount was 10 times less than the original amount, then the new amount would be 10% of the original amount.

Problem 30
Error Alert
Students may not realize that the bottom of the footstool does not need to be covered. Remind them to only consider five sides of the cube.

LOOKING FORWARD

Writing equations in slope-intercept form prepares students for

• **Lesson 52** Determining the Equation of a Line Given Two Points

• **Lesson 56** Identifying, Writing, and Graphing Direct Variation

• **Lesson 64** Identifying, Writing, and Graphing Inverse Variation

• **Lesson 65** Writing Equations of Parallel and Perpendicular Lines

LESSON 50

1 Warm Up

Problem 2
Remind students to use a variable in place of the phrase "a number."

2 New Concepts

In this lesson, students learn how to graph an inequality and to write an inequality from a graph.

Discuss how inequalities, unlike equations, are true for more than just one number.

Example 1

Error Alert Students might subtract before they multiply. Remind students to follow the order of operations.

Additional Example 1
Determine which of the values $\{0, 2, 4, 6\}$ are part of the solution set of the inequality $y - 4 \geq 2$. **6**

LESSON RESOURCES

Student Edition Practice Workbook 50
Reteaching Master 50
Adaptations Master 50
Challenge and Enrichment Master C50
Technology Lab Master 50

LESSON 50

Graphing Inequalities

Warm Up

1. **Vocabulary** A(n) _____ is a mathematical statement that compares quantities that are not equal. **inequality**

2. Translate the sentence below into an inequality.
   137 is at least 13 less than twice a number. $137 \geq 2x - 13$

Simplify.

3. $8y - 3 = 15$ $\frac{9}{4}$

4. $7 = 5x + 4$ $\frac{3}{5}$

New Concepts

A **linear inequality in one variable** is an inequality that can be written as $ax < b$, $ax > b$, $ax \leq b$, $ax \geq b$, or $ax \neq b$, where a and b are real numbers.

Unlike equations, inequalities can have more than one numeric solution.

The **solution of an inequality in one variable** is a value or set of values that satisfies the inequality. To determine if a value is a solution to an inequality, substitute the value of the variable into the equation and simplify. If the inequality statement is true, the value is part of the solution set.

Math Language
The expression $ax \neq 0$ means that x can equal any number except zero.

Example 1 Identifying Solutions to Inequalities

Determine which of the values $\{0, 2, 4, 6\}$ are part of the solution set of the inequality $4y - 5 \geq 11$.

SOLUTION

Substitute each value into the inequality.

$y = 0$ $\qquad$ $y = 2$
$4 \cdot 0 - 5 \geq 11$ $\qquad$ $4 \cdot 2 - 5 \geq 11$
$0 - 5 \geq 11$ $\qquad$ $8 - 5 \geq 11$
$-5 \geq 11$; false $\qquad$ $3 \geq 11$; false

$y = 4$ $\qquad$ $y = 6$
$4 \cdot 4 - 5 \geq 11$ $\qquad$ $4 \cdot 6 - 5 \geq 11$
$16 - 5 \geq 11$ $\qquad$ $24 - 5 \geq 11$
$11 \geq 11$; true $\qquad$ $19 \geq 11$; true

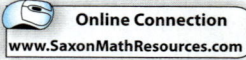
Online Connection
www.SaxonMathResources.com

The solution set for $4y - 5 \geq 11$ includes 4 and 6.

MATH BACKGROUND

Solutions to inequalities in one variable can be represented by graphing them on a number line. An infinite number of points, or solutions, can be represented by shading the line. Graphing inequalities in one variable prepares students for graphing inequalities in two variables. Inequalities in two variables are graphed on a coordinate grid. An infinite number of coordinate pairs can be represented by shading the grid.

Equivalent inequalities are inequalities that have the same solution set. It is not always reasonable to list all the values in a solution set. Instead, a graph on a number line can represent the solution set of an inequality. The graph shows the endpoint of the solution set as an open or closed circle. A heavy line and arrow indicate all values that are in the solution set.

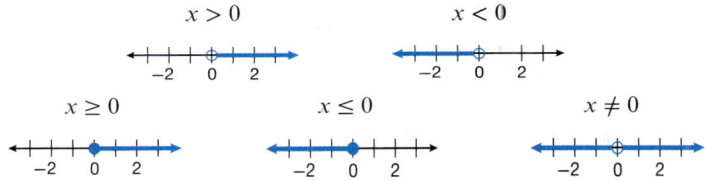

To create the graph of an inequality, first create a number line that includes the endpoint. Then determine if the endpoint should be shown with an open or closed circle. Finally, from the endpoint, draw a heavy line with an arrowhead to show the solution.

Math Reasoning

Write Why are the circles filled in for the graphs of the inequalities including ≥ and ≤?

Sample: The circles are filled in because the inequalities have "or equal to," making the value where the circle is shown part of the solution set.

Caution

When the variable is to the right of the inequality symbol, be careful to read the inequality correctly.

Example 2 Graphing Inequalities

Graph each inequality.

a. $g > 5.8$

SOLUTION

circle: open
arrowhead points to the right

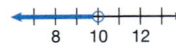

b. $v \geq 6$

SOLUTION

circle: closed
arrowhead points to the right

c. $x \leq -2$

SOLUTION

circle: closed
arrowhead points to the left

d. $10 > j$

SOLUTION

circle: open
arrowhead points to the left

The graph of an inequality can be translated to symbolic form. First identify the endpoint. If the endpoint is closed, the inequality includes that value and is represented using either ≥ or ≤. If the endpoint is open, the inequality does not include that value and is represented using either > or <.

Example 2

Graphing solutions to inequalities in one variable gives a visual representation that may help make the solution set clearer to students.

Additional Example 2

Graph each inequality.

a. $w < 7.9$

b. $p \geq 3$

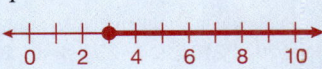

c. $y \leq -8$

d. $4 > t$

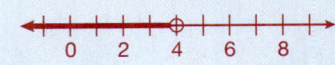

Lesson 50   315

ENGLISH LEARNERS

Explain the meaning of **symbolic form.** Draw a knife and fork on the chalkboard and below them write the words knife and fork. Say:

"**Symbolic form refers to how something is shown. For example, a knife and fork can be represented in symbolic form with a picture or with words.**"

Discuss which forms are most helpful in a public place.

Example 3
Additional Example 3
Write an inequality for each graph.

a.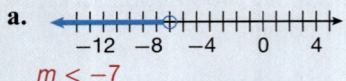
$m < -7$

b.
10 12 14 16 18 20
$n \leq 15$

c.
0 $1\frac{1}{3}$ $1\frac{2}{3}$ 1 $1\frac{1}{3}$ $2\frac{2}{3}$ $2\frac{1}{3}$ $2\frac{2}{3}$
$z > \frac{2}{3}$

d.
200 210 220 230 240 250
$q \geq 201$

TEACHER TIP
Encourage students to test their equations by substituting values shown on the graphs for the variable.

Example 4
Error Alert Students may graph values less than 0.5 to represent "at least." Remind them that "at least" means greater than or equal to.

Extend the Example
"If Marie practices more than half an hour, write an inequality to represent the number of hours that she practices." $h > 0.5$

Additional Example 4
The temperature on a winter day is no more than 40°F.

a. Write an inequality showing the possible temperatures on the winter day. $t \leq 40$

b. Graph the solution set of the inequality.

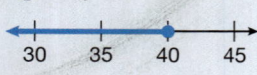

Example 3 Writing an Inequality from a Graph
Write an inequality for each graph.

a.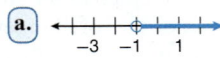

SOLUTION
endpoint: -1 inequality: $>$
$k > -1$

b.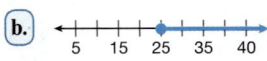

SOLUTION
endpoint: 25   inequality: $\geq$
$n \geq 25$

c.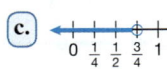

SOLUTION
endpoint: $\frac{3}{4}$ inequality: $<$
$r < \frac{3}{4}$

d.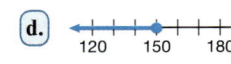

SOLUTION
endpoint: 150   inequality: $\leq$
$z \leq 150$

Math Reasoning
Analyze Although the graph of an inequality for a problem-solving situation includes a wide range of values, the problem will create some restrictions. What restrictions would be placed on this problem?

Sample: Marie probably will not practice for more than a few hours.

Example 4 Application: Practice Time
Marie does not take a break until she has practiced playing the violin for at least half an hour.

a. Write an inequality to represent the number of hours that Marie must practice before she takes a break.

SOLUTION Let h represent the number of hours that Marie practices. The phrase "at least" can be represented with $\geq$.
$h \geq 0.5$

b. Graph the solution set of the inequality.

SOLUTION Identify the endpoint (0.5), determine if the circle is open or closed (closed), and the direction in which the arrowhead points (to the right).

-1 0 1

Lesson Practice

a. Determine which of the values $\{-2, 0, 5, 11\}$ are part of the solution set
(Ex 1) of the inequality $3x + 4 < 19$. -2 and 0

Graph each inequality.

b. $u > -2$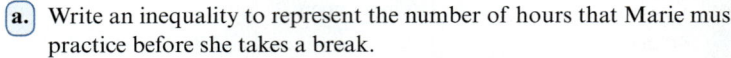
(Ex 2)

c. $t \geq 2.5$
(Ex 2)   1 2 3 4

316 **Saxon** Algebra 1

INCLUSION

When writing and graphing inequalities for word problems, it may be helpful for students to begin by drawing a number line and circling several allowable values until a pattern emerges. Then, have them write the inequality.

Have students write and graph an inequality showing that Frank has at least $5 in his wallet.

Draw the number line and circle several allowable values.

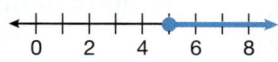

Once a pattern emerges, tell students to shade in the line and to write the inequality. $m \geq 5$

d. $y \leq 3\frac{1}{3}$ (Ex 2)

e. $0 > v$ (Ex 2)

Write an inequality for each graph.

f. (Ex 3) $m > 0.5$

g. (Ex 3) $n \geq 12$

h. (Ex 3) $g < 45$

i. (Ex 3) $p \leq \frac{2}{5}$

j. (Ex 4) **Chemistry** The boiling point of a liquid is the temperature at which it changes into a gas. The boiling point of water under normal atmospheric conditions is 100°C. Write an inequality to represent the temperatures for which water is a gas. Graph the solution set of the inequality. $t \geq 100$

Practice   Distributed and Integrated

Factor the greatest common factor.

1. (38) $6k^5m^2 - 2k^3m - km$ $km(6k^4m - 2k^2 - 1)$

2. (38) $mx^4y^2 - m^2x^3y^3 + 5m^2x^6y^2$ $mx^3y^2(x - my + 5mx^3)$

Simplify.

3. (40) $\left(\dfrac{2x}{3y^4}\right)^3$ $\dfrac{8x^3}{27y^{12}}$

4. (40) $(2x^3y^2)^4$ $16x^{12}y^8$

5. (1) True or False: The set of whole numbers is closed under subtraction. If false, give a counterexample.   false; $3 - 5 = -2$, and -2 is not a whole number.

6. (44) Determine the slope of the line shown in the graph. $m = \dfrac{9}{14}$

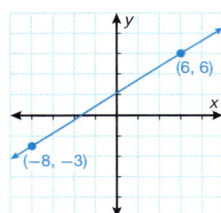

7. (35) Write $5x - 2 = 6y$ in standard form. $5x - 6y = 2$

8. (46) Write the expression $\sqrt[4]{y}$ with a fractional exponent. $y^{\frac{1}{4}}$

9. (33) **Probability** 7 cards labeled P, E, R, C, E, N, and T are in a jar. Find the probability of picking a P and then an E if the card drawn is not replaced. $\dfrac{1}{21}$

Lesson 50   317

Lesson Practice

Problem a

Error Alert Students might misread the inequality and think it is inclusive of 19. Remind them that if there is no underline under the greater-than sign, the inequality is exclusive.

Problem j

Scaffolding Before writing an inequality, suggest that students rephrase the problem. Sample: Water is a gas if its temperature is 100°C or higher.

Check for Understanding

The questions below help assess the concepts taught in this lesson.

"Explain how to identify if a number is part of a solution set for an inequality." Substitute the value into the inequality. Simplify the inequality and see if it is true or false. If it is true, the number is part of the solution set; if it is false, the number is not part of the solution set.

"Explain how to graph an inequality." Identify the endpoint and then determine if the point is open or closed. Then, determine which direction the arrow points.

3 Practice

Math Conversations

Discussion to strengthen understanding

Problem 8

Error Alert

Students may confuse fractional exponents with negative exponents. Remind them that a number raised to a negative exponent is equivalent to the inverse of the number raised to the positive exponent.

Lesson 50   317

Problem 10
Have students read carefully to find that the problem is asking for odds, not probability.

Problem 11
Encourage students to use the formula to find the fifth and twelfth terms. Use of the formula will help them recall it when working problems in which finding each term is tedious or time-consuming.

Problem 19
Since both lines pass through the origin, they are each the graph of a direct variation $y = ax$. Remind students that therefore, the ratio of y to x will be the slope of the line.

Problem 20
Extend the Problem
"Suppose Janis wants to know what 41% of 212 is. How could she find the percent using mental math?" Sample: She can find half of 10% and add it to 36% of 212.

---

10. (Vacation) At an amusement park, there are 5000 families. Ten families are chosen to have a meal with the park's owner each day. What are the odds that a family will be chosen?   1:499

11. Write a rule for the nth term of the sequence with $a_1 = 32$ and common difference $d = -6$. Then find the fifth and twelfth terms of the sequence.
$a_n = 32 + (n-1)(-6)$; 8; -34

*12. **Error Analysis** Two students wrote the equation $3x + 5y = 15$ in slope-intercept form. Which student is correct? Explain the error.   Student A; Sample: Student B solved the equation for x instead of for y.

Student A	Student B
$y = -\frac{3}{5}x + 3$	$x = -\frac{5}{3}y + 5$

*13. Determine which values in the set $\{-6, 0, 1, 6\}$ are solutions to the inequality $-2y + 3 < 0$.   6

*14. **Multiple Choice** Which of the following inequalities describes the graph?   A

A $x \leq 7$ B $7 < x$
C $x \geq 7$ D $x > 7$

*15. **Write** Explain how to graph the inequality $n \geq 12$.

15. Sample: Draw a number line and label several numbers, including 12. Draw a circle at the location of 12 and fill it in. Then shade the section of the number line to the right of the circle.

16. **Formulate** How could Yalda write the inequality $x \neq 2$ as two separate inequalities?
$x < 2, x > 2$, or the graph of $x \neq 2$ is all values except 2

17. **Multi-Step** The approximate diameter of Earth is 12,756,000 meters. The diameter of the Sun is approximately 695,900,000 meters.
   a. Write these distances in scientific notation. 1.2756×10^7; 6.959×10^8
   b. About how many times larger is the Sun than Earth in diameter?
   approximately 5.5×10^1, or about 55 times

18. (Physical Science) The formula $E = mc^2$ represents the amount of energy E, in joules, contained in an object with a given mass m, in kilograms. The variable c represents the speed of light, which is about 3×10^8 meters per second. Find the amount of energy in an object weighing 2 kg. 1.8×10^{17} joules

19. **Multi-Step** Ivan and Jed are both reading the same book for a school report. The graph shows the number of pages they read over time.
   a. What is Ivan's reading rate?   0.8 page/min
   b. What is Jed's reading rate?   0.9 page/min

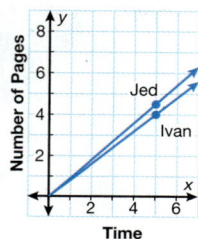

*20. **Justify** Janis is trying to find 36% of 212 using mental math. She knows how to find 25% of 212, 10% of 212, and 1% of 212. Can she use the sum of these percentages to find 36% of 212? Why or why not?   yes; Sample: Because of the Distributive Property of Multiplication, she can break the problem apart.

21. Simplify the rational expression $\frac{6x+30}{36x+6}$. State any excluded values. $\frac{x+5}{6x+1}, x \neq -\frac{1}{6}$

318   Saxon Algebra 1

⭐ CHALLENGE

Marie is planning a bowling party. The bowling alley allows no more than 12 players in 2 lanes. Ask students to explain if an inequality would be appropriate to represent this situation. An inequality is appropriate with a restriction of the domain being positive integers.

*22. **Personal Finance** Ricardo babysits his brother for $5 per hour. He wants to earn
(45) enough money to buy a new game console that costs $280. If he has already saved
$135, write an inequality that represents the least number of hours of babysitting
he needs to do to be able to buy the game console. **$5h + 135 \geq 280$, where h is the
number of hours**

23. **Multiple Choice** 49 changes to 45. Find the percent of increase or decrease. **B**
(47)
   A 4%   **B** 8%   **C** 2%   **D** 6%

24. **Write** Kwami's video game collection increased from 6 video games to 9 video
(47) games. Lisa's CD collection increased from 20 CDs to 28 CDs. Compare the
amount of increase and the percents of increase of both collections.

24. Sample: Kwami's collection increased by 3 which is a 50% increase. Lisa's collection increased by 8 which is a 40% increase.

*25. Troy recorded the number of minutes 11 people spent jogging: 25, 26, 18, 28, 20,
(48) 15, 27, 70, 32, 15, 21. Find the mean, median, and mode for the data.
mean: 27; median: 25; mode: 15

26. Two students looked at the following data that show the number of hospitals in
(48) each state. Find the range of the data. **412**

    108, 19, 62, 87, 361, 70, 35, 6, 203, 146, 24, 39, 191, 113, 115, 134, 105,
    131, 37, 50, 78, 144, 132, 93, 119, 54, 85, 30, 28, 80, 37, 206, 115, 40,
    166, 109, 58, 197, 11, 62, 51, 127, 418, 43, 14, 88, 85, 57, 121, 24

27. **Write** Doyle wrote the linear equation of a graphed line for a homework problem.
(49) Explain how a table of values for the graph of a linear equation can be used to
verify his answer. Sample: If he creates a table of values using the equation, he can
make sure that those ordered pairs are on the line in the original graph.

*28. **Geometry** Write an equation in slope-intercept form that shows the
(49) relationship between the perimeter of a square (y) and the length (x)
of a side. Graph the equation and find the coordinates of 3 points on
the line. $y = 4x$; Sample: (0, 0), (1, 4), (2, 8)

28.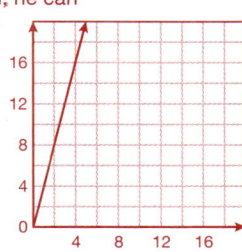

*29. **Hobbies** Jean Claude is making painted candles to sell at a local craft
(49) market. He purchased $185 in materials and sells each candle for $7.50.
   a. Write a linear equation in slope-intercept form that can be used to
     calculate his profit (y) based on the number of candles sold (x). $y = 7.5x - 185$
   b. Use a graphing calculator to graph the equation.
   c. How many candles must Jean Claude sell to make a profit? **25 candles**

29b.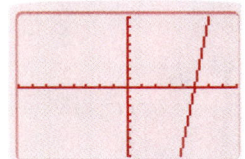

*30. **Chemistry** The freezing temperature of water at normal
(50) atmospheric conditions is 32°F. Write and graph an
inequality to model the temperatures at which water
freezes. $t \leq 32$;

Lesson 50   319

LOOKING FORWARD

Graphing inequalities prepares students for

- **Lesson 66** Solving Inequalities by Adding or Subtracting
- **Lesson 70** Solving Inequalities by Multiplying or Dividing
- **Lesson 73** Solving Compound Inequalities
- **Lesson 77** Solving Two-Step and Multi-Step Inequalities

Problem 25
Guide students by asking the following questions.

"How do you find the mean of the data?" Find the sum of the values and divide by the number of values.

"How could you arrange the numbers to find the median?" Sample: You could arrange the numbers from least to greatest.

"How do you find the mode of the data?" You find the number that occurs most frequently.

Problem 26
Suggest that students create a table to find the least and greatest data values. Have them write the first number in the list in the first row and column of the table. Then have them scan from that number on through the list for a smaller number and write it in the table below the first number. Students continue to scan and fill in the table until the least number is found. Have students find the greatest number in a similar manner.

Least	Greatest
~~108~~	~~108~~
~~19~~	~~361~~
6	418

$418 - 6 = 412$

Problem 28
Guide students by asking them the following question.

"If you know the length of 1 side of a square, how can you find the perimeter?" You can multiply the length by 4.

Lesson 50   319

INVESTIGATION 5

Using Logical Reasoning

Recall from Investigation 4 that a conditional statement has a hypothesis and a conclusion. For any conditional statement, a converse, inverse, and contrapositive can be written.

In the **converse** of a conditional statement the order of the hypothesis and conclusion of the original statement is reversed.

Original	Converse
If a figure is a triangle, then it has three sides.	If a figures has three sides, then it is a triangle.

Math Language
To **negate** a statement means to state its opposite using the word not.

The **inverse** of a conditional statement negates both the hypothesis and the conclusion.

Original	Inverse
If a figure is a triangle, then it has three sides.	If a figure is not a triangle, then it does not have three sides.

The **contrapositive** switches the hypothesis and the conclusion and negates both.

Original	Contrapositive
If a figure is a triangle, then it has three sides.	If a figure does not have three sides, then it is not a triangle.

Write the given statement in the form indicated. Note whether the new statement is true or false. If false, give a counterexample.

1. Write the converse. If a number ends in 5, then it is a multiple of 5.
   See Additional Answers.
2. Write the contrapositive. If two lines are parallel, then they do not meet.   If two lines meet, then they are not parallel.; true
3. Write the inverse. If it is Monday, then I will go to school.
   See Additional Answers.
4. Write the inverse. If a number is even, then it is divisible by two.
   If a number is not even, then it is not divisible by two.; true

The statement, "Dallas is the capital of New York," is false. However, saying "Dallas is not the capital of New York" is true. The truth value of a statement is either true or false.

5. Complete the table to compare the truth values of an original statement and its contrapositive.

Original	True or False	Contrapositive	True or False
If a figure is a square, then it is a rectangle.	true	If a figure is not a rectangle, then it is not a square.	true
If a number is odd, then it is divisible by 2.	false	If a number is not divisible by 2, then it is not odd.	false

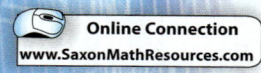
Online Connection
www.SaxonMathResources.com

INVESTIGATION 5

Discuss
Logical reasoning usually involves if/then statements. For example, "If it is snowing, then it must be below 32°F." These statements can be true or false. To show that a conditional statement is false, students need to change the statement to a converse, inverse, and contrapositive to show that the hypothesis is true but the conclusion is false.

Problem 1
Extend the Problem
Have students write a false mathematical statement. Have them write a converse, inverse, and contrapositive. Note whether the statement is true or false.
Sample: If two odd numbers are added together, then the sum of the two numbers is odd.
a. Converse: If the sum of two numbers is odd, then two odd numbers are added together.; false
b. Contrapositive: If the sum of two numbers is not odd, then two numbers that were not odd were added together.; false
c. Inverse: If two numbers that are not odd are added together, then the sum of the two numbers is not odd.; true

INVESTIGATION RESOURCES

Reteaching Master
Investigation 5

MATH BACKGROUND

Understanding the components of logical reasoning is necessary for proving and disproving statements. Mathematicians use geometric proofs to validate theorems and conjectures. The fields of law, science, and medicine, as well as the study of philosophy, also use logical reasoning. By breaking a conditional statement into a hypothesis and conclusion, one can test each part of the statement to prove its validity.

Logical reasoning can be helpful in spotting false claims in advertising and in learning to discuss ideas and issues articulately.

6. What is the relationship of the truth values of an original statement and its contrapositive?   Sample: They have the same truth values.

7. To compare the truth values of the converse and inverse, complete the table for each original statement.

   Original statement: If a figure is a square, then it is a rectangle.

		True or False
Converse	If a figure is a rectangle, then it is a square.	false
Inverse	If a figure is not a square, then it is not a rectangle.	false

   Original statement: If an object has wheels, then it is a bicycle.

		True or False
Converse	If an object is a bicycle, then it has wheels.	true
Inverse	If an object does not have wheels, then it is not a bicycle.	true

8. What is the relationship of the truth values of the converse and inverse of an original statement?   Sample: They have the same truth values.

Investigation Practice

Write the given statement in the form indicated.

Original statement: If it is raining, then it is cloudy.

a. Write the contrapositive.   If it is not cloudy, then it is not raining.
b. Write the converse.   If it is cloudy, then it is raining.
c. Write the inverse.   If it is not raining, then it is not cloudy.
d. **Generalize** If the original statement is true, what is the truth value of the contrapositive?   true
e. **Predict** If the converse of a statement is false, what is the truth value of the inverse of the statement?   false

f. contrapositive; The original statement and the contrapositive are true.

Identify Statement 2 as the converse, inverse, or contrapositive of Statement 1. Then indicate the truth value of each statement.

f. Statement 1: If a figure is a rectangle, then it is not a triangle.
   Statement 2: If a figure is a triangle, then it is not a rectangle.
g. Statement 1: If a figure is not a polygon, then it is not a right triangle.
   Statement 2: If a figure is a polygon, then it is a right triangle.
   inverse; The original statement is true, but the inverse is false.

Investigation 5   321

 ENGLISH LEARNERS

Explain the meaning of the word **original.** Say:

"Original means coming before all others in time or order. For example, the original story told is the first story that is told."

Ask a volunteer to tell about an original object with which they are familiar. Sample: I saw the original U.S. Constitution in Washington, D. C.

 LOOKING FORWARD

Using logical reasoning prepares students for

- **Investigation 10** Transforming Quadratic Functions
- **Investigation 11** Investigating Exponential Growth and Decay
- **Investigation 12** Multiplying Matrices

Discuss
Changing a conditional statement to the converse, inverse, and contrapositive, affects the wording, and in some instances, the truth of the statement.

Error Alert
Some students may only negate part of the statement when changing the statement to the inverse and contrapositive forms. Make sure they negate both the hypothesis and conclusion. No part of the statement is negated in the converse form.

Investigation Practice

Math Conversations
Discussion to strengthen understanding

Problem a
Scaffolding
Guide students by asking them the following questions.

"What is the hypothesis?" If it is raining

"What is the conclusion?" then it is cloudy

"What happens to the hypothesis and conclusion when the statement changes to a contrapositive?" They are switched and both negated.

Problem e
TEACHER TIP
Have students write a conditional statement that is true, then write the converse so that it is false. Have them use their example to determine the truth value of the inverse of the original statement.

Problem d
Error Alert Changing the statement to one of the four forms does not simply change it from true to false or vice versa. Remind students to read the statement again to determine its truth value.

Investigation 5   321

SECTION OVERVIEW

6

Lesson Planner

Lesson	New Concepts
51	Simplifying Rational Expressions with Like Denominators
52	Determining the Equation of a Line Given Two Points
53	Adding and Subtracting Polynomials
LAB 4	Graphing Calculator: Drawing Box-and-Whisker Plots
54	Displaying Data in a Box-and-Whisker Plot
LAB 5	Graphing Calculator: Calculating the Intersection of Two Lines
55	Solving Systems of Linear Equations by Graphing
	Cumulative Test 10, Performance Task 10
56	Identifying, Writing, and Graphing Direct Variation
57	Finding the Least Common Multiple
58	Multiplying Polynomials
59	Solving Systems of Linear Equations by Substitution
60	Finding Special Products of Binomials
	Cumulative Test 11, Performance Task 11
INV 6	Investigation: Transforming Linear Functions

Resources for Teaching

- Student Edition
- Teacher's Edition
- Student Edition eBook
- Teacher's Edition eBook
- Resources and Planner CD
- Solutions Manual
- Instructional Masters
- Technology Lab Masters
- Warm Up and Teaching Transparencies
- Instructional Presentations CD
- Online activities, tools, and homework help www.SaxonMathResources.com

Resources for Practice and Assessment

- Student Edition Practice Workbook
- Course Assessments
- Standardized Test Practice
- College Entrance Exam Practice
- Test and Practice Generator CD using ExamView™

Resources for Differentiated Instruction

- Reteaching Masters
- Challenge and Enrichment Masters
- Prerequisite Skills Intervention
- Adaptations for Saxon Algebra 1
- Multilingual Glossary
- English Learners Handbook
- TI Resources

Pacing Guide

 Resources and Planner CD for lesson planning support

45-Minute Class

Day 1	Day 2	Day 3	Day 4	Day 5	Day 6
Lesson 51	Lesson 52	Lesson 53	Lab 4 Lesson 54	Lab 5 Lesson 55	Cumulative Test 10
Day 7	**Day 8**	**Day 9**	**Day 10**	**Day 11**	**Day 12**
Lesson 56	Lesson 57	Lesson 58	Lesson 59	Lesson 60	Cumulative Test 11
Day 13					
Investigation 6					

Block: 90-Minute Class

Day 1	Day 2	Day 3	Day 4	Day 5	Day 6
Lesson 51 Lesson 52	Lesson 53 Lab 4 Lesson 54	Lab 5 Lesson 55 Cumulative Test 10	Lesson 56 Lesson 57	Lesson 58 Lesson 59	Lesson 60 Cumulative Test 11
Day 7					
Investigation 6 Lesson 61					

*For suggestions on how to implement Saxon Math in a block schedule, see the Pacing section at the beginning of the Teacher's Edition.

Differentiated Instruction

Below Level		Advanced Learners	
Warm Up	SE pp. 322, 329, 335, 345, 354, 361, 368, 375, 382, 390	Challenge	TE pp. 328, 334, 341, 351, 360, 366, 373, 380, 389, 395
Skills Bank	SE pp. 846–883	Extend the Example	TE pp. 324, 331, 338, 347, 356, 364, 371, 378, 386, 392
Reteaching Masters	Lessons 51–60, Investigation 6		
Warm Up Transparencies	Lessons 51–60	Extend the Exploration	TE pp. 337, 361, 376, 390
Prerequisite Skills Intervention	Skills 1, 2, 61, 62, 63, 64, 65, 75	Extend the Problem	TE pp. 327, 333, 334, 340, 341, 349, 358, 367, 373, 374, 379, 380, 381, 388, 394, 396, 397
		Challenge and Enrichment Masters	Challenge: 51–60; Enrichment: 58, 60

English Learners		Special Needs	
EL Tips	TE pp. 324, 332, 340, 348, 355, 365, 369, 376, 383, 391, 397	Inclusion Tips	TE pp. 325, 330, 336, 350, 357, 363, 371, 378, 384, 392
Multilingual Glossary	Booklet and Online	Adaptations for Saxon Algebra 1	Lessons 51–60, Cumulative Tests 10, 11
English Learners Handbook			

For All Learners			
Exploration	SE pp. 337, 361, 376, 390	Alternate Method	TE pp. 323, 331, 338, 346, 347, 356, 358, 370, 377, 386
Caution	SE pp. 335, 338, 371, 378, 384, 391	Manipulative Use	TE pp. 339
Hints	SE pp. 323, 324, 329, 330, 348, 362, 370, 383, 384, 386, 390, 396	Online Tools	
Error Alert	TE pp. 322, 325, 326, 328, 330, 331, 333, 335, 338, 339, 340, 341, 342, 346, 348, 349, 351, 356, 357, 358, 362, 365, 369, 372, 373, 377, 378, 379, 381, 386, 387, 391, 393, 394, 395, 397		

SE = Student Edition; TE = Teacher's Edition

Math Vocabulary

Lesson	New Vocabulary		Maintained	EL Tip in TE
51			GCF rational	exclude
52	point-slope form		slope slope formula x-coordinate y-coordinate	applicant
53	binomial degree of a monomial degree of a polynomial leading coefficient monomial	polynomial standard form of a polynomial trinomial	coefficient like terms term variable	inflation
54	box-and-whisker plot		mean median outlier	trainer
55	solution of a system of linear equations system of linear equations		slope-intercept form solution	system
56	constant of variation direct variation		constant proportional	manufacturer
57			multiple prime prime factor	LCM
58			binomial monomial trinomial	exploration
59			ordered pair solution	substitute
60	perfect-square trinomials		binomial polynomial	perfect-square trinomial
INV 6	family of functions parent function	reflection translation	linear function	transformations

Section Overview 6   322B

SECTION OVERVIEW 6

Math Highlights

Enduring Understandings – The "Big Picture"

After completing Section 6, students will understand:
- How to simplify rational expressions, add and subtract polynomials, and find special products of binomials.
- How to identify, write, and graph direct variation, and write the equation of a line given two points.
- How to solve a system of equation by graphing and substitution.
- How to use a box-and-whisker plot to display data.

Essential Questions

- When is a rational expression undefined and what are the excluded values?
- How can any two points on a line be used to write the equation of a line?
- When is a polynomial in standard form and when is a polynomial a perfect-square trinomial?
- What is the significance of the quartiles of a box-and-whisker plot and how can interquartiles be used to determine outliers?
- Why is the point of intersection of a system of equations the solution of that system?
- When does a linear equation represent a direct variation?

Math Content Strands		Math Processes	
Linear Equations and Functions		**Reasoning and Communication**	
• Lesson 52	Determining the Equation of a Line Given Two Points		*Lessons*
• Lesson 56	Identifying, Writing, and Graphing Direct Variation	• Analyze	51, 52, 56, 57, 58, Inv. 6
• Investigation 6	Transforming Linear Functions	• Connect	58
		• Error analysis	51, 52, 53, 54, 55, 56, 57, 58, 59, 60
Polynomials		• Estimate	55, 59
• Lesson 53	Adding and Subtracting Polynomials	• Formulate	54, 56, 58, 59
• Lesson 58	Multiplying Polynomials	• Generalize	53, 56, 57, Inv. 6
• Lesson 60	Finding Special Products of Binomials	• Justify	51, 57, 60
		• Math Reasoning	51, 52, 53, 54, 56, 57, 58, 59, 60, Inv. 6
Probability and Data Analysis		• Model	53, 56, 58
• Lesson 54	Displaying Data in a Box-and-Whisker Plot	• Multiple choice	51, 52, 53, 54, 55, 56, 57, 58, 59, 60
• Lab 4	Graphing Calculator: Drawing Box-and-Whisker Plots	• Multi-step	51, 52, 53, 54, 55, 56, 57, 58, 59, 60
		• Predict	52, 53, 57, Inv. 6
		• True or False	59
		• Verify	53, 55, 56, 57, 58, 59, 60
Rational Expressions and Functions		• Write	51, 52, 53, 54, 55, 56, 57, 58, 59, 60, Inv. 6
• Lesson 51	Simplifying Rational Expressions with Like Denominators		
• Lesson 57	Finding the Least Common Multiple	• Graphing Calculator	52, 53, 54, 55, 57
Systems of Equations and Inequalities		**Connections**	
• Lesson 55	Solving Systems of Linear Equations by Graphing	**In Examples:** Area of sandbox, Fencing a field, Gardening, Internet, Play tickets, Rate plans, Sales, Scheduling	
• Lesson 59	Solving Systems of Linear Equations by Substitution	**In Practice problems:** Advertisement, Astronomy, Automotive maintinance, Automotive performance, Baseball, Basketball, Biology, Business, Camping, Carpentry, Charity, Chemistry, Clocks, Currency, Energy, Finance, Fitness, Football, Framing, Games, Golf, Handicap ramps, Hobby, Installation, Law enforcement, Leisure time, Manufacturing, Market research, Meteorology, Painting, Phone rates, Phone service, Physics, Produce cost, Production design, Rockets, Running, Savings accounts, Simple interest, Soccer, Telecommunications, Tennis, Transportation, Travel, Water polo, Weather, Web design, Zoo	
• Lab 5	Graphing Calculator: Calculating the Intersection of Two Lines		
Connections in Practice Problems			
	Lessons		
Data Analysis	52, 58, 60		
Geometry	51, 52, 53, 54, 56, 57, 58, 59, 60		
Measurement	51, 53, 54, 56, 57, 58, 59, 60		
Probability	55		

Content Trace

Lesson	Warm Up: Prerequisite Skills	New Concepts	Where Practiced	Where Assessed	Looking Forward
51	Lessons 18, 38, 39	Simplifying Rational Expressions with Like Denominators	Lessons 52, 53, 54, 55, 56, 57, 58, 59, 60, 61, 64, 66, 67, 111, 112	Cumulative Tests 11, 12	Lessons 57, 78, 88, 90, 92, 99
52	Lessons 35, 36, 41	Determining the Equation of a Line Given Two Points	Lessons 53, 54, 55, 56, 58, 60, 61, 62, 65, 67, 68, 99	Cumulative Tests 11, 12, 13, 16	Lessons 56, 64, 65
53	Lessons 2, 32, 38	Adding and Subtracting Polynomials	Lessons 54, 55, 56, 57, 58, 59, 60, 61, 62, 63, 66, 68, 69, 98, 113	Cumulative Tests 11, 12, 17	Lessons 58, 60, 72, 75, 79, 83, 87, 93, 95
54	Lessons 11, 48	Displaying Data in a Box-and-Whisker Plot	Lessons 55, 56, 57, 58, 59, 60, 61, 62, 63, 64, 67, 69, 70	Cumulative Tests 11, 14	Lesson 62
55	Lessons 9, 30, 35, 49	Solving Systems of Linear Equations by Graphing	Lessons 56, 57, 60, 61, 62, 63, 64, 65, 68, 70, 71	Cumulative Test 11	Lessons 59, 63, 67, 97
56	Lessons 2, 25, 29	Identifying, Writing, and Graphing Direct Variation	Lessons 57, 58, 59, 60, 61, 62, 63, 64, 66, 69, 71, 72, 117	Cumulative Tests 12, 13, 16, 17	Lessons 64, 65, Investigations 6, 7, 8
57	Lesson 38	Finding the Least Common Multiple	Lessons 58, 59, 60, 61, 62, 63, 64, 65, 66, 67, 70, 72, 73, 101, 118	Cumulative Tests 12, 13, 15	Lessons 78, 88, 90, 92, 99
58	Lessons 15, 18, 53	Multiplying Polynomials	Lessons 59, 60, 61, 62, 63, 64, 65, 66, 67, 68, 71, 73, 74, 97, 102	Cumulative Tests 12, 13, 14, 17	Lessons 60, 72, 75, 79
59	Lessons 23, 26, 55	Solving Systems of Linear Equations by Substitution	Lessons 60, 61, 62, 63, 64, 65, 66, 67, 68, 69, 72, 74, 75, 103	Cumulative Tests 12, 13	Lessons 63, 67, 97, 109
60	Lessons 53, 58	Finding Special Products of Binomials	Lessons 61, 62, 63, 64, 65, 66, 67, 68, 69, 70, 73, 75, 76, 104, 105	Cumulative Tests 12, 13, 15, 16	Lessons 72, 75, 79, 83, 87
INV 6	N/A	Investigation: Transforming Linear Functions	Lessons 63, 66, 70, 89	Cumulative Test 12	Investigations 7, 8, 10, 11

SECTION OVERVIEW 6

Ongoing Assessment

	Type	Feature	Intervention *
BEFORE instruction	Assess Prior Knowledge	• Diagnostic Test	• Prerequisite Skills Intervention
BEFORE the lesson	Formative	• Warm Up	• Skills Bank • Reteaching Masters
DURING the lesson	Formative	• Lesson Practice • Math Conversations with the Practice problems	• Additional Examples in TE • Test and Practice Generator (for additional practice sheets)
AFTER the lesson	Formative	• Check for Understanding (closure)	• Scaffolding Questions in TE
AFTER 5 lessons	Summative	After Lesson 55 • Cumulative Test 10 • Performance Task 10 After Lesson 60 • Cumulative Test 11 • Performance Task 11	• Reteaching Masters • Test and Practice Generator (for additional tests and practice)
AFTER 20 lessons	Summative	• Benchmark Tests	• Reteaching Masters • Test and Practice Generator (for additional tests and practice)

* for students not showing progress during the formative stages or scoring below 80% on the summative assessments

Evidence of Learning – What Students Should Know

Because the Saxon philosophy is to provide students with sufficient time to learn and practice each concept, a lesson's topic will not be tested until at least five lessons after the topic is introduced.

On the Cumulative Tests that are given during this section of ten lessons, students should be able to demonstrate the following competencies:
- Graph a line given its equation in slope-intercept form.
- Write equations in slope-intercept form or point-slope form.
- Write a polynomial in standard form.
- Translate inequalities into words, and graph inequalities.
- Recognize and extend arithmetic sequences.
- Simplify rational expressions and expressions with higher-order roots.
- Solve percent problems.
- Identify outliers and find measures of central tendency.
- Analyze the effects of bias in sampling methods.
- Analyze box-and-whisker plots.

Test and Practice Generator CD using ExamView™

The Test and Practice Generator is an easy-to-use benchmark and assessment tool that creates unlimited practice and tests in multiple formats and allows you to customize questions or create new ones. A variety of reports are available to track student progress toward mastery of the standards throughout the year.

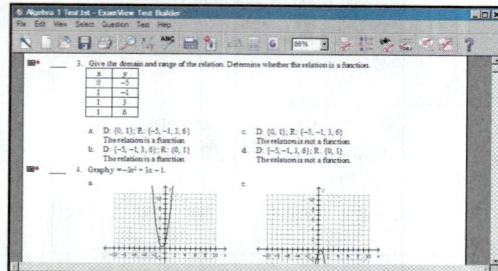
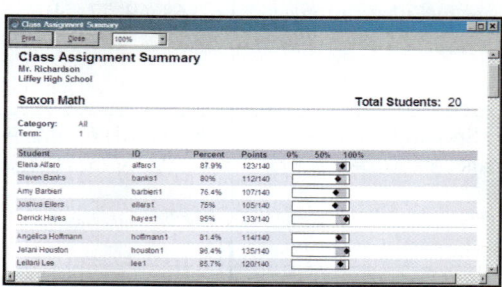

Saxon Algebra 1

Lessons 51–60, Investigation 6

Assessment Resources

Resources for Diagnosing and Assessing

- **Student Edition**
  - Warm Up
  - Lesson Practice

- **Teacher's Edition**
  - Math Conversations with the Practice problems
  - Check for Understanding (closure)

- **Course Assessments**
  - Diagnostic Test
  - Cumulative Tests
  - Performance Tasks
  - Benchmark Tests

Resources for Test Prep

- **Student Edition Practice**
  - Multiple-choice practice problems
  - Multiple-step and writing problems
  - Daily cumulative practice

- **Standardized Test Practice**

- **College Entrance Exam Practice**

- **Test and Practice Generator CD using ExamView™**

Resources for Intervention

- **Student Edition**
  - Skills Bank

- **Teacher's Edition**
  - Additional Examples
  - Scaffolding questions

- **Prerequisite Skills Intervention**
  - Worksheets

- **Reteaching Masters**
  - Lesson instruction and practice sheets

- **Test and Practice Generator CD using ExamView™**
  - Lesson practice problems
  - Additional tests

Cumulative Tests

The assessments in Saxon Math are frequent and consistently placed after every five lessons to offer a regular method of ongoing testing. These cumulative assessments check mastery of concepts from previous lessons.

Performance Tasks

The Performance Tasks can be used in conjunction with the Cumulative Tests and are scored using a rubric.

After Lesson 55

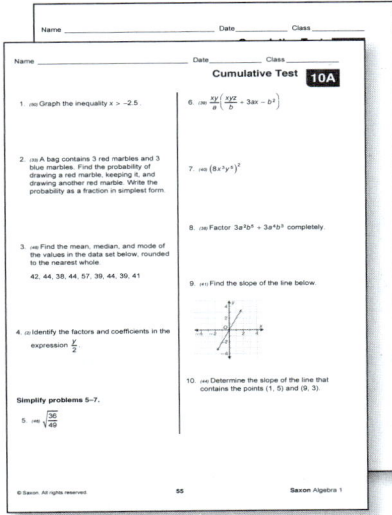

After Lesson 60

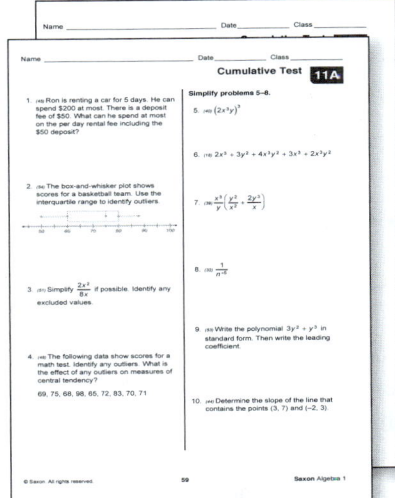

For use with Performance Tasks

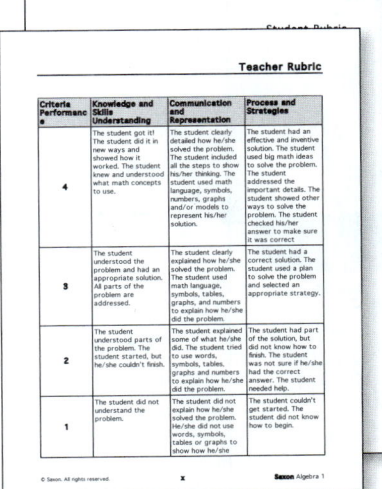

Section Overview 6   322F

LESSON 51

1 Warm Up

Problem 4
Remind students that the GCF can be a variable.

2 New Concepts

In this lesson, students learn to simplify rational expressions with like denominators. They also learn to identify excluded values.

Example 1

Students identify any excluded values of the expressions.

Additional Example 1
Find the excluded value(s) in each expression.

a. $\frac{5}{8p}$ $p \neq 0$

b. $\frac{6d}{c-6}$ $c \neq 6$

Error Alert In Additional Example 1b, students may try to cancel the 6's. Have them put parentheses around binomials like $c - 6$ to indicate that the terms in a binomial cannot be separated.

LESSON RESOURCES

Student Edition Practice
  Workbook 51
Reteaching Master 51
Adaptations Master 51
Challenge and Enrichment
  Master C51

LESSON 51

Simplifying Rational Expressions with Like Denominators

Warm Up

1. **Vocabulary** $\frac{2}{3x}$ is a(n) _____ expression.   **rational**

Simplify.

2. $5n - k + n$ $6n - k$

Factor each expression using the GCF.

3. $4x^2 + x$ $x(4x + 1)$
4. $w^2 - w$ $w(w - 1)$

5. **Multiple Choice** Which expression is equivalent to $6g^2 - 12g + 3$?   **D**
   A $3(g - 5)$
   B $6g(g - 2) + 1$
   C $3g(2g^2 - 4g + 1)$
   D $3(2g^2 - 4g + 1)$

New Concepts

Rational expressions have variables in the denominator. All values that would make the denominator equal zero are excluded.

Math Reasoning

Analyze Compare substituting a variable that makes the denominator equal to zero and dividing by zero.

Sample: A denominator equaling zero is the same as division by zero, which is undefined.

Example 1 Identifying Excluded Values

Find the excluded value(s) in each expression.

a. $\frac{3}{5m}$

SOLUTION

$5m = 0$ Set the denominator equal to zero.

$\frac{5}{5}m = \frac{0}{5}$ Divide both sides by 5.

$m = 0$

$m \neq 0$ 0 is an excluded value.

b. $\frac{5m}{m+1}$

SOLUTION

$m + 1 = 0$ Set the denominator equal to zero.

$-1 = -1$ Subtract 1 from both sides.

$m = -1$

$m \neq -1$ −1 is an excluded value.

Online Connection
www.SaxonMathResources.com

322   *Saxon Algebra 1*

MATH BACKGROUND

A rational expression has a variable in the denominator. Unless that variable has a value that makes the denominator equal to 0, the rational expression can be treated just like a fraction. Any value that makes the denominator equal 0 must be excluded.

When simplifying rational expressions, factoring is key. Expressions that seem to have no factors in common will look remarkably alike after factoring. Make sure that only like factors are divided out, not part of a binomial factor.

If integer exponents are involved, use the definition of negative exponents to rewrite the expressions with only positive exponents first. Then determine which, if any, values of the variable must be excluded, and simplify the expression.

Example 2 Simplifying Rational Expressions

Simplify each rational expression, if possible. Identify any excluded values.

a. $\dfrac{8h^2}{12h}$

SOLUTION

$12h = 0$	Set the denominator equal to zero.
$h = 0$	Solve.
$h \neq 0$	0 is the excluded value.

$\dfrac{8h^2}{12h}$

$= \dfrac{\cancel{4h}(2h)}{\cancel{4h}(3)}$ Factor out the GCF.

$= \dfrac{2h}{3}$ Simplify.

b. $\dfrac{2m - 6}{m - 3}$

SOLUTION

$m - 3 = 0$	Set the denominator equal to zero.
$m = 3$	Solve.
$m \neq 3$	3 is the excluded value.

$\dfrac{2m - 6}{m - 3}$

$= \dfrac{2\,\cancel{(m - 3)}}{\cancel{(m - 3)}}$ Factor the numerator. Divide out common factors.

$= 2$ Simplify.

c. $\dfrac{4y^2 + 8y}{y + 2}$

Hint

If there is more than one term in the numerator or denominator, begin by factoring.
$y + 2$ cannot be factored.
$4y^2 + 8y$ can be factored.

SOLUTION

$y + 2 = 0$	Set the denominator equal to zero.
$y = -2$	Solve.
$y \neq -2$	-2 is the excluded value.

$\dfrac{4y^2 + 8y}{y + 2}$

$= \dfrac{4y\,\cancel{(y + 2)}}{\cancel{(y + 2)}}$ Factor the numerator. Divide out common factors.

$= 4y$ Simplify.

Example 2

Students simplify rational expressions and identify any excluded values.

Additional Example 2

Simplify each rational expression, if possible. Identify any excluded values.

a. $\dfrac{6y^3}{24y}$ $\dfrac{y^2}{4}, y \neq 0$

b. $\dfrac{g - 2}{5g - 10}$ $\dfrac{1}{5}, g \neq 2$

c. $\dfrac{7d^2 + 21d}{d + 3}$ $7d, d \neq -3$

TEACHER TIP

Have students find the excluded values first. The excluded values are based on the original expression. Once students have simplified the expression, they tend to forget to return to the original expression to find the excluded values.

Lesson 51   323

ALTERNATE METHOD FOR EXAMPLE 2

When the numerator and denominator are both monomials, students can treat the expression like a fraction. Rather than factoring, they can reduce the numeric portion of the fraction. The algebraic part can be simplified using the Quotient Rule for Exponents.

In Example 2a, $\dfrac{8}{12} = \dfrac{2}{3}$ and $\dfrac{h^2}{h} = h$, so the rational expression simplifies to $\dfrac{2h}{3}$.

Example 3
Students simplify rational expressions with integer exponents.

Additional Example 3
Simplify each rational expression, if possible.

a. $\dfrac{2m}{n^2} - \dfrac{m}{n^2} \dfrac{m}{n^2}$

b. $s^{-3}t + \dfrac{12}{s^3 t^{-1}} \dfrac{13t}{s^3}$

Example 4
Students simplify rational expressions to solve real-world problems.

Extend the Example
The owner decides to just fence part of the field with length $\dfrac{3a}{3a+4}$. The width is still $\dfrac{8}{3a+4}$. What is the new amount of fencing needed? $\dfrac{6a+16}{3a+4}$

Additional Example 4
Two pieces of ribbon are missing from a pillow. One piece is $\dfrac{z}{3z+9}$ meters long and the other is $\dfrac{z+6}{3z+9}$ meters long. How much ribbon is needed to complete the pillow? $\dfrac{2}{3}$ meters

---

Example 3 Simplifying Expressions with Integer Exponents
Simplify each rational expression, if possible.

a. $\dfrac{b}{a^3} - \dfrac{2b}{a^3}$

SOLUTION

$\dfrac{b}{a^3} - \dfrac{2b}{a^3}$

$= -\dfrac{b}{a^3}$ The expressions have like denominators. Subtract the numerators.

Hint

pq^{-2} is the same as $\dfrac{p}{q^2}$.

b. $pq^{-2} - \dfrac{7}{p^{-1} q^2}$

SOLUTION

$pq^{-2} - \dfrac{7p}{q^2}$

$= \dfrac{p}{q^2} - \dfrac{7p}{q^2}$ Write the expression with only positive exponents.

$= -\dfrac{6p}{q^2}$ The expressions have like denominators. Subtract the numerators.

Example 4 Application: Fencing a Field

A rectangular field has length $\dfrac{6a}{3a+4}$ kilometers and width $\dfrac{8}{3a+4}$ kilometers. Find the amount of fencing needed to enclose all four sides.

SOLUTION

$P = 2(l + w)$ Write the formula for the perimeter of a rectangle.

$P = 2\left(\dfrac{6a}{3a+4} + \dfrac{8}{3a+4}\right)$ Substitute for the length and width.

$= 2\left(\dfrac{6a+8}{3a+4}\right)$ The expressions have like denominators. Add the numerators.

$= 2\left(\dfrac{2(3a+4)}{3a+4}\right)$ Factor the numerator. The GCF is 2.

$= 2(2)$ Simplify.

$= 4$

4 kilometers of fencing is needed.

ENGLISH LEARNERS

For this lesson, explain the meaning of the word **exclude**. Say:

"To exclude means to leave out."

Therefore, excluded values are those that must be left out of the solution set.

Discuss why each excluded value must be left out in Example 1. Explain that they make the denominator 0, and thus, the expression is undefined. Point out that the excluded value may work fine in the simplified expression, but because it did not work in the original expression, it must be left out. To indicate that it is excluded use the symbol $\neq$, which is read "cannot equal."

Lesson Practice

Find the excluded values in each expression.
(Ex 1)

a. $\dfrac{9}{4h}$ $h \neq 0$

b. $\dfrac{p+2}{p+4}$ $p \neq -4$

c. $\dfrac{g-5}{3g-15}$ $g \neq 5$

Simplify each rational expression, if possible. Identify any excluded values.
(Ex 2)

d. $\dfrac{4a^3}{2a^2}$ $a \neq 0, 2a$

e. $\dfrac{d+1}{d}$ $d \neq 0$, cannot be simplified

f. $\dfrac{3z^2 - 6z}{5z - 10}$ $z \neq 2, \dfrac{3z}{5}$

g. $\dfrac{5xy - 10x}{x^2 y^2}$ $x \neq 0, y \neq 0, \dfrac{5(y-2)}{xy^2}$

Simplify each rational expression, if possible.
(Ex 3)

h. $\dfrac{4f}{r^2} - \dfrac{2f}{r^2}$ $\dfrac{2f}{r^2}$

i. $6m^{-2}n^4 + \dfrac{3m^{-2}}{n^{-4}}$ $\dfrac{9n^4}{m^2}$

j. (Framing) A rectangular mirror has a frame with length $\dfrac{2x+5}{4y}$ inches and width $\dfrac{6-x}{4y}$ inches. Find the perimeter of the frame. $\dfrac{x+11}{2y}$ in.
(Ex 4)

Practice Distributed and Integrated

Simplify.

1. $\sqrt[4]{81}$ 3
(46)

2. $\sqrt[3]{-27}$ -3
(46)

3. $\sqrt[3]{64}$ 4
(46)

4. $\sqrt[3]{-64}$ -4
(46)

5. Write $7y = \dfrac{3}{8}x - 1$ in standard form. $3x - 56y = 8$
(35)

6. Simplify $\dfrac{12x^2 - 16x}{16xy}$. $\dfrac{3x - 4}{4y}$
(38)

Lesson 51   325

Add.

*7. $\dfrac{d\,m^{-2}}{3} + \dfrac{5d}{m^2}$ $\quad \dfrac{16d}{3m^2}$
(51)

*8. $\dfrac{8h^{-6}}{y^2} + \dfrac{y^{-2}}{h^6}$ $\quad \dfrac{9}{h^6 y^2}$
(51)

*9. Multiple Choice What is the excluded value for $\dfrac{h+3}{2h-6}$? **D**
(51)

  A $h \ne -2$ **B** $h \ne 0$

  C $h \ne 2$ **D** $h \ne 3$

*10. (Football) A NCAA football field has a width of $\dfrac{160 + 160f}{f+1}$ feet and a length
(51)
of $\dfrac{360 + 360f}{f+1}$ feet. A person walks the outside boundary line to mark it with chalk.
How far does the person walk? 1040 feet

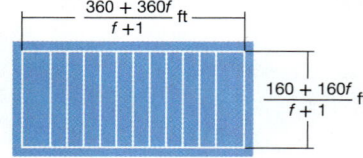

*11. Write Find the excluded value of the rational expression $\dfrac{5p}{p-6}$. Explain.
(51)

11. $p \ne 6$; Sample: A value of 6 would make the denominator equal to zero, and division by zero is undefined.

12. (Travel) You begin a long-distance trip along the highway at mile marker 21.
(34)
After 5 minutes, you pass mile marker 32. After another 5 minutes, you pass mile marker 43. You have been traveling at a constant rate. If you continue to travel at this constant rate, what mile marker will you be at after 60 minutes? (Hint: Consider marker 21 (after 0 minutes) to be a_1, marker 32 (5 minutes) to be a_2, marker 43 (after 10 minutes) to be a_3, and so on.) 153

13. Write the converse of the following statement: If a number is a whole number,
(Inv 5)
then the number is a natural number. Then determine whether the new statement is true or false. If false, give a counterexample. If a number is a natural number, then the number is a whole number; true

14. Multiple Choice The following data set shows the height in inches of 9 eighth
(48)
graders: 66, 62, 56, 64, 60, 62, 58, 57, 59. What is the range of the data? **B**

  A 7 **B** 10

  C 60 **D** 62

15. The scale factor of two similar triangles is 4:5. If one angle of the smaller triangle
(36)
measures 60°, what is the measure of its corresponding angle in the larger triangle? 60°

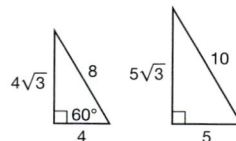

326 *Saxon Algebra 1*

16. **(Produce Cost)** Find the unit price of apples at the grocery store. $1.60/lb
(41)

Apples (lb)	1.5	2	3	3.5
Cost	$2.40	$3.20	$4.80	$5.60

Problem 16
To find the unit cost, divide the cost by the weight of the apples.

*17. **Multi-Step** Luca and Paolo buy old bikes for a few dollars each, and then fix them
(42) up so that they can sell them for a profit. If they bought a rare tandem bike for $8, spent an additional $150 on the bike for paint and parts, and sold it at a 285% profit, then how much money did they sell the bike for?
   a. Analyze If profit means the amount of money Luca and Paolo made after taking into account what they spent, write an equation to find how much the bike sold for. $285\% \cdot \$158 + \$158 = s$
   b. Solve the equation to find the sale price of the bike. $608.30

Problem 19
Choose two points on the graph. The slope is the difference in their y-values over the difference in their x-values.

*18. Write If a rational expression has values at which the numerator equals 0, are these points undefined for the expression? Explain.
(43)

18. no; Sample: A rational expression is undefined only when the denominator is zero because division by zero is undefined. If the numerator is zero and the denominator is a nonzero number, then the value of the rational expression is zero because zero divided by any nonzero number is zero.

19. Determine the slope of the line shown on the graph. $m = -\frac{9}{7}$
(44)

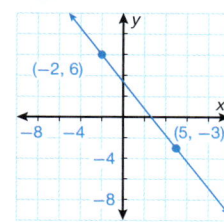

Problem 20
Scaffolding Guide the students by asking them the following questions.

"How do you know if it is an **increase or decrease?**" The price goes up, so it is an increase.

"How do you determine the **amount of change?**" Subtract the old price from the new price.

"What was the amount of **increase or decrease?**" $3200 increase

20. Find the percent of increase or decrease if the original price was $7000 and the
(47) new price is $10,200.   46% increase

21. Analyze Determine if the premise and the conclusion use inductive or deductive
(Inv 4) reasoning. Explain your choice.   deductive reasoning; The conclusion is based on the definition of a triangle.
Premise: The measures of two angles in a triangle add up to 80°.
Conclusion: The third angle is 100°.

*22. **(Astronomy)** The surface temperature of the sun is about 5880 kelvins. The
(50) sun's core is much hotter. Create a graph of an inequality that represents the temperature of the sun's core.

Problem 24
Extend the Problem
What are the mean and mode of the data set? The mean is 164.3 and the mode is 176.

23. $s \leq 900$;

*23. Geometry According to a city bylaw, the area of a store's sign cannot exceed
(50) 900 square decimeters. Write and graph an inequality to represent the situation.

24. Justify The numbers of students who bought lunch each day this month are
(48) listed below.

176, 134, 208, 170, 149, 153, 136,
200, 168, 150, 157, 141, 211, 176,
145, 155, 128, 199, 182, 148.

   a. How would you find the median of the set of data above?
   b. Find the median.   156

24a. Sample: First I would list the data in numeric order. Then I would count the number of data values (20). Because the number is even, I would find the average of the tenth and eleventh data values to determine the median.

Lesson 51   327

Problem 25
TEACHER TIP
Remind students that the slope-intercept form is $y = mx + b$.

Problem 27
TEACHER TIP
Substitute the possible values for x into the inequality and see if the inequality is true.

Problem 28
Error Alert
Students may assume that the inequality is less than because of the phrase "at least." Explain that "at least" means the smallest number possible. Therefore, greater than or equal to is the appropriate inequality.

25. Write the equation $5x + 3y = 9$ in slope-intercept form. $y = -\frac{5}{3}x + 3$
(49)

26. **Multiple Choice** Which equation has a slope of $-\frac{1}{2}$ and a y-intercept of -3? **C**
(49)
A $4x + 2y + 3 = 0$
B $3x + 6y + 6 = 0$
C $5x + 10y + 30 = 0$
D $6x + 2y + 1 = 0$

*27. Determine which values in the set $\{-1, 0, 1, 2\}$ are solutions to the inequality
(50) $x - 1 \geq 4$. none

28. **Error Analysis** Two students graphed the statement "A number is at least 9" as shown
(50) below. Which student is correct? Explain the error.

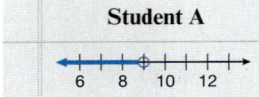
Student A

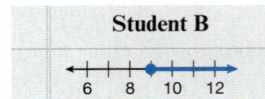
Student B

28. Student B; Sample: Student A graphed all numbers less than 9, and "at least 9" means that the number is equal to or greater than 9.

29. **Multi-Step** The graph shows that the temperature is now at least the temperature it
(50) was this morning. How can the current temperature be expressed with a sentence?

a. Write an inequality for the graph. $f \geq -15$
b. Translate the inequality into a sentence. Sample: The temperature is greater than or equal to negative fifteen.

30. **Measurement** The specifications for a housing development include that each
(50) lot has to be at least $1\frac{1}{2}$ acres. Write and graph an inequality to represent the situation.

$l \geq 1\frac{1}{2}$; ←++++♦++→
            0 1 2

328 **Saxon** Algebra 1

CHALLENGE

Write an expression that has more than one excluded value.

Sample: $\dfrac{3x + 1}{x(x - 2)(x + 3)}$

LOOKING FORWARD

Simplifying rational expressions with like denominators prepares students for

• **Lesson 57** Finding the Least Common Multiple
• **Lesson 78** Graphing Rational Functions
• **Lesson 88** Multiplying and Dividing Rational Expressions
• **Lesson 90** Adding and Subtracting Rational Expressions
• **Lesson 92** Simplifying Complex Fractions
• **Lesson 99** Solving Rational Equations

LESSON 52

Determining the Equation of a Line Given Two Points

Warm Up

1. **Vocabulary** The _____ is a measure of the steepness of a line. **slope**
2. Find the x-intercept in the equation $3x + y = 6$. **2**
3. Find the y-intercept in the equation $3x + y = 6$. **6**

Solve each proportion.

4. $\dfrac{2}{9} = \dfrac{4}{n}$ $n = 18$

5. $\dfrac{5}{x + 10} = \dfrac{1}{3}$ $x = 5$

New Concepts

A line can be graphed if the slope and any point on the line are known. For example, to graph a line that has a slope of $-\dfrac{2}{3}$ and passes through $(2, 4)$, begin by plotting the point $(2, 4)$. From the point $(2, 4)$, count down two units and to the right three units. Plot a point there. Then draw a line through the two points $(2, 4)$ and $(5, 2)$.

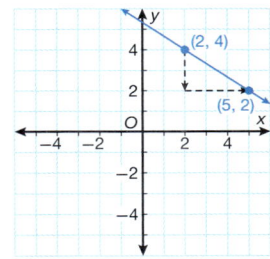

Example 1 Using Slope and a Point to Graph

a. Graph a line that has a slope of 4 and passes through point $(3, 5)$.

SOLUTION

Graph the point $(3, 5)$.

From the point $(3, 5)$, count up four units and to the right one unit. Graph a point there.

Sketch the line through the two points $(3, 5)$ and $(4, 9)$.

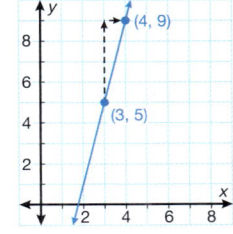

Hint

A slope of 4 is the same as $\dfrac{4}{1}$.

Math Language

The **slope** of a line represents a rate of change. A positive slope slants up to the right. A negative slope slants down to the right.

b. Graph a line that has a slope of 0 and passes through point $(2, 3)$.

SOLUTION

Graph the point $(2, 3)$.

A line with a slope of 0 is a horizontal line.

Sketch a horizontal line that passes through the point $(2, 3)$.

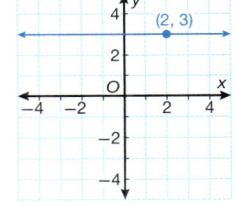

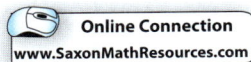
Online Connection
www.SaxonMathResources.com

Lesson 52   329

MATH BACKGROUND

Graphing lines is a critical component of algebraic skills. In order to graph a line, two pieces of information must be provided: a slope and a point. The slope may be given directly or it may need to be calculated from two points. Eventually it may even be given in terms of relationship to other lines (parallel or perpendicular).

A point is always needed. It also may be directly stated or given by an intercept.

Different forms of linear equations are used based on the information given. The most familiar form is slope-intercept form, $y = mx + b$. However, point-slope form is where to begin if the point given is not the intercept. When an equation is in point-slope form, solve for y to put it in slope-intercept form.

LESSON 52

1 Warm Up

Problem 2

Remind students that the x-intercept is the value of x when $y = 0$.

2 New Concepts

In this lesson, students learn to graph equations using a slope and a point, point-slope form, or two points.

Example 1

Students use a slope and a point to graph a line.

Additional Example 1

a. Graph line a that has slope 2 and passes through $(3, 4)$.

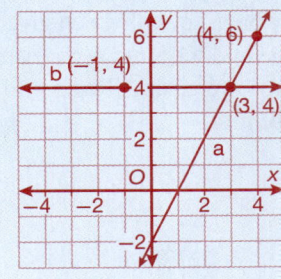

b. Graph line b that has a slope of 0 and passes through the point $(-1, 4)$.

LESSON RESOURCES

Student Edition Practice Workbook 52
Reteaching Master 52
Adaptations Master 52
Challenge and Enrichment Master C52

Lesson 52   329

Example 2

Students learn to write linear equations in point-slope form.

Additional Example 2

Write in point-slope form the equation of a line that has a slope of -3 and passes through point $(2, -7)$. $y + 7 = -3(x-2)$

Example 3

Students learn to write a linear equation given two points.

Additional Example 3

Write the equation of a line that passes through points $(15, -2)$ and $(-5, 6)$ in slope-intercept form. $y = -\frac{2}{5}x + 4$

Error Alert Students may not know where to begin when two points are given to write an equation of a line. Tell students that if they are given two points, they have actually been given the slope and a point. Whenever two points are given, always find the slope first.

Point-Slope Form

The form $y - y_1 = m(x - x_1)$, where m is the slope and (x_1, y_1) is a point on the line is called the point-slope form of a line.

Example 2 Writing an Equation in Point-Slope Form

Write the equation of a line that has a slope of 3 and passes through point $(2, 4)$ in point-slope form.

SOLUTION

$y - y_1 = m(x - x_1)$ Write the formula.

$y - 4 = 3(x - 2)$ Substitute $(2, 4)$ for (x_1, y_1) and 3 for m.

Example 3 Writing an Equation Using Two Points

Write the an equation of a line that passes through the points $(1, -3)$ and $(4, 5)$ in slope-intercept form.

SOLUTION

$m = \dfrac{y_2 - y_1}{x_2 - x_1}$ Write the slope formula.

$m = \dfrac{5 - (-3)}{4 - 1}$ Substitute $(1, -3)$ for (x_1, y_1) and $(4, 5)$ for (x_2, y_2).

$= \dfrac{8}{3}$ Simplify.

The slope is $= \dfrac{8}{3}$.

Hint
You can substitute either $(1, -3)$ or $(4, 5)$ for (x_1, y_1).

$y - y_1 = m(x - x_1)$ Write the point-slope formula.

$y - 5 = \dfrac{8}{3}(x - 4)$ Substitute $(4, 5)$ for (x_1, y_1) and $\dfrac{8}{3}$ for m.

$3(y - 5) = 3 \cdot \dfrac{8}{3}(x - 4)$ Multiply both sides by 3.

$3y - 15 = 8x - 32$ Distribute the 3 and 8.

$y = \dfrac{8}{3}x - \dfrac{17}{3}$ Solve for y.

Check

Graph $y = \dfrac{8}{3}x - \dfrac{17}{3}$.

The graph of $y = \dfrac{8}{3}x - \dfrac{17}{3}$ appears to go through the points $(1, -3)$ and $(4, 5)$.

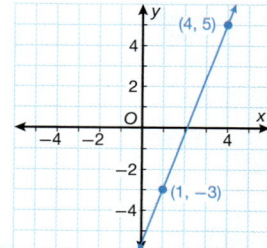

330   **Saxon** Algebra 1

🔺 INCLUSION

Use the following strategy with students who need help graphing by making connections between the words and the equations very clear. Make a color-coded chart to help associate the words and the equations. For example, write Point-Slope Form with "Point" in red and "Slope" in blue. Then write $y - y_1 = m(x - x_1)$, with m in blue and x_1 and x_2 in red.

Continue the coding with a graph where the point is in red and the dotted lines showing slope are in blue.

Example 4 Application: Sales

Rachel is selling seashells. She sold 1 for $5 and 2 for $8. What will Rachel charge for 5 seashells if she keeps selling the seashells at the same price rate?

Understand

The ordered pair (1, 5) represents "1 shell for $5."

The ordered pair (2, 8) represents "2 shells for $8."

The slope represents the price rate, which is constant.

Plan

Find the slope of the line.

Write an equation of the line that passes through (1, 5) and (2, 8).

Use the equation to find the value of y when $x = 5$.

Solve

$m = \dfrac{y_2 - y_1}{x_2 - x_1}$ Write the slope formula.

$= \dfrac{8 - 5}{2 - 1}$ Substitute (1, 5) for (x_1, y_1) and (2, 8) for (x_2, y_2).

$= 3$ Simplify.

$y - y_1 = m(x - x_1)$ Write the point-slope formula.

$y - 5 = 3(x - 1)$ Substitute (1, 5) for (x_1, y_1) and 3 for m.

$y - 5 = 3x - 3$ Distribute the 3.

$y = 3x + 2$ Solve for y.

$y = 3(5) + 2$ Substitute 5 for x.

$y = 17$

Rachel will sell 5 seashells for $17.

Check

Graph $y = 3x + 2$.

The graph representing $y = 3x + 2$ goes through the points (1, 5), (2, 8), and (5, 17).

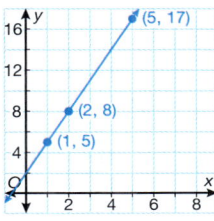

Math Reasoning

Predict Suppose Rachel sells some shells and receives $200. How many shells would she have sold if she had continued to sell the shells at the same price rate?

66 shells

Lesson Practice

a. Graph a line that has a slope of 2 and passes through the point (5, 6). (Ex 1)

b. Graph a line that has a slope of 0 and passes through the point (−1, 1). (Ex 1)

c. Write the equation of a line that has a slope of 6 and passes through the point (7, 9) in point-slope form. $y - 9 = 6(x - 7)$ (Ex 2)

d. Write the equation of a line that passes through the points (2, −3) and (7, 4) in slope-intercept form. $y = \tfrac{7}{5}x - \tfrac{29}{5}$ (Ex 3)

a.
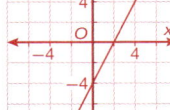

b.
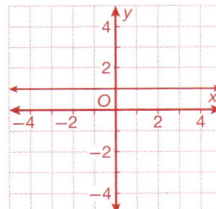

Example 4

Students use linear equations to solve sales problems.

Extend the Example

Rachel decides to have a sale. She reduces the price of every order by $1. What is the new equation? Does this change the price rate?
$y = 3x + 1$; no

Additional Example 4

Pete sells frozen lemonade at community baseball games. He sells 1 cup for $3 or 2 cups for $5. What will Pete charge for 6 cups if he keeps selling the lemonade at the same price rate? $13

Lesson Practice

Problem b

Error Alert Students may graph a vertical line for a line with a slope of 0. Explain to students that horizontal lines are flat, with 0 slope. Vertical lines are straight up and down; their slope is undefined.

ALTERNATE METHOD FOR EXAMPLE 4

Have students graph the points first and connect them with a line. Then have them find the value of y when $x = 5$ by looking at the line.

Discuss with students that this method is not as accurate as solving an equation. When the points are not at exact intersections on the coordinate plane, it is difficult to tell with accuracy what the answer is.

e. Trevor began a computer game with 3 points. After 1 minute he had −1 points, and after 2 minutes he had −5 points. How many points will he have after 3 minutes of playing the computer game if he continues losing at the same rate?   −9 points

Practice   Distributed and Integrated

Given the domain of a function, find the range.

1. $f(x) = 3x - 5$; domain: $\{0, 1, 2, 3\}$ $\{-5, -2, 1, 4\}$
2. $f(x) = \frac{1}{2}x + 3$; domain: $\{-2, 0, 2, 4\}$ $\{2, 3, 4, 5\}$

Write an inequality for each situation.

3. To qualify for the job, the applicants must have more than 3 years of experience in the field. $x > 3$

4. In 2005 the minimum wage in the United States was $5.15 per hour. $x \geq 5.15$

5. Divide $\frac{(3 \times 10^{-9})}{(4.8 \times 10^{-1})}$ and write the answer in scientific notation. 6.25×10^{-9}

*6. Graph the line that has a slope of −1 and passes through the point (3, 1).

7. The scale of a map is 1 in.:20 mi. Find the actual distance that corresponds to a map distance of 4 inches.   80 miles

8. (Carpentry) You are constructing a picnic table and are using a scale of 1 inch to 6 inches. If the length of the table on the drawing is 7 inches, what will the actual length of the table be?   42 inches

9. A box with a volume of $\frac{t^3}{y^4}\left(\frac{t^2}{y^2} + \frac{5y}{m}\right)$ receives a fixed postage rate.
   a. Simplify the expression above. $\frac{t^5}{y^6} + \frac{5t^3}{my^3}$
   b. Identify the variables that cannot equal zero. $y \neq 0, m \neq 0$

10. (Simple Interest) Simple interest is the amount of money the borrower pays based on the amount borrowed (the principal) for a given period of time (months or years). It is calculated this way: $I = prt$. If a person borrows $20,000 (p) to buy a car, pays 6.95% interest (r), and takes 5 years (t) to repay the loan, how much will the borrower pay in simple interest? $6950.00

11. **Analyze** The rational expression $\frac{x - 5}{15x^2 - 75x}$ is not defined for all real numbers.
    a. When is the denominator equal to 0?   It is 0 at $x = 0$ and at $x = 5$.
    b. When is the numerator equal to 0?   It is 0 at $x = 5$.
    c. When is the rational expression undefined?   It is undefined at $x = 0$ and at $x = 5$.

12. **Analyze** The slope of a line is 3. Two points on this line are (−1, −2) and (4, ?). Using the formula for slope, determine the missing y-value for the second point.   13

332   Saxon Algebra 1

13. Translate the following sentence into an inequality:

    The difference of −4 and an unknown number is less than or equal to 0. $-4 - x \leq 0$

14. Evaluate the expression for the given value.

    $-\sqrt{x}$ when $x = \frac{25}{16}$ $-1\frac{1}{4}$

*15. (Business) Arminda owns a ladies' bag business. The total cost of producing a group of bags is $1100. In addition, each bag costs $18 in materials. If Arminda sells each bag for $40, how many bags should Arminda sell to gain a profit of at least $2200? 150 bags

16. The data below are the weights of 10 newborns (to the nearest pound). Find the mean, median, and mode of the data. mean: 7; median: 7; mode: 8

    5, 8, 6, 5, 7, 8, 10, 7, 8, 6.

*17. **Data Analysis** Study the graph. It shows the cost of playing x number of games after renting equipment.
    a. Write an equation that represents the line of the graph in slope-intercept form. $y = 10x + 10$
    b. What is the cost of playing 5 games? $60

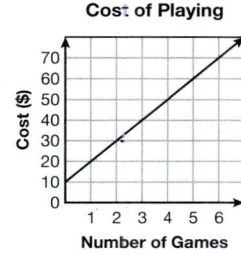

Cost of Playing

18. **Multi-Step** Murietta is planning a party at a bowling alley. She wants to rent two lanes. The rental fee for the two lanes is $40 plus the rental of $2 per pair of bowling shoes.
    a. Write an equation in slope-intercept form to represent this situation. $y = 2x + 40$
    b. Murietta is renting two lanes and inviting 9 people. If everyone including herself rents shoes, what will the cost of the party be? $60

19. Write an inequality for the graph below. $y \geq \frac{4}{5}$

*20. **Error Analysis** Two students graphed the inequality $2.5 > b$ as shown below. Which student is correct? Explain the error.

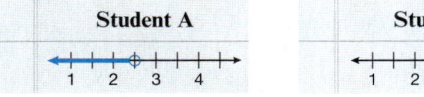

20. Student A; Sample: Student B graphed b as greater than 2.5, but should have graphed 2.5 as greater than b. Rewriting the inequality with the variable on the left, such as $b < 2.5$, would have been less confusing.

21. Find the excluded value in the expression $\frac{b^5}{b^3}$. $b \neq 0$

*22. (Soccer) In international play, the maximum length of a soccer field is $\frac{525x + 100}{5x + 1}$ meters and the maximum width is $\frac{400x + 85}{5x + 1}$ meters. Each linesman is responsible for watching half of the field's perimeter. How many meters along the border of the field must the linesman watch during the game? 185 meters

---

Problem 16
Error Alert
Students may forget that the data values must be in ascending order before determining the middle number, the median. Remind students to order the data values before determining the measures of central tendency.

Problem 18
Extend the Problem
If Murietta pays $104, how many people did she invite to the party? 31 people

Problem 19
Guide the students by asking them the following questions.

"What point is identified on the number line?" $\frac{4}{5}$

"What does the closed circle indicate?" equal to

"Is the shaded arrow indicating greater than or less than?" greater than

Problem 24
Write the expression with only positive exponents first.

Problem 25
Factor before simplifying.

Problem 26
TEACHER TIP
Remind students to add rational expressions like fractions. Combine the numerators, and keep the like denominator.

Problem 29
Extend the Problem
Michelle decides to continue knitting. She works for a total of 9 days. How long is the scarf?
96 inches

Problem 30
Extend the Problem
If John has already gone 195 miles, how long has he been traveling? 3 hours

---

*23. Write the inverse of the statement: "If a polygon is has four sides, then it is a quadrilateral." Then determine whether the new statement is true or false. If false, give a counterexample.
(Inv 5)

23. If a polygon does not have four sides, then it is not a quadrilateral.; True

24. **Error Analysis** Two students simplify the expression $-r^3s^{-4} + \frac{2s^{-4}}{r^{-3}}$. Which student is correct? Explain the error.
(51)

Student A	Student B
$-r^3s^{-4} + \frac{2s^{-4}}{r^{-3}}$	$-r^3s^{-4} + \frac{2s^{-4}}{r^{-3}}$
cannot simplify	$= \frac{-r^3}{s^4} + \frac{2r^3}{s^4}$
	$= \frac{r^3}{s^4}$

24. Student B; Sample: Student A forgot to rewrite each term with positive exponents before trying to combine like terms. As a result, the expressions did not appear to be like terms.

25. **Geometry** Two sides of a triangle measure $4x + 8$ and $x^2 + 2x$. Find the ratio of the first side to the second side. Simplify, if possible. $\frac{4}{x}$
(43)

26. A rectangular window has a length of $\frac{6a}{3a-1}$ meters and a width of $\frac{4}{3a-1}$ meters. How many feet of trim will be painted if the trim goes around three sides of the window (both lengths and one width)? $\frac{12a+4}{3a-1}$ meters
(51)

*27. **Multiple Choice** On the first day of the school play, Carlos sold four tickets. On the second day, he sold seven tickets. Which equation of a line represents the line that passes through the two points that represent the data in this problem? **A**
(52)

A $y = 3x + 1$ **B** $y = \frac{1}{3}x + 1$ **C** $y = -3x + 1$ **D** $y = 3x - 1$

*28. **Write** Find the slope of the line that passes through $(-1, 2)$ and $(3, 2)$. Explain. $m = 0$; Sample: It is a horizontal line, which has zero slope.
(52)

*29. Rachel and a Michelle are crocheting a baby blanket that will be 72 inches long. Rachel crochets the first 24 inches and then gives the blanket to Michelle to finish. Michelle expects to crochet at a rate of 8 inches per day. How many days will it take Michelle to finish the blanket?
(52)
  a. Write an equation giving the length y of the blanket (in inches) when crocheting for x days. $y = 8x + 24$
  b. Graph the equation using a graphing calculator.
  c. How long it will take Michelle to finish the blanket?   6 days

29b.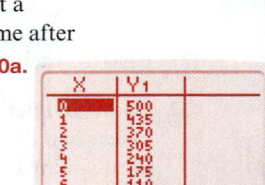

*30. **Transportation** John is 500 miles from home. He is traveling toward home at a constant rate of 65 miles per hour. The distance d (in miles) away from home after t (in hours) is given by the equation $d = 500 - 65t$.
(52)
  a. Use a graphing calculator to make a table of values with the values of t from 0 to 5 in increments of 1.
  b. How far away from home John is after 4 hours?   240 miles

30a.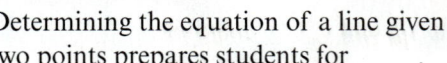

334   Saxon Algebra 1

CHALLENGE

Write the equation of a line that has no slope and an x-intercept of 22 in point-slope form. $x = 22$

LOOKING FORWARD

Determining the equation of a line given two points prepares students for

- **Lesson 56** Identifying, Writing, and Graphing Direct Variation
- **Lesson 64** Identifying, Writing, and Graphing Inverse Variation
- **Lesson 65** Writing Equations of Parallel and Perpendicular Lines

LESSON 53

Adding and Subtracting Polynomials

Warm Up

1. **Vocabulary** A part of an expression that is added to or subtracted from the other parts is called a _____.   **term**

Simplify.

2. $\left(\dfrac{4}{9}\right)^0$ **1**

3. $\left(\dfrac{12}{8}\right)^{-1}$ **$\dfrac{2}{3}$**

4. Find the GCF of $25b^3$, $50b^2$, and $100b$.   **$25b$**

New Concepts

A **monomial** is the product of numbers and/or variables with whole-number exponents.

Monomials	Not Monomials
$x,\ \dfrac{x^3}{2},\ -xy,\ 0.75x^2,\ 3$	$\dfrac{1}{x},\ \dfrac{2}{x^3},\ x-y,\ 0.75x^{-2}$

The **degree of a monomial** is the sum of the exponents of the variables in the monomial. A constant has a degree of 0.

Example 1   Finding the Degree of Monomials

Find the degree of each monomial.

a. $-7x^2yz^3$

SOLUTION

$-7x^2yz^3$ Find the sum of the exponents of the variables.

$2 + 1 + 3 = 6$

The degree of the monomial is 6.

b. $8xy^2z$

SOLUTION

$8xy^2z$ Find the sum of the exponents of the variables.

$1 + 2 + 1 = 4$

The degree of the monomial is 4.

c. 12^2ab^3c

SOLUTION

12^2ab^3c Find the sum of the exponents of the variables.

$1 + 3 + 1 = 5$

The degree of the monomial is 5.

Caution
Remember $y = y^1$

Caution
Be careful and do not include the exponent on the base 12. Use only the exponents of the variables to find the degree.

LESSON 53

1 Warm Up

Problem 1
Point out that a term can involve the operations of multiplication, division, and exponentiation (raising a variable to a power).

2 New Concepts

In this lesson, students learn the basic vocabulary needed to discuss polynomials, as well as the methods used to simplify polynomial expressions by adding or subtracting them.

Example 1
Students find the degree of a monomial by adding the exponents of the variables.

Error Alert Remind students that the exponent 1 is understood and not written; for example, m to the first power is written as simply m rather than m^1. So, the degree of the monomial xy^3 is 4, not 3.

Additional Example 1
Find the degree of each monomial.

a. $(3.5^4)abc^5$ **7**

b. $7xy^3z^2$ **6**

c. 10^2ab^3c **5**

LESSON RESOURCES

Student Edition Practice Workbook 53
Reteaching Master 53
Adaptations Master 53
Challenge and Enrichment Master C53
Technology Lab Master 53

MATH BACKGROUND

The general form of a monomial in x is ax^n where a is a nonzero real number and n is a positive integer. Values of 1 for a and n are usually omitted; that is, $1x^1$ is written as x. The number a is the numeric coefficient, or more simply the coefficient, of the monomial; the number n is the degree. A nonzero constant monomial such as -8 has degree zero. More than one variable may appear in a monomial. When this is the case, the degree is the sum of the exponents of the variables.

A string of monomials connected by plus signs is a polynomial. If no replacement sets for the variables are specified, the polynomial is an expression (rather than a number) and the variables are indeterminates. If real numbers are used as the replacement set for the variables, then, since the coefficients are also real numbers, the closure properties guarantee that a polynomial represents a real number for any replacement of the variable. Therefore, all properties of real numbers apply; specifically, those related to addition and subtraction.

Example 2

Students write polynomials in standard form by arranging the terms in descending order of degree.

Additional Example 2
Write each polynomial in standard form. Then find the leading coefficient.

a. $8 + 5x^2 - x + 7x^3$
$7x^3 + 5x^2 - x + 8; 7$

b. $3a^2b - 2b^4 + 5 - 6ab$
$-2b^4 + 3a^2b - 6ab + 5; -2$

c. $3xy - 2x^2y - 7x^3y^2$
$-7x^3y^2 - 2x^2y + 3xy; -7$

A **polynomial** is a monomial or the sum or difference of monomials.

Polynomials	
A polynomial with one term is a monomial.	$6x$
A polynomial with two terms is a **binomial**.	$6x + 10$
A polynomial with three terms is a **trinomial**.	$x^2 + 6x + 10$

The **degree of a polynomial** is the degree of the greatest-degree term in the polynomial.

The **leading coefficient** for a polynomial is the coefficient of the term with the greatest degree.

The **standard form of a polynomial** is a form of a polynomial where terms are ordered from greatest to least degree.

Example 2 Writing a Polynomial in Standard Form

Write each polynomial in standard form. Then find the leading coefficient.

a. $2n^2 + n^3$

SOLUTION

$2n^2$: degree 2

n^3 : degree 3

$n^3 + 2n^2$ is in standard form. The leading coefficient is 1.

b. $8xy^2 - 9 + 5x^3y^3z$

SOLUTION

$8xy^2$ — Add the exponents of the variables: $1 + 2 = 3$.

$5x^3y^3z$ — Add the exponents of the variables: $3 + 3 + 1 = 7$.

-9 — A constant has a degree of 0.

$5x^3y^3z + 8xy^2 - 9$
  ↓   ↓   ↓   Arrange the terms in descending order.
  7   3   0

$5x^3y^3z + 8xy^2 - 9$ is in standard form. The leading coefficient is 5.

c. $9x^2y - 3x^2y^2 - 5xy$

SOLUTION

$9x^2y$ — Add the exponents of the variables: $2 + 1 = 3$.

$-3x^2y^2$ — Add the exponents of the variables: $2 + 2 = 4$.

$5xy$ — Add the exponents of the variables: $1 + 1 = 2$.

$-3x^2y^2 - 9x^2y - 5xy$
  ↓   ↓   ↓   Arrange the terms in descending order.
  4   3   2

$-3x^2y^2 + 9x^2y - 5xy$ is in standard form. The leading coefficient is -3.

INCLUSION

Use this strategy with students who need help keeping track of exponents. Have students draw geometric shapes around the exponents of each variable of each term. Changes shapes for each term. Then have the students add the numbers in the matching shapes to find the degree of the term. Remind students that every variable should have a shape in the exponent's place. Students need to place a 1 in any empty shapes.

degree of first term: $2 + 1 = 3$
degree of second term: $2 + 3 = 5$
degree of third term: $3 + 1 = 4$

Exploration Using Algebra Tiles to Add or Subtract Polynomials

Use algebra tiles to find $(x^2 + 3x - 3) + (2x^2 - x + 2)$.

a. Model each expression using algebra tiles.

$(x^2 + 3x - 3)$ $(2x^2 - x + 2)$

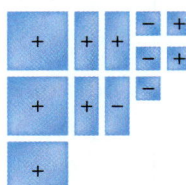

b. Rearrange tiles so that like terms are together.

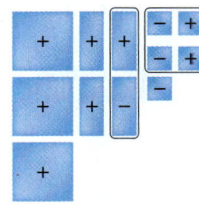

c. Remove the zero pairs.

d. The remaining tiles represent the sum.

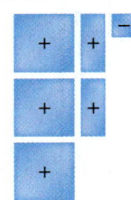

The sum is $3x^2 + 2x - 1$.

e. Model Use algebra tiles to find $(2x^2 + 3x) + (2x - x^2) - x^2$. $5x$

Exploration

Students use algebra tiles to model the addition and subtraction of polynomials. You may wish to introduce the term zero pair to describe tiles that are opposites. Three zero pairs are $+1$ and -1, x and $-x$, x^2 and $-x^2$. The principal method of simplifying an arrangement of algebra tiles is to remove all zero pairs.

Extend the Exploration
Use algebra tiles.

a. Add these polynomials.
$(-3x^2 - 4 + 2x)$
$+ (7 - 6x + x^2)$
$-2x^2 - 4x + 3$

b. Determine whether
$3x + (6 - x^2)$
$+ (5x - 8) + 2x^2$
is equivalent to $8x^2 + x - 2$.
no

Lesson 53   337

Example 3

Students add polynomials by adding the coefficients of like terms.

Additional Example 3

Add the polynomials. Write the answer in standard form.

a. $(-2a^4 + 3a^2 - 6a + 5) + (a^2 + a - 8)$ $-2a^4 + 4a^2 - 5a - 3$

b. $(3a - 2b + 5c) + (7a - 3c) + (-2b + 7c)$ $10a - 4b + 9c$

Error Alert Most students will make fewer errors if they write the problems in vertical form.

Example 4

Students subtract polynomials. They can do this by subtracting the coefficient of each term in the subtrahend from a like term in the minuend. An alternative to subtracting is adding the opposite.

Error Alert Remind students to write the opposite of every term in the polynomial they are subtracting.

Additional Example 4

Subtract the polynomials. Write the answer in standard form.

a. $(4z^2 - 5z + 3) - (2z^2 + 7z + 3)$ $2z^2 - 12z$

b. $(m^2 - 7m^3 - m - 3) - (10m^3 + m + 2 - m^2)$ $-17m^3 + 2m^2 - 2m - 5$

Extend the Example

Find a polynomial in standard form equivalent to the given expression.

a. $(2a + 3b) - (5b - 2c) + (3a - 7c)$ $5a - 2b - 5c$

b. $(8a + 5b) - (3b - 2a) - (3a + 5b)$ $7a - 3b$

To add or subtract polynomials, combine like terms. Polynomials can be added vertically or horizontally.

Example 3 Adding Polynomials

Add the polynomials. Write the answer in standard form.

a. $(-8x^3 + 4x^2 + x + 1) + (3x^3 - 2x^2 + 7)$

SOLUTION

$-8x^3 + 4x^2 + x + 1$ Arrange like terms in columns.
$\underline{+3x^3 - 2x^2 + 7}$
$-5x^3 + 2x^2 + x + 8$ Add like terms.

The polynomial $-5x^3 + 2x^2 + x + 8$ is in standard form.

b. $(x + 10 + 2x^3) + (3x^2 - 7x - 2)$

SOLUTION

$(x + 10 + 2x^3) + (3x^2 - 7x - 2)$
$x + 10 + 2x^3 + 3x^2 - 7x - 2$ Remove parentheses.
$2x^3 + 3x^2 + x - 7x - 2 + 10$ Arrange with like terms together.
$2x^3 + 3x^2 - 6x + 8$ Combine like terms.

The polynomial $2x^3 + 3x^2 - 6x + 8$ is in standard form.

Math Language

Like terms, such as $-8x^3$ and $3x^3$, have the same variables raised to the same powers.

Example 4 Subtracting Polynomials

Subtract the polynomials. Write the answer in standard form.

a. $(6x^2 + 4x + 2) - (2x^2 - x + 8)$

SOLUTION

$(6x^2 + 4x + 2) - (2x^2 - x + 8)$
$-2x^2 + x - 8$ Find the opposite of the second polynomial.

$6x^2 + 4x + 2$ Arrange like terms in columns.
$\underline{+ -2x^2 + x - 8}$
$4x^2 + 5x - 6$ Add like terms.

The polynomial $4x^2 + 5x - 6$ is in standard form.

Caution

Remember to multiply each term in the parentheses by -1.
$-1(2x^2 - x + 8)$.

 ALTERNATE METHOD FOR EXAMPLE 4

This method for subtracting polynomials uses horizontal rather than vertical form. For students who are more abstract thinkers, this method better emphasizes the application of the properties of real numbers than the same computation done in columns.

$(6x^2 + 4x + 2) - (2x^2 - x + 8) = (6x^2 + 4x + 2) + [-(2x^2 - x + 8)]$
$= (6x^2 + 4x + 2) + (-2x^2 + x - 8)$
$= (6 - 2)x^2 + (4 + 1)x + (2 - 8)$
$= 4x^2 + 5x - 6$

338 Saxon Algebra 1

Math Reasoning

Generalize When a polynomial is in standard form, is the leading coefficient always the coefficient of the first term?

Sample: Polynomials are in standard form when the terms are arranged from greatest to least degree, so the leading coefficient of a standard form polynomial is always the coefficient of the term with the greatest degree.

b. $(x^2 + 4x - 9) - (4x^2 - 5x + 11)$

SOLUTION

$(x^2 + 4x - 9) - (4x^2 - 5x + 11)$
$x^2 + 4x - 9 - 4x^2 + 5x - 11$ Remove the parentheses.
$x^2 - 4x^2 + 4x + 5x - 9 - 11$ Arrange like terms together.
$-3x^2 + 9x - 20$ Combine like terms.

The polynomial $-3x^2 + 9x - 20$ is in standard form.

Example 5 Application: Internet

For the years 1995 through 2001, the number of websites for businesses and education can be represented by the expressions below.

business websites: $0.333t^2 - 1.035t + 0.607$

education websites: $0.098t^2 - 0.121t + 0.296$

Write an expression for the total number of business and educational websites.

SOLUTION

$0.333t^2 - 1.035t + 0.607$
$+ 0.098t^2 - 0.121t + 0.296$
$0.431t^2 - 1.156t + 0.903$

The expression $0.431t^2 - 1.156t + 0.903$ represents the total number of websites.

Lesson Practice

Find the degree of each monomial.
(Ex 1)
a. $3x^2yz^6$ 9
b. -2^3xyz 3
c. $4^2xy^2z^3$ 6

Write each polynomial in standard form. Then find the leading coefficient.
(Ex 2)
d. $3w^2 - 2w^4$ $-2w^4 + 3w^2; -2$
e. $5ab^2 + 3a^2b^2 + 8ab - 1$ $3a^2b^2 + 5ab^2 + 8ab - 1; 3$
f. $2ab - 7 - 5a^2b$ $-5a^2b + 2ab - 7; -5$

Add the polynomials. Write each answer in standard form.
(Ex 3)
g. $(2x^2 + x + 8) + (x^2 + 4)$ $3x^2 + x + 12$
h. $(3n^2 + 7n - 1) + (-2n^2 - n + 1)$ $n^2 + 6n$

Subtract the polynomials. Write each answer in standard form.
(Ex 4)
i. $(12y^3 + 10) - (18y^3 - 3y^2 + 5)$ $-6y^3 + 3y^2 + 5$
j. $(c^2 + 6c - 2) - (c^2 - 2c + 6)$ $8c - 8$

Lesson 53   339

 MANIPULATIVE USE

Materials: algebra tiles for x^2, x, and 1

Remind students that to subtract a polynomial, they can add its opposite. Have students fold a piece of paper to make a mat with a positive top section and a negative bottom section, and have them shade the bottom section gray. Model $2x^2 - x - 3$. To find the opposite, students interchange the positions of the tiles, moving the tiles from top to bottom and vice versa. For $2x^2 - x - 3$, the opposite is $-2x^2 + x + 3$.

Have students use the manipulative model to find the opposites of polynomials such as these.

a. $3x^2 - 2$ $-3x^2 - 2$
b. $-4x^2 + x - 2$ $4x^2 - x + 2$
c. $-x^2 - 3x + 2$ $x^2 + 3x - 2$
d. $x - 2x^2 + 1$ $-x + 2x^2 - 1$

 **Example 5**

Students apply computation with polynomial expressions in a problem-solving situation.

Additional Example 5

The perimeter of an isosceles triangle is $8m - 11n$. The length of each of the two congruent sides is $3m - 8n$. Find a polynomial expression for the length of the third side of this triangle. $5n + 2m$

Lesson Practice

Problem e

Error Alert If students need help, have them focus on the variable a. Ask "In which term does the variable a have the greatest exponent?" $3a^2b^2$

Tell students that this term must come first when they write the polynomial in standard form.

Problems i and j

Scaffolding Have students begin by writing the opposite of each polynomial they are subtracting. $-18y^3 + 3y^2 - 5$, $-c^2 + 2c - 6$

Check for Understanding

The questions below help assess the concepts taught in this lesson.

"How do you recognize like terms?" Sample: They are numbers with no variables, or they have the same variable or product of variables with the same exponents for all like variables.

"What does it mean for a polynomial to be in standard form?" Sample: The terms are arranged so that their degrees are in descending order.

"How do you use the coefficients of the terms when you are adding or subtracting polynomials?" Samples: Combine like terms by adding their coefficients. Write the opposite of a polynomial by changing the signs of the coefficients.

Lesson 53   339

3 Practice

Math Conversations
Discussion to strengthen understanding

Problem 4
Extend the Problem
Write an inequality for this graph. Then describe the set of numbers in words.

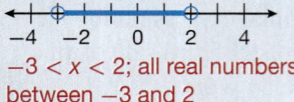

$-3 < x < 2$; all real numbers between -3 and 2

Problem 6
Error Alert
If students have trouble factoring, remind them that they can check their work by expanding the factored form:

$9ab^3c(2a - 5b^3) = 18a^2b^3c - 45ab^6c$

Problem 9
TEACHER TIP
Suggest that students begin by factoring both the numerator and denominator completely.

$\dfrac{40 + 6t}{20 + 10t} = \dfrac{2(20 + 3t)}{10(2 + t)}$

Extend the Problem
"For what real number is this expression not defined?" $t = -2$

"Why does this not matter for the situation described in the problem?" The variable t stands for time in seconds. In this problem, the time cannot be negative.

---

k. Hector throws a baseball up into the air, and at the same time, Jonas
(Ex 5) throws a another baseball upward. The expressions below represent the height of the baseballs at time t. $5t - 2$

Hector's baseball: $-16t^2 + 22t + 4$

Jonas's baseball: $-16t^2 + 17t + 6$

Write an expression for the difference in height between the two throws.

Practice Distributed and Integrated

Simplify each expression.

1. $18 - 12 + 4^2$ 22
(4)

2. $-2[7 + 6(3 - 5)]$ 10
(4)

3. Graph the inequality $x \leq 8$.
(50)

4. Write an inequality for the graph shown below. $x > 2.5$
(50)

5. Compare: 0.00304 ⓢ 3.04×10^{-4}.
(37)

6. Factor the polynomial $18a^2b^3c - 45ab^6c$ completely. $9ab^3c(2a - 5b^3)$
(38)

7. **Rockets** The formula $h = -16t^2 + 80t + 8$ can be used to find the height of a
(38) rocket that is launched into the air from 8 feet off the ground with an initial velocity of 80 feet/second. Write the formula by factoring the right side of the equation using the GCF. $h = -8(2t^2 - 10t - 1)$

8. Simplify the expression $(3a)(6a^2b)^3$. $648a^7b^3$
(40)

9. **Automotive Performance** The ratio $\dfrac{40 + 6t}{20 + 10t}$ compares the speeds of a car starting
(43) from two different cruising speeds after an acceleration lasting t seconds. What is the simplified form of the expression? $\dfrac{20 + 3t}{5(2 + t)}$

10. **Multi-Step** The inflation rate, the rate at which the things people buy and use
(44) increase in price, is constantly changing. During the first month of 2007, the inflation rate was 2.08%. By the sixth month, the rate had changed to 2.69%.
   a. Graph this information on a coordinate plane as 2 points connected by a line segment.
   b. What is the slope of the line segment? 0.122
   c. **Predict** Use the slope to predict the probable inflation rate for July of 2007. 2.812%

10a.

 11. **Write** What phrases can be used to indicate the inequality $\geq$? Sample: greater
(45) than or equal to, at least, no less than

12. Write the expression $-\sqrt{b}$ with a fractional exponent. $-b^{\frac{1}{2}}$
(46)

340 Saxon Algebra 1

ENGLISH LEARNERS

Discuss the word **inflation**.
Say,

"Inflation describes the increase in size of an object."

"What happens when you inflate a balloon with air?" The size of the balloon gets bigger.

"Inflation also can describe the increase in the cost of an item."

Have students describe objects that increase in size when inflated. Sample: tires, basketball

Have students describe items that have increased in price. Sample: gasoline, food

13. **Astronomy** The table shows the sidereal periods (the time it takes for a planet to orbit the sun) for the 8 planets of our solar system. What is the mean time it takes a planet in our solar system to revolve around the sun? What is the median time?
13,407.125 days; 2508 days

Planet	Sidereal Period (in days)
Mercury	88
Venus	225
Earth	365
Mars	687
Jupiter	4,329
Saturn	10,753
Uranus	30,660
Neptune	60,150

14. **Multiple Choice** Which of the following graphs is correct for $-3 \leq y$? A

A 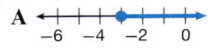 B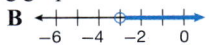

C  D

15. **Generalize** How can the graph of an inequality show if a number is in the solution set? Sample: Locate the number on the number line. If the number is in the region indicated by the shading, then it is part of the solution.

16. Find the percent of increase or decrease to the nearest percent if the original price was $48,763 and the new price is $39,400. 19% decrease

17. Identify the slope and y-intercept in the equation of a line given below.

$$1.5x + 3y - 6 = 0 \quad m = -0.5; b = 2$$

*18. Simplify the rational expression, if possible. Identify any excluded values.

$$\frac{2k+6}{k+2} \quad k \neq -2; \text{ cannot be simplified any further than } \frac{2(k+3)}{k+2}$$

*19. **Water Polo** A water-polo pool is $\frac{50x+150}{3x+5}$ meters long and $\frac{40x}{3x+5}$ meters wide. Find the perimeter of the pool. 60 meters

20. **Error Analysis** Two students simplify the expression $\frac{y+4}{y-2}$. Which student is correct? Explain the error.

Student A	Student B
$\frac{y+4}{y-2}$ cannot be simplified	$\frac{y+4}{y-2}$ $\frac{\cancel{y}+4}{\cancel{y}-2}$ $\frac{4}{-2}$ -2

Student A; Sample: Student B cancelled parts of a term. Only factors can be cancelled.

Problem 13
Extend the Problem
Pluto used to be considered a planet. It takes Pluto about 90,700 days to orbit the sun. How do the mean and median times change if Pluto is included in the chart? Sample: They both increase. The median becomes 4329 days. The mean becomes 21,995.2 days.

Problem 16
Error Alert
Remind students to divide the difference by the original price.

Problem 17
Error Alert
Students must first solve for y to transform the equation into the slope-intercept form $y = mx + b$. In that form, m is the slope and y is the y-intercept.

Lesson 53   341

CHALLENGE

A rectangular garden will be bordered by a stone walkway of width x. Use the diagram below to find the area of the walkway for the purpose of purchasing the stones. $84x^2$

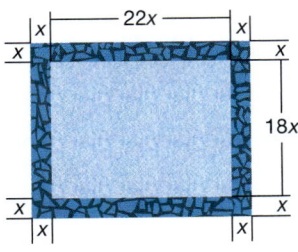

Lesson 53   341

Problem 23

Students will need the point-slope formula for the equation of a line.
$(y - y_1) = m(x - x_1)$

Error Alert

Caution students not to switch the values for y_1 and x_1. In this problem, -3 is used first in the formula even though it comes second in the given ordered pair.

Problem 24

Remind students that polynomials cannot have variables in the denominators of the terms. Then have them write answer choice **B** as an equivalent expression that does not use a negative exponent.
$x^2 + \frac{1}{x}$

---

21. Geometry Points A, B, and C are three vertices of a rectangle. Plot the three points. Then find the coordinates of the fourth point, D, to complete the rectangle. Finally, write the equation of the line that passes through points B and D and forms a diagonal of the rectangle.

$A(-2, 3)$, $B(4, 3)$, $C(4, -1)$ $D(-2, -1); y = \frac{2}{3}x + \frac{1}{3}$

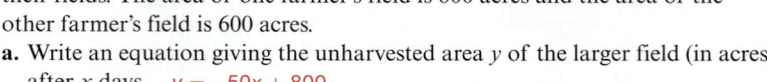

*22. Measurement Two farmers each harvested 50 acres of tomatoes per day from their fields. The area of one farmer's field is 800 acres and the area of the other farmer's field is 600 acres.

a. Write an equation giving the unharvested area y of the larger field (in acres) after x days. $y = -50x + 800$

b. Write an equation giving the unharvested area y of the smaller field (in acres) after x days. $y = -50x + 600$

c. What is the unharvested area of each field (in acres) after 10 days?   300 acres and 100 acres

*23. Write an equation of a line that passes through points $(6, -3)$ and has a slope of -2. $y = -2x + 9$

*24. Multiple Choice Which expression is not a polynomial?   **B**
A $-12b$
B $x^2 + x^{-1}$
C $y^2 - y + 6$
D -60

*25. (Advertisement) The polynomials below approximate the amount of dollars (in millions) one company spent on advertising children's books on the national and local level for each year during a certain period. In each polynomial, x represents the years since the company began its campaign. Write a polynomial that gives a combined amount spent each year on national and local advertising.
$-33x^3 + 670x^2 - 1695x + 31948$

national $= 59x^2 - 262x + 3888$
local $= -33x^3 + 611x^2 - 1433x + 28{,}060$

*26. What is the degree of $-a^2b^2c^3 + 5x^5$?   7

*27. A line passes through the points $(4, 5)$ and $(6, 4)$.
a. Write the equation of the line in point-slope form. $y - 5 = -\frac{1}{2}(x - 4)$ or $y - 4 = -\frac{1}{2}(x - 6)$
b. Write the equation of the line in slope-intercept form. $y = -\frac{1}{2}x + 7$ **27c.**
c. Graph the line using a graphing calculator.
d. Fill in the missing coordinates of the following points: $(x, 4)$ and $(3, y)$.

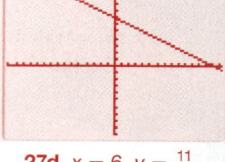

28. Write an equation of the line in point-slope form that has a slope of -1 and passes through the point $(3, 1)$. $y - 1 = -(x - 3)$

27d. $x = 6$, $y = \frac{11}{2}$

*29. Write Is 4 equal to $4x^0$? Explain.   yes; Sample: $x^0 = 1$ and $4 \times 1 = 4$.

*30. Verify What polynomial can be subtracted from $3x^2 + 7x - 6$ to get -6?

30. $3x^2 + 7x$;
Sample: $3x^2 + 7x - 6$
$\underline{-3x^2 - 7x}$
-6

342   Saxon Algebra 1

LOOKING FORWARD

Adding and subtracting polynomials prepares students for

- **Lesson 58** Multiplying Polynomials
- **Lesson 60** Finding Special Products of Binomials
- **Lesson 72** Factoring Trinomials: $x^2 + bx + c$
- **Lesson 75** Factoring Trinomials: $ax^2 + bx + c$
- **Lesson 79** Factoring Trinomials by Using the GCF
- **Lesson 83** Factoring Special Products
- **Lesson 87** Factoring Polynomials by Grouping
- **Lesson 93** Dividing Polynomials
- **Lesson 95** Factoring Polynomial Denominators

LAB 4

Drawing Box-and-Whisker Plots

Graphing Calculator Lab *(Use with Lesson 54)*

When making a box-and-whisker plot, remember to first place the given data in numeric order. Then separate that data into quartiles. Inadvertently omitting a value or listing the data out of order is a common error and will result in inaccurate quartiles. Use a graphing calculator to easily create a box-and-whisker plot based on a set of data, regardless of whether the data is given in numeric order.

The data listed are the ages of 16 students' oldest siblings. Make a box-and-whisker plot for the data.

10, 11, 15, 10, 9, 14, 12, 8, 9, 15, 7, 10, 10, 14, 18, 19

1. Press **STAT** and choose **1:Edit** to enter the data into L1 (List 1).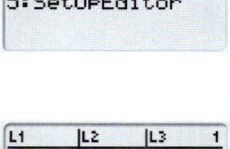

2. Clear any old data by pressing the ▲ key until L1 is selected and then by pressing **CLEAR** and then **ENTER**.

3. Enter the data one at a time. Press **ENTER** after keying in each value.

4. Press **2nd** **Y=** (STAT PLOT) and select **1:Plot1...** to open the plot setup menu.

5. Press **ENTER** to turn Plot1 **On** and then press the ▼ key once and the ▶ key four times to select the icon in the middle of the bottom row. The setting for **Xlist** should be L1 and **Freq** should be 1.

Online Connection
www.SaxonMathResources.com

Material
- graphing calculator

Discuss
A box-and-whisker plot is a way to display information that shows the relative spread of data. Tell students that the first quartile is the median of the first half of an ordered data set and that the third quartile is the median of the second half of an ordered data set.

6. Create a box-and-whisker plot by pressing **ZOOM** and selecting **9:ZoomStat**.

7. Use the **TRACE** key and then the ◀ and ▶ keys to view the statistical values.

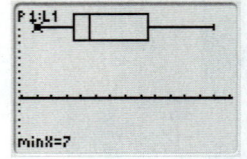

The minimum age is 7 years, the first quartile is 9.5 years, the median is 10.5 years, the third quartile is 14.5 years, and the maximum age is 19 years.

Lab Practice

a.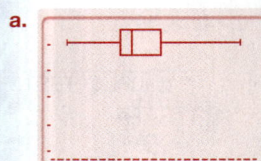

a. Use the data below to make a box-and-whisker plot for the maximum speeds of these animals.

Animal	Maximum Speed (mph)
Cheetah	70
Lion	50
Coyote	43
Hyena	40
Rabbit	35
Giraffe	32
Grizzly Bear	30
Cat	30
Elephant	25
Squirrel	12

The heights of 11 students in inches are as follows: 66, 60, 59, 67, 68, 63, 62, 61, 69, 64, and 61

b.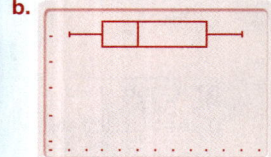

b. Make a box-and-whisker plot of the data.

c. What is the median height of the students?   63 inches

d. Between which heights do 50 percent of the students fall?
between 61 and 67 inches

LESSON 54

Displaying Data in a Box-and-Whisker Plot

Warm Up

1. **Vocabulary** A(n) _____ is a data value that is much greater or much less than the other values in the data set. **outlier**

2. Skateboards sell for $39.99, $32.99, $65.98, $38.99, $28.99, $31.00, $41.00. Find the mean price of the skateboards. (Round the answer to the nearest dollar.) **$40.00**

3. (**Space Exploration**) The data set shows the number of days each expedition crew was assigned to the International Space Station from 2000 to 2004.
140.98, 167.28, 128.86, 195.82, 184.93, 161.05, 184.93, 194.77, 185.66, 192.79

   a. Find the median of the data set. **184.93**
   b. Find the range of the data set. **66.96**

Evaluate.

4. $\dfrac{(8.2 + 3.7 + 9.1 + 3.8)}{4}$ **6.2**

5. $-\dfrac{7}{8} \div \left(-\dfrac{3}{4}\right)$ $\dfrac{7}{6}$ or $1\dfrac{1}{6}$

New Concepts

A **box-and-whisker plot** displays data that are divided into four groups.

A line inside the box shows the median, the ends of the box show the quartiles, and the ends of the whiskers show the minimum and maximum values.

In 15 hockey games, 1, 1, 1, 3, 4, 4, 4, 5, 6, 7, 7, 8, 8, 9, 9 goals were scored. The number of goals scored can be displayed in a box-and-whisker plot.

Math Language

The **median** is the middle number in a set of numbers that are arranged from least to greatest.

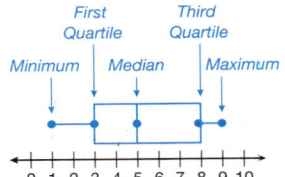

Hockey Goals

Half of the games had between 3 to 8 goals per game.

One-fourth of the games had between 1 and 3 goals per game.

The median number of goals scored was 5.

The greatest number of goals scored in one game was 9.

The quartiles divide the data into fourths. The first quartile is the median of the lower half of the data, and the third quartile is the median of the upper half of the data.

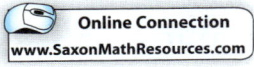
Online Connection
www.SaxonMathResources.com

Lesson 54   345

---

1 Warm Up

Problem 3a
Check that students remember how to find the median of a set of data. Remind them to put the values in order from least to greatest. If there are an odd number of values, the median is the middle number. If there is an even number of values, the median is the average, $\frac{1}{2}(a+b)$, of the two middle numbers.

2 New Concepts

In this lesson, students learn to interpret and make box-and-whisker plots. They will need to find the median, first and third quartiles, minimum and maximum values, and identify any outliers.

Discuss the five numbers used to make a box-and-whisker plot. Have 15 students tell the number of brothers and sisters each has. List these numbers in a row on the board. Have students order them from least to greatest. Then explain how to find the median, first quartile, and third quartile. These three values, along with the minimum and maximum, are those needed to make the plots.

LESSON RESOURCES

Student Edition Practice
 Workbook 54
Reteaching Master 54
Adaptations Master 54
Challenge and Enrichment
 Master C54
Technology Lab Master 54

Lesson 54   345

MATH BACKGROUND

A box-and-whisker plot, also known as a boxplot, is a convenient way to show the five-number summary for a data set. These five numbers are the least value, the lower quartile, the median, the upper quartile, and the greatest value. The box-and-whisker plot was introduced in 1977 by the American statistician John Tukey.

A quartile is any of the three values which divide an ordered data set into four equal parts. The second quartile is ordinarily called the median. Although there is no universal agreement on choosing the quartile values, most textbooks do not include the median value in either half of the data.

The interquartile range IQR is the difference between the upper and lower quartiles. A distinction can be made between "mild" and "extreme" outliers, represented on a box-and-whisker plot by closed and open dots, respectively. A mild outlier is between 1.5 · (IQR) and 3 · (IQR) from the first or third quartile; an extreme outlier is more than 3 · (IQR) away from either quartile.

Example 1

Students learn one definition of an outlier: a value more than $1.5 \cdot IQR$ away from either quartile.

Error Alert Make sure that students understand that the interquartile range IQR, not the range, is used to find outliers.

Additional Example 1

The box-and-whisker plot shows scores on a science test. Use the interquartile range to identify outliers.

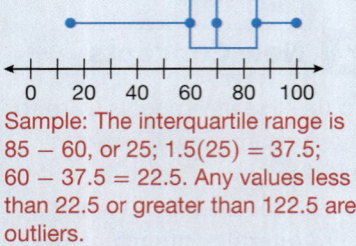

Sample: The interquartile range is $85 - 60$, or 25; $1.5(25) = 37.5$; $60 - 37.5 = 22.5$. Any values less than 22.5 or greater than 122.5 are outliers.

Example 2

Students make a box-and-whisker plot for a set of data. Emphasize that the right and left sides of the box contain one-half of the data points.

Error Alert Make sure students put the data in order before looking for the median and the quartiles.

Additional Example 2

Make a box-and-whisker plot to display the data of heights of plants (in centimeters) in a science experiment.

90, 118, 87, 114, 94, 85, 103, 89, 123, 94, 98, 124, 136, 72, 85
min = 72, Q_1 = 87, median = 94, Q_3 = 118, max = 136

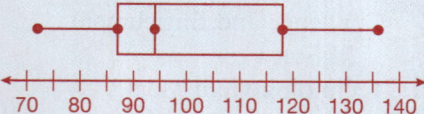

Math Language

An **outlier** is a data value that is much greater or much less than the other data values in the set.

Math Reasoning

Write In a box-and-whisker plot, what do Q_1, Q_2, and Q_3 represent in a data set?

Sample: Q_1 means the first quartile, which is the median of the lower half of the data set. Q_2 is the middle of the data set or the median. Q_3 means the third quartile which is the median of the upper half of the data set.

Determining Outliers

The interquartile range (IQR) is the difference between the third quartile (Q_3) and the first quartile (Q_1).

Outliers are any values x such that

$$x < Q_1 - 1.5(IQR) \quad \text{or} \quad x > Q_3 + 1.5(IQR)$$

Example 1 Analyzing a Box-and-Whisker Plot

The box-and-whisker plot shows scores on a history test. Use the interquartile range to identify outliers.

SOLUTION

first quartile (Q_1): 70   third quartile (Q_3): 90

interquartile range (IQR): $90 - 70 = 20 \rightarrow (1.5)20 = 30$

$$70 - 30 = 40 \qquad 90 + 30 = 120$$

No values are less than 40 or greater than 120, so there are no outliers.

Example 2 Displaying Data in a Box-and-Whisker Plot

Make a box-and-whisker plot to display the data of fish lengths (in millimeters) reported by the California Department of Fish and Game.

312, 210, 422, 323, 358, 511, 689, 722, 333, 301, 298, 755, 213, 245, 356

Half of the fish are between which lengths?

SOLUTION

Order the data from least to greatest. Then find the quartiles, median, minimum and maximum values.

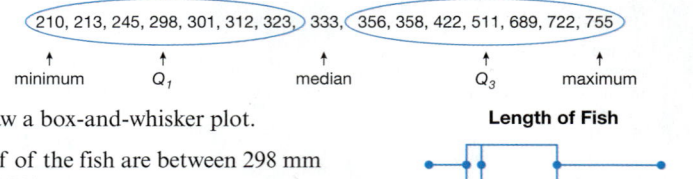

Draw a box-and-whisker plot.

Half of the fish are between 298 mm and 511 mm.

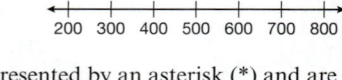

In a box-and-whisker plot, outliers are represented by an asterisk (*) and are not included in the whisker.

Example 3 Displaying Data Including Outliers

The speeds of 10 birds were recorded in miles per hour.

19, 20, 22, 24, 24, 26, 29, 30, 32, 47

Display the data using a box-and-whisker plot. Identify any outliers.

ALTERNATE METHOD FOR EXAMPLE 3

Use the bird speed data in Example 3.

19, 20, 22, 24, 24, 26, 29, 30, 32, 47

Draw a number line labeled in intervals of 5 on the board. Lead students through the steps to plot the data, ignoring the fact that 47 is probably an outlier. Have students label this Plot A. For Plot B, have students use the same median and quartiles, but mark 47 with an asterisk as an outlier. For Plot C, have students omit 47 before calculating the median and quartiles. Discuss how these three representations of the same data provide different types of information.

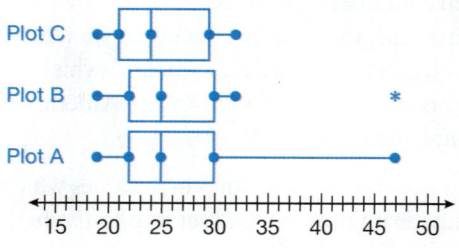

SOLUTION

Find the median, Q_1, Q_3, and IQR. Identify any outliers.

To find the median, calculate the mean of the two middle numbers.

$$\frac{24 + 26}{2} = 25$$

Q_1: 22 Q_3: 30 IQR: 8

$Q_1 - 1.5(IQR) = 22 - 1.5(8) = 10$ $Q_3 + 1.5(IQR) = 30 + 1.5(8) = 42$

47 is an outlier because it is greater than 42.

Make a box-and-whisker plot. The upper whisker will end at 32, and 47 will be represented by an asterisk.

Flight Speeds of Birds

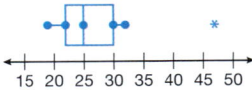

Example 4   Comparing Data Using a Box-and-Whisker Plot

The table shows the average number of rebounds per game for the Texan Runners during the 2006–07 season.

Rebounds Per Game, 2006–07	
B. Gracia	10.6
T. Chin	3.2
M. Barry	4.4
J. Carl	2.7
R. Iffla	2.1
B. Abena	2.7
J. Kunto	2.8
P. Herut	1.1
A. Carlos	4.7
C. Franca	3.4
P. Daniels	2.0
S. Roberts	1.1

a. Identify any outliers.

SOLUTION

$Q_1 - 1.5(IQR) = 2.05 - 1.5(1.85) = -0.725$
$Q_3 + 1.5(IQR) = 3.9 + 1.5(1.85) = 6.675$

10.6 is an outlier.

b. Use a graphing calculator to make a box-and-whisker plot with and without identifying the outlier. Which plot represents the data better?

Graphing Calculator Tip

For help with graphing box-and-whisker plots, see Graphing Calculator Lab 4 on page 343.

SOLUTION

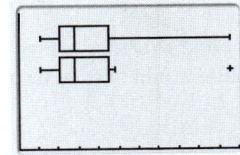

The plot that identifies the outlier is better. There are no values between 4.7 and 10.6. A whisker makes it look like data is distributed throughout that range. Using a plot that identifies the outlier shows that most of the data is very close to Q_3.

Lesson 54   347

Example 3
Students make a box-and-whisker plot that uses an asterisk to represent an outlier.

Extend the Example
Have students use the given data to find the mean with and without the outlier. with, 27.3; without, 25.11

Additional Example 3
The ages of the 14 members of the senior chess club are shown.

65, 60, 71, 70, 68, 70, 66, 67, 69, 88, 66, 73, 68, 70

Display the data using a box-and-whisker plot. Identify any outliers.

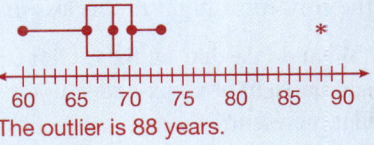

The outlier is 88 years.

Example 4
Students make and compare two box-and-whisker plots one with, and one without, an outlier.

Additional Example 4
This data set shows the distance (in miles) Vince ran on his running workouts last month.

4.2, 3.7, 3.4, 4.5, 3.6, 4.1, 6.2, 4.5, 3.3, 3.7, 4.1, 4.0, 3.5

a. Identify any outliers. 6.2 mi

b. Use a graphing calculator to make a box-and-whisker plot with and without identifying the outlier. Which plot represents the data better?
The plot that identifies the outlier is better.

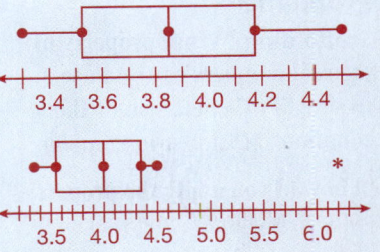

ALTERNATE METHOD FOR EXAMPLE 4

Explain to students that box-and-whisker plots can be made vertically as well as horizontally. When they are done vertically, they can be called a candlestick chart. Have students use the data in Example 4 to make a candlestick chart comparing two data sets, one with the outlier and one without.

Data Set A: 10.6, 3.2, 4.4, 2.7, 2.1, 2.7, 2.8, 1.1, 4.7, 3.4, 2.0, 1.1

Data Set B: 3.2, 4.4, 2.7, 2.1, 2.7, 2.8, 1.1, 4.7, 3.4, 2.0, 1.1

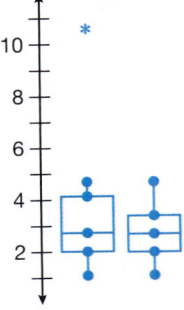

Lesson 54   347

Lesson Practice

Problem b

Error Alert Students may identify half the data above or below the median. Remind them that one-half of the data are between the first and third quartiles.

Problem c

Scaffolding Lead students through the first two steps.

"Start by putting the data in order. Underline the two middle numbers. Then find the median."
1, 18, 19, 19, 21, 22, <u>23, 27</u>, 28, 34, 37, 43, 44, 89; median = 25

✓ Check for Understanding

The questions below help assess the concepts taught in this lesson.

"What do the dots on the far left and far right of a box-and-whisker plot represent?" Sample: minimum and maximum values of the data set

"If you know the median and the first and third quartiles of a data set, what else do you need to know to make a box-and-whisker plot?" Sample: lowest and highest values of the data set

"If the whisker on the right side of a box-and-whisker plot is much longer than the one on the left. What does this tell you about the data?" Sample: The upper half of the data is much more dispersed or spread out than the lower half.

3 Practice

Math Conversations

Discussion to strengthen understanding

Problem 3

Scaffolding "What property of the real numbers can you use to simplify the left side of this equation?" Distributive Property

"How do you apply the property?" Sample: Multiply 4 times x, then multiply 4 times -2.

348 Saxon Algebra 1

---

b. **State Test Scores**

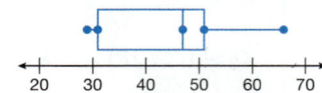

350 400 450 500 550 600 650

Hint
Don't forget to first put the numbers in order from least to greatest.

c. **Number of Yards Run**

0 10 20 30 40 50 60 70 80 90

d.

Lesson Practice

a. (Ex 1) A trainer made a box-and-whisker plot of the number of seconds her clients could stand on a balance pod. Use the interquartile range to identify outliers. **no outliers**

Number of Seconds on Balance Pod

20 30 40 50 60 70

b. (Ex 2) Make a box-and-whisker plot to display the data of scores on some state tests: 411, 507, 387, 475, 507, 477, 484, 605, 496, 504, 529, 585, 459, 586, 508, 589. Half the tests are between which scores? **476 and 557**

c. (Ex 3) A coach records the number of yards run by his players.
1, 22, 18, 34, 37, 89, 44, 43, 19, 28, 27, 23, 19, 21

Display the data using a box-and-whisker plot. Identify any outliers.

The populations of the 17 largest U.S. cities in 2005 are listed in millions.
0.7, 2, 0.9, 2.8, 1.5, 0.7, 1.3, 0.8, 0.7, 0.6, 0.8, 1.2, 3.8, 1.5, 0.7, 8.1, 0.9

d. (Ex 4) Identify any outliers. **3.8 and 8.1**

e. (Ex 4) Use a graphing calculator to make a box-and-whisker plot of this data with and without identifying the outlier. Which plot represents the data better?
Sample: The plot with the outlier represents the data better. There are no values between 3.8 and 8.1. A whisker makes it look like data are distributed throughout that range. Identifying an outlier shows that most of the data are less than 3.

Practice Distributed and Integrated

Solve each equation. Check your answer.

1. (26) $\frac{1}{2} + \frac{3}{8}x - 5 = 10\frac{1}{2}$ $x = 40$

2. (24) $0.02x - 4 - 0.01x - 2 = -6.3$ $x = -30$

3. (28) $x - 5x + 4(x - 2) = 3x - 8$ $x = 0$

Simplify.

4. (38) $\frac{2x^2 - 10x}{2x}$ $x - 5$

5. (39) $\frac{b^2}{d^{-3}}\left(\frac{db^{-2}}{4} - \frac{3f^{-3}d^2}{b^{-2}}\right)$ $\frac{d^4}{4} - \frac{3b^4d^6}{f^3}$

*6. (40) **Chemistry** Avogadro's number is represented by 6.02×10^{23}. Writing this number as a product, which value would have to be in the exponent of the expression $(6.02 \times 10^{15})(10^-)^2$?   **4**

7. (41) **Multi-Step** The formula to convert degrees Fahrenheit to degrees Celsius is $C = \frac{5}{9}(F - 32)$.
   a. On a separate sheet of paper, make a table of the equivalent Celsius temperature to -4, 32, 50, and 77 degrees Fahrenheit.
   b. Use the table to make a graph of the relationship.
   c. Find the slope of the graph. $\frac{5}{9}$

7a.
°F	−4	32	50	77
°C	−20	0	10	25

7b.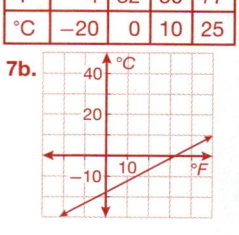

348 Saxon Algebra 1

---

eL ENGLISH LEARNERS

Explain the meaning of the word **trainer**. Say:

"A trainer is a person who teaches skills that often involve physical fitness. A trainer helps joggers perform better in races."

Discuss other types of athletic training with students. Have volunteers give some examples of sports in which a person might have a trainer. Sample: tennis, swimming, gymnastics

*8. A class makes a box-and-whisker plot to show how many children are in each
(54) family. Identify the median, upper and lower quartiles, upper and lower extremes, and the interquartile range.   LE: 1; Q_1: 2; median: 2.5; Q_3: 3; UE: 5; IQR: 1

Children per Family

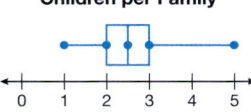

*9. A doctor makes a box-and-whisker plot to show the number of patients she
(54) sees each day. Identify the median, upper and lower quartiles, upper and lower extremes, and the interquartile range.   LE: 12; Q_1: 18; median: 25; Q_3: 27; UE: 30; IQR: 9

Patients per Day

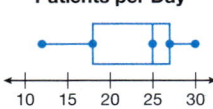

*10. Formulate Create a data set that meets the following criteria: lower extreme 62,
(54) lower quartile 70, median 84, upper quartile 86, and upper extreme 95.
Sample: 62, 64, 70, 70, 71, 84, 85, 86, 86, 90, 95

*11. Multiple Choice Using a box-and-whisker plot, which information can you
(54) gather?   **B**

   A the mode   **B** the range

   C the mean   **D** the number of data values

*12. (**Astronomy**) The planets' distances (in millions of miles) from the sun are as follows:
(54)

        36, 67, 93, 142, 484, 887, 1765, and 2791

Make a box-and-whisker plot of these distances and determine if any planet's distance is an outlier.   no outliers

13. Find the percent of increase or decrease to the nearest percent from the original
(47) price of $2175.00 to the new price of $2392.50.   10% increase

*14. Choose an appropriate measure of central tendency to represent the data set. Justify
(48) your answer.   Sample: the mean value of 90; The median value (91) is not a part of the data set and there is more than one mode (86, 92, 94).
12 quiz scores (in percents): 86, 92, 88, 100, 86, 94, 92, 78, 90, 96, 94, 84.

*15. (**Manufacturing**) A skateboard factory has 467 skateboards in stock. The factory can
(49) produce 115 skateboards per hour. Write a linear equation in slope-intercept form to represent the number of skateboards in inventory after so many hours if no shipments are made. $y = 115x + 467$

16. Write an inequality for the graph below. $x \leq -6$ 12. Planet Distance from the Sun (in millions of miles)
(50)

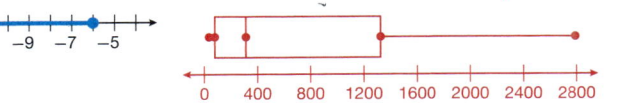

Lesson 54   349

Problem 20

Remind students that all three terms of this expression must have a common factor. So, to simplify the rational expression $\frac{2g}{2g+6}$, students divide each term by 2.

Problem 23

TEACHER TIP

Students will need to use the slope formula. $m = \frac{y_2 - y_1}{x_2 - x_1}$

Remind students to watch the positions of the x- and y-variables.

---

17. (Automotive Maintenance) The following chart shows the wear on a particular brand of tires every 10,000 miles. What is the average rate of wear for this brand of tires?

Mileage	Tread Depth
10,000	20 mm
20,000	16 mm
30,000	12 mm
40,000	8 mm

$m = \left(\frac{1}{2500}\right)$ mm/mi

18. The diagram shows types of transportation. Use the diagram to determine if each statement is true or false. If the statement is false, provide a counterexample.

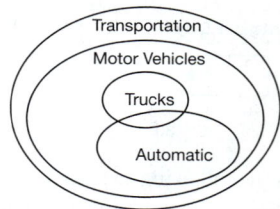

a. If a vehicle is a truck, then the vehicle is an automatic. false; Sample: A vehicle can be a standard truck.
b. All trucks are motor vehicles. true

19. Write Explain the difference between $\sqrt{-1}$ and $\sqrt{1}$. Sample: The square root of –1 is not a real number, whereas the square root of 1 is 1.

20. Write Explain why $\frac{2g}{2g+6}$ cannot be simplified to $\frac{1}{6}$.

20. Sample: In the denominator, the 2g and the 6 cannot be separated and canceled. The GCF of the numerator and the denominator is 2.

21. Multiple Choice Which expression is not equivalent to $3rd^{-1} - \frac{6}{r^{-1}d}$? **C**

A $-3rd^{-1}$ B $\frac{-3r}{d}$ C $\frac{-3d}{r}$ D $\frac{-3}{r^{-1}d}$

***22.** (Telecommunications) Jane bought a prepaid phone card that had 500 minutes. She used about 25 minutes of calling time per week. Write and graph an equation to approximate her remaining calling time y (in minutes) after 9 weeks.

22. $y = 500 - 25x$;

23. Find the slope of the line that passes through (1, 6) and (3, –4). -5

24. Describe a line that has a slope of 0 and passes through the point (–1, 1).
Sample: a horizontal line passing through (–1, 1)

25. Write an equation in slope-intercept form of a line that passes through the points (14, –3) and (–6, 9). $y = -\frac{3}{5}x + \frac{27}{5}$

26. Error Analysis Students were asked to find the sum of the polynomials vertically. Which student is correct? Explain the error. Student B; Student A didn't combine like terms.

Student A	Student B
$-6x^3 - 3x^2 + 5$	$-6x^3 - 3x^2 + 5$
$+\ 2x^3\ -\ x\ -7$	$+\ 2x^3\ -\ x\ -7$
$-4x^3 - 4x^2 - 2$	$-4x^3 - 3x^2 - x - 2$

350 Saxon Algebra 1

INCLUSION

Use the data set consisting of the numbers 1–15 to help students learn the concept of quartiles. List the numbers then put the box-and-whisker plot below them.

1, 2, 3, 4, 5, 6, 7, 8, 9, 10, 11, 12, 13, 14, 15

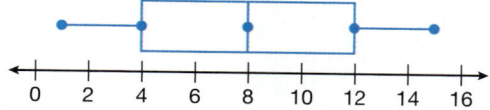

Have volunteers identify the minimum and maximum values in both the list and on the plot. Then ask, "What number is in the middle of this set?" 8

"Where is 8 on the box-and-whisker plot?" In the middle; It is shown by the line in the middle of the box.

Circle the 8 in the list of numbers. Repeat the discussion for the lower quartile 4 and the upper quartile 12.

27. Geometry Write a polynomial expression for the perimeter of the triangle. Simplify the polynomial and give your answer in standard form. $9x + 16$

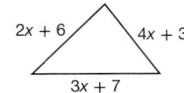

28. Measurement The length of the sidewalk that runs in front of Trina's house is $3x - 16$ and the width is $5x + 21$. Find the perimeter of the sidewalk. $16x + 10$

*29. Multi-Step The table shows the amounts that Doug and Jane plan to deposit in their savings account. Their savings account has the same annual growth rate g.

Date	1/1/04	1/1/05	1/1/06	1/1/07
Doug	$300	$400	$200	$25
Jane	$375	$410	$50	$200

a. On January 1, 2007, the value of Doug's account D can be modeled by $D = 300g^3 + 400g^2 + 200g + 25$, where g is the annual growth rate. Find a model for Jane's account J on January 1, 2007. $J = 375g^3 + 410g^2 + 50g + 200$

b. Find a model for the combined amounts of Doug and Jane's account on January 1, 2007. $675g^3 + 810g^2 + 250g + 225$

30. Find the sum of $(9x^3 + 12) + (16x^3 - 4x + 2)$ using a horizontal format. $25x^3 - 4x + 14$

Problem 28
TEACHER TIP
The perimeter formula $P = 2(l + w)$ may be easier for most students to use than $P = 2l + 2w$. They should start by adding the two binomials. Then they multiply by 2.

Problem 29
TEACHER TIP
Students may need help getting started. Suggest they compare the coefficients of Doug's polynomial with the numbers in his row of the chart.

Problem 30
Error Alert
If students make errors when using the horizontal format, tell them to cross out terms as they use them.

"Start with the cubic terms. Add their coefficients and cross out these two terms. Are there any terms with x squared?" no

"Write the x-term next. What are the two constant terms?" 12 and 2

"Finish by adding these terms."

CHALLENGE

John Wilder Tukey (1915–2000) was an American statistician born in Massachusetts. Have students research this important modern mathematician by finding the statistical graph he invented, as well as the two computer terms he is credited with coining. box-and-whisker plot, bit, software

LOOKING FORWARD

Displaying data in a box-and-whisker plot prepares students for

- **Lesson 62** Displaying Data in Stem-and-Leaf Plots and Histograms

LAB 5

Calculating the Intersection of Two Lines

Graphing Calculator Lab (*Use with Lesson 55*)

A graphing calculator can be used to find the intersection of two lines. Find the intersection of $y = 2x - 5$ and $2y + 3x = 6$.

Material
- graphing calculator

Discuss
Remind students that the point of intersection of two lines is the ordered pair that makes both equations true. Encourage students to verify their answers by substituting the solution into the original equations.

Caution
Equations entered into the Y = Editor should be solved for *y*.

Graphing Calculator Tip
For help with graphing equations, refer to Graphing Calculator Lab 3 on page 305.

Online Connection
www.SaxonMathResources.com

1. Enter the equations into the **Y = Editor**.

   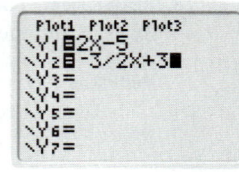

2. Graph the equations in a standard viewing window.

   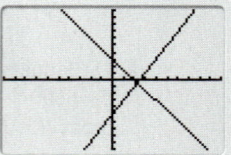

3. Approximate the intersection by tracing the line. Trace one of the lines by pressing TRACE. The ▼ and ▲ keys are used to move the cursor to another line. The ◄ and ► keys are used to move the cursor along a line. Use the keys to move the cursor to the intersection. The coordinates of the cursor are displayed at the bottom of the screen. The approximate intersection point of $y = 2x - 5$ and $2y + 3x = 6$ is about $(2.3, -0.3)$.

   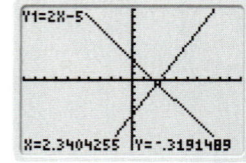

4. Calculate the exact intersection.

   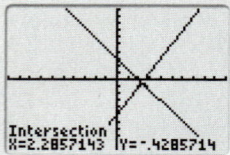

352 *Saxon Algebra 1*

Press **2nd** **TRACE** (CALC) and select **5:Intersection**. At the prompt "First Curve?," press **ENTER** to select the first line. At the next prompt, "Second Curve?," press **ENTER** to select the second line. Use the ◄ and ► keys to move the cursor near the intersection. At the prompt "Guess?," press **ENTER**. The solution is displayed as a decimal at the bottom of the screen.

5. Change to the x- and y-coordinates to fractions. Press **2nd** [QUIT] to return to the home screen. Press **X,T,θ,n** and **ENTER**, and then press **MATH** and select **1:▶Frac**. Press **ENTER**. Press **ALPHA** [Y] and **ENTER**, and then press **MATH** and select **1:▶Frac**. Press **ENTER**.

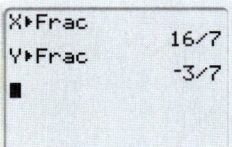

Lab Practice

a. 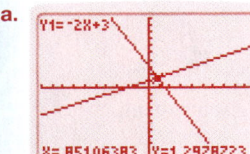 Use the trace feature to find the approximate intersection of $y = -2x + 3$ and $y = 0.5x + 1$. Sample: (0.851, 1.298)

b. Use the intersection feature to find the exact intersection of $y = -2x + 3$ and $y = 0.5x + 1$. (0.8, 1.4)

c. Use the graphing calculator to find the intersection of $y = -2x + 2$ and $3y - 4x = 12$. (−0.6, 3.2)

d. Use the intersection feature to find the exact intersection of $y = -\frac{3}{2}x - 5$ and $y = \frac{1}{3}x + 5$. Sample: $\left(-\frac{60}{11}, \frac{35}{11}\right)$

e. Use the graphing calculator to find the intersection of $y = 4x - 1$ and $2y + x = 2$. $\left(\frac{4}{9}, \frac{7}{9}\right)$

e.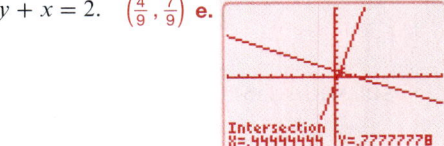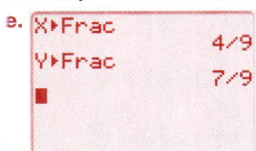

d.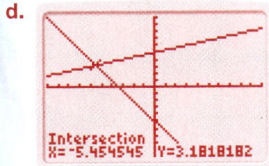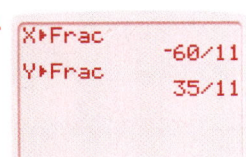

Lab 5   353

LESSON 55

1 Warm Up

Problem 3

Remind students that an ordered pair (x, y) is a solution to an equation if it makes the equation true.

2 New Concepts

In this lesson, students learn to solve systems of linear equations by graphing.

Discuss the definition of a system of linear equations. Explain if a system of linear equations has one solution that it is the point at which the two lines intersect on the coordinate plane, since the ordered pair must be a solution to both equations.

Example 1

Remind students that in Lesson 20 they learned to test an ordered pair to see whether it was a solution to an equation.

Additional Example 1

Tell whether the ordered pair is a solution of the given system.

a. (2, 3)
$x = 4y - 10$
$3x + 7y = 27$
yes

b. (1, 5)
$y = 4x + 1$
$y - 3x = 4$
no

LESSON RESOURCES

Student Edition Practice
  Workbook 55
Reteaching Master 55
Adaptations Master 55
Challenge and Enrichment
  Master C55
Technology Lab Master 55

LESSON 55

Solving Systems of Linear Equations by Graphing

Warm Up

1. **Vocabulary** The _____ of a linear equation is any ordered pair that makes the equation true. **solution**

2. Evaluate $18 + 3n$ for $n = 2$. **$n = 24$**

3. Is (3, 2) a solution to the equation $3x + 2y = 13$? Explain. **3. yes; Sample: Substituting the values for the variables makes the equation true.**

4. Write $2x + 3y = 6$ in slope-intercept form. $y = -\frac{2}{3}x + 2$

New Concepts

Math Language
A **linear equation** is an equation whose graph is a straight line.

A **system of linear equations** consists of two or more linear equations containing two or more variables. An example is shown below.

$$3x + y = 9$$
$$x + 2y = 8$$

A **solution of a system of linear equations** is any ordered pair that makes all the equations true.

Example 1 Identifying Solutions

Tell whether the ordered pair is a solution of the given system.

a. (1, 2); $\begin{array}{l} 3x + 2y = 7 \\ x = 7 - 3y \end{array}$

SOLUTION Substitute 1 for x and 2 for y in each equation.

$3x + 2y = 7$ $\quad\quad$ $x = 7 - 3y$
$3(1) + 2(2) \stackrel{?}{=} 7$ $\quad$ $1 \stackrel{?}{=} 7 - 3(2)$
$3 + 4 \stackrel{?}{=} 7$ $\quad\quad$ $1 \stackrel{?}{=} 7 - 6$
$7 = 7$ ✓ $\quad\quad$ $1 = 1$ ✓

The ordered pair (1, 2) makes both equations true.

A solution of the linear system is (1, 2).

b. (2, 3); $\begin{array}{l} 3x + 2y = 12 \\ x = 7 - 3y \end{array}$

SOLUTION Substitute 2 for x and 3 for y in each equation.

$3x + 2y = 12$ $\quad\quad$ $x = 7 - 3y$
$3(2) + 2(3) \stackrel{?}{=} 12$ $\quad$ $2 \stackrel{?}{=} 7 - 3(3)$
$6 + 6 \stackrel{?}{=} 12$ $\quad\quad$ $2 \stackrel{?}{=} 7 - 9$
$12 = 12$ ✓ $\quad\quad$ $2 \neq -2$ ✗

The ordered pair (2, 3) makes only one equation true.

(2, 3) is not a solution of the system.

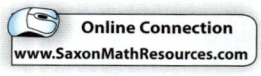
Online Connection
www.SaxonMathResources.com

354 Saxon Algebra 1

MATH BACKGROUND

The solutions to an equation of the form

$$Ax + By = C,$$

where A, B, and C are real numbers, form a line on the coordinate plane. With a system of two linear equations, an ordered pair is a solution only if it satisfies both equations. The ordered pair must lie on both lines, making it the point where the two lines intersect.

The solution to a system of linear equations is always a point, a line, or no solution at all. If the two equations are identical, then the intersection of the two equations is the entire line. The system will thus have an infinite number of solutions. If the two lines have the same slope but different y-intercepts (x-intercepts for vertical lines), then there will be no solution to the system.

All solutions of a linear equation can be found on its graph. Graphing each equation can solve a system of linear equations. If the system has one solution, the solution is the common point or the point of intersection.

Example 2 Solving by Graphing

Solve the system by graphing. Then check your solution.

$$y = x + 3$$
$$y = 2x + 1$$

SOLUTION Graph both equations on the same coordinate plane. Find the point of intersection.

Check that the ordered pair (2, 5) makes both equations true.

$y = x + 3$	$y = 2x + 1$
$5 \stackrel{?}{=} 2 + 3$	$5 \stackrel{?}{=} 2(2) + 1$
$5 = 5$ ✓	$5 \stackrel{?}{=} 4 + 1$
	$5 = 5$ ✓

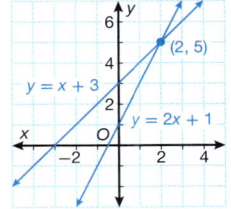

The ordered pair (2, 5) is a solution of each equation.

(2, 5) is a solution of the system.

Example 3 Writing Equations in Slope-Intercept Form

Solve the system by graphing. Then check your solution.

$$3x + y = 9$$
$$x + 2y = 8$$

SOLUTION Write the equations in slope-intercept form.

$$3x + y = 9 \qquad\qquad x + 2y = 8$$
$$\underline{-3x \quad\quad -3x} \qquad \underline{-x \qquad\quad -x}$$
$$y = -3x + 9 \qquad\quad 2y = -x + 8$$
$$\qquad\qquad\qquad\qquad\quad y = -\tfrac{1}{2}x + 4$$

Graph both equations on the same coordinate plane. Identify the point of intersection.

Check that the ordered pair (2, 3) makes both original equations true.

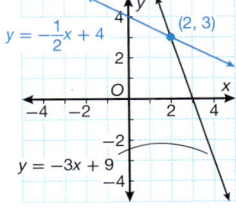

$3x + y = 9$	$x + 2y = 8$
$3(2) + 3 \stackrel{?}{=} 9$	$2 + 2(3) \stackrel{?}{=} 8$
$6 + 3 \stackrel{?}{=} 9$	$2 + 6 \stackrel{?}{=} 8$
$9 = 9$ ✓	$8 = 8$ ✓

The ordered pair (2, 3) is a solution of each equation.

(2, 3) is a solution of the system.

Example 2

Remind students that they learned to use intercepts to graph linear equations in Lesson 35. That is oftentimes the most expedient way of graphing a linear equation.

Additional Example 2

Solve the system by graphing. Then check your solution.

$$y = x + 5$$
$$y = 3x - 1$$
(3, 8)

Example 3

The slope-intercept form is very useful in graphing a linear equation. Have a volunteer explain what the slope of a line physically means.

Additional Example 3

Solve the system by graphing. Then check your solution.

$$4x + 3y = 1$$
$$7x + y = 6$$
(1, −1)

TEACHER TIP

Explain to students that the x- and y-axis can be represented by the equations $y = 0$ and $x = 0$, respectively. The x-intercept of a linear equation is the solution for the system consisting of the linear equation and $y = 0$.

ENGLISH LEARNERS

For this lesson, explain the meaning of the word **system.** Say:

"A system is a set of connected things or parts that form a complex whole."

Emphasize that a system must have smaller parts that form a whole. In mathematics, a system of equations consists of multiple equations.

Explain that a system does not imply that there must be a common solution. Systems can have parts that do not work together.

Discuss examples of systems where the parts work together (electrical systems and blood systems), and systems where the parts do not necessarily work together (political systems).

Example 4

Make sure that students know how to use their graphing calculators to graph equations and find the intersection.

Additional Example 4

Use a graphing calculator to solve the system and then check your solution.

$2x - y = 8$
$y = -2x$ (2, −4)

Example 5

Remind students to look closely at the units of the rates—that will determine how they define their variables.

Error Alert Students sometimes have difficulty keeping track of variables in word problems. Suggest that they write down how they are defining their variables before writing the equations.

Additional Example 5

Alex and Britney decide to open savings accounts. There are two banks to choose from near their school. Bank A gives a 4% annual interest rate and currently has a promotion where a $10 bonus is given if an amount of $1000 or more is deposited initially. Bank B offers no special promotion but has a higher annual interest rate of 5%. With an initial deposit of $1000, how long will it take for both banks to yield the same return? What is that amount? 1 year; $50

Extend the Example

Using only the graph of the two lines, ask students, "**When should they rent from Rent-a-Bike and when should they rent from Bike-o-Rama?**" Sample: They should rent from Bike-o-Rama when they need the bike for more than 2.5 hours and from Rent-a-Bike for less than 2.5 hours.

Example 4 Solving with a Graphing Calculator

Use a graphing calculator to solve the system and then check your solution.

$$2x + y = -2$$
$$y = -3x - 5$$

SOLUTION Write $2x + y = -2$ in slope intercept form.

$$2x + y = -2$$
$$\underline{-2x = -2x}$$
$$y = -2x - 2$$

> **Graphing Calculator Tip**
> For help with graphing systems, see the Graphing Calculator Lab 5 on page 352.

Graph both equations and then use the intersection command.

The intersection point is (−3, 4).

Check that the ordered pair (−3, 4) makes both original equations true.

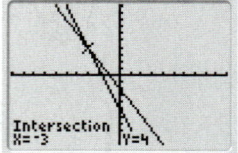

$2x + y = -2$ $y = -3x - 5$
$2(-3) + 4 \stackrel{?}{=} -2$ $4 \stackrel{?}{=} -3(-3) - 5$
$-6 + 4 \stackrel{?}{=} -2$ $4 \stackrel{?}{=} 9 - 5$
$-2 = -2$ ✓ $4 = 4$ ✓

The ordered pair (−3, 4) is a solution of each equation. (−3, 4) is a solution of the system.

Example 5 Application: Rate Plans

Beau and Celine decide to rent bikes. There are two shops from which to choose. Rent-a-Bike charges $10 per hour per bike. Bike-o-Rama charges only $4 per hour per bike, but with a deposit of $15 per bike. At what number of hours will both shops charge the same amount? What is that amount?

SOLUTION First write a system of equations.

Rent-a-Bike: amount charged = rate · hours
$$y = 10x$$

Bike-o-Rama: amount charged = rate · hours + deposit
$$y = 4x + 15$$

Graph the equations.

Find the intersection of the two lines using a graphing calculator.

intersection point: (2.5, 25)

At 2.5 hours, both shops will charge $25.

> **Graphing Calculator Tip**
> Adjust the graphing window to view the intersection.

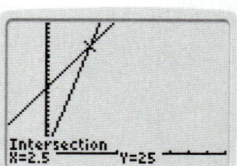

356   Saxon Algebra 1

🔺 ALTERNATE METHOD FOR EXAMPLE 4

Have students copy and complete the table for the system of equations.

Write the equations in slope-intercept form

$y = -2x - 2$
$y = -3x - 5$

x	$y = -2x - 2$	$y = -3x - 5$
0	−2	−5
−1	0	−2
−2	2	1
−3	4	4

Have students use the table to find the solution. (−3, 4)

c.
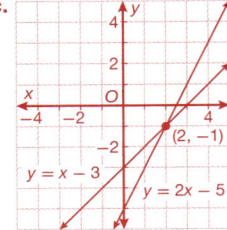

d.
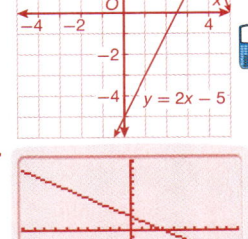

e.
[graphing calculator screen showing Intersection X=8.4 Y=-3.6]

Lesson Practice

Tell whether the ordered pair is a solution of the given system.
(Ex 1)

a. $(1, 3)$; $2x + y = 5$
$2x + 2y = 8$ Yes, (1, 3) is a solution to both equations.

b. $(3, 4)$; $2x + y = 5$
$2x + 2y = 8$ No, (3, 4) is not a solution of either equation.

Solve the system by graphing. Then check your solution.
(Ex 3)

c. $y = 2x - 5$
$y = x - 3$ $(2, -1)$

d. $y = 2x - 5$
$3x + y = 15$ $(4, 3)$

e. Use a graphing calculator to solve the system and then check your solution. $(8.4, -3.6)$
(Ex 4)
$2x + 3y = 6$
$y = x - 12$

f. (**Savings Accounts**) Jill has $20 in her savings account and plans to deposit $5 each week. Jose has $5 in his account and plans to deposit $10 each week. After how many weeks will they have the same amount of money in their accounts? What is that amount?   3 weeks; $35
(Ex 5)

Practice   Distributed and Integrated

Solve each equation. Check your answer.

1. $39.95 + 0.99d = 55.79$ $d = 16$
(24)

2. $12.6 = 4p + 1$ $p = 2.9$
(24)

3. $2(b - 4) = 8b - 11$ $b = \frac{1}{2}$
(28)

4. $1.8r + 9 = -5.7r - 6$ $r = -2$
(28)

Simplify.

5. $\frac{k^{-4}}{2}$ $\frac{1}{2k^4}$
(32)

6. $10r^{-3}t^4$ $\frac{10t^4}{r^3}$
(32)

7. $\frac{p^{-9}q^{-4}}{r^2s^{-3}}$ $\frac{s^3}{p^9q^4r^2}$
(32)

8. **Write** A student is conducting a class survey. Write each question so that it is not biased.
(Inv 3)

a. Doesn't milk taste better than the juice for lunch?   8a. Sample: Which beverage do you prefer to drink with your lunch?

b. Isn't math the best class?   Sample: What is your favorite class?

c. Shouldn't the class exercise in the morning?   Sample: When would be the best time for the class to exercise?

Lesson 55   357

3 Practice

Math Conversations
Discussion to strengthen understanding

Problem 10
Error Alert
A common mistake when applying the Law of Exponents is not applying the power to the coefficients in the parentheses. Show the following statements:

$(2xy^3)^2 \neq 2x^2y^6$

$(2xy^3)^2 = 4x^2y^6$

Problem 11
Guide the students by asking them the following questions.

"What is slope?" Sample: rise over run, or the change in y over the change in x

"What should be defined as the y-variable and the x-variable?" The height should be y and the distance should be x.

"How can you determine the maximum slope of the ramp?"
$\frac{1 \text{ foot}}{12 \text{ feet}} = \frac{1}{12}$

Problem 17
Extend the Problem

"If a law requires a student-to-teacher ratio of 4:1, write an equation to model the number of teachers employed by the preschool." $y = 125 + 5x$

"How many new teachers will the school have to hire per year?" 5

"Estimate the number of teachers at the school in 2005." 165

Problem 19
TEACHER TIP
Explain to students that graphing an equation in the slope-intercept form can be done without even finding solutions. To graph the equation $y = \frac{a}{b}x + c$, first locate the y-intercept $(0, c)$; and, using the slope, find the next point $(b, c + a)$. Then draw a line through the two points.

358   Saxon Algebra 1

---

9. Simplify $\frac{rs}{z^2}\left(\frac{pr^{-5}s^4}{z^{-7}} - 7p^{-2}s^{-1} + \frac{5}{z^{-3}}\right). \quad \frac{ps^5z^5}{r^4} - \frac{7r}{p^2z^2} + 5rsz$
(39)

10. Simplify $(2ab^2)^2(-2b^2)^2$. $16a^2b^8$
(40)

11. (**Handicap Ramps**) Building codes require that handicap ramps rise no more than
(41)   1 foot for every 12 feet of horizontal distance. What is the maximum allowable slope of a handicap ramp? $\frac{1}{12}$

12. **Multi-Step** Majid is hiking a total distance of 620 yards. He has already hiked
(42)   272.8 yards. What percentage of the total has Majid already completed?
   a. Write an equation to solve the problem.   Sample: $620x = 272.8$
   b. Find the solution.   44%
   c. Determine the reasonability of your solution.

12c. Sample: Round 272.8 up to 300. Round 620 down to 600. $300 \div 600 = 0.5 = 50\%$. Therefore, 44% is a reasonable answer compared to the estimate of 50%.

*13. (**Charity**) Gaby has $250 in donations, and she receives pledges of $40 for every mile
(45)   she walks in a charity walk-a-thon. She wants to have total donations of at least $500. Write an inequality to represent this situation. $40m + 250 \geq 500$, where m is the number of miles walked

14. **Multi-Step** A storage box in the shape of a cube is filled halfway with packing
(46)   material. There are 5324 cubic inches of packing material in the box.
   a. What is the volume of the box?   10,648 cubic inches
   b. What is the length of one side of the box?   22 inches

15. **Verify** Vickie's grade on her history report was 48 out of 60. Annie's grade on her
(47)   history report was 47 out of 60. How much greater was Vickie's percent grade than Annie's?   2% greater

16. The data represents the number of clocks in 9 households: 7, 5, 13, 5, 7, 10, 5,
(48)   5, 8. What measure of central tendency best describes the data?   the mode value of 5; Sample: This represents half of the values that fall below the median (7).

*17. **Estimate** In 1997 the enrollment in a preschool was approximately 500 students.
(49)   After that, the enrollment increased by approximately 20 students per year.
   a. Write an equation to model the school's enrollment y in terms of x, the number of years since 1997. $y = 20x + 500$
   b. Estimate the school's enrollment in 2005.   660

18. **Multiple Choice** A line through which of the following pairs of points has a
(52)   slope of 2?   **C**
   A (0, 0) (0, 4)
   B (0, 4) (6, 4)
   C (4, 0) (6, 4)
   D (6, 1) (2, 4)

*19. Graph the linear equation $2x - 7y + 5 = 0$ using slope-intercept form. Check
(49)   your graph with a graphing calculator.

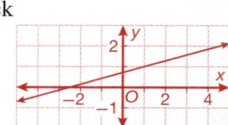

358   Saxon Algebra 1

ALTERNATE METHOD FOR PROBLEM 12

Students have learned in Lesson 36 how to use and solve problems with proportions. They should also know that a percentage could be expressed as follows:

$x\% = \frac{x}{100}$

Have students write the following proportion:

$\frac{272.8}{620} = \frac{x}{100}$

Remind them that since the problem asked for a percentage, and $x = 44$, their answer should be $\frac{44}{100} = 44\%$.

20. (Leisure Time) The current top score on Danielle's favorite arcade game is 13,468 points. Write an inequality expressing all the possible scores Danielle could score to not score lower than her top score. Graph the inequality. $s \geq 13,468$

***21.** Simplify the rational expression $\frac{5f^9}{20f^4}$, if possible. Identify any excluded values. $f \neq 0; \frac{f^5}{4}$

22. Error Analysis Students were asked to find the degree of the polynomial $2x^3 + 5x^2 - 3x + 1$. Which student is correct? Explain the error. Student A; Sample: Student B found the sum of all the exponents of each monomial.

Student A	Student B
The degree is 3.	The degree is 6.

***23. (Golf)** The height (in feet) of a golf ball t seconds after it is hit is given by the polynomial $-16t^2 + 100t$. What is the height of the golf ball 3 seconds after it is hit? 5 seconds after it is hit? 156 feet; 100 feet

24. Find the difference of the following expressions using a vertical form: $(3n^3 + 2n - 7) - (n^3 - n - 2)$. $2n^3 + 3n - 5$

***25.** A box-and-whisker plot is made to show the gas prices per gallon. Identify the median, upper and lower quartiles, upper and lower extremes, and the interquartile range. LE: 2.32; Q_1: 2.75; median: 2.89; Q_3: 2.94; UE: 3.02; IQR: 0.19

Gasoline Prices

26. Probability What is the probability that a data value will fall into the interquartile range? 50%

***27. Verify** Use a graphing calculator to find the solution to the linear system. Check your answer. (8, 0)

$$y = -\frac{1}{2}x + 4$$
$$y = \frac{1}{4}x - 2$$

***28. Multiple Choice** What is the solution of the linear system below? C

$$y = \frac{3}{4}x + 1$$
$$y = -\frac{1}{4}x - 3$$

A (4, −2)   **B** (−2, 4)
C (−4, −2)   **D** (4, 0)

Problem 28

Ask students, "**How can you solve this problem?**" Sample: Check whether each multiple-choice answer is a solution to the linear system, or solve the two equations and see which answer matches the calculated solution.

Lesson 55   359

*29. (**Phone Service**) A cell phone company named Talk-A-Lot charges $1.25 for a
(55) connection fee and $0.25 for each minute. Another company named Save-N-Talk
charges $0.50 for each minute but has no connection fee.
  a. Write a system of linear equations to represent the total cost for a phone call
     through each company.
     29a. Talk-A-Lot: $y = 0.25x + 1.25$
          Save-N-Talk $y: = 0.50x$
  b. Graph the system of equations using a graphing calculator and
     calculate the point of intersection. (5, 2.5); See Additional Answers.
  c. What does the point of intersection represent? Sample: Both phone companies
     will charge the same amount of $2.50 when 5 minutes are used.

*30. A dietician encourages students to eat lean meats. The table shows the fat grams
(54) of different types of meat.

Type of Meat (1 oz)	Fat Grams
White Meat Chicken	1
White Meat Turkey	1
Fresh Fish	1
Dark Meat Chicken	3
Dark Meat Turkey	3
Fish	3
Ground Beef	5
Beef	5
Pork	5
Lamb	5
Pork Sausage	8
Spare Ribs	8
Lunch Meat	8
Hot Dog (Turkey or Chicken)	8

  a. Make a box-and-whisker plot for the set of data.
  b. Why is this graph missing a whisker? The upper
     whisker is missing because the values of the whisker
     are contained in the upper quartile.

30a. **Fat Grams in Meat**

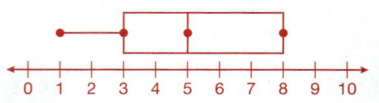

 CHALLENGE

Sometimes one or both equations in a
system will be nonlinear. The solution(s) to
these systems will still be at the points where
the graphs intersect. Solve this system by
graphing:

$y = x$
$x^2 + y^2 = 8$
(2, 2) and (−2, −2)

LOOKING FORWARD

Solving systems of linear equations by
graphing prepares students for

• **Lesson 59** Solving Systems of Linear
  Equations by Substitution

• **Lesson 63** Solving Systems of Linear
  Equations by Elimination

• **Lesson 67** Solving and Classifying Special
  Systems of Linear Equations

• **Lesson 97** Graphing Linear Inequalities

LESSON 56

Identifying, Writing, and Graphing Direct Variation

Warm Up

1. **Vocabulary** In the expression $3x + 7$, the coefficient is _____. 3

   Solve for y.

2. $3x + 2y = 8$ $y = -\frac{3}{2}x + 4$
3. $5y = 3x$ $y = \frac{3}{5}x$
4. Find the range of the function $y = \frac{3}{5}x$ for the domain $\{0, 5, 10\}$. $\{0, 3, 6\}$

New Concepts

Exploration Using Direct Variation

To make 1 pitcher of lemonade, 5 lemons are used.

a. **Model** Copy and complete the table to show how many lemons are needed to make each number of pitchers of lemonade.

Pitchers of Lemonade (x)	Lemons (y)	Ratio of Lemons to Pitchers
1	5	$\frac{5}{1} = 5$
2	10	$\frac{10}{2} = 5$
3	15	$\frac{15}{3} = 5$
4	20	$\frac{20}{4} = 5$
5	25	$\frac{25}{5} = 5$

b. **Formulate** Write a function rule for determining the number of lemons needed. $y = 5x$

c. How does the coefficient of x in the function rule compare to the ratio of lemons to pitchers?   It is the same.

d. Graph the function.

e. How many lemons are needed for 8 pitchers?   40 lemons

f. How many pitchers can be made from 47 lemons?   9 pitchers

Math Reasoning

Analyze Find the slope of the graph and compare it to the ratio.

The slope is 5, which is the same as the ratio.

Online Connection
www.SaxonMathResources.com

LESSON 56

1 Warm Up

Problem 2
Remind students that solving for y means writing the equation in terms of x.

2 New Concepts

In this lesson, students learn to identify, write, and graph direct variations.

Exploration

Point out to students that the ratios form a pattern.

Extend the Exploration

To redeem a free slinky at the arcades, 25 tickets are needed.

1. Copy and complete the following table.

Slinkies (x)	Tickets (y)	Tickets to Slinkies
1	25	$\frac{25}{1} = 25$
2	50	25
3	75	25

2. Write a function in terms of x. $y = 25x$

3. How does the coefficient of x compare to the ratio?   They are the same.

Lesson 56   361

LESSON RESOURCES

Student Edition Practice
    Workbook 56
Reteaching Master 56
Adaptations Master 56
Challenge and Enrichment
    Master C56
Technology Lab Master 56

MATH BACKGROUND

Direct variations are a special case of linear equations that students have learned already:

$Ay + Bx = C$,

where A and B are nonzero constants and $C = 0$, resulting in the form

$y = -\frac{B}{A}x$.

Since students are familiar with graphing and solving linear equations, they should be able to quickly identify and graph direct variations by knowing that there are no constants in the equations and that the graphs of the equations always go through $(0, 0)$.

A system of direct variations with different coefficients will have one, and only one, solution of $(0, 0)$.

Lesson 56   361

Example 1

Error Alert Students may not recognize the coefficient in the equation $y = kx$ as the constant of variation. Make sure that students know that the constant of variation is the coefficient, k, and not the constant, c, in $y = kx + c$.

Additional Example 1

Tell whether each equation represents a direct variation. If the equation is a direct variation, find the constant of variation.

a. $y + 5x = 1$ no

b. $\frac{y}{7} = x$
yes; The constant of variation is 7.

c. $xy = x$ no

TEACHER TIP

Explain to students that the only difference in equations representing direct variations is the slope. Since all of the graphs of direct variations go through the origin at (0, 0), the only thing that can change is the constants of variation, which are also the slopes of the lines.

When an equation has one variable that is equal to a constant times another variable, the equation represents a **direct variation**. The equation $y = kx$, where k is a nonzero constant called the **constant of variation**, shows a direct variation between x and y.

Direct Variation

Representation	Description
equation	$y = kx$; k is a nonzero constant.
graph	a line that always passes through (0, 0).
words	"y varies directly with x." "y is directly proportional to x."

Example 1 Identifying Direct Variation from an Equation

Tell whether each equation represents a direct variation. If the equation is a direct variation, find the constant of variation.

a. $y + 8x = 0$

SOLUTION

Transform the equation into $y = kx$ form.

$y + 8x = 0$

$\quad y = -8x \quad$ Subtract 8x from both sides.

This is a direct variation. The constant of variation is -8.

Hint
An equation that represents a direct variation is written in the form $y = kx$.

b. $\frac{y}{10} = x$

SOLUTION

Transform the equation into $y = kx$ form.

$\frac{y}{10} = x$

$\quad y = 10x \quad$ Multiply both sides by 10.

This is a direct variation. The constant of variation is 10.

c. $xy = 6$

SOLUTION

Transform the equation into $y = kx$ form.

$xy = 6$

$\quad y = \frac{6}{x} \quad$ Divide both sides by x.

This is not a direct variation. The constant is divided by x, not multiplied. It is not in the $y = kx$ form.

Hint
Remember that dividing by a number is the same as multiplying by its reciprocal.

Solving $y = kx$ for k gives a ratio for the constant of variation in a direct variation.

$y = kx$

$\dfrac{y}{x} = \dfrac{kx}{x}$ Divide both sides by x ($x \neq 0$).

$\dfrac{y}{x} = k$

Another way to decide if a relationship is a direct variation is to check whether the ratio $\dfrac{y}{x}$ is the same for each ordered pair (except where $x = 0$).

Example 2 Identifying Direct Variation from Ordered Pairs

Tell whether the set of ordered pairs represents a direct variation.

a. $(2, -14), (5, -35), (-3, 21)$

SOLUTION

Find the ratio $\dfrac{y}{x}$ for each ordered pair.

$\dfrac{-14}{2} = -7$ $\dfrac{-35}{5} = -7$ $\dfrac{21}{-3} = -7$

The ordered pairs represent a direct variation because the ratio $\dfrac{y}{x}$ is the same for each ordered pair.

b. $(2, 4), (3, 5), (5, 7)$

SOLUTION

Find the ratio $\dfrac{y}{x}$ for each ordered pair.

$\dfrac{4}{2} = 2$ $\dfrac{5}{3} = \dfrac{5}{3}$ $\dfrac{7}{5} = \dfrac{7}{5}$

The ordered pairs do not represent a direction variation because the ratio $\dfrac{y}{x}$ is not the same for each ordered pair.

To write an equation for a direct variation, one point other than the origin that lies on the graph of the equation is needed. First find the constant of variation, k, and then use the value of k to write an equation.

Example 3 Writing an Equation Given a Point

Write an equation for a direct variation that includes the point $(6, 24)$.

SOLUTION

$y = kx$	Begin with the equation for a direct variation.
$24 = k \cdot 6$	Substitute the x- and y-values from the point.
$4 = k$	Divide both sides by 6 to solve for k.
$y = 4x$	Write the direct variation equation and include the constant of variation, k.

Example 2

Similar to checking whether ordered pairs are solutions to a system of equations, a set of ordered pairs represents a direct variation only if all of the pairs have the same constants of variation.

Additional Example 2

Tell whether the set of ordered pairs represents a direct variation.

a. $(3, 12), (2, 8), (16, 4)$
no

b. $(4, 6), (2, 3), (24, 36)$
yes

Example 3

In a direct variation ordered pair (x, y), point out to students that the slope of the graph is $\dfrac{y}{x}$.

Additional Example 3

Write an equation for a direct variation that includes the point $(5, 30)$.
$y = 6x$

Lesson 56   363

 INCLUSION

Use this strategy to determine if a set of ordered pairs represents a direct variation. Use this set of ordered pairs:

$(3, 9), (5, 15) (6, 18)$

Have students make a table to organize the set of points. Then have them fill in the last column and compare the ratios.

x	y	$\dfrac{y}{x}$
3	9	3
5	15	3
6	18	3

Have students determine the constant of variation and write the equation that describes the direct variation. $k = 3$, $y = 3x$

Example 4
Point out to students that if the rate, or constant of variation, changes in a problem, it is not a direct variation.

Additional Example 4
The amount of water in a swimming pool is directly proportional to the time the water is left on. If the hose supplies 200 cubic feet of water per minute, how many cubic feet will be in the pool in half an hour? **6000 cubic feet**

Example 5
Remind students to think about what the range and domain are for word problems.

Extend the Example
If the grocery store has a special deal on lemons this week for 3 pounds for $0.85, what is the cost of 8 pounds of lemons? **$2.27**

Additional Example 5
The grocery store gives you $0.05 for every glass bottle that you recycle. Graph the relationship, and use the graph to estimate what you would get if you recycled 12 bottles. **$0.60**

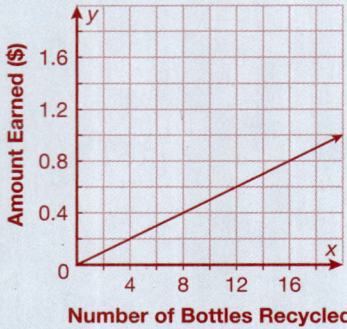

Example 4 Writing and Solving a Direct Variation Equation

The distance a person runs varies directly with the time spent running. If a person runs 12 miles in 2 hours, how many miles will the person run in 3 hours?

SOLUTION

Method 1: Because distance y varies directly with time x, the given point is (2, 12).

$y = kx$	Begin with the equation for direct variation.
$12 = k \cdot 2$	Substitute the x- and y-values from the point.
$6 = k$	Divide both sides by 2 to solve for k.
$y = 6x$	Write the direct variation equation with the constant of variation, k.
$y = 6 \cdot 3$	Substitute 3 for x.
$y = 18$ miles	Simplify and label the answer.

Method 2: Use a proportion.

$\frac{12}{2} = \frac{m}{3}$	Set up a proportion.
$12 \cdot 3 = 2m$	Cross multiply.
$18 = m$	Divide both sides by 2 and simplify.

She will run 18 miles in 3 hours.

Example 5 Graphing a Direct Variation

The grocery store sells 3 pounds of lemons for $1.00. Graph the relationship, and then use the graph to estimate the cost of 12 pounds of lemons.

SOLUTION Start with the point (3, 1.00). Choose another x-value. Use a proportion to find the corresponding y-value.

Let $x = 12$.

$\frac{1}{3} = \frac{y}{12}$	Set up a proportion.
$12 \cdot 1 = 3y$	Cross multiply.
$4 = y$	Divide both sides by 3 and simplify.

The second point is (12, 4).

Graph the two points and draw a line through them.

On the graph, find the y value when $x = 12$. When $x = 12$, the y value is 4. So, the cost of 12 pounds of lemons is $4.00.

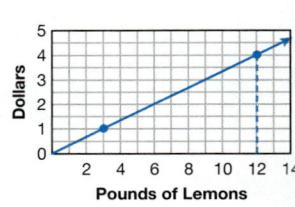

Math Reasoning

Write Why does the graph stop at (0, 0)?

Sample: You cannot buy a negative amount of lemons.

Lesson Practice

Tell whether each equation represents a direct variation. If the equation is a direct variation, find the constant of variation.
(Ex 1)

a. $y - 12 = x$ no

b. $\dfrac{y}{-3} = x$ yes, -3

c. $2xy = 8$ no

d. $3y = x$ yes, $\dfrac{1}{3}$

Tell whether each set of ordered pairs represents a direct variation.
(Ex 2)

e. (3, 10), (12, 40), (9, 30) yes

f. (10, 4), (12, 6), (14, 8) no

g. Write an equation for a direct variation that includes the point (9, 72). $y = 8x$
(Ex 3)

h. The number of boys in a class varies directly with the number of girls. One class has 6 girls and 18 boys. How many boys will be in a class with 8 girls? 24
(Ex 4)

i. The volume of a box with a fixed base area varies directly with its height. A box with a height of 4 centimeters has a volume of 29 cubic centimeters. Graph this relationship, and then use the graph to estimate the volume of a box that is 3 centimeters tall. See Additional Answers.
(Ex 5)

Practice Distributed and Integrated

Solve.

1. $-4\dfrac{3}{4} + 3\dfrac{3}{5}x = 13\dfrac{1}{4}$ $x = 5$
(26)

2. $0.3x - 0.02x + 0.2 = 1.18$ $x = 3.5$
(26)

3. Solve the following equation for p: $7p + 3w = w - 12 - 3p$. $p = -\dfrac{1}{5}w - \dfrac{6}{5}$
(29)

4. Write the prime factorization of 315. $315 = 3 \cdot 3 \cdot 5 \cdot 7$
(38)

5. What percent of 160 is 88?   55%
(42)

6. What number is 140 percent of 70?   98
(42)

7. Twenty percent of what number is 18?   90
(42)

*8. Tell whether the equation $\dfrac{y}{11} = x$ represents a direct variation.   yes
(56)

*9. Tell whether the equation $3y = x$ represents a direct variation.   yes
(56)

10. Simplify $\left(\dfrac{10x^3}{y}\right)^2 (-2x^2y^2)^3$. $-800x^{12}y^4$
(40)

11. (Market Research) An automobile manufacturer sent out 22,000 questionnaires to a sample of their customers who bought a new car from them this year. 63% of the customers who received the questionnaires filled them out and returned them. How many customers returned their questionnaires?   13,860 customers
(42)

Lesson 56   365

 ENGLISH LEARNERS

Discuss the word **manufacturer**. Say:

"A manufacturer is a group of people or a company that make things, usually by machine, to sell. The manufactured products are usually not unique and are made in stages. A car manufacturer is a company that builds cars to sell."

Ask:

"What are other items that are manufactured? Sample: phones, bikes

What are some items that are not manufactured?" Sample: vegetables grown at home

---

Lesson Practice

Problem c
Scaffolding Have students write the equation so that y is isolated.

Problem i
Error Alert Some students might be confused by the statement "The volume of a box varies directly with its height." Remind them that the box has a fixed base and that the formula for the volume of a box is $V = A \times h$.

 **Check for Understanding**

The questions below help assess the concepts taught in this lesson.

"Explain what makes a linear equation a direct variation."
Sample: The graph of the line crosses (0, 0), the equation is in the form $y = kx$, and y is directly proportional to x.

"How do you check whether a set of ordered pairs represents a direct variation?" Sample: Check and see if all the y-values of the ordered pairs are a constant multiple of the corresponding x-values.

3 Practice

Math Conversations
Discussion to strengthen understanding

Problem 7
Error Alert
Students may multiply the whole by the percent and not the value of the percent as a decimal. Remind students that twenty percent is 0.20.

Lesson 56   365

12. **Multi-Step** A circle with radius $10x$ is inscribed in a square.
    (43)
    a. Write an expression for the area of the circle. $\pi 100x^2$
    b. Write an expression for the area of the square. $400x^2$
    c. Form a simplified rational expression from the ratio of the two areas. Use the circle area as the numerator. $\frac{\pi}{4}$

*13. **Generalize** Explain why the graph of a direct variation will always go through the
     (56) origin (0, 0). Sample: The origin (0, 0) will always make the equation $y = kx$ true.

*14. **Multiple Choice** Which equation represents a direct variation? **D**
     (56)
     A $y = 2 - x$ **B** $x + 3 = y$ **C** $xy = -2$ **D** $3y = -2x$

*15. (**Currency**) The number of euros received varies directly with the number of dollars
     (56) exchanged. If $5.00 is exchanged for 3.65 euros, how many euros would be
     received for $8.00? 5.84 euros

16. Write the equation of the line in slope-intercept form.
    (49)
    $$-4y + x = 2 \quad y = \tfrac{1}{4}x - \tfrac{1}{2}$$

17. Write an inequality for the graph at right. $z \le 4.6$
    (50)

18. (**Camping**) A tent is in the shape of a triangular pyramid with a square footprint
    (46) (base). The tent is 6 feet high and has a volume of 128 cubic feet. What is the
    length of the base? 8 feet

19. **Model** Formulate a data set that has a mean value of 9, a median of 9, and a mode
    (48) of 12. Sample: 3, 7, 8, 9, 12, 12, 12

*20. (**Tennis**) An avid tennis player is painting lines to make a court at home. The tennis
     (51) court measures $\frac{150x + 200}{2x + 4}$ feet long and $\frac{60x + 220}{2x + 4}$ feet wide. How many feet did the
     tennis player paint to mark the outside lines of the court? 210 feet

*21. Write the equation of the line that has a slope of $\tfrac{1}{2}$ and passes through the point
     (52) (2, 8) in point-slope form. $y - 8 = \tfrac{1}{2}(x - 2)$

22. **Write** How is the degree of a polynomial determined? Sample: the degree of the
    (53) highest-degree term in the polynomial

23. **Multiple Choice** What is the degree of $a^2b^3 - a^3b^4 + 2ab$? **C**
    (53)
    A 14   **B** 2   **C** 7   **D** 5

24. Make a box-and-whisker plot to display the data titled "Average High
    (54) Temperature in Phoenix, AZ". See Additional Answers.

    66, 70, 75, 84, 93, 103, 105, 103, 99, 88, 75, 66

25. (**Running**) A group of friends run a marathon together. Their times in minutes are
    (54) shown below.

    201, 240, 236, 270, 245, 252, 239, 267, 241, 229, 360

    Make a box-and-whisker plot of these times and determine the outliers, if any.
    See Additional Answers.

366 *Saxon Algebra 1*

*26. Error Analysis Two students decide whether there is an outlier. Which student is correct? Explain the error.
(54)

grades on a math test: 100, 75, 80, 96, 77, 82, 88, 89, 79, 92, 100, 78, 95, 60

Student A	Student B
$78 - 1.5(95 - 78) = 52.5$	$78 - 1.5(85 - 78) = 67.5$
There is no outlier.	Yes, 60 is an outlier.

26. Student A; Sample: Student B used the median instead of Q_3 in the outlier formula.

*27. Measurement A square has side length s, while an equilateral triangle has length $s + 1$. Write and solve a system of linear equalities to determine the length of the side at which the perimeters of the triangle and the rectangle would be equal. **3**
(55)

$$P = 4s$$
$$P = 3(s + 1)$$

28. Error Analysis Two students used a graphing method to solve the system of equations.
(55)

$$-4x + 3y = 5$$
$$2x + 3y = -16$$

Student A; Sample: The solution of Student B is incorrect because it only satisfied one equation.

They used substitution to verify their solutions. Which student is correct? Explain the error.

Student A	Student B
$-4(-3.5) + 3(-3) = 5$	$-4(4) + 3(7) = 5$
$2(-3.5) + 3(-3) = -16$	$2(4) + 3(7) = -16$

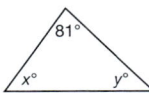
*29. Geometry The measure of the angles in a parallelogram total 360°. Write and solve a system of equations to determine the values of x and y.
(55)

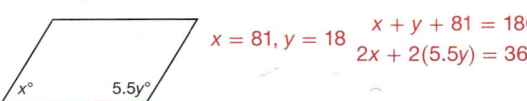

$x = 81, y = 18$

$x + y + 81 = 180$
$2x + 2(5.5y) = 360$

30. Multi-Step Thomas has a younger brother named Miguel. Thomas is 5 years older than Miguel. If Thomas's age is decreased by three years, it is equivalent to double Miguel's age.
(55)

a. **Formulate** Write a system of equations to represent the age of Thomas. Let t represent Thomas's age and m represent Miguel's age. $t = 2m + 3$
$t = m + 5$
b. Solve the system to determine the ages of Thomas and Miguel. Thomas is 7 years old and Miguel is 2 years old.
c. **Verify** Explain why your answer is reasonable. Sample: If 5 years were taken away from Thomas's age, the result would be 2 years, which is Miguel's age. If 3 years were taken away from Thomas's age, the result would be 4 years, which is equivalent to twice Miguel's age.

Problem 27
Extend the Problem
If the square is replaced with a rectangle that has a length of $2s$ and a width of s, and the equilateral triangle remains the same, determine the width of the rectangle at which the perimeters of the two figures are equal.
$P = 2(2s) + 2(s) = 6s$
$P = 3(s + 1)$
$(s, P) = (1, 6)$

Lesson 56   367

LOOKING FORWARD

Identifying, writing, and graphing direct variations prepare students for

- **Investigation 6** Transforming Linear Functions
- **Lesson 64** Identifying, Writing, and Graphing Inverse Variation
- **Lesson 65** Writing Equations of Parallel and Perpendicular Lines
- **Investigation 7** Comparing Direct and Inverse Variation
- **Investigation 8** Identifying and Writing Joint Variation

LESSON 57

1 Warm Up

Problems 2 and 3
Use the Warm Up to briefly review prime factorization in preparation for the lesson.

2 New Concepts

Students have previously found the least common multiple to add and subtract fractions. This lesson presents finding the LCM of variable expressions.

Example 1

This example demonstrates finding the LCM of two and three integers.

Additional Example 1

a. Find the LCM of 35 and 49.
   $5 \times 7 \times 7 = 245$

b. Find the LCM of 7, 8, and 13.
   LCM $= 2 \times 2 \times 2 \times 7 \times 13$
   $= 728$

LESSON RESOURCES

Student Edition Practice
   Workbook 57
Reteaching Master 57
Adaptations Master 57
Challenge and Enrichment
   Master C57

LESSON 57 — Finding the Least Common Multiple

Warm Up

1. **Vocabulary** A _____ (*prime, composite*) number has exactly two factors, itself and one.   **prime**

Find the prime factorization of each number.

2. 18 $2 \cdot 3 \cdot 3$
3. 110 $2 \cdot 5 \cdot 11$

Factor using the greatest common factor.

4. $(3x + 27)$ $3(x + 9)$
5. $(4x^3 + 14x)$ $2x(2x^2 + 7)$

New Concepts

The least number that is evenly divisible by each of the numbers in a set of numbers is called the least common multiple or LCM.

> **Finding the Least Common Multiple**
> 1. Write each number as a product of prime factors.
> 2. Use every factor of the given numbers as a factor of the LCM. Use each factor the greatest number of times it is a factor of any of the numbers or expressions.

Example 1 Identifying the LCM of a Set of Numbers

a. Find the LCM of 24 and 36.

Math Reasoning

Verify Show that 72 is the LCM of 24 and 36.

multiples of 24: 24, 48, 72
multiples of 36: 36, 72
The least multiple that 24 and 36 have in common is 72. ✓

www.SaxonMathResources.com

SOLUTION

Write each number as a product of prime numbers.

$24 = 2 \cdot 2 \cdot 2 \cdot 3$
$36 = 2 \cdot 2 \cdot 3 \cdot 3$

The number 2 is a factor of both 24 and 36. The greater number of times it appears is three times in 24, so it will appear three times in the LCM.

$2 \cdot 2 \cdot 2$

The number 3 is a factor of both numbers as well. The greater number of times it appears is two times in 36, so it will also appear in the LCM two times.

LCM $= 2 \cdot 2 \cdot 2 \cdot 3 \cdot 3$
LCM $= 72$

The LCM of 24 and 36 is 72.

MATH BACKGROUND

The least common multiple (LCM) of two or more numbers, terms, or expressions is the least number that contains the prime factorization of each number, term, or expression.

The LCM of the numbers 5, 8, and 12 can be found by first finding the prime factors of each number.

   5: 5
   8: $2 \times 2 \times 2$
   12: $2 \times 2 \times 3$

The LCM is found by multiplying each factor the most number of times in appears in one of the prime factorizations. The factors 5 and 3 only appear once, but the factor 2 appears three times in the factorization of 8.

The LCM of 5, 8, and 12 is found by multiplying $2 \times 2 \times 2 \times 3 \times 5 = 120$. 120 is the least number that can be evenly divided by 5, 8, and 12.

Math Reasoning

Analyze Why does 11 have only one prime factor?

Sample: The number 11 has two factors, 1 and 11. 1 is not prime, so 11 is the only prime factor.

b. Find the LCM of 11, 12, and 18.

SOLUTION

Write each number as a product of prime numbers.

$11 = 11$ $\qquad$ $12 = 2 \cdot 2 \cdot 3$ $\qquad$ $18 = 2 \cdot 3 \cdot 3$

The number 2 is a factor of both 18 and 12. The greater number of times it appears is two times in 12, so it will appear two times in the LCM.

$$2 \cdot 2$$

The number 3 is a factor of 12 and 18. The greater number of times it appears is two times in 18, so it will appear two times in the LCM.

$$2 \cdot 2 \cdot 3 \cdot 3$$

Because the number 11 is prime, its only prime factor is 11, so it will appear in the LCM one time.

$LCM = 2 \cdot 2 \cdot 3 \cdot 3 \cdot 11$

$LCM = 396$

The LCM of 11, 12, and 18 is 396.

In algebraic expressions, variables are included in the least common multiple. The number of times the variable appears in the least common multiple depends on the number of times it appears in each algebraic expression.

Finding the Least Common Multiple of Algebraic Expressions

1. Write each expression as a product of prime factors and factors with an exponent of 1.
2. Use every factor of the given numbers as a factor of the LCM. Use each factor the greatest number of times it is a factor of any of the numbers or expressions.

Example 2 **Identifying the LCM of Two Monomials**

Find the LCM of $10a^2c^4$ and $15a^3c^3$.

SOLUTION

Write each number as a product of prime numbers.

$10a^2c^4 = 2 \cdot 5 \cdot a \cdot a \cdot c \cdot c \cdot c \cdot c$

$15a^3c^3 = 3 \cdot 5 \cdot a \cdot a \cdot a \cdot c \cdot c \cdot c$

In the LCM, the factor 2 will appear one time, 3 will appear one time, and 5 will appear one time.

$$2 \cdot 3 \cdot 5$$

The greater number of times a appears is three times, so it will also appear three times in the LCM. The greater number of times c appears is four times, so it will appear four times in the LCM.

$LCM = 2 \cdot 3 \cdot 5 \cdot a \cdot a \cdot a \cdot c \cdot c \cdot c \cdot c$

The LCM is $30a^3c^4$.

Example 2

This example provides instruction on finding the LCM of two variable terms.

Additional Example 2

Find the LCM of $6x^2y^3$ and $9x^4y^4$. $18x^4y^4$

Error Alert Students confuse LCM with GCF and will sometimes switch back and forth between the two as they are finding the LCM. Emphasize that the LCM is the least number or term that the given numbers or terms will divide into.

 ENGLISH LEARNERS

Explain the meaning of the acronym **LCM.** Show the words Least Common Multiple, marking the letters L, C, and M heavily. Say:

"L, C, and M are the first letters of the words in the phrase 'Least Common Multiple.' The letters LCM are quick and easy to use."

Discuss other acronyms. Sample: BLT, SUV

Example 3

This example provides guidance in finding the LCM of three variable terms.

Additional Example 3

Find the LCM of $8a^2b^3$, $12b^2c$, and $18a^3bc^3$. $72a^3b^3c^3$

Example 4

This example demonstrates finding the LCM for two binomials, both prime in part **a** and neither prime in part **b**. Finding the LCM of two complex binomials is also shown.

Additional Example 4

a. Find the LCM of $(2m - 3)$ and $(5m + 7)$.
$(2m - 3)(5m + 7)$

b. Find the LCM of $(15p^2 - 5p)$ and $(24p - 8)$. $40p(3p - 1)$

c. Find the LCM of $(45h^2 + 30)$ and $(33h^4 + 22h^2)$.
$165h^2(3h^2 + 2)$

Hint

To be a factor of the LCM, a number does not need to be a factor of every number in the set. Simply being a factor of one number in the set makes it a factor of the LCM.

Math Reasoning

Justify Explain why the LCM of $(3x + 1)$ and $(2x + 9)$ is their product.

Sample: They are prime and they have no factors in common. Therefore, all the prime factors are used in the LCM. Their only factors are 1 and themselves, so the LCM is their product.

Caution

Be sure to factor all common factors, not just numeric factors.

Example 3 Identifying the LCM of Three Monomials

Find the LCM of $6p^2s^3$, $2m^2s^2$, and $8m^3p$.

SOLUTION

Write each expression as a product of prime numbers.

$6p^2s^3 = 2 \cdot 3 \cdot p \cdot p \cdot s \cdot s \cdot s$

$2m^2s^2 = 2 \cdot m \cdot m \cdot s \cdot s$

$8m^3p = 2 \cdot 2 \cdot 2 \cdot m \cdot m \cdot m \cdot p$

In the LCM, the factor 2 will appear three times and the factor 3 will appear one time.

$$2 \cdot 2 \cdot 2 \cdot 3$$

No one variable appears in all three expressions. The most the variable m appears is three times. The most the variable p appears is two times. The most the variable s appears is three times.

$LCM = 2 \cdot 2 \cdot 2 \cdot 3 \cdot m \cdot m \cdot m \cdot p \cdot p \cdot s \cdot s \cdot s$

The LCM is $24m^3p^2s^3$.

Example 4 Identifying the LCM of Polynomials

a. Find the LCM of $(3x + 1)$ and $(2x + 9)$.

SOLUTION

The binomials are prime. Their only factors are 1 and themselves. The LCM, then, is the product of the binomials.

The LCM is $(3x + 1)(2x + 9)$.

b. Find the LCM of $(7x^2 + 21x)$ and $(6x + 18)$.

SOLUTION

Factor each binomial, if possible.

The GCF of the terms in $(7x^2 + 21x)$ is $7x$. Factor it.

$(7x^2 + 21x) = 7 \cdot x(x + 3)$

The GCF of the terms in $(6x + 18)$ is 6. Factor it.

$(6x + 18) = 6(x + 3) = 2 \cdot 3(x + 3)$

$(x + 3)$ is a common factor, appearing one time in each binomial. The numbers 2, 3, and 7 are also factors, appearing one time. The variable x is also a factor.

$LCM = 2 \cdot 3 \cdot 7 \cdot x(x + 3)$

The LCM is $42x(x + 3)$.

370 **Saxon** Algebra 1

 ALTERNATE METHOD FOR EXAMPLE 3

After students gain some experience with finding the LCM of variable terms, they can simply list the factors of the numbers. They can list each variable in one column of a table and quickly determine the greatest exponent of each variable.

Find the LCM of $14m^3p^5$, $15m^6n^2p$ and $6m^4n^6p^3$.

Factors of Number		m	n	p
$14m^3p^5$	2×7	3		5
$15m^6n^2p$	3×5	6	2	1
$6m^4n^6p^3$	2×3	4	6	3

$LCM = 2 \times 3 \times 5 \times 7 \times m^6 \times n^6 \times p^5 = 210m^6n^6p^5$

c. Find the LCM of $(60x^3 + 24x)$ and $(45x^4 + 18x^2)$.

SOLUTION

Factor each binomial, if possible.

The GCF of the terms in $(60x^3 + 24x)$ is $12x$. Factor it.

$(60x^3 + 24x) = 2 \cdot 2 \cdot 3 \cdot x(5x^2 + 2)$

The GCF of the terms in $(45x^4 + 18x^2)$ is $9x^2$. Factor it.

$(45x^4 + 18x^2) = 3 \cdot 3 \cdot x \cdot x(5x^2 + 2)$

$(5x^2 + 2)$ is a common factor, appearing one time in each binomial. The numbers 2, 3, and the variable x are also factors, appearing at most two times.

$LCM = 2 \cdot 2 \cdot 3 \cdot 3 \cdot x \cdot x(5x^2 + 2)$

The LCM is $36x^2(5x^2 + 2)$.

> **Caution**
>
> Terms in parentheses are grouped and cannot be separated during factoring. The grouped terms make one factor.

Example 5 Application: Scheduling

A math test is given every 9 days. A history test is given every 14 days. A science test is given every 18 days. How many days into the school year will all three tests be given on the same day?

SOLUTION

Understand The frequency of the tests is a regular pattern. At some point the patterns will overlap and all three tests will be given on the same day.

Plan Math tests are given on days that are multiples of 9. History tests are given on days that are multiples of 14. Science tests are given on days that are multiples of 18. If the LCM of 9, 14, and 18 is found, it will show the day that all three tests will be given.

Solve Write each number as a product of prime numbers.

$9 = 3 \cdot 3$

$14 = 2 \cdot 7$

$18 = 3 \cdot 3 \cdot 2$

In the LCM, the factor 2 will appear one time, the factor 3 will appear two times, and the factor 7 will appear one time.

$LCM = 2 \cdot 3 \cdot 3 \cdot 7$

$LCM = 126$

So, all three tests will be given 126 days into the school year.

Check List the multiples of each number to 126.

9: 9, 18, 27, 36, 45, 54, 63, 72, 81, 90, 99, 108, 117, 126

14: 14, 28, 42, 56, 70, 84, 98, 112, 126

18: 18, 36, 54, 72, 90, 108, 126

The least multiple that appears in each list is 126. ✓

> **Math Reasoning**
>
> **Predict** If a school year is 180 days long, how many times will a student have a math and science test on the same day?
>
> 7 times

Lesson 57   371

Example 5

This example provides a frame of reference for real-world applications using the LCM.

Extend the Example

In addition to the math, history, and science test, an English test is given every 21 days. How many days into the school year will all three tests be given on the same day? LCM = 2 × 3 × 3 × 7 = 126 days into the school year

TEACHER TIP

For the Extend the Example, watch for students who take the answer to the original Example 5 and merely multiply by the factors of 21. Encourage students to start from the beginning by factoring all four of the numbers of days, and then have them find the LCM.

⚑ INCLUSION

Students who have a difficult time grasping the concept of least common multiple may benefit from reviewing the basic process using smaller numbers.

Have students find the LCM of numbers such as 15 and 18 by first finding the factors of each number. Students may benefit from using a tree diagram and dividing as they go.

Suggest that they start the search for prime factors with the number 2: is it divisible by 2; is it divisible by 3; is it divisible by 5?

After students have found the prime factors, have them circle the place where a given factor is listed the greatest number of times. For 15 and 18, 2 is listed once for 18 and 3 is listed twice for 18, and 5 is listed once for 15.

Have students multiply all these numbers, using a calculator if necessary. LCM = 90

Then have students divide the LCM by each of the given numbers 15 and 18. Does each number divide evenly into 90? yes

Lesson 57   371

Lesson Practice

Find the least common multiple of the numbers.
(Ex 1)
a. 16 and 42   336
b. 8, 12, and 17   408

Find the least common multiple of the algebraic expressions.
c. $6c^2d^7$ and $15c^5d$ $30c^5d^7$
(Ex 2)
d. $4k^4p^3n^2$, $5k^2p^3$, and $20n^4k^3$ $20n^4k^4p^3$
(Ex 3)

Find the least common multiple of the polynomials.
(Ex 4)
e. $(3x + 5)$ and $(2x - 7)$ $(3x+5)(2x-7)$
f. $(15c^2 - 3c)$ and $(35c - 7)$ $21c(5c-1)$
g. Find the LCM of $(8f^5 - 24f^2)$ and $(18f^3 - 54f^4)$. $72f^3(f^3-3)(1-3f)$

h. **Production Design** Every 24th backpack produced has a green stripe.
(Ex 5) Every 60th backpack produced has a big yellow dot. Every 36th backpack produced has a blue diamond. How many backpacks have been produced when a backpack has a green stripe, a big yellow dot, and a blue diamond?
360 backpacks

Practice   Distributed and Integrated

Solve each equation for the variable indicated.
1. $s + 4t = r$ for s $s = r - 4t$
(29)
2. $3m - 7n = p$ for m $m = \frac{p + 7n}{3}$
(29)

Solve each proportion.
3. $\frac{3}{4} = \frac{a+5}{21}$ $a = 10.75$
(36)
4. $\frac{3}{y-3} = \frac{1}{9}$ $y = 30$
(36)

Find each percent change. Tell whether it is a percent increase or decrease.
5. 50 to 20   60% decrease
(47)
6. 12 to 96   700% increase
(47)

7. **Sample:** The GCF uses the factors that appear in both numbers. The LCM uses all factors the greatest number of times they appear in either number.

*7. **Write** Explain how the processes for finding the LCM and the GCF of two numbers differ.
(57)

*8. Find the LCM of 24 and 84.   168
(57)

9. Find the GCF of 24 and 84.   12
(38)

10. Draw the horizontal and vertical lines passing through the point (6, 5).
(41)

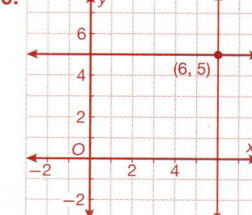

11. **Multi-Step** The graph at right shows the temperature measured at
(44) different times during a summer day. A weak cold front passed through in the early afternoon.
a. What was the rate of increase in temperature from 6:00 in the morning until noon?   2.17°F per hour
b. What was the rate of change in temperature from noon until 2:00 p.m.?   −3°F per hour
c. What would have been the rate of increase in temperature from 6:00 a.m. to 4:00 p.m. if those were the only times at which anyone had measured the temperature?   1.7°F per hour

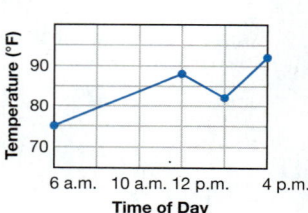

372   *Saxon Algebra 1*

12. **Multi-Step** Tenecia timed her classmates to see how many seconds they could jump up and down on one leg, and got these data results: 40, 33, 41, 36, 26, 38, 44, 46, 44, 35, 40, 37, 40, 31, 38, 41, 33, 51, 38, 40, 43, 35, 37, 38.
    a. Show Tenecia's data on a line plot.   See Additional Answers.
    b. **Analyze** Describe the overall shape of the line plot.   It is a bell curve.
    c. **Generalize** Make a statement about this data based on the line plot.   Sample: Most of the students could hop on one leg for 31 to 46 seconds.

13. (**Zoo**) The number of visitors at the petting zoo jumped from 600 in May to 900 in July. What is the percent of increase?   50%

14. Find the sum of $(-9z^3 - 3z) + (13z - 8z^2)$ using a vertical form. $-9z^3 - 8z^2 + 10z$

15. (**Phone Rates**) Ronnie is considering switching cell phone plans. The new plan would cost $5.95 per month plus $0.04 cents per minute.
    a. **Analyze** What are the restrictions on the domain and range of this situation?
    b. Write an equation in slope-intercept form to represent this situation.
    $y = 0.04x + 5.95$

    15a. Sample: The domain is whole numbers and the range is rational numbers greater than or equal to 5.95.

16. Simplify the rational expression, if possible. Identify any excluded values.
    $\frac{k-3}{7k-21}$ $\frac{1}{7}; k \neq 3$

17. Write an inequality for the graph. $2 \leq n$

18. (**Fitness**) After six weeks of participating in a fitness program, Joyce jogs 40 miles per week. Her average mile gain has been 2 miles per week. Write an equation that models Joyce's weekly mileage m in terms of the number of weeks w that she stays in the program. When will Joyce jog over 60 miles? $m = 2w + 40$; in 11 weeks

*19. **Verify** Verify that 221 is an outlier for the following data set that shows the number of dollars individuals have in a savings account.

    143, 95, 116, 169, 146, 131, 144, 150, 191, 127, 162, 221, 150

    19. $Q_3 + 1.5(IQR)$
    $= 165.5 + 1.5(36.5)$
    $= 220.25$ and
    $221 > 220.25$;
    Therefore, 221 is an outlier.

20. **Multiple Choice** What is the upper extreme in the box-and-whisker plot?   C

    Running Rate in mph

    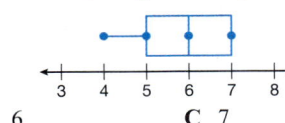

    A 5   B 6   C 7   D There is none.

*21. (**Basketball**) At the beginning of the third quarter of a basketball game, Stephen had 16 points and Robert had 14 points. During this quarter Stephen only attempted 2-point shots and Robert only attempted 3-point shots. For every shot Stephen made, Robert made a shot. At the end of the third quarter, they were tied.
    a. Write a system of linear equations to represent the total points earned by each player by the end of the third quarter. Let x be the number of shots that were made and y be the total number of points.
    b. How many shots would each player have to make so that the game would be tied?   2
    c. How many points had each player earned by the end of the third quarter?   20

    21a. $y = 2x + 16$
    $y = 3x + 14$

Lesson 57   373

Problem 8
Extend the Problem
Find the LCM of 24, 84, and 114.   3192

Problem 10
Guide students by asking them the following questions.

"What is the equation of the vertical line?" $x = 6$

"What is the equation of the horizontal line?" $y = 5$

Problem 12
Extend the Problem
Find the mean, median, mode, and range of the data set.   Mean: 38.542; modes: 38 and 40; median: 38; range: 25

Problem 18
Error Alert
Watch for students who simply solve the equation without considering the question asked in the problem. The problem asks for the point when Joyce jogs over 60 miles, which would be in Week 11. It is necessary to solve the equation and then answer the question asked.

Problem 21
Extend the Problem
Graph the equations.

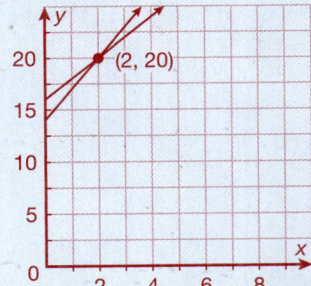

🌟 CHALLENGE

Find the LCM of
$22x^{-2}x^4yz^3$ and $26xy^{-3}y^5z$ and $34x^3y^3z^3$.
$4862x^3y^3z^3$

Lesson 57   373

Problem 22

"If you didn't have a graphing calculator, what other method could you use to solve this problem?" Sample: Use the elimination method: multiply the first equation by 3 and the second equation by 2; add the equations (this cancels the *x*-variable); solve for *y*; then substitute the values of *y* into each of the original equations and solve for *x*.

Problem 26

TEACHER TIP

Watch for students who have difficulty remembering the formula for the circumference of a circle $2\pi r$.

Problem 29

Extend the Problem

What is the LCM of $15k^{11}$, $36k^6$, and $56k^9$? $2520k^{11}$

Problem 30

Guide the students by asking them the following questions.

"What is this problem asking you to find?" Sample: the LCM for when the clocks go off

"If you multiplied the given number of minutes for each clock, would that give you a time the clocks would go off together? Is this the same as the LCM?" Sample: Yes, this would be one time the clocks go off together, but the problem asks for the first time they will go off together. This may or may not be the first time.

*22. Use a graphing calculator to solve the system of linear equations.   (0, 4)
(55)
$$2x + 3y = 12$$
$$-3x + 2y = 8$$

23. Tell whether the equation $7 + y = x$ represents a direct variation.   no
(56)

24. **Measurement** The number of centimeters varies directly with the number of inches.
(56) A table is 25 inches, or 63.5 centimeters, long. How many centimeters long is a book that is 9 inches?   22.86 centimeters

25. **Error Analysis** Two students solve the following problem:
(56)
A person's age in months is directly proportional to the number of years the person has been alive. A 3-year-old is 36 months old. How many months old is a 24-year-old?

Which student is correct? Explain the error.   Student B; Sample: Student A substituted 24 months instead of 24 years.

Student A	Student B
$y = kx$	$y = kx$
$36 = k \cdot 3$	$36 = k \cdot 3$
$12 = k$	$12 = k$
$24 = 12x$	$y = 12 \cdot 24$
$x = 2$	$y = 288$

*26. **Geometry** The circumference of a circle is directly proportional to the length of
(56) the radius. If the radius is 10 centimeters, the circumference is 20π centimeters. What is the circumference of a circle with a radius of 29 feet? 58π feet

*27. **Multi-Step** The fluid pressure on an object submerged in water varies directly with
(56) the depth of the object. At 2 feet below the surface of the water, there is a fluid pressure of 124.8 pounds per square feet.
   a. Write the equation that represents this relationship. $y = 62.4x$, where *x* represents feet below surface and *y* represents pressure in pounds per square feet
   b. Graph this relationship using a graphing calculator, and estimate the amount of pressure exerted on an object 9 feet below the surface.
   c. Use the graph to estimate how deep an object is that experiences 312 pounds per square foot of pressure.   5 feet

27b.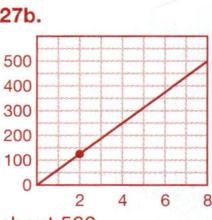
about 560 pounds per square foot

*28. **Write** Explain how the LCM is used when adding and subtracting fractions.
(57) Sample: The LCM is the least common denominator of the fractions.

*29. **Multiple Choice** What is the LCM of $15k^{11}$ and $36k^6$?   **C**
(57)
   A $3k^6$ **B** $180k^6$ **C** $180k^{11}$ **D** $540k^{17}$

*30. **Clocks** One clock chimes every $4x^3y^6$ minutes. Another clock cuckoos every
(57) $2xy^2$ minutes. A third clock rings every $6x^4y$ minutes. All the clocks just sounded together. How many more minutes will it be until they all go off together again?
$12x^4y^6$ minutes

374   *Saxon* Algebra 1

LOOKING FORWARD

Finding the LCM of rational expressions prepares students for

• **Lesson 78** Graphing Rational Functions

• **Lesson 88** Multiplying and Dividing Rational Expressions

• **Lesson 90** Adding and Subtracting Rational Expressions

• **Lesson 92** Simplifying Complex Fractions

• **Lesson 99** Solving Rational Equations

LESSON 58

Multiplying Polynomials

Warm Up

1. **Vocabulary** The polynomial $2x^2 + 3x - 6$ is a _____ (*binomial*, *trinomial*).   trinomial

   Simplify each expression.

2. $2xy^2(3x^2y + 5xy - 6x)$ $6x^3y^3 + 10x^2y^3 - 12x^2y^2$
3. $-3xy(x^3y^2 - 4xy - 7xy^2)$ $-3x^4y^3 + 12x^2y^2 + 21x^2y^3$
4. $3x^2 + 2x - 5x + 7$ $3x^2 - 3x + 7$
5. $6x^3 + 2x^2 - 10x - 15x^2 - 5x + 25$ $6x^3 - 13x^2 - 15x + 25$

New Concepts

When simplifying expressions, use the Distributive Property and the order of operations.

$$2(12 + 14)$$
$$2 \cdot 12 + 2 \cdot 14$$
$$24 + 28$$
$$52$$

The Distributive Property can be used when multiplying a polynomial by a monomial. To find the product of a monomial and polynomial, multiply the monomial by each term in the polynomial.

Math Language

A **monomial** is a polynomial with only one term.

Example 1 Multiplying a Polynomial by a Monomial

Find each product.

a. $3x(x^2 + y)$

SOLUTION

$3x(x^2 + y)$
$= 3x(x^2) + 3x(y)$ Distributive Property
$= 3x^3 + 3xy$ Simplify.

b. $-4xy(x^2 + y - 2z^2)$

SOLUTION

$-4xy(x^2 + y - 2z^2)$
$= -4xy(x^2) + (-4xy)(y) + (-4xy)(-2z^2)$ Distributive Property
$= -4x^3y - 4xy^2 + 8xyz^2$ Simplify.

Online Connection
www.SaxonMathResources.com

Lesson 58   375

MATH BACKGROUND

Multiplication of polynomials can be denoted in vertical or horizontal form. In vertical form, the multiplication closely resembles integer multiplication:

$$\begin{array}{r} (3x - 4) \\ \times (2x + 3) \\ \hline 9x - 12 \\ 6x^2 - 8x \\ \hline 6x^2 + x - 12 \end{array}$$

Each term is multiplied by both terms in the other expression.

The FOIL method regulates the order of the multiplication of binomials: the **F**irst terms of each binomial, the **O**uter terms, the **I**nner terms, and the **L**ast terms.

$(3x - 4)(2x + 3)$

First: $(3x)(2x) = 6x^2$

Outer: $(3x)(3) = 9x$

Inner: $(-4)(2x) = -8x$

Last: $(-4)(3) = -12$

Total the partial products: $6x^2 + x - 12$

---

1 Warm Up

Problems 2 and 3
These problems require multiplying polynomials by a monomial—a prerequisite skill for multiplying polynomials.

2 New Concepts

Students have multiplied polynomials in previous lessons, but only by single terms. This lesson introduces the methods for multiplying polynomials by binomials, with appropriate emphasis on the FOIL method.

Example 1
This example introduces multiplying a polynomial by a positive and a negative monomial.

Additional Example 1
Find each product.

a. $7x^2(2x - 3y^2)$
   $14x^3 - 21x^2y^2$

b. $-6ab^2(5a^2 + 3b - 2b^2c^2)$
   $-30a^3b^2 - 18ab^3 + 12ab^4c^2$

LESSON RESOURCES

Student Edition Practice Workbook 58
Reteaching Master 58
Adaptations Master 58
Challenge and Enrichment Master C58, E58

Lesson 58   375

Exploration

This Exploration helps students understand multiplying two binomials through the use of algebra tiles.

Extend the Exploration
Use algebra tiles to find the product of $(3x - 2)(2x + 2)$.
$6x^2 + 2x - 4$

Example 2a

This example introduces the use of the Distributive Property to multiply two binomials with positive terms and to multiply two binomials with positive and negative terms.

Additional Example 2
a. Find the product of $(a + 4)(a + 7)$.
$a^2 + 11a + 28$

b. Find the product of $(b - 6)(b - 3)$.
$b^2 - 9b + 18$

TEACHER TIP

Begin now to ask students to notice the pattern of signs according to the signs of the terms in binomials. If students learn early that they can reasonably predict the signs of the product, they will be able to more easily multiply and factor.

Materials
- algebra tiles

Math Reasoning

Connect What are the perimeter and area of a square with side lengths $(x + 1)$?

$4x + 4;\ x^2 + 2x + 2$

h.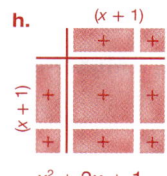

$x^2 + 2x + 1$

Exploration Modeling Products of Binomials

Use algebra tiles to find the product of $(2x + 2)(x + 3)$.

a. Make a rectangle using algebra tiles. Use the expressions $(2x + 2)$ and $(x + 3)$ to represent the length and width of the rectangle.

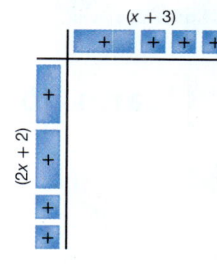

b. Multiply each term across the top by each term along the side.

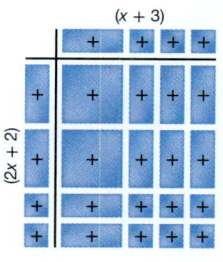

c. Which two terms have a product of x^2?   *x* and *x*

d. Why are there two x^2 tiles? $2x \cdot x = 2x^2$

e. How many *x*-tiles are there in all? Explain. $8;\ 2x \cdot 3 = 6x$ and $2 \cdot x = 2x,\ 6x + 2x = 8x$

f. Which two terms have a product of 6? $2 \cdot 3 = 6$

g. **Verify** If a rectangle has width $(x + 3)$ and length $(2x + 2)$, will the area be $(2x + 2)(x + 3)$?   Sample: $A = lw$, so the product of $(2x + 2)$ and $(x + 3)$ is equal to the area, which is $(2x + 2)(x + 3)$.

h. **Model** Use algebra tiles to find the product of $(x + 1)^2$.

Use the Distributive Property to find the product of two binomials. Every term in the first polynomial is multiplied by the second polynomial.

Example 2   Using the Distributive Property

a. Find the product of $(x + 7)(x + 3)$.

SOLUTION

$(x + 7)(x + 3)$

$x(x + 3) = x^2 + 3x$ Multiply the first term in the first binomial by the second binomial.

$7(x + 3) = 7x + 21$ Multiply the second term in the first binomial by the second binomial.

$x^2 + 3x + 7x + 21$ Add the two products.

$x^2 + 10x + 21$ Simplify.

ENGLISH LEARNERS

Explain the meaning of the word **exploration.** Say:

"An exploration is the act of investigating or studying. Explorations often involve a few activities that together teach an idea."

Discuss that a science experiment is an exploration. Ask for other examples of explorations. Sample: In English class, we did an exploration to find the kinds of books that students like to read.

b. Find the product of $(x - 5)(x - 7)$.

SOLUTION

$(x - 5)(x - 7)$

$x(x - 7) = x^2 - 7x$ Distribute first term in $(x - 5)$.

$-5(x - 7) = -5x + 35$ Distribute second term in $(x - 5)$.

$x^2 - 7x - 5x + 35$ Combine the products.

$x^2 - 12x + 35$ Simplify.

A second method of multiplying binomials is called the FOIL Method. FOIL stands for First, Outer, Inner, Last and is used as a tool to remember the steps for distributing the terms of the first binomial through the second binomial.

Math Reasoning

Analyze Compare using distribution and the FOIL method to multiply binominals.

The only difference in the two methods is the way in which they are shown. The order in which the variables are multiplied is the same.

The FOIL Method

First, Outer, Inner, Last

$(x + 2)(x + 3)$ First

$(x + 2)(x + 3)$ Outer

$(x + 2)(x + 3)$ Inner

$(x + 2)(x + 3)$ Last

Example 3   **Using the FOIL Method**

a. Find the product of $(2a + 5)(3a + 1)$.

SOLUTION

Each term of one polynomial must be multiplied by each term of the other polynomial.

$(2a)(3a) = 6a^2$ Find the product of the **First** terms.

$(2a)(1) = 2a$ Find the product of the **Outer** terms.

$(5)(3a) = 15a$ Find the product of the **Inner** terms.

$(5)(1) = 5$ Find the product of the **Last** terms.

$6a^2 + 2a + 15a + 5$ Add the four products.

$6a^2 + 17a + 5$ Simplify.

b. Find the product of $(8k - 1)(-3k - 5)$.

SOLUTION

$(8k - 1)(-3k - 5)$

    F   O   I   L

$(8k)(-3k) + (8k)(-5) + (-1)(-3k) + (-1)(-5)$ Use the FOIL method.

$-24k^2 - 40k + 3k + 5$ Simplify.

$-24k^2 - 37k + 5$ Combine like terms.

Example 3

This example introduces the FOIL method of multiplying binomials.

Additional Example

a. Find the product of $(4c + 3)(c + 5)$.
$4c^2 + 23c + 15$

b. Find the product of $(-6m - 3)(5m - 2)$.
$-30m^2 - 3m + 6$

Error Alert Watch for students who overlook the signs of the terms and write the products with positive terms only. Have these students circle negative terms before multiplying.

ALTERNATE METHOD FOR EXAMPLE 3A

Have students write out the entire multiplication horizontally before performing the operation:

$(2a + 5)(3a + 1)$

$(2a \cdot 3a) + (2a \cdot 1) + (5 \cdot 3a) + (5 \cdot 1)$

This allows students the opportunity to check that they have multiplied all the terms according to the FOIL method. They can then find each product and add or subtract to simplify the product.

Example 4

This example offers a pattern for multiplying a binomial and a trinomial.

Additional Example 4
Find the product of $(2x + 7)(2x^2 - 5x + 8)$.
$4x^3 + 4x^2 - 19x + 56$

Example 5

This example applies the principles learned in the lesson to a real-world problem.

Extend the Example
The sandbox has a depth of $(x + 4)$ inches. What is the volume of the sandbox?
$8x^4 + 66x^3 + 147x^2 + 2x - 168$

Additional Example 5
Find the area of a rectangular piece of matting that has a width of $3x^2 - 4x + 5$ inches and a length of $2x + 6$ inches.
$6x^3 + 10x^2 - 14x + 30$ in²

Lesson Practice

Problems e and f
Error Alert Some students will multiply all the factors, but will overlook that they need to simplify the partial product. Remind students to combine like terms whenever possible.

Problem h
Scaffolding Have students demonstrate how to write the problem in vertical form to be able to multiply. Check that the form is correct before allowing them to complete the problem.

Math Language
A **trinomial** is a polynomial with three terms.

Caution
Write polynomials in descending order before lining them up vertivcally.

Example 4 — Multiplying a Binomial and a Trinomial

Find the product of $(3x + 4)(x^2 - 4x - 6)$.

SOLUTION

Method 1: Use the Distributive Property.

$(3x + 4)(x^2 - 4x - 6)$

$3x(x^2 - 4x - 6) = 3x^3 - 12x^2 - 18x$ Multiply the first term of the binomial by each term of the trinomial.

$4(x^2 - 4x - 6) = 4x^2 - 16x - 24$ Multiply the second term of the binomial by each term of the trinomial.

$3x^3 - 12x^2 - 18x + 4x^2 - 16x - 24$ Add the products.

$3x^3 - 8x^2 - 34x - 24$ Simplify.

Method 2: Use vertical multiplication.

Align like terms. Multiply each term in the first row by the terms in the second row.

$$
\begin{array}{r}
x^2 - 4x - 6 \\
3x + 4 \\
\hline
4x^2 - 16x - 24 \\
+3x^3 - 12x^2 - 18x \\
\hline
3x^3 - 8x^2 - 34x - 24
\end{array}
$$

$\leftarrow 4(x^2 - 4x - 6)$
$\leftarrow 3x(x^2 - 4x - 6)$

Example 5 — Application: Area of Sandbox

Find the area of a rectangular sandbox that has a width of $2x^2 + 5x - 6$ inches and a length of $4x + 7$ inches.

SOLUTION.

$(4x + 7)(2x^2 + 5x - 6)$ Multiply length times width.

$4x(2x^2 + 5x - 6) = 8x^3 + 20x^2 - 24x$ Multiply the first term of the binomial by each term of the trinomial.

$7(2x^2 + 5x - 6) = 14x^2 + 35x - 42$ Multiply the second term of the binomial by each term of the trinomial.

$8x^3 + 20x^2 - 24x + 14x^2 + 35x - 42$ Add the products.

$8x^3 + 34x^2 + 11x - 42$ Simplify.

The area of the sandbox is $8x^3 + 34x^2 + 11x - 42$ in².

 INCLUSION

Students who prefer to multiply the polynomials vertically may also benefit from a more systematic method of vertical multiplication.

Find the product of $(4x - 3)(2x^2 + 4x - 7)$.

Have students first break apart the first binomial into two terms.

$(4x - 3)$ breaks apart into $4x$ and -3.

Now students can multiply the polynomial by one term, and then the other, and can use vertical notation to find the sum.

$$
\begin{array}{r}
(2x^2 + 4x - 7) \\
\times \quad 4x \\
\hline
8x^3 + 16x^2 - 28x
\end{array}
\qquad
\begin{array}{r}
(2x^2 + 4x - 7) \\
\times \quad -3 \\
\hline
-6x^2 - 12x + 21
\end{array}
$$

$$
\begin{array}{r}
8x^3 + 16x^2 - 28x \\
+ \quad -6x^2 - 12x + 21 \\
\hline
8x^3 + 10x^2 - 40x + 21
\end{array}
$$

The product is $8x^3 + 10x^2 - 40x + 21$.

Lesson Practice

Find each product.
(Ex 1)
a. $3x(x^2 + 3x - 7)$ $3x^3 + 9x^2 - 21x$ b. $-4x(x^2 + 2x - 3)$ $-4x^3 - 8x^2 + 12x$

Find each product using the Distributive Property.
(Ex 2)
c. $(x + 4)(x + 3)$ $x^2 + 7x + 12$ d. $(x - 5)(x - 2)$ $x^2 - 7x + 10$

Find each product using the FOIL Method.
(Ex 3)
e. $(x + 6)(x + 4)$ $x^2 + 10x + 24$ f. $(x - 8)(x - 1)$ $x^2 - 9x + 8$

g. Multiply $(2x + 2)(x^2 - 3x - 2)$ using the Distributive Property. $2x^3 - 4x^2 - 10x - 4$
(Ex 4)
h. Multiply $(5x - 2)(x^2 - 3x - 2)$ using vertical multiplication. $5x^3 - 17x^2 - 4x + 4$
(Ex 4)
i. Felipe added a rectangular porch to his house. The length of the porch is $(x + 6)$ inches and the width is $(x^2 + 4x - 2)$ inches. What is the area of the new porch? $x^3 + 10x^2 + 22x - 12$ in²
(Ex 5)

Practice Distributed and Integrated

Graph the inequalities on a number line.

1. $x \leq -2$
(50)

2. $x > 2$
(50)

Solve the equations. Check your answers.

3. $4(2x - 3) = 3 + 8x - 11$ no solution
(28)

4. $-5m + 2 + 8m = 2m + 11$ $m = 9$
(28)

*5. **Multiple Choice** Which product equals $6x^2 - 7x + 2$?   D
(58)
  A $(6x + 1)(x - 7)$ B $(2x - 1)(3x + 2)$
  C $(-6x + 1)(-x + 7)$ D $(-2x + 1)(-3x + 2)$

*6. **(Web Design)** Luke is designing a web page. At the top is a banner ad that is $3x^2 + 6x + 4$ inches high. The length is $x + 5$ inches. What is the area of the banner ad on Luke's web page? $3x^3 + 21x^2 + 34x + 20$ in²
(58)

*7. $(x - 2)(x + 3)$ $x^2 + x - 6$
(58)

*8. $(2x - 3)(2x + 3)$ $4x^2 - 9$
(58)

*9. **Analyze** Monroe says the product of x^2 and $x^3 + 5x^2 + 1$ is $x^6 + 5x^4 + x^2$. Do you agree? If not, explain your reasoning.   No; Sample: He multiplied the exponents instead of adding.
(58)

*10. Find the product of $5(x^2 + 3x - 7)$. $5x^2 + 15x - 35$
(58)

11. Find the LCM of 35, 60, and 100.   2100
(57)

*12. **Measurement** On a piece of plywood, there is a seam every 8 feet and a stud every 16 inches. After how many feet or how many inches is there a seam and a stud?   every 8 feet or 96 inches
(57)

Lesson 58   379

Check for Understanding

The questions below help assess the concepts taught in this lesson.

"What is the FOIL method?" Sample: This is a method for multiplying two binomials.

"How does the FOIL method work?" Sample: The FOIL method reminds you to multiply the first terms, then the outer terms, then the inner terms, and finally the last terms.

3 Practice

Math Conversations
Discussion to strengthen understanding

Problem 6
Extend the Problem
The web host charges $$(x - 2)$ per square inch to display the banner for a year. How much will Luke have to pay for his banner?
$$(3x^4 + 15x^3 - 8x^2 - 48x - 40)$

Problem 11
Guide the students by asking them the following questions.
"What is the first step needed to find the LCM of the numbers?"
Sample: Find the prime factorization of each number.

"What is the second step?"
Sample: Find the greatest number of each prime factor so that I can multiply them to find the LCM.

Problem 12
Error Alert
Watch for students who overlook the fact that one measure is given in inches and the other in feet. Remind students they need to convert one measure before they can find the answer.

Lesson 58   379

Problem 15
Extend the Problem
In addition to having blinking lights, glowing in the dark, and being waterproof, every 13th pair gets pink shoelaces. How many pairs of shoes are made before one pair blinks, glows, is waterproof, and has pink laces?
1560 pairs

Problem 16
Students may need to be reminded that the equation of a direct variation is $y = ax$.

Problem 20
Have students use simple division to find the percent.
$81 \div 108 = 0.75 = 75\%$

---

13. Error Analysis Two students are asked to find the LCM of $24x^5y^2$ and $32x^3y^6$. Which student is correct? Explain the error.

Student B; Sample: Student A only used factors that both expressions had in common—the GCF.

Student A
$24x^5y^2 = 2 \cdot 2 \cdot 2 \cdot 3 \cdot x \cdot x \cdot x \cdot x \cdot x \cdot y \cdot y$
$32x^3y^6 = 2 \cdot 2 \cdot 2 \cdot 2 \cdot 2 \cdot x \cdot x \cdot x \cdot y \cdot y \cdot y \cdot y \cdot y \cdot y$
$LCM = 2 \cdot 2 \cdot 2 \cdot x \cdot x \cdot x \cdot y \cdot y$
$LCM = 8x^3y^2$

Student B
$24x^5y^2 = 2 \cdot 2 \cdot 2 \cdot 3 \cdot x \cdot x \cdot x \cdot x \cdot x \cdot y \cdot y$
$32x^3y^6 = 2 \cdot 2 \cdot 2 \cdot 2 \cdot 2 \cdot x \cdot x \cdot x \cdot y \cdot y \cdot y \cdot y \cdot y \cdot y$
$LCM = 2 \cdot 2 \cdot 2 \cdot 2 \cdot 2 \cdot 3 \cdot x^5 \cdot y^6$
$LCM = 96x^5y^6$

*14. Geometry Write a counterexample for the statement: If the measures of the angles in a polygon add up to 360 degrees, then the polygon is a rectangle. The angles in a parallelogram add up to 360 degrees, but it is not a rectangle.

*15. Multi-Step A line of children's shoes are designed so that every 10th pair has blinking lights, every 24th pair glows in the dark, and every 15th pair is waterproof.
a. How many pairs of shoes are made before one pair blinks, glows, and is waterproof? **119**
b. If 2000 pairs of shoes are made, how many blink, glow, and are waterproof? **16**

16. Tell whether the set of ordered pairs $(9, 6)$, $(11, 8)$, and $(22, 19)$ represents a direct variation. **no**

*17. Meteorology The number of seconds between seeing a lightning flash and hearing the thunder is directly proportional to the number of kilometers between you and the lightning. When there are 27 seconds between the flash and the sound, you are 9 kilometers from the lightning. How far is the lightning if the time is 51 seconds?
17 kilometers

18. Error Analysis Two students are writing an equation for a direct variation that includes the point $(15, -5)$. Which student is correct? Explain the error.

Student A
$y = kx$
$-5 = k(15)$
$-\frac{1}{3} = k$
$y = -\frac{1}{3}k$

Student B
$y = kx$
$15 = k(-5)$
$-3 = k$
$y = -3k$

Student A; Sample: Student B reversed the original x- and y-values in the equation.

19. Data Analysis A box-and-whisker plot shows the number of signatures in yearbooks at the end of the school year. Identify the median, upper and lower quartiles, upper and lower extremes, and the interquartile range. LE: 3, Q_1: 14, median: 23, Q_3: 38, UE: 62, IQR: 24

Signatures in Yearbooks
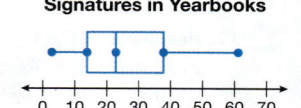

20. Use a proportion to find what percent of 108 is 81. **75%**

380   Saxon Algebra 1

CHALLENGE

Challenge students to find these products mentally. You may allow them to scribble notes on scratch paper, but actually writing the problem is not permitted.

$(m + 3)(m - 4)$ $m^2 - m - 12$

$(3p - 8)(5p + 4)$ $15p^2 - 28p - 32$

$(2a + 1)(3a^2 - 2a + 7)$
$6a^3 - a^2 + 12a + 7$

21. Simplify $\dfrac{9x - 81}{4x^2 - 36x}$. $\dfrac{9}{4x}, x \neq 0, 9$

22. Simplify $\dfrac{(x-4)(2x-3)}{7x-28}$. $\dfrac{2x-3}{7}, x \neq 4$.

23. **(Physics)** According to the Theory of Relativity, and as represented by the equation below, the mass of a particle changes with its velocity. When is the rational expression of the equation undefined? (Hint: Think of the fraction in the denominator as a single variable.) It is undefined at $\dfrac{v^2}{c^2} = 1$ or when the velocity equals the speed of light.

$$m^2 = \dfrac{m_0^2}{1 - \dfrac{v^2}{c^2}}, \ m_0 = \text{rest mass},\ v = \text{velocity},\ c = \text{speed of light}$$

24. **Multi-Step** The $5\tfrac{1}{2}$ cups of orange juice and half of the apricot juice left in the refrigerator added up to no more than 10 cups when combined in the pitcher.
 a. Translate the sentence into an inequality. $5\tfrac{1}{2} + \tfrac{1}{2}n \leq 10$
 b. Translate the inequality into words. The sum of $5\tfrac{1}{2}$ and half a number is no greater than 10.

25. **(Weather)** The table shows the total snowfall amounts for five months in Fargo, North Dakota, and St. Paul, Minnesota. Based on the measures of central tendency, which city receives less snow over the winter on average? St. Paul

Date	Fargo, North Dakota	St. Paul, Minnesota
November 2006	0.2 in.	0.2 in.
December 2006	5.4 in.	4.3 in.
January 2007	2.9 in.	5.5 in.
February 2007	10.9 in.	12.6 in.
March 2007	9.4 in.	3.6 in.

26. **Write** Create a table of values and a graph for the equation $4x - 2y = 10$. Explain how the three representations are related. See Additional Answers.

27. **(Energy)** The amount (in billions of dollars) spent on natural gas N and electricity E by a randomly selected country in a survey can be modeled by the equations below, where t is the number of years since the survey began. Write an expression that models the total amount A (in billions of dollars) spent on natural gas and electricity by this country's residents. $A = 1.417t^2 + 3.575t + 253.091$

$N = 1.521t^2 - 2.304t + 56.659$
$E = -0.104t^2 + 5.879t + 196.432$

28. **Formulate** Kami challenged her classmate to find the pattern in a logic puzzle. When she says 8, she means 9. When she says 16, she means 8. Find the equation of the line that passes through the two points that represent the data in the problem. Use the equation to predict what Kami means when she says -8. $y = -\tfrac{1}{8}x + 10; \ 11$

29. Simplify the rational expression $\dfrac{4m-8}{2m-4}$, if possible. Identify any excluded values. $2; m \neq 2$

30. **Analyze** Grace is making applesauce for a party. She has enough apples for 10 servings. If each guest gets 1 serving, how many guests could come to the party? Would a graph of this situation be helpful? Explain. 10 or fewer guests could come; Sample: A number line shows all the real number solutions for an inequality, and because the number of guests must be a natural number, the graph shows too many possible solutions.

Lesson 58 381

LOOKING FORWARD

Multiplying polynomials prepares students for

- **Lesson 60** Finding Special Products of Binomials
- **Lesson 72** Factoring Trinomials: $x^2 + bx + c$
- **Lesson 75** Factoring Trinomials: $ax^2 + bx + c$
- **Lesson 79** Factoring Trinomials by Using the GCF

LESSON 59

1 Warm Up

Problem 2
It is important that students understand that to be a solution to the system, the ordered pair must make both equations true.

2 New Concepts

In this lesson, students move from solving systems of equations using graphs to solving them algebraically.

Remind students of the definition of a system of linear equations: a set of linear equations with the same variables.

TEACHER TIP

Before introducing Example 1, use a simple set of equations to help students understand that if two expressions are equal then one can be replaced by other. For example, if $4 = y$ and $4 = 2 + 2$, then 4 can be replaced by y in the second equation to get $y = 2 + 2$.

Example 1

This example employs direct substitution without having to first isolate a variable.

LESSON RESOURCES

Student Edition Practice
    Workbook 59
Reteaching Master 59
Adaptations Master 59
Challenge and Enrichment
    Master C59

LESSON 59

Solving Systems of Linear Equations by Substitution

Warm Up

1. **Vocabulary** A (n) _____ to a system of linear equations is an ordered pair or set of ordered pairs that satisfies all the equations in the system.   **solution**

2. Is $(-1, 3)$ a solution to the system below?   **yes**
$$3x + 2y = 3$$
$$x - 3y = -10$$

Solve each equation.

3. $3x + 7 = 5x - 28$ $\frac{35}{2}$

4. $5x + 12 = 3x + 36$ 12

New Concepts

To be a solution to a system of equations, an ordered pair must satisfy both equations. One method for finding solutions to systems of equations is to use the substitution method.

Steps for Solving by Substitution
1. Rearrange one of the equations so that it is of the form $y = mx + b$, or $x = my + b$, if necessary.
2. Substitute the equivalent expression for the variable from the first step into the second equation of the system. The result is an equation with one unknown.
3. Solve the resulting equation from the second step for the variable.
4. Substitute the value of the variable from the third step into one of the original equations to find the value of the other unknown.
5. Write the values of the unknowns as an ordered pair.

Example 1 Using Substitution

Solve the system of equations by substitution.

$$y = 2x - 5$$
$$y = 5x + 7$$

SOLUTION

$y = 5x + 7$	Write the second equation.
$2x - 5 = 5x + 7$	Substitute $2x - 5$ for y.
$-5 = 3x + 7$	Subtract $2x$ from both sides.
$-12 = 3x$	Subtract 7 from both sides.
$-4 = x$	Divide both sides by 3.

MATH BACKGROUND

The systems in this lesson are restricted to the simplest systems: two linear equations in two variables where the equations are neither parallel nor the same line. When graphed, these equations will intersect in a point and the ordered pair associated with that point is a solution to both equations. By isolating one of the variables in one of the equations you obtain an equivalent expression that can be substituted for that variable in the other equation.

After substitution, the system is reduced to one equation with one unknown; which, by isolating the variable, is solvable. Once one of the variables is known, the value for that variable can be placed in either original equation, which again results in one equation with one unknown that is solvable for the remaining variable. The resulting ordered pair is the point of intersection of the two lines and a solution to the system of linear equations.

The value of x in the solution is -4. The y-value can be found by substituting -4 into either of the original equations.

First Equation	Second Equation
$y = 2x - 5$	$y = 5x + 7$
$y = 2(-4) - 5$	$y = 5(-4) + 7$
$y = -8 - 5$	$y = -20 + 7$
$y = -13$	$y = -13$

The solution to the system is $(-4, -13)$.

Example 2 Using the Distributive Property

Solve the system of equations by substitution. Check your answer.

$12x - 6y = 12$
$x = -2y + 11$

Hint
You can substitute for x or y. Choose the equation that is already solved for a variable.

SOLUTION

$12x - 6y = 12$	Write the first equation.
$12(-2y + 11) - 6y = 12$	Substitute $-2y + 11$ for x.
$-24y + 132 - 6y = 12$	Distribute.
$-30y + 132 = 12$	Combine like terms.
$-30y = -120$	Subtract 132 from both sides.
$y = 4$	Divide both sides by -30.

The value of y in the solution is 4. The x-value can be found by substituting 4 into either of the original equations.

First Equation	Second Equation
$12x - 6y = 12$	$x = -2y + 11$
$12x - 6(4) = 12$	$x = -2(4) + 11$
$12x - 24 = 12$	$x = -8 + 11$
$12x = 36$	$x = 3$
$x = 3$	

The solution to the system is $(3, 4)$.

Check To determine whether the ordered pair satisfies both of the original equations, substitute the x-value and y-value into the original equations.

First Equation	Second Equation
$12x - 6y = 12$	$x = -2y + 11$
$12(3) - 6(4) \stackrel{?}{=} 12$	$3 \stackrel{?}{=} -2(4) + 11$
$36 - 24 \stackrel{?}{=} 12$	$3 \stackrel{?}{=} -8 + 11$
$12 = 12$ ✓	$3 = 3$ ✓

Additional Example 1
Solve the system of equations by substitution. Check your answer.
$y = 2x - 3$
$y = x + 2$
The solution to the system is $(5, 7)$.

Example 2
This example illustrates that both equations do not have to be solved for a variable to use substitution. It also illustrates that either variable can be used for substitution.

TEACHER TIP
Encourage students to place parentheses around the expression that is equivalent to the isolated variable. This will help ensure that the entire expression is multiplied by the coefficient of the variable when it is replaced in the other equation.

Additional Example 2
Solve the system of equations by substitution. Check your answer.
$-5x + y = -7$
$y = -3x + 1$
The solution to the system is $(1, -2)$.

ENGLISH LEARNERS

The word **substitute** as it is used here may not be as familiar as the word replace. Point out that this method replaces a variable with its equivalent expression. Allow students to use replace instead of substitute for this lesson.

Example 3

This example involves having to isolate one of the variables in one of the equations.

Additional Example 3a

a. Solve the system of equations by substitution. Check your answer.

$2x + y = -6$
$3x + 2y = -10$

The solution to the system is $(-2, -2)$.

Hint

Use the variable with the coefficient of 1 whenever possible.

So far, every system of equations has had at least one equation of the form $y = mx + b$ or $x = my + b$. If neither equation is in this form, the first step is to rearrange one of the equations.

Example 3 Rearrange Before Substitution

a. Solve the system of equations by substitution. Check your answer.

$2x + y = -4$
$5x - 2y = -1$

SOLUTION

Because neither equation is in a form that can be used for substitution, one equation will need to be rearranged. The first equation can be rearranged to be in the form $y = mx + b$ easily because the coefficient of y is 1.

$2x + y = -4$	Write the first equation.
$y = -2x - 4$	Subtract $2x$ from both sides.

Now substitute $-2x - 4$ for y in the second equation.

Caution

Be sure to distribute the negative sign with the number.

$5x - 2y = -1$	Write the second equation.
$5x - 2(-2x - 4) = -1$	Substitute $-2x - 4$ for y.
$5x + 4x + 8 = -1$	Distribute.
$9x + 8 = -1$	Combine like terms.
$9x = -9$	Subtract 8 from both sides.
$x = -1$	Divide both sides by 9.

The value of x in the solution is -1. The y-value can be found by substituting -1 into either of the original equations.

First Equation	Second Equation
$2x + y = -4$	$5x - 2y = -1$
$2(-1) + y = -4$	$5(-1) - 2y = -1$
$-2 + y = -4$	$-5 - 2y = -1$
$y = -2$	$-2y = 4$
	$y = -2$

The solution to the system is $(-1, -2)$.

Check To check that this ordered pair satisfies both of the original equations, substitute the x-value and y-value into the original equations.

Hint

When neither variable has a coefficient of 1, choose a variable with a small coefficient or one that easily divides into the other coefficients and constants in the equation.

First Equation	Second Equation
$2x + y = -4$	$5x - 2y = -1$
$2(-1) + (-2) \stackrel{?}{=} -4$	$5(-1) - 2(-2) \stackrel{?}{=} -1$
$-2 + (-2) \stackrel{?}{=} -4$	$-5 + 4 \stackrel{?}{=} -1$
$-4 = -4$ ✓	$-1 = -1$ ✓

INCLUSION

The substitution method of solving systems requires adherence to a strict step-by-step procedure. While this can be a helpful strategy for some students, the complex wording of the instructions can cancel the beneficial nature of clearly defined steps. Encourage students to use a pattern to represent the steps: solve, replace, solve, replace.

In addition to placing parentheses around the equivalent expression for the isolated variable (see Teacher Tip for Example 2), encourage students to highlight both the equivalent expression and the variable it will be replacing in the other equation. This will help students replace the right variable in the right equation with the right expression.

b. Solve the system of equations by substitution. Check your answer.

$4x + 7y = 43$

$2x - 3y = -11$

SOLUTION

Again, one equation will need to be rearranged so that it can be used for substitution. None of the variables have a coefficient of 1, so solve the second equation for x.

$2x - 3y = -11$	Write the second equation.
$2x = 3y - 11$	Add $3y$ to both sides.
$x = \frac{3}{2}y - \frac{11}{2}$	Divide both sides by 2.

Now substitute $\frac{3}{2}y - \frac{11}{2}$ for the x in the first equation.

$4x + 7y = 43$	Write the first equation.
$4\left(\frac{3}{2}y - \frac{11}{2}\right) + 7y = 43$	Substitute $\frac{3}{2}y - \frac{11}{2}$ for x.
$\frac{12}{2}y - \frac{44}{2} + 7y = 43$	Distribute.
$6y - 22 + 7y = 43$	Simplify.
$13y - 22 = 43$	Combine like terms.
$13y = 65$	Add 22 to both sides.
$y = 5$	Divide both sides by 13.

The value of y in the solution is 5. Substitute 5 into either of the original equations to find x.

First Equation	**Second Equation**
$4x + 7y = 43$	$2x - 3y = -11$
$4x + 7(5) = 43$	$2x - 3(5) = -11$
$4x + 35 = 43$	$2x - 15 = -11$
$4x = 8$	$2x = 4$
$x = 2$	$x = 2$

The solution to the system is $(2, 5)$.

Check To determine whether the ordered pair satisfies both of the original equations, substitute the x-value and the y-value into the original equation.

First Equation	**Second Equation**
$4x + 7y = 43$	$2x - 3y = -11$
$4(2) + 7(5) \stackrel{?}{=} 43$	$2(2) - 3(5) \stackrel{?}{=} -11$
$8 + 35 \stackrel{?}{=} 43$	$4 - 15 \stackrel{?}{=} -11$
$43 = 43$ ✓	$-11 = -11$ ✓

Math Reasoning

Write When substituting the value of one variable to find the value of the other, only one equation needs to be used. So, why must both equations be used to check the answer?

A solution is only correct if it satisfies both equations.

Additional Example 3b

b. Solve the system of equations by substitution.

$2x - 3y = 8$

$3x + 4y = -5$

The solution to the system is $(1, -2)$.

Example 4

This example requires students to set up the system of equations by defining variables and translating the situation into two equations in two variables.

Extend the Example

The goal for the school play was to make $500 and to sell twice as many student's tickets as adult tickets. How many adult tickets would need to be sold? Use substitution to solve.
28 adult tickets

Additional Example 4

The cost of a cell phone includes the monthly fee plus the charge per minute for every minute over 500 minutes per month. The charge for 1000 minutes is $80. The charge for 1850 minutes is $131. How much is the monthly fee and how much is the charge per minute? **$50; $0.06**

Lesson Practice

Problem c

Scaffolding Ask students which variable in which equation would be easier to isolate.

Problem d

Error Alert This problem involves operations with fractions. It is important to differentiate whether a student is having difficulty with the process of substitution or with the mechanics of operating with fractions.

Hint
To determine how to define the variables, look at the question. The question will indicate what needs to be found; that is, what is unknown. Variables represent the unknown.

Example 4 Application: Play Tickets

A school play charged adults $8 and students $5 for tickets. There were 75 people who attended the play. The box office collected $444. How many adults and how many students attended the play? Use substitution to solve.

SOLUTION

First define the variables.

Let x = number of adults.

Let y = number of students.

Translate the situation into a system of equations.

$x + y = 75$ — Adults plus students equals the total number of people.

$8x + 5y = 444$ — The total amount of money collected can be found by multiplying the cost of the ticket by the number of people buying that kind of ticket.

Now use substitution to solve the system.

$y = -x + 75$ — Solve the first equation for y.

$8x + 5(-x + 75) = 444$ — Substitute $-x + 75$ for y in the second equation.

$8x - 5x + 375 = 444$ — Distribute.

$3x + 375 = 444$ — Combine like terms.

$3x = 69$ — Subtract 375 from both sides.

$x = 23$ — Divide both sides by 3.

$23 + y = 75$ — Substitute $x = 23$ into the first equation.

$y = 52$ — Subtract 23 from both sides.

The solution is (23, 52). There were 23 adults and 52 students at the play.

Check

First Equation	Second Equation
$x + y = 75$	$8x + 5y = 444$
$23 + 52 \stackrel{?}{=} 75$	$8(23) + 5(52) \stackrel{?}{=} 444$
$75 = 75$ ✓	$184 + 260 \stackrel{?}{=} 444$
	$444 = 444$ ✓

Lesson Practice

Solve each system of equations by substitution. Check your answer.

a. (Ex 1) $y = 4x - 3$
$y = 3x - 5$ $(-2, -11)$

b. (Ex 2) $x = 3y - 11$
$5x + 2y = -4$ $(-2, 3)$

c. (Ex 3) $4x + 3y = 2$
$2x + y = 6$ $(8, -10)$

d. (Ex 3) $4x + 3y = 19$
$7x - 6y = -23$ $(1, 5)$

ALTERNATE METHOD FOR PROBLEM d

When all of the variables have coefficients, isolating a variable will often result in fractional coefficients. Encourage students that have difficulty working with fractions to avail themselves of techniques that reduce the need to manipulate fractions. One such technique is to multiply through both sides of the equation by the LCD.

Problem **d:**

$4x + 3y = 19$
$7x - 6y = -23$

$x = -\dfrac{3}{4}y + \dfrac{19}{4}$

$7\left(-\dfrac{3}{4}y + \dfrac{19}{4}\right) - 6y = -23$

$-\dfrac{21}{4}y + \dfrac{133}{4} - 6y = -23$

$4\left[-\dfrac{21}{4}y + \dfrac{133}{4} - 6y = -23\right]$

$-21y + 133 - 24y = -92$

$-45y = -225$

$y = 5$

386 Saxon Algebra 1

e. (Finance) (Ex 4) The cost of 5 books and 10 pencils is $36. The cost of 2 books and 40 pencils is $18. How much do books cost and how much do pencils cost? **Books cost $7, and pencils cost $0.10.**

Practice   Distributed and Integrated

Solve.

1. (28) $-[-(-k)] - (-2)(-2 + k) = -k - (4k + 3)$ $k = \frac{1}{6}$

2. (26) $\frac{1}{3} + 5\frac{1}{3}k + 3\frac{2}{9} = 0$ $k = -\frac{2}{3}$

3. (13) Simplify $\sqrt{9} + \sqrt{16} - \sqrt{225}$. -8

4. (1) Give an example of a rational number that is not an integer.   Sample: $\frac{7}{4}$

5. (13) True or False: The number $\sqrt{49}$ is a rational number.   true

*6. (59) Solve by substitution: $y = 3x - 5$
$y = -2x + 15$. $(4, 7)$

*7. (59) Solve by substitution: $y = -8x + 21$
$y = -3x + 6$. $(3, -3)$

*8. (59) **Write** How do you know if a point is a solution to a system of equations?
Sample: The point satisfies every equation in the system.

*9. (59) **Multiple Choice** Which ordered pair is a solution to the system of equations?   **A**

$$4x + 9y = 75$$
$$8x + 6y = 66$$

A $(3, 7)$

B $(0, 11)$

C $(10, 4)$

D $(12, -5)$

*10. (59) The sum of two numbers is 64. Their difference is 14. Find each of the numbers. $(39, 25)$

11. (58) **Error Analysis** Students were asked to find the product of $2b^2(b^3 + 4)$. Which student is correct? Explain the error.

Student A	Student B
$2b^2(b^3 + 4)$	$2b^2(b^3 + 4)$
$2b^2(b^3) + 2b^2(4)$	$2b^2(b^3) + 2b^2(4)$
$2b^5 + 8b^2$	$2b^6 + 8b^2$

11. Student A; Sample: Student B multiplied the exponents instead of adding them.

Lesson 59   387

Check for Understanding

The questions below help assess the concepts taught in this lesson.

"Explain how to solve a system of equations by substitution."
Sample: Solve one of the equations for a variable. Substitute the equivalent expression for that variable for the same variable in the other equation. Solve that resulting equation. Substitute that solution into one of the original equations and solve for the remaining variable. The ordered pair is the solution of the system.

"Explain how to check a solution of a system of equations."
Sample: Substitute the values of the ordered pair into both equations to verify that they make both equations true.

3 Practice

Math Conversations
Discussion to strengthen understanding

Problem 1
Guide the students by asking them the following questions.

"To what does $-[-(-k)]$ simplify?" $-k$

"What is the expression for $(-2)(-2 + k)$ after distribution?" $(4 - 2k)$

"What is the expression for $-(4 - 2k)$ after distribution?" $-4 + 2k$

"What is the expression for $-(4k + 3)$ after distribution?" $-4k - 3$

"What does the equation look like now?" $-k - 4 + 2k = -k - 4k - 3$

Problem 4
Error Alert
Some students may think that any fraction is an acceptable answer. Remind them that if an improper fraction can be reduced to an integer, it does not satisfy the problem.

Lesson 59   387

*12. **Geometry** The length of a rectangular pool is four times the width. A
(58) four-foot-wide deck surrounds the pool. Write a polynomial expression for the
area of the pool and deck. Use the Distributive Property and write your answer in
standard form. $4x^2 + 40x + 64$ square feet

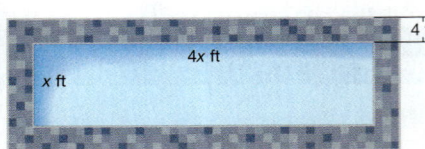

*13. **Multi-Step** Henry has a game that includes a number cube. The side length of the
(58) cube is $(5x + 1)$ inches. Find the volume of the number cube.
a. Find the area of the base. Multiply the length times the width. $25x^2 + 10x + 1$
b. Find the volume by multiplying the product found in part **a** by the height.
$125x^3 + 75x^2 + 15x + 1$ inches cubed

*14. **Measurement** Tim has a garden in the shape of a right triangle. The triangle has a
(58) base of $6x^2 + 8x + 12$ feet and a height of $(x - 1)$ feet. What is the area of Tim's
garden? $3x^3 + x^2 + 2x - 6$ square feet

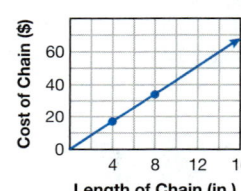

15. Find the product of $4x(x^2 + 2x - 9)$. $4x^3 + 8x^2 - 36x$
(58)

16. Write an equation of the line in slope-intercept form. The slope is 2; the
(49) y-intercept is -1. $y = 2x - 1$

17. What is the degree of $12x^4x^3 + 6xy + 41x^2y^3$? 7
(53)

18. **Baseball** The percentage of games won is used to determine a team's standing in
(54) the league. In the American League, the following percentages were recorded:

0.604, 0.540, 0.505, 0.465, 0.380, 0.600, 0.584, 0.505, 0.446,
0.430, 0.580, 0.545, 0.475, 0.451

18. Percentage of Games Won

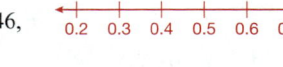

Make a box-and-whisker plot of these percentages and determine if there is an
outlier. There are no outliers.

*19. **Estimate** The cost of a chain is directly proportional to its length. Use the
(56) graph to estimate the cost of a chain that is 18 inches long.
Sample: $76.50

20. **Multiple Choice** Which point represents the same direct variation as $(3, -9)$? C
(56) **A** $(4, -8)$ **B** $(4, -7)$ **C** $(4, -12)$ **D** $(4, -16)$

21. Find the LCM of $16c^6$ and $24c^3$. $48c^6$

*22. **Games** Every $20x^3y$ turns, you win $500. Every $12xy^3c$ turns, you get to roll again. How many turns do you take before you win $500 and get to roll again on the same turn? $60x^3y^3c$

23. Find the LCM of $300d^2$ and $90d^4$.   LCM $= 2 \cdot 2 \cdot 3 \cdot 3 \cdot 5 \cdot 5 \cdot d \cdot d \cdot d \cdot d = 900d^4$

24. **Formulate** The equations $y = 3x - 24$ and $y = 24x + 9$ define two lines. Write a rational expression that represents the ratio of the first line to the second line. Simplify the expression, if possible. $\frac{x-8}{8x+3}$

25. Determine the slope of the line that goes through the points $(-1, 1)$ and $(1, -1)$. $m = -1$

26. **Biology** Write a counterexample for the following statement: If an animal has wings, then the animal is an insect.   A bird is an animal that has wings, but it is not an insect.

27. **Multi-Step** A canister of oatmeal has a height of 7 inches. Its volume is 28π cubic inches.
   a. Write an equation you can use to find the radius of the cylinder. $28\pi = 7\pi r^2$
   b. Find the radius of the canister.   2 inches

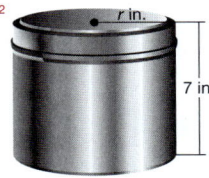

28. **Astronomy** The relative gravity on Jupiter is 2.34. This means that the weight of an object on Jupiter is 2.34 times greater than its weight on Earth. Identify the slope and the y-intercept of the equation representing this relationship and then write an equation for the situation in slope-intercept form.
   slope: 2.34; y-intercept: 0; $y = 2.34x$

29. **Verify** Write the converse of the following statement: If a number is an integer, then it is a rational number. Give an example to show that the converse is false.
   29. If a number is a rational number, then it is an integer; The number 0.5 is a rational number, but it is not an integer.

30. **Write** What is an excluded value for a rational expression? Why is it excluded?
   Sample: An excluded value is the value of the variable that makes the denominator equal 0. It is excluded because division by 0 is undefined.

Lesson 59   389

 CHALLENGE

Have students use the substitution method to try and solve the following system. Then have them graph the system and ask them to explain the relationship between their algebraic result and the graph.

$$y = x + 2$$
$$2y - 2x = 4$$

The equations are the same. The graphs are the same.

 LOOKING FORWARD

Solving systems of linear equations by substitution prepares students for

• **Lesson 63** Solving Systems of Linear Equations by Elimination

• **Lesson 67** Solving and Classifying Special Systems of Linear Equations

• **Lesson 97** Graphing Linear Inequalities

• **Lesson 109** Graphing Systems of Linear Inequalities

Lesson 59   389

LESSON 60

1 Warm Up

Problem 4
Remind students that because the second factor is a trinomial, they cannot use the FOIL method.

2 New Concepts

In this lesson, students learn to recognize special binomial factors and then employ patterns to find the product of the binomials without using the FOIL method. Students will also use these special binomial factors to find products mentally.

Exploration

The goal of the Exploration is to have students discover the patterns that produce the shortcuts for multiplying certain binomials.

Extend the Exploration
Square the following binomials:

a. $(x + 5)^2$ $x^2 + 10x + 25$

b. $(4x - 2)^2$ $16x^2 - 16x + 4$

Multiply the following binomials:

a. $(x + 7)(x - 7)$ $x^2 - 49$

b. $(2x + 5)(2x - 5)$ $4x^2 - 25$

LESSON RESOURCES

Student Edition Practice
   Workbook 60
Reteaching Master 60
Adaptations Master 60
Challenge and Enrichment
   Master C60, E60

LESSON 60

Finding Special Products of Binomials

Warm Up

1. **Vocabulary** Which polynomial is a trinomial?   **C**
   (53)
   A $3x^3 + 5$ **B** $7x^2 + 5 \cdot 4x$
   C $4x^2 + 6x - 9$ **D** $2x^3 + 5x^2 + 3x - 8$

Simplify.
(58)
2. $(2x + 3)(3x - 5)$ $6x^2 - x - 15$
3. $(3x + 7)(5x + 6)$ $15x^2 + 53x + 42$
4. $(3x - 2)(3x^2 - x + 7)$ $9x^3 - 9x^2 + 23x - 14$

New Concepts

Exploration Multiplying Binomials

Square the following binomials

1. $(2t + 2)^2$ $4t^2 + 8t + 4$

Hint
To square a binomial multiply it by itself.

2. $(4y + 3)^2$ $16y^2 + 24y + 9$

3. $(a + b)^2$ $a^2 + 2ab + b^2$

4. $(t - 5)^2$ $t^2 - 10t + 25$

5. $(2x - 3)^2$ $4x^2 - 12x + 9$

6. $(a - b)^2$ $a^2 - 2ab + b^2$

7. Sample: Square the first term, double the product of the first and second term, use the same sign, and then add the square of the last term.

7. Describe a pattern for $(a + b)^2$ and $(a - b)^2$.

Multiply the following binomials

8. $(3x + 4)(3x - 4)$ $9x^2 - 16$

9. $(x + 6)(x - 6)$ $x^2 - 36$

10. $(a + b)(a - b)$ $a^2 - b^2$

11. Describe a pattern for $(a + b)(a - b)$.   Sample: Square the first term and then subtract the square of the last term.

The square of a binomial $(a + b)^2$ or $(a - b)^2$ results in a perfect-square trinomial. Trinomials of the form $a^2 + 2ab + b^2$ and $a^2 - 2ab + b^2$ are **perfect-square trinomials** because they are the product of a factor times itself.

Online Connection
www.SaxonMathResources.com

390   Saxon Algebra 1

MATH BACKGROUND

Multiplying polynomials involves repeated use of the Distributive Property. When multiplying two binomials, the mnemonic FOIL is used to help students remember to multiply a total of four pairs of factors.

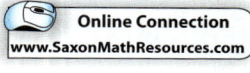

Certain binomials produce an interesting pattern when multiplied. Recognizing and taking advantage of these patterns leads to a shortcut for writing products for these special binomials that does not require distribution.

The product of a sum and difference of two binomials $(a - b)(a + b) = a^2 - b^2$ produces the difference of two squares.

Special Product of Binomials

Square of a Binomial	
Pattern	Example
$(a + b)^2 = a^2 + 2ab + b^2$	$(x + 5)^2 = x^2 + 10x + 25$
$(a - b)^2 = a^2 - 2ab + b^2$	$(2x - 4)^2 = 4x^2 - 16x + 16$

Sum and Difference	
Pattern	Example
$(a + b)(a - b) = a^2 - b^2$	$(3x - 2)(3x + 2) = 9x^2 - 4$

Example 1 Squaring Binomials in the Form $(a + b)^2$

a. Find the product: $(x + 2)^2$.

SOLUTION

$(a + b)^2 = a^2 + 2ab + b^2$ Write the pattern.
$(x + 2)^2 = (x)^2 + 2(x)(2) + 2^2$ Apply the pattern.
$= x^2 + 4x + 4$ Simplify.

b. Find the product: $(2x + 4)^2$.

SOLUTION

$(a + b)^2 = a^2 + 2ab + b^2$ Write the pattern.
$(2x + 4)^2 = (2x)^2 + 2(2x)(4) + 4^2$ Apply the pattern.
$= 4x^2 + 16x + 16$ Simplify.

Example 2 Squaring Binomials in the Form $(a - b)^2$

a. Find the product: $(x - 8)^2$.

SOLUTION

$(a - b)^2 = a^2 - 2ab + b^2$ Write the pattern.
$(x - 8)^2 = (x)^2 - 2(x)(8) + (8)^2$ Apply the pattern.
$= x^2 - 16x + 64$ Simplify.

b. Find the product: $(2x - 7)^2$.

SOLUTION

$(a - b)^2 = a^2 - 2ab + b^2$ Write the pattern.
$(2x - 7)^2 = (2x)^2 - 2(2x)(7) + (7)^2$ Apply the pattern.
$= 4x^2 - 28x + 49$ Simplify.

Caution

$(x - 5)^2 \neq x^2 + 25$

Remember to either use the pattern for squaring binomials or use the FOIL method.

$(x - 5)^2 = (x - 5)(x - 5)$
$= x^2 - 10x + 25$

TEACHER TIP

Remind students that when squaring a sum or difference, they have to write the binomial as a factor twice. In the Exploration, the FOIL method is used.

Example 1

This example focuses on squaring binomials in the form $(a + b)^2$. Students should recognize that when the binomial is a sum, the middle term of the resulting perfect-square trinomial will be positive.

Error Alert Be sure students understand that in the pattern, the a represents the first term of the binomial including the coefficient and not just the variable.

Additional Example 1

a. Find the product: $(x + 3)^2$.
$x^2 + 6x + 9$

b. Find the product: $(3x + 5)^2$. $9x^2 + 30x + 25$

Example 2

This example focuses on squaring binomials in the form $(a - b)^2$. Students should recognize that when the binomial is a difference, the last term will always be positive.

Additional Example 2

a. Find the product: $(x - 3)^2$.
$x^2 - 6x + 9$

b. Find the product: $(3x - 5)^2$.
$9x^2 - 30x + 25$

ENGLISH LEARNERS

To help students understand the term **perfect-square trinomial**, remind them that a square is a number that is the product of multiplying a number by itself. For example, 4, 9, 25, and 36 are all squares because they can be written respectively as follows: 2 · 2, 3 · 3, 5 · 5, and 6 · 6. A trinomial is a polynomial with three terms. So, a perfect-square trinomial is a trinomial that is the result of squaring.

Have students write each of the following expressions as a square and then have them use the FOIL method to show that the result is a trinomial.

a. $(x + 2)(x + 2)$ $(x + 2)^2$; $x^2 + 4x + 4$

b. $(x - 3)(x - 3)$ $(x - 3)^2$; $x^2 - 6x + 9$

c. $(2x + 1)(2x + 1)$ $(2x + 1)^2$; $4x^2 + 4x + 1$

Example 3

This example illustrates the difference of squares product.

Point out that when using FOIL to multiply products in the form $(a + b)(a - b)$ the outer and inner terms when added will be zero. So, the middle terms disappears

Additional Example 3

a. Find the product:
$(x + 9)(x - 9)$. $x^2 - 81$

b. Find the product:
$(6x + 4)(6x - 4)$. $36x^2 - 16$

Example 4

This example demonstrates how by using special product patterns and the knowledge that numbers are easier to multiply when they end in zero, you can compute products mentally.

Additional Example 4

a. Use mental math to find 31^2. 961

b. Use mental math to find the product of $37 \cdot 43$. 1591

Example 5

This example relates the difference-of-squares pattern to an application involving area: a formula that requires multiplying two factors.

Additional Example 5

Marcus built a 6-foot deck around his square house. A side of the house is $7x$ feet. Find the area of Marcus's house including the deck. $(7x + 12)^2 = 49x^2 + 168x + 144$ sq ft

Extend the Example

Roberto has another garden that is in the shape of a square. It has a side length of $2x - 5$ feet. Find the area of this garden.
$(2x - 5)^2 = 4x^2 - 20x + 25$ sq. ft

Example 3 Finding Products in the Form $(a + b)(a - b)$

a. Find the product: $(x + 3)(x - 3)$.

SOLUTION

$(a + b)(a - b) = a^2 - b^2$ Write the pattern.
$(x + 3)(x - 3) = (x)^2 - (3)^2$ Apply the pattern.
$\quad\quad\quad\quad\quad\, = x^2 - 9$ Simplify.

b. Find the product: $(5x + 4)(5x - 4)$.

SOLUTION

$(a + b)(a - b) = a^2 - b^2$ Write the pattern.
$(5x + 4)(5x - 4) = (5x)^2 - (4)^2$ Apply the pattern.
$\quad\quad\quad\quad\quad\quad\, = 25x^2 - 16$ Simplify.

Example 4 Mental Math

a. Use mental math to find 39^2. To use mental math, remember to use the special, product patterns.

SOLUTION

$(40 - 1)^2$ Write 39^2 as a square of binomial.
$= 40^2 - 2(40)(1) + (1)^2$ Apply the pattern.
$= 1600 - 80 + 1$
$= 1521$ Simplify.

b. Use mental math to find the product of $16 \cdot 24$. To use mental math, remember to use the special product patterns.

SOLUTION

$(20 - 4)(20 + 4) = 20^2 - 4^2$ Write $16 \cdot 24$ as the product of the difference and the sum.
$= 400 - 16$ Simplify.
$= 384$

Example 5 Application: Gardening

Roberto has a garden in the shape of a parallelogram. It has a height of $(x - 2)$ and a base length of $(x + 2)$. Find the area of Roberto's garden.

Math Reasoning

Write How could Roberto check his work?

Sample: He could have used the FOIL method.

SOLUTION

$A = bh$
$= (x - 2)(x + 2)$ Write as the product of difference and sum.
$= (x)^2 - (2)^2$
$= x^2 - 4$ Simplify.

392   Saxon Algebra 1

INCLUSION

Use the strategy below for students who have difficulty working horizontally. Have students set up the pattern for special products vertically. Then they should circle the result of each part of the pattern. The circled terms are combined for the product.

Find the product: $(3x + 4)^2$.

$(a + b)^2 = a^2 + 2ab + b^2$
$a^2 = (3x)^2 = \boxed{9x^2}$
$2ab = 2(3x)(4) = \boxed{24x}$
$b^2 = (4)^2 = \boxed{16}$
$(3x + 4)^2 = 9x^2 + 24x + 16$

Find the product: $(2x + 3)(2x - 3)$.

$(a + b)(a - b) = a^2 - b^2$
$a^2 = (2x)^2 = \boxed{4x^2}$
$b^2 = (3)^2 = \boxed{9}$
$(2x + 3)(2x - 3) = 4x^2 - 9$

(Remind students that this pattern subtracts the two terms.)

Lesson Practice

Find each product.

a. $(x + 9)^2$ $x^2 + 18x + 81$ (Ex 1)
b. $(3x + 5)^2$ $9x^2 + 30x + 25$ (Ex 1)
c. $(x - 1)^2$ $x^2 - 2x + 1$ (Ex 2)
d. $(8x - 6)^2$ $64x^2 - 96x + 36$ (Ex 2)
e. $(x + 8)(x - 8)$ $x^2 - 64$ (Ex 3)
f. $(3x + 2)(3x - 2)$ $9x^2 - 4$ (Ex 3)
g. (Ex 4) Use mental math to find 28^2.   784
h. (Ex 4) Use mental math to find the product of $58 \cdot 62$.   3596
i. (Ex 5) George is pouring a rectangular cement slab for his house. The length is $(x - 6)$ and the width is $(x + 6)$. Find the area of George's new slab. $x^2 - 36$

Practice   Distributed and Integrated

Simplify.

1. (53) $(3k + 2k^2 - 4) - (k^2 + k - 6)$ $k^2 + 2k + 2$
2. (53) $(-2m + 1) + (6m^2 - m - 2)$ $6m^2 - 3m - 1$
3. (58) $(x + 4)(x - 5)$ $x^2 - x - 20$
4. (58) $(x + 2)(6x^2 + 4x + 5)$ $6x^3 + 16x^2 + 13x + 10$

Find the square of each binomial.

*5. (60) $(3t - 1)^2$ $9t^2 - 6t + 1$
*6. (60) $(3t + 1)^2$ $9t^2 + 6t + 1$

*7. (60) **Painting** Dat is painting a picture for his grandmother. He wants a 3-inch-wide blue border around the square painting. Write a special product and simplify to find the area of the picture including the border.
$(3x + 6)(3x + 6) = (3x + 6)^2 = 9x^2 + 36x + 36$ square inches

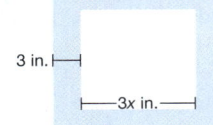

3 in.
3x in.

8. (59) Solve the linear system by substitution.   (5, 1)

$y = 2x - 9$
$8x - 6y = 34$

*9. (60) **Multiple Choice** Which of the following quadratic expressions is the product of $(6x + 7)^2$?   **C**

A $36x^2 + 42x + 49$
B $12x^2 + 84x + 49$
C $36x^2 + 84x + 49$
D $36x + 84x + 49$

Lesson 60   393

Problem 10
Extend the Problem
Verify the solution by graphing the ordered pair on a coordinate plane.

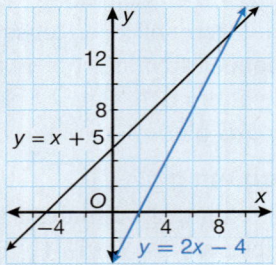

Problem 13
Error Alert
Students may forget what perimeter is or make the mistake of finding the area of the figure. Remind students that perimeter is $2(l + w)$ or $2l + 2w$.

Tell students to draw a rectangle and to label the drawing according to the description given.

Problem 16
Guide the students by asking the them following questions.

"If x represents the girl's age now and y represents the boy's age now, what equation would represent the first sentence of the problem?" $4x + 7y = 169$

"What equation would represent the second sentence of the problem?" $y = 2x + 1$

"How would you solve the two equations in two variables?" Sample: substitution

"Have you answered the problem once you find the values for x and y?" no; You have to find their ages 10 years from now.

Problem 19
TEACHER TIP
Remind students of the definition of LCM. LCM means least common multiple. It is the smallest nonzero multiple of two or more numbers.

---

10. Solve the linear system by substitution. (9,14)
    (59)
    $y = 2x - 4$
    $y = x + 5$

*11. **Write** How can you check your work when finding a product of two binomials using
    (60) special-product patterns? Sample: You can use the FOIL method to check your work.

*12. **Verify** Tell whether the statement $(9x + 8)(9x + 8) = 81x^2 + 64$ is true or false. If
    (60) false, explain why. false; $(9x + 8)(9x + 8) = 81x^2 + 144x + 64$

*13. **Measurement** The perimeter of a rectangle is 78 feet. The length is 3 feet more than
    (59) 3 times the width. Find the dimensions of the rectangle. The width is 9 feet. The length is 30 feet.

14. **Error Analysis** Two students are in the process of finding the solution to the system
    (59) of equations. Which student is correct? Explain the error. Student A; Sample: Student B did not distribute the 6 over the 19.

$x + 4y = 19$
$6x + 5y = 38$

Student A	Student B
$x = -4y + 19$	$x = -4y + 19$
$6(-4y + 19) + 5y = 38$	$6(-4y + 19) + 5y = 38$
$-24y + 114 + 5y = 38$	$-24y + 19 + 5y = 38$
$-19y = -76$	$-19y = 19$
$y = \frac{76}{19} = 4$	$y = -1$

15. **Installation** A contractor is installing some special light bulbs for two floors in a
    (55) building. For the first floor, she purchased 5 natural-light bulbs and 2 ceiling bulbs at a cost of $23. For the second floor, she purchased 3 natural-light bulbs and 4 ceiling bulbs at a cost of $25. How much does each type of bulb cost?
    $3 for each natural-light bulb, $4 for each ceiling bulb

*16. **Multi-Step** The sum of 4 times a girl's age and 7 times a boy's age is 169. The boy
    (59) is 1 year older than twice the age of the girl. Find how old each will be 10 years from now. girl: 19; boy: 29

*17. **Geometry** The perimeter of a rectangle is 24 centimeters. The length is 4 centimeters
    (59) less than 7 times the width. Find the dimensions of the rectangle. The width is 2 centimeters and the length is 10 centimeters.

18. **Data-Analysis** Display the data using a box-and-whisker plot titled "Average
    (54) Monthly Rainfall in Cloudcroft, NM (in inches)". Identify any outliers. See Additional Answers; 6.04 and 6.10 are outliers.

    1.68, 1.90, 1.54, 0.84, 1.35, 2.21, 6.10, 6.04, 3.11, 1.78, 1.58, 2.33

19. **Verify** Show that $12f^4$ is the LCM of $6f^4$ and $4f^2$. Sample: $6f^4 = 2 \cdot 3 \cdot f^4$ and
    (57) $4f^2 = 2 \cdot 2 \cdot f^2$, so the LCM $= 2^2 \cdot 3 \cdot f^4 = 12f^4$.

20. **Multiple Choice** What is the LCM of $(4x^4 - 14x^3)$ and $(6x^2 - 21x)$? A
    (57)
    A $6x^3(2x - 7)$ **B** $6x^4(2x - 7)$
    C $6(2x^4 - 7x^3)(2x^2 - 7x)$ **D** $(4x^4 - 14x^3)(6x^2 - 21x)$

394 Saxon Algebra 1

21. Tell whether the set of ordered pairs (2, 8), (4, 16), and (7, 28) represents a direct variation.   yes

22. (Tennis) A tennis court's dimensions can be represented by a width of $4x + 25$ feet and a length of $2x + 15$ feet. Write a polynomial for the area of the court.
$A = 8x^2 + 110x + 375$ sq. ft

23. Determine the slope of the line graphed below.   The slope is undefined.

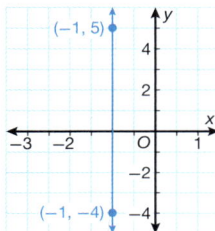

*24. Find the product of $(x + 2)(x + 9)$ using the FOIL method. $x^2 + 11x + 18$

25. Translate the inequality $x - 2.5 > 4.7$ into words.   Sample: The difference of a number and 2.5 is greater than 4.7.

26. (Hobby) Eleanor has more than twice as many football trading cards as José. Eleanor has 79 trading cards. What is the greatest number of trading cards José might have? $2t < 79$, where t is the number of José's cards, so José could have 39 cards.

27. **Multi-Step** The varsity football team started summer training with 85 players. 10 players dropped out after 1 week of training, and then 7 players dropped out after 2 weeks.
   a. What was the percent of decrease for the first week? What was the percent of decrease for the second week?   12%, 9%
   b. What was the total percent of decrease for the 2 weeks of summer training?   20%

28. (Law Enforcement) Arnold is using the graph to represent a speed limit of 45 miles per hour. What restrictions should also be placed on the graph?

28. Sample: The graph should only include non-negative numbers, because negative speed means moving backward and this cannot happen when driving legally on a road.

29. Before painting, the edges around a rectangular light fixture must be taped. The length of the fixture is $\frac{2a}{3a-2}$ yards, and the width is $\frac{a-2}{3a-2}$ yards. How much tape is needed?   2 yards

30. **Justify** Identify the slope and y-intercept of the line $y = x - 4$. Explain. $m = 1$; $b = -4$; Sample: Using the slope-intercept equation of a line, the slope is the coefficient of x and the y-intercept is the number added to or subtracted from x.

CHALLENGE

Factoring is the inverse of multiplying. Use your knowledge of special products to write each of the following expressions as a product of two binomials:

a. $x^2 - 64$ $(x + 8)(x - 8)$

b. $4x^2 - 25$ $(2x + 5)(2x - 5)$

c. $9a^2 - 16b^2$ $(3a + 4b)(3a - 4b)$

d. $x^2 + 14x + 49$ $(x + 7)^2$

e. $4a^2 + 12a + 9$ $(2a + 3)^2$

f. $9x^2 + 42xy + 49y^2$ $(3x + 7y)^2$

LOOKING FORWARD

Finding special products of binomials prepares students for

- **Lesson 72** Factoring Trinomials: $x^2 + bx + c$
- **Lesson 75** Factoring Trinomials by Using the GCF
- **Lesson 79** Factoring Trinomials: $ax^2 + bx + c$
- **Lesson 83** Factoring Special Products
- **Lesson 87** Factoring Polynomials by Grouping

Problem 21
TEACHER TIP
Remind students that the equation for a direct variation is $y = kx$.

Problem 23
Error Alert
Some students may not remember that a 0 in the denominator means that the slope is undefined.

Problem 27
TEACHER TIP
Remind students of the percent decrease formula:

$$\frac{\text{amount of decrease}}{\text{original amount}}$$

Emphasize that the amount of decrease is compared to the original amount.

INVESTIGATION 6

Transforming Linear Functions

A **family of functions** share common characteristics. A **parent function** is the simplest function in a family of functions. The parent function for a linear function is $f(x) = x$. Functions in the family are transformations of the parent function. The graph of $f(x) = x$ is shown below.

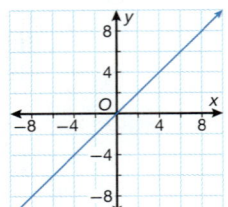

Sample: They all have the same basic form.

Hint
Function notation, $f(x)$, can be used in place of y.

Math Reasoning
Write Why do all linear functions belong to the same family of functions?

A **translation** shifts every point in a figure the same distance in the same direction. A translation can be thought of as a slide. A translation of a linear function is also referred to as a vertical change.

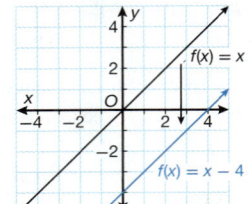 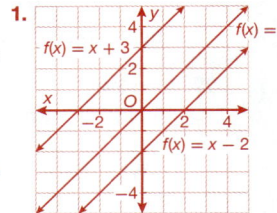

1. Graph $f(x) = x$, $f(x) = x + 3$, and $f(x) = x - 2$ on the same coordinate grid.

2. **Generalize** Compare the graphs of $f(x) = x + 3$ and $f(x) = x - 2$ to the parent function. Use the y-intercept in your comparison.

A vertical stretch or compression changes the rate of change of a linear equation.

2. Sample: The graph of $f(x) = x + 3$ shifts up 3 units from the graph of $f(x) = x$. The y-intercept shifts from (0, 0) to (0, 3); The graph of $f(x) = x - 2$ shifts down 2 units from the graph of $f(x) = x$; The y-intercept shifts from (0, 0) to (0, -2).

3.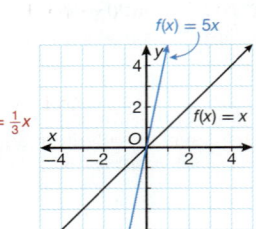

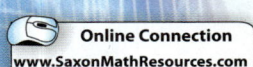
Online Connection
www.SaxonMathResources.com

3. Graph $f(x) = x$, $f(x) = 3x$, and $f(x) = \frac{1}{3}x$ on the same coordinate grid.

4. **Generalize** Discuss how the slope of a line is related to the steepness of a line. Sample: When a positive slope increases, the line is steeper than the original line. When a positive slope decreases and stays positive, the line is not as steep as the original line.

396   Saxon Algebra 1

INVESTIGATION 6

Material
• graph paper

Discuss
In this investigation, students recognize and graph transformations applied to the linear parent function $f(x) = x$.

Define **translation, rotation** and **reflection**.

Problem 2
Extend the Problem
Have students make tables for each function and compare the y-values for specific values of x.

INVESTIGATION RESOURCES

Reteaching Master
  Investigation 6
Technology Lab Master
  Investigation 6

MATH BACKGROUND

A graph can be predicted based on transformations of its parent function. All lines can be thought of as transformations of the graph $y = x$. For instance, $y = ax + b$ moves the graph up or down b units, rotates the graph towards the y-axis when $a > 1$ and away from the y-axis when $0 < a < 1$, and reflects $y = x$ over the y-axis when a is negative. For example, $y = -2x + 5$ moves the graph $y = x$ up 5 units, and reflects the line over the y-axis. Encourage students to use the words translation and reflection rather than slide and flip.

Math Reasoning

Analyze Describe how the value of *m* affects the steepness of the line.

Sample: When *m* is a positive number greater than [1], is ste[eper than] the g[raph of the] paren[t function;] when [m is a] positi[ve] fracti[on it] is not [steeper than] the gr[aph of the] paren[t function.]

5. **Predict** Will the graph of $f(x) = \frac{2}{3}x$ be steeper than the graph of the parent function? Explain.

A **reflection** produces a mirror image across a line. A reflection can be thought of as a flip.

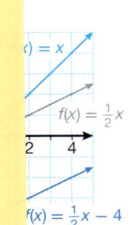

5. no; The slope of $\frac{2}{3}$ is less than the slope of 1 for the parent function.

[Handwritten note:]
translation - slide
Verticle stretch or compression — changes rate of change
reflection - flip

...the same coordinate plane.
...line is related to the reflection
...ransformation of the parent

6.

$f(x) = -4$
x

7. Graph... original line with the opposite slope results in a reflection of the line over the *y*-axis.

8. Graph $f(x) = x$ and $f(x) = 3x + 2$ on the same coordinate plane.

9. **Write** Describe the transformations from the graph of $f(x) = x$ to the graph of $f(x) = 3x + 2$. The graph of the line $y = 3x + 2$ is steeper than the graph of the line $y = x$ and is shifted up from the graph of the line $y = x$.

Investigation Practice

Graph each function on a coordinate plane with the parent function $f(x) = x$. Then describe the transformation.

a. $f(x) = x + 4$ See Additional Answers.

b. $f(x) = -x$ See Additional Answers.

c. $f(x) = \frac{1}{2}x$ See Additional Answers.

d. $f(x) = 4x - 2$ See Additional Answers.

8.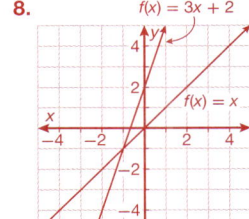

Investigation 6   397

Problem 8
Extend the Problem
Have students predict the changes to $y = x$ that will occur for $y = \frac{1}{2}x - 1$.

Discuss
Point out to students that if a rotation occurs after a translation of *b* units, the point of rotation is $(0, b)$.

Investigation Practice

Math Conversations
Discussion to strengthen understanding

Problem b
Error Alert Some students may be confused and think that the reflection is over the *x*-axis only. Although for $y = x$ the reflection is over both, point out the difference between the graphs of $y = -x + 1$ and $y = x + 1$. Have students reflect one line over the *x*-axis to show that the *y*-intercept changes. Remind them that in reflections over the *y*-axis the point on the *y*-axis does not move.

---

eL ENGLISH LEARNERS

For this lesson, explain the meaning of the word **transformations**. Say:

"A transformation means to move or change an object."

Discuss how this word applies to everyday situations. For example, a room in a house or a person's appearance can undergo a transformation.

LOOKING FORWARD

Transforming linear functions prepares students for

• **Investigation 7** Comparing Direct and Inverse Variation

• **Investigation 8** Identifying and Writing Joint Variation

• **Investigation 10** Transforming Quadratic Functions

• **Investigation 11** Investigating Exponential Growth and Decay

SECTION OVERVIEW 7

Lesson Planner

Lesson	New Concepts
61	Simplifying Radical Expressions
LAB 6	Graphing Calculator: Drawing Histograms
62	Displaying Data in Stem-and-Leaf Plots and Histograms
63	Solving Systems of Linear Equations by Elimination
64	Identifying, Writing, and Graphing Inverse Variation
65	Writing Equations of Parallel and Perpendicular Lines
	Cumulative Test 12, Performance Task 12
66	Solving Inequalities by Adding or Subtracting
67	Solving and Classifying Special Systems of Linear Equations
68	Mutually Exclusive and Inclusive Events
69	Adding and Subtracting Radical Expressions
70	Solving Inequalities by Multiplying or Dividing
	Cumulative Test 13, Performance Task 13
INV 7	Investigation: Comparing Direct and Inverse Variation

Resources for Teaching

- Student Edition
- Teacher's Edition
- Student Edition eBook
- Teacher's Edition eBook
- Resources and Planner CD
- Solutions Manual
- Instructional Masters
- Technology Lab Masters
- Warm Up and Teaching Transparencies
- Instructional Presentations CD
- Online activities, tools, and homework help www.SaxonMathResources.com

Resources for Practice and Assessment

- Student Edition Practice Workbook
- Course Assessments
- Standardized Test Practice
- College Entrance Exam Practice
- Test and Practice Generator CD using ExamView™

Resources for Differentiated Instruction

- Reteaching Masters
- Challenge and Enrichment Masters
- Prerequisite Skills Intervention
- Adaptations for Saxon Algebra 1
- Multilingual Glossary
- English Learners Handbook
- TI Resources

Pacing Guide

Resources and Planner CD for lesson planning support

45-Minute Class

Day 1	Day 2	Day 3	Day 4	Day 5	Day 6
Lesson 61	Lab 6 Lesson 62	Lesson 63	Lesson 64	Lesson 65	Cumulative Test 12
Day 7	**Day 8**	**Day 9**	**Day 10**	**Day 11**	**Day 12**
Lesson 66	Lesson 67	Lesson 68	Lesson 69	Lesson 70	Cumulative Test 13
Day 13					
Investigation 7					

Block: 90-Minute Class

Day 1	Day 2	Day 3	Day 4	Day 5	Day 6
Investigation 6 Lesson 61	Lab 6 Lesson 62 Lesson 63	Lesson 64 Lesson 65	Cumulative Test 12 Lesson 66	Lesson 67 Lesson 68	Lesson 69 Lesson 70
Day 7					
Cumulative Test 13 Investigation 7					

*For suggestions on how to implement Saxon Math in a block schedule, see the Pacing section at the beginning of the Teacher's Edition.

Lessons 61–70, Investigation 7

Differentiated Instruction

Below Level	
Warm Up	SE pp. 398, 406, 412, 418, 424, 430, 436, 443, 449, 455
Skills Bank	SE pp. 846–883
Reteaching Masters	Lessons 61–70, Investigation 7
Warm Up Transparencies	Lessons 61–70
Prerequisite Skills Intervention	Skills 53, 74, 75, 76

Advanced Learners	
Challenge	TE pp. 403, 410, 417, 423, 429, 435, 441, 448, 453, 460
Extend the Example	TE pp. 401, 407, 408, 414, 420, 426, 432, 439, 445, 451, 458
Extend the Exploration	TE pp. 399, 419
Extend the Problem	TE pp. 402, 410, 417, 423, 428, 434, 435, 441, 447, 453, 461, 462
Challenge and Enrichment Masters	Challange: 61–70; Enrichment: 64, 67

English Learners	
EL Tips	TE pp. 402, 407, 415, 421, 426, 431, 438, 444, 450, 458, 463
Multilingual Glossary	Booklet and Online English Learners Handbook

Special Needs	
Inclusion Tips	TE pp. 399, 409, 416, 422, 428, 432, 439, 446, 452, 456
Adaptations for Saxon Algebra 1	Lessons 61–70, Cumulative Tests 12, 13

For All Learners	
Exploration	SE pp. 399, 418, 463
Caution	SE pp. 407, 412, 426, 436, 457
Hints	SE pp. 407, 413, 415, 432, 450, 451, 455, 458
Error Alert	TE pp. 400, 401, 403, 407, 409, 410, 413, 415, 420, 421, 422, 425, 427, 432, 433, 434, 437, 439, 440, 444, 446, 447, 450, 451, 454, 456, 459, 460, 463
Alternate Method	TE pp. 400, 408, 413, 414, 425, 427, 434, 437, 451, 457
Manipulative Use Online Tools	TE pp. 419, 445

SE = Student Edition; TE = Teacher's Edition

Math Vocabulary

Lesson	New Vocabulary	Maintained	EL Tip in TE
61	radical expression	perfect square powers of ten prime factorization radical	igloo
62	histogram relative frequency stem-and-leaf plot	median mode range	stem-and-leaf
63		system of linear equations	eliminate
64	inverse variation	constant of variation direct variation	inverse
65	parallel lines perpendicular lines	parallel perpendicular slope slope-intercept form	reciprocal
66		inequality	endpoint
67	consistent system dependent equations dependent systems inconsistent equations independent system	system of linear equations parallel lines	system
68	inclusive events mutually exclusive events	outcome	probability
69	like radicals unlike radicals	like terms radicand radical	identify
70		inequality transformation	commission
INV 7		constant of variation direct variation inverse variation	variation

Section Overview 7   398B

SECTION OVERVIEW 7

Math Highlights

Enduring Understandings – The "Big Picture"

After completing Section 7, students will understand:
- How to simplify and add or subtract radical expressions.
- How to solve inequalities.
- How to identify an inverse variation.
- How to classify special systems of linear equations and use elimination to solve systems.
- How to write equations of parallel and perpendicular lines.
- How to display data using stem-and-leaf plots and histograms.
- How to find the probability of mutually exclusive and inclusive events.

Essential Questions

- How can the rules of radicals and exponents be applied to simplify expressions?
- What is the solution of an inequality?
- When is a relation a direct or inverse variation?
- How can it be determined whether two lines are parallel or perpendicular?
- How do stem-and-leaf plots and histograms display distribution of data?
- What is the nature of mutually exclusive and inclusive events?

Math Content Strands		Math Processes	
Inequalities		**Reasoning and Communication**	
• Lesson 66	Solving Inequalities by Adding or Subtracting		*Lessons*
• Lesson 70	Solving Inequalities by Multiplying or Dividing	• Analyze	61, Lab 6, 62, 64, 65, 67, 68, 69, 70, Inv. 7
		• Connect	70
Linear Equations and Functions		• Error analysis	61, 62, 63, 64, 65, 66, 67, 68, 69, 70
• Lesson 64	Identifying, Writing, and Graphing Inverse Variation	• Estimate	64, 69
		• Formulate	64, Inv. 7
• Lesson 65	Writing Equations of Parallel and Perpendicular Lines	• Generalize	61, 64, 69
		• Justify	64, 65, 66, 68, Inv. 7
• Investigation 7	Comparing Direct and Inverse Variation	• Math Reasoning	61, 63, 64, 65, 67, 68, 70, Inv. 7
Probability and Data Analysis		• Model	65, 65, 68, Inv. 7
• Lesson 62	Displaying Data in Stem-and-Leaf Plots and Histograms	• Multiple choice	61, 62, 63, 64, 65, 66, 67, 68, 69, 70
		• Multi-step	61, 62, 63, 64, 65, 66, 67, 68, 69, 70
• Lesson 68	Mutually Exclusive and Inclusive Events	• Predict	68
• Lab 6	Graphing Calculator: Drawing Histograms	• True or False	68
		• Verify	61, 63, 64, 67, 68
Radical Expressions and Functions		• Write	61, 62, 63, 64, 65, 66, 67, 68, 70
• Lesson 61	Simplifying Radical Expressions		
• Lesson 69	Adding and Subtracting Radical Expressions	• Graphing Calculator	61, 62, 63, 68, 70
Systems of Equations and Inequalities		**Connections**	
• Lesson 63	Solving Systems of Linear Equations by Elimination	**In Examples:** Business, Coin collecting, Coordinate Geometry, Digital music, Finding the perimeter of a swimming pool, Finding the perimeter of a triangle, Jogging, Length of a square room, Sports, Survey, Travel, Truck transportation	
• Lesson 67	Solving and Classifying Special Systems of Linear Equations		
Connections in Practice Problems		**In Practice problems:** Ages, Banking, Basketball, Box office sales, Boyle's Law, Budgeting, Building, Carpentry, Chemistry, Circular motion, City planning, Commerce, Construction, Consumer math, Cooking, Craft fair, Decibel levels, Discounts, Distance, Fantasy football, Football, Fundraising, Gardening, Golden Rectangle, Great Pyramid, Health, Hobbies, Investing, Job hunting, Landscaping, Life expectancy, Newspaper delivery, Paralympics, Physics, Produce purchase, Prom night, Rate, Recycling, Running, Sanitation, Sports, Transportation, Triathlon training, Velocity, Volleyball, Weather forecasting, World records	
	Lessons		
Coordinate Geometry	62, 65, 66, 67, 70		
Data Analysis	69		
Geometry	61, 62, 63, 64, 65, 66, 67, 68, 70		
Measurement	61, 65		
Probability	63, 67, 68		
Statistics	64		

Saxon *Algebra 1*

Lessons 61–70, Investigation 7

Content Trace

Lesson	Warm Up: Prerequisite Skills	New Concepts	Where Practiced	Where Assessed	Looking Forward
61	Lessons 13, 46	Simplifying Radical Expressions	Lessons 62, 63, 64, 65, 66, 67, 68, 69, 70, 71, 74, 76, 77, 100	Cumulative Tests 13, 14, 15, 17, 18	Lessons 69, 76, 103, 106, 114
62	Lesson 48	Displaying Data in Stem-and-Leaf Plots and Histograms	Lessons 63, 64, 65, 67, 70, 71, 72, 75, 77, 78	Cumulative Tests 13, 18	Lessons 71, 80
63	Lessons 3, 15, 18, 30	Solving Systems of Linear Equations by Elimination	Lessons 64, 65, 66, 67, 68, 69, 70, 71, 72, 73, 76, 78, 79, 106, 107	Cumulative Tests 13, 14, 15	Lessons 67, 97, 109
64	Lessons 19, 56	Identifying, Writing, and Graphing Inverse Variation	Lessons 65, 66, 67, 68, 69, 70, 71, 72, 73, 74, 77, 79, 80, 108	Cumulative Tests 13, 14, 17	Lesson 65, Investigations 7, 8
65	Lessons 49, 52	Writing Equations of Parallel and Perpendicular Lines	Lessons 66, 67, 68, 69, 70, 71, 72, 73, 74, 78, 80, 81, 83, 85, 98	Cumulative Tests 13, 14, 15, 17	Lessons 67, 109
66	Lessons 19, 45, 50	Solving Inequalities by Adding or Subtracting	Lessons 67, 68, 69, 70, 71, 72, 73, 74, 75, 76, 79, 81, 82, 83	Cumulative Tests 14, 15, 16	Lessons 70, 73, 81, 82
67	Lessons 49, 55, 65	Solving and Classifying Special Systems of Linear Equations	Lessons 68, 69, 70, 71, 72, 73, 74, 75, 76, 77, 80, 82, 83	Cumulative Tests 14, 15, 16	Lessons 97, 109, 112
68	Lessons 14, 33 Skills Bank 3	Mutually Exclusive and Inclusive Events	Lessons 69, 70, 71, 72, 73, 74, 75, 76, 77, 78, 81, 83, 84	Cumulative Tests 14, 16, 18, 19	Lessons 80, 111, 118, 120
69	Lessons 18, 61	Adding and Subtracting Radical Expressions	Lessons 70, 71, 72, 73, 74, 75, 76, 77, 78, 79, 82, 84, 85, 97, 109	Cumulative Tests 14, 16, 17, 18, 21	Lessons 76, 103, 106, 114
70	Lessons 21, 50	Solving Inequalities by Multiplying or Dividing	Lessons 71, 72, 73, 74, 75, 76, 77, 78, 79, 80, 83, 85, 86	Cumulative Tests 14, 15, 16, 18	Lessons 73, 81, 82
INV 7	N/A	Investigation: Comparing Direct and Inverse Variation	Lessons 75, 85, 100, 110	Cumulative Test 14	Lessons 71, 78, 99, Investigation 8

Section Overview 7

SECTION OVERVIEW 7

Ongoing Assessment

	Type	Feature	Intervention *
BEFORE instruction	Assess Prior Knowledge	• Diagnostic Test	• Prerequisite Skills Intervention
BEFORE the lesson	Formative	• Warm Up	• Skills Bank • Reteaching Masters
DURING the lesson	Formative	• Lesson Practice • Math Conversations with the Practice problems	• Additional Examples in TE • Test and Practice Generator (for additional practice sheets)
AFTER the lesson	Formative	• Check for Understanding (closure)	• Scaffolding Questions in TE
AFTER 5 lessons	Summative	After Lesson 65 • Cumulative Test 12 • Performance Task 12 After Lesson 70 • Cumulative Test 13 • Performance Task 13	• Reteaching Masters • Test and Practice Generator (for additional tests and practice)
AFTER 20 lessons	Summative	• Benchmark Tests	• Reteaching Masters • Test and Practice Generator (for additional tests and practice)

* for students not showing progress during the formative stages or scoring below 80% on the summative assessments

Evidence of Learning – What Students Should Know

Because the Saxon philosophy is to provide students with sufficient time to learn and practice each concept, a lesson's topic will not be tested until at least five lessons after the topic is introduced.

On the Cumulative Tests that are given during this section of ten lessons, students should be able to demonstrate the following competencies:
- Multiply and factor polynomials, and identify special products of binomials.
- Simplify radical expressions.
- Simplify rational expressions and determine when the expression is undefined.
- Solve inequalities and systems of linear equations.
- Use proportions to find measures in similar figures and solve percent problems.
- Determine slope of a line from a table, find the equation of a line given two points, and write an equation in point-slope form.
- Transform linear functions.
- Write equations of parallel and perpendicular lines and determine whether lines are parallel or perpendicular.
- Make a stem-and-leaf plot and a histogram.

Test and Practice Generator CD using ExamView™

The Test and Practice Generator is an easy-to-use benchmark and assessment tool that creates unlimited practice and tests in multiple formats and allows you to customize questions or create new ones. A variety of reports are available to track student progress toward mastery of the standards throughout the year.

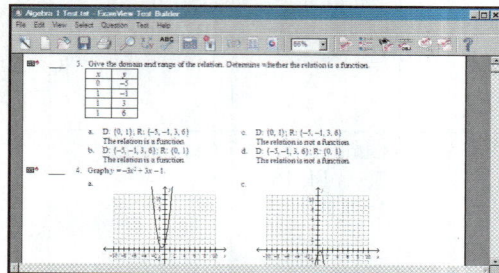
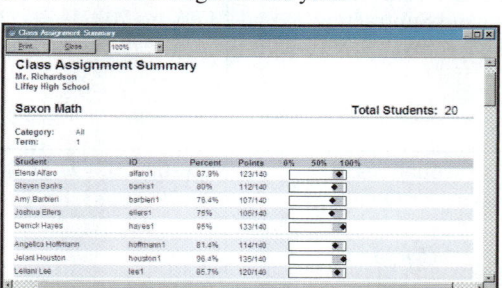

Saxon Algebra 1

Assessment Resources

Resources for Diagnosing and Assessing

- **Student Edition**
  - Warm Up
  - Lesson Practice

- **Teacher's Edition**
  - Math Conversations with the Practice problems
  - Check for Understanding (closure)

- **Course Assessments**
  - Diagnostic Test
  - Cumulative Tests
  - Performance Tasks
  - Benchmark Tests

Resources for Test Prep

- **Student Edition Practice**
  - Multiple-choice problems
  - Multiple-step and writing problems
  - Daily cumulative practice

- **Standardized Test Practice**

- **College Entrance Exam Practice**

- **Test and Practice Generator CD using ExamView™**

Resources for Intervention

- **Student Edition**
  - Skills Bank

- **Teacher's Edition**
  - Additional Examples
  - Scaffolding questions

- **Prerequisite Skills Intervention**
  - Skill worksheets

- **Reteaching Masters**
  - Lesson instruction and practice sheets

- **ExamView™ Test and Practice Generator CD**
  - Lesson practice problems
  - Additional tests

Cumulative Tests

The assessments in Saxon Math are frequent and consistently placed after every five lessons to offer a regular method of ongoing testing. These cumulative assessments check mastery of concepts from previous lessons.

Performance Tasks

The Performance Tasks can be used in conjunction with the Cumulative Tests and are scored using a rubric.

After Lesson 65

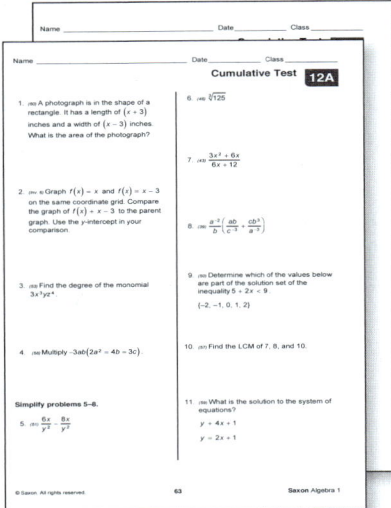

After Lesson 70

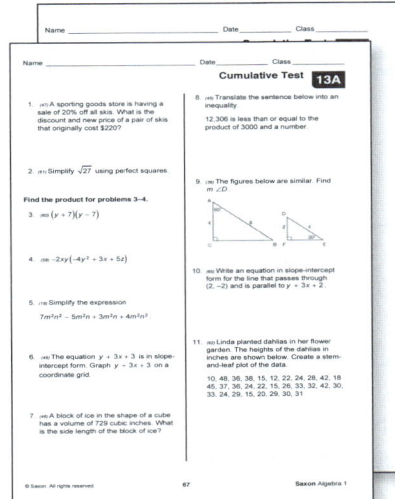

For use with Performance Tasks

Section Overview 7

LESSON 61

1 Warm Up

Problem 4

Remind students that since the radical symbol covers the whole fraction, they need to find the square root of both the numerator and the denominator.

2 New Concepts

In this lesson, students will learn methods for simplifying radicals of both numeric and algebraic expressions. This lesson restricts the radicals to square roots.

Example 1

One of the basic methods of simplifying a square root starts with identifying perfect squares among the factors of the expression under the radical. It may be helpful to work with students to generate a list of perfect squares for use in this lesson.

Additional Example 1

Simplify using perfect squares.

a. $\sqrt{196}$ 14

b. $\sqrt{320}$ $8\sqrt{5}$

LESSON RESOURCES

Student Edition Practice Workbook 61
Reteaching Master 61
Adaptations Master 61
Challenge and Enrichment Master C61

LESSON 61 Simplifying Radical Expressions

Warm Up

1. **Vocabulary** The _____ of x is the number whose square is x.   square root
   (13)

Simplify.

2. $\sqrt{36}$ 6
   (13)
3. $\sqrt{81}$ 9
   (13)
4. $\sqrt{\dfrac{1}{4}}$ $\dfrac{1}{2}$
   (46)
5. $\sqrt{54}$ is between which two consecutive integers?   7 and 8
   (13)

New Concepts

A **radical expression** is an expression containing a radical. Radical expressions can be simplified using the Product of Radicals Rule.

Product Property of Radicals
If a and b are non-negative real numbers, then $\sqrt{a}\,\sqrt{b} = \sqrt{ab}$ and $\sqrt{ab} = \sqrt{a}\,\sqrt{b}$.

Factoring a radicand into perfect squares is one way to determine if a radical expression can be simplified.

Example 1 Simplifying With Perfect Squares

Simplify using perfect squares.

Math Language
A **perfect square** is a number that is the square of an integer.

a. $\sqrt{225}$

SOLUTION

$\sqrt{225}$
$= \sqrt{9 \cdot 25}$ Find the perfect squares that are factors of 225.
$= \sqrt{9} \cdot \sqrt{25}$ Product of Radicals Rule
$= 3 \cdot 5$ Simplify the perfect squares.
$= 15$ Multiply.

b. $\sqrt{72}$

SOLUTION

$\sqrt{72}$
$= \sqrt{9 \cdot 4 \cdot 2}$ Find the perfect squares that are factors of 72.
$= \sqrt{9} \cdot \sqrt{4} \cdot \sqrt{2}$ Product of Radicals Rule
$= 3 \cdot 2\sqrt{2}$ Simplify.
$= 6\sqrt{2}$ Multiply.

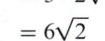 Online Connection
www.SaxonMathResources.com

MATH BACKGROUND

Roots and radicals are an important component of the real-number system. Students can simplify radical expressions by using the Product of Radicals rule. Numbers they can simplify to remove the root symbol are rational numbers, while those they cannot simplify to remove the root symbol are irrational numbers. Students need to simplify radical expressions so they can more easily perform operations with the expressions. They will also have an easier time finding the approximate value of an irrational expression when they have simplified the radical expression.

Exploration Finding Products of Square Roots

If a is equal to the area of a square, then $\sqrt{a}$ is the length of a side of the square. The formula for the area of a square is side length × side length, which can be written as $\sqrt{a} \cdot \sqrt{a} = a$.

a. Use the formula for the area of a square to write the area of a square that is 4 units squared. $\sqrt{4} \cdot \sqrt{4} = 4$

b. Simplify the formula for the area of a square that is 4 units² using the Product of Radicals Rule. $\sqrt{4 \cdot 4} = 4$

c. Simplify the product formed by the radicand. $\sqrt{16} = 4$

d. **Verify** Find the square root to show whether the equation is true. $\sqrt{16} = 4; 4 = 4$

The product of the square root of the area and the square root of the same area is equal to the area. This rule can be applied to all non-negative real numbers.

e. **Generalize** Write a rule for simplifying the expression $\sqrt{x} \cdot \sqrt{x}$, where x is a non-negative real number. If x is a non-negative real number, then the square root of x times the square root of x equals x.

f. Simplify $\sqrt{4} \cdot \sqrt{4}$ using the Product of Radicals Rule. $\sqrt{4 \cdot 4} = 4$

g. Simplify the radicand using the Product Property of Exponents. $\sqrt{4^2} = 4$

h. **Generalize** Write a rule for simplifying the expression $\sqrt{x^2}$, where x is a non-negative real number. If x is a non-negative real number, then the square root of x squared equals x.

Another way to simplify radical expressions is by factoring the radicand into prime numbers.

Example 2 Simplifying With Prime Factors

Simplify using prime factorization.

$\sqrt{180}$

SOLUTION

$\sqrt{180}$
$= \sqrt{2 \cdot 2 \cdot 3 \cdot 3 \cdot 5}$ Find the prime factorization.
$= \sqrt{2} \cdot \sqrt{2} \cdot \sqrt{3} \cdot \sqrt{3} \cdot \sqrt{5}$ Product Property of Radicals
$= 2 \cdot 3 \sqrt{5}$ Simplify.
$= 6\sqrt{5}$ Multiply.

Exploration
Use the Exploration to help students formulate rules for products of square-root pairs.

Extend the Exploration
Use the rule $\sqrt{x} \cdot \sqrt{x} = x$, $x \geq 0$, to simplify the following expressions.

a. $\sqrt{9} \cdot \sqrt{9}$ 9
b. $\sqrt{15} \cdot \sqrt{15}$ 15

Use the rule $\sqrt{x^2} = x$, $x \geq 0$, to simplify the expressions below.

c. $\sqrt{7^2}$ 7
d. $\sqrt{m^2}$ m

Example 2
When prime factors occur in pairs are they simplified by $\sqrt{m} \cdot \sqrt{m} = m$, $m \geq 0$.

Additional Example 2
Simplify $\sqrt{90}$ using prime factorization. $3\sqrt{10}$

INCLUSION

When simplifying radical expressions by prime factorization, it may be helpful to review the definitions of prime and composite numbers. Work with students to generate a chart of prime factors they can use if they are having difficulty with prime factorization.

Prime Factors			
2	3	5	7
11	13	17	19
23	29	31	37
41	43	47	53
59	61	67	71

Example 3

Powers of 10 can help form shortcuts for using exponents to simplify radical expressions.

Error Alert Students may use the number of place values to determine the exponent in powers of 10. Remind them that the number of zeros indicates the power of 10.

Additional Example 3
Simplify using powers of ten.

a. $\sqrt{1{,}000{,}000{,}000}$ $10{,}000\sqrt{10}$
b. $\sqrt{1{,}000{,}000}$ 1000

Example 4

Students should realize that when simplifying radicals they use the same rules for algebraic expressions as for numeric expressions. They can rewrite expressions as products, and can then apply rules of exponents and radicals to the individual factors.

Additional Example 4
Simplify. All variables represent non-negative real numbers.

a. $\sqrt{96g^3 f^6}$ $4gf^3\sqrt{6g}$
b. $\sqrt{54\,p^7 q^3}$ $3p^3 q\sqrt{6pq}$

Example 3 Simplifying With Powers of Ten

Simplify using powers of ten.

a. 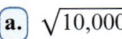 $\sqrt{10{,}000}$

SOLUTION Write the radicand as a power of ten. Then simplify.

$\sqrt{10{,}000}$
$=\sqrt{10^4}$ Write the radicand as a power of ten.
$=\sqrt{10^2 \cdot 10^2}$ Find factors that are perfect squares.
$=\sqrt{10^2} \cdot \sqrt{10^2}$ Product Property of Radicals
$= 10 \cdot 10$ Simplify.
$= 100$ Multiply.

b. $\sqrt{100{,}000}$

SOLUTION Write the radicand as a power of ten. Then simplify.

$\sqrt{100{,}000}$
$=\sqrt{10^5}$ Write the radicand as a power of ten.
$=\sqrt{10^2 \cdot 10^2 \cdot 10^1}$ Find factors that are perfect squares.
$=\sqrt{10^2} \cdot \sqrt{10^2} \cdot \sqrt{10^1}$ Product Property of Radicals
$= 10 \cdot 10 \cdot \sqrt{10}$ Simplify.
$= 100\sqrt{10}$ Multiply.

Math Reasoning

Generalize Find a pattern in the square roots of powers of ten.

Sample: Even powers are perfect squares. Odd powers are the product of a perfect square and $\sqrt{10}$.

The rules of radicals and exponents apply to variable expressions.

Example 4 Simplifying With Variables

Simplify. All variables represent non-negative real numbers.

a. $\sqrt{81x^4 y^3}$

SOLUTION Use the Product Property of Radicals. Then simplify.

$\sqrt{81x^4 y^3}$
$=\sqrt{81} \cdot \sqrt{x^4} \cdot \sqrt{y^3}$ Product Property of Radicals
$= 9 \cdot x^2 \cdot y\sqrt{y}$ Simplify.
$= 9x^2 y\sqrt{y}$ Multiply.

b. $\sqrt{162r^4 s^8}$

SOLUTION Use the Product Property of Exponents

$= \sqrt{162r^4 s^8}$
$= \sqrt{162} \cdot \sqrt{r^4} \cdot \sqrt{s^8}$ Product Property of Radicals
$= \sqrt{81} \cdot \sqrt{2} \cdot \sqrt{r^2} \cdot \sqrt{r^2} \cdot \sqrt{s^4} \cdot \sqrt{s^4}$ Find factors that are perfect squares.
$= 9 \cdot \sqrt{2} \cdot r^2 \cdot s^4$ Simplify.
$= 9r^2 s^4 \sqrt{2}$ Multiply.

400   Saxon Algebra 1

 ALTERNATE METHOD FOR EXAMPLE 3

Rather than separating the exponential form into squares, divide the exponent value by 2 and leave any remainder inside the radical.

$\sqrt{100{,}000}$

$\sqrt{10^5}$

$5 \div 2 = 2r1$

$\sqrt{10^5} = 10^2 \sqrt{10^1} = 10^2 \sqrt{10}$

Example 5 Application: Length of a Square Room

Idriana has a square bedroom. The area measures 48 square meters. Find the length of one side of Idriana's bedroom by simplifying $\sqrt{48 \text{ m}^2}$ using prime factorization.

SOLUTION

$s = \sqrt{48 \text{ m}^2}$ Simplify.
$= \sqrt{2 \cdot 2 \cdot 2 \cdot 2 \cdot 3} \text{ m}^2$ Product of Radicals Rule
$= 2 \cdot 2\sqrt{3} \text{ m}$ Simplify.
$= 4\sqrt{3} \text{ m}$ Multiply.

The length of one side of Idriana's bedroom is $4\sqrt{3}$ m.

Lesson Practice

Simplify using perfect squares.
a. $\sqrt{75}$ $5\sqrt{3}$ (Ex 1)
b. $\sqrt{63}$ $3\sqrt{7}$
c. Simplify $\sqrt{363}$ using prime factorization. $11\sqrt{3}$ (Ex 2)
d. Simplify. $\sqrt{1{,}000{,}000}$ using powers of ten. 1000 (Ex 3)

Simplify. All variables represent non-negative real numbers.
e. $\sqrt{90b^2c^4}$. $3bc^2\sqrt{10}$ (Ex 4)
f. $\sqrt{25x^3y^7}$. $5xy^3\sqrt{xy}$ (Ex 4)
g. Find the length of one side of a square room with an area of 80 square meters. $4\sqrt{5}$ m (Ex 5)

Practice   Distributed and Integrated

Simplify.

*1. $\sqrt{12}$ $2\sqrt{3}$ (61)

*2. $\sqrt{200}$ $10\sqrt{2}$ (61)

Evaluate.

3. $x^{\frac{1}{4}}$ when $x = -16$ not real (46)

4. $x^{\frac{1}{3}}$ when $x = 343$ 7 (46)

5. **Write** What does FOIL stand for in the term FOIL method? (58) First, Outer, Inner, Last

6. **(Basketball)** A basketball court is $\frac{144x}{x+3}$ feet long and $\frac{432}{x+3}$ feet wide. A team runs laps around the court. How far have they run after one lap?   288 feet (51)

7. **Error Analysis** Students were asked to use the sum and difference pattern to find the product of $(x-8)(x+8)$. Which student is correct? Explain the error.   Student A; Sample: Student B squared -8 instead of 8. (60)

Student A	Student B
$(x-8)(x+8)$	$(x-8)(x+8)$
$= x^2 - 8^2$	$= x^2 - 8^2$
$= x^2 - 64$	$= x^2 + 64$

Lesson 61   401

3 Practice

Math Conversations
Discussion to strengthen understanding

Problem 8
Extend the Problem
Have students expand the product of their answer to find a polynomial expression.
$2x^2 + 24x + 64$

Problem 10
Note that one of the equations is solved for the variable x. This means that students should substitute the equivalent expression for x in the other equation of the system.

Problem 17
Students may incorrectly set up the proportion to solve the problem. Guide students by asking, "How would you write the proportion in words before substituting values from the problem?"
$$\frac{\text{weight of 60-pound dog on moon}}{\text{weight of 60-pound dog on Earth}} = \frac{\text{weight of 25-pound dog on moon}}{\text{weight of 25-pound dog on Earth}}$$

---

8. Multiple Choice A rectangular picture is twice as long as it is wide. The picture has a 4-inch-wide mat around the picture. Let x represent the picture's width. Which product gives the area of the picture and mat? **C**
A $(2x)(x)$
B $(2x + 4)(x + 2)$
C $(2x + 8)(x + 8)$
D $(-2x + 6)(6 + 2)$

Solve the systems by the method given.

*9. Use a graphing calculator to solve.
$$-5x + 8y = 7$$
$$3y = -2x - 9 \quad (-3, -1)$$

10. Use substitution to solve.
$$2x - 3y = 3$$
$$x = 4y - 11 \quad (9, 5)$$

11. **World Records** In 2005, power-plant employees built the world's largest igloo in Quebec, Canada. The igloo is approximately in the shape of a half sphere and has a volume of about 1728π cubic feet. What is the igloo's approximate diameter? (Hint: The formula for the volume of a sphere is $V = \frac{4}{3}\pi r^3$.) about 27.5 ft

12. **Multi-Step** The following data shows the attendance at seven home games for a high school football team: 5846, 6023, 5921, 7244, 6832, 6496, 7012.
   a. Find the mean attendance value for the data set. 6482
   b. Suppose the stadium was almost filled to capacity for the homecoming game and that the data value 11,994 is now added to the data set. How does this outlier affect the mean of the data? Sample: The outlier raises the mean attendance value to 7171.

Simplify.

13. $(4b - 3)^2$ $16b^2 - 24b + 9$
14. $(-2x + 5)^2$ $4x^2 - 20x + 25$

*15. **Fundraising** At a school fundraiser, students charge $10 to wash a car and $20 to wash an SUV. They make $1700 by washing 105 vehicles. How many of each kind do they wash? 40 cars; 65 SUVs

16. **Multi-Step** Use these points (1, 3) and (2, 8) to answer the problems below.
   a. Find the slope of the line that passes through the points. 5
   b. Graph the line.
   c. Write the equation of the line in point-slope form. $y - 3 = 5(x - 1)$ or $y - 8 = 5(x - 2)$
   d. Write the equation of the line in slope-intercept form. $y = 5x - 2$
   e. Fill in the missing coordinates of the points $(x, -3)$ and $(-2, y)$. $x = -\frac{1}{5}, y = -12$

16.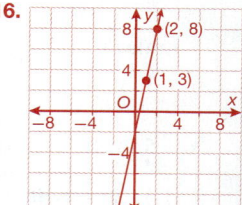

17. **Physics** An object's weight on the moon varies directly with its weight on Earth. A 60-pound dog would weigh 9 pounds on the moon. How much would a 25-pound dog weigh on the moon? 3.75 pounds

---

ENGLISH LEARNERS

Discuss the word **igloo**. Say:

"An igloo is a shelter made out of blocks of snow. The shape is similar to half of a ball. Igloos may be found in extremely cold places."

Say:

"An igloo is built using blocks of snow. This is similar to the way a brick house is built."

Ask,

"What other types of shelter do people use that is not common?" Sample: tents, huts

18. Multiple Choice Which point is a solution of to the linear system? **C**
$$y - 5x = 3$$
$$3x + 8y = 24$$
A (1, 8)   **B** (0, 0)   **C** (0, 3)   **D** (4, 1.5)

*19. Write Explain how to simplify $\sqrt{18a^2}$, $a \geq 0$.

*20. Geometry A triangle has a length of $(x - 4)$ inches and a height of $(x + 4)$ inches. What is the area of the triangle? $\frac{x^2 - 16}{2}$ square inches

21. Analyze What polynomial can be added to $x^2 + 5x + 1$ to get a sum of $4x^2 - 3$?
$3x^2 - 5x - 4$

19. Sample: I can write the radicand using prime factorization: $\sqrt{2 \cdot 3^2 \cdot a^2}$. Then, because squares and square roots are inverses, 3 and a can be removed from under the radical sign which leaves $3a\sqrt{2}$.

Find the LCM.

22. 21, 33, 13   3003

23. 8, 32, 12   96

*24. Multi-Step Laura is building on to her new pool house. Write an expression for the area of the non-shaded region. Find the area.
  a. Find the area of the large square.   9
  b. Find the area of the smaller square. x^2
  c. Write an expression for the area of the non-shaded region. $9 - x^2$

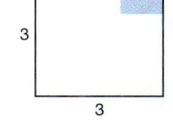

*25. Measurement Alan is building a square patio. He wants an 8-inch-wide border of flowers around his patio, and the total length of one side is $8x$. Write a polynomial that represents the area of the floor of the patio not including the border of flowers. $(8x - 16)^2 = 64x^2 - 256x + 256$ square inches

*26. Multi-Step The area of a circle is 20π cm². How long is the radius?
  a. Write an expression that can be used to find the length of the radius of a circle if given the area, A. $\sqrt{\frac{A}{\pi}}$
  b. Use the expression to find the length of the radius. $\sqrt{20}$ cm = $2\sqrt{5}$ cm

Translate each inequality into a sentence.

27. $\frac{n}{7} + 3 \geq 5$

28. $3g - 4 < -2$ Sample: The product of an unknown and 3 minus 4 is less than -2.

*29. Circular Motion The tangential velocity of an object in circular motion can be found using the expression $\sqrt{ar}$, where a is the centripetal acceleration and r is the path radius of the circle. What is the tangential velocity of an object with a path radius of 15 cm and a centripetal acceleration of 60 cm/s²?   30 cm/s

30. Make a box-and-whisker plot of the data below and title it "Shoe Sizes."

5, 10, 6, 7, 6.5, 7, 7, 8.5, 6.5, 8, 9, 7.5, 7

27. Sample: The quotient of an unknown and 7 plus 3 is greater than or equal to 5.

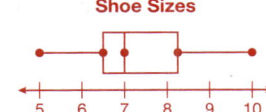

Shoe Sizes

Lesson 61   403

Problem 20
Error Alert
Some students may incorrectly divide the exponent of the variable with the denominator to simplify the expression to $x - 8$. Check that students are correctly simplifying the algebraic expression for area. An equivalent expression can be $\frac{x^2}{2} - 8$ because the fraction can be distributed across subtraction in the numerator.

Problem 26a
Guide students by asking them the following questions.

"What is the formula for the area of a circle?" $A = \pi r^2$

"Solve for r^2." $\frac{A}{\pi} = r^2$

"Since area is positive, we know that $\sqrt{r^2} = r$. Since $\frac{A}{\pi} = r^2$, use $\sqrt{\frac{A}{\pi}} = r$ to find the expression for the length of the radius."

CHALLENGE

Have students simplify radical algebraic expressions with roots greater than 2.

a. $\sqrt[3]{8g^3h^4}$ $2gh\sqrt[3]{h}$

b. $\sqrt[5]{32y^3z^8}$ $2z\sqrt[5]{y^3z^3}$

LOOKING FORWARD

Simplifying numeric and algebraic radical expressions prepares students for

• **Lesson 69** Adding and Subtracting Radical Expressions

• **Lesson 76** Multiplying Radical Expressions

• **Lesson 103** Dividing Radical Expressions

• **Lesson 106** Solving Radical Equations

• **Lesson 114** Graphing Square-Root Functions

LAB 6

Materials
- graphing calculator

Discuss
Before teaching students to create a histogram by using a graphing calculator, review what a bar graph is and the ways to display data on a graphing calculator.

Define range. Explain how knowing the range helps to define the intervals.

Discuss with students how making a histogram helps the teacher to better visualize the test scores for her class.

Ask students what the labels would be for the *x*- and *y*-axes.

LAB 6

Drawing Histograms

Graphing Calculator Lab (*Use with Lesson 62*)

A histogram is a vertical bar graph that organizes data into equally sized intervals. This makes it easy to see where the majority of data values fall in a measurement scale. Given a set of data, you can make a histogram with a graphing calculator.

A teacher has test scores for her class and wants to know how many students earned higher than 70 points. Use the data to make a histogram.

30, 33, 33, 34, 55, 56, 63, 65, 67, 71, 80, 82, 85, 88, 89, 90, 90, 97

Graphing Calculator Tip

For help with entering data into a list, see the graphing calculator keystrokes in Lab 4.

1. Enter the data into List 1.

2. Press [2nd] [STAT PLOT / Y=] and select **1:Plot1…** to open the plot setup menu.

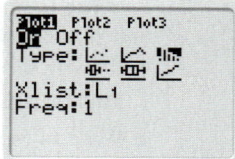

3. Press [ENTER] to turn Plot1 **On** and then press the ▼ key once and the ▶ key twice to select the type at the end of the first row. Press [ENTER]. The setting for **Xlist** should be L1 and **Freq** should be 1. If the **Xlist** setting is not L1, press the ▼ key once and then [2nd] [LIST / STAT] [ENTER].

4. Create a histogram by pressing [ZOOM] and selecting **9:ZoomStat**.

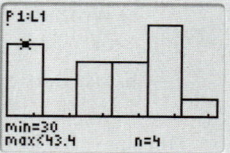

Press [TRACE]. The first interval has a minimum value of 30 and a maximum value of 43.4. To count the students who earned a score higher than 70 points, the intervals need to be graphed in multiples of 10 points.

5. Press [WINDOW] to change the intervals and window settings.

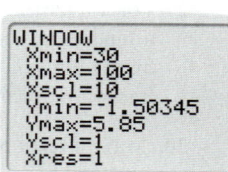

The lowest test score is 30, so press [ENTER] to accept **Xmin=30**. Since the test scores do not exceed 100 points, press **1 0 0** [ENTER]. To use intervals of 10 points, set **Xscl** by pressing **1 0** [ENTER].

404 *Saxon Algebra 1*

6. Press GRAPH to view the histogram in the new window.

7. Use TRACE and then use the ◄ and ► keys to view the statistical values. The "min=" and "max<" provide minimum and maximum values for each interval. The "n=" gives the number of test scores in the interval.

One student earned a score in the 70's, five students earned a score in the 80's, and three earned a score of at least 90 points. Therefore, of the 18 students, nine earned a score above 70 points on the test.

Lab Practice

1a. Sample:

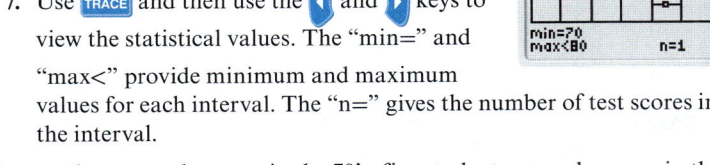

The data list the results of a words-per-minute typing test.

39, 41, 42, 47, 47, 50, 53, 55, 55, 57, 60, 62, 64, 68, 70, 71

a. Use a graphing calculator to make a histogram of the data using intervals of 5 words per minute.

b. According to the data, how many people type between 55 and 65 words per minute?   **6 people**

The histogram shows the ages of all members of a local orchestra.

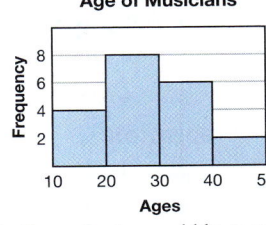

Age of Musicians

c. How many musicians in the orchestra could be teenagers?   **B**

A 2   B 4
C 6   D 8

d. **Analyze** The orchestra's conductor wants to give a prize to musicians in the age group that attends the most rehearsals. Based on the histogram, is he correct to give the prize to musicians who are between 20 and 29 years old? Explain.   **no; Sample: The histogram shows the frequency of ages of musicians, not the number of times musicians in each age group went to rehearsal.**

3 Practice

Problem a
Remind students to follow the same steps as they did in the initial lab.

Problem b
Guide students by asking, "What is meant by frequency in the label on the *y*-axis?" Sample: How many musicians are in each age group.

Lab 6   405

LESSON 62

1 Warm Up

Problem 3
Remind students that some data sets may have no mode.

2 New Concepts

In this lesson, two methods are shown for displaying the distribution of a data set. Stem-and-leaf plots include data points, but a histogram shows only distribution.

Example 1

Stem-and-leaf plots are useful for showing data when there is not a large spread of values.

Additional Example 1
Create a stem-and-leaf plot of the data.

Ages of Dance Instructors

19, 25, 34, 32, 48, 24, 28, 29, 26, 34, 17, 58, 47, 38, 27, 29

Stem	Leaves
1	7 9
2	4 5 6 7 8 9 9
3	2 4 4 8
4	7 8
5	8

4 | 7 = 47 years

LESSON RESOURCES

Student Edition Practice Workbook 62
Reteaching Master 62
Adaptations Master 62
Challenge and Enrichment Master C62
Technology Lab Master 62

LESSON 62

Displaying Data in Stem-and-Leaf Plots and Histograms

Warm Up

1. Vocabulary The sum of the values in a data set divided by the number of data values gives the _____. **A**

A mean   B median   C mode   D range

Find the mean, median, mode, and range.

2. 5, 3, 7, 6, 2, 4, 5, 8   5; 5; 5; 6

3. 12, 15, 20, 16, 14, 13   15; 14.5; no mode; 8

New Concepts

A **stem-and-leaf plot** is a data display that uses some digits as "stems" and others as "leaves". The "stems" have a greater place value than the "leaves." Stem-and-leaf plots are helpful in organizing data and displaying it to show the distribution of values.

stem ⟶ 2 3 ⟵ leaf

The digits other than the last digit are the stem. The last digit of a number is the leaf.

Example 1 Making a Stem-and-Leaf Plot

The high temperatures in degrees Fahrenheit for April 2007 in New Orleans, Louisiana, are shown. Create a stem-and-leaf plot of the data.

70, 83, 84, 77, 66, 67, 53, 55, 64, 69, 82, 78, 80, 81, 66,
71, 75, 76, 80, 78, 78, 81, 83, 83, 82, 81, 80, 85, 87, 87

SOLUTION

Step 1: There are two place values in each temperature in the data set, tens and ones. Organize the data by each tens value. Write each place-value group in ascending order. Include any values that repeat.

50's: 53, 55
60's: 64, 66, 66, 67, 69
70's: 70, 71, 75, 76, 77, 78, 78, 78
80's: 80, 80, 80, 81, 81, 81, 82, 82, 83, 83, 83, 84, 85, 87, 87

Math Language
All stem-and-leaf plots include a **key** to indicate how to read each stem and leaf. Place-value information and units are indicated.

Step 2: Use the tens digit of each group as the stem of a row on a stem-and-leaf plot. Write each ones digit as the leaf for the corresponding tens digit.

Step 3: Create a key to show how to read each entry in the plot.

8 | 5 = 85°F

High Temperatures (°F) April 2007 for New Orleans, LA

Stem	Leaves
5	3, 5
6	4, 6, 6, 7, 9
7	0, 1, 5, 6, 7, 8, 8, 8
8	0, 0, 0, 1, 1, 1, 2, 2, 3, 3, 3, 4, 5, 7, 7

Key: 5 | 3 = 53°F

406 *Saxon Algebra 1*

MATH BACKGROUND

Stem-and-leaf plots and histograms are typically taught together because they are very similar in how they display the distribution of data. A stem-and-leaf plot displays data that tend to have a small variance and will show all the data points. A histogram also tends to have a small variance but will show the curve of the data rather than the individual points.

Stem-and-leaf plots are typically used to show collected data, whereas a histogram is typically used to predict future data points.

When creating a histogram, it is often best to create a stem-and-leaf plot first. A stem-and-leaf plot, if turned on its side so that the stems represent the *x*-axis, will resemble a histogram.

Stem-and-leaf plots are used to show the distribution of data. In the stem-and-leaf plot for Example 1, there is an unequal distribution of temperatures in the 80's. This may not have been as obvious when the data was in a continuous list. When organizing the data by place values, it becomes easier to identify unequal distributions.

Stem-and-leaf plots are used to find measures of central tendency and other statistical measures because the actual data points are included in the plot. One of the many statistical measures that are helpful is relative frequency. In an experiment, the number of times an event happens divided by the total number of trials is the **relative frequency** of that event.

Example 2 Analyzing a Stem-and-Leaf Plot

Use the stem-and-leaf plot from Example 1 to find the following statistical measures.

a. median

SOLUTION

To find the median, find the middle value(s). For these data there are two middle values. The 15th and 16th values are 78 and 80. Find the average of 78 and 80.

$$\frac{78 + 80}{2} = \frac{158}{2} = 79$$

The median of the data is 79°F.

b. mode

SOLUTION

The mode is the value or values that occur most frequently. There are 4 values that occur 3 times: 78, 80, 81, and 83. These are the modes.

c. range

SOLUTION

The range is the difference between the greatest and least value in the set. The greatest data value is 87; the least data value is 53. The range is 34°F.

d. relative frequency of 80

SOLUTION

The data value 80 occurs 3 times. There are a total of 30 data values.

$$\frac{3}{30} = \frac{1}{10} = 0.10 = 10\%$$

Caution

The data must be in order before finding the middle value(s).

Hint

Relative frequency can be expressed as a fraction, a decimal, or a percent.

Online Connection
www.SaxonMathResources.com

Example 2

Point out that the measures could be computed without the stem-and-leaf plot, using only the data, but that the organization of the stem-and-leaf plot makes finding the statistical information easier.

Extend the Example

Have students find the mean of the data. mean ≈ 76°

"Explain how you could find the mean using the stem-and-leaf plot and the actual data." Sample: Each stem is the tens place value. Multiply each stem by the number of data points in it. Add those products. Then add the values of all the leaves. The total sum is the sum of the data points. Finally, divide by the number of leaves or data points.

Additional Example 2

Use the stem-and-leaf plot from Additional Example 1 to find the following statistical measures:
median: 29 years
mode: 29 and 34 years
range: 41 years

Error Alert Students may confuse the place values of the stems and leaves. Remind them to read the key carefully to find the correct place-value assignments, as well as the correct units for the data.

Lesson 62   407

ENGLISH LEARNERS

Students may not make a connection between a tree and a **stem-and-leaf** plot. This visual graph of part of a stem-and-leaf plot from Example 1 may be helpful. Say:

"**The stem of a tree supports the leaves. What numbers in the plot make up the stem? What numbers make up the leaf?**" the ten's digits; the one's digits

Discuss how the term stem-and-leaf plot is appropriate.

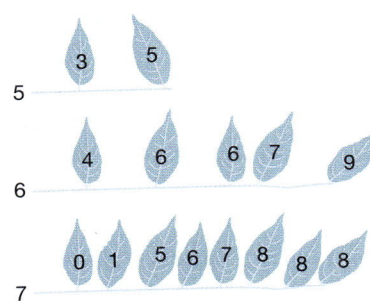

Lesson 62   407

Example 3

Remind students that creating histograms for data sets provides a visual representation of the distribution of the set, but does not provide any specific information about the data values.

Additional Example 3

Create a histogram of the data from Additional Example 1.

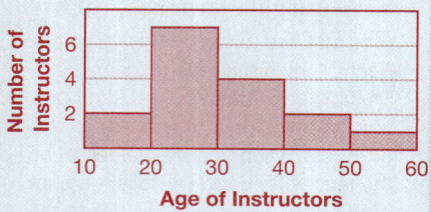

Example 4

Being able to use computer spreadsheet programs and graphing calculators can make the process of creating histograms and other plots for data much simpler.

Additional Example 4

Use the graphing calculator to create a histogram for the data in Additional Example 1, making only 4 intervals.

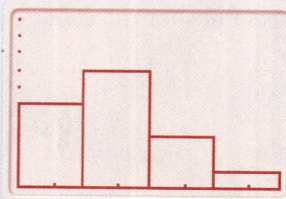

Extend the Example

Have students use the histogram to estimate the mean of the data values. Then have them calculate the actual mean. estimate: 11.5; actual: 11.34

Another display that can be used to show the distribution of numeric data is a histogram. A **histogram** is a bar graph that displays the frequency of data in equal intervals. Each bar must be the same width and should touch the bar(s) next to it.

Example 3 Making a Histogram

Create a histogram of the data from Example 1.

SOLUTION

The data from Example 1 are already organized into four intervals of 10. Create a graph showing the intervals and the number of data points in each interval.

High Temperatures April 2007 New Orleans, LA

Example 4 Application: Sports

The list below shows the results in meters of the first round triple jump from the 2007 NCAA women's outdoor track championships. Create a histogram of the data using a graphing calculator.

12.16, 11.77, 11.64, 11.50, 11.48, 11.45, 11.31, 10.94, 10.98, 9.88, 12.08, 11.58, 11.41, 11.5, 11.34, 11.24, 11.22, 11.13, 10.76

SOLUTION

Step 1: Enter the data into a list in the calculator.

> **Graphing Calculator Tip**
> Lists can be created using the home screen or using the STAT screen. Lists can only be edited in the STAT screen.

Step 2: Change the window settings to select intervals and to correctly view the data plot.

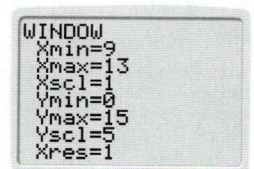

Step 3: On the STAT PLOT screen, select the histogram plot. Labels are not shown on the screen.

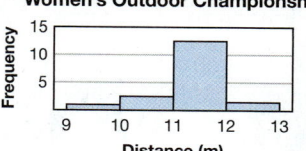

Triple Jump Results NCAA 2007 Women's Outdoor Championship

408 Saxon Algebra 1

ALTERNATE METHOD FOR EXAMPLE 3

For students having trouble directly creating the histogram, suggest that they take the stem-and-leaf plot from Example 1 and rotate it so the stems are on the *x*-axis. Ask them why this looks like a histogram.

Lesson Practice

a. The list shows the low temperatures in degrees Fahrenheit in New Orleans for the first 15 days of April 2007. Create a stem-and-leaf plot of the data.

65, 70, 69, 61, 56, 52, 43, 42, 51, 60, 63, 52, 60, 54, 50

b. Create a histogram of the data in problem **a.** See Additional Answers.

c. Use the stem-and-leaf plot to find the median, mode, and range of the low temperatures the last 15 days of April 2007 in New Orleans, LA.

a. Low Temperatures (°F) April 2007 for New Orleans, LA

Stem	Leaves
4	2, 3
5	0, 1, 2, 2, 4, 6
6	0, 0, 1, 3, 5, 9
7	0

Key: 5 | 6 = 56°F

Low Temperatures (°F) Last 15 Days April 2007 for New Orleans, LA

Stem	Leaves
4	5
5	4, 6, 7, 8, 9, 9
6	0, 3, 3, 4, 4, 8, 8
7	1

Key: 5 | 6 = 56°F

median: 60; mode: 59, 63, 64, 68; range = 26°

d. Use the stem-and-leaf plot in problem **c** to find the relative frequency of 64. $\frac{2}{15}$; $0.\overline{13}$; $13.\overline{3}\%$

e. Create a histogram of the data in problem **c** using a graphing calculator.

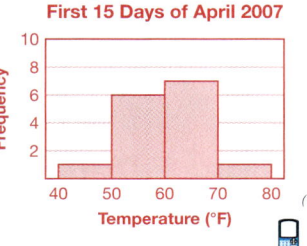

Low Temperatures in New Orleans First 15 Days of April 2007

Practice Distributed and Integrated

Find each of the following statistical measures using the data in the plot below.

Service Club Ages of Members

Stem	Leaves
2	5, 6
3	0, 2, 3, 4, 4, 4, 8, 9
4	1, 1, 2, 6, 7
5	2, 5, 7
6	0, 4

Key: 5 | 6 means 56 years old

*1. median 40 years

*2. mode 34 years

*3. range 39 years

*4. relative frequency of 41 10%

Simplify.

5. $\sqrt{88}$ $2\sqrt{22}$

*6. $\sqrt{720}$ $12\sqrt{5}$

7. $\sqrt{180}$ $6\sqrt{5}$

 8. **Write** Explain in your own words how to graph the equation $y = -\frac{1}{3}x + 2$.
Sample: Graph the point (0, 2) for the y-intercept. Then graph the point that is one unit down and 3 units to the right of that, or (3, 1), and draw a line between the two points.

*9. Error Analysis Students were asked to find the product $(2n - 5)^2$ using the square of a binomial pattern. Which student is correct? Explain the error. Student A; Sample: Student B used the wrong pattern to find the product.

Student A	Student B
$(2n - 5)^2$	$(2n - 5)^2$
$= (2n)^2 - 2(2n)(5) + (5)^2$	$= (2n)^2 - 5^2$
$= 4n^2 - 20n + 25$	$= 4n^2 - 25$

10. Analyze The solution to a system of equations is (4, 6). One equation in the system is $2x + y = 14$. One term in the other equation is $3x$. What could the equation be? Sample: $3x - 2y = 0$

11. Multiple Choice Which system of equations has a solution of $(2, -2)$? **C**

A $x + y = 0$
$2x - 3y = -2$

B $5x - 3y = 16$
$4x + 9y = 10$

C $9x - 2y = 22$
$3x + 6y = -6$

D $x + 2y = -2$
$2x + y = -2$

Multiply.

12. $-4(x^2 + 4x - 1)$ $-4x^2 - 16x + 4$

13. $(b - 8)^2$ $b^2 - 16b + 64$

14. $\left(x + \frac{1}{2}\right)\left(x + \frac{1}{4}\right)$ $x^2 + \frac{3}{4}x + \frac{1}{8}$

15. Consumer Math Consumers spend $95 million on Father's Day cards and $152 million on Mother's Day cards. What is the amount of increase or decrease from Mother's Day to Father's Day cards? What percentage of the combined total do consumers spend on Mother's Day cards? $57 million decrease; 62%

*16. Geometry The stem-and-leaf plot shows the diameters of a shipment of bicycle tires to a bicycle shop. Find the circumference of the tire with the median diameter in the data set. Use 3.14 for pi. 59.66 inches

Diameters of Bicycle Tires

Stem	Leaves
1	5, 5, 6, 7, 7, 8, 9, 9
2	0, 0, 0, 1, 2, 2, 4

Key: 1|5 means 15 inches

17. Solve the following system by graphing: $y = x + 6$
$y + 3x = 6$ (0, 6)

18. Write Explain what the whiskers in a box-and-whisker plot represent. Sample: the upper and lower quartiles of the data

*19. Fundraising The amount of money raised for a charity event by the homerooms at Jefferson High School are shown below. Create a stem-and-leaf plot of the data.

$150, $125, $134, $129, $106, $157, $108, $135, $144, $149

19. Money Raised in Homerooms

Stem	Leaves
10	6, 8
11	
12	5, 9
13	4, 5
14	4, 9
15	0, 7

Key: 10|5 means $105

410 Saxon Algebra 1

20. (**Commerce**) The weekly profit, p, in dollars at Bill's TV repair shop can be estimated by the equation $p = 30n - 400$, where n is the number of TVs repaired in a week. Graph the equation and predict the profit for a week if 50 TVs are repaired. **$1100**

Evaluate.

21. Evaluate $\sqrt[4]{x^2}$ when $x = 9$. **3**

22. Evaluate $\sqrt[3]{x^6}$ when $x = 2$. **4**

23. Write an equation for a direct variation that includes the point $(10, -90)$. $y = -9x$

24. Multi-Step Levi deposits $500 into a savings account that earns interest compounded annually. Let r be the annual interest rate. After two years, the balance from the first deposit is given by the polynomial $500 + 1000r + 500r^2$. A year after making the first deposit, Levi makes another deposit. A year later, the balance from the second deposit is $600 + 600r$.
 a. Find the balance of the accounts combined in terms of r after 2 years. $1100 + 1600r + 500r^2$
 b. Find the balance after two years when $r = 0.03$. **$1148.45**

Find the missing number.

25. original price: $68   **$87.72**
 new price: _____
 29% increase

26. original price: _____ $116.00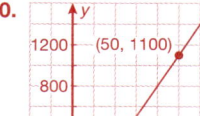
 new price: $98.60
 15% decrease

20.
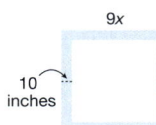

27. (**Triathlon Training**) Training for a triathlon involves running, swimming, and biking. The athlete runs every $(2r - 2s)$ days, swims every $(4r^2 - 4rs)$ days, and bikes every $(8rs - 8s^2)$ days. When would the athlete have all three activities on the same day? after $8rs(r - s)$ days

28. Multiple Choice Which of the following is not equivalent to $\sqrt{2800}$? **D**
 A $10\sqrt{28}$ **B** $2\sqrt{700}$ **C** $20\sqrt{7}$ **D** $40\sqrt{7}$

***29.** (**Gardening**) Isaac is planting a square flower garden. He wants a 10-inch-wide brick border around the outside edge of the garden. The total side length is $9x$. Write a special product that represents the area of the garden not including the brick border. Simplify. $(9x - 20)^2 = 81x^2 - 360x + 400$ square inches

***30. Coordinate Geometry** Lucia drew a square on grid paper that has an area of 25 units^2. What points could she have plotted? Sample: (0, 0), (0, 5), (5, 0), and (5, 5)

Lesson 62   411

LOOKING FORWARD

Learning to read and display data in stem-and-leaf plots and histograms prepares students for

• **Lesson 71** Making and Analyzing Scatter Plots

• **Lesson 80** Calculating Frequency Distributions

Problem 23
Remind students that the general form of a direct variation problem is $y = ax$.

Problem 29
Suggest that students draw a diagram and carefully label it to help visualize the information presented in the problem.

Lesson 62   411

LESSON 63

1 Warm Up

Problem 4
Remind students that when multiplying powers with the same base, they will add the exponents to simplify.

2 New Concepts

In this lesson, students learn another method of solving systems of linear equations. Review the substitution method and discuss when it may not be the best method to use. Explain that solving by elimination involves adding or subtracting the equations in the system.

Example 1
When adding equations, students will first remove a variable by combining like terms with opposite coefficients.

Additional Example 1
Solve the system by elimination and check the answer.

$3x + 7y = 16$

$6x - 7y = 11$

(3, 1); See student work.

LESSON RESOURCES

Student Edition Practice
   Workbook 63
Reteaching Master 63
Adaptations Master 63
Challenge and Enrichment
   Master C63

LESSON 63

Solving Systems of Linear Equations by Elimination

Warm Up

1. **Vocabulary** The graph of a _____ equation is a straight line. **linear**

Simplify.

2. $3(4x - 5)$ $(12x - 15)$

3. $4(7y + 12)$ $28y + 48$

4. $ky^2 k^3 k^2 y^5$ $k^6 y^7$

5. $xy - 3xy^2 + 5y^2 x - 4xy$ $-3xy + 2xy^2$

New Concepts

It is not always practical to isolate one of the variables in a system of linear equations in order to solve by substitution. Sometimes it is easier to eliminate one of the variables by combining the two equations using addition or subtraction.

Example 1 Adding Equations

Solve the system by elimination and check the answer.

$5x + 2y = 9$

$-5x + 6y = 7$

SOLUTION

The two equations have equal and opposite coefficients for one of the variables, so add the equations to eliminate that variable.

$5x + 2y = 9$
$\underline{-5x + 6y = 7}$
$8y = 16$ Add equations and combine like terms.
$y = 2$ Divide both sides by 8.

Substitute 2 for y in one of the original equations and solve for x.

$5x + 2(2) = 9$ Substitute 2 for y in the first equation.
$5x + 4 = 9$ Multiply.
$5x = 5$ Subtract 4 from both sides.
$x = 1$ Divide both sides by 5.

The solution is $(1, 2)$.

Caution
Be sure to list the values for x and y in the correct order, (x, y).

Check Substitute $(1, 2)$ for x and y in both of the original equations.

$-5x + 6y = 7$ $5x + 2y = 9$
$-5(1) + 6(2) \stackrel{?}{=} 7$ Substitute. $5(1) + 2(2) \stackrel{?}{=} 9$
$-5 + 12 \stackrel{?}{=} 7$ Multiply. $5 + 4 \stackrel{?}{=} 9$
$7 = 7$ ✓   Add. $9 = 9$ ✓

Online Connection
www.SaxonMathResources.com

MATH BACKGROUND

The elimination method solves systems of linear equations algebraically. The Addition Property of Equality states that if $a = b$, then $a + c = b + c$. Thus, if $a = b$ and $c = d$, then $a + c = b + d$. Students can use this property to solve systems of linear equations by elimination.

$ax + by = e$

$cx + dy = f$

$(ax + by) + (cx + dy) = e + f$

When using elementary operations on a system, replacing one equation with the sum of two equations yields an equivalent system. If either $a = -c$ or $b = -d$, then adding the two equations can form an equivalent system of one equation with only one variable. Since in a system of simultaneous equations all equations must be true at the same time, solving for one variable must yield a solution that applies to all equations in the system.

Example 2 Subtracting Equations

Solve the system by elimination. $7x + 3y = -5$
$2x + 3y = 5$

Hint
Subtracting is the same as adding the opposite.

SOLUTION

$7x + 3y = -5$ — Both equations have the same positive
$2x + 3y = 5$ — coefficient for one of the variables.
$5x = -10$ — Subtract the equations and combine like terms.
$x = -2$ — Divide both sides by 5.

Substitute -2 for x in one of the original equations and solve for y.

$2x + 3y = 5$
$2(-2) + 3y = 5$ — Substitute -2 for x in the second equation.
$-4 + 3y = 5$ — Multiply.
$3y = 9$ — Add 4 to both sides.
$y = 3$ — Divide both sides by 3.

The solution is $(-2, 3)$.

Sometimes it may be necessary to first multiply one or both of the equations by a number in order to have opposite coefficients.

Example 3 Multiplying One Equation

Solve the system by elimination. $5y = 8x - 2$
$4x - 3y = -2$

Hint
Make sure both equations are in standard form in order to easily combine like terms.

SOLUTION

$-8x + 5y = -2$ — Write the first equation in standard form.
$8x - 6y = -4$ — Multiply the second equation by 2.
$-y = -6$ — Add the equations and combine like terms.
$y = 6$ — Simplify.

Substitute 6 for y in one of the original equations and solve for x.

$5y = 8x - 2$
$5(6) = 8x - 2$ — Substitute 6 for y in the first equation.
$30 = 8x - 2$ — Multiply.
$32 = 8x$ — Add 2 to both sides.
$4 = x$ — Divide both sides by 8.

The solution is $(4, 6)$.

Lesson 63   413

Example 2

Explain that since subtraction is the same as adding the opposite, if there are like terms in each equation with similar signs, students can subtract to eliminate a variable.

Additional Example 2
Solve the system by elimination.

$-2x + 2y = 18$
$-2x - 7y = 9$
$(-8, 1)$

Example 3

Make sure students understand that eliminating a variable means that its coefficients must have a sum or difference of zero. Students may need to multiply an equation by a nonzero number to set up a system where this is possible.

Additional Example 3
Solve the system.

$3x - 6y = 18$
$5x = -2y + 6$
$(2, -2)$

Error Alert When multiplying an equation to solve a system by elimination, students may mistakenly multiply only one term in the equation. Remind them that for the equation to remain balanced, they need to multiply each side by a nonzero number, not just an individual term.

 ALTERNATE METHOD FOR EXAMPLE 2

Multiply the top equation by -1.

$-1(7x + 3y) = -1(-5)$

$-7x - 3y = 5$

Now add the two equations together.

$-7x - 3y = 5$
$2x + 3y = 5$
$\overline{-5x = 10}$

$\dfrac{-5x}{-5} = \dfrac{10}{-5}$

$x = -2$

Substitute -2 for x in one of the original equations and solve for y.

$7(-2) + 3y = -5$
$-14 + 3y = -5$
$+14 +14$
$3y = 9$
$y = 3$

The solution is $(-2, 3)$.

Lesson 63   413

Example 4

Students may need to multiply both equations in a system by a nonzero number in order to solve. Remind them to choose values that will create equivalent equations that they can add or subtract to eliminate a variable.

Additional Example 4

Solve the system of linear equations.

$2x + 2y = -8$

$-5x - 3y = 14$

$(-1, -3)$

Example 5

Extend the Example

"Carlos collected 18 new Buffalo nickels with and without dates. His collection is now worth $19.50. How many of his Buffalo nickels do not have dates on them?" 30 Buffalo nickels

Additional Example

A museum sells 280 tickets in one day for a special exhibit. A regular ticket costs $20 and a student ticket costs $14.50. How many student tickets did the museum sell if it made $4918? 124 student tickets

Math Reasoning

Write Is there another way to solve Example 4 by elimination? Explain.

yes; Sample: Multiply the first equation by 5 and the second equation by 3 and then add the two new equations.

Example 4 Multiplying Two Equations

Solve the system $4x - 3y = 15$ by elimination.
$6x + 5y = -25$

SOLUTION

Multiply the first equation by 3 and the second equation by -2 to get opposite coefficients for the variable x.

$3(4x - 3y = 15) \rightarrow 12x - 9y = 45$
$-2(6x + 5y = -25) \rightarrow -12x - 10y = 50$

$12x - 9y = 45$
$\underline{-12x - 10y = 50}$
$ -19y = 95$ Add the equations and combine like terms.
$y = -5$ Divide both sides by -19.

Substitute -5 for y in one of the original equations and solve for x.

$6x + 5y = -25$
$6x + 5(-5) = -25$ Substitute -5 for y in the second equation.
$6x - 25 = -25$ Multiply.
$6x = 0$ Add 25 to both sides.
$x = 0$ Divide both sides by 6.

The solution is $(0, -5)$.

Example 5 Application: Coin Collecting

Carlos has 32 Buffalo nickels, some with dates and some without dates. Buffalo nickels without dates are worth $0.15, and dated Buffalo nickels are worth $0.75. If Carlos's collection of Buffalo nickels is worth $10.80, how many of the coins have dates on them?

SOLUTION Write and solve a system of linear equations.

$u + d = 32$
$0.15u + 0.75d = 10.80$

Multiply the first equation by -15 and the second equation by 100 to get opposite coefficients for the variable x.

$-15(u + d = 32) \rightarrow -15u + (-15d) = -480$
$100(0.15u + 0.75d = 10.80) \rightarrow 15u + 75d = 1080$

$-15u + (-15d) = -480$ Distributive Property
$\underline{15u + 75d = 1080}$ Distributive Property
$60d = 600$ Add the equations and combine like terms.
$d = 10$ Divide both sides by 60.

Carlos has 10 Buffalo nickels with dates.

414   Saxon Algebra 1

ALTERNATE METHOD FOR EXAMPLE 4

Multiply the first equation by 5 and the second equation by 3 and add the two equations to eliminate the variable y.

$5(4x - 3y = 15)$
$3(6x + 5y = -25)$
$\overline{20x - 15y = 75}$
$\underline{18x + 15y = -75}$
$38x = 0$
$x = 0$

Substitute 0 for x in one of the original equations and solve for y.

$4(0) - 3y = 15$
$\dfrac{-3y}{-3} = \dfrac{15}{-3}$
$y = -5$

The solution is $(0, -5)$.

Lesson Practice

a. Solve the system by elimination and check the answer.
(Ex 1)
$$7x - 4y = -3$$
$$-3x + 4y = -1 \quad (-1, -1); \text{ See student work.}$$

Hint
When solving exercises a–d, look for the easiest way to solve the system.

Solve each system by elimination.

b. (Ex 2) $11x + 6y = 21$
$11x + 4y = 25 \quad (3, -2)$

c. (Ex 3) $-2x + 5y = 6$
$6x - 2y = 34 \quad (7, 4)$

d. (Ex 4) $-8x - 3y = 26$
$-5x - 2y = 16 \quad (-4, 2)$

e. (Ex 5) **Box Office Sales** A movie theater sells 540 tickets to a matinee showing of a new animated feature. A child matinee ticket costs $5.50 and an adult matinee ticket costs $6.00. If the movie theater made $3060 for that showing, how many adult tickets were sold? **180 adult tickets**

Practice Distributed and Integrated

Simplify.

1. (61) $\sqrt{256}$ **16**

2. (61) $\sqrt{108}$ $6\sqrt{3}$

3. (61) $\sqrt{294}$ $7\sqrt{6}$

4. (40) $\left(\dfrac{r^{-3}t^{\frac{1}{2}}e}{rg^4 t^{\frac{3}{2}}} \right)^2$ $\dfrac{e^2}{g^8 r^8 t^2}$

5. (39) **Sports** A sports court has area $\dfrac{t^3 n^{-2} s}{f^7 t b^5} \left(\dfrac{t^{-2}}{ns^3} - \dfrac{f^6 t^{-1}}{b} \right)$. Simplify. $\dfrac{1}{b^5 f^7 n^3 s^2} - \dfrac{st}{b^6 f n^2}$

6. (48) Find the range for these 6 house sizes in a neighborhood (in square feet):
1450, 1500, 2800, 1630, 1500, 1710   **1350**

7. (56) Tell whether the set of ordered pairs (5, 12), (3, 7.2), and (7, 16.8) represents a direct variation.   **yes**

Find the LCM.

8. (57) $2t^3 sv^5$, $6v^3 t^4$, and $10v^8 s^4$ $30s^4 t^4 v^8$

9. (57) $14dv^3$, $7s^2 v$, and $28s^7 v^5$ $28ds^7 v^5$

10. (60) **Multiple Choice** Which of the following polynomials is equal to $(x + 5)(x - 5)$?   **A**
A $x^2 - 25$ **B** $x^2 + 25$ **C** $x^2 - 5x + 25$ **D** $x^2 - 10x + 25$

11. (63) **Landscaping** Nasser wants to plant a 4-foot-high Yoshino Cherry tree near a 7-foot-high Snowdrift Crabapple tree. If the cherry tree grows at a rate of 16 inches a year and the crabapple tree grows at a rate of 13 inches per year, when will the two trees be the same height?   **in 12 years**

Lesson 63   415

Problem 12

Remind students to use the variable that is easiest to isolate when solving by substitution. Isolating variables with a coefficient other than 1 may require working with fractions to solve the system.

Problem 15

Guide students by asking them the following questions.

"What is the formula for the perimeter of a rectangle?"
$P = 2l + 2w$

"What property could you use to rewrite the expression for the sum of lengths of the rectangle?"
Distributive Property

"What equation could you write to find the perimeter of the rectangle?" $P = 2(3x - 6) + 2 \cdot 2x$

Problem 24

Remind students of the special-product patterns of binomials.

"What is similar about the product of $(a + b)^2$ and $(a - b)^2$?" Sample: Both a and b are positive when squared.

Solve each system of linear equations using the method indicated.

12. Solve by substitution: $6x - 2y = 12$. (2, 0)
$y = -5x + 10$

*13. Solve by elimination: $6x + 4y = 22$. (3, 1)
$-6x + 2y = -16$

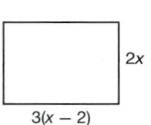*14. **Verify** Solve the system of linear equations by graphing: $\begin{array}{l} -x + y = 4 \\ 2x + y = 1 \end{array}$ Check your answer with a graphing calculator. (−1, 3)

14.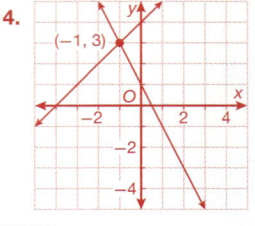

15. (**City Planning**) The city manager wants to build a rectangular walking track around the town's park. Below is a sketch of the new park. Write a polynomial expression for the perimeter of the rectangle. Simplify the polynomial. $10x - 12$

*16. **Multiple Choice** Which ordered pair is a solution of the system of equations? C
$9x - 3y = 20$
$3x + 6y = 2$

A $\left(-\frac{2}{3}, 2\right)$ B $\left(2, \frac{2}{3}\right)$ C $\left(2, -\frac{2}{3}\right)$ D $\left(-2, \frac{2}{3}\right)$

*17. **Verify** After solving a system of linear equations by elimination, how could you algebraically check your solution?

17. Sample: Substitute the values of the variables back into the original equations to ensure that they make both of the original equations true.

18. **Multi-Step** A group of 30 white-tailed deer all had 2 antler points at 1.5 years. At 4.5 years, their points were counted again.

Number of Points at 4.5 years	2	3	4	5	6	7	8	9
Number of Deer	1	0	4	3	7	4	10	1

a. Make a box-and-whisker plot for the data set at 4.5 years.

b. Can you predict how many points a deer would have at 4.5 years old if you know that it had 2 points at 1.5 years? no; Sample: There is a wide range on this graph.

*19. **Geometry** Main Market Square in Krakow, Poland has an area of 40,000 m². Find the length of one side of the square. 200 m

18a. Deer Antler Points at 4.5 Years

20. (**Football**) A football field's dimensions can be represented by a width of $3x + 15$ feet and a length of $x + 10$ feet. Write a polynomial expression for the area of the field.
$A = 3x^2 + 45x + 150$ square feet

Find the missing number.

21. original price: $1527
new price: _____
38% decrease $946.74

22. original price: $25,720
new price: _____
1.5% increase $26,105.80

23. original price: $10.25
new price: _____
215% increase $32.29

24. **Write** Write the two patterns for the square of a binomial. $\begin{bmatrix} (a+b)^2 = a^2 + 2ab + b^2 \\ (a-b)^2 = a^2 - 2ab + b^2 \end{bmatrix}$

416 Saxon Algebra 1

INCLUSION

Materials: algebra tiles

Have students use algebra tiles to model $5x + 2y = 9$ and $-5x + 6y = 7$.

Have them add the tiles vertically and remove the zero pairs. This leaves $8y = 16$. Have them solve for y. Then have them solve for x using substitution. (1, 2)

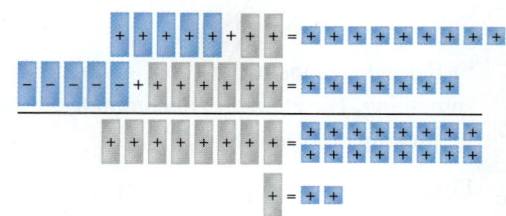

25. City Planning A city is planning to build a new park in a shape of a square in the business district. It has a side length of $2x + 6$ feet. Find the area of this park.
$4x^2 + 24x + 36$ square feet

*26. Multiple Choice Which of the following expressions is the simplest form of $\sqrt{76g^6}$? **A**

A $2g^3\sqrt{19}$ B $2g^4\sqrt{19}$ C $6g^3\sqrt{2}$ D $6g^4\sqrt{2}$

*27. Error Analysis Two students used the stem-and-leaf plot to find the mode height of the basketball players at their school. Which student is correct? Explain the error.

27. Student A; Sample: Student B found the stem with the most data points, 17 or 170.

Heights of Players on Team

Stem	Leaves
16	5, 7
17	1, 5, 6, 8, 8, 9
18	4, 5, 5, 5
19	2, 7
20	1

Key: 16 | 5 means 165 cm

Student A	Student B
The mode is 185 cm.	The mode is 170 cm.

*28. Write Explain how to solve the system of linear equations.

$3x - 2y = 10$
$-\dfrac{9}{2}x + 3y = -15$

28. Sample: The second equation is the first equation multiplied by $-\dfrac{3}{2}$, so the equations would be the same line on a graph. There are an infinite number of solutions.

29. What must be true about the coefficient of a linear function if that function experiences a vertical stretch of the parent function?   The absolute value of that coefficient would be greater than 1.

*30. Probability The histogram displays the number of hours students in Helene's homeroom average at their part-time jobs. What is the probability that a student randomly selected from the homeroom works 5–10 hours per week?   45%

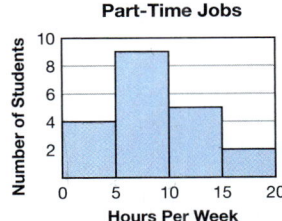

Part-Time Jobs

Problem 25
Extend the Problem

"Suppose a playground is to go in a corner of the park. If the playground is in the shape of a square and has a length of $x - 20$ feet, what is the area of the playground?"
$A = x^2 - 40x + 400$

"What is the difference between the area of the park and the area of the playground?"
$3x^2 + 64x - 364$

Lesson 63   417

CHALLENGE

Have students use elimination to solve for x, y, and z in the following system of equations.

$-x + 2y + 3z = 5$
$3y + 2z + 1 = x$
$z - x = 1$

$x = 3, y = -2, z = 4$

LOOKING FORWARD

Solving systems of linear equations by elimination prepares students for

- **Lesson 67** Solving and Classifying Special Systems of Linear Equations
- **Lesson 97** Graphing Linear Inequalities
- **Lesson 109** Graphing Systems of Linear Inequalities

Lesson 63   417

LESSON 64

1 Warm Up

Problem 4
Remind students that direct variation is modeled by $y = kx$, where k is the constant of variation and $k \neq 0$.

2 New Concepts

In this lesson, students learn about **inverse variation**. Explain that when y varies inversely with x, as one value increases, the other value will decrease to keep the product of xy constant.

Exploration

In the Exploration, students model inverse variation by drawing rectangles with the same area, but with different widths and lengths.

LESSON RESOURCES

Student Edition Practice
   Workbook 64
Reteaching Master 64
Adaptations Master 64
Challenge and Enrichment
   Master C64, E64
Technology Lab Master 64

LESSON 64

Identifying, Writing, and Graphing Inverse Variation

Warm Up

1. **Vocabulary** A(n) _____ "undoes" another operation.   **inverse**
   (19) operation

Suppose y varies directly as x. Find the constant of variation.

2. $y = 7x$ **7**
   (56)

3. $-4y = 12x$ **−3**
   (56)

Write an equation of the direct variation that includes the given point.

4. (3, 9)   Sample: $y = 3x$
   (56)

5. (−8, 4)   Sample: $y = -0.5x$
   (56)

New Concepts

Recall that direct variation occurs between two variables if $y = kx$ and $k \neq 0$.

Another type of variation, called inverse variation, may occur between two variables. **Inverse variation** is a relationship between two variables whose product is a constant. The equation $xy = k$ or $y = \frac{k}{x}$, where k is a nonzero constant, defines an inverse variation between x and y. The variable y is said to vary inversely with x.

Math Language
The letter k represents the **constant of variation.**

Exploration Modeling Inverse Variation

One example of inverse variation is the relationship between the length and width of a rectangle with a constant area.

a. Draw a rectangle that has a width of 1 unit and a length of 16 units on grid paper.

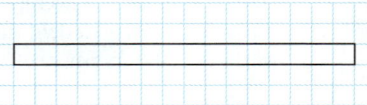

Continue to draw different rectangles with an area of 16 square units, changing the length and width for each.

b. Copy and complete the table after drawing each rectangle.

Width (x)	Length (y)	Area (xy)
1	16	16
2	8	16
4	4	16
8	2	16
16	1	16

c. Sample: As the width increases, the length decreases, so the product always equals 16.

c. What happens to the length of each rectangle as the width increases?

d. What will the product xy always equal?   **16**

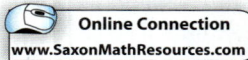
Online Connection
www.SaxonMathResources.com

e. Write an equation solved for y showing this relationship. $y = \frac{16}{x}$

MATH BACKGROUND

At this level, students are becoming familiar with various types of functions in order to represent relationships among different quantities. Previously they learned about direct variation, which represents a linear function with a slope, k. Inverse variations are an early introduction to nonlinear functions and are most often the first functions students graph that do not cross the x- or y-axis; nor do they pass through the origin. Since the constant of proportionality is the product of x and y ($xy = k$), when one value increases, the other decreases. Since $k \neq 0$, the curve of the graphed line approaches but does not cross either axis. Based on the Identity Property of Multiplication, every inverse variation will pass through the points $(1, y)$ and $(x, 1)$. This gives all inverse variation graphs the same basic shape.

In a direct variation, y is equal to the product of the constant of variation k and x; that is $y = kx$. However, in an inverse variation, y is equal to the quotient of the constant of variation k and x; in other words, $y = \frac{k}{x}$.

Example 1 Identifying an Inverse Variation

Tell whether each relationship is an inverse variation. Explain.

a. $\frac{y}{6} = x$

SOLUTION

Solve the equation for y.

$\frac{y}{6} \cdot 6 = x \cdot 6$

$y = 6x$ This is a direct variation.

b. $xy = 5$

SOLUTION

Solve the equation for y.

$\frac{xy}{x} = \frac{5}{x}$

$y = \frac{5}{x}$ This is an inverse variation.

For every ordered pair in an inverse variation, $xy = k$. This relationship can be used to find missing values in the relationship.

Product Rule for Inverse Variation
If (x_1, y_1) and (x_2, y_2) are solutions of an inverse variation, then $x_1y_1 = x_2y_2$.

Example 2 Using the Product Rule

If y varies inversely as x and $y = 3$ when $x = 12$, find x when $y = 9$.

SOLUTION

Use the product rule for inverse variation.

$x_1y_1 = x_2y_2$

$(12)(3) = x_2(9)$ Substitute the value 12 for x_1, 3 for y_1, and 9 for y_2.

$36 = 9x_2$ Multiply.

$4 = x_2$ Divide both sides by 9.

When $y = 9$, $x = 4$.

Math Reasoning

Formulate Find the k-value and write an equation that could be used to find x.

$y = \frac{36}{x}$

Lesson 64   419

Extend the Exploration

Draw different rectangles with an area of 24 square units. Copy and complete the table.

Length (x)	Width (y)	Area (xy)
1	24	24
2	12	24
3	8	24
4	6	24
6	4	24
8	3	24
12	2	24
24	1	24

Example 1

Remind students that they learned about direct variation in Lesson 56.

Additional Example 1

Tell whether each relationship is an inverse variation. Explain.

$x = \frac{36}{y}$ $\frac{y}{12} = x$

$x = \frac{36}{y}$ is an inverse variation, because $xy = 36$; $\frac{y}{12} = x$ is a direct variation because $y = 12x$.

Example 2

Discuss why the products of x_1y_1 and x_2y_2 are equal to each other.

Additional Example 2

If y varies inversely as x and $y = 5$ when $x = 12$, find x when $y = 3$. $x = 20$

🔶 MANIPULATIVE USE

Materials: Coordinate Grid Teacher Tool

Create a table of values for each equation in Example 1 and graph.

$\frac{y}{6} = x$

x	0	$\frac{1}{2}$	1	$1\frac{1}{2}$
y	0	3	6	9

$xy = 5$

x	$\frac{1}{2}$	1	$\frac{5}{2}$	5
y	10	5	2	1

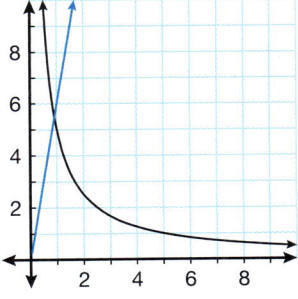

Lesson 64   419

Example 3

Point out that you only need to know one point on the graph of an inverse variation to determine the equation.

Additional Example 3

Write an inverse variation relating x and y when $x = 2$ and $y = 6$. Then graph the relationship. $y = \frac{12}{x}$

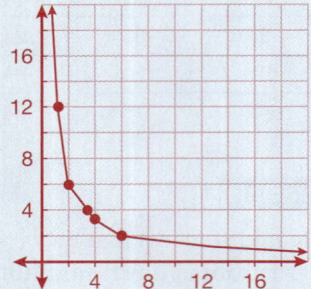

Error Alert When given the two values for an inverse variation, students may forget how to find the constant. Suggest that they remember that the words direct and divide each have six letters, and that division is used to find the constant in direct variation. The words inverse and product each have seven letters, and multiplication is used to find the constant in inverse variation.

Example 4

Remind students that with inverse variation, if $x_2 > x_1$ and $x_1 y_1 = x_2 y_2$, then $y_2 < y_1$.

Extend the Example

"Suppose the truck driver uses the same route on the way back from her delivery. The trip takes $17\frac{7}{8}$ hours because she drives at a slower rate. What is her rate of travel on the return trip?" 40 mi/h

Additional Example 4

If Maria is riding her bike at a rate of 12 miles per hour, it will take her $1\frac{3}{4}$ hours to reach her destination. How long will it take if she travels at a rate of 18 miles per hour? $1\frac{1}{6}$ hours

---

Math Reasoning

Write Does the inverse variation equation represent a function? Explain.

yes; Sample: For each value of x, there is only one value for y.

Math Reasoning

Verify Explain why k can be found by multiplying the values of x and y.

Sample: Solving the equation for an inverse variation, $y = \frac{k}{x}$, for k results in $k = xy$.

Math Reasoning

Analyze Would every value in the domain and range for the function this problem represents be a reasonable solution? Explain.

no; Sample: The truck driver should not drive over the speed limit or way under the speed limit for legal and safety reasons.

In a direct variation, if there is at least one known value for an x- and y-pair, the constant of variation, k, can be determined. The same holds true for an inverse variation; if at least one known value for an x- and y-pair exists, the constant of variation can be determined.

Example 3 Graphing an Inverse Variation

Write an inverse variation relating x and y when $y = 8$ and $x = 3$. Then graph the relationship.

SOLUTION

Find k.

$k = xy$
$k = 3(8)$ Substitute in the values for x and y.
$= 24$ Multiply.
$y = \frac{24}{x}$ Substitute 24 for k in the inverse variation equation.

The inverse variation relating x and y is $y = \frac{24}{x}$.

Use the equation to make a table of values.

x	−6	−4	−2	0	2	4	6
y	−4	−6	−12	Undefined	12	6	4

Plot the points. Then connect them with a smooth curve.

Check Use a graphing calculator to graph the equation $y = \frac{24}{x}$ and to verify that your graph is correct.

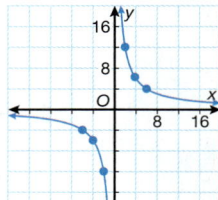

Example 4 Application: Truck Transportation

A truck driver is delivering goods from one state to another. Her speed is inversely related to her travel time. If she is traveling at 55 miles per hour, it will take her 13 hours to reach her destination. How long will it take her if she travels at 65 miles per hour?

SOLUTION Use the product rule for inverse variation to solve.

$x_1 y_1 = x_2 y_2$
$55 \cdot 13 = 65 \cdot y_2$ Substitute 55 for x_1, 13 for y_1, and 65 for x_2.
$715 = 65 y_2$ Multiply.
$11 = y_2$ Divide both sides by 65.

It will take the truck driver 11 hours if she travels at 65 miles per hour.

420   Saxon Algebra 1

Lesson Practice

Tell whether each relationship is an inverse variation. Explain.
(Ex 1)
a. $4y = x$
b. $3xy = 9$

(Ex 2) c. If y varies inversely as x and $y = 3.5$ when $x = 20$, find x when $y = 10$. $x = 7$

(Ex 3) d. Write an inverse variation relating x and y when $x = 8$ and $y = \frac{1}{2}$. Then graph the relationship. $y = \frac{4}{x}$

(Ex 4) e. Sierra found an inverse relationship between her hourly pay rate and the number of hours she must work to earn a set amount. If she works 7 hours for $8 an hour, how long will she work at $10 an hour to earn the same amount? 5.6 hours

a. This is not an inverse variation; Sample: The equation solved for y is $y = \frac{x}{4}$. This equation does not match the inverse variation equation $y = \frac{k}{x}$.

b. This is an inverse variation; Sample: The equation solved for y is $y = \frac{3}{x}$. This equation matches the inverse variation equation $y = \frac{k}{x}$.

Practice Distributed and Integrated

Find the LCM.

1. $8mn^4$ and $12m^5n^2$ $24m^5n^4$
(57)

2. $\frac{1}{2}wx^3$ and $\frac{1}{4}w^2x^6$ $\frac{1}{2}w^2x^6$
(57)

d.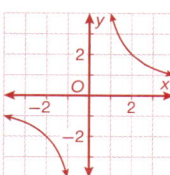

Tell whether each equation shows inverse variation. Write "yes" or "no".

*3. $y = \frac{x}{11}$ no
(64)

*4. $y = \frac{3}{x}$ yes
(64)

*5. **Estimate** If y varies inversely as x and $y = 24$ when $x = 99$, estimate the value of y when $x = 50$.   The value of y would be close to 50.
(64)

6. What is the minimum and maximum number of books read over the summer by 10 students: 10, 9, 8, 10, 1, 8, 11, 20, 9, 10?   1 and 20
(48)

7. (**Budgeting**) The cost of a cell phone plan includes a monthly fee plus a charge per minute. The charge for 200 minutes is $50. The charge for 350 minutes is $57.50. How much is the monthly fee and how much is the charge per minute? $40; $0.05
(52)

Find the product.

8. $(b + 2)^2$ $b^2 + 4b + 4$
(60)

9. $(x - 8)(x + 2)$ Use the FOIL method. $x^2 - 6x - 16$
(58)

*10. **Multi-Step** Darius drew a square on grid paper that covers 121 cm².
(61)
 a. Write an expression to find the side length. $\sqrt{a}$
 b. Substitute known values into the equation. $\sqrt{121 \text{ cm}^2}$
 c. Find the side length.   11 cm
 d. In which unit is the side length measured?   cm

Lesson 64   421

 ENGLISH LEARNERS

For this lesson, explain this meaning of the word **inverse**. Say:

"**Inverse means opposite.**"

Connect this meaning of inverse to the model for inverse variation by first discussing the model for direct variation, $y = kx$. Point out to students that they must multiply the constant k by the value of x to find the value of y. Now show the model for inverse variation, $y = \frac{k}{x}$. Point out that students must multiply k by the value $\frac{1}{x}$, the inverse of x, to find the value of y.

Discuss other uses of the word inverse, such as inverse operations. Inverse operations "undo" each other in equations. In direct variation, divide to find the constant, but in inverse variation, multiply to find the constant; these are inverse operations.

Lesson Practice

Problem a

Error Alert Students may identify the equation as an inverse variation because $y = \frac{x}{4}$ reminds them of $y = \frac{k}{x}$. Point out that the equation can be written as $y = \frac{1}{4} \cdot x$.

Problem e

Scaffolding Have students assign values to x_1, y_1, x_2, and y_2. Then have them substitute those values into the product rule for inverse variation.

✓ Check for Understanding

The questions below help assess the concepts taught in this lesson.

"How do the graphs of an inverse variation and a direct variation differ?" Sample: The graph of an inverse variation is two curves. The graph of a direct variation is a line of the form $y = mx$.

"What is the difference between a direct variation and an inverse variation?" Sample: In direct variation, the constant will be the quotient of x and y. In inverse variation, the constant will be the product of x and y.

3 Practice

Math Conversations

Discussion to strengthen understanding

Problem 2

Error Alert

Students may attempt to list the prime factors of the coefficients. They may mistakenly decide that the prime factorization of $\frac{1}{4}$ is $\left(\frac{1}{2}\right)\left(\frac{1}{2}\right)$. Students should list the multiples of the fractions instead and choose the LCM, one half.

Lesson 64   421

Problem 14
Error Alert

Students may forget to include the denominator when adding the side lengths of the sail, because each rational expression has the same common denominator and students are only working with adding the numerators. Remind them that when adding fractions with a common denominator, they must use that denominator in the sum.

Problem 15

Guide students by asking them the following questions.

"How many marketing associates are represented in the stem-and-leaf plot?" 23

"Which value would be the middle value of 23 data points?" the twelfth value

"How many values will fall above and below this middle value?" 11

"How would you use this information to find the median value?" Sample: Start at either the least value in the set and count up to find the twelfth data point, or start at the greatest value and count back to find the twelfth data point.

Problem 19

Suggest that students arrange the data values in numeric order before finding the maximum, minimum, median, and upper and lower quartiles of the set. Then they should sketch the box-and-whisker plot.

---

*11. **Multi-Step** Joseph lives 5 miles from the school and Maya lives 2 miles from the school. If Joseph walks from his house in an opposite direction from the school at a speed of 4 miles per hour, and Maya walks from her house in an opposite direction from the school at a speed of 6 miles per hour, after how long will they be the same distance from the school? What is that distance?   1.5 hours; 11 miles
(63)

*12. **Multiple Choice** If y varies inversely as x, and $y = 9$ when $x = 12$, what is y when $x = 4$?   C
(64)

   A 3   **B** 5.3   **C** 27   **D** 108

13. **Recycling** Use the table to compare the mean value of the amount of waste generated in the United States to the mean value of the amount of materials recovered for recycling from 1960 to 2005. Write a statement based on this comparison.
(48)

13. Sample: The mean value for waste generated is 192.125 million tons, and the mean value of materials recovered is 45.25. On average, the United States generates about 150 million tons of waste a year after recycling.

**Generation and Materials Recovery of Municipal Solid Waste, 1960–2005
(in millions of tons)**

Activity	1960	1970	1980	1990	2000	2003	2004	2005
Generation	88.1	121.1	151.6	205.2	237.6	240.4	247.3	245.7
Materials Recovery	5.6	8.0	14.5	33.2	69.1	74.9	77.7	79.0

14. **Multi-Step** A model sailboat calls for trim around the largest sail. The sail is triangular with side lengths $\frac{8}{2a^2 + 3a}$ centimeters, $\frac{5a + 1}{2a^2 + 3a}$ centimeters, and $\frac{3a + 3}{2a^2 + 3a}$ centimeters. How much trim will be used? $\frac{4}{a}$ centimeters
(51)

Find each of the statistical measures below using the data in the plot.

Annual Base Salary at Marketing Associates

Stem	Leaves
2	1, 1, 2, 2, 3, 3, 3, 6, 8
3	0, 1, 2, 6, 6, 9
4	2, 5, 8
5	3, 5, 7
6	4, 8

Key: 3 | 1 means $31,000

19.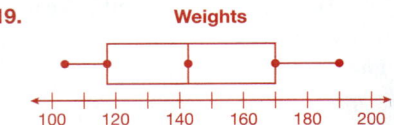

15. median $32,000
(62)

16. mode $23,000
(62)

17. range $47,000
(62)

18. relative frequency of $22,000   about 9%
(62)

19. **Health** To calculate a personal body mass index, students first had to report their weight in pounds. Make a box-and-whisker plot of the weights below and determine if there is an outlier.   no outliers
(54)

    140, 145, 170, 157, 130, 155, 190, 180, 175, 120, 116, 118, 112, 103

20. Identify Statement 2 as the converse, inverse, or contrapositive of Statement 1. Then indicate the truth value of each statement.
(Inv 5)

   Statement 1: If a figure is a rhombus, then it is not a rectangle.

   Statement 2: If a figure is a rectangle, then it is not a rhombus.   contrapositive; The original statement and the contrapositive are false.

422   *Saxon Algebra 1*

🔶 INCLUSION

Whole Number Pairs of Factors

Encourage students who have difficulty with written symbols or with abstract-concept processing to find all whole-number pairs of factors for the number 60.

    1 · 60   4 · 15
    2 · 30   5 · 12
    3 · 20   6 · 10

Have them use the values they found to answer the questions to the right.

"If you know the product of two numbers is 60, and one of the numbers is 4, what is the other number?" 15

"If one of the numbers is 15, what is the other number?" 4

"If one of the numbers is 12, what is the other number?" 5

"If one of the numbers is 5, what is the other number?" 12

*21. **Statistics** The standard deviation is the square root of the variance of a set of data. If the variance of a set of data is 24, what is the standard deviation in simplest form? $2\sqrt{6}$

22. Write $\sqrt{75}$ in simplest form. $5\sqrt{3}$

*23. **Error Analysis** Two students solved the following systems of equations. Which student is correct? Explain the error.

Student A	Student B
$2x + 11y = 13$	$2x + 11y = 13$
$2x + 9y = 11$	$2x + 6y = 8$
$20y = 24$	$5y = 5$
$y = 1.2$	$y = 1$
$(-0.1, 1.2)$	$(1, 1)$

23. Student B; Sample: Student A subtracted to eliminate the variable x, but then added the other terms in the equation.

24. **Geometry** The areas of two similar rectangles add up to 39 square units. Twice the area of Rectangle A plus one-third the area of Rectangle B equals 33 square units. What are the areas of Rectangles A and B? Rectangle A is 12 square units. Rectangle B is 27 square units.

25. Graph $9x - 1.5y + 12 = 0$ using slope-intercept form.

26. Solve the following system of linear equations: $-3x + 2y = -6$. $(-2, -6)$
$$-5x - 2y = 22$$

27. **Multi-Step** Use the system of linear equations to answer the problems below.
$$2x - y = 14$$
$$x + 4y = -2$$

a. Graph the system.

b. Determine the solution. $(6, -2)$

c. Check your answer by using substitution.

28. **Boyle's Law** In chemistry, Boyle's Law states that the volume of a sample of gas is inversely related to its pressure if the temperature remains constant. Jameka recorded the pressure of a sample of gas inside a 450-cubic millimeter container to be 95 kPa. If the pressure increased to 475 kPa, what would the new volume of the gas be? $90\ mm^3$

29. **Write** Describe a proportional situation that is represented by the equation $y = 6x$. Sample: The number of points varies directly with the number of touchdowns.

30. **Generalize** How would you describe the location of a graphed inverse variation based on the constant? Sample: When k is positive, the graph is in Quadrants I and III; when k is negative, the graph is in Quadrants II and IV.

27a.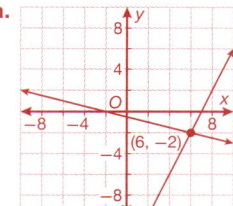

27c.
$2(6) - (-2) = 14$
$12 + 2 = 14$
$14 = 14$

$(6) + 4(-2) = -2$
$6 - 8 = -2$
$-2 = -2$

Lesson 64   423

Problem 25
Before graphing, ask, "How can you write the equation in slope-intercept form?" Sample: Solve the equation for y.

Problem 28
Extend the Problem
"If the volume of the container increased to 600 millimeters cubed, what would the pressure of the gas inside the container be?" 71.25 kPa

"What equation could Jameka write to model the inverse variation between the volume of her sample of gas and its pressure?" $y = \frac{42{,}750}{x}$

Problem 30
Guide students by reminding them that when multiplying numbers with the same sign, they will get a positive product; and when multiplying numbers with different signs, they will get a negative product. Ask, "In which quadrant does the point $(-2, -3)$ lie?" Quadrant III

"If these two values were inversely related, what would the constant of variation be?" 6

CHALLENGE

A number z varies directly with y and indirectly with x. When $y = 14$ and $x = 7$, $z = 8$. Write the equation that models this relationship. Then find z when $y = 32$ and $x = 8$. $z = \frac{4y}{x}$; $z = 16$

LOOKING FORWARD

Identifying, writing, and graphing inverse variations prepares students for

• **Lesson 65** Writing Equations of Parallel and Perpendicular Lines

• **Investigation 7** Comparing Direct and Inverse Variation

• **Investigation 8** Identifying and Writing Joint Variation

LESSON 65

1 Warm Up

Problem 2
Remind students that the equation $y = mx + b$ represents slope-intercept form, where m is the slope and b is the y-intercept.

2 New Concepts

In this lesson, students will use their knowledge of point-slope form to help them write equations of parallel and perpendicular lines.

Discuss the definitions of **parallel** and **perpendicular lines.** Explain that although any two lines with different slopes will eventually intersect, the slopes of perpendicular lines have a special relationship.

Example 1

Emphasize that lines are parallel if they have the same slope and different y-intercepts.

Additional Example 1
Determine if the equations represent parallel lines.
$2x - 5y = 10$ and $y = -\frac{2}{5}x + 10$
The slopes are not the same, so the lines are not parallel.

LESSON RESOURCES

Student Edition Practice
  Workbook 65
Reteaching Master 65
Adaptations Master 65
Challenge and Enrichment
  Master C65

LESSON 65

Writing Equations of Parallel and Perpendicular Lines

Warm Up

1. **Vocabulary** The _____ form for the equation of a line is $y - y_1 = m(x - x_1)$, where m is the slope and (x_1, y_1) is a point on the line.   **point-slope**

Find the slope and y-intercept.

2. $2x + y = -5$ $-2, -5$
3. $-9x + 3y = 12$ $3, 4$
4. Write an equation in slope-intercept form for a line that passes through the point $(0, -5)$ and has a slope of $\frac{2}{3}$. $y = \frac{2}{3}x - 5$

New Concepts **Parallel lines** are lines that are in the same plane but do not intersect.

Slopes of Parallel Lines
Two nonvertical lines are parallel if they have the same slope and are not the same line. Any two vertical lines are parallel. **Example** The equations $y = 2x + 7$ and $y = 2x - 1$ have the same slope, 2, and different y-intercepts. The graphs of the two lines are parallel.

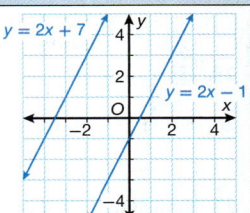

Example 1 **Determining if Lines are Parallel**

Determine if the equations represent parallel lines.

$y = -\frac{4}{3}x + 5$ and $4x + 3y = 6$

Math Reasoning

Analyze Will one ordered pair ever satisfy the equations of a pair of parallel lines? Explain.

no; Parallel lines never intersect, so they have no points in common.

SOLUTION

Write both equations in the slope-intercept form $y = mx + b$.

$y = -\frac{4}{3}x + 5$ The first equation is already in slope-intercept form.

Write the second equation in slope-intercept form by solving for y.

$4x + 3y = 6$
$\underline{-4x \qquad\quad = -4x}$
$3y = -4x + 6$
$\frac{3y}{3} = -\frac{4x}{3} + \frac{6}{3}$
$y = -\frac{4}{3}x + 2$

Since both lines have the same slope but have different y-intercepts, the two lines are parallel.

Online Connection
www.SaxonMathResources.com

424   Saxon Algebra 1

MATH BACKGROUND

The equation of a line that has slope m and contains the point (x_1, y_1) can be written using the point-slope form,
$y - y_1 = m(x - x_1)$.

Parallel lines never intersect, so they must have the same slope in order that they "rise" and "run" at the same rate. Perpendicular lines meet at right angles. So, one of the lines must rise and one must fall at reciprocal rate of changes. Therefore, the slopes of perpendicular lines are negative reciprocals of each other. The product of the slopes of two perpendicular lines is -1.

Knowing the slope of a line and a given point for the new line to pass through, it is always possible to write an equation for a line parallel or perpendicular to another line.

Example 2 Writing Equations of Parallel Lines

Write an equation in slope-intercept form for the line that passes through $(-1, 1)$ and is parallel to a line with equation $y = 2x - 1$.

SOLUTION

Determine the slope of the parallel line. Then substitute the slope and the point into the point-slope formula.

The slope of the line $y = 2x - 1$ is 2. Any line parallel to the given line has a slope of 2.

Substitute $m = 2$ and the point $(-1, 1)$ into the point-slope formula. Write the equation in slope-intercept form.

$y - y_1 = m(x - x_1)$
$y - 1 = 2(x + 1)$ Substitute the slope and point into the equation.
$y - 1 = 2x + 2$ Distributive Property
$y = 2x + 3$ Add 1 to both sides.

The equation of the line is $y = 2x + 3$.

Perpendicular lines are two lines that intersect at right angles.

> **Math Language**
>
> The **reciprocal** of a number n is $\frac{1}{n}$. The product of a number and its reciprocal is 1.

Slopes of Perpendicular Lines

Any two lines are perpendicular if their slopes are negative reciprocals of each other. A vertical and horizontal line are also perpendicular.

Example The slope of $y = 3x - 7$ is 3. The slope of $y = -\frac{1}{3}x + 3$ is $-\frac{1}{3}$. Since the slopes are negative reciprocals, the lines are perpendicular.

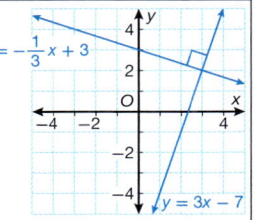

Example 3 Determining if Lines are Perpendicular

Determine if the lines passing through the given points are perpendicular.

line 1: $(-5, 4)$ and $(-3, 0)$ line 2: $(-2, -2)$ and $(-4, -3)$

SOLUTION

Find the slope of each line.

$m_1 = \dfrac{y_2 - y_1}{x_2 - x_1}$ $m_2 = \dfrac{y_2 - y_1}{x_2 - x_1}$

$= \dfrac{0 - 4}{-3 - (-5)}$ $= \dfrac{-3 - (-2)}{-4 - (-2)}$

$= \dfrac{-4}{2}$ $= \dfrac{-1}{-2}$

$= -2$ $= \dfrac{1}{2}$

Since -2 is the negative reciprocal of $\frac{1}{2}$, the lines are perpendicular.

 ALTERNATE METHOD FOR EXAMPLE 2

Use the slope-intercept form of the equation $y = 2x - 1$ to graph the line.

Since the line does not pass through the point $(-1, 1)$, a line parallel to it can be drawn through this point. Use the same slope ($m = 2$) to graph a line through this point. Note where the line crosses the y-axis and use this value to write the equation of the parallel line. $y = 2x + 3$

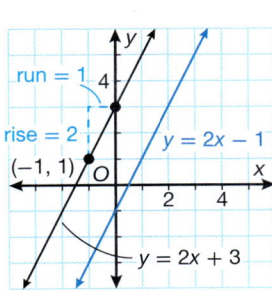

Example 4
Make sure students know how to find the negative reciprocal of the slope of the given line.

Additional Example 4
Write an equation in slope-intercept form for the line that passes through (1, 2) and is perpendicular to a line with equation $y = \frac{1}{6}x - 3$.
$y = -6x + 8$

Example 5
Extend the Example
"Suppose a point O is drawn at (1, 2) to create figure $LMNO$. Use the slopes of the line segments to determine that the shape is a parallelogram."
Sample: $LMNO$ is a parallelogram if $\overline{LO}$ is parallel to $\overline{MN}$ and $\overline{LM}$ is parallel to $\overline{ON}$. The slope of $\overline{LO}$ is $\frac{1}{4}$, and the slope of $\overline{MN}$ is $\frac{1}{4}$. The slope of $\overline{LM}$ is -4 and the slope of $\overline{ON}$ is -4. So, $\overline{LO}$ is parallel to $\overline{MN}$ and $\overline{LM}$ is parallel to $\overline{ON}$. Figure $LMNO$ is a parallelogram.

Additional Example 5
Use the slopes of the line segments to show that ABC is a right triangle.

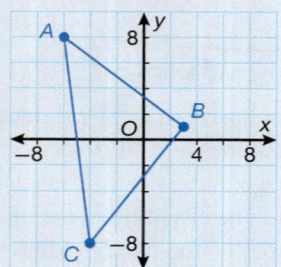

The slope of $\overline{AB}$ is $-\frac{7}{9}$ and the slope of $\overline{BC}$ is $\frac{9}{7}$. The slopes are negative reciprocals, so triangle ABC is a right triangle.

Caution
Pay attention to whether a problem is asking to write the equation for a parallel line or a perpendicular line.

Example 4 Writing Equations of Perpendicular Lines

Write an equation in slope-intercept form for the line that passes through $(-2, -3)$ and is perpendicular to a line with equation $y = -3x + 1$.

SOLUTION

The slope of $y = -3x + 1$ is -3. Any line perpendicular to the given line has a slope of $\frac{1}{3}$, which is a negative reciprocal of -3.

Substitute $m = \frac{1}{3}$ and the point $(-2, -3)$ into the point slope formula. Write the equation in slope-intercept form.

$$y - y_1 = m(x - x_1)$$

$y - (-3) = \frac{1}{3}(x - (-2))$ Substitute the slope and point into the equation.

$y + 3 = \frac{1}{3}x + \frac{2}{3}$ Simplify.

$y = \frac{1}{3}x - 2\frac{1}{3}$ Subtract 3 from both sides and simplify.

Example 5 Application: Coordinate Geometry

Use the slopes of the line segments to show that LMN is a right triangle.

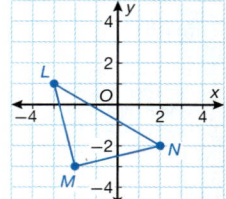

SOLUTION

LMN is a right triangle if $\overline{LM}$ is perpendicular to $\overline{MN}$. Find the slope of $\overline{LM}$ and $\overline{MN}$.

slope of $\overline{LM} = \frac{y_2 - y_1}{x_2 - x_1} = \frac{1 - (-3)}{-3 - (-2)} = \frac{4}{-1} = -4$

slope of $\overline{MN} = \frac{y_2 - y_1}{x_2 - x_1} = \frac{-3 - (-2)}{-2 - 2} = \frac{-1}{-4} = \frac{1}{4}$

The slopes of $\overline{LM}$ and $\overline{MN}$ are negative reciprocals, so the two sides are perpendicular. Therefore, LMN is a right triangle because it contains a right angle.

Lesson Practice

a. Determine if the equations represent parallel lines.
(Ex 1) no; The lines are perpendicular.
$y = \frac{2}{3}x + 5\frac{1}{3}$ and $\frac{3}{2}x + y = 1$

b. Write an equation in slope-intercept form for the line that passes
(Ex 2) through $(-3, 2)$ and is parallel to a line with equation $y = \frac{4}{7}x + \frac{5}{7}$.

b. $y = \frac{4}{7}x + 3\frac{5}{7}$

c. no; The lines are parallel.

c. Determine if the lines passing through the points are perpendicular.
(Ex 3) line 1: $(-2, 2)$ and $(2, -4)$ line 2: $(3, 6)$ and $(5, 3)$.

ENGLISH LEARNERS

For Example 4, explain the meaning of the word **reciprocal**. Say:

"In math, a reciprocal is an inverse, or opposite, relationship."

Explain that reciprocal can mean something that is mutual or shared. It can also mean something that is given in return.

Ask students why they think the word reciprocal is used in mathematics. Guide students by asking them if they notice anything that is mutual or shared between reciprocal numbers. Sample: 6 and $\frac{1}{6}$ share the number 6; $\frac{1}{6}$ is the inverse of 6.

d. $y = -\frac{7}{4}x + 1\frac{1}{4}$ (Ex 4)

d. Write an equation in slope-intercept form for the line that passes through $(-1, 3)$ and is perpendicular to a line with equation $y = \frac{4}{7}x + \frac{5}{7}$.

e. **Geometry** Use the slopes of the line segments to show that ABC is a right triangle.
(Ex 5)

Sample: The slope of $\overline{AB}$ is $-\frac{1}{2}$, the slope of $\overline{BC}$ is 2, and $(-\frac{1}{2})(2) = -1$. $\overline{AB} \perp \overline{BC}$. Therefore, ABC is a right triangle.

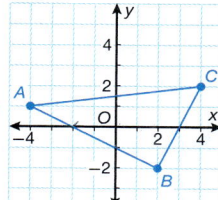

Practice Distributed and Integrated

Simplify.

1. $\sqrt{360}$ $6\sqrt{10}$
(61)

2. $\sqrt{252}$ $6\sqrt{7}$
(61)

3. $\sqrt{384}$ $8\sqrt{6}$
(61)

Find the product using the FOIL method.

4. $(x^2 + 5)^2$ $x^4 + 10x^2 + 25$
(58)

5. $(x - 2)(x - 9)$ $x^2 - 11x + 18$
(58)

6. Graph the inequality $c \geq -5$.
(50)

7. **Justify** Explain how you find the LCM of $2(x - 5)^3$ and $3(x - 5)^7$.
(57)

7. Sample: Treat the $(x - 5)$ like a single variable. Then, take each factor the greatest number of times it appears. LCM = $2 \cdot 3 \cdot (x - 5)^7 = 6(x - 5)^7$

8. **Multiple Choice** The key of a stem-and-leaf plot shows $2|9 = 2.9$ cm. What is the value of a data point with a leaf of 4 and a stem of 7? **B**
(62)
  A 4.7 cm   **B** 7.4 cm   **C** 47 cm   **D** 74 cm

*****9.** (**Sports**) The results in seconds for the men's 50-meter freestyle swimming finals at the NCAA Division II Championship in 2007 are listed below. Create a stem-and-leaf plot to organize the data.
(62)

20.43, 20.32, 20.36, 20.39, 20.67, 20.68, 20.68, 20.81, 20.62, 20.97, 21.07, 21.24, 21.25, 21.31, 21.45, 21.56

9. 2007 NCAA Division II Final Results Men's 50M Freestyle

Stem	Leaves
.203	2, 6, 9
204	3
206	2, 7, 8, 8
208	1
209	7
210	7
212	4, 5
213	1
214	5
215	6

Key: 201|7 = 20.17 seconds

10. **Multi-Step** The cost of parking at a concert is $22 for the first 2 hours and $4 for each additional hour. Write an equation that models the total cost y of parking a car in terms of the number of additional hours x. Using the linear equation, find the total cost of parking for 9 hours. $y = 4x + 22$; $50
(52)

11. **Error Analysis** Two students attempted to write an inverse variation equation relating x and y when $x = 5$ and $y = 10$. Which student is correct? Explain the error.
(64)

Student A	Student B
$y = \dfrac{50}{x}$	$y = 2x$

11. Student A; Sample: Student B wrote a direct variation equation.

Lesson 65   427

ALTERNATE METHOD FOR EXAMPLE 5

Use the graphed lines on the coordinate plane and the formula slope = $\frac{\text{rise}}{\text{run}}$ to find the slopes of $\overline{LM}$ and $\overline{MN}$.

Count the rise and the run for each line segment to find the rate of change. Line segment LM has a negative rise of 4 units and a run of 1 unit, making its slope -4. Line segment MN has a rise of 1 unit and a run of 4 units, making its slope $\frac{1}{4}$.

Since $-4 \cdot \frac{1}{4} = -1$, the slopes of the two line segments are negative reciprocals of each other. Therefore, line segment LM is perpendicular to line segment MN, and triangle LMN is a right triangle.

Lesson Practice

Problem d
Error Alert Students may only find the reciprocal or only the opposite of the slope of the given line. Have them check that the product of the slopes is equal to -1.

Problem e
Scaffolding Have students find the slopes of $\overline{AB}$ and $\overline{BC}$ by using the formula $m = \dfrac{y_2 - y_1}{x_2 - x_1}$ or by counting the rise and run of the graph of each segment.

Check for Understanding

The questions below help assess the concepts taught in this lesson.

"Write an equation for a line parallel to the graph of $-6x - 3y = 3$. How many equations are possible?"
Equations will vary; Sample: There are an infinite number of possible equations, with the exception of the line $y = -2x - 1$.

"How is it determined that the graph of a parallelogram is a rectangle?" Sample: Find out if the slopes of two pairs of adjacent legs of the parallelogram are negative reciprocals of each other. If so, the segments are perpendicular and the figure is a rectangle.

3 Practice

Math Conversations
Discussion to strengthen understanding

Problem 10
Error Alert
To find the cost of parking for 9 hours, students may multiply the total number of hours parked by 4. Remind them that the first 2 hours cost $22.

Lesson 65   427

Problem 16
Extend the Problem
"How much money will Ryan and Kathy have when they have saved the same amount of money?" $30

"After 6 weeks, Ryan begins to save $8 a week. Kathy deposits $20 more into her account and starts to save $6 a week. After how many more weeks will they have the same balance in their accounts?" 10 weeks

"What will be the total balance in their accounts?" $110

Problem 19
Remind students of the special-product pattern for the square of a binomial:
$(a - b)^2 = a^2 - 2ab + b^2$

Problem 20
Extend the Problem
"The school decides to add another $x + 4$ feet to the total length of the gym. Write a polynomial for the area of the court now, not including the tile border." $64x^2 - 320x + 400$

"If x is equal to 10 feet, what is the area of the entire gym, including the border?"
7056 square feet

---

*12. Measurement Giao wants to construct a picture frame made of wooden pieces that are 7 centimeters and 3 centimeters in length. He needs 20 pieces, and the total perimeter of the frame needs to be 108 centimeters. If Giao cuts eight 3-centimeter pieces first and is left with 0.8 meter of wood, will he have enough wood to cut the 7-centimeter pieces? Explain. no; Sample: He needs 84 centimeters of wood for the twelve 7-centimeter pieces, and he only has 80 centimeters of wood leftover.

Solve each system of linear equations by the method indicated.

13. Use graphing.
$2x - y = 3$
$3x + y = 2$ (1, −1)

14. Use elimination.
$5x + 7y = 41$
$3x + 7y = 47$
(−3, 8)

15. Use substitution.
$5x - 2y = 22$
$9x + y = 12$
(2, −6)

13.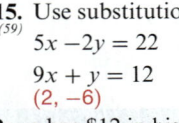

16. Banking Ryan and Kathy both have savings accounts. Ryan has $12 in his account and plans to add $3 each week to it. Kathy does not have any money in her account, but plans to add $5 each week. How many weeks will it take until Ryan and Kathy have the same amount of money? 6 weeks

*17. Multi-Step The results for the women's 3-meter diving finals at the NCAA Division II Championship in 2007 are listed below.

499.15, 429.15, 409.75, 405.90, 395.65, 382.15, 353.20, 351.75, 342.30, 333.75, 328.20, 325.75, 315.20, 302.85, 292.90, 277.90

a. **Write** Explain how to determine the intervals to create a histogram for the data. Identify the intervals. Sample: The range of the data is 221.25. To make it easier, I would create 5 intervals that are each 50 points apart.
b. Create a histogram for this data using the intervals from part **a.** See Additional Answers.
c. Is a histogram or a stem-and-leaf plot a better display for this data? Explain. Sample: A histogram is better. The data is so dispersed across a wide range that a stem-and-leaf plot would not be very useful.

18. Write the equation of the graphed line in slope-intercept form. $y = -2x + 6$

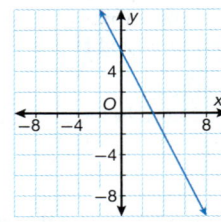

19. Investing Trey is making an investment of $(x - 11)$ dollars. The rate of interest on the investment is $(x - 11)$ percent. What is the interest gained after one year? (Hint: interest = principle × rate × time; $i = prt$) $(x - 11)(x - 11) = x^2 - 22x + 121$ dollars

20. Construction The school is constructing a new gym. They want a 12-foot-wide tile border around the outside edge of the square court, and the total side length is $7x$. Write a polynomial for the area of the court, not including the tile border. $(7x - 24)^2 = 49x^2 - 336x + 576$ square feet

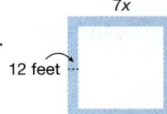

INCLUSION

For students who have difficulty with the abstract concepts involved in the lesson, choose and plot two points on the coordinate plane. Take another sheet of paper and place one of the corners so that the tip is on a third point of the coordinate grid. Make sure to choose a point so that each of the previously plotted points lies along a different edge of the paper coming off the corner. Plot the third point and draw two lines connecting the corner point to each of the first two points chosen. Write the equation of each line in slope-intercept form.

Ask:

"What kind of angle does the corner of a sheet of paper make?" a right angle

"What can you say about the edges of a sheet of paper?" They are perpendicular.

"What do you notice about the slopes of both equations you wrote?" They are negative reciprocals of each other.

"Are the lines perpendicular?" yes

21. Coordinate Geometry What kind of quadrilateral is the figure $WXYZ$? Justify your answer. *WXYZ is a parallelogram. The slopes of $\overline{WX}$ and $\overline{YZ}$ are both undefined, so $\overline{WX} \parallel \overline{YZ}$. The slopes of $\overline{WZ}$ and $\overline{XY}$ are the same, $\frac{3}{5}$, so $\overline{WZ} \parallel \overline{XY}$.*

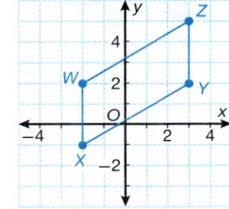

22. State whether the equation $5xy = 40$ shows inverse variation. Write "yes" or "no". **yes**

23. Write If line a is parallel to line b, could you find a line that makes lines a and b a reflection of each other? Explain.

24. Analyze How many parallel lines can be found for the line $y = 2x + 1$? *There are an infinite number of parallel lines for any given slope.*

25. Find the slope of a line that is parallel to the line $6x + 3y = 36$. *The slope of the parallel line is −2.*

26. Multi-Step Draw a coordinate grid, and number it from −5 to +5 along the x- and y-axis. Will a line passing through the points $(-4, 0)$ and $(4, 2)$ be parallel to $y = -\frac{1}{4}x - 3$?

 a. **Model** Graph the points $(-4, 0)$ and $(4, 2)$.

 b. Find the equation for the line that passes through both points. $y = \frac{1}{4}x + 1$

 c. **Justify** Is the line $y = -\frac{1}{4}x - 3$ parallel to the line you graphed? Explain.

23. yes; Sample: Choose two points along each line and find the midpoint between the corresponding points on each line. Use this point and the slope of lines a and b to create the line of reflection.

27. Error Analysis Two students solved the given system of equations. Which student is correct? Explain the error. *Student B; Sample: Student A tried to add the equations without aligning like terms first.*

26a.

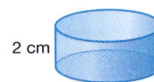

Student A	Student B
$3y = 2x + 8$	$3y = 2x + 8$
$8x = -2y + 24$	$8x = -2y + 24$
$11x = 32$	$14y = 56$
$x = 2\frac{10}{11}; \left(2\frac{10}{11}, 4\frac{20}{33}\right)$	$y = 4; (2, 4)$

28. Paralympics Suki is training in her wheelchair for the 100-meter race at the next Paralympics. In her initial acceleration phase, she averages a speed of 2.7 meters per second. At her maximum speed phase, she averages a speed of 6.6 meters per second. If she finishes a practice race in 18.1 seconds, how many meters long (to the nearest tenth of a meter) is her initial acceleration phase? **13.5 meters**

26c. no; Sample: The first line has a slope of $\frac{1}{4}$ and the second line has a slope of $-\frac{1}{4}$. They are not parallel.

29. Geometry The height h of a cylinder varies inversely with the area of the base B when the volume is constant. If the height of a cylinder is 6 centimeters when the area of the base is 12 square centimeters, what is the area of the base of the cylinder at right with the same volume? **36 cm²**

30. Multi-Step Tyson often rides his bike 8 miles to visit a friend. His speed varies inversely with the time it takes to cover that distance. Today he rode at 16 mph to get to his friend's house, and then he rode at a rate of 12 mph to get home. How much longer did it take him to get home than to get to his friend's house? **10 minutes**

Lesson 65   429

Problem 28
Guide students by asking the following questions.

"What equation can you write to model the total distance traveled in both the initial acceleration phase and the maximum speed phase?" $2.7x + 6.6y = 100$

"What equation can you write to model how long it takes Suki to travel the distance of the initial acceleration together with the distance of the maximum speed phase?" $x + y = 18.1$

"What is the name for these equations if there is one value for x and y that is a solution to both equations?" a system of equations

Problem 30
Have students find the constant of variation in the problem. 8

CHALLENGE

A rhombus is a quadrilateral with two pairs of parallel sides and perpendicular diagonals. Given that quadrilateral $QRST$ has vertices at $Q(1, 4)$, $R(2, 1)$, $S(-1, 0)$, and $T(-2, 3)$, show that $QRST$ is a rhombus.

Sample: The slopes of $\overline{QR}$ and $\overline{ST}$ are both −3, so they are parallel. The slopes of $\overline{RS}$ and $\overline{TQ}$ are both $\frac{1}{3}$, so they are parallel. The slope of $\overline{QS}$ is 2, and the slope of $\overline{RT}$ is $-\frac{1}{2}$. These are negative reciprocals of each other, so the diagonals are perpendicular. $QRST$ is a rhombus.

LOOKING FORWARD

Writing equations of parallel and perpendicular lines prepares students for

- **Lesson 67** Solving and Classifying Special Systems of Linear Equations
- **Lesson 109** Graphing Systems of Linear Inequalities

Lesson 65   429

LESSON 66

1 Warm Up

Problems 4 and 5
Remind students that ≥ and ≤ indicate that the circle in the graph should be shaded, but that < and > indicate that the circle should remain open.

2 New Concepts

In this lesson, students learn to solve inequalities by adding or subtracting.

Discuss with students the Addition Property of Inequality. Review the Subtraction Property of Inequality by reminding students that subtracting is the same as adding a negative.

Example 1

Tell students that when solving an inequality involving addition or subtraction, they will follow the same rules as when solving an equation.

Additional Example 1
Solve the inequality and graph the solution on a number line.
$x - 8 > -4$ $x > 4;$

LESSON RESOURCES

Student Edition Practice Workbook 66
Reteaching Master 66
Adaptations Master 66
Challenge and Enrichment Master C66
Technology Lab Master 66

LESSON 66

Solving Inequalities by Adding or Subtracting

Warm Up

1. **Vocabulary** A(n) _____ is a mathematical statement comparing quantities that are not equal.   **inequality**

Solve.

2. $x + 13 = 21$ **8**

3. $-26 + x = -9$ **17**

Graph.

4. $x < 2$

5. $x \geq -3$

New Concepts

Recall that you can add or subtract the same number from both sides of an equation and it remains a true statement. The same is true for inequalities. The Addition Property of Inequality states that when the same number is added to both sides of an inequality, the statement remains true.

Addition Property of Inequality
For any real numbers a, b, and c:
If $a < b$, then $a + c < b + c$.   If $a \leq b$, then $a + c \leq b + c$.
If $a > b$, then $a + c > b + c$.   If $a \geq b$, then $a + c \geq b + c$.

Example 1   Using the Addition Property of Inequality

Solve the inequality $x - 10 < -6$ and graph the solution on a number line.

SOLUTION

$x - 10 < -6$
$ +10 \phantom{<} +10$ Addition Property of Inequality
$ x < 4$ Simplify.

The solution includes all values less than, but not including, 4.

The solution to the inequality is $x < 4$.

Reading Math
An open circle on the graph of an inequality means that the value is not part of the solution.

Inequalities have an infinite number of solutions. This makes it impossible to check all the solutions. The endpoint and the direction of the inequality can be checked. For example, the solution in Example 1 can be checked using the steps on the following page.

Online Connection
www.SaxonMathResources.com

MATH BACKGROUND

Solving inequalities by adding or subtracting is similar to solving equations by adding or subtracting. Students may conceptualize solving equations as operations that keep a scale balanced. Help students conceptualize solving inequalities as operations that keep a scale proportionally out of balance.

Step 1: Check the endpoint.
The endpoint should be a solution of the related equation $x - 10 = -6$.

$x - 10 = -6$
$4 - 10 \stackrel{?}{=} -6$ Substitute 4 for x.
$-6 = -6$ ✓   Simplify.

Step 2: Check the inequality symbol.

Substitute a number less than 4 for x in the original inequality. The number chosen should be a solution of the inequality.

$x - 10 < -6$
$2 - 10 \stackrel{?}{<} -6$ Substitute a number less than 4 for x.
$-8 < -6$ ✓   Simplify.

Since the endpoint and the direction of the inequality are correct, the solution of $x - 10 < -6$ is $x < 4$.

Example 2 Checking Solutions

Solve the inequality $x - 3 \geq 5$. Then graph and check the solution.

SOLUTION

$x - 3 \geq 5$
$\underline{+3 \quad +3}$ Addition Property of Inequality
$x \geq 8$ Simplify.

Check The endpoint and direction of the inequality symbol should be checked to verify the solution.

Check the endpoint.

$x - 3 = 5$
$8 - 3 \stackrel{?}{=} 5$
$5 = 5$ ✓

Check the direction of the inequality. Choose a number greater than 8.

$x - 3 \geq 5$
$9 - 3 \stackrel{?}{\geq} 5$
$6 \geq 5$ ✓

Reading Math

A closed circle on the graph of an inequality means that the value is part of the solution.

Lesson 66   431

Example 2

Checking a solution set to an inequality is the best way for students to understand the meaning of inequalities.

Additional Example 2

Solve the inequality $x - 2 \leq 3$. Then graph and check the solution. $x \leq 5$;

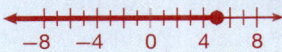

TEACHER TIP

If students find that the endpoint does not check, encourage them to re-solve the problem as an equation to find the correct endpoint.

ENGLISH LEARNERS

English learners may not know what **endpoint** refers to. Explain that the endpoint is the place on the graph of an inequality where numbers stop being part of the solution. Some students might think it is more natural to refer to this point as the "start point." Show students that either term is correct, as long as it is consistent with their explanation of the direction of the solution.

Lesson 66   431

Example 3

Error Alert Students might not correctly determine the direction of the inequality if the number they substitute for *x* makes the statement false. Point out that if substituted values for *x* make the inequality false, then the direction reverses.

Additional Example 3

Solve the inequality $x + 5 < 7$. Then graph and check the solution. $x < 2$;

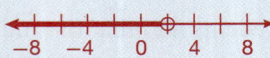

Example 4

Extend the Example

"Jared's sister has a suitcase that weighs 4 pounds. How much weight can Jared and his sister pack altogether?" $x \leq 91$ pounds

Additional Example 4

Michael's horse can carry no more than 200 pounds on its back. If Michael weighs 168 pounds, how much can his saddle weigh? $s \leq 32$ pounds

Just as you can add the same number to both sides of an inequality, you can also subtract the same number from each side. When equal quantities are subtracted from both sides of an inequality, the inequality remains true.

Subtraction Property of Inequality
For any real numbers *a*, *b*, and *c*:
If $a < b$, then $a - c < b - c$.   If $a \leq b$, then $a - c \leq b - c$.
If $a > b$, then $a - c > b - c$.   If $a \geq b$, then $a - c \geq b - c$.

Example 3 Using Subtraction

Solve the inequality $x + 2 > 3$. Then graph and check the solution.

SOLUTION

$x + 2 > 3$
$\underline{-2 -2}$ Subtraction Property of Inequality
$x > 1$ Simplify.

The solution is $x > 1$.

Check

Check the endpoint.   Check the direction of the inequality.

$x + 2 = 3$ $x + 2 > 3$
$1 + 2 \stackrel{?}{=} 3$ $2 + 2 \stackrel{?}{>} 3$
$3 = 3$ ✓ $4 > 3$ ✓

The solution of $x + 2 > 3$ is $x > 1$.

Example 4 Application: Travel

An airline allows a suitcase that weighs no more than 50 pounds when it is full. Jared's empty suitcase weighs 5 pounds. How much weight can Jared pack in his suitcase? Write an inequality to solve the problem. Check your solution.

SOLUTION

Write an inequality to represent the situation. Then solve the inequality.

$x + 5 \leq 50$
$x \leq 45$ Subtract 5 from both sides.

Jared can pack no more than 45 pounds.

Check

Hint
To check an inequality solution, try substituting in numbers that are part of the solution set.

Check the endpoint.   Check the direction of the inequality.

$x + 5 = 50$ $x + 5 \leq 50$
$45 + 5 \stackrel{?}{=} 50$ $44 + 5 \stackrel{?}{\leq} 50$
$50 = 50$ ✓ $49 \leq 50$ ✓

🔷 INCLUSION

Use this strategy if a student displays difficulty with directionality (working left to right or right to left).

When translating inequalities to symbolic form, students may confuse "at least" and "no more than". Using index cards, help students create an example of each phrase translated into symbolic form along with the graph of the inequality. Encourage students to refer to these examples when solving word problems.

a. $x > 3\frac{1}{2}$;

b. $z \geq 2\frac{1}{2}$;

c. $y \leq 2.1$;

1.5 1.6 1.7 1.8 1.9 2.0 2.1 2.2 2.3

Lesson Practice

a. Solve the inequality $x - \frac{1}{2} > 3$ and graph the solution on a number line. *(Ex 1)*

Solve each inequality. Then graph and check the solution.

b. $z - 2 \geq \frac{1}{2}$ *(Ex 2)*

c. $y + 1.1 \leq 3.2$ *(Ex 3)*

d. Rebecca wants to crochet a scarf that is at least 4.4 feet long. So far, she has completed 2.5 feet. How much more does Rebecca intend to crochet? Write an inequality to solve the problem. Check your solution. *(Ex 4)*
She intends to crochet at least 1.9 feet more; $x + 2.5 \geq 4.4$; $x \geq 1.9$

Practice   Distributed and Integrated

Simplify the rational expression, if possible.

1. $\dfrac{11p}{6s^4} + \dfrac{p}{6s^4} \cdot \dfrac{2p}{s^4}$ *(51)*

2. $\dfrac{4x}{5w^4} - \dfrac{5x}{5w^4} \cdot \dfrac{-x}{5w^4}$ *(51)*

3. $\dfrac{7y}{3x^4 + 1} + \dfrac{5y}{3x^4 + 1} \cdot \dfrac{12y}{3x^4 + 1}$ *(51)*

Solve the inequality.

*4. $z + 10 \geq 3$ $z \geq -7$ *(66)*

*5. $x - 4 \leq 9$ $x \leq 13$ *(66)*

6. Graph the inequality $z \leq 1\frac{2}{3}$.
(50)

 7. Write Explain the difference between $x > 5$ and $x \geq 5$.   See Additional Answers.
(66)

8. Define a linear function that has shifted upward 3 units. $f(x) = x + 3$
(Inv 6)

9. (**Sports**) In June 2000, the Russian Alexander Popov set a new world record of 21.64 seconds in men's freestyle swimming. Create the graph of an inequality that represents the times that could beat Popov's record. Explain any restrictions on the graph.   Sample: The graph would only include non negative numbers because there cannot be a negative time.
(50)
0 4 8 12 16 20 24

 10. Geometry In two similar triangles, the lengths of the sides of the larger triangle are directly proportional to the lengths of the corresponding sides of the smaller triangle. Find the length of x.   3 millimeters
(56)

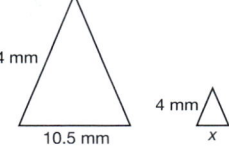

11. Multi-Step The total enrollment P and the female enrollment F of membership in a scholarship program (in thousands) can be modeled by the equations below, where t is the number of years since it was instituted.
(53)

$$P = 2387.74t + 155{,}211.46 \qquad F = 1223.58t + 79{,}589.03$$

a. Find a model that represents the male enrollment M in the scholarship program.

b. For the year 2010, the value of P is projected to be 298,475.86 and the value of F is projected to be 153,003.83. Use these figures to project the male enrollment in 2010. $M = 145{,}472.03$

11a. $M = 1164.16t + 75{,}622.43$

ALTERNATE METHOD FOR PROBLEM 10

Equations can be used to solve the problem.

$\dfrac{4a}{4} = \dfrac{14}{4}$ $\dfrac{3.5x}{3.5} = \dfrac{10.5}{3.5}$

$a = 3.5$ $x = 3$

The length of x is 3 millimeters.

Problem 14

Extend the Problem

"Suppose every tenth student likes green and every twenty-fifth student likes yellow. Which color is more popular?" green

Problem 16

Error Alert

Students might express the answer without units or with incorrect units. Remind them to perform their calculations with units. Point out that units cancel just like numbers and variables.

---

*12. **Multiple Choice** What is the solution to $3z + 2 \leq z - 4 + 2 + z$? A
  (66)
  A $z \leq -4$ **B** $z \leq 0$ **C** $z \leq 3$ **D** $z \leq 4$

*13. **Coordinate Geometry** Find a line that is both a line of symmetry for the
  (65) figure and also a perpendicular bisector of two of the sides.

14. **Multi-Step** In a student poll about yearbook covers, every 12th student likes
  (57) blue, every 16th student likes red, and every 28th student likes white.
  a. How many students are polled before one student likes red, white, and blue? 336 students
  b. If 1200 students are polled, how many like red, white, and blue? 3 students

15. Solve the system of equations by substitution.
  (59) (58, 6)

$$x = 10y - 2$$
$$2x - 18y = 8$$

13. Sample: $y = 3 - x$ is a line of symmetry for the figure. $y = 3 - x$ has a slope of -1 and is perpendicular to $\overline{AB}$ and $\overline{EF}$, which each have a slope of 1.

*16. **Velocity** The tangential velocity of an object in circular motion can be found using
  (61) the expression $\sqrt{\frac{Fr}{m}}$, where F is the centripetal force, r is the radius of the circle, and m is the mass of the object. What is the tangential velocity of an object with a path radius of 2 m, a centripetal force of 60 kgm/s², and a mass of 3 kg? $2\sqrt{10}$ m/s

17. **Multiple Choice** Which system of equations has a solution of $y = 5$? A
  (63)
  A $2x + 5y = 16$ **B** $2x + 5y = 19$
      $2x + y = -4$ $x - 5y = -13$
  C $2x + 5y = -4$ **D** $2x + 5y = 11$
      $-2x + y = -8$ $x - 5y = -17$

18. **Justify** Explain the steps that are used to solve this system of linear equations by
  (63) elimination.   See Additional Answers.

$$2x + 6y = 4$$
$$3x - 7y = 6$$

*19. **Coordinate Geometry** What kind of quadrilateral is *EFHG*? Justify your answer.
  (65)

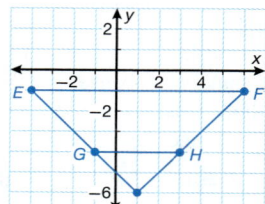

EFHG is a trapezoid because it has one pair of parallel sides. $\overline{EF} \parallel \overline{GH}$ because they have the equal slopes of 0. $\overline{EG}$ and $\overline{FH}$ are not parallel because they have different slopes.

434 Saxon Algebra 1

ALTERNATE METHOD FOR PROBLEM 17

The answer can be determined by finding the solution for each system of equations.

$$2x + y = -4$$
$$\underline{-2x \quad\quad -2x}$$
$$y = -2x - 4$$
$$2x + 5y = 16$$

$2x + 5(-2x - 4) = 16$
$2x - 10x - 20 = 16$
$-8x - 20 = 16$
$-8x = 36$
$x = -4.5$

$2(-4.5) + y = -4$
$-9 + y = -4$
$y = 5$

20. Error Analysis Two students are using the product rule below to find the missing value. Which student is correct? Explain the error.   Student B; Sample: Student A did not write down the product rule correctly.
(64)
If y varies inversely as x and $y = 0.2$ when $x = 100$, find y when $x = 4$.

Student A	Student B
$x_1 y_2 = x_2 y_1$	$x_1 y_1 = x_2 y_2$
$100 \cdot y_2 = 4 \cdot 0.2$	$100 \cdot 0.2 = 4 \cdot y_2$
$100 y_2 = 0.8$	$20 = 4 y_2$
$y_2 = 0.008$	$5 = y_2$

21. Write a direct-variation equation relating x and y when $x = 5$ and $y = 30$. $y = 6x$
(56)

22. Write an inverse-variation equation relating x and y when $x = 4$ and $y = 20$. $y = \frac{80}{x}$
(64)

Multiply.

23. $(2x - 3)(2x - 3)$ **24.** $(t - 12)(t + 12)$ **25.** $(y^3 - 4)^2$
(60) $4x^2 - 12x + 9$ (60) $t^2 - 144$ (60) $y^6 - 8y^3 + 16$

26. Justify Find the product of $(2y + 4)(3y + 5)$ using the Distributive Property.
(58) Then find the product using the FOIL method. Show that the answers are the same using either method.

26. Distributive Property:
$(2y + 4)(3y + 5)$
$(2y)(3y + 5) = 6y^2 + 10y$
$(4)(3y + 5) = 12y + 20$
$6y^2 + 22y + 20$

FOIL method:
$(2y + 4)(3y + 5)$
$6y^2 + 10y + 12y + 20$
$6y^2 + 22y + 20$

27. Life Expectancy For most mammals, there is an inverse relationship between life span and heart rate. Use the table below to write an inverse-variation equation to represent this relationship. Then find the life span in years, rounded to the nearest tenth, of a hamster with an average heart rate of 450 beats per minute. $y = \frac{1{,}000{,}000{,}000}{x}$; 4.2 years
(64)

Animal	Heart Rate (beats per minute)	Life Span (in minutes)
Guinea Pig	280	3,571,429
Rabbit	205	4,878,049
Dog	115	8,695,952
Rat	328	3,048,780

28. $m_{\overline{PQ}} = -2$, $m_{\overline{PR}} = \frac{1}{2}$, and $(-2)(\frac{1}{2}) = -1$; $\overline{PQ} \perp \overline{PR}$. Therefore, PQR is a right triangle.

*28. Coordinate Geometry Show that PQR is a right triangle.
(65)

*29. Justify True or False: The lines represented by $y = \frac{x}{3} - 1$ and $-4 = 12x + 4y$ are parallel. Explain.   false; Sample: The lines are perpendicular because their slopes are negative reciprocals: $\frac{1}{3}$, -3.
(65)

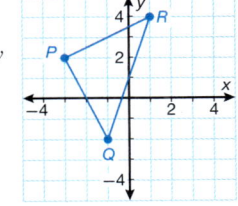

*30. Running John plans to run at least 5 miles more this week than he ran last week. He ran 25 miles last week. Write and solve an inequality describing the number of miles John plans to run this week. $x - 25 \geq 5$; $x \geq 30$ miles
(66)

Lesson 66   435

Problem 27
Extend the Problem
"If heart rate and life span are inversely related, how is life span determined when only the heart rate is known?" Sample: by finding the product of the heart rate and life span of another animal and dividing the product by the heart rate of the new animal

CHALLENGE

Sometimes a variable appears on both sides of an inequality. Determine which inequalities below are true by substituting values for x.

$x > x$ false

$x \leq x$ true

$x - 1 < x$ true

$x - 3 \geq x - 2$ false

LOOKING FORWARD

Solving inequalities by adding or subtracting prepares students for

- **Lesson 70** Solving Inequalities by Multiplying or Dividing

- **Lesson 73** Solving Compound Inequalities

- **Lesson 81** Solving Inequalities with Variables on Both Sides

- **Lesson 82** Solving Multi-Step Compound Inequalities

LESSON 67

1 Warm Up

Problem 5
Remind students that lines are perpendicular if their slopes are negative reciprocals of each other.

2 New Concepts

In this lesson, students learn how to manipulate systems of equations and to classify special systems as consistent and independent, consistent and dependent, or inconsistent.

Discuss with students how they have solved systems of linear equations before, using substitution and graphing.

Example 1

Remind students that in Lesson 59, they learned how to solve systems of linear equations using substitution. Now they will work with systems that have no solution.

Additional Example 1
Solve.

$y = 5x + 6$

$y = 5x$

There is no solution, so it is an inconsistent system.

LESSON RESOURCES

Student Edition Practice
   Workbook 67
Reteaching Master 67
Adaptations Master 67
Challenge and Enrichment
   Master C67, E67

LESSON 67

Solving and Classifying Special Systems of Linear Equations

Warm Up

1. **Vocabulary** A(n) _____ of linear equations is a set of linear equations with the same variables. **system**

Find the slope and y-intercept.

2. $y = 4x - 7$ **4, -7**
3. $6x - 2y = 18$ **3, -9**
4. Find the slope of a line parallel to $15x + 3y = 24$.   **-5**
5. Find the slope of a line perpendicular to $x + 4y = 7$.   **4**

New Concepts

Systems of linear equations can be classified by their common solutions. If no common solution exists, the system consists of **inconsistent equations.** The graphs of inconsistent equations never intersect. Therefore, since parallel lines never intersect, the graphs of inconsistent equations are the graphs of parallel lines.

Example 1   Solving Inconsistent Systems of Equations

Solve.

$-3x + y = -4$

$y = 3x$

Caution
Be sure to isolate a variable before using it to solve by substitution.

SOLUTION

Use substitution.

$y = 3x - 4$	Isolate y.
$y = 3x$	
$3x = 3x - 4$	Substitute 3x for y in the first equation.
$0 = -4$	Subtract 3x from both sides of the equation.

The statement is false. This means the system has no solution, so it is an inconsistent system.

Other systems of equations, known as **dependent systems,** can have an infinite number of solutions. The equations of a dependent system are called **dependent equations,** and they have identical solution sets. Since they have identical solution sets, the equations are the same.

Two methods can be used to solve dependent systems algebraically. One method shows that the equations are identical. The other method shows that the variables in dependent systems can be assigned any value. So, both equations have infinitely many solutions—an infinite set of ordered pairs.

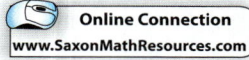
Online Connection
www.SaxonMathResources.com

436   Saxon Algebra 1

MATH BACKGROUND

There are only three possible solutions of a system of two linear equations. Graphically, the three possibilities are as follows:

1. The two lines will intersect at exactly one point.
2. The two lines are parallel and will never intersect.
3. The two lines overlap because they are the same line.

When the linear equations in a system are put into slope-intercept form it can be readily seen which one of these three situations exists.

Example 2 Solving Dependent Systems of Equations

Solve.
$x + 3y = 6$
$\frac{1}{3}x + y = 2$

SOLUTION Write the equations in slope-intercept form.

Method 1: $x + 3y = 6 \rightarrow y = -\frac{1}{3}x + 2$

$\frac{1}{3}x + y = 2 \rightarrow y = -\frac{1}{3}x + 2$

The equations are identical. Since the graphs would be the same line, there are infinitely many solutions. Any ordered pair (x, y) that satifies the equation $y = -\frac{1}{3}x + 2$.

SOLUTION

Method 2: $x + 3y = 6$

$\frac{1}{3}x + y = 2$

$y = 2 - \frac{1}{3}x$ Isolate y in the second equation.

$x + 3(2 - \frac{1}{3}x) = 6$ Substitute $2 - \frac{1}{3}x$ for y in the first equation.

$x + 6 - x = 6$ Distribute.

$6 = 6$ Simplify.

All variables have been eliminated. The last equation is true, $6 = 6$. This means that the original equations are true for all values of the variables. There are infinitely many solutions—an infinite set of ordered pairs.

A **consistent system** will have at least one common solution. An **independent system** will have exactly one solution. An independent system is also a consistent system. The graphs of the equations of an independent system will intersect at one point. Systems of linear equations can be classified into three different categories based on the number of solutions.

Math Reasoning

Analyze What is characteristic of systems of equations that are dependent?

One equation is a multiple of the other.

Systems of Linear Equations

Consistent and Independent	Consistent and Dependent	Inconsistent
Exactly One Solution	Infinitely Many Solutions	No Solution
The graphed lines intersect at a single point.	The graphed lines are the same line. The line is the solution.	The lines are parallel and do not intersect.

Lesson 67   437

Example 2

Remind students that in Lesson 49, they learned how to write equations in slope-intercept form.

Error Alert Unless students first put the equations in the form $y = mx + b$, they will not see that the lines are the same.

Additional Example 2

Solve.

$x - 4y = 8$
$\frac{1}{4}x - y = 2$

$x - 4y = 8 \longrightarrow y = \frac{1}{4}x - 2$
$\frac{1}{4}x - y = 2 \longrightarrow y = \frac{1}{4}x - 2$

infinitely many solutions—any ordered pair (x, y) that satisfies $y = \frac{1}{4}x - 2$

ALTERNATE METHOD FOR EXAMPLE 2

Students can use the Coordinate Grid transparency to graph the lines.

Have them fill in the table below to make ordered pairs.

This will allow them to see that the lines are the same, and therefore have an infinite number of solutions.

$x + 3y = 6$		$\frac{1}{3}x + y = 2$	
x	y	x	y
0	2	0	2
3	1	3	1
9	−1	9	−1

Lesson 67   437

Example 3

Explain to students that before they solve the system of equations using substitution, they should put the equations in $y = mx + b$ form.

Additional Example 3

Determine if each system of equations is consistent and independent, consistent and dependent, or inconsistent.

a. $x - 7y = 3$

$2x - 5y = 15$ (10, 1); consistent and independent

b. $8x - 5y = 16$

$y = 4x - 5$ $\left(\frac{3}{4}, -2\right)$; consistent and independent

TEACHER TIP

When solving systems of equations, it may be helpful to allow students to further verify their solutions using a graphing calculator.

Example 3 Classifying Systems of Equations

Determine if each system of equations is consistent and independent, consistent and dependent, or inconsistent.

a. $x - \frac{1}{4}y = \frac{3}{4}$

$2x + y = 1$

SOLUTION

Solve the system of equations.

$x - \frac{1}{4}y = \frac{3}{4} \longrightarrow y = 4x - 3$

$2x + y = 1 \longrightarrow y = -2x + 1$

Use substitution.

$y = 4x - 3$
$y = -2x + 1$
$-2x + 1 = 4x - 3$ Substitute $y = -2x + 1$ in the first equation.
$\frac{2}{3} = x$ Solve for x.

Substitute $\frac{2}{3}$ for x in one of the original equations and solve for y.

$2\left(\frac{2}{3}\right) + y = 1$ Substitute $\frac{2}{3}$ for x in the second equation.

$y = -\frac{1}{3}$ Solve for y.

The solution is $\left(\frac{2}{3}, -\frac{1}{3}\right)$. There is exactly one solution, so the system is consistent and independent.

Check Graph the lines and verify the solution.

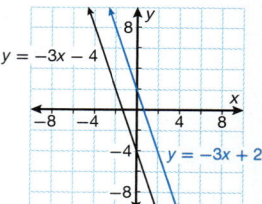

Math Reasoning

Write Why is there only one solution for a system of independent and consistent equations?

Sample: The lines described by the equations can only intersect at one point.

b. $3x + y = 2$

$y = -3x - 4$

SOLUTION Write the equations in slope-intercept form.

$3x + y = 2 \longrightarrow y = -3x + 2$
$y = -3x - 4$

The two equations have the same slope and different y-intercepts. The lines are parallel, so there is no solution. The system is inconsistent.

Check Graph the lines and verify the solution.

438   *Saxon Algebra 1*

ENGLISH LEARNERS

Explain to students what a **system** is. Say:

"A system can be parts of something that make a whole."

Ask students how a system of equations fits this definition. Explain that you have to work with both of the equations in the system to find an answer. For instance, if you are using substitution to solve a system of equations, you must substitute the second equation for y in the first equation. Both parts of the equation form the whole.

Ask students to come up with other types of systems and ask them why they think these are systems. Sample: ecosystem, respiratory system, and subway system

Math Reasoning

Analyze What does each equation represent?

Sample: $x =$ the number of hours jogged. The distance in miles y that Brandon jogged is shown by $4x + 1$. The distance in miles y that Anton jogged is shown by $4x$.

Example 4 Application: Jogging

Brandon started jogging at a rate of 4 miles per hour. After he jogged 1 mile, his friend Anton started jogging on the same path at a pace of 4 miles per hour. If they continue to jog at the same rate, will Anton ever catch up with Brandon? Explain.

SOLUTION Write a system of equations to represent the situation.

$y = 4x + 1$

$y = 4x$

The two equations have the same slope and different y-intercepts. The lines are parallel, so there are no solutions.

The boys are jogging at the same rate. Brandon had jogged 1 mile before Anton started. Anton will never catch up with Brandon.

Lesson Practice

Solve.

a. (Ex 1) $y = \frac{1}{2}x + \frac{1}{2}$
$y = \frac{1}{2}x + 7$ no solution

b. (Ex 2) $x + y = 10$
$-x - y = -10$ infinitely many solutions—any ordered pair (x, y) that satisfies the equation $y = -x + 10$.

Determine if the system of equations is consistent and independent, consistent and dependent, or inconsistent.

c. (Ex 3) $4y = 4x + 4$
$-4y = -4x - 4$ consistent and dependent

d. $-2x + y = 3$
$y = -x - 2$ $\left(-1\frac{2}{3}, -\frac{1}{3}\right)$; consistent and independent

e. (Ex 4) An emergency-road-service company offers different plans to its customers. Plan X offers service calls for $22 each. Plan Y offers a rate of $40 per month with an additional charge of $12 for each service call. For one month, how many service calls would it take for Plan Y to cost the same as Plan X? Explain.   4 service calls; Both plans cost $88 at 4 service calls.

Practice Distributed and Integrated

Find the product.

1. (60) $(2b - 3)^2$ $4b^2 - 12b + 9$

2. (60) $(-b^3 + 5)^2$ $b^6 - 10b^3 + 25$

Simplify.

3. (61) $\sqrt{25x^4}$ $5x^2$

4. (61) $\sqrt{144x^6y}$ $12x^3\sqrt{y}$

Lesson 67 **439**

Example 4

Extend the Example

"If Anton is running at a pace of 6 miles an hour, will he catch up with Brandon?"

$y = 4x + 1$

$y = 6x$

$\left(\frac{1}{2}, 3\right)$

Anton will catch up with Brandon in $\frac{1}{2}$ hour, or 3 miles into the run.

Additional Example 4

Hannah and her mother are going on a bike ride. Hannah's mother leaves the house traveling at 13 mph. Hannah leaves the house after her mother has biked 2 miles, and tries to catch up by traveling at a speed of 17 mph. Will Hannah catch up with her mother? If yes, when? yes; $\frac{1}{2}$ hour, or $6\frac{1}{2}$ miles after her mother started biking

Lesson Practice

Problem b

Error Alert Students may forget to change the signs when putting the second equation in $y = mx + b$ form.

Problem e

Scaffolding First ask students to write a system of equations with y as the total cost and x as the number of service calls. The x-value in their solution will be the answer.

Check for Understanding

The questions below help assess the concepts taught in this lesson.

"What kind of system would parallel lines be? Why?"
inconsistent system; Sample: Parallel lines never touch, so they cannot have a common solution.

"What kind of system would perpendicular lines be? Why?"
consistent and independent; Sample: Perpendicular lines meet at only one point and have exactly one solution.

Lesson 67 **439**

INCLUSION

Classifying Systems of Equations

Materials: ruler, coordinate grid

Use the following teaching strategy if students display difficulty with abstract concepts or weak conceptualization.

Give students a coordinate grid and have them graph the line $y = 2x + 5$.

Then give students other equations of lines that are parallel, that intersect, or that are the same line as $y = 2x + 5$.

Ask students to describe the relationship of the lines, how many solutions there would be to the system, and to identify the systems as consistent and dependent, consistent and independent, or inconsistent.

3 Practice

Math Conversations
Discussion to strengthen understanding

Problem 10
Error Alert
Some students may multiply 44 and 28, finding a multiple of the two numbers. Help them understand that since the problem asks for the next time both trains are at the station, the LCM is needed.

Problem 11
Remind students that the first step in making a box-and-whisker plot is organizing the data in order from least to greatest.

Problem 13
Remind students that to undo the +2, they need to subtract 2 from both sides.

---

5. Simplify the rational expression $\frac{3x}{y^2} + xy^{-2}$, if possible. $\frac{4x}{y^2}$
   (51)

6. In three hours, James read 18 pages of his history book. In four hours, he read
   (52) 21 pages. Write the equation of the line that passes through the two points that represent the data in the problem. Use the equation to predict how many pages James will read in six hours. $y = 3x + 9$; 27 pages

Solve the inequality.

7. $z - 3 \geq 10$ $z \geq 13$
   (66)

8. $z - 5 < -2$ $z < 3$
   (66)

9. **(Hobbies)** The stem-and-leaf plot shows the number of
   (62) cards each member of a baseball card enthusiasts' club has. What is the mode(s) of the data?
   324 cards and 356 cards

   Cards in Collection

Stem	Leaves
30	9
31	1, 4, 5, 7, 7, 9
32	0, 1, 4, 4, 4, 7, 8
33	5, 6
34	2, 8, 9
35	0, 4, 6, 6, 6, 7,

   Key: 31 | 5 means 315 cards

10. **(Transportation)** Two subway trains run through a station. One train goes through
    (57) the station every 44 minutes and the other train goes through the station every 28 minutes. If they just went through the station at the same time, how many minutes will it be until the next time they are both at the station at the same time? 308 minutes

11. **Multi-Step** A bank teller receives several deposits in one day. She tallies how
    (54) many of each amount she receives.
    a. Make a box-and-whisker plot for the set of data. See Additional Answers.
    b. List the lower extreme, lower quartile, median, upper quartile, and upper extreme of the data. LE: 25, Q1: 60, median: 75, Q3: 80, UE: 100

Amount	Tally
$25	4
$50	2
$60	6
$75	3
$80	7
$100	5

*12. Identify Statement 2 as the converse, inverse, or contrapositive of Statement 1.
 (Inv 5) Then indicate the truth value of each statement.

   Statement 1: If a figure is not a polygon, then it is not a square.

   Statement 2: If a figure is a polygon, then it is a square. inverse; The original statement is true, but the inverse is false.

13. **Error Analysis** Two students solve the inequality $x + 2 < 3$. Which student is correct?
    (66) Explain the error. Student B; Sample: You need to subtract 2 from each side to eliminate 2 from the left side.

Student A	Student B
$x + 2 < 3$	$x + 2 < 3$
$+2 \quad +2$	$-2 \quad -2$
$x < 5$	$x < 1$

440   Saxon Algebra 1

*14. (Sports) The ages of the players of the Eastern Conference team during the 2007 All-Star Game are listed below. Create a histogram of the data.   See Additional Answers.

$$25, 30, 24, 26, 30, 29, 21, 25, 33, 28, 34, 25$$

15. **Multi-Step** Find the volume of a toy building block that is in the shape of a cube with a side length of $(2x + 2)$ inches.
    a. Find the area of the base. Find the product of the length and the width. $4x^2 + 8x + 4$ in^2
    b. Find the volume by multiplying the product found in part **a** by the height.
       $8x^3 + 24x^2 + 24x + 8$ in^3

16. **Verify** Show that (20, 15) is a solution to the system of equations.
    Sample: $5(20) - 2(15) = 100 - 30 = 70$, and $3(20) + 4(15) = 60 + 60 = 120$.
    $$5x - 2y = 70$$
    $$3x + 4y = 120$$

*17. **Coordinate Geometry** For the figure at right, find two lines that are both a line of symmetry and a perpendicular bisector of the sides. $y = 1$ and $x = 3$ are both lines of symmetry; $y = 1$ is perpendicular to $\overline{DG}$ and $\overline{EF}$, and $x = 3$ is perpendicular to $\overline{DE}$ and $\overline{GF}$.

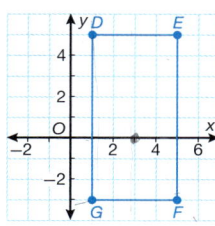

*18. (Job Hunting) Claudio is looking for a new job in sales. He interviews with Company A and they offer him a base salary of $32,000 plus a 1.5% bonus on his total sales for the year. When he interviews with Company B, they offer him a base salary of $26,000 plus a 3% bonus on his total sales for the year. How much would Claudio have to sell to make the same amount at each job? $400,000

*19. **Analyze** If an equation is multiplied by a number, a system of equations is formed that has infinitely many solutions. Classify the system formed by adding a number to a given equation.   inconsistent

Determine if the lines are parallel or perpendicular.

20. $y = 3x + 12$ and $y + 9 = 3x$ parallel

Solve each system of linear equations.

21. $2x - 3y = -17$
    $2x - 9y = -47$ $(-1, 5)$

*22. $y = x - 5$
     $y = -2x + 1$ $(2, -3)$

23. **Multiple Choice** If y varies inversely as x, and $y = 7.5$ when $x = 5$, what is the value of k?   **D**
    A 0   B 0.67   C 1.5   D 37.5

24. **Write** Will the graph of an inverse variation ever cross the x-axis? Explain.

24. no; Sample: The value of x can never equal 0 because that would mean the product of x and y would equal 0.

25. **Probability** A teacher allows students to draw from a bag of various prizes, four of which are new graphing calculators. If there are 24 students and each student chooses 3 items, what is the probability that the first student will choose a graphing calculator on his or her first draw? $\frac{1}{18}$

CHALLENGE

Write a system of equations in standard form with the given classification.

a. inconsistent   Sample: $-4x + y = -1$
                           $4x - y = 2$

b. consistent and dependent
   Sample: $x + 2y = 8$
           $\frac{1}{2}x + y = 4$

c. consistent and independent
   Sample: $2x + 3y = 3$
           $x - y = 4$

Problem 14
Guide students by asking the following questions.

"What is the first step in creating a histogram?" Sample: making a frequency table

"How do you break up the intervals?" Sample: They must be equal.

Problem 15
Remind students that the formula for volume is $V = l \cdot w \cdot h$.

Problem 16
Guide students by asking them the following questions.

"What is one way you could verify the solution to this system?" Sample: Substitute the solution into each equation.

"How could you use a graph?" Sample: I could graph both equations and see where they intersect.

Problem 18
Extend the Problem
"If Claudio only makes $100,000 in sales, which company would pay him more money?" Company A

Problem 20
Remind students that parallel lines have the same slope and that perpendicular lines have negative reciprocal slopes.

Problem 21
Remind students that they have a few options to solve systems of equations: graphing, addition, and substitution.

Problem 25
Guide students by asking them the following questions.

"How many chances are there to get the calculator?" 4 chances

"How many items are there in total?" 72 items

Problem 26

Watch for students who include 8 in the solution. Point out that since the sum of any two sides must be greater than the third side, 8 cannot be included in the solution.

Problem 29

Suggest to students that it may be helpful to first use the LCM to clear the fractions in $13x - \frac{1}{5}y = -3$.

---

26. Geometry The triangle inequality theorem states that the sum of the lengths of any two sides of a triangle must be greater than the length of the third side. Write an inequality for the length of the third side of the triangle. $x < 8$

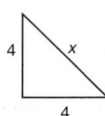

*27. Multi-Step Mr. Sanchez is planning a business trip. He estimates that he will have to drive 55 miles on one highway, 48 miles on another, and then 72 more miles to arrive at his destination. He starts with 25,000 miles on his car's odometer and later finds that his estimate was high.   **27a.** $x - 25{,}000 < 55 + 48 + 72$

a. Write an inequality to represent the odometer reading at the end of the trip.

b. Solve the inequality. $x < 25{,}175$

c. The inequality only considers the greatest amount the odometer could read. Write and solve an inequality for the least it could read. $x > 25{,}000$

*28. Error Analysis Two students checked the graph of a system of equations to see if it was consistent and independent, consistent and dependent, or inconsistent. Which student is correct? Explain the error.

28. Student B; Sample: Student A did not classify the graph correctly. Parallel lines have no common solutions.

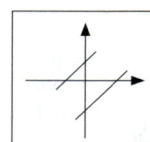

Student A	Student B
consistent and dependent	inconsistent

*29. Newspaper Delivery Mauricio and Aliyya are comparing their newspaper delivery speeds. Mauricio can deliver $y = 65x + 15$ papers per hour. Aliyya can deliver $13x - \frac{1}{5}y = -3$ papers per hour. Who delivers faster?   neither; Sample: These equations form a set of consistent and dependent equations.

*30. Verify Wanda determined that the system of equations below has one solution in common. Find the common solution and check your answer. $\left(\frac{5}{4}, 3\right)$

$$2y = 4x + 1$$
$$y = 8x - 7$$

442   Saxon Algebra 1

LOOKING FORWARD

Solving and classifying systems of equations prepares students for

- **Lesson 97** Graphing Linear Inequalities
- **Lesson 109** Graphing Systems of Linear Inequalities
- **Lesson 112** Graphing and Solving Systems of Linear and Quadratic Equations

LESSON 68

Mutually Exclusive and Inclusive Events

Warm Up

1. **Vocabulary** Events where the outcome of one event does not affect the probability of the other event are called _____. **independent events**

   Find the probability for one roll of a number cube.

2. $P(\text{less than } 4)$ $\frac{1}{2}$

3. $P(\text{multiple of } 3)$ $\frac{1}{3}$

   Simplify.

4. $\frac{2}{3} + \frac{1}{6}$ $\frac{5}{6}$

5. $\frac{3}{4} - \frac{1}{3}$ $\frac{5}{12}$

New Concepts

Probability describes the possibility of an event happening. In some cases, the events cannot happen at the same time. For example, when someone tosses a fair coin, there are two possible outcomes: heads or tails. Both outcomes cannot occur at the same time. Two events that cannot both occur in the same trial or experiment are **mutually exclusive events,** or disjoint events.

Math Reasoning

Write Give an example of mutually exclusive events.

Sample: rolling either an odd number or rolling an even number on a six-sided number cube

Probability of Mutually Exclusive Events
If A and B are mutually exclusive events, then $P(A \text{ or } B) = P(A) + P(B)$

Example 1 Finding the Probability of Mutually Exclusive Events

What is the probability of rolling either a sum of 6 or a sum of 11 using two different number cubes?

Roll of Cube 2

Roll of Cube 1	1	2	3	4	5	6
1	2	3	4	5	**6**	7
2	3	4	5	**6**	7	8
3	4	5	**6**	7	8	9
4	5	**6**	7	8	9	10
5	**6**	7	8	9	10	**11**
6	7	8	9	10	**11**	12

SOLUTION

Make a table of possible outcomes. Using two number cubes, it is not possible to roll both a sum of 6 and a sum of 11 at the same time.

Find the probability of each event and add them.

$P(A \text{ or } B) = P(A) + P(B)$

$P(6 \text{ or } 11) = P(6) + P(11)$

$\phantom{P(6 \text{ or } 11)} = \frac{5}{36} + \frac{2}{36}$

$\phantom{P(6 \text{ or } 11)} = \frac{7}{36}$

The probability of rolling either a sum of 6 or a sum of 11 is $\frac{7}{36}$.

LESSON 68

1 Warm Up

Problems 3 and 4

Check if students remember to find a common denominator before adding and subtracting fractions.

2 New Concepts

In this lesson, students learn how to determine the probability of mutually exclusive, or disjoint, events, and inclusive, or joint, events. Discuss with students how to find simple probabilities.

Example 1

Remind students that they have already learned how to find individual probabilities. Here, they just add probabilities together to find the probability of a mutually exclusive event.

Additional Example 1

What is the probability of rolling either a sum of 5 or a sum of 12 using two different number cubes? $\frac{5}{36}$

LESSON RESOURCES

Student Edition Practice Workbook 68
Reteaching Master 68
Adaptations Master 68
Challenge and Enrichment Master C68

MATH BACKGROUND

Students should understand how to find basic probabilities. Remind students that probability is the likelihood of an event happening, or $\frac{\text{favorable outcomes}}{\text{total outcomes}}$.

Discuss with students the difference between mutually exclusive events and inclusive events.

To explain mutually exclusive events, have students divide into two groups, girls and boys. Then, to explain inclusive events, ask them to divide into two additional groups, students with brothers and students with sisters.

Students should see that the groups in the first division cannot overlap because they are mutually exclusive (you cannot be both a boy and a girl), and that the groups in the second division may overlap because students can belong to both groups.

Example 2
Remind students that finding the probability of inclusive events is the same as finding the probability of mutually exclusive events and then subtracting out the outcomes the events have in common.

TEACHER TIP
Students may forget to subtract the probability of the common outcomes. Remind them that this is an inclusive event.

Additional Example 2
What is the probability of rolling at least one even number or a sum of 10 using two number cubes?

$\frac{27}{36} + \frac{3}{36} - \frac{2}{36}$ $= \frac{7}{9}$

In some instances it is possible for two events to occur at the same time. Two events are **inclusive events**, or joint events, if they can both occur at the same time.

Probability of Inclusive Events
If A and B are inclusive events, then
$P(A \text{ or } B) = P(A) + P(B) - P(A \text{ and } B)$

Math Reasoning

Write Give an example of inclusive events.

Sample: choosing a king or choosing a spade from a deck of cards

Example 2 Finding the Probability of Inclusive Events

What is the probability of rolling at least one odd number or a sum of 8 using two number cubes?

SOLUTION

Determine if the events are inclusive. List the possible outcomes for each event below.

rolling at least one odd number outcomes:

(1, 1), (1, 2), (1, 3), (1, 4), (1, 5), (1, 6), (3, 1), (3, 2), (3, 3), (3, 4), (3, 5), (3, 6), (5, 1), (5, 2), (5, 3), (5, 4), (5, 5), (5, 6), (2, 1), (4, 1), (6, 1), (2, 3), (4, 3), (6, 3), (2, 5), (4, 5), (6, 5)

rolling a sum of 8 outcomes:

(2, 6), (6, 2), (3, 5), (5, 3), (4, 4)

rolling at least one odd number and a sum of 8 outcomes:

(3, 5), (5, 3)

$P(A \text{ or } B) = P(A) + P(B) - P(A \text{ and } B)$

$P(\text{odd or } 8) = P(\text{odd}) + P(8) - P(\text{odd and } 8)$

$= \frac{27}{36} + \frac{5}{36} - \frac{2}{36}$

$= \frac{30}{36}$

$= \frac{5}{6}$

The probability of rolling either an odd number or a sum of 8 is $\frac{5}{6}$.

Example 3 Application: Survey

Briceson needs to randomly call 125 people from the state of Wyoming to conduct a short survey. The following data correspond to estimated values from 2005 describing the state's populace. Briceson assumes that everyone who is employed is younger than 75.

Total Population	Employed People	People 75 and Older
510,000	291,000	29,000

How many people can he expect to call who are either employed or are 75 or older?

444 Saxon Algebra 1

ENGLISH LEARNERS

Discuss the word **probability** with students. Explain that probability is the likeliness that something will happen.

Compare the words probability and probably. These two words may confuse students since they are spelled similarly. Say, **"In math, probability is a noun used to show the possibility that something will happen. Probably is an adverb used to show that something is likely to happen."**

Have students compare how these two words are similar and how they are different. Ask them to come up with sentences for each word.

444 Saxon Algebra 1

SOLUTION

Probability can be used to determine the number of people.

The events are mutually exclusive.

$$P(A \text{ or } B) = P(A) + P(B)$$
$$P(\text{employed or} \geq 75) = P(\text{employed}) + P(\geq 75)$$
$$= \frac{291}{510} + \frac{29}{510}$$
$$= \frac{32}{51}$$

Briceson can expect 32 out of 51 people to be employed or to be at least 75 years old. Multiply the probability by the 125 people.

$$125 \cdot \frac{32}{51}$$
$$= \frac{4000}{51}$$
$$\approx 78$$

Briceson can expect to call about 78 people who are either employed or 75 or older.

Math Reasoning

Verify Why is $\frac{4000}{51}$ rounded to the nearest whole number in Example 3?

Sample: The answer is rounded because Briceson cannot call part of a person.

Example 4 **Application: Digital Music**

Natalia has music from a variety of different artists on her MP3 player. There are 26 rock artists, 18 pop artists, 19 country artists, 10 alternative artists, and 7 crossover artists. The music by the crossover artists Natalia chose is on the pop and country charts. If Natalia's music player randomly selects the next artist, what is the probability that the artist will be singing a pop or country song?

SOLUTION

Find the total number of outcomes.

$$26 + 18 + 19 + 10 + 7 = 80$$

The events are inclusive events because the crossover artists are considered to be both country and pop artists.

$$P(A \text{ or } B) = P(A) + P(B) - P(A \text{ and } B)$$
$$P(\text{pop or country}) = P(\text{pop}) + P(\text{country}) - P(\text{pop and country})$$
$$= \frac{25}{80} + \frac{26}{80} - \frac{7}{80}$$
$$= \frac{11}{20}$$

There is an $\frac{11}{20}$ chance that the music player will choose a pop or country song next.

Example 3

Error Alert Students may find the probability and stop there. Remind them that the question is not looking for the probability, but for the actual number of people.

Extend the Example

"What if Briceson calls 450 people? About how many people will be either employed or over 75?"
~282 people

Additional Example 3

A town contains 5890 people planning to vote for Candidate A, 6910 planning to vote for Candidate B and 10,050 planning to vote for Candidate C. In a random gathering of 200 people, how many would you expect to be voting for Candidates A or B?
~112 people

Example 4

Remind students that this problem is about inclusive events.

Additional Example 4

Hayley has a bag of marbles. 13 are yellow, 16 are green, 23 are red, 8 are blue, and 6 are multicolor. The multicolored marbles are red and blue. If Hayley randomly selects a marble, what is the probability that the marble will have red or blue in it?
$\frac{29}{66} + \frac{14}{66} - \frac{6}{66} = \frac{37}{66}$

MANIPULATIVE USE

For Example 4, have students fill in a Venn Diagram to see that the crossover artists fit into both categories. Then have them subtract the crossover artists out so as not to count them twice.

Lesson Practice

Problem b
Error Alert Students may forget to subtract the overlapping events.

Problem d
Scaffolding First ask students if this is a mutually exclusive or inclusive event. Then ask them how this problem differs from Example 3. The events in problem d are inclusive. The events in Example 3 are mutually exclusive.

✓ Check for Understanding

The questions below help assess the concepts taught in this lesson.

"What are mutually exclusive events?" Sample: events that cannot happen at the same time

"What is an example of two mutually exclusive events?" Sample: getting 100% on a test and failing it

"What are inclusive events?" Sample: events that can happen at the same time

"What is an example of two inclusive events?" Sample: taking a math class and an English class

3 Practice

Math Conversations
Discussion to strengthen understanding

Problem 6
Remind students that an inverse variation is a relationship between two variables whose product is a constant. The equation $xy = k$ or $y = \frac{k}{x}$, where k is a nonzero constant, defines an inverse variation between x and y.

Lesson Practice

a. (Ex 1) What is the probability of rolling either a sum of 2 or a sum of 10 using two number cubes? $\frac{1}{9}$

b. (Ex 2) What is the probability of rolling at least one even number or a sum of 3 using two number cubes? $\frac{27}{36} = \frac{3}{4}$

c. (Ex 3) A digital music player randomly selects a song from a group of 12 rock, 12 pop, 5 country, and 3 alternative artists. What is the probability that the music player selects either a rock or alternative song? $\frac{15}{32}$

d. (Ex 4) Angelina uses Briceson's data from Example 3. She is planning to call 200 people from Wyoming. She assumes that 10,000 of the people who are 75 or older are also employed.

Total Population	Employed People	People 75 and Older
510,000	291,000	29,000

How many people would Angelina expect to call that are either employed or are 75 or older? about 122 people

Practice Distributed and Integrated

Determine the degree of each polynomial.

1. (53) $14x^2y^3z^4$ 9

2. (53) $12q^2r + 4r - 10q^2r^6$ 8

3. (53) $5x^4z^3 + 4xz$ 7

Simplify.

4. (61) $\sqrt{48}$ $4\sqrt{3}$

5. (61) $\sqrt{25x^4}$ $5x^2$

Tell whether each of the following equations shows inverse variation. Write "yes" or "no".

6. (64) $y = \frac{5}{x}$ yes

7. (64) $y = \frac{1}{2}x$ no

Solve each inequality.

8. (66) $x + 1 > 1.1$ $x > 0.1$

9. (66) $x - 2.3 \leq 7.6$ $x \leq 9.9$

Find the probability of the following events.

*10. (68) rolling a sum of 7 or a sum of 11 with two number cubes $\frac{2}{9}$

*11. (68) rolling a sum of 1 or a sum of 13 with two number cubes   0

12. (68) **Probability** A caterer is sorting silverware. There are 75 knives, 50 forks, and 75 spoons. Twenty of the forks and 30 of the spoons have red handles. If a piece of silverware is chosen at random, what is the probability that it will be a fork or have a red handle? Write and solve an expression to find the probability. $\frac{50 + 30}{75 + 50 + 75}; \frac{2}{5}$

446 Saxon Algebra 1

🔺 INCLUSION

Ask students who display weak conceptualization or difficulty with abstract concepts to draw a Venn Diagram like the one displayed below.

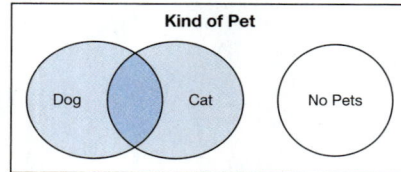
Kind of Pet — Dog, Cat, No Pets

Ask students if they have a dog, a cat, have both, or have neither. Write their names in the appropriate part of the Venn diagram.

Have students then use that information to create a frequency table. Make sure they include all students who are in each category, keeping in mind that a student can belong to more than one category.

Ask students to find the probability that a student has a dog, a cat, a dog and a cat, neither a dog nor a cat, or either a dog or a cat.

13. A car rental company charges a flat rate of $50 and an additional $.10 per mile to rent an automobile. Write an equation to model the total charge y in terms of x number of miles driven. Predict the cost after 100 miles driven.
$y = .10x + 50$; $60

14. (Chemistry) When Liquid A has a temperature of 0°F, Liquid B has a temperature of −8°F. When Liquid A has a temperature of 4°F, Liquid B has a temperature of −9°F. Write an equation of a line that passes through the two points that represent the data in this problem. Use the equation to predict the temperature of Liquid B if Liquid A has a temperature of −4°F. $B = -\frac{1}{4}A - 8$; −7°F

*15. Use the following system to answer the problems below.
$$x = y + 2$$
$$2x = y$$
a. Graph the system.   See Additional Answers.
b. Determine the solution. Verify the solution using your graphing calculator.
(−2, −4)

16. (Carpentry) Jorge is adding a rectangular family room onto his house. The dimensions of the room can be represented by a width of $(x + 6)$ feet and a length of $(2x + 5)$ feet. Write a polynomial expression for the area A of the new room.
$A = 2x^2 + 17x + 30$ square feet

17. **Multi-Step** The sum of 6 times a boy's age and 5 times a girl's age is 150. The girl is 2 years less than twice the boy's age. Find how old each was 5 years ago.
boy: 5 years old; girl: 13 years old

18. **Justify** True or False: $(a + b)(a + b) = a^2 + b^2$. Justify by giving an example.   See Additional Answers.

19. (Craft Fair) Celine sells her hand-painted chairs and tables at a local craft fair. She is selling her chairs for $30 a piece and her tables for $60 a piece. At the end of the day, she noted that she had sold 20 items for a total of $780. How many chairs did Celine sell? how many tables?   14 chairs; 6 tables

20. **Error Analysis** Two students want to find the equation of the line perpendicular to $y = -\frac{1}{5}x + 4$ that passes through $(1, -3)$. Which student is correct? Explain the error.

Student A	Student B
$y = 5x + b$	$y = 5x + b$
$1 = 5(-3) + b$	$-3 = 5(1) + b$
$1 = -15 + b$	$-3 = 5 + b$
$+15 \quad +15$	$-5 \quad -5$
$16 = b$	$-8 = b$
$y = 5x + 16$	$y = 5x - 8$

20. Student B; Sample: Student A did not correctly substitute the values of x and y from the known pair.

21. **Multi-Step** Draw a coordinate grid, numbering from −6 to +6 along the x- and y-axis. Will a line that passes through the points $(0, -4)$ and $(5, -2)$ be perpendicular to the line that passes through the points $(-2, 5)$ and $(0, 1)$?
a. **Model** Line 1 passes through the points $(0, -4)$ and $(5, -2)$. Line 2 passes through the points $(-2, 5)$ and $(0, 1)$. Graph the lines.   See Additional Answers.
b. Write an equation for both lines.   Line 1: $y = \frac{2}{5}x - 4$; Line 2: $y = -2x + 1$
c. **Justify** Are the lines perpendicular? Explain.   no; Sample: The slopes of line 1 and line 2 are not negative reciprocals.

Lesson 68   447

Problem 14
Guide students by asking the following questions.

"How do we find the slope of the line?" $m = \frac{y_2 - y_1}{x_2 - x_1}$ or
$m = \frac{-9 - (-8)}{4 - 0} = \frac{-1}{4}$

"How do we find the y-intercept?" Sample: Find the point where $x = 0$, which is the first point provided. The y-intercept is $(0, -8)$.

"How do we put it all together to get the equation?"
$y = mx + b$
$y = -\frac{1}{4}x - 8$

Problem 17
Error Alert
Students may forget to do the final step of subtracting 5 from each age.

Remind students to reread the question before writing their final answer, noting that this problem has 3 steps.

Problem 21
Guide students by asking the following question. "How are the slopes of perpendicular lines related?" Slopes of perpendicular lines are negative reciprocals of each other.

Extend the Problem
"Write the equation of a line perpendicular to line 1."
$y = -\frac{5}{2}x + 6$

Problem 24
Remind students that substitution would be a good choice for solving this system.

Problem 25
Remind students that a system with exactly one solution is called consistent and independent, a system with infinitely many solutions is called consistent and dependent, and a system with no solution is called inconsistent.

Problem 30
Remind students that with inclusive events, they have to subtract the probability of the common outcomes after adding the individual probabilities together, whereas with mutually exclusive events, they must simply add the two probabilities together.

---

22. Discounts A new pet store is selling dog food for $2 off. Another pet store is selling dog food for $14.99. Write and solve an inequality to represent the highest original price, before the discount, that will make the dog food at the new pet store cheaper. $x - 2 < 14.99; x < 16.99$

23. Error Analysis Two students solve and graph the inequality $x - 5 \leq -8$. Which student is correct? Explain the error. Student A; Sample: The solution of the equation is $x \leq -3$.

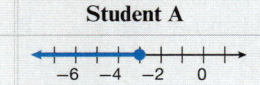 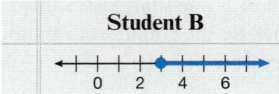

Student A   Student B

Find the common solution for each system of equations.

24. $y = \dfrac{3}{4}x + 3$
$y = x$ (12, 12)

25. Multi-Step Two satellite radio companies are offering different plans. One offers a flat fee of $15 per month for all stations. The second charges a rate of $y = 10 + 1.5x$, where x is the number of additional stations. Do the plans ever cost the same amount?
 a. How many stations can a consumer purchase from the second company before exceeding the flat fee of $15?   3
 b. Classify the system of equations for the plans offered by both companies. consistent and independent
 c. How is the classification of the equations misleading given the problem situation?
 d. Do the plans ever cost the same amount? no; Sample: There is no whole-number solution common to both equations.

25c. Systems of equations that are consistent and independent have a common solution. However, because that solution is a decimal number, and there can only be a whole number of stations, there is not a point where the plans cost the same amount.

26. Geometry Two secants to a circle are shown at right. Classify the system formed by the equations for these two lines. consistent and independent

★27. Predict If two standard number cubes are rolled 100 times, predict the number of times that a sum of 7 or 11 will be rolled. about 22

★28. Multiple Choice Which one of the following situations describes mutually exclusive events? **D**
 A rolling doubles or a sum of 4 with two number cubes
 B choosing an odd number or a multiple of 3
 C tossing a coin heads-up or rolling a 2 with a number cube
 D rolling two 5s or a sum of 12 with two number cubes

★29. Weather Forecasting On a winter day in Maine, there was a 30% chance of only freezing rain, a 45% chance of only rain, and a 25% chance of only snow. What was the chance of getting only freezing rain or snow? 55%

★30. Analyze Given two possible events, A and B, will the probability of either A or B occurring be higher if they are inclusive events or mutually exclusive events?
The probability is higher if A and B are mutually exclusive.

448   *Saxon* Algebra 1

CHALLENGE

Suppose Mariam needs to survey 200 residents to find out if they prefer paint or vinyl siding. Assume that of a local population of 320,000, 100,000 live in rented apartments, and 50,000 homeowners live in brick or stucco homes and have no preference for paint or vinyl siding. About how people can Mariam expect to call who prefer paint or vinyl siding? about 106 people

LOOKING FORWARD

Finding the probability of mutually exclusive and inclusive events prepares students for

- **Lesson 80** Calculating Probability Distributions

- **Lesson 111** Solving Problems Involving Permutations

- **Lesson 118** Solving Problems Involving Combinations

- **Lesson 120** Using Geometric Formulas to Find the Probability of an Event

LESSON 69

Adding and Subtracting Radical Expressions

Warm Up

1. **Vocabulary** Terms that have the same variable(s) raised to the same power(s) are called _____. **like terms**

Simplify.

2. $3s + 4t + 8s - 7t$ **$11s - 3t$**
3. $9wv - 4m + 13m - 17wv$ **$9m - 8wv$**
4. $\sqrt{72}$ **$6\sqrt{2}$**
5. $\sqrt{50}$ **$5\sqrt{2}$**

New Concepts

Combining radicals is similar to combining like terms. When combining radical expressions, use like radicals. **Like radicals** have the same radicand and index. **Unlike radicals** have different radicands and/or index numbers.

Math Language

A **radicand** is the number or expression under a radical symbol.

Example 1 Combining Like Radicals

Simplify. All variables represent non-negative real numbers.

a. $2\sqrt{7} + 4\sqrt{7}$

SOLUTION

Add the like radicals together.

$2\sqrt{7} + 4\sqrt{7} = (2 + 4)\sqrt{7}$ Combine coefficients of like radicals.
$= 6\sqrt{7}$

b. $4\sqrt{xy} - 6\sqrt{xy}$

SOLUTION

Subtract the like radicals.

$4\sqrt{xy} - 6\sqrt{xy} = (4 - 6)\sqrt{xy}$ Combine coefficients of like radicals.
$= -2\sqrt{xy}$

c. $6\sqrt{2} + 8\sqrt{11}$

SOLUTION

No simplification is possible since the radicands are not alike.

d. $\dfrac{2\sqrt{5q}}{7} + \dfrac{3\sqrt{5q}}{7} - \dfrac{4\sqrt{3r}}{7}$

SOLUTION

$\dfrac{2\sqrt{5q}}{7} + \dfrac{3\sqrt{5q}}{7} + \dfrac{4\sqrt{3r}}{7}$

$= \dfrac{(2 + 3)\sqrt{5q}}{7} - \dfrac{4\sqrt{3r}}{7}$ Combine the like radicals.

$= \dfrac{5\sqrt{5q} - 4\sqrt{3r}}{7}$ Simplify.

www.SaxonMathResources.com

Lesson 69   449

---

1 Warm Up

Problems 4 and 5

It may be helpful to use the divisibility rules when finding perfect squares.

2 New Concepts

Remind students that in Lesson 61, they learned how to simplify radical expressions. In this lesson, students learn how to add and subtract radical expressions.

Example 1

Tell students that like radicals can be treated like variables when adding and subtracting them. For example, $2\sqrt{7} + 4\sqrt{7}$ can be thought of as $2x + 4x$.

Additional Example 1

Simplify. All variables represent non-negative real numbers.

a. $3\sqrt{5} + 6\sqrt{5}$ **$9\sqrt{5}$**

b. $7\sqrt{ab} - 2\sqrt{ab}$ **$5\sqrt{ab}$**

c. $8\sqrt{5} + 9\sqrt{7}$ **$8\sqrt{5} + 9\sqrt{7}$**

d. $\dfrac{4\sqrt{6r}}{5} + \dfrac{8\sqrt{6r}}{5} - \dfrac{6\sqrt{2s}}{5}$

$\dfrac{12\sqrt{6r} - 6\sqrt{2s}}{5}$

LESSON RESOURCES

Student Edition Practice Workbook 69
Reteaching Master 69
Adaptations Master 69
Challenge and Enrichment Master C69

MATH BACKGROUND

Students have already learned how to simplify radical expressions. They will be using this knowledge to add and subtract like radicals.

Tell students to think of simplified radicals as variables. If variables are alike, then students simply add or subtract the coefficients and keep the variable (or radical) the same. If variables are unlike, students cannot combine them, and must just write a plus or a minus sign between them.

Sometimes unlike radicals can become like radicals when simplified. Remind students to always try to simplify when they have unlike radicals.

Lesson 69   449

Example 2

Remind students to find perfect squares in the radicands to help simplify and find like radicals.

Error Alert Students may forget that when they pull squares out of the radicals, they must pull out the square root of the number and not the whole number. To help them keep track, tell students to rewrite the radicand in factored form before they take the square root. They should, for example, rewrite $\sqrt{100}$ as $\sqrt{10^2}$.

Additional Example 2

a. $4\sqrt{20n^3} + 5\sqrt{5n} + 3\sqrt{5n}$
$(8n + 8)\sqrt{5n}$

b. $d\sqrt{48d} - \sqrt{75d^3}$ $-d\sqrt{3d}$

Example 3

See if students notice that all the radicands are perfect squares.

Additional Example 3

Find the perimeter of a rectangle if the length is $6\sqrt{16}$ inches and the width is $3\sqrt{121}$ inches.
114 inches

It is not always apparent that radicals are alike until they are simplified. All radicals should be simplified before trying to identify like radicals.

Example 2 Simplifying Before Combining

Simplify. All variables represent non-negative real numbers.

a. $3\sqrt{8m^3} + 2\sqrt{2m} + 4\sqrt{2m}$

SOLUTION

Hint
Use the **Product Property of Radicals.** If $a \geq 0$ and $b \geq 0$, then $\sqrt{ab} = \sqrt{a} \cdot \sqrt{b}$.

$3\sqrt{8m^3} + 2\sqrt{2m} + 4\sqrt{2m}$
$= 3\sqrt{4 \cdot m^2 \cdot 2m} + 2\sqrt{2m} + 4\sqrt{2m}$ Factor the first radicand.
$= 3\sqrt{4} \cdot \sqrt{m^2} \cdot \sqrt{2m} + 2\sqrt{2m} + 4\sqrt{2m}$ Product Property of Radicals
$= 6m\sqrt{2m} + 2\sqrt{2m} + 4\sqrt{2m}$ Simplify $3\sqrt{4} \cdot \sqrt{m^2}$.
$= (6m + 2 + 4)\sqrt{2m}$ Factor out $\sqrt{2m}$.
$= (6m + 6)\sqrt{2m}$ Simplify.

b. $c\sqrt{75c} - \sqrt{27c^3}$

SOLUTION

$c\sqrt{75c} - \sqrt{27c^3}$
$= c\sqrt{25} \cdot \sqrt{3c} - \sqrt{9} \cdot \sqrt{c^2} \cdot \sqrt{3c}$ Factor the radicands.
$= 5c\sqrt{3c} - 3c\sqrt{3c}$ Simplify each expression.
$= (5c - 3c)\sqrt{3c}$ Factor out $\sqrt{3c}$.
$= 2c\sqrt{3c}$ Simplify.

Example 3 Application: Finding the Perimeter of a Triangle

Find the perimeter of a right triangle if the lengths of the two legs are $4\sqrt{9}$ inches and $2\sqrt{64}$ inches, and the hypotenuse is $2\sqrt{100}$ inches.

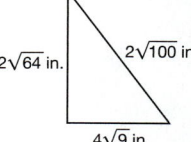

SOLUTION

The perimeter is the distance around the figure.

$P = 4\sqrt{9} + 2\sqrt{64} + 2\sqrt{100}$
$P = 4\sqrt{3^2} + 2\sqrt{8^2} + 2\sqrt{10^2}$ Factor each radicand.
$P = 4 \cdot 3 + 2 \cdot 8 + 2 \cdot 10$ Simplify each radical.
$P = 12 + 16 + 20$ Multiply.
$P = 48$ Add.

The perimeter is 48 inches.

ENGLISH LEARNERS

Explain the meaning of the word **identify**. Show a pen and a pencil to the students. Say:

"Identify means to find how something can be the same as or different from another thing. How can a pen or pencil be identified?"
Sample: Their shapes are alike, but one writes in lead, and the other in ink.

Discuss how other items found in the classroom can be identified.

Example 4 Application: Finding the Perimeter of a Swimming Pool

A rectangular swimming pool has a length of $\sqrt{800}$ feet and a width of $\sqrt{648}$ feet. What is its perimeter?

SOLUTION

Hint
Perimeter is the distance around a figure. Add the length of all 4 sides to find the perimeter of the pool.

Understand The length and width of a rectangle are given. Find the perimeter.

Plan Use the formula for perimeter and the length and width of the pool to write an equation.

Solve Perimeter $= l + l + w + w$

$P = \sqrt{800} + \sqrt{800} + \sqrt{648} + \sqrt{648}$
$P = \sqrt{20^2 \cdot 2} + \sqrt{20^2 \cdot 2} + \sqrt{18^2 \cdot 2} + \sqrt{18^2 \cdot 2}$ Factor each radicand.
$P = 20\sqrt{2} + 20\sqrt{2} + 18\sqrt{2} + 18\sqrt{2}$ Simplify each radical.
$P = 76\sqrt{2}$ feet   Add.

Check Square each simplified radical expression to make sure the radicals were simplified correctly.

$(20\sqrt{2})^2$ $\quad\quad\quad\quad\quad (18\sqrt{2})^2$
$\stackrel{?}{=} 20\sqrt{2} \cdot 20\sqrt{2}$ $\quad\quad \stackrel{?}{=} 18\sqrt{2} \cdot 18\sqrt{2}$
$\stackrel{?}{=} 400 \cdot 2$ $\quad\quad\quad\quad \stackrel{?}{=} 324 \cdot 2$
$= 800$ ✓ $\quad\quad\quad\quad\quad = 648$ ✓

The dimensions of the rectangular swimming pool are $\sqrt{800}$ and $\sqrt{648}$. So, the solution is correct.

Lesson Practice

Simplify. All variables represent non-negative real numbers.

a. $9\sqrt{5} + 8\sqrt{5}$ **$17\sqrt{5}$**
(Ex 1)

b. $11\sqrt{ab} - 23\sqrt{ab}$ **$-12\sqrt{ab}$**
(Ex 1)

c. $5\sqrt{7} + 3\sqrt{2}$ **$5\sqrt{7} + 3\sqrt{2}$**
(Ex 1)

d. $\dfrac{3\sqrt{2x}}{5} + \dfrac{2\sqrt{2x}}{5} - \dfrac{\sqrt{2x}}{5}$ **$\dfrac{4\sqrt{2x}}{5}$**
(Ex 1)

e. $4c\sqrt{3} - 8c\sqrt{2}$
f. $8\sqrt{10a}$
g. $6\sqrt{3} + 2\sqrt{15}$ meters

e. $4\sqrt{3c^2} - 8\sqrt{2c^2}$
(Ex 2)

f. $-11\sqrt{10a} + 3\sqrt{250a} + \sqrt{160a}$
(Ex 2)

g. Find the perimeter of a right triangle if the lengths of the two legs are $\sqrt{12}$ meters and $\sqrt{48}$ meters, and if the hypotenuse is $2\sqrt{15}$ meters.
(Ex 3)

h. A rectangular garden is $\sqrt{27a^2}$ feet wide and $\sqrt{75a^2}$ feet long. What is its perimeter? **$16a\sqrt{3}$ feet**
(Ex 4)

Lesson 69   451

Example 4
Extend the Example

"If the length of the swimming pool was $4\sqrt{8}$ feet shorter and the width was $3\sqrt{32}$ feet longer, what would the new perimeter be?" $84\sqrt{2}$ feet

Additonal Example 4
A rectangular backyard has a length of $3\sqrt{625}$ feet and a width of $2\sqrt{256}$ feet. What is its perimeter? 214 feet

Lesson Practice

Problem e
Scaffolding Ask students if they can simplify any of the radicals before they begin adding.

Problem g
Error Alert Students may forget that Perimeter $= l + l + w + w$ and only add the two radicals given. Students should write down the formula for perimeter to make sure they get all the numbers.

Check for Understanding

The questions below help assess the concepts taught in this lesson.

"What is necessary for adding and subtracting radical expressions?"
Sample: like radicals

"Can radical expressions without like radicals be added or subtracted?" Sample: only if the radicands can be simplified so that they are alike

---

ALTERNATE METHOD FOR EXAMPLE 4

It may help students to visualize the perimeter of the pool. Have students draw a rectangle and label the two lengths $\sqrt{800}$ ft and the two widths $\sqrt{648}$ ft. This will help them remember that the perimeter will be $P = l + l + w + w$. Some students might only add one length and one width to find the answer.

3 Practice

Math Conversations
Discussion to strengthen understanding

Problem 1
Remind students that when the radicals are alike, they should add or subtract the coefficients and keep the radical the same.

Problem 4
Remind students that the degree of a polynomial is the degree of the highest-degree term.

Problem 11
Guide students by asking them the following questions.

"What would *x* and *y* represent?"
Sample: *x* represents inches on the map and *y* represents miles.

"What is direct variation?"
Sample: a relationship between two variables whose ratio is constant

"What form does the equation take in a direct variation?"
Sample: The equation would be $y = kx$, where k is a nonzero constant.

Practice Distributed and Integrated

Add.

*1. $-6\sqrt{2} + 8\sqrt{2}$ $2\sqrt{2}$ *2. $-4\sqrt{7} - 5\sqrt{7}$ $-9\sqrt{7}$ *3. $2\sqrt{3} + 5\sqrt{3}$ $7\sqrt{3}$
(69)   (69)   (69)

Determine the degree.

4. $9x$ 1   5. $-3x^2 + 2x + 16$ 2   6. $xy + 2$ 2
(53)   (53)   (53)

Find the probability of the events described below.

*7. rolling a sum of 2 or a sum of 12 with two number cubes $\frac{1}{18}$
(68)

8. rolling a sum greater than 1 1
(68)

9. (Volleyball) A volleyball is hit upward from a height of 1.4 meters. The expression
(53) $-4.3t^2 + 7.7t + 1.4$ can be used to find the height (in meters) of the volleyball at time *t*. The ball was hit from a moving platform that has a height (in meters) of $-3t^2 + 5t + 6$. What is the combined height? $-7.3t^2 + 12.7t + 7.4$ meters

10. Display the data using a box-and-whisker plot titled "Hours a Candle Burns".
(54) Identify any outliers. 18 is an outlier.

4, 12, 3, 5, 7, 9, 4, 8, 3, 18, 5, 8, 4

11. **Multi-Step** The number of miles represented on a map varies directly with the
(56) number of inches on the map. In Texas, the distance from Austin to San Antonio is 79 miles; on a map, it is 5 inches.
a. Write the equation that represents this relationship.   11a. $y = 15.8x$, where *x* represents inches on a map and *y* represents miles.
b. Graph this relationship.
c. Estimate how far Waco is from Austin if they are $6\frac{1}{2}$ inches apart on a map. approximately 103 miles

12. (Produce Purchase) Bananas are $0.10 and apples are $0.25. The total cost for 35 pieces
(59) of fruit is $6.80. How many of each fruit were purchased? 13 bananas, 22 apples

13. **Multi-Step** Luke is building a new fence around his property.
(60) Write an expression for the area of the shaded region.
a. Find the area of the smaller square. x^2
b. Write an expression for the area of the larger square using special products. $(x + 10)(x + 10)$
c. Simplify part b. $x^2 + 20x + 100$
d. Write an expression for the area of the shaded region.
$x^2 + 20x + 100 - x^2 = 20x + 100$ square feet

14. **Generalize** Use examples to explain why $\sqrt{x^2} = -x$ for all negative values of *x*.
(61)

15. Solve the system of linear equations given below.
(63)
$$6x + 15y = 15$$
$$7x - 3y = -3$$ $(0, 1)$

11b.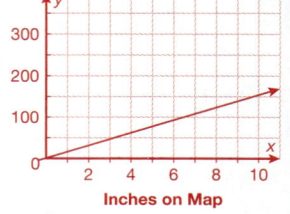

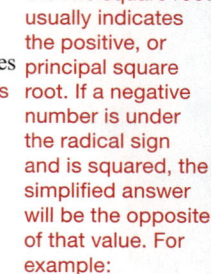
5 feet
5 feet

14. The square root usually indicates the positive, or principal square root. If a negative number is under the radical sign and is squared, the simplified answer will be the opposite of that value. For example:
$\sqrt{x^2} = -x$
$\sqrt{(-4)^2} = -(-4)$, when $x = -4$
$\sqrt{16} = 4$
$4 = 4$

10. Hours a Candle Burns
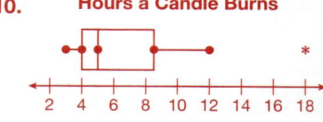

452 *Saxon Algebra 1*

INCLUSION

Students who have weak conceptualization or difficulty with abstract concepts may struggle with determining the like factors in a radical expression.

Have students read the radical expression aloud and listen for repeated words or phrases. Those that occur more than once in an expression likely indicate what to factor out of the expression using the Distributive Property.

16. Prom Night Jamal and his friends want to rent a limousine for prom night. The cost per person varies inversely with the number of people renting the limousine. If 4 people rent the limousine, it will cost them $180 each. How much would it cost per person if 12 people rented the limousine? **$60**

Determine if the lines are parallel or perpendicular.

17. $y = -\frac{3}{2}x + 8\frac{1}{2}$ and $y - \frac{2}{3}x = 0$ **perpendicular**

18. Data Analysis Rachel will receive an A in math for the semester if the mean of her test scores is at least 90. If her first two test scores are as shown in the table, write an inequality for the score Rachel needs on her third test to receive an A for the semester. $x \geq 90$

Test	Grade
Test 1	85
Test 2	95
Test 3	?

19. Analyze Graph the inequalities $x + 5 > 3$ and $x - 6 \leq -8$ on the same number line. What is true about their combined solutions?

20. Multiple Choice Which graph represents the solution to $x + 6 \geq 2x - 12$?   **B**

A 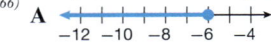   B 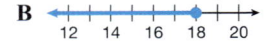   19. ;

C (same as A range -12 to -4)   D (range -20 to -12)

Sample: Together they include all real numbers but have no solutions in common.

21. Find the common solution for the system of equations given below.

$$-\frac{1}{4}x + y = -2$$
$$-x + 4y = -8$$

Any ordered pair (x, y) that satisfies the equation $y = \frac{1}{4}x - 2$.

22. Error Analysis Two students found a common solution for a system of equations. Which student is correct? Explain the error.   Student A; Sample: Student B did not interpret the solution correctly.

Student A	Student B
$y = -5x - 2$	$y = -5x - 2$
$6y = -30x - 12$	$6y = -30x - 12$
$-6y = +30x + 12$	$-6y = +30x + 12$
$6y = -30x - 12$	$6y = -30x - 12$
$0 = 0$	$0 = 0$
Solution:	Solution:
$y = -5x - 2$	$(0, 0)$

*23. Sanitation A garbage truck is on time with its collections if it maintains an average rate of $y = 75x + 5$. Currently, the truck is running at a rate of $\frac{1}{5}y - 15x = 1$. Is the garbage truck on schedule?   Sample: The equations are dependent, so the truck is on schedule.

Lesson 69   453

Problem 17
Remind students that parallel lines have the same slope and perpendicular lines have slopes that are negative reciprocals of each other.

Extend the Problem
"At which point do they intersect?"
$\left(3\frac{12}{13}, 2\frac{8}{13}\right)$

Problem 18
Guide students by asking, "How do you find the mean of a set of values?" Sample: Divide the sum of the values by the number of data values.

Problem 21
Remind students to put the equations in slope-intercept form. Guide them to see that both equations represent the same line and, therefore, have infinitely many solutions; the solution is the line.

CHALLENGE

Have students find the missing radicands in these true statements.

a. $\sqrt{\square} - \sqrt{3} = -\sqrt{3}$ **0**

b. $-2\sqrt{\square} = -6\sqrt{x}$ **9x**

c. $3x\sqrt{x} + \sqrt{\square} = 5x\sqrt{x}$ **4x³**

24. Error Analysis Two students found the probability of choosing either a black 2 or a king from a deck of cards. Which student is correct? Explain the error.

Student A	Student B
$P(A \text{ or } B) = \frac{2}{52} + \frac{4}{52}$	$P(A \text{ or } B) = \frac{2}{52} \cdot \frac{4}{52}$
$= \frac{6}{52}$	$= \frac{8}{2704}$
$= \frac{3}{26}$	$= \frac{1}{338}$

24. Student A; Sample: Student B multiplied the individual probabilities instead of adding them.

*25. Multi-Step Miranda baked several casseroles: 36 servings of chicken casserole, 24 servings of pasta casserole, 30 servings of beef casserole, and 28 servings of vegetarian casserole. She gives 1 serving to her brother. What is the probability that he will get a pasta casserole or a vegetarian casserole?
a. What is the probability that the serving will be pasta? $\frac{12}{59}$
b. What is the probability that the serving will be vegetarian? $\frac{14}{59}$
c. What is the probability that the serving will be pasta or vegetarian? $\frac{26}{59}$

26. If a circle is made into the spinner shown, what is the probability of landing on either a black space or a space worth 10 points? $\frac{5}{8}$

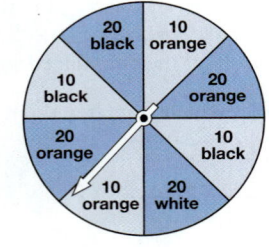

27. Analyze True or False: For the set of integers, $\sqrt{x^n}$ can be simplified when $x \geq 0$ and $n \geq 2$. Justify your answer.

27. true; Sample: If n is an even number greater than or equal to 2, the radical will be eliminated. If n is an odd number greater than 2, an x will remain under the radical.

*28. Error Analysis Ms. Nguyen asks her students if they can combine the radicals in the expression $\sqrt{13x} + \sqrt{23x} - \sqrt{33x}$. Student A says it is possible. Student B says that the radicals in the expressions $\sqrt{13x} + \sqrt{23x} - \sqrt{33x}$ do not combine. Which student is correct? Explain the error.

*29. Estimate Estimate the sum of $\sqrt{51} + \sqrt{63} + \sqrt{83} + \sqrt{104}$. Sample: 34

*30. Great Pyramid Each of the four sides of the base of the Great Pyramid measures 756 feet. If a scale model is made with the measurement of $\sqrt{756}$ inches for each side of the base, how many inches is the perimeter of the base of the scale model of the pyramid rounded to the nearest whole number? 110 in.

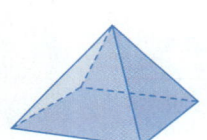

28. Student B; Sample: The radicals have different radicands and the radicands cannot be further simplified. Therefore, the radicals cannot combine.

454 Saxon Algebra 1

LOOKING FORWARD

Adding and subtracting radical expressions prepares students for

- **Lesson 76** Multiplying Radical Expressions
- **Lesson 103** Dividing Radical Expressions
- **Lesson 106** Solving Radical Equations
- **Lesson 114** Graphing Square-Root Functions

LESSON 70

Solving Inequalities by Multiplying or Dividing

Warm Up

1. **Vocabulary** The _____ of an inequality in one variable is a value or set of values that satisfies the inequality. **solution**
   (50)

Solve.

2. $12x = -84$ $x = -7$
   (21)

3. $-7x = -91$ $x = 13$
   (21)

Graph each inequality.

4. $x > -1$
   (50)

5. $x \leq 4$
   (50)

New Concepts

When multiplying an inequality by a positive value, the order of the inequality does not change.

$5 > 3$, so $5(2) > 3(2)$ $8 < 12$, so $8(4) < 12(4)$

Math Language

The **order of the inequality** refers to the direction of the inequality symbol. If $x > 2$ is rewritten $x < 2$, then the order of the inequality has changed.

Multiplication Property of Inequality for $c > 0$
For every real number a and b, and $c > 0$:
If $a > b$, then $ac > bc$.   If $a < b$, then $ac < bc$.
This property is also true for $\geq$ and $\leq$.

Example 1 Multiplying by a Positive Number

Solve, graph, and check the solution for the inequality $\frac{1}{2}x \leq 8$.

SOLUTION

Solve the inequality.

$\frac{1}{2}x \leq 8$

$(2)\frac{1}{2}x \leq 8(2)$ Multiplication Property of Inequality for $c > 0$

$x \leq 16$ Simplify.

Graph the solution on a number line.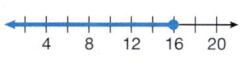

Hint

When checking the direction of an inequality, any value in the solution set can be substituted. Generally, it is best to select a value that can be easily computed.

Check

Check the endpoint.

$\frac{1}{2}x \stackrel{?}{=} 8$

$\frac{1}{2}(16) \stackrel{?}{=} 8$

$8 = 8$ ✓

Check the direction of the inequality.

$\frac{1}{2}x \stackrel{?}{\leq} 8$

$\frac{1}{2}(14) \stackrel{?}{\leq} 8$

$7 \leq 8$ ✓

Both statements are true, so the solution is correct.

Online Connection
www.SaxonMathResources.com

Lesson 70   455

MATH BACKGROUND

The solution set of an inequality can be written in interval notation. Interval notation consists of endpoints contained inside parentheses or square brackets. Parentheses are used to represent endpoints that are not included in the set. Square brackets are used to represent endpoints that are included in the set. The infinity symbols are used to indicate a set that is unbounded.

For instance, the solution set for the inequality $x < 2$ can be written as $(-\infty, 2)$. Parentheses are always used with infinity symbols. Intersection and union symbols are used to describe compound inequalities. The solution set for the compound inequality $-5 < x < 2$ or $x > 7$ can be written as $(-5, 2) \cup (7, \infty)$.

Example 2

Point out that the inequality sign reverses direction when both sides of the inequality are multiplied by a negative number.

Additional Example 2

Solve, graph, and check the solution for the inequality $\frac{-x}{2} < 7$. $x > -14$

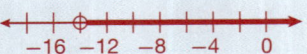

Error Alert Students may forget the negative sign when multiplying by the reciprocal. Remind students that the reciprocal of a negative number is also negative.

Math Language

A **transformation** is a change in a statement that is the result of an operation performed on an equality or inequality.

Hint

When the coefficient of a variable of an inequality is a fraction, multiply by the reciprocal to solve.

When solving an equation, the equality symbol never changes. Each transformation results in an equation equivalent to the previous equation. Multiplying an inequality by a positive value is similar to solving an equation because the symbol of inequality does not change, regardless of the operations required to solve the statement. However, when multiplying an inequality by a negative value, the order of the inequality does change.

$5 > 3$, so $5(-2) < 3(-2)$ because $-10 < -6$.
$8 < 12$, so $8(-4) > 12(-4)$ because $-32 > -48$.

Multiplication Property of Inequality for $c < 0$
For every real number a and b, and $c < 0$:
If $a > b$, then $ac < bc$.
If $a < b$, then $ac > bc$.
This property is also true for $\geq$ and $\leq$.

Example 2 Multiplying by a Negative Number

Solve, graph, and check the solution for the inequality $\frac{-x}{5} < 5$.

SOLUTION

Solve the inequality.

$$\frac{-x}{5} < 5$$

$$(-5)\frac{-x}{5} > 5(-5) \quad \text{Multiplication Property of Inequality for } c < 0$$

$$x > -25 \quad \text{Simplify.}$$

Graph the solution on a number line.

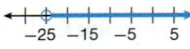

Check

Check the endpoint.

$$\frac{-x}{5} \stackrel{?}{=} 5$$

$$\frac{-(-25)}{5} \stackrel{?}{=} 5$$

$$\frac{25}{5} \stackrel{?}{=} 5$$

$$5 = 5 \checkmark$$

Check the direction of the inequality.

$$\frac{-x}{5} \stackrel{?}{<} 5$$

$$\frac{-(-20)}{5} \stackrel{?}{<} 5$$

$$\frac{20}{5} \stackrel{?}{<} 5$$

$$4 < 5 \checkmark$$

Both statements are true, so the solution is correct.

INCLUSION

To help students understand why the direction of an inequality switches when multiplying both sides of an inequality by a negative number, use two-color tiles to represent the situation. Use one color to show positive numbers and the other color to show negative numbers. Coach students as they act out the operation by reminding them about the rules for multiplying signed numbers.

When dividing an inequality by a positive value, the order of the inequality does not change.

$$6 > 4, \text{ so } \frac{6}{2} > \frac{4}{2}. \qquad 8 < 12, \text{ so } \frac{8}{4} < \frac{12}{4}.$$

Division Property of Inequality for $c > 0$

For every real number a and b, and $c > 0$:

If $a > b$, then $\frac{a}{c} > \frac{b}{c}$. 　　　If $a < b$, then $\frac{a}{c} < \frac{b}{c}$.

This property is also true for $\geq$ and $\leq$.

Example 3   Dividing by a Positive Number

Solve, graph, and check the solution for the inequality $18 > 3r$.

SOLUTION

Solve the inequality.

$18 > 3r$

$\frac{18}{3} > \frac{3r}{3}$　　Division Property of Inequality for $c > 0$

$6 > r$　　Simplify.

Graph the solution on a number line.

Check

Check the endpoint.　　　　　Check the direction of the inequality.

$18 \stackrel{?}{=} 3r$ 　　　　　　　　　　　$18 \stackrel{?}{>} 3r$

$18 \stackrel{?}{=} 3(6)$　　　　　　　　　　$18 \stackrel{?}{>} 3(5)$

$18 = 18$ ✓ 　　　　　　　　　$18 > 15$ ✓

Both statements are true so the solution is correct.

When dividing an inequality by a negative value, the order of the inequality changes.

$$6 > 4, \text{ so } \frac{6}{-2} < \frac{4}{-2}. \qquad 8 < 12, \text{ so } \frac{8}{-4} > \frac{12}{-4}.$$

Division Property of Inequality for $c < 0$

For every real number a and b, and $c < 0$:

If $a > b$, then $\frac{a}{c} < \frac{b}{c}$. 　　　If $a < b$, then $\frac{a}{c} > \frac{b}{c}$.

This property is also true for $\geq$ and $\leq$.

Caution

When the variable is on the right side of the inequality, be careful to read the inequality symbol correctly. $6 > r$ means that r is less than 6.

Example 3

Remind students that dividing both sides of an inequality by a positive number is the same as multiplying by the reciprocal of a positive number.

Additional Example 3

Solve, graph, and check the solution for the inequality $21 > 7x$. $3 > x$

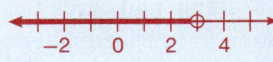

ALTERNATE METHOD FOR EXAMPLE 3

Students can use mental math to find the endpoint. Have students use their knowledge of basic facts to find a number that when multiplied by 3 equals 18.

Lesson 70

Example 4

Point out that the inequality sign reverses direction when both sides of the inequality are divided by a negative number, as with multiplication by a negative number. Remind them that this is true for $\geq$ and $\leq$ as well as $>$ and $<$.

Additional Example 4
Solve, graph, and check the solution for the inequality $-5x \leq 30$. $x \geq -6$

Example 5

Extend the Example
"Donald is looking for a job that pays at least $30,000. How much commission should the employment agency expect to make?" $c \geq \$4500$

Additional Example
A real estate agent receives a commission of 3% for every house sold. What price must a home be sold at in order for the agent to earn at least $6000? $h \geq \$200,000$

Example 4 Dividing by a Negative Number

Solve, graph, and check the solution for the inequality $-4m \geq 7$.

SOLUTION

Solve the inequality.

$-4m \geq 7$

$\dfrac{-4m}{-4} \leq \dfrac{7}{-4}$ Division Property of Inequality for $c < 0$

$m \leq -1\dfrac{3}{4}$ Simplify. Write the solution as a mixed number.

Graph the solution on a number line.

Check

Check the endpoint.

$-4m \stackrel{?}{=} 7$

$-4\left(-1\dfrac{3}{4}\right) \stackrel{?}{=} 7$

$7 = 7$ ✓

Check the direction of the inequality.

$-4m \stackrel{?}{\geq} 7$

$-4(-2) \stackrel{?}{\geq} 7$

$8 \geq 7$ ✓

Both statements are true, so the solution is correct.

Math Reasoning

Connect Solving inequalities is exactly the same as solving equations. Do you agree or disagree with the statement? Explain.

Sample: disagree; In an inequality, when you multiply or divide by a negative number, the comparison symbol is reversed. In an equation, when you multiply or divide by a negative number, the equal sign is unchanged.

Example 5 Application: Business

An employment agency charges a company 15% of the salary for every position filled. What salary must a company pay a new employee for the employment agency to earn a commission of at least $6000?

SOLUTION

Write and solve an inequality.

$0.15s \geq 6000$

$\dfrac{0.15s}{0.15} \geq \dfrac{6000}{0.15}$ Division Property of Inequality for $c > 0$

$s \geq 40,000$ Simplify.

Any salary of $40,000 or more will earn a commission of at least $6000.

Check

Check the endpoint.

$0.15s \stackrel{?}{=} 6000$

$0.15(40,000) \stackrel{?}{=} 6000$

$6000 = 6000$

Check the direction of the inequality.

$0.15s \stackrel{?}{\geq} 6000$

$0.15(50,000) \stackrel{?}{\geq} 6000$

$7500 \geq 6000$ ✓

Math Reasoning

Analyze When solving word problems with inequalities, think about what restrictions exist on the solution set. What are restrictions for this business application?

Sample: rational numbers up to the hundredths place

ENGLISH LEARNERS

English learners may not know what a **commission** is. Explain that a commission is usually money paid to an employee that is a percentage of the money the employee made for the company through a sale.

In the case of Example 5, a commission is the amount an employment agency charges for the service of finding an employee to fill a position. The company that needs a new worker pays a percentage of the amount the worker will receive in his first year. The worker receives the entire amount of the salary, but the company pays the employment agency a percentage of what they will pay the worker, so as not to have to do the searching for an employee on their own.

a. $n < 6$;

-2 0 2 4 6

See student work.

c. $w \leq 9\frac{1}{2}$;

6 7 8 9 10

See student work.

d. $-\frac{1}{8} \leq a$;

$-\frac{1}{8}$ 0 $\frac{1}{8}$ $\frac{2}{8}$ $\frac{3}{8}$ $\frac{4}{8}$ $\frac{5}{8}$ $\frac{6}{8}$ $\frac{7}{8}$ 1

See student work.

Lesson Practice

Solve, graph, and check the solution for each inequality.

a. (Ex 1) $\frac{1}{3}n < 2$

b. (Ex 2) $\frac{-x}{4} < 8$

c. (Ex 3) $6w \leq 57$

d. (Ex 4) $\frac{1}{2} \geq -4a$

e. (Ex 5) Barney earns a 4% commission on what he sells. How much does he need to sell to earn at least a $750 commission every month? **$18,750 or more**

b. $x > -32$;

-32 -30 -28

See student work.

Practice Distributed and Integrated

Find the probability of the following events.

1. (68) tossing a coin heads-up or rolling a 3 with a number cube $\frac{7}{12}$

2. (68) tossing a coin tails-up or rolling a number less than 4 on a number cube $\frac{3}{4}$

3. (33) tossing a coin tails-up and rolling a number greater than 6 on a number cube **0**

Solve the inequality.

4. (66) $y - 2 < \frac{1}{2}$ $y < 2\frac{1}{2}$

5. (66) $y + \frac{3}{2} < \frac{1}{4}$ $y < -1\frac{1}{4}$

Add.

*6. (69) $18\sqrt{3y} + 8\sqrt{3y}$ $26\sqrt{3y}$

7. (69) $\sqrt{3x} + 2\sqrt{3x}$ $3\sqrt{3x}$

8. (64) Write an inverse variation equation relating x and y when $x = 18$ and $y = 4.5$. $y = \frac{81}{x}$

9. (70) Determine if the inequality symbol needs to be reversed, and then solve.

$$-2a \geq -5 \quad \text{yes; } a \leq 2.5$$

*10. (54) A team scores 56, 42, 60, 43, 51, 22, 44, 55, and 49 points.

a. Identify any outliers. **22**

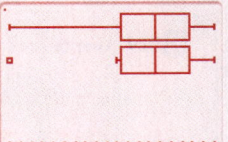

10b.

b. On the same screen of the graphing calculator, make one box-and-whisker plot of these data without identifying any outliers, and make another box-and-whisker plot that does identify any outliers.

c. How many points would you expect the team to score in the next game? Explain your answer. **Sample: about 50 points; Excluding the outlier, both the mean and median of the scores are 50 points.**

11. (54) (Ages) The ages at a family party are recorded. **See Additional Answers.**

5, 30, 33, 42, 36, 40, 1, 44, 29, 61, 82, 63, 29, 38, 6, 11

Make a box-and-whisker plot of these ages and determine if there is an outlier.

*12. (55) Use the graphing calculator to determine the solution to the following system. **(1, −3)**

$$x + y = -2$$
$$y = 4x - 7$$

Lesson 70   459

Lesson Practice

Problem b

Scaffolding Before solving, ask students to rewrite the left side of the inequality as a variable multiplied by a fraction.

Problem d

Error Alert Students might solve the problem by dividing the left side by 4, but not know how to divide a fraction by another number. Remind students that

$$\frac{\frac{x}{y}}{\frac{w}{z}} = \frac{x}{y} \cdot \frac{z}{w}$$

Check for Understanding

The questions below help assess the concepts taught in this lesson.

"Why check the solution of an inequality with a number that is not the endpoint?" Sample: to verify the direction of the inequality symbol

"Explain how to solve an inequality that involves multiplying or dividing by a negative number." Sample: Solve normally and reverse the inequality sign when multiplying or dividing by a negative number.

Lesson 70   459

3 Practice

Math Conversations
Discussion to strengthen understanding

Problem 13
Point out that in this problem, a ball can have more than one design.

Problem 15
Error Alert
Students may express the square of a square root of a number as the number raised to the second power. Help students remember that $\sqrt{w} \cdot \sqrt{w} = w$.

Problem 20
Encourage students to use mathematical reasoning to identify solutions. If two equations have a different number of terms, they cannot be multiples of each other.

---

13. Multi-Step Balls are printed in a pattern. Every 18th ball has stripes, every 15th ball (57) has polka dots, and every 30th ball has stars.

a. How many balls must be printed to get the first ball with stripes, polka dots, and stars? **90**

b. How many balls have been printed at that point that have only two of the designs? **2**

14. Building Jason is building a square deck around his home. His home is also in (60) the shape of a square. He wants the deck to be 9 feet wide around the outer edge of his house. The house has a total side length of $8x$. Write a special product and simplify to find the area of the house including the deck. $(8x + 18)^2 = 64x^2 + 288x + 324$ square feet

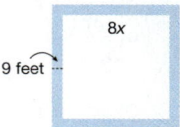

15. Golden Rectangle The length of a golden rectangle is equal to $x + x\sqrt{5}$. If $x = \sqrt{5}$, (61) what is the length of the golden rectangle? $\sqrt{5} + 5$

16. Multi-Step The data below show the number of customers served each day for (62) a month at a diner.

80, 86, 105, 109, 127, 148, 137, 148, 141, 140, 135, 146, 90, 95, 101, 83, 114, 148, 127, 86, 85, 91, 141, 136, 82, 148, 127, 149, 80, 86

a. Create a stem-and-leaf plot of the data.

b. **Analyze** Describe the distribution of the data. What conclusions can be drawn from this? Sample: The data is not distributed evenly; it is clustered at the upper and lower extremes. This means the diner is usually extremely busy or relatively slow.

16a.
Customers Served Per Day

Stem	Leaves
8	0, 0, 2, 3, 5, 6, 6, 6
9	0, 1, 5
10	1, 5, 9
11	4
12	7, 7, 7
13	5, 6, 7
14	0, 1, 1, 6, 8, 8, 8, 8, 9

Key : 10|1 means 101

17. Solve the following system using the elimination method.
(63)
$$-8x - 5y = -52$$
$$4x + 3y = 28$$ (4, 4)

18. Decibel Levels The relationship between the intensity of sound (W/m²) and the (64) distance from the source of the sound is represented by the equation $I = \frac{k}{d^2}$. If you sit only 1 meter away from the stage at a rock concert, the intensity of sound is about 0.1 W/m². If Vanessa does not want the sound intensity to be any more than 0.0001 W/m², how close to the stage can she sit? about 32 meters

*19. Coordinate Geometry Prove that $ABCD$ is a rectangle.
(65)

$m\overleftrightarrow{AB} = \frac{3}{2}$, $m\overleftrightarrow{CD} = \frac{3}{2}$, and $\overleftrightarrow{AB} \parallel \overleftrightarrow{CD}$. $m\overleftrightarrow{AD} = -\frac{2}{3}$, $m\overleftrightarrow{BC} = -\frac{2}{3}$, $\overleftrightarrow{AD} \parallel \overleftrightarrow{BC}$, and $\overleftrightarrow{AB} \perp \overleftrightarrow{AD} \perp \overleftrightarrow{CD} \perp \overleftrightarrow{BC} \perp \overleftrightarrow{AB}$. Therefore, $ABCD$ is a rectangle.

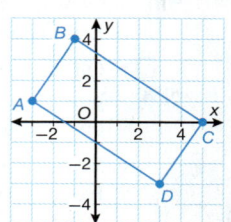

20. Multiple Choice Which one of the following systems has only one common (67) solution? **A**

A $y = 21x + 6$
   $y = -7x$

B $5x - 2y = 0$
   $\frac{5}{2}x - y = 0$

C $-y = 13x - 6$
   $-2y = 26x + 9$

D $x - 7y = 14$
   $\frac{1}{4}x - \frac{7}{4}y = \frac{7}{2}$

460 Saxon Algebra 1

CHALLENGE

Have students formulate and solve an inequality for the problem below.

At least 30% of a solution must be salt to form a usable solution. If there are only 7.8 grams of salt, then how many grams of solution can be formed? $0.3x \leq 7.8$; $x \leq 26$ grams

21. Write What kind of system is formed by two equations where one equation is a multiple of the other? Explain.   Sample: The system is consistent and dependent because both equations are the graph of the same line.

22. Error Analysis Two students found the probability of choosing either a black card or a face card from a deck of cards. Which student is correct? Explain the error.

22. Student B; Sample: Student A treated the events as being mutually exclusive.

Student A	Student B
$P(A \text{ or } B) = \frac{26}{52} + \frac{12}{52}$	$P(A \text{ or } B) = \frac{26}{52} + \frac{12}{52} - \frac{6}{52}$
$= \frac{38}{52}$	$= \frac{32}{52}$
$= \frac{19}{26}$	$= \frac{8}{13}$

*23. Fantasy Football In fantasy football, virtual teams are built by choosing from a pool of real players. In one pool of players, 72 play only defense, 65 play only offense, 8 play both, and 27 are on special teams. If at least one player must be chosen at random, what is the probability that the player will play either offense or special teams? $\frac{100}{172} = \frac{25}{43}$

24. Geometry One side of a square measures $2\sqrt{9}$ meters. What is its perimeter? 24 meters

*25. What must be true about the coefficient of a linear function if that function experiences a vertical compression of the parent function?   The absolute value of that coefficient would be between 0 and 1.

26. Multi-Step A flag displayed in the school measures $6\sqrt{4}$ feet by $5\sqrt{4}$ feet. If the school decides to display 8 flags, what is the total measurement of the sides of all the flags?   352 ft

*27. Multiple Choice Which graph shows the solution set of $5f > -10$?   A

A    C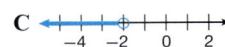

B    D

*28. Write Explain in your own words how to solve the inequality $-\frac{2}{5}g \leq 6$.   Multiply both sides by $-\frac{5}{2}$ and reverse the inequality sign.

*29. Analyze Kyle wants to spend at most $100 for birthday presents for the 4 other members of his family this year. He plans to spend the same amount on each person. Write and solve an inequality to represent the situation. What restrictions exist on the solution set? $4s \leq 100$; $s \leq 25$; The solutions are between 0 and 25 and are rational numbers to the hundredths place.

*30. Cooking Marianna can afford to buy at most 20 pounds of ground turkey. Write and solve an inequality to determine the number of burgers she can make if each patty uses $\frac{1}{3}$ pound of ground turkey. $\frac{1}{3}b \leq 20$; at most 60 burgers

Lesson 70   461

Problem 21
Extend the Problem
"Describe the graph of two equations when one equation is a multiple of the other." Sample: There is a single line.

Problem 22
Some students may not know the characteristics of a deck of cards. Use a deck to explain the different kinds of cards.

Problem 30
Extend the Problem
"If Marianna bought another 20 pounds of ground turkey, how could she use a proportion to find the greatest number of burgers she can make?" Sample: She can create a proportion to find the new endpoint of the graph. The direction of inequality will remain the same. $\frac{20}{60} = \frac{40}{x}$, $x = 120$, $x < 120$

LOOKING FORWARD

Solving inequalities by multiplying or dividing prepares students for

- **Lesson 73** Solving Compound Inequalities
- **Lesson 81** Solving Inequalities with Variables on Both Sides
- **Lesson 82** Solving Multi-Step Compound Inequalities

INVESTIGATION 7

Materials
- graphing calculator

Alternate Materials
- centimeter grid paper

Discuss
In this investigation, students compare direct and inverse variation using formulas, tables, and graphs.

Define variation and function. Explain that students can graph a function on their calculator to determine whether it is direct or inverse variation.

Problem 3
Extend the Problem

"If Alex starts walking at a constant rate of 4 miles per hour for $1\frac{1}{2}$ hours, how many miles will he have walked?" **6 miles**

"If you were to graph this variation, would the graph be linear or non linear?" **linear**

INVESTIGATION RESOURCES

Reteaching Master
 Investigation 7

INVESTIGATION 7

Comparing Direct and Inverse Variation

Math Language
The phrase **held constant** means that a variable is given a particular value. For example, if r is held constant with a value of 55, then $d = 55t$ in the expression $d = rt$.

Many situations involve direct or inverse variation. The formula $d = r \cdot t$, which relates distance, speed, and time, can represent either direct or inverse variation depending on the variable that is held constant.

A direct variation is a relationship between two variables whose ratio is constant. The equation $y = kx$, where k is a nonzero constant called the constant of variation, shows direct variation between variables x and y.

Identify the constant of variation, given that y varies directly with x. Then write the equation of variation.

1. y is 10 when x is 2. $k = 5; y = 5x$
2. y is 3 when x is 6. $k = \frac{1}{2}; y = \frac{1}{2}x$

The equation of direct variation can be written equivalently as $\frac{y}{x} = k$.

(Distance) Alex walks 3 miles per hour. If he walks at that rate for twice as long, he will travel twice as far. The ratio of the distance and time is always the same.

3. Identify the constant of variation. Rate is the constant of variation.; $k = 3$
4. **Model** Write an equation of direct variation that relates Alex's time to his distance traveled. $d = 3t; \frac{d}{t} = 3$

In inverse variation, when x increases, y decreases. An inverse variation describes a relationship between two variables whose product is a constant. The equation $xy = k$, where k is a nonzero constant, defines an inverse variation between x and y.

Identify the constant of variation, given that y varies inversely with x. Then write the equation of variation.

5. y is 1 when x is 3. $k = 3; xy = 3$
6. y is 4 when x is $\frac{1}{2}$. $k = 2; xy = 2$

The equation of inverse variation can be written equivalently as $y = \frac{k}{x}$.

Math Reasoning
Justify Show that the two equations for inverse variation are equivalent.

$xy = k$
$\frac{xy}{x} = \frac{k}{x}$
$y = \frac{k}{x}$

Notice the difference between the equations for inverse and direct variation. Inverse variation is the quotient of k and x, whereas direct variation is the product of k and x.

(Rate) Alex lives 4 miles from school. If he walks at a slower rate than normal, it will take him longer to reach his destination. In other words, the more time he spends walking home, the slower he is actually walking. This situation represents inverse variation.

7. Identify the constant of variation. Distance is the constant of variation.; $k = 4$
8. **Model** Write an equation of inverse variation that relates Alex's time to his rate of speed. $r = \frac{4}{t}$ or $r \cdot t = 4$

Online Connection
www.SaxonMathResources.com

MATH BACKGROUND

Direct and inverse variation statements are not always simple statements of direct variation or inverse variation. Often one variable will vary as the other variable squared or the other variable cubed.

For example, the distance D required to stop is directly proportional to the square of the velocity V. This statement is represented by the equation $D = kV^2$, where k is the constant of variation.

The weight W of a body varies inversely with the square of the distance D to the center of the earth. This statement is represented by the equation $W = \frac{k}{D^2}$ where k is the constant of variation. The equation $S = \frac{k}{R^3}$ represents the strength S of a field inversely proportional to the cube of the radius R.

These problems are solved just as simple variation problems are solved.

11. Sample: A direct-variation graph is linear and contains the origin. An inverse-variation graph is not linear and never intersects the *x*-axis.

Math Reasoning

Analyze Why will the graph of the inverse function never reach the *x*-axis as *x* increases?

If the graph reaches the *x*-axis, that means $y = 0$. Since the function takes on the form $y = \frac{k}{x}$ and $k \neq 0$, y will never equal zero. Thus, the graph will never touch or cross the *x*-axis.

Exploration: Determining Characteristics of Variation Graphs

Graph the functions on a graphing calculator and complete the table.
See Additional Answers.

	Direct or Inverse Variation	Linear or Not Linear	*x*–Intercept
9. $y = 3x$	Direct	Linear	(0, 0)
10. $y = \frac{1}{x}$	Inverse	Not Linear	None

11. What are the differences between the graph of a direct variation and an inverse variation?

Formulate Make a graph to determine whether the data show variation. If so, indicate the type of variation and write an equation of variation.

12. The table shows the force *F*, in Newtons, needed to move a rock a distance *d*, in meters, along the ground. inverse variation; $F = \frac{600}{d}$; See Additional Answers.

Distance	1	2	3	4	5
Force	600	300	200	150	120

13. The table shows an employee's pay *p* per number of hours worked *h*. direct variation; $p = 8.5h$; See Additional Answers.

Hours Worked (*h*)	1	2	3	4	5
Pay (*p*)	$8.50	$17.00	$25.50	$34.00	$42.50

Investigation Practice

Identify the constant of variation. Then write the equation of variation.

a. *y* varies directly with *x*; $y = 14$ when $x = 2$. $k = 7; y = 7x$

b. *w* varies inversely with *z*; $w = -8$ when $z = 3$. $k = -24; w = \frac{-24}{z}$

c. A recipe calls for 3 tomatoes to make 9 servings of salsa. Write an equation of variation where *t* represents the number of tomatoes and *s* represents the number of salsa servings. If Alex has 5 tomatoes, how many servings can he make? $s = 3t$; 15 servings

d. The table compares the pressure *P* in atmospheres to the volume of oxygen *V* in liters at 0°C. Make a graph to determine whether the data show direct or inverse variation. If so, find the equation of variation.
See Additional Answers.

Pressure	25	50	100	200	500
Volume	2.80	1.40	0.70	0.35	0.14

Investigation 7   463

Discuss

When using a table to determine variation, students should first make a graph to decide if they should write an inverse or direct-variation equation.

Investigation Practice

Math Conversations
Discussion to strengthen understanding

Problem a

Scaffolding
Guide students by asking them the following questions.

"Which equation shows direct variation between *x* and *y*?" $y = kx$

"How do you write this equation so that *k* is by itself?" Divide both sides by *x*; $k = \frac{y}{x}$

Problem b

Error Alert
Students may use the equation $y = kx$ instead of $k = xy$. Explain to students that for an inverse variation, the constant is the product of two variables.

Problem d
After students make a graph, remind them that direct variation is linear and that inverse variation is not linear.

 ENGLISH LEARNERS

Explain that **variation** is used to describe instances other than in math, such as variations in musical compositions or in sizes of different dog breeds. Say:

"Variation can be a slight change in something. For instance, aqua and navy blue are two different variations of the primary color blue."

Have volunteers describe other variations.
Sample: the same note played on different instruments, the size or intensity of rain drops

LOOKING FORWARD

Comparing direct and inverse variation prepares students for

- **Lesson 71** Making and Analyzing Scatter Plots
- **Lesson 78** Graphing Rational Expressions
- **Investigation 8** Identifying and Writing Joint Variation
- **Lesson 99** Solving Rational Equations

Investigation 7   463

SECTION OVERVIEW 8

Lesson Planner

Lesson	New Concepts
LAB 7	Graphing Calculator: Finding the Line of Best Fit
71	Making and Analyzing Scatter Plots
72	Factoring Trinomials: $x^2 + bx + c$
73	Solving Compound Inequalities
74	Solving Absolute-Value Equations
75	Factoring Trinomials: $ax^2 + bx + c$
	Cumulative Test 14, Performance Task 14
76	Multiplying Radical Expressions
77	Solving Two-Step and Multi-Step Inequalities
78	Graphing Rational Functions
79	Factoring Trinomials by Using the GCF
80	Calculating Frequency Distributions
	Cumulative Test 15, Performance Task 15
INV 8	Investigation: Identifying and Writing Joint Variation

Resources for Teaching
- Student Edition
- Teacher's Edition
- Student Edition eBook
- Teacher's Edition eBook
- Resources and Planner CD
- Solutions Manual
- Instructional Masters
- Technology Lab Masters
- Warm Up and Teaching Transparencies
- Instructional Presentations CD
- Online activities, tools, and homework help www.SaxonMathResources.com

Resources for Practice and Assessment
- Student Edition Practice Workbook
- Course Assessments
- Standardized Test Practice
- College Entrance Exam Practice
- Test and Practice Generator CD using ExamView™

Resources for Differentiated Instruction
- Reteaching Masters
- Challenge and Enrichment Masters
- Prerequisite Skills Intervention
- Adaptations for Saxon Algebra 1
- Multilingual Glossary
- English Learners Handbook
- TI Resources

Pacing Guide

 Resources and Planner CD for lesson planning support

45-Minute Class

Day 1	Day 2	Day 3	Day 4	Day 5	Day 6
Lab 7 Lesson 71	Lesson 72	Lesson 73	Lesson 74	Lesson 75	Cumulative Test 14

Day 7	Day 8	Day 9	Day 10	Day 11	Day 12
Lesson 76	Lesson 77	Lesson 78	Lesson 79	Lesson 80	Cumulative Test 15

Day 13
Investigation 8

Block: 90-Minute Class

Day 1	Day 2	Day 3	Day 4	Day 5	Day 6
Lab 7 Lesson 71 Lesson 72	Lesson 73 Lesson 74	Lesson 75 Cumulative Test 14	Lesson 76 Lesson 77	Lesson 78 Lesson 79	Lesson 80 Cumulative Test 15

Day 7
Investigation 8 Lesson 81

* For suggestions on how to implement Saxon Math in a block schedule, see the Pacing section at the beginning of the Teacher's Edition.

Lessons 71–80, Investigation 8

Differentiated Instruction

Below Level		Advanced Learners	
Warm Up	SE pp. 466, 474, 481, 487, 493, 500, 505, 510, 517, 523	Challenge	TE pp. 472, 479, 486, 492, 498, 504, 508, 515, 521, 527
Skills Bank	SE pp. 846–883	Extend the Example	TE pp. 469, 477, 482, 488, 496, 502, 507, 511, 512, 519, 525
Reteaching Masters	Lessons 71–80, Investigation 8	Extend the Exploration	TE pp. 474, 523
Warm Up Transparencies	Lessons 71–80	Extend the Problem	TE pp. 473, 479, 486, 491, 497, 498, 499, 503, 504, 508, 509, 514, 515, 521, 527, 528, 530
Prerequisite Skills Intervention	Skills 3, 4, 66, 67, 74	Challenge and Enrichment Masters	Challenge: 71–80; Enrichment: 72, 75

English Learners		Special Needs	
EL Tips	TE pp. 467, 479, 482, 491, 494, 503, 507, 511, 520, 524, 530	Inclusion Tips	TE pp. 469, 476, 484, 490, 495, 502, 506, 514, 519, 526
Multilingual Glossary	Booklet and Online English Learners Handbook	Adaptations for Saxon Algebra 1	Lessons 71–80, Cumulative Tests 14, 15

For All Learners			
Exploration	SE pp. 474, 523	Alternate Method	TE pp. 468, 477, 483, 488, 512, 518, 525
Caution	SE pp. 466, 475, 488, 494, 501, 502, 506, 507, 511, 517, 524, 530	Manipulative Use	TE pp. 497
Hints	SE pp. 467, 475, 477, 483, 488, 493, 495, 507, 511, 512, 513, 519, 524, 525	Online Tools	
Error Alert	TE pp. 467, 470, 471, 476, 478, 482, 483, 485, 489, 490, 492, 494, 497, 498, 499, 501, 502, 503, 504, 505, 507, 508, 511, 513, 514, 515, 516, 518, 520, 521, 522, 524, 526, 527, 529, 530, 531		

SE = Student Edition; TE = Teacher's Edition

Math Vocabulary

Lesson	New Vocabulary		Maintained		EL Tip in TE
71	correlation line of best fit negative correlation	positive correlation scatter plot trend line	slope slope formula		correlation
72			binomial constant term	factor trinomial	circular
73	compound inequality conjunction	disjunction	inequality		conjunction
74	absolute-value equation		absolute-value solution set		notch
75			binomial factor	term trinomial	completely
76			perfect square radical square root		guard
77			inequality inverse operation LCM		loan
78	asymptote excluded values	discontinuous function rational function	function horizontal	undefined vertical	rational expression rational function rational number
79			factor leading coefficient standard form of a polynomial		GCF
80	compound event discrete events	frequency distribution	frequency possible outcomes probability		experimental
INV 8	joint variation		direct variation inverse variation		variation

Section Overview 8 464B

SECTION OVERVIEW 8

Math Highlights

Enduring Understandings – The "Big Picture"

After completing Section 8, students will understand:

- Analyze scatter plots and calculate frequency distributions.
- Factor trinomials.
- Solve compound inequalities and graph conjunctions and disjunctions.
- Solve absolute-value equations.
- Multiply radical expressions.
- Graph rational functions and determine the vertical and horizontal asymptotes.

Essential Questions

- How does the line of best fit show the relationship of a scatter plot?
- How can trinomials be factored by reversing the FOIL method?
- When is the solution of a compound inequality a conjunction or disjunction?
- Why is the solution set of an absolute-value equation sometimes an empty solution set?
- When can the Product of Radicals Property be used to simplify radical expressions?
- When is a rational function undefined and how do the excluded values of the function determine the vertical asymptotes?
- How does a joint variation compare to a direct variation or an inverse variation?

Math Content Strands

Absolute-Value Equations and Inequalities
- Lesson 74 — Solving Absolute-Value Equations

Inequalities
- Lesson 73 — Solving Compound Inequalities
- Lesson 77 — Solving Two-Step and Multi-Step Inequalities

Linear Equations and Functions
- Investigation 8 — Identifying and Writing Joint Variation

Polynomials
- Lesson 72 — Factoring Trinomials: $x^2 + bx + c$
- Lesson 75 — Factoring Trinomials: $ax^2 + bx + c$
- Lesson 79 — Factoring Trinomials by Using the GCF

Probability and Data Analysis
- Lesson 71 — Making and Analyzing Scatter Plots
- Lesson 80 — Calculating Frequency Distributions
- Lab 7 — Graphing Calculator: Finding the Line of Best Fit

Rational Expressions and Functions
- Lesson 78 — Graphing Rational Functions

Radical Expressions and Functions
- Lesson 76 — Multiplying Radical Expressions

Connections in Practice Problems

	Lessons
Coordinate Geometry	72
Data Analysis	71, 76
Geometry	71, 72, 73, 74, 75, 76, 77, 78, 79, 80
Measurement	74, 75, 77, 78, 79
Probability	73, 80

Math Processes

Reasoning and Communication

	Lessons
Analyze	71, 72, 73, 74, 75, 76, 79, 80
Connect	78
Error analysis	71, 72, 73, 74, 75, 76, 77, 78, 79, 80
Formulate	72
Generalize	71, 72, 76, 77, 78, 80, Inv. 8
Justify	73, 74, 75, 76, 78, 79, 80
Math Reasoning	71, 72, 73, 74, 75, 76, 77, 78, 79, 80
Model	72, 73, 74, Inv. 8
Multiple choice	71, 72, 73, 74, 75, 76, 77, 78, 79, 80
Multi-step	71, 72, 73, 74, 75, 76, 77, 78, 79, 80
Predict	71, 74
Verify	74, 75, 77, 78, 79
Write	71, 72, 73, 74, 75, 76, 77, 79, Inv. 8
Graphing Calculator	71, 77, 80

Connections

In Examples: Carpeting, Golf, Loans, Population growth, Soccer, Technology

In Practice problems: Agriculture, Air traffic control, Art, Automotive care, Awards, Bakery, Baking, Biking, Body surface area, Books, Bowling, Budgeting, Carpentry, Cell phones, Chemistry, City parks, Climate, Construction, Demography, Dining, Elections, Fine arts, Fitness, Game play, Hobbies, Household security, Jewelry appraisal, Landscaping, Marketing, Noise, Nutrition, Party planning, Pendulum, Physics, Real estate, Sewing, Snowfall, Softball, Temperature, Vacation, Weaving, Web authoring

Lessons 71–80, Investigation 8

Content Trace

Lesson	Warm Up: Prerequisite Skills	New Concepts	Where Practiced	Where Assessed	Looking Forward
71	Lesson 49	Making and Analyzing Scatter Plots	Lessons 72, 73, 74, 75, 76, 77, 78, 79, 80, 81, 84, 86, 87	Cumulative Tests 15, 16	Lessons 96, 100, Investigation 11
72	Lessons 53, 58, 60	Factoring Trinomials: $x^2 + bx + c$	Lessons 73, 74, 75, 76, 77, 78, 79, 80, 81, 82, 85, 87, 88, 110, 111	Cumulative Tests 15, 16, 17	Lessons 75, 79, 83, 87, 93, 95, Investigation 9
73	Lessons 45, 66, 70	Solving Compound Inequalities	Lessons 74, 75, 76, 77, 78, 79, 80, 81, 82, 83, 86, 88, 89, 112	Cumulative Tests 15, 16, 17, 18, 19	Lessons 77, 81, 82
74	Lessons 5, 26, 28	Solving Absolute-Value Equations	Lessons 75, 76, 77, 78, 79, 80, 81, 82, 83, 84, 87, 89, 90, 113, 114	Cumulative Tests 15, 16, 18	Lessons 91, 94, 101, 107
75	Lessons 53, 58, 60, 72	Factoring Trinomials: $ax^2 + bx + c$	Lessons 76, 77, 78, 79, 80, 81, 82, 83, 85, 86, 88, 90, 91, 99	Cumulative Tests 15, 16, 17	Lessons 79, 87, 93, Investigation 9
76	Lessons 61, 69	Multiplying Radical Expressions	Lessons 77, 78, 79, 80, 81, 82, 83, 84, 85, 86, 89, 91, 92, 102	Cumulative Tests 16, 17, 18, 19, 20, 21	Lessons 103, 105, 106, 114
77	Lessons 21, 66, 70	Solving Two-Step and Multi-Step Inequalities	Lessons 78, 79, 80, 81, 82, 84, 85, 86, 87, 90, 92, 93	Cumulative Tests 16, 17, 18, 19	Lessons 81, 82, 91
78	Lessons 30, 39, 43	Graphing Rational Functions	Lessons 79, 80, 81, 82, 83, 84, 85, 86, 87, 88, 91, 93, 94, 117	Cumulative Tests 16, 17, 19	Lessons 88, 90, 92, 99
79	Lessons 53, 72, 75	Factoring Trinomials by Using the GCF	Lessons 80, 81, 82, 83, 84, 85, 86, 87, 88, 89, 92, 94, 95, 118	Cumulative Tests 16, 17, 19, 20, 21	Lessons 83, 87, 93, 95
80	Lessons 14, 48	Calculating Frequency Distributions	Lessons 81, 82, 83, 84, 86, 87, 88, 89, 90, 93, 95, 96, 100	Cumulative Tests 16, 17	Lessons 111, 118, 120
INV 8	N/A	Investigation: Identifying and Writing Joint Variation	Lessons 84, 90, 92, 93, 94, 96, 99	Cumulative Test 16	Investigations 9, 10, 11, 12

Section Overview 8

SECTION OVERVIEW 8

Ongoing Assessment

	Type	Feature	Intervention *
BEFORE instruction	Assess Prior Knowledge	• Diagnostic Test	• Prerequisite Skills Intervention
BEFORE the lesson	Formative	• Warm Up	• Skills Bank • Reteaching Masters
DURING the lesson	Formative	• Lesson Practice • Math Conversations with the Practice problems	• Additional Examples in TE • Test and Practice Generator (for additional practice sheets)
AFTER the lesson	Formative	• Check for Understanding (closure)	• Scaffolding Questions in TE
AFTER 5 lessons	Summative	After Lesson 75 • Cumulative Test 14 • Performance Task 14 After Lesson 80 • Cumulative Test 15 • Performance Task 15	• Reteaching Masters • Test and Practice Generator (for additional tests and practice)
AFTER 20 lessons	Summative	• Benchmark Tests	• Reteaching Masters • Test and Practice Generator (for additional tests and practice)

* for students not showing progress during the formative stages or scoring below 80% on the summative assessments

Evidence of Learning – What Students Should Know

Because the Saxon philosophy is to provide students with sufficient time to learn and practice each concept, a lesson's topic will not be tested until at least five lessons after the topic is introduced.

On the Cumulative Tests that are given during this section of ten lessons, students should be able to demonstrate the following competencies:
- Simplify radical expressions.
- Use the power rules for exponents to simplify expressions.
- Convert rates, use indirect measurements, and solve percent problems.
- Use the FOIL method and factor trinomials.
- Solve compound inequalities, and systems of equations.
- Recognize and extend arithmetic sequences.
- Compare direct and inverse variation.
- Analyze box-and-whisker plots.
- Graph a scatter plot and identify correlations.

Test and Practice Generator CD using ExamView™

The Test and Practice Generator is an easy-to-use benchmark and assessment tool that creates unlimited practice and tests in multiple formats and allows you to customize questions or create new ones. A variety of reports are available to track student progress toward mastery of the standards throughout the year.

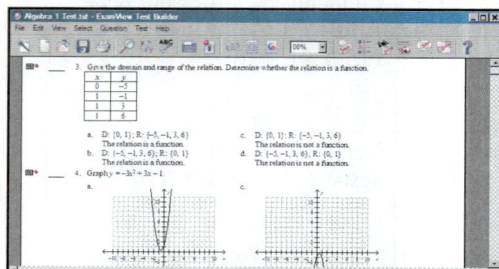 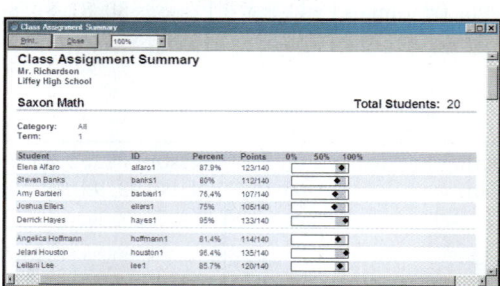

464E *Saxon Algebra 1*

Assessment Resources

Resources for Diagnosing and Assessing

- **Student Edition**
  - Warm Up
  - Lesson Practice

- **Teacher's Edition**
  - Math Conversations with the Practice problems
  - Check for Understanding (closure)

- **Course Assessments**
  - Diagnostic Test
  - Cumulative Tests
  - Performance Tasks
  - Benchmark Tests

Resources for Test Prep

- **Student Edition Practice**
  - Multiple-choice problems
  - Multiple-step and writing problems
  - Daily cumulative practice

- **Standardized Test Practice**

- **College Entrance Exam Practice**

- **Test and Practice Generator CD using ExamView™**

Resources for Intervention

- **Student Edition**
  - Skills Bank

- **Teacher's Edition**
  - Additional Examples
  - Scaffolding questions

- **Prerequisite Skills Intervention**
  - Worksheets

- **Reteaching Masters**
  - Lesson instruction and practice sheets

- **Test and Practice Generator CD using ExamView™**
  - Lesson practice problems
  - Additional tests

Cumulative Tests

The assessments in Saxon Math are frequent and consistently placed after every five lessons to offer a regular method of ongoing testing. These cumulative assessments check mastery of concepts from previous lessons.

Performance Tasks

The Performance Tasks can be used in conjunction with the Cumulative Tests and are scored using a rubric.

After Lesson 75

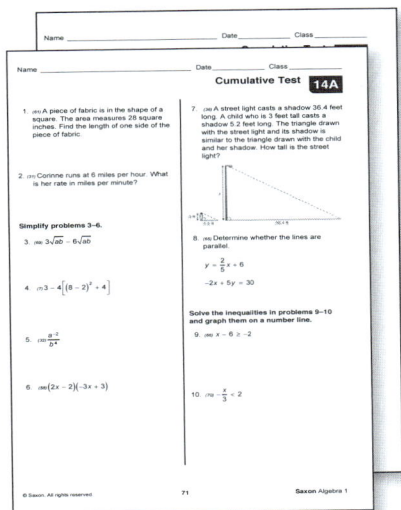

After Lesson 80

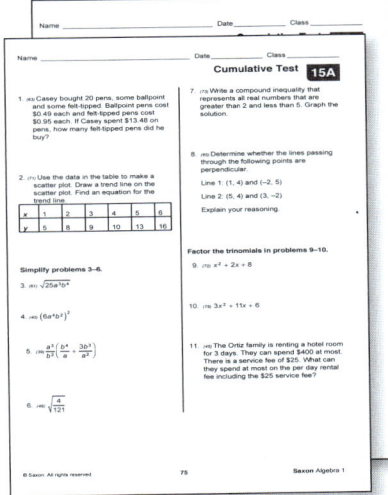

For use with Performance Tasks

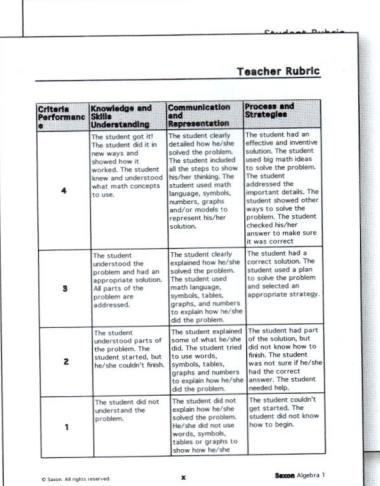

LAB 7

Materials
- graphing calculator

Discuss
Tell students that a line of best fit that rises quickly from left to right is called a positive correlation. A line of best fit that falls from left to right is called a negative correlation. Strong positive and negative correlations have data points very close to the line of best fit. Data points not clustered near the line have weak correlations.

LAB 7

Finding the Line of Best Fit

Graphing Calculator Lab (*Use with Lesson 71*)

A graphing calculator is often the easiest and most accurate method for making a scatter plot from a data set and then finding the equation of the line of best fit.

The following table gives the total number y in billions of movie admissions for x years after 1993.

Year (x)	1	2	3	4	5	6	7	8	9	10
Admissions (y)	1.29	1.26	1.34	1.39	1.48	1.47	1.42	1.49	1.63	1.57

Find a line of best fit for the data. According to the model, about how many billion movie admissions were there in 2004 ($x = 11$)?

Graphing Calculator Tip
For help with entering data into a list, see the graphing calculator keystrokes in Graphing Calculator Lab 4 on page 343.

1. Press **STAT** and choose **1:Edit.** Clear any old data by pressing the ▲ key until the list name is selected. Press **CLEAR** and then **ENTER**.

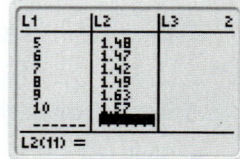

2. Enter the x-values as L1. Use the ▶ key to move to the next column and enter the y-values as L2.

3. Press **2nd** **Y=** (STAT PLOT) and select **1:Plot1…** to open the plot setup menu.

4. Press **ENTER** to turn **Plot1 On**. Then press the ▼ key once and then **ENTER** to select the first **Type**.

5. The default settings for **Xlist:** and **Ylist:** are L1 and L2, respectively. If these are not the current settings, then move the cursor next to **Xlist:**. Press **2nd** **STAT**. Select the list of independent variables, **1:L1**. To change the **Ylist:** setting, press **2nd** **STAT** and select **2:L2**, the list of dependent variables.

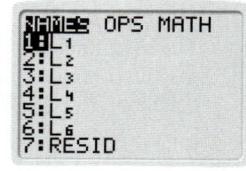

Online Connection
www.SaxonMathResources.com

6. Create a scatter plot by pressing **ZOOM** and selecting **9:ZoomStat**.

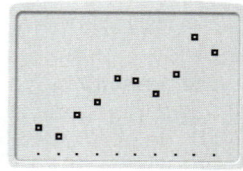

464 *Saxon Algebra 1*

7. Find the linear regression for the scatter plot. Press STAT and the ▶ key to highlight the CALC menu. Select **4:LinReg(ax+b)**.

8. Set the parameters for the linear regression. Press 2nd STAT (LIST) and choose **1:L1**. Then press , 2nd STAT (LIST) and choose **2:L2**.

9. To view the line of best fit with the scatter plot, press , VARS and the ▶ key to highlight Y-VARS. Then press ENTER twice to select Y1 as the destination for the equation.

10. Press ENTER. To write the equation of the line of best fit, the values of a and b are 0.036 and 1.236, respectively. The equation for the line of best fit is $y = 0.036x + 1.236$.

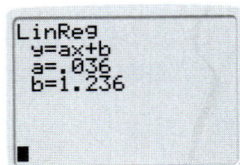

11. Press GRAPH to view the line of best fit with the scatter plot.

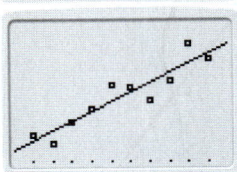

12. Predict the value of y when $x = 11$. Since $x = 11$ is outside the viewing window, press WINDOW and the ▼ key and type **11**.

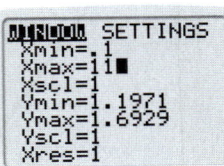

13. Press 2nd TRACE (CALC) and select **1:value**. Type **11** and press ENTER. When $x = 11$, the value of y is 1.632.

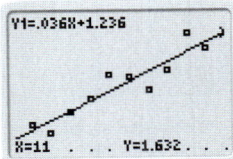

Therefore, according to the line of best fit, there would be about 1.632 billion movie admissions in the year 2004.

Lab Practice

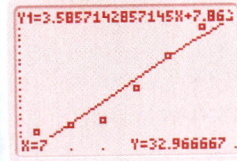

$y = 3.586x + 7.867$; about 33.0 megawatts

The table gives solar energy cell capacity y in megawatts for x years after 1989. Use a graphing calculator to create a scatter plot and to graph the line of best fit for the data. What is an equation for the line of best fit? Use the model to predict the solar-energy cell capacity in 1996 ($x = 7$).

Year (x)	1	2	3	4	5	6
Capacity (y)	13.8	14.9	15.6	21.0	26.1	31.1

Lab 7   465

LESSON 71

1 Warm Up

Problem 3
Remind students that in slope-intercept form, the coefficient of y must be 1. So, each term in the equation must be divided by -2.

2 New Concepts

In this lesson, students learn to make and analyze scatter plots.

Discuss the definition of a scatter plot and that two data sets are needed. Explain that scatter plots are discrete graphs and so the points are not connected.

Also discuss the definition of a trend line. Explain how a trend line can be used to model a set of ordered pairs that form a linear pattern. Only linear patterns are discussed in this lesson.

Example 1
Point out to students that depending on the points chosen, the trend lines will vary. However, as long as the trend line is drawn properly and the chosen points are on or near the trend line, the equations will graph to lines that are quite close to the trend line.

LESSON RESOURCES

Student Edition Practice Workbook 71
Reteaching Master 71
Adaptations Master 71
Challenge and Enrichment Master C71

LESSON 71

Making and Analyzing Scatter Plots

Warm Up

1. **Vocabulary** The constant m in the _____ form $y = mx + b$ is the slope of the line.   **slope-intercept**
2. The equation of a line is $y = -2x + 6$. What is the slope of the line?   **-2**
3. Write the equation $x - 2y = 4$ in slope-intercept form.   **$y = \frac{1}{2}x - 2$**
4. Write an equation in slope-intercept form for a line with slope $= \frac{3}{8}$ and y-intercept $= -4$.   **$y = \frac{3}{8}x - 4$**

New Concepts

One type of graph that relates two sets of data with plotted ordered pairs is called a **scatter plot**. Scatter plots are considered discrete graphs because their points are separate and disconnected. The points on scatter plots sometimes form a linear pattern. In these situations, a line can be drawn to model the pattern, which is called a trend line. A **trend line** is a line on a scatter plot, which shows the relationship between two sets of data.

Caution
A trend line does not have to go through any of the points on the scatter plot. It has to be drawn equally as close to one point as to another so that it models the approximate slope of the points.

Example 1 Graphing a Scatter Plot and a Trend Line

Use the data in the table.

x	1	2	3	4	5	6
y	4	10	12	18	23	29

a. Make a scatter plot of the data. Then draw a trend line on the scatter plot.

SOLUTION Plot the points on a coordinate plane. Then draw a straight line as near to as many of the points as possible.

b. Find an equation for the trend line.

Math Reasoning
Predict Using the table, the graph, or the equation from Example 1, what do you think would be a reasonable y-value for an x-value of 7?

Sample: 34

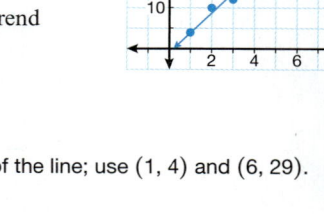

SOLUTION Use two points on or near the trend line to write an equation for the line.

$m = \dfrac{y_2 - y_1}{x_2 - x_1}$

$= \dfrac{29 - 4}{6 - 1}$ Find the slope of the line; use (1, 4) and (6, 29).

$= 5$

$(y - y_1) = m(x - x_1)$ Write the equation for the line.

$(y - 4) = 5(x - 1)$ Substitute $m = 5$ and (1, 4) for (x_1, y_1).

$y = 5x - 1$ Solve for y.

www.SaxonMathResources.com

466   Saxon Algebra 1

MATH BACKGROUND

Scatter plots are very useful in displaying two sets of data on the coordinate plane. scatter plots are sometimes called xy-graphs as well, since each data point is specified by an x-value and a y-value on the graph.

Scatter plots are most often used in displaying real-world data sets where the trend is not represented by a perfect line or equation.

How well a linear trend is modeled by a trend line can be described by the R^2 (R-squared) value. The closer it is to 1 or -1, the better the fit.

The R^2 value can be found using a graphing calculator. Under catalog, scroll down to **DiagnosticOn** and press **ENTER** twice. Then enter the data values and **STAT CALC 4: LinReg$(ax + b)$** to find the R^2 value.

Trend lines may vary. However, a trend line that shows the linear relationship of a scatter plot the most accurately is called the **line of best fit.** The equation of the line of best fit can be calculated on a graphing calculator. The line of best fit is also referred to as the regression line.

Example 2 Calculating a Line of Best Fit

The table shows the averages for homework grades and test scores for nine students. Use a graphing calculator to find the equation of the line of best fit.

Homework Grades and Test Scores

Average Homework Grade	75	85	94	88	91	95	76	84	90
Average Test Scores	83	87	95	93	88	91	83	80	92

Graphing Calculator Tip

For help with calculating a line of best fit, see Graphing Calculator Lab 7 on page 464.

SOLUTION

Step 1: Enter the data into your graphing calculator by pressing STAT ENTER to EDIT the data. Enter the average homework grades into L1 and the average test scores into L2. Then return to the home screen.

Step 2: Calculate the equation for the line of best fit by pressing STAT ▶ to access the CALC menu. Then press 4 to choose LinReg ($ax + b$). Type in L_1, L_2 and press ENTER to calculate the values used for writing the equation.

Hint

The calculator uses the variable a instead of m to represent the slope in the slope-intercept form of a line.

Step 3: Round the values for a and b to the nearest thousandth and write the equation for the line of best fit in slope-intercept form:
$y = 0.558x + 39.792$

Two sets of data may be related to each other. A **correlation** is a measure of the strength and direction of the association between data sets or variables. When the points tightly cluster in a linear pattern, then the correlation is strong.

Data can be positively correlated or negatively correlated. There is a **positive correlation** when the data values for both variables increase. There is a **negative correlation** when the data values for one variable increase while the data values for the other variable decrease.

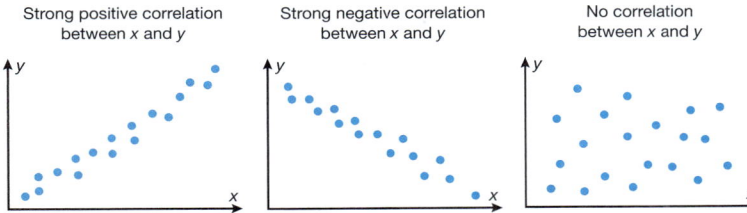

The direction of the association can be determined for scatter plots that have correlation. If the slope of the trend line is positive, then there is a positive correlation between the data values. If the slope of the trend line is negative, then there is a negative correlation between the data values.

Additional Example 1
Use the data in the table.

x	1	2	3	4	5	6
y	3	7	8	12	13	14

a. Make a scatterplot of the data. Then draw a trend line on the scatterplot.

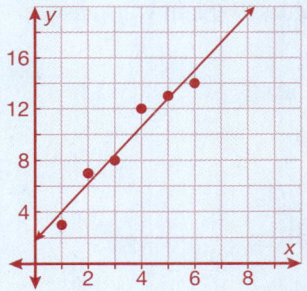

b. Find an equation for the trend line. Sample: $y = 2.5x + 0.5$

Example 2
This example makes students familiar with the use of a graphing calculator to determine the line of best fit.

Error Alert Students may inadvertently enter data incorrectly into the graphing calculator. Remind them to check their entries, as a change in the data can result in an incorrect equation for the line of best fit.

Additional Example 2
The table shows the length and weight of 6 carrots from a garden. Use a graphing calculator to find the equation for the line of best fit.

Weight (oz)	Length (in.)
1.1	5.3
1.3	5.6
1.2	5.4
1.4	5.7
1.6	6.1
1.5	5.8

$y = 1.514x + 3.606$

ENGLISH LEARNERS

For this lesson, explain the meaning of the word **correlation.** Say:

"A correlation is a mutual relationship or connection between two or more things."

Give examples of a correlation, such as the distance from a fire engine siren and its loudness. Ask:

"What correlation might relate to the grade made on a test?" Sample: the time spent studying

Example 3
Review the meaning of positive and negative correlations.

Additional Example 3
State whether there is a positive correlation, a negative correlation, or no correlation between the data values. Explain your answer.

a.

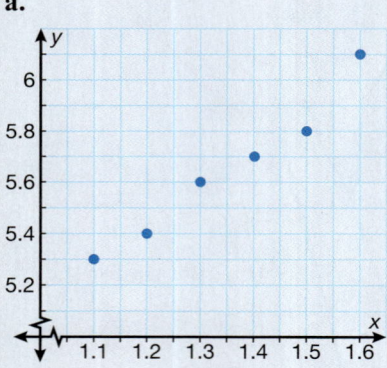

positive correlation.

b.

x	1	2	3	4	5
y	−2	−2.5	−3	−4	−5.5

negative correlation.

c. hours of sleep and alertness in school positive correlation.

d. test scores and eye color no correlation.

Example 4
This example draws on the students' experience with real world problems.

Additional Example 4
Match each situation with the scatter plot that models it best. Use the Example 4 graphs.

a. number of times one can lift a dumbbell and the weight of the dumbbell Graph 2

b. time spent reading novels and test scores on math exams Graph 3

c. number of classes taken and amount of homework Graph 1

Example 3 Identifying Correlations

State whether there is a positive correlation, a negative correlation, or no correlation between the data values.

a.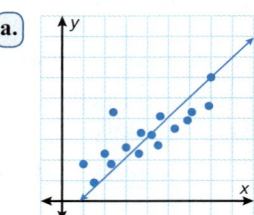

SOLUTION As the trend line rises from left to right, there is a positive correlation. Both sets of data values are increasing.

b.
x	10	9	8	7	6	5	4	3	2
y	60	63	72	75	77	81	83	89	92

SOLUTION Negative correlation: As x-values decrease the $y =$ values increase.

c. height and shoe size

SOLUTION Positive correlation: Taller people tend to have larger feet.

d. date of birth and shoe size

SOLUTION No correlation: date of birth and shoe size are not related to each other.

Example 4 Matching Situations to Scatter Plots

Match each situation with the scatter plot that models it best.

a. number of trucks on the road and number of days in a month

b. time spent driving and distance traveled

c. number of months you own a car and the value of the car

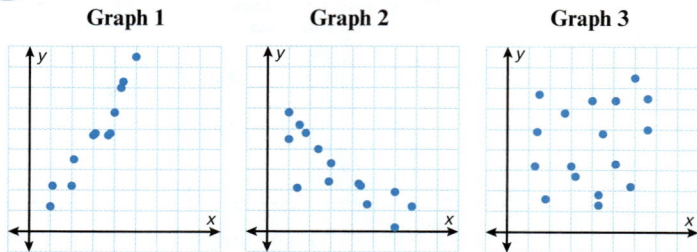

Graph 1   Graph 2   Graph 3

Math Reasoning

Generalize Explain the similarities between a positive or negative slope of a line and a positive or negative correlation among data.

Sample: In a positive correlation, both sets of data values increase, as do the data values on a line with a positive slope. In a negative correlation, one set of data values increases and the other decreases, as do the data values on a line with a negative slope.

ALTERNATE METHOD FOR EXAMPLE 4

Have students think of 3 ordered pairs for each situation:

a. number of trucks on the road and number of days in a month. Sample: (5, 28), (182, 30), (39, 31)

b. time spent driving and distance traveled
Sample: If going at 10 miles per hour: (1, 10), (3, 30), (4, 40)

c. number of months you own a car and the value of the car Sample: If initial value of car is $20,000: (1, $18,000), (3, $15,000), (5, $12,000)

Then have students match the situations with the scatter plots.

SOLUTION

a. Graph 3, as there is no correlation between the number of trucks on the road and the number of days in a month

b. Graph 1, as there is a positive correlation between time spent driving and distance traveled

c. Graph 2, as there is a negative correlation between the age of a car and its value

Estimations and predictions can be determined when there is a correlation, or a trend, between data values. **Interpolation** is a process of determining data points between given data points. **Extrapolation** is a process of determining data points that are beyond the given data points.

Example 5 Application: Population Growth

The table shows the population of the United States from the year 1960 through the year 2000.

U. S. Population

Year	1960	1965	1970	1975	1980	1985	1990	1995	2000
Population (in millions)	180	194	205	215	228	238	250	267	282

Math Reasoning

Analyze Why might a prediction determined by an equation for the line of best fit, be better than a prediction determined by a trend line?

A line of best fit most accurately models data with a linear relationship.

a. Draw a scatter plot and a trend line for the data.

SOLUTION Plot the points with the year on the horizontal axis and the population on the vertical axis. Draw a straight line as near to as many of the points as possible.

b. Use the trend line to make a prediction for the population in the year 2005.

SOLUTION From the graph, the population in the year 2005 will be about 290 million people.

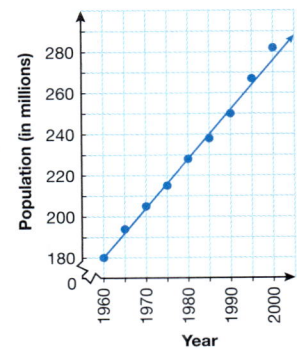

c. Find the equation for a line of best fit using a graphing calculator. Round the values for a and b to the nearest thousandth.

SOLUTION Use the LinReg ($ax + b$) feature on a graphing calculator to compute the values for the line of best fit.

The equation for the line of best fit is $y = 2.467x - 4655.222$.

d. Use the equation for the line of best fit to estimate the population in the year 2005. Round the answer to the nearest million.

SOLUTION

$y = 2.467x - 4655.222$
$y = 2.467(2010) - 4655.222$
$y \approx 291$ million

Lesson 71   469

Example 5

Scatter plots are commonly used to display scientific and statistical data.

Extend the Example

"With the same trend, make an estimate for the population in 1950." Sample: about 155 million people.

Additional Example 5

The table shows the average amount of carbon dioxide measured in the atmosphere.

Year	CO_2 concentration (ppm)
1960	317
1965	320
1970	326
1975	331
1980	339
1985	346
1990	354
1995	361
2000	369

a. Draw a scatter plot and a trend line for the data.

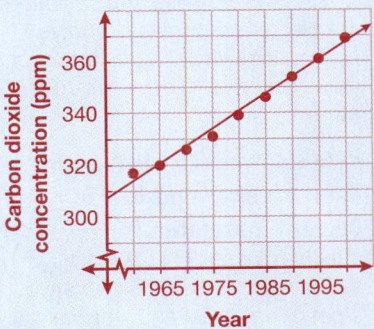

b. Use the trend line to make a prediction for the carbon dioxide concentration in the year 2005. Sample: about 375 ppm

c. Find the equation for a line of best fit using a graphing calculator. $y = 1.34x - 2312.867$

d. Use the equation for the line of best fit to estimate the carbon dioxide concentration in the year 2005. 373.833 ppm

INCLUSION

Use the following strategy with students who have difficulty with abstract concept processing. Have students choose a piece of clothing (e.g. hats, shorts, sweatshirts, sandals, etc.). Ask them if they see more, less, or no change in the number of classmates wearing that piece of clothing as the temperature outside gets colder as winter nears.

Then have them identify if each situation has a positive correlation, negative correlation, or no correlation.

Lesson 71   469

Lesson Practice

Problem b

Scaffolding Suggest that students draw the trend line so that, if possible, half of the points are on each side of the line.

Problem f

Error Alert Students may not clearly think of colder temperatures as decreasing and warmer temperatures as increasing. Suggest that they write down a few temperatures showing a decrease and a few showing an increase. Then have them associate those temperatures with the number of sweaters sold.

Check for Understanding

The questions below help assess the concepts taught in this lesson.

"What is the difference between scatter plots and graphs of equations?" Sample: The ordered pairs in a scatter plot are discrete data and there may not be a relationship between the data sets. With equations, the data are not discrete and there is always a relationship between the data sets (one value always depends on the other).

"How do you tell whether two data sets have a positive or negative correlation?" Sample: If the values of both datasets increase together, then they have a positive correlation; if the values for one data set increase while the other decreases, then they have a negative correlation.

Lesson Practice

a.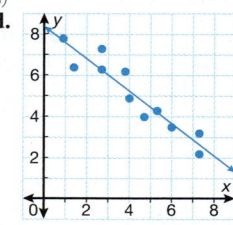

Use the data in the table. (Ex 1)

x	1	2	3	4	5	6
y	14	27	43	53	70	85

a. Make a scatter plot from the data in the table. Then draw a trend line on the scatter plot.

b. Find an equation for the trend line. Sample: $y = 14x$

c. Use a graphing calculator to find the equation of the line of best fit for the data in the table. $y = 1.486x + 10.048$ (Ex 2)

x	10	12	14	16	18	20
y	25	28	30	35	36	40

State whether there is a *positive correlation*, a *negative correlation*, or *no correlation* between the data values. (Ex 3)

d. 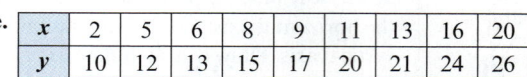 negative correlation

e.

x	2	5	6	8	9	11	13	16	20
y	10	12	13	15	17	20	21	24	26

positive correlation

f. negative correlation f. the outdoor temperature and the number of sweaters sold in a store

g. hair color and height   no correlation

Match each situation with the scatter plot that models it best. (Ex 4)

h. time spend exercising and calories burned.   Graph 2

i. the number of dishes washed and the number of ounces of detergent remaining in a bottle.   Graph 1

j. the population of a country and the number of states in the country.   Graph 3

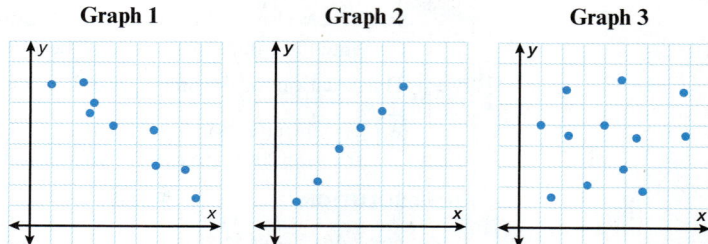

Graph 1   Graph 2   Graph 3

The table shows the number of people employed in agriculture in the United States from the year 1940 to the year 2000.

U. S. Agricultural Employment

Year	1940	1950	1960	1970	1980	1990	2000
Employment (in millions)	9.5	7.2	5.5	3.5	3.4	3.2	2.5

k. Draw a scatter plot and a trend line for the data.
(Ex 5)

l. Use the trend line to make a prediction for the population in the
(Ex 5) year 2010.   1.5 million

m. Find the equation for a line of best fit using a graphing calculator.
(Ex 5) Round the values for a and b to the nearest thousandth.
$y = -.111x + 223.782$

n. Use the equation for the line of best fit to estimate the population in the
(Ex 5) year 2010. Round the answer to the nearest half million.   0.5 million

k. (scatter plot: Population in millions vs Year 1940–2000)

Practice   Distributed and Integrated

1. Make a scatter plot from the data in the table.
(71)

x	1	2	3	4	5	6
y	26	24	21	14	9	5

Is the ordered pair (5, 2) a solution to the following systems?

2. $y = 7 - x$ yes
(55) $y = \frac{1}{5}x + 1$

3. $5y - x = 5$ yes
(55) $y = 2x - 8$

1.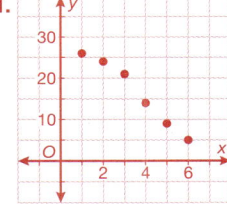

Subtract.

4. $31\sqrt{5} - 13\sqrt{5}$ $18\sqrt{5}$
(69)

*5. $\sqrt{27} - \sqrt{12}$ $\sqrt{3}$
(69)

Find the common solution for each system of equations.

6. $-y = x + 8$ no solution
(67) $y = -x + 1$

*7. $6y - x = 12$ Any ordered pair (x, y)
(67) $y = \frac{1}{6}x + 2$ that satisfies the equation $y = \frac{1}{6}x + 2$

Write an inverse variation equation relating x and y.

8. $x = \frac{2}{3}, y = 33$ $y = \frac{22}{x}$
(64)

9. $x = 6, y = 14$ $y = \frac{84}{x}$
(64)

*10. **Error Analysis** Two students solved the inequality $14 < -0.2k$ as shown below.
(70) Which student is correct? Explain the error.

Student A	Student B
$14 < -0.2k$	$14 < -0.2k$
$\frac{14}{0.2} > \frac{-0.2}{-0.2}k$	$\frac{14}{-0.2} > \frac{-0.2}{-0.2}k$
$70 > k$	$-70 > k$

10. Student B; Sample: Student A divided the left side by 0.2 instead of -0.2.

Lesson 71   471

3 Practice

Math Conversations
Discussion to strengthen understanding

Problem 4
Have students let $y = \sqrt{5}$. Then have them simplify the expression to get $18y$. By substituting $\sqrt{5}$ back in, they can get the solution.

Problem 6
Remind students that two lines on a graph will not intersect if they are parallel. The parallel lines will have the same slope and different y-intercepts.

Problem 8
Error Alert
Students often will not see immediately that the following statements are identical:

$y = \frac{22}{x}$

$x = \frac{22}{y}$

Remind students that they can multiply both sides by x or y and then divide by the other variable to have them swap places.

Lesson 71   471

Problem 14

Guide the students by asking them the following questions.

"How would you simplify $\sqrt{4}$?" Sample: 2

"How would you simplify $\sqrt{y^2}$?" Sample: $\sqrt{y^2} = y$

"How would you simplify $\sqrt{z^3}$?" Sample: $\sqrt{z^3} = \sqrt{z^2} \cdot z = z\sqrt{z}$

---

*11. **Multiple Choice** When one set of data values increases as the other set of data values decreases, what type of correlation does this represent? **B**
(71)
    A positive   **B** negative   **C** constant   **D** none

*12. (**Elections**) The table shows the voter turnout for National Federal Elections.
(71)

U.S. Voter Turnout (in millions)

Year	1990	1992	1994	1996	1998	2000	2002	2004
Number of Voters (in millions)	68	104	75	96	73	106	80	122

    a. Use the data to make a scatter plot.   See Additional Answers.

    b. Does the scatter plot show any trend in the data?   no; Sample: The data appear to show no correlation.

*13. **Generalize** If a scatter plot shows a negative correlation, what can you say about
(71) the relationship between the two sets of data values?   Sample: As one set of data values increases, the other set of data values decreases.

14. **Error Analysis** Student A and Student B combine the radicals. Which student is
(69) correct? Explain the error.   Student A; Sample: The square root of 4 is 2. Student B did not correctly calculate the square root of 4.

Student A	Student B
$8\sqrt{4y^2z^3} - 3yz\sqrt{49z}$	$8\sqrt{4y^2z^3} - 3yz\sqrt{49z}$
$= 8 \cdot 2yz\sqrt{z} - 3yz \cdot 7\sqrt{z}$	$= 8 \cdot 4yz\sqrt{z} - 3yz \cdot 7\sqrt{z}$
$= 16yz\sqrt{z} - 21yz\sqrt{z}$	$= 32yz\sqrt{z} - 21yz\sqrt{z}$
$= -5yz\sqrt{z}$	$= 11yz\sqrt{z}$

*15. (**Biking**) Randy biked $\sqrt{27}$ miles on the bike trail. He backtracked $\sqrt{3}$ miles, and
(69) then proceeded $\sqrt{12}$ miles to finish the trail. How far is Randy from his starting point? $4\sqrt{3}$ miles

16. **Multiple Choice** Which of the following situations describes inclusive events? **B**
(68)
    A rolling a sum of 5 or a sum of 4 with two number cubes

    B rolling a sum of 3 or a factor of 6 with two number cubes

    C rolling two 5's or a sum of 8 with two number cubes

    D rolling two 4's or a sum of 9 with two number cubes

17. **Write** If a fair coin is used, what is the probability that one toss will result in either
(68) heads or tails? Explain why your answer makes sense.

17. probability = 1; Sample: A probability of 1 means that the outcome is certain to happen. Since heads and tails are the only outcomes and are mutually exclusive, the coin is certain to land on either heads or tails.

*18. (**Nutrition**) Each day Paolo tries to consume at least 40 grams of protein. One day
(66) he has two soy shakes, each with 15 grams of protein, as well as a bowl of peanuts, containing 5 grams of protein. Write an inequality describing how much more protein Paolo should consume that day. $x + 15 + 15 + 5 \geq 40; x \geq 5$

19. Line 1 passes through the points $(2, -6)$ and $(4, 6)$. Line 2 passes through the
(65) points $(0, 1)$ and $(6, 0)$. Are the lines parallel or perpendicular?   perpendicular

472   Saxon Algebra 1

🏆 CHALLENGE

Even though a strong correlation may exist between sets of data values, one set does not necessarily cause the other. A positive correlation may exist between time spent studying and test grades, but time spent studying may be only one cause of the outcome. Have students explain what might be the reason for the positive correlations given.

a. time spent studying and test grades   Sample: An easy test may result in high grades; a difficult test in low grades.

b. the sale of swimsuits and the outside temperature   Sample: a discount swimsuit

c. the number of fans at a soccer game and the outside temperature   Sample: A particular player may be popular with the fans.

20. Data Analysis Use the table of values to draw a scatter plot.   See Additional Answers.

x	72	60	65	50	56	69
y	32	31	30	28	28	38

21. Determine if the inequality symbol in the inequality $11b < 5$ needs to be reversed, and then solve.   no; $b < \frac{5}{11}$

*22. Geometry JoAnna is making a banner the shape of an equilateral triangle. She has 36 inches of cording to put around the banner. Write and solve an inequality to find the range of measures of one side of the banner. $3s \leq 36$; 12 in. or less

23. Multi-Step A company spends 2% of its sales on marketing. How much money does the company need to earn to spend at least $250,000 on marketing?
a. Write an inequality to represent the situation. $0.02s \geq 250{,}000$
b. Solve the inequality. $s \geq 12{,}500{,}000$
c. How much money is needed to spend $250,000 on marketing?   at least $12,500,000

24. Generalize How would you choose which variable to eliminate when solving a system of linear equations?

24. Sample: If one variable had the same coefficient in each equation, I would eliminate that variable. If one of the coefficients of a variable in one equation is a multiple of a coefficient of the same variable in the other equation, I would multiply to eliminate that variable.

25. Use the table to determine if there is a positive correlation, a negative correlation, or no correlation between the data sets.   negative correlation

x	3	6	10	13	15	17
y	100	88	73	62	51	38

26. Write Is it possible to determine the mode of a data set using a histogram? Explain.

26. no; Sample: A histogram does not show exact values, but rather how the values are distributed within intervals. It would not be possible to determine exact values and find the mode given only a histogram.

27. Pendulum The period of a pendulum is equal to $2\pi\sqrt{\frac{l}{g}}$, where l is the length of the pendulum and g is the acceleration due to gravity. If the length of the pendulum is 40 m and the acceleration due to gravity is 10 m/s², what is the period of the pendulum? 4π s

*28. Demography The population of Fremont, California in 2005 was 200,770 and increased by 921 people by 2006. The population of Amarillo, Texas in 2005 was 183,106 and increased by 2419 people by 2006.
a. Write a system of linear equations to represent the population of these cities assuming that they continued to grow at these yearly rates. Let x be the number of years after 2005 and y be the population. $y = 921x + 200{,}770$
   $y = 2419x + 183{,}106$
b. Use a graphing calculator to solve the system of equations. At what year would the populations be equal?   2016

29. Write an equation for a direct variation that includes the point (6, 42). $y = 7x$

30. Multi-Step A cereal box is in the shape of a rectangular prism. Find the volume of a cereal box that has a width of $(2x + 2)$ inches, a length of $(5x + 1)$ inches, and a height of $(6x + 4)$ inches.
a. Multiply the length times the width. $10x^2 + 12x + 2$ inches squared
b. Multiply the height times the product found in part **a**. $60x^3 + 112x^2 + 60x + 8$ inches cubed

Lesson 71   473

Problem 27
Extend the Problem
"If the length of the pendulum was shortened to $\frac{1}{4}$ of the original length, will the period of it be longer or shorter? By how much?"
shorter; by half

Problem 30
Before calculating for the volume, ask students:

"How does one find the volume of a box? And what should the units be for volume?"

Sample: volume = area of base (inches squared) × height (inches); units for volume is thus cubic inches.

LOOKING FORWARD

- **Lesson 96** Graphing Quadratic Functions
- **Lesson 100** Solving Quadratic Equations by Graphing
- **Investigation 11** Investigating Exponential Growth and Decay

LESSON 72

1 Warm Up

Problems 2–4
When using the Distributive Property to simplify equations, remind students to multiply all the terms in the parentheses.

2 New Concepts

In this lesson, students learn to factor trinomials with the form $x^2 + bx + c$.

Discuss the definition of a trinomial. Explain that some trinomials can be factored into two linear factors.

Exploration

This exploration uses a hands-on method to introduce students to the concept of factoring trinomials.

Extend the Exploration
Use tiles to find the factors of $x^2 + 5x + 6$.

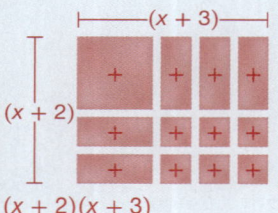

$(x + 2)(x + 3)$

LESSON RESOURCES

Student Edition Practice
  Workbook 72,
Reteaching Master 72
Adaptations Master 72
Challenge and Enrichment
  Master C72, E72

LESSON 72

Factoring Trinomials: $x^2 + bx + c$

Warm Up

1. **Vocabulary** A polynomial with two terms is a _____.   **binomial**
   (53)

   Simplify.
2. $(5x + 3)(2x - 4)$ $10x^2 - 14x - 12$
   (58)
3. $(5x - 6)^2$ $25x^2 - 60x + 36$
   (60)
4. $(x + 1)(x^2 + 3)$ $x^3 + x^2 + 3x + 3$
   (58)

New Concepts

The polynomial $x^2 + bx + c$ is a trinomial. Like numbers, some trinomials can be factored. One way to learn how to factor a trinomial is to model the terms of a trinomial with algebra tiles.

Math Reasoning

Generalize Why is $x^2 + bx + c$ classified as a trinomial?

Sample: It has three terms and *tri*-means three.

Exploration   Representing Trinomials with Algebra Tiles

The following tiles represent terms in the trinomial $x^2 + 3x + 2$.

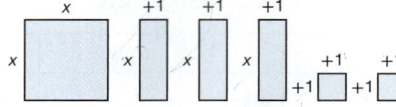

The tiles that represent some trinomials can be placed side by side to form rectangles. The tiles can be arranged to form a rectangle that has the dimensions $(x + 2)$ and $(x + 1)$.

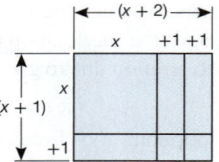

The area of the rectangle formed by the tiles can be represented as $(x + 2)(x + 1)$. By simplifying the product, the result will be the trinomial $x^2 + 3x + 2$. The binomials $x + 2$ and $x + 1$ are the factors of $x^2 + 3x + 2$.

a. **Model** Draw the tiles that represent the trinomial $x^2 + 4x + 3$.
   See Additional Answers.

b. Arrange the tiles into a rectangle.   See Additional Answers.

c. **Analyze** What are the dimensions of the rectangle? $(x + 3), (x + 1)$

d. **Formulate** Use the dimensions of the rectangle to calculate the area of the rectangle. $(x^2 + 4x + 3)$

e. **Analyze** What are the factors of $x^2 + 4x + 3$? $(x + 3), (x + 1)$

Online Connection
www.SaxonMathResources.com

474   Saxon Algebra 1

MATH BACKGROUND

Factorable trinomials in the form $x^2 + bx + c$ can be factored by using patterns. The two resulting linear binomial factors will each have a linear term x added to a constant term. The constants of the linear factors are determined by the sign of c. When c is positive, the constants of the linear factors are the factors of c whose sum is the coefficient b. When c is negative, the constants of the linear factors are the factors of c whose difference is the coefficient b.

The sign of c indicates the signs of the constants in the linear factors. When c is positive, the constant of the linear factors will have the same sign as b. When c is negative, the signs of the factors will be opposite and the "greater factor" will have the sign of b.

The trinomial $x^2 - 5x - 6$ factors into $(x - 6)(x + 1)$ because 6 and 1 are factors of 6 whose difference is 5. The signs of the constants are opposite and the constant 6 has a negative sign.

Hint

FOIL stands for First, Outer, Inner, Last.

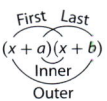

Tiling is a method for modeling the factoring of trinomials, but it is a slow method for finding the factors. Thinking about how factors are multiplied leads to a quicker method.

Binomials can be multiplied using the FOIL method. In each case, the product is a trinomial.

This procedure can be reversed to factor a trinomial into the product of two binomials. There is a pattern for factoring trinomials that are written in the standard form $ax^2 + bx + c$; that is, when $a = 1$.

1. The last term of the trinomial, c, is the product of the last terms of the binomials.
2. The coefficient of the middle term, b, is the sum of the last terms of the binomials.

Example 1 Factoring when c is Positive

Factor each trinomial.

a. $x^2 + 9x + 18$

SOLUTION

In this trinomial, b is 9 and c is 18. Because b is positive, it must be the sum of two positive numbers that are factors of c.

Caution

Pairs of numbers can have the same product but different sums.

Three pairs of positive numbers have a product of 18.

$(1)(18) = 18 \qquad (2)(9) = 18 \qquad (3)(6) = 18$

Only one pair of these numbers has a sum of 9.

$(1) + (18) = 19 \qquad (2) + (9) = 11 \qquad (3) + (6) = 9$

The constant terms in the binomials are 3 and 6.

$x^2 + 9x + 18 = (x + 3)(x + 6)$

The factored form of $x^2 + 9x + 18$ is $(x + 3)(x + 6)$.

b. $x^2 - 5x + 4$

SOLUTION

In this trinomial, b is -5 and c is 4. Because b is negative, it must be the sum of two negative numbers that are factors of c.

Two pairs of negative numbers have a product of 4.

$(-1)(-4) = 4 \qquad (-2)(-2) = 4$

Only one pair of these numbers has a sum of -5.

$(-1) + (-4) = -5 \qquad (-2) + (-2) = -4$

The constant terms in the binomials are -1 and -4.

$x^2 - 5x + 4 = (x - 1)(x - 4)$

The factored form of $x^2 - 5x + 4$ is $(x - 1)(x - 4)$.

TEACHER TIP

Emphasize that factoring a trinomial can be seen as solving a puzzle: "What two terms multiplied together will produce the trinomial?" By working backward, students can arrive at the factors again.

Example 1

Point out to students that factoring the constant term in the trinomial first can give insight into how to factor the trinomial.

Additional Example 1

Factor each trinomial.

a. $x^2 + 5x + 6$
$(x + 2)(x + 3)$

b. $x^2 - 8x + 15$
$(x - 5)(x - 3)$

TEACHER TIP

Emphasize that in factoring a trinomial, the sum of the factors of the constant term should be the coefficient of the middle term. Thus, if c is positive, the factors need to both be positive or both be negative; if c is negative, one must be negative and the other positive.

Example 2

Make sure that students know that the only way to multiply two real numbers to get a negative number is to have one positive number and one negative number.

Error Alert A common mistake that students make in factoring a negative number is to make both factors negative. Have students multiply the last terms of the factored expression to confirm that the product equals the constant of the expression.

Additional Example 2
Factor each trinomial.

a. $x^2 - 7x - 30$
$(x - 10)(x + 3)$

b. $x^2 + 3x - 54$
$(x - 6)(x + 9)$

Example 3

Remind students that factoring trinomials with two variables follows the same rules as factoring trinomials with one variable.

Additional Example 3
Factor each trinomial.

a. $x^2 + 4xy + 4y^2$
$(x + 2y)(x + 2y)$ or $(x + 2y)^2$

b. $x^2 - 7xy - 18y^2$
$(x + 2y)(x - 9y)$

Math Reasoning

Analyze How can the absolute value of the factors of c be used to find the last terms of the binomial factors?

Sample: By finding the sum or difference of the absolute values of the factors of c, the absolute value of b can be found quickly. Then find the appropriate sign for each factor so that the sum of the factors equals b.

Reading Math

The middle term of the trinomial is written $2xy$, not $2yx$, even though $2y$ is the value of b in the trinomial $x^2 + bx + c$.

Example 2 **Factoring when c is Negative**

Factor each trinomial.

a. $x^2 + 3x - 10$

SOLUTION

In this trinomial, b is 3 and c is -10.

Four pairs of positive and negative numbers have a product of -10.

$(-1)(10)$ $(1)(-10)$ $(-2)(5)$ $(2)(-5)$

The sum of only one of these pairs is 3.

$(-1) + 10 = 9$ $1 + (-10) = -9$ $(-2) + 5 = 3$ $2 + (-5) = -3$

The constant terms in the binomials are -2 and 5. So,

$x^2 + 3x - 10 = (x - 2)(x + 5)$

b. $x^2 - 7x - 8$

SOLUTION

In this trinomial, $b = -7$ and $c = -8$.

Four pairs of positive and negative numbers have a product of -8.

$(-1)(8)$ $(1)(-8)$ $(-2)(4)$ $(2)(-4)$

The sum of only one of these pairs is -7.

$(-1) + 8 = 7$ $1 + (-8) = -7$ $(-2) + 4 = 2$ $2 + (-4) = -2$

The constant terms in the binomial are 1 and -8. So,

$x^2 - 7x - 8 = (x + 1)(x - 8)$

Example 3 **Factoring with Two Variables**

Factor each trinomial.

a. $x^2 + 5xy + 6y^2$

SOLUTION In this trinomial, b and c have values of $5y$ and $6y^2$, respectively. Because both b and c are positive, b must be the sum of two positive terms that are factors of c.

Six pairs of positive terms have a product of $6y^2$.

$(1y^2)(6)$ $(1y)(6y)$ $(1)(6y^2)$ $(2y^2)(3)$ $(2y)(3y)$ $(2)(3y^2)$

Eliminate pairs of terms that contain y^2 because their sums cannot yield a term containing y. For example, $(1y^2)(6)$ has the sum $(y^2 + 6)$.

Only the pair $2y$ and $3y$ has a sum of $5y$, which is the value of b. So,

$x^2 + 5xy + 6y^2 = (x + 2y)(x + 3y)$

⚠ ALTERNATE METHOD FOR EXAMPLE 3a

Have students prepare the factors by placing an x and a y in the parentheses as follows: $(x \quad y)(x \quad y)$. Then have students find the factors of positive 6 that add to positive 5; these factors are positive 2 and positive 3.

Then have students place these numbers as the coefficients of the two y variables: $(x + 2y)(x + 3y)$.

b. $x^2 + 2xy - 3y^2$

SOLUTION

In this trinomial, b is $2y$ and c is $-3y^2$.

Four pairs of positive and negative terms have a product of $-3y^2$.

$$(-1)(3y^2) \quad (1)(-3y^2) \quad (-1y)(3y) \quad (1y)(-3y)$$

Only the pair $-1y$ and $3y$ has a sum of $2y$, which is the value of b. So,

$$x^2 + 2xy - 3y^2 = (x - y)(x + 3y)$$

Example 4 Rearranging Terms before Factoring

Factor the trinomial.

$$-21 - 4x + x^2$$

Hint

The terms of a trinomial are written in standard form when the terms contain descending powers of the variable.

SOLUTION

Write the trinomial in the standard form as $x^2 - 4x - 21$, where b is -4 and c is -21.

Four pairs of numbers have a product of -21.

$$(1)(-21) \quad (-1)(21) \quad (3)(-7) \quad (-3)(7)$$

Only the pair 3 and -7 has a sum of -4. So,

$$x^2 - 4x - 21 = (x + 3)(x - 7)$$

Example 5 Evaluating Trinomials

Evaluate $x^2 + 5x - 14$ and its factors for $x = 3$.

SOLUTION

In this trinomial, b is 5 and c is -14.

The number pair -2 and 7 has a sum of 5 and a product of -14.

So, $x^2 + 5x - 14 = (x - 2)(x + 7)$

Now evaluate $x^2 + 5x - 14$ and $(x - 2)(x + 7)$ for $x = 3$.

Trinomial	**Factors**
$x^2 + 5x - 14$	$(x - 2)(x + 7)$
$= (3)^2 + 5(3) - 14$	$= (3 - 2)(3 + 7)$
$= 9 + 15 - 14$	$= (1)(10)$
$= 10$	$= 10$

The results are the same. The trinomial is equal to the product of its binomial factors.

Example 4

Rearranging terms before factoring makes the factoring process much easier.

Additional Example 4

Factor the trinomial.

$-24 + 5x + x^2$ $(x + 8)(x - 3)$

Example 5

Point out that factoring a trinomial does not change the value of the expression; it just changes the way it looks. Using the factored form can make evaluating much quicker.

Extend the Example

Evaluate $x^2 + 5x - 14$ for $x = 2$. 0

Additional Example 5

Evaluate $x^2 + 9x - 52$ and its factors for $x = 1$. -42

 INCLUSION

When factoring a trinomial, students may find it helpful to make a chart to determine the constant terms of the binomial factors. For example, to factor $x^2 + 3x - 10$, have students copy and complete the table.

Factors	Product	Sum
-1	10	-10	9
1	-10	-10	-9
-2	5	-10	3
2	-5	-10	-3

Have students use the table to identify the factors of -10 whose sum is $+3$. Then have the students write the binomial factors $(x - 2)(x + 5)$.

Lesson Practice

Factor each trinomial.

a. $x^2 + 3x + 2$ $(x + 1)(x + 2)$
(Ex 1)

b. $x^2 - 10x + 16$ $(x - 2)(x - 8)$
(Ex 1)

c. $x^2 + 4x - 12$ $(x - 2)(x + 6)$
(Ex 2)

d. $x^2 - 5x - 36$ $(x - 9)(x + 4)$
(Ex 2)

e. $x^2 + 9xy + 20y^2$ $(x + 4y)(x + 5y)$
(Ex 3)

f. $x^2 - xy - 12y^2$ $(x - 4y)(x + 3y)$
(Ex 3)

g. $12x + 20 + x^2$ $(x + 2)(x + 10)$
(Ex 4)

h. $7x + x^2 - 44$ $(x - 4)(x + 11)$
(Ex 4)

i. Evaluate $x^2 + x - 6$ and its factors for $x = 4$.
(Ex 5) $x^2 + x - 6 = (x + 3)(x - 2)$;
$4^2 + 4 - 6 = 14$; $(4 + 3)(4 - 2) = (7)(2) = 14$

Practice   Distributed and Integrated

1. Solve the inequality $x + 2 + 3 > 6$. Then graph and check the solution.
(66) $x > 1$;

Find the probability of the following events.

2. choosing a vowel or a consonant from the alphabet   1
(68)

3. rolling a sum that is a multiple of 4 or a set of doubles with two number cubes $\frac{1}{3}$
(68)

Factor.

*4. $x^2 + 11x + 24$ $(x + 3)(x + 8)$
(72)

*5. $k^2 - 3k - 40$ $(k + 5)(k - 8)$
(72)

*6. $m^2 + 9m + 20$ $(m + 4)(m + 5)$
(72)

*7. $x^2 + 33 + 14x$ $(x + 3)(x + 11)$
(72)

*8. **Error Analysis** Two students are factoring the following trinomial. Which student is correct? Explain the error.   Student A; Sample: Student B incorrectly factored −6 and then subtracted the values rather than adding them to obtain b.
(72)

$$x^2 - 5x - 6$$

Student A	Student B
$(-6)(1) = -6$	$(-6)(-1) = -6$
$(-6) + 1 = -5$	$(-6) - (-1) = -5$
$x^2 - 5x - 6 = (x + 1)(x - 6)$	$x^2 - 5x - 6 = (x - 1)(x - 6)$

*9. (**Baking**) The area of the sheet-cake pans at a bakery are described by the trinomial
(72) $x^2 + 15x + 54$. What are the dimensions of a pan if $x = 11$? 17×20

*10. **Analyze** How many possible pairs of number factors does c have in the following
(72) trinomial?

$$x^2 + bx + 36 \quad 9$$

478   Saxon Algebra 1

*11. **Model** These tiles represent the trinomial $x^2 + x - 6$.
(72)

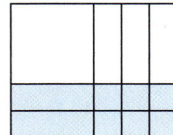

What does each of the shaded rectangles represent? the term $-1x$

12. Make a scatter plot from the data in the table.
(71)

x	5	10	15	20	25	30
y	11	13	16	20	21	25

12.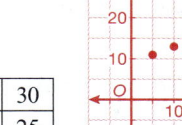

13. **Error Analysis** Two students are describing a trend line for a scatter plot but have different definitions. Which student is correct? Explain the error.
(71)

Student A	Student B
A trend line is a line on a scatter plot that goes through two data points and indicates a trend in the data.	A trend line is a line on a scatter plot that models the slope of the data points and indicates a trend in the data.

13. Student B; Sample: A trend line on a scatter plot does not have to contain any data points. It is used to indicate a trend in the data.

*14. **Geometry** Ten groups of students were given different circular objects. They measured the circumference and the diameter of the object. The table shows the results for each group.
(71)

Diameter (in.)	4	3.75	8	6.25	5.5	5	7	1.5	3	9
Circumference (in.)	12.1	12	25	19	16	16	21	4.5	9.5	28

a. Make a scatter plot of the data and draw a trend line. See Additional Answers.
b. Write an equation that models the data. Sample: $y = 3.1x + 0.2$
c. How does your equation compare to the formula for the circumference of a circle, $C = \pi d$? Sample: The equation is close to the formula since the slope of the line is approximately π and the y-intercept is very close to zero.

15. **Multi-Step** Use the scatter plot.
(71)
a. Use the trend line to estimate the corresponding y-value for an x-value of 18. Sample: 65
b. Use the trend line to estimate the x-value for a y-value of 50. Sample: 13

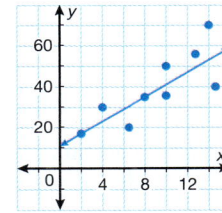

16. **Write** Can a perfect square have a negative square root? Explain. yes; Sample: Since the products of two negative numbers is a positive number, the square root of a perfect square can be negative. An example is $-7 \cdot -7 = 49$.
(69)

Lesson 72   479

Problem 13
Point out to students that a trend line is also called the line of best fit.

Problem 15
Extend the Problem
Determine the equation of the trend line by estimating the location of two points on or near the line. Sample: $y = 3x + 12$

Use the equation of the trend line to predict a y-value that corresponds to an x-value of 30. Sample: 102

ENGLISH LEARNERS

Discuss the meaning of **circular.** Draw a circle on the board or overhead. Say:

"An object is circular if it has the shape of a circle. Name a circular object." Sample: compact disc

Ask:

"How can the distance around a circular object be determined?" Sample: Use the formula $C = \pi d$.

CHALLENGE

Have students factor a trinomial with a constant term that has multiple factors. Factor $x^2 - 2x - 168$. $(x - 14)(x + 12)$

Lesson 72   479

Problem 27

Guide the students by asking them the following questions.

"How is the distance an object travels related to the time and the rate of travel?" Sample: distance = rate × time

"For how much time did the first object travel?" 35 seconds

"How far will the second object travel in that amount of time?" 175 meters

"What is another way of solving this problem?" Sample: Set up and solve the proportion: $\frac{3}{105} = \frac{5}{d}$.

---

17. **Air Traffic Control** An airplane approaching from the north is flying along a flight path of $y = 6x + 2$. The airport runway lies on the path $\frac{1}{2}y = 3x + 1$. Will the airplane be able to land on the runway if it continues on its current path? Explain.

18. **Coordinate Geometry** The triangle shown at right is formed by the intersection of three lines. The lines can be paired to form three separate systems of two equations. Classify these systems. Each system of paired equations will be consistent and independent.

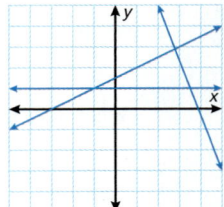

19. Determine if the lines described are parallel or perpendicular.

    Line 1 passes through the points $(-6, 3)$ and $(6, 1)$.

    Line 2 passes through the points $(-6, -2)$ and $(6, -4)$. parallel

20. **Model** Make a table that relates the length and width of a rectangle with a constant area of 100 square feet. See Additional Answers.

*21. **Multi-Step** Yoon has a number of dimes and quarters she wants to put into rolls. She has 124 coins in all that add up to $20.50. If a roll of quarters is equal to ten dollars, how many extra quarters does she have that will not fill up a roll? 14 quarters

22. Find the LCM of $(5x - 9)$ and $(3x + 8)$. $(5x - 9)(3x + 8)$

23. **Multiple Choice** Simplify $20\sqrt{7} - 12\sqrt{7} + 2\sqrt{7}$. **A**

    A $10\sqrt{7}$ **B** $18\sqrt{7}$ **C** $34\sqrt{7}$ **D** $-12\sqrt{7}$

24. **Hobbies** Enrique recorded his personal best times in minutes for completing different levels of a computer game in the stem-and-leaf plot shown. What is his median time for completing a level? 19 min

25. **Multi-Step** The sum of two numbers is 36. Their difference is 8. Find each of the numbers. What is their product? 22, 14; 308

26. Write an equation for a direct variation that includes the point $(13, 13)$. $y = x$

27. **Physics** The distance an object travels in a certain amount of time is directly proportional to its rate of travel. An object travels 105 meters at a rate of 3 meters per second. How far will an object travel if it travels at 5 meters per second for the same amount of time? 175 meters

28. Solve $2 < -4a$. $a < -\frac{1}{2}$

29. Solve $\frac{-1}{3} < \frac{-1}{9}p$. $p < 3$

30. **Real Estate** Donna and James have to pay 20% of the cost of a house as a down payment. They have $35,000 saved for the down payment. Write and solve an equation to determine the range for the sale price of a house they can make a down payment on. $0.20x \le 35{,}000$; $175,000 or less

17. yes; Sample: The equations for the flight path and runway form a set of consistent and dependent equations. The airplane is on the same path as the runway.

Personal Best Times for Completing Levels of Computer Game

Stem	Leaves
0	8, 9
1	1, 2, 3, 3, 8, 9
2	2, 2, 5, 6
3	0, 3
4	1

---

480 Saxon Algebra 1

LOOKING FORWARD

Factoring trinomials in the form $x^2 + bx + c$ prepare students for

- **Lesson 75** Factoring Trinomials: $ax^2 + bx + c$
- **Lesson 79** Factoring Trinomials by Using the GCF
- **Lesson 83** Factoring Special Products
- **Lesson 87** Factoring Polynomials by Grouping

- **Investigation 9** Choosing a Factoring Method
- **Lesson 93** Dividing Polynomials
- **Lesson 95** Combining Rational Expressions with Unlike Denominators

LESSON 73

Solving Compound Inequalities

Warm Up

1. **Vocabulary** A(n) _____ is a mathematical statement comparing quantities that are not equal. **inequality**

Solve.

2. $x + 7 < 0$ $x < -7$
3. $x - 3 \geq -5$ $x \geq -2$
4. $-x \geq 5$ $x \leq -5$
5. $\frac{-x}{4} \leq 3$ $x \geq -12$

New Concepts

Sometimes inequalities are described using two inequalities instead of just one. In these instances, a compound inequality is written to represent the situation. A **compound inequality** is two inequalities combined with the word AND or OR. A **conjunction** is a compound inequality that uses the word AND.

Reading Math

Read $-3 \leq x \leq 5$ as "x is greater than or equal to -3 and less than or equal to 5," or as "x is between -3 and 5, inclusive."

The statement $x \geq -3$ AND $x \leq 5$ is a conjunction. Because the word "AND" connects the two inequalities, the conjunction can also be written $-3 \leq x \leq 5$.

The graph of a conjunction is the intersection of the graphs of the two inequalities. That is, it includes all points common to both inequalities. For example, consider the graph of $x \geq -3$ AND $x \leq 5$.

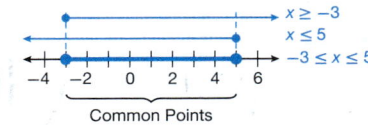

Common Points

Math Language

The phrase "less than" and "is less than" are often confused. For example, "six less than x" is translates to $x - 6$ while "six is less than x" translates to $6 < x$.

Example 1 Writing and Graphing Conjunctions

Write and graph a compound inequality to represent the statement.

a. all real numbers that are greater than 1 and less than 4

SOLUTION

$x > 1$ AND $x < 4$ or $1 < x < 4$

b. The winds of a hurricane range from 75 miles per hour to 200 miles per hour.

SOLUTION

$x \geq 75$ AND $x \leq 200$ or $75 \leq x \leq 200$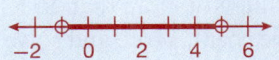

MATH BACKGROUND

Compound inequalities can also be seen as a system of inequalities. Systems of equations are all conjunctions: both equations must be satisfied. With compound inequalities, the system is either a conjunction or a disjunction depending on whether they are combined with the word AND or the word OR.

For a conjunction, both conditions must be satisfied; that is why it is acceptable to rewrite the compound inequality as a connected chain of inequalities. For a disjunction, it is sufficient that one of the inequalities is satisfied.

---

1 Warm Up

Problems 2–5

Remind students that multiplying and dividing by a negative number reverses the order of the inequality.

2 New Concepts

In this lesson, students learn to identify, write, and graph compound inequalities.

Example 1

A review of the inequality symbols may be helpful.

Additional Example 1

Write and graph a compound inequality to represent the statement below.

a. all real numbers that are greater than -1 and less than 5 $x > -1$ and $x < 5$ or $-1 < x < 5$

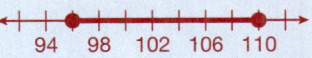

b. wind speeds ranging from 96 to 110 miles per hour $x \geq 96$ and $x \leq 110$ or $96 \leq x \leq 110$

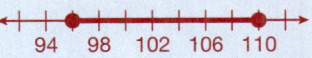

LESSON RESOURCES

Student Edition Practice Workbook 73
Reteaching Master 73
Adaptations Master 73
Challenge and Enrichment Master C73

Example 2
Error Alert When solving conjunctions using Method 2, students sometimes forget to operate on all three parts of the inequality. Point out that as with solving equations, what is done to one side of an inequality sign must be done to the other side. In these cases, there are three "sides".

Extend the Example
Another cellular phone contract increases the monthly fee by $10 and reduces the per-minute talk time by $0.05. Write a compound inequality that describes the situation. Solve the inequality to find the number of minutes that can be used to keep the monthly bill within the desired amounts of $30 and $40.
$30 \leq 20 + 0.05x \leq 40$;
$200 \leq x \leq 400$

Additional Example 2
A local moving company charges $60 an hour plus a $50 gasoline fee. They have a minimum charge of $140. Not more than $500 can be spent. Write and solve a conjunction that can be used to find the number of hours that will keep the bill within those limits.
$140 \leq 60x + 50 \leq 500$; $1.5 \leq x \leq 7.5$

Example 3

Additional Example 3
Write and graph a compound inequality to represent the statement.

a. all real numbers greater than 2 or less than −1 $x > 2$ OR $x < -1$;

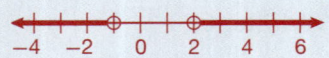

b. all real numbers no more than 3 and no less than 8 $x \leq 3$ OR $x \geq 8$;

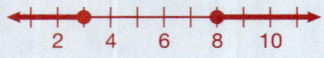

Reading Math
$<$ means is less than.
$>$ means is greater than and is more than.

$\leq$ means is less than or equal to, is at most, is no more than.

$\geq$ means is greater than or equal to, is at least, is no less than.

$\leq$ and $\geq$ are used with the word *inclusive* while $<$ and $>$ are used with the word *between*.

Math Reasoning
Justify Why is there no solution for the conjunction $x < -2$ AND $x > 3$?

The solution must include only numbers that satisfy both inequalities. Since the inequalities have no values in common, there is no solution for the conjunction.

Any number that satisfies both inequalities is a solution of a conjunction. A conjunction can be solved as two inequalities connected with AND or as an inequality with three parts, such as $8 \geq x \geq 3$.

Example 2 Solving Conjunctions
A cellular phone contract includes a monthly usage fee of $10 plus an additional $0.10 per minute of talk time. Suppose that the monthly cell phone bill is between $30 and $40. Write a compound inequality that describes the situation. Solve the inequality to find the number of minutes that can be used to keep the monthly bill within the desired amounts.

SOLUTION

Write and solve the conjunction as two separate inequalities connected with AND.

Method 1:

$30 \leq 10 + 0.10x$	AND	$10 + 0.10x \leq 40$
$20 \leq 0.10x$		$0.10x \leq 30$
$200 \leq x$	AND	$x \leq 300$

The solution is $200 \leq x \leq 300$. Between 200 and 300 minutes, inclusive, can be used monthly.

Method 2:
Write and solve the conjunction as $30 \leq 10 + 0.10x \leq 40$.

$30 \leq 10 + 0.10x \leq 40$
$20 \leq 0.10x \leq 30$ Subtract 10 from each part of the inequality.
$200 \leq x \leq 300$ Divide each part of the inequality by 0.10.

The solution is $200 \leq x \leq 300$. Between 200 and 300 minutes, inclusive, can be used monthly.

A **disjunction** is a compound inequality that uses the word OR. Disjunctions must be written as two separate inequalities connected with the word OR. A solution to these inequalities is any number that makes either inequality true.

Example 3 Writing and Graphing Disjunctions
Write and graph a compound inequality to represent the statement.

a. all real numbers greater than 9 or less than 3

SOLUTION
$x < 3$ OR $x > 9$

b. all real numbers no more than 7 and no less than 11

SOLUTION
$x \leq 7$ OR $x \geq 11$

ENGLISH LEARNERS

For this lesson, explain the meaning of the word **conjunction.** Say:

"A conjunction is the act of joining together. For example, the conjunction of two roads occurs where they cross."

Discuss that when law enforcement agencies and businesses work together, they are working in conjunction with each other.

Example 4 Solving Disjunctions

Solve the disjunction $x - 3 < -5$ OR $-2x < -6$.

SOLUTION

Solve the two inequalities separately.

$x - 3 < -5$ OR $-2x < -6$
$x < -2$ OR $x > 3$

The solution is $x < -2$ OR $x > 3$.

Hint
Remember that dividing by a negative number in an inequality reverses the order of the inequality.

Math Reasoning
Justify Why is "all real numbers" the solution of the disjunction $x > -2$ OR $x < 3$?

Sample: The solution must include any number that satisfies either inequality, so any real number must be part of the solution.

Example 5 Writing a Compound Inequality from a Graph

Write a compound inequality that describes each graph.

a.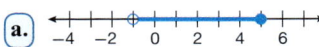

SOLUTION

The compound inequality is $-1 < x \le 5$ or $x > -1$ AND $x \le 5$.

b.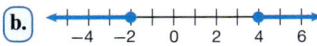

SOLUTION

The compound inequality is $x \le -2$ OR $x \ge 4$.

Lesson Practice

Write and graph a compound inequality to represent the statement. *(Ex 1)*
a. all real numbers that are greater than 5 and less than 10
b. a recommended cooking time for lasagna from 16 minutes to 20 minutes
c. A cellular phone company has a policy that charges a monthly fee of $20 plus $0.05 per minute of usage or text message. The monthly cell phone bill must be between $40 and $50. Write a compound inequality that describes the situation. Solve the inequality to find the number of minutes that can be used to keep the monthly bill within the desired amounts. $40 \le 20 + 0.05x \le 50$; $400 \le x \le 600$ *(Ex 2)*

Write and graph a compound inequality to represent the statement. *(Ex 3)*
d. all real numbers greater than 6 or less than 1
e. all real numbers greater than or equal to 5 or less than or equal to 0
f. Solve the disjunction $5x > -5$ OR $6x < -18$. $x < -3$ OR $x > -1$ *(Ex 4)*

Write a compound inequality that describes each graph. *(Ex 5)*

g.  $x \le 1$ OR $x > 2$

h. 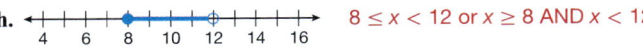 $8 \le x < 12$ or $x \ge 8$ AND $x < 12$

a. $x > 5$ AND $x < 10$ or $5 < x < 10$;
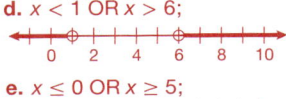

b. $16 \le t \le 20$;
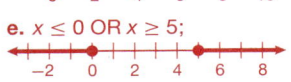

d. $x < 1$ OR $x > 6$;

e. $x \le 0$ OR $x \ge 5$;

Lesson 73 483

Example 4
The solution to a disjunction includes all numbers described in both inequalities.

Additional Example 4
Solve the disjunction $x + 6 < 7$ OR $-3x < -9$. $x < 1$ OR $x > 3$

Example 5
Review the meaning of closed and open circles on a number line.

Additional Example 5
Write a compound inequality that describes each graph.

a.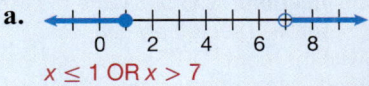
$x \le 1$ OR $x > 7$

b.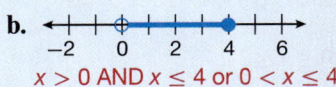
$x > 0$ AND $x \le 4$ or $0 < x \le 4$

Lesson Practice

Problems a and b
Scaffolding When graphing inequalities, suggest that students first graph the two points before shading the appropriate region(s).

Problems g and h
Error Alert Some students may overlook whether the circles are closed or open, resulting in an incorrectly written inequality. Remind them to read the graphs carefully.

⚠ ALTERNATE METHOD FOR PROBLEM a

Have the students graph both inequalities, one above the other above the same number line. Then have the students identify where the two inequalities overlap and have them graph the overlap on the number line.

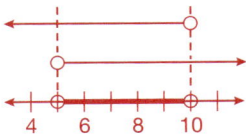

Finally, have the students write the inequality that describes the overlap. $5 < x < 10$

Check for Understanding

The questions below help assess the concepts taught in this lesson.

"What are the different types of compound inequalities?" Sample: a conjunction is joined by the word AND; a disjunction is joined by the word OR.

"Explain how to solve a conjunction." Sample: Write and solve the conjunction as two separate inequalities connected with AND or combine the inequalities and solve the resulting three-part inequality. The solutions are the values of the variable that make both inequalities true.

"Explain how to solve a disjunction." Sample: Write the two inequalities separately connected with the word "OR". Solve each inequality for the variable. The solutions are the values of the variable that make one inequality true.

3 Practice

Math Conversations
Discussion to strengthen understanding

Problems 1 and 2
To quickly determine if a system is inconsistent, write each equation in slope-intercept form. If the slopes are the same and the y-intercepts differ, then the system is inconsistent.

Practice — Distributed and Integrated

Determine if the systems of equations are consistent and independent, consistent and dependent, or inconsistent.

1. $-\frac{1}{2}x + y = 5$ consistent and independent
   $x + y = 5$
2. $y = 5x - 3$ inconsistent
   $2y - 10x = 8$

Solve the inequalities.

3. $x + 2 - 3 \leq 6$ $x \leq 7$
4. $z + 5 \geq 1.5$ $z \geq -3.5$
*5. $-15 \leq 2x + 7 \leq -9$ $-11 \leq x \leq -8$
*6. $x - 3 \geq 4$ OR $x + 2 < -5$ $x < -7$ OR $x \geq 7$

*7. Graph the compound inequality $-4 \leq x \leq 5$.

*8. Write a compound inequality that represents all real numbers that are no more than 1 or no less than 6. $x \leq 1$ OR $x \geq 6$

*9. **Multiple Choice** Which inequality describes the graph?   **A**

   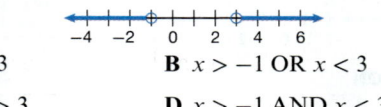

   A $x < -1$ OR $x > 3$
   B $x > -1$ OR $x < 3$
   C $x < -1$ AND $x > 3$
   D $x > -1$ AND $x < 3$

*10. (Noise) A human being cannot hear sound that is below 0 decibels and has a pain threshold of 120 decibels. Write a compound inequality that describes the decibel levels that human beings cannot hear or are too painful to hear.
   $x < 0$ OR $x > 120$

*11. **Write** Explain the difference between the use of the words AND and OR in a compound inequality.

11. Sample: Use AND when you are looking for the intersection of two inequalities or where two graphs overlap. Use OR when you are looking for the union of two inequalities or all numbers where two graphs are shaded.

12. Factor $x^2 - 12x + 32$. $(x - 4)(x - 8)$
13. Add $x\sqrt[3]{xy} + x\sqrt[3]{xy}$. $2x\sqrt[3]{xy}$

*14. **Geometry** The area of a rectangle is described by the trinomial $x^2 + 12x + 27$. What are the dimensions of the rectangle? $(x + 9)$ and $(x + 3)$

15. **Multi-Step** Factor the polynomial $8x + x^2 - 4 - 5x$. $(x - 1)(x + 4)$

16. **Multiple Choice** In which of the trinomials are the binomial factors equal?   **B**
   A $(x^2 + 7x - 8)$ **B** $(x^2 + 6x + 9)$ **C** $(x^2 + 9x + 8)$ **D** $(x^2 + 7x + 12)$

*17. Use the scatter plot and the trend line to write an equation of the line.   Sample: $y = 0.375x + 5.5$

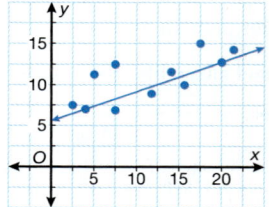

484   Saxon Algebra 1

INCLUSION

Use the following strategy for students who have difficulty with large group instruction. Have the students draw two identical number lines on separate transparencies and graph one inequality on each line. Then have the students write the inequalities for those graphs.

Have the students place the two number lines on top of each other and explain what the graph of the solution of the compound inequality should look like if they were joined by the word AND and then the word OR.

18. Error Analysis Two students are analyzing the data in the table and have drawn different conclusions. Which student is correct? Explain the error.

x	4	1	3	6	2	5
y	12	2	9	21	7	15

Student A	Student B
There is no correlation among the data because there is no constant increase or decrease in the data.	There is a positive correlation among the data because both sets of data values increase.

18. Student B; Sample: If the data are rearranged so that one set of data values are in ascending order, the corresponding data values in the other set also increase. A scatter plot of the data shows a positive correlation even though the data values are not in increasing order.

19. Chemistry The table shows atomic numbers and atomic mass for the first 10 elements of the periodic table of the elements. Make a scatter plot using the data values. See Additional Answers.

Atomic Symbol	H	He	Li	Be	B	C	N	O	F	Ne
Atomic Number	1	2	3	4	5	6	7	8	9	10
Atomic Weight	1.01	4.003	6.94	9.01	10.81	12.01	14.01	15.999	18.998	20.18

20. Which inequality is the solution of $-\frac{n}{12} < 36$? **B**

A $n < -432$ **B** $n > -432$ **C** $n < 432$ **D** $n > 432$

21. Analyze Consider the equation and inequality below. What parts of the solution steps are similar? What parts are different?

$$-2t = 4 \qquad -2t > 4$$

21. Sample: In both cases, divide by −2 to solve. For the inequality, the direction of the inequality needs to be switched because you are dividing by a negative number.

22. Marketing Four different collectible cards are being offered inside a cereal box. The probabilities of choosing a box with a given card are as follows: Card #1 (1 in 4), Card #2 (1 in 10), Card #3 (1 in 20), and Card #4 (6 in 10). If a box is chosen at random, what is the probability of getting either Card #3 or Card #4? $\frac{13}{20}$

23. Probability In some games, a single regular solid with 20 sides, labeled from 1 to 20, is used instead of a dot cube. What is the probability of rolling either a multiple of 2 or a multiple of 3 with a 20-sided solid? $\frac{13}{20}$

24. Multi-Step Draw a coordinate grid, and number it from −6 to +6 along the x- and y-axis. Will a line that passes through the points (−5, 1) and (−2, 4) be perpendicular to the line that passes through the points (−2, 2) and (2, −2)?

a. Model Line 1 passes through the points (−5, 1) and (−2, 4) and Line 2 passes through the points (−2, 2) and (2, −2). Graph the lines.

24a.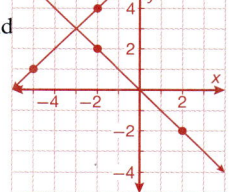

b. Write an equation for both lines.   line 1: $y = x + 6$; line 2: $y = -x$

c. Justify Are the lines perpendicular? Explain.   yes; Sample: The slopes of line 1 and line 2 have a product of −1.

Problem 29

Extend the Problem

Find the GCF of the two binomials. **(4r − d)**

25. **Multi-Step** There is an inverse square relationship between the electrostatic force
    (64) between two charged objects and the distance between the two objects, meaning
    that $F = \frac{k}{d^2}$. If two objects are 10 centimeters apart and have an attractive force
    of 0.512 newtons, how far apart are the two objects when they have an attractive
    force of 0.0142 newtons? Round to the nearest centimeter.   **60 cm**

*26. **Jewelry Appraisal** Maria has a white gold ring with a mass of 10.3 grams and a
    (63) volume of 0.7 cubic centimeters. White gold is made of nickel and gold. Nickel's
    mass is 9 grams per cubic centimeter and gold's mass is 19 grams per cubic
    centimeter. What is the volume of each metal in the ring?   **There are 0.4 cubic
    centimeters of gold and 0.3 cubic centimeters of nickel.**

27. **Multi-Step** Jack is building a rectangular barn. Write an expression for the area of
    (60) the region. Then find the area.   **$(x − 3)(x + 3)$; $x^2 − 9$ square units**

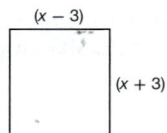

28. Find the product of $(x + 2)(x^2 + 2x + 2)$ using the Distributive Property.
    (58) **$x^3 + 4x^2 + 6x + 4$**

29. Find the LCM of $(24r − 6d)$ and $(20r − 5d)$.   **$30(4r − d)$**
    (57)

30. **Books** Every $14bn$ books donated to the library are nonfiction. Every $38b^9n$ books
    (57) donated are new. How many books have been donated when a new, nonfiction
    book is donated?   **$266b^9n$ books**

486   Saxon Algebra 1

CHALLENGE

Conjunctions can involve more than two inequalities. Although more complicated, the method to solving these compound inequalities is still the same. Solve this system:

$2x − 3 > 3$ AND $−x + 3 > −4$ AND

$3x − 4 \leq 11$

$3 < x \leq 5$

LOOKING FORWARD

Identifying, writing, and graphing compound inequalities prepare students for

• **Lesson 77** Solving Two-Step and Multi-Step Inequalities

• **Lesson 81** Solving Inequalities with Variables on Both Sides

• **Lesson 82** Solving Multi-Step Compound Inequalities

LESSON 74

Solving Absolute-Value Equations

Warm Up

1. **Vocabulary** The _____ of a number n is the distance from n to 0 on a number line. **absolute value**
$_{(5)}$

Solve.

2. $-5m + 6 = 8$ $-\frac{2}{5}$
$_{(23)}$

3. $\frac{2}{5}x - \frac{3}{10} = \frac{1}{2}$ 2
$_{(23)}$

4. $3m - 7m = 8m - 6$ $\frac{1}{2}$
$_{(28)}$

5. $-m - 6m + 4 = -2m - 5$ $\frac{9}{5}$
$_{(28)}$

New Concepts

The absolute value of a number n is the distance from n to 0 on a number line.

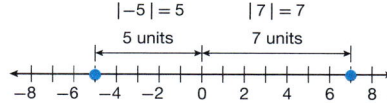

An equation that has one or more absolute-value expressions is called an **absolute-value equation**. There are two numeric values for x that have an absolute value of 5.

If $|x| = 5$, then $x = 5$ or $x = -5$.

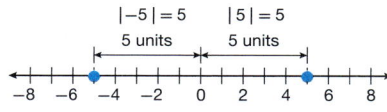

solution set: $\{5, -5\}$

In the equation $|x + 2| = 6$, $|x + 2|$ represents a distance of 6 units from the origin. The two numeric values for $(x + 2)$ that have an absolute value of 6 are 6 and -6.

If $|x + 2| = 6$, then $(x + 2) = 6$ or $(x + 2) = -6$.

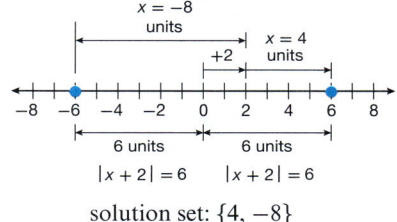

solution set: $\{4, -8\}$

Math Reasoning

Verify Use the definition of absolute value to verify that the absolute value of a number is never negative.

Sample: The absolute value of a number is its distance from zero. Distance cannot be negative.

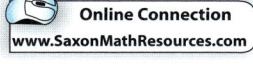
www.SaxonMathResources.com

Lesson 74   487

Example 1

These problems provide practice writing absolute-value equations without using the absolute-value symbol.

Additional Example 1
Solve.

a. $|x| = 4$ $\{4, -4\}$

b. $|x - 2| = 10$ $\{12, -8\}$

Example 2

TEACHER TIP
Emphasize that in general, absolute-value equations must be solved by first isolating the absolute-value term. If it is a special case where the isolated absolute value is equal to a negative number, the problem will have no solution.

Extend the Example 2a
Translate the equation into words using the definition of absolute value. **The distance from x to 0 times 5 equals 20.**

Additional Example 2
Solve.

a. $3|x| = 27$ $\{9, -9\}$

b. $5|x + 3| = 60$ $\{9, -15\}$

Example 1 Solving Absolute-Value Equations

Solve.

a. $|x| = 7$

SOLUTION Using the definition of absolute value, x is a number that is 7 units from 0. So, $|x| = 7$ means that $x = 7$ or that $x = -7$.

The solution is $\{7, -7\}$.

Check

$|x| = 7$ $\qquad$ $|x| = 7$
$|7| \stackrel{?}{=} 7$ $\qquad$ $|-7| \stackrel{?}{=} 7$
$7 = 7$ ✓ $\qquad$ $7 = 7$ ✓

b. $|x + 3| = 16$

SOLUTION Write $|x + 3| = 16$ as two equations.

$x + 3 = 16$ $\qquad$ or $\qquad$ $x + 3 = -16$
$x = 13$ Subtract 3 from both sides. $\qquad$ $x = -19$

The solution is $\{13, -19\}$.

Check

$|x + 3| = 16$ $\qquad$ $|x + 3| = 16$
$|13 + 3| \stackrel{?}{=} 16$ $\qquad$ $|-19 + 3| \stackrel{?}{=} 16$
$|16| \stackrel{?}{=} 16$ $\qquad$ $|-16| \stackrel{?}{=} 16$
$16 = 16$ ✓ $\qquad$ $16 = 16$ ✓

In some equations it is necessary to first isolate the absolute-value term.

Example 2 Isolating the Absolute Value

Solve.

a. $5|x| = 20$

SOLUTION

$\dfrac{5|x|}{5} = \dfrac{20}{5}$

$|x| = 4.$

The equation $|x| = 4$ means that $x = 4$ or that $x = -4$.

The solution set is $\{4, -4\}$.

Check

$5|x| = 20$ $\qquad$ $5|x| = 20$
$5|4| \stackrel{?}{=} 20$ $\qquad$ $5|-4| \stackrel{?}{=} 20$
$5 \cdot 4 \stackrel{?}{=} 20$ $\qquad$ $5 \cdot 4 \stackrel{?}{=} 20$
$20 = 20$ ✓ $\qquad$ $20 = 20$ ✓

Caution
When rewriting the absolute-value equation as two equations, do not use the absolute-value symbols.

Math Reasoning
Write Use the definition of absolute value to give the meaning of $|x + 3| = 16$.

Sample:
$|x + 3| = 16$ means that the distance from 0 to $(x + 3)$ is 16 units.

ALTERNATE METHOD FOR EXAMPLE 1b

Instead of rewriting the equation as two separate equations, have students write one single expression:

$|x + 3| = 16$

$x + 3 = \pm 16$

$x = \pm 16 - 3$

Then have students use the last equation to find the solution $\{13, -19\}$.

b. $4|x-2| = 80$

SOLUTION

Isolate the absolute value.

$\dfrac{4|x-2|}{4} = \dfrac{80}{4}$ Division Property of Equality

$|x-2| = 20$ Simplify.

Write $|x-2| = 20$ as two equations.

$x - 2 = 20$ or $x - 2 = -20$

$x = 22$ Add 2 to both sides. $x = -18$

The solution is $\{22, -18\}$.

Check

$4\|x-2\| = 80$	$4\|x-2\| = 80$
$4\|22-2\| \stackrel{?}{=} 80$	$4\|-18-2\| \stackrel{?}{=} 80$
$4\|20\| \stackrel{?}{=} 80$	$4\|-20\| \stackrel{?}{=} 80$
$4 \cdot 20 \stackrel{?}{=} 80$	$4 \cdot 20 \stackrel{?}{=} 80$
$80 = 80$	$80 = 80$

Example 3   Solving Special Cases

Solve.

a. $|x - 6| - 2 = -2$

SOLUTION

Isolate the absolute value.

$|x - 6| - 2 = -2$

$|x - 6| = 0$ Add 2 to both sides.

The absolute-value equation can be written as one equation: $(x - 6) = 0$.

$x - 6 = 0$

$x = 6$

The equation has only one solution. The solution is $\{6\}$.

b. $|x + 4| = -8$

SOLUTION

The expression $|x + 4|$ is equal to a negative value. Absolute value is a distance from 0, so it cannot be equal to a negative number. There is no solution. The solution is written as $\{\}$ or $\emptyset$, meaning that the solution set is empty.

Math Reasoning

Analyze Why does the absolute-value equation $|x - 6| = 0$ have only one solution?

Sample: The variable in the absolute value expression represents a point that is 0 units from 6. Only 1 number, 6, is 0 units from 6.

Error Alert When solving absolute-value equations, a common mistake is to treat the absolute-value bars like parentheses. Discuss the following statements:

$|x + 3| = 16$

$|x + 3 - 3| \neq 16 - 3$

Also, while $-(-7) = 7$, $-|-7| \neq 7$. The opposite of the absolute value of -7 is -7.

Example 3

Point out to students that there are two special cases with absolute-value equations: when the absolute value is equal to 0, or when it is set equal to a negative number.

Additional Example 3

Solve.

a. $|x + 3| + 4 = 4 \{-3\}$

b. $5|x - 2| = -1$ no solution or $\{\ \}$ or $\emptyset$

Lesson 74

Example 4 Application: Technology

The thermostat in a classroom is set at 21°C. The thermostat will turn on (or off) if the recorded temperature is ±1.2°C of this setting. What are the maximum and minimum temperatures for this classroom?

SOLUTION

Understand The thermostat will turn on or off if the difference between the recorded temperature, x, and the set temperature, 21°C, is 1.2° or $-1.2°$. This difference $(x - 21)$ can be thought of as the distance between the maximum (or minimum) temperature and the set temperature.

Plan The distance between the thermostat setting and the maximum (or minimum) temperature can be expressed by $|x - 21| = 1.2$.

Solve $|x - 21| = 1.2$

$$x - 21 = +1.2 \quad \text{or} \quad x - 21 = -1.2$$
$$x = 22.2 \quad \quad \quad x = 19.8$$

The solution is {22.2, 19.8}. With the thermostat set at 21°C, the temperature in the room could rise to a maximum of 22.2°C or fall to a minimum of 19.8°C.

Check $21°C + 1.2°C = 22.2°C \quad \quad 21°C - 1.2°C = 19.8°C$

Lesson Practice

Solve.

a. $|x| = 11$ (Ex 1)   b. $|q + 3| = 6$ (Ex 1)   c. $4|y| = 24$ {6, −6} (Ex 2)

d. $5|z - 3| = 20$ (Ex 2)   e. $|x - 5| + 3 = 3$ (Ex 3)   f. $|x - 5| = -1$ ∅ (Ex 3)

g.  A strawberry grower ships berries to a processing plant in 30-pound cases. The plant will not accept cases that differ from this weight by more than ±0.4 pound. Write and solve an absolute-value equation to find the minimum and maximum weights that the processing plant will accept. $|x - 30| = 0.4$; 29.6 lb, 30.4 lb

Practice Distributed and Integrated

Factor.

1. $x^2 + 12x - 28$ $(x - 2)(x + 14)$ (72)

2. $15x + 50 + x^2$ $(x + 5)(x + 10)$ (72)

3. $18 + x^2 + 11x$ $(x + 2)(x + 9)$ (72)

*4. $3x - 18 + x^2$ $(x - 3)(x + 6)$ (72)

Solve.

*5 $|n| = 13$ {13, −13} (74)

*6 Solve $|x + 7| = 3$. {−4, −10} (74)

*7. Find the common solution for the system of equations: $-2y + 3x = 4$. $y = \frac{3}{2}x - 2$
(67)
$$-y + \frac{3}{2}x = 2$$

*8. (Carpentry) The shelf in a cabinet is set into a notch at a height of 12 inches. So
(74) that the shelf can be adjusted to different heights, the cabinetmaker cuts notches at one-inch intervals above and below the shelf. Write and solve an absolute-value equation for the maximum and minimum heights of a shelf set two notches above or below the 12-inch height. $|h - 12| = 2$; 14 in., 10 in.

*9. **Write** Why does the equation $|x - 6| = 2x - 3$ have no solution for $x = -3$?
(74)

*10. **Model** Use a number line to diagram the solution of the absolute-value equation
(74) $|x - 3| = 5$. Then write the solution set to the absolute-value equation. See Additional Answers.; $\{-2, 8\}$

*11. **Measurement** The diameter of a circular clamp is 10 centimeters. Its diameter can
(74) be changed by changing its circumference.
   a. If the circumference of the clamp is changed by ± 5cm, write an equation to find the clamp's minimum and maximum diameters.   Sample: $|D - 10| = \frac{5}{\pi}$ or $\pi|D - 10| = 5$
   b. Solve the equation.   11.6 cm, 8.4 cm

12. Graph the compound inequality $x \geq 5$ OR $x < 0$.
(73)

13. Solve the inequality $6x < 12$ OR $3x > 15$. $x < 2$ OR $x > 5$
(73)

*14. **Error Analysis** Two students are solving $|z + 3| = 5$. Which student is correct? Explain the error.   Student B; Sample: Student A incorrectly isolated the absolute-value term as z; the term should be $z + 3$.
(74)

Student A	Student B	
$\|z + 3\| = 5$	$\|z + 3\| = 5$	
$\|z\| + 3 = 5$	$z + 3 = 5$	$z + 3 = -5$
$\|z\| = 5 - 3 = 2$	$z = 5 - 3$	$z = -5 - 3$
$z = 2 \quad z = -2$	$z = 2$	$z = -8$
The solution set is $\{2, -2\}$.	The solution set is $\{2, -8\}$.	

*15. **Geometry** The third side of a triangle must be greater than the difference of the
(73) other two sides and less than the sum of the other two sides. Suppose that two sides of a triangle have lengths 6 inches and 11 inches. Write a compound inequality that describes the possible values for the third side of the triangle. $5 < x < 17$

16. **Multi-Step** Use the compound inequality $3x > 45$ OR $-2x \geq 24$.
(73)
   a. Solve the compound inequality. $x > 15$ OR $x \leq -12$
   b. Graph the solution.

17. Factor the trinomial $x^2 - 3x - 40$. $(x - 8)(x + 5)$
(72)

18. (Landscaping) To beautify a city park, landscapers use two sets of plans to lay out
(72) rectangular flower beds. One set of plans for the area is described by the trinomial $x^2 + 9x + 20$. The other set is described by the trinomial $x^2 + 21x + 20$.
   a. Determine the binomial factors of each set. $(x + 4)(x + 5)$ and $(x + 1)(x + 20)$
   b. Which set can be used to lay out longer, narrower beds? Explain.

9. Sample: When the equation is evaluated at -3, the term on the right side of the equation has a value of -9. Such a solution would indicate that the absolute value of $|-3 - 6|$ is negative, which is not possible.

18b. the second set; Sample: The dimensions of the rectangles described by this trinomial are much longer than they are wide.

Lesson 74   491

3 Practice

Math Conversations
Discussion to strengthen understanding

Problem 18
Extend the Problem
"With the same two sets of plans for the flower beds, what are the areas of the flower beds?"
$x^2 + 9x + 20^2$;
$x^2 + 21x + 20^2$

"If $x \neq 0$, which plan will always take up more area?"
$x^2 + 21x + 20^2$

ENGLISH LEARNERS

For problem 8, explain the meaning of the word **notch**. Say:

"A notch is a v-shaped hole or cut. If a belt is too loose, a notch can be made to make it fit correctly."

Describe by drawing on the board how a carpenter would make notches to hold up shelves in a cabinet.

Lesson 74   491

Problem 20

Error Alert

A common mistake that students make when isolating the term with a fractional coefficient is to incorrectly multiply the other side by that coefficient and not the inverse. Remind students that the goal is to get a coefficient of 1, and to do that, you have to multiply by the multiplicative inverse.

Problem 27

Guide the students by asking them the following questions.

"If you increase the number of people will that increase or decrease the number of days to finish the house?" decrease

"If the number of days decreases when the number of people increases, is that a direct variation or an inverse variation?" inverse

"Write an inverse variation for the problem and solve for k."
$15 = \frac{k}{20}$ or $20 = \frac{k}{15}$; $k = 300$

"Use the value for k and an inverse-variation equation to solve the problem." $y = \frac{300}{5}$; 60 people

---

19. Multiple Choice A _____ is a graph made up of separate, disconnected points. **A**
(Inv 2)
A discrete graph B continuous graph C trend graph D linear graph

20. Determine if the inequality symbol in the expression $-\frac{2}{3}c \leq 6$ needs to be
(70) reversed, and then solve. yes; $c \geq -9$

21. If a square measures $\sqrt{144}$ inches on one side, what is the perimeter of the square?
(69) 48 in.

22. Determine the probability of rolling at least one odd number or a sum of 9 with
(68) two number cubes. $\frac{3}{4}$

23. Multi-Step The library charges a late fee based on the number of days a book is
(67) overdue. The equation for the fee is $y = \$0.25d + \$0.05$.
a. What is the fee for a book that is 10 days overdue? $2.55
b. Thirty days is the maximum number of days for which the library charges. What is the maximum amount the library charges? $7.55
c. Classify the system of equations for the library fee and $y = \$7.55$. consistent and independent

24. Justify If a, b, x, and y are all greater than 0 and $x > a$ and $y < b$, how does
(66) $\frac{x}{y}$ compare to $\frac{a}{b}$? Justify your answer. $\frac{x}{y}$ will always be greater than $\frac{a}{b}$ because $\frac{x}{y}$ will always have a larger numerator and smaller denominator than $\frac{a}{b}$.

*25. Predict Use the trend line to predict the corresponding y-value for an x-value of 40.
(71) $y \approx 7.9$

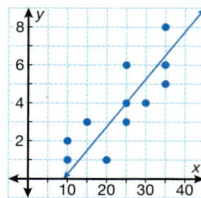

26. Justify True or False: The lines represented by $y = \frac{x}{4} - 2$ and $4y = x + 8$ are
(65) parallel. Explain.

26. true; Sample: The lines are parallel because they have the same slope of $\frac{1}{4}$ and different y-intercepts.

27. (**Construction**) To build Ariane's house will take a constant number of individual
(64) work days. If a construction crew of 15 people can build the house in 20 days, how many people does it take to finish the house in 5 days? 60 people

28. Multi-Step A container has a square base. The area is 800 cm². The size of a book is
(61) 25 cm by 30 cm. Can the book lie flat on the base of the container?
a. Find the side length of the container. $20\sqrt{2}$ cm
b. Compare the side length with the dimensions of the book. $20\sqrt{2}$ cm < 30 cm; $20\sqrt{2}$ cm > 25 cm
c. Use the comparison to determine if the book will fit. Sample: The book will not fit because one side of the container's dimensions is less than the book's dimensions.

29. Solve the system by substitution: $3x + y = 13$. (4, 1)
(59) $2x - 4y = 4$

30. Sue purchases a rectangular billboard sign for her new business. The length can
(58) be represented by $6x^2 + 6x + 6$ and the width is $(x + 8)$. What is the area of Sue's new billboard? $6x^3 + 54x^2 + 54x + 48$

492 Saxon Algebra 1

CHALLENGE

Translate and solve the following statement:
The distance from x to 3 times 2 plus 4 is 14.
$2|x - 3| + 4 = 14$; $\{8, -2\}$

LOOKING FORWARD

Solving absolute-value equations prepares students for

- **Lesson 91** Solving Absolute-Value Inequalities

- **Lesson 94** Solving Multi-Step Absolute-Value Equations

- **Lesson 101** Solving Multi-Step Absolute-Value Inequalities

- **Lesson 107** Graphing Absolute-Value Functions

LESSON 75

Factoring Trinomials: $ax^2 + bx + c$

Warm Up

1. **Vocabulary** A _____ is a polynomial with three terms.   **trinomial**

Factor.

2. $x^2 + 3x - 10$ $(x + 5)(x - 2)$
3. $x^2 - x - 42$ $(x + 6)(x - 7)$

Simplify.

4. $(4x + 5)(3x - 2)$ $12x^2 + 7x - 10$
5. $(2x + 5)^2$ $4x^2 + 20x + 25$

New Concepts

Recall that a pattern is used when factoring trinomials of the form $x^2 + bx + c$. A pair of numbers is found whose product is c and whose sum is b. When a trinomial takes the form $ax^2 + bx + c$, the pattern no longer works. When the leading coefficient a is not equal to 1 another pattern emerges.

Example 1 Factoring when b and c are Positive

Factor completely.

$2x^2 + 7x + 5$

SOLUTION

Since $2x^2$ is the product of $(2x)$ and (x), write $(2x)(x)$.

The third term of the trinomial, 5, is the product of the last terms in the binomials. List the pairs of numbers that result in a product of 5.

$(1)(5) \qquad (5)(1) \qquad (-1)(-5) \qquad (-5)(-1)$

Because the middle term, $7x$, is positive, eliminate the pairs of negative numbers. Check each of the other pairs to see which gives you $7x$.

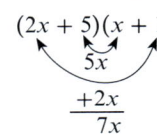

$(2x + 1)(x + 5)$ $(2x + 5)(x + 1)$
$1x$ $5x$
$+10x$ $+2x$
$\overline{11x}$ $\overline{7x}$

So, $2x^2 + 7x + 5 = (2x + 5)(x + 1)$.

Check Use FOIL to "undo" the factoring.

$(2x + 5)(x + 1) \stackrel{?}{=} 2x^2 + 2x + 5x + 5$
$ = 2x^2 + 7x + 5$ ✓

Hint
When c is positive, the second term in both binomials will have the same sign (negative or positive) depending on the sign of b.

Online Connection
www.SaxonMathResources.com

Lesson 75   493

MATH BACKGROUND

In a binomial of the form $x^2 + bx + c$, b is always the sum or difference of the factors of c.

To factor a trinomial in the form $ax^2 + bx + c$, the a coefficient must be taken into account. The b factor now becomes the sum or difference of the product of one a factor and one c factor, and the product of the other a factor and the other c factor. This opens up possibilities for many more combinations. Additionally, the signs of the factors must be considered.

To factor $12x^2 - 2x - 24$, the first coefficients must have a product of 12. The second terms of the binomials must have a product of -24. The second term of the trinomial is the product of one factor of 12 and one factor of 24 plus or minus the product of the second factor of 12 and the second factor of -24.

This presents a greater challenge finding the factors, but through experimentation the factors can be determined: $(3x + 4)(4x - 6)$.

Example 2

The example explains factoring a trinomial when one of the terms of each factor is negative.

Additional Example 2

Factor completely:

$4x^2 - 23x + 15$ $(x - 5)(4x - 3)$

Example 3

This example shows students how to factor a trinomial when one factor has a negative term that results in the second term of the trinomial being positive or negative.

Additional Example 3

Factor completely:

a. $6x^2 + 8x - 8$ $(2x + 4)(3x - 2)$

b. $2x^2 - 3x - 20$ $(2x + 5)(x - 4)$

Error Alert The most common error students make when factoring trinomials is to reverse the signs of the binomials. Encourage students to multiply the binomials in their solutions to check their answers.

TEACHER TIP

Most students will understand the concept of factoring the more complex trinomials, but they may be slow at first finding the correct solutions. Encourage them to list the possible factors on paper. Matching many factors can be time consuming. Allow a little extra time for students to work on this lesson.

Example 2 Factoring when *b* is Negative and *c* is Positive

Factor $6x^2 - 11x + 3$ completely.

SOLUTION

The first term of the trinomial, $6x^2$, is the product of $(6x)(x)$ or $(3x)(2x)$. So, write $(6x\ \ )(x\ \ )$ and $(3x\ \ )(2x\ \ )$.

The third term of the trinomial, 3, is the product of the last terms in the binomials. List the pairs of factors that result in a product of 3. Because *b* is negative, both factors will be negative.

$$(-1)(-3) \qquad (-3)(-1)$$

Check each of the pairs to see which results in the middle term, $-11x$.

Caution

After finding the pair that appears to work, check the other possibilities. If another answer is found, double-check your work.

Possibilities	Middle Term
$(6x - 1)(x - 3)$	$-19x$
$(6x - 3)(x - 1)$	$-9x$
$(3x - 1)(2x - 3)$	$-11x$ ✓
$(3x - 3)(2x - 1)$	$-9x$

So, $6x^2 - 11x + 3 = (3x - 1)(2x - 3)$.

Example 3 Factoring when *c* is Negative

Factor completely.

a. $4x^2 + 4x - 3$

SOLUTION

The first term of the trinomial, $4x^2$, is the product of $(4x)(x)$ and $(2x)(2x)$. So, write $(4x\ \ )(x\ \ )$ and $(2x\ \ )(2x\ \ )$.

The third term, -3, is the product of the last terms in the binomials. List the pairs of factors that result in the product -3.

$$(1)(-3) \qquad (-1)(3) \qquad (3)(-1) \qquad (-3)(1)$$

Check each of the pairs to see which results in the middle term, $4x$.

Possibilities	Middle Term
$(4x + 1)(x - 3)$	$-11x$
$(4x + 3)(x - 1)$	$-x$
$(4x - 1)(x + 3)$	$11x$
$(4x - 3)(x + 1)$	x
$(2x + 1)(2x - 3)$	$-4x$
$(2x + 3)(2x - 1)$	$4x$ ✓

So, $4x^2 + 4x - 3 = (2x + 3)(2x - 1)$.

ENGLISH LEARNERS

Explain the meaning of the word **completely**. Say:

"Completely describes the way that something is done. It means that a task is done so that all parts of the task have been fully carried out. For example, if all of the steps in a problem are shown, then the problem is completely shown."

Have students give other examples using the word completely.

b. $3x^2 - 11x - 4$

SOLUTION

Look at the first term of the trinomial. Since $3x^2 = (3x)(x)$, write $(3x \quad)(x \quad)$.

The last term is -4. List the pairs of factors whose product is -4.

$(-1)(4) \quad (1)(-4) \quad (-2)(2) \quad (-4)(1) \quad (4)(-1) \quad (2)(-2)$

Check each of the pairs to see which results in the middle term, $-11x$.

Possibilities	Middle Term
$(3x - 1)(x + 4)$	$11x$
$(3x - 4)(x + 1)$	$-x$
$(3x + 1)(x - 4)$	$-11x$
$(3x + 4)(x - 1)$	x
$(3x - 2)(x + 2)$	$4x$
$(3x + 2)(x - 2)$	$-4x$

So, $3x^2 - 11x - 4 = (3x + 1)(x - 4)$.

Hint

With a negative last term, if the middle term has the wrong sign, reverse the sign in both binomials.

Example 4 Factoring with Two Variables

Factor $2x^2 - 11xy + 5y^2$ completely.

SOLUTION

Since $2x^2 = (2x)(x)$, write $(2x \quad)(x \quad)$.

The last term, $5y^2$, is the product of $(-5y)$ and $(-y)$. Both factors are negative because the second term is negative.

Check the factors to see which order results in $-11xy$.

$(2x - 5y)(x - y)$

Add the product of the outer and inner terms to see if the sum is $-11xy$.

$(2x)(-y) + (-5y)(x)$
$= -2xy - 5xy$
$= -7xy$

Now check the middle term of $(2x - y)(x - 5y)$.

$(2x)(-5y) + (-y)(x)$
$= -10xy - xy$
$= -11xy$ ✓

So, $2x^2 - 11xy + 5y^2 = (2x - y)(x - 5y)$.

Hint

If there are two variables in the trinomial, one variable should descend in power while the other ascends.

Example 4

This example demonstrates how to factor a trinomial with two variables. Additionally, each factor includes a negative term.

Additional Example 4

Factor completely:

$(2x^2 - 5xy + 2y^2)$
$(2x - y)(x - 2y)$

Lesson 75   495

INCLUSION

Use the following strategy for students who have difficulty following multiple steps. Some students have a great deal of difficulty "un-multiplying" a trinomial, especially when the level of trinomials becomes more complex. Although it can be tedious, have students write lists of all the possible factors for the *a*- and *c*-terms in the trinomial. They can then check each possible combination to determine the correct terms for the binomial factors.

Factor completely: $4x^2 - 8x - 32$.

Factors of 4:
1 and 4
2 and 2

Factors of -32:
1 and -32 -2 and 16
-1 and 32   4 and -8
2 and -16 -4 and 8

By matching every possible combination until they find one that satisfies the conditions, students can develop good work habits and learn to factor the complex trinomials. $(2x - 8)(2x + 4)$

Lesson 75   495

Example 5

This example demonstrates how to reorder the terms of a trinomial so that it may be more easily factored.

Extend the Example

Have students evaluate the problem and the factors in parts **a** and **b** for $x = -2$.
$-17(-2) + 5 + 12(-2)^2 = 87$,
$(12(-2) - 5)(-2 - 1) = 87$;
$-2 - 7(-2) + 4(-2)^2 = 28$,
$(4(-2) + 1)(-2 - 2) = 28$

Additional Example 5

Factor completely.

a. $(32x + 8 + 14x^2)$
$(7x + 2)(2x + 4)$

b. $(-9 + 6x^2 - 3x)$
$(3x + 3)(2x - 3)$

Math Reasoning

Analyze Why are the terms rearranged before factoring?

Sample: Using the form $ax^2 + bx + c$ makes it easier to apply the factoring pattern.

Example 5 Rearranging Before Factoring

Factor completely.

a. $-17x + 5 + 12x^2$

SOLUTION

Before factoring, rearrange the terms so that they are in descending order according to the exponent.

$12x^2 - 17x + 5$

The first term, $12x^2$, can be factored as $(12x)(x)$, $(6x)(2x)$, and $(4x)(3x)$.

The last term, 5, can be factored as $(-5)(-1)$ and $(-1)(-5)$.

Check each pair to see which results in the middle term, $-17x$.

Possibilities	Middle Term
$(12x - 5)(x - 1)$	$-17x$ ✓
$(12x - 1)(x - 5)$	$-61x$
$(6x - 5)(2x - 1)$	$-16x$
$(6x - 1)(2x - 5)$	$-32x$
$(4x - 5)(3x - 1)$	$-19x$
$(4x - 1)(3x - 5)$	$-23x$

So, $12x^2 - 17x + 5 = (12x - 5)(x - 1)$.

b. $-2 - 7x + 4x^2$

SOLUTION

Rearrange the terms in the expression to $4x^2 - 7x - 2$.

The first term, $4x^2$, can be factored as $(4x)(x)$ and $(2x)(2x)$.

The last term, -2, can be factored as $(-2)(1)$, $(-1)(2)$, $(2)(-1)$, and $(1)(-2)$.

Check each pair to see which results in the middle term, $-7x$.

Possibilities	Middle Term
$(4x - 2)(x + 1)$	$2x$
$(4x - 1)(x + 2)$	$7x$
$(4x + 2)(x - 1)$	$-2x$
$(4x + 1)(x - 2)$	$-7x$ ✓
$(2x - 2)(2x + 1)$	$-2x$
$(2x - 1)(2x + 2)$	$2x$
$(2x + 2)(2x - 1)$	$2x$
$(2x + 1)(2x - 2)$	$-2x$

So, $4x^2 - 7x - 2 = (4x + 1)(x - 2)$.

496   Saxon Algebra 1

Lesson Practice

Factor completely.

a. $9x^2 + 38x + 8$ $(9x + 2)(x + 4)$ (Ex 1)
b. $10x^2 - 23x + 12$ $(5x - 4)(2x - 3)$ (Ex 2)
c. $3x^2 + 5x - 2$ $(3x - 1)(x + 2)$ (Ex 3)
d. $6x^2 - 5x - 4$ $(2x + 1)(3x - 4)$ (Ex 3)
e. $6x^2 + 11xy + 4y^2$ $(3x + 4y)(2x + y)$ (Ex 4)
f. $-13x + 14x^2 + 3$ $(2x - 1)(7x - 3)$ (Ex 5)

Practice — Distributed and Integrated

Factor completely.

*1. $6x^2 + 13x + 6$ $(3x + 2)(2x + 3)$ (75)

*2. $3x^2 - 14x - 5$ $(3x + 1)(x - 5)$ (75)

*3. $18 - 15x + 2x^2$ $(2x - 3)(x - 6)$ (75)

*4. $-15 + 7x + 2x^2$ $(2x - 3)(x + 5)$ (75)

Simplify.

5. $22c\sqrt{de} - 9\sqrt{de}$ $(22c - 9)\sqrt{de}$ (69)

6. $8\sqrt{7} - 4\sqrt{11} - 3\sqrt{7} + 7\sqrt{11}$ $5\sqrt{7} + 3\sqrt{11}$ (69)

 *7. **Write** Explain why b in $ax^2 + bx + c$ is not the sum of the factors of c.
(75)

7. Sample: Because the coefficient of the squared term is not 1, b is found by adding the product of factors of c and factors of a.

*8. **Justify** Show that $7x^2 - 12x + 10$ is prime (cannot be factored).
(75)

*9. **Multiple Choice** Evaluate $2x^2 - 10x + 14$ if $x = -2$. **C**
(75)
  A 2 **B** 10 **C** 42 **D** 50

*10. For a situation that represents a direct variation, what does the graph of that situation look like? a line
(Inv 7)

11. Solve $|z| = 5$. $\{5, -5\}$
(74)

12. **Geometry** Sliding-glass tubes form a square with a perimeter of 36 inches. Both the length and width of the square can be changed by ± 1.5 inches.
(74)
  a. Write an absolute-value equation to find the greatest and least perimeter of the square. Sample: $|x - 36| = 4(1.5)$
  b. What are the greatest and least perimeters? {42 in., 30 in.}

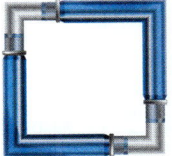

8. Sample: $(7x - 10)(x - 1) = 7x^2 - 17x + 10$, $(7x - 1)(x - 10) = 7x^2 - 71x + 10$, $(7x - 5)(x - 2) = 7x^2 - 19x + 10$, and $(7x - 2)(x - 5) = 7x^2 - 37x + 10$. These are all the possibilities and none are correct.

Lesson 75   497

MANIPULATIVE USE

Students who have difficulty factoring trinomials mentally may benefit from using algebra tiles. Have students make rectangles that show the different possible factors for the coefficient of the a-term and the c-term of the trinomial. They can derive a list of factors from this and check the possible combinations.

$24x^2 + 72x + 48$

Show the factors of 24:

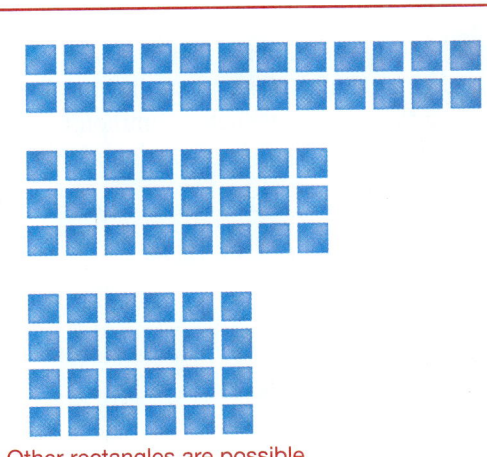

Other rectangles are possible.

Lesson Practice

Problem a

Scaffolding Have students make a list of all possible factors of $9x^2$ and a list of all possible factors of 8. Point out that the sign of the second term is positive, and have students explain how this helps eliminate some of the possible choices for factors.

Problem d

Error Alert Watch for students who think that because the second term of the trinomial is negative, then both second terms of the factors are negative.

 **Check for Understanding**

The questions below help assess the concepts taught in this lesson.

"What do the signs of a trinomial tell about the factors?" They give clues about the signs of the factors.

"If the middle term of a trinomial is negative, what is known about the signs of the second terms of the factors?" At least one second term of the factors is negative.

"When are both second terms of the factors negative?" If the third term of the trinomial is positive and the second term is negative, then the second terms of the factors are negative.

3 Practice

Math Conversations

Discussion to strengthen understanding

Problem 12

Extend the Problem

Find the greatest and least area of the square. greatest: 110.25 in²; least: 56.25 in²

Lesson 75   497

Problem 13
Error Alert
Watch for students who overlook that this is an absolute value equation and forget to solve two equations. Remind students that there are two valid solutions to the problem. They must write and solve two equations to find the complete solution.

Problem 15
Extend the Problem
Have students graph the results of the compound inequality to show the solution set.

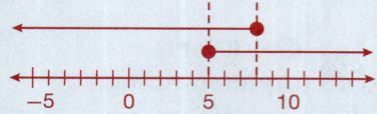

Problem 16
Guide the students by asking them the following questions.

"**What does the inequality tell you?**" that x is less than 1 and greater than -2

"**How should the signs of the inequality be shown in the solution graph?**" They should be shown as open circles on the graph.

"**How does the graph reflect the information given in the compound inequality?**" The compound inequality shows x between the two integers. The graph shows the line shaded between the two integers on the number line.

---

*13. **Multi-Step** Given the equation $|x + 2| + 6 = 17$, answer the questions below.
   a. Isolate the absolute value expression. $|x + 2| = 11$
   b. Use the definition of absolute value to rewrite the absolute-value equation as two equations. $x + 2 = 11, x + 2 = -11$
   c. What is the solution set? $\{9, -13\}$

*14. **Physics** A steel bar at a temperature of 300°C has the length L. If the temperature of the bar is raised or lowered 100°C, its length will increase or decrease by 0.12%, respectively. Write an absolute-value equation for the maximum and minimum lengths of the bar when it is heated to 400°C or cooled to 200°C.
$|x - L| = 0.0012L$

15. Solve the compound inequality $-14 \leq -3x + 10 \leq -5$. $5 \leq x \leq 8$

16. **Error Analysis** Two students graph the compound inequality $-2 < x < 1$ as shown. Which student is correct? Explain the error.

Student A 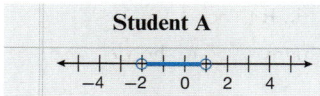   Student B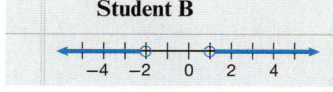

16. Student A; Sample: If you substitute 0 into the equation, it is a solution. Therefore, the points between the endpoints should be shaded since 0 is a solution.

17. **Temperature** The predicted high temperature for the day is 88°F and the predicted low temperature for the day is 65°F. Write a compound inequality that shows the range of temperatures predicted for the day. $65 \leq x \leq 88$; $x \geq 65$ AND $x \leq 88$

18. **Multiple Choice** Which binomial is a factor of $x^2 + 5x - 6$? **D**
   A $x + 1$ **B** $x + 2$ **C** $x + 3$ **D** $x + 6$

19. **Verify** Show that 2 is a solution of the compound inequality $x < 3$ OR $x > 6$.

20. Use the scatter plot and the trend line to write an equation of the line.

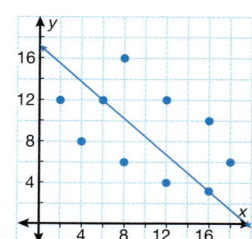

Sample: $y = -0.9x + 17.4$

19. Since $2<3$, 2 is a solution of the compound inequality because the inequality uses OR and the solution needs to be true only for one inequality.

21. **Measurement** Tyrone bought 24 quarts of juice for a party. He plans to serve the juice in $\frac{1}{4}$-quart cups. How many servings can he plan to make with the juice he has available? 96 servings or fewer

22. **Fitness** To make the swim team, Maria needs to swim 10 laps in under 8 minutes. Write and solve an inequality to find the maximum average time per lap she could swim to still make the team. less than 48 seconds

23. Suppose Carrie walks home from school at a rate of 4 miles per hour. Write an equation that relates Carrie's time to the distance traveled home. Is this a direct or indirect variation? What represents the constant of variation? $d = 4t$; direct; rate

498 Saxon Algebra 1

CHALLENGE

Challenge students to factor these higher level trinomials. Give them the hint that they can factor out any factor common to all the terms before factoring the trinomial itself.

1. $9p^2s - 30ps^2 + 25s^3$ $s(3p - 5s)(3p - 5s)$

2. $6k^3 + 5k^2 + k$ $k(2k + 1)(3k + 1)$

3. $30m^2 - 87m + 30$ $3(2m - 5)(5m - 2)$

4. $9a^3b - 24a^2b^2 + 16ab^3$ $ab(3a - 4b)(3a - 4b)$

5. $42x^3 + 45x^2 - 27x$ $3x(2x + 3)(7x - 3)$

24. Find the probability of choosing an odd number card from a pack of cards numbered 1 through 9 or the number 1. $\frac{5}{9}$

25. (Web Authoring) A company designs web sites and charges a fee of $y = \$250 + \$50w$. The charge includes a base fee of $250, plus a weekly fee based on the number of weeks the client requires full support. If the equation $y = 800$ represents the amount a company pays, for how many weeks do they receive full support?
11 weeks

26. Analyze The equation $y = 4$ describes a horizontal line with zero slope. The equation $x = 4$ describes a vertical line with infinite slope. Classify the system formed by these two equations.   consistent and independent

27. Multi-Step Charlene is shopping for used DVDs. She buys some DVDs from Bin A that cost $7 each and some from Bin B that cost $5 each. Charlene has $45.
  a. Write an inequality representing the situation. (Hint: You must use two different variables to represent DVDs from each bin.) $7a + 5b \leq 45$
  b. Can Charlene buy 4 DVDs from Bin A and 4 from Bin B? no
  c. Charlene decides to buy 3 DVDs from Bin A. How many can she choose from Bin B? 4

28. Multi-Step The amounts of measurable rain (in inches) per day recorded for Seattle in July 2007 are listed below.

0.06, 0.04, 0.01, 0.28, 0.01, 0.15, 0.21, 0.38, 0.30, 0.10
  a. Create a histogram of the data.
  b. Is this the best representation of the data for the entire month? Why or why not?

29. Find the product: $(4y - 4)(4y + 4)$. $16y^2 - 16$

30. Solve the system of equations by substitution.
$$5x + 3y = 1$$
$$8x + 4y = 4$$
$(2, -3)$

28a. Measurable Rainfall

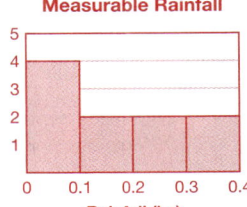

Rainfall (in.)

28b. No; Sample: the histogram only reports the days for which rainfall was measured. The frequency of days without rain would need to be represented as well for the plot to be accurate and fully useful.

Lesson 75   499

Problem 24
Error Alert
Watch for students who include the number 1 as a separate outcome and find the solution $\frac{6}{9}$.

The number 1 is already included as a possible outcome by virtue of being an odd number. The 1 should not be considered a separate outcome.

Problem 25
Extend the Problem
"What is the cost of 13 weeks of full support if 1 week of full support has a cost of $62?" $1,056

Problem 27
Guide the students by asking them the following questions.

"Why is an inequality written instead of an equation?" Charlene has $45, but she might spend less than that amount.

"Why are two different variables needed?" There are two different bins, and she might buy a different number of DVDs from each bin.

"How is the number of DVDs that can be chosen from Bin B in part c found?" Substitute the given number of DVDs from Bin A and solve the inequality for y.

LOOKING FORWARD

Factoring trinomials of the form $ax^2 + bx + c$ will prepare students for

- **Lesson 79** Factoring Trinomials by Using the GCF
- **Lesson 87** Factoring Polynomials by Grouping
- **Investigation 9** Choosing a Factoring Method
- **Lesson 93** Dividing Polynomials

Lesson 75   499

LESSON 76

1 Warm Up

Problems 4 and 5
Remind students that in order to add and/or subtract radical terms, the terms must have like radicals.

2 New Concepts

Students will learn how to apply the Product Property of Radicals in different situations.

Example 1

This example demonstrates using the Product Property to multiply simple radical expressions.

Additional Example 1

Simplify. All variables represent non-negative real numbers.

a. $\sqrt{2}\sqrt{50}$ **10**

b. $3\sqrt{2} \cdot 5\sqrt{7}$ **$15\sqrt{14}$**

c. $(4\sqrt{6})^2$ **96**

d. $3\sqrt{6x} \cdot \sqrt{2x}$ **$6x\sqrt{3}$**

LESSON RESOURCES

Student Edition Practice
 Workbook 76
Reteaching Master 76
Adaptations Master 76
Challenge and Enrichment
 Master C76

LESSON 76

Multiplying Radical Expressions

Warm Up

1. **Vocabulary** A _____ is an expression that contains a radical.
   (61) **radical expression**

   Simplify.

2. $\sqrt{50{,}000}$ **$100\sqrt{5}$**
   (61)

3. $\sqrt{108}$ **$6\sqrt{3}$**
   (61)

4. $2\sqrt{8} - 3\sqrt{32}$ **$-8\sqrt{2}$**
   (69)

5. $2\sqrt{18} + 4\sqrt{300} - \sqrt{72}$ **$40\sqrt{3}$**
   (69)

New Concepts

Math Reasoning

Generalize Why must a and b be greater than or equal to zero when finding $\sqrt{a} \cdot \sqrt{b}$?

Sample: There is no real number that when multiplied by itself results in a negative number.

Product Property of Radicals

The square root of a product equals the product of the square roots of the factors.

$$\sqrt{ab} = \sqrt{a} \cdot \sqrt{b} \text{ where } a \geq 0 \text{ and } b \geq 0.$$

This means, for example, that $\sqrt{(8)(2)}$ is the same as $\sqrt{8} \cdot \sqrt{2}$.

Example 1 Simplifying Radical Expressions

Simplify. All variables represent non-negative real numbers.

a. $\sqrt{8}\sqrt{2}$

SOLUTION

$\sqrt{8}\sqrt{2} = \sqrt{16}$ Use the Product Property of Radicals.

$\phantom{\sqrt{8}\sqrt{2}} = 4$ Simplify.

b. $6\sqrt{2} \cdot 4\sqrt{3}$

SOLUTION

$6 \cdot 4\sqrt{2 \cdot 3}$ Use the Product Property of Radicals.

$= 24\sqrt{6}$ Simplify.

c. $(6\sqrt{3})^2$

SOLUTION

$(6\sqrt{3})^2$

$= (6)^2(\sqrt{3})^2$ Power of a Product Property

$= 36\sqrt{9}$ Square each factor.

$= 36 \cdot 3$ Simplify.

$= 108$ Multiply.

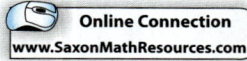
Online Connection
www.SaxonMathResources.com

MATH BACKGROUND

The Product Property of Radicals tells us that the square root of a product can be written as the product of its factors:

$$\sqrt{ab} = \sqrt{a} \cdot \sqrt{b}, \text{ where } a \geq 0 \text{ and } b \geq 0.$$

To multiply two radical expressions, write the product of the radicands with a radical sign:

$$\sqrt{a} \cdot \sqrt{b} = \sqrt{ab}$$

If the radical expression contains coefficients, they are multiplied as well, but remain as coefficients:

$$3\sqrt{a} \cdot 6\sqrt{b} = 18\sqrt{ab}$$

Radicals should always be simplified, so that there are no perfect squares as factors of the radicand.

$$\sqrt{200} = \sqrt{2}\sqrt{100} = 10\sqrt{2}$$

d. $2\sqrt{6x} \cdot \sqrt{4x}$

SOLUTION

$2\sqrt{6x} \cdot \sqrt{4x}$
$= 2\sqrt{24x^2}$ Multiply.
$= 4x\sqrt{6}$ Simplify.

Example 2 Applying the Distributive Property

Simplify.

a. $\sqrt{2}(3 + \sqrt{6})$

SOLUTION

$\sqrt{2}(3 + \sqrt{6})$
$= 3\sqrt{2} + \sqrt{12}$ Use the Distributive Property.
$= 3\sqrt{2} + 2\sqrt{3}$ Simplify.

b. $\sqrt{2}(\sqrt{6} - \sqrt{9})$

SOLUTION

$\sqrt{2}(\sqrt{6} - \sqrt{9})$
$= \sqrt{12} - \sqrt{18}$ Use the Distributive Property.
$= 2\sqrt{3} - 3\sqrt{2}$ Simplify.

Example 3 Multiplying Binomials with Radicals

Simplify.

a. $(4 + \sqrt{9})(2 - \sqrt{6})$

SOLUTION

$(4 + \sqrt{9})(2 - \sqrt{6})$
$= 8 - 4\sqrt{6} + 2\sqrt{9} - \sqrt{54}$ Use the Distributive Property or FOIL.
$= 8 - 4\sqrt{6} + 6 - 3\sqrt{6}$ Simplify the radicals.
$= 14 - 7\sqrt{6}$ Simplify by combining like terms.

b. $(6 - \sqrt{3})^2$

SOLUTION

$(6 - \sqrt{3})^2$
$= 36 - 12\sqrt{3} + \sqrt{9}$ Use the square of a binomial pattern.
$= 39 - 12\sqrt{3}$ Simplify the radical and combine like terms.

Caution

A number outside the radical and the radicand cannot be multiplied.

$2 \cdot \sqrt{3} \neq \sqrt{6}$
$2 \cdot \sqrt{3} = 2\sqrt{3}$

Example 2

This example serves as a model for applying the Distributive Property with a radical factor.

Additional Example 2

Simplify.

a. $\sqrt{3}(8 + \sqrt{6})$ $8\sqrt{3} + 3\sqrt{2}$

b. $\sqrt{3}(\sqrt{8} - \sqrt{5})$ $2\sqrt{6} - \sqrt{15}$

Example 3

This example illustrates multiplying binomials that contain radical terms. Students should note that the process is the same as with nonradical binomials.

Error Alert Watch for students who have difficulty remembering they have to find a perfect square as a factor, not the square root. Ask these students to tell what perfect squares they could look for when simplifying a radical expression.

Additional Example 3

Simplify.

a. $(3 + \sqrt{2})(6 - \sqrt{5})$
$18 - 3\sqrt{5} + 6\sqrt{2} - \sqrt{10}$

b. $(4 - \sqrt{8})^2$ $24 - 16\sqrt{2}$

Example 4

This example shows radical expressions that describe distance in a real-world setting.

Extend the Example

For another room, Chavez wants to install wall-to-wall carpeting. The room measures $(12 + \sqrt{8})$ feet by $(14 - \sqrt{3})$ feet. Find the amount of carpeting needed.
$168 - 12\sqrt{3} + 28\sqrt{2} - 2\sqrt{6}$ ft²

Additional Example 4

Find the area of a rectangular mat with a side length of $4 + \sqrt{3}$ feet and a width of $3 + \sqrt{2}$. What is the area of the mat?
$12 + 3\sqrt{3} + 4\sqrt{2} + \sqrt{6}$ square feet

Lesson Practice

Problem c

Error Alert Watch for students who square the radical term and overlook simplifying the product. Remind students that answers should always be written in simplest form.

Problem e

Scaffolding Ask students to write out the step that applies the Distributive Property before completing any calculations.

Check for Understanding

The questions below help assess the concepts taught in this lesson.

"Explain the method you would use to multiply two binomials that each contain a radical term."
I would use the FOIL method.

"Why is the product of two binomials with radical terms very often a four-term polynomial?"
The product of two binomials has four terms before simplifying. If the radicals are different, you cannot combine them, so the product may stay as four terms.

Example 4 **Application: Carpeting**

Chavez wants to find the area of a rectangular throw rug. The rug has a side length of $8 + \sqrt{5}$ feet and a width of $2 + \sqrt{2}$ feet. What is the area of the rug?

SOLUTION

$A = lw$
$= (8 + \sqrt{5})(2 + \sqrt{2})$
$= 16 + 8\sqrt{2} + 2\sqrt{5} + \sqrt{10}$

The area of the rug is $(16 + 8\sqrt{2} + 2\sqrt{5} + \sqrt{10})$ square feet.

Lesson Practice

Simplify. All variables represent non-negative real numbers.

a. $\sqrt{5}\sqrt{3}$ $\sqrt{15}$ (Ex 1)
b. $3\sqrt{7} \cdot 2\sqrt{3}$ $6\sqrt{21}$ (Ex 1)
c. $(3\sqrt{6})^2$ 54 (Ex 1)
d. $3\sqrt{3x} \cdot \sqrt{2x}$ $3x\sqrt{6}$ (Ex 1)
e. $\sqrt{7}(2 + \sqrt{4})$ $4\sqrt{7}$ (Ex 2)
f. $\sqrt{5}(\sqrt{4} - \sqrt{3})$ $2\sqrt{5} - \sqrt{15}$ (Ex 2)
g. $(5 + \sqrt{9})(4 - \sqrt{6})$ $32 - 8\sqrt{6}$ (Ex 3)
h. $(4 - \sqrt{7})^2$ $23 - 8\sqrt{7}$ (Ex 3)
i. The square dance floor at the local community building is being replaced. The floor's side length is $32 + \sqrt{13}$ feet. What is the area of the dance floor? $1037 + 64\sqrt{13}$ square feet (Ex 4)

Caution

$(4 - \sqrt{7})^2 \neq 16 + \sqrt{49}$

Remember to either use the square of a binomial pattern, the Distributive Property, or the FOIL method when squaring a binomial.

Practice   Distributed and Integrated

Solve.

1. $\dfrac{5}{6} \leq -2p$ $-\dfrac{5}{12} \geq p$ (70)
2. $|x + 4| = 5$ $\{1, -9\}$ (74)

Factor.

3. $12x^2 - 25x + 7$ $(3x - 1)(4x - 7)$ (75)
4. $x^2 + 10x - 39$ $(x - 3)(x + 13)$ (72)
5. $5z^2 + 2z - 7$ $(5z + 7)(z - 1)$ (75)
6. $3x^2 + 25x - 18$ $(3x - 2)(x + 9)$ (75)

Simplify.

*7. $4\sqrt{3} \cdot 6\sqrt{6} \cdot 3\sqrt{3} \cdot 2\sqrt{2}$ $864\sqrt{3}$ (76)
8. $-17\sqrt{7s} - 4\sqrt{7s}$ $-21\sqrt{7s}$ (69)
*9. $(4\sqrt{5})^2$ 80 (76)
*10. $3\sqrt{2} \cdot 4\sqrt{12} - 6\sqrt{54}$ $6\sqrt{6}$ (76)
11. $\sqrt{\dfrac{x^3}{60}}$ $\dfrac{x}{2}\sqrt{\dfrac{x}{15}}$ (61)

502   **Saxon** Algebra 1

INCLUSION

Have students complete a table when using the FOIL method to multiply binomials with radicals. Use Example 4 as a model. Then have the students copy and complete the chart.

×	2	$\sqrt{2}$
8	16	$8\sqrt{2}$
$\sqrt{5}$	$2\sqrt{5}$	$\sqrt{10}$

Students should distribute each term of the first binomial over each term of the second binomial. After the chart has been filled out, have them simplify each product and combine any like terms to write the final product.

12. Use mental math to find the product of 17 · 23.   **391**

*13. City Parks The City Works Department wants to build a new fence around the town's park. Write an expression for the area of the figure at right. Find the area. $(8 - \sqrt{4})^2$; 36 square feet

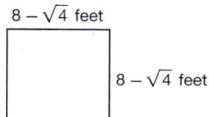
$8 - \sqrt{4}$ feet
$8 - \sqrt{4}$ feet

*14. Justify Explain how to find the product of $\sqrt{2}(\sqrt{3} - \sqrt{8})$.

14. Sample: Use the Distributive Property to multiply the radicals: $\sqrt{6} - \sqrt{16}$. Then simplify: $\sqrt{6} - 4$.

*15. Write Find two radical expressions that when multiplied together equal a perfect square.   Sample: $\sqrt{625} \cdot \sqrt{16}$

*16. Multiple Choice Which expression is not equivalent to $\sqrt{48}$?   **B**
   A $\sqrt{3 \cdot 16}$ **B** $16\sqrt{3}$ **C** $\sqrt{4^2 \cdot 3}$ **D** $4\sqrt{3}$

17. Vacation The cost of a vacation, in dollars, is represented by the expression $46x^2 - 9x + 95$, where x is the number of nights. What is the cost of a 3-night vacation?   **$482**

18. Error Analysis Two students factor $5x^2 - 6x - 8$. Which student is correct? Explain the error.

Student A	Student B
$(5x + 4)(x - 2)$	$(5x - 4)(x + 2)$

18. Student A; Sample: Student B's trinomial would have a middle term of 6x, not −6x.

*19. Geometry The sum of the squares of the two legs of a right triangle is $16x^2 - 40x + 25$. Factor the expression, and then take the square root to find the expression that represents the length of the hypotenuse. $(4x - 5)^2$; $(4x - 5)$

20. Multi-Step The area of a rectangular ottoman is represented by $2x^2 + 3x - 27$ square inches.
   a. Evaluate the expression for $x = 12$.   **297**
   b. Factor the expression completely. $(2x + 9)(x - 3)$

21. Error Analysis Two students are solving $|3x| = 6$. Which student is correct? Explain the error.

Student A	Student B
$\lvert 3x \rvert = 6$	$\lvert 3x \rvert = 6$
$3x = 6 \qquad 3x = -6$	$3x = 6 \qquad 3x = -6$
$3x - 3 = 6 - 3 \quad 3x - 3 = -6 - 3$	$\frac{3x}{3} = \frac{6}{3} \quad \frac{3x}{3} = \frac{-6}{3}$
$x = 3 \qquad x = -9$	$x = 2 \qquad x = -2$
The solution set of $\lvert 3x \rvert = 6$ is $\{6, -6\}$.	The solution set of $\lvert 3x \rvert = 6$ is $\{2, -2\}$.

21. Student B; Sample: Student A incorrectly isolated the absolute-value term by subtracting the coefficient 3 instead of dividing.

*22. Household Security A window guard is designed to be placed directly into windows that are 27 inches wide. The guard can be compressed or expanded with a tension spring to fit windows that are three inches narrower or wider than the standard width. Write and solve an absolute-value equation for the maximum and minimum width of windows in which the guard is designed to fit. $|w - 27| = 3$; 30 in., 24 in.

Lesson 76   503

Problem 23
Extend the Problem
Graph the three inequalities you did not select as the correct answer.

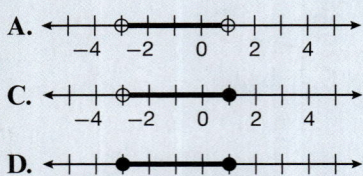

Problem 28
Extend the Problem
Another exercise club charges $45 per month, but all special services are included. If a regular member wants 3 special services, how much would that member save in a year by joining the second club? $60

Problem 30
Error Alert
The descriptions of the ages may be confusing to some students. Encourage them to make sketches or to write the inequalities they find as they read through the problem a second time. This should make solving the problem easier.

---

23. Multiple Choice Which inequality describes the graph? **B**
(73)

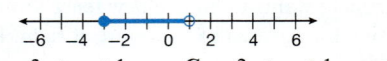

A $-3 < x < 1$ B $-3 \leq x < 1$ C $-3 < x \leq 1$ D $-3 \leq x \leq 1$

24. Analyze What are the solutions to the compound inequality $x > 3$ OR $x < 5$? Explain
(73) your answer. all real numbers; Every real number is more than three OR less than five.

*25. Climate The heat index displays apparent air temperatures in relation to the
(71) actual air temperature. The table shows the apparent air temperature for different humidity levels given that the actual air temperature is 85°.

Humidity Level (percent)	10	20	30	40	50	60	70	80	90	100
Apparent Air Temperature (°F)	80	82	84	86	88	90	93	97	102	108

a. Use the data to make a scatter plot.

b. Do the data values show a positive correlation, a negative correlation, or no correlation? positive correlation

25a.

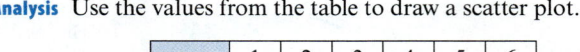

26. Data Analysis Use the values from the table to draw a scatter plot.
(71)

x	1	2	3	4	5	6
y	6	11	19	24	28	34

27. Analyze A book has 12 chapters about flying birds, 5 chapters about flying
(68) insects, 4 chapters about land insects, and 4 chapters about land mammals. If the probability of picking a chapter about certain types of animals is $\frac{8}{25}$, what type of animal is the chapter about? land animals

28. Multi-Step A new exercise facility recently opened up. Its initial promotional rate
(67) for new members, represented by $y = \$20 + \$6x$, includes a monthly fee plus an additional amount for x services.

a. How many services do new members receive before paying the same amount as a regular fee of $32? 2

b. Write an equation describing the regular rate for the facility. $y = \$32 + \$6x$

c. Classify the system of equations for the promotional and regular facility rates.
inconsistent

29. Snowfall In 1947, Mount Locke, Texas, had 23.5 inches of snow—its greatest yearly
(66) snowfall. The greatest monthly snowfall recorded was 20.5 inches, which occurred in January, 1958. Since the record wasn't broken in 1958, how many more inches of snow could Mount Locke, Texas, have had that year? less than 3 inches

30. Multi-Step The sum of Kaleigh and Dwayne's ages is 30. Three times Kaleigh's
(63) age minus twice Dwayne's age equals 5. How old is César if he is five years younger than Kaleigh? 8 years old

26.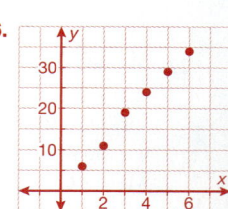

CHALLENGE
Have student use the FOIL method to multiply $(3x + \sqrt{5})(3x - \sqrt{5})$. $9x^2 - 5$

LOOKING FORWARD
Multiplying radical expressions prepares students for

• **Lesson 103** Dividing Radical Expressions

• **Lesson 105** Recognizing and Extending Geometric Sequences

• **Lesson 106** Solving Radical Equations

• **Lesson 114** Graphing Square-Root Functions

LESSON 77

Solving Two-Step and Multi-Step Inequalities

Warm Up

1. **Vocabulary** A(n) _____ is a mathematical statement with two equivalent expressions. **equation**

2.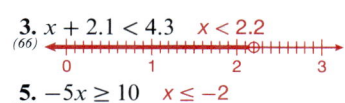

Solve and graph.

2. $x - \frac{1}{3} > 2$ $x > 2\frac{1}{3}$

3. $x + 2.1 < 4.3$ $x < 2.2$

4. $\frac{1}{2}x \leq -3$ $x \leq -6$

5. $-5x \geq 10$ $x \leq -2$

4.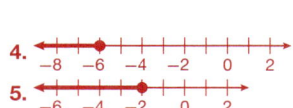

5.

New Concepts

Two-step and multi-step inequalities require more than one inverse operation to isolate the variable.

Reading Math
< less than
≤ less than or equal to
> greater than
≥ greater than or equal to

Example 1 Solving Two-Step Inequalities

Solve each inequality and graph the solutions.

a. $8m - 12 \leq -36$

SOLUTION

$8m - 12 \leq -36$

$8m \leq -24$ Add 12 to both sides.

$m \leq -3$ Divide both sides by 8.

To graph the solutions, place a closed circle on -3 and shade the number line to the left of the closed circle.

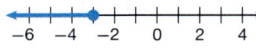

b. $9 - 3m > 21$

SOLUTION

$9 - 3m > 21$

$-3m > 12$ Subtract 9 from both sides.

$m < -4$ Divide both sides by -3 and reverse the direction of the inequality sign.

To graph the solutions, place an open circle on -4 and shade the number line to the left of the open circle.

Math Reasoning

Write Why is an inequality graphed on a number line?

Sample: It's a convenient way to represent all the real-number values that satisfy the inequality.

Before using inverse operations to isolate the variable, simplify each side of an inequality. Simplify by using the order of operations, distributing, combining like terms, or multiplying by the LCM of the denominators.

Lesson 77   505

MATH BACKGROUND

An inequality is an expression that contains the symbol <, ≤, >, or ≥. The inequality shows the relative magnitude of the two expressions. Expressions of the inequality may be numerical or variable expressions.

The solution set of an inequality is a set of numbers, each of which may be substituted for the variable to create a true inequality. Solution sets are graphed on a number line.

To solve an inequality, follow the same rules as solving an equation. The goal is to isolate a unit variable on one side of the sign. Any operation may be performed on one side of the inequality as long as it is also performed on the other side of the inequality.

The one new rule to remember for solving an inequality is that the sign must be reversed if both sides of the inequality are multiplied by or divided by a negative number.

LESSON 77

1 Warm Up

Problems 2–5
These inequalities review the basic skills needed to solve more complex inequalities.

2 New Concepts

Solving a complex inequality is similar to solving a complex equation. In the case of an inequality, the sign is reversed if both sides are divided or multiplied by a negative number.

Example 1

Error Alert If students forget to reverse the inequality sign when multiplying or dividing by a negative number, have them substitute a solution into the original inequality to check.

Additional Example 1

Solve each inequality and graph the solution.

a. $5p + 8 \geq -32$ $p \geq -8$

b. $-24 - 3x < 15$ $x > -13$

LESSON RESOURCES

Student Edition Practice
  Workbook 77
Reteaching Master 77
Adaptations Master 77
Challenge and Enrichment
  Master C77

Lesson 77   505

Example 2

This example demonstrates applying the Distributive Property to solve multi-step inequalities and solving a multi-step inequality with fractions.

Additional Example 2

Solve the inequality and graph the solution.

a. $-5x + 3 > -9 - 8$ $x < 4$

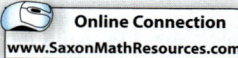

b. $4(x - 3) \leq 6^2$ $x \leq 12$

c. $\frac{5}{8}p - \frac{1}{3} \geq \frac{11}{12}$ $p \geq 2$

TEACHER TIP

Watch for students who inadvertently disregard the $\geq$ and $\leq$ sign, using only the $>$ and $<$ signs. Suggest that they preview the problems and underline those that would include the final number as part of the solution set ($\geq$ and $\leq$).

Caution

Use the inequality symbol to determine if the circle is open or a closed.
$\leq$ or $\geq$: closed circle
$<$ or $>$: open circle

Math Reasoning

Verify Show that the solution is the same if both sides of the inequality are divided by -6.

Sample:
$-6(4 - x) \geq -12^2$
$-6(4 - x) \geq -144$
$(4 - x) \leq 24$
$-x \leq 20$
$x \geq -20$

Online Connection
www.SaxonMathResources.com

Example 2 Solving Multi-Step Inequalities

Solve each inequality and graph the solutions.

a. $-8 + (-11) < -7d - 12$

SOLUTION

$-8 + (-11) < -7d - 12$
$-19 < -7d - 12$ Simplify the left side.
$-7 < -7d$ Add 12 to both sides.
$1 > d$ Divide both sides by -7 and reverse the direction of the inequality sign.

Place an open circle on 1. Shade the numbr line to the left of the circle.

b. $-6(4 - x) \geq -12^2$

SOLUTION

$-6(4 - x) \geq -12^2$
$-24 + 6x \geq -144$ Simplify both sides.
$6x \geq -120$ Add 24 to both sides.
$x \geq -20$ Divide by 6.

Place a closed circle on -20. Shade the number line to the right of the circle.

c. $\frac{3}{4}y + \frac{1}{2} < \frac{7}{10}$

SOLUTION

$\frac{3}{4}y + \frac{1}{2} < \frac{7}{10}$

$\frac{3(\overset{5}{\cancel{20}})}{\cancel{4}}y + \frac{1(\overset{10}{\cancel{20}})}{\cancel{2}} < \frac{7(\overset{2}{\cancel{20}})}{\cancel{10}}$ Multiply by the LCM, 20.

$15y + 10 < 14$ Simplify.
$15y < 4$ Subtract 10 from both sides.
$y < \frac{4}{15}$ Divide both sides by 15.

Since $\frac{4}{15}$ is a little less than $\frac{1}{3}$ the distance between 0 and 1, estimate that distance on the number line. Place an open circle on $\frac{4}{15}$. Then shade the number line to the left of the open circle.

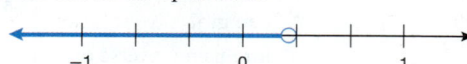

INCLUSION

Some students may have difficulty solving inequalities simply because they are unfamiliar or uncomfortable with inequalities.

Suggest that these students write the inequality as an equation and solve. They can then review the steps they used to check if they multiplied or divided by a negative number, and then can insert the correct sign accordingly.

Solve $7 - 3x \geq -5$.

write as equation: $7 - 3x = -5$
subtract 7: $-3x = -12$
divide by -3: $x = 4$

Review the steps:
• subtract 7 → no change in sign
• divide by -3 → reverse the sign

Insert the reverse of the original sign: $x \leq 4$.

Caution
Remember to change the direction of the inequality symbol when multiplying or dividing both sides by a negative number.

Hint
Explain the meaning of the solution after solving a real-world problem.

Example 3 Application: Loans

A student borrows $55 from his parents. They agree to subtract $3 from the loan for each hour he works in the yard. To find the number of hours, x, he needs to work before he owes less than $30, solve the inequality $55 - 3x < 30$.

SOLUTION

$55 - 3x < 30$

$-3x < -25$ Subtract 55 from both sides.

$x > \frac{25}{3}$ Divide both sides by -3.

$x > 8\frac{1}{3}$ Simplify.

He must work more than $8\frac{1}{3}$ hours.

Lesson Practice

Solve each inequality and graph the solutions.

a. (Ex 1) $4x + 29 \leq 25$ $x \leq -1$;

b. (Ex 1) $-36 - 7k < 6$ $k > -6$;

c. (Ex 2) $-18 + (-3) < -4f + 11$ $f < 8$;

d. (Ex 2) $-5(10 - 5p) > (-10)^2$ $p > 6$;

e. (Ex 2) $\frac{1}{12}y + \frac{2}{3} \geq \frac{5}{6}$ $y \geq 2$;

f. (Ex 3) **Athletics** A student runs a quarter-mile in 180 seconds. She improves her time by 5 seconds each week. To find the number of weeks w needed for her time to be at most 150 seconds, solve the inequality $180 - 5t \leq 150$. $t \geq 6$; Her time will be at most 150 seconds in 6 weeks.

Practice Distributed and Integrated

Use the stem-and-leaf plot to find the following statistical measures.

Average Milk Production

Stem	Leaves
3	5, 7
4	1, 6, 7, 7, 7, 8, 8, 9, 9
5	0, 2, 3, 6
6	1, 1

Key: 6 | 1 means 61 pounds

1. (62) Find the median.   48 lb

2. (62) Find the mode.   47 lb

3. (75) Factor the expression $6x^2 - 10x - 4$ completely. $2(3x + 1)(x - 2)$

4. (70) Solve $9 > 0.3r$. $r < 30$

*5. (77) Solve $5 + 4x > 37$, and then graph the solution. $x > 8$;

Lesson 77   507

ENGLISH LEARNERS

For Example 3, explain the meaning of the word **loan.** Say:

"Loan means to give something to another person for temporary use; that is, the item is returned. For example, the school library loans books."

Ask a volunteer to name other items that are commonly loaned. Sample: money, bicycles, MP3 players

Example 3

This example is a real-world application for solving multi-step inequalities.

Extend the Example
Graph the solution.

Additional Example 3

A student currently has a stamp collection with 326 unusual stamps. If an average of 3 new stamps is added to the collection every month, how many months will it take before there are at least 350 stamps in the collection? $x \geq 8$

Lesson Practice

Problem b
Error Alert Students may fill in the circle on the graph. Remind them to read the inequality symbol carefully.

Problem d
Scaffolding Review the order of operations with students. Ask them to explain how they would solve the problem before they begin work.

✓ Check for Understanding

The questions below help assess the concepts taught in this lesson.

"How can the fractions in an inequality be eliminated?" Sample: Multiply each term by the LCM of the denominators.

"What is the difference between the method for solving an equation and the method for solving an inequality?" Sample: You solve both the same way, but you have to remember to reverse the direction of the inequality if you multiply or divide both sides by a negative number.

Lesson 77   507

3 Practice

Math Conversations
Discussion to strengthen understanding

Problem 6
Error Alert
Watch that students remember to multiply all the terms by −3 as they simplify the inequality. Some may easily overlook the second term of the left side because it is already a whole number.

Problem 14
Extend the Problem
Jeff found another $5 bill in his coat pocket. He also needs 2 tubes of glue at $1.19 per tube and some paint at 59¢ per bottle. Solve the inequality $2(1.19) + 0.59p \leq 5$ to find how many bottles of paint Jeff can buy. $p \leq 4$

Problem 15
Allow students to use a calculator to find the square root of the two given radicals, $\sqrt{5184}$ and $\sqrt{32,400}$. Then have them multiply the two numbers to get the numerator of the fraction in the radical. Finally, have them divide using the calculator and extract the square root.

Problem 18
Error Alert
Watch for students who try to square the given value for the acceleration due to gravity. The exponent refers to the seconds, not the 9.8 meters.

Solve.

*6. $\frac{x}{-3} - 2 \leq 1$ $x \geq -9$

*7. $-3x + 2 \leq 1$ $x \geq \frac{1}{3}$

*8. $\frac{x}{5} - 4 > 9$ $x > 65$

9. $-5 < r - 6 < -2$ $1 < r < 4$

Simplify.

10. $4\sqrt{3x} \cdot \sqrt{4x}$ $8x\sqrt{3}$

11. $\sqrt{400g^6}$ $20g^3$

*12. **Generalize** Describe how solving inequalities is different from solving equations.

12. Sample: The only difference is having to remember to reverse the inequality sign when you multiply or divide both sides by a negative number.

*13. **Multiple Choice** What is the solution to $6 - 7y < 48$?   **B**
  A $y < -6$ **B** $y > -6$ **C** $y > -48$ **D** $y < -48$

*14. (Hobbies) Building ships in a bottle is Jeff's favorite hobby. He has $42 to purchase two ship kits and two bottles. Each ship kit is $18. To find how much he can spend on each bottle, solve the inequality $2(18) + 2b \leq 42$. $b \leq 3$; The bottles can cost at most $3 each.

15. (Body Surface Area) Physicians can estimate the body surface area of an adult (in square meters) using the formula $x = \sqrt{\frac{HW}{3125}}$ called BSA, where H is height in inches and W is weight is pounds. Find the BSA of a person who is $\sqrt{5184}$ inches tall and weighs $\sqrt{32,400}$ pounds. Round to the nearest whole number.   2 square meters

16. The brightness of a photograph is represented by the expression $12x^2 - 2x - 4$. Factor this expression completely. $2(3x - 2)(2x + 1)$

17. **Error Analysis** Students were asked to find the product of $\sqrt{75} \cdot \sqrt{2}$. Which student is correct? Explain the error.   Student A; Sample: Student B didn't correctly simplify $\sqrt{150}$.

Student A	Student B
$\sqrt{75} \cdot \sqrt{2}$	$\sqrt{75} \cdot \sqrt{2}$
$\sqrt{150}$	$\sqrt{150}$
$5\sqrt{6}$	$5\sqrt{30}$

*18. **Multi-Step** A tsunami is a big ocean wave that can be caused by underwater volcanic eruptions, earthquakes, or hurricanes. The equation $S = \sqrt{g \cdot d}$ models the speed of a tsunami, where g is the acceleration due to gravity, which is 9.8 meters/second^2, and where d is the depth of the ocean in meters.
  a. Suppose a tsunami begins in the ocean at a depth of 1000 meters. What is the speed of the tsunami? $70\sqrt{2}$ meters per second
  b. Suppose a tsunami begins in the ocean at a depth of 2000 meters. What is the speed of the tsunami?   140 meters per second

*19. **Geometry** A triangle has a base of $3 + \sqrt{15}$ inches and a height of $5 - \sqrt{20}$ inches. Find the area. $\frac{15 - 6\sqrt{5} + 5\sqrt{15} - 10\sqrt{3}}{2}$ square inches

---

CHALLENGE

Challenge students to solve these more complex inequalities:

1. $3[4(b - 2) - (1 - b)] > 5(b - 4)$
   $b > \frac{7}{10}$

2. $\frac{2}{3}(9m - 15) + 4 < 6 + \frac{3}{4}(4 - 12m)$
   $m < 1$

20. Error Analysis Two students factor $15x^2 + 16x - 15$. Which student is correct? Explain the error.   Student A; Sample: Student B's trinomial would have a middle term of $-16x$, not $16x$.

Student A	Student B
$(3x + 5)(5x - 3)$	$(3x - 5)(5x + 3)$

21. Multiple Choice Solve $|x - 3| + 2 = 0$.   **D**
A $\{5, 1\}$ B $\{4, -1\}$ C $\{1\}$ D $\emptyset$

22. Write Why is there no solution for the absolute-value equation $|x + 11| + 3 = 1$?

22. Sample: To solve the equation, the absolute value of $|x + 11|$ would be -2. However, an absolute value cannot be less than zero.

23. Weaving The area of rugs designed by a weaver are described by the trinomial $x^2 + 30x - 400$. What are the dimensions of a rug if x is 40? 30×80

24. State whether the data show a positive correlation, a negative correlation, or no correlation.   positive correlation

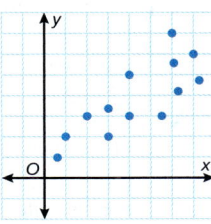

*25. Measurement A manufacturing company is making screws that have a width of 4 millimeters. Each screw must be made so that the actual width is ± 0.03 millimeters of the desired width. Write a compound inequality to represent this situation. $3.97 \leq x \leq 4.03$

26. Verify Verify that $3gh\sqrt{275g^7h^9}$ can be simplified to $15g^4h^5\sqrt{11gh}$.

26. $3gh\sqrt{275g^7h^9}$
$= 3gh\sqrt{275 \cdot g^7 \cdot h^9}$
$= 3gh\sqrt{25 \cdot 11}\sqrt{g^7}\sqrt{h^9}$
$= 3gh \cdot 5\sqrt{11} \cdot g^3\sqrt{g} \cdot h^4\sqrt{h}$
$= 15g^4h^5\sqrt{11gh}$

27. Multi-Step Gwynedd's piggy bank contains 57 quarters, 24 dimes, 35 nickels, and 60 pennies. Gwynedd turns her piggy bank over and one coin falls out. What is the probability that the coin will be worth more than 5 cents?
a. What is the probability that the coin is a quarter or dime? $\frac{81}{176}$
b. What is the probability that the coin is a quarter or worth more than 5 cents? $\frac{81}{176}$
c. Explain how the previous two answers are related.

28. Cell Phones Two different cell phone service plans are represented by the given equations. Classify this system of equations.   consistent and independent

$$p = 6x + 24$$
$$p = 8x + 20$$

27c. Sample: The answers are the same because the events describe the same set of possible outcomes, but in two different ways.

29. Multi-Step Anya has a number of square bricks with a side length of 1 foot that she wants to use to create a rectangular patio in her backyard. At first, she arranges them so the rectangle is 12 bricks long by 3 bricks wide, but then she decides she does not like that arrangement. How can Anya arrange the bricks if she would rather have a square-shaped patio?   6 bricks wide by 6 bricks long

30. Error Analysis Two students simplified the expression as shown. Which student is correct? Explain the error.

Student A	Student B
$\sqrt{80y^2z^2} = 16yz\sqrt{5}$	$\sqrt{80y^2z^2} = 4yz\sqrt{5}$

Student B; Sample: Student A removed the perfect-square factor rather than the square root of that factor.

Lesson 77   509

Problem 23
"What is the first step that needs to be completed in order to answer the question?" First factor the trinomial.

"What will the two binomials represent?" the length and width of the rug

"What is the second step needed to solve the problem?" Substitute the given value into the binomials and evaluate them.

Problem 27
Extend the Problem
Suppose the first coin was a quarter and that a second coin fell out of the bank when Gwynedd tipped it over. What is the probability that the second coin is worth more than 5¢? What is the probability that it is a dime?
$\frac{16}{35}$, $\frac{24}{175}$

LOOKING FORWARD

Solving two-step and multi-step inequalities will prepare students for

- **Lesson 81** Solving Inequalities with Variables on Both Sides
- **Lesson 82** Solving Multi-Step Compound Inequalities
- **Lesson 91** Solving Absolute-Value Inequalities

Lesson 77   509

LESSON 78

Graphing Rational Functions

1 Warm Up

Problem 1
Remind students that a rational expression is one that can be written as a ratio.

Warm Up

1. **Vocabulary** A _____ expression is an expression where the denominator contains a variable and the value of the variable cannot make the denominator equal to zero.   **rational**
2. True or False: The graph of the equation $x = -2$ is a vertical line.   **true**
3. True or False: The graph of the equation $y = -x$ is a horizontal line.   **false**
4. Determine when the expression $\frac{x+7}{3x}$ is undefined.   **when $x = 0$**

2 New Concepts

In this lesson, students learn to graph rational functions with equations of the form
$y = \frac{a}{x-b} + c.$
Discuss $y = \frac{1}{x}$, using it to introduce the terms **excluded value** and **asymptote**. Have students graph $y = \frac{1}{x}$ with their graphing calculators (or have them sketch the graph on the board). Have students identify the excluded value and describe what happens as values of x approach 0 or get very large or small.

New Concepts

A **rational function** is a function whose rule can be given as a rational expression. This means that a rational function has a variable in the denominator. Rational functions, like rational expressions, are undefined when the denominator is equal to zero.

A value of a variable for which an expression or a function is undefined is called an **excluded value**. For the function $y = \frac{7}{x+2}$, -2 is an excluded value; this is because when $x = -2$, the function is undefined.

Example 1   Determining Excluded Values

Find the excluded values.

$y = \frac{m-4}{3m-12}$

Math Reasoning

Verify Show that $m = 4$ without factoring out the GCF.

Sample: $3m - 12 = 0$
$3m = 12$
$m = 4$

Reading Math

$x \neq 6$ is read, "x is not equal to 6" or "x cannot equal 6".

Online Connection
www.SaxonMathResources.com

SOLUTION

Simplify the denominator by factoring out the GCF.

$3m - 12 = 3(m-4)$ The GCF is 3.

Set the denominator equal to zero and solve for m.

$3(m-4) = 0$	Set the denominator equal to zero.
$\frac{3(m-4)}{3} = \frac{0}{3}$	Divide both sides by 3.
$m - 4 = 0$	Simplify.
$+4 \quad +4$	Add 4 to both sides.
$m = 4$	Simplify.

The denominator equals zero when $m = 4$, so 4 is an excluded value.

$m \neq 4$

Example 1

Students identify the excluded values of rational expressions by finding numbers that make the denominator equal 0.

Additional Example 1
Find the excluded values.
$\frac{1+5a}{30+5a}$ $a \neq -6$

LESSON RESOURCES

Student Edition Practice Workbook 78
Reteaching Master 78
Adaptations Master 78
Challenge and Enrichment Master C78

MATH BACKGROUND

A rational function is formed when a polynomial is divided by another polynomial.

$f(x) = \frac{P(x)}{Q(x)}; Q(x) \neq 0$

All polynomial functions are also rational functions in which $Q(x) = 1$. Factoring the polynomials in a rational function helps to predict and understand its behavior; in particular, it shows the values for which the function is not defined—those that make the denominator equal 0. These values must be excluded from the domain of the function because the function is discontinuous at those points.

What happens to the graph of a rational function as x-values get very large or small is called its end behavior. Often the graph approaches an asymptote. Asymptotes can be vertical, horizontal, or oblique.

Rational functions are discontinuous functions. **Discontinuous functions** are functions that have a break or jump in the graph. A break or jump in the graph can be due to an asymptote. An **asymptote** is a boundary line that the graph of a function approaches but never touches or crosses.

Caution

Students may draw asymptotes as solid lines. However, asymptotes are usually shown with dashed lines because asymptotes are not part of the graph of the rational function.

When a graph of a rational function has a vertical asymptote, then there is an excluded value for the function. To determine where vertical asymptotes occur, find the excluded values for the function. Rational functions also have horizontal asymptotes. When the function is in the form $y = \frac{a}{x-b} + c$, the vertical asymptote occurs at $x = b$ and the horizontal asymptote occurs at $y = c$.

Example 2 Determining Asymptotes

Identify the asymptotes.

Hint

When $c = 0$ in the rational function $y = \frac{a}{x-b} + c$, the horizontal asymptote is the x-axis.

a. $y = \dfrac{2}{x-8}$

SOLUTION

$y = \dfrac{2}{x-8}$ a rational function in the form $y = \frac{a}{x-b} + c$, where $a = 2$, $b = 8$, and $c = 0$

Since $b = 8$, the equation of the vertical asymptote is $x = 8$.

Since $c = 0$, the equation of the horizontal asymptote is $y = 0$.

b. $y = \dfrac{4}{x+10} + 3$

SOLUTION

Hint

Compare the equation of the given rational function to $y = \frac{a}{x-b} + c$ to determine the correct sign of the asymptotes.

$y = \dfrac{4}{x+10} + 3$ a rational function in the form $y = \frac{a}{x-b} + c$, where $a = 4$, $b = -10$, and $c = 3$

$y = \dfrac{4}{x-(-10)} + (3)$

Since $b = -10$, the equation of the vertical asymptote is $x = -10$.

Since $c = 3$, the equation of the horizontal asymptote is $y = 3$.

Example 2

Students use the equations of rational functions in the form

$y = \dfrac{a}{x-b} + c$ to identify

asymptotes as lines with the equations $x = b$ and $y = c$.

Error Alert Some students may reverse the signs when reading the equations of the asymptotes from the rational equations. Suggest that these students write the equations in the form

$y - c = \dfrac{a}{x-b}$. The equation of the vertical asymptote is $x = b$, and the equation of the horizontal asymptote is $y = c$.

Extend the Example

Have students check their asymptotes by graphing the equations.

Additional Example 2

Identify the asymptotes.

a. $y = \dfrac{5}{x-1}$

 vertical asymptote: $x = 1$
 horizontal asymptote: $y = 0$

b. $y = \dfrac{6}{x-3} - 10$

 vertical asymptote: $x = 3$
 horizontal asymptote: $y = -10$.

TEACHER TIP

A parent function is a basic or simplified form of a function, one in which constants are set to 0 and coefficients to 1. For rational functions of the form $f(x) = \frac{a}{x-b} + c$, the parent function is $f(x) = \frac{1}{x}$. The parent function for quadratics is $f(x) = x^2$; for linear functions it is $f(x) = x$. Students should learn to recognize the general shape of the parent functions of different classes of functions.

Lesson 78   511

---

eL ENGLISH LEARNERS

Write the following expressions on the board:

$\dfrac{7}{4}$, 7 to 4, 7:4, 7 ÷ 4

Point out that the four expressions have the same value, but can be called by different names. Have students identify the fraction, the ratios, the quotients, and the rational number. Write the vocabulary words on the board as they are discussed. Erase all the expressions except for $\frac{7}{4}$. Explain that the top and bottom parts can have different names depending on whether $\frac{7}{4}$ is a fraction, a ratio, or a quotient. Write and discuss the words numerator, denominator, terms, dividend, and divisor.

Next to $\frac{7}{4}$ write $\frac{7}{x+4}$, explain that the first is a **rational number**, the second a **rational expression**. Change $\frac{7}{x+4}$ to $y = \frac{7}{x+4}$ and tell students you have turned the rational expression into a **rational function**.

Lesson 78   511

Example 3

Students graph rational equations in the form $y = \frac{a}{x-b} + c$ and identify vertical and horizontal asymptotes.

Extend the Example

What happens to the graph of $y = \frac{k}{x+2} + 5$ as you increase the value of k? Sketch some examples to show your answer. Sample: The asymptotes stay the same, but the curves bend more sharply away from the intersection of the asymptotes at $(-2, 5)$. For example, when $k = 10{,}000$, the graph looks like this:

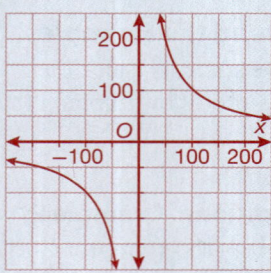

Additional Example 3

Identify the asymptotes and graph each function.

a. $y = \dfrac{5}{x-3}$

asymptotes: $x = 3, y = 0$

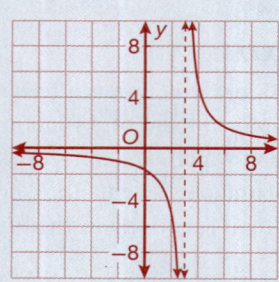

b. $y = \dfrac{3}{x+2} + 5$

asymptotes: $x = -2, y = 5$

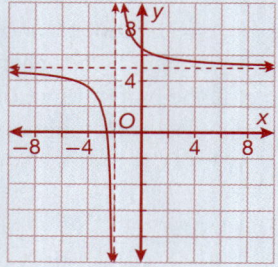

Math Reasoning

Connect What type of variation is a rational function?

An inverse variation; Sample: Its equation is $y = \frac{a}{x}$.

Math Reasoning

Generalize State the domain and range of the function $y = \frac{1}{x-4} - 2$.

The domain is all real numbers except 4. The range is all real numbers except -2.

Hint

Choose points that lie on either side of the vertical asymptote so that the curves of the graph will be more accurate.

The parent function for rational functions is $y = \frac{1}{x}$.

By identifying the asymptotes from the form $y = \frac{a}{x-b} + c$ and plotting a few points, the rational function can be graphed.

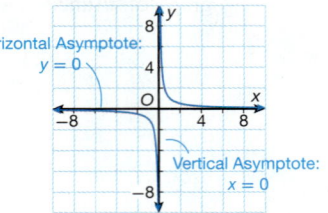

Example 3 Graphing Using Asymptotes

Identify the asymptotes and graph each function.

$y = \dfrac{1}{x-4} - 2$

SOLUTION

Step 1: Identify the vertical and horizontal asymptotes.

$y = \dfrac{1}{x-4} - 2 \qquad a = 1, b = 4, \text{ and } c = -2$

The equation of the vertical asymptote is $x = 4$.

The equation of the horizontal asymptote is $y = -2$.

Step 2: Graph the asymptotes using dashed lines.

Step 3: Make a table of values.

x	0	2	3	5	6
y	$-2\frac{1}{4}$	$-2\frac{1}{2}$	-3	-1	$-1\frac{1}{2}$

Step 4: Plot the points and connect them with smooth curves.

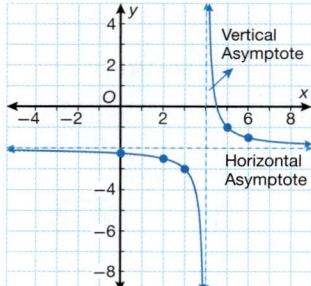

ALTERNATE METHOD FOR EXAMPLE 3

Present this general form of a rational equation:

$$y - k = \dfrac{a}{b(x-h)}$$

Explain that the values (x, y) are the ordered pairs that are graphed. The values a, b, h, and k are constants that can change to create new graphs. Have students work in small groups using graphing calculators to try out different values for a, b, h, and k. Ask the groups to prepare a summary report of their discoveries. Make sure students include what they learned about the lines $x = h$ and $y = k$. These two lines are the asymptotes.

$y + 3 = \dfrac{3}{2(x+5)}$

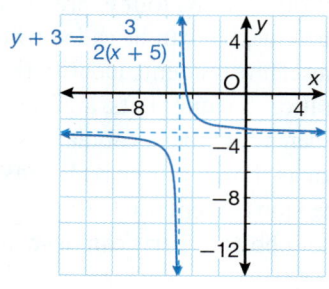

Example 4 Application: Soccer

The Soccer Administration plans to have 64 regular players on a team. The players will be divided equally among the coaches. There will be one backup player placed on each team at the beginning of the season in addition to the regular players. The number of players on each team, y, is given by $y = \frac{64}{x} + 1$, where x is the number of coaches.

a. Determine the vertical and horizontal asymptotes of the function.

SOLUTION

$y = \frac{64}{x} + 1 \qquad a = 64, b = 0, \text{ and } c = 1$

The equation of the horizontal asymptote is $y = 1$.

The equation of the vertical asymptote is $x = 0$.

Hint
When a rational function has no value for b in $y = \frac{a}{x-b} + c$, the vertical asymptote is the y-axis or $x = 0$.

b. If there are 4 coaches, how many players will each team have?

SOLUTION

$y = \frac{64}{x} + 1$

$y = \frac{64}{4} + 1 \qquad$ Replace x with 4.

$y = 17 \qquad$ Divide 64 by 4 and then add $16 + 1$.

There will be 17 players on each team.

Lesson Practice

Find the excluded values.
(Ex 1)

a. $y = \frac{4}{6m} \quad m \neq 0$ **b.** $y = \frac{6m}{m+2} \quad m \neq -2$ **c.** $y = \frac{m-3}{4m-8} \quad m \neq 2$

Identify the asymptotes.
(Ex 2)

d. $y = \frac{4}{x+1} \quad x = -1; y = 0$ **e.** $y = \frac{2}{x+7} + 6 \quad x = -7; y = 6$

Identify the asymptotes and graph each function.

f. $y = \frac{6}{x+4} \quad x = -4; y = 0$ **g.** $y = \frac{1}{x-6} - 5 \quad x = 6; y = -5$
(Ex 3)   (Ex 3)

A golf instructor has a budget of $5500 to buy new demonstration clubs. He will receive 5 free clubs when he places his order. The number of clubs, y, that he can buy is given by $y = \frac{5500}{x} + 5$, where x is the price per club.
(Ex 4)

h. Determine the vertical and horizontal asymptotes of the function. $x = 0; y = 5$

i. If each club costs $100, how many clubs will he receive? 60 clubs

f.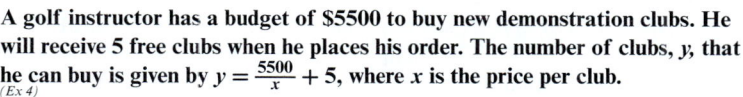

g.

Lesson 78 513

3 Practice

Math Conversations

Discussion to strengthen understanding

Problem 3
Error Alert
Students may try to factor out x or y from all three terms so that they will get a trinomial in one variable. Have them first factor $x^2 + 10x + 21$. $(x + 3)(x + 7)$ Change 3 to $3y$ and 7 to $7y$ in the binomial factors and ask what happens to the polynomial product. It changes from $x^2 + 10x + 21$ to $x^2 + 10xy + 21y^2$.

Now have students try again, using the factoring form $(x + \underline{\quad} y)(x + \underline{\quad} y)$.

Problem 7
Remind students that all vertical lines have equations in the form $x = a$, where a is the x-intercept.

Problem 8
Error Alert
Check that students use an open circle on their graphs. Open circles are used for $>$ and $<$; closed circles are used for $\geq$ and $\leq$.

Problem 11
Extend the Problem
How is the graph of the horizontal line $y = 5$ related to the graph of $y = \frac{1}{x} + 5$? The line with equation $y = 5$ is an asymptote for the graph.

Practice Distributed and Integrated

Solve each system of linear equations.

1. $3x - 2y = 17$ $(1, -7)$
(63) $-4x - 3y = 17$

2. $y = 2x + 4$ $(-3, -2)$
(63) $-x - 3y = 9$

Factor.

3. $x^2 + 10xy + 21y^2$ $(x + 3y)(x + 7y)$
(72)

4. $-30 - 13x + x^2$ $(x - 15)(x + 2)$
(72)

*5. Find the excluded values for $y = \frac{4}{7m}$. $m \neq 0$
(78)

*6. Find the excluded values for $y = \frac{m-2}{3m+9}$. $m \neq -3$
(78)

*7. Find the vertical asymptote for $y = \frac{5}{x-3} + \frac{2}{5}$. $x = 3$
(78)

8. Solve $3 - 9m < 30$ and graph the solution. $m > -3$;
(77)

9. Use the Distributive Property to find the product of $5(\sqrt{4} + \sqrt{36})$.   40
(76)

*10. (Awards) Jason plans to buy 20 prizes for the next school carnival and to divide
(78) them equally between the winners of the school trivia contest. There will also be an additional 6 prizes given to each winner at the awards assembly. The number of prizes for each winner, y, is given by $y = \frac{20}{x} + 6$, where x is the number of winners. Find the asymptotes and graph the function. $x = 0; y = 6$

*11. Verify Show that the value $y = 5$ will not satisfy the function $y = \frac{1}{x} + 5$.
(78)

*12. Justify What are the equations of the asymptotes in the graph of
(78) $y = \frac{2.3}{x+1.9} + 0.3$? $x = -1.9; y = 0.3$

*13. Multiple Choice What is the vertical asymptote for the rational function $y = \frac{6.1}{x+1.5} + 3.1$?   **C**
(78)
   A $x = 3.1$ **B** $x = 1.5$
   C $x = -1.5$ **D** $x = 6.1$

*14. (Budgeting) You have $30 to spend at the mall and your mother gives you an
(77) additional $15. You must buy a new shirt that is on sale for $12. You also would like to purchase 3 CDs. To find the maximum amount you can spend on each CD, solve the inequality $30 + 15 \geq 12 + 3c$. $11 \geq c$; You can spend at most $11 on each CD.

10.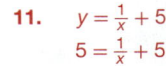

11. $y = \frac{1}{x} + 5$
$5 = \frac{1}{x} + 5$
$-5 \quad\quad -5$
$0 = \frac{1}{x}$
There is no value x such that $\frac{1}{x} = 0$.

514   Saxon Algebra 1

INCLUSION

Use the following strategy if students are confused by the concept of asymptotes. Have them graph $y = \frac{1}{x}$. Ask, "**How many parts does this graph have? What happens to the graph as x gets larger and larger?**" 2; It gets closer and closer to 0. Repeat for x-values getting smaller and those approaching 0 in both directions. Continue the discussion with the graphs of $y = \frac{-1}{x}$, $y = \frac{10}{x}$, and $y = \frac{-10}{x}$. Have students talk about how the graphs are the same and how they are different. Point out that the graphs all have the same asymptotes, the x-axis and the y-axis. Those with negative numerators are reflections across the x-axis.

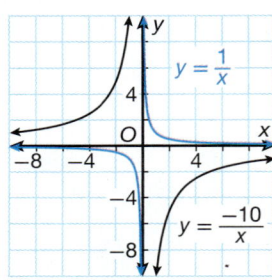

15. Error Analysis Two students solve $8p - 7 \leq 3p + 18$. Which student is correct? Explain the error.

Student A	Student B
$8p - 7 \leq 3p + 18$	$8p - 7 \leq 3p + 18$
$5p - 7 \leq 18$	$-7 \leq -5p + 18$
$5p \leq 25$	$-25 \leq -5p$
$p \leq 5$	$5 \leq p$

15. Student A; Sample: Student B did not reverse the inequality sign when dividing by -5.

 16. Geometry The triangle inequality theorem states that the sum of any two sides of a triangle must be greater than the third side. A triangle has sides $4g + 10$, $3g - 13$, and 46 as the longest side. Therefore, $(4g + 10) + (3g - 13) > 46$. Solve for g. $g > 7$

17. Multi-Step You can hike the trails at 2.5 miles per hour. You break for 1 hour to rest and eat lunch. You want to hike at least 15 miles. To find the number of hours you will hike, solve the inequality $2.5(h - 1) \geq 15$. $h \geq 7$; You will hike at least 7 hours.

18. Error Analysis Students were asked to find the product of $\sqrt{2}(7 + \sqrt{14})$. Which student is correct? Explain the error. Student B: Sample: Student A multiplied a radical and a whole number.

Student A	Student B
$\sqrt{2}(7 + \sqrt{14})$	$\sqrt{2}(7 + \sqrt{14})$
$\sqrt{14} + \sqrt{28}$	$7\sqrt{2} + \sqrt{28}$
$\sqrt{14} + 2\sqrt{7}$	$7\sqrt{2} + 2\sqrt{7}$

*19. **Art** Michael is submitting his first painting to the county fair art show. His painting has a side length of $7 + \sqrt{32}$ inches and a width of $9 + \sqrt{50}$ inches. What is the area of Michael's painting? $103 + 71\sqrt{2}$ square inches

20. Verify Show that $10x^2 - 11xy - 6y^2 = (2x - 3y)(5x + 2y)$.
Sample: $(2x - 3y)(5x + 2y) = 10x^2 + 4xy - 15xy - 6y^2 = 10x^2 - 11xy - 6y^2$

21. Multiple Choice Which expression is the factored form of $20x^2 + 49x + 9$? **C**
- **A** $(10x + 3)(2x + 3)$
- **B** $(20x + 3)(x + 3)$
- **C** $(5x + 1)(4x + 9)$
- **D** $(5x + 9)(4x + 1)$

22. Measurement The area of a rectangular tray is represented by $4x^2 - 16x + 16$ square inches. Evaluate the expression for $x = -3$. 100 square inches

23. Solve $|n| = 12$. $\{12, -12\}$

24. Dining A restaurant offers discounted meals to children 12 years old and under or to senior citizens who are at least 65 years old. Write a compound inequality that represents this situation. $x \leq 12$ OR $x \geq 65$

Problem 16
Extend the Problem
Find the shortest integer side lengths that could form this triangle. For $g = 8$, the sides are 42, 11, 46.

Problem 17
Extend the Problem
The time it takes for a 15-mile hike with a 1-hour rest stop can be given by the rational equation $y = \frac{15}{x} + 1$, where x is the speed in mi/h and y is the time in hours. Sketch the graph of the equation. Use it to find the time the hike takes if the speed is reduced to 2 mi/h. 8.5 hours

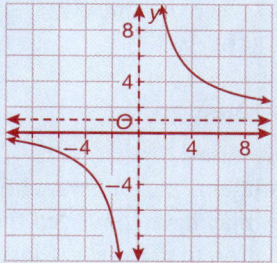

Problem 20
Students should multiply the binomials on the right side to show that their product equals the trinomial on the left side.

Error Alert
If the products that students find have four terms instead of three, remind them to combine like terms to create their final answer: $10x^2 + 4xy - 15xy - 6y^2 = 10x^2 - 11xy - 6y^2$.

CHALLENGE

Write this rational function on the board:
$$y = \frac{(x + 1)(x - 3)}{(x - 5)(x + 2)}$$

Ask students to describe as much as possible about the graph of this function without graphing it. Students can then check their predictions with a graphing calculator or a computer graphing utility. Sample: It has vertical asymptotes with equations $x = 5$ and $x = -2$. So, the graph will have three pieces. It has x-intercepts at -1 and 3 and a y-intercept at 0.3. As $|x|$ gets larger, y approaches $\frac{x^2}{x^2}$ or 1. So, there is a horizontal asymptote at $y = 1$.

Problem 27
Scaffolding Guide the students by asking them the following questions.

"If the side of a square is shown by the variable *s*, what are the formulas for the area and perimeter?" $A = s^2, P = 4s$

"Find a formula for the perimeter in terms of the area." $P = 4\sqrt{A}$

"Use A_1 and A_2 for the two given areas. Now find a formula for the combined perimeter."
$P = 4\sqrt{A_1} + 4\sqrt{A_2}$

Students can now substitute in the given areas. If necessary, remind them that $\sqrt{216} = \sqrt{6 \cdot 36} = 6\sqrt{6}$ and $\sqrt{125} = \sqrt{5 \cdot 25} = 5\sqrt{5}$.

Problem 29
Error Alert
If students pick answer choice **B**, they may have converted the equation to $x = \frac{1}{3}y - 1$ instead of to the slope-intercept form $y = 3x + 3$.

25. State whether the data show a positive correlation, a negative correlation, or no
(71) correlation.   no correlation

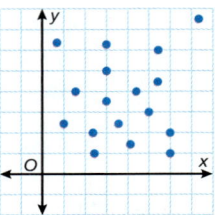

26. **Verify** Solve the inequality $\frac{n}{5} \leq -3$. Then select several values of *n* to substitute
(70) into the inequality to verify the answer. $n \leq -15$; See student work.

27. **Multi-Step** The larger square has an area of $216x^2$ and the smaller square has an area
(69) of $125x^2$. What is the combined perimeter of the two squares? $20x\sqrt{5} + 24x\sqrt{6}$

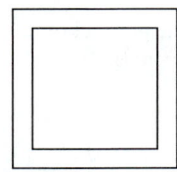

28. **Game Play** Derek is playing a board game with three number cubes. What is the
(68) probability of Derek rolling three of a kind or a sum that is an odd number? $\frac{111}{216}$

29. **Multiple Choice** What slope would the line parallel to $3x - y = -3$ have?   **C**
(65)
   A $-\frac{1}{3}$ **B** $\frac{1}{3}$
   C 3   **D** -3

30. Create a histogram to display the following data representing average daily
(62) milk production (in gallons) of seventeen dairies: 49, 41, 50, 47, 35, 47, 61, 49, 60, 46, 53, 48, 37, 47, 56, 52, 48. Use 35–39 as the starting interval.

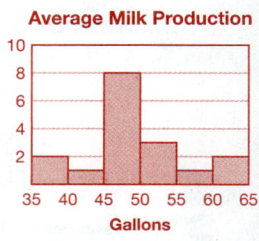

516   *Saxon* Algebra 1

LOOKING FORWARD

Graphing rational expressions prepares students for

• **Lesson 88** Multiplying and Dividing Rational Expressions

• **Lesson 90** Adding and Subtracting Rational Expressions

• **Lesson 92** Simplifying Complex Fractions

• **Lesson 99** Solving Rational Equations

LESSON 79

Factoring Trinomials by Using the GCF

Warm Up

1. **Vocabulary** A _____ is the sum or difference of monomials. **polynomial**

   Factor.

   2. $x^2 + 3x - 10$ $(x + 5)(x - 2)$
   3. $-13p + p^2 + 36$ $(p - 9)(p - 4)$
   4. $-11x - 21 + 2x^2$ $(2x + 3)(x - 7)$
   5. $5x^2 - 13x - 6$ $(5x + 2)(x - 3)$

New Concepts

The terms of a polynomial that is factored completely will have no common factors other than 1. To factor completely, begin by factoring out the greatest common factor, or GCF.

Example 1 Factoring Trinomials with Positive Leading Coefficients

Factor completely.

a. $x^4 + 5x^3 + 6x^2$

SOLUTION

Find the GCF of the terms. In this case, x^2 is the GCF.

$x^4 + 5x^3 + 6x^3$

$x^2(x^2 + 5x + 6)$ Factor out the GCF.

Find two numbers that have a product of 6 and a sum of 5.

$2 \cdot 3 = 6$ and $2 + 3 = 5$

$x^2(x^2 + 5x + 6) = x^2(x + 2)(x + 3)$

So, $x^4 + 5x^3 + 6x^2 = x^2(x + 2)(x + 3)$.

b. $4x^3 - 4x^2 - 80x$

SOLUTION

The GCF of the terms is $4x$.

$4x^3 - 4x^2 - 80x$

$4x(x^2 - x - 20)$ Factor out the GCF.

Find two numbers that have a product of -20 and a sum of -1.

$4 \cdot -5 = -20$ and $4 + (-5) = -1$

$4x(x^2 - x - 20) = 4x(x + 4)(x - 5)$

So, $4x^3 - 4x^2 - 80x = 4x(x + 4)(x - 5)$.

When the leading coefficient is negative, factor out a -1.

Caution

Include the GCF in the final factored form. The factored form equals the original trinomial if its factors are multiplied.

Math Language

The **leading coefficient** is the coefficient of the term with the greatest degree.

Lesson 79   517

LESSON 79

1 Warm Up

Problem 3

Use this problem to review factoring a trinomial with a leading coefficient of 1. Remind students to first put the trinomial in the standard form $p^2 - 13p + 36$.

2 New Concepts

In this lesson, students learn to factor a trinomial completely by first factoring out common factors from the terms. They then write the remaining trinomial factor as the product of two binomials.

Example 1

Students factor trinomials with positive leading coefficients. After common factors are removed from the terms, the resulting trinomial in this example has a leading coefficient of 1. Remind students that the leading coefficient is the first coefficient when the polynomial is arranged in standard form.

Additional Example 1

Factor completely.

a. $a^5 + 3a^4 - 18a^3$ $a^3(a - 3)(a + 6)$

b. $2m^4 - 16m^3 + 30m^2$ $2m^2(m - 3)(m - 5)$

LESSON RESOURCES

Student Edition Practice
   Workbook 79
Reteaching Master 79
Adaptations Master 79
Challenge and Enrichment
   Master C79

MATH BACKGROUND

A description of the topics of algebra might include solving equations, simplifying expressions, and graphing relations. Perhaps simplifying expressions seems to have no application. In a broad sense, simplifying expressions is done to solve equations, and equations are written to represent and learn more about phenomena in the natural world.

Factoring is meaningful only with reference to a specified set. For example, over the set of integers, 3 is not a factor of 5. But, over the set of rational numbers, 3 is a factor of 5 because $5 = 3 \cdot \frac{5}{3}$. It is customary to factor polynomials over the set of polynomials with integer constants. So, for example, $(x + 2)\left(x - \frac{1}{3}\right)$ is not an acceptable factored form. If a polynomial can be written as a product of polynomials of lower degree, it is reducible; polynomials that cannot are irreducible. An irreducible polynomial with a greatest common factor of 1 is prime.

TEACHER TIP

Encourage students to not write too small, or they are likely to make mistakes with exponents and dropped negative signs. Assure them it is fine if they get only two problems on a sheet of paper.

Example 2

Students factor trinomials with negative leading coefficients. After common factors are removed from the terms, the resulting trinomial has a leading coefficient of 1 in this example.

Error Alert When factoring out the common factor -1, remind students to write the opposite of every term in the trinomial.

Additional Example 2
Factor completely.

a. $-d^3 + 7d^2 - 6d$
   $-d(d - 6)(d - 1)$

b. $-5y^3 - 25y^2 - 20y$
   $-5y(y + 1)(y + 4)$

Example 3

Students factor trinomials with two variables. After common factors are removed from the terms, the resulting trinomial has one variable and a leading coefficient of 1.

Error Alert Students who are making frequent errors should be asked to check their answers by multiplying the factors. The product must exactly match the original polynomial.

Additional Example 3
Factor completely.

a. $pq^4 + 5pq^3 - 14pq^2$
   $pq^2(q - 2)(q + 7)$

b. $3a^3b - 12a^2b - 15ab$
   $3ab(a - 5)(a + 1)$

Example 2 — Factoring Trinomials with Negative Leading Coefficients

Factor completely.

a. $-x^2 + x + 56$

SOLUTION

The leading coefficient is -1, so factor out a -1.

$-x^2 + x + 56$
$-1(x^2 - x - 56)$ Factor out -1.

Find two numbers that have a product of -56 and a sum of -1.

$7 \cdot -8 = -56$ and $7 + (-8) = -1$
$-1(x^2 - x - 56) = -1(x + 7)(x - 8)$
So, $-x^2 + x + 56 = -(x + 7)(x - 8)$.

b. $-3x^3 - 6x^2 + 72x$

SOLUTION

The leading coefficient is -3. The GCF of the terms is $3x$. So, factor out $-3x$, which is $-1 \cdot 3x$.

$-3x^3 - 6x^2 + 72x$
$-3x(x^2 + 2x - 24)$ Factor out the GCF and -1.

Find two numbers that have a product of -24 and a sum of 2.

$-4 \cdot 6 = -24$ and $-4 + 6 = 2$
$-3x(x^2 + 2x - 24) = -3x(x - 4)(x + 6)$
So, $-3x^3 - 6x^2 + 72x = -3x(x - 4)(x + 6)$.

Math Reasoning

Analyze Explain why the product of $-(x + 7)(x - 8)$ and $-1(x + 7)(x - 8)$ are the same.

Sample: Taking the opposite of $(x + 7)$ is the same as multiplying it by -1.

Some polynomials have more than one variable. Factoring out the GCF first may be helpful.

Example 3 — Factoring Trinomials with Two Variables

Factor completely.

a. $bx^4 + 9bx^3 + 20bx^2$

SOLUTION

The GCF is bx^2.

$bx^4 + 9bx^3 + 20bx^2$
$bx^2(x^2 + 9x + 20)$ Factor out the GCF.

Find two numbers that have a product of 20 and a sum of 9.

$4 \cdot 5 = 20$ and $4 + 5 = 9$
$bx^2(x^2 + 9x + 20) = bx^2(x + 4)(x + 5)$
So, $bx^4 + 9bx^3 + 20bx^2 = bx^2(x + 4)(x + 5)$.

Online Connection
www.SaxonMathResources.com

 ALTERNATE METHOD FOR EXAMPLE 2

Show students how to use the factoring form $(-x + \_\_\_)(x + \_\_\_)$ for trinomials that begin with a negative x-squared term. If it is desired that all binomials begin with a positive term, students will need to factor a -1 out of one binomial like this:

$-x^2 + x + 56 = (-x + 8)(x + 7)$
$= (-1)(x - 8)(x + 7)$
$= -1(x - 8)(x + 7)$

This answer can also be written as $(8 - x)(x + 7)$, a form students might encounter on a standardized test. Point out that $(8 - x)$ is another way of writing $-(x - 8)$.

Repeat the discussion using the second problem in Example 2.

$-3x^3 - 6x^2 + 72x = 3x(-x^2 - 2x + 24)$
$= 3x(-x + 4)(x + 6)$
$= 3x(-1)(x - 4)(x + 6)$
$= -3x(x - 4)(x + 6)$

This answer can also be written as $3x(4 - x)(x + 6)$.

Reading Math

In the polynomial $5bx^3 + 5bx^2 - 60bx$, the coefficient of x^3 and x^2 is **5**. The coefficient of **x** is **−60**.

b. $5bx^3 + 5bx^2 - 60bx$

SOLUTION

The GCF is $5bx$.

$5bx^3 + 5bx^2 - 60bx$

$5bx(x^2 + x - 12)$ Factor out the GCF.

Find two numbers that have a product of -12 and a sum of 1.

$4 \cdot -3 = -12$ and $4 + (-3) = 1$

$5bx(x^2 + x - 12) = 5bx(x + 4)(x - 3)$

So, $5bx^3 + 5bx^2 - 60bx = 5bx(x + 4)(x - 3)$.

Rearrange the terms, if necessary, before factoring so that the polynomial is in standard form.

Hint

A polynomial is in standard form when the terms are ordered from greatest to least degree.

Example 4 Rearranging Terms Before Factoring

Factor completely.

$-105k - 14pk + 7p^2k$

SOLUTION

Before factoring, write the polynomial in standard form.

$-105k - 14pk + 7p^2k = 7p^2k - 14pk - 105k$

$7k(p^2 - 2p - 15)$ Factor out the GCF, $7k$.

Find two numbers that have a product of -15 and a sum of -2.

$-5 \cdot 3 = -15; -5 + 3 = -2$

$7k(p^2 - 2p - 15) = 7k(p + 3)(p - 5)$

So, $7p^2k - 14pk - 105k = 7k(p + 3)(p - 5)$.

Example 5 Application: Golf

The height of a golf ball hit from an elevated tee 40 meters above the hole is $-5t^2 + 35t + 40$, where t represents time. Factor the expression completely.

SOLUTION

The GCF of the terms is 5 and the leading coefficient is negative, so factor out -5, which is $-1 \cdot 5$.

$-5t^2 + 35t + 40$

$-5(t^2 - 7t - 8)$ Factor out the GCF and -1.

Find two numbers that have a product of -8 and a sum of -7.

$1 \cdot -8 = -8$ and $(1) + (-8) = -7$

$-5(t^2 - 7t - 8) = -5(t + 1)(t - 8)$

So, $-5t^2 + 35t + 40 = -5(t + 1)(t - 8)$.

Math Reasoning

Verify Show that $-5(t + 1)(t - 8)$ is equal to $-5t^2 + 35t + 40$.

$-5(t + 1)(t - 8)$
$= -5(t^2 - 7t - 8)$
$= -5t^2 + 35t + 40$

Lesson 79 519

Example 4

Students factor a trinomial with two variables after first writing it in standard form. After common factors are removed from the terms in this example, the resulting trinomial has one variable and a leading coefficient of 1.

Extend the Example

Factor completely. These problems are more difficult because after removing common factors, the resulting trinomials do not have a coefficient of 1.

a. $6x^3y - 36xy - 50x^2y$
 $2xy(3x + 2)(x - 9)$

b. $20ba - 35ba^2 - 10ba^3$
 $-5ab(2a - 1)(a + 4)$

Additional Example 4

Factor completely.

$2m^2n + 48n - 22mn$
$2n(m - 3)(m - 8)$

TEACHER TIP

In problems such as Example 4, some students may find it easier to first factor out common factors, and then to write the resulting trinomial in standard form.

Example 5

Students factor a trinomial expression that represents an application situation.

Additional Example 5

The number of feet a ball falls in t seconds is equal to $16t^2$. Five seconds after Sid drops a ball, Sally drops a ball. For her experiment, the distance fallen in terms of Sid's time is $16t^2 + 160t + 400$. Factor this expression completely.
$16(t + 5)(t + 5)$ or $16(t + 5)^2$

 INCLUSION

Some students may need a review of factoring all the terms of a polynomial. Start with the example $2x^2 + 4x + 6$. Ask, "What is the common factor?" 2

"What does each of the three terms become when you divide out the common factor 2?" $x^2, 2x, 3$

Have students write the two factors as a product. $(2)(x^2 + 2x + 3)$

Remind them they can remove the parentheses to get the simpler form $2(x^2 + 2x + 3)$.

Next discuss the example $2x^2y + 4xy + 6y$. Have students do this in two steps, first dividing out 2 and then dividing out y. $2(x^2y + 2xy + 3y); 2y(x^2 + 2x + 3)$

Emphasize that it is not necessary to divide out $2y$ in a single step. Two steps are fine. In this method students do not need to use the GCF. Finding the greatest common factor may be, in itself, too difficult for some students.

Lesson 79 519

Lesson Practice

Problem d
Scaffolding Have students identify the common factors in the three terms. Have students factor out $-5d$. $-5d(d^2 + 5d + 4)$
Ask, "What two numbers have a product of 4 and a sum of 5?"
1 and 4

"How are 1 and 4 used to factor $d^2 + 5d + 4$?"
$d^2 + 5d + 4 = (d + 4)(d + 1)$

Remind students to include $-5d$ as a factor in their final answers.

Problem e
Error Alert Students may factor out x or y rather than xy. Have them look at the third term, $-54xy$. Hint that it will be convenient to remove both variables from this term.

Check for Understanding
The questions below help assess the concepts taught in this lesson.

"What does it mean to factor a polynomial completely?" Sample: All common factors are pulled out from the terms. If a trinomial can be written as the product of two binomials, it is factored into that form.

"When can a trinomial not be written as the product of two binomials?" Sample: for a trinomial $x^2 + bx + c$: when it is impossible to find two integers such that their product equals the constant term c, and their sum equals the coefficient b of the x-term

---

Lesson Practice

Factor completely.

a. (Ex 1) $p^5 + 13p^4 + 12p^3$ $p^3(p + 12)(p + 1)$
b. (Ex 1) $6n^4 - 6n^3 - 12n^2$ $6n^2(n + 1)(n - 2)$
c. (Ex 2) $-r^2 + r + 30$ $-1(r + 5)(r - 6)$
d. (Ex 2) $-5d^3 - 25d^2 - 20d$ $-5d(d + 4)(d + 1)$
e. (Ex 3) $y^3x + 3y^2x - 54yx$ $xy(y + 9)(y - 6)$
f. (Ex 3) $5bx^3 - 5bx^2 - 60bx$ $5bx(x + 3)(x - 4)$
g. (Ex 4) $18fh - 240h + 6f^2h$ $6h(f - 5)(f + 8)$
h. (Ex 5) (**Construction**) A box is to be built in the shape of a rectangular prism. Its volume is represented by the expression $90x^3 + 450x^2 + 540x$. Factor the expression completely. $90x(x + 3)(x + 2)$

Practice Distributed and Integrated

Assuming that y varies inversely as x, find the missing value.

1. (64) If $y = 6$ and $x = 9$, what is y when $x = 12$? $y = 4.5$

Solve each system of linear equations.

2. (63) $5x = 2y + 10$
$-3y = -2x + 4$ (2, 0)

3. (63) $x - y = 2$
$y + 2x = 1$ (1, −1)

4. (73) Solve the compound inequality $3b - 2 < -8$ OR $4b + 3 > 11$. $b < -2$ OR $b > 2$

Factor.

5. (72) $x^2 - 4x - 45$ $(x - 9)(x + 5)$
*6. (79) $k^4 + 6k^3 + 8k^2$ $k^2(k + 4)(k + 2)$
7. (75) $5x^2 + 3x - 2$ $(5x - 2)(x + 1)$
*8. (79) $2x^3 + 16x^2 + 30x$ $2x(x + 3)(x + 5)$
*9. (79) $abx^2 - 5abx - 24ab$ $ab(x + 3)(x - 8)$
10. (79) $15mx^2 + 9mx - 6m$ $3m(5x - 2)(x + 1)$

11. (78) Find the excluded values for $y = \frac{9m}{m + 3}$. $m \neq -3$

12. (77) Solve $16 + (-6) \geq 2(d + 4)$ and graph the solution. $d \leq 1$;

*13. (79) **Write** Can you factor out the GCF after factoring a trinomial? yes; Sample: The answer will be the same, but factoring may be more difficult due to larger numbers.

*14. (79) **Justify** When asked to factor $3x^2 + 45x + 132$, one student writes $3(x + 4)(x + 11)$. Another student writes $3(x + 11)(x + 4)$. Show that both answers are correct. Explain your answer.

*15. (79) **Multiple Choice** Which expression is factored completely? D
  A $2(5x - 10)(x - 5)$
  B $10(x^2 - 7x + 10)$
  C $5(2x - 4)(x - 5)$
  D $10(x - 5)(x - 2)$

14. $3(x + 4)(x + 11) = 3(x^2 + 15x + 44) = 3x^2 + 45x + 132$ and $3(x + 11)(x + 4) = 3(x^2 + 15x + 44) = 3x^2 + 45x + 132$; Sample: By the Commutative Property of Multiplication, the order of the factors does not matter.

520 Saxon Algebra 1

ENGLISH LEARNERS

Review the meaning of the acronym **GCF**. Ask students what the three letters mean. greatest common factor Point out that this term is built up in three steps:

1. Define factor.
2. Define common factor.
3. Define greatest common factor.

Begin with factor.

"If a number can be written as the product of two other numbers, each of those is a factor."

Write $16 = 2 \cdot 8$ and ask what factors the equation shows. 2 and 8

Next, write $16 = 2 \cdot 8$ and underneath it $24 = 2 \cdot 12$. "What factor do 16 and 24 share?" 2 "So, 2 is a common factor of 16 and 24. Do 16 and 24 have any other common factors?" Yes: 1, 4, and 8 Have students prove these are common factors by writing the appropriate equations. Then have them identify the greatest common factor. 8 Show them the notation GCF(16, 24) = 8 as a way of recording this work.

*16. (Physics) An object is thrown from inside a hole. Its height after x seconds is represented by the expression $-16x^2 + 32x - 16$. Factor the expression completely. $-16(x-1)^2$

17. Error Analysis Students were asked to find the vertical asymptote of the expression $y = \frac{1}{x+2} + 8$. Which student is correct? Explain the error.

Student A	Student B
$x = -2$	$y = 8$

17. Student A; Sample: Student B wrote the horizontal asymptote.

*18. Multi-Step A band teacher has a budget of $50,000 to buy new instruments. He will receive 1 free instrument when he places his order. The number of instruments, y, that he can get is given by $y = \frac{50,000}{x} + 1$, where x is the price per instrument.
a. What is the horizontal asymptote of this rational function? $y = 1$
b. What is the vertical asymptote? $x = 0$
c. If the price per instrument is $1000, how many instruments will he receive? 51 instruments

19. (Party Planning) A party planner has a budget of $1350.00 to buy a steak dinner for the entire guest list for a company retirement party. The planner will receive 15 free dinners when she places the order. The number of steak dinners, y, that the planner can buy is given by $y = \frac{1350}{x} + 15$, where x is the price per steak dinner.
a. What is the horizontal asymptote of this rational function? $y = 15$
b. What is the vertical asymptote? $x = 0$
c. If the price per dinner is $25, how many dinners will the planner receive? 69 dinners

*20. Geometry Write a rational function that shows the relationship between the side lengths of the similar triangles shown. $\frac{5}{x-8} = \frac{y}{1}; \frac{5}{x-8} = y$

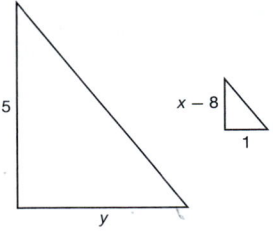

21. (Automotive Care) Steve's car is really dirty and is almost on empty. He has $20. A car wash is $7 and gas is $3 per gallon. To find how many gallons of gas he can buy with a car wash, solve the inequality $7 + 3g \le 20$. $g \le 4\frac{1}{3}$; He can buy up to $4\frac{1}{3}$ gallons.

22. Error Analysis Two students solve $3h + 15 > 6$. Which student is correct? Explain the error.

Student A	Student B
$3h + 15 > 6$	$3h + 15 > 6$
$3h > -9$	$3h > -9$
$h < -3$	$h > -3$

22. Student B; Sample: Student A reversed the inequality sign when dividing by a positive number.

 23. Write Explain the process for multiplying binomials with radicals. Sample: Use the FOIL method, simplify radicals, and then combine like terms.

Lesson 79   521

3 Practice

Math Conversations
Discussion to strengthen understanding

Problem 15
Error Alert
If students choose the wrong answer, tell them that the correct choice is D. Then ask them to explain why the other answer choices are wrong. Sample: In choices A and C, one of the binomials has terms with a common factor. In choice B, the trinomial factor can be factored into $(x - 2)(x - 5)$.

Problem 18
Extend the Problem
Explain how the horizontal asymptote of the rational function relates to the number of free band instruments. Sample: The equation of the horizontal asymptote is $y = n$, where n equals the number of free band instruments.

Problem 20
Sketch two right triangles on the board and label the legs a and b, c, and d. Ask, "If these two right triangles are similar, how are the legs related?" They are proportional.

"What proportion can you write for the legs?" $\frac{a}{c} = \frac{b}{d}$

Problem 23
Suggest that students use the example $(x + \sqrt{3})(x - 2\sqrt{5})$.

Guide the students by asking them the following questions.

"What is the product of the last terms?" $\sqrt{3}(-2\sqrt{5}) = -2\sqrt{15}$

"How many terms will there be in the product?" Most students will use four terms, writing the product as $x^2 + \sqrt{3}x - 2\sqrt{5}x - 2\sqrt{15}$ rather than $x^2 + (\sqrt{3} - 2\sqrt{5})x - 2\sqrt{15}$.

CHALLENGE

Explain that the greatest common factor of the terms of a binomial may be another binomial. Illustrate this with the example $x(x + 5) + 4(x + 5) = (x + 5)(x + 4)$.

Then have students factor these binomials.

a. $(xz - yz) + (2x - 2y)$
   $(x - y)(z + 2)$

b. $(q + pq) - (3 + 3p)$
   $(1 + p)(q - 3)$

Lesson 79   521

24. **Multiple Choice** Between which two numbers does $\sqrt{124}$ fall on a number line? **D**
    (76)
    A 9 and 11   **B** 8 and 11   **C** 12 and 14   **D** 11 and 13

25. **Measurement** Lou is building a square sandbox. The sandbox has a side length of
    (76) $6\sqrt{36}$ inches. What is the area of the sandbox? **1296 square inches**

26. **Fine Arts** In an antique shop, a painting is inclined on a display easel at an angle
    (74) of 65°. The angle of inclination can be increased or decreased by a maximum of 8°
    from the present setting by an adjustment screw. Write and solve an absolute-value
    equation for the maximum and minimum angles of inclination for the easel.
    $|x - 65| = 8$; 73°, 57°

27. **Write** Describe the characteristics of the trend line for scatter plots with a positive
    (71) correlation, a negative correlation, and no correlation.

    27. Sample: The trend line for a positive correlation rises from left to right. The trend line for a negative correlation falls from left to right. There is no trend line when there is no correlation.

28. **Multi-Step** The video store charges $4.80 per rental of a DVD. The store spends
    (70) $5100 on expenses each month. How many videos does the store have to rent to
    make more money than it spends on expenses?
    a. What are the total expenses of the store? **$5100**
    b. Write an inequality to show how many DVDs need to be rented to make a
    profit. **$4.80r > 5100$**
    c. Solve the inequality. **$r > 1062.5$**
    d. How many DVDs need to be rented a month to make a profit?
    at least 1063 DVDs per month

29. **Sewing** Deandra wants to put trimming around a rectangular tablecloth that
    (69) measures $2\sqrt{49}$ feet by $\sqrt{81}$ feet. How many feet of trimming will Deandra need?
    46 ft

*30. **Multi-Step** A fitness center has a small elevator for members to use and to move
    (66) fitness equipment. The elevator has a maximum capacity of 750 pounds.
    a. Troy weighs 185 pounds. Write an inequality representing how much more
    weight the elevator can carry if Troy uses the elevator. **$185 + x \leq 750$; $x \leq 565$**
    b. Alicia needs to move weight equipment to the second floor. She has four
    75-pound weights, four 50-pound weights, four 25-pound weights, and six
    20-pound weights. Will she be able to bring all of the weights up in one elevator
    trip? Explain. **no; Sample: The total weight of the weights is 720 pounds.
    This would mean that Alicia could weigh no more than 30 pounds, which is not
    reasonable.**

522   Saxon Algebra 1

LOOKING FORWARD

Factoring trinomials by using the GCF prepares students for

- **Lesson 83** Factoring Special Products
- **Lesson 87** Factoring Polynomials by Grouping
- **Lesson 93** Dividing Polynomials
- **Lesson 95** Combining Rational Expressions with Unlike Denominators

LESSON 80

Calculating Frequency Distributions

Warm Up

1. **Vocabulary** A _____ is a value that describes the center of a data set and includes the mean, median, and mode. **measure of central tendency**

Find the theoretical probability of each outcome.

2. flipping one coin and having it land tails up $\frac{1}{2}$ or 50%

3. randomly choosing a yellow marble from a bag of 3 yellow marbles and 7 blue marbles $\frac{3}{10}$ or 30%

4. rolling a 1 on a number cube labeled 1–6 $\frac{1}{6}$ or $16\frac{2}{3}$%

5. randomly choosing the letter A from the letters in MATH $\frac{1}{4}$ or 25%

New Concepts

Discrete events have a finite number of outcomes. A **compound event** is an event consisting of two or more simple events. A simple event could be tossing heads on a coin. A compound event could be tossing heads and then tails on a coin.

A **frequency distribution** shows the number of observations falling into several ranges of data values. Tables, graphs, tree diagrams, and lists are used to show frequency distributions.

Math Reasoning

Analyze Why is rolling cubes with a sum of 7 more likely than rolling any other sum?

Sample: There are more ways to roll a sum of 7 than any other sum.

Math Language

Frequency is how often something happens.

b. $\frac{1}{36}$; $\frac{2}{36}$ or $\frac{1}{18}$; $\frac{3}{36}$ or $\frac{1}{12}$; $\frac{4}{36}$ or $\frac{1}{9}$; $\frac{5}{36}$; $\frac{6}{36}$ or $\frac{1}{6}$; $\frac{5}{36}$; $\frac{4}{36}$ or $\frac{1}{9}$; $\frac{3}{36}$ or $\frac{1}{12}$; $\frac{2}{36}$ or $\frac{1}{18}$; $\frac{1}{36}$

c. Sample: 2, 1, 5, 6, 3, 14, 3, 6, 3, 4, 3; See Student Work.

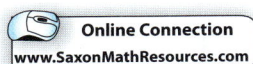
Online Connection
www.SaxonMathResources.com

Exploration Displaying Frequency Distributions

The likelihood of a particular sum, when two number cubes are rolled, is determined by the number of different sums that can be made with the two cubes.

a. Make a table or tree diagram to show the different possible sums, or outcomes. See Additional Answers.

b. Complete the table showing the probability of each sum, or outcome.

Sum	2	3	4	5	6	7	8	9	10	11	12
Probability											

c. Roll two differently colored number cubes 50 times. Use a frequency table to record the number of times each outcome occurs.

Sum	2	3	4	5	6	7	8	9	10	11	12
Frequency											

d. Use a bar graph to display your results. See Additional Answers.

e. Based on the theoretical probabilities you calculated, are your results what you expected? yes; Sample: I would have expected to roll 7 the most, and I did.

Lesson 80   523

MATH BACKGROUND

The frequency of an observation is the number of times the observation occurs in the data. A frequency distribution is the pattern of the frequencies. Frequency tables often show cumulative frequencies in either numeric or percentage format, or both.

Grade Range	Frequency (Number of Students)	Cumulative Frequency	Cumulative Percentage
0 to 40	3	3	5%
41 to 60	18	21	35%
61 to 80	27	48	80%
81 to 100	12	60	100%

A histogram is a bar graph in which each bar has a class interval as its base and a frequency of occurrence as its height.

LESSON 80

1 Warm Up

Problem 3
Remind students that the denominator of the fraction is the total number of marbles.

2 New Concepts

In this lesson, students use bar graphs to illustrate outcomes in probability experiments. They also calculate experimental and theoretical probabilities.

Discuss the difference between theoretical and experimental probability.

Exploration

Students roll a pair of number cubes 50 times and record the sums. They compare their results with those predicted using theoretical probabilities.

Extend the Exploration

Use the steps in the Exploration to find the experimental and theoretical probability of landing on 0, 1, 2, 3, and 4 heads when four coins are tossed. See Additional Answers.

LESSON RESOURCES

Student Edition Practice
   Workbook 80
Reteaching Master 80
Adaptations Master 80
Challenge and Enrichment
   Master C80

Lesson 80   523

Example 1

Students use a bar graph to illustrate the outcomes in a baseball season. They use the data to calculate experimental probabilities.

Error Alert Students may miscalculate the sum of the data values. Encourage them to check their work to avoid further errors when calculating probabilities.

Additional Example 1

A sailboat owner kept track of the weather for three months. Make a bar graph that shows the frequency distribution of the data. Find the experimental probability of each outcome.

Weather	No. of Days
sun and wind	42
no sun, wind	24
sun, no wind	18
no sun, no wind	8

Sun and wind $\frac{21}{46}$; no sun, wind $\frac{6}{23}$; sun, no wind $\frac{9}{46}$; no sun, no wind $\frac{2}{23}$; See Additional Answers.

Example 2

Students find the outcomes in a probability experiment with two independent events. They use this information to calculate theoretical probabilities.

Additional Example 2

The names of two students will be drawn at random from a four-person group that includes Jo, Ed, Dee, and Kim.

a. Make a table to show the possible outcomes in this experiment. See Additional Answers.

b. Find the theoretical probability of each possible outcome. $\frac{1}{6}$

Example 1 Using Experimental Probability

A baseball player bats multiple times in a season. The table shows the results of each at bat. Make a bar graph that shows the frequency distribution of the data. Find the experimental probability of each outcome.

Out	Walk	Single	Double	Triple	Home Run
30	36	20	9	3	1

SOLUTION

Understand A player bats multiple times. Make a bar graph showing the number of times each outcome occurs. Then state the probability of each outcome.

Hint
Probability is $\frac{\text{number of favorable outcomes}}{\text{total number of outcomes}}$. Use this to write the ratio for each result. For example, for outs, write the ratio of 30 to 99 because the player was out 30 times in 99 at bats.

Plan Calculate the total number of times at bat. Then find the probability of each outcome. Make a bar graph. Let each bar represent an outcome. The height of the bars will show the frequency of each outcome.

Solve The total number of times at bat is $30 + 36 + 20 + 9 + 3 + 1 = 99$.

$P(\text{out}) = \frac{30}{99} = \frac{10}{33}$ $P(\text{walk}) = \frac{36}{99} = \frac{4}{11}$

$P(\text{single}) = \frac{20}{99}$ $P(\text{double}) = \frac{9}{99} = \frac{1}{11}$

$P(\text{triple}) = \frac{3}{99} = \frac{1}{33}$ $P(\text{home run}) = \frac{1}{99}$

Caution
In a bar graph, the bars do not touch each other. All of the bars are the same width. Their heights may differ.

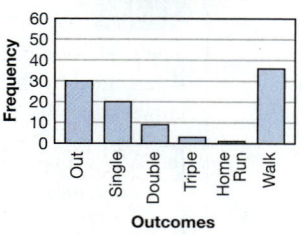

Results of At Bat

Check To check the probabilities, the numerators should match the data in the table. Each denominator is 99. Make sure fractions are reduced correctly.

To check the graph, make sure the heights of the bars match the data in the table. The sum of the heights of the bars should be 99, the total number of times at bat.

ENGLISH LEARNERS

Explain the meaning of the word **experimental.** Say:

"Experimental describes an action that is carried out to discover something or to show that something is true."

Discuss that when someone uses a new recipe, experimental learning occurs. The experiment lies in the act of trying a new recipe, not in the ingredients or the instructions the recipe requires.

Math Language

A **fair coin** has an equally likely chance of coming up heads or tails on the toss of the coin.

Example 2 Representing Data with a Table

A student spins the spinner and flips a fair coin.

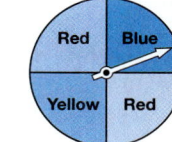

a. Make a table to show the possible outcomes in this experiment.

SOLUTION

The column headings are the possible colors for the spinner. Since there are two red sections on the spinner, there are two red columns.

The row headings are the possible sides of a coin, heads and tails.

The table is completed by recording all possible outcomes of a spin and a flip. Abbreviate the outcomes.

	Red	Blue	Red	Yellow
Heads	RH	BH	RH	YH
Tails	RT	BT	RT	YT

b. Find the theoretical probability of each possible outcome.

SOLUTION

The table shows that there are 8 possible outcomes.

$P(RH) = \frac{2}{8} = \frac{1}{4}$ $P(BH) = \frac{1}{8}$ $P(YH) = \frac{1}{8}$

$P(RT) = \frac{2}{8} = \frac{1}{4}$ $P(BT) = \frac{1}{8}$ $P(YT) = \frac{1}{8}$

Math Reasoning

Justify Why is the probability of spinning "red" $\frac{1}{2}$?

Sample: 2 of the 4 sections of the spinner are red; $\frac{2 \text{ favorable outcomes}}{4 \text{ total outcomes}} = \frac{1}{2}$

Reading Math

$P(RH)$ is the probability of spinning "red" and landing on "heads."

Example 3 Representing Data with a Graph

Suppose that eleven cards each contain one letter from the word MISSISSIPPI.

a. Make a bar graph to represent the frequency distribution for all possible outcomes.

SOLUTION

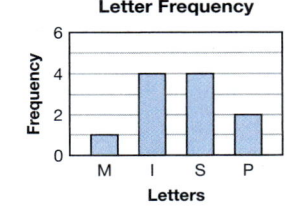

Hint

Although some letters are on more than one card, there will be only one bar on the graph for each letter.

b. Find the theoretical probability of each outcome.

SOLUTION

$P(M) = \frac{1}{11}$ $P(I) = \frac{4}{11}$ $P(S) = \frac{4}{11}$ $P(P) = \frac{2}{11}$

Lesson 80   525

Example 3

Students use a bar graph to illustrate the outcomes in a card-drawing application. They use the data to calculate theoretical probabilities.

Extend the Example

Have students refer to the bar graph.

"Assume this experiment with the letters from Mississippi is conducted 1000 times. What would a graph of the expected results look like?" Sample: It would look just like the "Letter Frequency" graph except that the vertical axis would be numbered 200, 400, and 600.

Additional Example 3

Suppose that 20 cards are put in a box for a drawing. There are 12 cards with hearts, 5 with circles, 2 with squares, and 1 with a star.

a. Make a bar graph to represent the frequency distribution for all possible outcomes.

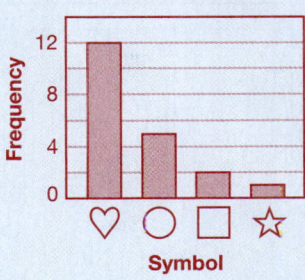

b. Find the theoretical probability of each outcome.
heart $\frac{3}{5}$, circle $\frac{1}{4}$, square $\frac{1}{10}$, star $\frac{1}{20}$

🚩 ALTERNATE METHOD FOR EXAMPLE 2

Sketch the four-part spinner on the board and label 2 parts red, 1 part blue, and 1 part yellow. Remind students that spinning the spinner and tossing a coin are two independent events. Say:

"When events A and B are independent, you can find the probability of A and B by multiplying the two separate probabilities."

Write on the board:
$P(A \text{ and } B) = P(A) \cdot P(B)$.

Say:

"What is the probability of spinning blue?"
1 out of 4, or $\frac{1}{4}$

"What is the probability of getting heads?"
1 out of 2, or $\frac{1}{2}$

Write on the board:

$P(\text{blue and heads}) = P(\text{blue}) \cdot P(\text{heads})$
$= \frac{1}{4} \cdot \frac{1}{2} = \frac{1}{8}$

Have students compute $P(\text{blue and tails})$ and $P(\text{red and heads})$ in the same way. $\frac{1}{8}, \frac{1}{4}$

Lesson 80   525

Lesson Practice

Problem a
Scaffolding Tell students that the bowler gets 10 turns per game.

"How many turns did he use for his data?" 50 "How will you use this number in calculating the probabilities?" It is the denominator in the probability fractions.

Problem b
Error Alert Make sure students understand that there are four possible outcomes, not three. The outcomes are HH, HT, TH, and TT. Two of these are the same.

Check for Understanding
The questions below help assess the concepts taught in this lesson.

"What are some different ways of displaying all the outcomes in a probability experiment?" Sample: bar graph, table

Sketch the graph below on the board. Ask, "How many outcomes are shown on this graph? How many different outcomes are shown?" 36, 11

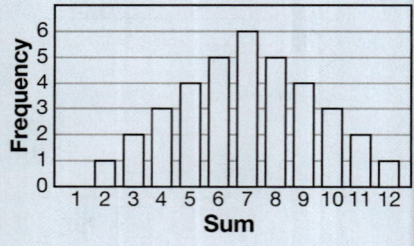
Sum of Two Cubes

---

a. See Additional Answers;
$P(0) = \frac{1}{50}, P(1) = \frac{0}{50} = 0,$
$P(2) = \frac{0}{50} = 0, P(3) = \frac{4}{50} = \frac{2}{25},$
$P(4) = \frac{1}{50}, P(5) = \frac{2}{50} = \frac{1}{25}, P(6) = \frac{0}{50} = 0, P(7) = \frac{6}{50} = \frac{3}{25}, P(8) = \frac{17}{50},$
$P(9) = \frac{8}{50} = \frac{4}{25}, P(10) = \frac{11}{50}$

b.

	Tails	Heads
Tails	TT	TH
Heads	TH	HH

c. $P(HH) = \frac{1}{4}, P(TH) = \frac{2}{4} = \frac{1}{2},$
$P(TT) = \frac{1}{4}$

e. $P(\text{tomato}) = \frac{3}{12} = \frac{1}{4},$
$P(\text{vegetable}) = \frac{6}{12} = \frac{1}{2},$
$P(\text{potato}) = \frac{2}{12} = \frac{1}{6},$
$P(\text{clam chowder}) = \frac{1}{12}$

Lesson Practice

a. (Bowling) A man bowls five games. He keeps track of how many pins he knocks down on the first try of each turn. Make a bar graph that shows the frequency distribution of the data. Find the experimental probability of each outcome.
(Ex 1)

Number of Pins	0	1	2	3	4	5	6	7	8	9	10
Frequency	1	0	0	4	1	2	0	6	17	8	11

A student flips two coins.
(Ex 2)
b. Make a table to show the possible outcomes in this experiment.

c. Find the theoretical probability of each outcome.

A toddler tears off the labels on several soup cans. There were 6 cans of vegetable soup, 3 cans of tomato soup, 2 cans of potato soup, and 1 can of clam chowder. One can is randomly chosen to open.
(Ex 3)
d. Make a bar graph to show the frequency distribution for all possible outcomes. See Additional Answers.

e. Find the theoretical probability of each outcome.

Practice   Distributed and Integrated

1. Write an equation for a line that passes through $(-1, 4)$ and is parallel to $2y + 10x = -36$. Sample: $y = -5x - 1$
(65)

Assuming that y varies inversely as x, find the missing value for each problem.

2. If $y = 108$ and $x = 3$, what is x when $y = 3$? $x = 108$
(64)

3. If $y = 56$ and $x = 7$, what is x when $y = 4$? $x = 98$
(64)

4. Find the horizontal asymptote: $y = \frac{7}{x+5}$. $y = 0$
(78)

5. Find the horizontal asymptote: $y = \frac{3}{2x+3} - 5$. $y = -5$
(78)

Solve.

6. $11|x| = 55$ $\{5, -5\}$
(74)

7. $x - 5 \geq 0$ OR $x + 1 < -2$ $x < -3$ OR $x \geq 5$
(73)

Factor.

*8. $c^{12} + 11c^{11} + 24c^{10}$ $c^{10}(c + 8)(c + 3)$
(79)

9. $42x^4 + 77x^3 - 70x^2$ $7x^2(3x - 2)(2x + 5)$
(79)

*10. $-3m^2 - 30m - 48$ $-3(m + 2)(m + 8)$
(79)

*11. $(x - 1)x^2 + 7x(x - 1) + 10(x - 1)$ $(x - 1)(x + 2)(x + 5)$
(79)

526   Saxon Algebra 1

INCLUSION

Materials: 8-part spinners showing 2 hearts, 3 circles, 1 square, and 2 stars

Demonstrate how to use the spinners. Say, "In eight spins, you might expect to get 1 square, 2 hearts, 2 stars, and 3 circles. Is that what is really going to happen?" Sample: Probably not. The number of trials is too small.

Relate the spinner to a simple bar graph. Have students use the spinners and record their results. Compile all the data. As the number of spins increases, the experimental results will begin to approach the theoretical ones.

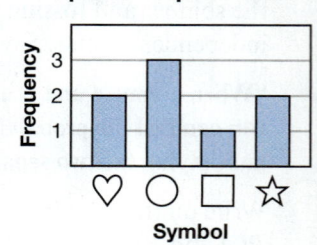
Spinner Experiment

*12. A student rolls a number cube, numbered 1–6, and spins the spinner. Make a table of the possible outcomes.

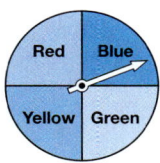

12.

	Red	Blue	Yellow	Green
1	R1	B1	Y1	G1
2	R2	B2	Y2	G2
3	R3	B3	Y3	G3
4	R4	B4	Y4	G4
5	R5	B5	Y5	G5
6	R6	B6	Y6	G6

*13. **Generalize** Explain when you would choose a graph or a table to show a frequency distribution. Sample: Use a table when organizing the data for further calculations. Use a graph to display the data.

14. **Multiple Choice** Which expression represents the probability of getting a 4 or 5 on three number cubes, numbered 1–6, and heads on four coins? **D**

A $P = \frac{4}{6} \cdot \frac{5}{6} \cdot \frac{4}{2}$

B $P = \frac{1}{6} \cdot \frac{1}{6} \cdot \frac{1}{2}$

C $P = \left(\frac{1}{6}\right)^2 \cdot \left(\frac{1}{2}\right)^4$

D $P = \left(\frac{1}{3}\right)^3 \cdot \left(\frac{1}{2}\right)^4$

15.

	Chemical	Physical
Success	CS	PS
Failure	CF	PF

*15. (**Chemistry**) Experiments in a chemistry lab either succeed or fail. They also can be characterized as chemical or physical reactions. Make a table to show all the possible outcomes.

*16. **Probability** A bag contains 3 red marbles and 7 blue marbles. A marble is drawn and replaced. Use an equation to show the probability of drawing 3 red marbles in a row. $P(\text{red, red, red}) = \left(\frac{3}{10}\right)^3 = \frac{27}{1000}$

17. (**Physics**) An object is thrown from a tower. The expression $-16x^2 + 32x + 48$ represents its height after x minutes. Factor this expression completely. $-16(x - 3)(x + 1)$

18. **Error Analysis** Two students factor $2x^2 - 2x - 12$. Which student is correct? Explain the error. Student B; Sample: Student A did not factor out the GCF, 2.

Student A	Student B
$(2x + 4)(x - 3)$	$2(x + 2)(x - 3)$

*19. **Geometry** A square has area $9m^4 - 54m^3 + 81m^2$ square inches. What is its side length? $3m(m - 3)$ inches

20. **Multi-Step** The volume of a rectangular cereal box is represented by the expression $3x^3 + 3x^2 - 18x$.
 a. Factor the expression completely. $3x(x - 2)(x + 3)$
 b. What are the dimensions of the box? $(3x) \times (x - 2) \times (x + 3)$

21. **Error Analysis** Students were asked to find the excluded values for $\frac{5m}{m+3}$. Which student is correct? Explain the error. Student B; Student A didn't change the sign when subtracting 3 from both sides after setting the denominator equal to 0.

Student A	Student B
$m + 3 \neq 0$	$m + 3 \neq 0$
$m \neq 3$	$m \neq -3$
$m \neq 3$	$m \neq -3$

Lesson 80   527

3 Practice

Math Conversations
Discussion to strengthen understanding

Problem 1
Scaffolding Guide the students by asking them the following questions.

"How is the slope of the given line found?" Sample: Solve the equation for y. The coefficient of the x is the slope of the line.

"Once the slope is found, what formula is used to solve the problem?" Sample: point-slope formula $y - y_1 = m(x - x_1)$

"What values are substituted into the formula?" Sample: 4 for y_1, -1 for x_1, and -5 for m

Problem 11
Scaffolding Guide the students by asking them the following questions.

"What are the three terms in this trinomial?" Sample: $(x - 1) x^2$, $7x(x - 1)$, and $10(x - 1)$

"What is the first step in factoring?" Sample: Factor out the common factor $(x - 1)$.

Problem 16
Extend the Problem
How does the probability change if the marble is not replaced? Use decimals in your answer. It decreases from 0.027 to 0.0083.

Problem 17
Error Alert
Some students may factor the expression without removing the GCF. This will be a good opportunity to show them that remembering to take out the GCF will make factoring the resulting trinomial easier.

Problem 20
Extend the Problem
The smallest dimension of this box is 8 centimeters. What are the other two dimensions? 13 cm, 30 cm

Lesson 80   527

CHALLENGE

Have students generalize the use of probability in making predictions by solving the given problem. Say:

"The probability of an outcome is p. Let n represent the number of trials in this experiment. Write an algebraic expression to make a prediction about the outcome."

Sample: This particular outcome will occur about $p \cdot n$ times in the next n trials.

Problem 23
Point out that 0 is a solution of $-6x < 42$, but not of $6x < -42$.

Extend the Problem
Have students sketch the graphs of both solution sets on the same number line.

"What number is not a member of either solution set?" -7

Problem 27
If students have difficulty, suggest that they first explain why they can eliminate 5 and 9 when factoring $x^2 + 18x + 45$. Sample: $5 \cdot 9 = 45$, but $5 + 9$ is not equal to 18. The correct pair is 3 and 15.

Problem 30
Point out that multiplying both sides of the second equation by 4 will show that the two equations are identical.

---

*22. (Bakery) Erica plans to buy 100 cookies for the parent-teacher conference and to divide them equally among the number of parents attending. There will also be an additional dozen cookies given to each parent at the end of school party. The number of cookies for each parent, y, is given by $y = \frac{100}{x} + 12$, where x is the number of parents. Find the asymptotes and graph the function. $x = 0; y = 12$

22.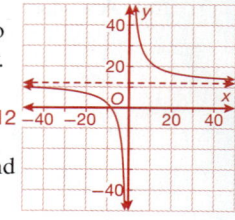

23. **Analyze** Explain why you would not reverse the inequality sign for $6x < -42$ and why you would for $-6x < 42$.

24. **Multiple Choice** What is the solution to $5 - 3(2 - m) \geq 29$? **D**
  A $m \leq -10$ **B** $m \geq -10$ **C** $m \leq 10$ **D** $m \geq 10$

25. Use the Distributive Property to find the product of $\sqrt{4}(3 + \sqrt{6})$. $6 + 2\sqrt{6}$

26. (Softball) The speed of a pitched ball is represented by the expression $9x^2 - 36x - 13$. Factor the expression completely. $(3x + 1)(3x - 13)$

27. **Justify** Why would you eliminate the factor pair $(5)(9z^2)$ in determining the binomial factors of $x^2 + 18xz + 45z^2$? Sample: The sum of $5 + 9z^2$ does not contain a factor of z, which is necessary for the coefficient b, $18z$.

28. **Multi-Step** Use the table of values.

x	40	100	120	20	80	60
y	80	161	196	34	141	105

  a. Enter the data into a graphing calculator and find an equation for the line of best fit. $y = 1.556x + 10.6$
  b. How can you tell if there is a positive or negative correlation for the data from the equation?

29. (Real Estate) A realtor gets 6.5% commission for each house sold. Write and solve an inequality to find the house prices that will give the realtor a commission of at least $20,000. $0.065x \geq 20{,}000$; any house with a sale price of $307,692 or greater

30. **Multi-Step** Two trains leave the rail yard at the same time. One travels east and the other west. The distance in miles traveled by the westbound train is $d = 40t + 12$. The distance in miles traveled by the eastbound train is $\frac{1}{4}d = 10t + 3$.
  a. Classify these two equations. consistent and dependent
  b. After a time of 10 hours, which train will have traveled farther?
  Neither train travels farther; they both travel the same distance because the equations are identical in slope-intercept form.

---

23. Sample: In the first inequality, you would solve by dividing both sides by positive 6. In the second, you would solve by dividing both sides by -6. It is what you are dividing by, not what is being divided, that determines whether the sign is reversed.

28b. Sample: Look at the value of the slope of the line (the coefficient of the x-term). If the slope is positive, then the correlation is positive. If the slope is negative, then the correlation is negative. In this example, there is a positive correlation.

LOOKING FORWARD

Calculating frequency distributions prepares students for

- **Lesson 111** Solving Problems Involving Permutations
- **Lesson 118** Solving Problems Involving Combinations
- **Lesson 120** Using Geometric Formulas to Find the Probability of an Event

INVESTIGATION 8

Identifying and Writing Joint Variation

Joint variation occurs when a quantity varies directly as the product of two or more other quantities. When y varies jointly with a set of variables, y is directly proportional to each variable taken one at a time. For example, if $y = kxz$ where k is the constant of variation and $k \neq 0$, then y varies jointly with x and z.

The equation $b = 3ac$ is a joint variation in which b varies jointly with a and c. The table of values below illustrates the relationship between the variables. Use the table to complete the statements that follow.

a	b	c
1	3	1
2	6	1
1	6	2
2	12	2

1. Doubling a causes b to change by a factor of _____.   **2**
2. _____ c causes b to change by a factor of two.   **doubling**
3. The statements above are true because b is _____ proportional to a, and b is directly proportional to _____.   **directly; c**
4. Doubling both _____ and _____ causes _____ to quadruple.   **a; c; b**

In each case, you must hold one variable constant to calculate changes in the other two variables.

If you know y varies jointly with x and z and also know one set of values, you can use the equation $y = kxz$ to find the equation of variation.

Suppose y varies jointly with x and z. Find y when $x = 8$ and $z = 3$, given that $y = 20$ when $x = 5$ and $z = 2$.

5. **Model** Set up an equation in the form $y = kxz$ using the given values. $20 = k \cdot 5 \cdot 2$
6. What is the value of k? $k = 2$
7. Use the value of k to write an equation of joint variation that relates x, y, and z. $y = 2xz$
8. Find y when $x = 8$ and $z = 3$. $y = 48$

Online Connection
www.SaxonMathResources.com

Discuss

In the activity on this page, students explore relationships in joint variation and find an equation for joint variation.

Before discussing joint variation, make sure that students remember the definitions of direct and inverse variation. The first is represented by equations of the form $y = kx$; the second is represented by equations of the form $y = \frac{k}{x}$. In both types of variation, k is the constant of variation.

Error Alert

Some students may need help to understand that the k in the equation $y = kxz$ represents a constant rather than a variable. Use an example students can visualize such as the volume of a box with a fixed height. The variation equation is $V = klw$, where the constant k is the fixed height of the box. If the height is 10 centimeters, the equation is $V = 10lw$ and the volume varies jointly with the length and the width. The volume is proportional to the product of the length and the width.

Investigation 8   529

MATH BACKGROUND

In direct variation $y = kx$, one variable is a constant multiple of the other. In inverse variation $y = \frac{k}{x}$, the product of the two variables is a constant. In most practical applications, k is positive. Functions of more than one variable can exhibit more than one type of variation. If y varies directly with x and also directly with z, the relationship $y = kxz$ is one of joint variation. In this type of variation, the first variable is proportional to the product of the others.

In combined variation, $y = \frac{kx}{z}$, the dependent variable varies directly with one variable and inversely with another variable. All problems in variation can be approached in a similar fashion. Use given numeric data to find the constant of variation. Then use the resulting equation to solve the problem.

INVESTIGATION RESOURCES

Reteaching Master
Investigation 8

Investigation 8   529

Problems 9–13

In the first activity on this page, students explore the ideal gas law using the variation equation $pV = nRT$. Make sure that students can identify the constant of variation R, the ideal gas constant. This constant depends on the units used in the formula. Another value for R is 8.314472 joules per mole per kelvin.

Error Alert

If students have difficulty with the ideal gas law problems, discuss these easier applications of joint variation:

(1) The area of a triangle varies jointly with the height and the base. The area formula is $A = \frac{1}{2}bh$ which shows that the constant of variation is $\frac{1}{2}$.

(2) The simple interest on a sum of money varies jointly as the rate and the time. The equation of variation is $i = krt$ and the constant of variation k is the fixed sum invested.

Problems 14–16

In the second activity on this page, students explore an example of combined variation. The variable P varies directly with the product WD^2 and inversely with the variable L. Point out that k would change both with the units of measurement used for the dimensions, as well as with the type of material used to construct the beam.

Extend the Problem

A beam of fixed length is 2 inches wide and 8 inches deep. If the safe load for this beam is 1200 pounds, find the safe load of a beam that is the same length but is 2 inches wide and 6 inches deep. **675 pounds**

Joint variation is found widely in scientific applications. An ideal gas can be characterized by three stated variables: absolute pressure P, volume V, and absolute temperature T. You can deduce the relationship between them from kinetic theory. This is called the ideal gas law. It is written as $PV = nRT$, where P is the absolute pressure in atmospheres, V is the volume of the vessel containing n moles of gas, n moles is the amount of substance of gas, R is the gas constant (0.08206), and T is the temperature in kelvins. Since R is a constant, the equation can be written as $PV = 0.08206nT$.

Use the ideal gas law to answer the questions.

9. $R = 0.08206$

9. What is the constant of variation in the ideal gas law equation?

10. How many moles of gas does it take to occupy 120 liters at a pressure of 2.3 atmospheres and a temperature of 340 K? Round the answer to the nearest tenth. **9.9 moles**

11. If a 50-liter container holds 45 moles of a gas at a temperature of 473.15 K, what is the pressure inside the container? Round the answer to the nearest tenth. **34.9 atm**

12. $P = \frac{0.08206nT}{V}$

12. Generalize Solve the ideal gas law for the absolute pressure P.

An equation in several variables can be written in terms of one variable, as in the previous exercise. This will produce a quotient on one side of the equal sign in the equation. You can describe the variation in terms of a joint and an inverse variation.

13. Write State the ideal gas law solved for P in words using the phrases jointly proportional to and inversely proportional to.

Caution
Sometimes there can be more than one type of variation in one situation. The type of variation depends on whether each variable is part of a product or quotient within the equation of variation.

By solving the ideal gas law for the absolute pressure P the equation is written as both a joint and an inverse variation. Many science applications involve more than one type of variation, as well as the square or square root of variable(s).

The load P in pounds that a horizontal beam can safely support varies jointly with the product of the width of the beam W in feet and the square of the depth D in feet, and inversely with the length L in feet.

14. Write an equation relating P, W, D, L, and a constant k. $P = \frac{kWD^2}{L}$

15. The load the beam can safely support is halved.

15. How does P change when the length of the beam is doubled?

16. How does P change when the width and the depth of the beam are cut in half? **The load the beam can safely support is divided by 8.**

13. Sample: The absolute pressure is jointly proportional to the number of moles of the gas and the temperature, and inversely proportional to the volume of the vessel.

ENGLISH LEARNERS

For this lesson, emphasize the fact that **variation** has a specific mathematical meaning different from other everyday meanings. Say, "In everyday language, variation is the amount or extent of change. It might be how much something differs from a given standard."

Use the following example to illustrate variation. There is a variation in the quality of the toys in this shipment. Yesterday there was a variation of 20 degrees in the temperature. Which variation of this carpet design do you like the best? Say:

"In mathematics, variation describes a certain way that variables are related. Variation is described using an equation in which the letter k stands for the constant of variation."

Investigation Practice

a. Write an equation for the relationship where s varies jointly with r and t and $k = 4$. $s = 4rt$

b. Write an equation for the relationship where m varies jointly with n and the square root of p and $k = \frac{1}{3}$. $m = \frac{1}{3} n \sqrt{p}$

The value of y varies jointly with w and x and inversely with z. If $w = 12$, $x = 9$, and $z = 15$, then $y = 36$.

c. Write an equation for the given relationship. $y = \frac{kwx}{z}$

d. Find the constant of variation. $k = 5$

e. What is the value of y, when $w = 16$, $x = 8$, and $z = 20$? $y = 32$

The ideal gas law is $PV = 0.08206nT$.

f. How many moles of gas are in a 30 liter scuba canister if the temperature in the canister is 300 K and the pressure is 200 atmospheres? Round the answer to the nearest tenth.   243.7 moles

g. Solve the ideal gas law for V. What type of variation exists between V and P? between V and n? $V = \frac{0.08206nT}{P}$; inverse; joint

The volume V of a right circular cone varies jointly with the square of the radius of the base r and the height of the cone h.

h. Write an equation relating the radius, height, and volume of a right circular cone. $V = kr^2h$

i. The volume of a right circular cone with a radius of 2 centimeters and a height of 4 centimeters is 16.76 cubic centimeters. Find the constant of variation to the nearest hundredth. $k = 1.05$

j. What is the volume of the cone pictured below?   66.15 cubic units

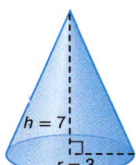

Investigation Practice

Math Conversations
Discussion to strengthen understanding

Problem b
Error Alert Make sure students understand that the fraction $\frac{1}{3}$ is a constant. Inverse and direct variations can be expressed with a variable in the denominator.

Problem c
Error Alert Check that students can translate the first sentence into the variation equation $y = \frac{kwx}{z}$.

Problem h
Some students may know the volume formula for a cone as $V = \frac{1}{3}\pi r^2 h$. Point out that in this problem, the constant of variation k is an approximation of $\frac{\pi}{3}$.

Investigation 8   531

LOOKING FORWARD

Identifying and writing joint variation prepares students for

- **Investigation 9** Choosing a Factoring Method
- **Investigation 10** Transforming Quadratic Functions
- **Investigation 11** Investigating Exponential Growth and Decay
- **Investigation 12** Investigating Matrices

SECTION OVERVIEW

9

Lesson Planner

Lesson	New Concepts
81	Solving Inequalities with Variables on Both Sides
82	Solving Multi-Step Compound Inequalities
83	Factoring Special Products
84	Identifying Quadratic Functions
85	Solving Problems Using the Pythagorean Theorem
	Cumulative Test 16, Performance Task 16
86	Calculating the Midpoint and Length of a Segment
87	Factoring Polynomials by Grouping
88	Multiplying and Dividing Rational Expressions
LAB 8	Graphing Calculator: Characteristics of Parabolas
89	Identifying Characteristics of Quadratic Functions
90	Adding and Subtracting Rational Expressions
	Cumulative Test 17, Performance Task 17
INV 9	Investigation: Choosing a Factoring Method

Resources for Teaching
- Student Edition
- Teacher's Edition
- Student Edition eBook
- Teacher's Edition eBook
- Resources and Planner CD
- Solutions Manual
- Instructional Masters
- Technology Lab Masters
- Warm Up and Teaching Transparencies
- Instructional Presentations CD
- Online activities, tools and homework help www.SaxonMathResources.com

Resources for Practice and Assessment
- Student Edition Practice Workbook
- Course Assessments
- Standardized Test Practice
- College Entrance Exam Practice
- Test and Practice Generator CD using ExamView™

Resources for Differentiated Instruction
- Reteaching Masters
- Challenge and Enrichment Masters
- Prerequisite Skills Intervention
- Adaptations for Saxon Algebra 1
- Multilingual Glossary
- English Learners Handbook
- TI Resources

Pacing Guide

 Resources and Planner CD for lesson planning support

45-Minute Class

Day 1	Day 2	Day 3	Day 4	Day 5	Day 6
Lesson 81	Lesson 82	Lesson 83	Lesson 84	Lesson 85	Cumulative Test 16
Day 7	**Day 8**	**Day 9**	**Day 10**	**Day 11**	**Day 12**
Lesson 86	Lesson 87	Lesson 88	Lab 8 Lesson 89	Lesson 90	Cumulative Test 17
Day 13					
Investigation 9					

Block: 90-Minute Class

Day 1	Day 2	Day 3	Day 4	Day 5	Day 6
Investigation 8 Lesson 81	Lesson 82 Lesson 83	Lesson 84 Lesson 85	Cumulative Test 16 Lesson 86	Lesson 87 Lesson 88	Lab 8 Lesson 89 Lesson 90
Day 7					
Cumulative Test 17 Investigation 9					

* For suggestions on how to implement Saxon Math in a block schedule, see the Pacing section at the beginning of the Teacher's Edition.

Lessons 81–90, Investigation 9

Differentiated Instruction

Below Level	
Warm Up	SE pp. 532, 538, 543, 550, 556, 563, 570, 576, 585, 592
Skills Bank	SE pp. 846–883
Reteaching Masters	Lessons 81–90, Investigation 9
Warm Up Transparencies	Lessons 81–90
Prerequisite Skills Intervention	Skills 32, 67, 73

Advanced Learners	
Challenge	TE pp. 536, 541, 548, 554, 562, 568, 575, 582, 591, 596, 599
Extend the Example	TE pp. 534, 539, 544, 552, 558, 565, 572, 578, 588, 594
Extend the Problem	TE pp. 536, 542, 549, 554, 562, 568, 574, 581, 582, 590, 596, 597, 598
Challenge and Enrichment Masters	Challenge: 81–90; Enrichment: 82, 83, 85

English Learners	
EL Tips	TE pp. 534, 540, 546, 551, 559, 565, 573, 581, 586, 593, 600
Multilingual Glossary	Booklet and Online English Learners Handbook

Special Needs	
Inclusion Tips	TE pp. 535, 539, 545, 553, 558, 564, 572, 577, 587, 594
Adaptations for Saxon Algebra 1	Lessons 81–90, Cumulative Tests 16, 17

For All Learners	
Exploration	SE pp. 556, 600
Caution	SE pp. 533, 538, 564, 572, 592
Hints	SE pp. 532, 538, 539, 544, 545, 557, 558, 564, 570, 576, 593, 594
Error Alert	TE pp. 533, 534, 537, 538, 540, 542, 545, 546, 547, 552, 553, 555, 557, 558, 559, 561, 564, 566, 567, 569, 571, 573, 574, 578, 579, 580, 586, 589, 590, 593, 595, 596, 597, 601
Alternate Method	TE pp. 533, 544, 552, 571, 593
Manipulative Use	TE pp. 574
Online Tools	

SE = Student Edition; TE = Teacher's Edition

Math Vocabulary

Lesson	New Vocabulary	Maintained	EL Tip in TE
81	contradiction	inequality solution set	registration
82		compound inequality	consistent inconsistent
83		binomial perfect-square trinomial	border
84	parabola quadratic function standard form of a quadratic function	domain range function	function
85	Pythagorean triple Converse of the Pythagorean Theorem	hypotenuse perfect square radical expression	positioned
86	midpoint	quadrilateral x-coordinate radical y-coordinate rhombus	midpoint
87		binomial GCF polynomial	score
88		rational expression	corner
89	axis of symmetry maximum of a function minimum of a function vertex of a parabola zero of a function	domain intercept parabola range real numbers	axis
90		factor LCM	common denominator
INV 9		perfect-square trinomial prime factorization prime number	monomial

Section Overview 9   532B

SECTION OVERVIEW 9

Math Highlights

Enduring Understandings – The "Big Picture"

After completing Section 9, students will understand:

- How to solve compound inequalities.
- How to factor trinomials.
- How to identify a quadratic function.
- How to use the Pythagorean theorem to find missing side lengths.
- How to use the midpoint and distance formulas.
- How to add, subtract, multiply, and divide rational expressions.

Essential Questions

- What are the solution sets of compound inequalities?
- When is a trinomial a perfect-square trinomial and how can it be factored?
- What are the characteristics of a quadratic function?
- How can Pythagorean triples be used to determine a right triangle?
- How can the Pythagorean theorem be used to find the distance between two points?
- How can rational expressions be simplified by factoring?

Math Content Strands

Inequalities
- Lesson 81 — Solving Inequalities with Variables on Both Sides
- Lesson 82 — Solving Multi-Step Compound Inequalities

Polynomials
- Lesson 83 — Factoring Special Products
- Lesson 87 — Factoring Polynomials by Grouping
- Investigation 9 — Choosing a Factoring Method

Quadratic Equations and Functions
- Lesson 84 — Identifying Quadratic Functions
- Lesson 85 — Solving Problems Using the Pythagorean Theorem
- Lesson 86 — Calculating the Midpoint and Length of a Segment
- Lesson 89 — Identifying Characteristics of Quadratic Functions
- Lab 8 — Graphing Calculator: Characteristics of Parabolas

Rational Expressions and Functions
- Lesson 88 — Multiplying and Dividing Rational Expressions
- Lesson 90 — Adding and Subtracting Rational Expressions

Connections in Practice Problems

	Lessons
Coordinate Geometry	90
Data Analysis	84
Geometry	81, 82, 83, 84, 85, 86, 87, 88, 89, 90
Measurement	81, 83, 86, 87, 88
Probability	82
Statistics	85

Math Processes

Reasoning and Communication

	Lessons
Analyze	81, 83, 84, 85, 86, 88, 89
Connect	86
Error analysis	81, 82, 83, 84, 85, 86, 87, 88, 89, 90
Estimate	81, 82, 90
Formulate	82, 84, 85, 86, 87
Generalize	83, 84, 86, 87, 88
Justify	83, 86, 88, 89, 90
Math Reasoning	81, 83, 84, 85, 86, 87, 88, 89, 90
Model	84, Inv. 9
Multiple choice	81, 82, 83, 84, 85, 86, 87, 88, 89, 90
Multi-step	81, 82, 83, 84, 85, 86, 87, 88, 89, 90
Predict	88, 90
Verify	81, 82, 83, 84, 85, 86, 87, 88, 89
Write	81, 83, 84, 85, 86, 87, 88, 90
Graphing Calculator	86

Connections

In Examples: Cell phone towers, Dog breeds, Football, Free fall, Garden planning, Height of a golf ball, Length of a ladder, Profit, Transportation, Zoology

In Practice problems: Art, Astronomy, Athletic directing, Baseball, Biology, Bridges, Business, Carpentry, Cell phones, Chess, Cholesterol levels, Communication, Computer electronics, Consumerism, Cost, Economics, Employment, Entertainment, Finances, Food packaging, Football, Games, Gardening, Grades, Health checks, Hiking, Hobbies, Home improvement, Length of a ladder, Marine biology, Murals, Music, Painting job, Paving, Personal finances, Profits, Quilting, Sail dimensions, Software, Space, Tennis, Tires, Traffic, Travel, Travel times, Water fountains, Woodworking

532C Saxon *Algebra 1*

Content Trace

Lesson	Warm Up: Prerequisite Skills	New Concepts	Where Practiced	Where Assessed	Looking Forward
81	Lessons 28, 70, 77	Solving Inequalities with Variables on Both Sides	Lessons 82, 83, 84, 85, 86, 87, 88, 89, 90, 94, 96, 97	Cumulative Tests 17, 18, 19, 20	Lessons 82, 91, 101
82	Lessons 73, 77, 81	Solving Multi-Step Compound Inequalities	Lessons 83, 84, 85, 86, 87, 88, 89, 90, 91, 92, 95, 97, 98	Cumulative Tests 17, 18, 20	Lessons 91, 97, 101, 109
83	Lessons 38, 60	Factoring Special Products	Lessons 84, 85, 86, 87, 88, 89, 90, 91, 92, 93, 96, 98, 99	Cumulative Tests 17, 18, 19	Lessons 87, 93, 98, Investigation 9
84	Lessons 9, 25, 29	Identifying Quadratic Functions	Lessons 85, 86, 87, 88, 89, 90, 91, 92, 93, 94, 97, 99, 100, 101	Cumulative Tests 17, 18, 19, 20	Lessons 89, 96, 98, 100
85	Lessons 13, 61	Solving Problems Using the Pythagorean Theorem	Lessons 86, 87, 88, 89, 90, 91, 92, 93, 94, 95, 98, 100, 101, 102, 103	Cumulative Tests 17, 18, 19, 20, 23	Lessons 86, 89, 96, 98
86	Lessons 4, 6, 20, 85	Calculating the Midpoint and Length of a Segment	Lessons 87, 88, 89, 90, 91, 92, 93, 94, 95, 96, 99, 101, 102, 104, 105	Cumulative Tests 18, 19, 20, 21	Lessons 89, 96, 98, 100
87	Lessons 38, 72, 75, 83	Factoring Polynomials by Grouping	Lessons 88, 89, 90, 91, 92, 93, 94, 95, 96, 100, 102, 103	Cumulative Tests 18, 19, 20	Lessons 93, 95, 98
88	Lessons 3, 32, 39, 43, 72	Multiplying and Dividing Rational Expressions	Lessons 89, 90, 91, 92, 93, 94, 95, 96, 97, 98, 101, 103, 104	Cumulative Tests 18, 19, 20	Lessons 90, 92, 95, 99
89	Lessons 9, 84	Identifying Characteristics of Quadratic Functions	Lessons 90, 91, 92, 93, 94, 95, 96, 97, 98, 99, 102, 104, 105	Cumulative Tests 18, 19, 20, 21	Lessons 96, 98, 100, 104
90	Lessons 2, 10, 18, 58	Adding and Subtracting Rational Expressions	Lessons 91, 92, 93, 94, 95, 96, 97, 98, 99, 100, 103, 105, 106	Cumulative Tests 18, 19, 22	Lessons 92, 95, 99
INV 9	N/A	Investigation: Choosing a Factoring Method	Lessons 91, 95, 96, 98, 102, 103, 104, 106, 109	Cumulative Test 18	Lessons 93, 95

SECTION OVERVIEW 9

Ongoing Assessment

	Type	Feature	Intervention *
BEFORE instruction	Assess Prior Knowledge	• Diagnostic Test	• Prerequisite Skills Intervention
BEFORE the lesson	Formative	• Warm Up	• Skills Bank • Reteaching Masters
DURING the lesson	Formative	• Lesson Practice • Math Conversations with the Practice problems	• Additional Examples in TE • Test and Practice Generator (for additional practice sheets)
AFTER the lesson	Formative	• Check for Understanding (closure)	• Scaffolding Questions in TE
AFTER 5 lessons	Summative	After Lesson 85 • Cumulative Test 16 • Performance Task 16 After Lesson 90 • Cumulative Test 17 • Performance Task 17	• Reteaching Masters • Test and Practice Generator (for additional tests and practice)
AFTER 20 lessons	Summative	• Benchmark Tests	• Reteaching Masters • Test and Practice Generator (for additional tests and practice)

* for students not showing progress during the formative stages or scoring below 80% on the summative assessments

Evidence of Learning – What Students Should Know

Because the Saxon philosophy is to provide students with sufficient time to learn and practice each concept, a lesson's topic will not be tested until at least five lessons after the topic is introduced.

On the Cumulative Tests that are given during this section of ten lessons, students should be able to demonstrate the following competencies:
- Factor trinomials and write a polynomial in standard form.
- Solve systems of equations, and two-step and multi-step inequalities.
- Write a compound inequality from a graph.
- Simplify radical expressions.
- Identify Pythagorean triples.
- Determine if lines are parallel or perpendicular.
- Graph rational functions and determine asymptotes.
- Calculate frequency distributions.

Test and Practice Generator CD using ExamView™

The Test and Practice Generator is an easy-to-use benchmark and assessment tool that creates unlimited practice and tests in multiple formats and allows you to customize questions or create new ones. A variety of reports are available to track student progress toward mastery of the standards throughout the year.

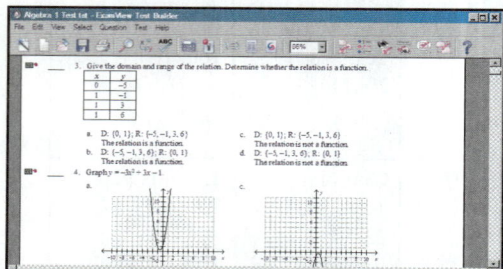
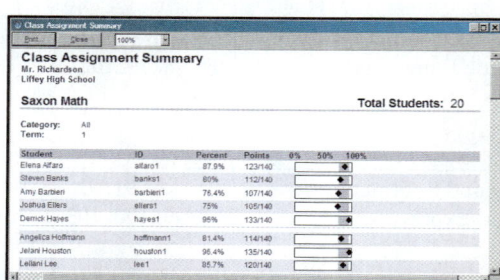

Lessons 81–90, Investigation 9

Assessment Resources

Resources for Diagnosing and Assessing

- **Student Edition**
  - Warm Up
  - Lesson Practice

- **Teacher's Edition**
  - Math Conversations with the Practice problems
  - Check for Understanding (closure)

- **Course Assessments**
  - Diagnostic Test
  - Cumulative Tests
  - Performance Tasks
  - Benchmark Tests

Resources for Test Prep

- **Student Edition Practice**
  - Multiple-choice problems
  - Multiple-step and writing problems
  - Daily cumulative practice

- **Standardized Test Practice**

- **College Entrance Exam Practice**

- **Test and Practice Generator CD using ExamView™**

Resources for Intervention

- **Student Edition**
  - Skills Bank

- **Teacher's Edition**
  - Additional Examples
  - Scaffolding questions

- **Prerequisite Skills Intervention**
  - Worksheets

- **Reteaching Masters**
  - Lesson instruction and practice sheets

- **Test and Practice Generator CD using ExamView™**
  - Lesson practice problems
  - Additional tests

Cumulative Tests

The assessments in Saxon Math are frequent and consistently placed after every five lessons to offer a regular method of ongoing testing. These cumulative assessments check mastery of concepts from previous lessons.

Performance Tasks

The Performance Tasks can be used in conjunction with the Cumulative Tests and are scored using a rubric.

After Lesson 85

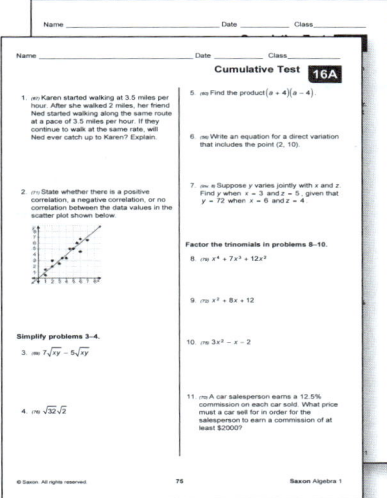

After Lesson 90

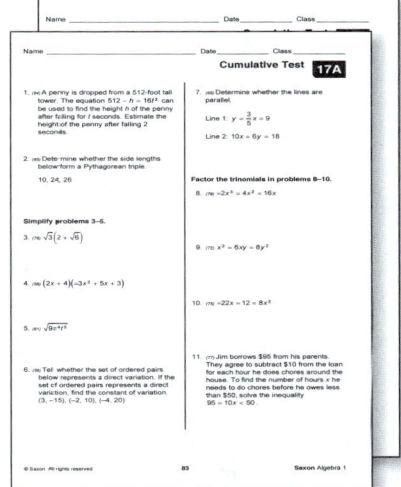

For use with Performance Tasks

Section Overview 9 532F

LESSON 81

1 Warm Up

Problem 3
Remind students that when $b \neq 0$, $\frac{ax}{b} = \frac{a}{b} \cdot x$, and when $a \neq 0$ and $b \neq 0$, $\frac{a}{b} \cdot \frac{b}{a} = 1$.

2 New Concepts

In this lesson, students learn to solve inequalities with variables on both sides of the inequality symbol.

Example 1

Have students solve the inequality using the same procedure they would use to solve an equation.

Additional Example 1
Solve and graph.

a. $4x + 1 < -x + 11$ $x < 2$;

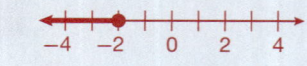

b. $\frac{4x}{9} + \frac{3}{18} \leq \frac{2x}{9} - \frac{5}{18}$ $x \leq -2$;

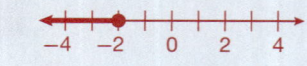

LESSON RESOURCES

Student Edition Practice Workbook 81
Reteaching Master 81
Adaptations Master 81
Challenge and Enrichment Master C81
Technology Lab Master 81

LESSON 81

Solving Inequalities with Variables on Both Sides

Warm Up

1. **Vocabulary** An equation or inequality that is always true is called a(n) _____ (identity, solution).   identity

Solve each inequality.

2. $6x \leq 42$ $x \leq 7$
3. $-\frac{3k}{4} > \frac{5}{8}$ $k < -\frac{5}{6}$
4. $2p + 3 < -25$ $p < -14$
5. $5x - 3 - 7x \leq -9$ $x \geq 3$

New Concepts

Sometimes an inequality will have a variable on both sides of the inequality sign. A solution to such an inequality is found by transforming the inequality so that the variable is isolated on one side of the inequality.

Example 1 Solving Inequalities with Variables on Both Sides

Solve and graph each inequality.

a. $2x + 7 > -5x + 21$

SOLUTION

$2x + 7 > -5x + 21$
$7x + 7 > 21$ Add $5x$ to both sides.
$7x > 14$ Subtract 7 from both sides.
$x > 2$ Divide both sides by 7.

Graph the inequality on a number line.

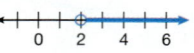

b. $-\frac{5b}{8} + \frac{5}{16} \geq \frac{b}{8} - \frac{9}{16}$

SOLUTION

$-\frac{5b}{8} + \frac{5}{16} \geq \frac{b}{8} - \frac{9}{16}$

$-\frac{6b}{8} + \frac{5}{16} \geq -\frac{9}{16}$ Subtract $\frac{b}{8}$ from both sides.

$-\frac{6b}{8} \geq -\frac{14}{16}$ Subtract $\frac{5}{16}$ from both sides.

$b \leq \frac{7}{6}$ Multiply both sides by $\frac{-8}{6}$.

Graph the inequality on a number line.

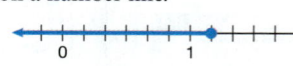

Hint
The order of the inequality is reversed when the inequality is multiplied or divided by a negative number.

Online Connection
www.SaxonMathResources.com

MATH BACKGROUND

For equations in the form $ax + b = cx + d$, when $a = c$, there is no value for x that makes the equation true when $b \neq d$. Inequalities, however, can be true for any value of x even when $a = c$ and $b \neq d$. For example, $4x - 10 < 4x + 2$ is true for all values of x. Inequalities can also be false for any value of x when $a = c$ and $b \neq d$. For example, $4x + 10 < 4x + 2$ is false for all values of x.

Example 2 Simplifying Each Side Before Solving

Solve and graph the inequality.

$2(x - 8) - 3x > 6 - 3(2x + 4)$

SOLUTION

$2(x - 8) - 3x > 6 - 3(2x + 4)$	
$2x - 16 - 3x > 6 - 6x - 12$	Distributive Property
$-x - 16 > -6x - 6$	Combine like terms.
$5x - 16 > -6$	Add $6x$ to both sides.
$5x > 10$	Add 16 to both sides.
$x > 2$	Divide both sides by 5.

Graph the inequality on a number line.

(number line showing open circle at 2, shaded to the right; marks at 0, 2, 4, 6)

Inequalities can be sometimes true, always true, or never true (false).

An inequality or equation that is always true is called an **identity**.

A **contradiction** is an inequality or an equation that is never true (false).

Example 3 Solving Special Cases

Determine whether each inequality is sometimes true, always true, or never true (false). If it is sometimes true, identify the solution set.

a. $3x + 4 - x > 2x + 7$

SOLUTION

$3x + 4 - x > 2x + 7$	
$2x + 4 > 2x + 7$	Combine like terms.
$\underline{-2x \quad\quad -2x}$	Subtraction Property of Inequality
$4 > 7$ ✗	

The inequality is never true (false), so it is a contradiction.

b. $3(2y - 6) \leq 6y + 4$

SOLUTION

$3(2y - 6) \leq 6y + 4$	
$6y - 18 \leq 6y + 4$	Distributive Property
$\underline{-6y \quad\quad -6y}$	Subtraction Property of Inequality
$-18 \leq 4$ ✓	

The inequality is always true, so it is an identity.

Caution

If the operation symbol in front of the term being distributed is subtraction, multiply all the terms inside the parentheses by the opposite of the term.

Math Language

The **solution set** is the set of values that makes an inequality true. If the inequality is a contradiction, then the solution set is empty, represented by ∅.

Example 2

Suggest to students that combining like terms on each side of the inequality will help them keep track of each term.

Additional Example 2

Solve and graph.

a. $4z + 1 - 8z > 3 - 2z + 4$
$z < -3$;

(number line showing open circle at -3, shaded to the left; marks at $-6, -4, -2, 0, 2$)

b. $3(5k - 4) \leq 30k + 3$ $-1 \leq k$;

(number line showing closed circle at -1, shaded to the right; marks at $-4, -2, 0, 2, 4$)

TEACHER TIP

Encourage students to check their solutions with the original inequality.

Example 3

Error Alert Students might not fully combine like terms when doing so removes the variable from the inequality. Remind them that when they remove the variable from the inequality, they are left with an inequality that is either always true or never true.

Additional Example 3

Determine whether each inequality is sometimes true, always true, or never true (false). If it is sometimes true, identify the solution set.

a. $2x + 1 + 2x > 4x + 10$
The inequality is never true (false), so it is a contradiction.

b. $2y + 3 - 2y < -7y + 9 + 7y$
The inequality is always true, so it is an identity.

 ALTERNATE METHOD FOR EXAMPLE 3

Write the inequality in the form $ax + b \bigcirc cx + d$. Determine if and when $a = c$ and $b \bigcirc d$ forms a true statement. If it does, the inequality is always true. If it does not, the inequality is never true.

$3x + 4 - x > 2x + 7$
$2x + 4 > 2x + 7$
never true

$3(2y - 6) \leq 6y + 4$
$6y - 18 \leq 6y + 4$
always true

Lesson 81

Example 4
Extend the Example
"If the trend continues, which year will be the last year rottweilers are at the show?" 2013

Additional Example 4
If the number of registered Rottweilers had decreased by 1100 fewer dogs, in what year would the number of registered Bernese mountain dogs have equaled or exceeded the number of registered rottweilers? 2016

Lesson Practice
Problem c
Scaffolding Suggest that students simplify each side of the inequality before doing any transformations. Then have them decide on which side of the inequality to isolate the variable. Remind students to check their answers by testing solutions in the original inequality.

Problem e
Error Alert Students may add x to both sides instead of adding $-x$ to both sides. Remind them that they must use inverse operations to isolate variables.

Check for Understanding
The questions below help assess the concepts taught in this lesson.

"In the process of solving an inequality, when is the solution set determined?" Sample: when the variable is isolated

"When is an inequality sometimes true?" Sample: when there is an isolated variable on one side of the inequality

---

Example 4 Application: Dog Breeds
The table shows the average number of American Kennel Club registrations (rounded to the nearest 100) for Bernese mountain dogs and rottweilers.

American Kennel Club Registrations, 2002–2006

Breed	2006 Registrations	Average Yearly Change
Bernese Mountain Dogs	3700	300
Rottweilers	14,700	−1900

If the trend continues, in which year will the number of registered Bernese mountain dogs be equal to or exceed the number of registered rottweilers?

SOLUTION

Write an expression for the number of registered dogs for y years after 2006.

Bernese mountain dogs: $3700 + 300y$

rottweilers: $14{,}700 - 1900y$

$3700 + 300y \geq 14{,}700 - 1900y$	Write an inequality.
$3700 + 2200y \geq 14{,}700$	Add $1900y$ to both sides.
$2200y \geq 11{,}000$	Subtract 3700 from both sides.
$y \geq 5$	Divide both sides by 2200.

The solution $y \geq 5$ does not answer the question. The variable y represents the years after 2006.

$2006 + 5 = 2011$

If the trend continues, the number of Bernese mountain dogs registered will be equal to or exceed the number of rottweilers registered in 2011.

Math Reasoning

Analyze In the year 2011, how does the number of rottweilers compare to the number of Bernese mountain dogs? Explain.

The number of both types of dogs will be the same. There will be 5200 of each type.

Lesson Practice
Solve and graph each inequality.

a. $4x - 8 > -2x + 4$ $x > 2$ (Ex 1)

b. $-\dfrac{3a}{5} + \dfrac{7}{10} \geq \dfrac{2a}{5} - \dfrac{9}{10}$ $a \leq 1\dfrac{3}{5}$ (Ex 1)

c. $4(x - 1) - 2x \leq 6 - 5(x + 2)$ $x \leq 0$; (Ex 2)

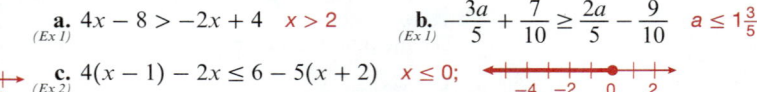

Determine whether each inequality is always true, sometimes true, or never true. If it is sometimes true, identify the solution set. (Ex 3)

d. $x + 5 + 3x > 4x + 19$ never true   e. $x + 5 > x - 3$ always true

f. The table shows the average number of cell phone minutes used by Ara and Lexi. (Ex 4)

User	January Average	Average Change, January–May
Ara	4000	500
Lexi	12,000	−500

If the trend continues, in which month will Ara's average minutes be equal to or greater than Lexi's? September

---

ENGLISH LEARNERS

For Example 4, explain the meaning of the word **registration**. Say:

"Registration is the process of putting items or persons on a list to show that they qualify for an activity or event. For example, the registration of a dog for a kennel club shows that the dog qualifies for a club event."

Discuss events for which students may have registered. Sample: a driver's license, summer camp, band camp

Practice Distributed and Integrated

Factor completely.

1. (72) $w^2 - 13w + 36$ $(w-4)(w-9)$
2. (79) $-q^2 + q + 42$ $-1(q-7)(q+6)$
3. (75) $30x^2 - 7xy - 2y^2$ $(5x-2y)(6x+y)$
4. (72) $x^2 - 11 + 6x - 44$ $(x-5)(x+11)$

Solve.

5. (74) $|x - 3| = 14$ $\{17, -11\}$
6. (74) $|x + 4| = 7.5$ $\{3.5, -11.5\}$
7. (77) $-5 - \frac{n}{8} \geq -6$ $n \leq 8$
8. (77) $12 - 3d \leq -3$ $d \geq 5$

Solve and graph. Then check the solution.

*9. (81) $6v + 5 > -2v - 3$ $v > -1$;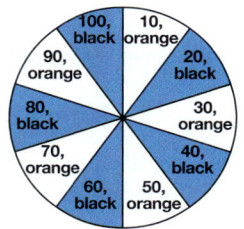
10. (66) $y + 4.5 < 10$ $y < 5.5$;

Write an equation for each of the lines described.

11. (65) a line that passes through $(1, -2)$ and is perpendicular to $y = 2x + 6$ Sample: $y = -\frac{1}{2}x - 1\frac{1}{2}$
12. (65) a line that passes through $(6, 5)$ and is parallel to $y = -x + 4$ $y = -x + 11$

13. (68) **Multi-Step** To win a game, Alvaro needs to spin a black section or the number 10.

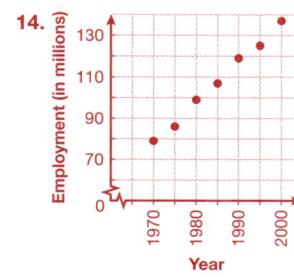

a. What is the probability of spinning a black section? $\frac{1}{2}$
b. What is the probability of spinning a 10? $\frac{1}{10}$
c. Are the events inclusive or mutually exclusive? mutually exclusive
d. What is the probability of Alvaro hitting a black section or the number 10? $\frac{3}{5}$

14. (71) (**Employment**) The table below shows the number of people employed in the United States. Make a scatter plot of the data.

U.S. Employment (in millions)

Year	1970	1975	1980	1985	1990	1995	2000
Employment (in millions)	79	86	99	107	119	125	137

15. (73) **Verify** Show that 2 is a solution of the compound inequality $x < 3$ OR $x > 6$.

16. (76) (**Gardening**) Debra is planting a square garden. The side length is $8 + \sqrt{8}$ inches. Write an expression to find the area of the garden, and then find the area.
$(8 + \sqrt{8})^2$; $72 + 32\sqrt{2}$ square inches

15. Since $2 < 3$, 2 is a solution of the compound inequality because the inequality uses OR and the solution needs to be true only for one inequality.

Lesson 81   535

3 Practice

Math Conversations
Discussion to strengthen understanding

Problems 11 and 12
Guide the students by asking them the following questions.

"If two lines are perpendicular what do you know about their slopes?" Sample: The slopes are negative reciprocals of each other. Their product is 1.

Problem 15
Remind students that the solutions for a compound inequality using OR includes all of the solutions to both inequalities while the solutions for a compound inequality using AND includes only those solutions that are common to both inequalities.

INCLUSION

Help students organize their work with the suggestions below.

- Using an index card to cover one side of the inequality, completely simplify the other side. Repeat the process for the un-simplified side.

- Once both sides of the inequality are simplified, determine on which side of the inequality to isolate the variable. Often it is easier to transform the inequality so that the isolated variable has a positive coefficient.

- To check for errors that may occur while solving, have students choose a value from their solution set to substitute back into the original inequality.

Lesson 81   535

Problem 17
Extend the Problem
"The area of the triangle is found with the formula $A = xh$, where A is the area of the triangle and h is the height of the triangle. What is the height of the triangle when the perimeter is 81 units and the area is more than 28 units squared?"
$2 < h$

Problem 18
Extend the Problem
Have students find the excluded values. b is an excluded value.

Problem 21
Remind students that to factor completely, the GCF must be factored out. While this can be done after the trinomial is factored into two binomials, the trinomial is easier to factor if the GCF is removed first.

Problem 23
Students may find it helpful to make a chart of all of the possible outcomes for the event of rolling two number cubes.

---

17. Measurement To find the values of x for which the triangle would have a perimeter of more than 81 units, solve the inequality $x + (x + 13) + (2x + 12) > 81$. $x > 14$

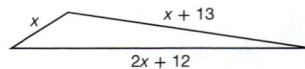

*18. **Write** How do changes to the value of b affect the graph of $y = \dfrac{a}{x-b} + c$?

*19. Two number cubes are rolled and their values are added. One number cube is labeled 1–6. The other has two of each of the numbers 1, 2, and 3. The possible outcomes are displayed in the table.

What is the theoretical probability of each possible sum?

18. Sample: The vertical asymptote of the graph will be moved horizontally to a value of b on the x-axis.

Cube 1

		1	2	3	4	5	6
Cube 2	1	2	3	4	5	6	7
	2	3	4	5	6	7	8
	3	4	5	6	7	8	9
	1	2	3	4	5	6	7
	2	3	4	5	6	7	8
	3	4	5	6	7	8	9

$P(2) = \frac{2}{36} = \frac{1}{18}, P(3) = \frac{4}{36} = \frac{1}{9},$
$P(4) = \frac{6}{36} = \frac{1}{6}, P(5) = \frac{6}{36} = \frac{1}{6},$
$P(6) = \frac{6}{36} = \frac{1}{6}, P(7) = \frac{6}{36} = \frac{1}{6},$
$P(8) = \frac{4}{36} = \frac{1}{9}, P(9) = \frac{2}{36} = \frac{1}{18}$

20. Multiple Choice What is the horizontal asymptote for the rational expression $y = \dfrac{7}{x-2} + 4$? **B**

A $y = -2$ **B** $y = 4$ **C** $y = -4$ **D** $y = 7$

21. (Football) A football is kicked into the air. In the expression $-5t^2 + 25t - 30$, t represents the time when the ball is 30 feet in the air. Factor the expression completely. $-5(t-2)(t-3)$

22. Error Analysis Two students factor $9m^2x^3 + 81mx^3 + 126x^3$. Which student is correct? Explain the error.   Student A; Sample: Student B did not include the GCF in the final factoring.

Student A	Student B
$9m^2x^3 + 81mx^3 + 126x^3$ $= 9x^3(m^2 + 9m + 14)$ $= 9x^3(m + 2)(m + 7)$	$9m^2x^3 + 81mx^3 + 126x^3$ The GCF is $9x^3$. Factor out $9x^3$. $m^2 + 9m + 14$ $= (m + 2)(m + 7)$

*23. (Games) Two number cubes are rolled and their values are added. Find the probability that the sum is less than or equal to 7. $\frac{7}{12}$

536 Saxon Algebra 1

CHALLENGE

Have students determine if an ordered pair is a solution to a system of inequalities.

For $x > 0$ and $y \leq 0$, is $(4, 0)$ a solution? Yes

For $x + 2 > 3$ and $3y < 9$, is $(1, 1)$ a solution? No

For $5x \leq 24 - x$ and $3y < 8 + y$, is $(-10, 4)$ a solution? No

*24. Geometry Students made five tetrahedrons, a three-dimensional figure with four triangular faces, and labeled the faces 1–4. Use an equation to find the probability that all five tetrahedrons land on 3. $P(\text{five 3s}) = \left(\frac{1}{4}\right)^5 = \frac{1}{1024}$

*25. Error Analysis Two students find the probability of rolling two number cubes and getting a sum less than 6. Which student is correct? Explain the error.

Student A; Sample: Student B included the sum of 6 but the question asked for less than 6.

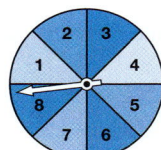
Student A
$\frac{10}{36} = \frac{5}{18}$

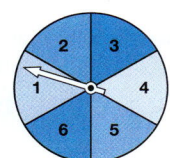
Student B
$\frac{15}{36} = \frac{5}{12}$

26. Multi-Step A game has two spinners. After spinning both spinners, the sum of the spins is found.

a. Make a table of all possible outcomes. See Additional Answers.

b. What is the probability that the sum is greater than 8? $\frac{7}{16}$

*27. Multiple Choice What is the first step in solving the inequality $2(x + 5) > x + 12$? **C**

A Combine the variables.

B Use the Addition Property of Inequality.

C Apply the Distributive Property.

D Use the Multiplication Property of Inequality.

*28. Travel A car rental company charges $40 a day with no additional mileage fees. Another company charges $24 each day plus $0.16 per mile. How many miles would have to be driven in one day for the first company to offer the better deal?
over 100 miles per day

*29. Write Explain how to solve the inequality $2x + 5 > -3(x - 15)$. Identify the solution.

29. Sample: Distribute −3 through the parentheses on the right side. Then add 3x to both sides. Then subtract 5 from both sides. Finally, divide both sides by 5. The solution is $x > 8$.

*30. Estimate During their freshman year, Malcolm averaged 17.3 points per game and Frederico averaged 15.2 points per game. In their sophomore year, Malcolm averaged 19.1 points per game and Frederico averaged 18.4 points per game. If the trend continues, in which years will Frederico have a better average than Malcolm? junior and senior years

---

Problem 26
Error Alert
Students might find the probability of the sum being greater than or equal to 8, instead of greater than 8. Encourage students to read the problem carefully.

Problem 30
Guide students by asking the following questions.

"How many more points did Malcolm score sophomore year than he did freshman year?" 1.8

"How many more points did Frederico score sophomore year than he did freshman year?" 3.2

Lesson 81   537

LOOKING FORWARD

Solving inequalities with variables on both sides prepares students for

- **Lesson 82** Solving Multi-Step Compound Inequalities

- **Lesson 91** Solving Absolute-Value Inequalities

- **Lesson 101** Solving Multi-Step Absolute-Value Inequalities

LESSON 82

1 Warm Up

Problem 5
Remind students they need to flip the inequality signs when they divide both sides by −2.

2 New Concepts

In this lesson, students learn to solve multi-step compound inequalities. Remind students that they learned how to solve compound inequalities in Lesson 73.

Example 1

Error Alert Students may have difficulty with problem **b** if they do not combine like terms first before isolating the variable.

Additional Example 1
Solve and graph each inequality.

a. $5x - 6 < 4$ OR $3x + 9 > 18$
$x < 2$ OR $x > 3$;

b. $-9 \leq 3x - 6 + 4x \leq 8$
$-\frac{3}{7} \leq x \leq 2$;

LESSON RESOURCES

Student Edition Practice
  Workbook 82
Reteaching Master 82
Adaptations Master 82
Challenge and Enrichment
  Master C82, E82

LESSON 82

Solving Multi-Step Compound Inequalities

Warm Up

1. **Vocabulary** A(n) _____ is made up of two inequalities combined with the word *and* or *or*. **compound inequality**

Solve each inequality.

2. $8x > 6x - 12$ $x > -6$
3. $-1 - (-7) \leq 3(y - 6)$ $y \geq 8$
4. $x - 2 < -7$ OR $2x \geq 11$ $x < -5$ OR $x \geq 5.5$
5. **Multiple Choice** Which compound inequality is equivalent to $6 \leq -2x < 22$?   **A**

   A $-11 < x \leq -3$ **B** $-11 > x \geq -3$
   C $8 \leq x < 24$ **D** $-24 < x \leq -8$

New Concepts

Inequalities can be solved in two or more steps using inverse operations. A compound inequality is made of two inequalities joined by the word AND or OR.

$$-2 < x \text{ AND } x \leq 5 \qquad x \leq -4 \text{ OR } x \geq 1$$

Hint
The term AND indicates that the solution must satisfy both inequalities. The term OR indicates that the solution must satisfy either inequality.

Example 1 Solving Multi-Step Compound Inequalities

Solve and graph each inequality.

a. $4x - 7 < 3$ OR $2x - 19 > -7$

SOLUTION Isolate the variable in both inequalities.

$4x - 7 < 3$ OR $2x - 19 > -7$

$+7 \quad +7$	$+19 \quad +19$	Addition Property of Inequality
$4x < 10$ OR $2x > 12$		Simplify.
$\frac{4x}{4} < \frac{10}{4}$ OR $\frac{2x}{2} > \frac{12}{2}$		Division Property of Inequality
$x < 2\frac{1}{2}$ OR $x > 6$		

Caution
Be sure to perform inverse operations on all three parts of the compound inequality.

b. $-9 \leq 3x - 4 + 2x \leq 11$

SOLUTION Isolate the variable between the inequality signs.

$-9 \leq 3x - 4 + 2x \leq 11$

$+4 \qquad +4 \qquad +4$	Addition Property of Inequality
$-5 \leq 3x + 2x \leq 15$	Simplify.
$\frac{-5}{5} \leq \frac{5x}{5} \leq \frac{15}{5}$	Division Property of Inequality
$-1 \leq x \leq 3$	

538 *Saxon Algebra 1*

MATH BACKGROUND

In order to understand how to solve multi-step compound inequalities, students must have a basic knowledge of inequalities and how to solve and simplify inequalities. In turn, solving multi-step compound inequalities prepares students for solving absolute-value inequalities.

There are many practical real-world applications of compound inequalities. These include finding the projected weight range for a baby when the average birth weight is known, or finding the maximum pH levels for a swimming pool.

The solutions of compound inequalities using AND can be related to the intersection of sets, where only elements common to each set are combined. The solutions of compound inequalities using OR can be related to the union of sets, where all elements of each set are combined.

Example 2 Simplifying Before Solving Inequalities

Solve the inequality. Justify each step.

a. $-15 \leq 3(2x - 1) \leq 39$

SOLUTION

$-15 \leq 3(2x - 1) \leq 39$	
$-15 \leq 6x - 3 \leq 39$	Distributive Property
$+3 \quad\quad +3 \quad +3$	Addition Property of Inequality
$-12 \leq 6x \leq 42$	Simplify.
$\frac{1}{6} \cdot -12 \leq \frac{1}{6} \cdot 6x \leq \frac{1}{6} \cdot 42$	Multiplication Property of Inequality
$-2 \leq x \leq 7$	Simplify.

b. $-12 \geq -6b - 18$ OR $-2(4 - b) \geq 10$

SOLUTION

$-12 \geq -6b - 18$ OR $-2(4 - b) \geq 10$	
$-12 \geq -6b - 18$ OR $-8 + 2b \geq 10$	Distributive Property
$+18 \quad\quad +18 \quad +8 \quad\quad +8$	Addition Property of Inequality
$6 \geq -6b$ OR $2b \geq 18$	Simplify.
$\frac{6}{-6} \leq \frac{-6b}{-6}$ OR $\frac{2b}{2} \geq \frac{18}{2}$	Division Property of Inequality
$-1 \leq b$ OR $b \geq 9$	Simplify.

Example 3 Application: Zoology

Zoologists randomly choose 5 zebras out of a herd of 20. Four zebras weigh 540 pounds, 550 pounds, 520 pounds, and 530 pounds, respectively. What could the weight of the fifth zebra be if the average weight of all 5 zebras is to be between 500 and 600 pounds?

SOLUTION Set up a compound inequality representing the situation and solve.

Minimum Weight	Mean Weight	Maximum Weight
greater than or equal to 500	$\frac{540 + 550 + 520 + 530 + x}{5}$	less than or equal to 600

$500 \leq \frac{540 + 550 + 520 + 530 + x}{5} \leq 600$

$500 \cdot 5 \leq \frac{2140 + x}{5} \cdot 5 \leq 600 \cdot 5$

$2500 \leq 2140 + x \leq 3000$

$-2140 \quad -2140 \quad\quad -2140$

$360 \leq x \leq 860$

The fifth zebra's weight could be between 360 lb and 860 lb, inclusive.

Hint

To find the mean (average) of a set of data, divide the sum of the data by the number of data in the set.

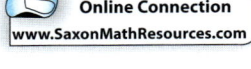

Online Connection
www.SaxonMathResources.com

Lesson 82   539

INCLUSION

Students who have trouble understanding the meaning of the word OR in solving compound inequalities may find it helpful to use a Venn diagram.

For problem b in Example 2, have students set up a Venn diagram with one oval being the values that solve the inequality $-12 \geq -6b - 18$ and the other oval being the values that solve the inequality $-2(4 - b) \geq 10$. Show them that, in this case, no values of b will solve both inequalities.

Ask:

"What can we assume about two inequalities connected with the word OR?" Sample: All values that satisfy either inequality are included in the solution set.

Example 2

Remind students how to use the Distributive Property when the terms within a set of parentheses are not like terms. Guide students to first simplify between the inequality signs before solving for the unknown variable.

TEACHER TIP

Suggest that students write any AND compound inequality as 2 separate inequalities and then that they solve each one separately.
$-4 < 2x \leq 6$
$-4 < 2x$ AND $2x \leq 6$

Additional Example 2

Solve the inequality. Justify your steps.

a. $-10 \leq 2(6x - 4) \leq 64$
$-\frac{1}{6} \leq x \leq 6$

b. $-16 \geq -8b - 32$ OR $-3(5 - b) \geq 24$
$-2 \leq b$ OR $b \geq 13$

Example 3

Extend the Example

"Suppose that one of the four zebras randomly chosen weighs 560 pounds instead of 530 pounds. What could be the possible weight of the fifth zebra?" $330 \leq x \leq 830$

Additional Example 3

Each of the 5 members of the Murillo family has a pet guinea pig. Four of the guinea pigs weigh 30, 31, 33, and 34 ounces, respectively. What could the weight of the fifth guinea pig be if the average weight of all 5 is between 30 and 35 ounces? The fifth guinea pig's weight could be between 22 and 47 ounces.

Lesson 82   539

Lesson Practice

Problem a
Error Alert Some students may always use a filled-in circle when graphing inequalities. Remind them to use an open circle to graph inequalities containing $>$ or $<$.

Problem e
Scaffolding Have students first determine the minimum and maximum weights so that they can begin to set up the compound inequality starting with the minimum weight.

Check for Understanding

The questions below help assess the concepts taught in this lesson.

"Is $-9 < x \le 6$ a compound inequality? Why or why not?" yes; Sample: The value of the variable must satisfy two inequalities at the same time.

"Explain the difference between $-13 \le x \le 8$ and $-13 \le x$ OR $x \le 8$."
Sample: The first inequality is an AND compound inequality, but the second inequality indicates that x can be either of the two solutions.

3 Practice

Math Conversations
Discussion to strengthen understanding

Problems 5 and 6
Guide students by asking them the following questions.

"What are excluded values?"
Sample: values that are not solutions for the variable

"How can you find the excluded value?" Sample: by determining the value of the variable that would result in a zero in the denominator, making the fraction undefined

---

Lesson Practice

Solve and graph each inequality.
(Ex 1)
a. $2x + 9 < 8$ OR $3x + 3 > 12$. $x < -\frac{1}{2}$ or $x > 3$;   a.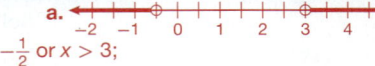
b. $24 \le 2x + 8 < 36$. $8 \le x < 14$

Solve the inequality. Justify each step.
(Ex 2)
c. $6 \le 2(x + 12) < 12$ See Additional Answers.
d. $-16 > 2(x - 2)$ OR $27 < 3(x + 2)$ See Additional Answers.

e. Of 4 babies born in a hospital in 1 night, 3 have weights of 5.2 pounds,
(Ex 3) 6.3 pounds, and 7.5 pounds, respectively. What could be the weight of the fourth baby if the average of all their weights fall within 6 and 8 pounds?
between 5 and 13 lb

Practice   Distributed and Integrated

Factor completely.
1. $2x^2 + 9xy + 7y^2$ $(x + y)(2x + 7y)$
(75)
2. $-4m^2 + 8mn + 5n^2$ $(2m + n)(-2m + 5n)$
(75)

Find the product.
3. $(\sqrt{3} - 12)^2$ $147 - 24\sqrt{3}$
(76)
4. $(2x + \sqrt{3})(2x - \sqrt{3})$ $4x^2 - 3$
(76)

Find the excluded values.
5. $\dfrac{m - 6}{2m - 10}$ $m \ne 5$
(78)
6. $\dfrac{y + 4}{-2y - 6}$ $y \ne -3$
(78)

Solve the inequality. Then graph and check the solution.
7. $2z - 6 \le z$ $z \le 6$;
(66)
8. Solve and graph $2x + 9 > -x + 18$. $x > 3$;
(81)

Determine if the following systems of equations are consistent and independent, consistent and dependent, or inconsistent.
9. $y = 10x - 2$
(67) $y = 10x + 8$ inconsistent
10. $y = 3x$
(67) $2y = 6x$ consistent and dependent

11. **Multi-Step** The perimeter of a square area rug is 48 feet. What is the length of each
(69) side? Express your answer as a radical number.   12 feet; Sample: One possible way to express the answer as a radical number is $6\sqrt{4}$.
12. (Quilting) A quilter uses a series of rectangular patterns to design quilt blocks. The
(72) area of the quilt block can be represented by the trinomial $(x^2 + 7x + 12)$ cm². If he plans a quilt block with x having a value of 20 centimeters, what is the dimension of the longer side of the block?   24 cm

13. **Multi-Step** A real number is less than 12 or is greater than 15.
(73) a. Write a compound inequality that represents the situation. $x < 12$ OR $x > 15$
b. Graph the solution.

540   Saxon Algebra 1

ENGLISH LEARNERS

Students may not understand the meanings of **consistent** and **inconsistent** in Problems 9 and 10. Say:

"Consistent means to be constant and predictable. This is in contrast to being inconsistent, which is its opposite, referring to being unpredictable and unreliable."

Give examples to further students' understanding. For example, if Matt always gets an A on his algebra quizzes, he is being consistent. If Lorinda always gets a C, she is consistent also. However, if Fiona gets an A, followed by a D, followed by a B, followed by a D, she is being inconsistent.

14. Estimate What is the lesser value of q in the solution set of $|q - 24.9| = 5.1$? 19.8

15. Cell Phones You pay $10 a month plus $0.30 per minute for your cell phone. You budget $20 each month for your bill. To find the maximum minutes you can use your phone, solve the inequality $10 + 0.3m \leq 20$. $33\frac{1}{3}$; You can talk at most 33 minutes.

16. Probability Write a rational function that expresses the following probability. Find the probability y of randomly choosing a red marble out of a bag full of x number of marbles that contains only one red marble. $y = \frac{1}{x}$

17. Verify Show that $-8u^5y + 56u^4y - 80u^3y = -8u^3y(u - 5)(u - 2)$.

17. Sample:
$-8u^5y + 56u^4y - 80u^3y$
$= -8u^3y(u^2 - 7u + 10)$
$= -8u^3y(u - 5)(u - 2)$

18. Multiple Choice Which expression is the complete factored form of $3x^6 + 6x^5 - 45x^4$?   **A**

A $3x^4(x - 3)(x + 5)$
B $x^4(3x - 9)(x + 5)$
C $x^4(x - 3)(3x - 15)$
D $(3x - 9)(x^5 + 5x^4)$

19. $P(A) = \frac{4}{28} = \frac{1}{7}$,
$P(B) = \frac{7}{28} = \frac{1}{4}$,
$P(C) = \frac{9}{28}$,
$P(D) = \frac{5}{28}$, $P(F) = \frac{3}{28}$

*19. Use the graph to find the theoretical probability of receiving each grade.

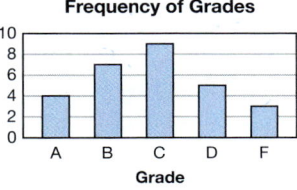

Frequency of Grades

21. Student B; Sample: Student A found the probability of rolling a 2 or 3 to be $\frac{1}{6} \cdot \frac{1}{6} = \frac{1}{36}$ when it is actually $\frac{2}{6} = \frac{1}{3}$.

20. Biology A Punnett square shows the probability distribution for genes. A short pea plant contributes two short genes, labeled "t." A tall pea plant contributes two tall genes, labeled "T." The plant will be short if it inherits the combination "tt." "TT" means the plant will be tall. The combination "Tt" also results in a tall plant. What is the probability that this plant will be short? Explain your answer.
0; Sample: "tt" does not occur in this chart.

	T	T
t	Tt	Tt
t	Tt	Tt

*21. Error Analysis Two students use an equation to find the probability of getting heads on four coin tosses and rolling a 2 or 3 on two number cubes labeled 1–6. Which student is correct? Explain the error.

Student A	Student B
$P(\text{4 heads and two 2 or 3}) =$	$P(\text{4 heads and two 2 or 3}) =$
$\left(\frac{1}{2}\right)^4 \cdot \left(\frac{1}{6} \cdot \frac{1}{6}\right)^2 = \frac{1}{20{,}736}$	$\left(\frac{1}{2}\right)^4 \cdot \left(\frac{1}{3}\right)^2 = \frac{1}{144}$

*22. Multi-Step Veejay is throwing a party. It costs $75 to rent a skating arena plus $3 per person to rent skates. It costs $100 to rent a bowling alley plus $2 per person to rent bowling shoes. How many people would Veejay have to invite to his party for the bowling alley to cost more than the skating arena?

a. Write an inequality to answer. $75 + 3p < 100 + 2p$
b. Solve the inequality. $p < 25$
c. Explain the correct domain of the solution set.

22c. Sample: The solution set is all natural numbers less than 25 since Veejay can only invite whole numbers of people, and at 25, the costs are equal.

Lesson 82   541

Problem 14
Error Alert
Remind students that there are two solutions to the absolute value equation. That is, there are two numbers that are 5.1 units from 24.9. One number is to the right of 24.9 and the other is to the left of 24.9.

Problem 17
Suggest that students begin by using FOIL to multiply the binomials, and then distribute $-8u^3y$ over the resulting trinomial. This approach may be easier than first distributing $-8u^3y$ over one of the binomials and then using FOIL to verify that the two expressions are the same.

Problem 18
Error Alert
Caution students that some multiple choice items may be partially correct, but do not answer the stated question. Choice **C** and **D** are correctly factored forms of the trinomial, but neither is completely factored.

Problem 23
Extend the Problem
"Suppose the total number of CDs that Amber listens to is at least 9 and no more than 24. Write a compound inequality that represents this situation."
$9 \leq c \leq 24$

Problem 24
"How do you write this as an inequality?" $4x + 7 > 5x - 2$

Problem 26
Error Alert
Some students may get $5 > x$ instead of $5 < x$. Remind them that they need to change the direction of the inequality sign when dividing by a negative number.

---

23. **(Music)** Amber normally listens to 1 new CD and 7 old CDs every day. She starts to listen to 2 more new CDs each day and 1 less old CD each day. How many days will it take her to listen to more new CDs than old CDs? 3 days

*24. **Geometry** The length of a rectangle is greater than its width. The length is $4x + 7$ and the width is $5x - 2$. What does the value of x have to be for this statement to be true? $x < 9$

*25. **Error Analysis** Two students are told to write an inequality that is a contradiction. Which student is correct? Explain the error.

Student A
$-2 + x > x + 3$

Student B
$2x + 24 < 3x + 24$

25. Student A; Sample: Student A is correct because $-2 + x > x + 3$ is an inequality that will never be true, while Student B wrote an inequality that is sometimes true.

*26. Solve the inequality. Justify your steps.   See Additional Answers.
$-17 > -2x - 7$ OR $27 > 3(x + 6)$

*27. **Multiple Choice** What is the solution to $32 < 7x + 11 < 39$?   **C**
A $21 > x > 28$ **B** $3 < x > 4$
C $3 < x < 4$ **D** $3 > x > 4$

*28. **(Cholesterol Levels)** An average level of HDL, a type of good cholesterol, for a person is usually no more than 60, and an unhealthy level is lower than 40. A doctor sees 4 patients and tests their HDL levels. The first 3 levels are 45, 52, and 60. What can the fourth patient's HDL level be if the average of all four patients' levels fall in the average, but not unhealthy, range of levels? $3 \leq c \leq 83$

*29. **Formulate** Half of Mr. Rubenstein's math class studied for the test and the other half did not. Everyone who studied for the test got a score no lower than 90; everyone who did not study got a score lower than 70. Write the scores of the class as an inequality. $x \geq 90$ OR $x < 70$

*30. **Estimate** Felipe wants to earn a grade between 90 and 100 in math. There are 4 major tests over the year, which are averaged to determine his final grade. Felipe scored 94, 88, and 91 on the first 3 tests. What must he score on the last test for his average grade to fall between 90 and 100? Round his scores to solve.   Felipe must score between 87 and 100 on his final test.

 CHALLENGE

In Problem 28, an average level of HDL for a person is no more than 60, and an unhealthy average level is lower than 40. Write a compound inequality that represents these averages. $c \leq 60$ OR $c < 40$

LOOKING FORWARD

Solving multi-step compound inequalities prepares students for

- **Lesson 91** Solving Absolute-Value Inequalities
- **Lesson 97** Graphing Linear Inequalities
- **Lesson 101** Solving Multi-Step Absolute-Value Inequalities
- **Lesson 109** Graphing Systems of Linear Inequalities

LESSON 83

Factoring Special Products

Warm Up

1. **Vocabulary** A trinomial that is the square of a binomial is called a(n) _____. **perfect-square trinomial**

Factor.

2. $3x^4 - 12x$ $3x(x^3 - 4)$

3. $48y^2 + 16y^3 - 56y^5$ $8y^2(6 + 2y - 7y^3)$

Multiply.

4. $(2b - 3)^2$ $4b^2 - 12b + 9$

5. $(3x + 7)(3x - 7)$ $9x^2 - 49$

New Concepts

Look for a pattern in the products.

$(x + 1)^2 = (x + 1)(x + 1) = x^2 + 2x + 1 \rightarrow x^2 + 2 \cdot 1x + 1^2$

$(x + 2)^2 = (x + 2)(x + 2) = x^2 + 4x + 4 \rightarrow x^2 + 2 \cdot 2x + 2^2$

$(x + 3)^2 = (x + 3)(x + 3) = x^2 + 6x + 9 \rightarrow x^2 + 2 \cdot 3x + 3^2$

$(x - 1)^2 = (x - 1)(x - 1) = x^2 - 2x + 1 \rightarrow x^2 - 2 \cdot 1x + (-1)^2$

$(x - 2)^2 = (x - 2)(x - 2) = x^2 - 4x + 4 \rightarrow x^2 - 2 \cdot 2x + (-2)^2$

Math Reasoning

Verify How can you check the products of these binomials?

Sample: You can use the FOIL method.

The pattern is:

Square the first term in the binomial.

Square the second term in the binomial.

Multiply the product of both terms by 2.

Recall that a perfect-square trinomial is a polynomial that is the square of a binomial. The trinomial has the form $a^2 + 2ab + b^2$ or $a^2 - 2ab + b^2$. When squaring binomials use the following patterns:

$(a + b)^2 = a^2 + 2ab + b^2$

$(a - b)^2 = a^2 - 2ab + b^2$

Use the same patterns to factor perfect-square trinomials.

Perfect-Square Trinomials
The factored form of a perfect-square trinomial is:
$a^2 + 2ab + b^2 = (a + b)^2$ **Example:** $x^2 + 12x + 36 = (x + 6)^2$
$a^2 - 2ab + b^2 = (a - b)^2$ **Example:** $x^2 - 12x + 36 = (x - 6)^2$

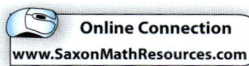
Online Connection
www.SaxonMathResources.com

Lesson 83   543

LESSON 83

1 Warm Up

Problem 4

Remind students that a binomial squared is the same as a binomial times itself.

2 New Concepts

In this lesson, students will factor special products, including perfect-square trinomials and differences of two squares. They will learn to recognize these products and to use the rules to factor them.

MATH BACKGROUND

The special products in this lesson are quadratic expressions. Quadratic expressions have related equations. If a quadratic equation is a perfect-square trinomial, then it has a double-root as a solution. If a quadratic equation is a difference of two squares, then it has solutions that are additive opposites of each other.

If a quadratic equation is a sum of two squares, then the equation is not factorable. Further, it has no real solutions. For example, the equation $0 = x^2 + 16$ is not factorable and it does not have any real solutions. It has the imaginary solutions $x = \pm 4i$.

LESSON RESOURCES

Student Edition Practice
  Workbook 83
Reteaching Master 83
Adaptations Master 83
Challenge and Enrichment
  Master C83, E83

Lesson 83   543

Example 1

Students will determine whether the polynomial is a perfect-square trinomial.

Additional Example 1

Determine whether each polynomial is a perfect-square trinomial. If it is, factor the trinomial.

a. $x^2 + 14x + 49$ yes; $(x + 7)^2$

b. $x^2 - 16x - 64$ no

c. $16x^2 - 24x + 9$ yes; $(4x - 3)^2$

Example 2

In this example, students will use a perfect-square trinomial to find an increase in signal range.

Extend the Example

"The coverage radius is later doubled. What area does the signal now cover?"
$\pi(2r + 10)^2$ square miles

Additional Example 2

Frida throws a rock into the center of a lake. After a second, the area inside the ripple is πr^2 square inches. After t seconds, the area inside the ripple is $\pi r^2 + 16\pi r + 64\pi$ square inches. How many inches has the radius increased? 8 inches

---

Example 1 Factoring Perfect-Square Trinomials

Determine whether each polynomial is a perfect-square trinomial. If it is, factor the trinomial.

a. $x^2 + 6x + 9$

SOLUTION

$x^2 + 6x + 9$
$= x^2 + 2 \cdot 3x + 3^2$ Write in perfect-square trinomial form.
$= (x + 3)^2$ It is a perfect-square trinomial.

b. $x^2 - 2x + 4$

SOLUTION

$x^2 - 2x + 4$
$\neq x^2 - 2 \cdot 1x + 2^2$ This is not equivalent to the perfect-square trinomial form. It is not a perfect-square trinomial.

c. $36x^2 - 48x + 16$

SOLUTION

$36x^2 - 48x + 16$
$= 4(9x^2 - 12x + 4)$ Factor out 4.
$= 4[(3x)^2 - 2 \cdot (3x)(2) + 2^2]$ Write in perfect-square trinomial form.
$= 4(3x - 2)^2$ It is a perfect-square trinomial.

Example 2 Application: Cell Phone Towers

A cellular phone tower's signal covers a circular area with a radius r in miles. The strength of the signal is increased, and now covers an area of $\pi r^2 + 10\pi r + 25\pi$ square miles. By how much did the radius of the coverage area increase?

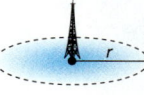

Hint

The original area covered by the phone tower signal was πr^2.

SOLUTION

Factor the expression for the new coverage area.

$\pi r^2 + 10\pi r + 25\pi$
$= \pi(r^2 + 10r + 25)$ Factor π out of the expression.
$= \pi(r^2 + 2 \cdot 5r + 5^2) = \pi(r + 5)^2$ Write in perfect-square trinomial form.

The radius of the new circle is $r + 5$.

The radius of the coverage area increased by 5 miles.

 ALTERNATE METHOD FOR EXAMPLE 2

Let x equal the increase in the radius. The area of the new coverage area, then, is $\pi(r + x)^2 = \pi r^2 + 2\pi rx + \pi x^2$. The given polynomial for the area is $\pi r^2 + 10\pi r + 25\pi$, so $2xr = 10$ and $x^2 = 25$; this means that $x = 5$.

Look for a pattern in the products.

$(x + 1)(x - 1) = x^2 - 1 \rightarrow (x \cdot x) - 1x + 1x - (1 \cdot 1) = x^2 - 1^2$
$(x + 2)(x - 2) = x^2 - 4 \rightarrow (x \cdot x) - 2x + 2x - (2 \cdot 2) = x^2 - 2^2$
$(x + 3)(x - 3) = x^2 - 9 \rightarrow (x \cdot x) - 3x + 3x - (3 \cdot 3) = x^2 - 3^2$
$(a + b)(a - b) = a^2 - b^2 \rightarrow (a \cdot a) - ab + ab - (b \cdot b) = a^2 - b^2$

The pattern can be used to factor the difference of two squares.

Difference of Two Squares
The factored form of a difference of two squares is:
$a^2 - b^2 = (a + b)(a - b)$ **Example:** $x^2 - 49 = (x + 7)(x - 7)$

Example 3 Factoring the Difference of Two Squares

Determine whether each binomial is the difference of two squares. If so, factor the binomial.

a. $4x^2 - 25$

SOLUTION

$4x^2 - 25$
$= (2 \cdot 2)(x \cdot x) - (5 \cdot 5)$ Factor each term.
$= (2x)^2 - 5^2$ Write as a difference of two squares.
$= (2x + 5)(2x - 5)$ Factor.

b. $9m^4 - 16n^6$

SOLUTION

$9m^4 - 16n^6$
$= (3 \cdot 3)(m^2 \cdot m^2) - (4 \cdot 4)(n^3 \cdot n^3)$ Factor each term.
$= (3m^2)^2 - (4n^3)^2$ Write as a difference of two squares.
$= (3m^2 + 4n^3)(3m^2 - 4n^3)$ Factor.

c. $x^2 - 8$

SOLUTION

$x^2 - 8$
$= (x \cdot x) - (4 \cdot 2)$ Factor each term.
$= x^2 - 8$ This is not a difference of two squares.

d. $-64 + z^8$

SOLUTION

$-64 + z^8 = z^8 - 64$ Write terms in descending order.
$= (z^4 \cdot z^4) - (8 \cdot 8)$ Factor each term.
$= (z^4)^2 - 8^2$ Write as a difference of two squares.
$= (z^4 + 8)(z^4 - 8)$ Factor.

Hint

Use exponent rules.
$m^4 = m^{2+2} = m^2 \cdot m^2$
$n^6 = n^{3+3} = n^3 \cdot n^3$

Example 3

Students must first determine whether the polynomial is a difference of two squares. You may want to further review this concept.

Error Alert Students may sometimes confuse the rule for the difference of two squares with that of a perfect-square trinomial. For example, in part **a** they may factor the polynomial as $(2x - 5)^2$. Encourage students to check their answers by multiplying.

Additional Example 3

Determine whether the binomial is a difference of two squares. If so, factor.

a. $100x^2 - 25$ yes; $(10x - 5)(10x + 5)$

b. $2x^6 - 288$ yes; $2(x^3 + 12)(x^3 - 12)$

c. $x^2 + 9$ no

d. $-36 + x^{10}$ yes; $(x^5 + 6)(x^5 - 6)$

INCLUSION

For factoring a difference of two squares, have students find the square root of the terms a^2 and b^2 before they begin to write the binomial as factors. First have them write the equivalency:

$a^2 - b^2 = (a + b)(a - b)$

Using Example 3a, have students determine if the binomial is factorable by setting up and solving the equations $a = \sqrt{4x^2}$ and $b = \sqrt{25}$. Explain to them why the binomial is a difference of two squares. Have them factor the binomial by setting up two empty sets of parentheses with opposite signs (to separate the terms) within each set. Using the equivalent square rooots, have them substitute the values a and b into the set of parentheses.

Example 4

This example uses a difference of two squares to find the differences in the areas of two squares.

Additional Example 4

A large square has an area of 121 square inches. A smaller square has a side length that is y inches. What is the polynomial representing the difference in the areas of the squares in factored form? $(11 + y)(11 - y)$

Lesson Practice

Problem b

Scaffolding Have students first identify what number they can factor out of the expression.

Problem e

Error Alert Students may subtract the larger square from the smaller square. Remind them that the order of the expression is important.

Check for Understanding

The questions below help assess the concepts taught in this lesson.

"Give an example of a perfect-square trinomial. Then factor."
Sample: $x^2 + 4x + 4$; $(x + 2)^2$

"Give an example of a binomial that is a difference of two squares. Then factor." Sample: $x^2 - 4$; $(x + 2)(x - 2)$

Math Reasoning

Analyze Suppose the side length of the larger square is double the side length of the pond. What is the area of the border?

675 ft²

Example 4 Application: Garden Planning

Ganesh is designing a square border around a square pond. The area of the pond is 225 square feet. Use the difference of two squares to write an expression that represents the area of the border.

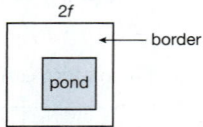

SOLUTION

Area of larger square:
$A = lw$
$= (2f)(2f)$

Area of pond:
$A = lw$
$225 = (15)(15)$

Find the difference between the area of the square surrounding the pond and the area of the pond.

$(2f)^2 - (15)^2$ Write as a difference of two squares.
$= (2f - 15)(2f + 15)$ Factor.

The area of the border is $(2f - 15)(2f + 15)$ ft².

Lesson Practice

Determine whether the polynomial is a perfect-square trinomial. If so, factor the trinomial.
(Ex 1)
a. $x^2 + 14x + 49$ yes; $(x + 7)^2$
b. $6n^4 - 12n^2 + 6$ yes; $6(n^2 - 1)^2$
c. $3g^2 + 9g + 9$ no

d. A radio tower's signal covers a circular area with a radius r in miles.
(Ex 2) The strength of the signal is increased, and now covers an area of $\pi r^2 + 12\pi r + 36\pi$ square miles. By how much did the radius of the coverage area increase? 6 miles

Determine whether the binomial is the difference of two squares. If so, factor the binomial.
(Ex 3)
e. $25x^2 - 4$ f. $9b^2 - 100a^2$
e. yes; $(5x + 2)(5x - 2)$
f. yes; $(3b + 10a)(3b - 10a)$
g. $x^2 - 14$ no   h. $-81 + x^{10}$ yes; $(x^5 + 9)(x^5 - 9)$

i. A square border is designed around a square pool.
(Ex 4) Use the difference of two squares to write and factor an expression that represents the area of the border.
$34^2 - s^2 = (34 - s)(34 + s)$ ft²

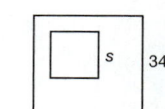

ENGLISH LEARNERS

For Example 4, explain the meaning of the word **border.** Say:

"A border is a part that forms the outer edge of something. A picture frame is a border of a picture."

Ask a volunteer to name other objects that have borders. Sample: bulletin board, garden

Practice Distributed and Integrated

Find the product.

1. $(7 + \sqrt{6})(4 - \sqrt{9})$ $7 + \sqrt{6}$
(76)

2. $(x + \sqrt{12})(x - \sqrt{3})$ $x^2 + x\sqrt{3} - 6$
(76)

Solve.

*3. $\dfrac{-b}{4} + \dfrac{3}{8} \geq \dfrac{3b}{4} - \dfrac{5}{8}$ $b \leq 1$
(81)

4. $11h + 9 \leq 5h - 21$ $h \leq -5$
(81)

Factor completely.

5. $3x^5 - 3x^4 - 216x^3$ $3x^3(x - 9)(x + 8)$
(79)

6. $-12x^3 - 48x$ $-12x(x^2 + 4)$
(79)

Determine whether the polynomial is a perfect-square trinomial or a difference of two squares. Then factor the polynomial.

*7. $x^2 + 10x + 25$ perfect-square trinomial; $(x + 5)^2$
(83)

*8. $x^2 + 12x + 36$ perfect-square trinomial; $(x + 6)^2$
(83)

9. Geometry Show that TUV is a right triangle.
(65)

$m_{\overline{TU}} = -1$, $m_{\overline{UV}} = 1$, and $(1)(-1) = -1$; $\overline{TU} \perp \overline{UV}$; Therefore, TUV is a right triangle.

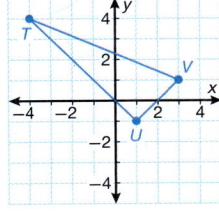

*10. Analyze The expression $-7x + 2y$ is one factor of a difference of two squares.
(83) What is the expanded polynomial? $49x^2 - 4y^2$ or $4y^2 - 49x^2$

11. Hiking Raul and his friends are hiking a 4-mile trail. After 2 hours of hiking,
(66) they turn off of the path to find a spot for lunch, and then hike back to the trail and continue to the end. Write an inequality to represent x, the total distance they hiked. $x > 4$

Determine if the following systems are consistent and independent, consistent and dependent, or inconsistent.

12. $y = 2x + 5$ inconsistent
(67) $y - 2x = 1$

13. $3y = 2x + 4$ consistent and dependent
(67) $3x = 4.5y - 6$

14. Find the probability of rolling a sum of 10 or a set of doubles with two
(68) number cubes. $\dfrac{2}{9}$

Lesson 83   547

Problem 20

Guide students by asking the following questions.

"What is the factored form of the polynomial?" $16m^4(m + 10)^2$

"What must you do to find the length of the hypotenuse?" Find the square root.

---

15. Multi-Step The local bank offers a savings account with a 3% annual interest rate. Alfred wants to earn at least $60 in interest. How much should he deposit?
(70)
  a. Write an inequality to represent the situation. $0.03d \geq 60$
  b. Solve the inequality. $d \geq 2000$
  c. How much should he deposit?   at least $2000
  d. Graph the solution.
  1000 2000 3000

16. (Food Packaging) The label of a certain cheese states that it weighs 8 ounces. The actual weight of the product sold is allowed to be 0.2 ounces above or below that.
(73)
Write a compound inequality that represents this situation. $7.8 \leq x \leq 8.2; x \geq 7.8$ AND $x \leq 8.2$

17. Multi-Step Solve $\frac{|x+3|}{4} = 6$.
(74)
  a. Isolate the absolute-value expression. $|x + 3| = 24$
  b. Use the definition of absolute value to rewrite the absolute-value equation as two equations. $x + 3 = 24; x + 3 = -24$
  c. What is the solution set? $\{21, -27\}$

18. Generalize When factoring a trinomial explain how you know if the second terms of binomial factors are both positive, both negative, or have opposite signs.
(75)

18. Sample: If c is positive, then both are the same sign as b: either both positive or both negative. If c is negative, then they have opposite signs.

19. (Consumerism) A preschool has a budget of $1000 to buy new outside toys. They will receive 1 free toy when they place the order. The number of toys, y, that they can get is given by $y = \frac{1000}{x} + 1$, where x is the price per toy.
(78)
  a. What is the horizontal asymptote of this rational function? $y = 1$
  b. What is the vertical asymptote? $x = 0$
  c. If the price per toy is $5, how many toys will they receive?   201 toys

20. Measurement The length of the hypotenuse of a right triangle is found by adding the squares of the two legs and then taking the square root. The sum of the squares of the legs is $16m^6 + 320m^5 + 1600m^4$. Find the length of the hypotenuse by factoring. $4m^2(m + 10)$
(79)

21. P(heads, heads) $= \left(\frac{1}{2}\right) \cdot \left(\frac{1}{2}\right) = \left(\frac{1}{2}\right)^2 = \frac{1}{4}$

21. Verify The table shows that the theoretical probability of landing on heads two times when flipping two coins is $\frac{1}{4}$. Use an equation to show that the probability is correct.
(80)

	Tails	Heads
Tails	TT	TH
Heads	HT	HH

22. Multiple Choice Using the table, what is the probability of rolling an even number and spinning a yellow or a green?   **A**
(80)

A $\frac{1}{3}$ **B** $\frac{1}{6}$ **C** $\frac{1}{18}$ **D** $\frac{1}{1944}$

	Red	Yellow	Green
1	1R	1Y	1G
2	2R	2Y	2G
3	3R	3Y	3G
4	4R	4Y	4G
5	5R	5Y	5G
6	6R	6Y	6G

***23. Write** Describe how factoring can help find $45^2 - 15^2$.   Sample: The expression is a difference of two squares. Factor as $(45 + 15)(45 - 15)$, which equals $60 \cdot 30 = 1800$.
(83)

548   Saxon Algebra 1

⭐ CHALLENGE

Factor $8x^4y^3 - 162x^2y$. $2x^2y(2xy + 9)(2xy - 9)$

*24. **Error Analysis** Beth claims that the inequality $12x + 67 \geq 52 + 5x + 15$ is always
(81) true for any value of x. Is Beth correct? Explain the error.   no; Sample: The
inequality is only true if x is 0 or greater.

25. (**Finances**) Chad works 20 hours each week. Juan works 10 hours and makes an
(81) additional $50 in tips each week. They both get paid the same amount per hour.
How much money do they each have to earn per hour for Chad to make more
money than Juan?   more than $5 an hour

26. **Error Analysis** Two students solve the following compound inequality. Which
(82) student is correct? Explain the error.

26. Student B; Sample: Student A forgot to change the direction of the inequality symbol when using the Multiplication Property of Inequality.

Student A	Student B
$10 < -2x + 2 < 16$	$10 < -2x + 2 < 16$
$-4 < x < -7$	$-4 > x > -7$

*27. **Multi-Step** Yvonne learns that a refrigerator should be kept at a temperature of no
(82) more than 40°F but warmer than 32°F.
  a. Write an expression to show the possible range of proper refrigerator
  temperatures. $32 < F \leq 40$
  b. Yvonne tests the temperatures of some refrigerators at an appliance store.
  The first 4 temperatures are 35°, 40°, 20°, and 45°. What should the last
  temperature be if the average of the temperatures is within the proper
  temperature range? $20 < F \leq 60$

*28. **Justify** Solve the inequality $28 < 2(x + 3) < 42$ and justify each step.
(82)

*29. **Multiple Choice** Which expression is a perfect-square trinomial?   D
(83)
  A $9x^2 + 49$ **B** $64x^2 - 100$
  C $6x^2 + 48x - 96$ **D** $49x^2 - 28x + 4$

*30. (**Home Improvement**) A square storage shed sits in the corner of a square deck that
(83) has a side length of s feet. The shed has a side length of 8 feet. Harper wants to
apply a coat of paint to the deck. Write and factor an expression to find the area
of the deck Harper will paint, not including the storage shed. $s^2 - 64$;
$(s + 8)(s - 8)$

28. $28 < 2(x + 3) < 42$
    $28 < 2x + 6 < 42$ Distributive Property of Inequality
    $22 < 2x < 36$ Addition Property of Inequality
    $11 < x < 18$ Multiplication Property of Inequality

Problem 25
Extend the Problem
This week, Juan worked an extra 5 hours and earned an additional $20 in tips. If they both earn $7 per hour, how many hours will Chad need to work to earn the same amount as Juan?
25 hours

Lesson 83   549

LOOKING FORWARD

Factoring special products prepares students for

• **Lesson 87** Factoring Polynomials by Grouping

• **Investigation 9** Choosing a Factoring Method

• **Lesson 93** Dividing Polynomials

• **Lesson 98** Solving Quadratic Equations by Factoring

Lesson 83   549

LESSON 84

1 Warm Up

Problems 2–4

The ability to evaluate the functions for several values of x is necessary for students to be able to graph quadratic functions.

2 New Concepts

In this lesson, students will learn to identify the equations and the graphs of quadratic functions, including the parent function in this family of functions. They will sketch graphs of these functions and learn that these graphs are parabolas that can open upward or downward.

TEACHER TIP

Review the relationship between equations and functions. Remind students that equations of the form $y = ax^2 + bx + c$ and $f(x) = ax^2 + bx + c$ both represent functions.

LESSON RESOURCES

Student Edition Practice Workbook 84
Reteaching Master 84
Adaptations Master 84
Challenge and Enrichment Master C84
Technology Lab Master 84

LESSON 84

Identifying Quadratic Functions

Warm Up

1. **Vocabulary** The equation $f(x) = 7x^2 - 3x + 1$ is written in _____ (*expanded, function*) notation.   **function**

Evaluate.

2. $6x^3$ for $x = 2$ **48**
3. $x^2 - 4x + 3$ for $x = -3$ **24**
4. $500 - 7x^2$ for $x = -10$ **−200**
5. **Multiple Choice** Solve $7x - y = 2 + 6x$ for y.   **B**

   A $y = \dfrac{7x - 2}{6}$ **B** $y = x - 2$ **C** $y = -x$ **D** $y = 13x + 2$

New Concepts

A function pairs each value in the domain with exactly one value in the range. A **quadratic function** is a function that can be written in the form $f(x) = ax^2 + bx + c$, where a is not equal to 0. So, quadratic functions must have a quadratic term, but they may also have a linear and/or a constant term.

Math Language

The table shows ways to describe the **domain** and **range**.

Domain	Range
x-values	y-values
Independent variable	Dependent variable
x	f(x)

$$f(x) = ax^2 + bx + c, \text{ where } a \neq 0$$

quadratic term — linear term — constant term

All quadratic functions consist of a polynomial expression with a degree of exactly 2. The degree of a polynomial is the same as the term with the greatest degree. The polynomial can be named by its highest degree.

Polynomial	Degree	Name Using Degree
$3x + 2$	1	Linear
$x^2 + 4x - 5$	2	Quadratic
$2x^3 - x^2 + 1$	3	Cubic

A quadratic function can be written in many ways; however, there is a standard way to write a quadratic function.

Math Language

Quadratic comes from the Latin word *quadratus*, which means "square."

Standard Form of a Quadratic Function
The **standard form of a quadratic function** is $f(x) = ax^2 + bx + c$, where a, b, and c are real numbers and $a \neq 0$.

If a function cannot be written in the standard form of a quadratic function, then the function is not quadratic.

MATH BACKGROUND

This lesson introduces quadratic functions and their graphs. In Lesson 25 students first learned about functions, but up to this point, the focus has been on linear functions. The general definition of a function, the pairing of an input value from the domain with exactly one output value from the range, still holds. The vertical-line test also holds for the parabolas formed when graphing quadratic functions.

Example 1 Identifying Quadratic Functions

Determine whether each function represents a quadratic function.

a. $y + 7x = 4x^2 - 6$

SOLUTION

$y + 7x = 4x^2 - 6$
$y = 4x^2 - 7x - 6$ Solve for y.

It is a quadratic function because it can be written in the standard form of a quadratic equation.

b. $y = 5 + 2x$

SOLUTION

$y = 5 + 2x$

Since there is no quadratic term, it is not a quadratic function.

c. $-2x^3 + y = -5x^3 + x^2$

SOLUTION

$-2x^3 + y = -5x^3 + x^2$
$y = -3x^3 + x^2$ Add $2x^3$ to both sides.

Since there is a cubic term, it is not a quadratic function.

Math Reasoning

Write What type of function is related to the equation $y = 5 + 2x$? Describe the graph that represents the equation.

linear function; Sample: The graph will be a straight line.

The graph of $f(x) = x^2$ is known as the quadratic parent function. Graph the parent function by making a table of values. Plot the points and connect them with a smooth U-shaped curve called a **parabola**.

x	−4	−2	0	2	4
y	16	4	0	4	16

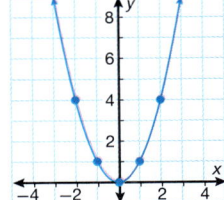

Example 2 Graphing Quadratic Functions Using a Table

Use a table to graph the function.

$f(x) = -3x^2$

SOLUTION

Plot the points in a coordinate plane and draw a smooth curve through the points.

x	−2	−1	0	1	2
y	−12	−3	0	−3	−12

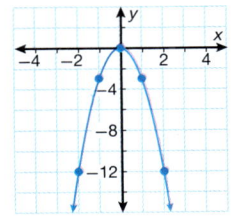

Math Reasoning

Analyze Compare the widths of the graphs representing $f(x) = x^2$ and $f(x) = -3x^2$.

The graph of $f(x) = -3x^2$ is narrower.

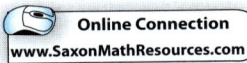
Online Connection
www.SaxonMathResources.com

Example 1

Students will write equations in standard form to determine if the function is quadratic.

Additional Example 1

Determine whether each equation represents a quadratic function.

a. $y - 15x^2 = 3 + 2x$ yes

b. $y - 62 = 3 - 2x$ no

c. $9x^4 - 9 = y + 8x$ no

Example 2

Students will graph simple quadratic functions.

Additional Example 2

Use a table to graph the function.

$f(x) = 5x^2 - 3$

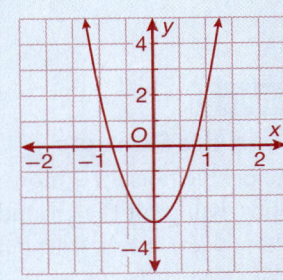

Lesson 84 551

---

eL ENGLISH LEARNERS

Explain the meaning of the word **function**. Say:

"Function means the action something performs or the purpose for which it exists. For example, the function of a car is to carry people from one place to another."

Ask a volunteer to give another example using the word function. Sample: The function of a CD player is to play music.

Lesson 84 551

Example 3

Students will determine if a parabola opens upward or downward by the value of the coefficient of the quadratic term.

Error Alert Some students may look at the coefficient of the first term to determine whether the parabola opens upward or downward. Tell them to make sure that the function is written in the standard form and to use the coefficient of the quadratic term to determine the direction that the parabola opens.

Additional Example 3

Determine whether the graph of each function opens upward or downward.

a. $f(x) = 3x^2 - 4x + 7$ upward

b. $f(x) = 15 - 10x - x^2$
downward

Example 4

Extend the Example

If the pebble falls for 2 more seconds, will it hit the ground? Explain. yes; Sample: If the pebble falls for 2 more seconds, then $t = 4$. When $t = 4$, $h = 0$. When the height is 0, the pebble has hit the ground.

Additional Example 4

Quan drops a marble from the top of a 33-foot tower. The equation $33 - h = 16t^2$ can be used to find the height h of the marble after t seconds. Find the height of the marble after it falls for 1 second. 17 feet

---

The direction of a parabola can be determined by value of the coefficient of the quadratic term.

Direction of a Parabola
For a quadratic function in standard form, $y = ax^2 + bx + c$:
If $a < 0$, the parabola opens downward.
If $a > 0$, the parabola opens upward.

Example 3 Determining the Direction of a Parabola

Determine whether the graph of each function opens upward or downward.

a. $f(x) = 3x^2 + 8$

SOLUTION

$f(x) = 3x^2 + 8 \qquad a = 3$

The graph opens upward because $a > 0$.

b. $f(x) = 3x - x^2 + 5$

SOLUTION

$f(x) = 3x - x^2 + 5$

$f(x) = -x^2 + 3x + 5 \qquad$ Write in standard form.

Since $a = -1$, $a < 0$ and the graph opens downward.

Example 4 Application: Free Fall

A pebble is dropped from a 256-foot-tall cliff. The equation $256 - h = 16t^2$ can be used to find the height h of the pebble after falling for t seconds. Find the height of the pebble after falling for 2 seconds.

Math Reasoning

Analyze If a pebble were dropped from a 144-foot-tall cliff, what would be a reasonable domain and range?

$0 \leq t \leq 3$;
$0 \leq h \leq 144$

SOLUTION

Understand Determine the height of the pebble using the function $256 - h = 16t^2$. Define the variables in the function.

$h =$ height in feet $\qquad t =$ time in seconds

Plan Solve the equation for height h, and then find h when $t = 2$.

Solve Solve the equation for height h.

$256 - h = 16t^2$

$h = -16t^2 + 256$

Find h when $t = 2$.

$h = -16t^2 + 256$

$= -16(2)^2 + 256$

$= 192$ feet

The height of the pebble after falling for 2 seconds is 192 feet.

 ALTERNATE METHOD FOR EXAMPLE 4

Solve the equation using square roots. When the pebble hits the ground, $h = 0$. The equation to find the time it takes to hit the ground is $256 = 16t^2$.

$256 = 16t^2$

$16 = t^2 \qquad$ Divide both sides by 16.

$4 = t \qquad$ Find the square root.

Check Make a table of values. Choose positive values for the number of seconds t.

t	0	1	2	3	4
h	256	240	192	112	0

From the table the range is $0 \leq h \leq 256$ and the answer was 192 feet, so the answer is reasonable.

Lesson Practice

Determine whether each function represents a quadratic function. (Ex 1)

a. $4 - y = x - 2x^2 - 3$ yes

b. $x = -x^2 + y$ yes

c. $4 = y$ no

Use a table of values to graph the function. (Ex 2)

d. $f(x) = 4x^2 - 3$

x	-2	-1	0	1	2
y	13	1	-3	1	13

Determine whether the graph of each function opens upward or downward. (Ex 3)

e. $f(x) = 2x^2 - 4$ upward

f. $f(x) = 2x - 5x^2$ downward

g. An acorn falls from a 16-foot-tall oak tree. The equation $h = -16t^2 + 16$ can be used to find the height h of the acorn after falling for t seconds. Find the height of the acorn after falling for 0.5 seconds.   12 feet

Practice   Distributed and Integrated

Determine whether the polynomial is a perfect-square trinomial or a difference of two squares. Then factor the polynomial.

1. $q^2 + 18q + 81$ perfect square trinomial; $(q + 9)^2$ (83)

*2. $36x^2 - 144$ difference of two squares; $(6x - 12)(6x + 12)$ (83)

Simplify.

3. $\sqrt{12} + \sqrt{48} - \sqrt{27}$ $3\sqrt{3}$ (69)

4. $\sqrt{18} + \sqrt{32} + \sqrt{50}$ $12\sqrt{2}$ (69)

Solve. Graph the solution.

5. $2p + 7 > p - 10$ $p > -17$; (77)

6. $16 < 2x + 8$ OR $15 > 7x + 1$ $4 < x$ OR $2 > x$ (82)

*7. Rewrite $x + 15x^2 - y = 4$ in the standard form of a quadratic function, if possible. $y = 15x^2 + x - 4$ (84)

3 Practice

Math Conversations
Discussion to strengthen understanding

Problem 8
Guide the students by asking the following questions.

"How many sections are on the spinner?" 10 sections

"How many are blue?" 4

"How many are labeled B?" 3

"How many are blue and labeled B?" 1

Problem 13
Extend the Problem
"The guesser predicts the weight of a patron to be 149 pounds. The patron receives a prize because the guess is 2 pounds over the acceptable error. How much does the patron weigh?" 144 pounds

---

Find the probability of the following events.

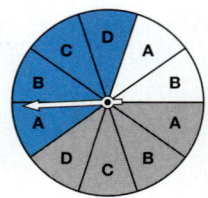

8. spinning a blue section or a letter B $\frac{3}{5}$
(68)

9. spinning a gray section or a letter D $\frac{1}{2}$
(68)

10. spinning a white section or a letter C $\frac{2}{5}$
(68)

11. **Computer Electronics** The failure rate for desktop computers is 5% for the first year
(68) of use. For notebooks it is 15%. If you purchase both a new computer and a notebook, what is the probability that either one will fail in the first year? $\frac{1}{5}$

12. **Multi-Step** Use the scatter plot.
(71)
   a. Using two points on the line, find an equation for the trend line. $y = 40x + 180$
   b. Does the graph show a positive correlation, a negative correlation, or no correlation? positive correlation

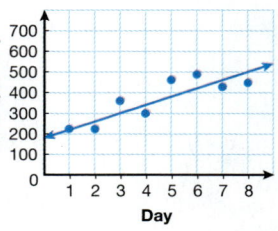

13. **Entertainment** People are often employed by amusement parks to
(74) predict the ages and weights of patrons. For a fee, one guesser claims she can predict a patron's weight within three pounds of the correct weight. If the guess is incorrect, the patron receives a prize. Write and solve an absolute-value equation for the maximum and minimum values of a correct guess for a person weighing 162 pounds.
$|W - 162| = 3$; 165 lb, 159 lb

14. **Multi-Step** The success rate on an exam is represented by $72x^2 - 156x + 72$.
(79)
   a. Evaluate the expression for $x = 2$. 48
   b. Factor the expression completely. $12(2x - 3)(3x - 2)$

15. **Verify** Show that $\sqrt{14} \cdot \sqrt{21} = 7\sqrt{6}$. $\sqrt{14} \cdot \sqrt{21} = \sqrt{14 \cdot 21} = \sqrt{2 \cdot 7 \cdot 3 \cdot 7} = 7\sqrt{6}$
(76)

16. Find the vertical asymptote: $y = \dfrac{1.6}{x + 2.5 + 7.8}$. $x = -10.3$
(78)

17. **Baseball** A pop fly is hit into the infield. In the expression $-5t^2 + 40t - 35$,
(79) t represents the time that the ball was 37 meters high. Factor the expression completely. $-5(t - 1)(t - 7)$

18. One student is selected from a school committee that has 12 seniors, 8 juniors,   See Additional
(80) 10 sophomores, and 4 freshmen. Make a graph showing the frequency distribution.   Answers.

19. **Data Analysis** Use the frequency distribution from the table to make a bar graph.   See Additional
(80)   Answers.

	Pasta Salad	Cucumber Salad	Caesar Salad	Carrot Salad
Number	12	16	22	10

*20. The value of a varies jointly with b and c. What is the constant of variation if
(Inv 8) $a = 18$, $b = 2$, and $c = 3$? Write an equation expressing the given relationship.
$k = 3$; $a = 3bc$

21. **Model** Graph the solution for $2(x + 9) - 14 > 3x + 7 + 2x$.
(81)

554   *Saxon Algebra 1*

CHALLENGE

Graph $y = x^2 + x + 1$.

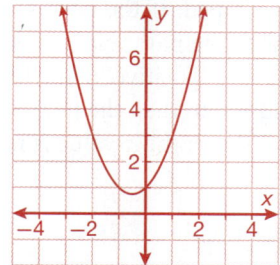

22. Multiple Choice What is the justification for subtracting 11 from all parts of the inequality $32 < 7x + 11 < 39$? **B**
(82)
A Combine the variable.
B Addition Property of Inequality
C Distributive Property of Inequality
D Multiplication Property of Inequality

23. (Health Checks) A borderline unhealthy cholesterol level is between 200 and 240.
(82) Five patients come to the doctor with borderline cholesterol levels. The first 4 have levels of 210, 230, 225, and 235. What could the fifth patient's level be if the average of all the patients' levels are within the borderline unhealthy range? $100 \leq c \leq 300$

*24. **Error Analysis** Ms. Cho asks two students to factor the polynomial only if it is a perfect-square trinomial. Which student is correct? Explain the error.
(83)

24. Student B; Sample: The trinomial is not of the form $a^2 + 2ab + b^2$ or $a^2 - 2ab + b^2$.

Student A	Student B
$x^2 + 8x - 16 = (x - 4)^2$	$x^2 + 8x - 16$ is not a perfect-square trinomial.

*25. **Multi-Step** A cylindrical thermos has a radius of r. Beneath the outer surface
(83) is an insulating layer. The volume, in cubic centimeters, that the thermos can hold is given by the expression $30\pi r^2 - 60\pi r + 30\pi$.
  a. Factor the polynomial representing the volume of the thermos. $30\pi(r-1)^2$
  b. How thick is the insulating layer?   1 cm
  c. What is the height of the thermos?   30 cm

*26. **Geometry** The surface area of a cube is given by the expression
(83) $6x^2 + 36x + 54$. What is the length of one side in terms of x? $x + 3$

*27. **Multiple Choice** Which function does the table of values represent?   **D**
(84)

x	−2	−1	0	1	2
y	6	6	4	0	−6

A $y = x + 8$
B $y = -x^2 + 12$
C $y = x^2 + 2$
D $y = -x^2 - 3x + 4$

*28. **Formulate** Write the equation of a function with degree 1 and of a function with
(84) degree 2.   Sample: $f(x) = -x + 3$; $f(x) = x^2 + x - 3$

*29. **Generalize** What is the relationship of the graph of $y = x^2$ to the graph of
(84) $y = -x^2$?   Sample: The shape of the parabolas is the same, but the graph of $y = x^2$ opens upward and the graph of $y = -x^2$ opens downward.

*30. (Water Fountains) A circular fountain sits in front of a city library. A pool of water
(84) surrounds a sculpture that sits on a circular platform in the middle. The radius of the sculpture is half the radius of the entire fountain. Write an equation to represent the area of the pool. Is the equation a quadratic function?
$A = \frac{3}{4}\pi r^2$; yes

Lesson 84   555

Problem 23
Error Alert
Students may first find the mean of the four given values and find the average of that number and the unknown to find the range. Have students write an equation for finding the mean of the 5 values.

Problem 26
Guide the students by asking the following questions.

"What is the formula for the surface area of a cube?" $6s^2$

"What common factor can be factored from the expression?" 6

TEACHER TIP
Generalizations in multiple-choice items can be difficult for some students. Encourage students to find concrete examples of items that can fit into categories. Introduce the strategy of choosing a few values to test. In problem 27, for example, substituting in 1 can eliminate choice **D**. Substituting in −1 can eliminate choices **A** and **C**. This strategy can prevent students from becoming overwhelmed with the number of values in the table.

LOOKING FORWARD

Identifying quadratic functions prepares students for

- **Lesson 89** Identifying Characteristics of Quadratic Functions
- **Lesson 96** Graphing Quadratic Functions
- **Lesson 98** Solving Quadratic Equations by Factoring
- **Lesson 100** Solving Quadratic Equations by Graphing

LESSON 85

Solving Problems Using the Pythagorean Theorem

Warm Up

1. **Vocabulary** The square of an integer is a _____ (*perfect square, radical expression*).   perfect square

Simplify.

2. $\sqrt{625}$ 25
3. $\sqrt{196}$ 14
4. $\sqrt{216}$ $6\sqrt{6}$

Estimate to the nearest tenth.

5. $\sqrt{389}$ 19.7

New Concepts

The Pythagorean Theorem states an important relationship among the lengths of the sides of any right triangle.

Math Language

The **hypotenuse** of a right triangle is the side opposite the right angle. The **legs** are the sides that form the right angle.

Pythagorean Theorem

If a triangle is a right triangle with legs of lengths a and b and hypotenuse of length c, then

$$a^2 + b^2 = c^2.$$

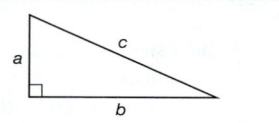

Exploration   Justifying the Pythagorean Theorem

The legs of the four blue congruent triangles form a square. The gray quadrilateral is also a square.

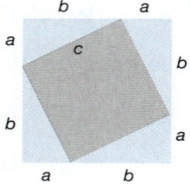

1. Explain why $(a + b)^2$ represents the area of the outer square formed by the blue triangles.

2. What area does the expression $\frac{1}{2}ab$ represent?

3. Write an algebraic expression for the area of the gray square. c^2

4. Use the expressions from problems **1**, **2**, and **3** to translate the statement below into an equation. $(a + b)^2 = 4\left(\frac{1}{2}ab\right) + c^2$

   Area of outer square = Area of 4 triangles + Area of gray square

5. Show that the equation you wrote in problem **4** simplifies to $a^2 + b^2 = c^2$.

Online Connection
www.SaxonMathResources.com

Answers (side margin):

1. Sample: The area of a square is the square of the length of a side of the square. The length of each side of the blue square is the sum of the two leg lengths a and b.

2. the area of each of the four congruent triangles

5. $a^2 + 2ab + b^2 = 2ab + c^2$
(Square the binomial. Multiply 4 times $\frac{1}{2}$.);
$a^2 + b^2 = c^2$
(Subtract $2ab$ from each side.)

556   *Saxon Algebra 1*

MATH BACKGROUND

Pythagoras was born in Greece (around 569–500 B.C.E.) and founded a group of mathematicians called the Pythagoreans. The Pythagoreans wrote many geometric proofs and have been given credit for discovering irrational numbers. A basic example for showing an irrational number is a right triangle with leg lengths of 1 unit each. This triangle has a hypotenuse with a length of $\sqrt{2}$ units, which is immeasurable with a ruler.

---

1 Warm Up

Problem 4
Remind students to use prime factorization to find perfect squares.

2 New Concepts

In this lesson, students use the Pythagorean Theorem to find missing side lengths.

Explain that the Pythagorean Theorem only applies to right triangles.

TEACHER TIP

Remind students that, no matter how they rotate the triangle, the hypotenuse will always be opposite the right angle.

LESSON RESOURCES

Student Edition Practice
  Workbook 85
Reteaching Master 85
Adaptations Master 85
Challenge and Enrichment
  Master C85, E85

556   *Saxon Algebra 1*

Example 1 Calculating Missing Side Lengths

Use the Pythagorean Theorem to find the missing side lengths.

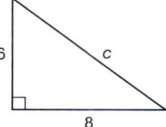

a. Find side length c.

SOLUTION

$a^2 + b^2 = c^2$	Pythagorean Theorem
$8^2 + 6^2 = c^2$	Substitute 8 for a and 6 for b.
$64 + 36 = c^2$	Simplify.
$100 = c^2$	Add.
$\sqrt{100} = c$	Take the square root of each side.
$10 = c$	Simplify. Because c is a length, c cannot be negative. The side length c is 10.

b. Find side length t to the nearest tenth.

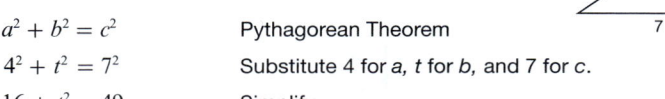

SOLUTION

$a^2 + b^2 = c^2$	Pythagorean Theorem
$4^2 + t^2 = 7^2$	Substitute 4 for a, t for b, and 7 for c.
$16 + t^2 = 49$	Simplify.
$t^2 = 33$	Subtract 16 from each side.
$t = \sqrt{33}$	Take the positive square root of each side.
$t \approx 5.7$	Estimate; round to the nearest tenth.

c. Find side length k.

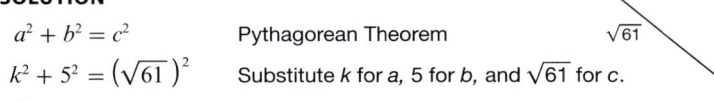

Hint

Recall that $(\sqrt{a})^2 = a$ for $a \geq 0$.

SOLUTION

$a^2 + b^2 = c^2$	Pythagorean Theorem
$k^2 + 5^2 = (\sqrt{61})^2$	Substitute k for a, 5 for b, and $\sqrt{61}$ for c.
$k^2 + 25 = 61$	Simplify.
$k^2 = 36$	Subtract 25 from each side.
$k = \sqrt{36}$	Take the positive square root of each side.
$k = 6$	Simplify.

d. Find side length m in simplest radical form.

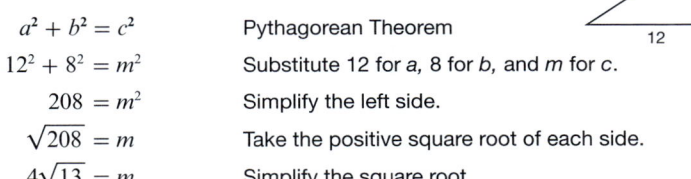

SOLUTION

$a^2 + b^2 = c^2$	Pythagorean Theorem
$12^2 + 8^2 = m^2$	Substitute 12 for a, 8 for b, and m for c.
$208 = m^2$	Simplify the left side.
$\sqrt{208} = m$	Take the positive square root of each side.
$4\sqrt{13} = m$	Simplify the square root.

Lesson 85   557

Example 1

Students learn to find a missing side length of a right triangle.

Additional Example 1

Use the Pythagorean Theorem to find the missing side lengths.

a. $20 = c$

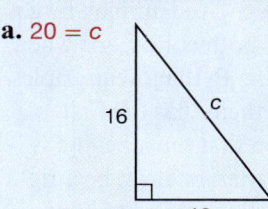

b. $4 = t$

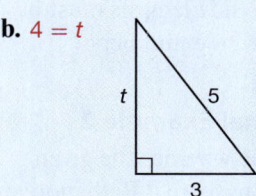

c. $24 = k$

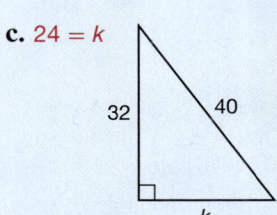

d. $10\sqrt{2} = m$

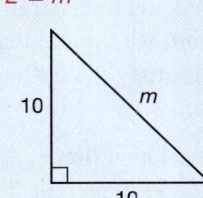

Error Alert Students may forget to square each term when they apply the Pythagorean Theorem. Remind them to use $a^2 + b^2 = c^2$ when they substitute values to check their work.

Lesson 85   557

Example 2

Students learn to identify right triangles using the converse of the Pythagorean Theorem and to identify special cases of right triangles called Pythagorean triples.

Error Alert Student may forget to check both conditions when identifying Pythagorean triples. Remind them that the first condition that must be met is that the triangle must be a right triangle. The second condition is that the side lengths must be nonzero whole numbers.

Additional Example 2

Determine whether the given side lengths form a Pythagorean triple.

a. 4, 5, 6 no

b. 9, 12, 15 yes

c. 15, 16, $\sqrt{481}$ no

Extend the Example

Have students to generate a list of nonzero whole-number values that will satisfy the Pythagorean Theorem.

"You have found that 6, 8, and 10 satisfy the Pythagorean Theorem. Identify five other nonezero whole-number triples that will work." 3, 4, 5; 9, 12, 15; 12, 16, 20; 15, 20, 25; 18, 24, 30

The **Converse of the Pythagorean Theorem** is also true; that is, if a triangle has side lengths a, b, and c that satisfy the equation $a^2 + b^2 = c^2$, then the triangle is a right triangle with legs of lengths a and b and hypotenuse of length c.

Pythagorean Triples
A **Pythagorean triple** is a group of three nonzero whole numbers a, b, and c that represent the lengths of the sides of a right triangle. Two triangles whose side lengths are Pythagorean triples are shown below. 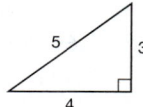 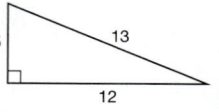

Example 2 Determining a Right Triangle

Determine whether the given side lengths form a Pythagorean triple.

a. 9, 40, 41

SOLUTION

Check whether 9, 40, and 41 satisfy the converse of the Pythagorean Theorem.

$9^2 + 40^2 \stackrel{?}{=} 41^2$ Substitute 9, 40, and 41 into $a^2 + b^2 = c^2$.

$81 + 1600 \stackrel{?}{=} 1681$ Simplify.

$1681 = 1681$ ✓   The equation is true.

Because 9, 40, and 41 are three nonzero whole numbers that satisfy $a^2 + b^2 = c^2$, they form a Pythagorean triple.

b. 8, 10, 12

SOLUTION

Check whether 8, 10, and 12 satisfy the converse of the Pythagorean Theorem.

$8^2 + 10^2 \stackrel{?}{=} 12^2$ Substitute 8, 10, and 12 into $a^2 + b^2 = c^2$.

$64 + 100 \stackrel{?}{=} 144$ Simplify.

$164 \neq 144$ The equation is false.

Because 8, 10, and 12 do not satisfy $a^2 + b^2 = c^2$, they do not form a Pythagorean triple.

c. 7, 11, $\sqrt{170}$

SOLUTION

Because $\sqrt{170}$ is not a nonzero whole number, the lengths 7, 11, and $\sqrt{170}$ do not form a Pythagorean triple.

Hint

Remember that since the hypotenuse is the longest side, the greatest number is subsituted for c.

Math Reasoning

Verify Show that the lengths 7, 11, and $\sqrt{170}$ determine a right triangle, even though they do not form a Pythagorean triple.

$7^2 + 11^2 = \left(\sqrt{170}\right)^2$

$49 + 121 = 170$

$170 = 170$

558 *Saxon Algebra 1*

INCLUSION

To determine whether the given lengths of a triangle form a Pythagorean triple have students draw a picture. While students label each part of the triangle, emphasize that the greatest side length is the hypotenuse. Then have the students assign values to each variable. Using Example 2b, let $a = 8$, $b = 10$, and $c = 12$. After values have been assigned, have students write the Pythagorean Theorem and substitute the values into the formula.

Additionally, students can construct triangles using the given lengths in any type of unit (inches, centimeters). Their constructions can be made with pencil and paper, cut-up drinking straws, or other available materials. This will allow them to see if the triangles are right.

Math Reasoning

Analyze The bottom of a ladder that satisfies the 1 in 4 rule is 3 feet from the base of a building. Find the length of the ladder.

$\sqrt{153}$ ft, or about 12.4 ft

Example 3 Application: Length of a Ladder

The ladder in the diagram satisfies the "1 in 4 rule," a rule of thumb for the safe use of ladders. This rule states that when the bottom of a ladder is positioned x feet from the base of a building, the top of the ladder should reach a point $4x$ feet off the ground. Find the length of the ladder in the diagram. Round your answer to the nearest tenth of a foot.

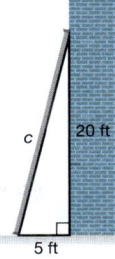

SOLUTION

The ladder is the hypotenuse of a right triangle. The lengths of the legs of the triangle are 5 feet and 20 feet. Use the Pythagorean Theorem to find the length c of the ladder.

$a^2 + b^2 = c^2$

$5^2 + 20^2 = c^2$ Substitute 5 for a and 20 for b.

$425 = c^2$ Simplify the left side.

$\sqrt{425} = c$ Take the positive square root of each side.

$5\sqrt{17} = c$ Simplify the square root.

$20.6 \approx c$ Estimate; round to the nearest tenth.

The length of the ladder is 20.6 feet.

Lesson Practice

Use the Pythagorean Theorem to find the missing side lengths.
(Ex. 1)

a. Find side length c.   20

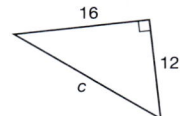

b. Find side length m to the nearest tenth.   10.8

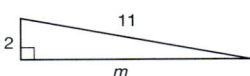

c. Find side length r.   7

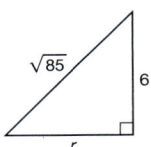

d. Find side length s in simplest radical form. $3\sqrt{10}$

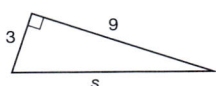

Lesson 85 559

Example 3

Additional Example 3
A ladder that leans against a building forms a right triangle with the ground. The ladder is positioned 6 feet from the building and reaches a height of 20 feet above the ground. Find the length of the ladder. Round your answer to the nearest tenth of a foot. **20.9 feet**

Lesson Practice

Problem a
Scaffolding Before students solve the problem, suggest that they identify a, b, and c in the problem. Then have them substitute values into the Pythagorean Theorem and solve the equation.

Problem b
Error Alert Some students may assume that the unknown value m is the hypotenuse. Remind them that the hypotenuse is the side opposite the right angle.

Check for Understanding

The questions below help assess the concepts taught in the lesson.

"Explain how to use the Pythagorean Theorem to find missing values." Sample: Substitute known values into the Pythagorean Theorem and solve for the missing value.

"Explain how to use the Pythagorean Theorem to determine if a triangle is a right triangle." Sample: Substitute values for a, b, and c into the Pythagorean Theorem to see if the statement is true. If it is true, then the triangle is a right triangle.

ENGLISH LEARNERS

For Example 3, explain the meaning of the word **positioned.** Say:

"To position something means to put something into place. The chairs were positioned in front of the stage."

Ask a volunteer to describe how to position a picture on a wall. Sample: Position a picture on the wall so that it is not tilted.

Determine whether the given side lengths form a Pythagorean triple.
(Ex. 2)
e. 5, 9, 11   no
f. 8, 15, 17   yes
g. 4, $\sqrt{65}$, 13   no

h. **Length of a Ladder** A ladder leaning against a building satisfies the "1 in
(Ex 3) 4 rule" for the safe use of ladders. The bottom of the ladder is 8 ft from
the base of the building. The top of the ladder touches the building
32 feet above the ground. Find the length of the ladder to the nearest
tenth.   33.0 ft

Practice   Distributed and Integrated

Simplify.

1. $3\sqrt{45} - \sqrt{5}$ $8\sqrt{5}$
(69)

2. $\dfrac{p^{-1}}{w}\left(\dfrac{wx}{cp^{-2}q^{-4}} + 5pq^{-3}\right)$ $\dfrac{pq^4x}{c} + \dfrac{5}{q^3w}$
(39)

Factor completely.

3. $-3t^3 - 27t^2 - 24t$ $-3t(t+8)(t+1)$
(79)

4. $4x^4 - 16x^2$ $4x^2(x-2)(x+2)$
(79)

5. $2x^2 + 14 - 9x - x^2$ $(x-7)(x-2)$
(72)

Determine whether the polynomial is a perfect-square trinomial or a difference of two squares. Then factor the polynomial.

6. $3g^2 - 12$
(83) difference of two squares; $3(g+2)(g-2)$

7. $9x^2 - 24x + 16$
(83) perfect-square trinomial; $(3x-4)^2$

Write the equations in the standard form of a quadratic function, if possible.

8. $4 + y = -8 + 16x$ not quadratic
(84)

9. $y + x^2 = 3x^2 - 10x + 12$ $y = 2x^2 - 10x + 12$
(84)

Solve.

10. $0.7 + 0.05y = 0.715$ $y = 0.3$
(24)

11. $\dfrac{1}{2} + \dfrac{3}{4}x = \dfrac{1}{6}x + 2$ $x = 2\dfrac{4}{7}$
(28)

12. Find the solution of $-1.2x \geq -4.8$. Then graph the solution set. $x \leq 4$;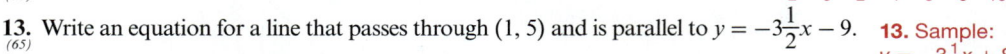
(70)

13. Write an equation for a line that passes through (1, 5) and is parallel to $y = -3\dfrac{1}{2}x - 9$.
(65)
13. Sample: $y = -3\dfrac{1}{2}x + 8\dfrac{1}{2}$

14. **Gardening** Niko wants to build a fence around his garden. If his garden measures
(69) $2\sqrt{4}$ feet by $\sqrt{25}$ feet, how many feet of fencing does Niko need?   18 ft

15. **Verify** Show that the solution to $\dfrac{x}{-5} + 6 \leq 10$ is $x \geq -20$.
(77)

15. Sample:
$\dfrac{x}{-5} + 6 \leq 10$
$\dfrac{x}{-5} \leq 4$
$x \geq -20$

560   Saxon Algebra 1

*16. Use the Pythagorean Theorem to find the missing side length. Give the answer in
(85) simplest radical form. $2\sqrt{5}$

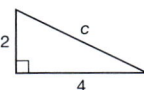

17. Find the vertical asymptote: $y = \dfrac{2.4}{x + 4.5} + 6.9$. $x = -4.5$
(78)

18. Given that y varies inversely with x, identify the constant of variation when
(Inv 7) $x = 4$ and $y = 2$. $k = 8$

19. **Statistics** In 2005 the population of North Dakota was about 635,000—a decrease
(81) of about 7000 from five years earlier. The population of Wyoming in 2005 was
509,000—an increase of about 15,000 from five years earlier. If this trend continues,
around what year will Wyoming's population exceed North Dakota's?   2034

*20. (**Sail Dimensions**) A main sail can be modeled by a right triangle whose sides are
(85) called the leach edge, the luff edge, and the foot. If the luff edge measures 27.5 feet
and the foot measures 10 feet, use the Pythagorean Theorem to estimate the length
of the leach edge to the nearest foot.   29 feet

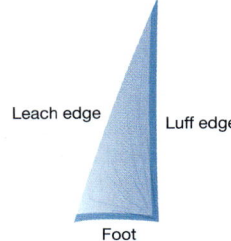

*21. **Multi-Step** In cooking school, Larissa learns that some foods should never be
(82) kept in the "danger zone": the temperature at which bacteria grow the fastest,
potentially causing food poisoning. She learns that the danger zone is 5°C to 60°C.

  a. Write an inequality that shows the temperatures that are in the danger zone in
  degrees Celsius. $5 \leq c \leq 60$

  b. Find an inequality that shows the temperatures that are in the danger zone in
  degrees Fahrenheit by substituting the expression $\frac{5}{9}(f - 32)$ for the variable
  used in the inequality from part a, and then solve for f. $41 \leq f \leq 140$

  c. Write an inequality to show at what temperature food should be kept in degrees
  Fahrenheit. $f < 41$ OR $f > 140$

22. **Verify** Solve the inequality $24 < 2x + 6 < 36$. Check to make sure that the
(82) equation really is an AND inequality. $9 < x < 15$; Sample: This is an AND
inequality since the solution falls within a specific range.

Lesson 85   561

Problem 17
Before finding the vertical
asymptote, ask the students,
"How can you find the values
for x that make the equation
undefined?" Solve $x + 4.5 = 0$.

Problem 20
Error Alert
Students may confuse the leach
edge length with the luff edge
length. Have students draw and
label each length before applying
the Pythagorean Theorem.

Problem 25
Extend the Problem

"What is the equation that that describes surface area of a cube?"
$y = 6x^2$

"What is the equation for the lateral surface area of a cube with side length x?" $y = 4x^2$

"Compare the graphs of the two functions. How are they different?" The parabola for the function $y = 4x^2$ is not as narrow as the parabola for the function $y = 6x^2$.

---

*23. **Error Analysis** Two students factor the polynomial. Which student is correct? Explain
(83) the error.   Student B; Sample: The polynomial is a difference of two squares.

Student A
$25x^2 - 36 = (5x - 6)^2$

Student B
$25x^2 - 36 = (5x - 6)(5x + 6)$

*24. (**Tires**) A truck's tire has an outside radius of r inches. The area of the side of the tire,
(83) not including the inside rim, is $\pi r^2 - 81\pi$ inches. What is the diameter of the rim?
18 inches

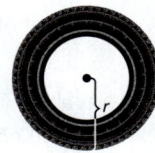

25. **Geometry** Graph the quadratic function representing the total surface area of a
(84) cube with side length x.

*26. **Write** Explain why the Pythagorean Theorem cannot be used to find the missing
(85) side length c.   Sample: The triangle is not a right triangle.

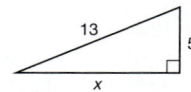

25. $y = 6x^2$
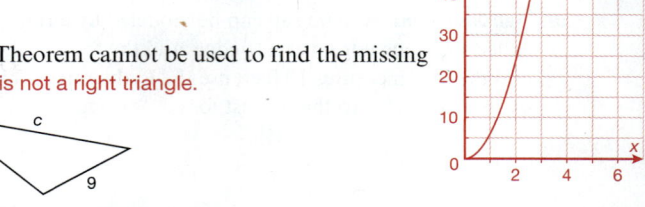

*27. **Formulate** One leg of a right triangle is twice the length of the other leg. The length
(85) of the hypotenuse is $\sqrt{45}$ centimeters. Let x represent the length of the shorter leg. $x^2 + (2x)^2 = 45$;
Use the Pythagorean Theorem to write and solve an equation to find the length of   3 cm and 6 cm
the legs.

*28. **Multiple Choice** What is the perimeter of the triangle to the nearest inch? **B**
(85)

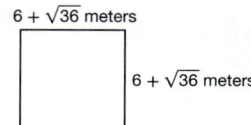

A 212 inches   **B** 30 inches   **C** 32 inches   **D** 12 inches

*29. (**Grades**) The grade a student earns on a project is represented by $-4x^2 + 48x - 63$,
(75) where x is the number of hours spent working on the project.
  a. Factor the polynomial. $(-2x + 3)(2x - 21)$
  b. What grade is earned when a student works 4 hours on the project?   65

*30. **Multi-Step** Write an expression for the area of the square. Then find the
(76) area. $(6 + \sqrt{36})^2$; 144 square meters

$6 + \sqrt{36}$ meters

$6 + \sqrt{36}$ meters

562   Saxon Algebra 1

CHALLENGE

Have students develop a formula for finding other Pythagorean triples, using the Pythagorean triple 3, 4, and 5.
$(3x)^2 + (4x)^2 = (5x)^2$, where x is a nonzero whole number

LOOKING FORWARD

Solving problems with the Pythagorean Theorem prepares students for

- **Lesson 86** Calculating the Midpoint and Length of Segments
- **Lesson 89** Identifying Characteristics of Quadratic Functions
- **Lesson 96** Graphing Quadratic Functions
- **Lesson 98** Solving Quadratic Functions by Factoring

LESSON 86

Calculating the Midpoint and Length of a Segment

Warm Up

1. **Vocabulary** In an ordered pair, the _____ (*x-coordinate*, *y-coordinate*) indicates the distance up or down from the origin.   **y-coordinate**

Simplify.

2. $-3.8 - 5.5$ **−9.3**

3. $(-6 - (-3))^2$ **9**

4. When viewed from the side, a skateboard landing ramp looks like a right triangle. What is the actual length of a ramp that is 2 feet tall if the base is 4 feet long? Round your answer to the nearest tenth.   **4.5 ft**

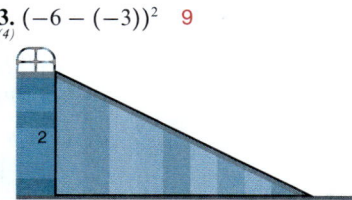

5. **Multiple Choice** Identify the coordinates of point *A*.
   A (4, 2)   **B** (−4, 2)
   C (2, −4)   **D** (4, −2)

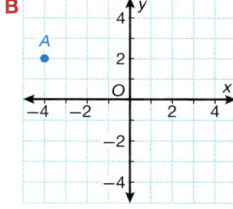

New Concepts

The Pythagorean Theorem is used to find distances that are difficult to measure directly.

Example 1 Calculating Distance Using the Pythagorean Theorem

The diagram shows a grid of city streets. A car travels from point *P* to point *Q* by moving east to point *R* and then south to point *Q*. What is the direct distance (in city blocks) from point *P* to point *Q*?

Math Reasoning

Analyze A crow flies directly from *P* to *Q*. How much farther does the car travel than the crow?

2 city blocks

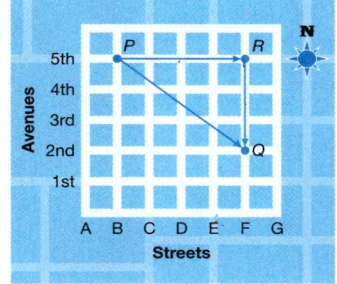

SOLUTION To find the direct distance (in city blocks) from *P* to *Q*, use the Pythagorean Theorem, written in the form $(PQ)^2 = (PR)^2 + (RQ)^2$.

$(PQ)^2 = (PR)^2 + (RQ)^2$ Pythagorean Theorem
$(PQ)^2 = 4^2 + 3^2$ Substitute 4 for *PR* and 3 for *RQ*.
$\sqrt{(PQ)^2} = \sqrt{4^2 + 3^2}$ Take the positive square root of each side.
$\sqrt{(PQ)^2} = \sqrt{25}$ Simplify under the radical.
$PQ = 5$ Simplify the square root.

Online Connection
www.SaxonMathResources.com

The direct distance from point *P* to point *Q* is 5 city blocks.

Lesson 86   563

---

1 Warm Up

Problem 4
Remind students to identify the hypotenuse before using the Pythagorean Theorem.

2 New Concepts

In this lesson, students use the distance formula and the midpoint formula.

Example 1
Make sure students correctly identify the unknown value as the hypotenuse.

Additional Example 1
Using the diagram of city streets, what is the direct distance (in city blocks) from the corner of C St. and 5th Ave. to the corner of G St. and 1st Ave.? Give the answer in simplest radical form. Use a calculator to approximate the answer to the nearest whole city block. $4\sqrt{2} \approx 6$ **city blocks**

LESSON RESOURCES

Student Edition Practice
  Workbook 86
Reteaching Master 86
Adaptations Master 86
Challenge and Enrichment
  Master C86
Technology Lab Master 86

MATH BACKGROUND

The distance formula can be derived using the Pythagorean Theorem. Find the distance between points $A(x_1, y_1)$ and $B(x_2, y_2)$.

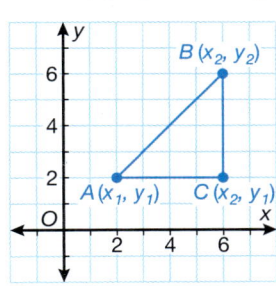

$c^2 = a^2 + b^2$

$(AB)^2 = (AC)^2 + (CB)^2$

$(AB)^2 = (x_2 - x_1)^2 + (y_2 - y_1)^2$

$\sqrt{(AB)^2} = \sqrt{(x_2 - x_1)^2 + (y_2 - y_1)^2}$

$AB = \sqrt{(x_2 - x_1)^2 + (y_2 - y_1)^2}$

The distance *d* between two points (x_1, y_1) and (x_2, y_2) is $d = \sqrt{(x_2 - x_1)^2 + (y_2 - y_1)^2}$.

Example 2
Make sure students substitute the correct value (with the correct sign) into the distance formula.

TEACHER TIP
Students may not know which point to use for (x_1, y_1) in the distance formula. Alternate the points in Example 2 to show them that it does not matter which point is used for (x_1, y_1).

Error Alert Students may take the square roots of the square of the simplified values and then find the sum of those square roots. Remind them to follow the order of operations to completely simplify the radicand before taking the square roots.

Additional Example 2
Find the distance between $(2, -2)$ and $(4, -3)$. $\sqrt{5}$

Example 3
Make sure students find all four side lengths before deciding if the quadrilateral is a rhombus.

Additional Example 3
Determine whether quadrilateral $ABCD$ is a rhombus.

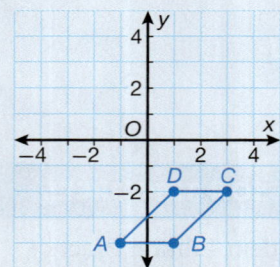

No; $ABCD$ is a quadrilateral but without four congruent sides, so $ABCD$ is not a rhombus

---

The Pythagorean Theorem can also be used to find the distance between two points in a coordinate plane. In the diagram for Example 1, let 1st Ave. be the x-axis and let A St. be the y-axis; then P is $(1, 4)$ and Q is $(5, 1)$. The lengths PR and RQ are found by subtracting coordinates.

Hint
Use absolute value when subtracting the coordinates so that the lengths PR and RQ will be positive numbers.

$(PQ)^2 = (PR)^2 + (RQ)^2$
$\sqrt{(PQ)^2} = \sqrt{(PR)^2 + (RQ)^2}$
$\sqrt{(PQ)^2} = \sqrt{|5-1|^2 + |1-4|^2}$
$\sqrt{(PQ)^2} = \sqrt{4^2 + 3^2}$
$\sqrt{(PQ)^2} = \sqrt{16 + 9}$
$\sqrt{(PQ)^2} = \sqrt{25}$
$PQ = 5$

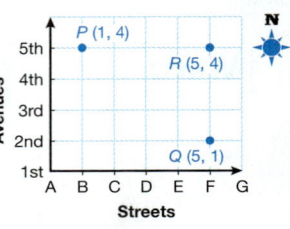

This method of finding the distance between two points leads to the distance formula.

The Distance Formula
The distance d between two points (x_1, y_1) and (x_2, y_2) is
$$d = \sqrt{(x_2 - x_1)^2 + (y_2 - y_1)^2}.$$

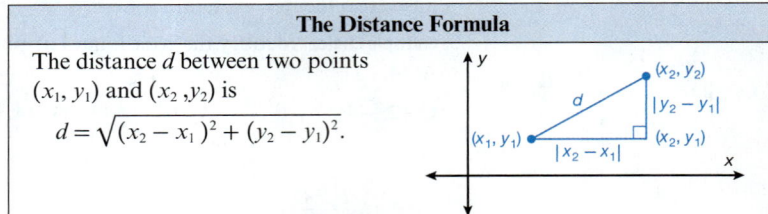

Example 2 Finding the Distance Between Two Points
Find the distance between $(3, -2)$ and $(6, 4)$.

SOLUTION Use the distance formula. Substitute $(3, -2)$ for (x_1, y_1) and $(6, 4)$ for (x_2, y_2).

Caution
Be careful when substituting negative numbers into the distance formula. Remember that $(4 - (-2)) = 4 + 2$.

$d = \sqrt{(x_2 - x_1)^2 + (y_2 - y_1)^2}$
$= \sqrt{(6 - 3)^2 + (4 - (-2))^2}$ Substitute.
$= \sqrt{3^2 + 6^2}$ Simplify inside parentheses.
$= \sqrt{9 + 36}$ Simplify powers.
$= \sqrt{45}$ Add.
$= 3\sqrt{5}$ Simplify the radical.

The distance between $(3, -2)$ and $(6, 4)$ is $3\sqrt{5}$.

Example 3 Classifying Polygons

Math Language
A **rhombus** is a quadrilateral with four congruent sides.

Determine whether quadrilateral $ABCD$ is a rhombus.

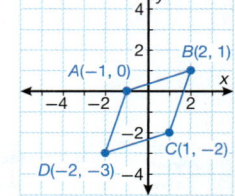

INCLUSION
Remind students who have a weak conceptualization of radicals that the prime factorization of the term under the radical will help them simplify the radical.

$\sqrt{45}$
$\sqrt{9 \cdot 5}$
$\sqrt{9} \cdot \sqrt{5}$
$\sqrt{3 \cdot 3} \cdot \sqrt{5}$
$3\sqrt{5}$

SOLUTION Use the distance formula to find the length of each side of $ABCD$.

$$AB = \sqrt{(x_2 - x_1)^2 + (y_2 - y_1)^2}$$
$$= \sqrt{(2 - (-1))^2 + (1 - 0)^2}$$
$$= \sqrt{3^2 + 1^2}$$
$$= \sqrt{9 + 1}$$
$$= \sqrt{10}$$

$$BC = \sqrt{(x_2 - x_1)^2 + (y_2 - y_1)^2}$$
$$= \sqrt{(2 - 1)^2 + (1 - (-2))^2}$$
$$= \sqrt{1^2 + 3^2}$$
$$= \sqrt{1 + 9}$$
$$= \sqrt{10}$$

$$CD = \sqrt{(x_2 - x_1)^2 + (y_2 - y_1)^2}$$
$$= \sqrt{(1 - (-2))^2 + (-2 - (-3))^2}$$
$$= \sqrt{3^2 + 1^2}$$
$$= \sqrt{9 + 1}$$
$$= \sqrt{10}$$

$$AD = \sqrt{(x_2 - x_1)^2 + (y_2 - y_1)^2}$$
$$= \sqrt{(-1 - (-2))^2 + (0 - (-3))^2}$$
$$= \sqrt{1^2 + 3^2}$$
$$= \sqrt{1 + 9}$$
$$= \sqrt{10}$$

$ABCD$ is a quadrilateral with four congruent sides, so $ABCD$ is a rhombus.

The **midpoint** of a line segment is the point that divides the segment into two equal-length segments. You can find the coordinates of the midpoint of a line segment by using the midpoint formula.

Math Reasoning

Connect How is finding a midpoint related to finding an average?

The x- and y-coordinates of the midpoint are the averages of the x- and y-coordinates of the endpoints.

The Midpoint Formula

The midpoint M of the line segment with endpoints (x_1, y_1) and (x_2, y_2) is

$$M = \left(\frac{x_1 + x_2}{2}, \frac{y_1 + y_2}{2}\right).$$

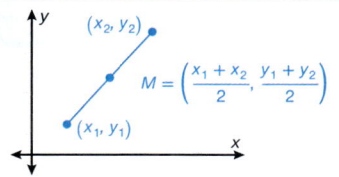

Example 4 Finding the Midpoint of a Segment

Find the midpoint of the line segment with the given endpoints.

$(3, 5)$ and $(7, -2)$

SOLUTION Use the midpoint formula. Substitute $(3, 5)$ for (x_1, y_1) and $(7, -2)$ for (x_2, y_2).

$$M = \left(\frac{x_1 + x_2}{2}, \frac{y_1 + y_2}{2}\right)$$

$$= \frac{3 + 7}{2}, \frac{5 + (-2)}{2} \quad \text{Substitute.}$$

$$= \left(\frac{10}{2}, \frac{3}{2}\right) \quad \text{Simplify.}$$

$$= \left(5, \frac{3}{2}\right) \quad \text{Simplify.}$$

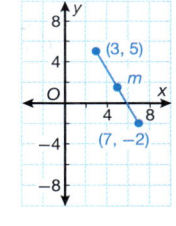

The midpoint of the line segment with endpoints $(3, 5)$ and $(7, -2)$ is $\left(5, \frac{3}{2}\right)$.

Math Reasoning

Generalize Does it make a difference as to which point is (x_1, y_1) or (x_2, y_2)? Explain.

no; Sample: Addition is commutative.

Lesson 86 565

Example 4

Finding the midpoint will have applications in the studies of triangles in geometry and conic sections in advanced algebra.

Extend the Example

Use the midpoint to write the equation of a line in slope intercept form that is perpendicular to the segment.
$y = \frac{4}{7}x - \frac{19}{14}$

TEACHER TIP

It may be helpful to tell the students that the line described in Extend the Example is called the perpendicular bisector of the segment.

Additional Example 4

Find the midpoint of the line segments with the given endpoints: $(7, 10)$ $(5, -4)$. $(6, 3)$

ENGLISH LEARNERS

Explore the meaning of the word **midpoint** in mathematics. Students may not know that midpoint is related to middle. Say:

"**The midpoint is the middle of the line.**"

Write midpoint on the board. Underneath, write the word middle so that the first three letters align. Say:

"**Midpoint and middle share the prefix *mid-*.**"

Brainstorm with students to find other words with *mid-* in them, such as midway, midtown, and midfield. Say:

"**What do all of these words have in common?**" Sample: All of these words have to do with the middle of a group or location.

Lesson 86 565

Example 5

Ask students to determine what they are trying to find before they begin to substitute numbers into a formula. They should respond that they are trying to find a distance between two points.

Additional Example 5

A quarterback is on the 30-yard line at (30, 20). He throws a pass to his receiver who is on the 50-yard line at (50, 10). Find the length of the pass as a radical in simplest form. Then use a calculator to estimate the length to the nearest yard. **$10\sqrt{5}$; 22 yards**

Lesson Practice

Problem b

Scaffolding Before students choose a formula, ask them to determine what they are trying to find. Then ask them to write out the appropriate formula.

Problem e

Error Alert Students may find the distance between yard lines and not the distance between players. Remind them that the ball must not only travel forward, but sideways as well.

Check for Understanding

The questions below help assess the concepts taught in the lesson.

"Explain how to find the distance between two points." Sample: Identify the right triangle that the two given points belong to. Then use the Pythagorean Theorem to find c or use the Distance Formula.

"Explain how to find the midpoint of a line." Sample: Find the average of the x-coordinates and the average of the y-coordinates.

Math Reasoning

Analyze If the pass is intercepted midway between the quarterback and the receiver, what are the coordinates of the player who intercepts the pass?

(40, 25)

Example 5 Application: Football

A coordinate plane can be used to model positions of players on a football field.

A quarterback is on the 30-yard line at (30, 10). He throws a pass to his receiver who is on the 50-yard line at (50, 40). Find the length of the pass as a radical in simplest form. Then use a calculator to estimate the length to the nearest yard.

SOLUTION Use the distance formula to find the distance between the quarterback and his receiver. Substitute (30, 10) for (x_1, y_1) and (50, 40) for (x_2, y_2).

$$d = \sqrt{(x_2 - x_1)^2 + (y_2 - y_1)^2}$$ Distance formula
$$= \sqrt{(50 - 30)^2 + (40 - 10)^2}$$ Substitute.
$$= \sqrt{20^2 + 30^2}$$ Simplify inside parentheses.
$$= \sqrt{400 + 900}$$ Simplify powers.
$$= \sqrt{1300}$$ Add.
$$= 10\sqrt{13} \approx 36$$ Simplify. Use a calculator to approximate.

The pass is about 36 yards long.

Lesson Practice

a. Use the diagram of city streets from Example 1. What is the direct (Ex 1) distance (in city blocks) from the corner of C St. and 2nd Ave. to the corner of D St. and 5th Ave.? Give your answer in simplest radical form. Use a calculator to approximate the answer to the nearest whole city block. **$\sqrt{10} \approx 3$ city blocks**

b. Find the distance between the points $(-3, -2)$ and $(4, 2)$. **$\sqrt{65}$**
(Ex 2)

c. Determine whether quadrilateral PQRS is a rhombus. **no**
(Ex 3)

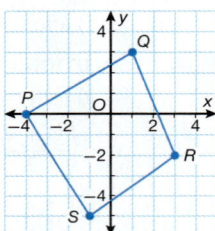

d. Find the midpoint of the line segment with endpoints $(-2, 3)$ and $(4, 7)$.
(Ex 4) **(1, 5)**

e. (**Football**) Use a coordinate plane like the one shown in Example 5. A
(Ex 5) quarterback is on the 20-yard line at (20, 33). He throws a pass to his receiver, who is on the opponent's 58-yard line at (58, 15). Find the length of the pass as a radical in simplest form. Then use a calculator to estimate the length to the nearest yard. **$2\sqrt{442} \approx 42$ yd**

566 Saxon Algebra 1

Practice   Distributed and Integrated

Solve and graph the solution set.

1. (70) $15y < 60$ $y < 4$;
2. (82) $16 < 6x + 10$ OR $-16 > 6x - 10$ $1 < x$ OR $-1 > x$;

Factor completely.

3. (79) $-2g^2 - 8g + 90$ $-2(g+9)(g-5)$
4. (75) $20b^2 + 21b - 5$ $(4b+5)(5b-1)$
5. (79) $-13w^2 + 38w - 25$ $-1(13w-25)(w-1)$

Write each equation in the standard form of a quadratic function, if possible.

6. (84) $y - 14x = -20x^2$ $y = -20x^2 + 14x$
7. (84) $x - 5x = -2x^2 + 7$ not possible

*8. (86) Find the distance between $(4, -1)$ and $(7, 3)$ using the distance formula.   5

9. (70) (**Personal Finance**) George's credit card company offers 4% cash back on all purchases. Write and solve an inequality to determine how many charges he needs to make in one year to earn at least $100 cash back. $0.04x \geq 100$; at least $2500

10. (71) Use the table to determine if there is a positive correlation, a negative correlation, or no correlation between the data sets.   positive correlation

x	2	4	6	8	10	12
y	12	25	40	51	61	75

11. (73) **Multi-Step** A real number is at most 13 and at least 5.
    a. Write two separate inequalities to describe the problem. $x \leq 13$ AND $x \geq 5$
    b. Write the two inequalities as one compound inequality. $5 \leq x \leq 13$
    c. Graph the compound inequality.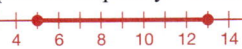

12. (76) (**Carpentry**) Louis is building a new rectangular room onto his house. The room has a side length of $3 + \sqrt{15}$ feet and a width of $4 + \sqrt{36}$ feet. What is the area of Louis's new room? $30 + 10\sqrt{15}$ square feet

13. (77) **Multi-Step** The temperature in Texas has never been above 120 degrees Fahrenheit. Describe this using Celsius temperature by solving the inequality $120 \geq \frac{9}{5}C + 32$.   13. $48\frac{8}{9} \geq C$; The temperature in Texas has never been above $48\frac{8}{9}$ degrees Celsius.

14. (78) **Write** How do changes to the value of c affect the graph of $y = \frac{a}{x-b} + c$?   Sample: The value of c determines vertical translation.

15. (80) A sandwich maker chooses a meat and a vegetable at random to put on a sandwich. There are three meats: turkey, ham, and chicken. There are 5 vegetables: lettuce, tomato, cucumber, onion, and peppers. Make a table of the possible outcomes.   See Additional Answers.

16. (81) (**Hobbies**) Kelly goes to a local store that has a monthly fee of $5 and rents games there for $1.75 a week. An online company has no monthly fee but rents games for $2.25 a week. How many games would Kelly have to rent per month for the local store to be the better deal?   11 games or more

Lesson 86   567

---

3 Practice

Math Conversations
Discussion to strengthen understanding

Problem 2
Ask students to identify a few numbers in the solution set before they graph the solution. After they graph, have them make sure that they have included the numbers they initially identified.

Problem 8
Students can use Pythagorean triples to find the distance. If a and b are members of the same Pythagorean triple, then c must be the member that completes the triple.

a	b	c
3	4	5
5	12	13
8	15	17

Since $a = 3$ and $b = 4$, $c = 5$.

Problem 11
Error Alert
Some students may reverse the inequality signs and their meanings. Before writing an inequality, ask students, "Does the small end of the inequality point toward the lesser or the greater amount?" lesser

Problem 12
The Distributive Property can be used instead of FOIL.

$$\begin{aligned} \text{Area} &= (3+\sqrt{15})(4+\sqrt{36}) \\ &= (3+\sqrt{15})(4+6) \\ &= (3+\sqrt{15})(10) \\ &= 30 + 10\sqrt{15} \end{aligned}$$

Lesson 86   567

Problem 17
Students may benefit from constructing squares with scissors and graph paper so that they can experiment with possible solutions to the problem.

Problem 20
Extend the Problem
"How do you know that $7x^2 + 24 = y - 6x(2 - 3x^2)$ is not quadratic?" When simplified, it has a variable raised to the third power.

"How could you graph this equation?" Substitute values for x and y.

"Find three values that make the equation true." $(0, 24)$, $(1, 25)$, and $(-1, 37)$

Problem 22
Guide the students by asking them the following questions.

"What values are equal to a, b, and c?" $a = n$, $b = \sqrt{84}$, $c = 10$

"Substitute values into the Pythagorean Theorem. What is the equation?" $n^2 + \left(\sqrt{84}\right)^2 = 10^2$

"What is the value of n?" 4

---

17. Measurement One square has an area of 16 square units and another square has an area of 36 square units. A third square has an area greater than that of the smaller square and less than that of the larger square. What are the possible lengths of the sides of the third square? $4 < s < 6$ units

18. Multiple Choice What is the factored form of $32x^2 - 50y^2$? **C**
A $2(4x + 5y)^2$
B $2(4x - 5y)^2$
C $2(4x + 5y)(4x - 5y)$
D $2(16x + 25y)(16x - 25y)$

*19. Verify Rewrite the expression $y^2 - x^2 - 8x - 41$ as a difference of two squares minus a perfect-square polynomial to show that $y^2 - x^2 - 8x - 41 = (y + 5)(y - 5) - (x + 4)^2$. $(y^2 - 25) - (x^2 + 8x + 16)$

20. Error Analysis Two students are asked if the equation $7x^2 + 24 = y - 6x(2 - 3x^2)$ is a quadratic function. Which student is correct? Explain the error. Student A; Sample: Student B did not use the Distributive Property correctly.

Student A	Student B
$y = -18x^3 + 7x^2 + 12x + 24$	$y = 10x^2 + 12x + 24$
no	yes

21. Economics A company has developed a new product. To determine the selling price, the company uses the function $y = -55x^2 + 1500x$ to predict the profit for selling the product for x dollars. Does the graph of this function open upward or downward? Explain why this might be given the context of the situation.

21. downward; Sample: If the price of the product is too low, people may buy a lot, but the company will not make much compared to its expenses. If the price of the product is too high, people will not buy it.

22. Use the Pythagorean Theorem to find the missing side length. Give the answer in simplest radical form. 4

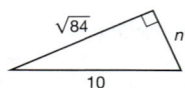

*23. Geometry A right isosceles triangle is a right triangle whose legs are equal in length.
a. Find the length of the hypotenuse of a right isosceles triangle with leg lengths of 3. $3\sqrt{2}$
b. Find the length of the hypotenuse of a right isosceles triangle with leg lengths of 5. $5\sqrt{2}$
c. **Formulate** Use the results of parts **a** and **b** to suggest a formula for the hypotenuse of a right isosceles triangle with legs of length a. $c = a\sqrt{2}$

*24. Error Analysis Two students use the Pythagorean Theorem to find length p. Which student is correct? Explain the error. Student B; Sample: Student A used p as the hypotenuse; 7 is the length of the hypotenuse.

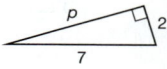

Student A	Student B
$2^2 + 7^2 = p^2$	$2^2 + p^2 = 7^2$
$4 + 49 = p^2$	$4 + p^2 = 49$
$53 = p^2$	$p^2 = 45$
$\sqrt{53} = p$	$p = \sqrt{45}$
	$p = 3\sqrt{5}$

568   Saxon Algebra 1

⭐ CHALLENGE

Have students find the perimeter of triangle ABC with vertices $A(1, 2)$, $B(4, 5)$, and $C(-7, -8)$. Round to the nearest hundredth. $3\sqrt{2} + \sqrt{290} + 2\sqrt{41}$; 34.08 units

*25. Use the diagram of city streets from Example 1 on page 563. What is the
(86) direct distance (in city blocks) from the corner of A St. and 4th Ave. to the corner
of E St. and 2nd Ave.? Give your answer in simplest radical form and to the nearest
tenth of a city block. $2\sqrt{5} \approx 4.5$ city blocks

*26. Multi-Step Marisol is flying a kite as shown in the diagram.
(85)
  a. Use the Pythagorean Theorem to find the length h.   80 ft
  b. How high is the kite off of the ground?   83 ft

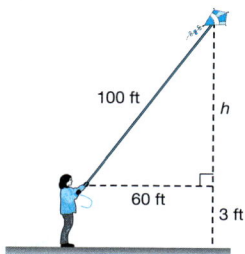

*27. Write To find the distance between (5, 3) and (−2, 9), Dan lets $(x_1, y_1) = (5, 3)$ in
(86) the distance formula. Dawn lets $(x_1, y_1) = (−2, 9)$. Explain why Dan and Dawn
will get the same result.

27. Sample: Dawn's values for $x_2 − x_1$ and $y_2 − y_1$ will be the opposite of Dan's values, but when the differences are squared, they will be the same positive numbers.

*28. Justify Is the triangle with vertices at (−3, 3), (1, 0), and (4, 4) a right triangle?
(86) Justify your answer.

*29. Multiple Choice Which points are not endpoints of a line segment with midpoint
(86) (7, −3)?   **B**
   A (1, 2) and (13, −8)   **B** (5, 0) and (9, −5)
   C (2, −9) and (12, 3)   **D** (4, −2) and (10, −4)

28. yes; Sample: Using the distance formula, the lengths of the sides of the triangle are 5, 5, and $5\sqrt{2}$; $5^2 + 5^2 = 25 + 25 = 50 = (5\sqrt{2})^2$. Because the lengths of the sides of the triangle satisfy the equation $a^2 + b^2 = c^2$, the triangle is a right triangle.

*30. Baseball A baseball diamond is a square that is 90 feet long on each side. Use
(86) a coordinate grid to model positions of players on the field; place home plate
at (0, 0), first base at (90, 0), second base at (90, 90), and third base at (0, 90).
An outfielder located at (50, 300) throws to the third-baseman. How long is the
throw? Round your answer to the nearest foot.   216 feet

Problem 26
Error Alert
Watch for students who let h equal the length of the hypotenuse. Point out that the hypotenuse is opposite the right angle and that its length is given in the diagram.

Problem 28
For students to further verify their conclusions, have them plot the points on a coordinate grid.

Lesson 86   569

LOOKING FORWARD

Solving problems calculating the midpoint and length of a segment prepares students for

• **Lesson 89** Identifying Characteristics of Quadratic Functions

• **Lesson 96** Graphing Quadratic Functions

• **Lesson 98** Solving Quadratic Functions by Factoring

• **Lesson 100** Solving Quadratic Equations by Graphing

LESSON 87

1 Warm Up

Problems 2–5
Remind students to factor the expressions completely by checking their answers to see if they are still factorable.

2 New Concepts

In this lesson, students learn ways to factor four-term polynomials by grouping.

Example 1
Additional Example 1
Factor $5x^2 + 10xy + 3x + 6y$. Check your answer.
$(5x + 3)(x + 2y)$

Example 2
Remind students to not only take out a common factor of the binomial, but to take out the GCF.

Additional Example 2
Factor $5x^2 - 12x^3 - 12x + 5$. Check your answer.
$(x^2 + 1)(5 - 12x)$

LESSON RESOURCES

Student Edition Practice Workbook 87
Reteaching Master 87
Adaptations Master 87
Challenge and Enrichment Master C87

LESSON 87

Factoring Polynomials by Grouping

Warm Up

1. **Vocabulary** For the terms in a polynomial, the product of the greatest integer that divides evenly into the coefficients and the greatest power of each variable that divides evenly into each term is the _____.
   greatest common factor

Factor each polynomial completely.

2. $90k^4 + 15k^3$ $15k^3(6k + 1)$
3. $x^2 - 8x + 15$ $(x - 3)(x - 5)$
4. $4n^2 + 5n - 21$ $(4n - 7)(n + 3)$
5. $81x^2 - 64y^2$ $(9x + 8y)(9x - 8y)$

New Concepts

Polynomials can be factored by grouping. When a polynomial has four terms, make two groups and factor out the greatest common factor from each group.

Hint
Factoring is the opposite of multiplying. Check the answer by multiplying. The product should be the original polynomial.

Example 1 Factoring Four-Term Polynomials

Factor $2x^2 + 4xy + 7x + 14y$. Check your answer.

SOLUTION

$2x^2 + 4xy + 7x + 14y$
$= (2x^2 + 4xy) + (7x + 14y)$ Group terms that have a common factor.
$= 2x(x + 2y) + 7(x + 2y)$ Factor out the GCF of each binomial.
$= (x + 2y)(2x + 7)$ Factor out $(x + 2y)$.

Check

$(x + 2y)(2x + 7)$
$\stackrel{?}{=} 2x^2 + 7x + 4xy + 14y$ Multiply using FOIL.
$= 2x^2 + 4xy + 7x + 14y$ ✓   Commutative Property

The product is the original polynomial.

Example 2 Rearranging before Grouping

Factor $3y^2 - 8y^3 - 8y + 3$. Check your answer.

SOLUTION

Use the Commutative and Associative Properties to rearrange terms to form two binomials with common factors.

$3y^2 - 8y^3 - 8y + 3$
$= 3y^2 + 3 - 8y^3 - 8y$ Group terms that have a common factor.
$= (3y^2 + 3) - (8y^3 + 8y)$ Group into two binomials.
$= 3(y^2 + 1) - 8y(y^2 + 1)$ Factor out the GCF of each binomial.
$= (y^2 + 1)(3 - 8y)$ Factor out $(y^2 + 1)$.

Hint
When rearranging terms, make sure the negative sign is distributed properly.

Online Connection
www.SaxonMathResources.com

570   Saxon Algebra 1

MATH BACKGROUND

The prime factorization of a polynomial can help to group terms. Terms that cannot group together do not have any common prime factors. Terms that best group together generally share the greatest possible number of prime factors.

$2x^2 + 4xy + 7x + 14y$.
$(2 \cdot x \cdot x) + (2 \cdot 2 \cdot x \cdot y) + (7 \cdot x) + (2 \cdot 7 \cdot y)$
$2x(x + 2y) + 7(x + 2y)$
$(x + 2y)(2x + 7)$

Check

$(y^2 + 1)(3 - 8y)$

$\stackrel{?}{=} 3y^2 - 8y^3 + 3 - 8y$ Multiply using FOIL.

$= 3y^2 - 8y^3 - 8y + 3$ ✓   Commutative Property

The product is the original polynomial.

Example 3   Factoring with the Greatest Common Factor

Factor $45a^3b - 15a^3 + 15a^2b - 5a^2$. Check your answer.

SOLUTION

$= 45a^3b - 15a^3 + 15a^2b - 5a^2$

$= 5a^2(9ab - 3a + 3b - 1)$ Factor out the GCF.

$= 5a^2[(9ab - 3a) + (3b - 1)]$ Group into two binomials.

$= 5a^2[(3a)(3b - 1) + 1(3b - 1)]$ Factor out the GCF of each binomial.

$= 5a^2[(3b - 1)(3a + 1)]$ Factor out $(3b - 1)$.

Check

$5a^2[(3b - 1)(3a + 1)]$

$\stackrel{?}{=} 5a^2[9ab + 3b - 3a - 1]$ Multiply using FOIL.

$\stackrel{?}{=} 45a^3b + 15a^2b - 15a^3 - 5a^2$ Distributive Property

$= 45a^3b - 15a^3 + 15a^2b - 5a^2$ ✓   Commutative Property

The product is the original polynomial.

Example 4   Factoring with Opposites

Factor $3a^2b - 18a + 30 - 5ab$ completely. Check your answer.

SOLUTION

$3a^2b - 18a + 30 - 5ab$

$= (3a^2b - 18a) + (30 - 5ab)$ Group into two binomials.

$= 3a(ab - 6) + 5(6 - ab)$ Factor the GCF from each binomial.

$= 3a(ab - 6) + 5(-1)(ab - 6)$ Take the opposite by multiplying by –1.

$= 3a(ab - 6) - 5(ab - 6)$ Simplify.

$= (ab - 6)(3a - 5)$ Factor out $(ab - 6)$.

Check

$(ab - 6)(3a - 5)$

$\stackrel{?}{=} 3a^2b - 5ab - 18a + 30$ Multiply using FOIL.

$= 3a^2b - 18a + 30 - 5ab$ ✓   Commutative Property

The product is the original polynomial.

Math Reasoning

Verify Show that $5(6 - ab)$ is equivalent to $-5(ab - 6)$.

$5(6 - ab) = 30 - 5ab$
Distributive Property;
$-5(ab - 6) = -5ab + 30$
Distributive Property;
$30 - 5ab = -5ab + 30$
Commutative Property

Example 3

Make sure students group the terms that share a common factor together.

Additional Example 3

Factor $54xz^3 + 6xz^2 - 18z^3 - 2z^2$. Check your answer.
$2z^2[(3x - 1)(9z + 1)]$

Example 4

Make sure students understand that removing the opposite will allow them to simplify further.

Additional Example 4

Factor $5x^2y - 3xy - 50x + 30$ completely. Check your answer.
$(xy - 10)(5x - 3)$

TEACHER TIP

Students may need to be prompted to simplify completely. Each of the examples has shown multiple steps toward simplification. At each stage, ask, "Is this expression completely simplified? Are there any other common factors?"

Error Alert Students sometimes factor -1 from a binomial expression without changing the signs of the terms in the binomial. Remind students to check the signs to make sure they took the opposite of each term.

⚠ ALTERNATE METHOD FOR EXAMPLE 3

In Example 3, have students solve $45a^3b - 15a^3 + 15a^2b - 5a^2$ without factoring $5a^2$ out first.

$45a^3b - 15a^3 + 15a^2b - 5a^2$

$(45a^3b - 15a^3) + (15a^2b - 5a^2)$

$15a^3(3b - 1) + 5a^2(3b - 1)$

$(15a^3 + 5a^2)(3b - 1)$

$5a^2(3a + 1)(3b - 1)$

A trinomial of the form $ax^2 + bx + c$ can also be factored by grouping. The trinomial is expressed as a polynomial with four terms so that it can be factored by grouping.

To express trinomials in the form $ax^2 + bx + c$ with four terms, first identify a, b, and c. For example, in the trinomial $2x^2 + 11x + 15$, $a = 2$, $b = 11$, and $c = 15$. Then, to factor a trinomial such as $2x^2 + 11x + 15$ by grouping, use the steps shown below.

Step 1: Find the product of ac.

$$2 \cdot 15 = 30$$

Step 2: Find two factors of ac with a sum equal to b.

$$6 \cdot 5 = 30 \text{ and } 6 + 5 = 11$$

Step 3: Write the trinomial using the sum. Replace $11x$ with $6x + 5x$.

$$2x^2 + 11x + 15 = 2x^2 + 6x + 5x + 15$$

Step 4: Factor by grouping.

$2x^2 + 11x + 15$
$= 2x^2 + 6x + 5x + 15$
$= (2x^2 + 6x) + (5x + 15)$
$= 2x(x + 3) + 5(x + 3)$
$= (x + 3)(2x + 5)$

Example 5 Factoring a Trinomial

Factor each trinomial by grouping.

a. $x^2 - 7x - 44$

SOLUTION

$ac = 1 \cdot -44 = -44$; Factors of -44 with a sum of -7 are -11 and 4.

$x^2 - 7x - 44$
$= x^2 - 11x + 4x - 44$ Replace $-7x$ with $-11x$ and $4x$.
$= (x^2 - 11x) + (4x - 44)$ Group into two binomials.
$= x(x - 11) + 4(x - 11)$ Factor out the GCF of each binomial.
$= (x - 11)(x + 4)$ Factor out $(x - 11)$.

b. $6k^2 - 17k + 10$

SOLUTION

$ac = 6 \cdot 10 = 60$; Factors of 60 with a sum of -17 are -5 and -12.

$6k^2 - 17k + 10$
$= 6k^2 - 12k - 5k + 10$ Replace $-17k$ with $-12k$ and $-5k$.
$= (6k^2 - 12k) - (5k - 10)$ Group into two binomials.
$= 6k(k - 2) - 5(k - 2)$ Factor out the GCF of each binomial.
$= (k - 2)(6k - 5)$ Factor out $(k - 2)$.

Caution

Remember to change the signs of terms within the parentheses when factoring out negative 1.

Example 5

Some students may find this method of factoring trinomials by grouping easier than using the guess-and-check method.

Additional Example 5

Factor each trinomial by grouping:

a. $x^2 - 4x - 21$ $(x - 7)(x + 3)$

b. $5k^2 - 13k + 6$ $(k - 2)(5k - 3)$

Extend the Example

"If $(x - 11)(x + 4)$ is multiplied by $3x$, how many terms are in the product?" 3 terms

---

INCLUSION

After grouping four terms into two binomials, if the terms of the two binomials are the same except for opposite signs, it may be helpful to relate the two binomials to additive inverses. Remind students that the sum of additive inverses is zero. When the two binomials appear similar except for their signs, have students check to see if their sum is zero. If so, a negative can be factored out of one of the binomials so that the factors match. Factor $10x - 5x^2 + x - 2$.

$(10x - 5x^2) + x - 2$ Group terms.
$5x(2 - x) + x - 2$ Factor out $5x$.

The factors $(2 - x)$ and $(x - 2)$ are additive inverses since their sum is zero. Factor -1 from one of the factors so that the factors are the same: $5x(2 - x) - (2 - x)$

The common binomial factor is $(2 - x)$. So, the factors of $10x - 5x^2 + x - 2$ are $(2 - x)(5x - 1)$.

Lesson Practice

Factor completely. Check your answer.

a. (Ex 1) $3y^2 + 6yz + 4y + 8z$ $(y + 2z)(3y + 4)$
b. (Ex 2) $3y^2 - 4y^3 + 3 - 4y$ $(y^2 + 1)(3 - 4y)$
c. (Ex 3) $99x^3y - 33x^3 + 33x^2y - 11x^2$ $11x^2[(3y - 1)(3x + 1)]$
d. (Ex 4) $3a^2b - 4ab + 20 - 15a$ $(ab - 5)(3a - 4)$

Factor each trinomial by grouping. (Ex 5)

e. $x^2 - 4x - 77$ $(x + 7)(x - 11)$

f. $6a^2 - 1a - 15$ $(2a + 3)(3a - 5)$

Practice Distributed and Integrated

Factor.

1. (72) $x^2 + 3xy - 54y^2$ $(x - 6y)(x + 9y)$
*2. (87) $64a^2b - 16a^3 + 18a^2b - 9$ $16a^2(4b - a) + 9(2a^2b - 1)$

Solve.

3. (81) $2g + 9 - 4g < 5 + 6g - 2$ $g > \frac{3}{4}$
4. (81) $6(k - 5) > 3k - 26$ $k > 1\frac{1}{3}$

Use an equation to find the probability of the event.

5. (80) rolling 4 on two number cubes and a coin landing on heads $P(4, 4, \text{heads}) = \left(\frac{1}{6}\right)^2 \cdot \frac{1}{2} = \frac{1}{72}$

6. (80) rolling a number less than 4 on two number cubes and a coin landing on heads
   $P(\text{less than 4, less than 4, heads}) = \left(\frac{1}{2}\right)^2 \cdot \frac{1}{2} = \frac{1}{8}$

Determine whether the polynomial is a perfect-square trinomial or a difference of two squares. Then factor the polynomial.

7. (83) $100 - c^6$
   difference of two squares; $(10 + c^3)(10 - c^3)$

8. (83) $4x^2 + 20x + 25$
   perfect-square trinomial; $(2x + 5)^2$

Find the distance between the given points. Give the answer in simplest radical form.

9. (86) $(1, 3)$ and $(4, 7)$ 5

*10. (86) $(2, -1)$ and $(6, 3)$ $4\sqrt{2}$

11. (71) Which situation would most likely be represented by a negative correlation: hours of practice and your golf score, hours of practice and the number of baskets you make in basketball, or hours of practice and the cost of a computer? Hint: In golf, the lower the score, the better.   hours of practice and your golf score

12. (71) (Entertainment) The table shows the average ticket price for a movie. Make a scatter plot from the data.   See Additional Answers.

Year	1990	1995	2000	2001	2002	2003	2004	2005
Ticket Price (dollars)	4.23	4.35	5.40	5.65	5.80	6.03	6.21	6.41

Lesson 87   573

 ENGLISH LEARNERS

In Problem 11, explain the meaning of the word **score.** Say:

"A score is a record of points in a game, contest, or test. For example, a football player gets a score of six points for making a touchdown."

Have volunteers give other examples using the word score. Sample: My score on the test was 100.

Lesson Practice

Problem a

Scaffolding Before students begin, ask them how they will group the terms. Then ask them to identify the common factors they will remove from each group.

Problem f

Error Alert Students may not remember to multiply the coefficients of *a* and *c* to see if the factors will add to the coefficient of *b*. Before they begin the problem, ask them what the product of *ac* is and why this is important.

 **Check for Understanding**

The questions below help assess the concepts taught in the lesson.

"How is grouping used to factor polynomials?" Sample: You can group terms that have a common number or variable before factoring.

"How can the factors be checked for accuracy?" Sample: You can use FOIL to multiply the expressions to see if they multiply to the original polynomial.

3 Practice

Math Conversations

Discussion to strengthen understanding

Problem 1

Encourage students to keep a list of factors that they have tested, so as not to repeat factors already tried.

Lesson 87   573

Problem 14
Extend the Problem

"What does each term in the inequality $2m + 5 \leq 9$ represent?"
Sample: $2m$ is the distance she hiked in m hours, 5 is the number of miles she has already hiked, and 9 is the greatest number of miles she wants to hike.

"Write an inequality representing that Heidi hiked at 3 miles per hour, had already hiked 5 miles, and wanted to hike no more than 12 miles." $3m + 5 \leq 12$

Problem 16
Error Alert

Students may not be able to generalize based on their experience with previous problems. Encourage them to create a table listing trinomials and the reasons they know they have factored the trinomial completely. Then have them look at their table to find what each case has in common.

---

13. **Multi-Step** A grower ships fruit to a processing plant in 50-pound cases. The plant (74) will not accept cases that differ from this weight by more than ±0.5 pound.
    a. Write an absolute-value equation to find the minimum and maximum weights of the cases that the processing plant will accept. $|x - 50| = 0.5$
    b. What are the maximum and minimum acceptable weights? 50.5 lb, 49.5 lb

14. (**Hiking**) Heidi can hike the mountains at 2 miles per hour. She has already hiked (77) 5 miles and wants to be sure to turn around before she hikes more than 9 miles. To find the number of hours she can hike before she needs to turn around, solve the inequality $2m + 5 \leq 9$. $m \leq 2$; She can hike at most 2 hours.

15. **Multi-Step** The local public library has a budget of $3000 to buy new children's (78) books. The library will receive 100 free books when it places its order. The number of books, y, that they can get is given by $y = \frac{3000}{x} + 100$, where x is the price per book.
    a. What is the horizontal asymptote of this rational function? $y = 100$
    b. What is the vertical asymptote? $x = 0$
    c. If the price per book is $20, how many books will the library receive? 250 books

16. **Generalize** How do you know when a trinomial is factored completely? Sample: (79) There are no common factors that can be factored out of any grouped terms.

17. (**Painting Job**) Marco paints walls and charges a $20 set-up fee. He charges at (82) least $60 per big wall, and for small walls he charges no more than $40 per wall. He has just completed a job painting either all big walls or all small walls. His invoice states that he received $2420 in payment. How many walls could he have painted? Sample: Marco painted either fewer than 40 big walls or more than 60 small walls.

18. **Measurement** A map has a scale 1 cm:500 m. A circular pond on the map has an (83) area of $9x^2\pi - 6x\pi + \pi$ square centimeters. What is the actual diameter of the pond? $3000x - 1000$ meters

19. **Multiple Choice** The graph of which function opens downward? C
    (84)
    A $-8y + 3x^2 = 4 + 7x$ **B** $-12x^2 + 15y = 18$
    C $-y + 36x = x^2 + 40$ **D** $-15 + 9y = 45x^2 - 3x$

*20. **Write** Explain how to graph a quadratic function such as $y + 28x - 3 = 50x^2 + 7$.   20. Sample: Rewrite the equation in the standard form of a quadratic function. Use the function to make a table of values. Plot the points from the table in a coordinate plane. Draw a smooth curve through the points.

21. Use the Pythagorean Theorem to find the missing side length. (85) Give the answer in simplest radical form. $\sqrt{6}$

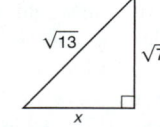

*22. Do the lengths 10, $5\sqrt{5}$, and 15 form a right triangle? yes; Using the Pythagorean (85) Theorem, $(10)^2 + (5\sqrt{5})^2 = (15)^2$.

23. (**Art**) Theresa is painting on a triangular canvas. The lengths of the sides of the (85) canvas are 24 inches, 32 inches, and 42 inches. Is her canvas a right triangle? no

574   Saxon Algebra 1

 MANIPULATIVE USE

In Problem 23, students may benefit from making squares on graph paper. The side lengths of the squares should measure 24 units, 32 units, and 42 units. When they have constructed their squares, they can then test to see if the area of the two smaller squares equals the area of the larger square.

24. Error Analysis Two students use the distance formula to find the length of the line segment with endpoints $(-1, 6)$ and $(4, -2)$. Which student is correct? Explain the error.

Student A	Student B
$d = \sqrt{(4+1)^2 + (-2-6)^2}$	$d = \sqrt{(4-1)^2 + (-2-6)^2}$
$d = \sqrt{25 + 64}$	$d = \sqrt{9 + 64}$
$d = \sqrt{89}$	$d = \sqrt{73}$

24. Student A; Sample: In calculating $x_2 - x_1$, Student B subtracted 1, instead of -1, from 4.

Problem 26
Guide the students by asking them the following questions.

"What are the points you need to find the distance between?"
(25, 10) and (30, 40); (25, 10) and (50, 20)

"What formula will help you solve parts a and b?" distance formula

*25. Geometry A midsegment of a triangle is a line segment joining the midpoints of two sides of the triangle. A triangle has vertices at $P = (3, 2)$, $Q = (3, 8)$, and $R = (7, 6)$.
  a. Find the endpoints M and N of the midsegment that joins sides $\overline{PQ}$ and $\overline{QR}$. (3, 5) and (5, 7)
  b. **Verify** Show that the length of the midsegment $\overline{MN}$ is half the length of $\overline{PR}$. $MN = 2\sqrt{2}$, $PR = 4\sqrt{2}$

26. Multi-Step Use a coordinate plane to model the following situation in a football game: A quarterback is on the 25 yard line at (25, 10); he has two receivers, one at (30, 40) and the other at (50, 20).
  a. Find the quarterback's distance to the receiver at (30, 40). Give your answer to the nearest yard. 30 yd
  b. Find the quarterback's distance to the receiver at (50, 20). Give your answer to the nearest yard. 27 yd
  c. Which receiver is closer to the quarterback? the receiver at (50, 20)

*27. Multi-Step The area of a right triangle is $x^2 + 2x$. The base, b, equals $x + 2$. What is the length of the height, h?
  a. Write the formula for the area of a triangle given the base and height. $\frac{1}{2}bh$
  b. Set the area equal to the product of the base and the height. $bh = 2A = 2(x^2 + 2x) = 2x^2 + 4x$
  c. Factor. $2x(x+2)$
  d. Divide by the length of the base to find the length of the height. $\frac{2x(x+2)}{(x+2)} = 2x$; The length of the height is $2x$.

*28. Write Is a binomial also a polynomial? Explain. yes; Sample: Any number of monomials expressed as a sum or difference is a polynomial.

*29. Formulate Write an expression to show the price of 2 discounted books when the first one is $20 + n$ and each one after that is $(20 + n)(n - 5)$. $(n - 4)(n + 20)$

*30. (Cost) The baseball team gets new uniforms. The first group of 5 costs $y^2 + 5$ dollars, and after that, each group of 5 costs $y + 1$ dollars. How much do the uniforms cost if the team buys 15? $(y^2 + 5) + 2(y + 1)$ dollars

CHALLENGE

Factor the polynomial completely.

$24x^3y - 28y^3 - 35x^2y^2 + 30x^5$
$(5x^2 + 4y)(6x^3 - 7y^2)$

LOOKING FORWARD

Factoring polynomials by grouping prepares students for

• **Lesson 93** Dividing Polynomials

• **Lesson 95** Combining Rational Expressions with Unlike Denominators

• **Lesson 98** Solving Quadratic Equations by Factoring

LESSON 88

1 Warm Up

Problem 3
Remind students to express their answer with only positive exponents.

2 New Concepts

In this lesson, students learn to multiply and divide rational expressions.

Discuss with students why simplifying rational expressions before multiplying or dividing makes finding the product or quotient easier.

Example 1

Students learn to multiply rational expressions that are formed by quotients of monomials.

Additional Example 1
Find each product.

a. $\dfrac{5x^2y}{12xy^5} \cdot \dfrac{2x^5y^3}{4x^4y^4}$ $\dfrac{5x^2}{24y^5}$

b. $\dfrac{8x^3}{5y^5} \cdot \dfrac{2x^2}{9y^3}$ $\dfrac{16x^5}{45y^8}$

LESSON RESOURCES

Student Edition Practice
   Workbook 88
Reteaching Master 88
Adaptations Master 88
Challenge and Enrichment
   Master C88

LESSON 88

Multiplying and Dividing Rational Expressions

Warm Up

1. **Vocabulary** A _____ (radical, rational) expression has at least one variable in its denominator. **rational**

Simplify. Assume that no denominator is equal to zero.

2. $x^6 x^2$ x^8

3. $\dfrac{8b^4}{12b^9}$ $\dfrac{2}{3b^5}$

4. $\dfrac{12y^4 - 18y^3}{28y^2 - 42y}$ $\dfrac{3y^2}{7}$

5. Factor $x^2 - 14x + 24$. $(x-2)(x-12)$

New Concepts

Multiplying and dividing rational expressions follows the same procedure as multiplying and dividing fractions.

Math Language
A **polynomial** is a monomial or a sum or difference of monomials.

Multiplying Rational Expressions	Dividing Rational Expressions
If a, b, c, and d are nonzero polynomials, $\dfrac{a}{b} \cdot \dfrac{c}{d} = \dfrac{ac}{bd}$.	If a, b, c, and d are nonzero polynomials, $\dfrac{a}{b} \div \dfrac{c}{d} = \dfrac{a}{b} \cdot \dfrac{d}{c} = \dfrac{ad}{bc}$.

Example 1 Multiplying Rational Expressions

Find each product.

a. $\dfrac{6x^4y}{21xy^3} \cdot \dfrac{7x^2y^2}{3x^3y^2}$

SOLUTION

$\dfrac{6x^4y}{21xy^3} \cdot \dfrac{7x^2y^2}{3x^3y^2}$

$= \dfrac{42x^6y^3}{63x^4y^5}$ Multiply the numerators and denominators.

$= \dfrac{2x^2}{3y^2}$ Simplify.

Hint
Remember, when multiplying powers, find the sum of the exponents.
$x^a \cdot x^b = x^{a+b}$

When dividing powers, subtract the exponents.
$\dfrac{x^a}{x^b} = x^{a-b}$

b. $\dfrac{6x^2}{5y^4} \cdot \dfrac{3x}{7y^2}$

SOLUTION

$\dfrac{6x^2}{5y^4} \cdot \dfrac{3x}{7y^2}$

$= \dfrac{18x^3}{35y^6}$ Multiply the numerators and denominators.

There are no common factors, so the product does not simplify any further.

Online Connection
www.SaxonMathResources.com

576 Saxon Algebra 1

MATH BACKGROUND

The Identity Property of Multiplication justifies dividing out like factors in the numerator and denominator of rational expressions. In the expression $\dfrac{3x(x+7)}{3x^2(2x+7)}$, the factor $3x$ in the numerator and denominator divides out because the factor $\dfrac{3x}{3x}$ equals 1.

However, the number 7 in the numerator and denominator cannot divide out. The number 7 is a term that belongs to each of the binomial factors. Since a term is formed by the sum or difference of monomials, it is not considered a factor and therefore cannot be divided out.

Example 2 Multiplying a Rational Expression by a Polynomial

Multiply $\dfrac{9}{3x-15} \cdot (x^2 - 2x - 15)$. Simplify your answer.

SOLUTION

$\dfrac{9}{3x-15} \cdot (x^2 - 2x - 15)$

$= \dfrac{9}{3x-15} \cdot \dfrac{(x^2 - 2x - 15)}{1}$ Write the polynomial with a denominator of 1.

$= \dfrac{9}{3(x-5)} \cdot \dfrac{(x-5)(x+3)}{1}$ Factor the trinomial.

$= \dfrac{\cancel{9}^{3}}{\cancel{3}(\cancel{x-5})_1} \cdot \dfrac{\cancel{(x-5)}(x+3)}{1}$ Divide out like factors.

$= 3(x+3)$ Simplify.

$= 3x + 9$ Distribute.

Math Reasoning

Justify How did you decide what binomials to factor the trinomial into?

Sample: I found two numbers whose product is −15 and whose sum is −2.

There is more than one way to find the product of two rational expressions. The factors can be multiplied first before being simplified. Another way to solve the problem would be to simplify each expression first, and then to multiply, simplifying again if necessary.

Example 3 Multiplying Rational Expressions Containing Polynomials

Multiply $\dfrac{8m^2n + 2mn}{2m} \cdot \dfrac{15}{24mn + 6n}$. Simplify your answer.

SOLUTION

Method 1: Multiply first.

$\dfrac{8m^2n + 2mn}{2m} \cdot \dfrac{15}{24mn + 6n}$

$= \dfrac{15(8m^2n + 2mn)}{2m(24mn + 6n)}$

$= \dfrac{120m^2n + 30mn}{48m^2n + 12mn}$

$= \dfrac{30mn(4m + 1)}{12mn(4m + 1)}$

$= \dfrac{\cancel{30mn(4m+1)}^{5}}{\cancel{12mn(4m+1)}_{2}}$

$= \dfrac{5}{2}$

Method 2: Factor first.

$\dfrac{8m^2n + 2mn}{2m} \cdot \dfrac{15}{24mn + 6n}$

$= \dfrac{2mn(4m + 1)}{2m} \cdot \dfrac{15}{6n(4m + 1)}$

$= \dfrac{\cancel{2mn}^{1}\cancel{(4m+1)}}{\cancel{2m}_{1}} \cdot \dfrac{\cancel{15}^{5}}{\cancel{6n}_{2}\cancel{(4m+1)}}$

$= \dfrac{5}{2}$

Example 2

Review factoring trinomials with students. Guide them to multiply their binomials to check that their products form the trinomial.

Additional Example 2

Multiply. Simplify your answer.

$\dfrac{16}{4x - 32} \cdot (x^2 - 5x - 24)$ $4(x + 3)$

Example 3

Students will factor polynomials to simplify rational expressions.

Additional Example 3

Multiply. Simplify your answer.

$\dfrac{3m^2n + 2mn}{2m} \cdot \dfrac{11}{24mn + 16n}$ $\dfrac{11}{16}$

INCLUSION

Students who have difficulty following multiple steps may not completely simplify rational expressions. Help students recognize actions that they can take to simplify a rational expression based on how the expression looks. For example, students should recognize three terms joined by addition or subtraction as a trinomial and factor it into two binomials. Encourage students to make a chart showing examples.

Form	$x^2 - 2x - 15$	$3x - 15$
Action	Factor into two binomials.	Use the Distributive Property.
Result	$(x - 5)(x + 3)$	$3(x - 5)$

Example 4

Students will divide rational expressions by multiplying by the reciprocal and then simplifying by dividing out like factors.

Extend the Example
Simplify the same expression by dividing out like factors before multiplying. Show your steps.
Sample:
$$\frac{5st^4}{4s^2t} \cdot \frac{2s^3t^2}{15s^2t}$$
$$\frac{t^3}{2} \cdot \frac{st}{3s}$$
$$\frac{t^3}{2} \cdot \frac{t}{3}$$
$$\frac{t^4}{6}$$

Additional Example 4
Find each quotient.

a. $\dfrac{3s^2t^5}{5s^4t^6} \div \dfrac{9s^3t^2}{10st^3}$ $\dfrac{2}{3s^4}$

b. $\dfrac{20r^2 - 10r}{35} \div (4r - 2)$ $\dfrac{r}{7}$

c. $\dfrac{x^2 - 5x - 14}{x^2} \div \dfrac{x+2}{x}$ $\dfrac{x-7}{x}$

Error Alert In Example 4c, students may think that the x in the numerator and denominator can divide out. Point out that only quotients of like factors can divide out.

TEACHER TIP
Encourage students to think about the terms in the expression before deciding to multiply or factor, and simplify first. Point out that sometimes partially completing each step may yield an expression that is easier to work with.

Example 4 — Dividing Rational Expressions

Find each quotient.

a. $\dfrac{5st^4}{4s^2t} \div \dfrac{15s^2t}{2s^3t^2}$

SOLUTION

$\dfrac{5st^4}{4s^2t} \div \dfrac{15s^2t}{2s^3t^2}$

$= \dfrac{5st^4}{4s^2t} \cdot \dfrac{2s^3t^2}{15s^2t}$ Write as multiplication by the reciprocal.

$= \dfrac{10s^4t^6}{60s^4t^2}$ Multiply the numerators and denominators.

$= \dfrac{t^4}{6}$ Simplify.

Math Reasoning

Verify How can you check your solution?

Sample: I can substitute real numbers for the variables x and y before and after dividing, and make sure I get the same answer.

b. $\dfrac{9r^2 - 12r}{27} \div (3r - 4)$

SOLUTION

$\dfrac{9r^2 - 12r}{27} \div (3r - 4)$

$= \dfrac{9r^2 - 12r}{27} \div \dfrac{(3r - 4)}{1}$ Write the polynomial with a denominator of 1.

$= \dfrac{9r^2 - 12r}{27} \cdot \dfrac{1}{(3r - 4)}$ Write as multiplication by the reciprocal.

$= \dfrac{3r(3r - 4)}{27} \cdot \dfrac{1}{(3r - 4)}$ Factor.

$= \dfrac{\cancel{3r}\cancel{(3r-4)}}{\underset{9}{\cancel{27}}} \cdot \dfrac{1}{\cancel{(3r-4)}}$ Divide out like factors.

$= \dfrac{r}{9}$ Simplify.

c. $\dfrac{x^2 + 4x + 3}{x^2} \div \dfrac{x+3}{x}$

SOLUTION

$\dfrac{x^2 + 4x + 3}{x^2} \div \dfrac{x+3}{x}$

$= \dfrac{x^2 + 4x + 3}{x^2} \cdot \dfrac{x}{x+3}$ Write as multiplication by the reciprocal.

$= \dfrac{\cancel{(x+3)}(x+1)}{x^{\cancel{2}\,1}} \cdot \dfrac{\cancel{x}^{\,1}}{\cancel{(x+3)}}$ Factor. Divide out like factors.

$= \dfrac{x+1}{x}$ Simplify.

Example 5 Application: Profit

A business makes a profit of $\dfrac{x^4}{100x^2 + 100x}$ dollars for each item sold. If $x^2 + 5x + 4$ items are sold, what is the total profit in terms of x?

SOLUTION

Multiply the profit for each item sold by the amount of items sold.

$\dfrac{x^4}{100x^2 + 100x} \cdot (x^2 + 5x + 4)$

$= \dfrac{x^4}{100x^2 + 100x} \cdot \dfrac{x^2 + 5x + 4}{1}$ Write the polynomial with a denominator of 1.

$= \dfrac{x^4}{100x(x + 1)} \cdot \dfrac{(x + 4)(x + 1)}{1}$ Factor.

$= \dfrac{x^{\cancel{4}3}}{100\cancel{x}(\cancel{x + 1})} \cdot \dfrac{(x + 4)\cancel{(x + 1)}}{1}$ Divide out like factors.

$= \dfrac{x^3(x + 4)}{100}$ Simplify.

Lesson Practice

Find each product.
(Ex 1)

a. $\dfrac{4z^5 q^8}{14qz^7} \cdot \dfrac{14qz^4}{3q^4 z}$ $\dfrac{4q^4 z}{3}$

b. $\dfrac{5x^2}{7y^4} \cdot \dfrac{4x^2}{9y^3}$ $\dfrac{20x^4}{63y^7}$

Multiply. Simplify your answer.

c. $\dfrac{6}{2x - 18} \cdot (x^2 - 6x - 27)$ $3(x + 3)$
(Ex 2)

d. $\dfrac{8m + 6m^2 n}{12} \cdot \dfrac{8m}{24m + 8mn}$ $\dfrac{m(4 + 3mn)}{6(3 + n)}$
(Ex 3)

Find each quotient.
(Ex 4)

e. $\dfrac{8j^2 k^7}{15k^7 j^4} \div \dfrac{6j^3 k}{5kj^6}$ $\dfrac{4j}{9}$

f. $\dfrac{x^2 + 7x + 12}{x + 5} \div (x + 3)$ $\dfrac{x + 4}{x + 5}$

g. $\dfrac{x^2 + 5x + 6}{x + 2} \div \dfrac{x + 3}{y^2}$ y^2

h. **(Profits)** Tran makes a profit of $\dfrac{x^2}{20x^2 + 10x}$ for each ticket he sells.
(Ex 5) What is his profit in terms of x if he sells $x^2 + 9x + 20$ tickets?
$\dfrac{x(x + 5)(x + 4)}{10(2x + 1)}$

Lesson 88

Practice Distributed and Integrated

1. Solve $6(x + 2) - 4x > 2 + x + 2$. $x > -8$

2. Solve and graph the inequality $4 \geq 2(x + 3)$ OR $23 < 8x + 7$. $x \leq -1$ OR $x > 2$;

Rewrite the equation in the standard form of a quadratic function, if possible.

3. $x(y - 2x) = 18x^2$ not quadratic

4. $2(y - 2x) = 6x^2$ $y = 3x^2 + 2x$

Find the distance between the given points. Give the answer in simplest radical form.

5. $(-4, -5)$ and $(2, -3)$ $2\sqrt{10}$

6. $(3, -2)$ and $(1, 0)$ $2\sqrt{2}$

Find the midpoint of the line segment with the given endpoints.

7. $(-4, -5)$ and $(2, -3)$ $(-1, -4)$

8. $(3, -2)$ and $(1, 0)$ $(2, -1)$

Find the product or quotient.

*9. $\dfrac{2y^2 + 10y}{y + 5} \cdot \dfrac{2x}{2x^3} \cdot \dfrac{2y}{x^2}$

*10. $\dfrac{6y}{x} \div \dfrac{x + y}{3y} \cdot \dfrac{18y^2}{x^2 + xy}$

*11. $\dfrac{7x}{y} \div \dfrac{4}{y}$ $\dfrac{7x}{4}$

Factor.

12. $7x - 60 + x^2$ $(x - 5)(x + 12)$

13. $64a^3b - 32a^3 + 16a^2b - 8a^2$ $8a^2(2b - 1)(4a + 1)$

14. (Woodworking) To inlay designs on the top of chest, a crafter uses a series of patterns. The area of the patterns are represented by the trinomial $x^2 + 4x - 21$. What are the dimensions of the patterns? $(x - 3) \times (x + 7)$

15. Write a compound inequality that describes the graph. $-2 < x < 2$

16. (Athletic Directing) An athletic director has a budget of $700 to buy uniforms. He will receive 5 free uniforms when he places his order. The number of uniforms, y, that he can get is given by $y = \dfrac{700}{x} + 5$, where x is the price per uniform.
   a. What is the horizontal asymptote of this rational function? $y = 5$
   b. What is the vertical asymptote? $x = 0$
   c. If the price per uniform is $50, how many uniforms will he receive?   19 uniforms
   d. Can the athletic director receive only 5 uniforms? Why or why not?

17. **Multi-Step** The area of a triangular sail in square feet is represented by the equation $\tfrac{1}{2}x^2 + \tfrac{7}{2}x + 5$.
   a. Factor this expression completely in terms of the area of a triangle.   17a. $\tfrac{1}{2}(x + 2)(x + 5)$
   b. Let $x = 3$. What is the area of the sail in square feet?   20 square feet

16d. no; Sample: The horizontal asymptote is $y = 5$. The value, 5, for y is undefined. The uniform company would not give away the five free uniforms unless other uniforms were purchased.

580   Saxon Algebra 1

18. **Write** Why is making tables and graphs a good way to show frequency distribution?
(80) Sample: They are easier to read than a long list of outcomes.

19. (Paving) A new restaurant is opening in a square building with a side length of
(83) s feet. A parking lot surrounds the building in the form of a larger square. The
restaurant sits in the middle of the lot. The plot of land on which the restaurant
and parking lot lie has an area of $9s^2 + 54s + 81$ square feet. How far does the
parking lot extend from the building? $\frac{2s + 9}{2}$ feet

*20. **Analyze** The figure shows the first four right triangles in the *Wheel of
(85) Theodorus* (named after a fifth-century Greek philosopher).

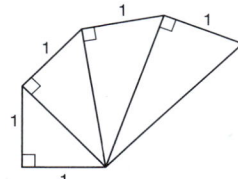

a. Find the length of the hypotenuse of each of the four triangles.

b. **Predict** Suppose the pattern of the triangles is continued until the figure
contains 10 triangles. Predict what the length of the hypotenuse of the tenth
triangle will be. $\sqrt{11}$ 20a. $\sqrt{2}$; $\sqrt{3}$; $\sqrt{4}$; $\sqrt{5}$.

21. **Multiple Choice** Which lengths represent the lengths of the sides of a right
(85) triangle? **C**

A 3, 4, 6   B $\sqrt{13}$, 5, 12

C $\sqrt{15}$, 7, 8   D 6, 8, 12

22. **Error Analysis** Students A and B find the midpoint of the line segment with
(86) endpoints $P = (12, -5)$ and $Q = (-2, 3)$. Student A says that the x-coordinate
of the midpoint is $\frac{12 - (-2)}{2} = \frac{14}{2} = 7$. Student B says that the x-coordinate of the
midpoint is $\frac{12 + (-2)}{2} = \frac{10}{2} = 5$. Which student is correct? Explain the error.

22. Student B; Sample: The midpoint formula involves adding the x-coordinates of the two points, not subtracting them.

23. (Software) A game designer is working on a computer basketball game. On the
(86) computer screen, the coordinates of the corners of the court are (20, 20), (20, 70),
(114, 70), and (114, 20). Find the length of a diagonal of the court to the nearest
tenth of a unit.   106.5

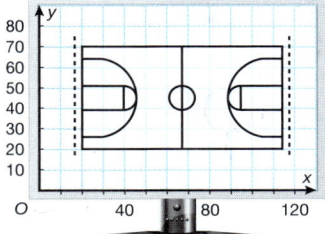

Lesson 88   581

Problem 21
Remind students that, by definition, c is the longest length.

Extend the Problem
"The longest length of a right triangle is 6 units and the shortest length is $\sqrt{14}$ units. Write a compound inequality using integers to show how long the third length is." $4 < a < 5$

ENGLISH LEARNERS

For Problem 23, explain the meaning of the word **corner.**

Say:

"A corner is a place or position where two edges or surfaces meet. The corner of the room is where the two walls meet the floor or where the two walls meet the ceiling."

Ask:

"What other items have corners?" Sample: desks, books, the end of a block on a street

Problem 24

Guide students by asking them the following questions.

"What are the dimensions of the original porch?" x by x

"What is the new length of the porch?" x + 5

"Write an equation that describes the area of the new porch." $(x + 5)(x) = 50$

Problem 30

Remind students that since $x \cdot x = x^2$, x^2 is a perfect square.

Extend the Problem

"If $x = 3$, what is the length of one side?" 25 feet

---

*24. **Measurement** Malik is adding 5 feet to the length of a screened-in porch. If the porch is originally a square room with area x^2 and the new area measures 50 square feet, what are the dimensions of the new porch?
(87)

*25. **Geometry** A rectangle has a length of $12x^2 + 3y$ and a width of $6x^2 + y$. What is its area? What is the simplest way to express the area?
(87)

26. **Multiple Choice** What is the result of a complete factoring of $25x^2 - 81$? **D**
(87)
  A $25(x + 9)(x - 9)$
  B $5x \cdot 5x - 81$
  C $5^2x^2 - 9^2$
  D $(5x + 9)(5x - 9)$

*27. **Generalize** What is the method for multiplying and dividing exponents when working with rational expressions?
(88)

*28. **Multiple Choice** Multiply $\frac{y^2 + 6y + 5}{y^2} \cdot \frac{y}{y + 1}$. **B**
(88)
  A $\frac{y + 5}{y^2}$
  B $\frac{y + 5}{y}$
  C $\frac{(y + 1)(y + 5)}{y^2}$
  D $y(y + 5)$

*29. **Murals** Lucy paints murals. She charges $10.00 per square foot. If she paints a mural that is $c^2 + 7c + 10$ ft by $\frac{1}{c + 5}$ ft, how much does Lucy charge for painting the mural? $10c + $20
(88)

30. **Multi-Step** The area of a square patio is represented by $81x^2 - 36x + 4$ square feet.
(75)
  a. Factor the expression completely. $(9x - 2)(9x - 2)$
  b. Why do you think this expression is called a perfect square? Sample: It is the product of an expression times itself.

24. width = 5 ft, length = 10 ft; $(x + 5)(x) = 50$, $x^2 + 5x - 50 = 0$, and $(x + 10)(x - 5) = 0$.

25. $3(24x^4 + 10x^2y + y^2)$; Sample: It is simpler to express the area as binomials before multiplying $(12x^2 + 3y)(6x^2 + y)$.

27. Sample: Add exponents when multiplying and subtract exponents when dividing.

582   Saxon Algebra 1

 CHALLENGE

Have students simplify the following expression using what they know about rational expressions and the order of operations.

$\frac{x^2 + 5x + 6}{x^2 + 13x + 42} \cdot \frac{x^2 + 8x + 7}{x^2 + 3x + 2}$

$\frac{(x + 3)}{(x + 6)}$

LOOKING FORWARD

Multiplying and dividing rational expressions prepares students for

- **Lesson 90** Adding and Subtracting Rational Expressions
- **Lesson 92** Simplifying Complex Fractions
- **Lesson 95** Combining Rational Expressions with Unlike Denominators
- **Lesson 99** Solving Rational Equations

LAB 8

Characteristics of Parabolas

Graphing Calculator Lab (Use with Lesson 89)

A zero of a function is an x-value where $f(x) = 0$. You can find the zeros of a parabola using a hand-drawn graph or algebraically using the equation. You can use a graphing calculator to compute approximate values, of any x-intercepts and the maximum or minimum of the parabola.

Find any x-intercepts and the maximum or minimum of the parabola $y = -2x^2 + 4x - 2$.

Graphing Calculator Tip

For help with entering an equation into the **Y =** editor, see the Graphing Calculator Lab 3 on page 305.

1. Enter the equation $y = -2x^2 + 4x - 2$ into the **Y=** editor.

2. Press 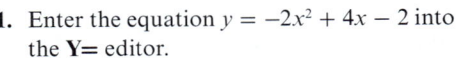 **6:ZStandard** to graph the equation.

3. Press **TRACE** and then use the ◀ and ▶ keys to move along the curve to the approximate x-intercept. The coordinates appear at the bottom of the screen. The x-intercept occurs close to the point (1.064, −0.008).

4. Find more accurate coordinates of the x-intercept.

   Press 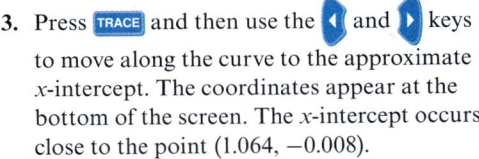 and select **2:zero**.

   Use the ◀ key to trace along the curve to a point to the left of the x-intercept and then press **ENTER**.

   Press the ▶ key to trace along the curve to a point to the right of the x-intercept and then press **ENTER**.

   Press the ◀ key to trace to a point near the x-intercept and then press **ENTER**.

   The approximate coordinates appear at the bottom of the screen. The x-intercept of the parabola occurs of about the point (1, 0).

   For this parabola, the x-intercept is also the maximum of the function.

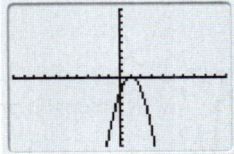
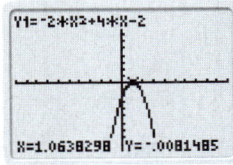
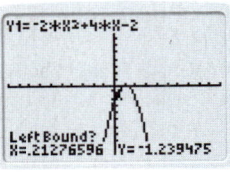
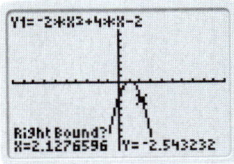
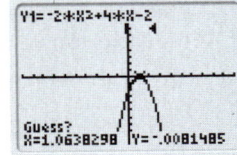
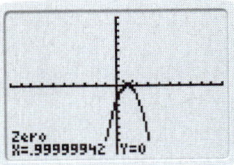

Online Connection
www.SaxonMathResources.com

Material
- graphing calculator

Discuss

Before teaching students to use a graphing calculator to graph parabolas, review quadratic functions.

Define a zero of a function.

Review with students what is meant by the x-intercept, and then give a sample coordinate for an x-intercept. Ask students if it is possible to have more than one x-intercept in a linear equation. Then ask them if it is possible to have more than one in a quadratic function.

Define maximum of a function and minimum of a function.

Ask students how graphing a quadratic function would help them to find the x-intercept, maximum, and minimum of that function.

Lab 8   583

Find any x-intercepts and the maximum or minimum of the parabola $y = x^2 - x - 2$.

5. Enter the equation $y = x^2 - x - 2$ into the **Y=** editor.

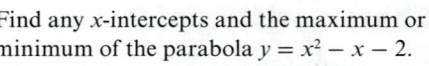

6. Press ZOOM **6:ZStandard** to graph the equation.

7. Use the keystrokes in Step 4 to find the coordinates of the two x-intercepts.

The x-intercepts of the parabola are $(-1, 0)$ and $(2, 0)$.

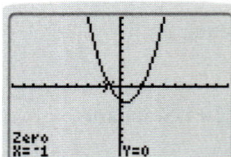 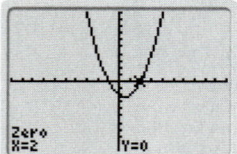

8. Find the minimum of the parabola.

Press 2nd TRACE (CALC) and select **3:minimum**.

Use the ◁ key to trace along the curve to a point on the left of the minimum and then press ENTER. Press the ▷ key to trace along the curve to a point to the right of the minimum and then press ENTER. Press the ◁ key to trace to a point near the minimum and then press ENTER.

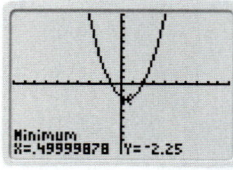

The approximate coordinates appear at the bottom of the screen. Decimal values may vary slightly. The minimum of the parabola occurs at about the point $(0.5, -2.25)$.

This parabola has three distinct characteristic points: two x-intercepts–or zeros–and one minimum.

Lab Practice

a. Graph the parabola $y = x^2 - 2x - 3$. Find any x-intercepts and the maximum or minimum of the parabola.

b. Graph the parabola $y = -x^2 - x + 6$. Find any x-intercepts and the maximum or minimum of the parabola.

a.

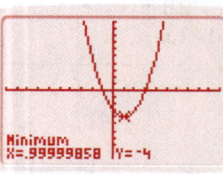

x-intercepts $(-1, 0)$ and $(3, 0)$ and minimum $(1, -4)$

b.

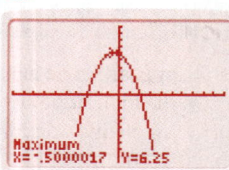

x-intercepts $(-3, 0)$ and $(2, 0)$ and maximum $(-0.5, 6.25)$

LESSON 89

Identifying Characteristics of Quadratic Functions

Warm Up

1. **Vocabulary** The U-shaped graph of a quadratic function is a(n) _____ (ellipse, parabola).   **parabola**

For each quadratic function, tell whether the graph opens upward or downward.

2. $y = -3x^2 + x - 11$ **downward**
3. $y = -8 - 7x + x^2$ **upward**
4. Evaluate $y = x^2 - 4x + 5$ for $x = -3$.   **26**
5. **Multiple Choice** Which of these functions is represented by this graph?   **C**

   A $y = 2x$
   B $y = -2x$
   C $y = 2x^2$
   D $y = -2x^2$

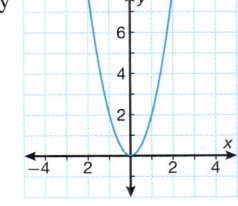

New Concepts

The **vertex of a parabola** is the highest or lowest point on a parabola. It is the parabola's "turning point."

The **minimum of a function** is the least possible value of a function and the **maximum of a function** is the greatest possible value of a function. It is the y-value of the lowest or highest point on the graph of a function. On a parabola, the minimum or maximum is the y-coordinate of the vertex.

Math Reasoning

Justify Why is the vertex a minimum when the parabola opens upward and a maximum when the parabola opens downward?

Sample: When the parabola opens upward, it has a low point, which is the vertex. When the parabola opens downward, it has a high point, which is the vertex.

Example 1 Identifying the Vertex and the Maximum or Minimum

Give the coordinates of each parabola's vertex. Then give the minimum or maximum value and the domain and range of the function.

a.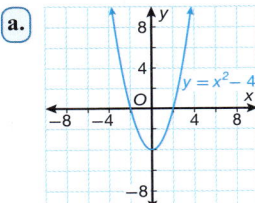

b.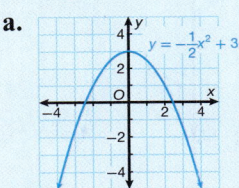

SOLUTION

The vertex appears to be at $(0, -4)$. It is the lowest point, so the minimum of the function is -4. The domain is the set of all real numbers; the range is the set of all real numbers greater than or equal to -4.

SOLUTION

The vertex appears to be at $(2, 5)$. It is the highest point, so the maximum of the function is 5. The domain is the set of all real numbers; the range is the set of all real numbers less than or equal to 5.

Lesson 89   585

MATH BACKGROUND

The domain of any quadratic function is all real numbers because any real number can be squared. The range is always restricted because the square of any real number is non-negative. In $y = x^2 + 4$, for instance, x^2 cannot be less than 0, so y cannot be less than 4.

There are two forms for writing quadratic functions: the standard form $y = ax^2 + bx + c$, $(a \neq 0)$ and the vertex form, $y = a(x - h)^2 + k$, where $(a \neq 0)$ and (h, k) is the vertex.

---

1 Warm Up

Problem 3
The equation is not written in standard form. Remind students to look at the coefficient of x^2 to determine the direction of the graph.

2 New Concepts

In this lesson, students learn about the characteristics of quadratic functions.

Example 1

Additional Example 1
Give the coordinates of each parabola's vertex. Then give the minimum or maximum value and the domain and range of the function.

a.

$(0, 3)$, maximum: 3; D: all real numbers; R: all real numbers ≤ 3

b.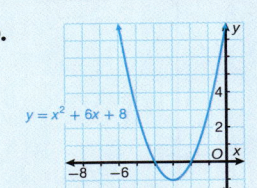

$(-3, -1)$; minimum: -1; D: all real numbers; R: all real numbers ≥ -1

LESSON RESOURCES

Student Edition Practice Workbook 89
Reteaching Master 89
Adaptations Master 89
Challenge and Enrichment Master C89
Technology Lab Master 89

Lesson 89   585

Example 2

The zeros of a function are the *x*-intercepts of the graph of the function. A quadratic function can have 0, 1, or 2 zeros.

Additional Example 2

Find the zeros of each function shown in the graph.

a. $y = x^2 + 2x - 8$

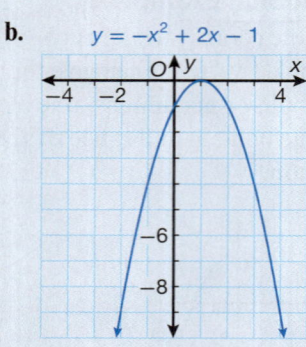

−4 and 2

b. $y = -x^2 + 2x - 1$

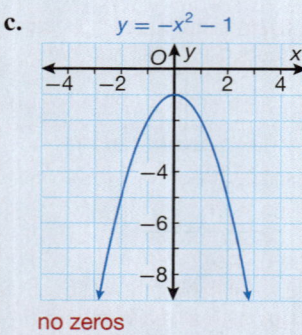

1

c. $y = -x^2 - 1$

no zeros

Error Alert For Additional Example 2c, a student may choose a *y*-intercept as a zero, especially when a graph has no *x*-intercepts. Remind them that the zero of a function must occur on the *x*-axis since the *y*-coordinates equal zero on the *x*-axis.

586   *Saxon Algebra 1*

Intercepts, zeros, and roots are related. An *x*-intercept of a function is the *x*-coordinate of the point where the graph of an equation intersects the *x*-axis. A **zero of a function** is the value of *x* that makes $f(x) = 0$, or $y = 0$. Because $y = 0$ for every value of *x* on the *x*-axis, the zeros of a function are the same as the *x*-intercepts.

Example 2 Finding Zeros from the Graph

Find the zeros of each function shown in the graph.

Math Language

The **zeros** of a quadratic function $f(x) = ax^2 + bx + c$ are the roots of the related equation

$$0 = ax^2 + bx + c.$$

a.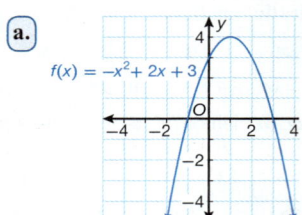

SOLUTION

The *x*-intercepts appear to be at −1 and 3. Check by substituting the ordered pairs (−1, 0) and (3, 0) into the function.

$y = -x^2 + 2x + 3$ $y = -x^2 + 2x + 3$

$0 \stackrel{?}{=} -(-1)^2 + 2 \cdot -1 + 3$ $0 \stackrel{?}{=} -(3)^2 + 2 \cdot 3 + 3$

$0 \stackrel{?}{=} -1 - 2 + 3$ $0 \stackrel{?}{=} -9 + 6 + 3$

$0 = 0$ ✓ $0 = 0$ ✓

The zeros are −1 and 3.

b.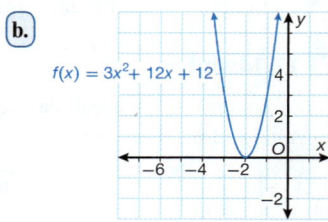

SOLUTION

The *x*-intercept appears to be at −2. Check by substituting the ordered pair (−2, 0) into the function.

$y = 3x^2 + 12x + 12$

$0 \stackrel{?}{=} 3(-2)^2 + 12 \cdot -2 + 12$

$0 \stackrel{?}{=} 12 - 24 + 12$

$0 = 0$ ✓

The zero is −2.

ENGLISH LEARNERS

For this lesson, explain the meaning of the word **axis.** Say:

"An axis is the center, often a line, around which something rotates."

Explain that the Earth spins on an imaginary axis that runs through the center of the Earth and the North and South Poles. Use a globe to illustrate, if one is available.

Likewise, an axis of symmetry runs through the center of a parabola. Draw a parabola and its axis of symmetry on the board or on a transparency. Pick two points with the same *y*-coordinates, other than the zeros, to show that they are the same distance from the axis.

Show how the *y*-axis serves as the axis of symmetry when the *x*-coordinate of the vertex is 0.

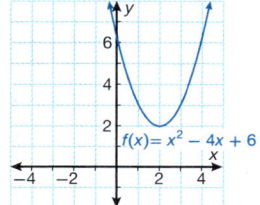

SOLUTION

The graph does not cross the x-axis, so there are no x-intercepts, and therefore no real zeros.

An **axis of symmetry** is a line that divides a figure or graph into two mirror-image halves. All parabolas have an axis of symmetry that passes through the vertex of the parabola.

In the figure, notice that the equation of the axis of symmetry includes the x-coordinate of the vertex, 2. Also notice that 2 is the average of the zeros, 1 and 3.

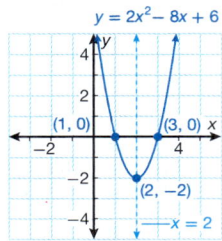

Example 3 Finding the Axis of Symmetry Using Zeros

Find the axis of symmetry for each graph.

Math Reasoning

Justify Why do the equations for the axes of symmetry begin with "$x =$" rather than "$y =$"?

Sample: They are vertical lines where every point has the same x-value.

a.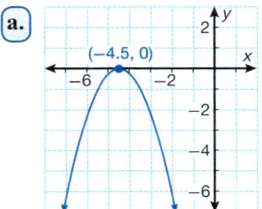

b.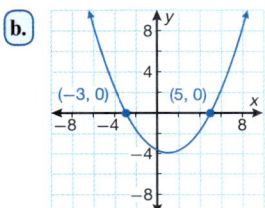

SOLUTION

When there is one zero, the zero occurs at the vertex point, so the vertex is at $(-4.5, 0)$. Use the x-coordinate of the vertex to identify the axis of symmetry: $x = -4.5$.

SOLUTION

Average the zeros to find the x-coordinate of the vertex: $\frac{-3 + 5}{2} = \frac{2}{2} = 1$. The x-coordinate of the vertex is 1. Since the axis of symmetry passes through the vertex, the equation for the axis of symmetry is $x = 1$.

Lesson 89   587

Example 3

Students can find the axis of symmetry by using the zeros of the function. Stress that all parabolas have an axis of symmetry, even those without zeros. For those without zeros, students must determine the axis of symmetry another way.

Additional Example 3

Find the axis of symmetry for each graph.

a.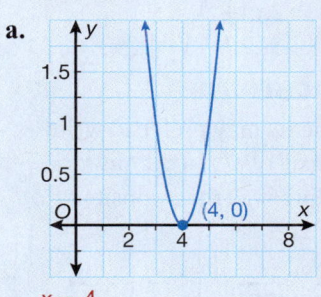

$x = 4$

b.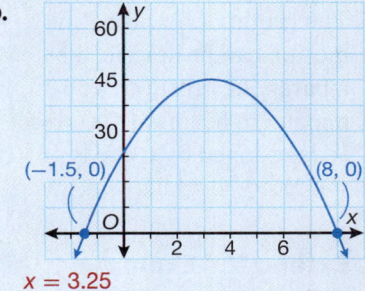

$x = 3.25$

TEACHER TIP

Point out that averaging the zeros is the same as finding the midpoint of the line segment whose endpoints are zeros.

INCLUSION

Some students can benefit from a more concrete presentation of the axis of symmetry. Before class, draw the graph of a parabola with no real solutions, such as $y = x^2 + 12x + 44$, on graph paper. Use a marker, and, if possible, thin paper that students can see through.

In class, have a student fold the graph over so that the two sides match up. Have the student make a good crease in the paper, open it up, and see where the line is. This line is the axis of symmetry.

You can run copies of the graph on a copy machine so that each student has his or her own.

Lesson 89   587

Example 4

When the function is given, students can find the axis of symmetry by using the coefficients of the quadratic and linear terms.

Additional Example 4

Find the axis of symmetry for the graph of each quadratic function.

a. $y = -x^2 - 4x + 3$ $x = -2$

b. $y = 3x^2 + 5x$ $x = 0$

TEACHER TIP

Students may prefer to write the axis of symmetry as $x = \frac{-b}{2a}$, reading it as the opposite of b over $2a$.

Example 5

The height of an object in motion can be described by a parabolic function. The maximum height of the object is determined by the axis of symmetry formula.

Extend the Example

"Find the height of the ball after 10 seconds." 10 feet

Additional Example 5

A boy standing on the roof of a building 75 feet above the ground throws a ball at 45 ft/s. Ignoring friction, the equation $y = -16t^2 + 45t + 75$ gives the height, y, as a function of time, t. Find the highest point the ball reaches. How many seconds does it take to reach this height? 106.641 ft, 1.406 s

---

The axis of symmetry can also be found by using a formula.

Math Reasoning

Analyze Describe the relationship between the vertex and the axis of symmetry.

The vertex is a point on the axis of symmetry. The axis of symmetry is a vertical line so its equation is $y =$ the x-coordinate of the vertex.

Axis of Symmetry Formula
The axis of symmetry for the graph of a quadratic equation $y = ax^2 + bx + c$ is $x = -\frac{b}{2a}$.

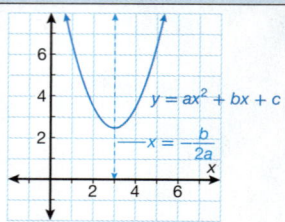

Example 4 Finding the Axis of Symmetry Using the Formula

Find the axis of symmetry for the graph of each quadratic function.

a. $y = x^2 + 6x + 5$

SOLUTION

$x = -\dfrac{b}{2a}$

$= -\dfrac{6}{2(1)}$ Substitute values.

$= -3$ Simplify.

The equation of the axis of symmetry is $x = -3$.

b. $y = -2x^2 + 3x - 1$

SOLUTION

$x = -\dfrac{b}{2a}$

$= -\dfrac{3}{2(-2)}$ Substitute values.

$= \dfrac{3}{4}$ Simplify.

The equation of the axis of symmetry is $x = \dfrac{3}{4}$.

Example 5 Application: Height of a Golf Ball

A golf ball is hit from an elevated platform 10 feet above the ground. It starts with a vertical speed of 160 feet per second. Ignoring friction, the equation $y = -16t^2 + 160t + 10$ gives the height, y, as a function of time, t. Find the highest point the ball reaches and how long it takes to reach it.

SOLUTION Find t at the vertex by using the formula for the axis of symmetry.

$t = -\dfrac{b}{2a}$ axis of symmetry formula

$= -\dfrac{160}{2(-16)}$ Use $a = -16$ and $b = 160$.

$= 5$ Simplify.

Substitute 5 for t in the equation to find the y-value of the vertex.

$y = -16t^2 + 160t + 10$

$= -16(5)^2 + 160(5) + 10$ Substitute 5 for t.

$= 410$ Simplify.

The vertex is at (5, 410). This means that 5 seconds after the golf ball is hit, it reaches a maximum height of 410 feet.

Lesson Practice

Give the coordinates of each parabola's vertex. Then give the minimum or maximum value and domain and range of the function. (Ex 1)

a. (−1, −4), maximum: −4;
D: all real numbers,
R: all real numbers less than or equal to −4

b. (5, −3), minimum: −3;
D: all real numbers,
R: all real numbers greater than or equal to −3

a.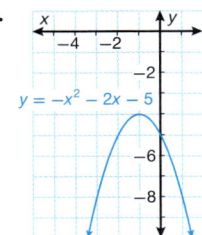

b.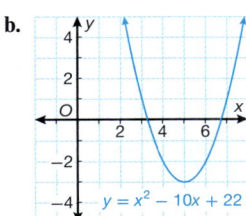

Find the zeros of each function. (Ex 2)

c. 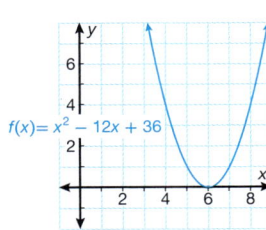 6

d. 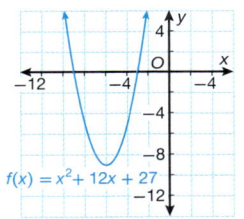 −9 and −3

e. 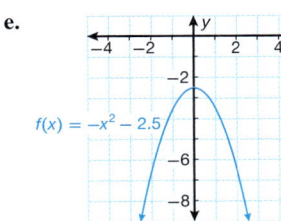 no zeros

Find the axis of symmetry for each graph. (Ex 3)

f. 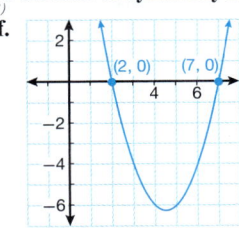 $x = 4.5$

g. 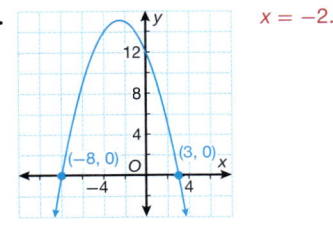 $x = -2.5$

Find the axis of symmetry for the graph of each quadratic function. (Ex 4)

h. $y = 3x^2 + 12x + 4$ $x = -2$

i. $y = -x^2 + 6x + 5$ $x = 3$

j. A chunk of lava flies out of a volcano from a height of 12,447 feet at a velocity of 608 feet per second. Find the highest point the lava reaches and how long it takes to reach it using the equation $y = -16t^2 + 608t + 12{,}447$.   18,223 ft; 19 seconds (Ex 5)

Lesson 89   589

3 Practice

Math Conversations
Discussion to strengthen understanding

Problem 1
Guide the students by asking them the following questions.

"How do you isolate the absolute-value expression?" Divide both sides by -2.

"How do you write the two equations without absolute-value symbols?" Set the expression inside the bars equal to 15 and -15.

Problem 3
Error Alert
If students graph $7 \leq x < 9$, they have not changed the direction of the inequality signs. Have students substitute a value from their graph into the equation to verify the solution set.

Problem 18
Extend the Problem
How much more expensive is the first plan when the consumer has used a total of 780 minutes? $1.40

Practice   Distributed and Integrated

Solve each equation and check your answer.

1. (74) $-2|r + 2| = -30$ $\{-17, 13\}$

2. (74) $3|r + 6| = 15$ $\{-11, -1\}$

3. (82) Solve and graph the inequality $35 < 3x + 8$ OR $72 \geq 9(x + 1)$. $x > 9$ OR $x \leq 7$;

Determine whether the polynomial is a perfect-square trinomial or a difference of two squares. Then factor the polynomial.

4. (83) $100y^2 - 80y + 16$.   perfect-square trinomial; $4(5y - 2)^2$

5. (83) $81x^2 - 1$ difference of two squares; $(9x + 1)(9x - 1)$

6. (83) Factor $9c^2 - 42c + 49$. $(3c - 7)^2$

7. (86) Find the distance between (2, 2) and the (4, 4). Give your answer in simplest radical form. $2\sqrt{2}$

Find the quotient or product.

8. (88) $\dfrac{15a + 5b}{5ab} \div (3a + b)$ $\dfrac{1}{ab}$

9. (88) $(4x + 2) \div \dfrac{2x + 1}{3y}$ $6y$

Find the axis of symmetry for the graph of each equation.

*10. (89) $y = x^2 + 4x + 6$ $x = -2$

*11. (89) $y = x^2 - x - 6$ $x = \dfrac{1}{2}$

*12. (89) **Analyze** Describe how you could use symmetry to graph a quadratic equation.

13. (73) **Traffic** You are driving on a highway that has a speed limit of 65 miles per hour and a minimum speed of 45 miles per hour. Write a compound inequality that describes this situation. $45 \leq x \leq 65$; $x \geq 45$ AND $x \leq 65$

14. (73) Use the graph to write a compound inequality as two separate inequalities. Then write a compound inequality without using the word AND. $x > 1$ AND $x \leq 5$; $1 < x \leq 5$

15. (76) **Multi-Step** Jordan is making a model of a trapezoid for her math class. Write an expression for the area of the trapezoid shown at right. Find the area.

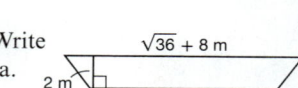

16. (79) **Tennis** A tennis ball is served at 87 miles per hour. In the expression $-16x^2 + 128x - 240$, x represents the time the ball is 246 feet high. Factor this expression completely. $-16(x - 5)(x - 3)$

17. (80) **Multi-Step** A spinner is spun 100 times. The spinner lands on brown 50 times, red 25 times, and yellow 25 times.   **17a.** $P(\text{brown}) = \dfrac{1}{2}$; $P(\text{red}) = \dfrac{1}{4}$; $P(\text{yellow}) = \dfrac{1}{4}$
a. Find the experimental probability for each color.
b. Draw a spinner that would also give this theoretical probability distribution.

17b.

18. (81) **Communication** A 400-anytime-minutes plan costs $35 plus $0.09 per minute overage. Another 400-anytime-minutes plan costs $45 plus $0.06 per minute overage. After how many overage minutes is the first plan more expensive?   334 minutes

---

15. $A = \dfrac{1}{2}h(b_1 + b_2)$

$A = \dfrac{1}{2}(2)\left[(\sqrt{49} + 4) + (\sqrt{36} + 8)\right]$

$A = (7 + 4) + (6 + 8)$

$A = 11 + 14$

$A = 25$ square meters

12. Sample: Use the formula for the axis of symmetry and sketch the axis on a graph. Substitute the x-value into the equation to find the y-value, and then plot the vertex. Use a table of ordered pairs to find values on the left (or right) side of the vertex, and then use symmetry to find the points that are mirror images of those points.

19. **Verify** Solve the inequality $2x + 8 > 2 + 5x + 6$. Then select some values of x and substitute them into the inequality to verify the solution set. See Additional Answers.

20. **Bridges** A footbridge follows the graph of the equation $y = -\frac{1}{9}x^2 + 1$. If the x-axis represents the ground and each unit on the graph represents 1 foot, what is the horizontal distance across the bridge? 6 ft

*21. **Geometry** A rectangular prism and a cylinder are both 10 inches tall. The base of the prism is a square with a side length x. The cylinder has a radius x. Graph the functions of the volumes of each solid in a coordinate plane. Then compare the graphs. See Additional Answers.

22. Use the Pythagorean Theorem to find the missing side length. Give the answer in simplest radical form. 15

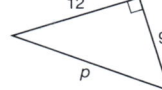

23. **Multiple Choice** Which point is the midpoint of the line segment joining $(3, 9)$ and $(-1, 2)$? **D**

   A $\left(2, \frac{11}{2}\right)$ **B** $\left(2, \frac{7}{2}\right)$ **C** $\left(-2, -\frac{7}{2}\right)$ **D** $\left(1, \frac{11}{2}\right)$

24. Describe the transformation of $f(x) = -4x$ from the linear parent function. The function is reflected about the x-axis and is vertically stretched by a factor of 4.

*25. **Multi-Step** A company is making various boxes to ship different-sized globes. The boxes have a volume of $\frac{6r^3h^2}{4r^2h} \cdot \frac{8rh^2}{3r^2h} \cdot \frac{2r^2h}{rh^2}$ and the globes have a volume of $\frac{4\pi rh}{3}$. What fraction of the boxes do the globes take up?

   a. Solve for the volume of the box. $8hr$

   b. Find the fraction of the box that the globes take up. $\frac{\pi}{6}$

*26. **Geometry** A rectangle has length $\frac{3x^2 + x}{y}$ and width $x + 2y$. What is its area? $\frac{(3x^3 + 6x^2y + x^2 + 2xy)}{y}$

*27. **Error Analysis** Two students are asked to solve the equation $\frac{6s^2 - 3s}{15} \div 2s - 1$. Which student is correct? Explain the error. Student B; Sample: Student A forgot to put the 1 in the numerator when switching to multiplication.

Student A	Student B
$\frac{6s^2 - 3s}{15} \div 2s - 1$	$\frac{6s^2 - 3s}{15} \div 2s - 1$
$\frac{6s^2 - 3s}{15} \cdot \frac{2s - 1}{1} = \frac{s(2s - 1)^2}{5}$	$\frac{6s^2 - 3s}{15} \cdot \frac{1}{2s - 1} = \frac{s}{5}$

*28. **Multiple Choice** What is the x-coordinate of the vertex of the graph of a quadratic function whose zeros are 0 and -8? **A**

   A -4 **B** 0   **C** 4   **D** 8

*29. **Space** If it were possible to play ball on Saturn, the function $y = -5.5x^2 + 44x$ would approximate the height of a ball kicked straight up at a velocity of 44 meters per second, where x is time in seconds. Find the maximum height of the ball and the time it takes the ball to reach that height. 88 meters in 4 seconds

*30. **Analyze** How does the value of a in a quadratic equation indicate if the graph of the equation has a minimum or a maximum? Sample: If the value of a is positive, the graph opens upward and has a minimum. If the value of a is negative, the graph opens downward and has a maximum.

Lesson 89   591

Problem 22
Guide the students by asking them the following questions.

"How do you find the missing side of a right triangle?" Use the Pythagorean Theorem.

"Is p the length of a leg or the length of the hypotenuse?" hypotenuse

"What are the values of a, b, and c?" Sample: a and b are 9 and 12 and c is p.

Problem 28
If the zeros are at 0 and -8, the x-coordinate of the vertex must be negative.

CHALLENGE

A farmer has 50 yards of fence to construct a rectangular kennel yard. The function $f(x) = 50x - 2x^2$ describes the areas that can be formed with x width. Find the maximum area that can be constructed.
321.5 square yards

LOOKING FORWARD

Identifying characteristics of quadratic functions prepares students for

- **Lesson 96** Graphing Quadratic Functions
- **Lesson 98** Solving Quadratic Equations by Factoring
- **Lesson 100** Solving Quadratic Equations by Graphing
- **Lesson 104** Solving Quadratic Equations by Completing the Square

LESSON 90

1 Warm Up

Problem 3
Remind students that like terms have the same variables and the same exponents.

2 New Concepts

In this lesson, students will add and subtract rational expressions with like and unlike denominators.

Example 1

A common denominator can have any number of variables or terms. As long as the denominators are alike, the numerators can be combined.

Additional Example 1
Add or subtract. Simplify your answers.

a. $\dfrac{7y}{4y^2} + \dfrac{3y}{4y^2}$ $\dfrac{5}{2y}$

b. $\dfrac{21 + 3g}{5 + g} - \dfrac{1 - g}{5 + g}$ 4

c. $\dfrac{2k^2}{k^2 + 5k - 24} - \dfrac{6k}{k^2 + 5k - 24}$
$\dfrac{2k}{k + 8}$

LESSON RESOURCES

Student Edition Practice Workbook 90
Reteaching Master 90
Adaptations Master 90
Challenge and Enrichment Master C90

LESSON 90

Adding and Subtracting Rational Expressions

Warm Up

1. **Vocabulary** One of two or more numbers or expressions that are multiplied to get a product is a(n) _____ of the product.   **factor**

2. Simplify $\dfrac{7}{12} + \dfrac{5}{18}$. $\dfrac{31}{36}$

3. Simplify $3x^4y + 7y^2 - 4x^4y$. $-x^4y + 7y^2$

4. Multiply: $6r^2(3r - 8)$. $18r^3 - 48r^2$

5. Multiply: $(x - 7)(x - 3)$. $x^2 - 10x + 21$

New Concepts

Adding and subtracting rational expressions follow the same rules as adding and subtracting fractions. If the denominators are the same, add the numerators and keep the common denominator. If the denominators are not the same, use the least common multiple of the denominators as the common denominator.

Example 1 Adding and Subtracting with Like Denominators

Add or subtract. Simplify your answers.

a. $\dfrac{2x^2}{20x} + \dfrac{3x^2}{20x}$

SOLUTION

$\dfrac{2x^2}{20x} + \dfrac{3x^2}{20x}$

$= \dfrac{5x^2}{20x}$ Add the numerators. Keep the denominator.

$= \dfrac{x}{4}$ Simplify.

b. $\dfrac{3a - 2}{a + 2} - \dfrac{a - 6}{a + 2}$

SOLUTION

$\dfrac{3a - 2}{a + 2} - \dfrac{a - 6}{a + 2}$

$= \dfrac{3a - 2 - (a - 6)}{a + 2}$ Subtract the numerators. Keep the denominator.

$= \dfrac{3a - 2 - a + 6}{a + 2}$ Distribute -1.

$= \dfrac{2a + 4}{a + 2}$ Combine like terms.

$= \dfrac{2(a + 2)}{a + 2}$ Factor and divide out common factors.

$= 2$

Caution
Not enclosing the numerator of the subtrahend in parentheses may result in sign errors.

Online Connection
www.SaxonMathResources.com

592   Saxon Algebra 1

MATH BACKGROUND

As with fractions, rational expressions need a common denominator before students can add or subtract them. Once the denominators are alike, students can combine the numerators and keep the same denominator for the sum or difference.

The same rules that applied to adding fractions apply to adding rational expressions: for $c \neq 0$, $\dfrac{a}{c} \pm \dfrac{b}{c} = \dfrac{a \pm b}{c}$.

Likewise, the same rules of factoring binomials and trinomials still apply: for $c \neq 0$, $\dfrac{a(x + b)}{c(x + b)} = \dfrac{a}{c}$.

c. $\dfrac{z^3 - 10z^2}{z^2 - 3z - 18} + \dfrac{4z^2}{z^2 - 3z - 18}$

SOLUTION

$\dfrac{z^3 - 10z^2}{z^2 - 3z - 18} + \dfrac{4z^2}{z^2 - 3z - 18}$

$= \dfrac{z^3 - 10z^2 + 4z^2}{z^2 - 3z - 18}$ Add the numerators. Keep the denominator.

$= \dfrac{z^3 - 6z^2}{z^2 - 3z - 18}$ Combine like terms.

$= \dfrac{z^2(z - 6)}{(z - 6)(z + 3)}$ Factor. Divide out common factors.

$= \dfrac{z^2}{z + 3}$ Simplify.

When the rational expressions being added or subtracted do not have common denominators, use the least common multiple (LCM) to rename each expression.

Example 2 Adding with Unlike Denominators

Add. Simplify your answers.

$\dfrac{2h^4}{6h} + \dfrac{4h^2}{2h^2}$

SOLUTION

Rename the expressions so that each has a denominator of $6h^2$.

$\dfrac{2h^4}{6h} + \dfrac{4h^2}{2h^2}$

$= \dfrac{2h^4}{6h}\left(\dfrac{h}{h}\right) + \dfrac{4h^2}{2h^2}\left(\dfrac{3}{3}\right)$ Multiply to get common denominators.

$= \dfrac{2h^5}{6h^2} + \dfrac{12h^2}{6h^2}$ Multiply. The LCD is $6h^2$.

$= \dfrac{2h^5 + 12h^2}{6h^2}$ Add the numerators. Keep the denominator.

$= \dfrac{2h^2(h^3 + 6)}{2h^2(3)}$ Factor and divide out the common factors.

$= \dfrac{h^3 + 6}{3}$ Simplify.

Hint

Remember to multiply the numerator and denominator by the same value when finding a common denominator.

Example 2

The product of the denominators is not necessarily the least common denominator. Using the LCD reduces the possibility of errors as well as the amount of simplifying to be done later in the problem.

Additional Example 2

Add or subtract. Simplify your answer.

$\dfrac{1}{5x^3} + \dfrac{4x}{10x}$ $\dfrac{1 + 2x^3}{5x^3}$

Error Alert Students may forget that they can only divide out factors. For instance, in Example 2, 6 is an addend, not a factor. If treated as a factor, the result is $h^3 + 2$. Encourage students to check their answers by substituting values in both the original expressions and their simplified expressions to see if the results are the same.

Lesson 90 593

ENGLISH LEARNERS

For this lesson, explain the meaning of the phrase **common denominator.** Say:

"A common denominator among a group of people is a characteristic that everyone in the group shares."

Discuss that a common denominator among a group of friends might be that they all enjoy watching soccer or playing chess. It is something that includes everyone.

ALTERNATE METHOD FOR EXAMPLE 2

Suggest to students that it is sometimes easier to simplify each expression first.

$\dfrac{2h^4}{6h} + \dfrac{4h^2}{2h^2}$

$\dfrac{\cancel{2} \cdot h^{\cancel{4}3}}{\cancel{6}3 \cdot \cancel{h}} + \dfrac{\cancel{4}2 \cdot \cancel{h^2}}{\cancel{2}1 \cdot \cancel{h^2}}$

$\dfrac{h^3}{3} + \dfrac{2}{1}$

$\dfrac{h^3}{3} + \dfrac{2(3)}{1(3)} = \dfrac{h^3 + 6}{3}$

Lesson 90 593

Example 3

Students will find a common denominator before subtracting.

Additional Example 3

$\dfrac{x+3}{x-1} - \dfrac{x+5}{x^2+8x-9}$ $\dfrac{x^2+11x+22}{(x-1)(x+9)}$

Example 4

Denominators are opposites, so multiply by −1 to find the common denominator.

Extend the Example

Check the answer by finding the value of both the simplified expression and the original expression when $v = 10$. $\dfrac{5}{6}$

Additional Example 4

$\dfrac{6}{a-3} + \dfrac{4a}{3-a}$ $\dfrac{2(2a-3)}{3-a}$

TEACHER TIP

Point out to students that it will not always be possible to divide out factors after the expressions are combined.

Example 5

When the distance formula is rearranged to solve for either rate or time, the resulting expression is a fraction. When solving for time, the numerator is distance. The value in the numerators will be the same for round trips.

Additional Example 5

The force Sarah exerts when paddling a canoe causes it to travel at an average rate of 2 mph. She paddles 8 miles upstream, turns around, and paddles 4 miles downstream. Write and simplify an expression for the total time Sarah is paddling assuming that the current speed c remains constant. $\dfrac{4(6+c)}{(2-c)(2+c)}$

Example 3 **Subtracting with Unlike Denominators**

Subtract. Simplify your answers.

$$\dfrac{x+3}{x-4} - \dfrac{2}{x^2+x-20}$$

SOLUTION

$\dfrac{x+3}{x-4} - \dfrac{2}{x^2+x-20}$

$= \dfrac{x+3}{x-4} - \dfrac{2}{(x-4)(x+5)}$ Factor the denominators.

$= \dfrac{x+3}{x-4}\left(\dfrac{x+5}{x+5}\right) - \dfrac{2}{(x-4)(x+5)}$ Write each expression using the LCD.

$= \dfrac{x^2+8x+15}{(x-4)(x+5)} - \dfrac{2}{(x-4)(x+5)}$ Multiply.

$= \dfrac{x^2+8x+13}{(x-4)(x+5)}$ Subtract.

The numerator cannot be factored; the expression is in simplified form.

Example 4 **Simplifying with Opposite Denominators**

Add. Simplify your answer.

$$\dfrac{8}{v-4} + \dfrac{v-7}{4-v}$$

SOLUTION

The denominators are opposites. Multiplying either denominator by −1 will make both denominators the same.

$\dfrac{8}{v-4} + \dfrac{v-7}{4-v}$

$= \dfrac{8}{v-4}\left(\dfrac{-1}{-1}\right) + \dfrac{v-7}{4-v}$ Multiply the numerator and denominator by −1.

$= \dfrac{-8}{4-v} + \dfrac{v-7}{4-v}$ Simplify.

$= \dfrac{-8+v-7}{4-v}$ Add numerators.

$= \dfrac{v-15}{4-v}$ Combine like terms.

Hint

A plane flying into a headwind is going against the wind, and is therefore slower. A plane with a tailwind is flying with the wind, and is therefore faster.

Example 5 **Application: Transportation**

A plane flies 2000 miles with a headwind and makes the return trip with a tailwind. Write and simplify an expression for the total time of the round-trip flight assuming that the wind speed w remains constant and the plane's rate averages 500 miles per hour.

 INCLUSION

In Example 5, help students organize their work by setting up a distance/rate/time table.

	Distance	Rate	Time
Going	2000	$500 - w$	$\dfrac{2000}{500-w}$
Returning	2000	$500 + w$	$\dfrac{2000}{500+w}$

SOLUTION

Rearrange the distance formula $t = \frac{d}{r}$, and use it to write expressions for the time of each flight. Then add the expressions.

$$\text{time going} = \frac{2000}{500 - w} \qquad \text{time returning} = \frac{2000}{500 + w}$$

$$\text{total time} = \frac{2000}{500 - w} + \frac{2000}{500 + w}$$

$$= \frac{2000}{500 - w}\left(\frac{500 + w}{500 + w}\right) + \frac{2000}{500 + w}\left(\frac{500 - w}{500 - w}\right)$$

$$= \frac{1{,}000{,}000 + 2000w}{(500 - w)(500 + w)} + \frac{1{,}000{,}000 - 2000w}{(500 - w)(500 + w)}$$

$$= \frac{2{,}000{,}000 + 2000w - 2000w}{(500 - w)(500 + w)} = \frac{2{,}000{,}000}{(500 - w)(500 + w)}$$

The expression $\frac{2{,}000{,}000}{(500 - w)(500 + w)}$, where w is the wind speed, represents the time of the round-trip flight.

Math Reasoning

Estimate About how long is the round-trip flight if the wind speed is 50 mph?

about 8 hours

Lesson Practice

Add or subtract. Simplify your answers.

a. (Ex 1) $\frac{4mn}{24m} + \frac{11mn}{24m}$ $\frac{5n}{8}$

b. (Ex 1) $\frac{7y - 2}{y + 6} - \frac{y - 38}{y + 6}$ 6

c. (Ex 1) $\frac{d^4 + 2d^3}{d^2 - 5d - 36} + \frac{2d^3}{d^2 - 5d - 36}$ $\frac{d^3}{d - 9}$

d. (Ex 2) $\frac{-3p}{6p^2} + \frac{2p^3}{p^4}$ $\frac{3}{2p}$

e. (Ex 3) $\frac{x}{x + 3} - \frac{3}{x^2 + 5x + 6}$ $\frac{x - 1}{x + 2}$

f. (Ex 4) $\frac{-1}{t^4 - 2} + \frac{t + 9}{2 - t^4}$ $\frac{-t - 10}{t^4 - 2}$

g. (Ex 5) A kayaker paddles 5 miles one way against the current and then makes the return trip with the current. Write and simplify an expression for the total time of the kayaking trip, assuming that the rate of the current remains constant and that the kayaker's paddling rate averages 1.5 miles per hour. $\frac{15}{(1.5 - c)(1.5 + c)}$

Practice Distributed and Integrated

Find the distance between the given points. Give the answer in simplest radical form.

1. (86) $(-3, -1)$ and $(4, 2)$ $\sqrt{58}$

2. (86) $(1, 1)$ and $(9, 1)$ 8

Factor completely.

3. (75) $12 + 17x + 6x^2$ $(2x + 3)(3x + 4)$

4. (75) $21t + 4t^2 - 49$ $(t + 7)(4t - 7)$

Determine whether the polynomial is a perfect-square trinomial or a difference of two squares. Then factor the polynomial.

5. (83) $9x^4 + 42x^2y + 49y^2$ perfect-square trinomial; $(3x^2 + 7y)^2$

6. (83) $x^6 + 16x^3 + 64$ perfect-square trinomial; $(x^3 + 8)^2$

Lesson 90   595

Problem 7
Students might be more comfortable seeing the function written as $y = -\frac{1}{2}x^2$.

Problem 16
Make a table for the amounts of each type of dog food for each day. Have students complete the table.

Day	Adult	Puppy
0	0	20
1	2	17
2	4	14
3	6	11

Then have students state the patterns they see. The numbers in the adult column increase by 2, the numbers in the puppy column decrease by 3. Have them translate these patterns into algebra, where the variable is the day number. adult = 2x and puppy = 20 - 3x

Extend the Problem
How many total ounces of food does Marisa's dog receive on Day 4? Day 5? Day 6?
16 oz, 15 oz, 14 oz

Problem 20
Error Alert
Some students may confuse finding a square root with dividing by 2. Have these students square their expression to see that it does not equal the original expression.

---

7. Graph the function $y = \frac{-x^2}{2}$. *(84)*

8. Multiply $\dfrac{2x - 16}{6x^2} \cdot \dfrac{3y^2 + 3x}{3x - 24}$. $\dfrac{y^2 + x}{3x^2}$ *(88)*

9. Solve $|n + 3| + 4 = 4$. $\{-3\}$ *(74)*

10. Find the axis of symmetry for the graph of the equation $y = -3x^2 + 8x + 1$. $x = 1\frac{1}{3}$ *(89)*

7.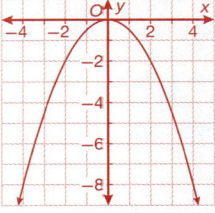

Add or subtract.

*11. $\dfrac{7x}{y} - \dfrac{2}{y}$ $\dfrac{7x-2}{y}$ *(90)*

*12. $\dfrac{4y}{x} - \dfrac{5y}{2x}$ $\dfrac{3y}{2x}$ *(90)*

13. **Marine Biology** A marine biologist netted a sample of wild sardines from the northern Pacific. In his analysis of the sample, the average length of an adult male fish was 210 millimeters. He noted that the greatest variation in length from the average length in the sample was ±33 millimeters. Write and solve an absolute-value equation to find the lengths of the longest and shortest sardines in the sample. $|x - 210| = 33$; 243 mm, 177 mm *(74)*

14. **Multi-Step** A student has grades 75 and 90 on his first two math tests. He wants to have an average of at least 80 after his third test. To find what score he needs, solve the inequality $\dfrac{75 + 90 + x}{3} \geq 80$. $x \geq 75$; Sample: He needs to make a score of 75 or better on his third test to have an 80 average. *(77)*

15. **Chess** All the chess pieces are put in a bag and one is drawn randomly. There are 2 kings, 2 queens, 4 rooks, 4 bishops, 4 knights, and 16 pawns. Make a graph to show the frequency distribution of the pieces. *(80)*

16b. Sample: The solution set is all whole numbers greater than 4, so after 4 days there will always be more adult formula than puppy formula.

16. **Multi-Step** Marisa is changing her dog's food from a puppy formula to an adult formula. The vet recommended that she exchange 2 ounces of adult formula for 3 ounces of puppy formula each day. Her dog usually eats 20 ounces of food per day. After how many days will the dog's daily diet include more adult formula than puppy formula? *(81)*
  a. Write and solve an inequality. $2f > 20 - 3f$; $f > 4$
  b. Explain the correct domain of the solution set.

15.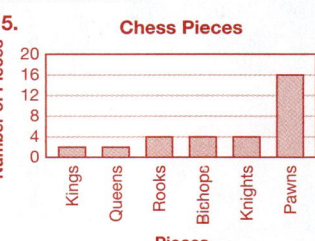

17. **Write** What does an AND inequality mean? Sample: that each inequality must be satisfied in the range of answers *(82)*

18. **Coordinate Geometry** Use the points (2, 2), (5, 2), and (2, −3). *(85)*
  a. **Write** Explain why the triangle is a right triangle.
  b. What are the lengths of the legs of the triangle? 5 and 3
  c. Use the Pythagorean Theorem to find the length of the hypotenuse. $\sqrt{34}$

19. **Astronomy** Eli is looking at three stars on a star map. He measures and records the distances between each pair of stars: 9 centimeters, 12 centimeters, and 15 centimeters. Do the stars on the map determine a right triangle? yes *(85)*

18a. Sample: The vertical segment joining (2, 2) and (2, −3) is perpendicular to the horizontal segment joining (2, 2) and (5, 2).

20. **Multi-Step** The area of a square is equal to $x^2 + 6x + 9$. What is the side length of the square? *(87)*
  a. Write the formula for the area of a square. s^2
  b. Factor the area. $(x + 3)(x + 3) = (x + 3)^2$
  c. Set the expressions equal to each other. $(x + 3)^2 = s^2$
  d. Find the square root of each side. $(x + 3) = s$

596   Saxon Algebra 1

🌟 CHALLENGE

Have advanced learners simplify this rational expression.

$$\dfrac{3x^6y}{x^4 + 2x^2y + y^2} + \dfrac{y}{x^5y + x^3y^2} \quad \dfrac{3x^9y + x^2 + y}{x^3(x^2 + y)^2}$$

21. The area of a triangle varies jointly with the base and height of the triangle. Given that the area of a triangle is 6 square feet, the base is 3 feet, and the height is 4 feet, find the constant of variation. Express the area of a triangle. $k = \frac{1}{2}; A = \frac{1}{2}bh$

22. Multiple Choice Divide $\frac{3mn^2}{4m^2n} \div \frac{9mn}{8m^3n^2}$. C

A $\frac{2mn^2}{3m}$ B $\frac{2mn}{3n^2}$ C $\frac{2mn^2}{3}$ D $\frac{27}{32m^3}$

23. (Travel Times) Use the formula $\frac{d}{r} = t$ to find how long it takes to travel a distance of $x^2 - 25$ miles at the rate of $x + 5$ miles per hour. $x - 5$ hours

24. Error Analysis Two students tried to find the axis of symmetry for the equation $y = x^2 - 4x - 3$. Which student is correct? Explain the error. Student B; Sample: Student A did not take the opposite of b.

Student A	Student B
$x = \frac{-b}{2a} = \frac{-4}{2(1)} = \frac{-4}{2} = -2$	$x = \frac{-(-4)}{2(1)} = \frac{4}{2} = 2$

*25. Multi-Step The population of Ireland between the years 1901 and 2006 can be approximated by the function $y = 0.000285x^2 - 0.0232x + 3.336$, where x is the number of years after 1900 and y is the population for that year in millions of people.

a. **Justify** Tell how you know the function has a minimum rather than a maximum.

b. **Estimate** What was the minimum population and when did it occur? Round to the nearest year.

c. **Predict** Use the function to predict the population of Ireland in 2020. about 4.66 million people

*26. Geometry The equation $y = -x^2 + 35x$ gives the area of a rectangle with a fixed perimeter of 70 units, where x is the width of the rectangle. Explain how to use the equation to find the greatest possible area of the rectangle.

*27. Multiple Choice Simplify $\frac{6}{9q^2} - \frac{3q}{9q^2}$. C

A $\frac{1}{3q}$ B $\frac{2}{3q}$ C $\frac{2-q}{3q^2}$ D $\frac{3(2-q)}{q^2}$

*28. (Business) Ms. Suarez owns a manufacturing company. Her total profits for one year are $x^2 + 44x + 420$, where x is the number of units manufactured. Her profits for the spring are $x^2 + 7x + 100$, while her profits for the winter are $17x + 40$. Write a simplified expression for the fraction of the total profits that come from the spring and winter seasons. $\frac{x+10}{x+30}$

*29. Justify When adding $\frac{5n}{n^4p^3} + \frac{6p}{n^2p^5}$, why multiply the first expression by $\frac{p^2}{p^2}$ and the second by $\frac{n^2}{n^2}$? Sample: Multiplying by these expressions makes each of the denominators equal to the LCD of n^4p^5.

*30. Write Describe the steps in adding and simplifying $\frac{2}{x^2+6x+9} + \frac{x}{x+3}$.

Sample: Factor the denominator of the first term: $(x+3)(x+3)$. Multiply the second expression by $\frac{x+3}{x+3}$. The numerator of the second expression becomes $x^2 + 3x$. The sum of the numerators is $x^2 + 3x + 2$, which factors into $(x+2)(x+1)$. No common factors cancel, so the answer is $\frac{(x+2)(x+1)}{(x+3)(x+3)} = \frac{(x+2)(x+1)}{(x+3)^2}$.

Problem 22
Error Alert
Students who answered **D** forgot to take the reciprocal of the second expression. Stress that there are two steps to dividing: changing the operation and taking the reciprocal.

Problem 25
Extend the Problem
What was the approximate population of Ireland in 1900?
3,336,000

25a. Sample: It has a minimum because the value of a is positive, which means it opens upward and the vertex is the lowest point.

25b. Sample: The minimum population occurred 41 years after 1900, or during 1941. The population was about 2.86 million people.

26. Sample: Find the axis of symmetry to find the x-coordinate of the vertex: $x = -\frac{35}{2(-1)} = 17.5$. Substitute 17.5 into the equation for x to find the area, y: $y = -x^2 + 35x = -(17.5)^2 + 35 \cdot 17.5 = 306.25$.

Lesson 90   597

LOOKING FORWARD

Adding and subtracting rational expressions prepares students for

- **Lesson 92** Simplifying Complex Fractions
- **Lesson 95** Combining Rational Expressions with Unlike Denominators
- **Lesson 99** Solving Rational Equations

Lesson 90   597

INVESTIGATION 9

Materials
- algebra tiles

Alternate Materials
- small squares of colored paper instead of algebra tiles

Discuss

In this investigation, students learn to factor polynomials by using a checklist and doing an activity.

Discuss greatest common factor, difference of two perfect squares, and perfect-square trinomials.

Remind students that an expression is not factored completely until all factors cannot be factored further.

Problem 4
Extend the Problem
Have students multiply out the factors to verify that they get the original polynomial.

TEACHER TIP

Students may not recognize that a polynomial is in quadratic form if the degree of the polynomial is even and greater than 2. Review the Power of a Power Property of exponents. Tell students to rewrite the power x^{2n} as $(x^n)^2$.

INVESTIGATION RESOURCES

Reteaching Master
Investigation 9

INVESTIGATION 9

Choosing a Factoring Method

Whole numbers can be factored into prime numbers. For example, 30 can be written as a product of its factors: $30 = 2 \cdot 3 \cdot 5$. A factorization can be verified as correct by multiplying the factors and verifying that the product is the same as the original whole number. Similarly, many polynomials, as shown below, can also be factored.

$$x^3y + 2xy^2 \qquad x^3 + 7x^2 + 2x + 14 \qquad x^2 - 4$$
$$x^2 + 16x + 64 \qquad x^2 + 8x + 15 \qquad 2x^2 + 7x + 3$$

The difference between factoring whole numbers and polynomials is that often the factors of polynomials are other polynomials and not whole numbers. Factorization can be checked through multiplication and simplification. If the original polynomial results after correctly multiplying and simplifying, the polynomial has been factored correctly. If not, try again, or the polynomial may in fact be prime.

Many possibilities and methods exist for factoring. To begin the factoring process, it is helpful to have a checklist.

Checklist Item 1: Look for the greatest common factor. Does each term have a common factor?

For example, factor $x^3y + 2xy^2$.

1. Write each term of the polynomial as a product of its factors.
   $x \cdot x \cdot x \cdot y + 2 \cdot x \cdot y \cdot y$
2. What does each term of the polynomial have in common? xy
3. Factor out the monomial from each term. $xy(x^2) + xy(2y)$
4. Now factor out the monomial from the polynomial. $xy(x^2 + 2y)$

Checklist Item 2: Look for a difference of two squares. Are there only two terms of the polynomial, and are they being subtracted? Are those two terms perfect squares?

For example, factor $x^2 - 4$.

5. To begin the process of factoring, start with the first item on the checklist and proceed. Is there a common factor for all terms in the binomial? no
6. Are there only two terms being subtracted? yes
7. The polynomial is a binomial of the form $a^2 - b^2$. What is the value of a? b? $a = x; b = 2$
8. Use the factorization of the difference of two squares, $a^2 - b^2 = (a + b)(a - b)$, to factor the binomial. $(x + 2)(x - 2)$
9. If the two terms of the binomial were perfect squares being added, $(x^2 + 4)$, could that binomial be factored similarly? no

Online Connection
www.SaxonMathResources.com

598 *Saxon Algebra 1*

MATH BACKGROUND

Students have already learned many different ways to factor binomials and trinomials. Here they are combining the different methods to factor polynomials.

They will also have a chance to model the factoring using algebra tiles, which will help kinesthetic learners to better visualize the factoring process.

Students should be able to recognize the special products and patterns by looking at them, and therefore be able to use them in factoring polynomials.

Checklist Item 3: Look for perfect-square trinomials. Are the first and last terms perfect squares? Is the second term the product of the square roots of the first and last term?

For example, factor $x^2 + 16x + 64$.

10. Is there a common factor for all terms in the polynomial? **no**
11. How many terms exist in the polynomial? **three**
12. Are the first and last terms perfect squares? If so, what are their respective square roots? **yes; x, 8**
13. Notice that the trinomial is of the form $a^2 + 2ab + b^2$. What is the value of a? b? **$a = x; b = 8$**
14. Use the formula $a^2 + 2ab + b^2 = (a + b)^2$ for factoring a perfect-square trinomial. **$(x + 8)^2$**
15. **Model** Is it possible to factor $x^2 + 8x + 32$ in a similar manner? Explain.

15. no; Sample: The value of a is x, but 32 is not a perfect square.

Checklist Item 4: Are there three terms of the polynomial, all of which are being added? Is the last term not a perfect square?

Some trinomials of the form $x^2 + bx + c$ that are not perfect-square trinomials can still be factored as the product of two binomials, such as $(x + j)(x + k)$, where $c = jk$ and $b = j + k$.

For example, factor $x^2 + 8x + 15$.

16. Is there a common factor for all terms in the polynomial? **no**
17. Is this a perfect-square trinomial? Explain.
18. Is the trinomial of the form $x^2 + (j + k)x + jk$? If so, find two values that add to 8 and multiply to 15. What is the value of j? k?
19. Factor the polynomial using the formula for factoring a trinomial that is not a perfect square. **$(x + 3)(x + 5)$**

17. no; Sample: 15 is not a perfect square.

18. yes; $j = 3$ and $k = 5$ or $j = 5$ and $k = 3$

Checklist Item 5: Are there four terms in the polynomial? If you have four terms with no GCF, try to group the terms into smaller polynomials. Then factor each group by its GCF.

For example, factor $x^3 + 7x^2 + 2x + 14$.

20. Is there a common factor for all terms in the polynomial? **no**
21. How many terms are in the polynomial? **four**
22. Use parentheses to group the first two terms and the last two terms.
23. Factor out the GCF of the first group of terms. **$x^2(x + 7)$**
24. Factor out the GCF of the second group of terms. **$2(x + 7)$**
25. Write the polynomial using the factored groups of terms.
26. What factor does each term have in common? **$(x + 7)$**
27. Factor out the common factor. **$(x + 7)(x^2 + 2)$**

22. $(x^3 + 7x^2) + (2x + 14)$

25. $x^2(x + 7) + 2(x + 7)$

Problems 5–9
Discuss with students examples of perfect squares, such as 4, 9, 16, 25, 36, 49, 64, 81, and 100.

Remind students that the formula for the difference of two perfect squares is as follows:

$a^2 - b^2 = (a + b)(a - b)$.

Problems 10–15
Remind students that the formulas for a perfect-square trinomial are as follows:

$a^2 + 2ab + b^2 = (a + b)^2$ and
$a^2 - 2ab + b^2 = (a - b)^2$.

Problem 19
Remind students that they can check their answer by using the FOIL method.

CHALLENGE

Have students explain why the following expressions are equal.

$$\frac{2x^2 + 24x + 70}{2x + 14} = (x + 5)$$

Sample: When factored, the numerator is $(2x + 14)(x + 5)$. $(2x + 14)$ divides out, resulting in $(x + 5) = (x + 5)$.

Problems 28–32

Guide students by asking them the following questions.

"If b and c are both positive in a trinomial in the form $ax^2 + bx + c$, what will the signs in the binomial factors be?" both positive

"If b is negative and c is positive in a trinomial in the form $ax^2 + bx + c$, what will the signs in the binomial factors be?" both negative

"If c is negative in a trinomial in the form $ax^2 + bx + c$, what will the signs in the binomial factors be?" one positive, one negative

---

Some trinomials of the form $ax^2 + bx + c$ can also be factored. The following activity will demonstrate this factorization through the use of algebra tiles.

Exploration Factoring Trinomials of the Form $ax^2 + bx + c$ Using Algebra Tiles

Factor $2x^2 + 7x + 3$.

Collect two x^2-tiles, seven x-tiles, and three 1-tiles.

28. Build a rectangle using the algebra tiles. Keep the x^2-tiles on the top row of the rectangle. Fill in the x-tiles horizontally below and vertically to the right of the x^2-tiles. Use the 1-tiles to fill in the gaps of the rectangle. Remember that the lines between the tiles must be completely vertical or horizontal across the entire pattern.

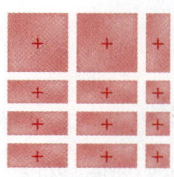

Observe that the top edge of the pattern represents the length of a rectangle. The side edge of the pattern represents the width of a rectangle.

29. Using the sides without the x^2-tiles, how can the length and width of the rectangle be represented? Sample: $2x + 1$; $x + 3$
30. How is the area of a rectangle calculated? Multiply the length times the width.
31. Write an expression for the area of the rectangle using the length and width previously found. $(2x + 1)(x + 3)$
32. What is the factored form of $2x^2 + 7x + 3$? $(2x + 1)(x + 3)$

To review factoring polynomials, first look for common factors of the terms. If there is a common factor, find the GCF, and then factor it out of the polynomial. After factoring out the GCF, look for patterns.

Pattern 1: If the polynomial has two terms, then look for the difference of two squares.

Pattern 2: If the polynomial has three terms, look for a perfect-square trinomial. If the trinomial is not a perfect square, try to factor using the method for general trinomials of the form $x^2 + bx + c$ or $ax^2 + bx + c$.

Pattern 3: If the polynomial has four terms, try to factor by grouping.

Examine the resulting polynomial factor(s) to determine if any can be factored further. If so, continue the process. If not, factoring is complete. Remember that the factored result can always be verified through multiplication and simplification.

600   Saxon Algebra 1

---

eL ENGLISH LEARNERS

Explain to students the meaning of the word **monomial**. Say:

"Mono means one, so a monomial is a single term in algebra."

Compare the word monomial with polynomial and binomial. Explain that poly- means many, which means there is more than one term and that bi- means two, which means that there are two terms.

Investigation Practice

Factor the polynomial.

a. $x^2 + 2x + 1$ $(x + 1)^2$

b. $3x^2 + xy - 12x - 4y$ $(3x + y)(x - 4)$

c. $9y^4 - 1$ $(3y^2 - 1)(3y^2 + 1)$

Identify the first step needed to factor the polynomial. Then use that method to factor the polynomial. List other methods used, if applicable.

d. $5x^4 - 5x^2$ GCF; $5x^2(x + 1)(x - 1)$; difference of squares

e. $9x^2 + 30x + 25$ perfect-square trinomial; $(3x + 5)^2$

f. $x^2 - 9$ difference of squares; $(x + 3)(x - 3)$

Use algebra tiles to factor the following polynomials. Verify the factorization through multiplication and simplification.

g. $3x^2 + 13x + 4$ $(3x + 1)(x + 4)$

h. $x^2 + 9x + 20$ $(x + 4)(x + 5)$

i. $2x^2 + 8x + 6$ $(2x + 2)(x + 3)$

Investigation Practice

Math Conversations
Discussion to strengthen understanding

Problem a

Scaffolding Guide the students by asking them the following questions.

"What kind of special polynomial is this?" perfect-square trinomial

"How can you recognize when a trinomial is a perfect-square trinomial?" c is a perfect square and $|b|$ is twice the square root of c.

"Use the formula $a^2 + 2ab + b^2 = (a + b)^2$ for factoring a perfect-square trinomial."

Problem d

Error Alert
Some students may stop after factoring out the GCF. Remind them that an expression is not completely factored until all factors, such as $x^2 - 1$ in this case, cannot be factored further.

LOOKING FORWARD

Choosing a factoring method prepares students for

• **Lesson 93** Dividing Polynomials

• **Lesson 95** Combining Rational Expressions with Unlike Denominators

SECTION OVERVIEW 10

Lesson Planner

Lesson	New Concepts
91	Solving Absolute-Value Inequalities
92	Simplifying Complex Fractions
93	Dividing Polynomials
94	Solving Multi-Step Absolute-Value Equations
95	Combining Rational Expressions with Unlike Denominators
	Cumulative Test 18, Performance Task 18
96	Graphing Quadratic Functions
LAB 9	Graphing Calculator Lab: Graphing Linear Inequalities
97	Graphing Linear Inequalities
98	Solving Quadratic Equations by Factoring
99	Solving Rational Equations
100	Solving Quadratic Equations by Graphing
	Cumulative Test 19, Performance Task 19
INV 10	Investigation: Transforming Quadratic Equations

Resources for Teaching
- Student Edition
- Teacher's Edition
- Student Edition eBook
- Teacher's Edition eBook
- Resources and Planner CD
- Solutions Manual
- Instructional Masters
- Technology Lab Masters
- Warm Up and Teaching Transparencies
- Instructional Presentations CD
- Online activities, tools and homework help www.SaxonMathResources.com

Resources for Practice and Assessment
- Student Edition Practice Workbook
- Course Assessments
- Standardized Test Practice
- College Entrance Exam Practice
- Test and Practice Generator CD using ExamView™

Resources for Differentiated Instruction
- Reteaching Masters
- Challenge and Enrichment Masters
- Prerequisite Skills Intervention
- Adaptations for Saxon Algebra 1
- Multilingual Glossary
- English Learners Handbook
- TI Resources

Pacing Guide

 Resources and Planner CD for lesson planning support

45-Minute Class

Day 1	Day 2	Day 3	Day 4	Day 5	Day 6
Lesson 91	Lesson 92	Lesson 93	Lesson 94	Lesson 95	Cumulative Test 18
Day 7	**Day 8**	**Day 9**	**Day 10**	**Day 11**	**Day 12**
Lesson 96	Lab 9 Lesson 97	Lesson 98	Lesson 99	Lesson 100	Cumulative Test 19
Day 13					
Investigation 10					

Block: 90-Minute Class

Day 1	Day 2	Day 3	Day 4	Day 5	Day 6
Lesson 91 Lesson 92	Lesson 93 Lesson 94	Lesson 95 Cumulative Test 18	Lab 9 Lesson 96 Lesson 97	Lesson 98 Lesson 99	Lesson 100 Cumulative Test 19
Day 7					
Investigation 10 Lesson 101					

* For suggestions on how to implement Saxon Math in a block schedule, see the Pacing section at the beginning of the Teacher's Edition.

Saxon Algebra 1

Differentiated Instruction

Below Level		Advanced Learners	
Warm Up	SE pp. 602, 609, 616, 624, 631, 638, 647, 655, 662, 669	Challenge	TE pp. 608, 614, 622, 630, 637, 644, 654, 660, 668, 674
Skills Bank	SE pp. 846–883	Extend the Example	TE pp. 605, 611, 620, 627, 629, 634, 641, 650, 657, 660, 665, 672
Reteaching Masters	Lessons 91–100, Investigation 10	Extend the Exploration	TE pp. 648
Warm Up Transparencies	Lessons 91–100	Extend the Problem	TE pp. 608, 613, 614, 622, 636, 642, 652, 653, 654, 666, 667, 668, 674, 675, 676
Prerequisite Skills Intervention	Skills 61, 81	Challenge and Enrichment Masters	Challenge: 91–100; Enrichment: 93

English Learners		Special Needs	
EL Tips	TE pp. 603, 610, 617, 627, 636, 643, 648, 656, 664, 670, 677	Inclusion Tips	TE pp. 604, 611, 619, 625, 632, 641, 649, 657, 663, 672
Multilingual Glossary	Booklet and Online English Learners Handbook	Adaptations for Saxon Algebra 1	Lessons 91–100, Cumulative Tests 18, 19

For All Learners			
Exploration	SE pp. 648	Alternate Method	TE pp. 605, 640
Caution	SE pp. 603, 618, 627, 633, 649, 657, 664, 671	Online Tools	
Hints	SE pp. 611, 617, 620, 624, 633, 639, 647, 648, 656, 663, 670, 672, 673		
Error Alert	TE pp. 603, 606, 607, 610, 612, 615, 617, 620, 622, 626, 627, 630, 632, 634, 637, 641, 642, 648, 651, 652, 654, 658, 659, 660, 665, 666, 667, 670, 673, 674, 675, 676, 677		

SE = Student Edition; TE = Teacher's Edition

Math Vocabulary

Lesson	New Vocabulary	Maintained	EL Tip in TE
91	absolute-value inequality	absolute value absolute-value expression	absolute
92	complex fraction	greatest common factor	reciprocal
93		coefficient rational expression	mono-, bi-, poly-
94		absolute value	ring
95		least common denominator least common multiple	cushion
96	standard form of a quadratic equation	axis of symmetry vertex y-intercept zero of a function	diver
97	solution of a linear inequality	coordinate plane linear equation ordered pair	shaded
98	root of an equation	quadratic function	root
99	rational equation extraneous solution	cross products least common denominator rational expression	extraneous
100		function notation parabola quadratic equation	related
INV 10		parent function quadratic function transformation	parent function

SECTION OVERVIEW 10

Math Highlights

Enduring Understandings – The "Big Picture"
After completing Section 10, students will understand:
- How to solve absolute-value equations.
- How to simplify complex fractions and solve rational equations.
- How to divide polynomials.
- How to graph quadratic functions and solve quadratic equations by graphing or factoring.

Essential Questions
- How do solutions of absolute-value inequalities relate to compound inequalities?
- How can the methods of simplifying fractions be applied to simplifying complex fractions?
- How can long division be applied to dividing algebraic expressions?
- How can the methods of adding and subtracting fractions be applied to simplifying complex fractions?
- What are elements of a parabola and how can any quadratic function be graphed using these elements?
- What is the difference between a quadratic function and a quadratic equation?
- How can the solutions of a quadratic equation be found by graphing the related function?

Math Content Strands	Math Processes

Polynomials
- Lesson 93   Dividing Polynomials

Rational Expressions and Functions
- Lesson 92   Simplifying Complex Fractions
- Lesson 95   Combining Rational Expressions with Unlike Denominators
- Lesson 99   Solving Rational Equations

Systems of Equations and Inequalities
- Lab 9   Graphing Calculator: Graphing Linear Inequalities
- Lesson 97   Graphing Linear Inequalities

Quadratic Equations
- Lesson 96   Graphing Quadratic Functions
- Lesson 98   Solving Quadratic Equations by Factoring
- Lesson 100   Solving Quadratic Equations by Graphing
- Investigation 10   Transforming Quadratic Functions

Absolute-Value Equations and Inequalities
- Lesson 91   Solving Absolute-Value Inequalities
- Lesson 94   Solving Multi-Step Absolute-Value Equations

Connections in Practice Problems
	Lessons
Data Analysis	100
Geometry	91, 92, 93, 94, 95, 96, 97, 98, 99, 100
Measurement	91, 95, 96, 98, 99
Probability	92, 93, 97, 99

Reasoning and Communication

	Lessons
Analyze	91, 93, 94, 95, 96, 98, 99, Inv. 10
Error analysis	91, 92, 93, 94, 95, 96, 97, 98, 99, 100
Estimate	91
Formulate	94, 99
Generalize	91, 95, 96, 97, 98, 99, 100, Inv. 10
Justify	91, 92, 93, 94, 95, 96, 98, 99
Math Reasoning	91, 92, 94, 95, 96, 98, 99, 100, Inv. 10
Multiple choice	91, 92, 93, 94, 95, 96, 97, 98, 99, 100
Multi-step	91, 92, 93, 94, 95, 96, 97, 98, 99, 100
Predict	Inv. 10
Verify	94, 96, 97, 99, 100
Write	91, 92, 93, 94, 95, 96, 97, 98, 99, 100
Graphing Calculator	93, 96, 97, 98, 100, Inv. 10

Connections

In Examples: Archery, Baseball, Carnival, Gardening, Length of a Garden, Painting, Physics, Polling, Speed Walking, Traveling

In Practice problems: Ages, Archeology, Architecture, Art, Band, Banking, Baseball, Basketball, Bike riding, Canoeing, Carpeting, Census, Commuting, Cost, Diving, Exercise, Flooring, Football, Geography, Hardiness zones, Hiking, Horseback riding, House painting, Housekeeping, Industry, Investments, Lawn care, Olympic swimming pool, Pendulums, Physics, Population, Profit, Rate, Refurbishing, Running, Shopping, Skating, Soccer, Space, Swimming, Track, Travel, United States flag, Vertical motion

Saxon Algebra 1

Lessons 91–100, Investigation 10

Content Trace

Lesson	Warm Up: Prerequisite Skills	New Concepts	Where Practiced	Where Assessed	Looking Forward
91	Lessons 5, 74	Solving Absolute-Value Inequalities	Lessons 92, 93, 94, 95, 96, 97, 98, 99, 100, 101, 104, 106, 107	Cumulative Tests 19, 20, 21, 22, 23	Lessons 94, 101, 107
92	Lessons 11, 57, 72, 83	Simplifying Complex Fractions	Lessons 93, 94, 95, 96, 97, 98, 99, 100, 101, 102, 105, 107, 108	Cumulative Tests 19, 20, 21, 22, 23	Lessons 95, 99
93	Lessons 38, 43, 53, 75, 83	Dividing Polynomials	Lessons 94, 95, 96, 97, 98, 99, 100, 101, 102, 103, 106, 107, 108, 109	Cumulative Tests 19, 20, 21, 22, 23	Lessons 95, 99
94	Lessons 5, 26	Solving Multi-Step Absolute–Value Equations	Lessons 95, 96, 97, 98, 99, 100, 101, 102, 103, 104, 107, 108, 109, 110	Cumulative Tests 19, 20, 21, 22, 23	Lessons 101, 107
95	Lessons 2, 57, 72, 75	Combining Rational Expressions with Unlike Denominators	Lessons 96, 97, 98, 99, 100, 101, 102, 103, 104, 105, 108, 110, 111	Cumulative Tests 19, 20, 21, 22, 23	Lesson 99
96	Lessons 9, 89	Graphing Quadratic Functions	Lessons 97, 98, 99, 100, 101, 102, 103, 104, 105, 106, 109, 110, 111, 112	Cumulative Test 20, 21	Lessons 98, 100, 102, 110
97	Lessons 49, 50	Graphing Linear Inequalities	Lessons 98, 99, 100, 101, 102, 103, 105, 106, 107, 110, 112, 113, 115	Cumulative Test 20, 21, 22	Lesson 109
98	Lessons 72, 75, 83, 89	Solving Quadratic Equations by Factoring	Lessons 99, 100, 101, 102, 103, 104, 105, 106, 107, 108, 111, 113, 114	Cumulative Test 20, 21, 22	Lessons 100, 102, 104, 110, 113
99	Lessons 39, 57	Solving Rational Equations	Lessons 100, 101, 102, 103, 104, 105, 106, 107, 108, 109, 112, 114, 115	Cumulative Test 20, 21, 22, 23	Lessons in other Saxon High School Math programs
100	Lessons 9, 84	Solving Quadratic Equations by Graphing	Lessons 101, 102, 103, 104, 105, 106, 107, 108, 109, 110, 113, 115, 116	Cumulative Test 20, 21	Lessons 102, 104, 110, 113
INV 10	N/A	Transforming Quadratic Functions	Lessons 101, 103, 106, 112, 113, 114, 116, 119	Cumulative Test 22	Lessons 107, 114, 119

SECTION OVERVIEW 10

Ongoing Assessment

	Type	Feature	Intervention *
BEFORE instruction	Assess Prior Knowledge	• Diagnostic Test	• Prerequisite Skills Intervention
BEFORE the lesson	Formative	• Warm Up	• Skills Bank • Reteaching Masters
DURING the lesson	Formative	• Lesson Practice • Math Conversations with the Practice problems	• Additional Examples in TE • Test and Practice Generator (for additional practice sheets)
AFTER the lesson	Formative	• Check for Understanding (closure)	• Scaffolding Questions in TE
AFTER 5 lessons	Summative	After Lesson 95 • Cumulative Test 18 • Performance Task 18 After Lesson 100 • Cumulative Test 19 • Performance Task 19	• Reteaching Masters • Test and Practice Generator (for additional tests and practice)
AFTER 20 lessons	Summative	• Benchmark Tests	• Reteaching Masters • Test and Practice Generator (for additional tests and practice)

* for students not showing progress during the formative stages or scoring below 80% on the summative assessments

Evidence of Learning – What Students Should Know

Because the Saxon philosophy is to provide students with sufficient time to learn and practice each concept, a lesson's topic will not be tested until at least five lessons after the topic is introduced.

On the Cumulative Tests that are given during this section of ten lessons, students should be able to demonstrate the following competencies:
- Solve multi-step compound inequalities, and absolute-value equations and inequalities.
- Graph quadratic functions, and identify the vertex, the maximum, and the minimum of a parabola.
- Simplify complex fractions.
- Multiply binomials with radicals.
- Factor polynomials, and divide polynomials by monomials.
- Use the Pythagorean Theorem, and find the distance between two points.
- Find the probability of mutually exclusive events.

Test and Practice Generator CD using ExamView™

The Test and Practice Generator is an easy-to-use benchmark and assessment tool that creates unlimited practice and tests in multiple formats and allows you to customize questions or create new ones. A variety of reports are available to track student progress toward mastery of the standards throughout the year.

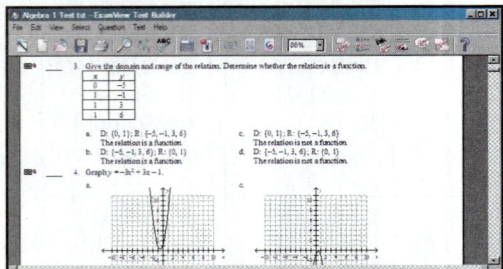
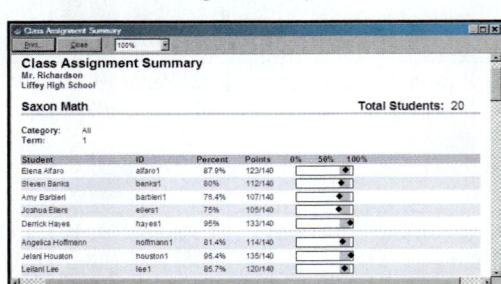

602E Saxon Algebra 1

Assessment Resources

Resources for Diagnosing and Assessing

- **Student Edition**
  - Warm Up
  - Lesson Practice

- **Teacher's Edition**
  - Math Conversations with the Practice problems
  - Check for Understanding (closure)

- **Course Assessments**
  - Diagnostic Test
  - Cumulative Tests
  - Performance Tasks
  - Benchmark Tests

Resources for Test Prep

- **Student Edition Practice**
  - Multiple-choice problems
  - Multiple-step and writing problems
  - Daily cumulative practice

- **Standardized Test Practice**

- **College Entrance Exam Practice**

- **Test and Practice Generator CD using ExamView™**

Resources for Intervention

- **Student Edition**
  - Skills Bank

- **Teacher's Edition**
  - Additional Examples
  - Scaffolding questions

- **Prerequisite Skills Intervention**
  - Worksheets

- **Reteaching Masters**
  - Lesson instruction and practice sheets

- **Test and Practice Generator CD using ExamView™**
  - Lesson practice problems
  - Additional tests

Cumulative Tests

The assessments in Saxon Math are frequent and consistently placed after every five lessons to offer a regular method of ongoing testing. These cumulative assessments check mastery of concepts from previous lessons.

Performance Tasks

The Performance Tasks can be used in conjunction with the Cumulative Tests and are scored using a rubric.

After Lesson 95

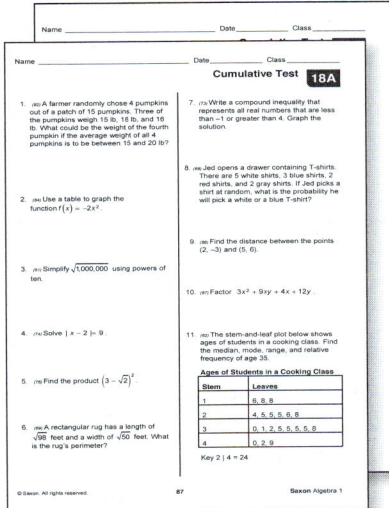

After Lesson 100

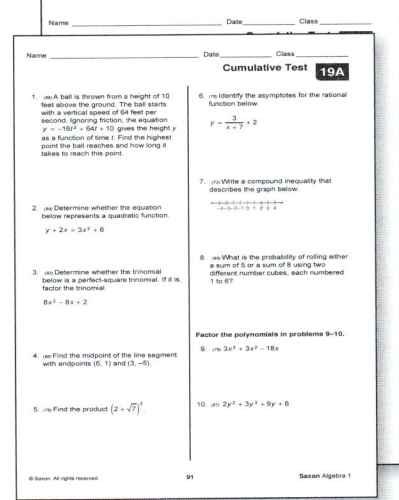

For use with Performance Tasks

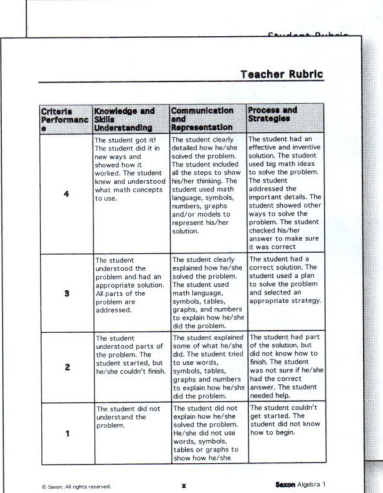

LESSON 91

Solving Absolute-Value Inequalities

1 Warm Up

Problems 2–5
Remind students that the expression inside the absolute-value bars can be negative, but the absolute value of any expression cannot be negative.

2 New Concepts

In this lesson, students learn to solve absolute-value inequalities.

Discuss the definition of an **absolute-value inequality**. Explain that the solution to an absolute-value inequality can be written as a compound inequality.

Example 1

Remind students that the absolute value of a number is its distance from zero on the number line.

Additional Example 1
Solve each inequality by graphing.

a. $|x| < 2.5$ $-2.5 < x < 2.5$;

b. $|x| > 10$ $x > 10$ OR $x < -10$;
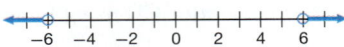

LESSON RESOURCES

Student Edition Practice Workbook 91
Reteaching Master 91
Adaptations Master 91
Challenge and Enrichment Master C91

Warm Up

1. **Vocabulary** An equation with one or more absolute-value expressions is called an _____. **absolute-value equation**

Simplify.

2. $|8 - 15|$ 7

3. $|-3 + 9|$ 6

Solve.

4. $|x - 4| = 7$ $x = 11, -3$

5. $|x + 7| = 2$ $x = -5, -9$

New Concepts

An **absolute-value inequality** is an inequality with at least one absolute-value expression. The solution to an absolute-value inequality can be written as a compound inequality.

Math Language
The **absolute value** of a number is its distance from zero on the number line.

The inequality $|x| < 6$ describes all real numbers whose distance from 0 is less than 6 units. The solutions are all real numbers between -6 and 6. The solution can be written $-6 < x < 6$ or as the compound inequality $x > -6$ AND $x < 6$.

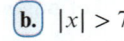

The inequality $|x| > 6$ describes all real numbers whose distance from 0 is greater than 6 units. The solutions are all real numbers less than -6 or greater than 6. The solution can be written as the compound inequality $x < -6$ OR $x > 6$.

Example 1 Solving Absolute-Value Inequalities by Graphing

Solve each inequality by graphing.

Reading Math
For the inequality $-4 < x < 4$, you can say, "x is between -4 and 4."

Math Reasoning
Analyze Why is the word "OR" used here to describe the solution?

Sample: A number cannot be both greater than 7 and less than -7.

a. $|x| < 4$

SOLUTION
If the absolute value of x is less than 4, then x is less than 4 units from zero on a number line.

The graph shows $x < 4$ AND $x > -4$. This can also be written $-4 < x < 4$.

b. $|x| > 7$

SOLUTION
If the absolute value of x is greater than 7, then x is more than 7 units from zero on a number line.

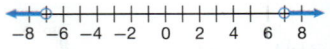

The graph shows $x > 7$ OR $x < -7$.

MATH BACKGROUND

In this lesson, the absolute-value inequalities have the form

$|x - a| > b$,

where a and b are constants. When graphed on the number line, the graph is always symmetric about the center point a.

In this case, the inequality can be understood as "the distance from x to a is greater than b." Students might have an easier time understanding why such graphs on the number line are symmetrical; one can take b steps from a in two directions.

Example 2 Isolating the Absolute Value to Solve

Solve and graph each inequality.

a. $|x| + 7.4 \leq 9.8$

SOLUTION

Begin by isolating the absolute value.

$$|x| + 7.4 \leq 9.8$$
$$\underline{\; -7.4 \quad -7.4} \quad \text{Subtraction Property of Inequality}$$
$$|x| \leq 2.4 \quad \text{Simplify.}$$

Since the absolute value of x is less than or equal to 2.4, it is 2.4 units or less from zero.

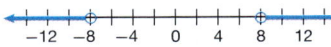

The solution can be written $x \geq -2.4$ AND $x \leq 2.4$ or $-2.4 \leq x \leq 2.4$.

b. $\dfrac{|x|}{4} > 2$

SOLUTION

Begin by isolating the absolute value.

$$\dfrac{|x|}{4} > 2$$
$$4 \cdot \dfrac{|x|}{4} > 2 \cdot 4 \quad \text{Multiplication Property of Inequality}$$
$$|x| > 8 \quad \text{Simplify.}$$

The absolute value of x is greater than 8, so it is more than 8 units from zero.

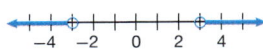

The solution is $x > 8$ OR $x < -8$.

c. $-2|x| < -6$

SOLUTION

Begin by isolating the absolute value.

$$-2|x| < -6$$
$$\dfrac{-2|x|}{-2} > \dfrac{-6}{-2} \quad \text{Division Property of Inequality}$$
$$|x| > 3 \quad \text{Simplify.}$$

Since the absolute value of x is greater than 3, it is more than 3 units from zero.

The solution is $x > 3$ OR $x < -3$.

Caution

Be sure to reverse the direction of the inequality sign if you multiply or divide by a negative number when solving the inequality.

Online Connection
www.SaxonMathResources.com

Example 2

Point out that in solving absolute-value inequalities, it is often easier to isolate the absolute value before solving for the variable.

Error Alert When graphing inequalities on the number line, students often will use open and closed circles incorrectly. Remind them to pay attention to what symbol is used in the expression.

Additional Example 2
Solve and graph each inequality.

a. $|x| - 2.2 \leq 7.8$ $-10 \leq x \leq 10$;

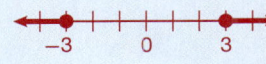

b. $3|x| > 2.7$ $x > 0.9$ OR $x < -0.9$;

c. $-3|x| \leq -9$ $x \geq 3$ OR $x \leq -3$;

ENGLISH LEARNERS

For this lesson, explain the meaning of the word **absolute.** Say:

"The word absolute means definite or final. It can describe something that exists independently and not in relation to other things."

Connect the meaning of absolute with absolute value by pointing to the definition of the absolute value and emphasizing that the distance from n to 0 is not relative to another value—it is absolute.

Discuss examples of other uses of the word absolute: the absolute-temperature scale Kelvin, absolute power, etc.

Example 3

Point out that the variable expression inside the absolute-value bars "shifts" the center of the graph. The expression $x + a$ shifts the center of the graph to $-a$ and the expression $x - b$ shifts the center of the graph to b when a and b are non-negative constants.

Additional Example 3

Solve each inequality. Then graph the solution.

a. $|x + 4| \leq 5$ $x \leq 1$ AND $x \geq -9$

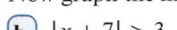

b. $|x - 2| > 3$ $x < -1$ OR $x > 5$

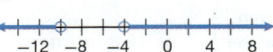

Some absolute-value inequalities have variable expressions inside the absolute-value symbols. The expression inside the absolute-value symbols can be positive or negative.

The inequality $|x + 1| < 3$ represents all numbers whose distance from -1 is less than 3.

The inequality $|x + 1| > 3$ represents all numbers whose distance from -1 is greater than 3.

Rules for Solving Absolute-Value Inequalities
For an inequality in the form $|K| < a$, where K represents a variable expression and $a > 0$, solve $-a < K < a$ or $K > -a$ AND $K < a$.
For an inequality in the form $|K| > a$, where K represents a variable expression and $a > 0$, solve $K < -a$ OR $K > a$.
Similar rules are true for $|K| \leq a$ or $|K| \geq a$.

Example 3 Solving Inequalities with Operations Inside Absolute-Value Symbols

Solve each inequality. Then graph the solution.

a. $|x - 5| \leq 3$

SOLUTION

Use the rules for solving absolute-value inequalities to write a compound inequality.

$|x - 5| \leq 3$

$x - 5 \geq -3$ AND $x - 5 \leq 3$ Write the compound inequality.

$\underline{+5 \quad +5} \qquad\qquad \underline{+5 \quad +5}$ Addition Property of Inequality

$x \geq 2$ AND $x \leq 8$ Simplify.

Now graph the inequality.

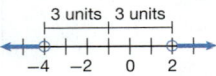

b. $|x + 7| > 3$

SOLUTION

Use the rules for solving absolute-value inequalities to write a compound inequality.

$|x + 7| > 3$

$x + 7 < -3$ OR $x + 7 > 3$ Write the compound inequality.

$\underline{-7 \quad -7} \qquad\qquad \underline{-7 \quad -7}$ Subtraction Property of Inequality

$x < -10$ OR $x > -4$ Simplify.

Now graph the inequality.

🔶 INCLUSION

Have students draw a number line from -5 to 5 with every whole number labeled and 1 inch apart. Have them locate the point 2, and with a ruler, have them then mark all the points that are less than 3 inches away from 2.

Lastly, have them show that the absolute-value inequality that represents the graph is $|x - 2| < 3$ and the solution is $-1 < x < 5$.

Example 4 Solving Special Cases

Solve each inequality.

a. $|x| + 6 \leq 4$

SOLUTION

$|x| + 6 \leq 4$

$|x| \leq -2$ Subtract 6 from both sides.

This inequality states that a number's distance from 0 is less than or equal to -2. No distance can be negative. Therefore, there are no solutions to this inequality. The solution is identified as { } or ∅, the empty set.

b. $|x| + 6 > 1$

SOLUTION

$|x| + 6 > 1$

$|x| > -5$ Subtract 6 from both sides.

This inequality states that a number's distance from 0 is greater than -5. Since all distances (and absolute values) are positive, all numbers on the number line are solutions. The solution is identified as $\mathbb{R}$, the set of all real numbers. It means that the inequality is an identity; it works for all real numbers.

Example 5 Application: Polling

A poll finds that candidate Garcia is favored by 46% of the voters surveyed and Jackson is favored by 44%. The poll has an accuracy of plus or minus 3%.

Math Reasoning

Justify According to the poll, Garcia and Jackson are in a "statistical dead heat"— a tie. Explain why the poll would not say that Garcia (46%) is leading Jackson (44%).

Sample: Because the accuracy of the poll is plus or minus 3%, either could actually be ahead. Garcia's percentage could actually be 3% less, at 43%. Jackson's percentage could actually be 3% more, at 47%, and Jackson would be leading Garcia.

a. Write an absolute-value inequality to show the true percentage of voters for Garcia.

SOLUTION

Let the true percentage of voters for Garcia be g.

For g to be within 3%, the distance from g to 46 must be less than or equal to 3. The distance is represented by the absolute value of their difference.

$|g - 46| \leq 3$

b. Solve the inequality to find the range for the true percentage of voters who support Garcia.

SOLUTION

$|g - 46| \leq 3$

$-3 \leq g - 46 \leq 3$ Write the inequality without an absolute value.

$43 \leq g \leq 49$ Add 46 to all 3 parts of the inequality.

The range is between 43% and 49%.

Lesson 91   605

Example 4

Remind students that they should always isolate the absolute value first to identify special cases.

Additional Example 4

Solve each inequality.

a. $|x| + 3 < 3$
{ } or ∅; There is no graph.

b. $|x| + 3 > 2$ $\mathbb{R}$;

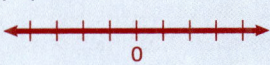

Example 5

Explain to students that a measurement, such as a poll, has an uncertainty or a range of values within which the true value lies.

Extend the Example

Let the true percentage of voters for Jackson be j. Write and solve an absolute-value inequality to show that j is within 3% of 44.
$|j - 44| \leq 3$
$41 \leq j \leq 47$

Additional Example 5

Jim and Tom went fishing and wanted to see who caught the biggest fish. Unfortunately, the scale they used was not very accurate and was only good to ±2 ounces. Jim's fish weighed in at 5 pounds 5 ounces and Tom's was 5 pounds 10 ounces.

a. Let the true weight of Jim's fish be j and Tom's fish be t. Write the absolute-value inequalities.
$|j - 85\ oz| \leq 2\ oz$
$|t - 90\ oz| \leq 2\ oz$

b. Can one confidently say that Tom's fish is bigger than Jim's?
yes

ALTERNATE METHOD FOR EXAMPLE 5

Instead of writing an absolute value inequality, have students think about the definition of accuracy. Since the problem states that the poll has an "accuracy of plus or minus 3%," have students write the range for the true percentage of voters that support Garcia.

The limits of the range will be 46 ± 3%, thus the range is between 43% and 49%.

Lesson Practice

Problem c
Scaffolding Before graphing the inequality, have students first isolate the absolute-value term and solve it completely before attempting to graph the solution.

Problem d
Error Alert Students may assume that there is no solution to an absolute value inequality when the expression containing the absolute value is related to a negative number. Remind them to isolate the absolute value, then consider whether there is a solution or not.

Check for Understanding
The questions below help assess the concepts taught in this lesson.

"Explain how to solve an absolute-value inequality." Sample: If the absolute-value term has a coefficient, isolate it first. Check for special cases. The expression inside the absolute-value bars can be positive and negative.

"Explain what absolute value means on the graph of an equation on the number line." Sample: The absolute value of a number n is the distance from n to 0.

Lesson Practice

a.–f. See Additional Answers.

a. (Ex 1) Solve and graph the inequality $|x| < 12$. $-12 < x < 12$
b. (Ex 1) Solve and graph the inequality $|x| > 19$. $x < -19$ OR $x > 19$
c. (Ex 2) Solve and graph the inequality $|x| + 2.8 \leq 10.4$. $-7.6 \leq x \leq 7.6$
d. (Ex 2) Solve and graph the inequality $\dfrac{|x|}{-5} < -1$. $x < -5$ OR $x > 5$
e. (Ex 3) Solve and graph the inequality $|x - 10| \leq 12$. $-2 \leq x \leq 22$
f. (Ex 3) Solve and graph the inequality $|x + 12| > 18$. $x < -30$ OR $x > 6$
g. (Ex 4) Solve the inequality $|x| + 21 \leq 14$. $\varnothing$
h. (Ex 4) Solve the inequality $|x| + 33 > 24$. $\mathbb{R}$

(Industry) A machine part must be 15 ± 0.2 cm in diameter.
(Ex 5)
i. $|m - 15| \leq 0.2$ **i.** Write an inequality to show the range of acceptable diameters.
j. Solve the inequality to find the actual range for the diameters. $14.8 \leq m \leq 15.2$

Practice   Distributed and Integrated

1. Find the axis of symmetry for the graph of the equation $y = -\tfrac{1}{2}x^2 + x - 3$.
(89) $x = 1$

Add or subtract.

2. $\dfrac{6rs}{r^2s^2} + \dfrac{18r}{r^2s^2}$ $\dfrac{6(s+3)}{rs^2}$
(90)

3. $\dfrac{b}{2b+1} - \dfrac{6}{b-4}$ $\dfrac{b^2 - 16b - 6}{(2b+1)(b-4)}$
(90)

Factor.

4. $-4y^4 + 8y^3 + 5y^2 - 10y$
(87) $-y(4y^2 - 5)(y - 2)$

5. $3a^2 - 27$ $3(a+3)(a-3)$
(83)

6. $4x^2 + 6x - 4$ $2(2x-1)(x+2)$
(75)

7. $9x^2 - 2x - 32$ $(9x+16)(x-2)$
(75)

*8. Solve and graph the inequality $|x| < 96$. $-96 < x < 96$;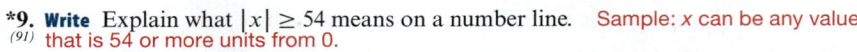
(91) $-96\ -48\ \ 0\ \ 48\ \ 96$

*9. Write Explain what $|x| \geq 54$ means on a number line.   Sample: x can be any value
(91) that is 54 or more units from 0.

*10. Justify When solving an absolute-value inequality, a student gets $|x| \geq -5$. Justify   **10.** Sample: No
(91) that any value for x makes this inequality true.   matter what I substitute for x, its absolute value is going to be greater than -5 because absolute value is always positive.

*11. Multiple Choice Which inequality is represented by the graph?   **B**
(91)

$-12\ -8\ -4\ \ 0\ \ 4\ \ 8\ \ 12$

A $|x| < 9$ **B** $|x| > 9$ **C** $|x| \leq 9$ **D** $|x| < -9$

*12. (Track) A runner finishes a sprint in 8.54 seconds. The timer's accuracy is plus or
(91) minus 0.3 seconds. Solve and graph the inequality $|t - 8.54| \leq 0.3$.
$8.24 \leq t \leq 8.84$
$\quad\quad\quad\quad\ \ $ 8.24 8.44 8.64 8.84

606   Saxon Algebra 1

*13. **Error Analysis** Two students simplified $\frac{2c}{c-6} + \frac{12}{6-c}$. Which student is correct? Explain the error.

Student A	Student B
$\frac{2c-12}{c-6}$	$\frac{2c+12}{c-6}$
$\frac{2(c-6)}{c-6} = 2$	$\frac{2(c+6)}{c-6} = -2$

13. Student A; Sample: Student B multiplied the denominator of one of the expressions by –1, but forgot to multiply the numerator of that expression by –1 also.

*14. **Multi-Step** A farmer has a rectangular plot of land with an area of $x^2 + 22x + 72$ square meters. He sets aside x^2 square meters for grazing and $2x - 8$ square meters for a chicken coop.
  a. Write a simplified expression for the total fraction of the field the farmer has set aside. $\frac{x-2}{x+18}$
  b. **Estimate** About what percent of the field has the farmer set aside if $x = 30$? about 60%

15. **Geometry** Write a simplified expression for the total fraction of the larger rectangle that the triangle and smaller rectangle cover. $\frac{2(x-1)}{5(x+9)}$

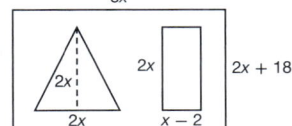

16. Find the product of $(\sqrt{4} - 6)^2$. 16

17. **Analyze** Why is it necessary to understand factoring when dealing with rational expressions? Sample: Factoring makes it easier to simplify complicated expressions.

18. **Multi-Step** The base of triangle ABC is $x^2 + y$. The height is $\frac{4x + 2xy}{x^3 + xy}$. What is the area of triangle ABC?
  a. Multiply the base of the triangle by its height. $2(2 + y)$
  b. Multiply the product from part **a** by $\frac{1}{2}$. $2 + y$

*19. **Error Analysis** Two students tried to find the axis of symmetry for the equation $y = 8x + 2x^2$. Which student is correct? Explain the error.

Student A	Student B
$x = \frac{-b}{2a} = \frac{-2}{2(8)} = \frac{-2}{16} = -\frac{1}{8}$	$x = \frac{-8}{2(2)} = \frac{-8}{4} = -2$

19. Student B; Sample: Student A used the wrong values for a and b. The equation in standard form is $y = 2x^2 + 8x$, so $a = 2$ and $b = 8$.

*20. **Space** If it were possible to play ball on Jupiter, the function $y = -13x^2 + 39x$ would approximate the height of a ball kicked straight up at a velocity of 39 meters per second, where x is time in seconds. Find the maximum height the ball reaches and the time it takes the ball to reach that height. (Hint: Find the time the ball reaches its maximum height first.) 29.25 feet in 1.5 seconds

21. **Measurement** The coordinates of two landmarks on a city map are $A(5, 3)$ and $B(7, 10)$. Each grid line represents 0.05 miles. Find the distance between landmarks A and B. 0.364 mile

3 Practice

Math Conversations
Discussion to strengthen understanding

Problem 16
Error Alert
A common mistake students make when multiplying expressions is not simplifying each expression first. Write the statement:

$(\sqrt{4} - 6)^2 = (\sqrt{4} - 6)(\sqrt{4} - 6)$
$= 4 - 12\sqrt{4} + 36$
$= 40 - 12\sqrt{4}$
$= 40 - 12(2)$
$= 16$

Compare with the statement:
$(\sqrt{4} - 6)^2 = (2 - 6)^2 = (-4)^2$
$= 16$

Remind students that it is often beneficial to simplify the expressions before multiplying them.

Problem 18
Guide the students by asking them the following questions.

"How can $x^3 + xy$ be factored?"
Sample: Put x outside of the parentheses: $x(x^2 + y)$

"How can the expression $(x^2 + y) \cdot \frac{4x + 2xy}{x(x^2 + y)}$ be simplified?" Sample: Divide out x and $x^2 + y$ from both the numerator and denominator: $4 + 2y$.

"What is the formula for the area of a triangle?" Sample: one half times the base times the height

Problem 27
Extend the Problem
"If the CDs cost $3 each at the used CD store, how many CDs can Roger buy?" 13 or fewer

22. (Archeology) Archeologists use coordinate grids to record locations of artifacts.
    (86) Jonah recorded that he found one old coin at (41, 37), and a second old coin at (5, 2). Each unit on his grid represents 0.25 feet. How far apart were the coins? Round your answer to the nearest tenth of a foot. **12.6 feet**

23. Find the length t to the nearest tenth. **5.3**
    (85)

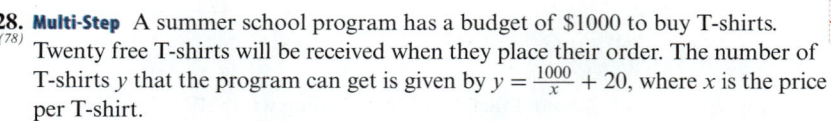

24. (House Painting) A house painter leans a 34-foot ladder against a house with
    (85) the bottom of the ladder 7 feet from the base of the house. Will the top of the ladder touch the house above or below a windowsill that is 33 feet off the ground? **above; $34^2 - 7^2 > 33^2$**

25. Graph the function $y = 4x^2$.
    (84)

26. **Generalize** What is the factored form of $a^{2m} + 2a^m b^n + b^{2n}$? **$(a^m + b^n)^2$**
    (83)

27. (Shopping) Roger has $40 to buy CDs. The CDs cost $5 each. He will definitely
    (82) buy at least 3 CDs. How many CDs can Roger buy? Use inequalities to solve the problems. **$x \geq 3$ and $5x \leq 40$; $3 \leq x \leq 8$**

28. **Multi-Step** A summer school program has a budget of $1000 to buy T-shirts.
    (78) Twenty free T-shirts will be received when they place their order. The number of T-shirts y that the program can get is given by $y = \frac{1000}{x} + 20$, where x is the price per T-shirt.
    a. What is the horizontal asymptote of this rational function? **$y = 20$**
    b. What is the vertical asymptote? **$x = 0$**
    c. If the price per T-shirt is $10, how many T-shirts can the program receive? **120**

*29. Suppose the area of a rectangle is represented by the expression $4x^2 + 9x + 2$.
 (Inv 9) Find possible expressions for the length and width of the rectangle. **width = $(4x + 1)$, length = $(x + 2)$ or width = $(x + 2)$ and length = $(4x + 1)$**

30. Simplify the expression $6\sqrt{8} \cdot \sqrt{5}$. **$12\sqrt{10}$**
    (76)

25.
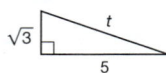

CHALLENGE

There are also compound absolute-value inequalities. Consider the inequalities:

$|x| < 6$ AND $|x - 2| > 6$

Have students solve the compound absolute-value inequalities. Sample: The solution will be the overlap of the two graphs on a number line, $-6 < x < -4$

LOOKING FORWARD

Solving absolute-value inequalities prepares students for

• **Lesson 94** Solving Multi-Step Absolute-Value Equations

• **Lesson 101** Solving Multi-Step Absolute-Value Inequalities

• **Lesson 107** Graphing Absolute-Value Functions

LESSON 92

Simplifying Complex Fractions

Warm Up

1. **Vocabulary** For any nonzero real number n, the _____ of the number is $\frac{1}{n}$. **reciprocal**

Identify the LCM.

2. $4x - 16$ and $x - 4$ $4(x - 4)$
3. $18x^2$ and $9x$ $18x^2$

Factor.

4. $x^2 - 4x - 77$ $(x + 7)(x - 11)$
5. $18x^2 + 12x + 2$ $2(3x + 1)(3x + 1)$

New Concepts

A **complex fraction** is a fraction that contains one or more fractions in the numerator or the denominator.

Complex Fractions

There are two ways to write a fraction divided by a fraction.

$$\frac{\frac{a}{b}}{\frac{c}{d}} = \frac{a}{b} \div \frac{c}{d}, \text{ when } b \neq 0, c \neq 0, \text{ and } d \neq 0.$$

A complex fraction can be written as a fraction divided by a fraction. The rules for dividing fractions can be applied to simplify complex fractions.

Example 1 Simplifying by Dividing

Simplify $\dfrac{\frac{a}{x}}{\frac{b}{a+x}}$.

SOLUTION

$$\frac{\frac{a}{x}}{\frac{b}{a+x}}$$

$$= \frac{a}{x} \div \frac{b}{a+x} \quad \text{Write using a division symbol.}$$

$$= \frac{a}{x} \cdot \frac{a+x}{b} \quad \text{Multiply by the reciprocal.}$$

$$= \frac{a(a+x)}{xb} \quad \text{Multiply.}$$

Math Reasoning

Write Explain why the complex fraction $\dfrac{\frac{a}{x}}{\frac{b}{a+x}}$ can be written as $\frac{a}{x} \div \frac{b}{a+x}$.

Sample: The fraction bar means divide, so the two expressions are equal.

Lesson 92   609

MATH BACKGROUND

The key to simplifying complex fractions is to remember that a fraction is just a way to write a series of division expressions. Take the complex fraction:

$$\frac{\frac{a}{x}}{\frac{b}{a+y}}$$

It is the same as the statement: "a divided by x is divided by b divided by $a + y$."

LESSON 92

1 Warm Up

Problems 2 and 3

Point out to students that factoring the expressions should always precede identifying the LCM.

2 New Concepts

In this lesson, students learn to simplify complex fractions.

Discuss the definition of a **complex fraction**.

Example 1

Remind students that dividing by a fraction is the same as multiplying by its reciprocal.

Additional Example 1

Simplify $\dfrac{\frac{b}{y}}{\frac{y}{a+y}}$. $\dfrac{b(a+y)}{y^2}$

LESSON RESOURCES

Student Edition Practice
    Workbook 92
Reteaching Master 92
Adaptations Master 92
Challenge and Enrichment
    Master C92

Lesson 92

Example 2

Students learn to use the reciprocal of the denominator to simplify complex fractions.

Additional Example 2

Simplify $\dfrac{\frac{bt}{as}}{\frac{r}{st}} \cdot \dfrac{bt^2}{ar}$

Error Alert A common mistake that students make when simplifying complex fractions is to divide out factors that are on the very top and very bottom of the fraction. Write the statements:

$\dfrac{\frac{ab}{x}}{\frac{y}{bx}} \neq \dfrac{\frac{a}{x}}{\frac{y}{x}}$

Remind students to write the fractions using a division symbol.

Example 3

Emphasize to students that factoring all the expressions before multiplying and dividing will make the problem easier to solve.

Additional Example 3

Simplify $\dfrac{\frac{x^2 - x}{9}}{\frac{x-1}{3x}} \cdot \dfrac{x^2}{3}$

The product of a number and its reciprocal is 1. To eliminate the fraction in the denominator of a complex fraction, multiply the numerator and the denominator by the reciprocal of the denominator.

Example 2   Simplifying Using the Reciprocal of the Denominator

Simplify $\dfrac{\frac{am}{n}}{\frac{x}{mn}}$.

SOLUTION

$\dfrac{\frac{am}{n}}{\frac{x}{mn}}$

$= \dfrac{\frac{am}{n} \cdot \frac{mn}{x}}{\frac{x}{mn} \cdot \frac{mn}{x}}$ Multiply by the reciprocal of the denominator.

$= \dfrac{\frac{am}{\cancel{n}} \cdot \frac{\cancel{mn}}{x}}{\frac{\cancel{x}}{\cancel{mn}} \cdot \frac{\cancel{mn}}{\cancel{x}}}$ Divide out common factors.

$= \dfrac{\frac{am^2}{x}}{1}$ Multiply.

$= \dfrac{am^2}{x}$ Simplify.

Example 3   Factoring to Simplify

Simplify $\dfrac{\frac{3x}{6x+12}}{\frac{9}{x+2}}$.

SOLUTION

$\dfrac{\frac{3x}{6x+12}}{\frac{9}{x+2}}$

$= \dfrac{3x}{6x+12} \div \dfrac{9}{x+2}$ Write using a division symbol.

$= \dfrac{3x}{6(x+2)} \cdot \dfrac{x+2}{9}$ Factor out the GCF and multiply by the reciprocal.

$= \dfrac{\cancel{3}x}{6\cancel{(x+2)}} \cdot \dfrac{\cancel{(x+2)}}{\cancel{9}_3}$ Divide out common factors.

$= \dfrac{x}{18}$ Simplify.

Online Connection
www.SaxonMathResources.com

ENGLISH LEARNERS

For this lesson, explain the meaning of the word **reciprocal.** Say:

"**The reciprocal of something is done for another in return for something else.**"

Connect the meaning of reciprocal with the fraction $\frac{1}{x}$ and its reciprocal x by emphasizing that the denominator and numerator swapped places.

Discuss examples of other uses of the word reciprocal. For example, when we treat people nicely, we can expect reciprocal comments or treatment.

Also mention that reciprocate is the verb form of the word. Have students come up with things that they do now and would like their friends to reciprocate, e.g., share their snacks.

Example 4 Combining Fractions to Simplify

Simplify $\dfrac{\frac{1}{x}}{1-\frac{1}{x}}$.

SOLUTION

Hint
Find the LCD of 1 and $\frac{1}{x}$ to subtract in the denominator.

$\dfrac{\frac{1}{x}}{1-\frac{1}{x}}$

$=\dfrac{\frac{1}{x}}{\frac{x-1}{x}}$ Subtract in the denominator.

$=\dfrac{1}{x} \div \dfrac{x-1}{x}$ Write using a division symbol.

$=\dfrac{1}{x} \cdot \dfrac{x}{x-1}$ Multiply by the reciprocal.

$=\dfrac{1}{\cancel{x}} \cdot \dfrac{\cancel{x}}{x-1}$ Divide out common factors.

$=\dfrac{1}{x-1}$ Simplify.

Example 5 Application: Speed Walking

It took Max $\dfrac{3x^2 - 12x}{3x}$ minutes to speed walk to the gym that was $\dfrac{5x-20}{x^3}$ miles away. Find his rate in miles per minute.

SOLUTION

Hint
Use the formula $d = rt$.

$r = \dfrac{d}{t}$ Solve for r.

$r = \dfrac{\frac{5x-20}{x^3}}{\frac{3x^2-12x}{3x}}$ Evaluate for d and t.

$= \dfrac{5x-20}{x^3} \div \dfrac{3x^2-12x}{3x}$ Write using a division symbol.

$= \dfrac{5x-20}{x^3} \cdot \dfrac{3x}{3x^2-12x}$ Multiply by the reciprocal.

$= \dfrac{5(x-4)}{x^3} \cdot \dfrac{3x}{3x(x-4)}$ Factor out any GCFs.

$= \dfrac{5}{x^3}$ miles per minute   Divide out common factors and simplify.

The expression $\dfrac{5}{x^3}$ represents Max's speed-walking rate in miles per minute.

Lesson 92   611

Example 4
Students learn to combine fractions to simplify complex fractions.

Additional Example 4

Simplify $\dfrac{1-\frac{1}{x+1}}{\frac{x}{2x}} \cdot \dfrac{2x}{(x+1)}$

TEACHER TIP
Emphasize that the long fraction bar between the numerator and denominator of a complex fraction indicates division and should be the last operation. The expressions in the numerator and denominator need to be simplified or evaluated separately first.

Example 5
Students learn to find a complex fraction that describes the rate of a person's walking speed.

Extend the Example
If it takes Max 25 minutes to walk to the grocery store that is 1 mile away, what is x? $x = 5$

Additional Example 5
On her bike, Emily can make it to her school that is x miles away in $3 + 4x$ minutes. If Jason's house is $\frac{1}{x}$ miles away from school, how long will it take Emily to get there from her school?
$\dfrac{3+4x}{x^2}$ minutes

  INCLUSION

Use the following strategy with students who have difficulty with complex operations. Have students write the expression below.

$\dfrac{\frac{1}{2}}{\frac{3}{4}}$

Then have them write the same expression replacing the fractions with their decimal equivalents.

Students should immediately see the order of operations:

$\dfrac{0.5}{0.75} = \dfrac{0.50}{0.75} = \dfrac{2}{3}$

Remind students that the method to simplify a complex fraction is the same.

Lesson 92   611

Lesson Practice

Problem d
Scaffolding Before writing the quotient using a division symbol, remind students to combine the fractions first.

Problem e
Error Alert Students will commonly calculate the rate incorrectly by dividing the time by the distance. Remind them that since speed has units of miles per minutes, it is "miles divided by minutes."

✓ Check for Understanding
The questions below help assess the concepts taught in this lesson.

"What is another way to write out the fraction ?" Sample: $\frac{a}{x} \div \frac{b}{y}$

"What can be done to a complex fraction to make the denominator equal to 1?" Sample: Multiply the numerator and denominators by the reciprocal of the denominator.

3 Practice

Math Conversations
Discussion to strengthen understanding

Problem 6
Before multiplying the expressions together, remind students to check for perfect squares.

Lesson Practice
Simplify.

a. (Ex 1) $\dfrac{\frac{x}{4}}{\frac{3(x-3)}{x}}$ $\dfrac{x^2}{12(x-3)}$

b. (Ex 2) $\dfrac{\frac{b}{cd}}{\frac{2b}{c}}$ $\dfrac{1}{2d}$

c. (Ex 3) $\dfrac{\frac{4x^2}{x-3}}{\frac{x}{3x-9}}$ $12x$

d. (Ex 4) $\dfrac{\frac{1}{m}+5}{\frac{2}{m}-\frac{x}{m}}$ $\dfrac{1+5m}{2-x}$

e. (Ex 5) It took Ariel $\dfrac{5x^2-45x}{5x}$ minutes to walk to school that was $\dfrac{3x-27}{x^3}$ miles away. Find her rate in miles per minute. $\dfrac{3}{x^3}$ miles per minute

Practice — Distributed and Integrated

Find the product or quotient.

1. (88) $\dfrac{15x^4}{x-4} \cdot \dfrac{x^2-10x+24}{3x^3+12x^2}$ $\dfrac{5x^2(x-6)}{(x+4)}$

2. (88) $\dfrac{x^2+12x+36}{x^2-36} \div \dfrac{1}{x-6}$ $x+6$

Solve.

3. (77) $-3(r-2) > -2(-6)$ $r < -2$

4. (77) $\dfrac{y}{4}+\dfrac{1}{2}<\dfrac{2}{3}$ $y<\dfrac{2}{3}$

Simplify.

*5. (92) $\dfrac{\frac{5x}{10x+20}}{\frac{15}{x+2}}$ $\dfrac{x}{30}$

6. (76) $8\sqrt{9} \cdot 2\sqrt{5}$ $48\sqrt{5}$

*7. (92) **Write** Under what conditions is a rational expression undefined? Sample: when the denominator equals zero

*8. (92) **Justify** Give an example to show $\dfrac{\frac{a}{b}}{\frac{c}{d}} = \dfrac{a}{b} \cdot \dfrac{d}{c} = \dfrac{ad}{bc}$. See Additional Answers.

*9. (92) **(Skating)** It took Jim $\dfrac{15}{x^2+2x-3}$ minutes to skate to the park that was $\dfrac{2x}{8x-8}+\dfrac{x}{4x+12}$ miles away. Find his rate in miles per minute. $\dfrac{x^2+x}{30}$ miles per minute

612   Saxon Algebra 1

*10. **Multiple Choice** Two fractions have a denominator of $x^2 + 6x + 9$ and $x^2 - 9$. What
(92) is the least common denominator? **D**
  A $x^2 + 9$
  B $x^2 + 6x + 9$
  C $2x^2 + 9$
  D $(x + 3)^2(x - 3)$

11. Solve and graph the inequality $|x| < 65$. $-65 < x < 65$;
(91)

*12. **Error Analysis** Two students solve the inequality $|x - 15| < -4$. Which student is
(91) correct? Explain the error.

Student A	Student B
$\|x - 15\| < -4$	$\|x - 15\| < -4$
$-4 < x - 15 < 4$	no solution
$11 < x < 19$	

Student B; Sample: Student A did not realize that an absolute value can never be less than -4 because absolute value is always positive.

*13. **Geometry** A triangle has sides measuring 16 inches and 23 inches. The triangle
(91) inequality states that the length of the third side must be greater than 7 inches and
less than 39 inches. Write this inequality and graph it. $7 < s < 39$;

*14. **Multi-Step** The grades on a math test were all within the range of 80 points plus or
(91) minus 15 points.
  a. Write an absolute-value inequality to show the range of the grades. $|x - 80| \leq 15$
  b. Solve the inequality to find the actual range of the grades. $65 \leq x \leq 95$

*15. **Error Analysis** Two students simplified $\frac{x + 2}{2x - 5} - \frac{3 - x}{2x - 5}$. Which student is correct?
(90) Explain the error.

Student A	Student B
$\frac{x + 2 - 3 + x}{2x - 5} = \frac{2x - 1}{2x - 5}$	$\frac{x + 2 - 3 - x}{2x - 5} = \frac{-1}{2x - 5}$

15. Student A; Sample: Student B did not fully distribute the negative sign through the numerator of the second expression.

*16. **Canoeing** Vanya paddled a canoe upstream for 4 miles. He then turned the canoe
(90) around and paddled downstream for 3 miles. The current flowed at a rate of
c miles per hour. Write a simplified expression to represent his total canoeing time
if he kept a constant paddling rate of 6 miles
per hour. $\frac{c + 42}{(6 - c)(6 + c)}$

17. **Multiple Choice** Which equation's graph has a maximum? **B**
(89)
  A $y = -5 + x^2$
  B $y = -x^2 + 5x$
  C $y = x^2 + 5$
  D $y = 5x^2 - 1$

18. **Write** Describe 2 ways to find the axis of symmetry for a parabola.
(89)

19. **Justify** Give an example of a quadratic function and an example of a function that
(84) is not quadratic. Explain why each function is or is not quadratic.
See Additional Answers.

18. Sample: One way is to use the zeros of the function. The axis of symmetry goes through the zero when there is 1 zero because the zero is contained in the vertex. It goes through the average of the 2 zeros when there are 2 zeros. The second way is to use the formula $x = -\frac{b}{2a}$. This is the only way to find the axis of symmetry when the function has no zeros.

Lesson 92   613

Problem 25

Extend the Problem

What is the probability of picking a red marble if there are 30 blue marbles in the bag? $\frac{1}{3}$

Does the probability of picking a red marble depend on the value of x? No, the probability is independent of x.

---

20. Find the length a to the nearest tenth. 10.5
    (85)

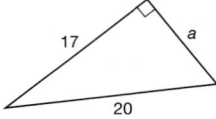

21. Subtract $\dfrac{5f + 6}{f^2 + 7f - 8} - \dfrac{f + 10}{f^2 + 7f - 8}$. $\dfrac{4}{f + 8}$
    (90)

22. Let $A = (-5, 3)$, $B = (0, 7)$, $C = (12, 7)$, and $D = (7, 3)$. Use the distance formula
    (86) to determine whether $ABCD$ is a parallelogram. yes

23. **(Geography)** Ithaca, New York is almost directly west of Oneonta, New York and
    (86) directly north of Athens, Pennsylvania. The three cities form a triangle that is nearly a right triangle. Use the distance formula to estimate the distance from Athens to Oneonta. Each unit on the grid represents 5 miles. about 83 miles

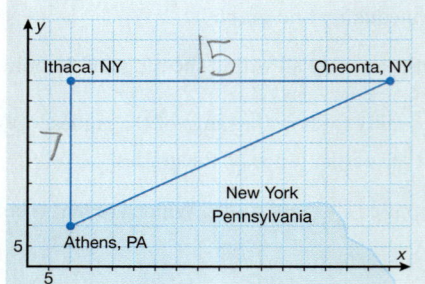

24. **Error Analysis** Two students factor the polynomial $(3x^2 + 6) - (4x^3 + 8x)$. Which
    (87) student is correct? Explain the error.

	Student A	Student B
	$3(x^2 + 2) - 4x(x^2 - 2)$	$3(x^2 + 2) - 4x(x^2 + 2)$
	$(3 - 4x)(x^2 - 4)$	$(3 - 4x)(x^2 + 2)$

Student B; Sample: Student A did not distribute the negative sign correctly.

25. **Probability** A bag has $2x + 1$ red marbles, $3x$ blue marbles, and $x + 2$ green
    (38) marbles. What is the probability of picking a red marble? $\frac{1}{3}$

26. **Multi-Step** A toolbox is 2 feet high. Its volume is represented by the expression
    (79) $2x^2 - 8x + 6$.

    a. Factor the expression completely. $2(x - 3)(x - 1)$

    b. Identify the expressions that represent the length and width of the toolbox.
    Sample: The length is $(x - 1)$ and the width is $(x - 3)$.

27. **(Hardiness Zones)** The state of Kansas falls into USDA hardiness zones 5b and
    (82) 6a. This means that plants in these zones must be able to tolerate an average minimum temperature range greater than or equal to $-15°F$, and less than $-5°F$. Write an inequality to represent the temperature range of the hardiness zones in Kansas. $-15 \leq t < -5$

CHALLENGE

Simplify:

$\dfrac{\frac{x^2 - 9}{x}}{\frac{x^2 + 5x + 6}{x^2}} \quad \dfrac{x(x - 3)}{x + 2}$

28. Multi-Step A rectangular playing field has a perimeter of $8x$ feet. Its length is 2 feet greater than $2x$.
(83)
   a. Write expressions for the length and width of the rectangle. length: $2x + 2$, width: $2x - 2$
   b. Write an expression for the area of the field. $4x^2 - 4$
   c. The playing field is in a city park. The park is a large square with a side length of x^2. Write and factor an expression for the area of the park that does not include the playing field. $x^4 - 4x^2 + 4 = (x^2 - 2)^2$

29. (Vertical Motion) The height h of an object t seconds after it begins to fall is given by
(83) the equation $h = -16t^2 + vt + s$, where v is the initial velocity and s is the initial height. When an object falls, its initial velocity is zero. Write an equation for the height of an object t seconds after it begins to fall from 14,400 feet. Then factor the expression representing the height. $h = -16t^2 + 14{,}400$; $16(30 + t)(30 - t)$

30. Given the equation $r = \frac{kst}{p}$, use the terms "jointly proportional to" and "inversely
(Inv 8) proportional to" to describe the relation in the equation such that k is the constant of variation. In the equation, r is jointly proportional to s and t, and inversely proportional to p.

Problem 30
Error Alert
Students can sometimes confuse the terms jointly and inversely. Remind them that if the value of a variable increases as the value of a related variable decreases, then the variables are inversely proportional.

LOOKING FORWARD

Solving complex fractions prepares students for

• **Lesson 95** Combining Rational Expressions with Unlike Denominators

• **Lesson 99** Solving Rational Equations

LESSON 93

1 Warm Up

Problem 5
Remind students that the difference of squares $a^2x^2 - b^2 = (ax + b)(ax - b)$.

2 New Concepts

In this lesson, students learn to divide polynomials.

Discuss the definition of a polynomial. Explain that division of polynomials is similar to division of whole numbers.

Example 1

Point out to students that a polynomial is the sum or difference of monomials, and that dividing a polynomial by a monomial can be done by dividing each term by the monomial.

Additional Example 1
Divide $(6x^4 + 4x^3 - 2x^2) \div 2x$.
$3x^3 + 2x^2 - x$

LESSON RESOURCES

Student Edition Practice Workbook 93
Reteaching Master 93
Adaptations Master 93
Challenge and Enrichment Master C93, E93

LESSON 93

Dividing Polynomials

Warm Up

1. Vocabulary A _____ is a monomial or the sum or difference of monomials. **polynomial**

Divide.

2. $\dfrac{72x^2 - 8x}{8x}$ $9x - 1$

3. $\dfrac{15x^2 - 3x}{5x - 1}$ $3x$

Factor.

4. $2x^2 + x - 3$ $(2x + 3)(x - 1)$

5. $25x^2 - 9$ $(5x + 3)(5x - 3)$

New Concepts

A polynomial division problem can be written as a rational expression. To divide a polynomial by a monomial, divide each term in the numerator by the denominator.

Example 1 Dividing a Polynomial by a Monomial

Divide $(8x^3 + 12x^2 + 4x) \div 4x$.

SOLUTION

$(8x^3 + 12x^2 + 4x) \div 4x$

$= \dfrac{(8x^3 + 12x^2 + 4x)}{4x}$ Write as a rational expression.

$= \dfrac{8x^3}{4x} + \dfrac{12x^2}{4x} + \dfrac{4x}{4x}$ Divide each term by the denominator.

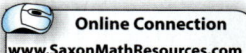 Divide out common factors.

$= 2x^2 + 3x + 1$ Simplify.

Division of a polynomial by a binomial is similar to division of whole numbers.

	Words	Numbers	Polynomials
Step 1	Factor the numerator and denominator, if possible.	$\dfrac{128}{4} = \dfrac{32 \cdot 4}{4}$	$\dfrac{x^2 + 4x + 3}{x + 1} = \dfrac{(x + 3)(x + 1)}{x + 1}$
Step 2	Divide out any common factors.	$\dfrac{32 \cdot \cancel{4}}{\cancel{4}}$	$\dfrac{(x + 3)\cancel{(x + 1)}}{\cancel{x + 1}}$
Step 3	Simplify.	32	$x + 3$

MATH BACKGROUND

The equation

$(ax^2 + bx + c) \div (x + d) = x + e$ can be written as a rational equation in the form:

$\dfrac{ax^2 + bx + c}{x + d} = x + e$

It can also be written in long-division form:

$x + d \overline{) ax^2 + bx + c}^{\,x + e}$

Regardless of the form, the quotient times the divisor is always equal to the dividend. This is a good way for students to learn to check their work.

Example 2 Dividing a Polynomial by a Binomial

Divide each expression.

a. $(x^2 - 6x + 9) \div (x - 3)$

SOLUTION

$(x^2 - 6x + 9) \div (x - 3)$

$= \dfrac{x^2 - 6x + 9}{x - 3}$ Write as a rational expression.

$= \dfrac{(x - 3)(x - 3)}{x - 3}$ Factor the numerator.

$= \dfrac{(x - 3)\cancel{(x - 3)}}{\cancel{(x - 3)}}$ Divide out common factors.

$= x - 3$ Simplify.

b. $(x^2 - 5x + 6) \div (2 - x)$

SOLUTION

$(x^2 - 5x + 6) \div (2 - x)$

$= \dfrac{x^2 - 5x + 6}{2 - x}$ Write as a rational expression.

$= \dfrac{(x - 3)(x - 2)}{2 - x}$ Factor the numerator.

$= \dfrac{(x - 3)(x - 2)}{-x + 2}$ Write the denominator in descending order.

$= \dfrac{(x - 3)(x - 2)}{-1(x - 2)}$ Factor out a -1 in the denominator.

$= \dfrac{(x - 3)\cancel{(x - 2)}}{-1\cancel{(x - 2)}}$ Divide out common factors.

$= -x + 3$ Simplify.

Hint
When the signs of the binomials, one in the numerator and one in the denominator, are opposites, factor out -1.

Just as with whole numbers, long division can also be used to divide polynomials.

$$\begin{array}{r} 27 \\ 21\overline{)567} \\ -42 \\ \hline 147 \\ -147 \\ \hline 0 \end{array} \qquad \begin{array}{r} x + 2 \\ x + 1\overline{)x^2 + 3x + 2} \\ -(x^2 + x) \\ \hline 2x + 2 \\ -(2x + 2) \\ \hline 0 \end{array}$$

Example 2

Remind students to factor the numerator and denominator, if possible.

Additional Example 2

Divide each expression.

a. $(x^2 + 5x - 14) \div (x + 7)$ $x - 2$

b. $(x^2 + 5x - 14) \div (2 - x)$
$-(x + 7)$

Error Alert A common mistake when dividing by a polynomial is to divide the numerator by each term in the denominator. Write the statement:

$$\dfrac{x}{x^2 + 3x - 4} \neq \dfrac{x}{x^2} + \dfrac{x}{3x} - \dfrac{x}{4}$$

Remind students that only terms in the numerator can be divided by the denominator.

Lesson 93

ENGLISH LEARNERS

For this lesson, explain the meanings of the prefixes **mono-, bi-,** and **poly-**. Say:

"Mono- means one, alone, or single, bi- means two, and poly- means many or much."

Connect the meaning of monomials and polynomials by the definition of polynomials. Emphasize that a polynomial is "an expression with one or multiple monomials."

Discuss examples of words that use mono-, bi-, and poly- and relate the use of the prefixes to their definitions, e.g. polygon, monopoly, bicycle, polymer, and monorail.

Example 3
Emphasize to students that long division can be used to divide polynomials.

Additional Example 3
Divide using long division.
$(13x^2 + 5x - 42) \div (x + 2)$
$13x - 21$

Example 4
Polynomial long division may have remainders. Students can multiply the divisor by the quotient and then add the remainder to that product to check their work.

Additional Example 4
Divide using long division.
$(4x^2 + 7x + 17) \div (x - 3)$
$4x + 19 + \frac{74}{x-3}$

TEACHER TIP
Emphasize that when using long division to divide polynomials, the remainder is a rational expression using the divisor as the denominator.

Caution
Be sure to put the divisor and dividend in descending order before dividing.

Example 3 Dividing a Polynomial Using Long Division

Divide using long division.
$(-25x + 3x^2 + 8) \div (x - 8)$

SOLUTION
$(-25x + 3x^2 + 8) \div (x - 8)$

$x - 8 \overline{) 3x^2 - 25x + 8 }$ — Write in long-division form with expressions in standard form.

$\, 3x$
$x - 8 \overline{) 3x^2 - 25x + 8x }$ — Divide the first term of the dividend by the first term of the divisor to find the first term of the quotient.

$\, 3x$
$x - 8 \overline{) 3x^2 - 25x + 8 }$
$\, 3x^2 - 24x$
— Multiply the first term of the quotient by the binomial divisor. Write the product under the dividend. Align like terms.

$\, 3x$
$x - 8 \overline{) 3x^2 - 25x + 8 }$
$\, -(3x^2 - 24x)$
$\, -x + 8$
— Subtract the product from the dividend. Then bring down the next term in the dividend.

$\, 3x - 1$
$x - 8 \overline{) 3x^2 - 25x + 8 }$
$\, -3x^2 + 24x$
$\, -x + 8$
$\, -(-x + 8)$
$\, 0$
— Repeat the steps to find each term of the quotient.

— The remainder is 0.

The quotient is $(3x - 1)$ remainder 0.

Check Multiply the quotient and the divisor.
$(3x - 1)(x - 8)$
$= 3x^2 - 24x - x + 8$
$= 3x^2 - 25x + 8$

The divisor is not always a factor of the dividend. When it is not, the remainder will not be 0. The remainder can be written as a rational expression using the divisor as the denominator.

Example 4 Long Division with a Remainder

Divide using long division.
$(2x^2 - 9 - 7x) \div (-4 + x)$

SOLUTION

$(2x^2 - 9 - 7x) \div (-4 + x)$

$x - 4 \overline{)2x^2 - 7x - 9}$ Write in long-division form with expressions in standard form.

$\begin{array}{r} 2x \\ x - 4 \overline{)2x^2 - 7x - 9} \end{array}$ Divide the first term of the dividend by the first term of the divisor to find the first term of the quotient.

$\begin{array}{r} 2x \\ x - 4 \overline{)2x^2 - 7x - 9} \\ 2x^2 - 8x \end{array}$ Multiply the first term of the quotient by the binomial divisor. Write the product under the dividend. Align like terms.

$\begin{array}{r} 2x \\ x - 4 \overline{)2x^2 - 7x - 9} \\ -(2x^2 - 8x) \\ \hline x - 9 \end{array}$ Subtract the product from the dividend. Then bring down the next term in the dividend.

$\begin{array}{r} 2x + 1 \\ x - 4 \overline{)2x^2 - 7x - 9} \\ -(2x^2 - 8x) \\ \hline x - 9 \\ -(x - 4) \\ \hline -5 \end{array}$ Repeat the steps to find each term of the quotient.

The quotient is $2x + 1 - \dfrac{5}{x - 4}$.

Example 5   Dividing a Polynomial with a Zero Coefficient

Divide $(-2x + 5 + 3x^3) \div (-3 + x)$.

SOLUTION

$(-2x + 5 + 3x^3) \div (-3 + x)$

$(3x^3 - 2x + 5) \div (x - 3)$ Write each polynomial in standard form.

$x - 3 \overline{)3x^3 + 0x^2 - 2x + 5}$ Write in long division form. Use $0x^2$ as a placeholder for the x^2-term.

$\begin{array}{r} 3x^2 + 9x + 25 \\ x - 3 \overline{)3x^3 + 0x^2 - 2x + 5} \\ -(3x^3 - 9x^2) \\ \hline 9x^2 - 2x \\ -(9x^2 - 27x) \\ \hline 25x + 5 \\ -(25x - 75) \\ \hline 80 \end{array}$

$3x^3 \div x = 3x^2$

Multiply $3x^2(x - 3)$. Then subtract.

Bring down $-2x$. $9x^2 \div x = 9x$

Multiply $9x(x - 3)$. Then subtract.

Bring down 5. $25x \div x = 25$

Multiply $25(x - 3)$. Then subtract.

The remainder is 80.

The quotient is $3x^2 + 9x + 25 + \dfrac{80}{x - 3}$.

Lesson 93   619

Example 5

Point out to students that when using long division to divide polynomials, it is very important to write the polynomial in standard form and to use 0 as the placeholder for any missing terms.

Additional Example 5

Divide $(6x^2 - 7 + 3x^3) \div (4 + x)$.

$3x^2 - 6x + 24 - \dfrac{103}{x + 4}$

INCLUSION

Using long division, have students divide the trinomial $x^2 - 3x - 18$ by the binomial $x - 6$ on grid paper to help them keep their work properly aligned.

Once the students have the answer, have them multiply the divisor by their answer to check that the product of the two expressons is equal to the dividend.

Next, have the students write a rational expression using the same polynomials.

$$\dfrac{x^2 - 3x - 18}{x - 6}$$

Have them factor and divide out like factors to find the quotient.

Point out that either method, finding the quotient using long division or using a rational expression and factoring, should result in the same quotient.

Lesson 93   619

Example 6

In this example, division of polynomials is used to solve a word problem.

Extend the Example

"What is the domain of x? How do you know?" $x > 6$; Since $x - 6$ is the width and $x - 5$ is the length of the garden, both have to be greater than zero for there to be a garden.

"If Jim added a fence around his garden and that added another foot to both the width and length, what is the new area?"
$(x - 5)(x - 4) =$
$x^2 - 9x + 20$ square feet

Additional Example 6

Jillian wants to find the radius of the circular fountain in the park. The area is $16\pi x^2 + 24\pi x + 9\pi$ square feet. What is the radius of the fountain? $4x + 3$ feet

Lesson Practice

Problem b
Scaffolding Have students write a rational expression, and then have them factor each term completely and divide out common factors.

Problem f
Error Alert Students may forget to include the divisor as the denominator of the remainder. Remind them that the remainder is a fractional part of the divisor.

Example 6 Application: Length of a Garden

Jim wants to find the length of the rectangular garden outside his office. The area is $(x^2 - 11x + 30)$ square feet. The width is $(x - 6)$ feet. What is the length of the garden?

SOLUTION

Hint
To find the length, solve the formula for the area of a rectangle, $A = lw$, for the length.

$l = \dfrac{A}{w}$ Solve for l.

$= \dfrac{x^2 - 11x + 30}{(x - 6)}$ Evaluate for A and w.

$= \dfrac{(x - 6)(x - 5)}{(x - 6)}$ Factor the numerator.

$= \dfrac{\cancel{(x - 6)}(x - 5)}{\cancel{(x - 6)}}$ Divide out common factors.

$= (x - 5)$ Simplify.

The length of the garden is $(x - 5)$ feet.

Lesson Practice

Divide each expression.

a. $(7x^4 + 7x^3 - 84x^2) \div 7x^2$ $x^2 + x - 12$ (Ex 1)

b. $(x^2 - 10x + 25) \div (x - 5)$ $x - 5$ (Ex 2)

c. $(3x^2 - 14x - 5) \div (5 - x)$ $-3x - 1$ (Ex 2)

Divide using long division.

d. $(8x^2 + x^3 - 20x) \div (x - 2)$ $x^2 + 10x$ (Ex 3)

e. $(-3x^2 + 6x^3 + x - 33) \div (-2 + x)$ $6x^2 + 9x + 19 + \dfrac{5}{x - 2}$ (Ex 4)

f. $(6x + 5x^3 - 8) \div (x - 4)$ $5x^2 + 20x + 86 + \dfrac{336}{x - 4}$ (Ex 5)

g. Carlos wants to find the width of his rectangular deck. The area is $(x^2 - 10x + 24)$ square feet and the length is $(x - 4)$ feet. What is the width? $(x - 6)$ feet (Ex 6)

Practice   Distributed and Integrated

1. Find the distance between $(-3, 2)$ and $(9, -3)$. Give the answer in simplest radical form.   13 (86)

2. Solve $\dfrac{5}{16}y + \dfrac{3}{8} \geq \dfrac{1}{2}$, and graph the solution. $y \geq \dfrac{2}{5}$; (77)

Factor.

3. $2x^2 + 12x + 16$ $2(x + 4)(x + 2)$ (79)

4. $3x^3 - 5x^2 - 9x + 15$ $(3x - 5)(x^2 - 3)$ (87)

*5. Find the quotient: $\dfrac{4x^3 + 42x^2 - 2x}{2x}$. $(2x^2 + 21x - 1)$
(93)

6. Find the axis of symmetry for the graph of the equation $y = x^2 - 2x$. $x = 1$
(89)

Simplify.

7. $\dfrac{\frac{7x^4}{4x+18}}{\frac{3x^2}{6x+27}}$ $\dfrac{7x^2}{2}$
(92)

*8. $\dfrac{\frac{1}{x^3}}{\frac{1}{x^3} + \frac{1}{x^3}}$ $\dfrac{1}{2}$
(92)

*9. **Write** Explain how to check that $(5x + 6)$ is the correct quotient of
(93) $(15x^2 + 13x - 6) \div (3x - 1)$. Sample: Multiply the divisor by the quotient. The product should equal the dividend.

*10. **Justify** Show that the quotient of $(x^2 - 4) \div (x + 2)$ can be found using two different methods.
(93)

10. Method 1:
$\dfrac{x^2 - 4}{x + 2} = \dfrac{(x-2)(x+2)}{(x+2)}$
$= (x - 2)$

Method 2:
$\,x - 2$
$x + 2\,\overline{)\,x^2 + 0x - 4}$
$\underline{-x^2 - 2x}$
$-2x - 4$
$\underline{+2x + 4}$
0

*11. (Swimming) The city has decided to open a new public pool. The area of the new rectangular pool is $(x^2 - 16x + 63)$ square feet and the width is $(x - 7)$ feet. What is the length? $(x - 9)$ feet
(93)

*12. **Multiple Choice** Simplify $\dfrac{x^3 - 7x + 3x^2 - 21}{x + 3}$. A
(93)

A $x^2 - 7$ B $x^3 - 7$
C -3 D $\dfrac{x^2 - 7}{2x}$

*13. **Error Analysis** Students were asked to simplify $\dfrac{\frac{6x^2 - 6x}{8x^2 + 8x}}{\frac{3x - 3}{4x^2 + 4x}}$. Which student is correct? Explain the error. Student A; Sample: Student B did not write solution in simplest form.
(92)

Student A	Student B
$\dfrac{6x^2 - 6x}{8x^2 + 8x} \cdot \dfrac{4x^2 + 4x}{3x - 3}$	$\dfrac{6x^2 - 6}{8x^2 + 8x} \cdot \dfrac{4x^2 + 4x}{3x - 3}$
$= \dfrac{6x(x-1)}{8x(x+1)} \cdot \dfrac{4x(x+1)}{3(x-1)}$	$= \dfrac{6x(x-1)}{8x(x+1)} \cdot \dfrac{4x(x+1)}{3(x-1)}$
$= x$	$= \dfrac{24x^2}{24x}$

14. **Multi-Step** Brent rode his scooter $\dfrac{8x^2 - 48x}{24x^5}$ minutes to get to baseball practice that
(92) was $\dfrac{7x - 42}{4x^2}$ miles away.

a. Find his rate in miles per minute. $\dfrac{21x^2}{4}$ miles per minute

b. If the rate is divided by $\dfrac{1}{x}$, what is the new rate? $\dfrac{21x^3}{4}$ miles per minute

*15. **Geometry** The area of a parallelogram is $\dfrac{m + n}{5}$ square inches and the height is
(92) $\dfrac{m^2 + n^2}{15}$ inches. What is the length of the base? $\dfrac{3(m + n)}{m^2 + n^2}$ inches

16. Solve and graph the inequality $|x| > 84$. $x < -84$ OR $x > 84$
(91)

Lesson 93   621

Check for Understanding

The questions below help assess the concepts taught in this lesson.

"Explain some of the first steps that should be taken before dividing a polynomial." Sample: Check if the polynomial can be factored, and write the polynomial in standard form.

"When doing long division, why are placeholders necessary for the missing terms in the polynomial?" Sample: Different places in the polynomial represent different powers of the variable.

3 Practice

Math Conversations
Discussion to strengthen understanding

Problem 7
Before students simplify the complex fractions, encourage them to factor the polynomials.

Lesson 93   621

*17. **Census** The census of England and Wales has a margin of error of ±104,000 people. The 2001 census found the population to be 52,041,916. Write an absolute-value inequality to express the possible range of the population. Then solve the inequality to find the actual range for the population.
$|x - 52,041,916| \leq 104,000$; $51,937,916 \leq x \leq 52,145,916$

18. **Error Analysis** Two students solve the inequality $|x + 11| > -15$. Which student is correct? Explain the error. Student A; Sample: Student B did not realize that all absolute values are greater than −15.

Student A	Student B
$|x + 11| > -15$ x can be any real number.	$|x + 11| > -15$ $x = \emptyset$

19. **Multiple Choice** When simplifying $\frac{1}{x^2 - 5x - 50} + \frac{1}{2x - 20}$, what is the numerator? **D**

A 1   **B** 2   **C** $x + 5$ **D** $x + 7$

*20. **Analyze** Explain what can be done so that $\frac{1}{3-r}$ and $\frac{5r}{r-3}$ have like denominators.

20. Sample: Multiply either of the expressions by $\frac{-1}{-1}$ because $-1(3-r) = -3+r = r-3$, or $-1(r-3) = -r+3 = 3-r$.

21. **Probability** Mr. Brunetti writes quadratic equations on pieces of paper and puts them in a hat, and then tells his students each to choose two at random. After each student picks, his or her two papers go back in the hat. The functions are $y = 4x^2 - 3x + 7$, $y = -7 + x^2$, $y = -2x + 6x^2$, $y = 0.5x^2 + 1.1$, and $y = -\frac{1}{2}x^2 + 7x + 5$. What is the probability of a student choosing two functions that have a minimum? $\frac{3}{5}$

22. **Error Analysis** Two students divide the following rational expression. Which student is correct? Explain the error. Student A; Sample: Student B did not multiply by the reciprocal of the rational expression.

Student A	Student B
$\frac{m^2}{6m^2} \div (m^2 + 2)$ $\frac{m^2}{6m^2} \cdot \frac{1}{m^2 + 2} = \frac{1}{6(m^2 + 2)}$	$\frac{m^2}{6m^2} \div (m^2 + 2)$ $\frac{m^2}{6m^2} \cdot \frac{m^2 + 2}{1} = \frac{m^2 + 2}{6}$

23. **Cost** A bakery sells specialty rolls by the dozen. The first dozen costs $6b + b^2$ dollars. Each dozen thereafter costs $4b + b^2$ dollars. If Marcello buys 4 dozen rolls, how much does he pay? $2b(9 + 2b)$ dollars

24. Find the vertical and horizontal asymptotes and graph $y = \frac{4}{x+2}$. $x = -2$; $y = 0$

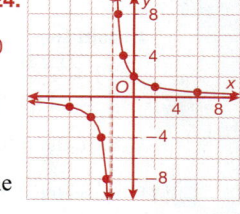

25. **Flooring** Theo is installing new kitchen tiles. The design on the tile includes a square within a square. The smaller square has a side length of s centimeters. The expression $4s^2 + 12s + 9$ describes the area of the entire tile. What is the difference between the length of the tile and the length of the square within the tile? $s + 3$ centimeters

26. Multi-Step Tony is sketching the view from the top of a 256-foot-tall observation
(84) tower and accidentally drops his pencil.
   a. Use the formula $h = -16t^2 + 256$ to make a table of values showing the height h
      of the pencil, 1, 2, and 3 seconds after it is dropped.   (1, 240), (2, 192), (3, 112)
   b. Graph the function.
   c. About how long does it take for the pencil to hit the ground?   about 4 seconds

27. (Pendulums) The time it takes a pendulum to swing back and forth depends on its
(84) length. The formula $l = 2.45\frac{t^2}{\pi^2}$ approximates this relationship. Graph the function
using 3.14 for π. Use the graph to estimate the time it takes a pendulum that is
1 meter long to swing back and forth.   about 2 sec

28. Write Explain how to determine whether a triangle with side lengths 5, 7, and 10 is
(85) a right triangle.

29. Multi-Step A bag of marbles contains 3 red, 5 blue, 2 purple, and 4 clear marbles.
(80) a. Make a graph that represents the frequency distribution.
   b. What is the probability of drawing a red or a clear marble? $\frac{7}{14} = \frac{1}{2}$

30. Given the following table, find the value of the constant of variation and
(Inv 8) complete the missing values in the table given that y varies directly with x and
inversely with z. $k = 3$

y	x	z
1	1	3
3	2	2
6	4	2
9	6	2
2	8	12

28. Sample: Substitute 5 for a, 7 for b, and 10 for c in the equation $a^2 + b^2 = c^2$ and simplify the equation. If the equation is true, then the triangle is a right triangle. If the equation is false, then the triangle is not a right triangle.

29.

Marbles

26 b.
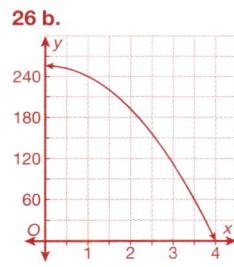

27.
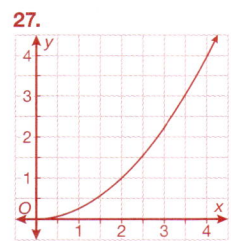

Problem 27
If students graph this function without a graphing calculator, tell them to use multiples of π for t to make the calculations easier. For example, let $t = 3 \cdot 3.14$. Then $(3 \cdot 3.14)^2 = 3^2 \cdot (3.14)^2$ and the $(3.14)^2$ will divide out.

Problem 30
A review of the definitions of direct and inverse variation may be helpful.

Lesson 93   623

LOOKING FORWARD

Dividing polynomials prepares students for

• **Lesson 95** Combining Rational Expressions with Unlike Denominators

• **Lesson 99** Solving Rational Equations

LESSON 94

1 Warm Up

Problem 2
Remind students that the absolute value of a number is its distance from zero. Distance is always positive.

2 New Concepts

In this lesson, students learn to solve multi-step absolute-value equations and to graph the solutions.

Example 1

Students solve equations involving two operations.

Additional Example 1
Solve each equation. Then graph the solution.

a. $\dfrac{|x|}{2} - 1 = 14$ $\{-30, 30\}$;

b. $-3|x| - 10 = -5$ Ø; There is no graph.

TEACHER TIP

Explain to students that the absolute-value symbol is a grouping symbol. Like parentheses, it must be isolated before it can be "undone" in an equation.

LESSON RESOURCES

Student Edition Practice Workbook 94
Reteaching Master 94
Adaptations Master 94
Challenge and Enrichment Master C94

LESSON 94

Solving Multi-Step Absolute-Value Equations

Warm Up

1. **Vocabulary** The _____ of a number *n* is the distance from *n* to 0 on a number line. **absolute value**

Simplify.

2. $|-9| - 5$ 4

3. $|12 - 23|$ 11

Solve.

4. $6x - 7 = 11$ $x = 3$

5. $11x + 8 = 41$ $x = 3$

New Concepts

To solve an absolute-value equation, begin by isolating the absolute value. Then use the definition of absolute value to write the absolute-value equation as two equations. Solve each equation, and write the solution set. There are often two answers to an absolute-value equation. The solutions can be graphed on a number line by placing a closed circle at each value in the solution set.

Math Language
The **absolute value** of a number *n* is the distance from 0 to *n* on a number line. The absolute value of 0 is 0.

Hint
Isolate the absolute value using inverse operations.

Example 1 Solving Equations with Two Operations

Solve each equation. Then graph the solution.

a. $\dfrac{|x|}{5} + 3 = 18$

SOLUTION

First isolate the absolute value. Write the equation so that the absolute value is on one side of the equation by itself.

$\dfrac{|x|}{5} + 3 = 18$

$\underline{\quad -3 = -3\quad}$ Subtraction Property of Equality

$\dfrac{|x|}{5} = 15$ Simplify.

$5 \cdot \dfrac{|x|}{5} = 5 \cdot 15$ Multiplication Property of Equality

$|x| = 75$ Simplify.

$x = 75$ or $x = -75$ Write as two equations without an absolute value.

The solution set is $\{-75, 75\}$.

Graph the solution on a number line.

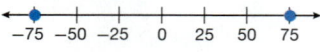

Online Connection
www.SaxonMathResources.com

624 *Saxon Algebra 1*

MATH BACKGROUND

Solving absolute-value equations involves many of the same steps as solving multi-step equations in order to isolate the absolute value. Then, the definition of absolute value is applied to find the solution set.

It is critical to understand that the absolute value of a number is its distance from zero. This distance can be to the left or right of 0. Even though the numbers are negative in one direction, the distance is still positive.

Beware of equations which simplify to an absolute value equal to a negative number. For these equations, there are no solutions because absolute value is never negative.

Emphasize to students that the absolute value expression must be isolated. The expression's distance from zero is given on the opposite side of the equal sign. If the absolute value has other operators on the same side with it, then the distance of the quantity in the absolute value symbol from zero is not clear.

b. $4|x| - 9 = 15$

SOLUTION

First isolate the absolute value.

$4|x| - 9 = 15$

$\quad 4|x| = 24$ Add 9 to both sides.

$\quad\quad |x| = 6$ Divide both sides by 4.

$x = 6 \quad$ and $\quad x = -6$ Write as two equations without an absolute value.

The solution set is $\{-6, 6\}$.

Graph the solution on a number line.

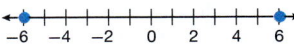

Example 2   Solving Equations with More than Two Operations

Solve each equation.

a. $\dfrac{5|x|}{2} + 4 = 4$

SOLUTION

$\dfrac{5|x|}{2} + 4 = 4$

$\dfrac{5|x|}{2} = 0$ Subtract 4 from both sides.

$5|x| = 0$ Multiply both sides by 2.

$|x| = 0$ Divide both sides by 5.

Since the absolute value is equal to zero, there is only one solution. The solution set is $\{0\}$.

b. $\dfrac{2|x|}{6} + 3 = 1$

SOLUTION

$\dfrac{2|x|}{6} + 3 = 1$

$\dfrac{2|x|}{6} = -2$ Subtract 3 from both sides.

$2|x| = -12$ Multiply both sides by 6.

$|x| = -6$ Divide both sides by 2.

By the definition of absolute value, we know that there are no solutions to this equation. The absolute value is never negative. The solution set is empty. You can write this as $\{\}$ or $\emptyset$.

Math Reasoning

Analyze Why can the absolute value never be negative?

Sample: A distance can only be represented by 0 or a positive number.

INCLUSION

Use the following strategy with students who have difficulty following multiple steps. The steps to solving these equations should be clearly identified.

1. Isolate the absolute value.
2. Set up two equations to show the definition of absolute value.
3. Solve the two equations.

Having students label their work with the steps will lead them through the steps in the appropriate order. Have a bulletin board or poster modeling these steps with an example problem for students to see as they work.

Example 3

Students learn to solve equations with operations inside the absolute-value symbols.

Additional Example 3

Solve each equation.

a. $|5x| - 10 = 25$ $\{-7, 7\}$

b. $2|x - 4| + 10 = 30$ $\{-6, 14\}$

c. $3\left|\dfrac{x}{2} - 1\right| = 18$ $\{-10, 14\}$

Error Alert Students may try to isolate the variable without isolating the absolute value first. Be sure to emphasize that once the absolute value is isolated, the definition of absolute value must be applied.

Example 3 Solving Equations with Operations Inside the Absolute-Value Symbols

Solve each equation.

a. $|2x| + 9 = 15$

SOLUTION

$|2x| + 9 = 15$

$|2x| = 6$ Subtract 9 from both sides.

Write the equation as two equations without the absolute value. Then solve both equations.

$2x = 6$ or $2x = -6$

$x = 3$ Divide both sides by 2. $x = -3$

The solution set is $\{3, -3\}$.

b. $6|x + 3| - 8 = 10$

SOLUTION

$6|x + 3| - 8 = 10$

$6|x + 3| = 18$ Add 8 to both sides.

$|x + 3| = 3$ Divide both sides by 6.

Write the equation as two equations without the absolute value and solve.

$x + 3 = 3$ or $x + 3 = -3$

$x = 0$ Subtract 3 from both sides. $x = -6$

The solution set is $\{0, -6\}$.

c. $5\left|\dfrac{x}{3} - 2\right| = 15$

SOLUTION

$5\left|\dfrac{x}{3} - 2\right| = 15$

$\left|\dfrac{x}{3} - 2\right| = 3$ Divide both sides by 5.

Write the equation as two equations without the absolute value and solve.

$\dfrac{x}{3} - 2 = 3$ or $\dfrac{x}{3} - 2 = -3$

$\dfrac{x}{3} = 5$ Add 2 to both sides. $\dfrac{x}{3} = -1$

$x = 15$ Multiply both sides by 3. $x = -3$

The solution set is $\{15, -3\}$.

Math Reasoning

Write Why do you often have to solve two equations without absolute value to find the solution to one equation with absolute value?

Sample: The definition of absolute value creates two possibilities for each absolute-value sign.

Example 4 Application: Archery

A 60-centimeter indoor archery target has several rings around a circular center. If the average diameter of a ring is d, and an arrow landing in that ring scores p points, the inner and outer diameters of the ring are given by the absolute-value equation $|d + 6p - 63| = 3$. Find the inner and outer diameters of the 8-point ring.

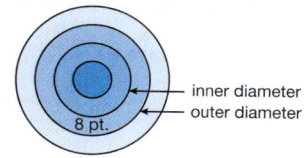

Caution
The absolute-value bars act as grouping symbols. Be sure to use the order of operations to simplify any expression within them.

SOLUTION

$|d + 6p - 63| = 3$
$|d + 6 \cdot 8 - 63| = 3$ Substitute 8 for p.
$|d + 48 - 63| = 3$ Multiply.
$|d - 15| = 3$ Subtract.

Write the absolute-value equation as two equations and solve.

$d - 15 = 3$ or $d - 15 = -3$
$d = 18$ Add 15 to both sides. $d = 12$

The inner diameter of the ring is 12 centimeters and the outer diameter of the ring is 18 centimeters.

Lesson Practice

Solve each equation. Then graph the solution. (Ex 1)

a. $\dfrac{|x|}{7} + 10 = 18$ {56, −56};

b. $3|x| - 11 = 10$ {7, −7};

Solve each equation.

c. $\dfrac{4|x|}{9} + 23 = 11$ ∅ (Ex 2)

d. $\dfrac{|x| + 3}{2} - 2 = 1$ {3, −3} (Ex 2)

e. $|7x| + 2 = 37$ {5, −5} (Ex 3)

f. $5|x + 1| - 2 = 23$ {4, −6} (Ex 3)

g. $9\left|\dfrac{x}{2} - 1\right| = 45$ {12, −8} (Ex 3)

h. **(Investments)** A factory produces items that cost $5 to make. The factory would like to invest $100 plus or minus $10 in the first batch. Use the equation $|5x - 100| = 10$ to find the least and greatest number of items the factory can produce.   18 items, 22 items (Ex 4)

Lesson 94

Example 4
Students use absolute-value equations to solve an archery problem.

Extend the Example
Find the inner and outer diameters of the 6-point ring. 24 cm and 30 cm

Additional Example 4
A family wants to spend $200 plus or minus $50 on a campsite for their entire trip. The campsite costs $25 per night. Use the equation $|200 - 25x| = 50$ to find the greatest and least number of nights the family can camp. 6 and 10 nights

Lesson Practice
Problem c
Error Alert Students need to stop when they isolate the absolute value and find that it equals a negative number. There is no need to go any further. There is no solution.

Problem f
Scaffolding Have students isolate the absolute value. Then apply the definition of absolute value.

Check for Understanding
The questions below help assess the concepts taught in this lesson.

"What are the steps for solving a multi-step absolute-value equation?" Sample: Isolate the absolute value. Apply the definition of absolute value. Set up two equations, and then solve them to find two solutions.

"What happens if the absolute value is equal to a negative number?" Sample: There is no solution.

ENGLISH LEARNERS

For Example 4, explain the meaning of the word **ring.** Tape a picture on the chalkboard and draw a circle around it. Say:

"This picture has a ring drawn around it. A ring is a circular line that surrounds an object. Circus acts are performed inside a large ring."

Ask volunteers to give examples of other types of rings. Sample: rings around a planet; a wedding ring

3 Practice

Math Conversations
Discussion to strengthen understanding

Problem 1
Combine the numerators, factor, and then cancel common factors in the numerator and denominator.

Problem 6
Remind students that when the droplet hits the ground, its height is 0.

Problem 7
Since the expression has 4 unlike terms, the students should factor by grouping. Factor pairs of terms rather than all four terms.

Practice Distributed and Integrated

Add or subtract.

1. (90) $\dfrac{m^2}{m-4} - \dfrac{16}{m-4}$ $m+4$

2. (90) $\dfrac{-66}{w^2 - w - 30} + \dfrac{w}{w-6}$ $\dfrac{w+11}{w+5}$

*3. **Write** Explain why some absolute-value equations have no solutions. (94)

*4. **Multiple Choice** The solution set $\{-12, 60\}$ correctly solves which absolute-value equation? **D** (94)

　A $\; 6\left|\dfrac{x}{4} - 1\right| = 42$ 　　　　B $\; -2\left|\dfrac{x}{4} - 1\right| = 16$

　C $\; 8\left|\dfrac{x}{3} - 2\right| = 48$ 　　　　D $\; -5\left|\dfrac{x}{6} - 4\right| = -30$

5. (**Refurbishing**) Rudy has $x + y$ junk cars in his lot. He fixes them up and sells (88) each car for $\dfrac{\$400 + \$100x}{y}$. If he sells 30% of them, how much profit will he make?

6. (**Physics**) The function $y = -16x^2 + 80x$ models the height of a droplet of water (89) from an in-ground sprinkler x seconds after it shoots straight up from ground level. Explain how you know when the droplet will hit the ground.

Factor.

7. (87) $2a^2 + 8ab + 6a + 24b$ $2(a+3)(a+4b)$

8. (79) $zx^{10} - 4zx^9 - 21zx^8$ $zx^8(x-7)(x+3)$

9. Find the product of $\dfrac{b-4}{b+9} \cdot (b^2 + 11b + 18)$. $(b-4)(b+2)$ (88)

*10. **Error Analysis** Students were asked to simplify $(15x^4 + 4x^2 + 3x^3) \div (x - 6)$. Which (93) student set their problem up correctly? Explain the error.   Student B; Sample: Student A did not put the dividend in descending order or insert a placeholder.

Student A	Student B
$(x-6)\overline{)(15x^4 + 4x^2 + 3x^3)}$	$(x-6)\overline{)(15x^4 + 3x^3 + 4x^2 + 0x + 0)}$

Simplify.

*11. (92) $\dfrac{\dfrac{-1}{10x-10}}{\dfrac{x^5}{10x^2 - 10}}$ $\dfrac{1-x}{x^5}$

12. (92) $\dfrac{\dfrac{2x}{3x+12}}{\dfrac{6x^2}{x^2 + 8x + 16}}$ $\dfrac{x+4}{9x}$

---

3. Sample: An absolute value cannot be negative, so any absolute-value equation that sets an absolute value equal to a negative number has no solution.

5. $\dfrac{30(x^2 + 4x + 4y + xy)}{y}$ dollars

6. Sample: The droplet is at ground level when $y = 0$. This first occurs at 0 seconds, before the water has shot out from the sprinkler. The maximum value occurs at $x = -\dfrac{b}{2a} = -\dfrac{80}{-32} = 2.5$. Because of symmetry, the droplet is at ground level 2.5 seconds before and after its maximum point, so it hits the ground 5 seconds after it shoots up.

628　Saxon Algebra 1

*13. (Canoeing) A canoe rental company charges $10 for the canoe and an additional
(94) charge per person. There are 4 people going on the trip and they have planned on
spending a total of $50. They hope that the total cost is within $20 of the planned
spending total. What is the minimum and maximum they can be charged per
person? **$5, $15**

Find the quotient.

14. $(1 + 4x^4 - 10x^2) \div (x + 2)$ $4x^3 - 8x^2 + 6x - 12 + \frac{25}{x+2}$
(93)

15. $\frac{25x^3 + 20x^2 - 5x}{5x}$ $(5x - 1)(x + 1)$
(93)

*16. Solve the equation $\frac{|x|}{11} + 9 = 15$ and graph the solution. $\{-66, 66\}$;
(94)

*17. **Justify** Show that the solution set to the equation $\frac{|x|}{-3} + 1 = 5$ is ∅.
(94)

17. Sample: Subtract 1 from both sides to get $\frac{|x|}{-3} = 4$. Then multiply both sides by −3 to get $|x| = -12$. Because absolute values cannot be negative, there are no solutions.

*18. **Multi-Step** Marty measured the area of his rectangular classroom. He determined
(93) that the area is $(-2x^2 + x^3 - 98 - 49x)$ square feet. The length is $(x + 6)$ feet.
   a. What is the width? $\left(x^2 - 8x - 1 - \frac{92}{x+6}\right)$ feet
   b. If the area is $(x^2 - 36)$ square feet, what is the width? $(x - 6)$ feet

19. **Geometry** The area of a triangle is $(10y^2 + 6y)$ square centimeters. The base is
(93) $(5y + 3)$ centimeters. What is the height? **4y centimeters**

*20. **Error Analysis** Students were asked to simplify $\frac{\frac{4x}{8x+16}}{\frac{12}{x+2}}$. Which student is correct?
(92) Explain the error.
Student B; Sample: Student A did not multiply by the reciprocal.

Student A	Student B
$\frac{4x}{8x+16} \cdot \frac{12}{x+2}$	$\frac{4x}{8x+16} \cdot \frac{x+2}{12}$
$= \frac{4x}{8(x+2)} \cdot \frac{12}{x+2}$	$= \frac{4x}{8(x+2)} \cdot \frac{x+2}{12}$
$= \frac{6x}{(x+2)(x+2)}$	$= \frac{x}{24}$

*21. (Commuting) It took Taylor $\frac{1}{x^2 + 3x - 40}$ minutes to get to work, which was
(92) $\frac{x^2}{6x + 48}$ miles away. Find his rate in miles per minute. $\frac{x^3 - 5x^2}{6}$ miles per minute

22. **Verify** Show that 0 is a solution to the inequality $|x - 14| < 30$. Sample:
(91) $|0 - 14| = |-14| = 14$ and $14 < 30$

23. **Multiple Choice** Which inequality is represented by the graph? **C**
(91)

  A $|x| \leq -21$ **B** $|x| < 21$
  C $|x| \leq 21$ **D** $|x| > 21$

24. **Analyze** When a line segment is horizontal, which expression under the radical in
(86) the distance formula is 0: $(x_2 - x_1)^2$ or $(y_2 - y_1)^2$? $(y_2 - y_1)^2$

Problem 15
Extend the Problem
Multiply the dividend by the divisor to verify that the solution is equal to the quotient.

Problem 17
Isolate the absolute value. Note that it is equal to a negative number.

Problem 19
The formula for the area of a triangle is $A = \frac{1}{2}bh$.

Problem 22
Substitute 0 into the equation and see if it makes the inequality true.

Lesson 94   629

25. **Multi-Step** Ornella hiked 8 miles on easy trails and 3 miles on difficult trails. Her hiking rate on the easy trails was 2.5 times faster than her rate on the difficult trails.
   a. Write a simplified rational expression for Ornella's total hiking time. $\frac{8}{2.5r} + \frac{3}{r} = \frac{15.5}{2.5r}$
   b. Find Ornella's hiking time if her hiking rate on the difficult trails was 2 miles per hour. 3.1 hours

26. Find the vertical and horizontal asymptotes and graph $y = \frac{1}{x-2} - 4$.

27. **Multi-Step** Phone Plan A costs $12 per month for local calls and $0.06 per minute for long-distance calls. Phone Plan B costs $15 per month for local calls plus $0.04 per minute for long-distance calls. How many minutes of long-distance calls would Jenna have to make for Plan B to cost less than Plan A?
   a. **Formulate** Write an inequality to answer. $12 + 0.06m > 15 + 0.04m$
   b. Solve the inequality and answer the question. $m > 150$; 150 minutes
   c. Graph the solution.

28. (United States Flag) An official American flag should have a length that is 1.9 times its width. The area of an official American flag can be found by the function $y = 1.9x^2$. Graph the function. Then use the graph to approximate the width of a flag that has an area of 47.5 square feet.

29. **Multi-Step** A rectangular garden that is 25 feet wide has a diagonal length that is 50 feet long.
   a. Find the length of the garden in simplest radical form. $25\sqrt{3}$ ft
   b. Find the perimeter of the garden to the nearest tenth of a foot. 136.6 ft

30. The volume of a sphere is $V = \frac{4}{3}\pi r^3$. Describe in words the relationship between the volume of a sphere and its radius. Identify the constant of variation. The volume of a sphere is directly proportional to the cube of its radius. The constant of variation is equal to $\frac{4}{3}\pi$.

28. 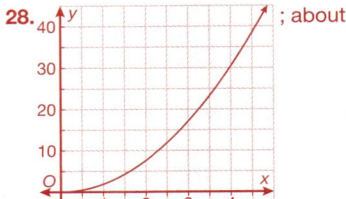 ; about 5 feet

26. $x = 2; y = -4$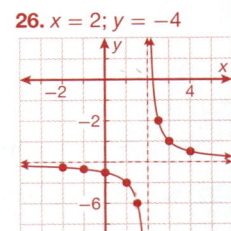

CHALLENGE

Write a multi-step absolute-value equation that has no solution.
Sample: $\left|\frac{x}{4} - 2\right| + 15 = 12$

LOOKING FORWARD

Solving multi-step absolute-value equations prepares students for

- **Lesson 101** Solving Multi-Step Absolute-Value Inequalities
- **Lesson 107** Graphing Absolute-Value Functions

LESSON 95

Combining Rational Expressions with Unlike Denominators

Warm Up

1. **Vocabulary** One of two or more numbers or expressions that are multiplied to get a product is called a (n) _____. **factor**

Find the LCM.

2. $8x^4y$ and $12x^3y^2$ $24x^4y^2$

3. $(9x - 27)$ and $(4x - 12)$ $36(x - 3)$

Factor.

4. $x^2 + 4x - 21$ $(x + 7)(x - 3)$

5. $10x^2 + 13x - 3$ $(5x - 1)(2x + 3)$

New Concepts

The steps for adding rational expressions are the same as for adding numerical fractions. Fractions with unlike denominators cannot be added unless you first find their least common denominator.

Example 1 Finding a Common Denominator

Find the least common denominator (LCD) for each expression.

Math Language

A **least common denominator** (LCD) is the least common multiple (LCM) of the denominators.

a. $\dfrac{3}{(x + 3)} - \dfrac{9}{(x^2 - 2x - 15)}$

SOLUTION

$\dfrac{3}{(x + 3)} - \dfrac{9}{(x^2 - 2x - 15)}$

$= \dfrac{3}{(x + 3)} - \dfrac{9}{(x + 3)(x - 5)}$ Factor each denominator, if possible.

To find the LCD of $(x + 3)$ and $(x + 3)(x - 5)$, use every factor of each denominator the greatest number of times it is a factor of either denominator. Each denominator has a factor of $(x + 3)$. One denominator also has a factor of $(x - 5)$. The product of these two factors is the LCD.

LCD = $(x + 3)(x - 5)$

b. $\dfrac{2x}{4x^2 - 196} + \dfrac{12x}{x^2 + x - 56}$

SOLUTION

$\dfrac{2x}{4x^2 - 196} + \dfrac{12x}{x^2 + x - 56}$

$= \dfrac{2x}{4(x - 7)(x + 7)} + \dfrac{12x}{(x - 7)(x + 8)}$ Factor each denominator completely.

LCD = $4(x - 7)(x + 7)(x + 8)$

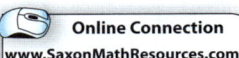
Online Connection
www.SaxonMathResources.com

Lesson 95   631

MATH BACKGROUND

Working with rational expressions can test the students' understanding of fractions. If the algorithm for adding and subtracting fractions is simply memorized, then adding and subtracting rational expressions can be challenging. Rational expressions can be treated as fractions. In order to add or subtract rational expressions, a common denominator must be found. Any common denominator will work, but the LCD is the most efficient. Keeping the terms simpler will help eliminate error.

Once a common denominator is found, each term must be multiplied by a factor equal to 1 so that equivalent fractions with a common denominator are found. Combine the fractions while keeping the denominator in factored form. After simplifying the numerator, it is important to factor the numerator to divide out factors that form quotients equal to one.

---

1 Warm Up

Problem 3
Remind students to factor first and then to find the LCM.

2 New Concepts

In this lesson, students combine rational expressions with unlike denominators.

Example 1
Students find a common denominator for rational expressions.

Additional Example 1
Find the least common denominator (LCD) for each expression.

a. $\dfrac{5}{x - 2} + \dfrac{6}{x^2 - x - 2}$
$(x - 2)(x + 1)$

b. $\dfrac{3x}{x^2 + 8x + 15} + \dfrac{4x}{5x^2 - 500}$
$5(x + 3)(x + 5)(x + 10)(x - 10)$

LESSON RESOURCES

Student Edition Practice
  Workbook 95
Reteaching Master 95
Adaptations Master 95
Challenge and Enrichment
  Master C95

Example 2

Students learn to use equivalent fractions to add rational expressions with unlike denominators.

Additional Example 2

Add $\dfrac{3x^2}{x^2-9} + \dfrac{x+2}{4x-12}$.

$\dfrac{13x^2 + 5x + 6}{4(x-3)(x+3)}$

Example 3

Students learn to use equivalent fractions to subtract rational expressions with unlike denominators.

Additional Example 3

Subtract $\dfrac{2x}{4x+16} - \dfrac{3x-4}{x^2-16}$.

$\dfrac{x^2 - 10x + 8}{2(x-4)(x+4)}$

Error Alert Students may forget to distribute the negative sign to each term in the numerator of the rational expression being subtracted. Putting parentheses around the terms in the numerator will help students to remember that they must subtract each term.

Example 2 Using Equivalent Fractions to Add with Unlike Denominators

Add $\dfrac{6x^2}{x^2-16} + \dfrac{x-1}{2x-8}$.

SOLUTION Factor each denominator.

$\dfrac{6x^2}{x^2-16} + \dfrac{x-1}{2x-8} = \dfrac{6x^2}{(x-4)(x+4)} + \dfrac{x-1}{2(x-4)}$

LCD $= 2(x-4)(x+4)$

Write an equivalent fraction for each addend with the LCD as a denominator.

Math Reasoning

Analyze What does it mean to write an equivalent fraction?

Sample: It means to multiply the numerator and denominator of a fraction by the same factor resulting in a fraction that is equal to the original fraction.

$\dfrac{6x^2}{(x-4)(x+4)} \cdot \dfrac{2}{2} = \dfrac{2(6x^2)}{2(x-4)(x+4)}$ Multiply the numerator and denominator of the first fraction by 2.

$\dfrac{x-1}{2(x-4)} \cdot \dfrac{x+4}{x+4} = \dfrac{(x-1)(x+4)}{2(x-4)(x+4)}$ Multiply the numerator and denominator of the second fraction by $\dfrac{x+4}{x+4}$.

$\dfrac{2(6x^2)}{2(x-4)(x+4)} + \dfrac{(x-1)(x+4)}{2(x-4)(x+4)}$ Write the sum of the equivalent fractions.

$= \dfrac{2(6x^2) + (x-1)(x+4)}{2(x-4)(x+4)}$ Add.

$= \dfrac{12x^2 + x^2 + 3x - 4}{2(x-4)(x+4)}$ Expand the numerator.

$= \dfrac{13x^2 + 3x - 4}{2(x-4)(x+4)}$ Combine like terms in the numerator.

Example 3 Using Equivalent Fractions to Subtract with Unlike Denominators

Subtract $\dfrac{4x^2}{9x-27} - \dfrac{2x-5}{x^2-9}$.

SOLUTION Factor each denominator.

$\dfrac{4x^2}{9x-27} - \dfrac{2x-5}{x^2-9} = \dfrac{4x^2}{9(x-3)} - \dfrac{2x-5}{(x-3)(x+3)}$

LCD $= 9(x-3)(x+3)$

$\dfrac{4x^2(x+3)}{9(x-3)(x+3)} - \dfrac{9(2x-5)}{9(x-3)(x+3)}$ Write the difference of the equivalent fractions.

$= \dfrac{4x^2(x+3) - 9(2x-5)}{9(x-3)(x+3)}$ Subtract.

$= \dfrac{4x^3 + 12x^2 - 18x + 45}{9(x-3)(x+3)}$ Expand the numerator.

There are no like terms, so the difference is $\dfrac{4x^3 + 12x^2 - 18x + 45}{9(x-3)(x+3)}$.

632   Saxon Algebra 1

 INCLUSION

To help students combine rational expressions, set up boxes. After students factor the denominators and determine the LCD for Example 3, have them draw unit factor boxes next to each term.

$\boxed{} \dfrac{(4x^2)}{9(x-3)} - \boxed{} \dfrac{(2x-5)}{(x-3)(x+3)}$

Then have the students compare the denominator of the terms to the LCD.

Say, "Since the first term is missing a factor of $(x+3)$, multiply by the unit factor $\dfrac{(x+3)}{(x+3)}$." Have students determine what to multiply the second term by. After the expression has been setup with common denominators it will be ready to simplify.

$\boxed{\dfrac{(x+3)}{(x+3)}} \dfrac{(4x^2)}{3 \cdot 3(x-3)} - \boxed{\dfrac{9}{9}} \dfrac{(2x-5)}{(x-3)(x+3)}$

Caution

Before factoring, write expressions in descending order.

Example 4 Adding and Subtracting with Unlike Denominators

a. Add $\dfrac{-35}{56 - 7x} + \dfrac{-6x - 2}{x^2 - 6x - 16}$.

SOLUTION

$\dfrac{-35}{56 - 7x} + \dfrac{-6x - 2}{x^2 - 6x - 16}$

$= \dfrac{-35}{-7(x - 8)} + \dfrac{-6x - 2}{(x - 8)(x + 2)}$ Factor each denominator.

$\text{LCD} = -7(x - 8)(x + 2)$ Find the LCD.

$\dfrac{-35(x + 2)}{-7(x - 8)(x + 2)} + \dfrac{-7(-6x - 2)}{-7(x - 8)(x + 2)}$ Write each fraction as an equivalent fraction.

$= \dfrac{-35(x + 2) + (-7)(-6x - 2)}{-7(x - 8)(x + 2)}$ Add.

$= \dfrac{7x - 56}{-7(x - 8)(x + 2)}$ Expand the numerator and collect like terms.

$= \dfrac{7(x - 8)}{-7(x - 8)(x + 2)}$ Factor the numerator.

$= -\dfrac{1}{x + 2}$ Divide out common factors.

b. Subtract $\dfrac{x - 5}{2x - 6} - \dfrac{x - 7}{4x - 12}$.

SOLUTION

$\dfrac{x - 5}{2x - 6} - \dfrac{x - 7}{4x - 12}$

$= \dfrac{x - 5}{2(x - 3)} - \dfrac{x - 7}{4(x - 3)}$ Factor each denominator.

$\text{LCD} = 4(x - 3)$ Find the LCD.

$\dfrac{2(x - 5)}{4(x - 3)} - \dfrac{(x - 7)}{4(x - 3)}$ Write each fraction as an equivalent fraction.

$= \dfrac{2(x - 5) - 1(x - 7)}{4(x - 3)}$ Subtract.

$= \dfrac{2x - 10 - x + 7}{4(x - 3)}$ Expand the numerator.

$= \dfrac{x - 3}{4(x - 3)}$ Collect like terms.

$= \dfrac{1}{4}$ Divide out common factors.

Hint

Always check to see if the numerator of the sum can be factored and if a common factor can be divided out.

Example 4

Students add and subtract rational expressions with unlike denominators. Then the sum or difference is simplified by dividing out like factors.

Additional Example 4

a. Add $\dfrac{-24}{32 - 8x} + \dfrac{4x + 1}{x^2 - 7x + 12}$.

$\dfrac{7x - 8}{(x - 4)(x - 3)}$

b. Subtract $\dfrac{x + 4}{3x + 9} - \dfrac{x + 9}{5x + 15}$.

$\dfrac{2x - 7}{15(x + 3)}$

Lesson 95

Example 5
Students add rational expressions to solve a rate problem.

Extend the Example
About how many hours does the trip take if the tailwind is 10 kilometers per hour? about 3.485 hours

Additional Example 5
Sarah biked $\frac{7x}{x^2 - 49}$ kilometers on Saturday. She biked $\frac{15}{5x + 35}$ kilometers on Sunday. How many kilometers did she bike altogether?  kilometers

Lesson Practice
Problem a
Scaffolding Factor both denominators completely. Then have students find the LCM of the denominator.

Problem f
Error Alert Students may not recognize x as a factor in the LCD. Remind them that every factor must be in the LCD.

Check for Understanding
The questions below help assess the concepts taught in this lesson.

"How do you find the LCD?" Sample: Factor each denominator. Find the LCM of the denominators. To find the LCM of the denominators, use every factor of each denominator the greatest number of times it is a factor of either denominator.

"When adding rational expressions with unlike denominators, what do you do after you find the LCD?" Sample: Find equivalent fractions with their denominators equal to the LCD.

Example 5 Application: Traveling

A pilot's single-engine aircraft flies at 230 kph if there is no wind. The pilot plans a round trip to a city that is 400 kilometers away. If there is a tailwind of w kilometers per hour, the time for the outbound flight is $\frac{400}{230 + w}$ hours. The time for the return flight with a headwind of w kilometers per hour is $\frac{400}{230 - w}$ hours. What is the total time for the round trip?

SOLUTION

$\frac{400}{230 + w} + \frac{400}{230 - w}$ Add to find the total time.

$\text{LCD} = (230 + w)(230 - w)$ Find the LCD.

$\frac{400(230 - w)}{(230 + w)(230 - w)} + \frac{400(230 + w)}{(230 + w)(230 - w)}$ Write equivalent fractions.

$= \frac{184{,}000}{(230 + w)(230 - w)}$ hours   Expand the numerator and collect like terms.

The round trip takes $\frac{184{,}000}{(230 + w)(230 - w)}$ hours.

Lesson Practice

Find the LCD for each expression.
(Ex 1)

a. $\frac{5x}{5x - 45} - \frac{44}{x^2 - 81}$ $\text{LCD} = 5(x - 9)(x + 9)$

b. $\frac{3x}{x + 4} - \frac{12}{x^2 + 2x - 8}$ $\text{LCD} = (x + 4)(x - 2)$

c. Add $\frac{3x^2}{x^2 - 25} + \frac{x - 1}{4x - 20}$. $\frac{13x^2 + 4x - 5}{4(x - 5)(x + 5)}$
(Ex 2)

d. Subtract $\frac{2x^2}{6x - 24} - \frac{3x - 4}{x^2 - 16}$. $\frac{x^3 + 4x^2 - 9x + 12}{3(x - 4)(x + 4)}$
(Ex 3)

e. Add $\frac{x - 1}{x^2 - 1} + \frac{2}{5x + 5}$. $\frac{7}{5(x + 1)}$
(Ex 4)

f. Subtract $\frac{2}{x^2 - 36} - \frac{1}{x^2 + 6x}$. $\frac{1}{x(x - 6)}$
(Ex 4)

g. Trenton hiked $\frac{4x}{x^2 - 64}$ miles on Saturday and $\frac{12}{7x - 56}$ miles on Sunday. How many miles did he hike altogether? $\frac{40x + 96}{7(x - 8)(x + 8)}$ miles
(Ex 5)

Practice Distributed and Integrated

Factor completely.

1. $3x^3 - 9x^2 - 30x$ $3x(x + 2)(x - 5)$
(Inv 9)

2. $8x^3y^2 + 4x^2y - 12xy^3$ $4xy(2x^2y + x - 3y^2)$
(Inv 9)

3. $32x^3 - 24x^4 + 4x^5$ $4x^3(x - 2)(x - 4)$
(79)

4. $mn^3 - 10mn^2 + 24mn$ $mn(n - 6)(n - 4)$
(79)

Find the quotient.

5. $\frac{4m}{17r} \div \frac{12m^2}{5r}$ $\frac{5}{51m}$

6. $(x^2 - 16x + 64) \div (x - 8)$ $(x - 8)$

7. Find the zeros of the function shown.   no zeros

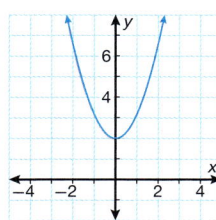

*8. Find the LCD of $\frac{4}{x+4} - \frac{8}{x^2+6x+8}$.   LCD $= (x+4)(x+2)$

*9. Add $\frac{2x}{2x^2 - 128} + \frac{5}{x^2 - 7x - 8}$. $\frac{x^2 + 6x + 40}{(x-8)(x+8)(x+1)}$

*10. Solve the equation $9|x| - 22 = 14$ and graph the solution. $\{-4, 4\}$;

11. **Error Analysis** Students were asked to subtract $\frac{6x^2}{x^2 + 6x - 16} - \frac{3}{8x - 16}$. Which student is correct? Explain the error.   Student A; Sample: Student B didn't distribute the negative all the way through the second numerator.

Student A	Student B
$\frac{6x^2}{x^2 + 6x - 16} - \frac{3}{8x - 16}$	$\frac{6x^2}{x^2 + 6x - 16} - \frac{3}{8x - 16}$
$\frac{6x^2}{(x+8)(x-2)} - \frac{3}{8(x-2)}$	$\frac{6x^2}{(x+8)(x-2)} - \frac{3}{8(x-2)}$
$\frac{6x^2(8)}{8(x+8)(x-2)} - \frac{3(x+8)}{8(x-2)(x+8)}$	$\frac{6x^2(8)}{8(x+8)(x-2)} - \frac{3(x+8)}{8(x-2)(x+8)}$
$\frac{48x^2 - 3x - 24}{8(x+8)(x-2)}$	$\frac{48x^2 - 3x + 24}{8(x+8)(x-2)}$

*12. **Generalize** Explain how to find the LCD of two algebraic rational expressions.

*13. **Running** Michele is training for a marathon. She ran $\frac{3x^2}{x^2 - 100}$ miles on Monday and $\frac{x-1}{2x-20}$ miles on Tuesday. How many miles did she run in all? $\frac{7x^2 + 9x - 10}{2(x+10)(x-10)}$ miles

*14. **Multi-Step** The girls' track team sprinted $\frac{2x}{4x^2 - 196}$ meters Thursday and $\frac{12x}{x^2 + x - 56}$ meters Friday.
   a. What was the total distance that the track team sprinted?
   b. If their rate was $\frac{2x}{x+8}$ meters per minute, how much time did it take them to sprint on Thursday and Friday? $\frac{25x + 176}{4(x-7)(x+7)}$ minutes

14a. $\frac{25x^2 + 176x}{2(x-7)(x+7)(x+8)}$ meters

12. Sample: Factor each denominator. The LCD must contain each factor of each denominator and use each factor the greatest number of times it occurs in either denominator.

3 Practice

Math Conversations

Discussion to strengthen understanding

Problem 5
To divide by a fraction is to multiply by its reciprocal. Before multiplying, divide out factors common to the numerator and denominator, if any.

Problem 9
Guide the students by asking them the following questions.

"What is the LCD of the fractions?" $2(x-8)(x+8)(x+1)$ or $(x-8)(x+8)(x+1)$

"How do you change the fractions so that they share the LCD?"
Sample: Multiply the numerator and denominator of each fraction by its missing factors of the LCD.

"Once the fractions share the LCD, what is the next step?"
Sample: Add the fractions.

Lesson 95   635

Problem 16
Extend the Problem
What is the greatest and least area the square can have?
64 square inches and 81 square inches

Problem 18
Remind students that when a term is within parentheses, it cannot be separated. In order to cancel these factors, they must both be identical.

Problem 19
Factor the expression that describes area. Then divide by the length to get the width.

Problem 22
Extend the Problem
Solve and graph $|x| \le 17$.
$-17 \le x \le 17$

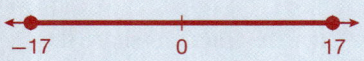

*15. **Error Analysis** Two students solve the equation $6|x+3| - 8 = -2$. Which student is correct? Explain the error.

Student A	Student B
$6|x+3| - 8 = -2$	$6|x+3| - 8 = -2$
no solution	$6|x+3| = 6$
Absolute values cannot equal a negative number.	$|x+3| = 1$
	$x+3 = 1$ and $x+3 = -1$
	$x = -2$ and $x = -4$

15. Student B; Sample: Student A did not isolate the absolute value and assumed that because the equation was equal to a negative number, the absolute value would be equal to a negative number.

 16. **Geometry** The perimeter of a square must be 34 inches plus or minus 2 inches. What is the longest and the shortest length each side can be? 8 inches, 9 inches

*17. **Multi-Step** A student budgets $35 for lunch and rides each week. He gives his friend $5 for gas and then pays for 5 lunches a week. He has a $2 cushion in his budget, meaning that he can spend $2 more or less than he budgeted.
 a. Write an absolute-value equation for the minimum and maximum he can spend on each lunch. $|5 + 5x - 35| = 2$
 b. What is the maximum and the minimum he can spend on each lunch? $5.60, $6.40

18. **Error Analysis** Students were asked to simplify $\frac{x^2 + 10x + 24}{x}$. Which student is correct? Explain the error. Student B; Sample: Student A canceled terms that were not common factors.

Student A	Student B
$\frac{(x+6)(x+4)}{x} = (x+6)(4)$	$\frac{(x+6)(x+4)}{x}$

*19. (**Carpeting**) The rectangular public library is getting new carpet. The area of the room is $(x^3 - 18x^2 + 81x)$ square feet. The length of the room is $(x-9)$ feet. What is the width? $(x^2 - 9x)$ feet

*20. **Justify** Give an example to show $\frac{a}{b} \cdot \frac{c}{d} = \frac{ac}{bd}$. Sample: $\frac{4}{2} \cdot \frac{3}{9} = 2 \cdot \frac{1}{3} = \frac{2}{3}$ and $\frac{4 \cdot 3}{2 \cdot 9} = \frac{12}{18} = \frac{2}{3}$

21. **Multiple Choice** Simplify: $\dfrac{\frac{x^2 - 9}{x^2 - 5x + 6}}{\frac{x^2 + 5x + 6}{x^2 - 4}}$. A

 A 1 **B** $\frac{(x-3)^2}{(x-2)^2}$ **C** -1 **D** $\frac{(x-3)}{(x-2)}$

22. Solve and graph the inequality $|x| > 17$. $x < -17$ or $x > 17$;

 23. **Measurement** When measuring something in centimeters, the accuracy is within 0.1 centimeter. A board is measured to be 15.6 centimeters. The accuracy of the measurement can be represented by the absolute-value inequality $|x - 15.6| \le 0.1$. Solve the inequality. $15.5 \le x \le 15.7$

636 Saxon Algebra 1

ENGLISH LEARNERS

In Problem 17, explain the meaning of the word **cushion**. Say:

"Cushioning provides or gives security or support to ensure safety. For example, the couch has cushions which provide comfort when we sit on it."

Explain to students that not only pillows can provide cushioning.

Say:

"Buying extra amounts of ingredients to bake a cake provides a cushion in case the cake doesn't come out correctly the first time."

Ask volunteers to give examples of other types of cushioning. Sample: bringing extra money to buy something when the price is estimated

24. **Multi-Step** Reggie has made a stew that is at a temperature of 100°F, and he either wants to heat it up to 165°F or cool it down to 45°F. To heat up the stew will take at most 45 minutes plus 1 minute for each degree the temperature is raised. To cool down the stew will take at least 10 minutes plus 2 minutes for each degree the temperature is lowered. How much time does Reggie need to allow for changing the food temperature either up or down?
   a. How many degrees up and down does the stew need to go?   65 degrees up or 55 degrees down
   b. How much time will it take to cool down or heat up the stew?   heat: $t \leq 110$ minutes; cool: $t \geq 120$ minutes
   c. Is it faster to heat up or cool down the stew?   To heat up the stew is faster.

25. (**Olympic Swimming Pool**) An Olympic swimming pool must have a width of 25 meters and a length of 50 meters. Find the length of a diagonal of an Olympic swimming pool to the nearest tenth of a meter.   55.9 meters

26. **Multi-Step** A graphing calculator screen is 128 pixels wide and 240 pixels long. The "pixel coordinates" of three points are shown.

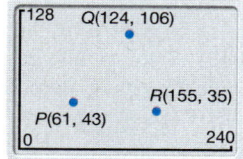

   a. Find the distance in pixels between each pair of points. $PQ \approx 89$ pixels, $QR \approx 77$ pixels, $PR \approx 94$ pixels
   b. List the line segments in order from shortest to longest. $\overline{QR}, \overline{PQ}, \overline{PR}$

27. **Write** Create a polynomial in which each term has a common factor of $4a$, and then factor the expression.   Sample: $8a^2b + 4a^3 + 12ab + 16ab^2$; $4a(2ab + a^2 + 3b + 4b^2)$

28. (**Hiking**) In celebration of getting to the top of Beacon Rock in southern Washington, Renata throws her hat up and off the top of Beacon Rock. The height of the hat x seconds after the throw (in meters) can be approximated by the function $y = -5x^2 + 10x + 260$. After how many seconds will the hat be at its maximum height? What is this height?   1 second; 265 feet

29. (**Commuting**) Mr. Shakour's round trip commute to and from work totals 30 miles. Because of traffic, his speed on the way home is 5 miles per hour less than what it is on the way to work. Write a simplified expression to represent Mr. Shakour's total commuting time. $\frac{15(2x-5)}{x(x-5)}$ hours where x is the rate in miles per hour.

30. A teacher randomly picks a shirt and a skirt from her closet to wear to school. Use the table to find the theoretical probability of the teacher choosing an outfit with a blue shirt and khaki skirt. $\frac{1}{10}$

		\multicolumn{5}{c}{Shirts}
		Red	Blue	Blue	White	White
Skirts	Khaki	KR	KB	(KB)	KW	KW
	Navy	NR	NB	NB	NW	NW
	Black	BR	BB	BB	BW	BW
	White	WR	WB	WB	WW	WW

Problem 25
Use the Pythagorean Theorem.

Problem 28
Error Alert
Students may set y equal to 0 to find the highest point. However, this is when the hat hits the ground. Remind students that the hat's maximum height is represented by the y-value at the vertex.

Problem 30
Remind students that the probability of an event is the number of desired outcomes over the total number of outcomes.

CHALLENGE

Find the LCD of $\frac{3}{mz^2 - mz}$, $\frac{6}{pz^2 - p^2z}$.

$mpz(z - 1)(z - p)$

LOOKING FORWARD

Combining rational expressions with unlike denominators prepares students for

Lesson 99 Solving Rational Equations

LESSON 96

1 Warm Up

Problem 3
Remind students that after substituting, (−2) should be squared and then the product should be multiplied by −1.

2 New Concepts

In this lesson, students graph quadratic functions.

Example 1
Students graph quadratics of the form $y = x^2 + bx + c$.

Additional Example 1
Graph the function $y = x^2 + 5x + 6$.

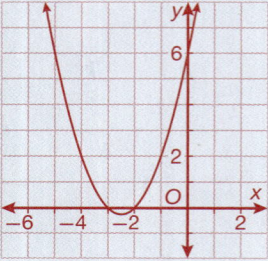

LESSON RESOURCES

Student Edition Practice
 Workbook 96
Reteaching Master 96
Adaptations Master 96
Challenge and Enrichment
 Master C96

LESSON 96

Graphing Quadratic Functions

Warm Up

1. **Vocabulary** A(n) _____ is a line that divides a figure or graph into two mirror-image halves. **axis of symmetry**

Evaluate for the given value.

2. $y = 4x^2 - 6x - 4$ for $x = \frac{1}{2}$ **−6**
3. $y = -x^2 + 5x - 6$ for $x = -2$ **−20**

Find the axis of symmetry using the formula.

4. $y = -2x^2 + 4x - 5$ $x = 1$
5. $y = x^2 - 3x - 4$ $x = \frac{3}{2}$

New Concepts

A quadratic function can be graphed using the axis of symmetry, the vertex, the y-intercept, and pairs of points that are symmetric about the axis of symmetry. The quadratic function in the standard form $f(x) = ax^2 + bx + c$ can be used to find these parts of the graph of the parabola.

The equation of the axis of symmetry and the x-coordinate of the vertex of a quadratic function is $x = -\frac{b}{2a}$. To find the y-coordinate of the vertex, substitute the x-coordinate of the vertex into the function. The y-intercept of a function is the point on the graph where $x = 0$. For quadratic functions in standard form, the y-intercept is c.

Math Reasoning

Analyze Why can *a* not equal 0 in the standard form of a quadratic equation?

Sample: If $a = 0$, then there is no x^2, or quadratic term. The function would no longer be a quadratic function.

Example 1 Graphing Quadratics of the Form $y = x^2 + bx + c$

Graph the function.
$y = x^2 + 4x + 5$

SOLUTION

Step 1: Find the axis of symmetry.

$x = -\frac{b}{2a}$ Use the formula.

$= -\frac{4}{2 \cdot 1} = -\frac{4}{2} = -2$ Substitute values for *b* and *a*.

The axis of symmetry is $x = -2$.

Step 2: Find the vertex.

$y = x^2 + 4x + 5$
$= (-2)^2 + 4(-2) + 5 = 1$ Substitute −2 for *x*.

The vertex is $(-2, 1)$.

Step 3: Find the y-intercept.

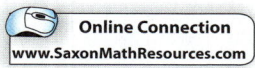

The y-intercept is *c*, or 5.

638 Saxon Algebra 1

MATH BACKGROUND

Graphing quadratic functions is a key element of algebra. The graph can help students analyze and solve problems that can be modeled by a quadratic function.

Begin by finding the equation of the axis of symmetry, which passes through the vertex. Then plot the y-intercept and one other point found by substituting a value of *x* into the function. Finally, reflect these points across the axis of symmetry. Connect all the points with a smooth curve.

Symmetry is an important characteristic of quadratic functions. By finding one point on the curve, a second point can be quickly identified by reflection across the axis of symmetry. Connecting the points with a smooth curve is critical. The graph of a quadratic function is different from a linear function because it is not straight. The vertex is a critical point because the y-value at the vertex represents the minimum or maximum value of the function.

Hint

Count how far the plotted point (1, 10) is from the axis of symmetry. Then check that the reflected point is the same distance from the axis of symmetry, but in the opposite direction.

Step 4: Find one point not on the axis of symmetry.

$y = x^2 + 4x + 5$

$y = (1)^2 + 4(1) + 5 = 10$ Substitute 1 for x.

A point on the curve is (1, 10).

Step 5: Graph.

Graph the axis of symmetry $x = -2$, the vertex $(-2, 1)$, the y-intercept $(0, 5)$. Reflect the point $(1, 10)$ over the axis of symmetry and graph the point $(-5, 10)$. Connect the points with a smooth curve.

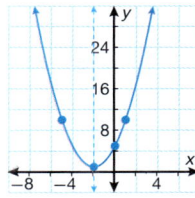

Example 2 Graphing Quadratics of the Form $y = ax^2 + bx + c$

Graph the function.

$y = 3x^2 + 18x + 13$

SOLUTION

Hint

Identify the values of a, b, and c first.

Step 1: Find the axis of symmetry.

$x = -\dfrac{b}{2a}$ Use the formula.

$= -\dfrac{18}{2(3)} = -3$ Substitute values for b and a.

The axis of symmetry is $x = -3$.

Step 2: Find the vertex.

$y = 3x^2 + 18x + 13$

$= 3(-3)^2 + 18(-3) + 13 = -14$ Substitute -3 for x.

The vertex is $(-3, -14)$.

Step 3: Find the y-intercept.

The y-intercept is c, or 13.

Step 4: Find one point not on the axis of symmetry.

$y = 3x^2 + 18x + 13$

$= 3(-1)^2 + 18(-1) + 13 = -2$ Substitute -1 for x.

A point on the curve is $(-1, -2)$.

Step 5: Graph.

Graph the axis of symmetry $x = -3$, the vertex $(-3, -14)$, the y-intercept $(0, 13)$. Reflect the point $(-1, -2)$ across the axis of symmetry to get the point $(-5, -2)$. Connect the points with a smooth curve.

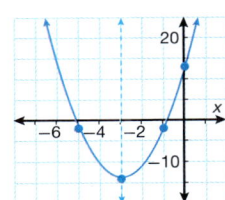

Lesson 96

Example 2

Students learn to graph quadratic functions of the form $y = ax^2 + bx + c$.

Additional Example 2

Graph the function.

$y = 5x^2 - 20x - 3$

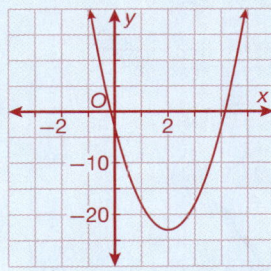

Example 3
Students learn to graph quadratic functions of the form $y = ax^2 + c$.

Additional Example 3
Graph the function $y = 8x^2 + 2$.

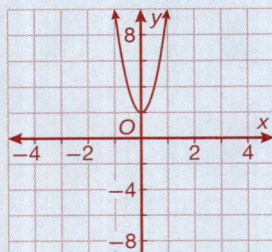

Example 3 Graphing Quadratics of the Form $y = ax^2 + c$

Graph the function.

$y = 5x^2 + 4$

SOLUTION

Step 1: Find the axis of symmetry.

$$x = -\frac{b}{2a} = -\frac{0}{2(5)} = 0$$

The axis of symmetry is $x = 0$.

Step 2: Find the vertex.

$y = 5x^2 + 4$
$= 5(0)^2 + 4 = 4$ Substitute 0 for x.

The vertex is (0, 4).

Step 3: Find the y-intercept.

The y-intercept is c, or 4.

Step 4: Find one point not on the axis of symmetry.

$y = 5x^2 + 4$.
$= 5(-1)^2 + 4 = 9$ Substitute −1 for x.

A point on the curve is (−1, 9)

Step 5: Graph.

Graph the axis of symmetry $x = 0$, the vertex (0, 4), the y-intercept (0, 4). Reflect the point (−1, 9) across the axis of symmetry to get the point (1, 9). Connect the points with a smooth curve.

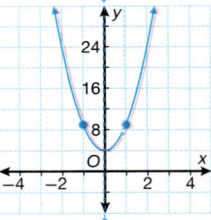

Math Language

A **zero of a function** is another name for an x-intercept of the graph.

A zero of a function is an x-value for a function where $f(x) = 0$. It is the point where the graph of the function meets or intersects the x-axis. The **standard form of a quadratic equation** $ax^2 + bx + c = 0$, where $a \neq 0$, is the related equation to the quadratic function. The quadratic equation is used to find the zeros of a quadratic function algebraically. Alternatively, a graphing calculator can help find zeros of a quadratic function.

Example 4 Finding the Zeros of a Quadratic Function

Graphing Calculator

For help with finding zeros, see graphing calculator keystrokes in Lab 8 on p. 583.

Find the zeros of the function.

a. $y = x^2 - 6x + 9$

SOLUTION

Use a graphing calculator to graph $y = x^2 - 6x + 9$.

The zero of the function is 3.

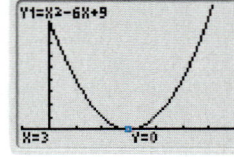

640   Saxon Algebra 1

 ALTERNATE METHOD

A table can be used to graph a quadratic function. Choose values for the x-coordinate and substitute them into the function to find the y-coordinates. Then plot the points and connect them with a smooth curve.

b. $y = x^2 - 3x - 10$

SOLUTION

Use a graphing calculator to graph $y = x^2 - 3x - 10$.

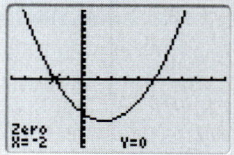 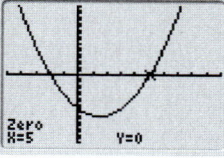

There are two zeros for this function, 5 and −2.

c. $y = -2x^2 - 3$

SOLUTION

Use a graphing calculator to graph $y = -2x^2 - 3$.

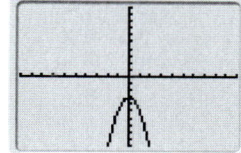

There are no real zeros for this function.

Math Language

If a quadratic function has **no real zeros**, then there are no real numbers that when substituted for x result in $y = 0$. The graph of such a function does not cross the x-axis.

When an object is thrown or kicked into the air, it follows a parabolic path.

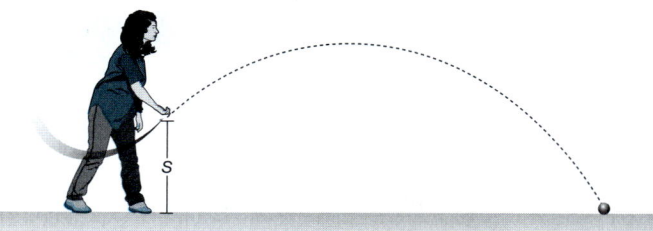

You can calculate its height in feet after t seconds using the formula $h = -16t^2 + vt + s$. The initial vertical velocity in feet per second is v, and s is the starting height of the object in feet.

Example 5 Application: Baseball

A baseball is thrown straight up with an initial velocity of 50 feet per second. The ball leaves the player's hand when it is 4 feet above the ground. At what time does the ball reach its maximum height?

SOLUTION Substitute the values given for the initial velocity and starting height into the formula $h = -16t^2 + vt + s$. Then find the x-coordinate of the vertex. Use the formula $x = -\frac{b}{2a}$.

$h = -16t^2 + 50t + 4$

$x = -\frac{b}{2a}$

$= -\frac{50}{2(-16)} = 1.5625$ Substitute values for b and a.

The ball reaches its maximum height 1.5625 seconds after it has been thrown.

Example 4

Students learn to find the zeros of a quadratic function.

Additional Example 4

Find the zeros of the function.

a. $y = x^2 - 16x + 64$ 8

b. $y = x^2 + 3x - 28$ 4 and −7

c. $y = 5x^2 + 9$ No real zeros

Error Alert Students may confuse the zeros of a function and the y-intercept. Explain that the zeros are the x-intercepts, and the y-intercept is where x equals zero.

Example 5

Students use quadratic functions to solve vertical motion problems.

Extend the Example

When does the baseball land on the ground? after about 3.2 seconds

Additional Example 5

An egg is thrown from the top of a wall that is 20 feet tall. Its initial velocity is 32 feet per second. How long will it take for the egg to reach its maximum height? 1 second

---

INCLUSION

Use the following strategy with students who have difficulty with graphing. To help them connect the algebraic representation with the graphical representation, create a color-coded chart. Color code each part of the graph and, in the same color, show how to find that part algebraically.

For example, show $x = \frac{-b}{2a}$ in red and then show the axis of symmetry in red on the graph. Do this for the vertex, the y-intercept, and a pair of symmetric points.

Lesson Practice

Graph each function.

a. $y = x^2 - 4x + 7$ (Ex 1)

b. $y = 2x^2 - 16x + 24$ (Ex 2)

c. $y = 2x^2 - 9$ (Ex 3)

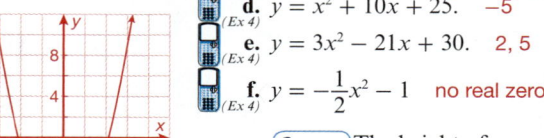

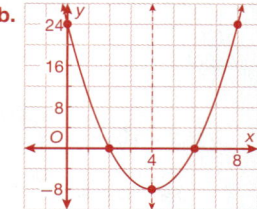

Find the zeros of each function.

d. $y = x^2 + 10x + 25$. -5 (Ex 4)

e. $y = 3x^2 - 21x + 30$. $2, 5$ (Ex 4)

f. $y = -\frac{1}{2}x^2 - 1$ no real zeros (Ex 4)

g. (Soccer) The height of a soccer ball that is kicked can be modeled by the function $f(x) = -8x^2 + 24x$, where x is the time in seconds after it is kicked. Find the time it takes the ball to reach its maximum height.   1.5 seconds (Ex 5)

Practice   Distributed and Integrated

1. Find the zeros of the function shown.   0 and 4
(89)

2. Add $\dfrac{25}{16x^2y} + \dfrac{xy}{32y^5}$. $\dfrac{50y^3 + x^3}{32x^2y^4}$
(90)

*3. Solve the equation $\dfrac{10|x|}{3} + 18 = 4$ and graph the solution.
(94)   ∅; no graph

4. Solve $-0.3 + 0.14n = 2.78$. $n = 22$
(24)

5. Solve $\dfrac{6}{x-3} = \dfrac{3}{10}$. $x = 23$
(31)

6. Find the LCD of $\dfrac{6}{x+6} - \dfrac{12}{x^2 + 8x + 12}$.   LCD $= (x+6)(x+2)$
(95)

7. The table lists the ordered pairs from a relation. Determine whether they form a function.   function
(25)

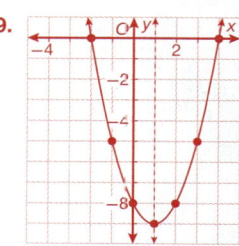

Domain (x)	Range (y)
10	15
11	17
8	11
9	13
5	5

8. Simplify $\dfrac{\frac{-x^5}{21x+3}}{\frac{5x^9}{28x+4}}$. $\dfrac{-4}{15x^4}$
(92)

*9. Graph the function $y = x^2 - 2x - 8$.
(96)

*10. **Write** Explain how to reflect a point across the axis of symmetry to get a second point on the parabola.   Sample: The second point will have the same y-value and will be the same horizontal distance from the axis of symmetry, but on the other side.
(96)

642   Saxon Algebra 1

*11. **Justify** Show that the vertex of $y = 4x^2 - 24x + 9$ is $(3, -27)$.
(96)

11. Sample: $x = \frac{-b}{2a} = \frac{24}{8} = 3$. Then, substitute 3 into the equation to get $4(3)^2 - 24(3) + 9 = -27$.

*12. **Multiple Choice** Which function has the vertex $(6, -160)$? **A**
(96)
  A $y = 6x^2 - 72x + 56$ **B** $y = 2x^2 - 8x + 48$
  C $y = 3x^2 + 42x - 12$ **D** $y = 5x^2 - 5x + 43$

*13. (Diving) A diver moves upward with an initial velocity of 10 feet per second.
(96) How high will he be 0.5 seconds after diving from a 6-foot platform? Use $h = -16t^2 + vt + s$. **7 feet**

14. **Multiple Choice** Find the LCD of $\frac{3}{2x - 10}$ and $\frac{5x}{2x^2 - 4x - 30}$. **A**
(95)
  A $2(x - 5)(x + 3)$ **B** $(x - 5)(x + 3)$
  C $(x + 5)(x - 3)$ **D** $\frac{2}{(x - 5)(x + 3)}$

*15. **Geometry** One side of a triangle is $\frac{2}{x + 2}$ yards and two sides are each $\frac{-5}{3x + 6}$ yards.
(95) Find the perimeter of the triangle. $\frac{-4}{3(x + 2)}$ yards

*16. **Measurement** Carrie measured a distance of $\frac{3x^2}{9x - 18}$ yards and Jessie
(95) measured a distance of $\frac{4x - 5}{x^2 - 4}$ yards. How much longer is Carrie's measurement than Jessie's? $\frac{x^3 + 2x^2 - 12x + 15}{3(x - 2)(x + 2)}$ yards

17. (Banking) The dollar amount in a student's banking account is represented by the
(91) absolute-value inequality $|x - 200| \leq 110$. Solve the inequality and graph the solution. $90 \leq x \leq 310$;

18. **Generalize** Why is a place holder needed for missing variables in a polynomial
(93) dividend? Sample: It helps line up like terms for the dividend and quotient.

19. **Multiple Choice** Simplify $(-5x + 2x^2 - 3) \div (x - 3)$. **B**
(93)
  A $2x - 1$ **B** $2x + 1$ **C** $\frac{x - 2}{2x}$ **D** $\frac{x^2 - 3}{5x}$

*20. (Physics) A family is going to see friends that live in two different towns. They will
(94) have to travel 100 miles plus or minus 10 miles to see either of them. They want to spend 2 hours in the car. What are the minimum and maximum rates that they need to go? **45 miles per hour; 55 miles per hour**

*21. **Error Analysis** Two students graph the solution to the equation $|2x + 10| = 8$.
(94) Which student is correct? Explain the error.

21. Student A; Sample: Student B graphed all values between -9 and -1 in addition to the solution set.

Student A
$\{-9, -1\}$
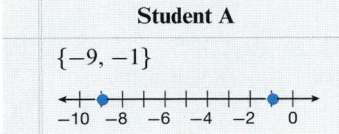

Student B
$\{-9, -1\}$
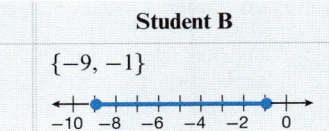

22. (Art) Jeremy's picture frame has an area of $x^2 - 18x + 80$ square inches. He has
(90) two square pictures in it, one measuring $\frac{1}{4}x$ inch on each side and the other measuring $\frac{1}{2}x$ inch on each side. Write a simplified expression for the total fraction of the frame covered by pictures. $\frac{0.3125x^2}{(x - 8)(x - 10)}$

Problem 14
Factor first. Then use the factors to find the LCD.

Problem 19
Order the powers in the trinomial in descending order before dividing.

Lesson 96   643

ENGLISH LEARNER

In problem 13, explain the meaning of the word **diver**. Say:

"A diver is a person who jumps into the water head first with his body straight and his arms out in front."

Ask volunteers to demonstrate how to position their arms to dive into the water.

Lesson 96   643

Problem 23

Write the division problem as the dividend times the reciprocal of the divisor. Factor each term and simplify.

Problem 25

Use the distance formula.

Problem 27

Test different types of numbers: positive, negative, zero, and fractions.

Problem 30

Remind students to be mindful of the signs when multiplying binomials.

---

23. Verify Divide the rational expression $\frac{3x^2 + 2x}{9y} \div \frac{y+2}{y}$. How can you check your answer? $\frac{x(3x+2)}{9(y+2)}$; Sample: Substitute real numbers for the variables x and y before and after dividing.

24. Multi-Step The volume of a prism is $6x^3 + 14x^2 + 4x$ cm³. Find the dimensions of the prism.
 a. Factor out common terms. $2x(3x^2 + 7x + 2)$
 b. Factor completely to find the dimensions. $2x(3x + 1)(x + 2)$

25. **Baseball** A baseball diamond is a square that is 90 feet long on each side. To use a coordinate grid to model positions of players on the field, place home plate at (0, 0), first base at (90, 0), second base at (90, 90), and third base at (0, 90). An outfielder located at (150, 80) throws to the first-baseman. How long is the throw? Round your answer to the nearest foot. **100 feet**

26. Multi-Step A square has a side length of a centimeters. A smaller square has a side length of b centimeters.
 a. If the difference in the areas of the squares is $a^2 - 16$, what is the value of b? **4 cm**
 b. If the area of the larger square is $36b^2 + 60b + 25$, what is the side length in terms of b? **$6b + 5$**
 c. Using your answers to parts **a** and **b**, find the side length and area of the larger square. **29 cm; 841 cm²**

27. Determine if the inequality $6x > 7x$ is never, sometimes, or always true. If it is sometimes true, identify the solution set. **sometimes true; It is true for all negative values of x.**

28. Use the graph to find the theoretical probability of choosing each color.

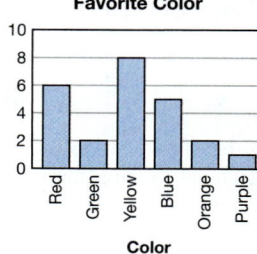

$P(red) = \frac{6}{24} = \frac{1}{4}$, $P(green) = \frac{2}{24} = \frac{1}{12}$,
$P(yellow) = \frac{8}{24} = \frac{1}{3}$, $P(blue) = \frac{5}{24}$,
$P(orange) = \frac{2}{24} = \frac{1}{12}$, $P(purple) = \frac{1}{24}$

29. Suppose d varies inversely with b and jointly with a and c. Find the constant of variation when $a = 4$, $b = 5$, $c = 2$, and $d = 8$. Express the relationship between these quantities. What is d when $a = 9$, $b = 15$, and $c = 6$? $k = 5$; $d = \frac{5ac}{b}$; $d = 18$

30. Is $(x + 10)(x - 2)$ the correct factorization for $x^2 - 8x - 20$? Explain. no; If $(x + 10)(x - 2)$ is multiplied, the result is $x^2 + 8x - 20$. Changing the signs to $(x - 10)(x + 2)$ would produce the correct factorization.

CHALLENGE

The height in feet of a dolphin as it jumps out of the water at an aquarium show can be modeled by the function $f(x) = -16x^2 + 32x$, where x is the time in seconds after it exits the water. Find how long the dolphin is in the air. **2 seconds**

LOOKING FORWARD

Graphing quadratic functions prepares students for

- **Lesson 98** Solving Quadratic Equations by Factoring
- **Lesson 100** Solving Quadratic Equations by Graphing
- **Lesson 102** Solving Quadratic Equations Using Square Roots
- **Lesson 110** Using the Quadratic Formula

LAB 9

Graphing Linear Inequalities

Graphing Calculator Lab (*Use with Lesson 97*)

Linear inequalities in two variables can be graphed by hand or with a graphing calculator. Begin by following the process used to graph a linear equation. Then change the settings to shade the region of the coordinate system that makes the inequality true.

Graph the solution set of the inequality $y > 2x - 7$.

Materials
- graphing calculator

Discuss
The solution set and graph for a linear inequality is a region of the rectangular coordinate system. Remind students that the graph of a linear equation is a straight line. The inequality sign extends the solution set to a region on a side of the line on the graph.

Graphing Calculator Tip

For help with entering an equation into the **Y=** editor, see the graphing calculator keystrokes in Lab 3 on page 305.

1. Enter the equation $y = 2x - 7$ into the **Y=** editor.

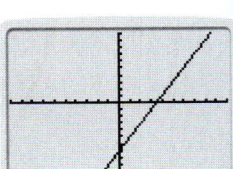

2. Graph the equation by pressing  and selecting **6:ZStandard**.

   The line represents the boundary of the solution set of the inequality $y > 2x - 7$. The solution set of the inequality is either the region above or the region below the line $y = 2x - 7$.

   Use a test point to determine which region makes the inequality true.

   Choose a test point that is not on the graph of the line $y = 2x - 7$.

   The point (0, 0) is a good test point because it does not fall on the boundary line.

   Substitute 0 for both x and y in the inequality. This substitution gives $0 > 2 \cdot 0 - 7$, or $0 > -7$, which is true.

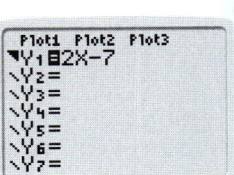

   Since the point (0, 0) satisfies the inequality, the solution set is the region that contains the point (0, 0).

3. Shade the region above the line $y = 2x - 7$.

   To graph this region, press 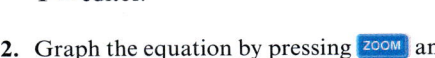. Then press the ◄ key twice. The cursor moves to the left of **Y1** over an icon that looks like a line segment, \.

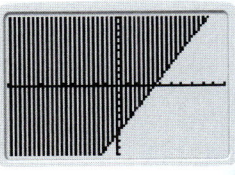

   Press 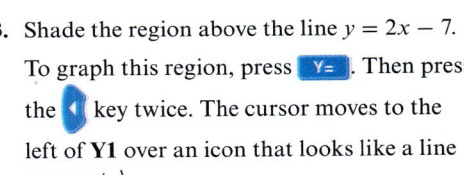 twice to choose the ◥ icon, which resembles a shaded region above a line.

Lab 9   645

(Pressing ENTER a third time allows you to choose the ◣ icon, which resembles a shaded region below a line.)

4. Press GRAPH to view the graph of the solution set.

All points in the shaded region are in the solution set of $y > 2x - 7$.

Note that the solution set does not include points on the line $y = 2x - 7$. The graph of the solution set of the inequality $y \geq 2x - 7$ does include points on the boundary line $y = 2x - 7$.

Lab Practice

a.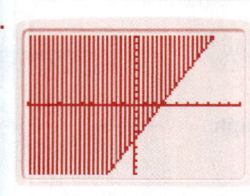

b.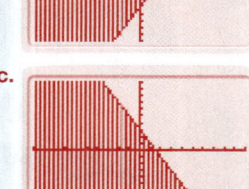

c.

Graph the solution set of each inequality.
a. $y < 3x + 5$; Is the point (1, 1) a solution of the inequality? yes

b. $y \geq 2x - 5$; Is the point (7, 2) a solution of the inequality? no

c. $y < -2x + 3$; Is the point (0, 0) a solution of the inequality? yes

LESSON 97

Graphing Linear Inequalities

Warm Up

1. **Vocabulary** The _____ of the equation of a line is $y = mx + b$, where m is the slope of the line and b is the y-intercept.   *slope-intercept form*

Determine the slope and the y-intercept of each equation.

2. $y = -\frac{1}{3}x - 5$ *slope is $-\frac{1}{3}$; y-intercept is -5*

3. $2x + 2y = 6$ *slope is -1; y-intercept is 3*

Graph each of the following inequalities on a number line.

4. $y < 3$

5. $x \geq -2$

New Concepts

A linear inequality is similar to a linear equation, except that a linear inequality has an inequality symbol instead of an equal sign. A **solution of a linear inequality** is any ordered pair that makes the inequality true.

You can evaluate an inequality with an ordered pair to find out if the ordered pair makes the inequality true and is a solution.

Example 1 Determining Solutions of Inequalities

Determine if each ordered pair is a solution of the given inequality.

a. $(0, 4); y > 5x - 1$

SOLUTION

$y > 5x - 1$

$4 > 5(0) - 1$ Evaluate the inequality for the point $(0, 4)$.

$4 > -1$ Simplify.

The inequality is true. The ordered pair $(0, 4)$ is a solution.

b. $(3, -3); y < -3x + 6$

SOLUTION

$y < -3x + 6$

$-3 < -3(3) + 6$ Evaluate the inequality for the point $(3, -3)$.

$-3 < -3$ Simplify.

The inequality is not true because -3 is not less than -3. The ordered pair $(3, -3)$ is not a solution.

c. $(-4, 8); y \leq 9$

SOLUTION

$y \leq 9$

$8 \leq 9$ Evaluate the inequality for the point $(-4, 8)$.

The inequality is true. The ordered pair $(-4, 8)$ is a solution.

Hint

The inequalities $y \leq 9$ and $y \leq 0x + 9$ are equivalent. If an ordered pair is a solution of the inequality, then the y-coordinate is less than or equal to 9, and the x-coordinate can be any real number.

Online Connection
www.SaxonMathResources.com

Lesson 97 647

LESSON 97

1 Warm Up

Problem 4
Remind students to represent the inequality using an open or closed circle.

2 New Concepts

In this lesson, students are introduced to graphing linear inequalities on the coordinate plane.

Example 1

This example shows whether a given ordered pair is or is not a solution of a linear inequality.

Additional Example 1

Determine if the ordered pair is a solution of the given inequality.

a. $(3, -2); y \leq 2x - 8$ *(3, −2) is a solution.*

b. $(2, -2); y > x - 3$ *(2, −2) is not a solution.*

c. $(-2, 8); x > -4$ *(−2, 8) is a solution*

LESSON RESOURCES

Student Edition Practice Workbook 97
Reteaching Master 97
Adaptations Master 97
Challenge and Enrichment Master C97

MATH BACKGROUND

The word solution means answer. For solutions of linear inequalities, there will be more than one ordered pair that will give a correct answer, or solution.

The graph of a simple inequality on a number line can be compared to the solution of a linear inequality. Note the differences: the linear inequality contains two variables while a simple inequality has only one variable. The solution of an inequality with only one variable has a linear solution. The solution of a linear inequality has an area as a solution.

Lesson 97 647

Exploration

This exploration will connect the shaded area of the graph with the solution of the inequality.

Extend the Exploration
Graph the equation $x = 3$. Where would you graph the inequality $x \leq 3$? Graph the points of the inequality to the left of the line for $x = 3$.

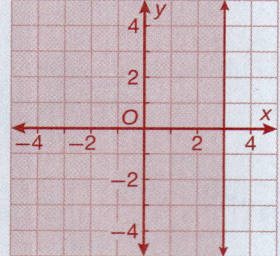

Example 2

This example introduces students to graphing a linear inequality on the coordinate plane.

Additional Example 2
Graph each inequality.

a. $y \leq \frac{1}{2}x + 2$

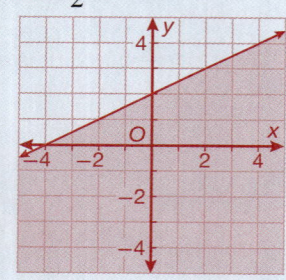

b. $y > 3$

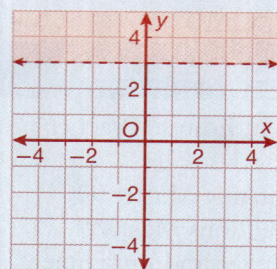

Error Alert Watch for students who identify the area to shade without checking. Have students verify their solutions using substitution.

---

a–c. Sample:

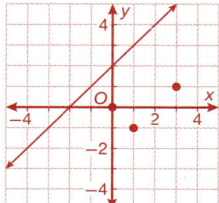

Exploration Graphing Inequalities

a. Graph the equation $y = x + 2$ on a coordinate plane.

b. Test three points that lie above the graph of $y = x + 2$. Substitute the coordinates of each point for the x- and y-values in the inequality $y < x + 2$. If the statement is true, mark the point of the graph.

c. Test three points that lie below the graph of $y = x + 2$. Substitute the coordinates of each point for the x- and y-values in the inequality $y < x + 2$. If the statement is true, mark the point of the graph.

d. To graph the inequality $y < x + 2$, would you choose points above or below $y = x + 2$? **below**

e. Would you graph points above or below the graph of $y = x - 3$ to graph the inequality $y > x - 3$? **above**

A linear inequality describes a region of a coordinate plane called a half-plane. The boundary line for the region is the related equation.

To graph an inequality, begin by graphing the boundary line. Test points are helpful in deciding which half-plane makes the inequality true.

The boundary line is a dashed line when the inequality contains the symbol $<$ or $>$. The boundary line is a solid line when the inequality contains the symbol $\leq$ or $\geq$.

Example 2 Graphing Linear Inequalities without Technology

Graph each inequality.

a. $y \geq -\frac{3}{4}x - 3$

SOLUTION

Graph the boundary line $y = -\frac{3}{4}x - 3$ using a solid line because the inequality contains the symbol $\geq$.

Next use an ordered pair as a test point to find which half-plane should be shaded on the coordinate plane.

Test $(0, 0)$.

Hint
The point $(0, 0)$ is a good test point if it is not on the boundary line.

$y \geq -\frac{3}{4}x - 3$

$0 \geq -\frac{3}{4}(0) - 3$ Evaluate for $(0, 0)$.

$0 \geq -3$ Simplify.

The point $(0, 0)$ satisfies the inequality, so it is a solution. The half-plane that contains the point should be shaded.

ENGLISH LEARNERS

Explain the meaning of a **shaded** area.
Say:

"An area that has been shaded is an area that has been darkened by coloring. To shade, artists may color more heavily in places."

Have students discuss other situations where artists use shading in their drawings.

b. $x < 4$

SOLUTION

Graph the boundary line $x = 4$ using a dashed line because the inequality contains the symbol $<$.

Test (0, 0).

$x < 4$

$0 < 4$ Evaluate for (0, 0).

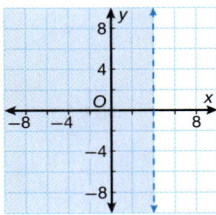

The point (0, 0) satisfies the inequality, so it is a solution. The half-plane that contains the point should be shaded.

To graph an inequality using a graphing calculator, the inequality must first be solved for y.

Example 3 Graphing Linear Inequalities with Technology

Graph each inequality using a graphing calculator.

a. $16x + 4y \leq 8$

SOLUTION

Solve for y.

$16x + 4y \leq 8$

$4y \leq -16x + 8$ Subtract 16x from both sides.

$\dfrac{4y}{4} \leq \dfrac{-16x}{4} + \dfrac{8}{4}$ Divide all three terms by 4.

$y \leq -4x + 2$ Simplify.

Enter the inequality into your graphing calculator to view the graph.

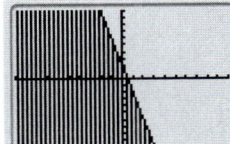

b. $3x - y < -4$

SOLUTION

Solve for y.

$3x - y < -4$

$-y < -3x - 4$ Subtract 3x from both sides.

$\dfrac{-y}{-1} > \dfrac{-3x}{-1} - \dfrac{4}{-1}$ Divide all three terms by -1.

$y > 3x + 4$ Simplify.

Enter the inequality into your graphing calculator to view the graph.

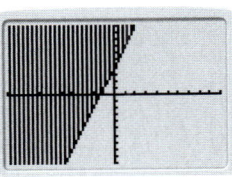

Graphing Calculator Tip

For help with graphing inequalities, see graphing calculator Lab 9 on p. 645.

Caution

Remember to reverse the inequality when multiplying or dividing both sides by a negative number.

Example 3

This example demonstrates graphing a linear inequality using a graphing calculator. Simplifying the inequality first is necessary.

Additional Example 3

Graph each inequality using a graphing calculator.

a. $2y - 8x > -6$

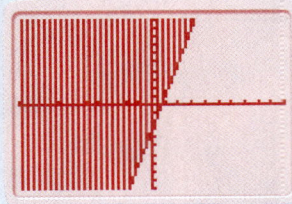

b. $5 - 2y \leq 3x$

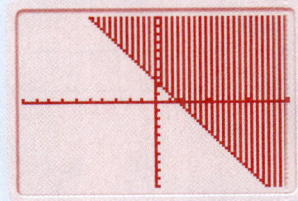

Lesson 97   649

INCLUSION

Students may have difficulty deciding which area to shade to represent the inequality. Once the equation of the related line is graphed, have them draw a dotted or solid line. For Example 3, copy and use the charts.

y	$\leq$	$-4x + 2$
output	$\leq$	line

Say, "Since the output is less than or equal to the y-values on the line, shade below the line to represent the output."

y	>	$3x + 4$
output	>	line

Say, "Since the output is greater than the y-values on the line, shade above the line to represent the output."

Lesson 97   649

Example 4

Students learn to formulate an inequality from a graph.

Additional Example 4
Write an inequality for the region graphed on each coordinate plane.

a.
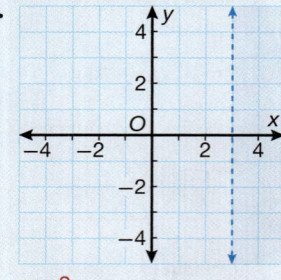
$x > 3$

b.
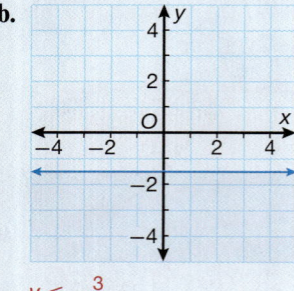
$y \leq -\dfrac{3}{2}$

Example 5

This example helps students formulate inequalities that describe maximum cost.

Extend the Example
Kia's father gave her an extra $5 for the carnival and her mother gave her an extra $8. Kia also learned that the cost of food items is $3.50 this year. Write a new inequality and graph the solution.
$2x + 3.5y \leq 25$;

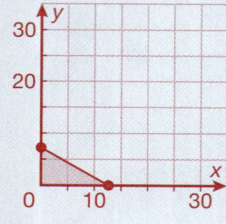

Example 4 — Writing a Linear Inequality Given the Graph

Write an inequality for the region graphed on each coordinate plane.

a.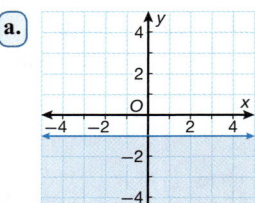

SOLUTION

Determine the equation of the boundary line. It is a horizontal line that cuts through the y-axis at -1.

The equation of the boundary line is $y = -1$.

Then decide which inequality symbol to use for this graph.

The graph is shaded below the solid boundary line, so the inequality contains the $\leq$ symbol.

The inequality shown on the graph is $y \leq -1$.

b.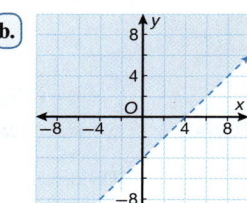

SOLUTION

Determine the equation of the boundary line. It has a y-intercept at -4 and a slope of 1.

The equation of the boundary line is $y = x - 4$.

Then decide which inequality symbol to use for this graph.

The graph is shaded above the dashed boundary line, so the inequality contains the $>$ symbol.

The inequality shown on the graph is $y > x - 4$.

Example 5 — Application: Carnival

Kia will attend a school carnival and she plans to spend no more than $12. Each game costs $2 and each item of food costs $3. Write and graph an inequality to describe the total cost of the carnival.

SOLUTION

Write the inequality that models the situation.

cost of games plus cost of food is no more than 12

$$2x + 3y \leq 12$$

Solve the inequality for y.

$2x + 3y \leq 12$

$\quad 3y \leq -2x + 12 \qquad$ Subtract $2x$ from both sides.

$\quad y \leq -\frac{2}{3}x + 4 \qquad$ Divide all three terms by 3 and simplify.

Graph the solutions.

Since Kia cannot buy a negative amount of games and food, use only Quadrant I. Graph the boundary line $y = -\frac{2}{3}x + 4$. Use a solid line for $\leq$.

Shade below the line. Kia must buy whole numbers of games and food items. All the points on or below the line with whole-number coordinates are the different combinations of games and food Kia can buy.

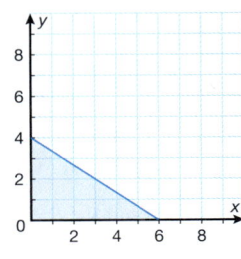

Caution

The graph of an inequality will represent all of the solutions of the inequality, but only selected points on the graph may represent solutions of the word problem.

Lesson Practice

Determine if each ordered pair is a solution of the given inequality.
(Ex 1)

a. $(2, 6); y > 3x - 2$ yes

b. $(4, 1); y < -4x + 1$ no

c. $(-6, 2); y \leq 5$ yes

Graph each inequality.
(Ex 2)

d. $4x + 5y \geq -10$

e. $x < 6$

Graph each inequality using a graphing calculator.
(Ex 3)

 f. $4x + 2y \leq 6$

g. $y > 2x + 6$

Write an inequality for the region graphed on each coordinate plane.
(Ex 4)

h.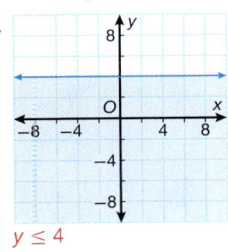
$y \leq 4$

i.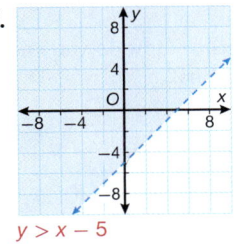
$y > x - 5$

e.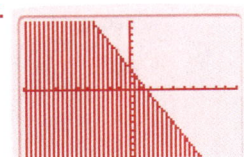

f.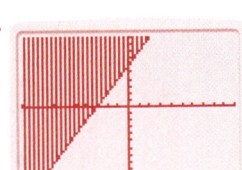

d.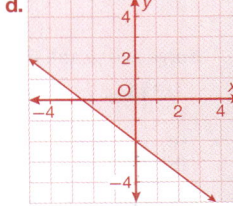

Additional Example 5

Student tickets for a play cost $5 and adult tickets cost $10. Write an inequality to describe the minimum number of tickets that need to be sold to earn $525 in sales. $5x + 10y \geq 525$

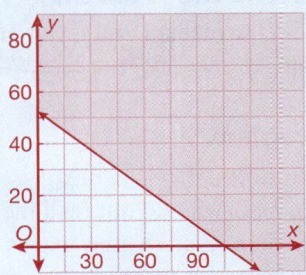

Lesson Practice

Problem c

Error Alert Make sure that students select the correct coordinate of the ordered pair to use in the inequality.

Problem f

Scaffolding Have students solve for y. Then enter the inequality into the graphing calculator.

✓ Check for Understanding

The questions below help assess the concepts taught in this lesson.

"Explain how to graph an inequality on the coordinate plane." Graph the boundary line. Then shade the area of the graph that contains the solution set of the inequality.

"How can you determine which area of the graph to shade to show the solution set?" Substitute an ordered pair into the inequality. If the point is a solution, then the points on that side of the line make up the solution set. If the point is not a solution, then the points on the other side make up the solution set.

Lesson 97   651

3 Practice

Math Conversations
Discussion to strengthen understanding

Problem 4
Extend the Problem
Find the median and mean of the data set. median: 31; mean: 32.$\overline{2}$

Problem 5
Error Alert
Students who do not read the problem carefully may expect a product with three terms. Caution students to be sure that they have copied the factors carefully before multiplying.

Problem 7
Guide the students by asking them the following questions.

"What is the first step needed to solve this problem?" Factor the denominator of the first expression.

"What are the factors of the denominator in the first expression?" The factors are $(x + 1)$ and $(x + 1)$.

"What is the LCD of the two expressions?" $(x + 1)(x + 1)$

---

j. Nila has plans to attend the school bookfair and she wants to spend no more than $25. Each book series costs $15 and each book costs $5. Write an inequality to describe the total cost of the books Nila can buy and graph the inequality. $15x + 5y \leq 25$; See Additional Answers.

Practice   Distributed and Integrated

Simplify.

1. $\dfrac{30x^{-2}y^{12}}{6y^{-5}}$ $\dfrac{5y^{17}}{x^2}$

2. $\sqrt{0.09q^2r} + q\sqrt{0.04r}$ $0.5q\sqrt{r}$

3. $\dfrac{16g^4}{2g+3} - \dfrac{81}{2g+3}$ $(4g^2 + 9)(2g - 3)$

4. Find the range of the data set that includes the ages of 9 members of a chess club: 23, 7, 44, 31, 18, 27, 35, 39, 66.   59

5. Find the product $(4x^2 + 8)(2x - 7)$ using the FOIL method. $8x^3 - 28x^2 + 16x - 56$.

*6. Add $\dfrac{9}{9x - 36} + \dfrac{-24}{3x^2 - 48}$. $\dfrac{1}{x+4}$

*7. Jim ran a total of $\dfrac{x}{x^2 + 2x + 1}$ miles in the gym and $\dfrac{x+2}{x+1}$ miles outside. How many more miles did he run inside? $\dfrac{-x^2 - 2x - 2}{(x+1)(x+1)}$ miles

8. Find the quotient of $(x^2 - 14x + 49) \div (x - 7)$. $(x - 7)$

Solve and graph the inequality.

9. $13 \leq 2x + 7 < 15$ $3 \leq x < 4$;

10. $\dfrac{|x|}{6} > 8$ $x < -48$ or $x > 48$;

11. Determine if the inequality $3x - 4x \geq 6 - x + 8$ is never, sometimes, or always true. If it is sometimes true, identify the solution set.   never true

*12. Determine if the ordered pair $(2, 6)$ is a solution of the inequality $y > 3x - 2$.   Yes, it satisfies the inequality.

*13. Graph the function. $y = x^2 + 2x - 24$

✎*14. **Write** What points on a graph of an inequality satisfy the inequality? Explain.

*15. **Generalize** How do you know which half-plane to shade for the graph of a linear inequality?

13.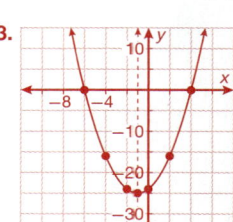

14. Sample: All the points that are on a solid boundary line and all the points that fall in the shaded half-plane satisfy the inequality.

15. Sample: Choose a test point and evaluate the inequality for that point. If the point satisfies the inequality, shade the half-plane that contains that point. If it does not satisfy the inequality, shade the remaining half-plane.

652   **Saxon** Algebra 1

*16. **Multiple Choice** Which inequality represents the graph on the coordinate plane? B
(97)

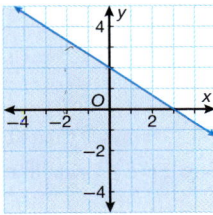

A $y \geq -\frac{2}{3}x + 2$

B $y \leq -\frac{2}{3}x + 2$

C $y \leq \frac{2}{3}x + 2$

D $y < -\frac{2}{3}x + 2$

17. **Football** Tickets for the school football game cost five dollars for adults and
(97) three dollars for students. In order to buy new helmets, at least $9000 worth of tickets must be sold. Write an inequality that describes the total number of tickets that must be sold in order to buy new helmets. $5x + 3y \geq 9000$

*18. **Error Analysis** Two students find the vertex for $y = x^2 - 6x + 19$. Which student is
(96) correct? Explain the error. Student B; Sample: Student A did not substitute the x-value into the original equation to find the y-value.

Student A	Student B
$\frac{-b}{2a} = \frac{6}{2} = 3$	$\frac{-b}{2a} = \frac{6}{2} = 3$
The vertex is (3, 0).	$3^2 - 6(3) + 19 = 10$
	The vertex is (3, 10).

*19. **Geometry** The area of a rectangle is 48 square inches. The length is three times
(96) the width. Find the width of the rectangle by finding the positive zero of the function $y = 3w^2 - 48$. 4 inches

*20. **Multi-Step** The height y of a golf ball in feet is given by the function $y = -16x^2 + 49x$.
(96)
a. What is the y-intercept? 0

b. What does this y-intercept represent? Sample: The ball starts on the ground.

c. What answer does the equation give for the height of the ball after 5 seconds? −155 feet

d. What does that height mean? Sample: After 5 seconds, the ball has already landed. It cannot have a negative height.

*21. **Commuting** Jeff traveled $\frac{1}{2x^2 - 4x}$ miles for his job on Monday and $\frac{1}{x^3 - 2x^2}$ miles for
(95) his job on Tuesday. How many more miles did he travel on Tuesday? $-\frac{1}{2x^2}$ miles

22. **Multiple Choice** Add $\frac{3y + 2}{y + z} + \frac{4}{2y + 2z}$. A
(95)

A $\frac{3y + 4}{y + z}$

B $\frac{y + 4}{y + z}$

C $\frac{6y}{4mn}$

D $\frac{3y - 4}{y - z}$

Lesson 97 653

Problem 16
Guide the students by asking them the following questions.

"Which choices can you immediately discard? Why?" Choice **D** because the line of the graph is solid; choice **A** because the shading of the graph is below the line.

"What is the y-intercept of the graph?" 2

"What is the slope of the graph?" $-\frac{2}{3}$

"What choice can you eliminate now? Why?" choice **C** because the slope of the graph is negative

Problem 17
Extend the Problem
Adult tickets to the game cost $15. Student tickets cost $6. If 432 adult tickets are sold, how many student tickets must be sold to reach the goal of $9000? 420

Lesson 97 653

Problem 26
Extend the Problem
Using the same tape measure, the carpenter measures the door opening at $31\frac{1}{4}$ inches. Find the range of possible measures by solving the inequality $|x - 31\frac{1}{4}| \le \frac{1}{32}$. $31\frac{7}{32} \le x \le 31\frac{9}{32}$

Problem 27
Guide the students by asking them the following questions.

"Think of the graph of a quadratic function. Under what circumstances would you say there is a zero of the function?" If the parabola touches or crosses the x-axis, there would be a zero in the function.

"Under what circumstances would there be one zero?" There would be one zero if the vertex was on the x-axis.

"When would there be two zeros?" There would be two zeros if the vertex was below the x-axis opening upward, or if the vertex was above the x-axis opening downward.

"When would there be no zeros?" There would be no zeros when the vertex is above the x-axis opening upward, or when the vertex is below the x-axis opening downward.

Problem 28
Error Alert
Watch for students who add instead of multiplying the given probabilities. Review how to find the probability of two independent outcomes.

---

23. **Verify** Show that -11 is a solution to the inequality $|3x| - 2 = 31$.
Sample: $|3(-11)| - 2 = |-33| - 2 = 33 - 2 = 31$

24. **Multiple Choice** Solve $4|x - 8| = 12$. **C**
   A $\{-5, 5\}$ B $\{11, -11\}$
   C $\{5, 11\}$ D $\{-20, 20\}$

25. **Bike Riding** Ron rode his bike for $\frac{10}{45x^2 + 4x - 1}$ minutes to get to his grandmother's house that was $\frac{1}{45x - 5} + \frac{2x}{25x + 5}$ miles away. Find his rate in miles per minute. $\frac{18x^2 + 3x + 1}{50}$ miles per minute

26. **Carpentry** A carpenter uses a measuring tape with an accuracy of $\pm\frac{1}{32}$ inches. He measures the height of a bookshelf to be $95\frac{5}{8}$ inches. Solve the inequality $|x - 95\frac{5}{8}| \le \frac{1}{32}$ to find the range of the height of the bookshelf. $95\frac{19}{32} \le x \le 95\frac{21}{32}$

27. **Generalize** How are the number of zeros of a function related to the location of the vertex of the function's parabola? See Additional Answers.

28. **Probability** The probability of winning a certain game is $\frac{2x^4y^2}{15xy^3}$. The probability of winning a different game is $\frac{5x^2y}{8x^3y^2}$. What is the probability of winning both games? $\frac{x^2}{12y^2}$

29. **Rate** An orange juice machine squeezes juice out of $x^2 + 30x$ oranges every hour. How much time in days will it take to squeeze 3000 oranges? $\frac{125}{x(x + 30)}$ days

30. **Multi-Step** A circle has a radius of x. Another circle has a radius of $3x$.
   a. Write equations for the areas of both circles. $A = \pi x^2$; $A = 9\pi x^2$
   b. Graph both functions in the same coordinate plane.
   c. Compare the graphs. Sample: The graph of the area of the larger circle is much narrower.

30b.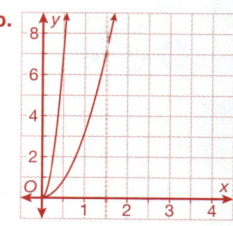

654 Saxon Algebra 1

CHALLENGE

Find the solution set to the system of inequalities by graphing. The solution set is the region where the areas overlap.

$$y < 3x - 5$$
$$2x - 3y \le 4$$

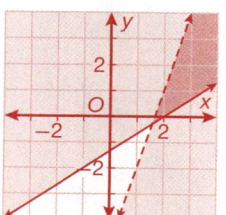

LOOKING FORWARD

Graphing linear inequalities prepares students for

- **Lesson 109** Graphing Systems of Linear Inequalities

LESSON 98

Solving Quadratic Equations by Factoring

Warm Up

1. **Vocabulary** A _____ is an x-value for the function where $f(x) = 0$.
   (89) zero of a function

   Factor.

   2. $x^2 + 3x - 88$ $(x + 11)(x - 8)$
   (72)

   3. $6x^2 - 7x - 5$ $(3x - 5)(2x + 1)$
   (75)

   4. $4x^2 + 28x + 49$ $(2x + 7)(2x + 7)$
   (83)

   5. $12x^2 - 27$ $3(2x + 3)(2x - 3)$
   (83)

New Concepts

A **root of an equation** is the solution to an equation. A quadratic equation can have zero, one, or two roots. The roots of a quadratic equation are the x-intercepts, or zeros, of the related quadratic function.

Math Language

The **roots** of a quadratic equation are the values of x that make $ax^2 + bx + c = 0$.

To find the roots of a quadratic equation, set the equation equal to 0. If the quadratic expression can be factored, the equation can be solved using the Zero Product Property.

Zero Product Property
If the product of two quantities equals zero, at least one of the quantities equals zero.

Math Reasoning

Analyze What is the difference between a quadratic function and a quadratic equation?

Sample: A quadratic equation has one variable, and a quadratic function has two variables.

Example 1 Using the Zero Product Property

Solve.

$(x - 4)(x + 5) = 0$

SOLUTION

By the Zero Product Property, one or both of these factors must be equal to 0. To find the solutions, set each factor equal to zero and solve.

$x - 4 = 0$ $x + 5 = 0$ Set each factor equal to zero.
$x = 4$ $x = -5$ Solve each equation for x.

Check Substitute each solution into the original equation to show it is true.

$(x - 4)(x + 5) = 0$ $(x - 4)(x + 5) = 0$
$(4 - 4)(4 + 5) \stackrel{?}{=} 0$ $(-5 - 4)(-5 + 5) \stackrel{?}{=} 0$
$0 \cdot 9 \stackrel{?}{=} 0$ $-9 \cdot 0 \stackrel{?}{=} 0$
$0 = 0$ ✓ $0 = 0$ ✓

Online Connection
www.SaxonMathResources.com

The solution set is $\{-5, 4\}$.

MATH BACKGROUND

The graph of a quadratic function is a parabola. The function is equal to 0 at the x-intercept(s).

Use this principle to set a quadratic equation equal to 0 and then to solve it. Factoring the equation produces two factors. By the Zero Product Property (or Principle of Zero Products), one of the factors must be equal to zero.

By setting each factor equal to zero and solving, the x-intercepts, or roots of the equation are determined.

Solutions can be checked by substituting one solution at a time into the original equation.

As a further check, have the students confirm their solutions using a graphing calculator. Have them graph the original function on the calculator and then use the calculator to find the x-intercepts. The x-intercepts and their solutions should be the same. Checking by graphing will also emphasize that the roots, solutions, and x-intercepts have the same meaning.

---

1 Warm Up

Problems 2–5

These problems review factoring quadratic expressions in preparation for solving quadratic equations by factoring.

2 New Concepts

This lesson introduces the Zero Product Property. Students are informally aware of this principle, but have not applied it.

This property shows that each factor is equal to zero.

Discuss the term **root of an equation.** Have students note that on the graph of the equation, any x-intercept, where y is equal to zero, is a solution of the equation.

Example 1

This example uses the Zero Product Property to solve a quadratic equation.

Additional Example 1

Solve.
$(x - 3)(x - 8) = 0$ $\{3, 8\}$

LESSON RESOURCES

Student Edition Practice Workbook 98
Reteaching Master 98
Adaptations Master 98
Challenge and Enrichment Master C98

TEACHER TIP

Encourage students to try to factor the equations mentally rather than listing all the possible combinations first. They may need to adjust their first guesses as they go along, but this will give them practice in mental math as well as help them gain familiarity with the factoring process.

Example 2

These examples demonstrate how to solve quadratic equations by factoring.

Additional Example 2

Find the roots.

a. $x^2 + 6 = -5x$
The roots are -3 and -2.

b. $3x^2 = 4x + 7$
The roots are $\frac{7}{3}$ and -1.

Example 2 Solving Quadratic Equations by Factoring

Find the roots.

a. $x^2 + 2x = 8$

Hint
Standard form for the equation is $ax^2 + bx + c = 0$.

SOLUTION

$x^2 + 2x = 8$
$x^2 + 2x - 8 = 0$ Set the equation equal to 0.
$(x + 4)(x - 2) = 0$ Factor.

Use the Zero Product Property to solve the equation.

$x + 4 = 0$ $\qquad$ $x - 2 = 0$ Set each factor equal to zero.
$x = -4$ $\qquad$ $x = 2$ Solve each equation for x.

Check

$x^2 + 2x = 8$ $\qquad\qquad$ $x^2 + 2x = 8$
$(-4)^2 + 2(-4) \stackrel{?}{=} 8$ $\qquad$ $(2)^2 + 2(2) \stackrel{?}{=} 8$
$16 - 8 \stackrel{?}{=} 8$ $\qquad\qquad$ $4 + 4 \stackrel{?}{=} 8$
$8 = 8$ ✓ $\qquad\qquad$ $8 = 8$ ✓

The roots are -4 and 2.

b. $7x^2 - 6 = 19x$

SOLUTION

$7x^2 - 6 = 19x$
$7x^2 - 19x - 6 = 0$ Set the equation equal to 0.
$(7x + 2)(x - 3) = 0$ Factor.
$7x + 2 = 0$ $\qquad$ $x - 3 = 0$ Set each factor equal to zero.
$7x = -2$ $\qquad$ $x = 3$ Solve each equation for x.
$x = -\frac{2}{7}$

Check

$7x^2 - 6 = 19x$ $\qquad\qquad$ $7x^2 - 6 = 19x$
$7\left(-\frac{2}{7}\right)^2 - 6 \stackrel{?}{=} 19\left(-\frac{2}{7}\right)$ $\qquad$ $7(3)^2 - 6 \stackrel{?}{=} 19(3)$
$\left(\frac{4}{7}\right) - 6 \stackrel{?}{=} -\frac{38}{7}$ $\qquad\qquad$ $63 - 6 \stackrel{?}{=} 57$
$-\frac{38}{7} = -\frac{38}{7}$ ✓ $\qquad\qquad$ $57 = 57$ ✓

The roots are $-\frac{2}{7}$ and 3.

ENGLISH LEARNERS

For this lesson, say and explain the meaning of **root**. Say:

"The word root means source or foundation. For example, the root of a tooth is under the gums."

Also relate the word root to the root of a tree, explaining that the roots are the foundation of a tree.

Example 3 Finding the Roots by Factoring Out the GCF

Find the roots.

$20 - 2x^2 = 70 - 20x$

SOLUTION

$2x^2 - 20x + 50 = 0$ Set the equation equal to zero.
$2(x^2 - 10x + 25) = 0$ Factor out the GCF.
$2(x - 5)(x - 5) = 0$ Factor the trinomial expression.

Disregard the factor of 2, since it can never equal 0.

The factor $(x - 5)$ appears twice, but it only needs to be set to equal zero once.

$x - 5 = 0$
$x = 5$

Check

$20 - 2x^2 = 70 - 20x$
$20 - 2(5)^2 \stackrel{?}{=} 70 - 20(5)$
$20 - 2(25) \stackrel{?}{=} 70 - 100$
$20 - 50 \stackrel{?}{=} -30$
$-30 = -30$ ✓

The root is 5.

Caution

When checking your answers, use the original equation, not the one that has been rearranged. Also, use the order of operations when simplifying each side of the equation.

Finding the values of x that satisfy the quadratic equation is another way of finding the roots of a quadratic equation.

Example 4 Application: Gardening

The area of a rectangular garden is 51 square yards. The length is 14 yards more than the width. What are the length and width of the garden?

SOLUTION

Let w be the width and $w + 14$ be the length.

$A = lw$ Area formula
$51 = (w + 14)w$ Substitute known values into the equation.
$51 = w^2 + 14w$ Distribute.
$0 = w^2 + 14w - 51$ Write the equation into standard form.
$0 = (w + 17)(w - 3)$ Factor.
$w + 17 = 0 \quad w - 3 = 0$ Use the Zero Product Property.
$w = -17 \quad w = 3$ Solve.

Because the width must be a positive number, the only possible solution is 3 yards. Since the width is 3 yards, the length is $w + 14$. So the length is $3 + 14$, which is 17 yards.

Math Reasoning

Justify How could you check your answers?

Sample: Multiply the length and width to see if the product is 51.

Example 3

This example requires that the GCF be first factored out of the quadratic equation. Then the equation is factored to solve.

Additional Example 3

Find the roots.
$6x^2 - 12 = -21x$.
The roots are $\frac{1}{2}$ and -4.

Example 4

This example shows how to solve an area problem using the Zero Product Property.

Extend the Example

The area of the garden is increased by 21 square yards. What are the dimensions of the expanded garden? The width is 4 yards and the length is 18 yards.

Additional Example 4

The area of a rectangular pasture is 58,500 square meters. The width is 320 meters less than the length. What are the length and width of the pasture? length = 450 meters; width = 130 meters

INCLUSION

Have students practice factoring quadratic expressions, including expressions for which the GCF can be factored out:

$x^2 - x - 12 \quad (x - 4)(x + 3)$

$6x^2 - 24x + 24 \quad 6(x - 2)(x - 2)$

$6x^3 - 2x^2 - 8x \quad 2x(3x - 4)(x + 1)$

Encourage students to identify which factors of their solutions would be used to find solutions for quadratic equations.

Help them understand that each factor containing a variable could be used to determine a root of an equation. For example, have students set each factor of $6x^2 - 24x + 24$ equal to zero. Point out the $6 \neq 0$. Then have them set each factor of $6x^3 - 2x^2 - 8x$ equal to zero. Point out that $x = 0$ is a solution of $2x = 0$.

Example 5

These examples demonstrate a method of solving that requires students to factor quadratic equations with missing terms.

Error Alert Some students may use incorrect signs in the solution. Encourage them to set each factor equal to zero and to solve the resulting equation. When the variable is isolated, the solution has the opposite sign of the term in the factor.

Additional Example 5

a. Solve $18x^2 + 9x = 0$.
   The solution set is $\{0, -\frac{1}{2}\}$.

b. Solve $9x^2 - 4 = 0$.
   The solution set is $\{-\frac{2}{3}, \frac{2}{3}\}$.

Example 5   Solving Quadratic Equations with Missing Terms

Solve.

a. $18x^2 = 8x$

SOLUTION

$18x^2 - 8x = 0$ Set the equation equal to zero.
$2x(9x - 4) = 0$ Factor out the GCF.

$2x = 0$ $9x - 4 = 0$ Set each factor equal to zero.

$x = 0$ $x = \frac{4}{9}$ Solve each equation for x.

Check

$18x^2 = 8x$ $18x^2 = 8x$

$18 \cdot (0)^2 \stackrel{?}{=} 8(0)$ $18\left(\frac{4}{9}\right)^2 \stackrel{?}{=} 8\left(\frac{4}{9}\right)$

$0 = 0$ ✓ $18\left(\frac{16}{81}\right) \stackrel{?}{=} 8\left(\frac{4}{9}\right)$

                              $\frac{32}{9} = \frac{32}{9}$ ✓

The solution set is $\{0, \frac{4}{9}\}$.

b. $4x^2 - 25 = 0$

SOLUTION

$4x^2 - 25 = 0$ Set the equation equal to 0.
$(2x - 5)(2x + 5) = 0$ Factor.

$2x - 5 = 0$ $2x + 5 = 0$ Set each factor equal to zero.
$2x = 5$ $2x = -5$ Solve each equation for x.
$x = 2.5$ $x = -2.5$

Check

$4x^2 - 25 = 0$ $4x^2 - 25 = 0$
$4(2.5)^2 - 25 \stackrel{?}{=} 0$ $4 \cdot (-2.5)^2 - 25 \stackrel{?}{=} 0$
$4(6.25) - 25 \stackrel{?}{=} 0$ $4(6.25) - 25 \stackrel{?}{=} 0$
$25 - 25 \stackrel{?}{=} 0$ $25 - 25 \stackrel{?}{=} 0$
$0 = 0$ ✓ $0 = 0$ ✓

The solution set is $\{-2.5, 2.5\}$.

Lesson Practice

a. Solve $(x - 3)(x + 7) = 0$.   3, –7
(Ex 1)

Find the roots.

b. $x^2 + 3x - 18 = 0$ 3, –6
(Ex 2)

c. $2x^2 + 13x + 15 = 0$ $-\frac{3}{2}$, –5
(Ex 2)

Solve.

d. $5x^2 - 20x = 10x - 45$ 3
(Ex 3)

e. $45x^2 = 27x$ $\{0, \frac{3}{5}\}$
(Ex 5)

f. $25x^2 - 16 = 0$ $\{-\frac{4}{5}, \frac{4}{5}\}$
(Ex 5)

g. (Architecture) A rectangular pool has an area of 360 square feet. The length is 6 feet more than three times the width. Find the dimensions of the pool.   The width is 10 feet, and the length is 36 feet.
(Ex 4)

Practice   Distributed and Integrated

Solve and graph the inequality.

1. $11 < 2(x + 5) < 20$
(82)
$\frac{1}{2} < x < 5$;

2. $|x| + 1.5 \leq 7.6$ $-6.1 \leq x \leq 6.1$;
(91)

3. Determine whether the polynomial $-121 + 9x^2$ is a perfect-square trinomial or a difference of two squares. Then factor the polynomial.   difference of two squares; $(3x + 11)(3x - 11)$
(83)

4. Graph the function $y = 2x^2 + 8x + 6$.
(96)

5. The number of Apples A and Oranges O grown in a certain fruit orchard can be modeled by the given expressions where x is the number of years since the trees were planted. Find a model that represents the total number of apples and oranges grown in this orchard. $S = 35x^3 + 28x - 24$
(53)

$A = 15x^3 + 17x - 20$

$O = 20x^3 + 11x - 4$

6. Write an equation for a line that passes through (1, 2) and is perpendicular to $y = -\frac{3}{4}x + 2\frac{3}{4}$.   Sample: $y = \frac{4}{3}x + \frac{2}{3}$
(65)

7. Solve the equation $\frac{4|x|}{9} + 3 = 11$ and graph the solution.
(94)
$\{18, -18\}$;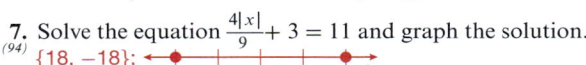

Simplify.

8. $\dfrac{\frac{3x + 6}{7x - 7}}{\frac{5x + 10}{14x - 14}}$ $\frac{6}{5}$
(92)

9. $(5xyz)^2(3x^{-1}y)^2$ $225y^4z^2$
(40)

*10. Determine if the ordered pair (5, 5) is a solution of the inequality $y < -5x + 4$.
(97)   no; It does not satisfy the inequality.

*11. Write Explain the Zero Product Property in your own words.   Sample: If two numbers multiplied together equal 0, then at least one of the numbers has to be 0.
(98)

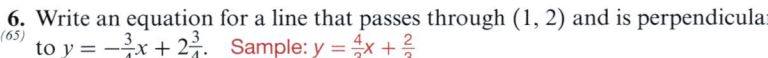

Lesson 98   659

Lesson Practice

Problem d

Error Alert Watch that students correctly combine the terms of the equation as they move all the terms to one side of the equation.

Problem e

Scaffolding Have students write the equation with all of the terms on one side of the equal sign. Have students explain how they decide on which side to isolate the zero.

✓ Check for Understanding

The questions below help assess the concepts taught in this lesson.

"What are some steps used to solve a quadratic equation by factoring?" Sample: Make sure that the equation is set equal to zero. Some terms may need to be moved from one side of the equation to the other so that the like terms can be combined.

"How is the Zero Product Property used when solving quadratic equations by factoring?" Sample: Since either factor may cause the equation to equal zero, each factor can be set equal to zero to find the solution(s).

3 Practice

Math Conversations

Discussion to strengthen understanding

Problem 1

Guide the students by asking them the following questions.

"Is this compound inequality combined with AND or OR?" AND

"How is the solution set found?" Sample: Include all values common to both inequalities.

Lesson 98   659

Problem 13

Error Alert

Encourage students who choose an incorrect solution to set each factor equal to zero and to carefully perform the operations necessary to isolate the variable. Then have them substitute their solutions into the respective factors and see if the result is zero.

Problem 14

Extend the Example

Have students solve the problem letting g represent the girl's age. Have them give the age of the mother in terms of g and explain how the solution compares to the solution of the original problem. Sample: The mother's age is $g + 27$. The solution is the same except that the girl's age is found first and is then used to find the age of her mother.

Problem 21

Remind students that the long division will be easier if a placeholder is used for the missing quadratic term.

---

*12. **Justify** What property allows you to use the following step when solving an equation? Sample: The Zero Product Property
(98)

$$(x + 4)(x + 5) = 0$$
$$x + 4 = 0 \quad x + 5 = 0$$

*13. **Multiple Choice** What is the solution set of $0 = (3x - 5)(x + 2)$? **A**
(98)

A $\left\{\frac{5}{3}, -2\right\}$ B $\left\{\frac{5}{3}, 2\right\}$ C $\left\{-\frac{5}{3}, -2\right\}$ D $\left\{-\frac{5}{3}, 2\right\}$

*14. (**Ages**) A girl is 27 years younger than her mother. Her mother is m years old. The product of their ages is 324. How old is each person? The mother is 36 years old and the girl is 9 years old.
(98)

*15. **Multi-Step** Seve plans to go shopping for new jeans and shorts. She plans to spend no more than $70. Each pair of jeans costs $20 and each pair of shorts costs $10.
(97)
   a. Write an inequality that describes this situation. $20x + 10y \leq 70$
   b. Graph the inequality. See Additional Answers.
   c. If Seve wants to spend exactly $70, what is a possible number of each she can spend her money on? Sample: 3 pairs of jeans and 1 pair of shorts

*16. **Geometry** The Triangle Inequality Theorem states that the sum of the lengths of any two sides of a triangle is greater than the length of the third side. The sides of a triangle are labeled $4x$ inches, $2y$ inches, and 8 inches. James wrote an inequality that satisfies the Triangle Inequality Theorem. He wrote the inequality $4x + 2y > 8$. Use a graphing calculator to graph the inequality. See Additional Answers.
(97)

*17. Solve $(x + 4)(x - 9) = 0$. $-4, 9$
(98)

18. **Error Analysis** Students were asked to write an inequality that results in a dashed horizontal boundary line. Which student is correct? Explain the error. Student A; Sample: Student B wrote an inequality with a solid horizontal line.
(97)

Student A	Student B
$y > -3$	$y \geq 4$

19. (**Horseback Riding**) It took Joe $\frac{2x - 10}{2x^5}$ minutes to ride his horse to Darrell's house that was $\frac{3x^2 - 15x}{3x}$ miles away. Find his rate in miles per minute. x^5 miles per minute
(92)

20. **Measurement** The area of a triangle can be expressed as $4x^2 - 2x - 6$ square meters. The height of the triangle is $x + 1$ meters. Find the length of the base of the triangle. $8x - 12$ meters
(92)

21. (**Art**) Michael bought a rectangular painting from a local artist. The area of the painting was $(20x + 5 + x^3)$ square inches. The width was $(x - 5)$ inches. What was the length? $\left(x^2 + 5x + 45 + \frac{230}{x-5}\right)$ inches
(93)

22. **Analyze** Should you find the LCD when multiplying or dividing rational fractions? Sample: No, the LCD is found in addition and subtraction problems so that parts of equal size can be added or subtracted.
(95)

660   *Saxon Algebra 1*

⭐ CHALLENGE

Factor and solve each quadratic equation. What do they have in common?

$x^2 + 12x + 36 = 0$

$16 = -24x - 9x^2$

$16x^2 + 48x = -48x - 144$

$81x^2 - 162x + 324 = 162x$

$-54x = -9x^2 - 81$

All these equations are products of squares. They have only one solution.

23. **Multi-Step** Erika and Casey started a new walking program. They walked $\frac{4x}{3x+9}$ miles Thursday and $\frac{16}{x^2+12x+27}$ miles Friday.
   a. What is the total distance that they walked? $\frac{4x^2+36x+48}{3(x+9)(x+3)}$ miles
   b. If their rate was $\frac{4x}{x+3}$ miles per hour, how much time did it take them to walk on Thursday and Friday? $\frac{x^2+9x+12}{3x(x+9)}$ hours

*24. **(Physics)** A ball is dropped from 100 feet in the air. What is its height after 2 seconds? Use $h = -16t^2 + vt + s$. (Hint: Its initial velocity is 0 feet per second.) 36 feet

*25. **Error Analysis** Two students find the zeros of the function $y = x^2 - 8x - 33$. Which student is correct? Explain the error. Student B; Sample: Student A found the y-intercept.

Student A	Student B
$y = x^2 - 8x - 33$	$0 = x^2 - 8x - 33$
$y = (0)^2 - 8(0) - 33$	$0 = (x - 11)(x + 3)$
$y = -33$	$x - 11 = 0$ or $x + 3 = 0$
$(0, -33)$	$x = 11$ or $x = -3$
	11 and -3

26. **Multi-Step** Hideyo has a picture frame that measures 20 centimeters by 26 centimeters. The frame is 1.5 centimeters wide.
   a. Find the length and width of the picture area. 23 cm; 17 cm
   b. Find the length of the diagonal of the picture area to the nearest tenth of a centimeter. 28.6 cm

27. **(Profit)** A business sold $x^2 + 6x + 5$ items. The profit for each item sold is $\frac{x^2}{100x}$ dollars.
   a. What is the profit in terms of x? $\frac{x(x+5)(x+1)}{100}$ dollars
   b. What is the profit (in dollars) if $x = 50$? $1402.50

28. **Multi-Step** Javed has a garden with an area of 36 square feet. The width of his garden is 9 feet less than the length. What are the dimensions of his garden?
   a. Write a formula to find the dimensions of the garden and describe how you will solve it. $x(x - 9) = 36$; Sample: The formula needs to be set in the form $ax^2 + bx + c = 0$ in order to solve for x.
   b. What are the dimensions of the garden? 12 feet long and 3 feet wide.

29. **Generalize** Describe the steps for subtracting $\frac{x-6}{x+5}$ from $\frac{x^2-x-30}{x+5}$.

30. The width of a rectangle is represented by the expression $(4x - 6)$ and the length $(8x + 7)$. Would the area of the rectangle be correctly expressed as $32x^2 + 20x - 42$? If not, what is the correct area? No. A sign error has occurred; The correct expression would be $32x^2 - 20x - 42$.

29. Sample: Distribute the negative sign so that you are subtracting x and adding 6 to $x^2 - x - 30$. Then combine like terms to get $x^2 - 2x - 24$. Finally, try to factor out $x + 5$ from the numerator. Since you can't, your answer in simplest form is $\frac{x^2 - 2x - 24}{x + 5}$.

Lesson 98 661

Problem 26
Guide the students by asking them the following questions.

"How many centimeters does the frame add to the width of the picture?" Sample: 3 cm

"What formula is used to find the length of the diagonal?" the Pythagorean Theorem

Problem 27
Have students check their work by substituting 50 for x in the original expressions for the number of items sold and the profit for each item. Then have them multiply the results to find the total profit.

LOOKING FORWARD

Solving quadratic equations by factoring prepares students for

- **Lesson 100** Solving Quadratic Equations by Graphing
- **Lesson 102** Solving Quadratic Equations by Using Square Roots
- **Lesson 104** Solving Quadratic Equations by Completing the Square
- **Lesson 110** Using the Quadratic Formula
- **Lesson 113** Interpreting the Discriminant

Lesson 98

LESSON 99

1 Warm Up

Problems 2–5
Review finding the LCM in preparation for finding the LCD to solve rational proportions.

2 New Concepts

Remind students of the definition of a rational number: a number that can be expressed as the quotient of two numbers. Introduce the term **rational equation** and have students look over the examples. Point out that all the terms have a variable in the denominator.

Explain that in this lesson, students will solve equations that contain rational terms.

Example 1

These examples introduce students to solving rational equations that take the form of a proportion.

Additional Example 1
Solve each equation.

a. $\dfrac{x}{5} = \dfrac{2x+4}{2}$
$x = -2.5$

LESSON RESOURCES

Student Edition Practice Workbook 99
Reteaching Master 99
Adaptations Master 99
Challenge and Enrichment Master C99

LESSON 99

Solving Rational Equations

Warm Up

1. **Vocabulary** The denominator of a _____ contains a variable. The value of the variable cannot make the denominator equal to zero. **rational expression**

Find the LCM.

2. $7x^2y$ and $3xy^3$ $\quad 21x^2y^3$
3. $(3x - 6)$ and $(9x^2 - 18x)$ $\quad 9x(x-2)$
4. $(x + 3)$ and $(2x - 1)$ $\quad (x+3)(2x-1)$
5. $(14x - 7y)$ and $(10x - 5y)$ $\quad 35(2x - y)$

New Concepts

A **rational equation** is an equation containing at least one rational expression. There are two ways to solve a rational equation: using cross products or using the least common denominator.

Math Language
A rational expression is a fraction with a variable in the denominator.

Either way may lead to an **extraneous solution**; that is, a solution that does not satisfy the original equation. The solution may satisfy a transformed equation, but make a denominator in the original equation equal 0. If an answer is extraneous, eliminate it from the solution set.

If a rational equation is a proportion, it can be solved using cross products.

Example 1 Solving a Rational Proportion

Solve each equation.

a. $\dfrac{3}{x} = \dfrac{5}{x-6}$

SOLUTION

$\dfrac{3}{x} = \dfrac{5}{x-6}$

$3(x - 6) = 5x$ Use cross products.
$3x - 18 = 5x$ Distribute 3 over $(x - 6)$.
$-18 = 2x$ Subtract $3x$ from both sides.
$-9 = x$ Divide both sides by 2.

Math Reasoning
Analyze Why is it necessary to keep the terms in the denominator grouped?

Sample: They are already grouped by the fraction bar. A set of parentheses is a reminder to distribute when cross multiplying.

Check Verify that the solution is not extraneous.

$\dfrac{3}{x} = \dfrac{5}{x-6}$

$\dfrac{3}{-9} \stackrel{?}{=} \dfrac{5}{-9-6}$ Substitute -9 for x in the original equation.

$\dfrac{3}{-9} \stackrel{?}{=} \dfrac{5}{-15}$ Simplify the denominator.

$-\dfrac{1}{3} = -\dfrac{1}{3}$ Simplify each fraction.

The solution is $x = -9$. ✓

662 Saxon Algebra 1

MATH BACKGROUND

For this lesson, consider any expression with a variable in the denominator to be a rational expression.

Rational equations can be solved using cross products or by finding the least common denominator to simplify all terms on both sides of the equation.

Using cross products to solve proportions can be applied to solving rational equations that have one term on each side.

Rational equations that contain more than two terms must be solved using the LCD.

Regardless of the method used to solve rational equations, the equations are transformed into the form of an equation, linear or quadratic, that the students already know how to solve.

b. $\frac{x}{4} = \frac{3}{x-1}$

SOLUTION

$\frac{x}{4} = \frac{3}{x-1}$

$x(x-1) = 12$ Use cross products.

$x^2 - x = 12$ Distribute x over $(x-1)$.

$x^2 - x - 12 = 0$ Subtract 12 from both sides.

$(x-4)(x+3) = 0$ Factor.

$x = 4$ or $x = -3$ Use the Zero Product Property to solve.

Check Verify that the solution is not extraneous.

$\frac{x}{4} = \frac{3}{x-1}; x = 4$ or $\frac{x}{4} = \frac{3}{x-1}; x = -3$

$\frac{4}{4} \stackrel{?}{=} \frac{3}{4-1}$ Substitute. $\frac{-3}{4} \stackrel{?}{=} \frac{3}{-3-1}$

$1 = 1$ ✓   Simplify each fraction. $-\frac{3}{4} = -\frac{3}{4}$ ✓

The solution set is $\{4, -3\}$.

If a rational equation includes a sum or difference, find the LCD of all the terms to solve.

Example 2   Using the LCD to Solve Addition Equations

Solve $\frac{3}{x} + \frac{16}{2x} = 11$.

SOLUTION

$\frac{3}{x} + \frac{16}{2x} = 11$

The LCD of the denominators is $2x$.

$(2x)\frac{3}{x} + (2x)\frac{16}{2x} = (2x)11$ Multiply each term by the LCD.

$6 + 16 = 22x$ Simplify each term.

$22 = 22x$ Add.

$1 = x$ Divide both sides by 22.

Check Verify that the solution is not extraneous.

$\frac{3}{x} + \frac{16}{2x} = 11$

$\frac{3}{1} + \frac{16}{2(1)} \stackrel{?}{=} 11$ Substitute 1 for x in the original equation.

$11 = 11$ ✓   Simplify.

The solution is $x = 1$.

Hint

To find the LCD of the terms, consider the denominator of the whole number to be 1.

b. $\frac{x}{3} = \frac{5}{x-2}$

$x = -3$ and $x = 5$

Example 2

This example demonstrates how to solve a rational equation involving addition by multiplying by the LCD.

Additional Example 2

Solve $\frac{9}{3x} + \frac{15}{x} = 6$. $x = 3$

Lesson 99   663

 INCLUSION

Use the following strategy with students who have difficulty with written symbols. Help students identify the terms needed to find the LCD of a rational equation. Since sometimes one denominator will be a factor of another, it is not necessary to multiply by that factor a second time.

Present students with these groups of rational terms. Have them identify the denominators used to find the LCD of the terms.

1. $\frac{3}{ab}; \frac{6}{bc}; \frac{12}{b}$ ab, bc

2. $\frac{9}{x+2}; \frac{13}{2x}; \frac{4}{x-3}$ $x+2$, $2x$, $x-3$

3. $\frac{18}{5m}; \frac{6}{2m+1}; \frac{3}{m}$ 5m, 2m + 1

4. $\frac{7}{x^2y^3}; \frac{9}{xy}; \frac{2}{xy^4}$ x^2y^3, xy^4

5. $\frac{5}{d-3}; \frac{1}{d-1}; \frac{4}{d^2}$ $d-3$, $d-1$, d^2

Lesson 99   663

Example 3

This example demonstrates how to solve a rational equation involving subtraction by multiplying by the LCD. Point out to students the caution note regarding distributing the negative sign over the new numerator in a subtraction equation.

Additional Example 3

Solve $\frac{12}{x} + \frac{15}{x+1} = \frac{72}{3x}$. $x = 4$

Example 4

This example shows students how an extraneous solution may occur and how such cases should be handled.

Additional Example 4

Solve the equation.

$\frac{3x-1}{x+3} = \frac{2x-4}{x-2}$ $x = 7$ and $x = 2$; 2 is an extraneous solution, so $x = 7$.

Error Alert Check that students fully understand that it is possible to get a solution that makes the equation false. Some students will assume they have made an error and continue trying to find a second valid solution.

Example 3 Using the LCD to Solve Subtraction Equations

Solve $\frac{3}{x-1} - \frac{2}{x} = \frac{5}{2x}$.

SOLUTION

$\frac{3}{x-1} - \frac{2}{x} = \frac{5}{2x}$

Caution
Remember to distribute the negative over the new numerator in a fraction following a subtraction sign.

The LCD is $2x(x-1)$.

$2x(x-1)\frac{3}{x-1} - 2x(x-1)\frac{2}{x} = 2x(x-1)\frac{5}{2x}$ Multiply each term by the LCD.

$6x - 4(x-1) = 5(x-1)$ Simplify each term.

$6x - 4x + 4 = 5x - 5$ Use the Distributive Property.

$2x + 4 = 5x - 5$ Collect like terms.

$4 = 3x - 5$ Subtract $2x$ from both sides.

$9 = 3x$ Add 5 to both sides.

$3 = x$ Divide both sides by 3.

Check Verify that the solution is not extraneous.

$\frac{3}{x-1} - \frac{2}{x} = \frac{5}{2x}$

$\frac{3}{3-1} - \frac{2}{3} \stackrel{?}{=} \frac{5}{2(3)}$ Substitute 3 for x in the original equation.

$\frac{5}{6} = \frac{5}{6}$ ✓ Simplify.

The solution is $x = 3$.

Example 4 Checking for Extraneous Solutions

Solve the equation.

$\frac{x-1}{x-2} = \frac{x+9}{2x-4}$

SOLUTION

$\frac{x-1}{x-2} = \frac{x+9}{2x-4}$

$(x-1)(2x-4) = (x-2)(x+9)$ Use cross products.

$2x^2 - 6x + 4 = x^2 + 7x - 18$ Multiply.

$x^2 - 13x + 22 = 0$ Subtract x^2, $7x$, and -18 from both sides.

$(x-11)(x-2) = 0$ Factor.

$x = 11$ or $x = 2$ Use the Zero Product Property to solve.

664 Saxon Algebra 1

ENGLISH LEARNERS

Explain the meaning of the word **extraneous**. Write the word on the board and underline "extra". Say:

"Extraneous means extra. Something that is extra is not needed. For example, the light from the window is extraneous lighting."

Have students give other examples using the word extraneous. Sample: He made an extraneous remark about the situation.

Math Reasoning

Justify Why do you have to check both solutions to the equation?

Sample: Either or both solutions could be extraneous.

Check Verify that the solutions are not extraneous.

$\dfrac{x-1}{x-2} = \dfrac{x+9}{2x-4}; x = 11$

$\dfrac{11-1}{11-2} \stackrel{?}{=} \dfrac{11+9}{2(11)-4}$ Substitute.

$\dfrac{10}{9} = \dfrac{10}{9}$ ✓ Simplify.

or

$\dfrac{x-1}{x-2} = \dfrac{x+9}{2x-4}; x = 2$

$\dfrac{2-1}{2-2} \stackrel{?}{=} \dfrac{2+9}{2(2)-4}$

$\dfrac{1}{0} = \dfrac{11}{0}$ ✗

2 is an extraneous solution.

The solution is $x = 11$.

Example 5 Application: Painting

It takes Samuel 7 hours to paint a house. It takes Jake 5 hours to paint the same house. How long will it take them if they work together?

SOLUTION

Understand The answer will be the number of hours h it takes for Samuel and Jake to paint the house.

Samuel can paint the house in 7 hours, so he can paint $\frac{1}{7}$ of the house per hour.

Jake can paint the house in 5 hours, so he can paint $\frac{1}{5}$ of the house per hour.

Plan The part of the house Samuel paints plus the part of the house Jake paints equals the complete job. Samuel's rate times the number of hours worked plus Jake's rate times the number of hours worked will give the complete time it will take them to paint the house. Let h represent the number of hours worked.

(Samuel's rate)h + (Jake's rate)h = complete job

$\frac{1}{7}h \quad + \quad \frac{1}{5}h \quad = \quad 1$

Math Reasoning

Verify Show that the solution $\frac{35}{12}$ hours satisfies the original equation.

Sample:

$\frac{1}{7}h + \frac{1}{5}h = 1$

$\frac{1}{7}\left(\frac{35}{12}\right) + \frac{1}{5}\left(\frac{35}{12}\right) = 1$

$\frac{5}{12} + \frac{7}{12} = 1$

$1 = 1$

Solve

$\frac{1}{7}h + \frac{1}{5}h = 1$

$(35)\frac{1}{7}h + (35)\frac{1}{5}h = (35)1$ Multiply each term by the LCD, 35.

$5h + 7h = 35$ Simplify each term.

$h = \dfrac{35}{12}$ Combine like terms; and divide both sides by 12.

Together, they can paint the house in $2\frac{11}{12}$ hours.

Example 5

This example solves a rate problem using rational expressions.

Extend the Example

Suppose that Samuel takes 1 hour less and Jake 1 hour more to paint a house. Will they still finish in the same amount of time as when they worked at their original rates? Explain. no; Sample: Both now have a rate of 6 hours to paint a house. Working together, it will take them 3 hours to paint the house.

Additional Example 5

It takes Bill 8 hours to mow the pasture. It takes Frank 10 hours to mow the same pasture. How long will it take them if they work together? Together, they can mow the pasture in $4\frac{4}{9}$ hours.

Lesson 99   665

Lesson Practice

Solve each equation.

a. (Ex 1) $\dfrac{6}{x} = \dfrac{7}{x-1}$ $x = -6$

b. (Ex 1) $\dfrac{2}{x+4} = \dfrac{x}{6}$ $x = 2, -6$

c. (Ex 2) $\dfrac{12}{2x} + \dfrac{16}{4x} = 5$ $x = 2$

d. (Ex 3) $\dfrac{4}{x-2} - \dfrac{2}{x} = \dfrac{1}{3x}$ $x = -\dfrac{14}{5}$

e. (Ex 4) $\dfrac{x+5}{x+4} = \dfrac{x-2}{2x+8}$ $x = -12$

f. (Ex 5) **Lawn Care** It takes John 2 hours to mow the yard. Sarah can do it in 3 hours. How long will it take them if they mow the yard together? $1\tfrac{1}{5}$ hours

Practice   Distributed and Integrated

Solve.

1. (99) $\dfrac{4}{x} = \dfrac{8}{x+4}$ $x = 4$

2. (98) $(x-13)(x+22) = 0$ $\{13, -22\}$

3. (94) **Physics** A student is biking to a friend's house. He bikes at 10 miles per hour. The friend lives 20 miles away, give or take 2 miles. What are the minimum and maximum times it will take him to get there?   1.8 hours, 2.2 hours

*4. (96) **Verify** Without graphing, show that the point $(2, -6)$ lies on the graph of $y = x^2 + x - 12$.   Sample: $y = (2)^2 + (2) - 12 = -6$

5. (92) Simplify: $\dfrac{\dfrac{4x}{12x-60} + \dfrac{1}{4x-16}}{\dfrac{-2}{9x-20-x^2}}$.

6. (75) Factor $x + 4x^2 - 5$. $(4x + 5)(x - 1)$

5.

7. (52) Larry weighed 180 pounds. He has lost 2 pounds a month for x months. Write a linear equation to model his weight after 8 months. $y = 180 - 2x$; 164 pounds

*8. (99) **Write** What is an extraneous solution?   Sample: It is an answer that solves the transformed equation, but not the original one.

9. (95) Find the LCD of $\dfrac{2x}{2x^2 - 72} - \dfrac{12}{x^2 + 13x + 42}$.   LCD $= 2(x-6)(x+6)(x+7)$

10. (89) **Population** The function $y = -0.0003x^2 + 0.03x + 1.3$ shows the population of Philadelphia County between the years 1900 and 1990, where x is the number of years after 1900 and y is the population for that year in millions of people. Find the vertex of the parabola that represents the function. What does it represent in terms of the scenario?   (50, 2.05); The population reached its maximum of about 2,050,000 people in 1950.

11. **Multi-Step** The coordinates of three friends' houses on a city map are $P(3, 3)$, $Q(5, 9)$, and $R(11, 3)$. The friends plan to meet at the point that is half-way between Q and the midpoint of $\overline{PR}$.
   a. Find the midpoint of $\overline{PR}$. (7, 3)
   b. Find the coordinates of the point where the friends plan to meet. (6, 6)

12. Find the quotient of $(18x^2 - 120 + 6x^5) \div (x - 2)$. $6x^4 + 12x^3 + 24x^2 + 66x + 132 + \frac{144}{x-2}$

13. What is the ratio of the volume of a cube with side lengths of 5 to the volume of a cube with side lengths of 3? $\frac{125}{27}$

*14. **Formulate** How can you quickly tell if a possible solution is extraneous using the denominators in the original equation? Sample: If it would cause one of the denominators to equal 0, the solution is extraneous.

*15. **Multiple Choice** Which of the following is an extraneous solution to the equation $\frac{x^2}{x-1} + \frac{4x^2 - 20x}{(x-1)(x-5)} = \frac{10}{2x-2}$? C and D
   A $x = -1$
   B $x = 0$
   C $x = 1$
   D $x = 5$

*16. (**Housekeeping**) It takes a man 8 hours to clean the house. His friend can clean it in 6 hours. How long will it take them if they clean together? $\frac{24}{7}$ hours

*17. **Error Analysis** Two students solve the equation $0 = (x - 5)(x + 11)$. Which student is correct? Explain the error.

17. Student A; Sample: Student B has the incorrect signs on both solutions.

Student A	
$x - 5 = 0$	$x + 11 = 0$
$x = 5$	$x = -11$

Student B	
$x - 5 = 0$	$x + 11 = 0$
$x = -5$	$x = 11$

18. **Geometry** The area of a triangle is 24 square centimeters. The height is four more than two times the base. Find the base and height of the triangle. The base is 4 centimeters and the height is 12 centimeters.

*19. **Multi-Step** The length of a lawn is twice the width. The lawnmower cuts 2-foot strips. One strip along the length and width has already been cut.

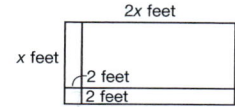

   a. Write expressions for the length and width of the area left to be cut. $2x - 2$ and $x - 2$
   b. The area left to be cut is 144 square feet. Find the width of the yard. 10 feet
   c. What is the length of the yard? 20 feet

20. **Generalize** How do you know when there is no solution to an absolute-value inequality? Sample: There is no solution when the absolute value is less than 0 because it would be a negative number.

21. (**Architecture**) Mia is designing a rectangular city hall. She accidentally spills water on her newly revised sketches. She is only able to determine the area, which is $(x^2 - 15x + 56)$ square feet, and the length, which is $(x - 7)$ feet. What is the width? $(x - 8)$ feet

---

Problem 14
Guide the students by asking them the following questions.

"What kind of denominator would not be allowed in a rational equation?" A denominator equal to 0.

"How could the denominator equal zero?" The value substituted for the variable causes the denominator to equal zero.

"What would this tell about the solution?" It would be an extraneous solution.

Problem 19
Error Alert
Make sure that students write the correct expressions for the length and width of the lawn yet to be cut. If students begin with erroneous expressions, they cannot arrive at the correct solution.

Problem 21
Extend the Problem
The height of the rectangular-prism-shaped city hall is $(3x + 5)$. What is the volume of the building?
$3x^3 - 40x^2 + 93x + 280$

Lesson 99   667

*22. **Multiple Choice** What are the zeros for the function $y = 4x^2 + 28x - 72$? **C**
(96)
A 0, 4
B 0, −4
C 2, −9
D 2, −76

*23. **Band** The school band is performing a music concert. Tickets cost $3 for adults and $2 for students. In order to cover expenses, at least $200 worth of tickets must be sold. Write an inequality that describes the graph of this situation. $3x + 2y \geq 200$

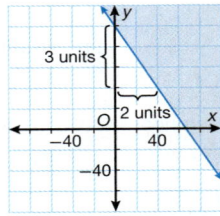

24. **Measurement** Jesse bought a new glass window to go in his front room. The area of
(93) the window is $(2 + 3x^3 - 8x)$ square inches. The width is $(x + 4)$ inches. What is the length? $\left(3x^2 - 12x + 40 - \frac{158}{x+4}\right)$ inches

*25. **Error Analysis** Students were asked to write an inequality that results in a solid, vertical boundary line. Which student is correct? Explain the error.

25. Student A; Sample: Student B wrote an inequality with a dashed vertical boundary line.

Student A	Student B
$x \leq 6$	$x < -2$

26. Graph the inequality $4x + 5y \geq -7$.
(97)

26.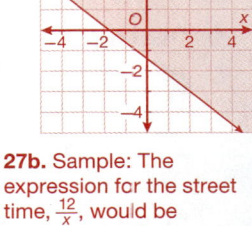

27. **Multi-Step** Pedro biked 6 miles on dirt trails and 12 miles on the street. His
(90) biking rate on the dirt trails was 25% of what it was on the street.
  a. Write a simplified expression for Pedro's total biking time. $\frac{9}{0.25x} = \frac{36}{x}$
  b. **Analyze** Explain how finding the simplified expression would change if Pedro's biking rate on the trails was 50% of what it was on the streets.

28. Graph the function $y - 3 = -x^2 + 3$.
(84)

27b. Sample: The expression for the street time, $\frac{12}{x}$, would be multiplied by $\frac{.5}{.5}$ instead of $\frac{.25}{.25}$, making the simplified expression $\frac{12}{.5x} = \frac{24}{x}$.

29. A square has a side length s. The square grows larger and has a new area
(83) of $s^2 + 16s + 64$. What is the new side length? $s + 8$

30. Write an equation where j is inversely proportional to m and n and directly
(Inv 8) proportional to p and q. $j = \frac{kpq}{mn}$

28.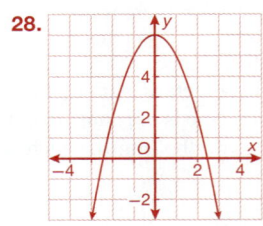

LESSON 100

Solving Quadratic Equations by Graphing

Warm Up

1. **Vocabulary** The U-shaped curve that results from graphing a quadratic function is called a(n) _____.   parabola

Evaluate each expression for the given values.

2. $3(x - y)^2 - 4y^2$ for $x = -5$ and $y = -2$ 11
3. $-x^2 - 3xy + y$ for $x = 3$ and $y = -1$ -1

Determine the direction that the parabola opens.

4. $f(x) = 3x^2 + x - 4$ upward
5. $f(x) = -2x^2 + x + 1$ downward

New Concepts

The solution(s) of a quadratic equation, $0 = ax^2 + bx + c$, can be found by graphing the related function, $f(x) = ax^2 + bx + c$. The U-shaped graph of a quadratic function is called a parabola. The solutions of the equation are called roots and can be found by determining the x-intercepts or zeros of the quadratic function. These zeros can be found by graphing the related function to see where the parabola intersects the x-axis.

Math Language

The same function is described by $y = 3x^2 - 5$ and $f(x) = 3x^2 - 5$.

The **function notation** for y is $f(x)$. It is read, "f of x."

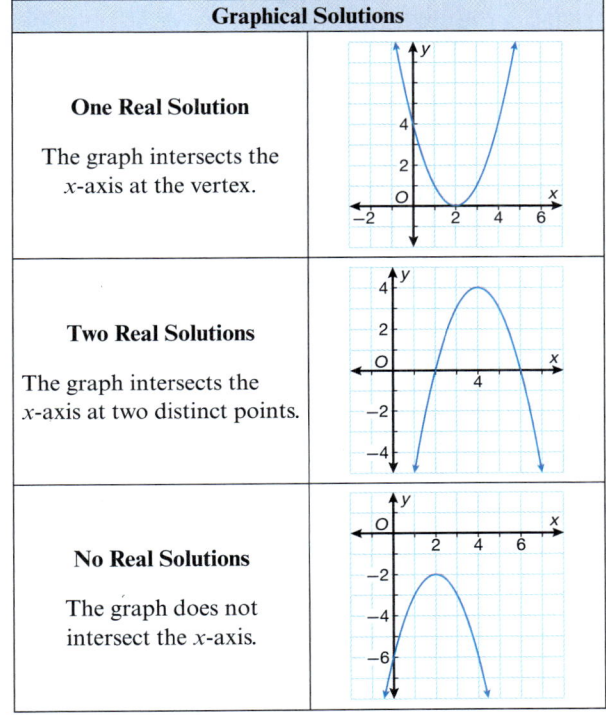

	Graphical Solutions
One Real Solution The graph intersects the x-axis at the vertex.	
Two Real Solutions The graph intersects the x-axis at two distinct points.	
No Real Solutions The graph does not intersect the x-axis.	

Online Connection
www.SaxonMathResources.com

Lesson 100   669

MATH BACKGROUND

To solve a quadratic equation, it is written in standard form, where the exponents are in descending order and the polynomial is set equal to zero: $0 = ax^2 + bx + c$.

Quadratic equations may have one real solution (when the vertex of the parabola is on the x-axis), two real solutions (when the parabola crosses the x-axis), or no real solutions (when the parabola does not interesect the x-axis). The x-intercepts shown by the graph are the solutions.

Take the opportunity with this lesson, to tell or remind students that when any type of equation is solved, the solution is the x-coordinate of the point where the graph of the equation crosses the x-axis.

Students have already solved linear, quadratic, and absolute-value equations in their study of algebra. In Section 10, they will solve rational and radical equations. In all cases, the graphical interpretation of the solution, or roots, will be the x-intercept(s).

Example 1

These examples introduce the concept of solving a simple quadratic equation through graphing the related function.

Error Alert Some students may locate points on only one side of the parabola. Encourage them to use the axis of symmetry to plot points on both sides of the parabola.

Additional Example 1

Solve each equation by graphing the related function.

a. $x^2 - 25 = 0$

The solutions are -5 and 5.

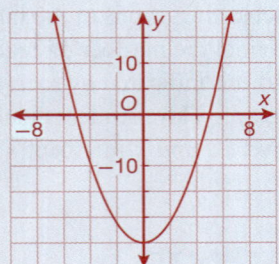

Example 1 Solving Quadratic Equations by Graphing

Solve each equation by graphing the related function.

a. $x^2 - 36 = 0$

SOLUTION

Step 1: Find the axis of symmetry.

$x = -\dfrac{b}{2a}$ Use the formula.

$x = -\dfrac{0}{2(1)} = 0$ Substitute values for a and b.

The axis of symmetry is $x = 0$.

Step 2: Find the vertex.

$f(x) = x^2 - 36$

$f(0) = (0)^2 - 36$ Evaluate the function for $x = 0$ to find the vertex.

The vertex is $(0, -36)$.

Step 3: Find the y-intercept.

The y-intercept is c, or -36.

Step 4: Find two more points that are not on the axis of symmetry.

$f(5) = 5^2 - 36$ $f(7) = 7^2 - 36$
$(5, -11)$ $(7, 13)$

Step 5: Graph.

Graph the axis of symmetry $x = 0$, the vertex and the y-intercept, both at coordinate $(0, -36)$. Reflect the points $(5, -11)$ and $(7, 13)$ over the axis of symmetry and graph the points $(-5, -11)$ and $(-7, 13)$. Connect the points with a smooth curve.

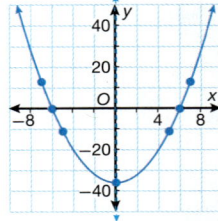

From the graph, the x-intercepts appear to be 6 and -6.

Check Substitute the values for x in the original equation.

$x^2 - 36 = 0; x = 6$ $x^2 - 36 = 0; x = -6$
$(6)^2 - 36 \stackrel{?}{=} 0$ $(-6)^2 - 36 \stackrel{?}{=} 0$
$36 - 36 \stackrel{?}{=} 0$ $36 - 36 \stackrel{?}{=} 0$
$0 = 0$ ✓ $0 = 0$ ✓

The solutions are 6 and -6.

Hint
When the coefficient of the x^2-term is positive, the parabola will open upward.
When the coefficient of the x^2-term is negative, the parabola will open downward.

Math Reasoning

Write Why are the x-intercepts substituted into the original equation?

The x-intercepts of the function are roots, or solutions, of the equation.

ENGLISH LEARNERS

For Example 1, explain the meaning of the word **related.** Say:

"Related means connected with. For example, we are related to the members of our family."

Have students give other examples using the word related in a sentence. Sample: The notes are related by the key signature of the music.

b. $-x^2 - 2 = 0$

SOLUTION

Graph the related function $f(x) = -x^2 - 2$.

axis of symmetry:	$x = 0$
vertex:	$(0, -2)$
y-intercept:	$(0, -2)$
two additional points:	$(1, -3)$ and $(3, -11)$

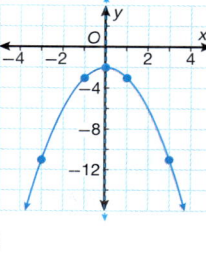

Reflect these two points across the axis of symmetry and connect them with a smooth curve.

From the graph, it can be seen that there is no x-intercept because the graph does not intersect the x-axis.

There is no real-number solution.

Caution

When a parabola does not cross the x-axis, there is no real-number solution to the quadratic equation.

c. $x^2 + 16 = 8x$

SOLUTION

Write the equation in standard form.

$x^2 - 8x + 16 = 0$

Graph the related function $f(x) = x^2 - 8x + 16$.

axis of symmetry:	$x = 4$
vertex:	$(4, 0)$
y-intercept:	$(0, 16)$
two additional points:	$(2, 4)$ and $(3, 1)$

Reflect these two points across the axis of symmetry and connect them with a smooth curve.

From the graph, the x-intercept appears to be 4.

Check Substitute 4 for x in the original equation.

$x^2 - 8x + 16 = 0; x = 4$

$(4)^2 - 8(4) + 16 \stackrel{?}{=} 0$

$16 - 32 + 16 \stackrel{?}{=} 0$

$0 = 0$ ✓

The solution is 4.

b. $0 = -x^2 - 3$ There are no real-number solutions.

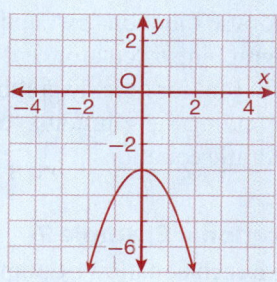

c. $x^2 - 3x - 18 = 0$
The solutions are 6 and -3.

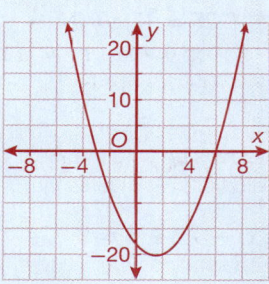

Lesson 100

Example 2

Once students have graphed quadratic functions by hand, the graphing calculator is a useful tool for quickly graphing and finding the solution(s) of quadratic equations.

Additional Example 2

Solve each equation by graphing the related function on a graphing calculator.

a. $x^2 + 28 = 11x$
   The solutions are 4 and 7. See Additional Answers.

b. $x^2 + 2x + 7 = 0$
   There is no solution. See Additional Answers.

c. $2x^2 - 7x + 3 = 0$
   The solutions are 3 and 0.5. See Additional Answers.

Example 3

The example provides a framework for a real-world application of solving quadratic equations by graphing.

Extend the Example

Suppose that Gill drops the baseball off of a platform twice the height of the original platform. How much longer does it take the baseball to hit the ground? about 0.8 second

Additional Example 3

Wendy dropped a golf ball from the top of a platform 102 feet off the ground. The height of the golf ball is described by the quadratic equation $h = -16t^2 + 102$, where h is the height in feet and t is the time in seconds. Find the time t when the golf ball hits the ground.
$t \approx 2.52$ seconds

Example 2 Solving Quadratic Equations Using a Graphing Calculator

Solve each equation by graphing the related function on a graphing calculator.

a. $-6x - 9 = x^2$

SOLUTION

Write the equation in standard form.

$-x^2 - 6x - 9 = 0$

Graph the related function
$f(x) = -x^2 - 6x - 9$.

The graph appears to have an x-intercept at -3.

Use the Table function to determine the zeros of this function.

The solution is -3.

b. $-6x = -x^2 - 13$

SOLUTION

Write the equation in standard form.

$x^2 - 6x + 13 = 0$.

Graph the related function $f(x) = x^2 - 6x + 13$.

The graph opens upward and does not intersect the x-axis.

There is no solution.

c. $-3x^2 + 5x = -7$

Round to the nearest tenth.

SOLUTION

Write the equation in standard form.

$-3x^2 + 5x + 7 = 0$

Graph the related function
$f(x) = -3x^2 + 5x + 7$.

The graph appears to have x-intercepts at 3 and -1.

Use the Zero function to determine the zeros of this function. Round to the nearest tenth.

The solutions are $x = 2.6$ and -0.9.

Hint

For help with graphing quadratic functions, see Graphing Calculator Lab 8: Characteristics of Parabolas on p. 583.

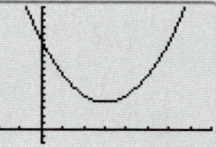

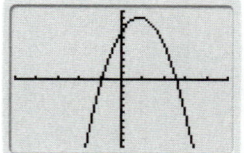

INCLUSION

Use the following strategy with students who have difficulty with abstract concept processing. Have students practice making tables in preparation for drawing graphs of quadratic equations. Help them decide which numbers to include in their tables. Have them find the vertex first using $\frac{-b}{2a}$. They should understand that since a parabola is symmetrical, their list of numbers should also be symmetrical about the axis of symmetry.

Students should be able to find the x-intercepts from the table. Any value of x for which the corresponding value of y is 0, is an x-intercept and thus a solution.

Once students have mastered making the table for the graph, help them plot the points and draw a smooth curve.

Example 3 Application: Physics

Gill drops a baseball from the top of a platform 64 feet off the ground. The height of the baseball is described by the quadratic equation $h = -16t^2 + 64$, where h is the height in feet and t is the time in seconds. Find the time t when the ball hits the ground.

Hint
The time t is plotted on the x-axis. The height h is plotted on the y-axis.

SOLUTION

Graph the related function $h(t) = -16t^2 + 64$ on a graphing calculator.

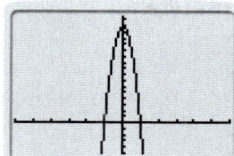

Height h is zero when the ball hits the ground. Use the Zero function of the graphing calculator to determine the zeros of this function.

There are two zeros for the given parabola: $t = 2$ and $t = -2$. Only values greater than or equal to zero are considered. So, $t = 2$ is the only solution.

The baseball hits the ground in 2 seconds.

Lesson Practice

Solve each equation by graphing the related function.
a. (Ex 1) $3x^2 - 147 = 0$ $x = 7$ and $x = -7$
b. $5x^2 + 6 = 0$ no solution
c. $x^2 - 10x + 25 = 0$ $x = 5$

Solve each equation by graphing the related function on a graphing calculator.
d. (Ex 2) $x^2 + 64 = 16x$ $x = 8$
e. (Ex 2) $x^2 + 4 = 2x$ no solution
f. (Ex 2) Round to the nearest tenth: $-7x^2 + 3x = -7$. $x = -0.8$ and 1.2
g. (Ex 3) Marcus shot an arrow while standing on a platform. The path of its movement formed a parabola given by the quadratic equation $h = -16t^2 + 2t + 17$, where h is the height in feet and t is the time in seconds. Find the time t when the arrow hits the ground. Round to the nearest hundredth. $t = 1.10$ seconds

a.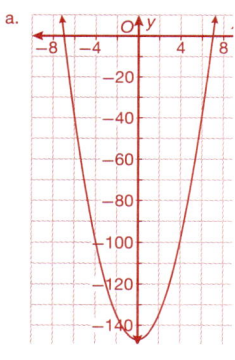

b.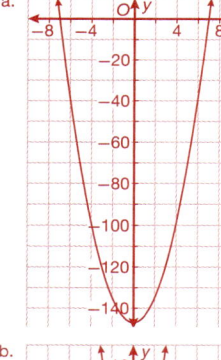

c.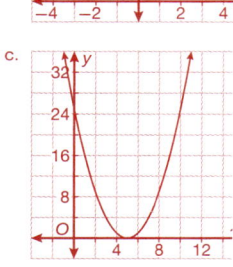

Practice Distributed and Integrated

Solve.
1. (98) $x(2x - 11) = 0$ $0, \frac{11}{2}$
2. (99) $\frac{12}{x - 6} = \frac{4}{x}$ $x = -3$

*3. (100) **Generalize** Using the path of a ball thrown into the air as an example, describe in mathematical terms each part of the graph the path of the ball creates. See Additional Answers.

*4. (100) **Generalize** What does the graph of a quadratic equation look like when there is no solution? one solution? two solutions? See Additional Answers.

Lesson 100   673

Lesson Practice

Problem a
Scaffolding To locate points on the parabola, first have students find the vertex and axis of symmetry. Then have them find two x-values to the left or right of the vertex and reflect them over the axis of symmetry.

Problem d
Error Alert Some students may not set the equation equal to zero. Remind them to write the equations in standard form.

✓ Check for Understanding

The questions below help assess the concepts taught in this lesson.

"Where on the graph of a quadratic equation are the solutions located?" Sample: where the graph intersects the x-axis

"What is another name for the solutions of a quadratic equation?" roots or x-intercepts

3 Practice

Math Conversations
Discussion to strengthen understanding

Problem 3
Guide the students by asking them the following questions.

"What is the name of the graph of a quadratic equation?" parabola

"What is the highest or lowest point on the graph called?" vertex

"What are the points where the graph crosses the horizontal axis?" x-intercepts or solutions

Lesson 100   673

Problem 12
Extend the Problem
Suppose Martha and Henry work the same job, but that this time, Martha begins one hour before Henry starts. How long do they work together? How long does Martha work? $1\frac{1}{7}$ hours; $2\frac{1}{7}$ hours

Problem 15
Error Alert
Make sure that students answer the question asked: the range of the number of objects she needs to sell, not the range of the amount of money she wants to make.

---

5. Given that y varies directly with x, identify the constant of variation such that when $x = 15$, $y = 30$. $k = 2$
(Inv 7)

*6. **Basketball** Ramero shoots a basketball into the air. The ball's movement forms a parabola given by the quadratic equation $h = -16t^2 + 7t + 7$, where h is the height in feet and t is the time in seconds. Find the maximum height of the path the basketball makes and the time t when the basketball hits the ground. Round to the nearest hundredth. $h = 7.77$ feet and $t = 0.92$ seconds
(100)

*7. **Multiple Choice** What is the equation of the axis of symmetry of the parabola defined by $y = \frac{1}{4}(x - 4)^2 + 5$? **B**
(100)
  A $x = 1$ B $x = 4$ C $x = 5$ D $x = -4$

*8. Solve $-7x^2 - 10 = 0$ by graphing. no solution
(100)

*9. Solve $\frac{6}{x} = \frac{8}{x + 7}$. $x = 21$
(99)

10. A deck of ten cards has 5 red and 5 black cards. Cards are replaced in the deck after each draw. Use an equation to find the probability of drawing a black card twice and rolling a 6 on a number cube. $P(\text{black, black, 6}) = \left(\frac{1}{2}\right)^2 \cdot \frac{1}{6} = \frac{1}{24}$
(80)

11. **Geometry** The altitude of the right triangle divides the hypotenuse into segments of lengths x units and 5 units. To find x, solve the equation $\frac{x+5}{6} = \frac{6}{x}$. 4 units
(99)

*12. **Multi-Step** Henry starts working a half-hour before Martha. He can complete the job in 4 hours. Martha can complete the same job in 3 hours.
(99)
  a. Let t represent the total time they work together. In terms of t, how long does Henry work? $t + 0.5$
  b. Use an equation to find how long they work together to complete the job. 1 hour 30 minutes
  c. How long does Henry work? 2 hours

13. Find the quotient of $\frac{a^2 + 10a - 24}{a - 2}$. 14. Simplify $\sqrt{49y^5}$. $7y^2\sqrt{y}$
(93) (a + 12) (61)

15. **Profit** An entrepreneur makes $3 profit on each object sold. She would like to make $270 plus or minus $30 total. What is the minimum and maximum number of objects she needs to sell? 80 objects, 100 objects
(94)

16. **Data Analysis** A student knows there will be 4 tests that determine her semester grade. She wants her average to be an 85, plus or minus 5 points. What is the minimum and maximum number of points she needs to earn during the semester? 320 points, 360 points
(94)

17. Solve the equation $|10x| - 3 = 87$. $\{-9, 9\}$
(94)

18. **Exercise** Tom ran a total of $\frac{7x}{x^2 + 3x - 18}$ miles in August and $\frac{2x + 1}{7x + 42}$ miles in September. How many more miles did he run in August? $\frac{-2x^2 + 54x + 3}{7(x - 3)(x + 6)}$ miles
(95)

19. Graph the function $y = 5x^2 - 10x + 5$.
(96)

*20. **Verify** A boundary line is a vertical line. The inequality contains a < symbol. Which half-plane should be shaded on the graph? Sample: Shade the half-plane to the left of the vertical line.
(97)

674 Saxon Algebra 1

⭐ **CHALLENGE**

Graph to find the ordered pair that is a solution to all the equations.

$2x^2 + 3x - 5 = 0$

$3x - 2y = 3$

$4x^2 + 3x - 4 = 3$

(1, 0)

21. **Multiple Choice** Which point does not satisfy the inequality $x + 2y < 5$? **D**
(97)
   A $(0, 0)$ **B** $(2, 1)$ **C** $(3, -4)$ **D** $(-1, 3)$

*22. (**Ages**) A boy is b years old. His father is 23 years older than the boy. The product
(98) of their ages is 50. How old is each person? The boy is 2 years old and the father is 25 years old.

*23. **Error Analysis** Two students find the roots of $3x^2 - 6x = 24$. Which student is
(98) correct? Explain the error.

23. Student B; Sample: Student A did not put the equation in standard form before factoring.

Student A	Student B
$3x^2 - 6x = 24$	$3x^2 - 6x = 24$
$3x(x - 2) = 24$	$3x^2 - 6x - 24 = 0$
$3x = 0 \quad x - 2 = 0$	$3(x^2 - 2x - 8) = 0$
$x = 0 \quad x = 2$	$3(x - 4)(x + 2) = 0$
	$x - 4 = 0 \quad x + 2 = 0$
	$x = 4 \quad x = -2$

24. Does the graph of $y + 2x^2 = 12 + x$ open upward or downward? downward
(84)

25. Do the side lengths 18, 80, and 82 form a Pythagorean triple? yes
(85)

26. **Multi-Step** The volume of a prism is $3x^3 + 12x^2 + 9x$. What are the possible
(87) dimensions of the prism?
   a. Factor out common terms. $3x(x^2 + 4x + 3)$
   b. Factor completely. $3x(x + 1)(x + 3)$
   c. Find the dimensions. $3x, x + 1, x + 3$

27. (**Travel**) The Jackson family drove 480 miles on Saturday and 300 miles on Sunday.
(90) Their average rate on Sunday was 10 miles per hour less than their rate was on Saturday. Write a simplified expression that represents their total driving time. $\frac{60(13x - 80)}{x(x - 10)}$

28. **Multi-Step** At the carnival, a man says that he will guess your weight within
(91) 5 pounds.
   a. You weigh 120 pounds. Write an absolute-value inequality to show the range of acceptable guesses. $|x - 120| \leq 5$
   b. Solve the inequality to find the actual range of acceptable guesses. $115 \leq x \leq 125$

29. **Verify** If the numerator of a rational expression is a polynomial and the
(92) denominator of the rational expression is a different polynomial, will factoring the polynomials always provide a way to simplify the expression? Verify your answer by giving an example.

29. no; Sample: If there are no common factors, the expression is in the simplest form; $\frac{x^2 - 4}{2x^2 + 12x + 18} = \frac{(x - 2)(x + 2)}{2(x + 3)(x + 3)}$

30. If a 9% decrease from the original price resulted in a new price of $227,500,
(47) what was the original price? $250,000

Lesson 100   675

LOOKING FORWARD

Solving quadratic equations by graphing prepares students for

- **Lesson 102** Solving Quadratic Equations Using Square Roots
- **Lesson 104** Solving Quadratic Equations by Completing the Square
- **Lesson 110** Using the Quadratic Formula
- **Lesson 113** Interpreting the Discriminant

Problem 21
Guide the students by asking them the following questions.

"Which choice can you eliminate immediately? Why?" Sample: choice **A**; The result of any calculations with two zeros will be less than 5.

"Which choice would you eliminate next? Why?" Sample: choice **C**; $3 + 2(-4)$ is a lot less than 5.

"What is the correct choice?" Sample: choice **D**; It is equal to 5, which means it is not less than 5.

Problem 25
Error Alert
Some students may believe that only multiples of the most common Pythagorean triple—3, 4, and 5—qualify as other Pythagorean triples. Remind students that any set of whole numbers that makes the Pythagorean Theorem true is considered a Pythagorean triple.

Problem 27
Guide the students by asking them the following questions.

"What formula do you have to use to solve the problem?" distance equals rate times time: $d = rt$

"How can you use this formula to find the driving time?" Rewrite the formula so that the time is isolated on one side of the equation: $\frac{d}{r} = t$.

"What LCD will you use to simplify the equation?" $(x)(x - 10)$

Problem 28
Extend the Problem
After looking at you, the man believes you weigh between 123 and 135 pounds. What is the probability of him choosing a weight from this range that is within 5 pounds of your actual weight? $\frac{3}{13}$

Lesson 100   675

INVESTIGATION 10

Transforming Quadratic Functions

A quadratic function is a function that can be written in the form $f(x) = ax^2 + bx + c$, where a is not equal to 0.

Math Reasoning
Analyze If $a = 0$, would the function still be quadratic? If not, what type of function would $f(x)$ be? **no; linear**

In Investigation 6, linear functions were graphed as transformations of the parent function $f(x) = x$. Similarly, you can graph a quadratic function as a transformation of the quadratic parent function $f(x) = x^2$.

Parameter Changes

Complete the table of values for $f(x) = x^2$ and graph the quadratic parent function.

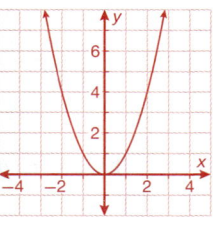

x	$f(x)$
-3	$(-3)^2 = 9$
-2	$(-2)^2 = 4$
-1	$(-1)^2 = 1$
0	$0^2 = 0$
1	$1^2 = 1$
2	$2^2 = 4$
3	$3^2 = 9$

As is the case for the linear parent function, the quadratic parent function $f(x) = x^2$ can be written as $f(x) = ax^2$, where $a = 1$. The graph changes when other values are substituted for a.

1. Graph $y = x^2$ and $y = 2x^2$ on the same set of axes. Compare the two graphs. **See Additional Answers.**

2. Graph $y = x^2$ and $y = \frac{1}{2}x^2$ on the same set of axes. Compare the two graphs. **See Additional Answers.**

3. Graph $y = x^2$ and $y = -x^2$ on the same set of axes. Compare the two graphs. **See Additional Answers.**

4. **Generalize** What is the effect of a on the graph of $y = ax^2$? **See Additional Answers.**

5. **Predict** How will the graph of $f(x) = \frac{2}{3}x^2$ change in relation to the quadratic parent function? **Sample: It's wider than the parent function.**

6. **Predict** How will the graph of $f(x) = -4x^2$ change in relation to the quadratic parent function? **Sample: It's narrower than the parent function and opens downward.**

The graph of a function of the form $f(x) = ax^2$ always crosses the y-axis at (0, 0). When $c \neq 0$, the graph of the function $f(x) = ax^2 + c$ does not pass through the point (0, 0).

7. Graph the quadratic parent function and the function $f(x) = x^2 + 1$ on the same set of axes. Compare the two graphs. **See Additional Answers.**

8. Graph the quadratic parent function and the function $f(x) = x^2 - 2$ on the same set of axes. **See Additional Answers.**

Online Connection
www.SaxonMathResources.com

676 Saxon Algebra 1

9. **Predict** How will the graph of $f(x) = x^2 + 7$ compare to the graph of the quadratic parent function? Sample: The new function moved up 7 units from the parent function.

Combinations of Parameter Changes

Predict How will each graph compare to the graph of the quadratic parent function? Verify your answer with a graphing calculator.

10. $f(x) = -x^2 + 2$ See Additional Answers.

11. $f(x) = \frac{1}{2}x^2 - 3$ See Additional Answers.

Investigation Practice

Describe how the graph for the given values of a and c changes in relation to the graph of the quadratic parent function. Verify your answer with a graphing calculator.

a. $f(x) = ax^2 + c$ for $a = 2$ and $c = 1$ The graph is narrower and moved 1 unit up.

b. $f(x) = ax^2 + c$ for $a = -3$ and $c = -2$ The graph is narrower, opens downward, and moved 2 units down.

c. $f(x) = ax^2 + c$ for $a = \frac{1}{2}$ and $c = 2$ The graph is wider and moved 2 units up.

d. $f(x) = ax^2 + c$ for $a = -\frac{1}{2}$ and $c = -1$ The graph opens downward, is wider, and moved 1 unit down.

Write an equation for the transformation described. Then graph the original function and the graph of the transformation on the same set of axes.

e. Shift $f(x) = 2x^2 - 4$ up 2 units.

f. Shift $f(x) = 3x^2 + 5$ down 4 units and open it downward.
$f(x) = -3x^2 + 1$;

e. $f(x) = 2x^2 - 2$;

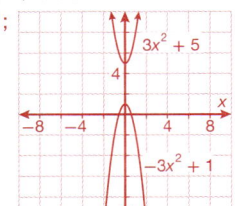

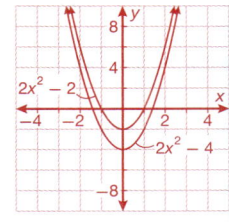

Investigation 10   677

ENGLISH LEARNERS

Discuss that children inherit some traits from their parents, but not all of them. Similarly, explain that a **parent function** has characteristics of any function of that type, but that other functions may look a little different. There are mathematical hints in the equation that indicate how different a transformed function will look.

LOOKING FORWARD

Transforming quadratic functions will prepare students for

- **Lesson 107** Graphing Absolute-Value Functions
- **Lesson 114** Graphing Square-Root Functions
- **Lesson 119** Graphing and Comparing Linear, Quadratic, and Exponential Functions

Discuss
The effect of each parameter in the equation on the graph of the function has been identified. Students will describe the transformations in the graph when multiple parameters are changed.

Investigation Practice

Math Conversations
Discussion to strengthen understanding

Problem a
Scaffolding Have students tell whether the function is wider or narrower, opens upward or downward, and moves up or down.

Problem b
Error Alert Students may forget the effect of the negative value of a. Remind students that a parabola opens down when $a < 0$.

Problems e and f
Guide the students by asking them the following questions.

"What value makes the graph move up or down?" c

"To move it down, will you add or subtract c?" subtract

"How do you make a parabola open downward?" Make a negative.

SECTION OVERVIEW
11

Lesson Planner

Lesson	New Concepts
101	Solving Multi-Step Absolute-Value Inequalities
102	Solving Quadratic Equations Using Square Roots
103	Dividing Radical Expressions
104	Solving Quadratic Equations by Completing the Square
105	Recognizing and Extending Geometric Sequences
	Cumulative Test 20, Performance Task 20
106	Solving Radical Equations
107	Graphing Absolute-Value Functions
108	Identifying and Graphing Exponential Functions
109	Graphing Systems of Linear Inequalities
110	Using the Quadratic Formula
	Cumulative Test 21, Performance Task 21
INV 11	Investigation: Investigating Exponential Growth and Decay

Resources for Teaching
- Student Edition
- Teacher's Edition
- Student Edition eBook
- Teacher's Edition eBook
- Resources and Planner CD
- Solutions Manual
- Instructional Masters
- Technology Lab Masters
- Warm Up and Teaching Transparencies
- Instructional Presentations CD
- Online activities, tools and homework help
  www.SaxonMathResources.com

Resources for Practice and Assessment
- Student Edition Practice Workbook
- Course Assessments
- Standardized Test Practice
- College Entrance Exam Practice
- Test and Practice Generator CD using ExamView™

Resources for Differentiated Instruction
- Reteaching Masters
- Challenge and Enrichment Masters
- Prerequisite Skills Intervention
- Adaptations for Saxon Algebra 1
- Multilingual Glossary
- English Learners Handbook
- TI Resources

Pacing Guide

 Resources and Planner CD for lesson planning support

45-Minute Class

Day 1	Day 2	Day 3	Day 4	Day 5	Day 6
Lesson 101	Lesson 102	Lesson 103	Lesson 104	Lesson 105	Cumulative Test 20
Day 7	**Day 8**	**Day 9**	**Day 10**	**Day 11**	**Day 12**
Lesson 106	Lesson 107	Lesson 108	Lesson 109	Lesson 110	Cumulative Test 21
Day 13					
Investigation 11					

Block: 90-Minute Class

Day 1	Day 2	Day 3	Day 4	Day 5	Day 6
Investigation 10 Lesson 101	Lesson 102 Lesson 103	Lesson 104 Lesson 105	Cumulative Test 20 Lesson 106	Lesson 107 Lesson 108	Lesson 109 Lesson 110
Day 7					
Cumulative Test 21 Investigation 11					

* For suggestions on how to implement Saxon Math in a block schedule, see the Pacing section at the beginning of the Teacher's Edition.

Lessons 101–110, Investigation 11

Differentiated Instruction

Below Level	
Warm Up	SE pp. 678, 684, 691, 697, 705, 712, 720, 727, 735, 742
Skills Bank	SE pp. 846–883
Reteaching Masters	Lessons 101–110, Investigation 11
Warm Up Transparencies	Lessons 101–110
Prerequisite Skills Intervention	Skills 81, 82

Advanced Learners	
Challenge	TE pp. 682, 690, 696, 704, 711, 719, 725, 734, 740, 748, 751
Extend the Example	TE pp. 680, 687, 692, 706, 708, 717, 723, 728, 738, 744
Extend the Exploration	TE pp. 698
Extend the Problem	TE pp. 681, 689, 690, 695, 701, 703, 710, 718, 719, 726, 733, 740, 746, 747, 749, 751
Challenge and Enrichment Masters	Challenge: 101–110; Enrichment: 104, 105, 109

English Learners	
EL Tips	TE pp. 680, 687, 694, 698, 709, 718, 721, 733, 736, 743, 750
Multilingual Glossary	Booklet and Online English Learners Handbook

Special Needs	
Inclusion Tips	TE pp. 679, 685, 693, 699, 710, 713, 724, 728, 729, 738, 744
Adaptations for Saxon Algebra 1	Lessons 101–110, Cumulative Tests 20, 21

For All Learners	
Exploration	SE pp. 698, 750
Caution	SE pp. 678, 685, 686, 708, 731, 736, 751
Hints	SE pp. 678, 680, 697, 698, 707, 715, 716, 722, 723, 727, 730, 743, 745, 751
Error Alert	TE pp. 680, 681, 682, 683, 685, 687, 689, 692, 694, 695, 699, 702, 703, 705, 707, 708, 710, 716, 717, 719, 721, 724, 726, 730, 731, 732, 733, 737, 738, 739, 743, 745, 747, 750, 751, 752
Alternate Method	TE pp. 686, 701, 706, 707, 708, 722, 723, 730, 731, 732, 737
Online Tools	

SE = Student Edition; TE = Teacher's Edition

Math Vocabulary

Lesson	New Vocabulary	Maintained	EL Tip in TE
101		Absolute-value compound inequality	acceptable
102		irrational number perfect square quadratic equation rational number	vinyl
103	conjugate of an irrational number rationalize	index number radical expression radicand	terminal
104	completing the square	binomial square perfect-square trinomial quadratic term	model
105	common ratio geometric sequence	sequence	sequence
106	radical equation	extraneous solution radical expression	bounce
107	absolute value function vertex of an absolute-value graph	axis of symmetry parent function translation vertex	translation
108	exponential function	common ratio exponent geometric sequence	accumulate accumulation
109	solution of a system of linear inequalities system of linear inequalities	system of linear equations	convenient
110	quadratic formula	completing the square standard form of a quadratic equation	rearrange
INV 11	doubling time exponential decay exponential growth half-life	exponent	share

Section Overview 11

SECTION OVERVIEW 11

Math Highlights

Enduring Understandings – The "Big Picture"

After completing Section 11, students will understand:

- How to solve multi-step absolute-value inequalities and graph absolute-value functions.
- Solve quadratic equations by using square roots, completing the square, and using the quadratic formula.
- How to rationalize the denominator of a radical expression.
- How to recognize and extend geometric sequences.
- How to solve radical equations and graph exponential functions.

Essential Questions

- What determines the solution set of an absolute–value inequality as AND or OR?
- When is a radical expression in simplest form?
- How is a perfect-square trinomial formed by completing the square?
- What is the quadratic formula and how can it be used to solve quadratic equations?
- When is a sequence an arithmetic or geometric sequence?
- What are the characteristics of absolute-value functions and exponential functions?
- How does the solution set of a system of linear equations compare to the solution set of a system of linear inequalities?

Math Content Strands	Math Processes
Absolute-Value Equations and Inequalities • Lesson 101 Solving Multi-Step Absolute-Value Inequalities • Lesson 107 Graphing Absolute-Value Functions **Functions and Relations** • Lesson 105 Recognizing and Extending Geometric Sequences • Lesson 108 Identifying and Graphing Exponential Functions • Investigation 11 Investigating Exponential Growth and Decay **Quadratic Equations and Functions** • Lesson 102 Solving Quadratic Equations Using Square Roots • Lesson 104 Solving Quadratic Equations by Completing the Square • Lesson 110 Using the Quadratic Formula **Radical Expressions and Functions** • Lesson 103 Dividing Radical Expressions • Lesson 106 Solving Radical Equations **Systems of Equations and Inequalities** • Lesson 109 Graphing Systems of Linear Inequalities **Connections in Practice Problems** 　　　　　　Lessons Coordinate Geometry　102, 104, 107 Data Analysis　103 Geometry　101, 103, 104, 105, 106, 107, 108, 109, 110 Measurement　101, 102, 104, 105, 110 Probability　109	**Reasoning and Communication** 　　　　　　　Lessons • Analyze　　101, 102, 103, 104, 105, 106, 107, 108, 110, Inv. 11 • Connect　　107 • Error analysis　101, 102, 103, 104, 105, 106, 107, 108, 109, 110 • Estimate　　102, 107 • Formulate　Inv. 11 • Generalize　102, 104, 105, 106, 108, 109, 110, Inv. 11 • Justify　　103, 104, 105, 106, 107, 108 • Math Reasoning　101, 102, 103, 104, 105, 106, 107, 108, 109, Inv. 11 • Multiple choice　101, 102, 103, 104, 105, 106, 107, 108, 109, 110 • Multi-step　101, 102, 103, 104, 105, 106, 107, 108, 109, 110 • Predict　　103, 110, Inv. 11 • Verify　　101, 102, 103, 104, 105, 106, 108, 109, Inv. 11 • Write　　101, 103, 105, 106, 107, 109, Inv. 11 • Graphing Calculator　101, 102, 105, 107, 108, 109, 110 **Connections** **In Examples:** Architecture, Basketball, Bounce height, Crafts, Employment, Object in motion, Population, Travel **In Practice problems:** Architecture, Area of a pool, Art supplies, Astronomy, Banking, Baseball, Basketball, Boating, Botany, Building, Business, Carbon, Cell phone, Chemistry, Compound interest, Construction, Dating, Depreciation, Design, Egg toss, Football, Fractals, Gardening, Horseshoes, Landscaping, Masonry, Meteorology, Office management, Oven temperature, Population, Printing, Projectile motion, Renovations, Road trip, Rocket, Running, School dance, Skydiving, Soccer, Sports, Stock exchange, Tennis, Time and distance, Traveling, Volleyball, Water balloons

Saxon *Algebra 1*

Content Trace

Lesson	Warm Up: Prerequisite Skills	New Concepts	Where Practiced	Where Assessed	Looking Forward
101	Lessons 7, 45, 77	Solving Multi-Step Absolute-Value Inequalities	Lessons 102, 103, 104, 105, 106, 107, 108, 109, 110, 111, 114, 116, 117	Cumulative Tests 21, 22, 23	Lesson 107
102	Lessons 13, 46	Solving Quadratic Equations Using Square Roots	Lessons 103, 104, 105, 106, 107, 108, 109, 110, 111, 112, 115, 117, 118	Cumulative Tests 21, 22, 23	Lessons 104, 110
103	Lessons 13, 61, 76	Dividing Radical Expressions	Lessons 104, 105, 106, 107, 108, 109, 110, 111, 112, 113, 116, 118, 119	Cumulative Tests 21, 22	Lessons 106, 114
104	Lessons 3, 4, 60, 98	Solving Quadratic Equations by Completing the Square	Lessons 105, 106, 107, 108, 109, 110, 111, 112, 113, 114, 117, 119, 120	Cumulative Tests 21, 22	Lessons 110, 112, 113
105	Lessons 3, 4, 32, 34	Recognizing and Extending Geometric Sequences	Lessons 106, 107, 108, 109, 110, 111, 112, 113, 114, 115, 118, 120	Cumulative Tests 21, 22	Lessons 108, 114, 115, Investigation 11
106	Lessons 61, 76, 98	Solving Radical Equations	Lessons 107, 108, 109, 110, 111, 112, 113, 114, 115, 116, 119	Cumulative Tests 22, 23	Lessons 108, 114
107	Lessons 5, 74, Inv. 6	Graphing Absolute-Value Functions	Lessons 108, 109, 110, 111, 113, 114, 115, 116, 120	Cumulative Tests 22, 23	Lessons 108, 114, 115, 119
108	Lesson 3	Identifying and Graphing Exponential Functions	Lessons 109, 110, 111, 112, 113, 114, 115, 116, 117	Cumulative Tests 22, 23	Lessons 114, 115, 119
109	Lessons 45, 97	Graphing Systems of Linear Inequalities	Lessons 110, 111, 112, 113, 114, 115, 116, 117, 118	Cumulative Tests 22, 23	Lessons 112, 114, 115, 119
110	Lessons 84, 104	Using the Quadratic Formula	Lessons 111, 112, 113, 114, 115, 116, 117, 118, 119	Cumulative Tests 22, 23	Lessons 112, 116, 119
INV 11	N/A	Investigation: Investigating Exponential Growth and Decay	Lessons 111, 112, 113, 114, 115, 116, 117, 118	Cumulative Test 23	Lessons 114, 115, 119

SECTION OVERVIEW 11

Ongoing Assessment

	Type	Feature	Intervention *
BEFORE instruction	Assess Prior Knowledge	• Diagnostic Test	• Prerequisite Skills Intervention
BEFORE the lesson	Formative	• Warm Up	• Skills Bank • Reteaching Masters
DURING the lesson	Formative	• Lesson Practice • Math Conversations with the Practice problems	• Additional Examples in TE • Test and Practice Generator (for additional practice sheets)
AFTER the lesson	Formative	• Check for Understanding (closure)	• Scaffolding Questions in TE
AFTER 5 lessons	Summative	After Lesson 105 • Cumulative Test 20 • Performance Task 20 After Lesson 110 • Cumulative Test 21 • Performance Task 21	• Reteaching Masters • Test and Practice Generator (for additional tests and practice)
AFTER 20 lessons	Summative	• Benchmark Tests	• Reteaching Masters • Test and Practice Generator (for additional tests and practice)

* for students not showing progress during the formative stages or scoring below 80% on the summative assessments

Evidence of Learning – What Students Should Know

Because the Saxon philosophy is to provide students with sufficient time to learn and practice each concept, a lesson's topic will not be tested until at least five lessons after the topic is introduced.

On the Cumulative Tests that are given during this section of ten lessons, students should be able to demonstrate the following competencies:
  • Find the distance between two points, the midpoint of a segment, and missing side lengths in triangles.
  • Identify the direction of a parabola, and find the axis of symmetry and zeros of a quadratic function.
  • Solve rational equations, quadratic equations, and absolute-value inequalities.
  • Add, subtract, multiply, and divide rational expressions with polynomials.
  • Simplify radical expressions.
  • Extend geometric sequences.

Test and Practice Generator CD using ExamView™

The Test and Practice Generator is an easy-to-use benchmark and assessment tool that creates unlimited practice and tests in multiple formats and allows you to customize questions or create new ones. A variety of reports are available to track student progress toward mastery of the standards throughout the year.

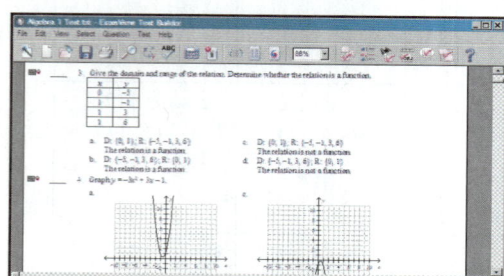
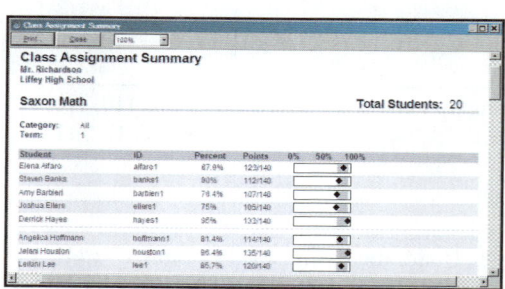

Saxon Algebra 1

Lessons 101–110, Investigation 11

Assessment Resources

Resources for Diagnosing and Assessing

- **Student Edition**
  - Warm Up
  - Lesson Practice

- **Teacher's Edition**
  - Math Conversations with the Practice problems
  - Check for Understanding (closure)

- **Course Assessments**
  - Diagnostic Test
  - Cumulative Tests
  - Performance Tasks
  - Benchmark Tests

Resources for Test Prep

- **Student Edition Practice**
  - Multiple-choice problems
  - Multiple-step and writing problems
  - Daily cumulative practice

- **Standardized Test Practice**

- **College Entrance Exam Practice**

- **Test and Practice Generator CD using ExamView™**

Resources for Intervention

- **Student Edition**
  - Skills Bank

- **Teacher's Edition**
  - Additional Examples
  - Scaffolding questions

- **Prerequisite Skills Intervention**
  - Worksheets

- **Reteaching Masters**
  - Lesson instruction and practice sheets

- **Test and Practice Generator CD using ExamView™**
  - Lesson practice problems
  - Additional tests

Cumulative Tests

The assessments in Saxon Math are frequent and consistently placed after every five lessons to offer a regular method of ongoing testing. These cumulative assessments check mastery of concepts from previous lessons.

Performance Tasks

The Performance Tasks can be used in conjunction with the Cumulative Tests and are scored using a rubric.

After Lesson 105

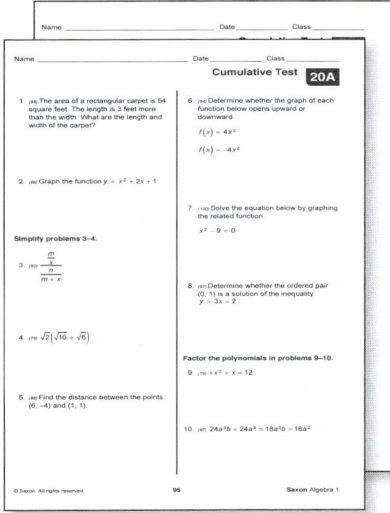

After Lesson 110

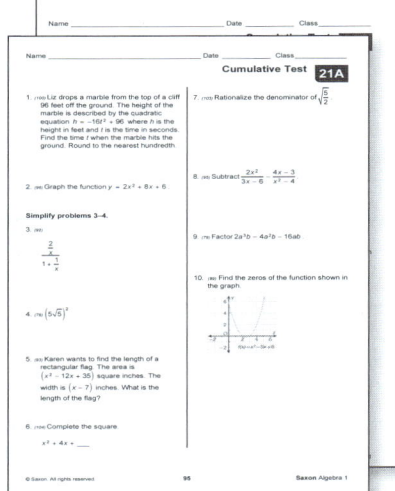

For use with Performance Tasks

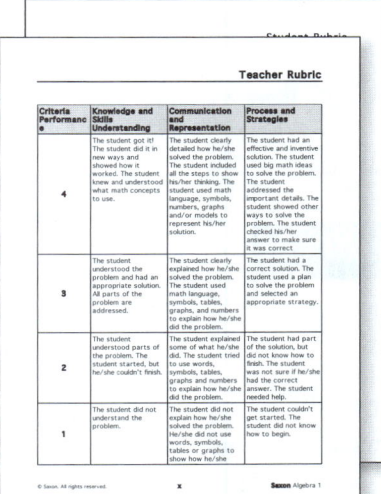

Section Overview 11   **678F**

LESSON 101

1 Warm Up

Problems 2 and 3
Remind students to follow the order of operations when simplifying expressions. Point out that they should treat absolute-value bars like parentheses.

2 New Concepts

In this lesson, students learn to solve multi-step absolute-value inequalities.

Example 1

Students solve absolute-value inequalities with operations outside the absolute-value symbols. The absolute value is isolated to solve the inequality.

Additional Example 1
Solve and graph each inequality.

a. $4|x| + 1 < 21$ $-5 < x < 5$;

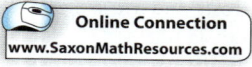

b. $\dfrac{|x|}{2} - 4 > 2$
$x < -12$ OR $x > 12$;

c. $-2|x| + 6 \geq 1$ $-2.5 \leq x \leq 2.5$;

LESSON RESOURCES

Student Edition Practice
   Workbook 101
Reteaching Master 101
Adaptations Master 101
Challenge and Enrichment
   Master C101

LESSON 101

Solving Multi-Step Absolute-Value Inequalities

Warm Up

1. **Vocabulary** A(n) _____ is a mathematical statement comparing quantities that are not equal. **inequality**

Simplify.

2. $|-8 + 5| - 7$ -4

3. $|2 \cdot -6| + 14$ 26

Solve.

4. $3x - 7 > 17$ $x > 8$

5. $-5x + 12 \geq 37$ $x \leq -5$

New Concepts

Recall that an absolute-value inequality is solved by first isolating the absolute-value expression. Then the inequality is written as a compound inequality with no absolute-value symbols. The compound inequality uses AND when the absolute-value inequality is a "less than" inequality. The compound inequality uses OR when the absolute-value inequality is a "greater than" inequality.

Caution
The absolute-value expression must be isolated to apply the rules:
AND ⟷ "less than"
OR ⟷ "greater than"

Example 1 Solving Multi-Step Absolute-Value Inequalities

Solve and graph each inequality.

a. $2|x| + 3 < 11$

SOLUTION

Isolate $|x|$ and then write the inequality as a compound inequality.

$2|x| + 3 < 11$

$\underline{-3 \quad -3}$ Subtraction Property of Inequality

$2|x| < 8$ Combine like terms.

$\dfrac{2|x|}{2} < \dfrac{8}{2}$ Division Property of Inequality

$|x| < 4$ Simplify.

$x > -4$ and $x < 4$ Write as a compound inequality.

The compound inequality can also be written as $-4 < x < 4$.

MATH BACKGROUND

Absolute value describes a number's distance from zero. The solutions to absolute-value inequalities describe values within a certain distance of zero. For $z = |ax - b|$, if $ax - b$ is a solution, then $-(ax - b)$ is also a solution, because both expressions describe the same distance from zero.

For $|ax - b| \leq, \geq, <,$ or $> z$, there are infinitely many solutions to the right and left of zero from $(ax - b)$ and from $-(ax - b)$.

The multi-step absolute value inequality with operators outside of the absolute value symbols requires isolating the absolute value symbols. This is so that the definition of absolute value may be applied to solve the inequality.

The use of a few test points from the solutions of the absolute-value inequalities will help students determine the accuracy of their work.

b. $\dfrac{|x|}{5} - 4 > -2$

SOLUTION

$\dfrac{|x|}{5} - 4 > -2$

$\dfrac{|x|}{5} > 2$ Add 4 to each side.

$|x| > 10$ Multiply each side by 5.

$x < -10$ OR $x > 10$ Write as a compound inequality.

c. $-10|x| + 54 \geq -21$

SOLUTION

$-10|x| + 54 \geq -21$

$-10|x| \geq -75$ Subtract 54 from each side.

$|x| \leq 7.5$ Divide each side by -10.

$-7.5 \leq x \leq 7.5$ Write as a compound inequality.

Hint

Reverse the direction of the inequality symbol when dividing each side of an inequality by a negative number.

Algebraic expressions within the absolute-value symbols may have one or more operations on the variable. So, after the absolute-value expression is isolated, solving the resulting compound inequality requires additional steps.

Example 2   **Solving Inequalities with One Operation Inside Absolute-Value Symbols**

Solve and graph the inequality.

$|x + 5| - 1 > 7$

SOLUTION

Isolate the absolute-value expression $|x + 5|$. Then write it as a compound inequality.

$|x + 5| - 1 > 7$

$|x + 5| > 8$ Add 1 to each side.

$x + 5 < -8$ OR $x + 5 > 8$ Write as a compound inequality.

Solve each part of the compound inequality for x.

$x < -13$ OR $x > 3$ Subtract 5 from each side of the two inequalities.

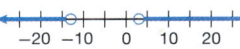

Lesson 101   **679**

Example 2

Students solve absolute-value inequalities with one operation outside and one inside the absolute-value symbols. Once the absolute value is isolated, the inequality is written as a compound inequality and the variable is isolated.

Additional Example 2

Solve and graph the inequality.

$|x + 2| - 1 > 11$
$x < -14$ OR $x > 10$;

INCLUSION

Students may need help relating what they have learned previously about absolute value inequalities to the inequalities presented in this lesson. Write the given inequalities on the chalkboard or overhead.

$|x| < 4$
$|x - 1| < 4$
$|x - 1| - 1 < 4$
$2|x - 1| < 4$

Help students solve the inequalities and graph the solutions on a number line.

Then discuss the similarities and differences between the problems and their solutions. For example, the absolute value must first be isolated and then written as a compound inequality.

Repeat the process writing the inequalities with a greater than symbol. Lastly, the two sets of inequalities can be contrasted as a reminder of those that are written as conjunctions and those that are written as disjunctions.

Lesson 101   **679**

Example 3

Students solve absolute-value inequalities with one operation outside and two inside the absolute-value symbols.

Additional Example 3

Solve and graph each inequality.

a. $\left|\frac{x}{2} + 3\right| + 4 \leq 6$ $-10 \leq x \leq -2$;

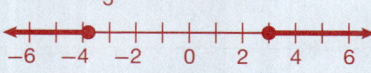

b. $|5x + 2| + 5 \geq 22$
$x \leq -\frac{19}{5}$ OR $x \geq 3$;

Error Alert Students may forget to reverse the inequality symbol when writing the compound inequality. Remind students to check their work.

TEACHER TIP

Encourage students to think of greater than and less than absolute-value statements as descriptions of magnitude (distance from zero).

Example 4

Extend the Example

"If the smallest acceptable circumference of the basketball is 29.5 inches, what is the smallest acceptable diameter to the nearest tenth?" 9.4 inches

Additional Example 4

The acceptable radius for a tire must not vary more than 1.4 centimeters from 33 centimeters. Write and solve an absolute-value inequality that models the acceptable radius of a tire. $|r - 33| \leq 1.4$; $31.6 \leq r \leq 34.4$

Math Reasoning

Verify For Example 3a, choose an x-value between −15 and 27. Show that it is a solution of the original inequality.

Sample: $x = 3$;

$\left|\frac{3}{3} - 2\right| + 12 < 19$

$|1 - 2| + 12 < 19$

$|-1| + 12 < 19$

$1 + 12 < 19$

$13 < 19$;
true

Hint

Look for a value that varies by some amount. The absolute-value expression will be $=, \geq,$ or $\leq$ the amount by which the value varies.

Example 3 Solving Inequalities with Two Operations Inside Absolute-Value Symbols

Solve and graph each inequality.

a. $\left|\frac{x}{3} - 2\right| + 12 \leq 19$

SOLUTION

$\left|\frac{x}{3} - 2\right| + 12 \leq 19$

$\left|\frac{x}{3} - 2\right| \leq 7$ Subtract 12 from each side.

$\frac{x}{3} - 2 \geq -7$ AND $\frac{x}{3} - 2 \leq 7$ Write as a compound inequality.

$\frac{x}{3} \geq -5$ AND $\frac{x}{3} \leq 9$ Add 2 to each side of the two inequalities.

$x \geq -15$ AND $x \leq 27$ Multiply each side by 3 in both inequalities.

$-15 \leq x \leq 27$

b. $|2x + 1| + 5 \geq 8$

SOLUTION

$|2x + 1| + 5 \geq 8$

$|2x + 1| \geq 3$ Subtract 5 from each side.

$2x + 1 \leq -3$ OR $2x + 1 \geq 3$ Write as a compound inequality.

$2x \leq -4$ OR $2x \geq 2$ Subtract 1 from each side of both inequalities.

$x \leq -2$ OR $x \geq 1$ Divide each side by 2 in both inequalities.

Example 4 Application: Basketball

NCAA rules require that the circumference c of a basketball used in an NCAA men's basketball game vary no more than 0.25 inch from 29.75 inches. Write and solve an absolute-value inequality that models the acceptable circumferences. What is the least acceptable circumference?

SOLUTION

The expression $|c - 29.75|$ represents the difference between the actual circumference and 29.75 inches. The absolute-value bars ensure that the difference is a positive number. The difference can be no more than 0.25 inches, so the acceptable circumference is modeled $|c - 29.75| \leq 0.25$.

$|c - 29.75| \leq 0.25$

$-0.25 \leq c - 29.75 \leq 0.25$ Write a compound inequality.

$29.5 \leq c \leq 30$ Add 29.75 to each side.

The least acceptable circumference is 29.5 inches.

ENGLISH LEARNERS

For Example 3, explain the meaning of the word **acceptable.** Say:

"**Acceptable means OK or all right. If an item is what is wanted or needed, then the item is acceptable. For example, the meal in the cafeteria was acceptable today.**"

Have volunteers share examples using the word **acceptable.** Sample: The CD was not acceptable because the plastic case was broken.

Lesson Practice

Solve and graph each inequality.

a. (Ex 1) $5|x| + 6 < 31$

b. (Ex 1) $\dfrac{|x|}{7} - 3 \geq 1$

a. $-5 < x < 5$;

b. $x \leq -28$ OR $x \geq 28$;

c. (Ex 1) $-4|x| + 9 > -1$

d. (Ex 2) $|x - 9| + 3 \leq 10$

c. $-2.5 < x < 2.5$;

d. $2 \leq x \leq 16$;

e. (Ex 3) $\left|\dfrac{x}{2} + 5\right| - 9 < -2$

f. (Ex 3) $|5x - 5| - 12 > -2$

e. $-24 < x < 4$;

f. $x < -1$ OR $x > 3$;

g. (Ex 4) **Basketball** NCAA rules require that the weight w of a basketball used in an NCAA men's basketball game vary no more than 1 ounce from 21 ounces. Write and solve an absolute-value inequality that models the acceptable weights. What is the largest acceptable weight?
$|w - 21| \leq 1$; $20 \leq w \leq 22$; 22 ounces

Practice Distributed and Integrated

*1. (101) Solve and graph the inequality $7|x| - 4 \geq 3$. $x \leq -1$ or $x \geq 1$;

*2. (101) **Error Analysis** Two students solve the inequality $|x - 4| + 2 \leq 6$. Which student is correct? Explain the error. Student A; Student B did not isolate the absolute-value expression before removing the absolute-value bars.

Student A	Student B
$\|x - 4\| + 2 \leq 6$	$\|x - 4\| + 2 \leq 6$
$\|x - 4\| \leq 4$	$-6 \leq x - 4 + 2 \leq 6$
$-4 \leq x - 4 \leq 4$	$-6 \leq x - 2 \leq 6$
$0 \leq x \leq 8$	$-4 \leq x \leq 8$

*3. (101) **Write** Describe the three steps needed to solve the inequality $\dfrac{|x|}{2} + 11 \leq 16$.

3. Sample: (1) Subtract 11 from each side. (2) Multiply each side by 2. (3) Rewrite as a compound inequality.

4. (39) Simplify $\dfrac{pt^{-2}}{m^3}\left(\dfrac{p^{-2}wt}{4m^{-1}} + 6t^4w^{-1} - \dfrac{w}{m^{-3}}\right)$. $\dfrac{w}{4ptm^2} + \dfrac{6pt^2}{wm^3} - \dfrac{pw}{t^2}$

*5. (101) **Analyze** Suppose that a, b, and c are all positive integers. Will the solution of the inequality $-a|x - b| \geq -c$ be a compound inequality that uses AND or a compound inequality that uses OR?   AND

*6. (101) **Oven Temperature** Liam's oven's temperature t varies by no more than 9°F from the set temperature. Liam sets his oven to 475°F. Write an absolute-value inequality that models the possible actual temperatures inside the oven. What is the highest possible temperature? $|t - 475| \leq 9$; $466 \leq t \leq 484$; 484°F

Problem 9
Make sure that students factor the binomials completely before they determine the LCM. Remind them to find the least expression that both binomials will divide into.

Problem 13
Error Alert
Some students may think that $2 - r$ and $r - 2$ are the same expression. Remind them that they are opposites because their sum is 0. So, -1 must be factored out of one of the expressions in order to have a common denominator and in order to add the rational expressions that represent how far Mia walked.

---

*7. **Error Analysis** Students were asked if a quadratic equation could have more than one solution. Which student is correct? Explain the error.
(100)

Student A	Student B
yes; A quadratic equation can have two solutions. When a parabola crosses the x-axis twice, there are two solutions.	no; A quadratic equation cannot cross the x-axis more than once. So, there can only be one solution.

7. Student A; Sample: A parabola can cross the x-axis once, twice, or not at all.

*8. **Multi-Step** Shaw hits a tennis ball into the air. Its movement forms a parabola given by the quadratic equation $h = -16t^2 + 2t + 9$, where h is the height in feet and t is the time in seconds.
(100)
   a. Find the maximum height of the arc the ball makes in its flight. Round to the nearest tenth. $h = 9.1$ feet
   b. Find the time t when the ball hits the ground. Round to the nearest hundredth. $t = 0.82$ seconds
   c. Find the time t when the ball is at its maximum height. Round to the nearest hundredth. $t = 0.06$ seconds

9. Find the LCM of $(6w^3 - 48w^5)$ and $(9w - 72w^3)$. $18w^3(1 - 8w^2)$
(57)

*10. **Geometry** A boy spills a cup of juice on the sidewalk. As time increases, the area of the spill changes. The area of the spill is given by the function $A = -2t^2 + 5t + 125$, where A is the area in square feet and t is the time in seconds. Find the time when the area is 60 square feet. Round to the nearest hundredth. $t = 7.09$ seconds
(100)

11. Solve $x^2 + 9 = -6x$ by graphing. $x = -3$
(100)

12. Solve the equation $|8x| + 4 = 28$. $\{-3, 3\}$
(94)

13. **(Traveling)** Mia walked $\frac{4}{r-2}$ miles to her neighbors' house on Monday and walked $\frac{r^2}{2-r}$ miles on Tuesday to go see her grandmother. How many miles total did she walk on Monday and Tuesday? $-(r + 2)$ miles
(95)

14. Subtract $\frac{5}{x-3} - \frac{2}{x-2}$. $\frac{3x-4}{(x-3)(x-2)}$
(95)

15. **(Soccer)** A soccer ball on the ground is passed with an initial velocity of 62 feet per second. What is its height after 3 seconds? Use $h = -16t^2 + vt + s$. 42 feet
(96)

16. **Measurement** A girl is 24 years younger than her mother. The product of their ages is 81. Find the mother's age by finding the positive zero of the function $y = x^2 - 24x - 81$. 27 years
(96)

17. Determine if the ordered pair $(-7, 2)$ is a solution of the inequality $y \leq 3$. Yes, it satisfies the inequality.
(97)

18. **Verify** Show that $\frac{3}{4}$ is a solution to $(4x - 3)(5x + 7) = 0$. Sample: $\left(4 \cdot \frac{3}{4} - 3\right)\left(5 \cdot \frac{3}{4} + 7\right) = 0\left(\frac{43}{4}\right) = 0$
(98)

19. **Multiple Choice** What are the roots of the equation $0 = x^2 - 10x - 39$? **D**
(98)
   A 0, 39   **B** 10, 0   **C** 3, -13   **D** 13, -3

CHALLENGE

Have students write an inequality that satisfies $x < 0$ OR $x > 0$ and that does not use absolute value. Sample: $x^2 > 0$

*20. Solve and check: $\frac{x}{11} = \frac{6}{x-5}$. $x = -6, 11$
(99)

21. Does the graph of $-8x^2 - 12 = 3 - y$ open upward or downward?   upward
(84)

22. **Office Management** Maria can complete all the copies in 1 hour. It takes Lachelle
(99) 2 hours. How long will it take them if they use two identical copiers and work
together? $\frac{2}{3}$ hours

23. **Error Analysis** Two students solve $\frac{x-8}{x+2} = \frac{x-6}{3x+6}$. Which student is correct? Explain
(99) the error.   Student A; Sample: Student B did not check to see that −2 is an extraneous solution.

Student A	Student B
$(x-8)(3x+6) = (x+2)(x-6)$	$(x-8)(3x+6) = (x+2)(x-6)$
$3x^2 - 18x - 48 = x^2 - 4x - 12$	$3x^2 - 18x - 48 = x^2 - 4x - 12$
$2x^2 - 14x - 36 = 0$	$2x^2 - 14x - 36 = 0$
$2(x-9)(x+2) = 0$	$2(x-9)(x+2) = 0$
$\{9\}$	$\{-2, 9\}$

24. Do the side lengths 3, $3\sqrt{3}$, and 6 form a Pythagorean triple?   no
(85)

25. Let $P = (-2, 1)$, $Q = (0, 2)$, $R = (1, -2)$, and $S = (-1, -3)$. Use the distance
(86) formula to determine whether $PQRS$ is a rhombus.   no

26. **Multi-Step** Find the product of $\frac{5x^2y^2}{3x^3y^3} \cdot \frac{9xy^2}{25xy^3}$ using two different methods.
(88)
a. Solve the expression by multiplying first and then simplifying.
b. Solve the expression by simplifying each factor and then multiplying.
c. Explain which method you prefer. $\frac{3}{5xy^2}$; Sample: simplifying before multiplying, because I can cancel out like terms before needing to multiply anything

27. **Road Trip** Carlos tracks the mileage for a road trip on his car's odometer. The
(91) total distance is 974.6 miles plus or minus 0.1 miles. Solve and graph the
inequality $|x - 974.6| \leq 0.1$. $974.5 \leq x \leq 974.7$;

28. **Multi-Step** Amy skipped for $\frac{3x-6}{9x}$ hours to get to her grandmother's house that
(92) was $\frac{2x^2-4x}{7x^3}$ miles away.
a. Find her rate in miles per hour.   miles per hour
b. If the rate is divided by $\frac{1}{x^2}$, what is the new rate? $\frac{6x}{7}$ miles per hour

29. How do you write a remainder of 5 for a division problem that has a divisor of
(93) $(3x^2 + 7x + 8)$? $\frac{5}{3x^2 + 7x + 8}$

*30. What is the parent quadratic function defined to be? What is the shape of its
(Inv 10) graph and where is it located on the coordinate system? $f(x) = x^2$; Its graph is a parabola opening upward with its vertex at the origin, (0, 0).

Lesson 101   683

LOOKING FORWARD

Solving multi-step absolute-value inequalities prepares students for

- **Lesson 107** Graphing Absolute-Value Functions

LESSON 102

Solving Quadratic Equations Using Square Roots

1 Warm Up

Problem 3
Remind students to be mindful of the negative sign.

2 New Concepts

In this lesson, students will solve quadratic equations by isolating the squared term and then taking the square root of each side of the equation. As with solving by factoring or graphing, there can be one, two, or no solutions. If $a > 0$, then there are two solutions. If $a = 0$, then there is one solution. If $a < 0$, then there is no solution. The solutions can be rational or irrational, depending on the value of the non-variable side of the equation after the squared term is isolated.

Example 1
Remind students that when quadratic terms equal non-negative numbers there is a positive and negative solution.

Additional Example 1
Solve.
a. $x^2 = 121$ $x = \pm 11$
b. $x^2 = -400$ no solution

LESSON RESOURCES

Student Edition Practice
  Workbook 102
Reteaching Master 102
Adaptations Master 102
Challenge and Enrichment
  Master C102

Warm Up

1. **Vocabulary** The _____ of x is the number whose square is x. square root

Simplify.

2. $\sqrt{81}$ 9
3. $-\sqrt{25}$ -5
4. $\sqrt{24}$ $2\sqrt{6}$
5. $\sqrt{\dfrac{9}{49}}$ $\dfrac{3}{7}$

New Concepts

Sometimes quadratic equations do not have linear terms. Quadratic equations in the form $x^2 = a$, can be solved by taking the square root of both sides.

Example 1 Solving $x^2 = a$

Solve each equation.

a. $x^2 = 25$

SOLUTION

Find the square root of both terms.

$x^2 = 25$
$\sqrt{x^2} = \pm\sqrt{25}$ Take the square root of both sides.
$x = 5$ or $x = -5$

You can combine the solutions using the $\pm$ symbol.

$x = \pm 5$

Check
$x^2 = 25$ $x^2 = 25$
$5^2 \stackrel{?}{=} 25$ $(-5)^2 \stackrel{?}{=} 25$
$25 = 25$ ✓ $25 = 25$ ✓

b. $x^2 = -16$

SOLUTION

Find the square root of both terms.

$x^2 = -16$
$\sqrt{x^2} = \pm\sqrt{-16}$ Take the square root of both sides.
$x \neq \pm\sqrt{-16}$ No real number squared can be negative.

There is no real-number solution.

Math Reasoning

Verify Show by factoring that the equation $x^2 = 25$ has the solution ± 5.

Sample: $x^2 = 25$
$x^2 - 25 = 0$
$(x + 5)(x - 5) = 0$
$x + 5 = 0$ $x - 5 = 0$
$x = -5$ $x = 5$

Math Reasoning

Analyze What is the relationship between squaring a number and taking the square root of a number?

Sample: Squaring and taking the root are inverse operations.

Online Connection
www.SaxonMathResources.com

When the quadratic equation is in the form $ax^2 + c = 0$, the square root can be taken after the variable is isolated.

MATH BACKGROUND

Students have solved quadratic equations by factoring and graphing, but these methods have limitations. If quadratic equations cannot be factored, or when a graphing calculator can only provide irrational solutions as approximations, then solving quadratic equations by using the definition of square roots may be a better method.

For any non-negative real number b, if $a^2 = b$, then $a = \pm\sqrt{b}$. So, if $x^2 = 10$, then $x = \pm\sqrt{10}$. These are real solutions, not approximations.

Note, however, that solving by using square roots also has limitations. It only works when the equation can be arranged so that one side of the equation is a quadratic term and the other side is a constant. The equation cannot contain any linear terms.

Example 2 Solving $ax^2 + c = 0$

Solve each equation.

a. $x^2 + 3 = 52$

SOLUTION

Isolate the variable and solve.

$x^2 + 3 = 52$
$\underline{-3 \quad -3}$ Subtraction Property of Equality
$x^2 = 49$ Simplify.
$\sqrt{x^2} = \pm\sqrt{49}$ Take the square root of both sides.
$x = \pm 7$ Simplify.

Check
$x^2 + 3 = 52$ $x^2 + 3 = 52$
$7^2 + 3 \stackrel{?}{=} 52$ $(-7)^2 + 3 \stackrel{?}{=} 52$
$49 + 3 = 52$ ✓ $49 + 3 = 52$ ✓

b. $4x^2 - 100 = 0$

SOLUTION

Isolate the variable and solve.

$4x^2 - 100 = 0$
$\underline{+100 = +100}$ Addition Property of Equality
$4x^2 = 100$ Simplify.
$\dfrac{4x^2}{4} = \dfrac{100}{4}$ Division Property of Equality
$x^2 = 25$ Simplify.
$\sqrt{x^2} = \pm\sqrt{25}$ Take the square root of both sides.
$x = \pm 5$ Simplify.

Check

$4x^2 - 100 = 0$ $4x^2 - 100 = 0$
$4(5)^2 - 100 \stackrel{?}{=} 0$ $4(-5)^2 - 100 \stackrel{?}{=} 0$
$4(25) - 100 \stackrel{?}{=} 0$ $4(25) - 100 \stackrel{?}{=} 0$
$100 - 100 \stackrel{?}{=} 0$ $100 - 100 \stackrel{?}{=} 0$
$0 = 0$ ✓ $0 = 0$ ✓

Numbers that are not perfect squares have irrational roots. Irrational solutions can be expressed in square root form: $\pm\sqrt{x}$. An approximate answer can be found using a calculator. To approximate $\sqrt{10}$ on a graphing calculator, press [2nd] [x^2], and then press [1] [0] [)] [ENTER].

√(10)
       3.16227766

> **Caution**
> When x^2 equals a number other than 0, the equation has two solutions. Use the $\pm$ symbol after taking the square root.

> **Math Reasoning**
> **Estimate** How can $\sqrt{10}$ be estimated?
> Sample: 10 is between the perfect squares 9 and 16. Since it is closer to 9 and $\sqrt{9} = 3$, then $\sqrt{10}$ is about 3.1 or 3.2.

> **Example 2**
> In order to take the square root of each side, one side must contain the squared term only. Use inverse operations to isolate x^2.
>
> **Error Alert** Students may rush to answer "no solution" when they see one side of the equation equal to a negative number. Stress the importance of working through inverse operations. Show that though $-x^2 = -16$ may first appear to have no solutions, when the student has divided both sides by -1, it will become clear that the solutions are -4 and 4.
>
> **Additional Example 2**
> Solve.
> **a.** $49 = x^2 - 15$ $x = \pm 8$
> **b.** $2x^2 + 5 = 77$ $x = \pm 6$

Lesson 102   685

⚠ INCLUSION

The following is useful for auditory and verbal learners.

To help students make the connection that squaring and taking the square root are inverse operations, ask the following questions in this order:

"What is 4 plus 3?" 7
"What is 7 minus 3?" 4
"What is 4 times 2?" 8
"What is 8 divided by 2?" 4
"What is 4 squared?" 16
"What is the positive square root of 16?" 4

Explain to students that they must use both square roots, positive and negative, when solving a quadratic equation, because both make the equation true.

Example 3

The square root of a number that is not a perfect square will be an irrational number; that is, a nonrepeating and nonterminating decimal number.

Additional Example 3

Solve.

a. $62 = x^2$ $x \approx \pm 7.874$

b. $4x^2 + 9 = 82$ $x \approx \pm 4.272$

TEACHER TIP

Point out that in Example 3a, $\pm 2\sqrt{10}$ are the exact solutions and ± 6.324 are the approximate solutions. Students should not consider $\sqrt{40}$ as the final solution because it is not in simplified form.

If no rounding instructions are given, round the approximation to the thousandths place.

Example 3 Approximating Solutions

Solve each equation.

a. $x^2 = 40$

SOLUTION

$x^2 = 40$

$\sqrt{x^2} = \pm\sqrt{40}$ Take the square root of both sides.

Simplify the square root.

$\sqrt{x^2} = \pm\sqrt{4 \cdot 10}$ Find a factor that is a perfect square.

$\sqrt{x^2} = \pm\sqrt{4} \cdot \sqrt{10}$ Product Property of Radicals

$x = \pm 2\sqrt{10}$ Simplify.

Use a calculator to find the approximate value of $\sqrt{10}$.

$x \approx 2 \cdot (3.16227766)$ Write the approximate value.

$x \approx \pm 6.32455532$ Multiply.

$x \approx \pm 6.325$ Round to the nearest thousandth.

Caution Round after all computations have been made.

Check $x^2 = 40$ $x^2 = 40$

$(6.325)^2 \stackrel{?}{\approx} 40$ $(-6.325)^2 \stackrel{?}{\approx} 40$

$40.006 \approx 40$ ✓ $40.006 \approx 40$ ✓

b. $8x^2 - 24 = 100$

SOLUTION

Begin by isolating x^2.

$8x^2 - 24 = 100$

$+24 +24$ Addition Property of Equality

$8x^2 = 124$ Combine like terms.

$\dfrac{8x^2}{8} = \dfrac{124}{8}$ Division Property of Equality

$x^2 = 15.5$ Simplify.

$\sqrt{x^2} = \pm\sqrt{15.5}$ Take the square root of both sides.

$x \approx \pm 3.937003937$ Find the approximate square root.

$x \approx \pm 3.937$ Round to the nearest thousandth.

Caution Remember to check both solutions.

Check $8x^2 - 24 = 100$ $8x^2 - 24 = 100$

$8(3.937)^2 - 24 \stackrel{?}{\approx} 100$ $8(-3.937)^2 - 24 \stackrel{?}{\approx} 100$

$8(15.499969) - 24 \stackrel{?}{\approx} 100$ $8(15.499969) - 24 \stackrel{?}{\approx} 100$

$123.999752 - 24 \stackrel{?}{\approx} 100$ $123.999752 - 24 \stackrel{?}{\approx} 100$

$99.999752 \approx 100$ ✓ $99.999752 \approx 100$ ✓

686 *Saxon Algebra 1*

ALTERNATE METHOD FOR EXAMPLE 3a

The approximation for $\sqrt{40}$ can be found without using a calculator.

$$x = \pm\sqrt{4 \cdot 10}$$

$$x = \pm 2 \cdot \sqrt{10}$$

The number 10 falls between the perfect squares 9 and 16. The square roots of each are 3 and 4, so students can reasonably estimate that the square root of 10 is between 3.1 and 3.2.

Example 4 Application: Crafts

Malik covered a cube with exactly 864 square inches of self-stick vinyl. What is the side length of the cube?

SOLUTION

Use the formula to find the surface area of a cube: $S = 6s^2$.

$S = 6s^2$

$864 = 6s^2$ Substitute 864 for S.

$\frac{864}{6} = \frac{6s^2}{6}$ Division Property of Equality

$144 = s^2$ Simplify.

$\pm\sqrt{144} = \sqrt{s^2}$ Take the square root of both sides.

$\pm 12 = s$ Simplify.

The longest possible side length of the cube is 12 inches.

Check $S = 6s^2$

$864 \stackrel{?}{=} 6(12)^2$

$864 \stackrel{?}{=} 6(144)$

$864 = 864$ ✓

Math Reasoning

Analyze Why is −12 square inch not a possible answer?

Sample: A linear measurement cannot be negative.

Lesson Practice

Solve each equation.

a. $x^2 = 81$ $x = \pm 9$ *(Ex 1)*

b. $x^2 = -36$ no real solution *(Ex 1)*

c. $x^2 + 5 = 54$ $x = \pm 7$ *(Ex 2)*

d. $3x^2 - 75 = 0$ $x = \pm 5$ *(Ex 2)*

e. $x^2 = 72$ $x = \pm 8.485$ *(Ex 3)*

f. $5x^2 - 60 = 0$ $x = \pm 3.464$ *(Ex 3)*

g. A golf ball is dropped from a height of 1600 feet. Use the equation $16t^2 - 1600 = 0$ to find how many seconds t it takes for the ball to hit the ground. 10 seconds *(Ex 4)*

Practice Distributed and Integrated

Simplify.

1. $4(2p^{-2}q)^2(3p^3q)^2$ $144p^2q^4$ *(40)*

2. $(7\sqrt{8})^2$ 392 *(76)*

ENGLISH LEARNERS

In Problem 13, explain the meaning of the word **vinyl**. Say:

"Vinyl is a type of plastic material that has many uses. It can be used to cover and protect the floor."

Ask students to describe other uses of vinyl. Sample: Toys and furniture are made of vinyl.

Example 4

Explain that the surface area of a cube equals $6s^2$ because there are six sides, each with an area of s^2 units. Remind students that since distances are always positive, they can disregard the negative solution.

Extend the Example

"Suppose that Malik does not want to cover the bottom of the cube because it will not be seen. Write and solve a quadratic equation to find the side length of the largest cube he can now cover." $864 = 5s^2$; $s \approx 13.145$ inches

Additional Example 4

Sue covers a cube with exactly 1536 square inches of self-stick vinyl. What is the side length of the largest cube that Sue can cover completely? 16 inches

Lesson Practice

Problem d

Scaffolding Ask students how they can isolate $3x^2$, then how they can isolate x^2, and finally, how they can isolate x.

Problem e

Error Alert Students might divide by 2 and answer $x = \pm 36$. A quick check of their answer will show that this is not correct.

Check for Understanding

The questions below help assess the concepts taught in this lesson.

"What type of quadratic equation can be solved by using square roots?" Sample: a quadratic that has no linear term

"What must be true about a if $x^2 = a$ does not have two solutions?" Sample: a is either 0 or negative.

Lesson 102 687

*3. Error Analysis Two students want to find the length of the sides of a square with an area that is 720 square meters less than 1161 square meters. Which student is correct? Explain the error.

Student A	Student B
$x^2 + 720 = 1161$	$x^2 + 720 = 1161$
$-720 -720$	$-720 -720$
$x^2 = 441$	$x^2 = 441$
$\sqrt{x^2} = \pm\sqrt{441}$	$\sqrt{x^2} = \pm\sqrt{441}$
$x = \pm 21$	$x = \pm 21$
The sides of the square are ± 21 m.	The sides of the square are 21 m.

3. Student B; Sample: Both have worked the problem correctly, but Student A did not realize that a negative measurement is impossible in this situation.

*4. Multi-Step Dominic wants to fence the perimeter of his property. The property is in the shape of a square. The area of the yard is 12,600 ft², and the area of the house is 1800 ft².
 a. Write an equation to find the length of the sides of the property. $x^2 = 12{,}600 + 1800$
 b. Solve the equation. $x = 120$ ft
 c. How many feet of fencing will Dominic need? 480 ft

*5. (Banking) Serena places $1000 in an interest-earning account where the interest compounds annually. After two years, there is $1123.60 in the account. Use the formula $\$1000(1 + r)^2 = \$1123.60$ to find the interest rate of the account. 6%

*6. Verify True or False: If $8x^2 - 72 = 0$, then $x = \pm 3$. If the answer is false, provide the correct answer. true

*7. Estimate Find the length of the side of a square with an area of 680 square kilometers. Round to the nearest thousandth. 26.077 km

8. Solve and graph the inequality $\frac{|x|}{3} + 6 < 13$. $-21 < x < 21$;

*9. Coordinate Geometry One side of a rectangle drawn in the coordinate plane has points whose y-coordinates are 7 and whose x-coordinates are the solutions of the inequality $|x + 1| - 8 \leq -4$. Another side has points whose x-coordinates are -5 and whose y-coordinates are solutions of the inequality $|y - 4| + 6 \leq 9$.
 a. Solve the inequality $|x + 1| - 8 \leq -4$. $-5 \leq x \leq 3$
 b. Solve the inequality $|y - 4| + 6 \leq 9$. $1 \leq y \leq 7$
 c. What are the coordinates of the four vertices of the rectangle? $(-5, 7), (3, 7), (3, 1), (-5, 1)$

10. Find the product of $(x - 7)(-7x^2 - x + 7)$ using the vertical method.
 $-7x^3 + 48x^2 + 14x - 49$

11. Graph the function $y = 4x^2 + 6$.

12. (Water Balloons) A water balloon is dropped from a third-story window. Its height in feet is represented by $h = -16t^2 + 30$. How high is the balloon after 1 second?
 14 feet

11.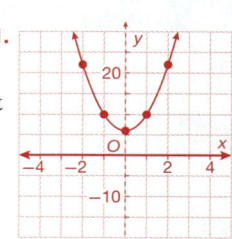

688 Saxon Algebra 1

*13. **Multi-Step** When the temperature t of the gas argon is within 1.65 degrees of
(101) $-187.65°C$, it will be in a liquid form. This can be modeled by the absolute-value
inequality $|t-(-187.65)| < 1.65$.

a. Solve and graph the inequality $|t-(-187.65)| < 1.65$. $-189.3 < t < -186$

13a.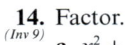

b. One endpoint of the graph represents the boiling point of argon—the
temperature at which argon changes from liquid to gas. The other endpoint
represents the melting point—the temperature at which argon turns from
solid to liquid. The higher temperature is the boiling point, and the lower
temperature is the melting point. What is the boiling point of argon? What is
the melting point? $-186°C; -189.3°C$

14. Factor.
(Inv 9)
a. $x^2 + 10x + 25$ $(x+5)^2$

b. $x^2 - 25$ $(x+5)(x-5)$

 15. **Measurement** The sides of a triangle are labeled $5x$ inches, $4y$ inches, and
(97) 20 inches. Jonas wrote an inequality that satisfies the Triangle Inequality
Theorem: $5x + 4y > 20$. Graph the inequality.

15.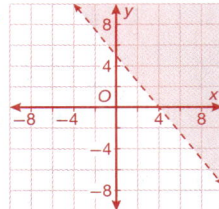

16. (**Art Supplies**) Tim plans to go shopping for new paper and paint for his students,
(97) and he does not want to spend more than $40. Each pack of paper costs $2, and
each set of paints costs $10. Write an inequality that describes this situation,
and graph it on a graphing calculator. $2x + 10y \le 40$

16.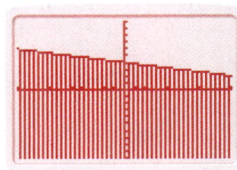

17. Solve $x(x + 12) = 0$. $\{0, -12\}$
(98)

18. **Verify** Show that $x = 1$ is an extraneous solution to $\frac{1}{x-1} = \frac{3}{2x-2}$.
(99)

19. **Multiple Choice** Solve $\frac{2}{x-3} = \frac{x}{9}$.   B
(99)

A $\{3, 6\}$ B $\{-3, 6\}$

C $\{3, -6\}$ D $\{6\}$

20. Add $\frac{m}{m^2-4} + \frac{2}{3m+6}$. $\frac{5m-4}{3(m+2)(m-2)}$
(95)

18. Sample: $\frac{1}{1-1} = \frac{3}{2(1)-2}; \frac{1}{0} = \frac{3}{0}$, which is undefined. This shows that 1 is an extraneous solution.

*21. **Error Analysis** Students were asked to write a quadratic equation that had no
(100) solution. Which student is correct? Explain the error.

Student A	Student B
$f(x) = x^2 - 3x + 12$	$f(x) = x^2 + 11x + 11$

 *22. (**Rocket**) Malachi shot a rocket for his science project. The path of the rocket's
(100) movement formed a parabola given by the quadratic equation $h = -16t^2 + 4t + 10$,
where h is the height in feet and t is the time in seconds. Find the maximum height
of the path the rocket makes and the time t when the rocket hits the ground. Round
to the nearest hundredth. $h = 10.25$ feet and $t = 0.93$ seconds

21. Student A; Sample: Student B wrote an equation that forms a parabola that
crosses the x-axis twice, so it has two solutions.

Lesson 102   689

Problem 15
Error Alert
Students may forget to use a dashed line instead of a solid line. Remind them to double-check the inequality symbol to see if the boundary line contains solutions.

Problem 16
Say, "If I do not want to spend more than $40, then I want to spend less than $40, but I'm also willing to spend exactly $40."

Problem 17
Error Alert
Students often forget to set a single x-factor equal to 0 because the equation formed by using the Zero Product Property does not require further steps. They should always write down $x = 0$, even if they think they will remember to include it at the end.

Problem 21
Extend the Problem
"Using the discriminant, how can you tell that the solutions of Student B's function will have a solution?" Sample: Because $b^2 - 4ac \ge 0$.

Problem 26
Extend the Problem
"Write an algebraic expression for the perimeter of the yard in terms of its width. What is the perimeter?" $4x + 14$; 50 feet

Problem 30
To help students form their answer, have them write and solve a simple equation of each type, such as $|x| + 2 = 6$ and $|x + 2| = 6$.

---

*23. Solve $x^2 + 12x + 40 = 0$ by graphing.   no solution
(100)

24. Find the midpoint of the line segment with the endpoints $(13, -3)$ and $(-7, -3)$.
(86) $(3, -3)$

25. Factor $-3y^3 - 9yz + 5y^2 + 15z$. $(-3y + 5)(y^2 + 3z)$
(87)

26. **Multi-Step** Mr. Tranh's lawn has an area of 144 square feet. The length of his yard
(89) is 7 feet more than the width. What are the dimensions of his yard?
   a. Write a formula to find the dimensions of the yard and describe how you will solve it.
   b. What are the dimensions of the yard?   16 feet long and 9 feet wide.

26. $x(x + 7) = 144$; Sample: the formula needs to be set in the form $ax^2 + bx + c = 0$ in order to solve for x

27. Do the side lengths 3, 7, and 8 form a Pythagorean triple?   no
(85)

28. **Running** It took Wayne $\frac{x}{2x^2 + x - 15}$ minutes to run to the gym that was
(92) $\frac{9x}{4x - 10} + \frac{5x^2}{3x + 9}$ miles away. Find his rate in miles per minute. $\frac{20x^2 - 23x + 81}{6}$ miles per minute

29. **Multi-Step** Raj is measuring the area of his rectangular living room. He determined
(93) that the area is $-64x + x^3 - 2x^2 + 128$ square feet. The width is $\frac{(x^2 - 64)}{(x + 8)}$ feet.
   a. Simplify the expression for the width of the living room. $(x - 8)$ feet
   b. Find the expression for the length. $x^2 + 6x - 16$ feet

30. **Generalize** What is the difference between solving an absolute-value equation with
(94) operations on the outside and solving absolute-value equations with operations on the inside?   Sample: When the operations are on the inside, write two equations to represent the absolute-value equation and solve them. When the operations are on the outside, isolate the absolute value first, then write two equations to represent the absolute-value equation and solve them.

 **CHALLENGE**

The area of a square is 225 square inches. Write an equation that can be used to find the dimensions of the square. Find the dimensions. $x^2 = 225$; 15 inches by 15 inches

 LOOKING FORWARD

Solving quadratic equations using square roots prepares students for

• **Lesson 104** Solving Quadratic Equations by Completing the Square

• **Lesson 110** Using the Quadratic Formula

LESSON 103

Dividing Radical Expressions

Warm Up

1. **Vocabulary** The number or expression under a radical symbol is called the _____. **radicand**

Simplify. All variables represent non-negative numbers.

2. $\sqrt{150}$ **$5\sqrt{6}$**
3. $3\sqrt{72}$ **$18\sqrt{2}$**
4. $\sqrt{48x^3}$ **$4x\sqrt{3x}$**
5. $\sqrt{12} \cdot \sqrt{15}$ **$6\sqrt{5}$**

New Concepts

When dividing radical expressions, use the Quotient Property of Radicals.

$$\sqrt[n]{\frac{a}{b}} = \frac{\sqrt[n]{a}}{\sqrt[n]{b}}, \text{ where } b \neq 0.$$

A radical expression in simplest form cannot have a fraction for a radicand or a radical in the denominator. To **rationalize** a denominator means to use a method which removes radicals from the denominator of a fraction. Using this method, a fraction is multiplied by another fraction that is equivalent to 1 in order to remove the radical from the denominator.

Math Language

In the expression $\sqrt[n]{\frac{a}{b}}$, $\frac{a}{b}$ is the **radicand** and n is the **index** number.

Math Reasoning

Verify Multiply $\frac{\sqrt{21}}{3}$ by $\frac{\sqrt{3}}{\sqrt{3}}$ to show that the product equals the original expression $\sqrt{\frac{7}{3}}$.

Sample: $\frac{\sqrt{21}}{3} \cdot \frac{\sqrt{3}}{\sqrt{3}}$

$= \frac{\sqrt{21 \cdot 3}}{3 \cdot \sqrt{3}} = \frac{\sqrt{63}}{3\sqrt{3}}$

$= \frac{\sqrt{9} \cdot \sqrt{7}}{3\sqrt{3}} = \frac{3\sqrt{7}}{3\sqrt{3}}$

$= \frac{\sqrt{7}}{\sqrt{3}} = \sqrt{\frac{7}{3}}$

Example 1 **Rationalizing the Denominator**

Simplify.

$\sqrt{\frac{7}{3}}$

SOLUTION

Use the quotient property. Then rationalize the denominator.

$\sqrt{\frac{7}{3}}$

$= \frac{\sqrt{7}}{\sqrt{3}}$ Quotient Property of Radicals

$= \frac{\sqrt{7}}{\sqrt{3}} \cdot \frac{\sqrt{3}}{\sqrt{3}}$ Multiply the expression by a factor of 1 that will make the radicand in the denominator a perfect square.

$= \frac{\sqrt{7 \cdot 3}}{\sqrt{3 \cdot 3}}$ Multiplication Property of Radicals

$= \frac{\sqrt{21}}{\sqrt{9}}$ Multiply.

$= \frac{\sqrt{21}}{3}$ Simplify the square root.

Lesson 103 691

---

1 Warm Up

Problem 3
Writing the radicand as a product of 36 times 2 is the quickest way to simplify the expression.

2 New Concepts

Radical expressions are in simplest form if there are no perfect square factors in a radicand, no fractions in a radicand, and no radicals in a denominator.

Example 1

The goal in rationalizing a denominator is to make the radicand in the denominator a perfect square. The student can achieve this by multiplying the numerator and denominator by the radical in the denominator.

Additional Example 1
Simplify $\sqrt{\frac{15}{2}} \cdot \frac{\sqrt{30}}{2}$

LESSON RESOURCES

Student Edition Practice Workbook 103
Reteaching Master 103
Adaptations Master 103
Challenge and Enrichment Master C103

MATH BACKGROUND

When a radical expression is not in simplest form because radicands contain perfect squares and there is a radical in the denominator, it is best to factor out the perfect squares before rationalizing the denominator.

To simplify an expression of the form $\frac{a}{\sqrt{b}}$, most students will multiply the numerator and denominator by $\sqrt{b}$ without much hesitation.

For example, $\frac{1}{\sqrt{8}}$ can be simplified by multiplying by $\frac{\sqrt{8}}{\sqrt{8}}$. However, multiplying by $\frac{\sqrt{2}}{\sqrt{2}}$ will also make the radicand in the denominator a perfect square.

$$\frac{1}{\sqrt{8}} \cdot \frac{\sqrt{2}}{\sqrt{2}} = \frac{\sqrt{2}}{\sqrt{16}} = \frac{\sqrt{2}}{4}$$

In this instance, using this method saves an extra step of simplifying in the numerator.

Example 2

In this example students rationalize a radical in a denominator with a variable as a radicand.

Additional Example 2

Simplify $\sqrt{\frac{7}{y}}$. All variables represent non-negative numbers. $\frac{\sqrt{7y}}{y}$

Example 3

Students learn to simplify radicals in the denominator before rationalizing the denominator.

Extend the Example

"Show that the simplified expression has the same value as the original expression by substituting 2 for x in each expression and finding the value. Round the value to the thousandths place." ≈ 0.894

Additional Example 3

Simplify $\frac{2\sqrt{50y^6}}{\sqrt{28y^5}}$. All variables represent non-negative numbers. $\frac{5\sqrt{14y}}{7}$

Error Alert Students may not extend a radical symbol far enough to completely cover the radicand. It may be helpful to have students draw the radical symbol so that the top right side drops down a bit, "enclosing" the radicand.

Example 2 Rationalizing a Variable Denominator

Simplify $\sqrt{\frac{5}{x}}$. All variables represent non-negative numbers.

SOLUTION

Use the quotient property. Then rationalize the denominator.

$\sqrt{\frac{5}{x}} = \frac{\sqrt{5}}{\sqrt{x}}$ Quotient Property of Radicals

$= \frac{\sqrt{5}}{\sqrt{x}} \cdot \frac{\sqrt{x}}{\sqrt{x}}$ Multiply the expression by a factor of 1 that will make the radicand in the denominator a perfect square.

$= \frac{\sqrt{5 \cdot x}}{\sqrt{x \cdot x}}$ Multiplication Property of Radicals

$= \frac{\sqrt{5x}}{\sqrt{x^2}}$ Multiply.

$= \frac{\sqrt{5x}}{x}$ Simplify the square root.

A radical expression is completely simplified when the radicand contains no perfect square factors other than 1, and there are no fractions in the radicand.

Example 3 Simplifying Before Rationalizing the Denominator

Simplify $\frac{\sqrt{72x^4}}{3\sqrt{20x^3}}$. All variables represent non-negative numbers.

SOLUTION

Simplify the numerator and denominator.

$\frac{\sqrt{72x^4}}{3\sqrt{20x^3}} = \frac{\sqrt{36 \cdot 2 \cdot x^2 \cdot x^2}}{3\sqrt{4 \cdot 5 \cdot x^2 \cdot x}}$ Factor out perfect squares, if possible.

$= \frac{6x^2\sqrt{2}}{2 \cdot 3 \cdot x\sqrt{5x}}$ Simplify the radical expressions.

$= \frac{6x^2\sqrt{2}}{6x\sqrt{5x}}$ Simplify the denominator.

$= \frac{x\sqrt{2}}{\sqrt{5x}}$ Divide out common factors in the numerator and denominator.

$= \frac{x\sqrt{2}}{\sqrt{5x}} \cdot \frac{\sqrt{5x}}{\sqrt{5x}}$ Rationalize the denominator.

$= \frac{x\sqrt{10x}}{5x}$ Simplify.

$= \frac{\sqrt{10x}}{5}$ Divide out common factors in the numerator and denominator.

Online Connection
www.SaxonMathResources.com

692   *Saxon* Algebra 1

The **conjugate of an irrational number** in the form $a + \sqrt{b}$ is $a - \sqrt{b}$. The conjugate is used to rationalize the denominator of a fraction when the denominator is a binomial with at least one term containing a radical.

Example 4 Using Conjugates to Rationalize the Denominator

Simplify.

a. $\dfrac{3}{4 + \sqrt{5}}$

SOLUTION

Find the conjugate of the denominator. Use the conjugate to write a factor equivalent to 1. Multiply the fraction by the factor.

$\dfrac{3}{4 + \sqrt{5}}$

$\dfrac{3}{4 + \sqrt{5}} \cdot \dfrac{(4 - \sqrt{5})}{(4 - \sqrt{5})}$ The conjugate of $4 + \sqrt{5}$ is $4 - \sqrt{5}$.

$= \dfrac{12 - 3\sqrt{5}}{16 - 4\sqrt{5} + 4\sqrt{5} - 5}$ Use the Distributive Property and the FOIL method to multiply numerators and denominators.

$= \dfrac{12 - 3\sqrt{5}}{11}$ Combine like terms and simplify.

$= \dfrac{12}{11} - \dfrac{3\sqrt{5}}{11}$ Write the solution as two fractions with the same denominator.

b. $\dfrac{2}{\sqrt{3} + 1}$

SOLUTION

$\dfrac{2}{\sqrt{3} + 1}$

$\dfrac{2}{\sqrt{3} + 1} \cdot \dfrac{(\sqrt{3} - 1)}{(\sqrt{3} - 1)}$ The conjugate of $\sqrt{3} + 1$ is $\sqrt{3} - 1$.

$= \dfrac{2\sqrt{3} - 2}{3 - \sqrt{3} + \sqrt{3} - 1}$ Use the Distributive Property and the FOIL method to multiply numerators and denominators.

$= \dfrac{2\sqrt{3} - 2}{2}$ Combine like terms and simplify.

$= \dfrac{\cancel{2}(\sqrt{3} - 1)}{\cancel{2}}$ Factor the numerator. Divide.

$= \sqrt{3} - 1$ Simplify.

Math Reasoning

Analyze Why must conjugates be used when rationalizing denominators with radicals containing binomials?

Sample: The denominator is rationalized to remove any radicals from the denominator. The product of conjugates does not contain any radicals.

Lesson 103   693

Lesson Practice

Simplify. All variables represent non-negative numbers.

a. (Ex 1) $\sqrt{\dfrac{5}{3}}$ $\dfrac{\sqrt{15}}{3}$

b. (Ex 2) $\sqrt{\dfrac{11}{x}}$ $\dfrac{\sqrt{11x}}{x}$

c. (Ex 3) $\dfrac{\sqrt{6x^6}}{\sqrt{27x}}$ $\dfrac{x^2\sqrt{2x}}{3}$

d. (Ex 4) $\dfrac{3}{5-\sqrt{6}}$ $\dfrac{15+3\sqrt{6}}{19}$ or $\dfrac{15}{19}+\dfrac{3\sqrt{6}}{19}$

e. (Ex 4) $\dfrac{3}{\sqrt{7}-1}$ $\dfrac{\sqrt{7}+1}{2}$ or $\dfrac{\sqrt{7}}{2}+\dfrac{1}{2}$

Practice Distributed and Integrated

*1. (103) Simplify $\dfrac{35}{\sqrt{7}}$. $5\sqrt{7}$

2. (99) Solve $\dfrac{8}{x-1}=\dfrac{x}{7}$. $x=-7, 8$

*3. (103) **Error Analysis** Two students simplified the following expression. Which student is correct? Explain the error.   Student A; Sample: Student B did not use a conjugate to rationalize the denominator.

Student A	Student B
$\dfrac{1}{3+\sqrt{2}}$	$\dfrac{1}{3+\sqrt{2}}$
$\dfrac{1}{3+\sqrt{2}}\cdot\dfrac{3-\sqrt{2}}{3-\sqrt{2}}$	$\dfrac{1}{3+\sqrt{2}}\cdot\dfrac{\sqrt{2}}{\sqrt{2}}$
$\dfrac{3-\sqrt{2}}{7}$	$\dfrac{\sqrt{2}}{3\sqrt{2}+2}$

*4. (103) **Skydiving** A 150-pound skydiver reaches terminal velocity after free-falling for a number of seconds. The formula for the terminal velocity V of a skydiver (in feet per second) can be estimated by the formula $V=\sqrt{\dfrac{2W}{0.0063}}$, where W equals the weight of the skydiver in pounds. Write a rational expression for the terminal velocity of the skydiver. $\dfrac{1000\sqrt{21}}{21}$ ft/s

5. (42) What is 400% of 40? Use a proportion to solve.   160

*6. (103) **Write** Is $\dfrac{2\sqrt{3}}{\sqrt{2}}$ in simplest form? Explain.   no; Sample: The radical in the denominator needs to be rationalized.

*7. (103) **Predict** If $2\div\sqrt{2}$ is $\sqrt{2}$, and $3\div\sqrt{3}$ is $\sqrt{3}$, what is a good prediction of what the quotient of $239\div\sqrt{239}$ might be? $\sqrt{239}$

8. (102) **Multi-Step** The area of a square is $9x^2$. The length of one of its sides plus 32 is 47.
 a. What is the length of one of its sides?   15 units
 b. What is the area of the square?   225 square units
 c. What is x?   5

694   Saxon Algebra 1

*9. (Time and Distance) A stone is dropped from a height of 450 feet. Use the equation
(102) $25t^2 - 450 = 0$ to find how many seconds it takes for the stone to hit the ground.
≈4.243 seconds

10. Solve $\begin{array}{l} 4x + 2y = 22 \\ 6x - 5y = 9 \end{array}$ by substitution. (4, 3)
(59)

*11. Verify True or False: $5x^2 + 125 = 0$; $x = \pm 5$. If the answer is false, provide the
(102) correct answer. false; The correct answer is $\pm 5\sqrt{-1}$.

Solve and graph the inequality.

12. $-6|x| + 20 \geq 2$ $-3 \leq x \leq 3$
(101)

13. $14x + 2y > 6$
(97)

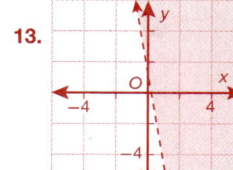

*14. Error Analysis Two students solve the inequality $-12|x| - 15 > -39$. Which student
(101) is correct? Explain the error.   Student B; Sample: Student A did not reverse the
inequality symbol when dividing each side by -12.

Student A	Student B
$-12\|x\| - 15 > -39$	$-12\|x\| - 15 > -39$
$-12\|x\| > -24$	$12\|x\| + 15 < 39$
$\|x\| > 2$	$12\|x\| < 24$
$x < -2$ OR $x > 2$	$\|x\| < 2$
	$-2 < x < 2$

*15. Geometry Find the length of the line segment that is the graph of the
(101) inequality $\left|\frac{x}{7} + 6\right| - 5 \leq 4$.   126

*16. (Tennis) The diameter d of a tennis ball should vary no more than $\frac{1}{16}$ inch
(101) from $2\frac{5}{16}$ inches. Write and solve an absolute-value inequality that models the
acceptable diameters. What is the greatest acceptable diameter?   16. $\left|d - 2\frac{5}{16}\right| \leq \frac{1}{16}$; $2\frac{1}{4} \leq d \leq 2\frac{3}{8}$; $2\frac{3}{8}$ inches

17. Graph the function $y = 10x^2 - 20$.
(96)

18. (Soccer) The height h in meters of a kicked soccer ball is represented by the
(98) function $h = -5t^2 + 20t$, where t stands for the number of seconds after the ball
is kicked. When is the ball on the ground?   It is on the ground at 0 and 4 seconds.

19. Data Analysis A teacher graphed the test grades. He found that the distribution
(98) formed a parabola. Solve the equation $0 = x^2 - 170x + 7000$ to find its roots.
70, 100

20. Write What are the other names for the x-intercepts of a function?   Sample: zeros
(100) or roots

21. Multiple Choice What is the equation of the parabola that passes through the points
(100) (0, 2), (−2, 6), and (6, 14)?   D
  A $y = x^2 - x + 2$
  B $y = -\frac{1}{2}x^2 - x + 2$
  C $y = \frac{1}{2}x^2 + x - 2$
  D $y = \frac{1}{2}x^2 - x + 2$

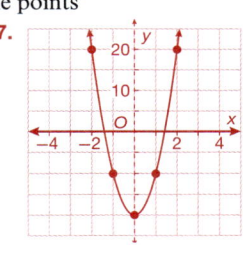

Lesson 103   695

Problem 15
Error Alert
Students may subtract the smaller absolute value from the larger when finding the length of the segment and get an answer of $105 - 21 = 79$. Tell them to subtract the value of the coordinate to the left of zero from the value of the coordinate to the right of zero: $21 - (-105) = 126$.

Problem 18
Extend the Problem
"When will the ball be at its maximum height? What is that height, given that it is being measured in meters?"   2 seconds, 20 meters

Problem 21
Students can eliminate choice C because the constant is the y-intercept, which is 2, not -2. They can also eliminate choice B by quickly sketching the three points to see that the parabola opens upward.

Problem 23
Because the coefficients are large, encourage students to first divide out common factors before multiplying.

Problem 27
Guide the students by asking them the following questions.

"What is the expression for the cost of one bike?" $8 + 10x$

"What is the expression for the cost of two bikes?" $2(8 + 10x)$

"Which goes inside the absolute-value bars with $2(8 + 10x)$: 66 or 10? Why?" 66; Sample: $66 is the budget, and the difference between the actual cost and the budget is what is limited.

---

22. Factor $2x^2y + 4xy - 7xyz - 14yz$. $(2xy - 7yz)(x + 2)$

23. Multiply $\frac{90}{24a} \cdot \frac{6a^2b^2}{25b}$. $\frac{9ab}{10}$

24. Do the side lengths 15, 36, and 39 form a Pythagorean triple?   yes

25. Multi-Step A plane left the airport and traveled west, with a tailwind, at a cruising speed of 230 miles per hour for 300 miles. After dropping passengers off, the plane traveled east at the same cruising speed, but into a headwind, for 220 miles before landing for fuel.
   a. **Justify** Write an expression for the time going west and another expression for the time going east. Explain how you came up with these expressions.
   b. Add the expressions and simplify. $\frac{119{,}600 - 80w}{(230 + w)(230 - w)}$
   c. What does the simplified expression represent?   Sample: the total time the plane flew in both directions

26. Gardening Jasmine has a rectangular garden with an area of $(x^2 - 14x + 45)$ square feet and a length of $(x - 5)$ feet. What is the width of her garden?
   $(x - 9)$ feet

27. Multi-Step A bike rental company charges $8 for each bike rental plus $10 for each hour it is rented. A couple has budgeted $66 for both of them to rent bikes. They hope that the total cost is within $10 of their budget.
   a. Write an absolute-value equation for the minimum and maximum number of hours the couple can ride bikes. $|2(8 + 10x) - 66| = 10$
   b. What is the minimum and maximum number of hours the couple can ride bikes?   2 hours, 3 hours

 28. Write How do you write $\frac{4y - 5}{6}$ as the difference of two rational expressions?

29. Can $x^2 + x + 1$ be factored? Explain.

30. If a quadratic function has been vertically stretched, does that mean the parabola is wider or narrower than the parent quadratic function, $f(x) = x^2$?   narrower

---

25a. west: $\frac{300}{230 + w}$; east: $\frac{220}{230 - w}$; Sample: The numerators represent distance and the denominators represent rate. Add the wind speed to the rate when the plane is going with the wind and subtract it from the rate when the plane is going against the wind.

28. Write each term in the numerator separately over the common denominator, and then simplify, if possible, to get $\frac{4y}{6} - \frac{5}{6}$ or $\frac{2y}{3} - \frac{5}{6}$.

29. It cannot be factored. The only whole-number factors of 1 are ±1, and neither will produce a middle term of x.

---

696   Saxon Algebra 1

CHALLENGE

Have advanced students simplify these expressions by making the radicand a perfect cube.

$$\frac{4}{\sqrt[3]{2}} \quad 2\sqrt[3]{4}$$

$$\frac{1}{\sqrt[3]{3}} \quad \frac{\sqrt[3]{9}}{3}$$

LOOKING FORWARD

Dividing radical expressions prepares students for

• **Lesson 106** Solving Radical Equations

• **Lesson 114** Graphing Square-Root Functions

LESSON 104

Solving Quadratic Equations by Completing the Square

Warm Up

1. **Vocabulary** A _____ is a trinomial that is the square of a binomial.
   (60) **perfect-square trinomial**

   Simplify.

   2. $\left(\dfrac{8}{3}\right)^2$ $\dfrac{64}{9}$
   (3)

   3. $\left(\dfrac{12}{3}\right)^2 - 5$ 11
   (4)

   Solve.

   4. $x^2 + 6x + 9 = 0$ $x = -3$
   (98)

   5. $x^2 - 18x + 81 = 0$ $x = 9$
   (98)

New Concepts

The product of a binomial square is a perfect-square trinomial.

Binomial Square	Perfect-Square Trinomial
$(x - 7)^2$	$x^2 - 14x + 49$
$(x + 3)^2$	$x^2 + 6x + 9$

Completing the square is a process used to form a perfect-square trinomial.

Hint

The last term of the binomial is doubled to get the coefficient of the middle term of the trinomial and squared to get the last term of the trinomial.

Completing the Square
Complete the square of $x^2 + bx$ by adding $\left(\dfrac{b}{2}\right)^2$ to the expression.

$x^2 + bx + \square$	Example: $x^2 + 6x + \square$
$x^2 + bx + \boxed{\left(\dfrac{b}{2}\right)^2}$	$x^2 + 6x + \boxed{\left(\dfrac{6}{2}\right)^2}$
$x^2 + bx + \left(\dfrac{b^2}{2^2}\right)$	$x^2 + 6x + (3)^2$
$\left(x + \dfrac{b}{2}\right)^2$	$x^2 + 6x + 9$
	$(x + 3)^2$

Example 1 Completing the Square

Complete the square.

$x^2 + 8x$

SOLUTION

$x^2 + 8x + \underline{}$

$x^2 + 8x + \left(\dfrac{8}{2}\right)^2$ Add the square of 8 divided by 2.

$x^2 + 8x + (4)^2$ Simplify the fraction.

$x^2 + 8x + 16$ Simplify.

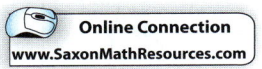
www.SaxonMathResources.com

Lesson 104   697

MATH BACKGROUND

Students have already learned that when solving quadratic equations there is a potential for more than one value of *x*. They have learned to factor trinomials.

For any real number *n*, there exists a value *x*, where $n + x$ will equal a perfect-square. If the expression $ax^2 + bx$ is treated the same as a real number, it can be assumed that there exists a value of *c* where $ax^2 + bx + c$ is a perfect-square trinomial. Turning the expression $ax^2 + bx$ into a perfect square makes it easier to find the square root and thus to isolate the variable *x*.

In Lesson 110, students learn that the quadratic formula is found by solving the general quadratic equation $ax^2 + bx + c = 0$ by completing the square. This lesson is prerequisite to the understanding of the derivation of the quadratic formula. Since any quadratic can be solved using the quadratic formula, it can also be solved by completing the square.

---

1 Warm Up

Problems 4 and 5
Remind students to factor and use the Zero Product Property.

2 New Concepts

In this lesson, students learn how to form a perfect-square trinomial to solve quadratic equations.

Example 1

Make sure students are dividing the value for *b* by 2 before squaring.

Additional Example 1
Complete the square.

$x^2 - 12x$ $x^2 - 12x + 36$

TEACHER TIP

For students who are having trouble understanding why they need to add $\left(\dfrac{b}{2}\right)^2$ to complete the square, have them find $\left(x + \dfrac{b}{2}\right)^2$ to get $x^2 + bx + \left(\dfrac{b}{2}\right)^2$.

LESSON RESOURCES

Student Edition Practice
 Workbook 104
Reteaching Master 104
Adaptations Master 104
Challenge and Enrichment
 Master C104, E104

Lesson 104   697

Exploration

In this Exploration, students use algebra tiles to see how a square is completed by adding $\left(\frac{b}{2}\right)^2$.

Extend the Exploration

Have students use algebra tiles to complete the square for $x^2 + 6x$.

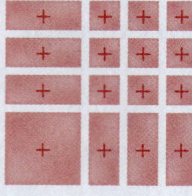

Exploration — Modeling Completing the Square

Algebra tiles are used to visualize the process of completing the square. Use algebra tiles to model $x^2 + 4x$.

a. Can these tiles be used to form a square? Explain. no; Sample: There is no way to organize the tiles to form a perfect square without 1-tiles.

b. What type of tile could be added to form a square? How many are needed? Make a drawing. four 1-tiles

c. What is the value of the tiles in this square? $x^2 + 4x + 4$

d. What is the factored form of the trinomial? What is the length of a side of the square? $(x + 2)^2$; $x + 2$

e. **Write** Does the sign of the coefficient of the x-term determine the sign of the constant? Explain. no; Sample: The last term will always be positive because the square of any nonzero real number is always positive.

Completing the square is used to solve quadratic equations. Once the square is completed, the equation is solved by finding the square root of both sides.

Math Reasoning

Analyze How would the drawing be different for completing the square of $x^2 - 4x$?

The x-squared tiles and 1-tiles would be the same, but the x-tiles have a "−" to indicate being negative.

Example 2 Solving $x^2 + bx = c$ by Completing the Square

Solve by completing the square.

a. $x^2 + 10x = 11$

SOLUTION

Complete the square.

$$x^2 + 10x = 11$$
$$x^2 + 10x + \underline{} = 11$$

$x^2 + 10x + \left(\frac{10}{2}\right)^2 = 11 + \left(\frac{10}{2}\right)^2$ Complete the square. Add the missing value to both sides of the equation.

$x^2 + 10x + (5)^2 = 11 + (5)^2$ Simplify the fraction.

$x^2 + 10x + 25 = 11 + 25$ Simplify.

$(x + 5)^2 = 36$ Factor the left side. Simplify the right side.

Math Reasoning

Analyze Why is 25 added to both sides of the equation?

Sample: to keep it equivalent to the original equation

Solve using square roots.

$\sqrt{(x + 5)^2} = \pm\sqrt{36}$ Take the square root of both sides of the equation.

$x + 5 = \pm 6$ Simplify.

$x + 5 = -6$ or $x + 5 = 6$ Write as two equations.

$\underline{-5 = -5}$ $\underline{-5 = -5}$ Subtraction Property of Equality

$x = -11$ or $x = 1$ Simplify.

Hint

The square root of a number squared is that number. So, $\sqrt{(x + 5)^2}$ $= \sqrt{(x + 5)(x + 5)}$ $= (x + 5)$.

698 *Saxon Algebra 1*

ENGLISH LEARNERS

For the exploration, explain the meaning of the word **model.** If possible, show students a road or city map. Say:

"A model is a pattern or example. A city map is a model of a city showing the location of homes and businesses."

Discuss other models such as those used in hobbies, architecture, and museums. Have volunteers give examples of models. Sample: model airplanes

Check $x^2 + 10x = 11$

$(-11)^2 + 10(-11) \stackrel{?}{=} 11$ Substitute -11 for x.

$121 - 110 \stackrel{?}{=} 11$ Simplify using the order of operations.

$11 = 11$ ✓   Subtract.

$x^2 + 10x = 11$

$(1)^2 + 10(1) \stackrel{?}{=} 11$ Substitute 1 for x.

$1 + 10 \stackrel{?}{=} 11$ Simplify using the order of operations.

$11 = 11$ ✓   Add.

b. $x^2 - 8x = 9$

SOLUTION

$x^2 - 8x = 9$

$x^2 - 8x + \left(\dfrac{8}{2}\right)^2 = 9 + \left(\dfrac{8}{2}\right)^2$ Complete the square. Add the missing value to both sides of the equation.

$x^2 - 8x + (4)^2 = 9 + (4)^2$ Simplify the fraction.

$x^2 - 8x + 16 = 9 + 16$ Simplify.

$(x - 4)^2 = 25$ Factor the left side. Simplify the right side.

$\sqrt{(x - 4)^2} = \pm\sqrt{25}$ Take the square root of both sides of the equation.

$x - 4 = \pm 5$ Simplify.

$x - 4 = -5$ or $x - 4 = 5$ Write as two equations.

$+4 = +4$ $+4 = +4$ Addition Property of Equality

$x = -1$ or $x = 9$ Simplify.

Check $x^2 - 8x = 9$

$(-1)^2 - 8(-1) \stackrel{?}{=} 9$ Substitute -1 for x.

$1 + 8 \stackrel{?}{=} 9$ Simplify using the order of operations.

$9 = 9$ ✓   Add.

$x^2 - 8x = 9$

$(9)^2 - 8(9) \stackrel{?}{=} 9$ Substitute 9 for x.

$81 - 72 \stackrel{?}{=} 9$ Simplify using the order of operations.

$9 = 9$ ✓   Add.

> **Math Language**
>
> The **quadratic term** is the x^2 term.

In Example 2 the coefficient of each quadratic term is 1. The coefficient of the quadratic term must be 1 in order to use the completing-the-square method for solving quadratic equations. However, the coefficient of the quadratic term is often not 1. In which case, each term must be divided by the coefficient a.

Example 2
Remind students to add $\left(\dfrac{b}{2}\right)^2$ to both sides of the equation.

Error Alert Students may think that $\sqrt{(x + 5)^2} = \pm(x + 5)$. Remind students that for the real number value of x, x^2 will always be a positive real number, so $\sqrt{x^2}$ will always be positive.

Additional Example 2
Solve by completing the square.

a. $x^2 + 12x = 13$
    $x = 1$ or $x = -13$

b. $x^2 - 16x = 36$
    $x = -2$ or $x = 18$

Lesson 104

INCLUSION

It may be helpful to provide students with a template for completing the square for equations given in the form $x^2 + ax = c$.

$\underline{\hspace{0.3cm}}\square\underline{\hspace{0.3cm}} = \underline{\hspace{0.5cm}}$

$\underline{\hspace{0.3cm}}\square\underline{\hspace{0.3cm}} + \left(\dfrac{\underline{\hspace{0.3cm}}}{2}\right)^2 = \underline{\hspace{0.5cm}} + \left(\dfrac{\underline{\hspace{0.3cm}}}{2}\right)^2$

$\underline{\hspace{0.3cm}}\square\underline{\hspace{0.3cm}} + \underline{\hspace{0.3cm}} = \underline{\hspace{0.3cm}} + \underline{\hspace{0.3cm}}$

$(\underline{\hspace{0.3cm}}\square\underline{\hspace{0.3cm}})^2 = \underline{\hspace{0.5cm}}$

Solve the equation $x^2 - 12x = 13$.

$x^2 \boxed{-} 12x = 13$

$x^2 \boxed{-} 12x + \left(\dfrac{12}{2}\right)^2 = 13 + \left(\dfrac{12}{2}\right)^2$

$x^2 \boxed{-} 12x + 36 = 13 + 36$

$(x \boxed{-} 6)^2 = 49$

Once students have a perfect square on both sides of the equal sign, they can take the square root and solve for x.

Lesson 104

Example 3

Remind students to divide both sides of the equation by a to get it into the form $x^2 + bx = c$.

Additional Example 3

Solve by completing the square.

a. $3x^2 + 12x = 42$
   $-2 \pm 3\sqrt{2}$; $-x = -6.243$
   or $x = 2.243$

b. $5x^2 - 40x = -85$
   $\emptyset$; There is no real number for x to solve the polynomial.

Example 3 Solving $ax^2 + bx = c$ by Completing the Square

Solve by completing the square.

a. $4x^2 + 16x = 8$

SOLUTION

Write the equation so that the coefficient of x^2 is 1. Then complete the square.

$$4x^2 + 16x = 8$$

$$\frac{4x^2 + 16x}{4} = \frac{8}{4}$$ Divide both sides by the coefficient of x^2.

$$x^2 + 4x = 2$$ Simplify.

$$x^2 + 4x + \left(\frac{4}{2}\right)^2 = 2 + \left(\frac{4}{2}\right)^2$$ Complete the square. Add the missing value to both sides of the equation.

$$x^2 + 4x + (2)^2 = 2 + (2)^2$$ Simplify the fraction.

$$x^2 + 4x + 4 = 2 + 4$$ Simplify.

$$(x + 2)^2 = 6$$ Factor the left side. Simplify the right side.

$$\sqrt{(x+2)^2} = \pm\sqrt{6}$$ Take the square root of both sides.

$$x + 2 = \pm\sqrt{6}$$ Simplify.

$x + 2 = -\sqrt{6}$ or $x + 2 = \sqrt{6}$ Write as two equations.

$\underline{-2 = -2}$ $\underline{-2 = -2}$ Subtraction Property of Equality

$x = -2 - \sqrt{6}$ or $x = -2 + \sqrt{6}$ Simplify.

$x \approx -4.450$ or $x \approx 0.450$ Use a calculator to find approximate values.

Check

$$4x^2 + 16x = 8$$

$4(-4.450)^2 + 16(-4.450) \stackrel{?}{\approx} 8$ Substitute -4.450 for x.

$4(19.8025) + 16(-4.450) \stackrel{?}{\approx} 8$ Square (-4.450).

$79.21 - 71.2 \stackrel{?}{\approx} 8$ Multiply.

$8.01 \approx 8$ ✓ Subtract.

$$4x^2 + 16x = 8$$

$4(0.450)^2 + 16(0.450) \stackrel{?}{\approx} 8$ Substitute 0.450 for x.

$4(0.2025) + 16(0.450) \stackrel{?}{\approx} 8$ Square (0.450).

$0.81 + 7.2 \stackrel{?}{\approx} 8$ Multiply.

$8.01 \approx 8$ ✓ Subtract.

b. $3x^2 - 12x = -54$

SOLUTION

$3x^2 - 12x = -54$	
$\dfrac{3x^2 - 12x}{3} = \dfrac{-54}{3}$	Divide both sides by the coefficient of x^2.
$x^2 - 4x = -18$	Simplify.
$x^2 - 4x + \left(\dfrac{-4}{2}\right)^2 = -18 + \left(\dfrac{-4}{2}\right)^2$	Complete the square. Add the missing value to both sides of the equation.
$x^2 - 4x + 4 = -18 + 4$	Simplify.
$(x - 2)^2 = -14$	Factor the left side. Simplify the right side.
$\sqrt{(x-2)^2} = \pm\sqrt{-14}$	Take the square root of both sides of the equation.
$x - 2 = \pm\sqrt{-14}$	Simplify.
$x = 2 \pm \sqrt{-14}$	Ø; No real number is the square root of a negative value.

Reading Math

A symbol for no solution is Ø.

Example 4 Finding Dimensions of a Rectangle

The length of a rectangle is 12 feet more than its width. The total area of the rectangle is 64 square feet. What are the dimensions of the rectangle?

SOLUTION

Write and solve an equation to find the dimensions.

$x =$ width; $x + 12 =$ length	Assign values for the length and width.
$w \cdot l = A$	Use the area formula.
$x(x + 12) = 64$	Substitute the width, length, and area.
$x^2 + 12x = 64$	Distribute.
$x^2 + 12x + \left(\dfrac{12}{2}\right)^2 = 64 + \left(\dfrac{12}{2}\right)^2$	Complete the square. Add the missing value to both sides.
$x^2 + 12x + 36 = 64 + 36$	Simplify.
$(x + 6)^2 = 100$	Factor and simplify.
$\sqrt{(x+6)^2} = \pm\sqrt{100}$	Take the square root of both sides.
$x + 6 = \pm 10$	Simplify.
$x + 6 = -10$ or $x + 6 = 10$	Write as two equations.
$x = -16$ or $x = 4$	Subtract 6 from both sides.

A negative length is not possible, so 4 feet is the solution. This means that the width of the rectangle is 4 feet and the length is $4 + 12$, or 16 feet.

Math Reasoning

Verify Show that $w = 4$ feet and $l = 16$ feet are the correct dimensions.

Sample: The dimensions are correct because the area of a 4-foot-by-16-foot rectangle is 64 ft².

Example 4

In application problems, solutions may be correct mathematically but may not make sense in the situation described in the problem.

Extend the Problem

Suppose that the total area is increased by 21 square feet. What are the new dimensions of the rectangle? $w = 5$ ft; $l = 17$ ft

Additional Example 4

The length of a rectangle is 8 inches more than its width. The total area of the rectangle is 384 square inches. What are the dimensions of the rectangle? $l = 24$ in.; $w = 16$ in.

ALTERNATE METHOD FOR EXAMPLE 4

Remind students that completing the square is not always the easiest method. Factoring may be a quicker method.

$x^2 + 12x = 64 \qquad x^2 + 12x - 64 = 0$

The factors of 64 are 1, 2, 4, 8, 16, 32, and 64.

Since $-4 + 16 = 12$, the equation $x^2 + 12x - 64 = 0$ can be factored as $(x - 4)(x + 16) = 0$.

Lesson Practice (sidebar)

Problems b–d
Scaffolding Remind students to check their answers by testing solutions in the original polynomial.

Problems b–e
Error Alert Students may forget to add $\left(\frac{b}{2}\right)^2$ to both sides of the equation. Remind them to think of an equation as a balance. If one number is added to one side, the same number needs to be added to the other side to maintain the balance.

Check for Understanding
The questions below help assess the concepts taught in this lesson.

"Explain why there are two values of x when solving $ax^2 + bx = c$."
Sample: When you take the square root of any positive real number, it can be positive or negative, so you have to use both values to solve for x.

"Could the completing the square method be used to solve $x^2 + 9x = 15$? Why or why not?"
yes; Sample: You would not be adding an integer to both sides of the equation. You would be adding a fraction.

3 Practice

Math Conversations
Discussion to strengthen understanding

Problem 7
Guide students by asking them the following questions.

"What is the probability of drawing a green card?" $\frac{6}{8}$

"If I remove one green card, what is left in the deck?" 5 green cards and 2 yellow cards

"What is the probability of drawing a yellow card out of the new deck?" $\frac{2}{7}$

Lesson Practice

a. Complete the square: $x^2 + 24x$. $x^2 + 24x + 144$
(Ex 1)

Solve by completing the square.

b. $x^2 + 2x = 8$ $x = 2$ or $x = -4$
(Ex 2)

c. $x^2 - 14x = 15$ $x = -1$ or $x = 15$
(Ex 2)

d. $3x^2 + 24x = -27$ $x = -4 + \sqrt{7}$ or $x = -4 - \sqrt{7}$; -6.646 or -1.354
(Ex 3)

e. $2x^2 + 6x = -6$ $\emptyset$
(Ex 3)

f. The base of a parallelogram is 8 centimeters more than its height. If the
(Ex 4) total area of the parallelogram is 20 square centimeters, what are the dimensions of the parallelogram? $h = 2$ cm, $b = 10$ cm

Practice   Distributed and Integrated

*1. Find the missing term of the perfect-square trinomial: $c^2 + 100c + $ ____.   2500
(104)

*2. Find the missing term of the perfect-square trinomial: $y^2 - 26y + $ ____.   169
(104)

*3. Multiple Choice What is the missing value for the perfect-square trinomial?
(104)
$$x^2 - 30x + \underline{} \quad \text{D}$$
A -225 **B** -15 **C** 15 **D** 225

*4. Justify Solve $6x^2 - 12x - 18 = 0$ by completing the square. Justify each step in
(104) your solution. Then check the answer(s).   See Additional Answers.

*5. Design The diagram shows the cutout for an open box. The height of
(104) the box is 3 inches. The length is 5 inches greater than the width. The area of the base of the box is 24 square inches. What are the dimensions of the box?   width: 3 in.; length: 8 in.; height: 3 in.

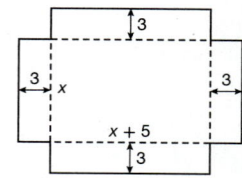

6. Simplify $\frac{\sqrt{3}}{\sqrt{11}}$. $\frac{\sqrt{33}}{11}$
(103)

7. A deck has 6 green cards and 2 yellow cards in it. What is the probability of
(33) drawing a green card, keeping it, and then drawing a yellow card? $\frac{3}{14}$

*8. Multi-Step A circle has an area of 6 square meters. Find the radius of the circle.
(103) Use $\frac{22}{7}$ for π. (Hint: Area of a circle $= \pi r^2$)
a. Write the formula for finding the radius of the circle. $r = \sqrt{\frac{A}{\pi}}$
b. Write the equation for finding the radius after substituting in $\frac{22}{7}$ for π. $r = \sqrt{\frac{7A}{22}}$
c. What is the radius of the circle? $\frac{\sqrt{231}}{11}$

*9. Coordinate Geometry A right triangle is plotted at points $A\left(\frac{\sqrt{5}}{3}, \frac{3\sqrt{3}}{4}\right)$, $B\left(\frac{\sqrt{5}}{3}, \frac{\sqrt{3}}{4}\right)$,
(86) and $C\left(\frac{2\sqrt{5}}{3}, \frac{\sqrt{3}}{4}\right)$, and line segment AC forms the hypotenuse of the triangle. What is the length of the hypotenuse of triangle ABC? $\frac{\sqrt{47}}{6}$

702   Saxon Algebra 1

10. **(Printing)** A photographer has printing paper that is 8 inches by 10 inches with a half-inch margin on the left and right side and a one-inch margin on the top and bottom. He can print out six square images. What are the dimensions of the image? **3 in. × 3 in.**

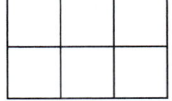

*11. **Geometry** The volume of a cylindrical container is 339.12 cubic meters. The formula representing the volume of the container is $(18\pi)r^2 = 339.12$. Find r, the radius of the container. Use 3.14 for π. **$r \approx 2.449$ m**

12. **Error Analysis** Two students were asked to find the LCD of $\frac{4x^2}{x^2 + 15x + 56} + \frac{7x + 1}{-3x + 21}$. Which student is correct? Explain the error.

12. Student A; Sample: Student B didn't correctly factor the GCF of −3 in the second denominator.

Student A	Student B
$\frac{4x^2}{x^2 + 15x + 56} + \frac{7x + 1}{-3x + 21}$	$\frac{4x^2}{x^2 + 15x + 56} + \frac{7x + 1}{-3x + 21}$
$\frac{4x^2}{(x + 7)(x + 8)} + \frac{7x + 1}{-3(x - 7)}$	$\frac{4x^2}{(x + 7)(x + 8)} + \frac{7x + 1}{-3(x + 7)}$
LCD = $-3(x - 7)(x + 7)(x + 8)$	LCD = $-3(x + 7)(x + 8)$

13. For which values is the rational expression $\frac{x - 6}{x}$ undefined? **$x = 0$**

14. Find the roots of $32x - 3x = 24 - 4x^2$. **$\{\frac{3}{4}, -8\}$**

15. Solve $x^2 = 100$. **$x = \pm 10$**

16. **(Football)** The height of a punted ball at time t is represented by the function $-32t^2 + 12t + 2 = h$, where t stands for the number of seconds after the ball is kicked. When does the ball land on the ground? **$\frac{1}{2}$ second**

17. **(Masonry)** Pedro can build a brick fence in 10 hours. His partner can build the same brick fence in 12 hours. How long would it take them to do the masonry work together? **$\frac{60}{11}$ hours**

18. Solve $x^2 + 81 = 18x$ by graphing. **$x = 9$**

19. **Measurement** A student uses indirect measurement to find the height of a flagpole. She writes a proportion relating the heights and lengths of the shadows. The equation she must solve is $\frac{x}{10} = \frac{x - 20}{2}$; where x is the height of the flagpole in feet. Find the height of the flagpole. **25 feet**

*20. **a.** Solve the inequality $-8|x + 7| \geq -24$. **$-10 \leq x \leq -4$**

b. Verify Choose two x-values in the solution set you found in part **a**. Verify that each x-value satisfies the original inequality. **See Additional Answers.**

*21. **Multiple Choice** Suppose a number n is a solution of the inequality $|5x - 2| < 9$. Which of the following inequalities does not have n as a solution? **B**
A $5x - 2 > -9$ **B** $5x - 2 > 9$ **C** $-9 < 5x - 2$ **D** $5x - 2 < 9$

Lesson 104   703

Problem 28

Have students write an inequality before trying to solve.

---

22. Find the zeros of the function shown. −6 and 2
(89)

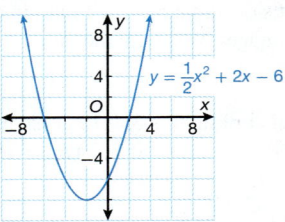

23. Find the quotient of $\frac{49x^2 + 21xy}{5x^2} \div \frac{14x}{25xy^2}$. $\frac{35xy^2 + 15y^3}{2x}$
(88)

24. Find the product $(6y - 3)(6y + 3)$. $36y^2 - 9$
(60)

25. Factor $4x^4 - 64$ completely. $4(x^2 + 4)(x + 2)(x - 2)$
(Inv 9)

26. Multi-Step When budgeting to purchase a new car, a student is willing to spend
(91) $3000 plus or minus $200.

   a. Write an absolute-value inequality to show the range of prices the student is willing to consider. $|x - 3000| \leq 200$

   b. Solve and find the range of the actual price the student might pay. $2800 \leq x \leq 3200$

27. Find the midpoint of the line segment with the endpoints $(-4, 3)$ and $(2, 4)$. $\left(-1, \frac{7}{2}\right)$
(86)

28. (**Cell Phone**) A student budgets $25 for his cell phone each month. He pays $10 for
(94) the service and $0.05 per minute. He knows that his budget can be off by $5 in either direction. What is the maximum and minimum number of minutes he can talk each month? 200 minutes, 400 minutes

29. Justify $\frac{a}{x} + \frac{a}{b} \neq \frac{2a}{x + b}$ Sample: The common denominator should be xb. Also,
(95) you have to have like denominators to be able to add the numerators without writing equivalent fractions.

30. Generalize When does a quadratic function only have one zero? Sample: It only
(96) has one zero when its vertex is on the x-axis.

---

704   **Saxon** Algebra 1

CHALLENGE

Have students complete the square to solve the quadratic equation $x^2 + 3x = 4$. Then have them check the answer using factoring. $\{1, -4\}$

LOOKING FORWARD

Solving quadratic equations by completing the square prepares students for

- **Lesson 110** Using the Quadratic Formula
- **Lesson 112** Graphing and Solving Systems of Linear and Quadratic Equations
- **Lesson 113** Interpreting the Discriminant

LESSON 105

Recognizing and Extending Geometric Sequences

Warm Up

1. **Vocabulary** A(n) _____ is a list of numbers that often follows a rule. **sequence**

Simplify

2. -2^5 -32
3. $(-3)^4$ 81
4. $15(-0.4)^2$ 2.4
5. 3^{-3} $\frac{1}{27}$

New Concepts

A **geometric sequence** is a sequence with a constant ratio between consecutive terms. The ratio between consecutive terms is known as the **common ratio**. In a geometric sequence, the ratio of any term divided by the previous term is the same for any two consecutive terms.

Math Language

A **sequence** is a list of numbers that often follows a rule.

geometric sequence: 3, 6, 12, 24, …

ratios: $\frac{6}{3} = \frac{12}{6} = \frac{24}{12}$

Example 1 Finding Common Ratios

Find the common ratio for each geometric sequence.

a. 4, 12, 36, 108, …

SOLUTION

4 → 12 → 36 → 108

$\frac{12}{4} = 3$ $\frac{36}{12} = 3$ $\frac{108}{36} = 3$

The common ratio is 3.

b. 320, −80, 20, −5, …

SOLUTION

320 → −80 → 20 → −5

$\frac{-80}{320} = -\frac{1}{4}$ $\frac{20}{-80} = -\frac{1}{4}$ $\frac{-5}{20} = -\frac{1}{4}$

The common ratio is $-\frac{1}{4}$.

c. 0.4, 1, 2.5, 6.25, …

SOLUTION

0.4 → 1 → 2.5 → 6.25

$\frac{1}{0.4} = 2.5$ $\frac{2.5}{1} = 2.5$ $\frac{6.25}{2.5} = 2.5$

The common ratio is 2.5.

Online Connection
www.SaxonMathResources.com

Lesson 105 705

LESSON 105

1 Warm Up

Problem 5
Point out that the exponent in the problem is negative and help students recall that $a^{-n} = \frac{1}{a^n}$.

2 New Concepts

Remind students that a sequence is a number pattern and that each number in the pattern is called a term of the sequence.

Discuss the meaning of a **common ratio** and how it defines a **geometric sequence**.

Example 1

Error Alert Some students may find only the ratio of the first two terms. Encourage them to check their work with each term.

Additional Example 1

Find the common ratio for each geometric sequence.

a. 5, 10, 20, 40, … **2**

b. 270, −90, 30, −10, … $-\frac{1}{3}$

c. 3, 4.5, 6.75, 10.125, … **1.5**

MATH BACKGROUND

A sequence of numbers is an ordered set or list of numbers arranged in such a way that you can determine the number preceding and following any term in the sequence according to a specified set of rules or a pattern. The pattern may be arithmetic, geometric, or neither.

In this lesson, students learn to recognize geometric sequences in which the ratio of successive terms is the same number, r, known as the common ratio.

The explicit formula for a geometric sequence ($a_n = a_1 \cdot r^{n-1}$) introduces students to exponential functions. The graph of a geometric sequence is exponential—increasing or decreasing rapidly.

Understanding different types of sequences also prepares students for more advanced algebra, when they will study series and learn to find the sum of a sequence of numbers.

LESSON RESOURCES

Student Edition Practice
  Workbook 105
Reteaching Master 105
Adaptations Master 105
Challenge and Enrichment
  Master C105, E105

Example 2

Have a volunteer give an example of an arithmetic sequence. Discuss how it differs from a geometric sequence.

Additional Example 2

Find the next four terms in the geometric sequence.

a. $36, 12, 4, \frac{4}{3}, \ldots$
   $\frac{4}{9}, \frac{4}{27}, \frac{4}{81}, \frac{4}{243}$

b. $2, -10, 50, -250, \ldots$
   $1250, -6250, 31{,}250, -156{,}250$

Example 3

As with an arithmetic sequence, a student can use a formula to find the value of the nth term when the previous term is unknown.

Extend the Example

"Suppose the common ratio in Example 3a is $\frac{1}{2}$. What would be the sixth term of the sequence?" $\frac{7}{32}$

"Use the same common ratio of $\frac{1}{2}$. What would be the sixth term of the sequence if the first term was 32?" 1

Additional Example 3

a. The first term of a geometric sequence is $\frac{1}{8}$ and the common ratio is 4. Find the eighth term in the sequence.
   2048

b. Find the fifth term of the geometric sequence.
   $-288, 48, -8, \ldots$ $-\frac{2}{9}$

c. Find the twelfth term of the geometric sequence.
   $2, 4, 8, 16, \ldots$ 4096

d. Find the sixth term of the geometric sequence.
   $2.3, 16.1, 112.7, 788.9, \ldots$
   $38{,}656.1$

Example 2 Extending Geometric Sequences

Find the next four terms in the geometric sequence.

a. $2, 8, 32, 128, \ldots$

SOLUTION

The common ratio is 4. Each term of the sequence is 4 times the previous term. Use the common ratio to find the next 4 terms.

$$128 \xrightarrow{\times 4} 512 \xrightarrow{\times 4} 2048 \xrightarrow{\times 4} 8192 \xrightarrow{\times 4} 32{,}768$$

The next 4 terms of the sequence are 512, 2048, 8192, and 32,768.

b. $250, -50, 10, -2, \ldots$

SOLUTION

Math Reasoning

Generalize When will the common ratio be negative?

Sample: when the sign of each term is the opposite of the term before and after it

The common ratio is $-\frac{1}{5}$. Use the common ratio to find the next 4 terms.

$$-2 \xrightarrow{\times\left(-\frac{1}{5}\right)} \frac{2}{5} \xrightarrow{\times\left(-\frac{1}{5}\right)} -\frac{2}{25} \xrightarrow{\times\left(-\frac{1}{5}\right)} \frac{2}{125} \xrightarrow{\times\left(-\frac{1}{5}\right)} -\frac{2}{625}$$

The next 4 terms of the sequence are $\frac{2}{5}, -\frac{2}{25}, \frac{2}{125},$ and $-\frac{2}{625}$.

Math Reasoning

Analyze Which operation is equivalent to multiplying by $-\frac{1}{5}$?

Sample: dividing by -5

Examine the terms of the sequence in Example 2a.

Term 1: $2 = 2 \cdot 1 = 2 \cdot 4^0$ Term 2: $8 = 2 \cdot 4 = 2 \cdot 4^1$
Term 3: $32 = 2 \cdot 4 \cdot 4 = 2 \cdot 4^2$ Term 4: $128 = 2 \cdot 4 \cdot 4 \cdot 4 = 2 \cdot 4^3$

The exponent on the common ratio 4 is 1 less than the number of the term. In general, the nth term of the sequence is $2 \cdot 4^{n-1}$.

Reading Math

In the expression 4^{n-1}, n represents the integers 1, 2, 3, 4, and so on.

Finding the nth Term of a Geometric Sequence
Let $A(n)$ equal the nth term of a geometric sequence, then $$A(n) = ar^{n-1}$$ where a is the first term of the sequence and r is the common ratio.

Example 3 Finding the nth Term of a Geometric Sequence

a. The first term of a geometric sequence is 7 and the common ratio is -3. Find the 6th term in the sequence.

SOLUTION

$A(n) = ar^{n-1}$ Use the formula.
$A(6) = 7(-3)^{6-1}$ Substitute 6 for n, 7 for a, and -3 for r.
$= 7(-3)^5$ Simplify the exponent.
$= 7(-243)$ Raise -3 to the 5th power.
$= -1701$ Multiply.

The 6th term in the sequence is -1701.

ALTERNATE METHOD FOR EXAMPLE 2b

Make a list of the terms of the sequence and their factors and look for a pattern.

Term	Factors
250	$-(2 \cdot -5^3)$
-50	$-(2 \cdot -5^2)$
10	$-(2 \cdot -5^1)$
-2	$-(2 \cdot -5^0)$

Continue the pattern to find the next four terms in the sequence.

$-(2 \cdot -5^{-1}) = -\left(2 \cdot -\frac{1}{5}\right) = \frac{2}{5}$

$-(2 \cdot -5^{-2}) = -\left(2 \cdot \frac{1}{25}\right) = -\frac{2}{25}$

$-(2 \cdot -5^{-3}) = -\left(2 \cdot -\frac{1}{125}\right) = \frac{2}{125}$

$-(2 \cdot -5^{-4}) = -\left(2 \cdot \frac{1}{625}\right) = -\frac{2}{625}$

b. Find the 7th term of geometric sequence.

$$\frac{1}{3}, -\frac{1}{9}, \frac{1}{27}, \ldots$$

SOLUTION

Find the common ratio: $-\frac{1}{9} \div \frac{1}{3} = -\frac{1}{9} \cdot \frac{3}{1} = -\frac{1}{3}$.

$A(n) = ar^{n-1}$ Use the formula.

$A(7) = \frac{1}{3}\left(-\frac{1}{3}\right)^{7-1}$ Substitute 7 for n, $\frac{1}{3}$ for a, and $-\frac{1}{3}$ for r.

$= \frac{1}{3}\left(-\frac{1}{3}\right)^{6}$ Simplify the exponent.

$= \left(\frac{1}{3}\right)\left(\frac{1}{729}\right)$ Raise $-\frac{1}{3}$ to the 6th power.

$= \frac{1}{2187}$ Multiply.

The 7th term in the sequence is $\frac{1}{2187}$.

c. Find the 9th term in the geometric sequence.

$$17, 8\frac{1}{2}, 4\frac{1}{4}, 2\frac{1}{8}, \ldots$$

> **Hint**
> Choose the two terms that are the easiest for finding the common ratio. Then use that ratio to check.

SOLUTION

Find the common ratio: $8\frac{1}{2} \div 17 = \frac{17}{2} \div 17 = \frac{17}{2} \cdot \frac{1}{17} = \frac{1}{2}$.

$A(n) = ar^{n-1}$ Use the formula.

$A(9) = 17\left(\frac{1}{2}\right)^{9-1}$ Substitute 9 for n, 17 for a, and $\frac{1}{2}$ for r.

$= 17\left(\frac{1}{2}\right)^{8}$ Simplify the exponent.

$= 17\left(\frac{1}{256}\right)$ Raise $\frac{1}{2}$ to the 8th power.

$= \frac{17}{256}$ Multiply.

The 9th term of the sequence is $\frac{17}{256}$.

d. Find the 5th term of the geometric sequence.

$$1.2, 7.2, 43.2, \ldots$$

SOLUTION

Find the common ratio: $7.2 \div 1.2 = 6$.

$A(n) = ar^{n-1}$ Use the formula.

$A(5) = 1.2(6)^{5-1}$ Substitute 5 for n, 1.2 for a, and 6 for r.

$= 1555.2$ Simplify.

The 5th term of the sequence is 1555.2.

TEACHER TIP

Emphasize that a sequence may be arithmetic, geometric, or neither. Suggest that students look for a common difference or a common ratio when first presented with a sequence.

Error Alert For students who multiply the ratio to the nth power instead of to $n - 1$, suggest that they make a table of values. Place the first few term numbers in one column and evaluate $a_1 \cdot r^n$ in the second column for each term number n. Now evaluate $a_1 \cdot r^{n-1}$ in a third column for the same values of n. Students can compare the value of each term to the original sequence to see that the first term in the sequence is left out when they only evaluate $a_1 \cdot r^n$.

$17, 8\frac{1}{2}, 4\frac{1}{4}, 2\frac{1}{8}, \ldots$

$a_1 = 17; r = \frac{1}{2}$

n	$a_1 \cdot r^n$	$a_1 \cdot r^{n-1}$
1	$8\frac{1}{2}$	17
2	$4\frac{1}{4}$	$8\frac{1}{2}$
3	$2\frac{1}{8}$	$4\frac{1}{4}$
4	$1\frac{1}{16}$	$2\frac{1}{8}$

ALTERNATE METHOD FOR EXAMPLE 3c

Make a table of each number's position in the sequence n, up to the ninth term in the sequence, and fill in the first four given terms.

Find the common ratio and multiply each value by the ratio to find the next term in the sequence until you have found the ninth term.

Position (n)	1	2	3	4	5	6	7	8	9
Term	17	$8\frac{1}{2}$	$4\frac{1}{4}$	$2\frac{1}{8}$	$1\frac{1}{16}$	$\frac{17}{32}$	$\frac{17}{64}$	$\frac{17}{128}$	$\frac{17}{256}$

Example 4

Explain that drawing a diagram can help students better understand this problem and problems similar to it.

Extend the Example

"Suppose the ball is now dropped from a height of 15 feet. A student standing nearby is 5 feet tall. After how many bounces will the ball height be less than the student's height?" after 6 bounces

Additional Example 4

A ball is dropped from a height of 3 meters. The height of each bounce is 90% of the height of the previous bounce. What is the height of the ball after 7 bounces? about 1.43 meters

Lesson Practice

Problem e

Error Alert Students may mistakenly treat a geometric sequence as an arithmetic sequence and use the difference between two terms to extend the pattern. Remind them that the difference between each term in an arithmetic sequence is constant. In a geometric sequence, the difference between each consecutive term varies.

Example 4 **Application: Bounce Height**

A ball is dropped from a height of 2 yards. The height of each bounce is 85% of the previous height. What is the height of the ball after 10 bounces?

SOLUTION

Understand A ball is dropped from a height of 2 yards. The height of each bounce is 85% of the height of the previous bounce. The common ratio is 85%, or 0.85.

> **Caution**
> The height of the first bounce is 1.7 yards. The first term of the sequence is 1.7, not 2. The height of the drop is 2 yards.

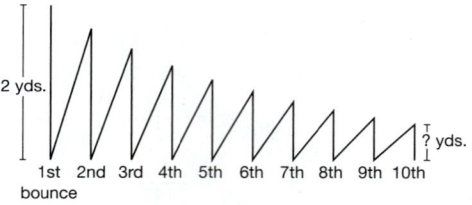

The heights of the bounces form a geometric sequence.

Plan Multiply the drop height of 2 yards by the common ratio 0.85 to find the height of the first bounce. This product is the 1st term of the sequence. Then use the formula $A(n) = ar^{n-1}$ to find the height of the 10th bounce. This is the 10th term in the sequence.

Solve Find the height of the 1st bounce: $2 \cdot 0.85 = 1.7$ yards.

So, the first term of the sequence is 1.7.

Use the formula $A(n) = ar^{n-1}$ to find the height of the 10th bounce.

$A(n) = ar^{n-1}$

$A(10) = 1.7(0.85)^{10-1}$ Substitute 1.7 for a, 10 for n, and 0.85 for r.

$\quad\quad\quad = 1.7(0.85)^9$ Simplify the exponent.

$\quad\quad\quad \approx 0.39$ yards   Simplify and round to the nearest hundredth.

The height of the 10th bounce is about 0.39 yards.

> **Math Reasoning**
> **Analyze** Why is 1.7 multiplied by 0.85 nine times instead of ten times?
>
> Sample: The height of the first bounce is 1.7 yards. There are 9 more bounces to get to the 10th bounce.

Check Multiply the height of the first bounce by 0.85 nine times.

$1.7 \times 0.85 \times 0.85 \times 0.85 \times 0.85 \times 0.85 \times 0.85 \times 0.85 \times 0.85 \times 0.85 \approx 0.39$ ✓

Lesson Practice

Find the common ratio for each geometric sequence. (Ex 1)

a. 2, 16, 128, 1024, ...   8

b. $-162, 54, -18, 6, ...$ $-\frac{1}{3}$

c. 0.7, 4.9, 34.3, 240.1, ...   7

Find the next four terms of each sequence. (Ex 2)

d. $5, -15, 45, -135, ...$ $405, -1215, 3645, -10{,}935$

e. $336, 168, 84, 42, ...$ $21, 10\frac{1}{2}, 5\frac{1}{4}, 2\frac{5}{8}$

🔺 ALTERNATE METHOD FOR EXAMPLE 4

Students can draw a diagram of the problem by starting where the ball drops from a height of 2 yards and sketching the path of 10 bounce heights.

Then they can multiply $2 \cdot 0.85$ and label the height of the first bounce: 1.7. They can continue multiplying each bounce height by 0.85 until they find the height of the tenth bounce. Have students explain why the answer differs from the example.

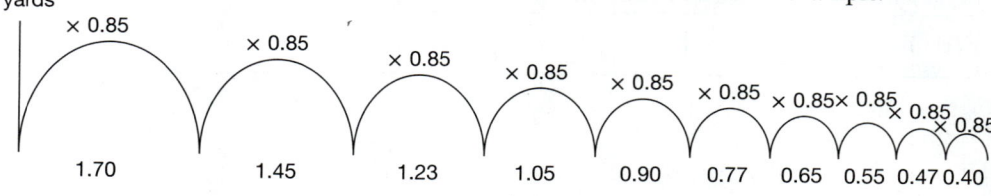

f. The first term of a geometric sequence is -3 and the common ratio is 4.
(Ex 3) Find the 6th term in the sequence. -3072

g. Find the 7th term in the geometric sequence.
(Ex 3)
$$-\frac{1}{2}, \frac{1}{8}, -\frac{1}{32}, \frac{1}{128}, -\frac{1}{512}, \ldots \quad -\frac{1}{8192}$$

h. Find the 8th term in the geometric sequence. -544
(Ex 3)
$$4\frac{1}{4}, -8\frac{1}{2}, 17, -34, \ldots$$

i. Find the 6th term of the geometric sequence 40, 32, 25.6, ...   13.1072
(Ex 2)

j. A fish tank is $\frac{9}{10}$ full. Every minute, $\frac{1}{3}$ of the water leaks out of the tank.
(Ex 4) After 5 minutes, how full is the tank? $\frac{16}{135}$

Practice   Distributed and Integrated

*1. Find the common ratio of the geometric sequence $-80, 20, -5, 1\frac{1}{4}, \ldots$. $-\frac{1}{4}$
(105)

*2. **Multiple Choice** Which rule can you use to find the nth term of the sequence
(105) 4, 6, 9, 13.5, ...?   **B**
  A $A(n) = 4(1.5)^n$ **B** $A(n) = 4(1.5)^{n-1}$
  C $A(n) = 4(2)^{n-1}$ **D** $A(n) = 3(1.5)^n$

*3. **Depreciation** Harper buys a car in 2007 for $20,000. Each year, the car decreases
(105) in value by 18%. How much will the car be worth in 2012? Round to the
nearest cent. $7414.80

*4. **Write** The third term of a sequence is 0. The first two terms are not 0. Can this
(105) be a geometric sequence? Explain.

4. no; Sample: The formula to find the third term of a geometric series is $A(n) = ar^2$. If the first term is not 0, then the only way any term of the series could equal 0 would be if $r = 0$. Since the second term is not 0, this cannot be true. So the sequence cannot be geometric.

5. Write a recursive formula for the arithmetic sequence with $a_1 = \frac{1}{2}$ and common
(34) difference $d = \frac{1}{2}$. Then find the first four terms of the sequence.

5. $a_1 = \frac{1}{2}$, $a_n = a_{n-1} + \frac{1}{2}$; $\frac{1}{2}, 1, 1\frac{1}{2}, 2$

*6. **Analyze** Write two possible rules for the nth term of the geometric sequence with a
(105) first term of 5 and a third term of 605. $5(11)^{n-1}$ or $5(-11)^{n-1}$

7. Find the missing term of the perfect-square trinomial: $x^2 + 18x + \underline{\quad}$.   81
(104)

8. **Error Analysis** Dominic stated that the missing value for completing the square of
(104) $g^2 + 28g + \underline{\quad}$ is 14. Is this correct? Explain.

8. no; Sample: The correct value is 196; 14 is the constant value in the factored form.

*9. **Multi-Step** A design for a rectangular flower bed is shown.
(104) The total area of the flower bed is 880 square feet.
  a. Write an equation to represent the problem.
  b. Write the quadratic equation in the form $x^2 + bx = c$.
  c. What is the width of the interior of the flower bed?   18 ft
  d. What is the area of the border?   232 ft^2

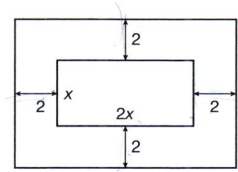

9a. $(x + 4)(2x + 4) = 880$
9b. $x^2 + 6x = 432$

Lesson 105   709

ENGLISH LEARNERS

For this lesson, discuss the meaning of the word **sequence.** Say:

"A sequence is a listing of items or objects that follow a set order or pattern."

Discuss other examples of sequences, such as the sequence of events students follow to get ready for school. Ask them if they could come to school before getting dressed in the morning or eat their breakfast before getting out of bed. There is a sequence they must follow to get from one event to the next.

Problem h
Scaffolding Before students solve, have them decide which two terms to use to determine the common ratio. The terms 17 and -34 make computation easy. After finding the common ratio, use it to evaluate the formula.

✓ Check for Understanding

The questions below help assess the concepts taught in this lesson.

"Write four terms of a geometric sequence. What is the formula that gives the value of a_n for your sequence?" Sample: 3, 12, 48, 192, ...; $a_n = 3 \cdot 4^{n-1}$

"How are a common difference and a common ratio similar? How are they different?" Sample: Neither changes within a sequence, but consecutive terms in an arithmetic sequence share a common difference and consecutive terms in a geometric sequence share a common ratio.

3 Practice

Math Conversations
Discussion to strengthen understanding

Problem 8
Remind students that the relationship to complete the square is $x^2 + bx + \left(\frac{b}{2}\right)^2$.

Lesson 105   709

Problem 11
Error Alert
A common error students may make is to leave the rational expression in the form $\frac{\sqrt{7}}{\sqrt{2}}$ or $\sqrt{\frac{7}{2}}$. Point out that a rational expression in simplest form will not have a radical as a denominator, nor have a fraction as a radicand. Guide students to find a fraction equivalent to 1 that can help them rationalize the denominator correctly.

Problem 15
Guide the students by asking them the following questions.

"What must a quadratic equation equal in order to find the roots?" 0

"How can the equation be written so that it is equal to 0?" $14x^2 + 19x - 3 = 0$

Problem 17
One way to mentally solve the problem is to square $(30 - 1)$ using the FOIL method.

$(30 - 1)(30 - 1) = 900 - 60 + 1 = 841$

Have a volunteer who found a different method demonstrate how he or she came to the solution.

Problem 19
Extend the Problem
"The water is collecting on Silvia's kitchen floor. The floor has an area of 100 square feet. If the area of the puddle becomes greater than the area of the kitchen floor, the room will flood. Using the function given in Problem 19, how long will it take for the kitchen to flood?" 6.31 s

"Silvia reacts quickly and begins to mop up the water after 4.2 seconds have passed. What was the area of the puddle of water as Silvia began to mop it up?" 16.52 square feet

Simplify.

10. (43) $\dfrac{11x + 22}{22x^2 + 44x}$ $\quad \dfrac{1}{2x}, x \neq 0, -2$

11. (103) $\dfrac{\sqrt{63}}{\sqrt{18}}$ $\quad \dfrac{\sqrt{14}}{2}$

*12. (104) **Geometry** The base of a right triangle is 14 units longer than its height. The hypotenuse is 26 units. What are the base and height measurements of the triangle? base = 24 units; height = 10 units

*13. (103) **Error Analysis** Two students simplified the given expression. Which student is correct? Explain the error. Student B; Sample: When rationalizing the denominator, Student A did not multiply by a factor of 1.

Student A	Student B
$\dfrac{5}{\sqrt{8}}$	$\dfrac{5}{\sqrt{8}}$
$\dfrac{5}{2\sqrt{2}} \cdot \dfrac{1}{\sqrt{2}}$	$\dfrac{5}{2\sqrt{2}} \cdot \dfrac{\sqrt{2}}{\sqrt{2}}$
$\dfrac{5}{4}$	$\dfrac{5\sqrt{2}}{4}$

*14. (103) **Architecture** In the city of Rotterdam, Netherlands, architect Piet Blom designed a group of cube-shaped houses that each sit upon its vertex. If the surface area of each cube measures $337\frac{1}{2}$ square meters, write a rational expression representing the edge length of the cube. (Hint: edge length = $\sqrt{\dfrac{A}{6}}$) $\dfrac{15}{2}$ meters

15. (98) Find the roots: $14x^2 - 2x = 3 - 21x$. $\left\{\dfrac{1}{7}, -\dfrac{3}{2}\right\}$

16. (99) **Construction** It takes a woman 3 hours to build a doghouse. Her husband can build it in 4 hours. How long will it take them if they build the doghouse together? $\dfrac{12}{7}$ hours

17. (60) Use mental math to find the product of 29^2. 841

18. (100) **Horseshoes** Shannon plays a game of horseshoes. The horseshoe's movement forms a parabola given by the quadratic equation $h = -16t^2 + 6t + 6$ where h is the height in feet and t is the time in seconds. Find the maximum height of the path the horseshoe makes and the time t when the horseshoe hits the ground. Round to the nearest hundredth. $h = 6.56$ feet and $t = 0.83$ seconds

19. (100) **Measurement** A puddle of water creates a shape on the ground. As time increases, the area of the puddle changes. The area of the puddle is given by the function $A = 3t^2 + 8t - 70$, where A is the area in square feet and t is the time in seconds. Find the time when the area is 55 square feet. Round to the nearest hundredth. $t = 5.26$ seconds

20. (101) Solve and graph the inequality $2|x| - 12 > -5$. $x < -3.5$ or $x > 3.5$;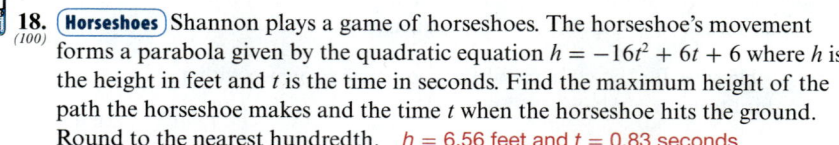

21. (102) **Verify** True or False: $4x^2 - 64 = 0$; $x = 4$. Verify that the answer is true. If the answer is false, provide the correct answer. false; The correct answer is ± 4.

710 Saxon Algebra 1

INCLUSION

Materials: large right isosceles triangles, circles or squares cut from sheets of construction paper, scissors

Have each student take a shape and sketch a picture of it. Ask them to label the drawing "a_1." Students will now fold their shapes in half, creating two congruent shapes, and cut the shapes apart on the fold. Tell them to make another sketch of the new shapes they have and to label this drawing "a_2." Place the shapes one on top of the other and repeat the process, labeling the next drawing "a_3."

Have students repeat the process once more and label the last drawing "a_4." Ask them to count and label how many shapes were in each drawing they made.

"What is the value of a_1? a_2? a_3? a_4?" 1, 2, 4, 8

"Is the difference between one number and the next always the same?" No, it changes.

"What pattern do you notice?" Each number is double the one before it.

*22. Error Analysis Student A and Student B want to find the length of the sides of a square with an area 460 square meters less than 685 square meters. Which student is correct? Explain the error. **Student A; Sample: Student B made a transformation error when attempting to isolate the variable and arrived at the wrong answer.**

Student A	Student B
$x^2 + 460 = 685$	$x^2 + 460 = 685$
$-460 \quad -460$	$+460 \quad +460$
$x^2 = 225$	$x^2 = 1145$
$\sqrt{x^2} = \sqrt{225}$	$\sqrt{x^2} = \sqrt{1145}$
$x = \pm 15$	$x \approx \pm 3.838$
The sides of the square are 15 m.	The sides of the square are about 3.838 m.

23. Give the coordinates of the parabola's vertex. Then give the minimum or maximum value. **(0, 0); maximum: 0**

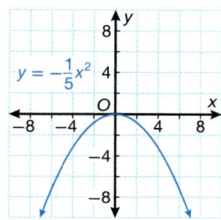

24. Add $\dfrac{d}{d-10} + \dfrac{10}{10-d}$. **1**

25. Solve and check: $\dfrac{18}{2x} - 4 = \dfrac{15}{3x}$. **$x = 1$**

26. Multi-Step Louis walked for $\dfrac{6x^2 - 24x}{6x}$ minutes to get to a grocery store that was $\dfrac{4x-16}{x^3}$ miles away.
  a. Find his rate in miles per minute. $\dfrac{4}{x^3}$ miles per minute
  b. If the rate is divided by $\dfrac{1}{x}$, what is the new rate? $\dfrac{4}{x^2}$ miles per minute

27. Football The school football team is going to a camp that is $\dfrac{8x^2}{x^2 - 11x + 18}$ miles away. The team traveled $\dfrac{2}{8x-72}$ miles on the first day. How many miles are left to travel? $\dfrac{32x^2 - x + 2}{4(x-2)(x-9)}$ miles

28. Find the midpoint of the line segment with the endpoints $(-5, 0)$ and $(1, 14)$. **(−2, 7)**

29. Multi-Step A ball is thrown into the air from the top of a cliff at an initial velocity of 32 feet per second. (Use $h = -16t^2 + vt + 0$.)
  a. How high is the ball after 2 seconds? **0 feet**
  b. What does this height represent? **Sample: the height the ball was thrown from**
  c. After 3 seconds, the ball is −48 feet. What does this height represent? **Sample: 48 feet below the top of the cliff**

30. Justify List the inequality symbols that result in graphs with dashed boundary lines and list the inequality symbols that result in graphs with solid boundary lines. **30. Sample: < and > are graphed with dashed lines and ≤ and ≥ are graphed with solid lines.**

Problem 27
Point out that students will need to find a common denominator so that they can subtract and find the miles left to travel. Have them first factor out any common factors, and then factor the trinomial into two binomials, if possible.

Lesson 105   711

CHALLENGE

The first three stages of Sierpinski's Triangle are shown below.

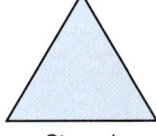
Stage 1   Stage 2   Stage 3

If the first triangle has an area of 1 square unit, what is the area of the shaded part of the second triangle? the third triangle? What is the area of the shaded part of a triangle at Stage n? $\dfrac{3}{4}$; $\dfrac{9}{16}$; Stage$_n = \left(\dfrac{3}{4}\right)^{n-1}$

LOOKING FORWARD

Recognizing and extending geometric sequences prepares students for

- **Lesson 108** Identifying and Graphing Exponential Functions
- **Investigation 11** Investigating Exponential Growth and Decay
- **Lesson 114** Graphing Square-Root Functions
- **Lesson 115** Graphing Cubic Functions

LESSON 106

1 Warm Up

Problems 2 and 3
Check to see if students remember that the square root of a number raised to the second power is equal to the number under the radical sign.

2 New Concepts

In this lesson, students learn to solve radical equations using inverse operations.

Discuss the definition of inverse operations and **radical equations.**

Example 1

Additional Example 1
Solve each equation.

a. $\sqrt{x} = 8$ $x = 64$

b. $\sqrt{2x} = 10$ $x = 50$

c. $\sqrt{x+7} = 11$ $x = 114$

d. $\sqrt{\frac{x}{3} + 4} = 5$ $x = 63$

LESSON RESOURCES

Student Edition Practice Workbook 106
Reteaching Master 106
Adaptations Master 106
Challenge and Enrichment Master C106

LESSON 106 Solving Radical Equations

Warm Up

1. **Vocabulary** Which of the following expressions is a radical expression? **B**
   (61)
   A $2x + 4$ B $\sqrt{x+1} + 2$ C $x^2 + 5$ D $2x^2 + 3x + 6$

Simplify.

2. $(\sqrt{5})^2$ 5
   (76)

3. $(\sqrt{x+2})^2$ $x + 2$
   (76)

Solve.

4. $x^2 + 5x + 6 = 0$ $x = -2, x = -3$
   (98)

5. $x^2 - 5x = 14$ $x = -2, x = 7$
   (98)

New Concepts

An equation containing a variable in a radicand is called a **radical equation**. Inverse operations are used to solve radical equations. The inverse of finding the square root of a term is squaring the term.

Math Language
Inverse operations are operations that undo each other.

Example 1 Solving Simple Radical Equations

Solve each equation.

a. $\sqrt{x} = 7$

SOLUTION

Use inverse operations.

$\sqrt{x} = 7$

$(\sqrt{x})^2 = 7^2$ Square both sides.

$x = 49$ Simplify.

Check $\sqrt{x} = 7$

$\sqrt{49} \stackrel{?}{=} 7$

$7 = 7$ ✓

Math Reasoning

Verify Show that simplifying $\sqrt{4x}$ before squaring will result in the same solution.

Sample:
$\sqrt{4x} = 12$
$2\sqrt{x} = 12$
$(2\sqrt{x})^2 = 12^2$
$4x = 144$
$x = 36$

b. $\sqrt{4x} = 12$

SOLUTION

Use inverse operations.

$\sqrt{4x} = 12$

$(\sqrt{4x})^2 = 12^2$ Square both sides.

$4x = 144$ Simplify.

$\frac{4x}{4} = \frac{144}{4}$ Division Property of Equality

$x = 36$ Simplify.

712 **Saxon** Algebra 1

MATH BACKGROUND

Radical equations may have extraneous solutions. The solution to $\sqrt{x-1} = x - 3$ is only $x = 5$, even though the extraneous solution $x = 2$ may have been found while solving for x. Since the principal square root of a real number is equal to a positive number, $x = 2$ does not make sense because it makes the right side of the equation negative. This misleading solution is the effect of squaring both sides of the equation when solving for x.

To verify that the solution is only $x = 5$, graph both sides of the equation as separate equations and find the point where the lines intersect.

Check $\sqrt{4x} = 12$

$\sqrt{4(36)} \stackrel{?}{=} 12$

$\sqrt{144} \stackrel{?}{=} 12$

$12 = 12$ ✓

c. $\sqrt{x+2} = 12$

SOLUTION

Use inverse operations.

$\sqrt{x+2} = 12$

$(\sqrt{x+2})^2 = 12^2$ Square both sides.

$x + 2 = 144$ Simplify.

$\underline{-2 \quad -2}$ Subtraction Property of Equality

$x = 142$ Simplify.

Check $\sqrt{x+2} = 12$

$\sqrt{142+2} \stackrel{?}{=} 12$

$\sqrt{144} \stackrel{?}{=} 12$

$12 = 12$ ✓

d. $\sqrt{\frac{x}{2} - 6} = 8$

SOLUTION

Use inverse operations.

$\sqrt{\frac{x}{2} - 6} = 8$

$\left(\sqrt{\frac{x}{2} - 6}\right)^2 = 8^2$ Square both sides.

$\frac{x}{2} - 6 = 64$ Simplify.

$\underline{+6 \quad +6}$ Addition Property of Equality

$\frac{x}{2} = 70$ Simplify.

$2 \cdot \frac{x}{2} = 70 \cdot 2$ Multiplication Property of Equality

$x = 140$ Simplify.

Check $\sqrt{\frac{x}{2} - 6} = 8$

$\sqrt{\frac{140}{2} - 6} \stackrel{?}{=} 8$

$\sqrt{70 - 6} \stackrel{?}{=} 8$

$\sqrt{64} \stackrel{?}{=} 8$

$8 = 8$ ✓

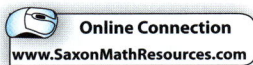
Online Connection
www.SaxonMathResources.com

Extend the Example
Have the students graph each equation in each part of the example with a graphing calculator. Tell them to use **Y=** to enter one side of the equation as Y_1 and the other side of the equation as Y_2. Then have them press **2nd** **TRACE** **5** to find the x-coordinate of the point of intersection. They can then verify that the solutions calculated by solving the equation algebraically and graphically are the same.

TEACHER TIP
Remind students that to solve the equation, they have to isolate the variable.

Example 2

Students learn to isolate the radical before they square both sides.

Additional Example 2

Solve each equation.

a. $\sqrt{x} - 6 = 5$ $x = 121$

b. $\sqrt{x} + 8 = 15$ $x = 49$

c. $4\sqrt{x} = 24$ $x = 36$

d. $\dfrac{\sqrt{x}}{3} = 12$ $x = 1296$

TEACHER TIP

For equations with one radical that is not isolated, have students write the problem and then use the eraser end of a pencil to cover the radical term. Any terms not covered will need to be moved to the opposite side of the equation and then simplified.

Sometimes the radical is not isolated in a radical equation. In those cases, inverse operations for addition, subtraction, multiplication, and division can be used to isolate the radical. Once the radical has been isolated, both sides of the equation can be squared.

Example 2 Solving by Isolating the Square Root

Solve each equation.

a. $\sqrt{x} - 5 = 8$

SOLUTION

Use inverse operations.

$\sqrt{x} - 5 = 8$

$\underline{+5 = +5}$ Addition Property of Equality

$\sqrt{x} = 13$ Simplify.

$(\sqrt{x})^2 = 13^2$ Square both sides.

$x = 169$ Simplify.

Check $\sqrt{x} - 5 = 8$

$\sqrt{169} - 5 \stackrel{?}{=} 8$

$13 - 5 \stackrel{?}{=} 8$

$8 = 8$ ✓

Math Reasoning

Analyze Is squaring first helpful in solving the equation $\sqrt{x} - 5 = 8$?

Sample: No, the left side of the equation still has a radical:
$x - 10\sqrt{x} + 25 = 64$.

b. $\sqrt{x} + 5 = 8$

SOLUTION

Use inverse operations.

$\sqrt{x} + 5 = 8$

$\underline{-5 = -5}$ Subtraction Property of Equality

$\sqrt{x} = 3$ Simplify.

$(\sqrt{x})^2 = 3^2$ Square both sides.

$x = 9$ Simplify.

$\sqrt{x} + 5 = 8$

$\sqrt{9} + 5 \stackrel{?}{=} 8$

$3 + 5 \stackrel{?}{=} 8$

$8 = 8$ ✓

c. $3\sqrt{x} = 21$

SOLUTION

Use inverse operations.

$3\sqrt{x} = 21$

$\dfrac{3\sqrt{x}}{3} = \dfrac{21}{3}$ Division Property of Equality

$\sqrt{x} = 7$ Simplify.

$(\sqrt{x})^2 = 7^2$ Square both sides.

$x = 49$ Simplify.

Check $3\sqrt{x} = 21$

$3\sqrt{49} \stackrel{?}{=} 21$

$3 \cdot 7 \stackrel{?}{=} 21$

$21 = 21$ ✓

d. $\dfrac{\sqrt{x}}{2} = 18$

SOLUTION

$\dfrac{\sqrt{x}}{2} = 18$

$\dfrac{\sqrt{x}}{2} \cdot \dfrac{2}{1} = 18 \cdot \dfrac{2}{1}$ Multiplication Property of Equality

$\sqrt{x} = 36$ Simplify.

$(\sqrt{x})^2 = 36^2$ Square both sides.

$x = 1296$ Simplify.

$\dfrac{\sqrt{x}}{2} = 18$

$\dfrac{\sqrt{1296}}{2} \stackrel{?}{=} 18$

$\dfrac{36}{2} \stackrel{?}{=} 18$

$18 = 18$ ✓

INCLUSION

Students who have difficulty with mental processing may not remember how to approach equations where the radical is not already isolated. These students may square each side before isolating, which results in a dead end. Encourage students to develop a process tree to help them remember the process.

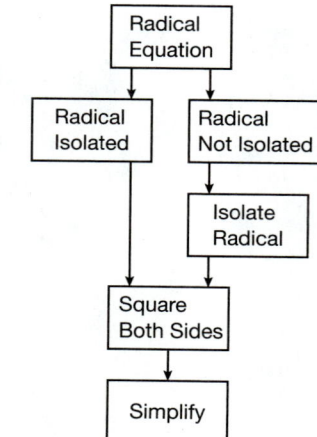

Some equations contain more than one radical expression. If possible, it is helpful to put the radical expressions on opposite sides of the equal sign.

Example 3 Solving With Square Roots on Both Sides

Solve each equation.

a. $\sqrt{x+2} = \sqrt{2x+4}$

SOLUTION

Use inverse operations.

$$\sqrt{x+2} = \sqrt{2x+4}$$
$$(\sqrt{x+2})^2 = (\sqrt{2x+4})^2 \quad \text{Square both sides.}$$
$$x + 2 = 2x + 4 \quad \text{Simplify.}$$
$$\underline{-2} = \underline{-2} \quad \text{Subtraction Property of Equality}$$
$$x = 2x + 2 \quad \text{Simplify.}$$
$$\underline{-2x} = \underline{-2x} \quad \text{Subtraction Property of Equality}$$
$$-x = 2 \quad \text{Simplify.}$$
$$x = -2 \quad \text{Multiply by } -1.$$

Check
$$\sqrt{x+2} = \sqrt{2x+4}$$
$$\sqrt{-2+2} \stackrel{?}{=} \sqrt{2(-2)+4}$$
$$\sqrt{0} \stackrel{?}{=} \sqrt{-4+4}$$
$$\sqrt{0} \stackrel{?}{=} \sqrt{0}$$
$$0 = 0 \checkmark$$

b. $\sqrt{x+2} - \sqrt{2x} = 0$

SOLUTION

Use inverse operations.

$$\sqrt{x+2} - \sqrt{2x} = 0$$
$$\underline{+\sqrt{2x}} = \underline{+\sqrt{2x}} \quad \text{Addition Property of Equality}$$
$$\sqrt{x+2} = \sqrt{2x} \quad \text{Simplify.}$$
$$(\sqrt{x+2})^2 = (\sqrt{2x})^2 \quad \text{Square both sides.}$$
$$x + 2 = 2x \quad \text{Simplify.}$$
$$\underline{-x} = \underline{-x} \quad \text{Subtraction Property of Equality}$$
$$2 = x \quad \text{Simplify.}$$

Check $\sqrt{x+2} - \sqrt{2x} = 0$
$$\sqrt{2+2} - \sqrt{2(2)} \stackrel{?}{=} 0$$
$$\sqrt{4} - \sqrt{4} \stackrel{?}{=} 0$$
$$0 = 0 \checkmark$$

Hint

When a single radical is on each side, begin by writing the equation without radical symbols.

Example 3

Explain to students that they must eliminate the radical symbols by squaring both sides.

Additional Example 3

Solve each equation.

a. $\sqrt{x+6} = \sqrt{2x+4}$ $x = 2$

b. $\sqrt{x+4} - \sqrt{3x} = 0$ $x = 2$

TEACHER TIP

As a class, it may be helpful to have students try to solve Example 2b by keeping the radicals on the same side of the equation. It not only will demonstrate to them that the equation becomes more complicated, it will sharpen skills that involve the FOIL method and multiplying radical expressions.

Lesson 106 715

Example 4

Error Alert Students may forget to square the right side of the equation. Remind them that in this case, they have to use the FOIL method.

Additional Example 4
Solve each equation.

a. $\sqrt{7x + 15} = x + 1$ $x = 7$

b. $\sqrt{x} + 6 = -3$ no solution

TEACHER TIP
Once students have solved a few problems of the type in Example 4b, ask them if they can identify under what conditions a radical equation will have no solution. They should respond that if the radical is isolated and equal to a negative number, then no solution will be possible as the square root of a real number is always positive.

Math Language
The **derived equation** is a new equation that results from squaring the original equation.

Hint
Remember that positive numbers have two square roots. By convention, $\sqrt{}$ returns the positive square root.

When both sides of an equation are squared to solve an equation, the resulting equation may have solutions that do not satisfy the original equation. Recall that an extraneous solution is a solution of a derived equation that does not satisfy the original equation.

Example 4 Determining Extraneous Solutions

Solve each equation.

a. $\sqrt{x - 1} = x - 3$

SOLUTION The radical expression is isolated. Use inverse operations.

$$\sqrt{x - 1} = x - 3$$
$$(\sqrt{x - 1})^2 = (x - 3)^2 \qquad \text{Square both sides.}$$
$$x - 1 = x^2 - 6x + 9 \qquad \text{Simplify.}$$
$$\underline{+1 = +1} \qquad \text{Addition Property of Equality}$$
$$x = x^2 - 6x + 10$$
$$\underline{-x = -x} \qquad \text{Subtraction Property of Equality}$$
$$0 = x^2 - 7x + 10 \qquad \text{Simplify.}$$
$$0 = (x - 2)(x - 5) \qquad \text{Factor.}$$
$$x - 2 = 0 \quad x - 5 = 0 \qquad \text{Write two equations.}$$
$$x = 2 \qquad x = 5 \qquad \text{Use inverse operations to simplify.}$$

Check $\sqrt{x - 1} = x - 3; x = 2$ $\qquad \sqrt{x - 1} = x - 3; x = 5$
$\sqrt{2 - 1} \stackrel{?}{=} 2 - 3 \qquad\qquad\qquad \sqrt{5 - 1} \stackrel{?}{=} 5 - 3$
$\sqrt{1} \stackrel{?}{=} -1 \qquad\qquad\qquad\qquad \sqrt{4} \stackrel{?}{=} 2$
$1 \neq -1 \quad \text{✗} \qquad\qquad\qquad\qquad 2 = 2 \quad \text{✓}$

The solution $x = 2$ is extraneous, so $x = 5$ is the only solution.

b. $\sqrt{x} + 5 = -2$

SOLUTION Use inverse operations to isolate the radical.

$$\sqrt{x} + 5 = -2$$
$$\underline{-5 = -5} \qquad \text{Subtraction Property of Equality}$$
$$\sqrt{x} = -7 \qquad \text{Simplify.}$$
$$(\sqrt{x})^2 = (-7)^2 \qquad \text{Square both sides.}$$
$$x = 49 \qquad \text{Simplify.}$$

Check $\sqrt{x} + 5 = -2$
$\sqrt{49} + 5 \stackrel{?}{=} -2$
$7 + 5 \stackrel{?}{=} -2$
$12 \neq -2 \quad \text{✗}$

The solution $x = 49$ is extraneous. There is no solution.

---

716 *Saxon Algebra 1*

Example 5 Application: Architecture

An architect is designing a performance center. If the area of the center is 30 square decameters, what is the area of the gallery?

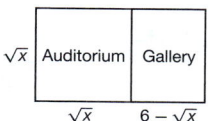

SOLUTION

total area = area of auditorium + area of gallery

$30 = (\sqrt{x})^2 + \sqrt{x}(6 - \sqrt{x})$

$30 = x + 6\sqrt{x} - x$ Simplify.

$30 = 6\sqrt{x}$ Combine like terms.

$5 = \sqrt{x}$ Divide both sides by 6.

$5^2 = (\sqrt{x})^2$ Square both sides.

$25 = x$ Simplify.

The area of the auditorium is 25 square decameters.

To find the area of the gallery, subtract the area of the auditorium from the total area.

$30 - 25 = 5$

The area of the gallery is 5 square decameters.

Math Reasoning

Analyze Is the answer reasonable?

yes; Sample: the sum of the areas of the gallery and the auditorium is the same as the area of the center: 5 dkm² + 25 dkm² = 30 dkm².

Lesson Practice

Solve each equation.

a. (Ex 1) $\sqrt{x} = 6$ $x = 36$
b. (Ex 1) $\sqrt{5x} = 15$ $x = 45$
c. (Ex 1) $\sqrt{x+3} = 12$ $x = 141$
d. (Ex 1) $\sqrt{4x - 15} = 7$ $x = 16$
e. (Ex 2) $\sqrt{x} - 8 = 5$ $x = 169$
f. (Ex 2) $\sqrt{x} + 8 = 15$ $x = 49$
g. (Ex 2) $6\sqrt{x} = 24$ $x = 16$
h. (Ex 2) $\frac{\sqrt{x}}{3} = 15$ $x = 2025$
i. (Ex 3) $\sqrt{x+4} = \sqrt{2x-1}$ $x = 5$
j. (Ex 3) $\sqrt{x+5} - \sqrt{6x} = 0$ $x = 1$
k. (Ex 4) $\sqrt{x-2} = x - 4$ $x = 6$
l. (Ex 4) $\sqrt{x} + 8 = -3$ no solution

m. (Ex 5) A breakfast nook has a planter along one side. The entire area of the nook is 42 square yards. What is the area of the planter?   6 yd²

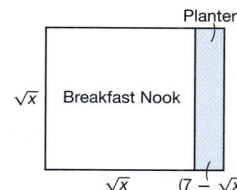

Practice Distributed and Integrated

1. (102) Solve $x^2 = 64$. $x = \pm 8$

2. (Inv 9) Factor $x^2 - 9x + 20$. $(x - 5)(x - 4)$

Lesson 106   717

Example 5

Extend the Example

"If the architect decreases the area of the center by $\frac{1}{3}$, what is the new area of the gallery?" $\frac{80}{9}$ dkm²

Additional Example 5

Linda is making a dollhouse for her little sister. If the area of the dollhouse is 216 square inches, what is the area of the kitchen in the dollhouse? 72 square inches

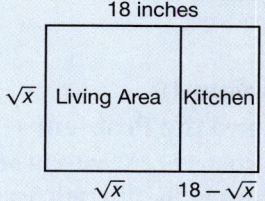

Lesson Practice

Problem i

Scaffolding Remind students to isolate the variables under the radical symbols by squaring both sides and combining like terms.

Problem k

Error Alert Make sure students check for extraneous solutions. In this case, $x = 3$ is extraneous.

Check for Understanding

The questions below help assess the concepts taught in this lesson.

"Why is it necessary to check every apparent solution of a radical equation in the original equation?" Sample: Sometimes there is an extraneous solution that does not work when it is substituted into the original equation.

"How do you solve a radical equation?" Sample: Isolate the radical, raise both sides to the same power to eliminate the radical, and then solve the equation.

3 Practice

Math Conversations
Discussion to strengthen understanding

Problem 4
Ask, "What operation is the inverse of division?" multiplication

Problem 5
Ask, "What is the first step needed to solve this problem?"
Square both sides to eliminate the radical signs.

Problem 10
Extend the Problem
Ask students, "What will be the area of the fifteenth figure?"
1,342,177,280 square feet

Problem 12
"Why should the equations be setup so that the coefficients of the x- or y-terms are opposites?"
Sample: so that the terms will cancel when the equations are added

"What should the first equation be multiplied by so that the x-terms are opposites? 3

"What should the second equation be multiplied by so that the x-terms are opposites? 5

---

3. Translate the inequality $3z + 4 < 10$ into a sentence. Sample: The sum of three times a number and 4 is less than 10.
(45)

*4. **Multiple Choice** Which of the following radical equations will require the use of division to isolate the radical? D
(106)

    A $\sqrt{x} - 12 = 2$ B $\sqrt{x} + 12 = 13$

    C $\dfrac{\sqrt{x}}{7} = 5$ D $14\sqrt{x} = 70$

5. no solution; When $x = -\frac{3}{2}$, the radicand is negative: $\sqrt{-\frac{3}{2} - 1} = \sqrt{-\frac{5}{2}}$.

*5. **Verify** Solve $\sqrt{x - 1} = \sqrt{3x + 2}$. Check your answer.
(106)

*6. **Justify** Solve $\dfrac{\sqrt{x}}{4} = 32$. Justify your answer. $x = 16{,}384$; $\dfrac{\sqrt{x}}{4} = 32$; $\sqrt{x} = 128$,
(106) multiplied both sides by 4; $x = 128^2$, squared both sides; $x = 16{,}384$.

*7. Find the common ratio of the geometric sequence $18, -9, 4\frac{1}{2}, -2\frac{1}{4}, \ldots$ $-\frac{1}{2}$
(105)

*8. Find the 6th term in the geometric series that has a common ratio of 2 and an initial term of 5.   160
(105)

9. **Multi-Step** Leila drops a ball from a height of 1 meter. The height of each bounce is 75% of the previous height.
(105)
   a. What is the ball's height after the first bounce?   0.75 meter
   b. What rule can be used to find the ball's height after n bounces? 0.75^n
   c. What is the height of the sixth bounce? Round your answer to the nearest hundredth.   0.18 meter

10. **Geometry** Each unit square in the figure represents 5 square feet. If the pattern continues, what will the area of the ninth figure be?   327,680 square feet
(105)

*11. **Botany** The growth of an ivy plant in feet can be described by $2\sqrt{x - 4}$. How many days x will it take for the ivy to reach a length of 20 feet? $x = 104$ days
(106)

12. Solve $\begin{array}{l} -5x + 4y = -37 \\ 3x - 6y = 33 \end{array}$ $(5, -3)$
(63)

*13. **Fractals** Fractals are geometric patterns that repeat themselves at smaller scales. The pattern shows fractals of equilateral triangles. How many unshaded triangles will be in the sixth figure?   243
(105)

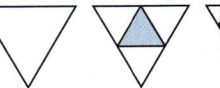

*14. Solve $x^2 + 9x = 4.75$ by completing the square. $x = 0.5$ or $x = -9.5$
(104)

15. **Error Analysis** Two students started solving the equation $2x^2 + 20x = -18$ as shown below. Which student is correct? Explain the error.
(104)

Student A; Sample: Student B did not divide all terms by 2 in the initial step.

Student A	Student B
$2x^2 + 20x = -18$	$2x^2 + 20x = -18$
$x^2 + 10x = -9$	$x^2 + 10x = -18$
$x^2 + 10x + 25 = -9 + 25$	$x^2 + 10x + 25 = -18 + 25$
$(x + 5)^2 = 16$	$(x + 5)^2 = 7$

718   Saxon Algebra 1

 ENGLISH LEARNERS

Explain the meaning of the word **bounce**. Say:

"A ball has bounced if a ball has been dropped or thrown, hit a surface, and traveled back in the opposite direction."

Ask students to name objects that can bounce. Sample: balls, putty, erasers

*16. **Business** The marketing group for a cosmetics company determined that the
(104) expression $u^2 - 0.8u$ represents the profit for every 1000 units u of mascara sold.
How many units need to be sold to have a profit margin of $0.33? **1100 units**

Solve each equation. Check your answer.

17. $x = 8$; $\frac{60}{4(8)} + \frac{45}{5(8)} = \frac{15}{8} + \frac{9}{8} = \frac{24}{8} = 3$

17. $\frac{60}{4x} + \frac{45}{5x} = 3$
(99)

*18. $\sqrt{x} = 9$ $x = 81$; $\sqrt{81} = 9$
(106)

19. **Egg Toss** Tyrese and Jameka were playing an egg-toss game. The egg's
(100) movement through the air formed a parabola given by the quadratic equation
$h = -16t^2 + 9t + 4$, where h is the height in feet and t is the time in seconds. Find
the maximum height of the path the egg makes and the time t when the egg hits
the ground. Round to the nearest hundredth. $h = 5.27$ feet and $t = 0.85$ seconds

20. Solve $x^2 - 16 = 0$ by graphing. $x = 4$ and $x = -4$
(100)

21. **Tennis** The weight w of a tennis ball should vary no more than $\frac{1}{12}$ ounce from $2\frac{1}{12}$
(101) ounces. Write an absolute-value inequality that models the acceptable weights.
What is the least acceptable weight? $\left|w - 2\frac{1}{12}\right| \leq \frac{1}{12}$; $2 \leq w \leq 2\frac{1}{6}$; 2 ounces

22. **Multiple Choice** Which is the simplest form of $\frac{18\sqrt{7}}{3\sqrt{28}}$?   **B**
(103)

A $\frac{3}{2}$ **B** 3   **C** $\frac{6\sqrt{7}}{\sqrt{28}}$ **D** $\frac{6\sqrt{7}}{7}$

23. **Write** Anton wants to estimate the quotient of $\frac{\sqrt{145}}{2\sqrt{9}}$. How should he do this?
(103)

24. Subtract $\frac{2r}{r-4} - \frac{6}{12-3r}$. $\frac{2(r+1)}{r-4}$
(90)

25. Solve and graph $|x - 16| \leq 12$. $4 \leq x \leq 28$;
(91)

26. Martha built a new playroom. She determined that the rectangular reading area
(93) is $(9x^2 + 44x - 5)$ square feet. The width is $(x + 5)$ feet. What is the length?
$(9x - 1)$ feet

27. **Volleyball** A server's hand is 3 feet above the floor when it hits the volleyball.
(96) After the volleyball is hit, it has an initial velocity of 23 feet per second. What is
its height after 1 second? Use $h = -16t^2 + vt + s$.   10 feet

23. Sample: Since $\sqrt{145}$ is close to $\sqrt{144}$, Anton should find the square root of 144 for the numerator (12) and multiply the square root of nine (3) by 2 in the denominator (6). The estimated quotient would be 2.

28. **Multi-Step** Tickets for the Valley High School production of *Romeo and Juliet* are
(97) $5 for adults and $4 for students. In order to cover expenses, at least $2500 worth
of tickets must be sold.
  a. Write an inequality that describes this situation. $5x + 4y \geq 2500$
  b. Graph the inequality.   See Additional Answers.
  c. If 200 adult and 400 student tickets are sold, will the expenses be covered?   yes

29. **Generalize** Consider the equation $(x - 5)(x + 8) = 0$. How can you quickly tell
(98) what the roots are?   Sample: The roots are the opposite of the constant term in
each factor.

30. The graph of $f(x) = x^2 + bx + 3$ has an axis of symmetry $x = 4$. What is the value
(Inv 10) of b? $b = -8$

Problem 22
Error Alert
Students may factor a 4 out of $\sqrt{28}$ instead of 2. Remind them to pull out the square root and not a factor of the radicand when factoring radicals.

Problem 28
Extend the Problem
"How much money would the drama club make if 200 adult and 400 student tickets were sold?"
$2600

Problem 29
Remind students that if either term is equal to zero, then the whole equation is equal to zero.

Lesson 106   719

 CHALLENGE

Solve $\sqrt{(x + 1)(x + 4)} = \sqrt{(x - 2)(x + 8)}$.
$x = 20$

LOOKING FORWARD

Solving radical equations prepares students for

• **Lesson 108** Identifying and Graphing Exponential Functions

• **Lesson 114** Graphing Square-Root Functions

Lesson 106   719

LESSON 107

1 Warm Up

Problem 5
If students do not see that there is no solution to this equation, ask them if $|x|$ can ever equal a negative number.

2 New Concepts

In this lesson, students learn how to graph absolute-value functions, using what they learn about the graph of the parent function to graph absolute value functions in other forms.

Example 1

Although an absolute-value function is nonlinear, its graph is two straight lines with opposite slopes that come to a shared point.

Additional Example 1
Graph the absolute-value function $f(x) = |-x|$. The graph will be the same as the graph in Example 1.

Have students explain why $y = |-x|$ will have the same table as the one shown in the solution of Example 1. Taking the absolute value of x or negative x will result in the same answer.

LESSON RESOURCES

Student Edition Practice
   Workbook 107
Reteaching Master 107
Adaptations Master 107
Challenge and Enrichment
   Master C107

LESSON 107

Graphing Absolute-Value Functions

Warm Up

1. **Vocabulary** A _____ is the simplest function of a particular type, or family. **parent function**

Simplify.

2. $3 \cdot 2 + 2|-5|$ **16**
3. $5 \cdot 8 - 4|-6|$ **16**
4. $4|x - 2| = 60$ **−13, 17**
5. $-3|x + 4| = 36$ **no solution**

New Concepts

A function whose rule has one or more absolute-value expressions is called an **absolute-value function**. The absolute-value parent function is $f(x) = |x|$.

Example 1 Graphing the Absolute-Value Parent Function

Graph the absolute-value parent function $f(x) = |x|$.

SOLUTION

Use a table to graph the function.

x	y
−2	2
−1	1
0	0
1	1
2	2

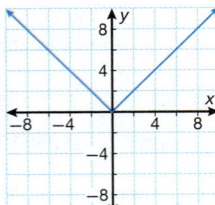

The absolute-value parent function forms the shape of a "V." The equation of the axis of symmetry of the absolute-value parent function is $x = 0$. The point on the axis of symmetry of the absolute-value graph, or the "corner" of the graph, is the **vertex of an absolute-value graph.**

The absolute-value function has two slopes. If the graph opens upward, the slope of the graph on the left of the axis of symmetry is −1. The slope of the graph on the right side of the axis of symmetry is 1.

Math Reasoning

Write Why is "axis of symmetry" an appropriate name?

Sample: One side of the graph is the mirror image of the other side of the graph over the axis of symmetry. The graph is symmetrical about the axis.

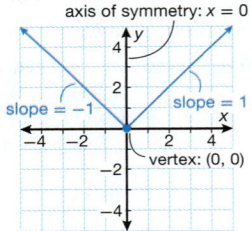

MATH BACKGROUND

First-degree equations generally only have one solution, but those with an absolute-value expression in them have more than one. Similar to quadratic equations, absolute-value equations have two solutions, which results in a nonlinear function when graphed.

The absolute-value function is defined by
$$|x| = \begin{cases} x & \text{if } x \geq 0 \\ -x & \text{if } x < 0 \end{cases}$$
This function is a composition of two other functions. If you take a number, square it, and then take its square root, you will find the absolute value of the number.

So, if $f(x) = x^2$ and $g(x) = \sqrt{x}$, then $g(f(x)) = \sqrt{x^2}$. The composition gives the graph of the function.

The domain of an absolute-value parent function is all real numbers, while the range is the interval $(0, \infty)$.

Absolute-value equations force a solution to be positive and are useful in computing standard deviations and distances.

Translations of Absolute-Value Graphs

The absolute-value parent function can be translated by adding or subtracting constants.

Vertical Translation	
If a constant k is added outside the absolute-value bars, the graph is translated up or down k units. For $f(x) = |x| + k$: • Graph translates up if $k > 0$. • Graph translates down if $k < 0$. • Coordinate of vertex is $(0, k)$.	The graph of $f(x) = |x| + k$, where $k = 1$, is shown. 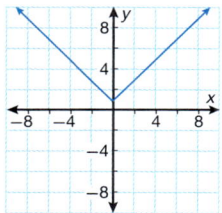 The graph of $f(x) = |x| + k$, where $k = -1$, is shown. 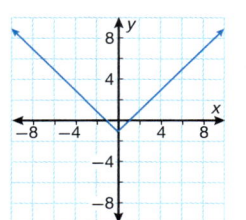
Horizontal Translation	
If a constant h is subtracted inside the absolute-value bars, the graph is translated right or left h units. For $f(x) = |x - h|$: • Graph translates right if $h > 0$. • Graph translates left if $h < 0$. • Coordinate of vertex is $(h, 0)$.	The graph of $f(x) = |x - h|$, where $h = 1$, is shown. 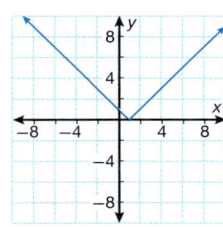 The graph of $f(x) = |x - h|$, where $h = -1$, is shown. 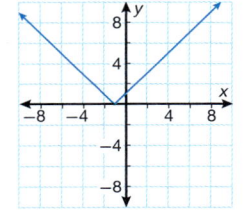

Reading Math

For positive h values, the graph moves right relative to the graph of the parent function and $f(x) = |x - h|$. For negative h values, the graph moves left and $f(x) = |x + h|$.

Online Connection
www.SaxonMathResources.com

Error Alert Students may choose to evaluate only positive values of x when they create a table of values for an absolute-value function. Make sure that they use a selection of numbers that include both negative and positive values so they correctly graph the function.

TEACHER TIP

Emphasize that a translation is simply a shift of a graph horizontally, vertically, or both. When students translate an absolute-value function, the result is a graph the same size and shape as the parent function, but in a different position. This can easily be demonstrated with a transparency on an overhead.

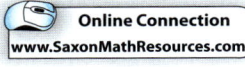 ENGLISH LEARNERS

For this lesson, explain the meaning of the word **translation**. Say:

"Translation comes from the word 'across' or 'change.' When a book written in English is then written in Spanish, a translation occurs. The language in which the book was written has changed, but the meaning of the words remains the same."

Discuss how 'translation' relates to shifts of the absolute-value parent function.

Example 2

Remind students that they can check their work by substituting ordered pairs from the graph into the equation.

Additional Example 2

Graph the function and give the coordinates of the vertex.

a. $f(x) = |x| + 3$

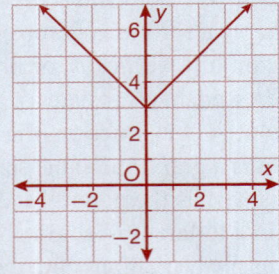

vertex: (0, 3)

b. $f(x) = |x - 4|$

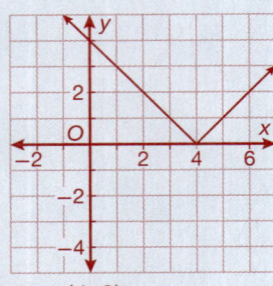

vertex: (4, 0)

Example 3

Remind students that they can check their work by substituting ordered pairs from the graph into the equation.

Additional Example 3

Graph the function and give the coordinates of the vertex.

$f(x) = |x + 2| - 1$

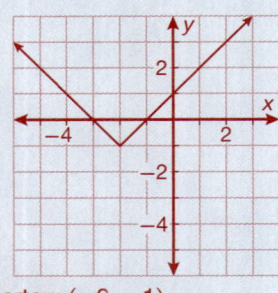

vertex: (−2, −1)

Example 2 Translating Absolute-Value Graphs

Graph the function and give the coordinates of the vertex.

a. $f(x) = |x| - 2$

SOLUTION

Use a table to graph the function.

x	−3	−2	−1	0	1	2	3
y	1	0	−1	−2	−1	0	1

The graph of the parent function is translated down 2 units. The vertex is (0, −2).

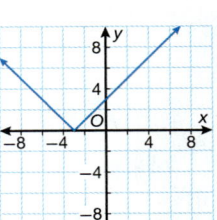

b. $f(x) = |x + 3|$

SOLUTION

Use a table to graph the function.

x	−6	−3	0	3	6
y	3	0	3	6	9

The graph of the parent function is translated left 3 units. The vertex is (−3, 0).

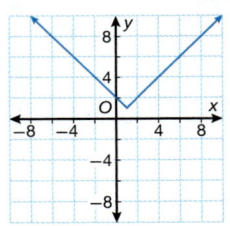

Multiple Translations of Absolute-Value Graphs

Vertical and Horizontal Translation	The graph of $f(x) = |x - h| + k$, where $h = 1$ and $k = 1$, is shown.
If a constant h is subtracted inside the absolute-value bars and a constant k is added outside the bars, as in $f(x) = |x - h| + k$. The graph is translated both vertically and horizontally. The vertex is at (h, k).	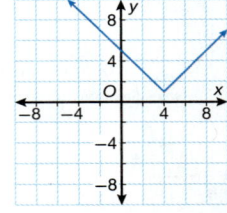

Example 3 Graphing Multiple Translations

Graph the function and give the coordinates of the vertex.

$f(x) = |x - 4| + 1$

Hint

Knowing how to translate the graph of $y = |x|$ using h and k can replace the use of a table of values to find points on the graph.

SOLUTION

The graph of the function is determined by translating the parent function. Evaluate how the function is different from the parent function.

The vertex is (4, 1).

ALTERNATE METHOD FOR EXAMPLE 3

Write and graph two linear equations using the definition of absolute value.

First isolate the absolute value.

$y = |x - 4| + 1$
$y - 1 = |x - 4|$

Now write one equation for when $x - 4 \geq 0$, and another for when $x - 4 < 0$.

$x - 4 \geq 0$ $x - 4 < 0$
$y - 1 = x - 4$ and $y - 1 = -(x - 4)$
$y = x - 3$ $y = -x + 5$

Graph each equation using the domain $x - 4 \geq 0$, or $x \geq 4$, for $y = x - 3$, and $x - 4 < 0$, or $x < 4$, for $y = -x + 5$.

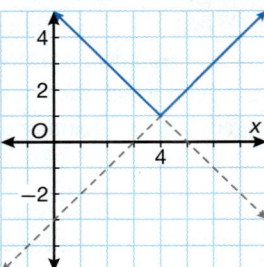

722 Saxon Algebra 1

Math Reasoning

Formulate What values are described by the inequality $|a| > 1$? $|a| < 1$?

Sample: $a > 1$ or $a < -1$; $-1 < a < 1$

Reflections, Stretches, and Compressions of Absolute-Value Graphs

The absolute-value parent function can be reflected, stretched, and compressed by multiplying by a constant a.

If $a < 0$, then the graph is reflected across the x-axis.
If $|a| > 1$, then the graph is stretched vertically, or away from the x-axis.
If $|a| < 1$, then the graph is compressed vertically, or toward the x-axis.

Example 4 Reflecting, Stretching, and Compressing Absolute-Value Graphs

Describe the graph of each function.

a. $f(x) = 3|x|$

SOLUTION

$a = 3$, so $|a| = 3$.

Since $|a| > 1$, the graph is stretched vertically.

b. $f(x) = -4|x|$

SOLUTION

$a = -4$, so $|a| = 4$.

Since $a < 0$, the graph is reflected across the x-axis.
Since $|a| > 1$, the graph is stretched vertically.

c. $f(x) = -0.2|x|$

SOLUTION

$a = -0.2$, so $|a| = 0.2$.

Since $a < 0$, the graph is reflected across the x-axis.
Since $|a| < 1$, the graph is compressed vertically.

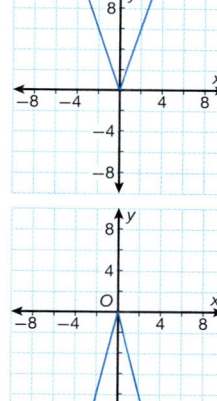
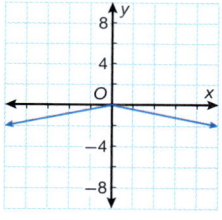
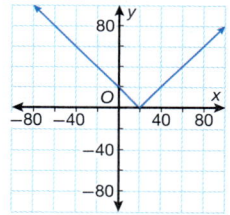

Hint

A function that is reflected can also be stretched or compressed.

Math Reasoning

Connect What other function is stretched or compressed vertically by changing the a value?

the quadratic function

Example 5 Application: Travel

A helicopter pilot is flying from town A to town B at 60 miles per hour. To make sure he is on course, he will fly over a landmark that he knows is 20 miles from town A. Write and graph the distance from the landmark as a function of minutes of flight time.

SOLUTION

Let a = rate = 60 mph = 1 mile per minute
Let h = time from landmark = $\frac{20}{1}$ = 20 minutes
Let k = closest distance to landmark = 0 miles

$f(x) = 1|x - 20| + 0$
$f(x) = 1|x - 20|$

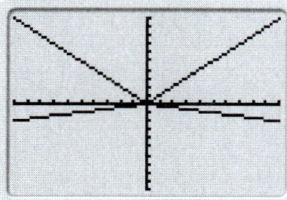

Lesson 107   723

Example 4

Absolute-value functions may be transformed in more than one way. Each transformation relates back to the parent function, $f(x) = |x|$.

Extend the Example

Challenge students to write an absolute-value function for $f(x) = |x|$ that meets the following parameters:

translated 2 units right and 3 units down and stretched vertically. any function $f(x) = a|x - 2| - 3$, where $a > 1$

Additional Example 4

Describe the graph of each function.

a. $f(x) = \frac{1}{4}|x|$ $a = \frac{1}{4}$, so $|a| = \frac{1}{4}$. Since $|a| < 1$, the graph is compressed vertically.

b. $f(x) = 8|x|$ $a = 8$, so $|a| = 8$. Since $|a| > 1$, the graph is stretched vertically.

c. $f(x) = -2.5|x|$ $a = -2.5$, so $|a| = 2.5$. Since $a < 0$, the graph is reflected across the x-axis. Since $|a| > 1$, the graph is stretched vertically.

Example 5

Additional Example 5

The path of a cue ball hitting the sidewall of a pool table is described by the function $f(x) = |x|$. For the next shot, the cue ball follows the same path except 12 inches to the right. Write and graph the function of the new path.

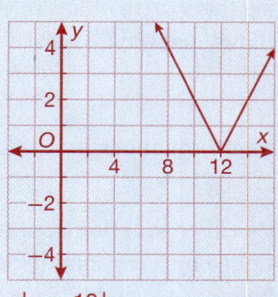

$f(x) = |x - 12|$

⚠️ **ALTERNATE METHOD FOR EXAMPLE 4c**

Graph the parent function $f(x) = |x|$ on a graphing calculator by using the absolute-value function and entering Y1 = abs(X). Now graph the function $f(x) = -0.2|x|$ using Y1 = -0.2abs(X). Compare the two graphs. Sample: The second graph is flipped over the x-axis and it is compressed vertically.

Lesson 107   723

Lesson Practice

Problem b
Error Alert If students mistakenly graph the vertex at (2, 0), remind them that they need to find a value for x that makes the expression within the absolute-value brackets equal to 0.

Problem f
Scaffolding First have students find the values for a and $|a|$, and then ask them where the graph is reflected if $a < 0$. Then ask how the value of a further changes the graph of the absolute-value parent function.

✓ Check for Understanding
The questions below help assess the concepts taught in this lesson.

"How is the vertex of an absolute-value function found?"
Sample: Find the values of h and k in the function and use (h, k).

"What are two different absolute-value functions that share the same vertex?" Sample: $y = |x|$; $y = |-x|$

3 Practice

Math Conversations
Discussion to strengthen understanding

Problem 8
Guide students by asking them the following questions.

"What is the best method for solving this system of linear equations, and why?" elimination; Sample: Solving by substitution would require computing with fractions.

"Are both equations in standard form?" no

"Does either equation need to be multiplied by a constant in order to eliminate a variable?" Yes, both equations need to be multiplied by a constant.

724 Saxon Algebra 1

Lesson Practice

Graph each function and give the coordinates of the vertex.

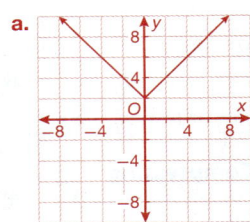

a. (Ex 2) $f(x) = |x| + 2$. (0, 2)
b. (Ex 2) $f(x) = |x + 2|$. (−2, 0); See Additional Answers.
c. (Ex 3) $f(x) = |x − 1| + 2$ (1, 2); See Additional Answers.

Describe the graph of each function.
d. (Ex 4) $f(x) = 4|x|$ Since $|a| > 1$, the graph is stretched vertically.
e. $f(x) = −2|x|$ Since $a < 0$, the graph is reflected across the x-axis. Since $|a| > 1$, the graph is stretched vertically.
f. $f(x) = −0.5|x|$

g. (Ex 5) The distance of a truck to a manhole cover is given by the function $f(t) = |t| + 25$. Write the function representing the distance of a truck starting at the same location, but traveling twice as fast. $f(t) = 2|t| + 25$

f. Since $a < 0$, the graph is reflected across the x-axis. Since $|a| < 1$, the graph is compressed vertically.

Practice   Distributed and Integrated

*1. **Estimate** Without graphing the function, which direction would the function (107) $f(x) = |x| − 6$ shift the parent function? down

2. Solve $\sqrt{2x} = 14$. Check your answer. $x = 98$; $\sqrt{2(98)} = \sqrt{196} = 14$
(106)

3. Write $5y − 29 = −14x$ in standard form. $14x + 5y = 29$
(35)

*4. **Multiple Choice** What absolute-value function is shown by the graph? C
(107)
   A $f(x) = 2|x|$ B $f(x) = 0.5|x|$
   C $f(x) = −5|x|$ D $f(x) = −0.5|x|$

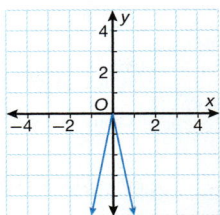

5. Translate the inequality $3b + \frac{2}{5} \geq 1\frac{3}{5}$ into a sentence. Sample: The sum of 3 times an unknown and $\frac{2}{5}$ is greater than or equal to $1\frac{3}{5}$.
(45)

*6. (Boating) The path of a sailboat is represented by the function
(107) $f(x) = \left|\frac{3}{5}x − 30\right| + 30$. At what point does the sailboat tack (turn)? (50, 30)

*7. **Write** Why does the graph of an absolute-value function not extend past the vertex?
(107)

8. Solve the system of linear equations: $\begin{matrix} 4y = −3x − 4 \\ 4x + 6 = −5y \end{matrix}$. (−4, 2)
(63)

*9. **Geometry** The perimeter of the square is 20 centimeters. Solve for x. $x = 25$ cm
(106)

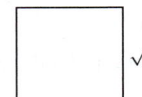

7. Sample: The absolute-value function has a minimum value and that is the y-value at the vertex.

724   Saxon Algebra 1

⬥ INCLUSION

Have students who are struggling with the lesson's concepts and abstractions graph the line $y = x$, but tell them that it cannot go below the x-axis. Then have them graph the line $y = −x$, and again give the condition that the line cannot go below the x-axis.

"At which point do these two lines meet?" (0, 0)

"In an absolute-value function, what is this point called?" the vertex

"What do all the values of y have in common?" They are all positive.

*10. Error Analysis Two students found the solution for a radical equation. Which
(106) student is correct? Explain the error.   Student A; Sample: Student B squared
incorrectly and should have subtracted seven from both sides, first.

Student A	Student B
$\sqrt{x} + 7 = 14$	$\sqrt{x} + 7 = 14$
$\sqrt{x} = 7$	$\sqrt{x} + 49 = 196$
$x = 49$	$\sqrt{x} = 147$
	$x = 21{,}609$

11. Jason built a new deck with an area of $(-20x + 100 + x^2)$ square feet. The width
(93) is $(x - 10)$ feet. What is the length? $(x - 10)$ feet

*12. Multi-Step A triangular brace is constructed in the shape of a right triangle. The
(106) two legs of the brace are $\sqrt{x + 5}$ and $\sqrt{x}$ units long.
  a. What expression could be used to solve for the length, l, of the third side
     of the brace? $(\sqrt{x+5})^2 + (\sqrt{x})^2 = l^2$
  b. Simplify the equation so it does not contain any radicals. $2x + 5 = l^2$
  c. Find the value of x for which the length of the third side of the brace is equal
     to 10. $x = \frac{95}{2}$

13. Coordinate Geometry Find the coordinates of the point(s) at which the graphs of
(106) $y = x$ and $y = \sqrt{x}$ intersect. (0, 0), (1, 1)

14. Find the next 3 terms of the sequence 125, 25, 5, 1.   0.2, 0.04, 0.008
(105)

*15. Carbon Dating Scientists can use the ratio of radioactive carbon-14 to carbon-12 to
(105) find the age of organic objects. Carbon-14 has a half-life of about 5730 years, which
means that after 5730 years, half the original amount remains. Carbon dating can date
objects to about 50,000 years ago, or about 9 half-lives. About what percent of the
original amount of carbon-14 remains in objects about 50,000 years old?   about 0.2%

*16. Error Analysis Two students find the 5th term in a geometric series that has a common
(105) ratio of $\frac{1}{2}$ and a first term of 6. Which student is correct? Explain the error.

Student A	Student B	
$A(n) = ar^{n-1}$	$A(n) = ar^{n-1}$	Student A; Student B incorrectly multiplied by 4 rather than using 4 as an exponent.
$= 6 \cdot \left(\frac{1}{2}\right)^4$	$= 6 \cdot \frac{1}{2} \cdot 4$	
$= \frac{3}{8}$	$= 12$	

17. Solve by graphing on a graphing calculator. Round to the nearest tenth.
(100)
$$-11x^2 + x = -4 \quad x = -0.6 \text{ and } 0.7$$

Solve and graph each inequality.

18. $|x - 4| + 15 \geq 21$ $x \leq -2$ OR $x \geq 10$ **19.** $|x| + 45 \leq 34$ $\{\varnothing\}$;
(101)   (91)

Problem 11
Have students write the area as
a trinomial in standard form,
and point out that they can use
what they learned about special
product patterns to factor the
trinomial into a perfect-square
binomial.

Students may need a reminder
that the square root of any
quantity squared is the quantity.
Use $(\sqrt{25})^2 = (5)^2 = 25$ as an
example.

Lesson 107   725

⭐ CHALLENGE

Have students graph the function
$f(x) = |x^2 - 2x - 4|$ using a table of values.

Describe how this graph differs from the
graph of the function $f(x) = x^2 - 2x - 4$.
Sample: Because there cannot be a negative
value for y, the points that fall below the x-axis
are "flipped," or reflected over the x-axis.

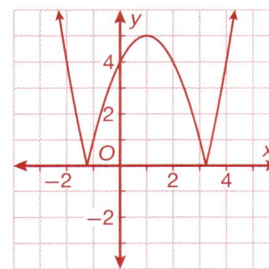

Lesson 107   725

Problem 21
Extend the Problem
"Maria wants to build a circular deck around her new pool that has a width of x meters. Write an expression to determine the area of the deck." $\pi(x+8)^2 - 200.96$

"If the area of the deck is equal to 113.04 square meters, what is the width of the deck?" 2 meters

Problem 25
Error Alert
Students may make errors if they miss a step while simplifying. Suggest they use the checklist:
1) Factor each denominator completely. 2) Find the LCD. 3) Write equivalent fractions. 4) Add the terms in the numerator. 5) Divide the expression in the numerator by the expression in the denominator.

Problem 28
Discuss with students the domain and range of the situation. Use only Quadrant 1 since a negative number of tickets cannot be sold. Since only a whole number of tickets can be sold, all the points with whole-number coordinates on or above the line are the different combinations of tickets that can be sold.

---

20. Football NCAA rules require that the circumference c of a football, measured around its widest part, 21 inches, to vary by no more than 0.25 inches. Write and solve an absolute-value inequality that models the acceptable circumferences. What is the least acceptable circumference? $|c - 21| \leq 0.25$; $20.75 \leq c \leq 21.25$; 20.75 inches

21. Area of a Pool Maria wants to increase the radius of a pool by 3 meters. The new area of the pool is 200.96 square meters.
a. Write a formula to find the original radius of the pool.
b. Solve the formula. $r = 5$ m $\quad \pi(r+3)^2 = 200.96$
c. What will the new diameter of the pool be? 16 m

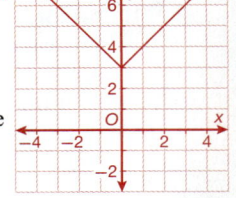

*22. Graph the function $f(x) = |x| + 3$.

22.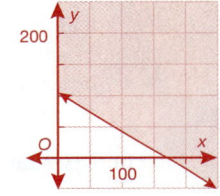

23. Multiple Choice Solve $-3x^2 + 24x = 36$. C
A $x = -8$ or 0 B $x = -6$ or 2 C $x = 2$ or 6 D $x = 0$ or 8

24. Analyze Determine what values of c would make the equation $x^2 - 50x = c$ have no solution. $c < -625$

Simplify.

25. $\dfrac{\dfrac{4x}{2x+12} + \dfrac{x}{3x+18}}{\dfrac{8x^2}{x^2+8x+12}}$ $\quad \dfrac{7(x+2)}{24x}$

26. $\sqrt{\dfrac{20}{3}}$ $\quad \dfrac{2\sqrt{15}}{3}$

27. Multi-Step A businessman makes $50 profit on each item sold. He would like to make $950 plus or minus $100 total each week.
a. Write an absolute-value equation for the minimum and maximum profit he desires. $|50x - 950| = 100$
b. What is the minimum and maximum number of items he needs to sell each week? 17 items, 21 items

28. School Dance Tickets for the school dance are $4 for middle school students and $6 for high school students. In order to cover expenses, at least $600 worth of tickets must be sold. Write an inequality that models this situation and graph it.

28. $4x + 6y \geq 600$;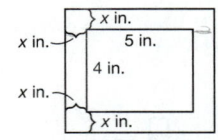

29. Multi-Step A painting is 5 inches by 4 inches. The frame around it is x inches wide.
a. Write expressions for the length and width of the picture with the frame.
b. The total area of the picture and frame is 42 square inches. What is the width of the frame? 1 inch

30. Justify Explain how to transform $\dfrac{x}{x-3} = \dfrac{4}{x}$ to $x^2 = 4x - 12$. Sample: cross multiply

29a. $5 + 2x$, $4 + 2x$

726 *Saxon Algebra 1*

LOOKING FORWARD

Graphing absolute-value functions prepares students for

- **Lesson 108** Identifying and Graphing Exponential Functions
- **Lesson 114** Graphing Square-Root Functions
- **Lesson 115** Graphing Cubic Functions
- **Lesson 119** Graphing and Comparing Linear, Quadratic, and Exponential Functions

LESSON 108

Identifying and Graphing Exponential Functions

Warm Up

1. **Vocabulary** In the expression 3^5, 5 is the _____. exponent

   Simplify.

2. 4^2 16
3. 6^{-3} $\frac{1}{216}$
4. $2 \cdot 5^{-2}$ $\frac{2}{25}$
5. $5 \cdot 2^{-1}$ $\frac{5}{2}$

New Concepts

In a geometric sequence, any term, except the first, can be found by multiplying the previous term by the common ratio. In the geometric sequence 2, 6, 18, 54, 162, …, the common ratio is 3.

The sequence can also be written like this: 2, $2(3)^1$, $2(3)^2$, $2(3)^3$, $2(3)^4$, …. Or, with a_1 representing the first term and r representing the common ratio, it can be written as a_1, $a_1(r)^1$, $a_1(r)^2$, $a_1(r)^3$, $a_1(r)^4$, ….

Using n as the term number, observe that the nth term of a geometric sequence can be found by using the rule $a_n = a_1 r^{n-1}$.

Notice that the independent variable n occurs in the exponent of the function rule. Any function for which the independent variable is an exponent is an **exponential function**.

Exponential Function
An exponential function is a function of the form $f(x) = ab^x$, where a and b are nonzero constants and b is a positive number not equal to 1.

Reading Math

The value of b in an exponential function is comparable to r in a geometric sequence.

Example 1 Evaluating an Exponential Function

Evaluate each function for the given values.

a. $f(x) = 5^x$ for $x = -3, 0,$ and 4.

SOLUTION

Use the order of operations.

$f(-3) = 5^{-3} = \frac{1}{5^3} = \frac{1}{125}$, $f(0) = 5^0 = 1$, $f(4) = 5^4 = 625$

b. $f(x) = 2(4)^x$ for $x = -1, 1,$ and 2.

SOLUTION

Use the order of operations. Evaluate exponents before multiplying.

$f(-1) = 2(4)^{-1} = 2 \cdot \frac{1}{4} = \frac{2}{4} = \frac{1}{2}$

$f(1) = 2(4)^1 = 2(4) = 8$

$f(2) = 2(4)^2 = 2(16) = 32$

Hint

$a^{-n} = \frac{1}{a^n}$

MATH BACKGROUND

By restricting the domain to the whole numbers, exponential functions can represent geometric sequences where each successive term is multiplied by the same value.

Exponential functions are nonlinear functions that have a variety of applications, including tracking growth, population changes, compound interest, and predicting decay, such as that studied in carbon dating and other half-life calculations.

LESSON 108

1 Warm Up

Problems 3–5

Remind students that a base with a negative exponent can be expressed as the reciprocal of the base to the opposite exponential value.

2 New Concepts

In this lesson, students will investigate exponential patterns and graph them. They will also look at applications of exponential functions, such as growth.

Example 1

In an exponential function, the value of the base of the exponent is constant and the exponent is the term that changes.

Additional Example 1

Evaluate each function for the given values.

a. $f(x) = (-3)^x$ for $x = -2, 0,$ and 3. $\frac{1}{9}$, 1, -27

b. $f(x) = 2(2)^x$ for $-2, 2,$ and 7. $\frac{1}{2}$, 8, 256

LESSON RESOURCES

Student Edition Practice Workbook 108
Reteaching Master 108
Adaptations Master 108
Challenge and Enrichment Master C108
Technology Lab Master 108

Example 2

Point out that the pattern of the outputs of the terms in an exponential function is multiplicative. If students were to look for the differences, they would not find a constant difference between successive terms.

Extend the Example

Using the formula for a geometric sequence, find the ordered pair with an x-coordinate of 5. −729

Additional Example 2

Determine if each set of ordered pairs satisfies an exponential function. Explain your answer.

a. $\{(2, 4), (1, 2), (4, 128), (3, 16)\}$ Because the ratios are not the same, the ordered pairs do not satisfy an exponential function.

b. $\{(12, 64), (4, 4), (16, 256), (8, 16)\}$ Because each ratio is the same, 4, the base $b = 4$. The set of ordered pairs satisfies an exponential function.

Reading Math

In the expression $f(x) = 4(2)^x$, 2 is the base and x is the exponent.

The common ratio of a geometric sequence is comparable to the base of an exponential function. For any exponential function, as the x-values change by a constant amount, the y-values change by a constant factor. For $f(x) = 4(2)^x$, as each x-value increases by 1, each y-value increases by a factor of 2.

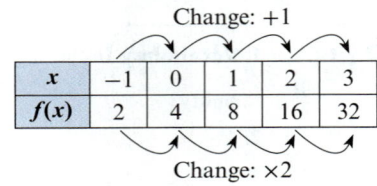

The base 2 of the exponential function $f(x) = 4(2)^x$ is the common ratio of the sequence 2, 4, 8, 16, 32, ….

Example 2 Identifying an Exponential Function

Determine if each set of ordered pairs satisfies an exponential function. Explain your answer.

a. $\left\{(0, -3), \left(-2, -\frac{1}{3}\right), (1, -9), (-1, -1)\right\}$

SOLUTION

Arrange the ordered pairs so that the x-values are increasing.

$\left\{\left(-2, -\frac{1}{3}\right), (-1, -1), (0, -3), (1, -9)\right\}$

The x-values increase by the constant amount of 1.

Divide each y-value by the y-value before it.

$-1 \div -\frac{1}{3} = -1 \times -3 = 3$

$-3 \div -1 = 3$

$-9 \div -3 = 3$

Because each ratio is the same, 3, the base $b = 3$. The set of ordered pairs satisfies an exponential function.

b. $\{(6, 150), (4, 100), (8, 200), (2, 50)\}$

SOLUTION

Arrange the ordered pairs so that the x-values are increasing.

$\{(2, 50), (4, 100), (6, 150), (8, 200)\}$

The x-values increase by the constant amount of 2.

Divide each y-value by the y-value before it.

$100 \div 50 = 2$

$150 \div 100 = 1\frac{1}{2}$

$200 \div 150 = 1\frac{1}{3}$

Because the ratios are not the same, the ordered pairs do not satisfy an exponential function.

Math Reasoning

Analyze What type of function do the ordered pairs in Example 2b satisfy, and why?

linear function; The range values increase by the constant amount of 50.

INCLUSION FOR EXAMPLE 2b

A table of values can be useful in helping visual learners identify any patterns in the values of the functions. If the pattern in the values is multiplicative, the function is exponential. Have students make a table like the one shown for Example 2b. Show them that the y-value does not change by the same ratio, and therefore is not an exponential function.

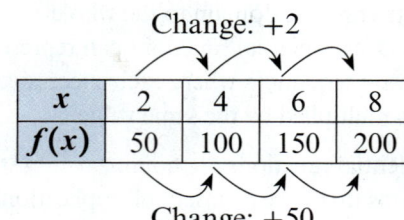

To graph an exponential function, make a table of ordered pairs and plot the points. The graph will always form a curve that comes close to, but never touches, the x-axis.

Example 3 Graphing $y = ab^x$

Graph each function by making a table of ordered pairs.

a. $y = 5(2)^x$

SOLUTION

Choose both positive and negative x-values.

x	y
−2	1.25
−1	2.5
0	5
1	10
2	20

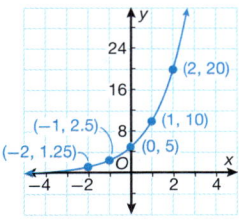

b. $y = -(3)^x$

SOLUTION

x	y
−1	$-\frac{1}{3}$
0	−1
1	−3
2	−9
3	−27

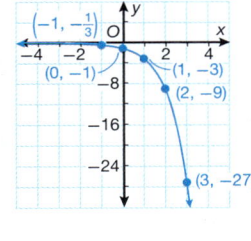

c. $y = 6\left(\dfrac{1}{2}\right)^x$

SOLUTION

x	y
−2	24
−1	12
0	6
1	3
2	1.5

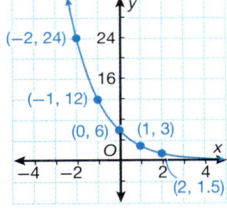

Caution

Due to limitations of scale, graphs of exponential functions often appear to touch the x-axis. The graph will approach but never touch the x-axis. Since $a \neq 0$ and $b \neq 0$, then $y \neq 0$.

Math Reasoning

Generalize Compare the domains and ranges of the functions in Examples 3a and 3b.

The domains for both are the same: all real numbers. In 3a, the range is real numbers greater than 0, in 3b it is real numbers less than 0.

Example 3

Creating a table of values is the best method for graphing an exponential equation without technology.

TEACHER TIP

Remind students to use the order of operations to simplify the expressions.

Additional Example 3

Graph each function by making a table of ordered pairs.

a. $y = -4^x$

x	−1	0	1	2	3
y	$-\frac{1}{4}$	−1	−4	−16	−64

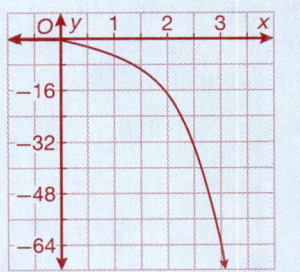

b. $y = 8(2)^x$

x	−2	−1	0	1	2
y	2	4	8	16	32

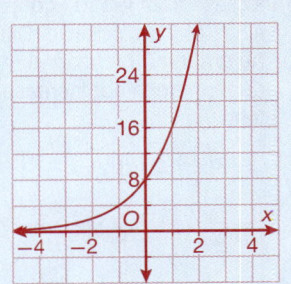

c. $y = 4\left(\dfrac{1}{4}\right)^x$

x	−1	0	1	2
y	16	4	1	$\frac{1}{4}$

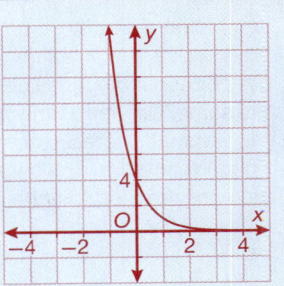

INCLUSION

Students may need additional help in organizing their work. Have them create a table of values. Offer them blank copies of the table at right to help show the substitution step. Give them space to simplify the expressions.

The function $y = 5(2)^x$ is evaluated for $x = -2$ as an example.

x	Substitute	Simplify	y
−2	$y = 5(2)^{-2}$	$y = 5\left(\frac{1}{4}\right)$	1.25

Example 4

Changes to the values of the coefficient or base of an exponential equation affect the shape and characteristics of the graph.

Error Alert Students may think that any function with an exponential term is an exponential function. Have them look carefully at the function and determine if the exponent has a variable term in it. If the exponent is constant, then it is not an exponential function.

Additional Example 4

Using a graphing calculator, graph each pair of functions on the same screen. Tell how the graphs are alike and how they are different.

a. $y = 2(2)^x$ and $y = \frac{1}{2}(2)^x$

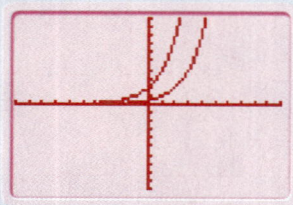

Sample: Alike: Both graphs increase from left to right and all values of y are positive. Different: The graph of the second equation does not increase as steeply as the first.

b. $y = 3\left(\frac{1}{2}\right)^x$ and $y = -3\left(\frac{1}{2}\right)^x$

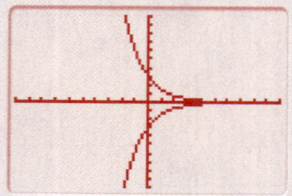

Sample: Alike: Both graphs are symmetric about the x-axis. For any x-value, the absolute value of the corresponding y-values are the same. Different: When $a = 3$, the y-values decrease from left to right. When $a = -3$, the y-values increase from left to right.

A graphing calculator is helpful with comparing graphs of functions and formulating rules based on the values of a and b.

Example 4 Comparing Graphs

Using a graphing calculator, graph each pair of functions on the same screen. Tell how the graphs are alike and how they are different.

a. $y = 3(2)^x$ and $y = -3(2)^x$

SOLUTION

Use **Y=** to enter the equations. Use **GRAPH** to graph the equations.

Hint
Use **ZOOM** 6 to set the intervals on the x-axis and y-axis from −10 to 10.

 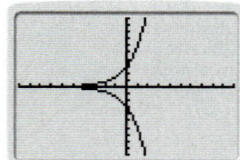

Alike: Both graphs are symmetric about the x-axis. For any x-value, the absolute values of the corresponding y-values are the same.

Different: When $a = 3$, the y-values increase from left to right. When $a = -3$, the y-values decrease from left to right.

Math Reasoning

Generalize For which values of b, 2 or $\frac{1}{2}$, do the y-values approach 0 as x increases? As x decreases?

$b = \frac{1}{2}$; $b = 2$

b. $y = 3(2)^x$ and $y = 3\left(\frac{1}{2}\right)^x$

SOLUTION

 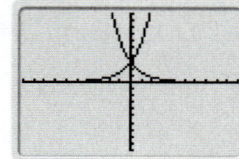

Alike: Both graphs are above the x-axis and symmetric about the y-axis. For any y-value, the absolute values of the corresponding x-values are the same.

Different: When $b = 2$, the y-values increase from left to right. When $b = \frac{1}{2}$, the y-values decrease from left to right.

Example 5 Application: Population

The exponential function $y = 12.28(1.00216)^x$ models the approximate population of Pennsylvania from 2000 to 2006, where x is the number of years after 2000 and y represents millions of people. Use a graphing calculator to find the approximate population of Pennsylvania in 2005. Assuming the model does not change, when will the population reach 13 million?

⚠ ALTERNATE METHOD FOR EXAMPLE 4a

Students can also compare pairs of functions by making tables instead of graphing.

$y = 3(2)^x$

x	−2	−1	0	1	2
y	0.75	1.5	3	6	12

$y = -3(2)^x$

x	−2	−1	0	1	2
y	−0.75	−1.5	−3	−6	−12

> **Caution**
> The variable y represents millions of people. The table entry $y_1 = 12.413$ means 12.413 million.

SOLUTION Enter the function rule into the Y= editor. Access the Table function by pressing [2nd] [GRAPH]. Since 2005 is 5 years after 2000, find the y-value for $x = 5$. The population was about 12,413,000. To find when the population will reach 13 million, scroll down until y equals 13 or more. It occurs during the 27th year after 2000, or 2027.

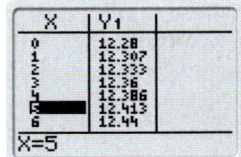   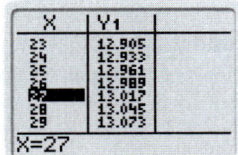

Lesson Practice

Evaluate each function for the given values.

(Ex 1)
a. Evaluate $f(x) = 2^x$ for $x = -4, 0$, and 5. $f(-4) = \frac{1}{16}, f(0) = 1, f(5) = 32$
b. Evaluate $f(x) = -3(3)^x$ for $x = -3, 1$, and 3. $f(-3) = -\frac{1}{9}, f(1) = -9, f(3) = -81$

Determine whether each set of ordered pairs satisfies an exponential function. Explain your answer.

(Ex 2)
c. $\{(3, -12), (6, -24), (12, -48), (9, -36)\}$ No, the y-values do not have a common ratio.
d. $\{(3, 108), (1, 12), (2, 36), (4, 324)\}$ Yes, as x increases by 1, the ratio of the y-values = 3.

Graph each function by making a table of ordered pairs.

(Ex 3)
e. $y = 2(3)^x$ f. $y = -4(2)^x$ g. $y = 2\left(\frac{1}{4}\right)^x$
See Additional Answers. See Additional Answers. See Additional Answers.

Using a graphing calculator, graph each pair of functions on the same screen. Tell how the graphs are alike and how they are different.

h. Sample: Alike: Both are symmetric about the x-axis. For any x-value, the absolute values of the y-values are the same. Different: When a is positive, all the range values are positive. When a is negative, all the range values are negative.

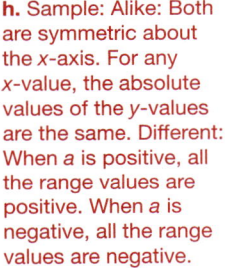

h. $y = \left(\frac{1}{3}\right)^x$ and $y = -\left(\frac{1}{3}\right)^x$
(Ex 4)

i. $y = -2(3)^x$ and $y = -2\left(\frac{1}{3}\right)^x$
(Ex 4)

i. Sample: Alike: Both graphs are below the x-axis and symmetic about the y-axis. Different: When b is 3, the y-values decrease as the x-values increase. When b is $\frac{1}{3}$, the y-values increase as the x-values increase.

j. The exponential function $y = 8.05(1.01683)^x$ models the approximate population of North Carolina from 2000 to 2006, where x is the number of years after 2000 and y represents millions of people. Use a graphing calculator to find the approximate population of North Carolina in 2006. Assuming the model does not change, when will the population reach 10 million? 8,897,900; 2013
(Ex 5)

Practice   Distributed and Integrated

*1. Evaluate the function $f(x) = 2(5)^x$ for $x = -2, 0$, and 2. $\frac{2}{25}$, 2, 50
(108)

2. Graph the function $f(x) = |x - 2|$. See Additional Answers.
(107)

Lesson 108   731

Example 5

Remind students that since the variable represents the years after 2000, they must determine a value and add 2000 to it to find the actual year. Also point out that y represents millions of people, so 12.28 means 12,280,000 people.

Additional Example 5

Assuming the model does not change, when will the population reach 15 million? **2092**

Lesson Practice

Problem b
Error Alert Remind students to evaluate the exponent before multiplying by the coefficient −3.

Problem c
Scaffolding Remind students to organize the data so that the first coordinates are in increasing order.

✓ Check for Understanding

The questions below help assess the concepts taught in this lesson.

"Use the number 2 and the variable x to create a linear equation. Describe its graph."
Sample: $f(x) = 2x$; The graph would be a straight line with a slope of 2, and a constant difference of 2 in the y-values.

"Use the number 2 and the variable x to create a quadratic equation. Describe its graph."
Sample: $f(x) = x^2$; The graph is a parabola and there is no constant difference or ratio in the y-values.

"Use the number 2 and the variable x to create an exponential equation. Describe its graph."
Sample: $f(x) = 2^x$; The graph is nonlinear and the constant ratio of the y-values is 2.

 ALTERNATE METHOD FOR EXAMPLE 5

Students could use a graphing calculator to solve the problem in Example 5.

They should graph the equation given as Y1. Then they should graph $y = 13$ as Y2, and use the CALC function to find the intersection and get an exact value. Since the x-value of the point of intersection is approximately 26.4, the population reaches 13 million during the 27th year.

Lesson 108   731

3 Practice

Math Conversations
Discussion to strengthen understanding

Problem 7
Have students draw each triangle before they identify corresponding sides and angles.

Problem 10
Error Alert
Some students may want to drop the negative sign when they solve because they are thinking about the principal square root. Remind them that the root they are looking for is odd, which maintains the negative value.

Problem 11
Students may need to graph a few points of the function $f(x)$ in order to determine why the function is in the shape of a "V".

---

*3. **Justify** Why is $f(x) = 4(1)^x$ not an exponential function?
(108)

*4. **Multiple Choice** Which could be the function graphed? B
(108)
  A $y = -\left(\frac{1}{2}\right)^x$
  B $y = \left(\frac{1}{2}\right)^x$
  C $y = -(2)^x$
  D $y = 2^x$

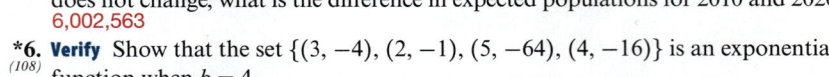

*5. (**Population**) The exponential function $y = 20.85(1.0212)^x$ can model the
(108) approximate population of Texas from 2000 to 2006, where x is the number of years after 2000 and y represents millions of people. Assuming the model does not change, what is the difference in expected populations for 2010 and 2020? 6,002,563

*6. **Verify** Show that the set $\{(3, -4), (2, -1), (5, -64), (4, -16)\}$ is an exponential
(108) function when $b = 4$.

7. Name the corresponding sides and angles if $\triangle RST \sim \triangle NVQ$. $\overline{RS}$ and $\overline{NV}$; $\overline{ST}$
(36) and $\overline{VQ}$; $\overline{RT}$ and $\overline{NQ}$; $\angle R$ and $\angle N$; $\angle S$ and $\angle V$; $\angle T$ and $\angle Q$

*8. **Multi-Step** Graph the parent function $f(x) = |x|$. Translate the function down
(107) by 2. Then reflect the function across the x-axis. What is the new function? $f(x) = -|x| - 2$

9. Is the graph an absolute-value function? Explain. no; Sample: There is no axis of symmetry.
(107)

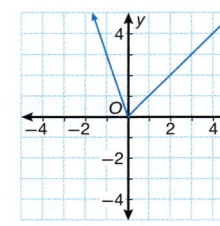

10. Evaluate $\sqrt[3]{x}$ when $x = (-4)^3$. -4
(46)

*11. **Geometry** Describe why the function $f(x) = |x|$ is in the shape of a "V".
(107) Sample: The output is the same for x and $-x$.

12. **Error Analysis** Two students found the solution to a radical equation. Which student
(106) is correct? Explain the error.

Student A	Student B
$\sqrt{x+3} = 6$	$\sqrt{x+3} = 6$
$x + 9 = 36$	$x + 3 = 36$
$x = 27$	$x = 33$

13. Solve $\sqrt{x} - 2 = 8$. Check your answer. $x = 100$; $\sqrt{100} - 2 = 10 - 2 = 8$
(106)

---

3. Sample: Because 1 raised to any power is 1, and 4 would be multiplied by 1 for every value of x, the resulting constant linear function is $f(x) = 4$.

6. Sample: When the ordered pairs are arranged so that the x-values are 2, 3, 4, and 5, then the y-values are -1, -4, -16, and -64; $-64 \div -16 = 4$, $-16 \div -4 = 4$ and $-4 \div -1 = 4$. Because the x-values increase by the constant amount of 1, the common ratio is the value of b.

12. Student B; Sample: Student A squared the number 3 within the radicand instead of squaring the expression $\sqrt{x+3}$.

732 Saxon Algebra 1

*14. Write the equation of the function graphed. $f(x) = -2|x - 2| + 3$
(107)

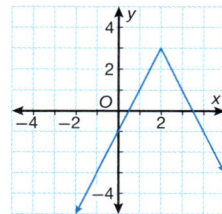

15. Assuming that y varies inversely as x, what is y when $x = 8$, if $y = 55$ when
(64) $x = 11.6$? $y = 79.75$

16. (Meteorology) In the mountains snow will accumulate quickly in winter. If the
(106) average accumulation can be described using the expression $12\sqrt{x}$, find the
value of x when the accumulation is equal to 108 inches. $x = 81$

17. Solve and graph the inequality $\frac{|x|}{8} - 10 < -9$. $-8 < x < 8$;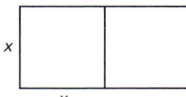
(101)

Solve.

18. $x^2 = -9$ no solution
(102)

19. $12|x + 9| - 11 = 1$ $\{-10, -8\}$
(94)

20. (Building) Tom's house has two square rooms. He knocks down a wall separating
(102) the rooms. The area of the new room is 338 square feet. What were the dimensions
of the original rooms? 13 ft × 13 ft

21. Simplify $\dfrac{\frac{24a^2b}{7c^2}}{\frac{8ab^2}{49c^2}}$. $\frac{21a}{b}$
(92)

22. Find the missing term of the perfect-square trinomial: $x^2 + 7x +$ _____. $\frac{49}{4} = 12.25$
(104)

*23. **Multiple Choice** What is the common ratio of the geometric sequence $-\frac{5}{8}, -\frac{5}{16},$
(105) $-\frac{5}{32}, -\frac{5}{64}, \ldots$? **C**

  A -2 **B** $-\frac{1}{2}$ **C** $\frac{1}{2}$ **D** 2

*24. (Landscaping) Li is designing a triangular flower bed in one corner of her
(103) rectangular yard. She plans on making one leg of the triangle $1\frac{11}{12}$ meters long
and the other leg $2\frac{5}{12}$ meters long. She wants to know how much edging material
she needs to buy to place along the hypotenuse of the triangle. Write a rational
expression to show how much material Li needs to buy.
$\frac{\sqrt{1370}}{12}$ meters

Lesson 108   733

Problem 15
Watch for students who work this problem as a direct variation. Discuss the differences in a direct and inverse variation. The constant in a direct variation is equal to the ratio of two numbers. The constant in an inverse variation is equal to the product of two numbers.

Problem 17
Error Alert
Some students may think that there is no solution since there is a negative number on the right side of the inequality symbol. Remind them that the absolute value must be isolated before solving.

Problem 20
Extend the Problem
The area of Tom's house is $2x^2 + 30x$. What is the area of Tom's house minus the area of the two rooms? 390 ft²

 ENGLISH LEARNERS

Explain the meaning of **accumulate** and **accumulation** in Problem 16. Say:

"Accumulate is a verb that means to build or pile up. Accumulation is a noun and means something that is gathered over a period of time."

Use snow as an example of accumulation. Explain that, when referring to snow, people say it accumulates, or piles up. Money that gathers interest in a bank is also an example of accumulation.

Lesson 108   733

Problem 26

Students should note that they can factor 3 out of the dividend first to make the division of the polynomial easier.

Problem 27

Guide the students by asking them the following questions.

"What must be found before adding the fractions?" Sample: Find the least common denominator

"How can the LCD be determined?" Sample: Factor each denominator, then use each factor that occurs in either denominator in the LCD. Factors common to both denominators should be used the greatest number of times that the factor occurs.

"How can Amber's time be found?" Sample: Use the formula $rt = d$. Use the total found in part **a** for the distance and the rate given in part **b** for the rate.

Problem 29

Guide students by asking them the following questions.

"How much of the work can Sherry do in 1 hour?" $\frac{1}{16}$

"How much of the work can Kim do in 1 hour?" $\frac{1}{x}$

"How can the total amount of work done by either girl be determined?" Sample: Multiply the rate of work by the amount of time worked.

---

25. Analyze Is the sequence $-72, -57.6, 46.08, 36.864, \ldots$ geometric? Explain.

25. no; Sample: The absolute values of the terms have a common ratio of $\frac{4}{5}$, but the signs of the terms do not follow a geometric pattern.

26. Find the quotient of $(36x + 12x^2 + 15) \div (2x + 1)$. $3(2x + 5)$

27. Multi-Step Amber drove $\frac{7x^2}{x^2 - 49}$ miles on Monday and $\frac{x - 1}{4x + 28}$ miles on Tuesday while delivering pizzas.
  a. What is the total distance she drove? $\frac{29x^2 - 8x + 7}{4(x + 7)(x - 7)}$ miles
  b. If her rate was $\frac{7}{7x + 49}$ miles per hour, how much time did it take her to deliver pizzas on Monday and Tuesday? $\frac{29x^2 - 8x + 7}{4(x - 7)}$ hours

28. Construction A box needs to be built so that its rectangular top has a length that is 3 more inches than the width, and so that its area is 88 square inches. Find the length and the width. The width is 8 inches, and the length is 11 inches.

29. Multi-Step Sherry can enter all weekly data into the computer in 16 hours. When she works with Kim, they complete the data entry in 9 hours 36 minutes.
  a. Convert 9 hours 36 minutes to hours. 9.6 hours
  b. Write an equation to find how long it would take Kim to enter the same data. $\frac{9.6}{16} + \frac{9.6}{K} = 1$
  c. How long would it take Kim to enter the data alone? 24 hours

30. Analyze If the y-coordinate of the ordered pair represents the maximum height of the path of a ball thrown into the air, what does the x-coordinate represent? Sample: It represents the time it takes for the ball to reach that height.

CHALLENGE

Have students do research to find some common exponential functions, such as half-life and compound interest. Then have them choose one function to create and solve their own problem. For example, the half-life of radioactive cobalt is 30 years. After 90 years, how much of 100 grams of cobalt remain?
12.5 grams

LOOKING FORWARD

Identifying and graphing exponential functions prepares students for

• **Lesson 114** Graphing Square-Root Functions

• **Lesson 115** Graphing Cubic Functions

• **Lesson 119** Graphing and Comparing Linear, Quadratic, and Exponential Functions

LESSON 109

Graphing Systems of Linear Inequalities

Warm Up

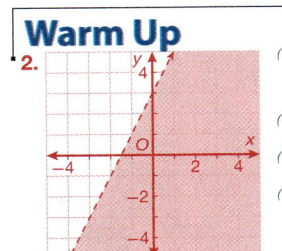

1. **Vocabulary** A(n) _____ (*inequality, equality*) is a mathematical statement comparing quantities that are not equal.   **inequality**
2. Graph $y < 2x + 3$.
3. Is the boundary of the graph of $y \leq 3x + 5$ solid or dashed?   **solid**
4. Is the shading above or below the boundary line on the graph of $y \geq 2x - 6$?   **above**

New Concepts

Recall that a system of linear equations is a set of two or more equations with the same variables.

The solution of the system below is (1, 2) because the ordered pair (1, 2) makes both equations true.

$y = x + 1$
$y = 2x$

$y = x + 1$	$y = 2x$
$2 = 1 + 1$	$2 = 2(1)$
$2 = 2$	$2 = 2$

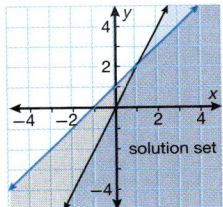

The coordinates also identify the point of intersection of the two lines.

Likewise, a **system of linear inequalities** is a set of linear inequalities with the same variables.

Math Reasoning

Verify Show that $(-4, -4)$ is not a solution of the system.

It does not satisfy $y \leq 2x$ because -4 is not less than or equal to -8.

In the system shown below, all of the ordered pairs in the overlapping region satisfy both inequalities. For example, (3, 2) lies in the overlapping region and makes both inequalities true.

$y \leq x + 1$
$y \leq 2x$

$y \leq x + 1$	$y \leq 2x$
$2 \leq 3 + 1$	$2 \leq 2(3)$
$2 \leq 4$	$2 \leq 6$

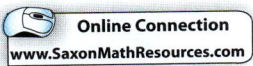

A **solution of a system of linear inequalities** is an ordered pair or set of ordered pairs that satisfy all the inequalities in the system. Therefore, all the ordered pairs in the overlapping region make up the solution of the system.

Lesson 109   735

Example 1
Additional Example 1
Graph each system.

a. $y < 3x + 2$
$y \leq \frac{1}{3}x + 10$.

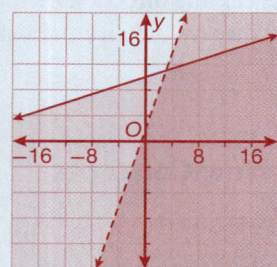

b. $y < 2x + 1$
$3y + 6 > -9x$.

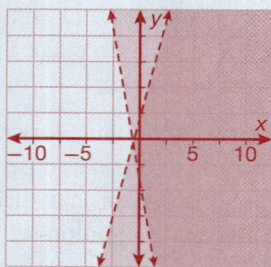

Example 2
Additional Example 2
Graph the system on a graphing calculator.

$y < \frac{1}{5}x + 2$
$y \geq \frac{1}{10}x + 5$

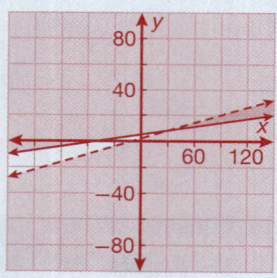

Example 1 Solving by Graphing

Graph each system.

a. $y > \frac{1}{4}x - 3$
$y \leq 3x + 4$.

SOLUTION

Graph each inequality on the same plane. Every point in the overlapping region is a solution.

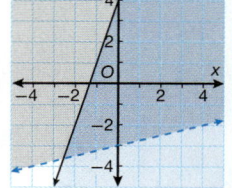

Check Substitute a point in the overlapping region to see that it satisfies both inequalities. The point $(0, 0)$ is convenient to substitute.

$y > \frac{1}{4}x - 3$ $\quad y \leq 3x + 4$

$0 > \frac{1}{4}(0) - 3$ $\quad 0 \leq 3(0) + 4$

$0 > -3$ ✓ $\quad 0 \leq 4$ ✓

b. $y < 4$
$2y + 2 > -6x$.

Caution
Do not forget to use a dashed line for the boundary line when the inequality has $<$ or $>$.

SOLUTION

Write the second inequality in slope-intercept form.

$2y + 2 > -6x$
$2y > -6x - 2$
$y > -3x - 1$

Check See if $(0, 0)$ satisfies both inequalities.

$y < 4$ $\quad 2y + 2 > -6x$

$0 < 4$ ✓ $\quad 2(0) + 2 > -6(0)$

$\quad\quad\quad\quad 2 > 0$ ✓

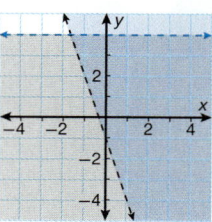

Example 2 Solving with a Graphing Calculator

Graph the system on a graphing calculator.

$y < \frac{3}{4}x + 2$

$y \geq -\frac{1}{5}x + 4$

Graphing Calculator Tip
For help with graphing inequalities, refer to the graphing calculator keystrokes in Graphing Calculator Lab 9 on p. 645.

SOLUTION Enter both functions. Use the arrow keys to move to the symbol to the left of Y_1 and press enter until the symbol shows the lower half of a plane shaded. For Y_2, select the symbol with the upper half shaded.

Note that for many graphing calculators, the option to choose between a strict and non-strict inequality does not exist.

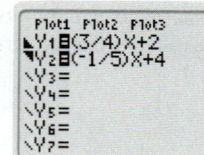 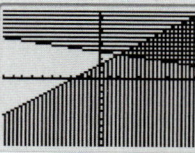

736 *Saxon Algebra 1*

---

eL ENGLISH LEARNERS

For Example 1 explain the meaning of **convenient**. Say:

"Convenient means easy. Usually, it means 'easy' at a particular time. If we are near a mall, it is convenient to shop there due to the variety of stores."

Ask a volunteer to use the word convenient in a sentence. Sample: It's convenient to do my homework while waiting for the bus.

Remember that a system of equations is inconsistent when there are no solutions. This occurs when the slopes of the lines are the same and the y-intercepts are different.

The system has no solutions because the lines are parallel.

$y = -\frac{2}{3}x - 2$

$y = -\frac{2}{3}x + 3$

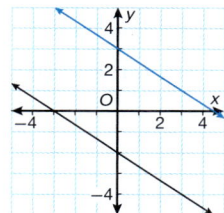

When the equal signs in these equations are replaced with inequality symbols, the system may or may not have a solution set.

Example 3 Solving Systems of Inequalities with Parallel Boundary Lines

Graph each system.

a. $y \leq -\frac{2}{3}x - 2$

$y \geq -\frac{2}{3}x + 3$

SOLUTION

The two solution sets do not intersect, so the system has no solution.

b. $y \geq -\frac{2}{3}x - 2$

$y \leq -\frac{2}{3}x + 3$

SOLUTION

The solution set is the region between the parallel lines.

c. $y \geq -\frac{2}{3}x - 2$

$y \geq -\frac{2}{3}x + 3$

SOLUTION

The solutions of $y \geq -\frac{2}{3}x + 3$ are a subset of the solutions of $y \geq -\frac{2}{3}x - 2$.

The solutions of the system are the same as the solutions of $y \geq -\frac{2}{3}x + 3$.

Math Reasoning

Generalize When the boundary lines are parallel, what must be true about the inequality symbols for one graph to be a subset of the other?

They must both include greater than or both include less than.

Example 3

Error Alert Students may think of the solution to these systems as any point that satisfies either inequality. Remind students that the solution is the set of points that satisfies both systems, where the graphs overlap.

Additional Example 3

Graph each system.

a. $y < 3x - 1$
$y > 3x + 1$

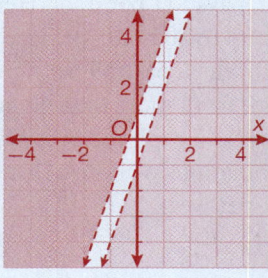

b. $y > 3x - 1$
$y < 3x + 1$

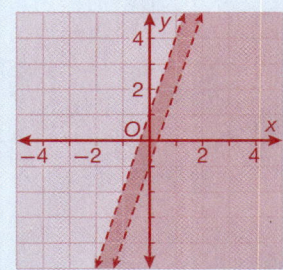

c. $y \leq 3x - 1$
$y \leq 3x + 1$

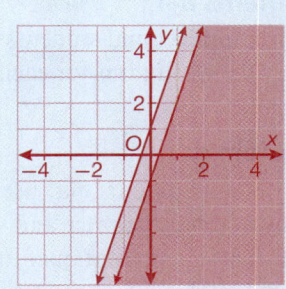

Lesson 109 737

ALTERNATE METHOD FOR EXAMPLE 3b

Have students determine the solution using test points from each region of the grid created by the boundary lines. In Example 3b use the test point $(3, -4)$ to determine if the region between the two lines is part of the solution set. Substitute the point into both inequalities.

$y \geq -\frac{2}{3}x - 2$ $y \leq -\frac{2}{3}x + 3$

$-4 \geq -\frac{2}{3}(3) - 2$ $-4 \leq -\frac{2}{3}(3) + 3$

$-4 \geq -2 - 2$ $-4 \leq -2 + 3$

$-4 \geq -4$ True $-4 \leq 1$ True

Since the inequalities are true, then all of the points in the region containing the test point are also solutions of the system. This region can be shaded. Students then select a checkpoint from each of the other two regions and substitute it into both inequalities. Any region for which the checkpoint makes both inequalities true is shaded. Any shaded area is part of the solution set for the system of inequalities.

Lesson 109 737

Example 4
Extend the Example
Lena worked 5 hours at Job A and 10 hours at Job B. Explain why this is not a solution to the system. Sample: The number of hours worked does not produce the minimum amount money of $210 that she has to earn.

Additional Example 4
Doug must earn at least $300 per week from two part-time summer jobs. Doug can work up to 20 hours per week at Job A, which pays $11 per hour. He can work up to 30 hours per week at Job B, which pays $9 per hour. He cannot work more than 40 hours per week. Graph the possible combinations of hours Doug can work per week.

$\begin{cases} x \leq 20 \\ y \leq 30 \\ 11x + 9y \geq 300 \\ x + y \leq 40 \end{cases}$

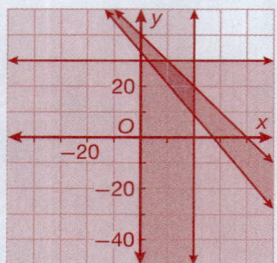

Lesson Practice
Problems a–f
Scaffolding Remind students to test their solutions for each inequality.

Problem g
Error Alert Students may use the x-axis to represent price and the y-axis to represent quantity. Remind students that they can write the quantity of pineapple in terms of the quantity of strawberries using the inequality: $3x + 2y \leq 30$.

Example 4 Application: Employment

Lena has to earn at least $210 per week from two part-time summer jobs. She can work up to 15 hours per week at Job A, which pays $12 per hour, and can work up to 35 hours per week at Job B, which pays $10 per hour. She is not allowed to work more than 40 hours per week. Graph the possible combinations of hours Lena can work per week.

SOLUTION

Write a system of inequalities where x is the number of hours worked per week at Job A, and y is the number of hours worked per week at Job B.

$x \leq 15$	no more than 15 hours at Job A
$y \leq 35$	no more than 35 hours at Job B
$12x + 10y \geq 210$	must earn at least $210 per week
$x + y \leq 40$	cannot work more than 40 hours per week

Math Reasoning
Verify Verify that Lena can make at least $210 working 9 hours at Job A and 20 hours at Job B.

$9(12) + 20(10) = 308$

The region where all four solution sets intersect shows the possible combinations of hours at each job. One possible combination is 9 hours at Job A and 20 hours at Job B.

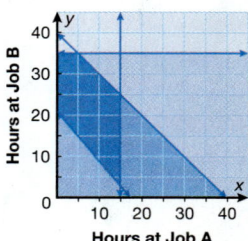

Lesson Practice

Graph each system.
(Ex 1)
a. $y > -2x - 1$
   $y \leq \frac{1}{5}x + 4$

b. $6y + 6 > -2x$
   $y < 2$

a.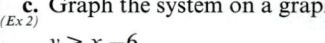

b.

c. Graph the system on a graphing calculator.
(Ex 2)
   $y \geq x - 6$
   $y \leq -x + 3$

c.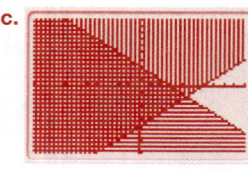

Graph each system. See Additional Answers.
(Ex 3)
d. $y > \frac{1}{2}x - 4$ e. $y < \frac{1}{2}x - 4$ f. $y > \frac{1}{2}x - 4$
   $y > \frac{1}{2}x$ $y > \frac{1}{2}x$ $y < \frac{1}{2}x$

g. Brett has $30 with which to buy dried strawberries and dried pineapple
(Ex 4) for a hiking trip. The dried strawberries cost $3 per pound and the dried pineapple costs $2 per pound. Brett needs at least 2 pounds of strawberries and 3.5 pounds of pineapple. Graph the possible combinations of pounds of each dried fruit that Brett can buy.
See Additional Answers.

738 *Saxon* Algebra 1

INCLUSION

Students who struggle with directionality may have difficulty with Example 4. Suggest to students that they think of the lines that slant up or down to the right as a tabletop. Have them associate above the line with the greater than symbol and below the line with the less than symbol. Help them determine "above" or "below" the line by telling them that if an object such as a paper clip could rest on the line, then that object is above the line. Otherwise, the object is below the line.

Practice Distributed and Integrated

*1. Multiple Choice Which system is represented in the graph? **A**
(109)

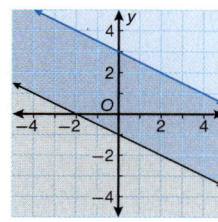

A. $y \le -0.5x + 3$
$y \ge -0.5x - 1$

B. $y \le -0.5x + 3$
$y \le -0.5x - 1$

C. $y \ge -0.5x + 3$
$y \ge -0.5x - 1$

D. $y \ge -0.5x + 3$
$y \le -0.5x - 1$

*2. (Sports) The requirements for a major league baseball are shown in
(109) the graph. Write the system of inequalities that matches the graph.
$x \ge 9$
$x \le 9.25$
$y \ge 5$
$y \le 5.25$

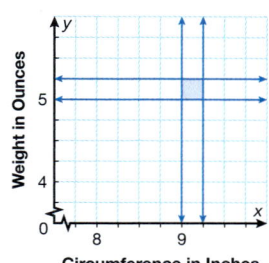

3. Graph the function $f(x) = -3|x|$.
(107)

*4. Write Explain how to represent the solution set of $\begin{array}{l}y \le -3x + 4\\y < 2x - 1\end{array}$.
(109)

4. Sample: Graph $y = -3x + 4$ with a solid line and shade below the line. On the same plane, graph $y = 2x - 1$ with a dashed line and shade below it. The solution set is represented by the region where the shadings overlap.

*5. Verify Graph the solution set of $\begin{array}{l}y \ge -x\\y \le 2x\end{array}$ to verify that $(1, -2)$ is not a
(109) solution of the system.

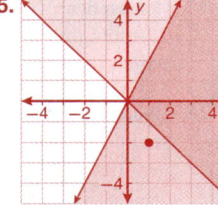

*6. Evaluate the function $f(x) = 3\left(\frac{1}{3}\right)^x$ for $x = -2, 0,$ and 2. $27, 3, \frac{1}{3}$
(108)

7. If the original price was increased 44% to a new price of $900, what was the
(47) original price? $625

Simplify. All variables represent non-negative real numbers.

8. $10\sqrt{8x^2y^3} - 5y\sqrt{98x^2y}$ $-15xy\sqrt{2y}$
(69)

9. $\sqrt{\dfrac{24y^8}{6x^3}}$ $\dfrac{2y^4\sqrt{x}}{x^2}$
(103)

Lesson 109   739

Check for Understanding

The question below help assess the concepts taught in this lesson.

"Explain how to use a graph to solve systems of inequalities."
Graph each inequality and identify the overlapping region.

"How is it determined whether the points on the boundary line are part of the solution set?" Sample: If the inequality symbols are $<$ or $>$, the points on the boundary line are not part of the solution set. If the inequality symbols are $\le$ or $\ge$ the points on the boundary line are part of the solution set.

3 Practice

Math Conversations
Discussion to strengthen understanding

Problem 7
Error Alert
Students may not realize that the new price is 144% of the original price instead of 44% of the original price. Encourage them to determine if 44% of the original value increases or decreases the price.

Lesson 109   739

Problem 16
Extend the Problem
"Curt can change the speed of his pitch by $|8|$ mph. If his slowest pitch is 72 mph, what is the speed of his fastest pitch?" 88 mph

Problem 18
Guide students by asking them the following questions.

"What should be the coefficient of the quadratic term when completing the square? 1

"What formula is used to find the constant term for a perfect square trinomial?" $\left(\frac{b}{2}\right)^2$

Extend the Problem
Explain why one of the solutions to the equation does not make sense. Sample: The situation described in the problem involves time, which cannot be negative. The other solution is negative

---

10. **Error Analysis** Student A said that the following set satisfies an exponential function because there is a common ratio of 3 among the y-values. Student B said that this is not so. Which student is correct? Explain the error.   Student B; Sample: The x-values do not increase by a constant amount.
$$\{(3, 1), (5, 3), (6, 9), (7, 27)\}$$

*11. **Multi-Step** Niall has a baseball card whose value, in dollars, x years after he acquired it, is represented by the function $f(x) = 4.8(1.25)^x$. If Niall bought the card in the year 2000, how much more is it worth in 2010 than it was in 2005? $30.06

*12. **Geometry** Mr. Flores gives the length of a rectangle, in inches, as $f(x) = 16\left(\frac{1}{2}\right)^x$, where x is the number of times he cuts the length in half. What is the length of the rectangle after Mr. Flores has cut it in half 4 times? 6 times? 0 times?   1 inch, $\frac{1}{4}$ inch, 16 inches

*13. **Probability** For the function $f(x) = 7(5)^x$, what is the probability that for a randomly chosen x-value from the domain of $\{0, 1, 2, 3, 4, 5\}$, $f(x)$ is a number between 100 and 1000? $\frac{1}{3}$

14. Is the graph an absolute-value function? Explain.   No; Sample: It does not make a V.

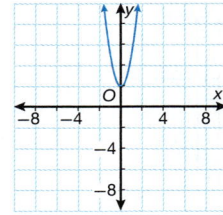

*15. Graph the system $\begin{array}{l} y > \frac{1}{4}x + 3 \\ y > -\frac{1}{4}x + 3 \end{array}$.

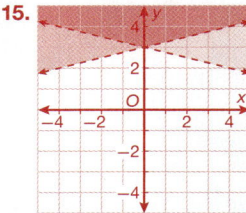

16. **Baseball** An outfielder catches a ball 120 feet from the pitcher's mound and throws it to home. If $d = |90t - 120|$ represents the ball's distance from the pitcher's mound, how would the graph change if the outfielder caught the ball 100 feet from the pitcher's mound?   The graph would shift to the left.

17. **Renovations** Nadia is using 48 tiles to cover a floor. The tiles come in 6-inch, 12-inch, and 13-inch sizes. If the total area of the floor is 6912 square inches, which tile size will fit best? $48x^2 = 6,912$; $x^2 = 144$; $x = 12$. The 12 in square tiles will work best.

18. **Projectile Motion** The equation for the time in seconds (t) it takes an object to strike the ground is $-4.9t^2 - 53.9t = -127.4$. When will the object strike the ground?   2 seconds

19. Find the next 3 terms of the sequence 5, 4.5, 4.05, 3.645, ...   3.2805, 2.95245, 2.657205

*20. **Multiple Choice** Which of the following radical equations has no solution?   C
 A $\sqrt{x - 3} = x - 9$ C $\sqrt{x} + 7 = -2$
 B $13\sqrt{x} = 65$ D $\sqrt{x + 10} = \sqrt{2x + 8}$

21. **Write** Why is it important to isolate the radical in a radical equation?   21. Sample: The equation is easier to solve if the radical is by itself, because squaring the equation then eliminates the radical.

740   Saxon Algebra 1

CHALLENGE

Have students create a system of inequalities whose solution is (1, 1).

Sample: $\begin{cases} y \geq 1 \\ y \leq 1 \\ x \geq 1 \\ x \leq 1 \end{cases}$

22. Jim's rectangular home gym has an area of $(x^2 - 144)$ square feet. The length
$_{(93)}$ is $(x - 12)$ feet. What is the width? **(x + 12) feet**

Solve.

23. $4|x + 2| - 9 = 19$ **24.** $x^2 = -49$ **no solution** **25.** $2\left|\dfrac{x}{4} - 6\right| = 8$ **{8, 40}**
$_{(94)}$ **{−9, 5}** $\quad\quad\quad _{(102)}$ $\quad\quad\quad\quad\quad\quad\quad\quad\quad _{(94)}$

26. Multi-Step A pitcher throws a softball. The height in feet is represented by the
$_{(96)}$ function $h = -16t^2 + 47t + 5$.
  a. How high is the ball after 1 second?   **36 feet**
  b. How high is the ball when it is released?   **5 feet**
  c. What is the initial velocity of the ball?   **47 feet per second**

27. (Gardening) It takes a boy 2 hours to pull all the weeds in the garden. It takes his sister
$_{(99)}$ 4 hours. How long will it take them if they pull weeds together? $\dfrac{4}{3}$ **hours**

28. Multi-Step Andrew hits a golf ball into the air. Its movement forms a parabola given by
$_{(100)}$ the quadratic equation $h = -16t^2 + 31t + 7$, where h is the height in feet and t is the time
in seconds.
  a. Find the time t when the ball is at its maximum height. Round to the nearest
  hundredth. $t = 0.97$ **seconds**
  b. Find the time t when the ball hits the ground. Round to the nearest
  hundredth. $t = 2.14$ **seconds**
  c. Find the maximum height of the arc the ball makes in its flight. Round to the nearest
  hundredth. $h = 22.02$ **feet**

29. Write Describe the similarities and differences between solving the inequality
$_{(101)}$ $2|x| + 1 < 7$ and solving the inequality $|2x + 1| < 7$.

30. If the area of a rectangle is represented by the expression $3x^2 + 22x - 45$ and
$_{(Inv\ 9)}$ the width by the expression $(x + 9)$, what would the length be?   **$(3x - 5)$**

Problem 29

"How does subtracting the 1 at a different stage impact the inequality?" It changes the solution from $-3 < x < 3$ to $-4 < x < 3$.

Problem 30

Encourage students to be systematic as they search for the factors that work. Tell them to keep a written record of the factors that they try, otherwise they may spend time unnecessarily retrying the same factors.

29. Sample: In both cases, subtract 1 from each side and divide each by 2. When solving $2|x| + 1 < 7$, do these operations before removing the absolute-value bars, but when solving $|2x + 1| < 7$, do these operations after writing as a compound inequality.

Lesson 109   741

LOOKING FORWARD

Graphing systems of linear inequalities prepares students for

- **Lesson 112** Graphing and Solving Systems of Linear and Quadratic Equations
- **Lesson 114** Graphing Square-Root Functions
- **Lesson 115** Graphing Cubic Functions
- **Lesson 119** Graphing and Comparing Linear, Quadratic, and Exponential Functions

Lesson 109   741

LESSON 110

1 Warm Up

Problem 4
Remind students to subtract the constant on both sides of the equation before completing the square.

2 New Concepts

In this lesson students will learn how the quadratic formula is derived and then apply it to solve quadratic equations. It is not always appropriate to apply other solution methods (graphing, factoring, or completing the square). Students can use the quadratic formula to solve any quadratic equation.

TEACHER TIP

Point out that if $a = 0$, the equation is not quadratic, so it makes sense that the quadratic formula is undefined when $a = 0$.

LESSON RESOURCES

Student Edition Practice
  Workbook 110
Reteaching Master 110
Adaptations Master 110
Challenge and Enrichment
  Master C110
Technology Lab Master 110

LESSON 110

Using the Quadratic Formula

Warm Up

1. **Vocabulary** A _____ equation can be written in the form $ax^2 + bx + c = 0$, where a is not equal to 0. **quadratic**

Find the value of c to complete the square for each expression.

2. $x^2 + 8x + c$ **16**

3. $x^2 + 9x + c$ $\frac{81}{4}$

4. Solve $x^2 + 10x = 24$ by completing the square. Check your answer. **2, −12**

New Concepts

Different methods are used to solve quadratic equations. One method is applying the **quadratic formula**. The quadratic formula is derived by completing the square of the standard form of the quadratic equation $ax^2 + bx + c = 0$.

$ax^2 + bx + c = 0$

$\frac{ax^2}{a} + \frac{bx}{a} + \frac{c}{a} = 0$ Divide by the coefficient of x^2.

$x^2 + \frac{bx}{a} = -\frac{c}{a}$ Subtract the constant $\frac{c}{a}$ from both sides.

$x^2 + \frac{bx}{a} + \left(\frac{b}{2a}\right)^2 = -\frac{c}{a} + \left(\frac{b}{2a}\right)^2$ Add $\left(\frac{b}{2a}\right)^2$ to complete the square.

$x^2 + \frac{bx}{a} + \frac{b^2}{4a^2} = -\frac{c}{a} + \frac{b^2}{4a^2}$ Simplify.

$\left(x + \frac{b}{2a}\right)^2 = \frac{b^2 - 4ac}{4a^2}$ Write the left side as a squared binomial and the other side with the LCD.

$\sqrt{\left(x + \frac{b}{2a}\right)^2} = \pm\sqrt{\frac{b^2 - 4ac}{4a^2}}$ Take the square root.

$x + \frac{b}{2a} = \pm\frac{\sqrt{b^2 - 4ac}}{2a}$ Simplify.

$x = \frac{-b \pm \sqrt{b^2 - 4ac}}{2a}$ Solve.

> **Math Language**
> A **quadratic equation** is an equation whose graph is a parabola.

Quadratic Formula
For the quadratic equation $ax^2 + bx + c = 0$, $$x = \frac{-b \pm \sqrt{b^2 - 4ac}}{2a}$$ when $a \neq 0$.

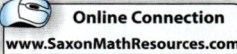
Online Connection
www.SaxonMathResources.com

The quadratic formula can be used to solve any quadratic equation.

742 *Saxon Algebra 1*

MATH BACKGROUND

The proof of the quadratic formula is a common algorithm used to show how the formula was developed. The quadratic formula is useful for all quadratic equations, especially when the equation is unfactorable or when the values of a and b make completing the square complicated. Although graphing calculators provide solutions to quadratic equations, sometimes the solutions are not exact numeric answers, but approximations. The quadratic formula will always give precise numeric answers that the student can round if necessary. This method may be preferred over factoring because there is no trial and error involved.

It may interest students to know that in Latin, *quadrum* means square, and in Middle English, *quadrat* means something square.

Example 1 Solving a Quadratic Equation in Standard Form

Use the quadratic formula to solve $x^2 - 9x + 20 = 0$ for x.

SOLUTION

$x = \dfrac{-b \pm \sqrt{b^2 - 4ac}}{2a}$ Use the quadratic formula.

$= \dfrac{-(-9) \pm \sqrt{(-9)^2 - 4(1)(20)}}{2(1)}$ Substitute 1 for a, -9 for b, and 20 for c.

$= \dfrac{9 \pm \sqrt{81 - 80}}{2}$

$= \dfrac{9 \pm \sqrt{1}}{2} = \dfrac{9 \pm 1}{2}$ Simplify.

$x = 5$ and 4

Check Verify that 5 and 4 make the original equation true.

$x^2 - 9x + 20 = 0$ $x^2 - 9x + 20 = 0$

$(5)^2 - 9(5) + 20 \stackrel{?}{=} 0$ $(4)^2 - 9(4) + 20 \stackrel{?}{=} 0$

$25 - 45 + 20 \stackrel{?}{=} 0$ $16 - 36 + 20 \stackrel{?}{=} 0$

$0 = 0$ ✓ $0 = 0$ ✓

Example 2 Rearranging Quadratic Equations before Solving

Use the quadratic formula to solve $-18x + x^2 = -32$ for x.

SOLUTION Rearrange the equation into the standard form $ax^2 + bx + c = 0$.

Hint
Rearrange terms and their corresponding signs to match the form $ax^2 + bx + c = 0$.

$x^2 - 18x + 32 = 0$ Write the equation in standard form.

$x = \dfrac{-b \pm \sqrt{b^2 - 4ac}}{2a}$ Use the quadratic formula.

$= \dfrac{-(-18) \pm \sqrt{(-18)^2 - 4(1)(32)}}{2(1)}$ Substitute 1 for a, -18 for b, and 32 for c.

$= \dfrac{18 \pm \sqrt{324 - 128}}{2}$

$= \dfrac{18 \pm \sqrt{196}}{2} = \dfrac{18 \pm 14}{2}$ Simplify.

$x = 16$ and 2

Check Verify the solutions for x.

$-18x + x^2 = -32$ $-18x + x^2 = -32$

$-18(16) + (16)^2 \stackrel{?}{=} -32$ $-18(2) + (2)^2 \stackrel{?}{=} -32$

$-288 + 256 \stackrel{?}{=} -32$ $-36 + 4 \stackrel{?}{=} -32$

$-32 = -32$ ✓ $-32 = -32$ ✓

Lesson 110

Example 1

Error Alert Students may not recognize both solutions of a quadratic equation. Remind students to simplify so that there are two distinct answers when using the quadratic formula.

Additional Example 1
Use the quadratic formula to solve for x.
$2x^2 + 6x + 4 = 0$ $x = -1$ or -2

Example 2

Students should equate quadratic equations to zero before identifying a, b, and c.

Additional Example 2
Use the quadratic formula to solve for x.
$3x^2 - x = 2$ $x = 1$ or $-\dfrac{2}{3}$

 ENGLISH LEARNERS

Explain the meaning of the word **rearrange**. Say:

"To arrange means to move or position items. To rearrange means to move or position the same items in a different way."

Ask:

"Why would someone rearrange a room of furniture?" Sample: because they may not like the way it was arranged the first time

Have students arrange a set of objects, and then have other students rearrange the objects.

Example 3

Not all quadratic equations have integer or rational solutions. Irrational solutions can be approximated using a calculator.

Additional Example 3

Use the quadratic formula to solve for x. Then use a graphing calculator to find approximate solutions and verify them.
$-x^2 - 10x + 5 = 0$
$\dfrac{10 \pm \sqrt{120}}{-2}$; $x \approx 0.477$ or -10.477

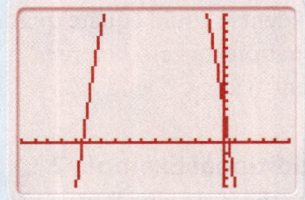

Example 4

Extend the Example

Have students graph the equation.

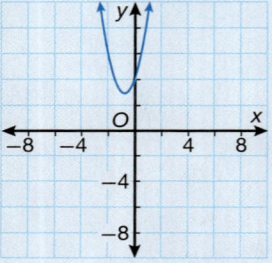

"How can you determine from the graph that there are no real solutions?" Sample: The graph does not intersect the x-axis.

Additional Example 4

Use the quadratic formula to solve $5x^2 + 4x + 2 = 0$ for x. ∅

Example 3 Finding Approximate Solutions

Use the quadratic formula to solve for x. Then use a graphing calculator to find approximate solutions and verify them.

$5x^2 - 3x - 1 = 0$

SOLUTION

$5x^2 - 3x - 1 = 0$

$x = \dfrac{-b \pm \sqrt{b^2 - 4ac}}{2a}$ Use the quadratic formula.

$= \dfrac{-(-3) \pm \sqrt{(-3)^2 - 4(5)(-1)}}{2(5)}$ Substitute the values for a, b, and c.

$x = \dfrac{3 \pm \sqrt{9 + 20}}{10} = \dfrac{3 \pm \sqrt{29}}{10}$

To find the approximate solutions, use a calculator with a square root key. Round the solutions to the nearest ten thousandth.

The solutions are $\dfrac{3 + \sqrt{29}}{10} \approx 0.8385$ and $\dfrac{3 - \sqrt{29}}{10} \approx -0.2385$.

Check

On a graphing calculator, graph the related function $y = 5x^2 - 3x - 1$ to check that the approximate solutions are the zeros of the graph.

Graphing Calculator Tip

For help with graphing quadratic equations, see the graphing calculator keystrokes in Lab 8 on p. 583.

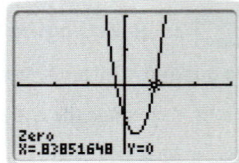 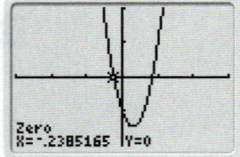

Example 4 Recognizing a Quadratic Equation With No Real Solutions

Use the quadratic formula to solve $2x^2 + 3x + 4 = 0$ for x.

SOLUTION

$x = \dfrac{-b \pm \sqrt{b^2 - 4ac}}{2a}$

$= \dfrac{-(3) \pm \sqrt{(3)^2 - 4(2)(4)}}{2(2)}$ Substitute the values for a, b, and c.

$x = \dfrac{-3 \pm \sqrt{9 - 32}}{4} = \dfrac{-3 \pm \sqrt{-23}}{4}$

The square root of a negative number cannot be taken, so there are no real solutions.

744   *Saxon* Algebra 1

🟥 INCLUSION

To ensure that students account for all negative signs when using the quadratic formula, have them write the quadratic formula with parentheses.

$x = \dfrac{-() + \sqrt{()^2 - 4()()}}{2()}$

Have students write the values for a, b, and c respectively inside the parentheses. Then have them simplify the equation.

Example 5 Application: Object in Motion

From an initial height s of 70 meters in a stadium, Luis tosses a ball up at an initial velocity v of 5 meters per second. Use the equation $-4.9t^2 + vt + s = 0$ to find the time t when the ball hits the ground.

SOLUTION

Substitute the values into the quadratic formula. Then solve.

$$-4.9t^2 + 5t + 70 = 0$$

$$t = \frac{-b \pm \sqrt{b^2 - 4ac}}{2a}$$

$$= \frac{-(5) \pm \sqrt{(5)^2 - 4(-4.9)(70)}}{2(-4.9)}$$

$$= \frac{-5 \pm \sqrt{25 + 1372}}{-9.8}$$

$$= \frac{-5 \pm \sqrt{1397}}{-9.8}$$

$$\approx \frac{-5 \pm 37.3765}{-9.8}$$

$t \approx -3.3037$ and $t \approx 4.3241$

Hint

When the solutions deal with time, we only consider positive values for solutions.

Check

$-4.9(4.3241)^2 + 5(4.3241) + 70 \approx -91.6194 + 21.6205 + 70 \approx 0$ ✓

The ball will land on the ground in approximately 4.3241 seconds.

Lesson Practice

a. (Ex 1) Use the quadratic formula to solve for x.
$x^2 + 3x - 18 = 0$ -6 and 3

b. (Ex 2) Use the quadratic formula to solve for x.
$-72 - 14x + x^2 = 0$ -4 and 18

c. (Ex 2) Use the quadratic formula to solve for x.
$x^2 + 80 = 21x$ 5 and 16

d. (Ex 3) Use the quadratic formula to solve for x. Then use a graphing calculator to find approximate solutions and verify them. Round the solutions to the nearest ten thousandth.
$9x^2 + 6x - 1 = 0$ $\frac{-1 \pm \sqrt{2}}{3} \approx 0.1381$ or -0.8047

e. (Ex 4) Use the quadratic formula to solve $4x^2 + 5x + 3 = 0$ for x.   no real solution

f. (Ex 5) From an initial height s of 50 meters on a cliff, Janet tosses a ball upward at an initial velocity v of 6 meters/second. At what point does the ball fall back to the ground? Round the solution to nearest ten thousandth.
3.8648 seconds

Example 5

Remind students that some solutions are not appropriate. In this example, a negative time has no meaning.

Additional Example 5

From an initial height s of 45 meters, Maria tosses a ball up at an initial velocity v of 7 meters/second. Find the time t when the ball hits the ground. Use the equation $-4.9t^2 + vt + s = 0$. about 3.8278 seconds

Lesson Practice

Problem a

Scaffolding Remind students to identify the values for a, b, and c including their signs.

Problem b

Error Alert Students may try to solve before ordering the terms. Remind students that the terms should be written in descending order by degree.

Check for Understanding

The questions below help assess the concepts taught in this lesson.

"Will all solutions to quadratic equations be integer values? Explain." No; Sample: Rational values may occur because of the fraction. Irrational values may occur because of the square root.

"What does the solution to a quadratic equation tell about the graph of the equation?" It tells where on the coordinate plane the graph crosses the x-axis.

3 Practice

Math Conversations
Discussion to strengthen understanding

Problem 7
Extend the Problem
Have students draw a stem-and-leaf plot to identify outliers.

Sample:

Stem	Leaf
0	1 1 1 1
0	2 2 2 2 2 2 2
0	3 3 3 3
0	
0	
0	6

Legend: 0 | 1 means 1

Practice   Distributed and Integrated

Use the quadratic formula to solve for x. Check the solutions.

*1. $x^2 - 2x - 35 = 0$ $-5, 7$
(110)

*2. $x^2 - 10x + 25 = 0$ 5
(110)

*3. **Multi-Step** Determine why $16h^2 + 25 = 40h$ has only 1 solution using the quadratic
(110) formula.
   a. Rearrange the equation into the $ax^2 + bx + c = 0$ form. $16h^2 - 40h + 25 = 0$
   b. What is different about $b^2 - 4ac$?   Sample: It equals zero.
   c. **Generalize** When will the equation $ax^2 + bx + c = 0$ have only 1 solution?
      when $b^2 = 4ac$

4. Compare: $12{,}000 \bigcirc 1.2 \times 10^3$. $12{,}000 > 1.2 \times 10^3$
(37)

5. Find the zeros of the function. $y = x^2 + 12x + 36$ -6
(96)

6. Describe the graph of an indirect variation when the constant of variation
(Inv 7) is positive.   a hyperbola with the x- and y-axes as asymptotes

7. Identify the outlier or outliers in the data set.
(48)
   number of cars for sixteen households: 3, 2, 2, 1, 2, 3, 6, 2, 1, 1, 3, 2, 2, 2, 1, 3   6

*8. **Predict** Use mental math to predict whether the quadratic formula is necessary to
(110) solve $3b^2 + 15b - 20 = 0$. Solve.   quadratic formula is necessary; $\frac{-15 \pm \sqrt{465}}{6}$

*9. (**Soccer**) A 1.5-meter-tall soccer player bounces a soccer ball off his head at a velocity
(110) of 7 meters per second upward. Use the formula $h = -4.9t^2 + v_0 t + h_0$ to estimate
how many seconds it will take the ball to hit the ground.   about 1.6 seconds

*10. **Error Analysis** For the system of inequalities graphed, Student A said that
(109) $(1, -4)$ is a solution of the system and Student B said that $(4, 2)$ is a solution of
the system. Which student is correct? Explain the error.   Student A; Sample: The
ordered pair (4, 2) is a solution to one of the inequalities, but not to both of them.

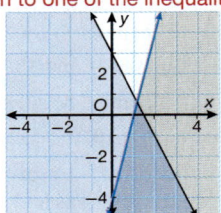

11. Graph the system $\begin{aligned} y &\leq 2 \\ x &\geq 2 \end{aligned}$.   See Additional Answers.
(109)

*12. **Multi-Step** A student group is planning on washing cars in an effort to raise at least
(109) $300. They want to charge $5 for a basic wash, which will take about 10 minutes, and
$15 for a detailed wash, which will take about 30 minutes. They have the car-wash
lot rented for 8 hours. Write and graph a system of linear inequalities to describe this
situation. Explain your findings.   See Additional Answers.

746   Saxon Algebra 1

13. Geometry Suppose the perimeter of a rectangle must be less than 50 units and
(109) the width must be greater than 5 units. Graph a system of linear inequalities to
describe this situation. Give one set of possible dimensions for the rectangle. See Additional Answers.

14. Evaluate the function $f(x) = -3(6)^x$ for $x = -2, 0,$ and 2. $-\frac{1}{12}, -3, -108$
(108)

15. Error Analysis Which student correctly evaluated $f(x) = 2(3)^x$ for $x = 2$? Explain
(108) the error.

Student A	Student B	Student B; Sample: Student A should not multiply 2 and 3 because 3 is the base of an exponent.
$f(x) = 2(3)^x$ $= 6^x$ $= 6^2 = 36$	$f(x) = 2(3)^x$ $= 2(3)^2$ $= 2(9) = 18$	

*16. Chemistry Amaro uses $f(x) = 10\left(\frac{1}{2}\right)^x$ to give the amount remaining from 10 grams
(108) of a radioactive substance after x number of half-lives. Which graph represents
this function? Graph A

Graph A Graph B Graph C

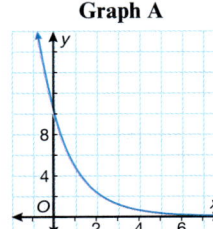
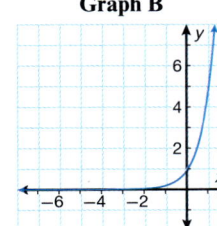
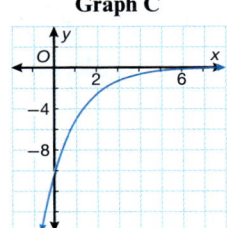

17. Simplify $\dfrac{\sqrt{15xy}}{3\sqrt{10xy^3}}$. $\dfrac{\sqrt{6}}{6y}$
(103)

18. Subtract $\dfrac{5x^2}{10x - 30} - \dfrac{2x - 5}{x^2 - 9}$. $\dfrac{x^3 + 3x^2 - 4x + 10}{2(x - 3)(x + 3)}$
(95)

19. Astronomy Astronomers can use the formula $T = \sqrt{d^3}$ to find the time T it takes a
(103) planet to orbit the Sun (in earth years), knowing the distance d of the planet from
the Sun (in astronomical units, AU). If Mars is about $\frac{3}{2}$ AU from the Sun, about
how long does it take Mars to orbit the Sun in earth years? Give your answer as a
rational expression. $\dfrac{3\sqrt{6}}{4}$

20. Multiple Choice What is the absolute-value function of the graph?   **B**
(107)

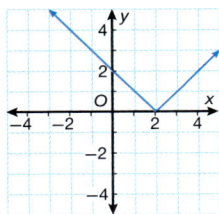

A $f(x) = |x + 2|$ **B** $f(x) = |x - 2|$

C $f(x) = |x| + 2$ **D** $f(x) = |x| - 2$

21. Solve $p^2 + 13p = -50$ by completing the square.   no real solutions
(104)

Lesson 110   747

Problem 14
Make sure that students are correctly applying the order of operations when simplifying.

Problem 18
Error Alert
Students may not simplify each fraction before finding a common denominator. Encourage them to factor the denominators as much as possible before finding a common denominator.

Problem 20
Extend the Problem
Have students describe a scenario that the graph and correct equation might represent.

Lesson 110   747

Problem 22
Be sure students use the order of operations after they substitute the values into the equation.

Problem 28
Make sure that students realize that they are identifying two distinct events, the maximum height and the time when the ball hits the ground where its height is 0.

*22. **Compound Interest** The formula for a fund that compounds interest is
$A_n = P\left(1 + \frac{r}{n}\right)^{nt}$, where A is the balance, P is the initial amount deposited, r is the annual interest rate, t is the number of years, and n is the number of times the interest is compounded per year. Gretchen deposits $1500 into an account that pays 4.5% interest compounded annually. Write the first 4 terms of the sequence representing Gretchen's balance after t years. Round to the nearest cent.
$1567.50, $1638.04, $1711.75, $1788.78

23. Solve $\sqrt{x + 11} = 16$. Check your answer. $x = 245; \sqrt{245 + 11} = \sqrt{256} = 16$

*24. **Analyze** Are the graphs for $f(x) = 5|x|$ and $f(x) = |5x|$ the same? Explain.

24. Yes; Sample: Multiplication does not change the absolute value like addition and subtraction do.

25. Solve the equation $9\left|\frac{x}{2} - 6\right| = 27$.   6, 18

26. Factor $x^2 + 42 + 13x$. $(x + 6)(x + 7)$

27. **Multi-Step** Lisa plans to shop for books and magazines and she plans to spend no more than $32. Each book costs $14 and each magazine costs $4.
   a. Write an inequality that describes this situation. $14x + 4y \leq 32$
   b. Graph the inequality.   See Additional Answers.
   c. If Lisa wants to spend exactly $32, what is a possible number of each she can spend her money on?   Sample: 2 books and 1 magazine

28. **Volleyball** Diego hits a volleyball into the air. The ball's movement forms a parabola given by the quadratic equation $h = -16t^2 + 3t + 14$ where h is the height in feet and t is the time in seconds. Find the maximum height of the path the volleyball makes and the time when the volleyball hits the ground. Round to the nearest hundredth. $h = 14.14$ feet and $t = 1.03$ seconds

29. **Multi-Step** When the temperature (t) of the gas neon is within 1.25° of −247.35°C it will be in a liquid form. This can be modeled by the absolute-value inequality $|t - (-247.35)| < 1.25$.
   a. Solve and graph the inequality $|t - (-247.35)| < 1.25$.

29a. $-248.6 < t < -246.1$;
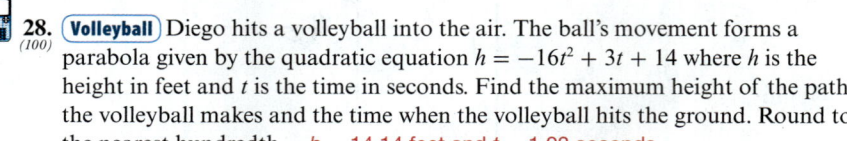

   b. One endpoint of the graph represents the boiling point of neon, the temperature at which neon changes from liquid to gas. The other endpoint represents the melting point, at which neon turns from solid to liquid. The higher temperature is the boiling point and the lower temperature is the melting point. What is the boiling point of neon? What is the melting point?   −246.1°C; −248.6°C

30. **Measurement** The following formula represents the area of circle A: $\pi r^2 - 165.05 \text{ m}^2 = 0$. What is the approximate measurement, in meters, of the radius r? Use 3.14 for π.   ≈7.249 m

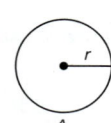

Saxon Algebra 1

 CHALLENGE

Have students write their own quadratic equation. It should have two real solutions. Then have them solve their equation using the quadratic formula.   See student work.

 LOOKING FORWARD

Using the quadratic formula prepares students for

• **Lesson 112** Graphing and Solving Systems of Linear and Quadratic Equations

• **Lesson 116** Solving Simple and Compound Interest Problems

• **Lesson 119** Graphing and Comparing Linear, Quadratic, and Exponential Functions

INVESTIGATION 11

Investigating Exponential Growth and Decay

Water Flow Rates

Water flows from a crack in the side of a swimming pool, initially releasing one gallon of water. The crack continues to widen as water continues to flow from the pool. For every second after that, the amount flowing from the pool doubles. The table below shows the relationship between time and the amount of water flowing.

Math Reasoning
Sample: The data values for the amount of water do not increase by a constant amount. The graph of the data is not a line.

Time (s)	Amount of Water (gal)
0	1
1	2
2	4
3	8

Math Reasoning
Analyze What characteristics of the data and the graph indicate that this data does not model a linear function?

1. Create a graph of the data. See Additional Answers.
2. **Predict** How many gallons of water flow from the pool in the fourth second? 16 gallons

Near the origin the graph looks similar to a parabola, however it grows much more quickly. The graph models exponential growth. **Exponential growth** is a situation where a quantity always increases by the same percent for a given time period.

Stock Exchange

The annual number of shares S in billions traded on the New York Stock Exchange from 1990 to 2000 can be approximated by the model $S = 39(1.2)^x$, where x is the number of years since 1990.

3. Create a table of values like the one below. Round each share to the nearest billion.

x	S
0	39
2	56
4	81
6	116
8	168
10	241

Math Reasoning
Sample: x represents time, so it must be 0 or positive. The domain is $x \geq 0$.

Math Reasoning
Analyze In the exponential growth equation $f(x) = kb^x$ what is the domain? Why?

Online Connection
www.SaxonMathResources.com

4. Plot the coordinates. Connect the points with a smooth curve. See Additional Answers.
5. Use the graph to estimate the number of shares traded in 1997. about 140 billion shares
6. **Verify** Use the equation to calculate the exact number of shares traded in 1997 algebraically. 139.74 billion shares

Investigation 11   749

INVESTIGATION 11

Materials
- several sheets of notebook paper
- graph paper

Discuss
In this investigation, students learn to find exponential growth and decay by graphing data and creating data tables. Remind them that they learned how to identify and graph exponential functions in Lesson 108.

Define **exponential growth**.

Water Flow Rates
Extend the Problem
Have students extend the table to show the amount of water that flows from the pool in the fourth through eighth seconds.

Time (s)	Amount of Water (gal)
4	16
5	32
6	64
7	128
8	256

Stock Exchange
Extend the Problem
Have students use the equation to estimate the number of shares traded in 1995. about 97 billion

INVESTIGATION RESOURCES

Reteaching Master
    Investigation 11
Technology Lab Master
    Investigation 11

MATH BACKGROUND

Banks pay interest to depositors in return for the use of the depositors' money. The interest depositors earn from a bank is usually compound interest, which means the bank pays based not only on the amount deposited in the bank, but also on the interest it has already paid.

For instance, if Marla deposits $500 into a bank that has an interest rate of 5% that is compounded annually, at the end of the first year she will have $525. This is 1.05 times Marla's $500 deposit.

To compound the interest, a bank will use an exponential growth formula, where k is the original deposit, b is the interest, and the exponent is the number of years the money stays in the bank:

$$y = kb^x$$
$$y = 500 \cdot 1.05^x$$

Investigation 11   749

Analyzing Different Values of *k* in the Exponential Growth Function

Discuss
Ask the students if they notice a pattern in the number of regions each time that they fold the paper. Discuss that the number of regions on the paper doubles with each fold. Connect this with the base of the exponential equation $f(x) = k2^x$.

Error Alert
Students may try to jump too quickly from the concrete to the abstract by filling in the tables without folding the paper, resulting in errors in their data. Encourage them to complete the paper folding for a thorough understanding of the concept.

Exponential growth is modeled by the function $f(x) = kb^x$, where $k > 0$. The percent of growth b, expressed as a decimal number, is greater than 1.

Exploration — Analyzing Different Values of *k* in the Exponential Growth Function

Materials
- several sheets of notebook paper

Step 1: Take one sheet of notebook paper. Fold it in half. Unfold the paper and count the number of rectangular regions formed. Record the number of folds and regions in a table like the one below.

Folds	Regions
0	1
1	2
2	4
3	8
4	16

Refold the paper along the initial crease you made and fold it in half again. Continue counting regions and folding in half at least four times.

Step 2: Take three sheets of notebook paper and stack them. Repeat Step 1. Create and complete a table like the one below.

Folds	Regions
0	3
1	6
2	12
3	24
4	48

Step 3: Take five sheets of notebook paper and stack them. Repeat Step 1. Create and complete a table like the one below.

Folds	Regions
0	5
1	10
2	20
3	40
4	80

Math Reasoning

Analyze Why are each of the three functions named using function notation?

Sample: It is convenient to refer to each function as *f*, *g*, or *h*. It would not be clear to call each exponential equation "*y*."

7. Plot the points on one coordinate plane. Let x = the number of folds. Let y = the number of regions. Connect the point for each set of data with a smooth curve. See Additional Answers.

The data in the Exploration are included in the graphs of the functions $f(x) = 2^x$, $g(x) = 3(2)^x$, and $h(x) = 5(2)^x$, respectively. All three functions are of the form $y = k(b)^x$.

8. What is the *y*-intercept of each function? Compare the *y*-intercept of each equation to $y = kb^x$. Name the *y*-intercept of $y = kb^x$. (0, 1); (0, 3); (0, 5); (0, *k*)

---

eL ENGLISH LEARNERS

Explain to students the meaning of a **share** of stock. Students already know that to share means to divide something among people, but may not know about a share of stock. Say:

"A share of stock is a part of a company and its profits that people can buy. Shares of stock are divided among people who invest in a company."

Discuss businesses with which the students may be familiar that sell shares of stock in the company.

9. **Generalize** How does changing the value of k affect the graph of the function? Sample: The y-intercept is k. Each graph has the same shape, but larger values of k cause the graph to curve upward more sharply.

10. **Formulate** As the number of folds increase, what happens to the number of regions on the folded paper? What is the b-value for each equation? Write an equation in the form $y = k(b)^x$ to model situations in which y doubles as x increases.

10. Sample: Every time the paper is folded in half, the number of regions doubles; 2; $y = k(2)^x$

11. For any function $y = k(b)^x$, what does k represent in any situation when $x = 0$? k represents the initial amount present.

The period of time required for a quantity to double in size or value is called **doubling time**. The equation will be of the form $y = k(2)^x$.

Just as data can grow exponentially, some data can model exponential decay. **Exponential decay** is a situation where a quantity always decreases by the same percent in a given time period.

Carbon-14 dating is used to find the approximate age of animal and plant material after it has decomposed. The half-life of carbon-14 is 5730 years. So, every 5730 years half of the carbon-14 in a substance decomposes. Find the amount remaining from a sample containing 100 milligrams of carbon-14 after four half lives.

Caution
Do not divide the original amount of a substance by 3 to calculate the amount of a substance left after three half-lives.

12. How many years are there in four half-lives?   22,920 years
13. Create and complete a table like the one below.

Number of Half-Lives	Number of Years	Amount of Carbon-14 Remaining (mg)
0	0	100
1	5730	50
2	11,460	25
3	17,190	12.5
4	22,920	6.25

Hint
Since x usually represents time in decay equations, $x > 0$.

14. How much of the sample remains after 22,920 years?   6.25 mg

Exponential decay is modeled by the function $f(x) = kb^x$, where $k > 0$ and $0 < b < 1$. Since the value of b is a positive number less than 1, as x increases, the value of $f(x)$ decreases by b.

Math Reasoning
Analyze Why does $f(x)$ decrease as x increases?

Sample: Since b is a fraction between 0 and 1, $f(x)$ decreases in value as b is raised to greater values of x.

An exponential decay function can model the amount of a substance in the body over time. Many diabetes patients take insulin. The exponential function $f(x) = 100 \left(\frac{1}{2}\right)^x$ describes the percent of insulin in the body after x half-lives. The **half-life** of a substance is the time it takes for one-half of the substance to decay into another substance.

15. About what percent of insulin would be left in the body after 8 half-lives?   0.39%

16. Sample: In each interval x, the amount of y remaining decreases by half.

16. **Write** Describe the effect that the b-value has on the amount of substance remaining as the number of half-lives x increases.

Investigation 11   751

CHALLENGE

The half-life of cobalt-60, an element used in some medical radiation therapies, is 5.26 years. If a sample of cobalt-60 is 550 milligrams, how many milligrams of cobalt-60 will remain after $31\frac{14}{25}$ years? Round to the nearest hundredths place if necessary.   8.59 mg

---

Problem 10
Extend the Problem
Have students use the formula $y = k(2)^x$ to find the amount of regions 6 pieces of paper would have if they were folded 7 times.
768 regions

Discuss
Define **doubling time** and **exponential decay**. Ask students why they think the value of b in the exponential decay formula $f(x) = kb^x$ is a positive number that is less than one.

Problem 15
Error Alert
Students may move the decimal place too far and get 39% as an answer. Remind them that they need to move the decimal only two decimal places to the right to get their answer.

17. **Predict** Graph the functions $f(x) = 100\left(\frac{1}{2}\right)^x$ and $g(x) = 50\left(\frac{1}{2}\right)^x$. How does the value of k in each equation compare to the y-intercept? How does the k-value affect the graph of the function? See Additional Answers.

Match the following exponential growth and decay equations to the graphs shown. Explain your choices.

18. $y = 2(0.5)^x$ See Additional Answers.
19. $y = 2(3)^x$ See Additional Answers.
20. $y = (0.25)^x$ See Additional Answers.
21. $y = 0.25(2)^x$ See Additional Answers.

Graph A
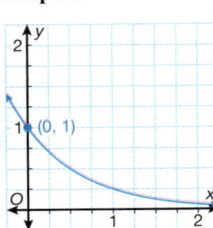

Graph B
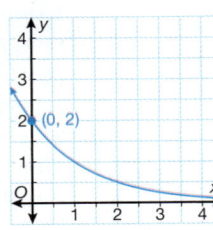

Graph C
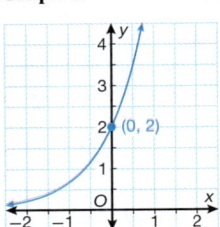

Graph D
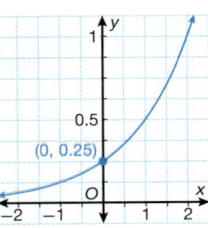

Investigation Practice

d. Both graphs have y-intercept (0, 1) and neither crosses the x-axis and both graphs show exponential decay. The graph of $y = \left(\frac{1}{3}\right)^x$ curves downward more sharply than the graph of $y = \left(\frac{1}{2}\right)^x$.

a. **Formulate** Alex invested $500 in an account that will double his balance every 8 years. How many times will the amount in the account double in 32 years? Write an equation to model the account balance y after x doubling times. What will his balance be in 32 years? 4 times; $y = 500(2)^x$; $8000

b. **Formulate** Radioactive glucose is used in cancer detection. It has a half-life of 100 minutes. How many half-lives are in 24 hours? Write an equation to model the amount y remaining of a 100 milligram sample after x half-lives. How much of a 100 milligram sample remains after 24 hours? d. 14.4 half-lives; $y = 100\left(\frac{1}{2}\right)^x$; about 0.0046 mg

Use the equation $f(x) = \left(\frac{1}{2}\right)^x$ to answer each problem.

c. Does the equation model exponential growth or exponential decay? Explain. decay; The value of b is 0.5, which is between 0 and 1.

d. How does the graph of $f(x) = \left(\frac{1}{2}\right)^x$ compare to the graph of $g(x) = \left(\frac{1}{3}\right)^x$?

e. How does the graph of $f(x) = \left(\frac{1}{2}\right)^x$ compare to the graph of $h(x) = 2^x$? See Additional Answers.

Match the following exponential growth and decay equations to the graphs shown. Explain your choices.

f. $y = 3(0.5)^x$ See Additional Answers.

g. $y = 3(2)^x$ See Additional Answers.

h. $y = (4)^x$ See Additional Answers.

i. $y = 2(0.25)^x$ See Additional Answers.

Graph A

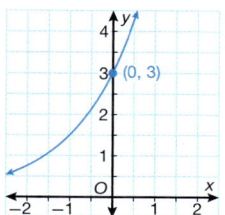

Graph B

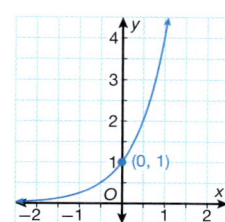

Graph C

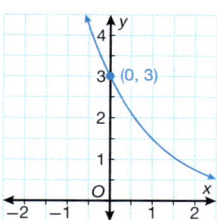

Graph D

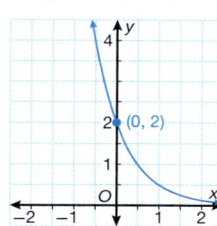

LOOKING FORWARD

Investigating exponential growth and decay prepares students for

- **Lesson 114** Graphing Square-Root Functions
- **Lesson 115** Graphing Cubic Functions
- **Lesson 119** Graphing and Comparing Linear, Quadratic, and Exponential Functions

SECTION OVERVIEW 12

Lesson Planner

Lesson	New Concepts
111	Solving Problems Involving Permutations
112	Graphing and Solving Systems of Linear and Quadratic Equations
113	Interpreting the Disciminant
LAB 10	Graphing Calculator: Graphing Radical Functions
114	Graphing Square-Root Functions
115	Graphing Cubic Functions
	Cumulative Test 22, Performance Task 22
116	Solving Simple and Compound Interest Problems
117	Using Trigonometric Ratios
118	Solving Problems Involving Combinations
119	Graphing and Comparing Linear, Quadratic, and Exponential Functions
120	Using Geometric Formulas to Find the Probability of an Event
	Cumulative Test 23, Performance Task 23
LAB 11	Graphing Calculator: Matrix Operations
INV 12	Investigation: Investigating Matrices

Resources for Teaching

- Student Edition
- Teacher's Edition
- Student Edition eBook
- Teacher's Edition eBook
- Resources and Planner CD
- Solutions Manual
- Instructional Masters
- Technology Lab Masters
- Warm Up and Teaching Transparencies
- Instructional Presentations CD
- Online activities, tools, and homework help
  www.SaxonMathResources.com

Resources for Practice and Assessment

- Student Edition Practice Workbook
- Course Assessments
- Standardized Test Practice
- College Entrance Exam Practice
- Test and Practice Generator CD using ExamView™

Resources for Differentiated Instruction

- Reteaching Masters
- Challenge and Enrichment Masters
- Prerequisite Skills Intervention
- Adaptations for Saxon Algebra 1
- Multilingual Glossary
- English Learners Handbook
- TI Resources

Pacing Guide

 Resources and Planner CD for lesson planning support

45-Minute Class

Day 1	Day 2	Day 3	Day 4	Day 5	Day 6
Lesson 111	Lesson 112	Lesson 113 Lab 10	Lesson 114	Lesson 115	Cumulative Test 22

Day 7	Day 8	Day 9	Day 10	Day 11	Day 12
Lesson 116	Lesson 117	Lesson 118	Lesson 119	Lesson 120	Cumulative Test 23

Day 13
Investigation 12 Lab 11

Block: 90-Minute Class

Day 1	Day 2	Day 3	Day 4	Day 5	Day 6
Lesson 111 Lesson 112	Lesson 113 Lesson 114 Lab 10	Lesson 115 Cumulative Test 22	Lesson 116 Lesson 117	Lesson 118 Lesson 119	Lesson 120 Cumulative Test 23

Day 7
Lab 11 Investigation 12

*For suggestions on how to implement Saxon Math in a block schedule, see the Pacing section at the beginning of the Teacher's Edition.

Lessons 111–120, Investigation 12

Differentiated Instruction

Below Level

Warm Up	SE pp. 754, 761, 769, 776, 782, 788, 796, 804, 809, 817
Skills Bank	SE pp. 846–883
Reteaching Masters	Lessons 111–120, Investigation 12
Warm Up Transparencies	Lessons 111–120
Prerequisite Skills Intervention	Skill 50

Advanced Learners

Challenge	TE pp. 760, 768, 774, 780, 787, 794, 802, 808, 816, 823
Extend the Example	TE pp. 757, 765, 771, 777, 784, 792, 799, 806, 812, 819
Extend the Exploration	TE pp. 756
Extend the Problem	TE pp. 760, 768, 773, 779, 780, 781, 786, 787, 794, 795, 802, 807, 814, 815, 816, 821, 826
Challenge and Enrichment Master	Challenge: 111–120; Enrichment: 115

English Learners

EL Tips	TE pp. 757, 766, 771, 777, 786, 789, 797, 805, 810, 822, 827
Multilingual Glossary	Booklet and Online
English Learners Handbook	

Special Needs

Inclusion Tips	TE pp. 756, 762, 772, 790, 778, 790, 799, 806, 811, 818, 820
Adaptations for Saxon Algebra 1	Lessons 111–120, Cumulative Tests 22, 23

For All Learners

Exploration	SE pp. 756, 827, 828
Caution	SE pp. 756, 762, 791, 797, 811, 827
Hints	SE pp. 776, 777, 783, 789, 790, 796, 800, 805, 806, 810, 817, 818
Error Alert	TE pp. 755, 757, 760, 763, 766, 768, 770, 771, 774, 777, 779, 780, 781, 785, 786, 787, 791, 792, 794, 795, 799, 800, 802, 803, 805, 806, 807, 811, 813, 815, 816, 819, 820, 823, 827, 828, 829
Alternate Method	TE pp. 812
Online Tools	

SE = Student Edition; TE = Teacher's Edition

Math Vocabulary

Lesson	New Vocabulary	Maintained	EL Tip in TE
111	factorial permutation	theoretical probability tree diagram	departure
112		quadratic equation system of linear equations	sprinkler
113	discriminant double root	quadratic formula vertex	discriminant
114	reflection square-root function	domain radical transformation	alteration
115	cubic function	degree of a polynomial linear function quadratic function	limb
116	compound interest simple interest	linear function exponential function	invested
117	cosecant sine cosine tangent cotangent trigonometric ratio secant	hypotenuse legs of a right triangle	adjacent opposite
118	combination	factorial permutation	choices
119		exponential function linear function parent function quadratic function	steep
120		complement of an event	unscramble
INV 12	element matrix	scale factor	transform

SECTION OVERVIEW 12

Math Highlights

Enduring Understandings – The "Big Picture"

After completing Section 12, students will understand:
- How to solve problems involving permutations and combinations.
- How to use trigonometric ratios.
- How to find the solution set of systems of linear and quadratic equations.
- How to interpret the discriminant.
- How to graph exponential functions.
- How to solve problems involving simple and compound interest.

Essential Questions

- How can the probability of an event be applied to the area of geometric figures?
- How do permutations and combinations differ?
- How can the discriminant be used to find the number of solutions to a quadratic equation, and how does this relate to the x-intercepts of the graph of the related function equation?
- How does the degree of a polynomial function determine the characteristics of its graph?
- How can trigonometric ratios be used to find missing side lengths and measures of angles?
- How do changes to the parent function affect the graph of the function?

Math Content Strands

Equations
- Lesson 117   Using Trigonometric Ratios

Functions and Relations
- Lesson 115   Graphing Cubic Functions
- Lesson 116   Solving Simple and Compound Interest Problems
- Lesson 119   Graphing and Comparing Linear, Quadratic, and Exponential Functions

Probability and Data Analysis
- Lesson 111   Solving Problems Involving Permutations
- Lesson 118   Solving Problems Involving Combinations
- Lesson 120   Using Geometric Formulas to Find the Probability of an Event

Quadratic Equations and Functions
- Lesson 113   Interpreting the Disciminant

Radical Expressions and Functions
- Lab 10   Graphing Calculator: Graphing Radical Functions
- Lesson 114   Graphing Square-Root Functions

Systems of Equations and Inequalities
- Lesson 112   Graphing and Solving Systems of Linear and Quadratic Equations
- Lab 11   Graphing Calculator: Matrix Operations
- Investigation 12   Investigating Matrices

Connections in Practice Problems

	Lessons
Coordinate Geometry	118
Geometry	111, 112, 113, 114, 115, 116, 117, 118, 119, 120
Measurement	111, 112, 114, 115, 116
Probability	113

Math Processes

Reasoning and Communication

	Lessons
Analyze	111, 112, 113, 114, 115, 116, 118, 119, 120
Error analysis	111, 112, 113, 114, 115, 116, 117, 118, 119, 120
Estimate	111, 118
Formulate	112, 115, 116, 119, Inv. 12
Generalize	111, 113, 115, 117, 120, Inv. 12
Justify	111, 116, 117, 119, 120
Math Reasoning	111, 112, 113, 114, 115, 116, 117, 118, 119, 120
Model	111, 113, 118, 120, Inv. 20
Multiple choice	111, 112, 113, 114, 115, 116, 117, 118, 119, 120
Multi-step	111, 112, 113, 114, 115, 116, 117, 118, 119, 120
Predict	111, Inv. 12
Verify	112, 113, 115, 118, 119, 120
Write	112, 114, 115, 116, 117, 118, 119, 120, Inv. 12
Graphing Calculator	112, 113, 115, 116, 117, Inv. 12

Connections

In Examples: Avalanches, Baseball, Horizon, Indirect measurement, Probability, Retirement investments, Uniform numbers, Volume of a cube, Zoning

In Practice problems: Accessories, Architecture, Astronomy, Aviation, Baking, Biking, Bonds, Business, Capacity, Chemistry, Construction, Credit cards, Dining, Engineering, Finance, Firefighting, Football, Fundraising, Games, Gardening, Interior decorating, Jewelry, Manufacturing, Mutual funds, Nature, Navigation, Nutrition, Oceanography, Oven temperatures, Packaging, Paper folding, Phone chains, Photography, Physics, Population, Projectile motion, Property, Puzzles, Retirement investments, Space Shuttle, Sports, Structural engineering, Temperature, Tennis, Video rental

Lessons 111–120, Investigation 12

Content Trace

Lesson	Warm Up: Prerequisite Skills	New Concepts	Where Practiced	Where Assessed	Looking Forward
111	Lessons 14, 15, 33	Solving Problems Involving Permutations	Lessons 112, 113, 114, 115, 117, 118, 119, 120	Cumulative Test 23	Lessons 118, 120
112	Lessons 9, 29, 55, 84	Graphing and Solving Systems of Linear and Quadratic Equations	Lessons 113, 114, 115, 116, 117, 118, 119, 120	Cumulative Test 23	Lesson 119
113	Lessons 9, 13	Interpreting the Disciminant	Lessons 114, 115, 116, 117, 118, 119, 120	Cumulative Test 23	Lesson 119
114	Lessons 69, 76	Graphing Square-Root Functions	Lessons 115, 116, 117, 118, 119, 120	Cumulative Test 23	Lessons 115, 119
115	Lessons 46, 53	Graphing Cubic Functions	Lessons 116, 117, 118, 119, 120	Cumulative Test 23	Lessons in other Saxon High School Math programs
116	Lessons 31, 42, Skills Bank 7	Solving Simple and Compound Interest Problems	Lessons 117, 118, 119, 120	Test and Practice Generator CD	Lessons in other Saxon High School Math programs
117	Lesson 85	Using Trigonometric Ratios	Lessons 118, 119, 120	Test and Practice Generator CD	Lessons in other Saxon High School Math programs
118	Lesson 111	Solving Problems Involving Combinations	Lessons 119, 120	Test and Practice Generator CD	Lessons in other Saxon High School Math programs
119	Lessons 49, 89	Graphing and Comparing Linear, Quadratic, and Exponential Functions	Lesson 120	Test and Practice Generator CD	Lessons in other Saxon High School Math programs
120	Lessons 14, 16	Using Geometric Formulas to Find the Probability of an Event	N/A	Test and Practice Generator CD	Lessons in other Saxon High School Math programs
INV 12	N/A	Investigation: Investigating Matrices	N/A	Test and Practice Generator CD	Lessons in other Saxon High School Math programs

SECTION OVERVIEW 12

Ongoing Assessment

	Type	Feature	Intervention *
BEFORE instruction	Assess Prior Knowledge	• Diagnostic Test	• Prerequisite Skills Intervention
BEFORE the lesson	Formative	• Warm Up	• Skills Bank • Reteaching Masters
DURING the lesson	Formative	• Lesson Practice • Math Conversations with the Practice problems	• Additional Examples in TE • Test and Practice Generator (for additional practice sheets)
AFTER the lesson	Formative	• Check for Understanding (closure)	• Scaffolding Questions in TE
AFTER 5 lessons	Summative	After Lesson 115 • Cumulative Test 22 • Performance Task 22 After Lesson 120 • Cumulative Test 23 • Performance Task 23	• Reteaching Masters • Test and Practice Generator (for additional tests and practice)
AFTER 20 lessons	Summative	• Benchmark Tests • End-of-Year Exam	• Reteaching Masters • Test and Practice Generator (for additional tests and practice)

* for students not showing progress during the formative stages or scoring below 80% on the summative assessments

Evidence of Learning – What Students Should Know

Because the Saxon philosophy is to provide students with sufficient time to learn and practice each concept, a lesson's topic will not be tested until at least five lessons after the topic is introduced.

On the Cumulative Tests that are given during this section of ten lessons, students should be able to demonstrate the following competencies:
- Simplify rational expressions.
- Translate graphs of quadratic functions and absolute–value functions.
- Divide polynomials.
- Use the discriminant to find the number of solutions without solving.
- Solve quadratic equations, radical equations, and absolute-value inequalities.
- Use the Fundamental Counting Principle.
- Solve systems of linear inequalities.
- Extend geometric sequences.

Test and Practice Generator CD using ExamView™

The Test and Practice Generator is an easy-to-use benchmark and assessment tool that creates unlimited practice and tests in multiple formats and allows you to customize questions or create new ones. A variety of reports are available to track student progress toward mastery of the standards throughout the year.

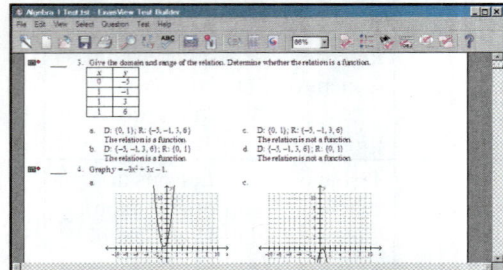
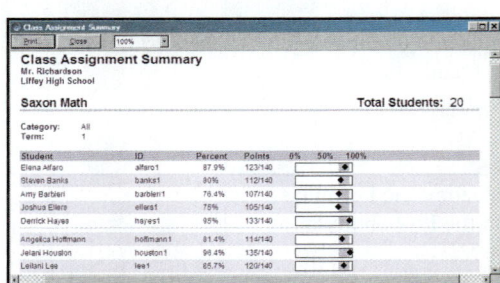

754E *Saxon Algebra 1*

Lessons 111–120, Investigation 12

Assessment Resources

Resources for Diagnosing and Assessing

- **Student Edition**
  - Warm Up
  - Lesson Practice

- **Teacher's Edition**
  - Math Conversations with the Practice problems
  - Check for Understanding (closure)

- **Course Assessments**
  - Diagnostic Test
  - Cumulative Tests
  - Performance Tasks
  - Benchmark Tests

Resources for Test Prep

- **Student Edition Practice**
  - Multiple-choice problems
  - Multiple-step and writing problems
  - Daily cumulative practice

- **Standardized Test Practice**

- **College Entrance Exam Practice**

- **Test and Practice Generator CD using ExamView™**

Resources for Intervention

- **Student Edition**
  - Skills Bank

- **Teacher's Edition**
  - Additional Examples
  - Scaffolding questions

- **Prerequisite Skills Intervention**
  - Worksheets

- **Reteaching Masters**
  - Lesson instruction and practice sheets

- **Test and Practice Generator CD using ExamView™**
  - Lesson practice problems
  - Additional tests

Cumulative Tests

The assessments in Saxon Math are frequent and consistently placed after every five lessons to offer a regular method of ongoing testing. These cumulative assessments check mastery of concepts from previous lessons.

Performance Tasks

The Performance Tasks can be used in conjunction with the Cumulative Tests and are scored using a rubric.

After Lesson 115

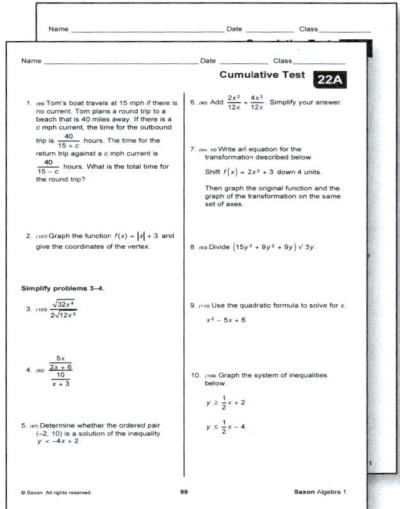

After Lesson 120

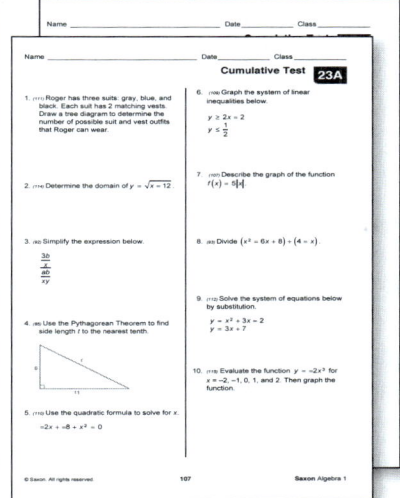

For use with Performance Tasks

Section Overview 12 754F

LESSON 111

1 Warm Up

Problems 4 and 5
Remind students of the difference between independent and dependent events.

2 New Concepts

In this lesson, students learn to solve problems involving permutations.

Example 1

Point out to students that using a tree diagram for reasonably sized sets can be very helpful to prevent counting errors.

Additional Example 1

A school basketball team uses three colors on their uniforms: red, blue, and white. Each uniform has a top and bottom. Determine the number of possible color combinations the team can have on their uniforms. **9**

LESSON RESOURCES

Student Edition Practice Workbook 111
Reteaching Master 111
Adaptations Master 111
Challenge and Enrichment Master C111
Technology Lab Master 111

LESSON 111 — Solving Problems Involving Permutations

Warm Up

1. **Vocabulary** _____ (*Experimental, Theoretical*) probability is found by analyzing a situation and finding the ratio of favorable outcomes to all possible outcomes. **Theoretical**

2. What is the probability of rolling a number greater than 3 on a number cube labeled 1–6? $\frac{1}{2}$

3. What is the probability of rolling a number greater than 7 on a number cube labeled 1–6? 0

Identify each set of events as independent or dependent.

4. Rolling a 5 on one number cube and a 3 on another. **independent**

5. Drawing a blue marble from a bag, keeping it, and then drawing a red marble. **dependent**

New Concepts

A tree diagram can be used to determine the number of ways 2 pairs of pants and 4 shirts can be arranged to make different outfits. However, the number of possible outcomes can be determined by multiplying the number of ways the first event can occur by the number of ways the second event can occur.

first event	second event	total possible outcomes
2 pairs of pants ×	4 shirts =	8 outfits

This method is an application of the Fundamental Counting Principle. The Fundamental Counting Principle can be used to determine the number of possible outcomes in situations involving independent events.

Fundamental Counting Principle

If an independent event M can occur in m ways and another independent event N can occur in n ways, then the number of ways that both events can occur is

$$m \cdot n.$$

Example: A restaurant offers 4 entrées and 5 vegetable dishes. How many meals with one entrée and one vegetable dish are possible?

20 meals may be ordered since $4 \cdot 5 = 20$.

Example 1 Using the Fundamental Counting Principle

A 1-topping pizza can be ordered with a choice of 4 different toppings: pepperoni, sausage, mushrooms, or onion. There is also a choice of different types of crust: thin, thick, or traditional. Find the number of ways that a 1-topping pizza can be ordered using the Fundamental Counting Principle.

Math Reasoning

Predict How many different pizzas would be possible if you had 5 choices for toppings and 2 choices for crust?

10 different pizzas

MATH BACKGROUND

It is very important for students to know the difference between permutations and combinations. The permutation and combination formulas:

$$_nP_r = \frac{n!}{(n-r)!} \qquad _nC_r = \frac{n!}{r!(n-r)!}$$

give the number of possible permutations/combinations of r objects from a set of n. Permutations have stricter requirements, such as the order, and will therefore have a larger number of possible outcomes than combinations. Students can remember this by:

$$_nP_r = {_nC_r} \cdot r!$$

SOLUTION

Determine the number of ways each event can occur and then find their product.

4 types of toppings × 3 types of crust = 12 possible pizza combinations

Check Use a tree diagram to verify that there are 12 possible pizza combinations.

Topping	Crust	Outcomes
Pepperoni	Thin / Thick / Traditional	Pepperoni Thin / Pepperoni Thick / Pepperoni Traditional
Sausage	Thin / Thick / Traditional	Sausage Thin / Sausage Thick / Sausage Traditional
Mushrooms	Thin / Thick / Traditional	Mushroom Thin / Mushroom Thick / Mushroom Traditional
Onions	Thin / Thick / Traditional	Onion Thin / Onion Thick / Onion Traditional

The tree diagram verifies that there are 12 possible outcomes.

When a group of people or objects are arranged in a certain order, the arrangement is called a **permutation.** The unique ways that 5 different colored blocks can be arranged are examples of permutations.

The factorial operation can be used to find different ways to arrange a set of n different items, where the first item may be selected n different ways, the second item may be selected $n - 1$ ways, and so on.

Reading Math

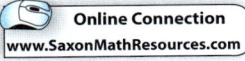

The expression 8! is read "eight factorial."

Factorial
The factorial $n!$ is defined for any natural number n as $n! = n(n-1)\ldots(2)(1)$.
Zero factorial is defined to be 1. $0! = 1$.
Example: $5! = 5 \cdot 4 \cdot 3 \cdot 2 \cdot 1$

There are $n!$ ways to position n students in a line. For example, the number of ways 6 students can be positioned in a line can be described by 6!. As each position in the line is filled, the number of students that can be chosen to fill each position decreases by 1.

1st	2nd	3rd ...
6 Students	5 Students	4 Students

Notice only 5 students can be chosen for the 2nd position because 1 student has already filled the 1st position. Continuing this pattern shows that 6 students can be arranged in order 6!, or $6 \cdot 5 \cdot 4 \cdot 3 \cdot 2 \cdot 1 = 720$, different ways.

Error Alert When drawing tree diagrams, a common mistake is to forget to apply the same number of choices to every independent event.

Remind students that for independent events, the tree diagram should be symmetrical.

Lesson 111

Example 2

Point out to students the shorthand, !, for factorials.

Additional Example 2
a. Find 9!. **362,880**

b. Find $\frac{3!}{7!}$. $\frac{1}{840}$

Exploration

Emphasize that using props and drawing pictures can be very helpful in solving problems involving probabilities.

Extend the Exploration

a. Given that a yellow ribbon is taken out of the set, list all possible ways that the three remaining colored ribbons can be arranged. **Sample: RBG, RGB, BGR, BRG, GBR, GRB**

b. List all possible way that any two of the three colored ribbons can be arranged. **6 ways; Sample: RB, BR, RG, GR, GB, BG**

Example 3

Remind students that the order matters in a permuation.

Additional Example 3

a. Eight people are competing in the 100-meter dash. In how many ways can the runners finish in first through eighth place? **40,320**

b. How many ways can the eight runners win a medal (finish in the top three places)? **336**

---

a. 24 ways; Sample with red, blue, yellow, and green ribbons: RBYG, RBGY, RYBG, RYGB, RGBY, RGYB, BRYG, BRGY, BYRG, BYGR, BGRY, BGYR, YRBG, YRGB, YBRG, YBGR, YGRB, YGBR, GRBY, GRYB, GBRY, GBYR, GYRB, GYBR

Materials
- index cards
- 4 different colored ribbons

Caution
Remember that 0! is equal to 1, not 0.

756 *Saxon* Algebra 1

Example 2 Simplifying Expressions with Factorials

a. Find 7!.

SOLUTION

$7!$
$= 7 \cdot 6 \cdot 5 \cdot 4 \cdot 3 \cdot 2 \cdot 1 = 5040$ Write the factors of 7! and multiply.

b. Find $\frac{9!}{4!}$.

SOLUTION

$\frac{9!}{4!}$

$= \frac{9 \cdot 8 \cdot 7 \cdot 6 \cdot 5 \cdot \cancel{4} \cdot \cancel{3} \cdot \cancel{2} \cdot \cancel{1}}{\cancel{4} \cdot \cancel{3} \cdot \cancel{2} \cdot \cancel{1}}$ Write the factors of 9! and 4!.

$= 9 \cdot 8 \cdot 7 \cdot 6 \cdot 5 = 15{,}120$ Multiply.

Exploration   Finding Possibilities When Order is Important

a. On an index card, list all possible ways that the 4 colored ribbons can be arranged.

b. On a second index card, list all possible ways that any two of the four colored ribbons can be arranged. **12 ways; Sample: RB, RG, RY, BR, BG, BY, YR, YG, YB, GR, GY, GB**

When choosing 3 of 8 contestants as finalists in a competition, order doesn't matter. However, in naming a first, second, and third place from the 8 contestants, the order does matter. Since order is important it is a permutation.

Permutation
The number of permutations of n objects taken r at a time is given by the formula $_nP_r = \frac{n!}{(n-r)!}$.

Example 3 Finding the Number of Permutations

a. Your school is running a recycling campaign in which 6 classes are competing to see who can collect the most recyclable materials. In how many ways can the classes finish in first through sixth place?

SOLUTION

This is a permutation of 6 things taken 6 at a time.

$_nP_r = \frac{n!}{(n-r)!}$ Write the formula.

$_6P_6 = \frac{6!}{(6-6)!} = \frac{6!}{0!}$ Simplify.

$= \frac{6 \cdot 5 \cdot 4 \cdot 3 \cdot 2 \cdot 1}{1}$ Write the factors of 6! and 0!.

$= 720$ Multiply.

756 *Saxon* Algebra 1

🛈 INCLUSION

Students may have difficulty with permutations. For Example **3a** have students draw blank lines on their paper to represent the places of the competition. Then ask,

"How many classes can fill first place?" **6**

Ask, "Once the first place position is filled, how many classes can fill second place?" **5**

Fill in the blank lines as the students answer the questions.

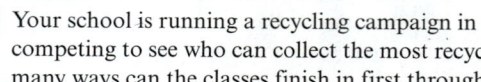

Then have the students fill in the rest of the blanks. Have them solve Example **3b** using the same method.

b. A total of 6 classes are competing to see who can collect the most recyclable materials. In how many different ways can the classes finish in first and second place?

SOLUTION

This is a permutation of 6 things taken 2 at a time.

$$_nP_r = \frac{n!}{(n-r)!}$$ Write the formula.

$$_6P_2 = \frac{6!}{(6-2)!} = \frac{6!}{4!}$$ Simplify.

$$= \frac{6 \cdot 5 \cdot \cancel{4} \cdot \cancel{3} \cdot \cancel{2} \cdot \cancel{1}}{\cancel{4} \cdot \cancel{3} \cdot \cancel{2} \cdot \cancel{1}} = 6 \cdot 5$$ Write the factors of 6! and 4!. Then simplify.

$$= 30$$ Multiply.

Math Reasoning

Generalize Another way to think about permutations of $_nP_r$ is to multiply the first r numbers of $n!$. So $_5P_3$ would be $5 \cdot 4 \cdot 3 = 60$. Explain how to find $_7P_2$ and then find its value.

Sample: Multiply 7 times 6; 42

Example 4 **Application: Uniform Numbers**

The 15 members of a softball team have uniform numbers 1 through 15. They are introduced randomly at a pep rally. What is the probability that the first 4 players introduced will have uniform numbers 1, 2, 3, and 4 in that order?

SOLUTION

Of the possible permutations only 1, 2, 3, 4 is favorable.

The probability is represented by:

$$\frac{\text{number of ways to choose 1, 2, 3, 4}}{\text{number of ways to choose 4 numbers}} = \frac{1}{_{15}P_4} = \frac{1}{15 \cdot 14 \cdot 13 \cdot 12} = \frac{1}{32{,}760}$$

Lesson Practice

a. While trying to schedule a flight for vacation, you are given two choices for departure and four choices for the return flight. How many ways can you schedule your flights for the trip? 8
(Ex 1)

b. A video game character has 6 choices each for hair color, face, attitude, and outfit as well as a choice of male or female. How many different characters are possible? 2592
(Ex 1)

c. Find 5!. 120
(Ex 2)

d. Find $\frac{6!}{3!}$. 120
(Ex 2)

e. You are selecting your class schedule for the school year. If there are 7 periods and each of the seven classes are taught each period, how many possible ways are there for your schedule to be determined? 5040
(Ex 3)

f. There are 10 people in the Activities Club. In how many different ways can a president, vice-president and treasurer be selected from the club members? 720
(Ex 3)

Lesson 111   757

Example 4

Explain to students that the probability of an event with one possible permutation is the reciprocal of the number of ways that event can happen.

Extend the Example

If the first 4 players that were introduced have uniform numbers 1, 2, 3, and 4, what is the probability that the next 4 being introduced will have numbers 5, 6, 7, and 8 in that order? $\frac{1}{7920}$

Additional Example 4

There are 10 people running for president of the student body government—each identified by a number. If the candidates are introduced randomly at a debate, what is the probability that the first 4 introduced will be candidates 10, 9, 8, 7 in that order? $\frac{1}{5040}$

Lesson Practice

Problem d

Scaffolding When simplifying a fraction involving factorials, suggest that students expand the factorials and divide out like terms one at a time.

Problem f

Error Alert It is possible that some students will attempt to draw the tree diagram for this problem. Remind students that with large numbers, the Fundamental Counting Principle is much more practical.

ENGLISH LEARNERS

Explain the meaning of the word **departure**. Say:

"The departure time of a flight is the time a plane is leaving the airport."

"Why should someone arrive at the airport several hours before the departure time?"
Sample: They will need to check in with the airline and go through security checkpoints.

Have students read a bus schedule to familiarize themselves with arrival and departure times.

Check for Understanding

The questions below help assess the concepts taught in this lesson.

"How many ways can 8 people be positioned in a line?" 8! or 40,320

"How can one find the number of permutations of r objects from a group of n?" Sample: $_nP_r = \frac{n!}{(n-r)!}$.

3 Practice

Math Conversations

Discussion to strengthen understanding

Problem 6

After factoring the expression to find the zeros, remind students that quadratic equations can have zero, one, or two solutions.

Problem 11

Guide the students by asking them the following questions.

"How is $y - 2.5 > 0$ graphed?" Sample: Graph the line $y = 2.5$ with a dashed line and shade the region above it.

"How is $y - 4 < -2x$ graphed?" Sample: Graph the line $y = -2x + 4$ with a dashed line and shade the region below the line.

---

g. A popular TV series ran for 10 seasons. You are buying the seasons (Ex 4) from an online DVD service. If each season arrives at random, what is the probability that the first 5 seasons you receive in the mail are the first 5 seasons that were made, in the correct order? $\frac{1}{30,240}$

Practice Distributed and Integrated

*1. Draw a tree diagram to represent the possible outcomes of flipping a coin (111) three times. See Additional Answers.

*2. **Multiple Choice** Evaluate 10!. A
(111)
   A 3,628,800   B 362,880   C 55   D 9

*3. (**Video Rental**) For movie night, you want to rent one drama, one comedy, and one (111) science fiction movie. The video store has 5 new releases for drama, 6 new releases for comedy, and 3 new releases for science fiction. How many possible movie combinations are there? 90

4. Simplify the rational expression $\frac{3d}{2x^3} - \frac{5d}{2x^3}$ if possible. $\frac{-d}{x^3}$
(51)

Find the zeros of each function.

5. $y = x^2 - 8x + 16$ 4
(96)

6. $y = 3x^2 + 36x - 39$ $-13, 1$
(96)

*7. **Model** Draw a tree diagram to determine the number of possible outcomes of (111) earning an A, B, or C in history, English, and math classes.
See Additional Answers.

*8. **Justify** Explain how to find the number of outfits possible if you have 5 shirts and (111) 4 pairs of pants to choose from. Sample: Multiply 5 times 4 to get 20 possible outfits.

*9. Use the quadratic formula to solve $c^2 + 16c - 36 = 0$. Check the solutions. 2, -18
(110)

*10. **Estimate** Find the best whole number estimate for the solutions to $70 - 52x = -x^2$.
(110) 1, 51

11. Find and correct the error the student made in graphing $\begin{array}{l} y - 2.5 > 0 \\ y - 4 < -2x \end{array}$.
(109)

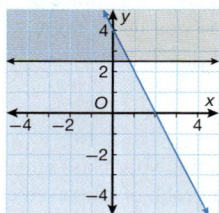

Sample: The student should have made both lines dashed because the points on the boundary lines are not solutions.

12. Graph the system $\begin{array}{l} 4x - 2y < 6 \\ y + 1 \geq 2x \end{array}$. See Additional Answers.
(109)

13. Solve $r^2 - 24r = -144$ by completing the square. $r = 12$
(104)

758   Saxon Algebra 1

*14. Error Analysis Two students used the quadratic formula to solve a quadratic equation. Which student is correct? Explain the error.
(110)

Student A	Student B
$8a = -10a^2 + 1$	$8a = -10a^2 + 1$
$8a - 10a^2 + 1 = 0$	$10a^2 + 8a - 1 = 0$
$x = \dfrac{-(-10) \pm \sqrt{-10^2 - 4(8)(1)}}{2(8)}$	$x = \dfrac{-8 \pm \sqrt{8^2 - 4(10)(-1)}}{2(10)}$
$x = \dfrac{10 \pm \sqrt{100 + 32}}{16}$	$x = \dfrac{-8 \pm \sqrt{64 + 40}}{20}$
$x = \dfrac{10 \pm \sqrt{132}}{16}$	$x = \dfrac{-8 \pm \sqrt{104}}{20}$
$x = \dfrac{10 \pm 2\sqrt{33}}{16}$	$x = \dfrac{-8 \pm 2\sqrt{26}}{20}$
$x = \dfrac{5 \pm \sqrt{33}}{8}$	$x = \dfrac{-4 \pm \sqrt{26}}{10}$

14. Student B; Sample: Student A did not substitute the correct values for a, b, and c and did not rearrange the equation correctly.

*15. Space Shuttle The external tank of the space shuttle separates after 8.5 minutes at a velocity of 28,067 kilometers per hour. Can the formula $-4.9t^2 + v_0 t + y_0 = 0$ be used to find the distance above earth? Explain. No. Sample: The formula involves the initial velocity and height.
(110)

16. Measurement The length of a piece of wood must measure between 15 and 17 centimeters and the width must measure between 9 and 11 centimeters. Write a system of linear inequalities to represent the possible dimensions of the wood piece, in inches, given that 1 inch is equal to 2.54 centimeters. $5.91 \leq l \leq 6.69$; $3.54 \leq w \leq 4.33$
(109)

17. Business The total profit on a particular skateboard is represented as $p^2 - 7p$ where p is the number of units sold in thousands. How many units need to be sold to have a profit of $23,750? Round to the nearest hundred. 157,700 units
(104)

18. Find the next 3 terms of the sequence $\dfrac{1}{2187}, \dfrac{1}{729}, \dfrac{1}{243}, \dfrac{1}{81}, \ldots$ $\dfrac{1}{27}, \dfrac{1}{9}, \dfrac{1}{3}$
(105)

19. Chemistry Oxygen evaporation from a body of water increases with the temperature. This process of oxygen depletion can be modeled by the expression $\dfrac{\sqrt{x}}{6}$ where x is the temperature in C°. What value of x corresponds to an evaporation of 9 cubic feet of oxygen? $x = 2916$
(106)

20. Graph the function $f(x) = 3|x|$. See Additional Answers.
(107)

21. Multiple Choice Which function is not an exponential function? **C**
(108)
  A $y = 4(3)^x$ **B** $y = -4(3)^x$ **C** $y = 4^3 x$ **D** $y = 4\left(\dfrac{1}{3}\right)^x$

22. Analyze For an exponential function with $a = 5$ and $b = 3$, why is it necessary to put parentheses around the 3 when writing the function rule? Sample: To show that the exponent of x only applies to the value of 3, and not to the product of 5 and 3.
(108)

23. Geometry The diagram shows a right triangle with a hypotenuse that is an irrational number. What set of numbers would include the hypotenuse? irrational, real numbers
(1)

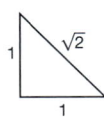

Problem 18

Guide the students by asking the following questions.

"What is happening to the numerators of the fractions as the position of the terms increase?" Sample: the numerators stay the same

"What is happening to the denominators of the fractions as the position of the terms increase?" Sample: the denominators decrease

"By how much are the denominators of the fractions decreasing?" By one third

"What is one third of 81?" 27

Lesson 111   759

Problem 25
Extend the Problem
"Is the setting on Jeannine's oven more accurate at 100°F or 450°F?"
Sample: It is more accurate at 450°F since ±9°F is a smaller fraction of the temperature at 450°F than at 100°F.

Problem 27
Error Alert
In part c, it is common for students to calculate the answer by $\frac{150}{0.5}$. That divides the length to 300 equal parts, but if Jasmine wants to plant tulips 6 inches apart, she will need $300 + 1 = 301$ tulips.

---

24. Evaluate $x^2 - 8x + 15$ and its factors for $x = -2$. $35 = (-5)(-7)$
    (72)

25. **Oven Temperature** The actual temperature (t) of Jeannine's oven varies by no more
    (101) than 9°F from the set temperature. Jeannine sets her oven to 350°F. Write an absolute-value inequality that models the possible actual temperatures inside the oven. What is the lowest possible temperature? $|t - 350| \leq 9$; $341 \leq t \leq 359$; 341°F

26. **Multi-Step** The length of a picture is 2 inches greater than
    (98) its width. A 3-inch-wide border is added to the bottom of
    the picture for a scrapbook page.
    a. Write expressions for the width and length of the
       picture with the border. $x + 3, x + 2$
    b. The area of the picture with the border is 110 square
       inches. Find the length and width of the original photo.
       8 inches by 10 inches

    $x + 2$ inches
    x inches
    3 inches

27. **Multi-Step** Jasmine wants to plant tulips around the perimeter of her property. The
    (102) property is the shape of a square. The area of the yard is 21,000 square feet and
    the area of the house is 1500 square feet.
    a. Write a formula to find the length of the sides of the property. $x^2 = 21,000 + 1500$
    b. Solve for x. $x = 150$ ft
    c. Jasmine changes her mind and decides to buy enough bulbs to plant them 6
       inches apart along just one edge of the property. How many bulbs will she need
       if she starts at the first corner and goes to the second corner?   301 bulbs

28. **Justify** Explain how to simplify $\frac{6}{\sqrt{5} - 7}$.
    (103)

29. Subtract $\frac{2x^2}{x^2 - 49} - \frac{x - 7}{x^2 - 6x - 7}$. $\frac{2x^3 + x^2 + 49}{(x - 7)(x + 7)(x + 1)}$
    (95)

*30. If $f(x) = \frac{1}{3}^x$ and $g(x) = 3^x$, which function represents exponential growth and
 (Inv. 11) which function represents exponential decay? $g(x)$ represents exponential growth and $f(x)$ represents exponential decay.

28. Sample: First, multiply by a factor of 1 using the conjugate of $\sqrt{5} - 7$, which is $\sqrt{5} + 7$. Then use the Distributive Property to multiply across the numerators, and the FOIL method to multiply across the denominators. Finally, combine like terms and simplify.

760   Saxon Algebra 1

 CHALLENGE

Ann, Bob, Charlie, and Denise are running for president of the Movie Club. The president will get to pick his/her vice-president. However, Ann and Bob don't know each other and won't choose the other. Charlie only wants to work with Ann or Denise. How many ways can the president and vice-president be chosen? Use a tree diagram to solve.
8 ways: (president, vice-president)(Ann, Charlie), (Ann, Denise)(Bob, Denise)(Charlie, Ann), (Charlie, Denise)(Denise, Ann), (Denise, Bob), (Denise, Charlie)

LOOKING FORWARD

Solving problems involving permutations prepares students for

• **Lesson 118** Solving Problems Involving Combinations

• **Lesson 120** Using Geometric Formulas to Find the Probability of an Event

LESSON 112

Graphing and Solving Systems of Linear and Quadratic Equations

Warm Up

1. **Vocabulary** A set of linear equations with the same variables is called a _____ of linear equations.   **system**

2. Write $2x^2 = -x + 8$ in standard form. $2x^2 + x - 8 = 0$

3. Solve $5x - y = 4 + 9x$ for y. $y = -4x - 4$

4. Evaluate $50 - 2x^2$ for $x = -5$. 0

5. **Multiple Choice** Which ordered pair is a solution of the system $\begin{array}{l} x - y = 7 \\ 2x + y = -1 \end{array}$?   **A**

   A $(2, -5)$ **B** $(6, -1)$ **C** $\left(\dfrac{8}{3}, -\dfrac{13}{3}\right)$ **D** $(3, -4)$

New Concepts

The equations $y = 14 - 4x$ and $y = x + 4$ are a system of linear equations. The solution $(2, 6)$ is a point at which the graphs of the equations intersect.

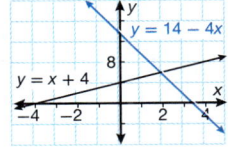

A system of equations can also consist of a linear equation and a quadratic equation. The graphs of three systems each consisting of a quadratic equation, $y = x^2$, and a linear equation are shown.

System A

$y = x^2$
$y = x + 6$

System A has two solutions because the graphs of the system intersect at two points.

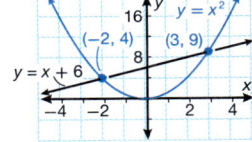

Math Reasoning

Analyze What are the cordinates of the vertex for every equation of the form $y = ax^2$?

$(0, 0)$

System B

$y = x^2$
$y = 2x - 1$

System B has only one solution.

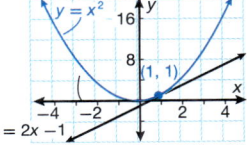

System C

$y = x^2$
$y = 3x - 5$

System C has no solution because the graphs do not intersect.

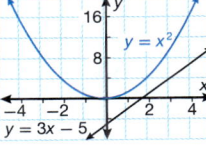

Online Connection
www.SaxonMathResources.com

MATH BACKGROUND

Students have learned how to solve systems of linear equations by graphing. They learned that the solution to a system of linear equations is the point at which the two lines intersect on the coordinate plane, so the ordered pair must be a solution to both equations. Solving with systems of equations consisting of linear and quadratic equations is similar to solving systems of linear equations.

However, when quadratic equations are involved, multiple solutions can be possible (including the special case of two identical equations in a system)—i.e. the graphs can intersect at multiple points.

A special case, where a line touches a parabola at a point without crossing over the parabola, is referred to as a tangent line.

Example 1

Remind students that the solution(s) to the system of equations is where the graph of the equations intersect.

TEACHER TIP

Emphasize that, in general, the graphing technique provides only approximate solutions. The estimated coordinates need to be checked by substituting them into each equation.

Additional Example 1

Solve each system of equations by graphing. Then check the solution.

a. $y = x^2$
$y = 9$

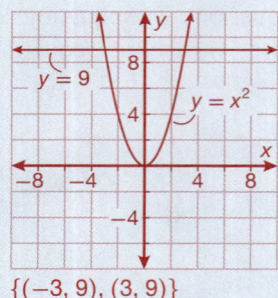

$\{(-3, 9), (3, 9)\}$

b. $y = x^2$
$y = 2x$

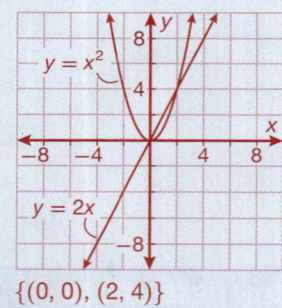

$\{(0, 0), (2, 4)\}$

c. $y = x^2 + 2$
$y = x$

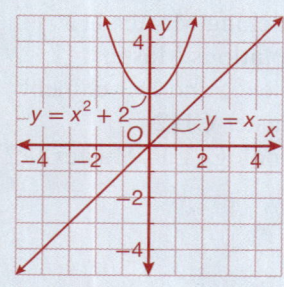

no solution

Example 1 Solving by Graphing

Solve each system of equations by graphing. Then check the solution.

a. $y = x^2$
$y = 4$

SOLUTION Graph the parabola $y = x^2$ and the horizontal line $y = 4$.

The line intersects the parabola at $(2, 4)$ and $(-2, 4)$. The solution of the system is the ordered pairs $(2, 4)$ and $(-2, 4)$.

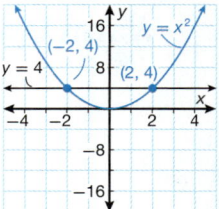

Check

$y = x^2$ $y = x^2$
$4 \stackrel{?}{=} (2)^2$ $4 \stackrel{?}{=} (-2)^2$
$4 = 4$ ✓ $4 = 4$ ✓

Caution

Be sure to check all solutions in both of the original equations of the system.

b. $y = x^2$
$y = -4x - 4$

SOLUTION Graph the parabola and the line.

The line intersects the parabola at only one point. The solution is $(-2, 4)$.

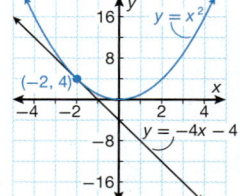

Check

$y = x^2$ $y = -4x - 4$
$4 \stackrel{?}{=} (-2)^2$ $4 \stackrel{?}{=} -4(-2) - 4$
$4 = 4$ ✓ $4 = 4$ ✓

c. $y = 2x^2 - 9$
$y = 4x - 9$

SOLUTION The graphs of $y = 2x^2 - 9$ and $y = 4x - 9$ show two points of intersection. The coordinates of those two points are $(2, -1)$ and $(0, -9)$.

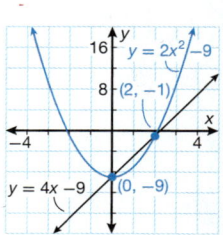

Check Verify that $(2, -1)$ is a solution.

$y = 2x^2 - 9$ $y = 4x - 9$
$-1 \stackrel{?}{=} 2(2)^2 - 9$ $-1 \stackrel{?}{=} 4(2) - 9$
$-1 = -1$ ✓ $-1 = -1$ ✓

Verify that $(0, -9)$ is a solution.

$y = 2x^2 - 9$ $y = 4x - 9$
$-9 \stackrel{?}{=} 2(0)^2 - 9$ $-9 \stackrel{?}{=} 4(0) - 9$
$-9 = -9$ ✓ $-9 = -9$ ✓

INCLUSION

Have students copy and complete the table for the system of equations:
$y = x^2$
$y = 4$

x	$y = x^2$	$y = 4$
-3	9	4
-2	4	4
-1	1	4
0	0	4
1	1	4
2	4	4
3	9	4

Have students use the table to find the solutions. $\{(-2, 4), (2, 4)\}$

Math Reasoning

Verify Use a graphing calculator to show that $\frac{x^2}{2} - 3$ is the same as $\left(\frac{x^2}{2}\right) - 3$. Explain.

Sample: The graphs are the same. The division bar acts as a grouping symbol. Since there are no terms added to the numerator or denominator, the parentheses are not necessary.

Graphing Calculator Tip

For help with graphing systems, refer to the graphing calculator keystrokes in Graphing Calculator Lab 5 on p. 352.

Example 2 Solving with a Graphing Calculator

Solve each system of equations by using a graphing calculator.

a. $y = \frac{x^2}{2} - 3$
$y = x - 3$

SOLUTION

Enter $Y_1 = \frac{x^2}{2} - 3$ and $Y_2 = x - 3$.

The display shows two graphs: a parabola and a line.

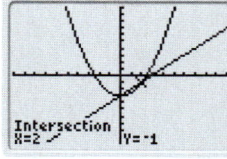

Use TRACE to approximate the solutions first. Then confirm the answers using INTERSECT.

The display shows the coordinates of the two points of intersection.

The first point of intersection is $(2, -1)$ and the second point of intersection is $(0, -3)$.

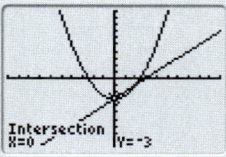

Check

Substitute $(2, -1)$ into both equations.

$y = \frac{x^2}{2} - 3$ $y = x - 3$
$-1 \stackrel{?}{=} \frac{(2)^2}{2} - 3$ $-1 \stackrel{?}{=} 2 - 3$
               $-1 = -1$ ✓
$-1 = -1$ ✓

Substitute $(0, 3)$ into both equations.

$y = \frac{x^2}{2} - 3$ $y = x - 3$
$-3 \stackrel{?}{=} \frac{(0)^2}{2} - 3$ $-3 \stackrel{?}{=} 0 - 3$
               $-3 = -3$ ✓
$-3 = -3$ ✓

b. $y = x^2$
$y = 2x - 2$

SOLUTION

Enter $Y_1 = x^2$ and $Y_2 = 2x - 2$.

The display shows two graphs: a parabola and a line.

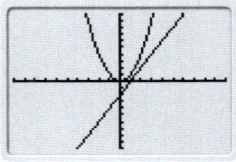

The display shows that the parabola and the line do not intersect, so there are no solutions to this system.

If the calculator is used to find a point of intersection, an error message is displayed.

Lesson 112   763

Example 2

Point out to students that entries into graphing calculators must be accurate for accurate results.

Error Alert Some students will forget to check the solution with both equations. Remind them that an ordered pair must be a solution to both equations to be a solution to the system.

Additional Example 2

Solve each system of equations by using a graphing calculator.

a. $y = x^2 - 3$
$y = x - 3$
$\{(0, -3), (1, -2)\}$

b. $y = -x^2$
$y = x + 1$
no solution

Lesson 112   763

Example 3

Point out to students that since a system of equations will have the same variables, they can substitute one into the other.

Additional Example 3

Solve each system of equations by substitution.

a. $y = x^2 + 3x + 3$
$y = -x - 1$
$\{(-2, 1)\}$

b. $y = x^2 + 2$
$y = 4x - 1$
$\{(1, 3), (3, 11)\}$

Math Reasoning

Verify Show that the ordered pairs $(-2, -7)$ and $(2, 13)$ are solutions to Example 3a and that the ordered pairs $(-2, -7)$ and $(-3, -9)$ are the solutions to Example 3b.

Example 3a:
$y = x^2 + 5x - 1$
$-7 \stackrel{?}{=} (-2)^2 + 5(-2) - 1$
$-7 \stackrel{?}{=} 4 - 10 - 1$
$-7 = -7$ ✓
$y = x^2 + 5x - 1$
$13 \stackrel{?}{=} (2)^2 + 5(2) - 1$
$13 \stackrel{?}{=} 4 + 10 - 1$
$13 = 13$ ✓

Example 3b:
$y = x^2 + 7x + 3$
$-7 \stackrel{?}{=} (-2)^2 + 7(-2) + 3$
$-7 \stackrel{?}{=} 4 - 14 + 3$
$-7 = -7$ ✓
$y = x^2 + 7x + 3$
$-9 \stackrel{?}{=} (-3)^2 + 7(-3) + 3$
$-9 \stackrel{?}{=} 9 - 21 + 3$
$-9 = -9$ ✓

Example 3 Solving Using Substitution

Solve each system of equations by substitution.

a. $y = x^2 + 5x - 1$
$y = 5x + 3$

SOLUTION

$x^2 + 5x - 1 = 5x + 3$ Substitute the quadratic equation into the linear equation.

$\underline{-5x - 3} \quad \underline{-5x - 3}$ Add the expression $-5x - 3$ to both sides.

$x^2 - 4 = 0$ Recognize the left side of the equation as a difference of squares.

$(x + 2)(x - 2) = 0$ Factor.

$x + 2 = 0$ and $x - 2 = 0$ Solve both equations.

$x = -2 \qquad x = 2$

Determine the corresponding values of y by substituting the values of x into either equation.

$y = 5x + 3 \qquad\qquad y = 5x + 3$
$y = 5(-2) + 3 \qquad y = 5(2) + 3$
$y = -10 + 3 \qquad\quad y = 10 + 3$
$y = -7 \qquad\qquad\quad y = 13$

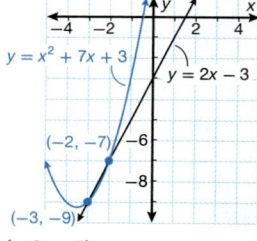

The solutions are the ordered pairs $(-2, -7)$ and $(2, 13)$. The solutions appear at the intersections of the two graphs.

b. $y = x^2 + 7x + 3$
$y = 2x - 3$

SOLUTION

$x^2 + 7x + 3 = 2x - 3$ Substitute the quadratic equation into the linear equation.

$\underline{-2x + 3} \quad \underline{-2x + 3}$ Add the expression $-2x + 3$ to both sides.

$x^2 + 5x + 6 = 0$ Recognize the left side of the equation as a trinomial that can be factored.

$(x + 3)(x + 2) = 0$ Factor.

$x + 3 = 0$ and $x + 2 = 0$ Solve both equations.

$x = -3$ and $x = -2$

Determine the values of y.

$y = 2x - 3 \qquad\qquad y = 2x - 3$
$y = 2(-3) - 3 \qquad y = 2(-2) - 3$
$y = -6 - 3 \qquad\quad y = -4 - 3$
$y = -9 \qquad\qquad\quad y = -7$

The solutions are the ordered pairs $(-3, -9)$ and $(-2, -7)$.

Example 4 Application: Avalanches

A ski patrol fires an explosive arrow to trigger a controlled avalanche. The path of the arrow is modeled by the equation $y = -\frac{x^2}{1600} + 2x$ and the shape of the mountainside is modeled by $y = \frac{3x}{4}$ where x is the horizontal distance and y is the vertical distance. At what altitude will the arrow strike the mountain? (Assume all dimensions are in feet.)

SOLUTION

Understand The path of the arrow is modeled by a parabola. The mountainside is modeled by a straight line.

$y = -\frac{x^2}{1600} + 2x$

$y = \frac{3x}{4}$

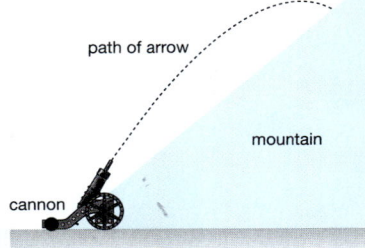

Plan The equation of the arrow's path and the equation of the shape of the mountain form a system of equations.

Solving this system will determine the points at which the two graphs intersect.

Solve One way of solving the system is by graphing the two equations. The cannon is located at the base of the mountain, so both graphs pass through (0, 0). The non-origin solution to the system is (2000, 1500). The altitude at which the arrow will strike the side of the mountain is 1500 feet.

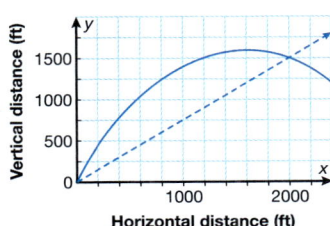

Check

$y = \frac{3x}{4}$

$1500 \stackrel{?}{=} \frac{3(2000)}{4}$

$1500 \stackrel{?}{=} \frac{6000}{4}$

$1500 = 1500$ ✓

$y = -\frac{x^2}{1600} + 2x$

$1500 \stackrel{?}{=} -\frac{2000^2}{1600} + 2(2000)$

$1500 \stackrel{?}{=} -\frac{4{,}000{,}000}{1600} + 4000$

$1500 \stackrel{?}{=} -2500 + 4000$

$1500 = 1500$ ✓

Math Reasoning

Write Describe the meaning of the x-coordinate in the solution (2000, 1500).

Sample: The arrow will strike the mountain at (2000 ft, 1500 ft). The arrow will be 2000 horizontal feet from the cannon when it strikes the mountain.

Lesson Practice

Solve each system of equations by graphing.
(Ex 1)

a. $y = x^2$
$y = 16$

b. $y = x^2$
$y = 6x - 9$

c. $y = x^2$
$y = -2x + 3$

See Additional Answers.

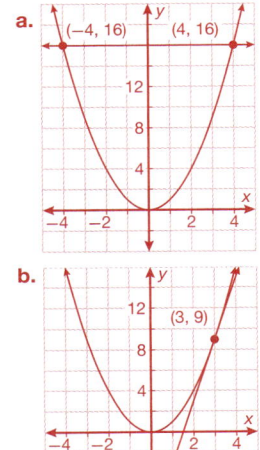

a. (−4, 16) (4, 16)

b. (3, 9)

Lesson 112   765

Lesson Practice

Problem e

Error Alert When entering the coefficients for equations on a graphing calculator, students sometimes will make the mistake of forgetting the minus sign of negative coefficients. Remind them to be careful and to double-check their inputs.

Problem f

Scaffolding After solving for x, suggest that students substitute the value of x into the linear equations to get y.

Check for Understanding

The questions below help assess the concepts taught in this lesson.

"Explain what the possible solutions are for a system of a linear and a quadratic equation." Sample: two points, one point, or no solution

"If an ordered pair is a solution to a system of two equations, what does that mean when the two equations are graphed?" Sample: The ordered pair will be the point where the two equations intersect.

3 Practice

Math Conversations

Discussion to strengthen understanding

Problem 3

Remind students that x^{-a} is the same as .

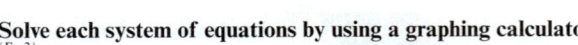 Solve each system of equations by using a graphing calculator.
(Ex 2)

d. $y = \frac{x^2}{2} + 1$
   $y = -\frac{3x}{2}$
   $(-1, 1.5)$ and $(-2, 3)$

e. $y = -2x^2 - 1$
   $y = -x - 2$
   $(1, -3)$ and $(-0.5, -1.5)$

Solve each system of equations by substitution.
(Ex 3)

f. $y = x^2 - 3x - 17$
   $y = -3x + 8$
   $(5, -7)$ and $(-5, 23)$

g. $y = x^2 + 7x + 5$
   $y = 2x - 1$
   $(-2, -5)$ and $(-3, -7)$

h. **Physics** A gardener places a sprinkler at the bottom of a gently rising
(Ex 4) hillside described by the equation $y = \frac{2x}{5}$. The equation $y = -\frac{x^2}{25} + x$ represents the path of the water. If the water splashes onto a rock on the hillside, what is the rock's altitude? (Assume all dimensions are in feet.)
6 feet

Practice Distributed and Integrated

*1. Solve this system by graphing: $\begin{array}{l} y = -x^2 + 12 \\ y = -x + 6 \end{array}$.
(112)

1.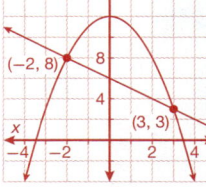

*2. **Multiple Choice** Which system of equations has no solution? C
(112)

A $\begin{array}{l} y = x^2 + 2 \\ y = 3 \end{array}$
B $\begin{array}{l} y = x^2 - 2 \\ y = 3 \end{array}$
C $\begin{array}{l} y = -x^2 + 2 \\ y = 3 \end{array}$
D $\begin{array}{l} y = -x^2 - 2 \\ y = -3 \end{array}$

3. Simplify the rational expression $c^{-2}f^{-5} + \frac{6}{c^2f^5}$, if possible. $\frac{7}{c^2f^5}$
(51)

4. Write a compound inequality that represents all real numbers that are greater than
(73) -4 and less than 8. $-4 < x < 8$

*5. **Architecture** In a European castle, a room with an arched ceiling is covered by a
(112) slanted roof. The ceiling is modeled by the equation $y = -x^2 + 4$ and the roofline by the equation $y = -2x + 5$. Assume that the dimensions are in meters. What are the coordinates for the point of intersection of the roof with the ceiling assuming that the vertex of the parabola is $(0, 4)$? $(1, 3)$

*6. **Analyze** A system of three equations consists of the quadratic equation $y = x^2$ and
(112) two linear equations that do not describe the same line. What is the maximum number of ordered pairs in the solution set? Explain.

7. A six-sided number cube is rolled three times. How many outcomes are possible?
(111) 216

*8. **Error Analysis** Two students are finding the value of $_6P_6$. Which student is correct?
(111) Explain the error. Student B; Sample: $0! = 1$, not 0.

Student A	Student B
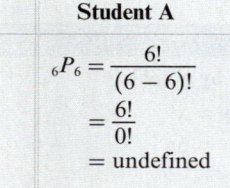	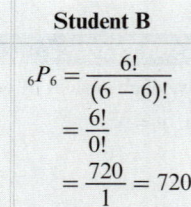

6. one; Sample: Because the two linear equations can only intersect at one point, that point must also be the point where they both intersect the parabola. So, the maximum number of points of intersection for all three equations is one.

766 Saxon Algebra 1

ENGLISH LEARNERS

Explain the meaning of the word **sprinkler**. Say:

"A sprinkler is a lawn tool that waters an area of lawn by spraying water."

Draw the parabolic path of a sprinkler on the board and show how it is able to water an area of a lawn. Say:

"What do the paths of the water from a lawn sprinkler look like?" Sample: a parabola

9. **Geometry** A triangle can be classified according to its sides or according to its angles. There are three side length categories—equilateral, isosceles, and scalene—and three angle categories—acute, obtuse, and right.
   a. How many possibilities are there for classifying triangles according to both sides and angles?   9
   b. How many of these triangles are not possible? Which ones are they?
   2; equilateral obtuse triangle and equilateral right triangle

10. **Multi-Step** There are 7 runners on the track team. Runners will be selected randomly for the first, second, third, and final positions on the 4-member relay team.
    a. How many different relay teams can be formed?   840 relay teams
    b. What is the probability that a runner at random is chosen to be on the relay team? $\frac{4}{7}$

11. Use the quadratic formula to solve $x^2 - 60 + 17x = 0$. Check the solutions.   3, −20

12. **Multiple Choice** What are the solutions to $2a^2 + 20a - 30 = 0$?   C
    A $20 \pm 4\sqrt{10}$
    B $-20 \pm \sqrt{10}$
    C $-5 \pm 2\sqrt{10}$
    D $-5 \pm \sqrt{10}$

*13. **Measurement** A rectangle has sides of length x feet and $2x + 2$ feet with an area of 24 square feet. Cassandra uses the quadratic formula and finds that x equals 3 and −4. She determines that this means the sides of the rectangle are −4 by −6 or 3 by 8. Why is she incorrect?   Sample: She's using measurements, therefore negative values of x are irrelevant.

14. **(Construction)** Suzanne would like to place a fence around her rectangular yard, which has a perimeter of 200 feet. The fencing for the front length of the yard will cost $5 per foot and the fencing for the side and back of the yard will cost $3 per foot. Her total cost is $720. What are the dimensions of her property?   40 feet by 60 feet

15. Find the next 3 terms of the sequence −0.032, 0.16, −0.8, 4, ….   −20, 100, −500

16. **(Paper Folding)** Solange folds a piece of paper, making two rectangles. When she folds it again, she makes 4 rectangles. Each fold doubles the number of rectangles. A sequence describing this process is 2, 4, 8, …. If someone folds a piece of paper 12 times, how many rectangles did the 12 folds form?   4096

17. Solve the equation $\frac{\sqrt{x}}{6} = 12$. Check your answer. $x = 5184$; $\frac{\sqrt{5184}}{6} = \frac{72}{6} = 12$

18. **(Population)** The exponential function $y = 11.35(1.00183)^x$ can model the approximate population of Ohio from 2000 to 2006, where x is the number of years after 2000 and y represents millions of people. What was the population in 2003?   11,412,000 people

19. Evaluate the function $f(x) = -2(4)^x$ for $x = -2, 0,$ and 2. $-\frac{1}{8}, -2, -32$

20. **Multiple Choice** Which system has no solutions?   D
    A $y < 2$; $y < 1$
    B $y > 2$; $y > 1$
    C $y < 2$; $y > 1$
    D $y > 2$; $y < 1$

Lesson 112   767

Problem 10
Guide students by asking them the following questions.

"How can the question be rephrased using the word permutation?"
Sample: How many permutations of 4 runners can be made from 7 total?

"What is the permutation formula? What are the values of n and r?" $_nP_r = \frac{n!}{(n-r)!}$; $n = 7, r = 4$

Problem 12
Guide the students by asking the following questions.

"When should the factoring method not be used to solve a quadratic equation?" Sample: when factors are difficult to find

"Name a method, other than factoring, that can be used to solve this equation." Sample: completing the square, substituting into the quadratic formula

Lesson 112   767

Problem 24
Extend the Problem

"If the girl's father takes 2 hours to complete the job and joins the three of them, how long will it take the four of them to finish the job?"

$\frac{t}{4} + \frac{t}{3} + \frac{t}{2} + \frac{t}{6} = 1$;

$t = \frac{4}{5}$ hours or 48 minutes.

Problem 28
Error Alert

A common mistake that students make when they divide to remove the negative coefficients of the x^2-term in quadratic equations is forgetting to change the signs of the other coefficients.

---

21. Analyze What inequality symbols should go into the boxes so that the solution set lies between the lines and does not include the boundary points?
Sample: The first inequality should have < and the second inequality should have >.

$y \;\square\; \frac{3}{5}x + 7$

$y \;\square\; \frac{3}{5}x + 1$

23.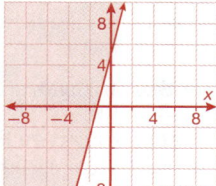

22. Find the zeros of the function $y = x^2 - 6x - 72$.   12, −6

23. Graph the inequality $4x - y \le -5$.

24. Multi-Step A girl takes 4 hours to complete a job. Her mother can complete the same job in 3 hours. Her little sister takes 6 hours to complete it.
  a. Write an equation representing how long it takes the three of them to complete the job working together. $\frac{t}{4} + \frac{t}{3} + \frac{t}{6} = 1$
  b. How long will it take to complete the job, in hours, if all three family members work together? $\frac{4}{3}$ hours
  c. How many minutes is that?   80 minutes

25. Biking Dustin and Roberto leave their house at the same time. Dustin rides his bike 49 feet east. Roberto rides his bike 81 feet south. Use the formula $(49)^2 + (81)^2 = x^2$ to find the distance between Dustin and Roberto.   ≈ 94.667 ft

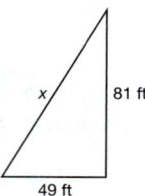

*26. Formulate In the system $\begin{matrix} y = x^2 - 3 \\ y = a \end{matrix}$, a is a real number. What is the minimum value of a so that the system will have two solutions? $a > -3$

27. Multi-Step A race-car driver is driving at a rate of $\sqrt{10{,}800}$ miles per hour. How long does it take the driver to go 85 miles? Give the answer as a rational expression in simplest form. (Hint: distance = rate times time)
  a. Write the equation to find the driver's travel time using the given values. $t = \frac{85}{\sqrt{10{,}800}}$
  b. Find the solution. $t = \frac{17\sqrt{3}}{36}$

28. Write Tell how to remove any coefficients of the x^2-term in a quadratic equation before completing the square.

*29. Describe the transformation of $f(x) = -x^2 + 2$ from the parent quadratic function.

*30. Charlotte invested $1000 in an account that doubles her balance every 7 years. Does this situation model exponential growth or decay? Express the function that represents this situation. After 42 years, how many times will her balance have doubled? What will that balance be after 42 years?   exponential growth; $f(x) = 1000 \cdot 2^x$; 6; $64,000

28. Sample: Divide each term of the quadratic equation by the coefficient of the quadratic term. The coefficient of the quadratic term must be 1 in order to complete the square.

29. The graph of the function is reflected about the x-axis (opens downward) and is shifted up two units.

CHALLENGE

A system of equations can consist of two quadratic equations. The solution(s) to these systems will still be at the points where the graphs intersect. Solve the system.

$y = x^2 + 2$
$y = -x^2 + 4$
$\{(1, 3), (-1, 3)\}$

LOOKING FORWARD

Graphing and solving systems of linear and quadratic equations prepare students for

• **Lesson 119** Graphing and Comparing Linear, Quadratic, and Exponential Functions

LESSON 113

Interpreting the Discriminant

Warm Up

1. **Vocabulary** The _____ is the number or expression under a radical symbol. **radicand**

Evaluate each expression for the given values.

2. $-x^2 - xy - y$ for $x = -5$ and $y = -1$ -29
3. $b^2 + 3ab - a$ for $a = -7$ and $b = -2$ 53
4. $ab - 5b^2$ for $a = 3$ and $b = 4$ -68
5. $7y^2z + 9$ for $y = -3$ and $z = -1$ -54

New Concepts

The quadratic formula is one method used to solve quadratic equations. Recall the quadratic formula for a quadratic equation of the form $ax^2 + bx + c = 0$ is:

$$x = \frac{-b \pm \sqrt{b^2 - 4ac}}{2a}$$

In the formula, the expression under the radical sign, $b^2 - 4ac$, is called the **discriminant**.

Consider the graphs below and the value of the discriminant for each equation.

$0 = x^2 - 4x + 3$
$b^2 - 4ac \qquad a = 1, b = -4, c = 3$
$= (-4)^2 - 4(1)(3)$ Substitute.
$= 4$

There are 2 x-intercepts. The discriminant is positive.

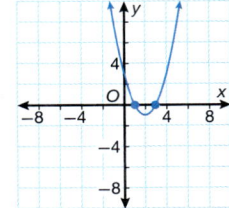

$0 = x^2 - 4x + 4$
$b^2 - 4ac \qquad a = 1, b = -4, c = 4$
$= (-4)^2 - 4(1)(4)$ Substitute.
$= 0$

There is one x-intercept. The discriminant is zero.

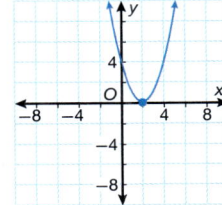

$0 = x^2 - 4x + 5$
$b^2 - 4ac \qquad a = 1, b = -4, c = 5$
$(-4)^2 - 4(1)(5)$ Substitute.
$= -4$

There are no x-intercepts. The discriminant is negative.

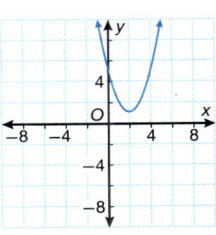

Online Connection
www.SaxonMathResources.com

---

1 Warm Up

Problems 2–5

Remind students that it is a good habit to place negative values in parentheses to avoid confusion when substituting into expressions.

2 New Concepts

In this lesson, students learn to interpret the discriminant in the quadratic formula.

Discuss the definition of the **discriminant**. Explain that the discriminant can be used to find the number of solutions to a quadratic equation, which represents the number of x-intercepts for its graph.

LESSON RESOURCES

Student Edition Practice
 Workbook 113
Reteaching Master 113
Adaptations Master 113
Challenge and Enrichment
 Master C113

MATH BACKGROUND

When the discriminant is a perfect square, there are one or two solutions to the equation $ax^2 + bx + c = 0$ because if $b^2 - 4ac \geq 0$, the square root can be taken, and it may be positive or negative. When factoring trinomials, the discriminant can be used to determine if the trinomial is factorable. If a polynomial with integer coefficients has a discriminant that is a perfect square, that polynomial is factorable over the integers. This knowledge can save time if students are having difficulty finding factors that work.

Example 1

Point out to students that, to avoid confusion, they should always write quadratic equations in standard form before calculating the discriminant.

Additional Example 1

Use the discriminant to find the number of real solutions to the equation. Then state the number of x-intercepts of the graph of the related function.

a. $x^2 - 3x + 4 = 0$
$b^2 - 4ac = -7$; there are no real solutions; $y = x^2 - 3x + 4$ has no x-intercepts

b. $2x^2 + 2x - 5 = 0$
$b^2 - 4ac = 44$; $y = 2x^2 + 2x - 5$ has two x-intercepts and two real solutions

c. $x^2 + 2x + 1 = 0$
$b^2 - 4ac = 0$; $y = x^2 + 2x + 1$ has one x-intercept and one real solution

Error Alert When calculating the discriminant, students can sometimes have problems keeping track of the sign of the $-4ac$ term. Remind them that the term is negative to start with and will change signs every time a negative value in a or c is introduced.

TEACHER TIP

Have students confirm the number of solutions by graphing the equations on their graphing calculators. Remind students that the solutions are the x-intercepts of the graph of the function.

Math Reasoning

Analyze What does the discriminant tell about the real solutions of a quadratic equation? What does the discriminant not tell about the solutions of a quadratic equation?

Sample: The discriminant tells the number and nature of the solutions of a quadratic equation. The discriminant does not tell the actual values of the solutions of a quadratic equation.

The value of the discriminant indicates the number of solutions.

Using the Discriminant
For the quadratic equation $ax^2 + bx + c = 0$ where $a \neq 0$, find the value of the discriminant, $b^2 - 4ac$, to determine the number of real solutions, which represents the number of x-intercepts of the graph of its related function.   If $b^2 - 4ac < 0$, then there are no real solutions and no x-intercepts.   If $b^2 - 4ac = 0$, then there is one real solution and one x-intercept.   If $b^2 - 4ac > 0$, then there are two real solutions and two x-intercepts.

If $b^2 - 4ac = 0$, then there is one real solution, which means there is one x-intercept. The real solution is the x value at the vertex of the parabola, which will be on the x-axis. The solution is called a **double root** of the equation.

Example 1 Finding the Number of Solutions Without Solving

Use the discriminant to find the number of real solutions to the equation. Then state the number of x-intercepts of the graph of the related function.

a. $x^2 - 3x + 9 = 0$

SOLUTION

$b^2 - 4ac$
$= (-3)^2 - 4(1)(9)$ Substitute.
$= 9 - 36$ Simplify.
$= -27$

There are no real solutions, so the graph has no x-intercepts.

b. $2x^2 - 3x - 4 = 0$

SOLUTION

$b^2 - 4ac$
$= (-3)^2 - 4(2)(-4)$ Substitute.
$= 9 + 32$ Simplify.
$= 41$

There are two real solutions, so the graph has two x-intercepts.

c. $x^2 + 8x + 16 = 0$

SOLUTION

$b^2 - 4ac$
$= 8^2 - 4(1)(16)$ Substitute.
$= 64 - 64$ Simplify.
$= 0$

There is one real solution, so the graph has one x-intercept.

Math Reasoning

Generalize What are the values of a, b, and c in the quadratic equation $x^2 - 4 = 0$?

$a = 1$, $b = 0$, and $c = -4$

Example 2 Application: Baseball

A baseball is thrown in the air with an initial velocity of 20 feet per second from 5 feet off the ground. Use the equation $h = -16t^2 + 20t + 5$ to model the situation. Will the ball reach a height of 30 feet?

SOLUTION

$h = -16t^2 + 20t + 5$

$30 = -16t^2 + 20t + 5$ Substitute 30 for h.

$0 = -16t^2 + 20t - 25$ Set the equation equal to 0.

Use the discriminant to determine if the ball will reach a height of 30 feet.

$b^2 - 4ac = 20^2 - 4(-16)(-25)$

$= 400 - 1600$

$= -1200$

Since the discriminant of the equation is negative, there are no solutions. The ball will not reach a height of 30 feet.

Lesson Practice

Use the discriminant to find the number of real solutions to the equation. Then state the number of x-intercepts of the graph of the related function.

a. (Ex 1) $x^2 - 2x - 35 = 0$ 144; 2 real solutions, 2 x-intercepts

b. (Ex 1) $4x^2 + 20x + 25 = 0$ 0; 1 real solution, 1 x-intercept

c. (Ex 1) $2x^2 - 3x + 7 = 0$ −47; no real solutions, no x-intercepts

d. (Ex 2) A football is punted from 2 feet off the ground with an initial velocity of 60 feet per second. Use the equation $y = -16t^2 + 60t + 2$ to model the situation. Will the ball reach a height of 45 feet?   The discriminant is 3728, so there are 2 real solutions. The ball will reach a height of 45 feet because its maximum height is 58.25 feet.

Practice Distributed and Integrated

*1. (113) Find the value of the discriminant of the equation $3x^2 - x + 2 = 0$.   −23

2. (53) The new rectangular basketball court at the high school has a width of $9x^2 + x + 36$ and a length of $4x^2 + 2x + 2$. What is the perimeter of the new court? $26x^2 + 6x + 76$

3. (74) Solve $6|z - 3| = 18$.   {0, 6}

 4. Find 8!.   40,320

Lesson 113   771

Example 2

Point out that y is the height of the baseball and t is the time after the ball is thrown.

Extend the Example

"What is the maximum height the baseball will reach?"

11.25 feet

Additional Example 2

If a baseball is thrown in the air with an initial velocity of 45 feet per second from 5 feet off the ground, will the ball reach a height of 30 feet?   yes

Lesson Practice

Problems a–c

Scaffolding Before calculating the discriminant, suggest that students write down what a, b, and c are equal to.

Problem d

Error Alert For this particular problem, students may forget that y is the height and leave out the 45 in the equation $45 = -16t^2 + 60t + 2$.

 **Check for Understanding**

The questions below help assess the concepts taught in this lesson.

"What is the standard form for a quadratic equation?"

$ax^2 + bx + c = 0$

"What is the discriminant?"

the radicand of the quadratic formula, $b^2 - 4ac$

"What does the discriminant tell you about the actual values of the solutions of the quadratic equation?" Sample: Nothing, it only tells you the number and nature of the solutions.

ENGLISH LEARNERS

For this lesson, explain the meaning of the word **discriminant**. Say:

"A discriminant is a characteristic that enables things, people, or classes to be distinguished from one another."

Connect the meaning of the vernacular use of discriminant with its mathematical use by explaining that the value of $b^2 - 4ac$ distinguishes the type of solution that a quadratic equation has.

Discuss the definition of "discriminate." Explain that discriminate does not necessarily imply a negativity or injustice.

Lesson 113   771

3 Practice

Math Conversations
Discussion to strengthen understanding

Problem 5
Emphasize that the discriminant only sheds light on the number and nature of solutions for the quadratic equation and tells nothing of the values of the solutions.

Problem 10
Point out to students that there are other ways they can solve this problem: by graphing or substitution.

*5. **Multiple Choice** Which is a possible value for the discriminant of the equation graphed? **A**
(113)

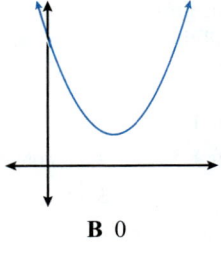

A −5 **B** 0
C 3 **D** 5

*6. **Model** Draw the graph of a quadratic equation that has a discriminant that is greater than zero.
(113)

6. Sample:

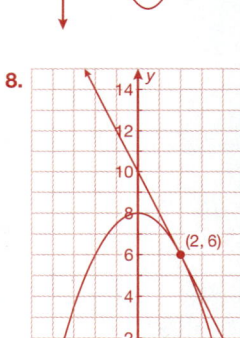

*7. **Generalize** Describe the values of the discriminant that indicate two real solutions. Sample: all positive values for $b^2 − 4ac$
(113)

*8. Solve this system $\begin{array}{l} y = -\frac{x^2}{2} + 8 \\ y = -2x + 10 \end{array}$ by graphing.
(112)

*9. **Error Analysis** Two students are solving the system of equations $\begin{array}{l} y = x^2 + 3 \\ y = -3x + 1 \end{array}$ by substitution. Which student is correct? Explain the error.
(112)

Student A	Student B
$y = x^2 + 3 \quad y = -3x + 1$	$y = x^2 + 3 \quad y = -3x + 1$
$x^2 + 3 = -3x + 1$	$x^2 + 3 - 3x + 1 = 0$
$x^2 + 3 + 3x - 1 = 0$	$x^2 - 3x + 4 = 0$
$x^2 + 3x + 2 = 0$	no solution
$(x + 2)(x + 1) = 0$	
So, $x = -2, x = -1$, and the solutions are $(-2, 7)$ and $(-1, 4)$.	

8.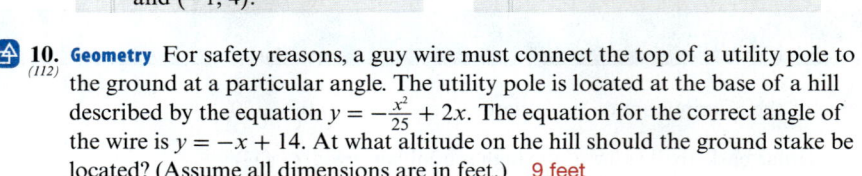

9. Student A; Sample: Student B added the linear equation to the quadratic equation rather than substituting it for y.

10. **Geometry** For safety reasons, a guy wire must connect the top of a utility pole to the ground at a particular angle. The utility pole is located at the base of a hill described by the equation $y = -\frac{x^2}{25} + 2x$. The equation for the correct angle of the wire is $y = -x + 14$. At what altitude on the hill should the ground stake be located? (Assume all dimensions are in feet.) **9 feet**
(112)

*11. In designing a necklace, a goldsmith places a gold wire on a workbench so that the wire takes on the shape of a parabola described by the equation $y = \frac{x^2}{2}$. The goldsmith then lays a straight wire across the first so that the second follows the equation $y = \frac{x}{6} + 6$. Use a graphing calculator to determine the coordinates for the points of intersection. Round answers to the nearest whole number. $(-3, 5)$ and $(4, 7)$
(112)

772 Saxon Algebra 1

INCLUSION

Use the following strategy with students who have difficulty with large group instruction. After students determine how many x-intercepts a quadratic equation has by calculating the discriminant, have them check by graphing it on their graphing calculators.

*12. **Error Analysis** Two students are finding the number of ways to choose a president
(111) and a vice president from a list of eight candidates. Which student is correct?
Explain the error. Student A; Sample: Student B did not use the correct formula for permutations.

Student A	Student B
$_8P_2 = \dfrac{8!}{(8-2)!}$	$_8P_2 = \dfrac{8!}{2!}$
$= \dfrac{8!}{6!}$	$= 20{,}160$
$= 56$	

17.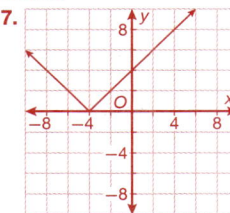

13. **Dining** A restaurant offers a choice of 3 sandwiches, 3 chips, and 5 soft drinks.
(111) How many different meal combinations are offered? 45

14. **Probability** A CD has 9 tracks. The CD player is set to play the songs randomly so
(111) that each song plays only once. What is the probability that the first 3 songs are
the first 3 tracks in order? $\dfrac{1}{504}$

15. Solve the equation $\sqrt{x} + 2 = 8$. Check your answer. $x = 36$; $\sqrt{36} + 2 = 6 + 2 = 8$
(106)

16. **Architecture** An architect is designing a structure that merges two different right
(106) triangles along the hypotenuse of each triangle. The hypotenuse of one triangle
is $\sqrt{x+2}$ units long and the hypotenuse of the second is $\sqrt{2x-4}$. At what value
of x are the two lengths equal? $x = 6$

17. Graph the function $f(x) = |x + 4|$.
(107)

*18. **Multi-Step** A plot of land is 143 square feet with dimensions of x and $x + 2$. What
(110) is the perimeter of the plot of land?
   a. Use the quadratic formula to find the dimensions of the plot of land. 11 feet by 13 feet
   b. What is the perimeter of the plot of land? 48 feet

19. **Multi-Step** Emmanuel throws a football into the air. Its movement forms a parabola
(100) given by the quadratic equation $h = -16t^2 + 14t + 50$, where h is the height in feet
and t is the time in seconds.
   a. Find the time t when the ball is at its maximum height. Round to the nearest hundredth. $t = 0.44$ seconds
   b. Find the time t when the ball hits the ground. Round to the nearest hundredth. $t = 2.26$ seconds
   c. Find the maximum height of the arc the ball makes in its flight. Round to the nearest tenth. $h = 53.1$ feet

20. **Firefighting** A forest ranger is stationed at the Delilah Lookout fire tower in the
(103) Sequoia National Forest in California. The distance d (in miles) he can see to
the horizon can be estimated by the formula $d = \sqrt{\dfrac{3h}{2}}$, where h is the height of
the observer's eyes (in feet) above sea level. If Delilah Lookout is located at an
elevation of 5176 feet above sea level, write a radical expression that shows the
distance the ranger can see to the horizon. $2\sqrt{1941}$ feet

Lesson 113   773

Problem 14
Extend the Problem
"Three of the tracks on the CD are instrumentals. What is the probability that the first three songs are all instrumentals?"
$\dfrac{3}{9} \cdot \dfrac{2}{8} \cdot \dfrac{1}{7} = \dfrac{1}{3} \cdot \dfrac{1}{4} \cdot \dfrac{1}{7} = \dfrac{1}{84}$

Problem 17
Error Alert Some students may translate the parent function $f(x) = |x|$ four units to the right since there is a plus sign in front of the 4. Show them that since the function to be graphed is $f(x) = |x + 4|$ then -4 is substituted for h in the function $f(x) = |x - h|$. Therefore, the parent function is translated 4 units to the left.

Problem 23
Error Alert

A common mistake that students make in identifying or graphing an inequality on the coordinate plane is the incorrect use of the solid or dotted line. Remind them that the dotted line is not included in the shaded region and is drawn when $<$ or $>$ is used.

Problem 25

Guide the students by asking them the following questions.

"What is the standard form for this equation?"
$9x^2 - 36x + 36 = 0$

"How can $9x^2 - 36x + 36 = 0$ be simplified?" Sample: divide both sides by 9; $x^2 - 4x + 4 = 0$

"How many real roots does it have?" Sample: The discriminant is zero, therefore it has one double root.

"How would you determine the root?" Sample: use the quadratic formula; factor the equation; graph the equation

---

21. Graph the system: $y \geq -\frac{3}{5}x + 3$
    $y \geq \frac{3}{4}x + 3$

22. **Analyze** Compare $-4.9t^2 + v_0 t + y_0 = 0$ and $-4.9t^2 + v_0 t = 0$.

23. Write the inequality that is graphed on the coordinate plane. $y > x - 6$

21.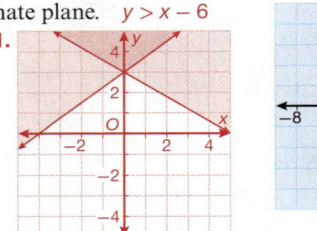

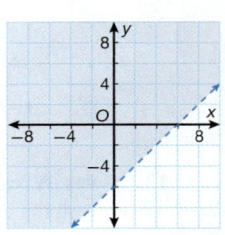

22. Sample: The first equation has a variable for the initial height while the second equation assumes that the initial height is 0.

*24. **Projectile Motion** A projectile is shot up in the air from the ground with an initial velocity of 84 feet per second. Using $y = -16t^2 + 84t$, write an equation to model the situation and use the discriminant to determine if the projectile will reach a height of 200 feet. Use the equation $200 = -16t^2 + 84t$. Since $0 = -16t^2 + 84t - 200$ and the discriminant is -5744, the projectile will not reach 200 feet.

25. Find the roots of $36x = 9x^2 + 36$. 2

26. **Finance** The amount of money Ricardo has after x years of investing $100 at his local bank is $f(x) = 100(1.065)^x$. Which graph could represent this function? **B**

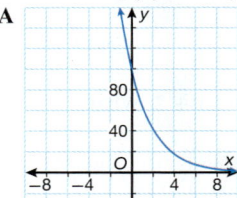 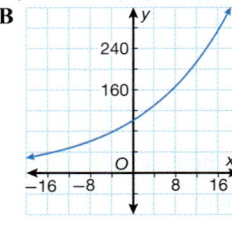 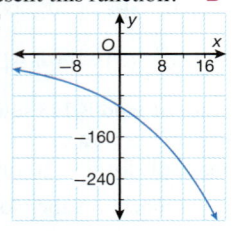

27. **Multi-Step** The time in minutes t it takes for a projectile to strike the ground is described by the equation $-4.9t^2 - 29.4t + 34.3 = 0$.
    a. Write the quadratic equation in the form $x^2 + bx = c$. $t^2 + 6t = 7$
    b. Find the real-number solutions by completing the square. $t = -7$ or 1
    c. At what time does the object strike the ground? Explain your answer.
       1 minute; Time cannot be negative.

28. **Verify** The fifth term of a geometric sequence is -1. The first is -81. Randy thinks the common ratio is $\frac{1}{3}$. Robin says it could be $-\frac{1}{3}$. Could both be correct? Explain.

29. If a quadratic function has been vertically compressed, does that mean the parabola is wider or narrower than the parent quadratic function $f(x) = x^2$? wider

30. For all real values of the domain, describe the relationship between the graphs of an exponential growth and an exponential decay function. They are mirror images of each other reflected about the y-axis.

28. yes; Sample: If the common ratio is $\frac{1}{3}$, the fifth term is $-81\left(\frac{1}{3}\right)^4 = -1$. If the common ratio is $-\frac{1}{3}$, the fifth term is $-81\left(-\frac{1}{3}\right)^4 = -1$.

774 Saxon Algebra 1

CHALLENGE

Mathematicians define the square root of a negative number to be "imaginary". The letter i is used to denote the square root of -1. So, $\sqrt{-1} = 1i$. For example, $\sqrt{-4} = 2i$, $\sqrt{-9} = 3i$, and so forth. Use the discriminant to find the number of real number solutions of the quadratic equation $x^2 + 1 = 0$. If there are no real number solutions, then find the imaginary solutions.
$\pm i$

LOOKING FORWARD

Interpreting the discriminant prepares students for

- **Lesson 119** Graphing and Comparing Linear, Quadratic, and Exponential Functions

LAB 10

Graphing Radical Functions

Graphing Calculator Lab (*Use with Lesson 114*)

A graphing calculator can be used to graph radical functions and to locate points on the graph.

Graph the function $y = 2\sqrt{x - 1}$.

1. To enter the equation into the **Y=** editor, press the `Y=` key. Then press 2 `2nd` `x²` `X,T,θ,n` `−` `1` `)`.

2. Graph the function by pressing `ZOOM` **6:ZStandard**.

3. Press `TRACE` and use the ▶ key to move along the x-axis until the cursor locates a point on the graph.

   The first point on the graph appears to be (1.064, 0.505).

4. Investigate actual points on the graph of $y = 2\sqrt{x - 1}$.

   Press `2nd` `WINDOW` `0` `ENTER` `1`. Then press `2nd` `GRAPH`.

   The first point on the graph is (1, 0). Note that this is different from (1.064, 0.505); the graph does not appear to pass through the point (1, 0). Therefore, it is important to use the Table feature to determine values of the function.

   a. 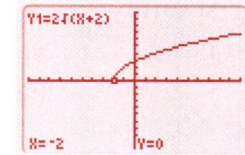 b.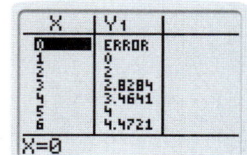

Materials
- graphing calculator

Discuss
Graphing radical equations may be the first time students consider the domain of the equation using the trace and table features.

Lab Practice

a. Graph the function $y = 3\sqrt{x + 2}$. At what point does the graph start?   (−2, 0)

b. Graph the function $y = 2\sqrt{x + 2}$. At what point does the graph start?   (−2, 0)

LESSON 114

1 Warm Up

Problems 2–5
Briefly review evaluating expressions with square roots prior to graphing functions that contain square roots.

2 New Concepts

In this lesson, students will graph square-root functions by using tables, transformations, and a graphing calculator.

Example 1

This example introduces students to graphing square-root functions.

Additional Example 1
Make a table of $y = 3\sqrt{x} - 2$. Then graph the function.

x	0	1	4	9	16
y	-2	1	4	7	10

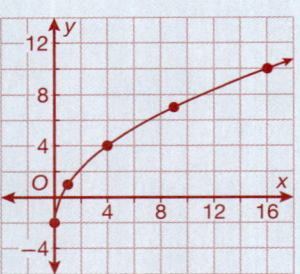

LESSON RESOURCES

Student Edition Practice
   Workbook 114
Reteaching Master 114
Adaptations Master 114
Challenge and Enrichment
   Master C114

776   Saxon Algebra 1

LESSON 114

Graphing Square-Root Functions

Warm Up

1. Vocabulary Radicals that have the same radicands and roots such as $2\sqrt{7} + 4\sqrt{7}$ are _____, and radicals that have different radicands and/or roots such as $4\sqrt{7} + 2\sqrt{11}$ are _____.   **like radicals, unlike radicals**

Add or subtract.

2. $-6\sqrt{2} + 8\sqrt{2}$ $2\sqrt{2}$ **3.** $31\sqrt{5} - 13\sqrt{5}$ $18\sqrt{5}$

Find each product.

4. $(7 + \sqrt{6})(4 - \sqrt{9})$ $7 + \sqrt{6}$ **5.** $(\sqrt{3} - 12)^2$ $147 - 24\sqrt{3}$

New Concepts

The square root of a number x is the number whose square is x.

$$\sqrt{9} = 3 \qquad 3^2 = 9$$

The square root of x can be a function. For the function $y = \sqrt{x}$ when x is 9, y is 3 since the square root of 9 is 3. Use the table to make connections with the graph.

Math Language
A **function** is a mathematical relationship that pairs each value in the domain with exactly one value in the range.

x	y
0	0
1	1
4	2
9	3
16	4

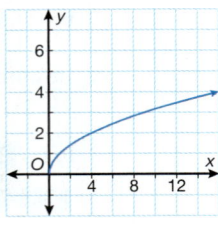

A **square-root function** is a function that contains a square root of a variable.

Example 1   Graphing a Square-Root Function

Make a table of $y = 2\sqrt{x} + 1$. Then graph the function.

SOLUTION

Evaluate the function when x is 0, 1, 4, and 9.

Hint
Try choosing x values that are perfect squares. This may make it easier to graph.

$y = 2\sqrt{0} + 1 = 2(0) + 1 = 1$
$y = 2\sqrt{1} + 1 = 2(1) + 1 = 3$
$y = 2\sqrt{4} + 1 = 2(2) + 1 = 5$
$y = 2\sqrt{9} + 1 = 2(3) + 1 = 7$

x	y
0	1
1	3
4	5
9	7

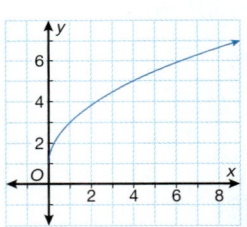

Online Connection
www.SaxonMathResources.com

In order for a square root to be a real number, the radicand cannot be negative.

776   Saxon Algebra 1

MATH BACKGROUND

A square root function contains a term that is the square root of a variable. A function that contains a square-root term without a variable is not considered a square-root function.

Equations with radicands containing variables must be evaluated in the same manner as other equations. However, the use of perfect squares in a table of values is recommended, as this will produce results more easily graphed.

The domain of a square-root function is the set of real numbers for which the radical expression is a real number. The radicand must be greater than or equal to zero to ensure the value will be a real number. If the radicand contains a negative number, then the square root is an imaginary number in the complex number system. The complex number system will be studied in more advanced mathematics courses.

Example 2 Determining the Domain of a Square-Root Function

a. Determine the domain of $y = \sqrt{x - 4}$.

SOLUTION

The domain is the values for x that make the radicand greater than or equal to zero. Solve $x - 4 \geq 0$.

$x - 4 \geq 0$ Set the radicand greater than or equal to 0.

$x \geq 4$ Solve for x by adding 4 to both sides.

The domain is the set of all real numbers greater than or equal to 4.

b. Determine the domain of $y = 3\sqrt{\frac{x}{2} + 4} - 7$.

SOLUTION

$\frac{x}{2} + 4 \geq 0$ Set the radicand greater than or equal to 0.

$\frac{x}{2} \geq -4$ Subtract 4 from both sides.

$x \geq -8$ Multiply both sides by 2.

The domain is the set of all real numbers greater than or equal to -8.

All square-root functions look similar to the graph of $y = \sqrt{x}$, which is called the parent function. A transformation of a function is an alteration of the parent function that produces a new function.

Compare the parent function $y = \sqrt{x}$ to the function $y = \sqrt{x} + 3$.

x	$y = \sqrt{x}$	$y = \sqrt{x} + 3$
0	0	3
1	1	4
4	2	5
9	3	6
16	4	7

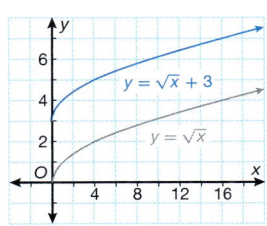

The function $y = \sqrt{x} + 3$ has been shifted 3 units up from the parent function $y = \sqrt{x}$. Transformations that involve vertical and horizontal shifting are called translations.

Transformations of the Graph of $f(x) = \sqrt{x}$

Vertical translation: The graph of $f(x) = \sqrt{x} + c$ is c units up from the parent graph if $c > 0$ and the graph is c units down from the parent graph if $c < 0$.

Horizontal translation: The graph of $f(x) = \sqrt{x - c}$ is c units to the right of the parent graph if $c > 0$ and the graph is c units to the left of the parent graph if $c < 0$.

Lesson 114   777

Example 3

These examples show how transformations are applied to square-root functions.

Additional Example 3

a. Describe the transformation applied to the parent function to form $y = \sqrt{x} + 2$.
translation of 2 units up from the parent function

b. Describe the transformation applied to the parent function to form $y = \sqrt{x - 4}$.
translation 4 units to the right of the parent function

Example 4

These examples investigate the effect of the inclusion of a negative sign in the function.

Additional Example 4

Describe the transformation applied to the parent function to form each of the given functions.

a. $f(x) = \sqrt{-x}$ reflected over the y-axis

b. $f(x) = \sqrt{-x - 5}$ reflected over the y-axis with a horizontal shift to the left 5 units; $f(x) = \sqrt{-x - 5} = \sqrt{-(x + 5)}$

Example 5

This example describes distance utilizing a square-root function.

Additional Example 5

When conditions are slightly foggy, the distance d (in kilometers) that Meliza can see from a height of h meters is approximately $d = \sqrt{12h}$. Find the distance she can see from a height of 1800 m. Round to the nearest kilometer. $d \approx 147$ km

---

Example 3 Translating the Square-Root Functions

a. Describe the transformations applied to the parent function to form $y = \sqrt{x} - 3$.

SOLUTION

This function can be written in the form $f(x) = \sqrt{x} + c$ by changing -3 to $+ (-3)$. The function can be written as $y = \sqrt{x} + (-3)$ which is a translation of the parent function that shifts the graph 3 units down.

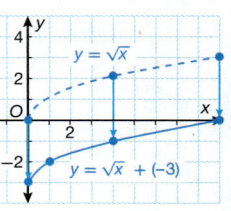

b. Describe the transformations applied to the parent function to form $y = \sqrt{x + 2}$.

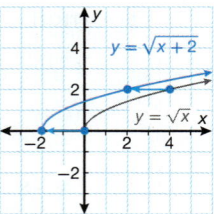

SOLUTION

This function $y = \sqrt{x + 2}$ is written in the form $f(x) = \sqrt{x - c}$, where c is -2, which is a translation of the parent function 2 units left.

Math Reasoning

Analyze What is the domain of $g(x) = \sqrt{-x}$?

$x \leq 0$

Reflections of the Graph of $f(x) = \sqrt{x}$
If $f(x) = \sqrt{x}$, then $g(x) = -\sqrt{x}$ is a reflection of the graph of f across the x-axis.
If $f(x) = \sqrt{x}$, then $g(x) = \sqrt{-x}$ is a reflection of the graph of f across the y-axis.

Example 4 Reflecting a Square-Root Function

a. Describe the transformations applied to the parent function to form $y = -\sqrt{x}$.

SOLUTION

The graph of $y = -\sqrt{x}$ is a reflection of the parent function over the x-axis.

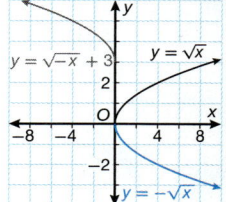

b. Describe the transformations applied to the parent function to form $y = \sqrt{-x} + 3$.

SOLUTION

The graph of $y = \sqrt{-x} + 3$ is a reflection of the parent function over the y-axis, and then a vertical shift of 3 units up.

INCLUSION

Use the following strategy with students who have memory difficulties. Have students use a graphing calculator to graph each of these basic square-root functions:

$y = \sqrt{x}$ $y = \sqrt{x} + 2$ $y = \sqrt{x} - 2$

$y = \sqrt{-x}$ $y = \sqrt{-x} + 2$ $y = \sqrt{-x} - 2$

$y = -\sqrt{x}$ $y = -\sqrt{x} + 2$ $y = -\sqrt{x} - 2$

Students can make sketches and label the graphs for future reference. Consulting these examples will help them determine the translations of other graphs in this lesson.

Example 5 Application: Horizon

The distance d (in kilometers) that Meliza can see on a clear day to the horizon from a height of h meters is approximately $d = \sqrt{15h}$. Find the distance she can see from a height of 2160 meters.

SOLUTION

Evaluate $d = \sqrt{15h}$ for $h = 2160$ m.

$d = \sqrt{15(2160)}$
$= \sqrt{32400} = 180$

180 km is the distance she can see from a height of 2160 m.

Lesson Practice

a. Graph $y = 3\sqrt{x} + 1$ using a table.
 (Ex 1)

Determine the domain of each of the following functions.
 (Ex 2)

b. $f(x) = \sqrt{\dfrac{x}{3}}$ $x \geq 0$ **c.** $f(x) = \sqrt{x-2}$ $x \geq 2$

Describe the transformations applied to the parent function to form the given function.

d. $f(x) = \sqrt{x} - 2$ **e.** $f(x) = \sqrt{x-2}$
 (Ex 3) *(Ex 3)*
f. $f(x) = -\sqrt{x} + 3$ **g.** $f(x) = \sqrt{-x} - 4$
 (Ex 4) *(Ex 4)*

h. (Physics) An acorn fell from a tree limb. The function $t = 0.45\sqrt{x}$
 (Ex 5) represents how many seconds it takes something to fall from a height of x meters to the ground. Estimate how long it would take the acorn to fall if the limb were 8 meters above the ground.   Sample: about 1.27 seconds

a.

x	y
−1	0
0	3
3	6
8	9
15	12

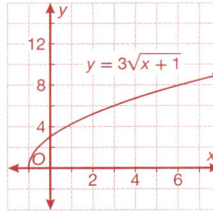

d. a shift of 2 units down

e. a shift of 2 units to the right

f. a reflection over the x-axis, then a shift of 3 units to the left

g. a reflection over the y-axis, then a shift of 4 units down

Practice Distributed and Integrated

Solve.

1. $|z + 5| + 11 = 10$ { }
 (74)
2. $10x^2 = 70x$ 0, 7
 (98)
3. $24x = 32x^2$ $0, \dfrac{3}{4}$
 (98)
4. $\dfrac{5}{x+1} - \dfrac{2}{x} = \dfrac{5}{10x}$ $x = 1$
 (99)

*5. Multiple Choice Evaluate the equation $y = \sqrt{x+6} - 1$ for $x = 2$.   **C**
 (114)
 A $\sqrt{2}$ **B** $\sqrt{7}$ **C** $2\sqrt{2} - 1$ **D** no solution

*6. (Oceanography) A good approximation of the speed of a wave in deep ocean water
 (114) is given by the equation $y = \sqrt{10d}$. In this equation, y is the wave's speed in meters per second and d is the ocean's depth in meters. What is the speed of a wave if the depth is 400 meters? Round to the nearest whole number.   ≈ 63 meters per second

*7. Analyze Given the function $f(x) = \sqrt{\dfrac{4x}{3}} - 1$, for what values of x will $f(x)$ be
 (114) greater than 5? Show your work.   See Additional Answers.

*8. Analyze Explain how to graph $f(x) = \sqrt{x-2} + 3$ in terms of its parent function.
 (114)

8. Sample: Translate the parent function, $f(x) = \sqrt{x}$, 2 units to the right and then translate the resulting graph 3 units up.

Lesson 114   779

Lesson Practice

Problem a

Scaffolding Have students discuss what values they would choose for the table. If opinions vary, allow groups of students to try each suggestion, then decide as a class which would be easiest to graph.

Problem h

Error Alert Make sure that students use a correct estimated value for $\sqrt{2}$. Consider finding this value as a class before students work to solve the problem.

Check for Understanding

The questions below help assess the concepts taught in this lesson.

What is the square-root parent function? $y = \sqrt{x}$

What is the purpose of a table in graphing a square-root function?
A table helps to organize and find values that can easily be graphed.

3 Practice

Math Conversations

Discussion to strengthen understanding

Problem 6
Extend the Problem

How does the speed of a wave at a depth of 175 meters compare with the speed of a wave at a depth of 400 meters? Round to the nearest whole number.
It is slower: 42 m/s < 63 m/s

Lesson 114   779

Problem 10
Extend the Problem
Ask students to graph the equation to check that there are two solutions. Yes, there are two x-intercepts;

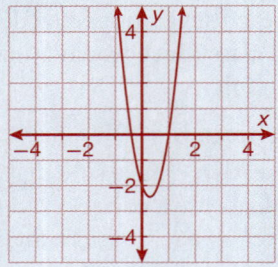

Problem 11
Error Alert
Students may use the quadratic formula and solve for x. Remind students that it is sufficient to only use the discriminant.

9. Find the value of the discriminant of the equation $2x^2 - 5x - 4 = 0$.   57
(113)

10. Student B; Sample: The values of a, b, and c are found when the equation is set equal to 0.

*10. **Error Analysis** Two students are using the discriminant to find the number of
(113) real solutions to the equation $5x^2 - 3x = 2$. Which student is correct? Explain the error.

Student A	Student B
$5x^2 - 3x = 2$	$5x^2 - 3x = 2$
$b^2 - 4ac = (-3)^2 - 4(5)(2)$	$5x^2 - 3x - 2 = 0$
$= 9 - 40$	$b^2 - 4ac = (-3)^2 - 4(5)(-2)$
$= -31$	$= 9 + 40$
	$= 49$
As the discriminant is negative, there are no x-intercepts.	As the discriminant is positive, there are two x-intercepts.

*11. **Geometry** The length of a rectangle is $x + 12$ inches and the width is $x + 8$ inches.
(113) Is there a value for x that makes the area of the rectangle 50 square inches? Explain your reasoning.   See Additional Answers.

*12. **Multi-Step** The equation $288 = (3 + x)(6 - x)$ can be used to determine if the base
(113) of a rectangular box with a length of $(3 + x)$ inches and a width of $(6 - x)$ inches can have an area of 288 square inches.
  a. Write the equation setting it equal to zero. $0 = -270 + 3x - x^2$
  b. Use the equation to find the values of a, b, and c. $a = -1$, $b = 3$, $c = -270$
  c. Find the value of the discriminant. -1071
  d. Can a box with these dimensions be made? Explain.   no; There is no base possible because the discriminant of the equation is negative.

13. Solve this system by graphing: $\begin{array}{l} y = x^2 + 3 \\ y = -2x + 3 \end{array}$.   See Additional Answers.
(112)

14. Student B; Sample: Student A did not add 4 to both sides when setting the equation equal to zero.

*14. **Error Analysis** Two students are solving the system of equations $\begin{array}{l} y = x^2 + 4x \\ y = -4 \end{array}$ by
(112) substitution. Which student is correct? Explain the error.

Student A	Student B
$y = x^2 + 4x \quad y = -4$	$y = x^2 + 4x \quad y = -4$
$x^2 + 4x = -4$	$x^2 + 4x = -4$
$(x^2 + 4x) - 4 = 0$	$(x^2 + 4x) + 4 = 0$
$x^2 + 4x - 4 = 0$	$x^2 + 4x + 4 = 0$
no solution	$(x + 2)(x + 2) = 0$ So, $x = -2$, and the solution is $(-2, -4)$.

*15. (**Physics**) Miguel is standing at the base of a ramp. He tosses a ball into the air. The
(112) path of the ball is described by the equation $y = -x^2 + 7x$. The equation $y = x$ represents the ramp. At what altitude does the ball strike the ramp? Assume that dimensions are in feet.   6 feet

16. **Measurement** On what scale would the distance between the x-coordinates in the
(112) solution set of the system $\begin{array}{l} y = \frac{x^2}{2} \\ y = 4x - 6 \end{array}$ be 8 centimeters?   1 unit:2 cm

780   Saxon Algebra 1

CHALLENGE

Use a graphing calculator to graph these functions:

$$f(x) = \sqrt[3]{x}$$
$$f(x) = \sqrt[4]{x}$$
$$f(x) = \sqrt[5]{x}$$
$$f(x) = \sqrt[6]{x}$$

Is there a pattern to the graphs? Explain your answer.   yes; Sample: Graphs of odd radicals fall on both sides of the y-axis. Graphs of even radicals fall only to the right of the y-axis.

17. Graph the function $f(x) = |x| - 2$. **See Additional Answers.**
(107)

18. **Temperature** The temperature outside yesterday was 65°. Today the temperature changed by 5°. Give the possible temperatures outside today. **60° or 70°**
(107)

19. Determine if the set of ordered pairs {(6, 3), (4, 2), (2, 1), (8, 4)} satisfies an exponential function. **no**
(108)

20. **Engineering** A small bridge has a weight limit of 8000 pounds. A photographer wants to photograph at least 5 vehicles on the bridge. The cars weigh about 1800 pounds each and the motorcycles weigh about 600 pounds each. There must be at least one car and four motorcycles in the photo. Graph a system of linear equations to describe the situation. Give two combinations of cars and motorcycles that are solutions. **See Additional Answers.**
(109)

21. Use the quadratic formula to solve $x^2 = 19x - 60$. Check the solutions. **4, 15**
(110)

22. **Multiple Choice** There are three numbers in a locker combination: 19, 22, and 28. How many different ways can the numbers be arranged? **B**
(111)
A 3   B 6   C 12   D 24

*23. **Write** Explain what types of situations apply to permutations.
(111)

24. **Multi-Step** In a bowling lane, the distance (d) from the foul line to the center of the Number 1 pin should be 60 feet and should vary from this length by no more than $\frac{1}{2}$ inch.
(101)
 a. Convert 60 feet to inches. **720 inches**
 b. Write and solve an absolute-value inequality that models the acceptable distances from the foul line to the center of the Number 1 pin.
 c. If the diameter of the base of the Number 1 pin is $4\frac{1}{8}$ inches, what is the shortest possible distance between the foul line and the front of the Number 1 pin? **$717\frac{7}{16}$ inches**

25. Evaluate $y = \sqrt{2x} + 3$ for $x = 8$. **7**
(114)

26. **Property** Mr. Kinsey's property is in the shape of a right triangle. The legal description states that the property has an area of 900 yd² and that the base of the property is 30 yards longer than the height. What are the actual dimensions of the property? **base: 60 yards, height: 30 yards**
(104)

27. **Multi-Step** A company gives its employees a 4% raise at the beginning of every year. This year, Jordan earns $32,000.
(105)
 a. Write a rule that can be used to find Jordan's salary after n years. **$32,000(1.04)^n$**
 b. How many years will it take for Jordan to earn $40,000? **6**
 c. What will Jordan's salary be in 12 years? Round to the nearest cent. **$51,233.03**

28. **Analyze** Write the radical equation $\sqrt{x+3} = 2x$ so that the equation has no radical and is equal to zero. **$4x^2 - x - 3 = 0$**
(106)

29. Has the graph of the parent quadratic function been stretched or compressed to produce the graph $f(x) = 4x^2 + 2$?
(Inv 10)

30. Describe the similarity and difference between the graphs of $f(x) = 3^x$ and $g(x) = 4 \cdot 3^x$.
(Inv 11)

23. Sample: When you are trying to find the number of ways to pick items and the order of the items matters.

24b. $|d - 720| \leq \frac{1}{2}$; $719\frac{1}{2} \leq d \leq 720\frac{1}{2}$

29. Because the coefficient of x^2, (i.e., 4) is greater than 1, the graph has been vertically stretched (which means the graph is narrower than the parent quadratic function).

30. Both are exponential functions with the same shape, but $g(x)$ has been vertically stretched by a factor of four.

Problem 21

Error Alert

Make sure that students have correctly written the equation in standard form before applying the quadratic formula. Check that they have identified a, b, and c correctly and copied them correctly into the formula.

Problem 27

Extend the Problem

Jordan's boss earned $82,431.12 this year and gets a 7% raise every year. What will she earn in 9 years? **$151,546.25**

Problem 29

Guide students by asking them the following questions.

"What is the parent function?" $y = x^2$

"Will the graph of this function be wider or narrower than that of the parent function? How do you know?" It will be narrower because the coefficient of the x^2 term is greater than 1.

Lesson 114   781

LOOKING FORWARD

Graphing square-root functions will prepare students for

• **Lesson 115** Graphing Cubic Functions

• **Lesson 119** Graphing and Comparing Linear, Quadratic, and Exponential Functions

Lesson 114   781

LESSON 115

Graphing Cubic Functions

Warm Up

1. **Vocabulary** The polynomial $x - 5x^2 + 3x^3 - 1$ written in _____ form is $3x^3 - 5x^2 + x - 1$. **standard**

Find the degree of each polynomial expression and write the polynomial in descending order.

2. $8 + x^2 + 2x$ $2; x^2 + 2x + 8$
3. $2x^3 - 6x + x^4$ $4; x^4 + 2x^3 - 6x$
4. Simplify $(125)^{\frac{1}{3}}$.   **5**
5. **Multiple Choice** Which value is equivalent to $\sqrt[3]{-343}$? **B**

   A 7   B −7   C 114.3   D −114.3

New Concepts

A **cubic function** is a polynomial function in which the greatest power of any variable is 3. In other words, a cubic function is a polynomial function of degree 3.

The degree of a polynomial function determines many characteristics of its graph.

Function Type	Graph	Degree	x-Intercepts (Maximum)	End Behavior
Linear		1	1	Ends go in opposite directions.
Quadratic		2	2	Ends go in the same direction.
Cubic		3	3	Ends go in opposite directions.

Reading Math

The equation $y = x^3$ is read, "y is equal to x cubed" or "y is equal to x to the third power."

Online Connection
www.SaxonMathResources.com

782 Saxon Algebra 1

MATH BACKGROUND

The degree of a polynomial function determines the general shape of its graph, the maximum number of possible solutions of the function, and along with the coefficient of the highest degreed term, the end behavior of its graph.

When the leading coefficient of a polynomial function with an even degree is positive, the end behavior of the function is $y \longrightarrow +\infty$ as $x \longrightarrow \pm\infty$. If it is negative, the end behavior of the function is $y \longrightarrow -\infty$ as $x \longrightarrow \pm\infty$.

When the leading coefficient of a polynomial function with an odd degree is positive, the end behavior of the function is $y \longrightarrow +\infty$ as $x \longrightarrow +\infty$, and $y \longrightarrow -\infty$ as $x \longrightarrow -\infty$. When the leading coefficient is negative, the end behavior of the function is $y \longrightarrow -\infty$ as $x \longrightarrow +\infty$, and $y \longrightarrow +\infty$ as $x \longrightarrow -\infty$.

Once the end behavior of a function is determined, it can be used to help graph the function.

The parent function for cubic polynomials is $y = x^3$. The graph of $y = -x^3$ is related to the graph of the parent function $y = x^3$.

Example 1 Graphing Cubic Functions

Evaluate the cubic parent function $y = x^3$ and the function $y = -x^3$ for $x = -2, -1, 0, 1,$ and 2. Then graph the functions.

SOLUTION Make tables of values. Then plot points to graph the functions.

x	-2	-1	0	1	2
y	-8	-1	0	1	8

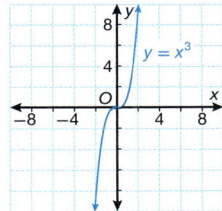

Math Reasoning

Generalize Which transformation changes the graph of $y = x^3$ into the graph of $y = -x^3$?

Sample: a reflection over the y-axis

x	-2	-1	0	1	2
y	8	1	0	-1	-8

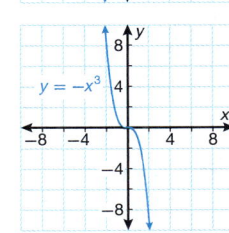

Example 2 Solving Cubic Equations by Graphing

a. Solve $0 = x^3 - 1$ by graphing.

SOLUTION

To solve $0 = x^3 - 1$, begin by graphing the related function $y = x^3 - 1$.

Then find the x-intercepts of $y = x^3 - 1$ since these are the x-values where $y = 0$.

The only x-intercept is near 1, so the approximate solution to $0 = x^3 - 1$ is $x \approx 1$.

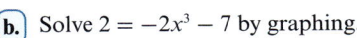

Math Reasoning

Verify In Example 2a, how can you check whether $x = 1$ is the exact solution or not?

Sample: Substitute $x = 1$ into the original equation and see whether the resulting equation is true.

b. Solve $2 = -2x^3 - 7$ by graphing.

SOLUTION

Write $2 = -2x^3 - 7$ so that one side is equal to zero. Then graph the related function and find its x-intercepts.

Subtracting 2 from both sides of $2 = -2x^3 - 7$ gives the equation $0 = -2x^3 - 9$. To solve $0 = -2x^3 - 9$, graph the related function $y = -2x^3 - 9$.

The only x-intercept is between -1 and -2, at about -1.7.

The approximate solution to $2 = -2x^3 - 7$ is $x \approx -1.7$.

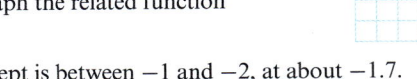

Hint

Another way to solve $2 = -2x^3 - 7$ is to graph $y = -2x^3 - 7$ and $y = 2$, and then to find the x value(s) at their point(s) of intersection.

Lesson 115

Example 1

Whenever students are not familiar with a given function, a table of values can be used to find points to plot to determine the shape of the graph.

Additional Example 1

Evaluate the function $y = 2x^3$ for $x = -2, -1, 0, 1,$ and 2. Then graph the function.

x	-2	-1	0	1	2
y	-16	-2	0	2	16

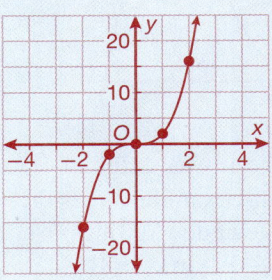

Example 2

These examples show students how a cubic equation can be solved by graphing the related function.

Additional Example 2

a. Solve $0 = x^3 + 2$ by graphing. $x \approx -1.25$

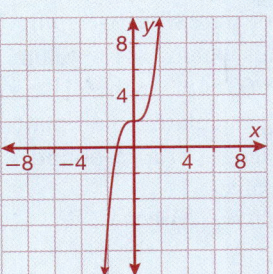

b. Solve $4 = -3x^3 + 6$ by graphing. $x \approx 0.9$

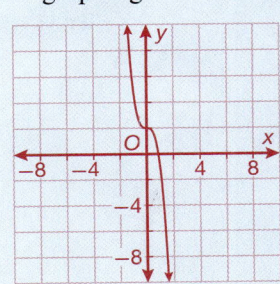

Lesson 115

Example 3

This example focuses on the use of a graphing calculator to solve cubic equations.

Additional Example 3

Solve $3 = -\frac{2}{3}x^3 + 6x^2$ by graphing on a graphing calculator. The x-intercepts are approximately -0.68176, 0.73801, and 8.94374.

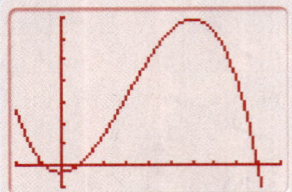

Note: The answer graph in Additional Example 3 uses the following window settings: $X\text{min} = -2$, $X\text{max} = 10$, $X\text{scl} = 1$, $Y\text{min} = -10$, $Y\text{max} = 69$, $Y\text{scl} = 10$, and $X\text{res} = 1$.

Example 4

This example shows how a cubic equation can describe the volumes of different sized cubes.

Additional Example 4

A cube of pure silver weighing 25 pounds would have a volume of about 66 cubic inches. Use a graphing calculator to estimate the side length of a 25-pound cube of silver.
side length ≈ 4.09 inches

Example 3 Solving Cubic Equations Using a Graphing Calculator

Solve $-2x^2 = \frac{1}{2}x^3 - 1$ by graphing on a graphing calculator.

SOLUTION

Write $-2x^2 = \frac{1}{2}x^3 - 1$ so that one side is equal to zero. Then graph the related function and find its x-intercepts.

Adding $2x^2$ to both sides of the original equation gives the equation $0 = \frac{1}{2}x^3 + 2x^2 - 1$. Use the graphing calculator to graph the related function $y = \frac{1}{2}x^3 + 2x^2 - 1$.

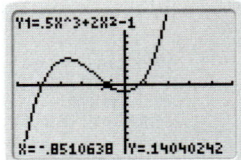

The graph shows that there are three x-intercepts. Trace to estimate their values.

The approximate solutions are $x \approx -3.9$, $x \approx -0.8$, and $x \approx 0.7$.

For better estimates, use the Zero function. To the nearest hundredth, the solutions are $x \approx -3.87$, $x \approx -0.79$, and $x \approx 0.66$.

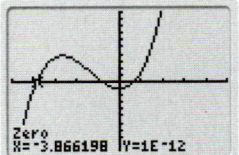

Graphing Calculator Tip

For help with graphing functions, refer to the graphing calculator keystrokes in Lab 3 on p. 305.

Math Language

Remember that the **zeros** of a function are its x-intercepts or solutions.

Example 4 Application: Volume of a Cube

A cube of pure gold weighing 100 pounds would have a volume of about 143 cubic inches. Use a graphing calculator to estimate the side length of a 100-pound cube of gold.

SOLUTION

The formula for the volume of a cube is $V = s^3$. To graph this equation on a graphing calculator, let y represent V and x represent s. Then graph $y = x^3$.

Adjust the window to make sure that 143 is included in the y-values.

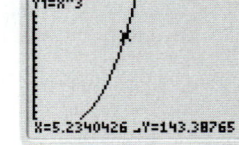

Window Settings

$X\text{min} = 0$

$X\text{max} = 12$

$Y\text{min} = 0$

$Y\text{max} = 200$

Trace to estimate the x-value where $y = 143$.

When $y = 143$, $x \approx 5.2$.

The side length of a cube of gold weighing 100 pounds would be about 5.2 inches—about the width of a DVD case.

a.

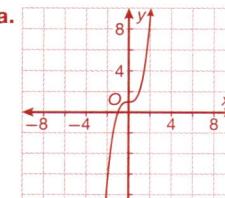

Lesson Practice

a. Graph $y = x^3 + 1$.
(Ex 1)

b. Solve $0 = -4x^3$ by graphing.   See Additional Answers.
(Ex 2)

c. Solve $3 = -x^3 + 8$ by graphing.   See Additional Answers.
(Ex 2)

d. Solve $x^2 - \frac{1}{4} = \frac{1}{4}x^3$ by graphing on a graphing calculator.
(Ex 3)   See Additional Answers.

e. The volume of a rectangular prism is represented by the equation
(Ex 4) $V = x^3 + 4$. Use a graphing calculator to find the volume when $x = 25.5$ units.   See Additional Answers.

Practice   Distributed and Integrated

Solve and check.

1. $\frac{x-2}{x+7} = \frac{x-6}{3x+21}$ $x = 0$
(99)

2. $\frac{x-4}{x+1} = \frac{x+5}{2x+2}$ $x = 13$
(99)

3. ; $x = 0$

*3. Graph the cubic function $y = \frac{1}{3}x^3$. Use it to solve the equation $0 = \frac{1}{3}x^3$.
(115)

*4. Multiple Choice Which equation represents a cubic function?   **C**
(115)
  A $y = 3x - 4y$
  B $y = 6x^2 + 2$
  C $y = x^3 - 4x + 1$
  D $y = 10x^4 + 3x^2 - 5$

*5. (Capacity) The volume of a box is represented by the equation $V = x^3 - 4$. Use a
(115) table or graph to find the value of x that corresponds to a volume of 23 cubic units. $x = 3$

*6. (Games) The volume of a whiffle ball is represented by the equation $V = \frac{4}{3}\pi r^3$. Use
(115) a graphing calculator to graph the equation and then use the graph to estimate the volume of air in a ball with a radius of 2 inches.

*7. Write Describe the characteristics of the graph of a cubic function.
(115)

*8. Formulate Write an example of a cubic function.   Sample: $y = 10x^3$
(115)

9. Evaluate $y = \sqrt{4x} - 5$ for $x = 3$. Round to the nearest tenth. $y \approx -1.5$
(114)

*10. Error Analysis Two students are evaluating the equation $y = \sqrt{2x - 5} + 2$ for
(114) $x = 6$. Which student is correct? Explain the error.   Student B; Sample: Student A incorrectly subtracted the 5 from 6.

7. Sample: The ends of the graph go in opposite directions, it is a smooth curve, and the graph crosses the x-axis at least once and at most three times.

Student A	Student B
$y = \sqrt{2x - 5} + 2$	$y = \sqrt{2x - 5} + 2$
$y = \sqrt{2 \cdot 6 - 5} + 2$	$y = \sqrt{2 \cdot 6 - 5} + 2$
$y = \sqrt{2} + 2$	$y = \sqrt{12 - 5} + 2$
	$y = \sqrt{7} + 2$

6. 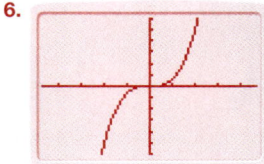 ;

33.51 cubic inches

Lesson 115   785

Lesson Practice

Problem a

Scaffolding Have students make a table of values before drawing their graphs.

Problem d

Error Alert Remind students that they will have to insert parentheses around the fractions. Omitting the parentheses will cause an error in the calculation.

✓ Check for Understanding

The questions below help assess the concepts taught in this lesson.

"On the graph of a cubic equation, what is represented by the x-intercept(s)?" The x-intercept(s) represent the solution(s) or zero(s) of the equation.

"In general, describe the graph of a cubic function." The ends always go in opposite directions (up and down); there can be 1, 2, or 3 x-intercepts or solutions.

3 Practice

Math Conversations

Discussion to strengthen understanding

Problem 4

Guide the students by asking them the following questions.

"What characteristic identifies a cubic function?"
A cubic function has a degree of 3.

"Does choice A include a cubic term?" No

"Does choice D include a cubic term?" No

"Which choice is correct?"
Choice C

Problem 9

Error Alert

Make sure that students do not include -5 as part of the radicand.

Lesson 115   785

Problem 14
Error Alert
Students may not multiply the binomials. Remind students to write the product in standard form before finding the discriminant.

Problem 19
Guide the students by asking them the following questions.

"Use a graphing calculator to show these graphs: $y = 2x^3$, $y = 8x^3$, and $y = 5.5x^3$. What do these graphs have in common?" The x-intercept for each is 0.

"Predict the x-intercept of the function $y = 6\frac{1}{3}x^3$." The x-intercept would be 0.

"Write a cubic function with an x-intercept of 0." $y = 4x^3$

Problem 20
Extend the Problem
A zip code consists of five digits 0–9. If the first digit must be a 6 or 7, the second digit must be less than 8, and the fourth digit cannot be a 3, 5, or 6, how many zip codes are possible? 11,200

---

11. Multi-Step An apple fell from a tree limb. The function $t = 0.45\sqrt{x}$ represents how long it takes an object to fall from a height of x meters.
(114)
  a. Graph the function. (Hint: Increment the x-axis by 1 and the y-axis by 0.1, and if a graphing calculator is not used, then use the following values for x: 0, 4, 9, and 16.) See Additional Answers.
  b. Use the graph to estimate how long it took the apple to fall if the limb was 12 meters above the ground. Sample: ≈1.6 seconds

12. Use the discriminant to find the number of real solutions of the equation
(113) $6x^2 + 2x - 1 = 0$. $d = 28$; two real solutions

***13. Error Analysis** Two students are using the discriminant to find the number of real solutions to the equation $2x^2 + 3x - 4 = 0$. Which student is correct? Explain the error. Student B; Sample: The value of c is -4, not 4.
(113)

Student A	Student B
$2x^2 + 3x - 4 = 0$	$2x^2 + 3x - 4 = 0$
$b^2 - 4ac = 3^2 - 4(2)(4)$	$b^2 - 4ac = 3^2 - 4(2)(-4)$
$= 9 - 32$	$= 9 + 32$
$= -23$	$= 41$
As the discriminant is negative, there are no x-intercepts.	As the discriminant is positive, there are two x-intercepts.

14. Gardening The length of a garden is $6 + x$ meters and the width is $10 - x$ meters. Write an equation to model the area of the garden, and use the discriminant to determine if there is a value for x that will allow the area of the garden to be 50 square meters. $A = (6 + x)(10 - x)$; $50 = 60 + 4x - x^2$ and the discriminant is 56; Yes, the garden can have an area of 50 square meters.
(113)

15. Measurement The length of a fence is $15 - x$ feet and the width is $12 + x$ feet. Can the fence enclose an area of 200 square feet? Explain.
(113)

16. Determine if the set of ordered pairs $\left\{\left(-3, \frac{1}{8}\right), \left(-1, \frac{1}{2}\right), \left(-2, \frac{1}{4}\right), \left(-4, \frac{1}{16}\right)\right\}$ satisfies an exponential function. yes
(108)

17. Graph the system $\begin{array}{l} 21x + 7y \geq -14 \\ \frac{1}{2}y \leq -x + 2 \end{array}$. See Additional Answers.
(109)

18. Geometry If the area of the triangle is 48 square units, what are the lengths of the base and the height to the nearest whole number? $h = 8$ units, $b = 12$ units
(110)

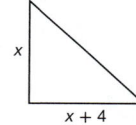

15. no; Sample: The equation $200 = (15 - x)(12 + x)$ represents the area of the rectangle; $200 = 180 + 3x - x^2$ and $0 = -x^2 + 3x - 20$. The discriminant of this equation is $3^2 - 4(-1)(-20) = 9 - 80 = -71$. Since the discriminant is negative, there is no value for x that makes the equation true.

***19.** Graph the cubic function $y = 3x^3$. Use it to solve the equation $0 = 3x^3$.
(115) See Additional Answers.

20. A new 3-digit area code is being created for new telephone numbers. If the first digit must be even but not 0, the second digit is 0 or 1, and the third digit can be any number except 0, how many new area codes are possible? 72 area codes
(111)

786 Saxon Algebra 1

ENGLISH LEARNERS

For problem 11 explain the meaning of the word **limb.** Say:

"A tree limb is a part of a tree that extends out from the trunk of the tree. It can have leaves and fruit on it."

Draw a tree on the board and label the larger branches limbs. Then draw a stick person on the board. Say:

"The arms and legs on a person are also called limbs because they extend from the body."

Have students use the word limb in a sentence. Sample: Lightning struck the tree limb.

21. **Multiple Choice** Which system of equations has the solution $(-1, 1)$? **C**
(112)
   A $y = x^2$
   $y = x + 6$

   B $y = x^2$
   $y = 6$

   C $y = x^2$
   $y = -2x - 1$

   D $y = x^2$
   $y = -x + 6$

*22. **Analyze** A system of three equations consists of a quadratic, given by
(112) $y = x^2 - 3$, and two linear equations. One linear equation intersects the parabola at two points. If the second linear equation is parallel to the first, how many solutions does the system have? Explain.

22. none; Sample: The second parallel line could intersect the parabola at least once. However, since it never intersects the other linear equation, there can be no solution to the system.

23. (**Accessories**) Candida has plans to shop for hair bows and does not plan on
(97) spending more than $20. Each big bow costs $5 and each small bow costs $2. Write an inequality and graph it to describe the situation.   See Additional Answers.

24. Solve $-x^2 + 2 = -7x$ by using a graphing calculator. Round to the nearest tenth.
(100) $x = -0.3$ and 7.3

25. **Multiple Choice** Solve $x^2 + 7 = -42$. **C**
(102)
   A 7   **B** ±7   **C** no solution   **D** $\pm 7\sqrt{1}$

26. (**Phone Chains**) In order to relay information quickly, staff at a school use a phone
(105) chain. The superintendent first notifies 3 people of a snow day. In the second set of calls, these 3 people each call 2 people. Each person called then calls 2 other people. How many sets of calls need to be made to notify 96 people?   6 sets of calls

27. **Multi-Step** A square frame is to be made so that its side length is $\sqrt{x+1}$.
(106)
   a. What is the perimeter of the square? $4\sqrt{x+1}$ units
   b. For what value of x will the perimeter of the frame be equal to 8 units? $x = 3$

28. **Generalize** Look at the function $f(x) = -0.5|x|$. How can you find the direction of
(107) the "V" without graphing it?   Sample: The negative sign indicates that the "V" will open downward.

29. (**Football**) The distance d from the goal post in feet of a football during a field goal
(107) kick is represented by the function $d = |60t - 90|$ where t is the time in seconds. If the ball were kicked at 80 feet per second how would the graph change?   The graph would be compressed.

30. Write, in order, the function that grows the slowest to the one that grows the
(Inv 11) fastest: exponential, linear, quadratic.   linear, quadratic, exponential

Problem 23
Error Alert
Students may not use two variables to represent the two kinds of bows. Remind them that the bows have different prices and cannot be represented by the same variable.

Problem 25
Guide the students by asking them the following questions.

"What is the degree of the equation?" The variable is squared, so the degree is 2.

"How can x^2 be isolated?" Subtract 7 from both sides of the equation to get $x^2 = -49$.

"What answer choice or choices can be eliminated at this point? Why?" All answer choices except C can be eliminated. The term x^2 is equal to -49. There is no real number that when squared will equal a negative number.

Problem 27
Extend the Problem
For what value of x will each side of the frame be equal to 8 units? $x = 63$

Lesson 115   787

CHALLENGE

Describe the end behavior of each graph:
   linear equation ends go in opposite directions
   quadratic equation ends go in the same direction
   cubic equation ends go in opposite directions

Use this knowledge to predict the end behavior of the graph of $y = x^4$. Then graph $y = x^4$ to check your prediction. ends go in the same direction

LOOKING FORWARD

Graphing cubic functions will be further developed in other Saxon Secondary Mathematics courses.

Lesson 115   787

LESSON 116

Solving Simple and Compound Interest Problems

Warm Up

1. **Vocabulary** Two equivalent ratios form a _____. proportion
2. Change 24% to a fraction and a decimal. $\frac{6}{25}$, 0.24
3. Change $\frac{1}{40}$ to a decimal and a percent. 0.025, 2.5%
4. Find 25% of 250. 62.5
5. 36 is what percent of 1125? 3.2%

New Concepts

Money that is borrowed or invested is called principal. Interest is money paid for the use of that money. If money is borrowed, interest is paid. If money is invested, interest is earned.

Simple interest is interest paid on the principal only. To find simple interest, use the formula $I = Prt$.

Simple Interest Formula	
$I = Prt$	
I	the amount of interest
P	the principal
r	the annual rate, a percent expressed as a decimal
t	the time in years

Math Language

Even though the account value grows as interest is earned, **simple interest** is only paid on the original amount deposited into the account.

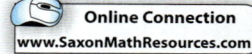

Example 1 Finding Simple Interest

(a.) An account is opened with $4000. The bank pays 5% simple interest annually. How much interest will be earned in 3 years?

SOLUTION

Use the simple interest formula.

The principal P is 4000. The rate r is 5%, or 0.05. The time t is 3.

$I = Prt$ Write the formula, then evaluate.

$= 4000(0.05)(3)$ Substitute the values of the variables.

$= 600$ Simplify.

The account will earn $600 interest in 3 years.

788   Saxon Algebra 1

b. $12,500 is invested for 15 years at 4% simple interest. How much money will be in the account after 15 years?

SOLUTION

Use the simple interest formula.

The principal P is 12,500. The rate r is 4%, or 0.04. The time t is 15.

$I = Prt$	Write the formula, then evaluate.
$= 12,500(0.04)(15)$	Substitute the values of the variables.
$= 7500$	Simplify.

The account will earn $7500 interest in 15 years.

Add this interest to the original amount invested to find the total amount in the account.

$12,500 + 7500 = 20,000$

There will be $20,000 in the account after 15 years.

c. $6000 is borrowed at 8.5% simple interest. The total amount of interest paid is $2040. For how many years was the money borrowed?

SOLUTION

Use the simple interest formula and solve for t.

The principal P is 6000. The interest I is 2040. The rate r is 8.5% or 0.085.

$I = Prt$	Write the formula.
$2040 = 6000(0.085)t$	Substitute the values of the variables.
$2040 = 510t$	Simplify.
$4 = t$	Divide both sides by 510.

The money was borrowed for 4 years.

d. After 18 months, $738 had been earned on an $8200 investment. What was the interest rate?

SOLUTION

Use the simple interest formula and solve for r.

The principal P is 8200. The interest I is 738. The time t is $\frac{18}{12} = 1.5$ years.

$I = Prt$	Write the formula.
$738 = 8200 \cdot r \cdot 1.5$	Substitute the values of the variables.
$738 = 12,300r$	Simplify.
$0.06 = r$	Divide both sides by 12,300.

Convert 0.06 to a percent. The interest rate was 6%.

Hint

The time in the simple interest formula must be in years. There are 12 months in 1 year. To change the units from months to years, divide by 12.

Example 1

This example demonstrates the application of the formula for finding simple interest.

Additional Example 1

a. An account is opened with $3500. The bank pays 4.5% simple interest annually. How much interest will be earned in 8 years? **$1260.00**

b. $15,000 is invested for 30 years at 6.25% simple interest. How much will be in the account after 30 years? **$43,125**

c. $7500 is borrowed at 7.75% simple interest. The total amount of interest paid is $3487.50. For how many years was the money borrowed? **6 years**

d. After 66 months, $1384.62 had been earned on an investment of $5750. What was the interest rate? **4.4%**

ENGLISH LEARNERS

For Example 1b, explain the meaning of the word **invested.** Say:

"**Invested means that money has been put into a business, real estate, stocks, or bonds in order to make more money.**"

Discuss ways that money is invested by the purchase of land or homes. Explain that stocks are investments in privately owned companies, and that bonds are investments in a government agency.

TEACHER TIP

Students should realize that while the formula for simple interest gives a result that shows the interest earned, the formula for compound interest yields a cumulative account balance (principal plus interest). Help students recognize this difference so they can more accurately answer the questions.

Example 2

Discuss with students the difference in the value of the investment when compounded annually and quarterly.

Additional Example 2

a. $13,000 is invested at 4.5% compounded annually. Find the value of the investment after 8 years. **$18,487.31**

b. $7500 is invested at 5.8% compounded semi-annually. Find the value of the investment after 20 years. **$23,532.94**

The amount in an account grows faster with **compound interest**. Compound interest is interest that is paid on both principal and on previously-earned interest. The compound interest formula gives the total amount accumulated after a given number of years.

Compound Interest Formula

$$A = P\left(1 + \frac{r}{n}\right)^{nt}$$

A	the total amount after t years
P	the principal
r	the annual rate, a percent expressed as a decimal
t	the time in years
n	the number of times interest is compounded each year

Math Reasoning

Justify Explain why the formula for interest compounded annually is $A = P(1 + r)^t$.

Sample: When interest is compounded annually, it is compounded once a year; $n = 1$. So,

$A = P\left(1 + \frac{r}{n}\right)^{nt}$
$= P\left(1 + \frac{r}{1}\right)^{1t}$
$= P(1 + r)^t$

Hint

Use a calculator to evaluate the power and to multiply the result by the principal.

Example 2 Finding Compound Interest

a. $5000 is invested at 6% compounded annually. Find the value of the investment after 10 years.

SOLUTION

The principal P is 5000. The rate r is 6% or 0.06. The time t is 10 years.

$A = P(1 + r)^t$ Write the formula, then evaluate.
$= 5000 \cdot (1 + 0.06)^{10}$ Substitute the values of the variables.
$= 5000 \cdot (1.06)^{10}$ Simplify inside the parentheses.
$= 5000 \cdot 1.790847697$ Simplify the power, and do not round.
$= 8954.24$ Multiply, and round to the nearest penny.

The value of the investment will be $8954.24.

b. $5000 is invested at 6% compounded quarterly. Find the value of the investment after 10 years.

SOLUTION

The principal P is 5000. The rate r is 6% or 0.06. The time t is 10 years and $n = 4$ because quarterly means four times per year.

$A = P\left(1 + \frac{r}{n}\right)^{nt}$ Write the formula, then evaluate.

$= 5000\left(1 + \frac{0.06}{4}\right)^{4(10)}$ Substitute the values of the variables.

$= 5000 \cdot (1.015)^{40}$ Use the order of operations to simplify.
$= 5000 \cdot 1.814018409$ Simplify the power and do not round.
$= 9070.09$ Multiply and round to the nearest penny.

The value of the investment will be $9070.09.

INCLUSION

Use the following strategy with students who have difficulty with written symbols. Help students remember the formulas by writing out the formulas using complete words.

The formula for simple interest would look like this:

Interest = Principal × rate × time

For students who may need further help, write out the formula to find factors other than the interest paid:

$$\frac{\text{Interest}}{\text{Principal} \times \text{rate}} = \text{time}$$

$$\frac{\text{Interest}}{\text{Principal} \times \text{time}} = \text{rate}$$

Allow students to refer to these diagrams as needed during the lesson.

Example 3 Comparing Simple and Compound Interest

a. An account has $1000 and earns 20% simple interest. Make a table to find the total amount in the account after 1, 2, 5, and 10 years.

SOLUTION

Years	$Prt = I$		Total in Account	
1	$(1000)(0.20)(1)$	$= 200$	$\$1000 + \$200$	$= \$1200$
2	$(1000)(0.20)(2)$	$= 400$	$\$1000 + \$400$	$= \$1400$
5	$(1000)(0.20)(5)$	$= 1000$	$\$1000 + \$1000$	$= \$2000$
10	$(1000)(0.20)(10)$	$= 2000$	$\$1000 + \$2000$	$= \$3000$

Caution

Be sure to add the interest paid to the original principal to find the total amount in the account.

b. An account has $1000 and earns 20% interest compounded annually. Make a table to find the total amount in the account after 1, 2, 5, and 10 years.

SOLUTION

Years	$A = P(1 + r)^t$	Total in Account
1	$A = 1000(1 + 0.20)^1$	$1200
2	$A = 1000(1 + 0.20)^2$	$1440
5	$A = 1000(1 + 0.20)^5$	$2488.32
10	$A = 1000(1 + 0.20)^{10}$	$6191.74

c. Use the table in **a** to graph the account earning simple interest and the table in **b** to graph the account earning compound interest on the same coordinate plane. Compare the growth of the two accounts over time.

SOLUTION

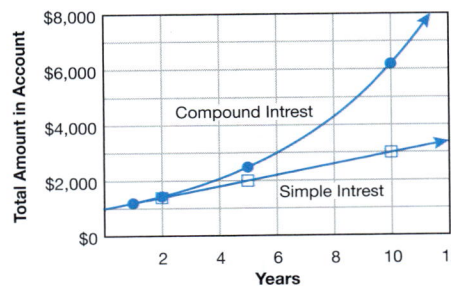

Simple interest grows *linearly* because it adds the same amount each year. Compound interest grows *exponentially* because it pays interest on the previously-earned interest as well as the principal. The account earning compound interest grows more rapidly than the account earning simple interest.

Lesson 116   791

Example 4

Have students find the amount of each investment when compounded quarterly in order to compare compounding for different intervals of time.
woman's: $32,102.35; man's: $20,031.96

Extend the Example

What amount would the man have to invest for the value of his investment at his retirement to equal the value of the woman's investment at her retirement?
$7739.37

Additional Example 4

A 30-year-old man invests $4000 in a bond that pays 5.5% interest per year, compounded semi-annually. How much will the investment be worth at his retirement age of 65? $26,717.03

Lesson Practice

Problem b

Error Alert Make sure that students remember to add the amount of interest to the principal to correctly answer the question. Suggest that students write the formula to emphasize that it computes interest only.

Problem d

Scaffolding Have students first write the formula for simple interest, transforming it to show how they would find the interest rate:

$\frac{I}{Pt} = r$. They can then substitute the given information and find the solution.

Math Reasoning

Analyze Why was the man's account value less than the woman's?

Sample: The man had 20 fewer years of compounded interest.

Example 4 Application: Retirement Investments

Two people plan to retire at age 65. A 25-year-old woman invests $2000 in a bond that pays 7% per year, compounded annually. A 45-year-old man invests $5000 in a bond that pays 7% per year, also compounded annually. Whose investment will be worth more when they reach retirement age and by how much?

SOLUTION

Use $A = P(1 + r)^t$ to calculate the value of the investment for each person.

For the 25-year-old woman, $P = 2000$, $r = 0.07$, and $t = 40$.

$A = 2000(1 + 0.07)^{40}$ Substitute.
$A = 2000(1.07)^{40}$ Add inside the parentheses.
$A = 29,948.92$ Simplify using the order of operations.

The total value of her account will be $29,948.92.

For the 45-year-old man, $P = 5000$, $r = 0.07$, and $t = 20$.

$A = 5000(1 + 0.07)^{20}$ Substitute.
$A = 5000(1.07)^{20}$ Add inside the parentheses.
$A = 19,348.42$ Simplify using the order of operations.

The total value of his account will be $19,348.42. The woman's investment will be worth $10,600.50 more.

Lesson Practice

a. An account is opened with $5600. The bank pays 4% simple interest annually. How much interest will be earned in 10 years? $2240
(Ex 1)

b. $25,000 is invested for 12 years at 6% simple interest. How much will be in the account after 12 years? $43,000
(Ex 1)

c. $4500 is borrowed at 2.5% simple interest. The total amount of interest paid is $562.50. For how many years was the money borrowed? 5 years
(Ex 1)

d. After 15 months, $130 had been earned on a $2600 investment. What was the interest rate? 4%
(Ex 1)

e. $12,000 is invested at 4% compounded annually. Find the value of the investment after 30 years. $38,920.77
(Ex 2)

f. $12,000 is invested at 4% compounded quarterly. Find the value of the investment after 30 years. $39,604.64
(Ex 2)

g. An account has $2500 and earns 12% simple interest. Complete the table to find the total amount in the account after 1, 2, 5, and 10 years.
(Ex 3)

Years	$Prt = I$	Total Amount in Account
1	$300	$2800
2	$600	$3100
5	$1500	$4000
10	$3000	$5500

i.

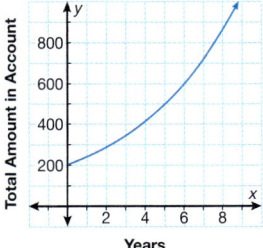

The account earning compound interest increases more rapidly.

h. A second account has $2500 and earns 12% compounded annually. Complete the table to find the total amount in each account after 1, 2, 5, and 10 years.
(Ex 3)

Principal	Rate	Years	Total Amount in Account
$2500	12%	1	$2800
$2500	12%	2	$3136
$2500	12%	5	$4405.85
$2500	12%	10	$7764.62

i. Use the table in problem g to graph the account earning simple interest and the table in problem h to graph the account earning compound interest on the same coordinate plane. Compare the growth of the two accounts over time.
(Ex 3)

j. (Retirement Investments) Two people plan to retire at age 60. A 30-year-old man invests $4000 in a bond that pays 5% per year, compounded annually. A 40-year-old man invests $6000 in a bond that pays 5% per year, also compounded annually. Whose investment will be worth more when they reach retirement age and by how much? The 30-year-old man's investment will be worth more by $1367.98.
(Ex 4)

Practice Distributed and Integrated

*1. $900 is invested at 3% simple interest for 5 years. How much interest is earned? $135
(116)

*2. Write Explain the difference between simple and compound interest.
(116)

2. Sample: Simple interest is just paid on the principal. Compound interest is paid on the principal and interest earned.

*3. Formulate The graph shows the value of a money market account that pays compound interest. How much principal was originally invested? $200
(116)

4. (Population) The exponential function $y = 3.45(1.00617)^x$ can model the approximate population of Oklahoma from 2000 to 2006, where x is the number of years after 2000 and y represents millions of people. Assuming the model does not change, predict when the population will reach 4 million? 2025
(108)

Lesson 116   793

Check for Understanding

The questions below help assess the concepts taught in this lesson.

What is the difference between simple interest and compound interest? Simple interest is paid on the principal only; compound interest is paid on the principal and any interest earned.

How can the formula for compound interest be used to find the principal? Write the formula. Divide the amount in the account (A) by the rate and time portion of the formula: $\frac{A}{\left(1 + \frac{r}{n}\right)^{nt}}$.

3 Practice

Math Conversations

Discussion to strengthen understanding

Problem 1

Guide the students by asking them the following questions.

"What is the principal in this problem?" $900

"What is the interest rate? 3%

What is the period of time?" 5 years

"How is this information substituted into the formula?" The P stands for the principal, or $900. The r stands for the interest rate of 3%, or 0.03. The t stands for the length of time of the investment, or 5.

Lesson 116   793

Problem 6
Error Alert
Make sure that students remember to change the percent to a decimal before completing the calculations.

Problem 12
Extend the Problem
What is the speed in feet per second of a coin that is dropped from the roof of a building 450 feet tall? **169.7 feet per second**

Problem 16
Have students give the answer in simplest radical form for practice simplifying radical expressions.
$-8 + 3\sqrt{2}, -8 - 3\sqrt{2}$

---

*5. Multiple Choice $600 is invested at 11% simple interest. What is the value of the investment after 14 years? **B**
A $924   B $1524   C $2586.26   D $92,400

*6. Mutual Funds Over the past 20 years, a mutual fund averages paying 10% interest compounded annually. If a woman had invested $3000 originally, how much would her account be worth now? **$20,182.50**

*7. Graph the cubic function $y = -3x^3$. Use the graph to find the roots of the equation.

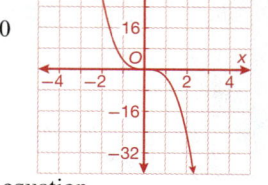
7. ; $x = 0$

8. Error Analysis Two students write the equation "y equals x cubed plus five." Which student is correct? Explain the error. **Student A; Sample: The word "cubed" means to the third power, not to the second power.**

Student A	Student B
$y = x^3 + 5$	$y = x^2 + 5$

9. Geometry The formula for the volume of a cube is $V = s^3$. Graph the equation and find the volume of the cube if the side length is 2 units.

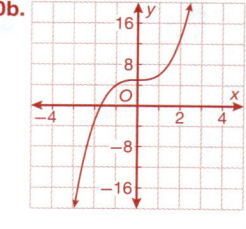
9. ; 8 cubic units

*10. Multi-Step The volume of a packing container is given by the function $y = x^3 + 5$.
a. Make a table of values for the equation.
b. Graph the equation.
c. Find the volume when x is 3 feet. **32 cubic feet**

10a.
x	y
-2	-3
-1	4
0	5
1	6
2	13

10b.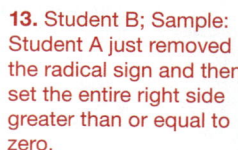

11. Evaluate $y = 3\sqrt{7x+2} - 7$ for $x = 2$. **5**

12. Physics The speed at which an object in free fall drops is modeled by the equation $y = 8\sqrt{x}$. In this equation, y is the speed in feet per second and x is the distance fallen in feet. What is the speed of an apple after it falls a distance of 8 feet? Round to the nearest tenth. **≈ 22.6 feet per second**

*13. Error Analysis Two students are determining the domain and range of the function $f(x) = \sqrt{x-5} + 1$. Which student is correct? Explain the error.

Student A	Student B
$f(x) = \sqrt{x-5} + 1$	$f(x) = \sqrt{x-5} + 1$
$x - 4 \geq 0$	$x - 5 \geq 0$
$x \geq 4; y \geq 0$	$x \geq 5; y \geq 1$

13. Student B; Sample: Student A just removed the radical sign and then set the entire right side greater than or equal to zero.

14. Measurement The function $s = \sqrt{A}$ gives the side length of a square with area A. What is the side length of a square that has an area of 625 square feet? **25 feet**

15. Graph the system $\begin{array}{l} y \geq \frac{2}{5}x - 4 \\ y \leq 0 \end{array}$.

15.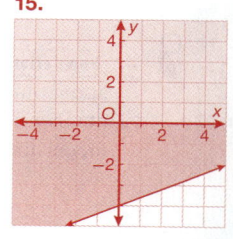

16. Use the quadratic formula to solve $46 + 16x = -x^2$. Find approximate answers to four decimal places. **−3.7574, −12.2426**

CHALLENGE

Have students solve this problem:

Antwaan deposited $5000 in a savings account that paid 5.75% interest compounded semi-annually. After 6 years, he withdrew $2500. What is the total amount in the account 13 years after the account was opened? **$6730.10**

17. **(Sports)** The American League Central Division in Major League Baseball has
    (111) 5 teams. How many different ways are there for the teams to finish first through
    fifth? 120

18. Solve this system by graphing: $y = 2x^2 - 6x + 1$
    (112) $y = -x - 4$.

18. no solution;
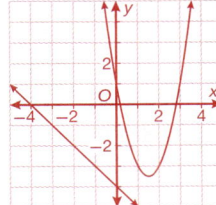

19. **Multiple Choice** How many x-intercepts does the equation $y = 4x^2 + 8x - 2$ have?
    (113)
    A 0   **B** 1   **C** 2   **D** 3   **C**

20. **Write** Explain what the discriminant tells about the graph of a quadratic
    (113) equation. Sample: The discriminant tells how many times the graph of a
    quadratic equation crosses or touches the x-axis.

21. Solve $4x^2 + 8 = -6x$ by using a graphing calculator. Round to the nearest tenth.
    (100) no solution

22. Solve and graph the inequality $|4x - 3| + 1 > 10$. $x < -1.5$ OR $x > 3$;
    (101)
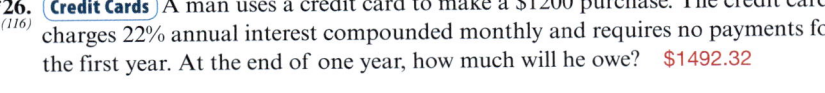

23. **(Structural Engineering)** The water pressure p on a dam is a function of the depth
    (106) of the water x behind the dam: $p = 4905\sqrt{x}$. For what value of x is the pressure
    equal to 44,145? $x = 81$

24. **Multi-Step** Graph the function $f(x) = |x| - 4$, and then translate the function to
    (107) the left by 2. What is the vertex of this new function? $(-2, -4)$

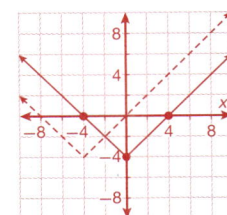

*25. $4500 is borrowed at 3.5% simple interest. The total amount of interest paid is
    (116) $1260. For how many years was the money borrowed?   8 years

*26. **(Credit Cards)** A man uses a credit card to make a $1200 purchase. The credit card
    (116) charges 22% annual interest compounded monthly and requires no payments for
    the first year. At the end of one year, how much will he owe? $1492.32

27. **Justify** Why is $f(x) = 4(-2)^x$ not an exponential function?
    (108)

28. **Multi-Step** Study the numbers in the sequence.
    (103)
    $$3, \sqrt{3}, 1, \frac{\sqrt{3}}{3}, \frac{1}{3}, \ldots$$

    27. because b is negative;
    Sample: The range values
    are not all positive or all
    negative. For example,
    $f(2) = 16$ and $f(3) = -32$.

    a. Find the pattern.   Divide each term by $\sqrt{3}$.
    b. What is the next term in the sequence? $\frac{\sqrt{3}}{9}$

29. If $f(x) = 3x^2 - 12x + 2$, where is the axis of symmetry located? Give the x- and
    (Inv 10) y-coordinates of the vertex. $x = 2$, $(2, -10)$

30. Identify which function is linear, quadratic, exponential growth, and exponential
    (Inv 11) decay: $f(x) = \left(\frac{1}{5}\right)^x$, $g(x) = x^2$, $h(x) = 5^x$, and $j(x) = 5x$. $f(x)$ is exponential decay,
    $g(x)$ is quadratic, $h(x)$ is exponential growth, and $j(x)$ is linear.

Problem 19
Guide the students by asking them the following questions.

"What is an x-interceept?" A point at which the line of a graph crosses the x-axis.

"What is the shape of this graph?" A parabola that opens upward.

"Where is the vertex located?" The vertex is below the x-axis.

"How many x-intercepts does the equation produce?" 2

Problem 21
Error Alert
Some students may not enter the function correctly into their calculators. Remind them that the function must be in standard form and that, depending on the side of the equal sign to which the terms are gathered, sign changes will occur.

Problem 23
Extend the Problem
What is the water pressure on the dam at a depth of 225 feet? 73,575 psi

---

LOOKING FORWARD

Solving simple and compound interest problems will be further developed in other Saxon Secondary Mathematics courses.

LESSON 117

1 Warm Up

Problem 4
Remind students that the hypotenuse is always the longest side, no matter in what order the sides are listed.

2 New Concepts

In this lesson, students find trigonometric ratios and use them to find missing side lengths. They use trigonometry to find missing angle measures.

TEACHER TIP

Emphasize which sides of a right triangle are legs and which side is the hypotenuse. In addition, for each acute angle in the triangle, have students identify the adjacent and opposite sides.

LESSON RESOURCES

Student Edition Practice Workbook 117
Reteaching Master 117
Adaptations Master 117
Challenge and Enrichment Master C117
Technology Lab Master 117

LESSON 117

Using Trigonometric Ratios

Warm Up

1. **Vocabulary** A ratio is the comparison of two quantities using _____. division
2. If the two legs of a right triangle measure 9 inches and 12 inches, find the length of the hypotenuse. 15 in.
3. In a right triangle, one leg measures 10 inches and the hypotenuse measures 17 inches. Find the length of the other leg. $3\sqrt{21}$ in. or ≈ 13.75 in.

Decide if the following are Pythagorean triples or not.

4. 6, 10, 8   yes
5. 8, 12, 20   no

New Concepts

Recall that a right triangle has one right angle and two acute angles. In the triangle, $\angle C$ is the right angle and $\angle A$ and $\angle B$ are the acute angles.

Using $\angle A$ in the triangle, the leg across from the angle is called the opposite leg and the leg next to $\angle A$ is called the adjacent leg. The hypotenuse is always opposite the right angle and is always the longest side of the triangle.

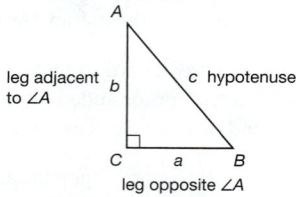

Hint
The three trigonometric ratios of sine, cosine, and tangent can be remembered using the mnemonic device:

SOH-CAH-TOA
(pronounced "sew-ka-toe-a"). **S**ine equals **O**pposite leg over **H**ypotenuse, **C**osine equals **A**djacent leg over **H**ypotenuse, and **T**angent equals **O**pposite leg over **A**djacent leg. This can also be written as $S\frac{o}{h}\ C\frac{a}{h}\ T\frac{o}{a}$.

Online Connection
www.SaxonMathResources.com

In any right triangle, there are six **trigonometric ratios** that can be written using two side lengths of the triangle in relation to the angles of the triangle. The three most common trigonometric ratios are sine, cosine, and tangent, abbreviated sin, cos, and tan, respectively.

Sine, Cosine, and Tangent
sine of $\angle A = \dfrac{\text{length of leg opposite } \angle A}{\text{length of hypotenuse}} = \dfrac{a}{c}$
cosine of $\angle A = \dfrac{\text{length of leg adjacent to } \angle A}{\text{length of hypotenuse}} = \dfrac{b}{c}$
tangent of $\angle A = \dfrac{\text{length of leg opposite } \angle A}{\text{length of leg adjacent to } \angle A} = \dfrac{a}{b}$

MATH BACKGROUND

The word trigonometry derives from Greek words meaning "triangle measurement."

Trigonometric ratios are used to find angle and side measurements in right triangles. In a right triangle, the hypotenuse is the longest side and is opposite the right angle. The legs are the two sides adjacent to the right angle. Each angle other than the right angle has a leg that is opposite it and a leg that is adjacent to it. These relationships are used in the definition of the trigonometric ratios: sine, cosine, and tangent. The reciprocals of each of the trigonometric ratios are cosecant, secant, and cotangent, respectively.

When an angle measurement and side length are known, these ratios can be used to find the lengths of the other sides. If the side lengths are known, the inverse functions can be used to find the angle measures.

In addition to the three trigonometric ratios previously discussed, there are three other trigonometric ratios called cosecant, secant, and cotangent, abbreviated csc, sec, and cot, respectively.

Math Reasoning

Generalize Explain the relationship between sine and cosecant; cosine and secant; and tangent and cotangent ratios.

They are reciprocals of each other.

Cosecant, Secant, and Cotangent
cosecant of $\angle A = \dfrac{\text{length of hypotenuse}}{\text{length of leg opposite } \angle A} = \dfrac{c}{a}$
secant of $\angle A = \dfrac{\text{length of hypotenuse}}{\text{length of leg adjacent to } \angle A} = \dfrac{c}{b}$
cotangent of $\angle A = \dfrac{\text{length of leg adjacent to } \angle A}{\text{length of leg opposite } \angle A} = \dfrac{b}{a}$

Caution

Writing "$\sin = \frac{5}{13}$" is not a valid trigonometric ratio because there is no angle measure included with sine.

Example 1 Finding Trigonometric Ratios

a. Using the right triangle, find $\sin B$, $\cos B$, and $\tan B$.

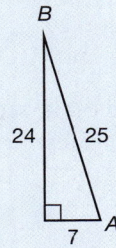

SOLUTION

$\sin B = \dfrac{\text{opposite leg}}{\text{hypotenuse}} = \dfrac{5}{13}$

$\cos B = \dfrac{\text{adjacent leg}}{\text{hypotenuse}} = \dfrac{12}{13}$

$\tan B = \dfrac{\text{opposite leg}}{\text{adjacent leg}} = \dfrac{5}{12}$

b. Using the right triangle, find all six trigonometric ratios for $\angle A$.

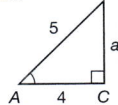

SOLUTION

First find the length of side a using the Pythagorean Theorem.

$a^2 + b^2 = c^2$

$a^2 + 4^2 = 5^2$

$a^2 + 16 = 25$

$a^2 = 9$

$a = 3$

Caution

Although $a = \pm 3$, only the positive value is used because a represents length.

$\sin A = \dfrac{a}{c} = \dfrac{3}{5}$ $\cos A = \dfrac{b}{c} = \dfrac{4}{5}$

$\tan A = \dfrac{a}{b} = \dfrac{3}{4}$ $\csc A = \dfrac{c}{a} = \dfrac{5}{3}$

$\sec A = \dfrac{c}{b} = \dfrac{5}{4}$ $\cot A = \dfrac{b}{a} = \dfrac{4}{3}$

Example 1

Students find the trigonometric ratios for a right triangle.

Additional Example 1

a. Using the right triangle, find $\sin B$, $\cos B$, and $\tan B$.

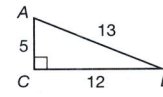

$\sin B = \dfrac{7}{25}$; $\cos B = \dfrac{24}{25}$; $\tan B = \dfrac{7}{24}$

b. Using the right triangle, find all six trigonometric ratios for $\angle A$.

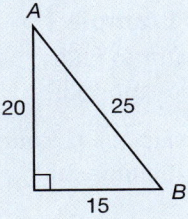

$\sin A = \dfrac{3}{5}$, $\cos A = \dfrac{4}{5}$,

$\tan A = \dfrac{3}{4}$, $\csc A = \dfrac{5}{3}$,

$\sec A = \dfrac{5}{4}$, $\cot A = \dfrac{4}{3}$

Lesson 117

ENGLISH LEARNERS

For this lesson, explain and contrast the meaning of the words **adjacent** and **opposite**. Using four volunteers, stand two students next to each other and the other two students opposite each other.

Discuss that adjacent means "next to" and opposite means "across from."

Have students identify objects in the classroom that are opposite each other and adjacent to each other.

Example 2
Students find the value of trigonometric ratios using a calculator.

Additional Example 2

a. If $\angle A = 38°$, find $\sin A$, $\cos A$, and $\tan A$ to the nearest ten-thousandth. **0.6157, 0.7880, 0.7813**

b. If $\angle A = 51°$, find $\csc A$, $\sec A$, and $\cot A$ to the nearest ten-thousandth. **1.2868, 1.5890, 0.8098**

Example 3
Students use trigonometric ratios to find missing side lengths.

Additional Example 3
Use a calculator to find trigonometric ratio values.

a. Find the value of x. Round to the nearest hundredth.

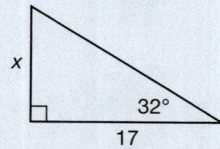

$x \approx 10.62$

b. Find the value of x and y. Round to the nearest hundredth.

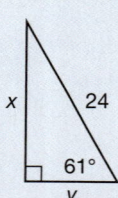

$x \approx 20.99, y \approx 11.64$

Example 2 Using a Calculator with Trigonometric Ratios

a. If $\angle A = 42°$, find $\sin A$, $\cos A$, and $\tan A$ to the nearest ten-thousandth.

SOLUTION

Use a calculator to find the value of the trigonometric ratios.

[SIN] 42 [ENTER] $\sin A \approx 0.6691$
[COS] 42 [ENTER] $\cos A \approx 0.7431$
[TAN] 42 [ENTER] $\tan A \approx 0.9004$

b. If $\angle A = 33°$, find $\csc A$, $\sec A$, and $\cot A$ to the nearest ten-thousandth.

SOLUTION

Use a calculator.

[SIN] 33 [ENTER] [x^{-1}] [ENTER]   OR   1 [÷] [SIN] 33 [ENTER]
$\csc A \approx 1.8361$

[COS] 33 [ENTER] [x^{-1}] [ENTER]   OR   1 [÷] [COS] 33 [ENTER]
$\sec A \approx 1.1924$

[TAN] 33 [ENTER] [x^{-1}] [ENTER]   OR   1 [÷] [TAN] 33 [ENTER]
$\cot A \approx 1.5399$

Example 3 Using Trigonometry to Find Missing Side Lengths

Use a calculator to find trigonometric ratio values.

a. Find the value of x. Round to the nearest hundredth.

SOLUTION

Since the missing side is opposite the angle and the adjacent side length is given, use the tangent ratio.

$\tan 28° = \dfrac{x}{9}$

$9 \cdot \tan 28° = x$

$4.79 \approx x$

b. Find the value of x and y. Round to the nearest hundredth.

SOLUTION

$\sin A = \dfrac{\text{opposite leg}}{\text{hypotenuse}}$ $\cos A = \dfrac{\text{adjacent leg}}{\text{hypotenuse}}$

$\sin 52° = \dfrac{x}{12}$ $\cos 52° = \dfrac{y}{12}$

$12 \cdot \sin 52° = x$ $12 \cdot \cos 52° = y$

$9.46 \approx x$ $7.39 \approx y$

Inverse trigonometric functions can be used to find missing angle measures. On a calculator, these are $\sin^{-1}$, $\cos^{-1}$, and $\tan^{-1}$. Because they are inverse functions, $\sin^{-1}(\sin A) = A$, and the same principle follows for cosine and tangent.

Math Reasoning

Generalize When do you use the sine function and when do you use the inverse sine ($\sin^{-1}$) function?

Sample: Use the sine function when you know the angle and want to find the side length. Use the inverse sine function when you want to find the angle and you know the side length.

Hint

You can also find the measure of the second acute angle of a right triangle by subtracting the first angle from 90°. For example, if m∠A = 21.80°, then m∠B = 90° − 21.80° = 68.20°.

Example 4 Using Trigonometry to Find Missing Angle Measures

a. Find the measure of ∠A. Round to the nearest hundredth of a degree.

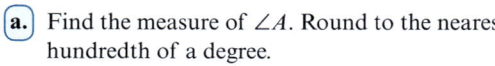

SOLUTION

Use the cosine ratio since you know the adjacent leg and the hypotenuse.

$$\cos A = \frac{6}{11}$$

$$\cos^{-1}(\cos A) = \cos^{-1}\left(\frac{6}{11}\right)$$

$$\angle A \approx 56.94°$$

b. Find the measures of ∠A and ∠B. Round to the nearest hundredth of a degree.

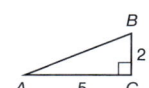

SOLUTION

Use the tangent ratio since you know the lengths of the legs.

$$\tan A = \frac{2}{5} \qquad \tan B = \frac{5}{2}$$

$$\tan^{-1}(\tan A) = \tan^{-1}\left(\frac{2}{5}\right) \qquad \tan^{-1}(\tan B) = \tan^{-1}\left(\frac{5}{2}\right)$$

$$\angle A \approx 21.80° \qquad \angle B \approx 68.20°$$

Example 5 Application: Indirect Measurement

If an airplane takes off at a 35° angle with the ground, how far has the plane traveled horizontally when it reaches an altitude of 10,000 feet?

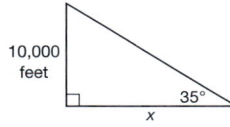

SOLUTION

Use the tangent ratio since the problem involves both legs.

$$\tan 35° = \frac{10{,}000}{x}$$

$$x \cdot \tan 35° = \frac{10{,}000}{x} \cdot x$$

$$x \cdot \tan 35° = 10{,}000$$

$$x = \frac{10{,}000}{\tan 35°} \approx 14{,}281$$

The plane has traveled about 14,281 feet horizontally.

Lesson 117   799

INCLUSION

Have students create a poster of a 3-4-5 right triangle. They can highlight each side of the triangle in a different color and label the acute angles *A* and *B*. Then have students list the 6 trigonometric ratios for each angle using the corresponding color when writing each side length.

Example 4

Students find missing angle measures using trigonometric ratios and inverse trigonometric functions.

Error Alert Students may confuse the word inverse with reciprocal. Emphasize that inverse is used to find the measure of an angle.

Additional Example 4

a. Find the measure of ∠A. Round to the nearest hundredth of a degree.

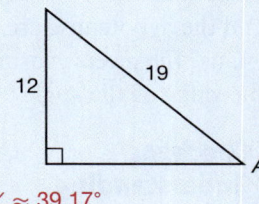

∠ ≈ 39.17°

b. Find the measures of ∠A and ∠B. Round to the nearest hundredth of a degree.

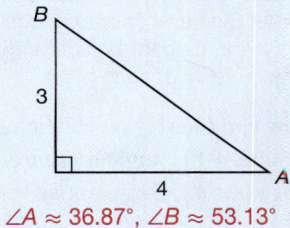

∠A ≈ 36.87°, ∠B ≈ 53.13°

Example 5

Students apply trigonometric ratios to indirect measurement.

Extend the Example

When the plane is at 10,000 feet, how far is the plane from where it left the ground? Round to the nearest foot. approximately 17,434 feet

Additional Example 5

A tree falls over and rests against a wall 10 feet off the ground. The tree now forms a 28° angle with the ground. How tall was the tree? Round to the nearest tenth of a foot. about 21.3 feet

Lesson 117   799

Lesson Practice

Problem d
Error Alert Students may take the reciprocal of 67 and then find the sine. Emphasize that sin 67° must be found. Then, the reciprocal of that value is the cosecant.

Problem h
Scaffolding Draw a picture of the situation. Label the angle A. The hypotenuse should be labeled 10, and the adjacent side, or ground distance, should be labeled 4. Because the adjacent side and the hypotenuse are known, use the inverse cosine to find the value of the angle.

Check for Understanding

The questions below help assess the concepts taught in this lesson.

"Explain the relationship among the six trigonometric ratios."
Sample: Sine and cosecant, cosine and secant, tangent and cotangent are reciprocals of each other.

"How can the trigonometric ratios be useful if the angle measure is not known?" Sample: Use the ratios with the inverse trigonometric functions to find the angle measure.

---

a. $\sin A = \frac{12}{13}$, $\cos A = \frac{5}{13}$, $\tan A = \frac{12}{5}$

b. $\sin B = \frac{4}{5}$, $\cos B = \frac{3}{5}$, $\tan B = \frac{4}{3}$, $\csc B = \frac{5}{4}$, $\sec B = \frac{5}{3}$, $\cot B = \frac{3}{4}$

Lesson Practice

a. Using the right triangle, find $\sin A$, $\cos A$, and $\tan A$.
(Ex 1)
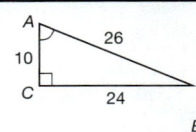

b. Using the right triangle, find all six trigonometric ratios for $\angle B$.
(Ex 1)
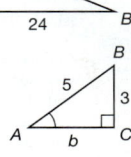

c. If $\angle A = 49°$, find $\sin A$, $\cos A$, and $\tan A$. Round to the nearest ten-thousandth. $\sin 49° \approx 0.7547$, $\cos 49° \approx 0.6561$, $\tan 49° \approx 1.1504$
(Ex 2)

d. If $\angle A = 67°$, find $\csc A$, $\sec A$, and $\cot A$. Round to the nearest ten-thousandth. $\csc 67° \approx 1.0864$, $\sec 67° \approx 2.5593$, $\cot 67° \approx 0.4245$
(Ex 2)

e. Find the value of x. Round to the nearest hundredth. $x \approx 29.06$
(Ex 3)
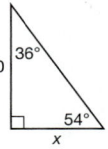

f. Find the value of x and y. Round to the nearest hundredth. $x \approx 12.63$; $y \approx 11.38$
(Ex 3)
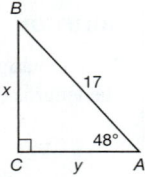

g. Find $\angle A$ and $\angle B$. $\angle A \approx 32.28°$; $\angle B \approx 57.72°$
(Ex 4)
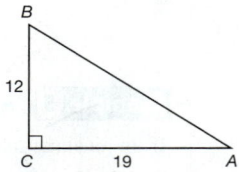

h. A 10-foot ladder is placed on the side of a building 4 feet away from the base of the building along the ground. Find the measure of the angle the ladder makes with the ground.   66.42°
(Ex 5)

Practice Distributed and Integrated

*1. Find $\sin A$, $\cos A$, and $\tan A$.
(117)
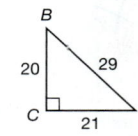

*2. Find $\sin A$, $\cos A$, and $\tan A$.
(117)
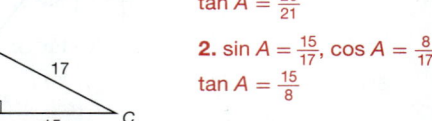

1. $\sin A = \frac{20}{29}$, $\cos A = \frac{21}{29}$, $\tan A = \frac{20}{21}$

2. $\sin A = \frac{15}{17}$, $\cos A = \frac{8}{17}$, $\tan A = \frac{15}{8}$

3. Write an equation for a direct variation that includes the point, (24, 3). $y = \frac{1}{8}x$
4. sin 77° ≈ 0.9744, cos 77° ≈ 0.2250, tan 77° ≈ 4.3315

*4. If $\angle A = 77°$, find sin A, cos A, and tan A to the nearest ten-thousandth.

*5. **Error Analysis** Two students are finding the measure of $\angle A$. Which student is correct? Explain the error.

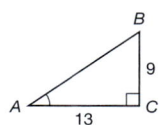

Student A	Student B
$\tan A = \frac{9}{13}$	$\tan A = \frac{13}{9}$
$\tan^{-1}(\tan A) = \tan^{-1}\left(\frac{9}{13}\right)$	$\tan^{-1}(\tan A) = \tan^{-1}\left(\frac{13}{9}\right)$
$A \approx 34.7°$	$A \approx 55.3°$

5. Student A; Sample: The tangent ratio is the opposite leg over the adjacent leg and Student B used adjacent over opposite.

 *6. **Geometry** In a right isosceles triangle, the acute angles are congruent. Find the measures of the acute angles. Then use the sine or cosine ratio to find the length of a leg of a right isosceles triangle to the nearest hundredth if the hypotenuse is 5 centimeters.   45°; 3.54 cm

*7. **Multi-Step** You are standing on the roof of a 70-foot-tall building looking across at another building. Use the picture to answer the questions.
   a. Find the distance from the bottom of the building where you are standing to the top of the other building.   250 feet
   b. Find the measure of $\angle A$.   16.26°

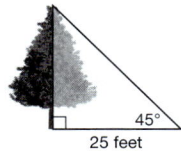

*8. **Nature** A tree casts a shadow of 25 feet along the ground. The angle from the ground to the top of the tree is 45°. How tall is the tree?   25 feet tall

9. If $1100 is borrowed for 2 years at 9% simple interest, how much interest is paid? $198

*10. **Navigation** A submarine begins diving from the water's surface at an angle of 7°. How far below the water's surface is the submarine after it has traveled 3.4 miles?

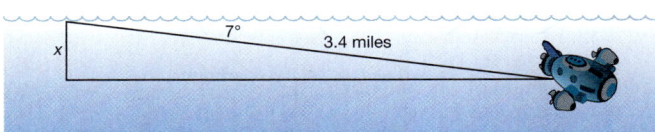

10. about 0.41 miles below the water's surface

*11. **Generalize** Explain the meaning of opposite leg and adjacent leg to an acute angle in a right triangle.   Sample: The opposite leg is the leg of a right triangle that is opposite the acute angle and the adjacent leg is the leg that is next to the acute angle, but not the hypotenuse.

Lesson 117   801

3 Practice

Math Conversations

Discussion to strengthen understanding

Problem 3
Have students substitute values of x and y into the equation $y = kx$ to find k.

Problem 6
Suggest that students draw a right isosceles triangle and label the hypotenuse with the given length, 5 centimeters. Ask them if trigonometry is needed to find the measure of the acute angles in the triangle. no; The acute angles measures can be determined without trigonometry because the sum of the measures of the angles in any triangle is 180°.

Problem 7
Guide the students by asking them the following questions.

"What formula is used to find the distance from the bottom of the building to the top of the other building?" the Pythagorean Theorem

"How is the trigonometric ratio determined for finding the measure of $\angle A$?" Since the length of the sides opposite and adjacent to $\angle A$ are given, the tangent ratio is used.

Problem 9
Remind students that the formula for simple interest is $I = Prt$.

Lesson 117   801

12. **Error Analysis** A $1500 investment earns 8% simple interest. Two students find the value of the account after 25 years. Which student is correct? Explain the error.

Student A	Student B
$I = Prt$	$I = Prt$
$I = 1500 \cdot 0.08 \cdot 25$	$I = 1500(0.08)(25)$
$I = 3000$	$I = 3000$
3000	$3000 + 1500 = 4500$
	4500

13. **Multi-Step** A boy plans to invest $100 in an account that pays 10% interest compounded annually for 10 years. Another option is an account that earns 20% interest compounded annually for 5 years. Which will earn him more money, and how much more?   10% for 10 years earns $10.54 more.

14. Graph the cubic function $y = x^3 + 3$. Use the graph to evaluate the equation for $x = 0$.   See Additional Answers.

15. **Error Analysis** Two students draw a graph of the equation $y = 2x^3$. Which student is correct? Explain the error.   Student B; Sample: Student A graphed the parent function.

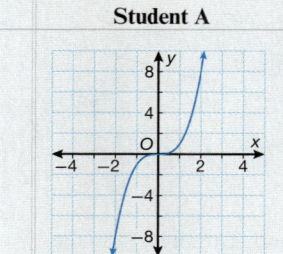
Student A

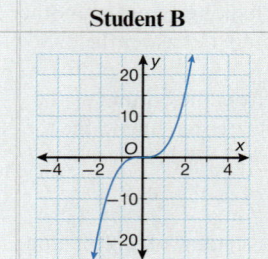
Student B

16. **Packaging** A rectangular box has a volume of $V = x^3 + 3$ cubic units. Use a table or graph to find the value of x that corresponds to a volume of 30 cubic units. $x = 3$

17. Use the quadratic formula to solve $2x^2 + 9 = 9x$. Check the solutions. $x = 3$ or $x = 1.5$

18. Find $_{12}P_3$.   1320

19. Solve $x^2 + 5 = 9$. $x = \pm 2$

20. **Astronomy** Near a planet, a satellite follows a trajectory described by the equation $y = \frac{x^2}{8} + \frac{7}{4}$. The trajectory is intercepted by a radio signal represented by the line $y = -\frac{9x}{8}$. At what coordinates will the radio signal intersect the trajectory? $\left(-2, \frac{9}{4}\right)$ and $\left(-7, \frac{63}{8}\right)$

21. Use the discriminant to find the number of real solutions of the equation $x^2 + 2x - 2 = 0$. $d = 12$; two real solutions

22. **Multiple Choice** What is the domain of the function $f(x) = 2\sqrt{x+6} - 1$?   **B**
   A $x \geq -5$ **B** $x \geq -6$ **C** $x \geq 6$ **D** $x \geq 0$

23. **Write** Describe the graph of $f(x) = \sqrt{x+4}$ in terms of its parent function.

24. Solve and graph the inequality $3|8x + 2| < 12$. $-0.75 < x < 0.25$ See Additional Answers.

802   Saxon Algebra 1

CHALLENGE

Identify trigonometric ratios that have the value $\frac{5}{12}$.

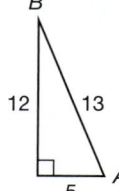

tan B, cot A

25. Multi-Step The sum of the squares of two consecutive odd numbers is 74.
(104)
  a. Write expressions for two consecutive odd numbers. x and $x + 2$
  b. Write an equation to represent the problem. $x^2 + (x + 2)^2 = 74$
  c. What is the possible solution(s)?   5 and 7 or −5 and −7

*26. If $\angle A = 81°$, find csc A, sec A, and cot A to the nearest ten-thousandth.
(117) csc 81° ≈ 1.0125, sec 81° ≈ 6.3925, cot 81° ≈ 0.1584

27. Multi-Step Anita figures that the value of her car, in thousands of dollars,
(108) can be approximated by $f(x) = 15\left(\frac{4}{5}\right)^x$, where x is the number of years after the car's manufacture. Evaluate the function for $x = 0, 1,$ and 2 and then sketch the function.   See Additional Answers.

28. Justify Explain why $\begin{matrix} y > 4 \\ y < 4 \end{matrix}$ has no solutions but $\begin{matrix} y \geq 4 \\ y \leq 4 \end{matrix}$ does.   See Additional
(109) Answers.

29. What does a half-life mean? If a substance's half-life is 25 hours, how many
(Inv 11) half-lives are there in 150 hours?   A half-life is the amount of time it takes for half of a substance to remain; 6 half-lives

30. (Tennis) A tennis instructor has a budget of $2000 to buy new rackets. He will
(78) receive 2 free rackets when he places his order. The number of rackets, y, that he can get is given by $y = \frac{2000}{x} + 2$, where x is the price per racket.
  a. What is the horizontal asymptote of this rational function? $y = 2$
  b. What is the vertical asymptote? $x = 0$
  c. If the price per racket is $200, how many rackets will he receive?   12 rackets

Problem 25
Error Alert
When writing an expression for two consecutive odd numbers, students may write x and $x + 1$, rather than $x + 2$. Remind them that consecutive odd numbers differ by 2.

Problem 30
The horizontal asymptote of an equation in the form
$y = \frac{a}{x - b} + c$ occurs where $y = c$. The vertical asymptote occurs at values for which the domain is undefined, when $x = b$.

Lesson 117   803

LOOKING FORWARD

Using trigonometric ratios will be further developed in other Saxon Secondary Mathematics courses.

LESSON 118

Solving Problems Involving Combinations

Warm Up

1. **Vocabulary** A _____ (*permutation, factorial*) is an arrangement of outcomes in which the order does matter.   **permutation**

Simplify.

2. $7!$ **5040**

3. $\dfrac{6!}{4!}$ **30**

Simplify.

4. $_7P_3$ **210**

5. $_9P_4$ **3024**

New Concepts

In Lesson 111, you learned about permutations, a selection of items where order does matter. In some cases, however, the final group of items is all that matters, not the order in which the items were selected. A **combination** is a grouping of items where order does not matter.

Example 1 Comparing Combinations to Permutations

A teacher puts 4 essay questions on a test. They are labeled A, B, C, and D. Students are required to choose 3 questions to answer.

a. How many permutations of the 3 questions are possible?

SOLUTION

First, find the number of permutations.

$$_4P_3 = \dfrac{4!}{(4-3)!} = \dfrac{4!}{1!}$$

$$= \dfrac{4 \cdot 3 \cdot 2 \cdot 1}{1} = 24.$$

There are 24 permutations of the 3 test questions.

Math Reasoning

Analyze Why are there more permutations than combinations?

Sample: When order matters, there are more results.

b. How many combinations of the 3 questions are possible?

SOLUTION

As the order of the questions chosen does not matter, choosing ABC is the same as ACB, CAB, CBA, BCA, and BAC. So, to find the number of combinations, list the 24 permutations and then cross out the duplicate sets.

ABC	ABD	~~ACB~~	ACD	~~ADB~~	~~ADC~~
~~BAC~~	~~BAD~~	~~BCA~~	BCD	~~BDA~~	~~BDC~~
~~CAB~~	~~CAD~~	~~CBA~~	~~CBD~~	~~CDA~~	~~CDB~~
~~DAB~~	~~DAC~~	~~DBA~~	~~DBC~~	~~DCA~~	~~DCB~~

That leaves 4 combinations of the 3 test questions.

LESSON 118

1 Warm Up

Problem 3

Cancel common factors in the numerator and denominator to simplify the expression.

2 New Concepts

In this lesson, students solve problems involving combinations.

Example 1

Students find the number of permutations and combinations.

Additional Examples

Five students volunteer to work a problem on the board. The teacher selects a student for each of 4 problems.

a. How many permutations of the students are possible?   **120**

b. How many combinations of the 4 students are possible?   **5**

TEACHER TIP

Analyze with the students a variety of situations to determine when order matters. That is, determine whether the situation requires permutations or combinations.

LESSON RESOURCES

Student Edition Practice
   Workbook 118
Reteaching Master 118
Adaptations Master 118
Challenge and Enrichment
   Master C118
Technology Lab Master 118

MATH BACKGROUND

Combinations are the number of ways a group of objects can be selected when order does not matter. For example, if you are chosen to be on a committee, whether you are chosen first or last does not affect the makeup of the committee. Similarly, if grouping 3 letters, ABC is the same group as BCA. When compared to permutations, with which order does matter, there will be fewer possible groups. With a permutation, ABC is different from BCA.

It may be helpful to make a list of key words that are associated with a permutation and with a combination. However, be careful when instructing students to look for key words. For example, choosing 3 out of 5 people to be in a group is a combination, while choosing 3 out of 5 people to be in 1st, 2nd, and 3rd place is a permutation. It is most important to determine whether or not order matters in the situation.

In Example 1, there are 6 times as many permutations as combinations. For each set of 3 letters, there are $3 \cdot 2 \cdot 1 = 6$ different ways to order the letters. To find the number of combinations, $_nC_r$, when selecting r out of n items, divide the number of permutations, $_nP_r$, by the number of ways to order r items, $r!$.

Math Language

$_nC_r$ is read "n choose r." So, $_4C_3$ is read, "Four choose three."

That is, $_nC_r = \dfrac{_nP_r}{\text{number of ways to order } r \text{ items}} = \dfrac{\frac{n!}{(n-r)!}}{r!} = \dfrac{n!}{r!(n-r)!}$.

Combination Formula

The number of combinations of n items taken r at a time is

$$_nC_r = \dfrac{n!}{r!(n-r)!}.$$

Example 2 Finding the Number of Combinations

a. At a restaurant 2 side dishes may be chosen. There is a total of 6 side dish choices. How many combinations are there?

SOLUTION

$_nC_r = \dfrac{n!}{r!(n-r)!}$ Use the combination formula.

$_6C_2 = \dfrac{6!}{2!(6-2)!}$ Substitute $n = 6$ and $r = 2$.

$= \dfrac{6!}{2!4!}$ Simplify inside parentheses.

$= \dfrac{720}{2 \cdot 24} = 15$ Simplify.

There are 15 ways to choose 2 side dishes.

b. A company delivers fruit to its customers every month. There are 16 different types of fruit. Each customer can choose 12 types of fruit each year. How many combinations can each customer make?

SOLUTION

$_nC_r = \dfrac{n!}{r!(n-r)!}$ Use the combination formula.

$_{16}C_{12} = \dfrac{16!}{12!(16-12)!}$ Substitute 16 for n and 12 for r.

$= \dfrac{16!}{12!4!}$ Simplify inside parentheses.

$= \dfrac{16 \cdot 15 \cdot 14 \cdot 13 \cdot 12!}{12!4!}$ Rewrite 16! as $16 \cdot 15 \cdot 14 \cdot 13 \cdot 12!$.

$= \dfrac{16 \cdot 15 \cdot 14 \cdot 13}{4!}$ Cancel 12!.

$= 1820$ Simplify.

There are 1820 ways to choose 12 fruits.

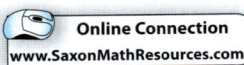
Online Connection
www.SaxonMathResources.com

Example 2
Students find the number of combinations.

Error Alert Students may confuse permutations and combinations. Emphasize that a general group means a combination. A group with specific positions or titles would mean permutations.

Additional Examples

a. In class, there are 8 report topics. A student must research 3 of them during the year. How many combinations are there for the student? 56

b. At a salad bar, there are 20 types of food. Each customer is allowed to choose 15 of them. How many combinations of plates can be made? 15,504

Lesson 118   805

ENGLISH LEARNERS

For Example 2, explain the meaning of the word **choices.** Say:

"Choices means the best or most wanted items. For example, favorite color choices for baby girl's clothing are pink and yellow."

Have students think about their choices of lunch foods, entertainers, or books. Have them share their thoughts with the class using the word choices in a complete sentence.

Lesson 118   805

Example 3
Students use combinations to find the probability of an event.

Extend the Example
What is the probability that those three will not be chosen together? $\frac{1139}{1140}$

Additional Example 3
A student has 20 stickers and wants to trade 10 of them. A friend randomly chooses 10 of them. What is the probability that those were her favorite 10 stickers? $\frac{1}{184,756}$

Lesson Practice
Problems a and b
Scaffolding First, find $_5P_2$. Then, find $_5C_2$. Compare to make sure that the number of combinations is less than the number of permutations.

Problem e
Error Alert Students may find the number of permutations because they think about selecting the ingredients in a particular order. The order in which they were chosen does not matter.

✓ Check for Understanding
The questions below help assess the concepts taught in this lesson.

"Explain the difference between a permutation and combination." Sample: There are more possibilities with a permutation because order does matter. With combinations, order does not matter.

"Explain how to find the probability of a particular group being chosen from a larger population." Sample: Find the number of ways the number in the group can be chosen from the larger population using combinations. Because there is only one way to form that group, the probability is 1 out of the number of possibilities.

Example 3 Application: Probability
An animal shelter has 20 dogs. Each month 3 of the dogs are randomly chosen to be pets-of-the-month on the website.

What is the probability that Jumbo, Fluffy, and Max will be selected?

SOLUTION

Note that the order in which the dogs are chosen does not matter, so it is a combination.

$_{20}C_3 = \dfrac{20!}{3!(20-3)!}$ Use the formula. Substitute 20 for n and 3 for r.

$= \dfrac{20!}{3!17!} = 1140$ Simplify.

There are 1140 ways 3 dogs can be chosen, but only one way that a particular set of 3 dogs, {Jumbo, Fluffy, and Max}, can be chosen. So, the probability of choosing that set is $\frac{1}{1140}$.

Hint
Remember, the theoretical probability of an event is
$\dfrac{\text{\# of favorable outcomes}}{\text{total number of outcomes}}$

Lesson Practice
A teacher selects 2 students from a group of 5 students.

a. How many permutations of the 2 students are possible? **20 permutations** *(Ex 1)*

b. How many combinations of the 2 students are possible? **10 combinations** *(Ex 1)*

c. To color a map, each student chooses 4 markers from a box of 8. How many combinations are there? **70** *(Ex 2)*

d. To pick a parent committee for his class, the teacher chooses 9 parents out of the 22 volunteers. How many combinations can the teacher make? **497,420** *(Ex 2)*

e. A cook has 18 possible ingredients for soup. He only uses 4 ingredients. What is the probability he will pick beans, corn, rice, and carrots? $\frac{1}{3060}$ *(Ex 3)*

Practice Distributed and Integrated

*1. (Photography) A photographer wants to take a picture of a group of 4 students from a class of 15. How many different pictures could she take? **1365** *(118)*

Calculate each combination.

*2. $_{11}C_4$ **330** *(118)*

3. $_9C_7$ **36** *(118)*

4. $_{12}C_5$ **792** *(118)*

*5. **Write** Explain the difference between permutations and combinations. *(118)*

5. Sample: With permutations order matters, but with combinations, order does not matter.

*6. **Verify** Show that $_8C_3 = \dfrac{_8P_3}{\text{number of ways to order 3 items}}$. *(118)*

Sample: $_8C_3 = \dfrac{8!}{3!(8-3)!} = \dfrac{8!}{(8-3)!} \cdot \dfrac{1}{3!} = \dfrac{\frac{8!}{(8-3)!}}{3!} = \dfrac{_8P_3}{\text{number of ways to order 3 items}}$

806 Saxon Algebra 1

INCLUSION

Materials: pattern blocks

Use pattern blocks to make groups of particular shapes or colors. Then, use them to make particular patterns. Have students use the blocks to show the number of different ways the groups or combinations can be made. Discuss each time whether the order mattered or not, and thus, whether it would be a permutation or combination. Show, each time, that the number of permutations is greater than the number of combinations.

*7. **Multiple Choice** Find $_5C_3$. **A**
(118)
 A 10   B 12   C 20   D 60

*8. (**Nutrition**) Teenage girls need 3 servings of dairy products per day. How many
(118) combinations can a girl make from 10 different dairy products? 120

9. Find the LCM of $(15x - 10)$ and $(3x - 2)$. $5(3x - 2)$
(57)

*10. **Geometry** How many straight line segments can be formed by connecting any 2 of
(118) 8 points? 28

*11. **Multi-Step** A student chooses 9 stuffed animals to give to a charity. He had a total
(118) of 25 stuffed animals.
  a. How many combinations of 9 animals could be chosen? 2,042,975
  b. If one stuffed animal has already been chosen, then what is the probability that
     he chooses his 8 favorite animals. $\frac{1}{735,471}$

*12. Find the six trigonometric ratios for $\angle A$.
(117) $\sin A = \frac{24}{25}$, $\cos A = \frac{7}{25}$, $\tan A = \frac{24}{7}$, $\csc A = \frac{25}{24}$, $\sec A = \frac{25}{7}$, $\cot A = \frac{7}{24}$

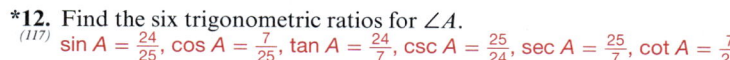

13. **Multi-Step** A kite is caught in the top of a 12-foot tree and a string 20 feet
(117) long is stretched out to the ground.
  a. Find the distance along the ground from the base of the tree to the end
     of the string. 16 feet
  b. Find $\angle A$, the angle the string makes with the ground. 36.87°

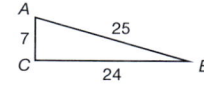

14. **Coordinate Geometry** A right triangle has coordinate $A(2, 1)$, $B(8, 9)$, and $C(8, 1)$.
(117) Plot the points and find the measure of acute angle A. 53.13°

15. If $9200 is borrowed for 3 years at 5% simple interest, how much money will be
(116) owed after 3 years? $10,580

16. (**Bonds**) A woman invests $20,000 in a bond that pays 6% interest compounded
(116) annually. How much interest will she earn in 5 years? $6764.51

*17. **Error Analysis** A CD earns 4% interest compounded quarterly. A woman
(116) deposits $10,000 for 20 years. Two students find the value of her account.
Which student is correct? Explain the error.

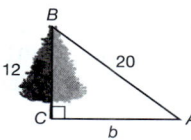

Student A	Student B
$A = 10,000(1 + 0.01)^{80}$	$A = 10,000(1 + 0.04)^{20}$
$A = 10,000(1.01^{80})$	$A = 10,000(1.04^{20})$
$A = 22,167.15$	$A = 21,911.23$
$22,167.15	$21,911.23

17. Student A; Sample: Student B used interest compounded annually, not quarterly.

18. Find $\frac{10!}{5!}$. 30,240
(111)

19. Simplify $\frac{4}{\sqrt{3} - 2}$. $-4\sqrt{3} - 8$
(103)

20. Solve this system by substitution: $y = x^2 - 5$, $y = 4x$. $(-1, -4)$ and $(5, 20)$
(112)

Lesson 118 807

---

3 Practice

Math Conversations
Discussion to strengthen understanding

Problem 9
Remind students to factor first.

Problem 13
Guide the students by asking them the following questions.

"What lengths do you know?" the height of the tree and the length of the string

"What theorem will help you find the distance on the ground?" Pythagorean

"What will you use to find the measure of the angle?" inverse sine

Problem 14
Error Alert
When finding the length of the sides, students may count the number of lines. Explain that a distance is measured by the number of spaces.

Problem 15
Remind students to change the percent to a decimal before multiplying.

Problem 16
Extend the Problem
How much more interest would be earned if it were calculated semi-annually? $113.82

Problem 19
Check that students multiply by $\frac{\sqrt{3} + 2}{\sqrt{3} + 2}$ to remove the radical from the denominator.

Lesson 118 807

Problem 22

Remind students that the radical sign acts as a grouping symbol. Simplify inside the radical before taking the square root.

Problem 27

Guide students to understand that one equation will represent the number of tickets sold. The other equation will represent the number of dollars earned.

21. (**Football**) A punter kicks a football straight up in the air from 2 feet off the ground
(113) with an initial velocity of 75 feet per second. Using $y = -16t^2 + 75t + 2$, write an equation to model the situation and use the discriminant to determine if the ball will reach a height of 45 feet.

21. Use the equation $45 = -16t^2 + 75t + 2$. Then $0 = -16t^2 + 75t - 43$ and the discriminant is 2873, so the ball will reach a height of 45 feet.

22. Evaluate $y = \sqrt{\frac{3}{x} + 2}$ for $x = 6$. Round to the nearest tenth. $y \approx 1.6$
(114)

23. **Multiple Choice** What is the solution to the equation $x^3 - 27 = 0$? **A**
(115)   **A** 3   **B** 9   **C** 27   **D** 0

24. **Model** What is the equation for the parent function of a cubic equation? $y = x^3$
(115)

25. Find the solution of $x^2 = 45$. Round the answer to three decimal places. $x \approx \pm 6.708$
(102)

26. **Multi-Step** Colin is experimenting with a type of cell that multiplies by 5 each day.
(105)   a. At the end of the day on Monday, there are 500 cells. If all cells survive, how many are there on Friday? 312,500

  b. Approximately one fourth of the cells die off each day. If the cells still multiply at the same rate, what rule represents a geometric sequence to represent the number of cells remaining each day? $500\left(3\frac{3}{4}\right)^{n-1}$

  c. Use the rule to find the number of cells on Friday if there are 500 on Monday. about 98,877

27. **Multi-Step** Tickets to a school play are sold to teachers for $3 each and to students
(109) for $0.50 each. The drama class hopes to earn at least $200 from the ticket sales. The theater seats 250 people.

  a. Write and graph a system of linear inequalities to describe the situation.

  b. If 15 teachers buy tickets, is it possible for the drama class to meet their goal? Explain. No; Sample: There is no ordered pair with 15 teachers that is in the solution set.

28. **Estimate** Estimate to the nearest whole number the value of the zeros for the
(110) equation $2v^2 + 20v = 21$. 1 and −11

29. Factor completely $-88z^3 - 2r^2z^3 - 30rz^3$. $-2z^3(r+11)(r+4)$
(79)

30. Radioactive glucose is used in cancer detection. It has a half-life of 100 minutes. How
(Inv 11) much of a 320 mg sample remains in the body after 10 hours? First determine how many half-lives there are in a 10-hour period if the half-life is 100 minutes.
6 half-lives; 5 mg

27a. $\begin{cases} 3x + \frac{1}{2}y \geq 200 \\ x + y \leq 250 \end{cases}$;

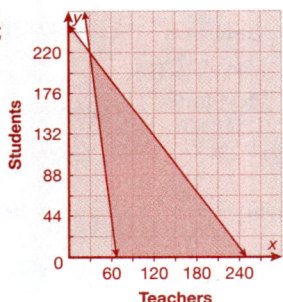

CHALLENGE

There are 13 different toppings available at a pizza place. A family chooses 3 different toppings. What is the probability that the toppings are three of the following: pineapple, mushrooms, olives, tomatoes, or peppers? $\frac{10}{286} = \frac{5}{143}$

LOOKING FORWARD

Solving problems involving combinations will be further developed in other Saxon Secondary Mathematics courses.

LESSON 119

Graphing and Comparing Linear, Quadratic, and Exponential Functions

Warm Up

1. **Vocabulary** The highest or lowest point (turning point) on a parabola is called the _____ of the parabola. **vertex**

2. Find the axis of symmetry for the graph of $y = 2x^2 + 8x + 2$. $x = -2$

Determine the slope and the y-intercept of each equation.

3. $y = 0.5x - 3.5$ $m = 0.5; b = -3.5$
4. $-8x + 2y = 10$ $m = 4; b = 5$

5. **Multiple Choice** Which is the zero of the function $y = x^2 + x - 2$? **B**
   A $x = 2$ **B** $x = -2$ **C** $x = -1$ **D** $x = 3$

New Concepts

A function family is a set of functions whose graphs have similar characteristics. A function family can be formed through transformations of one function, called the parent function. Transformations of the parent function can cause the graph of the function to move vertically or horizontally, be stretched or compressed, or be reflected across an axis.

Math Reasoning

Write In your own words, describe a parent function.

Sample: A parent function is a basic graph that can be changed in many ways to form a function family.

The following chart gives three examples of parent functions, along with the characteristics of each parent function. Those characteristics can be helpful in identifying functions within that family.

	Linear Function	Quadratic Function	Exponential Function
Parent Function	$f(x) = x$	$f(x) = x^2$	$f(x) = b^x$
Graph	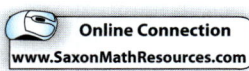		
Domain	real numbers	real numbers	real numbers
Range	real numbers	real numbers ≥ 0	real numbers > 0
Maximum/ Minimum	none	vertex	none
Rate of Change	constant	not constant	not constant

Online Connection
www.SaxonMathResources.com

MATH BACKGROUND

The study of functions begins with linear functions because they are the simplest. They are defined over all real numbers with a constant rate of change. They are straight lines. Quadratics are a bit more complicated. Their rate of change is not constant and they are not straight lines. In fact, their range is restricted and each one has a maximum or minimum. They are symmetric. Exponential functions have even more limitations. They are not straight lines or symmetric in their shape.

Each type of function has a parent function that shows the characteristics of its family. Understanding the basic shape is critical to recognizing to which family a function belongs. Learning how changes in the equation affect the appearance of the graph is explored further in other Saxon High School Math courses.

Example 1

Students match function families with their graphs.

Additional Example 1

a. Which of the graphs from Example 1 represents a quadratic function? A

b. Use the graph to identify the function family. exponential

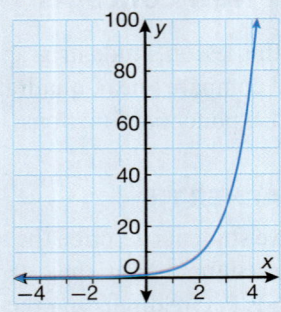

c.

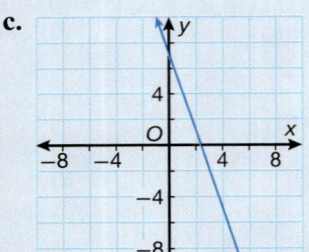

Use the graph to identify the function family. linear

Hint

Recall that $y = 6x^2$ and $f(x) = 6x^2$ describe the same function. The form that uses $f(x)$ is called **function notation**.

Example 1 Matching Function Families and Graphs

a. Which of the following graphs represents an exponential function?

Graph A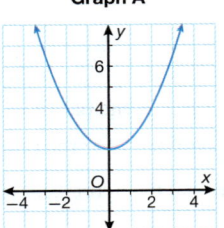

Graph B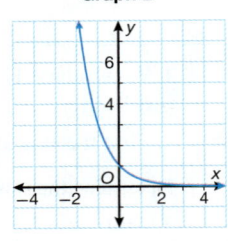

Graph C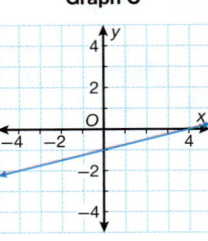

SOLUTION

Graph B displays the shape of an exponential function.

b. Use the graph to identify the function family.

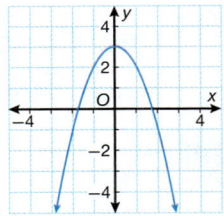

SOLUTION

This graph has the shape of the quadratic function. It is the graph of $f(x) = -x^2 + 3$.

c. Use the graph to identify the function family.

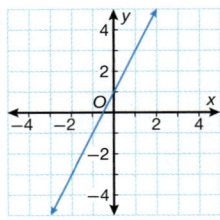

SOLUTION

This graph has the shape of a linear function. It has a slope of 2 and a y-intercept of 1. It is the graph of $f(x) = 2x + 1$.

Example 2 Matching Function Families and Tables

Use each table of values to identify the function family.

a.
x	−3	−2	−1	0	1	2	3
$f(x)$	$\frac{1}{27}$	$\frac{1}{9}$	$\frac{1}{3}$	1	3	9	27

SOLUTION

Plot the points on a graph and connect them using a smooth curve. From the graph you can tell that the function belongs to the exponential function family. It is a graph of $f(x) = 3^x$. The values for $f(x)$ increase more steeply as x increases, so it shows exponential growth.

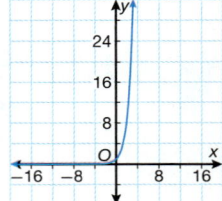

Math Reasoning

Analyze Is there a maximum number of functions that can be in a function family? Explain.

no; Sample: A parent function can be transformed in an infinite number of ways by adding different numbers to it or multiplying it by different numbers.

ENGLISH LEARNERS

For Example 2, explain the meaning of the word **steep**. Draw a picture of two mountains on the chalkboard. Be sure one mountain is steep and the other is not steep. Say:

"A steep mountain is difficult to walk up because of its sharp incline."

Have the students decide which mountain in the drawing is steeper.

Next have students use grid paper to draw two lines with positive slopes. Ask:

"Which line is steeper? Which line has the greater slope?"

Explain to students how the slope of a line and the steepness of a line are directly related.

b.

x	−3	−2	−1	0	1	2	3
$f(x)$	8	3	0	−1	0	3	8

SOLUTION

Plot the points on a graph and connect them using a smooth curve.

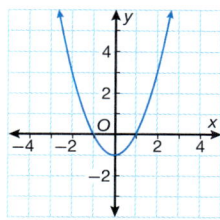

You can see that this function has a graph similar to the graph of $f(x) = x^2$, but it is translated down one unit. This function belongs to the quadratic function family. It is the graph of $f(x) = x^2 - 1$.

c. Identify the table of values that shows a linear function family.

Table 1

x	−3	−2	−1	0	1	2	3
$f(x)$	−9	−4	−1	0	−1	−4	−9

Table 2

x	−3	−2	−1	0	1	2	3
$f(x)$	$\frac{1}{125}$	$\frac{1}{25}$	$\frac{1}{5}$	1	5	25	125

Table 3

x	−3	−2	−1	0	1	2	3
$f(x)$	0	2	4	6	8	10	12

SOLUTION

For a function to be linear, it must have a constant rate of change. Determine which of these tables shows a constant rate of change of $f(x)$ as x increases by 1.

Table 1: In the first row, $f(-3) = -9$ and $f(-2) = -4$, which is a difference of 5. But the difference between $f(-2)$ and $f(-1)$ is only 3. This is not a constant rate of change, so the function is not linear.

Table 2: The difference between $f(1)$ and $f(2)$ is 20, but the difference between $f(2)$ and $f(3)$ is 100, so this function is also not linear.

Table 3: $f(-3) = 0$ and $f(-2) = 2$, which is a difference of 2. Each time x increases by 1, the value of $f(x)$ increases by 2. This is a constant rate of change.

Table 3 shows a linear function.

 Caution

A constant rate of change does not have to be a positive number. In the function $f(x) = -3x$, the constant rate of change is −3. Each time x increases by 1, $f(x)$ decreases by 3.

Lesson 119 811

Example 2

Students use a table of values to identify the function family.

Additional Example 2

Use each table of values to identify the function family.

a.

x	−2	−1	0	1	2	3
$f(x)$	0.01	0.1	1	10	100	1000

exponential

b.

x	−2	−1	0	1	2	3
$f(x)$	40	10	0	10	40	90

quadratic

c. Identify the table of values that shows a linear function.

Table 1

x	−2	0	1	5	7	8
$f(x)$	7	9	11	13	15	17

Table 2

x	−2	−1	0	1	2	3
$f(x)$	−4	−6	−8	−10	−12	−14

Table 3

x	−2	0	1	5	7	8
$f(x)$	−3	−2	0	3	7	11

Table 2

Error Alert Students may decide that the ordered pairs in a table of values represent a line based only on the $f(x)$ values. Point out to students that linear functions can be identified by their constant rate of change. Remind students that the rate of change is found by comparing the change in $f(x)$ values with the change in corresponding x values.

INCLUSION

Give each student a card with each of the three parent functions on it. Have students trace each new function that they must categorize on a sheet of thin paper. Then, have them translate, rotate, or flip it until it lines up with the general shape of a parent function. Emphasize that it will not match identically, but when their shapes look similar, then the functions belong to the same family.

Lesson 119 811

Example 3 Identifying the Function Family from a Description

For each description, state whether the description best fits a linear, quadratic, or exponential function.

(a.) The rate of change is always the same. The graph is always decreasing.

SOLUTION

Because the rate of change is always the same, the function is linear.

(b.) The rate of change is not always the same. The graph is always increasing. The graph is a curve that gets steeper as the x-values increase.

SOLUTION

The rate of change is not always the same, so the function family is not linear. The graph is always increasing, so it is not quadratic.

The function is exponential.

(c.) The rate of change is not always the same. The graph changes direction at a minimum point at which $y = -1$.

SOLUTION

The rate of change is not constant, so the function family is not linear. It has a minimum point at which $y = -1$ where the graph changes direction, so it is quadratic.

(d.) The graph is always decreasing. The graph is a curve that gets less steep as the x-values increase.

SOLUTION

The graph is always decreasing, so it is not quadratic.

The graph is a curve that gets less steep as x increases, so it is exponential.

Linear, quadratic, and exponential functions can be used to model real-world situations.

Linear models apply to situations with a constant rate of change. An example of a function with a positive rate of change is the distance traveled by a train that travels at a constant speed. An example of a function with a negative rate of change is the amount of water left in a bucket with a constant leak.

Quadratic models may apply in situations with a maximum or minimum value because the graph of a quadratic function changes direction at the vertex. For example, if a ball is thrown up in the air, its height at time t is modeled by a quadratic function.

Exponential models can be used for situations where values are always increasing or always decreasing, but not at a constant rate. Examples of exponential situations are population growth and radioactive decay.

Math Reasoning

Justify The graph of a function crosses the x-axis twice. Could the function be linear? Explain.

no; Sample: A linear function always increases or always decreases, so once it crosses the x-axis, it cannot cross it again.

Example 3
Students identify the function family from a description.

Additional Example 3
For each description tell whether the description best fits a linear, quadratic, or exponential function.

a. The function is always increasing. Its rate of change is 2. linear

b. The range is restricted to real numbers greater than or equal to 0. quadratic

c. The rate of change is not constant. In fact, sometimes the graph is increasing and sometimes it is decreasing. quadratic

d. The function is always increasing. Its rate of change is not constant. exponential

Example 4
Students identify an appropriate model for a real-world situation.

Extend the Example
Write an equation for the number of bacteria cells in the laboratory dish. $y = 1(2)^{x-1}$

Additional Example 4
a. The number of people who hear the news doubles every hour. exponential

b. the wage of a dog walker who earns $2 per hour linear

c. the height of a disc that is thrown upward from a 2-meter tall wall quadratic

---

 ALTERNATE METHOD FOR EXAMPLE 3

Have student sketch a graph that fits all of the characteristics given. Then, based on the sketch, determine to which family function it belongs.

Example 4 Identifying an Appropriate Model

Identify the appropriate model for each of the following situations.

a. the height of a ball thrown upward from an initial height of 5 feet

SOLUTION

When a ball is thrown upward, it goes up for a short time and then changes direction and comes down again. Its height has a maximum value. Therefore, a quadratic function models this situation.

b. the cost of a tank of gas when gas costs $3.25 per gallon

SOLUTION

The cost of gas is a constant rate. For every additional gallon, the price of the tank of gas increases by $3.25. Therefore, a linear function models this situation.

Math Reasoning

Formulate Write a function that could be used to find the cost of gas in Example 4b.

$f(x) = 3.25x$

c. the number of bacteria cells in a laboratory dish when each cell divides into two cells every day

SOLUTION

Imagine the first day there was only one cell in the dish. The next day, there would be 2 cells, and the following day, 4 cells. The number of cells doubles every day, so it is not a constant rate of change but an increasing rate of change. Therefore, an exponential function models this situation.

Lesson Practice

Identify the function family represented by each graph.
(Ex 1)

a. linear
b. quadratic
c. exponential

a. 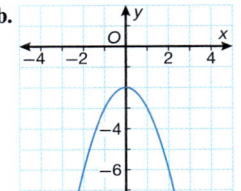 b. 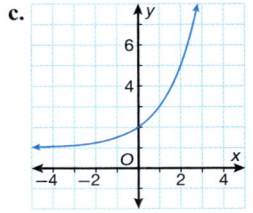 c.

Use the table of values to identify the function family.
(Ex 2)

d.
x	−2	−1	0	1	2
$f(x)$	4	7	10	13	16

linear

e.
x	−2	−1	0	1	2
$f(x)$	4	2	0	2	4

quadratic

Tell whether the function family is linear, quadratic, or exponential.
(Ex 3)

f. The graph is always increasing with a constant rate. linear

g. The graph changes direction at a maximum of 3. quadratic

h. The graph is always increasing and it gets steeper as x increases. exponential

Lesson 119

Lesson Practice

Problem a

Scaffolding First determine whether the rate of change is constant. Then, if not, see if the graph is always increasing or decreasing.

Problem h

Error Alert Students may decide that the graph represents a linear function from the first part of the statement. Point out that the function is not constant as indicated in the second part of the statement.

Check for Understanding

The questions below help assess the concepts taught in this lesson.

"What is a family of functions?"
Sample: Functions that have the same general shape.

"Describe the characteristics of a linear function." Sample: It is always increasing or decreasing at a constant rate of change. It has no maximum or minimum.

"How do quadratic and exponential functions differ?"
Sample: The range of the exponential parent function does not include 0. Exponential functions are always increasing or decreasing. Quadratic functions have a maximum or minimum.

3 Practice

Math Conversations
Discussion to strengthen understanding

Problem 1
Point out to students that the function written by Student A has a binomial factor that is raised to the second power. Have them use the FOIL method to see that the function contains a quadratic term.

Problem 5
Extend the Problem
Find the cost of carpeting a room with a side length of 13 feet. $2528

Identify the appropriate model for each of the following situations.
(Ex 4)

i. the height of an arrow that is shot upwards from the edge of a cliff   quadratic

j. the number of radioactive particles remaining in a sample when, at the end of each hour, the number of radioactive particles is half of what it was at the beginning of the hour   exponential

k. the amount of money you can earn babysitting when you charge $5 per hour of babysitting   linear

Practice   Distributed and Integrated

*1. **Error Analysis** Students were asked to write an equation that has a quadratic
(119) parent function. Which student is correct? Explain the error.

Student A	Student B
$f(x) = 2(x-1)^2 - 4$	$f(x) = 2x + 5$

1. Student A; Sample: Student B wrote an equation that does not have an x^2 term in it.

*2. Identify the function family.   exponential
(119)

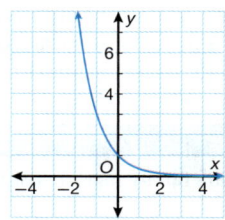

*3. Identify the function family.   quadratic
(119)

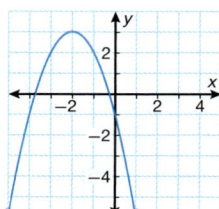

*4. **Write** How can a parent function be used to graph a family of functions?   Sample:
(119) Graph the parent function and then graph a series of transformations of it.

*5. (**Interior Decorating**) A type of carpet sells for $12 per square foot. Installation is an
(119) additional $500. A function can be written to determine the price for installing carpet in a square room with floor x feet in length. Identify the function family and the parent function.   quadratic; $f(x) = x^2$

814   *Saxon Algebra 1*

6. Error Analysis Two students find $_{18}C_5$. Which student is correct? Explain the error.
(118)

Student A	Student B
$_{18}C_5 = \dfrac{18!}{5!(18-5)!}$ $= 8568$	$_{18}C_5 = \dfrac{18!}{(18-5)!}$ $= 1{,}028{,}160$

6. Student A; Sample: Student B used the formula for permutations.

Problem 6
Remember that the number of combinations is less than the number of permutations.

*7. Multi-Step A restaurant charges $16 for a large pizza plus $1.50 per topping.
(119)
 a. Which type of function best describes the cost of a pizza? linear
 b. Write a function that describes the cost of a pizza with x toppings. $f(x) = 1.5x + 16$

8. Jewelry A jewelry store sells necklaces for the cost of the chain plus the cost of the
(119) beads. Chains cost $20 each, and beads cost $7.50 each. To which function family does the equation that describes the cost of a necklace with x beads belong? linear

Problem 8
Extend the Problem
What is the cost of a necklace with 5 beads? $57.50

*9. Multiple Choice Which of the following describes the graph of $y = 5^x$? **C**
(119)
 A quadratic   **B** linear   **C** exponential   **D** none of these

*10. Geometry A triangle has base b and height $b - 4$. If its area is written as a function,
(119) to which function family does the function belong? quadratic

Problem 11
Rearrange the equation to be in the form $y = mx + b$.

11. Identify the function family to which $y = 2 - 1100x$ belongs. linear
(119)

*12. Write A fair coin is flipped many times in a row. The probability of all flips
(119) resulting in heads is given by $P(\text{all heads}) = \left(\dfrac{1}{2}\right)^x$, where x is the number of flips. What type of function is this? exponential

Problem 13
Error Alert
Students may try to use the formula for permutations. Remind them that with a group of four helpers, the order does not matter.

13. Multi-Step A teacher randomly selects 4 helpers from her class of 22.
(118)
 a. How many ways can 4 helpers be selected? 7315
 b. What is the probability that Shawn, Tonia, Torie, and Reid are all chosen? $\dfrac{1}{7315}$

*14. If $\angle A = 14°$, find sin A, cos A, and tan A to the nearest ten-thousandth. sin 14° $\approx$
(117) 0.2419, cos 14° $\approx$ 0.9703, tan 14° $\approx$ 0.2493

Problem 15
Review the acronym SOH–CAH–TOA to help students remember the trignometric ratios.

15. Error Analysis Two students are finding the value of x in the figure. Which student
(117) is correct? Explain the error.

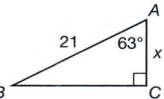

Student A	Student B
$\sin 63° = \dfrac{x}{21}$ $21 \cdot \sin 63° = x$ $18.71 \approx x$	$\cos 63° = \dfrac{x}{21}$ $21 \cdot \cos 63° = x$ $9.53 \approx x$

15. Student B; Sample: The cosine ratio is the adjacent leg over the hypotenuse and x represents the adjacent leg.

*16. Aviation An airplane begins making its descent at an
(117) angle of 11° with the horizontal. If the plane is at an altitude of 8000 feet and will remain at this angle throughout its descent, how far away is the plane from its landing point? about 41,927 feet

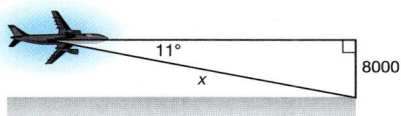

Lesson 119   815

Problem 17
Remember the solution to a system of equations is where the graphs intersect.

Problem 19
Remind students that the radicand must be positive.

Problem 22
Extend the Problem
How much interest has been earned? $1701.48

Problem 24
Use the conjugate to take the radical out of the denominator.

Problem 27
Error Alert
Students may want to describe this as a cubic function because there is a 3 in the exponent. Because there is a variable, x, in the exponent, it must be an exponential function.

Problem 29
Extend the Problem
What is $_6C_2$? 15

Problem 30
Encourage students to substitute values for a and b that fit the criteria given. Then, analyze the general shape of the graph.

---

17. Solve this system by graphing: $\begin{aligned} y &= x^2 - 2 \\ y &= 2x - 5 \end{aligned}$ no solution.

18. Use the discriminant to find the number of real solutions of the equation $9x^2 - 24x + 16 = 0$. $d = 0$; one real solution

19. Business A baseball-card seller models the costs for attending a sale as the function $y = \$250 + \$0.25\sqrt{n + 30}$. In this function, n represents the number of cards sold and 30 is the number of cards given out free as prizes. What is the domain of the function? Explain. $n \geq 0$; Sample: The domain is $n \geq -30$, but in the context of the problem the number of cards cannot be negative.

20. Graph the cubic function $y = x^3 - 2$. Use the graph to evaluate the equation for $x = 0$.

21. Verify Show that a $500 investment earning 6% interest compounded annually for 3 years will earn more than earning 6% simple interest for 3 years.

22. Multiple Choice $1000 is invested in an account paying 5% interest compounded quarterly. What is the value of the account after 20 years? **D**
A $1282.04 B $2000 C $2653.30 D $2701.48

23. Find $_8C_3$. 56

24. Simplify $\dfrac{6}{\sqrt{7} - 3\sqrt{5}}$. $-\dfrac{3\sqrt{7}}{19} - \dfrac{9\sqrt{5}}{19}$

25. Solve $-2m^2 - 12m = 10$ by completing the square. $m = -1$ or $m = -5$

26. Multi-Step The expression $-\sqrt{x - 4}$, where x is the time in seconds, represents the change in temperature as water cools when ice cubes are placed in a glass of water.
a. For what value of x is the temperature change equal to -4? $x = 20$
b. What must be done to isolate the radical when solving for x?
c. Graph the radical equation $y = -\sqrt{x - 4}$.

27. Identify the function family to which $y = 100^{(-3x)}$ belongs. exponential

28. Write Explain why you would not use the quadratic formula for the equation $x^2 - x - 2 = 0$? Sample: It can be easily factored so the quadratic formula would be unnecessary work.

29. Verify Use the formula for permutations to verify that $_6P_2 = 30$.

30. Given the function $f(x) = ax^2 + bx + c$, describe the general shapes of the graphs of $f(x)$ when: parabola; line; parabola; horizontal line
a. $a \neq 0$ and $b \neq 0$;
b. $a = 0$ and $b \neq 0$;
c. $a \neq 0$ and $b = 0$;
d. $a = 0$ and $b = 0$.

17.

20.

26c.

26 b. Sample: To isolate the radical, both sides of the equation must be multiplied by -1.

29. $_6P_2 = \dfrac{6!}{(6-2)!} = \dfrac{6!}{4!} = \dfrac{6 \cdot 5 \cdot \cancel{4} \cdot \cancel{3} \cdot \cancel{2} \cdot \cancel{1}}{\cancel{4} \cdot \cancel{3} \cdot \cancel{2} \cdot \cancel{1}} = 6 \cdot 5 = 30$

21. Sample: The amount for simple interest results in $I = 500(0.06)(3) = 90$ for an account balance of $590, but compound interest is $A = 500(1.06)^3 = 595.51$ for an account balance of $595.51.

CHALLENGE
Describe a situation that can be modeled by an exponential function. Sample: The number of pairs of rabbits multiplies every month.

LOOKING FORWARD
Graphing and comparing linear, quadratic, and exponential functions will be further developed in other Saxon Secondary Mathematics courses.

LESSON 120

Using Geometric Formulas to Find the Probability of an Event

Warm Up

1. **Vocabulary** In probability, the set of all outcomes that are not in an event is the _____ (*complement, converse*) of that event.   **complement**

2. If the probability of an event happening is $\frac{3}{4}$ what is the probability of the complement of the event happening? $\frac{1}{4}$

3. What is the probability of tossing a number cube and getting a number greater than 4? $\frac{1}{3}$

4. Find the area of a rectangle with length of 25 inches and width of 5 inches.   **125 sq in.**

5. Find the area of a circle with a radius of 2 inches. Use 3.14 for π.   **12.56 sq in.**

New Concepts

In Lesson 14, you learned that the theoretical probability of an event is the ratio of the number of favorable outcomes to the total number of outcomes. The same definition applies to geometric probability when working with the area of geometric shapes.

Example 1 Finding Geometric Probability with Rectangles

A rectangular vegetable garden is 10 feet by 15 feet. Tomatoes are planted in a rectangular area that is 3 feet by 12 feet. A bird lands in the garden. What is the probability that it lands in the tomato area?

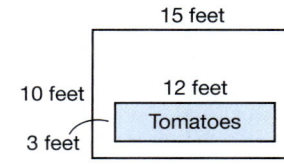

Hint
The favorable outcome is the area with tomatoes. The area of the entire garden represents all possible outcomes.

SOLUTION

$$\frac{\text{favorable outcomes}}{\text{total outcomes}} = \frac{\text{area with tomatoes}}{\text{area of entire garden}}$$

$$= \frac{3 \cdot 12}{10 \cdot 15} \qquad \text{Use } A = l \cdot w \text{ to find the area of each figure.}$$

$$= \frac{36}{150} \qquad \text{Multiply.}$$

$$= \frac{6}{25} \qquad \text{Simplify.}$$

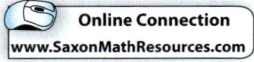

The probability of a bird landing in the area with tomatoes is $\frac{6}{25}$.

LESSON 120

1 Warm Up

Problem 2
Remind students that the sum of the probability of an event and its complement is 1.

2 New Concepts

In this lesson, students use geometric formulas to find the probability of an event.

Example 1
Students find geometric probability.

Additional Example 1
A sheet of paper, 12 inches by 9 inches, is lying on a table. The table is 15 inches by 18 inches. What is the probability that a fly will land on the paper?

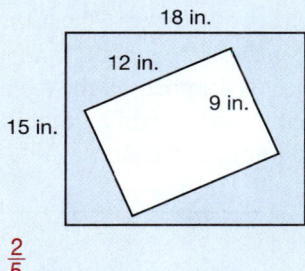

$\frac{2}{5}$

MATH BACKGROUND

Geometric probability combines two different branches of mathematics, geometry and probability. Geometric figures are used to describe a situation. Then, based on those figures, a probability can be calculated. As usual, the probability of an event is the ratio of favorable outcomes to total outcomes. Drawing a picture and shading the favorable area is one strategy for working these problems.

Geometric probability can incorporate any geometric figure. In addition, any skill in probability can be required. So, it is a review of previously-learned concepts applied in a new way.

LESSON RESOURCES

Student Edition Practice Workbook 120
Reteaching Master 120
Adaptations Master 120
Challenge and Enrichment Master C120

Example 2
Additional Example 2

A parachutist jumps from a plane. The target area for his landing is a circle with diameter 40 meters. There is one large pond that covers an area with a diameter of 10 meters. What is the probability that he lands in the water?

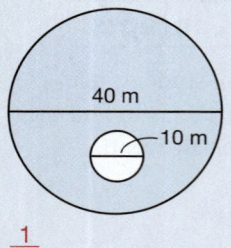

$\frac{1}{16}$

Example 3

Students learn to use geometric formulas to find the probability of the complement of an event.

Additional Example 3

a. A rectangular train table is 48 inches by 24 inches. The train is 2 inches by 6 inches. If an object is dropped on the table, what is the probability that it will not hit the train?

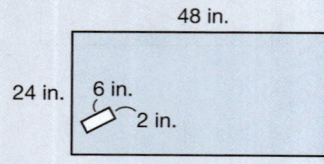

$\frac{95}{96}$

b. On the front of a tent is a two-foot square door. The base of the tent is 5 feet and the height is 4 feet. A bird flies at the tent. What is the probability that it does not hit the door?

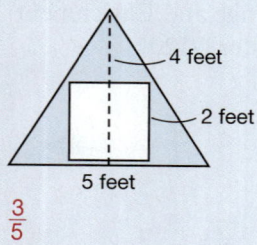

$\frac{3}{5}$

Example 2 **Finding Geometric Probability with Circles**

A target is made of two concentric circles. The outer circle has a radius of 12 inches. The inner circle has a radius of 4 inches. What is the probability that a dart will land in the inner circle?

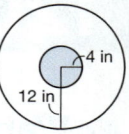

Hint
When finding the ratio of the areas of two circles, leave the areas in terms of π to make simplification easier.

SOLUTION

$$\frac{\text{favorable outcomes}}{\text{total outcomes}} = \frac{\text{shaded area}}{\text{entire area}}$$

$$= \frac{\pi(4)^2}{\pi(12)^2} \quad \text{Use } A = \pi r^2 \text{ to find the areas.}$$

$$= \frac{16\pi}{144\pi} = \frac{1}{9} \quad \text{Simplify.}$$

The probability that a dart will land in the inner circle is $\frac{1}{9}$.

Recall that the formula for the complement of an event is:
$1 - P(A) = P(\text{not } A)$

Example 3 **Finding the Probability of the Complement**

Math Language
The **complement** of an event is all the outcomes in the sample space that are not included in the event.

a. A town is represented by a circle with a diameter of 50 miles. There is a square park with side length 5 miles located within the town. What is the probability that a raindrop would land in the town, but not the park?

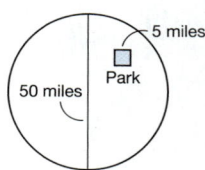

SOLUTION

Find the probability of the complement of the raindrop landing in the park.

$P(\text{not landing in the park}) = 1 - P(\text{landing in the park})$

$$= 1 - \frac{\text{area of park}}{\text{area of town}}$$

$$= 1 - \frac{5^2}{\pi(25)^2} \quad \text{Use the area formulas.}$$

$$= 1 - \frac{25}{625\pi} \quad \text{Simplify the powers.}$$

$$\approx 0.99 \quad \text{Subtract.}$$

The probability of a raindrop landing in the town but not the park is 99%.

b. A carnival game has the player release an air-filled balloon towards a square wall. In the middle of the wall is a triangular target. What is the probability that the balloon will not hit the target?

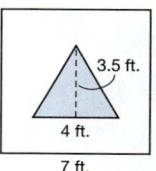

818 *Saxon* Algebra 1

INCLUSION

To find the complement of an event, the probability of the event can be subtracted from 1. When working with geometric probability, some students may prefer to subtract the areas to find the favorable area, and then use it to find the probability directly.

For example, in Example 3a, students could find the area of the town that excludes the park by subtracting the area of the park from the area of the town. Then, the result is the favorable area and the area of the town is the total area.

SOLUTION

Find the probability of the complement of the balloon hitting the target.

$P(\text{not hitting the target}) = 1 - P(\text{hitting the target})$

$= 1 - \dfrac{\text{area of the triangle}}{\text{area of square wall}}$

$= 1 - \dfrac{\frac{1}{2} \cdot 4 \cdot 3.5}{7^2}$ Use the area formulas.

$= 1 - \dfrac{7}{49}$ Multiply and square 7.

$= 1 - \dfrac{1}{7}$ Simplify the fraction.

$= \dfrac{6}{7}$ Subtract.

The probability of not hitting the target is $\frac{6}{7}$.

Example 4 Application: Zoning

A new school is being built. All students live within a 4-mile radius of the school, and homes are evenly distributed throughout the area. Planners think that students who live within 0.5 mile of the school would walk to school. Students who live between 0.5 and 2 miles would ride a bike, a city bus, or a private car to school. Students who live between 2 and 4 miles from the school would ride the school bus. What is the probability of a student not walking to school?

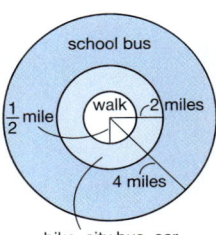

SOLUTION

Find the complement of a student walking to school.

$P(\text{not walking to school}) = 1 - P(\text{walking to school})$

$= 1 - \dfrac{\text{area of walking circle}}{\text{total area}}$

$= 1 - \dfrac{\pi (0.5)^2}{\pi (4)^2}$ Use the area formulas.

$= 1 - \dfrac{0.25\pi}{16\pi}$ Simplify the powers.

$= 1 - \dfrac{1}{64}$ Simplify the fraction.

$= \dfrac{63}{64}$ Subtract.

The probability of not walking to school is $\frac{63}{64}$.

Math Reasoning

Analyze When calculating with the area of circles, why are some answers exact and some approximate?

Sample: When π cancels, the answer is exact, but when π is multiplied or divided, the answer is approximated.

TEACHER TIP

Treat these problems as multi-step rather than putting the geometric formulas in a probability formula. Have students first calculate the area using geometric formulas. Then substitute those values into a probability formula.

Example 4

Students apply geometric probability to solve a problem involving zones.

Extend the Example

What is the probability that a student rides the school bus? $\frac{3}{4}$

Additional Example 4

A tile border has a pattern of three triangles that repeats inside a rectangle. When paint splatters on the wall, what is the probability that it will not hit one of the triangles?

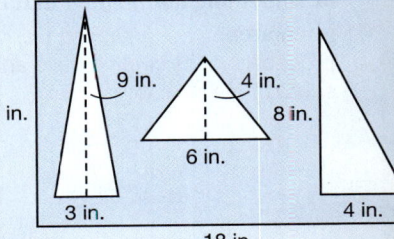

$\dfrac{313}{396}$

Error Alert Students may try to estimate the probability by just looking at the picture. Explain that the pictures are labeled correctly but may not be drawn to scale.

Lesson Practice

Problem b

Scaffolding Remember that a 10-inch plate has a 10-inch diameter. First find the area of the plate and the center. Then write the probability.

Problem c

Error Alert Students may look at the picture and assume they are finding the probability of the popcorn hitting the mouth. Have students read each problem carefully and shade the area the words describe before working the problem.

✓ Check for Understanding

The questions below help assess the concepts taught in this lesson.

"What is geometric probability?"
Sample: It is using geometry formulas to help solve probability problems.

"How do you find the probability of something not landing in the given area?" Sample: Find the probability of its landing there and subtract the probability from 1.

Lesson Practice

a. (Ex 1) A rectangular swimming pool is 15 feet by 30 feet. A raft in the pool is 2 feet by 3 feet. A beach ball is thrown randomly into the pool. What is the probability that the ball hits the raft? $\frac{1}{75}$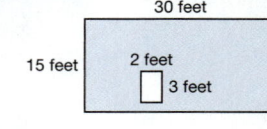

b. (Ex 2) A child's crown is made by cutting the 6-inch center out of a 10-inch paper plate. The plate is then decorated by sprinkling it with glitter. What is the probability that a piece of glitter misses the crown? $\frac{9}{25}$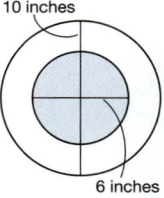

c. (Ex 3) A round piece of cardboard with radius 4 inches is used to make a mask. A two-inch square hole is cut for a mouth piece. If a piece of popcorn is tossed at the mask, what is the probability that it will miss the mouth hole? $1 - \frac{4}{16\pi} \approx 0.92$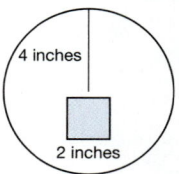

d. (Ex 3) A rectangular yard is 10 feet by 15 feet. Tulips are planted in a triangular area that has a 5-foot base and a height of 6 feet. A bird lands in the yard. What is the probability that it does not land in the tulip garden? $1 - \frac{15}{150} = 0.9$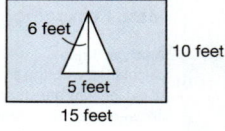

e. (Ex 4) **Puzzles** A rug in the kindergarten class has various shapes on it. One student steps onto the rug. What is the probability that he is not standing on the square? $\frac{11}{12}$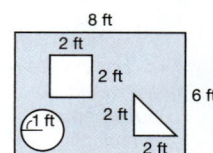

Practice   Distributed and Integrated

*1. (120) Find the probability of landing in the shaded area. $\frac{15}{64}$

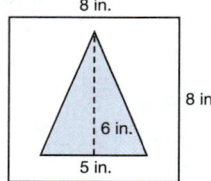

2. (120) **Write** Explain what geometric probability is.   Sample: using geometric formulas to calculate the favorable and total outcomes.

3. **Generalize** A system of equations consists of a quadratic and a linear equation. If
(112) the graphs of the two equations do not intersect, what can you conclude about the
solution to the system? The system has no solution.

*4. **Verify** Show that the probability of landing in the shaded region is $\frac{1}{2}$.
(120)

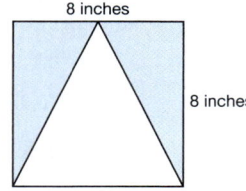

Sample:
$1 - \frac{\frac{1}{2} \cdot 8 \cdot 8}{8 \cdot 8} = 1 - \frac{32}{64} = \frac{32}{64} = \frac{1}{2}$

5. Find $_7C_2$ 21
(118)

6. **(Manufacturing)** A number cube is made with side lengths of 5 centimeters.
(115) Use the function $V = s^3$ to find the volume of plastic that is contained in the
number cube.   125 cubic centimeters

*7. **Multiple Choice** A parachutist will land in a rectangular field with a circular landing
(120) area as her target. What is the probability that she will land on target?   **B**

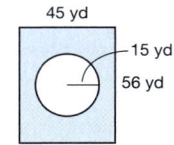

A ≈ 0.09   **B** ≈ 0.28   **C** ≈ 0.72   **D** ≈ 0.92

8. **(Jewelry)** To make a friendship bracelet, 8 beads are used. How many different
(118) combinations of beads could be on the bracelet if there are 20 different beads?
125,970

*9. **(Puzzles)** A children's stacking puzzle teaches shapes. A child randomly points to the
(120) puzzle. What is the probability that the child's finger lands on the shaded part of
the square? $\frac{36 - \frac{1}{2}(4)(5)}{64\pi} \approx 0.13$

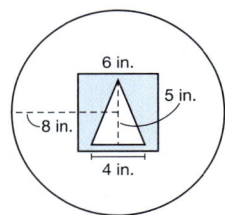

10. **Model** Draw right $\triangle ABC$ with right angle C so that $\sin A = \frac{3}{5}$ and $\cos A = \frac{4}{5}$.
(117)

11. What is the domain of $f(x) = 3\sqrt{x} - 5$? $x \geq 0$
(114)

12. Find the 4th term in the geometric series that has a common ratio of -1.1 and a
(105) first term of 7. -9.317

10. Any right triangle with sides that are similar to a 3-4-5 right triangle is valid where the shorter leg is opposite angle A.

Lesson 120   821

Problem 17

Guide the students by asking the following questions.

"What is the formula for finding the geometric probability of an event?" favorable area divided by the total area

"What is the area of the shaded region?" 16 square inches

"What is the area of the triangle?" 60 square inches

---

*13. **(Baking)** After rolling the dough into a 9-inch by 12-inch rectangle, a boy cuts as
(120) many biscuits with a 3-inch diameter as possible. His little sister comes and touches
the dough. What is the probability that she did not touch a biscuit? ≈ 0.21

*14. **Error Analysis** Two students find the probability of landing in the shaded region.
(120) Which student is correct? Explain the error.

Student A	Student B
$A = \frac{1}{2}(10)(7) = 35$	$A = \frac{1}{2}(10)(7) = 35$
$A = 13^2 = 169$	$A = 13^2 = 169$
$P(shaded) = \frac{35}{169}$	$P(shaded) = 1 - \frac{35}{169} = \frac{134}{169}$

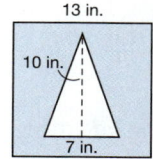

14. Student B; Sample: Student A found the probability of landing on the triangle.

*15. **Justify** Find the probability of landing in the shaded region and explain your steps.
(120) Sample: Using $A = s^2$, the area of the square is 49 square centimeters. The radius of
the circle is half the diameter or 3 centimeters. Using $A = \pi r^2$, the area of the circle is
9π. Find the probability of not landing in the circle by finding the complement of the
probability of landing in the circle. The formula is $1 - \frac{9\pi}{49}$ which is approximately 0.42.

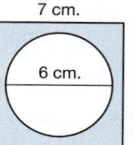

*16. **Geometry** A spinner is divided into equal sectors. The red sector is 120°. What is the
(120) probability of not landing on a red sector? $\frac{2}{3}$

17. Find the probability of landing in the shaded square. $\frac{4}{15}$
(120)

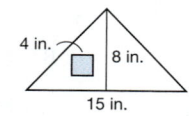

*18. **Multi-Step** A game uses a large square game board that is divided into congruent
(120) smaller squares. The probability of landing on one of those smaller squares is $\frac{1}{4}$.
Each of the smaller squares has area 49 square millimeters.
   a. What is the probability of not landing on that square the next time? $\frac{3}{4}$
   b. What is the area of the larger square? 196 square millimeters

19. **Error Analysis** Students were asked to sketch an example of a linear function. Which
(119) student is correct? Explain the error.

Student A
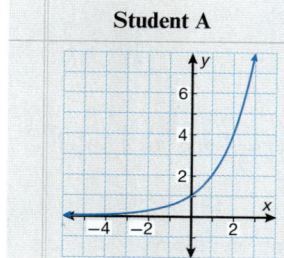

Student B
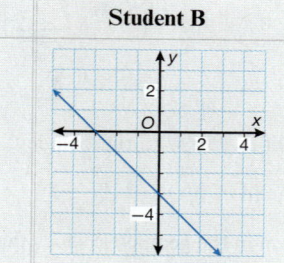

19. Student B; Sample: A linear function must have a constant rate of change. Student A's graph does not have a constant rate of change; it gets steeper as x increases.

822   Saxon Algebra 1

ENGLISH LEARNERS

For Problem 30, Explain the meaning of the word **unscramble.**

Say:

"To scramble something means mix something up. Eggs are scrambled when the clear and yellow parts are mixed together. However, to unscramble means to sort or order a set of objects."

Have students write the letters A, C, S, and T on equal sized sheets of paper. Have them scramble the papers. Ask the students if the scrambled papers form a word. If not, have the students unscramble the letters to form a word.

Ask:

"Why can the letters be unscrambled, but eggs cannot?" because once the eggs are mixed the parts are permanently combined

*20. **Multi-Step** The graph shows the height in feet, h, of a
(119) tennis ball hit into the air with initial velocity of 30 feet
per second at time t seconds.
  a. What type of function is this? How do you know?
  b. Use the graph to approximate the maximum height
     that the ball reaches. Round to the nearest foot.
     14 feet

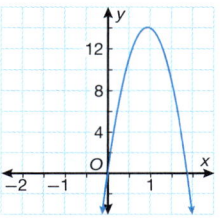

20a. quadratic;
Sample: The graph
is a parabola.

21. Identify the function family: $y = 4x^2 + 2$. quadratic
(119)

22. **Error Analysis** Two students are asked to list all the possible combinations choosing
(118) 2 letters from A, B, and C. Which student is correct? Explain the error. Student A;
Sample: Student B made order count.

Student A	Student B
AB, AC, BC	AB, AC, BA, BC, CA, CB

23. Use the discriminant of the equation $-x^2 + 2x + 1 = 0$ to find the number of real
(113) solutions. $d = 8$; two real solutions

24. Find the probability of a randomly tossed dart landing in
(120) the shaded area. ≈ 0.42

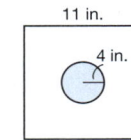

25. An investment of $2600 is made for 7 years at 8% simple interest. How much will
(116) be in the account after 7 years? $4056

26. **Multi-Step** Graph the function $f(x) = |x + 2|$, then translate the function up by 3.
(107) What function does this graph now represent? $f(x) = |x + 2| + 3$

27. **Multiple Choice** Find $\angle A$ if $\cos A = \frac{5}{7}$. A
(117)
  A 44.4°   **B** 45.6°   **C** 0.71°   **D** 1.00°

28. Solve $3x^2 + 9x = 5.25$ by completing the square. $x = 0.5$ or $x = -3.5$
(104)

29. Find the probability of a randomly tossed bean bag not landing in
(120) the shaded area. ≈ 0.99

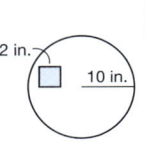

30. **Multi-Step** To work a word jumble the letters P, S, A, C, M, and H need to be
(111) unscrambled.
  a. How many different arrangements of the letters are possible? 720
  b. What is the probability of writing the word CHAMPS on the first try if each
     letter is equally likely to be chosen? $\frac{1}{720}$

Problem 21
Choose from linear, quadratic, or exponential.

Problem 25
Error Alert
The simple interest formula results in just that, the interest. To find the total amount in the account, the interest must be added to the principal.

Problem 26
To shift a function up 3, add 3 to $f(x)$.

Problem 27
Use $\cos^{-1} \frac{5}{7}$.

Problem 28
Divide all terms by 3 before completing the square.

Lesson 120   823

CHALLENGE

A rectangular garden has a length twice as long as its width. In the middle of the garden is a triangular fountain with height and base equal to the garden's width. What is the probability that a bird would land on the fountain?

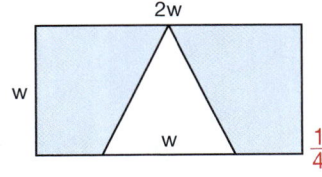

LOOKING FORWARD

Using geometric formulas to find the probability of an event will be further developed in other Saxon Secondary Mathematics courses.

LAB 11

Materials
- graphing calculator

Discuss
Addition and subtraction of matrices can only be done with matrices of the same dimensions. Have students verify this by attempting to add or subtract matrices with different dimensions on a graphing calculator.

When multiplying by a scalar, the dimensions of the matrix do not matter as each element of the matrix is multiplied by the scalar.

When multiplying matrices, the number of columns in the first matrix must match the number of rows in the second matrix.

Multiplying matrices will be studied in future mathematics courses.

LAB 11

Matrix Operations

Graphing Calculator Lab (*Use with Investigation 12*)

You can enter and store one or more matrices in a graphing calculator. Then you can use the calculator to perform matrix operations such as addition, subtraction, and scalar multiplication.

Let $A = \begin{bmatrix} 4 & -6 \\ 2 & 3 \end{bmatrix}$ and $B = \begin{bmatrix} -3 & 7 \\ 5 & -9 \end{bmatrix}$. Use a graphing calculator to find $A + B$, $A - B$, and $2A$.

1. Press `2nd` `x⁻¹` ◄ to highlight the **EDIT** menu.

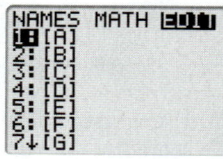

2. Select 1: [A].

3. Matrix A has two rows and two columns. Press 2 `ENTER` 2 `ENTER`.

4. Enter each element of matrix A, starting with the element in the first row, first column. Press 4 `ENTER` `(−)` 6 `ENTER` 2 `ENTER` 3 `ENTER`.

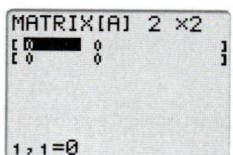

5. Press `2nd` `x⁻¹` ◄ to highlight the **EDIT** menu.

6. Select 2: [B].

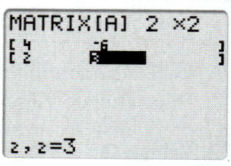

7. Matrix B has two rows and two columns. Press 2 `ENTER` 2 `ENTER`.

8. Enter each element of matrix B, starting with the element in the first row, first column. Press `ENTER` after keying in each value.

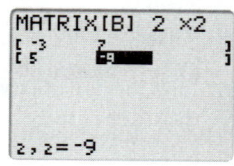

9. Press `2nd` `MODE` to return to the home screen.

10. Find the sum of $A + B$. Press `2nd` `x⁻¹` 1 `+` `2nd` `x⁻¹` 2 `ENTER`.

The sum is $A + B = \begin{bmatrix} 1 & 1 \\ 7 & -6 \end{bmatrix}$.

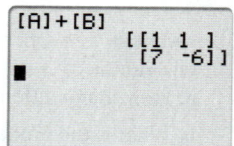

824 *Saxon Algebra 1*

11. Find the difference of $A - B$.

    Press CLEAR 2nd x^{-1} (MATRX) 1 − 2nd x^{-1} (MATRX) 2 ENTER.

    The difference is $A - B = \begin{bmatrix} 7 & -13 \\ -3 & 12 \end{bmatrix}$.

12. Find $2A$.

    Press CLEAR 2 2nd x^{-1} (MATRX) 1 ENTER.

    So, $2A = \begin{bmatrix} 8 & -12 \\ 4 & 6 \end{bmatrix}$.

Lab Practice

Let $A = \begin{bmatrix} 3 & 2 & 4 \\ -1 & 4 & 0 \end{bmatrix}$ and $B = \begin{bmatrix} 2 & 8 & -3 \\ 5 & -9 & 2 \end{bmatrix}$. Use a graphing calculator to find each value.

a. $A + B$

b. $A - B$

c. $3B$

d. $B - A$

e. $-2A$

INVESTIGATION 12

Materials
- graphing calculator
- graph paper

Alternate Materials
Function-Graphing Program for a computer

Discuss
In this investigation, students explore the characteristics of matrices. They see how matrices can be used to solve real-world problems and transform geometric shapes.

Define **matrix**.

Fundraiser
Extend the Problem
Have students write a matrix that could be used to show how much money the school made from each item sold. Sample:

Item	Medium	Large
T-shirts	$12	$15
Hats	$8	$10
Sweat shirts	$15	$18

$$\begin{bmatrix} 12 & 15 \\ 8 & 10 \\ 15 & 18 \end{bmatrix}$$

INVESTIGATION RESOURCES

Reteaching Master
Investigation 12

INVESTIGATION 12

Investigating Matrices

Materials
- graph paper
- graphing calculator

The table shows the price of tickets sold at a local movie theater.

Type	Matinee	Regular
Child	$5	$7
Student	$6	$8
Adult	$9	$11

Use a matrix to organize data, such as the price of movie tickets. A **matrix** is a rectangular array of numbers in horizontal rows and vertical columns. Each number in a matrix is called an element. An **element** is any individual object or member belonging to a set.

Below is a matrix for the ticket prices.

$$\begin{bmatrix} 5 & 7 \\ 6 & 8 \\ 9 & 11 \end{bmatrix}$$

Notice that the entries in the table above correspond to the elements in the matrix.

(**Fundraiser**) The table below shows the number of items sold during the first day of a school fundraiser.

Items Sold on First Day

Item	Medium	Large
T-shirts	10	7
Hats	3	2
Sweatshirts	4	9

1.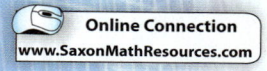

1. **Model** Use the data in the table to create a matrix that represents the situation.

2. Explain how to use the matrix to calculate the total number of sweatshirts sold during the first day of the fundraiser. How many sweatshirts were sold? Sample: Add the numbers in the third row.; 13 sweatshirts

The dimensions of a matrix with m rows and n columns are $m \times n$. Each element has a specific position in the matrix that is relative to its row and column.

Complete the statements. Refer to the matrix of the number of items sold during the school fundraiser's first day.

3. The matrix has _____ rows and _____ columns. 3, 2

4. The dimensions of the matrix are _____. 3×2

Online Connection
www.SaxonMathResources.com

826   Saxon Algebra 1

MATH BACKGROUND

Matrices are used to organize data in a clear, concise format. Operations with matrices are used to solve problems. For example, matrices and diagrams are used to represent communication networks and grids such as those that model the delivery of electricity.

Matrices are also used for transformations of geometric figures in a coordinate plane. Addition translates, or shifts, the shape on the coordinate plane without changing its shape and size. Scalar multiplication dilates, or shrinks or enlarges, a shape on a coordinate plane while preserving its shape.

5. The element in the third row, second column is _____. **9**

6. Describe the dimensions of a matrix representing data about a school fundraiser with five types of items available in four different sizes.
The matrix would have five rows and four columns.

Since matrices are a method of organizing information, sometimes they are added or subtracted to get new information. Matrices that have the same dimensions can be added subtracted.

Caution
Matrices can be added or subtracted only if they have the same number of rows *and* the same number of columns.

The table shows the number of items sold during the second day of the fundraiser.

Items Sold on Second Day

Item	Medium	Large
T-shirts	8	3
Hats	1	5
Sweatshirts	4	7

8. Put the data from each table into a matrix and then find the sum of the values in the second row and second column of each matrix.

7. **Sample: Add the number of large hats sold on the first day, 2, to the number of large hats sold on the second day, which is 5.**

7. **Generalize** Explain how to find the total number of large hats sold during the first two days of the fundraiser.

8. **Formulate** Explain how to use matrices to find the total number of large hats sold during the first two days of the fundraiser.

Graphing Calculator Tip
For help with adding matrices, see the Graphing Calculator Lab 11 on page 824.

9. Use matrices to model the sum of the items sold during the first two days. Then add the matrices using a graphing calculator. **See Additional Answers.**

10. Find the difference between the two matrices. How many more medium hats were sold on the first day than on the second day? **2 hats**
10. See Additional Answers.

Matrix addition also has a geometric application.

Exploration Using Matrix Addition to Transform Geometric Figures

11. Complete the following table by finding the coordinates of the vertices of △ABC.

	Point A	Point B	Point C
x-coordinate	−1	−2	2
y-coordinate	2	−1	−2

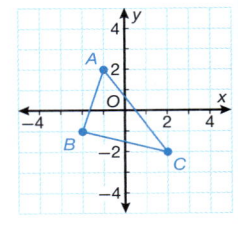

12. Use the data in the table to create matrix A. **See Additional Answers.**

13. Using a graphing calculator find the sum $A + B$, when $B = \begin{bmatrix} 3 & 3 & 3 \\ 2 & 2 & 2 \end{bmatrix}$. **See Additional Answers.**

14. Use the elements of $A + B$ as the coordinates of the vertices of △A'B'C'. Plot the vertices of △A'B'C' to create a graph of the triangle.

15. **Write** Describe the relationship between △ABC and △A'B'C'.

16. What matrix would translate △ABC one unit to the left and three units down? $\begin{bmatrix} -1 & -1 & -1 \\ -3 & -3 & -3 \end{bmatrix}$

14. See Additional Answers.

15. **Sample: The matrix addition $A + B$ translates △ABC three units to the right and two units up.**

Problems 11–16
Error Alert
When writing a matrix that transforms a shape, students may write a 2 × 1, where the first row shows what happens to the x-coordinate and the second row shows the change in the y-coordinate. In order for matrices to be added, they must have exactly the same number of rows and columns, even if each column is the same.

Investigation 12

---

eL ENGLISH LEARNERS

For the exploration, explain the meaning of the word **transform.** Say:

"Transform means to change the form or appearance of something. The job of a make-up artist is to transform the face."

Discuss how moving furniture in a room can transform the appearance of the room. Have volunteers use the word transform in a sentence. **Sample: We will transform the room with decorations.**

Problems 18–22

Error Alert

To enlarge or reduce a figure, students may try to add or subtract, respectively, a value to each element in the matrix. Discuss the phrase "How many times as big ..." to show that multiplication is the correct operation to be used. To shrink a figure, division or multiplication by a fraction can be used.

17. What matrix was used to translate $\triangle ABC$ to $\triangle A'B'C'$ using matrix addition? $\begin{bmatrix} 5 & 5 & 5 \\ 2 & 2 & 2 \end{bmatrix}$

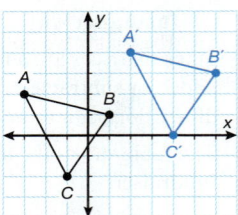

You can also transform a geometric figure through scalar multiplication. **Scalar multiplication** multiplies a matrix A by a scalar c. To find the resulting matrix cA, multiply each element of A by c.

Exploration Using Scalar Multiplication to Transform Geometric Figures

18. **Predict** Use matrix A from the previous Exploration. What would be the effect of multiplying each element in matrix A by 2?

    18. Sample: The coordinates of the vertices would double so the transformed triangle would be four times as big as $\triangle ABC$.

19. Find the matrix $2A$ using a graphing calculator.   See Additional Answers.

20. Use the elements of $2A$ as the coordinates of the vertices of $\triangle A''B''C''$. Plot the vertices of $\triangle A''B''C''$ to create a graph of the triangle.
    See Additional Answers.

21. **Write** Describe the relationship between $\triangle ABC$ and $\triangle A''B''C''$.

    21. Sample: Scalar multiplication $2A$ quadrupled the size of $\triangle ABC$.

22. What matrix would create a triangle one-fourth the size of $\triangle ABC$?
    See Additional Answers.

23. Describe the relationship between $\triangle ABC$ and $\triangle A'B'C'$.
    Sample: $\triangle ABC$ was transformed by scalar multiplication using scalar 3.

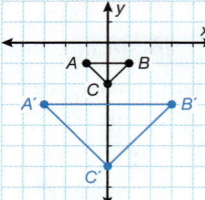

Investigation Practice

The first table shows how much money Abram and two friends earned doing chores last summer. The second table shows how much money they made this summer.

Money Earned Last Summer

	Mowing Lawns	Washing Cars	Babysitting
Abram	$15	$55	$0
Paul	$75	$10	$30
Leila	$20	$40	$35

Money Earned This Summer

	Mowing Lawns	Washing Cars	Babysitting
Abram	$25	$60	$10
Paul	$85	$20	$35
Leila	$30	$60	$40

a. Put the data in each table above into a matrix. Label the first table matrix A and the second matrix B. Subtract the data in matrix A from matrix B.

a. How can matrices be used to calculate how much more money each person made during the second summer?

b. Use a matrix operation to display the additional money each person made during the second summer. How much more money did Paul make during the second summer than the first? **$25**

c. Use scalar multiplication to find the vertices of a quadrilateral whose area is one-fourth of the quadrilateral shown.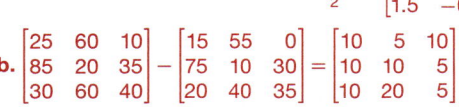

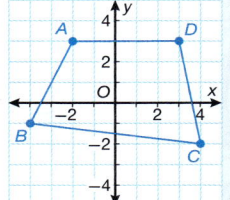

b. $\begin{bmatrix} 25 & 60 & 10 \\ 85 & 20 & 35 \\ 30 & 60 & 40 \end{bmatrix} - \begin{bmatrix} 15 & 55 & 0 \\ 75 & 10 & 30 \\ 20 & 40 & 35 \end{bmatrix} = \begin{bmatrix} 10 & 5 & 10 \\ 10 & 10 & 5 \\ 10 & 20 & 5 \end{bmatrix}$

Investigation 12   **829**

LOOKING FORWARD

Using matrices will be further developed in other Saxon Secondary Mathematics courses.

Investigation Practice

Math Conversations
Discussion to strengthen understanding

Problem a
Guide the students by asking them the following questions.

"What is used to represent the data from the tables?" matrices

"What dimensions will each matrix have?" 3×3

"What operation should be used to find how much more money was made?" subtraction

"Which matrix would come first in the subtraction problem?" matrix B

Problem b
Error Alert
Students may forget to add each element in Paul's row. Remind them that Paul earned money in three different ways.

Problem c
Scaffolding First form a matrix where each column represents a point, and each row represents one of the coordinates of those points. Then multiply each element in the matrix by $\frac{1}{2}$.

Investigation 12   **829**

APPENDIX LESSONS

APPENDIX LESSON 1

Graphing and Solving Nonlinear Inequalities

New Concepts

A quadratic inequality in two variables can be written in four different forms

$$y < ax^2 + bx + c \qquad y \le ax^2 + bx + c$$
$$y > ax^2 + bx + c \qquad y \ge ax^2 + bx + c$$

Using a procedure similar to graphing linear equalities a quadratic inequality can be graphed.

Example 1 Graphing a Quadratic Inequality

a. Graph $y > x^2 + 4x - 5$.

SOLUTION

Step 1: Graph $y = x^2 + 4x - 5$ as a boundary. Use a dashed curve because the inequality symbol is $>$.

Step 2: Shade inside the parabola since the solution consists of y-values greater than the y-values on the parabola for the corresponding x-values.

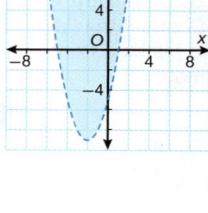

Check Test a point in the solution region. Substitute $(1, 3)$ into the inequality

$y > x^2 + 4x - 5$

$3 \overset{?}{>} (1)^2 + 4(1) - 5$

$3 \overset{?}{>} 1 + 4 - 5$

$3 > 0$ ✓

b. Graph $y \le x^2 + 2x - 8$.

SOLUTION

Step 1: Graph $y \le x^2 + 2x - 8$ as a boundary. Use a solid curve because the inequality symbol is $\le$.

Step 2: Shade below the parabola since the solution consists of y-values less than the y-values on the parabola for the corresponding x-values.

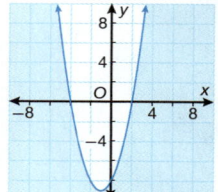

Check To verify the solution region test a point. Substitute $(3, -4)$ into the inequality.

$y \le x^2 + 2x - 8$

$-4 \overset{?}{\le} (3)^2 + 2(3) - 8$

$-4 \overset{?}{\le} 9 + 6 - 8$

$-4 \le 7$ ✓

A quadratic inequality in one variable can be written in four different forms

$$ax^2 + bx + c < 0 \quad ax^2 + bx + c \leq 0$$
$$ax^2 + bx + c > 0 \quad ax^2 + bx + c \geq 0$$

Quadratic inequalities can be solved using tables, graphs, or algebraic methods.

Example 2 Solving with a Table

Solve $x^2 - 2x \leq 3$ using a table.

SOLUTION

Step 1: Write the inequality as $x^2 - 2x - 3 \leq 0$.

Step 2: Make a table of values.

x	-5	-4	-3	-2	-1	0	1	2	3	4	5
$x^2 - 2x - 3$	32	21	12	5	0	-3	-4	-3	0	5	12

The inequality $x^2 - 2x - 3 \leq 0$ is true for values of x between -1 and 3 inclusively. The solution of the inequality is $-1 \leq x \leq 3$.

Example 3 Solving with a Graphing Calculator Table

Solve $x^2 - x - 4 \leq 2$ using a graphing calculator.

SOLUTION

Step 1: Use a graphing calculator to graph each side of the inequality. Set **Y1** equal to $x^2 - x - 4$ and set **Y2** equal to 2.

Step 2: View the table comparing the two equations.

Step 3: Identify the values of x where $\mathbf{Y1} = x^2 - x - 4$ are less than or equal to the values of $\mathbf{Y2} = 2$.

The solution set is $-2 \leq x \leq 3$.

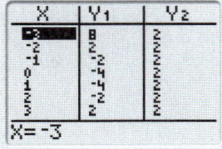

Appendix Lesson 1   831

Example 4 Solving with a Graphing Calculator Graph

Solve $x^2 + 2x - 6 < 2$ using a graphing calculator.

SOLUTION

Step 1: Use a graphing calculator to graph each side of the inequality. Set **Y1** equal to $x^2 + 2x - 6$ and set **Y2** equal to 2.

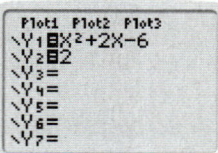

Step 2: Calculate the points of intersection.

Step 3: Identify the values of x where **Y1** ≤ **Y2**.

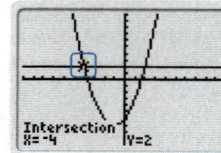 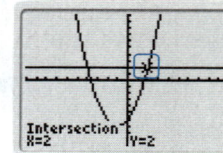

The solution set is $-4 < x < 2$.

Lesson Practice

a. Graph $y > x^2 - 6x + 8$.
(Ex 1)

b. Graph $y \leq x^2 - 4x - 5$.
(Ex 1)

c. Solve $x^2 - 3x \leq 4$ using a table. $-1 \leq x \leq 4$
(Ex 2)

d. Solve $x^2 - 5x + 10 \leq 4$ using a graphing calculator. $2 \leq x \leq 3$
(Ex 3)

e. Solve $x^2 - 6x - 5 < 2$ using a graphing calculator. $-1 < x < 7$
(Ex 4)

a.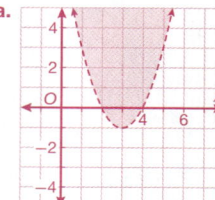

b.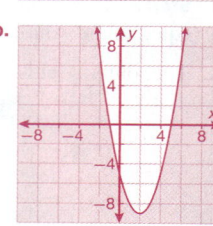

APPENDIX LESSON 2

Graphing Piecewise and Step Functions

New Concepts

When a function has a different rule for different pieces of its domain, it is called a **piecewise function**. This kind of function is a combination of two or more functions. It assigns a different value to each domain interval. A piecewise function that is constant for each part of the domain is called a **step function**.

Example 1 Evaluating a Step Function

Evaluate the function for $x = -4$, $x = -2$, and $x = 6$.

$$f(x) = \begin{cases} 10 \text{ if } x \leq -2 \\ 8 \text{ if } x > -2 \end{cases}$$

SOLUTION

When $x = -4$, then $f(-4) = 10$ because $-4 \leq -2$.

When $x = -2$, then $f(-2) = 10$ because $-2 \leq -2$.

When $x = 6$, then $f(6) = 8$ because $6 > -2$.

Example 2 Evaluating a Piecewise Function

Evaluate the function for $x = -4$, $x = -2$, and $x = 6$.

$$f(x) = \begin{cases} 2x - 1 & \text{if } x < 6 \\ 8x^2 & \text{if } x \geq 6 \end{cases}$$

SOLUTION

When $x = -4$, then $x < 6$. Use the piece of the function, $f(x) = 2x - 1$.

$f(-4) = 2(-4) - 1$ Substitute -4 for x into $f(x)$.

$\quad\quad = -8 - 1$ Multiply 2 and -4.

$\quad\quad = -9$ Simplify.

When $x = -2$, then $x < 6$. Use the piece of the function, $f(x) = 2x - 1$.

$f(-2) = 2(-2) - 1$ Substitute -2 for x into $f(x)$.

$\quad\quad = -4 - 1$ Multiply 2 and -2.

$\quad\quad = -5$ Simplify.

When $x = 6$, then $x \geq 6$. Use the piece of the function, $f(x) = 8x^2$.

$f(6) = 8 \cdot 6^2$ Substitute 6 for x into $f(x)$.

$\quad\quad = 8 \cdot 36$ Simplify the exponent.

$\quad\quad = 288$ Multiply.

Example 3 Graphing a Step Function

Graph the function.

$$f(x) = \begin{cases} -1 & \text{if } x \leq 4 \\ 3 & \text{if } x > 4 \end{cases}$$

SOLUTION

Graphing a step function is a lot like graphing inequalities. You will use open circles to indicate $>$ or $<$ and closed circles to show $\leq$ or $\geq$.

Begin by considering the function at $x = 4$. This is where the "steps" separate. Because $f(4) = -1$, graph the point $(4, -1)$ with a closed circle. $f(x) = -1$ for $x \leq 4$. Draw a ray from the point extending to the left, along the line $y = -1$. This is one horizontal step.

Next consider the other piece, $f(x) = 3$ for $x > 4$.

At $(4, 3)$, draw an open circle because $f(4) \neq 3$. Draw a ray going to the right. This is another horizontal step.

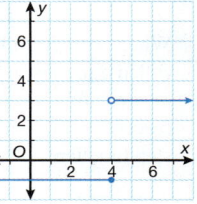

Example 4 Graphing a Piecewise Function

Graph the function.

$$f(x) = \begin{cases} -2x + 3 & \text{if } x \leq -1 \\ -5x & \text{if } -1 < x \leq 2 \\ x^2 - 10 & \text{if } x > 2 \end{cases}$$

SOLUTION

The function is made of two linear pieces and a quadratic piece with a domain divided at $x = -1$ and $x = 2$. Find the value of the two surrounding functions for these values to see if the graph is continuous.

Use a table to find points and graph each piece. The shaded regions are coordinates that will not be included in the graph of $f(x)$.

x	$f(x) = -2x + 3$	$f(x) = -5x$	$f(x) = x^2 - 10$
-3	9		
-2	7		
-1	5	5	
0		0	
1		-5	
2		-10	-6
3			-1
4			6
5			15

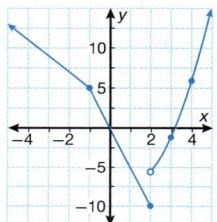

Graph each value. There will be an open circle at $(2, -6)$ and a closed circle at $(2, -10)$ to clearly show the value of the function at $x = 2$. No open circle is needed at $x = -1$ because the function is connected at that point by the two pieces of the function.

Saxon Algebra 1

Example 5 **Application: Ticket Prices**

At an amusement park, children under three years of age are free. Ages 3 to 12 pay $20. Everyone older than 12 pays $30. Write the function that represents this information, and graph the function.

SOLUTION

First, identify the intervals for the independent variables. Let x represent age in years.

under three $\quad x < 3$

ages 3 to 12 $\quad 3 \leq x \leq 12$

older than 12 $\quad x > 12$

Then, write the function rule. $f(x)$ is the price of the ticket.

$$f(x) = \begin{cases} 0 & \text{if } x < 3 \\ 20 & \text{if } 3 \leq x \leq 12 \\ 30 & \text{if } x > 12 \end{cases}$$

Graph the function.

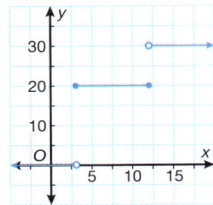

Lesson Practice

Evaluate each step function for the values given.
(Ex 1)

a. $f(x) = \begin{cases} -2 & \text{if } x \leq 1 \\ 4 & \text{if } x > 1 \end{cases}$ for $x = -3$ and $x = 10$. $f(-3) = -2, f(10) = 4$

b. $f(x) = \begin{cases} 6 & \text{if } x < 9 \\ -11 & \text{if } x \geq 9 \end{cases}$ for $x = 8$ and $x = 9$. $f(8) = 6, f(9) = -11$

Evaluate each piecewise function for the values given.
(Ex 2)

c. $f(x) = \begin{cases} 2x^3 & \text{if } x < 0 \\ 10 - 3x & \text{if } x \geq 0 \end{cases}$ for $x = 4$ and $x = -1$. $f(4) = -2, f(-1) = -2$

d. $f(x) = \begin{cases} 3x & \text{if } x \leq -1 \\ x - 5 & \text{if } x > -1 \end{cases}$ for $x = -5$ and $x = 1$. $f(-5) = -15, f(1) = -4$

Graph each step function.
(Ex 3)

e. $f(x) = \begin{cases} 7 & \text{if } x < 5 \\ 2 & \text{if } x \geq 5 \end{cases}$

f. $f(x) = \begin{cases} 3 & \text{if } x < -3 \\ 0 & \text{if } -3 \leq x < 3 \\ -3 & \text{if } x \geq 3 \end{cases}$

e.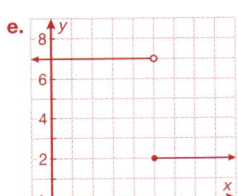

f.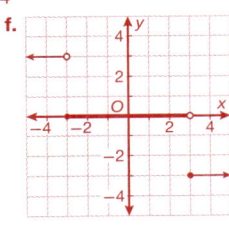

Appendix Lesson 2

Graph each piecewise function.
(Ex 4)

g. $f(x) = \begin{cases} 4x & \text{if } x < -2 \\ 2x + 2 & \text{if } x \geq -2 \end{cases}$

h. $f(x) = \begin{cases} 3x & \text{if } x \leq 1 \\ 6x - 3 & \text{if } 1 < x < 2 \\ -x^2 & \text{if } x \geq 2 \end{cases}$

i. **Allowance** A child less than 5 years old does not get an allowance.
(Ex 5) Starting at 5 years old, he gets 3 times his age per month. At 10 years, the rate increases to 4 times his age per month. Write the function that represents this information, and graph the function.

j. **Rides** At an amusement park, there are 15 rides that have no height
(Ex 5) requirement. If a person is at least 4 feet tall, there are a total of 20 available rides. To be granted access to all 24 rides in the park, a person must be at least 4.5 feet tall. Write a function that represents the number of available rides based on a person's height. Sketch a graph of that function.

g.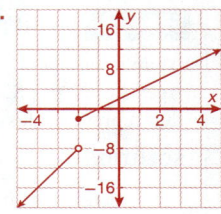

h.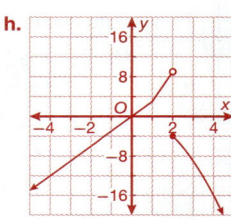

i.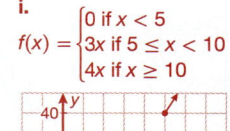
$f(x) = \begin{cases} 0 & \text{if } x < 5 \\ 3x & \text{if } 5 \leq x < 10 \\ 4x & \text{if } x \geq 10 \end{cases}$

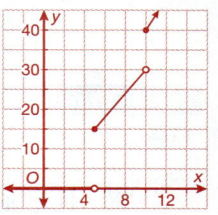

j.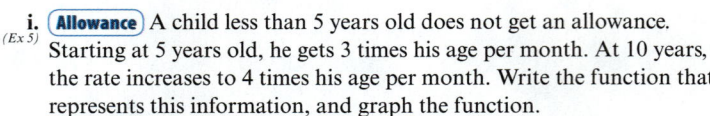
$f(x) = \begin{cases} 15 & \text{if } x < 4 \\ 20 & \text{if } 4 \leq x < 4.5 \\ 24 & \text{if } x \geq 4.5 \end{cases}$

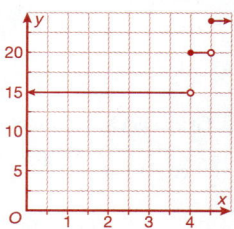

836 **Saxon** Algebra 1

APPENDIX LESSON 3

Understanding Vectors

New Concepts

To say that you biked 3 miles tells how far you went, but to say that you biked 3 miles north tells how far you went and in what direction. **A vector** is a quantity with both magnitude (size) and direction. "3 miles north" can be represented by a vector.

A vector is represented by a line segment with a half-arrow that indicates direction, not a continuation of the segment infinitely as in a ray. This vector can be named $\overrightarrow{MN}$ or $\vec{v}$.

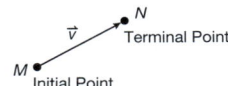

Component form is also used to name a vector. It identifies the horizontal change (x) and vertical change (y) from the initial point to the terminal point in the form, $\langle x, y \rangle$. The horizontal change is positive to the right and negative to the left. The vertical change is positive up and negative down.

Example 1 Writing Vectors in Component Form

Write each vector in component form.

a. $\overrightarrow{AB}$

SOLUTION

The horizontal change from A to B is 5.

The vertical change from A to B is -2.

The component form of $\overrightarrow{AB}$ is $\langle 5, -2 \rangle$.

b. $\overrightarrow{RS}$ with $R(-1, 4)$ and $S(6, 3)$.

SOLUTION

$\overrightarrow{RS} = \langle x_2 - x_1, y_2 - y_1 \rangle$ Horizontal change is $x_2 - x_1$ and vertical change is $y_2 - y_1$.

$\overrightarrow{RS} = \langle 6 - (-1), 3 - 4 \rangle$ Substitute the coordinates of the given points. Subtract the initial point's coordinates from the terminal point's coordinates.

$\overrightarrow{RS} = \langle 7, -1 \rangle$ Simplify.

The length of the vector is called its magnitude. It is written $|\overrightarrow{EF}|$ or $|\vec{v}|$. Derived from the distance formula, the formula for the length of a vector is

$$|\langle a, b \rangle| = \sqrt{a^2 + b^2}.$$

Appendix Lesson 3   837

Example 2 Finding the Magnitude of a Vector

Find the magnitude of the vector to the nearest tenth.

$\langle -3, 5 \rangle$

SOLUTION

$$|\langle a, b \rangle| = \sqrt{a^2 + b^2}$$
$$|\langle -3, 5 \rangle| = \sqrt{(-3)^2 + 5^2}$$
$$= \sqrt{9 + 25}$$
$$= \sqrt{34}$$
$$\approx 5.8$$

The direction of a vector is the angle formed by it and a horizontal line. Begin at the positive x-axis and measure counterclockwise to the vector. Then, use inverse trigonometric functions to find the angle.

Example 3 Finding the Direction of a Vector

Find the direction of the vector to the nearest degree.

A boat's velocity is given by the vector $\langle 4, 8 \rangle$.

SOLUTION

First, draw the vector on a coordinate plane. Use the origin as the initial point.

The horizontal change and the vertical change make right triangle FGH. $\angle G$ is the angle formed by the vector and the x-axis.

$\tan G = \frac{8}{4}$.

So $m\angle G = \tan^{-1}\left(\frac{8}{4}\right) \approx 63°$.

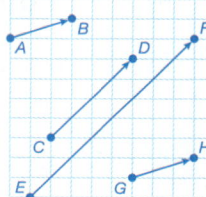

Equal vectors are two vectors that have the same magnitude and direction. They do not have to have the same initial and terminal points.

Parallel vectors may have different magnitudes, but have the same or opposite direction. Equal vectors are always parallel vectors.

Example 4 Identifying Equal and Parallel Vectors

a. Identify equal vectors.

SOLUTION

Equal vectors have the same magnitude and direction.

$\overrightarrow{AB} = \overrightarrow{GH}$

b. Identify parallel vectors.

SOLUTION

Parallel vectors have the same or opposite directions.

$AB \| GH$ and $CD \| EF$

Lesson Practice

Write each vector in component form.

a. Write the vector in component form. ⟨4, 8⟩

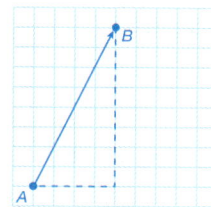

b. Write the vector in component form. ⟨−4, −5⟩

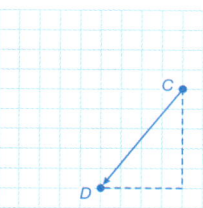

Write each vector in component form.

c. $\overrightarrow{PQ}$ with $P(2, -6)$ and $Q(1, -1)$. ⟨−1, 5⟩

d. $\overrightarrow{JK}$ with $J(3, 7)$ and $K(8, -2)$. ⟨5, −9⟩

Find the magnitude of each vector to the nearest tenth.

e. ⟨2, −9⟩   9.2

f. ⟨6, 12⟩   13.4

g. (Water Current) The river's current is given by the vector ⟨3, 1⟩. Find the direction of the vector to the nearest degree.   18°

h. Identify the equal vectors. $\overrightarrow{DE} = \overrightarrow{FG}$

i. Identify the parallel vectors. $\overrightarrow{DE} \parallel \overrightarrow{FG}$ and $\overrightarrow{NM} \parallel \overrightarrow{LK}$

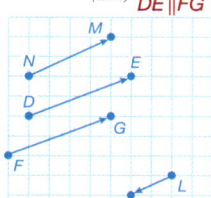

Appendix Lesson 3   839

APPENDIX LESSON 4

Using Variation and Standard Deviation to Analyze Data

New Concepts

$$\{1, 2, 3, 4, 5, 6, 7, 8, 9\}$$

The mean of the data set is 5. **Standard deviation** measures how the data is spread from the mean. It is a measure of variation.

The **variance**, represented by the symbol σ^2, is the average of the squared differences from the mean. To calculate the variance,

- Find the mean of the data.
- Subtract each value from the mean and square the result.
- Find the average of the squared results.

The standard deviation, represented by the symbol σ, is the square root of the variance.

Example 1 Finding the Standard Deviation

Ten students are asked how many CDs they own. Their responses are recorded in the data set.

$$\{10, 15, 13, 20, 8, 11, 10, 9, 14, 16\}$$

Find the standard deviation of the data.

SOLUTION

First, find the mean of the data by adding the data and dividing by 10.

$$\frac{10 + 15 + 13 + 20 + 8 + 11 + 10 + 9 + 14 + 16}{10} = \frac{126}{10} = 12.6$$

Next, subtract each value in the data set from the mean and square the result.

Value (x)	10	15	13	20	8	11	10	9	14	16
Difference ($12.6 - x$)	2.6	−2.4	−0.4	−7.4	4.6	1.6	2.6	3.6	−1.4	−3.4
Difference Squared ($12.6 - x$)^2	6.76	5.76	0.16	54.76	21.16	2.56	6.76	12.96	1.96	11.56

Now, find the average of the differences squared.

$$\frac{6.76 + 5.76 + 0.16 + 54.76 + 21.16 + 2.56 + 6.76 + 12.96 + 1.96 + 11.56}{10}$$

$$= \frac{124.4}{10} = 12.44.$$

Finally, take the square root to get the standard deviation. $\sqrt{12.44} \approx 3.53$

The standard deviation describes the spread of the data. When the standard deviation is low, the data tends to be close to the measure of central tendency, or mean. When the standard deviation is high, the data is more spread out.

An outlier is a number that is much greater or much less than the other values in the data set. Outliers have a great impact on the mean and standard deviation and can cause them to misrepresent the data set. One way to determine whether a value is an outlier is to see if it is more than 3 standard deviations from the mean.

Example 2 Examining Outliers

The population of southern states is shown. Find the mean and standard deviation of the data. Identify any outliers, and if one is found, explain how it affects the mean.

State	TX	OK	AK	LA	MS	AL	FL	GA	NC	SC	VA	WV	MD	DE	KY	TN
Population in millions	22.9	3.5	2.8	4.5	2.9	4.6	17.8	9.1	8.7	4.2	7.6	1.8	5.6	0.8	4.1	6.0

SOLUTION

First, find the mean of the state populations.

$$\frac{22.9 + 3.5 + 2.8 + 4.5 + 2.9 + 4.6 + 17.8 + 9.1 + 8.7 + 4.2 + 7.6 + 1.8 + 5.6 + 0.8 + 4.1 + 6.0}{16}$$

≈ 6.7

Next, subtract each value in the data set from the mean and square the result.

Now, find the average of the difference squared, $\frac{518.89}{16} \approx 32.43$, and take the square root to get the standard deviation.

$\sqrt{32.43} \approx 5.69$

An outlier would be outside the 3 standard deviations from the mean, $6.7 \pm 3(5.69)$.

Negative population would not make sense, so check to see if any state has a greater population than $6.7 + 3(5.69) = 23.77$ million.

There are no outliers in this data because there are no populations larger than 23.77 million. All data is within 3 standard deviations of the mean.

Population x	Difference $(6.7 - x)$	Difference Squared $(6.7 - x)^2$
22.9	−16.2	262.44
3.5	3.2	10.24
2.8	3.9	15.21
4.5	2.2	4.84
2.9	3.8	14.44
4.6	2.1	4.41
17.8	−11.1	123.21
9.1	−2.4	5.76
8.7	−2	4
4.2	2.5	6.25
7.6	−0.9	0.81
1.8	4.9	24.01
5.6	1.1	1.21
0.8	5.9	34.81
4.1	2.6	6.76
6.0	0.7	0.49

Appendix Lesson 4

Some data is said to be normally distributed. The shape of the data looks like a bell, so it is often called a "bell-shaped curve." The mean is at the center.

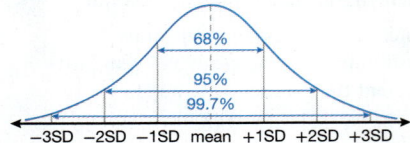

As the graph indicates, 68% of the data falls within one standard deviation of the mean. 95% of the data falls within two standard deviations of the mean, and 99.7% of the data falls within three standard deviations of the mean.

Example 3 Using the Normal Distribution

The ages of people at a park are normally distributed. The mean is 18 years and the standard deviation is 6 years. Between what two ages do 95% of the ages fall?

SOULTION

Because it is a normal distribution, 95% of the data falls within 2 standard deviations of the mean.

$$18 \pm 2(6) = 18 \pm 12$$

95% of the ages fall between 6 and 30.

Lesson Practice

Find the standard deviation of the data.

a. An ATM machine records the values of the withdrawals made in one day. $\sigma \approx 50.6$
(Ex 1)
$\{20, 100, 20, 200, 20, 20, 100, 20, 80, 20, 20, 40, 100, 40, 100\}$

b. A group of students is asked how many movies they watched in the last month. Their responses are recorded in the data set. $\sigma \approx 7.68$
$\{4, 10, 6, 8, 4, 5, 30, 4, 2, 3, 1\}$

Find the mean and standard deviation of the data. Identify any outliers, and if one is found, explain how it affects the mean.

c. Twelve students are asked how many books they read last year. Their responses are recorded in the data set.
(Ex 2)
$\{12, 15, 30, 14, 13, 9, 10, 10, 11, 12, 14, 8\}$

c. mean ≈ 13.2, $\sigma \approx 5.47$, 30 is an outlier and it makes the mean larger.

d. A teacher records the scores on a test.
(Ex 1)
$\{90, 95, 90, 85, 80, 80, 90, 40, 95, 90, 85, 90, 95, 80, 100\}$

d. mean ≈ 85.7, $\sigma \approx 13.5$, 40 is an outlier and makes the mean smaller.

e. **Test Results** The results on a test are normally distributed with a mean of 85 and a standard deviation of 5. Between what two scores are 68% of the scores? between 80 and 90
(Ex 3)

f. **Salaries** The salaries of educators are normally distributed with a mean of $35,000 and a standard deviation of $10,000. Between what two scores are 99.7% of the salaries? between $5,000 and $65,000
(Ex 3)

APPENDIX LESSON 5

Evaluating Expressions with Technology

New Concepts

A graphing calculator can help you evaluate expressions for several values of the variable.

Example 1 Using a Graphing Calculator to Evaluate Expressions

a. Use a graphing calculator to evaluate $3x^2 + 2x - 1$ for $x = 50, 150, 250, 350$ and 450.

SOLUTION

Press **Y=**.

Enter $3x^2 + 2x - 1$ for Y_1.

Press **2nd** **WINDOW** (TBLSET) to set the table values.

Enter the first value of x, 50, for **TblStart**.

For **ΔTbl**, enter the difference in the x-values, 100.

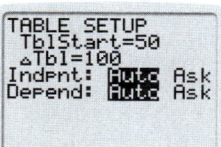

Press **2nd** **GRAPH** (TABLE).

In the first column, you will see the values of x.

The second column shows the value of the expression for each value of x.

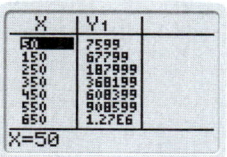

b. Use the table to find the value of the expression when $x = 550$.

SOLUTION

Find 550 in the first column, and look across from it. The value is 908,599.

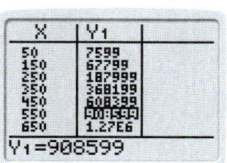

c. Use the table to find the value of x if the expression is equal to 368,199.

SOLUTION

Find 368,199 in the second column. It is next to $x = 350$.

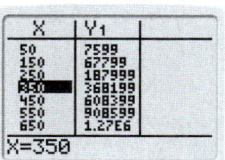

Appendix Lesson 5

A spreadsheet can also be used to evaluate expressions.

Example 2 Using a Spreadsheet to Evaluate an Expression

Evaluate $5x^2 - 12x - 16$ for $x = 11, 13, 15, 17$, and 19.

SOLUTION

Enter 11, 13, 15, 17, and 19 in the first column, A1 to A5.

	A	B	C	D	E	F	G
1	11						
2	13						
3	15						
4	17						
5	19						
6							

Enter the expression in cell B1, using A1 instead of a variable.

The expression should be typed as $= 5 * \text{A1}^\wedge 2 - 12 * \text{A1} - 16$

	A	B	C	D	E	F	G
1	11	=5*A1^2-12*A1-16					
2	13						
3	15						
4	17						
5	19						
6							

After pressing **enter**, the value of the expression appears in the cell.

	A	B	C	D	E	F	G
1	11	457					
2	13						
3	15						
4	17						
5	19						
6							

Copy the expression by clicking on the bottom right corner of B1.

Hold the mouse while you drag to highlight the cells B2 through B5.

Column B will be filled with the values of the expression.

	A	B	C	D	E	F	G
1	11	457					
2	13						
3	15						
4	17						
5	19						
6							

B1 = =5*A1^2-12*A1-16

The spreadsheet will automatically evaluate the expression using the corresponding value of x in column A.

	A	B	C	D	E	F	G
1	11	457					
2	13	673					
3	15	929					
4	17	1225					
5	19	1561					
6							

B1 = =5*A1^2-12*A1-16

b. Use the spreadsheet to find the value of the expression when $x = 22$.

	A	B	C	D	E	F	G
1	11	457					
2	13	673					
3	15	929					
4	17	1225					
5	19	1561					
6	22	2140					

B6 = =5*A6^2-12*A6-16

SOLUTION

Enter 22 in the first column, and copy the expression into the corresponding row of column B. The value is 2140.

Lesson Practice

Use a graphing calculator to evaluate $-x^2 - 7x + 9$ for the given values.
(Ex 1)
    a. $x = 22$ -629 **b.** $x = 42$ -2049 **c.** $x = 62$ -4269

Use a graphing calculator to evaluate $6x^2 + x - 13$ for the given values.
(Ex 1)
    d. $x = 48$ $13{,}859$ **e.** $x = 78$ $36{,}569$ **f.** $x = 108$ $70{,}079$

Use a spreadsheet to evaluate $-2x^2 + 8x - 4$ for the given values.
(Ex 2)
    g. $x = 6$ -28 **h.** $x = 12$ -196 **i.** $x = 18$ -508

Use a spreadsheet to evaluate $x^2 + 14x - 21$ for the given values.
(Ex 2)
    j. $x = 4$ 51 **k.** $x = 9$ 186 **l.** $x = 14$ 371

SKILLS BANK

Skills Bank

Compare and Order Rational Numbers

Skills Bank Lesson 1

A **rational number** is a number that can be written as a ratio of two integers.

Example 1 Comparing Rational Numbers

Compare $\frac{7}{10}$ and $\frac{5}{12}$. Write <, >, or =.

SOLUTION

Method 1: Multiply to find a common denominator.

$10 \cdot 12 = 120$ Multiply the denominators.

$\frac{7}{10} \cdot \frac{12}{12} \bigcirc \frac{5}{12} \cdot \frac{10}{10}$ Write fractions with a common denominator.

$\frac{84}{120} > \frac{50}{120}$, so $\frac{7}{10} > \frac{5}{12}$

Method 2: Find the least common denominator (LCD).

$\frac{7}{10} \cdot \frac{6}{6} \bigcirc \frac{5}{12} \cdot \frac{5}{5}$ Write fractions using the LCD of 60.

$\frac{42}{60} > \frac{25}{60}$, so $\frac{7}{10} > \frac{5}{12}$

Example 2 Ordering Rational Numbers

Order the numbers $-\frac{5}{4}$, 2.75, -3, $2\frac{1}{2}$, $-\frac{14}{5}$ from least to greatest.

SOLUTION Write each fraction as a decimal. Graph the numbers on a number line.

$-\frac{5}{4} = -1.25$, $2\frac{1}{2} = 2.5$, $-\frac{14}{5} = -2.8$

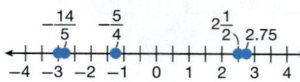

Read the numbers from left to right: $-3, -\frac{14}{5}, -\frac{5}{4}, 2\frac{1}{2}, 2.75$.

The numbers are in order from least to greatest.

Skills Bank Practice

Compare. Use >, <, or =.

a. $\frac{5}{8} \;\;\bigcirc>\;\; \frac{7}{12}$

b. $\frac{3}{11} \;\;\bigcirc<\;\; \frac{3}{10}$

c. $-\frac{3}{7} \;\;\bigcirc>\;\; -\frac{4}{5}$

Order from least to greatest.

d. $-2, \frac{7}{8}, 0.8, 2.1, 1\frac{1}{3}$
$-2, 0.8, \frac{7}{8}, 1\frac{1}{3}, 2.1$

e. $0.7, -1, -\frac{5}{4}, \frac{4}{3}, -2.3, -\frac{9}{2}$
$-\frac{9}{2}, -2.3, -\frac{5}{4}, -1, 0.7, \frac{4}{3}$

Decimal Operations

Skills Bank Lesson 2

To add or subtract decimals, align the numbers at their decimal points. Then perform the operation the same way as adding or subtracting whole numbers.

Example 1 Adding and Subtracting Decimals

a. Find the sum of 24.5 and 1.235.

SOLUTION

$24.5 + 1.235$

$$\begin{array}{r} 24.500 \\ +\ 1.235 \\ \hline 25.735 \end{array}$$

Write the problem vertically.
Align the decimal points.

b. Find the difference of 36.762 and 4.2.

SOLUTION

$36.762 - 4.2$

$$\begin{array}{r} 36.762 \\ -\ 4.200 \\ \hline 32.562 \end{array}$$

To multiply decimals, multiply first. Then place the decimal so that the product has the same number of decimal places as the total number of decimal places in the two factors. To divide decimals, multiply the divisor and the dividend by a power of 10 in order to make the divisor a natural number. Then divide as with whole numbers.

Example 2 Multiplying and Dividing Decimals

a. Find the product of 1.25 and 2.7.

SOLUTION

1.25×2.7

$$\begin{array}{r} 1.25 \\ \times 2.7 \\ \hline 3.375 \end{array}$$

Write the problem vertically.

Since the factors have a total of 3 decimal places, there should be 3 decimal places in the product.

b. Find the quotient of 3.72 and 0.3.

SOLUTION

$3.72 \div 0.3$

$0.3\overline{)3.72} = 12.4$

Multiply the divisor and dividend by 10 so the divisor is a natural number.

Skills Bank Practice

a. Find the sum of 19.3 and 24.54.
43.84

b. Find the difference of 55.755 and 30.93.
24.825

c. Find the product of 4.28 and 0.216.
0.92448

d. Find the quotient of 0.756 and 0.06.
12.6

Simplify.

e. $176.4 - 23.72$
152.68

f. $24.6 + 18.76$
43.36

g. 84.7×6.2
525.14

h. $7.95 \div 1.5$
5.3

Fraction Operations

Skills Bank Lesson 3

To add or subtract fractions with unlike denominators, first find a common denominator.

Example 1 Adding and Subtracting Fractions

a. Add $\frac{5}{6}$ and $\frac{3}{8}$.

SOLUTION

Method 1: Multiply to find a common denominator.

$6 \cdot 8 = 48$

$\frac{5}{6}\left(\frac{8}{8}\right) + \frac{3}{8}\left(\frac{6}{6}\right)$ Multiply by fractions equal to 1.

$= \frac{40}{48} + \frac{18}{48}$ Add.

$= \frac{58}{48}$ Simplify.

$= \frac{29}{24}$ or $1\frac{5}{24}$

Method 2: Find the lowest common denominator (LCD).

Multiples of 6: 6, 12, 18, 24, ...
Multiples of 8: 8, 16, 24, ...
The LCD is 24.

$\frac{5}{6}\left(\frac{4}{4}\right) + \frac{3}{8}\left(\frac{3}{3}\right)$ Multiply by fractions equal to 1.

$= \frac{20}{24} + \frac{9}{24}$ Add.

$= \frac{29}{24}$ or $1\frac{5}{24}$

b. Subtract $\frac{1}{2}$ from $\frac{7}{8}$.

SOLUTION

$\frac{7}{8} - \frac{1}{2}\left(\frac{4}{4}\right)$ Write equivalent fractions using a denominator of 8.

$= \frac{7}{8} - \frac{4}{8} = \frac{3}{8}$

Example 2 Multiplying and Dividing Fractions

a. Multiply $\frac{2}{3} \cdot \frac{5}{6}$.

SOLUTION

Multiply the numerators and denominators. Then simplify if possible.

$\frac{2}{3} \cdot \frac{5}{6} = \frac{10}{18}$

$= \frac{5}{9}$

b. Divide $\frac{5}{4} \div \frac{3}{5}$.

SOLUTION

Write the reciprocal of $\frac{3}{5}$ and then multiply.

$\frac{5}{4} \cdot \frac{5}{3} = \frac{25}{12}$ Multiply by $\frac{5}{3}$.

$= \frac{25}{12}$ or $2\frac{1}{12}$

Skills Bank Practice

Add, subtract, multiply, or divide. Simplify if possible.

a. $\frac{7}{12} + \frac{3}{8}$ $\frac{23}{24}$ **b.** $\frac{9}{10} - \frac{4}{5}$ $\frac{1}{10}$ **c.** $\frac{5}{9} \cdot \frac{3}{4}$ $\frac{5}{12}$ **d.** $\frac{2}{16} \div \frac{9}{8}$ $\frac{1}{9}$ **e.** $\frac{5}{8} - \frac{5}{16}$ $\frac{5}{16}$ **f.** $\frac{7}{10} + \frac{8}{15}$ $\frac{37}{30}$ or $1\frac{7}{30}$

Divisibility

Skills Bank Lesson 4

A number is **divisible** by another number if the quotient is a whole number without a remainder.

Divisibility Rules
A number is divisible by …
2 if its last digit is even (0, 2, 4, 6, or 8).
3 if the sum of its digits is divisible by 3.
4 if its last two digits are divisible by 4.
5 if its last digit is 0 or 5.
6 if it is divisible by both 2 and 3.
9 if the sum of its digits is divisible by 9.
10 if its last digit is 0.

Example 1 Determining the Divisibility of Numbers

a. Determine whether 24 is divisible by 2, 3, 4, 5, and 6.

SOLUTION

2	The last digit is even.	24	divisible
3	The sum of the digits is divisible by 3.	$2 + 4 = 6$	divisible
4	The last two digits are divisible by 4.	24	divisible
5	The last digit is not 0 or 5.	24	not divisible
6	The number is divisible by both 2 and 3.		divisible

24 is divisible by 2, 3, 4, and 6.

b. Determine whether both the numerator and denominator in the fraction $\frac{16}{60}$ are divisible by 2, 3, 4, and 5.

SOLUTION

2	The last digit is even.	16	60	both divisible
3	The sum of the digits in 16 is not divisible by 3.	$1 + 6 = 7$	$6 + 0 = 6$	not both divisible
4	The last two digits are divisible by 4.	16	60	both divisible
5	The last digit in 16 is not 0 or 5.	16	60	not both divisible

Both the numerator and denominator in $\frac{16}{60}$ are divisible by 2 and 4.

Skills Bank Practice

Determine whether each number is divisible by 2, 3, 4, 5, 6, 9, and 10.

a. 90   2, 3, 5, 6, 9, 10   **b.** 830   2, 5, 10   **c.** 1024   2, 4

d. Determine whether both the numerator and denominator in the fraction $\frac{12}{54}$ are divisible by 2, 3, 4, 5, and 6.   2, 3, 6

Equivalent Decimals, Fractions, and Percents

Skills Bank Lesson 5

Numbers can be written as decimals, fractions, and percents. The table shows common fractions and their equivalent decimals and percents.

Fraction	Decimal	Percent
$\frac{1}{4}$	0.25	25%
$\frac{1}{2}$	0.5	50%
$\frac{3}{4}$	0.75	75%
$\frac{1}{5}$	0.2	20%
$\frac{1}{8}$	0.125	12.5%

Example 1 Writing Fractions As Decimals and Percents

Find the equivalent decimal and percent for each fraction.

a. $\frac{7}{10}$

SOLUTION

$10\overline{)7.0}$ gives 0.7 — Find the equivalent decimal. Divide the numerator by the denominator.

$0.70 = 70\%$ — Find the equivalent percent. Move the decimal two places to the right.

$\frac{7}{10}$ is equivalent to 0.7 and 70%.

b. $\frac{2}{9}$

SOLUTION

$2 \div 9 = 0.\overline{2}$ Divide the numerator by the denominator.

$0.\overline{2} = 22.\overline{2}\%$ Move the decimal two places to the right.

$\frac{2}{9}$ is equivalent to $0.\overline{2}$ and $22.\overline{2}\%$.

Skills Bank Practice

Write the equivalent decimal and percent for each fraction.

a. $\frac{3}{5}$ 0.6, 60%

b. $\frac{4}{10}$ 0.4, 40%

c. $\frac{3}{8}$ 0.375, 37.5%

d. $\frac{5}{11}$ $0.\overline{45}$ and $45.\overline{45}\%$

e. $\frac{7}{9}$ $0.\overline{7}, 77.\overline{7}\%$

f. $\frac{3}{4}$ 0.75, 75%

Saxon Algebra 1

Repeating Decimals and Equivalent Fractions

Skills Bank Lesson 6

A **terminating decimal,** such as 0.75, has a finite number of decimal places.

A **repeating decimal,** such as 0.333... and 0.353535..., has one or more digits after the decimal point repeating indefinitely. A repeating decimal can be written with three dots or a bar over the digit or digits that repeat, such as $0.\overline{3}$ and $0.\overline{35}$.

Example 1 Writing an Equivalent Fraction for a Terminating Decimal

Write each decimal as a fraction in simplest form.

a. 0.35

SOLUTION

$0.35 = \dfrac{35}{100}$ The decimal is in the hundredths place, so use 100 as the denominator.

$\dfrac{35}{100} = \dfrac{7}{20}$ Simplify.

b. 1.9

SOLUTION

$1.9 = 1\dfrac{9}{10}$ The decimal is in the tenths place, so use 10 as the denominator.

Example 2 Writing an Equivalent Fraction for a Repeating Decimal

Write 0.272727... as a fraction.

SOLUTION

To eliminate the repeating decimal, subtract the same repeating decimal.

$n = 0.272727...$ Let n represent the fraction equivalent to 0.272727...

$100n = 27.272727...$ Since 2 digits repeat, multiply both sides of the equation by 10^2 or 100.

$100n = 27.272727...$
$\underline{-n = -0.272727...}$ Subtract the original equation.
$99n = 27$ Combine like terms.
$n = \dfrac{27}{99} = \dfrac{3}{11}$ Divide both sides by 99 and simplify.

0.272727... is equivalent to $\dfrac{3}{11}$.

Skills Bank Practice

Write an equivalent fraction in simplest form for each decimal.

a. 0.85 $\dfrac{17}{20}$
b. 1.75 $1\dfrac{3}{4}$
c. 0.575757... $\dfrac{19}{33}$
d. $0.\overline{81}$ $\dfrac{9}{11}$
e. 0.48 $\dfrac{12}{25}$
f. 1.25 $1\dfrac{1}{4}$
g. 0.363636... $\dfrac{4}{11}$
h. $0.44\overline{4}$ $\dfrac{4}{9}$

Equivalent Fractions

Skills Bank Lesson 7

Fractions that represent the same amount or part are called **equivalent fractions**.

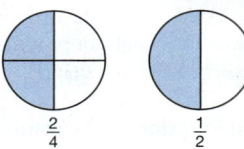

$$\frac{2}{4} \qquad \frac{1}{2}$$

Example 1 Finding Equivalent Fractions

For each fraction, write two equivalent fractions.

a. $\frac{3}{4}$ **b.** $\frac{36}{40}$

SOLUTION

Choose any whole number. Multiply the numerator and the denominator by that number.

$$\frac{3}{4} = \frac{3 \cdot 3}{4 \cdot 3} = \frac{9}{12}$$

$$\frac{3}{4} = \frac{3 \cdot 5}{4 \cdot 5} = \frac{15}{20}$$

$\frac{3}{4}$ is equivalent to $\frac{9}{12}$ and $\frac{15}{20}$.

SOLUTION

Find a number that is a factor of the numerator and the denominator. Divide both by that number.

$$\frac{36}{40} = \frac{36 \div 4}{40 \div 4} = \frac{9}{10}$$

$$\frac{36}{40} = \frac{36 \div 2}{40 \div 2} = \frac{18}{20}$$

$\frac{36}{40}$ is equivalent to $\frac{9}{10}$ and $\frac{18}{20}$.

Example 2 Writing Fractions in Simplest Form Using the GCF

Simplify.

$$\frac{24}{48}$$

SOLUTION

Find the greatest common factor (GCF) of 24 and 48. The GCF is 24.

$$\frac{24}{48} = \frac{24 \div 24}{48 \div 24} = \frac{1}{2} \qquad \text{Divide the numerator and denominator by 24.}$$

Skills Bank Practice

For each fraction, write two equivalent fractions.

a. $\frac{3}{7}$ Sample: $\frac{6}{14}$ and $\frac{15}{35}$ **b.** $\frac{1}{5}$ Sample: $\frac{5}{25}$ and $\frac{7}{35}$ **c.** $\frac{54}{72}$ Sample: $\frac{27}{36}$ and $\frac{9}{12}$ **d.** $\frac{120}{360}$ Sample: $\frac{12}{36}, \frac{1}{3}$

Simplify.

e. $\frac{14}{24}$ $\frac{7}{12}$ **f.** $\frac{30}{36}$ $\frac{5}{6}$ **g.** $\frac{75}{100}$ $\frac{3}{4}$

h. $\frac{48}{60}$ $\frac{4}{5}$ **i.** $\frac{90}{360}$ $\frac{1}{4}$

Estimation Strategies

Skills Bank Lesson 8

To estimate is to find an approximate answer. Rounding numbers is one way to estimate.

Rounding Rules	
If the digit to the right of the rounding digit is > 5, round up.	Round 35,679 to the nearest thousand. 35,679 rounds up to 36,000.
If the digit to the right of the rounding digit is < 5, round down.	Round 35,479 to the nearest thousand. 35,479 rounds down to 35,000.
If the digit to the right of the rounding digit = 5, then round up.	Round 35,579 to the nearest thousand. 35,579 rounds up to 36,000.

Compatible numbers are numbers that are close in value to the actual numbers and are easy to add, subtract, multiply, or divide. Compatible numbers can be used to estimate. An overestimation is an estimate greater than the exact answer. An underestimation is an estimate less than the exact answer.

Example 1 Estimate by Rounding

a. Sally has $23 to buy two shirts. One shirt is $9.75, and the other shirt is $10.95. Explain whether Sally should overestimate or underestimate the total cost. Then estimate the total cost and tell whether Sally has enough money to buy both shirts.

SOLUTION Sally should overestimate. If her estimate is more than the actual cost, then she has enough money to buy both shirts.

$9.75 + $10.95   To overestimate, round each number up.

$10.00 + $11.00 = $21.00

The actual cost will be less than $23.00, so Sally has enough money.

b. Alan plans to drive 575 miles to his aunt's house. He can drive 65 mi/hr. About how long will the trip take?

SOLUTION Alan should underestimate his speed.

Round 575 up to 600. Round 65 mi/hr down to 60.

600 ÷ 60 = 10   Distance divided by rate is equal to time.

It will take Alan about 10 hours to drive to his aunt's house.

Skills Bank Practice

a. Rico has $30 to buy school supplies. He wants to buy 2 packages of pens for $2.75 each, a backpack for $12.50, and 4 notebooks for $1.99 each. Tell whether Rico should overestimate or underestimate the total cost. Then estimate the total and tell whether Rico has enough money.   overestimate; $27; Rico has enough money.

b. Jordan drives 120 miles. If his car gets 32 miles per gallon of gas, about how much gas will he use?   about 4 gal

Greatest Common Factor (GCF)

Skills Bank Lesson 9

The **greatest common factor,** or **GCF,** is the largest factor two or more given numbers have in common. For example, 2 and 5 are common factors of 10 and 20, but 5 is the greatest common factor.

One way to find the GCF is to make a list of factors and choose the greatest factor that appears in each list. Another way is to divide by prime factors.

Example 1 Finding the GCF

a. Find the GCF of 24 and 60.

SOLUTION

24: 1, **2, 3, 4, 6,** 8, **12,** 24 List the factors of each number.
60: 1, **2, 3, 4,** 5, **6,** 10, **12,** 15, 20, 30, 60 Find the greatest common factor.
2, 3, 4, 6, and 12 are common factors.

The GCF of 24 and 60 is 12.

b. Find the GCF of 54 and 72.

SOLUTION

$$\begin{array}{c|cc} 2 & 54 & 72 \\ \hline 3 & 27 & 36 \\ \hline 3 & 9 & 12 \\ \hline & 3 & 4 \end{array}$$

Divide both numbers by the same prime factor.
Keep dividing until there is no prime factor that divides into both numbers without a remainder.

$2 \cdot 3 \cdot 3$ or $2 \cdot 3^2 = 18$

The GCF of 54 and 72 is 18.

Example 2 Using the GCF to Simplify Fractions

a. Write $\frac{21}{28}$ in simplest form.

SOLUTION Divide 21 and 28 by the GCF, 7.

$$\frac{21}{28} = \frac{21 \div 7}{28 \div 7} = \frac{3}{4}$$

b. Write $1\frac{9}{12}$ in simplest form.

SOLUTION Divide 9 and 12 by the GCF, 3.

$$\frac{9}{12} = \frac{9 \div 3}{12 \div 3} = \frac{3}{4}$$

$$1\frac{9}{12} = 1\frac{3}{4}$$

Skills Bank Practice

Find the GCF.

a. 72 and 60 **12**
b. 54 and 89 **1**
c. 21 and 56 **7**
d. 120 and 960 **120**
e. 3, 6, and 12 **3**
f. 7, 21, and 49 **7**
g. 4, 22, and 40 **2**
h. 20, 45, and 80 **5**

Write each fraction in simplest form.

i. $\frac{8}{12}$ **$\frac{2}{3}$**
j. $\frac{15}{25}$ **$\frac{3}{5}$**
k. $\frac{16}{64}$ **$\frac{1}{4}$**
l. $\frac{110}{150}$ **$\frac{11}{15}$**
m. $\frac{52}{65}$ **$\frac{4}{5}$**

Least Common Multiple (LCM) and Least Common Denominator (LCD)

Skills Bank Lesson 10

The **least common multiple,** or **LCM,** is the smallest whole number, other than zero, that is a multiple of two or more given numbers.

Example 1 Finding the LCM

a. Find the LCM of 6 and 10.

SOLUTION

List the multiples of each number.

Multiples of 6: 6, 12, 18, 24, **30**, 36, 42, 48, 54, **60**, …

Multiples of 10: 10, 20, **30**, 40, 50, **60**, …

30 and 60 are common multiples.   Find the common multiples that are in both lists.

The LCM of 6 and 10 is 30.   Find the least common multiple.

b. Find the LCM of 12 and 18.

SOLUTION

2	12	18	Divide both numbers by the same prime factor.
3	6	9	Keep dividing until there is no prime factor that divides into both
	2	3	numbers without a remainder.

$2 \cdot 3 \cdot 2 \cdot 3$ or $2^2 \cdot 3^2 = 36$. The LCM of 12 and 18 is 36.

The **least common denominator,** or **LCD,** is the least common multiple of two or more denominators.

Example 2 Finding the LCD and Writing Equivalent Fractions

Find the LCD of $\frac{3}{8}$ and $\frac{5}{12}$. Use the LCD to write equivalent fractions.

SOLUTION The LCM of 8 and 12 is 24, so 24 is the LCD.

$\frac{3}{8} = \frac{3 \cdot 3}{8 \cdot 3} = \frac{9}{24}$ Write an equivalent fraction using a denominator of 24.

$\frac{5}{12} = \frac{5 \cdot 2}{12 \cdot 2} = \frac{10}{24}$ Write an equivalent fraction using a denominator of 24.

$\frac{3}{8}$ and $\frac{5}{12}$ are equivalent to $\frac{9}{24}$ and $\frac{10}{24}$.

Skills Bank Practice

Find the LCM.

a. 9 and 15   45   **b.** 20 and 25   100   **c.** 24 and 48   48   **d.** 14 and 21   42

e. 25, 50, and 100   100   **f.** 8, 16, and 48   48   **g.** 2, 3, and 20   60

h. Use the LCD to write equivalent fractions for $\frac{1}{2}$ and $\frac{7}{15}$. $\frac{15}{30}$ and $\frac{14}{30}$

Mental Math

Skills Bank Lesson 11

Mental math means to find an exact answer quickly in your head. Mental math strategies use number properties.

Example 1 Using Properties to Add or Multiply Whole Numbers

a. Find the sum of $32 + 3 + 48 + 57$.

SOLUTION

$32 + 3 + 48 + 57$	Look for sums that are multiples of 10.
$= 3 + 57 + 32 + 48$	Use the Commutative Property.
$= (3 + 57) + (32 + 48)$	Use the Associative Property.
$= 60 + 80$	Add.
$= 140$	

b. Find the product of $2 \cdot 44 \cdot 5$.

SOLUTION

$2 \cdot 44 \cdot 5$	Look for products that are multiples of 10.
$= 2 \cdot 5 \cdot 44$	Use the Commutative Property.
$= (2 \cdot 5) \cdot 44$	Use the Associative Property.
$= 10 \cdot 44$	Multiply.
$= 440$	

c. Find the product of $8 \cdot 47$.

SOLUTION

$8 \cdot 47$	
$8 \cdot 47 = 8 \cdot (40 + 7)$	"Break apart" 47 into $40 + 7$.
$= (8 \cdot 40) + (8 \cdot 7)$	Use the Distributive Property.
$= 320 + 56$	Multiply.
$= 376$	Add.

Skills Bank Practice

Find each sum or product.

a. $24 + 15 + 16 + 15$ 70
b. $6 \cdot 12 \cdot 5$ 360
c. $58 \cdot 4$ 232
d. $6 + 31 + 34 + 9$ 80
e. $34 \cdot 7$ 238
f. $4 \cdot 62 \cdot 25$ 6200
g. $8 + 67 + 12 + 3$ 90
h. $33 \cdot 9$ 297

Prime and Composite Numbers and Prime Factorization

Skills Bank Lesson 12

A **prime number** is a number that has exactly two factors, 1 and itself. For example, 5 is a prime number because its only factors are 1 and 5.

A **composite number** has more than two factors. For example, 8 is a composite number because its factors are 1, 2, 4, and 8.

The number 1 is neither prime nor composite.

Example 1   Determining Whether a Number is Prime or Composite

Determine whether each number is prime or composite.

a. 18

SOLUTION

1, 2, 3, 6, 9, 18   List the factors.

18 is a composite number.

b. 13

SOLUTION

1, 13   List the factors.

13 is a prime number.

Every composite number can be written as the product of two or more prime numbers. This product is called the **prime factorization** of a number.

Example 2   Using a Factor Tree to Find the Prime Factorization

36

SOLUTION

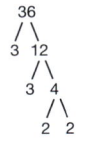

Choose any two factors of 36. Continue to factor until each branch ends in a prime number.

The prime factorization of 36 is $2 \cdot 2 \cdot 3 \cdot 3$ or $2^2 \cdot 3^2$.

Skills Bank Practice

Determine whether each number is prime or composite.

a. 17   prime
b. 15   composite
c. 32   composite
d. 29   prime

Find the prime factorization of each number.

e. 72 $2 \cdot 2 \cdot 2 \cdot 3 \cdot 3$ or $2^3 \cdot 3^2$
f. 28 $2 \cdot 2 \cdot 7$ or $2^2 \cdot 7$
g. 34 $2 \cdot 17$
h. 24 $2 \cdot 2 \cdot 2 \cdot 3$ or $2^3 \cdot 3$
i. 76 $2 \cdot 2 \cdot 19$ or $2^2 \cdot 19$
j. 32 $2 \cdot 2 \cdot 2 \cdot 2 \cdot 2$ or 2^5
k. 45 $3 \cdot 3 \cdot 5$ or $3^2 \cdot 5$
l. 52 $2 \cdot 2 \cdot 13$ or $2^2 \cdot 13$

Classify Angles and Triangles

Skills Bank Lesson 13

You can classify an angle by its measure.

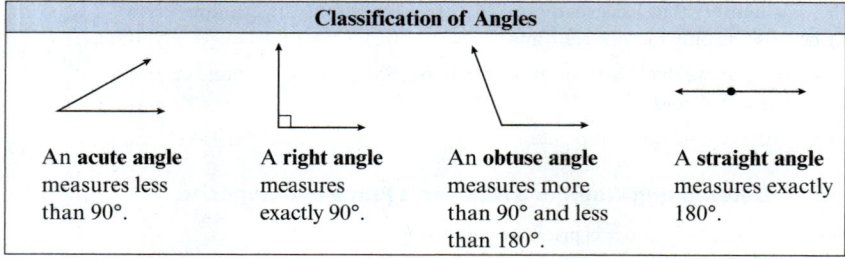

Classification of Angles
An **acute angle** measures less than 90°. A **right angle** measures exactly 90°. An **obtuse angle** measures more than 90° and less than 180°. A **straight angle** measures exactly 180°.

You can classify a triangle by its angle measures.

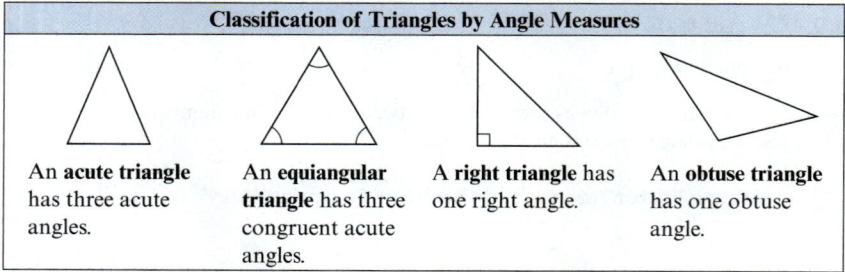

An **acute triangle** has three acute angles. An **equiangular triangle** has three congruent acute angles. A **right triangle** has one right angle. An **obtuse triangle** has one obtuse angle.

You can also classify a triangle by its side lengths.

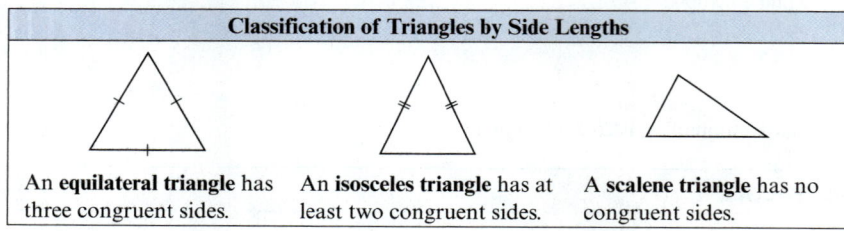

An **equilateral triangle** has three congruent sides. An **isosceles triangle** has at least two congruent sides. A **scalene triangle** has no congruent sides.

Example 1 Classifying Angles

Classify each angle according to its measure.

a.

SOLUTION

This is a straight angle, because the figure is a line and the angle measures 180°.

b.

SOLUTION

This is an obtuse angle, because the angle measure is greater than 90° but less than 180°.

c.

SOLUTION

This is an acute angle because the angle measure is less than 90°.

d.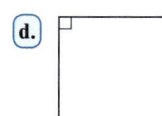

SOLUTION

This is a right angle because the angle measure is equal to 90°.

Example 2 Classifying Triangles

Classify each triangle according to its angle measures and side lengths.

a.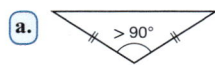

SOLUTION

The figure has one obtuse angle and at least 2 congruent sides. So, this is an obtuse isosceles triangle.

b.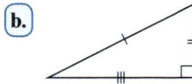

SOLUTION

The figure has one right angle and no congruent sides. So, this is a right scalene triangle.

Skills Bank Practice

Classify each angle according to its measure.

a.

right angle

b.

obtuse angle

c.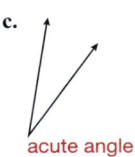

acute angle

Classify each triangle according to its angle measures and side lengths.

d.

acute scalene

e.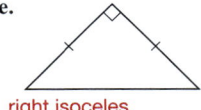

right isoceles

f.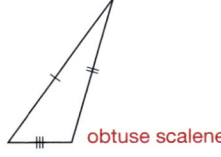

obtuse scalene

Classify Quadrilaterals

Skills Bank Lesson 14

A **quadrilateral** is a two-dimensional figure with four sides and four angles. The table shows five special quadrilaterals and their properties.

Parallelogram Opposite sides are parallel and congruent. Opposite angles are congruent.	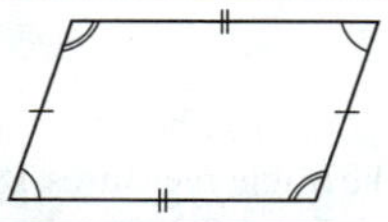
Rectangle Parallelogram with four right angles	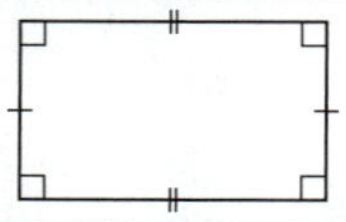
Rhombus Parallelogram with four congruent sides	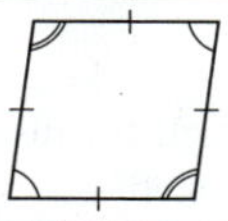
Square Rectangle with four congruent sides	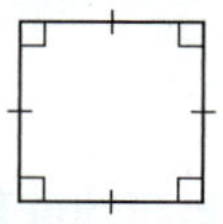
Trapezoid Quadrilateral with exactly two parallel sides May have two right angles	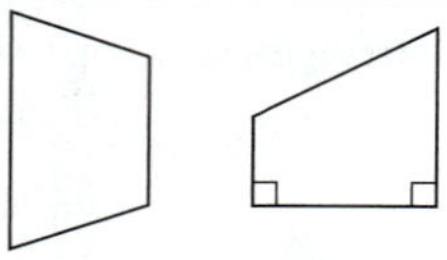

Example 1 Classifying Quadrilaterals

a. Identify which statement is always true.

- A trapezoid is also a parallelogram.
- A square is also a rhombus.
- A parallelogram is also a rectangle.
- A rectangle is also a square.

SOLUTION

A square is also a rhombus is true, because a square is a parallelogram with four congruent sides.

b. Identify which statement is not always true.

- A quadrilateral has 4 sides.
- A quadrilateral has 4 angles.
- A quadrilateral has straight sides.
- A quadrilateral has right angles.

SOLUTION

A quadrilateral does not always have right angles.

Skills Bank Practice

Complete each statement.

a. A square is also a __rectangle or rhombus__   b. A rhombus is sometimes a __square__.

c. All trapezoids are also __quadrilaterals__.

d. A __quadrilateral__ is any two-dimensional figure with four straight sides and four angles.

Complementary and Supplementary Angles

Skills Bank Lesson 15

Two angles with measures that have a sum of 90° are **complementary angles**.
Two angles with measures that have a sum of 180° are **supplementary angles**.

Example 1 Identifying Complementary and Supplementary Angles

a. Are $\angle A$ and $\angle B$ complementary or supplementary angles?

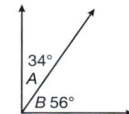

SOLUTION

$m\angle A + m\angle B = 34° + 56° = 90°$

$\angle A$ and $\angle B$ are complementary.

b. Are $\angle K$ and $\angle L$ complementary or supplementary angles?

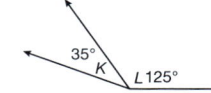

SOLUTION

$m\angle K + m\angle L = 35° + 125° = 160°$

$\angle K$ and $\angle L$ are neither complementary nor supplementary.

Example 2 Finding Missing Angle Measures

a. $\angle M$ and $\angle N$ are supplementary angles. Find $m\angle N$.

SOLUTION

$38° + m\angle N = 180°$

$m\angle N = 180° - 38°$

$m\angle N = 142°$

b. $\angle E$ and $\angle F$ are complementary angles. Find $m\angle F$.

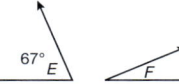

SOLUTION

$67° + m\angle F = 90°$

$m\angle F = 90° - 67°$

$m\angle F = 23°$

Skills Bank Practice

Classify each pair of angles as complementary or supplementary. Then find the missing angle measure.

a. complementary, 24°

66°, x

b. supplementary, 152°

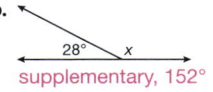

28°, x

c. supplementary, 46°

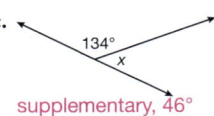

134°, x

d. $\angle D$ and $\angle E$ are complementary angles. If the measure of $\angle D$ is 50°, what is the measure of $\angle E$?   40°

e. $\angle W$ and $\angle T$ are supplementary angles. If the measure of $\angle W$ is 50°, what is the measure of $\angle T$?   130°

Congruence

Skills Bank Lesson 16

Congruent segments are segments that have the same length.

Congruent angles are angles that have the same measure.

Figures are congruent if all of their corresponding angles and sides are congruent.

Hint
The symbol for congruent is ≅.

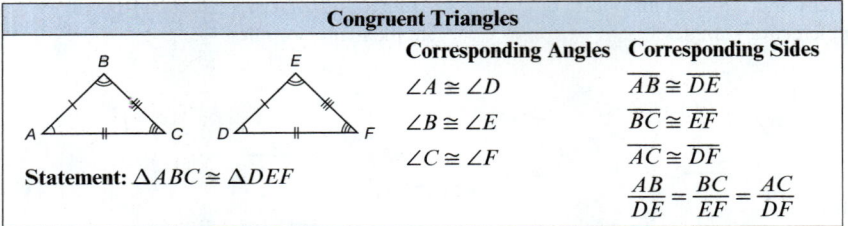

Congruent Triangles

Corresponding Angles	Corresponding Sides
∠A ≅ ∠D	$\overline{AB} \cong \overline{DE}$
∠B ≅ ∠E	$\overline{BC} \cong \overline{EF}$
∠C ≅ ∠F	$\overline{AC} \cong \overline{DF}$
	$\frac{AB}{DE} = \frac{BC}{EF} = \frac{AC}{DF}$

Statement: △ABC ≅ △DEF

In a congruence statement, the order of the letters shows which angles and sides are congruent.

Example 1 Identifying the Corresponding Angles and Sides

Find the congruent angles and sides. Then write a congruence statement.

SOLUTION

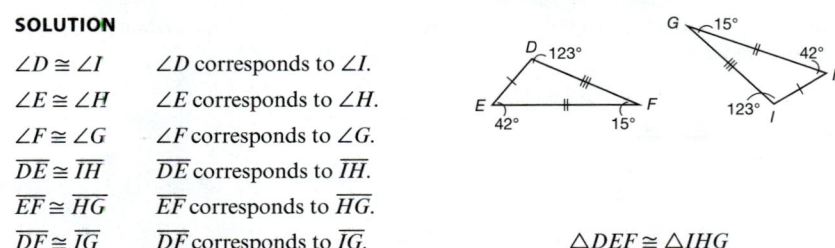

∠D ≅ ∠I   ∠D corresponds to ∠I.
∠E ≅ ∠H   ∠E corresponds to ∠H.
∠F ≅ ∠G   ∠F corresponds to ∠G.
$\overline{DE} \cong \overline{IH}$ $\overline{DE}$ corresponds to $\overline{IH}$.
$\overline{EF} \cong \overline{HG}$ $\overline{EF}$ corresponds to $\overline{HG}$.
$\overline{DF} \cong \overline{IG}$ $\overline{DF}$ corresponds to $\overline{IG}$.

△DEF ≅ △IHG

Skills Bank Practice

Write a congruence statement for each pair of figures.

a.

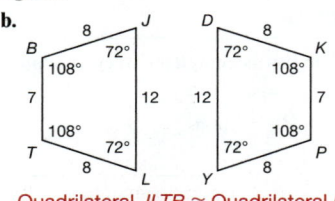

△LKJ ≅ △PQT

b.

Quadrilateral JLTB ≅ Quadrilateral DYPK

862 *Saxon Algebra 1*

Estimate the Perimeter and Area of Figures

Skills Bank Lesson 17

Perimeter is the distance around a figure. The perimeter of a polygon is the sum of its side lengths. The **area** of a figure is the amount of surface it covers.

Perimeter and Circumference Formulas	Area Formulas
Rectangle $P = 2l + 2w$ or $P = 2(l + w)$	Rectangle $A = lw$
Circle $C = 2\pi r$ or $C = \pi d$	Circle $A = \pi r^2$

Example 1 Estimating Perimeter

a. Estimate the perimeter of the figure.

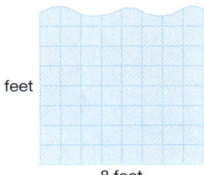

8 feet

8 feet

b. Estimate the perimeter of the trapezoid.

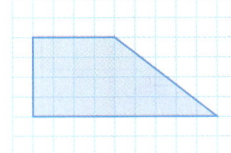

SOLUTION

Estimate the length of the top, sides, and bottom of the figure.

right and left: ≈ 8 feet

bottom: 8 feet

top: ≈ 8 feet

$P \approx 4(8)$

The perimeter is about 32 feet.

SOLUTION

Find the length of the top, side, and bottom of the trapezoid.

top: 4 units

left: 4 units

bottom: 9 units

Estimate the length of the diagonal line.

diagonal line: ≈ 5 units

$P \approx 4 + 4 + 9 + 5 \approx 22$

The perimeter is about 22 units.

Example 2 Estimating Area

Estimate the area of the circle.

SOLUTION

Estimate the area by counting the squares.

12 full squares   4 almost full squares

8 quarter full squares: ≈ 2 8 corners: ≈ 1

The area of the circle is about 19 units².

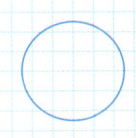

Skills Bank Practice

a. Estimate the perimeter of the figure. $P \approx 22$ units
b. Estimate the area of the figure. $A \approx 23$ units²

Nets

Skills Bank Lesson 18

A **net** is a two-dimensional representation of a solid that can be folded to form a three-dimensional figure.

A **polygon** is a closed plane figure formed by three or more line segments.

Example 1 **Identifying a Net of a Three-Dimensional Figure**

Draw the net that represents the pizza box.

SOLUTION

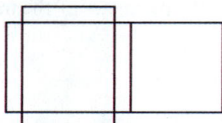

Example 2 **Drawing a Three-Dimensional Figure from a Net**

Draw the three-dimensional figure that the net represents.

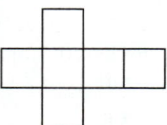

SOLUTION

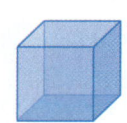

Skills Bank Practice

a. Draw the net that represents the can.

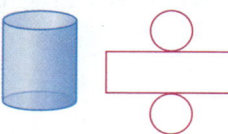

b. Draw the three-dimensional figure that the net represents.

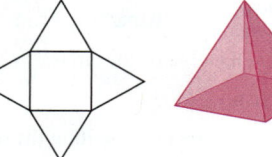

Parts of a Circle

Skills Bank Lesson 19

A **circle** is the set of points in a plane that are a fixed distance from a given point, the center.

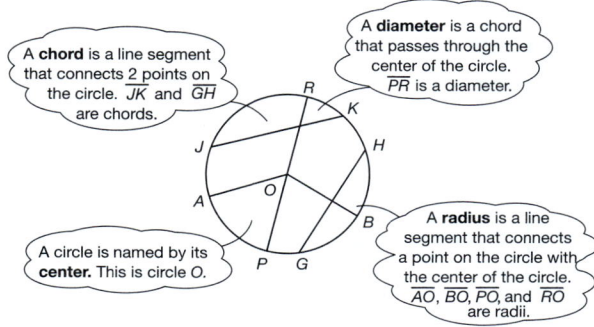

A **chord** is a line segment that connects 2 points on the circle. $\overline{JK}$ and $\overline{GH}$ are chords.

A **diameter** is a chord that passes through the center of the circle. $\overline{PR}$ is a diameter.

A circle is named by its **center**. This is circle O.

A **radius** is a line segment that connects a point on the circle with the center of the circle. $\overline{AO}$, $\overline{BO}$, $\overline{PO}$, and $\overline{RO}$ are radii.

Example 1 Naming Parts of a Circle

Name the center, radii, diameters, and chords.

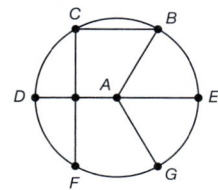

SOLUTION

Center A
Radii $\overline{AB}$, $\overline{AD}$, $\overline{AE}$, $\overline{AG}$ The plural of radius is radii.
Diameters $\overline{DE}$
Chords $\overline{CF}$, $\overline{CB}$, $\overline{DE}$ A diameter is also a chord.

Skills Bank Practice

Name the center, radii, diameters, and chords of each circle.

a. 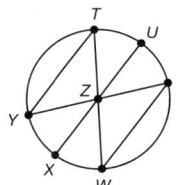   **center Z, radii $\overline{ZY}$, $\overline{ZT}$, $\overline{ZU}$, $\overline{ZV}$, $\overline{ZW}$, $\overline{ZX}$, diameters $\overline{TW}$, $\overline{YV}$, $\overline{XU}$, chords $\overline{TW}$, $\overline{YV}$, $\overline{XU}$, $\overline{YT}$, $\overline{WV}$**

b. 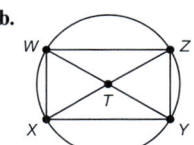   **center T, radii $\overline{WT}$, $\overline{XT}$, $\overline{YT}$, $\overline{ZT}$, diameters $\overline{WY}$, $\overline{XZ}$, chords $\overline{WX}$, $\overline{WY}$, $\overline{WZ}$, $\overline{XY}$, $\overline{XZ}$, $\overline{YZ}$**

Perspective Drawing

Skills Bank Lesson 20

You can see up to three sides of a figure when drawing a three-dimensional object. This means you have to visualize how a figure looks from other angles. Orthogonal views show how a figure looks from different perspectives. For figures constructed with cubes, the orthogonal views will be groups of squares.

Example 1 Drawing a Figure from Different Perspectives

Draw the front, top, and side views of the figure.

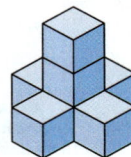

SOLUTION

From the front and all side views, there appears to be 3 stacked cubes, with 2 cubes on each side. The top view shows that 4 cubes are on the sides of the bottom cube.

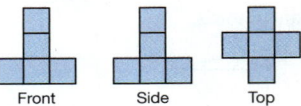

Front   Side   Top

Skills Bank Practice

a. Draw the front, top, and side views of the figure.

  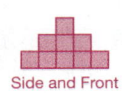

Top   Side and Front

Surface Area of Prisms and Pyramids

Skills Bank Lesson 21

The **surface area**, S, is the total area of the two-dimensional surfaces that make up the figure.

Formulas for Surface Area of Prisms and Pyramids		
Prism	$S = 2B + Ph$	B: area of base P: perimeter of base h: height
Pyramid	$S = B + \frac{1}{2}Pl$	B: area of base P: perimeter of base l: slant height

Example 1 Finding the Surface Area of Prisms and Pyramids

Find the surface area of each figure.

a.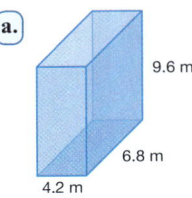
9.6 m, 6.8 m, 4.2 m

b.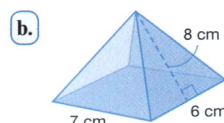
8 cm, 7 cm, 6 cm

SOLUTION

$S = 2B + Ph$
$= 2(4.2 \cdot 6.8) + (22) \cdot (9.6)$
$= 2(28.56) + 211.2$
$= 57.12 + 211.2$
$= 268.32 \text{ m}^2$

SOLUTION

$S = B + \frac{1}{2}Pl$
$= (7 \cdot 6) + \frac{1}{2}(26)(8)$
$= 42 + 104$
$= 146 \text{ cm}^2$

Skills Bank Practice

Find the surface area of each figure.

a. 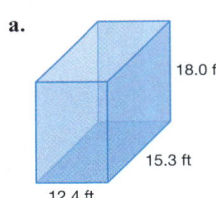 1376.64 ft²
18.0 ft, 15.3 ft, 12.4 ft

b. 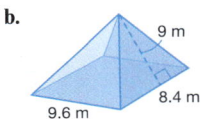 242.64 m²
9 m, 8.4 m, 9.6 m

Skills Bank 867

Tessellations

Skills Bank Lesson 22

A tessellation is a pattern of plane figures that completely covers a plane with no gaps or overlays.

Example 1 Creating Tessellations

Determine whether each figure can be used to create a tessellation.

 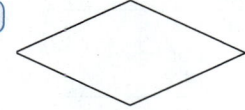   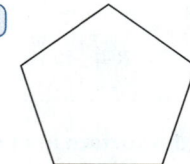

SOLUTION

The rhombus can create a tessellation. There are no gaps or overlays.

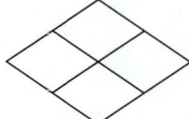

SOLUTION

A pentagon cannot create a tessellation. There will be gaps and overlays.

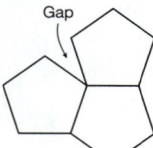

Skills Bank Practice

Determine whether each figure can be used to create a tessellation. If not, explain why not.

a. (circle) — No you cannot create a tessellation because there will be gaps.

b. (hexagon) — Yes, you can create a tessellation.

c. (octagon) — No, you cannot create a tessellation because there will be overlap.

868 *Saxon Algebra 1*

Three-Dimensional Figures

Skills Bank Lesson 23

A **polyhedron** is a three-dimensional figure that is made up of polygons which are called **faces**. A polyhedron has flat faces and straight edges. The faces intersect at **edges**. A **vertex** is any point in which three or more edges intersect.

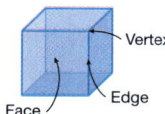

Some three dimensional figures are not polyhedra because they are not made up of polygons.

Example 1 Determining Whether a Three-Dimensional Shape Is a Polyhedron

Determine whether the three-dimensional shape is a polyhedron. If yes, tell how many faces, edges, and vertices the shape has.

SOLUTION

This shape is not a polyhedron.

SOLUTION

This shape is a polyhedron. There are 6 faces, 12 edges, and 8 vertices.

Skills Bank Practice

Determine whether the three-dimensional shape is a polyhedron. If yes, tell how many faces, edges, and vertices the shape has.

a. 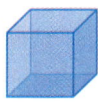 Yes, this shape is a polyhedron. There are 6 faces, 12 edges, and 8 vertices.

b.  No, this shape is not a polyhedron.

Transformations in the Coordinate Plane

Skills Bank Lesson 24

A **transformation** is a change in the size or position of a figure. If you transform the preimage, or original figure ABC, then the transformed figure, or image, is named $A'B'C'$. Transformations include translations or slides, reflections or flips, and rotations or turns. Preimages and images are congruent for all transformations.

Example 1 Finding Transformations

a. Reflect $\triangle ABC$ across the y-axis.

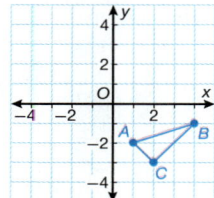

b. Translate $\triangle ABC$ 3 units left and 4 units down.

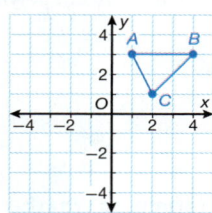

SOLUTION

The y-axis is a line of symmetry.

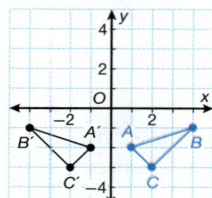

SOLUTION

Move each vertex 3 units left and 4 units down.

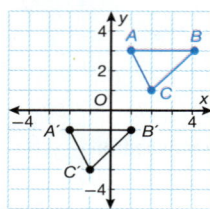

Skills Bank Practice

a. Reflect $\triangle ABC$ across the y-axis.

b. Give the coordinates for the points that describe the translation 5 units left.

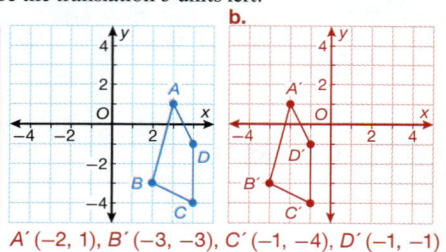

$A'(-2, 1), B'(-3, -3), C'(-1, -4), D'(-1, -1)$

870 *Saxon Algebra 1*

Vertical Angles

Skills Bank Lesson 25

When two lines intersect, the nonadjacent angles are called **vertical angles**. Vertical angles always have the same measure, so they are congruent angles.

Example 1 Finding the Measure of Vertical Angles

Find m$\angle WVY$, m$\angle YVZ$, and m$\angle ZVX$, where m$\angle XVW = 70°$.

a.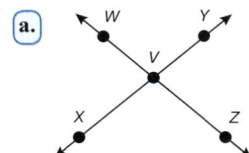

SOLUTION

m$\angle XVW$ + m$\angle WVY = 180°$ $\quad$ $\angle XVW$ and $\angle WVY$ are supplementary.

$70°$ + m$\angle WVY = 180°$ $\quad$ Substitute.

m$\angle WVY = 110°$

m$\angle YVZ$ = m$\angle XVW$ $\quad$ Vertical angles have the same measure.

m$\angle YVZ = 70°$

m$\angle ZVX$ = m$\angle WVY$ $\quad$ Vertical angles have the same measure.

m$\angle ZVX = 110°$

Skills Bank Practice

a. Name the two pairs of vertical angles.

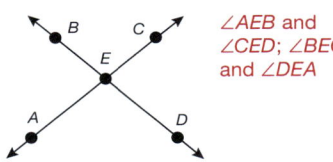

$\angle AEB$ and $\angle CED$; $\angle BEC$ and $\angle DEA$

b. Find m$\angle ABQ$, m$\angle ABC$, and m$\angle CBR$.

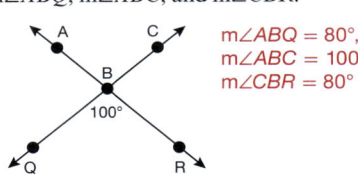

m$\angle ABQ = 80°$,
m$\angle ABC = 100°$,
m$\angle CBR = 80°$

c. Find m$\angle EFG$, m$\angle GFH$, and m$\angle HFI$, where m$\angle EFI = 20°$.

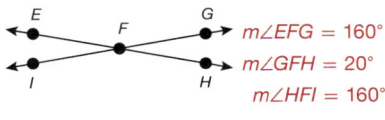

m$\angle EFG = 160°$
m$\angle GFH = 20°$
m$\angle HFI = 160°$

d. Find m$\angle BAC$, m$\angle DAE$, and m$\angle EAB$, where m$\angle CAD = 140°$.

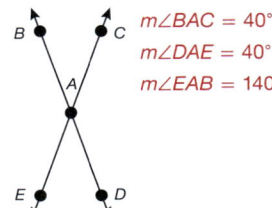

m$\angle BAC = 40°$
m$\angle DAE = 40°$
m$\angle EAB = 140°$

Volume of Prisms and Cylinders

Skills Bank Lesson 26

The **volume** is the amount of space a solid occupies. Volume is measured in cubic units. To estimate volume, imagine unit cubes filling a figure.

Formulas for the Volume of Prisms and Cylinders		
Prism	$V = Bh$	B: area of base h: height of prism
Cylinder	$V = \pi r^2 h$	r: radius h: height

Example 1 Finding the Volume of Prisms and Cylinders

Find the volume of each figure. Use 3.14 for π. Round to the nearest hundredth.

a.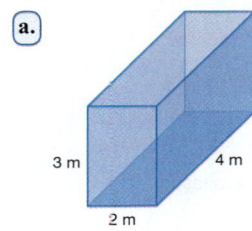

b.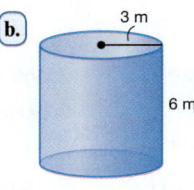

SOLUTION

$V = Bh$
$= (4 \cdot 2) \cdot 3$
$= 8 \cdot 3$
$= 24 \text{ m}^3$

SOLUTION

$V = \pi r^2 h$
$\approx 3.14 \cdot (3^2) \cdot 6$
$= 3.14 \cdot (9) \cdot 6$
$= 169.56 \text{ m}^3$

Skills Bank Practice

Find the volume of each figure. Use 3.14 for π. Round to the nearest hundredth.

a. 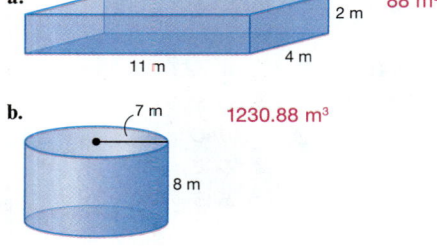   88 m³

b.   1230.88 m³

Saxon Algebra 1

Making Bar and Line Graphs

Skills Bank Lesson 27

In a bar graph, bars are used to represent and compare data. The bars can be horizontal or vertical.

In a line graph, points that represent data values are connected using segments. Line graphs often show a change in data over time.

Example 1 Making a Bar or Line Graph

a. Use the data to make a bar graph.

Favorite Activities

Activity	Golf	Movie	Amusement Park
Number of People	35	45	20

SOLUTION

- Find the appropriate scale.
- Use the data to determine the length of the bars.
- Title the graph and label the axes.

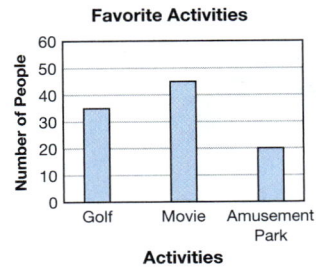

b. Use the data to make a line graph.

U.S. Households with a Computer

Year	1984	1989	1993	1997
Percent	8%	15%	22%	36%

SOLUTION

- Find the appropriate scale.
- Make a point for each data value. Connect the points with line segments.
- Title the graph and label the axes.

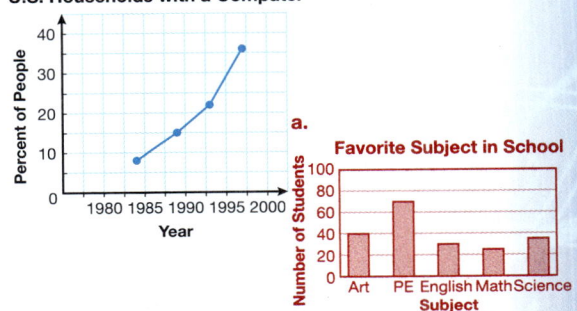

Skills Bank Practice

a. Use the data to make a bar graph.

Favorite Subject in School

Subject	Art	PE	English	Math	Science
Number of Students	40	70	30	25	35

b. Use the data to make a line graph.

Average High Temperature in Palm Beach, Florida

Month	March	April	May	June
Temperature	80	83	85	88

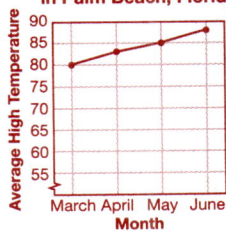

Skills Bank 873

Making Circle Graphs

Skills Bank Lesson 28

A **circle graph** compares part of the data set to the whole set of data.

In a circle graph, data is displayed as sections of a circle. Each section has an angle at the center. The total measure of the angles at the center of the circle is 360°. The entire circle represents all of the data.

Example 1 Making a Circle Graph

Use the data in the table to make a circle graph.

SOLUTION

Step 1: Find the angle measures by multiplying each percent by 360°.

Cheese: 40% · 360° = 0.40 · 360° = 144°

Supreme: 10% · 360° = 0.10 · 360° = 36°

Pepperoni: 50% · 360° = 0.50 · 360° = 180°

Favorite Pizza Toppings

Toppings	Students in Class
Cheese	40%
Supreme	10%
Pepperoni	50%

Step 2: Use a compass to draw a circle.

Step 3: Draw a circle and radius with a compass and straightedge. Then use a protractor to draw the first angle, 144°. Then draw the second and third angles, 36° and 180°.

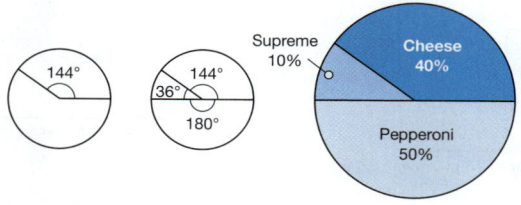

Favorite Pizza Toppings

Step 4: Label the graph and give it a title.

Skills Bank Practice

a. In a survey, people were asked what kind of pet they owned. The table shows the results of the survey. Use the table to make a circle graph.

Pet Owners	
Dog	36%
Cat	25%
Fish	15%
No pets	24%

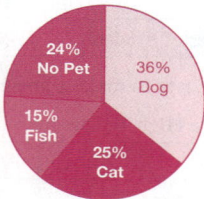

Pet Owners

Making Line Plots

Skills Bank Lesson 29

How often a data value occurs in a data set is called its frequency. A line plot is a graph made up of a number line and columns of x's. Other markers can be used to show a frequency. A cluster is a group of data values that are grouped together.

Example 1 Making a Line Plot

 In a survey, 28 people waiting at a bus stop were asked their age. Their ages are shown in the frequency table below. Make a line plot. Identify any gaps or clusters in the data set.

Age	Frequency	Age	Frequency
15	3	16	2
17	0	18	0
19	5	20	6
21	4	22	1
23	2	24	4
25	1	26	0
27	0	28	0

SOLUTION

Draw a number line that includes the minimum and maximum age. Use an x to represent each person. Title the graph and the axis.

There is a gap between 16 and 19.

There is a cluster between 19 and 25.

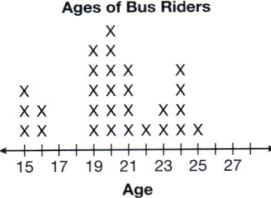

Skills Bank Practice

a. Make a line plot of the lowest temperatures for the last two weeks.

55°F, 60°F, 65°F, 65°F, 65°F, 60°F, 60°F, 70°F, 65°F, 65°F, 70°F, 65°F, 65°F, 60°F

b. What are the minimum and maximum temperatures that were recorded? 55°F and 70°F

c. What was the most common temperature? 65°F

a. Lowest Temperature Each Day For Two Weeks

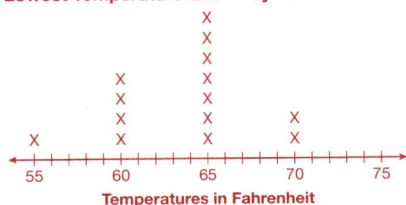

Skills Bank 875

Venn Diagrams

Skills Bank Lesson 30

A **Venn diagram** shows the relationship between sets.

Example 1 Making a Venn Diagram

167 people taste tested two new brands of cereal. 7 people did not like either brand, 100 people liked Brand A, and 110 people liked Brand B. How many people only liked Brand A? Make a Venn diagram to represent the data.

SOLUTION

Draw and label two intersecting circles to show the set of people that liked Brand A and Brand B.

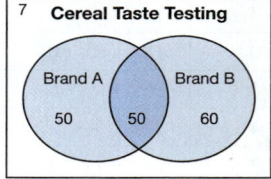

There must be people that liked both brands of cereal, because $100 + 110 + 7 = 217$, and only 167 people taste tested the cereal.

The overlap is $217 - 167 = 50$.

This means 50 people were counted twice because 50 people liked both Brand A and Brand B.

Out of 100 people who liked Brand A, 50 of them also liked Brand B. So, 50 people liked only Brand A.

Skills Bank Practice

Out of a group of 133 people, 55 people carpool to work, 67 take the bus to work, and 30 do not carpool or take the bus to work. Make a Venn diagram. Then use the Venn diagram to find how many people use both a carpool and a bus.   **19 people use both a carpool and a bus.**

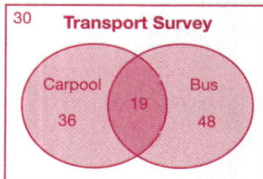

Problem-Solving Strategies

Skills Bank Lesson 31

Sometimes it helps to **draw a diagram** when solving problems.

Example 1 Drawing a Diagram to Solve a Problem

A landscaper is designing a garden. It will have a rectangular flower border around a rectangular fountain. The flower border will be a 3-foot wide border. The water fountain is 7 feet long and 5 feet wide. What is the area of the border?

Understand

You need to find the area of the flower border surrounding the water fountain.

- The flower border and the fountain are both rectangles.
- Fountain: 7 ft × 5 ft
- Border: 3 ft wide

Plan

Draw and label a diagram of the water fountain with the surrounding border. Subtract the area of the fountain from the entire area of the garden.

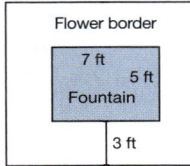

Solve

Find the length and width of the garden.
length: 3 ft + 7 ft + 3 ft = 13 ft
width: 3 ft + 5 ft + 3 ft = 11 ft

Find the area of the garden.   Find the area of the fountain.
$A = lw$ 13 · 11 = 143 ft² $A = lw$ 7 · 5 = 35 ft²

The area of the garden is 143 ft².   The area of the fountain is 35 ft².

Find the area of the flower border.

Subtract area of fountain from the area of the garden.

$$143 \text{ ft}^2 - 35 \text{ ft}^2 = 108 \text{ ft}^2$$

Check

The area of the fountain and the border is equal to the area of the entire garden.

$$108 \text{ ft}^2 + 35 \text{ ft}^2 = 143 \text{ ft}^2$$

Skills Bank Practice

a. Sajio is building a new rectangular deck around his rectangular pool. The pool is 40 feet long and 30 feet wide. The deck is 6 feet wide. What is the area of the deck? **984 ft²**

When a problem has a sequence of numbers or objects, **find a pattern** to solve the problem.

Example 2 Finding a Pattern to Solve a Problem

Brian created the following sequence of small squares. How many small squares are in the 7th position?

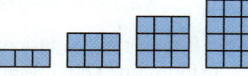

Understand

The diagram shows the number of small squares in the first, second, third, and fourth position. Find the number of boxes in the 7th position.

Plan

Count the small squares in the first 4 positions. Use the information to determine a pattern.

Solve

Position	1	2	3	4	5	6	7
Number of small squares	3	6	9	12	?	?	?

Look for a pattern in the table. Multiply the position by the number of small squares in the first row.

A possible pattern is to multiply by 3.

$$1 \cdot 3 = 3, 2 \cdot 3 = 6, 3 \cdot 3 = 9, 4 \cdot 3 = 12, \ldots \text{ and } 7 \cdot 3 = 21$$

There will be 21 boxes in the 7th position.

Check

Look for another pattern. With each position the number of small squares increases by 3.

$$0 + 3 = 3, 3 + 3 = 6, 6 + 3 = 9, 9 + 3 = 12, 12 + 3 = 15, 15 + 3 = 18, 18 + 3 = 21$$

Skills Bank Practice

The table shows part of a shuttle schedule.

Shuttle stop	1	2	3	4	5	6
Time	5:45 a.m.	6:10 a.m.	6:35 a.m.	?	?	?

Use the table to answer each question.

a. What time should the shuttle make its 6th stop?   7:50 a.m.

b. What time should the shuttle make its 10th stop?   9:30 a.m.

The **guess-and-check** method can be used when you cannot think of another way to solve a problem or not enough information has been given to simplify the solution process.

Example 3 Using Guess and Check to Solve a Problem

The Drama Team made $534 for their fall festival. They sold 130 tickets. The tickets were $5 for adults and $3 for children. How many of each type of ticket were sold?

Understand

Find the number of each type of ticket sold.

- Cost of adult ticket: $5
- Cost of child ticket: $3
- Number of tickets sold: 130
- Total sales: $534

Plan

Make a first guess for each type of ticket. The sum of tickets must be 130 and the total cost must be exactly $534. Multiply each guess by the cost of each ticket. Compare the total to $534. Adjust your guess until you find the solution.

Solve

	Adult Ticket	Child Ticket	Total Tickets	Total Cost
1st guess	65	65	130	65($5) + 65($3) = $520
2nd guess	55	75	130	55($5) + 75($3) = $500
3rd guess	72	58	130	72($5) + 58($3) = $534

72 adult tickets and 58 child tickets were sold.

Check

The total spent was $534, and the total number of tickets sold was 130. So, the solution is correct.

Skills Bank Practice

a. A local bus tour sold 65 tickets. Senior citizen tickets cost $10 and regular tickets cost $15. The total sales were $855. How many of each type of ticket were sold? *24 senior citizen tickets and 41 regular-priced tickets were sold.*

You can **make a table** to solve problems. A table can help you recognize patterns or relationships.

Example 4 Making a Table to Solve a Problem

Sam opened a bank account with $450. At the end of each year, the account earns 5% interest on the balance. If Sam does not deposit or withdraw any money, how much money will he have at the end of 10 years?

Understand

Find the total amount of money Sam will have at the end of 10 years.
- The starting balance is $450.
- Add 5% interest to the balance at the end of every year.

Plan

Make a table with the starting balance and the total amount of interest added at the end of the 1st year. Continue building the table until you have the balance at the end of the 10th year.

Solve

Sam will have $733.02 at the end of 10 years.

Check

The interest each year is increasing. The balance each year is increasing.

Suppose the balance was constant over 10 years.

$22.50 \cdot 10 = $225.

$450 + $225 = $675.

Sam's balance of $733.02 is close to $675, so the answer is reasonable.

End of Year	Add 5% of the balance	Balance
1	$450 + $22.50	$472.50
2	$472.50 + $23.63	$496.13
3	$496.13 + $24.81	$520.94
4	$520.94 + $26.05	$546.99
5	$546.99 + $27.35	$574.34
6	$574.34 + $28.72	$603.06
7	$603.06 + $30.15	$633.21
8	$633.21 + $31.66	$664.87
9	$664.87 + $33.24	$698.11
10	$698.11 + $34.91	$733.02

Skills Bank Practice

Make a table to solve the problem.

a. Gas from an 8550 ft³ gas tank is used at a rate of 475 ft³ per day. Gas from a 7200 ft³ gas tank is used at a rate of 250 ft³ per day. If no gas is replaced, how much gas will be in each tank when the two tanks hold equal amounts of gas? **5700 ft³**

End of Day	Gas Amount in First Tank (in ft³)	Gas Amount in Second Tank (in ft³)
0	8550	7200
1	8075	6950
2	7600	6700
3	7125	6450
4	6650	6200
5	6175	5950
6	5700	5700

Sometimes there are so many numbers in a problem that it can be confusing to solve. To solve **a simpler problem,** rewrite the numbers so they are easier to compute.

Example 5 Writing a Simpler Problem to Solve a Problem

In a cycling race, Elio cycled 128 blocks. One block is 1.9 kilometers. If Elio finished in 5.9 hours, what was his average speed?

Understand

Find Elio's average speed.

- Distance: 128 blocks each 1.9 km long
- Time: 5.9 hours

Plan

Find Elio's average speed by using simpler numbers to compute.

Solve

$(128)(1.9)$	Find the total distance of the race.
$= (128)(2 - 0.1)$	Write 1.9 as $2 - 0.1$.
$= 128(2) - 128(0.1)$	Use the Distributive Property.
$= 256 - 12.8$	
$= 243.2$ km	

$d = rt$	Use the distance formula.
$243.2 = r(5.9)$	Solve for r.

$\dfrac{243.2}{5.9} \approx 41.2$ km/hr

Elio's average speed was about 41.2 km/hr.

Check

Each block is close to 2 miles and 128 is close to 130.

The total distance rounds to 260 kilometers.

Round the time to 6 hours and divide into the distance.

$260 \div 6 \approx 43.3$ km/hr. This is close to 41.2 km/hr.

Skills Bank Practice

a. Frank walked 9 laps around the track. One lap is 1312 feet. Frank walked at a rate of 4 mi/hr. How many minutes did it take him to walk 9 laps? about 33.5 minutes

Use **logical reasoning** when you are given many facts in a problem.

Example 6 Using Logical Reasoning to Solve a Problem

Janie, Christa, Lisa, and Brandi had golf scores of 110, 123, 78, and 86. Christa did not shoot a 110. The person who shot an 86 is Janie's sister and Christa's aunt. Brandi shot a 123. What did Christa shoot?

Understand

Find Christa's golf score.

- There are 4 scores and 4 people.
- Some information on who shot what score is given.

Plan

Organize the information in a table. Start with the fact that Brandi shot a 123 and Christa did not shoot a 110.

Brandi shot a 123, so no other player had that score.

Janie's sister and Christa's aunt shot an 86, so Janie and Christa cannot have that score.

Solve

Enter a Y for *yes* or N for *no* in the table.

Once you enter a Y in a cell, enter a N in the remaining cells for that row or that column.

Score	110	123	78	86
Janie	Y	N	N	N
Christa	N	N	Y	N
Lisa	N	N	N	Y
Brandi	N	Y	N	N

Christa shot a 78.

Check

Complete the table. Read the problem again while looking at the table to make sure all the information entered is correct.

Skills Bank Practice

a. Bill, John, Marc, and Terry all have different color eyes (green, brown, blue, and hazel). Marc does not have hazel eyes. The person who has blue eyes is Bill's brother and Marc's uncle. Terry has green eyes. What is the color of each person's eyes? Bill:hazel, John:blue, Marc:brown, Terry:green

One way to solve a problem when you know the ending value is to **work backward.**

Example 7 Working Backward to Solve a Problem

A plane left Tulsa, Oklahoma and flew for 5 hours and 45 minutes to Orlando, Florida, where there was a layover for 3 hours and 10 minutes. From Orlando, Florida, the plane flew 1 hour and 20 minutes and arrived in the Bahamas at 10:00 a.m. on Monday. The Bahamas time is 1 hour ahead of the Tulsa time. What time did the plane leave Tulsa, Oklahoma?

Understand

Find the time the plane left Tulsa, Oklahoma.

You know when the plane landed in the Bahamas, the lengths of the stops that were made, and the time difference between Tulsa and the Bahamas.

Plan

Start at the end of the trip when the plane landed in the Bahamas.

Work backward from the time the plane landed in the Bahamas.

Then apply the time difference between the two cities.

Solve

Subtract the length of time it took to fly from Orlando, Florida, to the Bahamas.

10:00 − 1 hour and 20 minutes = 8:40 a.m.   Monday

Subtract the layover in Orlando, Florida.

8:40 − 3 hours and 10 minutes = 5:30 a.m.   Monday

Subtract the length of the flight from Tulsa to Orlando.

5:30 − 5 hours and 45 minutes = 11:45 p.m.   Sunday

Since the Bahamas is 1 hour ahead of Tulsa time, subtract the difference.

11:45 − 1 hour = 10:45 p.m.   Sunday

The plane left Tulsa at 10:45 p.m. Sunday night.

Check

Work forward to check your answer.

Sunday:

10:45 p.m. + 1 hour + 5 hours 45 minutes + 3 hours 10 minutes + 1 hour 20 minutes = 10:00 a.m. The flight arrived in the Bahamas at 10:00 a.m. on Monday.

Skills Bank Practice

a. A bus arrives in Dallas, Texas, at 11:00 on Saturday morning. The bus started from San Francisco, California, and took 16 hours to arrive in Tulsa, Oklahoma. From Tulsa it took 6 hours to get to Dallas. What time did the bus leave San Francisco? (Note: There is a two-hour difference in time zones, with California being two hours earlier than both Oklahoma and Texas.)   Friday, 11:00 a.m.

Properties and Formulas

Properties

Addition Property of Equality
(19)

For every real number a, b, and c, if $a = b$, then $a + c = b + c$.

Addition Property of Inequality
(66)

For every real number a, b, and c, if $a < b$, then $a + c < b + c$.

Also holds true for $>$, $\leq$, $\geq$, and $\neq$.

Associative Property of Addition
(12)

For every real number a, b, and c,
$(a + b) + c = a + (b + c)$.

Associative Property of Multiplication
(12)

For every real number a, b, and c,
$(a \cdot b) \cdot c = a \cdot (b \cdot c)$.

Commutative Property of Addition
(12)

For every real number a and b, $a + b = b + a$.

Commutative Property of Multiplication
(12)

For every real number a and b, $a \cdot b = b \cdot a$.

Converse of Pythagorean Theorem
(85)

If a triangle has side lengths a, b, and c, and $a^2 + b^2 = c^2$, then the triangle is a right triangle with a hypotenuse of length c.

Cross Products Property
(31)

For every real number a, b, c, and d, where $b \neq 0$ and $d \neq 0$, if $\frac{a}{b} = \frac{c}{d}$, then $ad = bc$.

Distributive Property
(15)

For all real numbers a, b, and c,

$a(b + c) = ab + ac$ and $(b + c)a = ab + ac$.

$a(b - c) = ab - ac$ and $(b - c)a = ab - ac$.

Discriminant
(113)

The discriminant of a quadratic equation $ax^2 + bx + c = 0$, is $b^2 - 4ac$.

If $b^2 - 4ac > 0$, there are two real solutions.

If $b^2 - 4ac = 0$, there is one real solution.

If $b^2 - 4ac < 0$, there are no real solutions.

Division Property of Equality
(21)

For every real number a, b, and c, where $c \neq 0$, if $a = b$, then $\frac{a}{c} = \frac{b}{c}$.

Division Property of Inequality
(70)

For every real number a, b, and c, where $c > 0$, if $a < b$, then $\frac{a}{c} < \frac{b}{c}$.

For every real number a, b, and c, where $c < 0$, if $a < b$, then $\frac{a}{c} > \frac{b}{c}$.

Also holds true for $>$, $\leq$, $\geq$, and $\neq$.

Identity Property of Addition
(12)

For every real number a, $a + 0 = a$.

Identity Property of Multiplication
(12)

For every real number a, $1 \cdot a = a$.

Inverse Property of Addition
(6)

For every real number a, $a + (-a) = 0$.

Saxon Algebra 1

Inverse Property of Multiplication
(11)

For every real number $\frac{a}{b}$, where $a \neq 0$ and $b \neq 0$, $\frac{a}{b} \cdot \frac{b}{a} = 1$.

Multiplication Property of Equality
(21)

For every real number a, b, and c, if $a = b$, then $ac = bc$.

Multiplication Property of Inequality
(70)

For every real number a, b, and c, where $c > 0$, if $a < b$, then $ac < bc$.

For every real number a, b, and c, where $c < 0$, if $a < b$, then $ac > bc$.

Also holds true for $>$, $\leq$, $\geq$, and $\neq$.

Multiplication Property of Zero
(11)

For every real number a, $a \cdot 0 = 0$.

Multiplication Property of -1
(11)

For every real number a, $-1 \cdot a = -a$.

Negative Exponent Property
(32)

For any nonzero real number x and integer n, $x^{-n} = \frac{1}{x^n}$ and $\frac{1}{x^{-n}} = x^n$.

Order of Operations
(4)

To evaluate expressions:
1. Work inside grouping symbols.
2. Simplify powers and roots.
3. Multiply and divide from left to right.
4. Add and subtract from left to right.

Power of a Power Property
(40)

If x is any nonzero real number and m and n are integers, then $(x^m)^n = x^{mn}$.

Power of a Product Property
(40)

If x and y are any nonzero real numbers and m is an integer, then $(xy)^m = x^m y^m$.

Power of a Quotient Property
(40)

If x and y are any nonzero real numbers and m is an integer, then $\left(\frac{x}{y}\right)^m = \frac{x^m}{y^m}$.

Product Property of Exponents
(3)

If x is any nonzero real number and m and n are integers, then $x^m \cdot x^n = x^{m+n}$.

Product Property of Radicals
(61)

If m and n are non negative real numbers, then $\sqrt{m}\sqrt{n} = \sqrt{mn}$ and $\sqrt{mn} = \sqrt{m}\sqrt{n}$.

Pythagorean Theorem
(85)

If a triangle is a right triangle with legs of lengths a and b and hypotenuse of length c, then $a^2 + b^2 = c^2$.

Quotient Property of Exponents
(32)

If x is any nonzero real number and m and n are integers, then $\frac{x^m}{x^n} = x^{m-n}$.

Quotient Property of Radicals
(103)

If $m \geq 0$ and $n > 0$, then $\frac{\sqrt{m}}{\sqrt{n}} = \sqrt{\frac{m}{n}}$ and $\sqrt{\frac{m}{n}} = \frac{\sqrt{m}}{\sqrt{n}}$.

Scientific Notation
(37)

A number written as $a \times 10^n$, where $1 \leq a < 10$ and n is an integer.

Subtraction Property of Equality
(19)

For every real number a, b, and c, if $a = b$, then $a - c = b - c$.

Subtraction Property of Inequality
(66)

For every real number a, b, and c, if $a < b$, then $a - c < b - c$.

Also holds true for $>$, $\leq$, $\geq$, and $\neq$.

Zero Exponent Property
(32)

For every nonzero number x, $x^0 = 1$.

Zero Product Property
(98)

For every real number a and b, if $ab = 0$, then $a = 0$ and/or $b = 0$.

Formulas

Perimeter

Rectangle	$P = 2l + 2w$ or $P = 2(l + w)$
Square	$P = 4s$

Circumference

Circle	$C = \pi d$ or $C = 2\pi r$

Area

Rectangle	$A = lw$
Triangle	$A = \frac{1}{2}bh$
Trapezoid	$A = \frac{1}{2}(b_1 + b_2)h$
Circle	$A = \pi r^2$

Surface Area

Cube	$S = 6s^2$
Cylinder	$S = 2\pi r^2 + 2\pi rh$
Cone	$S = \pi r^2 + \pi rl$

Volume

Where B is the area of the base of a solid figure,

Prism or cylinder	$V = Bh$
Pyramid or cone	$V = \frac{1}{3}Bh$

Linear Equations

Slope formula	$m = \frac{y_2 - y_1}{x_2 - x_1}$
Slope-intercept form	$y = mx + b$
Point-slope form	$y - y_1 = m(x - x_1)$
Standard form	$Ax + By = C$

Quadratic Equations

Standard form	$ax^2 + bx + c = 0$
Axis of symmetry	$x = -\frac{b}{2a}$
Discriminant	$b^2 - 4ac$
Quadratic formula	$x = \frac{-b \pm \sqrt{b^2 - 4ac}}{2a}$

Sequences

nth term of an arithmetic sequence

$$a_n = a_1 + (n - 1)d$$

nth term of an geometric sequence

$$a_n = a_1 \cdot r^{n-1}$$

Trigonometric Ratios

$$\text{sine of } \angle A = \frac{\text{length of leg opposite } \angle A}{\text{length of hypotenuse}}$$

$$\text{cosine of } \angle A = \frac{\text{length of leg adjacent to } \angle A}{\text{length of hypotenuse}}$$

$$\tan \text{ of } \angle A = \frac{\text{length of leg opposite } \angle A}{\text{length of leg adjacent to } \angle A}$$

Percents

$$\text{Percent of change} = \frac{\text{amount of change}}{\text{original amount}}$$

Permutations and Combinations

P(n, r)   permutation of n things taken r at a time

$$_nP_r = \frac{n!}{(n-r)!}$$

C(n, r)   combination of n things taken r at a time

$$_nC_r = \frac{n!}{r!(n-r)!}$$

n! $n! = n \cdot (n-1) \cdot (n-2) \cdot \ldots \cdot 3 \cdot 2 \cdot 1$

Probability

$$P(\text{event}) = \frac{\text{number of favorable outcomes}}{\text{total number of outcomes}}$$

P(A)   probability of event A

Probability of complement

$$P(\text{not event}) = 1 - P(\text{event})$$

Probability of independent events

$$P(A \text{ and } B) = P(A) \cdot P(B)$$

Probability of dependent events

$$P(A \text{ then } B) = P(A) \cdot P(B \text{ after } A)$$

Probability of mutually exclusive events

$$P(A \text{ or } B) = P(A) + P(B)$$

Probability of inclusive events

$$P(A \text{ or } B) = P(A) + P(B) - P(A \text{ and } B)$$

Additional Formulas

Direct variation $y = kx$

Inverse variation $y = \frac{k}{x}; x \neq 0$

Distance formula $d = \sqrt{(x_2 - x_1)^2 + (y_2 - y_1)^2}$

Distance traveled $d = rt$

Exponential decay $y = kb^x; k > 0, 0 < b < 1$

Exponential growth $y = kb^x; k > 0, b > 1$

Midpoint of a segment $M = \left(\frac{x_1 + x_2}{2}, \frac{y_1 + y_2}{2}\right)$

Symbols

Comparison Symbols

$<$	less than
$>$	greater than
$\leq$	less than or equal to
$\geq$	greater than or equal to
$\neq$	not equal to
$\approx$	approximately equal to

Geometry

$\cong$	is congruent to
$\sim$	is similar to
$\circ$	degree(s)
$\angle ABC$	angle ABC
$m\angle ABC$	the measure of angle ABC
$\triangle ABC$	triangle ABC
$\overleftrightarrow{AB}$	line AB
$\overline{AB}$	segment AB
$\overrightarrow{AB}$	ray AB
AB	length of $\overline{AB}$
∟	right angle
$\perp$	is perpendicular to
$\parallel$	is parallel to

Real Numbers

$\mathbb{R}$	the set of real numbers
$\mathbb{Q}$	the set of rational numbers
$\mathbb{Z}$	the set of integers
$\mathbb{W}$	the set of whole numbers
$\mathbb{N}$	the set of natural numbers

Additional Symbols

$\pm$	plus or minus
$a \cdot b$, ab or $a(b)$	a times b
$\|-5\|$	the absolute value of -5
%	percent
π	pi, $\pi \approx 3.14$, or $\pi \approx \frac{22}{7}$
$f(x)$	function notation: f of x
a^n	a to nth power
a_n	nth term of a sequence
(x, y)	ordered pair
$x{:}y$	ratio of x to y, or $\frac{x}{y}$
$\{\ \}$	set braces
$\sqrt{x}$	nonnegative square root of x

Table of Metric Measures

Length

1 kilometer (km) = 1000 meters (m)

1 meter = 100 centimeters (cm)

1 centimeter = 10 millimeters (mm)

Capacity and Volume

1 liter (L) = 1000 milliliters (mL)

Mass

1 kilogram (kg) = 1000 grams (g)

1 gram = 1000 milligrams (mg)

Table of Customary Measures

Length

1 mile (mi) = 5280 feet (ft)

1 mile = 1760 yards (yd)

1 yard = 3 feet

1 yard = 36 inches (in.)

1 foot = 12 inches

Capacity and Volume

1 gallon (gal) = 4 quarts (qt)

1 quart = 2 pints (pt)

1 pint = 2 cups (c)

1 cup = 8 fluid ounces (fl oz)

Weight

1 ton = 2000 pounds (lb)

1 pound = 16 ounces (oz)

Customary and Metric Measures

1 inch = 2.54 centimeters

1 yard $\approx$ 0.9 meters

1 mile $\approx$ 1.6 kilometers

Time

1 year = 365 days

1 year = 12 months

1 month $\approx$ 4 weeks

1 year = 52 weeks

1 week = 7 days

1 day = 24 hours

1 hour (hr) = 60 minutes (min)

1 minute = 60 seconds (s)

GLOSSARY

English/Spanish Glossary

English	Example	Spanish
absolute value (5) — The absolute value of x is the distance from zero to x on a number line, denoted $\|x\|$. $\|x\| = \begin{cases} x \text{ if } x \geq 0 \\ -x \text{ if } x < 0 \end{cases}$	$\|4\| = 4$ $\|-4\| = 4$	**valor absoluto** (5) — El valor absoluto de x es la distancia desde cero hasta x en una recta numérica y se expresa $\|x\|$. $\|x\| = \begin{cases} x \text{ if } x \geq 0 \\ -x \text{ if } x < 0 \end{cases}$
absolute-value equation (74) — An equation that contains absolute-value expressions.	$\|x + 5\| = 8$	**ecuación de valor absoluto** (74) — Ecuación que contiene expresiones de valor absoluto.
absolute-value function (107) — A function whose rule contains absolute-value expressions.	$\|x + 5\| = y$	**función de valor absoluto** (107) — Función cuya regla contiene expresiones de valor absoluto.
absolute-value inequality (91) — An inequality that contains absolute-value expressions.	$\|x + 5\| > 8$	**desigualdad de valor absoluto** (91) — Desigualdad que contiene expresiones de valor absoluto.
additive inverse (6) — The opposite of a number. Two numbers are additive inverses if their sum is zero.	The additive inverse of 6 is −6. The additive inverse of −6 is 6.	**inverso aditivo** (6) — El opuesto de un número. Dos números son inversos aditivos si su suma es cero.
algebraic expression (9) — An expression that contains at least one variable.	$4x + 2y$ $5x$	**expresión algebraica** (9) — Expresión que contiene por lo menos una variable.
arithmetic sequence (34) — A sequence whose successive terms differ by the same nonzero number d, called the *common difference*.	5, 9, 13, 17, 21, … The common difference is 4.	**sucesión aritmética** (34) — Sucesión cuyos términos sucesivos difieren en el mismo número distinto de cero d, denominado *diferencia común*.

Glossary 889

A

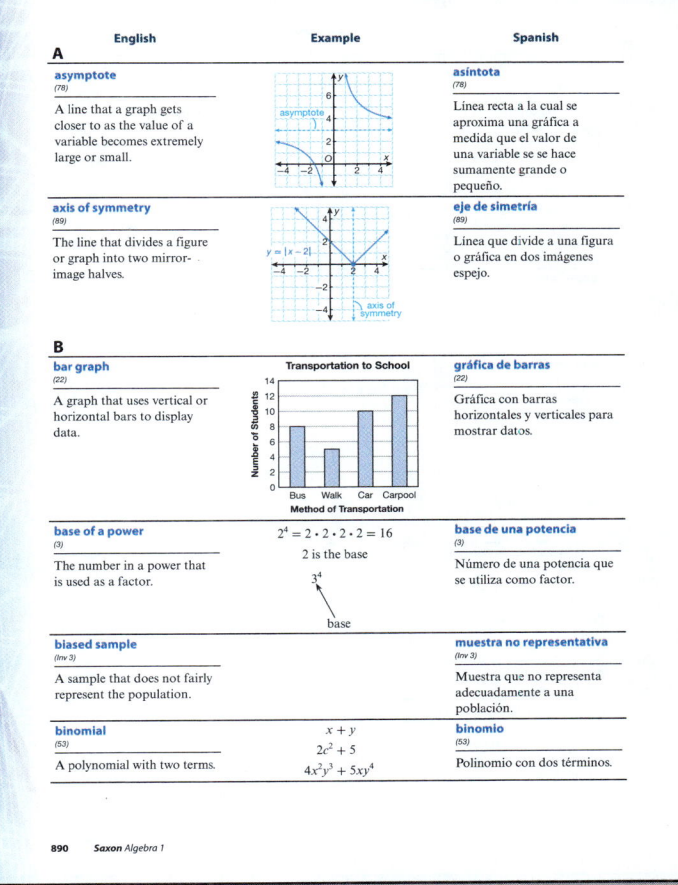

English	Example	Spanish
asymptote (78) — A line that a graph gets closer to as the value of a variable becomes extremely large or small.		**asíntota** (78) — Línea recta a la cual se aproxima una gráfica a medida que el valor de una variable se se hace sumamente grande o pequeño.
axis of symmetry (89) — The line that divides a figure or graph into two mirror-image halves.		**eje de simetría** (89) — Línea que divide a una figura o gráfica en dos imágenes espejo.

B

bar graph (22) — A graph that uses vertical or horizontal bars to display data.	Transportation to School	**gráfica de barras** (22) — Gráfica con barras horizontales y verticales para mostrar datos.
base of a power (3) — The number in a power that is used as a factor.	$2^4 = 2 \cdot 2 \cdot 2 \cdot 2 = 16$ 2 is the base 3^4 base	**base de una potencia** (3) — Número de una potencia que se utiliza como factor.
biased sample (Inv 3) — A sample that does not fairly represent the population.		**muestra no representativa** (Inv 3) — Muestra que no representa adecuadamente a una población.
binomial (53) — A polynomial with two terms.	$x + y$ $2c^2 + 5$ $4x^2y^3 + 5xy^4$	**binomio** (53) — Polinomio con dos términos.

890 Saxon Algebra 1

B

English	Example	Spanish
box-and-whisker plot (54) — A method of showing how data is distributed by using the median, quartiles, and minimum and maximum values; also called a *box plot*.		**gráfica de mediana y rango** (54) — Método para demostrar la distribución de datos utilizando la mediana, los cuartiles y los valores mínimos y máximos; también llamado *gráfica de caja*.

C

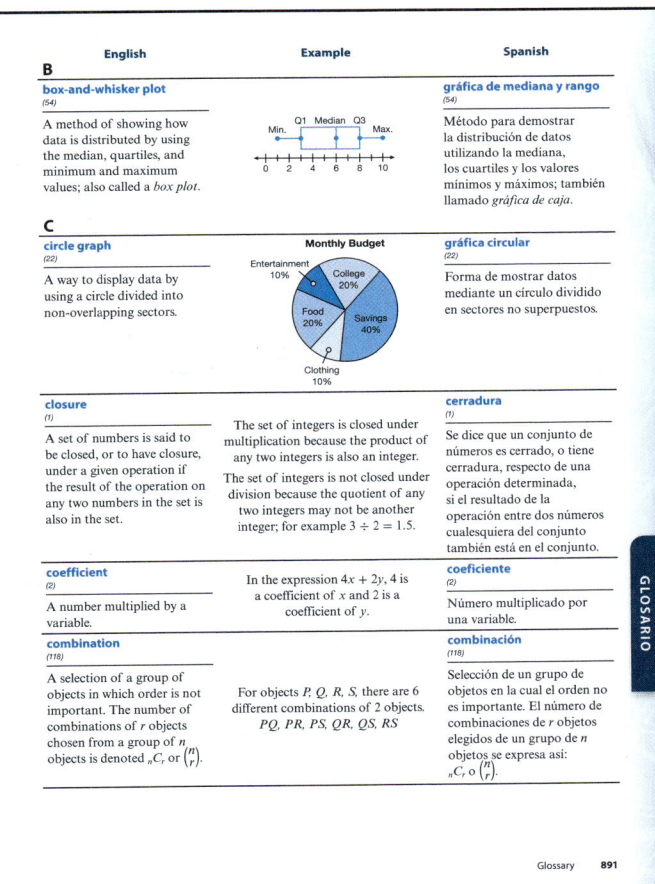

circle graph (22) — A way to display data by using a circle divided into non-overlapping sectors.	Monthly Budget	**gráfica circular** (22) — Forma de mostrar datos mediante un círculo dividido en sectores no superpuestos.
closure (1) — A set of numbers is said to be closed, or to have closure, under a given operation if the result of the operation on any two numbers in the set is also in the set.	The set of integers is closed under multiplication because the product of any two integers is also an integer. The set of integers is not closed under division because the quotient of any two integers may not be another integer; for example $3 \div 2 = 1.5$.	**cerradura** (1) — Se dice que un conjunto de números es cerrado, o tiene cerradura, respecto de una operación determinada, si el resultado de la operación entre dos números cualesquiera del conjunto también está en el conjunto.
coefficient (2) — A number multiplied by a variable.	In the expression $4x + 2y$, 4 is a coefficient of x and 2 is a coefficient of y.	**coeficiente** (2) — Número multiplicado por una variable.
combination (118) — A selection of a group of objects in which order is not important. The number of combinations of r objects chosen from a group of n objects is denoted $_nC_r$ or $\binom{n}{r}$.	For objects P, Q, R, S, there are 6 different combinations of 2 objects. PQ, PR, PS, QR, QS, RS	**combinación** (118) — Selección de un grupo de objetos en la cual el orden no es importante. El número de combinaciones de r objetos elegidos de un grupo de n objetos se expresa así: $_nC_r$ o $\binom{n}{r}$.

Glossary 891

C

English	Example	Spanish
common difference (34) — In an arithmetic sequence, the nonzero constant difference of any term and the previous term.	In the arithmetic sequence 4, 6, 8, 10, …, the common difference is 2.	**diferencia común** (34) — En una sucesión aritmética, diferencia constante distinta de cero entre cualquier término y el término anterior.
common ratio (105) — In a geometric sequence, the constant ratio of any term and the previous term.	In the geometric sequence 64, 32, 16, 8, 4, …, the common ratio is $\frac{1}{2}$.	**razón común** (105) — En una sucesión geométrica, la razón constante entre cualquier término y el término anterior.
complement of an event (14) — All outcomes in the sample space that are not in event A, denoted $\overline{A}$.	The complement of rolling an even number on a number cube is rolling an odd number.	**complemento de un suceso** (14) — Todos los resultados en el espacio muestral que no están en el suceso A y se expresan $\overline{A}$.
completing the square (104) — A process used to form a perfect-square trinomial. To complete the square of $x^2 + bx$, add $\left(\frac{b}{2}\right)^2$.	$x^2 + 8x + \square$ Add $\left(\frac{8}{2}\right)^2 = 16$ $x^2 + 8x + 16$	**completar el cuadrado** (104) — Proceso utilizado para formar un trinomio cuadrado perfecto. Para completar el cuadrado de $x^2 + bx$, hay que sumar $\left(\frac{b}{2}\right)^2$.
complex fraction (92) — A fraction that contains one or more fractions in the numerator, the denominator, or both.	$\dfrac{2}{\frac{1}{2} + \frac{1}{3}}$	**fracción compleja** (92) — Fracción que contiene una o más fracciones en el numerador, el denominador, o en ambos.
compound event (80) — An event made up of two or more simple events.	In the experiment of rolling a number cube and tossing a coin, a compound event is the number cube landing on 5 and the coin landing on tails.	**suceso compuesto** (80) — Suceso formado por dos o más sucesos simples.
compound inequality (73) — Two inequalities that are combined into one statement by the word *and* or *or*.	$x \geq 1$ AND $x < 5$ (also written $1 \leq x < 5$)	**desigualdad compuesta** (73) — Dos desigualdades unidas en un enunciado por la palabra *y* u *o*.

892 Saxon Algebra 1

C

English	Example	Spanish
compound interest (116) Interest earned or paid on both the principal and previously earned interest. The formula for compound interest is $A = P\left(1 + \frac{r}{n}\right)^{nt}$, where A is the final amount, P is the principal, r is the interest rate expressed as a decimal, n is the number of times interest is compounded, and t is the time.		**interés compuesto** (116) Intereses ganados o pagados sobre el capital y los intereses ya devengados. La fórmula de interés compuesto es $A = P\left(1 + \frac{r}{n}\right)^{nt}$, donde A es la cantidad final, P es el capital, r es la tasa de interés expresada como un decimal, n es la cantidad de veces que se capitaliza el interés y t es el tiempo.
conclusion (Inv 4) The part of a conditional statement following the word *then*.		**conclusión** (Inv 4) Parte de un enunciado condicional que sigue a la palabra *entonces*.
conditional statement (Inv 4) A logical statement that can be written in "if-then" form.	If a polygon has three sides, then it is a triangle.	**enunciado condicional** (Inv 4) Una afirmación lógica que puede ser escrita en la forma "si-entonces".
congruent (36) Having the same size and shape, denoted by $\cong$.	$\overline{AB} \cong \overline{CD}$	**congruente** (36) Que tiene el mismo tamaño y forma, expresado por $\cong$.
conjugate of an irrational number (103) The conjugate of a number in the form $a + \sqrt{b}$ is $a - \sqrt{b}$.	The conjugate of $1 + \sqrt{5}$ is $1 - \sqrt{5}$.	**conjugado de un número irracional** (103) El conjugado de un número en la forma $a + \sqrt{b}$ es $a - \sqrt{b}$.
conjunction (73) A compound statement that uses the word *and*.	$x \geq 2$ AND $x < 6$	**conjunción** (73) Enunciado compuesto que contiene la palabra *y*.
consistent system (67) A system of equations or inequalities that has at least one solution.	$x + y = 8$ $x - y = 2$ solution: (5, 3)	**sistema consistente** (67) Sistema de ecuaciones o desigualdades que tiene por lo menos una solución.

C

English	Example	Spanish
constant (2) A value that does not change.	$4, 0, \pi$	**constante** (2) Valor que no cambia.
constant of variation (56) The constant k in a direct variation equation.	$y = kx$ $y = 6x$ 6 is the constant of variation	**constante de variación** (56) La constante k en una ecuación de variación directa.
continuous graph (Inv 2) A graph made up of connected lines or curves.		**gráfica continua** (Inv 2) Gráfica compuesta por líneas rectas o curvas conectadas.
contradiction (81) An equation or inequality that is never true.	$x + 2 = x$ $2 = 0$ never true	**contradicción** (81) Ecuación o desigualdad que nunca es verdadera.
contrapositive (Inv 5) The conditional statement formed by exchanging the hypothesis and conclusion and negating both.	Statement: If a figure is a triangle, then it has three sides. Contrapositive: If a figure does not have three sides, then it is not a triangle.	**contrapositivo** (Inv 5) El enunciado condicional formado al intercambiar la hipótesis y la conclusión y negar las dos.
converse (Inv 5) The statement formed by exchanging the hypothesis and conclusion of a conditional statement.	Statement: If a figure is a triangle, then it has three sides. Converse: If a figure has three sides, then it is a triangle.	**expresión recíproca** (Inv 5) Enunciado que se forma intercambiando la hipótesis y la conclusión de un enunciado condicional.
coordinate (20) A number used to identify the location of a point. On a number line, one coordinate is used. On a coordinate plane, two coordinates are used, called the x-coordinate and the y-coordinate. In space, three coordinates are used, called the x-coordinate, the y-coordinate, and the z-coordinate.	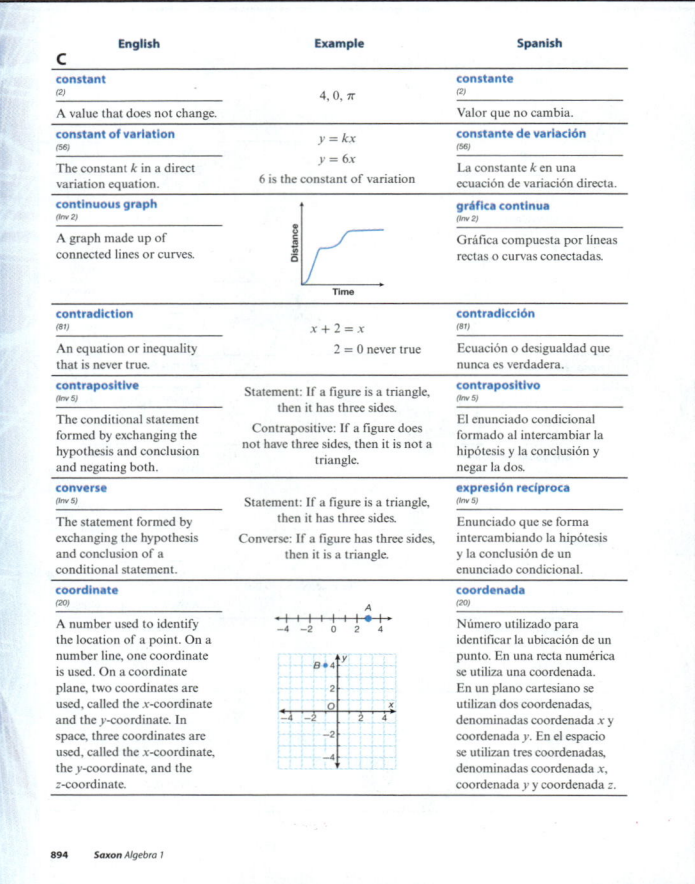	**coordenada** (20) Número utilizado para identificar la ubicación de un punto. En una recta numérica se utiliza una coordenada. En un plano cartesiano se utilizan dos coordenadas, denominadas coordenada x y coordenada y. En el espacio se utilizan tres coordenadas, denominadas coordenada x, coordenada y y coordenada z.

C

English	Example	Spanish
coordinate plane (20) A plane that is divided into four regions by a horizontal line called the x-axis and a vertical line called the y-axis.		**plano cartesiano** (20) Plano dividido en cuatro regiones por una línea horizontal denominada eje x y una línea vertical denominada eje y.
correlation (71) A measure of the strength and direction of the relationship between two variables or data sets.	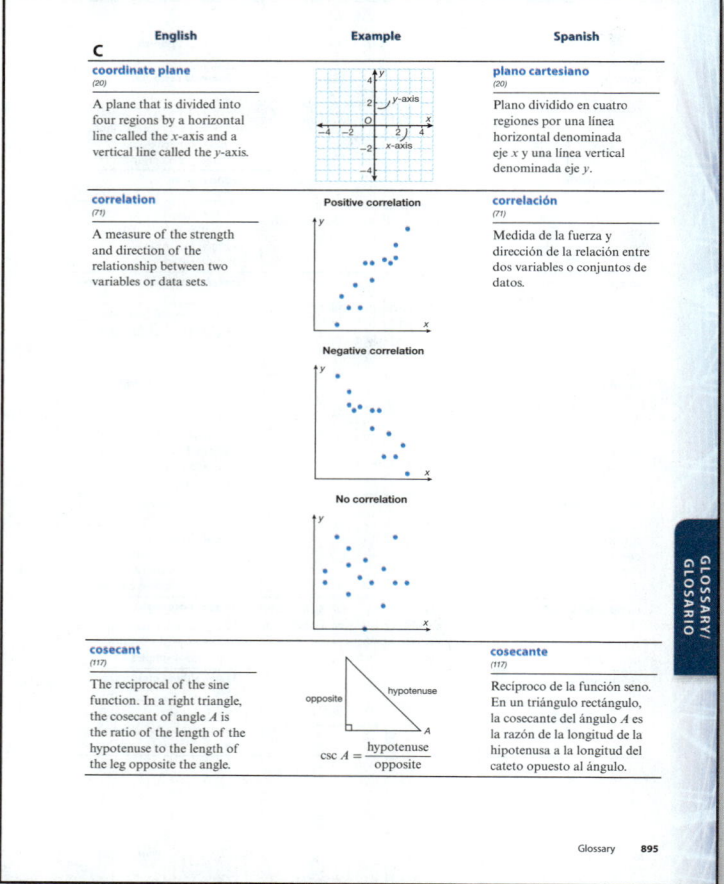 Positive correlation / Negative correlation / No correlation	**correlación** (71) Medida de la fuerza y dirección de la relación entre dos variables o conjuntos de datos.
cosecant (117) The reciprocal of the sine function. In a right triangle, the cosecant of angle A is the ratio of the length of the hypotenuse to the length of the leg opposite the angle.	$\csc A = \dfrac{\text{hypotenuse}}{\text{opposite}}$	**cosecante** (117) Recíproco de la función seno. En un triángulo rectángulo, la cosecante del ángulo A es la razón de la longitud de la hipotenusa a la longitud del cateto opuesto al ángulo.

C

English	Example	Spanish
cosine (117) In a right triangle, the cosine of angle A is the ratio of the length of the leg adjacent to the angle to the length of the hypotenuse.	$\cos A = \dfrac{\text{adjacent}}{\text{hypotenuse}}$	**coseno** (117) En un triángulo rectángulo, el coseno del ángulo A es la razón entre la longitud del cateto adyacente al ángulo y la longitud de la hipotenusa.
cotangent (117) The reciprocal of the tangent function. In a right triangle, the cotangent of angle A is the ratio of the length of the leg adjacent to the angle to the length of the leg opposite the angle.	$\cot A = \dfrac{\text{adjacent}}{\text{opposite}}$	**cotangente** (117) Recíproco de la función tangente. En un triángulo rectángulo, la cotangente del ángulo A es la razón de la longitud del cateto adyacente al ángulo a la longitud del cateto opuesto al ángulo.
counterexample (1) An example that proves that a conjecture or statement is false.	Statement: If a number is divisible by 5, its ones digit is a 5. Counterexample: 10 is divisible by 5.	**contraejemplo** (1) Ejemplo que demuestra que una conjetura o enunciado es falso.
cross products (31) In the statement $\frac{a}{b} = \frac{c}{d}$, the product of the means bc and the product of the extremes ad are called the cross products.	$\frac{1}{2} = \frac{4}{8}$ Cross products: $1 \cdot 8 = 8$ and $2 \cdot 4 = 8$.	**productos cruzados** (31) En el enunciado $\frac{a}{b} = \frac{c}{d}$, el producto de los valores medios bc y el producto de los valores extremos ad se denominan productos cruzados.
cube root (46) A number, written as $\sqrt[3]{x}$, whose cube is x.	$\sqrt[3]{8} = 2$, because $2^3 = 8$; 2 is the cube root of 8.	**raíz cúbica** (46) Número, expresado como $\sqrt[3]{x}$, cuyo cubo es x.
cubic function (115) A polynomial function of degree 3.	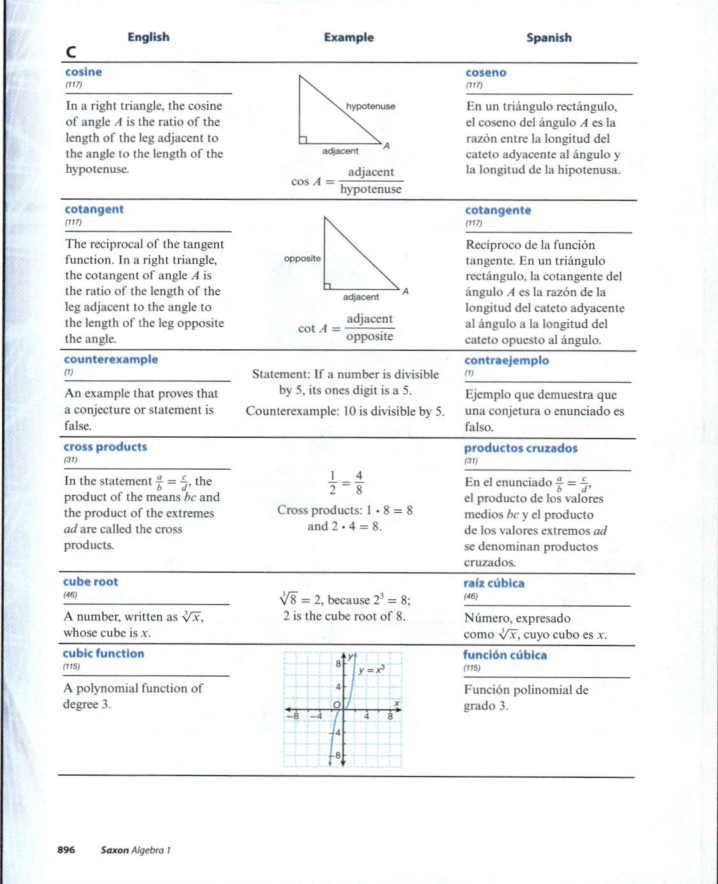 $y = x^3$	**función cúbica** (115) Función polinomial de grado 3.

English	Example	Spanish
D		
deductive reasoning (Inv 4)		**razonamiento deductivo** (Inv 4)
The process of using logic to draw conclusions.		Proceso en el que se utiliza la lógica para sacar conclusiones.
degree of a monomial (53)	$5x^2y^4z^3$ Degree: $2 + 4 + 3 = 9$	**grado de un monomio** (53)
The sum of the exponents of the variables in the monomial.		Suma de los exponentes de las variables del monomio.
degree of a polynomial (53)	$2xy^2 + 3x^2y^4 + 6x^2y^2$ 1st term degree 3; 2nd term degree 6; third term degree 4; Polynomial Degree: 6	**grado de un polinomio** (53)
The degree of the term of the polynomial with the greatest degree.		Grado del término del polinomio con el grado máximo.
dependent equations (67)	$x + y = 4$ $3x + 3y = 12$	**ecuaciones dependientes** (67)
Simultaneous equations whose solution sets are identical.		Ecuaciones simultáneas cuyos conjuntos solución son idénticos.
dependent events (33)	From a bag containing 4 green marbles and 2 red marbles, drawing a green marble, and then drawing a red marble without replacing the first marble.	**sucesos dependientes** (33)
Events for which the occurrence or nonoccurrence of one event affects the probability of the other event.		Dos sucesos son dependientes si el hecho de que uno de ellos se cumpla o no afecta la probabilidad del otro suceso.
dependent system (67)	$x + y = 4$ $3x + 3y = 12$	**sistema dependiente** (67)
A system of equations that has infinitely many solutions.		Sistema de ecuaciones que tiene infinitamente muchas soluciones.
dependent variable (20)	For $y = 3x + 2$, y is the dependent variable.	**variable dependiente** (20)
The output of a function; a variable whose value depends on the value of the input, or independent variable.		Salida de una función; variable cuyo valor depende del valor de la entrada, o variable independiente.

English	Example	Spanish
D		
direct variation (56)	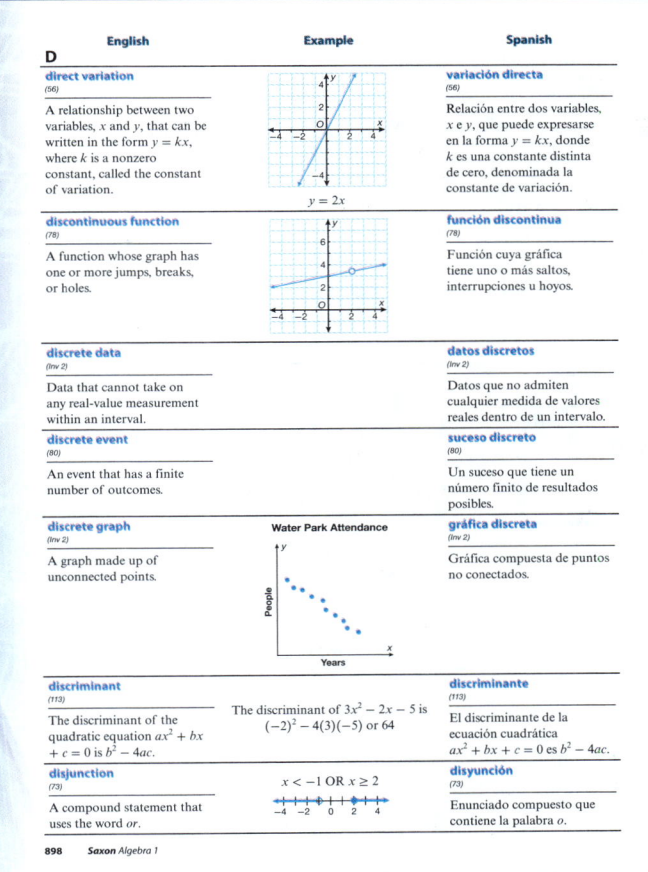 $y = 2x$	**variación directa** (56)
A relationship between two variables, x and y, that can be written in the form $y = kx$, where k is a nonzero constant, called the constant of variation.		Relación entre dos variables, x e y, que puede expresarse en la forma $y = kx$, donde k es una constante distinta de cero, denominada la constante de variación.
discontinuous function (78)		**función discontinua** (78)
A function whose graph has one or more jumps, breaks, or holes.		Función cuya gráfica tiene uno o más saltos, interrupciones u hoyos.
discrete data (Inv 2)		**datos discretos** (Inv 2)
Data that cannot take on any real-value measurement within an interval.		Datos que no admiten cualquier medida de valores reales dentro de un intervalo.
discrete event (80)		**suceso discreto** (80)
An event that has a finite number of outcomes.		Un suceso que tiene un número finito de resultados posibles.
discrete graph (Inv 2)	Water Park Attendance	**gráfica discreta** (Inv 2)
A graph made up of unconnected points.		Gráfica compuesta de puntos no conectados.
discriminant (113)	The discriminant of $3x^2 - 2x - 5$ is $(-2)^2 - 4(3)(-5)$ or 64	**discriminante** (113)
The discriminant of the quadratic equation $ax^2 + bx + c = 0$ is $b^2 - 4ac$.		El discriminante de la ecuación cuadrática $ax^2 + bx + c = 0$ es $b^2 - 4ac$.
disjunction (73)	$x < -1$ OR $x \geq 2$	**disyunción** (73)
A compound statement that uses the word *or*.		Enunciado compuesto que contiene la palabra *o*.

English	Example	Spanish
D		
domain (25)	The domain of $y = \sqrt{x}$ is $x \geq 0$.	**dominio** (25)
The set of input values of a function or relation.		Conjunto de valores de entrada de una función o relación.
double root (113)	$x^2 - 4x + 4 = 0$ $x = 2, 2$	**raíz doble** (113)
Two equal roots in a quadratic equation are sometimes called a double root.		Dos raíces iguales en una ecuación cuadrática a veces son llamadas una raíz doble.
double-bar graph (22)		**gráfica de doble barra** (22)
A graph that shows two bar graphs together and compares two related sets of data.		Una gráfica que muestra dos gráficas de barras juntas y compara los conjuntos de datos relacionados.
double-line graph (22)	Stamp Collections	**gráfica de línea doble** (22)
A graph with two line graphs together that compare two related sets of data.		Una gráfica con dos gráficas lineales juntas que comparan dos conjuntos de datos relacionados.
doubling time (Inv 11)		**tiempo de duplicación** (Inv 11)
The period of time required for a quantity to double in size or value.		El período de tiempo requerido para que una cantidad duplique su tamaño o valor.
E		
element of a set (Inv 12)		**elemento de un conjunto** (Inv 12)
An item in a set.		Componente de un conjunto.

English	Example	Spanish
E		
empty set (1)	The solution set of $|x| < -1$ is the empty set, { }, or ∅.	**conjunto vacío** (1)
A set with no elements.		Conjunto sin elementos.
equation (19)	$x + 5 = 7$ $4 + 3 = 8 - 1$ $(x - 2)^2 + (y - 3)^2 = 4$	**ecuación** (19)
A mathematical sentence that shows that two expressions are equivalent.		Enunciado matemático que indica que dos expresiones son equivalentes.
equivalent equations (19)	$x + 2 = 4; x = 2$ $2x + 4 = 8; x = 2$	**ecuaciones equivalentes** (19)
Equations that have the same solution set.		Ecuaciones que tienen el mismo conjunto solución.
equivalent inequalities (50)	$x + 3 < 5; x < 2$ $2x + 6 < 10; x < 2$	**desigualdades equivalentes** (50)
Inequalities that have the same solution set.		Desigualdades que tienen el mismo conjunto solución.
event (Inv 1)	In the experiment of rolling a number cube, the event of "an even number" consists of 2, 4, and 6.	**suceso** (Inv 1)
An outcome or set of outcomes in a probability experiment.		Resultado o conjunto de resultados en un experimento de probabilidades.
excluded values (78)	The excluded values of $f(x) = \dfrac{(x + 3)}{(x + 1)(x - 4)}$ are $x = -1$ and $x = 4$, which would make the denominator equal to 0.	**valores excluidos** (78)
Values of x for which a function or expression is not defined.		Valores de x para los cuales no está definida una función o expresión.
experimental probability (Inv 1)		**probabilidad experimental** (Inv 1)
The ratio of the number of times an event occurs to the number of trials, or times, that an activity is performed.		Razón entre la cantidad de veces que ocurre un suceso y la cantidad de pruebas, o veces, que se realiza una actividad.
exponent (3)	$2^4 = 2 \cdot 2 \cdot 2 \cdot 2 = 16$ 4 is the exponent $3^4 \leftarrow$ exponent	**exponente** (3)
The number that indicates how many times the base in a power is used as a factor.		Número que indica la cantidad de veces que la base de una potencia se utiliza como factor. $3^4 \leftarrow$ exponente

English	Example	Spanish
E		
exponential decay (Inv 11) An exponential function of the form $f(x) = ab^x$ in which $0 < b < 1$. If r is the rate of decay, then the function can be written $y = a(1 - r)^t$, where a is the initial amount and t is the time.	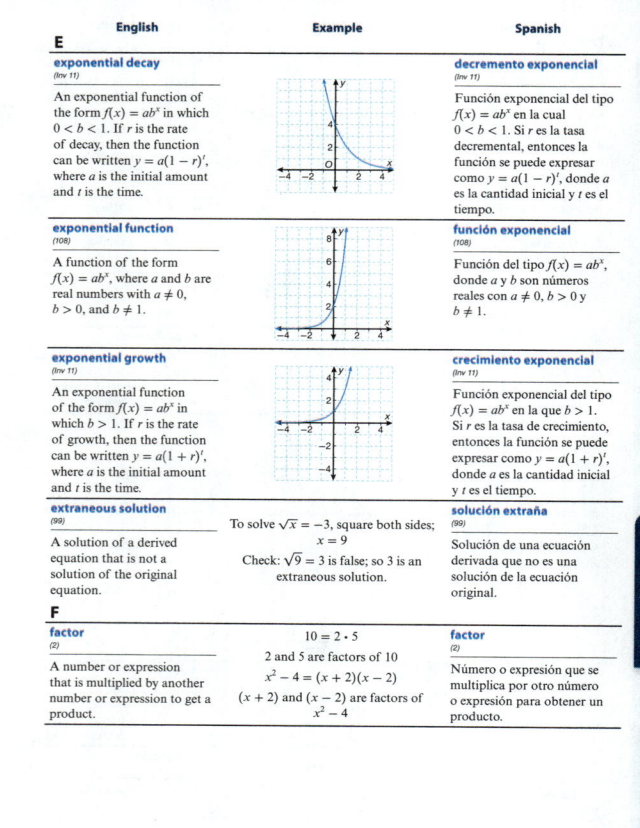	**decremento exponencial** (Inv 11) Función exponencial del tipo $f(x) = ab^x$ en la cual $0 < b < 1$. Si r es la tasa decremental, entonces la función se puede expresar como $y = a(1 - r)^t$, donde a es la cantidad inicial y t es el tiempo.
exponential function (108) A function of the form $f(x) = ab^x$, where a and b are real numbers with $a \neq 0$, $b > 0$, and $b \neq 1$.		**función exponencial** (108) Función del tipo $f(x) = ab^x$, donde a y b son números reales con $a \neq 0$, $b > 0$ y $b \neq 1$.
exponential growth (Inv 11) An exponential function of the form $f(x) = ab^x$ in which $b > 1$. If r is the rate of growth, then the function can be written $y = a(1 + r)^t$, where a is the initial amount and t is the time.		**crecimiento exponencial** (Inv 11) Función exponencial del tipo $f(x) = ab^x$ en la que $b > 1$. Si r es la tasa de crecimiento, entonces la función se puede expresar como $y = a(1 + r)^t$, donde a es la cantidad inicial y t es el tiempo.
extraneous solution (99) A solution of a derived equation that is not a solution of the original equation.	To solve $\sqrt{x} = -3$, square both sides; $x = 9$ Check: $\sqrt{9} = 3$ is false; so 3 is an extraneous solution.	**solución extraña** (99) Solución de una ecuación derivada que no es una solución de la ecuación original.
F		
factor (2) A number or expression that is multiplied by another number or expression to get a product.	$10 = 2 \cdot 5$ 2 and 5 are factors of 10 $x^2 - 4 = (x + 2)(x - 2)$ $(x + 2)$ and $(x - 2)$ are factors of $x^2 - 4$	**factor** (2) Número o expresión que se multiplica por otro número o expresión para obtener un producto.

Glossary 901

English	Example	Spanish
F		
factorial (111) If n is a positive integer, then n factorial, written $n!$, is $n \cdot (n-1) \cdot (n-2) \cdot \ldots \cdot 2 \cdot 1$. The factorial of 0 is defined to be 1.	$6! = 6 \cdot 5 \cdot 4 \cdot 3 \cdot 2 \cdot 1 = 720$	**factorial** (111) Si n es un entero positivo, entonces el factorial de n, expresado como $n!$, es $n \cdot (n-1) \cdot (n-2) \cdot \ldots \cdot 2 \cdot 1$. Por definición, el factorial de 0 es 1.
family of functions (Inv 6) A set of functions whose graphs have basic characteristics in common.	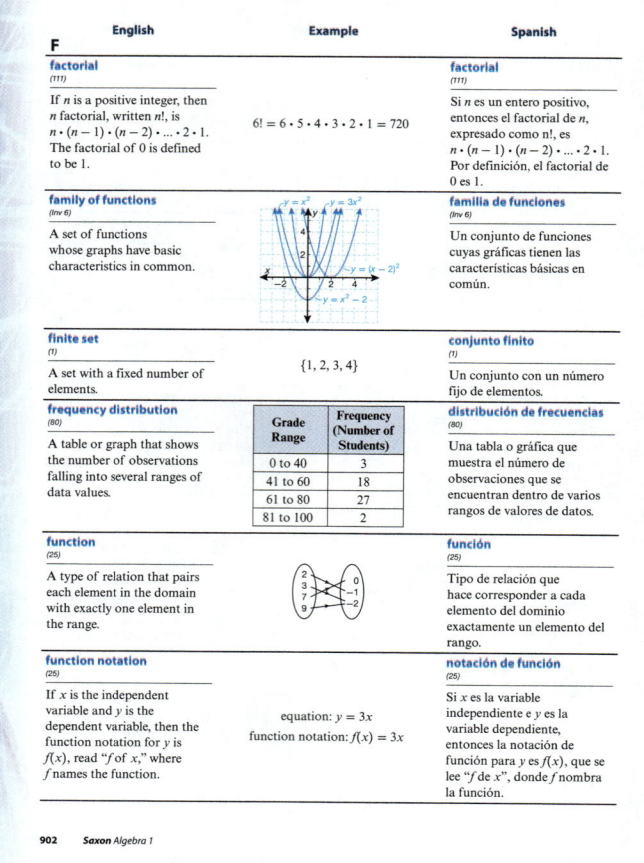	**familia de funciones** (Inv 6) Un conjunto de funciones cuyas gráficas tienen las características básicas en común.
finite set (1) A set with a fixed number of elements.	$\{1, 2, 3, 4\}$	**conjunto finito** (1) Un conjunto con un número fijo de elementos.
frequency distribution (80) A table or graph that shows the number of observations falling into several ranges of data values.	Grade Range / Frequency (Number of Students): 0 to 40 / 3; 41 to 60 / 18; 61 to 80 / 27; 81 to 100 / 2	**distribución de frecuencias** (80) Una tabla o gráfica que muestra el número de observaciones que se encuentran dentro de varios rangos de valores de datos.
function (25) A type of relation that pairs each element in the domain with exactly one element in the range.		**función** (25) Tipo de relación que hace corresponder a cada elemento del dominio exactamente un elemento del rango.
function notation (25) If x is the independent variable and y is the dependent variable, then the function notation for y is $f(x)$, read "f of x," where f names the function.	equation: $y = 3x$ function notation: $f(x) = 3x$	**notación de función** (25) Si x es la variable independiente e y es la variable dependiente, entonces la notación de función para y es $f(x)$, que se lee "f de x", donde f nombra la función.

902 Saxon Algebra 1

English	Example	Spanish
G		
geometric sequence (105) A sequence in which the ratio of successive terms is a constant r, called the common ratio, where $r \neq 0$ and $r \neq 1$.	3, 6, 12, 24, … The ratio is 2.	**sucesión geométrica** (105) Sucesión en la que la razón de los términos sucesivos es una constante r, denominada razón común, donde $r \neq 0$ y $r \neq 1$.
greatest common factor (GCF) of an expression (38) The product of the greatest integer and the greatest power of each variable that divides evenly into each term of the expression.		**máximo común divisor (MCD) de una expresión** (38) Producto del entero mayor y la potencia mayor de cada variable que divide exactamente cada término de la expresión.
H		
half-life (Inv 11) The half-life of a substance is the time it takes for one-half of the substance to decay into another substance.		**vida media** (Inv 11) La vida media de una sustancia es el tiempo que tarda la mitad de la sustancia en desintegrarse y transformarse en otra sustancia.
histogram (62) A bar graph used to display data grouped in class intervals. The width of each bar is proportional to the class interval, and the area of each bar is proportional to the frequency.	Age of Visitors (histogram)	**histograma** (62) Gráfica de barras utilizada para mostrar datos agrupados en intervalos de clases. El ancho de cada barra es proporcional al intervalo de clase y el área de cada barra es proporcional a la frecuencia.
hypothesis (Inv 4) The part of a conditional statement following the word *if*.		**hipótesis** (Inv 4) La parte de un enunciado condicional que sigue a la palabra *si*.
I		
identity (28) An equation that is true for all values of the variables.	$2x + 6 = 2(x + 3)$	**identidad** (28) Ecuación verdadera para todos los valores de las variables.

Glossary 903

English	Example	Spanish
I		
inclusive events (68) Events that have one or more outcomes in common.	In the experiment of rolling a number cube, rolling an odd number and rolling a number less than 3 are inclusive events because both contain the outcome 1.	**sucesos inclusivos** (68) Sucesos que tienen uno o más resultados en común.
inconsistent system (67) A system of equations or inequalities that has no solution.	$x + y = 2$ $x + y = 1$	**sistema inconsistente** (67) Sistema de ecuaciones o desigualdades que no tiene solución.
independent events (33) Events for which the occurrence or non-occurrence of one event does not affect the probability of the other event.	From a bag containing 4 green marbles and 2 red marbles, drawing a green marble, replacing it, and then drawing a red marble.	**sucesos independientes** (33) Dos sucesos son independientes si el hecho de que ocurra o no uno de ellos no afecta la probabilidad del otro suceso.
independent system (67) A system of equations that has exactly one solution.	$x + y = 6$ $x - y = 2$ Solution: (4, 2)	**sistema independiente** (67) Sistema de ecuaciones que tiene sólo una solución.
independent variable (20) The input of a function; a variable whose value determines the value of the output, or dependent variable.	For $y = 3x + 2$, x is the independent variable.	**variable independiente** (20) Entrada de una función; variable cuyo valor determina el valor de la salida, o variable dependiente.
inductive reasoning (Inv 4) The process of reasoning that a rule or statement is true because specific cases are true.		**razonamiento inductivo** (Inv 4) Proceso de razonamiento por el que se determina si una regla o enunciado es verdadero porque ciertos casos específicos son verdaderos.
inequality (45) A statement that compares two expressions by using one of the following signs $<$, $>$, $\leq$, $\geq$, or $\neq$.	$x \geq 3$	**desigualdad** (45) Enunciado que compara dos expresiones utilizando uno de los siguientes signos: $<$, $>$, $\leq$, $\geq$, o $\neq$.
infinite set (1) A set with an unlimited, or infinite, number of elements.	Set of Integers $\{\ldots, -3, -2, -1, 0, 1, 2, 3, \ldots\}$	**conjunto infinito** (1) Conjunto con un número de elementos ilimitado o infinito.

904 Saxon Algebra 1

English	Example	Spanish
I		
integer (1)	..., −3, −2, −1, 0, 1, 2, 3, ...	**entero** (1)
A member of the set of whole numbers and their opposites.		Miembro del conjunto de números cabales y sus opuestos.
intersection of sets (1)	$A = \{1, 2, 3\}$ $B = \{2, 3, 4, 5\}$ $A \cap B = \{2, 3\}$	**intersección de conjuntos** (1)
The intersection of two sets is the set of all elements that are common to both sets, denoted by ∩.		La intersección de dos conjuntos es el conjunto de todos los elementos que son comunes a ambos conjuntos, expresado por ∩.
inverse (Inv 5)	Statement: If a figure has three sides, then it is a triangle. Inverse: If a figure does not have three sides, then it is not a triangle.	**inverso** (Inv 5)
A conditional statement formed by negating both the hypothesis and the conclusion.		Un enunciado condicional formado al negar tanto la hipótesis como la conclusión.
inverse operations (19)	Addition and subtraction are inverse operations: $4 + 3 = 7, 7 − 4 = 3$ Multiplication and division are inverse operations: $2 \cdot 4 = 8, 8 \div 2 = 4$	**operaciones inversas** (19)
Operations that undo each other.		Operaciones que se anulan entre sí.
inverse variation (64)	$y = \frac{6}{x}$	**variación inversa** (64)
A relationship between two variables, x and y, that can be written in the form $y = \frac{k}{x}$, where k is a nonzero constant and $x \neq 0$.		Relación entre dos variables, x e y, que puede expresarse en la forma $y = \frac{k}{x}$, donde k es una constante distinta de cero y $x \neq 0$.
irrational number (1)	$\sqrt{3}, \pi$	**número irracional** (1)
A real number that cannot be written as a ratio of integers.		Número real que no se puede expresar como una razón de enteros.

English	Example	Spanish
J		
joint variation (Inv 8)		**variación conjunta** (Inv 8)
A relationship among three variables that can be written in the form $y = kxz$, where k is a nonzero constant.		Relación entre tres variables que se puede expresar en la forma $y = kxz$, donde k es una constante distinta de cero.
L		
leading coefficient (53)	$4x^2 + 2x + 5$ 4 is the leading coefficient	**coeficiente principal** (53)
The coefficient of the first term of a polynomial in standard form.		Coeficiente del primer término de un polinomio en forma estándar.
like radicals (69)	$5\sqrt{3x}$ and $\sqrt{3x}$	**radicales semejantes** (69)
Radical terms having the same radicand and index.		Términos radicales que tienen el mismo radicando e índice.
like terms (18)	$2x^2y^3$ and $5x^2y^3$	**términos semejantes** (18)
Terms with the same variables raised to the same powers.		Términos con las mismas variables elevadas a los mismos exponentes.
line graph (22)	Car Acceleration	**gráfica lineal** (22)
A graph that uses line segments to show how data changes.		Gráfica que utiliza segmentos de líneas para mostrar cambios en los datos.
line of best fit (71)		**línea de mejor ajuste** (71)
The line that comes closest to all of the points in a data set.		Línea que más se acerca a todos los puntos de un conjunto de datos.
linear equation (30)		**ecuación lineal** (30)
An equation whose graph is a line.		Un enunciado cuya gráfica es una línea.

English	Example	Spanish
L		
linear function (30)		**función lineal** (30)
A function that can be written in the form $y = mx + b$, where x is the independent variable and m and b are real numbers. Its graph is a line.		Función que puede expresarse en la forma $y = mx + b$, donde x es la variable independiente y m y b son números reales. Su gráfica es una línea.
linear inequality in one variable (50)	$2x + 4 \leq 3(x + 5)$	**desigualdad lineal en una variable** (50)
An inequality that can be written in one of the following forms: $ax < b$, $ax > b$, $ax \leq b$, $ax \geq b$ or $ax \neq b$, where a and b are constants and $a \neq 0$.		Una desigualdad que puede expresarse de una de las siguientes formas: $ax > b$, $ax \leq b$, $ax \geq b$ o $ax \neq b$, donde a y b son constantes y $a \neq 0$.
linear inequality in two variables (97)	$4x + 2y > 7$	**desigualdad lineal en dos variables** (97)
An equation that can be written in one of the following forms: $y < mx + b$, $y > mx + b$, $y \leq mx + b$, $y \geq mx + b$, or $y \neq mx + b$, where m and b are real numbers.		Ecuación que puede expresarse de una de las siguientes formas: $y < mx + b$, $y > mx + b$, $y \leq mx + b$, $y \geq mx + b$, o $y \neq mx + b$, donde m y b son números reales.
literal equation (29)	$d = rt$ $A = \frac{1}{2}bh$	**ecuación literal** (29)
An equation that contains two or more variables.		Ecuación que contiene dos o más variables.
M		
matrix (Inv 12)	$\begin{bmatrix} 1 & 0 & 3 \\ -2 & 4 & 5 \\ 0 & 7 & -3 \end{bmatrix}$	**matriz** (Inv 12)
A rectangular array of numbers enclosed in brackets.		Arreglo rectangular de números encerrados entre corchetes.
maximum of a function (89)		**máximo de una función** (89)
The y-value of the highest point on the graph of the function.		Valor de y del punto más alto en la gráfica de la función.

English	Example	Spanish
M		
mean (48)	Data set: 4, 5, 6, 7 Mean: $\frac{4 + 5 + 6 + 7}{2} = 11$	**media** (48)
The sum of all the values in a data set divided by the number of data values. Also called the average.		Suma de todos los valores de un conjunto de datos dividido por el número de valores de datos. También llamada promedio.
measure of central tendency (48)	mean, median, or mode	**medida de tendencia central** (48)
A measure that describes the center of a data set.		Medida que describe el centro de un conjunto de datos.
median (48)	Data set: 7, 8, 10, 12, 14 Median: 10 Data set: 4, 6, 7, 10, 11, 12 Median: $\frac{7 + 10}{2} = 8.5$	**mediana** (48)
If there are an odd number of data values, the median is the middle value. If there are an even number of values, the median is the average of the two middle values.		Dado un número impar de valores de datos, la mediana es el valor del medio. Dado un número par de valores, la mediana es el promedio de los dos valores del medio.
midpoint (86)		**punto medio** (86)
The point that divides a segment into two congruent segments.		Punto que divide un segmento en dos segmentos congruentes.
minimum of a function (89)		**mínimo de una función** (89)
The y-value of the lowest point on the graph of the function.		Valor de y del punto más bajo en la gráfica de la función.
mode (48)	Data set: 3, 5, 7, 7, 10 Mode: 7 Data set: 2, 4, 4, 6, 6, Modes: 4 and 6 Data set: 2, 4, 5, 8, 9 No mode	**moda** (48)
The value or values that occur most frequently in a data set. If all values occur with the same frequency, the data set is said to have no mode.		El valor o los valores que se presentan con mayor frecuencia en un conjunto de datos. Si todos los valores se presentan con la misma frecuencia, se dice que el conjunto de datos no tiene moda.

English	Example	Spanish
M		
monomial (53)		**monomio** (53)
A number or a product of numbers and variables with whole-number exponents, or a polynomial with one term.	$5x^3y^2$	Número o producto de números y variables con exponentes de números cabales, o polinomio con un término.
multiplicative inverse of a number (11)	The multiplicative inverse of 6 is $\frac{1}{6}$.	**inverso multiplicativo de un número** (11)
The reciprocal of the number.		Recíproco de un número.
mutually exclusive events (68)		**sucesos mutuamente excluyentes** (68)
Two events are mutually exclusive if they cannot both occur in the same trial of an experiment.	In the experiment of rolling a number cube, rolling a 2 and rolling an odd number are mutually exclusive events.	Dos sucesos son mutuamente excluyentes si ambos no pueden ocurrir en la misma prueba de un experimento.
N		
natural number (1)		**número natural** (1)
A counting number.	1, 2, 3, 4, 5, …	Número que se utiliza para contar.
negative correlation (71)		**correlación negativa** (71)
Two data sets have a negative correlation if one set of data values increases as the other set decreases.		Dos conjuntos de datos tienen una correlación negativa si un conjunto de valores de datos aumenta a medida que el otro conjunto de datos disminuye.
numeric expression (9)		**expresión numérica** (9)
An expression that contains only numbers and operations.	$2 \cdot 5 + (6 - 8)$	Expresión que contiene únicamente números y operaciones.

English	Example	Spanish
O		
odds (33)		**posibilidades** (33)
A comparison of favorable and unfavorable outcomes. The odds in favor of an event are the ratio of the number of favorable outcomes to the number of unfavorable outcomes. The odds against an event are the ratio of the number of unfavorable outcomes to the number of favorable outcomes.	The odds in favor of rolling a 4 on a number cube are 1:5.	Comparación de los resultados favorables y desfavorables. Las posibilidades a favor de un suceso son la razón entre la cantidad de resultados favorables y la cantidad de resultados desfavorables. Las posibilidades en contra de un suceso son la razón entre la cantidad de resultados desfavorables y la cantidad de resultados favorables.
opposite (6)		**opuesto** (6)
The opposite of a number a, denoted $-a$, is the number that is the same distance from zero as a, on the opposite side of the number line. The sum of opposites is 0.	⟵4 units⟶⟵4 units⟶ -4 -2 0 2 4	El opuesto de un número a, expresado $-a$, es el número que se encuentra a la misma distancia de cero que a, del lado opuesto de la recta numérica. La suma de los opuestos es 0.
order of magnitude (3)		**orden de magnitud** (3)
The order of magnitude of a quantity is the power of 10 nearest the quantity.		El orden de magnitud de una cantidad es la potencia de diez más cercana a la cantidad.
order of operations (4)		**orden de las operaciones** (4)
A rule for evaluating expressions: First, perform operations in parentheses or other grouping symbols. Second, evaluate powers and roots. Third, perform all multiplication and division from left to right. Fourth, perform all addition and subtraction from left to right.		Regla para evaluar las expresiones: Primero, realizar las operaciones entre paréntesis u otros símbolos de agrupación. Segundo, evaluar las potencias y las raíces. Tercero, realizar todas las multiplicaciones y divisiones de izquierda a derecha. Cuarto, realizar todas las sumas y restas de izquierda a derecha.

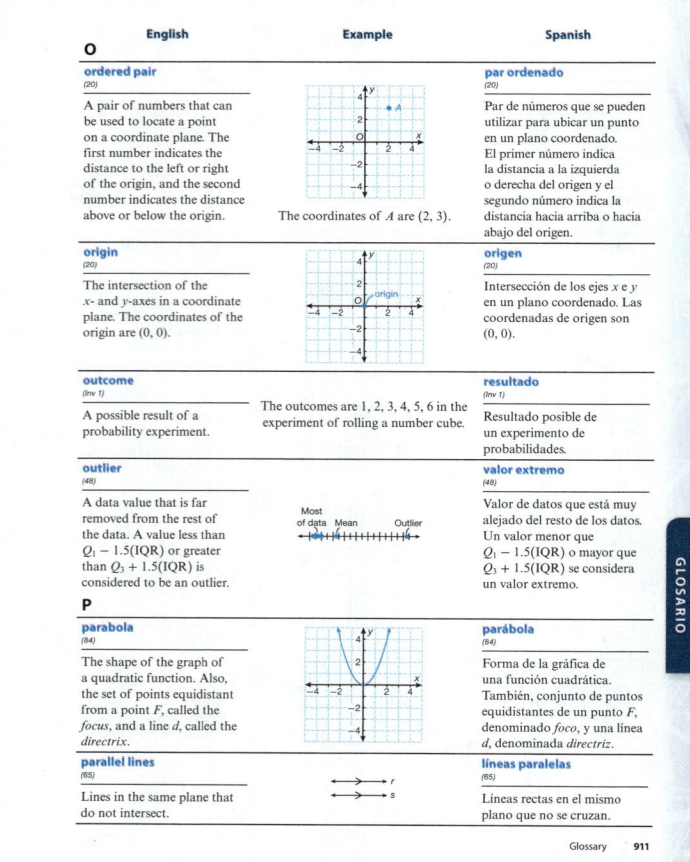

English	Example	Spanish
O		
ordered pair (20)		**par ordenado** (20)
A pair of numbers that can be used to locate a point on a coordinate plane. The first number indicates the distance to the left or right of the origin, and the second number indicates the distance above or below the origin.	The coordinates of A are (2, 3).	Par de números que se pueden utilizar para ubicar un punto en un plano coordenado. El primer número indica la distancia a la izquierda o derecha del origen y el segundo número indica la distancia hacia arriba o hacia abajo del origen.
origin (20)		**origen** (20)
The intersection of the x- and y-axes in a coordinate plane. The coordinates of the origin are (0, 0).		Intersección de los ejes x e y en un plano coordenado. Las coordenadas de origen son (0, 0).
outcome (Inv 1)	The outcomes are 1, 2, 3, 4, 5, 6 in the experiment of rolling a number cube.	**resultado** (Inv 1)
A possible result of a probability experiment.		Resultado posible de un experimento de probabilidades.
outlier (48)		**valor extremo** (48)
A data value that is far removed from the rest of the data. A value less than $Q_1 - 1.5(IQR)$ or greater than $Q_3 + 1.5(IQR)$ is considered to be an outlier.	Most of data Mean Outlier	Valor de datos que está muy alejado del resto de los datos. Un valor menor que $Q_1 - 1.5(IQR)$ o mayor que $Q_3 + 1.5(IQR)$ se considera un valor extremo.
P		
parabola (84)		**parábola** (84)
The shape of the graph of a quadratic function. Also, the set of points equidistant from a point F, called the focus, and a line d, called the directrix.		Forma de la gráfica de una función cuadrática. También, conjunto de puntos equidistantes de un punto F, denominado foco, y una línea d, denominada directriz.
parallel lines (65)		**líneas paralelas** (65)
Lines in the same plane that do not intersect.	⟷ r ⟷ s	Líneas rectas en el mismo plano que no se cruzan.

English	Example	Spanish
P		
parent function (Inv 6)		**función madre** (Inv 6)
The most basic function of a family of functions, or the original function before a transformation is applied.	$f(x) = x^2$ is the parent function for $h(x) = x^2 + 5$.	La función más básica de una familia de funciones o la función original antes de aplicar una transformación.
percent (42)		**porcentaje** (42)
A ratio that compares a number to 100.	$\frac{16}{100} = 16\%$	Razón que compara un número con 100.
percent of change (47)		**porcentaje de cambio** (47)
An increase or decrease given as a percent of the original amount. Percent increase describes an amount that has grown. Percent decrease describes an amount that has been reduced.		Incremento o disminución dada como un porcentaje de la cantidad original. El porcentaje de incremento describe una cantidad que ha aumentado. El porcentaje de disminución describe una cantidad que se ha reducido.
perfect square (13)		**cuadrado perfecto** (13)
A number whose positive square root is a whole number.	49 is a perfect square because $\sqrt{49} = 7$.	Número cuya raíz cuadrada positiva es un número cabal.
perfect-square trinomial (60)		**trinomio cuadrado perfecto** (60)
A trinomial whose factored form is the square of a binomial. A perfect-square trinomial has the form $a^2 - 2ab + b^2 = (a - b)^2$ or $a^2 + 2ab + b^2 = (a + b)^2$.	$x^2 + 10x + 25$ is a perfect-square trinomial, because $x^2 + 10x + 25 = (x + 5)^2$.	Trinomio cuya forma factorizada es el cuadrado de un binomio. Un trinomio cuadrado perfecto tiene la forma $a^2 - 2ab + b^2 = (a - b)^2$ o $a^2 + 2ab + b^2 = (a + b)^2$.
permutation (111)	For objects P, Q, R, S, there are 12 different permutations of 2 objects. PQ, PR, PS, QR, QS, RS, QP, RP, SP, RQ, SQ, SR	**permutación** (111)
An arrangement of a group of objects in which order is important.		Arreglo de un grupo de objetos en el cual el orden es importante.
perpendicular lines (65)		**líneas perpendiculares** (65)
Lines that intersect at 90° angles.		Líneas que se cruzan en ángulos de 90°.

English	Example	Spanish
P		
point-slope form (52)		**forma de punto y pendiente** (52)
$y - y_1 = m(x - x_1)$ where m is the slope and (x_1, y_1) is a point on the line.	$y - 4 = 2(x - 5)$	$y - y_1 = m(x - x_1)$, donde m es la pendiente y (x_1, y_1) es un punto en la línea.
polynomial (53)		**polinomio** (53)
A monomial or a sum or difference of monomials.	$3x^2 + 4xy - 8y^2$	Monomio o suma o diferencia de monomios.
positive correlation (71)		**correlación positiva** (71)
Two data sets have a positive correlation if both sets of data values increase.		Dos conjuntos de datos tienen correlación positiva si los valores de ambos conjuntos de datos aumentan.
principal square root (46)		**raíz cuadrada principal** (46)
The positive square root of a number, indicated by the radical sign.	$\sqrt{64} = 8$	Raíz cuadrada positiva de un número, expresada por el signo de radical.
probability (Inv 1)		**probabilidad** (Inv 1)
A number from 0 to 1 (or 0% to 100%) that describes how likely an event is to occur.	A bag contains 4 green marbles and 5 purple marbles. The probability of randomly choosing a purple marble is $\frac{5}{9}$.	Número entre 0 y 1 (o entre 0% y 100%) que describe cuán probable es que ocurra un suceso.
proportion (31)		**proporción** (31)
An equation that states that two ratios are equal.	$\frac{3}{4} = \frac{9}{12}$	Ecuación que establece que dos razones son iguales.
Pythagorean triple (85)		**Tripleta de Pitágoras** (85)
A set of three nonzero whole numbers a, b, and c such that $a^2 + b^2 = c^2$.	The numbers 3, 4, and 5 are a Pythagorean triple because $3^2 + 4^2 = 5^2$.	Conjunto de tres números cabales distintos de cero a, b y c tal que $a^2 + b^2 = c^2$.

Glossary 913

English	Example	Spanish
Q		
quadrant (20)		**cuadrante** (20)
One of the four regions into which the x- and y-axes divide the coordinate plane.	Quadrant II, Quadrant I, Quadrant III, Quadrant IV	Una de las cuatro regiones en las que los ejes x e y dividen el plano coordenado.
quadratic function (84)		**función cuadrática** (84)
A function that can be written in the form $f(x) = ax^2 + bx + c$, where a, b, and c are real numbers and $a \neq 0$, or in the form $f(x) = a(x - h)^2 + k$, where a, h, and k are real numbers and $a \neq 0$.	$f(x) = x^2 - 5x + 6$	Función que se puede expresar como $f(x) = ax^2 + bx + c$, donde a, b y c son números reales y $a \neq 0$, o como $f(x) = a(x - h)^2 + k$, donde a, h y k son números reales y $a \neq 0$.
R		
radical equation (106)		**ecuación radical** (106)
An equation that contains a variable within a radical.	$\sqrt{x + 2} + 5 = 9$	Ecuación que contiene una variable dentro de un radical.
radical expression (61)		**expresión radical** (61)
An expression that contains a radical sign.	$\sqrt{x + 2} + 5$	Expresión que contiene un signo de radical.
radicand (13)		**radicando** (13)
The number or expression under a radical sign.	Expression: $\sqrt{x + 7}$ Radicand: $x + 7$	Número o expresión debajo del signo de radical.
random event (Inv 1)		**suceso aleatorio** (Inv 1)
An event whose outcome cannot be predicted.		Un suceso para el cual no se pueden predecir sus resultados posibles.
random sample (Inv 3)		**muestra aleatoria** (Inv 3)
A sample selected from a population so that each member of the population has an equal chance of being selected.		Muestra seleccionada de una población tal que cada miembro de ésta tenga igual probabilidad de ser seleccionada.

914 Saxon Algebra 1

English	Example	Spanish
R		
range (25)		**rango** (25)
The set of output values of a function or relation.		Conjunto de los valores de salida de una función o relación.
range of a function (25)		**rango de una función** (25)
The set of all possible output values of a function.	The range of $y = 2x^2$ is $y \geq 0$.	Conjunto de todos los valores de salida posibles de una función o relación.
range of a set of data (48)		**rango de un conjunto de datos** (48)
The difference between the greatest and least values in the data set.	The data set {2, 4, 6, 8, 10} has a range of $10 - 2 = 8$.	La diferencia entre los valores mayor y menor en un conjunto de datos.
rate (31)		**tasa** (31)
A ratio that compares two quantities measured in different units.	$\frac{65 \text{ miles}}{1 \text{ hour}} = 65$ mi/hr	Razón que compara dos cantidades medidas en diferentes unidades.
rate of change (41, 44)		**tasa de cambio** (41)
A ratio that compares the amount of change in the dependent variable to the amount of change in the independent variable.		Razón que compara la cantidad de cambio de la variable dependiente con la cantidad de cambio de la variable independiente.
ratio (31)		**razón** (31)
A comparison of two numbers by division.	$\frac{1}{3}$ or 1:3	Comparación de dos números mediante una división.
rational equation (99)		**ecuación racional** (99)
An equation that contains one or more rational expressions.	$\frac{x + 3}{x^2 - 2x - 3} = 2$	Ecuación que contiene una o más expresiones racionales.
rational expression (39)		**expresión racional** (39)
An algebraic expression whose numerator and denominator are polynomials and whose denominator has a degree ≥ 1.	$\frac{x + 3}{x^2 - 2x - 3}$	Expresión algebraica cuyo numerador y denominador son polinomios y cuyo denominador tiene un grado ≥ 1.

Glossary 915

English	Example	Spanish
R		
rational function (78)		**función racional** (78)
A function whose rule can be written as a rational expression.	$f(x) = \frac{x + 3}{x^2 - 2x - 3}$	Función cuya regla se puede expresar como una expresión racional.
rational number (1)		**número racional** (1)
A number that can be written in the form $\frac{a}{b}$, where a and b are integers and $b \neq 0$.	$4, 2.75, 0.\overline{4}, -\frac{4}{5}, 0$	Número que se puede expresar como $\frac{a}{b}$, donde a y b son números enteros y $b \neq 0$.
rationalizing the denominator (103)		**racionalizar el denominador** (103)
A method of rewriting a fraction by multiplying by another fraction that is equivalent to 1 in order to remove radical terms from the denominator.	$\frac{1}{\sqrt{3}} \cdot \frac{\sqrt{3}}{\sqrt{3}} = \frac{\sqrt{3}}{3}$	Método que consiste en escribir nuevamente una fracción multiplicándola por otra fracción equivalente a 1 a fin de eliminar los términos radicales del denominador.
real number (1)		**número real** (1)
A rational or irrational number. Every point on the number line represents a real number.		Número racional o irracional. Cada punto de la recta numérica representa un número real.
reciprocal (11)		**recíproco** (11)
For a real number $a \neq 0$, the reciprocal of a is $\frac{1}{a}$. The product of reciprocals is 1.	The reciprocal of 2 is $\frac{1}{2}$.	Dado el número real $a \neq 0$, el recíproco de a es $\frac{1}{a}$. El producto de los recíprocos es 1.
reflection (Inv 6)		**reflexión** (Inv 6)
A transformation across a line, called the line of reflection. The line of reflection is the perpendicular bisector of each segment joining a point and its image.		Transformación sobre una línea, denominada la línea de reflexión. La línea de reflexión es la mediatriz de cada segmento que une un punto con su imagen.
relation (25)		**relación** (25)
A set of ordered pairs.	{(2, 3), (3, 4), (4, 5), (6, 7)}	Conjunto de pares ordenados.

916 Saxon Algebra 1

English	Example	Spanish
R		
relative frequency (62)		**frecuencia relativa** (62)
In an experiment, the number of times an event happens divided by the total number of trials.		En un experimento, el número de veces de ocurrencia de un suceso dividido entre el número total de intentos.
root of an equation (98)		**raíz de una ecuación** (98)
Any value of the variable that makes the equation true.	4 is a root of $2x + 3 = 11$.	Cualquier valor de la variable que transforme la ecuación en verdadera.
S		
sample space (14)	The sample space in the experiment of rolling a number cube is $\{1, 2, 3, 4, 5, 6\}$.	**espacio muestral** (14)
The set of all possible outcomes of a probability experiment.		Conjunto de todos los resultados posibles de un experimento de probabilidades.
scale (36)	1 cm : 6 mi	**escala** (36)
The ratio of any length in a drawing to the corresponding actual length.		Razón entre una longitud cualquiera en un dibujo y la longitud real correspondiente.
scale drawing (36)	Scale: 1 in.: 5 ft	**dibujo a escala** (36)
A drawing that uses a scale to represent an object as smaller or larger than the original object.		Dibujo que utiliza una escala para representar un objeto como más pequeño o más grande que el objeto original.
scale factor (36)	Scale Factor: $\frac{9}{6} = 1.5$	**factor de escala** (36)
The ratio of a side length of a figure to the corresponding side length of a similar figure.		La razón de la longitud de un lado de una figura a la longitud del lado correspondiente de una figura similar.

Glossary 917

English	Example	Spanish
S		
scatter plot (71)		**diagrama de dispersión** (71)
A graph with points plotted to show a possible relationship between two sets of data.		Gráfica con puntos dispersos para demostrar una relación posible entre dos conjuntos de datos.
scientific notation (37)	$1{,}420{,}000{,}000 = 1.42 \times 10^9$	**notación científica** (37)
A method of writing very large or very small numbers, by using powers of 10, in the form $m \times 10^n$, where $1 \leq m < 10$ and n is an integer.		Método que consiste en escribir números muy grandes o muy pequeños utilizando potencias de 10 del tipo $m \times 10^n$, donde $1 \leq m < 10$ y n es un número entero.
secant of an angle (117)		**secante de un ángulo** (117)
The reciprocal of the cosine function. In a right triangle, the secant of angle A is the ratio of the length of the hypotenuse to the length of the leg adjacent to the angle.	$\sec A = \frac{\text{hypotenuse}}{\text{adjacent}}$	Inversa de la función coseno. En un triángulo rectángulo, la secante del ángulo A es la razón de la longitud de la hipotenusa a la longitud del cateto adyacente al ángulo.
sequence (34)	$1, 2, 4, 8, 16, \ldots$	**sucesión** (34)
A list of numbers that often form a pattern.		Lista de números que generalmente forman un patrón.
set (1)		**conjunto** (1)
A collection of items called elements.		Grupo de componentes denominados elementos.
similar (36)		**semejantes** (36)
Two figures that have the same shape, but not necessarily the same size.		Dos figuras con la misma forma pero no necesariamente del mismo tamaño.
simple event (14)	The event of rolling a die and it landing on 4 is a simple event.	**suceso simple** (14)
An event resulting in a single outcome.		Suceso que tiene sólo un resultado.

918 Saxon Algebra 1

English	Example	Spanish
S		
simple interest (116)		**interés simple** (116)
A fixed percent of the principal. For principal P, interest rate r, and time t in years, the simple interest is $I = Prt$.		Porcentaje fijo del capital. Dado el capital P, la tasa de interés r y el tiempo t expresado en años, el interés simple es $I = Prt$.
simplify (4)	$12 - 10 + 8$ $2 + 8$ 10	**simplificar** (4)
To perform all indicated operations.		Realizar todas las operaciones indicadas.
simulation (Inv 1)		**simulación** (Inv 1)
A model of an experiment, often one that would be too difficult or time-consuming to actually perform.		Modelo de un experimento; generalmente se recurre a la simulación cuando realizar dicho experimento sería demasiado difícil o llevaría mucho tiempo.
sine (117)	$\sin A = \frac{\text{opposite}}{\text{hypotenuse}}$	**seno** (117)
In a right triangle, the sine of angle A is the ratio of the length of the leg opposite the angle to the length of the hypotenuse.		En un triángulo rectángulo, el seno del ángulo A es la razón entre la longitud del cateto opuesto al ángulo y la longitud de la hipotenusa.
slope (41, 44)	$m = \frac{y_2 - y_1}{x_2 - x_1} = \frac{0 - 4}{-3 - 3} = \frac{-4}{-6} = \frac{2}{3}$	**pendiente** (41, 44)
A measure of the steepness of a line. If (x_1, y_1) and (x_2, y_2) are any two points on the line, the slope of the line, known as m, is represented by the equation $m = \frac{y_2 - y_1}{x_2 - x_1}$.		Medida de la inclinación de una línea. Dados dos puntos (x_1, y_1) y (x_2, y_2) en una línea, la pendiente de la línea, denominada m, se representa por la ecuación $m = \frac{y_2 - y_1}{x_2 - x_1}$.
slope-intercept form (49)	$y = -3x + 5$ The slope is -3. The y-intercept is 5.	**forma de pendiente-intersección** (49)
A line with slope m and y-intercept b can be written in the form $y = mx + b$.		Una línea con pendiente m e intersección con el eje y en b se puede expresar como $y = mx + b$.

Glossary 919

English	Example	Spanish
S		
solution of a linear equation in two variables (35)	$(2, 3)$ is a solution of the equation $3x + 4y = 18$.	**solución de una ecuación lineal de dos variables** (35)
An ordered pair or set of ordered pairs that satisfies the equation.		Un par ordenado o conjunto de pares ordenados que satisfacen la ecuación.
solution of a linear inequality in two variables (97)	$(1, 4)$ is a solution of the inequality $3x + 4y > 18$.	**solución de una desigualdad lineal de dos variables** (35)
An ordered pair or set of ordered pairs that satisfies the inequality.		Un par ordenado o conjunto de pares ordenados que satisfacen la desigualdad.
solution of a system of linear equations (55)	$(7, 1)$ is a solution of $\begin{array}{l}x - y = 6\\ x + y = 8\end{array}$	**solución de un sistema de ecuaciones lineales** (55)
An ordered pair or set of ordered pairs that satisfies all the equations in the system.		Un par ordenado o conjunto de pares ordenados que satisfacen todas las ecuaciones en el sistema.
solution of a system of linear inequalities (109)	$(2, 1)$ is a solution of $\begin{array}{l}x - y < 6\\ x + y < 8\end{array}$	**solución de un sistema de desigualdades lineales** (109)
An ordered pair or set of ordered pairs that satisfies all the inequalities in the system.		Un par ordenado o conjunto de pares ordenados que satisfacen todas las desigualdades en el sistema.
solution of an equation in one variable (19)	6 is a solution of $2x + 3 = 15$.	**solución con una variable de una ecuación** (19)
A value of the variable that makes the equation true.		Un valor de la variable que satisface la ecuación.
solution of an equation in two variables (49)	$(2, 3)$ is a solution to the equation $x + y^2 = 11$.	**solución de una ecuación con dos variables** (19)
An ordered pair or set of ordered pairs that satisfies the equation.		Un par ordenado o conjunto de pares ordenados que satisface la ecuación.
solution of an inequality in one variable (50)	4 is a solution of $x + 3 < 10$.	**solución con una variable de una desigualdad** (50)
A value or set of values that satisfies the inequality.		Un valor de la variable que satisface la desigualdad.

920 Saxon Algebra 1

S

English	Example	Spanish
solution of an inequality in two variables (97) An ordered pair or set of ordered pairs that satisfies the inequality.	(2, 3) is a solution of $x + y > 2$.	**solución de una desigualdad de dos variables** (97) Un par ordenado o conjunto de pares ordenados que satisface la desigualdad.
square root (13) A number that is multiplied by itself to form a product is called a square root of that product.	$\sqrt{25}$ is 5 because $5^2 = 5 \cdot 5 = 25$.	**raíz cuadrada** (13) El número que se multiplica por sí mismo para formar un producto se denomina la raíz cuadrada de ese producto.
square-root function (114) A function whose rule contains a variable under a square-root sign.	$y = \sqrt{5x} - 6$	**función de raíz cuadrada** (114) Función cuya regla contiene una variable bajo un signo de raíz cuadrada.
standard form of a linear equation (35) $Ax + By = C$, where A, B, and C are real numbers.	$3x + 5y = 6$	**forma estándar de una ecuación lineal** (35) $Ax + By = C$, donde A, B y C son números reales.
standard form of a polynomial (53) A polynomial in one variable is written in standard form when the terms are in order from greatest degree to least degree.	$3x^4 - 2x^3 - 6x^2 + 2x - 1$	**forma estándar de un polinomio** (53) Un polinomio de una variable se expresa en forma estándar cuando los términos se ordenan de mayor a menor grado.
standard form of a quadratic equation (96) $ax^2 + bx + c = 0$, where a, b, and c are real numbers and $a \neq 0$.	$3x^2 + 4x - 1 = 0$	**forma estándar de una ecuación cuadrática** (96) $ax^2 + bx + c =$, donde a, b y c son números reales y $a \neq 0$.
standard form of a quadratic function (84) $f(x) = ax^2 + bx + c$, where a does not equal 0.	$f(x) = 2x^2 - 3x + 5$	**forma estándar de una función cuadrática** (84) $f(x) = ax^2 + bx + c$, donde a no es igual a 0.

S

English	Example	Spanish
stem-and-leaf plot (22) A graph used to organize and display data by dividing each data value into two parts, a stem and a leaf.	Stem | Leaves 2 | 2, 4, 5, 6 3 | 1, 2, 4 4 | 4, 7, 9 Key: 3|1 means 3.1	**diagrama de tallo y hojas** (22) Gráfica utilizada para organizar y mostrar datos dividiendo cada valor de datos en dos partes, un tallo y una hoja.
system of linear equations (55) A system of equations in which all of the equations are linear.	$2x + 4y = 2$ $x - 2y = 5$	**sistema de ecuaciones lineales** (55) Sistema de ecuaciones en el que todas las ecuaciones son lineales.
system of linear inequalities (109) A system of inequalities in two or more variables in which all of the inequalities are linear.	$y \leq x + 1$ $y < -x + 3$	**sistema de desigualdades lineales** (109) Sistema de desigualdades en dos o más variables en el que todas las desigualdades son lineales.

T

English	Example	Spanish
tangent of an angle (117) In a right triangle, the tangent of angle A is the ratio of the length of the leg opposite the angle to the length of the leg adjacent to the angle.	$\tan A = \dfrac{\text{opposite}}{\text{adjacent}}$	**tangente de un ángulo** (117) En un triángulo rectángulo, la tangente del ángulo A es la razón entre la longitud del cateto opuesto al ángulo y la longitud del cateto adyacente al ángulo.
term of an expression (2) A part of an expression to be added or subtracted	$4x^2 + 3x$ $4x^2$ and $3x$ are terms.	**término de una expresión** (2) Parte de una expresión que debe sumarse o restarse.
term of a sequence (34) An element or number in the sequence.	6 is the third term in the sequence 2, 4, 6, 8, …	**término de una sucesión** (34) Elemento o número de una sucesión.

T

English	Example	Spanish
theoretical probability (14) The ratio of the number of equally likely outcomes in an event to the total number of possible outcomes.	In the experiment of rolling a number cube, the theoretical probability of rolling an even number is $\frac{3}{6} = \frac{1}{2}$.	**probabilidad teórica** (14) Razón entre el número de resultados igualmente probables de un suceso y el número total de resultados posibles.
translation (Inv 6) A transformation in which all the points of a figure move the same distance in the same direction; the figure is moved along a vector so that all of the segments joining a point and its image are congruent and parallel.		**traslación** (Inv 6) Transformación en la que todos los puntos de una figura se mueven la misma distancia en la misma dirección; la figura se mueve a lo largo de un vector de forma tal que todos los segmentos que unen un punto a su imagen son congruentes y paralelos.
trend line (71) A line on a scatter plot that helps show the correlation between data sets more clearly. See also line of best fit.	Tea Consumption	**línea de tendencia** (71) Línea en un diagrama de dispersión que sirve para mostrar la correlación entre conjuntos de datos más claramente. Ver también línea de mejor ajuste.
trigonometric ratio (117) A ratio of two sides of a right triangle.	$\sin A = \dfrac{a}{c}$, $\cos A = \dfrac{b}{c}$, $\tan A = \dfrac{a}{b}$	**razón trigonométrica** (117) Razón entre dos lados de un triángulo rectángulo.
trinomial (53) A polynomial with three terms.	$4x^2 + 2xy - 7y^2$	**trinomio** (53) Polinomio con tres términos.

U

English	Example	Spanish
union (1) The union of two sets is the set of all elements that are in either set, denoted by $\cup$.	$A = \{1, 2, 3\}$ $B = \{2, 3, 4, 5\}$ $A \cup B = \{1, 2, 3, 4, 5\}$	**unión** (1) La unión de dos conjuntos es el conjunto de todos los elementos que se encuentran en ambos conjuntos, expresado por $\cup$.
unit rate (31) A rate in which the second quantity in the comparison is one unit.	$\dfrac{60 \text{ mi}}{1 \text{ h}} = 60 \text{ mi/h}$	**tasa unitaria** (31) Tasa en la que la segunda cantidad de la comparación es una unidad.
unlike radicals (69) Radicals with a different quantity under the radical.	$3\sqrt{5}$ and $2\sqrt{6}$	**radicales distintos** (69) Radicales con cantidades diferentes debajo del signo del radical.
unlike terms (18) Terms with different variables or the same variables raised to different powers.	$3xy^2$ and $4x^2y$	**términos distintos** (18) Términos con variables diferentes o las mismas variables elevadas a potencias diferentes.

V

English	Example	Spanish
variable (2) A symbol used to represent a quantity that can change.	In the expression $x + 5$, x is the variable.	**variable** (2) Símbolo utilizado para representar una cantidad que puede cambiar.
vertex of a parabola (89) The highest or lowest point on a parabola.		**vértice de una parábola** (89) Punto más alto o más bajo de una parábola.
vertex of an absolute-value graph (107) The point on the axis of symmetry of the graph.		**vértice de una gráfica de valor absoluto** (107) Punto en el eje de simetría de la gráfica.

English	Example	Spanish
V		
vertical-line test (25)		**prueba de la línea vertical** (25)
A test used to determine whether a relation is a function. If any vertical line crosses the graph of a relation more than once, the relation is not a function.	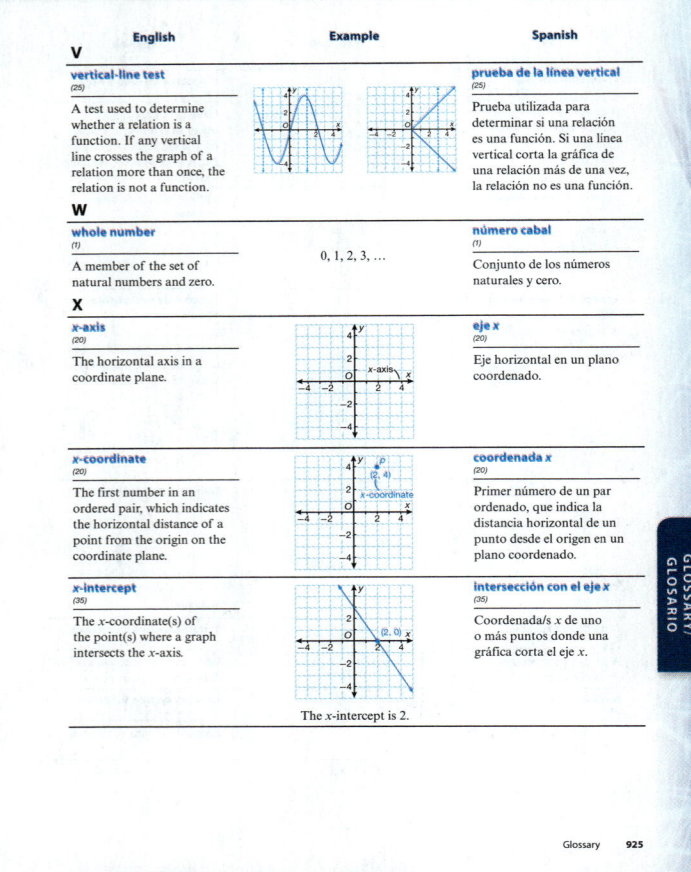	Prueba utilizada para determinar si una relación es una función. Si una línea vertical corta la gráfica de una relación más de una vez, la relación no es una función.
W		
whole number (1)	0, 1, 2, 3, …	**número cabal** (1)
A member of the set of natural numbers and zero.		Conjunto de los números naturales y cero.
X		
x-axis (20)		**eje x** (20)
The horizontal axis in a coordinate plane.		Eje horizontal en un plano coordenado.
x-coordinate (20)		**coordenada x** (20)
The first number in an ordered pair, which indicates the horizontal distance of a point from the origin on the coordinate plane.		Primer número de un par ordenado, que indica la distancia horizontal de un punto desde el origen en un plano coordenado.
x-intercept (35)		**intersección con el eje x** (35)
The x-coordinate(s) of the point(s) where a graph intersects the x-axis.		Coordenada/s x de uno o más puntos donde una gráfica corta el eje x.

The x-intercept is 2.

English	Example	Spanish
Y		
y-axis (20)		**eje y** (20)
The vertical axis in a coordinate plane.	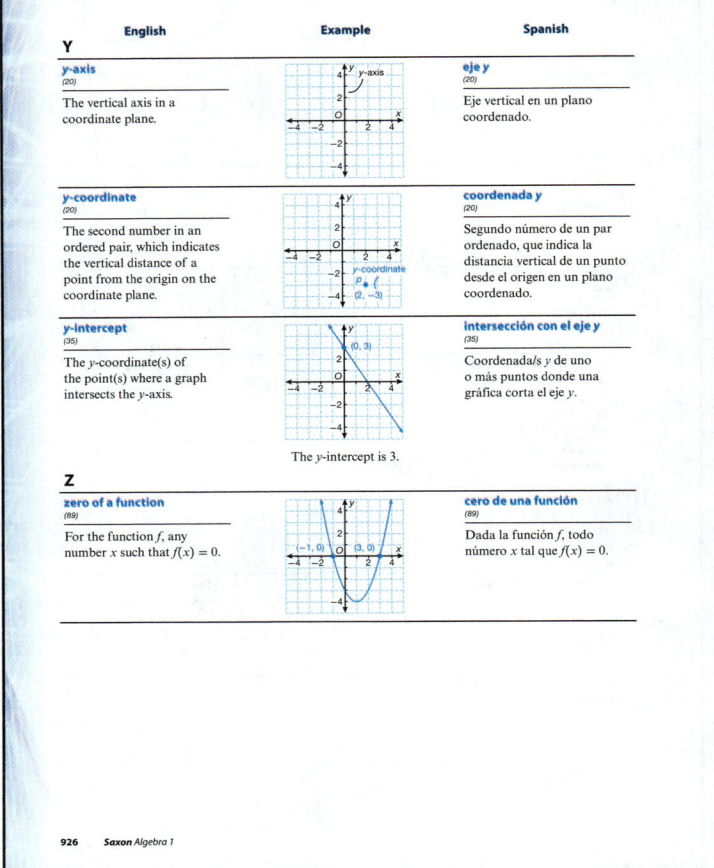	Eje vertical en un plano coordenado.
y-coordinate (20)		**coordenada y** (20)
The second number in an ordered pair, which indicates the vertical distance of a point from the origin on the coordinate plane.		Segundo número de un par ordenado, que indica la distancia vertical de un punto desde el origen en un plano coordenado.
y-intercept (35)		**intersección con el eje y** (35)
The y-coordinate(s) of the point(s) where a graph intersects the y-axis.		Coordenada/s y de uno o más puntos donde una gráfica corta el eje y.

The y-intercept is 3.

English	Example	Spanish
Z		
zero of a function (89)		**cero de una función** (89)
For the function f, any number x such that $f(x) = 0$.		Dada la función f, todo número x tal que $f(x) = 0$.

Lesson 4

Lesson Practice

a. $45 - (2 + 4) \cdot 5 - 3$
  $= 45 - 6 \cdot 5 - 3$ Simplify inside parentheses.
  $= 45 - 30 - 3$ Multiply.
  $= 12$ Subtract.

b. $9 \cdot 2^3 - 9 \div 3$
  $= 9 \cdot 8 - 9 \div 3$ Simplify the exponent.
  $= 72 - 3$ Multiply and divide from left to right.
  $= 69$ Subtract.

c. $\frac{15 - 3^2 + 4 \cdot 2}{7}$
  $= \frac{15 - 9 + 4 \cdot 2}{7}$ Simplify exponents.
  $= \frac{15 - 9 + 8}{7}$ Multiply.
  $= \frac{14}{7}$ Add and subtract left to right in numerator.
  $= 2$ Divide.

Lesson 7

Lesson Practice

d. Sample:
  $4(1+2)^2 \div 6 + \frac{8 \cdot 3}{2}$
  $= 4 \cdot 3^2 \div 6 + \frac{8 \cdot 3}{2}$ Simplify inside parentheses.
  $= 4 \cdot 3^2 \div 6 + \frac{24}{2}$ Simplify the numerator.
  $= 4 \cdot 3^2 \div 6 + 12$ Simplify the fraction.
  $= 4 \cdot 9 \div 6 + 12$ Simplify the exponent.
  $= 6 + 12$ Multiply and divide from left to right.
  $= 18$ Add.

Lesson 12

Practice

11. $x + 5 + 15$ Commutative Property of Addition
  $= x + (5 + 15)$ Associative Property of Addition
  $= x + 20$ Add.
  or
  $5 + 15 + x$ Commutative Property of Addition
  $= (5 + 15) + x$ Associative Property of Addition
  $= 20 + x$ Add.

Lesson 15

Practice

21. $7 \cdot 8x$ Commutative Property of Multiplication
  $(7 \cdot 8)x$ Associative Property of Multiplication
  $56x$ Multiply.
  or
  $x \cdot 7 \cdot 8$ Commutative Property of Multiplication
  $x(7 \cdot 8)$ Associative Property of Multiplication
  $x \cdot 56$ Multiply.

24.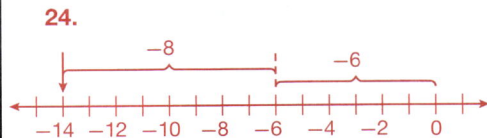

Lesson 20

Lesson Practice

a–f.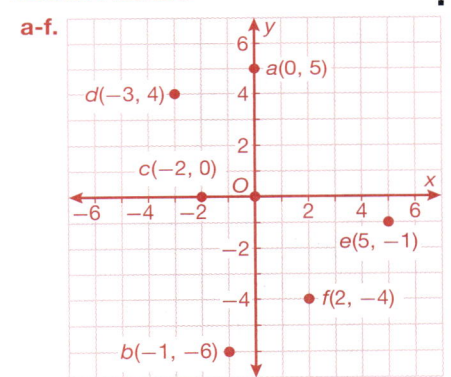

Practice

12a.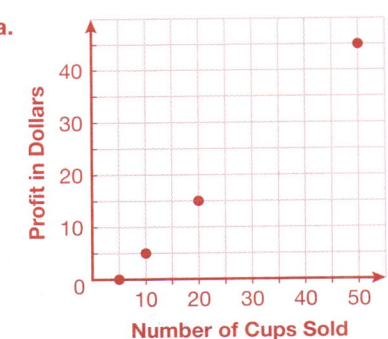

Lesson 21

Practice

20a.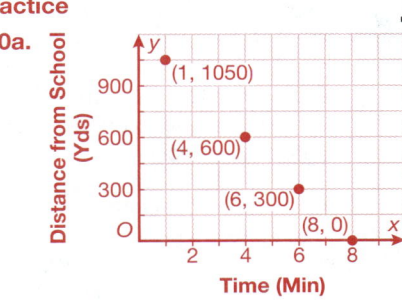

20b. Sample: It takes her 8 minutes to get from home to school.

25.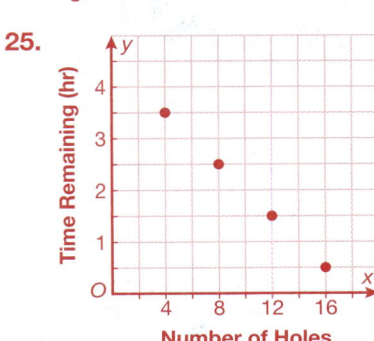

x	y
4	3.5
8	2.5
12	1.5
16	0.5

Lesson 22

Practice

10. Sample: The lap times have become faster since 1960.

Fastest Lap Times in the Indianapolis 500

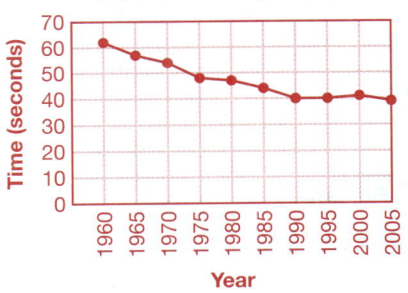

Additional Answers T899

19. Sample: There are more threatened and endangered mammals, birds, and reptiles in other countries, but the total number of threatened and endangered animals in the United States is greater than the total for other countries.

Threatened and Endangered Animals

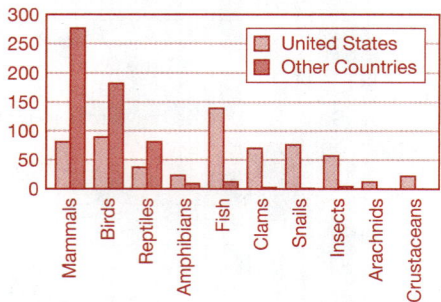

Lesson 23

Practice

10.

Favorite Vacation Destinations

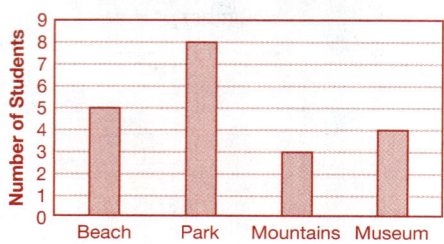

Lesson 24

Practice

13.

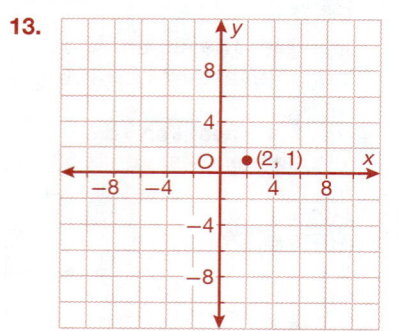

Lesson 25

Practice

2a. Sample:
$$103 + x = 99$$
$$103 + (-4) = 99$$
$$103 - 4 = 99$$
$$99 = 99$$

2b. Sample:
$$\frac{1}{2} - x = \frac{3}{4}$$
$$\frac{1}{2} - \left(-\frac{1}{4}\right) = \frac{3}{4}$$
$$\frac{1}{2} + \frac{1}{4} = \frac{3}{4}$$
$$\frac{2}{4} + \frac{1}{4} = \frac{3}{4}$$
$$\frac{3}{4} = \frac{3}{4}$$

3. Sample: This equation is a function.

Domain (x)	Range (y)
−2	0
0	2
2	4
4	6
5	7

19.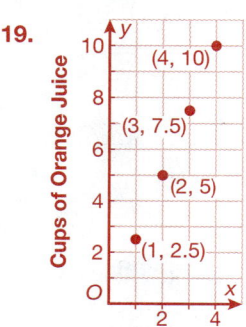

Lesson 26

Lesson Practice

a. $3x + 2 - x + 7 = 16$
$2x + 9 = 16$ Collect like terms.
$\underline{-9 = -9}$ Subtraction Property of Equality
$2x = 7$ Simplify.
$x = 3\frac{1}{2}$ Division Property of Equality

b. $6(x - 1) = 36$
$6x - 6 = 36$ Distributive Property
$\underline{+6 = +6}$ Addition Property of Equality
$6x = 42$ Simplify.
$x = 7$ Divide both sides by 6.

c. $5x - 3(x - 4) = 22$
$5x - 3x + 12 = 22$ Distributive Property
$2x + 12 = 22$ Combine like terms.
$\underline{-12 = -12}$ Subtraction Property of Equality
$2x = 10$ Simplify.
$x = 5$ Division Property of Equality

Practice

7. $-15x + 35 + 11 = 1$ Distributive Property.
$-15x + 46 = 1$ Combine like terms.
$-15x = -45$ Subtraction Property of Equality
$x = 3$ Division Property of Equality

Lesson 27

Practice

8. Sample: The title does not specify that the animals listed are only 5 of the 10 species in the petting zoo.

12. Sample: Machine 4 appears to produce about 3 times more parts than Machine 2 each day. Machine 2 appears to be less efficient.

Lesson 28

Lesson Practice

a. $6x = 3x + 27$
$\underline{-3x = -3x}$ Subtraction Property of Equality
$3x = 27$ Simplify.
$\frac{3x}{3} = \frac{27}{3}$ Division Property of Equality
$x = 9$ Simplify.

Check

$6(9) \stackrel{?}{=} 3(9) + 27$
$54 = 54$

b. $2 + 3(3x - 6) = 5(x - 3) + 15$
$2 + 9x - 18 = 5x - 15 + 15$
　　　　　　　　　　Distributive Property
$9x - 16 = 5x$　　　Simplify.
$\underline{-9x = -9x}$　Subtraction Property of Equality
$-16 = -4x$　　　Simplify.
$\frac{-16}{-4} = \frac{-4x}{-4}$　　　Division Property of Equality
$4 = x$　　　　　Simplify.

Check
$2 + 3[3(4) - 6] \stackrel{?}{=} 5[(4) - 3] + 15$
$2 + 3[12 - 6] \stackrel{?}{=} 5[1] + 15$
$2 + 18 \stackrel{?}{=} 5 + 15$
$20 = 20$

c. $2(x + 3) = 3(2x + 2) - 4x$
$2x + 6 = 6x + 6 - 4x$
　　　　　　　Distributive Property
$2x + 6 = 2x + 6$　Simplify.
$\underline{-2x = -2x}$　Subtraction Property of Equality
$6 = 6$　　　Simplify. Always true!

d. $3(x + 4) = 2(x + 5) + x$
$3x + 12 = 2x + 10 + x$
　　　　　　　Distributive Property
$3x + 12 = 3x + 10$　Simplify.
$\underline{-3x = -3x}$　Subtraction Property of Equality
$12 = 10$　　　Simplify. Never true!

Practice
11a. Sample:

Average Home Prices

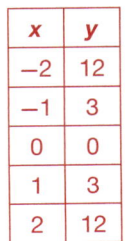

22.

Method 1	Method 2
$8(10 - 4)$	$8(10 - 4)$
$= 8(10) - 8(4)$	$= 8(6)$
$= 80 - 32$	$= 48$
$= 48$	

Lesson 30

Practice
22.

24. Sample:
$18 \cdot \frac{1}{6} x$　Commutative Property of Multiplication
$= \left(18 \cdot \frac{1}{6}\right)x$　Associative Property of Multiplication
$= 3x$

25. $3.6 + 4.08 + 8$　Subtract from left to right.
$= 7.68 + 8$　Add from left to right.
$= 15.68$　Add from left to right.

27. Sample:
$3 + \left(\frac{3}{4} + 2^2\right)$　symbol of inclusion
$= 3 + \left(\frac{3}{4} + 4\right)$　powers
$= 3 + 4\frac{3}{4}$　symbols of inclusion
$= 7\frac{3}{4}$　addition

Teacher's Edition Additional Example 1b.
b.

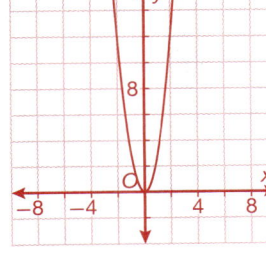

Challenge

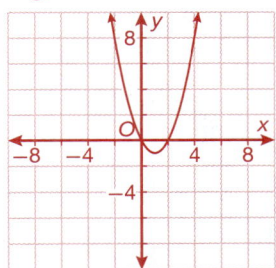

The graph is a nonlinear function.

Lesson 31

Practice
21.

x	-2	-1	0	1	2
y	3	0	-1	0	3

Domain: all real numbers
Range: $y \geq -1$

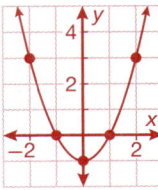

Lesson 35

Practice
14.

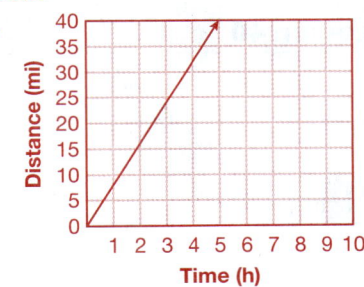

Lesson 36

Practice
30.
$34 - 2(x + 17) = 23x - 15 - 3x$
$34 - 2x - 34 = 23x - 15 - 3x$
　　　　　　Distributive Property
$-2x = 20x - 15$
　　　　　　Combine like terms.
$\underline{-20x = -20x}$
　　　　　　Subtraction Property of Equality
$-22x = -15$
$-\frac{1}{22} \cdot -22x = -15 \cdot -\frac{1}{22}$
　　　　　　Multiplication Property of Equality
$x = \frac{15}{22}$
　　　　　　Multiply.

Additional Answers　T901

Lesson 37

Practice

13.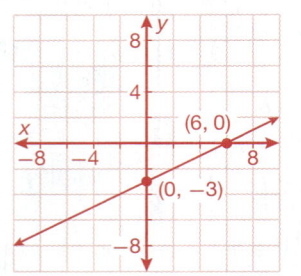

Lesson 38

Practice

4.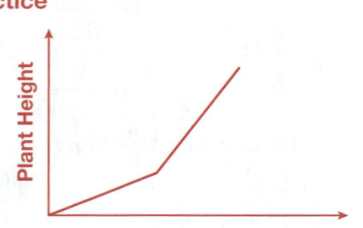

5.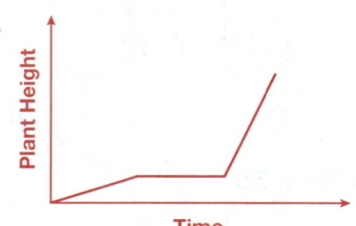

Lesson 40

Practice

20a.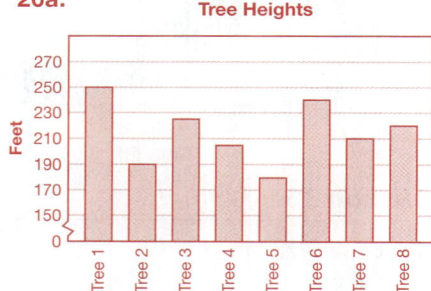

20b.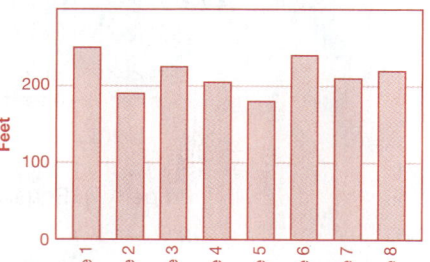

Investigation 4

1. inductive reasoning; Sample: The conclusion is based on the student's previous performance on tests.

Lesson 46

Practice

20. $27x^2y^3z = 3 \cdot 3 \cdot 3 \cdot x \cdot x \cdot y \cdot y \cdot y \cdot z$ and $12xy^2z = 2 \cdot 2 \cdot 3 \cdot x \cdot y \cdot y \cdot z$, so both terms have $3 \cdot x \cdot y \cdot y \cdot z$ in common and the GCF is $3xy^2z$; $3xy^2z(9xy + 4)$

Lesson 49

Lesson Practice

g.

Investigation 5

1. If a number is a multiple of 5, then it ends in 5.; false; Sample: 10 is a multiple of 5 but does not end in 5.

3. If it is not Monday, then I will not go to school.; false; Sample: If it is Tuesday, I will go to school.

Lesson 55

Practice

29b.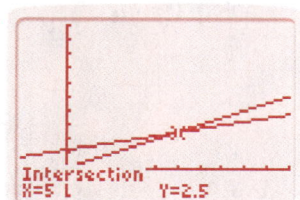

Lesson 56

Lesson Practice

i.

21.75 cubic centimeters

Practice

24.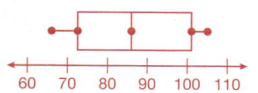
Average High Temperature in Phoenix, AZ

25.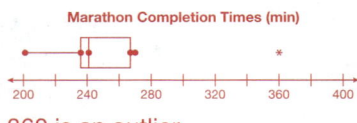
Marathon Completion Times (min)

360 is an outlier.

Lesson 57

Practice

12a.

Lesson 58

Practice

26. Sample:

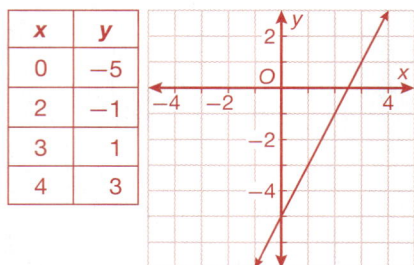

x	y
0	−5
2	−1
3	1
4	3

The pairs of values that satisfy the equation are recorded in the table of values and form coordinates that are points on the line in the graph.

Lesson 60

Practice

18.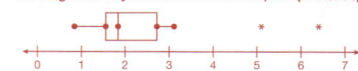
Average Monthly Rainfall in Cloudcroft, NM (in inches)

Investigation 6

Practice

a.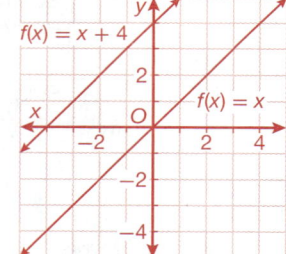

Sample: The graph of $f(x) = x$ is shifted up 4 units.

b.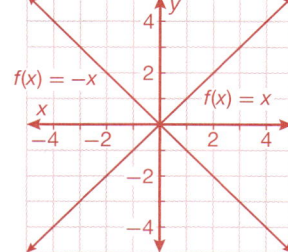

Sample: The graph of $f(x) = x$ is reflected over the y-axis.

c.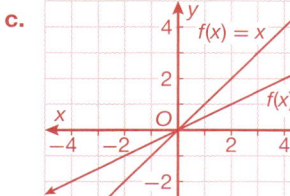

Sample: The graph of $f(x) = \frac{1}{2}x$ is not as steep as the graph of $f(x) = x$.

d.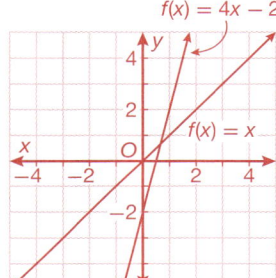

Sample: The graph is 4 times as steep as $f(x) = x$ and is shifted down 2 units.

Lesson 62

Lesson Practice

b.
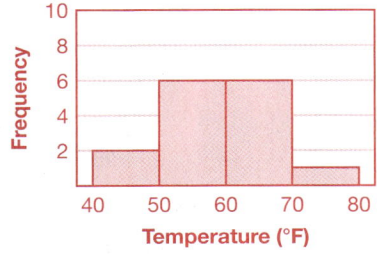

Lesson 65

Practice

17b. 2007 NCAA Division II Championship Women's 3-Meter Diving Results
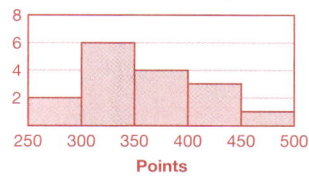

Lesson 66

Practice

7. The inequality $x > 5$ does not include 5. The inequality $x \geq 5$ does include 5. When graphing $x > 5$ starts with an open circle and $x \geq 5$ starts with a closed circle.

18. Sample: First I would multiply the first equation by 3, and then I would multiply the second equation by 2. Then I would subtract the second equation from the first, eliminating the variable x. After solving for y, I would substitute the y-value into one of the original equations to solve for x.

Lesson 67

Practice

11a. Deposits Received
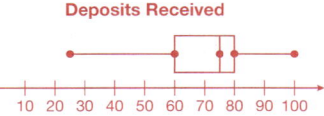

14. Ages of Players on Eastern Conference Team for NBA 2007 All-Star Game
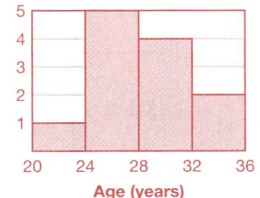

Lesson 68

Practice

15a.
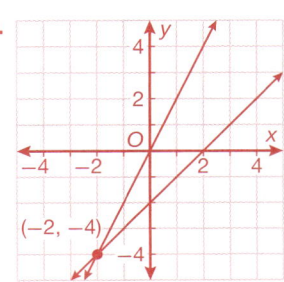

18. false; Sample: $(x + 2)(x + 2) = (x)^2 + 2^2 = x^2 + 4$

Check work by using the FOIL method:

$(x + 2)(x + 2) =$
$x^2 + 2x + 2x + 4 =$
$x^2 + 4x + 4 \neq x^2 + 4$

21a.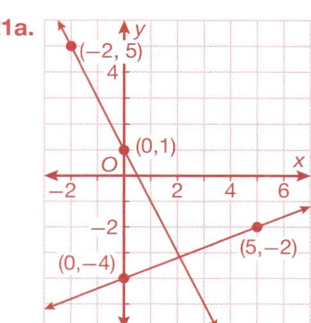

Lesson 70

Practice

11. Ages at a Family Party
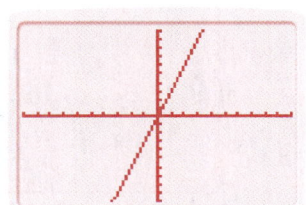

outlier: 82

Investigation 7

9.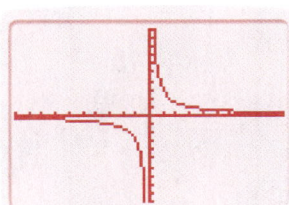

10.

12.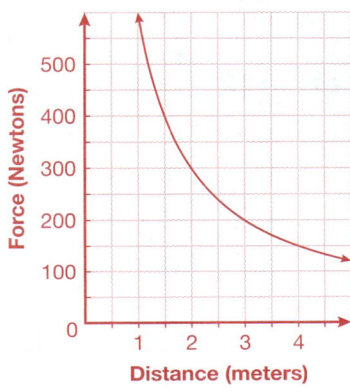

13.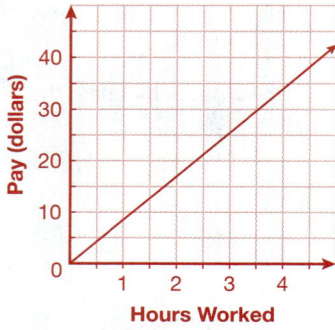

Investigation Practice

d.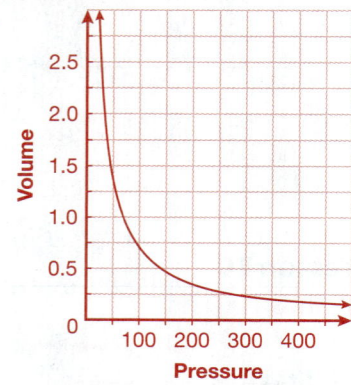
inverse variation; $P = \frac{70}{V}$

Lesson 71

Practice

12a.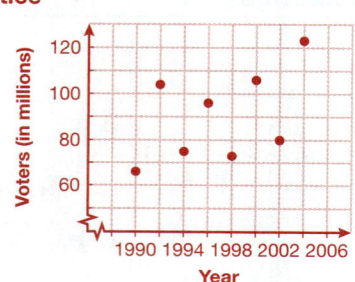

20.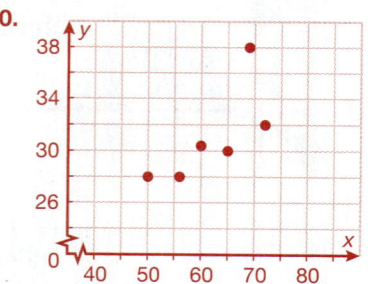

Lesson 72

Exploration

a.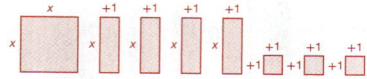

b.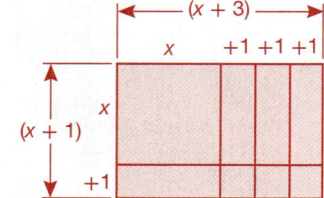

Practice

14a.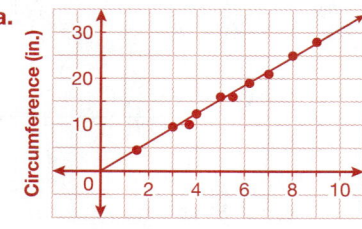

20.

Length	Width	Area
1	100	100
2	50	100
4	25	100
5	20	100
10	10	100
20	5	100
25	4	100
50	2	100
100	1	100

Lesson 73

Practice

19.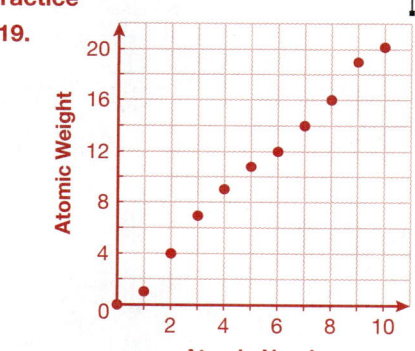

Lesson 74

Practice

10.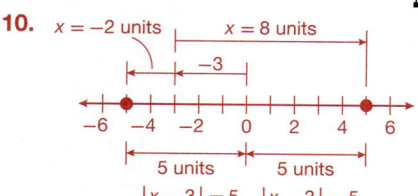

Lesson 80

Exploration

a.

		Cube 1					
		1	2	3	4	5	6
Cube 2	1	2	3	4	5	6	7
	2	3	4	5	6	7	8
	3	4	5	6	7	8	9
	4	5	6	7	8	9	10
	5	6	7	8	9	10	11
	6	7	8	9	10	11	12

d. Sample:

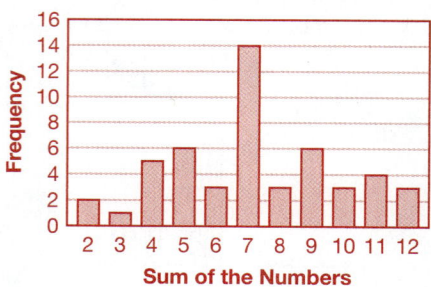

TE Additional Exploration

a.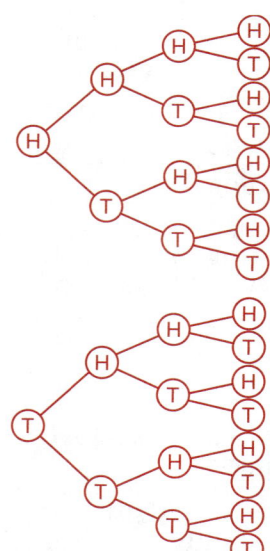

b.

Number of Heads	0	1	2	3	4
Probability	$\frac{1}{16}$	$\frac{4}{16}$	$\frac{6}{16}$	$\frac{4}{16}$	$\frac{1}{16}$

c. The answers depend on the results of the experiment.

d. The answers depend on the results of the experiment. The graph shows the expected results of 80 tosses based on theoretical probabilities.

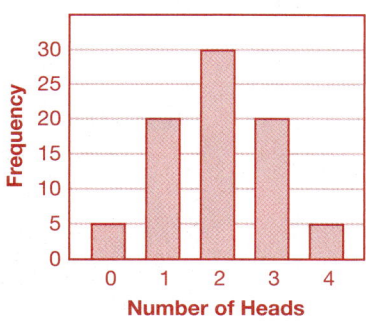

e. The answers will depend on the results of the experiment.

TE Additional Example 1

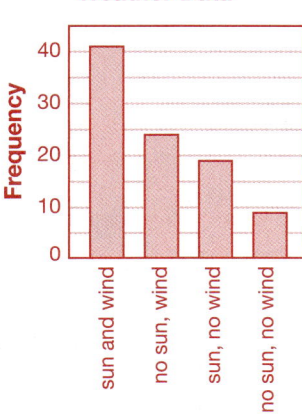

TE Additional Example 2a

	Jo	Ed	Dee	Kim
Jo	--	JE	JD	JK
Ed	EJ	--	ED	EK
Dee	DJ	DE	--	DK
Kim	KJ	KE	KD	--

Lesson Practice

a.

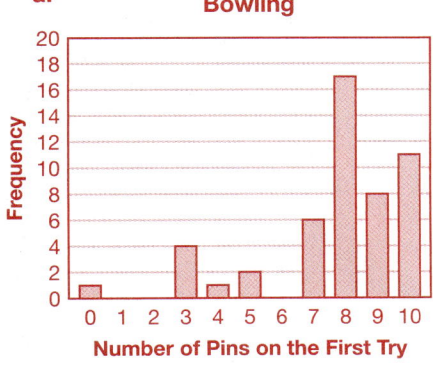

d.

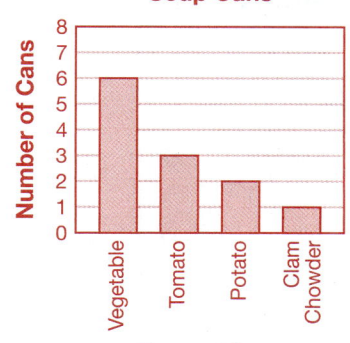

Lesson 81

Practice

26a.

Sum of Two Spins

	1	2	3	4	5	6	7	8
1	2	3	4	5	6	7	8	9
2	3	4	5	6	7	8	9	10
3	4	5	6	7	8	9	10	11
4	5	6	7	8	9	10	11	12
5	6	7	8	9	10	11	12	13
6	7	8	9	10	11	12	13	14

Lesson 82

Lesson Practice

c. $6 \leq 2(x + 12) < 12$

$6 \leq 2x + 24 < 12$ Distributive Property

-24 -24 -24 Subtraction Property of Inequality

$-18 \leq 2x < -12$ Simplify.

$\frac{-18}{2} \leq \frac{2x}{2} < \frac{-12}{2}$ Division Property of Inequality

$-9 \leq x < -6$ Simplify.

d. $-16 > 2(x - 2)$ OR $27 < 3(x + 2)$

$-16 > 2x - 4$ OR $27 < 3x + 6$

  Distributive Property

$+4$ $+4$ $+(-6)$
$+(-6)$

  Addition Property of Inequality

$-12 > 2x$ OR $21 < 3x$

  Simplify.

$\frac{-12}{2} > \frac{2x}{2}$ OR $\frac{21}{3} < \frac{3x}{3}$

  Division Property of Inequality

$-6 > x$ OR $7 < x$

  Simplify.

Practice

26. Sample:

$-17 > -2x - 7$ OR $27 > 3(x + 6)$

$-17 > -2x - 7$ OR $27 > 3x + 18$

   Distributive Property

$+7$ $+7$ -18 -18

   Addition Property of Inequality

$-10 > -2x$ OR $9 > 3x$

   Simplify.

$\frac{-10}{-2} < \frac{-2x}{-2}$ OR $\frac{9}{3} > \frac{3x}{3}$

   Division Property of Inequality

$5 < x$ OR $3 > x$

   Simplify.

$x > 5$ OR $x < 3$

   Write with the variable on the left.

Lesson 84

Practice

18.

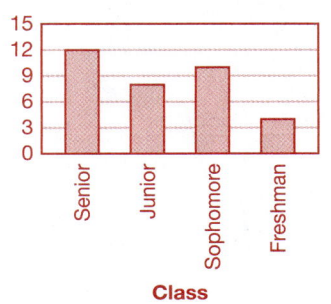

19.

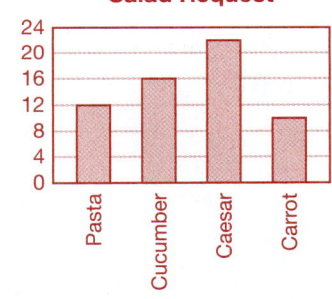

Lesson 86

Practice

15.

	Turkey	Ham	Chicken
Lettuce	TL	HL	CL
Tomato	TT	HT	CT
Cucumber	TC	HC	CC
Onion	TO	HO	CO
Peppers	TP	HP	CP

Lesson 87

Practice

12.

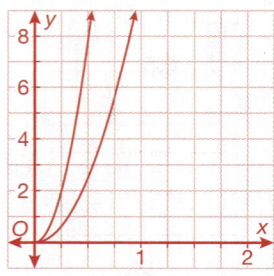

Lesson 89

Practice

19. $x < 0$;

$2(0) + 8 > 2 + 5(0) + 6$,
$8 \not> 8$

$2(-1) + 8 > 2 + 5(-1) + 6$,
$6 > 3$

$2(-3) + 8 > 2 + 5(-3) + 6$
$2 > -7$

21.

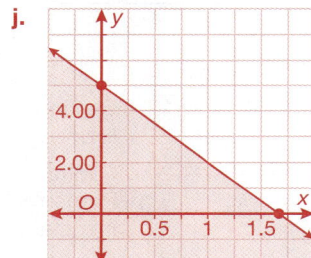

Sample: The volume of the cylinder increases faster than that of the rectangular prism.

Lesson 91

Lesson Practice

a.
```
-12 -8 -4 0 4 8 12
```
b.
```
-24 -16 -8 0 8 16 24
```
c.
```
-12 -8 -4 0 4 8 12
```
d.
```
-6 -4 -2 0 2 4 6
```
e.
```
-4 0 4 8 12 16 20 24
```
f.
```
-30 -20 -10 0 10
```

Lesson 92

Practice

8. Sample: $\dfrac{\frac{8x^2y}{15a^2b}}{\frac{2xy}{5ab^4}}$

$= \dfrac{8x^2y}{15a^2b} \cdot \dfrac{5ab^4}{2xy}$

$= \dfrac{8 \cdot 5 \cdot x^2 \cdot y \cdot a \cdot b^4}{15 \cdot 2 \cdot x \cdot y \cdot a^2 \cdot b}$

$= \dfrac{4b^3x}{3a}$

and

$\dfrac{8x^2y \cdot 5ab^4}{15a^2b \cdot 2xy}$

$= \dfrac{40x^2yab^4}{30a^2bxy}$

$= \dfrac{4b^3x}{3a}$

19. Answers will vary. Accept any function that can be written in the standard form of a quadratic function and any function that cannot. Students should explain that they must be able to write the function in standard quadratic form for it to be quadratic.

Lesson 97

Lesson Practice

j.

Practice

27. Sample: When the vertex is on the x-axis, there is 1 zero. When the vertex is not on the x-axis, the related function could have either no zeros or 2 zeros. There are no zeros when the vertex is above the x-axis and opening upward, or below the x-axis and opening downward. There are 2 zeros when the vertex is above the x-axis and opening downward or below the x-axis and opening upward.

Lesson 98

Practice

15b.

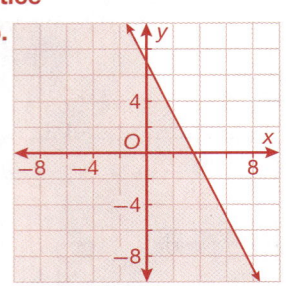

16.

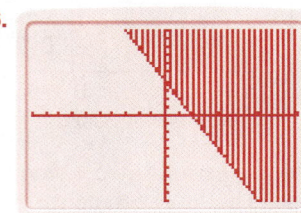

Lesson 100

Practice

3. Sample: The path creates a parabola that opens downward. The maximum point on the parabola shows the maximum height. The positive zero shows the time that the ball hits the ground (when height is zero).

4. Sample: The graph does not cross the x-axis when there is no solution. The graph has its vertex on the x-axis when there is one solution. The graph crosses the x-axis two times when there are two solutions.

TE Additional Example 2

a.

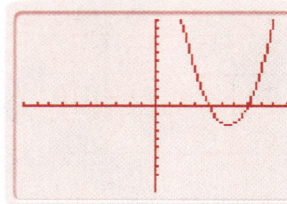

b.

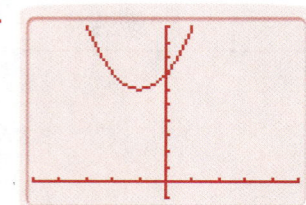

T906 Saxon Algebra 1

c.
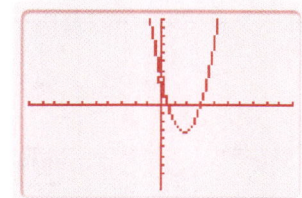

Investigation 10

Practice

1.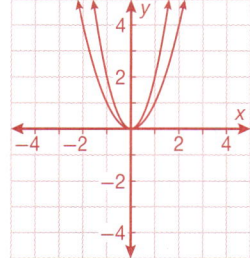

Sample: The graph of $y = 2x^2$ is narrower than the parent function.

2.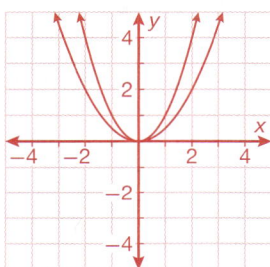

Sample: The graph of $y = \frac{1}{2}x^2$ is wider than the parent function.

3.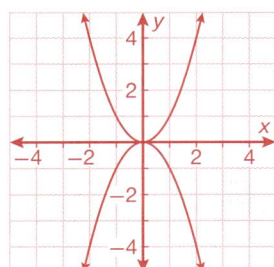

Sample: The graph of $y = -x^2$ opens in the opposite direction (downward) of the parent function.

4. Sample: It makes the graph wider or narrower and changes the direction in which the parabola opens.

7.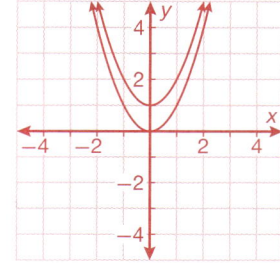

Sample: The new function moved up 1 unit from the parent function.

8.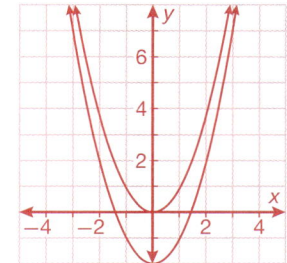

Sample: The new function shifts down 2 units from the parent function.

10. moved up 2 units and opens downward;

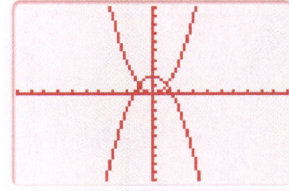

11. moved down 3 units and is wider;

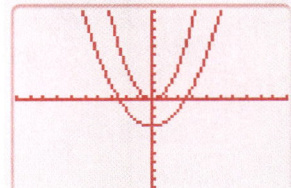

Lesson 104

Practice

4. $6x^2 - 12x = 18$ Add 18 to both sides.
$x^2 - 2x = 3$ Divide both sides by 6.
$x^2 - 2x + 1 = 3 + 1$ Complete the square.
$(x - 1)^2 = 4$ Write in factored form.
$\sqrt{(x - 1)^2} = \pm\sqrt{4}$ Take the square roots.

$x - 1 = \pm 2$
$x = -1$ or $x = 3$ Solve both equations.

To check substitute each value into the original equation.

$6(-1)^2 - 12(-1) - 18 = 0$
$6 + 12 - 18 = 0$
$0 = 0$

AND

$6(3)^2 - 12(3) - 18 = 0$
$54 - 36 - 18 = 0$
$0 = 0$

20b.
Sample: $x = -5$:
$-8|-5 + 7| = -8|2| = -8 \cdot 2 = -16$
$-16 \geq -24$;

$x = -7$:
$-8|-7 + 7| = -8|0| = -8 \cdot 0 = 0$
$0 \geq -24$

Lesson 106

Practice

28b.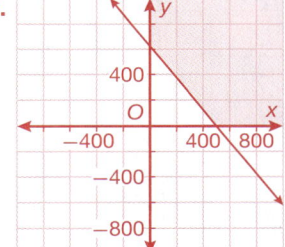

Lesson 107

Lesson Practice

b.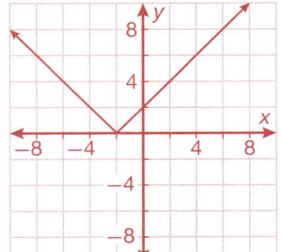

c.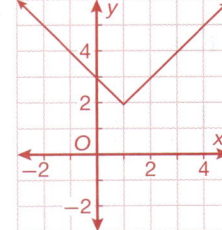

Lesson 108

Lesson Practice

e.

x	y
−2	$\frac{2}{9}$
−1	$\frac{2}{3}$
0	2
1	6
2	18

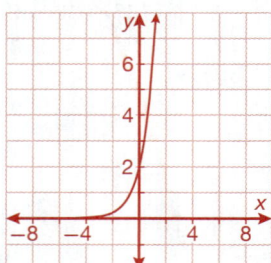

f.

x	y
−2	−1
−1	−2
0	−4
1	−8
2	−16

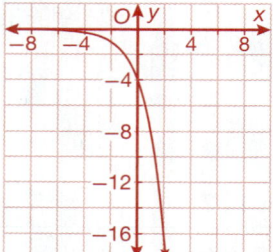

g.

x	y
−2	32
−1	8
0	2
1	$\frac{1}{2}$
2	$\frac{1}{8}$

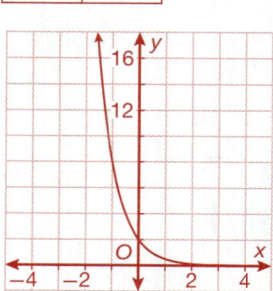

Practice

2.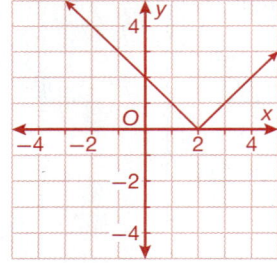

Lesson 109

Lesson Practice

d.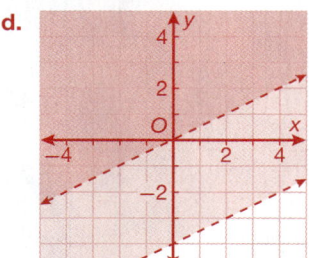

e.

f.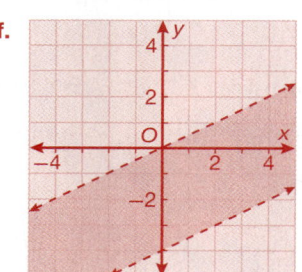

g.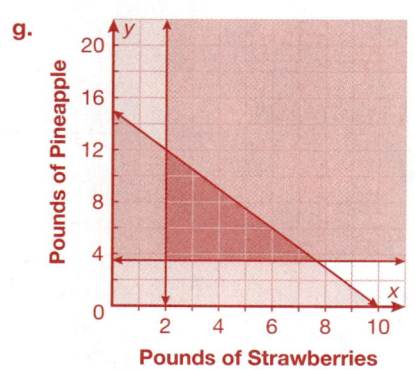

Lesson 110

Practice

11.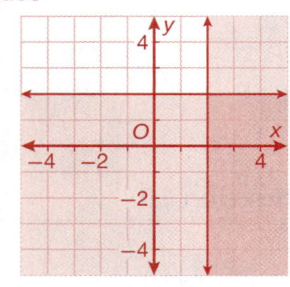

12. $5x + 15y \geq 300$
$10x + 30y \leq 480$;

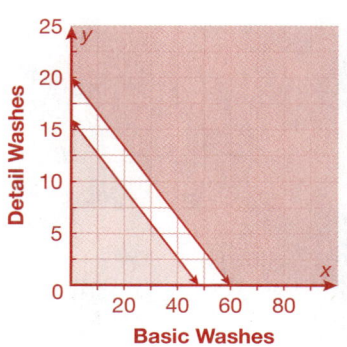

Sample: With these conditions, the goal will never be met because the system has no solutions.

13. 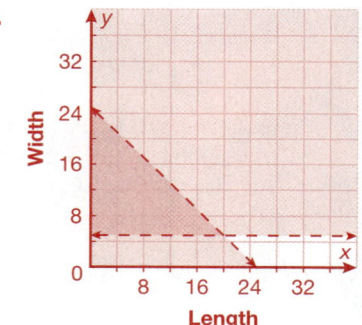 ;

Sample: length 14 units and width 9 units

27b.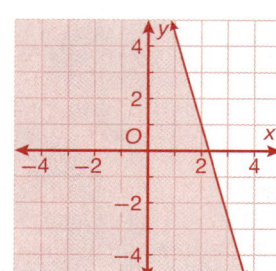

Investigation 11

1. Flow of Water

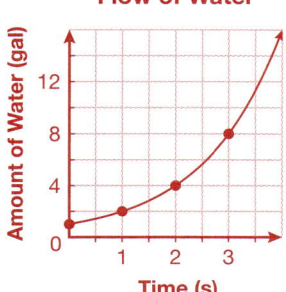

4. Stocks Traded on the NYSE

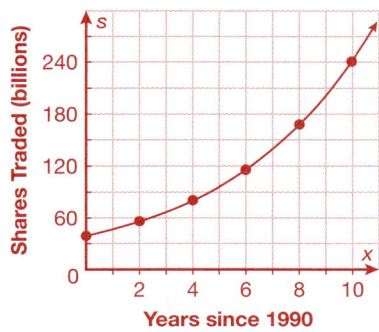

7. Exponential Growth

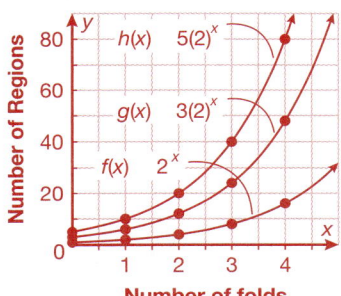

17. Sample: The k value and the y-intercept are the same. The exponential decay graphs have y-intercept $(0, k)$. The y-intercept of f is $(0, 100)$. The y-intercept of g is $(0, 50)$. The graphs have the same shape, but a larger value of k causes the graph to curve downward more sharply.

Exponential Decay

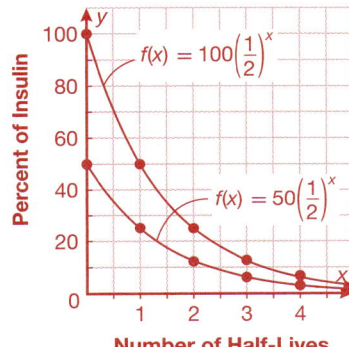

18. Graph B; The y-intercept is 2 because $k = 2$. The value of b is 0.5, which is greater than zero and less than one, so the equation is exponential decay—as x increases, y decreases.

19. Graph C; The y-intercept is 2 because $k = 2$. The value of b is 3 and is greater than one, so the equation is exponential growth—as x increases, y increases.

20. Graph A; The y-intercept is 1 because $k = 1$. The value of b is 0.25 which is greater than zero and less than one, so the equation is exponential decay—as x increases, y decreases.

21. Graph D; The y-intercept is 0.25 because $k = 0.25$. The value of b is 2 and is greater than one so the equation is exponential growth—as x increases, y increases.

Investigation Practice

e. Both graphs have y-intercept $(0, 1)$ and neither crosses the x-axis. The graph of $f(x) = \left(\frac{1}{2}\right)^x$ represents exponential decay. The graph of $h(x) = 2^x$ represents exponential growth. The graphs are mirror images of each other reflected over the y-axis.

f. Graph C; The y-intercept is 3 because $k = 3$. The value of b is 0.5 which is greater than zero and less than one, so the equation is exponential decay—as x increases, y decreases.

g. Graph A; The y-intercept is 3 because $k = 3$. The value of b is 2 and is greater than one, so the equation is exponential growth—as x increases, y increases.

h. Graph B; The y-intercept is 1 because $k = 1$. The value of b is 4 and is greater than one, so the equation is exponential growth—as x increases, y increases.

i. Graph D; The y-intercept is 2 because $k = 2$. The value of b is 0.25 which is greater than zero and less than one, so the equation is exponential decay—as x increases, y decreases.

Lesson 111

Practice

1.

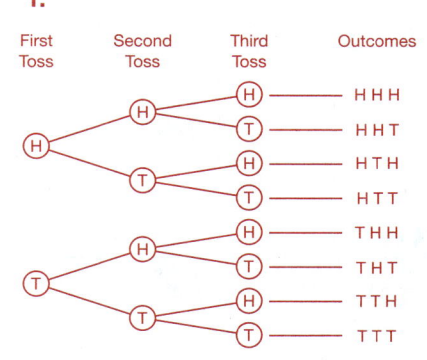

7.

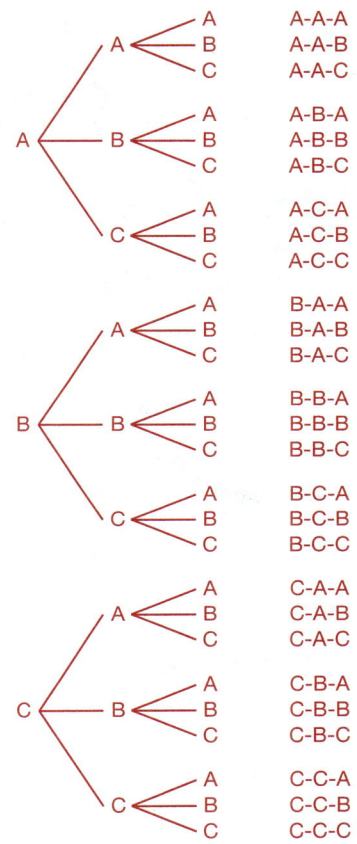

12.

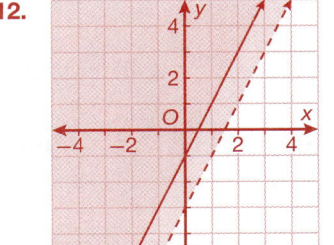

20.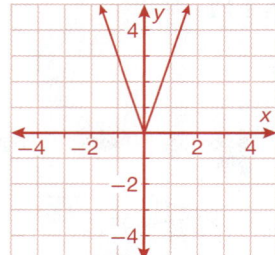

Lesson 112

Lesson Practice

c.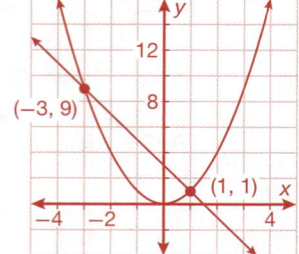

Lesson 114

Practice

7. $x > 19.5$; Sample:

$(f(x))^2 < \left(\sqrt{\frac{4x}{3} - 1}\right)^2$,

$5^2 < \frac{4x}{3} - 1$, $25 < \frac{4x}{3} - 1$, $26 < \frac{4x}{3}$,

$78 < 4x$, $19.5 < x$

11. yes; Sample: The equation $50 = (x + 12)(x + 8)$ represents the area of the rectangle. Then $50 = x^2 + 20x + 96$ and $0 = x^2 + 20x + 46$. The discriminant of this equation is $20^2 - 4(1)(46) = 400 - 184 = 216$. Since the discriminant is positive, there is a value for x that makes the equation true.

13.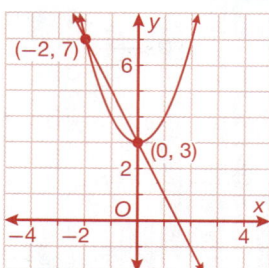

17.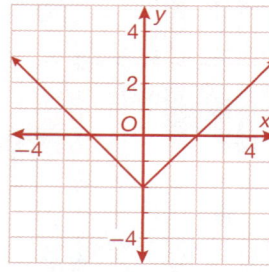

20.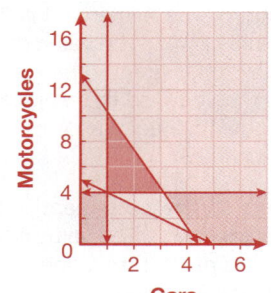

Sample: 2 cars and 6 motorcycles or 3 cars and 4 motorcycles

Lesson 115

Lesson Practice

b. 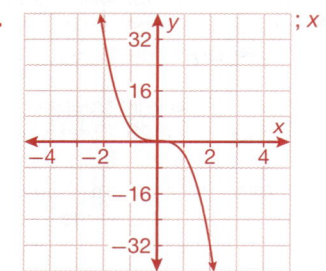; $x = 0$

c.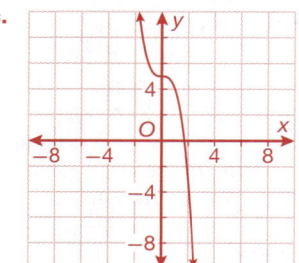

$x \approx 1.70998$

d. 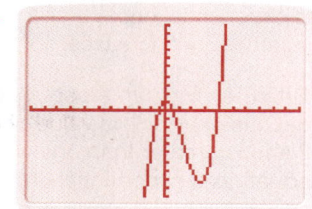;

$x \approx -0.47$, $x \approx 0.54$, $x \approx 3.94$

e. 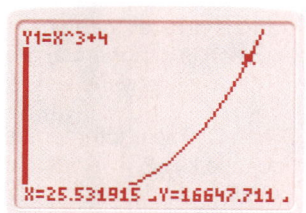;

$V \approx 16{,}648$ cubic units

Practice

11a.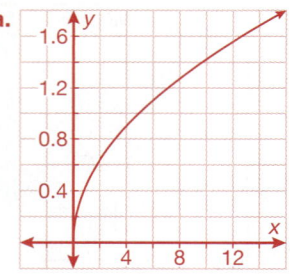

17.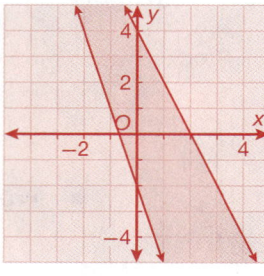

19. 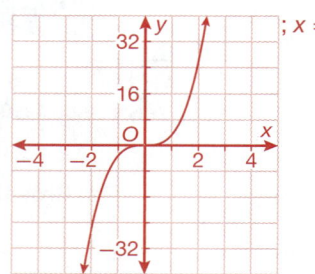; $x = 0$

23. $5x + 2y \leq 20$;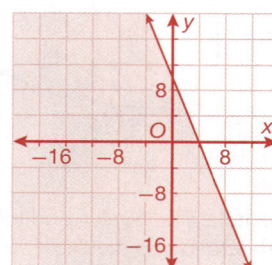

Lesson 117

Practice

14. 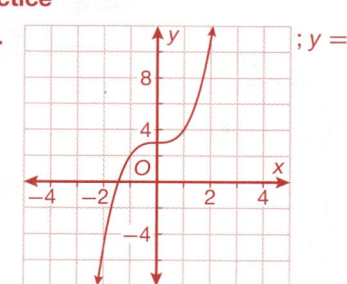; $y = 3$

24. ←|—⊕—|—|—|—⊕—|—|→
    −1 −0.5   0   0.5   1

27. $f(0) = 15$, $f(1) = 12$, $f(2) = 9\frac{3}{5}$

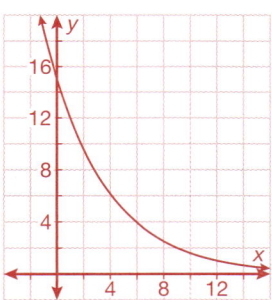

28. Sample: In the second system, the points on the boundary line are solutions to the system, and the boundary lines, which intersect, are solid. In the first system, the boundary line is dashed because the points on that line are not solutions. They do not intersect.

Investigation 12

9. $\begin{bmatrix} 10 & 7 \\ 3 & 2 \\ 4 & 9 \end{bmatrix} + \begin{bmatrix} 8 & 3 \\ 1 & 5 \\ 4 & 7 \end{bmatrix} = \begin{bmatrix} 18 & 10 \\ 4 & 7 \\ 8 & 16 \end{bmatrix}$

10. $\begin{bmatrix} 10 & 7 \\ 3 & 2 \\ 4 & 9 \end{bmatrix} - \begin{bmatrix} 8 & 3 \\ 1 & 5 \\ 4 & 7 \end{bmatrix} = \begin{bmatrix} 2 & 4 \\ 2 & -3 \\ 0 & 2 \end{bmatrix}$

12. $A = \begin{bmatrix} -1 & -2 & 2 \\ 2 & -1 & -2 \end{bmatrix}$

13. $A + B = \begin{bmatrix} 2 & 1 & 5 \\ 4 & 1 & 0 \end{bmatrix}$

14.

19. $2A = \begin{bmatrix} -2 & -4 & 4 \\ 4 & -2 & -4 \end{bmatrix}$

20.

22. $\frac{1}{2}A = \begin{bmatrix} -\frac{1}{2} & -1 & 1 \\ 1 & -\frac{1}{2} & -1 \end{bmatrix}$

INDEX

A

Absolute value, 22, 487

Absolute-value equations
  defined, 487
  isolating the, 488–489
  with more than two operations, 625
  multi-step, 624–625
  solving, 488
  special cases, 488
  with two operations, 624–625

Absolute-value functions
  defined, 720
  graphing, 720

Absolute-value graphs
  reflections, stretches and compression of, 723
  translations of, 721–722

Absolute-value inequalities
  defined, 602
  graphing, 602–603
  isolating to solve, 603–604
  solving, 602
  solving multi-step, 678
  special cases, 605

Absolute-value symbols
  operations inside of, 626–627
  solving with operations inside, 604–605
  as symbols of inclusion, 31

Addition
  in algebraic expressions, 93
  associative property of, 63
  commutative property of, 63
  distributing over, 243
  of equations, 412
  equations solved by, 105
  fraction equations solved by, 106
  identity property of, 63
  inequalities solved by, 430
  inverse property of, 27
  of polynomials, 338
  of rational expressions with like denominators, 592
  of rational expressions with unlike denominators, 593, 633, 663
  rules for, with real-numbers, 23

Addition and subtraction
  of fractions and decimals, 47
  of polynomials, 338
  of real numbers, 47–48

Addition property
  of equality, 104
  of inequalities, 430

Additive inverse, 27

Analyze. *See* **Math Reasoning**

Algebraic expressions
  comparison of, 44
  evaluating and comparing, 43–44
  evaluation of, 43
  with exponents, 43–44
  least common multiple (LCM) of, 369
  vs. numeric expressions, 43–44
  simplification of, 81
  translating into words, 93

Alternate Method, 4, 9, 13, 19, 24, 28, 32, 38, 44, 57, 70, 76, 99, 122, 129, 149, 154, 166, 167, 180, 183, 184, 191, 205, 212, 214, 219, 233, 238, 239, 244, 250, 258, 264, 278, 289, 295, 300, 309, 323, 331, 338, 346, 347, 356, 358, 370, 377, 386, 400, 408, 413, 414, 425, 427, 433, 434, 437, 451, 457, 468, 477, 483, 488, 512, 518, 525, 533, 544, 552, 571, 593, 605, 640, 686, 701, 706, 707, 708, 722, 723, 730, 731, 732, 737, 812

Applications, 6, 9, 11, 14, 16, 19, 21, 24, 26, 28, 29, 30, 33, 34, 35, 38, 40, 41, 42, 44, 45, 46, 48, 50, 51, 54, 55, 59, 61, 62, 65, 67, 68, 70, 72, 73, 76, 78, 79, 82, 83, 84, 88, 91, 92, 94, 95, 96, 97, 99, 100, 101, 102, 106, 107, 109, 113, 114, 116, 117, 118, 123, 124, 125, 126, 130, 131, 132, 136, 137, 138, 139, 142, 143, 144, 145, 149, 150, 151, 152, 155, 156, 157, 158, 160, 162, 163, 166, 167, 169, 170, 173, 174, 176, 182, 183, 184, 185, 186, 187, 188, 193, 194, 195, 196, 200, 201, 202, 203, 209, 210, 214, 216, 220, 221, 222, 225, 226, 227, 228, 229, 232, 233, 234, 235, 240, 241, 242, 245, 246, 247, 248, 251, 252, 253, 258, 260, 261, 262, 264, 265, 266, 267, 268, 272, 273, 274, 278, 279, 280, 281, 284, 285, 286, 287, 290, 291, 292, 293, 295, 297, 298, 301, 302, 303, 311, 312, 313, 316, 317, 318, 319, 324, 325, 326, 327, 331, 332, 334, 339, 340, 341, 342, 343, 345, 348, 349, 350, 356, 357, 358, 359, 360, 365, 366, 371, 372, 373, 374, 378, 379, 380, 381, 386, 387, 388, 389, 392, 393, 394, 395, 401, 402, 403, 408, 410, 411, 414, 415, 416, 417, 420, 421, 422, 423, 426, 427, 428, 429, 432, 433, 434, 435, 439, 440, 441, 442, 444, 445, 447, 448, 450, 451, 452, 453, 454, 458, 459, 460, 461, 462, 469, 472, 473, 478, 480, 484, 485, 486, 490, 491, 492, 498, 499, 502, 503, 504, 507, 508, 509, 513, 514, 515, 516, 519, 520, 521, 522, 526, 527, 528, 534, 535, 536, 537, 539, 540, 541, 542, 544, 546, 547, 548, 549, 552, 554, 555, 559, 560, 561, 562, 566, 567, 568, 569, 573, 574, 575, 579, 580, 581, 582, 588, 590, 591, 594, 596, 597, 605, 606, 607, 608, 611, 612, 613, 614, 615, 620, 621, 622, 623, 627, 628, 629, 630, 634, 635, 636, 637, 641, 642, 643, 644, 650, 653, 654, 657, 659, 660, 661, 665, 666, 667, 668, 673, 674, 675, 680, 681, 682, 683, 687, 688, 689, 690, 694, 695, 696, 702, 703, 704, 708, 709, 710, 711, 717, 718, 719, 723, 724, 725, 726, 730, 732, 733, 734, 738, 739, 740, 741, 745, 746, 747, 748, 749, 757, 758, 759, 760, 765, 766, 767, 768, 771, 773, 774, 779, 780, 781, 784, 785, 786, 787, 792, 793, 794, 795, 799, 801, 802, 806, 807, 808, 814, 815, 816, 819, 820, 821, 822, 826

Area
  converting units of, 38
  similar figures ratio of, 226

Arithmetic sequences, 211
  finding the nth term of, 213
  formula for, 212
  recognition of, 211

Associative property
  of addition, 63
  of multiplication, 63

Asymptotes
  defined, 511
  determination of, 511–512
  graphing using, 512

Axis of symmetry, 587
  finding from formula, 588
  using zeros to find, 587–588

B

Bar graphs, 127–128, 159

Binomials, 336
  mental math, 392
  multiplication of, 390
  multiplication with trinomial, 378
  polynomial division by, 617–618
  product of sum and difference of, 391
  special products of, 390
  square of, 391

Binomial squares, 697

Box-and-whisker plot
  analyzing, 346
  comparing data with, 347
  data including outliers, 346
  defined, 345
  displaying data in, 345–346

Boxplot. *See* **box-and-whisker plot**

Braces, 31

Brackets
  simplifying expressions with, 32
  as symbols of inclusion, 31

C

Calculator. *See* **Graphing Calculator**

Central tendency
  measures of, 299
  outliers effect on, 300

Challenge, 6, 10, 16, 21, 26, 30, 35, 41, 46, 51, 61, 68, 72, 79, 85, 91, 96, 101, 108, 116, 126, 131, 139, 144, 152, 158, 162, 169, 176, 186, 189, 196, 203, 209, 216, 222, 228, 235, 242, 248, 253, 262, 269, 273, 281, 287, 292, 298, 303, 312, 318, 328, 334, 341, 351, 360, 366, 373, 380, 389, 395, 403, 410, 417, 423, 429, 435, 441, 448, 453, 460, 472, 479, 486, 492, 498, 504, 508, 515, 521, 527, 536, 541, 548, 554, 562, 568, 575, 582, 591, 596, 599, 608, 614, 622, 630, 637, 644, 654, 660, 668, 674, 682, 690, 696, 704, 711, 719, 725, 734, 740, 748, 751, 760, 768, 774, 780, 787, 794, 802, 808, 816, 823

Chance, 76

Check for Understanding (Closure), 5, 9, 14, 19, 25, 29, 34, 39, 44, 49, 59, 66, 71, 77, 82, 89, 95, 100, 107, 113, 123, 130, 137, 142, 149, 155, 161, 167, 174, 183, 193, 200, 208, 215, 221, 227, 233, 241, 246, 251, 259, 266, 272, 278, 284, 290, 296, 302, 310, 317, 325, 332, 339, 348, 357, 365, 372, 379, 387, 393, 401, 409, 415, 421, 427, 433, 439, 446, 451, 459, 470, 478, 484, 490, 497, 502, 507, 513, 520, 526, 534, 540, 546, 553, 559, 566, 573, 579, 589, 595, 606, 612, 621, 627, 634, 642, 651, 659, 666, 673, 681, 687, 694, 702, 709, 717, 724, 731, 739, 745, 758, 766, 771, 779, 785, 793, 800, 806, 813, 820

Circle graphs, 130
  misleading, 160

Circumference, 226

Closed sets, 4
  under addition, 24
  under subtraction, 28

Closure, 4

Closure. *See also* **Check for Understanding**

Index **T913**

Coefficients, 7
Combinations
    compared to permutations, 804
    defined, 804
    finding number of, 805
    formula for, 805
    probability, 806
Combining like terms, 153
    with and without exponents, 98–99
Common denominators, 631
Common difference, 211
Common factors, 271
Common ratio, 705
Commutative property
    of addition, 63
    of multiplication, 63
Comparison
    of algebraic expressions, 44
    of algebraic expressions with exponents, 44
    of rational expressions, 48
Completing the square process, 697–700
Complex fractions
    defined, 609
    factoring to simplify, 610
    simplification by dividing, 609–610
    simplification by using the reciprocal of the denominator, 610
    simplification of, 609–611
Compound events, 523
Compound inequalities
    defined, 481
    multi-step, 678
    writing from a graph, 483
Compound interest, 790
    vs. simple interest, 791
Compression, 723
Conclusions, 254
Conditional statements, 254
    contrapositive of, 320
    converse of, 320
    inverse of, 320
Congruent angles, 223
Conjugates
    of irrational numbers, 693
    used to rationalize denominators, 693
Conjunction
    defined, 481
    solving, 482
    writing, 481–482
Connections. *See* **Math to Math Connections**
Consistent systems, 437
Constant of variation, 462
    defined, 362
Constants, 7
Continuous data, 118
Continuous graph, 118
Contrapositive, 320
Convenience sampling method, 187
Converse, 320
Conversion factor, 36
Coordinate, 110

Coordinate plane
    defined, 110
    graphing on, 110–111
Correlation
    defined, 467
    identification of, 468
    lack of, 467
    positive and negative, 467
Cosecant, 797
Cosine, 796
Cotangent, 797
Counterexample, 4
Cross products, 191
Cross products property, 191
Cubic functions
    defined, 782
    graphing, 783–784
    solving by graphing, 783
    solving with graphing calculator, 784
Currency, 39

D

Data
    comparing, 300
    misleading, 159–160
    range of set of, 300
Decimal equations
    solving, 140
    two-step, 141
Decimal parts, 141
Deductive reasoning, 254
Degree of monomials, 335
Degree of polynomials, 336
Denominators
    conjugate used to rationalize, 693
    rationalization of, 691–692
    simplifying before rationalization of, 692
    simplifying with opposite, 594
Dependent equations, 436
Dependent events
    calculating probability of, 206
    defined, 204
    probability of, 204–205
    situations involving, 205
Dependent systems of equations
    defined, 436
    solving for, 437
Dependent variables
    defined, 111
    determination of, 112
    identification of, 111
Difference of two squares, 545
Direction
    of a parabola, 552
Direct variation
    defined, 362, 462
    vs. inverse variation, 462–463
    from ordered pairs, 363
Direct variation equation
    graphing, 364
    writing and solving, 364
Discontinuous functions, 511
Discounts, 295

Discrete data, 118
Discrete events, 523
Discrete graphs, 118
Discriminant
    determination of, 769
    use of, 770
Disjunction
    defined, 482
    solving, 483
    writing, 482–483
Distance
    calculating with Pythagorean theorem, 563–564
    between two points, 564
Distributing over addition, 243
Distributing over multiple operations, 245
Distributing over subtraction, 244
Distributive property
    polynomials and, 375
    radical expressions, 501
    simplifying expressions with, 80–81
    to simplify rational expressions, 243
    used in substitution, 383
    using, 154
Division
    in algebraic expressions, 93
    distributing over, 245
    of inequalities by a negative number, 458
    of inequalities by a positive number, 457
    of numbers in scientific notation, 232
    one-step equations solved by, 120–122
    of polynomials, 617–618
    of polynomials with a zero coefficient, 619
    of positive and negative fractions, 58
    of radical expressions, 691–692
    of rational expressions, 578
    of signed numbers, 58
    simplification of complex fractions by, 609–610
    solving equations by, 122
Division properties
    of equality, 120
    of an inequality, 457
Domain, 146, 181
Double-bar graphs, 128
Double-line graphs, 128–129
Double root, 770

E

Elements, 2, 826
Ellipsis, 211
English Learners, 3, 8, 14, 18, 24, 28, 34, 37, 45, 48, 54, 56, 64, 69, 75, 81, 88, 94, 98, 104, 113, 118, 124, 130, 138, 143, 148, 155, 161, 168, 172, 181, 188, 193, 200, 208, 212, 218, 224, 230, 237, 245, 251, 257, 265, 272, 280, 284, 290, 296, 301, 310, 315, 321, 324, 332, 340, 348, 355, 365, 369, 376, 383, 391, 397, 402, 407, 415, 421, 426, 431, 438, 444, 450, 458, 463, 467, 479, 482, 491, 494, 503, 507, 511, 520, 524, 530, 534, 540, 546, 551, 559, 565, 573, 581, 586, 593, 600, 603, 610, 617, 627, 636, 643, 648, 656, 664, 670, 677, 680, 687, 694, 698, 709, 718, 721, 733, 736, 743, 750, 757, 766, 771, 777, 786, 789, 797, 805, 810, 822, 827

Equation of a line
  given two points, 330
  from a graph, 309
  in point slope form, 330
  in slope-intercept form, 307
  in standard form, 217

Equations
  absolute-value, 487–488
  addition of, 412
  classifying systems of, 438
  defined, 103
  equivalent, 103
  evaluation and solution of, 134
  of line of best fit, 464–465, 467
  matching to graphs, 180–181
  multiplication of one, 413
  multiplication of two, 414
  of parallel lines, 424–425
  of perpendicular lines, 426
  roots of, 655
  in slope-intercept form, 307
  solution of, in one variable, 103
  solved by addition, 105
  solved by division, 122
  solved by multiplication, 121
  solved by subtraction, 105
  subtraction of, 413
  of two variables, 308
  with variables on both
      sides, 164–165
  writing, given a point, 363

Equivalent equations, 103

Equivalent fractions
  to add with unlike denominators, 632, 633
  to subtract with unlike denominators, 632, 633, 664

Equivalent inequalities, 315

Error Alert, 3, 5, 6, 8, 9, 10, 11, 12, 14, 18, 19, 21, 24, 25, 26, 28, 29, 30, 33, 35, 39, 41, 43, 44, 45, 47, 49, 50, 54, 55, 57, 59, 60, 64, 66, 70, 71, 73, 76, 77, 79, 80, 81, 82, 85, 88, 89, 90, 92, 94, 95, 97, 99, 100, 102, 105, 106, 107, 109, 110, 113, 114, 115, 118, 119, 122, 123, 124, 128, 130, 133, 135, 136, 137, 139, 141, 142, 143, 145, 147, 149, 151, 155, 157, 158, 161, 163, 165, 167, 169, 172, 174, 175, 182, 183, 184, 188, 191, 192, 193, 194, 195, 196, 198, 200, 202, 207, 208, 210, 213, 214, 215, 216, 218, 220, 222, 225, 227, 231, 233, 234, 235, 237, 240, 241, 243, 246, 250, 251, 252, 254, 255, 257, 259, 260, 264, 266, 268, 271, 272, 273, 274, 276, 278, 280, 281, 283, 284, 285, 287, 288, 289, 290, 293, 294, 296, 297, 301, 303, 308, 310, 311, 313, 314, 316, 317, 321, 322, 325, 326, 328, 330, 331, 333, 335, 338, 339, 340, 341, 342, 346, 348, 349, 351, 356, 357, 358, 362, 365, 369, 372, 373, 377, 378, 379, 381, 386, 387, 391, 393, 394, 395, 397, 400, 401, 403, 407, 408, 409, 410, 413, 415, 420, 421, 422, 425, 427, 432, 433, 434, 437, 439, 440, 444, 446, 447, 450, 451, 454, 456, 459, 460, 463, 467, 470, 471, 476, 478, 482, 483, 485, 489, 490, 492, 494, 497, 498, 499, 501, 502, 503, 504, 505, 507, 508, 511, 513, 514, 515, 516, 518, 520, 521, 522, 524, 526, 527, 529, 530, 531, 533, 534, 537, 538, 540, 542, 545, 546, 547, 552, 553, 555, 557, 558, 559, 561, 564, 566, 567, 569, 571, 573, 574, 578, 579, 580, 586, 589, 590, 593, 595, 596, 597, 601, 603, 606, 607, 610, 612, 615, 617, 620, 622, 626, 627, 630, 632, 634, 637, 641, 642, 648, 651, 652, 654, 658 659 660, 665, 666, 667, 670, 673, 674, 675, 676, 677, 680, 681, 682, 683, 685, 687, 689, 692, 694, 695, 697, 699, 702, 703, 705, 707, 708, 710, 716, 717, 719, 721, 724, 726, 730, 731, 732, 733, 737, 738, 739, 743, 745, 747, 750, 751, 752, 755, 757, 760, 763, 766, 768, 770, 771, 774, 777, 779, 780, 781, 782, 785, 786, 787, 791, 792, 794, 795, 799, 800, 802, 803, 805, 806, 807, 811, 813, 815, 816, 819, 820, 823, 827, 828, 829

Estimate. *See* **Math Reasoning**

Error Analysis, 5, 11, 15, 20, 25, 30, 35, 41, 42, 45, 46, 50, 51, 60, 61, 67, 68, 73, 78, 79, 83, 84, 85, 91, 92, 96, 97, 101, 102, 107, 108, 115, 126, 131, 137, 143, 151, 156, 157, 167, 168, 175, 185, 196, 201, 209, 216, 221, 228, 234, 247, 248, 252, 261, 268, 273, 281, 287, 293, 297, 298, 304, 312, 313, 318, 328, 333, 334, 341, 350, 359, 367, 374, 380, 387, 394, 401, 410, 417, 423, 427, 429, 435, 440, 442, 447, 448, 453, 454, 461, 471, 472, 478, 479, 485, 491, 498, 503, 508, 509, 515, 521, 527, 536, 537, 541, 542, 549, 555, 562, 568, 575, 581, 591, 597, 607, 612, 613, 614, 621, 622, 628, 629, 635, 636, 643, 653, 660, 661, 667, 668, 675, 681, 682, 683, 688, 689, 694, 695, 703, 709, 710, 711, 718, 725, 732, 740, 746, 747, 759, 766, 772, 773, 780, 785, 786, 794, 801, 802, 807, 814, 815, 822, 823

Estimation of square roots, 70

Evaluate, 43

Excluded values, 322
  determining, 510

Experimental probability, 53–54, 524

Exploration, 23, 37, 53, 74, 121, 127, 164, 225, 230, 249, 256, 337, 361, 376, 390, 399, 418, 474, 523, 648, 698, 756

Exponential decay, 751
  defined, 751

Exponential form, 200

Exponential functions
  evaluating, 727–728
  identifying and graphing, 728, 729

Exponential growth, 749

Exponential growth and decay, 749–753

Exponential growth function, 750

Exponents, 12
  algebraic expressions with, 43, 44
  square and cubic roots as fractional, 91

Expressions
  with absolute-value symbols and
      parentheses, 31
  comparing, 18
  with exponents, evaluation of, 88
  with fractional exponents, 289
  with integer and zero exponents, 197–198
  multiple variable, simplification and
      evaluation of, 86–87
  with powers, simplification of, 251
  with scientific notation, 231
  simplification before evaluation of, 87
  simplifying and comparing with symbols
      of inclusion, 31
  simplifying rational, 270
  simplifying with greatest common factor
      (GCF), 239

  undefined, 270

Extend the Example, 3, 8, 14, 19, 24, 28, 33, 39, 44, 48, 59, 65, 69, 75, 82, 88, 93, 99, 106, 111, 112, 123, 129, 136, 142, 148, 155, 160, 166, 172, 182, 193, 200, 206, 214, 220, 225, 226, 232, 240, 245, 251, 257, 258, 264, 270, 278, 284, 290, 295, 301, 310, 316, 324, 331, 338, 347, 356, 364, 371, 378, 386, 392, 401, 407, 408, 414, 420, 426, 432, 439, 445, 451, 458, 469, 477, 482, 488, 496, 502, 507, 511, 512, 519, 525, 534, 539, 544, 552, 558, 565, 572, 578, 588, 594, 600, 605, 611, 620, 627, 634, 641, 650, 657, 660, 664, 665, 672, 680, 687, 692, 706, 708, 717, 723, 728, 738, 744, 757, 765, 771, 777, 784, 792, 799, 806, 812, 819

Extend the Exploration, 32, 37, 53, 121, 187, 337, 361, 376, 390, 399, 419, 474, 523, 648, 698, 756

Extend the Problem, 6, 10, 16, 21, 26, 29, 35, 41, 46, 50, 51, 54, 60, 68, 73, 78, 85, 91, 95, 97, 101, 102, 108, 109, 116, 118, 124, 131, 133, 138, 144, 150, 151, 157, 158, 162, 163, 174, 176, 184, 186, 195, 203, 210, 215, 222, 228, 233, 234, 235, 241, 248, 254, 255, 261, 267, 268, 274, 279, 280, 286, 287, 292, 297, 303, 304, 312, 318, 320, 327, 333, 334, 340, 341, 349, 358, 367, 373, 374, 379, 380, 381, 388, 394, 396, 397, 402, 410, 417, 423, 428, 434, 435, 441, 447, 453, 461, 462, 473, 479, 486, 491, 497, 498, 499, 503, 504, 508, 509, 514, 515, 521, 527, 528, 530, 535, 536, 542, 549, 554, 562, 568, 574, 581, 582, 590, 596, 597, 608, 613, 614, 622, 629, 636, 642, 652, 653, 654, 666, 667, 668, 674, 675, 676, 681, 689, 690, 695, 701, 703, 710, 718, 719, 726, 733, 740, 746, 747, 749, 751, 760, 768, 773, 779, 780, 781, 786, 787, 794, 795, 802, 807, 814, 815, 816, 821, 826

Extraneous solution, 716

F

Factorials, 755–756

Factoring
  combining fractions to simplify, 611
  difference of two squares, 545
  four term polynomials, 570
  with greatest common factor (GCF), 571
  with opposites, 571
  perfect square trinomials, 543
  polynomials, 238
  polynomials by grouping, 570–571
  quadratic equations by, 655–657
  to simplify complex fractions, 610
  special products, 543–545
  trinomials, 474–477, 517–518, 572

Factor, 7

Family of functions, 396

FOIL (first, outer, inner, last) method, 377

Formula solving, for a variable, 172

Formulate. *See* **Math Reasoning**

Fractional exponents, 289

Fraction bars as symbols of inclusion, 31

Fraction equations
  solved by addition, 106
  solved by subtraction, 106

Index **T915**

Fractions
    division of, positive and negative, 58
    simplification of complex, 609–611
    two-step equations with, 136

Fractions and decimals, 47

Frequency distributions
    calculating, 523–524
    defined, 523

Function notation, 669

Functions
    defined, 146
    families and tables, 810
    family of, 396
    graphs of, 179–180, 809–812
    identification of graphs as, 148
    linear vs. quadratic vs. exponential, 809–811
    maximum of, 585
    minimum of, 585
    ordered pairs of, 147
    parent, 396
    vs. relations, 147
    writing, 148

Fundamental counting principle, 754

G

Generalize. *See* **Math Reasoning**

Geometric sequences
    defined, 705
    finding nth term of, 706–707
    formula for, 706
    recognizing and extending, 705–706

Graphing. *See also* **graphs**
    absolute-value functions, 720
    absolute-value inequalities, 602–603
    using asymptotes, 512
    on coordinate plane, 110–111
    cubic functions, 782–784
    direct variation equations, 364
    exponential functions, 729–730
    inequalities, 315
    inverse variation, 420
    linear and quadratic equations, 761
    linear inequalities, 647–649, 735
    linear inequalities without technology, 648–649
    linear inequalities with technology, 649
    quadratic equations solutions by, 669–671
    quadratic functions, 638–640
    quadratic functions using a table, 551
    radical functions, 775
    rational functions, 510–512
    scatter plots, 466
    slope (of a line) from, 276
    with a slope and a point, 329
    square root functions, 776
    using standard form for, 219
    trend line, 466
    x-intercept, 218
    y-intercept, 218

Graphing calculator. *See also* **labs,** 33, 52, 54, 55, 56, 72, 91, 133, 145, 156, 158, 176, 177, 178, 179, 182, 195, 210, 215, 267, 285, 305–306, 319, 334, 342, 343, 344, 347, 352, 353, 356, 357, 358, 360, 374, 402, 404, 405, 408, 409, 416, 447, 459, 464, 465, 467, 473, 528, 566, 583, 584, 640, 642, 645, 646, 649, 651, 660, 672, 673, 674, 677, 682, 685, 689, 710, 725, 730, 731, 736, 738, 741, 744, 745, 748, 763, 766, 772, 773, 775, 784, 787, 793, 795, 798, 800, 824, 825, 827, 829

Graphs. *See also* **graphing**
    bar, 127
    bar, misleading, 159
    circle, 130
    circle, misleading, 160
    comparing, 730
    continuous, 118
    double-bar, 128–129
    double-line, 128–129
    finding zeros from, 586–587
    of functions, 179–180
    identification of, as a function, 148
    identification of, as a relation, 148
    identifying domain and range, 181
    identifying range, 181
    line, 128–129
    line, misleading, 159
    matching equations to, 180
    matching to tables, 179–180
    of relationships, 117
    representing data with, 525
    statistical, 127–128
    stem and leaf plots, 128

Greatest common factor (GCF)
    of algebraic expressions, 238
    factoring trinomials using, 517
    factoring with, 571
    of monomials, 237
    simplifying expressions with, 239

Grouping polynomials, 570–571

H

Half-life, 751

Higher-Order Thinking Skills. *See also* **Math Reasoning**

Histograms
    creating, 408
    defined, 408
    drawing lab, 404–405

Horizontal lines, 258

Horizontal translations, 777

Hypothesis, 254

I

Identification
    of dependent variables, 111
    of independent variables, 111
    of ordered pairs, as a function, 147
    of ordered pairs, as a relation, 147
    of properties, 64
    of quadratic equations, 550–551

Identity, defined, 165

Identity property
    of addition, 63
    of multiplication, 56, 63

Inclusion, 3, 9, 15, 20, 25, 29, 33, 40, 45, 50, 59, 66, 71, 78, 82, 89, 95, 100, 106, 111, 121, 123, 128, 137, 142, 147, 151, 156, 160, 165, 173, 182, 192, 199, 206, 213, 220, 225, 232, 240, 246, 252, 259, 267, 271, 276, 283, 291, 297, 302, 308, 316, 325, 330, 336, 350, 357, 363, 366, 371, 378, 384, 392, 399, 409, 415, 416, 422, 428, 432, 439, 446, 452, 456, 469, 476, 484, 490, 495, 502, 506, 514, 519, 526, 535, 539, 545, 553, 558, 564, 570, 572, 577, 587, 594, 604, 611, 612, 619, 625, 632, 641, 649, 657, 663, 672, 679, 685, 693, 699, 710, 713, 724, 726, 728, 729, 738, 744, 756, 762, 772, 778, 790, 799, 806, 811, 818

Inclusive events, defined, 444

Inconsistent equations, 436

Independent events
    defined, 204
    probability of, 204–205
    situations involving, 204

Independent system, 437

Independent variables, 146
    defined, 111
    identification of, 111

Indirect measurement, 224

Inductive reasoning, defined, 254

Inequalities
    addition property of, 430
    compound, 481–482
    defined, 282
    division of, by negative numbers, 458
    division of, by positive numbers, 457
    equivalent, 315
    graphing, 314–315
    linear, of one variable, 314
    multiplication property of, 455
    multi-step absolute-value, 678
    multi-step compound, 538
    with operations inside absolute-value symbols, 679–680
    simplifying before solving, 533
    solving by addition, 430
    solving by multiplication, 455
    solving by subtraction, 432
    special cases, 533
    subtraction property of, 432
    translating sentences into, 282
    translating words into, 283
    with variables on both sides, 532–533
    and words, 282
    writing from a graph, 316

Infinite set, defined, 2

Input variables. *See* **independent variables**

Integer exponents, 324

Integers, defined, 2

Intercepts, 217

Interest, 788–792

Interquartile range (IQR), 346

Intersection of sets, 4

Inverse of conditional statements, 321

Inverse operations, 104, 165, 712–713
    defined, 120
    use of, 121

Inverse property of multiplication, 56

Inverse variation
    defined, 418, 462
    vs. direct variation, 462–463
    graphing, 420
    identifying, 419
    modeling, 418
    product rule for, 419

Investigations
  analyzing bias in sampling, surveys, and bar graphs, 187–189
  choosing a factoring method, 598–601
  comparing direct and inverse variations, 462–463
  using deductive and inductive reasoning, 254–256
  determining probability of event, 53–54
  on experimental probability, 54
  identifying and writing joint variation, 529–531
  investigating exponential growth and decay, 749–753
  investigating matrices, 826–829
  using logical reasoning, 320–321
  transforming linear functions, 396–399
  transforming quadratic functions, 676–677

Irrational numbers
  conjugate of, defined, 693
  defined, 2

J

Joint variations, 529–531

Justify. *See* **Math Reasoning**

L

Labs
  calculating intersection of two lines, 352–353
  characteristics of parabolas, 583–584
  creating a table, 177–178
  drawing box-and-whisker plots, 343–344
  drawing histograms, 404–405
  finding the line of best fit, 464–465
  graphing linear functions, 305–306
  graphing linear inequalities, 645–646
  graphing radical functions, 775
  matrix operations, 824–825

Leading coefficient, 336

Least common multiple (LCM)
  of algebraic expressions, 369
  finding and identifying, 368
  of monomials, 369
  of polynomials, 370
  of three monomials, 370

Like radicals
  combining, 449
  defined, 449
  simplifying before combining, 450

Like terms, 338
  combining, 153
  combining, with exponents, 99
  combining, without exponents, 98

Linear and quadratic equation solutions, 761–764

Linear equations
  defined, 179
  elimination method solution, 412–413
  with graphing calculator, 356
  graphing quadratic equations and, 761–764
  graphing solutions, 355–356
  in slope-intercept form, 355
  solution of a system of, 354
  standard form of, 217
  by substitution, 382
  systems of, 354, 436–437
  with two variables, 217

Linear inequalities
  defined, 647
  determining solutions of, 647
  graphing, 647–649
  midpoint and segment of, 563–564
  in one variable, 314
  solution of a system of, 735
  solving by graphing, 736
  solving with a calculator, 736–737
  solving with parallel boundary lines, 737
  system of, 735
  writing, given the graph, 650

Line graphs, 128–129
  misleading, 159

Line of best fit calculation, 467

Lines, slope and *y*-intercept of, 307

Literal equations
  defined, 171
  solutions to, 171–172

Long division, 618–619

M

Manipulative use, 5, 60, 77, 105, 135, 136, 141, 150, 174, 241, 339, 419, 445, 497, 574

Markups, 295

Math Background, 2, 7, 12, 17, 22, 27, 31, 36, 43, 47, 53, 56, 63, 69, 74, 80, 86, 93, 98, 103, 110, 117, 120, 127, 134, 140, 146, 153, 159, 164, 171, 179, 187, 190, 197, 204, 211, 217, 223, 230, 236, 243, 249, 254, 256, 263, 270, 275, 282, 288, 294, 299, 307, 314, 320, 322, 329, 335, 345, 354, 361, 368, 375, 382, 390, 396, 398, 406, 412, 418, 424, 430, 436, 443, 449, 455, 462, 466, 474, 481, 487, 493, 500, 505, 510, 517, 523, 529, 532, 538, 543, 550, 556, 563, 570, 576, 585, 592, 598, 602, 609, 616, 624, 631, 638, 647, 655, 662, 669, 676, 678, 684, 691, 697, 705, 712, 720, 727, 735, 742, 749, 754, 761, 769, 776, 782, 788, 796, 804, 809, 817, 826

Math Language, 3, 24, 28, 31, 43, 53, 63, 74, 75, 110, 120, 136, 141, 146, 153, 165, 187, 197, 200, 211, 217, 226, 254, 307, 314, 320, 329, 338, 345, 346, 354, 375, 378, 398, 406, 418, 425, 449, 455, 456, 462, 481, 517, 523, 525, 533, 550, 556, 564, 576, 586, 602, 624, 631, 640, 655, 662, 669, 691, 699, 705, 712, 716, 742, 776, 777, 784, 788, 805, 818

Math Reasoning (Higher-Order Thinking Skills)
  analyze, 27, 38, 42, 44, 56, 62, 64, 70, 76, 92, 111, 115, 116, 117, 118, 125, 126, 132, 150, 151, 157, 162, 175, 176, 186, 187, 189, 192, 199, 203, 209, 231, 241, 242, 247, 248, 253, 260, 272, 273, 275, 283, 289, 295, 297, 298, 303, 304, 310, 311, 313, 316, 322, 327, 332, 361, 369, 373, 377, 379, 381, 397, 403, 405, 410, 420, 424, 429, 437, 439, 441, 448, 453, 454, 458, 460, 461, 463, 469, 474, 476, 478, 485, 489, 496, 499, 504, 518, 523, 528, 534, 546, 547, 551, 552, 559, 563, 566, 581, 588, 590, 591, 602, 607, 622, 625, 629, 632, 638, 655, 660, 662, 668, 676, 681, 684, 687, 693, 698, 706, 708, 709, 714, 717, 726, 728, 734, 748, 749, 750, 751, 759, 761, 766, 768, 770, 774, 778, 779, 781, 787, 792, 804, 810, 819
  connect, 7, 171, 376, 456, 512, 565, 723
  estimate, 13, 61, 91, 118, 124, 169, 193, 235, 291, 312, 358, 388, 421, 454, 537, 541, 542, 595, 597, 607, 685, 688, 724, 758, 808
  formulate, 25, 69, 167, 235, 236, 248, 274, 304, 318, 349, 381, 389, 419, 463, 474, 542, 555, 562, 568, 575, 667, 723, 751, 752, 768, 785, 793, 813, 827
  generalize, 13, 57, 94, 112, 132, 145, 150, 168, 176, 179, 186, 212, 216, 225, 241, 246, 249, 252, 268, 277, 278, 281, 287, 309, 321, 339, 341, 366, 373, 399, 400, 423, 452, 468, 472, 473, 474, 500, 508, 512, 527, 530, 548, 555, 565, 574, 582, 608, 635, 643, 652, 654, 661, 667, 673, 676, 690, 704, 706, 719, 729, 730, 737, 746, 751, 757, 771, 772, 783, 787, 797, 798, 801, 821, 827
  justify, 30, 34, 37, 41, 60, 68, 73, 78, 84, 92, 94, 95, 97, 98, 100, 101, 102, 105, 109, 118, 125, 137, 143, 145, 156, 162, 163, 176, 186, 188, 196, 206, 215, 229, 235, 241, 244, 246, 251, 253, 292, 318, 327, 370, 395, 423, 427, 429, 434, 435, 447, 462, 482, 483, 485, 492, 497, 503, 514, 520, 525, 528, 549, 569, 577, 585, 587, 597, 605, 606, 612, 613, 621, 629, 636, 643, 657, 660, 665, 696, 704, 711, 718, 726, 732, 758, 760, 790, 795, 803, 812, 822
  model, 25, 29, 50, 62, 71, 79, 84, 116, 139, 157, 186, 209, 287, 366, 376, 429, 447, 462, 474, 479, 480, 485, 491, 529, 554, 599, 758, 772, 808, 821
  predict, 53, 55, 101, 113, 127, 129, 130, 184, 194, 203, 209, 215, 234, 235, 242, 257, 280, 321, 331, 340, 371, 397, 448, 466, 492, 581, 597, 676, 677, 694, 746, 752, 754, 828
  true or false, 6, 10, 15, 20, 25, 34, 41, 45, 50, 60, 66, 71, 72, 83, 95, 101, 131, 162, 168, 170, 209, 216, 227, 246, 251, 387, 447, 492
  verify, 5, 6, 10, 15, 20, 25, 26, 34, 45, 54, 60, 68, 72, 79, 80, 85, 87, 102, 103, 116, 121, 125, 128, 131, 132, 137, 138, 141, 143, 144, 149, 152, 156, 157, 163, 170, 175, 176, 182, 184, 196, 197, 201, 214, 216, 220, 222, 226, 228, 234, 240, 248, 252, 260, 267, 268, 274, 275, 342, 358, 359, 367, 368, 373, 376, 389, 394, 399, 416, 420, 441, 442, 445, 487, 498, 506, 509, 510, 514, 515, 516, 519, 535, 541, 543, 548, 554, 558, 560, 561, 568, 571, 575, 578, 591, 629, 644, 654, 665, 666, 674, 675, 680, 682, 684, 688, 689, 691, 695, 701, 703, 710, 712, 718, 732, 735, 738, 739, 763, 764, 774, 783, 806, 816, 821
  write, 6, 10, 15, 20, 25, 26, 29, 34, 37, 40, 46, 51, 64, 68, 79, 84, 92, 95, 97, 107, 108, 109, 115, 118, 119, 124, 125, 126, 132, 133, 135, 137, 139, 144, 145, 149, 150, 151, 152, 154, 156, 163, 165, 170, 174, 186, 188, 196, 200, 201, 204, 209,

210, 213, 215, 216, 218, 221, 222, 233, 239, 241, 243, 246, 250, 255, 261, 266, 273, 275, 280, 285, 286, 297, 302, 303, 312, 315, 318, 319, 326, 327, 334, 340, 342, 346, 350, 357, 364, 366, 372, 374, 381, 385, 387, 389, 392, 394, 396, 397, 401, 403, 409, 410, 414, 416, 417, 420, 423, 428, 429, 433, 438, 441, 443, 444, 461, 472, 473, 479, 484, 488, 491, 497, 503, 505, 509, 520, 521, 522, 530, 536, 537, 548, 551, 562, 567, 569, 574, 575, 581, 596, 597, 606, 609, 612, 613, 621, 623, 626, 628, 637, 642, 652, 659, 666, 670, 681, 694, 695, 696, 709, 719, 720, 724, 739, 740, 741, 751, 765, 768, 781, 785, 793, 795, 802, 806, 809, 814, 815, 816, 820, 828

Math to Math connection
   coordinate geometry, 298, 411, 426, 429, 434, 435, 441, 460, 480, 596, 688, 702, 725, 807
   data analysis, 45, 222, 297, 302, 333, 380, 394, 453, 473, 504, 554, 674, 695
   geometry, 6, 10, 16, 21, 26, 29, 30, 35, 42, 46, 50, 62, 67, 77, 85, 90, 96, 102, 108, 115, 124, 125, 133, 138, 145, 152, 155, 158, 162, 168, 173, 174, 175, 185, 194, 201, 210, 215, 221, 228, 234, 241, 247, 252, 261, 269, 274, 281, 285, 286, 293, 304, 313, 319, 327, 334, 342, 351, 367, 374, 380, 388, 394, 403, 410, 416, 423, 427, 429, 433, 442, 448, 461, 473, 479, 484, 491, 497, 503, 508, 515, 521, 527, 537, 542, 547, 555, 562, 568, 575, 582, 591, 597, 607, 613, 621, 629, 636, 643, 653, 660, 667, 674, 682, 695, 703, 710, 718, 724, 726, 732, 740, 747, 759, 767, 772, 780, 786, 794, 801, 807, 815, 822
   measurement, 6, 10, 15, 20, 25, 29, 35, 51, 91, 97, 99, 102, 125, 143, 152, 163, 170, 176, 185, 224, 229, 234, 241, 253, 261, 292, 328, 342, 351, 367, 374, 379, 388, 394, 403, 428, 491, 498, 509, 515, 522, 536, 548, 568, 574, 582, 607, 636, 643, 644, 660, 668, 682, 689, 703, 710, 748, 759, 767, 780, 786, 794, 799
   statistics, 116, 138, 163, 215, 302, 423, 561
   probability, 62, 73, 85, 97, 102, 109, 125, 133, 139, 144, 157, 158, 170, 176, 195, 222, 247, 274, 281, 312, 317, 359, 417, 441, 446, 485, 527, 541, 614, 622, 654, 740, 773

Matrix, defined, 826

Maximum
   of functions, 585
   identifying, 585–586

Mean, 299

Measures of central tendency, 299

Median, 299
   defined, 345

Midpoint
   of a line, 563–564, 565
   of a segment, 565

Midpoint formula, 565

Minimum
   of functions, 585
   identifying, 585–586

Mode, 299

Model, *See also* **Math Reasoning,** 23, 25, 29,

50, 62, 71, 79, 84, 104, 116, 139, 157, 164, 186, 209, 287, 366, 376, 429, 447, 462, 474, 479, 480, 485, 491, 554, 758, 772, 808, 812, 821, 826

Monomials
   defined, 335, 375
   degree of, 335
   least common multiple (LCM) of, 369
   polynomials division by, 616
   polynomials multiplied by, 375

Multiple Choice, 6, 11, 16, 20, 21, 26, 29, 30, 35, 40, 41, 45, 50, 60, 66, 67, 71, 72, 73, 77, 78, 83, 90, 91, 95, 100, 102, 107, 108, 109, 114, 115, 119, 124, 125, 132, 137, 138, 139, 142, 143, 150, 151, 153, 155, 156, 161, 167, 169, 174, 184, 185, 194, 196, 202, 209, 215, 216, 221, 222, 227, 229, 233, 234, 241, 242, 246, 247, 252, 253, 260, 266, 268, 273, 274, 281, 285, 291, 292, 297, 303, 304, 311, 318, 319, 322, 326, 328, 334, 341, 342, 349, 350, 358, 359, 366, 373, 374, 379, 387, 388, 393, 394, 402, 403, 410, 411, 415, 416, 417, 422, 427, 434, 441, 448, 453, 460, 461, 472, 480, 484, 492, 497, 498, 503, 504, 508, 509, 514, 515, 516, 520, 522, 527, 528, 536, 537, 541, 542, 548, 549, 555, 562, 563, 568, 569, 574, 581, 582, 591, 597, 606, 613, 621, 622, 628, 629, 636, 643, 653, 654, 660, 667, 668, 674, 675, 682, 689, 695, 702, 703, 709, 718, 719, 724, 726, 732, 733, 739, 740, 747, 758, 759, 766, 767, 772, 779, 781, 785, 794, 795, 802, 807, 808, 815, 816, 821, 823

Multiple variable expressions, 86–87

Multiplication
   in algebraic expressions, 93
   associative property of, 63
   of binomial and a trinomial, 378
   of binomials, 390
   of binomials with radical expressions, 501
   commutative property of, 63
   identity property of, 56, 63
   of inequalities by a negative number, 456
   of inequalities by a positive number, 455
   inverse property of, 56
   of numbers in scientific notation, 231
   of one equation, 413
   one-step equations solved by, 120–121
   of polynomials, 375
   by powers of ten, 140
   of rational expressions, 576–577
   scalar, 828
   of signed numbers, 57
   solving equations by, 121
   of two equations, 414

Multiplication properties of equality, 120

Multiplication property of inequalities, 455–456

Multiplication Property of −1, 56

Multiplication property of zero, 56

Multi-step, 6, 10, 16, 21, 26, 30, 35, 41, 42, 46, 50, 51, 61, 67, 72, 83, 84, 90, 91, 92, 96, 101, 102, 108, 109, 115, 116, 125, 126, 133, 138, 139, 144, 145, 151, 157, 158, 162, 163, 168, 175, 184, 185, 186, 194, 195, 196, 202, 203, 210, 216, 222, 228, 229, 235, 241, 242, 247, 261, 262, 267, 269, 273, 274, 280, 281, 286, 287, 291, 292, 297, 298, 302, 303, 311, 312, 313, 318, 327, 328, 333, 340, 348, 351, 358, 366, 367, 372, 373, 374, 380, 381, 388, 389, 394, 395, 402, 403, 411, 416, 421, 422, 423,

427, 428, 429, 433, 434, 440, 441, 442, 447, 448, 452, 454, 460, 461, 473, 479, 480, 484, 485, 486, 491, 492, 498, 499, 503, 504, 508, 509, 515, 516, 521, 522, 527, 528, 535, 537, 540, 541, 548, 549, 554, 555, 561, 562, 567, 569, 574, 575, 580, 582, 590, 591, 596, 597, 607, 608, 613, 614, 615, 621, 623, 629, 630, 635, 636, 637, 644, 653, 654, 660, 661, 667, 668, 674, 675, 683, 688, 689, 690, 694, 696, 702, 704, 709, 711, 718, 719, 725, 726, 732, 734, 740, 741, 746, 748, 760, 767, 768, 773, 774, 780, 781, 786, 787, 794, 795, 801, 802, 803, 807, 808, 815, 816, 822, 823

Multi-step absolute-value inequalities, 678

Multi-step compound inequalities, 538–539
   defined, 538

Multi-step equations, 153–154

Multi-step inequalities, 506

Multi-step proportions, 192

Mutually exclusive events
   defined, 443
   probability of, 443

N

Natural numbers, defined, 2

Negative coefficients, 135

Negative correlation, 467–468

Negative exponents
   evaluation of expressions with, 198
   property of, 197
   simplifying, 198
   simplifying with, 244

Numbers
   decimal parts of, 141
   rules for adding with different signs, 23
   rules for adding with same sign, 23

Numeric coefficients, 7

Numeric expressions vs. algebraic expressions, 43–44

O

Odds
   calculating, 207
   defined, 206

One-step equations
   algebra tiles to solve, 104
   solved by addition or subtraction, 103
   solved by multiplication or division, 120–121

Opposites, 27
   factoring with, 571

Ordered pairs
   defined, 110, 217
   direct variation from, 363
   identification of, as a function, 147

Order of magnitude, defined, 13

Order of operations rules, 17

Origin, defined, 110

Outliers, 300, 346
   box-and-whisker plot with, 346
   effects of, 300

Output variables. *See* **dependent variables**

P

Parabola, 551
   direction of, 552
   vertex of, 585

Parallel lines
   defined, 424
   determining, 424
   equations of, 424–425

Parent functions, 396, 809

Parentheses
   simplifying expressions with, 17
   as symbols of inclusion, 31

Parentheses and absolute value symbols, 31

Percent, defined, 263

Percentage
   defined, 263
   using an equation to find, 263

Percent of change
   defined, 294
   increase or decrease, 294

Percent problems, 263

Perfect squares
   defined, 69
   simplifying with, 398

Perfect square trinomials, 543, 697
   factored form of, 543
   factoring, 544

Perimeter
   defined, 226
   similar figures ratio of, 226

Permutations, 754–756
   combinations compared to, 804
   defined, 756

Perpendicular lines
   described, 110
   determining, 425
   equations of, 425–426
   slope (of a line) of, 425

Pie graphs/charts. *See* **circle graphs**

Point-slope form, 330

Polygons, classification of, 564–565

Polynomials
   addition and subtraction of, 338
   addition of, 338
   defined, 336
   degree of, 336
   distributive property and, 376
   division of, 617–619
   division of, by binomials, 617–618
   division of, by long division, 618–619
   division of, by monomials, 616
   factoring by grouping, 570–572
   factoring of, 238
   four-term, 570
   least common multiple (LCM) of, 370
   multiplication by a monomial, 375
   multiplication of, 375
   multiplication of rational expressions containing, 577
   products of, 376
   rearranging before grouping, 570–571
   standard form of, 336
   subtraction of, 338
   with a zero coefficient, division of, 619

Population, 187

Positive and negative fractions, division of, 58

Positive coefficients, two-step equations with, 135

Positive correlation, 467–468

Possibilities, 756

Power, 12

Power property of exponents, 13

Powers
   raising numbers to, 57
   simplifying expressions with, 251

Powers of ten
   multiplication by, 140
   simplifying with, 400

Power of a power, 249–250

Power of a product, 250

Power of a quotient, 251

Predict. *See* **Math Reasoning**

Prime factorization, 236–237

Prime numbers, 236

Principal, 788

Principal square roots, 288

Probability
   combinations, 804–806
   dependent events calculation, 205
   of independent and dependent events, 204–205
   multi-step problems involving, 207
   of mutually exclusive events, 443
   of inclusive events, 444

Probability of event, 53–54

Product property of exponents, 198

Product rule, 197
   of exponents, 13
   for inverse variation, 419

Product property of radicals, 500

Properties
   of addition and multiplication, 63
   of equality, 104, 120
   identification of, 64
   use of, 64

Properties of equality
   division, 120
   multiplication, 120

Proportions
   cross products solution to, 191
   defined, 191
   to find a percentage, 264
   multi-step, 192
   writing and solving, 223

Pythagorean theorem, 556–557
   calculating distance with, 563–564
   converse of, 558
   justification of, 556
   missing side lengths calculation, 557

Pythagorean triple, 558

Q

Quadrants, defined, 110

Quadratic equations
   approximating solutions, 686
   completing the square to solve, 697–700
   graphing linear equations and, 761
   identification of, 550–551
   missing terms, 657
   solutions by graphing, 669–671
   solutions by graphing calculator, 671–672
   solving by factoring, 655, 656
   solving using square roots, 684–685

Quadratic formula
   approximate solutions to, 744
   defined, 742
   rearranging before solving, 743–744
   recognizing, with no real solutions, 744
   standard form, 743

Quadratic functions
   defined, 550
   finding zeros of, 640–641
   graphing, 638–639
   graphing using a table, 551
   identifying characteristics of, 585–586
   standard form of, 550, 638

Quotient property for exponents, 199

R

Radical equations, 712–715
   solving by isolating square roots, 714
   solving with square roots on both sides, 715

Radical expressions, 500–501
   addition of, 449
   distributive property, 501
   division of, 691–692
   multiplication of binomials with, 501
   simplifying, 398–399, 500

Radical functions, 775

Radicand, 69

Random number generator, 52

Random sampling method, 187

Range, 146
   of functions, identifying in graphs, 181

Range of set of data, 300

Rates
   converting, 190
   defined, 190

Rates of change
   defined, 256
   determination from a graph, 256
   determination from a table, 257

Rational equations
   defined, 662
   solving for, using LCD, 663

Rational expressions
   addition and subtraction of, 592–593
   common denominators for, 631
   common factors, 271
   comparison of, 48
   defined, 243
   distributive property to simplify, 243
   division of, 578
   with like denominators, 322
   multiplication and division of, 576–577
   simplifying, 270, 323
   with unlike denominators, 632–633

Rational functions
   defined, 510
   graphing, 511–512

Rationalization
   defined, 691
   of denominator, 691–692

Rational numbers
defined, 2
multiplication of, 57
ordering, 48
simplifying expressions with, 32

Rational proportions, 662–663

Ratios, defined, 190

Reading Math, 2, 22, 59, 75, 81, 99, 106, 111, 122, 148, 223, 224, 282, 283, 430, 431, 476, 481, 482, 505, 510, 519, 525, 602, 701, 706, 721, 727, 728, 755, 782

Real-number addends, 23

Real numbers
addition and subtraction of, 47–48
classification of, 2–3
defined, 2
division of, 58
multiplication of, 56
properties of, used to simplify expressions, 63
rules for adding, 23
sets of, closed under addition, 24
subsets of, 2–3
subtraction of, 27

Real World Connections. *See* **Applications**

Reasoning. *See* **Math Reasoning**

Reciprocals, 136, 797

Rectangles, 701

Recursive formulas, 212

Reflections, 397
of absolute-value graphs, 723
of square-root functions, 778

Relation
defined, 146
determining domain and range of, 146
ordered pairs of, 147

Relationships, 117

Relations vs. functions, 146

Relative frequency, 407

Roots. *See also* **square roots**
of equations, 655
higher-order, 289
simplifying, 289

S

Sample, 187

Sample spaces, 74–75

Sampling, 187

Scalar multiplication, 828

Scale drawing, 225

Scale factor, 223

Scatter plots
defined, 466
graphing, 466
making and analyzing, 466–467
matching situations to, 468

Scientific notation
comparing expressions with, 232
division of numbers in, 232
multiplying numbers in, 231
vs. standard form, 230
writing numbers in, 231

Secant, 797

Segment of a line, 563–564

Sequences
arithmetic, 211
defined, 211
term of, 211

Sets
defined, 2
intersection of, 4
union of, 4

Signed numbers
division of, 58
multiplication of, 57

Similar figures, 223
finding measures in, 224
ratio of perimeter, area and volume in, 226

"Similar to" symbol, 223

Simple event, 74

Simple interest, 788–789
vs. compound interest, 791

Simple random sampling method, 187

Simplify/simplification
defined, 43
vs. evaluate/evaluation, 43

Sine, 796

Slope (of a line)
defined, 257, 329
determination from a graph, 257
from a graph, 276
of parallel lines, 424
of perpendicular lines, 425
using slope formula, 275
from a table, 276
from two points, 275

Slope formula, 275

Slope-intercept form
defined, 307
equation of a line in, 308
equations in, 307

Special products, 543–544

Square-root functions
defined, 776
determining domain of, 777
graphing, 776
reflections of, 778
translations of, 778

Square roots, 288
calculating and comparing, 69–70
comparing expressions involving, 70
estimation of, 70
finding products of, 399
of perfect squares, 69
positive and negative values of, 288
principal, 288
solving by isolating, 714

Standard form
of linear equations, 217
of polynomials, 336
of quadratic functions, 550
vs. scientific notation, 231
used to graph, 218

Stem-and-leaf plots, 128
analyzing, 407
creating, 406

Stratified random sampling method, 187

Stretches of absolute-value graphs, 723

Subsets, 2

Substitution
distributive property used in, 383
linear and quadratic equations system solved by, 764
linear equations solved by, 382
rearranging before, 384
steps for solving by, 382

Subtraction
closed sets under, 28
distributing over, 244
of equations, 413
equations solved by, 105
fraction equations solved by, 106
inequalities solved by, 432
of polynomials, 338
of rational expressions with like denominators, 592
of rational expressions with unlike denominators, 594, 633, 664
of real numbers, 27

Subtraction property
of equality, 104
of inequalities, 432

Symbols of inclusion
comparing expressions with, 32
simplifying and comparing expressions with, 31

Symmetry, 587

Systematic random sampling method, 187

Systems of linear equations, 437
solving by elimination, 412–414
solving by graphing, 355–356
solving by substitution, 382–386
solving special systems, 436–439

T

Tables
to graph functions, 179–180
representing data with, 525
slope (of a line) from, 276

Tangent, 796

Technology
See also **Graphing Calculator.**
See also **Labs.**
spreadsheets, 843–845

Term, 7, 8

Term of a sequence, defined, 211

Terms of an expression, 8

Theoretical probability
calculating, 75
finding, 74

Transformations, 777

Translations, 396, 777
of absolute-value functions, 721–722
of square-root functions, 778

Tree diagrams, 205

Trend lines, 466

Trigonometric ratios, 796–797

Trigonometry
finding missing angle measures, 798–799
finding missing side lengths, 798

Trinomial, 336

Trinomials
   evaluating, 477
   factoring, 474–477, 493–496, 517–518, 572
   multiplication with binomial, 378
   with tiles, 474–475

Two points
   equation of a line given, 330
   writing an equation using, 330

Two-step decimal equations, 141

Two-step equations
   with fractions, 136
   with negative coefficients, 135
   with positive coefficients, 135
   solutions to, 134

Two-step inequaltities, 505

Two variables, equations of, 308

U

Undefined expressions, 270
Union of sets, 4
Unit analysis, 36–39
Unit equivalency, 37
Unit rate, defined, 190
Unlike denominators
   adding and subtracting with, 633–665
   using equivalent fractions to subtract, 664
Unlike radicals, defined, 449

V

Variable expressions
   multiple, simplification and evaluation of, 86–88
Variables, 7
   on both sides, solving for, 172
   simplifying with, 400
   solved a formula for, 172
   solving for, 171
Variation graphs, 463
Vectors, 22
Venn Diagram, 2, 4
Vertex
   identifying, 585–586
   of absolute-value function, 720
   of parabola, 585
Vertical lines, 258
Vertical line test, 146
Vertical line test, 147
Vertical translations, 777
Volume
   converting units of, 38
   similar figures ratio of, 226
Voluntary sampling method, 187

W

Whole numbers, defined, 2
Word problems
   translating between algebraic expressions and, 94
   words and phrases to algebraic expressions, 93

Words
   and inequalities, 282
   translating into algebraic expressions, 93
Write. *See* **Math Reasoning**

X

x-**axis,** 110
x-**coordinate,** 110
x-**intercept**
   finding, 217
   graphing, 218
   locating on graph, 218

Y

y-**axis,** 110
y-**coordinate,** 110
y-**intercept**
   finding, 217
   graphing, 218
   locating on graph, 218
   and slope of a line, 307

Z

Zero exponents, 197–198
Zero of the function, 583
Zero product property, 655
Zeros
   finding, from axis of symmetry, 587–588
   finding from graphs, 586–587
   multiplication property of, 56